The Good Pub Guide 2008

The Good Pub Guide 2008

Edited by

Alisdair Aird and Fiona Stapley

Managing Editor: Karen Fick
Senior Associate Editor: Robert Unsworth
Associate Editor: Tim Locke
Editorial Assistance: Fiona Wright

EBURY PRESS
LONDON

Please send reports on pubs to

The Good Pub Guide
FREEPOST TN1569
WADHURST
East Sussex
TN5 7BR

or contact our website:
www.goodguides.co.uk

Good Guide publications are available at special discounts for bulk purchases or for sales promotions or premiums. Special editions, including personalised covers, excerpts of existing Guides and corporate imprints, can be created in large quantities for special needs. Enquiries should be sent to the Sales Development Department, Random House, 20 Vauxhall Bridge Road, London SW1V 2SA (020 7840 8400).

Published in 2007 by Ebury Press, an imprint of Ebury Publishing

A Random House Group Company

The Random House Group Limited Reg. No. 954009

Addresses for companies within the Random House Group can be found at www.randomhouse.co.uk

A CIP catalogue record for this book is available from the British Library

Mixed Sources
Product group from well-managed
forests and other controlled sources
www.fsc.org Cert no. TT-COC-2139
© 1996 Forest Stewardship Council

Typeset from authors' disks by Clive Dorman
Edited by Pat Taylor Chalmers
Project managed by Nicky Thompson

Printed in the UK by CPI Cox & Wyman, Reading, RG1 8EX

ISBN 9780091918361

To buy books by your favourite authors and register for offers visit www.rbooks.co.uk

Contents

Introduction

Already, people eat out in pubs far more than in restaurants. We eat 1,100 million pub meals a year. That's more than half as much again as in restaurants. With the new smoking ban now in force, the pub industry is hoping for an influx of new customers – the many people who would not even have considered a pub as somewhere to eat can now think again. The big pub chains are all gearing up for this, often now serving food all day (Wetherspoons even opening pubs from 9 in the morning to catch the coffee and breakfast trade, for example, or Vintage Inns 'unbranding' some of their pubs to make them more like individually run upscale brasseries). And the great majority of pubs in this *Guide* depend increasingly on their food sales.

ARE PUBS KILLING THE GOOSE THAT LAYS THEIR GOLDEN EGGS?

The quality of pub food needs no apology these days. We have already charted the extraordinary improvement in cooking standards over the last decade or so, and the much more recent and dramatic reliance on carefully sourced genuinely local produce, sometimes home-grown. Now, virtually all the main entries, not just the smart dining pubs but the simple more homely places, use the best quality ingredients they can track down, as locally as possible.

But what does now need apology is pub food pricing. In the last year or two the cost of pub meals has soared. For this edition, we have scrutinised well over a thousand pub menus, heard about many thousands of pub meals eaten by our reader/reporters, and eaten a great many ourselves.

Our country-wide analysis of pub food prices shows that the average price of a typical quick and unassuming pub dish such as steak and kidney pie is now £10.50. To see what a middle-price pub lunch costs now, we checked 1,069 menus, taking from each the average of its cheapest and most expensive starter, and the average of its cheapest and most expensive main dish. This came to £16.76.

With a single glass of wine, this bill for a middle-of-the-road pub lunch now adds up to £20

So it's no surprise to us that many pub customers are getting worried. A common theme in their reports to us is that, to quote a typical reader, *'the food just seems to get increasingly expensive'*. This is not yet a customer rebellion. But the rumblings of discontent about price have started.

The price of pub food **can** be kept down. One in twelve of the main entries in this edition have won our Bargain Award, in recognition of their keen pricing. A few of these specialise in snacks rather than meals – but delicious and tremendous value. Top examples are the Bell at Aldworth (Berkshire) with its filled hot rolls inspiring many dozens of congratulatory reports from readers over the years, and the Pineapple at Dorney (Buckinghamshire) with its seemingly limitless array of inventive sandwiches. Others do hot meals too. On average, the most popular dish in each of these price-friendly pubs costs around £6.25, and tends to be the same sort of thing as in our other main entries – steak and ale pie, fish and chips and so forth. That's to say, these bargain pubs are selling their food for little more than half the price of the national average. Taking the average price charged by these bargain pubs as a fair yardstick, that means most pubs are now overcharging for their food by around 67%. No wonder one reader said they must be members of the Robber Barons Union.

Even at the prices charged by these bargain pubs, the quality can be high. Meals have been winning strong applause at the Brewery Tap and the Charters in Peterborough (Cambridgeshire), the Old Ale House in Truro (Cornwall), the John Thompson near Melbourne (Derbyshire), the Digby Tap in Sherborne (Dorset), the White Horse in Hertford (Hertfordshire), the Lincolnshire Poacher and the Keans Head in Nottingham

(Nottinghamshire), the Basketmakers Arms in Brighton and the Six Bells at Chiddingly (Sussex), the Fat Cat in Sheffield (Yorkshire), and the Pen-y-Gwryd up above Llanberis (Wales). With its interesting specials such wild boar casserole, goat curry or braised armenian lamb shanks, and a great value Sunday lunch, the White Horse in Hertford is **Bargain Pub of the Year 2008**.

With the increasing flow of people visiting and eating out in France, is it wishful thinking to hope that price examples there may help to put a lid on pub meal costs here? One reader, a great enthusiast for british pubs who has been reporting on them to us for many years, recently told us of a 'pub lunch' he'd had in Brittany, in a *restaurant ouvrier* – the spotless plain locals' restaurants which are very much the french equivalent of lunch pubs. The menu was a three-course buffet, as much as you wanted, with the choice of half a crab, coquille st jacques, salamis, rillettes, egg mayonnaise and around ten salads; then mussels or a big breton stew; then a choice of four or five puddings. With a litre of wine, mineral water and coffee, the bill was 10 euros – around £6.50!

Pubs can't hope to attract a great many new diners – or even keep all their old faithfuls – unless they rein in their rising food prices. Pubs may well be tempted to push their prices up further, by the present rise in the cost of the raw ingredients. But that represents only a very small fraction of the prices charged by them. And even as things are, we'd see the £40 typical cost of a meal for two as quite a deterrent.

What is certain is that if you are paying anything like that you should aim to get something really special. In this edition, over 250 pubs have qualified for our Food Award. Their food does tend to cost rather more than the average – typically, £2 extra for a main course. Given the quality, this seems fair, for this top tier of exceptional dining pubs.

This year's best pub meals can be found in the Swan in Denham (Buckinghamshire), the Old Bridge in Huntingdon (Cambridgeshire), the Punch Bowl at Crosthwaite and the Gate at Yanwath (Cumbria), the Drewe Arms at Broadhembury (Devon), the Museum at Farnham (Dorset), the Bathurst Arms at North Cerney and the Fox at Lower Oddington (Gloucestershire), the Wykeham Arms in Winchester (Hampshire), the Stagg at Titley (Herefordshire), the Inn at Whitewell (Lancashire), the Olive Branch at Clipsham (Leicestershire and Rutland), the George of Stamford (Lincolnshire), Woods in Dulverton (Somerset), the Parrot at Forest Green (Surrey), the Appletree at Marton and the Three Acres near Shelley (Yorkshire), the Hope & Anchor in South London, and the Applecross Inn (Scotland). For a special meal, book at the Appletree at Marton in Yorkshire. Their almost obsessive concentration on good ingredients, grown by themselves or produced for them specially by local farmers, then given imaginative treatment by the landlord himself, really pays off. For the quality, their prices compare favourably with their relatively few competitors in this premier league. The Appletree is **Dining Pub of the Year 2008**.

WHERE'S CHEAP, WHERE'S NOT
In Surrey a pint of beer costs 31% more than in the West Midlands
Drinks prices vary very widely from area to area. Our annual price survey, running now for over 20 years, compares prices in over 1,000 pubs of similar quality, country-wide. It gives the most reliable analysis of how prices change from year to year, as each year it compares the price in each pub with the price in that pub the previous year – the only survey which does this. The Table (opposite) shows how prices vary this year, from area to area.

Pub food prices follow a broadly similar pattern, with some exceptions. The West Midlands is again the cheapest area, followed by Staffordshire, Derbyshire, Nottinghamshire, Scotland and Northumbria. The most expensive are – starting from the top – Warwickshire, Gloucestershire, Kent, Sussex, Berkshire, Oxfordshire and Buckinghamshire. London pub food prices tend to be rather lower than the national average – certainly much lower than you'd expect from drinks prices there.

HOW BEER PRICES VARY	£/pint
extraordinarily cheap	
West Midlands	2.05
very cheap	
Lancashire, Staffordshire	2.20
Nottinghamshire	2.21
Cumbria, Derbyshire	2.22
Cheshire	2.24
Yorkshire	2.25
Northumbria	2.26
quite cheap	
Channel Islands	2.28
Worcestershire	2.29
Shropshire	2.31
Herefordshire	2.33
Cornwall, Somerset	2.35
Lincolnshire	2.36
average	
Wales	2.37
Wiltshire	2.38
Devon, Northamptonshire	2.39
Dorset	2.42
Essex, Cambridgeshire, Gloucestershire, Leicestershire and Rutland	2.43
Warwickshire	2.44
Norfolk	2.45
quite expensive	
Hertfordshire	2.48
Hampshire, Suffolk, Scotland	2.49
Isle of Wight, Kent, Oxfordshire	2.51
Bedfordshire	2.52
Sussex	2.53
very expensive	
Buckinghamshire	2.58
Berkshire	2.60
London	2.67
Surrey	2.69

BEER

Beer now averages £2.41 a pint – that's up by nearly 4% since last year: where can you find the best buys?

Almost all the pubs in this *Guide* stock cask conditioned ales – 'real ales' – and keep them well. Around one-third of the main entries now qualify for our Beer Award, because of their superb cellarmanship. Often they have particularly interesting beers, changing frequently – sometimes, an exceptional range. Happily, this is one time where top quality doesn't cost you any extra. In fact, on average these Beer Award pubs charge at least 10p a pint *less* than pubs whose beer didn't qualify for the award.

Pubs which stand out as really special for beer are the Charters in Peterborough (Cambridgeshire), the Bhurtpore at Aston (Cheshire), the Old Ale House in Truro (Cornwall), the Watermill at Ings (Cumbria), the Bridge in Topsham (Devon), the Brunswick in Derby (Derbyshire), the Old Spot in Dursley (Gloucestershire), the Hawkley Inn (Hampshire), the Marble Arch in Manchester (Lancashire), the Fat Cat in Norwich (Norfolk), the Crown Posada in Newcastle (Northumbria), the Victoria in Beeston and the Bell in Nottingham (Nottinghamshire), the Crown at Churchill (Somerset), the Nags Head in Malvern (Worcestershire), the New Barrack in Sheffield and the Marton Arms in Thornton in Lonsdale (Yorkshire), the Market Porter in South London, and the Guildford Arms in Edinburgh and the Bon Accord in Glasgow (Scotland). The Fat Cat in Norwich, with up to two or three dozen different ales on at any one time, and a helpful landlord, takes the top title of **Beer Pub of the Year 2008** – and it's one of the increasingly rare pubs where you can still get a pint for under £2.

Nearly four dozen of the main entries now brew their own beer. This makes for big savings. Typically, these beers are 30p cheaper per pint than the local competition. Almost always, they are interesting, and often very good indeed. Brew pubs which delight the choosiest aficionados are the Brewery Tap in Peterborough (Cambridgeshire), the Kirkstile Inn at Loweswater (Cumbria), the John Thompson near Melbourne (Derbyshire), the Marble Arch in Manchester and the Church Inn at Uppermill (Lancashire), the Grainstore in Oakham (Leicestershire and Rutland), the Keelman in Newburn (Northumbria), the Six Bells and the Three Tuns, both in Bishop's Castle (Shropshire), the Burton Bridge Inn in Burton (Staffordshire), the Beacon in Sedgley (Warwickshire chapter), the New Inn at Cropton, the Queens Arms at Litton and the Fat Cat in Sheffield (Yorkshire), and the Moulin in Pitlochry (Scotland). The Keelman, an unusual conversion of a distinguished Victorian industrial building in Newburn up on the edge of Newcastle, brewing its fine range of splendid Big Lamp beers, is **Own Brew Pub of the Year 2008**.

Of course, most pubs have to get their beers from outside breweries. There is relentless financial pressure for consolidation in the brewing industry. Big breweries tend to get bigger by swallowing smaller ones. Greene King has acquired a continuing stream of breweries such as Ruddles, Morlands, Ridleys, Belhaven and Hardys & Hansons, usually closing them. Marstons now includes Banks's, Burtonwood and Jennings. Other breweries amalgamate: Charles Wells and Youngs now have all their beers produced at the single Wells & Youngs brewery. So it is refreshing that newcomers start up in competition with these growing giants, and succeed. We remember, on a Cornwall inspection trip in 1994, arriving at the Crown in Lanlivery to see a van delivering a cask of a beer quite new to us. We tried it and liked it. It turned out to be from a Cornish brewery which had just started, called Sharps. Now, Sharps beers are quite widely available right across the south of England. This year we found them in over 50 of our main entries, usually at below-average prices – it was the lowest-priced beer in nearly half the pubs. Sharps are **Brewery of the Year 2008**.

Two pub groups, Punch and Enterprise, dominate the pub scene, owning many thousands. Over a hundred of our main entries belong to them. This sounds a lot, but in fact does not speak highly for the quality of their pubs. Between them, they own about one in four of the UK's pubs. But they own only about one in nine of our main entry Good Pubs. What's more, their pubs – effectively bought on credit – are expensive. A proportion of what you pay in their pubs is soaked up by the financial groups which have put up the money to build these pub chains. Compared with the average, we found Punch and Enterprise pubs were charging about 5% more for beer.

Very much smaller pub groups can be very much better value. A prime example is Tynemill, based in Nottingham. Their cheerful and distinctive pubs offer tremendous value. Their food, simple and tasty, is always well priced. Their beers are around 20% cheaper than the national average. Tynemill is **Pub Group of the Year 2008.**

WINE
Among the thousands of reports readers send us each year, nearly one in ten now mentions wine

Pubs take their wine increasingly seriously these days – so do our readers. Most good pubs now have a choice of half a dozen or more decent wines by the glass. With some pubs, the quality is extremely high. With others, the range is remarkably interesting. Our favourites this year have been the French Horn at Steppingley (Bedfordshire), the Swan in Denham and the Royal Oak at Bovingdon Green (Buckinghamshire), the Drunken Duck near Hawkshead and the Punch Bowl at Crosthwaite (Cumbria), the Culm Valley at Culmstock, the Nobody Inn at Doddiscombsleigh and the Harris Arms at Portgate (Devon), the Museum at Farnham and the Cow in Poole (Dorset), the Rose at Peldon (Essex), the Bathurst Arms at North Cerney (Gloucestershire), the Wykeham Arms in Winchester (Hampshire), the Stagg at Titley (Herefordshire), the Inn at Whitewell (Lancashire), the Olive Branch at Clipsham, the Kings Arms at Wing and the Chequers at Woolsthorpe (Leicestershire and Rutland), the Wig & Mitre in Lincoln and the George of Stamford (Lincolnshire), the Old Ram at Tivetshall St Mary (Norfolk), the Duke of Cumberlands Head and the Royal Oak at Ramsden (Oxfordshire), Woods in Dulverton and the Helyar Arms at East Coker (Somerset), the Crown in Southwold (Suffolk), the White Horse at Chilgrove (Sussex), and the Vine Tree at Norton (Wiltshire). With reasonable prices for its big glasses of carefully chosen and often interesting wines, not to mention its well organised tutored tastings, the Vine Tree at Norton is **Wine Pub of the Year 2008.**

WHISKY
There's one pub where it would take you 18 years to get through all their whiskies

For most people, whisky is now not a drink they look for in a pub. But a minority of our readers – about one in two hundred – really enjoy a wee dram, and prize the pubs which offer a great choice. In Scotland most good pubs stock a fine range: outstanding among them are the Bow Bar in Edinburgh, the Bon Accord in Glasgow and the Fox & Hounds in Houston. South of the border, two welsh pubs do us proud: the Pant-yr-Ochain in Gresford and the Goose & Cuckoo tucked away at Rhyd-y-Meirch. English pubs with dozens and dozens of interesting malt whiskies are the Bhurtpore at Aston, the Combermere Arms at Burleydam and the Old Harkers Arms in Chester (Cheshire), the Nobody Inn at Doddiscombsleigh (Devon), the Britons Protection in Manchester (Lancashire chapter), the Victoria in Beeston (Nottinghamshire), and the Marton Arms at Thornton in Lonsdale (Yorkshire). The Nobody Inn has a staggering choice. At the last count, we worked out that, having a glass a day, getting through the whole of their current range would take us at least 18 years. The Nobody Inn at Doddiscombsleigh is **Whisky Pub of the Year 2008.**

UNSPOILT PUBS
Escape from piped music, mobile phones and plastic food to the pubs where time stopped in 1950 or earlier, and a sandwich is still a sandwich

This *Guide* includes a host of truly unspoilt pubs, unaffected and genuine places which are a refreshing contrast to the recent influx of chic faux-rustic gastropubs. A surprising number of these have been in the same family for generations, sometimes even centuries. You can find them both in towns and out in the countryside. With many, the sheer sense of timelessness is enough on its own to delight you: pubs like the Magpie & Parrot in Shinfield (Berkshire), the White Horse at Hedgerley (Buckinghamshire), the Olde Gate at Brassington and the Barley Mow at Kirk Ireton (Derbyshire), the Bridge Inn in Topsham (Devon), the Square & Compass at Worth Matravers (Dorset), the Red Lion at Ampney St Peter and the Boat at Ashleworth Quay (Gloucestershire), the Three Horseshoes at Warham (Norfolk), the Black Horse at Checkendon (Oxfordshire), the Tuckers Grave at Faulkland and Rose & Crown at Huish Episcopi (Somerset), the Case is Altered at Five Ways (Warwickshire chapter), the Monkey House at Defford (Worcestershire), the Birch Hall at Beck Hole (Yorkshire), and the Plough & Harrow at Monknash (Wales).

Some unspoilt gems do offer suprisingly good food – usually very simple, but of its type unbeatable: homely hearty soups, first-class plain sandwiches, perhaps a hot dish or two of the day. Our private shortlist includes the Bell at Aldworth (Berkshire), the Red Lion at Chenies (Buckinghamshire), the Rugglestone near Widecombe (Devon), the Vine at Pamphill (Dorset), the Harrow at Steep (Hampshire), the Gate at Boyden Gate (Kent), the Crown at Churchill and the London at Molland (Somerset), and the Cricketers Arms at Berwick (Sussex). Still doing the glorious thick pea and ham soup which won us over some 25 years ago, the idyllic Harrow at Steep, run by the same family for over 70 years, is **Unspoilt Pub of the Year 2008.**

CITY PUBS
Forget drunken louts and binge drinking, and discover the town-centre treats where traditional values still matter
The unspoilt favourites mentioned so far are all in or on the edge of the country. In towns and cities, it's a real pleasure to come across such genuine places, almost cheek by jowl with noisy sports bars and the like. Our favourites are the Turf in Bloxwich (Warwickshire chapter), the Rose & Crown and the Turf Tavern in Oxford (Oxfordshire), the White Horse in Beverley and the Olde White Harte in Hull (Yorkshire), the Lamb and the Olde Cheshire Cheese in Central London, and the Colton Arms in West London.

Other city pubs which, if not exactly 'unspoilt', have great appeal because of their character and atmosphere are the Eagle in Cambridge, the Albion in Chester (Cheshire), the Alexandra and the Brunswick in Derby, the Wykeham Arms in Winchester (Hampshire), the Sun in Lancaster and the Britons Protection in Manchester (Lancashire chapter), the Wig & Mitre in Lincoln, the Victoria in Durham (Northumbria chapter), the Armoury in Shrewsbury (Shropshire), the Old Green Tree in Bath (Somerset), the Nutshell in Bury St Edmunds (Suffolk), the Haunch of Venison in Salisbury (Wiltshire), the Nags Head in Malvern (Worcestershire), the Maltings in York, and the Bow Bar in Edinburgh (Scotland). With good food and drink, great atmosphere, a charming layout and friendly staff, the Old Green Tree in Bath is **Town Pub of the Year 2008.**

PUBBY BARS IN COMFORTABLE HOTELS
Coupling a smart hotel's facilities and style with a warm local atmosphere – quite an achievement
The Gumstool outside Tetbury, one of our main entries, is an adjunct to the comfortable Calcot Manor country house hotel. Other good hotels occasionally have more integral pubby bars – a real plus. Places which successfully carry off this difficult trick are the Pheasant at Bassenthwaite Lake (Cumbria), the Snooty Fox in Tetbury (Gloucestershire), the Feathers in Ledbury (Herefordshire), the George of Stamford (Lincolnshire), the Morritt Arms at Greta Bridge (Northumbria), the Cock & Hoop, part of the Lace Market Hotel in Nottingham (Nottinghamshire), the White Swan in Middleham, the White Swan in Pickering and the Boars Head at Ripley (Yorkshire), the Moulin in Pitlochry (Scotland), and the Penhelig Arms in Aberdovey and the Olde Bulls Head in Beaumaris (Wales). The bar in the Pheasant at Bassenthwaite Lake puts you straight into the pages of a 1930s novel – perhaps Graham Greene in an unusually sunny mood: it is **Hotel Bar of the Year 2008.**

NEW FINDS
Hundreds of new entries – which is the best?
This edition of the *Guide* includes 1,793 new additions to the Lucky Dip sections at the end of each chapter (not including those in the Overseas section at the back of the book). Many of these had at least crossed our radar at some time in the past, often many years ago. Over 300 of them were completely new to us, and some of these seem really promising.

We have also added over a hundred pubs to the large-print main entries. Outstanding among these newcomers are the Swan at Radwell (Bedfordshire), the Snooty Millstone at Barnack (Cambridgeshire), the Combermere Arms at Burleydam (Cheshire), the Gurnards Head Hotel (Cornwall), the Sun in Kirkby Lonsdale and the Horse & Farrier at Threlkeld (Cumbria), the Golden Lion at Tipton St John (Devon), the Three Horseshoes at Powerstock and the Ship at West Stour (Dorset), the Horse & Groom at Bourton-on-the-Hill, the Westcote Inn at Nether Westcote and the Churchill Arms at Paxford

(Gloucestershire), the Hampshire Bowman at Dundridge and the Willow Tree in Winchester (Hampshire), the Saracens Head at Symonds Yat (Herefordshire), the Fox in Willian (Hertfordshire), the Timber Batts at Bodsham and the Granville at Lower Hardres (Kent), the Rams Head near Denshaw and the Highwayman at Nether Burrow (Lancashire), the Samuel Pepys at Slipton (Northamptonshire), the Greyhound on Gallowstree Common, the Rose & Crown at Shilton and the Swan at Swinbrook (Oxfordshire), the George at Croscombe and the Lord Poulett Arms at Hinton St George (Somerset), the Hand & Trumpet at Wrinehill (Staffordshire), the Fountain at Tuddenham (Suffolk), the Royal Oak at East Lavant and the Half Moon at Warninglid (Sussex), the Blue Boar in Aldbourne, the Castle Inn in Castle Combe and the Cross Keys at Upper Chute (Wiltshire), the Gray Ox at Hartshead (Yorkshire), the Narrow in East London, the Greenwich Union in South London and the Fat Badger in West London, and the Royal Oak at Gladestry (Wales). Under its friendly Canadian landlord, the George at Croscombe in Somerset is **New Pub of the Year 2008.**

INN OF THE YEAR
Twenty-two lovely places to stay in
More than one-third of the main entries have bedrooms; of these, about half qualify for our Stay Award. This award means that either we or trusted reader/reporters have stayed there and enjoyed themselves. The award covers the whole range of places to stay from simple cheap country inns to the much more stylish and even luxurious. This system seems to work well – we believe it is better than flowery descriptions which can mislead and disappoint. Proof of this is that it is very rare for us to have to remove a Stay Award once it has been given.

Places which have been much enjoyed this year are the Port Gaverne Inn near Port Isaac (Cornwall), the Pheasant at Bassenthwaite Lake and the Punch Bowl at Crosthwaite (Cumbria), the Museum at Farnham (Dorset), the Trooper near Petersfield (Hampshire), the Stagg at Titley (Herefordshire), the Inn at Whitewell (Lancashire), the Olive Branch at Clipsham (Leicestershire and Rutland), the George of Stamford (Lincolnshire), the Hoste Arms in Burnham Market (Norfolk), the Rose & Crown at Romaldkirk (Northumbria), the Lord Poulett Arms at Hinton St George and the Royal Oak at Luxborough (Somerset), the Castle in Castle Combe (Wiltshire), the Charles Bathurst near Langthwaite, the Star at Harome, the White Swan in Pickering and the Sportsmans Arms at Wath (Yorkshire), the Applecross Inn (Scotland), the Griffin at Felinfach and the Groes at Ty'n-y-groes (Wales), and the Fleur du Jardin at King's Mills on Guernsey. The half-dozen lovely rooms at the Olive Branch are in a house just opposite the pub: a super place for a treat, with a great supper then a particularly good breakfast. The Olive Branch at Clipsham in Rutland is **Inn of the Year 2008.**

THE TOP LANDLORDS AND LANDLADIES
Very british, running a pub – though in fact the best licensees come from all over, including one from Canada and two from South Africa
Ever since this *Guide* started, our first requirement for a good pub has been that it should feel welcoming. Obviously, other things too will make it memorable, and all those qualities, like the welcome, depend on the landlords and landladies. It takes a special talent to keep a pub in the top rank, given all its customers' very varied wants. With a great many of our main entries, the licensees keep everything running well without your being aware of how much they put into the task. In some pubs, though, they are very much centre-stage. Their friendly enthusiasm is a big part of the pub's appeal. These are the star landladies and landlords.

Shining examples are Frank Adams in the Winterbourne Arms at Winterbourne (Berkshire), Niki and Andrew Law at the Kings Head in Ruan Lanihorne (Cornwall), Jamie Stuart and Pippa Hutchinson in the Duke of York at Iddesleigh (Devon), Paul Crisp at the George in Chideock, and John Ford, Karen Trimby, Ron Hobson and Cherry Ball in the Greyhound at St Nicholas (Dorset), John Barnard in the Red Lion at Ampney St Peter, Tony and Gill Burreddu in the Queens Arms at Ashleworth, André and Liz Large at the Cross House in Doynton, Jo and Jon Carrier of the Five Mile House at Duntisbourne Abbots, James Walker in the Bathurst Arms at North Cerney and Paul Davidson and Pat LeJeune at the Bell in Sapperton (Gloucestershire), Mary Holmes in the Sun at Bentworth, Hassan Matini at the Trooper near Petersfield and George and Sonia Humphrey in the Cross Keys at Upper Chute

(Hampshire), Richard and Liz Gresko of the Riverside Inn at Aymestrey (Herefordshire), Chris Smith in the Gate Inn at Boyden Gate and John Elton and Claire Butler of the Harrow at Ightham Common (Kent), Bob and Josie Dyer at the Wheatsheaf in Dry Doddington (Lincolnshire), Lucille and Barry Carter in the Woolpack at Terrington St John (Norfolk), Maggie Chandler at the George in Kilsby (Northamptonshire), Assumpta and Peter Golding of the Chequers at Churchill and Andrew Hill and Eilidh Ferguson of the Half Moon at Cuxham (Oxfordshire), Paul and Jo Stretton-Downes in the Bottle & Glass at Picklescott (Shropshire), Peter and Veryan Graham in the George at Croscombe (Somerset), Ann and Bill Cross at the Castle Inn in Castle Combe (Wiltshire), Judith Fish in the Applecross Inn (Scotland), and the Key family at the Nags Head in Usk (Wales). There must be something in the Gloucestershire air for the county to house so many of our top licensees. And it is two of these who take the title of **Licensees of the Year 2008**: Paul Davidson and Pat LeJeune of the Bell in Sapperton.

PUB OF THE YEAR
Britain's top ten pubs – and the winner is...
This year's top pubs are the Duke of York at Iddesleigh (Devon), the Bell in Sapperton (Gloucestershire), the Royal Oak at Fritham and the Wykeham Arms in Winchester (Hampshire), the Lord Nelson in Southwold (Suffolk), the Parrot at Forest Green (Surrey), the Griffin at Fletching and the Queens Head at Icklesham (Sussex), the Nags Head in Malvern (Worcestershire), and the Appletree at Marton (Yorkshire). The Nags Head in Malvern, a proper pub full of interest, with a great range of drinks and a buoyant friendly atmosphere, is **Pub of the Year 2008**.

What is a Good Pub?

The main entries in this *Guide* have been through a two-stage sifting process. First of all, some 2,000 regular correspondents keep in touch with us about the pubs they visit, and double that number report occasionally. We also get a flow of reports through our www.goodguides.co.uk website. This keeps us up to date about pubs included in previous editions – it's their alarm signals that warn us when a pub's standards have dropped (after a change of management, say), and it's their continuing approval that reassures us about keeping a pub as a main entry for another year. Very important, though, are the reports they send us on pubs we don't know at all. It's from these new discoveries that we make up a shortlist, to be considered for possible inclusion as new main entries. The more people that report favourably on a new pub, the more likely it is to win a place on this shortlist – especially if some of the reporters belong to our hard core of about 600 trusted correspondents whose judgement we have learned to rely on. These are people who have each given us detailed comments on dozens of pubs, and shown that (when we ourselves know some of those pubs too) their judgement is closely in line with our own.

This brings us to the acid test. Each pub, before inclusion as a main entry, is inspected anonymously by one of the editorial team. They have to find some special quality that would make strangers enjoy visiting it. What often marks the pub out for special attention is good value food (and that might mean anything from a well made sandwich, with good fresh ingredients at a low price, to imaginative cooking outclassing most restaurants in the area). The drinks may be out of the ordinary – maybe several hundred whiskies, remarkable wine lists, interesting ciders, or a wide range of well kept real ales, possibly with some home-brewed, or bottled beers from all over the world. Perhaps there's a special appeal about it as a place to stay, with good bedrooms and obliging service. Maybe it's the building itself (from centuries-old parts of monasteries to extravagant Victorian gin-palaces), or its surroundings (lovely countryside, attractive waterside position, an extensive well kept garden), or what's in it (charming furnishings, extraordinary collections of bric-a-brac).

Above all, though, what makes the good pub is its atmosphere – you should be able to feel at home there, and feel not just that *you're* glad you've come but that *they're* glad you've come. A good landlord or landlady makes a huge difference here – they can make or break a pub.

It follows from this that a great many ordinary locals, perfectly good in their own right, don't earn a place in the *Guide*. What makes them attractive to their regular customers (an almost clubby chumminess) may even make strangers feel rather out-of-place.

Another important point is that there's not necessarily any link between charm and luxury. A basic unspoilt village tavern, with hard seats and a flagstone floor, may be worth travelling miles to find, while a deluxe pub-restaurant may not be worth crossing the street for. Landlords can't buy the Good Pub accolade by spending thousands on thickly padded banquettes, soft music and elaborate menus – they can only win it, by having a genuinely personal concern for both their customers and their pub.

Using the *Guide*

NEW FORMAT
This year you will notice that we have introduced a new format for the main entries, which we think will make the *Guide* easier to use. We hope these changes will make it easier for you to quickly decide if that particular pub is what you're looking for. We've broken the text down into three helpful segments: the banner gives a brief summary of what you might expect in that pub, the next part – the description – goes into more depth, and the new separate food section tells you about the style of cooking with examples of the sort of snack or meal on offer, with a price range for each course.

THE COUNTIES
England has been split alphabetically into counties. Each chapter starts by picking out the pubs that are currently doing best in the area, or are specially attractive for one reason or another.

The county boundaries we use are those for the administrative counties (not the old traditional counties, which were changed back in 1976). We have left the new unitary authorities within the counties that they formed part of until their creation in the most recent local government reorganisation. Metropolitan areas have been included in the counties around them – for example, Merseyside in Lancashire. And occasionally we have grouped counties together – for example, Rutland with Leicestershire, and Durham with Northumberland to make Northumbria. If in doubt, check the Contents.

Scotland, Wales and London have each been covered in single chapters. Pubs are listed alphabetically (except in London which is split into Central, East, North, South and West), under the name of the town or village where they are. If the village is so small that you probably wouldn't find it on a road map, we've listed it under the name of the nearest sizeable village or town. The maps use the same town and village names, and additionally include a few big cities that don't have any listed pubs – for orientation.

We list pubs in their true county, not their postal county. Just once or twice, when the village itself is in one county but the pub is just over the border in the next-door county, we have used the village county, not the pub one.

STARS ★
Really outstanding pubs are awarded a star, and in a few cases two: these are the aristocrats among pubs. The stars do NOT signify extra luxury or specially good food – in fact some of the pubs which appeal most distinctively and strongly of all are decidedly basic in terms of food and surroundings. The detailed description of each pub shows what its particular appeal is, and this is what the stars refer to.

FOOD AWARD 🍴
Pubs where food is quite outstanding.

STAY AWARD ⇥
Pubs that are good as places to stay at (obviously you can't expect the same level of luxury at £60 a head as you'd get for £100 a head). Pubs with bedrooms are marked on the maps as a dot within a square.

WINE AWARD ♀
Pubs with particularly enjoyable wines by the glass – often a good choice.

BEER AWARD 🍺
Pubs where the quality of the beer is quite exceptional, or pubs which keep a particularly interesting range of beers in good condition.

BARGAIN AWARD £
Pubs with decent snacks at £3.50 or less, or worthwhile main dishes at £6.50 or less.

RECOMMENDERS
At the end of each main entry we include the names of readers who have recently recommended that pub (unless they've asked us not to).

Important note: the description of the pub and the comments on it are our own and not the recommenders'; they are based on our own personal inspections and on later verification of facts with each pub. A good pub which has no reader recommenders, or one that we judge deserves to stay in the main entries despite a very recent management change includes the acronym BOB (buyer's own brand) as a recommender.

LUCKY DIPS
The Lucky Dip section at the end of each county chapter includes brief descriptions of pubs that have been recommended by readers in the year before the *Guide* goes to print and that we feel are worthy of inclusion. We do not include a pub unless readers' descriptions make the nature of the pub quite clear, and give us good grounds for trusting that other readers would be glad to know of the pub. A bare mention that food is served shouldn't be taken to imply a recommendation of the food. The same is true of accommodation and so forth. At the end of the entry we print the recommenders' names. BB means we have inspected a pub and found nothing against it and LYM means the pub was a main entry in a previous edition of the *Guide*. In both these cases, the description is our own; in others, it's based on the readers' reports. This year, we have deleted many previously highly rated pubs from the *Guide* simply because we have no very recent reports on them. This may well mean that we have left out some favourites – please tell us if we have!

LUCKY DIPS WITH ☆
Roughly speaking these pubs are as much worth considering as some of the main entries themselves.

All the Lucky Dips, but particularly the starred ones, are under consideration for inspection for a future edition so please let us have any comments you can make on them using the report forms in this *Guide*, by writing to us at The Good Pub Guide, FREEPOST TN1569, WADHURST, East Sussex TN5 7BR or contacting us through our website **www.goodguides.co.uk**.

LOCATING PUBS
To help readers who use digital mapping systems we include a **postcode** for every pub.

Pubs outside London are given a British Grid four-figure **map reference**. Where a pub is exceptionally difficult to find, we include a six-figure reference in the directions. The map number (main entries only) refers to the map in our *Guide*.

MOTORWAY PUBS
If a pub is within four or five miles of a motorway junction we give special directions for finding it from the motorway. The Special Interest Lists at the end of the book include a list of these pubs, motorway by motorway.

PRICES AND OTHER FACTUAL DETAILS
The *Guide* went to press during the summer of 2007, after each pub was sent a checking sheet to verify up-to-date food, drink and bedroom prices and other factual information. By the summer of 2008 prices are bound to have increased, but if you find a significantly different price please let us know.

Breweries or independent chains to which pubs are 'tied' are named at the beginning of the rubric after the food description of each main entry. That generally means the pub has to get most if not all of its drinks from that brewery or chain. If the brewery is not an independent one but just part of a combine, we name the combine in brackets. When the pub is tied, we have spelled out whether the landlord is a tenant, has the pub on a lease, or is a manager. Tenants and leaseholders of breweries generally have considerably greater freedom to do things their own way, and in particular are allowed to buy drinks including a beer from sources other than their tied brewery.

Free houses are pubs not tied to a brewery. In theory they can shop around but in practice many free houses have loans from the big brewers, on terms that bind them to sell those breweries' beers. So don't be too surprised to find that so-called free houses may be stocking a range of beers restricted to those from a single brewery.

Real ale is used by us to mean beer that has been maturing naturally in its cask. We do not count as real ale beer which has been pasteurised or filtered to remove its natural yeasts. If it is kept under a blanket of carbon dioxide to preserve it, we still generally mention it – as long as the pressure is too light for you to notice any extra fizz, it's hard to tell the difference. (For brevity, we use the expression 'under light blanket pressure' to cover such pubs; we do not include among them pubs where the blanket pressure is high enough to force the beer up from the cellar, as this does make it unnaturally fizzy.)

Other drinks We've also looked out particularly for pubs doing enterprising non-alcoholic drinks (including good tea or coffee), interesting spirits (especially malt whiskies), country wines, freshly squeezed juices, and good farm ciders.

Bar food usually refers to what is sold in the bar, we do not describe menus that are restricted to a separate restaurant. If we know that a pub serves sandwiches we say so – if you don't see them mentioned, assume you can't get them. Food listed is an example of the sort of thing you'd find served in the bar on a normal day and we try to indicate any difference we know of between lunchtime and evening.

Children If we don't mention children at all, assume that they are not welcome. All but one or two pubs allow children in their garden if they have one. 'Children welcome' means the pub has told us that it lets them in with no special restrictions. In other cases we report exactly what arrangements pubs say they make for children. However, we have to note that in readers' experience some pubs make restrictions that they haven't told us about (children only if eating, for example). If you come across this, please let us know, so that we can clarify with the pub concerned for the next edition. The absence of any reference to children in a Dip entry means we don't know either way. Children's Certificates exist, but in practice children are allowed into some part of most pubs in this *Guide* (there is no legal restriction on the movement of children over 14 in any pub). Children under 16 cannot have alcoholic drinks. Children aged 16 and 17 can drink beer, wine or cider with a meal if it is bought by an adult and they are accompanied by an adult.

Dogs If main entry licensees have told us they allow dogs in their pub or bedrooms we say so. Absence of reference to dogs means dogs are not welcome. If you take a dog into a pub you should have it on a lead. We also mention in the text any pub dogs or cats (or indeed other animals) that we've come across ourselves, or heard about from readers.

Parking If we know there is a problem with parking we say so; otherwise assume there is a car park.

Credit cards We say if a pub does **not** accept them; some which do may put a surcharge on credit card bills, to cover charges made by the card company. We also say if we know that a pub tries to retain customers' credit cards while they are eating. This is a reprehensible practice, and if a pub tries it on you, please tell them that all banks and card companies frown on it – and please let us know the pub's name, so that we can warn readers in future editions.

Telephone numbers are given for all main entries that are not ex-directory.

Opening hours are for summer; we say if we know of differences in winter, or on particular days of the week. In the country, many pubs may open rather later and close earlier than their details show (if you come across this, please let us know – with details). Pubs are allowed to stay open all day if licensed to do so. However, outside cities many english and welsh pubs close during the afternoon. We'd be grateful to hear of any differences from the hours we quote.

Bedroom prices normally include full english breakfasts (if available), VAT and any automatic service charge. If we give just one price, it is the total price for two people sharing a double or twin-bedded room for one night. Otherwise, prices before the / are for single occupancy, prices after it for double. A capital B against the price means that it includes a private bathroom, a capital S a private shower. As all this coding packs in quite a lot of information, some examples may help to explain it:

£70	on its own means that's the total bill for two people sharing a twin or double room without private bath; the pub has no rooms with private bath, and a single person might have to pay that full price.
£70B	means exactly the same – but all the rooms have a private bath
£65(£70B)	means rooms with private baths cost £5 extra
£40/£65(£70B)	means the same as the last example, but also shows that there are single rooms for £40, none of which has a private bathroom

If there's a choice of rooms at different prices, we normally give the cheapest. If there are seasonal price variations, we give the summer price (the highest). During the winter, many inns, particularly in the country, will have special cheaper rates. And at other times, especially in holiday areas, you will often find prices cheaper if you stay for several nights. On weekends, inns that aren't in obvious weekending areas often have bargain rates for two- or three-night stays.

Meal times Bar food is commonly served from 12-2 and 7-9, at least from Monday to Saturday (food service often stops a bit earlier on Sundays). If we don't give a time against the *Bar food* note at the bottom of a main entry you should be able to get bar food at those times. However, we do spell out the times if we know that bar food service starts after 12.15 or after 7.15; if it stops before 2 or before 8.45; or if food is served for significantly longer than usual (say, till 2.30 or 9.45).

Though we note days when pubs have told us they don't do food you should play safe on Sundays, and check before you visit. Also, out-of-the-way pubs often cut down on cooking during the week, especially the early part of the week, if they're quiet – as they tend to be, except at holiday times. Please let us know if you find anything different from what we say!

Disabled access Deliberately, we do not ask pubs about this, as their answers would not give a reliable picture of how easy access is. Instead, we depend on readers' direct experience. If you are able to give us help about this, we would be particularly grateful for your reports.

SAT NAV AND ELECTRONIC ROUTE PLANNING
Garmin now sell a version of their Nüvi 310 sat nav device loaded with *The Good Pub Guide*. It will tell you the nearest pubs to your current location, or you can get it to track down a particular pub, and it will then direct you to your choice. Readers using a trial version found it led them painlessly to even the most remote Lucky Dips. Computer users may also like to know of a route-finding programme, Microsoft® AutoRoute™, which shows the location of *Good Pub Guide* pubs on detailed maps, works out the quickest routes for journeys, adds diversions to nearby pubs – and shows our text entries for those pubs on screen.

OUR WEBSITE (www.goodguides.co.uk)
Our Internet website uses material from *The Good Pub Guide* in a way that gives people who do not yet know it at least a taste of it. It includes a map to find each pub, and you

can use it to send us reports – this way they get virtually immediate attention. We are hoping for major developments to the site in the forthcoming year.

CHANGES DURING THE YEAR – PLEASE TELL US

Changes are inevitable during the course of the year. Landlords change, and so do their policies. We very much hope that you will find everything just as we say but if not please let us know, using the tear-out card in the middle of the book, the report forms at the back of the book, or just a letter. You don't need a stamp: the address is The Good Pub Guide, FREEPOST TN1569, WADHURST, East Sussex TN5 7BR. As we have said, you can also send us reports by using our website **www.goodguides.co.uk**

Authors' Acknowledgements

This *Guide* would be impossible to produce without the hugely generous help we have from the many thousands of readers who report to us on the pubs they visit, often in great detail. For the special help they have given us this year, we are deeply grateful to the Didler, Joe Green, Steve Whalley, N R White, Ian Phillips, Guy Vowles, Tracey and Stephen Groves, Kevin Thorpe, Peter Meister, Paul Humphreys, George Atkinson, Michael Dandy, Dr and Mrs M E Wilson, Phil Bryant, Bruce Bird, Keith and Sue Ward, Gerry and Rosemary Dobson, Susan and John Douglas, Colin Moore, Michael Doswell, W W Burke, Martin and Karen Wake, Roland and Wendy Chalu, Phil and Jane Hodson, Michael and Jenny Back, Dennis Jenkin, Joan and Michel Hooper-Immins, JJW, CMW, Donna Madeloff, Roger Huggins, Ewan McCall, Tom McLean, Dave Irving, Ann and Colin Hunt, Pete Baker, Howard Dell, LM, Phil and Sally Gorton, Tony and Wendy Hobden, John Wooll, Reg Fowle, Helen Rickwood, Val and Alan Green, Simon and Mandy King, Derek and Sylvia Stephenson, Rona Murdoch, Richard Fendick, Chris Flynn, David and Sue Smith, Andy and Jill Kassube, Andy and Claire Barker, Brian and Anna Marsden, Tom and Jill Jones, David Handforth, Dr and Mrs C W Thomas, Keith and Chris O'Neill, Bob and Margaret Holder, Wendy Jones, JCW, Nick Holding, Tom Evans, Comus and Sarah Elliott, Mike Gorton, Barry and Anne, Paul and Ursula Randall, Roger and Lesley Everett, Gordon Ormondroyd, Phyl and Jack Street, John Saville, Tony and Jill Radnor, John Beeken, Penny Simpson, Dr and Mrs A K Clarke, Michael Butler, Liz and Brian Barnard, David Barnes, R T and J C Moggridge, Simon Collett-Jones, B and M Kendall, Margaret Dickinson, KC, MLR, Charles and Pauline Stride, Tony Hobden, Alan and Eve Harding, Jeremy King, Alan Thwaite, Neil and Anita Christopher, M G Hart, Edward Mirzoeff, Ted George, Richard and Jean Green, Terry Buckland, Rob and Catherine Dunster, Denys Gueroult, Les and Sandra Brown, Heather and Dick Martin, Ross Balaam, Bill Strang, Stuart Pearson, Clive and Fran Dutson, Mike and Sue Loseby, Paul A Moore, Dennis Jones, Brian and Janet Ainscough, Carol and Colin Broadbent, Dave Braisted, WW, Julian and Janet Dearden, Lynda and Trevor Smith, MDN, P and J Shapley, John Evans, David Crook, Dick and Madeleine Brown, John Tav, Mike Ridgway, Sarah Miles, Chris and Ann Coy, Michael and Alison Sandy, Mayur Shah, Tina and David Woods-Taylor, Meg and Colin Hamilton, Noel Grundy, Jenny and Brian Seller, DWAJ and P and D Carpenter.

Warm thanks too to John Holliday of Trade Wind Technology, who built and looks after our database.

Alisdair Aird and Fiona Stapley

Authors
Acknowledgments

England

Bedfordshire

It's been very rewarding watching the huge improvements that have taken place during recent times in the quality of food served at pubs in Bedfordshire. The last few years have each seen us able to add one or two good new entries, to what was not so long ago a rather lacklustre county for dining. What's more, pub food prices here are typically a little lower than prices in many other areas for similar quality. One doesn't have to go too far back in the *Guide's* history to years when there wasn't really a proper competition for the Bedfordshire Dining Pub Award. This year, for the first time, we were happy to face a difficult decision. The cheery Plough at Bolnhurst, well run and stylish, with thoughtfully sourced ingredients and sensibly imaginative menu, put up a real challenge, but for one year more at least, the Hare & Hounds at Old Warden is the best in the county for a celebratory meal out. Good news, too, is that after a short blip in performance, the civilised Knife & Cleaver at Houghton Conquest has settled down enough to earn back its Food Award. A newcomer which looks particularly promising for the future is the pretty little Swan at Radwell, and the Birch on the edge of Woburn is a smart place for a really good meal. For a jolly enjoyable but more pubby meal the comfortable Falcon at Bletsoe is the place to head for, and the new licensees at the Crown in Northill make it one to watch. The companionable Engineers Arms in Henlow deserves a special mention for its impressive range of drinks, which includes ten real ales. Prices here are relatively good, too. The county as a whole tends to be rather more expensive than the national average for drinks. The main local brewer, Charles Wells, has merged its brewing activities with the London firm Youngs, and now produces not only their beers as well, but Courage ales as well. Suffolk-based Greene King also has a strong presence in the county. Finally, three pubs to look out for particularly in the Lucky Dip section at the end of the chapter: the Black Horse at Ireland, Live & Let Live at Pegsdon, and Three Fyshes at Turvey, all inspected and approved by us.

BIDDENHAM   TL0249   MAP 5

Three Tuns

Village signposted from A428 just W of Bedford; MK40 4BD

Homely thatched village pub with fairly priced traditional food, and good children's play area in big garden

The pleasant low-beamed lounge here has wheelback chairs round dark wood tables, window seats and pews on a red turkey carpet, and country paintings. The green-carpeted oak panelled public bar has photographs of local sports teams, also darts, skittles, cards and dominoes; piped music. On handpump, Greene King Abbot is kept under light blanket pressure alongside a guest such as Brains Rev James. There are seats in the attractively sheltered spacious garden, lots of picnic-sets on a big decked terrace, and swings and a climbing frame.

🍴 Served in generous helpings, enjoyable food runs from soup, sandwiches and ploughman's, to steak and kidney pie, poached salmon, and lamb shank in red wine and mint sauce with horseradish mash. *Starters/Snacks: £4.00 to £6.50. Main Courses: £7.00 to £9.50. Puddings: £4.00*

Greene King ~ Tenant Kevin Bolwell ~ Real ale ~ Bar food (not Sun evening) ~ (01234) 354847 ~ Children in dining room and lounge bar ~ Dogs allowed in bar ~ Open 11.30-2.30, 6-11; 12-3, 7-10.30 Sun

Recommended by John Taylor, Mr and Mrs John Taylor, Colin and Janet Roe, John Saville, M and GR

BLETSOE
TL0157   MAP 5

Falcon �

Rushden Road (A6 N of Bedford); MK44 1QN

Cheerfully relaxed beamed old place with kind service, good value tasty food, a decent range of drinks, and a nice riverside garden

The welcoming carpeted bar has low beams and joists, a pleasant mix of sturdy dark tables, seating that ranges from cushioned wall/window seats to high-backed settles, and in winter a couple of open fires – in summer the brick inglenook on the left is instead decorated with copperware and fat church candles. A little side snug on the right has a couple of chairs and stools, and through on the left is a quiet and comfortable beamed and timbered dining room. They have Wells & Youngs Eagle and Bombardier on handpump, with a guest such as Adnams, a decent choice of just over a dozen wines by the glass, and good coffee; daily papers and unobtrusive piped music. French doors lead out on to a sheltered terrace overlooking the slow River Ouse, and a big garden which has plenty of trees and shrubs, and perhaps strolling peafowl. Picnic-sets in the main garden area include one stone table and seats, and a couple of teak seats on a lower stretch of grass, which works its way down to the water.

🍴 Besides good lunchtime sandwiches and ploughman's, the menu (on a lectern in the bar) includes pubby standards such as steak and kidney pie or cod and chips, along with just a few dishes like seared scallops with bacon and roasted bass. Puddings are fairly traditional, and they've a thoughtfully annotated english cheeseboard. *Starters/Snacks: £3.95 to £6.95. Main Courses: £8.75 to £14.95. Puddings: £4.35 to £5.95*

Charles Wells ~ Tenants Jonathan Seaton-Reid, Lisa Sutcliffe and Lianne Poole ~ Real ale ~ Bar food ~ Restaurant ~ (01234) 781222 ~ Children welcome in dining areas till 8pm ~ Jazz bank hol Mons ~ Open 12-3, 6-11; 12-11 Sat, Sun

Recommended by Michael Dandy

BOLNHURST
TL0858   MAP 5

Plough ♟

Kimbolton Road; MK44 2EX

Stylish conversion of fine old building; thriving atmosphere, charming staff, very good food and drinks (a lot of thought goes into both), and attractive garden

Helpful staff cope happily with the buzzing crowd that fills this very well run place. The ancient building was cleverly and painstakingly restored some time ago after a fire, with fine old timbers set off nicely by the light and airy contemporary décor, and you can see into the smart stainless kitchen. An interesting range of drinks includes Batemans XB, Potton Village Bike and a guest such as Caledonian Deuchars IPA on handpump, a very good wine list including well over a dozen by the glass, home-made lemonade (in summer) and tomato juice, and local apple juice. The lovely tree-shaded garden looks on to a pond where you can still see the remains of the moat that used to surround the pub.

🍴 Beautifully presented inventive food (from a well balanced changing menu) is prepared using thoughtfully sourced ingredients, and served with complimentary home-made bread. Dishes work their way up from tasty canapés such as devils on horseback to starters such as crab risotto with chilli and lemon or beef carpaccio, and main courses which range from sausage and mash to spinach, mascarpone and black truffle lasagne or belly of pork with roast summer squash, pak choi, ginger and sesame; imaginative puddings and very good cheese platter; reasonably priced set lunch menu too. *Starters/Snacks: £4.50 to £8.50. Main Courses: £9.95 to £17.50. Puddings: £4.95 to £5.95*

Free house ~ Licensees Martin and Jayne Lee and Michael Moscrop ~ Real ale ~ Bar food (12-2, 6.30-9.30) ~ Restaurant ~ (01234) 376274 ~ Children welcome ~ Dogs allowed in bar ~ Open 12-3(4 Sun), 6.30-11; closed Sun evening, Mon and first two weeks in Jan

Recommended by Michael Sargent, Ryta Lyndley, Eithne Dandy, John Saul, John and Gillian Browne, Dr Brian and Mrs Anne Hamilton, Ken Carr-Brion, K Carr-Brion

BROOM   TL1743   MAP 5

Cock ★ £

High Street; from A1 opposite northernmost Biggleswade turn-off follow Old Warden 3, Aerodrome 2 signpost, and take first left signposted Broom; SG18 9NA

Simple and well loved unchanging village green pub with straightforward tasty food, beers tapped straight from the cask; garden, and caravanning and camping facilities

Little changes from year to year at this small old-fashioned pub. There's no bar counter, so the Greene King IPA, Abbot and Ruddles County are tapped straight from casks by the cellar steps off a central corridor. Original latch doors lead from one cosy little room to the next (four in all), inside which you'll find warming winter open fires, low ochre ceilings, stripped panelling, and farmhouse tables and chairs on antique tiles; piped (perhaps classical) music, darts and board games. There are picnic-sets and flower tubs on the terrace by the back lawn.

🍴 **Well liked bar food includes sandwiches, soup, ploughman's, scampi, vegetarian curry and filled yorkshire pudding.** *Starters/Snacks: £3.25 to £3.95. Main Courses: £5.95 to £8.95. Puddings: £3.45 to £3.85*

Greene King ~ Tenants Gerry and Jean Lant ~ Real ale ~ Bar food (12-2.30, 7-9; not Sun evening) ~ Restaurant ~ (01767) 314411 ~ Children welcome ~ Dogs allowed in bar ~ Open 12-3(4 Sat), 6-11; 12-4, 7-10.30 Sun

Recommended by Derek and Sylvia Stephenson, Pete Baker, R T and J C Moggridge, Mrs Jane Kingsbury, John Robertson, Michael Dandy, the Didler

HENLOW   TL1738   MAP 5

Engineers Arms 🍺 £
A6001 S of Biggleswade; High Street; SG16 6AA

Good choice of drinks including fabulous range of up to nine beautifully kept guest ales at charmingly spick and span traditional pub; snacks (all day) only

Besides their house beer (Everards Tiger), real ales will probably be from smaller far-flung brewers such as Archers, Buntingford, Cottage, Newby Wyke and Potton. They also stock four ciders and a perry, many belgian bottled beers, decent wines by the glass, a good value wine of the month by the bottle and Tyrrells crisps; good coffee. If you're struggling to choose from this great range, the helpful staff are very knowledgeable. The pub holds quarterly bank holiday beer festivals, and a bigger one in mid-October. The comfortable green-carpeted front room has lots of old local photographs on its green fleur-de-lys wallpaper, tidily kept and interesting bric-a-brac collections, traditional green-cushioned wall seats, settles and other dark seats, armchair-style bar stools, daily papers and a good log fire. A small tiled inner area has wide-screen sports TV, and beyond is a step up to another comfortable carpeted area, with a second TV, juke box, silenced fruit machine, board games and other games such as table football; the good-natured spaniel is called Chico. The back terrace has picnic-sets and heaters.

Smoking is not allowed inside any pub.

🍽 **Light snacks, including sausage rolls, pies and pizzas, are served most of the time they are open.** *Starters/Snacks: £1.00 to £2.40*

Free house ~ Licensees Kevin Machin and Claire Sturgeon ~ Real ale ~ Bar food (snacks when open) ~ No credit cards ~ (01462) 812284 ~ Children welcome in back room till 8pm ~ Dogs allowed in bar ~ Live blues Fri ~ Open 12-midnight(1 Fri, Sat, no admission after 12)

Recommended by Bruce Bird, Michael Dandy

HOUGHTON CONQUEST   TL0441   MAP 5
Knife & Cleaver 🍽 ♀
Between B530 (old A418) and A6, S of Bedford; MK45 3LA

Nice-looking comfortably civilised 17th-c dining pub with thoughtfully prepared food, a good range of drinks, including lots of wines by the glass, and friendly service

---

The rather lovely dark panelling in the bar here is reputed to have come from nearby ruined Houghton House. Maps, drawings and old documents on the walls, as well as lamps, comfy seating and a blazing winter fire add a cosy feel. An airy white-walled conservatory restaurant has rugs on the tiled floor and lots of hanging plants. There's also a family room, and tables on a terrace alongside a neatly kept attractive garden; unobtrusive piped music. Batemans XB and Potton Village Bike are on handpump alongside Stowford Press farm cider, they've around 30 good wines by the glass, and over 20 well aged malt whiskies.

🍽 **With emphasis on carefully sourced good ingredients (some of the vegetables come from the family garden), the food here is very well prepared, and they make their own bread. You may have to book, and do be aware that they may not serve bar meals if the restaurant is full on Saturday evenings and Sunday lunchtimes. The seasonally changing menu might include smoked queen scallop chowder, fried veal kidneys with toasted onion bread and creamy mustard sauce and antipasti to start, with main courses such as minute steak baguette, mushroom, cheese and hazelnut parcels with sweet red pepper sauce, grilled bass with sweetcorn and chive fritters and yoghurt and ginger sauce, and venison meatballs with redcurrant and bacon sauce and noodles. Puddings could be orange treacle tart, baked date sponge or apple amaretto sponge with meringue topping, also home-made ice-creams.** *Starters/Snacks: £4.00 to £7.95. Main Courses: £6.95 to £8.95. Puddings: £4.25*

Free house ~ Licensees David and Pauline Loom ~ Real ale ~ Bar food (12-2.30(2 Sat), 7-9.30; not Sun evening; see note in text about weekends) ~ Restaurant ~ (01234) 740387 ~ Children welcome ~ Dogs allowed in bedrooms ~ Open 12-2.30(2 Sat, 3 Sun), 6.30-11; closed Sun evening, 27-30 Dec ~ Bedrooms: £59B/£74B

Recommended by Michael Dandy, Dr and Mrs Michael Smith, Lyndsey Millar, Mr and Mrs D S Price, Mr and Mrs John Taylor, Roger and Lesley Everett

KEYSOE   TL0763   MAP 5
Chequers
Pertenhall Road, Brook End (B660); MK44 2HR

Down-to-earth village local with good value simple but tasty food, and garden with play area

---

Two simple beamed rooms at this homely yellow and cherry brown painted house (usually fairly quiet at lunchtime unless a group is in) are divided by a stone-pillared fireplace. Carpets and furnishings are fairly well worn and piped local radio or music lends a homely 1960s air. Fullers London Pride is served from a handpump on the stone bar counter, they have a few malt whiskies, and their short wine list is very reasonably priced. Tables and chairs on the back terrace look over the garden which has a play tree and swings.

🍽 **The straightforward bar food takes in pub standards such as sandwiches, ploughman's, chilli and steaks, with a few blackboard specials.** *Starters/Snacks: £4.00 to £5.00. Main Courses: £7.00 to £9.00*

Free house ~ Licensee Jeffrey Kearns ~ Real ale ~ Bar food ~ No credit cards ~ (01234) 708678 ~ Children welcome ~ Open 11.30-2.30, 6.30-11; 12-2.30, 7-10.30 Sun; closed Tues

Recommended by Michael and Jenny Back, R T and J C Moggridge, JJW, CMW, Mr and Mrs John Taylor

MILTON BRYAN
SP9730   MAP 4

Red Lion ♀
Toddington Road, off B528 S of Woburn; MK17 9HS

Beamed pub quite near Woburn Abbey and Safari Park; pretty views from garden

This attractive old pub is well positioned in a pretty little country village. In summer, a plethora of carefully tended floral hanging baskets makes a spectacular show, and there are plenty of tables, chairs and picnic-sets out on the terrace and lawn, which looks across to a delightful row of thatched black and white timbered cottages. The immaculately kept beamed bar area has cream-coloured walls, some exposed brickwork, polished wood and part flagstoned floors, with cheery fresh flowers on the round wooden tables. Greene King IPA, Abbot and Old Speckled Hen are kept under a light blanket pressure, and ten wines and a local apple juice are sold by the glass.

🍴 **Using some thoughtfully sourced ingredients, bar food includes sandwiches, thai fishcakes, ploughman's, caramelised onion and cherry tomato tartlet with taleggio cheese, toulouse sausage and crème fraîche mash, steak and kidney pudding, smoked haddock fillet on cabbage with poached egg and butter sauce, and puddings such as summer fruit pudding or warm chocolate fudge brownie with preserved cherries and mascarpone cream.** *Starters/Snacks: £4.95 to £7.95. Main Courses: £8.50 to £15.00. Puddings: £4.50 to £5.50*

Greene King ~ Lease Paul Ockleford ~ Real ale ~ Bar food (12-2.30(3 Sun), 7-9.30) ~ Restaurant ~ (01525) 210044 ~ Children welcome ~ Open 11.30-3, 6-11; 12-4 Sun; closed Mon in winter, Sun evening

Recommended by Michael Dandy, Andrea and Guy Bradley, Dr S Lightfoot, Mrs Nading Ridgeway, F D Smith, N R White, John Saville

NORTHILL
TL1446   MAP 5

Crown
Ickwell Road; village signposted from B658 W of Biggleswade; SG18 9AA

Prettily situated village pub with nice old interior, warmly relaxed atmosphere, enjoyable food, and a big garden

Just across from the church, in a green and peaceful village, this old pub has large tables under cocktail parasols out in front looking over the village pond. The smallish bar has a big open fire, flagstones, heavy low beams and comfortable bay window seats. Greene King IPA, Abbot and Old Speckled Hen and a guest such as Highwood Bomber County are served on handpump from the copper-topped counter. On the left is a small dining area, while on the right, the airy main dining room has elegantly laid tables on bare boards, with steps up to a smaller more intimate side room. The atmosphere throughout is warm and relaxed with friendly service and fairly unobtrusive piped music. A sheltered side terrace (with picnic-sets) opens into a very large garden with a few widely spaced canopied tables, plenty of trees and shrubs, a good play area, and masses of room for children to run around.

🍴 **Bar food includes a sound range of dishes from sandwiches (lunchtimes only), sausage and mash, beef stew and dumplings, duck in oriental spices and calves liver with smoked bacon to daily specials such as seafood tagliatelle and lemon peppered pork steak.** *Starters/Snacks: £3.95 to £5.95. Main Courses: £7.95 to £9.95. Puddings: £4.50*

Greene King ~ Tenant Kevin Blois ~ Real ale ~ Bar food (12-2.30(3 Sun), 6.30-9.30; not Sun evening) ~ Restaurant ~ (01767) 627337 ~ Children welcome away from main bar ~ Dogs allowed in bar ~ Open 11.30-3, 6-11; 11.30-midnight Sat; 11.30-11 Sun; 11.30-4, 7-midnight(11 Sun) weekends winter

Recommended by Michael Dandy, Pete Baker

OLD WARDEN

TL1343   MAP 5

Hare & Hounds 🍴 ♀

Village signposted off A600 S of Bedford and B658 W of Biggleswade; SG18 9HQ

BEDFORDSHIRE DINING PUB OF THE YEAR

Comfortably elegant dining pub with delicious food served by thoughtful well turned out staff; lovely gardens

Painted in cosy reds and creams and rambling around a central servery, four beautifully kept beamed rooms have dark standing timbers, upholstered armchairs and sofas on stripped flooring, light wood tables and coffee tables, a woodburning stove in an inglenook fireplace and fresh flowers on the bar. Prints and photographs displayed on the walls depict historic aircraft in the famous Shuttleworth Collection just up the road. Courage Directors and Wells & Youngs Eagle and Bombardier are on handpump, with eight or so wines by the glass including some from a local vineyard. Although the accent is very much on dining, you can pop in for just a drink; piped music. The village and pub form part of the Shuttleworth Estate which was built about 200 years ago in a swiss style, and a glorious sloping garden (with tables on a terrace) which stretches up to pine woods behind the pub dates back to the same period and was desiged in the same style. Though there's an ample car park, you may need to use the village hall parking as an overflow. There are some substantial walks nearby.

🍴 Food here is beautifully prepared and presented. They make an effort to use local and even organic ingredients (such as pork from the Shuttleworth Estate), the breads and ice-cream are home made, and they sell a small range of home-made larder goods. The changing menus might include whitebait, rabbit and pistachio ravioli, salmon tagliatelle, braised wild venison with sausage dumplings, mackerel fillet with roast garlic polenta and steak with rocket and basil salad, with puddings such as warm bakewell tart or vanilla crème brûlée, and british cheeses. *Starters/Snacks: £3.95 to £6.95. Main Courses: £9.95 to £16.95. Puddings: £5.95*

Charles Wells ~ Lease Jane Hasler ~ Real ale ~ Bar food (12-2(3 Sun), 6.30-9; not Sun evening) ~ Restaurant ~ (01767) 627225 ~ Children welcome in family room ~ Dogs allowed in bar ~ Open 12-3, 6-11; 12-10.30 Sun; closed Mon except bank hols

Recommended by David and Ruth Shillitoe, Geoff and Carol Thorp, John and Patricia White, Michael Dandy, Peter and Margaret Glenister, Mr and Mrs D S Price, Alain and Rose Foote, P Waterman

RADWELL

TL0057   MAP 4

Swan ♀

Village signposted off A6 Bedford—Rushden; Felmersham Road; MK43 7HS

Small thatched dining pub, friendly and comfortably unpretentious, with enterprising snacks and meals

The friendly young couple who took over in 2006 have given the low-ceilinged flagstoned bar an appealingly simple décor; it has bucket seats around just three tables, a coal-effect fire, Wells & Youngs Eagle and perhaps one or two related guest beers such as Special or Courage Directors on handpump, and a dozen good wines by the glass. There's usually an attractive flower arrangement on the counter, and may be piped music. Light and airy bare-boards black-beamed rooms on either side have fresh modern prints. It's usually quiet at lunchtime, but busy on weekend evenings – best to book ahead for Saturday. The pleasantly informal garden, with shrubs and a weeping willow, has picnic-sets and a play area – as well as a productive vegetable patch; attractive village.

🍴 Warm filled lunchtime ciabattas and bagels, starters such as lemon grass king prawn skewers on noodles with sweet chilli sauce or duck and port pâté, main courses such as emmental and mushroom ravioli in a mediterranean sauce, smoked haddock and spring onion fishcakes with pesto mayonnaise, lamb steaks in cranberry and balsamic marinade, and 14oz rib-eye steak, and puddings such as bread and butter pudding or rhubarb and apple crumble. *Starters/Snacks: £3.95 to £5.95. Main Courses: £7.45 to £25.00. Puddings: £3.95 to £5.95*

Charles Wells ~ Tenants Kevin and Julie Tyrrell ~ Real ale ~ Bar food ~ Restaurant ~ (01234) 781351 ~ Children welcome ~ Open 12-3, 7-11.30; 12-4, 7-10.30 Sun; closed Mon
Recommended by Mr and Mrs G Swire, John Saville, Michael Dandy

RISELEY
TL0462   MAP 5

Fox & Hounds
High Street; village signposted off A6 and B660 N of Bedford; MK44 1DT

Steaks are the speciality at this cheery bustling pub, though other dishes are available; decent drinks range; pleasant garden

A relaxing lounge area, with comfortable leather chesterfields, lower tables and wing chairs, contrasts with the more traditional pub furniture spread among timber uprights under the heavy low beams; unobtrusive piped classical or big band piped music. A decent range of drinks takes in Wells & Youngs Eagle and Bombardier on handpump, bin-end wines and a range of malts and cognacs. Service is normally very attentive and friendly, but it does get busy, and, as they don't take bookings on Saturday night you may have to wait for your table and food. An attractively decked terrace with wooden tables and chairs has outside heating, and the pleasant garden has shrubs and a pergola.

🍴 **You get to choose your own piece of steak here (you pay by weight), and you can then watch it cooked on an open grill. If you don't want steak, other good food (listed on blackboards) might include parsnip and ginger soup, ploughman's, steak and stilton pie, salmon in champagne sauce, and puddings such as jam roly poly or spotted dick and custard. Even if you don't see anything you fancy, it's worth asking as they're very obliging and will try to cope with particular food requests.** *Starters/Snacks: £3.25 to £5.50. Main Courses: £6.95 to £16.20. Puddings: £3.75*

Charles Wells ~ Lease Jan and Lynne Zielinski ~ Real ale ~ Bar food ~ Restaurant ~ (01234) 708240 ~ Children welcome ~ Dogs allowed in bar ~ Open 11.30-2.30, 6.30-11; 12-3, 7-10.30 Sun
Recommended by Michael Dandy, Philip Denton, Michael Sargent

STANBRIDGE
SP9623   MAP 4

Five Bells
Station Road, at junction with A505 – and pub signposted off A5 N of Dunstable; LU7 9JF

Big beamed place with comfortable modern interior, large well tended garden and decent food

This cream-fronted pub, with some striking grey woodwork, appears to be a perfectly traditional pub from the outside, but inside it has been comprehensively updated with a stylish, contemporary look. The very low exposed old beams are complemented by careful spotlighting, rugs on wooden floors, armchairs and sofas and neatly polished tables. An elegantly airy restaurant leads into a large garden which has plenty of good wooden tables and chairs, and big perfectly mown lawns with fruit trees. They offer about ten wines by the glass, as well as Fullers Discovery and London Pride which are served on handpump; one reader found the piped music obtrusive.

🍴 **Very good bar food might include sandwiches (not Sunday), tagliatelle with grilled cajun chicken breast and arrabiata sauce, vegetable lasagne, beef and ale pie and grilled bass with herb butter, and puddings such as chocolate brownie or pecan pie.** *Starters/Snacks: £3.75 to £5.50. Main Courses: £7.55 to £15.25. Puddings: £4.95*

Fullers ~ Manager Laura Jones ~ Real ale ~ Bar food (12-9.30(9 Sun)) ~ Restaurant ~ (01525) 210224 ~ Children welcome ~ Open 12-midnight (10.30 Sun)
Recommended by Gerry and Rosemary Dobson, David and Ruth Shillitoe, Michael Dandy, Dave Braisted

Tipping is not normal for bar meals, and not usually expected.

STEPPINGLEY   TL0135   MAP 5

French Horn ♀
Village signposted off A507 just N of Flitwick; Church End; MK45 5AU

Modish leather furniture in minimalist open plan exposed beam interior, short choice of elaborate snack meals in the bar, lots of wines by the glass, garden with good children's play area

---

Going into this old pub, snuggled down below the quiet village's church, brings a real surprise. Yes, there are the low heavy beams you'd expect, the flagstones and the inglenook fireplace (with a solid fuel stove), and staff are friendly and interested in the proper old-fashioned way. But the style of the place is thoroughly up to date, with big brown leather bucket armchairs, comfortable bar stools to match, squishy leather sofas in a jungly back corner of lilies and house plants, and a bright bare-boards dining area with a couple of big abstracts on plain cream walls. They have Greene King IPA and a guest on handpump, around 52 wines by the glass; piped music and TV for major sporting events only. The little public bar on the left is a nice exercise in modernity, too, with its minimalist décor and admirably blocky dark seats and tables. There are tables outside front and back, with a good children's play area at the back, and this is fairly handy for Woburn.

🍴 **They serve only light but interesting snacks such as soup, fried pigeon breast with puy lentils and poached quails egg, tartare of salmon, seared scottish scallops and a range of filled ciabattas or sandwiches in the bar, with a more extensive (not cheap) restaurant menu.** *Starters/Snacks: £5.50 to £8.95. Puddings: £6.95*

Greene King ~ Lease Gary McCarthy ~ Real ale ~ Bar food (12-3, 6.30-9.30; 12-4 Sun) ~ Restaurant ~ (01525) 712051 ~ Children welcome ~ Open 12-3, 5.30-11; 12-midnight Sat; 12-10.30 (may close Sun evening in winter) Sun

Recommended by Geoff and Carol Thorp, Michael Dandy

WOBURN   SP9433   MAP 4

Birch ♀
3.5 miles from M1 junction 13; follow Woburn signs via A507 and A4012, then in village turn right and head out on A5130 (Newport Road); MK17 9HX

Well run stylishly upscale dining establishment right in Woburn, focus on good imaginative food, good wines and attentive service

---

Modern prints on cream walls and handsome flower arrangements decorate the bar, which loops around the front servery and is furnished with soft brown leather sofas, bar stools and deep armchairs on good dark hardwood flooring. The carefully lit back part consists of an extensive and comfortable dining area, the central part of which is given an airy conservatory feel by its ceramic tile floor, lightly ragged plank panelling and glazed pitched roof, with a step up either side to carpeted or bare-boards sections with attractive artwork on their soft canary walls; unobtrusive piped music and daily papers. They keep a good range of interesting wines by the glass as well as Adnams and Fullers London Pride on handpump. Service by neatly dressed staff is helpful and efficient. There are tables out on a sheltered deck.

🍴 **The changing menu might include prawn, crab and dill tortellini with lemon grass cream, rocket, tomato and parmesan risotto, smoked haddock with poached egg, spinach and hollandaise, battered fish of the day, or roast rump of lamb with rosemary potato cake.** *Starters/Snacks: £4.95 to £7.25. Main Courses: £9.95 to £14.50. Puddings: £5.50*

Free house ~ Licensee Mark Campbell ~ Real ale ~ Bar food (12-2.30, 6-10) ~ Restaurant ~ (01525) 290295 ~ Children welcome ~ Open 11.30-11; 12-5 Sun; closed Sun evening

Recommended by Michael Dandy, Michael Sargent, Mr and Mrs C Prentis

LUCKY DIP

Besides the fully inspected pubs, you might like to try these Lucky Dips recommended to us and described by readers (if you do, please send us reports: www.goodguides.co.uk).

AMPTHILL [TL0338]
Prince of Wales MK45 2NB [Bedford St (B540 N from central crossroads)]: Good imaginative food, Wells & Youngs Eagle and Bombardier, good choice of wines by the glass, cheerful and helpful staff, small bar with easy chairs and settees, larger flagstoned dining room, contemporary décor; piped music *(Stephen Cavender, Michael Dandy)*

BEDFORD [TL0550]
Park MK40 2PF [Park Ave/Kimbolton Rd]: Large modernised pub with mix of furnishings inc leather sofas in partly flagstoned linked areas, Wells & Youngs Eagle and Bombardier, good coffee, daily papers, conservatory eating area; piped music; sizeable garden with tables on decking, open all day *(Eithne Dandy)*

BROMHAM [TL0050]
Swan MK43 8LS [Bridge End; nr A428, 2 miles W of Bedford]: Comfortable beamed dining pub, relaxed atmosphere, wide choice from sandwiches to seafood specials, good separate restaurant menu, quick friendly service, well kept Greene King IPA and Abbot, good choice of wines by the glass, evening log fire, lots of pictures, locals' bar; children welcome, disabled access, picnic-sets out by car park *(Michael Tack)*

CLOPHILL [TL0838]
Stone Jug MK45 4BY [N on A6 from A507 roundabout, after 200 yds 2nd turn on right into Back St]: Secluded stone-built local, cosy and welcoming, with good value lunchtime food from sandwiches and baked potatoes up, well kept B&T Shefford, Courage Directors or John Smiths and interesting changing ales, pleasantly unpretentious comfortable bar with family area and darts in small games extension; piped music; small pretty back terrace, roadside picnic-sets too *(Michael Dandy, Geoff and Carol Thorp)*

EVERSHOLT [SP9832]
Green Man MK17 9DU [Church End]: Refurbished under new management, some settees and open fire, part of carpeted bar screened off for eating, second dining room, pubby food from baguettes and baked potatoes up, Adnams, Fullers London Pride and Greene King IPA; back terrace tables with trees and shrubs, picturesque village handy for Woburn Abbey *(Michael Dandy)*

GREAT BARFORD [TL1351]
Anchor MK44 3LF [High St; off A421]: Open-plan bar with Wells & Youngs Bombardier and guests such as Everards Tiger and Mansfield, friendly staff, usual food from sandwiches and baked potatoes up, back restaurant; piped music; roadside picnic-sets looking over River Ouse by medieval bridge and church, bedrooms *(Michael Dandy)*

HARROLD [SP9456]
Muntjac MK43 7BJ [High St]: Some booth seating in long carpeted front bar, changing ales such as Potton Village Bicycle and Bill Suttons, pubby bar lunches from sandwiches and toasted paninis up, quick helpful service, contemporary back restaurant; pavement tables, bedrooms *(Michael Dandy)*

Oakley Arms MK43 7BH [between A6 and A428, E of Northampton; High St]: Cosy recently refurbished beamed pub with several linked areas around central bar, well kept Wells & Youngs and guest ales, good value changing food; quiet garden tables, bedrooms *(Revd R P Tickle)*

HENLOW [TL1738]
Crown SG16 6BS [High St]: Small Chef & Brewer with their usual décor and food, Adnams Broadside, Courage Best or Directors and a guest beer, good coffee and choice of wines by the glass, nice log fire, daily papers; piped music, games machine; terrace and small garden, open all day *(Michael Dandy)*

HOUGHTON CONQUEST [TL0342]
☆ *Chequers* MK45 3JP [B530 towards Ampthill]: Recently spaciously extended and refurbished in pleasant contemporary style, nice and airy, with good choice of reasonably priced food from baguettes and baked potatoes to venison casserole, Fullers London Pride, Greene King IPA, Wells & Youngs Bombardier and good choice of wines by the glass, quick friendly service; terrace tables, open all day *(Dudley and Moira Cockroft, Michael Dandy)*

IRELAND [TL1341]
☆ *Black Horse* SG17 5QL [off A600 Shefford—Bedford]: Smart busy dining pub in picturesque building, good range of enjoyable food from ciabattas and interesting light dishes up, wider evening menu, welcoming efficient staff, comfortable mix of furniture and plenty of space including stylish garden-view extension, Fullers London Pride, Greene King IPA and a local guest beer, good range of wines and good coffee; plenty of tables on attractive terracing, play area, cottage bedrooms – nice peaceful rural setting *(Michael Sargent, BB, Eithne Dandy, Giles Barr, Eleanor Dandy, Jill and Julian Tasker, Peter and Margaret Glenister, John Saul, Michael Dandy)*

KEMPSTON [TL0347]
Slaters Arms MK43 8RS [Box End Rd (A5134, off A4218 W of Bedford)]: Comfortably modern carpeted bar and family restaurant area, wide choice of pub food from generous sandwiches and baguettes up using some local and organic ingredients, cut-price Sun lunch for children, Greene King ales, speciality coffees; picnic-sets in big back tree-shaded garden with plenty for children inc well equipped fenced-off play area, pets corner, summer barbecues and ice-cream bar, open all day *(Michael Dandy,*

Mike Ridgway, Sarah Miles)
LANGFORD [TL1840]
Plough SG18 9QA [Church St]: Simple comfort in small two-bar pub with Greene King ales and good choice of wines by the glass from central servery, wide food choice from good sandwiches and baguettes up, quick service; may be piped music, TV; good-sized garden, bedrooms *(Michael Dandy)*
LINSLADE [SP9126]
Globe LU7 2TA [off A4146 nr bridge on outskirts]: 19th-c pub nicely set below Grand Union Canal, lots of rooms, beams and flagstones, log and coal fires, Greene King ales, usual food (not winter Sun evening), pleasant service; piped music; children welcome in eating areas, tables up on embankment and in garden, open all day *(Charles and Pauline Stride, LYM)*
MAULDEN [TL0538]
Dog & Badger MK45 2AD [Clophill Rd]: Attractive thatched village pub, refurbished bare-boards bar, steps down to two carpeted areas and restaurant, changing ales such as Bass and Flowers, wide food choice inc lunchtime sandwiches, friendly service; piped music; tables in front garden *(Michael Dandy)*
White Hart MK45 2DH [Ampthill Rd]: Thatch and low beams, big fireplace dividing bar, wide food choice from good value hot ciabattas and baked potatoes up, friendly helpful service, Caledonian Deuchars IPA, Greene King IPA and Timothy Taylors Landlord, good choice of wines by the glass, large well divided dining area; piped music; plenty of tables in sizeable gardens with pleasant back decking, open all day wknds *(Michael Dandy)*
MILLBROOK [TL0138]
Chequers MK45 2JB: Two-room village pub opp golf club, log fire and plate collection in small low-beamed carpeted bar, Flowers IPA and Stonehenge Pigswill, good coffee, reasonably priced food lunch deals, quick service, back restaurant; piped music *(Michael Dandy)*
PEGSDON [TL1130]
☆ *Live & Let Live* SG5 3JX [B655 W of Hitchin]: Neatly kept dining pub with wide choice of enjoyable food, friendly staff, real ales such as Adnams, Brakspears, Fullers London Pride and Theakstons, good wine choice, snug traditional tiled and panelled core; piped music; lovely garden below Deacon Hill, open all day *(Michael Dandy, LYM, David and Ruth Shillitoe, Mr and Mrs John Taylor)*
POTTON [TL2249]
Royal Oak SG19 2LU [Biggleswade Rd]: Neatly kept traditional thatched pub with large bar and spacious dining areas, food from sandwiches and pubby favourites to restaurant dishes, Greene King and a guest ale, decent wines by the glass; garden tables *(anon)*
RAVENSDEN [TL0754]
Horse & Jockey MK44 2RR [Church End]:

Village pub doing well under new ownership, friendly service, good food, extensively refurbished bar and restaurant *(D C Poulton)*
RIDGMONT [SP9736]
Rose & Crown MK43 0TY [2 miles from M1 junction 13: A507, follow Ampthill signs – High St]: Useful off-motorway standby with open fire in neat comfortable lounge, traditional public bar, well kept Adnams and Wells & Youngs ales, usual food from sandwiches and baked potatoes up (not Sun evening); piped music and machines, darts; children and dogs allowed, good wheelchair access, long and attractive sheltered back garden, camping and caravanning, open all day wknds *(Philip Denton, Dave Braisted, Andy Lickfold, Michael Dandy, LYM, Geoff and Carol Thorp)*
SALFORD [SP9338]
Red Lion MK17 8AZ [Wavendon Rd]: Wells & Youngs Eagle and Bombardier, good choice of wines, soft drinks and fresh food, log fire, dining room; piped music; garden tables, bedrooms *(JJW, CMW)*
SHARPENHOE [TL0630]
☆ *Lynmore* MK45 4SH [Sharpenhoe Rd]: Reworked as open-plan contemporary gastropub, familiar and more exotic food from ciabattas and lunchtime deli board up, Adnams and Fullers London Pride, good choice of wines by the glass, pleasant service, modern furniture on bare boards, fine views of The Clappers (NT); piped music; tables out on decking, good walks *(Michael Dandy)*
SHILLINGTON [TL1234]
Crown SG5 3LP [High Rd, S end]: Small flagstoned bar and attractive lounge area, Greene King and a guest beer, good choice of wines by the glass, good value generous straightforward food from baguettes up, quick friendly service; pleasant garden with heaters *(Michael Dandy)*
Musgrave Arms SG5 3LX [Apsley End Rd, towards Pegsdon and Hexton]: Low-beamed village local with settles, tables, prints and horsebrasses in friendly and civilised lounge, woodburner in comfortable public bar, small dining room, Greene King IPA and Abbot, generous home-made pubby food from sandwiches and baked potatoes up, cheerful service, daily papers; piped music; big back garden with picnic-sets, cl Mon lunchtime *(Geoff and Carol Thorp, Michael Dandy)*
SILSOE [TL0835]
☆ *Star & Garter* MK45 4DR [High St]: Smart pub by village church, large bar and raised dining area, wide choice of usual bar food from sandwiches and baguettes up, separate evening menu, efficient service and reasonable prices, well kept Adnams, B&T Two Brewers and Greene King IPA, darts; may be piped music; good-sized attractive terrace *(John Saul, Michael Dandy)*
SOULDROP [SP9861]
Bedford Arms MK44 1EY [High St; off A6 Rushden—Bedford]: Pleasant rambling beamed village pub under new licensees,

friendly atmosphere, good value food and Greene King ales, large central stone fireplace and several bright and cheerful linked areas; children welcome, good garden with play area *(BB, D C Poulton)*

SOUTHILL [TL1441]

White Horse SG18 9LD [off B658 SW of Biggleswade]: Well run and comfortable country pub with extensive eating area, wide range of enjoyable generous food from baguettes and baked potatoes up, welcoming staff, several changing well kept ales, good wine choice; piped music; lots of tables in large pleasant neatly kept garden with good play area *(LYM, Michael Dandy, Peter and Margaret Glenister)*

STANFORD [TL1541]

Green Man SG18 9JD [Southill rd]: L-shaped bar with big fireplace, adjoining games area with pool, attractively priced bar food from generous sandwiches, baguettes and baked potatoes up, smart restaurant with beams and stripped brick, Courage Best and Theakstons; terrace with barbecue, big garden with play area, 11 bedrooms in chalet block *(Michael Dandy)*

STOTFOLD [TL2236]

Chequers SG5 4NX [Queen St]: Low beams, lots of photographs and ornaments, nice fireplace in lounge, Greene King IPA and Old Speckled Hen, several wines by the glass, lunchtime bar food inc wraps and salads, wide good value evening choice, quick helpful service; sizeable garden with play area *(Michael Dandy)*

TEMPSFORD [TL1652]

Wheatsheaf SG19 2AN [Church St]: 18th-c village pub with open fire in cosy lounge, Special Operations Executive memorabilia (nearby World War II base), friendly service, wide choice of good value straightforward pub food from sandwiches and baked potatoes up, small helpings available, Courage and Greene King IPA, pleasant restaurant; may be piped music; tables on decking and in big garden (some traffic noise) *(Michael Dandy)*

TODDINGTON [TL0128]

Angel LU5 6DE [Luton Rd]: Contemporary furnishings inc a log-fire area with sofas and comfortable seats, Greene King and a guest beer, good coffee and choice of wines by the glass, wide range of food, quick helpful service, daily papers, pub games; tables in garden with terrace and heaters, overlooking village pond and green *(Michael Dandy)*

TURVEY [SP9452]

Three Cranes MK43 8EP [off A428 W of Bedford]: Two-level pub with quickly served pub food all day, Greene King and a guest beer, log fire, darts and games; two TVs; children in restaurant area, tables in secluded tree-shaded garden with climber, bedrooms *(LYM, Michael Dandy, George Atkinson, B C Robertson)*

☆ *Three Fyshes* MK43 8ER [A428 NW of Bedford; Bridge Street, W end of village]: Early 17th-c beamed pub with plenty of character, big inglenook log fire, mix of easy chairs and upright chairs around tables on carpet or ancient flagstones, good friendly service, Caledonian Deuchars IPA, Fullers London Pride, Greene King IPA and a guest beer, good coffee, very wide choice of pub food from baguettes and baked potatoes up, daily paper; decking and canopy in charming garden overlooking bridge and mill on Great Ouse *(Michael Dandy, George Atkinson, Mr and Mrs D Price, Sarah Flynn, LYM, Michael Tack)*

WESTONING [SP0332]

Chequers MK45 5LA [Park Rd (A5120 N of M1 junction 12)]: Multi-gabled thatched pub with black bargeboards, well kept Fullers London Pride and Greene King IPA, good choice of wines by the glass, good coffee, enjoyable pub food from ciabattas up, attentive service, cask tables in small low-beamed front bar, good-sized back bar inc some settees, big stables restaurant; piped music; courtyard tables, open all day *(Dudley and Moira Cockroft, Michael Dandy)*

WHIPSNADE [TL0018]

Old Hunters Lodge LU6 2LN [B4540 E, nr B4521 junction]: Olde-worlde extended thatched pub with sofas in carpeted bar, roomy dining area in beamed original core dating from 15th c, unpretentious food from sandwiches and baguettes up (they could be more flexible about the fillings), more extensive restaurant menu, Greene King and perhaps a guest beer, good wines by the glass, cheery young staff; piped music may obtrude; handy for zoo, with tables in good-sized pleasant and sheltered garden, bedrooms, open all day Sun *(Paul Humphreys, Peter and Anne Hollindale, Neil Hardwick, Michael Dandy)*

WOBURN [SP9433]

Bell MK17 9QJ [Bedford St]: Small beamed bar area, longer bare-boards dining lounge up steps, pleasant décor and furnishings, generous all-day pubby food from sandwiches and baked potatoes up, attentive service, Greene King IPA and a related guest beer, good choice of wines by the glass, good coffee; piped music, games; children welcome at lunchtime, tables on back terrace, hotel part across busy road, handy for Woburn Park *(Michael Dandy, Paul Humphreys, George Atkinson)*

☆ *Black Horse* MK17 9QB [Bedford St]: Good lively atmosphere in smartly updated 19th-c pub with cheerful friendly staff, all-day food inc good value cold cut platters and wide choice of other dishes, Greene King ales, good choice of wines by the glass, coal fire, several bare-boards areas with contemporary furnishings inc some settees, steps down to pleasant back restaurant; piped music; children in eating areas, summer barbecues in attractive sheltered back courtyard, open all day *(Mr and Mrs John Taylor, LYM, Paul Humphreys, Michael Dandy)*

Flying Fox MK17 9HD [Sheep Lane (actually

A5 Bletchley—Hockcliffe, well away from village)]: Well run Vintage Inn dining pub with hop-hung beams, pictures and artefacts in well arranged linked areas, pleasant atmosphere and attentive service, attractively priced food from sandwiches to steaks, fine choice of wines by the glass, Greene King IPA and Old Speckled Hen and Wells & Youngs Bombardier; piped music, pub games; tables out on lawn *(B H and J I Andrews, Michael Dandy)*

Inn at Woburn MK17 9PX [George St]: Attractive Georgian hotel with sofas and high-backed leather seats in beamed bar, Wells & Youngs Bombardier and Eagle, friendly service, up-to-date bar food inc baguettes, good choice of wines by the glass, brasserie-style restaurant; nice bedrooms *(Michael Dandy)*

Magpie MK17 9QB: Small low-ceilinged traditional bar, sofas in small lounge, Marstons Pedigree, sensible food from sandwiches and pubby things to popular restaurant dishes; TV; tables in neatly kept back courtyard, bedrooms, open all day *(Michael Dandy)*

WRESTLINGWORTH [TL2547]

Chequers SG19 2EP [High St]: Carpeted bar with Greene King IPA from central servery, lunchtime food from sandwiches up, wider evening choice, open fire, side dining area, pool and darts in games end; garden tables *(Michael Dandy)*

YIELDEN [TL0166]

Chequers MK44 1AW [High St]: Welcoming village local with good choice of real ales and two farm ciders, good value house wine and good soft drinks range, wide choice of enjoyable food (not Sun evening; freshly made so can take a while), afternoon snacks too, World War II mementoes fom nearby Chelveston USAF base, pool room and skittles; garden behind, open all day, cl Tues lunchtime and Mon *(JJW, CMW)*

Post Office address codings confusingly give the impression that some pubs are in Bedfordshire, when they're really in Buckinghamshire or Cambridgeshire (which is where we list them).

Berkshire

If it's unspoilt pubs you're after, you'd be hard-pushed to find anywhere more charming than the Bell at Aldworth, in the same family for over 200 years and a particular favourite with us as well as with a great many of our readers. The cosy little Magpie & Parrot near Shinfield, expanded a bit this year, is a chatty and relaxing home from home, and the Hobgoblin in Reading is a cheerful town tavern whose friendly landlord keeps his eight real ales in tip-top condition. By contrast, pubs majoring on good food include the handsome Hinds Head in Bray (interesting dishes, super wines, and under the same ownership as the famous Fat Duck restaurant nearby), the Pot Kiln at Frilsham (unusual and imaginative game dishes), and the Little Angel in Remenham (a new Food Award this year, for its increasingly popular modern choices). It's the Hinds Head in Bray which takes the title of Berkshire Dining Pub of the Year. Other pubs currently on particularly good form are the Sun in the Wood at Ashmore Green (very enthusiastic licensees and a really good mix of customers of all ages), the Crown & Garter at Inkpen (hard-working, hands-on landlady and in a nice spot), the Royal Oak in Ruscombe (bustling and consistently friendly), the Bull in Stanford Dingley (both drinkers and diners are made very welcome), and the Winterbourne Arms at Winterbourne (a really nice place with good food and wine). New licensees have brought us a couple of interesting new entries this year: the Hinds Head at Aldermaston, most appealing after its careful refurbishment; and the Belgian Arms in Holyport, now a smart dining pub. In the Lucky Dip section at the end of the chapter, this year's stars are the gently upgraded Flower Pot at Aston, the Olde Red Lion at Chieveley, Chequers in Cookham Dean, Swans at Great Shefford and at Inkpen, restaur“ant Hare near Lambourn, unusual Sweeney & Todd in Reading, Pheasant at Shefford Woodlands, Bull in Sonning, Bell at Waltham St Lawrence and Carpenters Arms in Windsor. This is an expensive county both for pub food and for drinks; a thriving local brewery, West Berkshire (which actually started in the Pot Kiln but has moved and expanded), often undercuts other beer prices here and is well worth looking out for – good ale, good value for money.

ALDERMASTON   SU5865   MAP 2
Hinds Head
Wasing Lane; RG7 4LX

Newly refurbished old inn with welcoming licensees and enjoyable food and drink; nice bedrooms

Dominating the centre of the village, this is an interesting creeper-clad 17th-c inn taken in hand by friendly and efficient new licensees. It's been carefully refurbished recently and the homely but civilised bar is now rather upmarket and has some cosy corners, neat staff, Fullers ESB and London Pride and a changing guest on handpump, a good choice of wines by the glass and quite a collection of malt whiskies. Seats outside in the fine garden and the bedrooms have been attractively redone. This is one of the few inns to have its own gaol situated behind – it was last used in 1865.

🍽 **Well liked bar food now includes sandwiches, soup, smoked haddock topped with welsh rarebit, goats cheese, tomato and aubergine stack, battered haddock fillet, sausage and mash with onion gravy, mushroom and asparagus risotto, calves liver and bacon, chicken supreme stuffed with brie wrapped in bacon in a rich tomato sauce and slow-roasted shoulder of lamb in red wine and thyme.** *Starters/Snacks: £4.95 to £6.15. Main Courses: £9.25 to £14.95. Puddings: £5.25*

Fullers ~ Managers Louis and Laura Thaker ~ Real ale ~ Bar food (12-2.30(3 Sun), 6-9(8 Sun)) ~ Restaurant ~ (0118) 971 2194 ~ Children allowed until 6pm ~ Open 11.30-11; 12-10.30 Sun ~ Bedrooms: £67.50B/£80B

Recommended by Wendy Arnold, Sara Fulton, Roger Baker

ALDWORTH   SU5579   MAP 2

Bell ★ ♀ 🍺 £

A329 Reading—Wallingford; left on to B4009 at Streatley; RG8 9SE

Outstanding unspoilt pub run by the same family for over 200 years, super value limited food, fair-priced beers, good quality house wines, lovely friendly atmosphere, and nice garden

'The benchmark by which all pubs should be marked' wrote one enthusiastic reader – and we feel he is probably right. It's been run by the same family for over 200 years and remains a favourite with a wide mix of customers who love the fact that mobile phones, piped music and games machines are banned. Quite unspoilt and unchanging, the rooms have benches around the panelled walls, an ancient one-handed clock, beams in the shiny ochre ceiling, and a woodburning stove – and rather than a bar counter for service, there's a glass-panelled hatch. Well priced Arkells BBB and Kingsdown are superbly kept alongside Old Tyler, Maggs Magnificent Mild and a monthly guest on handpump from the local West Berkshire Brewery; Upton farm cider; no draught lager. They also serve good house wines and spiced porter at Christmas. Darts, shove-ha'penny, and dominoes. The quiet, old-fashioned cottagey garden is by the village cricket ground, and behind the pub there's a paddock with farm animals. In summer there may be occasional morris dancers, while at Christmas local mummers perform in the road by the ancient well-head (the shaft is sunk 365 feet through the chalk). It tends to get very busy at weekends; dogs must be kept on leads.

🍽 **Excellent value bar food is limited to filled hot crusty rolls and a variety of ploughman's; in winter they also do home-made soup.** *Starters/Snacks: £2.50 to £5.00*

Free house ~ Licensee H E Macaulay ~ Real ale ~ Bar food (11-2.30, 6-10; 12-2.45, 7-9.30 Sun; not Mon) ~ No credit cards ~ (01635) 578272 ~ Well behaved children in Tap Room ~ Dogs welcome ~ Open 11-3, 6-11; 12-3, 7-10.30 Sun; closed Mon and Mon bank hol evenings

Recommended by Thomas Lane, Guy Vowles, I H G Busby, Andrew Hollingshead, Pete Baker, Mike Vincent, Rob Winstanley, N R White, Ian Phillips, Ray J Carter, Dick and Madeleine Brown, Anthony Longden, Dr and Mrs A K Clarke, Richard Endacott, Mr and Mrs H J Langley, the Didler, Tracey and Stephen Groves, Mark and Diane Grist

ASHMORE GREEN   SU4969   MAP 2

Sun in the Wood ♀

At A34 Robin Hood roundabout, take B4009 (Shaw Road) off A339 then right on to Kiln Road, then left on to Stoney Lane. Pub is 1 mile on left; RG18 9HF

Popular and well run country pub with a genuine mix of customers, plenty of room, enjoyable food, beer and wine, and friendly licensees

Particularly at weekends, there's a really good mix of customers of all ages at this very popular country pub. It's run by enthusiastic and hard-working licensees who – along with their team of staff – offer a genuinely warm welcome to all. The high-beamed front bar has bare boards on the left, carpet on the right, and a mix of nice old chairs, padded dining chairs and stripped pews around sturdy tables. It opens into a big back dining area which has the same informal feel, candles on tables, and some interesting touches like the big stripped bank of apothecary's drawers. There's a small conservatory sitting area by the side entrance. Well kept Wadworths JCB and 6X, and a guest such as Badger Tanglefoot on handpump, and a fine choice of wines by the glass. The decked terrace has outdoor heaters, plenty of flowers and old-fashioned street lights, there's a big woodside garden with lots of picnic-sets, and a small child-free area. The nine-hole woodland crazy golf pitch is a big hit with families. It's hard to believe the pub is only a few minutes away from the centre of Newbury.

🍴 Enjoyable bar food such as good freshly baked filled baguettes (Tuesday-Saturday lunchtimes), home-made soup, tempura king prawns, calves liver on spring onion mash with bacon and onion sauce, cajun spiced tuna on herby couscous and black olive polenta with roasted fennel and butternut squash, mozzarella and pesto cream sauce; puddings like mango and passion fruit crème brûlée, a children's menu, and two- and three-course Sunday lunches. *Starters/Snacks: £4.00 to £6.00. Main Courses: £7.00 to £16.00. Puddings: £4.95*

Wadworths ~ Tenant Philip Davison ~ Real ale ~ Bar food (12-2(2.30 Sat), 6(5.30 Sat)-9.30(9.45 Sat); 12-4 Sun; not Mon) ~ Restaurant ~ (01635) 42377 ~ Children welcome ~ Open 12-2.30, 5.30-11; 12-11 Sat; 12-10.30 Sun; closed Mon, winter Sun evening, 25-26 Dec, 1 Jan

Recommended by Sue and Roger Bourne, Angus and Rosemary Campbell, Peter and Jean Hoare, Ray J Carter, Martin and Karen Wake

BRAY

SU9079   MAP 2

Crown

1¼ miles from M4 junction 9; A308 towards Windsor, then left at Bray signpost on to B3028; High Street; SL6 2AH

Low-beamed, busy pub with roaring log fires in knocked-through rooms, enjoyable food, and helpful service

Mainly set up for eating, though there are tables for drinkers too, this bustling 14th-c pub has lots of beams (some so low you have to mind your head), plenty of old timbers handily left at elbow height where walls have been knocked through, and three roaring winter log fires. The partly panelled main bar has oak tables and leather backed armchairs, and one dining area has photographs of WWII aeroplanes. To be sure of a place it's best to arrive early or book in advance – especially in the restaurant. Well kept Brakspears Special, and Courage Best and Directors on handpump along with a decent choice of wines. There are tables and benches out in a sheltered flagstoned front courtyard (which has a flourishing grape vine), and in the large back garden. There's a smokers' shelter.

🍴 Popular – if not cheap – food such as home-made soup, goats cheese on peppered pineapple, moules marinière and frites, home-made beef and Guinness pie, oriental warm chicken salad, tagliatelle with fresh tomato, mushrooms, basil and chilli, and smoked haddock with wholegrain mustard sauce. *Starters/Snacks: £4.80 to £9.25. Main Courses: £9.30 to £17.95. Puddings: £4.50*

Scottish Courage ~ Lease John and Carole Noble ~ Real ale ~ Bar food (not Sun or Mon evenings) ~ Restaurant ~ (01628) 621936 ~ Children at weekends only in restaurant and eating area of bar ~ Open 11-3, 6-11; 12-3, 7-10.30 Sun; closed 25 and 26 Dec, 1 Jan

Recommended by Ray J Carter, Michael Dandy, R T and J C Moggridge, Susan and John Douglas, Dr K P Tucker, Julia Morris

---

Food details, prices, timing etc refer to bar food (if that's separate and different from any restaurant there).

Hinds Head ⑪ ♈

High Street; car park opposite (exit rather tricky); SL6 2AB
BERKSHIRE DINING PUB OF THE YEAR

Beautifully flavoured food in traditionally furnished gastro pub, a fine choice of drinks, and efficient service

Given that this handsome old pub is under the same ownership as the highly praised Fat Duck restaurant nearby, readers have been happily surprised by the relaxed and informal atmosphere here. Most customers come to enjoy the simple but brilliant food though there is a thoroughly traditional L-shaped bar with dark beams and panelling, polished oak parquet, blazing log fires, red-cushioned built-in wall seats and studded leather carving chairs around small round tables, and latticed windows. They have a dozen interesting wines by the glass including two champagnes, well kept Greene King IPA and Abbot and a couple of guests such as Everards Tiger and Rebellion Mutiny on handpump, 24 malt whiskies, an excellent bloody mary, Sheppy's farm cider and a fine choice of tea and coffee. A spacious restaurant area spreads off to the left.

⑪ **Superbly executed, the delicious bar food includes lunchtime snacks like scotch quail eggs or devils on horseback and lunchtime sandwiches, as well as soup, rabbit and bacon terrine, soused herrings with beetroot and horseradish, steamed mussels with garlic, lemon and parsley, gloucester old spot pork chop with pease pudding, lancashire hotpot, oxtail and kidney pudding and whole sea bream with fennel, and puddings like sherry trifle or quaking pudding.** *Starters/Snacks: £4.50 to £9.50. Main Courses: £7.75 to £18.50. Puddings: £5.95*

Free house ~ Licensees Mr and Mrs A Proctor ~ Real ale ~ Bar food (12-2.30, 6.30-9.30; Sun 12-4; not Sun evening) ~ Restaurant ~ (01628) 626151 ~ Children welcome ~ Dogs allowed in bar ~ Open 11-11; 12-10.30 Sun; closed 25 and 26 Dec

Recommended by Michael Dandy, John Urquhart, Ray J Carter, Paul Humphreys, David Tindal, Michael and Alison Sandy, Maggie Atherton, Howard Dell, David and Sue Smith, P Waterman, Dr K P Tucker

FRILSHAM   SU5573   MAP 2

Pot Kiln ⑪ ◀

From Yattendon take turning S, opposite church, follow first Frilsham signpost, but just after crossing motorway go straight on towards Bucklebury ignoring Frilsham signposted right; pub on right after about half a mile; RG18 0XX

Imaginative modern cooking in country dining pub but still with a little locals' bar for the good choice of ales; suntrap garden

It's certainly essential to book ahead to be sure of table in this extremely popular dining pub. They do still offer West Berkshire Brick Kiln Bitter, Mr Chubbs Lunchtime Bitter and Maggs Magnificent Mild with guests like Crouch Vale Brewers Gold on handpump in the little bar where friendly locals gather, but the emphasis is very much on the imaginative restauranty food. The bar area has dark wooden tables and chairs on bare floorboards, and a good winter log fire, and the extended lounge is open-plan at the back and leads into a large, pretty dining room with a nice jumble of old tables and chairs, and an old-looking stone fireplace; darts and cards. This is a charming rural spot, and seats in the big suntrap garden have good views of the nearby forests and meadows; plenty of nearby walks.

⑪ **As well as game dishes like terrine of muntjac deer, saddle of hare and venison stew, the food might include sandwiches or ploughman's, home-made soup, shepherd's pie, warm pigeon salad, ham hock with pease pudding, rolled shoulder of lamb, and hot passion fruit soufflé.** *Starters/Snacks: £2.95 to £3.50. Main Courses: £8.00 to £9.50. Puddings: £6.00*

Free house ~ Licensees Mr and Mrs Michael Robinson ~ Real ale ~ Bar food (not Sun evening) ~ Restaurant ~ (01635) 201366 ~ Children welcome ~ Dogs allowed in bar ~ Open 12-3, 6-11; 12-11 Sat; 12-10.30 Sun

Recommended by I H G Busby, G Coates, Mr and Mrs G S Ayrton, Franklyn Roberts, Andrew Given, Robert Jamieson, the Didler

HOLYPORT
SU8977 MAP 2

Belgian Arms
Handy for M4 junction 8/9, via A308(M) and A330; SL6 2JR

Recently refurbished and rather smart dining pub with friendly staff, good food and seats on new decked area

Overlooking the village ponds, this bustling place has had a complete makeover and is now a smart dining pub. The low-ceilinged bar has been tidied up and has better spaced tables and chairs on the stripped wooden floor, interesting cricketing memorabilia on the walls, a china cupboard in one corner, a log fire and a discreetly placed flat TV screen. The old cellar room is now a dining area and the conservatory has had a half wall removed to create the illusion of more space. Friendly, humorous staff serve Brakspears Bitter and Special and a guest beer on handpump and there are quite a few wines by the glass. There's a new terrace with good quality wooden furniture on decking amongst pretty flowering terracotta tubs.

🍴 **Good bar food includes sandwiches, interesting soups, soft boiled duck egg with parma ham and wild garlic salad, grilled chicken caesar salad, moules marinière, a pasta dish of the day, burgers topped with smoked cheese, mayo and bacon, cumberland sausages with onion jus, beef bourguignon with garlic mash, chargrilled tuna steak with sour cream potato salad and pesto, daily specials, and puddings such as chocolate brownie with hot fudge sauce and banana split with marmalade ice-cream.** *Starters/Snacks: £5.95 to £8.00. Main Courses: £8.95 to £14.00. Puddings: £4.50 to £5.95*

Brakspears ~ Lease Jamie Sears ~ Real ale ~ Bar food (12-2, 6.30-9; 12-4 Sun; not Sun evening) ~ Restaurant ~ (01628) 634468 ~ Well behaved children welcome ~ Dogs allowed in bar ~ Open 11-3, 5.30-11; 11-midnight Fri and Sat; 12-11 Sun

Recommended by Simon Collett-Jones, Stan Edwards

HURST
SU8074 MAP 2

Green Man
Hinton Road, off A321 just outside village; RG10 0BP

An interesting mix of bars in bustling pub with well liked food, and plenty of space outside on terrace and in big garden

Bustling and friendly, this partly 17th-c pub has plenty of atmosphere in its old-fashioned bar. There are black standing timbers and dark oak beams around cosy alcoves, cushioned wall seats and built-in settles around copper-topped and other pub tables, and attractive prints, Edwardian enamels and decorative plates on cream or terracotta walls; it's warmed by a hot little fire in one fireplace and a nice old iron stove in another. Beyond is a light and airy dining room and the appealing cellar room has just four tables and lots of pictures on its cream-painted brickwork. Well kept Brakspears PA, Special, and a seasonal ale on handpump, and half-a-dozen wines by the glass. The sheltered, heated terrace has tables under giant umbrellas, there are picnic-sets under big oak trees in the large garden, and a good sturdy children's play area.

🍴 **Reliably good and reasonably priced bar food such as sandwiches, soup, deep-fried camembert with cranberry coulis, crab millefeuille, salmon fishcakes, mexican chilli, steak in ale pie, mushrooms and red pepper stroganoff, nice daily specials, and a daily home-made pudding; all day Sunday and special occasion menus too.** *Starters/Snacks: £3.25 to £4.95. Main Courses: £5.95 to £14.45. Puddings: £3.45 to £4.95*

Brakspears ~ Tenants Simon and Gordon Guile ~ Real ale ~ Bar food (12-2.30, 6-9.30; 12-9 Sun (roasts until 4)) ~ Restaurant ~ (0118) 934 2599 ~ Children welcome until 8.30pm ~ Open 11-3, 5.30-11; 12-10.30 Sun

Recommended by Ian Phillips, Paul Humphreys, Nina Randall, Kevin Thomas, M G Hart, R Lake, Kim Mead, June and Robin Savage, Kevin Thomas, Nina Randall, Mark and Diane Grist, Fred and Kate Portnell

---

Pubs with outstanding views are listed at the back of the book.

INKPEN
SU3764   MAP 2

Crown & Garter 🍺 🛏️

Inkpen signposted with Kintbury off A4; in Kintbury turn left into Inkpen Road, then keep on into Inkpen Common; RG17 9QR

Remote-feeling pub with appealing layout, lovely garden and nearby walks, local ales and tasty food in nicely lit bars, and friendly licensees

This year, a new front terrace for outside eating has been added to this 16th-c brick pub and inside, the bar area has been panelled and separated from the restaurant. It's run by a welcoming landlady and is surprisingly substantial for somewhere so remote-feeling. The appealing low-ceilinged and relaxed bar keeps West Berkshire Mr Chubbs Lunchtime Bitter and Good Old Boy plus a guest such as Archers Golden, Arkells Moonlight or Timothy Taylors Landlord on handpump, decent wines by the glass, and several malt whiskies. Three areas radiate from here; our pick is the parquet-floored part by the raised log fire which has a couple of substantial old tables, a huge old-fashioned slightly curved settle, and a neat little porter's chair decorated in commemoration of the Battle of Corunna (the cats' favourite seat – they've two). Other parts are slate and wood with a good mix of well spaced tables and chairs, and nice lighting. There's a lovely long side garden with picnic-sets and a play area, and plenty of good downland walks nearby. In a separate single-storey building, the bedrooms form an L around a pretty garden. James II is reputed to have used the pub on his way to visit his mistress locally.

🍴 **Enjoyable bar food includes home-made soup, red onion and goats cheese tart, steak and kidney pudding, venison and cranberry sausages, tandoori chicken with onion bhaji, spinach, leek and cheese tortellini, whole grilled lemon sole with parsley butter, and puddings such as Tia Maria and fresh fruit brûlée or profiteroles.** *Starters/Snacks: £4.95 to £6.95. Main Courses: £9.95 to £17.95. Puddings: £4.95 to £6.75*

Free house ~ Licensee Gill Hern ~ Real ale ~ Bar food (not Sun evening, not Mon-Tues lunchtime) ~ Restaurant ~ (01488) 668325 ~ Children allowed away from bar; not encouraged after 9pm ~ Dogs allowed in bar ~ Open 12-3, 5.30-11; 12-5, 7-10.30 Sun; closed Mon and Tues lunchtimes ~ Bedrooms: £59.50B/£90B

Recommended by Pam and John Smith, Mary Rayner, C R Crofton, Jeff and Wendy Williams, Pat and Tony Martin, Michael Dallas, Mr and Mrs H J Langley, Jane and Emma Macdonald, J Stickland, Douglas and Ann Hare, Sue Demont, Tim Barrow

OAKLEY GREEN
SU9276   MAP 2

Olde Red Lion 🛏️

4 miles from M4 junction 8 (and also junction 6); B3024, off A308 just W of Windsor; SL4 4PZ

Attractive pub filling quickly at weekends, attentive service, several dining areas and enjoyable food – the breakfasts are good too

Particularly popular at weekends (and certainly worth booking for Sunday lunch), this tiled and black-shuttered pub is run by friendly people. The low-ceilinged bar has Adnams and Bass on handpump, a decent range of wines by the glass, good coffee, and piped music; service is attentive and friendly. On the right a snugly narrow sloping-ceiling side area has white tablecloths on its tables but is designated for drinking as well as eating. On the left, past a cosy corner with a brown leather sofa and coal-effect fire, is an extensive carpeted dining area. A good-sized sheltered back garden has plenty of picnic-sets under cocktail parasols on the grass and there are more seats on a terrace under a fairy-lit arbour; biggish front car park.

🍴 **Enjoyable food includes a commendable range of sandwiches, soup, chicken liver pâté with red onion marmalade, thai crab cake with mango chilli salsa, tomato and basil tortellini, steak and Guinness pudding, baked salmon in a white wine and dill sauce and slow-baked half shoulder of lamb, with puddings such as raspberry crème brûlée or sticky toffee pudding with butterscotch sauce.** *Starters/Snacks: £5.00 to £10.00. Main Courses: £10.00 to £20.00. Puddings: £4.75*

Punch ~ Tenant Andrew Deeley ~ Real ale ~ Bar food (12-2.30, 6.30-10; 12-5 Sun (not Sun evening)) ~ Restaurant ~ (01753) 863892 ~ Well behaved children in restaurant only ~ Dogs allowed in bar ~ Open 11-11; 12-10 Sun ~ Bedrooms: /£60B

Recommended by June and Robin Savage, Andy Blackburn, Simon Collett-Jones

READING

SU7173   MAP 2

Hobgoblin

2 Broad Street; RG1 2BH

Eight quickly changing ales in no-frills backstreet pub with small panelled rooms and a cheerful atmosphere

Pump clips cover practically every inch of the walls and ceiling of the simple bare-boards bar in this basic and cheerful pub – a testament to the enormous number of brews that have passed through the pumps over the past few years (now over 5,350). They keep up to eight regularly changing real ales including three from the West Berkshire Brewery alongside five interesting guests: Church End Wild Thing, Crouch Vale Amarillo, Hop Back Back Row, Itchen Valley Engine Driver, and Spinning Dog Doggy Fashion. If that isn't enough, they've also lots of different bottled beers, czech lager on tap, Weston's farm cider and perry, and country wines. Up a step is a small seating area, but the best places to sit are the three or four tiny panelled rooms reached by a narrow corridor leading from the bar; cosy and intimate, each has barely enough space for one table and a few chairs or wall seats, but they're very appealing if you're able to bag one; the biggest also manages to squeeze in a fireplace. It does get very busy, especially at weekends. They don't do any food at all, and they don't allow children or mobile phones. Piped music (very much in keeping with the rough and ready feel of the place), and TV.

🍴 **No food.**

Community Taverns ~ Manager Rob Wain ~ Real ale ~ No credit cards ~ (0118) 950 8119 ~ Open 11-11; 12-10.30 Sun

Recommended by Mark and Diane Grist, Catherine Pitt, Mike Vincent, Pete Walker, the Didler

REMENHAM

SU7682   MAP 2

Little Angel 🍴 🍷

A4130, just over bridge E of Henley; RG9 2LS

Relaxed linked contemporary areas plus attractive conservatory, good modern bar food, helpful service, and a dozen wines by the glass

The atmosphere in this attractive pub is buzzy yet civilised and several areas link openly together so you feel part of what's going on, though each has its own distinct individual feel. There are well spaced seats and tables on the bare boards or ochre tiles, and furnishings are mainly in pale fabrics or soft suede, running from comfortable bar seats through tub chairs to deep sofas, with new artwork on the walls. In one corner a case of art books and the like helps to set the tone. The conservatory has been refurbished. The attractive curved bar counter has a good choice of a dozen wines by the glass (plus champagne), smoothies and cocktails, and Brakspears Bitter and Wychwood January Sale on handpump; board games, unobtrusive piped music, TV, and friendly and efficient young staff. A sheltered floodlit back terrace has tables under cocktail parasols, looking over to the local cricket ground.

🍴 **Very good food using local estate game and organic fruit and vegetables includes lunchtime food such as sandwiches, hand-made pie of the day, port and stilton on toast with fries, and a plate of mixed antipasti, plus home-made soup, eggs benedict, king scallops with truffle mash and chive butter sauce, cauliflower, broccoli and dolcelatte lasagne, calves liver, mushy pea mash and pancetta, slow-roast shoulder of lamb with chorizo, baby onion and potato cassoulet, and puddings like treacle apple sponge with vanilla crumble ice-cream.** *Starters/Snacks: £4.95 to £7.50. Main Courses: £8.95 to £15.95. Puddings: £5.00 to £6.50*

Brakspears ~ Lease Douglas Green ~ Real ale ~ Bar food (12-3, 6.45-10; 12-4, 7-9.30 Sun) ~ Restaurant ~ (01491) 411008 ~ Children allowed but must be well behaved ~ Dogs welcome ~ Live sax/acoustic guitar Weds ~ Open 11-11(midnight Sat)

Recommended by Ray J Carter, Andy and Claire Barker, Chris Glasson, Michael Dandy, Ian Phillips, Tracey and Stephen Groves, Stephen P Edwards, Simon Rodway

RUSCOMBE   SU7976   MAP 2

Royal Oak

Ruscombe Lane (B3024 just E of Twyford); RG10 9JN

Wide choice of popular food in smart village pub with interesting furnishings and paintings, and quite a choice of drinks

You can be sure of a warm welcome from the friendly licensees and their staff in this bustling village pub. Throughout, it's open plan and carpeted (not the cheerful side garden room), and well laid out so that each bit is fairly snug, yet keeps the overall feel of a lot of people enjoying themselves. A good variety of furniture runs from dark oak tables to big chunky pine ones, with mixed seating to match – the two sofas facing one another are popular. Contrasting with the exposed ceiling joists, mostly unframed modern paintings and prints decorate the walls, mainly dark terracotta over a panelled dado. Brakspears Bitter and Fullers London Pride, and maybe a guest beer like Loddon Ferrymans Gold on handpump, and half a dozen nicely chosen wines. Picnic-sets are ranged around a venerable central hawthorn in the garden behind (where there are ducks and chickens); summer barbecues, spit roasts and morris dancing.

🍴 Bar food is popular and as well as lunchtime snacks such as sandwiches and paninis, ploughman's, beer-battered fish, stilton and bacon burger and bangers and mash, there's home-made soup, king prawns in garlic citrus butter, shank of lamb with red wine and rosemary jus, savoury mushroom bread and butter pudding and daily specials like smoked salmon and scrambled eggs, red thai chicken and prawn on noodles, and home-made steak in ale pie; two- and three-course set menu, too. *Starters/Snacks: £3.95 to £6.95. Main Courses: £9.95 to £16.00. Puddings: £3.25 to £5.25*

Enterprise ~ Lease Jenny and Stefano Buratta ~ Real ale ~ Bar food (12-2.30, 7-9.30; 12-4 Sun; not Sun or Mon evenings) ~ Restaurant ~ (0118) 934 5190 ~ Children welcome ~ Dogs welcome ~ Open 12-3, 7-11; 12-4 Sun; closed Sun and Mon evenings

Recommended by Tracey and Stephen Groves, Mr and Mrs C R Little, Paul Humphreys, Mrs L M Beard, Simon Collett-Jones, Fred and Kate Portnell

SHINFIELD   SU7367   MAP 2

Magpie & Parrot 🍺

2.6 miles from M4 junction 11, via B3270; A327 just SE of Shinfield – heading out on Arborfield Road, keep eyes skinned for small hand-painted green Nursery sign on left, and Fullers 'bar open' blackboard; RG2 9EA

Most unusual and homely little roadside cottage with warm open fire, lots of bric-a-brac in cosy small bar, and hospitable landlady

A second room has been opened up in what was a private lounge – creating much welcome extra space in this little roadside cottage. You go in through the lobby (with its antiquated telephone equipment), and find a cosy and inviting high-raftered room with a handful of small polished tables – each with a bowl of peanuts (they don't do any food) – and a comfortable mix of individualistic seats from Georgian oak thrones to a red velveteen sofa, not to mention the armchair with the paw-printed cushion reserved for Aitch the new pub dog. It's a charming and relaxed place to while away an hour or so in the afternoon beside the warm open fire. Everything is spick and span, from the brightly patterned carpet to the plethora of interesting bric-a-brac covering the walls: miniature and historic bottles, dozens of model cars, veteran AA badges and automotive instruments, and mementoes of a pranged Spitfire (ask about its story – they love to chat here). Well kept Fullers London Pride and a changing guest on handpump from the small corner counter, a good range of malt whiskies and of soft drinks; very hospitable landlady. There are teak tables on the back terrace and an immaculate lawn beyond. Hog roasts and morris men at various summer events and two beer festivals in June and December with 22 real ales; aunt sally. Note the unusual opening hours; no children inside.

⑪ No food.

Free house ~ Licensee Mrs Carole Headland ~ Real ale ~ No credit cards ~ (0118) 988 4130 ~ Dogs welcome ~ Open 12-7; 12-3 Sun; closed Sun evening

Recommended by R T and J C Moggridge, Mayur Shah, Mark and Diane Grist, Jeremy Woods, Tracey and Stephen Groves

STANFORD DINGLEY   SU5771   MAP 2

Bull 🛏

Off A340 via Bradfield, coming from A4 just W of M4 junction 12; RG7 6LS

Run by licensees with an interest in classic cars (the décor reflects this) and with good beers and tasty food

An excellent break from the M4, this attractive 15th-c brick pub has a good bustling atmosphere and a happy mix of drinkers and diners. The main part of the building has an old brick fireplace, cushioned seats carved out of barrels, a window settle, wheelback chairs on the red quarry tiles, and an old station clock; a carpeted section has an exposed wattle and daub wall. The half-panelled lounge bar reflects the motorsport and classic car interests of the licensees, and on the third Saturday of the month owners of classic cars and motorcycles gather in the grounds. The beamed tap room is firmly divided into two by standing timbers hung with horsebrasses. Brakspears Bitter, West Berkshire Good Old Boy and Skiff (exclusive to the pub), and maybe Scattor Rock Old Blossom on handpump, and seven wines by the glass. The dining room has waitress service at weekends only; dominoes, ring-the-bull and piped music. In front of the building are some big rustic tables and benches, and to the side the big garden has plenty of seats. Morris men visit several times a year including St George's Day and New Year's Day.

⑪ Well liked food such as lunchtime home-made soup, sandwiches, filled baguettes and ploughman's as well as nachos with guacamole, chilli, and bull fries, twice-baked goats cheese soufflé, home-made chilli or fishcakes, beer-battered cod, venison sausages and daily specials such as lamb shank with garlic and rosemary mash, tagliatelle with olive, mushroom, chilli and garlic cream sauce, and cajun blackened cod; also, two- and three-course set meals. *Starters/Snacks: £4.50 to £6.50. Main Courses: £7.00 to £17.00. Puddings: £3.50 to £5.00*

Free house ~ Licensees Robert and Kate Archard ~ Real ale ~ Bar food (12-2.30, 6.30-9.30; not Sun evening) ~ (0118) 974 4409 ~ Children allowed but must be well behaved ~ Dogs allowed in bar ~ Folk second Weds of month and blues fourth Fri of month ~ Open 12-3, 6-11; 12.30-3, 7-10.30 Sun ~ Bedrooms: £70S/£87.50S

Recommended by MDN, Martin and Pauline Jennings, Simon Collett-Jones, Dick and Madeleine Brown, David and Sue Smith, I H G Busby

Old Boot

Off A340 via Bradfield, coming from A4 just W of M4 junction 12; RG7 6LT

Rural views from garden behind neat pub with country furnishings inside, and bar and restaurant food cooked by a team of French chefs

As the kitchen here is now staffed by a team of French chefs, food is very much the draw – so to be sure of a table you must book in advance, especially at weekends. It's a stylish, very neatly kept 18th-c pub, and the beamed bar has two welcoming fires (one in an inglenook), fine old pews, settles, old country chairs, and polished tables. There are some striking pictures and hunting prints, boot ornaments in various sizes, and fresh flowers. A couple of beers from West Berkshire and a guest like Fullers London Pride on handpump and around ten wines by the glass. There are seats in the quiet sloping back garden or on the terrace, and pleasant rural views; more tables out in front.

🍴 As well as tasty bar food such as **filled baguettes, fresh cod and chips, game stew and risotto, there are more elaborate dishes too: deep-fried brie with red fruit compote, moules marinière, seared scallops, gressingham duck breast with blackcurrant sauce, venison in port wine and chestnuts, winter casseroles, best end of lamb, and steak with a stilton and mushroom sauce.** *Starters/Snacks: £5.50 to £8.50. Main Courses: £6.50 to £13.50. Puddings: £5.50*

Free house ~ Licensees John and Jeannie Haley ~ Real ale ~ Bar food ~ Restaurant ~ (0118) 974 4292 ~ Children welcome ~ Dogs allowed in bar ~ Open 11(12 Sun)-3, 6-11
Recommended by Paul Humphreys, I H G Busby, John and Joan Nash

WHITE WALTHAM   SU8477   MAP 2
Beehive 🍺
Waltham Road (B3024 W of Maidenhead); SL6 3SH

Honest bar food, changing real ales and welcoming staff in neatly kept country local

This is a smartened up village local with lots of space on the right, country kitchen chairs around sturdy tables in several comfortably carpeted areas, and a conservatory. The neat bar to the left is brightened up by cheerful scatter cushions on its comfortable seats – built-in wall seats, captain's chairs and a leather wing armchair. Brakspears, Fullers London Pride, Greene King Abbot and a changing guest such as Loddons Ferrymans Gold on handpump and a good choice of soft drinks, nuts and so forth; piped music, games machine, and board games. Besides the few picnic-sets and teak seats out by the topiary on the front grass, there are more on a good-sized sheltered back lawn. It's just by the village cricket field. Good disabled access and facilities.

🍴 Honest bar food includes **sandwiches and ploughman's, soup, calamari in home-made batter, home-cooked ham and eggs, spicy beanburger, home-made thai-style fishcakes, steak and kidney pie, braised lamb shank, and puddings like belgian chocolate mousse** *Starters/Snacks: £3.25 to £6.95. Main Courses: £7.95 to £16.95. Puddings: £3.25 to £4.50*

Enterprise ~ Lease Guy Martin ~ Real ale ~ Bar food (12-2.30, 5.30-9.30; all day weekends) ~ Restaurant ~ (01628) 822877 ~ Children welcome ~ Dogs welcome ~ Open 11-3, 5-11; 11-12 Sat; 12-10.30 Sun
Recommended by Paul Humphreys, Dr and Mrs A K Clarke, Alan and Carolin Tidbury

WINTERBOURNE   SU4572   MAP 2
Winterbourne Arms 🍷
3.7 miles from M4 junction 13; A34 N, bear immediately left up slip road for Chieveley towards North Heath when the main road bends round to the right, and follow Winterbourne signs; RG20 8BB

Charming and friendly with country furnishings, lots of wines by the glass and enjoyable bar food; large landscaped garden

You can be sure of a warm welcome from the friendly landlord and his staff in this pretty black and white village house. The bars have a collection of old irons around the fireplace, early prints and old photographs of the village, and a log fire; piped music. The peaceful view over the rolling fields from the big bar windows cleverly avoids the quiet road, which is sunken between the pub's two lawns. There's a good wine list with 20 by the glass (served in elegant glasses and including sparkling and sweet wines), and Fullers London Pride, Ramsbury Gold, Wadworths 6X, and West Berkshire Good Old Boy on handpump. Seats outside in the large landscaped side garden and pretty flowering tubs and hanging baskets. The surrounding countryside here is lovely and there are nearby walks to Snelsmore Common and Donnington. More reports please.

🍴 Enjoyable bar food includes **filled baguettes and ploughman's, soup, garlic mushrooms**

in a white wine cream sauce on toasted brioche, thai fishcakes with coriander sweet chilli, home-made burger, cannelloni with ricotta cheese, spinach and bechamel sauce, gammon and eggs, and steak and kidney pie, with more elaborate evening choices and popular Sunday brunch. *Starters/Snacks: £3.25 to £8.95. Main Courses: £8.95 to £19.95. Puddings: £3.25 to £5.95*

Free house ~ Licensee Frank Adams ~ Real ale ~ Bar food (12-2.30, 6-10; 12-3.30, 6-9.30 Sun) ~ Restaurant ~ (01635) 248200 ~ Children welcome away from bar service area ~ Dogs allowed in bar ~ Open 12-3, 6-11; 12-10.30 Sun

Recommended by Mark and Joanna, John Robertson, Dave Braisted, V B Side, Mr and Mrs J S Roberts, Mr and Mrs J P Blake, Ray J Carter, Martin and Karen Wake, Mark and Ruth Brock, Mike and Sue Loseby

LUCKY DIP

Besides the fully inspected pubs, you might like to try these Lucky Dips recommended to us and described by readers (if you do, please send us reports: www.goodguides.co.uk).

ALDWORTH [SU5579]
☆ **Four Points** RG8 9RL [B4009 towards Hampstead Norreys]: Attractive thatched pub with low beams and standing timbers, good value home-made food from baguettes up, Adnams Best and Wadworths 6X, quick service, fresh flowers on tidy array of polished tables in good-sized eating area (bar area not so big), no piped music, games room; children very welcome, neat garden over road *(Mrs Ann Gray, LYM, I H G Busby)*
ASTON [SU7884]
☆ **Flower Pot** RG9 3DG [small signpost off A4130 Henley—Maidenhead at top of Remenham Hill]: Roomy country pub with roaring log fire, array of stuffed fish and fishing prints on dark green walls of opened-up dining area with new tables and chairs on its newly laid floorboards, snug traditional bar with more fishing memorabilia and life-like fox curled up on one settle, Brakspears ales with guests such as Hook Norton Old Hooky and Wychwood Dirty Tackle, reasonably priced food from sandwiches to lots of fish and game in season, friendly service; may be unobtrusive piped music, very busy with walkers and families wknds; lots of picnic-sets giving quiet country views from nice big dog-friendly orchard garden, side field with chickens, ducks and guinea fowl *(Bob and Laura Brock, BB, P Waterman, Roy Hoing, Susan and John Douglas, Michael Dandy)*
BAGNOR [SU4569]
☆ **Blackbird** RG20 8AQ [quickest approach is from Speen on edge of Newbury]: Chatty country pub in peaceful setting nr Watermill Theatre (pre-show menu, discount for actors and stage hands), friendly licensees, changing ales inc West Berkshire, home-made pubby food, simple unfussy traditional bar with log fire and old farm tools and firearms, more formal eating area off; tables in pleasant side garden and on green in front *(Emma Newsome, Paul Humphreys, BB)*
BEECH HILL [SU6964]
Elm Tree RG7 2AZ [3½ miles from M4 junction 11: A33 towards Basingstoke, turning off into Beech Hill Rd after about

2 miles]: Five carefully furnished and decorated rooms, one with dozens of clocks, Hollywood photographs and blazing fire, nice views especially from simply furnished more modern barn-style restaurant and conservatory, quick friendly staff, enjoyable food (all day wknds) from hearty baguettes up inc some unusual dishes, well kept Fullers London Pride, Greene King IPA and Old Speckled Hen and a guest beer, amazing ladies'; children welcome away from bar, benches and tables on front decking in nice setting, open all day *(David and Sue Smith, LYM)*
BINFIELD [SU8271]
Warren RG40 5SB [Forest Rd (B3034 W)]: Well laid out family dining pub, roomy and comfortably refurbished, with good friendly service even when busy, enjoyable food from enterprising ciabattas up, quite a few italian dishes, good range of wines and of soft and hot drinks; plenty of garden tables *(R Lake, P J Ridley, Alistair Forsyth)*
BISHAM [SU8585]
Bull SL7 1RR: Good-sized L-shaped bar with some booth seating and wide choice of enjoyable pubby food, Brakspears and Greene King IPA, good choice of wines by the glass, good service, separate small bar for sizeable french restaurant; piped music; pleasant garden *(Michael Dandy)*
BRACKNELL [SU8566]
Golden Retriever RG12 7PB [Nine Mile Ride (junction A3095/B3430)]: Beams galore in largely thatched Vintage Inn with comfortable farmhouse-style décor in maze of linked rooms (was a boarding kennels until a few years ago), decent food all day, Bass and Fullers London Pride, plenty of wines by the glass, lots of young attentive staff, log fires, daily papers; open all day *(Ian Phillips, P J Ridley, R Lake, David and Sue Smith)*
BURCHETTS GREEN [SU8381]
Crown SL6 6QZ [side rd from A4 after Knowl Green on left, linking to A404]: Above-average upmarket food in restauranty pub (though there is a small bar, with well kept Greene King IPA), lots of wines by the glass,

high-backed chairs; soft piped music; tables out in pleasant quiet garden *(Mrs Ann Gray, LYM, P J Ridley, Ray J Carter)*

CHADDLEWORTH [SU4177]

Ibex RG20 7ER [Main St]: Quiet village pub with enjoyable food from good baguettes up, welcoming landlady and friendly staff, good choice of beers and soft drinks, good coffee, traditional games in public bar; wheelchair access, dogs and walkers welcome, tables out on sheltered lawn and floodlit terrace *(Andrew Jones, LYM, Paul Humphreys)*

CHIEVELEY [SU4773]

☆ *Olde Red Lion* RG20 8XB [handy for M4 junction 13 via A34 N-bound; Green Lane]: Attractive village pub with welcoming log fire, friendly landlord and staff, buoyant local atmosphere, well kept Arkells ales, good choice of unpretentious yet imaginative food, low-beamed L-shaped bar with lots of brassware, back restaurant with paintings for sale; piped music, games machine, TV *(J V Dadswell, Stewart Rigby, Stan Edwards, BB, T R and B C Jenkins)*

COLD ASH [SU5169]

Spotted Dog RG18 9PR [Gladstone Lane]: Good reliable food choice giving honest value in comfortable modern pub, bright and roomy, with properly pubby atmosphere, several well kept ales and friendly efficient young staff, small restaurant off bar *(Stan Edwards)*

COOKHAM [SU8985]

Ferry SL6 9SN [Sutton Rd]: Splendidly placed riverside pub with stylish modern décor, enjoyable if not cheap food (very popular Sun lunchtime), obliging staff, real ale and some interesting lagers, contemporary artwork, blue sofas and armchairs, solid teak furnishings in light and airy Thames-view dining areas upstairs and down, dark décor and small servery in beamed core; piped music, children welcome, extensive decking overlooking river *(BB, Simon Collett-Jones, David Tindal, Roy Hoing)*

COOKHAM DEAN [SU8785]

☆ *Chequers* SL6 9BQ [Dean Lane]: Cosy pleasantly refurbished brasserie with consistently good imaginative food and buoyant atmosphere, good value wines, real ale, good friendly service, beams, flagstones, fine old fireplace, traditional furniture and decorations, sofas in bar area, back conservatory; garden picnic-sets *(Ron and Kathy Durnford, P Waterman, Fred and Kate Portnell)*

☆ *Jolly Farmer* SL6 9PD [Church Rd, off Hills Lane]: Traditional pub owned by village consortium, old-fashioned unspoilt bars with open fires, friendly staff, labrador and cat, prompt service, real ales such as Brakspears and Hop Back Summer Lightning, decent wines and coffee, stylishly simple back dining room (sandwiches and baguettes too, even on Sun), pub games, no music or machines; well behaved children welcome away from bar, tables out in front and in good quiet garden with play area

(John Saville, LYM, Paul Humphreys)

CRAZIES HILL [SU7980]

☆ *Horns* RG10 8LY [Warren Row Rd off A4 towards Cockpole Green, then follow Crazies Hill signs]: New brother-and-sister team in comfortable and individual beamed pub, Brakspears ales, good choice of wines by the glass, good value bar snacks and promising enterprising restaurant meals (can take a while, veg extra), stripped furniture and open fires, prints for sale on warm-coloured walls, raftered barn dining room; pleasant seats in large informal garden with civilised barbecues and play area *(LYM, David and Sue Smith, Paul Humphreys, June and Robin Savage)*

CURRIDGE [SU4871]

☆ *Bunk* RG18 9DS [handy for M4 junction 13, off A34 S]: More restaurant than pub, with wide choice of good interesting food (not cheap, and they add a service charge) inc Fri paella night, well kept ales inc Fullers London Pride, reasonably priced wines by the glass, buoyant atmosphere, smart stripped-wood tiled-floor bar, spacious dining conservatory overlooking meadows and woods; plenty of tables in neat garden, fine woodland walks nearby *(Richard Marjoram, Guy Vowles, BB, Dr and Mrs R E S Tanner)*

DONNINGTON [SU4668]

☆ *Castle Inn* RG14 3AA [Oxford Rd (B4494 N of Newbury; handy for M4 junction 13)]: Smart open-plan pub with good pubby bar lunches from baguettes up, wider evening menu, good choice of real ales, decent wines by the glass, attentive and welcoming young staff, plenty of pleasant nooks and corners; no dogs; tables under cocktail parasols on attractive suntrap walled terrace *(Mark and Ruth Brock, John and Rosemary Haynes)*

EAST ILSLEY [SU4981]

☆ *Crown & Horns* RG20 7LH [Just off A34, about 5 miles N of M4 junction 13; Compton Road]: Bustling pub in horse-training country, lots of interesting racing pictures, well worn in rambling beamed rooms, blazing log fire, well kept Adnams Regatta, Brakspears and Timothy Taylors Landlord, massive whisky choice, bar food and four dining rooms; piped music, TV and games machine; children and dogs allowed, comfortable tables in pretty courtyard, modern bedroom extension, open all day *(Robert and Jill Kennedy, LYM, Mrs S A Brooks, John Cook, P Price, Chris Kay, Angus and Carol Johnson, David Coleman)*

EASTBURY [SU3477]

Plough RG17 7JN: Large lively locals' bar, quieter lounge and contemporary restaurant, changing real ales, friendly staff, good value food from snacks and midweek bargains to more ambitious dishes; children welcome *(Mark and Ruth Brock)*

ETON [SU9677]

Crown & Cushion SL4 6AF [High St]: Old pub much refurbished under new management, enjoyable sensibly priced pubby bar food, unpretentious cheerful staff, mainstream beers, new restaurant *(Mike and Sue Richardson)*

George SL4 6AF [High St]: Neat dining tables on stripped wood, Brakspears, Fullers London Pride and Wadworths 6X (order from your table), good wine choice; piped music; children welcome, big back terrace with heaters *(Mike and Sue Richardson, Derek and Sylvia Stephenson)*

☆ *Gilbeys* SL4 6AF [High St]: Not a pub, but well worth knowing for imaginative home-made bar meals, nice house wines inc one from their own vines (bottled beers), cheerful helpful family service; can be very busy if there's an event at the school, best to book for light and airy back restaurant down long corridor *(Peter Smith, Judith Brown, Mike and Sue Richardson, Alistair Forsyth, BB)*

Henry VI SL4 6BD: Light and airy, with some stripped brickwork, log fire, rugs on bare boards, some comfortable leather sofas, reasonably priced home-made pubby food, Wells & Youngs Bombardier, lots of old Eton photographs; piped music, live wknds, no children or dogs; tables out on decking with own servery and barbecue *(Michael and Alison Sandy, BB)*

New College SL4 6BL [High St]: Pleasantly refurbished local with bare boards, lots of panelling and glazed partitions, college blue décor, enjoyable straightforward sensibly priced food from baguettes up, Brakspears and Fullers London Pride, friendly staff; may be piped music; nice terrace *(Michael and Alison Sandy, Pete Coxon)*

☆ *Watermans Arms* SL4 6BW [Brocas St]: Large friendly dark-panelled pub facing Eton College boat house, horseshoe servery with real ales such as Brakspears, Fullers London Pride, Hogs Back TEA and/or Wychwood Hobgoblin, prompt friendly service, good usual food (all day Fri/Sat, not Sun eve) from sandwiches to fresh fish, bargain prices, roomy back dining area, overhead Thames map and lots of old river photographs; children welcome, covered tables outside *(Bruce Bird, LYM, Ian Phillips, Michael and Alison Sandy, Derek and Sylvia Stephenson)*

FIFIELD [SU9076]

Fifield Inn SL6 2NX [just off B3024 W of Windsor; Fifield Rd]: Neat and attractive old stone-built village local with welcoming staff, Greene King IPA and Abbot, lots of wines by the glass, good value fresh restaurant and bar food inc interesting dishes (no snacks on Sun), daily papers, flame-effect fire; live jazz Sun evening; children welcome, picnic-sets in lovely garden *(June and Robin Savage)*

FINCHAMPSTEAD [SU7963]

Queens Oak RG40 4LS [Church Lane, off B3016]: Relaxed and friendly country local, largely open-plan, with good mix of simple seats and tables, some in airy parquet-floored area on right, well kept Brakspears Bitter and Special, pleasant helpful staff,

separate dining room where children allowed; picnic-sets, some sheltered, in good-sized garden with aunt sally, play area, Sun lunchtime barbecues, and perhaps wild rabbits; open all day at least in summer *(BB, Dr and Mrs Jackson)*

GREAT SHEFFORD [SU3875]

☆ *Swan* RG17 7DS [2 miles from M4 junction 14 – A338 towards Wantage (Newbury Rd)]: Low-ceilinged bow-windowed pub with good welcoming service, pleasant décor and furnishings, good log fire, enjoyable baguettes and hot dishes inc pubby favourites, real ales inc local Butts and Fullers London Pride, good wine choice, daily papers, well laid out river-view dining room; soft piped music; good wheelchair access, children in eating areas, tables on attractive waterside lawn and terrace *(John and Jill Perkins, Simon Jones, Simon Collett-Jones, Mr and Mrs J S Roberts, Mark and Ruth Brock, Colin and Janet Roe, LYM)*

HALFWAY [SU4068]

Halfway Inn RG20 8NR [A4 Hungerford—Newbury]: Nicely refurbished Badger dining pub with well divided back dining area, wide choice of enjoyable food inc some imaginative dishes, good range of wines and beers, smiling helpful landlady, daily papers and log fire in attractive rambling bar; may be faint piped music; picnic-sets on side terrace and neat back lawn *(BB)*

HOLYPORT [SU8977]

George SL6 2JL [1½ miles from M4 junction 8/9, via A308(M)/A330; The Green]: Welcoming new mother-and-daughter team doing enjoyable food inc enterprising dishes and good fresh veg in pleasant open-plan low-beamed pub with nice old fireplace, Adnams, Courage Best and Fullers London Pride, good service; picnic-sets on attractive terrace, lovely village green *(C L Metz, Sue Strachan, Michael and Alison Sandy, Michael Dandy)*

Sun & Stars SL6 2NN [Forest Green Rd]: Popular for its traditional pubby food, also some more upmarket dishes, small cosy bar and several linked eating rooms *(Paul Humphreys)*

HUNGERFORD [SU3468]

Downgate RG17 0ED [Down View, Park St]: Prettily placed and relaxing, with decent food, friendly efficient service, Arkells real ale, two linked areas overlooking common, small lower room with open fire *(J Woolf)*

HURLEY [SU8183]

Black Boys SL6 5NQ [Henley Rd (A4130 E of Henley)]: Restaurant not pub now (you can't just drop in for a drink), clean, bright and smart in the modern bare-boards style, well executed modern cooking esp fresh west country fish, Brakspears Bitter, great range of wines by the glass, woodburner separating main eating area from small bar; piped music; garden tables, walks to Thames, nine bedrooms *(Michael Dandy, David Tindal, Mr and Mrs Gordon Turner, P Waterman)*

Dew Drop SL6 6RB [small yellow sign to pub

off A4130 just W]: Country pub tucked away in nice rustic setting, popular food from good baguettes up, friendly newish landlord and good service, Brakspears ales, traditional games; children in eating area, french windows to courtyard and attractive sloping garden with barbecue, good walks *(Paul Humphreys, LYM)*

☆ *Red Lyon* SL6 5LH [A4130 SE, just off A404]: Several warmly traditional linked low-beamed and partly quarry-tiled areas, two log fires, attractive medley of seating, lots of pewter and bric-a-brac, friendly helpful service, decent food from open sandwiches and generous light dishes up, Brakspears, Greene King Old Speckled Hen and a changing guest beer, good wine and coffee choice; piped music (can be turned down for your table); children welcome, picnic-sets in good-sized garden behind, open all day *(Susan and John Douglas, Michael Dandy)*

INKPEN [SU3564]

☆ *Swan* RG17 9DX [Lower Inkpen; coming from A338 in Hungerford, take Park St (first left after railway bridge, coming from A4)]: Rambling beamed country pub with strong organic leanings in its wines as well as the food from sandwiches and pubby things to more upscale dishes (the farming owners also have an interesting organic shop next door), cosy corners, three log fires, friendly helpful service, good Butts and West Berkshire ales, local farm cider, pleasant restaurant, flagstoned games area; piped music; well behaved children welcome in eating areas, picnic-sets out in front, small quiet garden, well equipped bedrooms, open all day in summer *(Guy Vowles, LYM, Pete Baker, Betsy and Peter Little)*

KINTBURY [SU3866]

☆ *Dundas Arms* RG17 9UT [Station Rd]: Fine summer pub, with tables out on deck above Kennet & Avon Canal and pleasant walks; well kept Adnams Best, West Berkshire Mr Chubbs and a couple of changing guest beers, good coffee and wines by the glass (but pricy soft drinks), generally enjoyable home-made food (not Sun), evening restaurant; well behaved children allowed, comfortable bedrooms with own secluded waterside terrace, good breakfast, cl Sun evening *(Bruce and Sharon Eden, Chris Smith, John Robertson, Paul Humphreys, Jeff and Wendy Williams, Evelyn and Derek Walter, Lynn Sharpless, Mrs J H S Lang, Mr and Mrs P R Thomas, Franklyn Roberts, LYM, Rob Winstanley, Phyl and Jack Street, Hunter and Christine Wright, Philip and June Caunt, Colin Wood)*

KNOWL HILL [SU8178]

☆ *Bird in Hand* RG10 9UP [A4, quite handy for M4 junction 8/9]: Relaxed, civilised and roomy, with cosy alcoves, heavy beams, panelling and splendid log fire in tartan-carpeted main area, enjoyable home-made straightforward food even Sun evening from sandwiches and baguettes up (children allowed in buffet), several real ales, good

wines by the glass, good choice of other drinks, polite prompt staff in colourful waistcoats, much older side bar, smart restaurant; tables out on front terrace, tidy modern bedrooms *(Simon Collett-Jones, LYM, Mark and Diane Grist)*

☆ *Royal Oak* RG10 9YE [Pub signed off A4 in village; coming from E, first unmarked turning on left by St Peter's Church just after limit sign, after Shottesbrooke turn-off]: Perhaps more bistro than pub with a French chef/patron, though corner bar has Loddon Ferrymans Gold and Hoppit on handpump and interesting wines by the glass; by the bar is a brown leather fireside sofa but otherwise the softly lit carpeted room is all pale wood modern dining tables with comfortable rather elegant matching chairs; simple décor limited to candles, an intriguingly techno clock and just a couple of monochrome prints on buttery walls; well reproduced piped music; good, imaginative bistro-style food well up to main entry standard; good-sized informal garden with picnic-sets and sturdy play installation in a meadow; no food Sun evening or Mon; children welcome *(Brian England, Paul Humphreys, Susan and John Douglas, Simon Collett-Jones, LYM)*

LAMBOURN [SU3175]

☆ *Hare* RG17 7SD [aka Hare & Hounds; Lambourn Woodlands, well S of Lambourn itself (B4000/Hilldrop Lane)]: Restaurant rather than pub now, with good enterprising food from short choice of sophisticated light lunches to more elaborate evening menu, several nicely individual rooms inc a proper bar, elegant décor, furnishings, glass and china, welcoming landlord and friendly efficient service, Bass and Wadworths IPA or 6X, nice wines, exemplary lavatories; piped music; children welcome, garden behind with decent play area, cl Sun evening *(D R Ellis, LYM, Dr D and Mrs B Woods, Mark and Ruth Brock)*

LITTLEWICK GREEN [SU8379]

Cricketers SL6 3RA [not far from M4 junction 9; A404(M) then left on to A4, from which village signed on left; Coronation Rd]: Proper old-fashioned pub with well kept Badger ales, good choice of wines by the glass, daily papers, darts, lots of cricketing prints, friendy local atmosphere, pubby food (not Sun evening); piped music, sometimes closes for private functions; charming spot opp cricket green, bedrooms, open all day wknds *(Susan and John Douglas, LYM, Paul Humphreys, Michael Dandy)*

Novello SL6 3RX [A4, W of A404(M)]: Former Ring o' Bells, renamed for local 'We'll Gather Lilacs' song writer, friendly service, enjoyable pub food (all day wknds) from good enterprising sandwiches and light dishes to full meals, real ales such as Loddon and Marlow Rebellion from horseshoe bar, comfortable sofas, pleasant décor; open all day *(Paul Humphreys)*

Shire Horse SL6 3QA [Bath Rd; 3 miles from

M4 junction 9; A404(M) then left on to A4]: Chef & Brewer taking its name from Courage's former adjoining shire horse centre, comfortable and attractive linked areas with old beams and tiled floors, good choice of sensibly priced wines by the glass, cafetière coffee, decent food all day inc good value baguettes served promptly by young staff (who comment you to 'enjoy'); tables out on side lawn *(Paul Humphreys, LYM)*

MAIDENHEAD [SU9082]

Boulters Lock SL6 8PE [Boulters Lock Island (bridge access – best to park back in visitors' car park off Ray Mead Rd/A4094)]: Recently reopened waterside hotel on small Thames eyot, bright new décor in bar, good waitress service, restaurant; balcony tables, handy for charming park on same islet, 19 bedrooms *(Susan and John Douglas)*

Lemon Tree SL6 6NW [Golden Ball Lane, Pinkneys Green – off A308 N]: Low-beamed linked rooms and good-sized smart airy dining area, pubby food from interesting sandwiches to steaks, good service, Marlow Rebellion and Smuggler, good coffee and choice of wines by the glass; picnic-sets out on grass behind, open all day *(Michael and Alison Sandy, Michael Dandy)*

MARSH BENHAM [SU4267]

☆ *Red House* RG20 8LY [off A4 W of Newbury]: Attractive restaurant rather than pub (they no longer serve real ale), with enjoyable modern food, good staff and atmosphere, appealing library-style front room lined with bookcases and paintings, lots of wines by the glass; piped music; terrace with teak tables and chairs over long lawns sloping to water meadows and the River Kennet, cl Sun evening and Mon *(LYM, James A Waller)*

MORTIMER [SU6464]

Turners Arms RG7 3TW [Fairfield Park, West End Rd, Mortimer Common]: Recently reopened, with Brakspears ales, nice coffee and decent wines by the glass from central bar, lounge with log fire on left, dining area on right with interesting food inc thai dishes; garden tables *(J V Dadswell)*

NEWBURY [SU4766]

King Charles RG14 5BX [Cheap St]: Enjoyable food, friendly landlord and staff, real ale, imaginative décor *(anon)*

Queens RG14 5BD [Market Pl]: Lots of pictures in former coaching inn's suitably furnished linked areas, wide choice of low-priced all-day food inc OAP bargains, real ale *(W W Burke)*

OLD WINDSOR [SU9774]

Union SL4 2QY [Crimp Hill Rd, off B3021 – itself off A308/A328]: Friendly and comfortable old pub, good reasonably priced traditional bar food from sandwiches and omelettes up, well kept Courage Best, Marstons Pedigree and Theakstons Best, consistently good service from long-serving staff, big woodburner, dated black and white show-business photographs, bank notes on beams, good copper-decorated restaurant; soft piped music, fruit machine; tables under

cocktail parasols on heated front terrace, country views; comfortable bedrooms with own bathrooms *(BB, D M and B K Moores)*

PALEY STREET [SU8675]

Bridge House SL6 3JS: Small black and white pub with comfortably refurbished beamed bar, friendly long-serving landlady, cheerful helpful service even when busy, Brakspears SB and Fullers London Pride, good value home-made food from lunchtime baguettes and baked potatoes up, pleasant back dining room; children welcome, big garden *(June and Robin Savage, Paul Humphreys)*

PANGBOURNE [SU6376]

☆ *Cross Keys* RG8 7AR [Church Rd, opp church]: Linked beamed rooms and open fires, new oak floors in dining rooms, new chef/landlord doing enjoyable bar food (all day wknds) from good baguettes to steaks, own-baked bread, interesting restaurant menu, Greene King and guest ales; good back terrace with heated pergola and decorative japanese bridge over little River Pang, open all day *(Paul Humphreys)*

Swan RG8 7DU [Shooters Hill]: Attractive Thames-side pub dating from 17th c, good choice of wines by the glass, Greene King ales, friendly staff, lounge with open fire, river-view dining balcony and conservatory (food all day); piped music, sports TV; picnic-sets on terrace overlooking weir and moorings, open all day *(Roy and Lindsey Fentiman, Bob and Angela Brooks)*

PEASEMORE [SU4577]

☆ *Fox & Hounds* RG20 7JN [off B4494 Newbury—Wantage]: Genuine country local tucked away in racehorse country, good honestly priced home-made food, particularly good house wines, well kept West Berkshire ales, good service, welcoming log fire *(LYM, Stan Edwards, Mark and Ruth Brock)*

READING [SU7273]

☆ *Fishermans Cottage* RG1 3DW [Kennet Side – easiest to walk from Orts Rd, off Kings Rd]: Friendly local in nice spot by canal lock and towpath; good value lunches inc lots of hot or cold sandwiches (very busy then but service quick), full Fullers beer range, small choice of wines, modern furnishings, pleasant stone snug behind woodburning range, light and airy conservatory, small darts room; SkyTV; dogs allowed (not in garden), waterside tables, lovely big back garden *(the Didler, Susan and John Douglas)*

Red Cow RG4 5BE [Star Rd, Caversham]: Local doing well under friendly new couple, home-made bar lunches, welcoming atmosphere, darts and pool, lots of activities; garden with play area and barbecues, open all day *(Terry Tozer)*

☆ *Retreat* RG1 4EH [St Johns St]: Friendly 1960ish backstreet local with good choice of particularly well kept changing ales, farm ciders, reasonable prices, back bar with darts; open all day Fri-Sun *(Mark and Diane Grist, John Slade, the Didler)*

☆ *Sweeney & Todd* RG1 7RD [Castle St]: Cross between café and pub with exceptional value home-made pies all day, also ploughman's, casseroles and roasts, in warren of little period-feel alcoves and other areas on various levels, cheery staff, small well stocked bar with Adnams Best, Badger Tanglefoot, Wadworths 6X and a changing guest beer, children welcome in restaurant area, open all day (cl Sun and bank hols) *(Ray J Carter, LYM, the Didler, Susan and John Douglas)*

SHEFFORD WOODLANDS [SU3673]

☆ *Pheasant* RG17 7AA [less than ½ mile from M4 junction 14 – A338 towards Wantage then 1st left on to B4000]: Tucked-away country pub with lots of horse-racing pictures and cartoons and horsey customers, enjoyable regularly changing traditional food in end dining area with burgundy décor and bistro atmosphere, welcoming old-school landlord and friendly staff, worthwhile real ales, log fires, four neat rooms inc public bar with games inc ring the bull; attractive views from pleasant garden *(LYM, I H G Busby, John Urquhart)*

SONNING [SU7575]

☆ *Bull* RG4 6UP [off B478, by church; village signed off A4 E of Reading]: Unchanging old-world inn in pretty setting nr Thames, low heavy beams, cosy alcoves, cushioned antique settles and low-slung chairs, inglenook log fires, well kept Fullers ales, enjoyable food from grand baguettes to steaks, quick friendly service by neat waistcoated staff, back dining area (children allowed); large TV in small public bar; charming courtyard, five attractive bedrooms, open all day summer wknds *(Simon Collett-Jones, John and Joan Nash, G Robinson, LYM, Susan and John Douglas, Mike and Heather Watson)*

STOCKCROSS [SU4368]

Rising Sun RG20 8LG [Ermin St]: Traditional village pub tied to West Berkshire, their ales well kept inc a Mild, friendly licensees with motor-cycling and folk music interests (Sun folk night), lunchtime ploughman's and enjoyable hearty home-made food (not Sun night) such as faggots, pies and chops, entertaining dog called The Luggage and cat called Star, darts, simple carpeted dining room; picnic-sets in enclosed garden, open all day Sat *(Mark and Ruth Brock)*

STREATLEY [SU5980]

Bull RG8 9JJ [Reading Rd (A417/B4009)]: Pleasantly olde-worlde refurbishment (in fact dates from Tudor times), friendly staff, real ales inc Brakspears; tables in tree-sheltered garden, good walks, bedrooms *(N R White)*

SUNNINGHILL [SU9568]

Belvedere Arms SL5 7SB [London Rd]: Thoughtfully modernised with enjoyable smart food, well kept beer, good service, fancy furnishings; large split-level garden with stream *(Piotr Chodzko-Zajko)*

SWALLOWFIELD [SU7364]

☆ *George & Dragon* RG7 1TJ [Church Rd, towards Farley Hill]: Restauranty pub, but relaxed and cottagey, with fresh hearty food

inc some good interesting recipes, Brakspears, Fullers London Pride and Youngs, good reasonably priced wines, big log fire, stripped beams, red walls, rugs on flagstones and plenty of character and atmosphere; very popular with business diners, piped music; well behaved children welcome, open all day *(KC, David and Sue Smith, LYM, PL, R and H Fraser, Richard Endacott)*

THEALE [SU6168]

☆ *Winning Hand* RG7 5JB [A4 W, opp Sulhamstead turn; handy for M4 junction 12]: Enjoyable reasonably priced food from sandwiches, baguettes and light meals up inc particularly good fish and chips, good friendly service, Arkells and Hook Norton, varied wine list, restaurant; quiet piped music; bright gardens, four bedrooms *(John Baish, Bob and Margaret Holder)*

TIDMARSH [SU6374]

Greyhound RG8 8ER [A340 S of Pangbourne]: Thatched pub, prettily restored after a fire, with good service, enjoyable food, Fullers ales inc seasonal ones, back dining extension; good walks nearby *(Robert Turnham, Dr and Mrs A K Clarke)*

UPPER BASILDON [SU5976]

Red Lion RG8 8NG [Aldworth Rd]: Small open-plan Victorian pub with enjoyable upmarket food in bar and dining room, well kept Brakspears and Fullers London Pride, friendly staff, decent house wines, interesting pictures; weekly live music, popular with young people then; large garden with play area *(I H G Busby)*

WALTHAM ST LAWRENCE [SU8376]

☆ *Bell* RG10 0JJ [B3024 E of Twyford; The Street]: Heavy-beamed and timbered village local doing well under current cheerful landlord, chatty regulars too, good log fires, efficient friendly service, good value pubby bar food (not Sun evening) from good sandwiches and focaccias up inc interesting pizzas, small choice of main dishes, well kept changing local ales such as Loddon and West Berkshire, plenty of malt whiskies, good wine, daily papers, compact panelled lounge; children and dogs welcome, tables in back garden with extended terrace, open all day wknds *(Simon Collett-Jones, LYM, Paul Humphreys, Tracey and Stephen Groves, Mark and Diane Grist)*

Star RG10 0HY [Broadmoor Rd]: Neat and quiet old pub with enjoyable food from good if not cheap sandwiches and substantial starters to restauranty dishes, friendly licensees, beams, brasses, daily papers, open fire, Wadworths ales; Mon quiz night *(Paul Humphreys, Mr and Mrs A Silver)*

WARGRAVE [SU7878]

White Hart RG10 8BU: Low-beamed lounge bar of some character, friendly helpful staff, well kept Fullers London Pride, good value wines, enjoyable unpretentious food with some novel touches, restaurant on right *(LYM, Paul Humphreys)*

WEST ILSLEY [SU4782]

Harrow RG20 7AR [signed off A34 at E Ilsley

slip road]: Appealing country pub in peaceful spot overlooking cricket pitch and pond, Victorian prints in deep-coloured knocked-through bar, some antique furnishings, log fire, Greene King ales, good choice of wines by the glass; children in eating areas, dogs allowed in bar, picnic-sets in big garden, more seats on pleasant terrace, cl Sun evening (I H G Busby, Tony and Wendy Hobden, F D Smith, Bridget Nichols, A G Marx, J and F Gowers, LYM)

WINDSOR [SU9676]

51 SL4 1DE [Peascod St]: Contemporary décor and furnishings in modern bar with John Smiths, pubby food inc Sun roast, John Smiths, daily papers; nice sheltered side courtyard (Michael Dandy)

☆ *Carpenters Arms* SL4 1PB [Market St]: Town pub ambling around central servery with particularly well kept changing ales such as Adnams, Greene King Old Speckled Hen, Marlow Rebellion and Wadworths 6X, good value pubby food all day from sandwiches and baked potatoes up (can take a while when busy), good choice of wines by the glass, sturdy pub furnishings and Victorian-style décor inc two pretty fireplaces, family areas up a few steps, also downstairs beside former tunnel entrance with suits of armour; piped music, no nearby parking; tables out on cobbled pedestrian alley opp castle, handy for Legoland bus stop, open all day (Michael and Alison Sandy, Pete Coxon, Bruce Bird, Michael Dandy, BB, Keith and Janet Morris, David and Sue Smith, Derek and Sylvia Stephenson)

Greene Oak SL4 5UW [Dedworth Rd]: Latest reincarnation of former Nags Head, lately Hungry Horse: now a smart Greene King dining pub with upmarket food, pleasant informal service, traditional furnishings with a modern slant (Simon Collett-Jones)

Three Tuns SL4 1PB [Market St]: Courage Best and Directors from central servery, kind helpful service, sensibly priced pubby food from good sandwiches up, lots of games; piped music; tables out on pedestrianised street (Pete Coxon, Michael Dandy)

☆ *Two Brewers* SL4 1LB [Park St]: Three compact bare-board rooms, Courage Best, Fullers London Pride and Wadworths 6X, quite a few wines by the glass, friendly staff and thriving old-fashioned pub atmosphere, daily papers; no children inside; tables out by pretty Georgian street next to Windsor Park's Long Walk, has been open all day (Michael Dandy, Mr and Mrs J P Blake, Ian Phillips, John Saville, Ray J Carter, Fr Robert Marsh, LYM, Michael and Alison Sandy)

Vansittart Arms SL4 5DD [Vansittart Rd]: Busy but relaxed three-room Victorian pub, interesting local prints, some old furniture and cosy corners, efficient service, well kept Fullers ales, enjoyable reasonably priced food, home-made and chip-free, good choice of wines by the glass; quiet piped music;

children welcome, pleasant terrace tables (Bruce Bird)

Windsor Castle SL4 2AP [Kings Rd]: Pleasant informal atmosphere, emphasis on enjoyable food without discouraging drinkers, four real ales such as Adnams, Brakspears, Caledonian Deuchars IPA and Hogs Back TEA, good choice of wines by the glass, helpful staff, log fire; sports TV; dogs very welcome (handy for the Park with view over Royal Paddocks to Frogmore House), good parking (a real bonus here), small outside deck (John Millwood, Michael Dandy, Dr R W Pickles)

Windsor Lad SL4 5HQ [Maidenhead Rd (A308)]: Useful two-level Harvester with uncramped standard seating, wide food range, ample helpings, upper-level salad bar (go back as often as you like), good friendly service; unobtrusive piped music; children welcome (Ron and Sheila Corbett)

WINNERSH [SU7871]

☆ *Wheelwrights Arms* RG10 0TR [off A329 Reading—Wokingham at Winnersh crossroads by Sainsburys, signed Hurst, Twyford; then right into Davis Way]: Cheerfully bustling beamed local with big woodburner, bare black boards and flagstones, Wadworths IPA, 6X and guest beers, great value lunchtime food from huge doorstep sandwiches up, quick friendly service, cottagey dining area; may keep your credit card; children welcome, disabled parking and facilities, picnic-sets in smallish garden with terrace, open all day wknds (Paul Humphreys, R T and J C Moggridge, John Baish, BB)

WOODSIDE [SU9271]

Duke of Edinburgh SL4 2DP [Woodside Rd (narrow turn off A332 Windsor—Ascot S of B3034)]: Welcoming local with Arkells 2B, 3B and Kingsdown, good choice of wines by the glass, friendly service, sofas in roomy and civilised middle lounge, usual bar food from good range of proper sandwiches up, separate dining room, solidly furnished main locals' bar; big-screen TV, quiz night; children welcome, tables out in front and in pleasant garden with summer marquee (John and Joyce Snell, Tracey and Stephen Groves)

☆ *Rose & Crown* SL4 2DP [Woodside Rd, Winkfield, off A332 Ascot—Windsor]: Thriving pub with low-beamed bar and extended dining area, good attentive service, enjoyable food (not Sun or Mon evening) using good ingredients from lunchtime sandwiches and baguettes to more elaborate evening restaurant dishes and popular Sun lunch, Greene King ales, interesting affordable wines; piped music, games machine; children in eating areas, tables and swing in side garden backed by woodland, bedrooms, open all day, cl Sun evening (Lesley and Barbara Owen, LYM, Jack and Sandra Clarfelt, Mrs Ann Gray)

WOOLHAMPTON [SU5766]

Rowbarge RG7 5SH [Station Rd]: Big canalside family dining pub under new management, good range of fresh food, well kept Greene King ales, good log fire in attractively refurbished beamed bar, panelled side room, large water-view conservatory; tables out by water and in roomy garden with fishpond, moorings not far *(LYM, Angus and Rosemary Campbell)*

YATTENDON [SU5574]

☆ *Royal Oak* RG18 0UG [The Square; B4009 NE from Newbury; turn right at Hampstead Norreys, village signposted on left]: Handsome civilised inn with panelled and prettily decorated brasserie/bar (quite expensive, no food Sun evening), nice log fire and striking flower arrangements, West Berkshire beers, several wines by the glass; well behaved children welcome, tables in pleasant walled garden, more in front by peaceful village square, attractive bedrooms, open all day *(the Didler, Dr and Mrs A K Clarke, LYM, Richard Atherton, Bob and Margaret Holder, Gerald and Gabrielle Culliford)*

Post Office address codings confusingly give the impression that some pubs are in Berkshire, when they're really in Buckinghamshire, Oxfordshire or Hampshire (which is where we list them).

Buckinghamshire

There's a fine choice of proper friendly country pubs in pretty walking country here – as well as some very smart dining pubs. Pubs on top form this year include the Three Horseshoes at Bennett End (the new licensee/chef is working hard, smartening up rooms and the garden), the welcoming Royal Oak at Bovingdon Green (a fantastic choice of pudding wines), the Red Lion at Chenies (run by long-standing and friendly people), the Swan at Denham (super imaginative food), the much enjoyed Palmers Arms at Dorney (more of a dining pub with impeccably presented food), the Royal Standard of England at Forty Green (particularly for its historic interior), the White Horse at Hedgerley (lots of real ales in a real country local), the cheerfully run and simple Crown at Little Missenden, the bustling Polecat at Prestwood (a good local following), the very popular Frog at Skirmett (a super pub run by cheerful people), and the civilised Boot at Soulbury. Many of the pubs specialise in good food; the top title of Buckinghamshire Dining Pub of the Year is awarded to the Swan at Denham. After rather a lot of new entries over the last few years, this year we have restricted ourselves to just one here: the beautifully placed Chequers at Fingest, back in the *Guide* after all too long a break. Three pubs in the Lucky Dip section at the end of the chapter particularly worth looking out for are the Red Lion at Bradenham, Ivy House in Chalfont St Giles and Cowpers Oak at Weston Underwood. On the expensive side for pub food, this county tends to be pricy for drinks, too: Rebellion, Vale and Chiltern are local beers to look out for, often featuring as the cheapest a pub here has on offer.

AYLESBURY

SP8113   MAP 4

Kings Head ◀

Kings Head Passage (narrow passage off Bourbon Street), also entrance off Temple Street; no nearby parking except for disabled; HP20 2RW

Handsome and carefully restored town centre pub with civilised atmosphere, good local ales (used in the food, too), and friendly service

Only a part of this handsome, 15th-c National Trust-owned building is used as a pub – other parts include a coffee shop, arts and crafts shop, and conference rooms, and besides striking early Tudor window lighting, the former Great Hall has even more ancient stained glass showing the Royal Arms of Henry VI and Margaret of Anjou. The three rooms have been restored with careful and unpretentious simplicity – stripped boards, cream walls with little decoration, gentle lighting, a variety of seating which includes upholstered sofas and armchairs, cushioned high-backed settles and little dove-grey café chairs. Most of the bar tables are of round glass, supported on low cask tops; the left-hand room has simple modern pale dining tables and chairs. It's all nicely low-key – not smart, but thoroughly civilised. The neat corner bar has Chiltern Ale, Beechwood Bitter, 300s Old Ale, and a guest on handpump (there will be several beer festivals during the summer with pig roasts and jazz), and some interesting bottled beers, service is friendly, and there's no piped music or machines; disabled access and facilities. The original cobbled courtyard has teak seats and tables, some under cover of a pillared roof, and there's now a florist and (in the old panelled dining room) Aylesbury Tourist Information. No children inside. Several undercover outdoor areas for smokers.

🍴 Their own beer is included in much of the food: home-made soup, sandwiches, ploughman's with beer cheese and beer bread, three different sausages made with three different beers and spiced ale gravy, and a proper steak in ale pie, and puddings such as barley wine fruit cake and peach and cherry crumble. *Starters/Snacks: £3.40 to £6.00. Main Courses: £4.95 to £15.95. Puddings: £2.50 to £7.50*

Chiltern ~ Manager Claire Bignell ~ Real ale ~ Bar food (12-2(3 Sat), 6-8; 1-4 Sun; not Sun or Mon evenings) ~ (01296) 718812 ~ Occasional live music ~ Open 11-11; 12-10.30 Sun

Recommended by Tim and Ann Newell, Caren Harris, Adam F Padel, Ann Griffiths, Mike Pugh, Roger Shipperley

BENNETT END   SU7897   MAP 4

Three Horseshoes

Horseshoe Road; from Radnage follow unclassified road towards Princes Risborough and turn left into Bennett End Road, then right into Horseshoe Road; HP14 4EB

Several seating areas in quietly set country pub with quite an emphasis on interesting meals

Close to the M40 but in a tranquil spot, this old country inn is a popular and friendly place. There are several separate seating areas: to the left of the entrance (mind your head) is the flagstoned and darkly-lit snug bar with a log fire in the raised stone fireplace and original brickwork and bread oven. To the right of the entrance are two further sitting areas, one with a long wooden winged settle and the other enclosed by standing timbers with wooden flooring and a woodburning stove. The two-part light and airy dining room (now modern and minimalist in design) overlooks the garden and valley beyond. Fullers London Pride and a couple of changing guests on handpump, several wines by the glass including local champagne, summer Pimms and winter mulled wine, all served by smart uniformed staff. Seats in the garden and a rather endearing red telephone box that is gradually sinking into one of the duck ponds. Some of the bedrooms have been newly refurbished.

🍴 Well liked bar food such as sandwiches, soup, tiger prawns with indian spiced risotto, smoked ham hock and parsley terrine with caper and gherkin dressing, poached smoked haddock with bubble and squeak and soft poached egg, chicken breast with gorgonzola polenta, leeks and sage jus, roast rump of lamb with niçoise vegetables, and puddings such as crème brûlée with rhubarb and ginger compote or bread and butter pudding with marmalade ice-cream; two- and three-course set lunchtime menus. *Starters/Snacks: £4.50 to £9.00. Main Courses: £9.50 to £18.00. Puddings: £4.50 to £6.00*

Free house ~ Licensee Simon Crawshaw ~ Real ale ~ Bar food (not winter Sun evening or winter Mon) ~ Restaurant ~ (01494) 483273 ~ Children welcome ~ Dogs allowed in bar ~ Monthly live jazz ~ Open 12-3, 6-11; 12-8 Sun; closed winter Sun evening (except for residents) and all day Mon ~ Bedrooms: £75S/£110B

Recommended by Tracey and Stephen Groves, Janet Cameron, Colin and Janet Roe, Brian Young, Tim and Ann Newell, Susan and John Douglas, Brian Root, Stephen Moss, Ken and Pat Headley, Paul Humphreys, Howard Dell, Roy Hoing, Mrs Ann Gray

BOVINGDON GREEN   SU8386   MAP 2

Royal Oak 🍴 ♀

¾ mile N of Marlow, on back road to Frieth signposted off West Street (A4155) in centre; SL7 2JF

Fantastic choice of wines by glass and popular food in civilised and attractively decorated pub

Run by people who really care, this rather civilised old whitewashed pub is enjoyed by a good mix of people – locals in for a chat and a pint, couples out for a special meal, and walkers with their dogs seeking some basic sustenance. Several attractively decorated areas open off the central bar, the half-panelled walls variously painted in pale blue, green or cream: the cosiest part is the low-beamed room closest to the car park, with three small tables, a woodburner in an exposed brick fireplace, and a big pile of logs. Throughout there's a mix of church chairs, stripped wooden tables and chunky wall seats, with rugs on the partly wooden, partly flagstoned floors, co-ordinated cushions and curtains, and a very bright, airy feel; thoughtful extra touches set the tone, with a big, square bowl of olives on the bar, carefully laid out newspapers and fresh flowers or candles on the tables. Brakspears Bitter, Fullers London Pride, and local Rebellion IPA on handpump, 18 wines and ten pudding wines by the glass and quick, helpful service; board games, and piped music. A terrace with good solid tables leads to an appealing garden with plenty more, and there's a smaller garden at the side as well. The pub is part of a little group which comprises the Alford Arms in Frithsden (see Hertfordshire main entries), the Old Queens Head in Penn (Buckinghamshire), and the Swan at Denham (see Buckinghamshire main entries). Sheltered area next to bar for smokers.

🍴 Popular bar food includes home-made soup, salt hake brandade with salsa verde, bubble and squeak with oak smoked bacon, poached egg and hollandaise, slow-roast pork belly on cumin mash with apple compote and cider cream sauce, wild mushroom and spiced courgette strudel with caraway cream sauce, baked gilt-head bream with roast garlic, thyme and paprika, roast lamb rump on lemon and garlic hummus with candied beetroot and red wine jus, and puddings such as warm chocolate cake with rocky road ice-cream or vanilla bean crème brûlée with brandy ginger snaps. A good few tables may have reserved signs (it's worth booking ahead, especially on Sundays). *Starters/Snacks: £3.75 to £6.75. Main Courses: £10.75 to £14.75. Puddings: £4.25 to £6.50*

Salisbury Pubs ~ Lease Trasna Rice Giff ~ Real ale ~ Bar food (12-2.30(4 Sun), 7-10) ~ Restaurant ~ (01628) 488611 ~ Children welcome ~ Dogs allowed in bar ~ Open 11-11; 12-10.30 Sun; closed winter Sun evening (except for residents) and all day Mon

Recommended by Mike and Nicky Pleass, Stephen Moss, A J Murray, Mrs Ann Gray, Tracey and Stephen Groves, Jeff and Wendy Williams, Geoff Simms, Michael Dandy, Simon Collett-Jones, Maggie Atherton

CADMORE END
SU7892 MAP 4

Old Ship 🍺
B482 Stokenchurch—Marlow (Marlow Road); HP14 3PN

Small and unspoilt with simply furnished bars, and decent food and beer

There's plenty of unpretentious charm in the two little low-beamed rooms of the bar in this tiny and carefully restored 17th-c cottage. They are separated by standing timbers and simply furnished with scrubbed country tables and bench and church chair seating (one still has a hole for a game called five-farthings); warm coal fire. Well kept Brakspears, Hook Norton and Youngs tapped straight from the cask down in the cellar and carried upstairs; piped music and TV. Outside, there are seats in the sheltered garden with a large pergola, and a terrace at the end of the bar with cushioned seats and clothed tables. Parking is on the other side of the road.

🍴 Simple, tasty bar food under the new licensee includes a good range of filled baguettes and ploughman's, local ham and eggs or local sausages, salmon and cod fishcakes, hand-made pies, and puddings such as treacle sponge. *Starters/Snacks: £3.95 to £5.95. Main Courses: £7.95 to £11.95. Puddings: £4.95*

Free house ~ Licensee Richard O'Neill ~ Real ale ~ Bar food (not Sun evening, not Mon) ~ Restaurant ~ (01494) 883496 ~ Children allowed but with restrictions ~ Open 12-2.30, 5.30-11; 12-3, 7-10.30 Sun; closed Mon

Recommended by Michael Dandy, Edmund Coan, Pete Baker, B and M Kendall, Alan and Anne Driver, the Didler, Brian and Rosalie Laverick

---

Looking for a pub with a really special garden, or in lovely countryside, or with an outstanding view, or right by the water? They are listed separately, at the back of the book.

CHALFONT ST GILES   SU9893   MAP 4

White Hart ⑪

Three Households (main street, W); HP8 4LP

Bustling place with quite an emphasis on food, modern but comfortable furnishings, neatly dressed staff

---

The emphasis here is on the interesting, modern – but not cheap – food, though they do keep Greene King IPA, Morlands Original, Speckled Hen and Ruddles County on handpump. The civilised bar has chocolate leather seats and sofas and contemporary artwork on the mushroom coloured walls. The extended, spreading dining room (similarly furnished to the bar) is mainly bare boards – the bright acoustics make for a lively medley of chatter – and it can be on the noisy side when very busy. Several wines by the glass, broadsheet daily papers, piped music, and neatly dressed young staff. A sheltered back terrace has squarish picnic-sets under cocktail parasols, with more beyond in the garden. Please note, no under 21s (but see below for children). More reports please.

⑪ As well as sandwiches and daily specials, the menu might include **pressing of confit suckling pig, marinated foie gras, sauternes fig chutney and toasted brioche, potted brown shrimps with spiced avocado, deep-fried goats cheese with tapenade, walnut and olive salad, a trio of sausages with bacon crisps and caramelised onion gravy, monkfish tails, prawn and dill mousse, wrapped in savoy cabbage and parma ham with champagne fish sauce and roasted guinea fowl, raisin and thyme farce and redcurrant and thyme jus; puddings such as orange crème brûlée or sticky toffee pudding with butterscotch sauce, banana and coconut ice-cream.** *Starters/Snacks: £4.50 to £10.95. Main Courses: £9.25 to £17.95. Puddings: £4.95 to £5.75*

Greene King ~ Lease Scott MacRae ~ Real ale ~ Bar food (12-2(2.30 Sat and Sun), 6.30-9.30) ~ Restaurant ~ (01494) 872441 ~ Children allowed if with an adult ~ Dogs allowed in bar ~ Open 11.30-2.30, 5.30-11(11.30 Sat); 12-10.30 Sun ~ Bedrooms: £77.50S/£97.50S

Recommended by Mr and Mrs A Curry, Howard Dell, Roy Hoing

CHENIES   TQ0298   MAP 3

Red Lion ★ ◀

2 miles from M25 junction 18; A404 towards Amersham, then village signposted on right; Chesham Road; WD3 6ED

Traditional pub with long-serving licensees, a bustling atmosphere, and very well liked food

---

Readers love the fact that this splendid small village pub changes so little. It's run by long-serving and welcoming licensees and the bustling, unpretentious L-shaped bar has comfortable built-in wall benches by the front windows, other traditional seats and tables, and original photographs of the village and traction engines; there's also a small back snug and (hopefully) by the time this edition is published, a new restaurant. Very well kept Rebellion Lion Pride (brewed for the pub), Vale Best Bitter, Wadworths 6X, and a guest beer on handpump, 13 wines by the glass and some nice malt whiskies. The hanging baskets and window boxes are pretty in summer, and there are picnic-sets on a small side terrace. No children, games machines or piped music.

⑪ Very popular and reasonably priced food includes **home-made pâté, fishcake with horseradish and beetroot dip, mushroom and mixed pepper stroganoff, bangers with red wine gravy and mash of the day, roast pork belly with crackling and apple sauce, coq au vin, a curry of the day, their much loved home-made lamb pie, and home-made puddings.** *Starters/Snacks: £3.65 to £5.95. Main Courses: £7.50 to £11.95. Puddings: £2.95 to £4.25*

Free house ~ Licensee Mike Norris ~ Real ale ~ Bar food (12-2, 7-10; 12-2.30, 6.30-9.30 Sun) ~ Restaurant ~ (01923) 282722 ~ Dogs allowed in bar ~ Open 11-2.30, 5.30-11; 12-3, 6.30-10.30 Sun; closed 25 Dec

Recommended by Michael Dandy, Howard Dell, Colin and Alma Gent, Jarrod and Wendy Hopkinson, Brian P White, Kevin Thorpe, Stuart and Doreen Ritchie, Ian Phillips, Roy Hoing, Joan York

DENHAM

TQ0487   MAP 3

Swan 🍴 ♀

¾ mile from M40 junction 1 or M25 junction 16; follow Denham Village signs; UB9 5BH
BUCKINGHAMSHIRE DINING PUB OF THE YEAR

So popular, it's best to book in advance – civilised dining pub with a fine choice of wines and interesting food

With very good food and friendly, helpful staff, this civilised dining pub is, not surprisingly, very popular and it's best to book a table in advance. The rooms are stylishly furnished with a nice mix of antique and old-fashioned chairs and solid tables, individually chosen pictures on the cream and warm green walls, rich heavily draped curtains, inviting open fires (usually lit), newspapers to read, and fresh flowers. A smashing choice of 17 wines plus ten pudding wines by two sizes of glass, and Courage Best, Rebellion IPA, and Wadworths 6X on handpump; piped music. The extensive garden is floodlit at night, and leads from a sheltered terrace with tables to a more spacious lawn. It can get busy at weekends, and parking may be difficult. The wisteria is very pretty in May. The pub is part of a little group which comprises the Royal Oak, Bovingdon Green and the Old Queens Head in Penn (also in Buckinghamshire) and the Alford Arms in Frithsden (see Hertfordshire main entries).

🍴 Promptly served and particularly good, the bar food includes soup, guinea fowl and foie gras ballotine with cranberry and orange chutney, crab and tomato risotto with crispy seaweed, toad in the hole with grain mustard mash and red onion gravy, butternut squash, sweet potato and celeriac wellington with lentil cream, braised lamb shank on moroccan vegetable ragoût, beer-battered pollack on pea purée, chargrilled rib-eye steak with dijon mustard butter, and puddings like chocolate truffle doughnuts with vanilla milkshake or plum crème brûlée with pistachio tuile. Best to book to be sure of a table. *Starters/Snacks: £3.75 to £6.75. Main Courses: £10.75 to £14.75. Puddings: £4.25 to £6.50*

Salisbury Pubs ~ Lease Mark Littlewood ~ Real ale ~ Bar food (12-2.30(4 Sun), 7-10) ~ Restaurant ~ (01895) 832085 ~ Children welcome ~ Dogs allowed in bar ~ Open 11-11; 12-10.30 Sun; closed 25 and 26 Dec

Recommended by Ian Phillips, Philip Clouts, Mrs Hazel Rainer, John Saville, Martin and Karen Wake, Grahame Brooks, Phil and Gill Wass, Kevin Thomas, Nina Randall

DORNEY

SU9279   MAP 2

Palmer Arms 🍴 ♀

2.7 miles from M4 junction 7; turn left on to A4, then left on B3026; Village Road; SL4 6QW

Well presented food in smart dining pub including good value set menus and Sunday lunch with jazz; attractive garden

As this extended and smartly modernised dining pub is in an attractive conservation village and close to the M4, it can get pretty busy. They do keep Greene King IPA and Abbot on handpump and have 20 wines by the glass, but it's the good food that draws in most customers. The bar is civilised and relaxed with several separate-seeming areas around a central counter: a nicely polished wooden floor, newspapers, a couple of fireplaces and the occasional sofa, fresh flowers, mirrors, and art for sale on the walls. At the back is a more elegant dining room, with exposed brick walls, long red curtains, solid wooden tables and brown leather armchairs. The terrace overlooks a very attractively landscaped palm-filled garden, with plenty of stylish tables and chairs. The drive from here to Eton throws up splendid views of Windsor Castle.

🍴 Lunchtime choices such as a cheese platter, trio of local sausages and ham terrine with pineapple chutney and poached egg, plus home-made soup, stilton, celery, port and walnut pâté, vegetable moussaka, fish pie, well hung rib-eye steak with garlic butter, and seared duck breast with parsnip purée and raspberry and cassis sauce, with puddings like chocolate, strawberry and turkish delight fool or lemon brûlée with citrus shortbread; two- and three-course set meals, too. *Starters/Snacks: £5.00 to £9.50. Main Courses: £9.00 to £18.00. Puddings: £5.00 to £6.00*

Greene King ~ Lease Elizabeth Dax ~ Real ale ~ Bar food (12-2.30, 6.30-9.30; 12-4 Sun; not Sun evening) ~ Restaurant ~ (01628) 666612 ~ Children allowed in restaurant before 8pm ~ Jazz first Sun of month ~ Open 11-11; 12-6 Sun; closed Jan1-4; Sun evening

Recommended by Ian Phillips, Susan and John Douglas, Michael Dandy, A J Murray, Mike and Sue Richardson, Simon Collett-Jones, Kevin Thomas, Nina Randall, Gerald and Gabrielle Culliford

Pineapple ◖

2.4 miles from M4 junction 7; turn left on to A4, then left on B3026 (or take first left off A4 at traffic lights, into Huntercombe Lane S, then left at T junction on main road – shorter but slower); Lake End Road; SL4 6QS

Fantastic choice of interesting sandwiches in unpretentious pub

This is a nicely old-fashioned and unpretentious pub with low shiny Anaglypta ceilings, black-panelled dados and sturdy country tables – one very long, another in a big bow window. There is a woodburning stove at one end, a pretty little fireplace in a second room and china pineapples join the decorations on a set of shelves in one of three cottagey carpeted linked rooms on the left. It's bare boards on the right where the bar counter has Black Sheep Bitter, Fullers London Pride and Greene King IPA on handpump and several wines by the glass; friendly staff and piped music. A roadside verandah has some rustic tables, and there are plenty of round picnic-sets out in the garden, some on fairy-lit decking under an oak tree; the nearby motorway makes itself heard out here.

🍴 **A remarkable choice of up to 1,000 varieties of sandwiches in five different fresh breads that come with your choice of hearty vegetable soup, salad or chips, run from cream cheese with beetroot, smoked salmon and cream cheese to chicken, avocado, crispy bacon and lettuce with a honey and mustard dressing; well liked Sunday roasts.** *Starters/Snacks: £6.25 to £6.95*

Punch ~ Lease Stuart Jones ~ Real ale ~ Bar food (12-9) ~ (01628) 662353 ~ Children welcome ~ Dogs welcome ~ Open 11-11; 12-10.30 Sun

Recommended by Bob and Laura Brock, Karen Keen, Ian Phillips, Tracey and Stephen Groves, Paul Humphreys, Michael Dandy, Mike and Sue Richardson

EASINGTON   SP6810   MAP 4

Mole & Chicken   🛏

From B4011 in Long Crendon follow Chearsley, Waddesdon signpost into Carters Lane opposite the Chandos Arms, then turn left into Chilton Road; HP18 9EY

Lovely views and sunsets from wooden decking area and garden, nice open-plan layout, and excellent food

The views and sunsets over the Thames Valley from this inviting pub are lovely and you can make the most of them from seats in the garden. Inside, the open-plan layout is cleverly done, so that all the different parts seem quite snug and self-contained without being cut off from what's going on, and the atmosphere is relaxed and sociable. The beamed bar curves around the serving counter in a sort of S-shape, and there are oak and pine tables on flagstones, rag-washed terracotta walls with lots of big antique prints, lit candles and good winter log fires. A thoughtful choice of wines (with decent french house ones), over 40 malt whiskies, and Fullers London Pride, Greene King IPA and Vale Notley Ale on handpump; piped music. One reader's disappointing evening in spring 2007 could perhaps have been eased by more sympathetic management; this seems to have been an uncharacteristic temporary lapse.

🍴 **Consistently excellent food might include sandwiches, soup, chicken and prawn skewers with peanut dip and chilli garlic mayonnaise, deep-fried breaded brie with redcurrant jelly, sun-dried tomato and asparagus tart with grilled goats cheese, duck and bacon salad with a warm plum and red wine sauce, beef, ale and mushroom pie, rack of ribs in barbecue sauce, thai prawn curry, crispy gressingham duck with orange sauce, and seasonal puddings.** *Starters/Snacks: £3.50 to £6.95. Main Courses: £8.95 to £14.95. Puddings: £4.95*

Free house ~ Licensees A Heather and S Ellis ~ Real ale ~ Bar food (all day Sun) ~ Restaurant ~ (01844) 208387 ~ Children welcome ~ Open 12-3, 6-11; 12-10.30 Sun; closed 25 Dec ~ Bedrooms: £50B/£65B

Recommended by Dennis and Doreen Haward, John Tyrle, Julia and Richard Tredgett, Graham Oddey, Cathryn and Richard Hicks, Andy Dale, K S Whittaker, Dr A McCormick, Donna and Roger, Paul Humphreys, Dr David C Price

FINGEST
SU7791   MAP 2

Chequers
Village signposted off B482 Marlow—Stokenchurch; RG9 6QD

Friendly, spotlessly kept old pub with big garden, good food and new sunny dining extension

Readers have been particularly enthusiastic about their visits to this 15th-c pub over the last year. A sunny new back dining extension has been added with french doors opening out on to the terrace where there are plenty of picnic-sets and this leads on to the big garden with fine view down the Hambleden valley; beyond here, quiet pastures slope up to beech woods. Inside, several spotless old-fashioned rooms have pewter tankards, horsebrasses and pub team photographs on the walls, large open fires, Brakspears Bitter and Special and Wychwood Hobgoblin on handpump, a dozen wines by the glass, jugs of Pimms and several malt whiskies; good friendly service. Board games. Over the road is a unique Norman twin-roofed church tower – probably the nave of the original church.

▥ **Reasonably priced, enjoyable bar food includes sandwiches, soup, mushroom or pork pâté, popular ploughman's, sausages with creamy mash, super shepherd's pie, sweet chicken and pineapple curry with almonds and peppers, steak in ale pie, grilled pear and halloumi salad, baked brown trout with fennel and garlic, and puddings such as chocolate brownies or rhubarb crumble.** *Starters/Snacks: £4.75 to £6.75. Main Courses: £7.95 to £14.50. Puddings: £2.95 to £3.95*

Brakspears ~ Tenants Ray Connelly and Christian Taubert ~ Real ale ~ Bar food (not Sun or Mon evenings) ~ Restaurant ~ (01491) 638335 ~ Children welcome ~ Dogs allowed in bar ~ Open 12-3, 6-11; 12-10.30 Sun

Recommended by Derek Harvey-Piper, Paul Humphreys, Howard Dell, Sharon Hancock, Peter Saville, the Didler, Roy Hoing

FORD
SP7709   MAP 4

Dinton Hermit ⊞ ⇌
SW of Aylesbury; HP17 8XH

Carefully furnished inn, perhaps more restaurant than pub, with attractively presented food and nicely decorated bedrooms in converted barn

This is a nice place to stay – the bright, well decorated bedrooms are in a sympathetically converted barn – and the breakfasts are especially good. It's a carefully extended 16th-c stone building with quite an emphasis on the first class food but they do keep Adnams Bitter, Batemans XB Bitter and Brakspears Bitter on handpump; a decent choice of wines. The bar has scrubbed tables and comfortable cushioned and wicker-backed mahogany-look chairs on a nice old black and red tiled floor, a huge inglenook fireplace, and white-painted plaster on very thick uneven stone walls. There's an old print of John Bigg, the supposed executioner of King Charles I and the man later known as the Dinton Hermit. The back dining area has similar furniture on quarry tiles. A nice touch is the church candles lit throughout the bar and restaurant and there are hundreds of bottles of wine decorating the walls and thick oak bar counter. Plenty of picnic sets in the garden.

> Post Office address codings confusingly give the impression that some pubs are in Buckinghamshire, when they're really in Bedfordshire or Berkshire (which is where we list them).

⚑ The particularly good food includes filled ciabatini, marinated seared scallops with brussels sprouts, bacon and horseradish potato cake, dill oil and carrot crisps, twice-roasted duck and bacon salad with plum compote, roasted turbot fillet with home-made lemon pasta, herb crust and crayfish sauce and beef rossini with carrot and parsnip rösti and foie gras. *Starters/Snacks: £3.95 to £7.50. Main Courses: £13.85 to £18.50. Puddings: £4.50 to £6.50*

Free house ~ Licensees John and Debbie Colinswood ~ Real ale ~ Bar food (12-2, 7-9(till 7 summer Sun, till 4 winter Sun)) ~ Restaurant ~ (01296) 747473 ~ Well behaved children allowed under supervision ~ Open 11am-midnight; 11-10.30(8.30 winter) Sun ~ Bedrooms: /£100S

Recommended by J Sugarman, Howard Dell, Mr and Mrs J Jennings

FORTY GREEN   SU9291   MAP 2

Royal Standard of England 🍺

3½ miles from M40 junction 2, via A40 to Beaconsfield, then follow sign to Forty Green, off B474 ¼ mile N of New Beaconsfield; keep going through village; HP9 1XT

Ancient place with lots of history and fascinating antiques in the rambling rooms

Said to be the oldest free house in England and trading for nearly 900 years, this very well run pub remains a favourite with many of our readers. There's certainly lots to look at – both in the layout of the building itself and in the fascinating collection of antiques which fills it. The rambling rooms have huge black ship's timbers, finely carved old oak panelling, roaring winter fires with handsomely decorated iron firebacks, and there's a massive settle apparently built to fit the curved transom of an Elizabethan ship; you can also see rifles, powder-flasks and bugles, ancient pewter and pottery tankards, lots of brass and copper, needlework samplers, and stained glass. A fine choice of real ales on handpump might include Brakspears Bitter, Marstons Pedigree, Rebellion IPA and Mild, and guests such as Hop Back Entire Stout and Vale Black Beauty Porter; a good range of bottled beers, too, 11 wines by the glass, Thatcher's and Stowford's cider, and Weston's perry; shove-ha'penny. Seats outside in a neatly hedged front rose garden or in the shade of a tree.

⚑ They have been championing mutton recently but other popular dishes include lunchtime sandwiches and daily specials, grilled sardines on fried toast, home-made terrine or parfait, soup, spinach and butternut squash lasagne, their own sausages, honey-roast ham and eggs, steak and kidney pudding, smoked haddock, kedgeree and poached egg, welsh lamb chops, and puddings like treacle tart or fruit crumble. *Starters/Snacks: £3.95 to £6.95. Main Courses: £7.95 to £16.95. Puddings: £2.95 to £4.95*

Free house ~ Licensee Matthew O`Keeffe ~ Real ale ~ Bar food (all day every day) ~ Restaurant ~ (01494) 673382 ~ Children welcome ~ Dogs welcome ~ Open 11-11.30; 12-11 Sun

Recommended by Paul Humphreys, Susan and John Douglas, T R and B C Jenkins, Anthony Longden, Tracey and Stephen Groves, the Didler, Piotr Chodzko-Zajko, E V Lee, Keith Barker, Heather Couper, Simon Collett-Jones, John and Glenys Wheeler, Chris Smith

GROVE   SP9122   MAP 4

Grove Lock 🍷 🍺

Pub signed off B488, on left just S of A505 roundabout (S of Leighton Buzzard); LU7 0QU

Modern open-plan pub by Grand Union Canal with plenty of room inside and on terraced waterside garden

Usefully open all day at weekends and overlooking the Grand Union Canal, this modern open-plan pub has a partly terraced garden with plenty of circular picnic-sets both there and on canopied decking. Inside, the extensive main area has diagonal oak floor boarding, a lofty high-raftered pitched roof, a big open-standing winter log fire under an impressive steel chimney canopy and a choice of seating between pleasant modern dining tables (all with flowers) and more laid-back seating such as squishy brown leather sofas, bucket chairs and drum stools around low tables. Steps take you up to a further three-room restaurant area, partly flagstoned, looking down on the narrow canal lock. Fullers London Pride, ESB and Discovery, Gales HSB and a guest beer on handpump and several wines by the glass; efficient young staff, piped music (not too obtrusive) and disabled access and facilities. Games machine and TV for sports. More reports please.

🍴 **Under the new licensee, bar food includes sandwiches and wraps, a trio of crab and prawn fishcakes with sweet chilli dressing, baked rustic bread stuffed with mixed peppers and chargrilled halloumi, vegetable linguini, hoi sin chicken with rice noodles, seared tuna steak with stir-fried vegetables and wasabi, popular seafood salad with lime mayonnaise, and puddings such as chocolate and almond torte and passion fruit and raspberry bavarois.** *Starters/Snacks: £4.00 to £6.50. Main Courses: £9.00 to £18.50. Puddings: £4.95*

Fullers ~ Manager Luke Davy ~ Real ale ~ Bar food (12-3, 6-9.30; all day weekends) ~ Restaurant ~ (01525) 380940 ~ Children welcome ~ Open 11.30-11(midnight Sat); 12-10.30 Sun

Recommended by Michael Dandy

HADDENHAM   SP7408   MAP 4

Green Dragon 🍴 ⛾

Village signposted off A418 and A4129, E/NE of Thame; then follow Church End signs; HP17 8AA

Good imaginative food is the draw here though drinkers are made welcome too; pretty village

They do keep Vale Wychert Ale (brewed in the village) plus Caledonian Deuchars IPA and Wadworths 6X on handpump in this well run place, but most customers are here to enjoy the particularly good, imaginative food. The neatly kept opened-up bar, in colours of pale olive and antique rose, has an open fireplace towards the back of the building and attractive furnishings throughout; the dining area has a fine mix of informal tables and chairs. A dozen wines plus champagne by the glass and friendly, competent service. A big sheltered gravel terrace behind the pub has white tables and picnic-sets under cocktail parasols, with more on the grass, and a good variety of plants. This part of the village is very pretty, with a duck pond unusually close to the church.

🍴 **The particularly good food might include sandwiches, soup, gravadlax with crayfish and avocado with a caper and mustard dressing, salmon and prawn fishcakes with sweet chilli, butternut squash risotto, steak and kidney suet pudding, seared bass fillet with crab velouté, pheasant with bacon sauce, braised lamb shank, and puddings like iced chocolate and hazelnut parfait with hazelnut praline or orange and lemon tart.** *Starters/Snacks: £4.50 to £8.00. Main Courses: £9.95 to £17.95. Puddings: £4.95 to £6.95*

Enterprise ~ Lease Peter Moffat ~ Real ale ~ Bar food ~ Restaurant ~ (01844) 291403 ~ Children must be over 7 in evening ~ Open 12-2.30, 6.30-11(11.30 Sat); 12-2.30 Sun; closed Sun evening, 25 Dec

Recommended by Ms D Smith, Mike and Sue Richardson, Peter and Jan Humphreys, Jill and Julian Tasker, Jack and Sandra Clarfelt

HAWRIDGE COMMON   SP9406   MAP 4

Full Moon 🍺

Hawridge Common; left fork off A416 N of Chesham, then follow for 3.5 miles towards Cholesbury; HP5 2UH

Especially fine in summer with outside heaters and awning, six real ales, and enjoyable food; plenty of nearby walks

On fine days, you can sit outside this attractive country pub in the garden or on the heated and covered terrace and gaze over the fields or windmill behind; lots of walks over the common. The six real ales on handpump are also quite a draw: Adnams, Bass, Brakspears Special, and Fullers London Pride plus Shepherd Neame Spitfire and Timothy

Taylors Landlord. Several wines by the glass, good service, and cribbage. The low-beamed rambling bar is the heart of the building, with oak built-in floor-to-ceiling settles, ancient flagstones and flooring tiles, hunting prints and an inglenook fireplace.

🍴 Enjoyable lunchtime food such as filled baguettes and baked potatoes, home-made soup, smoked bacon and cheddar tartlet, roast vegetable lasagne, chicken thai green curry and home-made pie of the day, with evening choices like seared scallops with pesto dressing, chicken liver pâté or antipasti, chicken and porcini stroganoff, salmon fricassee, moroccan lamb shank, and venison niçoise; puddings that might include fresh fruit trifle or chocolate brownies with chocolate sauce, daily specials, and Sunday roasts. *Starters/Snacks: £4.50 to £5.95. Main Courses: £9.25 to £16.95. Puddings: £4.50 to £4.95*

Enterprise ~ Lease Peter and Annie Alberto ~ Real ale ~ Bar food ~ Restaurant ~ (01494) 758959 ~ Children welcome ~ Dogs allowed in bar ~ Open 12-11; 12-10.30 Sun

Recommended by Tracey and Stephen Groves, Maggie Atherton, Mike Pugh, Roy Hoing

HEDGERLEY
SU9687   MAP 2

White Horse ★ 🍺

2.4 miles from M40 junction 2; at exit roundabout take Slough turn-off then take Hedgerley Lane (immediate left) following alongside M40; after 1.5 miles turn right at T junction into Village Lane; SL2 3UY

Old-fashioned drinkers' pub with good jolly mix of customers, fine real ales and regular beer festivals

Happily unchanging, this remains a proper country local with a good mix of customers and a fine range of real ales. The cottagey main bar has plenty of character, with lots of beams, brasses and exposed brickwork, low wooden tables, some standing timbers, jugs, ballcocks and other bric-a-brac, a log fire, and a good few leaflets and notices about future village events. There is a little flagstoned public bar on the left. On the way out to the garden, which has tables and occasional barbecues, they have a canopy extension to help during busy periods. Tapped from the cask in a room behind the tiny hatch counter, the well kept ales include Greene King IPA and Rebellion IPA and five daily changing guests from anywhere in the country, with good farm cider and perry, and belgian beers too; their regular ale festivals are very popular. The atmosphere is jolly with warmly friendly service from the cheerful staff. In front are lots of hanging baskets and a couple more tables overlooking the quiet road. There are good walks nearby, and the pub is handy for the Church Wood RSPB reserve. It can get crowded at weekends.

🍴 Lunchtime bar food such as sandwiches, ploughman's, cold meats and quiches, and changing straightforward hot dishes. *Starters/Snacks: £3.95 to £5.00. Main Courses: £5.50 to £8.95. Puddings: £3.00*

Free house ~ Licensees Doris Hobbs and Kevin Brooker ~ Real ale ~ Bar food (lunchtime only) ~ (01753) 643225 ~ Children in canopy extension area ~ Dogs allowed in bar ~ Open 11-2.30, 5-11; 11-11 Sat; 12-10.30 Sun

Recommended by Susan and John Douglas, Chris Glasson, Anthony Longden, Mrs Ann Gray, N R White, Keith Barker, Brian Young, Paul Humphreys, the Didler, Tracey and Stephen Groves, Dennis Jenkin, Mr and Mrs John Taylor, Bob and Laura Brock, Roy Hoing, Simon Rodway

LEY HILL
SP9901   MAP 4

Swan 🍺

Village signposted off A416 in Chesham; HP5 1UT

Charming, old-fashioned pub with chatty customers and decent food

Once you have discovered this charming little timbered 16th-c pub, you will want to come back again and again. It's run by friendly, enthusiastic licensees who keep everything spic and span and the atmosphere is relaxed and chatty. The main bar has black beams (mind your head) and standing timbers, an old range, a log fire and a collection of old local photographs; there's a cosy snug. Adnams, Brakspears, Fullers

London Pride, Timothy Taylors Landlord and maybe a guest from Tring on handpump, and several wines by the glass. In front of the pub amongst the flower tubs and hanging baskets are some picnic-sets, with more in the large back garden. There's a cricket pitch, a nine-hole golf course, and a common opposite. More reports please.

🍴 Well liked bar food includes sandwiches, baked brie wrapped in filo pastry with cranberry sauce, chicken pasta, wild mushroom risotto, a couple of fish dishes, fillet steak with a blue cheese crust, and puddings; two-course set menu, too. *Starters/Snacks: £2.25 to £3.95. Main Courses: £6.95 to £8.95. Puddings: £4.25 to £4.95*

Punch ~ Lease Nigel Byatt ~ Real ale ~ Bar food (12-2, 7-9; 12-3.30 Sun; not Sun evening) ~ Restaurant ~ (01494) 783075 ~ Children welcome ~ Various jazz and blues evenings ~ Open 12-3.30, 5.30-11(midnight Sat); 12-4, 5.30-10.30 Sun

Recommended by Tracey and Stephen Groves, Joe and Agnes Walker, Wilma Hooftman, Richard Harris, Roy Hoing

LITTLE MISSENDEN
SU9298 MAP 4

Crown ★ ◫ £
Crown Lane, SE end of village, which is signposted off A413 W of Amersham; HP7 0RD

Long-serving licensees and a cheerful pubby feel in little brick cottage; attractive garden

For more than 90 years the same family have run this small brick cottage. The friendly landlord keeps things spotless and the bustling bars have a cheery, traditional feel. Adnams, Brakspears, Exmoor Gold, Hook Norton Bitter, and St Austell Tribute on handpump or tapped from the cask, farm cider and several malt whiskies. There are old red flooring tiles on the left, oak parquet on the right, built-in wall seats, studded red leatherette chairs, and a few small tables; darts and board games. The large attractive sheltered, garden behind has picnic-sets and other tables, and the interesting church in the pretty village is well worth a visit. No children. More reports please.

🍴 Straightforward bar food such as winter soup, good fresh sandwiches, buck's bite (a special home-made pizza-like dish), filled baked potatoes, ploughman's, and steak and kidney pie. *Starters/Snacks: £3.00 to £4.75. Main Courses: £4.75 to £5.25*

Free house ~ Licensees Trevor and Carolyn How ~ Real ale ~ Bar food (lunchtime only, not Sun) ~ No credit cards ~ (01494) 862571 ~ Open 11-2.30, 6-11; 12-3, 7-10.30 Sun

Recommended by Brian Root, Paul Humphreys, Tracey and Stephen Groves

OVING
SP7821 MAP 4

Black Boy
Village signposted off A413 out of Whitchurch, N of Aylesbury; HP22 4HN

Extended 16th-c pub with lots of room, plenty of fresh flowers and candles, quite a choice of popular food, and impressive garden

The old front parts of this distinctive 16th-c pub are perhaps the most atmospheric, especially the cosy red and black-tiled area around the enormous inglenook. The low heavy beams have mottoes chalked on them and, up a couple of steps, another snug corner has a single table, some exposed stonework, and a mirror over a small brick fireplace. The long, light wooden bar counter is covered with posters advertising sales of agricultural land; opposite, two big, comfortable leather armchairs lead into the lighter, more modern dining room, with good-sized country kitchen pine tables set for eating, and picture windows offering the same view of the gardens. Throughout are plenty of candles and fresh flowers. Brakspears Bitter, Rebellion IPA and maybe a guest such as Gales Swing Low or Timothy Taylors Landlord on handpump, and a dozen wines by the glass; piped music. The impressive garden has tables on its spacious sloping lawns and terrace with remarkable views down over the Vale of Aylesbury. The licensees breed and train chocolate labradors. More reports please.

🍴 With some emphasis on food, there might be lunchtime sandwiches, filled baked potatoes and omelettes, plus soup, black pudding and haggis stack with fried egg, roquefort, leek and walnut tart, home-cured ham and eggs, steamed thai-style bass fillets, chicken and bacon on creamed leeks, liver and bacon with mustard mash, beef in red wine, and daily specials. *Starters/Snacks: £4.50 to £7.50. Main Courses: £8.50 to £17.75. Puddings: £4.75 to £5.50*

Free house ~ Licensees Sally and David Hayle ~ Real ale ~ Bar food (12-2, 6-9; 12-3.30 Sun; not Sun evening or all day Mon) ~ Restaurant ~ (01296) 641258 ~ Well behaved children welcome ~ Dogs welcome ~ Open 12-3, 6-11; 12-11 Sat; 12-4.30 Sun; closed Sun evening and all day Mon (exc bank hols)

Recommended by Gerry and Rosemary Dobson, Brian Root

PRESTWOOD SP8799 MAP 4

Polecat 🍽

170 Wycombe Road (A4128 N of High Wycombe); HP16 0HJ

Enjoyable food in several smallish civilised rooms, chatty atmosphere, and attractive sizeable garden

The garden here is most attractive with lots of spring bulbs and colourful summer hanging baskets, tubs, and herbaceous plants; quite a few picnic-sets under parasols on neat grass out in front beneath a big fairy-lit pear tree, with more on a big well kept back lawn. Inside, it's friendly and rather civilised with chatty middle-aged diners at lunchtime and more of a broad mix of customers in the evening. Opening off the low-ceilinged bar are several smallish rooms with an assortment of tables and chairs, various stuffed birds as well as the stuffed white polecats in one big cabinet, small country pictures, rugs on bare boards or red tiles, and a couple of antique housekeeper's chairs by a good open fire. Brakspears Bitter, Flowers IPA, Greene King Old Speckled Hen, and Marstons Pedigree on handpump, quite a few wines by the glass, and 20 malt whiskies; piped music.

🍽 Popular and enjoyable bar food such as lunchtime sandwiches, filled baked potatoes and ploughman's, as well as fresh soup, pâté with onion marmalade, crab cakes rolled in lemon crumbs with chilli jam, cumberland sausages, vegetable stroganoff, chicken madras, seafood hotpot, tender rack of lamb, daily specials, and puddings like sherry trifle or chocolate and hazelnut tart with fudge sauce. *Starters/Snacks: £3.70 to £5.25. Main Courses: £9.20 to £13.80. Puddings: £4.50*

Free house ~ Licensee John Gamble ~ Real ale ~ Bar food (not Sun evening) ~ (01494) 862253 ~ Children in Gallery Room and Drovers Bar only ~ Dogs allowed in bar ~ Open 11.30-2.30, 6-11; 12-3 Sun; closed Sun evening, evenings 24 and 31 Dec, all day 25 and 26 Dec and 1 Jan

Recommended by Tracey and Stephen Groves, Howard Dell, Peter Saville, Michael Dandy, Paul Humphreys, Brian P White, Roy Hoing, Phil Bryant

SKIRMETT SU7790 MAP 2

Frog 🍺 🛏

From A4155 NE of Henley take Hambleden turn and keep on; or from B482 Stokenchurch— Marlow take Turville turn and keep on; RG9 6TG

Bustling, brightly decorated pub with a good mix of locals and visitors, modern cooking and wide choice of drinks; lovely garden and nearby walks

There's a really friendly, bustling atmosphere in this country pub. The neatly kept beamed bar area has a mix of comfortable furnishings, a striking hooded fireplace with a bench around the edge (and a pile of logs sitting beside it), big rugs on the wooden floors and sporting and local prints around the salmon painted walls. The function room leading off is sometimes used as a dining overflow. Although brightly modernised, there is still something of a local feel with leaflets and posters near the door advertising raffles and so forth; piped music. Adnams Bitter, Rebellion IPA, and Sharps Doom Bar on handpump, 16 wines by the glass (including champagne), and 20 malt whiskies. A side gate leads to a lovely garden with a large tree in the middle, and the unusual five-sided tables are well placed for attractive valley views. Plenty of nearby hikes, Henley is close by, and just down the road is the delightful Ibstone windmill. There's a purpose-built outdoor heated area for smokers.

🍴 **Well liked food includes fresh soup, warm potato rösti, black pudding and smoked salmon with poached egg, linguini with wild mushrooms, shallots, artichoke hearts and parmesan, supreme of chicken with crostini of wild mushrooms, pancetta and watercress, calves liver and bacon with caramelised onion gravy, breast of duck with honey and a red wine jus, daily specials, and puddings like mascarpone and fruit crème brûlée or knickerbocker glory.** *Starters/Snacks: £2.95 to £7.25. Main Courses: £10.50 to £14.50. Puddings: £3.50 to £5.25.*

Free house ~ Licensees Jim Crowe and Noelle Greene ~ Real ale ~ Bar food (12-2.30, 6.30-9.30; not winter Sun evening) ~ Restaurant ~ (01491) 638996 ~ Children welcome ~ Occasional live entertainment ~ Open 11-3, 6-11; 12-10.30(4pm in winter) Sun; 11-4 Sun in winter ~ Bedrooms: £55B/£70B

Recommended by David Collison, Dr and Mrs P Reid, Mike and Sue Richardson, Andy and Claire Barker, Paul Humphreys, Michael Dandy, T R and B C Jenkins, J and F Gowers, Fred and Kate Portnell

SOULBURY   SP8826   MAP 4

Boot ♀

B4032 W of Leighton Buzzard; LU7 0BT

Smart, attractive and individually furnished, super choice of wine and champagne by glass, and pubby food plus daily specials

This civilised village pub has been redecorated throughout in pale blue and cream and the restaurant has been refurbished with smart new tables and chairs. The partly red-tiled bar has a light, sunny feel with a nice mix of individual furnishings, sporting prints and houseplants, and Courage Directors, Greene King IPA, and Shepherd Neame Spitfire on handpump from the modern, light wood bar counter; fantastic choice of around 40 wines and a couple of champagnes by the glass. One end of the room, with a fireplace and wooden floors, is mostly set for diners, and then at the opposite end, by some exposed brickwork, steps lead down to a couple of especially cosy rooms for eating; piped music. Overlooking peaceful fields, there are tables behind in a small garden and on a terrace (with heaters for cooler weather), and a couple more in front.

🍴 **Good food (starters are offered in regular or large sizes) includes lunchtime sandwiches, soup, moules marinière, chicken liver, brandy and peppercorn pâté, organic pizzas and sausages, ham with organic eggs, steak and mushroom pie, seafood platters and fresh fish dishes, steaks, puddings like lemon and lime brûlée with coconut muffin or rich chocolate and rum truffle torte, and Sunday roasts.** *Starters/Snacks: £4.50 to £8.95. Main Courses: £8.25 to £20.75. Puddings: £4.50*

Pubmaster ~ Lease Greg Nichol, Tina and Paul Stevens ~ Real ale ~ Bar food (12-2.30, 6.30-9.30; all day Sun) ~ Restaurant ~ (01525) 270433 ~ Children welcome ~ Open 11-11; 12-10.30 Sun; closed 25-26 Dec

Recommended by Andy and Claire Barker, Mrs Julie Thomas, John Branston, John Baish

STOKE MANDEVILLE   SP8310   MAP 4

Woolpack

Risborough Road (A4010 S of Aylesbury); HP22 5UP

Stylish, with contemporary furnishings in knocked-through areas, good modern food, and obliging staff

A new licensee has taken over this partly thatched and stylish old pub. The original stripped beams, timbers and massive inglenook log fireplace comfortably jostle for attention with gleaming round copper-topped tables, low leather armchairs, and rich purple walls. In the comfortable, knocked-through front areas by the bar it's the wood and low beams that make the deepest impression, but there are also substantial candles artfully arranged around the fireplace, and illuminated Mouton Rothschild wine labels (designed by top artists) on the walls. Beyond here is a big, busily chatty dining room with chunky wooden tables, a dividing wall made up of logs of wood, thick columns with ornate woodcarvings, and a real mix of customers. Fullers London Pride and Timothy Taylors Landlord on handpump, decent wines, and piped music. Tables in the neatly landscaped back garden and on the front heated terrace; large car park. More reports please.

🍽 **The good modern food now includes soup, sharing plates of greek mezze or tapas, crab cakes with mango and chilli, chicken caesar salad, a daily risotto, blue cheese tortellini with broccoli, cream and walnut pesto, beer-battered haddock, pork fillet with blue cheese dauphinoise, duck confit with spiced orange sauce, fish of the day, and steaks with bloody mary butter or horseradish crème fraîche.** *Starters/Snacks: £4.00 to £10.00. Main Courses: £8.50 to £17.50. Puddings: £4.25 to £5.75*

Mitchells & Butlers ~ Manager Ben Pentony ~ Real ale ~ Bar food (12-3, 6-10; Sun 12-7) ~ Restaurant ~ (01296) 615970 ~ Children allowed but must be quiet and well behaved ~ Open 11-11; 11-10 Sun

Recommended by Adam F Padel

TURVILLE   SU7691   MAP 2

Bull & Butcher ♀

Off A4155 Henley—Marlow via Hambleden and Skirmett; RG9 6QU

Timbered pub, a handy all-day stop in this lovely village

This is a lovely village and popular with television and film companies; *The Vicar of Dibley*, *Midsomer Murders* and *Chitty Chitty Bang Bang* were all filmed here – not surprisingly, this pub does get crowded at weekends. There are two low-ceilinged, oak-beamed rooms both with inglenook fireplaces and the bar, with cushioned wall settles and a tiled floor, has a very deep well incorporated into a glass-topped table. Brakspears Bitter, Special, and a seasonal guest, and Hook Norton Hooky Dark on handpump, Addlestone's cider and a fair choice of wines by the glass; piped music and TV. There are seats on the lawn by fruit trees in the attractive garden, and plenty of walks in the lovely Chilterns valley.

🍽 **Bar food includes soup, chicken liver pâté, bangers with onion jam, vegetable lasagne, roast chicken with mustard sauce, shin of beef stew, and daily specials.** *Starters/Snacks: £5.00 to £7.00. Main Courses: £9.00 to £15.00. Puddings: £4.00 to £6.00*

Brakspears ~ Tenant Lydia Botha ~ Real ale ~ Bar food (12-2.30(3 Sat), 6.30-9.30; 12-4, 7-9 Sun and bank hol Mon) ~ Restaurant ~ (01491) 638283 ~ Children allowed but away from bar ~ Dogs allowed in bar ~ Open 12-11; 12-10.30 Sun

Recommended by Andy and Claire Barker, Tom and Jill Jones, Michael Dandy, R T and J C Moggridge, Tim Maddison

WOOBURN COMMON   SU9087   MAP 2

Chequers

From A4094 N of Maidenhead at junction with A4155 Marlow road keep on A4094 for another ¾ mile, then at roundabout turn off right towards Wooburn Common, and into Kiln Lane; if you find yourself in Honey Hill, Hedsor, turn left into Kiln Lane at the top of the hill; OS Sheet 175 map reference 910870; HP10 0JQ

Sizeable wine list, thriving hotel and restaurant side but with friendly, bustling bar

The busy, friendly bar here has a good mix of local customers and those drawn in from the thriving hotel and restaurant side. Standing timbers and alcoves break up the low-beamed room that is furnished with comfortably lived-in sofas (just right for settling into) on its bare boards, a bright log-effect gas fire, and various pictures, plates, a two-man saw, and tankards. They offer a sizeable wine list (with champagne and good wines by the glass), a fair range of malt whiskies and brandies, and Greene King Abbot, IPA, Old

Speckled Hen and a guest such as Rebellion Smuggler on handpump; piped music. The spacious garden, set away from the road, has cast-iron tables. The bedroom rate given below is for a weekend stay; the weekly rate is quite a bit more expensive.

🍴 **Bar food includes sandwiches, ploughman's, chicken caesar salad, slow-roasted lamb shank, tuna steak with tomato salsa, confit of duck, and puddings such as chocolate brownie with chocolate sauce.** *Starters/Snacks: £3.95 to £6.95. Main Courses: £8.95 to £19.95. Puddings: £4.50 to £5.25*

Free house ~ Licensee Peter Roehrig ~ Real ale ~ Bar food (12-2.30, 6.30-9.30; all day Sat, Sun and bank hols) ~ Restaurant ~ (01628) 529575 ~ Children welcome ~ Open 11-12.30am; closed evenings 25 Dec and 1 Jan ~ Bedrooms: £82.50B/£87.50B

Recommended by Paul Humphreys, Simon Collett-Jones, Kevin Thomas, Nina Randall, David Tindal, Mrs Deborah Chalmers, W K Wood, Michael Dandy, Mrs Jane Kingsbury, Mike and Heather Watson, Roy Hoing

LUCKY DIP

Besides the fully inspected pubs, you might like to try these Lucky Dips recommended to us and described by readers (if you do, please send us reports: www.goodguides.co.uk).

AMERSHAM [SU9698]
Boot & Slipper HP6 5JN [Rickmansworth Rd]: Chef & Brewer with their usual food and décor in plenty of cosy corners, wide choice of wines by the glass, changing ales such as Adnams Broadside, Brains Rev James, Caledonian Deuchars IPA, Fullers HSB and St Austell Tribute, good coffee, daily papers; piped music, games; tables on back terrace *(Michael Dandy, Roy Hoing)*
Crown HP7 0DH [Market Sq]: Small plushly modernised hotel bar, leather, polished wood and beams, interesting 16th-c features in comfortable lounge, starched table linen in pleasant dining area, short choice of bar food from sandwiches up, young helpful staff, real ale, good range of wines by the glass; nearby parking may be difficult; attractive split-level outside seating area with cobbled courtyard and plant-filled garden, comfortable bedrooms *(BB, Tracey and Stephen Groves)*
Eagle HP7 0DY [High St]: Rambling low-beamed pub with decent food, quick friendly service even when busy, Adnams, Fullers London Pride and Greene King Old Speckled Hen, good choice of wines by the glass, log fire, simple décor with a few old prints, pub games; pleasant streamside walled back garden *(Michael Dandy)*
☆ *Saracens Head* HP7 0HU [Whielden St (A404)]: Neat and friendly 17th-c beamed local, massive inglenook with log fire in ancient decorative fire-basket, interesting décor, good fresh food from sandwiches and baked potatoes up, Greene King real ales, good choice of wines by the glass, pleasant staff, cheery chatty landlord; soft piped music; little back courtyard, bedrooms *(LYM, Michael Dandy, Steve and Liz Tilley)*
ASTWOOD [SP9547]
☆ *Old Swan* MK16 9JS [Main Rd]: Appealing and stylish low-beamed pub with helpful friendly service, Everards Tiger and Beacon and Timothy Taylors Landlord, interesting choice of enjoyable fairly priced food,

flagstones, inglenook woodburner and nice collection of blue china, two attractive dining areas, warm cosy atmosphere; large garden *(LYM, Michael Dandy)*
AYLESBURY [SP8114]
Hop Pole HP19 9AZ [Bicester Rd]: Open-plan pub now tied to Vale and completely refurbished, their Best and lots of guest beers, good value food; open all day *(Roger Shipperley)*
BLEDLOW [SP7702]
Lions of Bledlow HP27 9PE [off B4009 Chinnor—Princes Risboro; Church End]: Great views from bay windows of well worn Chilterns pub with low 16th-c beams, ancient floor tiles, inglenook log fires and a woodburner, well kept ales such as Marlow Rebellion and Wadworths 6X, good value bar food from sandwiches up, games room; well behaved children allowed, picnic-sets out in attractive sloping garden with sheltered terrace, nice setting, good walks *(LYM, the Didler, Peter J and Avril Hanson)*
BOURNE END [SU8987]
Bounty SL8 5RG [Cock Marsh, actually across the river along the Cookham towpath, but shortest walk – still about ¼ mile – is from Bourne End, over the railway bridge]: Friendly pub tucked away in outstanding setting on the opposite bank of the Thames, well kept Marlow Rebellion ales, decent unpretentious food; children and walkers welcome, tables in recently reworked garden *(David Tindal)*
Spade Oak SL8 5PS [Coldmoorholme Lane (off A4155 towards Thames)]: Good choice of food in much refurbished pub, at least one real ale; smartly contemporary outdoor eating area *(D and M T Ayres-Regan)*
BRADENHAM [SU8297]
☆ *Red Lion* HP14 4HF [on corner of Walters Ash turn off A4010]: Enjoyable food (not Sun evening or Mon lunchtime) from good baguettes to popular Sun lunch under friendly new landlord, well kept ales such as Wells & Youngs, pleasant décor, Sun jazz

nights, restaurant, unspoilt National Trust village; no under-10s; cl Mon lunchtime (Ross Balaam)

BUCKINGHAM [SP6933]

Villiers MK18 1BS [Castle St]: Pub part of this large comfortable hotel formerly known as Swan & Castle, with own courtyard entrance, big inglenook log fire, panelling and stripped masonry in flagstoned bar, limited choice of good lunchtime bar food, real ale, friendly attentive largely French staff, more formal lounge and restaurant; tables out in pretty cobbled courtyard, open all day (George Atkinson)

BUTLERS CROSS [SP8407]

Russell Arms HP17 0TS [off A4010 S of Aylesbury, at Nash Lee roundabout; or off A413 in Wendover, passing stn; Chalkshire Rd]: Civilised pub with wide choice of good food in beamed and flagstoned bar and separate modern light and roomy restaurant, real ales, two open fires; small sheltered garden, well placed for Chilterns walks (Mrs Deborah Chalmers, LYM, Andy Dale)

CALVERTON [SP7939]

Shoulder of Mutton MK19 6ED [just S of Stony Stratford]: Friendly open-plan L-shaped pub with brasses and pewter mugs on beams, stripped brickwork, wide food range from sandwiches up inc wkdy bargain lunches and lots of curries, half a dozen or more good real ales, good choice of other drinks, quick attentive service, decorative plates in nicely laid out dining area, darts; piped music, TV, games machines, live music Fri; picnic-sets in big attractive back garden with pleasant view and play area, well equipped bedrooms, open all day wknds (JJW, CMW, George Atkinson)

CHALFONT ST GILES [SU9893]

Fox & Hounds HP8 4PS [Silver Hill]: Small quietly set 16th-c local with limited choice of good value lunchtime food (not Sun), quick friendly service, open fire in simple unspoilt interior, darts and pool; pleasant garden behind with play area (R K Phillips)

☆ *Ivy House* HP8 4RS [A413 S]: Smart and attractive open-plan dining pub, wide range of good if not cheap freshly cooked food (can take a while), friendly young staff, good wines by the glass, changing ales such as Archers, espresso coffee, comfortable fireside armchairs in carefully lit and elegantly cosy L-shaped tiled bar, lighter flagstoned dining extension; pleasant terrace and sloping garden (can be traffic noise), five bedrooms (Tracey and Stephen Groves, BB, Roy Hoing)

COLESHILL [SU9594]

Mulberry Bush HP7 0LU [Magpie Lane/A355]: Modern family-friendly roadside dining pub with wide range of generous pubby food all day from sandwiches and melts up inc good children's choice, staff cheerful and helpful even when busy, full range of Marlow ales, good tea and coffee; piped music; children welcome, disabled facilities, large fenced garden with terrace and good play area, walking country, open all day (Michael Dandy, James Orme)

☆ *Red Lion* HP7 0LH [Village Rd]: Small traditional local, relaxed, individual and warmly welcoming, with wide choice of good value pubby food (not Sun eve) from sandwiches and baked potatoes up, changing ales such as Wells & Youngs Bitter and Vale Wychert, quick service, interesting helpful long-serving licensees, two open fires, thriving darts and dominoes teams; TV for racing, fruit machine; front and back gardens, sturdy climbing frames, good walks, open all day wknds (BB, Michael B Griffith, Michael Dandy, Mrs Ann Gray, Roy Hoing)

COLNBROOK [TQ0277]

Ostrich SL3 0JZ [1¼ miles from M4 junction 5 via A4/B3378, then 'village only' rd; High St]: Spectacular timbered Elizabethan building (with even longer gruesome history), recently given contemporary makeover with comfortable sofas on stripped wood and a startling red plastic and stainless bar counter, real ales such as Courage Directors, Fullers London Pride and Greene King Old Speckled Hen, good friendly service, upscale food and restaurant – bar serving largely as ante-room for diners; soft piped music, music and comedy nights upstairs (LYM, Pete Coxon, Ian Phillips, Simon Collett-Jones, D and M T Ayres-Regan)

CRYERS HILL [SU8796]

White Lion HP15 6JP [Cryers Hill Rd: A4128]: Enjoyable sensibly priced food, well kept Fullers London Pride, efficient friendly staff (Ross Balaam)

CUDDINGTON [SP7311]

☆ *Crown* HP18 0BB [village signed off A418 Thame—Aylesbury; Spurt St]: Small convivial thatched village pub, olde-worlde charm, candles, low beams, good tables, nicely cushioned settles, pleasant décor and inglenook log fires, efficient friendly service, unusual choice of good food inc interesting hot sandwiches and specials, Fullers ales; appealing small terrace, open all day Sun (Giles and Annie Francis, Craig Turnbull, Mike and Jennifer Marsh)

DENHAM [TQ0487]

Green Man UB9 5BH [Village Rd]: Warm and lively 18th-c pub, beams and flagstones in original part, well kept Fullers London Pride, Greene King IPA and Abbot and Wells & Youngs Bombardier, good value generous food from sandwiches and baked potatoes up, decent wines, cheerful willing service, conservatory dining extension; piped music; picnic-sets under cocktail parasols on small back terrace, many more in quiet garden beyond (Revd R P Tickle)

DINTON [SP7610]

Seven Stars HP17 8UL [signed off A418 Aylesbury—Thame, nr Gibraltar turn-off; Stars Lane]: Welcoming new management in pretty pub with inglenook bar, comfortable beamed lounge and spacious dining room, real ales such as Fullers London Pride, good choice of reasonably priced food; tables under cocktail parasols in sheltered garden with terrace, pleasant village, handy for Quainton Steam Centre (LYM, David Lamb)

DOWNLEY [SU8495]

☆ *Le De Spencers Arms* HP13 5YQ [The Common]: Unpretentious and softly lit 18th-c Fullers local hidden away from High Wycombe on Chilterns common, their good beers, prompt cheerful service, good value bar food, big pine tables, pictures and bric-a-brac, some stripped masonry, low ceilings; fairy-lit loggia overlooking lawn with picnic-sets, woodland walks to nearby Hughenden Manor (Tracey and Stephen Groves, LYM, Roy Hoing)

FRIETH [SU7990]

Prince Albert RG9 6PY [off B482 SW of High Wycombe]: Old-fashioned cottagey Chilterns local with low black beams and joists, high-backed settles, big black stove in inglenook, big log fire in larger area on the right, pubby food from baguettes up, Brakspears; children and dogs welcome, nicely planted informal side garden with views of woods and fields, open all day (Paul Humphreys, Pete Baker, LYM, the Didler)

GREAT BRICKHILL [SP9029]

☆ *Red Lion* MK17 9AH [Ivy Lane]: Friendly pub with reasonably priced food from baguettes to monkfish, Fullers London Pride and Greene King IPA, good choice of wines by the glass, quick service, daily papers, log fire in small bar, woodburner in restaurant, simple décor; piped music; fabulous view over Buckinghamshire and beyond from neat walled back lawn (Eithne Dandy, Lynne Carter, LYM)

GREAT HAMPDEN [SP8401]

☆ *Hampden Arms* HP16 9RQ [off A4010 N and S of Princes Risborough]: Nicely placed dining pub opp village cricket pitch, good range of enjoyable reasonably priced food made by landlord from lunchtime sandwiches to substantial main dishes, speedy civilised service, Adnams, a seasonal Vale ale and Addlestone's cider from small corner bar, good choice of wines by the glass, big woodburner in more spacious back room; children and dogs welcome, tree-sheltered garden, good walks nearby (LYM, John Franklin, Charles Gysin, Paul Humphreys, Peter Saville, Jarrod and Wendy Hopkinson)

GREAT HORWOOD [SP7630]

Swan MK17 0QN [B4033 N of Winslow]: Well modernised old coaching inn, low beams, pictures and two feature fireplaces (one a big inglenook) in open-plan lounge/dining area, Wells & Youngs Eagle and a guest beer such as Mauldons, usual food from sandwiches up inc OAP wkdy lunches, friendly landlord and staff, back bar with darts and pool; TV; nice side garden, open all day wknds (George Atkinson, Michael Dandy)

GREAT LINFORD [SP8442]

Black Horse MK14 5AJ [from Newport Pagnell take Wolverton Rd towards Stony Stratford]: Reopened under newish licensees

and back to its proper name after a spell as Proud Perch, large pub rambling through different levels, good value food in bar and upstairs restaurant, interesting nooks and crannies devoted to Grand Union Canal alongside – drinks can be taken out on the towpath (good walks along here), and sizeable lawn with well spaced picnic-sets; children welcome (Charles and Pauline Stride, LYM)

GREAT MISSENDEN [SP8901]

☆ *Cross Keys* HP16 0AU [High St]: Relaxed and unspoilt beamed bar divided by standing timbers, bric-a-brac, traditional furnishings inc high-backed settle and open fire in huge fireplace, Fullers ales, good wines, good interesting modern food from tasty baguettes up, attractive and spacious beamed restaurant (children allowed here), cheerful helpful staff; back terrace (John Baish, LYM, Mrs Ann Gray, Roy Hoing)

HAMBLEDEN [SU7886]

☆ *Stag & Huntsman* RG9 6RP [off A4155 Henley—Marlow]: Handsome brick and flint pub in pretty Chilterns village, congenial old-fashioned front public bar with masses of beer mats, big fireplace in low-ceilinged partly panelled lounge bar, Rebellion IPA, Wadworths 6X and a guest beer, farm cider, good wines, friendly efficient staff, decent food (not Sun evening), darts, dominoes, cribbage, shove-ha'penny, secluded dining room; piped music; provision for children and dogs, spacious and attractive garden with some raised areas and decking, good walks, bedrooms (Tracey and Stephen Groves, LYM, Michael Dandy, Tim Maddison, Roy Hoing)

HAVERSHAM [SP8242]

Greyhound MK19 7DT [High St]: Quiet 17th-c village pub in attractive countryside, some stripped stone and beams, Greene King IPA and Abbot, good choice of wines by the glass, enjoyable food inc meal deals, friendly staff, woodburner in lounge, darts in games room; small garden with picnic-sets (JJW, CMW)

HAWRIDGE [SP9505]

☆ *Rose & Crown* HP5 2UG [signed from A416 N of Chesham; The Vale]: Roomy open-plan pub dating from 18th c, wide choice of good value home-made food from sandwiches and baguettes up, well kept Fullers London Pride and two guest beers, good range of wines, enthusiastic young licensees and friendly efficient staff, big log fire, peaceful country views from upper restaurant area; children welcome, broad terrace with lawn dropping down beyond, play area, open all day wknds (Geoff and Elaine Colson, LYM, Ross Balaam)

HUGHENDEN VALLEY [SU8697]

Harrow HP14 4LX [Warrendene Rd, off A4128 N of High Wycombe]: Pretty roadside pub with pleasant Chilterns views, smart café-style main bar with bright homely carpeted eating area and cosy cabin-like low-ceilinged back bar, chatty licensees, real ales inc local Marlow Rebellion, good atmosphere; tables out in front, more in good-sized garden with play area, water feature and sculptures, good walks *(Tracey and Stephen Groves)*

HYDE HEATH [SU9300]

Plough HP6 5RW [village signed off B485 Great Missenden—Chesham]: Prettily placed pub getting popular locally under friendly newish landlord for good value food in bar and new evening restaurant extension, real ales such as Adnams, Fullers London Pride and Wells & Youngs, open fires *(LYM, Roy Hoing)*

IVER [TQ0281]

Red Lion SL0 0JZ [Langley Park Rd (B470 W)]: Cheerful efficient staff, three real ales inc a guest beer, good choice of wines, enjoyable food *(John Branston)*

KINGSWOOD [SP6819]

Plough & Anchor HP18 0RD [Bicester Rd (A41 NW of Aylesbury)]: Wide choice of enjoyable lunchtime food from sandwiches up (cooked to order so may be a wait if busy), simple smart décor, variety of well spaced heavy wooden tables, beams and flagstones, friendly staff, real ales such as Fullers London Pride and Greene King, good wine list; music nights; children welcome *(Mrs Jean Mitchell, David Lamb)*

☆ *Pink & Lily* HP27 0RJ [from A4010 High Wycombe—Princes Risboro follow Loosley sign, then Gt Hampden, Gt Missenden one]: Charming little old-fashioned tap room (a Rupert Brooke favourite – see his tipsy poem framed here) in much-extended Chilterns pub with airy and plush main dining bar/conservatory, well presented good food (all day Sun), real ales such as Brakspears, Fullers London Pride and Wychwood Hobgoblin, good well priced wines, bar nibbles, friendly efficient staff, log fires, dominoes, cribbage, ring the bull; piped music; children and dogs welcome, conservatory, big garden *(LYM, the Didler, Jennifer Banks, Jarrod and Wendy Hopkinson, Roy Hoing)*

Whip HP27 0PG [Pink Rd]: Cheery and attractive local welcoming walkers, mix of simple traditional furnishings in small front bar and larger downstairs area, reliable food from good lunchtime soup and sandwiches to Sun lunches, good choice of well kept ales inc local Chiltern, Oct beer festival with jazz, copious coffee, friendly service; fruit machine, TV; tables in sheltered garden looking up to windmill *(Tracey and Stephen Groves, BB, Adam F Padel)*

LAVENDON [SP9153]

Green Man MK46 4HA [A428 Bedford—Northampton]: Handsome 17th-c thatched pub in pretty village, roomy and relaxed open-plan wood-floored bar with beams, lots of stripped stone and open woodburner, Greene King IPA, Abbot and Old Speckled Hen, good choice of wines by the glass, good coffee, generous standard food from soup and sandwiches up, friendly attentive service even when busy, big carpeted

evening/wknd restaurant; piped music; children welcome, tables and heaters outside, open all day *(Michael Dandy, George Atkinson)*

☆ *Horseshoe* MK46 4HA [A428 Bedford—Northampton; High St]: Polished low-beamed village pub with log fire and plush banquettes, airy dining extension, enjoyable food from baguettes and baked potatoes up, lots of fish from good fresh haddock to all sorts of exotics (ex-fisherman landlord), Wells & Youngs Eagle and Bombardier, good value small but interesting wine list, quick cheerful service, skittles in public bar; piped music; appealing good-sized garden behind with terrace, decking and play area, cl Sun evening *(BB, Michael Dandy, Howard and Margaret Buchanan)*

LITTLE CHALFONT [SU9997]

Sugar Loaves HP7 9PN [Chalfont Station Rd]: Bright spacious dining pub, wide choice from light dishes up, real ales as well as good choice of wines by the glass, helpful service; attractive outdoor area *(anon)*

LITTLE HAMPDEN [SP8503]

☆ *Rising Sun* HP16 9PS [off A4128 or A413 NW of Gt Missenden; OS Sheet 165 map ref 856040]: Comfortable dining pub in delightful out-of-the-way setting, opened-up bar with woodburner and log fire, good food inc interesting dishes and popular Sun lunch (can be very busy wknds), Adnams and Shepherd Neame Spitfire, good short wine list, may be home-made mulled wine and spiced cider in winter, friendly service; piped music; tables out on terrace, lovely walks, bright newly decorated bedrooms, cl Sun evening and Mon *(Mrs Ann Gray, Mark Farrington, LYM, Roy Hoing)*

LITTLE KINGSHILL [SU8999]

Full Moon HP16 0EE [Hare Lane]: Picturesque country pub with current friendly licensees doing good value generous fresh food, Adnams, Fullers London Pride and Wells & Youngs, good choice of wines by the glass, pleasantly traditional front bar and bigger carpeted side room, quiet on wkdy lunchtimes, buoyant atmosphere evenings and wknds; neat attractive garden *(Steve Langbridge, Barney Drake)*

LITTLE MARLOW [SU8788]

☆ *Kings Head* SL7 3RZ [A4155 about 2 miles E of Marlow; Church Rd]: Long flower-covered pub with open-plan low-beamed bar, wide blackboard choice of good value food from plenty of sandwiches, paninis and baked potatoes to popular Sun roasts, smart dining room, Adnams Broadside, Fullers London Pride and Timothy Taylors Landlord, quick cheerful service even though busy, log or coal fires, Sun bar nibbles, cricket memorabilia; children welcome; big attractive walled garden behind popular with families, nice walk down to church *(D and M T Ayres-Regan, Ian Phillips, Paul Humphreys, BB, Michael Dandy)*

☆ *Queens Head* SL7 3RZ [Church Rd/Pound Lane; cul de sac off A4155 nr Kings Head]:

Charming small tucked-away pub with wide food choice from chunky rustic rolls to some interesting main dishes (not Sun-Tues evenings), real ales such as Adnams Broadside and Jennings Cumberland, quick friendly service, cosy lighter dining room on right with biggish back extension, lots of books in saloon; darts and TV in public bar on left, no dogs; picnic-sets in appealing cottagey front garden, a couple more tables on secluded terrace across lane – short walk from River Thames *(BB, Paul Humphreys, Roy Hoing)*

LITTLE TINGEWICK [SP6432]
Red Lion MK18 4AG [off A421 SW of Buckingham, over the Oxon border]: 16th-c stone-built pub restored after a thatch fire, some emphasis on good gently upmarket food choice, full Fullers beer range at a price, decent wines by the glass, helpful service, big log fire, low beams, mixed simple new furniture on wood floor; piped music; tables out in front and in small garden behind, open all day wknds *(Colin and Jo Howkins, George Atkinson, Michael Dandy)*

LITTLEWORTH COMMON [SU9386]
Jolly Woodman SL1 8PF [2 miles from M40 junction 2; off A355]: Good site by Burnham Beeches, pleasant atmosphere, Brakspears, Fullers London Pride and interesting changing ales, fresh food from sandwiches and baked potatoes up (blackboard choice narrows as things run out – often a good sign), rambling beamed and timbered linked areas with log fire, central woodburner and rustic woody décor, pub games; piped pop music may obtrude; picnic-sets outside, open all day *(LYM, Michael Dandy, Peter and Eleanor Kenyon)*

LONG CRENDON [SP6808]
Angel HP18 9EE [Bicester Rd (B4011)]: Partly 17th-c restaurant-with-rooms rather than pub, though still has something of the flavour of a pub, particularly in the civilised pre-meal menu-perusing lounge with sofas and easy chairs; most enjoyable interesting meals (lunchtime open sandwiches and baguettes too), well kept Hook Norton, good house wines, appealing dining areas inc a conservatory; may be piped music; garden tables, good bedrooms *(LYM, William Goodhart)*

Chandos Arms HP18 9EE [Bicester Rd (B4011)]: Handsome thatched pub under new management, pleasant low-beamed linked areas, good choice of reasonably priced food inc OAP bargains, separate restaurant menu, real ales inc Brakspears, log fire *(David Lamb)*

LUDGERSHALL [SP6617]
Bull & Butcher HP18 9NZ [off A41 Aylesbury—Bicester; The Green]: Keen and helpful new licensees in small beamed country pub, short blackboard choice of reasonably priced food, back dining room; tables in nice front garden, attractive setting *(David Lamb)*

MAIDS MORETON [SP7035]
Wheatsheaf MK18 1QR [Main St, just off A413 Towcester—Buckingham]: Attractive thatched and low-beamed old-world pub, friendly atmosphere and service, wide choice of good attractively priced food from sandwiches up, Hook Norton Best and changing guest beers such as Tring and Wadworths, farm cider, decent choice of wines, lots of pictures and bric-a-brac in old part, two inglenooks, settles and chairs, conservatory restaurant with woodburner; unobtrusive piped music; pleasant quiet enclosed garden behind *(Michael Clatworthy, George Atkinson)*

MARLOW [SU8486]
☆ *Hand & Flowers* SL7 2BP [West St (A4155)]: Restaurant rather than pub now (Greene King IPA and Abbot from bar counter, but not a place to sit with a drink), well worth knowing for very good but expensive meals inc short choice of lunchtime bar food, pleasant rustic no-frills furnishings and careful decorations, informal service, log fire; piped music; tables in small garden *(Cindy Cottman, Kevin Deacon, Michael Dandy)*

☆ *Two Brewers* SL7 1NQ [St Peter St, first right off Station Rd from double roundabout]: Busy low-beamed pub with shiny black woodwork, nautical pictures, gleaming brassware and interesting layout, most tables set for good food inc particularly good choice of sandwiches and light snacks, Brakspears, Fullers London Pride, Hook Norton Old Hooky and Marlow Rebellion, good wines, cafetière coffee, good friendly service, relaxed atmosphere; children in eating area, may be unobtrusive piped music; tables in sheltered back courtyard with covered area, front seats with glimpse of the Thames – pub right on Thames Path *(Paul Humphreys, LYM, Michael Dandy)*

MARSWORTH [SP9114]
Red Lion HP23 4LU [village signed off B489 Dunstable—Aylesbury; Vicarage Rd]: Low-beamed partly thatched village pub with real ales such as Fullers and Vale, decent wines, good value food from enterprising baguettes up, slight coffee-shop feel in quiet lounge with two open fires, steps up to snug parlour and games area, nice variety of seating inc traditional settles; sheltered garden, not far from impressive flight of canal locks *(LYM, Paul Humphreys, Roy Hoing)*

MENTMORE [SP9019]
Stag LU7 0QF [The Green]: This pretty former village pub, a previous main entry, has now become an italian restaurant *(LYM)*

MILTON KEYNES [SP9137]
Wavendon Arms MK17 8LJ [not far from M1 junctions 13 and 14]: Pleasant front bar with mix of modern furniture, airy contemporary tiled-floor restaurant, Wells & Youngs Bombardier, good choice of wines by the glass, up-to-date food, efficient service; tables out in back garden with terrace, more in front *(Michael Dandy)*

MOULSOE [SP9141]
Carrington Arms MK16 0HB [1¼ miles from M1 junction 14: A509 N, first right signed Moulsoe; Cranfield Rd]: Wide food choice inc chargrilled meats sold by weight from refrigerated display, Fri fish night, Greene King IPA and Old Speckled Hen and a guest ale, friendly helpful staff, open-plan layout with comfortable mix of wooden chairs and cushioned banquettes; children allowed, long pretty garden behind, decent bedrooms in adjacent block (Alan Sutton, Michael Dandy, LYM)

NEWTON LONGVILLE [SP8431]
☆ ***Crooked Billet*** MK17 0DF [off A421 S of Milton Keynes; Westbrook End]: Thatched pub with good enterprising restaurantly food, lunchtime sandwiches and wraps too, Greene King ales, brightly modernised extended pubby bar with games, log-fire dining area; piped music, TV; dogs in bar (no children), tables out on lawn, cl Mon lunchtime, open all day Sat (Graham Oddey, LYM, Ian Phillips, Hunter and Christine Wright, Michael Dandy)

OLNEY [SP8851]
Bull MK46 4EA [Market Pl/High St]: Two small front bar rooms, big airy bare-boards eating area on the right, popular quickly served pubby food from sandwiches and baguettes up, well kept Wells & Youngs ales with a guest beer such as Everards Beacon, flourishing Aug bank hol beer festival, good coffee, friendly staff and chatty landlord, log-effect gas fires, lots of games; small courtyard (no dogs), big back garden with big climbing frame; HQ of the famous Shrove Tuesday pancake race (Ted George)

PENN [SU9193]
☆ ***Crown*** HP10 8NY [B474 Beaconsfield—High Wycombe]: Good value Chef & Brewer dining pub perched opp 14th-c church on high ridge with distant views, friendly helpful service, interesting décor and attractive furnishings in the various areas carefully extended from its low-ceilinged medieval core, wide choice of generous food all day from sandwiches up, real ales such as Fullers London Pride, Greene King Old Speckled Hen, Ringwood Old Thumper and Timothy Taylors Landlord, good choice of wines by the glass, two roaring log fires; piped music, games machine; children welcome, lots of tables in attractive gardens with good play area, open all day (Tracey and Stephen Groves, Brian P White, Mrs Ann Gray, Kevin Thomas, Nina Randall, Susan and John Douglas, LYM, Geoff and Sylvia Donald, Roy Hoing)

PENN STREET [SU9295]
☆ ***Hit or Miss*** HP7 0PX [off A404 SW of Amersham, then keep on towards Winchmore Hill]: Well laid out low-beamed pub with own cricket ground, freshly made food (can take a while when busy) inc good fish and popular all-day Sun lunch (not cheap but worth booking), Badger ales, decent wines, friendly helpful young staff, cheerful atmosphere in three clean linked rooms, log fire, charming décor inc interesting cricket

and chair-making memorabilia; piped music; picnic-sets out in front, pleasant setting, open all day (Kevin Thomas, Nina Randall, Di and Mike Gillam, Mrs Ann Gray, LYM, Howard Dell)
Squirrel HP7 0PX: Friendly open-plan bar with flagstones, log fire, comfortable sofas as well as tables and chairs, good value home-made traditional food from baguettes up (not Sun evening), good children's meals, well kept changing ales such as Hydes, good service, free coffee refills, bric-a-brac and cricketing memorabilia, darts; big garden with good play area, handy for lovely walks (and watching cricket), open all day wknds (Paul Humphreys, Mary Priest, Ross Balaam, Roy Hoing)

SPEEN [SU8399]
☆ ***Old Plow*** HP27 0PZ [Flowers Bottom Lane, from village towards Lacey Green and Saunderton Stn]: Restaurant not pub (they won't serve drinks unless you're eating – you can have just one course), but very good if pricy food in both relaxing and charmingly cottagey bistro and more formal dining room, friendly, with log fires, fine service, a real ale as well as good wines; children welcome, pretty lawns, lovely countryside, cl Sun evening and Mon (Mr and Mrs A Curry, LYM)

ST LEONARDS [SP9107]
White Lion HP23 6NW [Jenkins Lane: edge of Buckland Common – village signed off A4011 Wendover—Tring]: Neat open-plan pub, highest in the Chilterns, with old black beams, well kept ales such as Batemans and Greene King, good value pub food, friendly service, log-effect gas fire; children and dogs welcome, attractive sheltered garden, good walks (BB, Roy Hoing)

STOKE GOLDINGTON [SP8348]
☆ ***Lamb*** MK16 8NR [High St (B526 Newport Pagnell—Northampton)]: Proper chatty village pub with three or four good interesting changing ales, Weston's farm cider, good generous home-made food (all day Sat, not Sun evening) at appealing prices from baguettes to several bargain Sun roasts, welcoming landlady, prompt service even when busy, good public bar with table skittles and two small pleasant dining rooms, quiet lounge with log fire and sheep decorations; quiet piped radio, TV; terrace and sheltered garden behind, open all day wknds (JJW, CMW, BB, Steve Willis)

STOKE POGES [SU9885]
Fox & Pheasant SL2 4EZ [Gerrards Cross Rd (B416, Stoke Common)]: Reasonably priced carvery restaurant, usual other food too, quick friendly service, small quiet bar with Wells & Youngs Bombardier (Geoff and Sylvia Donald, David Lamb)

STONE [SP7912]
Bugle Horn HP17 8QP [Oxford Rd, Hartwell (A418 SW of Aylesbury)]: Long low 17th-c stone-built family dining pub, warm and friendly series of comfortable rooms, pleasant furnishings, good choice of

modestly priced home-made food from good daytime sandwiches and Brakspears and Hook Norton Old Hooky, lots of wines by the glass, quick efficient service, several log fires, prettily planted well furnished conservatory; tables on attractive terrace, lovely trees in large pretty garden, horses grazing in pastures beyond, open all day *(Tim and Ann Newell, E A and D C T Frewer)*

STONY STRATFORD [SP7840]

Old George MK11 1AA [High St]: Attractive and lively beamed and timbered inn, cosily pubby, with good value food at any time inc roast of the day, quick friendly staff, real ales such as Fullers London Pride and Greene King IPA, good coffee, small dining room up at the back; piped music, lavatories up rather awkward stairs; tables in courtyard behind, bedrooms *(George Atkinson)*

TAPLOW [SU9185]

Feathers SL1 8NS [Taplow Common, opp Cliveden entrance]: Rambling olde-worlde Chef & Brewer family dining pub opp Cliveden entrance (NT), sensibly priced all-day food in roomy beamed eating areas, Fullers London Pride, John Smiths, Theakstons Old Peculier and Wells & Youngs Bombardier, good choice of decent wines, good coffee, helpful service; piped music, games; charming courtyard, large garden with play area (dogs allowed only by front picnic-sets), open all day *(Roy and Lindsey Fentiman, Michael Dandy)*

THE LEE [SP8904]

Cock & Rabbit HP16 9LZ [back roads 2½ miles N of Great Missenden, E of A413]: Warmly welcoming Italian-run dining pub, stylish and comfortable, with reasonably priced home-made food (not Sun or Mon evenings) inc good fresh fish, pasta, real ales such as Fullers and Greene King, decent wines, good lively staff, panelled bar, two separate back dining areas welcoming children; big garden with tables on verandah, terraces and lawn *(LYM, Paul Humphreys, Roy Hoing)*

WADDESDON [SP7416]

☆ *Five Arrows* HP18 0JE [High St (A41)]: Small hotel/restaurant rather than pub, linked light and airy well furnished high-ceilinged rooms with Rothschild family portrait engravings and lots of old estate-worker photographs, excellent wines (Fullers London Pride and Discovery too), good coffee, ciabattas and baguettes as well as light dishes and full meals; children allowed, appealing back garden, comfortable bedrooms, handy for Waddesdon Manor *(Michael Dandy, John Robertson, LYM, Mrs Deborah Chalmers)*

Lion HP18 0JD [High St]: Friendly welcome, good range of beers, good carefully cooked food in lively bar and smart linked bistro-style dining areas *(George Tucker)*

WESTON TURVILLE [SP8510]

Chequers HP22 5SJ [Church Lane]: Cosy two-level traditional bar with good welcoming long-serving staff, Adnams, Boddingtons,

Fullers London Pride and HSB and Wadworths 6X, enjoyable bar food, large log fire, flagstones, low beams and stylish solid wooden furniture, adjoining restaurant with good food esp fish; tucked away in attractive part of village, tables in nice garden *(Mrs Deborah Chalmers, Peter and Jan Humphreys, Roy Hoing)*

WESTON UNDERWOOD [SP8650]

☆ *Cowpers Oak* MK46 5JS [signed off A509 in Olney; High St]: Attractive family-friendly wisteria-covered beamed pub in pretty thatched village, generous good value food (all day wknds) from tasty choice of imaginative soups up, well kept Fullers London Pride, Greene King IPA, Oxfordshire Marshmellow and Theakstons Old Peculier, nice medley of old-fashioned furnishings, woodburners, dark red walls, dark panelling and some stripped stone, back restaurant (best to book Sun), good games room with darts, bar billiards, hood skittles and table football, daily papers; piped music, TV; children very welcome, dogs in main bar, small suntrap front terrace, more tables on back decking and in big orchard garden (no dogs) with play area and farm animals, bedrooms, open all day wknds *(LYM, Michael Sargent, George Atkinson, Colin and Janet Roe, David Campbell, Vicki McLean)*

WHADDON [SP8034]

Lowndes Arms MK17 0NA [off A421; High St]: Small bar with inglenook fireplace, beams, brasses and bric-a-brac, well kept ales such as Black Sheep, Brains, Fullers London Pride and Greene King IPA and Abbot, good choice of wines by the glass, enterprising range of food, attractive restaurant; piped music; tables on small heated terrace, small garden with great views, refurbished bedroom block *(Michael Dandy, MLR)*

WINCHMORE HILL [SU9394]

Plough HP7 0PA [The Hill]: Smart restaurant rather than pub now, carefully cooked enterprising meals rather than snacks inc good value set lunch, flagstones and low beams but contemporary furnishings and décor in leather-seated bar and linked dining area, neat helpful staff, fashionable imported lagers, good coffee; piped music; tables on lawn with wishing well *(BB, Michael Dandy)*

WOOBURN COMMON [SU9387]

☆ *Royal Standard* HP10 0JS [about 3½ miles from M40 junction 2]: Well kept changing ales such as Caledonian Deuchars IPA, Dark Star, Fullers London Pride, Hop Back Summer Lightning, Inveralmond and Wells & Youngs in busy low-ceilinged local with good value pubby food from baguettes and baked potatoes up, welcoming helpful staff, well chosen wines, open fire, lots of daily papers and crossword reference books, neat dining area; picnic-sets on pretty roadside terrace and in back garden, open all day *(Michael Dandy, LYM, Nina Randall, Kevin Thomas, P Waterman, Roy Hoing)*

Cambridgeshire

Real ale pubs feature strongly here, with a growing number of pubs even brewing their own. The Cambridge Blue and Live & Let Live, both in Cambridge, keep up to seven real ales each, the bustling Blue Bell at Helpston has half a dozen, the Brewery Tap and Charters in Peterborough both keep a dozen (and the Brewery Tap also brews its own), and the Dyke's End at Reach has just started brewing its own. Also, quite a number of places making a name for their fantastic food go out of their way to make those just wanting a drink very welcome too. These include the Chequers at Fowlmere, the Cock at Hemingford Grey and the stylish Old Bridge Hotel in Huntingdon. Other particularly good dining pubs are the restauranty Pheasant at Keyston and the Three Horseshoes, Madingley; the Snooty Millstone, an interesting new entry in Barnack, looks very promising on the food side, too, as does another new entry, the George & Dragon at Elsworth. For a special meal out the Old Bridge Hotel in Huntingdon takes some beating, and is our Cambridgeshire Dining Pub of the Year. In the Lucky Dip section at the end of the chapter, pubs on a rising tide of good form are the Crown at Broughton, Kingston Arms in Cambridge, White Horse in Eaton Socon, Cutter near Ely and Tavern on the Green at Great Staughton. Pub food prices in the county, given similar quality, are broadly in line with prices elsewhere. Drinks prices, though, are generally a shade above the national average. The Brewery Tap in Peterborough and Dyke's End at Reach, both brewing their own beer, are much cheaper, as is Charters, the Brewery Tap's floating offshoot. Besides Oakham (the Brewery Tap's beer brand), other more or less local ales we found featuring as the cheapest on offer in the area's pubs were Earl Soham, Fenland, Adnams (from Suffolk, but very widely available in the better pubs here), Nethergate, Digfield and City of Cambridge; Greene King is the dominant regional brewer.

BARNACK TF0704 MAP 5

Snooty Millstone ♀ 🍺

Off B1443 SE of Stamford, via School Lane into Millstone Lane; PE9 3ET

New management has brought good cooking and a fresh new look to this stone-built pub in a picturesque village; good range of drinks, too

Recently given a contemporary makeover in a smart clean-cut pared-down style, this stone-built pub still has welcoming fires and cosy corners in its timbered bar, now joined by some bold oil paintings by local artists. They have Adnams Bitter and Everards Tiger and Original on handpump, nine wines by the glass from a thoughtful list, several malt whiskies, and a good choice of bottled beers including belgian fruit beers. There's a lovely enclosed courtyard for outside dining. Burghley House, home of the famous horse trials, is nearby. This is one of the four pubs in the Snooty Inns Group. More reports please; if initial promise is confirmed, this is well in line for a Food Award.

🍴 Cooked by one of the licensees, the well thought-of bar food includes sandwiches, ploughman's soup, carpaccio of aberdeenshire beef with rocket and parmesan, baked camembert for two with fruit chutney, potato gnocchi with tomatoes, roasted peppers and buffalo mozzarella, free-range pork sausages and onion gravy, cottage pie, seared lambs liver with mustard mash and smoked bacon, slow-cooked pork belly with black pudding mash, good steaks using dry-aged aberdeenshire beef, and puddings such as vanilla panna cotta with poached rhubarb and banoffi trifle. *Starters/Snacks: £3.95 to £6.95. Main Courses: £7.95 to £22.00. Puddings: £4.25 to £6.25*

Everards ~ Tenants Clive Dixon and David Hennigan ~ Real ale ~ Bar food (12-2(2.30 Sun), 6.30-9.30) ~ Restaurant ~ (01780) 740296 ~ Children welcome ~ Dogs allowed in bar ~ Open mike session first Tues of month ~ Open 12-11; closed evenings 25 and 26 Dec and 1 Jan

Recommended by Roy Bromell, Ian Stafford

CAMBRIDGE
TL4658   MAP 5

Cambridge Blue 🍺 £
85 Gwydir Street; CB1 2LG

Friendly backstreet pub, simply decorated with lots to look at, and interesting ales

A fine choice of real ales in this friendly back street pub might include Adnams Bitter, City of Cambridge Hobsons Choice, Elgoods Black Dog, Woodfordes Wherry and changing guests such as Nethergate Augustinian Ale and Oakham JHB on handpump; quite a choice of malt whiskies as well. There's an attractive little conservatory and two peaceful rooms that are simply decorated with old-fashioned bare-boards style furnishings, candles on the tables, and a big collection of oars; there's also the bow section of the Cambridge boat that famously rammed a barge and sank before the start of the 1984 boat race, and such a nice selection of rowing photographs you feel you're browsing through someone's family snaps. Board games, cards and dominoes. The big back garden is surprisingly rural feeling.

🍴 Straightforward bar food includes home-made soup, filled ciabatta rolls and baked potatoes, nut roast, chilli, sausages, daily specials and Sunday pies. *Starters/Snacks: £2.25 to £3.25. Main Courses: £5.50 to £7.25. Puddings: £1.25 to £2.75*

Free house ~ Licensees Chris and Debbie Lloyd ~ Real ale ~ Bar food (12-2.30, 6-9.30) ~ (01223) 505110 ~ Children welcome in conservatory ~ Dogs welcome ~ Open 12-2.30(3 Sat), 5.30-11; 12-3, 6-10.30 Sun; closed evening 25 and 26 Dec

Recommended by Jerry Brown, Helen McLagan, Mark Farrington, Dr David Cockburn, the Didler, Andy and Jill Kassube

Eagle 🍷 £
Bene't Street; CB2 3QN

Standard food served all day in rambling rooms with original features; cobbled and galleried courtyard

To appreciate the many original architectural features in the rambling rooms here, try to avoid peak times as the pub is nearly always extremely busy. There are two medieval mullioned windows and the remains of two possibly medieval wall paintings, two fireplaces dating back to around 1600, lovely worn wooden floors and plenty of pine panelling. Don't miss the high dark red ceiling which has been left unpainted since World War II to preserve the signatures of British and American airmen worked in with Zippo lighters, candle smoke and lipstick. Creaky old furniture is nicely in keeping with it all and drinks include Greene King IPA, Abbot, Old Speckled Hen and a changing guest beer on handpump, and around a dozen wines by the glass. An attractive cobbled and galleried courtyard, screened from the street by sturdy wooden gates and with heavy wooden seats and tables, heaters and pretty hanging baskets, takes you back through the centuries – especially at Christmas, when they serve mulled wine and you can listen to the choristers from King's College.

🍴 Straightforward bar food includes filled baguettes and baked potatoes, steak in ale pie, ham and eggs, lasagne and giant battered cod. *Starters/Snacks: £5.45. Main Courses: £6.56 to £11.95. Puddings: £3.50*

Greene King ~ Managers Steve Ottley and Sian Crowther ~ Real ale ~ Bar food (12-10(8 Fri and Sat)) ~ (01223) 505020 ~ Children allowed if with parents and if eating ~ Open 11-11; 12-10.30 Sun

Recommended by Andy and Jill Kassube, John Saville, Peter and Pat Frogley, Rosanna Luke, Matt Curzon, Dr David Cockburn, Michael Dandy, D P and M A Miles, the Didler, Barry Collett, Simon Watkins

Free Press £
Prospect Row; CB1 1DU

Quiet and unspoilt with some interesting local décor, and good value food

Well off the tourist track, this unspoilt little pub has a suntrap sheltered and paved back garden which is popular in summer, whilst in winter you can sit peacefully reading a newspaper by the log fire (no piped music, mobile phones or games machines). In a nod to the building's history as home to a local newspaper, the walls of its characterful bare-board rooms are hung with old newspaper pages and printing memorabilia, as well as old printing trays that local customers are encouraged to top up with little items. Well kept Greene King IPA, Abbot and Mild and a guest or two such as Batemans XXXB and Greene King Morlands Original on handpump, and around 20 malt whiskies; quite a few assorted board games.

🍴 Bar food is tasty but straightforward: filled ciabattas, soup, ploughman's, stuffed peppers, gammon with bubble and squeak, and lamb shank. *Starters/Snacks: £3.25. Main Courses: £5.95 to £7.95. Puddings: £3.25*

Greene King ~ Tenant Craig Bickley ~ Real ale ~ Bar food (12-2(2.30 Sat and Sun), 6-9; not Sun evening) ~ (01223) 368337 ~ Children welcome till 9pm ~ Dogs welcome ~ Open 12-2.30, 6-11; 12-11 Sat; 12-3, 7-10.30 Sun; closed 25 and 26 Dec, 1 Jan

Recommended by Michael Dandy, John Wooll, Dr David Cockburn, the Didler

Live & Let Live 🍴 £
40 Mawson Road; off Mill Road SE of centre; CB1 2EA

Fine real ales in popular local, a relaxed atmosphere, and homely food

Being a real ale enthusiast, the landlord at this down-to-earth but popular old local usually has at least seven very well kept real ales on handpump or tapped from the cask: Everards Tiger, Nethergate Umbel Magna and guests from Castle Rock, Loddon and Tring, a draught belgian beer plus a big choice of bottled belgian beers and differing local ciders. The atmosphere is relaxed and friendly, and the heavily timbered brickwork rooms have sturdy varnished pine tables with pale wood chairs on bare boards, and real gas lighting. An assortment of collectables takes in lots of interesting old country bric-a-brac and some steam railway and brewery memorabilia, and posters advertise local forthcoming events; cribbage and dominoes. More reports please.

🍴 Good value straightforward food might include sandwiches and filled baked potatoes, home-made soup, ploughman's, sausage or ham and eggs, vegetable lasagne, and beef bourguignon. *Starters/Snacks: £2.75 to £4.00. Main Courses: £6.50 to £9.50. Puddings: £3.00 to £4.00*

Burlison Inns ~ Lease Peter Wiffin ~ Real ale ~ Bar food (12-2, 6(7 Sun)-9) ~ (01223) 460261 ~ Children in eating area of bar ~ Dogs welcome ~ Open 11.30-2.30, 5.30(6 Sat)-11; 12-3, 7-11 Sun

Recommended by Helen McLagan, Richard J Stanley, Dr David Cockburn, Revd R P Tickle

---

Children – if the details at the end of a main entry don't mention them, you should assume that the pub does not allow them inside.

ELSWORTH   TL3163   MAP 5

George & Dragon

Off A14 NW of Cambridge, via Boxworth, or off A428; CB3 8JQ

Busy dining pub with quite a choice of interesting food served by efficient staff

The weekday lunchtime and evening set menus in this bustling brick-built dining pub are very popular so it's best to book a table in advance. A pleasant panelled main bar with lots of shiny brassware opens on the left to a slightly elevated dining area with flowers on comfortable tables, and a good woodburning stove. From here, steps lead down to a garden room behind with tables overlooking attractive garden terraces. On the right is a more formal restaurant. Greene King IPA and Old Speckled Hen and a guest beer on handpump and decent wines; polite, neat staff.

🍴 As well as their themed menu choices such as pie, fish, steak and so forth, the well liked food might include lunchtime sandwiches, filled baguettes and ploughman's as well as home-made chicken liver pâté, home-made soup, warm tomato and brie tart, spinach and four cheese tortellini with tomato and basil sauce, haddock and prawn mornay, gammon and eggs, chicken in bacon and mushroom sauce, and aberdeen angus steaks. *Starters/Snacks: £3.75 to £5.95. Main Courses: £7.50 to £17.00*

Free house ~ Licensees Paul and Karen Beer ~ Real ale ~ Bar food ~ Restaurant ~ (01954) 267236 ~ Children welcome ~ Dogs allowed in bar ~ Open 11-3, 6-11; 12-2.30 Sun; closed 25 and 26 Dec

Recommended by Michael and Jenny Back, J Jennings, Keith and Janet Morris

ELTON   TL0893   MAP 5

Black Horse ♀

B671 off A605 W of Peterborough and A1(M); Overend; PE8 6RU

Well run dining pub with country furnishings, good food, and super views from big garden

This is a handsome honey brick dining pub with roaring log fires, hop-strung beams, a homely and comfortable mix of furniture (no two tables and chairs seem the same), antique prints, and lots of ornaments and bric-a-brac including an intriguing ancient radio set. Dining areas at each end of the bar have parquet flooring and tiles, and the stripped stone back lounge towards the restaurant has an interesting fireplace. Bass, Digfield Barnwell Bitter and Shacklebush and Everards Tiger on handpump and 15 wines by the glass. The big garden has super views across to Elton Hall park and the village church, there are seats on the terrace and a couple of acres of grass for children to play. More reports please.

🍴 Good, but not cheap, food ranges from bar snacks such as filled baked potatoes, sandwiches, ploughman's and home-made pie of the day, to bangers and mash, pork medallions stuffed with garlic and herbs wrapped in bacon with stilton sauce or tuna loin with red pesto sauce; they sometimes offer afternoon snacks in summer. They may ask you to leave your credit card behind the bar or pay on ordering. *Starters/Snacks: £4.25 to £6.95. Main Courses: £11.95 to £17.95. Puddings: £4.95*

Free house ~ Licensee John Clennell ~ Real ale ~ Bar food (12-2.30, 6-9) ~ Restaurant ~ (01832) 280240 ~ Children welcome ~ Dogs allowed in bar ~ Open 12-11(midnight Fri and Sat, 6pm Sun); closed Sun evening

Recommended by M and GR, J C M Troughton, Fiona McElhone

Bedroom prices normally include full english breakfast, VAT and any inclusive service charge that we know of. Prices before the '/' are for single rooms, after for two people in double or twin (B includes a private bath, S a private shower). If there is no '/', the prices are only for twin or double rooms (as far as we know there are no singles). If there is no B or S, as far as we know no rooms have private facilities.

ELY   TL5380   MAP 5

Fountain ◀

Corner of Barton Square and Silver Street; CB7 4JF

Happily escaping tourists but close to cathedral

All very neatly kept and with no music, fruit machines or even food, this is a simple yet genteel 19th-c pub very close to the cathedral and with a good mix of chatty customers. Old cartoons, local photographs, regional maps and mementoes of the neighbouring King's School punctuate the elegant dark pink walls, and neatly tied-back curtains hang from gold colour rails above the big windows. Above one fireplace is a stuffed pike in a case, and there are a few antlers dotted about. An extension at the back provides much needed additional seating. Adnams Bitter and Broadside, Woodfordes Wherry and a guest such as Everards Tiger on handpump. Note the limited opening times below. More reports please.

📷 **No food served.**

Free house ~ Licensees John and Judith Borland ~ Real ale ~ No credit cards ~ (01353) 663122 ~ Children welcome away from bar until 8pm ~ Dogs welcome ~ Open 5-11; 12-2, 6-11.30 Sat; 12-2, 7-10.30 Sun; closed weekday lunchtimes
Recommended by the Didler, Dr Andy Wilkinson

FEN DITTON   TL4860   MAP 5

Ancient Shepherds

Off B1047 at Green End, The River signpost, just NE of Cambridge; CB5 8ST

Beamed and comfortable with coal fires and homely food

This solidly beamed old pub offers a friendly welcome to both locals and visitors. Perhaps the nicest room here is the softly lit central lounge, where you can't fail to be comfortable on one of the big fat dark red button-back leather settees or armchairs which are grouped round low dark wood tables. The warm coal fire and heavy drapes around the window seat with its big scatter cushions add to the cosiness. Above a black dado, the walls (and ceiling) are dark pink, and decorated with comic fox and policeman prints and little steeplechasing and equestrian ones. On the right the smallish more pubby bar, with its coal fire, serves Adnams and Greene King IPA, while on the left is a pleasant restaurant (piped music in here). The licensee's west highland terrier, Billie, might be around outside food service times.

📷 **Generously served and fairly priced bar food such as home-made soup, lunchtime filled baguettes, ploughman's, ham, egg and chips, beef and Guinness pie, and daily specials.**
Starters/Snacks: £4.50 to £6.95. Main Courses: £8.95 to £16.95. Puddings: £4.75

Punch ~ Tenant J M Harrington ~ Real ale ~ Bar food (12-2(2.30 Sun), 6.30-9) ~ Restaurant ~ (01223) 293280 ~ Children in lounge and dining room only ~ Dogs allowed in bar ~ Open 12-2.30, 6-11; 12-5 Sun; closed Sun evening
Recommended by R T and J C Moggridge, Gordon Tong, Dr Phil Putwain

FORDHAM   TL6270   MAP 5

White Pheasant ♀

A142 (may be bypassed by the time this edition is published) at junction with B1102 to Burwell, north of Newmarket; Market Street; CB7 5LQ

Unassuming from outside but with simple, stylish rooms, a restaurant feel but with relaxed friendliness, and enjoyable food

Although there is quite an emphasis on the popular food here, the staff create a warm, friendly and relaxed atmosphere that's more akin to a proper pub. It's open-plan and light and airy with an attractive mix of well spaced big farmhouse tables and chairs on bare boards, some stripped brickwork, and a cheery log fire at one end. One or two steps lead down to a small similarly furnished but carpeted room; piped music. Fenland Rabbit Poacher and a guest like Milton Jupiter on handpump, four ciders and perry, and a dozen carefully chosen wines (including champagne) by the glass served from the horseshoe bar that faces the entrance.

⑪ As well as filled breads and salads, the enjoyable food might include deep-fried crispy whitebait, tiger prawns in chilli butter with avocado and cream cheese galette, ham and eggs, sausage and mustard mash, wild mushroom stroganoff, slow-braised shin of beef, local pheasant breasts wrapped in prosciutto, marmalade-glazed gressingham duck breast, and daily specials. *Starters/Snacks: £4.50 to £9.95. Main Courses: £9.95 to £19.95. Puddings: £4.50 to £5.50*

Free house ~ Licensee Elizabeth Trangmar ~ Real ale ~ Bar food (12-2.30, 6-9.30(7-9 Sun)) ~ Restaurant ~ (01638) 720414 ~ Well behaved children welcome until 8pm ~ Open 12-3, 6-11; 12-3, 7-10 Sun; closed 26-28 Dec, 1 Jan

Recommended by John Saville, George Atkinson, Sally Anne and Peter Goodale, Ryta Lyndley

FOWLMERE
TL4245   MAP 5

Chequers
B1368; SG8 7SR

First-rate food in lovely coaching inn, comfortable bars, and lots of wines by the glass

Rather smart and attractive, this 16th-c country pub is just the place for a special meal – though they do keep Adnams Broadside and a couple of guests from brewers such as Nethergate on handpump, 18 wines by the glass and 30 malt whiskies. Two comfortably furnished downstairs rooms are warmed by an open log fire, and upstairs there are beams, wall timbering and some interesting moulded plasterwork above the fireplace. The airy conservatory overlooks tables with cocktail parasols on a terrace and flowers and shrub roses in the neatly kept floodlit garden. Historic aeroplanes from Duxford fly over here during the summer months.

⑪ As well as starters and light meals like soup, scallops with wilted spinach on a red pepper and smoked garlic jus, stilton, port and walnut terrine, and baked smoked haddock with cream, tomatoes and cheese, the imaginative dishes might include freshwater prawn and mango curry, roast barbary duck in ginger, garlic and soy with stir-fried pak choi and oriental sauce, pasta with artichoke hearts, red peppers, chestnuts, cherry tomatoes, basil and cream, game pie and lamb tagine, with puddings such as hot date sponge with hot toffee sauce and cold lemon tart with Cointreau flavoured mascarpone. *Starters/Snacks: £4.60 to £7.95. Main Courses: £10.95 to £19.95. Puddings: £4.60 to £5.50*

Free house ~ Licensee Paul Beaumont ~ Real ale ~ Bar food (12-2, 7-9.30(9 Sun)) ~ Restaurant ~ (01763) 208369 ~ Children in conservatory only ~ Open 12-3, 6-11(7-10.30 Sun); closed 25 Dec, evenings 26 Dec and 1 Jan

Recommended by Mrs Jane Kingsbury, Pat Flynn, Adele Summers, Alan Black, Mrs P J Pearce, Michael Butler, Mrs Joyce Ferguson, Jeremy Whitehorn, Andy Millward, Peter and Jean Hoare, Jennie Challacombe, K S Whittaker, Roy Hoing

GODMANCHESTER
TL2470   MAP 5

Exhibition
London Road; PE29 2HZ

Interesting and amusingly decorated rooms with fresh flowers, candles and fairy lights

There's an attractive choice of rooms here – which is rather a surprise given the rather ordinary exterior. The main bar has its walls humorously decorated with re-created shop-fronts – a post office, gallery, and wine and spirit merchant – complete with doors and stock in the windows. It's cosy with big flagstones on the floor, cushioned wall benches, fresh flowers and candles on each of the tables and white fairy lights on some of the plants; piped music. The dining room has smart candelabra and framed prints. Fullers London Pride and Greene King IPA on handpump. There are picnic-sets on the back lawn, some shaded by pergolas, and a couple in front as well. More reports please.

🍴 Lunchtime bar food includes sandwiches, soup, wild boar pâté, chargrilled burger in a seeded bun, pasta or pie of the day, lasagne and wild mushroom risotto, with evening dishes like pork loin wrapped in pancetta with spring onion mash, lemon sole with thai vegetables and coconut sauce and venison steak with berry compote, and puddings such as crème brûlée or lemon tart. *Starters/Snacks: £3.95 to £6.95. Main Courses: £7.95 to £15.95. Puddings: £4.95*

Enterprise ~ Lease Paul Dyer ~ Real ale ~ Bar food (12-3, 6.30-9.30) ~ Restaurant ~ (01480) 459134 ~ Children in restaurant ~ Dogs allowed in bar ~ Open 11.30-11(12 Thurs-Sat); 12-11 Sun

Recommended by Michael Dandy, M and GR, Derek and Sylvia Stephenson, R T and J C Moggridge, Peter and Jean Hoare, Mick Miller, Mrs Jane Kingsbury, Christopher Turner

HELPSTON   TF1205   MAP 5

Blue Bell 🍺
Woodgate; off B1443; PE6 7ED

Bustling and friendly, fine choice of beers, and tasty food including good value OAP lunch

There's always a cheerful, bustling atmosphere in this particularly well run pub and a warm welcome to all from the hard-working and knowledgeable landlord. Comfortable cushioned chairs and settles, plenty of pictures, ornaments, mementoes and cart-wheel displays, and piped music give a homely atmosphere to the lounge, parlour and snug. The dining extension is light and airy with a sloping glass roof. Well kept Adnams Broadside, Batemans Hooker, Grainstore Cooking Bitter and Ten Fifty, North Yorkshire Flying Herbert, and Timothy Taylors Landlord on handpump; pool, piped music and cribbage. A sheltered and heated terrace has plastic seats and garden tables and a new awning; pretty hanging baskets and wheelchair access.

🍴 As well as a good value OAP two-course lunch, the very popular food includes sandwiches, steak in ale pie, five-cheese cannelloni, baked egg on ham and potato hash, lasagne, chicken breast in creamy tarragon sauce, salmon and dill fishcakes, and steaks. *Starters/Snacks: £2.90 to £4.25. Main Courses: £8.25 to £10.95*

Free house ~ Licensee Aubrey Sinclair Ball ~ Real ale ~ Bar food (not Sun or Mon evenings) ~ Restaurant ~ (01733) 252394 ~ Children in snug and dining areas until 9pm ~ Dogs allowed in bar ~ Open 11.30-2.30, 5-11; 11.30-3, 6-12 Sat; 12-9 Sun

Recommended by Michael and Jenny Back, Ian Stafford, Eddie and Lynn Jarrett, Ben and Helen Ingram

HEMINGFORD GREY   TL2970   MAP 5

Cock 🍴 🍷 🍺
Village signposted off A14 eastbound, and (via A1096 St Ives road) westbound; High Street; PE28 9BJ

Imaginative food in pretty pub, extensive wine list plus other drinks, bustling atmosphere, and smart restaurant

If you wish to enjoy the very good imaginative food at this pretty little pub, you must eat in the restaurant as they have sensibly kept the public bar on the left for drinking only. It's a traditional room with an open woodburning stove on the raised hearth, bar stools, wall seats, and a carver, steps that lead down to more seating below black beams, and Earl Soham Victoria, Woodfordes Wherry and a couple of guests such as Nethergate Stinger and Wolf Golden Jackal on handpump, alongside 15 good wines by the glass from an extensive list. In marked contrast, the stylishly simple spotless restaurant on the right – you must book to be sure of a table – has clattery pale bare boards, canary walls above a powder-blue dado, and another woodburning stove. There's a friendly, bustling atmosphere and a good mix of locals and visitors. Tables out behind in a neat garden.

⊞ As well as a very useful two- and three-course lunch menu, changing dishes might include sandwiches (not listed so you have to ask), soup, duck parcel with sweet and sour cucumber, seared scallops with crayfish tails and winter fruit salsa, sautéed chicken livers, spring onions, and pecan nuts, home-made sausages, tagliatelle with ricotta cheese, sun blush tomatoes and mint, halibut fillet with garlic, chilli and mint risotto and sweet basil yoghurt, and roasted lamb chump, puy lentils, caramelised shallots and blood orange relish, with puddings such as chocolate nut truffle cake or apple and lemon tart with berry coulis. *Starters/Snacks: £3.95 to £7.95. Main Courses: £6.95 to £15.95. Puddings: £4.95 to £5.50.*

Free house ~ Licensees Oliver Thain and Richard Bradley ~ Real ale ~ Bar food (12-2.30, 6.30-9(9.30 Fri and Sat; 8.30 Sun)) ~ Restaurant ~ (01480) 463609 ~ Children in restaurant only but must be over 5 in evening ~ Dogs allowed in bar ~ Open 11.30-3, 6-11; 12-4, 6.30-10.30 Sun

Recommended by Margaret and Roy Randle, Howard and Margaret Buchanan, Gordon Ormondroyd, Chris Bell, MJB, R T and J C Moggridge, J Stickland, Michael Dandy, Jim and Sheila Prideaux

HEYDON
TL4339   MAP 5

King William IV
Off A505 W of M11 junction 10; SG8 8PW

Rambling rooms with fascinating rustic jumble, quite a few vegetarian dishes on sizeable menu, and pretty garden

The beamed nooks and crannies in this neatly kept dining pub are filled with ploughshares, yokes and iron tools, cowbells, beer steins, samovars, brass or black wrought-iron lamps, copper-bound casks and milk ewers, harness, horsebrasses, and smith's bellows – as well as decorative plates, cut-glass and china ornaments; winter log fire and piped music. Adnams Best, Fullers London Pride, Greene King IPA and Timothy Taylors Landlord on handpump and helpful staff. A wooden deck has teak furniture and outdoor heaters, and there are more seats in the pretty garden.

⊞ Well liked bar food includes quite a few vegetarian choices as well as sandwiches, soup, mussels, fish pie, grilled pork chops with apple and cider sauce, baked bass with thai spices and stir-fried vegetables, and puddings such as apple and rhubarb crumble. *Starters/Snacks: £5.95 to £6.95. Main Courses: £10.95 to £17.95. Puddings: £5.95 to £6.25.*

Free house ~ Licensee Elizabeth Nicholls ~ Real ale ~ Bar food (12-2(3 Sun), 6.30-9.30) ~ Restaurant ~ (01763) 838773 ~ Children welcome with restrictions ~ Dogs allowed in bar ~ Open 11.30-2.30, 6-11; 12-3, 7-11 Sun

Recommended by Richard Siebert, Gillian Grist, M S Pizer, Mrs Margo Finlay, Jörg Kasprowski

HINXTON
TL4945   MAP 5

Red Lion
2 miles off M11 junction 9 northbound; take first exit off A11, A1301 N, then left turn into village – High Street; a little further from junction 10, via A505 E and A1301 S; CB10 1QY

Pink-washed and handy for Duxford and M11, friendly staff, and neat, big garden

A welcome break from the nearby M11 and close to the Imperial War Museum at Duxford, this carefully extended pink-washed old inn has a friendly, bustling atmosphere. Its dusky, mainly open-plan beamed bar has leather chesterfields on wooden floors, an old wall clock, a dark green fireplace and Adnams Bitter, Greene King IPA, Woodfordes Wherry and a guest such as City of Cambridge Hobsons Choice or Nethergate Augustinian Ale on handpump, 12 wines by the glass, and Aspall's cider. Off here there are high-backed upholstered settles in an informal dining area and pictures and assorted clocks in the smart restaurant. The neatly kept big garden has a pleasant terrace with picnic-sets, a dovecote and views of the village church.

⊞ Popular bar food, served by friendly helpful staff, might include sandwiches and filled baked potatoes and baguettes, soup, smoked goose and redcurrant compote, potted venison, lunchtime steak in ale pie or ham and free range egg, chicken curry, roast cashew and pine nut wellington, roast partridge wrapped in bacon with thyme jus, pork tenderloin in cider, and puddings like steamed chocolate and Cointreau pudding or raspberry fool. *Starters/Snacks: £4.00 to £6.00. Main Courses: £8.00 to £16.00. Puddings: £4.00 to £6.00.*

Free house ~ Licensee Alex Clarke ~ Real ale ~ Bar food (12-2, 7-9(9.30 Fri, Sat); 12-2.30, 7-9 Sun) ~ Restaurant ~ (01799) 530601 ~ Well behaved children welcome ~ Dogs allowed in bar ~ Open 11-3, 6-11; 12-4, 7-10.30 Sun

Recommended by Mrs M Hatwell, Roy Bromell, David Cosham, Keith Widdowson, Mrs Hazel Rainer, Louise Medcalf, Kevin Thorpe, B C Robertson, Charles Gysin

HUNTINGDON
TL2471   MAP 5

Old Bridge Hotel ★ ⑪ ♀ ⊨

1 High Street; ring road just off B1044 entering from easternmost A14 slip road; PE29 3TQ

CAMBRIDGESHIRE DINING PUB OF THE YEAR

Georgian hotel with smartly pubby bar, splendid range of drinks, and excellent food

The bar in this very civilised ivy-covered Georgian hotel has fine polished floorboards, a good log fire and a quietly chatty atmosphere, and is still somewhere customers like to drop into for a drink: Adnams Bitter, City of Cambridge Hobsons Choice, and Digfield Barnwell Bitter on handpump, 18 wines by the glass, ten sweet ones and two champagnes. But it's the imaginative food served by excellent staff that most people come to enjoy which can be eaten in the big airy Terrace (an indoor room, but with beautifully painted verdant murals suggesting the open air) or in the slightly more formal panelled restaurant. The building is tucked away in a good spot by the River Great Ouse with its own landing stage, and tables on waterside terraces.

⑪ **Beautifully presented, the modern bar food might include sandwiches, interesting soups, spaghetti with clams, chilli, garlic and parsley, salad of confit pheasant leg with chicory, orange and pistachio, spinach, nutmeg and ricotta ravioli with sage butter, pork sausages with onion gravy, rack of cornish lamb with herb crust and chateau potatoes, hake with spring onion mash and mustard cream, slow-braised blade of beef with mushroom and red wine risotto, and puddings such as vanilla panna cotta with chocolate and grappa sauce or apple and hazelnut crumble; nice nibbles like home-made crisps and focaccia with olives, confit garlic and olive oil and two- and three-course set menus.** *Starters/Snacks: £4.95 to £9.75. Main Courses: £10.95 to £23.00. Puddings: £4.95 to £7.95*

Huntsbridge ~ Licensee John Hoskins ~ Real ale ~ Bar food (12-2.15, 6.30-9.30) ~ Restaurant ~ (01480) 424010 ~ Children welcome ~ Open 11.30-11 ~ Bedrooms: £95B/£125B

Recommended by Mrs Margo Finlay, Jörg Kasprowski, Lesley and Barbara Owen, Michael Dandy, J F M and M West, Martin and Pauline Jennings, Mr and Mrs Ladley, MJB, Michael Sargent

KEYSTON
TL0475   MAP 5

Pheasant ⑪ ♀

Just off A14 SE of Thrapston; village loop road, off B663; PE28 0RE

Essentially a restaurant with modern, highly thought-of food and excellent range of drinks

By the time this edition is published, new licensees will have taken over the running of this long low thatched inn – though in fact they had been managers for a while beforehand. Mr Scrimshaw is also the chef and as well as using tip-top local produce for his exceptional modern cooking, there are helpful notes on some of the more unusual menu terms. The immaculately kept spacious oak-beamed bar has a comfortably civilised atmosphere, open fires, simple wooden tables and chairs and country paintings and maybe some guns on the pale walls. Adnams Bitter, Oakham JHB and Potton Village Bike on handpump, 16 wines by the glass (plus eight sweet wines and two champagnes), and fine port and sherry; very good service. There are seats out in front of the building.

⑪ **Served by friendly and helpful young staff, the delicious food might include sandwiches, soup, razor clams with chilli, garlic, mint and sherry, halloumi cheese with** nashi pear, red onion and parsley salad, leek and goats cheese tart, roast leg of mutton with potato pancake, guinea fowl with pancetta and borlotti bean broth and a dumpling, soy and palm sugar glazed ham hock with a mango, ginger, chilli and coriander salad, and roast monkfish with smoked sausage and wild mushrooms; two- and three-course menus, **too.** *Starters/Snacks: £4.95 to £6.95. Main Courses: £9.75 to £17.95. Puddings: £4.95 to £5.95*

Free house ~ Licensee Taffeta Scrimshaw ~ Real ale ~ Bar food (12-2, 6.30-9.30(8.30 Sun)) ~ Restaurant ~ (01832) 710241 ~ Children welcome ~ Dogs allowed in bar ~ Open 11.30-11(10.30 Sun); closed Sun evenings Jan-Mar

Recommended by Michael Sargent, J F M and M West, Mrs Roxanne Chamberlain, Ryta Lyndley, M and GR, Dave Braisted, Paul and Margaret Baker, Dr and Mrs M E Wilson, Bill and Marian de Bass

KIMBOLTON TL0967   MAP 5

New Sun ♀
High Street; PE28 0HA

Several interesting bars and rooms, tapas menu plus other good food, and pleasant back garden

A new conservatory has been added to this nice old pub with doors opening on to the terrace where there's now smart new furniture under giant umbrellas. Inside, the low-beamed front lounge is perhaps the cosiest room, with a couple of comfortable armchairs and a sofa beside the fireplace, standing timbers and exposed brickwork, and books, pottery and brasses. This leads into a narrower locals' bar, with Wells & Youngs Bombardier and Eagle, and a guest such as Greene King Old Speckled Hen on handpump, and about a dozen wines by the glass; piped music and games machine. The dining room opens off here. This is a lovely village main street. Do note that some of the nearby parking spaces have a 30-minute limit.

🍴 **As well as lunchtime sandwiches and filled baked potatoes, the well liked food includes popular hot and cold tapas, king prawns in hot garlic and ginger oil, bubble and squeak, bacon, poached egg and hollandaise, roast butternut squash and sage risotto with grilled goats cheese, home-made steak and kidney pudding, braised lamb shank, whole grilled dover sole, daily specials, and puddings such as Malteser cheesecake or sticky toffee pudding with butterscotch sauce.** *Starters/Snacks: £3.25 to £6.95. Main Courses: £8.95 to £18.25. Puddings: £3.75 to £5.75*

Charles Wells ~ Lease Stephen and Elaine Rogers ~ Real ale ~ Bar food (12-2.15(2.30 Sun), 7-9.30; not Sun or Mon evenings) ~ Restaurant ~ (01480) 860052 ~ Children allowed in front bar and eating areas ~ Dogs allowed in bar ~ Open 11.30-2.30, 6-11; 12-10.30 Sun

Recommended by John Picken, Mrs Margo Finlay, Jörg Kasprowski, Michael Dandy

MADINGLEY TL3960   MAP 5

Three Horseshoes 🍴 ♀
Off A1303 W of Cambridge; High Street; CB3 8AB

Sophisticated (if not cheap) italian cooking in civilised dining pub – best to book in advance – outstanding wine list, and efficient service

As this civilised thatched dining pub is so popular for its interesting italian cooking, you must book to be sure of a table. The pleasantly relaxed little airy bar (which can be a bit of a crush at busy times) has an open fire, simple wooden tables and chairs on bare floorboards, stools at the bar and pictures on green walls; there's also a pretty conservatory restaurant. Adnams Southwold and a guest such as City of Cambridge Hobsons Choice on handpump and an outstanding wine list with over 16 by the glass, plus sweet wines and ports.

🍴 **The excellent, carefully prepared food might include risotto with brown shrimps, peas, chives, ricotta, prosecco and lemon, hand-rolled pasta stuffed with gorgonzola and mascarpone with sage butter and parmesan, roast chicken breast wrapped in pancetta with grilled courgettes, new potatoes, mint and salsa verde, roast monkfish with italian** sprue and white asparagus, thyme salmoriglio and fagioli beans cooked with garlic and olive oil and slow-cooked pork shin with saffron risotto, gremolata and baby carrots; two-, three- and five-course set meals also available. *Starters/Snacks: £4.50 to £7.95. Main Courses: £7.50 to £10.50. Puddings: £3.50 to £5.50*

Huntsbridge ~ Licensee Richard Stokes ~ Real ale ~ Bar food (12-2(2.30 Sun), 6.30-9.30(8.30 Sun)) ~ Restaurant ~ (01954) 210221 ~ Children welcome ~ Open 11.30-3, 6-11.30; 12-3.30, 6-10.30 Sun; closed 1 and 2 Jan

Recommended by Michael Dandy, Bob Sadler, Sally Anne and Peter Goodale, B and M Kendall, Michael Butler, Adele Summers, Alan Black, John and Elisabeth Cox, Eamonn and Natasha Skyrme, John and Joan Calvert

NEWTON
TL4349 MAP 5

Queens Head ★ ◼ £

2½ miles from M11 junction 11; A10 towards Royston, then left on to B1368; CB2 5PG

Lovely traditional and cosy pub in the same family for many years, simple very popular food and fair choice of drinks

'The jewel in the Cambridgeshire crown' is how one reader describes this exceptional old pub. It's been run by the same genuinely welcoming family for three generations and thankfully, has changed little. Comfortably worn and low key, but always spotlessly clean, the peaceful main bar has a low ceiling and crooked beams, bare wooden benches and seats built into the cream walls, paintings, and bow windows. A curved high-backed settle stands on yellow tiles, a loudly ticking clock marks the unchanging time, and a lovely big log fire crackles warmly. The little carpeted saloon is similar but even cosier. Adnams Bitter and Broadside and a seasonal guest tapped from the cask and farm cider. Darts, shove-ha'penny, table skittles, dominoes, cribbage and nine men's morris. There are seats in front of the pub, with its vine trellis. This is a popular place so you will need to get here early for a seat during peak times, and there may be a queue of people waiting for the doors to open on a Sunday.

🍴 A limited range of basic but well liked food, which comes in hearty and very fairly priced helpings: toast and beef dripping, lunchtime sandwiches (including things like banana with sugar and lemon or herb and garlic), a mug of their famous home-made soup and filled Aga-baked potatoes; evening and Sunday lunchtime plates of excellent cold meat, smoked salmon, cheeses and pâté. *Starters/Snacks: £3.00 to £3.50. Main Courses: £2.40 to £5.50*

Free house ~ Licensees David and Robert Short ~ Real ale ~ Bar food (12-2.15, 7-9.30) ~ No credit cards ~ (01223) 870436 ~ Very well behaved children welcome in games room ~ Dogs welcome ~ Open 11.30-2.30, 6-11; 12-2.30, 7-10.30 Sun; closed 25 and 26 Dec

Recommended by Mr and Mrs W Mills, Michael Butler, Helen McLagan, Mr and Mrs T B Staples, Steve Williamson, Keith and Janet Morris, Louise Gibbons, Mrs Margo Finlay, Jörg Kasprowski, R T and J C Moggridge, Conor McGaughey

PETERBOROUGH
TL1899 MAP 5

Brewery Tap ◼ £

Opposite Queensgate car park; PE1 2AA

Fantastic range of real ales including its own brews and popular thai food in huge conversion of old labour exchange

The first thing that will probably grab your attention in this striking modern conversion of an old labour exchange is the vast two-storey high glass wall that divides the bar and brewery, giving fascinating views of the massive copper-banded stainless brewing vessels. From here they produce their own Oakham beers (Bishops Farewell, JHB, and White Dwarf) but also keep nine guests from thoughtfully chosen countrywide brewers as well; also, a good number of bottled belgian beers and quite a few wines by the glass. There's an easy going relaxed feel to the open-plan contemporary interior, with an expanse of light wood and stone floors for drinkers, blue-painted iron pillars holding up a steel-corded mezzanine level, and hugely enlarged newspaper cuttings on light orange or burnt red walls. It's stylishly lit by a giant suspended steel ring with bulbs running around the rim, and steel-meshed wall lights. A band of chequered floor tiles traces the path of the long sculpted light wood bar counter, which is boldly backed by an impressive display of bottles in a ceiling-high wall of wooden cubes. A sofa seating area downstairs provides a comfortable corner for a surprisingly mixed bunch of customers from young to old; there's a big screen TV for sporting events, piped music and games machines and DJs or live bands at the weekends. It gets very busy in the evening. The pub is owned by the same people as Charters (see below).

🍴 The thai food is very good and extremely popular and runs from snacks such as chicken satay or tempura vegetables to soups like aromatic crispy duck noodle or tom yum and to main courses such as curries, noodle and rice dishes, salads and stir fries. *Starters/Snacks: £2.99 to £3.99. Main Courses: £3.99 to £6.99*

Own brew ~ Licensees Stuart Wright, Jessica Loock, Paul Hook ~ Real ale ~ Bar food (12-2.30, 6-9.30; 12-10.30 Fri, Sat) ~ Restaurant ~ (01733) 358500 ~ Children welcome during food service times ~ Dogs allowed in bar ~ DJs or live bands weekends ~ Open 12-11; 12-10.30 Sun; closed 25 and 26 Dec, 1 Jan

Recommended by Ben and Helen Ingram, Andy and Jill Kassube, Rona Murdoch, the Didler, Mike and Sue Loseby, P Dawn, Joe Green

Charters 🍺 £

Town Bridge, S side; PE1 1FP

Remarkable conversion of dutch grain barge with impressive real ales and good value oriental-style food

Once a barge working on the rivers and canals of Holland, Belgium and Germany and now moored on the River Nene, this remarkable conversion houses a sizeable timbered bar on the lower deck and an oriental restaurant on the upper deck. Old wooden tables and pews provide plenty of seating and there's an impressive range of real ales including three Oakham beers and around nine quickly changing guests from an interesting variety of brewers. They also keep around 30 foreign bottled beers, and hold regular beer festivals; piped music, games machines and darts. Adjacent to the mooring is what is thought to be the biggest pub garden in the city, making this a great place for a summer visit.

🍴 Good value oriental-style food includes filled pitta bread, various starters like tempura prawns, spring rolls or dim sum, vegetarian choices, special fried rice, noodle and wok dishes, curries, and seafood. *Starters/Snacks: £3.25 to £4.65. Main Courses: £4.65 to £9.65*

Free house ~ Licensees Stuart Wright, Paul Hook ~ Real ale ~ Bar food (12-2.30, 6-10) ~ Restaurant ~ (01733) 315700 ~ Children welcome ~ Dogs allowed in bar ~ Live bands Fri and Sat ~ Open 12-11(1 Fri, Sat)

Recommended by Joe Green, P Dawn, the Didler, Ben and Helen Ingram, Rona Murdoch, Andy and Jill Kassube, Barry Collett

REACH   TL5666   MAP 5

Dyke's End 🍺

From B1102 E of A14/A1103 junction, follow signpost to Swaffham Prior and Upware – keep on through Swaffham Prior (Reach signposted from there); Fair Green; CB5 0JD

Peaceful, candle-lit rooms in former farmhouse, enjoyable food, and decent drinks

This looks every inch the classic village pub with its well-worn inn sign, big front yew tree and charming village-green setting. Inside, a high-backed winged settle screens off the door, and the simply decorated ochre-walled bar has stripped heavy pine tables and pale kitchen chairs on dark boards with one or two rugs, a few rather smarter dining tables on parquet flooring in a panelled section on the left, and on the right a step down to a red-carpeted bit with the small red-walled servery, and sensibly placed darts at the back. All the tables have lit candles in earthenware bottles, and there may be a big bowl of lilies to brighten up the serving counter. As well as their own-brewed Buntingford Flying Coach and Devils Dyke No 7, they might keep Adnams Bitter or Woodfordes Wherry on handpump alongside a good wine, and Old Rosie cider. There are picnic-sets under big green canvas parasols out in front on the grass and Banger, the dachshund, may have pride of place on a rug spread on the lawn.

🍴 **Tasty bar food includes sandwiches and interestingly filled baked potatoes, soup, chickpea and goats cheese bruschetta, local sausages with onion gravy, home-cooked ham and egg, pasta with wild mushrooms and parmesan, rack of lamb with parsley crust, smoked haddock with spinach and poached egg, a slow braise of the day, fillet steak with pink peppercorn sauce, puddings like rich chocolate pot or zesty lemon posset, and Sunday lunch.** *Starters/Snacks: £4.95 to £6.95. Main Courses: £6.95 to £14.95. Puddings: £3.95*

Free house ~ Licensee Simon Owers ~ Real ale ~ Bar food (not Sun evening or all day Mon) ~ Restaurant ~ (01638) 743816 ~ Children in restaurant ~ Dogs allowed in bar ~ Occasional impromptu folk jam Sun evenings ~ Open 12-3, 6-11; 12-3, 7-10.30 Sun; closed Mon lunchtime

Recommended by John and Bettye Reynolds, Sally Anne and Peter Goodale, M and GR, Chris Bell, Marion and Bill Cross, R T and J C Moggridge, Paul Humphreys, Mrs P J Pearce

ST NEOTS
TL1859   MAP 5

Chequers
St Marys Street, Eynesbury (B1043 S of centre); PE19 2TA

Charming old pub with a fair choice of food and drink

A new licensee has taken over this charming 16th-c pub. The small carpeted bar has lots of traditional character with its dark heavy beams, an appealing mix of seats including an unusually shaped rocking chair, and a log fire in a big inglenook fireplace. Archers IPA and Nethergate Lounge Lizard on handpump and several wines by the glass. The busy communicating back restaurant area has attractively set tables, fresh flowers throughout, and rugs on its brick floor; piped music. There are tables out in the sheltered garden behind and more on a terrace.

🍴 **Good food now includes sandwiches, soup, chicken liver pâté, aubergine and cheese bake, sausages of the day, beer-battered haddock, steak and mushroom pie, rack of lamb with rosemary jus, daily specials, and puddings.** *Starters/Snacks: £3.95 to £6.95. Main Courses: £6.75 to £12.95*

Free house ~ Licensee Stephen Lamb ~ Real ale ~ Bar food (not Sun evening) ~ Restaurant ~ (01480) 472116 ~ Children in restaurant ~ Open 12-2.30, 7-11; 12-4 Sun; closed Sun evenings

Recommended by Mrs Jane Kingsbury, Martin and Alison Stainsby, Michael Dandy, R T and J C Moggridge

STILTON
TL1689   MAP 5

Bell ♀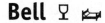
High Street; village signposted from A1 S of Peterborough; PE7 3RA

Fine coaching inn with several civilised rooms including a residents' bar, well liked food, and very pretty courtyard

A lovely example of a 17th-c coaching inn on the Great North Road between London and York, this elegant and civilised hotel has two neatly kept bars with a relaxed and informal atmosphere, Fullers London Pride, Greene King IPA and Abbot, and Oakham JHB on handpump or tapped from the cask and a dozen wines by the glass. These rooms have bow windows, sturdy upright wooden seats on flagstone floors as well as plush button-back built-in banquettes, and a good big log fire in one handsome stone fireplace; one bar has a large cheese press. The partly stripped walls have big prints of sailing and winter coaching scenes, and there's a giant pair of blacksmith's bellows hanging in the middle of the front bar. Also, a bistro, restaurant and residents' bar. Through the fine coach arch is a very pretty sheltered courtyard with tables, and a well which supposedly dates back to Roman times.

🕮 Bar food might include soup, chicken liver parfait, roast pepper and gorgonzola risotto, boiled smoked gammon with poached egg and parsley butter sauce, pasta with wild mushrooms, roasted chestnuts and herbs in garlic, parmesan and white wine sauce, coq au vin with wild mushroom dumplings, bass fillet on thyme-roasted pumpkin and sweet potato with mild chilli sauce, and puddings such as triple chocolate mousse terrine with pistachio ice-cream and crème brûlée with passion fruit jellies. *Starters/Snacks: £3.95 to £6.95. Main Courses: £10.50 to £15.95. Puddings: £4.75*

Free house ~ Licensee Liam McGivern ~ Real ale ~ Bar food (12-2, 6.30-9.30; 12-2.30, 7-9 Sun) ~ Restaurant ~ (01733) 241066 ~ Children in eating area of bar only ~ Open 12-2.30(3 Sat), 6-11(midnight Fri and Sat); 12-3, 7-11 Sun ~ Bedrooms: £72.50B/£99.50B

Recommended by Jerry Brown, Phil and Jane Hodson, Matt Anderson, David Glynne-Jones, John Roots, Ray and Winifred Halliday, Michael Dandy, Martin and Karen Wake, John Saville

SUTTON GAULT   TL4279   MAP 5

Anchor 🍴 ♀

Village signed off B1381 in Sutton; CB6 2BD

Tucked away inn with charming candlelit rooms, good modern food, and thoughtful wine list

We do hope this appealing inn is not becoming too much of a restaurant nowadays. The emphasis is on the modern cooking but they have City of Cambridge Hobsons Choice and Boathouse Bitter tapped from the cask and a dozen wines by the glass (including champagne). Four heavily timbered rooms are stylishly simple with two log fires, antique settles and well spaced candlelit scrubbed pine tables on gently undulating old floors, and good lithographs and big prints on the walls. There are nice walks along the high embankment by the river and the bird-watching is said to be good. Seats outside; more reports please.

🕮 As well as a two-course weekly set menu, the well liked food might include soup, tian of crayfish and guacamole with citrus mayonnaise, smoked duck breast with an orange reduction, pasta with fresh pesto, leeks, and sunblush tomatoes, chicken supreme on forestière potatoes and a madeira cream sauce, pork fillet with ginger cake stuffing wrapped in parma ham with sage and onion sauce, and puddings like lemon grass panna cotta with sweet chilli and coconut sorbet or chocolate tart. *Starters/Snacks: £4.00 to £7.00. Main Courses: £8.50 to £19.50. Puddings: £4.00 to £6.50*

Free house ~ Licensees Carlene Bunten and Adam Pickup ~ Real ale ~ Bar food (12-2, 7-9; 6.30-9.30 Sat) ~ Restaurant ~ (01353) 778537 ~ Children welcome ~ Open 12-2.30, 7(6.30 Sat)-11(11.30 Sat); 12.30-3, 7-10.30 Sun ~ Bedrooms: £59.50S/£75(£79.50S)(£115B)

Recommended by John Wooll, B N F and M Parkin, Sally Anne and Peter Goodale, Stephen Woad, Anthony Longden, M and GR, Derek Thomas, Ryta Lyndley, Jeff and Wendy Williams, Mrs Carolyn Dixon, A J Bowen

THRIPLOW   TL4346   MAP 5

Green Man

3 miles from M11 junction 10; A505 towards Royston, then first right; Lower Street; SG8 7RJ

Comfortable and cheery with homely food and changing ales

Handy for Duxford, this cheery Victorian pub is comfortably laid out with modern tables and attractive high-backed dining chairs and pews, and there are some small pictures on deeply coloured walls; two arches lead through to a restaurant on the left. Four regularly changing real ales are likely to be from brewers such as Archers, Dark Star and Nethergate; darts. The exterior is painted a striking dark blue, with window boxes and potted plants looking particularly nice against this strong background. There are tables and an outdoor heater outside.

🕮 Hearty helpings of homely bar food include lunchtime baguettes, home-made burger and sausage and mash, evening chicken, duck, salmon or stuffed pepper with a choice of sauces, and daily specials like pork loin with cider gravy or roast lamb shoulder with minted gravy. *Starters/Snacks: £4.50 to £7.00. Main Courses: £7.00 to £14.50. Puddings: £4.50 to £6.00*

Free house ~ Licensen Ian Parr ~ Real ale ~ Bar food (Sun evening or Mon) ~ Restaurant ~ (01763) 208855 ~ Children welcome away from the bar ~ Open 12-3, 6-11; closed Sun evening, all day Mon, Easter weekend and Christmas week

Recommended by Christine and Phil Young, Stan Edwards, Mark Farrington, Louise Gibbons, KC, Gerry and Rosemary Dobson

LUCKY DIP

Besides the fully inspected pubs, you might like to try these Lucky Dips recommended to us and described by readers (if you do, please send us reports: www.goodguides.co.uk).

ABINGTON PIGOTTS [TL3044]
Pig & Abbot SG8 0SD: Thriving L-shaped bar with food from good hot beef baguettes to ample Sun lunches, attentive staff, Adnams, Fullers London Pride and two guest beers, open woodburner in inglenook; pretty village with good walks, open all day wknds *(David and Pam Wilcox)*

BOURN [TL3256]
Willow Tree CB3 7SQ [High St]: Recently attractively refurbished and relaxed dining pub locally popular for good unpretentious food with enterprising veg, friendly efficient staff, good wines by the glass and soft drinks choice, Greene King IPA and Shepherd Neame Spitfire, log fire, medley of furnishings from plain pine tables and chairs to leather sofas on tiled floors; may be piped jazz; children welcome, garden with floodlit willow, tables on decking and play area *(Richard Atherton)*

BOXWORTH [TL3464]
Golden Ball CB3 8LY [High St]: Attractive 16th-c thatched pub/restaurant, open-plan contemporary bar with pine tables on tiles, sizeable restaurant in original core, friendly well trained young staff, enjoyable generous food inc baguettes, baked potatoes and interesting light dishes, Adnams and Greene King IPA, good range of wines; big well kept garden and heated terrace, pastures behind (good walks), 11 good bedrooms in new block *(J Jennings, Michael Dandy)*

BRANDON CREEK [TL6091]
☆ *Ship* PE38 0PP [A10 Ely—Downham Market]: Lovely spot on Norfolk border at confluence of Great and Little Ouse, plenty of tables out by the moorings; welcoming helpful staff, good choice of enjoyable pub food, real ales such as Adnams, Shepherd Neame Spitfire and St Austell, spacious tastefully modernised bar with massive stone masonry in sunken former forge area, big log fire one end, woodburner the other, interesting old photographs and prints, evening restaurant; bedrooms *(George Atkinson, LYM, R C Vincent)*

BROUGHTON [TL2877]
☆ *Crown* PE28 3AY [off A141 opp RAF Wyton; Bridge Rd]: Attractively tucked away opp church (pub owned by village consortium),

fresh and airy décor, sturdy furnishings inc nicely set dining end, good enterprising food, good service, real ales such as Elgoods Black Dog; disabled access and facilities; tables out on big stretch of grass behind, cl Mon/Tues, open all day wknds *(J Stickland, BB)*

BUCKDEN [TL1967]
☆ *George* PE19 5XA [Old Gt North Rd]: Stylish and elegant modern revamp of handsome former coaching inn with medieval origins (wonderful fan beamwork in bar, which is still well used by regulars), friendly helpful staff, brasserie food all day inc good lunchtime baguettes, wide range of good wines (and choice of champagnes) by the glass, Adnams and a guest ale, coffee by the pot, log fire; large integral boutique, tables out on sheltered pretty terrace, nice bedrooms – they bring you morning tea *(Mr and Mrs Staples, Mike and Mary Carter, Michael Dandy, BB, Michael Sargent, Paul Humphreys)*

☆ *Lion* PE19 5XA [High St]: Partly 15th-c coaching inn, black beams and big inglenook log fire in airy and civilised bow-windowed entrance bar with plush bucket seats, wing armchairs and settees, decent bar food inc good value lunchtime sandwiches, good choice of wines, Greene King IPA and a guest such as Skinners, friendly staff, no music or machines, panelled back dining room beyond latticed window partition; children welcome, bedrooms *(David and Ruth Shillitoe, Michael Dandy, BB)*

CAMBRIDGE [TL4458]
Bath CB2 3QN [Bene't St]: Unpretentious pub with Ringwood ale, sensibly priced pubby food, good atmosphere for watching sports TV; shame the old beams have been covered, near the bar *(Giles and Annie Francis)*

☆ *Castle* CB3 0AJ [Castle St]: Large airy bare-boards pub, several simple and pleasantly decorated rooms, full Adnams ale range and lots of guest beers, wide range of good value quick pubby food from sandwiches up inc a popular bargain burger, friendly staff, peaceful upstairs (downstairs can be noisy, with piped pop music – live jazz Sun night); picnic-sets in good walled back courtyard

(Dr David Cockburn, the Didler, Michael Dandy)

Clarendon Arms CB1 1JX [Clarendon St]: Partly flagstoned, with interesting wall hangings and other collectables, friendly attentive service, bustling local atmosphere, Greene King and unusual guest beers, wide choice of reasonably priced food (unusual timed pricing, eg steak £6 at six o'clock, £8 at eight), carpeted dining area, books and daily papers, darts, cribbage; piped music may obtrude; simple good value bedrooms, open all day *(Dr David Cockburn, P and D Carpenter, Tony and Jill Radnor)*

Flying Pig CB2 1LQ [Hills Rd]: Individual small local with pig emblems everywhere, young friendly staff, well kept Adnams, Fullers London Pride and Greene King Old Speckled Hen, daily papers, back games room with pool; eclectic piped music; seats outside front and back *(Colin McKerrow, Dr David Cockburn)*

☆ **Kingston Arms** CB1 2NU [Kingston St]: Unpretentious U-shaped pub, tidy and attractive, with fine choice of real ales inc four or five changing guest beers, enjoyable food freshly made from good ingredients (many tables booked for the popular light lunches), thriving atmosphere, good choice of wines by the glass, friendly service, simple stools and plain tables, no music or children inside; wkdy lunchtime free internet access (two terminals and wireless access); small pretty back terrace, torch-lit and heated, open all day Fri-Sun *(James Crouchman, Dr David Cockburn, John Wooll, Jerry Brown)*

Mitre CB2 1UF [Bridge St, opp St Johns Coll]: Welcoming homely atmosphere with soft lighting and old-fashioned tavern décor, tasty honest food inc good bargain puddings, friendly service, well priced wines by the glass, good range of real ales, farm cider, log-effect fire *(Maggie Atherton)*

☆ **Old Spring** CB4 1HB [Ferry Path; car park on Chesterton Rd]: Extended Victorian pub, roomy and airy, with smartly old-fashioned scrubbed-wood décor, bare boards, gas lighting, lots of old pictures, enjoyable food inc good vegetarian options and Sun roasts, quick pleasant service, well kept Greene King IPA and Abbot, good coffee and choice of wines by the glass, two log fires, long back conservatory; no children; large heated well planted terrace, summer barbecues *(Mrs Jane Kingsbury, LYM, Keith and Janet Morris, John Wooll)*

CASTOR [TL1298]

Prince of Wales Feathers PE5 7AL [off A47]: Newish landlord, landlady doing limited range of enjoyable good value lunchtime food (not Mon), well kept Adnams *(Ian Stafford)*

CHATTERIS [TL3986]

Cross Keys PE16 6BA [Market Hill]: Comfortable and warmly relaxing 16th-c coaching inn opp church in fenland market town, good friendly service, good

attractively priced food in bar and candlelit restaurant from soup and sandwiches to good Sun lunches, long bar with fireside armchairs, Greene King beers, inexpensive wine, tea and coffee; pleasant back courtyard, good bedrooms *(Robert Turnham, R T and J C Moggridge)*

CLAYHITHE [TL5064]

Bridge Hotel CB5 9HZ [Clayhithe Rd]: Well run Chef & Brewer dining pub with small bar area, beams and timbers, attentive service; picturesque spot by River Cam with pretty waterside garden, comfortable bedroom extension *(LYM, Trevor Swindells, Simon Watkins)*

CONINGTON [TL3266]

☆ **White Swan** CB3 8LN [signed off A14 (was A604) Cambridge—Huntingdon; Elsworth Rd]: Attractive and quietly placed Victorian country local with friendly helpful staff, fairly priced straightforward food from baps, generous baguettes and baked potatoes up, well kept Greene King ales tapped from the cask, cheerful simple bar, neat eating areas, games inc bar billiards and darts on left; good big front garden with terrace, play area and play house, open all day *(Michael Dandy, Keith and Janet Morris, David Campbell, Vicki McLean)*

COTON [TL4158]

Plough CB3 7PL [just off M11 junction 13; High St]: Well reworked, with plenty of space, interesting tasty food from tapas and other light dishes to full meals (all day wknds), helpful staff, Fullers London Pride, Greene King IPA and a guest beer, clean-cut contemporary décor with pale wood, pastel colours, sofas and log fires; sizeable garden, open all day *(Colin and Sally French, LYM)*

CROYDON [TL3149]

☆ **Queen Adelaide** SG8 0DN [off A1198 or B1042; High St]: Wide range of enjoyable food inc upmarket dishes, friendly prompt service, mainstream real ales such as Greene King IPA, impressive array of spirits, big beamed main area with standing timbers dividing off part with settees, banquettes and stools; garden, play area *(R T and J C Moggridge, P and D Carpenter)*

EATON SOCON [TL1658]

Crown PE19 8EN [Gt North Rd (B4128, nr A1/A428 interchange)]: Chef & Brewer with linked low-beamed areas, moderately priced food from sandwiches and baked potatoes up, Courage Directors, Everards Tiger and Theakstons, good coffee, two coal-effect gas fires; games machine, piped music; garden, comfortable bedroom block *(Michael Dandy)*

☆ **White Horse** PE19 8EL [Gt North Rd (B4128)]: Rambling, comfortable and interestingly furnished low-beamed rooms dating from 13th c, nice high-backed traditional settles around big inglenook log fire in end room, relaxing atmosphere, enjoyable bargain food from sandwiches and baked potatoes up, good value Sun lunch, Adnams, Flowers IPA and Fullers London Pride, decent wines, quick friendly service, daily papers, pub games; play area in back garden, children in eating areas, refurbished bedrooms, open all day Fri-Sun *(Conor McGaughey, Michael Dandy, Marion and Bill Cross, LYM)*

ELSWORTH [TL3163]

Poacher CB3 8JS [Brockley Rd]: Unpretentious 17th-c thatched and beamed pub with polished pine and neat pews and settles on bare boards, lots of carving inc nicely done birds on bar front, nice pictures, Adnams Broadside, Greene King IPA and Old Speckled Hen and Shepherd Neame Spitfire, cheerful staff, popular traditional food from baguettes and baked potatoes up; piped music; plenty of tables in pretty garden with play area and barbecues, good walks *(Keith and Janet Morris, Michael Sargent, BB)*

ELTISLEY [TL2759]

Leeds Arms PE19 6TG [signed off A428; The Green]: Traditional beamed bar overlooking peaceful village green, three or four real ales, Stowford Press cider, huge log fire, daily papers, darts, decent bar and restaurant food; piped music; children in eating area, attractive garden with play area, simple comfortable bedrooms in separate block *(Michael Dandy, D and M T Ayres-Regan, LYM)*

ELY [TL5479]

☆ *Cutter* CB7 4BN [Annesdale, off Station Rd just towards centre from A142 roundabout; or walk S along Riverside Walk from Maltings car park]: Current management doing well in beautifully placed riverside pub with enjoyable reasonably priced generous food inc good value Sun roasts in carpeted dining bar and smart newish restaurant, cheerful staff, Greene King Abbot, Shepherd Neame Spitfire and Woodfordes Wherry, decent wines by the glass, fairly lively bare-boards front bar; plenty of tables outside *(Dr Andy Wilkinson, Revd John Hibberd, LYM, John Wooll, Ryta Lyndley)*

Minster Tavern CB7 4EL [Minster Pl]: Interestingly worn in Victorian/Edwardian décor in older beamed building, popular bargain Sun roasts served quickly as well as usual wkdy lunchtime food, Greene King ales *(John Wooll)*

Prince Albert CB7 4JF [Silver St]: Spotless traditional two-bar local with half a dozen well kept mainly Greene King ales inc their XX Mild, bargain straightforward lunchtime food (not Sun) from sandwiches up, friendly long-serving landlord and staff, books for sale; trim and attractive garden with two aviaries, cl Tues lunchtime *(Pete Baker, Victor Perry, Dr Andy Wilkinson)*

FENSTANTON [TL3168]

King William IV PE28 9JF [off A14 nr St Ives; High St]: Hospitable low-beamed pub with wide choice of above-average food from sandwiches up, Greene King ales, good range of wines, cosy bar with adjoining restaurant; pretty outside *(P and D Carpenter, Robert W Buckle)*

GOREFIELD [TF4111]

Woodmans Cottage PE13 4NB [Main St; off B1169 W of Wisbech]: Roomy bar with beams and open fires, stripped brick side dining area, opened through to pitched-ceiling restaurant, good value generous pubby food from low-priced baguettes to vast array of home-made puddings, Greene King IPA and Old Speckled Hen from central servery; piped music; children in eating areas, tables on front verandah and sheltered back terrace, play area *(LYM, Michael and Jenny Back)*

GRANTCHESTER [TL4355]

Blue Ball CB3 9NQ [Broadway]: Small quiet and friendly bare-boards village local, said to be the oldest in the area and given plenty of character by its landlord, good log fire, particularly well kept Adnams and a guest such as Timothy Taylors Landlord, cards and traditional games inc shut the box and ring the bull, lots of books; dogs welcome, tables on small terrace with lovely views to Grantchester meadows a short stroll away, nice village *(Oliver J Brown, Pete Baker, Ian Frowe, Conor McGaughey)*

☆ *Green Man* CB3 9NF [High St]: Friendly helpful current management doing enjoyable good value food in heavily beamed pub dating from 16th c, log fire and individual furnishings, good choice of ales such as Adnams and Greene King, separate dining room; disabled facilities, tables out behind *(Andrei, LYM, DC)*

Rupert Brooke CB3 9NQ [Broadway; junction Coton rd with Cambridge—Trumpington rd]: Open-plan pub with enjoyable if not cheap food from good lunchtime sandwiches and light dishes up, Greene King Old Speckled Hen and Charles Wells Bombardier, good choice of wines by the glass, generally efficient friendly young staff, central log fire in small comfortable bar, simple extended family dining area; young staff, piped music *(MJB, Tony and Margaret Cross)*

GRAVELEY [TL2463]

Three Horseshoes PE19 6PL [High St]: Pleasantly furnished long narrow bar with two fish tanks, good choice of usual food from baguettes to steaks, Adnams, Fullers London Pride and Theakstons XB, low-beamed restaurant; piped music; a few tables outside *(Michael Dandy)*

GREAT STAUGHTON [TL]

☆ *Tavern on the Green* PE19 5DG [The Green; B645/B661]: Comfortably up-to-date and uncluttered open-plan layout, now calling itself Snooty Fox Tavern, in same small group as Millstone, Barnack, and Snooty Fox, Lowick (Northants) – see main entries; good and not over-generous fresh food from sandwiches, ploughman's and appealing light dishes up, good range of wines by the glass, Greene King ales; may be unobtrusive piped music; children welcome, some picnic-sets outside *(Michael Dandy, Fr Robert Marsh, BB)*

GUYHIRN [TF3903]

☆ *Oliver Twist* PE13 4EA [follow signs from

A47/A141 junction S of Wisbech]: Comfortable open-plan lounge with buoyant local atmosphere, good cheap generous home-made food from crusty baguettes to steaks, cheerful attentive service, interesting changing real ales, big open fires, neat sturdy furnishings, restaurant; may be piped music; six bedrooms *(Barry Collett, BB, Phil and Jane Hodson, R T and J C Moggridge)*

HADDENHAM [TL4675]
Three Kings CB6 3XD [Station Rd]: Popular village pub, well run and friendly, with nice staff, well kept Greene King IPA and Old Speckled Hen, enjoyable varied home-made food with fresh veg *(K Christensen, Simon Watkins)*

HARDWICK [TL3758]
Blue Lion CB3 7QU [signed off A428 (was A45) W of Cambridge; Main St]: Friendly and attractive old local with lots of beams, inglenook log fire and woodburner, good food from lunchtime sandwiches and baguettes to wide choice of home-made dishes in bar, extended air-conditioned dining area with pleasant conservatory (evening booking recommended), children's helpings, cheerful helpful staff, Greene King IPA and Abbot tapped from the cask, old farm tools, games and TV on lower level; may be piped music; pretty roadside front garden, play area and pets corner, handy for Wimpole Way walkers *(Michael Dandy, Mr and Mrs John Taylor, BB)*

HARLTON [TL3852]
Hare & Hounds CB23 1ES [High St]: Popular and welcoming village pub, sensibly priced food, three well kept beers; tables out on quiet street *(Keith and Janet Morris)*

HEMINGFORD ABBOTS [TL2870]
Axe & Compass PE28 9AH [High St]: Quietly welcoming 15th-c two-bar thatched pub with flagstones and inglenook seats, contemporary fittings in extension dining areas, friendly staff, changing ales such as Adnams, Greene King IPA and Oakham JHB, good choice of wines by the glass, good value fresh pubby lunchtime food from baguettes and good ploughman's up, wider evening menu, tea and a cake too, pool and bar billiards; piped music, TV, quiz or live music nights; garden tables, quiet and pretty village, open all day *(Ian Blake, Michael Dandy, Paul Humphreys)*

HILDERSHAM [TL5448]
☆ ***Pear Tree*** CB1 6BU [off A1307 N of Linton]: Spotless and friendly Victorian pub in picturesque thatched village, odd crazy-paved floor and plenty of curios, good value food from ploughman's to straightforward home cooking, daily papers, board games; children welcome, tables and aviary in garden behind, cl Mon lunchtime *(Stephen Woad, BB, Jane Elliott)*

HISTON [TL4363]
Red Lion CB4 9JD [High St]: Popular and friendly, with half a dozen well kept

changing ales (spring and early autumn beer festivals), lots of bottled belgian beers, good value generous pub lunches, proper character landlord, lots of pubby memorabilia, comfortably well used lounge, games and sports TV in plain and unyobby public bar; big garden, open all day Sat *(Jerry Brown)*

HOLYWELL [TL3370]
Old Ferry Boat PE27 4TG [signed off A1123]: Partly thatched chain pub in lovely setting, much refurbished yet interesting, with low beams, open fires and side areas, dozens of carpenter's tools, window seats overlooking Great Ouse, Greene King ales, decent wines by the glass, good coffee, reasonably priced food (all day in summer – service well organised to cope with crowds); quiet piped music, games; children welcome, plenty of tables and cocktail parasols on front terrace and riverside lawn, moorings, bedrooms, open all day wknds *(Robert Turnham, Ian Blake, Michael Dandy, LYM)*

HORSEHEATH [TL6147]
Old Red Lion CB1 6QF [Linton Rd]: Well refurbished and neatly kept, with hard-working staff under good newish licensees, sensibly priced food, Greene King ales; comfortable bedroom cabins *(Mr and Mrs T B Staples)*

LITTLE WILBRAHAM [TL5458]
☆ ***Hole in the Wall*** CB1 5JY [off A14 at Stow cum Quy turn, turning right off A1303 Newmarket rd; High St]: Appealing 15th-c pub with impressive if not cheap food, charming service, good choice of wines by the glass, real ales such as Courage Best and Elgoods Golden Newt, plenty of atmosphere, heavy beams, timbering and stripped brickwork, log fire in big fireplace, restaurant; sturdy seats and tables in pretty garden, interesting fenland walks nearby, cl Mon *(P and D Carpenter)*

LONGSTOWE [TL3154]
☆ ***Red House*** CB3 7UT [Old North Road; A1198 Royston—Huntingdon, S of village]: Creeper-covered pub with dark red décor and sporting theme, red-tiled bar with big log fire, lower part with chintzy easy chairs and settees, Cottage Atlantic, Fullers London Pride and Slaters Original, several wines by glass, straightforward food; piped music; children and dogs welcome, sheltered little garden with picnic-sets, open all day wknds *(Edward Mirzoeff, Russell and Alison Hunt, Michael Dandy, LYM, O K Smyth)*

MARCH [TL4196]
George PE15 9JJ [High St]: Neat and tidy, with plush banquettes, good choice of bar food (not Mon/Tues evenings) from snacks up inc OAP bargains, Flowers IPA, friendly staff, games room; impressive floral displays, garden tables *(Tony and Wendy Hobden)*

PAMPISFORD [TL4948]
Chequers CB2 4ER [Town Lane, off A505 E of M11 junction 10]: Picturesque, low-beamed and cosy, recently comfortably refurbished, with friendly helpful licensees, efficient

service, good value food inc fresh fish and Sun lunch (popular, so get there early), OAP lunch Weds, Greene King ales; lovely window boxes and hanging baskets, tables in pleasant garden *(D and M T Ayres-Regan, Roy and Lindsey Fentiman)*

PETERBOROUGH [TL1998]

Bogarts PE1 2RA [North St]: Half a dozen well kept ales mainly from small breweries in friendly open-plan Victorian pub with central bar, good value simple food noon–6 (9 Sun), helpful staff, daily papers, fine mix of customers, lots of Humphrey Bogart pictures; silent TV, games machine, quiz nights; handy for Westgate shopping centre, tables out on small terrace, open all day *(Joe Green)*

Coalheavers Arms PE2 9BH [Park St, Woodston]: Small and friendly, proper old-fashioned flagstoned local, well kept Milton and guest beers, farm cider, good range of continental imports and malt whiskies; pleasant garden, cl Mon-Weds lunchtimes, open all day wknds *(Ben and Helen Ingram, Joe Green, the Didler)*

Palmerston Arms PE2 9PA [Oundle Rd]: Partly 17th-c stone-built pub with Batemans and lots of guest ales tapped from the cask, good choice of malt whiskies, good pork pies, welcoming service, well worn-in furnishings in lounge and tiled-floor public bar, no music or machines; step down into pub, steps to lavatory; picnic-sets in small garden, open all day *(the Didler, Joe Green, P Dawn)*

Wortley Almshouses PE1 1QA [Westgate]: Attractive conversion of old stone-built almshouses (among modern buildings), with well kept bargain Sam Smiths, appropriately robust furnishings and simple décor in several appealing rooms off corridor; open all day *(the Didler)*

SHEPRETH [TL3947]

Plough SG8 6PP [signed just off A10 S of Cambridge; High St]: Smart and airy upmarket wine bar/restaurant, low black cubic sofas, black wood and chrome, pale sage walls, good stylish food (not Sun evening) from ciabattas up, attentive service, good choice of wines by the glass, Adnams; tidy back garden with stylish furnishings, fairy-lit arbour and pond *(BB)*

SPALDWICK [TL1372]

☆ *George* PE28 0TD [just off A14 W of Huntingdon]: 16th-c pub with good individual up-to-date food (they bake their own bread), cool stylish décor, sofas in bar, larger bistro area, lots of wines by the glass and a couple of real ales; children welcome *(LYM, P Berry)*

ST IVES [TL3171]

Oliver Cromwell PE27 5AZ [Wellington St]: Friendly traditional two-bar pub with good value lunchtime food (not Sun) inc good homely dishes, half a dozen well kept changing ales inc Adnams, Oakham JHB and Woodfordes Wherry; pleasant garden with stylish terrace, open all day *(Andy Littley)*

White Hart PE27 5AH [Sheep Market]: Small

local with enjoyable sensibly priced home cooking, good helpings, warm friendly service and atmosphere *(Robert Turnham)*

STAPLEFORD [TL4751]

Longbow CB2 5DS [Church St]: Welcoming bright local, comfortable and roomy, with five well kept changing ales, local Cassels' cider, good wholesome sensibly priced food inc unusual specials (they call the restaurant side Papillon), well chosen reasonably priced wines, pleasant staff, darts and pool; some live music; open all day Fri *(Jerry Brown)*

STILTON [TL1689]

Talbot PE7 3RP [North St]: Two-bar pub taken in hand by local couple, well kept beer, enjoyable pubby food inc pizzas and other italian dishes *(Andrew Berry)*

STRETHAM [TL5072]

Lazy Otter CB6 3LU [Elford Closes, off A10 S of Stretham roundabout]: Big rambling nicely furnished family pub in fine spot on the Great Ouse, with good views from waterside conservatory and tables in big garden with neat terrace; real ales such as Greene King and Nethergate, reasonably priced generous food, friendly staff, warm fire; piped music; bedroom annexe, open all day *(LYM, Frank W Gadbois, R M Chard)*

SWAFFHAM PRIOR [TL5663]

Red Lion CB5 0LD [B1102 NE of Cambridge; High St]: Attractive and spotless ancient building, wide range of enjoyable and generous fresh food from sandwiches up, friendly efficient staff, good value house wines, Greene King Old Speckled Hen and Abbot, comfortably divided dining area, interesting old local photographs; tables in big back courtyard *(Stephen Woad)*

UFFORD [TF0904]

☆ *White Hart* PE9 3BH [back rd Peterborough—Stamford, just S of B1443; Main St]: 17th-c village pub brewing its own Ufford ales (not unlike Adnams in style), guest beers too, enjoyable food all day using local organic supplies and their own free range eggs, good wines by the glass, leather sofas, log fire and railway memorabilia in busy stripped stone and flagstoned bar, plain tables in rustic back dining area and conservatory; children welcome, big garden with terrace and play area, newish bedroom block, open all day *(Jeff and Wendy Williams, LYM, Ray and Winifred Halliday, the Didler)*

WANSFORD [TL0799]

Haycock PE8 6JA [just off A1 W of Peterborough]: Hugely extended old coaching inn now a big hotel and conference centre, useful break for bar food all day from generous but pricy sandwiches and ciabattas up, Adnams, Bass and a guest beer, good wine choice, variety of seating areas with plenty of character, big log fire, restaurant with airy conservatory; children in eating areas, attractive courtyard and garden near river, dogs allowed in bar and comfortable bedrooms, open all day *(Michael Dandy, LYM, Eithne Dandy, David Glynne-Jones)*

Paper Mills PE8 6JB [London Rd]: Front bar with two woodburners, Bass, Hancocks and a guest such as Greene King Old Speckled Hen, usual bar food inc good baguettes and baked potatoes, good friendly service, separate menu for larger back restaurant; piped music; tables out in front and on back terrace *(Michael Dandy)*

WHITTLESFORD [TL4648]
Tickell Arms CB2 4NZ [off B1379 S of Cambridge, handy for M10 junction 10, via A505; North Rd]: Great building and atmosphere, with ornate heavy furnishings, soft lighting, good log fire, attractive flower-filled Victorian-style conservatory overlooking ducks and black swans on pond in formal terraced garden, cheerful staff, wide range of good imaginative food (they add an optional 12½% service charge), good wines by the glass, well kept Adnams, lovely log fire; may be well reproduced classical music *(LYM, Ryta Lyndley)*

WITCHFORD [TL5078]
Village Inn CB6 2HQ [Main St]: Sizeable Victorian pub, friendly and recently refitted, with cheerful landlady, enjoyable reasonably priced food inc some smaller helpings and good choice for children, freshly made so may take a while, two real ales; piped music may obtrude; disabled facilities, tables out behind *(Keith and Janet Morris)*

WOODDITTON [TL6558]
Three Blackbirds CB8 9SQ [signed off B1063 at Cheveley]: Pretty thatched and low-beamed pub with attractively old-fashioned flagstoned bar on left, second bar opening into large dining area with more tables upstairs, enterprising food inc local game, good service, Greene King IPA and Old Speckled Hen, racing photographs and cartoons; TV; children welcome, pretty garden; cl first Tues of month *(Stephen Woad, LYM, Simon Watkins)*

Post Office address codings confusingly give the impression that some pubs are in Cambridgeshire, when they're really in the Leicestershire or Midlands groups of counties (which is where we list them).

Cheshire

This county has a splendid variety of good pubs – everything from the very traditional, to pubs with a great range of beers, to leading-edge dining pubs. More than a fair share are in particularly pleasing settings, too. One of the best and most loved all-rounders here is the distinctive Bhurtpore at Aston, with its fantastic range of drinks and astonishing turnover of real ales from all sorts of far-flung brewers, its great curries and really warm welcome. The charming old White Lion at Barthomley confounds the pessimists who worry about the future of simple and genuinely traditional pubs – it's living proof that, when well run, they still attract plenty of business. The very successful small Brunning & Price pub group grows again this year with the addition (in this, the company's home county) of the appealingly renovated Combermere Arms at Burleydam. As with the other well run pubs in the chain, it offers an extensive range of drinks and carefully prepared good food in an attractive layout, chatty and relaxed. The other pubs in the chain (in this county the Grosvenor Arms at Aldford, the Dysart Arms at Bunbury and the waterside Old Harkers Arms in Chester) are all run along the same lines, but very much as independent places – they give no sense of being part of a larger organisation. Talking of individuality, mention has to be made of the mildly eccentric and very well liked Albion in Chester – a very grown-up pub with a calm restful appeal, hearty traditional food and well kept beer. After a short break, the Boot at Willington is back in the *Guide* as a main entry. It's enjoyable as a dining pub, and its suntrap terrace is not to be missed on a fine day. Another pub on winning form this year is the stylish Roebuck in Mobberley; it gains a Wine Award for its carefully chosen reasonably priced wine list. Competition for the county Dining Pub Award came down to a shortlist of three: the Dysart Arms at Bunbury, the Grosvenor Arms in Aldford and the Pheasant at Burwardsley, with its new Food Award. The award this year goes to the Grosvenor Arms in Aldford, the Brunning & Price flagship – it's given readers from Cheshire and further afield a year of faultless pleasure. In general pub food prices here are broadly in line with the national average; by comparison, the Albion in Chester and White Lion at Barthomley both offer some real food bargains. The Lucky Dip section at the end of the chapter shows an increasing number of pubs here doing food throughout the day at weekends – a helpful trend. And it includes a good many attractive places. Ones currently showing special appeal are the Mill in Chester, Ring o' Bells in Frodsham, Calveley Arms at Handley, Swan at Kettleshulme, Duke of Portland at Lach Dennis, Leathers Smithy at Langley, Golden Pheasant and Smoker, both at Plumley, and Swettenham Arms at Swettenham. Cheshire drinks prices are comfortably below the national average, with Hydes beers (particularly in the Plough at Eaton and Legh Arms in Prestbury) offering great value at well below £2 a pint, and the regional brewer Robinsons generally very fairly priced too. Though not notably low-priced, local beers such as Weetwood and Oak Beauty are well worth looking out for – and when a pub does stock them they tend to be cheaper than beers from elsewhere.

ALDFORD
SJ4259   MAP 7

Grosvenor Arms ★
B5130 Chester—Wrexham; CH3 6HJ
CHESHIRE DINING PUB OF THE YEAR

Plenty of character and life, impressive range of drinks, well balanced sensibly imaginative menu, good service; lovely big terrace and gardens

A buoyantly chatty atmosphere fills spacious cream-painted areas, which are sectioned by big knocked-through arches and a variety of wood, quarry tile, flagstone and black and white tiled floor finishes – some good richly coloured Turkey rugs look well against these natural materials. Good solid pieces of traditional furniture, plenty of interesting pictures and attractive lighting keep it all intimate enough. The huge panelled library room has tall bookshelves lining one wall, and lots of substantial tables well spaced on the handsomely boarded floor. Lovely on summer evenings, the airy terracotta-floored conservatory has lots of gigantic low hanging flowering baskets and chunky pale wood garden furniture. This opens on to a large elegant suntrap terrace (delightful for a summer evening drink), and a neat lawn with picnic-sets, young trees and a tractor. The rather fine looking bar counter stocks a comprehensive range of drinks including around 16 wines (largely new world and all served by the glass), a tempting range of whiskies (including 100 malts, 30 bourbons, and 30 irish whiskeys), as well as Caledonian Deuchars IPA, Weetwood Eastgate, Thwaites and a couple of interesting guests from brewers such as St Austell. Attentive service is friendly and reliable, and they keep a good selection of board games.

🍴 Food is very good, and the well balanced changing menu includes something to please most tastes. As well as sandwiches, there might be duck spring rolls, wild mushroom risotto, ham, egg and chips, ploughman's, monkfish wrapped in parma ham with pea and saffron risotto, pork loin steak with apple and celeriac mash and calvados cream and steaks; puddings such as bread and butter pudding and raspberry and lemon cheesecake. *Starters/Snacks: £4.50 to £7.50. Main Courses: £7.25 to £18.95. Puddings: £4.95 to £5.50*

Brunning & Price ~ Managers Gary Kidd and Jeremy Brunning ~ Real ale ~ Bar food (12-10 (9 Sun and bank hols)) ~ (01244) 620228 ~ Children welcome till 7pm, no prams or pushchairs ~ Dogs allowed in bar ~ Open 11.30-11; 12-10.30 Sun

Recommended by Revd D Glover, Phil and Gill Wass, Paul Boot, R G Stollery, J S Burn, Clive Watkin, Mrs Maricar Jagger, Steve Whalley, Maurice and Gill McMahon, Bruce and Sharon Eden

---

ASTBURY
SJ8461   MAP 7

Egerton Arms 🛏
Village signposted off A34 S of Congleton; CW12 4RQ

Cheery village pub with decent straightforward bar food, good value OAP lunches; front garden and nice bedrooms

This welcoming family-run place is in a pretty spot overlooking an attractive old church. Rambling around the bar, the cream-painted rooms are decorated with the odd piece of armour and shelves of books. Mementoes of the Sandow Brothers who performed as 'the World's Strongest Youths' are particularly interesting as one of them was the landlady's father. In summer dried flowers fill the big fireplace. Robinsons Double Hop, Hartleys XB and Unicorn are well kept on handpump; piped music, fruit machine, TV. You'll find a few well placed tables out in front, and a play area with a wooden fort. Despite the large car park you might struggle to get a place Sunday lunchtime. More reports please.

⏚ **The traditional menu includes sandwiches, sausage and chips, steak and kidney pudding, battered haddock and vegetable stroganoff.** *Starters/Snacks: £3.25 to £4.95. Main Courses: £7.25 to £13.50. Puddings: £3.50 to £4.00*

Robinsons ~ Tenants Alan and Grace Smith ~ Real ale ~ Bar food (11.30-2, 6(6.30 Sat, Sun)-9) ~ Restaurant ~ (01260) 273946 ~ Children welcome ~ Open 11.30-11; 11.30-3, 6.30-11 Sun ~ Bedrooms: £45S/£65B

Recommended by Liz Blackadder, Ross Balaam, Dr D J and Mrs S C Walker

ASTON
SJ6146   MAP 7

Bhurtpore ★ ♉ ◖
Off A530 SW of Nantwich; in village follow Wrenbury signpost; CW5 8DQ

Fantastic range of drinks (especially real ales) and tasty curries in warm-hearted pub with some unusual artefacts; big garden

Each year, over 1,000 different superbly kept real ales – anything from Abbeydale Absolution to Salopian Cock & Bull – pass through the 11 handpumps at this enthusiastically run red brick free house. They also stock dozens of unusual bottled beers and fruit beers, a great many bottled ciders and perries, over 100 different whiskies, and carefully selected soft drinks, and they have a good wine list. If you're a very keen real ale enthusiast, it's worth going during their summer beer festival. The pub takes its unusual name from the town in India, where a local landowner, Lord Combermere, won a battle. This explains why a collection of exotic artefacts in the carpeted lounge bar has an indian influence – a turbaned statue behind the counter proudly sports any sunglasses left behind by customers; also good local period photographs, and some attractive furniture. Tables in the comfortable public bar are reserved for people not eating; darts, dominoes, cribbage, pool, TV and games machine. At lunchtime and early weekday evenings the atmosphere is cosy and civilised, and on weekends, when it gets packed, the cheery staff cope superbly.

⏚ **The enjoyable menu has sandwiches and paninis (not Friday or Saturday night), a choice of five tasty curries, traditional dishes such as sausage, egg and chips, cheese and leek cakes with creamy dijon sauce, steak and kidney pie and steaks. Daily changing specials might include pork and black pudding patties on mustard and apple sauce and monkfish in red wine sauce with mushrooms and bacon; puddings such as banoffi pie with toffee sauce.** *Starters/Snacks: £3.50 to £4.95. Main Courses: £7.95 to £12.95. Puddings: £4.25*

Free house ~ Licensee Simon George ~ Real ale ~ Bar food (12-9 Sun) ~ Restaurant ~ (01270) 780917 ~ Children welcome till 8.30pm ~ Dogs allowed in bar ~ Folk third Tues ~ Open 12-2.30(3 Sat), 6.30-11.30(midnight Sat); 12-11 Sun

Recommended by Dave Webster, Sue Holland, the Didler, Andy Chetwood, Rick Capper, Jeremy King, Ann and Tony Bennett-Hughes, Malcolm Pellatt, Selwyn Roberts

BARTHOMLEY
SJ7752   MAP 7

White Lion ★ £
A mile from M6 junction 16; from exit roundabout take B5078 N towards Alsager, then Barthomley signposted on left; CW2 5PG

Charming 17th-c thatched village tavern with classic period interior and good value straightforward lunchtime food

The welcoming main bar here has a timelessly informal feel, with its blazing open fire, heavy low oak beams (dating back to Stuart times), attractively moulded black panelling, cheshire watercolours and prints on the walls, latticed windows and thick wobbly old tables. Up some steps, a second room has another welcoming open fire, more oak panelling, a high-backed winged settle, a paraffin lamp hinged to the wall, and shove-ha'penny, cribbage and dominoes; local societies make good use of a third room and look out for the cat here – one reader told us it is totally mad! Beers, which are on electric pump, include Marstons Bitter and Pedigree and Mansfield and a couple of guests such as Jennings Cocker Hoop and Snecklifter. Outside, seats and picnic-sets on the cobbles have a charming view of the attractive village, and the early 15th-c red sandstone church of St Bertiline across the road is well worth a visit.

🍴 **The short traditional menu might include sandwiches, staffordshire oakcakes with cheese, onions, tomatoes and beans, ploughman's, sausage and mash, hotpot and beef and mushroom pie.** *Starters/Snacks: £3.50 to £5.50. Main Courses: £4.95 to £7.95*

Marstons ~ Tenant Laura Condliffe ~ Real ale ~ Bar food (lunchtime only) ~ (01270) 882242 ~ Children welcome with restrictions ~ Open 11.30-11; 12-10.30 Sun

Recommended by Simon and Sally Small, MLR, Dr and Mrs M E Wilson, Clare Rosier, David Green, Leslie G Smith, Dr and Mrs A K Clarke, Richard Smith, G K Smale, Dave Webster, Sue Holland, Louise English, Paul Humphreys, Jo Lilley, Simon Calvert, Rob Stevenson, Dave Braisted, the Didler, Edward Mirzoeff, Piotr Chodzko-Zajko, Tracey and Stephen Groves, Maurice and Gill McMahon

BICKLEY MOSS
SJ5550   MAP 7

Cholmondeley Arms ♀

Cholmondeley; A49 5½ miles N of Whitchurch; the owners would like us to list them under Cholmondeley Village, but as this is rarely located on maps we have mentioned the nearest village which appears more often; SY14 8HN

Imaginatively converted high-ceilinged schoolhouse with decent range of real ale and wines, jolly nice food, and sizeable gardens

The cross-shaped lofty bar, high gothic windows, huge old radiators and old school desks on a gantry above the bar all leave no doubt that this was once a schoolhouse. Well used chairs in all shapes and forms – some upholstered, some bentwood, some with ladderbacks and some with wheelbacks – are set in groups round an almost equally eclectic mix of tables, all on comfy carpets. There's a stag's head over one of the side arches, an open fire and lots of Victorian portraits and military pictures on colourwashed walls. Mallard Spittin' Feather, local Woodland and a couple of guests such as Adnams and Weetwood on handpump are served from a pine clad bar, alongside around eight interesting and reasonably priced wines by the glass, all listed on a blackboard. There are seats outside on the sizeable lawn, and more in front overlooking the quiet road. The pub is handy for Cholmondeley Castle Gardens.

🍴 **Readers very much enjoy the food here, which runs from lunchtime sandwiches and steak baguettes, lasagne and steaks, to daily specials such as warm goats cheese mousse, steak and ale pie, duck breast with black cherry and mint sauce, morrocan lamb tagine, roast mediterranean vegetables with tagliatelle and bass fillet with shallot, rosemary and white wine sauce. Yummy home-made puddings might include syrup tart, chocolate hazelnut charlotte, bakewell tart and temptingly flavoured ice-creams.** *Starters/Snacks: £3.95 to £6.25. Main Courses: £8.95 to £16.75. Puddings: £3.95 to £4.75*

Free house ~ Licensee Carolyn Ross-Lowe ~ Real ale ~ Bar food ~ (01829) 720300 ~ Children welcome ~ Dogs welcome ~ Open 10-3.30, 6-11 ~ Bedrooms: £50S(£50B)/£70S(£70B)

Recommended by Rob and Catherine Dunster, Richard Smith, Ray and Winifred Halliday, M Thomas, K S Whittaker, Edward Leetham, Mrs P J Carroll, Kay and Alistair Butler, Richard Cole, Mr and Mrs J Freund

BUNBURY
SJ5658   MAP 7

Dysart Arms ♀

Bowes Gate Road; village signposted off A51 NW of Nantwich; and from A49 S of Tarporley – coming this way, coming in on northernmost village access road, bear left in village centre; CW6 9PH

Civilised chatty dining pub attractively filled with good furniture in thoughtfully laid out rooms; very enjoyable food, lovely garden with pretty views.

There's a relaxed social atmosphere throughout the immaculately kept knocked-through cream-walled rooms which ramble around the pleasantly lit central bar at this well run country pub. Each is nicely furnished with an appealing variety of well spaced sturdy wooden tables and chairs, a couple of tall filled bookcases, just the right amount of carefully chosen bric-a-brac and properly lit pictures. Under deep venetian red ceilings, some areas have good winter fires, red and black tiles, some stripped boards and some carpet. They've lowered the ceiling in the more restaurant end room (with its book-lined back wall), and there are lots of plants on the window sills. Service is efficient and friendly. Thwaites and Weetwood Eastgate and a couple of guests such as Phoenix Arizona and Rudgate Viking are very well kept on handpump, alongside a good selection of 16 malts by the glass, just over 20 malts and fresh apple juice. Sturdy wooden tables on the terrace and picnic sets on the lawn in the neatly kept slightly elevated garden are lovely in summer, with views of the splendid church at the end of the pretty village, and the distant Peckforton Hills beyond.

🍴 **From a changing menu, food is tasty, just imaginative enough, attractively presented, and fairly priced. As well as sandwiches, there might be pheasant terrine, smoked trout and herb tartlet, steak burger or sausage and mash, thai coconut and chilli beef, grilled bass with saffron creamed potatoes, lemon and garlic chicken breast with lemon risotto, grilled rib-eye steak, and puddings such as sticky toffee and date pudding, white chocolate cheesecake with fruit and elderflower sorbet and rhubarb fool with shortbread biscuits.** *Starters/Snacks: £4.25 to £7.50. Main Courses: £8.95 to £14.95. Puddings: £4.25 to £6.50*

Brunning & Price ~ Managers Darren and Elizabeth Snell ~ Real ale ~ Bar food (12-9.30(9 Sun)) ~ (01829) 260183 ~ Children away from bar, no under-10s after 6pm ~ Dogs allowed in bar ~ Open 11.30-11; 12-10.30 Sun

Recommended by Mrs P J Carroll, J S Burn, Clive Watkin, Mr Tarpey, Ann and Tony Bennett-Hughes, Dave Webster, Sue Holland, Revd D Glover, Rob Stevenson, Roger Yates, Dr Phil Putwain, Bruce and Sharon Eden, Richard Smith, Mr and Mrs Gerry Price, Derek and Sylvia Stephenson, Maurice and Gill McMahon

BURLEYDAM   SJ6042   MAP 7

Combermere Arms 🍺

A525 Whitchurch—Audlem; SY13 4AT

Roomy and attractive beamed pub successfully mixing good drinking side with good imaginative all-day food; garden

Now part of the same successful little chain that runs other very good Cheshire pubs, this 18th-c beamed place has been under that umbrella for some three years. A very good conversion of its attractive traditional interior feels nice and roomy but still cosy with nooks and crannies, open fires, rugs on wooden floors and lots of pictures. Linked areas have an equally comfortable atmosphere for drinkers as well as diners – both aspects of the business seem to do well here. Half a dozen real ales, often from local brewers, might be from Black Sheep, Flowers, Northumberland, Okells, Weetwood and Woodlands. They also stock three ciders, 100 whiskies, and 15 wines by the glass from an extensive list; a few board games. During summer evenings, they put candles on tables in the established garden.

🍴 **Most of the bar food is home made from carefully sourced, often local, ingredients. Dishes from the snack menu might include ploughman's, interesting sandwiches, tortilla or italian breads and cheshire cheese, onion and potato pasty. Starters might be soup, ham hock and black pudding cake with a poached egg and blackened mackerel fillet with piccalilli potato salad, and main courses could be battered cod, lentil and mushroom shepherd's pie, coriander marinated chicken breast with spinach and chickpea cake, roast loin of venison wrapped in air-dried ham with fondant potato and red wine sauce, with puddings such as banana toffee crumble tart, summer pudding and chocolate brownie with white chocolate ice-cream; english cheeseboard.** *Starters/Snacks: £4.25 to £6.25. Main Courses: £8.95 to £20.95. Puddings: £5.00*

Brunning & Price ~ Licensee John Astle Rowe ~ Real ale ~ Bar food (12-9.30(10 Thurs-Sat, 9 Sun)) ~ (01948) 871223 ~ Children welcome ~ Dogs allowed in bar ~ Open 12-11(10.30 Sun)

Recommended by D Weston, Philip Hesketh, Dave Webster, Sue Holland, Ann and Tony Bennett-Hughes, Alun Jones

---

Prices of main dishes sometimes now don't include vegetables – if in doubt ask.

BURWARDSLEY   SJ5256   MAP 7

Pheasant 🍴 ♟

Higher Burwardsley; signposted from Tattenhall (which itself is signposted off A41 S of Chester) and from Harthill (reached by turning off A534 Nantwich—Holt at the Copper Mine); follow pub's signpost on up hill from Post Office; OS Sheet 117 map reference 523566; CH3 9PF

Fantastic views, local beer and good range of very enjoyable food at heavily beamed and roomily fresh conversion of old inn

Views from this half-timbered and sandstone 17th-c pub really are tremendous. On a clear day the telescope on the terrace (with nice hard wood furniture) lets you make out the pier head and cathedrals in Liverpool, while from inside you can see right across the Cheshire plain. The nicely timbered interior has an airy modern feel, with wooden floors and well spaced furniture, including comfy leather armchairs and nice old chairs. They say the see-through fireplace houses the largest log fire in the county, and there's a pleasant restaurant. Three local Weetwood beers and a guest from a brewer such as Hanby are served on handpump alongside a selection of bottled beers, nine wines by the glass and around 20 malts; piped music, daily newspapers. A big side lawn has picnic-sets, and on summer weekends they sometimes have barbecues. Popular with walkers, the pub is well placed for the Sandstone Trail along the Peckforton Hills.

🍴 **Besides sandwiches and paninis, the imaginative menu includes something for most tastes, from soup, ploughman's, caesar salad, steak and kidney or fish pie, steak burger and battered cod, to crispy duck with hoi sin and crispy vegetables in a filo basket, wild mushroom and asparagus risotto and lamb shank with mint and redcurrant glaze, with daily specials such as calamari in cajun batter, chicken breast stuffed with mozzarella and wrapped in bacon with black pudding mash, and red snapper in rosemary crust with mussels and prawns in saffron broth with dill.** *Starters/Snacks: £3.95 to £8.95. Main Courses: £8.50 to £18.95. Puddings: £3.95 to £5.50*

Free house ~ Licensee Andrew Nelson ~ Real ale ~ Bar food (12-3, 6-9.30 Mon; 12-9.30 (10 Fri, Sat, 8.30 Sun)) ~ (01829) 770434 ~ Children welcome till 6pm ~ Dogs allowed in bar and bedrooms ~ Open 11-11(midnight Sat, 10.30 Sun) ~ Bedrooms: £65B/£85B

Recommended by Brian and Anna Marsden, Edward Leetham, John and Hazel Williams, Rita and Keith Pollard, Richard Cole, Alan and Eve Harding, Margaret and Roy Randle, Mark and Ruth Brock, Peter Craske

CHESTER   SJ4066   MAP 7

Albion ★

Albion Street; CH1 1RQ

Strongly traditional Victorian pub with comfortable period décor and captivating World War I memorabilia; hearty food and good drinks

With a layout that's little changed since Victorian times, this slightly eccentric pub is tucked away on a quiet street corner just below the Roman Wall, and has been leased by the same landlord for some 35 years. Most unusually, it's the officially listed site of four war memorials and attracts a handful of veterans during commemorative events. Throughout its tranquil rooms (no games machines or children here) you'll find an absorbing collection of World War I memorabilia, from big engravings of men leaving for war, and similarly moving prints of wounded veterans, to flags, advertisements and so on. The post-Edwardian décor is appealingly muted, with dark floral William Morris wallpaper (designed on the first day of World War I), a cast-iron fireplace, appropriate lamps, leatherette and hoop-backed chairs, a period piano and cast-iron-framed tables; there's an attractive side dining room too. Service is friendly, though this is a firmly run place: groups of race-goers are discouraged (opening times may be limited during meets), and they don't like people rushing in just before closing time. Three or four well kept real ales on handpump might be from brewers such as Batemans, Black Sheep, Exmoor and Titanic. They also stock new world wines, fresh orange juice, over 25 malt whiskies and a good selection of rums.

🍴 Served in generous helpings, wholesome good value bar food includes doorstep sandwiches, filled staffordshire oatcakes, cottage pie, creamy coconut chicken and rice, lambs liver, bacon and onions in cider gravy, daily specials such as hot thai chicken curry, and puddings such as chocolate torte or bread and butter pudding with marmalade. *Main Courses: £4.95 to £7.85. Puddings: £3.75*

Punch ~ Lease Michael Edward Mercer ~ Real ale ~ Bar food (12-2, 5-8(6-8.30 Sat); not Sun evening) ~ No credit cards ~ (01244) 340345 ~ Dogs allowed in bar ~ Open 12-3, 5(5.30 Mon, 6 Sat)-11; 12-11 Fri; 12-3, 7-10.30 Sun ~ Bedrooms: £65B/£75B

Recommended by Rob and Catherine Dunster, Mrs Philippa Wilson, J S Burn, Joe Green, Chris and Heather Street, Maurice and Gill McMahon, J and F Gowers, the Didler, Nigel Epsley, Mr and Mrs Gerry Price, Ann and Tony Bennett-Hughes, Dave Webster, Sue Holland, Graham Findley

Old Harkers Arms 🍺 🍴

Russell Street, down steps off City Road where it crosses canal – under Mike Melody antiques; CH3 5AL

Well run spacious but intimately laid out canalside building with great range of drinks (including lots of changing real ales) and good value tasty food

You can watch canal and cruise boats glide past from this big early Victorian warehouse. It takes its name from a Mr Harker, who once ran a canal-boat chandler's here. Lofty ceilings and tall windows give an appealing light and airy feel, though tables are carefully arranged to create a sense of privacy and cheery staff spread a happy bustle. Walls are covered with frame to frame old prints, and the usual Brunning & Price wall of bookshelves feature at one end. Attractive lamps add cosiness, and the bar counter is apparently constructed from salvaged doors. A great choice of around nine real ales on handpump includes Flowers, Timothy Taylors Landlord, Thwaites Original, Weetwood Cheshire Cat, with regularly changing guests from brewers such as Hereford, Mallard, Titanic and Wye Valley. They also do around 100 malt whiskies, decent well described wines (with around 40 by the glass), farmhouse ciders and local apple juice.

🍴 As well as a good range of sandwiches, nicely presented bar food, from a changing menu, could include starters and snacks such as roast tomato and black olive soup, aubergine and goats cheese fritter, cheshire cheese tart and ploughman's. Main courses might be sweet potato and spinach curry, duck breast with potato and celeriac rösti, sausages with leek mash, battered haddock, smoked salmon and tiger prawn linguini and rump steak with dauphinoise potatoes and red wine sauce, with puddings such as chocolate brownie with chocolate sauce, apple tart and locally made ice-creams, and a cheeseboard. *Starters/Snacks: £4.25 to £6.95. Main Courses: £8.95 to £14.75. Puddings: £4.50 to £5.25*

Brunning & Price ~ Manager Paul Jeffery ~ Real ale ~ Bar food (12-9.30(9 Sun)) ~ (01244) 344525 ~ Supervised children till 5pm, no pushchairs ~ Dogs allowed in bar ~ Open 11.30-11; 12-10.30 Sun

Recommended by Joe Green, Bruce and Sharon Eden, Simon J Barber, Lawrence Pearse, David Collison, Nigel Epsley, Mr and Mrs Gerry Price, Mrs Maricar Jagger, Steve Whalley, Mrs Hazel Rainer, Dave Webster, Sue Holland, Tony Hobden, Roger Yates, Graham Findley

COTEBROOK   SJ5765   MAP 7

Fox & Barrel

A49 NE of Tarporley; CW6 9DZ

Changing hands as we went to press, this neatly kept old place has a cosy bar, appealing restaurant and uniformed staff

The original part of this pretty white cottage comprises a snug little bar, which is dominated by a big log fireplace and interestingly furnished with a good mix of tables and chairs (including two seats like Victorian thrones), a comfortable banquette corner, and rather nice ornaments and china jugs; unobtrusive piped music, TV and board games. The much bigger uncluttered candlelit dining area is a later addition to the building, and has attractive rugs on bare boards, rustic tables, comfortable dining chairs, rustic pictures above the panelled dado, and an extensively panelled section. Neatly turned out staff serve well kept Jennings Cumberland, John Smiths, Marstons Pedigree and a guest such as Greene King Abbot through a sparkler (though you can ask for it to be taken off).

🍴 As we went to press the recently simplified menu included lunchtime sandwiches, ploughman's and burgers; the fairly traditional bar food might now include soup, tandoori chicken salad, steak, ale and mushroom pie, chicken stroganoff, sausage and mash, braised lamb shank and 8oz fillet; Sunday roast. *Starters/Snacks: £3.95 to £6.25. Main Courses: £7.95 to £16.95. Puddings: £3.95 to £6.25*

Punch ~ Lease Darren Melville ~ Real ale ~ Bar food (12-9(10 Sat, 7 Sun)) ~ Restaurant ~ (01829) 760529 ~ Children welcome ~ Dogs allowed in bar ~ Open 12-midnight
Recommended by Ray and Winifred Halliday, J C Clark, Lucien Perring

EATON   SJ8765   MAP 7

Plough 🛏️
A536 Congleton—Macclesfield; CW12 2NH

Neat and cosy village pub with four interesting beers, bar food, views from big attractive garden, and good bedrooms

The carefully converted bar at this attractive 17th-c inn has plenty of beams and exposed brickwork, a couple of snug little alcoves, comfortable armchairs and cushioned wooden wall seats on red patterned carpets, long red curtains, mullioned windows, and a big stone fireplace. Moved here piece by piece from its original home in Wales, the heavily raftered barn at the back is a striking restaurant. Beers include Hydes Bitter (very reasonably priced) and three guests from brewers such as Copper Dragon, Moorehouses and Storm. The decent wine list includes ten by the glass. Service is friendly and attentive, and look out for Thunder, the resident black labrador; piped music, TV. The big tree-filled garden is attractive, with good views of nearby hills, and there are picnic-sets on the lawn and a smaller terrace. The appealingly designed bedrooms are in a converted stable block.

🍴 It's advisable to book if you are eating. Food includes lunchtime sandwiches, as well as soup, prawns in garlic butter, steak and kidney pudding, thai green curry, 10oz rib-eye steak and some interesting daily specials; three-course Sunday lunch. *Starters/Snacks: £3.25 to £6.95. Main Courses: £7.95 to £18.95. Puddings: £3.95 to £5.95*

Free house ~ Licensee Mujdat Karatas ~ Real ale ~ Bar food (12-2, 7-9; 12-8 Sun) ~ Restaurant ~ (01260) 280207 ~ Children welcome ~ Dogs allowed in bedrooms ~ Live music last Fri of the month ~ Open 11(12 Sun)-11(midnight Sat) ~ Bedrooms: £55B/£70B
Recommended by Dr David Clegg, David and Ros Hanley, Mark and Ruth Brock, Mrs P J Carroll

HAUGHTON MOSS   SJ5855   MAP 7

Nags Head 🍴 🍷
Turn off A49 S of Tarporley into Long Lane, at 'Beeston, Haughton' signpost; CW6 9RN

Spotlessly kept with nice traditional décor, log fires, popular tasty food including good value lunchtime buffet, and big garden

Dating back in parts to the 16th c, this black and white pub is nicely tucked away down winding country lanes. It has gleaming black and white tiles by the serving counter, pews and a heavy settle by the fire in a small quarry-tiled room on the left, and button-back wall banquettes in the carpeted room on the right, which also has logs burning in a copper-hooded fireplace. Below heavy black beams are shelves of pewter mugs, attractive Victorian prints and a few brass ornaments, and the front window of the pub is full of charmingly arranged collector's dolls. On the right is a sizeable carpeted dining area. An oak beamed conservatory extension also serves as the dining room; maybe very quiet piped music. Drinks include a well chosen wine list (with 18 by the glass), a dozen malts, and Flowers and Greene King Abbot and a guest such as Abbeydale Moonshine on handpump. A big immaculately kept garden has well spaced picnic-sets and a bowling green.

⊞ The generously served tasty bar food does draw the crowds, particularly between 12 and 2 on weekdays when they run the bargain-priced self-service buffet. Other dishes include soup, sandwiches, ploughman's, tasty whitebait, roasted peppers filled with vegetable risotto, half a roast chicken, pork medallions with cider and cream sauce, mixed seafood in a cream sauce with tagliatelle, steak with port and brandy sauce, and daily specials such as smoked trout salad with citrus mayonnaise, guinea fowl with berry compote, and on Fridays quite a few fresh fish dishes such as bass and shark; there's a puddings trolley and various ice-cream sundaes. *Starters/Snacks: £3.60 to £6.75. Main Courses: £8.60 to £16.50. Puddings: £3.55 to £4.50*

Free house ~ Licensees Rory and Deborah Keigan ~ Real ale ~ Bar food (12-10) ~ Restaurant ~ (01829) 260265 ~ Children welcome ~ Open 11-midnight

Recommended by Herbert and Susan Verity, Mr and Mrs M Stratton, David A Hammond, J Roy Smylie, M Thomas, Maurice and Gill McMahon

LANGLEY

SJ9569   MAP 7

Hanging Gate ♀

Meg Lane, Higher Sutton; follow Langley signpost from A54 beside Fourways Motel, and that road passes the pub; from Macclesfield, heading S from centre on A523 turn left into Byrons Lane at Langley, Wincle signpost; in Sutton (½ mile after going under canal bridge, ie before Langley) fork right at Church House Inn, following Wildboarclough signpost, then 2 miles later turning sharp right at steep hairpin bend; OS Sheet 118 map reference 952696; SK11 0NG

Remotely set old place with fires in traditional cosy rooms, lovely views from airy extension and terrace, and bar food

This welcoming old drover's inn was first licensed around 300 years ago, though it's thought to have been built long before that. Given its remote location high on a Peak District ridge, it's not surprising that it's popular with hikers. Still in their original layout, its three cosy little low-beamed rooms are simply furnished, and have attractive old prints of Cheshire towns, and big coal fires. The first simple room houses the bar (with well kept Hydes Bitter, Jekylls Gold and a Hydes seasonal beer on handpump, quite a few malt whiskies and ten wines by the glass) and is so small there's ample space for seating, the second room has a section of bar in the corner and three or four tables, and the third appealing snug is blue, and has a little chaise longue. Down some stone steps, an airy garden room extension has panoramic views over a patchwork of valley pastures to distant moors and the tall Sutton Common transmitter above – seats out on the crazy-paved terrace also have terrific views; piped music. It does get busy so it's best to book on weekends.

⊞ Under the new licensee, bar food from the menu and changing blackboard could include soup, fresh sardines, fish broth, thai green curry, steak and ale pie, fish and chips and steaks. *Starters/Snacks: £3.50 to £6.50. Main Courses: £7.95 to £17.95. Puddings: £4.95*

Hydes ~ Tenants Ian and Luda Rottenbury ~ Real ale ~ Bar food (12-2.30(3 Sat, 3.30 Sun), 6.45-9.30) ~ Restaurant ~ (01260) 252238 ~ Children welcome away from snug bar ~ Open 12-3, 5-11; 12-11(10.30 Sun) Sat

Recommended by Mr and Mrs Colin Roberts, the Didler, Alun Jones

---

A very few pubs try to make you leave a credit card at the bar, as a sort of deposit if you order food. They are not entitled to do this. The credit card firms and banks which issue them warn you not to let them out of your sight. If someone behind the counter used your card fraudulently, the card company or bank could in theory hold you liable, because of your negligence in letting a stranger hang on to your card. Suggest instead that if they feel the need for security, they 'swipe' your card and give it back to you. And do name and shame the pub to us.

MOBBERLEY

SJ7879 MAP 7

Roebuck ♀

Mill Lane; down hill from sharp bend on B5085 at E edge of 30mph limit; WA16 7HX

Stylish and airy country interior, warm welcome and service, very good food, good wine list, courtyard, garden, and children's play area

A comfortable mix of furnishings, from cushioned long wood pews that were rescued from a redundant welsh chapel to scrubbed pine farmhouse tables and a mix of old chairs, as well as old tiled and boarded floors, give a relaxed country feel to this popular white-painted pub which is in a quiet spot down a bypassed lane. The wine list is short but well chosen and very reasonably priced, with about a dozen by the glass; also Greene King Old Speckled Hen, Tetleys, Timothy Taylors Landlord and a guest such as Adnams Broadside. Staff are polite, friendly and helpful; piped music. A cobbled courtyard has benches and tables and there are picnic-sets in an enclosed beer garden (and more by the car park); also a play area for small children with a sandpit and play equipment.

🍴 **The enjoyable food is thoughtfully prepared and includes traditional dishes with an appealing twist. As well as interesting sandwiches (not evenings), dishes might include soup, scallops, steak and ale pie, avocado and crème fraîche soufflé omelette, chicken breast with savoury tarragon bread and butter pudding, lamb shank with bubble and squeak cake, fillet steak with foie gras, and puddings such as warm chocolate brownie with mascarpone ice-cream or strawberry risotto with basil ice-cream. You will probably need to book.** *Starters/Snacks: £4.25 to £8.25. Main Courses: £9.25 to £18.95. Puddings: £3.95 to £5.30*

Free house ~ Licensee Jane Marsden ~ Real ale ~ Bar food (12-2.30, 6-9.30; 12-9.30 Sat; 12-8 Sun) ~ Restaurant ~ (01565) 873322 ~ Children welcome ~ Open 12-3, 5-11; 12-11 Sat; 12-10.30 Sun

Recommended by Mrs P J Carroll, Rob and Catherine Dunster

PEOVER HEATH

SJ7973 MAP 7

Dog 🍺

Off A50 N of Holmes Chapel at the Whipping Stocks, keep on past Parkgate into Wellbank Lane; OS Sheet 118 map reference 794735; note that this village is called Peover Heath on the OS map and shown under that name on many road maps, but the pub is often listed under Over Peover instead; WA16 8UP

Cheerful and pleasant dining pub with interesting range of beers and generous traditional food

It's worth arriving early to try for a seat in the slightly more spacious feeling main bar. This is comfortably furnished with easy chairs and wall seats (including one built into a snug alcove around an oak table), and two wood-backed seats built in either side of a coal fire. There's also a log fire in an old-fashioned black grate; games machine, darts, pool, dominoes, board games, TV and piped music. The five reasonably priced and very well kept real ales here are likely to include Copper Dragon Scotts 1816, Hydes, Moorhouses Black Cat and Weetwood Cheshire Cat. They also have Addlestone's cider, 35 different malt whiskies and eight wines by the glass. There are picnic-sets beneath colourful hanging baskets on the peaceful lane, and more out in a pretty back garden. It's a pleasant walk from here to the Jodrell Bank Centre and Arboretum; recently refurbished bedrooms.

🍴 **Bar food includes many pub standards, such as soup, sandwiches, hot baguettes, ploughman's, curry or sausage of the day and mash, steak and ale pie, oakcakes stuffed with leeks, mushrooms and cheese, giant cod with chips and mushy peas, roast beef, and puddings such as strawberry pavlova or pecan and lemon cheesecake.** *Starters/Snacks: £3.25 to £5.95. Main Courses: £10.25 to £15.95. Puddings: £3.95*

Please let us know of any pubs where the wine is particularly good.

Free house ~ Licensee Steven Wrigley ~ Real ale ~ Bar food (12-2.30, 6-9; 12-8.30 Sun) ~
Restaurant ~ (01625) 861421 ~ Children welcome in dining rooms ~ Dogs allowed in bar ~
Live music monthly Fri ~ Open 11.30-3, 4.30-11; 11.30-midnight Sat; 12-11 Sun ~ Bedrooms:
£60B/£80B

*Recommended by Martin Hann, Steve Whalley, Gerry and Rosemary Dobson, Tom and Jill Jones, Mike and
Linda Hudson, Dr Phil Putwain, P J and R D Greaves, Brian and Janet Ainscough*

PRESTBURY   SJ8976   MAP 7

Legh Arms 🛏

A538, village centre; SK10 4DG

**Comfortable and immaculately kept inn with good food, appealingly individual bar,
terraced garden, and beautiful bedrooms**

Elegantly worked in a smart traditional style with plenty of soft furnishings, the relaxing
bar, though opened up, is well divided into several distinctive areas, with muted tartan
fabric over a panelled dado on the right, ladderback dining chairs, good solid dark tables,
stylish french steam train prints, italian costume engravings and a glass case of china
and books. On the left there are brocaded bucket seats around more solid tables tables,
antique steeplechase prints, staffordshire dogs on the stone mantelpiece, all warmed by a
good coal fire; a snug panelled back part has cosy wing armchairs and a grand piano, and
a narrow side offshoot has pairs of art deco leather armchairs around small granite
tables, and antique costume prints of French tradesmen. The bar, towards the back on the
left, has well kept Robinsons Unicorn and Hatters Mild on handpump and nice house
wines (eight by the glass), a good range of malts and whiskies, good coffee, and maybe
genial regulars perched on the comfortable leather bar stools; this part looks up to an
unusual balustraded internal landing. There are daily papers on a coffee table, and
magazines on an antique oak dresser; piped music. A garden behind has a terrace with
outdoor heating, tables and chairs.

🍴 **Very tasty bar food might include soup, spicy fishcakes with sweet chilli sauce, a
selection of dips, oysters, thai chicken curry, fish and chips, tomato risotto, steak and ale
pie, seared tuna steak on niçoise salad, and puddings such as chocolate torte and sticky
toffee pudding. The pricier menu in the sumptuous restaurant is more elaborate.**
Starters/Snacks: £3.50 to £8.95. Main Courses: £7.50 to £17.95. Puddings: £3.95

Robinsons ~ Tenant Peter Myers ~ Real ale ~ Bar food (12-2, 7-10; 12-9.30 Sun) ~ Restaurant ~
(01625) 829130 ~ Children welcome within reason ~ Open 11-11(midnight Sat) ~
Bedrooms: /£95B

Recommended by Mrs P J Carroll, Ian Legge, Joan York, Howard Dell, Rob Stevenson

TARPORLEY   SJ5562   MAP 7

Rising Sun

High Street; village signposted off A51 Nantwich—Chester; CW6 0DX

Quaint, bustling and friendly, with wide range of generously served homely food

The appealingly aged brick frontage of this family-run pub opens into a suitably nice old
interior. It's cosily furnished with well chosen tables surrounded by eye-catching old
seats (including creaky 19th-c mahogany and oak settles), an attractively blacked iron
kitchen range, and sporting and other old-fashioned prints on the walls. There are one or
two seats in a tiny side bar where they might put on a portable TV for major sporting
events; piped music. Happy to please staff serve Robinsons Double Hop, Hartleys XB and
Unicorn from handpumps.

🍴 **Good value bar food includes soup, sandwiches, toasties, filled baked potatoes, half a
dozen tasty pies, fish and chips, poached salmon with prawn and tomato sauce, a dozen
spicy dishes such as fruit beef curry, over a dozen vegetarian dishes such as vegetable
stroganoff, and 12oz sirloin.** *Starters/Snacks: £2.95 to £4.95. Main Courses: £6.35 to £14.95.
Puddings: £3.25 to £3.75*

Robinsons ~ Tenant David Robertson ~ Real ale ~ Bar food (11.30-2, 5.30-9.30; 12-9 Sun; 11.30-9.30 bank hols) ~ Restaurant (evening) ~ (01829) 732423 ~ Children welcome away from small bar ~ Open 11.30-3, 5.30-11; 11.30-11 bank hols and Sat; 12-10.30 Sun

Recommended by the Didler, Bob Broadhurst

WETTENHALL   SJ6261   MAP 7

Boot & Slipper

From B5074 on S edge of Winsford, turn into Darnhall School Lane, then right at Wettenhall signpost: keep on for 2 or 3 miles; OS Sheet 118 map reference 625613; CW7 4DN

Low-beamed old place with very friendly welcome, straightforward food, and tables on front terrace

The chatty licensee couple and staff at this traditional pub seem genuinely interested in their customers. The knocked-through beamed main bar has three shiny old dark settles, straightforward chairs, and a fishing rod above the deep low fireplace with its big warming log fire. The modern bar counter also serves the left-hand communicating beamed room, which has shiny pale brown tiled floors, a cast-iron-framed long table, a panelled settle and bar stools; darts and piped music. An unusual trio of back-lit arched pseudo-fireplaces forms one stripped-brick wall, and there are two further areas on the right, as well as an attractive back restaurant with big country pictures. Drinks include Bass and Tetleys on handpump, a good choice of malt whiskies and a decent wine list. There are picnic-sets out on the cobbled front terrace by the big car park; children's play area.

Traditional food could include soup, prawn cocktail, breaded brie, pie and curry of the day, cheese and broccoli bake, 10oz rump steak, and puddings such as sherry trifle or sticky toffee pavlova. *Starters/Snacks: £2.50 to £5.95. Main Courses: £8.50 to £16.95. Puddings: £2.00 to £3.95*

Free house ~ Licensee Joan Jones ~ Real ale ~ Bar food (12-8 Sun) ~ Restaurant ~ (01270) 528238 ~ Children welcome till 8pm ~ Open 12-3, 5.30-11.30; 12-midnight Sat; 12-10.30 Sun ~ Bedrooms: £40S/£60S

Recommended by Ann and Tony Bennett-Hughes, Dr Phil Putwain

WILLINGTON   SJ5367   MAP 7

Boot

Boothsdale, off A54 at Kelsall; CW6 0NH

Enjoyable dining pub (you may need to book at weekends) with suntrap terrace, charming restaurant and tasty food

In a terrific setting on a wooded hillside (with views across the Cheshire plain to the Welsh Hills), this lovely old place has been carefully converted from a row of attractive sandstone cottages. The interior has been opened up around the central bar, leaving small unpretentiously furnished room areas, with lots of original features, and there's a woodburning stove. The charming flagstoned restaurant (with a roaring log fire) has wheelback chairs around plenty of tables. Friendly staff serve Greene King IPA, Tetleys and a guest from the local Weetwood brewery from handpumps; they keep 30 malt whiskies and have a decent wine list. An extension with french windows overlooks the garden (the three donkeys, and Sooty and Sweep the cats are popular with children), and picnic-sets in front on the raised stone terrace are an idyllic suntrap in summer.

Besides tasty regularly changing specials such as spicy crab fishcakes, bass, smoked haddock with rarebit topping or pork belly, other good dishes could include soup, olives and bread, sandwiches, steak and ale or fisherman's pie, fillet steak, and puddings such as sticky toffee pudding or rhubarb crumble. *Starters/Snacks: £3.30 to £8.00. Main Courses: £8.90 to £16.90. Puddings: £4.50*

> Planning a day in the country? We list pubs in really attractive scenery at the back of the book.

Punch ~ Lease Mike and Jon Gollings ~ Real ale ~ Bar food (10-2.30, 6-9.30; 10-9.30 Fri-Sun) ~ Restaurant ~ (01829) 751375 ~ Children welcome ~ Open 10-midnight
Recommended by Mrs Jane Kingsbury, Ann and Tony Bennett-Hughes

WINCLE   SJ9665   MAP 7

Ship 🍺

Village signposted off A54 Congleton—Buxton; SK11 0QE

Popular sandstone village pub in good walking country, thoughtful staff, small but interesting range of beers, good inventive food, and little garden

A sympathetically designed extension into the old stables should ease the weekend bustle at this attractive 16th-c pub. It's in an area of lovely countryside so can get very busy with walkers (they sell their own book of local walks, £3) and tourists. Two simple little tap rooms have an enjoyably welcoming atmosphere, thick stone walls and a coal fire, and the stable extentsion, with its flagstone floors, beams and log burning stove blends in nicely. A couple of thoughtfully sourced guest beers from brewers such as Batemans and Thornbridge are well kept alongside Fullers London Pride, Moorhouses Premier, belgian beers, Weston's farm cider and fruit wines. A small garden has wooden tables.

🍴 As well as imaginative sandwiches such as brie with roasted mediterranean vegetables and pesto, tasty bar food could include parsnip and pear soup, thai kebabs, seared wood pigeon stuffed with dolcelatte and wrapped in parma ham with wild mushroom and pigeon jus, wild mushroom and asparagus tagliatelle with broccoli pesto and parmesan wafer, chicken and leek pie, confit of duck with pak choi and plum sauce, grilled red snapper with hollandaise, and puddings such as crème brûlée or banoffi pie. *Starters/Snacks: £3.50 to £7.50. Main Courses: £9.95 to £17.95. Puddings: £3.95 to £4.95*

Free house ~ Licensee Giles Henry Meadows ~ Real ale ~ Bar food (12-2.30(3 Sat, 3.30 Sun), 6.30-9(9.30 Sat); not Sun evening) ~ Restaurant ~ (01260) 227217 ~ Children in family room till 8pm ~ Dogs allowed in bar ~ Live jazz third Thurs ~ Open 12-3, 6.30(5.30 Fri)-11; 12-11 Sat; 12-10.30 Sun; closed Mon
Recommended by DJH, Richard, Ian Dutton, Mrs Ann Gray, Rob Stevenson, Mrs P J Carroll, B and M Kendall, Jeremy Whitehorn, the Didler, Maurice and Gill McMahon

WRENBURY   SJ5947   MAP 7

Dusty Miller

Village signposted from A530 Nantwich—Whitchurch; Cholmondeley Road; CW5 8HG

Generous food and views of busy canal from bars and terrace of big mill conversion

This substantial brick building, right next to the Shropshire Union Canal, is a neatly converted 19th-c corn mill – you can still see the old lift hoist up under the rafters. The River Weaver runs in an aqueduct under the canal at this point, and it was the river that once powered the millrace. These days a constant stream of boats slipping through the striking counter-weighted canal drawbridge, just outside here, provides entertainment if you're sitting at picnic-sets among rose bushes on the gravel terrace or at one of the tables inside by the series of tall glazed arches. The atmosphere is low-key restaurary, with some emphasis on the generously served food, though drinkers are welcome, and in summer the balance may even tip. The very spacious modern feeling main bar area is comfortably welcoming and furnished with a mixture of seats (including tapestried banquettes, oak settles and wheelback chairs) round rustic tables. Further in, a quarry-tiled part by the bar counter has an oak settle and refectory table. Friendly staff serve three well kept Robinsons beers on handpump; eclectic piped music.

🍴 The monthly changing menu might include soup, port and stilton pâté with pear chutney, smoked salmon and gravadlax cream cheese roulade, thai potato curry, beef braised in ale, blackened salmon fillet with horseradish cream and fried new potatoes, honey-glazed roast duck with orange and mango salad, grilled rib-eye, and puddings such as baked rice pudding and sticky toffee pudding, with british cheeses. *Starters/Snacks: £3.95 to £5.25. Main Courses: £7.95 to £14.50. Puddings: £3.95 to £5.25*

Robinsons ~ Tenant Mark Sumner ~ Real ale ~ Bar food (12-2, 6.30-9.30(7-9 Sun); not Mon in winter) ~ Restaurant ~ (01270) 780537 ~ Children in dining area ~ Dogs allowed in bar ~ Open 12-3, 6.30(7 Sun)-11; closed Mon lunchtime in winter

Recommended by JCW, Frank and Chris Sharp, Gerry Price

LUCKY DIP

Besides the fully inspected pubs, you might like to try these Lucky Dips recommended to us and described by readers (if you do, please send us reports: www.goodguides.co.uk).

ALDERLEY EDGE [SJ8479]
Merlin SK9 7QN [Harden Park]: Substantial Victorian building with pleasant modern décor in bar and eating areas (emphasis on popular food from snacks up), well kept Timothy Taylors Landlord, interesting continental beers on tap and good choice of wines by the glass; tables on terrace by riverside garden, Innkeepers Lodge bedrooms *(Andy and Claire Barker)*
ALLGREAVE [SU9767]
Rose & Crown SK11 0BJ [A54 Congleton—Buxton]: Small and friendly, in remote upland spot with good Dane valley views, well kept Robinsons, good value food, pleasant landlord; great walking country, three refurbished bedrooms *(Tom and Jill Jones)*
ALPRAHAM [SJ5759]
Travellers Rest CW6 9JA [A51 Nantwich—Chester]: Unspoilt four-room country local with friendly staff and veteran landlady (same family for three generations), well kept Caledonian Deuchars IPA and Tetleys Bitter and Mild, low prices, leatherette, wicker and Formica, some flock wallpaper, fine old brewery mirrors, darts and dominoes, back bowling green; no machines, piped music or food (apart from crisps and nuts), cl wkdy lunchtimes *(the Didler, Pete Baker, Dave Webster, Sue Holland)*
ALTRINCHAM [SJ7688]
☆ *Victoria* WA14 1EX [Stamford St]: Reopened as civilised dining pub, sensibly short choice of proper food made with fresh country ingredients from good local farm shops and the like, real ales such as Flowers IPA and Greene King Old Speckled Hen, friendly service, comfortable fireside settees on right, spruce and airy restaurant on left; open all day *(Sarah Attwater, Chris Wilding)*
ALVANLEY [SJ4973]
White Lion WA6 9DD [Manley Rd; handy for M56 junction 14]: Comfortable 16th-c Chef & Brewer dining pub with low beams, cosy corners and candlelight, good friendly service, real ales, good choice of wines by the glass; tables on terrace, play area, duck pond *(LYM, D Watson)*
ANDERTON [SJ6475]
Stanley Arms CW9 6AG [just NW of Northwich; Old Rd]: Busy friendly local by Trent & Mersey Canal in pleasant surroundings overlooking amazing restored Anderton boat lift, wide choice of good value generous pubby food, well kept John

Smiths and Tetleys, agreeable family dining area; children welcome, tables in attractive yard with grassy play area, overnight mooring *(Tony Hobden)*
ASHTON [SJ5069]
Golden Lion CH3 8BH [Kelsall Rd (B5393, off A54 nr Tarvin)]: Village pub with well furnished three-tier layout inc modern eating areas, enjoyable fresh food, efficient service, real ales such as Caledonian Deuchars IPA; children welcome *(Alan and Eve Harding)*
BRERETON GREEN [SJ7764]
Bears Head CW11 1RS [handy for M6 junction 17; set back off A50 S of Holmes Chapel]: Beautiful and thoughtfully developed heavily timbered inn, welcoming and civilised linked rooms with old-fashioned furniture, flagstones, carpets and hop-hung low beams, enjoyable fresh food inc big sandwiches (till 5pm) and varying sizes of hot dishes, good service, well kept ales and decent wines by the glass, cheerful log fires, daily papers; open all day, good value bedrooms in modern block *(LYM, Bob and Angela Brooks)*
CALVELEY [SJ5958]
Davenport Arms CW6 9JN: Friendly pub under newish management, good range of generous good value food; children welcome, garden tables *(Trevor Whitaker)*
CHESTER [SJ4166]
☆ *Mill* CH1 3NF [Milton St]: Early 19th-c mill converted to hotel, neat and comfortable sizeable bar on right, five regular beers inc ones brewed for them by Coach House and Phoenix, up to nine changing guest ales, reasonable prices, good value ciabattas and enjoyable hot dishes till late evening, charming service, relaxed mix of customers, canalside restaurant and dining barge; quiet piped music, unobtrusively placed big-screen sports TV, jazz Mon; children looked after well, benches out by water, good bedrooms, open all day *(the Didler, BB, Nigel Epsley, Joe Green, Colin Moore, Dave Webster, Sue Holland)*
Olde Boot CH1 1LQ [Eastgate Row N]: Down-to-earth pub in lovely 17th-c Rows building, heavy beams, lots of dark woodwork, oak flooring, flagstones, some exposed Tudor wattle and daub, black-leaded kitchen range in lounge beyond decent lunchtime food servery (not Tues), old-fashioned settles and oak panelling in upper area popular with families, good service, bargain Sam Smiths

OB; piped music; children allowed
*(Michael Dandy, the Didler, Nigel Epsley,
Joe Green, LYM, Ian Legge)*
Spital Vaults CH3 5DB [Spital Walk]: Local
with warmly welcoming new young landlord,
two real ales, bar snacks, pub games; tables
outside *(G Harrison)*
Union Vaults CH1 3ND [Francis St/Egerton
St]: Basic local notable for its reasonably
priced changing ales inc Caledonian and
Phoenix, friendly knowledgeable staff,
bagatelle, dominoes, cards and back games
room with pool, two quieter upper rooms
with old local photographs; piped music, two
TV sports channels; open all day *(Joe Green,
Nigel Epsley, Dave Webster, Sue Holland,
the Didler)*
☆ **CHILDER THORNTON** [SJ3678]
White Lion CH66 5PU [off A41 S of M53
junction 5; New Rd]: Low two-room
whitewashed country pub, old-fashioned and
unpretentious, with welcoming atmosphere
and staff, good value sensible lunches (not
Sun) from good ciabattas and hot filled rolls
up, well kept Thwaites Bitter, Mild and
Lancaster Bomber, open fire, framed
matchbooks, no music or machines (small TV
for big matches); children welcome, tables
out in covered front area and secluded back
garden, play area, open all day *(MLR)*
CHURTON [SJ4156]
White Horse CH3 6LA [Chester Rd (B5130)]:
Small village pub doing well under new
licensees, friendly atmosphere in three
attractively furnished linked areas, enjoyable
food, real ales *(Barry Hayes)*
COMBERBACH [SJ6477]
Spinner & Bergamot CW9 6AY [Warrington
Rd]: Comfortably plush beamed pub doing
well under current newish tenants, enjoyable
food, several real ales inc rarities for the
area, daily papers, log fires, hunting prints
and lots of toby jugs and brasses, softly lit
back dining room with country-kitchen
furniture and big inglenook, red-tiled public
bar; piped music; picnic-sets on sloping
lawn, lots of flowers, bowling green
(Simon J Barber)
CONGLETON [SJ8663]
Beartown Tap CW12 1RL [Willow St (A54)]:
Tap for nearby Beartown small brewery, their
interesting beers well priced and perhaps a
guest microbrew, changing farm cider,
bottled belgians, bare boards in friendly
down-to-earth bar and two light and airy
rooms off, no food, games or music;
upstairs lavatories; open all day Fri-Sun
(Tony Hobden, Rob Stevenson, the Didler)
Castle CW12 3LP [Castle Inn Rd (A527 SE)]:
Attractive early 19th-c cottage-row
conversion, enjoyable if not cheap food, well
kept mainstream and other real ales, Tues
quiz night; children welcome in restaurant,
open all day *(Tony and Wendy Hobden)*
Queens Head CW12 3DE [Park Lane]: Friendly
licensees, good choice of well kept ales,
limited choice of basic food; by Macclesfield
Canal, steps up from towpath to large garden

with play area, bedrooms, open all day
(Tony and Wendy Hobden)
CREWE [SJ7055]
Angel CW1 2PU [Victoria Centre]: Surprising
basement pub with bargain Barnsley Bitter,
wide reasonably priced menu, good friendly
service, lively atmosphere, pool *(John Tav)*
Borough Arms CW1 2BG [Earle St]:
Interesting grown-up pub, recently
refurbished to incorporate a barber's, with
changing ales from its own microbrewery,
several good guest beers, belgian beers on
tap and dozens in bottle, friendly
enthusiastic landlord, two small rooms off
central bar; sports TV, no under-21s; tables
outside, has been cl wkdy lunchtimes
(the Didler, Selwyn Roberts, Rob Stevenson)
British Lion CW2 6AL [Nantwich Rd]: Snug
local known as the Pig, genuine and friendly,
with comfortable partly panelled bar, back
snug, well kept Tetleys and guest beers,
good friendly staff, darts; no food, cl wkdy
lunchtimes *(John Tav)*
DARESBURY [SJ5782]
Ring o' Bells WA4 4AJ [B5356, handy for
M56 junction 11]: Thriving Chef & Brewer
with wide choice of inexpensive food all day
from sandwiches, baguettes and baked
potatoes up, plenty of helpful young staff,
several real ales, lots of wines by the glass,
generous coffee, comfortable library-style
areas and part more suited to walkers (canal
is not far); children in eating areas, good
disabled access, plenty of tables in long
partly terraced garden, pretty village, church
with *Alice in Wonderland* window, open all
day *(LYM, Glenwys and Alan Lawrence,
Mrs Hazel Rainer, Mrs Phoebe A Kemp,
Mart Lawton, Dr and Mrs A K Clarke,
Frank and Chris Sharp)*
DAVENHAM [SJ6670]
Bulls Head CW9 8NA [London Rd]:
Picturesque old coaching inn, clean and
bright, with friendly helpful staff, changing
real ales, decent wines, several low-beamed
rooms, nicely placed tables, sympathetic
décor, interesting prints, small library under
stairs, upstairs dining room; back terrace
tables *(Mr and Mrs John Taylor)*
DELAMERE [SJ5667]
☆ **Fishpool** CW8 2HP [A54/B5152]: Popular for
food (very busy lunchtime), with good
service, real ales such as Tetleys and Wells &
Youngs, good relaxed atmosphere in four
small linked areas with bright china and
brasses; well behaved children allowed,
picnic-sets on peaceful lawn, good spot nr
pike-haunted lake and Delamere Forest, open
all day *(J Roy Smylie, LYM)*
DUDDON [SJ5164]
Headless Woman CW6 0EW [A51 NW of
Tarporley]: Neatly renovated beamed
country pub, smart minimalist contemporary
décor, sofas and logs in bar area, enjoyable
food (all day wknds) inc interesting light
dishes here and in nicely laid out
restaurant, games room *(Ann and
Tony Bennett-Hughes)*

DUTTON [SJ5779]
Tunnel Top WA4 4JY [Northwich Rd]: Former
Talbot Arms, getting its new name from
nearby air vent for Trent & Mersey Canal
tunnel, wide food choice all day, Coach
House Dick Turpin in distinct pubby bar
area well used by regulars *(Tony and
Wendy Hobden)*

FRODSHAM [SJ5177]
Helter Skelter WA6 6PN [Church St]:
Interesting well kept beers from small
breweries inc one brewed locally for the pub
from long counter on right, imported beers
too, wide range of freshly made imaginative
food (not Sun evening), neatly kept, airy
and comfortable, with tall stools, leaning-
post seating, window tables and raised back
area, real fire, upstairs restaurant Thurs-Sat;
open all day *(Tony Hobden, Lynne Carter,
J S Burn)*
Netherton Hall WA6 6UL [A56 towards
Helsby]: Large converted town-edge
farmhouse with good imaginative well
presented food all day, nice sandwiches after
2, friendly obliging service, changing real
ales such as Timothy Taylors Landlord, good
choice of wine by the glass, calm relaxed
atmosphere, 'library' room as seems so
popular in Cheshire; well behaved children
welcome, nice setting *(Pat and Tony Hinkins,
Alan and Eve Harding, Derek and
Sylvia Stephenson)*
☆ *Ring o' Bells* WA6 6BS [Bellemonte Rd,
Overton – off B5152 at Parish Church sign;
M56 junction 12 not far]: Charming early
17th-c pub in attractive spot, little rambling
rooms, antique seating and prints, beams,
dark oak panelling and stained glass,
friendly staff and cats, three changing real
ales from old-fashioned hatch-like central
servery, dozens of malt whiskies, good value
lunchtime bar food, games room; children in
eating areas, secluded back garden with
pond, colourful hanging baskets *(LYM,
Ann and Tony Bennett-Hughes)*

GAWSWORTH [SJ8869]
☆ *Harrington Arms* SK11 9RJ [Church Lane]:
Rustic 17th-c farm pub with two small basic
rooms (children allowed in one), bare boards
and panelling, fine carved oak bar counter,
Robinsons Best and Hatters Mild, friendly
new landlord, simple bar snacks such as pork
pies; Fri folk night; sunny benches on small
front cobbled terrace *(the Didler, LYM)*

GRAPPENHALL [SJ6386]
Parr Arms WA4 3EP [nr M6 junction 20; A50
towards Warrington, left after 1½ miles;
Church Lane]: Charming pub in picture-
postcard setting with tables out by church,
good friendly service, wide choice of
enjoyable home-made traditional food (all
day Fri-Sun) from sandwiches up, big
helpings and reasonable prices, well kept
Thwaites and a guest beer such as Marstons
Pedigree or Tetleys, several different areas
off central bar, bulldog pictures and
brassware *(Alan and Eve Harding,
Edward Mirzoeff, Julian and Janet Dearden)*

GREAT BUDWORTH [SJ6677]
George & Dragon CW9 6HF [signed off A559
NE of Northwich; High St]: Attractive and
unusual 17th/18th-c building in delightful
village, rambling panelled lounge, beams
hung with copper jugs, interesting old
pictures, red plush button-back banquettes
and older settles, three good changing ales
such as local Weetwood, farm cider, decent
coffee, sensibly priced bar food inc good Sun
lunch and (not Sun) two-for-one early
evening bargains, upstairs restaurant and
family dining area, back games room; open
all day Fri-Sun *(LYM, Tony Hobden)*

HANDLEY [SJ4657]
☆ *Calveley Arms* CH3 9DT [just off A41 S of
Chester]: Black and white beamed country
pub licensed since 17th c and thriving under
newish owners, good fresh home cooking
using local supplies, friendly efficient staff,
changing real ales, good wines by the glass
and nice soft drinks, open fire in appealing
attractively decorated old-world bar with
cosy alcove seating; tables in secluded
garden *(LYM, Jean and Douglas Troup,
Linda Fletcher)*

HELSBY [SJ4874]
☆ *Helsby Arms* WA6 0JE [Chester Rd (A56,
handy for M56 junction 14)]: Under new
management and freshly refurbished keeping
traditional pubby feel, welcoming young
staff, short daily-changing choice of good
value food inc popular Sun lunch, well kept
Black Sheep and three changing ales, good
wine choice, lovely log fire *(S Chambers,
Myke and Nicky Crombleholme, Pete Wright,
Jo Finley)*

HOLMES CHAPEL [SJ7667]
George & Dragon CW4 7EA [Middlewich Rd]:
Enjoyable pubby food inc good puddings,
helpful staff, well kept Robinsons, decent
house wines, choice of coffees, comfortable
and pleasantly decorated *(R S Talbot)*

KETTLESHULME [SJ9879]
☆ *Swan* SK23 7QU [Macclesfield Rd (B5470)]:
Delightful little traditional beamed 16th-c
pub run by consortium of locals inc former
main-entry landlord of Oddfellows in Mellor,
well kept Marstons and two interesting
changing guest beers, enjoyable food from
good lunchtime soup and sandwiches to very
popular Sun lunch with very rare beef and
other meats, log fires, old settles and pews,
Dickens prints; children welcome, garden
tables, good walks, cl Mon lunchtime, open
all day wknds *(Dennis Jones, Roger Yates,
Brian and Anna Marsden, Ian and Liz Rispin)*

KINGSLEY [SJ5574]
Red Bull WA6 8AN [The Brow]: Open-plan
village pub with half a dozen changing ales,
bar food (not Sun evening), Tues quiz night
(Tony and Wendy Hobden)

LACH DENNIS [SJ7072]
☆ *Duke of Portland* CW9 7SY [Holmes Chapel
Rd (B5082, off A556 SE of Northwich)]:
Stylish and relaxing country dining pub
locally very popular for beautifully presented
fresh traditional and more unusual food (all

day Sun) using good local supplies from interesting sandwiches and light lunches to splendid sticky toffee pudding, super chips made with local potatoes, young attentive helpful staff, four or more changing ales inc Marstons Pedigree and Weetwood, good choice of wines by the glass, daily papers, attractive L-shaped bar with leather seats and sofas and balustraded eating areas, little dance floor for special nights, Sun jazz nights; children welcome only till 6.30, open all day wknds *(Mr and Mrs John Taylor, Alun Jones, Mrs P J Carroll, Brian Scanlon, Jonathon Reed)*

Three Greyhounds WA16 9JY [B5082 Northwich rd off A50]: Enjoyable food and good service, getting to be more of a dining pub but still has a busy proper bar area, well supported Tues quiz night and live music most Weds *(Tom and Jill Jones)*

LANGLEY [SJ9471]

☆ *Leathers Smithy* SK11 0NE [off A523 S of Macclesfield, OS Sheet 118 map ref 952715]: Isolated pub up in fine walking country, well kept Theakstons Best, Timothy Taylors Landlord, Wells & Youngs Bombardier and a guest beer, lots of whiskies, may be winter glühwein, enjoyable bar food (all day Sun) from sandwiches up, good cheerful service, pleasant relaxing atmosphere, log fire, spotless flagstoned bar and carpeted dining room, interesting local prints and photographs; unobtrusive piped music; no dogs, picnic-sets in garden behind and on grass opposite *(LYM, David Crook, Edward Leetham)*

LITTLE BUDWORTH [SJ5867]

Cabbage Hall CW6 9ES [Forest Rd (A49)]: Smart new dining pub opened by restaurateur Francis Carroll (no relation to our recommender), handy for Cheshire Polo Club (has a helipad), good wines by the glass and top-drawer list, beautifully presented restaurant food, friendly staff, squashy sofas and plush chairs in bar still used by drinkers, thriving atmosphere; garden tables *(Mrs P J Carroll)*

LITTLE LEIGH [SJ6076]

Holly Bush CW8 4QY [A49 just S of A533]: Ancient timbered and thatched pub, good value food (all day wknds) in plush turkey-carpeted restaurant with courtyard tables, busy young staff, Tetleys and guest beers; good big play area, 13 bedrooms in converted back barn, open all day *(LYM, David Abbot)*

LOWER PEOVER [SJ7474]

Bells of Peover WA16 9PZ [just off B5081; The Cobbles]: Chef & Brewer in charming spot, lovely wisteria-covered building with plenty of old-fashioned character inside, panelling, antiques and good coal fire, well kept Timothy Taylors Landlord and Wells & Youngs Bombardier; piped music, no children now unless eating full meal in dining room; terrace tables and big side lawn with trees, rose pergolas and a little stream, on quiet cobbled lane opposite fine black and white 14th-c church, open all day *(Michael Dugdale, Revd D Glover, Rob Stevenson, Ann and Tony Bennett-Hughes, LYM, Stan and Hazel Allen, Revd Michael Vockins, the Didler, Dr Phil Putwain)*

Crown WA16 9QB [B5081, off A50]: Comfortable and attractive L-shaped bar with two rooms off, good food (all day Sun), fresh-cooked so can take a while, Boddingtons, Flowers, Greene King Old Speckled Hen, Timothy Taylors Landlord and two guest beers, quick friendly service, low beams and flagstones, lots of bric-a-brac inc interesting gooseberry championship memorabilia, darts and dominoes; tables outside, open all day Sun *(Tom and Jill Jones)*

LYMM [SJ6988]

Farmers Arms WA13 9RD [Rushgreen Rd (A6144 out towards Heatley)]: Large old-fashioned rambling pub with good value bar food, well kept Black Sheep and other ales, good sturdy tables *(Dave Braisted)*

☆ *Spread Eagle* WA13 0AG [not far from M6 junction 20; Eagle Brow (A6144, in centre)]: Big cheerful rambling beamed pub, charming black and white façade, good value home-made food all day from sandwiches and baguettes through two-course bargains to steaks, particularly well kept Lees Bitter and Red Dragon, good choice of wines, good service, comfortable two-level lounge, proper drinking area by central bar, coal fire, lots of brasses, separate games room with pool; piped music; attractive village, open all day *(BB, Pete Baker)*

MACCLESFIELD [SJ9272]

Hollins SK11 7JY [Black Rd, off A537 Buxton Rd]: Recently refurbished former Beehive, by Macclesfield Canal, with commendably short and simple choice of enjoyable food, Black Sheep, Caledonian Deuchars IPA and Courage Directors; children welcome, waterside garden and moorings *(Dr D J and Mrs S C Walker)*

Railway View SK11 7JW [Byrons Lane (off A523)]: Half a dozen or more unusual changing ales in pair of 1700 cottages knocked into roomy pub with attractive snug corners, farm cider, good value simple home-made food, friendly service; back terrace overlooking railway, remarkably shaped gents'; cl lunchtime Mon-Thurs and Sat, open all day Fri and Sun *(the Didler)*

Sutton Hall Hotel SK11 0HE [Leaving Macclesfield southwards on A523, turn left into Byrons Lane signposted Langley, Wincle, then just before canal viaduct fork right into Bullocks Lane; OS Sheet 118 map reference 925715]: Delightful building bought by Brunning & Price and cl until summer 2008 for total reworking; we would expect their usual combination of well prepared food, good drinks range and helpful service in a well thought out and attractive environment *(LYM)*

Waters Green Tavern SK11 6LH [Waters Green, opp stn]: Quickly changing and interesting largely northern real ales in roomy L-shaped open-plan local, home-made lunchtime food (not Sun), friendly staff and locals, back pool room; open all day *(the Didler)*

MARBURY [SJ5645]

☆ *Swan* SY13 4LS [NNE of Whitchurch]: Old-fashioned farmhouse pub doing well under present welcoming landlords, good fresh fairly priced food in roomy partly panelled lounge and pretty candlelit restaurant, good range of good value wines by the glass, local Woodlands ales, log fire in copper-canopied fireplace; venerable oak on green opposite, delightful village a half-mile's country walk from the Llangollen Canal, Bridges 23 and 24 *(LYM, John and Joyce Farmer, Liz Webster, Edward Leetham, John Goodison)*

MARTON [SJ8568]

Davenport Arms SK11 9HF [A34 N of Congleton]: Comfortable, roomy and tasteful, with good choice of freshly made food from ciabattas and baguettes up in bar and newly refurbished dining room inc their speciality venison and black pudding salad and good value Sun lunch, friendly obliging service, Courage Directors, Theakstons and a more or less local guest such as Copper Dragon, Storm or Weetwood; no dogs; nr ancient half-timbered church (and Europe's widest oak tree) *(Mrs P J Carroll)*

MOBBERLEY [SJ8079]

☆ *Bird in Hand* WA16 7BW [Knolls Green; B5085 towards Alderley]: Low-beamed traditional pub, cosy and well managed, with good plain honest fairly priced food, bargain Sam Smiths OB, lots of malt whiskies, decent house wines, linked rooms with comfortably cushioned heavy wooden seats, warm coal fires, small pictures on Victorian wallpaper, little panelled snug, good top dining area, pub games; children allowed, picnic-sets on pleasant sunny front terrace with awning, open all day *(Noel Grundy, Mrs P J Carroll, LYM, Dr Phil Putwain)*

☆ *Plough & Flail* WA16 7DB [Paddock Hill; small sign off B5085 towards Wilmslow]: Good atmosphere, light and airy, with impressive and enterprising home-made food (they even bake the biscuits for your coffee), lunchtime sandwiches too, attentive cheerful service, good wines by the glass, Bass and Boddingtons; children very welcome, good garden with play area *(UN, Mrs P J Carroll, Helen Cobb, P J and R D Greaves)*

MOULDSWORTH [SJ5170]

Goshawk CH3 8AJ [Station Rd (B5393)]: Comfortable family dining pub with masses of pictures and nice mix of largely pine furniture in extensive series of rooms, attentive young manager and uniformed staff, prompt service even when busy, enjoyable generous food from sandwiches to restauranty dishes using local supplies (all day wknds; free rail travel from Chester if you eat), enterprising wines by the glass, real ales such as Timothy Taylors Landlord

and Wells & Youngs Bombardier; piped music; good spot nr Delamere Forest with big outdoor area inc good play area and bowling green *(Tom and Jill Jones, Mr and Mrs A H Young)*

NANTWICH [SJ6452]

☆ *Black Lion* CW5 5ED [Welsh Row]: Three little rooms alongside main bar, old-fashioned nooks and crannies, beams, bare floors and timbered brickwork, big grandfather clock, coal fire; three local Weetwood ales and a guest beer, farm cider, may be cheap sandwiches; dogs welcome, open all day from 4 (1 Fri-Sun) *(the Didler, Rob Stevenson, Pete Baker, BB)*

Crown CW5 5AS [High St, free public parking behind]: Striking and attractively placed three-storey timbered Elizabethan hotel with overhanging upper galleries, cosy rambling beamed bar with antique tables and chairs on sloping creaky floors, enjoyable generous food from sandwiches and baked potatoes up inc evening italian restaurant dishes, well kept Boddingtons and Flowers IPA; busy wknd evenings, piped music, fruit machine and TV; children very welcome, open all day, comfortable bedrooms *(Dave Webster, Sue Holland, LYM)*

NESS [SJ3076]

Wheatsheaf CH64 4AP [Neston Rd]: Large Thwaites roadhouse overlooking Dee Estuary by Ness Gardens, sturdy comfortable furnishings in open-plan L-shaped bar with spacious alcoves, 1940s stained glass, cheerful family food from good value baguettes up, friendly staff; sports TVs, games; picnic-sets on lawn, play area, open all day *(Paul Humphreys)*

NESTON [SJ2976]

☆ *Harp* CH64 0TB [Quayside, SW of Little Neston; keep on along track at end of Marshlands Rd]: Tucked-away country local with new licensees, well kept changing ales such as Holts, Mallard Spittin' Feathers, Timothy Taylors Landlord and Titanic Iceberg, good malt whiskies, good value home-made wknd lunchtime food, woodburner in pretty fireplace, pale quarry tiles and simple furnishings (children allowed in room on right); picnic-sets up on grassy front sea wall look out over the Dee marshes to Wales, glorious sunsets with wild calls of wading birds; open all day *(Ann and Tony Bennett-Hughes, BB, Paul Humphreys, Dr Phil Putwain, MLR)*

Hinderton Arms CH64 7TA [Chester High Rd (A540)]: Large Chef & Brewer all-day dining pub, well divided and tastefully decorated, with friendly staff, Courage Directors, splendid choice of wines by the glass, sensibly priced soft drinks *(Paul Humphreys, Tom and Jill Jones)*

NORTHWICH [SJ6873]

Old Broken Cross CW9 7EB [Broken Cross (B5082 E); byTrent & Mersey Canal, Bridge 184]: Lively family pub/restaurant, hearty cheap food all day, Marstons and Greenalls, games room; children and dogs welcome, some waterside tables *(Tony and Wendy Hobden)*

Penny Black CW9 5AB [Witton St]: High-ceilinged Wetherspoons with black and white timbered façade, their usual beer and food range *(Tony and Wendy Hobden)*

OAKGROVE [SJ9169]

Fools Nook SK11 0JF [Leek Rd (A523 S of Macclesfield)]: Well refurbished by good new landlord (from the Hanging Gate in Langley), good plain country cooking, good choice of beers and wines, friendly staff; cottagey garden *(John and Barbara Hirst)*

PARKGATE [SJ2778]

Boathouse CH64 6RN [village signed off A540]: Black and white timbered pub with well spaced tables in several attractively refurbished linked rooms, friendly staff, good choice of good value wines, Tetleys, generous food from snack lunches to wider evening choice, popular Sun lunch, big conservatory with spectacular views to Wales over estuary and silted marshes *(Paul Humphreys)*

Ship CH64 6SA [The Parade]: Bow-window estuary views from long cheery bar of large hotel, good changing beer range, good value bar food inc local fish (and afternoon teas), quick pleasant service, open fire, restaurant; 24 bedrooms, open all day *(Paul Humphreys)*

PLUMLEY [SJ7275]

☆ *Golden Pheasant* WA16 9RX [Plumley Moor Lane (off A556 by the Smoker)]: Civilised, friendly and spacious, with well kept Lees Bitter and Mild and decent food in comfortable lounge areas, wider menu in roomy restaurant and conservatory, dark timbering of extensions blending well with older part; children welcome, spacious gardens inc play area and bowling green, good well equipped bedrooms *(LYM, Paul and Margaret Baker)*

☆ *Smoker* WA16 0TY [A556 S of M6 junction 19]: Attractive and spotless 16th-c pub with dark panelling, open fires in impressive period fireplaces, deep sofas as well as other comfortable seats in three linked areas, good choice of wines and whiskies, Robinsons and a guest ale, friendly staff helpful with special diets, food (all day Sun) from sandwiches up in bar and restaurant; piped music; children welcome, good-sized garden with good play area, open all day Sun *(LYM, Kay and Alistair Butler, Piotr Chodzko-Zajko, Mart Lawton, Alan Bulley)*

RAINOW [SJ9678]

☆ *Highwayman* SK10 5UU [A5002 Whaley Bridge—Macclesfield, NE of village]: Warmly welcoming 17th-c moorside pub with good value generous food from good sandwiches up, Thwaites Original and Lancaster Bomber, cosy low-beamed rooms with lovely log fires, plenty of atmosphere, grand views; open all day Thurs-Sun *(LYM, the Didler, Brian and Anna Marsden)*

RAVENSMOOR [SJ6250]

Farmers Arms CW5 8PR [Barracks Lane]: Popular dining pub, Timothy Taylors Landlord

and two seasonal beers, choice of wines by the glass, fresh home-made food, pool; tables outside *(Edward Leetham)*

RODE HEATH [SJ8057]

Broughton Arms ST7 3RU [Sandbach Rd (A533)]: By Trent & Mersey Canal, bar food, Burton Bridge and Marstons Pedigree, Tues quiz night; picnic-sets on heated terrace and waterside lawn *(Tony and Wendy Hobden)*

Royal Oak ST7 3RW [A533; a walk from Trent & Mersey Canal, Bridge 141/142]: Family all-day dining pub with wide choice inc OAP lunches and Tues evening bargains for two, big helpings, various areas off central bar inc back games room with sports TV, Greene King Abbot, Tetleys, Wells & Youngs Bombardier and three guest beers, plenty of brass, ornaments and pictures; outside tables with play area *(Tony Hobden)*

RUNCORN [SJ5081]

Prospect WA7 4LD [Weston Rd, Weston, just off A557 expressway]: Cains and four other good ales inc a Mild, good value standard food lunchtime and early evening and two open fires in two-bar village local with darts, dominoes, cribbage and pool in good public bar; tables outside, open all day *(Colin Boardman, Pete Baker)*

SPROSTON GREEN [SJ7366]

Fox & Hound CW4 7LW [very handy for M6 junction 18 – A54 towards Middlewich]: Attractive haven with low beams and varnished flagstones, welcoming service, decent food in bar and dining area, well kept real ale, open fire *(B and F A Hannam)*

STRETTON [SJ6282]

☆ *Stretton Fox* WA4 4NU [Spark Hall Cl, Tarporley Rd, just off M56 junction 10 exit roundabout]: Particularly good Vintage Inn in spaciously converted farmhouse, surprisingly rural setting, interesting variety of rooms pleasantly done in their usual faux-old style, generous well priced food, cheerful efficient young staff, real ales and good choice of wines *(Roger Noyes, Roger and Anne Newbury)*

STYAL [SJ8383]

Ship SK9 4JE [B5166 nr Ringway Airport]: Friendly helpful staff, good simple reasonably priced food (long wknd lunches); children welcome, seats out in front, attractive NT village, walks in riverside woods, open all day *(Mrs P J Carroll)*

SWETTENHAM [SJ7967]

☆ *Swettenham Arms* CW12 2LF [off A54 Congleton—Holmes Chapel or A535 Chelford—Holmes Chapel]: Attractive old country pub in pretty setting by scenic Quinta wildlife arboretum, imaginative choice of good food from sandwiches up in immaculate line of individually furnished rooms from sofas and easy chairs to dining area (must book Sun) with well spaced tables, fine range of well kept changing real ales, good wine choice, efficient friendly service, log fires; may have two evening sittings, 7.15 and 9.15; children welcome, picnic-sets on quiet side lawn, open all day Sun *(LYM, Brian and Anna Marsden, Selwyn Roberts, Mrs P J Carroll)*

TARPORLEY [SJ5562]

Crown CW6 0AT [High St]: Traditional family-run country inn, welcoming relaxed atmosphere, wide choice of hearty home cooking, real ales, good service, log fires, lots of pictures, conservatory, amiable pub dog called Duncan; dogs welcome, good walks, bedrooms *(Mrs Jane Kingsbury, Emma Goldstone)*

WHEELOCK [SJ7559]

Nags Head CW11 3RL [A534 Sandbach—Crewe]: Food (not Sat/Sun evenings) in comfortable bar or adjacent café-style eating area, well kept Coach House Honeypot; children and dogs welcome, secluded walled garden, good canalside and country walks, bedrooms *(Tony Hobden)*

WILDBOARCLOUGH [SJ9868]

Crag SK11 0BD: Straightforward old stone-built pub notable for its position in charming little sheltered valley below the moors (good walk up Shutlingsloe for great views), good basic fresh home cooking using local ingredients, well kept Worthington and a guest beer, help-yourself coffee; walkers welcome (boot covers available), tables on pretty terrace *(LYM, Maurice and Gill McMahon)*

Post Office address codings give the impression that some pubs are in Cheshire, when they're really in Derbyshire (and therefore included in this book under that chapter) or in Greater Manchester (see the Lancashire chapter).

Cornwall

This county has plenty of pubs of real character, run by hard-working licensees who manage to run tight ships even under huge pressure at peak holiday times. There's a good range of styles, too, from highly traditional fishermen's taverns to more contemporary food-oriented places – and this is mirrored in this year's interesting batch of new entries, all three pubs which have featured in the *Guide* some years ago, and which now return to it in their latest guise. These are the newly refurbished Gurnards Head Hotel, just a breezy stroll from the Atlantic and now with super food; the Ship in Mousehole, a well run, bustling local right by the pretty harbour; and the Kings Head in Ruan Lanihorne – good food and drink, tucked away down country lanes. Other pubs doing well this year include the Blisland Inn at Blisland (a fantastic range of real ales kept in tip-top condition), the Old Ferry at Bodinnick (simply furnished, and in a lovely spot by the Fowey river), the Halzephron near Helston (super landlady and a great place to stay), the Pandora at Mylor Bridge (an idyllic setting and plenty of character), the Port Gaverne Inn near Port Isaac (chatty and cheery bar with a good mix of customers), the Ship in Porthleven ('a treasure', say readers), Blue in Porthtowan (not a traditional pub, but a very popular and relaxed bar by a beautiful beach), the Eliot Arms at Tregadillett (lots of interesting things to see), and the bustling Old Ale House in Truro (a marvellous mix of customers, excellent cheap food and well kept ales). The Lucky Dip section at the end of the chapter has a particularly rich range of worthwhile pubs, a high proportion of them already inspected and approved by us. Current stars are the Napoleon in Boscastle, Queens Arms at Botallack (but it was up for sale as we went to press), Maltsters Arms at Chapel Amble, Smugglers Den at Cubert, Chain Locker in Falmouth, King of Prussia and Ship in Fowey, Fox & Hounds at Lanner, Bush at Morwenstow, Old Coastguard in Mousehole, London in Padstow, Cornish Arms at Pendoggett, Victoria at Perranuthnoe, Weary Friar at Pillaton, Sloop in St Ives, Rising Sun and Victory in St Mawes, Springer Spaniel at Treburley, New Inn at Veryan, Bay View at Widemouth, and Turks Head on St Agnes in the Isles of Scilly (its rather special owners have just retired, but we have high hopes of the new people there). Drinks prices in Cornwall are only a shade below the national average now. Sharps, Skinners and St Austell are the main local brewers, and one of these will usually be the lowest-price beer you'll find in any pub here; it's also worth looking out for the smaller local Organic beer. Pub food prices do tend to be a bit lower than the national average; if it's real quality you want, our choice as Cornwall Dining Pub of the Year is the Gurnards Head Hotel.

If you stay overnight in an inn or hotel, they are allowed to serve you an alcoholic drink at any hour of the day or night.

ALTARNUN

SX2083   MAP 1

Rising Sun 🍺

Village signposted off A39 just W of A395 junction; pub itself NW of village, so if coming instead from A30 keep on towards Camelford; PL15 7SN

Straightforward Bodmin pub with cheerful locals and decent food and beer

A new licensee has taken over this rustic pub on the edge of Bodmin Moor and the bedrooms have been upgraded and a restaurant added. But the low-beamed L-shaped main bar is still popular with friendly locals (with their dogs) and has plain traditional furnishings, bare boards and polished delabole slate flagstones, some stripped stone, guns on the wall and a couple of coal fires. Up to five real ales on handpump: Cotleigh Golden Eagle and Tawny, Flowers Original, Greene King IPA, Sharps Doom Bar and Skinners Betty Stogs. Pool, games machine, darts, juke box and piped music; they were searching for a bar billiards table as we went to press. Seats out on a terrace with more in the garden opposite. There's a field for camping screened off by high evergreens. The village itself (with its altarless church – hence the village name) is well worth a look.

🍴 **Bar food includes sandwiches, ploughman's, soup, potted pork and venison pâté with apple jelly, wild mushrooms on toast, omelettes, ham and eggs, bangers and mash with sage and onion gravy, cod in parsley sauce and daily specials; in the evening they offer a two- and three-course set menu.** *Starters/Snacks: £3.95 to £5.00. Main Courses: £7.95 to £12.00. Puddings: £3.95*

Free house ~ Licensee Andy Mason ~ Real ale ~ Bar food (restaurant closed Sun evening and Mon) ~ Restaurant ~ (01566) 86636 ~ Children welcome but may be restricted to certain times in restaurant ~ Dogs allowed in bar ~ Open 11-11; 12-10.30 Sun

Recommended by Dennis Jenkin, Lynda Bentley, Di and Mike Gillam, the Didler, P J Checksfield

BLISLAND

SX1073   MAP 1

Blisland Inn 🍺

Village signposted off A30 and B3266 NE of Bodmin; PL30 4JF

Super choice of real ales and beer-related memorabilia in welcoming local; home-made food, and cheerful service

Every inch of the beams and ceiling in this chatty and welcoming local is covered with beer badges (or their particularly wide-ranging collection of mugs), and the walls are similarly filled with beer-related posters and memorabilia. Up to eight real ales are kept at any one time, tapped from the cask or on handpump. Two are brewed for the pub by Sharps – King Buddha Blisland Special and Bulldog – and the other six come from all over the country and change constantly: 'You think of it, we will stock it,' says the landlord. They also have a changing farm cider, fruit wines, and real apple juice; service is cheerful and friendly. The carpeted lounge has a number of barometers on the walls, a rack of daily newspapers for sale, and a few standing timbers, and the family room has pool, table skittles, euchre, cribbage and dominoes; piped music. Plenty of picnic-sets outside. The popular Camel Trail cycle path is close by – though the hill up to Blisland is pretty steep. As with many pubs in this area, it's hard to approach without negotiating several single-track roads.

🍴 **Tasty, hearty home-made food includes filled lunchtime baguettes, lasagne, moussaka, leek and mushroom bake and various pies like rabbit or steak in ale.** *Starters/Snacks: £2.50 to £4.05. Main Courses: £4.25 to £7.95. Puddings: £3.75*

Free house ~ Licensees Gary and Margaret Marshall ~ Real ale ~ Bar food ~ (01208) 850739 ~ Children in family room only ~ Dogs welcome ~ Live music Sat evening ~ Open 11.30-11; 12-10.30 Sun

Recommended by Rona Murdoch, David Crook, R V T Pryor, Barry and Sue Pladdys, W F C Phillips, Dr and Mrs M W A Haward, Lynda Bentley, Andrea Rampley, Peter Meister, Pauline and Philip Darley, the Didler

BODINNICK   SX1352   MAP 1

Old Ferry

Across the water from Fowey; coming by road, to avoid the ferry queue turn left as you go down the hill – car park on left before pub; PL23 1LX

Bustling local across the water from Fowey, simple little rooms with nautical bits and pieces, and lots of summer customers

The position of this popular old inn is splendid and seats on the front terrace or from the homely little restaurant make the most of the pretty Fowey river views. Three simply furnished little rooms have quite a few bits of nautical memorabilia, a couple of half model ships mounted on the wall, and several old photographs, as well as wheelback chairs, built-in plush pink wall seats, and an old high-backed settle; there may be several friendly cats and a dog. The family room at the back is actually hewn into the rock; piped music and TV. Sharps Own and in summer, Sharps Coaster, on handpump, kept under light blanket pressure. The lane beside the pub, in front of the ferry slipway, is extremely steep and parking is limited, and some readers suggest parking in the public car park in Fowey and taking the small ferry to the pub. Lovely circular walks. Mobile phones are banned and a 50p fine goes to the RNLI.

🍴 **Bar food includes sandwiches, pasties, ploughman's, soup, home-cooked ham and egg, home-made steak, kidney and ale pie or chilli, cheese and broccoli pasta bake, daily specials, and puddings.** *Starters/Snacks: £4.00 to £6.50. Main Courses: £6.00 to £15.95. Puddings: £3.95 to £5.00*

Free house ~ Licensees Royce and Patricia Smith ~ Real ale ~ Bar food (12-3, 6-9; 12-2.30, 6.30-8.30 in winter) ~ Restaurant ~ (01726) 870237 ~ Children welcome ~ Dogs allowed in bar and bedrooms ~ Open 11-11; 12-10.30 Sun; closed 25 Dec ~ Bedrooms: £70S/£60(£75B)

Recommended by Roger Thornington, Mrs Margo Finlay, Jörg Kasprowski, Mayur Shah, David Crook, Phil and Sally Gorton, MB, Nick Lawless, Dave Webster, Sue Holland, Peter Salmon

CADGWITH   SW7214   MAP 1

Cadgwith Cove Inn

Down very narrow lane off A3083 S of Helston; no nearby parking; TR12 7JX

Fine walks in either direction from old-fashioned inn at the bottom of fishing cove

In summer, it might be best to park at the top of this charming village and walk down to the pub in its fishing cove setting – but it's a very steep hike up again. The two snugly dark front rooms have plain pub furnishings on their mainly parquet flooring, a log fire in one stripped stone end wall, lots of local photographs including gig races, cases of naval hat ribands and of fancy knot-work and a couple of compass binnacles. Some of the dark beams have ships' shields and others have spliced blue rope hand-holds. Flowers IPA, Sharps Doom Bar, Skinners Betty Stogs and maybe a guest on handpump. A plusher pink back room has a huge and colourful fish mural and the left-hand room has darts, euchre, and maybe piped music. A good-sized front terrace has green-painted picnic-sets, some under a fairy-lit awning, looking down to the fish sheds by the bay. Fine coastal walks in either direction.

🍴 **Bar food includes sandwiches (the crab are well liked), soup, lasagne, stilton and broccoli quiche, daily specials, and puddings; best to check food times in winter.** *Starters/Snacks: £4.10 to £6.95. Main Courses: £5.00 to £11.00. Puddings: £4.00*

Punch ~ Lease David and Lynda Trivett ~ Real ale ~ Bar food ~ (01326) 290513 ~ Children welcome away from main bar ~ Dogs allowed in bar ~ Open 12-3, 6-midnight; midday-1am Sat; 12-10.30 Sun ~ Bedrooms: £47.50S/£55(£75S)

Recommended by Derek and Heather Manning, Victoria Hatfield, Barry and Anne, Dave Webster, Sue Holland

---

Pubs with particularly interesting histories, or in unusually interesting buildings, are listed at the back of the book.

DULOE

Olde Plough House

B3254 N of Looe; PL14 4PN

Popular food in neat, communicating rooms, friendly service, and local beer and cider

The three communicating rooms in this neatly kept and friendly pub have lovely dark polished delabole slate floors, some turkey rugs, a mix of pews, modern high-backed settles and smaller chairs, foreign banknotes on the beams, and three woodburning stoves. The décor is restrained – prints of waterfowl and country scenes, copper jugs and a fat wooden pig perched on a window sill. There's a small more modern restaurant; piped music. Butcombe Bitter and Sharps Doom Bar on handpump, nine wines by the glass and local cider. Some picnic-sets out by the road. The friendly jack russells are both called Jack, and the cat Tia.

🍴 As well as lunchtime filled baguettes, pasties and ploughman's, the well liked bar food might include soup, local sausages, vegetable lasagne, home-cooked ham and egg, a daily roast and evening half roast duck with orange and Cointreau sauce, local fish, steak cooked on pre-heated grillstones and roast lamb rump with port sauce. *Starters/Snacks: £3.45 to £5.65. Main Courses: £8.25 to £14.95. Puddings: £3.75*

Free house ~ Licensees Gary and Alison Toms ~ Real ale ~ Bar food ~ Restaurant ~ (01503) 262050 ~ Children welcome away from main bar ~ Dogs allowed in bar ~ Open 12-2.30, 6.30-11; 12-2.30, 7-10.30 Sun; closed 25 Dec, evening 26 Dec

Recommended by Paul and Shirley White, Ray and Winifred Halliday, Nick Lawless, Julia and Richard Tredgett, John and Alison Hamilton, Lynda Bentley, John and Joan Calvert, P and J Shapley, Jacquie Jones, Mrs M N Grew

EGLOSHAYLE

Earl of St Vincent

Off A389, just outside Wadebridge; PL27 6HT

Lots of interest including 200 antique clocks in tucked away local

The summer flowering baskets and tubs outside this pretty pub are really quite a sight and you can enjoy them from picnic-sets in the lovely garden, too. There's plenty of interest inside – golfing memorabilia, art deco ornaments, all sorts of rich furnishings, and around 200 antique clocks, all in working order. St Austell HSD, Tinners and Tribute on handpump; piped music.

🍴 Bar food includes sandwiches, ploughman's, soup, mushroom and broccoli au gratin, ham and egg, fish dishes and grills. *Starters/Snacks: £2.50 to £7.50. Main Courses: £7.00 to £15.00. Puddings: £3.50 to £4.50*

St Austell ~ Tenants Edward and Anne Connolly ~ Real ale ~ Bar food (not Sun evening) ~ (01208) 814807 ~ Well behaved children allowed at lunchtime ~ Open 11-3, 6.30-11; 12-3, 7-10.30 Sun

Recommended by Mayur Shah, R V T Pryor, M A Borthwick, John Tyrle, Brian and Bett Cox, the Didler, Jacquie Jones

FALMOUTH

5 Degrees West ♀

Grove Place, by the main harbourside car park; TR11 4AU

Modern, airy open-plan bar with décor to match, a fine choice of drinks, enjoyable food, and friendly young staff

Of course this is not a traditional pub – it's a modern, light and airy bar with a relaxed and informal atmosphere and neatly dressed friendly young staff. There are several different areas, all open-plan with an expanse of stripped wood flooring: squashy sofas around low tables, some contemporary leatherette cushioned dining chairs around chunky pine tables, a few leather-topped high steel benches and stools dotted about (one table has a nice metal fish leg), and a log fire in a driftwood-effect fireplace. The artwork and photographs are local, there's lots of steel and etched glass, and good lighting. From the long bar counter they serve St Austell Tribute on handpump and bottle conditioned beers, 14 good wines by the glass (local ones and fizz), lots of coffees and teas, and hot chocolate with marshmallows and a flake. A back dining area is similar in style with long built-in side pews and a couple of little semi-open booths; doors lead to an attractive and sheltered back terraced area with picnic-sets under umbrellas. A side ramp gives good wheelchair access; disabled facilities. There's a useful short-term car park across the road by the marina.

🍽 **Popular food includes nibbles and tapas, filled toasted ciabattas, a local cheeseboard, soup, king prawns in thai butter, pork and apple sausages with cider and apple gravy, home-made vegetarian pancake, caribbean-style chicken, lambs liver and bacon with brandy cream sauce, cajun salmon, and puddings like hot chocolate sponge with chocolate sauce or gin and lemon sorbet.** *Starters/Snacks: £2.50 to £6.95. Main Courses: £7.95 to £12.95. Puddings: £2.50 to £4.50*

St Austell ~ Manager Justine Stockton ~ Real ale ~ Bar food (all day) ~ (01326) 311288 ~ Children welcome ~ Dogs welcome ~ Open 12-11.30pm (midnight Fri and Sat); 12-11 Sun; closed 25 Dec

Recommended by N Taylor, Dr and Mrs M E Wilson, Andy and Claire Barker

GURNARDS HEAD   SW4337   MAP 1

Gurnards Head Hotel 🍽 🛏

B3306 Zennor—St Just; TR26 3DE

CORNWALL DINING PUB OF THE YEAR

Interestingly renovated inn close to the sea with very good food and wine, and comfortable bedrooms

Back in the *Guide* after a 'spirited refurbishment', this handsome building is some 500 yards from the Atlantic in outstanding bleak National Trust scenery and surrounded by glorious walks – both inland and along the cliffy coast. The bar rooms are painted in bold, strong colours, there's an interesting mix of furniture, paintings by local artists, open fires, and an informal, friendly atmosphere. Skinners Betty Stogs and Heligan Honey and St Austell Tribute on handpump and up to ten wines by the glass from a carefully chosen list; piped music, darts and board games. Seats in the large garden behind and the comfortable bedrooms either have views of the rugged moors or of the sea. This is under the same ownership as the civilised Griffin at Felinfach (see our Wales chapter). Reports on the changes, please.

🍽 **Excellent food which may be eaten in either the bar, restaurant or garden might include at lunchtime home-made pork pie, cheese platter with home-made bread and home-made water biscuits, kippers and toast, proper sausages, beef stroganoff and various stews with evening dishes like salami and rillettes, cured beef with remoulade sauce, pilchards with herb crème fraîche, courgette and mint risotto, fish stew with aïoli, roast lamb rump with confit of new season's garlic, fillet of beef with béarnaise sauce, and puddings such as chocolate torte with clotted cream or tunisian orange cake.** *Starters/Snacks: £4.50 to £6.50. Main Courses: £6.50 to £11.00. Puddings: £4.50 to £5.50*

Free house ~ Licensee Charles Inkin ~ Real ale ~ Bar food (12.30-2.30, 6-9.30) ~ Restaurant ~ (01736) 796928 ~ Children welcome ~ Dogs allowed in bar and bedrooms ~ Guitar duo Mon evenings ~ Open 12-11 ~ Bedrooms: £45S/£82S

Recommended by Sue Demont, Tim Barrow, Darren and Kirstin Arnold

HELSTON   SW6522   MAP 1

Halzephron 🍷 🛏

Gunwalloe, village about 4 miles S but not marked on many road maps; look for brown sign on A3083 alongside perimeter fence of RNAS Culdrose; TR12 7QB

Book in advance to be sure of a table in popular, well run inn with lovely nearby walks; nice to stay in

Mrs Thomas continues to run a tight ship here. It's a lovely place and very popular but it does get packed at peak times so you must book to be sure of a table. Seating is comfortable, the rooms are neatly kept with copper on the walls and mantelpiece, and there's a warm winter fire in the big hearth. The family room is being refurbished. Organic Halzephron Gold (this local brewer supplies only organic beers), Sharps Special, Doom Bar and Wills Resolve, and St Austell Tribute on handpump, seven wines by the glass, and 40 malt whiskies; darts and board games. There are lots of fine surrounding unspoilt walks with views of Mount's Bay. Gunwalloe fishing cove is just 300 yards away, Church Cove with its sandy beach is a mile away, and the church of St Winwaloe (built into the dunes on the seashore) is also only a mile away, and well worth a visit.

🍽 **Popular bar food includes lunchtime sandwiches, platters of cheese, gammon and shellfish, tagliatelle bolognese and daily specials such as soup, smoked salmon pâté, spanish pork casserole, mushroom and nut stroganoff, thai cod with mussels and crayfish and caramelised duck breast with sweet cherry sauce.** *Starters/Snacks: £4.50 to £7.95. Main Courses: £8.50 to £17.00. Puddings: £3.50 to £5.25*

Free house ~ Licensee Angela Thomas ~ Real ale ~ Bar food ~ Restaurant ~ (01326) 240406 ~ Children in family room ~ Open 11-2.30, 6(6.30 winter)-11; 12-2.30, 6(6.30 in winter)-10.30 Sun ~ Bedrooms: £48B/£84B

Recommended by John and Joan Nash, Andrew Shore, Maria Williams, W M Paton, Derek and Heather Manning, John Brough, Colin and Alma Gent, Brian and Bett Cox, Sue Demont, Tim Barrow, Jacquie Jones, Andrea Rampley, Martin and Pauline Jennings, Matthew Hegarty, R V T Pryor, Paul Boot, Walter and Susan Rinaldi-Butcher, Barry and Anne, Roger Brown, Andy and Claire Barker, Dr Phil Putwain

LANLIVERY   SX0759   MAP 1

Crown 🍺

Signposted off A390 Lostwithiel—St Austell (tricky to find from other directions); PL30 5BT

Chatty atmosphere in nice old pub, old-fashioned rooms, and well liked food and drink; the Eden Project is close by

One of Cornwall's oldest pubs and at its liveliest in the evening, this is a proper old-fashioned place. The small, dimly lit public bar has heavy beams, a slate floor and a mix of tables and chairs, and there's an attractive alcove of seats in the dark former chimney. A much lighter room leads off, with beams in the white boarded ceiling, cushioned black settles, and a little fireplace with an old-fashioned fire; a small room is similarly furnished. Sharps Doom Bar and Atlantic IPA, and Skinners Betty Stogs on handpump, seven wines by the glass, and local cider; board games. The slate-floored porch room has lots of succulents and a few cacti and wood-and-stone seats, and at the far end of the restaurant is a sun room full of more plants, with tables and benches. Seats in the sheltered garden. The Eden Project is only 10 minutes away.

🍽 **Decent bar food includes lunchtime pasties and sandwiches as well as chicken liver pâté, caesar salad, steak in ale or apricot, mushroom and chestnut pies, braised shoulder of lamb, chicken with bacon, cheese and barbecue sauce, and steaks; puddings such as bread and butter pudding or lemon tart.** *Starters/Snacks: £2.95 to £7.95. Main Courses: £6.95 to £15.95. Puddings: £3.95 to £4.95*

Wagtail Inns ~ Licensee Andrew Brotheridge ~ Real ale ~ Bar food (12-2(3 in summer), 6.30(6 in summer)-9) ~ Restaurant ~ (01208) 872707 ~ Children welcome but must be away from bar ~ Dogs allowed in bar ~ Live music Sun lunchtime ~ Open 12-11; 12-10.30 Sun; 12-3, 6-11 in winter ~ Bedrooms: /£79.95S

Recommended by Jacquie Jones, Mrs Frances Pennell, Ron and Sheila Corbett, Ian Wilson, Paul Rampton, Ian Phillips, Tom and Rosemary Hall, R V T Pryor, P and J Shapley, Colin and Peggy Wilshire, Nick and Meriel Cox, R and S Bentley, B and M A Langrish, Brian and Bett Cox, P R Waights, Andy and Claire Barker, Dennis Jenkin, Mike and Mary Carter

LOSTWITHIEL   SX1059   MAP 1

Globe ♀ 🍺

North Street (close to medieval bridge); PL22 0EG

Unassuming bar in traditional local, interesting food and drinks and friendly staff; suntrap back courtyard with outside heaters

Just a stone's throw from the lovely, ancient river bridge, this traditional local is run by friendly licensees. The cheerfully relaxed and unassuming bar is long and somewhat narrow with a good mix of pubby tables and seats, customers' photographs on pale green plank panelling at one end, nice more or less local prints (for sale) on canary walls above a coal-effect stove at the snug inner end, and a small red-walled front alcove. The ornately carved bar counter, with comfortable chrome and leatherette stools, dispenses well kept Crouch Vale Brewers Gold, Fullers London Pride, Sharps Doom Bar and Skinners Betty Stogs from handpump, with 12 reasonably priced wines by the glass. Piped music, darts, board games and TV. The sheltered back courtyard, with a dogs' water bowl, is not large, but has some attractive and unusual pot plants, and is a real suntrap (with an extendable overhead awning, the first of its kind in the UK, and outside heaters).

🍴 As well as lunchtime snacks, the enjoyable bar food might include soup, scallops and bacon, confit of duck with honey, ginger and orange, venison sausages with red wine and juniper berry sauce, brie and redcurrant tart, a trio of local fish, pot-roasted shoulder of lamb, steak and stilton pie and thai chicken curry. *Starters/Snacks: £4.00 to £6.95. Main Courses: £7.95 to £16.95. Puddings: £3.50 to £4.50*

Free house ~ Licensee William Erwin ~ Real ale ~ Bar food ~ Restaurant ~ (01208) 872501 ~ Children welcome ~ Dogs allowed in bar ~ Cornish music Weds ~ Open 12-2.30, 6(7 Sun)-11(midnight Sat) ~ Bedrooms: /£70B

Recommended by PL, Evelyn and Derek Walter, Bob Monger, Dave Webster, Sue Holland

Royal Oak 🍺

Duke Street; pub just visible from A390 in centre – best to look out for Royal Talbot Hotel; PL22 0AG

A fine choice of bottled beers, real ales and tasty food in friendly town local

New licensees have taken over this friendly, busy town local but happily little seems to have changed. They keep a fine choice of bottled beers from around the world and Bass, Fullers London Pride, Sharps Doom Bar and a changing guest on handpump. The neat lounge is spacious and comfortable with captain's chairs and high-backed wall benches on its patterned carpet and a couple of wooden armchairs by the log-effect gas fire; there's also a delft shelf, with a small dresser in one inner alcove. The flagstoned and beamed back public bar has darts, fruit machines, TV, juke box and board games. On a raised terrace by the car park are some picnic-sets.

🍴 Tasty bar food includes sandwiches, soup, ploughman's, field mushrooms, bacon and goats cheese on toast, deep-fried haddock, pork chop with black pudding and apple sauce, steaks, and daily specials. *Starters/Snacks: £5.00 to £7.00. Main Courses: £7.00 to £18.00. Puddings: £4.00 to £6.00*

Punch ~ Lease Adam Bannister and Colin Phillips ~ Real ale ~ Bar food (12-2(2.30 Sun), 6(7 Sun)-9) ~ Restaurant ~ (01208) 872552 ~ Children welcome ~ Dogs allowed in bar ~ Open 11-11; 12-10.30 Sun ~ Bedrooms: £45B/£79.50B

Recommended by Ron and Sheila Corbett, Simon Fox, Dennis and Gill Keen, Mick and Moira Brummell, Ray and Winifred Halliday, Ian Phillips, Andy and Claire Barker, Colin and Peggy Wilshire, John and Pat Morris, Edward Mirzoeff, Dave Webster, Sue Holland, Mrs Angela Graham

---

Please keep sending us reports. We rely on readers for news of new discoveries, and particularly for news of changes – however slight – at the fully described pubs. No stamp needed: The Good Pub Guide, FREEPOST TN1569, Wadhurst, E Sussex TN5 7BR or send your report through our website: www.goodguides.co.uk

MITCHELL
SW8554 MAP 1

Plume of Feathers 🛏

Just off A30 Bodmin—Redruth, by A3076 junction; take the southwards road then turn first right; TR8 5AX

Light modern bars and quite a choice of daily specials in well run dining pub; comfortable bedrooms

This friendly and well run dining pub has appealing and contemporary bars with Farrow & Ball pastel-coloured walls, paintings by local artists, stripped old beams, painted wooden dado, and two fireplaces. Courage Directors, Sharps Doom Bar and a couple of guests like Greene King Ruddles County and Skinners Betty Stogs on handpump and several wines by the glass; piped music, games machine and TV. The well planted garden areas have plenty of seats and the bedrooms are comfortable.

🍴 As well as quite a choice of evening specials, bar food includes home-made italian bread with olive oil and balsamic vinegar, greek mezze, chicken liver parfait with spiced pear chutney, pasta with wild mushrooms, truffle oil and parmesan, aberdeen angus beefburger, confit duck leg with sherry vinegar dressing, and puddings such as sticky toffee pudding or raspberry and blueberry cheesecake. *Starters/Snacks: £2.25 to £5.50. Main Courses: £7.50 to £14.95. Puddings: £1.40 to £5.00*

Free house ~ Licensee Joe Musgrove ~ Real ale ~ Bar food (12-5, 6-10) ~ Restaurant ~ (01872) 510387/511125 ~ Children welcome but must be away from bar ~ Dogs allowed in bar and bedrooms ~ Open 10-midnight ~ Bedrooms: £48.75S(£56.25B)/£65S(£75B)

Recommended by Phil and Sally Gorton, Mrs B J Pugh, David Rule, Bernard Stradling, Dr and Mrs A K Clarke, M G Hart, Ian Wilson, Andy and Claire Barker, Michael and Maggie Betton, Will and Kay Adie, R V T Pryor, Dr Peter Andrews, Mrs Sheela Curtis, David Swift, John and Bettye Reynolds

MITHIAN
SW7450 MAP 1

Miners Arms

Just off B3285 E of St Agnes; TR5 0QF

Cosy pub with open fires in several smallish rooms and friendly staff

Several cosy little rooms and passages in this 16th-c pub are warmed by winter open fires, and the small back bar has an irregular beam and plank ceiling, a wood block floor and bulging squint walls (one with a fine old wall painting of Elizabeth I). Another small room has a decorative low ceiling, lots of books and quite a few interesting ornaments. Adnams Broadside, Bass, and Sharps Doom Bar on handpump; piped music, darts and board games. Seats outside on the back terrace with more on the sheltered front cobbled forecourt.

🍴 Served by friendly staff, the bar food includes lunchtime sandwiches, ploughman's, ham and egg, steak in ale pie, wild mushroom and courgette risotto, calves liver and bacon, steaks, and daily specials. *Starters/Snacks: £3.95 to £6.25. Main Courses: £8.95 to £16.95. Puddings: £4.95 to £5.95*

Punch ~ Lease Dyanne Hull and Chris Mitchell ~ Real ale ~ Bar food (12-3, 6-9; not Mon evenings in Jan and Feb) ~ Restaurant ~ (01872) 552375 ~ Children allowed until 9pm ~ Dogs allowed in bar ~ Open 12-midnight(1am Sat); 12-11.30 Sun

Recommended by Steve Harvey, Roger Brown, Mick and Moira Brummell, Michael Saunders, N Taylor, Dennis Jenkin, Lynda Bentley, Ted George, Andrea Rampley, Tim and Joan Wright

---

Stars after the name of a pub show exceptional quality. One star means most people (after reading the report to see just why the star has been won) would think a special trip worth while. Two stars mean that the pub is really outstanding – for its particular qualities it could hardly be bettered.

MOUSEHOLE   SW4626   MAP 1

Ship

Harbourside; TR19 6QX

Bustling harbourside local in lovely village

Run by friendly licensees, this is a bustling local just across the road from the harbour in
a lovely village. The opened-up main bar has black beams and panelling, built-in wooden
wall benches and stools around the low tables, photographs of local events, sailors' fancy
ropework, granite flagstones, and a cosy open fire; piped music. St Austell IPA, Tinners,
HSD and Tribute on handpump and several malt whiskies. The elaborate harbour lights at
Christmas are worth a visit; best to park at the top of the village and walk down (traffic
can be a bit of a nightmare in summer).

🍴 **Tasty bar food includes sandwiches, soup, steak and kidney pie, chargrilled vegetables
with pasta, fresh local fish dishes, and daily specials.** *Starters/Snacks: £3.95 to £5.95. Main
Courses: £5.95 to £13.50. Puddings: £4.25 to £4.95*

St Austell ~ Managers Colin and Jackie Perkin ~ Real ale ~ Bar food (12-3(2.30 in winter),
6-9(8.30 in winter); light snacks available all day) ~ Restaurant ~ (01736) 731234 ~ Children
welcome ~ Dogs allowed in bar ~ Occasional live music ~ Open 11-11.30; 11.30-11 Sun ~
Bedrooms: £40S/£65S

*Recommended by Alan Johnson, Pete Walker, Julie Russell-Carter, Michael B Griffith, Bruce and Penny Wilkie,
David Gunn, Stuart Turner, Colin Gooch, JCW*

MYLOR BRIDGE   SW8137   MAP 1

Pandora ★★ ♀

*Restronguet Passage: from A39 in Penryn, take turning signposted Mylor Church, Mylor
Bridge, Flushing and go straight through Mylor Bridge following Restronguet Passage signs;
or from A39 further N, at or near Perranarworthal, take turning signposted Mylor,
Restronguet, then follow Restronguet Weir signs, but turn left down hill at Restronguet
Passage sign; TR11 5ST*

**Beautifully placed waterside inn with seats on long floating pontoon, low-ceilinged
beamed and flagstoned rooms; maybe afternoon teas as well as bar food**

The position of this lovely medieval thatched pub is very special, and in fine weather you
can sit with your drink on the long floating pontoon and watch children crabbing and
visiting dinghies pottering about in the sheltered waterfront. Inside, the several
rambling, interconnecting rooms have low wooden ceilings (mind your head on some of
the beams), beautifully polished big flagstones, cosy alcoves with leatherette benches
built into the walls, old race posters, model boats in glass cabinets, and three large log
fires in high hearths (to protect them against tidal floods). St Austell HSD, Tinners and
Tribute on handpump, and a dozen wines by the glass. It does get very crowded and
parking is difficult at peak times.

🍴 **Popular bar food includes lunchtime sandwiches (the crab is well liked) and filled
baked potatoes, as well as soup, local mussels and sausages, crab cakes, pasta with
spinach and mushrooms with sun-dried tomatoes, beer-battered cod, chicken with white
bean cassoulet, smoked bacon and basil pesto, and puddings like warm coconut, lemon
and treacle tart or sugar-glazed banana brûlée; maybe afternoon teas.** *Starters/Snacks:
£4.25 to £7.95. Main Courses: £9.50 to £14.95. Puddings: £4.75 to £5.25*

St Austell ~ Tenant John Milan ~ Real ale ~ Bar food (12-3, 6.30-9) ~ Restaurant ~
(01326) 372678 ~ Children welcome away from bar area ~ Dogs allowed in bar ~ Jazz winter
Sun, quiz Weds ~ Open 10am-midnight; 10.30am-11pm in winter

*Recommended by Neil Whitehead, Victoria Anderson, Martin Hann, David Rule, R V T Pryor, Steve Harvey,
Dennis Jenkin, Gary Rollings, Bruce and Sharon Eden, Dr and Mrs M E Wilson, Colin and Alma Gent, the Didler,
Peter Johnson, Neil and Anita Christopher, Andrea Rampley, David Crook, Andy and Claire Barker, Julie Russell-
Carter, Paul and Shirley White, M Bryan Osborne*

PENZANCE   SW4730   MAP 1

Turks Head

At top of main street, by big domed building (Lloyds TSB), turn left down Chapel Street;
TR18 4AF

**Cheerfully run pub, the oldest in town, with a good, bustling atmosphere, and decent food
and beer**

Locals and holiday-makers mix happily in this relaxed and friendly old pub. The bustling
bar has old flat irons, jugs and so forth hanging from the beams, pottery above the
wood-effect panelling, wall seats and tables, and a couple of elbow-rests around central
pillars; piped music. Adnams Broadside, Sharps Doom Bar, Skinners Betty Stogs,
Wadworths 6X, and maybe a guest on handpump; helpful service. The suntrap back garden
has big urns of flowers. There has been a Turks Head here for over 700 years – though
most of the original building was destroyed by a Spanish raiding party in the 16th c.

🍴 **Bar food includes lunchtime sandwiches, baguettes and filled baked potatoes, soup, a
pie of the day, sizzler dishes and white crabmeat salad.** *Starters/Snacks: £3.75 to £6.95.
Main Courses: £6.95 to £15.45. Puddings: £3.95 to £4.95*

Punch ~ Lease Jonathan and Helen Gibbard ~ Real ale ~ Bar food (12-2.30, 6-10) ~ Restaurant
~ (01736) 363093 ~ Children welcome ~ Dogs allowed in bar ~ Open 10.30-midnight; 12-11
Sun; 11-3, 5.30-11 in winter

*Recommended by Bruce and Penny Wilkie, Andrea Rampley, Clifford Blakemore, Alan Johnson, Paul and
Shirley White*

PERRANWELL   SW7739   MAP 1

Royal Oak ♀

Village signposted off A393 Redruth—Falmouth and A39 Falmouth—Truro; TR3 7PX

**Welcoming and relaxed with quite an emphasis on well presented food, and thoughtful
wines**

With friendly staff and a gently upmarket and relaxed atmosphere, this pretty and quietly
set stone-built village pub remains a popular place for a meal or a drink. The roomy,
carpeted bar has horsebrasses and pewter and china mugs on its black beams and joists,
plates and country pictures on the cream-painted stone walls, and cosy wall and other
seats around candlelit tables. It rambles around beyond a big stone fireplace (with a
good log fire in winter) into a snug little nook of a room behind, with just a couple more
tables. Bass, Sharps Special and Skinners Betty Stogs on handpump from the small
serving counter, good wines by the glass and cocktails; piped music, shove-ha'penny and
board games. There are tables out in front and in a secluded canopied garden.

🍴 **Well presented, interesting bar food includes a tapas board, sandwiches, fried scallops
and chorizo in saffron cream, smoked salmon and crayfish gateau, teriyaki chicken, beer-
battered cod, seafood linguini, gressingham duck breast with summer fruit sauce, and
daily specials.** *Starters/Snacks: £3.50 to £6.75. Main Courses: £9.50 to £14.95. Puddings: £2.25
to £4.95*

Free house ~ Licensee Richard Rudland ~ Real ale ~ Bar food (12-2.30, 7-9.30) ~ Restaurant ~
(01872) 863175 ~ Children in dining areas only ~ Dogs allowed in bar ~ Open 11-3,
6-midnight; 12-3.30, 6-11 Sun

Recommended by J K and S M Miln, R V T Pryor, Julie Russell-Carter, David Gunn

---

If a service charge is mentioned prominently on a menu or accommodation terms, you
must pay it if service was satisfactory. If service is really bad, you are legally
entitled to refuse to pay some or all of the service charge as compensation
for not getting the service you might reasonably have expected.

POLKERRIS   SX0952   MAP 1

Rashleigh

Signposted off A3082 Fowey—St Austell; PL24 2TL

Popular pub by splendid beach with outside heaters on sizeable sun terrace, and well liked food and beer

In fine weather you can really make the best of this pub's lovely position. There's a front sun terrace with seats under the big heated awning and views towards the far side of St Austell and Mevagissey bays and a splendid beach with restored jetty that's only a few steps away. Inside, the bar is cosy and the front part has comfortably cushioned seats and between three and six real ales on handpump: Otter Bitter, Sharps Doom Bar and Timothy Taylors and perhaps guests such as Doghouse Seadog, Skinners Figgys Brew and Wooden Hand Cornish Mutiny. A couple of farm ciders and several wines by the glass. The more basic back area has local photographs on the brown panelling and a winter log fire. There's plenty of parking either at the pub's own car park or the large village one. This whole section of the Cornish Coast Path is renowned for its striking scenery.

🍴 **Changing frequently, bar food includes sandwiches, crab and prawn cocktail, fried mushrooms stuffed with pâté, steak in ale or fish pies, chicken curry, vegetable korma, beer-battered cod, duck breast in orange and Grand Marnier sauce, and puddings like apple, rhubarb and ginger crumble or Baileys crème brûlée.** *Starters/Snacks: £3.60 to £5.75. Main Courses: £5.95 to £15.50. Puddings: £3.50 to £4.25*

Free house ~ Licensees Jon and Samantha Spode ~ Real ale ~ Bar food (12-2, 6-9; cream teas and snacks during the afternoon) ~ Restaurant ~ (01726) 813991 ~ Children welcome ~ Piano player Sat evening ~ Open 11-11; 12-10.30 Sun

Recommended by Bob and Margaret Holder, Gary Rollings, Mayur Shah, Meg and Colin Hamilton, Edward Mirzoeff, Andrew York, Rob Stevenson, the Didler, Darren and Kirstin Arnold, Andy and Claire Barker, David Crook, Colin and Peggy Wilshire, Dave Webster, Sue Holland, Conor McGaughey

POLPERRO   SX2050   MAP 1

Blue Peter

Quay Road; PL13 2QZ

Hard-working licensees in friendly pub overlooking pretty harbour, fishing paraphernalia, and paintings by local artists

In a picturesque village with a pretty working harbour, this bustling little pub is run by friendly licensees. The cosy low-beamed bar has fishing regalia and photographs and pictures by local artists for sale on the walls, traditional furnishings including a small winged settle and a polished pew on the wooden floor, candles everywhere, a solid wood bar counter, and a simple old-fashioned local feel despite being in such a touristy village. One window seat looks down on the harbour, another looks out past rocks to the sea. St Austell Tribute and a couple of guest beers on handpump and local cider. A few seats outside on the terrace and more in an upstairs amphitheatre-style area. The pub is quite small, so it does get crowded at peak times.

🍴 **Enjoyable bar food includes filled baguettes (the crab is popular), tempura-battered fresh cod, vegetable medley, chicken curry, seafood stew, pies such as steak and plum or lamb and pear, and Sunday roasts.** *Starters/Snacks: £3.95 to £6.95. Main Courses: £5.95 to £11.95. Puddings: £3.50*

Free house ~ Licensees Steve and Caroline Steadman ~ Real ale ~ Bar food ~ (01503) 272743 ~ Children in upstairs family room ~ Dogs welcome ~ Live music in summer ~ Open 11-midnight; 11-11 Sun

Recommended by Rob Stevenson, the Didler, Mrs Margo Finlay, Jörg Kasprowski, John and Joan Calvert, Dr and Mrs M E Wilson, Jonathan Brown

PORT ISAAC

SX0080 MAP 1

Port Gaverne Inn ♀ 🛏

Port Gaverne signposted from Port Isaac, and from B3314 E of Pendoggett; PL29 3SQ

Lively bar with plenty of chatty locals in popular small hotel close to sea and fine cliff walks

There's always a good bustling atmosphere and a happy mix of locals and visitors in the bar of this 17th-c inn, set just back from the sea. As well as big log fires, this room has low beams, flagstones as well as carpeting, some exposed stone, and genuinely helpful, friendly staff. In spring, the lounge is usually filled with pictures from the local art society's annual exhibition, and at other times there are interesting antique local photographs. You can eat in the bar or the 'Captain's Cabin' – a little room where everything is shrunk to scale (old oak chest, model sailing ship, even the prints on the white stone walls. St Austell Tribute, Sharps Doom Bar and Cornish Coaster and a guest beer on handpump, a good wine list and several whiskies; cribbage and dominoes. There are seats in the terraced garden and splendid clifftop walks all around.

🍴 **Bar food includes sandwiches, crab soup, chicken liver pâté, ploughman's with home-made rolls, ham and eggs, roasted mediterranean vegetable lasagne, fishcakes, local crab salad (in season), more elaborate evening choices, and puddings.** *Starters/Snacks: £4.00 to £7.00. Main Courses: £6.00 to £14.00. Puddings: £4.95*

Free house ~ Licensee Graham Sylvester ~ Real ale ~ Bar food ~ Restaurant ~ (01208) 880244 ~ Children allowed away from bar area ~ Dogs allowed in bar and bedrooms ~ Open 11-11; 12-10.30 Sun ~ Bedrooms: £60B/£100B

Recommended by Darren and Kirstin Arnold, Bob and Margaret Holder, Peter and Margaret Glenister, David Tindal, John and Gloria Isaacs, John and Alison Hamilton, Geoff and Brigid Smithers, Adrian Johnson, R G Glover, Theo, Anne and Jane Gaskin, Peter Salmon, Betsy Brown, Nigel Flook, David J Cooke, Conor McGaughey

PORTHLEVEN

SW6225 MAP 1

Ship

Village on B3304 SW of Helston; pub perched on edge of harbour; TR13 9JS

Fisherman's pub built into cliffs, fine harbour views from seats on terrace, and tasty bar food

From seats inside this friendly old fisherman's pub – it is actually built into the steep cliffs – you can watch the sea only yards away from the window as it pounds the harbour wall. There are tables out in the terraced garden that make the most of the view too, and at night the harbour is interestingly floodlit. The knocked-through bar has a relaxed atmosphere, welcoming log fires in big stone fireplaces and some genuine individuality. The family room is a conversion of an old smithy with logs burning in a huge open fireplace; piped music, games machine, cards and dominoes. The candlelit dining room also looks over the sea. Courage Best and Sharps Doom Bar and a couple of summer guests on handpump.

🍴 **Good bar food includes sandwiches or toasties, tasty crab soup, ploughman's, smoked fish platter, chicken tikka masala, mediterranean vegetable bake, home-made chilli, minted lamb casserole, local crab claws (when available), steaks, and puddings like syrup sponge or treacle tart.** *Starters/Snacks: £3.10 to £6.75. Main Courses: £9.95 to £20.95. Puddings: £4.50 to £4.95*

Free house ~ Licensee Colin Oakden ~ Real ale ~ Bar food ~ (01326) 564204 ~ Children in family room only ~ Dogs allowed in bar ~ Open 11.30-11; 12-10.30 Sun

Recommended by Stuart Turner, the Didler, Andrea Rampley, Lynda Bentley, Michael Saunders, Derek and Heather Manning, Barry and Anne, Dr and Mrs Ellison, Clifford Blakemore, Paul and Shirley White, Andy and Claire Barker, Theo, Anne and Jane Gaskin, Gary Rollings

PORTHTOWAN   SW6948   MAP 1

Blue

Beach Road, East Cliff; use the car park (fee in season), not the slippy sand; TR4 8AW

Informal, busy bar – not a traditional pub – right by wonderful beach with modern food and drinks, and lively staff and customers

---

Despite not serving real ale and by no means a traditional pub, this light and airy bar is much enjoyed by our readers. There's a really easy, informal atmosphere and a genuinely interesting range of customers (and dogs) of all ages and as it's right by a fantastic beach – huge picture windows look across the terrace to the huge expanse of sand and sea – it tends to be busy all year. The front bays have built-in pine seats and throughout are chrome and wicker chairs around plain wooden tables on the stripped wood floor, quite a few high-legged chrome and wooden bar stools, and plenty of standing space around the bar counter; powder blue painted walls, ceiling fans, some big ferny plants, two large TVs showing silent surfing videos, and fairly quiet piped music; pool table. Quite a few wines by the glass, cocktails and shots, and giant cups of coffee; perky, helpful young staff.

🍴 **Good modern bar food includes lunchtime filled baps, soup, caramelised leek and brie tartlet, mezze platter to share, home-made burger, butternut squash, apple and cheddar gratin, cajun chicken, nice pizzas, chargrilled local sardines with lemon and chive mayonnaise, daily specials, and puddings like hot chocolate brownie with chocolate cream or apple and cinnamon crumble.** *Starters/Snacks: £4.00 to £5.50. Main Courses: £7.50 to £12.50. Puddings: £4.00 to £5.50*

Free house ~ Licensees Tara Roberts, Luke Morris and Alexandra George ~ Bar food (12-3, 6-9; 10-4, 6-9 weekends) ~ Restaurant ~ (01209) 890329 ~ Children welcome ~ Dogs welcome ~ Live bands Sat evening and jazz last Sun evening of month ~ Open 11-11; 10-midnight Sat; 10-10.30pm Sun; closed all Jan

Recommended by Tim and Ann Newell, Dr R A Smye, Andy Sinden, Louise Harrington, David Crook, Andy and Claire Barker, Steve Pocock

RUAN LANIHORNE   SW8942   MAP 1

Kings Head

Off A3078; TR2 5NX

Friendly country pub with good popular food and beer, and welcoming licensees

---

Down country lanes in a pleasant out-of-the-way village, this neatly kept and attractive pub is run by friendly licensees. The bustling bar has beams, a winter roaring fire, a mix of seats including a comfortable sofa, and a relaxed atmosphere. Skinners Betty Stogs, Cornish Knocker and a beer named for the pub on handpump, and several wines by the glass; piped music. Seats in the suntrap, sunken garden with outside heaters for chillier evenings, and views down over the pretty convolutions of the River Fal's tidal estuary.

🍴 **Good bar food includes sandwiches, ploughman's, soup, garlic tiger prawns, herb-crusted marinated salmon, a trio of local sausages with red onion marmalade, home-made pesto pasta, roast lamb rump with plum and rosemary sauce, roast duckling with quince sauce, daily specials, and puddings like orange and chocolate mousse pot or hot apple and gingerbread pudding.** *Starters/Snacks: £4.60 to £6.80. Main Courses: £7.95 to £13.75. Puddings: £4.50*

Free house ~ Licensees Andrew and Niki Law ~ Real ale ~ Bar food (12.30-2, 6.30-9; not Sun evening or winter Mon) ~ Restaurant ~ (01872) 501263 ~ Children welcome away from bar area ~ Dogs allowed in bar ~ Open 12-2.30, 6-11; 12-2.30, 7-10.30 Sun; closed Mon in winter

Recommended by Michael Saunders, M Bryan Osborne, Jennifer Sheridan, Christopher Wright, Guy Vowles, Andrew Clive, Richard Hussey

---

Please let us know what you think of a pub's bedrooms. No stamp needed:
The Good Pub Guide, FREEPOST TN1569, Wadhurst, E Sussex TN5 7BR.

SENNEN COVE   SW3526   MAP 1

Old Success
Off A30 Land's End road; TR19 7DG

Looking over Whitesands Bay and close to Land's End, with lifeboat memorabilia in unpretentious bar

From seats in the terraced garden or from inside this traditional seaside hotel, there are smashing views over Whitesands Bay; Land's End is a pleasant walk away. The unpretentious beamed and timbered bar has plenty of lifeboat memorabilia, including an RNLI flag hanging on the ceiling; elsewhere are ship's lanterns, black and white photographs, dark wood tables and chairs, and a big ship's wheel that doubles as a coat stand. The restaurant has been refurbished this year. A couple of real ales from Sharps and Skinners on handpump; piped music, TV and darts. Bedrooms are basic but comfortable, enjoying the sound of the sea, and they have four self-catering flats. It does get crowded at peak times.

🍴 **Straightforward bar food includes sandwiches, local pasties, filled baked potatoes, ploughman's, gammon and pineapple, steak and kidney pie, lasagne, beer-battered cod, daily specials, and puddings such as chocolate fudge cake.** *Starters/Snacks: £3.95 to £5.95. Main Courses: £6.95 to £15.00. Puddings: £3.50 to £4.50*

Free house ~ Licensee Martin Brooks ~ Real ale ~ Bar food (all day school summer hols) ~ Restaurant ~ (01736) 871232 ~ Children welcome ~ Dogs allowed in bar ~ Live music some Sat evenings ~ Open 11-11; 11.30-10.30 Sun ~ Bedrooms: £35(£45B)/£90B

Recommended by Julie Russell-Carter, Gaynor Gregory, Matthew Hegarty, Paul Goldman, Andy and Claire Barker, J and D Waters, Roger Brown

ST KEW   SX0276   MAP 1

St Kew Inn
Village signposted from A39 NE of Wadebridge; PL30 3HB

Grand-looking pub with neat bars and big garden

The neatly kept bar in this rather grand-looking old stone building has winged high-backed settles and varnished rustic tables on the lovely dark delabole flagstones, black wrought-iron rings for lamps or hams hanging from the high ceiling, and a handsome window seat; there's also an open kitchen range under a high mantelpiece decorated with earthenware flagons. St Austell HSD, Tinners and Tribute tapped from wooden casks behind the counter (lots of tankards hang from the beams above it), a couple of farm ciders and several malt whiskies. The big garden has seats on the grass and picnic-sets on the front cobbles.

🍴 **Bar food includes sandwiches, pasties, ploughman's, filled baked potatoes, mushroom risotto, lasagne, fish or steak and kidney pies, steaks, and puddings.** *Starters/Snacks: £4.25 to £6.50. Main Courses: £9.00 to £14.00. Puddings: £4.25 to £4.50*

St Austell ~ Tenant Justin Mason ~ Real ale ~ Bar food ~ (01208) 841259 ~ Children in dining room ~ Open 11-2.30, 5-11(all day July and Aug); 12-3, 7-10.30(all day in July and Aug) Sun

Recommended by M Bryan Osborne, Andrea Rampley, Michael B Griffith, Tony Allwood, Geoff and Brigid Smithers, Mick and Moira Brummell, M A Borthwick, Ian Wilson, the Didler, David Rule, Barry and Sue Pladdys, Conor McGaughey

ST MAWGAN

Falcon

NE of Newquay, off B3276 or A3059; TR8 4EP

Peaceful garden by old stone inn, log fires, falcon pictures, and popular food

Popular locally, the neatly kept big bar in this wisteria-clad old stone inn has a log fire, large antique coaching prints and falcon pictures on the walls, and St Austell HSD, Tinners, and Tribute on handpump; piped music, darts and pool. There are seats on the front cobbled courtyard and more in a peaceful garden with a wishing well. The bedrooms have been refurbished. This is a pretty village.

🍴 **Lunchtime bar food includes filled baguettes and baked potatoes, soup, seafood and broccoli mornay, ham and egg, steak, stilton and mushroom pie, and vegetarian pasta, with evening choices like chilli or curry, speciality sausages, and wild mushroom and stilton moussaka.** *Starters/Snacks: £3.95 to £6.25. Main Courses: £7.75 to £15.95. Puddings: £3.95 to £5.50*

St Austell ~ Manager Andy Marshall ~ Real ale ~ Bar food (12-2.30(2 winter Sun, 6-9.30)) ~ Restaurant ~ (01637) 860225 ~ Children welcome ~ Dogs allowed in bar ~ Open 11am-midnight; 12-midnight Sun; 11-3, 6-midnight weekdays and 12-5, 7-11 Sun in winter ~ Bedrooms: /£78S(£88B)

Recommended by R V T Pryor, David Eberlin, Andrew Curry, Theo, Anne and Jane Gaskin, Mr and Mrs A J Hudson, Brian and Bett Cox, Rona Murdoch, David Crook

TREGADILLETT

Eliot Arms

Village signposted off A30 at junction with A395, W end of Launceston bypass; PL15 7EU

Fantastic collection of antique clocks and snuffs in creeper-covered pub

The series of small rooms in this friendly, creeper-covered inn are full of interest: 72 antique clocks (including seven grandfathers), 400 snuffs, hundreds of horsebrasses, old prints, old postcards or cigarette cards grouped in frames on the walls, quite a few barometers, and shelves of books and china. Also, a fine old mix of furniture on the delabole slate floors, from high-backed built-in curved settles, through plush Victorian dining chairs, armed seats, chaise longues and mahogany housekeeper's chairs, to more modern seats, and open fires. Courage Best, Sharps Doom Bar and a guest like Fullers London Pride on handpump; piped music, games machine and darts. There are seats in front of the pub and at the back of the car park.

🍴 **Enjoyable bar food under the new licensee includes soup, whitebait, chargrilled burgers, ham and egg, a pie and a curry of the day, spinach and mushroom lasagne, lamb chops with mint sauce, steaks, combo meals, and daily specials.** *Starters/Snacks: £2.95 to £5.50. Main Courses: £5.95 to £15.95. Puddings: £3.95*

S&N ~ Lease Chris Hume ~ Real ale ~ Bar food ~ Restaurant ~ (01566) 772051 ~ Children in front two bars ~ Dogs allowed in bar ~ Open 11.30-11(midnight Sat); 12-10.30 Sun; 11.30-3, 5-midnight in winter ~ Bedrooms: £45B/£70S(£65B)

Recommended by the Didler, Jude Wright, George A Rimmer, Michael Saunders, Roger Thornington, John Urquhart, Chris Glasson, John Evans, Colin and Alma Gent, Nick Lawless, Peter Salmon, Rod and Chris Pring, Pauline and Philip Darley, Betsy and Peter Little, Paul Goldman, Sue Demont, Tim Barrow

---

'Children welcome' means the pub says it lets children inside without any special restriction. If it allows them in, but to restricted areas such as an eating area or family room, we specify this. Places with separate restaurants often let children use them, hotels usually let them into public areas such as lounges.
Some pubs impose an evening time limit – let us know if you find this.

TRESCO

SV8815 MAP 1

New Inn ♀ 🍺 🛏️

New Grimsby; Isles of Scilly; TR24 0QG

Close to quay and very attractive with chatty bar and light dining extension, enjoyable food and drinks, and sunny terrace

---

Once a row of fishermen's cottages and handy for the quay and ferries, this neat and attractive inn does get very busy in high season. There is a little locals' bar but visitors tend to head for the main bar room or the light, airy dining extension: comfortable old sofas, banquettes, planked partition seating, and farmhouse chairs and tables, a few standing timbers, boat pictures, a large model sailing boat, a collection of old telescopes, and plates on the delft shelf. The Pavilion extension has cheerful yellow walls and plenty of seats and tables on the blue wooden floors and looks over the flower-filled terrace with its teak furniture, huge umbrellas and views of the sea. Ales of Scilly Natural Beauty, St Austells Tribute and Skinners Betty Stogs and Tresco Tipple on handpump, interesting wines by the glass and several coffees; piped music, darts, pool, and board games.

🍴 Good bar food at lunchtime includes sandwiches, soup, salmon fishcakes with chive fish cream, shepherd's pie, and corn-fed chicken with wild mushrooms with evening choices such as roast rack of herb-crusted lamb with lavender jelly and pork loin cutlet with apple mash and honey and mustard sauce, daily specials, and puddings like knickerbocker glory with chocolate sauce or steamed treacle sponge. *Starters/Snacks: £4.50 to £8.00. Main Courses: £8.50 to £20.00. Puddings: £5.00*

Free house ~ Licensee Robin Lawson ~ Real ale ~ Bar food (12-3, 6-9; 12-2, 7-9 in winter) ~ Restaurant ~ (01720) 422844 ~ Children welcome ~ Dogs allowed in bar ~ Open 11-11; 12-10.30 Sun; 11-3, 6-11 weekdays in winter ~ Bedrooms: £157.50B/£210B

Recommended by Bernard Stradling

TRURO

SW8244 MAP 1

Old Ale House 🍺 £

Quay Street; TR1 2HD

Eight real ales and good value, wholesome food in particularly well run, bustling place

---

With eight well kept real ales on handpump, a fantastic atmosphere and a really good mix of customers, it's not surprising that this well run pub remains so popular. Changing every day and tapped from the cask or on handpump there might be Adnams Broadside, Courage Directors, Greene King Old Speckled Hen, St Austell HSD, Sharps Doom Bar, Skinners Kiddlywink, Wold Top Falling Stone and Wooden Hand Cornish Mutiny; they hold two beer festivals a year with up to 26 ales. Eleven wines by the glass and quite a few country wines. The dimly lit bar has an engaging diversity of furnishings, some interesting 1920s bric-a-brac, beer mats pinned everywhere, matchbox collections, and newpapers and magazines to read. There's now an upstairs room with pool and table football; piped music.

🍴 Tasty wholesome bar food prepared in a spotless kitchen in full view of the bar includes open sandwiches, 'hands' or half bloomers with toppings such as bacon, onions and melted cheese or tuna, mayonnaise and melted cheese, sautéed potatoes with bacon and mushrooms in a creamy garlic sauce, cauliflower and broccoli bake, various sizzling skillets, a pie of the day, lamb and mint hotpot and beef stew. *Main Courses: £4.25 to £8.50. Puddings: £3.25*

Enterprise ~ Tenants Mark Jones and Beverley Jones ~ Real ale ~ Bar food (12-3, 6.30-9; not Sat or Sun evenings) ~ (01872) 271122 ~ Children allowed but away from bar ~ Jazz every second Weds, live band last Thurs of month ~ Open 11-11(midnight Fri and Sat); 12-11 Sun; closed 26 Dec

Recommended by Dr and Mrs A K Clarke, the Didler, David Crook, Brian and Bett Cox, Mr and Mrs A J Hudson, Alan Johnson, Andrew Curry, Ted George, Tim and Ann Newell, Jacquie Jones, Lynda Bentley, Barry Collett, Jeff Davies

ZENNOR   SW4538   MAP 1

Tinners Arms
B3306 W of St Ives; TR26 3BY

Good mix of customers, friendly atmosphere, and tasty food

There are some fine nearby coastal walks and in good weather you can sit on benches in the sheltered front courtyard or at tables on a bigger side terrace. It's an ancient, friendly pub with wooden-ceilings, cushioned settles, benches, and a mix of chairs around wooden tables, antique prints on the stripped plank panelling, and a log fire in cool weather. Sharps Doom Bar and a beer named for the pub, and St Austell Tinners on handpump.

🍴 **Tasty bar food at lunchtime includes sandwiches, good soup, ploughman's, vegetable lasagne and steak and kidney pie with evening choices like chicken stuffed with brie and wrapped in bacon, a fresh fish dish and steaks.** *Starters/Snacks: £4.50 to £7.50. Main Courses: £6.50 to £14.50. Puddings: £3.75 to £4.75*

Free house ~ Licensees Grahame Edwards and Richard Motley ~ Real ale ~ Bar food (12-2.30(3 Sun), 6.30-9) ~ (01736) 796927 ~ Children welcome away from main bar ~ Dogs allowed in bar ~ Open 11-11; 12-10.30 Sun; 11-3, 6.30-11 Mon-Fri in winter ~ Bedrooms: £40/£70S

Recommended by Pete Walker, George A Rimmer, Roger Brown, the Didler, David Gunn, Paul and Shirley White, Alan Johnson, Roger and Anne Newbury, Stuart Turner, Richard, Jacquie Jones, Steve Pocock

---

LUCKY DIP

Besides the fully inspected pubs, you might like to try these Lucky Dips recommended to us and described by readers (if you do, please send us reports: www.goodguides.co.uk).

ANGARRACK [SW5838]
☆ *Angarrack Inn* TR27 5JB [Steamers Hill]: Welcoming pub tucked below railway viaduct, enjoyable country cooking with local produce inc Newlyn fish, good choice changing daily (worth booking Sun lunch and evenings in season), great atmosphere, St Austell beers kept well, friendly landlord, log fire, comfortable well divided bar with interesting bric-a-brac and a couple of cockatiels; children and dogs welcome, picnic-sets outside, quiet pretty village in little secluded valley (*Keith and Chris Tindell, Stanley and Annie Matthews*)

BODMIN [SX0767]
Hole in the Wall PL31 2DS [Crockwell St]: Former debtors' prison, masses of bric-a-brac inc old rifles, pistols and swords, arched 18th-c stonework, Bass, Sharps Doom Bar and a guest beer, good value fresh local food (not Mon), upstairs dining bar; well planted yard with small stream running past, open all day (*the Didler*)

BOLVENTOR [SX1876]
☆ *Jamaica Inn* PL15 7TS [signed just off A30 on Bodmin Moor]: Genuinely 18th-c main bar with oak beams, stripped stone, massive log fire and well kept Sharps Doom Bar (here it's easy to ignore the big all-day cafeteria, games machines, souvenir shop and tourist coaches), young enthusiastic staff, bar food, plaque commemorating murdered landlord Joss Merlyn, great Daphne du Maurier connection; pretty secluded garden with

play area, bedrooms, moorland setting (*David Crook*)

BOSCASTLE [SX0991]
☆ *Cobweb* PL35 0HE [B3263, just E of harbour]: Cosily dim-lit two-bar pub with plenty of character, hundreds of old bottles hanging from heavy beams, two or three high-backed settles, flagstones and dark stone walls, cosy log fire, St Austell real ales, wide blackboard choice of generous popular food at good prices, quick friendly service, decent wine choice, pub games, sizeable family room with a second fire; dogs welcome, open all day (*LYM, David Eagles, Lynda Bentley, Ted George, the Didler, Di and Mike Gillam*)

☆ *Napoleon* PL35 0BD [High St, top of village]: Good atmosphere in low-beamed 16th-c pub with good value generous blackboard bar food, St Austell ales tapped from the cask, decent wines, good coffee, friendly service, log fires, interesting Napoleon prints, slate floors and cosy rooms on different levels inc small evening bistro, traditional games; piped music; children welcome, picnic-sets on small covered terrace and in large sheltered garden, steep climb up from harbour (splendid views on the way), open all day (*LYM, Peter and Margaret Glenister, Mrs E M Richards, Dr and Mrs M W A Haward, the Didler*)

Wellington PL35 0AQ [Harbour]: Long low-beamed bar impressively restored in 1800s style after 2004 floods, upstairs balcony area, several Skinners ales and St Austell Tribute kept well, enjoyable food (interesting without being too fancy), log fire; children welcome, big secluded garden, comfortable bedrooms *(Peter Meister, BB, Ian and Deborah Carrington)*

BOTALLACK [SW3632]

☆ *Queens Arms* TR19 7QG: Friendly and unpretentious, with good food choice from generous BLT to good local seafood and Sun lunch, well kept Sharps Doom Bar, a Skinners ale brewed for the pub and guest beers, cheerful helpful staff, log fire in unusual granite inglenook, comfortable settles and other dark wood furniture, tin mining and other old local photographs on stripped stone walls, attractive family extension; tables out in front and pleasant back garden with owl refuge, wonderful clifftop walks nearby, open all day wknds; for sale as we go to press – news please *(Mick and Moira Brummell, Ian and Joan Blackwell, Jeff Davies)*

BOTUSFLEMING [SX4061]

Rising Sun PL12 6NJ [off A388 nr Saltash]: Convivial low-ceilinged rural local, lively games bar, smaller quieter stripped stone room with two good coal fires, changing real ales; picnic-sets in garden looking over quiet valley to church, has been cl Mon-Thurs lunchtimes, open all day wknds *(Phil and Sally Gorton)*

BREAGE [SW6128]

Queens Arms TR13 9PD [3 miles W of Helston]: L-shaped local with friendly new landlord, Caledonian Deuchars IPA, Sharps Doom Bar and up to four guest beers, farm cider, decent wines by the glass, wide range of good value food from baguettes up, daily papers, good coal fires, plush banquettes, back games area with pool, paperback sales for silver band, restaurant area; piped music; dogs welcome, some picnic-sets outside, bedrooms, medieval wall paintings in church opp, open all day Sun *(Dennis Jenkin, Revd R P Tickle, BB, R V T Pryor)*

CALLINGTON [SX3569]

Bulls Head PL17 7AQ [Fore St]: Ancient local with handsome black timbering inside, St Austell HSD *(Giles and Annie Francis)*

CALSTOCK [SX4368]

☆ *Boot* PL18 9RN [off A390 via Albaston; Fore St]: 17th-c, stylishly brought up to date as evening restaurant rather than pub now, wide choice of good food, menu changing frequently, cheerful attentive service, thriving local atmosphere, carefully chosen wines by the glass; little nearby parking; cl Mon-Weds, and for sale as we go to press – news please *(E Bridge, BB)*

Tamar PL18 9QA [Quay]: Spotless comfortable bars in lovely setting yards from the river, good generous straightforward food at bargain prices, well kept changing ales such as Marstons Pedigree, Sharps Doom Bar and St Austell, impressive helpful service, darts and pool, separate dining room; shiny tables and chairs on sunny decking, hilly

walk or ferry to Cotehele (NT) *(Barry Gibbs, David Crook)*

CAMBORNE [SW6437]

☆ *Old Shire* TR14 0RT [Pendarves; B3303 towards Helston]: Largely extended traditional family dining pub with decent generous food based on popular carvery, Bass, pleasant wines, friendly hands-on landlady and long-serving staff, modern back part with lots of easy chairs and sofas, pictures for sale and roaring coal fire, conservatory; picnic-sets on terrace, summer barbecues *(Eamonn and Natasha Skyrme, Mr and Mrs Richard Wells, Colin Gooch)*

CAWSAND [SX4350]

☆ *Cross Keys* PL10 1PF [The Square]: Pretty pub in picturesque square opp boat club, friendly and simple-smart, with wide range of enjoyable generous food esp seafood (well worth booking in season) in small bar and large attractive stripped-pine dining room, reasonable prices, changing ales such as Archers, Dawlish and Greene King Abbot, flexible service; pool, may be piped music, no nearby parking; children and dogs welcome, some seats outside, pleasant bedrooms *(Roger Brown, Andrew Gardner)*

CHAPEL AMBLE [SW9975]

☆ *Maltsters Arms* PL27 6EU [off A39 NE of Wadebridge]: Busy country food pub, welcoming attentive staff, thriving atmosphere, enjoyable food from sandwiches and baguettes to enterprising proper cooking, Sharps and St Austell Tribute, splendid fire, beams, panelling, stripped stone and partly carpeted flagstones, upstairs family room, attractive restaurant; picnic-sets out in sheltered sunny corner *(Rachel, M Hosegood, Mick and Moira Brummell, Peter and Margaret Glenister, M A Borthwick, David Eberlin, Jacquie Jones, LYM, Mrs Angela Graham)*

CONSTANTINE [SW7229]

☆ *Trengilly Wartha* TR11 5RP [Nancenoy; off A3083 S of Helston, via Gweek then forking right]: Popular tucked-away inn with cheerful and helpful newish licensees, generally good food (particularly, if you're staying, the breakfasts) though things may run out, good choice for children, Sharps Cornish Coaster, Skinners Betty Stogs and perhaps a guest beer, good wines by the glass, long low-beamed main bar with woodburner and attractive built-in high-backed settles boxing in heavy wooden tables, bright family conservatory; children and dogs welcome, pretty garden with boules and lots of surrounding walks, has been open all day wknds *(Dennis Jenkin, Dr A McCormick, David Rule, Mrs M Godolphin, Brian and Anita Randall, Eamonn and Natasha Skyrme, LYM, Brian and Bett Cox, M A Borthwick, Paul Boot, Robin and Joyce Peachey, Andy and Claire Barker, Dr and Mrs M E Wilson, Michael Lamm)*

CRACKINGTON HAVEN [SX1496]

☆ *Coombe Barton* EX23 0JG [off A39 Bude—

Camelford]: Much-extended old inn in beautiful setting overlooking splendid sandy bay, welcoming modernised thoroughly pubby bar with plenty of room for young summer crowds, neat and pleasant young staff, wide range of simple bar food inc local fish, Sharps Safe Haven (brewed for the pub) and St Austell, good wine choice, lots of local pictures, surfboard hanging from plank ceiling, big plain family room, enjoyable no smoking restaurant; darts, glazed-off pool table, fruit machines, piped music, TV; dogs allowed in bar, side terrace with plenty of tables, good cliff walks, roomy bedrooms, open all day Sun, also Sat in school hols *(Peter and Margaret Glenister, Roger Brown, G K Smale, Julie Russell-Carter, LYM, Pete Walker)*

CRANTOCK [SW7960]
☆ *Old Albion* TR8 5RB [Langurroc Rd]: Picture-postcard thatched village pub, low beams, flagstones and open fires, old-fashioned small bar with brasses and low lighting, larger more open room with local pictures, informal atmosphere, generous if not cheap basic home-made bar lunches inc good sandwiches and giant ploughman's, Sharps and Skinners real ales, farm cider, decent house wines, pool and darts at back of lounge; staff may look dressed ready for beach and surf, loads of summer visitors, souvenirs sold; dogs welcome, tables out on small terrace, open all day *(Gloria Bax, Adrian Johnson, Colin Gooch, LYM)*

CREMYLL [SX4553]
☆ *Edgcumbe Arms* PL10 1HX: Super setting by foot-ferry to Plymouth, with good Tamar views and picnic-sets out by water; attractive layout and décor, with slate floors, big settles, comfortable fireside sofas and other old-fashioned furnishings, old pictures and china, plentiful food from sandwiches up, St Austell ales, good wines by the glass, cheerful staff, good family room/games area; pay car park some way off; children in eating area, dogs allowed in one bar, bedrooms, open all day *(LYM, Shirley Mackenzie, Dennis Jenkin)*

CRIPPLES EASE [SW5036]
Engine TR20 8NF [B3311 St Ives—Penzance]: Family-friendly former tin-mine counting house in superb moorland location, views of the sea on all sides from nearby hill (very popular summer evenings), cheerful landlady, enjoyable food from sandwiches up, real ales such as Greene King Old Speckled Hen, Marstons Pedigree and Sharps Doom Bar, pool; good value bedrooms *(Stuart Turner)*

CUBERT [SW7857]
☆ *Smugglers Den* TR8 5PY [village signed off A3075 S of Newquay, then brown sign to pub (and Trebellan holiday park) on left]: Big open-plan 16th-c thatched pub, neat ranks of tables (worth booking), dim lighting, stripped stone and heavy beam and plank ceilings, west country pictures and seafaring memorabilia, small barrel seats, steps down

to further area with enormous inglenook woodburner, another step to big side family dining room; neat helpful friendly staff, fresh generous enjoyable food inc local seafood, Sharps, Skinners and St Austell ales, well lit pool area, darts; piped music, fruit machine; dogs welcome, picnic-sets in small courtyard and on lawn with climbing frame, has been cl winter Mon-Weds lunchtime *(Adrian Johnson, Peter Salmon, Steve Harvey, Paul and Shirley White, the Didler, R V T Pryor, BB, Chris Reading, Steve Pocock)*

DEVORAN [SW7938]
☆ *Old Quay* TR3 6NE [Quay Rd – brown sign to pub off A39 Truro—Falmouth]: Two light and fresh rooms off bar, enjoyable food inc nice lunchtime sandwiches and enterprising specials, well kept ales such as Flowers IPA, Fullers London Pride and Sharps Doom Bar, interesting wines by the glass, good friendly young staff, big coal fire, daily papers, boating bric-a-brac, some attractive prints, evening restaurant; they may try to keep your credit card while you eat; imaginatively terraced suntrap garden behind making the most of the idyllic spot – peaceful creekside village, lovely views, walks nearby, and this ends a coast-to-coast cycle way; dogs welcome, open all day in summer *(Ian and Joan Blackwell, Dr and Mrs M E Wilson, BB, Dennis Jenkin, Roger E F Maxwell, Norman and Sarah Keeping)*

EDMONTON [SW9672]
☆ *Quarryman* PL27 7JA [off A39 just W of Wadebridge bypass]: Welcoming three-room beamed bar, part of a small holiday complex around courtyard of former quarrymen's quarters; interesting decorations inc old sporting memorabilia, Sharps, Skinners and a couple of good guest beers, some good individual cooking besides generous pubby lunchtime food inc good baguettes, salads and fish and chips, good curry night Tues, attentive staff; pool, cribbage and dominoes, cosy bistro; well behaved dogs and children welcome, open all day *(Lynda Bentley, LYM, J Kirkland)*

FALMOUTH [SW8033]
Boathouse TR11 2AG [Trevethan Hill/Webber Hill]: Interesting two-level local with buoyant young atmosphere, lots of woodwork, nautical theme, log fire, two or three real ales, friendly bar staff; piped music can be loud; children welcome, smart chrome tables outside, upper deck with awning, heaters and great estuary views *(Dr and Mrs M E Wilson)*
☆ *Chain Locker* TR11 3HH [Custom House Quay]: Fine spot by inner harbour with window tables (pub dog likes the seats here) and lots outside, real ales such as Sharps Doom Bar and Skinners Cornish Knocker, generous bargain food from sandwiches and baguettes to fresh local fish, bargains for two, quick service, masses of nautical bric-a-brac, darts alley; games machine, piped music; well behaved children welcome, self-

catering accommodation, open all day
(Dr and Mrs M E Wilson, Neil and Anita
Christopher, LYM, Rona Murdoch, Colin Gooch)
Grapes TR11 3DS [Church St]: Spacious
family-friendly refurbished pub with fine
harbour view (beyond car park) from the
back, beams, comfortable armchairs, sofas,
lots of ships' crests and nautical
memorabilia, plenty of tables, wide range of
cheap food esp fish from adjoining servery,
helpful friendly young staff, local real ales,
games room; piped music, steep stairs to
lavatories (Dr and Mrs M E Wilson)
Quayside Inn & Old Ale House TR11 3LH
[ArwenackSt/Fore St]: Bare-boards dark-
panelled bar with Fullers London Pride,
Sharps Doom Bar and Skinners, decent
wines, efficient service, good value food (all
day in summer) from doorstep sandwiches to
Sun roasts, friendly helpful staff, tall tables,
upstairs harbour-view lounge with armchairs
and sofas one end; lots of pub games, piped
music, big-screen TV, busy with young
people evenings – esp Fri/Sat for live music;
children welcome, plenty of waterside picnic-
sets, open all day (Dr and Mrs M E Wilson,
LYM, Mike Gorton, Colin Gooch, Barry Collett)
Seaview TR11 3EP [Wodehouse Terr]:
Convivial maritime local above 111-step
Jacob's Ladder (so off the tourist beat), lots
of dark oak and appropriate bric-a-brac,
stunning harbour and dockyard view from
picture windows and a few tables outside,
good range of local beers; big-screen sports
TV; bedrooms (Dr and Mrs M E Wilson)
☆ **Seven Stars** TR11 3QA [The Moor (centre)]:
Quirky 17th-c local, unchanging and
unsmart, with long-serving and entertaining
vicar-landlord, no gimmicks (nor machines or
mobile phones), warm welcome, Bass, Sharps
and Skinners tapped from the cask, home-
made rolls, chatty regulars, big key-ring
collection, quiet back snug; corridor hatch
serving tables on prime-site roadside
courtyard (the Didler, Dave Webster,
Sue Holland, BB)
FOWEY [SX1251]
Galleon PL23 1AQ [Fore St; from centre
follow Car Ferry signs]: Superb spot
overlooking harbour and estuary, good ale
range inc local microbrews, generous food
from good sandwiches to plenty of fish,
reasonable prices, fast service, modern
nautical décor with lots of solid pine, dining
areas off; pool, jazz Sun lunchtime, and
evenings can get loud with young people;
children welcome, disabled facilities, tables
out on attractive extended waterside terrace
and in sheltered courtyard with covered
heated area, estuary-view bedrooms
(Margaret and Roy Randle, Colin and
Peggy Wilshire, Andrew York, BB,
Dave Webster, Sue Holland)
☆ **King of Prussia** PL23 1AT [Town Quay]:
Handsome quayside building with good
welcoming service in roomy and neatly
refreshed upstairs bar, bay windows looking
over harbour to Polruan, good pubby bar

food, St Austell ales, sensibly priced wines,
splendid local seafood in side family
restaurant; may be piped music; seats
outside, open all day at least in summer, six
pleasant bedrooms (Rob Stevenson,
Edward Mirzoeff, Michael and Alison Sandy,
LYM, Alan Johnson, Phil and Sally Gorton,
Margaret and Roy Randle, Dave Webster,
Sue Holland)
Lugger PL23 1AH [Fore St]: Friendly and
relaxing family pub with good mix of locals
and visitors in unpretentious bar,
comfortable small candlelit back dining area,
well kept St Austell ales, wide choice of
generous food inc good simply prepared fish
specials, big waterfront mural; piped music;
children welcome, pavement tables,
bedrooms (BB, Peter Meister, Margaret and
Roy Randle, the Didler, Dave Webster,
Sue Holland)
Safe Harbour PL23 1BP [Lostwithiel St]:
Quiet local, relaxing and homely, with
St Austell ales, welcoming new landlord,
horsebrasses and old local prints (Ash Waller,
Phil and Sally Gorton)
☆ **Ship** PL23 1AZ [Trafalgar Sq]: Bustling local
with friendly staff, good choice of good
value generous food from sandwiches up inc
fine local seafood, well kept St Austell ales,
coal fire and banquettes in tidy bar with lots
of yachting prints and nauticalia, steps up to
family dining room with big stained-glass
window, pool/darts room; piped music, small
TV for sports; dogs allowed, comfortably old-
fashioned bedrooms, some oak-panelled
(Phil and Sally Gorton, LYM, Mike and
Heather Watson, Rob Stevenson,
Peter Meister, Nick Lawless, Margaret and
Roy Randle, Michael and Alison Sandy,
Dave Webster, Sue Holland)
GOLANT [SX1254]
☆ **Fishermans Arms** PL23 1LN [Fore St
(B3269)]: Bustling partly flagstoned
waterside local with lovely views across River
Fowey from front bar and terrace, good value
generous home-made food inc good crab
sandwiches and seafood, all day in summer
(cl Sun afternoon), Sharps Doom Bar and
Ushers Best, good wines by the glass,
friendly staff and cat, log fire, interesting
pictures, back family room; piano, TV;
pleasant garden (the Didler, Dr and
Mrs M E Wilson, BB, Edward Mirzoeff,
Rob Stevenson, Dave Webster, Sue Holland)
GOLDSITHNEY [SW5430]
Crown TR20 9LG [B3280]: Friendly bustling
local, roomy and comfortable, with good
value simple food inc local fresh fish and
bargain Thurs and Sun lunches, well kept
Sharps and a guest such as St Austell
Dartmoor, decent house wines, good service,
L-shaped beamed bar and small attractive
dining room; pretty suntrap glass-roofed
front loggia and pavement tables, masses of
hanging baskets (Nigel Long)
GORRAN CHURCHTOWN [SW9942]
Barley Sheaf PL26 6HN [follow Gorran Haven
signs from Mevagissey]: Welcoming old pub,

reputedly haunted but extensively modernised, central servery for three areas, back pool room, long-serving landlord, good food choice in bar and restaurant inc Fri fish and chips, real ales such as Flowers IPA and Original, Skinners Betty Stogs and Sharps Doom Bar, good range of ciders; children welcome, disabled facilities, garden with summer barbecues, nice village *(Christopher Wright)*

GWITHIAN [SW5840]
Red River TR27 5BW [Prosper Hill]: Former Pendarves Arms refitted in clean-cut contemporary style, sofa and stools around pubby tables on stripped boards, pine dado, neat dining area with pews and wheelback chairs, several well kept ales, enjoyable food; picnic-sets in small garden across road, delightful village near dunes, beach and coastal path *(Simon Menneer)*

HELFORD [SW7526]
☆ *Shipwrights Arms* TR12 6JX [off B3293 SE of Helston, via Mawgan]: Thatched pub overlooking beautiful wooded creek, at its best at high tide, terraces making the most of the view, plenty of surrounding walks – and there's a summer foot ferry from Helford Passage; nautical décor, winter open fire, separate dining area; has had real ale, a decent wine list, bar food inc summer barbecues and lunchtime buffet platters, but up for sale as we go to press, with possible threat of residential development – news please; quite a walk from nearest car park, has been cl winter Sun and Mon evenings *(the Didler, LYM, Andrea Rampley, Paul and Shirley White, Derek and Heather Manning)*

HELSTON [SW6527]
☆ *Blue Anchor* TR13 8EL [Coinagehall St]: 15th-c no-nonsense thatched local, highly individual, with quaint rooms off corridor, flagstones, stripped stone, low beams and simple old-fashioned furniture, traditional games, family room, cheap lunchtime food (perhaps better then for a visit than the evening), ancient back brewhouse still producing their own distinctive Spingo IPA, Middle and specials; seats out behind, bedrooms, open all day *(the Didler, David Crook, LYM, Clifford Blakemore, Dave Webster, Sue Holland, Pete Walker)*

HESSENFORD [SX3057]
Copley Arms PL11 3HJ [A387 Looe—Torpoint]: Emphasis on good food from sandwiches, baguettes and baked potatoes to popular Sun lunch and restaurant dishes using local produce in modernised linked areas, St Austell ales, nice wine choice, variety of teas and coffee, log fires, one part with sofas and easy chairs; piped music, dogs allowed in one small area, big plain family room; sizeable and attractive streamside garden and terrace (but by road), play area, bedrooms *(John and Joan Calvert, Brian P Kirby)*

HOLYWELL [SW7658]
Treguth TR8 5PP [signed from Cubert, SW of Newquay]: Comfortable and cosy thatched

local nr big beach, several unpretentious low-beamed rooms, real ales, local farm cider, home-cooked food inc vegetarian dishes and good value three-course set menu, friendly service, real fire, darts; handy for camp sites *(Chris Reading)*

KINGSAND [SX4350]
☆ *Halfway House* PL10 1NA [Fore St, towards Cawsand]: Attractive well sited inn with simple mildly Victorian bar rambling around huge central fireplace, low ceilings and soft lighting, Sharps Doom Bar and guest beers, decent wines, bar food from crab sandwiches and baguettes up, pleasant service, morning coffee, perhaps summer afternoon teas, restaurant; car park not close; children and dogs warmly welcome, picturesque village, marvellous walks, bedrooms, open all day in summer *(W F C Phillips, Neil Hammacott, Ian and Joan Blackwell, LYM)*

LAMORNA [SW4424]
☆ *Lamorna Wink* TR19 6XH [off B3315 SW of Penzance]: Great collection of warship mementoes, sea photographs, nautical brassware, hats and helmets in proper no-frills country local with particularly well kept Sharps Doom Bar and Eden, nice house wine, swift friendly service, enormous lunchtime sandwich platters and the like from homely kitchen area (may not be available out of season), coal fire, pool table, books and perhaps lots of local produce for sale; children in eating area, picnic-sets outside, short stroll above beautiful cove with good coast walks *(Paul Rampton, Paul and Shirley White, LYM, Thomas Lane)*

LANNER [SW7339]
☆ *Fox & Hounds* TR16 6AX [Comford; A393/B3298]: Cosily comfortable rambling low-beamed pub with top-notch friendly service, good choice of generous fresh food from sandwiches to massive steaks, St Austell ales tapped from the cask, good house wines, warm fires, high-backed settles and cottagey chairs on flagstones, stripped stone and dark panelling; pub games, piped music; children welcome in dining room, dogs in bar, disabled access and facilities, great floral displays in front, neat back garden with pond and play area, open all day wknds *(Paul and Shirley White, David Crook, LYM, Michael Saunders)*

LAUNCESTON [SX3384]
West Gate PL15 7AD [Westgate St]: Bustling well run town pub with well kept St Austell Tribute, bargain food, old timbers *(Giles and Annie Francis)*

LELANT [SW5436]
☆ *Old Quay House* TR27 6JG [Griggs Quay, Lelant Saltings; A3047/B3301 S of village]: Large neatly kept modern pub in marvellous spot overlooking bird sanctuary estuary, good value wholesome usual food inc good salad bar, real ales such as Bass, Sharps Doom Bar and St Austell Tribute, good service, dining area off well divided open-plan bar, children allowed upstairs; garden tables, decent motel-type bedrooms, open all

day in summer (John and Jackie Chalcraft, Mr and Mrs C R Little)

Watermill TR27 6LQ [Lelant Downs; A3074 S]: Mill-conversion family dining pub, working waterwheel behind with gearing in dark-beamed central bar opening into brighter airy front extension and gallery evening restaurant area with racks of wine, good atmosphere, quick friendly service, real ales such as Sharps Doom Bar and Skinners Green Hop, sensibly priced food inc good generous baguettes, decent wines (off-sales too), good coffee; dark pink pool room, may be piped music; tables out under pergola and among trees in good-sized pretty streamside garden, open all day (BB, David and Teresa Frost)

LERRYN [SX1356]

☆ **Ship** PL22 0PT [signed off A390 in Lostwithiel; Fore St]: Lovely spot esp when tide's in (boats from Fowey then, can radio your order ahead), real ales such as Bass, Skinners and Sharps Eden, local farm cider, good wines, fruit wines and malt whiskies, huge woodburner, attractive adults-only dining conservatory (booked quickly evenings and wknds), games room with pool; dogs on leads and children welcome, picnic-sets and pretty play area outside, nr famous stepping-stones and three well signed waterside walks, decent bedrooms in adjoining building (Andrew Shore, Maria Williams, Nick Lawless, Mike Abbott, Mike and Heather Watson, LYM, Peter Salmon)

LIZARD [SW7012]

☆ **Top House** TR12 7NQ [A3083]: Neat pub with lots of good local sea pictures, fine shipwreck relics and serpentine craftwork (note the handpumps), good log fire, real ales inc Sharps Doom Bar, reasonably priced wines, simple choice of generous food), darts, pool, no piped music – occasional live); tucked-away fruit machine; dogs welcome, tables on sheltered terrace, interesting nearby serpentine shop (Paul and Shirley White, BB, Dave Webster, Sue Holland, Dave Braisted)

LOOE [SX2553]

Decker PL13 1BS [Higher Market St]: Comfortable big-windowed holiday bar with café-style eating room, wide range of good value food, St Austell Tribute, nostalgic film memorabilia; well reproduced piped music, upstairs nightclub (Michael and Alison Sandy)

LUDGVAN [SW5033]

☆ **White Hart** TR20 8EY [off A30 Penzance—Hayle at Crowlas]: Proper old-fashioned 19th-c pub, friendly and well worn-in, with great atmosphere in small unspoilt beamed rooms, paraffin lamps, masses of mugs, jugs and pictures, rugs on bare boards, two big blazing woodburners, Bass, Flowers IPA and Marstons Pedigree tapped from the cask, sensibly priced home cooking (not Mon exc high season) from sandwiches to prized treacle tart, no piped music (Alan and Pat Newcombe, Paul and Shirley White, Gaynor Gregory, the Didler, LYM)

MALPAS [SW8442]

☆ **Heron** TR1 1SL [Trenhaile Terrace, off A39 S of Truro]: Suntrap slate-paved front terrace making the best of lovely creekside position, well kept and attractively priced St Austell beers, several wines by glass, bar food, light and airy narrow bar with blue and white décor, warming flame-effect fire, modern yacht paintings and heron pictures; parking difficult at peak times; children welcome (Ian Phillips, R V T Pryor, LYM, Andy and Claire Barker, Peter Salmon)

MANACCAN [SW7624]

New Inn TR12 6HA [down hill signed to Gillan and St Keverne]: Small thatched pub in attractive setting above sea and popular with sailing folk, bar with beam and plank ceiling, comfortably cushioned built-in wall seats and other chairs, helpful staff, real ales inc Sharps Doom Bar, basic food, cribbage, dominoes; children and dogs welcome, picnic-sets in rose-filled garden, bedrooms (LYM, the Didler, Gloria Bax, Geoff Calcott, Ian and Deborah Carrington, Steve Pocock)

MEVAGISSEY [SX0144]

Fountain PL26 6QH [Cliff St, down alley by Post Office]: Unpretentious and interesting fishermen's pub, low beams, slate floor and some stripped stone, well kept St Austell ales, good coal fire, lots of old local pictures, small fish tank, enjoyable food from simple lunchtime dishes to fresh local fish, back locals' bar with glass-topped cellar (and pool, games machine and sports TV), upstairs evening restaurant; occasional sing-songs; dogs welcome, bedrooms, pretty frontage, open all day in summer (the Didler, Ted George, Christopher Wright, Adrian Johnson, Alan and Paula McCully, BB, Andy and Claire Barker)

Kings Arms PL26 6UQ [Fore St]: Small welcoming local with real ales such as Sharps Doom Bar (Christopher Wright)

☆ **Ship** PL26 6UQ [Fore St, nr harbour]: Lively yet relaxed 16th-c pub with interesting alcove areas in big open-plan bar, low beams and flagstones, nice nautical décor, open fire, cheerful efficient uniformed staff, good range of generous quickly served pubby food esp fresh fish, small helpings available, full St Austell range kept well, back pool table; games machines, piped music, occasional live; children welcome in two front rooms, comfortable bedrooms, open all day in summer (Andy Sinden, Louise Harrington, Rona Murdoch, Christopher Wright, Alan and Paula McCully, Michael and Alison Sandy)

MORWENSTOW [SS2015]

☆ **Bush** EX23 9SR [signed off A39 N of Kilkhampton; Crosstown]: Beautifully placed unpretentious beamed pub near interesting village church and great cliff walks, updated pastel décor with light and tidy contemporary-feel dining room and conservatory, but keeping the bar's massive flagstones and fireplace (in fact it's partly Saxon and one of Britain's most ancient pubs, with a serpentine Celtic basin in one wall), real ales, enjoyable food using local seasonal produce; garden with good views and solid wooden play things, two new bedrooms *(John Lane, Nigel Long, Nevill Pike, LYM, Jeremy Whitehorn, the Didler, Conor McGaughey)*

MOUSEHOLE [SW4726]

☆ *Old Coastguard* TR19 6PR [The Parade (edge of village, Newlyn coast rd)]: More hotel/restaurant than pub, though they do keep real ales and a fair choice of wines by the glass; lovely position with neat and attractive sizeable mediterranean garden by rocky shore with marble-look tables out on decking, good up-to-date food, polite service, light and airy modern bar with potted plants, lower dining part with glass wall giving great view out over garden to Mounts Bay; children in eating areas, comfortable sea-view bedrooms, good breakfast, open all day *(Stuart Turner, Roger Price, David Gunn, LYM, P R Waights, Dr R A Smye, Matthew Hegarty, I A Herdman)*

MULLION [SW6719]

☆ *Old Inn* TR12 7HN [Churchtown – not down in the cove]: Extensive thatched and beamed family food pub with central servery doing generous good value food (all day July/Aug) from good doorstep sandwiches to pies and evening steaks, linked eating areas with lots of brasses, plates, clocks, nautical items and old wreck pictures, big inglenook fireplace, Sharps Doom Bar, Skinners Cornish Knocker and John Smiths, lots of wines by the glass; children welcome, open all day Sat/Sun and Aug; picnic-sets on terrace and in pretty orchard garden, good bedrooms, open all day *(LYM, David and Alison Walker, Gloria Bax)*

NOTTER [SX3860]

Notter Bridge Inn PL12 4RW [signed just off A38 Saltash—Liskeard]: Lovely spot just off trunk road, tables in conservatory and fairy-lit garden looking down on sheltered stream, neatly kept open-plan dining lounge, wide choice of pubby food inc good curries, welcoming bustling atmosphere, well kept Bass, Courage Best and Greene King Abbot, decent wines by the glass; may be unobtrusive piped music; open all day wknds, very handy for nearby holiday parks *(J F M and M West, BB)*

PADSTOW [SW9175]

Golden Lion PL28 8AN [Lanadwell St]: Cheerful black-beamed locals' bar, high-raftered back lounge with plush banquettes against ancient white stone walls, well kept ales inc Sharps Doom Bar, reasonably priced simple bar lunches inc good crab sandwiches, evening steaks and fresh seafood, prompt friendly service, coal fire; pool in family area, piped music, games machines; terrace tables, bedrooms, open all day *(Dr and Mrs M W A Haward, the Didler, Michael B Griffith, BB)*

☆ *London* PL28 8AN [Llanadwell St]: Down-to-earth fishermen's local with flower-filled façade, lots of pictures and nautical

memorabilia, jolly atmosphere, good staff, well kept St Austell ales, decent choice of malt whiskies, wknd lunchtime bar food inc good if pricy crab sandwiches, fresh local fish, more elaborate evening choice (small back dining area – get there early for a table), great log fire; can get very busy, games machines but no piped music – home-grown live music Sun night; dogs welcome (if the resident collies approve), open all day, good value bedrooms *(Sue and Dave Harris, LYM, Ted George, Lynda Bentley, Andrew Curry)*

Metropole PL28 8DB [Station Rd]: Enjoyable if not cheap bar food from sandwiches up (service charge added) in hotel's comfortable bar lounge, friendly staff, decent wines by the glass, big windows overlooking estuary; well behaved dogs welcome in bar, bedrooms *(Dennis Jenkin)*

Old Custom House PL28 8BL [South Quay]: Large bright and airy open-plan seaside bar, comfortable and well divided, with rustic décor and cosy corners, bare boards, raised section, big family area and conservatory, good food choice from baguettes to bargain deals for two, St Austell ales, good friendly service, adjoining fish restaurant, pool; big-screen TV, some live music; good spot by harbour, open all day, attractive sea-view bedrooms *(BB, John and Alison Hamilton, Ted George, Stephen Allford)*

Old Ship PL28 8AE [Mill Sq, just off North Quay/Broad St]: Cheery mix of locals and visitors in hotel's bustling open-plan bar with St Austell ales, good range of reasonably priced food from sandwiches to plenty of good seafood, upstairs restaurant; good live music Fri/Sat, back games room with SkyTV, may be piped radio, parking only for people staying; dogs welcome, tables in heated front courtyard tucked away just off harbour, open all day from breakfast on at least in summer, 15 simple bedrooms *(BB, Chris Glasson, Pete Walker)*

Shipwrights PL28 8AF [North Quay; aka the Blue Lobster]: Big low-ceilinged quayside bar, stripped brick, lots of wood, flagstones, lobster pots and nets, quick popular food, well kept St Austell ales, friendly service, further upstairs eating area; busy with young people evenings; dogs welcome, a few tables out by water, more in back suntrap garden *(BB, Paul and Shirley White, Lynda Bentley)*

PAR [SX0754]

☆ *Royal* PL24 2AJ [Eastcliffe Rd (close to station, off A3082)]: Light and airy open-plan refurbishment, solid pale country furniture on flagstones and bare boards, some stripped stone, log-effect fire, restaurant opening into slate-floored conservatory, good food, Cotleigh Golden Eagle, Sharps Doom Bar and Skinners Cornish Knocker, good choice of wines by the glass, darts and pool; piped pop music may be on the loud side, big-screen TV, games machine; disabled access, picnic-sets on small heated terrace, comfortable bedrooms *(BB)*

PAUL [SW4627]

☆ *Kings Arms* TR19 6TZ: Appealing beamed local opp church, cosy bustling atmosphere and friendly licensees (landlord is talking of retirement), St Austell ales, enjoyable sensibly priced food; dogs welcome, decent simple bedrooms *(Dr R A Smye, Paul and Karen Cornock, Stuart Turner)*

PELYNT [SX2054]

☆ *Jubilee* PL13 2JZ [B3359 NW of Looe]: Recently refurbished 16th-c beamed inn with well kept St Austell Tribute, good wines by the glass, wide choice of food from good sandwiches up, interesting Queen Victoria mementoes, some handsome antique furnishings and log fire in big stone fireplace, separate public bar with darts, pool and games machine; children and dogs welcome, picnic-sets under cocktail parasols in inner courtyard with pretty flower tubs, good play area, 11 comfortable bedrooms, open all day wknds *(LYM, Dennis Jenkin)*

PENDOGGETT [SX0279]

☆ *Cornish Arms* PL30 3HH [B3314]: Picturesque and friendly old coaching inn with traditional oak settles on civilised front bar's handsome polished slate floor, fine prints, above-average food from good soup and sandwiches to fresh fish, splendid steaks and great Sunday lunch, particularly welcoming service, well kept Bass and Sharps Doom Bar, good wines by the glass, comfortably spaced tables in small dining room, proper back locals' bar with woodburner and games; provision for children, disabled access (staff helpful), terrace with distant sea view, open all day, bedrooms *(Gloria Bax, Michael B Griffith, M A Borthwick, LYM, Tony Allwood, Mrs Angela Graham)*

PENELEWEY [SW8140]

☆ *Punch Bowl & Ladle* TR3 6QY [B3289]: Thatched dining pub in picturesque setting handy for Trelissick Gardens, comfortable olde-worlde bar with big settees, rustic bric-a-brac, several room areas, wide choice of generous sensibly priced home-made food from good sandwiches up (Thurs very popular with elderly lunchers), children's helpings, efficient helpful service, St Austell ales, good wine choice; unobtrusive piped music; children and dogs on leads welcome, small back sun terrace, open all day summer *(Paul and Shirley White, LYM, Clifford Blakemore, Tony Allwood)*

PENZANCE [SW4730]

☆ *Admiral Benbow* TR18 4AF [Chapel St]: Well run rambling pub, full of life and atmosphere and packed with interesting nautical gear, friendly thoughtful staff, good value above-average food inc local fish, real ales such as Sharps, Skinners and St Austell, decent wines, cosy corners, downstairs restaurant, upper floor with pool, pleasant view from back room; children welcome, open all day summer *(LYM, Margaret and Roy Randle, Matthew Hegarty, David Tindal)*

☆ *Dolphin* TR18 4EF [The Barbican; Newlyn road, opp harbour after swing-bridge]: Roomy and welcoming, part old-fashioned pub and part bistro, with attractive nautical décor, good harbour views, good value food from good lunchtime sandwiches and baguettes to steaks and fresh local fish (landlady's husband is a fisherman), St Austell ales, good wines by the glass, helpful service, great fireplace, dining area a few steps down, cosy family room; big pool room with juke box etc, no obvious nearby parking; pavement picnic-sets, open all day *(LYM, the Didler, Dr R A Smye, Peter Salmon)*

☆ *Globe & Ale House* TR18 4BJ [Queen St]: Small low-ceilinged tavern with changing real ales inc Bass, Sharps and Skinners, some tapped from the cask, lots of old pictures and artefacts, bare boards and dim lighting, enthusiastic helpful landlord, enjoyable simple prompt food; TV sports *(Pete Walker, the Didler)*

PERRANARWORTHAL [SW7738]

☆ *Norway* TR3 7NU [A39 Truro—Penryn]: Large pub doing well under enterprising current licensees, quietly efficient helpful service, good value carefully prepared sensible food using local produce, all-day Sun carvery, three St Austell real ales, good choice of wines by the glass, half a dozen linked areas, beams hung with farm tools, lots of prints and rustic bric-a-brac, old-style wooden seating and big tables on slate flagstones, open fires; tables outside, open all day *(BB, David Crook)*

PERRANUTHNOE [SW5329]

☆ *Victoria* TR20 9NP [signed off A394 Penzance—Helston]: Comfortable low-beamed bar and good-sized dining room, good interesting food from freshly baked lunchtime baguettes and doorstep sandwiches through enterprising main dishes to great puddings, fully fledged dining pub evenings, friendly efficient service, well kept ales such as Bass and Sharps Doom Bar, nice wine choice, neat coal fire, some stripped stonework, coastal and wreck photographs; quiet piped music; picnic-sets in sheltered pretty sunken garden, good bedrooms, handy for Mounts Bay *(Nigel Long, Bruce and Sharon Eden, LYM)*

PHILLEIGH [SW8739]

Roseland TR2 5NB [Between A3078 and B3289, NE of St Mawes just E of King Harry ferry]: Up for sale as we went to press, this little pub is handy for King Harry ferry and Trelissick Garden; two bar rooms (one with flagstones and the other carpeted) with wheelback chairs, built-in red-cushioned seats, open fires, old photographs, and some giant beetles and butterflies in glass cases; tiny lower back area is liked by locals, separate restaurant, Adnams Best, Sharps Doom Bar and Skinners Betty Stogs on handpump and a dozen wines by glass; seats in paved front courtyard; dogs in bar, children welcome *(Mr and Mrs Bentley-Davies, David Crook, Adrian Johnson, Michael Cooper,*

LYM, Walter and Susan Rinaldi-Butcher, Andrea Rampley, Christopher Wright, Clifford Blakemore, P R Waights, John and Jackie Chalcraft, Steve Harvey, Pete Walker, Andy and ClaireBarker, Barry Collett)

PILLATON [SX3664]

☆ *Weary Friar* PL12 6QS [off Callington—Landrake back road]: Pretty tucked-away 12th-c pub doing well under current enthusiastic and welcoming management, enjoyable food in bar and big back restaurant, good service, real ales such as Bass and Sharps Eden, farm cider, four spotless and civilised knocked-together rooms, appealing tastefully updated décor, comfortable seating on easy chairs one end, log fire; children in eating area (no dogs inside), tables outside, Tues bell-ringing in church next door, comfortable bedrooms with own bathrooms (Gerry Price, LYM, Ted George)

POLGOOTH [SW9950]

☆ *Polgooth Inn* PL26 7DA [well signed off A390 W of St Austell; Ricketts Lane]: Popular country food pub with efficiently produced generous food from sandwiches to some contemporary dishes (only roasts on Sun), children's helpings and appealing prices, well kept St Austell ales, good wine choice, eating area around sizeable bar with woodburner, good big family room; fills quickly in summer (handy for nearby caravan parks); steps up to play area, tables out on grass, pretty countryside (Michael and Jean Hockings, Stephen and Jean Curtis, LYM, Mick and Moira Brummell, Andy and Claire Barker)

POLPERRO [SX2051]

☆ *Crumplehorn Mill* PL13 2RJ [top of village nr main car park]: Converted mill well reworked by new owners, keeping beams, flagstones and some stripped stone, snug lower beamed bar leading to long neat and attractively furnished main room with further cosy end eating area, top-notch service, enjoyable food, well kept ales, log fire; families welcome, good value bedrooms (Ted George, BB)

Noughts & Crosses PL13 2QU [Lansallos St; bear right approaching harbour]: Large streamside back dining bar with low beams and tiled floor, vast food choice from baguettes and baked potatoes to plenty of seafood, well kept ales such as Sharps Doom Bar, Skinners Betty Stogs and St Austell Tribute, hospitable and unpretentious flagstoned front bar (Michael and Alison Sandy, BB)

POLRUAN [SX1250]

Lugger PL23 1PA [The Quay; back roads off A390 in Lostwithiel, or passenger/bicycle ferry from Fowey]: Beamed waterside local with high-backed wall settles, big model boats etc, open fires, good views from upstairs rooms, good generous fish and chips from bar food servery, reasonably priced wines and St Austell ales, restaurant; children welcome, good walks, open all day

(LYM, Brian and Bett Cox, Dave Webster, Sue Holland)

Russell PL23 1PJ [West St]: Fishermen's local, lively yet relaxing, with sensibly priced straightforward food using local produce from good sandwiches up, St Austell beers, friendly staff, log fire, large tidy bar with interesting photographs; lovely hanging baskets (Edward Mirzoeff, A Truelove, Dave Webster, Sue Holland)

PORT ISAAC [SX9980]

Edge PL29 3SB [New Rd]: Clifftop bar/restaurant with picture-window coast views (may see basking sharks), light oak modern interior, up-to-date food, Sharps Doom Bar tapped from the cask, good wine selection; children looked after well (Simon Rhodes, David Tindal)

☆ *Golden Lion* PL29 3RB [Fore Street]: Bustling local atmosphere in simply furnished old rooms, open fire in back one, window seats and three balcony tables looking down on rocky harbour and lifeboat slip far below, straightforward food inc good fish range, St Austell Tinners, HSD and Tribute, darts, dominoes, cribbage; piped music, games machine; children in eating areas, dramatic cliff walks from the door, open all day (LYM, the Didler, John and Alison Hamilton, Mrs Julie Thomas, Rob Stevenson, David Tindal, Betsy Brown, Nigel Flook)

Old School PL29 3RD [Fore St]: Hotel not pub, but well worth knowing for good food inc seafood in former period school hall, pleasant modern bar; spacious clifftop terrace overlooking harbour, 15 bedrooms (David Tindal)

Slipway PL29 3RH [Middle St]: Small hotel just across from delightful village's slipway and beach, small unpretentious cellar-like bar with low dark beams, flagstones and some stripped stonework, Sharps Doom Bar and Cornish Coaster, decent wines by the glass, nice bar food, appealing watercolours for sale, good restaurant; leave car at top of village unless you enjoy a challenge; children welcome, crazy-paved heated terrace with awning, refurbished bedrooms, open all day in summer (Kevin and Jane O'Mahoney, John and Alison Hamilton, LYM)

PORTHLEVEN [SW6225]

Harbour Inn TR13 9JB [Commercial Rd]: Large neatly kept pub/hotel in outstanding harbourside setting, pleasant well organised service, expansive newly fitted out lounge and bar with impressive dining area off, St Austell ales, comprehensive wine list; quiet piped music; picnic-sets on big quayside terrace, decent bedrooms, some with harbour view, good breakfast (Mick and Moira Brummell, Charles Gysin, Sue Demont, Tim Barrow)

PORTLOE [SW9339]

☆ *Ship* TR2 5RA: Friendly new licensees in comfortably bright L-shaped local with reasonably priced straightforward food from well filled sandwiches to local seafood, well kept St Austell ales, farm cider, decent wines, good prompt service, interesting nautical and local memorabilia and photographs; piped music; sheltered and attractive streamside picnic-sets over road, pretty fishing village with lovely cove and coast path above, open all day Fri-Sun in summer (Christopher Wright, BB, Guy Vowles, Neil Whitehead, Victoria Anderson, Paul and Shirley White, David J Cooke)

PORTMELLON COVE [SX0143]

Rising Sun PL26 6PL [Just S of Mevagissey]: A new licensee for this black-shuttered seaside pub; black beams, small old local photographs, a variety of nautical hardware on ochre walls above dark panelled dado and an unusual log fire at the far end; Blue Anchor Spingo and Wooden Hand Cornish Buccaneer and Cornish Mutiny on handpump, standard bar food; side restaurant, conservatory; a few seats out by side entrance steps with more modern tables on small front terrace; the sandy rock cove is very peaceful out of season; bedrooms (some overlook the water); dogs in bar, children until 6pm and must be over 12 in restaurant (BB, Roger Brown, Gary Rollings, Alan and Paula McCully, LYM)

PORTSCATHO [SW8735]

Plume of Feathers TR2 5HW [The Square]: Cheerful largely stripped stone pub in pretty fishing village, friendly service, well kept St Austell and other ales, pubby food from sandwiches up, bargain fish night Fri, sea-related bric-a-brac in comfortable linked room areas, side locals' bar (can be very lively evenings), restaurant; very popular with summer visitors but perhaps at its best with warm local atmosphere out of season; dogs welcome, open all day in summer (and other times if busy), lovely coast walks (Dr and Mrs M E Wilson, Paul and Shirley White, LYM, David J Cooke, Tim and Joan Wright)

REDRUTH [SW6842]

Tricky Dickys TR15 3TA [Tolgus Mount; OS Sheet 203 map ref 686427]: Part of hotel/fitness complex in isolated former tin-mine buildings, well used bar in dark cheerfully converted ex-smithy, with forge bellows, painting of how it might have looked, buoyant atmosphere, seven beers such as Ring o' Bells and Sharps, good wines and spirits choice, helpful friendly staff, good value food; piped music, games machines; children welcome, partly covered terrace, bedroom block (Dr and Mrs M E Wilson)

SCORRIER [SW7244]

Fox & Hounds TR16 5BS [B3298, off A30 just outside Redruth]: Long partly panelled well divided bar, big log or coal fires each end, red plush banquettes, hunting prints, stripped stonework and creaky joists, wide choice of generous food, Sharps Doom Bar; unobtrusive piped music; picnic-sets out in front, handy for Portreath—Devoran cycle trail (Helen and Brian Edgeley, LYM)

SLADESBRIDGE [SX0171]

Slades House PL27 6JB: Neatly kept and friendly, with decent pub food inc very popular Sun roast, good quick service even when busy, well kept St Austell ales; children welcome (Lynda Bentley)

ST ANNS CHAPEL [SX4170]

Rifle Volunteer PL18 9HL [A390]: Under new management after sale to national local chain, two bars with pews, country kitchen chairs and log fires, good wines by the glass, Sharps Cornish Coaster and Doom Bar and a guest beer, friendly helpful staff, food drom good baguettes up, modern back dining room with picture-window views to Tamar estuary and Plymouth; dogs allowing in public bar, outside tables; more reports on new regime, please (LYM, Dennis Jenkin)

ST BREWARD [SX0977]

☆ *Old Inn* PL30 4PP [off B3266 S of Camelford; Churchtown]: Broad slate flagstones, low oak beams, stripped stonework, two massive granite fireplaces dating from 11th c, straightforward bar food, Bass and Sharps Doom Bar and Eden, lots of wines by the glass, sensibly placed darts, roomy extended restaurant with tables out on deck; piped music, games machine; provision for dogs and children, moorland behind (cattle and sheep wander into the village), open all day Fri-Sun and summer (Gloria Bax, the Didler, Jacquie Jones, LYM, Conor McGaughey)

ST DOMINICK [SX4067]

Who'd Have Thought It PL12 6TG [off A388 S of Callington]: Large comfortable country pub with superb Tamar views esp from conservatory, cosily plush lounge areas with open fires, enjoyable food from sandwiches and baked potatoes to steaks, efficient friendly staff, well kept St Austell ales; dogs allowed in public bar, garden tables, handy for Cotehele (NT) (Ted George, LYM)

ST ERTH PRAZE [SW5735]

Smugglers TR27 6EG [Calais Rd (B3302)]: Large old pub sympathetically refurbished under new management, enjoyable food using local produce and seafood, sensible wine list, good service; frequent live music (anon)

ST EWE [SW9746]

☆ *Crown* PL26 6EY [off B3287]: Low-beamed pub with 16th-c flagstones, traditional furnishings, lovely log fire, voluble parrot and some nice decorative touches, St Austell full beer range, good house wines, helpful attentive licensees, generous but pricy food (can take a while) from crab sandwiches up, large back dining room up steps (heavily booked in season); outside gents', no dogs even in garden; children in eating areas, stone tables in good garden, geese and ducks outside, handy for the Lost Gardens of Heligan, one bedroom, open all day in summer (LYM, David Eberlin, Jack Pridding, Andy Sinden, Louise Harrington, Dr and Mrs M W A Haward, Alan and Paula McCully, Nick Lawless, Christopher Wright, Mike Gorton, Gary Rollings, George Murdoch)

ST IVES [SW5140]

Lifeboat TR26 1LF [Wharf Rd]: Refurbished quayside pub, good atmosphere, wide choice of good value all-day food, three St Austell ales, friendly helpful staff, well spaced harbour-view tables and cosier corners, nautical theme; sports TV; dogs welcome, good disabled access and facilities, open all day *(Michael Saunders, Alan Johnson)*

☆ *Sloop* TR26 1LP [The Wharf]: Busy low-beamed, panelled and flagstoned harbourside pub with bright St Ives School pictures and attractive portrait drawings in front bar, booth seating in back bar, good value food from sandwiches and interesting baguettes to lots of fresh local fish, quick friendly service even though busy, Greene King Old Speckled Hen and Ruddles County and Sharps Doom Bar, good coffee; piped music, TV; children in eating area, a few beach-view seats out on cobbles, open all day (breakfast from 9am), cosy bedrooms, handy for Tate Gallery *(LYM, Alan Johnson, Bruce and Sharon Eden, Steve Harvey, Jarrod and Wendy Hopkinson, Adrian Johnson, Tim and Ann Newell, the Didler)*

ST JUST IN PENWITH [SW3731]

Kings Arms TR19 7HF [Market Sq]: Unpretentious local with St Austell ales, some tapped from the cask, friendly relaxed service, comfortable elderly furniture and local photographs, good value bar meals from baguettes up; popular live music nights; dogs welcome, tables out in front, good value bedrooms with big breakfast, open all day *(the Didler)*

☆ *Star* TR19 7LL [Fore St]: Relaxed and informal dimly lit low-beamed local with good value home-made food from sandwiches and pasties up, St Austell ales, farm cider in summer, mulled wine in winter, coal fire; traditional games inc bar billiards, nostalgic juke box, singalong Mon; tables in attractive back yard, simple bedrooms, good breakfast *(the Didler, LYM)*

ST MAWES [SW8433]

☆ *Rising Sun* TR2 5DJ [The Square]: Long nicely updated bare-boards bar, light, airy and civilised, with prized bow-window seat, good coal fire, well kept St Austell ales, decent wines and whiskies, good coffee, prompt service, emphasis on interesting choice of reasonably priced good food here and in classy restaurant with pleasant conservatory, good crab sandwiches and unusual seafood snacks, great puddings; dogs and children welcome, teak seats and slate-topped tables on handsome sunny terrace just across lane from harbour wall, charming bedrooms, good breakfast, open all day summer *(Mrs M Ainley, Matthew Shackle, Sarah Eley, Helen Sharpe, LYM, David J Cooke, Andy and Claire Barker)*

☆ *Victory* TR2 5DQ [Victory Hill]: Proper local bare-boards bar on left, dining area on right, real ales such as Sharps Doom Bar, friendly staff and locals, enjoyable if pricy food from

good crab sandwiches to carefully cooked fresh local fish, warm log fires, plain wooden seating, upstairs dining room in season; piped music; pleasant picnic-sets outside, good value bedrooms, open all day *(LYM, Dennis Jenkin, J D O Carter, Adrian Johnson, Brian and Genie Smart, Gordon Tong, Barry Collett)*

ST MERRYN [SW8874]

Cornish Arms PL28 8ND [Churchtown (B3276 towards Padstow)]: Well kept St Austell ales and good value generous pubby food inc good fresh fish and steaks (can take a while if busy), also more extensive evening menu, in recently refurbished family-oriented pub with friendly staff, good choice of wines by the glass, log fire, fine slate floor, some 12th-c stonework and RNAS memorabilia; children and dogs welcome, picnic-sets under cocktail parasols on sunny terrace *(LYM, Peter and Margaret Glenister, Lynda Bentley)*

ST TUDY [SX0676]

Cornish Arms PL30 3NN [off A391 nr Wadebridge]: Attractive low-beamed 16th-c local with Bass, Sharps and St Austell, decent food in flagstoned front bar and restaurant, pool room; children welcome *(the Didler)*

STRATTON [SS2306]

☆ *Tree* EX23 9DA [just E of Bude; Fore St]: Rambling and softly lit 16th-c beamed local with interesting old furniture and colourful décor, chatty staff, friendly locals and relaxed atmosphere, great log fires, well kept ales inc Sharps Doom Bar and St Austell Tinners, good coffee, good value generous home-made food using supplies from local farms, character Elizabethan-style evening restaurant with old paintings; big-screen sports TV; children welcome in back bar, seats alongside unusual old dovecote in attractive ancient coachyard, bedrooms *(Jeremy Whitehorn, Ryta Lyndley, Pauline and Philip Darley, BB)*

TINTAGEL [SX0588]

Old Malthouse PL34 0DA [Fore St]: Dark-beamed bar with panelling and inglenook woodburner, friendly atmosphere, wide choice of food inc good local seafood, half a dozen local real ales, carpeted restaurant hung with jugs; tables on roadside terrace, seven bedrooms *(Barry and Sue Pladdys)*

TREBARWITH [SX0586]

☆ *Mill House* PL34 0HD [signed off B3263 and B3314 SE of Tintagel]: Marvellously placed in own steep streamside woods above sea, convivial black-beamed bar with fine delabole flagstones, mix of furnishings from sofas to long tables and chairs, light and airy restaurant area alongside, generally good rather upmarket food (service, normally helpful, can slow right down), Sharps and other real ales; piped music; dogs and children welcome, tables out on sunny terrace and in attractive streamside garden, 12 bedrooms, open all day *(Lynda Bentley, Peter Meister, John Coatsworth, BB)*

Port William PL34 0HB [Trebarwith Strand]: Lovely seaside setting with glorious views, waterside picnic-sets across road and on covered terrace, fishing nets, fish tanks and maritime memorabilia inside, gallery with local artwork, well kept St Austell Tinners and HSD, farm cider; pool and other games, piped music, limited nearby parking; children in eating area, well equipped comfortable bedrooms, open all day *(LYM, John Coatsworth)*

TREBURLEY [SX3477]

☆ *Springer Spaniel* PL15 9NS [A388 Callington—Launceston]: Friendly new licensees, well kept fairly priced Sharps and Skinners real ales, good service, nice décor, with a very high-backed settle by the woodburner, high-backed farmhouse chairs and other seats, olde-worlde stage-coach pictures, further cosy room with big solid teak tables, attractive restaurant up some steps; dogs very welcome in bar, children in eating areas, good tables out on terrace *(Barry and Sue Pladdys, Giles and Annie Francis, Lynda Bentley, LYM)*

TREEN [SW3923]

Logan Rock TR19 6LG [just off B3315 Penzance—Lands End]: Low-beamed traditional bar with inglenook seat by hot coal fire, pricy St Austell HSD and other ales, courteous service, wide choice of standard food all day in summer from sandwiches up, smaller more enterprising choice out of season, lots of games in family room, small back snug with excellent cricket memorabilia – landlady eminent in the county's cricket association; may be piped music, no children inside; tables in small and pretty sheltered garden, good coast walks *(Stuart Turner, LYM, David Crook, the Didler, Richard, JCW)*

TREGONY [SW9244]

Kings Arms TR2 5RW [Fore St (B3287)]: 16th-c pub with long traditional main bar, St Austell ales, good value food using local produce, keen welcoming service and chatty landlord, woodburners in two beamed and panelled front rooms, one for families, back games room; tables in pleasant garden, charming village, open all day *(Christopher Wright, Stephen and Jean Curtis, Tim and Joan Wright)*

TREMATON [SX3960]

☆ *Crooked Inn* PL12 4RZ [off A38 just W of Saltash]: Quietly set down a long drive, this laid-back and decidedly not smart place has free-roaming horses, a pig and sheep, and swings, slides and a trampoline for children; more or less open-plan bar with lower lounge leading to conservatory and doors on to decked area overlooking garden and valley; beams, straightforward furnishings, open fire, several well kept ales such as Sharps and Skinners, decent wines by the glass, cheerful service, wide food choice; children and dogs welcome, bedrooms overlook courtyard, nice breakfast, open all day *(J F M and M West, LYM, Ian Phillips,*

Ted George, Roger and Anne Newbury, Richard May)

TREVAUNANCE COVE [SW7251]

☆ *Driftwood Spars* TR5 0RT [off B3285 in St Agnes; Quay Rd]: Big friendly nautical-theme pub just up from beach and dramatic cove, great coastal walks; slate, granite and massive timbers, lots of nautical and wreck memorabilia, log fires, garden tables across road, and bedrooms; has been popular, with up to half a dozen or so mainly cornish ales, over 100 malt whiskies, Addlestone's cider, lots of wines by the glass, friendly efficient service, and food from bar food (all day in summer) to new fish restaurant, welcoming children and dogs, but changed hands as we went to press – so news please *(LYM)*

TRURO [SW8244]

Try Dower TR1 2LW [Lemon Quay]: New Wetherspoons in former newspaper offices, eight real ales at bargain prices, their usual meal deals, fast efficient service, pastel décor with appropriate prints, sofas, family tables and quiet areas; TV news *(David Crook)*

TYWARDREATH [SX0854]

New Inn PL24 2QP [off A3082; Fore St]: Relaxed local atmosphere, Bass tapped from the cask and St Austell ales on handpump, caring landlord, games and children's room; large secluded garden behind, nice village setting, bedrooms *(Ian and Joan Blackwell, the Didler, BB)*

UPTON CROSS [SX2772]

Caradon Arms PL14 5AZ [B3254 N of Liskeard]: Welcoming country pub with built-in banquettes and dark chairs, carpet over 17th-c flagstones, woodburner, pewter hanging from joists, decorative plates, good cheerful service, wide choice of enjoyable reasonably priced food (not Weds) inc some unusual dishes, Sharps and guest real ales, games room with pool; children welcome, some picnic-sets outside *(Michael and Alison Sandy, BB, Nick and Meriel Cox)*

VERYAN [SW9139]

☆ *New Inn* TR2 5QA [village signed off A3078]: Neat and comfortably homely one-bar beamed local very popular for good generous nourishing food using local produce inc Sun lunch (must book), well kept St Austell Tinners and Tribute, good value house wines and good coffee, leisurely atmosphere, inglenook woodburner, lots of polished brass and old pictures, friendly helpful licensees, quick service even when very busy; piped music, nearby parking unlikely in summer; quiet garden behind the pretty house, charming comfortable bedrooms, good breakfast, interesting partly thatched village not far from nice beach *(Guy Vowles, J D O Carter, Roger Brown, the Didler, BB, Nick Lawless, Christopher Wright, Norman and Sarah Keeping, Michael Lamm)*

WATERGATE BAY [SW8464]

Beach Hut TR8 4AA: Stylish modern beachside bar, relaxed and ultra-cool, with great food (not winter evenings) esp seafood and puddings, good wines, coffee and hot chocolate, comfortable wicker bucket seats, friendly staff and customers, stunning view; children welcome, open all day *(Ryta Lyndley)*

WIDEMOUTH [SS1902]

☆ *Bay View* EX23 0AW [Marine Drive]: Open-plan family-friendly pub, lively and interesting, overlooking magnificent stretch of sand, gorgeous sunset views, wide choice of tasty good value food inc good cream teas in roomy dining area, light and summery, neat staff, cheerful and helpful even when busy, well kept Sharps Doom Bar and Own, Skinners Betty Stogs and a beer brewed by them for the pub; tables on heated front decking, comfortably modernised bedrooms, open all day in summer *(Carrie Wass, Ryta Lyndley, the Didler, G K Smale, Gloria Bax, J R Storey)*

ZELAH [SW8151]

Hawkins Arms TR4 9HU [A30]: 18th-c beamed stone-built local doing well under friendly newish owners, good value food, well kept real ales such as Skinners, log fire, copper and brass in bar and dining room; children welcome, pleasant back terrace *(Neil and Jill Butcher, Steve Pocock)*

ISLES OF SCILLY

ST AGNES [SV8808]

☆ *Turks Head* TR22 0PL [The Quay]: Good service and enjoyable food from pasties up from friendly new ex-restaurateur licensees, following John and Pauline Dart's retirement, for one of the UK's most beautifully placed pubs, with idyllic sea and island views from the garden terrace; no longer lets bedrooms, has been cl winter, open all day other times; more reports on this promising new regime, please *(LYM, Shirley Sandilands)*

ST MARY'S [SV9010]

☆ *Atlantic Inn* TR21 0HY [The Strand; next to but independent from Atlantic Hotel]: Spreading and hospitable dark bar with St Austell ales, enjoyable sea-view restaurant, friendly efficient service, low beams, hanging boat and lots of nautical bits and pieces, flowery-patterned seats, mix of locals and tourists – busy evenings, quieter on sunny lunchtimes; darts, pool, fruit machines; nice raised verandah with green cast-iron furniture and wide views over harbour, good bedrooms in adjacent hotel side *(David Swift, C A Hall, BB, Richard Tosswill)*

Cumbria

The countryside here is of course magnificent, so it's a bonus that so many of the good pubs in this area welcome walkers – and often their dogs, too. Beer is a strong point, and pubs doing well for real ales, often brewing their own, include Wainwrights at Chapel Stile, the Bitter End in Cockermouth (one of the own-brew specialists), the Drunken Duck near Hawkshead (a sophisticated inn but with several own brews), the Old Crown at Hesket Newmarket (owned by a co-operative of locals, and also brewing its own beer), the Watermill at Ings (up to 16 ales including their own), the Kirkstile Inn at Loweswater (popular with walkers, and more own brews), the Eagle & Child at Staveley (good ales, and also a nice place to stay), and the Farmers Arms in Ulverston (appealingly modernised, with half a dozen good beers). We have an interesting clutch of four new main entries here this year – in some cases pubs which we've known in the past, and where more recent changes have been very well received. These are the cheery and attractively furnished Punch Bowl, beautifully sited at Askham; the lively old Sun at Bassenthwaite (good value); the ancient Sun in Kirkby Lonsdale, handsomely updated as a good dining pub, and the Horse & Farrier at Threlkeld, a comfortable dining pub in an enviable spot. Other pubs doing particularly well at the moment are the Pheasant by Bassenthwaite Lake (a civilised hotel with an exceptionally nice pubby little bar), the White Hart at Bouth (a good lakeland atmosphere and very well run), the Blacksmiths Arms at Broughton Mills (despite its remoteness it's deservedly very popular), the Punch Bowl at Crosthwaite (classy and stylish, and with enough bar life to keep it pubby), the Highland Drove at Great Salkeld (a nice place with a particularly friendly, helpful landlord), the Three Shires at Little Langdale (enjoyable food and fine views), the Blacksmiths Arms at Talkin (a good mix of customers and extremely busy), and the Gate Inn at Yanwath (run by a friendly landlord, and much loved for its food). Some exceptionally good food can be found at the Gate, and also at the Pheasant at Bassenthwaite Lake, the Punch Bowl at Crosthwaite, the Highland Drove at Great Salkeld, the Drunken Duck near Hawkshead, the Queens Head at Troutbeck, and the Bay Horse and Farmers Arms both in or near Ulverston. Our choice as Cumbria Dining Pub of the Year is the Punch Bowl at Crosthwaite. This, like several of these other short-listed foodie pubs, also has super bedrooms – excellent, if you want a really self-indulgent meal without having to worry about driving afterwards. The Lucky Dip section at the end of the chapter is rich in appealing pubs, often in prime spots. We'd particularly pick out the warm-hearted Kings Head at Ravenstonedale, a fine all-rounder these days, the Fox & Pheasant at Armathwaite, Bradylls Arms in Bardsea, New Inn at Blencogo (a good food oasis in an area where that's particularly welcome), Brook House at Boot, Oddfellows Arms at Caldbeck, Black Bull and Sun in Coniston, Sun at Crook, Horse & Farrier at Dacre, Bower House at Eskdale Green, Travellers Rest in Grasmere, Dalesman in Sedbergh, Greyhound at Shap,

Kings Arms at Stainton and Church House at Torver. Generally, Cumbrian pub food prices tend to be rather lower than the national average (and helpings are often very hearty). Drinks prices, too, tend to be comfortably below the national norm, with the pubs that brew their own often setting appealing prices, and small local brewers such as Hawkshead, Yates, Tirril, and the Drunken Duck and Old Crown's breweries (Hawkshead and Hesket Newmarket), often providing a pub's best-priced beers. The main local brewery, Jennings, now part of Marstons, is also good value.

AMBLESIDE NY3704 MAP 9

Golden Rule

Smithy Brow; follow Kirkstone Pass signpost from A591 on N side of town; LA22 9AS

Simple town local with cosy, relaxed atmosphere, real ales, and snacks

Walker and dog friendly, this no-frills town local remains happily unchanging. The bar area has built-in wall seats around cast iron-framed tables, horsebrasses on the black beams and assorted pictures decorating the butter-coloured walls; there's a warm winter fire and a relaxed, chatty atmosphere. Also, a back room with TV (not much used), a left-hand room with darts, dominoes, cards and games machine, and a further room down a few steps on the right with lots of seats. Robinsons Hatters Dark, Hartleys XB, Cumbrian Way, Old Stockport, Unicorn, Double Hop and a seasonal ale on handpump. The back yard has some benches and especially colourful window boxes. The golden rule referred to in its name is a brass measuring yard mounted over the bar counter. They will be providing a proper smoking shelter.

🍴 **Snacks such as pork pies, jumbo scotch eggs and filled rolls.** *Starters/Snacks: £0.55 to £2.50*

Robinsons ~ Tenant John Lockley ~ Real ale ~ Bar food ~ No credit cards ~ (015394) 32257 ~ Children welcome away from bar until 9pm ~ Dogs welcome ~ Open 11am-midnight

Recommended by Andy and Jill Kassube, Mike and Sue Loseby, Bob Broadhurst, Edward Leetham, Michael Butler, Pierre Richterich, David and Sue Smith, Helen Clarke

ARMATHWAITE NY5046 MAP 10

Dukes Head

Off A6 S of Carlisle; CA4 9PB

Popular for enjoyable food in comfortable lounge, heated outside area and day fishing tickets

The good food here continues to draw in contented visitors. The comfortable lounge bar has oak settles and little armchairs among more upright seats, oak and mahogany tables, antique hunting and other prints, and some brass and copper powder-flasks above the open fire. Jennings Cumberland and Marstons Pedigree on handpump and home-made lemonade and ginger cordial; separate public bar with darts and table skittles. Seats on a heated outside area and more on the lawn behind; boules. Day tickets for fishing are available.

🍴 **As well as sandwiches and ploughman's, the interesting bar food includes soup, pork, duck and apricot terrine, butter bean and black olive pâté with pesto dressing, hot potted shrimps, filo parcels filled with roasted red pepper, red onion and goats cheese, steak in ale pie, cod goujons in a light basil and olive crumb with home-made tartare sauce, baked salmon on leeks with dry vermouth and prawns, popular roast duckling, and daily specials.** *Starters/Snacks: £3.65 to £5.95. Main Courses: £8.75 to £14.95. Puddings: £2.95 to £3.75*

Punch ~ Tenant Henry Lynch ~ Real ale ~ Bar food ~ Restaurant ~ (016974) 72226 ~ Children welcome ~ Dogs allowed in bar and bedrooms ~ Open 11.30am-midnight; closed 25 Dec ~ Bedrooms: £38.50B/£58.50B

Recommended by Helen Clarke, Alan and Eve Harding, Lee and Liz Potter, Christine and Phil Young, Richard J Holloway, Ann and Tony Bennett-Hughes, B I Mason, Bill and Sheila McLardy

ASKHAM
NY5123   MAP 9

Punch Bowl 🛏

4.5 miles from M6 junction 40; village signposted on right from A6 4 miles S of Penrith; CA10 2PF

Cheery well furnished inn with good choice of different areas, good food and service, log fires; in a lovely spot

Quietly set facing a charming village green (the lower of two), this attractive inn well combines civilised comforts for people staying or wanting a leisurely meal with the warm relaxed atmosphere of a good-hearted local. The spreading main bar has good-sized round and oblong tables with spindle-back chairs and comfortable leather tub chairs on its turkey carpet, an antique settle by the log fire in its imposing stone fireplace, local photographs and prints, and coins stuck into the cracks of the dark wooden beams (periodically taken out and sent to charity). They have Hawkshead Red on handpump, and under the hospitable landlord service is kind and attentive – they are nice to children, too. The lively locals' area has sturdy wooden stools, wall benches and window seats, with darts, dominoes, cribbage and pool in the games room; piped music, games machine. A snug separate lounge has button-back leather settees and easy chairs, and there's an attractive beamed formal dining room with regency striped wallpaper. There are tables out on a flower-filled terrace and a marquee. The bedrooms have been recently refurbished.

🍴 **Good seasonal food includes nice lunchtime sandwiches, cumberland sausage, a vegetarian dish and gammon and egg as well as soup, teriyaki pork tenderloin with egg noodles, pak choi and coriander, home-smoked chicken breast with chorizo, thyme risotto and tomato chutney, pink bream on a beef tomato with roasted pepper, feta cheese and tarragon dressing, organic salmon supreme with smoked salmon and mussel fishcake and a creamy tapenade sauce, guinea fowl breast stuffed with garlic, ginger and spring onion wrapped in pancetta with stir-fried bean sprouts and chilli, rack of local lamb with haggis, ratatouille and honey and mint fondant potatoes, and puddings such as summer pudding and Baileys cheesecake with fresh fruit; they do a good cheeseboard and their Sunday spit roasts are particularly popular.** *Starters/Snacks: £3.95 to £7.95. Main Courses: £9.50 to £19.50. Puddings: £4.75*

Free house ~ Licensees Louise and Paul Smith ~ Real ale ~ Bar food ~ Restaurant ~ (01931) 712443 ~ Children welcome until 8.30pm ~ Dogs welcome ~ Live music some weekends ~ Open 10-midnight ~ Bedrooms: £59.50B/£79.50B

Recommended by Robert Turnham, Phil Bryant, Graham and Elizabeth Hargreaves

BASSENTHWAITE
NY2332   MAP 9

Sun

Off A591 N of Keswick; CA12 4QP

Bustling old pub with tasty, good value food, real ales, and cheerful service

Friendly and cheerful licensees run this ex-farmhouse. The rambling bar has low 17th-c black oak beams, two good stone fireplaces with big winter log fires, built-in wall seats and plush stools around heavy wooden tables and areas that stretch usefully back on both sides of the servery. Jennings Bitter, Cumberland Ale, Sneck Lifter and Mountain Man on handpump and some interesting whiskies. A huddle of white houses looks up to Skiddaw and other high fells, and you can enjoy the view from the tables in the pub's front yard by the rose bushes and honeysuckle; there's a new covered gazebo. The pub is handy for osprey viewing at Dodd Wood.

🍴 **Generous helpings of fairly priced food include soup, lunchtime filled baguettes, chicken liver pâté, garlic mushrooms, local cumberland sausage, vegetable lasagne, smoked haddock fishcakes on tomato sauce, steak in ale pie, braised lamb shank, steaks and daily specials; the landlord loves pickles and you can sample pickled eggs, chillis and so forth.** *Starters/Snacks: £2.95 to £5.00. Main Courses: £6.95 to £14.00. Puddings: £3.50*

Jennings (Marstons) ~ Lease Ali Tozer and Richard McLean ~ Real ale ~ Bar food (12-2, 6-8.45) ~ (017687) 76439 ~ Children welcome ~ Dogs allowed in bar ~ Open 12-11(11.30 Sat); 4.30-11 Mon; closed until 4.30 Mon (except bank hols)

Recommended by Sylvia and Tony Birbeck, D Miller, Helen Clarke, B I Mason

BASSENTHWAITE LAKE

NY1930 MAP 9

Pheasant ★ 🍴 🍷 🛏

Follow Pheasant Inn sign at N end of dual carriageway stretch of A66 by Bassenthwaite Lake; CA13 9YE

Charming, old-fashioned bar in smart hotel with enjoyable bar food and fine range of drinks; excellent restaurant, and attractive surrounding woodlands

This is an exceptional place to stay overnight and enjoy the excellent restaurant food so it is a wonderful added bonus that the civilised little bar remains as pleasantly old-fashioned and pubby as ever, with plenty of customers enjoying a quiet pint or an informal lunch. There are mellow polished walls, cushioned oak settles, rush-seat chairs and library seats, hunting prints and photographs, and Bass, Jennings Cumberland and Theakstons Best on handpump; 12 good wines by the glass and over 60 malt whiskies. Several comfortable lounges have log fires, lovely flower arrangements, fine parquet flooring, antiques, and plants. Dogs are allowed in the residents' lounge at lunchtime and they do let them into the bar during the day too, unless people are eating. There are seats in the garden, attractive woodland surroundings, and plenty of walks in all directions.

🍴 **Enjoyable lunchtime bar food includes very good freshly made soup with home-made bread, stilton, walnut and apricot pâté, open sandwiches with home-made crisps, ploughman's, their own potted silloth shrimps, baked goats cheese tartlet with red onion marmalade, shepherd's pie, smoked haddock on buttered spinach with light cheese sauce and poached egg, daily specials, and puddings such as white chocolate mousse or poached pears in white wine with almond parfait; excellent breakfasts.** *Starters/Snacks: £4.35 to £7.25. Main Courses: £8.95 to £11.95. Puddings: £5.35*

Free house ~ Licensee Matthew Wylie ~ Real ale ~ Bar food (not in evening – restaurant only then) ~ Restaurant ~ (017687) 76234 ~ Children in eating area of bar if over 8 ~ Dogs allowed in bar and bedrooms ~ Open 11.30-2.30, 5.30-10.30(11 Sat); 12-2.30, 5.30-10.30 Sun; closed 24 and 25 Dec ~ Bedrooms: £82B/£144B

Recommended by Julian and Janet Dearden, W K Wood, Geoff and Brigid Smithers, Pat and Stewart Gordon, Mrs Sheila Stothard, Paul Humphreys, Dr and Mrs S G Barber, Mike and Sue Loseby, K S Whittaker, Tina and David Woods-Taylor, B I Mason, Helen Clarke, Neil Ingoe, Revd D Glover, Christine and Phil Young, Sylvia and Tony Birbeck, Jane and Alan Bush, W W Burke, Gordon Ormondroyd

BEETHAM

SD4979 MAP 7

Wheatsheaf 🍷 🛏

Village (and inn) signposted just off A6 S of Milnthorpe; LA7 7AL

17th-c inn with handsome timbered cornerpiece, lots of beams and candles, and a good choice of food and drink

In a quiet village and opposite a pretty 14th-c church, this neatly kept old coaching inn is very striking. Inside, there's an opened-up front lounge bar with fresh flowers and candles on the tables and lots of exposed beams and joists. The main bar (behind on the right) has an open fire, Jennings Cumberland and a couple of guest beers like Hawkshead Lakeland Gold and Tirril Academy Ale on handpump, a dozen wines by the glass, and quite a few malt whiskies. Two upstairs dining rooms are open only at weekends; piped music.

🍽 Under the new licensees bar food now includes open sandwiches, soup, local potted shrimps, chicken liver pâté with apple marmalade, cumberland sausage with sage and red onion mash, mediterranean chargrilled vegetable tart, fillet of cod with a pine nut and basil crust, pork fillet stuffed with apricots and brandy, red snapper fillet on a prawn and mussel chowder and half a duck with a mixed spice and citrus syrup; two- and three-course Early Bird menu Monday-Thursday. *Starters/Snacks: £3.95 to £7.50. Main Courses: £8.95 to £14.95. Puddings: £4.95 to £5.95*

Free house ~ Licensees Mr and Mrs Skelton ~ Real ale ~ Bar food (12-2, 6-9(8.30 Sun); all day Sat) ~ Restaurant ~ (015395) 62123 ~ Children in restaurant before 7pm ~ Open 11-11; 12-10.30 Sun ~ Bedrooms: £65B/£75B

Recommended by Michael Doswell, Dr and Mrs T E Hothersall, Anthony Waters, Brian and Janet Ainscough, G Dobson, Karen Eliot, Maurice and Gill McMahon, Chris Smith, Jo Lilley, Simon Calvert, W K Wood, W W Burke

BOUTH
SD3285 MAP 9

White Hart 🍺
Village signposted off A590 near Haverthwaite; LA12 8JB

A fine range of well kept real ales, tasty bar food, and plenty of bric-a-brac in cheerful lakeland inn; good surrounding walks

There's a friendly and bustling atmosphere in this well run, traditional inn – and a fine range of real ales too: Black Sheep, Jennings Cumberland and guests like Hawkshead Bitter and Lakeland Gold, Titanic Mild and Ulverston UXB are well kept on handpump and they also have 25 malt whiskies and several wines by the glass. The sloping ceilings and floors show the building's age, and there are lots of old local photographs and bric-a-brac – farm tools, stuffed animals, a collection of long-stemmed clay pipes – and two woodburning stoves. The games room (where dogs are allowed) has darts, pool, dominoes, fruit machine, TV and juke box; piped music. Some seats outside and fine surrounding walks.

🍽 Good bar food includes sandwiches, soup, five-bean chilli, home-made steak and Guinness pie, halibut steak in garlic and parsley butter, cumberland sausage with rich onion and cranberry gravy, rare breed sirloin steak, nice daily specials and a good children's menu. *Starters/Snacks: £4.75 to £6.25. Main Courses: £9.25 to £14.75. Puddings: £4.25 to £4.75*

Free house ~ Licensees Nigel and Peter Barton ~ Real ale ~ Bar food (12-2, 6-8.45; not Mon or Tues lunchtime except bank hols) ~ (01229) 861229 ~ Children in bar until 9pm ~ Dogs allowed in bedrooms ~ Live music every other Fri and occasionally on Sun ~ Open 12-2, 6-11; 12-11(10.30 Sun) Sat; closed Mon and Tues lunchtimes (except bank hols) ~ Bedrooms: £47.50S(£37.50B)/£80S(£60B)

Recommended by Michael Doswell, Ann and Tony Bennett-Hughes, Dr Peter Crawshaw, Andy and Jill Kassube, Alain and Rose Foote, Lee and Liz Potter, Bob Ellis, Ron Gentry, Pip King, Dr and Mrs A K Clarke, JDM, KM

BRAMPTON
NY6723 MAP 10

New Inn 🍺
Note: this is the small Brampton near Appleby, not the bigger one up by Carlisle. Off A66 N of Appleby – follow Long Marton 1 signpost then turn right at church; village also signposted off B6542 at N end of Appleby; CA16 6JS

Traditional village inn with decent beer and food, and Pennine views from seats in garden

Well cared for and traditional, this is an 18th-c black and white slated village inn. There's an open-plan bar with a mix of wooden dining chairs around straightforward pub tables on the wood-boarded floor, some upholstered cushions, photographs of the pub and country pictures on the wall, Tirril Bewshers, Brougham Ale and Old Faithful on handpump and local juices. Piped music, darts, pool, cards and dominoes. The interesting low-beamed and flagstoned dining room has an ancient cooking range by a massive old oak settle. Picnic-sets in the garden and views over the Pennines. More reports please.

🍴 **Tasty bar food includes lunchtime filled ciabattas and baked potatoes, soup, garlic mushrooms, a pie of the day, goats cheese tart, cumberland sausage, battered cod, lasagne, evening steaks, daily specials, and puddings such as home-made sticky toffee pudding.** *Starters/Snacks: £3.75 to £6.00. Main Courses: £7.95 to £14.95. Puddings: £2.95 to £3.95*

Free house ~ Licensee Dan Ingham ~ Real ale ~ Bar food (12-2.30, 6-9.30; all day weekends; not Tues and Weds lunchtime) ~ Restaurant ~ (017683) 51231 ~ Children welcome until 9pm ~ Dogs allowed in bar ~ Open 12-2.30, 6-11; 12-11(10.30 Sun) Sat; closed Tues and Weds lunchtime

Recommended by Tony and Betty Parker

BROUGHTON MILLS
SD2190   MAP 9

Blacksmiths Arms
Off A593 N of Broughton-in-Furness; LA20 6AX

Good food, local beers and open fires in charming small pub liked by walkers

With friendly, cheerful staff and warm log fires, this charming little pub is just the place to head for after a fine walk. Three of the four simply but attractively decorated small rooms have straightforward chairs and tables on ancient slate floors, Barngates Tag Lag, Dent Aviator and Jennings Cumberland on handpump and summer farm cider. There are three smallish dining rooms; darts, board games, dominoes and cards. Pretty summer hanging baskets and tubs of flowers in front of the building.

🍴 **Good, often interesting bar food includes lunchtime sandwiches or ciabattas and ploughman's, soup, duck terrine with spiced red onion jam, potted shrimps with toasted sourdough bread, beer-battered cod, chargrilled lime and coriander chicken with beetroot, carrot and chickpea salad, slow-braised shoulder of minted lamb, braised rabbit with roasted sweet potatoes and mustard sauce, butternut squash and thyme risotto, daily specials, and puddings like panna cotta with blueberry compote or sticky toffee pudding with butterscotch sauce.** *Starters/Snacks: £3.95 to £4.45. Main Courses: £7.85 to £13.95. Puddings: £3.95*

Free house ~ Licensees Mike and Sophie Lane ~ Real ale ~ Bar food (12-2, 6-9; not Mon lunchtime) ~ Restaurant ~ (01229) 716824 ~ Children welcome ~ Dogs welcome ~ Open 12-11(5-11 Mon); 12-10.30 Sun; 12-2.30, 5-11 Tues-Fri in winter; closed Mon lunchtime

Recommended by Peter F Marshall, Derek Harvey-Piper, Tina and David Woods-Taylor, Julie and Bill Ryan, the Didler

BUTTERMERE
NY1716   MAP 9

Bridge Hotel
Just off B5289 SW of Keswick; CA13 9UZ

Wonderful walks close to bustling coaching inn usefully open all day

As Crummock Water and Buttermere are just a stroll away and there is unrestricted walking for all levels nearby, this bustling 18th-c coaching inn is, not surprisingly, very popular with walkers. The beamed bar has built-in wooden settles and farmhouse chairs around traditional tables, a panelled bar counter, and a few horsebrasses – as well as a dining bar with plush armchairs around copper-topped tables and brass ornaments hanging from the beams, and a guest lounge. Black Sheep, Hawkshead Gold, Theakstons Old Peculier and a guest beer on handpump, several malt whiskies, and a decent wine list; hot drinks are usefully sold all day. Outside, a flagstoned terrace has seats by a rose-covered sheltering stone wall. As well as comfortable bedrooms there are some self-catering apartments too (where dogs are allowed).

🍴 **As well as lunchtime filled baked potatoes or hot paninis, open sandwiches and home-made burgers, bar food includes cumberland sausage and egg, a hotpot, chicken liver pâté, mushroom stroganoff, chicken and mushroom pie, steak and kidney pudding and daily specials.** *Starters/Snacks: £3.00 to £5.00. Main Courses: £6.00 to £14.95. Puddings: £3.25 to £4.25*

Free house ~ Licensees Adrian and John McGuire ~ Real ale ~ Bar food (all day) ~ Restaurant ~ (017687) 70252 ~ Children welcome but must be over 7 in evening dining room ~ Open 9.15am-11.30pm(10.30 Sun) ~ Bedrooms: £60B/£120B

Recommended by Dr and Mrs Michael Smith, Sylvia and Tony Birbeck, Comus and Sarah Elliott, Kay and Alistair Butler, Louise English, Margaret Whalley, Lindsley Harvard, the Didler

CARTMEL

SD3778 MAP 7

Kings Arms
The Square; LA11 6QB

Timbered pub in ancient village with seats facing lovely village square

In an ancient village with a grand priory church, this little black and white pub has seats outside that make the most of the lovely square. Inside, the rambling bar has small antique prints on the walls, a mixture of seats including old country chairs, settles and wall banquettes, and tankards hanging over the bar counter. Barngates Tag Lag, Black Sheep, Hawkshead Bitter and Marstons Pedigree on handpump and ten wines by the glass; piped music. The pub is close to a fine medieval stone gatehouse and the race track is 200 yards away. More reports please.

🍽 **Bar food includes lunchtime sandwiches, nut roast, gammon and egg, venison and cranberry sausage, chicken, ham and mushroom pie, beer-battered cod, and daily specials.** *Starters/Snacks: £3.25 to £5.95. Main Courses: £7.95 to £13.95. Puddings: £2.00 to £4.25*

Enterprise ~ Lease Richard Grimmer ~ Real ale ~ Bar food (12-2.30, 5.30-8.30; 12-8.45 weekends) ~ Restaurant ~ (01539) 536220 ~ Children in restaurant and snug until 9pm ~ Dogs allowed in bar ~ Open 11-11(10.30 Sun); closed 25 Dec

Recommended by A and B D Craig, Alain and Rose Foote, Alan and Paula McCully, Michael Doswell

CARTMEL FELL

SD4189 MAP 9

Masons Arms
Strawberry Bank, a few miles S of Windermere between A592 and A5074; perhaps the simplest way of finding the pub is to go uphill W from Bowland Bridge (which is signposted off A5074) towards Newby Bridge and keep right then left at the staggered crossroads – it's then on your right, below Gummer's How; OS Sheet 97 map reference 413895; LA11 6NW

Plenty of character in beamed bar, good food, real ales plus many foreign bottled beers, and fine views from terrace

In beautiful surroundings, this is a charming little pub run with care and thought. The main bar has plenty of character with low black beams in the bowed ceiling and country chairs and plain wooden tables on polished flagstones. A small lounge has oak tables and settles to match its fine Jacobean panelling, there's a plain little room beyond the serving counter with pictures and a fire in an open range, a family room with an old-parlourish atmosphere, and an upstairs dining room; piped music and board games. Black Sheep, Hawkshead Bitter and Ulverston Laughing Gravy on handpump and a wide range of foreign bottled beers. Comfortable self-catering cottages and apartments behind. The view down over the Winster Valley to the woods below Whitbarrow Scar is really quite special and can be enjoyed from the rustic benches and tables on the terrace.

🍽 **Good, enjoyable bar food includes sandwiches, soup, chicken or hazelnut and brown lentil pâté, duck sausage and black pudding salad topped with a soft poached egg, popular spare ribs with sticky sauce, roasted red pepper and goats cheese melt, slow-cooked minted lamb, beef in ale or game pie, chicken tikka masala, daily specials, and puddings like warm chocolate fudge cake with chocolate sauce or apple crumble.** *Starters/Snacks: £3.95 to £6.99. Main Courses: £9.99 to £13.99. Puddings: £2.50 to £4.75*

Free house ~ Licensees John and Diane Taylor ~ Real ale ~ Bar food (12-2.30, 6-9; all day in summer and on winter weekends) ~ Restaurant ~ (015395) 68486 ~ Children welcome ~ Open 11.30-11; 12-10.30 Sun

*Recommended by Tina and David Woods-Taylor, Rob & Sue Hastie, M J Winterton, Helen and Brian Edgeley,
Tessa Allanson, Chris Evans, David and Sue Atkinson, Kay and Alistair Butler, Jo Lilley, Simon Calvert, Andy and
Jill Kassube, Walter and Susan Rinaldi-Butcher, Helen Clarke, Jenny and Peter Lowater, Mr and Mrs
Richard Osborne, Maurice Ricketts*

CASTERTON
SD6279   MAP 7

Pheasant ♀

*A683 about 1 mile N of junction with A65, by Kirkby Lonsdale; OS Sheet 97 map reference
633796; LA6 2RX*

Neat beamed rooms in pleasant inn, and seats in attractive garden with fell views

The beamed rooms of the main bar in this traditional 18th-c inn are neatly kept and
attractively modernised, with wheelback chairs, cushioned wall settles, a nicely arched
oak framed fireplace (gas-effect fires now), and Dent Aviator, Greene King Old Speckled
Hen, Theakstons Bitter and Timothy Taylors Landlord on handpump; over 25 malt
whiskies, an extensive wine list and courteous, friendly staff. Piped music and board
games. There are some tables under cocktail parasols outside by the road, with more in
the pleasant garden. The nearby church (built for the girls' school of Brontë fame here)
has some attractive pre-Raphaelite stained glass and paintings.

🍴 Bar food includes sandwiches, soup, smoked mackerel mousse, deep-fried breaded
mushrooms with garlic butter, spinach, feta cheese and mushroom strudel, spiced lamb,
pork fillet in pepper cream sauce, roast topside with yorkshire pudding and horseradish
sauce, seafood mixed grill, daily specials, and puddings. *Starters/Snacks: £3.50 to £5.95.
Main Courses: £8.25 to £19.00. Puddings: £4.00 to £4.50*

Free house ~ Licensee the Dixon family ~ Real ale ~ Bar food (12-2, 6-9) ~ Restaurant ~
(015242) 71230 ~ Children allowed during food serving times ~ Open 12-3, 6-11(10.30 Sun) ~
Bedrooms: £38B/£86B

*Recommended by Margaret and Roy Randle, Bill Gallon, Roger Thornington, John and Yvonne Davies, G Dobson,
Tom and Jill Jones, Mr and Mrs Ian King, William and Ann Reid, John and Sylvia Harrop*

CHAPEL STILE
NY3205   MAP 9

Wainwrights ◀

B5343; LA22 9JH

Fine choice of beers, lovely views, and surrounding walks

This white-rendered lakeland house is useful after one of the good surrounding walks and
you can enjoy the views from the picnic-table sets out on the terrace. It's been
refurbished inside since they had to close after a fire but the slate-floored bar still has
plenty of room and it is here that walkers and their dogs are welcomed. There's a relaxed
atmosphere, an old kitchen range, cushioned settles and Thwaites Original, Lancaster
Bomber and Thoroughbred and guests like Barngates Tag Lag, Black Sheep, Caledonian
Deuchars IPA and Yates Sun Goddess on handpump and quite a range of bottled beers.
Piped music, TV and games machine. More reports please.

🍴 Bar food includes sandwiches, garlic mushrooms, tex mex vegetarian chilli, salads,
burgers, steak in ale pie, cumberland sausage, fish and chips, and puddings.
Starters/Snacks: £3.25 to £7.50. Main Courses: £7.50 to £9.75. Puddings: £3.75

Free house ~ Licensees Mrs C Darbyshire and B Clarke ~ Real ale ~ Bar food (12-2, 6-9) ~
(015394) 38088 ~ Children allowed away from bar ~ Dogs welcome ~ Open 11.30-11;
12-11 Sun

*Recommended by Irene and Derek Flewin, Louise English, Tony and Penny Burton, David and Katharine Cooke,
Julie and Bill Ryan*

Pubs brewing their own beers are listed at the back of the book.

COCKERMOUTH

NY1230 MAP 9

Bitter End ◖

Kirkgate, by cinema; CA13 9PJ

Own-brewed beers and lots of bottled beers in three interesting bars

As well as brewing their own two real ales, this friendly, bustling pub also keeps three regulars and three guests: Cuddy Lugs and Cockermouth Pride from their own little brewery plus Hawkshead Red, Jennings Bitter and Cumberland, Keswick Thirst Pitch, O'Hanlon's Firefly and Roosters Yankee on handpump in good condition. Quite a few bottled beers from around the world and eight wines by the glass. The three cosy main rooms have a different atmosphere in each – from quietly chatty to sporty, with the décor reflecting this, such as unusual pictures of a Cockermouth that even Wordsworth might have recognised, to more up-to-date sporting memorabilia, various bottles, jugs and books, and framed beer mats; welcoming log fire, piped music and quiz night on Tuesdays. The public car park round the back is free after 7pm.

🍴 **Good value traditional bar food includes sandwiches, steak in ale pie, cumberland sausage with caramelised onion sauce, goats cheese, tomato, red onion and garlic in puff pastry with home-made tomato sauce, fish in beer batter, lasagne, steaks, and puddings.** *Starters/Snacks: £3.25 to £4.75. Main Courses: £6.95 to £14.50. Puddings: £3.25*

Own brew ~ Licensee Susan Askey ~ Real ale ~ Bar food (12-2, 6-8.45) ~ (01900) 828993 ~ Children allowed during food service only ~ Open 12-2.30, 6-11.30; 11.30-midnight Sat; 12-3, 6-11 Sun; 11.30-3, 6-midnight Sat in winter

Recommended by Edward Mirzoeff, Peter Smith, Judith Brown, Pat and Stewart Gordon, GSB, Kevin Flack, Andy and Jill Kassube, Helen Clarke, Julia Morris, the Didler

CROSTHWAITE

SD4491 MAP 9

Punch Bowl

Village signposted off A5074 SE of Windermere; LA8 8HR

CUMBRIA DINING PUB OF THE YEAR

Nicely uncluttered and stylish dining pub with wide choice of super food, good wine and real ales; lovely bedrooms, and seats on terrace overlooking valley

We've had a lot of warm feedback from our readers on this carefully and stylishly refurbished place. And although there's no doubt that much emphasis is placed on the marvellous food, there is still enough bar life to call it a pub. They keep four real ales on handpump served by friendly, attentive staff – Barngates Cat Nap, Tag Lag and Westmorland Gold (brewed at their sister pub the Drunken Duck near Hawkshead) as well as Coniston Bluebird – a wide range of malt whiskies, and 18 wines by the glass plus eight champagnes. The enlarged raftered and hop-hung bar has a couple of eye-catching rugs on flagstones and bar stools by the slate-topped counter, and this opens on the right into two linked carpeted and beamed rooms with well spaced country pine furnishings of varying sizes, including a big refectory table. The walls, painted in restrained neutral tones, have an attractive assortment of prints, with some copper objects, and there's a dresser with china and glass; winter log fire and daily papers. On the left is the wooden-floored restaurant area, also attractive, with comfortable leather seating. Throughout, the pub feels relaxing and nicely uncluttered. There are some tables on a terrace stepped into the hillside, overlooking the Lythe Valley. This is a lovely place to stay.

🍴 **Some sort of food is served all day and it is extremely good: sandwiches, soup with home-made bread, chicken caesar salad, warm vegetable terrine with pear and raspberry chutney, roasted local quail with squash mash, caraway and bacon, chicken breast with baby spinach mousse and a light chicken cream, noisettes of herdwick lamb with wild mushrooms and minted potato purée, spinach and ricotta pancakes, steamed sea bream with samphire and prawn broth and sweet potato mash, and puddings like Valrhona chocolate fondant, Horlicks ice-cream, beetroot syrup and chocolate crisps or apple crème brûlée with granny apple sorbet and blackberry compote.** *Starters/Snacks: £6.00 to £7.75. Main Courses: £13.00 to £17.95. Puddings: £6.00 to £9.00*

Free house ~ Licensee Stephen Carruthers ~ Real ale ~ Bar food (12-3, 6-9; light lunches all afternoon) ~ Restaurant ~ (015395) 68237 ~ Children welcome ~ Dogs allowed in bar ~ Open 12-11(10.30 Sun) ~ Bedrooms: £75B/£110B

Recommended by Hugh Roberts, Leslie G Smith, Richard Greaves, Rob Bowran, Brian and Pat Wardrobe, W K Wood, Dr K P Tucker, Tessa Allanson, Michael Doswell, Helen Clarke, Dr and Mrs A K Clarke, Simon and Mandy King

ELTERWATER
NY3204 MAP 9

Britannia
Off B5343; LA22 9HP

Well run pub, extremely popular at peak times and surrounded by wonderful walks and scenery

As this old-fashioned and friendly walkers' pub is in such a beautiful part of the Lake District, close to the central lakes and with tracks over the fells, there are inevitable queues at peak times. There's a small and traditionally furnished back bar and a front one with a couple of window seats looking across to Elterwater itself through the trees: winter coal fires, oak benches, settles, windsor chairs, a big old rocking chair, and Caledonian Deuchars IPA, Coniston Bluebird, Jennings Bitter, Oakham JHB and Timothy Taylors Landlord on handpump; quite a few malt whiskies and mulled wine. The lounge is comfortable and there's a hall and dining room. Plenty of seats outside and summer morris and step and garland dancers.

🍴 **Tasty home-made bar food includes lunchtime filled rolls, soup, garlic mushrooms, beer-battered fresh haddock, steak in ale pie, cumberland sausage with onion gravy, wild mushroom stroganoff, braised minted lamb with rosemary gravy, daily specials, and puddings such as apple and raspberry crumble or blueberry brûlée.** *Starters/Snacks: £3.60 to £5.25. Main Courses: £8.00 to £15.00. Puddings: £4.00 to £5.25*

Free house ~ Licensee Clare Woodhead ~ Real ale ~ Bar food (all day) ~ Restaurant ~ (015394) 37210 ~ Children welcome but must leave bar by 9pm ~ Dogs allowed in bar and bedrooms ~ Open 10am-11pm ~ Bedrooms: £80S/£110S(£90B)

Recommended by David and Jean Hall, Dr David Clegg, Arthur Pickering, John and Jackie Walsh, Tina and David Woods-Taylor, Tom and Jill Jones, Paul Humphreys, David and Sue Smith, Jarrod and Wendy Hopkinson, Chris Willers, Malcolm and Jane Levitt, C J Pratt, Jo Lilley, Simon Calvert

GREAT SALKELD
NY5536 MAP 10

Highland Drove
B6412, off A686 NE of Penrith; CA11 9NA

Smashing place with a cheerful mix of customers, good food in several dining areas, fair choice of drinks, and fine views from upstairs verandah

Run by a convivial and helpful landlord and liked by both drinkers and diners, this is a bustling and deservedly popular pub. The chatty main bar has sandstone flooring, stone walls, cushioned wheelback chairs around a mix of tables and an open fire in a raised stone fireplace. The downstairs eating area has cushioned dining chairs around wooden tables on the pale wooden floorboards, stone walls and ceiling joists and a two-way fire in a raised stone fireplace that separates this room from the coffee lounge with its comfortable leather chairs and sofas. There's also an upstairs restaurant. Best to book to be sure of a table. John Smiths, Theakstons Black Bull and a guest such as Archers Bobs Your Uncle on handpump, 14 wines by the glass and 25 malt whiskies. Piped music, TV, juke box, darts, pool and games machine. The lovely views over the Eden Valley and the Pennines are best enjoyed from seats on the upstairs verandah. As we went to press, they were building a back terrace.

🍴 **As well as sandwiches, the enjoyable food in the downstairs bar might include soup, spiced devilled mushrooms with a puff pastry crown, a charcuterie plate, home-made burger, ham and egg, beer-battered haddock, cottage pie and chicken chasseur, with upstairs choices like smoked haddock pâté with apple and tarragon dressing, cheese and tomato tart with rocket pesto, noisette of lamb with apricot and prune stuffing and** minted orange jus, and nile perch with a tian of lemon and crab mash and chilli, lime and coconut sauce; puddings such as toffee and banana crumble or trio of chocolate. *Starters/Snacks: £2.95 to £7.25. Main Courses: £7.95 to £19.50. Puddings: £4.25 to £5.95*

Free house ~ Licensees Donald and Paul Newton ~ Real ale ~ Bar food (12-2, 6-9; not Mon lunchtime) ~ Restaurant ~ (01768) 898349 ~ Children welcome with restrictions ~ Dogs allowed in bar ~ Open 12-3, 6-midnight; 12-midnight Sat; 12-3, 6-midnight Sun in winter; closed Mon lunchtime; 25 Dec ~ Bedrooms: £35B/£65B

Recommended by Les and Sandra Brown, Dr K P Tucker, Richard J Holloway, Phil Bryant, Kevin Tea, Helen Clarke, Michael Doswell, John and Jackie Walsh, K S Whittaker, Robert and Susan Phillips, B I Mason, Comus and Sarah Elliott, Peter Tanfield, Peter Craske

HAWKSHEAD   NY3501   MAP 9

Drunken Duck ⌘ ♀ ◧ ⇌

Barngates; the hamlet is signposted from B5286 Hawkshead—Ambleside, opposite the Outgate Inn; or it may be quicker to take the first right from B5286, after the wooded caravan site; OS Sheet 90 map reference 350013; LA22 0NG

Stylish small bar, several restaurant areas and lovely bedrooms in civilised inn with own-brewed beers, imaginative food, and stunning views

There is a small, smart bar in this civilised inn with seating for around thirty, and as well as their own-brewed beers, they now offer hot bar meals in addition to sandwiches – and locals do drop in for a pint and a chat. But there is no doubt that a great many of their customers (and a lot of our readers) are here to enjoy the imaginative modern cooking in the three restaurant areas and the beautifully appointed bedrooms (the ones across the courtyard have been newly refurbished). The bar has beams and oak floorboards, leather-topped bar stools by the slate-topped bar counter, leather club chairs, photographs, coaching prints and hunting pictures, and some kentish hop bines. They keep four of their own brews on handpump, usually Barngates Cat Nap, Cracker, Tag Lag and Red Bull Terrier but you could also choose from Chesters Strong & Ugly, K9 (to mark the occasion of their 1,000th brew), Pride of Westmorland and Westmorland Gold. 18 wines plus three pudding wines by the glass, a fine choice of spirits and belgian and german draught beers. New wooden tables and benches on the grass bank opposite the building offer spectacular views across the fells, and there are thousands of spring and summer bulbs.

⌘ As well as sandwiches using their own white bread, home-cooked meats, local cheeses and free-range eggs, the modern bar food includes soup, ploughman's, crab ravioli with basil and caper pesto, foie gras cake with mulled wine and gingerbread, crispy duck salad with pickled rhubarb, organic salmon cakes with togarashi mayonnaise, beef in ale suet pudding, and puddings such as white chocolate and stilton ice-cream or warm rice pudding with spiced quince. The excellent and imaginative à la carte menu is a great deal more expensive. *Starters/Snacks: £3.75 to £6.95. Main Courses: £4.25 to £7.95. Puddings: £5.95*

Own brew ~ Licensee Steph Barton ~ Real ale ~ Bar food (12-4(2.15 restaurant), 6-9) ~ Restaurant ~ (015394) 36347 ~ Children must leave restaurant by 8pm ~ Dogs allowed in bar ~ Open 11.30-11; 12-10.30 Sun ~ Bedrooms: £71.25B/£95B

Recommended by Leslie G Smith, Tina and David Woods-Taylor, Mrs Suzy Miller, Mr and Mrs P Eastwood, Peter and Lesley Yeoward, Noel Grundy, Richard Cole, Mike and Sue Loseby, P Briggs, W M Lien, K S Whittaker, Roger Yates, David and Sue Atkinson, Dr K P Tucker, John and Sylvia Harrop

Kings Arms
The Square; LA22 0NZ

Some fine original features in 16th-c inn, decent drinks, homely food, and free fishing permits for residents

In summer, the best place to sit is on the terrace outside this 16th-c inn and look over the central square of its lovely Elizabethan village. Inside, there are some fine original features, traditional pubby furnishings, and an open log fire: Black Sheep, Coniston Bluebird, Hawkshead Bitter and Moorhouses Pride of Pendle on handpump, 30 malt whiskies, a decent wine list, farm cider and winter mulled wine. Piped music, games machine, darts, dominoes, cards and board games. As well as bedrooms, they offer self-catering cottages. There are free fishing permits for residents. More reports please.

🍴 **Decent lunchtime bar food such as filled baguettes, ciabatta and open sandwiches, soup, fish and chips, vegetarian quiche and cumberland sausages and evening choices like steak in ale pie, parmesan and coriander chicken and minted lamb chops.** *Starters/Snacks: £2.95 to £5.25. Main Courses: £4.25 to £12.50. Puddings: £4.25*

Free house ~ Licensees Rosalie and Edward Johnson ~ Real ale ~ Bar food (12-2.30, 6-9.30) ~ Restaurant ~ (015394) 36372 ~ Children welcome ~ Dogs allowed in bar and bedrooms ~ Live music third Thurs in month ~ Open 11-midnight ~ Bedrooms: £46S/£82S

Recommended by Alan and Paula McCully, Nick Lawless, Robert Wivell, Margaret Whalley, Lindsley Harvard

Queens Head
Main Street; LA22 0NS

Lovely timbered pub, liked by locals and visitors, with bustling atmosphere, and decent food and drinks

With a good mix of locals and visitors, this lovely black and white timbered pub has a good bustling atmosphere. The low-ceilinged bar has heavy bowed black beams, red plush wall seats and plush stools around heavy traditional tables, lots of decorative plates on the panelled walls, and an open fire; a snug little room leads off. Robinsons Cumbria Way, Double Hop, Unicorn, and a guest beer on handpump; piped music, dominoes, cards and board games. As well as bedrooms in the inn, they have three holiday cottages to rent in the village. The summer window boxes are very pretty and there are plenty of seats outside. Residents can get a parking pass from the inn for the public car park about 100 yards away.

🍴 **Meals can be eaten either in the bar or the more formal restaurant: sandwiches, soup, duck liver pâté, leek and blue cheese tart, beer-battered haddock, chicken breast stuffed with garlic, mozzarella and ham, golden coated, slow-roasted shoulder of lamb, venison with an orange and apricot sauce, steaks, and daily specials.** *Starters/Snacks: £3.25 to £6.50. Main Courses: £12.00 to £20.00. Puddings: £3.50 to £4.75*

Robinsons ~ Tenants Mr and Mrs Tony Merrick ~ Real ale ~ Bar food (12-2.30, 6.15-9.30; all day Sun) ~ Restaurant ~ (015394) 36271 ~ Children welcome ~ Open 10am-midnight ~ Bedrooms: £60B/£90B

Recommended by Tom and Jill Jones, Jarrod and Wendy Hopkinson, David and Ros Hanley, Arthur Pickering, Mr and Mrs P Eastwood, Alan and Paula McCully, Ian and Jane Irving, W W Burke

HESKET NEWMARKET   NY3438   MAP 10
Old Crown 🍺
Village signposted off B5299 in Caldbeck; CA7 8JG

Straightforward local with own-brewed beers, in attractive village

New licensees have taken over the running of this unfussy local – still owned by a co-operative of more than a hundred local people. The own-brewed beers remain well kept on handpump: Hesket Newmarket Blencathra Bitter, Doris's 90th Birthday Ale, Great Cockup Porter, Haystacks, Helvellyn Gold, Skiddaw Special Bitter, Old Carrock Strong Ale, Catbells Pale Ale and Scafell Blonde. The little bar has a few tables, a log fire, bric-a-brac, mountaineering kit and pictures and a friendly atmosphere; darts, pool, juke box, board games and dominoes. There's also a dining room and garden room. The pub is in a pretty setting in a remote, attractive village. You can book up tours to look around the brewery, £10 for the tour and a meal.

🍴 **Bar food includes lunchtime sandwiches as well as cumberland sausage with onion gravy, vegetarian or meaty curries, beef in ale pie, barnsley chop with mint sauce, daily specials, and puddings such as syrup sponge or apple crumble.** *Starters/Snacks: £2.95 to £4.95. Main Courses: £6.25 to £10.75. Puddings: £3.95*

Own brew ~ Tenants Pat and Malcolm Hawksworth ~ Real ale ~ Bar food ~ Restaurant ~ (016974) 78288 ~ Children welcome ~ Dogs allowed in bar ~ Regular folk music ~ Open 12-11(10.30 Sun)
Recommended by B I Mason, Helen Clarke, Adam F Padel, Mike and Sue Loseby

INGS   SD4498   MAP 9

Watermill ◀

Just off A591 E of Windermere; LA8 9PY

Busy, cleverly converted pub with fantastic range of real ales including own brew

As well as their own-brewed Watermill Collie Wobbles, A Bit'er Ruff and W'Ruff Night, there's an amazing choice of up to 16 well kept real ales on handpump in this popular pub: Atlas Latitude, Clarks Classic Blonde, Coniston Bluebird, Hawkshead Bitter, Keswick Thirst Pitch, Lancaster Duchy, Moorhouses Black Cat, Oakham JHB, Theakstons Best and Old Peculier, Triple fff Moondance, Ulverston Another Fine Mess and Yates Fever Pitch. Also, 60 foreign bottled beers and over 50 whiskies. The building is cleverly converted from a wood mill and joiner's shop, and the bars have a friendly, bustling atmosphere, a happy mix of chairs, padded benches and solid oak tables, bar counters made from old church wood, open fires and interesting photographs and amusing cartoons by a local artist. The spacious lounge bar, in much the same traditional style as the other rooms, has rocking chairs and a big open fire. Darts and board games. Seats in the gardens, and lots to do nearby.

🍴 **Bar food usefully served virtually all day includes lunchtime sandwiches and rolls, filled baked potatoes and ploughman's, lasagne, beer-battered fresh haddock, mediterranean pasta bake, cumberland sausage, beef in ale pie, lamb shoulder in mint, garlic and red wine, daily specials such as goats cheese tartlet with red onion marmalade and scrumpy pork casserole, and puddings like home-made sticky toffee pudding with butterscotch sauce.** *Starters/Snacks: £3.50 to £4.95. Main Courses: £6.50 to £14.95. Puddings: £3.95 to £4.75*

Free house ~ Licensee Brian Coulthwaite ~ Real ale ~ Bar food (12-4.30, 5-9) ~ (01539) 821309 ~ Children in lounge area ~ Dogs allowed in bar and bedrooms ~ Storytelling first Tues of month ~ Open 12-11(10.30 Sun); closed 25 Dec ~ Bedrooms: £38S/£70B

Recommended by David and Ruth Shillitoe, G Dobson, Tom and Jill Jones, Mr and Mrs Maurice Thompson, Dennis Jones, Helen Clarke, P Dawn, Julian and Janet Dearden, Phil and Jane Hodson, Jo Lilley, Simon Calvert, Gwyneth and Salvo Spadaro-Dutturi, Andy and Jill Kassube, Dr David Clegg, Neil Ingoe, Adrian Johnson, Pam and John Smith, J S Burn, Len Beattie, Paul Boot, Alain and Rose Foote, Mr and Mrs J N Graham, Tim Maddison, Lee and Liz Potter, MLR, Andrew and Christine Gagg, Ray and Winifred Halliday, Bob Broadhurst, Maurice and Gill McMahon, Mike and Sue Loseby, Margaret Whalley, Lindsley Harvard, Ian and Sue Wells, W W Burke, the Didler

KESWICK   NY2623   MAP 9

Dog & Gun ◀

Lake Road; CA12 5BT

Unpretentious town pub with popular food and drink

A proper pub where walkers are welcome and with a good bustling atmosphere. The homely bar has low beams, a partly slate floor (the rest are carpeted or bare boards), some high settles, a fine collection of striking mountain photographs by the local firm G P Abrahams, brass and brewery artefacts, and coins in beams and timbers by the fireplace (which go to the Mountain Rescue Service). Well kept Theakstons Best and Old Peculier, Yates Bitter and a couple of guests from Keswick on handpump, and a dozen wines by the glass.

🍴 **Tasty bar food includes soup, filled baked potatoes, big pies, lasagne, sausage and mash, barbecue chicken, a vegetarian dish, their not-to-be-missed famous goulash, daily specials, and puddings; they may stop food service early if not busy** *Starters/Snacks: £2.95 to £4.25. Main Courses: £6.95 to £9.95. Puddings: £2.95 to £3.95*

Scottish Courage ~ Manager Peter Ede ~ Real ale ~ Bar food (all day – usually) ~ (017687) 73463 ~ Children allowed if dining ~ Dogs welcome ~ Open 12-11

Recommended by Mary McSweeney, Louise English, Mr and Mrs Maurice Thompson, Fred and Lorraine Gill, Patrick Renouf, Phil Merrin, P Dawn, Mike and Sue Loseby, Brian and Anna Marsden, Adrian Johnson

KIRKBY LONSDALE   SD6178   MAP 7

Sun ♀ 🛏️

Market Street (B6254); LA6 2AU

Recently well reworked as dining pub, nice contrast between mellow bar and stylish contemporary restaurant, good interesting food, comfortable bedrooms

Looking very 17th-c on its steep cobbled alley, this white-painted stone inn has an upper floor supported on two or three sturdy pillars above the pavement and modest front door. Inside, the attractive rambling bar, with Jennings Cumberland Ale, Marstons, Timothy Taylors Landlord and a guest beer on handpump, an enterprising choice of wines by the glass and plenty of malt whiskies, has a warm log fire and seats of some character, from cosy window seats and pews to armchairs. It has beams, flagstones and stripped oak boards, nice lighting, and big landscapes and country pictures on the cream walls above its handsome panelled dado; there's also a back lounge with a leather sofa and comfortable chairs. Service is efficient and welcoming, with spotless housekeeping; there may be piped music. The back dining room is very up to date: comfortable tall-backed seats and pale tables on new woodstrip flooring, a clean-cut cream and pink décor with a modicum of stripped stone, attractive plain modern crockery (you can eat in any part of the establishment). Some of the bedrooms are in a stone barn with lovely views across the Barbon Fells.

🍴 **Marrying good country ingredients with up-to-date cooking, the food might include lunchtime sandwiches, cumberland sausage and burger as well as interesting dishes such as their own gravadlax served with char pâté and rollmops, venison terrine with prune and apple chutney, crab and avocado salad, wild mushroom open ravioli, rabbit steamed pudding, old spot pork loin with sautéed potatoes, chorizo and roast peppers, monkfish with creamed spinach and chive potato cake, guinea fowl stuffed with chestnuts and apricots, and puddings like chocolate and pear pancakes and fig and honey crème brûlée.** *Starters/Snacks: £3.50 to £6.95. Main Courses: £8.95 to £19.95. Puddings: £3.95 to £5.95*

Free house ~ Licensee Mark Fuller ~ Real ale ~ Bar food ~ Restaurant ~ (015242) 71965 ~ Children welcome ~ Dogs allowed in bar and bedrooms ~ Open 11-11; 12-10.30 Sun ~ Bedrooms: /£70B

Recommended by John and Yvonne Davies, Alun and Stephanie Llewellyn, Michael Doswell, Paul Davies

LANGDALE   NY2806   MAP 9

Old Dungeon Ghyll 🍺

B5343; LA22 9JY

Straightforward place in lovely position with fine walks

Even on particularly sodden, chilly days there's always a boisterous atmosphere and plenty of fell walkers and climbers in this straightforward local. It is at the heart of the Great Langdale Valley and surrounded by fells including the Langdale Pikes flanking the Dungeon Ghyll Force waterfall. The whole feel of the place is basic but cosy and there's no need to remove boots or muddy trousers – you can sit on seats in old cattle stalls by the big warming fire and enjoy well kept Black Sheep Special, Jennings Cumberland Ale, Theakstons Old Peculier and XB, Yates Bitter and a couple of changing guests on handpump; up to 30 malt whiskies, and farm cider. Darts and board games. It may get lively on a Saturday night (there's a popular National Trust camp site opposite).

🍴 **Good helpings of traditional food such as soup, lunchtime sandwiches, curries, stews, lasagne or pie of the day.** *Starters/Snacks: £2.50 to £3.75. Main Courses: £7.00 to £9.95. Puddings: £2.50 to £3.75*

Free house ~ Licensee Neil Walmsley ~ Real ale ~ Bar food (12-2, 6-9) ~ Restaurant ~ (015394) 37272 ~ Children welcome ~ Dogs welcome ~ Folk first Weds of month ~ Open 11-11; closed Christmas ~ Bedrooms: £45/£90(£96S)

Recommended by Russell and Alison Hunt, Len Beattie, Irene and Derek Flewin, David and Sue Smith, David and Katharine Cooke, Jarrod and Wendy Hopkinson, Dr David Clegg, Helen Clarke, Tim Maddison, the Didler

LEVENS
SD4987 MAP 9

Strickland Arms ♀ ◖
4 miles from M6 junction 36, via A590; just off A590, by Sizergh Castle gates; LA8 8DZ

Friendly, open-plan National Trust place popular for home-made food and local ales

Owned by the National Trust, this carefully refurbished dining pub is largely open plan with a light and airy contemporary feel. There are oriental rugs on the flagstones of the bar on the right, which has a log fire and keeps Thwaites Original and Lancaster Bomber and guests such as Coniston Bluebird and Hawkshead Gold on handpump, 30 malt whiskies and good wines by the glass. On the left are polished boards and another log fire and throughout, there's a nice mix of sturdy country furniture, candles on tables, hunting scenes and other old prints on the walls, heavy fabric for the curtains and some staffordshire china ornaments; a further dining room upstairs, piped music and board games. Service is friendly and personal and they have disabled access and facilities. Seats out in front on a flagstone terrace. The Castle, in fact a lovely partly medieval house with beautiful gardens, is open in the afternoon (not Friday/Saturday) from April to October.

🍴 **As well as lunchtime filled baguettes, the generous helpings of enjoyable food might include soup, their own meat loaf with a honey and redcurrant sauce, organic pork ribs with sweet chilli dipping sauce, steak in ale pie, smoked haddock fillet with rosemary butter, leek, fennel and cherry tomato bake with savoury crumb, roast chump of fell-bred lamb with port caramelised shallot sauce, daily specials, and puddings like gooseberry pie or rum, raisin and white chocolate torte.** *Starters/Snacks: £3.95 to £6.95. Main Courses: £8.95 to £15.95. Puddings: £5.00*

Free house ~ Licensees Kerry Parsons and Martin Ainscough ~ Real ale ~ Bar food (12-2(2.30 Sat), 6-9; all day Sun) ~ (015395) 61010 ~ Children welcome ~ Dogs welcome ~ Monthly Sun afternoon jazz, Weds evening quiz ~ Open 11.30-11(10.30 Sun); 11.30-3, 5.30-11 weekdays in winter

Recommended by John and Sylvia Harrop, Susan Street, Ray and Winifred Halliday, Bruce Braithwaite, Michael Doswell, Louise English, Margaret and Jeff Graham

LITTLE LANGDALE
NY3103 MAP 9

Three Shires 🛏
From A593 3 miles W of Ambleside take small road signposted The Langdales, Wrynose Pass; then bear left at first fork; LA22 9NZ

Friendly inn with valley views from seats on terrace, good lunchtime bar food with more elaborate evening meals, and comfortable bedrooms

Friendly and with a good welcome for walkers, this stone-built inn has lovely views from seats on the terrace over the valley to the partly wooded hills below Tilberthwaite Fells; more seats on a well kept lawn behind the car park, backed by a small oak wood. Inside, the comfortably extended back bar has a mix of grey lakeland stone and homely pink patterned wallpapered walls (which works rather well), stripped timbers and a beam-and-joist stripped ceiling, antique oak carved settles, country kitchen chairs and stools on its big dark slate flagstones, and lakeland photographs; a couple of warm fires. An arch leads through to a small, additional area and there's a front dining room. Well kept Black Sheep Best and Jennings Cumberland Ale and a couple of guests like Coniston Old Man or Hawkshead Red on handpump, over 50 malt whiskies and a decent wine list; darts and board games. The three shires are the historical counties Cumberland, Westmorland and Lancashire, which meet at the top of the nearby Wrynose Pass. The summer hanging baskets are very pretty. Please note, opening hours in December and January are restricted; best to phone then.

⑪ Generous helpings of honest lunchtime bar food include sandwiches, filled baguettes or ploughman's, home-made fishcake with lime and cucumber crème fraîche and cumberland sausage or beef in ale pie; evening choices such as baked melting brie with honey and thyme and chunks of rustic bread, tagliatelle with wild mushrooms, parmesan and cream sauce, garlic and mint marinated lamb with port wine reduction, salmon fillet with lemon grass, spinach and ginger en-papillote, lovely duckling with orange and thyme glaze, daily specials, and puddings such as sticky toffee pudding. *Starters/Snacks: £3.75 to £6.50. Main Courses: £7.95 to £15.00. Puddings: £3.95 to £6.00*

Free house ~ Licensee Ian Stephenson ~ Real ale ~ Bar food (12-2, 6-8.45; restricted evening meals Dec and Jan) ~ Restaurant ~ (015394) 37215 ~ Children welcome until 9pm ~ Dogs allowed in bar ~ Open 11-10.30(11 Fri and Sat); 12-10.30 Sun; 11-3, 8-10.30(Sun-Thurs) and 11-3, 6-11 (Fri and Sat) in winter ~ Bedrooms: /£78B

Recommended by Irene and Derek Flewin, Tony and Penny Burton, Tina and David Woods-Taylor, Simon and Mandy King, Arthur Pickering, Ron Gentry, Dr David Clegg, R M Corlett, Michael Doswell, J S Burn, Paul Humphreys, Louise English, David and Sue Atkinson, JDM, KM

LOWESWATER   NY1421   MAP 9

Kirkstile Inn ◨ ⛏

From B5289 follow signs to Loweswater Lake; OS Sheet 89 map reference 140210; CA13 0RU

Busy bar in popular inn surrounded by stunning peaks and fells; own-brewed beers and tasty food

Even though this friendly little country pub is off the beaten track – in a glorious spot between Loweswater and Crummock Water – it's always very busy and full of walkers. The fine view can be enjoyed from picnic-sets on the lawn, from the very attractive covered verandah in front of the building and from the bow windows in one of the rooms off the bar. The bustling main bar is low-beamed and carpeted, with a good mix of customers, a roaring log fire, comfortably cushioned small settles and pews and partly stripped stone walls; slate shove-ha'penny board. As well as their own-brewed and well kept Loweswater Grasmere Dark, Kirkstile Gold and Melbreak Bitter, guests include Coniston Bluebird, and Yates Bitter on handpump; ten wines by the glass.

⑪ As well as filled baguettes and baked potatoes, bar food includes soup, locally smoked trout parfait, beer-battered black pudding, pasta carbonara, steak in ale pie, cumberland sausage, goats cheese en croûte, lamb shoulder in honey and mint, daily specials, and puddings like treacle tart or home-made crumble. *Starters/Snacks: £3.00 to £5.00. Main Courses: £7.00 to £12.00. Puddings: £4.00 to £5.00*

Own brew ~ Licensee Roger Humphreys ~ Real ale ~ Bar food (12-2, 6-9) ~ (01900) 85219 ~ Children welcome ~ Dogs allowed in bar ~ Occasional jazz ~ Open 11-11; 12-10.30 Sun; closed 25 Dec ~ Bedrooms: £57.50B/£83B

Recommended by Sylvia and Tony Birbeck, Dr and Mrs Michael Smith, Richard Tosswill, David Morgan, Comus and Sarah Elliott, Patrick Renouf, Pat and Stewart Gordon, Mr and Mrs John Taylor, Bob and Sue, Marcus Byron, Edward Mirzoeff, Peter Smith, Judith Brown, GSB, Glenwys and Alan Lawrence, Mike and Sue Loseby, Tim Maddison, Dr K P Tucker, Christopher Turner, the Didler, Gordon Ormondroyd

MUNGRISDALE   NY3630   MAP 10

Mill Inn

Off A66 Penrith—Keswick, a bit over 1 mile W of A5091 Ullswater turn-off; CA11 0XR

Bustling pub in fine setting with marvellous surrounding walks, and known for its interesting pies

In the lea of the Blencathra fell range, this partly 16th-c inn is surrounded by stunning scenery and spectacular walks; in fine weather you can sit in the garden by the little river. The traditionally furnished and neatly kept bar has a wooden bar counter with an old millstone built into it, an open log fire in the stone fireplace, and Jennings Bitter and Cumberland Ale on handpump; over 30 malt whiskies and seven wines by the glass.

They also own the Pie Mill in Threlkeld which makes their popular pies. Please note that there's a quite separate Mill Hotel here.

⑪ **Lunchtime bar food includes filled rolls, open sandwiches, soup, fishcakes, spicy chicken salad, battered haddock and one of their popular home-made pies; evening choices such as chicken liver pâté, black pudding scotch egg, home-made ravioli, roasted vegetable lasagne, lamb shank, chicken breast with a mushroom, stilton, white wine and cream sauce, and puddings like cinder toffee chocolate cheesecake or apple and pear crumble.** *Starters/Snacks: £3.10 to £5.25. Main Courses: £8.00 to £18.00. Puddings: £3.95 to £5.25*

Free house ~ Licensees Jim and Margaret Hodge ~ Real ale ~ Bar food (12-2, 6-8.30) ~ Restaurant ~ (017687) 79632 ~ Children welcome ~ Dogs allowed in bar and bedrooms ~ Open 12-11(may shut earlier winter weekday evenings); 12-10.30 Sun; closed 25 and 26 Dec ~ Bedrooms: £47.50B/£75B

Recommended by David J Cooke, Helen Clarke, J S Burn, Mike and Sue Loseby, Robert Turnham, Pip King, Dr and Mrs Michael Smith, Dennis Jones, John and Jackie Walsh, Patrick Renouf, Tina and David Woods-Taylor, Jed Scott, Eileen McCall, Glenwys and Alan Lawrence, Jack and Rosalin Forrester, Karen Hands, Christopher Turner, Gordon Ormondroyd

NEAR SAWREY
SD3795 MAP 9

Tower Bank Arms 🍺
B5285 towards the Windermere ferry; LA22 0LF

Backing on to Beatrix Potter's farm with a good range of ales, and redecorated bedrooms

The bedrooms in this little country inn have been redecorated and readers have enjoyed staying here, and the garden has been tidied up giving more seating space from which to enjoy the pleasant views of the wooded Claife Heights. The low-beamed main bar has plenty of rustic charm, seats on the rough slate floor, game and fowl pictures, a grandfather clock, an open fire, and fresh flowers; the restaurant now has a new oak floor. Many illustrations in the Beatrix Potter books can be traced back to their origins in this village, including this pub which features in *The Tale of Jemima Puddleduck*. Well kept Barngates Cat Nap, Hawkshead Bitter, Hesket Newmarket Catbells Pale Ale, Keswick Thirst Run and Yates Sun Goddess on handpump; board games and darts (on request).

⑪ **Lunchtime bar food includes sandwiches, soup, a trio of sausages with onion gravy, freshly battered haddock and beef in ale stew with dumplings; in the evening there might be chicken liver pâté, mussels in chilli, lime and lemon grass, chicken and mushroom tagliatelle, mediterranean pasta, local trout stuffed with prawns and duck with a sweet plum and ginger sauce.** *Starters/Snacks: £3.95 to £6.75. Main Courses: £9.50 to £12.75. Puddings: £2.95 to £3.95*

Free house ~ Licensee Anthony Hutton ~ Real ale ~ Bar food (12-2, 6-9) ~ Restaurant ~ (015394) 36334 ~ Children welcome until 9pm ~ Dogs allowed in bar and bedrooms ~ Open 10am-11pm; 12-10.30 Sun; 10-3, 5-11 weekdays in winter ~ Bedrooms: £45B/£75B

Recommended by Arthur Pickering, Dr A J and Mrs Tompsett, Peter F Marshall, David S Clark, Ron Gentry, Alice Carruthers, Jason Caulkin, R E McEleney

SANDFORD
NY7316 MAP 10

Sandford Arms 🛏
Village and pub signposted just off A66 W of Brough; CA16 6NR

New licensee in neat little former farmhouse in tucked away village

A new licensee has taken over this neat little inn, tucked away in a very small village and the opening hours are now far less restricted. There's an L-shaped carpeted main bar with stripped beams and stonework, a collection of Royal Doulton character jugs and some Dickens ware; Black Sheep, Jennings Cocker Hoop and a guest on handpump, and a fair range of malt whiskies. The compact and comfortable dining area is on a slightly raised balustraded platform at one end, there's a more formal separate dining room and a second bar area with broad flagstones, charming heavy-horse prints, an end log fire, and darts, board games, TV and piped music. Tables out in front and in the courtyard. More reports please.

🍴 Bar food includes sandwiches, soup, grilled black pudding with mustard sauce, cumberland sausage with onion gravy, steak in ale pie, a vegetarian dish, chicken with mushrooms, smoked bacon and cream, steaks, and puddings. *Starters/Snacks: £3.25 to £5.50. Main Courses: £7.25 to £17.95. Puddings: £3.75 to £4.25*

Free house ~ Licensee Steven Porter ~ Real ale ~ Bar food (not Tues) ~ Restaurant ~ (017683) 51121 ~ Children welcome until 9pm ~ Dogs allowed in bar ~ Open 12-3, 6-11; 12-11(10.30 Sun) Sat; closed Tues lunchtime in winter ~ Bedrooms: £50B/£60B

Recommended by Richard Gibbs

SANTON BRIDGE
NY1101   MAP 9

Bridge Inn
Off A595 at Holmrook or Gosforth; CA19 1UX

A good choice of drinks and well liked food, cheerful atmosphere, and plenty of surrounding walks

Our readers enjoy staying at this bustling black and white hotel run by friendly, helpful licensees. The turkey-carpeted bar is popular with locals and has stripped beams, joists and standing timbers, a coal and log fire, and three rather unusual timbered booths around big stripped tables along its outer wall. Bar stools line the long concave bar counter, which has Jennings Bitter, Cocker Hoop, Cumberland Ale, and Sneck Lifter and a couple of guest beers on handpump; good big pots of tea, speciality coffees, and six wines by the glass. Piped music, games machine, darts and board games. As well as an italian-style bistro, there's a small reception hall with a rack of daily papers and a comfortable more hotelish lounge on the left. Fell views and seats out in front by the quiet road and plenty of surrounding walks; more reports please.

🍴 Well liked bar food includes filled baguettes, soup, cumberland sausage, curry of the day or steak and kidney pie, lamb samosas, teriyaki red snapper, and daily specials. *Starters/Snacks: £2.50 to £5.95. Main Courses: £8.95 to £15.95. Puddings: £3.95*

Marstons ~ Lease John Morrow and Lesley Rhodes ~ Real ale ~ Bar food (12-2.30, 6-9(9.30 in summer)) ~ Restaurant ~ (01946) 726221 ~ Children welcome ~ Dogs allowed in bar and bedrooms ~ Open 11-11(midnight Sat) ~ Bedrooms: £58S/£70B

Recommended by W K Wood, Helen Clarke, Mr and Mrs Maurice Thompson, J S Burn, David Heath, Phil and Jane Hodson, Helen Rowett

SCALES
NY3426   MAP 9

White Horse
A66 W of Penrith; CA12 4SY

Usefully open all day in summer and – given the position – plenty of walkers

A new licensee and his family have taken over this traditional lakeland pub and have opened up a beer garden; the flowering window boxes and tubs are pretty in summer. Inside, the comfortable beamed bar has warm winter fires, hunting pictures and photographs of the pub on the walls, and the little snug and old kitchen have all sorts of implements such as butter churns, kettles, a marmalade slicer and a black range. Camerons Castle Eden Ale and a changing guest on handpump. From the cluster of pub and farm buildings, tracks lead up into the splendidly daunting and rocky fells with names like Foule Crag and Sharp Edge; muddy boots should be left outside. More reports please.

🍴 Bar food might include sandwiches, soup, spinach pancake with cheese sauce, ploughman's, steak in ale pie and chicken in tarragon and cream or pork fillets in brandy sauce. *Starters/Snacks: £3.95 to £5.95. Main Courses: £6.95 to £14.00. Puddings: £3.95 to £5.95*

Camerons ~ Tenant Malcolm Vassallo ~ Real ale ~ Bar food ~ Restaurant ~(017687) 79241 ~ Children welcome ~ Open 10am-11pm; 12-4, 6-10.30 in winter

Recommended by Patrick Renouf, David J Cooke, Tracey and Stephen Groves

SEATHWAITE   SD2295   MAP 9

Newfield Inn 🍺

Duddon Valley, near Ulpha (ie not Seathwaite in Borrowdale); LA20 6ED

Climbers' and walkers' cottagey inn with genuine local feel and hearty food

Even when this cottagey 16th-c inn is full of walkers and climbers it still manages to keep a relaxed and genuinely local atmosphere. The slate-floored bar has wooden tables and chairs, some interesting pictures and Black Sheep Bitter and Emmerdale, Jennings Cumberland Ale and Theakstons Old Peculier on handpump; several malt whiskies. There's a comfortable side room and a games room with shove-ha'penny and board games; piped music. Tables outside in the nice garden have good hill views. The pub owns and lets the next-door self-catering flats and there are fine walks from the doorstep.

🍴 Good value, home-made bar food includes filled rolls, lunchtime snacks like beans on toast and home-cooked ham and eggs, cumberland sausage, steak pie, battered cod, spicy bean casserole, lasagne, and puddings such as home-made pear and chocolate crumble. *Starters/Snacks: £2.40 to £4.95. Main Courses: £3.50 to £17.00. Puddings: £1.90 to £3.95*

Free house ~ Licensee Paul Batten ~ Real ale ~ Bar food (12-9) ~ (01229) 716208 ~ Children welcome ~ Dogs allowed in bar ~ Open 11-11

Recommended by Mr and Mrs Maurice Thompson, Christine and Phil Young, Rona Murdoch, Julie and Bill Ryan

STAVELEY   SD4797   MAP 9

Eagle & Child 🍺 🛏

Kendal Road; just off A591 Windermere—Kendal; LA8 9LP

Welcoming inn with warming log fires, well kept beers and home-made food

As well as being a popular place to stay, this bustling little inn has a good pubby atmosphere and friendly staff. The roughly L-shaped flagstoned main area has plenty of separate parts to sit in, a welcoming fire under an impressive mantelbeam, and pews, banquettes, bow window seats and some high-backed dining chairs around polished dark tables. Also, police truncheons and walking sticks, some nice photographs and interesting prints, a few farm tools, a delft shelf of bric-a-brac and another log fire. Barngates Cat Nap, Hawkshead Bitter, Yates Bitter, and guests like Caledonian Great Slot and Copper Dragon Golden Pippin on handpump, several wines by the glass and farm cider. An upstairs barn-theme dining room (with its own bar for functions and so forth) doubles as a breakfast room. There are picnic-sets under cocktail parasols in a sheltered garden by the River Kent, with more on a good-sized back terrace, and second garden behind.

🍴 Good bar food includes sandwiches, soup, home-made smoked trout and spinach terrine, local deep-fried cheeses with tomato jam and herb yoghurt dip, vegetable pie, a trio of local sausages with red wine onion gravy, gammon and egg, shepherd's pie, fresh cod in anchovy, cracked black pepper and parsley butter, slow-roasted lamb shank and duck breast in a rich orange and madeira sauce; there might be special lunch deals. *Starters/Snacks: £2.95 to £5.95. Main Courses: £6.95 to £14.95. Puddings: £4.50 to £5.50*

Free house ~ Licensees Richard and Denise Coleman ~ Real ale ~ Bar food (12-2.30(3 weekends), 6-9) ~ Restaurant ~ (01539) 821320 ~ Children welcome ~ Dogs allowed in bar ~ Open 11-11(midnight Sat) ~ Bedrooms: £40B/£60B

Recommended by Bob Broadhurst, P Dawn, Michael Doswell, Dennis Jones, Jo Lilley, Simon Calvert, Julian and Janet Dearden, John and Joan Nash, Dave Braisted, Janet and Peter Race, RJH, the Didler

---

If you know a pub's ever open all day, please tell us.

STONETHWAITE   NY2513   MAP 9

Langstrath 🍺 🛏

Off B5289 S of Derwent Water; CA12 5XG

Civilised little place in lovely spot with interesting food and drink

The bedrooms in this civilised little inn have been refurbished this year and now all have their own bathrooms. The neat and simple bar (at its pubbiest at lunchtime) has a welcoming coal and log fire in a big stone fireplace, just a handful of cast-iron-framed tables, plain chairs and cushioned wall seats, and on its textured white walls maybe quite a few walking cartoons and attractive lakeland mountain photographs. Black Sheep and Jennings Bitter and a couple of guests such as Coniston Bluebird or Hesket Newmarket Doris's 90th Birthday Ale on handpump served by friendly staff, 25 malt whiskies and eight wines by the glass; quite a few customers also drop in for tea and coffee. Board games. A little oak-boarded room on the left is a bit like a doll's house living room in style – this is actually the original cottage built around 1590; there's also a residents' lounge. Outside, a big sycamore shelters a few picnic-sets and there are fine surrounding walks as the pub is in a lovely spot in the heart of Borrowdale and en route for the Cumbrian Way and the Coast to Coast Walk. As opening hours are limited in December and January, you must phone before setting out.

🍴 Good bar food includes sandwiches, soup, morecambe bay potted shrimps, pork terrine with apricot chutney, courgette and hazelnut roast with tomato salsa, salmon and haddock fishcakes, slow-roasted lamb with rosemary and red wine gravy, steak in ale pie, gressingham duck breast with puy lentils and thyme jus, and puddings like warm chocolate brownie or spiced apple crumble; best to book to be sure of a table. *Starters/Snacks: £4.50 to £5.50. Main Courses: £9.50 to £16.50. Puddings: £4.25 to £4.50*

Free house ~ Licensees Sara and Mike Hodgson ~ Real ale ~ Bar food (12-3, 6-9(not Mon lunchtime)) ~ Restaurant ~ (017687) 77239 ~ No children under 5 in bar and children must leave by 8pm ~ Open 12.30-11(4-11 Mon); closed summer Mon lunchtime; Mon-Weds during Nov, Feb and Mar ~ Bedrooms: £30(£37.50B)/£39.50S(£42.50B)

Recommended by Tina and David Woods-Taylor, Malcolm and Jane Levitt, Christine and Phil Young, J and F Gowers, Dr and Mrs D Ash, Mrs Sheila Stothard, Tracey and Stephen Groves

TALKIN   NY5457   MAP 10

Blacksmiths Arms 🍷 🛏

Village signposted from B6413 S of Brampton; CA8 1LE

Neatly kept and welcoming, and a nice place to stay

This is a smashing place with a good mix of locals and visitors and a cheerful, bustling atmosphere. It's well run and friendly and in an attractive village green setting; good surrounding walks. The neatly kept, warm lounge is on the right with a log fire, upholstered banquettes, tables and chairs, and country prints and other pictures on the walls; the restaurant to the left is pretty, there's a long lounge opposite the bar with smaller round tables, and a well lit garden room. Jennings Cumberland Ale, Yates Bitter, and a couple of guests from breweries like Copper Dragon or Hawkshead on handpump, 20 wines by the glass and 25 malt whiskies; piped music and darts. There are a couple of picnic-sets outside the front door with more in the back garden.

🍴 As well as lunchtime sandwiches, toasties and filled baked potatoes, the reasonably priced, enjoyable food might include soup, chicken and pistachio paté, fresh haddock in beer batter, steak and kidney pie or mushroom stroganoff, chicken curry, beef stroganoff, daily specials, and Sunday roast. *Starters/Snacks: £3.95 to £4.95. Main Courses: £5.95 to £16.95. Puddings: £3.95*

Free house ~ Licensees Donald and Anne Jackson ~ Real ale ~ Bar food (12-2, 6-9) ~ Restaurant ~ (016977) 3452 ~ Children welcome ~ Open 12-3, 6-midnight ~ Bedrooms: £40B/£55B

Recommended by Roy and Lindsey Fentiman, Ken Richards, Tony and Maggie Harwood, David and Katharine Cooke, Alun and Stephanie Llewellyn, UN, Ian and Jane Irving, John and Sylvia Harrop, Di and Mike Gillam, Ian and Sue Wells

THRELKELD   NY3225   MAP 9

Horse & Farrier
A66 Penrith—Keswick; CA12 4SQ

Well run 17th-c fell-foot dining pub with good food and drinks, good value bedrooms

---

The civilised and neatly fitted out mainly carpeted bar of this lakeland inn has sturdy farmhouse and other nice tables, and a mix of comfortably padded seats from pubby chairs and stools to bigger housekeeper's chairs and wall settles, with country pictures on its white walls, one or two stripped beams, and some flagstones. They have three well kept Jennings ales on handpump, such as Bitter, Cumberland, Cockerhoop and Crag Rat, usually a couple of guests such as Adnams Explorer, a good range of wines by the glass, and winter open fires. Service is efficiently organised and unstuffy. The partly stripped stone restaurant is smart and more formal, with quite close-set tables. They have good disabled access and facilities, and a few picnic-sets outside, with inspiring views up to Blease and Gategill Fells behind the pretty white-painted inn, or over to Clough Head behind the houses opposite; good walks straight from this attractive village. If you stay, they do a good breakfast.

🍽 **Bar food includes good open sandwiches and baguettes, staples such as baked potatoes, vegetarian lasagne or chilli, steak pie, big burger, cod and mushy peas, scampi, cumberland sausage and steak, and their good speciality dish of slow-cooked beer-marinated local shoulder of lamb, with a somewhat grander evening choice that might take in guinea fowl and roast duck.** *Starters/Snacks: £3.25 to £5.95. Main Courses: £6.95 to £14.95. Puddings: £3.95*

Jennings (Marstons) ~ Lease Ian Court ~ Real ale ~ Bar food (12-2.30, 5.30-9 Mon-Thurs; 12-9 Fri-Sun) ~ Restaurant ~ (017687) 79688 ~ Children welcome ~ Dogs welcome ~ Open 7.30am-midnight ~ Bedrooms: £35B/£70B

Recommended by David Morgan, Fred and Lorraine Gill, Ann and Tony Bennett-Hughes, Steve Godfrey, J A Hooker, Rob and Catherine Dunster, Gordon Ormondroyd

TROUTBECK   NY4103   MAP 9

Queens Head ★
A592 N of Windermere; LA23 1PW

Civilised inn with several rambling rooms, interesting food and real ales, and comfortable bedrooms

---

Readers do enjoy their overnight stays in this popular and rather upmarket old inn and the bedroom refurbishments will continue throughout the year. The big rambling original U-shaped bar has a very nice mix of old cushioned settles and mate's chairs around some sizeable tables, beams and flagstones and a log fire in the raised stone fireplace with horse harness and so forth on either side of it; there's also a coal fire, some trumpets, cornets and saxophones on one wall with country pictures on others, stuffed pheasants in a big glass case, and a stag's head with a tie around his neck. A massive Elizabethan four-poster bed is the basis of the finely carved counter where they serve up to six real ales on handpump such as Black Sheep Bitter, Boddingtons Bitter, Coniston Bluebird, Hawkshead Gold and Jennings Cumberland Ale. The newer dining rooms are similarly decorated to the main bar, with oak beams and stone walls, settles along big tables, and an open fire. Piped music. Seats outside have a fine view over the Troutbeck valley to Applethwaite moors.

🍽 **The particularly good, interesting food is cheaper at lunchtime when it might include filled rolls, soup, spicy sweet potato cake on wilted pak choi with satay sauce, smooth parfait of mackerel with toasted home-made brioche, szechuan pepper and lemon chutney, lamb hotpot with pickled red cabbage and cornfed chicken on sweetcorn and crab pancake with sweet chilli dressing; evening choices like terrine of aubergine, red pepper and courgette with goats cheese fondant and gazpacho, confit leg of guinea fowl with herbed puy lentils and balsamic syrup, risotto of mussels, king prawn and saffron dusted with parmesan, roast fillet of pork and home-made black pudding with creamy cider sauce and roast breast and leg of magret duck with a sweet plum and spring onion sauce; puddings** such as bramley apple nut crumble with lancashire cheese ice-cream and custard and pavlova with hot chocolate sauce, chantilly cream and a cappuccino froth; a three-course set menu, and well liked breakfasts. *Starters/Snacks: £3.95 to £8.50. Main Courses: £11.95 to £15.95. Puddings: £5.25 to £6.25*

Free house ~ Licensees Mark Stewardson and Joanne Sherratt ~ Real ale ~ Bar food (12-9) ~ Restaurant ~ (015394) 32174 ~ Children welcome ~ Dogs allowed in bar ~ Open 11-11; 12-10.30 Sun ~ Bedrooms: /£105B

Recommended by Michael Butler, Steve Whalley, Revd D Glover, Tina and David Woods-Taylor, Paul Boot, Liz and Tony Colman, Arthur Pickering, Adrian Johnson, B I Mason, John and Joan Nash, Linda and Rob Hilsenroth, Noel Grundy, Pierre Richterich, J C Clark, Chris Willers, Michael Doswell, Margaret and Jeff Graham, Dr and Mrs R G J Telfer, Ann and Tony Bennett-Hughes, Helen Clarke, Kay and Alistair Butler, Stuart and Doreen Ritchie, Louise English, Mr and Mrs Richard Osborne

ULVERSTON   SD3177   MAP 7

Bay Horse

Canal Foot signposted off A590 and then you wend your way past the huge Glaxo factory; LA12 9EL

Civilised waterside hotel at its most relaxed at lunchtime, with super food, wine and beer, and a nice, smart place to stay

---

Lunchtime is when this smart and civilised hotel – on the water's edge of the Leven Estuary – is at its most informal. The bar has a relaxed atmosphere despite its smart furnishings: attractive wooden armchairs, some pale green plush built-in wall banquettes, glossy hardwood traditional tables, blue plates on a delft shelf, a huge stone horse's head and black beams and props with lots of horsebrasses. Magazines are dotted about, there's an open fire in the handsomely marbled green granite fireplace, and decently reproduced piped music; board games and cards. Jennings Cumberland Ale and Cocker Hoop and Moorhouses Pendle Witches Brew on handpump, and a dozen wines by the glass (champagne, too) from a carefully chosen and interesting wine list. The conservatory restaurant has fine views over Morecambe Bay (as do the newly refurbished bedrooms) and there are some seats out on the terrace.

🍽 Imaginative lunchtime bar food might include sandwiches and filled ciabattas, baguettes or baked potatoes, button mushrooms in a tomato, cream and brandy sauce on a peanut butter croûton, chicken liver pâté with cranberry and ginger purée, fresh crab and salmon fishcakes, cumberland sausage with date chutney, peppers stuffed with mushroom and onion pâté on a tomato provençale with a garlic and chive cream and breadcrumb and pine nut topping, steak and kidney pie, lamb shank braised in red burgundy, and home-made puddings; good breakfasts. *Starters/Snacks: £3.95 to £7.50. Main Courses: £10.50 to £17.00. Puddings: £5.75 to £7.00*

Free house ~ Licensee Robert Lyons ~ Real ale ~ Bar food (12-2(not Mon lunchtime); only restaurant food at night) ~ Restaurant ~ (01229) 583972 ~ Children in eating area of bar but must be over 12 in evening ~ Dogs allowed in bar and bedrooms ~ Open 11-11; 12-10.30 Sun ~ Bedrooms: £80B/£95B

Recommended by Dave Braisted, Andrew Beardsley, Alison Lawrence, Mr and Mrs P Eastwood, Carol and Dono Leaman, Neil Ingoe, M J Winterton, K S Whittaker, W K Wood

Farmers Arms

Market Place; LA12 7BA

Appealingly modernised town pub with quickly changing real ales, a dozen wines by the glass, and good food

---

A fine range of real ales here might include Coniston Bluebird, Courage Directors, Greene King Old Speckled Hen, Hawkshead Bitter, Theakstons Best and Yates Bitter, all on handpump. It's a straightforward looking town pub that has been appealingly modernised and extended. The original fireplace and timbers blend in well with the more contemporary furnishings in the front bar – mostly wicker chairs on one side, comfortable sofas on the other; the overall effect is rather unusual, but somehow it still feels like a proper village pub. A table by the fire has newspapers, glossy magazines and local information, and a second smaller bar counter leads into a big raftered eating area; a dozen wines by the glass and piped music. In front is a very attractive terrace with outdoor heaters, plenty of good wooden tables looking on to the market cross and lots of colourful plants in tubs and hanging baskets. If something's happening in town, the pub is usually a part of it, and they can be busy on Thursday market day. More reports please.

🍴 **Good food includes lunchtime hot and cold sandwiches, soup, chicken caesar salad with parmesan and croûtons, greek mezze, home-made burger with bacon, pineapple and salsa, grilled salmon topped with whole green beans stir fried in chilli marmalade, stir-fried cajun chicken and pasta with leeks, mushrooms, wine and cream.** *Starters/Snacks: £3.75 to £4.95. Main Courses: £8.95 to £12.95. Puddings: £3.00 to £3.95*

Free house ~ Licensee Roger Chattaway ~ Real ale ~ Bar food (10-3, 5.30-8.30) ~ Restaurant ~ (01229) 584469 ~ Children allowed if eating ~ Open 9.30am-11pm(midnight Sat); 10am-11pm Sun

Recommended by BOB

YANWATH
NY5128   MAP 9

Gate Inn 🍴 ⏐

2¼ miles from M6 junction 40; A66 towards Brough, then right on A6, right on B5320, then follow village signpost; CA10 2LF

Emphasis on imaginative food but with local beers and thoughtful wines, a pubby atmosphere, and warm welcome from helpful staff

A favourite with a great many of our readers, this bustling 17th-c inn is particularly well run and you can be sure of a warm welcome from the helpful and cheerful staff. There is quite an emphasis on the very good, imaginative food but the atmosphere is relaxed and pubby; they keep Keswick Thirst Run, Hesket Newmarket Doris's 90th Birthday Ale, and Tirril Bewshers Bitter on handpump, a dozen wines by the glass, scrumpy cider, and organic soft drinks. The cosy bar has country pine and dark wood furniture, lots of brasses on the beams, church candles on all the tables and a good log fire in the attractive stone inglenook. Two restaurant areas have oak floors, panelled oak walls and heavy beams; piped music. There are seats on the terrace and in the garden.

🍴 **Excellent, interesting bar food at lunchtime includes soup, chicken, bacon and pistachio terrine, griddled stuffed aubergine, a good platter, fish in cider batter and chips, spaghetti with mussels and clams and lamb and rosemary burger, with evening choices such as black pudding and haggis with poached egg and grain mustard sauce, hot smoked salmon rillette with crostinis and smoked paprika rouille, thai-style pumpkin and coconut curry, glazed pork belly, chorizo and toulouse sausage cassoulet and goosnargh corn-fed duck with orange and chilli marinade, chinese greens and noodles; puddings like sticky date pudding with toffee sauce or chocolate and brandy bread and butter pudding with tonka bean anglaise.** *Starters/Snacks: £5.00 to £11.00. Main Courses: £13.00 to £24.00. Puddings: £5.00 to £9.00*

Free house ~ Licensee Matt Edwards ~ Real ale ~ Bar food (12-2.30, 6-9) ~ Restaurant ~ (01768) 862386 ~ Children welcome ~ Dogs allowed in bar ~ Open 12-11

Recommended by David and Katharine Cooke, John Watson, Lucien Perring, Dr J R Norman, Richard J Holloway, Marcus Byron, Peter Mueller, J S Burn, Christine and Neil Townend, Sylvia and Tony Birbeck, Helen Clarke, Kerry Law, Comus and Sarah Elliott, Maurice and Gill McMahon, Jed Scott, Walter and Susan Rinaldi-Butcher, C and H Greenly, Tina and David Woods-Taylor, David J Cooke, Nick Holding, Dr K P Tucker, John Urquhart, Bill and Pauline Critchley

---

Real ale to us means beer which has matured naturally in its cask – not pressurised or filtered. We name all real ales stocked. We usually name ales preserved under a light blanket of carbon dioxide too, though purists – pointing out that this stops the natural yeasts developing – would disagree (most people, including us, can't tell the difference!).

LUCKY DIP

Besides the fully inspected pubs, you might like to try these Lucky Dips recommended to us and described by readers (if you do, please send us reports: www.goodguides.co.uk).

ALSTON [NY7146]
Cumberland CA9 3HX [Townfoot]: Real ales such as Allendale, Derwent, Jennings and Theakstons, friendly staff, food in second room; terrace with great views from picnic-sets, quoits pitch, good value bedrooms *(Mr and Mrs Maurice Thompson)*
Nent Hall CA9 3LQ [Nenthall; A689 E]: Coach House bar with enjoyable pubby food inc children's, smart separate restaurant; attractive area, bedrooms *(Keith and Chris O'Neill)*
AMBLESIDE [NY4008]
☆ *Kirkstone Pass Inn* LA22 9LQ [A592 N of Troutbeck]: Lakeland's highest pub, in grand scenery, hiker-friendly décor of flagstones, stripped stone and simple furnishings with lots of old photographs and bric-a-brac, two log fires, welcoming staff, cheap hearty food all day from 9.30, changing ales such as Carlisle State, daily papers, games and books; piped music, pool room; dogs welcome, tables outside, three bedrooms, open all day *(David and Sue Smith, Tina and David Woods-Taylor, LYM, Di and Mike Gillam)*
☆ *Wateredge* LA22 0EP [Borrans Rd]: Lovely spot with sizeable garden running down to the edge of Windermere, lots of tables out here, same splendid view through big windows in much-modernised bar with real ales such as Coniston Bluebird and Theakstons and several wines by the glass (drinks somewhat pricy), quickly served generous food, cosy beamed area down steps with fireside sofa; piped music; children welcome in eating areas, open all day, comfortable bedrooms *(Michael Butler, LYM, Chris and Amy Johnson, Neil Ingoe, Dennis Jones, Dr and Mrs R G J Telfer, Julia Morris)*
APPLEBY [NY6819]
☆ *Royal Oak* CA16 6UN [B6542/Bongate is E of the main bridge over the River Eden]: Old beamed and timbered coaching inn given a younger feel under current licensees, popular bar food (all day Sun), real ales such as Hawkshead, Jennings and John Smiths, friendly young staff, log fire in panelled bar, armchair lounge with carved settle, traditional snug, attractively refurbished dining room; TV opposite bar, piped music; children and dogs welcome, terrace tables, good-sized bedrooms, good breakfast, open all day *(LYM, Ian and Jane Irving)*
ARMATHWAITE [NY5045]
☆ *Fox & Pheasant* CA4 9PY: Friendly new licensees in spotless and attractive Victorian coaching inn dating from 18th c, River Eden views, sensibly short choice of good reasonably priced fresh food, Robinsons ales, decent wines by the glass, inglenook log fire in main beamed and flagstoned bar, another in second bar, charming small dining room; picnic-sets outside, comfortable bedrooms

(Comus and Sarah Elliott, Angus Lyon)
ASPATRIA [NY1140]
Miners Arms CA7 2LP [Prospect – A596 W]: Useful main-road stop, small and friendly, with darts and pool *(Gwyneth and Salvo Spadaro-Dutturi)*
BAMPTON GRANGE [NY5218]
Crown & Mitre CA10 2QR: Welcoming new couple, imaginatively cooked local food (steaks particularly good), Black Sheep and local guest beers, fresh modern décor for two-room main bar with some comfortable wall seats and log fire, smaller bar with pool, stripped wood furniture in cheerful red-walled dining room; eight comfortably modernised bedrooms *(David and Katharine Cooke)*
BARBON [SD6282]
☆ *Barbon Inn* LA6 2LJ [off A683 Kirkby Lonsdale—Sedbergh]: New owners in 2006 for this charmingly set fell-foot village inn, several rooms off simple friendly bar, some sofas, armchairs and antique carved settles, food from baguettes and morecambe bay shrimps to local game, real ales such as Greene King Old Speckled Hen, attractive restaurant; children welcome, sheltered pretty garden, good walks, bedrooms being refurbished; more reports on new regime please *(LYM, John and Joan Nash)*
BARDSEA [SD3074]
☆ *Bradylls Arms* LA12 9QT [Main St]: Enjoyable food inc fresh seafood and some particularly good authentic portuguese specialities (portuguese night Tues), good choice of locally brewed ales and of wines, welcoming relaxed atmosphere, plush seating and some stripped stone, popular richly decorated back conservatory restaurant with lovely Morecambe Bay views; garden with play area, very attractive village nr sea *(Stephen R Holman, BB)*
BLENCOGO [NY1948]
☆ *New Inn* CA7 0BZ [signed off B5302 Wigton—Silloth]: Very good food, with interesting choice, good helpings and reasonable prices, in bright and simply modernised country pub, log fire, real ale, decent wines and whiskies, a few big Cumbrian landscapes, pleasant service; well worth booking; cl Mon *(Helen Clarke, Michael and Helen Braithwaite, BB)*
BOOT [NY1701]
Boot Inn CA19 1TG [aka Burnmoor; signed just off the Wrynose/Hardknott Pass rd]: Comfortably modernised beamed pub with ever-burning fire, Black Sheep, Jennings Bitter and Cumberland and a guest beer, decent wines and malt whiskies, good mulled wine, reasonably priced home-made lunchtime bar food from sandwiches and baked potatoes up, restaurant and dining conservatory; games room with pool and TV; children and dogs welcome, seats out on

sheltered front lawn with play area, good walks, lovely surroundings, open all day *(Christine and Phil Young, LYM, Kevin Flack)*

☆ **Brook House** CA19 1TG: Converted small Victorian hotel with good views, friendly family service, wide choice of good generous home-made food inc some interesting dishes (breakfast for nearby campers too), several well kept ales such as Black Sheep, Coniston, Theakstons and Yates, decent wines, log fires, small plushly modernised bar, comfortable hunting-theme lounge, peaceful separate restaurant; tables outside, handy for Ravenglass railway and great walks, seven good fell-view bedrooms (and good drying room), open all day *(Kevin Flack, J S Burn, the Didler)*

Woolpack CA19 1TH [Bleabeck, midway between Boot and Hardknott Pass]: Last pub before the notorious Hardknott Pass, up to five well kept real ales and by now maybe their own brew, generous home-made food, woodburner, hunting prints, brasses and fresh flowers; children welcome, nice garden with mountain views, bedrooms and bunkhouse, open all day at least in summer *(Mr and Mrs Maurice Thompson)*

BOTHEL [NY1839]

Greyhound CA7 2HS: Hard-working current landlord winning strong local support for his enjoyable food (proper shortcrust pies, best real chips in the area), Jennings Cumberland, good choice of wine *(Helen Clarke)*

BOWNESS-ON-WINDERMERE [SD4096]

Albert LA23 3BY [Queens Sq]: No-frills bar with well kept Robinsons Hartleys, good value food and wide choice of reasonably priced wines in separate restaurant; comfortable bedrooms *(Dennis Jones)*

☆ **Hole in t' Wall** LA23 3DH [Lowside]: Friendly bustle in ancient beamed pub, stripped stone and flagstones, lots of country bric-a-brac and old pictures, enjoyable home-made food, well kept Robinsons ales, splendid log fire under vast slate mantelpiece, upper room with attractive plasterwork; very busy in tourist season; children welcome, no dogs or prams, sheltered picnic-sets in tiny flagstoned front courtyard *(Robert Wivell, LYM, Margaret Whalley, Lindsley Harvard)*

Royal Oak LA23 3EG [Brantfell Rd]: Decent town pub with well kept beers, reasonably priced food, friendly efficient service; children welcome, tables out in front, bedrooms with own bathrooms *(Dennis Jones)*

BRAITHWAITE [NY2323]

Coledale Hotel CA12 5TN [signed off A66 W of Keswick, pub then signed left off B5292]: Small Victorian hotel below Whinlatter Pass, two bustling bars, real ales such as Jennings, Keswick and John Smiths, reasonably priced hearty food, friendly efficient staff, coal fire, little 19th-c lakeland engravings, plush banquettes and studded tables, darts and dominoes, big dining room; piped music; fine Skiddaw views, garden with slate terrace and

sheltered lawn, pretty bedrooms, open all day *(A J Bowen, David J Cooke, LYM, Brian and Anna Marsden, W W Burke)*

Royal Oak CA12 5SY: Well worn in flagstoned bar with bustling local atmosphere, good choice of enjoyable food (best to book evenings) inc small helpings for children, prompt helpful service, well kept Jennings ales; dogs welcome exc at mealtimes *(W M Lien, A J Bowen, Dr and Mrs Michael Smith, Brian and Anna Marsden)*

BRIGSTEER [SD4889]

☆ **Wheatsheaf** LA8 8AN: Attractive dining pub with good food inc interesting sandwiches, fresh fish, game and good value Sun lunch inc splendid fish hors-d'oeuvre, nice breads baked here, takeaways some nights, cheerful attentive staff, real ales such as Jennings and an unusual distant guest beer, good choice of wines by the glass, charming dining room; pretty village *(Ray and Winifred Halliday, Alan and Carolin Tidbury, Michael Doswell, Jenny and Peter Lowater, Clive Gibson)*

BROUGHTON-IN-FURNESS [SD2187]

Black Cock LA20 6HQ [Princes St]: Well run olde-worlde pub dating from 15th c, largely given over to the enjoyable reasonably priced food, also comfortable and convivial bar with well kept ales; tables out in front and in attractive courtyard, pleasant bedrooms *(Angus Lyon)*

☆ **Manor Arms** LA20 6HY [The Square]: Outstanding choice of interesting changing well priced ales in neat and comfortable open-plan pub on quiet sloping square, flagstones and nice bow window seats in front bar, coal fire in big stone fireplace, chiming clocks, good sandwiches, pizzas and bockwurst sausages, winter soup, pool table; children allowed, stairs down to lavatories (ladies' has baby-changing); well appointed good value bedrooms, big breakfast, open all day *(Angus Lyon, BB, Ben and Helen Ingram)*

Old Kings Head LA20 6HJ [Church St]: Smart but relaxed family-run pub with son cooking enjoyable food, friendly obliging service, good choice of well kept ales, stone fireplace, chintz and knick-knacks, separate games area, small cosy restaurant; attractive garden behind with covered heated terrace, comfortable bedrooms *(Angus Lyon)*

BUTTERMERE [NY1716]

Fish CA13 9XA: Spacious, fresh and airy former coaching inn on NT property between Buttermere and Crummock Water, fine views, up to half a dozen or so changing ales inc Jennings, wide range of good value food, good mature staff, pleasant atmosphere; terrace tables, bedrooms *(BB, J and F Gowers, the Didler)*

CALDBECK [NY3239]

☆ **Oddfellows Arms** CA7 8EA [B5299 SE of Wigton]: Unpretentious split-level pub popular for generous good value home cooking from lunchtime sandwiches up inc good proper chips, well kept Jennings ales, good choice of wines by the glass, affable landlord, quick pleasant service, fine old photographs and woodburner in comfortable front bar full of locals and visitors, big back dining room; piped music, games area with darts, pool and TV; children welcome, open all day Fri-Sun and summer, low-priced bedrooms, nice village *(Helen Clarke, B I Mason, Mrs C E Godfrey, Adam F Padel)*

CARLISLE [NY4056]

Howard Arms CA3 8ED [Lowther St]: Well kept Theakstons and a guest beer, several linked rooms, traditional fittings and memorabilia; big-screen sports TV; open all day *(the Didler)*

Kings Head CA3 8RF [Fishergate]: Enjoyable cheap bar lunches, well kept Jennings and Yates, comfortable atmosphere, upstairs dining room; open all day *(the Didler)*

Woodrow Wilson CA1 1QS [Botchergate]: Civilised Wetherspoons with fine range of real ales inc local Geltsdale, their usual bargain food; attractive terrace, open all day *(the Didler)*

CARTMEL [SD3778]

☆ *Cavendish Arms* LA11 6QA [Cavendish St, off main sq]: Friendly local atmosphere, promptly served bar food from sandwiches up, real ales, good coffee, great log fire (not always lit), restaurant; children truly welcome, tables out in front and behind by stream, ten comfortable bedrooms, good walks, open all day *(Alain and Rose Foote, Ann and Tony Bennett-Hughes, Mr and Mrs P Eastwood, Michael Doswell, R Davies, LYM)*

CASTLE CARROCK [NY5455]

☆ *Weary Sportsman* CA8 9LU: Smart modern pub/brasserie with comfortable sofas and bucket chairs on bare boards of refreshingly light and airy bar, ambitious choice of good upmarket food, good lunchtime sandwiches too, a real ale such as Black Sheep or Greene King, interesting wines, welcoming service, good modern prints and wall of glassware and objets, conservatory dining room; good tables in back japanese garden, comfortable well equipped bedrooms *(Michael Doswell, Maurice and Gill McMahon, Dr K P Tucker, B I Mason, A J Bowen)*

CONISTON [SD3097]

☆ *Black Bull* LA21 8DU [Yewdale Rd (A593)]: Unpretentiously welcoming, with good Coniston Bluebird, XB and Old Man brewed here, bustling flagstoned back area, banquettes and open fire in relaxed carpeted lounge bar, simple good value food inc children's, good sandwiches and more enterprising specials, farm ciders, quite a few bottled beers and malt whiskies, lots of Donald Campbell water-speed memorabilia, separate restaurant; children and dogs welcome, tables out in suntrap former coachyard, bedrooms, open all day *(Maggie Chandler, Carl Van Baars, Irene and Derek Flewin, Arthur Pickering, Stephen R Holman, Dave Braisted, LYM, Jill Littlewood, Christopher Joinson)*

Ship LA21 8HB [Bowmanstead, tucked away off A593 S]: Olde-worlde pub in pretty

hamlet, popular with walkers and campers from lakeside camp sites for good-sized helpings of good value food, well kept ales, friendly service *(Russell and Alison Hunt)*

☆ *Sun* LA21 8HQ: 16th-c pub in terrific setting below dramatic fells, interesting Donald Campbell and other lakeland photographs in old-fashioned back bar with beams, flagstones, good log fire in 19th-c range, cask seats and old settles, big conservatory restaurant off carpeted lounge, good generous food, Coniston Bluebird, Hawkshead and three good guest beers, decent wines, darts, cribbage, dominoes; children and dogs welcome, tables with great views on pleasant front terrace, big tree-sheltered garden, comfortable bedrooms, good hearty breakfast, open all day *(Jarrod and Wendy Hopkinson, Jo Lilley, Simon Calvert, Malcolm and Jane Levitt, Arthur Pickering, Chris Evans, LYM, M Thomas, Tina and David Woods-Taylor, Michael J Caley, Margaret Whalley, Lindsley Harvard)*

CROOK [SD4695]

☆ *Sun* LA8 8LA [B5284 Kendal—Bowness]: Good bustling atmosphere in low-beamed bar with two dining areas off, good varied traditional food (all day wknds) from unusual sandwiches to enterprising hot dishes, winter game and lovely puddings, reasonable prices, prompt cheerful helpful service, well kept Coniston Bluebird and Hawkshead, good value wines, roaring log fire, fresh flowers *(Lee and Liz Potter, Janet and Peter Race, Hugh Roberts, Ray and Winifred Halliday, Mrs Sheila Stothard, LYM, Margaret and Roy Randle, Michael Doswell, Tony and Penny Burton, Julian and Janet Dearden, David and Jean Hall)*

CROSBY ON EDEN [NY4459]

Stag CA6 4QN [A689 NE of Carlisle]: Good value food from baguettes up, pleasant service; tables outside *(Monica Shelley)*

DACRE [NY4526]

☆ *Horse & Farrier* CA11 0HL [between A66 and A592 SW of Penrith]: 18th-c village pub under new licensees, good local home-made food (not Sun evening), well kept Jennings ales, cheerful atmosphere, lovely fire in front room's big old-fashioned range, nice beam-and-plank ceiling, more modern dining extension down steps on the left, darts and dominoes; children welcome, integral post office, pretty village, cl Mon lunchtime *(David and Katharine Cooke, BB)*

DALTON-IN-FURNESS [SD2376]

☆ *Black Dog* LA15 8JP [Broughton Rd, well N of town]: Unpretentious country local handy for South Lakes Wild Animal Park, with fine range of interesting changing ales, log fires, simple tiled and flagstoned low-beamed bar, hearty good value food all day, traditional games; children welcome, side terrace tables, bedrooms, open all day, cl Mon, till 4 Tues *(Andrew Beardsley, Alison Lawrence, LYM)*

DENT [SD7086]

Sun LA10 5QL [Main St]: Popular old-fashioned local with four Dent ales brewed nearby, decent simple food from sandwiches up, good atmosphere in well worn in beamed traditional bar with coal fire and darts; children welcome, open all day in summer (LYM, Dudley and Moira Cockroft, Margaret Dickinson, John Coatsworth)

DOCKRAY [NY3921]

Royal CA11 0JY [A5091, off A66 or A592 W of Penrith]: Bright open-plan bar, well kept Black Sheep, Dent and Jennings, straightforward food from bargain sandwiches up, two dining areas, walkers' part with stripped settles on flagstones, darts, cribbage and dominoes; piped music; picnic-sets in large peaceful garden, great setting, open all day, comfortable bedrooms (J Hudson, Mr and Mrs Maurice Thompson, LYM, John and Gloria Isaacs, David J Cooke)

ENNERDALE BRIDGE [NY0615]

☆ *Shepherds Arms* CA23 3AR [off A5086 E of Egremont]: Comfortable walkers' inn well placed by car-free dale, with footpath plans, weather-forecast blackboard and helpful books, lots of pictures, log fire and woodburner, Coniston Bluebird, Jennings, Timothy Taylors Landlord and guest beers, good wine choice, panelled dining room and conservatory; may be piped music; children and dogs welcome, bedrooms, open all day (may be winter afternoon break Mon-Thurs) (LYM, Sylvia and Tony Birbeck, Tina and David Woods-Taylor, GSB)

ESKDALE GREEN [NY1200]

☆ *Bower House* CA19 1TD [½ mile W]: Civilised old-fashioned stone-built inn with friendly mix of walkers, locals and businessmen, helpful obliging staff, real ales such as Hesket Newmarket, good value pubby food, good log fire in main lounge bar extended around beamed and alcoved core, biggish restaurant; may be piped music; nicely tended sheltered garden by cricket field, charming spot with great walks, bedrooms, open all day (Mr and Mrs Maurice Thompson, Tina and David Woods-Taylor, LYM)

FAR SAWREY [SD3795]

☆ *Sawrey Hotel* LA22 0LQ: Comfortable, warm and welcoming stable bar with tables in wooden stalls, harness on rough white walls, even water troughs and mangers, big helpings of good value simple lunchtime bar food, well kept Black Sheep, Jennings and Theakstons, good coffee, pleasant staff, appealingly relaxed and old-fashioned second bar in main hotel, log fires in both, restaurant; seats on nice lawn, beautiful setting, walkers, children and dogs welcome, good bedrooms (G Coates, LYM, Dennis Jones, Janet and Peter Race)

FOXFIELD [SD2085]

☆ *Prince of Wales* LA20 6BX [opp stn]: Cheery bare-boards pub with half a dozen good changing ales inc bargain beers brewed in the former stables here and at their associated Tigertops brewery, bottled imports, farm cider and regular beer festivals, enthusiastic licensees, enjoyable home-made food (can take a long while) inc lots of unusual pasties, hot coal fire, maps, customer snaps and beer awards, pub games inc bar billiards, daily papers and beer-related reading matter, back room with one huge table; children very welcome, games for them; steps up to door; reasonably priced bedrooms with own bathrooms, cl Mon/Tues, opens mid-afternoon Weds/Thurs, open all day Fri-Sun (BB, MLR, the Didler)

GRASMERE [NY3406]

Travellers Rest LA22 9RR [A591 just N]: Comfortable and cheery, with settles, banquettes, upholstered armchairs and log fire, local watercolours, old photographs, suggested walks, friendly staff, Jennings ales, bar food (all day in summer) from sandwiches with crisps up; piped music may be loud, and the big games end may not appeal to all; provision for children and dogs, good quiet bedrooms, good breakfast, open all day (Mr and Mrs Maurice Thompson, John and Joan Nash, Mr and Mrs John Taylor, John and Sylvia Harrop, Walter and Susan Rinaldi-Butcher, Arthur Pickering, LYM, Ian and Sue Wells)

Tweedies LA22 9SW [part of Dale Lodge Hotel]: Big square bar, warm and cosy, with lively atmosphere, plenty of young people, attractively updated traditional décor, sturdy furnishings in adjoining flagstoned family dining room, helpful welcoming staff, enjoyable food from pizzas and lunchtime baguettes to steak, braised pheasant and Sun roast (which is free for under-8s), five changing real ales, farm cider, wide choice of wines by the glass; children, walkers and dogs welcome, picnic-sets out in large pleasant garden, bedrooms (Alice English)

HAVERTHWAITE [SD3284]

Anglers Arms LA12 8AJ [just off A590]: Busy split-level pub with up to ten real ales, friendly helpful staff, good choice of fairly priced generous fresh food from sandwiches to steak, sports memorabilia, separate upstairs dining room, lower area with pool (Ron Gentry, Mr and Mrs Maurice Thompson, Dennis Jones)

HEVERSHAM [SD4983]

Blue Bell LA7 7FH [A6]: Beamed and partly panelled lounge bar with bow-windowed eating area, warm log fire, pubby food (all day during hols), friendly service, low-priced Sam Smiths OB, plenty of character, long public bar (games, TV, piped music), separate restaurant; children and dogs welcome, comfortable roomy bedrooms, open all day (L and D Webster, Sylvia and Tony Birbeck, LYM, Neil Ingoe, A and B D Craig)

IRTHINGTON [NY4961]

Salutation CA6 4NJ: Unpretentious local with good value creative bar food using local produce, efficient service, Thwaites ale (C and H Greenly)

KENDAL [SD5292]

Ring o' Bells LA9 5AF [Kirkland]: Two bars, little snug in between, three real ales, separate dining room (Edward Leetham)

KESWICK [NY2623]

Bank Tavern CA12 5DS [Main St]: Low-beamed L-shaped carpeted bar, spotless and well run, with Jennings and guest ales, simple pub food (very popular for this at lunchtime), lots of nooks and crannies, log-effect gas fire, children's room; dogs welcome, bedrooms, open all day *(Kevin Flack, Mr and Mrs Maurice Thompson, Fred and Lorraine Gill)*

Four in Hand CA12 5BZ [Lake Rd]: Pleasantly unassuming traditional two-room pub with impressively panelled hushed back lounge, brighter front part, stage-coach bric-a-brac, lots of brasses and old photographs, decent-sized tables in dining room, full Jennings range kept well, enjoyable pubby lunchtime food, wider evening choice; very busy in summer *(Phil Bryant)*

☆ *George* CA12 5AZ [St Johns St]: Handsome old place with attractive traditional black-panelled side room, open-plan main bar, old-fashioned settles and modern banquettes under Elizabethan beams, daily papers, four Jennings ales, big log fire, restaurant; piped music, service can slow when busy; children welcome in eating areas, dogs in bar, bedrooms with own bathrooms, open all day *(LYM, Steve Godfrey, P Dawn)*

Keswick Lodge CA12 5HZ [Main St]: Hotel lounge bar with three Thwaites real ales, wide choice of reasonably priced bar food all day, pleasant service; 20 bedrooms with own bathrooms *(Mr and Mrs Maurice Thompson)*

☆ *Swinside Inn* CA12 5UE [Newlands Valley, just SW]: Brilliant peaceful valley setting, long bright public bar, traditionally furnished, with Jennings Cumberland, Theakstons Best and a guest beer, pleasant service, generous pubby food at popular prices, games area beyond central log fire (two more elsewhere); piped music; children and dogs welcome, tables in garden and on upper and lower terraces giving fine views across to the high crags and fells around Grisedale Pike, bedrooms, open all day *(Mark Lubienski, Sylvia and Tony Birbeck, David J Cooke, J S Burn, Edward Mirzoeff, LYM, Stephen R Holman, David and Katharine Cooke, Brian and Anna Marsden)*

KIRKBY LONSDALE [SD6278]

Snooty Fox LA6 2AH [Main St (B6254)]: Rambling partly panelled pub with interesting pictures and bric-a-brac, country furniture, two coal fires, dining annexe, Timothy Taylors Landlord, Theakstons Best and a guest beer, several country wines, reasonably priced straightforward food; piped music, machines; children in eating areas, tables in pretty garden, open all day *(LYM, A Benson)*

LANGWATHBY [NY5633]

Shepherds CA10 1LW [A686 Penrith—Alston]: Welcoming open-plan beamed village pub with good quickly served reasonably priced food, friendly efficient service, well kept ales such as Black Sheep, decent wine choice, comfortable banquettes, bar down steps from lounge, games room;

tables and chairs on big back terrace, attractive spot on huge green of Pennines village, play area *(Len Beattie, Sarah and Peter Gooderham)*

LINDALE [SD4180]

Lindale Inn LA11 6LJ [B5277 N of Grange-over-Sands]: Smartly reworked in dark green and cherry red, with new licensees, wide choice of food from interesting baguettes to venison and smoked game, Black Sheep and guest beers such as Everards Beacon, decent wines, sofas and polished flagstones in informal softly lit beamed bar, lighter carpeted dining room; good value comfortable bedrooms *(Michael Doswell)*

☆ *Royal Oak* LA11 6LX: Spacious open-plan village pub with good home-made food using local ingredients, wider evening choice, modestly priced wines, Robinsons ales such as Hartleys XB. blue banquettes and padded chairs in carpeted bar, wood-floored dining areas either side, restrained décor with a few modern prints, pleasant atmosphere *(John Lane, Michael Doswell, Peter Burton)*

LORTON [NY1526]

☆ *Wheat Sheaf* CA13 9UW [B5289 Buttermere—Cockermouth]: Good relaxed atmosphere, affable landlord, four Jennings ales, good generous food (not Mon-Weds lunchtimes) from sandwiches up using fresh local produce, good value wines, neatly furnished bar with roaring fire, good-sized dining area, pool, no piped music; children welcome, tables outside, camp site behind *(Sylvia and Tony Birbeck, BB, Tim Maddison)*

LOW HESKET [NY4646]

Rose & Crown CA4 0HG [A6 Carlisle-Penrith]: Warmly welcoming, with enjoyable home-made no-nonsense food, Jennings ale, comfortable new dining room extension *(Bill and Pauline Critchley)*

LOWICK GREEN [SD3084]

☆ *Farmers Arms* LA12 8DT [just off A5092 SE of village]: Cosy public bar with heavy beams, huge slate flagstones, big open fire, cosy corners and pub games, some interesting furniture and pictures in plusher hotel lounge bar across yard, nice atmosphere, tasty reasonably priced food in bar and restaurant, well kept local ales; unobtrusive piped music; children and dogs welcome, open all day, comfortable bedrooms *(LYM, Julie and Bill Ryan)*

LUPTON [SO5581]

Plough LA6 1PJ [A65, nr M6 junction 36]: Impressive oak beams and stonework, Black Sheep, good home-made food, attractive conservatory; disabled access, garden tables, beautiful spot *(Margaret Dickinson)*

MELMERBY [NY6137]

Shepherds CA10 1HF [A686 Penrith—Alston]: Popular country pub with comfortable heavy-beamed eating area off flagstoned bar, spacious end room with woodburner, generous food, Black Sheep, Jennings Cumberland and John Smiths, quite a few malt whiskies, games area with darts and pool; juke box; children welcome, terrace tables *(Mr and Mrs Maurice Thompson, LYM)*

NEWBY BRIDGE [SD3686]
Newby Bridge Hotel LA12 8NA: Panelled and flagstoned hunting-theme hotel bar popular with locals and tourists, enjoyable food all day from sandwiches and baguettes up inc some interesting dishes, real ales such as Hawkshead, friendly efficient staff; bedrooms *(Alice English)*

ORTON [NY6208]
George CA10 3RJ [2 miles from M6 junction 38; B6261 towards Penrith]: Roomy bar in attractive old inn, enjoyable food inc good specials, welcoming log fire, four real ales, wonderful peaceful setting on coast-to-coast walk; seven comfortable bedrooms *(Clive Gibson)*

OUSBY [NY6134]
Fox CA10 1QA: Well placed for walkers and pleasantly updated inside by current owners, with good service, generous and enjoyable pubby food, well kept local ales, open fire, pool table, separate dining room; bedrooms, caravan site, has been cl lunchtime exc Sun *(Bill and Sheila McLardy)*

OUTGATE [SD3599]
☆ *Outgate Inn* LA22 0NQ [B5286 Hawkshead—Ambleside]: Attractively placed, neatly kept and very hospitable country pub with three pleasantly modernised rooms, good food from sandwiches through popular favourites to some unusual specialities, well kept Robinsons ales, friendly licensees and helpful staff, popular food inc sandwiches; trad jazz Fri (very busy then); terrace picnic-sets, three bright comfortable bedrooms, good breakfast, nice walks, open all day summer wknds *(BB, Maggie Chandler, Carl Van Baars, Mr and Mrs M Wall)*

PAPCASTLE [NY1131]
Belle Vue CA13 0NT [Belle Vue]: Unpretentious choice of consistently enjoyable food, friendly helpful service *(Dr and Mrs S G Barber)*

PATTERDALE [NY3915]
Patterdale Hotel CA11 0NN: Large hotel's bar popular with locals, residents and walking parties, Hesket Newmarket Helvellyn Gold and Timothy Taylors Landlord; bedrooms *(Mr and Mrs Maurice Thompson)*

PENRITH [NY5130]
Gloucester Arms CA11 7DE [Great Dockray/Cornmarket]: Ancient low-beamed and panelled local with comfortable settles, big open fire, changing ales such as Caledonian Deuchars IPA and Timothy Taylors Landlord, bargain bar food inc good sandwiches and baked potatoes, friendly if not swift service, daily papers, appropriate Richard III portraits; no dogs, open all day *(Rona Murdoch, Fred and Lorraine Gill)*

PORT CARLISLE [NY2462]
Hope & Anchor CA7 5BU: Bright, cheerful and lively front locals' bar, Jennings ales, current licensees doing enjoyable food in new back restaurant with good service *(Monica Shelley)*

RAVENGLASS [SD0894]
Ratty Arms CA18 1SN: Extended former waiting room a 200-metre walk over the footbridge from the Ravenglass & Eskdale terminus and rail museum (and right on main-line platform), well kept Jennings ales, good value pub food, quick friendly service, pool table in busy public bar; children welcome, open all day wknds and summer, big courtyard *(LYM, John Tav)*

RAVENSTONEDALE [SD7401]
☆ *Fat Lamb* CA17 4LL [Crossbank; A683 Sedbergh—Kirkby Stephen]: Attractively isolated, with pews in cheerful relaxing bar, coal fire in traditional black inglenook range, good local photographs and bird plates, friendly helpful staff, wide choice of good proper food from filled baguettes to enjoyable restaurant meals, Tetleys, decent wines; facilities for disabled, children welcome, tables out by nature-reserve pastures, good walks, bedrooms *(BB, John and Yvonne Davies, Mrs Ann Gray, Helen and Brian Edgeley)*

☆ *Kings Head* CA17 4NH [Pub visible from A685 W of Kirkby Stephen]: Traditional country inn well refurbished after dire 2005 flood, friendly helpful staff, well kept Black Sheep, Dent and two guest ales, farm cider, good range of enjoyable food using local produce from good sandwiches up, comfortable carpeted lounge and bar, roaring log fires, sizeable dining room with shelves of whisky-water jugs, lower games room with traditional games and pool; children and dogs welcome, picnic-sets out in front, by stream across lane, and in garden with red squirrel feeders, three comfortable bedrooms, open all day *(Christopher Beadle, Adam F Padel, LYM, Simon Marley)*

ROSTHWAITE [NY2514]
Scafell CA12 5XB [B5289 S of Keswick]: Plain slate-floored bar in back extension, a few tables out overlooking beck, well kept ales such as Barngates Westmorland Gold and Theakstons XB, blazing log fire, usual food from sandwiches up, efficient service even when packed with walkers (weather forecasts up on a board); afternoon teas, piped music, pool; separate entrance to rather plush hotel with appealing cocktail bar/sun-lounge and dining room, bedrooms not big but good *(Mr and Mrs Maurice Thompson, BB, J and F Gowers, Brian and Anna Marsden)*

RYDAL [NY3606]
Glen Rothay Hotel LA22 9LR [A591]: Attractive small olde-worlde hotel with enjoyable pubby lunchtime food from baguettes up in popular and well furnished back bar, fireside armchairs in beamed lounge bar, real ales such as Barngates Pride of Westmorland and Thwaites Liberation, restaurant; tables in pretty garden, boats for residents on nearby Rydal Water, comfortable bedrooms *(LYM, Mr and Mrs Maurice Thompson, Alan and Paula McCully)*

SEATOLLER [NY2413]

Yew Tree CA12 5XN: Enjoyable food inc authentic south african specialities (esp evening) in attractive low-ceilinged dining area, well kept Hesket Newmarket, good whisky choice, cosy beamed and slate-floored back bar with open range, relaxed service; piped music may be loud; interesting garden behind *(J and F Gowers)*

SEDBERGH [SD6592]

Bull LA10 5BL [Main St]: Welcoming and unpretentious bar in rather rambling hotel, well kept ales such as Black Sheep, bar food, popular with locals and walkers; dogs welcome, bedrooms *(Dr D J and Mrs S C Walker, John Coatsworth)*

Dalesman LA10 5BN [Main St]: Linked rooms well used by visitors, stripped stone and beams, log fire, sporting prints, quickly served good value traditional food (all day Sun) from sandwiches to aberdeen angus steaks, big helpings, well kept Peak Dalesman and Tetleys, dominoes; piped music, monthly jazz 1st Mon; children welcome, picnic-sets out in front, bedrooms, open all day *(Michael Doswell, John and Yvonne Davies, Andy and Jill Kassube, LYM, Rob Bowran, David and Sue Atkinson, Nick and Meriel Cox)*

Red Lion LA10 5BZ [Finkle St (A683)]: Cheerful family-run beamed local, down to earth and comfortable, with good value generous home-made food from baguettes to bargain Sun lunch using local meats, full Jennings range kept well, helpful friendly staff, splendid coal fire, sports TV; very busy wknds, no dogs *(BB, John and Yvonne Davies, Dr D J and Mrs S C Walker)*

SHAP [NY5614]

Greyhound CA10 3PW [A6, S end]: Unpretentious newly refurbished former coaching inn, good sensible food from sandwiches through particularly good carefully cooked local meats to imaginative puddings in open-plan bar or restaurant (chefs happy to share their recipes), hearty helpings, well kept Jennings and up to half a dozen guest beers, good reasonably priced house wines, cheerful bustle and friendly helpful young staff; may be unobtrusive piped classical music, resident collie, dogs welcome; nine comfortable bedrooms, good breakfast, popular with coast-to-coast walkers *(J S Burn, Michael Doswell)*

STAINTON [NY4828]

Kings Arms CA11 0EP [village signed off A66, handy for M6 junction 40]: Friendly new father-and-son landlords settling in well at pleasant open-plan pub, good reasonably priced pubby food, well kept ales such as Black Sheep and Shepherd Neame Spitfire, thriving local atmosphere, darts; children welcome in eating areas, tables on small lawn and nice heated side terrace with gazebo *(Revd John Hibberd, Geoff and Angela Jacques, LYM)*

STAVELEY [SD4798]

Hawkshead Brewery Bar LA8 9LR [Staveley

Mill Yard, Back Lane]: Spacious modern span-roof beer hall with full Hawkshead beer range in top condition from long counter, local farm cider, good wine and soft drinks choice, friendly staff happy to talk beer, long tables and benches and comfortable groups of leather sofas on new oak boards, view down into brewery, food from adjoining café, T-shirts etc for sale; brewery tours available, open 12-5, occasionally later *(the Didler)*

TIRRIL [NY5026]

☆ *Queens Head* CA10 2JF [B5320, not far from M6 junction 40]: Buoyant atmosphere, low beams, black panelling, flagstones, bare boards, high-backed settles and four open fireplaces inc a roomy inglenook, good Tirril ales (formerly brewed here, now from Appleby), fairly priced generous food in bar and restaurant; piped music (may be loud) and pool in back bar; children welcome in eating areas, bedrooms, open all day Fri-Sun *(Michael and Maggie Betton, Christine and Neil Townend, Rona Murdoch, LYM, B I Mason, Tracey and Stephen Groves)*

TORVER [SD2894]

☆ *Church House* LA21 8AZ [A593/A5084 S of Coniston]: Attractive rambling building dating from 14th c, lots of low beams, new chef/landlord doing reasonably priced good local food, warmly welcoming hands-on landlady, well kept Adnams, Barngates Tag Lag and Hawkshead, fine log fire in cheerful flagstoned bar with interesting bric-a-brac, another in comfortable lounge with dark red walls, separate dining room, splendid hill views (if weather allows); children and dogs welcome, picnic-sets in big well tended garden, six bedrooms, has been open all day at least in summer *(John and Hilary Penny, Dennis Jones, John Arnold)*

TROUTBECK [NY4103]

☆ *Mortal Man* LA23 1PL [A592 N of Windermere; Upper Rd]: Partly panelled beamed hotel bar with welcoming efficient staff, food with carefully sourced ingredients from doorstep sandwiches to some interesting dishes, real ales such as Jennings, John Smiths and Theakstons Best, big log fire, mix of seats inc a cushioned settle, copper-topped tables, picture-window restaurant, darts, dominoes; piped music, TV room, Sun folk/blues night; children welcome, great views from sunny garden, lovely village, comfortable bedrooms, open all day *(Dr and Mrs R G J Telfer, Paul Humphreys, Bruce Braithwaite, LYM)*

ULDALE [NY2436]

Snooty Fox CA7 1HA: Comfortable two-bar village inn with wide choice of good generous food using local ingredients, changing real ales inc one brewed for them in Hesket Newmarket, good wines by the glass; good value bedrooms with own bathrooms *(Steve Godfrey)*

WABERTHWAITE [SD1093]

Brown Cow LA19 5YJ [A595]: Unpretentious pleasantly refurbished pub with enjoyable simple food using local ingredients, local

real ales, warm friendly atmosphere
(Dr J R Norman, J and E Dakin)

WALTON [NY5264]

Centurion CA8 2DH: Artfully simple and comfortable refurbishment, with big informal flagstoned bar, good value simple lunchtime snacks from sandwiches and baguettes up, more ambitious evening choice of good inventive food – also good value – using local produce inc sausages from their own rare breed pigs, attractive Pennine views, Jennings Cumberland, one of their seasonal beers and Timothy Taylors Landlord, decent wines, small entrance lounge with sofa and daily papers, restaurant extension; large terrace, cl winter wkdy lunchtimes
(Dr and Mrs R G J Telfer, Monica Shelley, Kevin Jeavons, Alison Turner, Michael Doswell)

WASDALE HEAD [NY1807]

Wasdale Head Inn CA20 1EX [NE of West Water]: Mountain hotel worth knowing for its stunning fellside setting and the interesting Great Gable beers it brews, available in taster glasses; roomy walkers' bar with side hot food counter (all day in summer, may be restricted winter), decent choice of wines and malt whiskies, striking mountain photographs, traditional games, old-fashioned residents' bar, lounge and restaurant; children welcome, dogs allowed in bar, open all day (Ben and Helen Ingram, LYM, Mr and Mrs Maurice Thompson, the Didler)

WATERMILLOCK [NY4523]

☆ *Brackenrigg* CA11 0LP [A592, Ullswater]: Opened-up 19th-c inn in lovely spot, local real ales such as Coniston and Jennings, decent bar food from generous lunchtime filled rolls and sandwiches up, willing and cheery if not always speedy staff, pleasant partly panelled bar with log fire and darts, carpeted lounge, spectacular Ullswater and mountain views, stylish good-sized dining room (restaurant meals are on the pricy side); no dogs inside, no children after teatime; front roadside tables, ten bedrooms, self-catering (BB, Dr D J and Mrs S C Walker, David Morgan, Richard J Holloway, Tina and David Woods-Taylor, Mrs A J Robertson, Dave and Sue Mitchell, Tracey and Stephen Groves)

WEST CURTHWAITE [NY3248]

Royal Oak CA7 8BG: Unpretentious pub with young chef/landlord doing wide choice of good fresh food using local produce, Jennings Cumberland, good choice of wines with strong australian leanings, friendly landlady and efficient service (B I Mason, Helen Clarke)

WINSTER [SD4193]

☆ *Brown Horse* LA23 3NR [A5074 S of Windermere]: Open-plan dining pub with enjoyable food inc interesting dishes and good Sun lunch, friendly helpful service, Jennings and Timothy Taylors ales, decent wines, log fire, pleasantly up-to-date mediterranean-style décor, roomy dining area not too cut off from bar; big-screen sports TV; children and walkers welcome, country-view tables outside, handy for Blackwell Arts & Crafts House, reasonably priced bedrooms with good breakfast, has been cl wkdy lunchtimes out of season
(Margaret Dickinson, Kevin Flack, LYM)

WREAY [NY4349]

Plough CA4 0RL: Saved from proposed demolition for housing development, now reopened after careful restoration, with heavy beams, sturdy furnishings on flagstones, enjoyable reasonably priced food, well kept changing ales inc Theakstons Best, buoyant relaxed atmosphere; cl Mon/Tues (Colin and Anne Glynne-Jones, N Tunstall)

The letters and figures after the name of each town are its Ordnance Survey map reference. 'Using the *Guide*' at the beginning of the book explains how it helps you find a pub, in road atlases or on large-scale maps as well as in our own maps.

Derbyshire

Three features stand out particularly for our selection of Derbyshire pubs: interesting beers, fine scenery, and character. A good number of our featured pubs are in the Peak District and in marvellous country for walking – see in particular the entries for Earl Sterndale, Fenny Bentley, Foolow, Hassop, Hathersage, Hayfield, Hope, Ladybower Reservoir, Litton, Monsal Head, Over Haddon, Sheldon and Wardlow. Some are in buildings that are themselves really special: those particularly worth knowing for their unspoilt character include the Bear at Alderwasley, the Olde Gate at Brassington, the Quiet Woman at Earl Sterndale, the Barley Mow at Kirk Ireton (also impressive for its range of beers), and the Three Stags Heads at Wardlow (but watch out for the limited opening times). Other pubs liked especially for beer include three that brew their own – the Old Poets Corner at Ashover (its microbrewery is a recent addition), the Brunswick in Derby (a railway-age beer palace) and the John Thompson near Melbourne (efficiently run, and with decent, unpretentious bar food). Other beer specialists are the Alexandra in Derby, the Bulls Head at Foolow, the Dead Poets at Holbrook (with a noticeable absence of music or similar intrusions; also has farm cider), the Monsal Head Hotel (friendly and efficient, and memorably perched above Monsal Dale) and the Lathkil at Over Haddon (well placed for exploring Lathkill Dale). Other pubs currently doing well here are the Eyre Arms at Hassop (a stone-built 17th-c house with lovely views from the garden) and the Red Lion at Litton (flourishing under its new landlady). This year, no single pub has stood out above others here as the obvious Dining Pub of the Year for Derbyshire. There are some promising possibilities among those pubs that offer more ambitious food, and it will be interesting to see which emerges as the outstanding choice for dining in the months to come. Ones already winning some strong support include the Bell at Alderwasley, the Old Pump at Barlow, the Plough and the Scotsmans Pack around Hathersage, and the Monsal Head Hotel. Derbyshire is one of the best value areas for pub food, with two-course pub meals typically costing a pound or two less than in most areas, for equivalent quality, and plenty of starters or light dishes around for under £5. Expect generous helpings here. Drinks prices, too, are comfortably below the national average. Turning to the Lucky Dip section at the end of the chapter, pubs to note particularly here are the Bulls Head at Ashford in the Water, Devonshire Arms at Beeley, Old Sun in Buxton, Abbey Inn and Olde Dolphin in Derby, Shire Horse at Edlaston, Barrel near Foolow, Hardwick Inn near Hardwick Hall, Devonshire Arms at Hartington, Bulls Head at Monyash, Royal Oak in Ockbrook, Old Crown at Shardlow, Smisby Arms at Smisby, Derby Tup in Whittington Moor and Bowling Green at Winster.

ALDERWASLEY

SK3153 MAP 7

Bear ★ ♀

Village signposted with Breanfield off B5035 E of Wirksworth at Malt Shovel; inn ½ mile SW of village, on Ambergate—Wirksworth high back road; DE56 2RD

Friendly unspoilt pub with plenty of character in low-beamed cottagey rooms

'A lovely pub in beautiful nowhere,' remarked one reader of this popular country inn. The dark, low-beamed rooms have a cheerful miscellany of antique furniture including high-backed settles and locally made antique oak chairs with derbyshire motifs, and there are staffordshire china ornaments, old paintings and engravings, and a trio of grandfather clocks; roaring open fires. One little room is filled right to its built-in wall seats by a single vast table. It's all very easy-going with dominoes players clattering about beside canaries trilling in a huge Edwardian-style white cage (elsewhere look out for the budgerigars and talkative cockatoos). Bass, Black Sheep, Greene King Old Speckled Hen, Marstons Pedigree and Whim Hartington Bitter on handpump, and several wines by the glass; darts and board games. Well spaced picnic-sets out on the side grass with peaceful country views. There's no obvious front door – you get in through the plain back entrance by the car park.

🍽 **There's a large choice of food: sandwiches, soup, smoked salmon fishcakes, haunch of venison, pork and black pudding sausages or vegetable stew with cheddar mash, slow-cooked lamb in red wine, monkfish tails in a creamy thai curry sauce, and puddings such as lemon tart or bakewell pudding. You must book to be sure of a table.** *Starters/Snacks: £3.95 to £5.95. Main Courses: £8.95 to £17.95. Puddings: £3.95 to £5.95*

Free house ~ Licensee Nicky Fletcher-Musgrave ~ Real ale ~ Bar food (12-9.30) ~ (01629) 822585 ~ Children welcome away from bar areas ~ Dogs welcome ~ Open 12-11.30 ~ Bedrooms: £55S/£75S

Recommended by John and Karen Wilkinson, Richard Cole, Tony and Tracy Constance, Derek and Sylvia Stephenson, Peter F Marshall, Alan Bowker, Gerald and Gabrielle Culliford, Cathryn and Richard Hicks, the Didler, Brian and Jean Hepworth, Janet and Peter Race, Theocsbrian, Jeff and Wendy Williams, Ken and Barbara Turner, Deb and John Arthur, Rob and Catherine Dunster, John and Enid Morris, Annette Tress, Gary Smith, Dean Rose, Maurice and Gill McMahon

ASHOVER

SK3462 MAP 7

Old Poets Corner 🍺 🛏

Butts Road (B6036, off A632 Matlock—Chesterfield); S45 0EW

A fine range of interesting real ales in a simple village pub with enthusiastic owners

Readers praise the friendly welcome at this comfortably unpretentious village pub, in lovely countryside for walkers. The most obvious draw is the range of perfectly kept real ales, never fewer than six and often running to eight, typically including beers from the pub's own microbrewery, which produces Ashover Light Rale and Poet's Tipple, as well as Greene King Abbot, Timothy Taylors Landlord and rapidly changing brews like Sarah Hughes Dark Ruby and beers from the Titanic Brewery. Other carefully chosen drinks include at least four farm ciders, a dozen bottled belgian beers and a good choice of malt whiskies and fruit wines. They have regular beer festivals. The landlord's other chief interest is very much in evidence with one or two music nights a week (mostly acoustic, folk and blues), and posters around the walls list the range of what's coming up, the busy calendar also taking in weekly quiz nights and occasional poetry evenings and morris dancers. We visited on a quieter winter Saturday night, when there was a steady murmur of laid-back chat, and candles in bottles flickering on the tables. With a cosy, lived-in feel, the bar has a mix of chairs and pews with well worn cushions, a pile of board games by a piano, a big mirror above the fireplace, plenty of blackboards, and lots of hops around the counter; there's also a simple dining room. A small room opening off the bar has another fireplace, a stack of newspapers and vintage comics and a french door leading to a tiny balcony with a couple of tables. The bedrooms are attractive, and they also have a holiday cottage sleeping up to eight people.

🍴 Good honest bar food includes soup, hot baguettes, meat pie, a good choice of vegetarian dishes like butternut squash and ginger bake, haddock and chips, a Sunday carvery and specials such as steak or sausage platter; good helpings of nice breakfasts. *Starters/Snacks: £3.25 to £4.50. Main Courses: £5.95 to £10.50. Puddings: £1.50 to £3.95*

Free house ~ Licensees Kim and Jackie Beresford ~ Real ale ~ Bar food (12-2(3 Sat), 6.30-9; not Sun evening) ~ (01246) 590888 ~ Children welcome away from bar area ~ Dogs allowed in bar ~ Live music Sun and Tues evenings ~ Open 12-3, 5-11; 12-11 Fri-Sun ~ Bedrooms: /£65S

Recommended by Tony Mills, Keith and Chris O'Neill, JJW, CMW, the Didler, Derek and Sylvia Stephenson, Dr and Mrs M W A Haward

BARLOW   SK3474   MAP 7

Old Pump
B6051 (Hackney Lane) towards Chesterfield; S18 7TD

Dining pub with chatty atmosphere and a garden

New licensees took over this dining pub in 2007, and have started making more use of the side garden, which is sheltered by hedges but overlooks fields. There's a reddish hue to the long, narrow beamed bar, which has fresh flowers, quite a few dark tables and stools, and a tiny alcove with a single table tucked beside the neatly curtained windows. It's book-ended by the dining room and two comfortably traditional little rooms, the first with big cushioned wall-benches, the other with salmon-painted walls and more substantial wooden tables for larger groups; tables are candlelit at night. Two monthly changing real ales from brewers such as Black Sheep and Jennings on handpump; several malt whiskies. There are a few tables outside in front. Barlow is well known for its August well-dressing festivities, and there are good walks nearby. More reports please.

🍴 Bar food includes lunchtime sandwiches, soup, field mushrooms in blue cheese, fillet or rump steak, a pie of the day, fish dishes such as bass or salmon. *Starters/Snacks: £3.50 to £6.00. Main Courses: £7.00 to £14.50. Puddings: £3.95 to £4.50*

Union Pub Company ~ Lease Ken Redfearn ~ Real ale ~ Bar food (12-2, 6-9(12-9 Sun)) ~ (0114) 289 0296 ~ Children welcome ~ Quiz night Mon ~ Open 12-3, 6-11; 12-11 Sun ~ Bedrooms:/50B

Recommended by Keith and Chris O'Neill

BRASSINGTON   SK2354   MAP 7

Olde Gate ★
Village signposted off B5056 and B5035 NE of Ashbourne; DE4 4HJ

Just the place to head for on a Peak District walk, with a timeless and beautifully unspoilt interior, candlelit at night

It's a treat taking in the details at this old tavern, with its fine ancient wall clock, rush-seated old chairs and antique settles, including one ancient black solid oak one. Log fires blaze away, gleaming copper pots sit on a 17th-c kitchen range, pewter mugs hang from a beam, and a side shelf boasts a collection of embossed Doulton stoneware flagons. To the left of a small hatch-served lobby, another cosy beamed room has stripped panelled settles, scrubbed-top tables, and a blazing fire under a huge mantelbeam. Marstons Pedigree and a guest such as Marstons Wranghams Station Master are on handpump, and there is a good selection of malt whiskies; board games. Stone-mullioned windows look out across lots of tables in the pleasant garden to small silvery-walled pastures, and there are some benches in the small front yard. Maybe Sunday evening boules in summer and Friday evening bell-ringers. Although the date etched on the building reads 1874, it was originally built in 1616, from magnesian limestone and timbers salvaged from Armada wrecks, bought in exchange for locally mined lead. Carsington Water is a few minutes' drive away.

🍴 Bar food typically includes well presented lunchtime sandwiches and baguettes and steak and kidney suet pudding, with evening meals like fisherman's crumble, lamb tagine and rib-eye steaks. *Starters/Snacks: £4.50 to £7.50. Main Courses: £7.50 to £15.00. Puddings: £4.50*

Marstons ~ Lease Paul Burlinson ~ Real ale ~ Bar food (12-1.45, 7-8.45; not Sun evening or Mon) ~ (01629) 540448 ~ Children over 10 only ~ Dogs welcome ~ Open 12-2.30, 6-11; 12-3, 7-11 Sun; closed Mon; 25 Dec, 26 Dec evening, 1 Jan evening

Recommended by John Dwane, Richard, Derek and Heather Manning, the Didler, John and Fiona McIlwain, Peter F Marshall, John and Enid Morris, Maurice and Gill McMahon

DERBY   SK3635   MAP 7

Alexandra 🍺 £
Siddals Road, just up from station; DE1 2QE

Railway-themed paraphernalia in a town pub well liked for its range of drinks

The staff cope admirably well under pressure here, and readers have been impressed with the friendliness of the knowledgeable landlord, who keeps a very wide range of drinks. In addition to six well kept and constantly changing real ales from all sorts of small countrywide breweries, there is also a big range of continental bottled beers and belgian and german beers on tap; quite a few malt whiskies, too. Two simple rooms have a buoyantly chatty atmosphere, good heavy traditional furnishings on dark-stained floorboards, shelves of bottles, breweriana, and lots of railway prints and memorabilia about Derby's railway history. Darts and fruit machine; there is also a yard with plants in pots and in borders. Derby station is just a few minutes away.

🍴 Bar food is confined to tasty filled rolls, available during opening times. *Starters/Snacks: £2.00*

Tynemill ~ Licensee Jonathan Hales ~ Real ale ~ No credit cards ~ (01332) 293993 ~ Children in lounge until 8.30 ~ Dogs allowed in bar ~ Open 11.45-11; 7-10.30 Sun ~ Bedrooms: /£40S
Recommended by the Didler, P Dawn, MP, Mark and Diane Grist, David Carr, R T and J C Moggridge, C J Fletcher

Brunswick 🍺 £
Railway Terrace; close to Derby Midland station; DE1 2RU

One of Britain's oldest railwaymen's pubs, now something of a treasure trove of real ales, with its own microbrewery adjacent

Not far from Derby Midland railway station and beside a terrace of former railway workers' cottages stands this 1840s tower that was sympathetically restored by a local trust in the 1980s. Of some 16 beers on handpump or tapped straight from the cask, seven or eight real ales brewed here are on offer, such as Father Mikes, Old Accidental, Railway Porter, Triple Hop and Usual), with eight others including Everards Beacon, Marstons Pedigree and Timothy Taylors Landlord and regularly changing guests like Burton Bridge Bridge Bitter and Oakham JHB. You can tour the brewery – £7.50 including a meal and a pint. The welcoming high-ceilinged bar has heavy well padded leather seats, whisky-water jugs above the dado, and a dark blue ceiling and upper wall, with squared dark panelling below. Another room is decorated with little old-fashioned prints and swan's neck lamps, and has a high-backed wall settle and a coal fire; behind a curved glazed partition wall is a chatty family parlour narrowing to the apex of the triangular building. Informative wall displays tell you about the history and restoration of the building, and there are interesting old train photographs. There are two outdoor seating areas, including a terrace behind. They'll gladly give dogs a bowl of water.

🍴 Straightforward lunchtime bar food includes toasties, filled baguettes, home-made soup, home-made quiche and home-made beef stew. *Starters/Snacks: £2.00 to £6.00*

Pubs in outstandingly attractive surroundings are listed at the back of the book.

Everards ~ Tenant Graham Yates ~ Real ale ~ Bar food (11.30-2.30 Mon-Thurs; 12-5 Fri and Sat) ~ No credit cards ~ (01332) 290677 ~ Children allowed in two rooms ~ Dogs welcome ~ Live jazz Thurs ~ Open 11-11; 12-10.30 Sun

Recommended by Kevin Blake, Brian and Jean Hepworth, Pam and John Smith, the Didler, Andrew Birkinshaw, MP, Mark and Diane Grist, P Dawn, David Carr, C J Fletcher, Brian and Rosalie Laverick

EARL STERNDALE   SK0966   MAP 7

Quiet Woman

Village signposted off B5053 S of Buxton; SK17 0BU

Unspoilt, friendly and splendidly unpretentious village local

There's a real time-warp quality about this unchanged rural pub, in lovely countryside in the Peak District. It's very simple inside, with hard seats, plain tables (including a sunken one for dominoes or cards), low beams, quarry tiles, lots of china ornaments and a coal fire. There's a pool table in the family room (where you may be joined by a friendly jack russell eager for a place by the fire), darts, bar skittles and board games. Jennings Dark Mild and Marstons Best and Pedigree, and a couple of guests such as Archers and Leek Brewery Staffordshire Gold are on handpump. They also sell gift packs of their own-label bottled beers: Quiet Woman Old Ale, Quiet Woman Headless and Nipper Ale – the latter named after one of their jack russells who passed away in 2007 (you can also buy Nipper or Quiet Woman woollen sweaters and polo shirts). You can buy free-range eggs, local poetry books and even silage here, and sometimes local dry-cured bacon and raw sausages; they have a caravan for hire in the garden, and you can also arrange to stay at the small camp site next door. There are picnic-sets out in front, and the budgies, hens, turkeys, ducks and donkeys help keep children entertained. Needless to say, it's a popular place with walkers, with some very rewarding hikes across the Dove valley towards Longnor and Hollinsclough.

🍽 **Bar food is limited to locally made pork pies.**

Free house ~ Licensee Kenneth Mellor ~ Real ale ~ No credit cards ~ (01298) 83211 ~ Children allowed in pool room if accompanied ~ Dogs allowed in bar ~ Open 12-3(Sat 4, Sun 5.30), 7-1am

Recommended by DC, the Didler, John Dwane, Rona Murdoch, P Dawn, Barry Collett

FENNY BENTLEY   SK1750   MAP 7

Coach & Horses

A515 N of Ashbourne; DE6 1LB

Cosy former coaching inn with pretty country furnishings and roaring open fires

Readers enjoy the welcoming atmosphere and food at this 17th-c rendered stone house. In the main part of the building are exposed brick hearths, flagstone floors, and hand-made pine furniture that includes flowery-cushioned wall settles; wagon wheels hang from the black beams amid horsebrasses, pewter mugs and prints. There's also a recently added conservatory dining room; quiet piped music, cards, board games and dominoes. Two or three real ales are on hand pump, with Marstons Pedigree and guests such as Abbeydale Moonshine or Peak Ales Swift Nick; 25 malt whiskies. Outside, there are views across fields from picnic-sets in the side garden by an elder tree, and wooden tables and chairs under cocktail parasols on the front terrace. The ever-popular Tissington Trail is a short stroll away.

🍽 **Served by efficient uniformed staff, the well liked bar food might include lunchtime sandwiches, baguettes and ploughman's, soup, smoked salmon and cream cheese roulade with melba toast, steak and kidney pie, rib-eye steak, sausages and mash, duck breast with port and wild berry sauce, and vegetable balti; puddings; they also do fish specials such as smoked haddock with mustard mash on Fridays, and Sunday roasts.** *Starters/Snacks: £3.50 to £4.75. Main Courses: £6.50 to £12.95. Puddings: £3.75 to £4.25*

Free house ~ Licensees John and Matthew Dawson ~ Real ale ~ Bar food (12-9) ~
(01335) 350246 ~ Children welcome ~ Open 11-11; 12-10.30 Sun

Recommended by Mrs Tessa Hibbert, P Dawn, Andrew Beardsley, Alison Lawrence, Martin and Alison Stainsby, I J and S A Bufton, Cathryn and Richard Hicks, P M Newsome, the Didler, Mr and Mrs John Taylor, Dudley Newell, Maurice and Gill McMahon

FOOLOW

SK1976 MAP 7

Bulls Head 🍺

Village signposted off A623 Baslow—Tideswell; S32 5QR

A cheerfully run tavern by a village green, with well kept ales and decent food

According to a sign outside, this friendly village pub welcomes 'dogs, muddy boots and children on leads': it is an enjoyable place to stop at on a country walk – from here you can follow paths out over rolling pasture enclosed by dry-stone walls, and the plague village of Eyam is not far away, or you can just stroll round the green and duck pond. It has a simply furnished flagstoned bar plus a couple of quieter areas for eating. A step or two takes you down into what may once have been a stables with its high ceiling joists, stripped stone and woodburning stove. On the other side, a smart dining room has more polished tables set in cosy stalls. Interesting photographs include a good collection of Edwardian naughties. Adnams, Black Sheep, Peak Ales and a guest beer such as Shepherd Neame Spitfire are well kept on handpump; piped music and darts. The west highland terriers are called Holly and Jack. Picnic-sets at the side have nice views.

🍴 **Tasty bar food includes lunchtime snacks such as sandwiches, hot filled baps and ploughman's, as well as soup, thai fishcakes with sweet chilli sauce, sausages with yorkshire pudding, steak and kidney pie, rump steak, and chicken curry; in the evenings they also do starters like warm salad of black pudding and chorizo sausage or duck and mango salad, and main courses like roasted bass with fennel, mediterranean vegetable hotpot or pork fillet with mustard sauce.** *Starters/Snacks: £4.50 to £6.00. Main Courses: £7.50 to £13.00. Puddings: £4.25 to £4.50*

Free house ~ Licensee William Leslie Bond ~ Real ale ~ Bar food (12-2, 6.30-9; 12-2, 5-8 Sun) ~ Restaurant ~ (01433) 630873 ~ Children welcome ~ Dogs allowed in bar ~ Live folk Fri evening ~ Open 12-3, 6.30-11; 12-10.30 Sun; closed Mon ~ Bedrooms: £50S/£70S

Recommended by Derek and Sylvia Stephenson, Richard, Mrs J Clarke-Williams, Peter F Marshall, Sean A Smith, Russell Grimshaw, Kerry Purcell, Barbara Ronan, Eddie Edwards

HASSOP

SK2272 MAP 7

Eyre Arms

B6001 N of Bakewell; DE45 1NS

Gracious stone pub adorned with hanging baskets, and with pretty views from the garden

The creeper on this 17th-c stone former farmhouse bursts into a spectacular colour in autumn while hanging baskets make a fine display in the summer months. The Eyre coat of arms (painted above the stone fireplace) dominates the beamed dining bar. There's also a longcase clock, cushioned settles around the walls, comfortable plush chairs and lots of brass and copper. A smaller public bar has an unusual collection of teapots and another fire. Black Sheep Special, Marstons Pedigree and Theakstons Black Bull on handpump, and several wines by the glass; piped classical music, darts, board games. A fountain gurgles in the small garden, where tables look out over beautiful Peak District countryside.

🍴 **Bar food includes sandwiches, soup, thai-style crab cakes, fried garlic mushrooms, breaded plaice, steak and kidney pie, mushroom stroganoff, steaks, and specials.** *Starters/Snacks: £3.85 to £6.85. Main Courses: £7.75 to £13.75. Puddings: £4.25 to £4.50*

Free house ~ Licensee Lynne Smith ~ Real ale ~ Bar food (12-2, 6.30-9) ~ (01629) 640390 ~ Well behaved children welcome if dining ~ Open 11-3, 6.30-11(10.30 Sun); closed Mon evenings in winter

Recommended by DC, Malcolm Pellatt, Peter F Marshall, A N Duerr, the Didler, Annette and John Derbyshire, Martin and Alison Stainsby, Kevin Blake, Susan and John Douglas

HATHERSAGE   SK2380 MAP 7

Plough 🍴 ♀ 🛏

Leadmill; B6001 towards Bakewell, OS Sheet 110 map reference 235805; S32 1BA

Comfortable inn usefully placed for exploring the Peak District

Although they put the emphasis on accommodation and upmarket dining here, it is somewhere you can pop in for a drink, with Adnams, Batemans, Theakstons and Youngs on handpump, 17 wines (plus champagne) by the glass and 40 malt whiskies. One attractive room, on two levels, has dark wood tables and chairs on a turkey carpet, with a big log fire at one end and a woodburning stove at the other; friendly staff, piped music and TV. There are picnic-sets in the pretty secluded, suntrap garden, which goes right down to the River Derwent. The bedrooms are comfortable and the breakfasts good. More reports please.

🍴 As well as lunchtime sandwiches, there are bar meals such as a toad in the hole, lasagne or roast of the day, plus more elaborate choices such as smoked trout, leek, mustard and crème fraîche tartlet, goats cheese terrine with jerusalem artichoke, hotpot of pheasant with puy lentils, game or fish of the day, and rib-eye steak. *Starters/Snacks: £4.25 to £7.95. Main Courses: £8.95 to £16.95. Puddings: £4.50 to £5.95*

Free house ~ Licensees Bob, Cynthia and Elliott Emery ~ Real ale ~ Bar food (11.30-2.30, 6.30-9.30 Mon-Fri; 11.30-9.30 Sat; 12-9 Sun) ~ Restaurant ~ (01433) 650319 ~ Children welcome ~ Open 11-11; 12-10.30 Sun ~ Bedrooms: £60B/£90B

Recommended by DC, Tom and Ruth Rees, Brian and Jacky Wilson, Richard Marjoram, Cathryn and Richard Hicks, B and M Kendall, Jo Lilley, Simon Calvert, Avril Burton, Susan and Nigel Brookes, Mrs L Aquilina, Bob, Paul Wilson, Roger Yates, DFL, Fred and Lorraine Gill, John and Sarah Webb, Christine Shepherd, Darren and Kirstin Arnold, W W Burke, Annette and John Derbyshire, Richard and Emily Whitworth

Scotsmans Pack 🛏

School Lane, off A6187; S32 1BZ

A perennially popular inn that strikes just the right note for food, service, beer and general attitude

Walkers are made to feel very welcome at this civilised inn, and it's a good place to stay. Perhaps the nicest area is on the left as you enter, with a fireplace and patterned wallpaper somewhat obscured by a splendid mass of brasses, stuffed animal heads and the like. Elsewhere there's plenty of dark panelling, lots of mugs and plates arranged around the bar, and a good few tables, many with reserved signs (it's worth booking ahead, particularly at weekends). Jennings Bitter and Cumberland, Marstons Pedigree, and a couple of changing guests such as Bass and Brains St Davids are served under light blanket pressure on handpump or electric pump; service remains prompt and cheery even when busy; piped music, games machine, TV, board games and darts. Outside is a small but very pleasant terrace, next to a trout-filled stream (one reader was sceptical about the idea that a stream could be filled with trout, but his scepticism was confounded after watching it for five minutes). This is close to the church where Little John is said to be buried.

🍴 Good, enjoyable food (booking for dinner is recommended) includes sandwiches, home-made soup, button mushrooms in a peppercorn, cream and brandy sauce, feta cheese, parma ham and plum salad, home-made lasagne, a sausage of the day, peppers filled with aromatic couscous on a tomato sauce or niçoise salad, home-made steak in ale pie, gammon with pineapple and egg, grilled salmon steak with tomato and herb hollandaise, and 10oz sirloin steak or chicken in leek and stilton sauce. *Starters/Snacks: £3.25 to £5.95. Main Courses: £7.25 to £16.95. Puddings: £3.80 to £4.50*

Marstons ~ Lease Nick Beagrie, Steve Bramley and Susan Concannon ~ Real ale ~ Bar food (12-2, 6-9; 12-5, 6-9 Sat and Sun) ~ (01433) 650253 ~ Children welcome ~ Jazz first Mon evening of month ~ Open 11.30-3, 5.30-11; 11-11.30 Sat; 12-11 Sun ~ Bedrooms: £40S/£70B

HAYFIELD   SK0388   MAP 7

Lantern Pike 🛏

Glossop Road (A624 N) at Little Hayfield, just N of Hayfield; SK22 2NG

Run by enthusiastic licensees, an unpretentious retreat from the surrounding moors of Kinder Scout

Near the bar of this cheerfully run pub are photos of the original *Coronation Street* cast with a letter from Tony Warren stating that he wrote many episodes here, nearly 50 years ago. The sweeping views might well have inspired him: the tables on a stonewalled terrace look over a big-windowed weaver's house towards the hill of Lantern Pike, and there are plenty of challenging walks on to the moors of Kinder Scout. The bar is unpretentious but cosy with a warm fire, plush seats, flowers on the tables, and lots of brass platters, china and toby jugs; Black Sheep and Timothy Taylors Landlord on handpump, and one or two guests such as Howard Town Wrens Nest, and several malt whiskies; TV and piped music; covered heated area for smokers. There are five bedrooms.

🍴 **Reasonably priced bar food includes home-made soup, sandwiches and changing specials such as baked goats cheese, black pudding and bacon tart, fried bass, lamb shank, salmon hollandaise, seafood and vegetable pasta, dutch apple pie and bread, butter and toffee pudding. They also have food theme nights, such as fresh fish or curry suppers.** *Starters/Snacks: £3.25 to £3.95. Main Courses: £6.95 to £12.95. Puddings: £3.25 to £3.50*

Enterprise ~ Lease Stella and Tom Cunliffe ~ Real ale ~ Bar food (12-9(12-6, 6-9 Sun)) ~ Restaurant ~ (01663) 747590 ~ Children welcome ~ Open 12-11; 5-11 Mon in winter ~ Bedrooms: £40B/£55B

Royal

Market Street, just off A624 Chapel-en-le-Frith—Buxton; SK22 2EP

Very much at the centre of things, with a well sourced choice of real ales

At this bustling, no-frills inn real ales on handpump include Hydes and five guest ales, such as Buffy's, Enville, Howard Town, Osset or York on handpump, and there is a beer festival in October. As a former vicarage the building has many original features: there's lots of dark panelling in the separate-seeming areas around the central island bar counter, as well as several fireplaces, bookshelves, brasses and house plants, and newspapers to read; piped music (which one reader found too noisy). On fine days, drinkers spill out on to the terrace in front which has lots of picnic-sets. The River Sett runs alongside the car park, and the pub's a useful base for exploring the local scenery. More reports please; we would like to hear from any readers who have stayed here.

🍴 **Straightforward bar food includes sandwiches, soup, double spinach pancake, cod and chips, roast of the day and sirloin steak.** *Starters/Snacks: £3.50 to £5.00. Main Courses: £6.50 to £14.00. Puddings: £3.95*

Free house ~ Licensee David Ash ~ Real ale ~ Bar food (12-2.30, 6-9; 12-9 Sat, Sun) ~ Restaurant ~ (01663) 742721 ~ Children in restaurant and family room ~ Open 10am-11pm (10.30 Sun) ~ Bedrooms: £45B/£60B

HOLBROOK

Dead Poets 🍺 £

Village signposted off A6 S of Belper; Chapel Street; DE56 OTQ

Reassuringly pubby and unchanged, with an excellent range of real ales and simple, cottagey décor

Friendly chatter fills this unspoilt place, and readers enjoy its unpretentious atmosphere. Although there's a range of basic snacks, beer is the thing here, with eight well kept real ales on handpump or served in a jug from the cellar: Caledonian Deuchars, Greene King Abbot and Marstons Pedigree with guests from breweries such as Abbeydale, Adnams, Brains, Kelham Island and Woodefordes. They also serve Old Rosie farm cider and country wines. It's quite a dark interior with low black beams in the ochre ceiling, stripped stone walls and broad flagstones, although there is a lighter conservatory at the back. There are candles on scrubbed tables, a big log fire in the end stone fireplace, high-backed winged settles forming snug cubicles along one wall, and pews and a variety of chairs in other intimate corners and hideaways. The décor makes a few nods to the pub's present name (it used to be the Cross Keys) including a photo of W B Yeats and a poem dedicated to the pub by Les Baynton, and there are old prints of Derby; quiet piped music. Behind is a sort of verandah room with lanterns, heaters, fairy lights and a few plants, and more seats out in the yard.

🍴 Alongside cobs (nothing else on Sundays), bar food is limited to a few good value hearty dishes such as home-made soup and chilli con carne or casserole. *Starters/Snacks: £2.00 to £5.00*

Everards ~ Tenant William Holmes ~ Real ale ~ Bar food (12-2 only) ~ No credit cards ~ (01332) 780301 ~ Children welcome, with restrictions ~ Dogs welcome ~ Open 12-3, 5-midnight; 12-midnight Fri-Sat; 12-11.30 Sun

Recommended by Rona Murdoch, JJW, CMW, Kerry Law, the Didler

HOPE

Cheshire Cheese 🛏

Off A6187, towards Edale; S33 6ZF

Up-and-down, oak-beamed old stone pub warmed by coal fires, in an attractive Peak District village

It does get really busy at this 16th-c pub, and parking can be a problem, so it might be worth considering arriving on foot: there is a glorious range of local walks, taking in the summits of Lose Hill and Win Hill, or the cave district of the Castleton area, and the village of Hope itself is worth strolling around. The friendly chatty landlord will make you feel welcome; each of the three very snug oak-beamed rooms is on a different level and has its own coal fire. Black Sheep Bitter and Whim Hartington plus guests from brewers like Bradfield and Salamander on handpump, and a good range of spirits and several wines by the glass; piped music. The pub takes its name from the payments that were made in the form of cheese for an overnight stop, and you can still stay here. More reports please.

🍴 As well as lunchtime snacks such as sandwiches and ploughman's, food includes soup, grilled black pudding, steak pie, mixed grill, cream cheese and broccoli bake and roasted lamb shank in minted gravy, and puddings such as spotted dick or chocolate pudding in chocolate sauce, as well as specials such as a trio of sausages, chicken curry or battered haddock. *Starters/Snacks: £3.50 to £6.50. Main Courses: £6.95 to £11.95. Puddings: £3.50*

Free house ~ Licensee David Helliwell ~ Real ale ~ Bar food (12-3(2.30 Sat), 6.30-9; 12-8.30 Sun) ~ Restaurant ~ (01433) 620381 ~ Children not allowed in bar ~ Dogs allowed in bar ~ Open 12-3, 6.30-11; 12-midnight Sat; 12-10.30 Sun ~ Bedrooms: £50S/£65S(£75B)

Recommended by Malcolm Pellatt, Dr Ann Henderson, Pete Baker, the Didler, Peter F Marshall

KIRK IRETON

SK2650 MAP 7

Barley Mow 🍺 🛏️

Village signed off B5023 S of Wirksworth; DE6 3JP

Wonderfully timeless, chatty, character-laden inn that focuses on real ale rather than food

This striking three-storey 17th-c Jacobean inn is spotlessly kept, and although they don't serve cooked food it's a lovely place for a drink. The dimly lit passageways and narrow stairwells have a timeless atmosphere, helped along by traditional furnishings and civilised old-fashioned service. It's a place to sit and chat and there's a good mix of customers of all ages. The small main bar has a relaxed pubby feel, with antique settles on the tiled floor or built into the panelling, a roaring coal fire, four slate-topped tables and shuttered mullioned windows. Another room has built-in cushioned pews on oak parquet and a small woodburning stove, and a third room has more pews, a tiled floor, beams and joists, and big landscape prints. In casks behind a modest wooden counter are six or seven well kept, often local and reasonably priced changing real ales such as Archers, Burton Bridge, Cottage, Peak Ales, Storm, Thornbridge and Whim Hartington IPA; farm cider too. There's a good-sized garden, and a couple of benches out in front, and a post office in what used to be the pub stables. The hilltop village is very pretty, and within walking distance of Carsington Water, and the bedrooms are comfortable.

🍽 **Very inexpensive lunchtime filled rolls are the only food; the decent evening meals are reserved for those staying here.** *Starters/Snacks: £0.95*

Free house ~ Licensee Mary Short ~ Real ale ~ Bar food (lunchtime only) ~ No credit cards ~ (01335) 370306 ~ Children lunchtime only ~ Dogs allowed in bar and bedrooms ~ Open 12-2, 7-11(10.30 Sun); closed 25 Dec and 1 Jan ~ Bedrooms: £35S/£55B

Recommended by David Martin, Simon Fox, John Dwane, the Didler, David and Sue Smith, T Stone, Pete Baker

LADYBOWER RESERVOIR

SK2084 MAP 7

Yorkshire Bridge 🛏️

A6013 N of Bamford; S33 0AZ

Comfortably old-fashioned hotel close to the Upper Derwent Valley Reservoirs

In dramatic country, beneath forested and moorland slopes just south of the Ladybower Reservoir dam, stands this pleasantly run inn. One area has a country cottage feel with floral wallpaper, sturdy cushioned wall settles, staffordshire dogs and toby jugs above a big stone fireplace, china on delft shelves, and a panelled dado. Another extensive area, also with a fire, is lighter and more airy with pale wooden furniture, good big black and white photographs and lots of polished brass and decorative plates on the walls. The Bridge Room (with yet another coal-effect fire) has oak tables and chairs, and the Garden Room gives views across a valley to steep larch woods. Black Sheep, Copper Dragon Best Bitter and Golden Pippin, and Theakstons Old Peculier on handpump; darts, dominoes, games machine and piped music; disabled lavatories. Note that they don't allow dogs here during food service times.

🍽 **Well liked bar food includes soup, salads, quiche, battered haddock, pot-roasted lamb with minted gravy, steak and kidney pie, and sirloin steak.** *Starters/Snacks: £3.25 to £5.50. Main Courses: £8.75 to £13.95. Puddings: £4.00 to £4.25*

Free house ~ Licensees Trevelyan and John Illingworth ~ Real ale ~ Bar food (12-2, 6-9(9.30 Fri, Sat); 12-8.30 Sun) ~ (01433) 651361 ~ Children in dining areas only until 9.30pm ~ Dogs allowed in bedrooms ~ Open 10am-11pm ~ Bedrooms: £45B/£55B

Recommended by Andrew Beardsley, Alison Lawrence, Brian Brooks, Malcolm Pellatt, James A Waller, Hilary Forrest, Mike and Sue Loseby

Post Office address codings confusingly give the impression that a few pubs are in Derbyshire, when they're really in Cheshire (which is where we list them).

LITTON   SK1675   MAP 7

Red Lion

Village signposted off A623, between B6465 and B6049 junctions; also signposted off B6049; SK17 8QU

Good new landlady in convivial all-rounder with unspoilt charm, prettily placed by village green

Standards have been admirably maintained, even given a boost, at this 18th-c village pub since it was recently taken over by a new licensee. The two inviting homely linked front rooms have low beams and some panelling, and blazing log fires. There's a bigger back room with good-sized tables, and large antique prints on its stripped stone walls. The small bar counter has Oakwell Barnsley and Timothy Taylors Landlord on handpump, plus two guests from breweries such as Kelham Island and Whim Hartington, with decent wines and several malt whiskies; darts and board games; tasty bar food. A particularly rewarding time to visit is during the annual village well-dressing carnival (usually the last weekend in June), when villagers create a picture from flower petals, moss and other natural materials, and at Christmas a brass band plays carols. It's such a small pub that it's not ideal for children, but there is seating outside on the pretty village green, which is covered in daffodils in early spring.

🍴 **Well liked bar food includes filled baguettes, soup, cock-a-leekie pie, steak, ale and mushroom casserole, cumberland or vegetarian sausage and mash, and specials such as garlic and rosemary lamb shank and trout fillet with cream and herb sauce.** *Starters/Snacks: £2.80 to £4.95. Main Courses: £4.50 to £9.95. Puddings: £3.00 to £4.25*

Enterprise ~ Lease Suzy Turner ~ Real ale ~ Bar food (12-2, 6-8; 12-8.30 Thurs-Sun) ~ (01298) 871458 ~ No children under 6; no children under 18 after 9pm ~ Dogs allowed in bar ~ Open 12-11(midnight Fri, Sat); 12-10.30 Sun

Recommended by B and M Kendall, Peter F Marshall, Hazel Matthews, Susan and John Douglas, the Didler

MELBOURNE   SK3427   MAP 7

John Thompson 🍺 £

Ingleby, which is NW of Melbourne; turn off A514 at Swarkestone Bridge or in Stanton by Bridge; can also be reached from Ticknall (or from Repton on B5008); DE73 7HW

Strikes the right balance between attentive service, roomy comfort, good value food and well kept own-brew beer

Everything ticks along perfectly here. Named after its owner, this pub has its own micro-brewery, and readers continue to be enthusiastic about the quality of the beer and food, and the friendly and efficient staff. The layout is simple but comfortable, and the big modernised lounge has ceiling joists, some old oak settles, button-back leather seats, sturdy oak tables, antique prints and paintings, and a log-effect gas fire; piped music. A couple of smaller cosier rooms open off; piano, fruit machine, TV, and pool in the conservatory. From the JT brewery behind, they serve three from JT 80, JTS XXX, Gold, Rich Porter and St Nick's; sometimes they have a guest ale from another brewery such as Shardlow. Outside are lots of tables by flowerbeds on the neat lawns or you can sit on the partly covered terrace.

🍴 **The menu is very short but the food is decidedly tasty, and service is efficient:** sandwiches, soup, beef, ham or cheese salads, very reasonably priced roast beef with yorkshire pudding, and puddings like crumble or dark chocolate and pecan fudge brownie. *Starters/Snacks: £2.50. Main Courses: £5.00 to £6.00. Puddings: £2.50 to £2.75*

Own brew ~ Licensee Nick Thompson ~ Real ale ~ Bar food (lunchtime only – not Sun or Mon) ~ (01332) 862469 ~ Children welcome in conservatory until 9pm ~ Open 11-2.30, 6-11; 11-11 Sat; 12-10.30 Sun; closed Mon lunchtime

Recommended by Rob Berridge, P Dawn, N R White, Pete Baker, Pat and Peter Grove, C D Bowring, Margaret and Allen Marsden, the Didler, Brian and Jacky Wilson, Annette Tress, Gary Smith, Mr and Mrs T Wilkinson, Michael Lamm

MONSAL HEAD
SK1871 MAP 7

Monsal Head Hotel 🍴 🛏

B6465; DE45 1NL

Hilltop inn winning consistent praise for food, beer and friendly staff, and well worth seeking out for the view alone

One of the classic Derbyshire views is from this very spot, looking down to a bend in steep-sided Monsal Dale with its huge railway viaduct, which is now crossed by the Monsal Trail. It's the cosy stable bar (once housing the horses that used to pull guests and their luggage up from the station at the other end of the steep valley) that readers head for – and walkers and their dogs are welcome here too: stripped timber horse-stalls, harness and brassware, and lamps from the disused station itself all hint at those days. There's a big warming open fire, and cushioned oak pews around the tables on the flagstones. They keep between six and eight real ales on handpump with Lloyds Monsal Bitter, Theakstons Best and Old Peculier and Timothy Taylors Landlord alongside a few guests often from local breweries such as Thornbridge or Whim Hartington; a good choice of german bottled beers, and at least a dozen wines by the glass. There are a spacious restaurant and residents' lounge as well as a beer garden. The best places to admire the terrific view are from the big windows in the lounge, the garden, and from four of the seven bedrooms.

🍴 **Well liked bar food, using herbs grown from their own garden, includes lunchtime sandwiches and fajitas, soup, double-baked goats cheese soufflé, slow-roasted pork belly, smoked duck and sweet potato salad, cod and chips, spicy thai vegetable curry, rib-eye steak, beef and smoked bacon and ale pie, with puddings such as lemon posset with a ginger biscuit topping.** *Starters/Snacks: £2.00 to £6.00. Main Courses: £6.00 to £14.00. Puddings: £3.00 to £6.00*

Free house ~ Licensee Philip Smith ~ Real ale ~ Bar food ~ Restaurant ~ (01629) 640250 ~ Children welcome ~ Dogs allowed in bar and bedrooms ~ Open 11.30-11.30; 12-10.30 Sun; closed 25 Dec ~ Bedrooms: £55B/£50S(£70B)

Recommended by Pam and John Smith, Greta and Guy Pratt, David Martin, Andrew Wallace, N R White, the Didler, Paul and Margaret Baker, Mike and Sue Loseby, Fred and Lorraine Gill, Dr David Clegg, Peter F Marshall, Russell Grimshaw, Kerry Purcell, Janet and Peter Race, Brian and Jacky Wilson, DFL, P Dawn, Keith and Chris O'Neill, Bruce and Sharon Eden, Susan and John Douglas, Mark and Diane Grist

OVER HADDON
SK2066 MAP 7

Lathkil 🍴

Village and inn signposted from B5055 just SW of Bakewell; DE45 1JE

Hiker-friendly, well placed for Lathkill Dale, super views from the garden, and cheerfully efficient staff get all the details right

Popular with locals and walkers, this pub continues to provide a winning formula as it has for many years – the licensees have been here now for a quarter of a century. Dogs are welcome, too, though muddy boots are not and must be left in the lobby. The airy room on the right as you go in has a nice fire in the attractively carved fireplace, old-fashioned settles with upholstered cushions and chairs, black beams, a delft shelf of blue and white plates, original prints and photographs, and big windows. On the left, the spacious and sunny dining area doubles as an evening restaurant. Well kept Everards Tiger and Whim Hartington Bitter plus three guests like Lloyds Best Bitter, Peak Ales Swift Nick and Thornbridge Blackthorn on handpump, a few unusual malt whiskies, and decent range of wines. More elaborate restaurant food in the evening. Piped music, darts, bar billiards, shove-ha'penny, dominoes and board games. The walled garden is a good place to sit and soak in the views over the bewitchingly secretive surroundings of Lathkill Dale.

🍴 **The popular buffet-style lunch menu includes filled rolls, soup, broccoli and cauliflower crumble, steak and kidney pie, a good range of cold meats and tasty salads, venison and blackberry casserole, daily specials, and good puddings; children's menu.** *Starters/Snacks: £3.25 to £4.10. Main Courses: £6.50 to £7.95. Puddings: £3.25 to £3.50*

Free house ~ Licensee Robert Grigor-Taylor ~ Real ale ~ Bar food (12-2(2.30 Sun)) ~ Restaurant ~ (01629) 812501 ~ Children allowed away from bar ~ Dogs allowed in bar ~ Open 11.30-11; 12-10.30 Sun; 11.30-3, 6.30-11 Mon-Fri in winter ~ Bedrooms: £45B/£65S(£80B)

Recommended by John and Karen Wilkinson, Hilary Forrest, Richard and Margaret McPhee, Dr and Mrs R G J Telfer, Jo Lilley, Simon Calvert, Peter F Marshall, Richard, the Didler, Dr D J and Mrs S C Walker, Malcolm Pellatt, Mrs P J Carroll, Russell Grimshaw, Kerry Purcell, R M Chard, Roderick Braithwaite

SHELDON
SK1768   MAP 7

Cock & Pullet £
Village signposted off A6 just W of Ashford; DE45 1QS

Well run village local with an appealingly unpretentious atmosphere and good value bar food

At the back of this family-run place is a pleasant little terrace with tables and a water feature, while inside an array of 30 clocks greets you within the cosy little rooms. As well as low beams, exposed stonework, flagstones, scrubbed oak tables and pews, and an open fire, there's a cheerful assembly of deliberately mismatched furnishings. It looks like it's been a pub for many decades, but it was only converted into a pub a dozen years ago. A fireplace is filled with flowers in summer, and around it are various representations of poultry, including some stuffed. A plainer room has pool and a TV; there's also a snug; darts and dominoes. Thornbridge Lord Marples and a couple of guests such as Black Sheep are on handpump. The pub is a year-round favourite with walkers (it can be busy at weekends); the pretty village is just off the Limestone Way.

🍽 **Very reasonably priced bar food includes soup, sandwiches, fish pie, a curry of the day, a vegetarian dish, steak in ale pie, minted lamb casserole and specials; Sunday roast.** *Starters/Snacks: £2.75 to £4.50. Main Courses: £4.50 to £9.75. Puddings: £2.75*

Free house ~ Licensees David and Kath Melland ~ Real ale ~ Bar food (12-2.30, 6-9) ~ No credit cards ~ (01629) 814292 ~ Children allowed in dining area until 8pm ~ Dogs allowed in bar ~ Open 11-11; 12-11 Sun ~ Bedrooms: /£60B

Recommended by Martin Sherwood, Richard, J and E Dakin, Dave Webster, Sue Holland, DC, John Yates, Peter F Marshall, Martin Peters, Brian and Jacky Wilson, Brian and Anna Marsden

WARDLOW
SK1875   MAP 7

Three Stags Heads 🍺
Wardlow Mires; A623 by junction with B6465; SK17 8RW

Full of character, no frills, with flagstoned floors, a chatty bar and old country furniture

This cottagey, delightfully basic place was originally a farmhouse, or longhouse, and its exterior walls are painted white in accordance with an ancient derbyshire tradition, where a white-painted building signified a pub. It's situated in a natural sink, so don't be surprised to find the floors muddied by boots in wet weather (and the dogs even muddier). Warmed right through by a cast-iron kitchen range, the tiny flagstoned parlour bar has old leathercloth seats, a couple of antique settles with flowery cushions, two high-backed windsor armchairs and simple oak tables (look out for the petrified cat in a glass case). Abbeydale Absolution, Black Lurcher (brewed for the pub at a hefty 8% ABV), Brimstone and Matins on handpump, and lots of bottled continental and english beers. The front terrace looks across the main road to the distant hills. Please note the opening times.

🍽 **Hearty seasonally changing food might include soup, pork and stilton hotpot, fish pie and local game such as roast pheasant or rabbit and pigeon pie; the hardy plates are home made.** *Starters/Snacks: £4.50. Main Courses: £8.50 to £10.50*

Free house ~ Licensees Geoff and Pat Fuller ~ Real ale ~ Bar food (12.30-3.30, 7-9, when open) ~ No credit cards ~ (01298) 872268 ~ Children welcome if under control ~ Dogs welcome ~ Folk music some Sat evenings ~ Open 7-11 Fri; 12-11 Sat, Sun and bank hols; closed Mon-Thurs and Fri lunchtime

Recommended by Pete Baker, Chris Reading, John Dwane, P Dawn, the Didler, Mark and Diane Grist

WOOLLEY MOOR

SK3661   MAP 7

White Horse

Badger Lane, off B6014 Matlock—Clay Cross; DE55 6FG

Prettily set country pub in an attractive old stone building

In very attractive, rolling countryside, this popular old pub looks over the Amber Valley. There's a buoyantly chatty feel to the tap room; there is piped music in the lounge and conservatory, which gives great views of Ogston Reservoir (which in 1958 submerged the village of Woolley, the inhabitants of which moved up the hill to Woolley Moor); dominoes. Black Sheep, St Austell Tribute and Timothy Taylors Landlord are on handpump. In the garden are a boules pitch, picnic-sets, and a children's play area with a wooden train, boat, climbing frame and swings, and there is a covered area for smokers. A sign outside shows how horses and carts carried measures of salt along the toll road in front – the toll bar cottage still stands at the entrance of the Badger Lane (a badger was the haulier who transported the salt).

🍴 Besides lunchtime sandwiches, **tasty bar food includes soup, field mushrooms filled with stilton and wrapped in parma ham, steak and ale pie, sirloin steak, duck breast and fried fillet of bass with basil, olive-crushed potatoes and white wine sauce, with puddings like chocolate brownie.** *Starters/Snacks: £3.20 to £4.90. Main Courses: £6.95 to £12.50. Puddings: £3.95*

Free house ~ Licensee John Parsons ~ Real ale ~ Bar food (12-2, 5-9; not Sun evening) ~ (01246) 590319 ~ Children welcome ~ Dogs allowed in bar ~ Open 12-3, 5-11; 12-10.30 Sun; closed Mon

Recommended by Michael and Maggie Betton, MP, Phil and Jane Hodson

---

LUCKY DIP

Besides the fully inspected pubs, you might like to try these Lucky Dips recommended to us and described by readers (if you do, please send us reports: www.goodguides.co.uk).

AMBERGATE [SK3451]
Hurt Arms DE56 2EJ [Derby Rd (A6)]: Large pub with smart lounge and adjoining restaurant, Courage Directors, Marstons Pedigree and Ruddles County; pleasant spot by river, nr cricket ground *(C J Fletcher)*
ASHBOURNE [SK1846]
☆ *Smiths Tavern* DE6 1GH [bottom of market place]: Neatly kept traditional pub, chatty and relaxed, stretching back from heavily black-beamed bar through lounge to attractive light and airy end dining room, friendly efficient staff, above-average sensibly priced food using local produce from fresh sandwiches up, Banks's, Marstons Pedigree and a guest beer, lots of whiskies and vodkas, daily papers, traditional games; children welcome, open all day summer Sun *(I J and S A Bufton, LYM, John and Yvonne Davies, David Carr)*
ASHFORD IN THE WATER [SK1969]
Ashford Arms DE45 1QB [Church St]: Good range of real ales, enjoyable food (not Sun evening) inc good Weds steak night, reasonable prices and friendly staff in attractive place with pleasant modern furnishings and two dining areas; children welcome, plenty of tables outside *(Martin Peters, BB)*
☆ *Bulls Head* DE45 1QB [Church St]: Cosy and comfortable two-bar beamed pub dating

from 16th c, friendly old-school landlord, well kept Banks's and Robinsons, good proper food from lunchtime sandwiches up inc some unusual dishes, reasonable prices, daily papers; may be piped music; plastic overshoes for walkers, tables out behind and by front car park, attractive village *(Martin and Alison Stainsby, Annette and John Derbyshire, Martin Peters, the Didler, Peter F Marshall, Mr and Mrs Staples, DJH)*
ASHOVER [SK3463]
Crispin S45 0AB [Church St]: Tastefully extended old building with very welcoming landlord, reasonably priced enjoyable food, Marstons-related real ale, log fires, several areas from beamed original core to back conservatory *(Robert F Smith, Barry Steele-Perkins)*
BAKEWELL [SK2168]
Castle Inn DE45 1DU [Bridge St]: Bay-windowed Georgian-fronted 17th-c pub with good service, full range of Greene King ales kept well, enjoyable food inc good specials, friendly staff, daily papers, three candlelit rooms with two real fires, flagstones, stripped stone and lots of pictures; dogs welcome, tables outside, four bedrooms *(Russell Grimshaw, Kerry Purcell, Derek and Sylvia Stephenson, Mr and Mrs Staples)*
Peacock DE45 1DS [Bridge St]: Neat and bright, popular even Mon lunchtime for good

value plentiful food, Theakstons and guest beers, quick cheerful staff *(David and Sue Smith, Bob, Janet and Peter Race, Mike Dean, Lis Wingate Gray)*

BEELEY [SK2667]

☆ *Devonshire Arms* DE4 2NR [B6012, off A6 Matlock—Bakewell]: Contrast between black beams, flagstones, stripped stone and traditional settles of original part and boldly colourful contemporary furnishings of light brightly decorated bistro/conservatory delights many (but not all), well kept changing ales inc Black Sheep and Theakstons, good range of malt whiskies, wide choice of all-day food (not that cheap) from big sandwiches up, big log fires, no music; children welcome, attractive rolling scenery nr Chatsworth, good modish new bedrooms, open all day *(Roger Hobson, LYM, Kerry Law, Maurice and Janet Thorpe, A Darroch Harkness, Mike and Sue Loseby, John and Enid Morris, Susan and John Douglas, Keith and Chris O'Neill)*

BELPER [SK3547]

Cross Keys DE56 1FZ [Market Pl]: Two-room pub with well kept Bass, Batemans and a guest beer, bar food, coal fire in lounge, bar billiards; open all day *(the Didler)*

Queens Head DE56 1FF [Chesterfield Rd]: Warm and cosy three-room pub with five real ales such as Caledonian Deuchars IPA, Carlsberg Burton and Tetleys, nourishing rolls, constant coal fire, local photographs; good upstairs wknd band nights, beer festivals; good views from terrace tables, open all day *(the Didler, C J Fletcher)*

BIRCH VALE [SK0186]

☆ *Sycamore* SK22 1AB [Sycamore Rd; from A6015 take Station Rd towards Thornsett]: Reliable dining pub with attractive four-room layout, wide choice of good value food (all day Sun) from big filled baguettes up, well kept John Smiths and Timothy Taylors Landlord, good choice of wines by the glass, friendly helpful service, fountain in downstairs drinking bar, restaurant; may be piped music; children welcome, spacious streamside gardens with good play area and summer bar, handy for Sett Valley trail *(Doug Christian, LYM)*

BIRCHOVER [SK2362]

☆ *Druid* DE4 2BL [off B5056; Main St]: Neatly kept two-storey dining pub with four spacious areas, very wide choice of good food, friendly helpful staff (good service even when very busy), real ale such as Marstons Pedigree, good choice of malt whiskies and wines; piped music, no dogs; children welcome, picnic-sets out in front, good area for walks, has been cl Mon *(B and M A Langrish, Eddie and Lynn Jarrett, LYM, Margaret and Jeff Graham)*

BONSALL [SK2758]

Barley Mow DE4 2AY [off A6012 Cromford—Hartington; The Dale]: Friendly tucked-away pub with well kept Whim Hartington, Greene King Abbot and guest beers, fresh sandwiches and other decent plain food,

character furnishings, coal fire, tiny pool room; live music Sat inc landlord playing accordion or keyboards, runs local walks and idiosyncratic special events; small front terrace, cl wkdy lunchtimes and Mon, open all day wknds *(Kevin Blake, the Didler, Richard)*

BUXTON [SK1266]

☆ *Bull i' th' Thorn* SK17 9QQ [Ashbourne Rd (A515) 6 miles S of Buxton, nr Flagg and Hurdlow]: Medieval hall doubling as straightforward roadside dining pub, all sorts of antique features to look at, handsome panelling, old flagstones and big open fire, friendly licensees, wide range of food all day from baguettes to restaurant dishes, Robinsons Best, plain games room and family room; children and dogs welcome, terrace and big lawn, bedrooms, big breakfast, open all day from 9.30am, may be cl Mon *(Mr and Mrs John Taylor, the Didler)*

☆ *Old Sun* SK17 6HA [33 High St]: Charming old building with friendly landlady and helpful service, five good ales inc Banks's and Marstons Best and Pedigree, good value wines by the glass, farm cider, bargain food from good sandwiches and baked potatoes up usefully served till 10, several small and interesting traditional linked areas, low beams and soft lighting, open fires, bare boards or tiles, stripped wood screens, old local photographs; piped music, TV; children in back bar, open all day *(the Didler, Andy and Cath Pearson, LYM, Peter and Pat Frogley, Barry Collett, Bruce and Sharon Eden, M G Hart)*

BUXWORTH [SK0282]

☆ *Navigation* SK23 7NE [S of village towards Silkhill, off B6062]: Popular and cheery pub by restored canal basin, linked low-ceilinged flagstoned rooms with canalia and brassware, lacy curtains, coal and log fires, flagstone floors, good attractively priced changing ales, summer farm ciders, winter mulled wine, enjoyable generous bar food all day from nice sandwiches up, restaurant, games room; quiet piped music; tables on sunken flagstoned terrace, play area and pets corner, open all day *(Bob and Laura Brock, LYM, J and E Dakin)*

CALVER [SK2474]

Bridge Inn S32 3XA [Calver Bridge, off A623 N of Baslow]: Unpretentious two-room stone-built village pub, short choice of good value plain food (not Mon evening or winter Sun evening), small separate eating area, particularly well kept Hardys & Hansons ales, quick friendly service, cosy comfortable corners, coal fires, bank notes on beams, local prints and bric-a-brac inc old fire-fighting equipment in lounge; picnic-sets in nice big garden by River Derwent *(Malcolm Pellatt)*

CASTLETON [SK1582]

☆ *Bulls Head* S33 8WH [Cross St (A6187)]: Roomy and attractively decorated, with good reasonably priced food, well kept Robinsons,

helpful service, log fire; four bedrooms
(Tony Goff, Ian Thurman, Paul McQueen)
Castle Hotel S33 8WG [High St/Castle St]:
Pleasant and roomy Vintage Inn useful for
all-day food from good sandwiches up, good
choice of real ales and of wines by the glass,
log fires, stripped-stone walls, beams and
some ancient flagstones; piped music;
children welcome, heated terrace,
comfortable bedrooms, open all day
(Peter and Pat Frogley, LYM, Brian Brooks,
Sharon Hancock, David Carr,
Diana Lockwood)
☆ **George** S33 8WG [Castle St]: Busy but
relaxed and friendly, good value food from
hearty sandwiches to imaginative main
dishes, four well kept ales such as Black
Sheep, Greene King Abbot and Timothy
Taylors Landlord, two good-sized rooms, one
mainly for eating, ancient beams and
stripped stone, no music; tables on wide
forecourt, lots of flower tubs; dogs, children
and muddy boots welcome, may be cl Mon
lunchtime (Gwyn and Anne Wake, David Carr,
Jenny, Keith and Chris O'Neill)
Peak S33 8WJ [How Lane, off A625]: Well
kept real ales such as Black Sheep, Greene
King Abbot and Timothy Taylors Landlord,
wide choice of enjoyable reasonably priced
food, friendly service, airy lounge, smaller
bar and dining room with high ceiling and
picture-window hill view; dogs welcome,
bedrooms (Jenny)
CHAPEL-EN-LE-FRITH [SK0581]
Cross Keys SK23 0QQ [Chapel Milton]: Neatly
kept old family pub with good value
generous standard food (all day Sun), well
kept beers inc Timothy Taylors Landlord,
friendly service, smartly decorated small
restaurant; children welcome, cl wkdy
lunchtimes (Malcolm Pellatt)
CHELMORTON [SK1170]
Church Inn SK17 9SL [between A6 and A515
SW of Buxton]: Comfortable and convivial
split bar with good range of enjoyable
generous food, reasonable prices, Adnams,
Marstons Pedigree and a guest beer, friendly
landlord and golden labrador, lots of bric-a-
brac and woodburners in dining area; piped
music, outside lavatories; nice spot at top of
village with pleasant sloping garden and
terrace tables, superb walking country
(J R Ringrose, Peter F Marshall)
CHESTERFIELD [SK3871]
Barley Mow S40 1JR [Saltergate]:
Companionable and civilised, with wide
choice of enjoyable food from sandwiches,
cobs, baguettes and baked potatoes up, low
prices, well kept ales such as Black Sheep,
Greene King IPA, Marstons Pedigree and
John Smiths, good hot drinks, original Wards
stained glass; sunny picnic-sets outside
(Keith and Chris O'Neill)
Portland S40 1AY [New Sq]: Well laid out
Wetherspoons in handsome building, their
usual food, good range of changing ales;
nicely planted terrace, bedrooms, open all
day (Keith and Chris O'Neill)

Rutland S40 1XL [Stephenson Pl]:
Unpretentious proper pub next to crooked-
spire church, thriving atmosphere, Badger
Best, Timothy Taylors Landlord and up to
half a dozen or more interesting guest beers,
Weston's farm cider, low-priced pub food all
day from sandwiches and baguettes up,
friendly polite service even when busy, rugs
and assorted wooden furniture on bare
boards, old photographs, darts; piped music;
children welcome, open all day (Keith and
Chris O'Neill, Alan Johnson)
Spa Lane Vaults S41 7TH [St Marys Gate]:
Reliable Wetherspoons, their usual pricing,
food and good beer choice, smart lavatories
(Mrs Hazel Rainer)
CHINLEY [SK0382]
Old Hall SK23 6EJ [Whitehough]: Friendly
16th-c inn locally popular for good unusual
food, Adnams ales; dogs welcome, four good
bedrooms (JT)
COMBS [SK0378]
Beehive SK23 9UT: Roomy, neat and
comfortable, very popular for good generous
pubby food (all day Sun) from sandwiches to
steaks, well kept ales such as Black Sheep,
decent house wines, log fire, heavy beams
and copperware; quiet piped jazz, live music
Fri, quiz night Tues; bedrooms, tables
outside, by lovely valley tucked away from
main road (Malcolm Pellatt, J and E Dakin)
COWERS LANE [SK3147]
Railway Inn DE56 2LF [Ashbourne Rd
(A517/B5023 W of Belper)]: Comfortable
traditional pub under friendly and hard-
working newish licensees, good choice of
enjoyable food, good wines, friendly staff,
real fire, separate dining area; tables and
play area outside (Mrs Tessa Hibbert)
CRICH [SK3454]
Cliff DE4 5DP [Cromford Rd, Town End]: Cosy
and unpretentious two-room pub with
Greene King ales, reliable straightforward
food, friendly service, open fire; children
welcome, great views, handy for National
Tramway Museum (the Didler)
CROMFORD [SK2956]
Boat DE4 3QF [Scarthin, off Mkt Pl]:
Traditional 18th-c pub with changing ales
such as Black Sheep, Derby Falstaff,
Springhead and Whim Hartington, relaxed
atmosphere, coal fire, long narrow low-
beamed bar with stripped stone and bric-a-
brac, darts and pool area, cool cellar bar
(used for easter and Nov beer festivals); TV;
children and dogs welcome, back garden,
open all day wknds (Rona Murdoch, BB,
the Didler, JJW, CMW, Paul J Robinshaw)
DALE ABBEY [SK4338]
Carpenters Arms DE7 4PP [Dale Lane, off
A6096 Derby rd]: Attractive spot nr abbey
ruins, Hermit's Cave and remarkable All Saints
church (part of which used to be the village
inn); decent range of drinks, good choice of
enjoyable pub food (Peter and Jean Hoare)
DERBY [SK3538]
☆ **Abbey Inn** DE22 1DX [Darley St, Darley
Abbey]: Interesting former abbey gatehouse

opp Derwent-side park (pleasant riverside walk out from centre), pleasant service, bargain Sam Smiths and lunchtime bar food, massive 15th-c or older stonework remnants, brick floor, studded oak doors, coal fire in big stone inglenook, stone spiral stair to upper bar with handsome oak rafters and tapestries (and the lavatories with their beams, stonework and tiles are worth a look too); piped music; children welcome, open all day wknds *(LYM, the Didler, R T and J C Moggridge)*

Babington Arms DE1 1TA [Babington Lane]: Large well run open-plan Wetherspoons with uncommonly good choice of real ales, good welcoming service, well priced food, comfortable seating with steps up to relaxed back area; attractive verandah, open all day *(the Didler, C J Fletcher)*

Falstaff DE23 6UJ [Silver Hill Rd, off Normanton Rd]: Basic unpretentious local aka the Folly, brewing its own good value ales, guest beers too; left-hand bar with games and occasional discos, right-hand lounge with coal fire usually quieter; open all day *(the Didler)*

☆ *Flower Pot* DE1 3DZ [King St]: Extended real ale pub with up to a dozen or more good reasonably priced changing beers mainly from small breweries (glazed panels show cellarage, and own microbrewery should be up and running by now), friendly staff, three linked rooms inc comfortable back bar with lots of books, side area with old Derby photographs and brewery memorabilia, good value basic bar food, daily papers, pub games; piped music/juke box, separate concert room – good live bands Thurs-Sat and busy then; disabled access and facilities, tables on small cherry-tree terrace, open all day *(David Carr, Bob, the Didler)*

☆ *Olde Dolphin* DE1 3DL [Queen St]: Quaint 16th-c timber-framed pub, four small dark unpretentious rooms, big bowed black beams, shiny panelling, opaque leaded windows, lantern lights and coal fires, well kept ales such as Adnams, Bass, Black Sheep, Caledonian Deuchars IPA, Greene King Abbot, Jennings Cumberland, and Marstons Pedigree, bargain simple food all day, good value upstairs steak restaurant (not always open); no children, terrace tables, open all day *(LYM, the Didler, Kevin Blake, Mark and Diane Grist, Brian and Rosalie Laverick)*

Rowditch DE22 3LL [Uttoxeter New Rd (A516)]: Traditional two-bar friendly local with well kept Marstons Pedigree and guest beers, country wines, attractive small snug on right, coal fire, Sat piano-player, occasional downstairs cellar bar; small pleasant back garden *(the Didler)*

☆ *Smithfield* DE1 2BH [Meadow Rd]: Friendly and comfortable bow-fronted local with big bar, snug, back lounge with traditional settles, old prints, curios and breweriana, up to ten well kept changing ales, filled rolls and hearty lunchtime meals, real fires, daily

papers; piped music, games room with table skittles, board games, TV and machines (children welcome here), quiz nights, live bands; riverside terrace with wknd barbecues, open all day *(C J Fletcher, the Didler)*

☆ *Standing Order* DE1 3GL [Irongate]: Spacious Wetherspoons in grand and lofty-domed former bank, central bar, booths down each side, elaborately painted plasterwork, pseudo-classical torsos, high portraits of mainly local notables; usual popular food all day, good range of real ales, reasonable prices, daily papers, neat efficient young staff; very busy wknds; good disabled facilities, open all day *(Bob, the Didler, BB, David Carr, Kevin Blake)*

Station Inn DE1 2SN [Midland Rd, below station]: Friendly local, simple and neatly kept, with good food lunchtime and early evening in large back lounge and dining area, particularly well kept Bass (in jugs from cellar) and other ales such as Black Sheep and Caledonian Deuchars IPA, long panelled and quarry-tiled bar, side room with darts, pool and TV, ornate façade; piped music; open all day Fri *(the Didler)*

DRONFIELD [SK3479]

Coach & Horses S18 2GD [Sheffield Rd (B6057)]: Reopened after comfortable refurbishment by Thornbridge microbrewery as showcase for their interesting beers, friendly staff informative about them, enjoyable home-made food (plans for new barn restaurant), pleasant civilised furnishings inc sofas; open all day *(the Didler)*

EDALE [SK1285]

Rambler S33 7ZA: Recently refurbished stone-built country hotel with extensive bar rambling through linked rooms, flagstones, quarry tiles, bare boards and carpet, good solid furnishings, cosy informal dining room, enjoyable food all day from sandwiches to some good and imaginative cooking, well kept real ales; children welcome, lots of picnic-sets in garden with play area, bedrooms *(David Hoult)*

EDLASTON [SK1842]

☆ *Shire Horse* DE6 2DQ [off A515 S of Ashbourne, just beside Wyaston]: Rambling timbered pub run by hospitable sisters, blazing fires and gleaming brass in civilised and well furnished long beamed bar with unusual slate-roofed counter and cottagey areas off, good very popular bar food and some interesting recipes for evening conservatory restaurant, reasonable prices, efficient attentive service, Bass, Marstons Pedigree and a guest beer; piped music; children welcome, tables out in front and in back garden with terrace, peaceful spot *(Dr David Clegg, Peter and Jean Hoare, BB)*

ELMTON [SK5073]

Elm Tree S80 4LS [off B6417 S of Clowne]: Softly lit and popular country pub with good value unpretentious bar food all day, Black Sheep and Wells & Youngs, quietly welcoming service, stripped stone and panelling, back barn restaurant (Fri/Sat evening and for good Sun lunch); children welcome if eating, garden tables, open all day Weds-Sun *(Keith and Chris O'Neill, Ian and Nita Cooper)*

ELTON [SK2260]

☆ *Duke of York* DE4 2BW [village signed off B5056 W of Matlock; Main St]: Old-fashioned local kept spotless by very long-serving friendly landlady, lovely little quarry-tiled back tap room with hot coal fire in massive fireplace, glazed bar and hatch to flagstoned corridor, nice prints and more fires in the two front ones – one like private parlour with piano and big dining table (no food, just crisps), the other with pool; Adnams Broadside, Black Sheep and Marstons Pedigree, welcoming regulars, darts, dominoes; outside lavatories; in charming Peak District village, open 8.30am-11pm, and Sun lunchtime *(the Didler, Pete Baker, John Dwane)*

EYAM [SK2276]

Miners Arms S32 5RG [off A632 Chesterfield—Chapel-en-le-Frith; Water Lane]: Three-roomed pub with good value food (not Sun evening) from good sandwiches to some interesting dishes, friendly efficient service, well kept beers such as Caledonian Deuchars IPA, Greene King Old Speckled Hen and Theakstons Best, plush beamed rooms, stone fireplaces, restaurant, darts; TV, piped music; children and dogs welcome, tables outside, decent walks nearby especially below Froggatt Edge, open all day *(J and E Dakin, John Tav, LYM, Dr and Mrs R G J Telfer, Pete Coxon)*

FENNY BENTLEY [SK1850]

Bentley Brook DE6 1LF [A515 N of Ashbourne]: Sizeable place with good real ales inc its own Leatherbritches brews, central log fire and big open-plan bare-boards bar/dining room with communicating restaurant (service can take a while); piped music; terrace picnic-sets, barbecue, good play area, open all day *(LYM, John Tav, Malcolm Pellatt, Eddie and Lynn Jarrett)*

FOOLOW [SK2078]

☆ *Barrel* S32 5QD [Bretton, N of village]: Perhaps the best views from any pub in England from this stone-roofed turnpike inn, lots of pictures and end log fire in old-fashioned low-beamed bar, well kept real ales, amiable chef doing decent bar food, pleasant young staff; they may turn you out on the dot at the end of lunchtime, to finish your drinks outside; piped music, may be live Weds; children and dogs welcome, front terrace and courtyard garden, good walking, four neat simple bedrooms, good breakfast, open all day wknds *(Malcolm Pellatt, LYM, Darren and Kirstin Arnold, Jo Lilley, Simon Calvert, Eddie and Lynn Jarrett, Mrs J Clarke-Williams, Sean A Smith, Susan and John Douglas, Mrs M E Mills, Eddie Edwards)*

FROGGATT EDGE [SK2476]

☆ *Chequers* S32 3ZJ [A625, off A623 N of Bakewell]: Smart and busy dining pub with

good if not cheap interesting food (all day wknds) from unusual sandwiches up, solid country furnishings in civilised and cosily attractive dining bar with antique prints and longcase clock, changing ales such as Black Sheep, Caledonian Deuchars IPA or Wells & Youngs Bombardier, good choice of wines by the glass; piped music; children welcome, peaceful back garden with Froggatt Edge just up through the woods behind, comfortable bedrooms (quarry lorries use the road), good breakfast, open all day wknds *(Mr and Mrs M Wall, W M Lien, LYM, Adrian White, Richard, Phil and Gill Wass, Bob, Malcolm Pellatt, James A Waller, Annette and John Derbyshire, Roger Yates, Noel Dinneen)*

Grouse S11 7TZ [Longshaw, off B6054 NE of Froggatt]: Plush front bar, log fire and wooden benches in back bar, big dining room, good home cooking from sandwiches to imaginative dishes, good value smaller helpings, well kept Caledonian Deuchars IPA, Banks's and Marstons Pedigree, friendly service, handsome views; verandah and terrace, neat bedrooms, good moorland walking country, open all day *(Mr and Mrs Staples, C J Fletcher)*

GLOSSOP [SK0294]

Globe SK13 8HJ [High St W]: Good changing ales inc its own microbrew, local Howard Town and other interesting slightly less local ones, farm cider and perry, comfortable relaxed atmosphere, friendly licensees, frequent live music; cl lunchtime and Tues, open till late Fri-Sun *(the Didler)*

Star SK13 7DD [Howard St]: Good changing real ales such as local Howard Town, Pictish, Shaws and Whim and farm cider in friendly bare-boards alehouse opp station, interesting layout inc taproom with hatch service, helpful staff, old local photographs; piped music; bedrooms, open all day *(Dennis Jones, the Didler)*

GREAT HUCKLOW [SK1777]

Queen Anne SK17 8RF: Comfortable and friendly 17th-c stone-built pub, low beams, big log fire and gleaming brass and copper, Adnams and changing guest beers such as Storm, good soft drinks choice, good simple food (may be just soup and sandwiches, winter lunchtimes), walkers' bar, pub games; piped music; dogs welcome, french windows to small back terrace and charming garden with picnic-sets and lovely views, two quiet bedrooms, good walks, cl Tues lunchtime *(John Dwane, the Didler)*

GREAT LONGSTONE [SK1971]

☆ *Crispin* DE45 1TZ [Main St]: Spotless pub with welcoming and particularly obliging landlord, buoyant atmosphere, good choice of generous food inc OAP lunches, Robinsons ales, log fire; picnic-sets out in front, nice spot at top of *Peak Practice* village *(Peter F Marshall, Iain Greenhalgh)*

HARDWICK HALL [SK4663]

☆ *Hardwick Inn* S44 5QJ [quite handy for M1, junction 29; Doe Lea]: Handsome 17th-c golden stone building in lovely setting just a walk from Elizabethan Hardwick Hall, several linked rooms, fine range of some 220 malt whiskies and of wines by the glass, Greene King Old Speckled Hen and Ruddles County, Marstons Pedigree and Theakstons XB and Old Peculier, all-day food operation; piped music; children allowed, pleasant back garden, more tables out in front, open all day (Andrew Beardsley, Alison Lawrence, Brian and Jacky Wilson, Jill and Julian Tasker, Mark and Diane Grist, Susan and Nigel Wilson, John Saville, A J Ward, LYM, DFL, Michael Dandy, the Didler, John and Helen Rushton, Peter F Marshall)

HARTINGTON [SK1260]

☆ *Devonshire Arms* SK17 0AL [Market Pl]: Attractive and relaxing old pub with good choice of well kept real ales, new chef doing good food in cosy lounge bar and smart daytime teashop/evening restaurant, efficient helpful staff, log fire, flagstoned public bar welcoming walkers and dogs; tables out in front facing village duck pond, more in small garden behind, good walks (Chris Reading, Alan Johnson, Keith and Chris O'Neill, H G H Stafford)

HARTSHORNE [SK3221]

Old Mill Wheel DE11 7AS [Ticknall Rd]: Recently refurbished former screw mill, huge working water wheel, some sofas and open fires in main bar area, more extensive dining area upstairs, well kept changing ales such as Oakham, friendly attentive staff, enjoyable food inc good value wkdy lunches; bedrooms (Steve Piggott)

HOGNASTON [SK2350]

☆ *Red Lion* DE6 1PR [Village signposted off B5035 Ashbourne—Wirksworth]: Open-plan beamed bar with three open fires, attractive mix of old tables, old-fashioned settles and other comfortable seats on ancient flagstones, Marstons Pedigree and changing guest beers, nice wines by the glass, food inc imaginative dishes in bar and conservatory restaurant; piped music; handy for Carsington Water; bedrooms (Derek and Sylvia Stephenson, Mrs P J Carroll, LYM, Philip and Susan Philcox, John Robertson, Dr David Clegg, Colin McKerrow, Brian and Jean Hepworth)

HOLYMOORSIDE [SK3369]

Lamb S42 7EU [Loads Rd, just off Holymoor Rd]: Small village pub in leafy spot, friendly licensees, up to half a dozen or so particularly well kept ales such as Adnams, Black Sheep, Fullers London Pride, John Smiths and Timothy Taylors Landlord, charming lounge, coal fire, pub games in neat bar; tables outside, cl wkdy lunchtimes (the Didler)

HORSLEY WOODHOUSE [SK3944]

Old Oak DE7 6AW [Main St (A609 Belper—Ilkeston)]: Attractively basic two-bar beamed pub tied to Leadmill, their interesting ales and guest beers inc good Columbus from related Bottle Brook (just along the A609 in Kilburn), farm ciders, may be cobs and pork pies, friendly staff and

locals, candles and coal fires, back rooms with toys, games and pool, no piped music (occasional live); children and dogs welcome, hatch to covered courtyard tables, cl wkdy lunchtimes, open all day wknds (Rona Murdoch, the Didler, A and P Lancashire)

HULLAND WARD [SK2647]

Black Horse DE6 3EE [Hulland Ward; A517 Ashbourne—Belper]: 17th-c pub with good fresh food at sensible prices inc local game in low-beamed quarry-tiled bar or back country-view dining room, popular Sun carvery, Bass, Harviestoun Bitter & Twisted and other changing ales, friendly licensees; children welcome, garden tables, comfortable bedrooms, nr Carsington Water, open all day Fri-Sun (Martin and Alison Stainsby, the Didler)

ILKESTON [SK4643]

Bridge Inn DE7 8RD [Bridge St, Cotmanhay; off A609/A6007]: Welcoming pub by Erewash Canal, popular with fishermen and boaters for early breakfast and sandwich lunches, low-priced Hardys & Hansons Bitter and Mild, interesting railway photographs in lounge, darts and dominoes in locals' bar; TV; well behaved children allowed, nice back garden with play area, open all day (the Didler)

Ilford DE7 5LJ [Station Rd]: Welcoming roadside local with interesting range of well kept local and other small-brewery ales, bottled imports, filled rolls at wknds, pool and other games; TV; tables on pleasant terrace, open all day Sun, cl wkdy lunchtimes (the Didler)

Poacher DE7 5QQ [South St]: Recently reopened two-bar pub with Black Sheep, Nottingham Rock, Wells & Youngs Bombardier and good guest beer range, friendly staff, back snug; sports TV; small back terrace, open all day (the Didler)

Spanish Bar DE7 5QJ [South St]: Busy café-bar with sensibly priced changing ales inc Fun Fair, Mallard and Whim Hartington, bottled belgians, friendly efficient service even when busy, log fire, Tues quiz night, popular Sun lunchtime card games with free nibbles; video juke box; small garden, skittle alley, open all day (the Didler)

LADYBOWER RESERVOIR [SK1986]

Ladybower Inn S33 0AX [A57 Sheffield—Glossop, junction with A6013]: Fine views of attractive reservoir from open-plan stone-built pub, clean and spacious, with friendly staff, enjoyable food, real ales, red plush seats; parking across road – take care; children welcome, low stone seats and tables outside, good walks, good value bedrooms, good breakfast (Richard, Mrs Jane Kingsbury, Sean A Smith)

LITTLE LONGSTONE [SK1971]

☆ *Packhorse* DE45 1NN [off A6 NW of Bakewell via Monsal Dale]: Three recently refurbished linked beamed rooms, pine tables and flagstone floor, welcoming and enthusiastic new landlord, simple yet interesting substantial food (Sat breakfast from 8.30), well kept Black Sheep and Marstons, good choice of wines by the glass, coal fire; hikers welcome (on Monsal Trail), terrace in steep little back garden *(LYM, DC, Bruce and Sharon Eden)*

LONGFORD [SK2237]

Ostrich DE6 3AH: Pleasantly placed weathered brick country pub with Marstons Pedigree, Titanic Iceberg and Tom Woods, sensibly priced home-made food, prompt friendly service, darts and pool; games machines; large garden *(Deb and John Arthur)*

LULLINGTON [SK2513]

☆ *Colvile Arms* DE12 8EG [off A444 S of Burton; Main St]: Neatly preserved 18th-c village pub with high-backed settles in simple panelled bar, cosy beamed lounge with soft seats and scatter cushions, pleasant atmosphere, friendly staff, four well kept ales inc Bass, Marstons Pedigree and a Mild, good value food; may be piped music; picnic-sets on small sheltered back lawn overlooking bowling green, cl wkdy lunchtimes *(LYM, the Didler)*

MAKENEY [SK3544]

☆ *Holly Bush* DE56 0RX [from A6 heading N after Duffield, 1st right after crossing River Derwent, then 1st left]: Down-to-earth two-bar village pub with bags of character, three blazing coal fires (one in old-fashioned range by snug's curved high-backed settle), flagstones, beams, black panelling and tiled floors, lots of brewing advertisements, five well kept changing ales (some brought from cellar in jugs), cheap food from lunchtime rolls up inc Thurs steak night, may be local cheeses for sale; games lobby; children allowed in basic hatch-served back conservatory, picnic-sets outside, dogs welcome, open all day wknds *(Rona Murdoch, BB, the Didler)*

MATLOCK BATH [SK2958]

Temple DE4 3PG [Temple Walk]: 18th-c hotel with wonderful Derwent valley views, comfortable bar, dining area and restaurant, two well kept changing real ales from more or less local small breweries, enjoyable food; children welcome, tables outside, summer barbecues, bedrooms *(the Didler)*

MAYFIELD [SK1444]

☆ *Rose & Crown* DE6 2JT [Main Rd (B5032 off A52 W of Ashbourne)]: Comfortable pub with enterprising choice of good food, Marstons Pedigree and good range of reasonably priced wines by the glass, good friendly service, log fire in thriving carpeted bar, restaurant; children welcome, garden tables, local walks leaflets, four good bedrooms *(John and Karen Wilkinson, Roderick Braithwaite)*

MELBOURNE [SK3825]

Blue Bell DE73 8EJ [Church St]: Warm-hearted little two-bar pub in attractive country town, full range of good local Shardlow ales kept well, substantial bar food inc wide range of hot rolls and ciabattas,

friendly staff, pleasant chatty atmosphere, sporting pictures, games in public bar; sports TV in both bars; terrace tables *(Pete Baker, N R White)*

MILLERS DALE [SK1473]

Anglers Rest SK17 8SN [just down Litton Lane; pub is PH on OS Sheet 119, map ref 142734]: Two-bar pub in lovely quiet riverside setting on Monsal Trail, wonderful gorge views and riverside walks (though it's more of a foody than a rough-and-ready ramblers' place now); enjoyable food, well kept ales such as Storm Damage, efficient service, open fire, dining room; children welcome, attractive village *(Peter F Marshall, Matthew Shackle, David Crook, the Didler)*

MILLTOWN [SK3561]

☆ *Miners Arms* S45 0HA [off B6036 SE of Ashover; Oakstedge Lane]: Good properly sensible home cooking (best to book) in appealing L-shaped pub with friendly service, Archers and Greene King Abbot, warm-hearted local atmosphere, quieter eating area further back; may be quiet piped classical music; children welcome, attractive country walks right from the door, cl Sun evening, Mon/Tues, winter Weds, and 10 days Aug *(the Didler, LYM)*

MONYASH [SK1566]

☆ *Bulls Head* DE45 1JH [B5055 W of Bakewell]: Unpretentious high-ceilinged local with good changing home cooking at sensible prices, well kept real ales and good choice of wines by the glass, good log fire, unpretentious furnishings, horse pictures, shelf of china, mullioned windows, two-room dining room, darts, dominoes, pool in small back bar; may be quiet piped music; children and muddy dogs welcome, gate to nice new village play area, simple bedrooms, fine walking country, open all day *(Mrs Deborah Chalmers, BB, Pam and John Smith, Eddie and Lynn Jarrett, Mrs M Shardlow, Mike Wass)*

Royal Oak SK17 9QJ [Hurdlow, W of Monyash, on opposite side of A515 – towards Crowdecote]: Friendly beamed stone-built country pub with good choice of good value home-made food all day, esp pies and Thurs steak night, chatty local atmosphere, well kept Bass and Marstons Pedigree, lower dining area; camp site with new camping barn and stables, handy for High Peak/Tissington Trail, open all day *(John and Jackie Walsh)*

MORLEY [SK3941]

Three Horseshoes DE7 6DF: Friendly open-plan stone-built pub with wide choice of decent generous food (not Sun evening), Marstons and interesting guest beers from central bar, good service, dining one end, darts, TV and games machine the other; may be quiet piped music; children welcome, picnic-sets in small garden with play area *(JJW, CMW, Derek and Sylvia Stephenson)*

NEW MILLS [SJ9886]

Fox SK22 3AY [Brookbottom; OS Sheet 109 map ref 985864]: Tucked-away traditional country local with good long-serving landlord, particularly well kept Robinsons, good value simple food (not Tues evening) from sandwiches up, log fire, darts and pool; children welcome, lots of tables outside, good walking area (so can get crowded wknds – open all day then) *(John Fiander, David Hoult, Bob Broadhurst, the Didler)*

Pack Horse SK22 4QQ [Mellor Rd]: Popular and friendly family-run country pub with lovely views across broad Sett valley to Kinder Scout, plentiful good value food, well kept Tetleys and guest beers, sensibly priced wine, warm atmosphere; bedrooms, open all day *(Jan and Roger Ferris)*

OCKBROOK [SK4236]

☆ *Royal Oak* DE72 3SE [village signed off B6096 just outside Spondon; Green Lane]: Quiet 18th-c village local run by same friendly family for half a century, bargain honest food (not wknd or Tues evenings) from super lunchtime rolls to steaks, Sun lunch and OAP meals, Bass and three interesting guest beers, good soft drinks choice, tiled-floor tap room, turkey-carpeted snug, inner bar with Victorian prints, larger and lighter side room, nice old settle in entrance corridor, open fires, darts and dominoes, charity book sales, no music or machines; tables in sheltered cottage garden, more on cobbled front courtyard, separate play area *(Robert F Smith, Pete Baker, BB, the Didler, JJW, CMW)*

OLD GLOSSOP [SK0494]

Queens SK13 7RZ [Shepley St]: Open-plan dining pub with quick service even when busy, small bar area too with well kept Black Sheep, upstairs restaurant; picnic-sets out in front *(Len Beattie)*

OSMASTON [SK1943]

Shoulder of Mutton DE6 1LW [off A52 SE of Ashbourne]: Snug and inviting down-to-earth pub with enjoyable generous home-made food, well kept Bass, Marstons Pedigree and a guest beer; attractive garden, peaceful pretty village with thatched cottages, duck pond and good walks *(Edward Leetham)*

PADFIELD [SK0396]

Peel Arms SK13 1EX [Temple St]: Small stone-built village pub with split-level lounge and cosy public bar, well kept changing ales, enjoyable food, three real fires, panelling, nice brass and china, pleasant views; good bedrooms *(Piotr Chodzko-Zajko)*

PARWICH [SK1854]

Sycamore DE6 1QL: Chatty old country pub with good log fire in simple but comfortable main bar, generous wholesome food lunchtimes and most Weds-Sat evenings, Bass, Marstons and a guest beer, cheerful service, lots of old local photographs, hatch-served tap room with games; tables out in front and on grass by car park, quiet village not far from Tissington, good walks *(the Didler, Pete Baker)*

PENTRICH [SK3852]

☆ *Dog* DE5 3RE [Main Rd (B6016 N of Ripley)]:

Extended traditional pub, cosy and smartly fitted out, very popular for its fresh up-to-date food (best to book), reasonable prices, Bass, Marstons Pedigree and a guest beer, nice wines by the glass, friendly and attentive well turned out staff, beams and panelling; tables in attractive garden behind, quiet village, good walks *(the Didler, John E Robson, Robert F Smith, Derek and Sylvia Stephenson)*

PILSLEY [SK2371]

Devonshire Arms DE45 1UL [off A619 Bakewell—Baslow; High St]: Good homely food, generous and attractively priced, from sandwiches to popular fresh fish and Thurs-Sat evening carvery (may need to book), pleasant staff, cosy and appealing lounge bar with bric-a-brac and open fire, another in walkers'/family bar area, well kept ales inc local Peak; quiz and music nights; bedrooms, handy for Chatsworth farm and craft shops, lovely village *(Stephen Woad, Ian and Jane Irving, Peter F Marshall)*

RIPLEY [SK3950]

Pear Tree DE5 3HR [Derby Rd (B6179)]: Blazing coal fires in both rooms, Greene King ales inc Hardys & Hansons, friendly chatty staff, darts and dominoes; open all day *(the Didler)*

ROWARTH [SK0189]

☆ *Little Mill* SK22 1EB [pub now signed well locally; off A626 in Marple Bridge at Mellor sign, sharp left at Rowarth sign]: Beautifully tucked-away family pub with continuing improvements under newish landlord, good choice of real ales, popular reasonably priced food from sandwiches and baked potatoes up in roomy open-plan bar and upstairs restaurant, big log fire, unusual features inc working waterwheel, pub games; frequent live music; children welcome, pretty garden dell across stream great for them, with good recently extended play area, picnic-sets on decking, vintage Pullman-carriage bedrooms, open all day *(David Hoult, LYM, Dennis Jones)*

ROWSLEY [SK2565]

Grouse & Claret DE4 2EB [A6 Bakewell—Matlock]: Attractive and spotless family dining pub in old stone building, spacious and comfortable, with friendly helpful staff, enjoyable food (all day wknd) from sandwiches and pubby things to more enterprising dishes, decent wines, open fires, taproom popular with walkers; tables outside, good value bedrooms *(David Carr, Malcolm Pellatt)*

SHARDLOW [SK4430]

Malt Shovel DE72 2HG [3½ miles from M1 junction 24, via A6 towards Derby; The Wharf]: Busy old-world beamed pub in 18th-c former maltings, interesting odd-angled layout, changing ales inc Marstons Pedigree, quick friendly service, good value food (not Sat evening) from baguettes and baked potatoes up, good central open fire, farm tools and bric-a-brac; no small children; lots of tables out on terrace by Trent &

Mersey Canal, pretty hanging baskets and boxes *(the Didler, John Beeken, LYM)*

☆ **Old Crown** DE72 2HL [off A50 just W of M1 junction 24; Cavendish Bridge, E of village]: Good value interesting pub with wide choice of pubby food (not wknd evenings) from sandwiches and baguettes up, half a dozen or more well kept Marstons and related ales, nice choice of malt whiskies, friendly service and atmosphere, beams hung with masses of jugs and mugs, walls covered with other interesting bric-a-brac and breweriana, big inglenook fireplace; children and dogs welcome, simple good value bedrooms (with videos inc children's ones), good breakfast, open all day *(the Gray family, Kevin Blake, the Didler, LYM, Michael J Caley, Mr and Mrs John Taylor, Blaise Vyner, John and Enid Morris, P J Holt, John Cook)*

SMALLEY [SK4044]

Bell DE7 6EF [A608 Heanor—Derby]: Small comfortable two-room village pub with lots of breweriana, half a dozen or more well kept low-priced changing ales such as Mallard and Oakham, good choice of wines, pots of tea or coffee, smart efficient friendly staff, dining area with good value fresh food (not Sun evening); quiet piped music; post office annexe, tables out in front and on big relaxing lawn with play area, beautiful hanging baskets, attractive bedrooms behind, open all day wknds *(JJW, CMW)*

SMISBY [SK3419]

☆ **Smisby Arms** LE65 2UA [Nelsons Sq]: Ancient low-beamed village pub doing well under helpful new father-and-son landlords, good pub food all freshly cooked to order at bargain prices, friendly efficient service, well kept ales such as Greene King Abbot, Marstons Pedigree and Timothy Taylors Landlord, pleasantly bright little dining extension *(John and Hazel Williams, Dr J H Bulmer, Brian and Jean Hepworth, Annette Tress, Gary Smith, Paul J Robinshaw, Derek and Sylvia Stephenson)*

SPONDON [SK3935]

☆ **Malt Shovel** DE21 7LH [off A6096 on edge of Derby, via Church Hill into Potter St]: Unspoilt traditional pub with decent cheap food, well kept Bass and changing guest beers from hatch in tiled corridor with cosy panelled and quarry-tiled or turkey-carpeted rooms off, cheap food, old-fashioned décor, huge inglenook, steps down to big games bar with full-size pool table; lots of picnic-sets, some under cover, in big well used back garden with good play area *(the Didler, BB)*

STANTON IN PEAK [SK2364]

Flying Childers DE4 2LW [off B5056 Bakewell—Ashbourne; Main Rd]: Cosy and unspoilt beamed right-hand bar with fireside settles, larger comfortable lounge, Adnams, Black Sheep, Wells & Youngs Bombardier and interesting local guest beers, friendly service, good value lunchtime soup and rolls, dominoes and cribbage; in delightful steep stone village overlooking rich green valley, good walks, cl Mon/Tues lunchtimes (winter

Weds/Thurs lunchtimes too) *(the Didler)*

STARKHOLMES [SK3058]

White Lion DE4 5JA [Starkholmes Rd]: Open-plan village pub in exceptional location, views over Matlock Bath and Derwent valley, decent reasonably priced food, Burtonwood, Marstons Pedigree, Whim Hartington and a guest beer, low ceilings and stripped stone, coal fire in restaurant; pleasant tables outside, boules, bedrooms (with fridge for good self-serve continental breakfast), open all day wknds *(David and Sue Smith, Derek and Sylvia Stephenson)*

STONEY MIDDLETON [SK2375]

Moon S32 4TW [Townend (A623)]: Sensibly priced food inc hugely garnished sandwiches and OAP lunchtime bargains, Banks's, Marstons Pedigree and a couple of guest beers, reasonably priced wines, friendly staff, nice décor with old photographs; picnic-sets outside, handy for dales walks *(Gwyn and Anne Wake, Richard)*

TANSLEY [SK3159]

Royal Oak DE4 5FY [A615 Matlock—Mansfield]: Pleasant village pub with enjoyable simple food cooked to order, friendly staff *(Trevor and Sylvia Millum)*

THORPE [SK1650]

Dog & Partridge DE6 2AT: Welcoming country pub with good range of good value food, well kept Black Sheep, prompt friendly service, bright comfortable lounge; handy for Dovedale *(John Tav)*

TIDESWELL [SK1575]

George SK17 8NU [Commercial Rd (B6049, between A623 and A6 E of Buxton)]: Unpretentious L-shaped bar/lounge and linked dining room, choice of real ales, modestly priced wines, generous food, open fires, paintings by local artists, separate bar with darts and pool; piped music; children and dogs welcome, by remarkable church, tables in front overlooking pretty village, sheltered back garden, pleasant walks *(BB, Michael Butler, the Didler, Alan Johnson, H G H Stafford)*

Horse & Jockey SK17 8JZ [Queen St]: Well reworked in appealing old-fashioned style, with beams, flagstones, cushioned wall benches and coal fire in small public bar's traditional open range, bare boards, button-back banquettes and woodburner in lounge, changing ales such as Kelham Island and Theakstons, modestly priced food, stripped stone and flagstones in sparely decorated dining room; dogs welcome, four newly done bedrooms, good walks *(Michael Butler, Eddie Edwards)*

TINTWISTLE [SK0297]

☆ **Bulls Head** SK13 1JY [Old Rd (off A628, N side)]: Low-beamed Tudor pub tucked away in pretty stone-built village, good food, enterprising without being too fancy, very friendly staff, well kept ales, big log fire, plenty of character and furnishings to suit its age, no machines; children, dogs and walking groups welcome, handy for Woodhead Pass *(GLD)*

WENSLEY [SK2661]
Red Lion DE4 2LH [Main Rd (B5057 NW of Matlock)]: Friendly and utterly unspoilt farm pub run by chatty brother and sister, assorted 1950s-ish furniture, piano in main bar (landlord likes sing-songs), unusual tapestry in second room (usually locked, so ask landlady), no games or piped music, just bottled beer, tea, coffee, soft drinks and filled sandwiches or home-baked rolls perhaps using fillings from the garden – may be their fruit for sale, too; outside gents'; open all day *(Richard and Margaret McPhee, Pete Baker, the Didler)*
WHATSTANDWELL [SK3255]
Homesford Cottage DE4 5HJ [Homesford; A6 towards Cromford]: Friendly and comfortable, good helpings of fair-priced lunchtime bar food from good filled rolls up, well kept real ales and decent wines by the glass, separate restaurant; open all day *(John and Helen Rushton)*
WHITTINGTON [SK3875]
Cock & Magpie S41 9QW [Church Street N, behind museum]: Old stone-built dining pub with new landlord, his three chef children cooking enjoyable food from sandwiches and OAP bargains up (best to book Sun lunch), friendly well organised service, well kept Banks's and Marstons Pedigree, good soft drinks choice, conservatory, separate public bar with games room; piped music, no dogs; children welcome in dining areas, next to Revolution House museum *(Keith and Chris O'Neill)*
WHITTINGTON MOOR [SK3873]
☆ *Derby Tup* S41 8LS [Sheffield Rd; B6057 just S of A61 roundabout]: Spotless no-frills Tynemill pub with good changing ales such as Archers, Peak and Thornbridge from long line of gleaming handpumps, good choice of other drinks, pleasant service, simple furniture, coal fire and lots of standing room as well as two small side rooms (children allowed here), daily papers, good value basic bar lunches; can get very busy wknd evenings (Sun quiz night); dogs welcome, open all day Fri-Sun *(P Dawn, LYM, Peter F Marshall, the Didler)*

Red Lion S41 8LX [Sheffield Rd (B6057)]: Simple friendly two-room 19th-c stone-built local tied to Old Mill with their real ales, hard-working landlady, thriving atmosphere, old local photographs; juke box, sports TV; open all day *(P Dawn, the Didler)*
WINSTER [SK2460]
☆ *Bowling Green* DE4 2DS [East Bank, by NT Market House]: Classic traditional pub with good chatty atmosphere, character landlord and welcoming efficient service, enjoyable generous reasonably priced food, changing well kept ales such as Abbeydale, Theakstons and Thornbridge, end log fire, dining area and family conservatory; open all day wknds, cl Mon/Tues *(John Knighton, Theocsbrian, Andrew Beardsley, Alison Lawrence, N R White, Diana Lockwood, Sharon and Alan Corper)*
WIRKSWORTH [SK2854]
Royal Oak DE4 4FG [North End]: Traditional small backstreet local with proper friendly licensees, well kept changing ales inc Bass, Timothy Taylors Landlord and Whim Hartington, dominoes, may be good filled cobs, key fobs, old copper kettles and other bric-a-brac, interesting old photographs; opens 8pm, cl lunchtime exc Sun *(the Didler)*
YOULGREAVE [SK2064]
Farmyard DE45 1UW [Main St]: Comfortable low-ceilinged local, warm and welcoming, with good well priced food, attentive landlord, well kept real ales, fire in impressive stone fireplace, old farm tools, big upstairs restaurant; children, walkers and dogs welcome, TV, tables in garden *(Mr and Mrs R Duys)*
☆ *George* DE45 1WN [Alport Lane/Church St]: Handsome 17th-c stone-built inn opp Norman church, friendly landlord and locals, wide range of good straightforward low-priced home-made food all day inc game, well kept John Smiths, Theakstons Mild and a local guest beer, comfortable banquettes, flagstoned tap room (walkers and dogs welcome), games room; attractive village handy for Lathkill Dale and Haddon Hall, roadside tables, simple bedrooms, open all day *(Pete Baker, the Didler, Russell Grimshaw, Kerry Purcell)*

Anyone claiming to arrange or prevent inclusion of a pub in the *Guide* is a fraud. Pubs are included only if recommended by genuine readers and if our own anonymous inspection confirms that they are suitable.

Devon

This big county has a remarkable variety of good pubs – many of them in lovely countryside or by the water and with fine nearby walks. It's one of Britain's best areas for the pub lover, usually with a warm welcome for visitors, not just from licensees but from locals too. West Country beers feature strongly, you can still find good local cider, and many pubs have a fantastic number of wines by the glass from interesting lists. Places doing especially well this year include the Durant Arms at Ashprington (a very nice place to stay, really more of a small hotel), the Turtley Corn Mill at Avonwick (a large converted mill house with good modern food), the Drewe Arms at Broadhembury (exceptional fish dishes, at a price), the charming Drake Manor at Buckland Monachorum (the long-serving landlady makes everyone feel really at home), the Five Bells at Clyst Hydon (bustling and friendly, with a lovely garden), the Anchor at Cockwood (incredibly popular for its fish), the Wild Goose at Combeinteignhead (a good all-rounder, and always enjoyed by people finding it for the first time through the *Guide*), the Culm Valley at Culmstock (eccentric and even on the scruffy side, but interesting, with super food), the Nobody Inn at Doddiscombsleigh (a quite amazing choice of drinks), the Turf near Exminster (half the fun is getting there), the Dartmoor Union at Holbeton (civilised, with something of a wine bar feel), the Duke of York at Iddesleigh (a favourite with many, and so friendly), the Cleave at Lustleigh (again, with friendly licensees), the Bridge Inn on the edge of Topsham (wonderfully unspoilt, and with fine beers), the Old Church House at Torbryan (lots of real character), the Start Bay near Torcross (always packed out for its fantastic fish), and the Diggers Rest at Woodbury Salterton (a bustling village pub with good food). The numbers of these top Devon pubs are swollen this year by five interesting new entries, in some cases returning to these pages under go-ahead new management, after quite a long break: the Cricket, a well run all-rounder by the sea at Beesands, the handsome old Ring o' Bells in Chagford (interesting food under its new landlord), the ancient Royal Oak by the green at Meavy (another pub put on a winning streak by a newish landlord), the Church House at Stokenham (good food in this unspoilt country pub), and the friendly Golden Lion at Tipton St John (good food here too). In this county, with its marvellous range of carefully raised livestock, the top food pubs tend now to get their supplies from local farms, and with this richness on their doorstep can afford to choose the absolute best. Many of the pubs mentioned above are great for super meals out, and to these we'd add the Merrie Harriers at Clayhidon, the New Inn at Coleford, the Church House at Marldon, the Jack in the Green at Rockbeare, the Tower in Slapton (though there may be new people by the time this edition is published), the Kings Arms at Strete and the Rose & Crown at Yealmpton. From this splendidly contested field, it's the Drewe Arms at Broadhembury that wins the award of Devon Dining Pub of the Year. Despite the top quality of pub food in Devon, it is if anything a little cheaper than in many areas, so you can generally expect really good food value. Drinks prices are fairly close to the national average; the Imperial in Exeter is a bargain for beers, and the Duke of York at Iddesleigh has been holding down its drinks prices very well indeed. More or less local beers such as Sharps, Teignworthy, Branscombe Vale, Blackawton, Butcombe, St Austell and, particularly, Otter and Cotleigh tend to offer the best value in Devon pubs. In the Lucky Dip section at the end of the chapter, current stars are the Beaver in Appledore, Exeter Inn at Bampton, Bearslake at Lake, Ferry Boat in Dittisham, Fingle Bridge Inn near Drewsteignton, Rock at Georgeham, Rising Sun in Lynmouth, Ring of Bells at North Bovey, Lamb at Sandford, Old Ship in Sidmouth, Globe in Topsham, Northmore Arms at Wonson, and out on the island of Lundy the Marisco. We have hopes that the Blue Ball at Sidford will reopen this year, rebuilt after fire damage; up until the disaster it had featured as a main entry in every single edition of the *Guide*.

ASHPRINGTON
SX8157   MAP 1

Durant Arms 🛏

Village signposted off A381 S of Totnes; OS Sheet 202 map reference 819571; TQ9 7UP

Small Victorian country hotel with little bar, busy dining room and comfortable bedrooms

Run by charming and helpful licensees, this attractive Victorian gabled place is more of a small country hotel than a pub but it is extremely popular with our readers. Sadly we heard it was up for sale just as we went to press. There is a busy dining side and attached bar with St Austell Dartmoor Best and Tribute on handpump and local wines. The three linked and turkey carpeted areas are spotlessly clean with comfortably upholstered red dining chairs around clothed tables and a small corner bar counter in one area with a couple of bar stools in front; piped music. Good, attentive service. The dining room is hung with lots of oil paintings and watercolours by local artists on the walls. There are teak seats and tables in the flagged back courtyard and the bedrooms are carefully decorated and comfortable.

🍽 **The well liked food might include sandwiches, soup, chicken liver pâté, fresh crab cocktail, moussaka, roast rib of local beef with yorkshire pudding or smoked haddock and broccoli bake, steak and kidney pie, fresh poached salmon in prawn sauce, venison fillet with shallots and port, and puddings such as rhubarb crumble or bread and butter pudding; best to book to be sure of a table.** *Starters/Snacks: £4.00 to £6.75. Main Courses: £6.75 to £18.00. Puddings: £4.50*

Free house ~ Licensees Graham and Eileen Ellis ~ Real ale ~ Bar food ~ Restaurant ~ (01803) 732240 ~ Children in own room ~ Dogs allowed in bar ~ Open 11.30-2.30, 6.30-11; 12-2.30, 7-10.30 Sun; closed evenings 25 and 26 Dec ~ Bedrooms: £45B/£80B

Recommended by Gerry and Rosemary Dobson, Michael B Griffith, P and J Shapley, Mr and Mrs A R Maden, Howard and Lorna Lambert

---

AVONWICK   SX6958   MAP 1

Turtley Corn Mill ♀

½ mile off A38 roundabout at SW end of S Brent bypass; TQ10 9ES

Careful conversion of tall mill house with interestingly furnished spreading areas, local beers, modern cooking, and huge gardens

This careful conversion of a large, tall mill house (with its waterwheel now standing idle) gives a spreading series of linked areas – each with some individuality: bookcases, fat church candles and oriental rugs in one area, dark flagstones by the bar, a strategic woodburning stove dividing one part, a side enclave with a modern pew built in around a really big table, and so on. Throughout, lighting is good, with plenty of big windows looking out over the grounds, a pleasant array of prints and some other decorations (framed 78rpm discs, elderly wireless sets, house plants) on pastel walls, and a mix of comfortable dining chairs around heavy baluster-leg tables in a variety of sizes. They have a commendable range of wines and sherries including good french house wines, Princetown Jail, St Austell Tribute and Summerskills Tamar with a guest or two such as Butcombe Blonde on handpump, 50 malt whiskies and decent coffee; board games. The extensive gardens, leading down to a lake, have well spaced picnic-sets and a giant chess set. The only serious minus is that they try to keep your credit card if you eat outside.

🍴 **Enjoyable food includes sandwiches, soup, chicken caesar salad, local haddock in beer batter, sweet potato fritters with avocado purée, steak burger with gruyère and bacon, bass fillets on chorizo mash, braised lamb shank with dauphinoise potatoes, cornish scallops topped with crispy bacon, duck breast with rhubarb sauce on stir-fried egg noodles, and puddings like a trio of chocolate or seasonal fruit crumble.** *Starters/Snacks: £4.50 to £9.50. Main Courses: £8.50 to £17.50. Puddings: £5.25 to £5.75*

Free house ~ Licensees Lesley and Bruce Brunning ~ Real ale ~ Bar food (12-9.30(9 Sun)) ~ Restaurant ~ (01364) 646100 ~ Children welcome until 7.30pm ~ Dogs welcome ~ Open 11-11; 12-10.30 Sun

Recommended by John Evans, Andrew York, Dudley and Moira Cockroft, Andy and Claire Barker

BEESANDS   SX8140   MAP 1

Cricket

About 3 miles S of A379, from Chillington; in village turn right along foreshore road; TQ7 2EN

Welcoming small pub by beach with enjoyable food and beer

Popular with South Devon Coastal Path walkers, this is a friendly little pub by Start Bay beach; the bedrooms have fine sea views. It's neatly kept and open-plan with dark traditional pubby furniture (carpeted in the dining part and with a stripped wooden floor in the bar area), some nice, well captioned photographs of local fisherpeople, knots and fishing gear on the walls and a couple of small fireplaces. Fullers London Pride and Otter Bitter on handpump, a dozen wines by the glass and local cider; piped music and darts. The cheerful black labrador is called Brewster. Picnic-sets outside by the sea wall; good wheelchair access.

🍴 **As well as very good fresh local fish and shellfish, the well liked bar food includes lunchtime sandwiches, super crab soup, smoked mackerel and horseradish pâté, home-made pie or vegetable bake, pasta in spicy tomato sauce and chicken breast in red wine, shallot and bacon sauce.** *Starters/Snacks: £5.00 to £6.50. Main Courses: £7.60 to £16.50. Puddings: £4.50*

Heavitree ~ Tenant Nigel Heath ~ Real ale ~ Bar food (not winter Sun evening) ~ Restaurant ~ (01548) 580215 ~ Children allowed with some restrictions ~ Dogs allowed in bar ~ Open 11(12 summer Sun)-11; 11-3, 6-11 weekdays in winter ~ Bedrooms: /£65S

Recommended by M G Hart, Phil and Anne Nash, David and Karen Cuckney, Jenny and Brian Seller, Roger Wain-Heapy

BRANSCOMBE   SY1888   MAP 1

Fountain Head 🍺

*Upper village, above the robust old church; village signposted off A3052 Sidmouth—
Seaton, then from Branscombe Square follow road up hill towards Sidmouth, and after
about a mile turn left after the church; OS Sheet 192 map reference SY188889; EX12 3BG*

Old-fashioned stone pub with unspoilt rooms and own-brewed beers

The new licensee of this old-fashioned and unspoilt stone pub will continue brewing their
own Branscombe Vale Branoc, Jolly Geff and Summa That, and the annual beer festival in
June should still take place. The room on the left – formerly a smithy – has forge tools
and horseshoes on the high oak beams, a log fire in the original raised firebed with its
tall central chimney, and cushioned pews and mate's chairs. On the right, an irregularly
shaped, more orthodox snug room has another log fire, white-painted plank ceiling with
an unusual carved ceiling-rose, brown-varnished panelled walls, and rugs on its
flagstone-and-lime-ash floor. Darts, cards and dominoes. There are seats out on the front
loggia and terrace, and a little stream rustling under the flagstoned path; pleasant
nearby walks.

🍴 **As well as lunchtime sandwiches and ploughman's, the bar food now includes soup,
chicken liver pâté, home-cooked ham and eggs, beer-battered cod fillet, beef in ale pie,
mushroom stroganoff, chicken topped with bacon and melted cheese with barbecue sauce
and calves liver in sage butter.** *Starters/Snacks: £3.95 to £5.25. Main Courses: £7.25 to
£15.00. Puddings: £3.95*

Own brew ~ Licensees Jon Woodley and Teresa Hoare ~ Real ale ~ Bar food ~ Restaurant ~
(01297) 680359 ~ Children in dining room and one other room ~ Dogs welcome ~ Open
11-2.30, 6-11; 12-10.30 Sun; 12-3, 6-10.30 Sun in winter

*Recommended by Di and Mike Gillam, Pete Walker, Bruce Horne, Sue and Keith Campbell, Wendy Straker,
Richard Pitcher, Revd R P Tickle, Kerry Law, Phil and Sally Gorton, Gary Rollings, the Didler, Jeremy Whitehorn,
Jill Healing, Mike Gorton, Lynne James, JP, PP*

Masons Arms 🍷 🍺 🛏️

Main Street; signed off A3052 Sidmouth—Seaton, then bear left into village; EX12 3DJ

**Rambling low-beamed rooms, woodburning stoves and good choice of real ales and wines
in 14th-c longhouse; quiet terrace and garden**

Travellers have been coming to this pretty longhouse for nearly seven centuries now. The
rambling main bar is the heart of the building and has ancient ships' beams, a massive
central hearth in front of the roaring log fire (where spit roasts are held) and comfortable
seats and chairs on slate floors. The Old Worthies bar also has a slate floor, a fireplace
with a two-sided woodburning stove and woodwork that has been stripped back to the
original pine. There's also the original restaurant (warmed by one side of the
woodburning stove) and another beamed restaurant above the main bar. Branscombe Vale
Branoc, Otter Bitter, St Austell Tribute, Teignworthy Beachcomber and a beer named for
the pub on handpump, 14 wines by the glass and 33 malt whiskies; darts, shove-
ha'penny, cribbage, and dominoes. Outside, the quiet flower-filled front terrace has tables
with little thatched roofs, extending into a side garden. They may insist that you leave
your credit card behind the bar. The only disappointment we've come across here is from
a reader visiting on a quiet afternoon who felt that, retrieved from pressure, the staff
seemed to be taking things too easy.

🍴 **Good bar food includes lunchtime sandwiches, paninis and ploughman's, soup, goats
cheese panna cotta with spicy guacamole, steamed mussels provençale, beer-battered cod,
fresh gnocchi with wilted spinach, garlic and parmesan cream, pork and black pepper
sausages with mustard mash, salmon, mussel, cod and leek stew, garlic-roasted shank of
lamb with root vegetable dauphinoise, daily specials, and puddings like chocolate and
orange crème brûlée or chilled berry soup with clotted cream.** *Starters/Snacks: £3.50 to
£6.25. Main Courses: £9.50 to £13.50. Puddings: £3.50 to £4.25*

Smoking is not allowed inside any pub.

Free house ~ Licensees Colin and Carol Slaney ~ Real ale ~ Bar food ~ Restaurant ~ (01297) 680300 ~ Children in bar with parents but not in restaurant ~ Dogs allowed in bar and bedrooms ~ Open 11-11; 12-10.30 Sun; 11-3, 6-11 weekdays in winter ~ Bedrooms: /£75B

Recommended by Mike and Shelley Woodroffe, Barry Steele-Perkins, Pete Walker, Kerry Law, the Didler, Wendy Straker, Gary Rollings, Di and Mike Gillam, Neil and Lorna Mclaughlan, Lawrence Pearse, Mike Gorton, Dennis Jenkin, Peter Titcomb, John and Enid Morris, MB, Richard Pitcher, Mrs L Aquilina, Tracey and Stephen Groves, Pat and Roger Davies, Michael Doswell, Jo Rees, John and Fiona McIlwain, Peter Craske

BRIXHAM
SX9256   MAP 1

Maritime

King Street (up steps from harbour – nearby parking virtually non-existent); TQ5 9TH

Informal little one-bar pub with friendly landlady and lots to look at

This is a very informal and relaxed little pub and the one bar is crammed full of interest: hundreds of key fobs and chamber-pots hang from the beams, there's a binnacle by the door, cigarette cards and pre-war ensigns from different countries, toby jugs and horsebrasses, mannequins, pictures of astronomical charts and plenty of mugs and china jugs. Both the african grey parrot (mind your fingers) and the lively terrier may be around, and there are two warming coal fires, cushioned wheelback chairs and pink-plush cushioned wall benches, flowery swagged curtains. The small TV might be on if there's something the landlady wants to watch; darts, piped music and board games. Badger Best and Fursty Ferret, and St Austell Dartmoor on handpump (though only one in winter), 78 malt whiskies, and home-made smoothies; no food. Fine views down over the harbour and almost non-existent nearby parking. More reports please.

🍴 **No food.**

Free house ~ Licensee Mrs Pat Seddon ~ Real ale ~ No credit cards ~ (01803) 853535 ~ Well behaved children allowed ~ Dogs allowed in bar ~ Open 11-3, 6.30-midnight; 12-3, 7-midnight Sun ~ Bedrooms: £20/£40

Recommended by BOB

BROADHEMBURY
ST1004   MAP 1

Drewe Arms ★

Signposted off A373 Cullompton—Honiton; EX14 3NF

DEVON DINING PUB OF THE YEAR

Fantastic fish dishes in civilised and rather smart inn, helpful service, and super wines

It's the delicious fish dishes that most customers are here to enjoy in this civilised and well run place – though locals do still drop in for just a drink. The small bar has neatly carved beams in its high ceiling and handsome stone-mullioned windows (one with a small carved roundabout horse). On the left, a high-backed stripped settle separates off a little room with flowers on the three sturdy country tables, plank-panelled walls painted brown below and yellow above with attractive engravings and prints, and a roaring winter fire in the big black-painted fireplace with bric-a-brac on a high mantelpiece (a plump labrador may have pride of place in front of the fire); some wood carvings, walking sticks and framed watercolours for sale. The flagstoned entry has a narrow corridor of a room by the servery with a couple of tables, and the cellar bar has simple pews on the stone floor. Best to book to be sure of a table. Otter Bitter, Ale and Bright are tapped from the cask and the very good wine list is laid out extremely helpfully – several by the glass. There are picnic-sets in the lovely garden which has a lawn stretching back under the shadow of chestnut trees towards a church with its singularly melodious hour-bell. Thatched and very pretty, the 15th-c pub is in a charming village of similar cream-coloured cottages.

🍴 **Unfailingly good (if not cheap), the food might include open sandwiches, smoked haddock chowder, cornish mussels marinière, squid with garlic, herbs and chilli, john dory with anchovies and capers, whole lemon sole with herb butter, fillet of turbot with**

hollandaise, langoustines, crab and lobster, a few meaty choices, and puddings such as compote of preserved fruits with preserved ginger ice-cream or crème brûlée. *Starters/Snacks: £5.00 to £10.00. Main Courses: £10.30 to £18.00. Puddings: £5.00*

Free house ~ Licensees Kerstin and Nigel Burge ~ Real ale ~ Bar food (not winter Sun evening) ~ Restaurant ~ (01404) 841267 ~ Children in eating area of bar, restaurant and family room ~ Dogs allowed in bar ~ Open 11-3, 6-11; 12-4, 6-10 Sun; closed Sun evening in winter

Recommended by Kerry Law, Philip and Susan Philcox, John and Enid Morris, Bob and Laura Brock, Revd D E and Mrs J A Shapland, Pete Walker, Gary Rollings, Robin and Ann Taylor, Jacquie Jones, John and Fiona Merritt, Jo Lilley, Simon Calvert, MB, Richard Pitcher, Alan Cowell, Mike Gorton, John Urquhart, Mike Turner, the Didler, Philip and Jude Simmons, Steve and Liz Tilley, Dr Ian S Morley, Anthony Barnes, Peter Craske

BUCKFAST
SX7467 MAP 1

Abbey Inn ♀

Just off A38 at A384 junction; take B3380 towards Buckfastleigh, but turn right into Buckfast Road immediately after bridge; TQ11 0EA

Rather decorous place with tables on terrace overlooking River Dart, neat rooms, well liked bar food, and St Austell beers

If you stay here, try to get one of the bedrooms overlooking the River Dart; the tables on the terrace make the most of this riverside spot, too. The pub is a sizeable, pleasant place and the bar has partly panelled walls with some ships' crests there and over the gantry (Mr Davison was in the Royal Navy for many years), two chequered green and beige wooden-armed settees, a mix of high-backed chairs and captain's chairs around a few circular tables, and a woodburning stove in an ornate fireplace. The big dining room also has a woodburning stove, as well as more panelling and river views. St Austell Dartmoor Best, HSD and Tribute on handpump, 13 wines by the glass and local cider; piped music and board games. The pub is reached down a steep little drive from the car park.

🍴 Good quality bar food includes sandwiches, soup, chicken liver pâté, lemon and thyme risotto, home-made steamed chicken and ham suet pudding, local sausages with onion gravy, trout fillets with roasted hazelnut butter, nut loaf with wild mushroom sauce, lamb shank with spring onion mash, and puddings like warm chocolate brownies or sticky toffee pudding with toffee sauce. *Starters/Snacks: £3.25 to £5.25. Main Courses: £8.95 to £12.50. Puddings: £4.50*

St Austell ~ Tenants Terence and Elizabeth Davison ~ Real ale ~ Bar food ~ Restaurant ~ (01364) 642343 ~ Children in bar until 9pm; must be accompanied on riverside terrace ~ Dogs allowed in bar and bedrooms ~ Open 11(11.30 Sun)-11(midnight Fri and Sat); 11-2.30, 6-11 Mon-Thurs in winter; closed 24-26 Dec ~ Bedrooms: £50S/£80S

Recommended by Mike Gorton, Brian and Anita Randall, Mayur Shah, Evelyn and Derek Walter

BUCKLAND BREWER
SS4220 MAP 1

Coach & Horses

Village signposted off A388 S of Monkleigh; OS Sheet 190 map reference 423206; EX39 5LU

Friendly old village pub with good mix of customers, open fires, and decent food and beer; good nearby walks

In the same friendly family for 20 years, this thatched old village pub remains popular with both regulars and visitors. The heavily beamed bar has comfortable seats (including a handsome antique settle) and a woodburning stove in the inglenook – there's also a good log fire in the big stone inglenook of the cosy lounge. A small back room has darts and pool. Well kept Cotleigh Golden Eagle, Fullers London Pride, and Shepherd Neame Spitfire on handpump, and around eight wines by the glass; games machine, skittle alley (that doubles as a function room), piped music, and occasional TV for sports. Tables on a terrace in front and in the side garden and nearby moorland walks and the beaches of Westward Ho!

⏣ Tasty bar food such as sandwiches, ham and egg, pork in honey and mustard, creamy spiced chicken, beef and stilton pie, bream fillets with tomato and pepper salsa and beef in wild mushroom sauce. *Starters/Snacks: £2.95 to £4.50. Main Courses: £6.50 to £14.95. Puddings: £2.95 to £3.95*

Free house ~ Licensees Oliver Wolfe and Nicola Barrass ~ Real ale ~ Bar food ~ Restaurant ~ (01237) 451395 ~ Well behaved children welcome ~ Dogs allowed in bar ~ Open 12-3, 6(7 Sun)-midnight; closed evenings 25 and 26 Dec

Recommended by Tony and Jill Radnor, the Didler, Brian and Karen Thomas, Revd D E and Mrs J A Shapland, Ryta Lyndley, Jean Barnett, David Lewis, Peter and Margaret Glenister, Bob and Margaret Holder

BUCKLAND MONACHORUM   SX4968   MAP 1

Drake Manor ⬤

Off A386 via Crapstone, just S of Yelverton roundabout; PL20 7NA

Nice little village pub with snug rooms, popular food, decent drinks, and pretty back garden

You can be sure of a friendly welcome from the long-serving landlady in this charming little pub and there's usually a good mix of both locals and those from further afield. The heavily beamed public bar on the left has brocade-cushioned wall seats, prints of the village from 1905 onwards, some horse tack and a few ship badges on the wall, and a really big stone fireplace with a woodburning stove; a small door leads to a low-beamed cubbyhole. The snug Drakes Bar has beams hung with tiny cups and big brass keys, a woodburning stove in an old stone fireplace, horsebrasses and stirrups, a fine stripped pine high-backed settle with a partly covered hood, and a mix of other seats around just four tables (the oval one is rather low). On the right is a small, beamed dining room with settles and tables on the flagstoned floor. Shove-ha'penny, darts, games machine and euchre. Courage Best, Greene King Abbot and Sharps Doom Bar on handpump, around 40 malt whiskies, and nine wines by the glass. The sheltered back garden – where there are picnic-sets – is prettily planted, and the floral displays in front are very attractive all year round.

⏣ As well as some interesting daily specials, the carefully sourced, popular bar food includes lunchtime baguettes, ploughman's and snacks like sausage and chips plus soup, a pâté of the day, sweet potato, spicy parsnip and chestnut bake, lasagne or chilli, steak and kidney pie, salmon fillet with spinach and pesto risotto, chicken wrapped in bacon with three cheeses, white wine and cream, and puddings such as sticky toffee pudding or gooseberry crunch. *Starters/Snacks: £3.50 to £4.75. Main Courses: £6.50 to £12.75. Puddings: £3.25 to £3.75*

Punch ~ Lease Mandy Robinson ~ Real ale ~ Bar food (12-2, 7-10(9.30 Sun)) ~ (01822) 853892 ~ Children in restaurant and cellar bar if eating ~ Dogs allowed in bar ~ Open 11.30-2.30 (3 Sat), 6.30-11; 12-10.30 Sun

Recommended by Emma Kingdon, Dr Peter Andrews, Tracey and Stephen Groves, Dr and Mrs P Truelove

CHAGFORD   SX7087   MAP 1

Ring o' Bells

Off A382 Moretonhampstead—Whiddon Down; TQ13 8AH

Friendly old pub with new landlord, good wine list and interesting bar food

A new licensee took over this quietly civilised old black and white pub just as we were going to press. There will be quite a few changes to the food side of things but it will remain a fine place for a quiet pint, too, with Butcombe Bitter, Fullers London Pride and a changing guest like Timothy Taylors Gold on handpump; the landlord is very keen on wine so the wine list will be greatly expanded. The oak-panelled bar has comfortable seats and tables, a log fire in the big fireplace and maybe some interesting old photographs. There's a sunny walled garden behind the pub and walks on the nearby moorland. Dogs are made at home with fresh water and perhaps a free dog biscuit. The bedrooms were on the point of being upgraded so no prices were available. A proper shelter for smokers will be up and running by the time this edition is published.

🍴 **Decent bar food includes sandwiches and ploughman's, soup, whitebait, deep-fried brie wedges with cranberry dressing, mushroom risotto, mussels in cider and cream, smoked pork steak with dijonnaise sauce, game pie or steak and kidney pudding, roast lamb with mint sauce, and puddings like chocolate and pear sponge or treacle tart.** *Starters/Snacks: £3.50 to £5.50. Main Courses: £8.95 to £12.95. Puddings: £3.50 to £3.95*

Free house ~ Licensee Tony Fey ~ Real ale ~ Bar food (12-2, 6-9) ~ (01647) 432466 ~ Children welcome ~ Dogs allowed in bar and bedrooms ~ Guitar player most Suns ~ Open 10.30-midnight ~ Bedrooms: /£50S

Recommended by Prof Keith and Mrs Jane Barber, Ken Flawn, John Stirrup, Michael and Ann Cole, Mr and Mrs D Moir

CHERITON BISHOP
SX7792 MAP 1

Old Thatch Inn
Village signposted from A30; EX6 6JH

Welcoming old pub, handy for the A30 with good food and beer, and a pretty garden

Closed for a while after a bad fire, this old-fashioned and friendly place has now been re-thatched and carefully refurbished. The traditionally furnished lounge and rambling beamed bar are separated by a large open stone fireplace (lit in the cooler months), and they keep Otter Ale, Sharps Doom Bar and a couple of guests like O'Hanlons Yellowhammer or Princetown Jail Ale on handpump and ten wines by the glass. The sheltered garden has lots of pretty flowering baskets and tubs.

🍴 **Good bar food includes lunchtime filled ciabattas, soup, terrine of wild boar with red onion confit, mussels in white wine and garlic cream, beer-battered cod, goats cheese and asparagus filo parcel with tomato coulis, chicken breast stuffed with leeks and peppers with chardonnay sauce, slow-braised lamb shank with rosemary jus, venison fillet with butterbean potato cake and spiced pear chutney, and puddings such as dark chocolate tart with Cointreau coulis or strawberry crème brûlée.** *Starters/Snacks: £4.50 to £7.95. Main Courses: £8.50 to £17.50. Puddings: £4.95*

Free house ~ Licensees David and Serena London ~ Real ale ~ Bar food ~ Restaurant ~ (01647) 24204 ~ Children welcome away from bar area ~ Dogs allowed in bar ~ Open 11.30-3, 6-11; 12-3, 6.30-10.30 Sun; closed 25 and 26 Dec ~ Bedrooms: £45B/£60B

Recommended by Dave Braisted, Ross and Christine Loveday, Andrew Curry, David and Ruth Shillitoe, Neil and Anita Christopher, Mr and Mrs A R Maden, Dr and Mrs M W A Haward, Martin and Pauline Jennings, David Crook, W M Paton, Dr and Mrs M E Wilson, Norman and Sarah Keeping, Mrs M N Grew

CLAYHIDON
ST1817 MAP 1

Merry Harriers 🍴 ♟ 🍺
3 miles from M5 junction 26: head towards Wellington; turn left at first roundabout signposted Ford Street and Hemyock, then after a mile turn left signposted Ford Street; at hilltop T junction, turn left towards Chard – pub is 1½ miles on right; EX15 3TR

Bustling dining pub with imaginative food, several real ales and quite a few wines by the glass; sizeable garden

By the time this edition is published the licensees here hope to have built an extension which will add new dining space and a disabled lavatory. There are several small linked green-carpeted areas with comfortably cushioned pews and farmhouse chairs, candles in bottles, a woodburning stove with a sofa beside it, and plenty of horsey and hunting prints and local wildlife pictures. Two dining areas have a brighter feel with quarry tiles and lightly timbered white walls. Cotleigh Harrier Lite and Otter Head and a couple of guests like Exmoor Hound Dog and St Austell Proper Job on handpump, 14 wines by the glass, local cider, 25 malt whiskies and a good range of spirits. Picnic-sets on a small terrace, with more in a sizeable garden sheltered by shrubs and the popular skittle alley; this is a good walking area.

▥ **Imaginative bar food using very carefully sourced local produce (they name all their suppliers on a special sheet) includes lunchtime sandwiches and ploughman's, soup, a plate of antipasti, potted duck liver and cranberry terrine with spiced orange chutney, tagliatelle with wild mushrooms, rocket and parmesan in a white wine and mushroom sauce, organic pork and apple sausages with onion gravy, lamb korma with home-made chutney, game casserole, fresh brixham cod in beer batter with home-made tartare sauce, duck breast stuffed with pheasant and a redcurrant sauce, daily specials, and puddings like chocolate tiramisu roulade or raspberry and vanilla crème brûlée.** *Starters/Snacks: £4.00 to £6.00. Main Courses: £6.00 to £10.00. Puddings: £4.00 to £4.50*

Free house ~ Licensees Peter and Angela Gatling ~ Real ale ~ Bar food (not Sun evening or Mon) ~ Restaurant ~ (01823) 421270 ~ Children welcome ~ Dogs allowed in bar ~ Open 12-3, 6.30-11; 12-3 Sun; closed Sun evening, Mon; 25 and 26 Dec

Recommended by Philip and Jude Simmons, PLC, Martin and Pauline Jennings, G K Smale, Mike Gorton, Revd D E and Mrs J A Shapland, C J Baker, I H G Busby, John and Enid Morris, Stuart Turner, Heather Coulson, Neil Cross, Bob and Margaret Holder

CLYST HYDON
ST0201 MAP 1

Five Bells

West of the village and just off B3176 not far from M5 junction 28; EX15 2NT

Attractive thatched pub with several distinctive, different areas, well liked food and drink, and carefully planted cottagey garden

Reached down narrow lanes, this attractive thatched pub is run by friendly licensees. The bar is divided at one end into different seating areas by brick and timber pillars: china jugs hang from big horsebrass-studded beams, there are many plates lining the shelves, lots of copper and brass, and a nice mix of dining chairs around small tables, with some comfortable pink plush banquettes on a little raised area. Past the inglenook fireplace is another big (but narrower) room they call the Long Barn, with a series of prints on the walls, a pine dresser at one end, and similar furnishings. Cotleigh Tawny, O'Hanlon's Royal Oak, and Otter Bitter on handpump, local farm cider and several wines by the glass; piped music, board games and books and toys for children. The immaculate cottagey front garden is a fine sight with its thousands of spring and summer flowers, big window boxes and pretty hanging baskets; up some steps is a sizeable flat lawn with picnic-sets, a play frame, and pleasant country views.

▥ **Popular bar food includes soup, filled baguettes, ploughman's, pheasant and chicken terrine with cranberry relish, crab cakes with sweet chilli dip, roasted mediterranean vegetable tart, steak and kidney suet pudding, beer-battered cod, a curry of the week, lamb shank with redcurrant and red wine sauce, duck breast with pink peppercorn sauce, and daily specials.** *Starters/Snacks: £3.95 to £5.50. Main Courses: £6.95 to £15.75. Puddings: £4.75 to £5.50*

Free house ~ Licensees Mr and Mrs R Shenton ~ Real ale ~ Bar food ~ (01884) 277288 ~ Children welcome away from bar ~ Live jazz second Weds of the month and folk duo fourth Weds of month ~ Open 11.30-3, 6.30-11; 12-3, 6.30-10.30 Sun; evening opening 7pm in winter

Recommended by Ian Phillips, Mike Gorton, Philip and Jude Simmons, Mike and Mary Carter, Ian and Deborah Carrington, Mr and Mrs A R Maden, Dr and Mrs A K Clarke, Alistair Forsyth

COCKWOOD
SX9780 MAP 1

Anchor ♀ ◀

Off, but visible from, A379 Exeter—Torbay; EX6 8RA

Extremely popular dining pub specialising in seafood (other choices available), with six real ales too

As popular as ever, this very well run place is almost as busy on a cold winter's day as it is in peak season – so you must arrive early to be sure of a table (and even a parking space). There's often a queue to get in but they do two sittings in the restaurant on winter weekends and every evening in summer to cope with the crowds. But despite the emphasis on food, there's still a pubby atmosphere, and they keep six real ales on handpump: Adnams Bitter and Broadside, Bass, Greene King Abbot, Otter Ale and Timothy Taylors Landlord. Also, a fine wine list of 300 (bin ends and reserves and 12 by the glass), 20 brandies and 20 ports, and 130 malt whiskies; lots of liqueur coffees too. The small, low-ceilinged, rambling rooms have black panelling, good-sized tables in various alcoves, and a cheerful winter coal fire in the snug; piped music and games machine. From the tables on the sheltered verandah you can look across the road to the bobbing yachts and crabbing boats in the harbour.

🍽 **Fantastic fish dishes include 30 different ways of serving mussels, 13 ways of serving scallops and five ways of serving oysters, as well as crab and brandy soup, smoked haddock steam pudding, seafood pancakes and various platters to share. Non-fishy dishes feature as well such as sandwiches, stilton and Guinness pâté, mushroom and asparagus wellington, chicken wrapped in bacon stuffed with garlic and herb cheese, lamb cutlets with port and redcurrant sauce, steak and kidney pudding; daily specials, and puddings.** *Starters/Snacks: £3.50 to £8.95. Main Courses: £4.95 to £13.75. Puddings: £4.25*

Heavitree ~ Tenants Mr Morgan and Miss Sanders ~ Real ale ~ Bar food (all day) ~ Restaurant ~ (01626) 890203 ~ Children in snug and restaurant ~ Dogs allowed in bar ~ Open 11-11; 12-10.30 Sun; closed evening 25 Dec

Recommended by Norman and Sarah Keeping, Graham and Glenis Watkins, Hugh Roberts, Gary Rollings, Meg and Colin Hamilton, Dr Ian S Morley, Di and Mike Gillam, Richard Fendick, Peter and Margaret Lodge, R J Walden, Mr and Mrs A R Maden, the Didler, John and Fiona McIlwain

COLEFORD
SS7701   MAP 1

New Inn 🍽 ♟ 🛏
Just off A377 Crediton—Barnstaple; EX17 5BZ

Thatched 13th-c inn with interestingly furnished areas, good food and real ales

At 600 years old, this must be one of the oldest 'new' inns around. It's an L-shaped building with the servery in the 'angle', and interestingly furnished areas leading off it: ancient and modern settles, spindleback chairs, plush-cushioned stone wall seats, some character tables – a pheasant worked into the grain of one – and carved dressers and chests; also, paraffin lamps, antique prints and old guns on the white walls and landscape plates on one of the beams, with pewter tankards on another. The chatty resident parrot Captain is most vocal when it's quieter. Exmoor Ale, Otter Ale and Sharps Doom Bar on handpump, local cider and several wines by the glass; good, cheerful service, piped music and darts. There are chairs, tables and umbrellas on decking under the willow tree along the stream with more on the terrace.

🍽 **Good bar food includes filled baguettes and ciabattas, ploughman's, soup, duck liver and orange pâté, smoked fish platter, local pork and garlic sausages with onion marmalade, gratinated brie, mushroom and onion pancake with tomato coulis, steak, kidney and mushroom pie, chicken supreme on a pâté croûton with madeira sauce and white chocolate cheesecake with orange jelly topping and profiteroles with clotted cream and chocolate sauce. The end-of-the-month pig roasts are popular.** *Starters/Snacks: £4.00 to £5.95. Main Courses: £5.95 to £15.50. Puddings: £3.50 to £5.95*

Free house ~ Licensees Simon and Melissa Renshaw ~ Real ale ~ Bar food (12-2, 7-10(9.30 Sun)) ~ Restaurant ~ (01363) 84242 ~ Children allowed away from bar ~ Dogs allowed in bar ~ Open 12-3, 6-11; 12-3, 7-10.30 Sun; closed 25 and 26 Dec ~ Bedrooms: £60B/£75B

Recommended by Mike and Mary Carter, Peter and Margaret Lodge, Peter Craske, Peter Burton, Bob and Angela Brooks, Betsy Brown, Nigel Flook, Mrs L M Lefeaux, Derek Harvey-Piper, Dennis Jenkin, John Robertson, Di and Mike Gillam

---

'Children welcome' means the pub says it lets children inside without any special restriction. If it allows them in, but to restricted areas such as an eating area or family room, we specify this. Some pubs may impose an evening time limit. We do not mention limits after 9pm as we assume children are home by then.

COMBEINTEIGNHEAD

SX9071 MAP 1

Wild Goose ♀ ◖

Just off unclassified coast road Newton Abbot—Shaldon, up hill in village; TQ12 4RA

Fine choice of real ales in well run, friendly pub with outdoor heaters in attractive garden

The sheltered and walled back garden here – beneath the 14th-c church tower – has plenty of seats and there are outdoor heaters for chillier evenings. Inside, the back beamed spacious lounge has a mix of wheelbacks, red plush dining chairs, a decent mix of tables, and french windows to the garden, with nice country views beyond. The front bar has seats in the window embrasures of the thick walls, flagstones in a small area by the door, some beams and standing timbers, and a step down on the right at the end, with dining chairs around the tables and a big old fireplace with an open log fire. There's a small carved oak dresser with a big white goose, piped music and board games and also a cosy section on the left with an old settee and comfortably well used chairs. A fine choice of regularly changing real ales on handpump from West Country breweries such as Otter, Palmers, O'Hanlons, Red Rock, Sharps, Skinners and Teignworthy, two village ciders and several wines by the glass.

🍴 **Homely bar food includes sandwiches, ploughman's, soup, garlic mushrooms, ham and egg, leek and mushroom crumble, fresh haddock in herb batter, steak and kidney pie, beef curry, daily specials and puddings.** *Starters/Snacks: £2.00 to £6.75. Main Courses: £5.00 to £16.25. Puddings: £3.95 to £4.50*

Free house ~ Licensees Jerry and Kate English ~ Real ale ~ Bar food ~ (01626) 872241 ~ Well behaved children in restaurant ~ Dogs allowed in bar ~ Live music Fri evenings ~ Open 11-2.30(3 Sat), 5.30-11(midnight Sat); 12-3, 7-11 Sun

Recommended by John and Helen Rushton, Ken Flawn, Mike and Mary Carter, Gerry and Rosemary Dobson, Prof H G Allen

CORNWORTHY

SX8255 MAP 1

Hunters Lodge

Off A381 Totnes—Kingsbridge ½ mile S of Harbertonford, turning left at Washbourne; can also be reached direct from Totnes, on the Ashprington—Dittisham road; TQ9 7ES

Friendly pub with good food cooked by the landlord, local beer, and nice garden

Well run and friendly, this bustling village pub is liked by both locals and visitors. The small low-ceilinged bar has two rooms with an engagingly pubby feel and a combination of wall seats, settles and captain's chairs around heavy elm tables; there's also a small and pretty cottagey dining room with a good log fire in its big 17th-c stone fireplace. Teignworthy Reel Ale and maybe Skinners Heligan Honey on handpump, 50 malt whiskies, a dozen wines by the glass, and local Hogwash cider. In summer, there is plenty of room to sit outside, either at the picnic-sets on a big lawn with extensive views or on the flower-filled terrace closer to the pub.

🍴 **Cooked by the landlord, the good food might include lunchtime sandwiches and ploughman's as well as soup, chicken and date pâté with apricot chutney, breaded whitebait with sweet chilli dipping sauce, sesame battered brixham cod fillet, a trio of sausages with mustard mash and onion gravy, wild mushroom tagliatelle with garlic, pesto and parmesan, gammon and eggs, and puddings such as walnut, stem ginger and dark chocolate terrine with rasberry coulis or rosemary crème brûlée.** *Starters/Snacks: £3.00 to £6.95. Main Courses: £6.95 to £17.95. Puddings: £3.00 to £4.50*

Free house ~ Licensees J Reen and G Rees ~ Real ale ~ Bar food ~ Restaurant ~ (01803) 732204 ~ Children welcome ~ Dogs welcome ~ Open 11.30-3, 6.30-11; 12-3, 7-10.30 Sun

Recommended by J P Greaves, Neil Ingoe, Simon Hollis, M G Hart, Richard and Sheila Brooks, Simon Rodway, John Day

---

We say if we know a pub allows dogs.

CULMSTOCK   ST1013   MAP 1

Culm Valley 🍴 🍷 ☕

B3391, off A38 E of M5 junction 27; EX15 3JJ

Quirky dining pub with imaginative food, up to ten real ales, a fantastic wine list, and outside seats overlooking River Culm

There's a good lively atmosphere and friendly, helpful staff in this unfussy country pub. It's not the place for those who like everything neat and tidy – and indeed it's actually rather idiosyncratic and scruffy but that, as far as many of our readers feel, is part of its appeal. The salmon-coloured bar has a hotch-potch of modern and unrenovated furnishings, a big fireplace with some china above it, newspapers, and a long elm bar counter; further along is a dining room with a chalkboard menu, a small front conservatory, and leading off here, a little oak-floored room with views into the kitchen. A larger back room has paintings by local artists for sale. Board games and a small portable TV for occasional rugby, rowing and racing events. The landlord and his brother import wines from smaller french vineyards, so you can count on a few of those (they offer 50 wines by the glass), as well as some unusual french fruit liqueurs, somerset cider brandies, vintage rum, good sherries and madeira, local ciders, and up to ten well kept real ales tapped from the cask: Blackawton Original Bitter, Branscombe Vale Branoc, Cotleigh 25, Cottage Frosty Whippet, Hop Back Crop Circle, O'Hanlons Yellowhammer, St Austell Tribute and Spire Stonehenge. They hold an end of May bank holiday weekend beer festival with 23 different ales; chess, cribbage, Spoof and boules. Outside, tables are very attractively positioned overlooking the bridge and the River Culm. The gents' is in an outside yard. They may be building a special shed for smokers; boules is planned.

🍽 **Enjoyable, imaginative food using as much free-range and organic local produce as possible includes sandwiches, soup, a selection of tapas, duck terrine with prunes and armagnac, scallops with pancetta and celeriac purée, moules marinière, chicken breast with mushrooms, ham and goats cheese butter, poached cod with puy lentils and salsa verde, beef braised in red wine with horseradish mash, whole grilled lemon sole with lemon grass butter, and puddings like treacle and lemon tart and iced hazelnut parfait.** *Starters/Snacks: £5.00 to £8.00. Main Courses: £8.00 to £16.00. Puddings: £5.00*

Free house ~ Licensee Richard Hartley ~ Real ale ~ Bar food (not Sun evening) ~ Restaurant ~ No credit cards ~ (01884) 840354 ~ Children allowed away from main bar ~ Dogs welcome ~ Occasional impromptu piano and irish music ~ Open 12-3, 6-11(may open all day on fine summer days); 11-11 Sat; 12-10.30 Sun ~ Bedrooms: £30B/£55B

Recommended by MB, David Collison, S G N Bennett, Michael Cleeve, Brian and Anita Randall, John and Fiona Merritt, Tony and Tracy Constance, Jacquie Jones, Adrian Johnson, Sue Demont, Tim Barrow, John and Fiona McIlwain, Peter Craske, Dennis and Gill Keen

DALWOOD   ST2400   MAP 1

Tuckers Arms

Village signposted off A35 Axminster—Honiton; keep on past village; EX13 7EG

Pretty, thatched inn with long-serving licensees and lovely summer hanging baskets and tubs

In summer, the hanging baskets, flowering tubs and window boxes in front of this pretty, cream-washed and thatched old inn are lovely and there's a covered pergola with outdoor heating. Inside, the fine flagstoned bar has a lot of atmosphere, plenty of beams, a random mixture of dining chairs, window seats, and wall settles (including a high-backed winged black one) and a log fire in the inglenook fireplace. The back bar has an enormous collection of miniature bottles. Greene King Old Speckled Hen, Otter Bitter and Wadworths 6X on handpump, a dozen wines by the glass and farm cider; food service can slow down at peak times. Piped music and skittle alley.

🍽 **Well liked bar food includes filled baguettes or granary torpedos, soup, home-made pâté, kidneys in garlic or smoked haddock rarebit, pork sausages with black pudding and eggs, steaks, and puddings such as date and banana sponge pudding or treacle and walnut tart; from a more elaborate menu they offer two- and three-course set menus.** *Starters/Snacks: £4.25 to £6.95. Main Courses: £8.95 to £17.95. Puddings: £4.25*

Free house ~ Licensees David and Kate Beck ~ Real ale ~ Bar food ~ Restaurant ~
(01404) 881342 ~ Children in restaurant ~ Open 12-3, 6.30-11; 12-3, 7-10.30 Sun ~
Bedrooms: £42.50S/£69.50S

Recommended by Frogeye, MB, Stephen and Jean Curtis, Pete Walker, Mr and Mrs W Mills, Anthony Longden,
Bob and Margaret Holder, Mike Gorton, Anthony Freemantle

DARTMOUTH   SX8751   MAP 1

Cherub
Higher Street; TQ6 9RB

**Handsome old building with bustling bar and plenty of atmosphere; can get busy at peak
times**

In summer this striking old inn – Dartmouth's oldest building – is full of visiting
holidaymakers; locals prefer it at quieter times. The bustling bar has tapestried seats
under creaky heavy beams, leaded-light windows, a big stone fireplace with a
woodburning stove, and Sharps Doom Bar, a beer named for the pub and a changing
guest on handpump; quite a few malt whiskies and 14 wines by the glass. Upstairs is the
fine, low-ceilinged restaurant; piped music. The building is a fine sight with each of the
two heavily timbered upper floors jutting further out than the one below; the hanging
baskets are very pretty.

🍴 **Good bar food includes sandwiches (the crab ones are well liked), soup, smoked
haddock in a saffron and herb sauce topped with cheese, local scallops, beer-battered
cod, lambs liver and bacon on bubble and squeak, bangers and mash with apple and
honey sauce and pasta with langoustines, pancetta, basil and sunblush tomatoes.**
Starters/Snacks: £4.95 to £7.95. Main Courses: £9.95 to £14.95. Puddings: £4.95

Free house ~ Licensee Laurie Scott ~ Real ale ~ Bar food ~ Restaurant ~ (01803) 832571 ~
Children allowed only in restaurant and must be over 5 ~ Dogs allowed in bar ~ Open 11
(12 Sun)-11; 11-2.30, 5-11 in winter

Recommended by Paul and Shirley White, John and Helen Rushton, David Carr, Di and Mike Gillam,
Emma Kingdon, P Dawn, John Evans, Sue Heath, Dr and Mrs M E Wilson, Jenny and Brian Seller, W W Burke,
John Day

DODDISCOMBSLEIGH   SX8586   MAP 1

Nobody Inn ★ ♀ 🍺
Village signposted off B3193, opposite northernmost Christow turn-off; EX6 7PS

**Extraordinary choice of wines and whiskies plus local ciders and beer in popular old pub
with long-serving landlord**

Many of our readers tend to come back to this fine old pub again and again and it's a
popular place to stay too. They keep an extraordinary range of drinks and the pub wine
cellar must be one of the best in the country: around 700 wines by the bottle and 20 by
the glass, 260 whiskies, Red Rock, Teignworthy Reel Ale and a beer named for the pub on
handpump or tapped from the cask, local straw-pressed cider, local organic apple juice
and real lemonade. The two rooms of the lounge bar have handsomely carved antique
settles, windsor and wheelback chairs, benches, carriage lanterns hanging from the
beams, and guns and hunting prints in a snug area by one of the big inglenook
fireplaces. There are picnic-sets on the terrace with views of the surrounding wooded hill
pastures. As well as offering B&B bedrooms (which are being refurbished), there is a self-
catered tithe barn too. The medieval stained glass in the local church is some of the best
in the West Country. No children.

🍴 **Carefully locally sourced bar food (which includes up to 75 west country cheeses) such
as sandwiches, ploughman's, soup, duck liver pâté, faggots and beer gravy, fish pie, roasted
mediterranean vegetables with couscous and goats cheese, belly pork with savoy cabbage,
smoked bacon and mustard sauce, steak and kidney suet pudding, venison casserole, and
puddings like warm treacle tart of passion fruit crème brûlée with coconut shortbread.**
Starters/Snacks: £4.50 to £6.90. Main Courses: £6.90 to £11.00. Puddings: £3.50 to £4.50

Free house ~ Licensee Nick Borst-Smith ~ Real ale ~ Bar food (12-2, 7-10) ~ Restaurant ~ (01647) 252394 ~ Open 12-2.30, 6-11; 12-3, 7-10.30 Sun; closed 25 Dec, evening 26 Dec, 1 Jan ~ Bedrooms: £25(£45B)/£40(£80B)

Recommended by J L Wedel, Andrew Shore, Maria Williams, Adrian Johnson, Gene and Kitty Rankin, Peter Burton, J D O Carter, Betsy Brown, Nigel Flook, Simon Fox, Phyl and Jack Street, Tracey and Stephen Groves, Gareth Lewis, Steve Whalley, the Didler, Richard J Mullarkey, Sue Demont, Tim Barrow, Mrs Bridget Cushion, John Brooks, Dr and Mrs M E Wilson, Lynn Sharpless

EAST BUDLEIGH

SY0684   MAP 1

Sir Walter Raleigh

High Street; EX9 7ED

Lively local in pretty village with low-beamed chatty bar, good food and decent beers

Run by a friendly young landlady, this is an unfussy little local with a good bustling atmosphere. The low-beamed bar has lots of books on shelves, Adnams Broadside, Otter Bitter and St Austell Tribute on handpump and plenty of chatty customers. There's an attractive restaurant down a step from the bar and seats in the attractive garden. The fine village church has a unique collection of carved oak bench ends and the pub is handy for Bicton Park gardens. Raleigh himself was born at nearby Hayes Barton, and educated in a farmhouse 300 yards away. Parking is about 100 yards away. No children.

🍴 **Good, popular bar food includes sandwiches, soup, sardines in garlic butter, baked goats cheese en croûte, mushroom, spinach and stilton tagliatelle, smoked chicken and pickled cucumber, steak, mushroom and Guinness pudding, trout fillets with a medley of shellfish, lamb shank with minted mash, and puddings such as syrup sponge and custard and raspberry soufflé.** *Starters/Snacks: £3.75 to £5.25. Main Courses: £7.95 to £11.95. Puddings: £3.95*

Enterprise ~ Lease Lindsay Mason ~ Real ale ~ Bar food (12-2, 6-9; not Sun evening) ~ Restaurant ~ (01395) 442510 ~ Dogs allowed in bar ~ Open 11.45-2.30, 6-11; 12-2.30, 7-10.30 Sun

Recommended by Dr and Mrs M E Wilson, John and Enid Morris, Mr and Mrs A R Maden, Mike Gorton, Steve Whalley, Paul and Shirley White

EXETER

SX9193   MAP 1

Imperial 🏚 £

New North Road (St David's Hill on Crediton/Tiverton road, above St David's station); EX4 4AH

19th-c mansion in own grounds with interesting seating areas and cheap food and drink; very popular with students

The setting for this early 19th-c mansion is impressive – it stands in its own six-acre hillside park and is reached along a sweeping drive; plenty of picnic-sets in the grounds and elegant garden furniture in the attractive cobbled courtyard. Inside, there's a light and airy former orangery with an unusual lightly mirrored end wall, and various different areas including a couple of little clubby side bars, a left-hand bar that looks into the orangery, and a fine ex-ballroom filled with elaborate plasterwork and gilding brought here in the 1920s from Haldon House (a Robert Adam stately home that was falling on hard times). The furnishings give Wetherspoons' usual solid well spaced comfort, and there are plenty of interesting pictures and other things to look at; readers this year have felt some housekeeping is in order. They always have Greene King Abbot and Marstons Pedigree on handpump plus Exmoor Stag, O'Hanlons Yellowhammer, Otter Bright, Sharps Doom Bar and up to nine other guests. The place is often hopping with students. Two outside sheltered and heated smoking areas.

🍴 **Standard bar food includes filled paninis, meaty or vegetarian burgers (the price also includes a pint), battered cod, ham and eggs, mediterranean pasta bake and sausages and mash.** *Starters/Snacks: £1.99 to £4.69. Main Courses: £4.99 to £7.39. Puddings: £1.49 to £2.89*

Wetherspoons ~ Manager Paul Dixey ~ Real ale ~ Bar food (all day) ~ (01392) 434050 ~
Children allowed away from bar until 9pm ~ Open 9am-midnight(1am Sat)

*Recommended by R T and J C Moggridge, Donna and Roger, Mike Gorton, Ian Phillips, the Didler, Dr and Mrs
A K Clarke, Pete Walker*

EXMINSTER
SX9686   MAP 1

Turf Hotel ★

*Follow the signs to the Swan's Nest, signposted from A379 S of village, then continue to
end of track, by gates; park, and walk right along canal towpath – nearly a mile; there's a
fine seaview out to the mudflats at low tide; EX6 8EE*

**Remote but very popular waterside pub with fine choice of drinks, super summer
barbecues and lots of space in big garden**

You cannot reach this very popular, isolated pub by car. You must either walk (which
takes about 20 minutes along the ship canal) or cycle and or catch a 60-seater boat
which brings people down the Exe estuary from Topsham quay (15-minute trip, adult £3,
child £2); there's also a canal boat from Countess Wear Swing Bridge every lunchtime.
Best to phone the pub for all sailing times. For those arriving in their own boat there is a
large pontoon as well as several moorings. It's not huge inside so you must get there
early to be sure of a seat and the tables in the bay windows are much prized; the sea and
estuary birds are fun to watch at low tide. The end room has a slate floor, pine walls,
built-in seats, lots of photographs of the pub, and a woodburning stove; along a corridor
(with an eating room to one side) is a simply furnished room with wood-plank seats
around tables on the stripped wooden floor. Otter Bitter and Ale, O'Hanlons
Yellowhammer, Red Rock and Topsham & Exminster Ferryman tapped from the cask. Also,
local Green Valley cider, local juices, 20 wines by the glass (and local wine too), and jugs
of Pimms. The main outdoor barbecue area is much used in good weather and there are
plenty of picnic-sets spread around the big garden. The children's play area was built
using a lifeboat from a liner that sank off the Scilly Isles around 100 years ago. Although
the pub and garden do get packed in good weather and there are inevitable queues, the
staff remain friendly and efficient.

🍴 **Interesting bar food using organic and local produce includes lunchtime sandwiches,
toasties and filled baked potatoes as well as various tapas, soup, antipasti platters, thai
fishcakes with lime mayonnaise, spicy chilli on tortilla chips with melted cheese, soured
cream and jalapenos, beer-battered hake, mushroom, spinach and ricotta cannelloni, thai
chicken curry and bass on a potato and chorizo cream; puddings such as sticky toffee
pudding or fruit crumble.** *Starters/Snacks: £4.25 to £7.95. Main Courses: £7.95 to £12.95.
Puddings: £4.00*

Free house ~ Licensees Clive and Ginny Redfern ~ Real ale ~ Bar food (12-2(3 weekends),
7-9(9.30 Fri and Sat); not Sun evening) ~ (01392) 833128 ~ Children welcome ~ Dogs welcome
~ Open 11.30-11; 12-10.30 Sun; closed Dec-Feb

*Recommended by Dr and Mrs M E Wilson, Mike Gorton, J D O Carter, the Didler, Phyl and Jack Street, Neil and
Lorna Mclaughlan, Peter Salmon*

HAYTOR VALE
SX7777   MAP 1

Rock ★ 🍴 🛏

*Haytor signposted off B3387 just W of Bovey Tracey, on good moorland road to Widecombe;
TQ13 9XP*

**Civilised Dartmoor inn at its most informal at lunchtime; super food, comfortable
bedrooms, and pretty garden**

At lunchtime this civilised and neatly kept place gives a nod towards pubbiness. It's on
the edge of Dartmoor National Park and is much enjoyed by our readers after a walk for a
pint of St Austell Dartmoor Best or changing guest beer on handpump and an informal
meal. In the evening though it becomes a restaurant-with-rooms with all space given

over to the excellent food. The two communicating, partly panelled bar rooms have lots of dark wood and red plush, polished antique tables with candles and fresh flowers, old-fashioned prints and decorative plates on the walls, and warming winter log fires (the main fireplace has a fine Stuart fireback. There are seats in the large, pretty garden opposite the inn, with tables and chairs on a small terrace next to the pub itself. The bedrooms are comfortable with good facilities but some are up steep stairs. Parking is not always easy.

🍴 Served by helpful, welcoming staff the lunchtime bar food includes filled ciabatta or focaccia bread, ploughman's, soup, chicken liver parfait with red onion marmalade, local pork and apple sausages with red wine gravy, wild mushroom and chestnut risotto, beef in ale pie, chicken curry, bass with chilli and lemon butter and puddings like white chocolate panna cotta and treacle and walnut tart. *Starters/Snacks: £4.95 to £7.00. Main Courses: £11.95 to £16.00. Puddings: £5.25*

Free house ~ Licensee Christopher Graves ~ Real ale ~ Bar food ~ Restaurant ~ (01364) 661305 ~ Children welcome ~ Dogs allowed in bedrooms ~ Open 10.30(12 Sun)-11; closed 25 and 26 Dec ~ Bedrooms: £66.95B/£95.95B

Recommended by Mike Gorton, Dr Ian S Morley, Frank Plater, Lesley Piekielniak, B J Harding, Mr and Mrs D J Nash, Mr and Mrs A R Maden, Brian and Bett Cox, Peter and Margaret Lodge, Doug Kennedy, Pat and Robert Watt, Barry and Anne, James and Ginette Read, M G Hart, Lisa Robertson, Mrs Viv Haigh, Tom and Ruth Rees, Bill Smith

HOLBETON   SX6150   MAP 1

Dartmoor Union
Village signposted off A379 W of A3121 junction; Fore Street; PL8 1NE

Stylish spreading bar with contemporary furnishings and smart flower arrangements, own-brewed beers, modern food and neat staff

The microbrewery behind this civilised place is now up and running and producing Union Pride and Jacks and they also keep Otter Ale and St Austell Dartmoor IPA on handpump; nine wines by the glass from a carefully chosen list. The rather chic spreading bar has a nice mix of dining chairs around several wooden tables on the stripped wood floor, squashy leather sofas and armchairs in front of the log fire in the brick fireplace, witticisms and old photographs of the village on the elegant, pale yellow walls, and a dark wood, brass and black slate bar counter; board games. The restaurant leads off here with big yachting photographs by Beken on the dark red walls and close-set white-clothed tables and high-backed leather dining chairs; stylish flower arrangements. The atmosphere is chatty and relaxed, there's a good mix of customers and neat young staff all dressed in black. Smart teak furniture on a sheltered back terrace. There's a back car park that may not be signed from the street and no inn sign – just a brass plaque.

🍴 Good modern bar food includes sandwiches, soup, tempura soft shell crab with mango salsa, seared scallops with smoked haddock brandade, crispy bacon and lemon mayonnaise, tagliatelle with roasted butternut squash, spinach, mascarpone and walnut pesto, monkfish wrapped in prosciutto with romesco sauce, lamb chump with braised lamb belly, chickpea purée and spinach and rosemary jus, saddle of wild venison with chocolate jus and puddings such as hot chocolate fondant with chocolate ice-cream or vanilla panna cotta with rhubarb soup; set two- and three-course lunch too.
Starters/Snacks: £3.95 to £5.95. Main Courses: £8.95 to £16.95. Puddings: £4.25 to £5.25

Wykeham Inns ~ Licensee Tony Richardson ~ Real ale ~ Bar food ~ Restaurant ~ (01752) 830288 ~ Children in restaurant and bar until 9pm ~ Dogs allowed in bar ~ Open 12-3, 5.30-11; 12-10.30 Sun
Recommended by John Evans, Keith and Margaret Kettell, David M Cundy, John Lane, J Crosby

---

Stars after the name of a pub show exceptional character and appeal.
They don't mean extra comfort. And they are nothing to do with food quality, for which
there's a separate knife-and-fork symbol. Even quite a basic pub
can win stars, if it's individual enough.

HOLNE

SX7069   MAP 1

Church House

Signed off B3357 W of Ashburton; TQ13 7SJ

Medieval inn on Dartmoor with pubby food, real ales, and log fires in simply furnished bars

A new licensee has taken over this medieval inn but readers are happy to report that little has changed. It's just five minutes from open moorland and there are fine views from the pillared porch and plenty of good surrounding walks. The lower bar has stripped pine panelling and an 18th-c curved elm settle, and is separated from the lounge bar by a 16th-c heavy oak partition; open log fires in both rooms. Butcombe Bitter and Teignworthy Reel Ale on handpump, several wines by the glass, and organic cider, apple juice and ginger beer; darts. There may be morris men and clog dancers in the summer. Charles Kingsley (of *Water Babies* fame) was born in the village. The church is well worth a visit.

🍴 Bar food includes lunchtime sandwiches and snacks and evening choices such as soup, greek salad, smoked haddock fishcake, rabbit casserole, braised lamb shank, fish pie, venison steak with marsala gravy, daily specials, and puddings. *Starters/Snacks: £3.95 to £6.25. Main Courses: £6.50 to £15.00. Puddings: £3.95*

Free house ~ Licensee A Wright ~ Real ale ~ Bar food (not Sun evening or Mon in winter) ~ Restaurant ~ (01364) 631208 ~ Children welcome but not in bar after 8pm ~ Dogs welcome ~ Open 12-3, 6.30-11(11.30 Sat); winter evening opening Mon-Sat 7pm, Sun 9pm ~ Bedrooms: £34S/£58(£68B)

Recommended by P and J Shapley, Gerry and Rosemary Dobson, Mike Gorton, Phil and Sally Gorton, R J Walden

HORNDON

SX5280   MAP 1

Elephants Nest 🍺

If coming from Okehampton on A386 turn left at Mary Tavy Inn, then left after about ½ mile; pub signposted beside Mary Tavy Inn, then Horndon signposted; on the Ordnance Survey Outdoor Leisure Map it's named as the New Inn; PL19 9NQ

Isolated old inn surrounded by Dartmoor walks, some interesting original features, and decent beers and food

The garden behind this 400-year-old inn is being extended this year to provide extra seating. From here you look over dry-stone walls to the pastures of Dartmoor's lower slopes and the rougher moorland above; plenty of surrounding walks. Inside, the bar has original stone walls, flagstones, three woodburning stoves and a beam-and-board ceiling; there's also a dining room and garden room. Palmers IPA and Copper Ale, Princetown Jail Ale and a guest like Cotleigh Golden Seahawk on handpump, farm cider and a few wines by the glass; piped music. More reports please.

🍴 Bar food at lunchtime includes soup, goats cheese and roasted vegetable ciabatta, home-made burger with onion marmalade and fresh beer-battered haddock with evening choices like chicken liver parfait, antipasti plate, steak and kidney pudding, pork tenderloin in dijon mustard and cranberry cream fish pie, and puddings such as treacle tart or steamed chocolate pudding with chocolate sauce. *Starters/Snacks: £3.95 to £6.95. Main Courses: £8.95 to £16.95. Puddings: £4.25 to £4.75*

Free house ~ Licensee Hugh Cook ~ Real ale ~ Bar food (12-2.15, 6.30-9) ~ (01822) 810273 ~ Children welcome ~ Dogs welcome ~ Open 12-3, 6.30-11 ~ Bedrooms: /£75B

Recommended by Peter and Margaret Lodge, Emma Kingdon, John and Bernadette Elliott

---

Bedroom prices normally include full english breakfast, VAT and any inclusive service charge that we know of. Prices before the '/' are for single people, after for two people in double or twin (B includes a private bath, S a private shower). If there is no '/', the prices are only for twin or double rooms (as far as we know there are no singles).

IDDESLEIGH

SS5608 MAP 1

Duke of York ★ ♀

B3217 Exbourne—Dolton; EX19 8BG

Unfussy and exceptionally friendly pub with simply furnished bars, popular food, fair choice of drinks, and quirky bedrooms

For many people, this is just how pubs should be. Friendly, chatty locals in their wellies (with maybe a dog or two) sitting around a roaring log fire, a warmly welcoming and hospitable landlord and flower posies on the tables. The enjoyably unspoilt bar has a lot of homely character: rocking chairs, cushioned wall benches built into the wall's black-painted wooden dado, stripped tables and other simple country furnishings and well kept Adnams Broadside, Cotleigh Tawny, and Sharps Doom Bar or Teignworthy Reel Ale tapped from the cask, and quite a few wines by the glass. It does get pretty cramped at peak times; darts. There's also a dining room. Through a small coach arch is a little back garden with some picnic-sets. The bedrooms are quirky and in some cases very far from smart, so their appeal is very much to people who enjoy taking the rough with the smooth.

🍴 Good, honest, fairly priced bar food – using the landlord's own rare-breed beef – includes sandwiches, ploughman's, soup, chicken liver pâté, sausage or ham with eggs, liver and bacon, leek and mushroom bake, steak and kidney or fish pie, various curries and casseroles, double lamb chop with rosemary and garlic gravy and puddings. *Starters/Snacks: £4.00 to £7.00. Main Courses: £6.50 to £13.50. Puddings: £3.50 to £4.50*

Free house ~ Licensees Jamie Stuart and Pippa Hutchinson ~ Real ale ~ Bar food (all day) ~ Restaurant ~ (01837) 810253 ~ Children welcome ~ Dogs allowed in bar and bedrooms ~ Open 11-11(midnight Sat); 12-10.30 Sun; closed evening 25 Dec ~ Bedrooms: £40B/£70B

Recommended by Anthony Longden, Steve Crick, Helen Preston, R J Walden, the Didler, John Urquhart, Paul and Ursula Randall, Sara Fulton, Roger Baker, Rona Murdoch, P and J Shapley, Mrs Susan Clifford, Ruth Hooper, Mayur Shah, John and Mary Ling, PL, Jamie Turner, Peter Craske, Maurice Ricketts, Ken and Janet Bracey

KINGSTON

SX6347 MAP 1

Dolphin 🛏

Off B3392 S of Modbury (can also be reached from A379 W of Modbury); TQ7 4QE

Peaceful old pub with walks down to the sea, cheerful atmosphere, and decent drinks and food

This is a peaceful little 16th-c inn not far from the sea and with nice surrounding tracks to walk along. Several knocked-through beamed rooms have amusing drawings and photographs on the walls and rustic tables and cushioned seats and settles around their bared stone walls. The cheerful landlady offers a warm welcome to all. Courage Best, Sharps Doom Bar and maybe Teignworthy Springtide on handpump. There are some seats and tables outside. More reports please.

🍴 Bar food at lunchtime includes sandwiches, ploughman's, soup, steak in ale pie, beer-battered cod, pasta with fresh tomato sauce and curry with evening dishes like garlic and chilli king prawns, crispy belly of pork on onions, apple and sage and fillet steak with roquefort sauce, and puddings such as bread and butter pudding. *Starters/Snacks: £5.25 to £7.95. Main Courses: £10.25 to £16.95. Puddings: £4.25 to £5.75*

Punch ~ Lease Janice Male ~ Real ale ~ Bar food (12-2.30, 6-9; not Sun evening or Mon Jan/Feb) ~ (01548) 810314 ~ Children welcome ~ Open 12-3, 6-11; 12-3, 7-10.30 Sun ~ Bedrooms: £42.50B/£60B

Recommended by Alan and Anne Driver, Roger Wain-Heapy, Keith and Margaret Kettell, Tracey and Stephen Groves

LUSTLEIGH

SX7881   MAP 1

Cleave

Village signposted off A382 Bovey Tracey—Moretonhampstead; TQ13 9TJ

In a popular beauty spot so best to arrive early at this thatched pub with its roaring log fire and well liked food and drink; pretty summer garden

The licensees of this charming thatched pub offer a warm welcome to all their customers and readers report that they are genuinely kind to children too. The low-ceilinged lounge bar has a roaring log fire, attractive antique high-backed settles, cushioned wall seats and wheelback chairs around the tables on its patterned carpet and granite walls. A second bar has similar furnishings, a large dresser, harmonium, an HMV gramophone, and prints and there's a family room with toys for children. Adnams Explorer, Otter Ale and Wadworths 6X on handpump, quite a few malt whiskies, several wines by the glass and local organic soft drinks. In summer, you can sit in the sheltered garden and the hanging baskets and flower beds are lovely. Until the car parking field in the village is opened during the summer, parking can be very difficult.

🍴 **Attractively presented bar food includes sandwiches, soup, grilled goats cheese on mixed leaves, tiger prawn cocktail, home-cooked ham with fries, spinach, hazelnut, field mushroom and truffle oil pie, smoked haddock and bacon fishcakes with lemon and tarragon sauce, calves liver with red wine and rosemary gravy, roast beef and yorkshire pudding and half honey-roast duckling with orange sauce.** *Starters/Snacks: £2.95 to £5.95. Main Courses: £6.50 to £14.95. Puddings: £3.95 to £4.95*

Heavitree ~ Tenant A Perring ~ Real ale ~ Bar food (not Mon) ~ (01647) 277223 ~ Children in family room ~ Dogs allowed in bar ~ Open 11.30-3, 6(6.30 winter Sat)-11; 11.30-11(10.30 Sun) Sat; 11.30-4 Sun in winter; closed Mon
Recommended by James and Ginette Read, Mr and Mrs D J Nash, Glenn and Gillian Miller, David and Paula Russell, Dr and Mrs M E Wilson

LYDFORD

SX5184   MAP 1

Castle Inn

Off A386 Okehampton—Tavistock; EX20 4BH

Pink-washed old inn next to ruined castle with plenty of character in two bars, homely food and fair choice of drinks

After a walk in the beautiful nearby river gorge (owned by the National Trust; closed November-Easter), this pleasant pink-washed Tudor inn is just the place for a drink. The twin-roomed bar has country kitchen chairs, high-backed winged settles and old captain's chairs around mahogany tripod tables on big slate flagstones. One room has low lamp-lit beams, a sizeable open fire, masses of brightly decorated plates, some Hogarth prints, and, near the serving counter, seven Lydford pennies hammered out in the old Saxon mint in the reign of Ethelred the Unready, in the 11th c. The bar area has a bowed ceiling with low beams, a polished slate flagstone floor, and a stained-glass door with the famous Three Hares; there's also a snug with high-backed settles. Bass, Fullers London Pride and Otter Ale on handpump, and several wines by the glass; darts and board games.

🍴 **Bar food includes sandwiches, filled baked potatoes, ploughman's and pubby dishes such as steak and kidney pie, wild boar and apple burger with bacon and smoked cheese and scampi but you can also eat off the more elaborate menu: prawn and crab salad, butternut squash and feta cheese strudel, chicken in wild mushroom sauce on a potato and leek rösti, rump of lamb with white wine, orange and thyme sauce, and puddings like lemon brioche or sticky toffee pudding with fudge sauce.** *Starters/Snacks: £4.25 to £5.95. Main Courses: £9.25 to £13.95. Puddings: £3.95*

Heavitree ~ Tenant Richard Davies ~ Real ale ~ Bar food ~ Restaurant ~ (01822) 820241 ~ Children allowed in snug, restaurant and lounge ~ Dogs allowed in bar and bedrooms ~ Open 11.30-11; 12-10.30 Sun ~ Bedrooms: £45B/£65B
Recommended by Dr Nigel Bowles, James and Ginette Read, Andrea Rampley, Mrs M Ainley, Michael and Ann Cole, David and Paula Russell, Mrs J H S Lang, Tony and Tracy Constance, David Eberlin, Dr and Mrs A K Clarke

MARLDON

SX8663 MAP 1

Church House 🍴 ♈

Just off A380 NW of Paignton; TQ3 1SL

Spreading bar plus several other rooms in pleasant inn, well liked drinks and bar food, and seats on three terraces

This year, a new restaurant displaying art by local artists has been opened in an old barn next to this attractive inn. In the main building, the spreading bar has several different areas that radiate off the big semi-circular bar counter. There are interesting windows, some beams, dark pine chairs around solid tables on the turkey carpet and yellow leather bar chairs; leading off here is a cosy little candlelit room with just four tables on the bare-board floor, a dark wood dado and stone fireplace. There's also a restaurant with a large stone fireplace. At the other end of the building, a similarly interesting room is split into two parts with a stone floor in one bit and a wooden floor in another (which has a big woodburning stove). Bass, Fullers London Pride, Otter Ale, and St Austell Dartmoor Best on handpump, and ten wines by the glass; piped music. Picnic-sets on three grassy terraces behind the pub. More reports please.

🍴 **Well liked bar food includes sandwiches, soup, coarse pâté with apple and cranberry chutney, warm potato and spinach tartlet topped with cornish brie, chicken supreme with tarragon cream sauce, pork loin steak with spicy sauce, pasta with courgettes, tomatoes and parmesan, slow-cooked lamb shoulder with port, orange and redcurrant sauce and king prawns in garlic butter.** *Starters/Snacks: £5.50 to £7.50. Main Courses: £9.00 to £18.50. Puddings: £5.50 to £7.50*

Enterprise ~ Lease Julian Cook ~ Real ale ~ Bar food (12-2, 6.30-9.30) ~ Restaurant ~ (01803) 558279 ~ Children welcome ~ Dogs allowed in bar ~ Open 11.30-2.30, 5-11; 11.30-3, 5.30-11.30 Sat; 12-3, 5.30-10.30 Sun
Recommended by Simon Fox, Chris Howland-Harris

MEAVY

SX5467 MAP 1

Royal Oak

Off B3212 E of Yelverton; PL20 6PJ

Pleasant old pub with friendly landlord, country furnishings and decent food and drink

In a pretty Dartmoor-edge village, this partly 15th-c pub has seats on the green in front and by the building itself. Inside, the heavy-beamed L-shaped bar has pews from the church, red plush banquettes, and old agricultural prints and church pictures on the walls; a smaller bar – where the locals like to gather – has flagstones, a big open hearth fireplace and side bread oven. Princetown Jail Ale, St Austell IPA and Tribute and Sharps Doom Bar on handpump; friendly service. The ancient oak from which the pub gets its name is just close by. No children inside.

🍴 **Decent bar food includes filled baguettes, chicken liver pâté, breaded camembert with raspberry coulis, courgette, brie and almond crumble, chicken wrapped in bacon and stuffed with stilton with a port and walnut sauce, steak in ale pie, fillet of bass topped with prawns and parsley butter, and puddings such as bread and butter pudding and strawberry pavlova.** *Starters/Snacks: £3.50 to £5.25. Main Courses: £6.50 to £11.50. Puddings: £3.00 to £3.75*

Free house ~ Licensee Matthew Smith ~ Real ale ~ Bar food ~ (01822) 852944 ~ Dogs allowed in bar ~ Open 11.30-3, 6-11; 11.30(12 Sun)-11 Sat
Recommended by Tracey and Stephen Groves, Jacquie Jones, J F Stackhouse

---

Please keep sending us reports. We rely on readers for news of new discoveries, and particularly for news of changes – however slight – at the fully described pubs. No stamp needed: The Good Pub Guide, FREEPOST TN1569, Wadhurst, E Sussex TN5 7BR or send your report through our website: www.goodguides.co.uk

MOLLAND   SS8028   MAP 1

London 🍺

Village signposted off B3227 E of South Molton, down narrow lanes; EX36 3NG

A proper Exmoor inn with customers and their dogs to match, a warm welcome from the licensees, honest food, farm cider and real ales

A bit quirky and very much huntin', shootin' and fishin', with a water bowl by the good log fire for the working dogs that come in with their keepers, this is a proper, traditional Exmoor pub. You can be sure of a genuinely warm welcome from the licensees and they keep farm cider as well as Cotleigh Tawny and Exmoor Ale tapped from casks. The two small linked rooms by the old-fashioned central servery have lots of local stag-hunting pictures, tough carpeting or rugs on flagstones, cushioned benches and plain chairs around rough stripped trestle tables, a table of shooting and other country magazines, ancient stag and otter trophies, and darts and board games. On the left an attractive beamed room has accounts of the rescued stag which lived a long life at the pub some 50 years ago, and on the right, a panelled dining room with a great curved settle by its fireplace has particularly good hunting and gamebird prints, including ones by McPhail and Hester Lloyd. A small hall with stuffed birds and animals and lots of overhead baskets has a box of toys, and there are good country views from a few picnic-sets out in front. The low-ceilinged lavatories are worth a look, with their Victorian mahogany and tiling (and in the gents' a testament to the prodigious thirst of the village cricket team). And don't miss the next-door church, with its untouched early 18th-c box pews – and a spring carpet of tenby daffodils in the graveyard. Readers in tune with the down-to-earth style of the pub have enjoyed staying here.

🍽 **Honest bar food at lunchtime includes sandwiches, ploughman's, soup, ham and egg, excellent savoury pancakes and a dish of the day such as cottage or steak and kidney pie or curry; evening choices such as steak, pigeon and mushroom pie, tuna steak chargrilled with salsa verde or lamb chop with port and redcurrant sauce.** *Starters/Snacks: £3.80 to £5.50. Main Courses: £7.00 to £12.50. Puddings: £3.80*

Free house ~ Licensees Mike and Linda Short ~ Real ale ~ Bar food (not Sun evening) ~ Restaurant ~ No credit cards ~ (01769) 550269 ~ Children in own room or lower bar until 9pm ~ Dogs welcome ~ Open 11-2.30, 6-11; 12-2.30, 7-11 Sun ~ Bedrooms: /£60B

Recommended by Dave Braisted, MB, Mrs J C Pank, Angus and Rosemary Campbell, Martin and Pauline Jennings, the Didler, Heather and Dick Martin, George Atkinson, Jeremy Whitehorn, Bob and Margaret Holder, Conor McGaughey, Tom Evans

NEWTON ABBOT   SX8468   MAP 1

Two Mile Oak 🍺

A381 2 miles S, at Denbury/Kingskerswell crossroads; TQ12 6DF

Relaxed and pleasant old place with traditional furnishings, well liked food and real ales

Under a new licensee, this pleasant old coaching inn remains thankfully unchanged. There's a beamed lounge and an alcove just for two, a mix of wooden tables and chairs and a fine winter log fire. The beamed and black-panelled bar is traditionally furnished, again with a mix of seating, lots of horsebrasses and another good log fire. Bass and Otter Ale tapped from the cask and decent wines. Piped music, TV, games machine, and darts. Picnic-sets on the terrace and a lawn with shrubs and tubs of flowers. More reports please.

🍽 **Bar food includes filled baguettes, ploughman's, soup, ham and eggs, lasagne, lamb curry, steak and kidney pudding, and daily specials.** *Starters/Snacks: £3.95 to £5.95. Main Courses: £6.95 to £14.95. Puddings: £3.95 to £4.35*

Heavitree ~ Manager Tony Pitcher ~ Real ale ~ Bar food ~ Restaurant ~ (01803) 812411 ~ Children allowed in lounge bar ~ Dogs allowed in bar ~ Open 11-11; 12-10.30 Sun

Recommended by Mr and Mrs Colin Roberts, the Didler

NEWTON FERRERS

SX5447   MAP 1

Dolphin

Riverside Road East – follow Harbour dead end signs; PL8 1AE

Terraces looking down over the River Yealm, a simply furnished bar, traditional food and local ales

This 18th-c pub is now owned by Badger and has new licensees. What won't change is the grandstand view of the boating action on the busy tidal River Yealm from the two terraces across the lane. Inside, the L-shaped bar has a few low black beams, slate floors, some white-painted plank panelling, and simple pub furnishings including cushioned wall benches and small winged settles. It can get packed in summer. Badger Tanglefoot and First Gold on handpump or tapped from the cask and ten wines by the glass; board games and Tuesday evening quiz in winter. Parking by the pub is very limited, with more chance of a space either below or above. More reports please.

Ⓜ Bar food now includes chunky sandwiches, ploughman's, local fish pie, goats cheese and roasted vegetable tartlet, honey and mustard ham with free-range eggs, fresh battered haddock, local mussels and oysters when available, sausage and cheddar mash with onion gravy, daily specials and puddings like white chocolate and lime mascarpone cheesecake or sticky toffee pudding. *Starters/Snacks: £3.95 to £5.95. Main Courses: £7.50 to £11.00. Puddings: £4.25 to £5.00*

Badger ~ Tenants Jackie Cosens and Adrian Jenkins ~ Real ale ~ Bar food (12-3, 6-9.30; all day weekends; not winter Sun evening) ~ (01752) 872007 ~ Children welcome ~ Dogs welcome ~ Open 11-11(1.30 Sun); 12-2.30(3 Sat, 3.30 Sun), 6-11 in winter; closed winter Sun evening

Recommended by David M Cundy

NOMANSLAND

SS8313   MAP 1

Mount Pleasant

B3137 Tiverton—South Molton; EX16 8NN

Three fireplaces and a mix of furnishings in long bar, interesting food, a fair choice of drinks, and friendly service

By the time this edition is published, the long-standing licensees may well have sold this friendly pub. The long bar is divided into three with huge fireplaces each end, one with a woodburning stove under a low dark ochre black-beamed ceiling, the other with a big log fire, and there are tables in a sizeable bay window extension. A nice mix of furniture on the patterned carpet includes an old sofa with a colourful throw, old-fashioned leather dining chairs, pale country kitchen chairs, and tables all with candles in attractive metal holders; country prints and local photographs including shooting parties. The public bar, with plenty of bar stools, has Cotleigh Tawny and Sharps Doom Bar on handpump, eight wines by the glass and Weston's Old Rosie cider. On the left, a high-beamed stripped stone dining room was once a smithy and still has the raised forge fireplace. Piped music, darts and board games. There are some picnic-sets under smart parasols in the neat back garden.

Ⓜ Bar food includes sandwiches, chicken liver pâté, sausages and onion gravy, steak and kidney pie, mushroom stroganoff, chicken breast with a choice of sauces, lamb shank with redcurrant and orange sauce, daily specials, and puddings such as treacle tart or chocolate brownie. *Starters/Snacks: £4.95 to £6.00. Main Courses: £5.95 to £14.95. Puddings: £3.95 to £4.50*

Free house ~ Licensees Anne, Karen and Sarah Butler ~ Real ale ~ Bar food (all day) ~ Restaurant ~ (01884) 860271 ~ Children welcome ~ Dogs allowed in bar ~ Open 11.30-11; 12-10.30 Sun; closed 26 Dec, 1 Jan

Recommended by Bob and Margaret Holder, R J Walden, Jeremy Whitehorn, Rona Murdoch, Conor McGaughey, Ken and Janet Bracey

---

Pubs close to motorway junctions are listed at the back of the book.

NOSS MAYO SX5447 MAP 1

Ship ♀ ◖

Off A379 via B3186, E of Plymouth; PL8 1EW

Popular pub with new owners, seats overlooking the inlet and visiting boats, thick-walled bars with log fires, west country beers and friendly atmosphere

New owners took over this popular pub just as we went to press – but they are no strangers to this *Guide* and a couple of years ago ran the chatty Chequers in Smarden, Kent. They have told us of no changes and the two thick-walled bars have a happy mix of dining chairs and tables on the wooden floors, log fires, bookcases, dozens of local pictures, maybe newspapers and magazines to read, and a chatty atmosphere; board games. Butcombe Blonde, Princetown Jail Ale, St Austell Tribute and Summerskills Tamar on handpump, lots of malt whiskies, and quite a few wines by the glass. The front terrace is extremely popular in fine weather – you can sit at the octagonal wooden tables under parasols and look over the inlet, and visiting boats can tie up alongside (with prior permission); there are outdoor heaters for cooler evenings. Parking is restricted at high tide. More reports on the new regime, please.

🍴 **Bar food now includes sandwiches, ploughman's, soup, goats cheese and bramley apple tartlet, chicken liver pâté with red onion marmalade, local haddock in beer batter, steak burger with gruyère and bacon, pork and leek sausages with black pudding and gravy, roasted nut loaf with a light mornay sauce, dressed local crab and braised lamb shank with roasted mediterranean vegetables.** *Starters/Snacks: £5.00 to £8.95. Main Courses: £10.00 to £18.00. Puddings: £5.75*

Free house ~ Licensees Charlie and Lisa Bullock ~ Real ale ~ Bar food (all day) ~ (01752) 872387 ~ Children allowed before 8pm ~ Dogs allowed in bar ~ Open 11-11; 12-11 Sun; closed Mon Nov-March

Recommended by Tracey and Stephen Groves, Graham Oddey, Mrs Bridget Cushion, John Evans, Bruce Bird, Jennifer Sheridan, Lynda and Trevor Smith, David Rule, Dr and Mrs M E Wilson, John Smart, Gerry and Rosemary Dobson

PARRACOMBE SS6644 MAP 1

Fox & Goose ♀

Village signposted off A39 Blackmoor Gate—Lynton (actually a short cut, but winding and rather narrow); EX31 4PE

Friendly licensees in quiet Exmoor inn with tasty food, local cider and beer, and dining room overlooking small stream

There's a proper Exmoor feel to the informal and relaxed bar of this quietly placed and friendly inn with its hunting and farming memorabilia. Seating is mainly wheelback carvers around solid tables and there are some interesting black and white photographs of the local area and an open log fire. Cotleigh Barn Owl and Exmoor Fox on Handpump, ten wines by the glass and farm cider. The dining room on the right looks down on a little stream and the front verandah has hanging baskets and flower tubs and a couple of picnic-sets. There are seats in a new streamside terraced garden with raised flower beds and this leads to a garden room. Please note, they no longer offer bed and breakfast.

🍴 **Tasty bar food might include sandwiches, soup, chicken liver pâté, garlic mushrooms, dressed crab salad, game and wild mushroom pie, butternut squash risotto, venison casserole, local plaice with lemon and parsley butter, bouillabaisse, lamb steak with mint gravy, and puddings like baked chocolate cheesecake or sponge pudding with rich toffee sauce.** *Starters/Snacks: £3.95 to £6.25. Main Courses: £10.95 to £18.95. Puddings: £3.95 to £5.25*

Free house ~ Licensees N Baxter and P Houle ~ Real ale ~ Bar food (12-2, 6(7 winter Sun)-9) ~ (01598) 763239 ~ Children welcome ~ Dogs allowed in bar ~ Open 12-3, 6-11(10.30 Sun); Sun evening opening 7pm in winter

Recommended by MB, Margit Severa, Felicity Stephens, David Fox, David and Carole Sayliss, Janice and Phil Waller, Mehefin, Ian Phillips, Tom Evans

SX5177 MAP 1

Peter Tavy Inn ♀

Off A386 near Mary Tavy, N of Tavistock; PL19 9NN

Old stone inn with pretty garden, bustling bar with beams and big log fire, and good choice of food and drink

From the picnic-sets in the pretty garden here, there are peaceful views of the moor rising above nearby pastures. Inside, the low-beamed bar has high-backed settles on the black flagstones by the big stone fireplace (a fine log fire on cold days), smaller settles in stone-mullioned windows, and a good bustling atmosphere; there's also a snug dining area and restaurant. Blackawton Original Bitter, Princetown Jail Ale, Sharps Doom Bar and maybe St Austell Tribute on handpump; local cider, 20 malt whiskies and ten wines by the glass; piped music.

🍽 **Good food at lunchtime might include filled ciabattas and baguettes, ploughman's, soup, stilton and pear pâté, ham and egg, mixed meat salad, thai chicken curry, roasted vegetable and ricotta cheesecake and stuffed roast lamb shoulder with minted pear with evening dishes such as breaded camembert with cranberry sauce, chicken liver, tequila and cranberry pâté, duck breast with honey and ginger sauce, game casserole with stilton dumplings, mexican fajita with either chicken, pork or vegetables and monkfish with creamy garlic sauce.** *Starters/Snacks: £4.25 to £6.55. Main Courses: £6.25 to £17.95. Puddings: £3.75 to £4.50*

Free house ~ Licensees Chris and Joanne Wordingham ~ Real ale ~ Bar food (not 25, 26, 31 Dec) ~ Restaurant ~ (01822) 810348 ~ Children welcome ~ Dogs welcome ~ Open 12-3(3.30 Sat and Sun), 6-11(10.30 Sun)

Recommended by Mick and Moira Brummell, Jacquie Jones, Peter and Margaret Lodge, Dr and Mrs M W A Haward, Leo and Barbara Lionet, R and H Fraser, Helen and Brian Edgeley, Alistair Caie, Andrea Rampley, Peter Craske, George Murdoch

SX4185 MAP 1

Harris Arms ♀

Turn off A30 E of Launceston at Broadwoodwidger turn-off (with brown Dingle Steam Village sign), and head S; Launceston Road (old A30 between Lewdown and Lifton); EX20 4PZ

Enthusiastic, well travelled licensees in roadside pub with exceptional wine list (they also have their own vines)

The chatty and friendly licensees here are both qualified award-winning wine-makers and are more than happy to help you through their eclectic wine list. With helpful notes and 20 of their favourites by the glass, there are plenty of gems to choose from. The bar has burgundy end walls and cream ones in between, some rather fine photographs, a huge table at one end (brought back from New Zealand), a long red-plush built-in wall banquette and a woodburning stove; afghan saddle-bag cushions are scattered around a mixture of other tables and dining chairs. On the left, steps lead down to the dining room with elegant beech dining chairs (and more afghan cushions) around stripped wooden tables, and some unusual paintings on the walls collected by the Whitemans on their travels. Sharps Doom Bar and a beer from Exe Valley on handpump, Luscombe organic soft drinks, summer cider, and a pile of country magazines. Seats under umbrellas, pots of lavender and outdoor heaters on a decked area and plenty of picnic-sets in the sloping back garden looking out over the rolling wooded pasture hills. They are growing 24 vines.

🍽 **As well as a set lunchtime menu (not Sunday), the carefully sourced bar food includes seasonal soups, home-cured gravadlax, home-made terrine with spiced pear chutney, english snails in garlic butter, bangers and mash with beer and onion gravy, ham and eggs, home-made burgers with beetroot and red wine relish, evening dishes like braised lamb shank in plum and orange sauce or chicken breast with thyme and onion potatoes and a wild mushroom and wine jus, daily specials, and puddings such as brandied plum crème brûlée or chocolate torte with berry compote.** *Starters/Snacks: £5.75 to £8.50. Main Courses: £8.50 to £9.50. Puddings: £4.50 to £5.50*

Free house ~ Licensees Andy and Rowena Whiteman ~ Real ale ~ Bar food ~ Restaurant ~
(01566) 783331 ~ Children welcome ~ Dogs allowed in bar ~ Open 12-3, 6(6.30 in winter)-11;
12-3, 7-10.30 Sun; closed Mon all day and winter Sun evenings

*Recommended by R J Walden, Mr and Mrs Ron Patterson, Alistair Caie, Andy and Claire Barker, Lynne Carter,
Charles and Isabel Cooper, M and R Thomas, Lesley and Peter Barrett*

POSTBRIDGE   SX6780   MAP 1

Warren House

B3212 ¾ mile NE of Postbridge; PL20 6TA

Straightforward old pub, relaxing for a drink or snack after a Dartmoor hike

One of the fireplaces in the cosy bar of this straightforward place is said to have been
kept alight almost continuously since 1845 and is most welcome after a hike on
Dartmoor. There are simple furnishings like easy chairs and settles under the beamed
ochre ceiling, old pictures of the inn on the partly panelled stone walls, and dim lighting
(fuelled by the pub's own generator); a family room also. Butcombe Gold, Otter Ale and
Sharps Doom Bar on handpump, local farm cider and malt whiskies; piped music, darts
and pool. They may try to keep your credit card while you eat. The picnic-sets on both
sides of the road have moorland views.

🍴 **Bar food includes filled baguettes and baked potatoes, ploughman's, pasties, spicy
vegetable burger, local jumbo sausage, rabbit pie, breaded plaice, daily specials, and
puddings like sticky toffee pudding with toffee sauce.** *Starters/Snacks: £2.60 to £5.95.
Main Courses: £6.25 to £17.00. Puddings: £4.50*

Free house ~ Licensee Peter Parsons ~ Real ale ~ Bar food (all day but more restricted winter
Mon and Tues) ~ (01822) 880208 ~ Children in family room ~ Dogs allowed in bar ~
Open 11-11; 12-10.30 Sun; 11-5 Mon and Tues during Nov-Feb winter

*Recommended by Anthony Longden, Ken Flawn, John Robertson, Andrea Rampley, Roger E F Maxwell, Phil and
Sally Gorton*

POUNDSGATE   SX7072   MAP 1

Tavistock Inn

B3357 continuation; TQ13 7NY

Friendly old pub with some original features; lovely scenery and plenty of walkers

In a Dartmoor-edge village, this picturesque old pub is popular with walkers (and their
dogs) as moorland hikes start and finish here or pass it en route. There are tables on the
front terrace and pretty flowers in stone troughs, hanging baskets and window boxes and
more seats (and ducks) in the quiet back garden; lovely scenery. Inside, some original
features include a narrow-stepped granite spiral staircase, flagstones, ancient log
fireplaces, and beams, and there's a friendly atmosphere and a good mix of locals and
visitors. Courage Best, Otter Ale, St Austell Dartmoor Best and Wychwood Hobgoblin Best
on handpump and several malt whiskies. Sir Arthur Conan Doyle wrote *The Hound of the
Baskervilles* while staying here.

🍴 **Traditional bar food includes filled baguettes and baked potatoes, home-made lasagne
or vegetarian pasta bake, locally made burger and beef in ale pie.** *Starters/Snacks: £4.15 to
£4.35. Main Courses: £5.90 to £11.90. Puddings: £4.25*

Punch ~ Lease Peter and Jean Hamill ~ Real ale ~ Bar food (all day in summer) ~ Restaurant ~
(01364) 631251 ~ Children welcome away from bar ~ Dogs allowed in bar ~ Open 11-11;
12-10.30 Sun; 11-3, 6-11 winter

Recommended by JHW, Dr R C C Ward, Bob and Angela Brooks, Mrs S Wallis, Paul and Shirley White, Simon Rodway

---

Places with gardens or terraces usually let children sit there – we note in
the text the very few exceptions that don't.

RATTERY   SX7461   MAP 1

Church House

Village signposted from A385 W of Totnes, and A38 S of Buckfastleigh; TQ10 9LD

One of Britain's oldest pubs with some fine original features, pubby food, and peaceful views

The craftsmen who built the Norman church were probably housed in the original building here – parts of it still survive, notably the spiral stone steps behind a little stone doorway on your left. There are massive oak beams and standing timbers in the homely open-plan bar, large fireplaces (one with a little cosy nook partitioned off around it), windsor armchairs, comfortable seats and window seats, and prints on the plain white walls; the dining room is separated from this room by heavy curtains and there's also a lounge area too. Otter Ale, Princetown Jail Ale, Skinners Betty Stogs and St Austell Dartmoor Best on handpump, quite a few malt whiskies and eight wines by the glass; obliging service. The garden has picnic benches on the large hedged-in lawn, and peaceful views of the partly wooded surrounding hills.

🍴 Bar food includes sandwiches, toasties and filled baguettes, ploughman's, soup, **mushroom pot, vegetable lasagne, sausage and mash with onion gravy, battered cod, a fry-up, chicken in whisky cream sauce, daily specials, and puddings like lemon meringue pie or double chocolate fudge cake.** *Starters/Snacks: £4.25 to £8.95. Main Courses: £6.95 to £13.95. Puddings: £3.50 to £4.95*

Free house ~ Licensee Ray Hardy ~ Real ale ~ Bar food ~ Restaurant ~ (01364) 642220 ~ Children welcome ~ Dogs allowed in bar ~ Open 11.30-2.30, 6-11; 12-2.30, 6-10.30 Sun

Recommended by Hugh Roberts, Dudley and Moira Cockroft, Bob and Angela Brooks, Rona Murdoch, MP, Mrs J H S Lang, JT, Tracey and Stephen Groves, Clare Rosier

ROCKBEARE   SY0195   MAP 1

Jack in the Green

Signposted from new A30 bypass E of Exeter; EX5 2EE

Neat dining pub with traditionally furnished bars and imaginative meals

The particularly good food remains the main draw to this big, neatly kept roadside dining pub. It's a friendly place and the comfortable good-sized bar has wheelback chairs, sturdy cushioned wall pews and varying-sized tables on its dark blue carpet, a dark carved oak dresser, and sporting prints and nice decorative china; piped music. The larger dining side is similarly traditional in style: some of its many old hunting and shooting photographs are well worth a close look and there are button-back leather chesterfields by the big woodburning stove. O'Hanlons Yellowhammer and Otter Ale on handpump, and ten wines by the glass. There are some tables out behind by a dark skittle alley.

🍴 Top quality bar food using local, seasonal, if not cheap, ingredients includes snacks like ploughman's, soup, chicken liver and foie gras parfait, bangers and mash with onion gravy, tomato risotto with chorizo and basil, braised faggot with red onion marmalade and truffle mash and fresh fish pie; there are more elaborate dishes such as sesame tuna with crushed potato, roasted mediterranean vegetable tartlet, chicken breast with smoked bacon tortellini and jerusalem artichoke purée and fillet of brill with provençale vegetables and pistou; puddings like sticky toffee pudding and apple and pear trifle, and they also have two- and three-course set menus. *Starters/Snacks: £4.25 to £8.50. Main Courses: £9.50 to £18.50. Puddings: £5.25 to £7.25*

Free house ~ Licensee Paul Parnell ~ Real ale ~ Bar food (all day Sun) ~ Restaurant ~ (01404) 822240 ~ Well behaved children in one bar only ~ Open 11-3, 5.30(6 Sat)-11; 12-10.30 Sun; closed 25 Dec-4 Jan

Recommended by Hugh Roberts, Mike and Heather Watson, John and Julie Moon, Rod Stoneman, Gene and Tony Freemantle, Lucien Perring, Dr D and Mrs B Woods, Dr and Mrs A K Clarke, Ian Phillips, Dr Donald Ainscow, Andy and Claire Barker, John and Fiona McIlwain

SANDY PARK   SX7189   MAP 1

Sandy Park Inn 🛏

A382 Whiddon Down—Moretonhampstead; TQ13 8JW

Busy little thatched inn with snug bars and attractive bedrooms

A new licensee has taken over this little thatched inn but doesn't plan any major changes. The small bar on the right has rugs on the black-painted composition floor, black beams in the cream ceiling, varnished built-in wall settles forming separate areas around nice tables, and high stools by the chatty bar counter with Otter Ale, St Austell Tribute and maybe O'Hanlons Original Port Stout and Yellowhammer on handpump and a decent choice of wines by the glass; big blow-ups of old golfing pictures and some smaller interestingly annotated Dartmoor photographs. The back snug has one big table that a dozen people could just squeeze around, stripped stone walls, and a cream-painted bright-cushioned built-in wall bench. On the left is a small dining room with golfing and other prints on the red walls and just a few tables, and an inner private dining room with lots of prints, and one big table. Board games. There are seats by outdoor heaters in a large garden with fine views. Reports on the new regime, please.

🍴 **Enjoyable food includes sandwiches, soup, local sausages and mash, roasted red pepper and asparagus risotto, lambs liver and bacon, beer-battered cod, braised lamb shank and sirloin steak with blue cheese.** *Starters/Snacks: £4.50 to £7.00. Main Courses: £8.50 to £14.00. Puddings: £4.50*

Free house ~ Licensee Nic Rout ~ Real ale ~ Bar food (12-2.30(4 Sun), 6.30-9) ~ Restaurant ~ (01647) 433267 ~ Children allowed at lunchtime and up to 7pm in restaurant ~ Dogs allowed in bar and bedrooms ~ Occasional folk and blues evenings ~ Open 11-11; 12-10.30 Sun ~ Bedrooms: /£98B

Recommended by Mr and Mrs A R Maden, Donna and Roger, Andrea and Guy Bradley, Derek Allpass, Julie Russell-Carter, Will and Kay Adie, John and Bettye Reynolds

SIDBURY   SY1496   MAP 1

Hare & Hounds 🍺

3 miles N of Sidbury, at Putts Corner; A375 towards Honiton, crossroads with B3174; EX10 0QQ

Large well run roadside pub with log fires, beams and attractive layout, popular daily carvery, efficient staff, and big garden

So much bigger inside than you could have guessed from outside, this is an extremely popular and very well run roadside pub. There are two good log fires (and rather unusual wood-framed leather sofas complete with pouffes), heavy beams and fresh flowers throughout, some oak panelling, plenty of tables with red leatherette or red plush-cushioned dining chairs, window seats and well used bar stools too; it's mostly carpeted, with some bare boards and stripped stone walls. At the opposite end, on the left, another big dining area has huge windows looking out over the garden. Branscombe Vale Summa That and Otter Ale and Bright tapped from the cask; a side room has a big-screen sports TV. The big garden, giving nice valley views, has picnic-sets, a children's play area and a marquee; maybe a small strolling flock of peafowl.

🍴 **It's the good daily carvery counter with a choice of joints and enough turnover to keep up a continuous supply of fresh vegetables that is so enjoyable here. Other food includes sandwiches or baguettes, soup, chicken liver pâté, pie of the day and a curry or nut roast.** *Starters/Snacks: £3.95 to £5.95. Main Courses: £7.25 to £14.95. Puddings: £2.65 to £4.25*

Free house ~ Licensee Peter Cairns ~ Real ale ~ Bar food (all day) ~ Restaurant ~ (01404) 41760 ~ Children in two bars ~ Dogs allowed in bar ~ Live music Sun lunchtimes in marquee ~ Open 10.30am-11pm; 12-10.30 Sun

Recommended by Richard Wyld, Mrs P Bishop, Rod Stoneman, Edna Jones, Louis Hertzberg

> If we know a pub has an outdoor play area for children, we mention it.

SLAPTON   SX8245   MAP 1

Tower ★

Signposted off A379 Dartmouth—Kingsbridge; TQ7 2PN

Imaginative food in bustling old place, beams and log fires, good beers and wines, and pretty back garden

As we went to press we heard that this atmospheric old place was up for sale. It's been much enjoyed by our readers – mainly as somewhere to eat – so we are keeping our fingers crossed that things won't change too much. The low-ceilinged beamed bar has armchairs, low-backed settles and scrubbed oak tables on the flagstones or bare boards, open log fires, Badger Tanglefoot, Butcombe Bitter and St Austell Tribute on handpump, a couple of ciders and several wines by the glass; piped music. The picnic-sets on the neatly kept lawn in the pretty back garden are overlooked by the ivy-covered ruin of a 14th-c chantry – lovely in summer. The lane up to the pub is very narrow and parking is difficult. We'd be grateful for reports on any changes.

🍴 **Imaginative lunchtime food has included sandwiches, soup, chicken liver and wild mushroom pâté with curried fruit chutney, a plate of antipasti, smoked haddock, mozzarella and spring onion fishcake with chive crème fraîche, trio of local sausages with onion gravy, beef, ale and mushroom pie, pasta with smoked cheddar, spinach and pine nut cream sauce and lamb shank with rosemary jus; extra evening dishes like chicken breast in a white wine and tarragon cream sauce with a gruyère crust, bass fillets with a lemon and coriander dressing and fillet steak tournedos rossini.** *Starters/Snacks: £4.50 to £7.00. Main Courses: £9.00 to £18.00. Puddings: £5.50*

Free house ~ Licensees Annette and Andrew Hammett ~ Real ale ~ Bar food ~ Restaurant ~ (01548) 580216 ~ Children not allowed in bar ~ Dogs allowed in bar ~ Open 12-3, 6-11; 12-3, 7-10.30 Sun; closed Sun evening and Mon in winter ~ Bedrooms: £50S/£70S

Recommended by Mike Gorton, Andrew and Debbie Ettle, Lynda and Trevor Smith, David Eberlin, Peter and Giff Bennett, Mayur Shah, Mrs Carolyn Dixon, Gerry and Rosemary Dobson, Alan and Anne Driver, Wendy and Carl Dye, the Didier, Mike and Shelley Woodroffe, Dr R C C Ward, Terry and Linda Moseley, Bob and Margaret Holder, Roger Wain-Heapy

STOCKLAND   ST2404   MAP 1

Kings Arms ♀

Village signposted from A30 Honiton—Chard; and also, at every turning, from N end of Honiton High Street; EX14 9BS

Pleasant old inn with elegant bar, cosy restaurant, and local beers and cider

New licensees have taken over this 16th-c inn. The dark beamed, elegant Cotley Bar has had solid refectory tables and settles, attractive landscapes, a medieval oak screen (which divides the room into two), and a great stone fireplace across almost the whole width of one end. The cosy restaurant has a huge inglenook fireplace and bread oven. Exmoor Ale and Otter Ale and a monthly changing guest such as O'Hanlons Yellowhammer on handpump, quite a few malt whiskies and decent wines. At the back, a flagstoned bar has cushioned benches and stools around heavy wooden tables; there's also a darts area, a room with more tables, and a neat ten-pin skittle alley; bar billiards and board games. There are tables under parasols on the terrace in front of the white-faced thatched pub and a lawn enclosed by trees and shrubs. More reports on any changes, please.

🍴 **Bar food at lunchtime now includes sandwiches, soup, omelettes, local pork sausages with caramelised red onion gravy, mexican chicken in pitta bread, steak, mushroom and blue cheese pie and beer-battered cod; a more elaborate menu serves duck liver pâté, crab cakes with lemon, lime and chilli dressing, roasted and stuffed whole peppers in a tomato and herb coulis, beef stroganoff, slow-roasted minted lamb shoulder and king prawns in a cream thermidor sauce.** *Starters/Snacks: £4.00 to £5.00. Main Courses: £5.00 to £14.00*

Free house ~ Licensee Tom Richards ~ Real ale ~ Bar food ~ Restaurant ~ (01404) 881361 ~ Children in restaurant ~ Dogs allowed in bar and bedrooms ~ Open 12-3, 6-11.20; 12-11.20(10.30 Sun) Sat ~ Bedrooms: £45S/£70S

Recommended by John Evans, Michael B Griffith, Gene and Tony Freemantle, Bob and Margaret Holder, Derek and Heather Manning, D Restarick, John and Wendy Hamilton, Mike Gorton, John and Julie Moon, John and Fiona Merritt, Malcolm and Jane Levitt

STOKE GABRIEL
SX8457 MAP 1

Church House

Village signposted from A385 just W of junction with A3022, in Collaton St Mary; can also be reached from nearer Totnes; TQ9 6SD

Busy local with fine medieval ceiling and huge fireplace, little public bar, and honest pubby food

This early 14th-c pub has a bustling atmosphere and plenty of customers. The lounge bar has an exceptionally fine medieval beam-and-plank ceiling, as well as a black oak partition wall, window seats cut into the thick butter-coloured walls, decorative plates and vases of flowers on a dresser, and a huge fireplace still used in winter to cook the stew; darts. The mummified cat in a case, probably about 200 years old, was found during restoration of the roof space in the verger's cottage three doors up the lane – one of a handful found in the West Country and believed to have been a talisman against evil spirits. Bass, Exe Valley Bitter and a changing guest on handpump and 20 malt whiskies. Euchre in the little public locals' bar. There are picnic-sets on the small terrace in front of the building. The church is very pretty, and relations with the Church of England and this pub go back a long way – witness the priest hole, dating from the Reformation, visible from outside. Parking is very limited. No children.

🍴 **Straightforward, good value bar food includes a big choice of sandwiches and toasties, filled baked potatoes, ploughman's, soup, steak and kidney pie, wild mushroom ravioli, chicken curry and lamb shank.** *Starters/Snacks: £2.95 to £4.95. Main Courses: £6.95 to £8.40. Puddings: £3.75*

Free house ~ Licensee T G Patch ~ Real ale ~ Bar food (11-3, 6-9.30; 12-3, 7-9.30 Sun) ~ (01803) 782384 ~ Dogs allowed in bar ~ Open 11-11; 12-11 Sun

Recommended by Di and Mike Gillam, Dr and Mrs M E Wilson, Simon Fox, Peter Titcomb, David and Karen Cuckney

STOKENHAM
SX8042 MAP 1

Church House ♀

Opposite church, N of A379 towards Torcross; TQ7 2SZ

Good food and ales in bustling, unspoilt pub; pretty countryside

For centuries this well run pub has been associated with the ancient Norman church next door. It's in lovely countryside and looks out on to a common where sheep graze; seats in the attractive garden. Inside, three rambling, low-beamed open-plan areas connected by archways have a good, bustling atmosphere, Brakspears Bitter, Greene King Abbot, Otter Ale and Timothy Taylors Landlord on handpump, local ciders and several whiskies; friendly, efficient service. Piped music, darts, cards and euchre.

🍴 **Good bar food includes sandwiches, soup, a daily changing tartlet, local crab cocktail, herby sausages with caramelised onions, vegetarian or lamb and mint pudding, roasted salmon with teriyaki sauce, chicken breast with red and yellow pepper sauce, steak, kidney and Guinness in a yorkshire pudding, lambs liver with watercress and orange sauce, daily specials, and puddings such as chocolate tart with ginger ice-cream or plum frangipane with clotted cream.** *Starters/Snacks: £3.95 to £6.50. Main Courses: £7.50 to £13.95. Puddings: £3.95*

Heavitree ~ Tenants Richard Smith and Simon Cadman ~ Real ale ~ Bar food (12-2, 6-9) ~ Restaurant ~ (01548) 580253 ~ Children allowed until 9pm ~ Dogs allowed in bar ~ Live jazz Weds evening ~ Open 11-2.30, 6-11; 11-11 Sat; 12-2.30, 6-10.30 Sun

Recommended by Mr and Mrs G Owens, Jennifer Sheridan, David and Karen Cuckney, Mrs D Shoults, B J Harding, Roger Wain-Heapy, MP

STRETE   SX8446   MAP 1

Kings Arms 🍴 ♀

A379 SW of Dartmouth – car park is S of pub; TQ6 0RW

Super fish dishes in pretty pub with civilised little dining room and views over Start Bay from back garden

Although they do offer Adnams Best and Otter Ale on handpump, it's the seafood that most customers come to enjoy. The L-shaped bar has country kitchen chairs and tables, some comfortable brocaded dining chairs, very nice fish prints on the dark salmon pink walls, and bar stools by the attractively carved oak bar counter where the chatty locals gather; piped music. Up some stairs is a little restaurant decorated in cool blue/green colours with dark green padded plush and pale wood chairs around wooden tables. The wrought-iron work and canopied upper balcony are pretty and there's a back terrace and garden with views over Start Bay. The pub is on the South West Coastal Path.

🍽 **Fresh local and seasonal fish dishes from Start Bay and Brixham such as crab bisque, moules marinière, black bream fillet, bass with chorizo mash, and fish in beer batter with home-made tartare sauce; non-fishy dishes, too.** *Starters/Snacks: £6.00 to £9.50. Main Courses: £9.50 to £18.00. Puddings: £5.00 to £6.00*

Heavitree ~ Tenant Rob Dawson ~ Real ale ~ Bar food (12-2(3 Sun), 6.30-9.30) ~ Restaurant ~ (01803) 770377 ~ Children welcome ~ Dogs allowed in bar ~ Open 11-11; 12-10.30 Sun; closed Sun evening

Recommended by M G Hart, Michael B Griffith, R D Howard, Jenny and Brian Seller, Paul Boot, Alastair Beck, Dr and Mrs M W A Haward

TIPTON ST JOHN   SY0991   MAP 1

Golden Lion

Signed off B3176 Sidmouth—Ottery St Mary; EX10 0AA

A good mix of diners and drinkers in friendly village pub; attractive garden with evening jazz on summer Sundays

The friendly owners of this attractive village pub are keen that diners and drinkers can mix happily and even keep a few tables reserved for those just wanting a chat and a pint. There's a relaxed, comfortable atmosphere in the main bar area, which is split into two, and in the back snug and throughout there are paintings from West Country artists, art deco prints, tiffany lamps, and hops, copper pots and kettles hanging from the beams. Bass, Greene King IPA and Otter Ale on handpump, ten wines by the glass and local organic soft drinks; piped music, cribbage and board games. There are seats on the terracotta-walled terrace with outside heaters and grapevines and more seats on the grass edged by pretty flowering borders; summer Sunday evening jazz out here.

🍽 **Popular bar food at lunchtime includes sandwiches, ploughman's, soup, home-cooked ham and egg, a vegetarian dish, cod in batter, lots of nice salads and steak in ale pie with evening choices such as home-cured gravadlax, marinated seafood salad, chicken in a creamy sherry sauce, pork tenderloin with prunes and armagnac and duck breast with star anise, honey and orange segment sauce; daily specials, and puddings.** *Starters/Snacks: £4.50 to £7.50. Main Courses: £8.50 to £16.50. Puddings: £4.50*

Heavitree ~ Tenants François and Michelle Teissier ~ Real ale ~ Bar food ~ Restaurant ~ (01404) 812881 ~ Children welcome ~ Jazz summer Sun evenings ~ Open 12-2.30(3 Sat and Sun), 6-11(11.30 Sat and Sun); closed Sun evening Oct-Mar ~ Bedrooms: /£40S

Recommended by Dr and Mrs M E Wilson, Julie Cox, Colin Wright, Tracey and Stephen Groves, John Kent

---

Ideas for a country day out? We list pubs in really attractive scenery at the back of the book – and there are separate lists for waterside pubs, ones with really good gardens, and ones with lovely views.

TOPSHAM   SX9688   MAP 1

Bridge Inn ★ ⬤

*2¼ miles from M5 junction 30: Topsham signposted from exit roundabout; in Topsham
follow signpost (A376) Exmouth on the Elmgrove Road, into Bridge Hill; EX3 0QQ*

**Wonderful old drinkers' pub with eight real ales, in the landlady's family for five
generations**

For those who love utterly old-fashioned pubs – in both character and layout – this
remains a firm favourite. The very friendly landlady is the fifth generation of her family
to run it and the atmosphere is chatty and relaxed with no noisy games machines, music
or mobile phones to spoil that. Of course, the perfectly kept eight real ales are a big
draw too and are helpfully described on the daily changing list. Tapped from the cask,
these might include Adnams Broadside, Blackawton Merryweather, Branscombe Vale
Branoc and Summa That, Jollyboat Plunder and Privateer and O'Hanlons Royal Oak and
Yellowhammer; country wines, non-alcoholic pressés, and decent wines by the glass.
There are fine old traditional furnishings (true country workmanship) in the little lounge
partitioned off from the inner corridor by a high-backed settle; log fire, and a bigger
lower room (the old malthouse) is open at busy times. Outside, riverside picnic-sets
overlook the weir.

🍽 **Simple, tasty bar food such as pasties, sandwiches, a hearty winter soup and various
ploughman's.** *Starters/Snacks: £2.50 to £5.90*

Free house ~ Licensee Mrs C Cheffers-Heard ~ Real ale ~ Bar food (lunchtime only) ~ No credit
cards ~ (01392) 873862 ~ Children in two rooms ~ Dogs allowed in bar ~ Open 12-2, 6(7 Sun)-
10.30(11 Fri/Sat)

*Recommended by Mike Gorton, Donna and Roger, Philip and Jude Simmons, David Swift, the Didler, Dr and Mrs
M E Wilson, Phil and Sally Gorton, Pete Baker, R T and J C Moggridge, Peter Titcomb, Will and Kay Adie, Dr and
Mrs A K Clarke, Barry Steele-Perkins, Richard Pitcher, Tony and Jill Radnor, OPUS, Peter Craske*

TORBRYAN   SX8266   MAP 1

Old Church House

Most easily reached from A381 Newton Abbot—Totnes via Ipplepen; TQ12 5UR

**Ancient inn with lovely original features, neat rooms, friendly service and well liked tasty
food**

This is a smashing old pub with lots of atmosphere. One couple were surprised to find a
man in the bar with a barn owl on his shoulder and others have found the folk sessions
and the welcoming locals who attend them great fun. The particularly attractive bar on
the right of the door is neatly kept and bustling and has benches built into the fine old
panelling as well as a cushioned high-backed settle and leather-backed small seats
around its big log fire. On the left there is a series of comfortable and discreetly lit
lounges, one with a splendid deep Tudor inglenook fireplace with a side bread oven;
piped music. Skinners Betty Stogs and Cornish Knocker on handpump, 30 malt whiskies,
and several wines by the glass; friendly service. Plenty of nearby walks.

🍽 **Generous helpings of good bar food include soup, sandwiches, filled baguettes,
ploughman's, mushroom risotto, lasagne, beef in ale pie, haddock mornay and rack of
lamb.** *Starters/Snacks: £3.95 to £5.95. Main Courses: £6.95 to £15.00. Puddings: £3.95 to £4.50*

Free house ~ Licensees Kane and Carolynne Clarke ~ Real ale ~ Bar food ~ Restaurant ~
(01803) 812372 ~ Children in lounge and restaurant ~ Dogs allowed in bar ~ Acoustic guitar
Thurs evening and sometimes Fri/Sat; open music night Sun ~ Open 11-11 ~ Bedrooms:
£54B/£69B

*Recommended by Peter and Margaret Lodge, Andrew Shore, Maria Williams, J D O Carter, Kevin and
Jane O'Mahoney, Mike Gorton, Graham and Glenis Watkins, Jane and Martin Headley*

TORCROSS   SX8242   MAP 1

Start Bay

A379 S of Dartmouth; TQ7 2TQ

Fresh local fish dishes in exceptionally popular dining pub; seats outside overlooking the beach

If fresh fish is what you are after, then this extremely popular dining pub is just the place to head for. It's delivered to the door by local fishermen (who work off the beach in front of the pub). Queues usually form even before the doors open and the straightforward main bar is always packed. It is very much set out for eating with wheelback chairs around plenty of dark tables or (round a corner) back-to-back settles forming booths; country pictures and some photographs of storms buffeting the pub on the cream walls, and a winter coal fire. A small chatty drinking area by the counter has a brass ship's clock and barometer and there's more booth seating in a family room with sailing boat pictures. Pool and darts in the winter. Bass, Flowers Original and Otter Ale on handpump, local Heron Valley juice and local wine from the Sharpham Estate. They do warn of delays in food service at peak times but the staff remain friendly and efficient. There are seats (highly prized) outside that look over the three-mile pebble beach, and the freshwater wildlife lagoon of Slapton Ley is just behind the pub.

▥ Their speciality is fish in light batter: cod or haddock (medium, large or jumbo), plaice, lemon sole and other fish dishes as available; also, sandwiches, filled baked potatoes, ploughman's, vegetable lasagne and steaks. *Starters/Snacks: £3.50 to £5.80. Main Courses: £5.80 to £13.90. Puddings: £2.70 to £3.90*

Heavitree ~ Tenant Stuart Jacob ~ Real ale ~ Bar food (11.30-2(2.15 weekends), 6-10 (9.30 in winter); some food all day in high summer) ~ (01548) 580553 ~ Children in large family room ~ Open 11.30-11; 12-10.30 Sun; 11.30-2.30, 6-11 in winter

Recommended by Mike Gorton, P and J Shapley, Jenny and Brian Seller, Mayur Shah, M Thomas, Mike and Mary Carter, Mr and Mrs A R Maden, Mr and Mrs G Owens

TOTNES   SX8059   MAP 1

Steam Packet

St Peters Quay, on W bank (ie not on Steam Packet Quay); TQ9 5EW

Seats outside overlooking the quay, as well as an interesting inside layout, popular food and drink, and friendly staff

Overlooking the River Dart, the terrace in front of this bustling pub has plenty of modern tables and chairs, flowering tubs, and outdoor heaters. Inside it is interestingly laid out with stripped wood floors throughout. The end part has an open coal fire, fancy knotwork in a case above the fireplace, a squashy leatherette sofa with lots of cushions against a wall of books, and a similar seat built into a small curved brick wall (which breaks up the room). The main bar has built-in wall benches and plenty of stools and chairs around traditional pubby tables, and a further section with another small fire and plain dark wooden chairs and tables leads into the conservatory restaurant. Butcombe Bitter, Courage Best, Otter Bright and a guest like Princetown Jail Ale on handpump and ten wines by the glass; friendly staff. Piped music and board games.

▥ Enjoyable bar food includes lunchtime sandwiches, toasties, wraps and paninis and ploughman's, interesting soup, chargrilled chicken caesar salad, venison burger, thai green chicken curry, warm stilton and roasted pepper tart, cumberland sausages with onion and balsamic vinegar, slow-roasted lamb shank, chinese spiced duck breast with cranberry gravy, daily specials, and puddings like chocolate Malteser cappuccino or apple tarte tatin with honeycomb ice-cream. *Starters/Snacks: £4.50 to £6.00. Main Courses: £8.50 to £16.00. Puddings: £4.50*

> Virtually all pubs in this book sell wine by the glass. We mention wines if
> they are a cut above the average.

Buccaneer Holdings ~ Manager James Pound ~ Real ale ~ Bar food (12-2.30, 6-9.30(9 Sun)) ~ Restaurant ~ (01803) 863880 ~ Children welcome ~ Dogs allowed in bar ~ Live jazz every second Sun lunchtime ~ Open 11-11; 12-10.30 Sun ~ Bedrooms: £59.50B/£79.50B

Recommended by P Dawn, Frogeye, Mrs M Tee, Mike Gorton, Dr and Mrs M E Wilson, John and Alison Hamilton, Lesley and Peter Barrett, David Crook, Jo Rees

TUCKENHAY   SX8156   MAP 1

Maltsters Arms ♀

Take Ashprington road out of Totnes (signed left off A381 on outskirts), keeping on past Watermans Arms; TQ9 7EQ

Lovely spot by wooded creek with tables by the water, a good choice of drinks and varied food

This is a lovely creekside spot and there are tables on the terrace by the water with outdoor heaters and an outside bar. Inside, the long, narrow bar links two other rooms – a small snug one with an open fire and plenty of bric-a-brac and another with red-painted vertical seats and kitchen chairs on the wooden floor; there are nautical charts and local photographs on the walls. Blackawton 44 Special, Princetown Dartmoor IPA, Robinsons Old Tom and maybe South Hams Eddystone on handpump, quite a few wines by the glass, a dozen malt whiskies and a couple of local farm ciders. Several readers have felt the welcome from staff could be a lot friendlier. Darts, board games and TV for sports. More reports on service and housekeeping, please.

🍴 As well as lunchtime sandwiches and ploughman's, bar food includes soup, fried local squid in sweet spices with tomato and basil, pot-roasted pigeon in elderberry and red wine, potato gnocchi in tomato, olive and caper sauce, blackened cajun chicken, local dab with lemon and herb butter, half a duckling in honey and spices, and puddings like treacle tart or pear and madeira bread and butter pudding. *Starters/Snacks: £4.25 to £6.25. Main Courses: £9.25 to £18.95. Puddings: £4.25 to £4.75*

Free house ~ Licensees Denise and Quentin Thwaites ~ Real ale ~ Bar food (12-3(4 Sun), 7-9.30) ~ Restaurant ~ (01803) 732350 ~ Children welcome away from bar ~ Dogs welcome ~ Live music first and third Fri of month ~ Open 11-11 ~ Bedrooms: /£65S(£95B)

Recommended by Michael B Griffith, Gareth Lewis, Peter Burton, MP, Mike Gorton, Sue Heath, Alan and Anne Driver, OPUS, Hannah Selinger, John Day

WIDECOMBE   SX7276   MAP 1

Rugglestone

Village at end of B3387; pub just S – turn left at church and NT church house, OS Sheet 191 map reference 720765; TQ13 7TF

Unspoilt local near busy tourist village with just a couple of bars, cheerful customers and homely food

New licensees have taken over this unspoilt local but the place remains as busy as ever. It's in rural surroundings – though just up the road from the bustling tourist village – and if you sit outside in the field, across the little moorland stream, where there are lots of picnic-sets, you might be joined by some wild dartmoor ponies. Tables and chairs in the garden, too. The small bar has a strong country atmosphere and plenty of cheerful customers, just four small tables, a few window and wall seats, a one-person pew built into the corner by the nice old stone fireplace, and a rudimentary bar counter dispensing Butcombe Bitter, Cotleigh Kookaburra and St Austell Dartmoor Best tapped from the cask; local farm cider and a decent little wine list. The room on the right is a bit bigger and lighter-feeling with another stone fireplace, beamed ceiling, stripped pine tables, and a built-in wall bench. There's also a small room which is used for dining.

Pubs in outstandingly attractive surroundings are listed at the back of the book.

🍽 Good, straightforward bar food now includes filled baguettes and baps, pasties, filled baked potatoes, soup, home-made chicken liver and cranberry pâté, stilton and mushroom quiche, steak and kidney pie, fish pie, ham and eggs, beer-battered fresh haddock and lambs liver with bacon and onion gravy. *Starters/Snacks: £3.75 to £5.95. Main Courses: £7.95 to £9.95. Puddings: £3.50 to £4.50*

Free house ~ Licensees Richard Palmer and Vicky Moore ~ Real ale ~ Bar food ~ (01364) 621327 ~ Children allowed but must be away from bar area ~ Dogs welcome ~ Open 11.30-3, 6.30-midnight; 11.30(12 Sun)-midnight Sat

Recommended by J D O Carter, Theocsbrian, R J Walden, Lynne Carter, Donna and Roger, Michael and Ann Cole, David and Paula Russell, the Didler, Geoff and Carol Thorp, Mr and Mrs A R Maden, Mike Gorton, Ken Flawn, JHW, Dr and Mrs M E Wilson, Peter Craske

WINKLEIGH   SS6308   MAP 1

Kings Arms

Village signposted off B3220 Crediton—Torrington; Fore Street; EX19 8HQ

Friendly pub with woodburning stoves in beamed bar and popular pubby food served all day

Bustling and friendly, this thatched village pub has a good mix of both locals and visitors. The attractive beamed main bar has some old-fashioned built-in wall settles, scrubbed pine tables and benches on the flagstones and a woodburning stove in a cavernous fireplace; another woodburning stove separates the bar from the dining rooms (one has military memorabilia and a mine shaft). Butcombe Bitter and Sharps Cornish Coaster and Doom Bar on handpump, local cider and decent wines; darts, board games, shut-the-box, and dominoes. There are seats out in the garden.

🍽 Popular bar food includes sandwiches, soup, chicken liver pâté, mushrooms in creamy garlic sauce, vegetable shepherd's pie, haddock and chips, ham or sausages and eggs, lambs liver and bacon with onion gravy, curry of the day, pork medallions in cider sauce, mixed grill and loin of lamb with rosemary and redcurrant sauce; cream teas served all day. *Starters/Snacks: £2.00 to £4.50. Main Courses: £5.95 to £13.95. Puddings: £3.50 to £4.50*

Enterprise ~ Lease Chris Guy and Julia Franklin ~ Real ale ~ Bar food (all day) ~ Restaurant ~ (01837) 83384 ~ Children welcome ~ Dogs welcome ~ Open 11-11(midnight Sat); 12-10.30 Sun

Recommended by Mr and Mrs Syson, Mayur Shah, John Lane, R J Walden, Alan and Ruth Hooper, W M Paton, Mark Flynn

WOODBURY SALTERTON   SY0189   MAP 1

Diggers Rest 🍽

3½ miles from M5 junction 30: A3052 towards Sidmouth, village signposted on right about ½ mile after Clyst St Mary; also signposted from B3179 SE of Exeter; EX5 1PQ

Bustling village pub with emphasis on good food (welcome for drinkers too), and lovely views from terraced garden

There are always plenty of customers in this well run thatched village pub. Readers like the main bar with its antique furniture, local art on the walls, and cosy seating area by the open fire with its extra large sofa and armchair. The modern extension is light and airy and opens on to the garden with contemporary garden furniture under canvas parasols on the terrace and lovely countryside views. Butcombe Bitter, Otter Bitter and Scatter Rock Scatty Bitter on handpump and 15 wines by the glass; efficient service from young antipodean staff; piped music.

🍽 Even by Devon's high standards, the Diggers take enormous care over the quality and provenance of what goes into their good, popular food. This includes sandwiches, nibbles such as home-made red pepper hummus and tzatziki with crudités, soup, coarse country pâté, warm red onion and goats cheese tart, fresh haddock and herb fishcakes with crème fraîche and dill tartare sauce, free-range pork sausages with onion gravy, pasta in a mushroom, garlic, parmesan and cream sauce, lamb casserole with wild mushroom dumplings, local venison with butternut purée and pear chutney, daily specials, and puddings like rich chocolate brownie with hot chocolate sauce or crème brûlée. *Starters/Snacks: £3.85 to £6.95. Main Courses: £8.75 to £15.50. Puddings: £4.75*

Free house ~ Licensee Stephen Rushton ~ Real ale ~ Bar food (all day weekends) ~ (01395) 232375 ~ Children welcome ~ Dogs allowed in bar ~ Open 11-3, 6-11; 11-11 Sun and Sat

Recommended by Mike Gorton, John and Jackie Chalcraft, Tracey and Stephen Groves, J Kirkland, M G Hart, Paul and Shirley White, John Evans, Dr and Mrs M E Wilson, Emma Kingdon, David and Pauline Brenner, Mr and Mrs A R Maden, Hugh Roberts, Mr and Mrs W Mills, Richard Wyld, Joan and Michel Hooper-Immins, Gene and Tony Freemantle

YEALMPTON   SX5851   MAP 1

Rose & Crown ✗🍴 ♈

A379 Kingsbridge—Plymouth; PL8 2EB

Smart modern place with plenty of dark wood and heavy brass, neat staff, and contemporary food plus attractive adjacent seafood restaurant

Part of Wykeham Inns (along with the Dartmoor Union over at Holbeton), this is a civilised and stylish place for a drink or a meal. The big central bar counter, all dark wood and heavy brass with good solid leather-seated bar stools, has Courage Best, Fullers London Pride, Otter Ale and Sharps Doom Bar on handpump, ten wines by the glass and a fine choice of other drinks too; quick, friendly service by neatly aproned black-dressed staff. There's an attractive mix of tables and old dining chairs, good lighting, and some leather sofas down on the left. With its stripped wood floor and absence of curtains and other soft furnishings, the open-plan bar's acoustics are lively; beige carpeting keeps the two dining areas on the right rather quieter and here smart leather high-backed dining chairs, flowers on the tablecloths and framed 1930s high-life posters take you a notch or two upscale. They also have an attractive adjacent seafood restaurant with super big fishing photographs, lobster pots and nets on decking, and high-backed powder blue cushioned dining chairs around white clothed tables.

🍴 Modern restauranty food includes sandwiches, pressing of chicken, pheasant and parma ham with honey jelly and prune purée, local crab with sweet pepper coulis and pesto, scallops, roasted cantaloupe melon, coriander pesto and curry oil, wild mushroom risotto with aged parmesan and white truffle oil, roast duck breast with vanilla purée and armagnac, braised turbot with shellfish nage and lettuce sauce, and puddings such as hot chocolate fondant with white chocolate mousse or iced mandarin parfait with poached clementines and melon soup *Starters/Snacks: £3.00 to £9.00. Main Courses: £6.00 to £12.00. Puddings: £4.25 to £5.00*

Free house ~ Licensee Simon Warner ~ Real ale ~ Bar food (12-2(3 Sun), 6.30-9) ~ Restaurant ~ (01752) 880223 ~ Children welcome ~ Dogs allowed in bar ~ Open 12-11(10.30 Sun)

Recommended by John Evans, Richard and Deborah Morisot, J Crosby, Richard Beharrell

LUCKY DIP

Besides the fully inspected pubs, you might like to try these Lucky Dips recommended to us and described by readers (if you do, please send us reports: www.goodguides.co.uk).

ABBOTSHAM [SS4226]
Thatched Inn EX39 5BA Extensively refurbished family pub popular at lunchtime for good value pubby food from sandwiches and baked potatoes to fresh fish and Sun lunch, friendly staff, Fullers London Pride and Greene King Old Speckled Hen, mix of modern seating and older features (dates from 15th c); garden tables, handy for the Big Sheep *(Mark Flynn, June and Robin Savage)*

APPLEDORE [SS4630]
☆ *Beaver* EX39 1RY [Irsha St]: Relaxed good-humoured harbourside pub, good value generous honest cooking esp fresh local fish and good puddings, friendly helpful staff, Bideford Mainbrace and St Austell Tribute, farm cider, decent house wines, great range of whiskies, cuddly beaver toys on bar shelves, lovely estuary view from popular raised dining area; pool in smaller games room; children and dogs welcome, disabled

access (but no nearby parking), tables on small sheltered water-view terrace *(Rona Murdoch, Bob and Margaret Holder, Peter and Margaret Glenister, R J Walden, Roger Brown, John and Fiona McIlwain, Paul and Ursula Randall)*

Royal George EX39 1RY [Irsha St]: Good choice of real ales, thriving narrow bar (dogs allowed) with attractive pictures and well worn in front room, simple fresh food inc local fish, decent wines, dining room with superb estuary views; disabled access (but no nearby parking), picnic-sets outside, picturesque street sloping to sea *(Roger Brown, Rona Murdoch, Tom Evans)*

AVONWICK [SX7158]

Avon TQ10 9NB [off A38 at W end of South Brent bypass]: Comfortable light and airy dining pub with French chef/landlord doing good food in restaurant and bar, realistic prices, relaxed atmosphere, smart polite staff, real ales such as Badger Best and Teignworthy, decent wine choice, log fire; picnic-sets in meadow by River Avon, adventure playground *(LYM, John Evans, David Wharfe)*

AXMOUTH [SY2591]

☆ **Harbour Inn** EX12 4AF [B3172 Seaton—Axminster]: Prettily set thatched pub doing well under hard-working and popular newish owners (she's Spanish), low beams, flagstones, traditional settles and big log fires, good proper cooking, adventurous without being too fancy, from plenty of sandwiches, baguettes and snacks to good value Sun roast (food all day then), real ales, friendly staff, big simple summer family bar; children very welcome, disabled access and facilities, tables in neat back garden *(LYM, Penny Simpson)*

BAMPTON [SS9520]

☆ **Exeter Inn** EX16 9DY [A396 some way S, at B3227 roundabout]: Long low stone-built roadside pub under steep hill overlooking River Exe, fairly handy for Knightshayes Court, several friendly and comfortable linked rooms, mainly flagstoned, sensible choice of good reasonably priced bar food inc plenty of fresh fish, large pleasant restaurant, Cotleigh Tawny and Exmoor Ale and a monthly guest beer tapped from the cask, decent coffee, welcoming helpful landlord, quick bar service, log fire, daily papers, no piped music; tables out in front, good value bedrooms, good breakfast, open all day *(Paul Rampton, Martin and Pauline Jennings, BB, Dr A McCormick)*

BANTHAM [SX6643]

Sloop TQ7 3AJ [off A379/B3197 NW of Kingsbridge]: Popular updated beamed and flagstoned pub in great spot across dunes from lovely beach, character bar with big-screen TV, woodburner and sofa, real ales, good wines, good friendly young staff, sturdy tables in ship-shaped dining room (two evening sittings, 6.30 and 8.30), lots of children; dogs warmly welcomed, seats outside, bedrooms, plenty of surrounding

walks *(Lynda and Trevor Smith, M Thomas, Bob and Margaret Holder, Stephen Wood, MP, Theocsbrian, H G H Stafford, David Barnes, LYM)*

BARNSTAPLE [SS5533]

Panniers EX31 1RX [Boutport St]: Busy reliable Wetherspoons with good value beers and cider, simple appetising food all day *(Dr and Mrs M E Wilson)*

BEER [ST2289]

☆ **Anchor** EX12 3ET [Fore St]: Neat and spacious sea-view dining pub with enjoyable food from sandwiches and baked potatoes to good local and brixham fish, Greene King IPA and Abbot and Otter, decent wines, genial management, prompt and friendly young staff, rambling open-plan layout with old local photographs, large eating area; sports TV, piped music; reasonably priced bedrooms, lots of tables in attractive clifftop garden over road, delightful seaside village – parking may not be easy *(Rod and Chris Pring, Pat and Tony Martin, Lawrence Pearse, Mr and Mrs P A Stevens, LYM, Neil and Lorna Mclaughlan, Penny Simpson)*

☆ **Barrel o' Beer** EX12 3EQ [Fore St]: Lively and informal family-run pub with good interestingly cooked local fish and seafood (they cure and smoke their own) as well as simpler more straightforward dishes, sandwiches too (the crab's good), Exe Valley Bitter and Devon Glory and a guest beer, choice of ciders, log fire, very small back dining area; piped music; dogs welcome, open all day *(Howard and Margaret Buchanan, George Atkinson, Mike Gorton, BB)*

☆ **Dolphin** EX12 3EQ [Fore St]: Open-plan local quite near sea, old-fashioned décor, oak panelling, nautical bric-a-brac and interesting nooks inc marvellous old distorting mirrors and antique boxing prints in corridors leading to back antique stalls, very wide choice of good value food from lunchtime sandwiches to good local fish, Cotleigh real ales, decent wine, cheery staff; piped music; children and dogs welcome, one or two tables out by pavement, bedrooms *(LYM, Mike Gorton, Joan and Michel Hooper-Immins)*

BERRYNARBOR [SS5546]

☆ **Olde Globe** EX34 9SG [off A399 E of Ilfracombe]: Rambling dim-lit rooms, low ceilings and ancient walls and flagstones, high-backed oak settles, cushioned cask seats around antique tables, lots of old pictures, cutlasses, swords, shields and rustic bric-a-brac, Golden Hill Exmoor, Shepherd Neame Spitfire and Wadworths 6X, reasonably priced straightforward food, darts and pool; piped music; dogs and children welcome in parts, crazy-paved front terrace, play area, pretty village *(Lisa Robertson, John and Alison Hamilton, Lynda and Trevor Smith, LYM)*

BIDEFORD [SS4526]

Kings Arms EX39 2HW [The Quay]: Cheerful old-fashioned 16th-c local with Victorian harlequin floor tiles in alcovey front bar, friendly staff, local ales such as Jollyboat Grenvilles Favourite, decent wines by the glass, reasonably priced usual food (not Fri/Sat evenings) from filled rolls to steaks, back raised family area; piped music; dogs welcome, pavement tables *(John and Alison Hamilton, Dennis Jenkin)*

BIGBURY [SX6647]

Royal Oak TQ7 4AP Welcoming multi-level village pub with good value food inc local fish, good choice of wines by the glass, Sharps Doom Bar, eager-to-please management, good atmosphere, restaurant; attractive flowers outside *(Lynne Carter)*

BISHOP'S TAWTON [SS5629]

☆ *Chichester Arms* EX32 0DQ [signed off A377 outside Barnstaple; East St]: Friendly 15th-c cob and thatch pub with well priced good generous food from home-made soup and sandwiches to fresh local fish and seasonal game (all meat from named local farms), quick obliging service even when crowded, Greene King Abbot and other ales, decent wines, heavy low beams, large stone fireplace with log fire, restaurant; children welcome, disabled access not good but staff very helpful, picnic-sets on front terrace and in back garden, open all day *(LYM, Mark Flynn, B M Eldridge, Mrs Angela Graham)*

BOVEY TRACEY [SX8178]

Old Thatched TQ13 9AW [Station Rd]: Attractive 15th-c pub with wide choice of good value food, welcoming landlady and staff, good beer; gets busy at holiday times *(Ken Flawn, Dudley and Moira Cockroft)*

BOW [SS7101]

White Hart EX17 6EN [A3072 W of Crediton]: Beamed bar with friendly helpful newish licensees, enjoyable food, good beers and wines, settles and huge inglenook log fire, small dining room; tables in big back garden *(Ken Flawn, BB)*

BRAYFORD [SS7235]

☆ *Poltimore Arms* EX36 3HA [Yarde Down; 3 miles towards Simonsbath]: Old-fashioned 17th-c two-bar beamed local, so remote it generates its own electricity, friendly landlord and cheerful obliging staff, enticing good value blackboard food inc good Sun roast, real ales such as Adnams, Cotleigh Tawny and Exmoor and Greene King Abbot tapped from the cask, good wines by the glass, basic traditional furnishings, fine woodburner in inglenook, interesting ornaments, two attractive restaurant areas; children welcome, also dogs on leads (pub has own dogs), picnic-sets in side garden, has been cl winter lunchtimes *(LYM, Stan and Hazel Allen, Andrew Scott, George Atkinson, B M Eldridge)*

BRENDON [SS7547]

☆ *Rockford Inn* EX35 6PT [Rockford; Lynton—Simonsbath rd, off B3223]: Small linked rooms in unspoilt and interesting 17th-c beamed inn by East Lyn river, friendly staff, limited low-priced homely food from good proper sandwiches and baked potatoes up,

cream teas (all day in summer), Cotleigh Barn Owl and a beer brewed for the pub tapped from the cask, Addlestone's cider, good house wines and choice of malt whiskies, farm cider, woodburners, lots of local pictures, traditional games, restaurant; children in eating areas, quiet dogs on leads welcome (sweet resident springer), good walks, bedrooms, cl Sun evening and Mon out of season *(George Atkinson, Sheila Topham, LYM, B M Eldridge)*

☆ *Staghunters* EX35 6PS Welcoming new licensees in idyllically set newly renovated hotel with gardens by East Lyn river, neat bar with woodburner, good value food, good log fire, Exmoor Ale and Gold, restaurant; can get very busy; walkers and dogs welcome, twelve good value bedrooms *(Lynda and Trevor Smith, Mrs Carolyn Dixon, George Atkinson)*

BRIDESTOWE [SX5287]

Fox & Hounds EX20 4HF [A386 Okehampton—Tavistock]: Popular and friendly moors-edge local, old-fashioned and well worn in, good value generous food (all day at least in summer) inc good steaks and specials (two dining rooms), good range of real ales; TV in extension public bar; dogs welcome, bedrooms, open all day *(BB, JCW)*

BRIXHAM [SX9256]

Blue Anchor TQ5 8AH [Fore St/King St]: Attractive harbourside pub with Dartmoor Best, Greene King Abbot and a guest beer, banquettes and plenty of nautical hardware, cheerfully served food from good value sandwiches to low-priced hot meals in two small dining rooms with some interesting old photographs – one a former chapel, down some steps; open all day *(Richard Fendick)*

BROADHEMPSTON [SX8066]

☆ *Coppa Dolla* TQ9 6BD Good ambitious food at sensible prices inc two-in-one pies and fine steaks, children's helpings, welcoming hands-on landlord, real ale such as Fullers London Pride tapped from the cask, good choice of wines by the glass, log fires, small comfortable bar and dining area divided by sturdy timber props, more tables upstairs; well spaced picnic-sets in attractive garden with country views *(Gary Marchant, BB, Mrs Bridget Cushion, Gerry and Rosemary Dobson)*

BUCKFASTLEIGH [SX7466]

Kings Arms TQ11 0BT [Fore St]: Small and welcoming, with genial landlord, short choice of good value food, Marstons Old Peculier; dogs welcome, beautiful garden, bedrooms *(Michael and Ann Cole)*

BUDLEIGH SALTERTON [SY0681]

Feathers EX9 6LE [High St]: Good bustling atmosphere, well kept ales at reasonable prices, nice mix of customers *(Dr and Mrs M E Wilson, Mr and Mrs A R Maden)*

☆ *Salterton Arms* EX9 6LX [Chapel St]: Recently refurbished, with partly divided open-plan layout, enjoyable reasonably priced food in bar and roomy upstairs gallery restaurant, thriving friendly atmosphere, three real ales, farm cider, darts on right; children welcome, open all day wknds *(LYM, Dr and Mrs M E Wilson)*

BURGH ISLAND [SX6444]

Pilchard TQ7 4BG [300 yds across tidal sands from Bigbury-on-Sea; walk, or summer Tractor if tide's in – unique bus on stilts]: Sadly the splendid beamed and flagstoned upper bar with its lanterns, parrot and roaring log fire is now reserved for people staying in the associated flamboyantly art deco hotel, but the more utilitarian roadside lower bar is still worth a visit for the unbeatable setting high above the sea swarming below this tidal island; Sharps, Thwaites Lancaster Bomber and an ale brewed for the pub, local farm cider, friendly chatty staff, lunchtime baguettes; tables outside, some down by beach *(Donna and Roger, Graham Oddey, LYM, the Didler)*

CALIFORNIA CROSS [SX7053]

☆ *California* PL21 0SG Thoughtfully modernised 18th-c or older pub with beams, panelling, stripped stone and log fire, wide choice of good sensibly priced food from sandwiches to steaks in dining bar and family area, good menu for new restaurant, small separate snug, friendly efficient staff, well kept local ales as well as Fullers London Pride and Greene King Old Speckled Hen, decent wines, local farm cider; children and dogs welcome, attractive garden and back terrace, open all day *(Pam Williams, Neil and Anita Christopher, Jonathan Bell, Bob and Margaret Holder)*

CHALLACOMBE [SS6941]

☆ *Black Venus* EX31 4TT [B3358 Blackmoor Gate—Simonsbath]: Low-beamed 16th-c pub with good varied food from sandwiches and baguettes to blackboard specials, friendly staff, two changing ales, Thatcher's farm cider, pews and comfortable chairs, woodburner and big open fire, roomy and attractive dining area; garden tables, grand countryside *(Stan and Hazel Allen, BB, B M Eldridge)*

CHUDLEIGH [SX8679]

Bishop Lacey TQ13 0HY [Fore St, just off A38]: Quaint partly 14th-c low-beamed church house with cheerful obliging landlady and staff, good choice of changing largely local real ales, enjoyable food using local produce cooked by landlord, good strong coffee, two log fires, dark décor, dining room; live bands in next-door offshoot; children welcome, garden tables, winter beer festival, bedrooms, open all day *(John Urquhart, the Didler)*

CHUDLEIGH KNIGHTON [SX8477]

Claycutters Arms TQ13 0EY [just off A38 by B3344]: Attractive 17th-c thatched two-bar village pub with real ales such as Fullers London Pride and Otter, home-made food from sandwiches and baguettes up (can take a while), polite service, decent wines by the glass, stripped stone, interesting nooks and crannies, pleasant restaurant; piped pop

music; dogs and children welcome, tables on side terrace and in orchard *(Alain and Rose Foote, LYM, Mr and Mrs D J Nash)*

CHURCHSTOW [SX7145]

Church House TQ7 3QW [A379 NW of Kingsbridge]: New management in long pub dating from 13th c, much refurbished though keeping heavy black beams and stripped stone, helpful staff, sturdy food, local ales, decent wines, back conservatory with floodlit well feature; well behaved children welcome, tables outside *(David Barnes, LYM, B J Harding)*

CHURSTON FERRERS [SX9056]

☆ *Churston Court* TQ5 0JE [off A3022 S of Torquay; Church Rd]: Interesting converted manor house, largely early 17th-c, in pretty spot next to ancient church; warren of candlelit rooms, plenty of beams, flagstones and open fires inc a massive inglenook, suits of armour, historic portraits, faded tapestries, long wooden tables, sofas, gilt-framed mirrors, Greene King Abbot, Princetown Dartmoor and Jail, friendly service, food inc Sun lunchtime carvery; children allowed, lots of tables in attractive walled lawn, quirky individual bedrooms, good walks nearby, open all day *(Dr and Mrs M E Wilson, LYM, P Dawn)*

CLEARBROOK [SX5265]

Skylark PL20 6JD [village signed down dead end off A386 Tavistock—Plymouth]: Simple two-room pub in pretty cottage row tucked right into Dartmoor, enjoyable usual food running up to big steaks, well kept ales, log fire; piped music; pleasant family room in big back garden with plenty of picnic-sets and other seats, small adventure play area, wandering ponies *(BB, Ted George, Richard May)*

CLOVELLY [SS3225]

New Inn EX39 5TQ [High St]: Attractive old inn halfway down the steep cobbled street, simple easy-going lower bar with flagstones and bric-a-brac (narrow front part has more character than back eating room), well kept Sharps Cornish Coaster and a beer brewed for the pub by local Country Life, upstairs restaurant; quiet piped music; bedrooms *(Mrs Hazel Rainer, Bruce Bird)*

Red Lion EX39 5TF [The Quay]: Rambling building in lovely position on curving quay below spectacular cliffs, beams, flagstones and interesting local photographs in character back bar, well kept Sharps Doom Bar and a beer from local Country Life, bar food and upstairs restaurant; simple attractive bedrooms *(Bruce Bird)*

CLYST ST GEORGE [SX9888]

St George & Dragon EX3 0QJ Spaciously extended open-plan Vintage Inn, fresh and cheerful décor, with careful lighting, low beams and some secluded corners, log fires, welcoming and helpful young staff, real ales, good choice of wines by the glass; good value bedrooms in adjoining Innkeepers Lodge, open all day *(Dr and Mrs M E Wilson)*

CLYST ST MARY [SX9791]

☆ *Half Moon* EX5 1BR [under a mile from M5 junction 30 via A376]: Attractive and genuine old pub next to disused multi-arched bridge (Devon's oldest) over Clyst, generous reasonably priced home-made food inc interesting dishes, cheerful attentive service, Bass, Fullers London Pride and Otter, friendly unpretentious local atmosphere, red plush seating, log fire; wheelchair access, bedrooms *(Dr and Mrs M E Wilson, Mr and Mrs A Green)*

COFFINSWELL [SX8968]

☆ *Linny* TQ12 4SR [just off A380 at Kingskerswell S of Newton Abbot]: Very pretty partly 14th-c thatched country pub in picturesque village, wide choice of good generous food inc lots of fresh fish, good steaks and fine local cheeseboard, friendly attentive service, Bass and Fullers London Pride, big beamed bar with traditional settles and other comfortable and individual seats, smaller areas off, cosy log fires, lots of twinkling brass, children's room, upstairs restaurant extension; tables outside *(Philip Kingsbury, Mr and Mrs Colin Roberts, BB, Darren and Jane Staniforth)*

COLYFORD [SY2492]

White Hart EX24 6QF [A3052 Exeter—Lyme Regis, by tramway stn]: Popular riverside pub with wide standard menu from good baguettes up, good fish choice, large main bar, interesting and well kept changing real ales, wide choice of wine, log fires, skittle alley, restaurant; garden tables *(Steve and Liz Tilley)*

COLYTON [SY2494]

Gerrard Arms EX24 6JN [St Andrews Sq]: Unpretentious open-plan local with Bass, Branscombe Vale Branoc and a guest beer tapped from the cask, skittle alley, lunchtime food inc Sun roasts; tables in courtyard and informal garden *(the Didler, Pete Walker)*

☆ *Kingfisher* EX24 6NA [off A35 and A3052 E of Sidmouth; Dolphin St]: Low-beamed village pub with enjoyable food from popular baguettes and ploughman's to fresh local crab, well kept Badger ales, farm cider, good wines by the glass, big open fire, stripped stone, plush seats and elm settles, pub games, upstairs family room, skittle alley; parking can be a problem, outside gents'; tables out on terrace, garden with water feature *(Alun Evans, LYM, Meg and Colin Hamilton, Pete Walker, the Didler, LM)*

COMBE MARTIN [SS5747]

Dolphin EX34 0AW [Seaside]: Well placed pub long in same family, enjoyable fresh food inc local fish, good friendly staff, well kept beer, lots of whiskies and liqueurs, log fire, upstairs restaurant; may be quiet piped music; bedrooms *(Mr and Mrs C Gulvin)*

DARTINGTON [SX7861]

Cott TQ9 6HE [Cott signed off A385 W of Totnes, opp A384 turn-off]: Lovely long 14th-c thatched pub with plenty of potential in its heavy-beamed flagstoned core, well

kept Greene King IPA and Abbot, dining area with close-set tables for the popular daily carvery, wide choice of other food from sandwiches and baked potatoes up; children and dogs on leads welcome, picnic-sets in garden and on pretty terrace, open all day at least in summer *(Clifford Blakemore, Mr and Mrs A R Maden, David M Cundy, LYM)*

White Hart Bar TQ9 6EL [Dartington Hall]: Light bright modern décor and open fires in the college's bar (open to visitors), good low-priced food here and in baronial hall, well kept Otter ales, matter-of-fact service; very special atmosphere sitting out in the famously beautiful grounds *(Giles and Annie Francis)*

DARTMOUTH [SX8751]

Floating Bridge TQ6 9PQ [Coombe Rd]: Recently renovated in contemporary bistro style, with Greene King IPA and Old Speckled Hen and Otter, good range of reasonably priced food from enjoyable lunchtime sandwiches to fish and seafood, good Dart views and roof terrace *(Gerry and Rosemary Dobson, Ken Flawn)*

☆ *Royal Castle Hotel* TQ6 9PS [the Quay]: Rambling 17th-c or older hotel behind Regency façade overlooking inner harbour, traditional bar on right with dining area for all-day food from plain sandwiches to good steaks, perhaps winter lunchtime spit-roasts from their 300-year-old Lidstone range, bustling more contemporary bar on left (TV, piped music may be a bit loud, dogs very welcome – no children), pleasant efficient staff, Bass, Courage Directors and St Austell Dartmoor Best, restaurant; 25 comfortable bedrooms with secure parking, open all day *(David Carr, Keith and Margaret Kettell, Hugh Roberts, LYM, David and Karen Cuckney, W W Burke)*

DAWLISH [SX9676]

Exeter Inn EX7 9PN [Beach St]: Cosy linked bars, welcoming landlord, well kept Adnams, bar food, games room with pool across alley *(Phil and Sally Gorton)*

DENBURY [SX8268]

Union TQ12 6DQ [The Green]: Nice atmosphere in comfortable low-beamed pub under new landlord, good choice of real ales, enjoyable reasonably priced food, two eating areas; tables in garden by green of quietly pretty sheltered village *(BB, Ray Crabb)*

DITTISHAM [SX8654]

☆ *Ferry Boat* TQ6 0EX [Manor St; best to park in village – steep but attractive walk down]: Well refurbished family-friendly pub in idyllic waterside setting, big windows making the most of it, good choice of enjoyable home-made food using local produce from baguettes to fresh fish, home-made cakes, real ales such as Bass, Wychwood Hobgoblin and Youngs, organic drinks, beams and bare boards, lots of interesting bric-a-brac, warmly welcoming landlord and family; no parking, quite a walk down; nr little foot-ferry you call by bell, good walks, open all day *(Emma Kingdon, LYM, Peter and*

Giff Bennett, Sue Heath, Di and Mike Gillam, John Day)

DOWN THOMAS [SX5049]

Mussel PL9 0AQ Long low building, very welcoming, with good value food, attractive layout, eating area in split-level lower end, restaurant up beyond central bar; garden with huge well equipped playground (Margaret and Roy Randle)

DREWSTEIGNTON [SX7390]

☆ *Drewe Arms* EX6 6QN [off A30 NW of Moretonhampstead]: Popular old thatched pub with enjoyable food from pubby things to enterprising dishes using local ingredients, real ales such as Bass, Gales and Otter from casks in back tap room, charming old-fashioned layout, log fire, plenty of locals, sizeable back restaurant (children welcome); open all day, handy for Castle Drogo (Glenwys and Alan Lawrence, Ian and Joan Blackwell, Tom and Rosemary Hall, LYM, Andrea Rampley, Peter and Margaret Lodge, Colin and Peggy Wilshire)

☆ *Fingle Bridge Inn* EX6 6PW [E of village; OS Sheet 191 map ref 743899 – may be shown under its former Anglers Rest name]: Idyllic wooded Teign valley spot by 16th-c pack-horse bridge, lovely walks and a magnet for summer visitors; much extended former tea pavilion, tourist souvenirs and airy café feel, Exe Valley and Teignworthy ales, reliable substantial food from baguettes and good local cheese ploughman's up, Sun carvery, friendly helpful service, log fire; children and dogs welcome, waterside picnic-sets, has been cl winter evenings (Robert Gomme, Dr and Mrs M E Wilson, LYM)

DUNSFORD [SX8189]

Royal Oak EX6 7DA [signed from Moretonhampstead]: Well worn-in village inn with good generous food cooked to order, good choice of changing ales inc Princetown and Sharps, local farm cider, friendly landlord, light and airy lounge bar with woodburner and view from small sunny dining bay, simple dining room, steps down to games room with pool; quiz nights, piped music; children welcome, sheltered tiered garden, good value bedrooms in converted barn (the Didler, LYM)

EAST DOWN [SS5941]

Pyne Arms EX31 4LX [off A39 Barnstaple—Lynton nr Arlington]: Darkly appealing low-beamed bar with lots of alcoves, small galleried loft, enjoyable food inc good Sun lunch, real ales, good value house wines, flagstoned games area; handy for Arlington Court, good walks (Philip and Jude Simmons, LYM)

EXETER [SX9490]

Countess Wear EX2 6HE [on B3181 ring rd roundabout, Topsham Rd]: Well run Beefeater with reliable low-priced food, real ales such as Greene King Old Speckled Hen and Wadworths 6X, pleasant staff, good quick service even though busy; good value comfortable bedrooms in attached Travel Inn (Dr and Mrs A K Clarke, Dr and Mrs M E Wilson)

Double Locks EX2 6LT [Canal Banks, Alphington, via Marsh Barton Industrial Estate; OS Sheet 192 map ref 933901]: Remote and unpretentious refuge by ship canal, Youngs and guest ales often tapped straight from the cask, Gray's farm cider in summer, good value plain home-made bar food from sandwiches and hot filled rolls up all day; piped music, live wknds; children welcome in eating areas, dogs very welcome too, seats out on decking with distant view to city and cathedral (nice towpath walk out – or hire a canoe at the Quay), good big play area, camping, open all day (the Didler, LYM, Pete Walker, Peter Titcomb, Dr and Mrs A K Clarke)

Georges Meeting House EX1 1ED [South St]: Comfortable and vibrant Wetherspoons in grand former 18th-c chapel dominated by tall pulpit one end; stained glass, original pews in three-sided gallery, some leather settees, their usual food and good west country cheese, fish and meat, half a dozen real ales, good wine choice; children welcome when eating, quality furniture in attractive side garden, open all day (Dr and Mrs A K Clarke, John Fiander, Philip and Jude Simmons)

☆ *Great Western* EX4 4NU [St Davids Hill]: Up to a dozen or so changing real ales usually inc Adnams, Bass, Exmoor, Fullers London Pride and Teignworthy in large hotel's small split-level convivial bar, wholesome good value fresh food all day from sandwiches and generous baked potatoes up (kitchen also supplies the hotel's restaurant), daily papers, no music; 35 bedrooms, open all day (Phil and Sally Gorton, Colin Gooch, Dr and Mrs A K Clarke, the Didler)

☆ *Hour Glass* EX2 4AU [Melbourne St, off B3015 Topsham Rd]: Thriving bistro-feel 19th-c pub with interesting blackboard food inc delicatessen meats and good fish, also good tapas and nibbles, Adnams Broadside, Otter and Sharps Doom Bar, good choice of wines by the glass, cheerful helpful young staff, beams, bare boards, panelling, candles and open fire (Mike Gorton, Dr and Mrs A K Clarke, the Didler, Dr and Mrs M E Wilson)

Prospect EX2 4AN [The Quay (left bank, nr rowing club)]: Good quayside spot, good value up-to-date bar food from baguettes with chips and baked potatoes up, Adnams and Otter, friendly helpful young staff, plenty of comfortable tables inc raised river-view dining area, modern colour-scheme and prints contrasting with the old building's beams; gentle piped music; tables out by historic ship-canal basin (Peter Titcomb, Roger Thornington, Dr and Mrs A K Clarke, Peter Salmon)

Ship EX1 1EY [Martins Lane, nr cathedral]: Pretty 14th-c building with genuine dark heavy beams, done up inside in olde-worlde city pub style, with thriving friendly atmosphere, well kept Bass, Greene King Old Speckled Hen and Marstons Pedigree, farm cider; food can take a while (comfortable

upstairs restaurant) *(Andrew York, LYM)*
Welcome EX2 8DU [Haven Banks, off Haven Rd (which is first left off A377 heading S after Exe crossing)]: Two-room pub little changed since the 1960s (ditto the juke box), gas lighting and flagstones, very friendly old-school landlady, changing real ales; a few tables out overlooking basin on Exeter Ship Canal, and can be reached on foot via footbridges from The Quay *(Dr and Mrs A K Clarke, the Didler)*
Well House EX1 1HB [Cathedral Yard, attached to Royal Clarence Hotel]: Big windows looking across to cathedral in open-plan bar divided by inner walls and partitions, good choice of local ales such as Otter, quick service, wide range of reasonably priced upscale lunchtime food inc good sandwiches and salads, daily papers, sofa, lots of interesting Victorian prints, Roman well below (can be viewed when pub not busy); may be piped music; open all day *(Pete Walker, BB, Meg and Colin Hamilton, Dr and Mrs M E Wilson, Dr and Mrs A K Clarke)*
EXMINSTER [SX9587]
Swans Nest EX6 8DZ [Station Rd, just off A379 on outskirts]: Huge well arranged food pub very popular for grand carvery display of reasonably priced meats, pies and salads, also sandwiches and hot dishes from baked potatoes up, friendly staff, Otter Best and Youngs Special, comfortable seating – especially good for family groups; handy for M5 *(Keith and Margaret Kettell, LYM, Alain and Rose Foote, David Carr)*
EXMOUTH [SX9980]
Beach EX8 1DR [Victoria Rd]: Popular old quayside local with Bass, Greene King Old Speckled Hen and Otter, food, friendly landlord and staff, shipping and lifeboat memorabilia and photographs, beams, posts and panelling, cast-iron framed tables *(Dr and Mrs M E Wilson, Mrs Hazel Rainer)*
Imperial EX8 2SW [Esplanade]: Large Shearings hotel on seafront, comfortable lounge bar popular with older people, good value simple bar lunches though limited on the drinks side; plenty of garden and terrace tables, bedrooms *(MB)*
GEORGEHAM [SS4639]
Lower House EX33 1JJ [B3231 Croyde—Woolacombe]: Former Kings Arms entirely reworked by current owners, sofas, clean-cut décor, woodburner and flat-screen TV downstairs, friendly service, well kept St Austell and local guest ales such as Barum and Exmoor, reasonably priced wines by the glass, daily papers, good food in comfortably modern new restaurant upstairs; tables out on small front terrace screened from road *(Paul and Ursula Randall, John and Fiona McIlwain)*
☆ **Rock** EX33 1JW [Rock Hill, above village]: Well kept ales such as Cotleigh Golden Eagle, Fullers London Pride, Greene King Abbot and St Austell Tribute in welcoming beamed pub with friendly quick-witted landlady and cheerful staff, wide range of good value

generous food from baguettes to plenty of fish, local farm cider, open fire, old red quarry tiles, pleasant mix of rustic furniture, lots of bric-a-brac, separate vine-adorned back family conservatory (children allowed in pool room too); piped music, darts, fruit machine, juke box; dogs welcome, tables under cocktail parasols on flower-decked front terrace *(Peter and Margaret Glenister, Paul and Ursula Randall, Philip and Jude Simmons, Mark Flynn, BB, B M Eldridge)*
GOODLEIGH [SS5934]
New Inn EX32 7LX Welcoming pubby atmosphere, chatty locals, two well kept changing ales, good blackboard choice of enjoyable reasonably priced food cooked to order, log fire *(Gordon Tong)*
GOODRINGTON [SX8959]
Inn on the Quay TQ4 6LP [Tanners Rd]: Huge comfortable Brewers Fayre family dining pub, good atmosphere and service, well supervised play room and outdoor play area, baby-changing, disabled facilities; quiet TV and piped music; dogs allowed in non-food areas, garden, handy for beach and Quaywest, open all day *(John Wassell)*
HATHERLEIGH [SS5404]
George EX20 3JN [A386 N of Okehampton; Market St]: Timbered pub with huge oak beams, enormous fireplace, easy chairs, sofas and antique cushioned settles in original core, more modern main bar, more settles and woodburner in L-shaped beamed back bar, good value simple generous food, cheery staff, Bass, St Austell Dartmoor Best and a beer named for the pub, lots of malt whiskies, farm cider, restaurant; children in eating area, dogs in bar, rustic tables in pretty courtyard and walled cobbled garden, bedrooms, open all day *(the Didler, LYM, Ryta Lyndley)*
☆ **Tally Ho** EX20 3JN [Market St (A386)]: Attractive heavy-beamed and timbered linked rooms, sturdy furnishings, big log fire and woodburner, ample enjoyable food from lunchtime sandwiches up, local Clearwater ales, welcoming staff, traditional games, restaurant; may be piped music; tables in nice sheltered garden, three pretty bedrooms *(LYM, the Didler, David Ashton)*
HEXWORTHY [SX6572]
Forest Inn PL20 6SD [signed off B3357 Tavistock—Ashburton, E of B3212]: Gorgeous Dartmoor setting, roomy plush-seated open-plan bar and back walkers' bar, short daily-changing choice of generous bar and restaurant food using fresh local produce, prompt service, well kept Teignworthy ales with a guest such as Otter, local cider, friendly helpful staff, real fire, daily papers; dogs and boots welcome, comfortable bedrooms (also bunkhouse), fishing permits, good walking and riding *(M G Hart, LYM)*
HOLBETON [SX6150]
Mildmay Colours PL8 1NA [off A379 W of A3121]: Local beers inc one brewed for the pub by Skinners, local farm cider, generous

food from sandwiches and baguettes up (and chinese restaurant behind), stripped stone and timbers, woodburner, small family room, games area; piped music, TV, fruit machine; dogs and children welcome, colourful front terrace, well kept back garden, comfortable bedrooms, good breakfast *(LYM, Margaret and Roy Randle, Jeremy Whitehorn, B J Harding, Tracey and Stephen Groves)*

HOLCOMBE [SX9575]
Castle Inn EX7 0LF [Fordens Lane, off A379]: Small and friendly, with enjoyable and reasonably priced sensible food using local ingredients, well kept Greene King Old Speckled Hen, lovely views; no dogs or credit cards; nice courtyard *(Michael and Ann Cole)*

HOLSWORTHY [SS3403]
Kings Arms EX22 6EB [Fore St/The Square]: 17th-c village pub with Victorian fittings, etched windows and coal fires in three interesting traditional bars, friendly regulars, well kept Bass and Sharps Doom Bar, food inc proper fresh sandwiches, old pictures and photographs, 40s and 50s beer advertisements, lots of optics behind ornate counter with snob screens; dogs welcome, open all day, Sun afternoon closure *(Dennis Jenkin, the Didler)*
Rydon Inn EX22 7HU [Rydon (A3072 W)]: Enjoyable food in comfortable dining pub with two dining rooms; disabled access and facilities, dogs welcome by arrangement in part of bar, garden tables *(Dennis Jenkin)*

HONITON [SY1198]
Holt EX14 1LA [High St]: Short choice of good interesting up-to-date food, well kept Otter *(Michael B Griffith)*
Red Cow EX14 1PW [High St]: Welcoming local, very busy on Tues and Sat market days, scrubbed tables, pleasant alcoves, log fires, real ales such as local Otter, decent wines and malt whiskies, good value quickly served no-nonsense food from sandwiches up in restaurant part, lots of chamber-pots and big mugs on beams; pavement tables, bedrooms *(BB, B J Harding)*

HOPE COVE [SX6740]
☆ **Hope & Anchor** TQ7 3HQ Cheerfully unpretentious inn, friendly and comfortably unfussy in lovely seaside spot, good open fire, kind quick service, good value straightforward food inc good crab sandwiches, well kept St Austell Dartmoor and a beer brewed for the pub, reasonably priced wines, flagstones and bare boards, great bay views to Burgh Island from dining room, big separate family room; piped music; children and dogs welcome, sea-view tables out on decking, great coast walks, bedrooms, open all day *(Mr and Mrs G Owens, LYM, Michael and Ann Cole, David and Karen Cuckney)*

HORNS CROSS [SS3823]
☆ **Hoops** EX39 5DL [A39 Clovelly—Bideford, W of village]: Picturesque thatched inn with oak settles, beams and inglenook log fires in pleasant bar, enjoyable food, well kept Sharps and other ales tapped from the cask inc one brewed for the pub, local farm cider,

good wine choice, good welcoming service, daily papers, darts; what we call piped music (actually separate CD players in bar and restaurant), TV; well behaved children in eating area till 8, dogs allowed in bar, tables in small courtyard, bedrooms, open all day *(Nick Lawless, Peter and Margaret Lodge, LYM, Peter and Margaret Glenister, Mr and Mrs A J Hudson, John and Jackie Chalcraft, R J Walden)*

HORSEBRIDGE [SX4074]
☆ **Royal** PL19 8PJ [off A384 Tavistock—Launceston]: Cheerful slate-floored rooms, interesting bric-a-brac and pictures, simple good value food from baguettes and baked potatoes to fresh scallops, friendly landlord and staff, well kept Bass, Blackawton and Sharps Doom Bar and Special, Rich's farm cider, log fire, bar billiards, cribbage, dominoes, café-style side room, no music or machines; no children in evening, picnic-sets on back terrace and in big garden, quiet rustic spot by lovely old Tamar bridge *(LYM, Mrs J H S Lang, Alistair Caie, R M Yard, Peter Craske)*

IDE [SX8990]
☆ **Poachers** EX2 9RW [3 miles from M5 junction 31, via A30; High St]: Friendly and individual, with nice non-standard mix of old chairs and sofas, good generous food, both traditional and inventive, from sandwiches to good fish choice (worth booking evenings), Bass, Branscombe Vale Branoc, Otter and one brewed locally for the pub, good value house wines, big log fire; picnic-sets in pleasant garden, attractive and comfortable bedrooms, small quaint village, cl Mon lunchtime *(Cheryl Haddy, Phil and Sally Gorton, the Didler)*

IDEFORD [SX8977]
☆ **Royal Oak** TQ13 0AY [2 miles off A380]: Unpretentious 16th-c thatched and flagstoned village local with friendly helpful service, Bass, Timothy Taylors Landlord and two guest beers, good generous simple food inc bargain steaks, interesting Nelson and Churchill memorabilia, big log fireplace; children and dogs welcome, tables out by car park over road *(Darren and Jane Staniforth, the Didler, Phil and Sally Gorton)*

ILFRACOMBE [SS5247]
George & Dragon EX34 9ED [Fore St]: Oldest pub here, handy for harbour, with good local atmosphere, helpful friendly staff, Brakspears, Courage and Shepherd Neame Spitfire, decent wines, low-priced pubby food, attractive olde-worlde décor with stripped stone, open fireplaces, lots of ornaments, china etc; piped music, cash machine but no credit cards *(Philip and Jude Simmons, Miss J F Reay, Dave Braisted)*

INSTOW [SS4730]
Wayfarer EX39 4LB [Lane End]: Refurbished under new management, tucked away nr dunes and beach, welcoming staff, well kept ales tapped from the cask, enjoyable food using local fish and meats; children and dogs welcome, enclosed garden behind,

smartly redone bedrooms (some with sea view), open all day *(Colin Canavan)*

KINGSBRIDGE [SX7344]

Dodbrooke Inn TQ7 1DB [Church St, Dodbrooke]: Cosy and comfortably traditional local with unfussy welcome, well kept ales such as Arundel Castle, Bass, Palmers and Youngs, local farm cider, wide choice of enjoyable well priced food inc enterprising specials and puddings, log fire, good local evening atmosphere; unobtrusive piped music *(J Iorwerth Davies, MP)*

KINGSTEIGNTON [SX8773]

Old Rydon TQ12 3QG [Rydon Rd]: Dining pub with big log fire in small cosy heavy-beamed bar with upper gallery, roomy vine-draped dining conservatory, ample above-average pub food, good choice of beers and wines, welcoming staff; piped music; tables on terrace and in nice sheltered garden *(David and Sue Smith, LYM)*

KINGSWEAR [SX8851]

Royal Dart TQ6 0AA [The Square]: Fine setting by ferry and Dart Valley Railway terminal, great view of Dartmouth from balcony outside upstairs restaurant, enjoyable food inc seafood here and in modern bar, South Hams ale *(P Dawn, Dave Braisted)*

Ship TQ6 0AG [Higher St]: Tall and attractive old two-bar pub with interesting décor, quiet little lounge, well kept ales such as Adnams, Greene King IPA, Fullers London Pride and Otter, farm cider, nice wines, welcoming service, usual food inc good fresh fish (best views from upstairs restaurant); a couple of tables outside, open all day *(P Dawn, Pete Walker, Ted Watts)*

Steam Packet TQ6 0AD [Fore St]: Small local with friendly staff, well kept Exmoor, Otter and Sharps Doom Bar, pubby food in bar and restaurant with good views across to Dartmouth *(David Sizer)*

LAKE [SX5288]

☆ *Bearslake* EX20 4HQ [A386 just S of Sourton]: Welcoming family in rambling thatched stone-built Dartmoor inn dating from 13th c, beams, flagstones, inglenook fireplace, pews and plenty of local atmosphere, wide choice of reliably good home-made food from generous baguettes to restaurant dishes, mainstream and local real ales, good friendly service; picnic-sets in sizeable streamside garden with terrace, six comfortably olde-worlde bedrooms, filling breakfast *(Peter and Margaret Lodge, Keith and Sally Jackson, Mick and Moira Brummell)*

LAPFORD [SS7308]

Old Malt Scoop EX17 6PZ Extended from coaching-inn core with mix of genuinely old and newer, friendly atmosphere, huge log fire, real ales, good choice of pubby food (not Sun evening or Mon), darts, pool and skittle alley *(Conor McGaughey)*

LIFTON [SX3885]

☆ *Arundell Arms* PL16 0AA [Fore St]: Consistently good interesting lunchtime bar food in substantial country-house fishing hotel, warmly welcoming and individual, with rich décor, nice staff and sophisticated service, good choice of wines by the glass, evening restaurant; can arrange fishing tuition – also shooting, deer-stalking and riding; pleasant bedrooms *(Mrs J H S Lang)*

LITTLEHEMPSTON [SX8162]

Pig & Whistle TQ9 6LT [Newton Rd (A381)]: Large former coaching inn with friendly efficient staff, satisfying food from generous sandwiches to good value set meals, Sharps Special and Wells & Youngs Bombardier, long bar with beams, stripped brick and comfortable pews boxing in large old table,, extensive dining area; pleasant little front terrace *(Peter Burton, Steve Whalley)*

Tally Ho! TQ9 6NF [off A381 NE of Totnes]: Low-beamed 14th-c pub, neat and cosy, with interesting mix of chairs and settles, lots of cheerful bric-a-brac on stripped stone walls, some panelling, helpful friendly family service, food from sandwiches to steaks, duck and tuna, Greene King IPA and perhaps a guest beer, restaurant, pub cat called Thomas; piped music; children welcome, flower-filled terrace, bedrooms (main rail line nearby) *(LYM, Mrs J Gowan)*

LOWER ASHTON [SX8484]

☆ *Manor Inn* EX6 7QL [Ashton signposted off B3193 N of Chudleigh]: Bistro-style reworking and extension of what used to be known as a cheery real ale local, still has half a dozen or more well kept ales but now more of a wine bar feel, with good if more costly food and friendly young staff; children and dogs welcome, picnic-sets in pleasant garden, open all day *(Mr and Mrs A R Maden, Barry Steele-Perkins, David Hall, LYM, the Didler)*

LUPPITT [ST1606]

☆ *Luppitt Inn* EX14 4RT [back roads N of Honiton]: Unspoilt little basic farmhouse pub, amazing survivor of past times, friendly chatty landlady who keeps it open because she (and her cats) like the company; tiny room with corner bar and a table, another not much bigger with fireplace, cheap Otter tapped from the cask, intriguing metal puzzles made by neighbour, no food or music, lavatories across the yard; cl lunchtime and Sun evening *(the Didler, Richard Pitcher)*

LUTTON [SX5959]

☆ *Mountain* PL21 9SA [pub signed off Cornwood—Sparkwell rd]: Simply furnished 18th-c beamed pub with four well kept changing ales, farm cider, traditional bar food, friendly service, log fire, some stripped stone, a high-backed settle, no piped music or machines; children welcome, tables on verandah and vine-arbour terrace, open all day exc Tues *(D Cheesbrough, LYM)*

LYDFORD [SX5285]

☆ *Dartmoor Inn* EX20 4AY [Downton, A386]: Attractive restaurant-with-rooms, several small civilised and relaxed stylishly decorated contemporary areas, good wines by the glass, good recent reports on the food (priced at restaurant levels); children welcome, dogs allowed in small front log-fire bar, terrace tables, cl Sun evening, Mon (*Andrea Rampley, Jacquie Jones, R W Brooks, Victoria Hatfield, LYM*)

LYMPSTONE [SX9984]

☆ *Redwing* EX8 5JT [Church Rd]: Bustling village local with good value food inc lots of local fish and good puddings, Greene King Abbot, Otter, Palmers and a guest beer, local farm cider, good house wines, helpful efficient service, brightly painted lounge, thriving bar and neat little dining area; may be discreet piped music, regular live music; pretty enclosed garden behind, unspoilt village with shore walks, open all day wknds (*the Didler, BB, Dr and Mrs M E Wilson, Kevin Flack, Donna and Roger*)

LYNMOUTH [SS7249]

☆ *Rising Sun* EX35 6EG [Harbourside]: Wonderful position overlooking harbour, bustling bar with Exmoor ales, farm cider, imaginative if not cheap blackboard food inc plenty of good fish, pleasant service, good fire, friendly and upmarket hotel side with attractive cosy restaurant; piped music, parking can be a problem – expensive by day, sparse at night; children and dogs welcome, bedrooms in cottagey old thatched building stepped up hills, gardens up behind (*Julie Russell-Carter, Nick Lawless, P Dawn, Edward Leetham, LYM, Lynda and Trevor Smith, B M Eldridge, Miss J F Reay*)

LYNTON [SS7148]

Bridge Inn EX35 6NR [B3234 just S]: Good choice of food, well kept ales, friendly accommodating licensees, pleasant straightforward décor, churchy Victorian windows, dining room overlooking West Lyn gorge; glorious coast views from terrace, footbridge to wooded NT walks up to Watersmeet or even the Rockford Inn at Brendon – and there's a lovely short walk from Lynton centre, on the Lynway (*Andy Cleverdon*)

Crown EX35 6AG [Market St/Sinai Hill]: Relaxing hotel lounge bar, five well kept ales such as St Austell, farm cider, chatty locals, decent reasonably priced bar food all day from baguettes up, open fire, small comfortable restaurant; no pushchairs allowed, even for disabled children; a few covered tables outside, good bedrooms, open all day (*Tim and Rosemary Wells, Stan and Hazel Allen*)

MAIDENCOMBE [SX9268]

Thatched Tavern TQ1 4TS [Steep Hill]: Much extended three-level thatched building under new management, wide choice of good value generous food in two eating areas, pubby bar with Badger ales; children allowed, nice garden with small thatched huts, small attractive village above small beach (*M G Hart, Mike and Mary Carter*)

MALBOROUGH [SX7039]

Royal Oak TQ7 3RL [Higher Town]: Cosy well worn in local with interesting choice of

enjoyable food, good beer and wine, friendly service, log fire; some folk nights (*John and Julie Moon*)

MANATON [SX7580]

Kestor TQ13 9UF Modern Dartmoor-edge inn in splendid spot nr Becky Falls, warm-hearted family giving it a welcoming homely feel, good range of enjoyable food from good lunchtime sandwiches up, real ales, farm cider, good wine choice, open fire, attractive dining room; piped music; nice bedrooms (*Alan Swann, Barry and Anne, Dennis and Jean Bishop*)

MARLDON [SX8762]

Old Smokey House TQ3 1NN [Vicarage Rd]: Pleasantly laid out old pub, welcoming staff, food inc good fresh crab, help-yourself salads and carvery (*Keith and Margaret Kettell*)

MARSH [ST2510]

Flintlock EX14 9AJ [pub signed just off A303 Ilminster—Honiton]: Long smartly kept dining pub popular for wide choice of good varied reasonably priced food inc well cooked Sun lunches, Fullers London Pride and Otter, neat furnishings, woodburner in stone inglenook, beamery and mainly stripped stone walls, plenty of copper and brass; piped music may obtrude; cl Mon (*BB, Brian and Bett Cox, Dr and Mrs M E Wilson*)

MERRIVALE [SX5475]

☆ *Dartmoor Inn* PL20 6ST [B3357, 4 miles E of Tavistock]: Hotel in tranquil spot with high Dartmoor views, pleasant beamed bar, generous lunchtime food from good baguettes up, quick friendly service, guest beers such as Black Sheep, decent wines, water from their 36-metre (120-ft) deep well, log fire; dogs on leads allowed, good views from tables out in front (very popular summer evenings), good walks – nr bronze-age hut circles, stone rows and pretty river, bedrooms, open all day (*Dennis Jenkin*)

MODBURY [SX6551]

White Hart PL21 0QW [Church St]: Roomy bar and pleasant dining room with up-to-date minimalist décor, Tetleys and two guest beers, wide choice of wines, welcoming staff, enjoyable food (*Keith and Margaret Kettell*)

MORCHARD BISHOP [SS7607]

London Inn EX17 6NW [signed off A377 Crediton—Barnstaple]: Prettily placed open-plan low-beamed 16th-c village coaching inn, helpful friendly service, good generous traditional home-made food, real ales such as Fullers London Pride and Sharps Doom Bar, big carpeted red plush bar with rather dark décor and woodburner in large fireplace, thriving local atmosphere, pool, darts and skittles, small dining room (*Miss A G Drake, Peter Craske*)

MORETONHAMPSTEAD [SX7586]

White Hart TQ13 8NF [A382 N of Bovey Tracey; The Square]: Smart small hotel well placed for Dartmoor, cheery stripped floor back bar with log fire, helpful friendly service, real ales, good choice of wines by the glass, enjoyable bar food (not Mon), elegant relaxing lounge, attractive brasserie; courtyard tables, 13 well equipped country-style bedrooms *(LYM, Alec and Barbara Jones)*

MORTEHOE [SS4545]
Chichester Arms EX34 7DU [off A361 Ilfracombe—Braunton]: Wide choice of pubby food, quick friendly service, real ales such as local Barum Original, reasonably priced wine, plush and leatherette panelled lounge, comfortable dining room, pubby locals' bar with darts and pool, interesting old local photographs; skittle alley and games machines in summer children's room, tables out in front and in shaded pretty garden, good coast walks *(Stan and Hazel Allen, Felicity Stephens, David Fox, B M Eldridge)*
Ship Aground EX34 7DT [signed off A361 Ilfracombe—Braunton]: Comfortably worn in open-plan beamed village pub, real ales such as Cotleigh Tawny and Greene King Abbot, decent wine, wide choice of food from good crab sandwiches up, upstairs carvery some days, big log fires, massive rustic furnishings, interesting nautical brassware, children allowed in big back family room with pool in games area; tables on sheltered sunny terrace with good views, by interesting church, wonderful walking on nearby coast footpath *(GSB, Rona Murdoch, Chris Reading, LYM, Felicity Stephens, David Fox)*

NEWTON ABBOT [SX8571]
Dartmouth TQ12 2JP [East St]: Genuine old place with low ceilings, dark woodwork, roaring log fire, interesting changing local real ales, farm cider, decent wines; piped music; children welcome till 7, tables and barbecues in nice outside area, open all day *(the Didler, Dr and Mrs M E Wilson)*
Locomotive TQ12 2JP [East St]: Cheerful traditional town pub with friendly staff, well kept real ales, linked rooms inc games room with pool; TV, juke box; open all day *(the Didler)*
☆ ***Olde Cider Bar*** TQ12 2LD [East St]: Basic old-fashioned cider house with casks of interesting low-priced farm ciders (helpful long-serving landlord may give you samples), a couple of perries, more in bottles, good country wines from the cask too, baguettes and pasties etc, great atmosphere, dark stools made from cask staves, barrel seats and wall benches, flagstones and bare boards; small back games room with machines; terrace tables *(the Didler, Meg and Colin Hamilton)*

NEWTON ST CYRES [SX8798]
☆ ***Beer Engine*** EX5 5AX [off A377 towards Thorverton]: Welcoming helpful licensees in cheerful and roomy pub brewing its own good beers, with good home-made bar food esp fish and very popular Sun lunch (children welcome in eating area), traditional games; verandah and large sunny garden, popular summer barbecues, open all

day *(Philip and Jude Simmons, LYM, Mr and Mrs A R Maden)*

NORTH BOVEY [SX7483]
☆ ***Ring of Bells*** TQ13 8RB [off A382/B3212 SW of Moretonhampstead]: Attractive bulgy-walled 13th-c thatched inn doing well under current management, low beams, flagstones, big log fire, sturdy rustic tables and winding staircases, good interesting fresh food strong on local produce, sensible prices, Otter, St Austell Dartmoor Best and Wadworths 6X, Gray's farm cider, pleasant carpeted dining room, longer more functional room with pool and TV; attractive garden by lovely tree-covered village green below Dartmoor, good walks from the door, five big comfortable bedrooms *(Prof Keith and Mrs Jane Barber, LYM, Geoff and Carol Thorp, Tom and Rosemary Hall, Dr and Mrs M E Wilson, Mr and Mrs A R Maden, Cameron and Stephanie Hestler)*

NOSS MAYO [SX5447]
☆ ***Swan*** PL8 1EE [off B3186 at Junket Corner]: Very family-friendly small two-room beamed pub right on the creek, lovely harbour views and good terraces facing the sunset, with wide choice of enjoyable food inc good low-priced fresh fish, Sharps Doom Bar, good-humoured landlord and chatty locals, open fire, unpretentiously traditional décor with plenty of individuality; can get crowded, with difficult parking; dogs on leads and children welcome, terrace tables facing the sunset *(Hugh Roberts, Michael Lamm)*

OTTERTON [SY0885]
Kings Arms EX9 7HB [Fore St]: Big open-plan pub handy for families from extensive nearby caravan site, quick food service from doorstep sandwiches up (big linen napkins), Fullers London Pride and Otter, friendly staff; TV and darts in carpeted lounge, good skittle alley doubling as family room; dogs welcome, beautiful evening view from picnic-sets on good-sized attractive back garden with play area, bedrooms, charming village *(Meg and Colin Hamilton, Dr and Mrs M E Wilson)*

OTTERY ST MARY [SY0995]
London Inn EX11 1DG [Gold St]: Rambling two-bar village local, beams, timbers and brasses, reasonably priced standard food from sandwiches, baked potatoes and good ploughman's to mixed grill, Adnams Bitter and Broadside and Bass, cheerful informal service, open fires; large back terrace, bedrooms *(Colin and Peggy Wilshire)*

PARKHAM [SS3821]
Bell PL39 5PL Cheerful thatched village pub with large comfortable family eating areas, good value food cooked to order using local produce inc fresh fish, lots of nooks and crannies, log fire, pleasant friendly staff, real ales *(Mrs J Hindley, LYM)*

PLYMOUTH [SX4854]
☆ ***China House*** PL4 0DW [Sutton Harbour, via Sutton Rd off Exeter St (A374)]: Attractive conversion of Plymouth's oldest warehouse, super boaty views day and night over

harbour and Barbican, great beams and flagstones, bare slate and stone walls, good log fire, good choice of real ales and wines by the glass; piped music; good parking and disabled access and facilities, tables out on waterside balconies, open all day *(Mick and Moira Brummell, Gareth Lewis, LYM, Hugh Roberts, Meg and Colin Hamilton)*

Dolphin PL1 2LS [Barbican]: Basic local with good range of beers inc Bass tapped from the cask, coal fire (not always lit), Beryl Cook paintings inc one of the friendly landlord; open all day *(the Didler)*

Minerva PL4 0EA [Looe St (nr Barbican)]: Lively low-ceilinged backstreet pub dating from 16th c, good choice of mainstream and less common ales, coal fire, good nostalgic juke box; quite small so can get packed; open all day *(the Didler)*

Navy PL1 2LE [Southside St, Barbican]: Daytime recommendation for no-nonsense waterside local with popular bargain fry-up, polite efficient service, Wells & Youngs Bombardier, cosy corner seats; sports TV, and this area gets yobby in the evening; tables out on balcony, handy for aquarium *(David Crook, Meg and Colin Hamilton)*

Thistle Park PL4 0LE [Commercial Rd]: Welcoming bare-boards pub nr National Maritime Aquarium, South Hams ales (used to be brewed next door), tasty food all day, friendly service, interesting décor, live music wknds; children welcome, open all day till late *(the Didler)*

Waterfront PL1 3DQ [Grand Parade]: Pleasant café-bar in good spot by Plymouth Sound, big dining areas; plenty of outside seating *(Margaret and Roy Randle)*

POSTBRIDGE [SX6578]

East Dart PL20 6TJ [B3212]: Central Dartmoor hotel by pretty river, in same family since 1861; big comfortable open-plan bar, good value generous food using local ingredients from sandwiches with chips up, St Austell ales, good wines by the glass, good fire, hunting murals and horse tack, pool room; can take coaches; dogs welcome, tables out in front and behind, decent bedrooms, some 30 miles of fishing *(Dennis Jenkin, BB, Mike Turner)*

PRINCETOWN [SX5973]

☆ *Plume of Feathers* PL20 6QQ [central mini-roundabout]: Bustling extended four-room local with wide choice of good value generous food inc Sun carvery, cheerful attentive service even when busy, real ales inc Princetown Jail, good choice of wines by the glass, two log fires, solid slate tables, big family room; children welcome, play area, good value bedrooms, also bunkhouse and good camp site, open all day *(Dr and Mrs M E Wilson, Ken Flawn, David and Karen Cuckney)*

RINGMORE [SX6545]

☆ *Journeys End* TQ7 4HL [signed off B3392 at Pickwick Inn, St Anns Chapel, nr Bigbury; best to park up opp church]: Ancient village inn with character panelled lounge,

enjoyable food, good friendly service, half a dozen changing local ales from casks behind bar, local farm cider, decent wines, log fires, bar billiards (for over-16s), sunny back family dining conservatory with board games; pleasant big terraced garden with boules, attractive setting nr thatched cottages not far from the sea, bedrooms antique but comfortable and well equipped *(LYM, Edward Leetham, the Didler)*

SALCOMBE [SX7438]

Ferry Inn TQ8 8JE [off Fore St nr Portlemouth Ferry]: Splendid location, breathtaking estuary views from three floors of stripped-stone bars rising from sheltered and attractive flagstoned waterside terrace, inc top one opening off street (this may be only one open out of season), middle dining bar, classic seaside pub menu inc good crab sandwiches, Palmers and farm cider, good house wines, friendly young staff; piped music, can get busy, no nearby parking, outside gents'; may be cl part of winter *(Peter and Giff Bennett, Ken Flawn, B J Harding, Jenny and Brian Seller, LYM)*

Victoria TQ8 8BU [Fore St]: Neat and attractive 19th-c pub opp harbour car park, colourful window boxes, comfortable furnishings, usual food from sandwiches up, St Austell ales, decent wines, good coffee, nautical décor; piped music; large sheltered tiered garden behind with good play area, bedrooms *(Roger Wain-Heapy, John and Julie Moon)*

SANDFORD [SS8202]

☆ *Lamb* EX17 4LW [The Square]: Relaxed informal local with small choice of interesting and very reasonably priced good food (bar snacks all day from 9.30), well kept local and guest ales, village farm cider, good value wines by the glass, friendly efficient service, log fire, fresh flowers, daily papers, books and magazines; upstairs skittle alley/cinema; tables in attractive sheltered garden, open all day *(Dr and Mrs J Mitchell, Miss N Myers, David J Cooke)*

SANDY GATE [SX9690]

☆ *Blue Ball* EX2 7JL [from M5 junction 30, take A376 and double back from A376/A3052 roundabout, turning off left towards Topsham just before getting back to M5 junction]: Extended thatched dining pub, handy and relaxing escape from the M5, warm and friendly, with good rather upmarket food, good helpings, old wood and tile floors, beams, candles and lovely settles, big inglenook log fire, O'Hanlons Yellowhammer and Otter, well priced wine, friendly attentive young staff; good gardens inc good play area *(BB, Dr and Mrs M E Wilson, Mr and Mrs A R Maden)*

SHEBBEAR [SS4309]

Devils Stone Inn EX21 5RU [off A3072 or A388 NE of Holsworthy]: Tucked-away 16th-c village pub with big oak-beamed bar, three other rooms, good value sensible food, cheerful staff and regulars, good range of well kept beers, may be winter mulled wine, small restaurant area with huge inglenook log fire, family room; handy for Tarka Trail; garden with play area, simple bedrooms *(LYM, Ryta Lyndley)*

SHEEPWASH [SS4806]

Half Moon EX21 5NE [off A3072 Holsworthy—Hatherleigh]: Ancient fisherman's hotel with 10 miles of fishing on River Torridge (salmon, sea trout and brown trout), rod and drying rooms and fishing supplies; big log fire in beamed bar, good sandwiches and other simple lunchtime snacks, Courage Best and Greene King Ruddles County, farm cider, reasonably priced wines, fine choice of malt whiskies, black oak woodwork polished to perfection in attractive evening dining room, games room; children in eating areas, comfortable annexe bedrooms, good breakfast *(S G N Bennett, LYM)*

SIDFORD [SY1389]

☆ *Blue Ball* EX10 9QL [A3052 just N of Sidmouth]: As we go to press rebuilding work after the 2006 fire is proceeding so well that there is a good chance this fine old pub, a main entry for many years, will be open again before this edition of the *Guide* is in the shops; when open, it should be well worth a visit – still under the same family after five generations, with enjoyable food, well kept local and other real ales, plenty of character, and a warm welcome; children welcome, comfortable bedrooms, open all day *(LYM)*

SIDMOUTH [ST1287]

Anchor EX10 8LP [Old Fore St]: Well refurbished high-ceilinged pub on two floors, increasingly popular locally for its seafood and other good value food; tables in good outdoor area, open all day – plenty of folk music in festival week *(Marjorie Bretherton)*

Bowd EX10 0ND [junction B3176/A3052]: Big thatched family dining pub with wide choice of enjoyable food in bar and restaurant, good friendly service, real ales; children welcome, tables in big garden with play area, open all day *(Mick and Moira Brummell, LYM)*

Dukes EX10 8AR [Market Pl]: Good central spot nr esplanade, long bar on left, linked areas with low modern leather sofas and armchairs around low tables, conservatory and flagstoned eating area, three well kept ales such as Branscombe Vale, Fullers London Pride and Otter, pubby food all day inc good lunchtime crab sandwiches, pleasant efficient staff, daily papers; big-screen TV, may be a queue to order in summer; prom-view terrace tables, bedrooms in adjoining Elizabeth Hotel, open all day *(Dr and Mrs M E Wilson, Steve Whalley, Joan and Michel Hooper-Immins)*

☆ *Old Ship* EX10 8LP [Old Fore St]: Partly 14th c and nicely traditional in style, with low beams, mellow black woodwork inc early 17th-c carved panelling, sailing ship prints, good inexpensive food (not Sun evening)

from simple snacks and huge crab sandwiches to local fish and some adventurous dishes, well kept Branscombe Vale Branoc, Otter, St Austell Tribute and Wadworths 6X, decent wine choice, prompt friendly service even when busy, no piped music; close-set tables – raftered upstairs family area is more roomy; dogs allowed, in pedestrian zone just moments from the sea (note that around here parking is limited to 30 mins) *(Meg and Colin Hamilton, Phil and Sally Gorton, Dr and Mrs M E Wilson, Steve Whalley, BB, Gary Rollings, Tracey and Stephen Groves)*

☆ *Swan* EX10 8BY [York St]: Cheerful old-fashioned local, well kept Wells & Youngs Bitter, Special and Waggledance, good value food from doorstep sandwiches up, helpful long-serving licensees, lounge bar with interesting pictures and memorabilia, darts and warm coal fire in bigger light and airy public bar with boarded walls and ceilings, separate dining area; dogs welcome, nice small flower-filled garden *(Di and Mike Gillam, MB, Mike Gorton)*

SILVERTON [SS9503]

Lamb EX5 4HZ [Fore St]: Friendly flagstoned local with two or three changing real ales tapped from the cask, food from sandwiches to good steaks, helpful family service, separate eating area; handy for Killerton (NT), open all day wknds *(the Didler)*

Three Tuns EX5 4HX [Exeter Rd]: 17th-c or older, with comfortable settees, period furniture and log fire in attractively old-fashioned beamed lounge, food here or in cosy restaurant welcoming children, Exe Valley and guest beers, fair-sized public bar; lovely flower displays, tables in pretty inner courtyard, handy for Killerton (NT) *(the Didler)*

SLAPTON [SX8245]

☆ *Queens Arms* TQ7 2PN Warm welcome in neatly modernised village local with snug comfortable corners, good inexpensive straightforward food using local suppliers, well kept Teignworthy and Otter ales, interesting World War II pictures and brassware, dominoes and draughts; parking needs skill; children and dogs welcome, plenty of tables in lovely suntrap stepped back garden *(Mr and Mrs A R Maden, Bob and Margaret Holder, MP)*

SOURTON [SX5390]

☆ *Highwayman* EX20 4HN [A386, S of junction with A30]: Fantastical décor in warren of dimly lit stonework and flagstone-floored burrows and alcoves, all sorts of things to look at, even a make-believe sailing galleon; local farm cider (perhaps a real ale in summer), organic wines, good proper sandwiches or pasties, friendly chatty service, old-fashioned penny fruit machine, 40s piped music; outside has fairy-tale pumpkin house and an old-lady-who-lived-in-the-shoe house – children allowed to look around pub but can't stay inside; period bedrooms with four-posters and half-testers,

bunk rooms for walkers and cyclists
(Richard Baldwin, Clive Godwin, LYM,
Richard Atherton, the Didler)

SOUTH POOL [SX7740]

☆ *Millbrook* TQ7 2RW [off A379 E of
Kingsbridge]: Charming little creekside pub
with dining area off cheerful compact bar,
good food using much local produce from
generous lunchtime crab sandwiches,
ploughman's and so forth to wider range of
interesting simple modern evening cooking,
with well kept ales such as Bass and South
Hams Devon Pride tapped from the cask,
local farm cider, no piped music; children
and dogs welcome, covered seating and
heaters for front courtyard and waterside
terrace, bedrooms (MP, LYM, Roger Wain-
Heapy)

SOUTH ZEAL [SX6593]

☆ *Oxenham Arms* EX20 2JT [off A30/A382]:
Stately and interesting building with elegant
mullioned windows and Stuart fireplaces in
friendly beamed and partly panelled front
bar enjoyed by locals, small beamed family
room with another open fire, Sharps and
guest ales tapped from the cask, quite a few
wines by the glass; dogs allowed in bar,
imposing garden with lovely views, bedrooms
with own bathrooms (David Carr, Pete Baker,
Michael and Ann Cole, David Rule, LYM,
Phil and Sally Gorton, the Didler,
Paul Williams, Dr and Mrs P Truelove,
Peter Craske)

ST ANNS CHAPEL [SX4170]

☆ *Old Chapel* TQ7 4HQ [B3392 Modbury—
Bigbury-on-Sea]: Chunky furnishings,
stripped stone and stylish chapel
photographs in candlelit beamed bar, Sharps
Doom Bar and South Hams Devon Pride,
good wines by the glass, big log fire,
separate restaurant in airy modern
extension; children and dogs welcome,
picnic-sets in neat back terraced garden, five
bedrooms furnished in character, cl Sun
evening and Mon (John Smart, LYM)

ST GILES IN THE WOOD [SS5420]

Cranford EX38 7LA [off B3227 NE of
Torrington]: Friendly pub, unexpectedly
pretty inside, with good service, worthwhile
food from ciabattas up, well kept Fullers
London Pride and St Austell Tribute,
attractive dining room (Mark Flynn)

STAPLE CROSS [ST0320]

Staplecross Inn TA21 0NH [Holcombe
Rogus—Hockworthy]: Simple Exmoor-edge
village pub sensitively renovated under
friendly newish landlady, short choice of
good value honest food, well kept local ales,
pleasant wooded setting (Michael Cleeve)

STAVERTON [SX7964]

☆ *Sea Trout* TQ9 6PA [off A384 NW of Totnes]:
New licensees in smartly kept and much
extended beamed village inn, friendly staff,
enjoyable food, well kept Palmers real ales,
good choice of wines by the glass, neat and
comfortable bars with fishing memorabilia,
open fire; children welcome, seats under
parasols in attractive paved back garden,

comfortable quiet bedrooms; more reports on
new regime please (LYM, John Smart)

STICKLEPATH [SX6494]

Devonshire EX20 2NW [off A30 at Whiddon
Down or Okehampton]: Old-fashioned 16th-c
thatched village local next to foundry
museum, low-beamed slate-floored bar with
big log fire, longcase clock and easy-going
old furnishings, sofa in small snug, Bass and
St Austell ales tapped from the cask, farm
cider, good value sandwiches, bookable Sun
lunches and evening meals, games room with
piano and bar billiards, lively folk night 1st
Sun in month; dogs welcome, open all day
Fri/Sat, bedrooms, good walks (the Didler,
LYM, Phil and Sally Gorton)

STOKE FLEMING [SX8648]

☆ *Green Dragon* TQ6 0PX [Church St]: Relaxed
village pub with yachtsman landlord, beams
and flagstones, boat pictures and burmese
cats, snug with sofas and armchairs, adult
board games, grandfather clock, open fire,
Flowers IPA, Otter and Wadworths 6X, good
choice of wines by the glass, food from
lunchtime baguettes to restaurant meals;
children and dogs welcome, tables out on
partly covered heated terrace, climbing
frame (LYM, John and Fiona Merritt,
Dennis Jenkin)

STOKENHAM [SX8042]

☆ *Tradesmans Arms* TQ7 2SZ [just off A379
Dartmouth—Kingsbridge]: Picturesque
15th-c thatched and low-beamed pub
overlooking village green, good pubby
atmosphere, enjoyable reasonably priced
food from traditional favourites to lots of
local fish, good Sun roasts and puddings,
four good ales such as Brakspears and South
Hams Devon Pride, local farm cider, well
chosen wines, woodburner, nice antique
tables and interesting old pictures, lovely
cat called Mr Black, separate dining room;
attractive garden (Mrs J Ekins-Daukes,
Mrs Carolyn Dixon, Wendy and Carl Dye,
Torrens Lyster, Roger Wain-Heapy, David and
Karen Cuckney, LYM, Paul Boot)

SWIMBRIDGE [SS6229]

Jack Russell EX32 0PN [nr Barnstaple]: Well
reworked under new owners, enjoyable food
from generous doorstep sandwiches up,
Winkleigh farm cider, smart dining room;
terrace, opp the eponymous 19th-c parson's
church in pleasant village (D P and
M A Miles)

TAVISTOCK [SX4975]

Trout & Tipple PL19 0JS [Parkwood Rd,
towards Okehampton]: Good food with great
emphasis on trout (nearby trout farm), well
kept Princetown Jail and two or three
quickly changing guest beers, decent wines
(friendly licensees may offer samples),
attractive bar décor with fly-fishing theme,
nice log fire, ex-stables dining room
(Emma Kingdon, Ken Flawn)

TEDBURN ST MARY [SX8194]

Kings Arms EX6 6EG [off A30 W of Exeter]:
Picturesque traditional thatched pub, open-
plan but comfortable and quietly welcoming,

with enjoyable pubby food, Otter and St Austell ales, local farm cider, efficient neatly dressed staff, heavy-beamed and panelled L-shaped bar, lantern lighting and snug stable-style alcoves, big log fire, lots of brass and hunting prints, modern restaurant, end games bar with pool (and big-screen TV); piped pop music may obtrude; children in eating area, tables on renovated back terrace, garden, bedrooms (J J B Rowe, LYM, Dr and Mrs M E Wilson)

Red Lion EX6 6EQ Friendly village pub with good local atmosphere, honest satisfying food inc Sun roasts, good range of real ales, light polished woodwork and fresh décor, end dining area; tables outside (Dr and Mrs M E Wilson, Philip Kingsbury)

THURLESTONE [SX6743]

Village Inn TQ7 3NN [part of Thurlestone Hotel]: Small much refurbished pub attached to smart family hotel and emphasising wide food choice from sandwiches (particularly good crab) to blackboard hot dishes from open kitchen behind servery, efficient friendly service, up to four real ales inc Sharps Doom Bar, comfortable country-style furnishings, dividers forming alcoves, darts, Tues quiz night; children and dogs catered for, handy for coast path (Richard and Deborah Morisot)

TOPSHAM [SX9687]

☆ *Globe* EX3 0HR [Fore St; 2 miles from M5 junction 30]: Substantial traditional inn dating from 16th c, solid comfort in heavy-beamed bow-windowed bar (very popular with the locals), good interesting home-cooked food from tasty sandwiches and toasties up, reasonable prices, Bass, Sharps Doom Bar and guest beers, good value house wines, prompt service, log-effect gas fire, compact dining lounge, good value separate restaurant, back extension; children in eating area, open all day, well priced attractive bedrooms (Dr and Mrs M E Wilson, LYM, the Didler, Barry Steele-Perkins)

☆ *Lighter* EX3 0HZ [Fore St]: Big comfortable pub with tall windows and balcony looking out over tidal flats, quickly served food from good sandwiches and light dishes to fresh fish, some small helpings available, Badger ales, nautical décor, panelling and central log fire, friendly staff, good children's area; games machines, piped music; handy for antiques centre, a mass of tables out in lovely spot on old quay (Dr and Mrs M E Wilson, the Didler, Pete Walker, Edward Leetham, B J Harding, BB, Barry Steele-Perkins)

☆ *Passage House* EX3 0JN [Ferry Rd, off main street]: New licensees yet again, but this attractive 18th-c pub still has good fresh fish choice and other pubby food from sandwiches up, thriving atmosphere even in winter, real ales, good wines, traditional black-beamed and slate-floored lower bistro area; peaceful terrace looking over moorings and river (lovely at sunset) to

nature reserve beyond, has been open all day wknds and summer (Philip and Jude Simmons, LYM, Dr and Mrs M E Wilson, the Didler)

TORQUAY [SX9166]

Crown & Sceptre TQ1 4QA [Petitor Rd, St Marychurch]: Friendly two-bar local in 18th-c beamed and stone-built coaching inn, eight mainstream and other changing ales, interesting naval memorabilia and chamber-pot collection, good-humoured long-serving landlord, basic good value lunchtime food (not Sun), snacks any time, frequent wknd jazz; dogs very welcome, children too (the Didler)

TOTNES [SX8060]

King William IV TQ9 5HN [Fore St]: Roomy and comfortable town-centre pub popular (esp with older people) for enjoyable bargain main dishes, quick cheerful young staff, real ales such as Fullers London Pride and St Austell, new world wines, colourful décor, stained-glass windows; big-screen sports TV; bedrooms (Glenwys and Alan Lawrence, Joan and Michel Hooper-Immins, Mr and Mrs Colin Roberts)

Royal Seven Stars TQ9 5DD [Fore St, The Plains]: Civilised old hotel with roomy and cosy bay-windowed bars off flagstoned reception hall (former coach entry) with imposing staircase and sunny skylight, Courage Best and Greene King Old Speckled Hen, cheerful helpful service, reasonably priced bar food, pretty restaurant; tables out in front – ideal on a Tues market day when the tradespeople wear Elizabethan dress; bedrooms, river on other side of busy main road (Dr and Mrs M E Wilson)

TURNCHAPEL [SX4953]

Clovelly Bay PL9 9TB [Boringdon Rd]: Former New Inn, refurbished and renamed under new owners, attractive waterside position with great views across to Plymouth, good atmosphere, well kept ales such as Bass, Princetown Jail and Sharps Doom Bar, log fires; juke box; five bedrooms, has been open all day wknds (Dino Riccobono)

WEST ALVINGTON [SX7243]

Ring o' Bells TQ7 3PG Extended modernised pub under new management, wide views, relaxing atmosphere, bar food, Sharps Doom Bar; children welcome, terrace tables, comfortable bedrooms in motel-style upper bedroom wing (B J Harding, Bob and Margaret Holder, BB)

WESTON [ST1400]

☆ *Otter* EX14 3NZ [off A373, or A30 at W end of Honiton bypass]: Busy family pub with heavy low beams, reasonably priced enjoyable food from light dishes to substantial meals and popular Sun carvery, OAP specials, quick cheerful helpful service, Fullers London Pride and Otter, good value wines, good log fire; piped music; children welcome, disabled access, picnic-sets on big lawn leading to River Otter and its ducks and skipping-rocks, play area (Bob and

Margaret Holder, Nicholas and Dorothy Stephens, LYM, B Pike)

WHIMPLE [SY0497]

☆ **New Fountain** EX5 2TA [off A30 Exeter—Honiton; Church Rd]: Attractive and civilised two-bar beamed village pub, warmly welcoming, with bustling local atmosphere, good inexpensive food inc interesting starters, well kept changing beers inc O'Hanlons brewed in the village, woodburner; well behaved dogs welcome (LYM, Dr and Mrs M E Wilson, Gene and Tony Freemantle)

WHITCHURCH [SX4972]

Whitchurch Inn PL19 9ED [village signed off A386 just S of Tavistock, then keep on up into Church Hill]: Beamed local owned by the church, neatly renovated with woodburner each end, friendly competent service, long sparklingly kept bar for the Princetown and other local ales, nice changing choice of wines by the glass, good food choice (particularly local meats), comfortable furnishings, butter-coloured plaster crisply cut away to show stonework (R and H Fraser, BB)

WILMINGTON [ST2199]

White Hart EX14 9JQ [A35 Honiton—Axminster]: Warmly welcoming newish licensees in well furnished and attractively restored pub keeping beams, flagstones and log fires, good choice of reasonably priced food inc some stylish imaginative dishes and OAP wkdy lunches, Cotleigh or Courage Directors and Otter tapped from the cask, local farm ciders, spacious bar with rooms off; disabled access, three bedrooms (Maggie, Anthony Double, Mr and Mrs R B Berry)

WONSON [SX6789]

☆ **Northmore Arms** EX20 2JA [A30 at Merrymeet roundabout, take first left on old A30, through Whiddon Down; new roundabout and take left on to A382; then right down lane signposted Throwleigh/Gidleigh. Continue down lane over hump-back bridge; turn left to Wonson; OS Sheet 191 map reference 674903]: Far from smart and greatly enjoyed by readers who value character more than mod cons, with two simple old-fashioned rooms, log fire and woodburner, low beams and stripped stone, well kept Adnams Broadside, Cotleigh Tawny and Exe Valley Dobs tapped from the cask, good house wines, cheap plain food (all day Mon-Sat), darts and board games; children and dogs welcome, picnic-sets outside, two modest bedrooms, beautiful remote walking country, normally open all day (R J Walden, Michael and Ann Cole, the Didler, LYM, Anthony Longden, Paul Goldman, Dr and Mrs A K Clarke)

WOODBURY [SY0087]

White Hart EX5 1HN [3½ miles from M5 junction 30; A376, then B3179; Church St]: Good choice of good value straightforward

food (not Sun) in unpretentious local with Bass and Everards Tiger, decent wines, log fire, comfortable dining lounge, plain public bar, no piped music; attractive small walled garden with aviary, skittle alley, nice spot by church in peaceful village (Dr and Mrs M E Wilson)

WOODLAND [SX7869]

☆ **Rising Sun** TQ13 7JT [village signed off A38 just NE of Ashburton, then pub usually signed, nr Combe Cross]: New licensees again in surprisingly plush and expansive softly lit beamed pub, snug corner by log fire, bar food from sandwiches to some enterprising main dishes and good seafood, Princetown Jail Ale and a local guest beer, good choice of wines by the glass, Luscombe farm cider, family area, restaurant; picnic-sets and play area in spacious garden, children and dogs welcome, four comfortable bedrooms, cl Mon; more reports on new regime please (Charlie and Chris Barker, Donna and Roger, David and Christine Francis, LYM)

WOOLACOMBE [SS4543]

Red Barn EX34 7DF Modern seaside bar and restaurant with wide choice of reasonably priced enjoyable food all day, well kept St Austell and guest ales (early Dec beer festival), pleasant service, surfing pictures and memorabilia; children and dogs welcome, open all day (Bob and Margaret Holder)

YARCOMBE [ST2408]

Yarcombe Inn EX14 9BD [A30 2 miles E of A303]: Interesting 14th-c thatched pub under new licensees, fresh and attractive layout, flagstones and ancient stonework, St Austell ales, good wines by the glass, friendly staff, food from good baguettes up; dogs welcome, small back terrace overlooking churchyard, bedrooms (Dennis Jenkin)

LUNDY

LUNDY [SS1344]

☆ **Marisco** EX39 2LY One of England's most isolated pubs (yet full every night), great setting (steep trudge up from landing stage where the boat with you and perhaps 250 others docks), galleried interior with lifebelts and other paraphernalia from local shipwrecks; two St Austell ales labelled for the island, also Lundy spring water on tap, good value house wines, welcoming staff, good basic food (all day from breakfast on) using island produce and lots of seafood fresh from immaculate kitchen, open fire, fine views, no music, TV or machines; children welcome, tables outside, self catering and camping available; souvenir shop, and doubles as general store for the island's few residents (Dave Braisted, D Cheesbrough, Michael Roper, Phil and Sally Gorton, B M Eldridge)

Dorset

Food in pubs here can be extremely good, making the best of the local fish and seafood. It's not particularly cheap, indeed pub food prices in Dorset tend to be a shade higher than the national norm, and certainly higher than over the border in Devon, for equivalent quality. So this is a county where it particularly pays to know the pubs which give good value. Fortunately, we have tracked down a goodly number of well run value-conscious – if not necessarily cheap – pubs here, with hard-working licensees giving a really friendly welcome to both locals and visitors. Four are pubs newly upgraded to this edition's main entries: the picturesque old Fox at Corscombe (super food); the Three Horseshoes at Powerstock (friendly licensees, interesting and rewarding food); the Ship at West Stour (a pretty building, smart yet relaxed, another with super food); and the Green Man in Wimborne Minster (hard-working young licensees who give it a bustling, friendly feel, and popular pubby food). Others on top form this year are the Cock & Bottle at East Morden (successful dining pub with a proper pubby bar too), the Museum at Farnham (exceptionally well run, with interesting food – a marvellous all-rounder), the Marquis of Lorne at Nettlecombe (some refurbishment this year, with a nice, friendly landlord and noteworthy food), the Vine at Pamphill (lovely bustling unspoilt atmosphere, carefully nurtured over many decades by the same family), the Greyhound at Sydling St Nicholas (warmly welcoming and well cared for, with most enjoyable food), and the Square & Compass at Worth Matravers (a delightful time machine, takes you back a century or so, to when the landlord's family first took it on). As we've implied, several of these places are rather special for a meal out; the award of Dorset Dining Pub of the Year goes to the Museum at Farnham. In the Lucky Dip section at the end of the chapter, noteworthy pubs are the Anchor and the Three Horseshoes in Burton Bradstock, Fox & Hounds at Cattistock, Winyards Gap at Chedington, Olde George in Christchurch, Blue Raddle in Dorchester, Drovers at Gussage All Saints, White Horse at Litton Cheney, Royal Standard and Victoria in Lyme Regis, Crown at Puncknowle, Skippers in Sherborne, Bankes Arms at Studland, Bull at Sturminster Newton, Crown at Uploders and Manor Hotel at West Bexington. Drinks prices here are closely in line with the national average. The county's two main brewers are Badger (who have a good many reliable mainstream dining pubs here now), and Palmers (who have over the years built up a notable cadre of good tenants, running their pubs with real affection and individuality). Both tend to have good wines by the glass in their pubs. It's well worth looking out too for Ringwood beers here, brewed just over the border in Hampshire, but featuring as the cheapest on offer in many Dorset pubs.

CERNE ABBAS   ST6601   MAP 2

Royal Oak
Long Street; DT2 7JG

Bustling dining pub with enjoyable food in panelled communicating rooms

The stone walls and ceilings in the three flagstoned communicating rooms of this friendly and chatty pub are packed with all sorts of small ornaments from local photographs to antique china and brasses and farm tools. They also have sturdy oak beams, lots of shiny black panelling, an inglenook with an oven, and warm winter log fires; candles on tables, fresh flowers and occasional piped music. Badger K&B, First Gold, Tanglefoot and a guest beer on handpump from the uncommonly long bar counter and quite a few wines by the glass from an extensive wine list; good service. The enclosed back garden is very pleasant, with comfortable chairs and tables under cocktail parasols and outdoor heaters on purbeck stone terracing and cedarwood decking. On sunny summer afternoons they sometimes serve drinks and snacks out here. Parking can be a problem at busy times.

🍴 **Good bar food (cooked by the son of the licensees) includes lunchtime paninis and ploughman's, soup, goats cheese and tomato tart, hand-dived scallops, slow-cooked lamb shank, venison bourguignon, bass, daily specials, and puddings.** *Starters/Snacks: £3.95 to £6.50. Main Courses: £8.95 to £17.95. Puddings: £4.25*

Badger ~ Tenants Maurice and Sandra Ridley ~ Real ale ~ Bar food (12-3, 7-9) ~ (01300) 341797 ~ Children welcome ~ Dogs welcome ~ Open 11.30-3.30, 6.30-12.30; 11-3, 6.30-11 in winter

Recommended by John Coatsworth, P Dawn, Andy and Yvonne Cunningham, Andrew Turnbull, Mrs J H S Lang, John and Sheila Packman, the Didler, Simon Fox

CHIDEOCK   SY4292   MAP 1

George
A35 Bridport—Lyme Regis; DT6 6JD

Comfortable local with well liked food and some interesting photographs and drawings

There's quite a collection of brassware hanging from the beams and masses of tools on the white walls of the back bar in this thatched 17th-c inn. The chatty landlord is very welcoming and keeps his ales well: Palmers Copper Ale, IPA, Palmers 200 and either Dorset Gold or Tally Ho on handpump from the horseshoe-shaped counter. Several wines by the glass, too. The dark-beamed lounge bar has comfortable blue plush stools and wall and window seats, pewter tankards hanging from the mantelpiece above the big fireplace (with a good winter log fire), hundreds of banknotes pinned to the beams, boat drawings and attractively framed old local photographs on its cream walls and high shelves of bottles, plates, mugs and so forth. The snug is liked by locals; piped music and TV. In summer you can eat out on the terrace.

🍴 **Good bar food at lunchtime includes sandwiches, filled baguettes and baked potatoes, ploughman's, home-cooked ham or local sausages with free-range eggs and nice beer-battered haddock, with evening choices such as soup, local scallops, creamy garlic mushrooms, thai-style chicken, fish pie, vegetable lasagne, barnsley lamb chops, barbary duck breast, and puddings like hot chocolate pudding or lemon and lime cheesecake.** *Starters/Snacks: £4.45 to £6.95. Main Courses: £9.95 to £18.95. Puddings: £4.25*

Palmers ~ Tenant Paul Crisp ~ Real ale ~ Bar food (12-2, 6-9.30; 12-3, 6-9 Sun) ~ Restaurant ~ (01297) 489419 ~ Children allowed in most areas ~ Dogs allowed in bar ~ Live folk country, jazz or rock every second Sat evening ~ Open 11(11.30 winter weekdays)-2.30, 6-11(11.30 Sat); 12-3, 6-11 Sun

Recommended by Bruce Bird, Terry and Linda Moseley, Dave Mower, Gene and Kitty Rankin, Louise English, John and Fiona McIlwain, Peter Craske, Roland and Wendy Chalu

---

If we know a pub does summer barbecues, we say so.

CHURCH KNOWLE

SY9381   MAP 2

New Inn ♀

Village signposted off A351 just N of Corfe Castle; BH20 5NQ

A wide choice of food (plenty of fish) and wines in attractively furnished rooms; good walks

In a pretty little village, this partly thatched 16th-c inn was once part of a working farm and is run by friendly, cheerful people. The two main areas, linked by an arch, are attractively furnished with farmhouse chairs and tables, lots of bric-a-brac (including stuffed pheasants and a glass case with some interesting memorabilia, including ration books and Horlicks tablets) and a log fire at each end. You can choose wines (with help from the staff if you wish) from a tempting display in the walk-in wine cellar and there are several by the glass and a wine of the month. Flowers Original, Greene King Old Speckled Hen and Wadworths 6X on handpump. There are disabled facilities, though there's a step down to the gents'. They've recently opened a function room with its own bar and dance floor. The good-sized garden has plenty of tables and fine views of the Purbecks and you can camp in two fields behind (you must book); fine surrounding walks.

🍴 **Good popular food includes lunchtime sandwiches and ploughman's as well as soup, smoked haddock and salmon pot, chicken liver pâté, asparagus and gruyère tart, battered fresh cod fillet, game casserole, steak in ale pie, a roast of the day, braised lamb shank, and puddings such as lemon sponge with lemon sauce or Baileys cheesecake; best to book, especially at weekends.** *Starters/Snacks: £4.50 to £6.50. Main Courses: £7.95 to £19.00. Puddings: £4.50 to £5.50.*

Badger ~ Tenants Maurice and Rosemary Estop ~ Real ale ~ Bar food (12-2.15, 6-9.15) ~ (01929) 480357 ~ Children allowed in main bar ~ Dogs allowed in bar ~ Open 11(12 Sun)-3, 6-11; closed Mon evening Jan-March

Recommended by Pat and Robert Watt, Pat and Roger Davies, Clive Watkin, Mike and Sue Loseby, John and Joan Calvert, Janet Whittaker, Joan and Michel Hooper-Immins, Peter and Margaret Glenister, Charles and Pauline Stride, D R Robinson, JDM, KM

CORSCOMBE

ST5205   MAP 2

Fox 🍴

Towards Halstock; DT2 0NS

Attractive country inn with beams, flagstones and ingelnooks and interesting food

In a country setting just out of the village with seats across a quiet lane on a lawn by a little stream, this is an attractive cream-washed old inn with rustic charm. In the left-hand room there are built-in settles, candles on the blue-and-white gingham tablecloths or barrel tables, an assortment of chairs, lots of horse prints, antlers on the beams and an L-shaped wall settle by the inglenook fireplace. A flagstoned room on the right has harness hanging from the beams, hunting and other prints, Spy cartoons of fox hunting gentlemen and two open fires with large inglenooks. There's also a conservatory with plants and a dining room. Butcombe Bitter and Exmoor Ale on handpump and several wines by the glass; polite, friendly service.

🍴 **High quality food using produce from named suppliers might include sandwiches, soup, ploughman's, pigeon breasts with roasted pancetta and a grain mustard dressing, crab and gruyère tartlet with a lemon and honey dressed salad, five-spice duck with red wine and cranberry sauce, pork and leek sausages with mustard mash and onion gravy, risotto with asparagus and chargrilled fennel with a truffle dressed rocket salad, rack of lamb with pea and mint purée and rosemary jus, chicken with aged cheddar and sautéed leeks wrapped in smoked bacon, daily fresh fish dishes, and puddings such as dark chocolate torte and treacle tart.** *Starters/Snacks: £4.75 to £7.95. Main Courses: £9.50 to £17.00. Puddings: £4.95*

Free house ~ Licensee Clive Webb ~ Real ale ~ Bar food ~ Restaurant ~ (01935) 891330 ~ Children over 5 in dining areas ~ Open 12-3, 7-11; 10.30am-11pm Sun ~ Bedrooms: £55B/£80B

Recommended by Dr A McCormick, J S Burn, Alan M Pring, Andy Booth, Gene and Kitty Rankin, Mrs J H S Lang, Roland and Wendy Chalu

EAST CHALDON   SY7983   MAP 2

Sailors Return

Village signposted from A352 Wareham—Dorchester; from village green, follow Dorchester,
Weymouth signpost; note that the village is also known as Chaldon Herring; OS sheet 194
map reference 790834; DT2 8DN

Just the place for a drink after a walk; gets busy at weekends

Although fairly isolated, this thatched country local does get busy at weekends,
especially in fine weather and there are picnic-sets, benches and log seats on the grass
in front of the pub that look down over fields to the village. Inside, the flagstoned bar
still keeps much of its original rural-tavern character, while the newer part has unfussy
furnishings, old notices for decoration, and open beams showing the roof; some of the
older beams are very low. Hampshire Strongs Best and Ringwood Best with guests such as
Dorset Durdle Door and Palmers Dorset Gold on handpump, Weston's cider and several
malt whiskies. The restaurant has solid old tables in nooks and corners; darts and piped
music. You can walk over the downs and join the coast path above the cliffs between
Ringstead Bay and Durdle Door.

⦿ **Straightforward bar food includes sandwiches, ploughman's, filled baked potatoes, ham
and egg, breaded plaice, and daily specials.** *Starters/Snacks: £2.95 to £4.95. Main Courses:*
£7.25 to £12.95. Puddings: £2.50 to £3.95

Free house ~ Licensees Mike Pollard and Claire Kelly ~ Real ale ~ Bar food (12-2, 6-9(9.30
weekends)) ~ Restaurant ~ (01305) 853847 ~ Children in restaurant ~ Dogs allowed in bar ~
Open 11.30-11; 12-10.30 Sun; 11.30-2, 6-11 in winter; closed 25 Dec

Recommended by Mark Flynn, Sue Heath, JT, Alan Cowell, Pat and Robert Watt, Mike and Sue Loseby, Edna Jones,
Pat and Roger Davies, Roland and Wendy Chalu

EAST MORDEN   SY9194   MAP 2

Cock & Bottle

B3075 between A35 and A31 W of Poole; BH20 7DL

**Character dining areas with cosy corners, interesting vintage car and motorcyle bric-a-brac,
and imaginative food**

Although many customers do come to this busy dining pub to enjoy the good, interesting
food, there's a proper pubby bar with plenty of locals, Badger First Gold, Tanglefoot and a
seasonal beer on handpump, several wines by the glass, and a fruit machine and sensibly
placed darts. The rest of the interior is made up of two dining areas with heavy rough
beams, some stripped ceiling boards, squared panelling, a mix of old furnishings in
various sizes and degrees of antiquity, small Victorian prints and some engaging bric-a-
brac; some of this reflects the landlord's passion for vintage cars and motorcycles (the
pub hosts meetings for such vehicles in summer). There's a roaring log fire, and
comfortably intimate corners, each with just a couple of tables. Outside are a few picnic-
sets, a garden area and an adjoining field with a nice pastoral outlook.

⦿ **Imaginative, if not cheap, food might include mussel and leek chowder, ham hock,
duck and chicken liver terrine with home-made tomato chutney, crisp marinated duck
spring roll with spiced mango jam and cucumber salad, local crab and scallop tart with
prawn sauce, smoked haddock with parmesan cheese mash, poached egg and pesto
dressing, pork tenderloin with walnut, stilton and port sauce, lamb loin with mini
shepherd's pie and redcurrant jus, and puddings such as Baileys panettone bread and
butter pudding or pina colada cheesecake with pineapple compote.** *Starters/Snacks: £4.95*
to £7.50. Main Courses: £8.25 to £16.50. Puddings: £4.75 to £6.25

Badger ~ Tenant Peter Meadley ~ Real ale ~ Bar food (12-2, 6(7 Sun)-9) ~ Restaurant ~ (01929)
459238 ~ Children in restaurant only ~ Dogs allowed in bar ~ Open 11-2.30, 6-11; 12-3,
7-10.30 Sun

Recommended by Pat and Robert Watt, Pat and Roger Davies, John and Joan Nash, W W Burke, Peter Titcomb,
M Joyner, Clive and Janice Sillitoe

FARNHAM   ST9515   MAP 2

Museum 🍴 🍷 🍺 🛏

Village signposted off A354 Blandford Forum—Salisbury; DT11 8DE
DORSET DINING PUB OF THE YEAR

Stylish and civilised inn with innovative food, appealing rooms (and a bustling bar), and super bedrooms

This is a lovely place to stay overnight and our readers particularly enjoy the very comfortable, well appointed bedrooms in the main building. The food – including the stylish breakfast – is exceptionally good too and served by attentive but unobtrusive staff. But what we like so much is that the little flagstoned bar remains a real focus for locals of all ages and has a lively atmosphere, light beams, a big inglenook fireplace, good comfortably cushioned furnishings and fresh flowers on all the tables. The attractively extended building has been opened up into a series of appealing interconnecting rooms and cheery yellow walls and plentiful windows give the place a bright, fresh feel. To the right is a dining room with a fine antique dresser, while off to the left is a cosier room, with a very jolly hunting model and a seemingly sleeping stuffed fox curled in a corner. Another room feels rather like a contemporary baronial hall, soaring up to a high glass ceiling, with dozens of antlers and a stag's head looking down on a long refectory table and church-style pews. This leads to an outside terrace with more wooden tables. An excellent choice of wines with a dozen by the glass and Hop Back Summer Lightning, Ringwood Best Bitter and Timothy Taylors Landlord on handpump.

🍴 **The delicious food – using organic, free-range and local seasonal produce – might include soup, lunchtime sandwiches, lightly pickled local mackerel with garlic aïoli, pink fir apple potato salad and crunchy vegetables, smoked haddock fishcake, creamed leek and split pea velouté, cauliflower, blue cheese and sage risotto, fish stew with rouille croûtes and saffron potatoes, roasted local estate venison loin with butternut squash mash, honey-glazed parsnips and sour cherry jus, rack of lamb with ratatouille vegetables, aubergine purée and garlic and rosemary jus, and puddings like cappuccino-style crème brûlée and prune and armagnac pudding with butterscotch sauce. The restaurant is open only Friday and Saturday evenings and for Sunday lunch.** *Starters/Snacks: £6.00 to £8.00. Main Courses: £14.00 to £17.50. Puddings: £5.00 to £6.50*

Free house ~ Licensees Vicky Elliot and Mark Stephenson ~ Real ale ~ Bar food (12-2.30, 7-9.30) ~ Restaurant (Fri and Sat evenings and Sun lunch) ~ (01725) 516261 ~ Children over 8 only ~ Dogs allowed in bar and bedrooms ~ Open 12-3, 6-11; 12-3, 7-10.30 Sun; closed 25 Dec, 1 Jan evening ~ Bedrooms: £85B/£95B

Recommended by Phil Bryant, Noel Grundy, Andrea Rampley, Dr A J and Mrs Tompsett, Steve Whalley, P Dawn, Mrs J H S Lang, John Robertson, R J Davies, Terry and Linda Moseley, Tony Orman, Pat and Robert Watt, I H Curtis, Colin and Janet Roe

LANGTON HERRING   SY6182   MAP 2

Elm Tree

Signed off B3157; DT3 4HU

Pretty summer flowering tubs and baskets and lots of copper and brass in bustling pub

As we went to press we heard that this colourwashed, extended place was up for sale. There's a lot of character in the main beamed and carpeted rooms (where the Portland spy ring is said to have met) which have walls festooned with copper, brass and bellows, cushioned window seats, red leatherette stools, windsor chairs and lots of big old kitchen tables; one has some old-fashioned settles and an inglenook. The traditionally furnished extension gives more room for diners. Adnams Best Bitter and Courage Directors on handpump and a dozen wines by the glass; piped music and darts. Outside, there are flower tubs, hanging baskets and a very pretty flower-filled sunken garden with outdoor heaters. A track leads down to the Dorset Coast Path, which here skirts the eight-mile lagoon enclosed by Chesil Beach.

🍴 **Bar food has included sandwiches, ploughman's, soup, lasagne, steak in ale pie, cod florentine, vegetable bake, daily specials, and puddings such as treacle tart or chocolate rum pot.** *Starters/Snacks: £3.50 to £5.95. Main Courses: £7.95 to £12.95. Puddings: £4.95*

Punch ~ Lease Paul and Jo-Ann Riddiough ~ Real ale ~ Bar food (12-2.15(3 Sun), 6.30-9.30; 12-3, 7-9.15 Sun) ~ (01305) 871257 ~ Children welcome except at bar ~ Folk music night first Tues in month, jazz every second Sun lunchtime ~ Open 11.30-3, 6-11; 12-3, 7-10.30 Sun; closed Mon evenings 1 Jan-1 April
Recommended by Janet Whittaker, Pat and Roger Davies, Peter J and Avril Hanson, Roland and Wendy Chalu

MARSHWOOD
SY3799 MAP 1

Bottle
B3165 Lyme Regis—Crewkerne; DT6 5QJ

Unchanging local, tasty food, summer beer festival and big back garden

This is an enjoyably straightforward local with Otter Bitter and Ale and guest beers like Branscombe Vale On The Rocks and O'Hanlons Royal Oak on handpump. The simple cream-walled interior has down-to-earth furnishings including cushioned benches and one high-backed settle and there's an inglenook fireplace with (usually) a big log fire in winter. Pool, games machine, TV, a skittle alley and piped music in a more modern extension. A good big back garden has a play area and beyond it is a field for camping. This is attractive rolling country and the pub is set beneath Lambert's Castle, one of several imposing iron-age hill forts in the area; good surrounding walks. The annual world stinging-nettle eating championships are held at the same time as their beer festival, on the weekend before the summer solstice. More reports please.

🍴 **Tasty bar food includes filled baguettes and baked potatoes, soup, ploughman's, a vegetarian pie or roast of the day, salmon fillet with hollandaise, medallions of pork fillet with stilton sauce, chicken breast stuffed with smoked salmon in whisky, cream and mustard sauce, and puddings.** *Starters/Snacks: £3.95 to £5.95. Main Courses: £7.25 to £15.45. Puddings: £2.75 to £4.25*

Free house ~ Licensees Shane and Ellen Pym ~ Real ale ~ Bar food (12-2, 6.30-9; not Mon (except during summer hols)) ~ (01297) 678254 ~ Children welcome ~ Open 12-3, 6.30-11(and winter weekends); 12-midnight(11 Sun) Sat; closed Mon except bank hols
Recommended by R J Townson, Pat and Tony Martin, David Eberlin, Terry and Linda Moseley

MIDDLEMARSH
ST6607 MAP 2

Hunters Moon
A352 Sherborne—Dorchester; DT9 5QN

Plenty of bric-a-brac in several linked areas, reasonably priced food, and a good choice of drinks

We gather that some time during this year, the friendly licensee of this peaceful village pub will be moving on. The comfortably welcoming interior rambles around in several linked areas, with a great variety of tables and chairs, plenty of bric-a-brac from decorative teacups, china ornaments and glasses through horse tack and brassware, to quite a collection of spirits miniatures. Beams, some panelling, soft lighting from converted oil lamps, three log fires (one in a capacious inglenook), and the way that some attractively cushioned settles form booths all combine to give a cosy relaxed feel. St Austell Tinners and Sharps Doom Bar on handpump, several wines by the glass and a dozen malt whiskies; faint piped music. A neat lawn has circular picnic-sets as well as the more usual ones, and the bedrooms are in what was formerly a skittle alley and stable block.

🍴 **Bar food includes sandwiches, soup, salmon and cod fishcakes, spinach and mascarpone lasagne, meat or game pies, lamb shank, daily specials, maybe some 'smaller appetite meals', and puddings.** *Starters/Snacks: £3.50 to £6.25. Main Courses: £6.95 to £12.75. Puddings: £2.95 to £8.25*

Free house ~ Licensee Brendan Malone ~ Real ale ~ Bar food ~ (01963) 210966 ~ Children welcome ~ Dogs allowed in bar ~ Open 11-3, 6-11; 12-3, 6-10.30 Sun ~ Bedrooms: £55S/£60S

Recommended by Joan and Michel Hooper-Immins, Dave Braisted, R J Townson, John A Barker, M G Hart

MUDEFORD
SZ1792   MAP 2

Ship in Distress ♀
Stanpit; off B3059 at roundabout; BH23 3NA

Wide choice of fish dishes, nautical décor, and friendly staff in cheerful cottage

Much more fun inside than out, this 300-year-old smugglers' pub is full of entertaining bits and pieces, with nautical bric-a-brac from rope fancywork and brassware through lanterns, oars and ceiling nets and ensigns, to an aquarium, boat models (we particularly like the Mississippi steamboat), and the odd piratical figure. Besides a good few boat pictures, the room on the right has masses of snapshots of locals caught up in various waterside japes, under its glass tabletops. Adnams, Greene King Old Speckled Hen, Ringwood Best Bitter, Shepherd Neame Spitfire on handpump and six wines by the glass served by pleasant staff; darts, games machine, a couple of TV sets and piped music. A spreading two-room restaurant area, as cheerful in its way as the bar, has a light-hearted mural sketching out the impression of a window open on a sunny boating scene. There are tables out on the back terrace.

🍴 **Enjoyable fresh local fish and seafood is the thing here: sandwiches, breton-style fish soup, fish and chips, seafood pancake, tagliatelle with wild mushroom, garlic, parsley, lemon and truffle oil, fried smoked haddock fishcake on rocket and tomato salad with poached egg and chive butter sauce, smoked trout and asparagus risotto, and puddings such as Cointreau orange mascarpone cheesecake or banana tarte tatin.** *Starters/Snacks: £4.95 to £6.95. Main Courses: £8.95 to £20.00. Puddings: £4.50 to £6.00*

Punch ~ Tenants Colin Pond and Maggie Wheeler ~ Real ale ~ Bar food ~ Restaurant ~ (01202) 485123 ~ Children welcome ~ Dogs allowed in bar ~ Open 10am-11pm; 11-11 Sun; closed 25 Dec

Recommended by Chris Flynn, Wendy Jones, Janet Whittaker, Mrs C Sleight, Martin and Karen Wake, Colin Wood

NETTLECOMBE
SY5195   MAP 2

Marquis of Lorne 🍺 🛏
Off A3066 Bridport—Beaminster, via W Milton; DT6 3SY

Tasty food and beer in country pub with large, mature garden

The bedrooms in this attractive country inn have been upgraded this year and the kitchen refurbished, too. The comfortable bustling main bar has a log fire, mahogany panelling and old prints and photographs around its neatly matching chairs and tables; two dining areas lead off, the smaller of which has another log fire. The wooden-floored snug (liked by locals) has cribbage, dominoes, board games and table skittles; gentle piped music. Four real ales from Palmers are on handpump, with Copper, IPA and 200 alongside Gold in summer or Tally Ho in winter, and Thatcher's Gold cider or perhaps a cloudy farm cider; a decent wine list with several by the glass and several malt whiskies. The maturing big garden is full of pretty herbaceous borders, and has a rustic-style play area among the picnic-sets under its apple trees.

🍴 **In addition to tasty sandwiches, filled baguettes and winter ploughman's, bar food includes soup, chicken and pork pâté with plum chutney, local scallops with herb risotto and pesto dressing, ham and egg, beer-battered fresh cod, lasagne, pork tenderloin with apple and red onion in cider sauce and noisettes of lamb on mint mash with madeira sauce.** *Starters/Snacks: £4.50 to £7.00. Main Courses: £8.50 to £16.00. Puddings: £4.50*

Post Office address codings confusingly give the impression that some pubs are in Dorset, when they're really in Somerset (which is where we list them).

Palmers ~ Tenants David and Julie Woodroffe ~ Real ale ~ Bar food (12-2.30, 7-9.30(9 winter))
~ Restaurant ~ (01308) 485236 ~ Children in eating area of bar and restaurant ~ Dogs allowed
in bar ~ Open 12-2.30, 6.30-midnight ~ Bedrooms: £50S/£90S

*Recommended by Michael Bayne, Pete Walker, Alan and Pat Newcombe, Brian Lord, Terry and Linda Moseley,
Roland and Wendy Chalu*

PAMPHILL

ST9900   MAP 2

Vine 🍺

*Off B3082 on NW edge of Wimborne: turn on to Cowgrove Hill at Cowgrove signpost, then
turn right up Vine Hill; BH21 4EE*

Charming and unchanging, run by the same family for three generations

This is a smashing little place with really friendly licensees and plenty of local customers
– though visitors are made very welcome too. It's now been run by the same family for
three generations but is actually owned by the National Trust as part of the Kingston
Lacy estate. Its two tiny bars have that well cared-for feel that makes small places like
this seem so special. One, with a warm coal-effect gas fire, has only three tables, the
other just half a dozen or so seats on its lino floor, some of them huddling under the
stairs that lead up via narrow wooden steps to an upstairs games room; darts and board
games. Local photographs (look out for the one of the regular with his giant pumpkin)
and notices decorate the painted panelling; quiet piped music. Fullers London Pride,
Hidden Pint and Palmers 200 on handpump, and farm cider. There are picnic-sets and
benches out on a sheltered gravel terrace and more share a fairy-lit, heated verandah
with a grapevine. Round the back a patch of grass has a climbing frame; outside
lavatories. The National Trust estate includes Kingston Lacy house and the huge Badbury
Rings iron-age hill fort (itself good for wild flowers), and there are many paths. They
don't accept credit cards or cheques.

🍽 **Lunchtime bar snacks such as good, fresh sandwiches and ploughman's.** *Starters/Snacks:
£2.50 to £4.50*

Free house ~ Licensee Mrs Sweatland ~ Real ale ~ Bar food (11(12 Sun)-2; not evenings) ~
No credit cards ~ (01202) 882259 ~ Well behaved children in upper room ~ Dogs welcome ~
Open 11(12 Sun)-3, 7-10.30(11 Thurs-Sat)

*Recommended by Peter Titcomb, M R Phillips, the Didler, David Parker, Emma Smith, Pat and Roger Davies,
W W Burke, Alan Wright*

PLUSH

ST7102   MAP 2

Brace of Pheasants

Off B3143 N of Dorchester; DT2 7RQ

**Fairly smart but relaxed pub with friendly service, good beers, and decent garden; nearby
walks**

Once two cottages and the village smithy, this handsome 16th-c thatched country pub
has a rather smart but relaxed atmosphere. The airy beamed bar has good solid tables,
windsor chairs, fresh flowers, a huge heavy-beamed inglenook at one end with cosy
seating inside, and a good warming log fire at the other. Otter Bitter, Ringwood Best and
Timothy Taylors Landlord tapped from the cask and several wines by the glass; friendly
service, skittle alley. A decent-sized garden and terrace includes a lawn sloping up
towards a rockery. The pub lies alongside Plush Brook, and an attractive bridleway behind
goes to the left of the woods and over to Church Hill. They hope to open bedrooms some
time during this year.

🍽 **Bar food – using village grown and other local produce – includes sandwiches, soup,
warm goats cheese salad with roasted pine nuts, home-cooked ham and egg, beer-
battered plaice, venison sausages, roulade of pancakes with vegetable mousse and tomato
and basil sauce, local rabbit pie, and salmon fishcake with sorrel sauce.** *Starters/Snacks:
£4.00 to £8.00. Main Courses: £8.00 to £16.00. Puddings: £5.00 to £7.00*

Free house ~ Licensees Phil and Carol Bennett ~ Real ale ~ Bar food (12.30-2.30, 7.30-9.30;
not winter Sun evening) ~ Restaurant ~ (01300) 348357 ~ Children welcome ~ Dogs allowed in
bar ~ Open 12-3, 7-11(10.30 Sun); closed Mon exc bank hols

*Recommended by Maggie Chandler, Carl Van Baars, Rob Winstanley, Edward Mirzoeff, Mike and Sue Loseby,
the Didler, Pat and Robert Watt*

POOLE   SZ0391   MAP 2

Cow ♀

Station Road, Ashley Cross, Parkstone; beside Parkstone Station; BH14 8UD

Interesting one-bar pub with contemporary décor, good modern food, and fine wines

Don't be put off by the unpromising exterior and location next to the railway station: the
décor inside comes as a pleasant surprise. Ochre ragged walls are hung with a vintage
songsheet of 'Three Acres and a Cow', Twickenham Rugby Museum replicas of 1930s and
1940s rugby prints and big modern cow prints in bright pinks, yellows and blues. There is
a mix of wooden tables and dining chairs, a couple of low tables by some comfortable
squashy sofas with huge colourful cushions and high leatherette bar chairs. A gas-effect
coal fire in a brick fireplace, with another in the entrance hall and quite a discreet flat-
screen TV in one corner; piped music, board games and a good array of newspapers.
Fullers London Pride, Ringwood Best and a guest such as Batemans Valiant on handpump,
and an extensive wine list with about ten wines by the glass and many remarkable
bottles (the most expensive being a Château Pétrus at £650). In the evening you can eat
in the sizeable bistro where there are more heavy stripped tables on bare boards and
plenty of wine bottles lining the window sills. Seats outside on the enclosed and heated
terrace area. More reports please.

🍴 From a sensibly short menu, the good modern lunchtime bar food includes sandwiches
and filled baguettes, soup, sausages and mash with onion gravy, bacon, bubble-and-
squeak and free-range eggs, fishcakes, sweet chilli beef stir fry, fried fillet of bass, and
puddings such as dark chocolate mousse or warmed lemon and almond sponge pudding.
Starters/Snacks: £4.50 to £6.95. Main Courses: £9.50 to £17.95. Puddings: £5.00

Free house ~ Licensee David Sax ~ Real ale ~ Bar food (12-2.30(4 Sun), 7-10; not Sun evening)
~ Restaurant ~ (01202) 749569 ~ Children allowed in bistro, and in bar until 7pm ~ Dogs
allowed in bar ~ Open 11-11; 12-midnight(10.30 Sun) Sat

Recommended by W W Burke, Terry and Linda Moseley, Andy and Claire Barker, Janet Whittaker, JDM, KM

POWERSTOCK   SY5196   MAP 2

Three Horseshoes ♀

Off A3066 Beaminster—Bridport via W Milton; DT6 3TF

**Friendly inn in fine countryside with imaginative food and a fair choice of drinks; walks
nearby**

With plenty of surrounding hikes and dogs welcome, this Victorian inn is, not
surprisingly, popular with walkers. Smart teak seats and tables under large parasols on
the back terrace (steps down to it) have a lovely uninterrupted view towards the sea and
there's a big sloping garden. Inside, the L-shaped bar has good log fires, magazines and
newspapers to read, stripped panelling, country furniture including settles, Palmers IPA
and Copper on handpump, and several wines by the glass served by friendly staff. There
are local paintings for sale in the dining roopm; piped music and board games. Two of
the bedrooms have fine valley views.

We mention bottled beers and spirits only if there is something unusual about them –
imported belgian real ales, say, or dozens of malt whiskies; so do
please let us know about them in your reports.

⏍ Cooked by the landlord/chef and using home-grown vegetables and herbs, the enterprising food might include lunchtime filled rolls, ploughman's with maybe pigeon terrine, interesting soup, seared scallops with coconut and galangal broth, rabbit casserole with chorizo dumplings, wild mushroom risotto, smoked haddock and artichoke gratin, lamb shank with rosemary and redcurrant jus and mustard mash, fillet of bass with a banana and chilli cream, guinea fowl with elderberries and Cointreau jus, and puddings such as strawberry and basil crème brûlée or baked chocolate and raspberry torte. *Starters/Snacks: £5.85 to £6.95. Main Courses: £7.95 to £15.95. Puddings: £4.25 to £4.85*

Palmers ~ Tenants Andy and Marie Preece ~ Real ale ~ Bar food ~ Restaurant ~ (01308) 485328 ~ Children welcome ~ Dogs welcome ~ Open 11-3, 6.30-11.30; 12-3, 6.30-11 Sun ~ Bedrooms: /£80B

Recommended by A J King, Noel Grundy, B D Nunn, Roland and Wendy Chalu

---

SHAVE CROSS   SY4198   MAP 1

Shave Cross Inn

On back lane Bridport—Marshwood, signposted locally; OS Sheet 193 map reference 415980; DT6 6HW

Caribbean touches to food and drink in 14th-c pub; carefully tended garden

This is one of those off the beaten track pubs that take a little effort tracking down but it's worth seeking out as it's a very attractive historic flint and thatch inn, dating back to the 14th c. The original timbered bar is a lovely flagstoned room, surprisingly roomy and full of character, with country antiques, two armchairs either side of a warming fire in an enormous inglenook fireplace and hops round the bar – a scene little altered from the last century. Branscombe Vale Branoc, their own-label 4Ms and a guest from the Dorset Brewery on handpump, alongside half a dozen wines by the glass, two farm ciders, several vintage rums and a caribbean beer; piped music (jazz or caribbean). Pool, darts, juke box (a real rarity now), dominoes, cards and a popular skittle alley. Lovingly tended, the sheltered flower-filled garden with its thatched wishing-well, carp pool and children's play area is very pretty.

⏍ With some caribbean influence, the bar food might include filled baguettes and ploughman's, caribbean chicken, ham and free-range eggs, sausage and mash, guyanaise pork stew, aubergine, pepper and caribbean vegetable bake, tobago baked fish, creole duck breast with black cherry compote, and puddings such as chocolate truffle torte or crème brûlée; there's also a two- and three-course set restaurant menu. *Starters/Snacks: £4.50 to £6.95. Main Courses: £9.95 to £16.50. Puddings: £4.95*

Free house ~ Licensee Mel Warburton ~ Real ale ~ Bar food (12-2.30, 6-9; not winter Sun evening) ~ Restaurant (7-9.30) ~ (01308) 868358 ~ Children welcome ~ Dogs allowed in bar ~ Folk club third Thurs of month ~ Open 11-3, 6-1am; 12-1am Sun; 11-3, 6-1am Sat and 12-3, 7-1am Sun in winter; closed Mon except bank hols

Recommended by Fred and Lorraine Gill, Michael Doswell, Pat and Roger Davies, Terry and Linda Moseley, Gene and Kitty Rankin, Roland and Wendy Chalu

---

SHERBORNE   ST6316   MAP 2

Digby Tap ⏍ £

Cooks Lane; park in Digby Road and walk round corner; DT9 3NS

Regularly changing ales in simple tavern, usefully open all day; close to abbey

There's a good mix of chatty customers in this delightfully unpretentious alehouse. Its simple flagstoned bar is full of character and the four well priced real ales on handpump change regularly: Church End Cuthberts, Isle of Purbeck Fossil Fuel, Sharps Cornish Coaster and Teignworthy Beachcomber. A little games room has pool and a quiz machine, and there's a TV room. There are some seats outside and the pub is only a couple of minutes' walk from the famous abbey.

⏍ Good value, straightforward bar food includes sandwiches, filled baguettes and baked

potatoes, chilli beef, and maybe liver and bacon, mixed grill or plaice stuffed with prawns; no puddings apart from ice-cream. *Main Courses: £3.25 to £4.50. Ice-cream: £2.50*

Free house ~ Licensees Oliver Wilson and Nick Whigham ~ Real ale ~ Bar food (12-1.45, not Sun) ~ No credit cards ~ (01935) 813148 ~ Children welcome lunchtimes only ~ Dogs welcome ~ Open 11-11; 12-3, 7-11 Sun

Recommended by JT, Theo, Anne and Jane Gaskin, Guy Vowles, Pat and Tony Martin, Michael B Griffith, Phil and Sally Gorton, Donna and Roger

SHROTON
ST8512 MAP 2

Cricketers ♀ 🍺 🛏

Off A350 N of Blandford (village also called Iwerne Courtney); follow signs; DT11 8QD

Well run pub with neatly uniformed and friendly staff, well liked food, and lots of wines by the glass; walks and nice views nearby

This is a pleasant, red-brick pub facing the village green. The bright divided bar has a big stone fireplace, alcoves and cricketing memorabilia and Greene King IPA and Old Speckled Hen, Palmers Dorset Gold and Charles Wells Bombardier from pumps made into little cricket bats. They've also a dozen wines by the glass, and quite a few malt whiskies; good friendly service from the attentive landlord and his neatly uniformed staff. The comfortable back restaurant overlooks the garden and has a fresh neutral décor, and a sizeable games area has pool, darts, board games, games machine and piped music. The garden is secluded and pretty with big sturdy tables under cocktail parasols, well tended shrubs and a well stocked (and well used) herb garden by the kitchen door. There are good walks from here over Hambledon Hill with its fine views (though you must leave your boots outside).

🍴 As well as filled baguettes, the well liked bar food might include soup, garlic mushrooms, butternut squash, roasted red onion and goats cheese filo parcels, caribbean cod cakes with chilli dressing, pork fillet with prunes, apples and cider and grain mustard sauce, beef curry, pheasant breast with apple, sage and bacon, and puddings such as fresh blueberry and apple crumble or chocolate torte with an almond ice and warm chocolate fudge sauce. *Starters/Snacks: £3.95 to £5.25. Main Courses: £7.95 to £13.95. Puddings: £4.25*

Free house ~ Licensees George and Carol Cowie ~ Real ale ~ Bar food ~ Restaurant ~ (01258) 860421 ~ Children welcome ~ Open 11.30-2.30, 6.30-11; 12-3, 6.30(7 in winter)-11 Sun; closed evenings 25 and 26 Dec ~ Bedrooms: £45S/£75S

Recommended by Terry and Linda Moseley, J Stickland, Pat and Robert Watt, Colin and Janet Roe, Stan Edwards, P and J Shapley, Peter Salmon

SYDLING ST NICHOLAS
SY6399 MAP 2

Greyhound 🍽 ♀ 🛏

Off A37 N of Dorchester; High Street; DT2 9PD

Genuinely welcoming staff, attractively presented food, good range of drinks, and country décor in beamed rooms

You can be sure of a warm welcome from the friendly staff in this attractively kept and very well run village inn. The beamed and flagstoned serving area is airy and alluring with big bowl of lemons and limes, a backdrop of gleaming bottles and copper pans, and plenty of bar stools, with more opposite ranging against a drinking shelf. On one side a turkey-carpeted area with a warm coal fire in a handsome portland stone fireplace has a comfortable mix of straightforward tables and chairs and country decorations such as a stuffed fox eyeing a collection of china chickens and a few farm tools. Greene King Old Speckled Hen, St Austell Tinners and Wadworths 6X on handpump and a dozen wines by the glass; fairly unobtrusive piped music and board games. At the other end, a cosy separate dining room with smart white table linen has some books and a glass-covered well set into its floor and a garden room with succulents and other plants on its sills has simple modern café furniture. The small front garden has a wooden climber and slide alongside its picnic-sets. The bedrooms are in a separate block; this is a quiet and very pretty streamside village.

🍴 **Extremely good, if not cheap, bar food includes lunchtime sandwiches, filled baguettes and ploughman's, mediterranean fish soup, chicken, bacon and leek terrine, seared scallops and chorizo sausage with hazelnut coriander butter, chicken tagine, steak and kidney pudding, marinaded lamb chop on champ mash, honey-roasted ham hock with parsnip sauce, halibut steak with anchovies, capers and garlic, daily specials, and puddings like treacle tart and chocolate terrine; vegetables are extra.** *Starters/Snacks: £3.95 to £7.25. Main Courses: £9.50 to £17.95. Puddings: £4.25 to £4.95*

Free house ~ Licensees John Ford, Karen Trimby, Ron Hobson, Cherry Ball ~ Real ale ~ Bar food (12-2(2.30 Sun), 6.30-9; not Sun evening) ~ Restaurant ~ (01300) 341303 ~ Children welcome ~ Dogs allowed in bar ~ Open 11-2.30, 6-11; 12-3 Sun; closed Sun evening ~ Bedrooms: /£70S(£80B)

Recommended by Brian Thompson, Geoffrey Leather, Barbara Wright, Kerry Murray, Dennis Buckland, Mr and Mrs Peter Larkman, Donna Mason, Neil and Sue Cumming, Ian Malone, N M Penfold, Roland and Wendy Chalu

TARRANT MONKTON   ST9408   MAP 2

Langton Arms 🍴 🛏

Village signposted from A354, then head for church; DT11 8RX

Paintings (for sale) and fresh flowers in light rooms, attractive bistro, good children's play area, and comfortable bedrooms

This is a very attractive 17th-c thatched dining inn, prettily placed next to the village church. The beamed bar has flagstone floors, a light oak counter with recessed lighting, fresh flowers on the wooden tables, paintings for sale (by a local artist) and Hidden Pint, Ringwood Best and a couple of changing guest beers on handpump; juke box and TV in the public bar. The bistro restaurant is in an attractively reworked barn and the skittle alley doubles as a family room during the day; piped music. There's a very good wood-chip children's play area in the garden and the comfortable ensuite bedrooms are in a modern block at the back; good breakfasts. They are licensed for weddings. Tarrant Monkton is a charming village (with a ford that can flow quite fast in wet weather), and is well located for local walks and exploring the area.

🍴 **Popular – if not cheap – bar food includes lunchtime filled baguettes and baked potatoes, ploughman's, home-cooked ham and eggs and local sausages as well as rustic breads with local butter, home-made hummus and marinated olives, soup, smoked fish and crayfish tartlet, broccoli, brie and mushroom lasagne, steak in ale pie, local faggots in rich onion gravy, chicken curry, beer-battered haddock, local venison in green peppercorn sauce, and puddings such as three-tier chocolate mousse or banana mousse with brownie biscuits.** *Starters/Snacks: £4.25 to £7.95. Main Courses: £7.95 to £16.50. Puddings: £4.95 to £6.75*

Free house ~ Licensees Barbara and James Cossins ~ Real ale ~ Bar food (11.30-2.30, 6-9.30; all day Sat and Sun) ~ Restaurant ~ (01258) 830225 ~ Children in restaurant and family room ~ Dogs allowed in bedrooms ~ Open 11.30-midnight; 12-10.30 Sun ~ Bedrooms: £60B/£80B

Recommended by Colin and Janet Roe, John A Barker, Gene and Kitty Rankin, P and J Shapley, Graham Holden, Julie Lee, Bruce and Sharon Eden, M G Hart, Peter Titcomb, Pat and Robert Watt, Julie Cox, W W Burke

WEST STOUR   ST7822   MAP 2

Ship 🍷 🛏

A30 W of Shaftesbury; SP8 5RP

Good imaginative fresh food in civilised and neatly updated roadside inn

The bar on the left, with a cool sage green décor and big sash windows, has a mix of seats around nice stripped tables on the dark boards or flagstones of its two smallish rooms; the gossipy inner one has a good log fire, and its bow window looks beyond the road and car park to a soothing view of rolling pastures. They have good wines by the glass, and Palmers Dorset Gold and Ringwood Best and Shepherd Neame Spitfire on handpump; the neatly dressed staff give good service. On the right two carpeted dining rooms, with stripped pine dado and shutters, are furnished in a similar pleasantly informal style, and have some attractive contemporary nautical prints. The bedlington terrier is called Douglas. As there's a sharp nearby bend, keep your fingers crossed that drivers are obeying the 30mph limit when you walk from or to the car park opposite.

🍴 The imaginative food is a main draw here, with a wide choice of lunchtime sandwiches and paninis and a fresh fish board: soup, a changing pâté or terrine, cornish mussels in garlic, herbs and white wine, roasted piedmont peppers on parmesan rocket pasta, beer-battered cod with minted pea purée, whole baked trout with prawn and caper butter, lamb and mint suet pudding with spring onion mash and rich onion and rosemary gravy, rabbit casserole in cider and mustard cream sauce, duck breast with sloe gin and cherry sauce, daily specials, and puddings such as white chocolate and mango cheesecake with fruit coulis or apple and cherry flapjack pudding with custard. *Starters/Snacks: £3.95 to £6.25. Main Courses: £8.95 to £17.95. Puddings: £4.50 to £6.95*

Free house ~ Licensee Gavin Griggs ~ Real ale ~ Bar food (12-2.30, 6-9) ~ Restaurant ~ (01747) 838640 ~ Children welcome ~ Dogs allowed in bar ~ Open 12-3, 6-11; 12-10.30 Sun ~ Bedrooms: £50B/£70B

Recommended by Neil Crux, Alan M Pring, Colin and Janet Roe, Pat and Robert Watt

WIMBORNE MINSTER
SZ0199   MAP 2

Green Man £
Victoria Road at junction with West Street (B3082/B3073); BH21 1EN

Cosy and warm-hearted town pub with bargain simple food

Quick cheerful service and loads of copper and brass ornaments brighten up this welcoming and relaxed pub's muted warm tones – soft lighting, dark red walls, maroon plush banquettes and polished dark pub tables in four small linked areas. One of these has a log fire in a biggish brick fireplace, another has a coal-effect gas fire, and they have two darts boards (the games machine is silenced, but they have piped music). Even early in the day quite a few regulars drop in for a coffee and chat, Wadworths IPA, 6X or Bishops Tipple, or perhaps Weston's farm cider; there's a nice little border terrier called Cooper. A back terrace has a couple of picnic-sets, and in summer the floral displays well deserve the prizes they win.

🍴 As well as a very popular breakfast, they do light snacks such as baked beans on toast as well as a wide choice of sandwiches, filled rolls and baked potatoes and simple pubby lunchtime dishes such as fish and chips or ham and egg; good Sunday roasts *Starters/Snacks: £1.50 to £4.75. Main Courses: £4.50 to £6.95. Puddings: £2.50*

Wadworths ~ Tenants Kate Webster and Andrew Kiff ~ Real ale ~ Bar food (lunchtime only) ~ Restaurant ~ (01202) 881021 ~ Children allowed but must be seated when in bar ~ Dogs allowed in bar ~ Live music Fri, Sat and Sun evenings ~ Open 10am-12.30am(1.30am Fri and Sat)

Recommended by W W Burke

WORTH MATRAVERS
SY9777   MAP 2

Square & Compass ★ 🍺
At fork of both roads signposted to village from B3069; BH19 3LF

Unchanging country tavern, masses of character, in the same family for many years; lovely sea views and fine nearby walks

From benches out in front of this charming, old-fashioned pub there's a fantastic view down over the village rooftops to the sea between the East Man and the West Man (the hills that guard the coastal approach) and out beyond Portland Bill; there may be free-roaming hens, chickens and other birds clucking around your feet. The pub has been in the hands of the Newman family for 100 years now and to this day there's no bar counter, so Ringwood Best and guests like Cottage Golden Arrow and White Star Battleaxe and up to ten ciders are tapped from a row of casks and passed to you in a drinking corridor through two serving hatches; several malt whiskies. A couple of basic unspoilt rooms opposite have simple furniture on the flagstones, a woodburning stove and a loyal crowd of friendly locals; darts, cribbage, shove-ha'penny and table skittles. A little museum (free) exhibits local fossils and artefacts, mostly collected by the current friendly landlord and his father; mind your head on the way out. There are wonderful walks from here to some exciting switchback sections of the coast path above St Aldhelm's Head and Chapman's Pool; you will need to park in the public car park 100 yards along the Corfe Castle road (which has a £1 honesty box).

🍴 **Bar food is limited to tasty home-made pasties and pies, served till they run out.** *Starters/Snacks: £2.50*

Free house ~ Licensee Charlie Newman ~ Real ale ~ Bar food (all day) ~ No credit cards ~ (01929) 439229 ~ Children welcome ~ Dogs welcome ~ Live music most Sats ~ Open 12-11; 12-3, 6-11 in winter

Recommended by the Didler, John and Joan Nash, Jeremy Whitehorn, P Dawn, Richard Siebert, Steve Derbyshire, Pete Baker, Chris Flynn, Wendy Jones, Mike and Sue Loseby, Bernard Stradling, Mrs Maricar Jagger, C J Fletcher, JDM, KM

LUCKY DIP

Besides the fully inspected pubs, you might like to try these Lucky Dips recommended to us and described by readers (if you do, please send us reports: www.goodguides.co.uk).

ABBOTSBURY [SY5785]
Ilchester Arms DT3 4JR [Market St (B3157)]: Rambling stone-built pub with old pine tables and settles, lots of rustic bric-a-brac, prints of the famous swans, well kept ales such as Courage Best, Gales HSB and Wychwood, wide food choice from doorstep sandwiches and baked potatoes up, good house wines in three glass sizes, large games room, conservatory restaurant; quiet piped music, TV, games machine; children in eating areas, nice views from suntrap terrace picnic-sets, ten bedrooms, open all day *(W W Burke, George Atkinson, LYM, Colin Gooch, Roland and Wendy Chalu)*
ALDERHOLT [SU1112]
Churchill Arms SP6 3AA [Daggons Rd (back rd Fordingbridge—Cranborne)]: Thriving local with brass cannons by fireplace of panelled bar, darts in second bar, family/games room with more darts, usual food from sandwiches and baked potatoes up, Badger Best and Tanglefoot, skittle alley; garden tables *(June and Robin Savage)*
ALMER [SY9098]
☆ *Worlds End* DT11 9EW [B3075, just off A31 towards Wareham]: Handsome thatched Badger family dining pub, plenty of individuality in long busy beamed and flagstoned bar with panelled alcoves and candles, very wide choice of enjoyable reasonably priced food all day (you can choose generous or smaller helpings), Badger ales, pleasant helpful hard-working staff (lots of tables, even so you may have to wait); open all day, picnic-sets and heaters out in front and behind, outstanding play area *(BB, Steve Crick, Helen Preston, Mrs Ruth Lewis, Jennifer Banks, Stuart Turner)*

ANSTY [ST7603]
Fox DT2 7PN [NW of Milton Abbas]: Hotel rather than pub but with flourishing recently refurbished high-ceilinged bar side, lots of toby jugs, Badger Best, Tanglefoot and a seasonal beer, good wines by the glass, very wide choice of inexpensive food; piped music, separate locals' bar with pool and TV, skittle alley; children welcome in restaurant, garden tables, bedrooms, attractive countryside, open all day *(Pat and Robert Watt, LYM, Pat and Roger Davies)*
ASKERSWELL [SY5393]
☆ *Spyway* DT2 9EP [off A35 Bridport—Dorchester]: Good value mainly pubby food from sandwiches and baguettes to tasty main dishes with lightly cooked fresh veg in prettily set beamed country pub, charming family service, real ales such as Dorset Weymouth Best and Otter, old-fashioned high-backed settles, cushioned wall and window seats, old-world décor, local pictures for sale, dining area with steps down to overflow area; disabled access, children in eating areas, spectacular views from back terrace and large attractive garden, good walks, comfortable bedrooms *(Peter Neate, Mrs Hilarie Taylor, LYM, Roland and Wendy Chalu)*
BEAMINSTER [ST4801]
Greyhound DT8 3AW [A3066 N of Bridport; The Square]: Well run compact local on market square, cheerful landlord, wide blackboard choice of reasonably priced standard food from sandwiches and baked potatoes up, full Palmers ale range, farm cider, daily papers, flagstones and simple furnishings on right, plusher on left, open fires, local paintings for sale, small back family room, darts; may be piped music;

dogs welcome (Christine and Neil Townend, John A Barker, BB, Roland and Wendy Chalu, Joan and Michel Hooper-Immins)

BERE REGIS [SY8494]

Drax Arms BH20 7HH [West St; off A35 bypass]: Neatly kept village local with cheerful helpful service, well kept Badger Best and farm cider, good value generous home-made food from sandwiches up, esp pies and casseroles, big open fire on left, small dining area (busy in summer); dogs welcome, good walking nearby (John and Joan Nash)

BLANDFORD FORUM [ST8806]

Crown DT11 7AJ [West St]: Best Western hotel's well furnished spacious bar areas used by locals as pub, spacious adjacent informal eating area, Badger beers from nearby brewery, good range of reasonably priced straightforward bar food inc good sandwiches and light meals, separate restaurant; bedrooms (W W Burke)

Dolphin DT11 7DR [East St]: Interesting and friendly old market-town local, well kept changing ales, fruit wines, reasonably priced standard food, bare boards, rugs and panelling, pews, fireside sofa (Stan Edwards)

BLANDFORD ST MARY [ST8805]

Hall & Woodhouse DT11 9LS Visitor centre for Badger brewery, their full beer range in top condition inc interesting bottled beers, varied food from well filled baguettes up, friendly staff; spectacular chandelier made of Badger beer bottles, lots of memorabilia in centre and upper gallery; popular brewery tours; likely to close some time in 2008 when the present brewery gives way to its new nearby replacement (Joan and Michel Hooper-Immins)

BOURNEMOUTH [SZ0791]

Pig & Whistle BH2 6BE [Queens Rd]: Recently opened, with lavish Victorian/Edwardian décor, comfortable bar and substantial restaurant, sensibly priced pubby lunches, more ambitious evening menu, Ringwood beers, friendly service; open all day (W W Burke)

BOURTON [ST7731]

☆ *White Lion* SP8 5AT [High St, off old A303 E of Wincanton]: The newish tenants who were winning a good reputation for the food in this 18th-c beamed and stripped stone dining pub moved on again in 2007; it's an appealing place, with fine inglenook log fire in pubby bar, two cosy rooms off, real ales such as Fullers London Pride and Greene King IPA, farm ciders and good wines, and good-sized restaurant; well spaced tables in pleasant garden, two neat bedrooms with own bathrooms; reports on new regime please (LYM)

BRIDPORT [SY4692]

George DT6 3NQ [South St]: Cheery unpretentious two-bar town local, traditional dark décor, assorted furnishings and floor rugs, bargain home-made pub lunches (not Sun) cooked in sight, filling sandwiches, well kept Palmers ales, good choice of wines by

the glass, efficient service, hot coal fire, hatch-served family room; piped radio, upstairs lavatories; dogs welcome, open all day, from 9am for popular wkdy breakfast or coffee (LYM, Roland and Wendy Chalu)

BROADWINDSOR [ST4302]

☆ *White Lion* DT8 3QD [The Square (B3163/B3164)]: Comfortable 17th-c stone-built pub with enjoyable meals using local meat and fish (no sandwiches or baguettes), well kept Palmers ales, decent wines by the glass, cheerful landlord, pews and flagstones on left, pine booth seating, attractively set tables and big inglenook with log fire in carpeted dining area on right, no machines or music; disabled facilities, picnic-sets in small courtyard (BB, Brian Roe, Michael David Doyle, Frank and Pat Shepherd)

BUCKHORN WESTON [ST7524]

Stapleton Arms SP8 5HS [Church Hill]: Former village local reworked into more of a bistro dining pub, enjoyable up-to-date food at a price from sandwiches up, Ringwood and other good local beers; tables outside, pleasant countryside (Richard Wyld)

BURTON BRADSTOCK [SY4889]

☆ *Anchor* DT6 4QF [B3157 SE of Bridport]: Cheerful new landlord and staff, pricy but good seafood restaurant, wide choice of other generous food inc pub lunches from baguettes and baked potatoes up, lively village pub part too (games and sports TV), several real ales such as Ushers Best and Wychwood Hobgoblin, Thatcher's farm cider, lots of malt whiskies, decent wines by the glass; children and dogs welcome, comfortable bedrooms, open all day; more reports on new regime please (LYM, Roland and Wendy Chalu)

☆ *Three Horseshoes* DT6 4QZ [Mill St]: Attractive thatched inn reopened under friendly new licensees after extensive comfortable refurbishment, sensibly shortish lunchtime choice of enjoyable pubby food from sandwiches to fish, somewhat wider evening range, quick cheerful service, Palmers complete ale range particularly well kept (head brewer lives nearby), good wines by the glass, thriving atmosphere in cottagey low-beamed L-shaped bar with log fire in big inglenook, rustic tables (mainly laid for eating) and lots of pictures, passage to pretty dining room; may be piped music; dogs welcome, picnic-sets out on back terrace and lawn, charming village, pleasant shingle beach a few minutes' drive away (with NT car park) (LYM, George Atkinson, Bob and Margaret Holder, Roland and Wendy Chalu)

CATTISTOCK [SY5999]

☆ *Fox & Hounds* DT2 0JH [off A37 N of Dorchester]: Good atmosphere in attractive 17th-c or older pub, friendly helpful service, enjoyable food from baguettes to enterprising specials and generous OAP meals, Palmers ales from attractively carved counter, Taunton cider, good value wine choice, flagstones and nicely moulded

Jacobean beams, stripped stone, log fire in huge inglenook, minimal décor, table skittles, pleasant side dining room, back public bar with well lit darts and TV, immaculate skittle alley; piped pop music, live some Sats; dogs allowed on back terrace, comfortable bedrooms, cl Mon lunchtime, open all day wknds *(Pat and Roger Davies, R T and J C Moggridge, W F C Phillips, BB)*

CERNE ABBAS [ST6601]

☆ *New Inn* DT2 7JF [14 Long Street]: Handsome Tudor inn with mullioned window seats in nicely spruced up beamed bar, revised range of enjoyable food inc good basic bar lunches, Palmers ales, nice wine choice, helpful staff, comfortable restaurant; children welcome, lots of tables on raised coachyard platform and attractive sheltered lawn behind, play area, eight bedrooms with own bathrooms, open all day wknds and summer *(Rosanna Luke, Matt Curzon, LYM, John Coatsworth, Richard and Jean Green, Alan Johnson)*

CHEDINGTON [ST4805]

☆ *Winyards Gap* DT8 3HY [A356 Dorchester—Crewkerne]: Attractive and neatly kept dining pub, good choice of generous enjoyable food inc popular OAP lunches, sensible prices, relaxed atmosphere and good cheerful service, Cotleigh, Exmoor and perhaps guest ales, dining area welcoming children, skittle alley; spectacular view over Parrett Valley and into Somerset from tables out in front, good walks nearby *(LYM, Mr and Mrs Peter Larkman, Bob and Margaret Holder)*

CHICKERELL [SY6480]

Turks Head Inn DT3 4DS [6 East St (separate from the Turks Head Hotel in front, at number 8)]: Large traditional stone-built village pub with well kept ales inc Courage Directors, good choice of generous food, pleasant beamed bar with lots of old local photographs, cheerful efficient service, spacious simply furnished eating area (former skittle alley); children welcome *(Tim and Rosemary Wells)*

CHIDEOCK [SY4191]

Anchor DT6 6JU [Seatown signed off A35 from Chideock]: Unpretentious and well worn-in seaside pub in outstanding spot, with dramatic sea and cliff views and big front terrace, well kept Palmers ales, good choice of wines by the glass, local farm cider, generous reasonably priced basic food (all day in summer) from lunchtime sandwiches up, woodburners, interesting local photographs; unobtrusive piped music, and they may try to keep your credit card while you eat; children and dogs welcome, open all day in summer *(LYM, Miss A G Drake, PRT, W W Burke, R J Townson, David Thornton, Sue Heath, Edna Jones, Di and Mike Gillam, Fred and Lorraine Gill, Roland and Wendy Chalu)*

CHRISTCHURCH [SZ1592]

☆ *Olde George* BH23 1DT [Castle St]: Bustling and cheerfully old-fashioned 17th-c pub with

friendly efficient staff, snug little front bars, two well kept Ringwood ales and interesting changing guest beers, good choice of sensibly priced home-made food all day with unusual puddings, Sun carvery and different evening menu; the nice old dog's called Sophie; lots of teak seats and tables in heated character coach yard, open all day *(D W Stokes, BB)*

CORFE CASTLE [SY9682]

Bankes Arms BH20 5ED [East St]: Big, busy and welcoming, on attractive village square, with flagstones and comfortable traditional décor, subtle lighting, enjoyable food, good choice of wines by the glass, well kept ales, restaurant; piped music; children and dogs welcome, tables on terrace and in long garden with end play area overlooking steam railway, bedrooms *(Peter Salmon)*

Castle Inn BH20 5EE [East St]: Neatly refurbished unpretentious two-room pub mentioned in Hardy's *Hand of Ethelberta*, enjoyable home cooking inc Sun lunches, friendly staff, Ringwood ales, good value wines, flagstone floors; popular terrace garden *(John and Joan Calvert)*

Fox BH20 5HD [West St]: Very much an old-fashioned take-us-as-you-find us stone-built local with tiny front bar dominated by bar-stool regulars, real ales such as Timothy Taylors Landlord and Wadworths 6X tapped from the cask, good log fire in early medieval stone fireplace, glassed-over well in lounge (many tables reserved for the plain if not cheap food); dogs but not children allowed inside, informal castle-view garden *(the Didler, J S and S Chadwick, Joan and Michel Hooper-Immins, M Joyner, LYM)*

☆ *Greyhound* BH20 5EZ [A351]: Bustling and picturesque old pub in centre of tourist village, three small low-ceilinged panelled rooms, steps and corridors, well kept changing ales such as Ringwood and Timothy Taylors Landlord, Aug beer festival, generous food from baguettes to steaks, friendly well managed staff, traditional games inc purbeck long board shove-ha'penny, family room; piped music, live Fri; garden with fine castle and countryside views, pretty courtyard opening on to castle bridge, open all day wknds and summer *(LYM, W W Burke, Peter and Margaret Glenister, the Didler)*

CORFE MULLEN [SY9798]

☆ *Coventry Arms* BH21 3RH [A31 W of Wimborne; Mill St]: Civilised four-room dining pub with enjoyable bistro-style meals (named suppliers, local fish, their own herbs, some unusual dishes and enterprising children's things), changing real ales such as Butcombe, Isle of Purbeck and Timothy Taylors Landlord tapped from the cask, decent wines, large central open fire, low ceilings, flagstones, bare boards, evening candles and fishing décor; tables out by small river *(Pat and Robert Watt, Gerald and Gabrielle Culliford, M R Phillips, Mike and Shelley Woodroffe)*

DORCHESTER [SY6990]

☆ **Blue Raddle** DT1 1JN [Church St, nr central short stay car park]: Current owners doing good interesting food from generous sandwiches to game and good Sun roast in cheery unpretentious pub with friendly service, Otter, Sharps Doom Bar and guest beers such as Timothy Taylors Landlord, good wines, open fire; piped music; disabled access, but one step, cl Mon lunchtime *(Mr and Mrs D Renwick, Joan and Michel Hooper-Immins, Gene and Kitty Rankin, Pat and Roger Davies, the Didler, BB)*

Kings Arms DT1 1HF [High East St]: Hotel bar with thriving atmosphere, appealing old-world décor, Courage Directors and guest beers, decent wines, enjoyable food from sandwiches up, two-for-one deals and Sun carvery, attentive service, open fire; close associations with Nelson and Hardy's *Mayor of Casterbridge*; bedrooms (the Lawrence of Arabia suite and the Tutenkhamen are pretty striking) *(LYM, the Didler)*

Tom Browns DT1 1HU [High East St]: Under new owners still brewing their own Goldfinch ales in back microbrewery, perhaps an occasional guest beer too, welcoming staff, friendly locals and traditional games in bare-boards L-shaped bar, lightly refurbished but kept thoroughly unpretentious, back juke box; garden extended down to river, open all day Fri/Sat *(Joan and Michel Hooper-Immins, BB)*

EAST BURTON [SY8287]

Seven Stars DT2 8RL Comfortable old country pub with dining conservatory, good choice of generous if not cheap food (can be a wait – can get packed in summer), Greene King Abbot and Old Speckled Hen, nice fairly priced wine list, friendly welcome for families, lots of prints, stuffed fish and copper bric-a-brac; tables outside, play area, handy for Bovington Tank Museum and Monkey World, parking for caravans *(David Lamb, Joan and Michel Hooper-Immins)*

EAST KNIGHTON [SY8185]

Countryman DT2 8LL [signed off A352 Dorchester—Wareham]: Big bustling family food pub with quick service by friendly young staff, enjoyable food, some comfortable sofas in bar area, log fires, well kept ales such as Greene King and Ringwood, farm cider, good value wines; piped music; good provision for disabled, peaceful setting, comfortable spacious bedrooms, good breakfast *(John and Joan Calvert, John and Joan Nash, Andy and Yvonne Cunningham, LYM, K Sloan)*

EVERSHOT [ST5704]

Acorn DT2 0JW [off A37 S of Yeovil]: Charmingly placed upmarket inn with Branscombe Vale and Fullers London Pride, good choice of wines by the glass inc champagne, restaurant front part with up-to-date décor as well as log fires and oak panelling, bar snacks from interesting open

sandwiches to salads and pubby hot dishes in beamed and flagstoned back bar with games and juke box, skittle alley; they may try to keep your credit card while you eat; children allowed in eating areas, dogs in bar, terrace with dark oak furniture, bedrooms, pretty village, good surrounding walks, open all day *(Rob Winstanley, Edna Jones, LYM, Bob and Angela Brooks, Alan Johnson, OPUS, Roland and Wendy Chalu)*

EYPE [SY4491]

New Inn DT6 6AP Unassuming two-bar village local, cheerful landlord, staff and african grey parrot, well kept Palmers, enjoyable popular food, coal fire, darts, two steps down to cottagey dining room; may be piped music; level access, magnificent views from back terrace, steps down to lawn *(John Coatsworth, Roland and Wendy Chalu)*

FIDDLEFORD [ST8013]

Fiddleford Inn DT10 2BX [A357 Sturminster Newton—Blandford Forum]: Three linked smartly simple areas looked after well by young staff, nice atmosphere, ancient flagstones, some stripped stone, Ringwood Best, Timothy Taylors Landlord and Wells & Youngs, generous standard food (not Sun evening) from sandwiches up; unobtrusive piped music; big pleasant garden with play area safely fenced from busy road *(Richard and Jean Green, LYM)*

FONTMELL MAGNA [ST8616]

☆ **Crown** SP7 0PA Emphasis on enjoyable reasonably priced food using fresh local supplies from bar snacks to full meals in three smallish linked areas with pleasant mix of furnishings on tiled floors, country prints on sage green walls, friendly service, interesting wines, well kept Badger ales; lavatories outside (nice covered walkway over little sparkling brook); terrace tables, bedrooms *(BB, Paul and Caroline Marland, Mrs G C Kohn)*

GILLINGHAM [ST7926]

Buffalo SP8 4NJ [off B3081 at Wyke 1 mile NW of Gillingham, pub 100 yds on left]: Busy and welcoming Badger local surrounded by new housing, their ales kept well, sensibly priced food (not Sun evening) from sandwiches and baked potatoes up, stripped stone and brick in three smartly refurbished linked rooms with popular back restaurant; picnic-sets on back terrace, open all day Sun *(Edward Mirzoeff, Ian Phillips)*

Dolphin SP8 4HB [Peacemarsh (B3082)]: Friendly and popular dining pub with well kept Badger beers, pleasant beamed bar and restaurant area; garden with play area *(Pat and Robert Watt, BB, Roy Hoing)*

GUSSAGE ALL SAINTS [SU0010]

☆ **Drovers** BH21 5ET [8 miles N of Wimborne]: Partly thatched pub with good value generous home-made food from snacks to full meals, well kept Ringwood ales and a guest such as Fullers London Pride, friendly staff, good log fire and pleasantly simple country furnishings, public bar with piano and darts; quiet village, tables on pretty front lawn with views across the Dorset hills *(LYM, Pat and Robert Watt, W W Burke, Richard and Sue Fewkes)*

HIGHCLIFFE [SZ2193]

Hinton Oak BH23 5EA [Lymington Rd]: Pleasant dining pub with interesting changing ale choice, good range of enjoyable home-made food all day, conservatory; terrace tables, open all day *(A D Lealan)*

HOLT [SU0304]

Old Inn BH21 7DJ Busy and well run beamed Badger dining pub, their real ales, helpful friendly service, good well priced food inc many oriental dishes and fresh fish, small helpings available, plenty of comfortable tables, winter fires, good atmosphere; children welcome *(M R Phillips, M and R Thomas, June and Robin Savage, Stan Edwards)*

HOLT HEATH [SU0604]

Cross Keys BH21 7JZ Unreconstructed village pub, welcoming and pleasantly set, with usual food inc reasonably priced specials, well kept Badger ales, games room behind small bar; colourful garden *(John and Angela Main)*

IWERNE MINSTER [ST8614]

Talbot DT11 8QN [Blandford Rd]: Well refurbished pub well run by sociable and experienced new licensees, emphasis on enjoyable food from sandwiches up inc popular Sun lunch, Badger ales, sensibly priced wines by the glass, friendly local atmosphere, candlelit tables in pleasant dining area, public bar with darts and pool; TV; tables and chairs on heated terrace, five bedrooms also comfortably updated, good breakfast *(M R Eavis)*

KINGSTON [SY9579]

Scott Arms BH20 5LH [West St (B3069)]: Much-used rambling holiday pub mixing plain eating tables and chairs with sofas and easy chairs, beams, stripped stone and log fires, Courage Best and Ringwood Best, lots of wines, popular food inc summer cream teas, family dining area; darts, dominoes, pool and games machine, piped music; attractive garden with outstanding views of Corfe Castle and the Purbeck Hills, good walks *(Peter Meister, LYM, the Didler)*

LITTON CHENEY [SY5490]

☆ *White Horse* DT2 9AT Relaxed and unpretentious, with good value food from sandwiches and traditional dishes to imaginative cooking with good fresh local ingredients, particularly well kept Palmers ales, decent reasonably priced wines by the glass, pleasant efficient service, big woodburner, lots of pictures, some pine panelling, stripped stone and flagstones, country kitchen chairs in dining area, table skittles; may be piped jazz; children and dogs welcome, disabled access, good spot on quiet lane into quaint village, picnic-sets on pleasant streamside front lawn *(BB, Dr Peter Andrews, Gavin Robinson, Edna Jones, C and R Bromage, Roland and Wendy Chalu)*

LODERS [SY4994]

Loders Arms DT6 3SA [off A3066 just N of Bridport]: Extended 17th-c stone-built pub, relaxed and unspoilt, with well kept Palmers, good value changing food from huge baguettes up inc some innovative dishes, polite efficient service, good choice of wines by the glass, Taunton farm cider, log fire, magazines and daily papers, thousands of corks on ceiling, pretty dining room, skittle alley; children in eating areas, pleasant views from picnic-sets in small informal back garden, pretty thatched village, comfortable bedrooms, open all day Sun *(LYM, Steve Derbyshire, Roland and Wendy Chalu)*

LONGBURTON [ST6412]

☆ *Rose & Crown* DT9 5PD [A352 Sherborne—Dorchester]: Extended thatched Badger dining pub with pubby furnishings in maroon-walled bar, enjoyable food (limited Mon), freshly made and generous, from sandwiches to imaginative restaurant dishes inc unusual puddings, Badger beers, decent wines by the glass, big inglenook with woodburner, pool and darts one end, attractive back dining room with booth seating and well feature, skittle alley; easy disabled access, picnic-sets on back grass, bedrooms *(Jean and David Darby, BB, Richard and Jean Green, Jason Muxworthy, Mrs Angela Graham)*

LYME REGIS [SY3391]

Cobb Arms DT7 3JF [Marine Parade, Monmouth Beach]: Lively spaciously refurbished local with well kept Palmers ales, wide range of reasonably priced generous bar food inc local fish, decent wines, quick service even when busy, good value cream teas, interesting ship pictures and marine fish tank; popular with local young people till late; next to harbour, beach and coastal walk, children welcome, open all day, tables on small back terrace, bedrooms, good breakfast *(Steve and Liz Tilley)*

☆ *Harbour Inn* DT7 3JF [Marine Parade]: Good pubby food from lunchtime sandwiches up, plenty of fresh local fish (great fish soup), friendly efficient service, good choice of wines by the glass, Otter and St Austell real ale, farm cider, clean-cut modern décor keeping original flagstones and stone walls (so can be a bit noisy when busy), thriving family atmosphere, big paintings for sale, sea and coast views from front windows; piped music; disabled access from street, verandah tables *(Bruce Horne, JT, Roland and Wendy Chalu, Joan and Michel Hooper-Immins)*

☆ *Pilot Boat* DT7 3QA [Bridge St]: Popular and reliable modern all-day family food place nr waterfront, long-serving licensees and bright young staff, good value food, well kept Palmers ales, good choice of wines by the glass, plenty of tables in cheery nautically themed areas, skittle alley; piped music; children and dogs welcome, tables out on terrace, open all day *(Joan and Michel Hooper-Immins, Sue and Mike Todd,*

LYM, Steve Crick, Helen Preston, Pat and Tony Martin, Richard Pitcher)

Royal Lion DT7 3QF [Broad St]: Coaching inn dating from 17th c, comfortably old-fashioned many-roomed bar with log fire and dark panelling, well kept Bass and guest beers, good value pub meals, efficient service, games room, upstairs restaurant (JT, Sue and Mike Todd, LYM)

☆ **Royal Standard** DT7 3JF [Marine Parade, The Cobb]: Right on broadest part of beach, properly pubby bar with fine built-in stripped high settles and even old-fashioned ring-up tills, quieter eating area with stripped brick and pine, quick friendly service, three Palmers ales, good choice of wines by the glass, popular food from good crab sandwiches inc local fish, good cream teas, log fire, darts, prominent pool table; may be piped pop; children welcome, good-sized sheltered suntrap courtyard with own servery and wendy house – and you can keep an eye on your children on the beach just feet away (Mr and Mrs G Ives, Gene and Kitty Rankin, Sue and Mike Todd, BB, Dave Mower, Steve and Liz Tilley)

Ship DT7 3PY [Coombe St]: Pleasant local with well kept Palmers ales; sports TV (Steve and Liz Tilley)

☆ **Victoria** DT7 3LP [Uplyme Rd (B3165)]: Well updated and pleasantly unpretentious Victorian pub/hotel, good reasonably priced food from lunchtime paninis (not Mon) and other bar meals to well prepared and imaginative restaurant dishes (can be eaten in bar too) strong on fresh local seafood and carefully chosen local produce from named farms, reasonable prices, well kept Fullers London Pride, Greene King Abbot and Ushers, good wines by the glass, friendly licensees and staff, attractive neatly kept open-plan bar, big-windowed restaurant looking down on town; may be faint piped music; nicely planted sheltered terrace, bedrooms (Terry and Linda Moseley, Mr and Mrs P Stephens, BB, Steve and Liz Tilley)

LYTCHETT MINSTER [SY9693]

St Peters Finger BH16 6JE [Dorchester Rd]: Well run two-part beamed Badger roadhouse with plenty of friendly efficient staff, sensibly priced food from sandwiches and baguettes up, small helpings available, real ale inc Tanglefoot, cottagey mix of furnishings in different sections and end log fire giving a cosy feel despite its size; good skittle alley, tables on big terrace, part covered and heated (Douglas and Ann Hare, B and K Hypher)

MARNHULL [ST7719]

☆ **Blackmore Vale** DT10 1JJ [Burton St, via Church Hill off B3092]: Comfortably modernised pub with good generous freshly made food inc OAP lunches Tues and Thurs, friendly service, three Badger beers, good choice of reasonably priced wines, pleasantly opened-up beamed and flagstoned dining bar with woodburner, cosy smaller bar with log fire, settles, sofas and pub games; piped

music; children welcome, tables in attractively reworked garden, open all day wknds (B and K Hypher, Pat and Robert Watt, LYM)

MARTINSTOWN [SY6488]

Brewers Arms DT2 9LB Extended village local under welcoming new licensees, enjoyable food (not Sun evening or Mon lunchtime) from baguettes up, real ales, lively atmosphere, restaurant, pool and skittle alley; well behaved children and dogs welcome (friendly resident lurchers), garden picnic-sets (Sam and Ann Salmon)

MELPLASH [SY4897]

☆ **Half Moon** DT6 3UD [A3066 Bridport—Beaminster]: Friendly and cottagey 18th-c thatched pub, beams, brasses and pictures of local scenes and animals, landlord doing good range of good value standard food from sandwiches up, well kept Palmers ales, cheerful landlady, good choice of wines, log fire, carpeted bar, eating area and evening dining room (worth booking); may be unobtrusive piped music; tables and chairs in good-sized attractive garden with water feature, shares car park with cricket club next door (George Atkinson, Roland and Wendy Chalu)

MOTCOMBE [ST8426]

Coppleridge SP7 9HW Enjoyable food from sandwiches to speciality steaks, Boddingtons and Butcombe, decent wines and welcoming service in former 18th-c farmhouse's bar/lounge and two smallish dining rooms; big airy beams, good-sized grounds (Colin and Janet Roe, Pat and Robert Watt)

MUDEFORD [SZ1891]

☆ **Haven House** BH23 4AB [beyond huge seaside car park at Mudeford Pier]: Popular much-extended pub in great spot on beach with superb views and bird watching, good value food from good crab sandwiches and winter soup up, well kept Ringwood and other ales, cheerful efficient service, popular linked family cafeteria (all day in summer); nice in winter with old-fashioned feel in quaint little part-flagstoned core and lovely seaside walks (dogs banned from beach May-Sept); tables on sheltered terrace (D W Stokes, LYM)

OSMINGTON [SY7282]

Sunray DT3 6EU [A353 Weymouth—Wareham]: Good-sized pub with good friendly service and hardworking landlord, hearty good value food (small helpings available), well kept Butcombe, Flowers IPA and Ringwood Best and Fortyniner, relaxing atmosphere and pleasant contemporary décor, card games; children welcome, large garden and terrace, play area (Pat and Roger Davies, Joan and Michel Hooper-Immins)

OSMINGTON MILLS [SY7381]

☆ **Smugglers** DT3 6HF [off A353 NE of Weymouth]: Good atmosphere in pretty part-thatched pub, well extended, with cosy dark corners, two open woodburners, old local pictures, nautical decorations and shiny black panelling, well kept Badger beers, nice wines by the glass, discreet games area; a managed pub, so food (served all day) and service may vary with management changes, piped music, can be very crowded in summer (holiday settlement nearby), disabled access tricky; children welcome, streamside garden with good play area and thatched summer bar, fine position a short stroll up from the sea, good cliff walks, four comfortable bedrooms, open all day *(LYM, the Didler, Ian Phillips)*

PIDDLEHINTON [SY7197]

☆ *Thimble* DT2 7TD [High St (B3143)]: Friendly well organised partly thatched pub with two handsome fireplaces and deep glazed-over well in attractive low-beamed core, well kept Badger, Palmers and Ringwood ales, quite a few fruit wines, pleasant staff, straightforward bar food from sandwiches and baked potatoes up, interesting bottle collection, darts and cribbage; children and dogs welcome, floodlit garden with summer house, barbecues, stream and little bridge *(David Thornton, David Billington, LYM, P and J Shapley, Mrs Diane M Hall, M G Hart, Joan and Michel Hooper-Immins, John Coatsworth, M Joyner, Bill Smith, Phil and Jane Hodson, Gordon Tong, Dennis Jenkin, John A Barker)*

PIDDLETRENTHIDE [SY7198]

☆ *European* DT2 7QT Unpretentious traditional beamed pub now taken over and renovated by former landlord of Trout at Tadpole Bridge (Oxon), emphasis on sound local country cooking at sensible prices (some produce from their own farm), real ales such as Ringwood Best, good wines by the glass, cheerful service, log fire in attractive fireplace; dogs very welcome, tables in neatly kept front garden, newly fitted bedrooms with good views *(BB, Dennis Jenkin)*

☆ *Poachers* DT2 7QX [B3143 N of Dorchester]: Good atmosphere and friendly licensees, Butcombe, Palmers Tally Ho and Ringwood Fortyniner, generous food, bright up-to-date décor, comfortable lounge end, three linked beamed dining areas with local artwork for sale; piped music; dogs welcome, garden with tables on decking and stream at bottom, 20 comfortable good value motel-style bedrooms around residents' heated swimming pool, good breakfast, open all day *(Richard Marjoram, Rob Winstanley, Joan and Michel Hooper-Immins)*

PIMPERNE [ST9009]

☆ *Anvil* DT11 8UQ [well back from A354]: Attractive 16th-c thatched family pub with wide choice of appetising food from enterprising and generous lunchtime baguettes and ciabattas to piping hot substantial main dishes, good ales such as Butcombe, Palmers and Timothy Taylors Landlord, cheerful efficient young staff, bays of plush seating in bright and welcoming bar, neat black-beamed dining areas; fruit machine, piped music; good garden with fish

pond and big weeping willow, 12 bedrooms with own bathrooms, nice surroundings *(Stan Edwards, John and Joan Nash, BB)*

POOLE [SZ0190]

☆ *Angel* BH15 1NF [Market St, opp Guildhall which is signed off A348]: Well run, spacious and relaxed, with fresh modern décor, good lighting, friendly efficient staff, enjoyable up-to-date food 12-7 (just lunchtime Sun), four Ringwood ales from visible cellar, decent wines; disabled facilities, colourful and attractive heated back courtyard, modern bedrooms *(LYM, David Billington, G Coates)*

Inn in the Park BH13 6JS [Pinewood Rd, off A338 towards Branksome Chine, via The Avenue]: Popular open-plan bar in substantial Edwardian villa (now a small hotel), Wadworths and other ales, good value generous standard food (not Sun evening) from good sandwiches to fresh seafood, cheerful young staff, log fire, oak panelling and big mirrors, airy and attractive restaurant (children allowed) and Sun carvery; tables on small sunny terrace, comfortable bedrooms, quiet pine-filled residential area just above sea, open all day *(W W Burke, LYM, JDM, KM)*

Nightjar BH13 7HX [Ravine Rd, Canford Cliffs]: Comfortable and well run Ember Inn with leather armchairs, sofas and so forth, several separate areas, good wines by the glass, Bass and other good ales such as Fullers London Pride and Wells & Youngs Bombardier from long bar, occasional beer festivals, usual food from sandwiches up; piped music, machines, two quiz nights; picnic-sets on pleasant shaded lawn, nice quiet spot in upmarket district *(W W Burke, Betsy Brown, Nigel Flook, JDM, KM)*

Queen Mary BH15 1LD [West St]: Generous wholesome pub food from well filled proper sandwiches up, pleasant staff, two well kept Ringwood ales and a guest beer, roaring fire, traditional dark wood furnishings and usual nautical pictures and bric-a-brac, darts; disabled access *(Mrs Hilarie Taylor)*

PORTLAND [SY6873]

Cove House DT5 1AW [follow Chiswell signposts – is at NW corner of Portland]: Pleasantly refurbished low-beamed and bare-boarded 18th-c pub in superb position effectively built into the sea defences just above the miles-long Chesil pebble beach, great views from three-room bar's bay windows, reasonably priced usual food from huge sandwiches, baguettes and baked potatoes to good value local fish and seafood, mainstream real ales, friendly efficient service; quiet piped music, steep steps down to gents'; picnic-sets out by sea wall *(LYM, Mike and Linda Hudson, Roland and Wendy Chalu)*

George DT5 2AP [Reforne]: Cheery 17th-c stone-built local mentioned by Thomas Hardy and reputed to have smugglers' tunnels running to the cliffs, very low doorways and beams, flagstones, small rooms, old scrubbed tables carved with names of generations of sailors and quarrymen, interesting prints and mementoes, Greene King Abbot and and a guest such as Otter, Addlestone's cider, children's room, pool room and newer end bar; the chatty local landlord planned to leave as we went to press – news please; picnic-sets in pleasant back garden, open all day *(Joan and Michel Hooper-Immins, Ian Phillips)*

PORTLAND BILL [SY6768]

Pulpit DT5 2JT Welcoming extended traditional pub at end of Weymouth bus route in great spot nr Pulpit Rock, picture-window views, dark beams and stripped stone, a real ale such as Fullers London Pride or Ringwood Best, friendly long-serving licensees, generous quickly served food from good crab sandwiches through pubby favourites to lobster (they shout your name when it's ready); may be piped music; tiered sea-view terrace, short stroll to lighthouse and cliffs *(Meg and Colin Hamilton, A and B D Craig, Colin Gooch, Joan and Michel Hooper-Immins)*

PUNCKNOWLE [SY5388]

☆ *Crown* DT2 9BN [off B3157 Bridport—Abbotsbury]: 16th-c thatched inn, recently refurbished yet pleasantly unpretentious, with warm welcome, good value pubby food from lunchtime sandwiches and baked potatoes to several casseroles and steaks, full Palmers ale range kept well, a dozen wines by the glass, nice coffee, inglenook log fires each end of low-beamed stripped stone lounge, steps up to public bar with books, magazines and another log fire, children's books in family room, local paintings for sale; no credit cards; views from peaceful pretty back garden, good walks, bedrooms *(Alan Johnson, LYM, R J Townson, Terry and Linda Moseley, Peter Titcomb, Roland and Wendy Chalu)*

PYMORE [SY4794]

Pymore Inn DT6 5PN [off A3066 N of Bridport]: New licensees in attractive Georgian beamed and stone-built pub with good atmosphere, enjoyable food inc good fish choice (most tables laid for eating), friendly prompt service, St Austell ales, good choice of wines by the glass, prints on panelled walls, old settles and woodburner, small pretty dining room; wheelchair access, large pleasant garden *(Fred and Lorraine Gill, Roland and Wendy Chalu)*

SHAFTESBURY [ST8722]

Half Moon SP7 8BS [Salisbury Rd (A30 E, by roundabout)]: Comfortable and pleasantly extended family dining pub with wide choice of good value generous food inc popular Sun lunch, well kept Badger beers, quick helpful service, spotless housekeeping; garden with adventure playground *(Rodger and Yvonne MacDonald)*

Two Brewers SP7 8HE [St James St]: Nicely tucked away below steep famously photogenic Gold Hill, friendly well divided open-plan plush-seated bar, lots of decorative plates, pleasant staff, Fullers London Pride, Greene King Old Speckled Hen, Ringwood Best and Fortyniner and one from Sharps or St Austell, good value wines, food from baguettes up (children's helpings of any dish), back dining room, skittle alley; children in eating areas, dogs in bar, picnic-sets in attractive good-sized garden with pretty views *(Pat and Roger Davies, LYM, John A Barker)*

SHERBORNE [ST6316]

☆ *Skippers* DT9 3HE [A352 link rd, W of centre; Terrace View, Horsecastles]: Good relaxed atmosphere in comfortable extended pub with rather close-set tables in long stripped-stone bar, good value food inc generous fresh fish and (not Sun) bargain OAP lunch, Butcombe and Wadworths IPA and 6X, good service, daily papers, coal-effect gas fire, lively décor inc interesting helicopter and other mainly RNAS photographs; may be unobtrusive piped radio; children welcome in eating areas, tables outside *(LYM, Richard and Jean Green, Muriel and John Hobbs)*

SHIPTON GORGE [SY4991]

New Inn DT6 4LT [off A35/B3157 E of Bridport]: Reopened after refurbishment by villagers, smart décor with a couple of sofas and dark blue carpet, friendly licensees, well kept Palmers ales, good wines by the glass, enjoyable generous pubby food from lunchtime sandwiches and baguettes to steaks and mixed grill, extension dining area; piped music; small garden *(Roland and Wendy Chalu)*

STOBOROUGH [SY9286]

Kings Arms BH20 5AB [B3075 S of Wareham; Corfe Rd]: Well kept Ringwood and other ales, late May beer festival, enjoyable food with good choice of specials inc local fish in bar and restaurant, good service and atmosphere; disabled access, garden with terrace by River Frome, open all day wknds *(Gerry and Rosemary Dobson, Ross Balaam, JT, Alan M Pring)*

STOKE ABBOTT [ST4500]

New Inn DT8 3JW [off B3162 and B3163 2 miles W of Beaminster]: 17th-c thatched pub with friendly licensees and pleasant efficient service, well kept Palmers ales, traditional bar food from sandwiches up, log fire in big inglenook, beams, brasses and copper, paintings for sale, some handsome panelling, flagstoned dining room; occasional piped music; wheelchair access, children welcome, picnic-sets in neat and attractive sizeable garden, unspoilt quiet thatched village, good walks, bedrooms *(LYM, Roland and Wendy Chalu)*

STOURPAINE [ST8609]

White Horse DT11 8TA [Shaston Rd; A350 NW of Blandford]: Traditional country pub carefully extended from original core, landlord/chef doing good choice of food from lunchtime sandwiches and bar meals to ambitious dishes (particularly evenings), friendly young staff, Badger ales, nice layout

and décor, scrubbed tables; bedrooms
(Stan Edwards)

STOURTON CAUNDLE [ST7115]

Trooper DT10 2JW [village signed off A30 E
of Milborne Port]: Stone-built pub in lovely
village setting, good value basic pub food,
friendly service, a real ale such as Fullers
London Pride, tiny low-ceilinged bar,
stripped stone dining room, darts, cribbage,
dominoes, shove-ha'penny, skittle alley;
piped music, TV, outside gents'; children and
dogs welcome, a few picnic-sets out in front
and in side garden, has been open all day
summer wknds, cl Mon lunchtime *(Mr and
Mrs W D Borthwick, LYM)*

STRATTON [SY6593]

Saxon Arms DT2 9WG [off A37 NW of
Dorchester; The Square]: Traditional but
recently built thatched local, open-plan,
bright and spacious, with open fire, part
flagstones, part carpet, light oak tables and
comfortable settles, pleasant prompt service,
well kept ales inc Ringwood Best, good value
wines, wide choice of generous food, large
comfortable dining section on right,
traditional games; piped music; children and
dogs welcome, tables out overlooking village
green *(C and R Bromage, M G Hart, LYM,
John and Tania Wood)*

STUDLAND [SZ0382]

☆ *Bankes Arms* BH19 3AU [off B3351, Isle of
Purbeck; Manor Rd]: Very popular spot above
fine beach, outstanding country, sea and
cliff views from huge pleasant garden over
road with masses of seating; comfortably
basic and easy-going big bar with raised
drinking area, impressive range of well kept
changing ales inc its own Isle of Purbeck
ones brewed here, local farm cider, good
wines by the glass, very wide choice of food
(at a price) all day from baguettes to local
fish and good crab salad, helpful young
staff, great log fire, darts and pool in side
games area; they try to keep your credit card
while you eat, can get very busily trippery
wknds and in summer, parking in season can
be complicated or expensive if you're not a
NT member, piped music, machines, big-
screen sports TV; children and dogs welcome,
just off Coast Path, big comfortable
bedrooms *(Steve Derbyshire, Peter Meister,
Bernard Stradling, John and Joan Calvert,
Andy and Yvonne Cunningham, M Joyner,
Maurice and Gill McMahon, Betsy Brown,
Nigel Flook, Keith Widdowson, JDM, KM)*

STURMINSTER MARSHALL [SY9500]

☆ *Red Lion* BH21 4BU [opp church; off A350
Blandford—Poole]: Attractive and civilised
village pub opp handsome church, good
friendly relaxed atmosphere, good value home-
made food from sandwiches and substantial
interesting starters up, neat and welcoming
staff, well kept Badger Best and Tanglefoot,
old-fashioned roomy U-shaped bar with log
fire, team photographs and caricatures,
cabinet of sports trophies and round corner,
adjoining dining room for busier times
(BB, Pat and Roger Davies, JT, W W Burke)

STURMINSTER NEWTON [ST7813]

☆ *Bull* DT10 2BS [A357, S of centre]: Busy
thatched 16th-c country inn by River Stur,
low beams and plenty of character, friendly
staff, good bar food, Badger real ales, soft
lighting; children welcome in eating area,
roadside picnic-sets out in front, more in
pleasant secluded back garden *(Mr and Mrs
W D Borthwick, LYM, W W Burke,
Stan Edwards)*

SWANAGE [SZ0278]

☆ *Red Lion* BH19 2LY [High St]: Low-beamed
17th-c two-bar local doing well under
friendly helpful landlord, good value simple
food, wonderful choice of ciders, reasonably
priced ales such as Caledonian Deuchars IPA,
Flowers, Ringwood and Timothy Taylors
Landlord; piped music, some live; children's
games in large barn, picnic-sets in extended
garden with partly covered back terrace,
comfortable bedrooms in former back coach
house, open all day *(Mr and Mrs M Clark,
Dave Braisted, JMM, Ian Sortwell, the Didler)*

SYMONDSBURY [SY4493]

☆ *Ilchester Arms* DT6 6HD [signed off A35 just
W of Bridport]: Attractive partly thatched
old pub with short choice of traditional
lunchtime food from sandwiches up, wider
evening range inc local fish and more exotic
things, friendly chatty landlady, well kept
Palmers ales, Taunton farm cider, limited
choice of wines by the glass, snugly rustic
open-plan low-beamed bar with high-backed
settle built in by inglenook log fire, pretty
restaurant with another fire (worth booking
wknds – food not served in bar Sat night),
colourful flower displays, pub games, skittle
alley doubling as family room (no children in
bar); fairly quiet piped music; level entrance
(steps from car park), tables in nice informal
brookside back garden with play area,
peaceful village, good walks nearby *(LYM,
Neil and Anita Christopher, Malcolm and
Kate Dowty, Roland and Wendy Chalu,
Joan and Michel Hooper-Immins)*

TARRANT KEYNSTON [ST9204]

True Lovers Knot DT11 9JG [B3082
Blandford—Wimborne]: Light and spacious
extended Badger pub, their ales from long
L-shaped counter in largely carpeted bar
with some beams and flagstones, helpful
friendly service, generous straightforward
pubby food using local supplies, some small
helpings available, uncluttered open-plan
dining area; children welcome, picnic-sets in
good-sized garden with enclosed play area
and camp site, four well equipped bedrooms
(some road noise) *(B and K Hypher)*

THREE LEGGED CROSS [SU0905]

Old Barn Farm BH21 6RE [Ringwood Rd,
towards Ashley Heath and A31]: Picturesque
thatched Vintage Inn, long and low, with
their usual food presented well, pleasant
rambling layout, friendly attentive young
staff, decent wines, real ale; lots of tables
on attractive terrace and front lawn by fish
pond, some children's amusements, handy
for Moors Valley Country Park *(Phyl and*

Jack Street, Pat and Roger Davies, June and Robin Savage)

UPLODERS [SY5093]

☆ *Crown* DT6 4NU [signed off A35 E of Bridport]: Appealing low-beamed flagstoned pub with friendly landlord, good country food from sandwiches and baguettes to fresh local seafood, well kept Palmers ales, ten wines by the glass, prompt service, cheerful décor, candles, fresh flowers and log fires, daily papers, steps down to pretty evening restaurant, table skittles; may be piped music; picnic-sets in small attractive two-tier garden *(Terry and Linda Moseley, G F Couch, Peter Neate, LYM, John Saul, Roland and Wendy Chalu)*

UPWEY [SY6684]

Riverhouse DT3 5QB [B3159, nr junction A354]: Coal-effect gas fireplace dividing flagstoned bar side from neat carpeted dining side, charming licensees and friendly staff, main emphasis on wide range of quickly served enjoyable food from lunchtime baguettes through familiar and less familiar dishes to good choice of showy puddings, good relaxed gently upmarket atmosphere, Courage Best and Directors, adventurous wine choice, good coffees; well reproduced piped music; disabled access, sizeable garden with play area and water for dogs, cl Sun evening *(Elizabeth and Gordon Foote, BB, Jean Barnett, David Lewis, M G Hart)*

VERWOOD [SU0808]

Monmouth Ash BH31 6DT [Manor Rd (B3082 S)]: Helpful friendly staff, enjoyable food from lunchtime snacks to evening meals, good choice of well kept ales inc Ringwood Best, nice pine tables and settles; children welcome *(June and Robin Savage)*

WAREHAM [SY9287]

Antelope BH20 4JS [West St]: Town local, good beer, some sofas, youngish crowd; may be sports TV *(JT)*

Black Bear BH20 4LT [South St]: Well worn inn bow-windowed 18th-c hotel with old local prints and lots of brass in individual and convivial bar off through corridor, lounge with settees and easy chairs, well kept Ringwood Best, nice choice of keenly priced generous food from good baguettes up, decent coffee, efficient service, back eating room and restaurant; piped classical music; picnic-sets in pleasant flower-filled back yard, bedrooms, open all day *(BB, Steve Derbyshire, Richard and Jean Green)*

Kings Arms BH20 4AD [North St (A351, N end of town)]: Traditional thatched town local thriving under new landlady, well kept real ales, good value pubby food, friendly staff, back serving counter and two bars off flagstoned central corridor; back garden *(JT, LYM)*

WAYTOWN [SY4797]

Hare & Hounds DT6 5LQ [between B3162 and A3066 N of Bridport]: Attractive 18th-c country local up and down steps, well kept Palmers ales tapped from the cask, good

value straightforward food from sandwiches, baguettes and baked potatoes up inc popular Sun lunch, friendly licensees and staff, coal fire, two small cottagey rooms and pretty dining room, no music; lovely Brit Valley views from picnic-sets in sizeable and unusual garden with good play area *(Fred and Lorraine Gill, Roland and Wendy Chalu)*

WEST BAY [SY4690]

Bridport Arms DT6 4EN Large light and airy two-level seaside bar, pleasantly stripped down rooms around original inglenook flagstoned core, well kept Palmers, good friendly service, quite a food operation majoring on fish, baguettes and pubby bar lunches too; piped music; picnic-sets outside, paying public car park, bedrooms in adjoining hotel with own entrance *(Pat and Robert Watt, Rosanna Luke, Matt Curzon, BB, Fred and Lorraine Gill, Roland and Wendy Chalu)*

George DT6 4EY [George St]: Roomy simple bar with mixed furniture inc some corner armchairs, masses of shipping pictures, some model ships and nautical hardware, games room enjoyed by young people, separate back restaurant, wide food choice from sandwiches up, well kept Palmers IPA and Gold, Thatcher's farm cider, cheery helpful staff; children and dogs welcome, picnic-sets outside, bedrooms *(BB, Roland and Wendy Chalu)*

☆ *West Bay* DT6 4EW [Station Rd]: Comfortable seaside pub very popular for its food esp fresh local fish (book well ahead for wknds), wide choice of other dishes from sandwiches to steaks, pleasant atmosphere, well kept Palmers ales, good house wines and whiskies, polite service; piped music; children welcome in restaurant, dogs in bar, disabled access, garden tables, bedrooms *(John and Liz Wheeler, James A Waller, David Parker, Emma Smith, Tony Baldwin, B and F A Hannam, PRT, Dave Braisted, Charles Gysin, Gaynor Gregory, LYM, W W Burke, Pat and Tony Martin, Terry and Linda Moseley, Marje Sladden, David and Julie Glover, George Atkinson, Peter and Andrea Jacobs, Nigel B Thompson, Roland and Wendy Chalu)*

WEST BEXINGTON [SY5386]

☆ *Manor Hotel* DT2 9DF [voff B3157 SE of Bridport; Beach Rd]: Relaxing quietly set hotel with long history and fine sea views, comfortable log-fire lounge and bustling black-beamed cellar bar with another log fire, helpful friendly staff kind to children, good seasonal bar food from sandwiches to some enterprising country cooking, cream teas, Butcombe Gold and Quay Harbour Master, organic cider, quite a few malt whiskies and several wines by the glass, wide choice of hot drinks, good restaurant with smart Victorian-style conservatory; piped music, service can slow at busy times; dogs allowed in bar, charming well kept garden with plenty of picnic-sets, comfortable bedrooms, open all day *(LYM, Peter Nuttall, Gordon Prince, Andy and Yvonne Cunningham, Judith Davies, Roland and Wendy Chalu)*

WEST KNIGHTON [SY7387]

New Inn DT2 8PE [off A352 E of Dorchester]: Good-sized neatly kept pub with good value food, friendly attentive staff, real ales, country wines, small restaurant, skittle alley, good provision for children; big colourful garden, pleasant setting in quiet village with wonderful views *(Pat and Roger Davies)*

WEST LULWORTH [SY8280]

Castle Inn BH20 5RN [B3070 SW of Wareham]: Pretty thatched inn in lovely spot nr Lulworth Cove, good walks and lots of summer visitors; quaintly divided flagstoned bar concentrating on food (not cheap, and may take a while) from sandwiches to local crab, friendly chatty staff, real ales such as Gales HSB and Ringwood Best, decent house wines, farm cider, maze of booth seating divided by ledges for board games and jigsaws, cosy more modern-feeling separate lounge bar and pleasant restaurant, splendid ladies'; piped music, video game; long attractive garden behind on several levels, front terrace too, giant chess boards, boules and barbecues, bedrooms *(Robert Gomme, LYM, George Atkinson)*

WEYMOUTH [SY6778]

Boot DT4 8JH [High West St]: Friendly two-bar partly bare-boards local nr harbour dating from early 1600s, sloping beams, panelling and hooded stone-mullioned windows, well worn comfort, well kept Ringwood ales with a guest such as Exmoor Gold from fine brass handpumps, Cheddar Valley farm cider; disabled access, pavement tables, open all day *(Joan and Michel Hooper-Immins, Dave Webster, Sue Holland, the Didler, Roland and Wendy Chalu)*

George DT4 8BE [Custom House Quay]: Unpretentious quayside pub with good fresh local seafood at tempting prices, Badger Best and Tanglefoot, dining lounge bar with linked back extension *(David Morgan)*

☆ *Nothe Tavern* DT4 8TZ [Barrack Rd]: Roomy and comfortable local with good atmosphere, wide range of enjoyable food inc local fresh fish and good value roast lunches, friendly service, Courage Best, Ringwood Best, Otter and Wadworths 6X, decent wines, good choice of malt whiskies, lots of whisky-water jugs on ceiling, interesting prints and photographs, children welcome in restaurant with distant harbour glimpses; may be quiet piped music; garden tables *(M G Hart, Dave Webster, Sue Holland, Joan and Michel Hooper-Immins, BB)*

☆ *Red Lion* DT4 8TR [Hope Sq]: Bare-boards pub with Courage Best and Dorset beers from smart touristy complex in former brewery opp, quickly served bargain lunches, good crab sandwiches too, interesting RNLI and fishing stuff all over the walls and ceiling (even two boats), coal fire, daily papers, friendly laid-back atmosphere, good staff,

darts; may be piped music; dogs welcome, plenty of picnic-sets on sunny front terrace (more than inside), open all day wkdays, food all day then too *(Pete Walker, PRT, BB, the Didler)*

Sailors Return DT4 8AD [St Nicholas St]: Old-fashioned local with RNLI and naval memorabilia, enjoyable food from baguettes through up-to-date snacks to bargain meals for two, Courage and other ales *(Dave Webster, Sue Holland)*

Spa DT3 5EQ [Dorchester Rd, Radipole; off A354 at Safeway roundabout]: Large open-plan family pub, good choice of generous food (all day Sun) inc pasta, curries, fish and grills, Marstons Bitter and Pedigree, peaceful picture-window back restaurant; good garden with terrace and play area, open all day *(Joan and Michel Hooper-Immins)*

Wellington Arms DT4 8PY [St Alban St]: Handsome green and gold 19th-c tiled façade, newly refurbished and quite ornate inside, with carpets, banquettes, mirrors, panelling and lots of old local photographs, well kept Marstons Bitter, Pedigree and a related or more local guest beer panelled town pub, bargain pubby food from sandwiches up inc a daily roast; children welcome in back dining room, disabled access, open all day *(Joan and Michel Hooper-Immins, Roland and Wendy Chalu)*

WIMBORNE MINSTER [SZ0199]

Kings Head BH21 1JG [The Square]: Popular brasserie/bar in old-established hotel, enjoyable quickly served food, plenty of room for drinkers in roomy bar areas; comfortable bedrooms *(Pat and Roger Davies)*

Oddfellows Arms BH21 1JH [Church St]: Compact pub kept spotless by friendly newish landlord, well kept Badger Best, enjoyable lunchtime snacks *(M R Phillips)*

Olive Branch BH21 1PF [Hanham Rd/East Borough]: Opened-up 18th/19th-c town house, airy contemporary décor and coloured vases alongside handsome panelling and ceilings, welcoming service, up-to-date approach to enjoyable bistro food using local ingredients, Badger ales, nicely served coffee, big conservatory dining area; children welcome, picnic-sets on lawn running down to small river *(Joan and Michel Hooper-Immins)*

White Hart BH21 1JL [Corn Market]: Cheerful old-fashioned low-beamed bar in pedestrian precinct a few steps from minster, well kept Marstons ales, good range of fresh popular food from good baguettes up in eating area, reasonable prices, good welcoming service *(Colin and Janet Roe)*

WINFRITH NEWBURGH [SY8085]

Red Lion DT2 8LE [A352 Wareham—Dorchester]: Comfortable Badger family dining pub with wide choice of generous enjoyable food inc fresh fish, good friendly service, real ales, reasonably priced wines, beamy décor and candlelit tables to give old-fashioned atmosphere; TV room, piped music; tables in big sheltered garden (site for caravans), good bedrooms *(Brian and Bett Cox, M Joyner, John and Tania Wood)*

WINKTON [SZ1696]

Fishermans Haunt BH23 7AS [B3347 N of Christchurch]: Big-windowed bar, neat and well divided, with relaxed friendly atmosphere, good value standard food from sandwiches and filled baked potatoes up, Gales/Fullers HSB, Butser and London Pride, wknd restaurant; they may try to keep your credit card while you eat; disabled facilities, children and dogs welcome, well kept gardens, comfortable bedrooms, open all day *(LYM, Joan and Michel Hooper-Immins)*

WINTERBOURNE ABBAS [SY6190]

Coach & Horses DT2 9LU Big roadside pub with extensive lounge bar and long side dining area, wide choice of pubby food (all day Sun) from well filled rolls to carvery, Palmers and Ringwood Best, sensibly priced wines by the glass, pleasant service, unusual pictures, games end with darts and pool; piped music; children welcome, a few picnic-sets outside with play area and aviary, bedrooms *(BB, Phil and Jane Hodson, Roland and Wendy Chalu)*

WOOL [SY8486]

Ship BH20 6EQ [Dorchester Rd (A352)]: Roomy open-plan thatched and timbered family pub, generous reasonably priced all-day food from baguettes and baked potatoes up, small helpings available, low-ceilinged linked areas and plush back restaurant, friendly prompt service, well kept Badger ales, decent wines, good coffee; quiet piped music; picnic-sets overlooking railway in attractive fenced garden with terrace and play area, handy for Monkey World and Tank Museum, pleasant village *(Gloria Bax, Phil and Jane Hodson)*

Please tell us if any Lucky Dips deserve to be upgraded to a main entry – and why. No stamp needed: The Good Pub Guide, FREEPOST TN1569, Wadhurst, E Sussex TN5 7BR.

Essex

Essex is rather a poor relation to many other counties, as far as pubs are concerned. On the whole, pubs here don't inspire quite so much enthusiasm among our readers as pubs elsewhere – certainly, by comparison with other places we get fewer reports from readers on pubs here, and would very much like to receive more. We have not found any newcomers here whose sheer quality demands addition to the main entries this year. But if you know where to look the county does indeed have some really worthwhile pubs. And a good point is that pub meals in Essex tend to give better value than in many places, with food prices rather below the national average, for equivalent quality. Pubs that currently do inspire plenty of praise from readers include the friendly Three Willows at Birchanger (lots of cricket memorabilia to browse, and the food's good too), the Bell in Castle Hedingham (an interesting old place, with a turkish slant to some of the cooking), the Sun in Dedham (in the heart of Constable country, a stylish dining inn that takes care with its selection of seasonal ingredients as well as its wines), the Henny Swan by the river at Great Henny (another stylish place for a smart meal out), the restauranty Bell in Horndon-on-the-Hill (which has a good range of beer and wine), the friendly Shepherd & Dog at Langham, the Crown at Little Walden, the Viper at Mill Green (excellent range of beers, some from local microbreweries, as well as very reasonably priced bar food), the Mole Trap at Stapleford Tawney (with its entourage of rescued animals as well as some interesting beers), the Hoop at Stock (with one of its six real ales specially brewed for the pub), and the nicely pubby Green Dragon at Youngs End. Enjoyable food is a major part of the appeal of most of these places: the title of Essex Dining Pub of the Year goes to the Rose at Peldon. On the drinks side, Suffolk-based Greene King is the area's dominant brewer, supplying at least half the county's good pubs. Good beers from Adnams, also in Suffolk but much smaller, are widely available. It's not quite so easy to find beers actually brewed in Essex, such as Nethergate, Mighty Oak, Crouch Vale, Saffron and Mersea Island – all worth looking out for. Essex is not vintage territory for walking but does have some very attractive villages for pottering in, particularly in the north of the county, such as Castle Hedingham, Clavering, Dedham – all with worthwhile main entries. Pubs with particularly enticing outlooks or in specially character-laden buildings include the riverside White Harte in Burnham-on-Crouch, the Swan at Chappel (with its view of a spectacular railway viaduct), the Queens Head at Fyfield, the Green Man at Little Braxted, the nicely unchanged Punchbowl at Paglesham and the 15th-c White Horse at Pleshey. The Lucky Dip section at the end of the chapter is also well worth a close look. Pubs we'd single out here are the Axe & Compasses at Arkesden, Alma in Chelmsford (too much of a restaurant now for the main entries) and Queens Head there, Sun at Feering, Pheasant at Gestingthorpe, Swan at Little Totham and Blue Boar in Maldon.

BIRCHANGER

TL5122 MAP 5

Three Willows

Under a mile from M11 junction 8: A120 towards Bishops Stortford, then almost immediately right to Birchanger Village; don't be waylaid earlier by the Birchanger Services signpost! CM23 5QR

Full of cricketing memorabilia, a happy, civilised place serving consistently good food

Earning high praise from readers for its food and friendly, efficient staff, this popular cricket-themed pub is handily placed for Stansted Airport. The spacious, carpeted main bar is full of cricketing prints, photographs, cartoons and other memorabilia. A small public bar has pool and sensibly placed darts, and there's a fruit machine. Friendly attentive staff serve well kept Greene King Abbot and IPA and a guest on handpump, and there are decent house wines. The generously served food draws quite a crowd, so it's best to arrive early if you want to eat. Booking is a good idea. There are picnic-sets out on a terrace (with heaters) and on the lawn behind, which also has a sturdy climbing frame, swings and a basketball hoop (you can hear the motorway and airport out here). Children are not allowed inside.

🍴 **Besides a wide selection of more standard bar food such as lunchtime sandwiches, filled baked potatoes and ploughman's, the main focus is on fish, with about a dozen dishes including cod, tuna steak, crab salad and lemon sole; other dishes feature steak and ale pie, steaks and vegetable curry; puddings include raspberry and hazelnut meringue and jaffa puddle pudding.** *Starters/Snacks: £2.50 to £8.95. Main Courses: £8.95 to £14.95. Puddings: £2.50 to £3.90*

Greene King ~ Tenants Paul and David Tucker ~ Real ale ~ Bar food (12-2, 6-9.30(9 Mon), not Sun evening) ~ (01279) 815913 ~ Open 11.30-3, 6-11; 12-3, 7-10.30 Sun; closed 26 Dec, 1 Jan

Recommended by Charles Gysin, David and Sue Smith, Gordon Tong, B N F and M Parkin, KC, Marion and Bill Cross, A J Andrews, Mrs Margo Finlay, Jörg Kasprowski, Mrs Hazel Rainer, Martin Wilson, Roy Hoing, J Crosby

BURNHAM-ON-CROUCH

TQ9495 MAP 5

White Harte

The Quay; CM0 8AS

Lovely waterside position, and with an aptly nautical twist to the décor

This comfortably old-fashioned hotel is the perfect place to relax on a summer's evening with a drink in hand, contemplating the sound of the water lapping against their private jetty and the sight of yachts in the River Crouch. Inside, the relaxed partly carpeted bars (cushioned seats around oak tables) carry assorted nautical bric-a-brac and hardware, from models of Royal Navy ships, to a ship's wheel and a barometer, to a compass set in the hearth. The other traditionally furnished high-ceilinged rooms have sea pictures on panelled or stripped brick walls. An enormous log fire makes it cosy in winter. Adnams and Crouch Vale Best are on handpump.

🍴 **Bar food includes lunchtime sandwiches, soup, steak and kidney pie, a choice of three fish (cod, plaice and skate) and specials such as baked lamb chops.** *Starters/Snacks: £3.50 to £5.20. Main Courses: £6.80 to £9.80. Puddings: £3.30*

Free house ~ Licensee G John Lewis ~ Real ale ~ Bar food ~ Restaurant ~ (01621) 782106 ~ Children in eating area of bar ~ Dogs welcome ~ Open 11-11; 12-10.30 Sun ~ Bedrooms: £25(£59B)/£50(£79B)

Recommended by John Wooll, Sean A Smith

We checked prices with the pubs as we went to press in summer 2007. They should hold until around spring 2008 – when our experience suggests that you can expect an increase of around 10p in the £.

CASTLE HEDINGHAM   TL7835   MAP 5

Bell

B1058 E of Sible Hedingham, towards Sudbury; CO9 3EJ

Nicely unchanged in its series of interesting rooms and lovely garden, and with well kept real ales and a turkish touch to some dishes

The delightful big walled garden is a special highlight of this pleasant old place, with an acre or so of grass, trees and shrubs, as well as toys for children, and there are more seats on a heated vine-covered terrace. Inside, little has changed over the 40 years the family has been in charge. The beamed and timbered saloon bar is furnished with Jacobean-style seats and windsor chairs around sturdy oak tables, and beyond standing timbers left from a knocked-through wall, steps lead up to an unusual little gallery. Behind the traditionally equipped public bar, a games room has dominoes, cribbage, shove-ha'penny and other board games; piped music. Each of the rooms has a warming log fire. During their mid-July beer festival they bring in around 15 real ales, but the rest of the year you'll find well kept Adnams, Greene King IPA and Mighty Oak Maldon Gold, along with a guest or two such as Oakham JHB, tapped from the cask, and they stock a good selection of malts and several wines by the glass. Dogs are welcome but you must phone first. Close by in the village are the impressive 12th-c castle keep and Colne Valley Railway.

Ⅱ **Tasty, good value bar food includes lunchtime paninis, soup, ploughman's, steak and ale or fish pie, spinach and red pepper lasagne, mostly turkish daily specials such as chicken or lamb casserole, and roasted aubergine, courgettes and peppers in tomato sauce with garlic yoghurt, and puddings like vanilla and poppyseed cheesecake.** *Starters/Snacks: £3.95 to £6.95. Main Courses: £6.95 to £11.95. Puddings: £3.50 to £4.25*

Grays ~ Tenants Penny Doe and Kylie Turkoz-Ferguson ~ Real ale ~ Bar food (12-2(2.30 Sat, Sun), 7-9.30(9 Sun)) ~ (01787) 460350 ~ Children welcome ~ Dogs welcome ~ Live acoustic music Fri evening and trad jazz last Sun in month ~ Open 11.45-3, 6-11; 11.45-12 Fri; 12-11.30(11 Sun) Sat
Recommended by John Saville, Mrs Margo Finlay, Jörg Kasprowski, G Dobson

CHAPPEL   TL8928   MAP 5

Swan

Wakes Colne; pub visible just off A1124 Colchester—Halstead; CO6 2DD

Oak-beamed pub specialising in sea food, with spreading riverside garden

Although this pub prides itself on serving fish dishes, it is somewhere regulars enjoy a drink. As well as just under two dozen malt whiskies and a dozen wines by the glass, they keep Greene King IPA and Abbot and a guest on handpump. The low-beamed rambling bar at this spacious old pub has standing oak timbers dividing off side areas, plenty of dark wood chairs around lots of dark tables for diners, a couple of swan pictures and plates on the white and partly panelled walls, and a few attractive tiles above the very big fireplace. The central bar area keeps a pubbier atmosphere; fruit machine and piped music. The River Colne runs through the garden from where you can see a splendid Victorian viaduct. Flower tubs and french street signs lend the suntrap cobbled courtyard a continental feel, and gas heaters mean that even on cooler evenings, you can sit outside. The Railway Centre (a must for train buffs) is only a few minutes' walk away. More reports please.

Ⅱ **The menu features a good range of fresh fish, served in generous helpings, like prawns wrapped in smoked salmon, fried squid, scallops grilled with bacon, and fried rock eel. Other bar food includes sirloin or fillet steak, sweet and sour chicken with rice; puddings; they also have a children's menu.** *Starters/Snacks: £2.95 to £6.95. Main Courses: £3.95 to £16.95. Puddings: £3.25 to £4.25*

Free house ~ Licensee Terence Martin ~ Real ale ~ Bar food (12-2.30, 6.30-9.30(10 Fri, Sat); 12-8 Sun) ~ Restaurant ~ (01787) 222353 ~ Children welcome away from bar ~ Dogs allowed in bar ~ Open 11-3, 6-11; 11-11 Sat; 12-10.30 Sun
Recommended by Michael Butler, Marion and Bill Cross, Colin and Dot Savill, Mrs P J Pearce, Charles Gysin

CLAVERING TL4832 MAP 5

Cricketers ⑪ ⇔
B1038 Newport—Buntingford, Newport end of village; CB11 4QT

An attractive place to stay, a dining pub that draws a well heeled set

Run by the parents of celebrity chef Jamie Oliver, this pub places much emphasis on food: they use free-range pork, organic salmon and free-range corn-fed chickens here, and fish dishes feature widely among the specials. The roomy L-shaped beamed bar is very traditional, in appearance at least, with standing timbers resting on new brickwork, and pale green plush button-backed banquettes, stools and windsor chairs around shiny wooden tables on a pale green carpet, gleaming copper pans and horsebrasses, dried flowers in the big fireplace (open fire in colder weather), and fresh flowers on the tables; piped music. Adnams Bitter and Broadside are well kept on handpump alongside a guest such as Greene King IPA, and they've decent wines (15 by the glass) and freshly squeezed juices. It can get very busy; piped music. The attractive front terrace has picnic-sets and umbrellas among colourful flowering shrubs, and the bedrooms are comfortable. Signed copies of Jamie Oliver's cookbooks are on sale.

🍴 From a seasonally changing menu, there might be sandwiches, soup, wild rabbit ravioli in artichoke pesto, herb and potato gnocchi with wild mushrooms, roasted loin of pork sliced on to apple and mustard sauce with fried sage leaves, red mullet fillets and baked ricotta cheese tart with marjoram, fennel and courgette; puddings like warm treacle tart or dark chocolate mousse with slices of navel oranges; there's also a short children's menu. *Starters/Snacks: £4.50 to £8.25. Main Courses: £9.50 to £17.25. Puddings: £5.00 to £5.25*

Free house ~ Licensee Trevor Oliver ~ Real ale ~ Bar food (12-2, 7-9.30) ~ Restaurant ~ (01799) 550442 ~ Children welcome ~ Open 10-11; closed 25, 26 Dec ~ Bedrooms: £65B/£110B

Recommended by John Saville, Les and Sandra Brown, Mrs Margo Finlay, Jörg Kasprowski, Paul Humphreys, Roy and Lindsey Fentiman, Dr and Mrs A K Clarke

DEDHAM TM0533 MAP 5

Sun ⑪ ♇ ◗
High Street (B2109); CO7 6DF

Stylish Tudor inn in Constable country, with individuality, thoughtfully prepared food and an impressive wine selection

Part of the reason for coming to this elegant dining pub is just to enjoy the architecture: furnished with high settles and easy chairs, this fine old coaching inn has high carved beams, squared panelling, wall timbers and big log fires in splendid fireplaces. Young staff offer friendly relaxed but efficient service. Adnams Broadside and Crouch Vale Brewers Gold are well kept on handpump alongside a couple of guests from brewers such as Dark Star, Phoenix and West Berkshire, and they've a very good selection of more than 70 wines (20 by the glass) and some interesting soft drinks. A window seat in the bar looks across to the church which is at least glimpsed in several of Constable's paintings; piped music, TV and board games. In the archway annexe is their fruit and vegetable shop, Victoria's Plums, with local, seasonal and organic produce. On the way out to picnic-sets on the quiet and attractive back lawn, notice the unusual covered back staircase, with what used to be a dovecote on top. If you have time, beautiful walks into the heart of Constable country lead out of the village, over water meadows towards Flatford Mill. The panelled bedrooms are nicely done and have abundant character; we would welcome reports from any readers who have stayed here.

🍴 The food places much emphasis on seasonal game, fish, fruit and vegetables. The daily changing menu might include mussel soup, seared pigeon breast salad, confit of free-range leg of duck with lentils, pancetta and rocket; grilled tuscan-style sausages with roast celeriac, squash and fennel, slow-cooked lamb in red wine with winter vegetables and wet polenta, and puddings such as lemon tart or chocolate cake. They also sell picnics. *Starters/Snacks: £5.50 to £8.50. Main Courses: £8.50 to £15.00. Puddings: £4.50 to £6.00*

Free house ~ Licensee Piers Baker ~ Real ale ~ Bar food (12-2.30(3 Sat and Sun), 6.30-9.30) ~ (01206) 323351 ~ Children welcome ~ Dogs allowed in bar ~ Open 12-11; closed 25, 26 Dec ~ Bedrooms: £60B/£130B

Recommended by Marion and Bill Cross, Bernard Phelvin, Robert and Susan Phillips, Trevor and Sheila Sharman, John Saville, Adrian White, Peter Guy, Peter and Margaret Glenister, John Wooll, N R White, Jill Franklin, A D Cross

FYFIELD   TL5706   MAP 5

Queens Head ♀ ◖

Corner of B184 and Queen Street; CM5 0RY

Very friendly 15th-c pub with the accent firmly on food

The main focus of this spotless 15th-c pub is the very good food, served by friendly staff, and at the back a neat little prettily planted garden by a weeping willow has a teak bench and half a dozen picnic-sets under canvas parasols, with the sleepy River Roding flowing past beyond. A pubby balance is maintained by their good range of real ale: Adnams Bitter and Broadside are well kept on handpump alongside four guests from brewers such as Cottage, Dark Star, Hop Back and Nethergate. They've also Weston's Old Rosie farm cider, and good wines by the glass including champagne – most of the pictures have a humorous wine theme, including a series of Ronald Searle cartoons. The low-beamed, compact L-shaped bar has some exposed timbers in the terracotta-coloured walls, fresh flowers and pretty lamps on its nice sturdy elm tables, and comfortable seating, from button-back wall banquettes to attractive and unusual high-backed chairs, some in a snug little side booth. Two facing log fireplaces have lighted church candles instead in summer; the licensees have a cat and two dogs; piped music. Note that children are not allowed inside.

🍴 Besides good lunchtime sandwiches and toasted baguettes, and baked potatoes or ploughman's, dishes from the daily changing menu might include soup, monkfish cooked with thai spice, baked goats cheese with mediterranean vegetables, steak and kidney pie, roast garlic rack of lamb or fillet steak. *Starters/Snacks: £4.75 to £8.50. Main Courses: £10.50 to £16.95. Puddings: £4.50*

Free house ~ Licensees Daniel Lemprecht and Penny Miers ~ Real ale ~ Bar food (12-2.30, 7-9.30; not Sun evenings) ~ (01277) 899231 ~ Open 11-3.30, 6-11; 12-3.30, 7-10.30 Sun

Recommended by Richard Siebert, Lucy Moulder, Dave Lowe, Tina and David Woods-Taylor, H O Dickinson, Reg Fowle, Helen Rickwood, David Twitchett

GREAT HENNY   TL8738   MAP 5

Henny Swan 🍴 ♀

Henny Street, signposted off A131 at traffic lights just SW of Sudbury, at the bottom of Ballingdon Hill; OS Sheet 155 map reference 879384; CO10 7LS

Very restauranty, a stylish place for a meal, with contemporary furnishings and a riverside garden

A good number of customers arrive by boat at this dining pub, which occupies a converted barge-house by the River Stour. The smallish L-shaped contemporary bar has soft leather settees, armchairs and drum stools, with carefully lit big bright modern prints contrasting with its stripped beams and dark walls, a woodburning stove in a big brick fireplace, Adnams and Greene King IPA on handpump, good coffee, and a fine choice of wines by the glass including a champagne and a pudding wine. They do a good jug of Pimms. The restaurant is bigger, bright and airy – thanks to french windows along two walls. It has comfortable rather elegant modern dining chairs and tables well spaced on polished oak boards, more modern artwork, and another woodburning stove; disabled access and facilities. There are stylish metal tables and chairs, some under canvas parasols, out on the good-sized side terrace with heaters, and picnic-sets across the quiet lane on a large informal lawn, beside which the River Stour flows gently past the willow trees and over a low weir. In summer they have monthly jazz outside on Sundays.

🍽 Food includes lunchtime sandwiches, and other dishes could include soup, grilled avocado filled with stilton and crushed walnuts, cumberland sausage and mash, lemon sole and scallop filo parcels on basmati rice with saffron cream sauce, butternut squash filled with spinach and pine nuts and topped with goats cheese, and tasty puddings like sticky toffee pudding or pecan pie. *Starters/Snacks: £3.95 to £8.95. Main Courses: £9.25 to £13.50. Puddings: £4.50*

Punch ~ Lease Harry and Sofia Charalambous ~ Real ale ~ Bar food (12-2.30, 6.30-9.30; 12-4 Sun) ~ Restaurant ~ (01787) 269238 ~ Children welcome ~ Jazz outside summer Suns ~ Open 11-3, 6-11; 11-11(11-3, 6-11 in winter) Sat; 12-10 (12-4 in winter) Sun

Recommended by Adele Summers, Alan Black, Dave and Chris Watts, Rosemary McRobert, John and Enid Morris

HASTINGWOOD
TL4807   MAP 5

Rainbow & Dove £

¼ mile from M11 junction 7; Hastingwood signposted after Ongar signs at exit roundabout; CM17 9JX

Useful for the motorway, a pleasantly traditional low-beamed pub with attentive staff

This welcoming 16th-c cottage makes a very useful stop if you want a break from the nearby M11. Of its three little low-beamed rooms opening off the main bar area, the one on the left is particularly beamy, with the lower part of its wall stripped back to bare brick and decorated with brass pistols and plates. Adnams Broadside, Greene King IPA and a guest such as Shepherd Neame Bishops Finger are on handpump; piped music, winter darts and occasional jazz nights. In the evening it often gets busy with people dining here. Hedged off from the car park, a stretch of grass has picnic-sets (one reader found sitting out here rather unappealing), and you can also eat outside in front of the pub.

🍽 Served by friendly and helpful staff who cope well even at busy times, bar food includes lunchtime sandwiches, fresh crab and prawn cocktail, meat or vegetable lasagne, mushroom tortellini, sausage and mash, and grilled wing of skate, with puddings such as apple pie or spotted dick. *Starters/Snacks: £3.25 to £5.45. Main Courses: £5.60 to £11.95. Puddings: £3.60 to £4.00*

Punch ~ Lease Andrew Keep and Kathryn Chivrall ~ Real ale ~ Bar food (12-2(3 Sun), 7-9) ~ (01279) 415419 ~ Children welcome ~ Dogs allowed in bar ~ Open 11.30-3, 6-11; 12-3.30, 6-11 Sat; 12-4 Sun; closed Sun evening

Recommended by H O Dickinson, Donna and Roger, Mrs Hazel Rainer, Sally Anne and Peter Goodale, John Robertson, B N F and M Parkin, W W Burke, Adele Summers, Alan Black, Malcolm and Barbara Lewis

HORNDON-ON-THE-HILL
TQ6783   MAP 3

Bell 🍷 🍺 🛏

M25 junction 30 into A13, then left into B1007 after 7 miles, village signposted from here; SS17 8LD

Ancient pub with heavily beamed bar, mostly restaurant food and a wide drinks selection

The list of drinks here is really impressive: they keep Bass, Greene King IPA and five guests from brewers such as Archers, Crouch Vale, Shepherd Neame and St Austell (the pub holds occasional beer festivals) and over a hundred well chosen wines from all over the world, including 16 by the glass. The heavily beamed bar maintains a strongly pubby appearance with some antique high-backed settles and benches, rugs on the flagstones or highly polished oak floorboards, and a curious collection of ossified hot cross buns hanging from a beam. Note the accommodation is divided between five suites in the pub and 11 doubles in a separate building 100 yards away.

🍽 You will need to book for food. As well as a short bar menu (from which it's cheaper to eat items in the bar than in the restaurant) with lunchtime sandwiches and dishes such as fishcakes with poached egg and hollandaise, and pot-roast lamb shank with black pudding mash, there are more elaborate items (available in the restaurant or the bar; not cheap) from a daily menu which might feature hot and cold local oysters, fried scallops with roasted spring onions, garlic mash and tempura of red mullet, or field mushroom bread cannelloni with braised salsify and mushroom velouté. *Starters/Snacks: £4.95 to £8.10. Main Courses: £8.50 to £14.95. Puddings: £5.95 to £8.10*

Free house ~ Licensee John Vereker ~ Real ale ~ Bar food (12-1.45(2.30 Sun), 6.30(7 Sun)-9.45; not bank hol Mon) ~ Restaurant ~ (01375) 642463 ~ Children in eating area of bar and restaurant ~ Dogs allowed in bar and bedrooms ~ Open 11-2.30(3 Sat), 5.30(6 Sat)-11; 12-4, 7-10.30 Sun ~ Bedrooms: /£64B

Recommended by David and Ruth Shillitoe, Adrian White, Andy and Jill Kassube, John and Enid Morris

LANGHAM
TM0231   MAP 5

Shepherd & Dog

Moor Road/High Street; village signposted off A12 N of Colchester – coming from S, keep straight on the Langham road for about a mile then turn right at T junction, bearing right at fork; coming from N, turn right at T junction in village, then first left; CO4 5NR

Proper pub well liked for food and service, a nice all-rounder

Cheerfully chatty, this bustling village pub has an entertaining miscellany of items, including collections of continental bottled beers and brass and copper fire extinguishers. Greene King IPA, Abbot and three seasonal beers are on handpump; piped music. In summer, there are very pretty window boxes, and a shaded bar in the enclosed side garden.

🍴 **Bar food includes sandwiches, ploughman's, salads, and up to a couple of dozen main courses such as haddock or cod and chips, tuna steaks on chilled fettuccine with apple salsa, and goats cheese, honey and pine nut parcels on mediterranean salad; they've recently started doing indian curries too.** *Starters/Snacks: £3.25 to £5.95. Main Courses: £7.25 to £16.95. Puddings: £3.50 to £4.25*

Free house ~ Licensee Sav Virdi ~ Real ale ~ Bar food (12-2.15, 6-9.30(10 Fri, Sat); 12-9 Sun) ~ Restaurant ~ (01206) 272711 ~ Children welcome ~ Dogs allowed in bar ~ Open 11-3, 5.30-11; 12-10.30 Sun

Recommended by Gill Brice, Liz and Brian Barnard, N R White, Marion and Bill Cross, Gordon Prince

LITTLE BRAXTED
TL8413   MAP 5

Green Man £

Kelvedon Road; village signposted off B1389 by NE end of A12 Witham bypass – keep on patiently; OS Sheet 168 map reference 848133; CM8 3LB

Prettily traditional brick-built pub with a garden and reasonably priced food

There's a feeling of cosy isolation here, tucked as it is along a country lane. The traditional little lounge has an interesting collection of bric-a-brac, including 200 horsebrasses, some harness, mugs hanging from a beam, and a lovely copper urn; it's especially appealing in winter, when you'll really feel the benefit of the open fire. The tiled public bar has books, darts, cribbage and dominoes; two Greene King beers and a monthly changing guest from a brewer such as Batemans; picnic sets in pleasant sheltered garden. More reports please.

🍴 **Reasonably priced bar food includes lunchtime sandwiches and warm baguettes, soup, ploughman's, baked potatoes, sausage and mash, and specials such as lamb shank in redcurrant gravy or steak and kidney pudding; they always have a couple of vegetarian dishes.** *Starters/Snacks: £3.55 to £4.95. Main Courses: £4.95 to £8.95. Puddings: £3.25*

Greene King ~ Tenant Neil Pharaoh ~ Real ale ~ Bar food (not on first Sun of month) ~ (01621) 891659 ~ No children under 8 ~ Dogs allowed in bar ~ Open 11.30-3, 6-11.30; 12-4, 7-11 Sun

Recommended by John and Bettye Reynolds, David Twitchett

LITTLE WALDEN
TL5441   MAP 5

Crown

B1052 N of Saffron Walden; CB10 1XA

Low-ceilinged 18th-c cottage with a warming log fire and hearty food

You have a choice of around four beers at this bustling pub, normally Adnams, City of Cambridge Boathouse, Greene King Abbot and IPA and possibly a guest from a brewery such as Brandon or Woodfordes are tapped straight from casks racked up behind the bar. The 18th-c country building has three brick fireplaces, and at chillier times a log fire is lit in one of them. Bookroom-red walls, flowery curtains and a mix of bare boards and navy carpeting add to the homely snugness. Seats ranging from high-backed pews to little cushioned armchairs are spaced around a good variety of closely arranged tables, mostly big, some stripped. The small red-tiled room on the right has two little tables; piped music; toilet with disabled access. There is a restaurant, and in summer you can eat outside at tables on the terrace, whilst taking in the tranquil countryside. They may offer accommodation some time in the future.

🍴 Hearty bar food is popular, so you may need to book at weekends: sandwiches (not Sun), soup, lasagne, sirloin steak, and a changing seasonal menu that could include avocado and crayfish tails, curries and half a dozen fish dishes. *Starters/Snacks: £4.25 to £7.95. Main Courses: £7.95 to £13.95. Puddings: £3.95 to £4.50*

Free house ~ Licensee Colin Hayling ~ Real ale ~ Bar food (not Sun or Mon evening) ~ (01799) 522475 ~ Children welcome ~ Dogs welcome ~ Trad jazz Weds evening ~ Open 11.30-3, 6-11; 12-10.30 Sun ~ Bedrooms: £55B/£70B
Recommended by Ken Millar, Mrs Margo Finlay, Jörg Kasprowski, the Didler, Simon Watkins

MILL GREEN
TL6401   MAP 5

Viper 🍺 £

The Common; from Fryerning (which is signposted off north-east bound A12 Ingatestone bypass) follow Writtle signposts; CM4 0PT

Timeless and charmingly unspoilt, with local ales, simple pub food and no modern intrusions

There's an easy-going welcoming atmosphere at this delightful old local, which is quietly tucked away in the woods, and it's the kind of place where you're quite likely to fall into casual conversation with the sociable locals or welcoming licensee. There is an interesting range of five well kept beers on handpump: Viper (produced for the pub by Nethergate), and local microbrewery Mighty Oak Hissed Off and Jake the Snake, and a couple of quickly changing guests from thoughtfully sourced microbrewers such as Maldon and Nethergate; Wilkins' farm cider, straight from the barrel. The timeless cosy lounge rooms have spindleback seats, armed country kitchen chairs, and tapestried wall seats around neat little old tables, and there's a log fire. Booted walkers are directed towards the fairly basic parquet-floored tap room, which is more simply furnished with shiny wooden traditional wall seats and a coal fire, and beyond that another room has country kitchen chairs and sensibly placed darts; darts, dominoes, cribbage; the pub cat is Millie and the white west highland terrier is Jimmy. Tables on the lawn overlook a beautifully tended cottage garden which is a dazzling mass of colour in summer, further enhanced at the front by overflowing hanging baskets and window boxes. Morris men often dance here. Note that the pub doesn't take credit cards.

🍴 Simple but tasty bar snacks might include sandwiches, soup, steak and ale pie, curry and lasagne; Sunday roasts. The tasty bread comes from a local baker a mile or so down the road. They do a popular barbecue at summer weekends and bank holidays, weather allowing. *Starters/Snacks: £3.25 to £4.95. Main Courses: £4.95 to £7.95. Puddings: £3.25 to £3.50*

The 🍺 symbol shows pubs which keep their beer unusually well, have a particularly good range or brew their own.

Free house ~ Licensees Peter White and Donna Torris ~ Real ale ~ Bar food (12-2(3 Sat, Sun);
not evenings) ~ No credit cards ~ (01277) 352010 ~ Dogs allowed in bar ~ Open 12-11; 12-11
Sat; 12-10.30 Sun; 12-3, 6-11 weekdays in winter

*Recommended by Richard Pitcher, Bob Richardson, Philip Denton, Andy and Jill Kassube, Dave Lowe, the Didler,
David Twitchett, Pete Baker, Sally and Mark Bramall, Ian Phillips, Donna and Roger*

PAGLESHAM   TQ9293   MAP 5

Punchbowl

*Church End; from the Paglesham road out of Rochford, Church End is signposted on the left;
SS4 2DP*

A secluded traditional favourite, with a woodburner giving a cosy glow in winter

From the little garden in front of this pretty partly weatherboarded pub (originally a
sailmaker's loft), tables take in a lovely rural view. Inside, the cosy beamed bar has
exposed brick walls, low beams, pews, barrel chairs and other seats, and lots of pictures
and memorabilia. In winter, a woodburner warms its darker corners. A lower room is laid
out for dining. Besides Adnams, they usually have beers from Cottage and Nethergate,
and one other brewery; cribbage, darts and piped music playing mostly 1960s and 70s
classic hits. Be warned that they sometimes close a few minutes early at lunchtime
during the week. More reports please, particularly on the food.

🍴 **Straightforward but fairly priced bar food includes sandwiches, ploughman's, Sunday
roasts, rump steak, lasagne, steak and stout pie, a fresh fish board (not Sunday), and
puddings like bakewell tart or raspberry trifle.** *Starters/Snacks: £3.25 to £4.25. Main Courses:
£5.95 to £10.50. Puddings: £3.25 to £3.75*

Free house ~ Licensees Bernie and Pat Cardy ~ Real ale ~ Bar food ~ Restaurant ~
(01702) 258376 ~ Children welcome in restaurant area ~ Open 11.30(12 Sun)-3, 6.30-11(10.30
Sun, Mon)

Recommended by Sean A Smith, Stuart and Doreen Ritchie

PELDON   TM0015   MAP 5

Rose 🍴 ♟ 🛏

B1025 Colchester—Mersea; CO5 7QJ
ESSEX DINING PUB OF THE YEAR

**Friendly dining pub in an appealing building – good food, thoughtful staff and great wine
choice**

Reassuringly traditional, this appealing pastel-coloured old inn has a delightful interior,
with standing timbers supporting the heavy low ceilings with their dark bowed 17th-c
oak beams, alcoves that conjure up smugglers discussing bygone contraband, little
leaded-light windows, and brass and copper on the mantelpiece of a gothic-arched brick
fireplace. There are creaky close-set tables, and some antique mahogany and padded wall
banquettes. The very spacious airy conservatory dining area, with views over the garden,
has a much more modern feel. On handpump are Adnams Best and Broadside, Greene King
IPA and a weekly guest such as Thwaites Original; as the pub is run by the family-owned
Essex wine merchant Lay & Wheeler, they have a very good wine list, with about 25 by
the glass, listed with helpful descriptions on a blackboard. Staff are friendly and
efficient, though as it does get very busy you may need to book. The spacious garden is
very relaxing, with good teak seats and a nice pond with white ducks. More reports
please.

🍴 **Bar food from a weekly changing menu might include sandwiches, chargrilled local
asparagus, chicken and baby vegetable terrine, smoked salmon with celeriac remoulade,
baked pork chop on mustard mash, fried escalopes of monkfish on a bed of linguini, or
baked spinach, pine nut and ricotta cheese parcels, with puddings like golden apple
streusel tart with almond ice-cream.** *Starters/Snacks: £1.95 to £6.25. Main Courses: £8.25 to
£14.45. Puddings: £1.40 to £4.25*

Lay & Wheeler ~ Licensee Craig Formoy ~ Real ale ~ Restaurant ~ (01206) 735248 ~ Children welcome away from bar ~ Open 11-11; 12-10.30 Sun; 12-7 Sun in winter ~ Bedrooms: £40S/£60S

Recommended by John Wooll, Janice and Phil Waller, Richard C Morgan

PLESHEY   TL6614   MAP 5

White Horse ♀
The Street; CM3 1HA

Packed to the gills with knick-knacks and crafts, an ancient inn nicely placed in a pretty village

Just opposite the church in an attractive village, this 15th-c pub is crammed with a cheerful clutter, and sells crafts, locally made preserves, greetings cards and gifts too. It even has its own little art gallery, with works by local artists. All around are jugs, tankards, antlers, miscellaneous brass, prints, books, bottles and an old ship's bell. Furnishings take in wheelback and other chairs and tables with cloths, and a fireplace has an unusual curtain-like fireguard. Glass cabinets in the big sturdily furnished dining room are filled with lots of miniatures and silverware, and there are flowers on tables. A snug room by the tiny bar counter has brick and beamed walls, a comfortable sofa, some bar stools and a table with magazines to read. Mighty Oak IPA or Maldon Gold is on handpump, and they've several wines by the glass; piped music. Doors from here open on to a terrace and a grass area with trees, shrubs and tables. The pub hosts monthly jazz buffets (not in summer) and a midsummer barbecue.

🍴 **At lunchtime you can choose from bar snacks such as toasted sandwiches, tasty herring roes fried in butter, ploughman's, or steak and kidney pie, or you can eat from the more elaborate lunchtime and evening à la carte menu, which includes dishes such as duck, bass, lamb casserole or almond nut roast with creamy mushroom sauce. Puddings feature home-made fruit crumble or bread and butter pudding; two-course set Sunday lunchtime menu.** *Starters/Snacks: £2.50 to £6.00. Main Courses: £7.50 to £15.00. Puddings: £3.95*

Free house ~ Licensees Mike and Jan Smail ~ Real ale ~ Bar food (12-2.30 Tues, Weds; 12-2.30, 7.9.30 Thu, Fri, Sat; 12-4 Sun) ~ Restaurant ~ (01245) 237281 ~ Dogs allowed in bar ~ Open 11.30-3, 6.30-11.30; closed Tues and Weds evening, and all day Mon

Recommended by David Twitchett, Richard Siebert, Paul and Ursula Randall, Mrs Margo Finlay, Jörg Kasprowski, Roy and Lindsey Fentiman

RICKLING GREEN   TL5129   MAP 5

Cricketers Arms
Just off B1383 N of Stansted Mountfichet; CB11 3YG

Attractive timbered pub with a relaxed atmosphere, handy for Stansted Airport

Run by pleasant, cheerful staff, this Elizabethan dining pub makes a comfortable and convenient place to stay if you're flying from nearby Stansted Airport. The atmosphere is pleasantly mellow, with leather sofas and stripped pine trunks as coffee tables on stone floors, an open fire, a handful of carefully selected prints on cream walls, thoughtful lighting and modern stools at the counter. Greene King IPA, Jennings Cumberland and a guest such as Jennings Sneck Lifter are racked behind the bar and tapped straight from the cask. You can eat in the bar but they encourage you to eat in one of the two smallish restaurants, which are gently contemporary with softly coloured walls and solid uniform wood tables and chairs on well finished (if slightly clattery) newish wooden floors; piped music. Outside on a decked area, trellis screening and clusters of plants in pots partition off private little areas which are set out with wood and metal tables and chairs. More reports please.

🍴 **Food includes a lunchtime menu with items such as steak baguette, an italian stew of sausage and white bean cassoulet, and smoked chicken tagliatelle, as well as a more expensive menu (available lunchtime and evening) which could include soup, crayfish**

risotto, fried fillet of bass, rib-eye steak or a vegetable assiette with stuffed artichoke, courgette and beef tomato. *Starters/Snacks: £5.95 to £9.75. Main Courses: £9.75 to £16.50. Puddings: £5.75*

Punch ~ Lease Barry Hilton ~ Real ale ~ Bar food (12-2.30(3 Sun), 6-9.30(10.30 Fri, Sat; 9 Sun)) ~ Restaurant ~ (01799) 543210 ~ Children welcome away from the bar ~ Open 12-11 ~ Bedrooms: £65B/£95B

Recommended by Dr and Mrs D A Blackadder, Les and Sandra Brown, Mrs Roxanne Chamberlain, Grahame Brooks, Michael and Maggie Betton

STAPLEFORD TAWNEY   TL5001   MAP 5

Mole Trap 🍺

Tawney Common, which is a couple of miles away from Stapleford Tawney and is signposted off A113 just N of M25 overpass – keep on; OS Sheet 167 map reference 500013; CM16 7PU

Tucked away but humming with customers; interesting selection of guest beers

---

Run with considerable individuality, this little isolated country pub is especially cosy in winter, when you can fully appreciate the three blazing coal fires. As well as Fullers London Pride on handpump, they have three constantly changing guests from smaller brewers such as Buntingford, Crouch Vale and Green Jack. It fills up quickly at lunchtimes, so it's worth getting here early if you want to eat. The smallish carpeted bar (mind your head as you go in) has black dado, beams and joists, brocaded wall seats, library chairs and bentwood elbow chairs around plain pub tables, and steps down through a partly knocked-out timber stud wall to a similar area. There are a few small pictures, 3-D decorative plates, some dried-flower arrangements and (on the sloping ceiling formed by a staircase beyond) some regulars' snapshots, with a few dozen beermats stuck up around the serving bar; quiet piped radio. Outside are some plastic tables and chairs and a picnic-set, and a happy tribe of resident animals, many rescued, including friendly cats, rabbits, a couple of dogs, hens, geese, a sheep, goats and horses. Food service on Sunday may occasionally end earlier than times stated. Do make sure children behave well here if you bring them, and note that the pub doesn't take cheques or credit cards.

🍴 **Besides sandwiches and popular Sunday roasts, bar food includes ploughman's, soup, lasagne, steak and kidney pie, ham, egg and chips and a vegetarian option like quiche, with puddings like cherry and apple pie.** *Starters/Snacks: £3.50 to £3.95. Main Courses: £6.95 to £9.95. Puddings: £3.95*

Free house ~ Licensees Mr and Mrs Kirtley ~ Real ale ~ Bar food (till 3 Sun, not Sun and Mon evening) ~ No credit cards ~ (01992) 522394 ~ Children welcome ~ Open 11.30-2.30, 6-11; 12-4, 6.30-10.30 Sun

Recommended by David Twitchett, the Didler, Mrs Ann Gray, N R White, H O Dickinson, Evelyn and Derek Walter

STOCK   TQ6999   MAP 5

Hoop 🍺

B1007; from A12 Chelmsford bypass take Galleywood, Billericay turn-off; CM4 9BD

Weatherboarded pub with large garden, keeping an interesting range of beers

---

'No piped music, just the relaxing murmur of pubby conversation,' reported one reader of this well liked weatherboarded pub. Adnams and Hoops, Stock and Barrel (brewed for the pub by Brentwood) are on handpump with four guests from brewers such as Archers, Crouch Vale and Green Tye; several wines by the glass. Standing timbers and beams in the open plan bustling bar indicate the building's age and original layout as a row of three weavers' cottages. Stripped floors, a big brick fireplace, brocaded settles and stools and dark wood tables keep it feeling pubby; there is also an upstairs restaurant in the timbered eaves. Prettily bordered with flowers, the large sheltered back garden has picnic-sets and a covered seating area. Parking can be difficult. Dogs are allowed in the right-hand bar only.

▥ Tasty bar food includes sandwiches, soup, chargrilled sirloin steak, toad in the hole and various pies, while a more expensive à la carte menu features dishes like goats cheese and red onion marmalade tart, bass with braised fennel and basil mash, slow-braised lamb shank, and puddings such as hot chocolate fondant. *Starters/Snacks: £3.95 to £6.95. Main Courses: £6.95 to £12.00. Puddings: £3.95 to £4.95*

Free house ~ Licensee Michelle Corrigan ~ Real ale ~ Bar food (12-2.30, 6-9; 12-5 Sun; not Sun or Mon evenings) ~ Restaurant ~ (01277) 841137 ~ Children welcome in back bar and restaurant ~ Dogs allowed in bar ~ Open 11-11(12 Sat); 12-10.30 Sun

Recommended by Evelyn and Derek Walter, John Saville, Ian Phillips, Paul A Moore, MJVK, Simon and Mandy King, R T and J C Moggridge, Clare Rosier

STOW MARIES
TQ8399 MAP 5

Prince of Wales ◪

B1012 between S Woodham Ferrers and Cold Norton Posters; CM3 6SA

Unfussy local, recently refitted, with a good range of drinks

The bar has undergone a fresh refitting and as we went to press bed and breakfast accommodation was due to open, with two rooms in the side barn and four ensuite rooms adjoining the conservatory (which will double as a breakfast room for guests and a dining area for the pub). Elsewhere the low-ceilinged rooms have kept much of their old feel. Few have space for more than one or two tables or wall benches on their tiled or bare-boards floors, though the room in the middle squeezes in quite a jumble of chairs and stools. On handpump, as well as two real ales from Adnams, they have four guests from brewers such as Dark Star, Farmers, Hopback and Maldon, and you'll also find bottled and draught belgian beers as well as several bottled fruit beers. There are seats and tables in the back garden, and between the picket fence and the pub's white weatherboarded frontage is a terrace, with herbs in Victorian chimneypots, sheltered by a huge umbrella. There are live bands on most bank holidays and some Sundays. More reports please.

▥ Besides sandwiches or paninis, the bar menu includes fish and chips, whitebait and burgers, with a choice of eight specials like steaks, fish pies, steak and kidney pie, and roasted vegetable bake. On Thursday evenings in winter they fire up the old bread oven to make pizzas in the room that used to be the village bakery, and on some summer Sundays, they barbecue steaks and all sorts of fish such as mahi-mahi and black barracuda. *Starters/Snacks: £3.45 to £4.95. Main Courses: £6.95 to £10.70. Puddings: £3.50*

Free house ~ Licensee Rob Walster ~ Real ale ~ Bar food (12-2.30, 6.30-9.30, 12-9.30 Sun) ~ (01621) 828971 ~ Children in family room ~ Live music Sun afternoons and bank hols ~ Open 11-11(12 Fri, Sat); 12-11 Sun

Recommended by David Twitchett, Adrian White, Reg Fowle, Helen Rickwood

YOUNGS END
TL7319 MAP 5

Green Dragon

Former A131 Braintree—Chelmsford (off new bypass), just N of Essex Showground; CM77 8QN

Nicely pubby character, and makes considerable efforts with its food

This busy dining pub has received consistent praise from readers for its interesting food, but it has still kept the feel of a local. Greene King Abbot and IPA and a guest such as Hardy and Hansons Olde Trip are on handpump; unobtrusive piped jazz. Two bars have cheery yellow walls and ordinary pub furnishings, and there's an extra low-ceilinged snug just beside the serving counter. A lawn at the back has lots of picnic-sets under cocktail parasols, a terrace with outdoor heaters, and a budgerigar aviary.

Waterside pubs are listed at the back of the book.

〖¶〗 Lunchtime dishes include sandwiches and baguettes, soup, cottage pie and ploughman's. Specials might feature mutton and apricot casserole, seared tuna steak and confit of duck; also curry of the day, beefsteak, ale and mushroom pie, seasonal items like game pie, and a seafood menu offering perhaps loch duart salmon supreme with asparagus spears and hollandaise sauce. *Starters/Snacks: £3.50 to £7.00. Main Courses: £6.00 to £21.00. Puddings: £4.00 to £4.50*

Greene King ~ Lease Bob and Mandy Greybrook ~ Real ale ~ Bar food (12-2.30, 5-9.30, 12-10 Sat, 12-9 Sun) ~ Restaurant ~ (01245) 361030 ~ Children welcome till 8pm ~ Open 12-3, 5.30-11(12-11 Sat, Sun)

Recommended by Adrian White, Ian Phillips, Evelyn and Derek Walter, Mrs Margo Finlay, Jörg Kasprowski, Peter and Jean Hoare

LUCKY DIP

Besides the fully inspected pubs, you might like to try these Lucky Dips recommended to us and described by readers (if you do, please send us reports: www.goodguides.co.uk).

ARDLEIGH [TM0429]
☆ *Wooden Fender* CO7 7PA [A137 towards Colchester]: Pleasantly extended and furnished old pub with friendly attentive service, beams and log fires, Greene King and a guest ale, decent wines; children welcome in large dining area, good-sized garden with water feature and play area *(N R White, LYM, David Eberlin)*

ARKESDEN [TL4834]
☆ *Axe & Compasses* CB11 4EX [off B1038]: Thatched village pub with easy chairs, upholstered oak and elm seats, open fire and china trinkets in cosy lounge bar, built-in settles in smaller public bar with darts and board games, good choice of wines by the glass, Greene King IPA and Old Speckled Hen and a guest beer, usual bar food, more elaborate menu in restaurant allowing children; pretty hanging baskets, seats on side terrace *(Charles Gysin, LYM, Ross and Christine Loveday, Simon Watkins, Gordon Neighbour)*

BELCHAMP ST PAUL [TL7942]
Half Moon CO10 7DP [Cole Green]: Thatched pub with generous good value home-made food, quick friendly service, snug beamed lounge, cheerful locals' bar, restaurant, real ales; children welcome, tables out in front and in back garden *(LYM, Lynn Ward)*

BILLERICAY [TQ6893]
Duke of York CM11 2PR [Southend Rd, South Green]: Pleasant beamed local with good choice of food (not wknd evenings) from sandwiches to great homely puddings in old front bar and modern restaurant, well kept Greene King IPA and Abbot and Shepherd Neame Spitfire, long-serving licensees, good service, real fire, longcase clock, local photographs, upholstered settles and wheelback chairs; evenings can get loud and lively; a few roadside picnic-sets *(Stuart Paulley)*

BLACKMORE [TL6001]
Leather Bottle CM4 0RL [The Green]: Comfortable furniture on millstone floors, nice décor, helpful efficient staff, well kept ales such as Adnams Bitter and Broadside,

Cottage Normans Conquest and Greene King IPA, fresh tasty food inc lunch deals, restaurant and dining conservatory; dogs warmly welcomed, picnic-sets in sheltered garden behind *(Paul and Ursula Randall)*

BOREHAM [TL7509]
Six Bells CM3 3JE [Main Rd (B1137)]: Well run dining pub with good value food cooked to order in comfortably opened-up bar and neat front restaurant, cheerful polite staff, well kept Greene King IPA, Abbot and a related guest beer; play area in garden *(Paul and Ursula Randall)*

BULMER TYE [TL8438]
Fox CO10 7EB [A131 S of Sudbury]: Well refurbished, with welcoming bustling staff, good range of food inc interesting dishes, Greene King IPA from small bar on left, pleasant conservatory; terrace tables *(MDN)*

BUMBLES GREEN [TL4105]
King Harolds Head EN9 2RY: Friendly, welcoming and quite spacious traditional pub, with comfortable beamed and carpeted bar and dining areas, locally popular for enjoyable reasonably priced food (all day Sun); picnic-sets outside, pretty flower-baskets and window boxes *(James Isaacs)*

BURNHAM-ON-CROUCH [TQ9596]
Ship CM0 8AA [High St]: Welcoming Adnams pub with efficient friendly service, enjoyable generous food inc Sun lunch, attractive nautical-theme interior; can be noisy; comfortable bedrooms *(Sean A Smith, Richard Burton)*

CHELMSFORD [TL7107]
☆ *Alma* CM1 7RG [Arbour Lane, off B1137]: Restaurant rather than pub now, with airy contemporary décor, food from lunchtime ciabattas and bar dishes through bargain off-season lunches to sophisticated meals, polite service, open fires, leather sofas and flagstones in bar with real ales such as Adnams Broadside and Greene King IPA as well as good choice of wines by the glass, smart dining area; piped music; pleasant tables outside, children welcome in restaurant, open all day *(Ian Phillips, LYM, Mrs Margo Finlay, Jörg Kasprowski, Paul and*

Ursula Randall, Sheila Robinson-Baker, Miss E Thorne)

☆ **Queens Head** CM2 0AS [Lower Anchor St]: Lively well run Victorian backstreet local with half a dozen or more changing ales inc Caledonian Deuchars IPA, three from Crouch Vale and Mauldons Micawbers Mild, summer farm cider, good value wines, friendly staff, winter log fires, bargain cheerful lunchtime food (not Sun) from separate counter; children welcome, terrace tables, open all day (Joe Green, the Didler, the Gray family, Dave Lowe)

Railway Tavern CM1 1LW [Duke St]: Small railway-theme real ale pub with bargain simple lunchtime food (Joe Green)

☆ **Riverside** CM2 6LJ [Victoria Rd]: Open-plan weatherboarded watermill conversion, low heavy beams, dark corners and some mill gearing, good choice of generous food, not cheap but good value and interesting, from open sandwiches up, well kept Wells & Youngs ales, impressive friendly service, separate restaurant; tables and picnic-sets on attractive waterside terrace and decking, well thought out bedrooms (Joe Green)

COGGESHALL [TL8224]

☆ **Compasses** CM77 8BG [Pattiswick, signed off A120 W]: Attractively reworked country dining pub with wide choice of good food, interesting variations on familiar favourites, keen attentive staff, neatly comfortable spacious beamed bars and barn restaurant; children warmly welcome, plenty of lawn and orchard tables, rolling farmland beyond (LYM, Francis Nicholls)

COOPERSALE STREET [TL4701]

☆ **Theydon Oak** CM16 7QJ [off B172 E of Theydon Bois; or follow Hobbs Cross Open Farm brown sign off B1393 at N end of Epping]: Attractive weatherboarded dining pub very popular esp with older lunchers for ample good value quickly served straightforward food from sandwiches up inc plenty of bargain specials, Sun roasts and puddings cabinet, well kept Black Sheep and Greene King IPA, friendly staff, long convivial beamed bar with masses of brass, copper and old brewery mirrors, decorative antique tills, interesting old maps, log fire, no piped music; no credit cards, no dogs; tables on side terrace and in garden with small stream (may be ducks), lots of hanging baskets, wknd barbecues and separate play area (N R White, Quentin and Carol Williamson, BB)

DANBURY [TL7705]

Griffin CM3 4DH [A414, top of Danbury Hill]: Former Chef & Brewer, spacious and well divided, wide range of food, well kept Adnams Broadside and guest beers, 16th-c beams and some older carved woodwork, good log fires, pleasant service; piped music; children welcome, open all day (Tina and David Woods-Taylor)

DEBDEN [TL5533]

White Hart CB11 3LE [High St]: Country pub with three real ales such as local Saffron

Muntjac, lunchtime sandwiches and basic hot dishes, more elaborate evening menu; picnic-sets out in front (MLR)

DUTON HILL [TL6026]

☆ **Three Horseshoes** CM6 2DX [off B184 Dunmow—Thaxted, 3 miles N of Dunmow]: Traditional village local with friendly proper landlord, Everards and two guest beers, masses of bottled beers, late spring bank hol beer festival, central fire, aged armchairs by fireplace in homely left-hand parlour, interesting theatrical and 1940s memorabilia, breweriana and enamel signs; darts and pool in small public bar, pleasant views and pond in garden, cl lunchtimes Mon-Weds (BB, Dave Lowe, Pete Baker, the Didler)

EAST MERSEA [TM0514]

Dog & Pheasant CO5 8TP [East Rd]: Country pub handy for Cudmore Grove country park, three real ales inc Mersea Island Yo Boy, usual food from sandwiches up; good coastal walks, open all day (MLR)

ELMDON [TL4639]

Elmdon Dial CB11 4NH [Heydon Lane]: Reopened after handsome refurbishment and kept gleaming, charming staff, good food from sandwiches, baguettes and unpretentious pubby things up, well kept ales such as Adnams and Fullers London Pride, bar, snug and restaurant; cl Mon (Mr and Mrs T B Staples, M R D Foot)

EPPING [TL4602]

George & Dragon CM16 4AQ [High St (nr police stn)]: Comfortable Ember Inn in 1600s building, good choice of pubby food, changing real ales such as Black Sheep, Caledonian, Timothy Taylors, Wells & Youngs and Wyre Piddle, friendly staff; piped music; terrace tables, open all day (Robert Goodall)

FEERING [TL8720]

☆ **Sun** CO5 9NH [Feering Hill, B1024]: Interesting old pub with 16th-c beams (watch out for the very low one over the inner entrance door), plenty of bric-a-brac, woodburners in huge inglenook fireplaces, nice carved bar counter with Wolf and other good real ales, pleasant helpful staff, wide food choice from sandwiches up, daily papers, board games; well behaved children allowed, tables out on partly covered paved terrace and in attractive garden behind, some wknd barbecues (the Didler, LYM, Comus and Sarah Elliott, Matthew Shackle, John Allen, the Gray family)

FINGRINGHOE [TM0220]

☆ **Whalebone** CO5 7BG [off A134 just S of Colchester centre, or B1025]: Attractively airy rooms with cream-painted tables on oak floors, Wells & Youngs Bombardier, Woodfordes Wherry and a guest beer, changing food choice with some interesting cooking; TV, piped music, no children; charming back garden with peaceful valley view from picnic-sets, tables and chairs on front terrace, open all day wknds (Dr and Mrs Michael Smith, R T and J C Moggridge, Bob Richardson, Tina and David Woods-Taylor, LYM)

GESTINGTHORPE [TL8138]
☆ *Pheasant* CO9 3AU [off B1058]: Attractively refurbished under new owners, fresh and enjoyable proper bar food, friendly service, real ales such as Greene King and Mauldons, farm cider, good value wines by the glass, neat and simple décor, log fires; children welcome, picnic-sets in garden with terrace and quiet country views *(LYM, Mrs Hilarie Taylor, David Twitchett)*

GOSFIELD [TL7829]
Green Man CO9 1TP [3 miles N of Braintree]: New licensees doing occasional theme nights such as caribbean or greek, otherwise more straightforward bar food, Greene King IPA and Abbot, two little beamed bars, one with an inglenook fireplace, pool, restaurant; juke box, games machine; children welcome, garden tables, open all day Sat *(Tina and David Woods-Taylor, LYM)*

GREAT CHESTERFORD [TL5142]
Crown & Thistle CB10 1PL [just off M11 junction 9 (A11 exit roundabout); High St]: Busy recently upgraded pub/restaurant in affluent village, enjoyable if not cheap food, friendly staff, good atmosphere, range of wines by the glass, smartly served tea and coffee, well kept Greene King ales, log fire, fresh flowers, simple heavy furnishings on bare boards; Thurs quiz night; new simple bedrooms *(Mrs Margo Finlay, Jörg Kasprowski, Roy Bromell)*

GREAT EASTON [TL6126]
Green Man CM6 2DN [Mill End Green; pub signed 2 miles N of Dunmow, off B184 towards Lindsell]: Recently reopened after thorough refurbishment as dining pub, comfortable armchairs and crisp up-to-date décor in linked beamed rooms and conservatory, bar food (not Fri/Sat evening or Sun lunch) from sandwiches up, two real ales such as Fullers London Pride, restaurant meals; good-sized attractive garden with terrace, pleasant rural setting *(Paul and Ursula Randall)*

GREAT SALING [TL7025]
☆ *White Hart* CM7 5DR [village signed from A120; The Street]: Friendly and distinctive Tudor pub with ancient timbering and flooring tiles, lots of plates, brass and copperware, scarecrows in upper gallery, good reasonably priced food from speciality giant filled baps to steaks and fresh fish, Greene King IPA and Abbot, decent wines, good service; no credit cards; well behaved children welcome, tables outside *(Roy and Lindsey Fentiman, LYM)*

GREAT TOTHAM [TL8613]
Compasses CM9 8BZ [Colchester Rd]: Appealing village pub with reasonably priced food from very long-serving cook, welcoming service *(Roy Hoing)*

GREAT WALTHAM [TL7013]
Rose & Crown CM3 1AG [about ¾ mile from Ash Tree Corner, old A130/A131]: Friendly and comfortable little 16th-c local with particularly well kept Fullers London Pride and changing ales from small breweries,

cheerful and popular ex-farmer landlord, good lunchtime bar food; ghost said to use gents' *(Paul and Ursula Randall)*

GREAT YELDHAM [TL7637]
☆ *White Hart* CO9 4HJ [Poole St (A1017 Halstead—Haverhill)]: Striking old black and white timbered dining room, stone and wood floors, some dark oak panelling, lovely old fireplace, emphasis on the food from light lunches up, Adnams and one or two guest beers; children welcome, attractive garden with well tended lawns and pretty seating, 11 bedrooms, open all day *(Marion and Bill Cross, Michael Dandy, LYM, Adele Summers, Alan Black)*

HATFIELD HEATH [TL5115]
Thatchers CM22 7DU [Stortford Rd (A1005)]: Olde-worlde beamed and thatched pub with lovely log fire, copper kettles, jugs, brasses, plates and pictures in L-shaped bar, Greene King IPA and Wells & Youngs Bombardier from long counter, decent house wines, wide choice of good value fresh pubby food from sandwiches up, back dining area; no children in bar, may be piped music; at end of large green, tables out in front under cocktail parasols *(Mrs Margo Finlay, Jörg Kasprowski, Eddie Edwards)*

HERONGATE [TQ6391]
Boars Head CM13 3PS [Billericay Rd, just off A128]: Picturesque low-beamed all-day dining pub with pleasant nooks and crannies, up to five changing real ales, reasonably priced wines, friendly staff; relaxing garden overlooking big attractive reed-fringed pond with ducks, swans and moorhens *(Roy and Lindsey Fentiman, DFL)*

HEYBRIDGE BASIN [TL8706]
Old Ship CM9 4RX [Lockhill]: Decent food inc breakfast all morning, friendly service, pale wood chairs and tables, upstairs restaurant with estuary views; dogs and children welcome, seats outside, some overlooking water by canal lock with lovely views of the saltings and across to Northey Island, open all day 8am-midnight *(John Wooll)*

HOWE STREET [TL6914]
Green Man CM3 1BG [just off A130 N of Chelmsford]: Spacious heavily beamed and timbered building dating from 14th c, reworked under new licensees as more of a bistro pub, good value wholesome food inc traditional dishes, Greene King ales, log fire; garden being brought into more use *(Paul and Ursula Randall, Roy and Lindsey Fentiman)*

HOWLETT END [TL5834]
White Hart CB10 2UZ [Thaxted Rd (B184 SE of Saffron Walden)]: Recently reopened after contemporary redecoration, good choice of home-made food and of wines ('taste then decide'), helpful service by landlady *(Mrs Carol Oxley)*

INWORTH [TL8817]
Prince of Wales CO5 9SP [Kelvedon Rd]: Good if not cheap food, efficient friendly service, real ales such as Greene King Abbot, decent house wines, recent refurbishment

with plain pine tables and chairs and leather sofas; tables out on attractive front lawn (Adele Summers, Alan Black)

LEIGH-ON-SEA [TQ8385]

☆ **Crooked Billet** SS9 2EP [High St]: Homely old pub with waterfront views from big bay windows, Adnams, Bass and a guest beer, good spring and autumn beer festivals, friendly attentive staff, log fires, beams and bare boards, local fishing pictures and bric-a-brac; piped music, live music nights, no under-21s; open all day, side garden and terrace, seawall seating over road shared with Osbornes good shellfish stall; pay-and-display parking (free Sat/Sun) by fly-over (N R White, LYM, John and Enid Morris, Andy and Jill Kassube)

LITTLE BADDOW [TL7807]

Generals Arms CM3 4SX [The Ridge; minor rd Hatfield Peverel—Danbury]: Friendly newish management in pleasantly furnished pub, roomy and airy, with well kept Shepherd Neame Spitfire, good range of pubby food from sandwiches up, reasonably priced wines; tables on terrace and back lawn with play area, good walks nearby (LYM, John Saville)

LITTLE DUNMOW [TL6521]

Flitch of Bacon CM6 3HT [off A120 E of Dunmow; The Street]: Hard-working friendly licensees in informal country local, Courage Best, Greene King IPA and a local guest beer such as Mauldons, short but varied choice of enjoyable bar food from baguettes up (not Sun evening), simple and attractive small timbered bar kept spotless, flowery-cushioned pews and ochre walls, children welcome in back eating area with french windows to terrace; piped music; a few picnic-sets outside, peaceful views, bedrooms (Joe Green, LYM)

LITTLE TOTHAM [TL8811]

☆ **Swan** CM9 8LB [School Rd]: Country local worth finding for its good changing range of real ales tapped from the cask such as Adnams, Crouch Vale, Mauldons and Mighty Oak, farm ciders and country wines, welcoming service, enjoyable straightforward food (not Sun evening), low 17th-c beams, coal fire, tiled games bar with darts and bar billiards, dining extension, June beer festival; children and dogs welcome, small terrace and picnic-sets under cocktail parasols on sizeable front lawn, open all day (Adrian White, Mrs Roxanne Chamberlain, the Didler)

LITTLEY GREEN [TL6917]

Compasses CM3 1BU [off A130 and B1417 SE of Felsted]: Unpretentiously quaint and old-fashioned country pub with big huffers, ploughman's and baked potatoes, Greene King IPA and Ruddles Best tapped from cellar casks, interesting irish whiskeys, darts and old-fashioned board games, no machines, occasional folk music, friendly cat called Mocha; tables in big back garden, benches out in front, good walks (the Didler, Reg Fowle, Helen Rickwood)

MALDON [TL8407]

☆ **Blue Boar** CM9 4QE [Silver St; car park round behind]: Quirky cross between coaching inn and antiques or auction showroom, most showy in the main building's lounge and dining room, interesting antique furnishings and pictures also in the separate smallish dark-timbered bar and its spectacular raftered upper room, their own Farmers ales brewed at the back (to take away too), Crouch Vale guest beers, enjoyable fresh food, friendly helpful staff; open all day (Mrs Roxanne Chamberlain, LYM)

Jolly Sailor CM9 5HP [Church St/The Hythe]: Charming timber-framed quayside pub, three Greene King ales and great choice of wines by the glass, friendly helpful landlady and staff, food from rolls, sandwiches and baked potatoes to plenty of fish; piped music; tables out overlooking Thames barges, play area and parakeet aviary (John Wooll)

Queens Head CM9 5HN [The Hythe]: Greene King IPA and Abbot and Mighty Oak Burntwood and Maldon Gold, reasonably priced standard food, back lounge overlooking Thames barges on River Blackwater and leading out to good-sized quayside terrace (Tony and Wendy Hobden)

MARGARETTING [TL6601]

Red Lion CM4 0EQ [B1002 towards Mountnessing]: Busy beamed and timbered dining pub popular with families and older people, hard-working friendly landlady, Greene King ales; eclectic piped music; good wheelchair access, pretty in summer, with picnic-sets and play area (Adrian White, Paul and Ursula Randall)

MARGARETTING TYE [TL6801]

☆ **White Hart** CM4 9JX [The Tye]: Good value unpretentious food from sandwiches up, well kept Adnams Bitter and Broadside, Mighty Oak IPA and local guest beers, occasional beer festivals, cheerful friendly service, pleasant L-shaped bar, bright and comfortable conservatory-roofed dining room – nice for families; attractive garden with robust play area, well fenced duck pond and birds and animals to look at (Paul and Ursula Randall, John and Enid Morris)

MATCHING GREEN [TL5310]

Chequers CM17 0PZ: Victorian pub comprehensively modernised as contemporary upmarket pub/restaurant, not cheap but enjoyable traditional and mediterranean-style food from ciabattas up, pleasant staff, well kept Greene King IPA, candles on pine tables, lounge with sofas and open fire, american-style central bar; garden, quiet spot with picnic-sets overlooking pretty cricket green, cl Mon (Tina and David Woods-Taylor)

MATCHING TYE [TL5111]

Fox CM17 0QS [The Green]: Attractive low-beamed 17th-c pub opp peaceful village green, good choice of pub food inc OAP specials, Greene King IPA and Shepherd Neame Spitfire, pleasant staff, comfortable dark wood furniture, brasses, model vehicles,

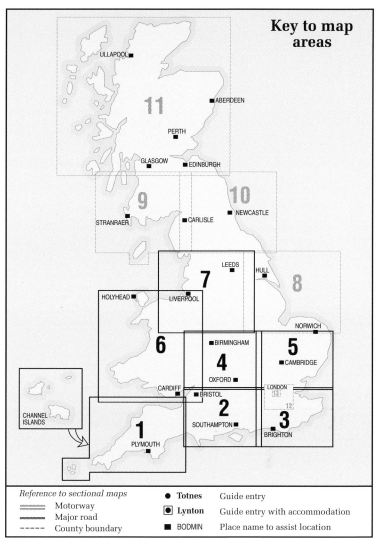

Key to map areas

ULLAPOOL

ABERDEEN

11

PERTH

GLASGOW   EDINBURGH

9   10

STRANRAER   CARLISLE   NEWCASTLE

LEEDS   HULL

7

HOLYHEAD   LIVERPOOL   8

BIRMINGHAM   5

6   4   CAMBRIDGE

OXFORD

CARDIFF   BRISTOL   LONDON   13   12

2   3

CHANNEL
ISLANDS   SOUTHAMPTON   BRIGHTON

1

PLYMOUTH

Reference to sectional maps

▦ Motorway	● **Totnes** Guide entry
━ Major road	◉ **Lynton** Guide entry with accommodation
- - - County boundary	■ BODMIN Place name to assist location

MAPS IN THIS SECTION

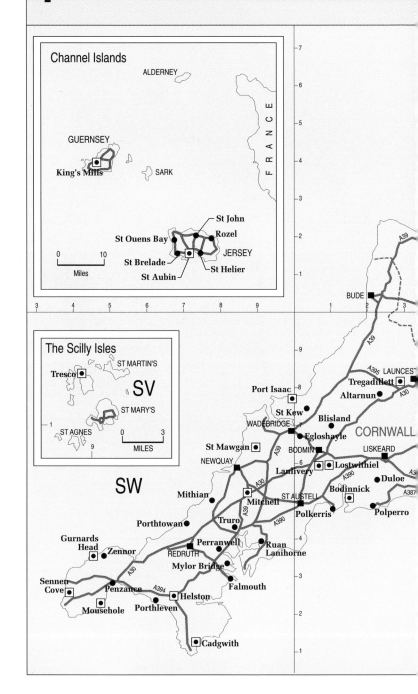

1

Channel Islands

ALDERNEY

GUERNSEY

King's Mills

SARK

FRANCE

St John
Rozel
St Ouens Bay
St Brelade
St Helier
St Aubin

JERSEY

0 — 10
Miles

BUDE

The Scilly Isles

ST MARTIN'S

Tresco

SV

ST MARY'S

ST AGNES

0 — 3
MILES

SW

LAUNCES
Tregadillett
Altarnun

A395
A30

Port Isaac

St Kew

Blisland

WADEBRIDGE

Egloshayle

CORNWALL

St Mawgan

BODMIN

LISKEARD

NEWQUAY

Lanivery

Lostwithiel

Duloe

A390

A3

Mithian

Mitchell

ST AUSTELL

Bodinnick

A387

Porthtowan

Truro

A30

A390

Polkerris

Polperro

Perranwell

Ruan
Lanihorne

Gurnards
Head

Zennor

REDRUTH

Mylor Bridge

Sennen
Cove

Penzance

A394

Helston

Falmouth

Mousehole

Porthleven

Cadgwith

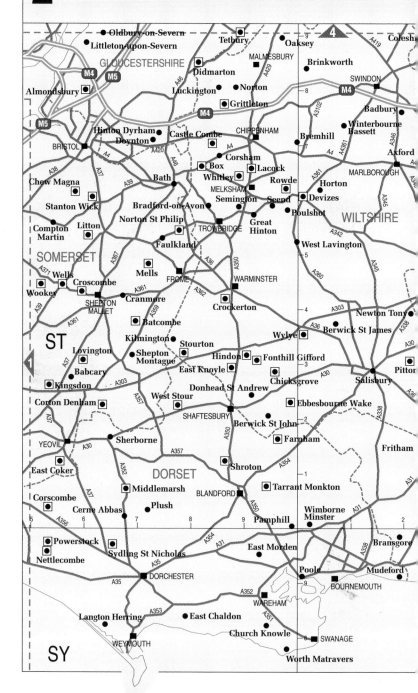

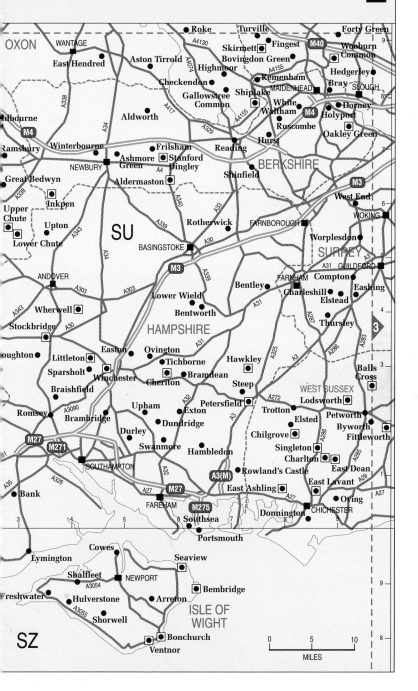

OXON
WANTAGE
East Hendred
Roke
Turville
Forty Green
Skirmett
Fingest
M40
Wooburn Common
Aston Tirrold
Bovingdon Green
Highmoor
Hedgerley
Checkendon
Remenham
Bray
SLOUGH
Gallowstree Common
Shiplake
MAIDENHEAD
Aldworth
White Waltham
Dorney
Holyport
M4
Ruscombe
Oakley Green
dbourne
M4
Winterbourne
Frilsham
Reading
Ramsbury
Ashmore Green
Stanford Dingley
Hurst
BERKSHIRE
NEWBURY
A4
Great Bedwyn
Aldermaston
Shinfield
Inkpen
M3
Upton
West End
Upper Chute
Rotherwick
FARNBOROUGH
WOKING
Lower Chute
SU
Worplesdon
BASINGSTOKE
SURREY
ANDOVER
M3
GUILDFORD
Lower Wield
Bentley
FARNHAM
Compton
Eashling
Wherwell
Charleshill
Elstead
Stockbridge
Bentworth
Thursley
HAMPSHIRE
oughton
Littleton
Easton
Ovington
Hawkley
Balls Cross
Sparsholt
Tichborne
Winchester
Cheriton
Bramdean
Steep
WEST SUSSEX
Braishfield
Upham
Petersfield
Lodsworth
Romsey
Exton
Trotton
Petworth
Brambridge
Dundridge
Elsted
Byworth
Durley
Chilgrove
Fittleworth
M27
Swanmore
Singleton
M271
Hambledon
Charlton
East Dean
SOUTHAMPTON
Rowland's Castle
East Lavant
Bank
East Ashling
M27
FAREHAM
Oving
M275
Donnington
CHICHESTER
Southsea
Portsmouth

Cowes
Seaview
Lymington
Shalfleet
NEWPORT
Bembridge
Freshwater
Hulverstone
Arreton
Shorwell
ISLE OF WIGHT
SZ
Bonchurch
Ventnor

0   5   10
MILES

SU
SZ

3

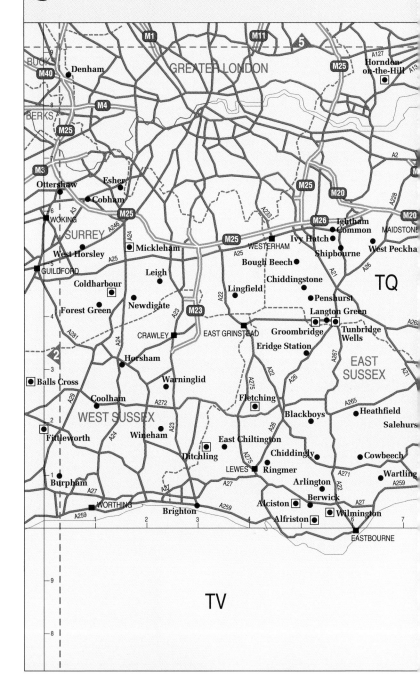

TV

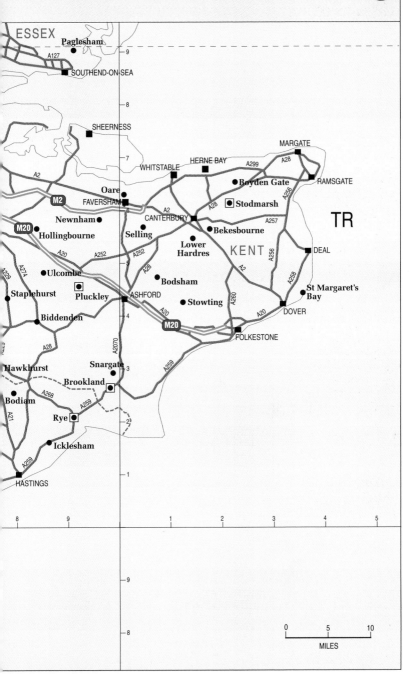

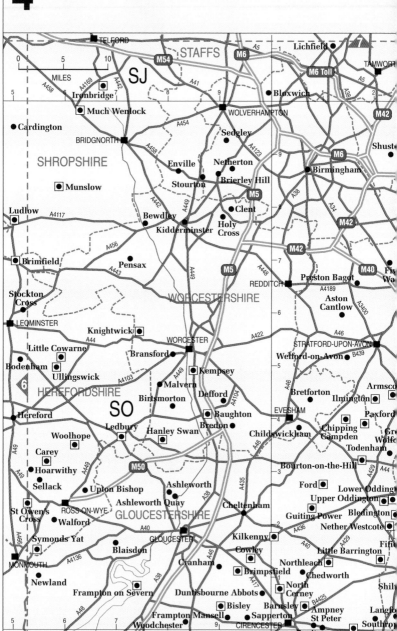

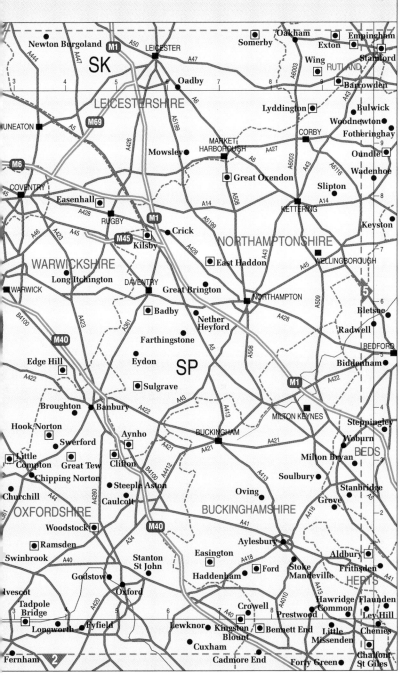

4

Newton Burgoland
M1
A50
LEICESTER
SK
A444
A447
A47
Oadby
LEICESTERSHIRE
A6
Somerby
Oakham
Empingham
Exton
Wing
RUTLAND
Stamford
Barrowden
Lyddington
Bulwick
Woodnewton
Fotheringhay
Oundle
Wadenhoe

M69
A5
A426
A5199
Mowsley
MARKET HARBOROUGH
Great Oxendon
CORBY
A427
A6
A6003
A43
A6116
Slipton

M6
COVENTRY
Easenhall
A428
RUGBY
M1
Crick
M45
Kilsby
A428
East Haddon
A14
A5199
A508
KETTERING
A14
NORTHAMPTONSHIRE
A43
WELLINGBOROUGH
Keyston

WARWICKSHIRE
Long Itchington
DAVENTRY
Great Brington
A45
A5
NORTHAMPTON
A509
Bletsoe
WARWICK
A46
A423
A45
A423
Badby
Nether Heyford
A428
Radwell
BEDFORD

B4100
M40
Edge Hill
A422
A361
Farthingstone
Eydon
SP
A508
Biddenham

Sulgrave
A5
M1
Broughton
Banbury
A422
A43
A413
MILTON KEYNES
Steppingley
Hook Norton
Aynho
BUCKINGHAM
A421
Woburn
BEDS
Swerford
A421
A421
A423
Milton Bryan
Little Compton
Great Tew
Clifton
A421
A4260
B4100
A4412
Soulbury
Stanbridge
Chipping Norton
Steeple Aston
A413
Oving
Grove
Churchill
A44
Caulcott
BUCKINGHAMSHIRE
A418
A5
OXFORDSHIRE
Woodstock
M40
A41
A418

Ramsden
A34
Stanton St John
Easington
Aylesbury
Aldbury
Swinbrook
A40
Ford
Frithsden
Godstow
Haddenham
Stoke Mandeville
HERTS
Ivescot
Oxford
A4010
Hawridge Common
Flaunden
A413
A41
Tadpole Bridge
A420
Crowell
Prestwood
Ley Hill
Longworth
Fyfield
A40
Lewknor
Kingston Blount
Bennett End
Little Missenden
Chenies
Cuxham
Chalfont St Giles
Fernham
2
Cadmore End
Forty Green

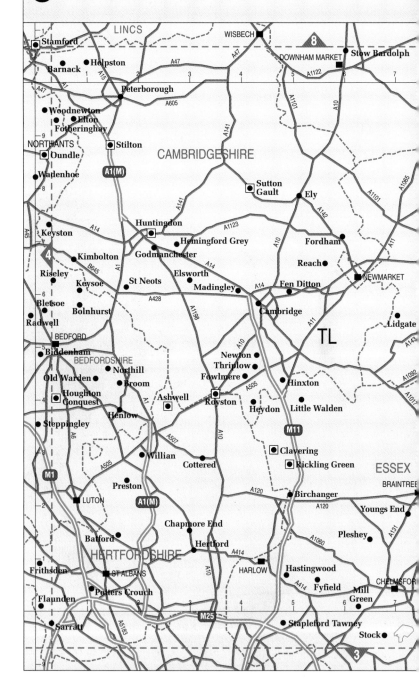

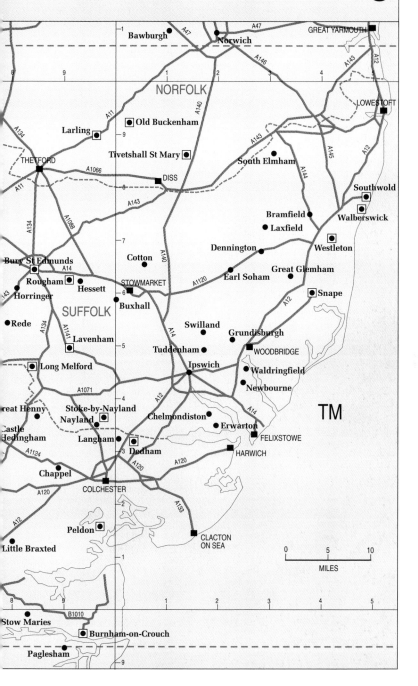

5

GREAT YARMOUTH

Bawburgh
Norwich
A47
A47
A146
A143
A12

NORFOLK

LOWESTOFT

A11
A34
Larling
Old Buckenham
A140
A143
A145
A12

THETFORD
A1066
Tivetshall St Mary
South Elmham
A144
Southwold

A11
A1088
DISS
A143
Bramfield
Laxfield
Walberswick

A134
Cotton
A140
Dennington
Westleton

Bury St Edmunds
A14
STOWMARKET
A1120
Earl Soham
Great Glemham

Rougham
Hessett
A12
Snape

Horringer
SUFFOLK
Buxhall

Rede
A134
A1141
Lavenham
A14
Swilland
Grundisburgh

Tuddenham
Ipswich
WOODBRIDGE

Long Melford
Waldringfield

A1071
A12
Newbourne

reat Henny
Stoke-by-Nayland
Chelmondiston
A14
TM

Nayland
Erwarton

Castle
Hedingham
Langham
FELIXSTOWE

A1124
Dedham
A120
HARWICH

Chappel
A120
A120

COLCHESTER

A12
A133

Peldon
CLACTON
ON SEA

Little Braxted

0   5   10
MILES

Stow Maries
B1010

Burnham-on-Crouch

Paglesham

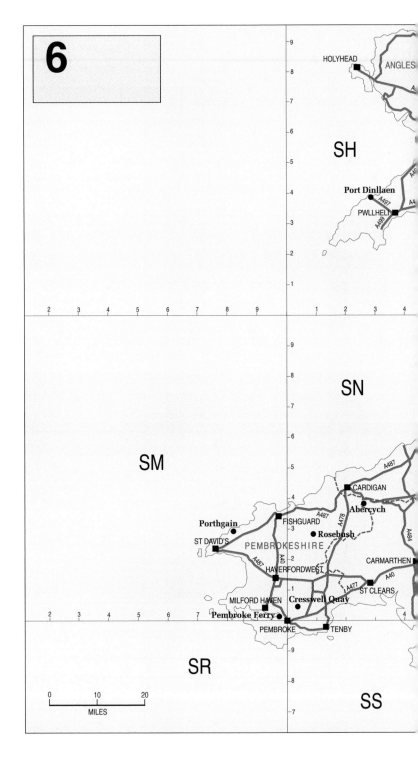

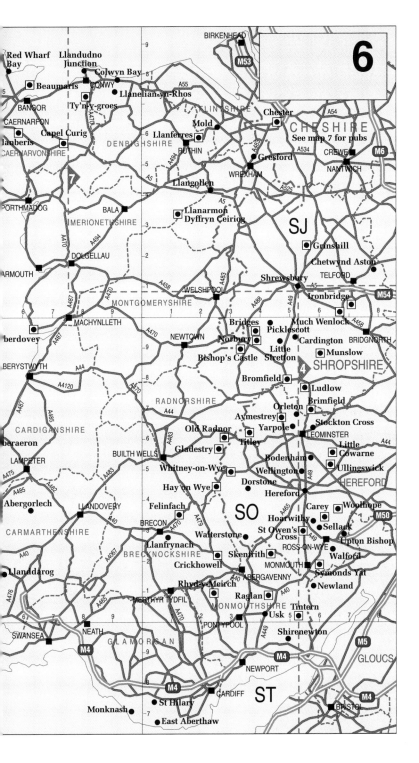

6

Red Wharf Bay
Llandudno Junction
Colwyn Bay
CONWY
Llanelian-yn-Rhos
Beaumaris
Ty'n-y-groes
BANGOR
BIRKENHEAD
M53
A55
Chester
CHESHIRE
A54
See map 7 for pubs
FLINTSHIRE
Mold
Llanferres
RUTHIN
Gresford
WREXHAM
CREWE
M6
NANTWICH
A534
A483
A525
CAERNARFON
Capel Curig
Llanberis
CAERNARVONSHIRE
DENBIGHSHIRE

Llangollen
A5
PORTHMADOG
BALA
MERIONETHSHIRE
Llanarmon Dyffryn Ceiriog
SJ
A494
A470
Grinshill
Chetwynd Aston
TELFORD
M54

DOLGELLAU
BARMOUTH
WELSHPOOL
Shrewsbury
Ironbridge
MONTGOMERYSHIRE
A458
A483
A5
A49
BRIDGNORTH
A458
MACHYNLLETH
aberdovey
A487
A470
NEWTOWN
Bridges
Picklescott
Norbury
Cardington
Much Wenlock
Munslow
SHROPSHIRE
Bishop's Castle
Little Stretton
A488
ABERYSTWYTH
A44
A4120
Bromfield
Ludlow
Brimfield
RADNORSHIRE
A44
Orleton
Aymestrey
Yarpole
Stockton Cross
LEOMINSTER
Little Cowarne
Ullingswick
A44
CARDIGANSHIRE
A485
Old Radnor
Titley
aberaeron
LAMPETER
A475
A482
A485
BUILTH WELLS
A483
Gladestry
Whitney-on-Wye
Bodenham
Wellington
A49
HEREFORD
Abergorlech
A44
Hay on Wye
Dorstone
Hereford
SO
Carey
Woolhope
M50
Hoarwithy
Sellack
St Owen's Cross
ROSS-ON-WYE
Upton Bishop
LLANDOVERY
Felinfach
BRECON
A40
A479
A470
Watterstone
CARMARTHENSHIRE
A40
A4067
Llanfrynach
BRECKNOCKSHIRE
Skenfrith
Walford
Symonds Yat
MONMOUTH
Crickhowell
Newland
Llanddarog
A476
A40
A465
Rhyd-y-Meirch
ABERGAVENNY
Raglan
MERTHYR TYDFIL
A470
MONMOUTHSHIRE
Tintern
Usk
A449
A40
A465
GLAMORGAN
Shirenewton
M5
SWANSEA
M4
NEATH
M4
GLOUCS
PONTYPOOL
A4042
NEWPORT
M4
CARDIFF
ST
St Hilary
Monknash
East Aberthaw
BRISTOL
M4

9

Ulverston

Beetham
Cartmel
Nether
Yealand Burrow
Conyers Tunstall

Casterton
Kirkby
Lonsdale Chape
le Dal
Thornton
in Lonsdale

A683

M6

A65

Long Presto

BARROW-IN-FURNESS

SD

Lancaster

LANCASHIRE

0   10   20

MILES

Bay Horse

A6

Whitewell
Chipping

Sawley

Rimingto

Great Mitton
Longridge

Fenc

BLACKPOOL

M55

Broughton
Goosnargh

Ribchester

BLACKBURN

M65

BURNLE

Lytham

A584

PRESTON

Brindle
Wheelton

Bu

SOUTHPORT

A59

Bispham Green

M61

GREATER
MANCHESTE

A6

M58

WIGAN

5   6   7

M6

M6

8   9

1   2   3

4

5   6

MERSEYSIDE

M6

A580

M60

BIRKENHEAD

Liverpool

M62

WARRINGTON

M56

Llandudno
Junction

Barnston

M53

ELLESMERE
PORT

RUNCORN

CHESHIRE

Mobberle

CONWY

Colwyn Bay

A55

A540

M56

NORTHWICH

Peov
Hea

Ty'n-y-groes

Llanelian
-yn-Rhos

A525

PLINTSHIRE

Chester

Willington
Cotebrook

M6

A470

Mold

A494

Tarporley

Wettenhall

Bartholm

A5

Llanferres
RUTHIN

Aldford
Burwardsley

Bunbury

CREWE

Gresford

A534

Haughton
Moss

NANTWICH

DENBIGHSHIRE

A5

WREXHAM

Bickley Moss

Wrenbury

Wrinehi

SJ

Aston

BALA

Llangollen

Burleydam

MERIONETHSHIRE

A5

Llanarmon
Dyffryn Ceiriog

A483

A41

A53

A494

6

A528

A49

A41

A51

Grinshill

SHROPSHIRE

A495

MONTGOMERYSHIRE

A5

Chetwynd Aston

Shrewsbury

TELFORD

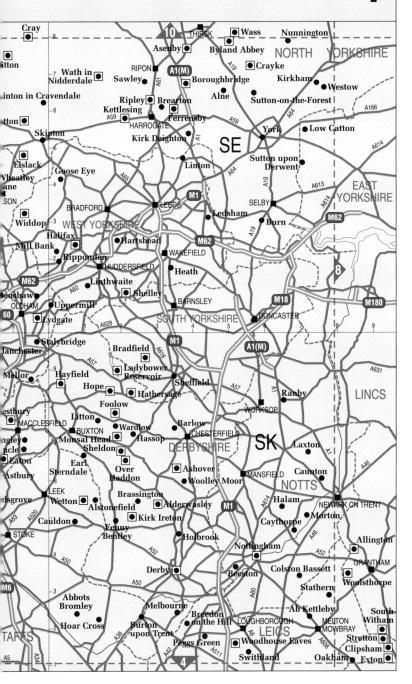

Cray
itton
itton
inton in Cravendale
tton
Skipton
Elslack
Wheatley
ane
SON
Widdop
Mill Bank
Ripponden
enshaw
OLDHAM
60
Lydgate
Stalybridge
lanchester
Mellor
esthury
MACCLESFIELD
ngley
ncle
Eaton
Astbury
sgrove
LEEK
STOKE
M6
M62
TAFFS
A5
A34

Wath in Nidderdale
Sawley
RIPON
Ripley
Kettlesing
HARROGATE
Brearton
Ferrensby
Kirk Deighton
Goose Eye
BRADFORD
Halifax
Hartshead
HUDDERSFIELD
Linthwaite
Shelley
Uppermill
Bradfield
Hayfield
Hope
Foolow
Litton
BUXTON
Monsal Head
Sheldon
Earl
Sterndale
Over
Haddon
Brassington
Wetton
Alstonefield
Cauldon
Fenny
Bentley
Abbots
Bromley
Hoar Cross
Ladybower
Reservoir
Hathersage
Wardlow
Hassop
Ashover
Woolley Moor
Alderwasley
Kirk Ireton
Holbrook
Melbourne
Burton
upon Trent
Pegs Green

THIRSK
10
Asenby
A1(M)
Boroughbridge
Alne
Linton
LEEDS
M1
WAKEFIELD
M62
Heath
BARNSLEY
SOUTH YORKSHIRE
M1
Sheffield
Barlow
CHESTERFIELD
DERBYSHIRE
MANSFIELD
M1
Nottingham
Beeston
Derby
Breedon
on the Hill
LOUGHBOROUGH
Woodhouse Eaves
Swithland

Wass
Byland Abbey
Crayke
Sutton-on-the-Forest
York
Ledsham
Burn
Ledsham
SE
Sutton upon
Derwent
SELBY
M62
M18
DONCASTER
A1(M)
WORKSOP
Ranby
LINCS
SK
Laxton
Caunton
NOTTS
Halam
NEWARK ON TRENT
Caythorpe
Morton
Colston Bassett
Stathern
Ab Kettleby
MELTON
MOWBRAY
LEICS
Oakham

Nunnington
NORTH YORKSHIRE
Kirkham
Westow
Low Catton
EAST
YORKSHIRE
8
Allington
GRANTHAM
Woolsthorpe
South
Witham
Stretton
Clipsham
Exton
4

FIND THE NEAREST GOOD PUB
ANYTIME, ANYWHERE!

Good Pub Guide Mobile – Text GOODPUB to 87080*

Receive full details of your nearest good pub direct to your mobile. Our brand-new enhanced mobile phone system provides a complete description, contact details, map and directions, all displayed within our intuitive mobile phone application.

Visit **www.goodguides.co.uk/mobile** for full details.

* Texts cost 50p plus standard network charges

The Good Pub Guide 2008 Sat Nav Edition

A digital version of *The Good Pub Guide* is now available on a special edition Garmin satellite navigation system.

The Garmin nüvi 310 with Good Pub Guide enables drivers to find their nearest good pub, or locate a specific pub just by touching their sat nav screen. It will then direct you to the pub as you drive, anywhere in the UK!

Visit **www.goodguides.co.uk/satnav** for full details.

www.goodguides.co.uk

Search for good pubs and events, sign up for the newsletter and find full details of all good pub products and services.

You can purchase *The Good Pub Guide* and many other leading travel guides direct from the publisher at

www.rbooks.co.uk

Browse more than 10,000 titles from the UK's leading publishers

cricket and transport pictures, restaurant; big-screen TV, games machine; tables in big garden *(Keith and Janet Morris)*

MILL GREEN [TL6301]

Cricketers CM4 0RH: Low beams, interesting cricketing memorabilia, enjoyable bar food, well kept Greene King IPA, Abbot and a seasonal beer tapped from the cask, decent wines, friendly attentive staff, newly refurbished restaurant; children very welcome, picturesque setting, plenty of picnic-sets on big front terrace and in extensive tree-shaded garden behind, cl winter Sun evenings *(Tina and David Woods-Taylor)*

MISTLEY [TM1131]

☆ *Thorn* C011 1HE [High St (B1352 E of Manningtree)]: Bistro-style restaurant-with-rooms rather than pub, with short daily-changing choice of enterprising food inc local seafood (American chef/landlady does cookery classes here), interesting sandwiches too, friendly service, good choice of wines by the glass, Adnams, smart bar, light and airy eating areas with contemporary pictures for sale; evening booking recommended; children welcome, pavement tables, five well equipped bedrooms, great breakfast, open all day wknds *(MDN, Tony and Shirley Albert, Adrian White, Judi Bell, N R White, A D Cross)*

Waggon C011 2AP [New Rd, Mistley]: Reopened by new management as dining pub, good fresh up-to-date food cooked to order (so may be a wait), spare minimalist décor *(Tom Gondris)*

MOLE HILL GREEN [TL5624]

Three Horseshoes CM22 6PQ [off A120, E of M11 junction 8]: Quaint thatched pub on the edge of Stansted Airport, low oak beams, antique settles, big fireplaces, comfortable relaxed atmosphere, well kept Greene King IPA, friendly staff, good value pubby food, corner bar for locals *(Chris and Mike Sobey)*

MORETON [TL5307]

Nags Head CM5 0LF [signed off B184, at S end of Fyfield or opp Chipping Ongar school]: Cosy and friendly country pub with good blackboard choice of good value food from tasty lunchtime sandwiches up, friendly service, Greene King ales, three big log fires, comfortable mix of tables and medley of salvaged rustic beams and timbers, restaurant; children welcome, picnic-sets on side grass *(Gordon Neighbour, B N F and M Parkin, H O Dickinson, Roger and Pauline Pearce)*

MOUNT BURES [TL9031]

Thatchers Arms C08 5AT: New licensees doing good freshly made country food using local game and meats, midweek meal deals, Adnams and local guest ales, good wines by the glass and spirits range, friendly service, peaceful Stour valley views from dining room; plenty of picnic-sets out on the grass, cl Mon, open all day wknds *(Sarah Mennell)*

NEWNEY GREEN [TL6506]

☆ *Duck* CM1 3SF [W of Chelmsford]: Attractive rambling dining bar, dark beams, timbering,

panelling and interesting bric-a-brac, comfortable furnishings, enjoyable food inc good value set lunches, well kept Shepherd Neame ales, decent wines by the glass, attentive service; tables out on pleasant terrace *(Paul and Ursula Randall, Roy and Lindsey Fentiman, LYM)*

NORTH WEALD [TL4903]

Kings Head CM16 6BU [B181]: Pretty timber-framed 16th-c Vintage Inn, rambling linked areas with flagstones, low beams, timber partitions, log fires, pews and other old furnishings, plenty of pictures, reasonably priced food from good value sandwiches up, quick friendly service, wide choice of wines by the glass, changing real ales; piped music; tables out on large grassy area *(Mrs P J Pearce)*

PAGLESHAM [TQ9492]

Plough & Sail SS4 2EQ [East End]: Relaxed 17th-c dining pub in pretty spot, low beams and big log fires, pine tables, lots of brasses and pictures, enjoyable food from sandwiches through familiar favourites to interesting specials inc fresh fish, well kept Greene King IPA and a guest beer, decent house wines, good friendly service, traditional games; unobtrusive piped music; tables and finch aviary in attractive garden, open all day Sun *(Sean A Smith, LYM, John Saville)*

RIDGEWELL [TL7340]

White Horse C09 4SG [Mill Rd (A1017 Haverhill—Halstead)]: Friendly and comfortable low-beamed village pub with good value range of well kept ales tapped from the cask on cooled stillage, good value generous food with changing separate bar and restaurant menus, friendly service, fireside sofa, no music; no dogs; terrace tables, newish bedroom block with good disabled access, open all day *(Adele Summers, Alan Black, MLR, Pam and David Bailey)*

ROMFORD [TQ5189]

Coach House RM1 3DL [Main Rd (A118)]: Hotel with good italian food in cheerful bar, conservatory and more formal restaurant, good range of beers and wine, friendly efficient staff; terrace tables, comfortable bedrooms, open all day from breakfast on *(Karen Eliot)*

ROWHEDGE [TM0321]

Anchor C05 7ES [off A134 just S of Colchester; High St]: Well kept local and other ales, reasonably priced wines by the glass, enjoyable freshly made food inc puddings made here, friendly licensees and staff, attractive flagstoned bar and pine furniture in nicely decorated tiled bistro, picture-window views over marshes and tidal River Colne with its swans, gulls and yachts; large waterside terrace, lovely lunchtime or summer evening setting *(Mr and Mrs Brabants)*

ROXWELL [TL6508]

Hare CM1 4LU [Bishops Stortford Rd (A1060)]: Tasty sensibly priced straightforward food cooked to order, Adnams, Courage Directors and Greene King IPA, cheerful staff, comfortably worn in rustic décor in beamed panelling-effect lounge, separate public bar, dining conservatory; piped music, small TV, games machine; children welcome, attractive garden with wendy house, swings and climber *(Reg Fowle, Helen Rickwood, Paul and Ursula Randall)*

STISTED [TL7923]

☆ *Dolphin* CM77 8EU [A120 E of Braintree, by village turn]: Friendly heavily beamed and timbered bar, popular well priced straightforward food (not Tues or Sun evenings), log fire, bright eating area on left (children allowed here), Greene King ales; tables in pretty garden, nice hanging baskets *(LYM, the Didler, Pete Baker)*

STURMER [TL6944]

Red Lion CB9 7XF [A1017 SE of Haverhill]: Attractive thatched and beamed pub run by mother and three daughters, enjoyable fresh food inc light lunchtime dishes in bar, dining area, pleasant conservatory and small dining room, good service, well kept real ales, well spaced tables with solid cushioned chairs, big fireplace; level access, large appealing garden *(Adele Summers, Alan Black)*

TENDRING [TM1326]

Tendring Tavern CO16 0BX [Heath Rd]: Well run pub with keen new landlady, good smiling service, good interesting food *(David M Smith)*

TILBURY [TQ6475]

Worlds End RM18 7NR [Fort Rd – follow signs to Tilbury Fort]: Weatherboarded 17th-c waterside local alongside Tilbury Fort, interesting views of Gravesend and of the docks up river, three fireplaces, original flagstones, well kept Greene King Abbot and Mighty Oak Bitter and IPA, helpful friendly staff, simple good value food; children welcome, play area in small garden behind *(Mike and Mary Clark)*

UPSHIRE [TL4100]

Horseshoes EN9 3SN [Horseshoe Hill, E of Waltham Abbey]: Friendly Victorian local, simple and clean, with popular reasonably priced food (not Mon), McMullens ales; tidy garden overlooking Lea Valley, more tables

out in front, good walks *(N R White, Roger and Pauline Pearce)*

WENDENS AMBO [TL5136]

☆ *Bell* CB11 4JY [B1039 just W of village]: Small cottagey low-ceilinged pub with friendly service, bar food (not Sun/Mon evenings) from hearty baguettes up, Adnams, Woodfordes Wherry and a couple of changing guest beers, good value coffee, open fire, ancient timbers, snug alcoves, quite a few pictures, cribbage and dominoes; piped music; children welcome in restaurant and family room, dogs in bar, big tree-sheltered garden with terrace and plenty to keep children occupied, handy for Audley End, open all day Fri-Sun *(LYM, Paul Humphreys)*

WEST MERSEA [TM0012]

Coast CO5 8NA [Coast Rd]: Two-bar pub in attractive spot opp creek and mudflats, Greene King IPA and a guest beer, half a dozen wines by the glass, generous enjoyable food with quite a few fish dishes, friendly service, back dining extension; a few tables out in front *(John Wooll)*

WICKEN BONHUNT [TL4933]

Coach & Horses CB11 3UG: Attractive partly thatched traditional two-bar pub with friendly new licensees, enjoyable and genuine homely food from good sandwiches up, well kept Greene King ales, fresh flowers, beams and brasses, open fire, dining room *(M R D Foot, Mrs Margo Finlay, Jörg Kasprowski)*

WIVENHOE [TM0321]

Black Buoy CO7 9BS [off A133]: Attractive open-plan partly timbered bar (16th-c behind the more recent façade), good cheerful service, wide choice of good generous food inc local fish, well kept ales inc Adnams and Greene King, decent wines by the glass, open fires, upper dining area glimpsing river over roofs; own parking (useful here), pleasant village *(Giles Barr, Eleanor Dandy, BB)*

WRITTLE [TL6706]

Wheatsheaf CM1 3DU [The Green]: Thriving traditional two-room 19th-c local, Greene King, Mighty Oak and Mauldon ales, friendly knowledgeable landlord; terrace tables, open all day wknds *(the Didler)*

Gloucestershire

For pub lovers, this is a smashing county. It has some real gems, ranging from delightfully unspoilt through stylish bars attached to smart hotels to carefully run, lovely golden stone inns with delicious food, super drinks and comfortable bedrooms. And there's a lot of enthusiasm from our many readers for the pubs in this area, too. With their help, and after our usual programme of careful and anonymous editorial inspection, we have been able to add a fat batch of interesting new entries this year. These are the Horse & Groom at Bourton-on-the-Hill (enthusiastically run by two hard-working young brothers), the Black Horse at Cranham (an engaging and unassuming country pub with friendly staff), the Bull at Hinton Dyrham (interesting food in this friendly, well run ancient village pub), the Kilkeney Inn at Kilkenny (a smartly modernised dining pub), the beautifully refurbished Westcote Inn at Nether Westcote (thoroughly up to date in both style and food), the smart Wheatsheaf in Northleach (good all round under the three sisters who run it now), the Churchill Arms at Paxford (creative food and comfortable bedrooms), the Swan at Southrop (consistently good food yet keeping a proper village bar too), and the Ram at Woodchester (a cheerful all-rounder with good beers and great views). Other pubs currently getting top-notch ratings from readers include the bustling and popular Bowl in Almondsbury, the charmingly unspoilt Red Lion at Ampney St Peter (such a lovely landlord), the riverside Boat at Ashleworth Quay (in the same family for hundreds of years), the Kings Head at Bledington (popular always, and at its best when the landlord himself is there), the Five Mile House at Duntisbourne Abbots (particularly well run and very highly thought of), the Old Spot in Dursley (marvellous beers and a cheerful landlord), the Inn for all Seasons at Little Barrington (a handsome inn with a fine choice of food and drink), the first-rate Fox at Lower Oddington (a tip-top all-rounder), the enjoyable Weighbridge just outside Nailsworth (their two-in-one pies are much liked), the friendly Bathurst Arms at North Cerney (a proper pub but with nice bedrooms and good food and wines), the Anchor in Oldbury-on-Severn (always busy and with a great atmosphere), the Bell at Sapperton (a brilliant place for food, drink and welcome), the stylish Gumstool just outside Tetbury (attached to an upmarket hotel but with an informal feel and good food and drink), and the Farriers Arms at Todenham (friendly landlady and an informal and enjoyable atmosphere). For a special meal out you really are spoilt for choice here – but be warned, this is a pricy area for pub food, with prices tending to be noticeably above what you'd pay for the same sort of thing in most places elsewhere. Those pubs at the top of the list for food quality are the Queens Head at Ashleworth, the Village Pub at Barnsley, the Kings Head at Bledington, the Five Mile House at Duntisbourne Abbots, the White Horse at Frampton Mansell, the Inn For All Seasons at Little Barington, the Fox at Lower Oddington, the Weighbridge near Nailsworth, the Bathurst Arms at North Cerney, the Bell at Sapperton, and the Gumstool and Trouble House, both near Tetbury. The Bathurst Arms in

North Cerney is our Gloucestershire Dining Pub of the Year. It's reassuring to find local beers featuring strongly in most of the pubs in this county – as do quite an interesting range of soft drinks. Drinks prices tend to be around average, perhaps a very few pence above the national norm, with more or less local Donnington and Hook Norton quite widely available at bargain price, and the local Uley and Wickwar also good value. Other local ales to look out for include Stroud and Nailsworth. Particularly noteworthy Lucky Dips (at the end of the chapter) are the hotelish Swan in Bibury, Bakers Arms in Broad Campden, Lygon Arms in Chipping Campden, Twelve Bells in Cirencester, Tunnel House at Coates, Plough at Cold Aston, Puesdown Inn at Compton Abdale, Ebrington Arms, Fossebridge Inn, Hunters Hall at Kingscote, Trout in Lechlade, Catherine Wheel in Marshfield, Dog at Old Sodbury, Cat & Custard Pot at Shipton Moyne, Queens Head in Stow-on-the-Wold and Rose & Crown at Wick.

ALMONDSBURY   ST6084   MAP 2

Bowl

1¼ miles from M5 junction 16 (and therefore quite handy for M4 junction 20); from A38 towards Thornbury, turn left signposted Lower Almondsbury, then first right down Sundays Hill, then at bottom right again into Church Road; BS32 4DT

Bustling, friendly and handy for the motorway; quite a few real ales and fairly priced food

Handy for the M5 but with plenty of local customers as well, this is a bustling pub with a relaxed, friendly atmsophere. The long beamed bar is neatly kept, with traditional settles, cushioned stools and mate's chairs around elm tables, horsebrasses on stripped bare stone walls and a big winter log fire at one end with a woodburning stove at the other. Up to seven real ales are well kept on handpump: Bass, Butcombe Bitter, Courage Best, Moles Best and Rucking Mole, and a couple of changing guests; piped music. This is a pretty setting with the church next door and lovely flowering tubs, hanging baskets and window boxes. You will be asked to leave your credit card behind the bar.

🍴 Reasonably priced bar food includes filled baguettes or club sandwiches, poached pear, walnut and blue cheese salad, warm duck confit salad with honey, orange and sesame dressing, spinach and mushroom pasta with parmesan, steak and mushroom steamed pudding, battered haddock, hay-baked lamb and spicy sausage casserole, salmon goujons, and puddings such as lemon tart with raspberry coulis or sticky toffee pudding. *Starters/Snacks: £4.75 to £8.95. Main Courses: £7.75 to £13.95. Puddings: £3.95*

Free house ~ Licensee Mrs J Stephenson ~ Real ale ~ Bar food (12-2.30, 6-10; all day weekends) ~ Restaurant ~ (01454) 612757 ~ Children welcome ~ Dogs allowed in bar and bedrooms ~ Open 11.30-3, 5-11; 11.30-11 Sat; 12-10.30 Sun; closed 25 Dec ~ Bedrooms: £51.50S/£79S

Recommended by Len Clark, Dave Braisted, Bruce and Sharon Eden, Matthew Hegarty, Bob and Margaret Holder, Ian Phillips, Dr and Mrs A K Clarke, Roy and Lindsey Fentiman, Gerry and Rosemary Dobson, Bob and Angela Brooks, Comus and Sarah Elliott, John and Helen Rushton, Donna and Roger

---

If a pub tries to make you leave a credit card behind the bar, be on your guard. The credit card firms and banks which issue them condemn this practice. After all, the publican who asks you to do this is in effect saying: 'I don't trust you'. Have you any more reason to trust his staff? If your card is used fraudulently while you have let it be kept out of your sight, the card company could say you've been negligent yourself – and refuse to make good your losses. So say that they can 'swipe' your card instead, but must hand it back to you. Please let us know if a pub does try to keep your card.

AMPNEY ST PETER
SP0801 MAP 4

Red Lion 🍺
A417, E of village; GL7 5SL

Friendly long-serving landlord in charmingly unspoilt little pub; note the limited opening hours

For lovers of totally unspoilt pubs, this smashing little place should not be missed. It's run by a very friendly, long-serving landlord who will draw you into conversation with both him and the chatty locals – one group of readers found themselves helping people they had never met before to compile part of their quiz. A central corridor, served by a hatch, gives on to the little right-hand tile-floor public bar. This has just one table, a wall seat, and one long bench facing a small open fire. Behind this bench is an open servery (no counter, just shelves of bottles and – by the corridor hatch – handpumps for the well kept Hook Norton Best plus weekend guest; reasonably priced wine. There are old prints on the wall, and on the other side of the corridor is a small saloon with panelled wall seats around its single table, old local photographs, another open fire, and a print of Queen Victoria one could believe hasn't moved for a century – rather like the pub itself. There are seats in the side garden. Please note the limited opening hours.

🍴 **No food.**

Free house ~ Licensee John Barnard ~ Real ale ~ No credit cards ~ (01285) 851596 ~ Children and dogs in the tiny games room ~ Open 6-10; 12-2, 6(7 Sun)-10 Sat; closed weekday lunchtimes
Recommended by E McCall, T McLean, D Irving, R Huggins, Ray J Carter, Richard Endacott, the Didler

ASHLEWORTH
SO8125 MAP 4

Queens Arms 🍴 🍷 🍺
Village signposted off A417 at Hartpury; GL19 4HT

Neatly kept pub with civilised main bar, interesting food, thoughtful wines and ales, and sunny courtyard

The friendly licensees here continue to work very hard to keep this low-beamed country dining pub in tip-top condition. It's spotlessly kept and consistently well run and remains a favourite with many of our readers. The comfortably laid out and civilised main bar has faintly patterned wallpaper and washed red ochre walls, big oak and mahogany tables and a nice mix of farmhouse and big brocaded dining chairs on a red carpet; at night it is softly lit by fringed wall lamps and candles. Brains Reverend James, Donnington BB, and Timothy Taylors Landlord on handpump, a dozen wines by the glass from a thoughtful wine list (including south african choices), and 22 malt whiskies; maybe summer home-made lemonade or winter mulled wine. Piped music, board games and (by arrangement) a skittle alley; Bonnie, the little black pub cat, may entertain customers with her ping-pong football antics. Two perfectly clipped mushroom shaped yews dominate the front of the building. There are cast-iron tables and chairs in the sunny courtyard.

🍴 **Very popular, the good interesting bar food might include filled baguettes, nice soups, deep-fried brie and stilton croquettes with cranberry sauce, sautéed scallops with parma ham and a creamy brandy sauce, chicken, ham and leek pie, poached fresh smoked haddock with a poached egg, chive mash and wholegrain mustard sauce, spinach and mushroom crêpes with tomato sauce, pork schnitzel, a south african spicy lamb stew, super steaks, and puddings such as a light custard tart sprinkled with cinnamon and walnut and fudge pudding with fudge sauce.** *Starters/Snacks: £4.95 to £7.50. Main Courses: £7.75 to £18.95. Puddings: £4.50 to £5.50*

Free house ~ Licensees Tony and Gill Burreddu ~ Real ale ~ Bar food (not Sun evening) ~ Restaurant ~ (01452) 700395 ~ Well behaved children allowed ~ Open 12-3, 7-11(10.30 Sun); 12-3 Sun; closed Sun evening; 25 and 26 Dec
Recommended by Dr A J and Mrs Tompsett, Dr and Mrs C W Thomas, Bernard Stradling, Mrs Jill Wyatt, Paul Gavaghan, Michael Dallas, Denys Gueroult, Tony and Tracy Constance, Dave Kenward, J Crosby

ASHLEWORTH QUAY

SO8125 MAP 4

Boat ★ ◀

Ashleworth signposted off A417 N of Gloucester; quay signed from village; GL19 4HZ

Delightful and unchanging Severn-side pub with swiftly changing beers – and in the same family for hundreds of years

This quaint and unpretentious pub is set back from the embankment of a peaceful curve in the River Severn. It remains as unchanging as ever and has been in the same family since it was originally granted a licence by Charles II. The little front parlour has a built-in settle by a long scrubbed deal table that faces an old-fashioned open kitchen range with a side bread oven and a couple of elderly fireside chairs; there are rush mats on the scrubbed flagstones, houseplants in the window, fresh garden flowers, and old magazines to read; cribbage and dominoes in the front room. Two antique settles face each other in the back room where four or five swiftly changing beers from breweries such as Archers, Church End, RCH, Slaters and Whittingtons are tapped from the cask, along with a full range of Weston's farm ciders. The front suntrap crazy-paved courtyard is bright with plant tubs in summer, with a couple of picnic-sets under cocktail parasols; there are more seats and tables under cover at the sides.

🍴 **Lunchtime filled rolls during the week and maybe cake.** *Starters/Snacks: £1.60*

Free house ~ Licensees Ron, Elisabeth and Louise Nicholls ~ Real ale ~ Bar food (lunchtime only; not Mon and Weds) ~ No credit cards ~ (01452) 700272 ~ Children welcome ~ Folk band once a month ~ Open 11.30-2.30(3 Sat), 6.30-11; 12-3, 7-10.30 Sun; evening opening 7 in winter; closed all day Mon, Weds lunchtime

Recommended by the Didler, Matthew Shackle, Dr W J M Gissane, Mike and Mary Carter, Pete Baker, Phil and Sally Gorton

BARNSLEY

SP0705 MAP 4

Village Pub 🍴 ♀

B4425 Cirencester—Burford; GL7 5EF

Good mix of customers in civilised communicating rooms, candles and newspapers, and enjoyable food; comfortable bedrooms

The interesting modern cooking remains the mainstay in this smart and civilised country pub, but if you go to eat you shouldn't expect pub prices, or indeed pub quantities for their bar snacks. Instead, soak up the comfortably civilised old-world atmosphere. The low-ceilinged communicating rooms have flagstones and oak floorboards, oil paintings, plush chairs, stools, and window settles around polished candlelit tables, three open fireplaces and country magazines and newspapers to read. Hook Norton Bitter, Donningtons BB and a guest beer on handpump, and an extensive wine list with over a dozen by the glass. The sheltered back courtyard has plenty of good solid wooden furniture under umbrellas, outdoor heaters and its own outside servery. More reports please.

🍴 **Contemporary bar food includes soup, a plate of salami with home-made chutney, marinated quail, mushrooms, green beans and sweet mustard dressing, risotto of fresh peas, asparagus and poached duck egg, rare beef, beetroot and green bean salad, roast monkfish with creamed lentils and potato gnocchi, chicken with celeriac, broad beans and lardons, calves liver, bacon and sautéed potatoes, and puddings such as rhubarb sponge with ginger ice-cream or warm rice pudding with home-made jam.** *Starters/Snacks: £4.00 to £7.00. Main Courses: £10.00 to £16.00. Puddings: £6.00*

Free house ~ Licensees Tim Haigh and Rupert Pendered ~ Real ale ~ Bar food (12-2.30(3 weekends), 7-9.30(10 Fri and Sat)) ~ Restaurant ~ (01285) 740421 ~ Children welcome but with restrictions ~ Dogs allowed in bar ~ Open 11-3, 6-11; 11-11 Sat; 11-10.30 Sun ~ Bedrooms: £75S/£105S(£115B)

Recommended by Mr and Mrs G S Ayrton, Noel Grundy, Graham Oddey, Derek Thomas, Bernard Stradling, E McCall, T McLean, D Irving, R Huggins, J Crosby

BISLEY

S09006   MAP 4

Bear ◀

Village signposted off A419 just E of Stroud; GL6 7BD

Friendly 16th-c inn with decent food and beer, and garden across quiet road

New licensees have taken over this elegantly gothic 16th-c inn and have refurbished the bedrooms. The meandering L-shaped bar has a friendly, bustling atmosphere, a long shiny black built-in settle and a smaller but even sturdier oak settle by the front entrance, and an enormously wide low stone fireplace (not very high – the ochre ceiling's too low for that); the separate stripped-stone area is used for families. Tetleys and Wells & Youngs Bombardier and Special on handpump; darts and board games. A small front colonnade supports the upper floor of the pub, and the sheltered little flagstoned courtyard made by this has a traditional bench. The garden is across the quiet road, and there's quite a collection of stone mounting-blocks. The steep stone-built village is attractive. More reports please.

Ⓜ Bar food now includes lunchtime filled baguettes, soup, sautéed potato and onions with various toppings, vegetable pasty stuffed with fennel, mushrooms and pine kernels, fish and chips with mushy peas, steak in ale pie, salmon steak with mediterranean vegetables, daily specials, and puddings. *Starters/Snacks: £4.50 to £5.25. Main Courses: £7.50 to £12.95. Puddings: £4.95*

Punch ~ Lease Kate Gibbons ~ Real ale ~ Bar food (12-2(3 Sat), 7-9(6-9.30 Sat); 12-6 Sun) ~ (01452) 770265 ~ Children welcome ~ Dogs allowed in bar ~ Open 12-11(midnight Sat); 12-10.30 Sun; 12-3, 6-11 weekdays in winter ~ Bedrooms: £45S/£70S

Recommended by E McCall, T McLean, D Irving, R Huggins, Paul and Shirley White, Tom and Ruth Rees, Guy Vowles, Brian McBurnie, David Morgan, Brian and Jacky Wilson, Evelyn and Derek Walter, Brian and Rosalie Laverick, Nick and Meriel Cox

BLAISDON

S07016   MAP 4

Red Hart ◀

Village signposted off A4136 just SW of junction with A40 W of Gloucester; OS Sheet 162 map reference 703169; GL17 0AH

Relaxed and friendly, some interesting bric-a-brac in attractive rooms, and several real ales

There's a fair choice of real ales in this bustling and friendly pub. Kept on handpump, they might include Adnams Broadside, Cotleigh Tawny, Hook Norton Bitter, Otter Ale and Tetley; a decent wine list, too. The flagstoned main bar has cushioned wall and window seats, traditional pub tables, a big sailing-ship painting above the log fire and a thoroughly relaxing atmosphere – helped along by well reproduced piped bluesy music and maybe Spotty the jack russell (who is now eleven). On the right, there's an attractive, beamed two-room dining area with some interesting prints and bric-a-brac, and on the left, you'll find additional dining space for families; board games and table skittles. There are some picnic-sets in the garden and a children's play area, and at the back of the building is a terrace for barbecues. The little church above the village is worth a visit.

Ⓜ Bar food includes sandwiches, soup, pork pâté with red onion chutney, king prawns in garlic butter, vegetable lasagne, steak in ale pie, liver and bacon, chicken in a creamy mustard seed and sherry sauce, poached salmon with lemon and dill sauce, daily specials, and puddings such as treacle sponge or chocolate mousse. *Starters/Snacks: £3.95 to £6.25. Main Courses: £5.25 to £12.95. Puddings: £3.95*

Free house ~ Licensee Guy Wilkins ~ Real ale ~ Bar food ~ Restaurant ~ (01452) 830477 ~ Children allowed but must be well behaved ~ Dogs allowed in bar ~ Open 12-2.30, 6-11; 12-3, 7-10.30 Sun

Recommended by Guy Vowles, Dr A J and Mrs Tompsett, M J Winterton, Mr and Mrs A J Hudson, A and B D Craig, Dave Braisted, Michael Doswell, Graham and Glenis Watkins, Susan and Nigel Brookes, MLR, John and Tania Wood

BLEDINGTON

SP2422 MAP 4

Kings Head

B4450; OX7 6XQ

Beams and atmospheric furnishings in rather smart old place, super wines by the glass, interesting food, and comfortable bedrooms

Many of our readers enjoy staying overnight at this rather smart 500-year-old inn and the breakfasts are very good. The main bar is full of ancient beams and other atmospheric furnishings (high-backed wooden settles, gateleg or pedestal tables) and there's a warming log fire in the stone inglenook where a big black kettle hangs. To the left of the bar a drinking space for locals has benches on the wooden floor and a woodburning stove. Hook Norton Best and three changing guests on handpump, an excellent wine list with ten by the glass, 20 malt whiskies and interesting bottled ciders; piped music. There are seats at the front and in the back courtyard garden, and the pub is set back from the village green where there are usually ducks pottering about.

🍴 Very well liked food at lunchtime includes sandwiches, toasted paninis, potted shrimps with lemon butter, devilled lambs kidneys with mushrooms and fried bread, warm oyster mushroom, spinach and roasted pine nut salad, gloucester old spot sausages, with red onion marmalade, red wine jus and mustard mash and beef in ale hotpot with evening main courses such as smoked haddock and crayfish pie, chargrilled vegetable, basil and feta rigatoni, roasted lamb chop with fresh herb rösti and rosemary jus and bass with herb crushed potatoes and cucumber and dill relish; puddings like chocolate caramel brownie and banoffi cheesecake, and good british cheeses. *Starters/Snacks: £4.50 to £6.95. Main Courses: £9.50 to £17.50. Puddings: £4.75*

Free house ~ Licensees Nicola and Archie Orr-Ewing ~ Real ale ~ Bar food ~ Restaurant ~ (01608) 658365 ~ Children allowed but away from bar area ~ Dogs allowed in bar ~ Open 11.30-3, 6-11; 11.30-11 Sat; 12-11 Sun; closed 25 and 26 Dec ~ Bedrooms: £55B/£70B

Recommended by Jacques and Huguette Laurent, Jane McKenzie, John and Jackie Chalcraft, Richard Greaves, Mr and Mrs J Brown, Keith and Sue Ward, M and GR, Noel Grundy, Di and Mike Gillam, Lynda and Roy Mills, Simon Fox, Graham Oddey, Sean A Smith, A G Marx, Mr and Mrs John Taylor, Richard Wyld, Mr and Mrs A J Hudson

BOURTON-ON-THE-HILL

SP1732 MAP 4

Horse & Groom

A44 W of Moreton-in-Marsh; GL56 9AQ

Refurbished Georgian inn with a relaxed, friendly atmosphere, super food, thoughtful choice of drinks, and fine views from seats outside; comfortable bedrooms

With a family connection to the Howard Arms in Ilmington (see our Warwickshire main entries), this honey-coloured stone inn is run with some enthusiasm by two brothers. There are plenty of original period features, a bustling and friendly atmosphere and the light and airy bar has a nice mix of wooden chairs and tables on bare boards, stripped stone walls, a good log fire. Hook Norton Cotswold Lion, Purity Brewing Company Pure Ubu and Wye Valley Dorothy Goodbody on handpump and a sensibly short wine list with 13 by the glass; friendly young staff. There's a high-ceilinged bistro, too. Plenty of seats under smart umbrellas in the large back garden for eating and drinking, and fine views over the surrounding countryside. We expect the well equipped bedrooms to be very comfortable and hope to hear from readers who have stayed here.

🍴 Changing daily, the particularly good food includes interesting soup, home-made scotch quail eggs with mustard cream sauce, roast butternut squash, spinach and ricotta roulade, thai broth of diver-caught scallops, prawns, steamed mussels and noodles, griddled old spot pork chop with cider cream sauce and apple compote, roast stuffed duck breast with madeira jus, mozzarella and chilli-stuffed free-range chicken supreme in barbecue sauce, and puddings such as apple and blueberry flapjack crumble and chocolate nemesis. *Starters/Snacks: £3.50 to £7.50. Main Courses: £10.00 to £15.00. Puddings: £4.50 to £6.00*

There are report forms at the back of the book.

Free house ~ Licensee Tom Greenstock ~ Real ale ~ Bar food (not Sun evening or Mon lunchtime) ~ (01386) 700413 ~ Children welcome ~ Open 11-2(2.30 Sat), 6-11; 12-3 Sun; closed Sun evening and Mon lunchtime ~ Bedrooms: £70B/£98B

Recommended by Chris Glasson, Roger Braithwaite, Michael and Anne Brown, Susan and Nigel Brookes, Martin and Pauline Jennings, Ian and Joan Blackwell

BOX   SO8500   MAP 4

Halfway House

Edge of Minchinhampton Common; from A46 S of Stroud follow Amberley signpost, then after Amberley Inn turn right towards Box, then left along common edge as you reach Box; OS Sheet 162 map reference 856003; can also be reached from Brimscombe on A419 SE of Stroud; GL6 9AE

Light, airy bars and downstairs restaurant, several real ales, and interesting bar food

New licensees again for this tall 300-year-old house. The open-plan bars are light and airy and ramble around the central serving bar and there are simple sturdy blond wooden chairs around good wooden tables, a built-in wall seat and stripped wooden floors. The bar has yellowy cream walls and ceiling, the dining area is mainly a warm terracota, there are windows with views to the common and an unusual pitched-roof area. Downstairs, the restaurant has enclosures where customers can adjust the lighting or volume of music to suit their personal tastes. Butcombe Blond, Nailsworth Artists Ale, Stroud Tom Long, Timothy Taylors Landlord and Wickwar BOB on handpump and decent wines; piped music. There are seats in the landscaped garden. More reports please.

🍴 **Interesting bar food includes soup, seared medallions of ostrich fillet with tarragon and red onion butter, pheasant liver pâté with calvados and home-made caramelised onion chutney, spiced coconut thai-style mushrooms on pilau rice, seared hand-dived scallops and lardons of gloucester old spot bacon finished with a steamed cockle, white wine and cream sauce, free-range gressingham duck breast with beetroot purée and apple, quince and cinnamon compote, slow-cooked lamb shank moroccan tagine and seared venison steak with balsamic vinegar and shallot jus.** *Starters/Snacks: £4.60 to £6.50. Main Courses: £7.50 to £19.75. Puddings: £4.95 to £5.25*

Free house ~ Licensees Chris Cowcher and Jessica Trerise ~ Real ale ~ Bar food (12-2(3 Sun), 6.30-9.30) ~ Restaurant ~ (01453) 832631 ~ Children welcome ~ Dogs allowed in bar ~ Open 10am-midnight

Recommended by Neil and Jenny Dury, Tom and Ruth Rees, E McCall, T McLean, D Irving, R Huggins, Andy and Claire Barker

BRIMPSFIELD   SO9413   MAP 4

Golden Heart ♀

Nettleton Bottom (not shown on road maps, so we list the pub instead under the name of the nearby village); on A417 N of the Brimpsfield turning northbound; GL4 8LA

Nice old-fashioned furnishings in several cosy areas, big log fire and fair choice of food and drink; suntrap terrace and nearby walks

Bustling and popular, this is an enjoyable roadside pub of some genuine character. The main low-ceilinged bar is divided into five cosily distinct areas; there's a roaring log fire in the huge stone inglenook fireplace in one, traditional built-in settles and other old-fashioned furnishings throughout, and quite a few brass items, typewriters, exposed stone and wood panelling; newspapers to read. A comfortable parlour on the right has another decorative fireplace, and leads into a further room that opens on to the terrace. Archers Best Bitter, Jennings Cumberland, Timothy Taylors Golden Best and Youngs Winter Warmer on handpump, and quite a few wines by the glass. From the rustic cask-supported tables on the suntrap terrace, there are pleasant views down over a valley; nearby walks. If you are thinking of staying here, bear in mind that the nearby road is a busy all-night link between the M4 and M5.

🍴 A fair choice of bar food includes doorstep sandwiches, filled baked potatoes, ploughman's, soup, devilled whitebait, battered cod, vegetarian nut roast, chicken curry, steak and kidney pie, slow-cooked lamb shank, and puddings such as treacle tart and trio of chocolate tower. *Starters/Snacks: £3.95 to £6.50. Main Courses: £8.95 to £14.95. Puddings: £4.25*

Free house ~ Licensee Catherine Stevens ~ Real ale ~ Bar food (12-3, 6-10; all day Sun) ~ (01242) 870261 ~ Children welcome ~ Dogs welcome ~ Open 11-3, 5.30-11; 11-11 Sat; 12-10 Sun; closed 25 Dec ~ Bedrooms: £35S/£55S

Recommended by Colin Moore, E McCall, T McLean, D Irving, R Huggins, Michael Doswell, Guy Vowles, R T and J C Moggridge, R B Gardiner, Nigel and Sue Foster, Mike Vincent, N R White, Chris Flynn, Wendy Jones, Bob and Angela Brooks, Theocsbrian, Martin and Karen Wake, Ian Phillips, Di and Mike Gillam

CHEDWORTH   SP0512   MAP 4

Seven Tuns ♀

Village signposted off A429 NE of Cirencester; then take second signposted right turn and bear left towards church; GL54 4AE

Handy for nearby Roman villa and with several open fires, lots of wines by the glass, decent food, and plenty of seats outside

After a visit to the famous nearby Roman villa, you'll find this friendly little 17th-c pub is just the place to drop in for drink. The small snug lounge on the right has comfortable seats and decent tables, sizeable antique prints, tankards hanging from the beam over the serving bar, a partly boarded ceiling, and a good winter log fire in a big stone fireplace. Down a couple of steps, the public bar on the left has an open fire and this opens into a dining room with another open fire. Wells & Youngs Bombardier and Special and a seasonal guest on handpump, 14 wines by the glass and 13 malt whiskies; darts, TV, skittle alley, dominoes and piped music. One sunny terrace has a boules pitch and across the road there's another little walled raised terrace with a waterwheel and a stream; plenty of tables and seats. There are nice walks through the valley.

🍴 Well liked bar food includes sandwiches, ploughman's, coarse chicken liver pâté with red onion confit, roast mediterranean vegetable tagliatelle topped with goats cheese, ham and egg, beer-battered fish, tiger prawn and pineapple stir fry with chilli and lime basmati rice, oriental-style crispy duck salad and chicken supreme with butternut squash and garlic mash. *Starters/Snacks: £4.50 to £5.95. Main Courses: £7.95 to £14.95. Puddings: £3.95 to £4.95*

Youngs ~ Tenant Mr Davenport-Jones ~ Real ale ~ Bar food (12-2.30(3 Sun), 6.30-9.30) ~ Restaurant ~ (01285) 720242 ~ Children welcome ~ Dogs allowed in bar ~ Open 12-midnight (2am Fri and Sat); 12-11 Sun; 12-3, 6-midnight weekdays in winter

Recommended by Mrs Roxanne Chamberlain, Keith and Sue Ward, D P and M A Miles, Guy Vowles, KC, E McCall, T McLean, D Irving, R Huggins

CHELTENHAM   SO9624   MAP 4

Royal Oak ♀ 🍺

Off B4348 just N of Cheltenham; The Burgage, Prestbury; GL52 3DL

Handy for Cheltenham race course, with a newly reworked garden, enjoyable food and drink (Sunday lunch all day), and enthusiastic friendly staff

The sheltered garden behind this attractive cotswold stone building has been completely reworked and re-turfed this year and there are seats and tables under canopies on the new heated terrace. The skittle alley has been upgraded too and can now also be used as a function room (which you can hire). Although there is quite an emphasis on the enjoyable bar food, the licensees are very keen to remain a proper pub and keep Bath Ales Gem, Malvern Hills Black Pear and Timothy Taylors Landlord on handpump; they also hold an ale and sausage festival in May, a cider and perry and cheese one in August and a stout and oyster weekend in November. Nine wines by the glass and local soft drinks;

friendly, efficient service. The congenial low-beamed carpeted bar has fresh flowers and polished brasses, a comfortable mix of seating from country chairs and a cushioned pew to dark green wall banquettes built in on either side of its stone fireplace; there are some interesting pictures on the ochre walls. Dining room tables are nicely spaced so that you don't feel crowded; the restaurant has piped music. This is the closest pub to Cheltenham race course so it does get busy on race days.

🍴 **Enjoyable bar food at lunchtime includes filled warm baguettes and ciabattas, chicken, mushroom and tarragon pie, smoked haddock fishcake with dill mayonnaise, three-bean vegetable enchilada with guacamole and ham and egg, with evening choices such as chicken liver and duck confit pâté with berry compote, moules marinière, steak and mushroom pudding, chicken breast stuffed with merguez sausage and chunky tomato sauce, braised shoulder of lamb with creamed aubergine and smoked garlic, daily specials, and puddings like lemon and ginger cheesecake and brioche bread and butter pudding; Sunday roasts all day.** *Starters/Snacks: £4.50 to £7.50. Main Courses: £9.95 to £16.95. Puddings: £4.50 to £5.00*

Enterprise ~ Lease Simon and Kate Daws ~ Real ale ~ Bar food (all day Sun) ~ Restaurant ~ (01242) 522344 ~ Children in bar before 7pm, in restaurant before 8pm ~ Open 11.30-2.30, 5.30(6 Sat)-11; 12-10.30 Sun; closed 25 Dec

Recommended by M Thomas, Keith and Sue Ward, Theocsbrian, Michael Sargent

CHIPPING CAMPDEN   SP1539   MAP 4

Eight Bells

Church Street (which is one way – entrance off B4035); GL55 6JG

Handsome inn with massive timbers and beams, log fires, and seats in large terraced garden; handy for Cotswold Way

Inset into the floor of the dining room in this handsome old inn is a glass panel showing part of the passage from the church by which Roman Catholic priests could escape from the Roundheads. The bars have heavy oak beams, massive timber supports and stripped stone walls with cushioned pews and solid dark wood furniture on the broad flagstones and log fires in up to three restored stone fireplaces; daily papers to read. Goffs Jouster, Hook Norton Best and Old Hooky and Wye Valley Butty Bach on handpump from the fine oak bar counter, quite a few wines by the glass, Old Rosie cider and country wines. Piped music, darts and board games. There's a large terraced garden with plenty of seats, and striking views of the almshouses and church. The pub is handy for the Cotswold Way walk to Bath.

🍴 **Bar food includes lunchtime sandwiches, soup, fishcakes with tomato and basil coulis, warm goats cheese and sun-dried tomato tartlet with basil pesto, lamb and coriander burger with cajun mayonnaise, butternut and pumpkin risotto with dolcelatte, lambs liver on rosemary mash with red onion gravy, pork and leek sausages with grain mustard sauce, and puddings such as lemon posset with red berry coulis and dark chocolate cheesecake with orange syrup.** *Starters/Snacks: £4.75 to £7.25. Main Courses: £10.00 to £16.00. Puddings: £5.25*

Free house ~ Licensee Neil Hargreaves ~ Real ale ~ Bar food (12-2(2.30 Fri and Sat), 6.30-9(9.30 Fri and Sat); 12-2.30, 7-9 Sun) ~ Restaurant ~ (01386) 840371 ~ Children must be well behaved and supervised by parents ~ Dogs allowed in bar ~ Open 12-11(10.30 Sun); closed 25 Dec ~ Bedrooms: £55S/£95B

Recommended by Jude Wright, W W Burke, Dru and Louisa Marshall, Michael Dandy, David Howe, David and Jean Hall, Tracey and Stephen Groves, Graham Oddey, Gerry and Rosemary Dobson, Noel Grundy

---

'Children welcome' means the pub says it lets children inside without any special restriction. If it allows them in, but to restricted areas such as an eating area or family room, we specify this. Places with separate restaurants often let children use them, hotels usually let them into public areas such as lounges.
Some pubs impose an evening time limit – let us know if you find this.

COWLEY   SO9714   MAP 4

Green Dragon ⇐

Off A435 S of Cheltenham at Elkstone, Cockleford signpost; OS Sheet 163 map reference 970142; GL53 9NW

Cosy and old-fashioned bars with winter fires, real ales, and terraces overlooking Cowley Lake; comfortable bedrooms

This attractive stone-fronted pub is an enjoyable place to stay with very comfortable and well equipped bedrooms and good breakfasts. The two beamed bars have a cosy and genuinely old-fashioned feel with big flagstones and wooden boards, winter log fires in two stone fireplaces, candlelit tables, a woodburning stove and Butcombe Bitter, Courage Directors and Hook Norton on handpump. The furniture and the bar itself in the upper Mouse Bar were made by Robert Thompson, and little mice run over the hand-carved chairs, tables and mantelpiece; there's also a larger Lower Bar and upstairs restaurant; piped music and skittle alley. Terraces outside overlook Cowley Lake and the River Churn, and the pub is a good centre for the local walks.

🍴 Bar food includes lunchtime sandwiches, smoked haddock and spring onion fishcakes, omelettes, turkey and mushroom pie, steak and kidney suet pudding, garlic and mustard pork fillet with sweet apple jus and barbary duck breast with stir-fried vegetables, egg noodles and chilli plum sauce. *Starters/Snacks: £5.25 to £8.95. Main Courses: £9.95 to £15.95. Puddings: £4.50 to £5.50*

Buccaneer Holdings ~ Licensees Simon and Nicky Haly ~ Real ale ~ Bar food (12-2.30(3 Sat, 3.30 Sun), 6-10(9 Sun)) ~ Restaurant ~ (01242) 870271 ~ Children welcome ~ Dogs allowed in bar ~ Open 11(12 Sun)-11 ~ Bedrooms: £65B/£85B

Recommended by Michael Doswell, Russell Grimshaw, Kerry Purcell, E McCall, T McLean, D Irving, R Huggins, Stuart Turner, Keith and Sue Ward, Guy Vowles, Bruce and Sharon Eden, Mike Vincent, KC, Ian Phillips, J Crosby

CRANHAM   SO8912   MAP 4

Black Horse 🍺

Village signposted off A46 and B4070 N of Stroud; look out for small sign up village side turning; GL4 8HP

Friendly, old-fashioned country inn with obliging staff, homely food and real ales

Popular locally – though there's a warm welcome for visitors too – this old-fashioned and unassuming 17th-c inn is tucked away down narrow lanes. A cosy little lounge has just three or four tables, the main bar has window seats and other traditional furniture and a good log fire, and the atmosphere is friendly and convivial; there are a couple of upstairs dining rooms, too (they take bookings up here but not in the bar or lounge). Bath Ales Gem, Hancocks HB, Wells & Youngs Bombardier and Wickwar BOB on handpump. Tables in the sizeable garden behind have a good view out over the steep village and wooded valley. They have a successful pub cricket team.

🍴 Popular homely bar food includes sandwiches, soup, smoked mackerel pâté, melted brie, bacon and walnut salad, fishcakes, vegetarian pasta bake, cumberland sausage and mash, pies such as fish, cottage or beef in Guinness, various casseroles, lamb kleftiko, and puddings like lemon shortcake or fruit filled meringues. *Starters/Snacks: £3.25 to £4.50. Main Courses: £6.50 to £11.95. Puddings: £3.75*

Free house ~ Licensees David and Julie Job ~ Real ale ~ Bar food (not Sun evening or Mon) ~ Restaurant ~ (01452) 812217 ~ Children welcome if well behaved ~ Open 12-2.30, 6.30-11; 12-3 Sun; closed Sun evening and all day Mon

Recommended by Andrew Shore, Maria Williams, Dennis and Gill Keen, Guy Vowles, Mrs L Ferstendik, Pete Baker, E McCall, T McLean, D Irving, R Huggins

---

Smoking is not allowed inside any pub. Some pubs now have outdoor shelters, open on two sides and sometimes heated, where smoking is allowed.

DIDMARTON
ST8187   MAP 2

Kings Arms ♀ ⇌
A433 Tetbury road; GL9 1DT

Busy pub, close to Westonbirt Arboretum, with knocked-through rooms, refurbished restaurant, pleasant back garden, and self-catering cottages

New licensees yet again for this busy pub. They have painted the outside and refurbished the restaurant, but the several knocked-through bar rooms have not changed. These work their way around a big central counter with deep terracotta walls above a dark green dado, a pleasant mix of chairs on bare boards, quarry tiles and carpet, hops on beams, and a big stone fireplace. Moles Rucking Mole, Otter Ale and Uley Bitter on handpump and ten wines by the glass; darts and piped music. There are seats out in the pleasant back garden, and they have self-catering cottages in a converted barn and stable block. The pub is close to Westonbirt Arboretum. More reports please.

🍴 Bar food now includes sandwiches, soup, wild mushroom and pepper tagliatelle, cajun chicken, home-cooked ham and free-range eggs, gloucester old spot sausages and mash, beer-battered haddock, calves liver with red wine jus, beef casserole, chargrilled duck breast with juniper berries, and daily specials. *Starters/Snacks: £4.25 to £8.00. Main Courses: £8.00 to £16.00. Puddings: £5.00 to £7.00*

Free house ~ Licensees R A and S A Sadler ~ Real ale ~ Bar food (12-2.30, 6-9.30; all day Sun) ~ Restaurant ~ (01454) 238245 ~ Children allowed away from bar ~ Dogs allowed in bar ~ Open 11(12 Sun)-11.30 ~ Bedrooms: £55S/£80S

Recommended by Matthew Shackle, Pamela and Alan Neale, Tom and Ruth Rees, Dr and Mrs C W Thomas, Simon Jones, Jonathan Martin, Derek and Sylvia Stephenson, Bernard Stradling, Alec and Barbara Jones, Stephen Woad, Rod Stoneman, Dr A McCormick, Donna and Roger, Roger Price, J Crosby

DOYNTON
ST7174   MAP 2

Cross House ◖
Village signposted with Dyrham off A420 Bristol—Chippenham just E of Wick; High Street; BS30 5TF

Friendly staff and customers, honest food and beers and 15 wines by the glass; close to Dyrham Park and walking country

You can be sure of a warm welcome from the friendly staff in this pleasant village pub. There's a good mix of both locals and visitors and the softly lit carpeted bar has some beams and stripped stone, simple pub furniture brightened up with cheerful scatter cushions, a woodburning stove in a big stone fireplace and a chatty atmosphere. Two or three steps take you down to a cottagey candlelit dining room. A fair choice of beers such as Bath Ales Gem Bitter, Courage Best, Greene King Old Speckled Hen, Timothy Taylors Landlord and Wickwar BOB on handpump and 15 decent wines by the glass; darts, games machine, TV and piped music. There are picnic-sets out by the road. This is fine walking country, and Dyrham Park is quite close.

🍴 Good, reasonably priced homely bar food includes sandwiches, chicken liver pâté, steak and kidney or rabbit pie, faggots, salmon, broccoli and chilli fishcakes, chicken wrapped in bacon with red wine and leg of lamb with barbecue sauce. *Starters/Snacks: £3.50 to £5.95. Main Courses: £7.95 to £10.30. Puddings: £3.50 to £3.95*

Unique (Enterprise) ~ Lease Andre and Liz Large ~ Real ale ~ Bar food (11.30-2, 6-9(10 Sat); 12-2, 7-9 Sun) ~ (0117) 937 2261 ~ Children welcome ~ Dogs allowed in bar ~ Open 11.30-3, 6-11; 12-4, 7-10.30 Sun

Recommended by Michael Doswell, Andrew Shore, Maria Williams, John and Gloria Isaacs, Dr and Mrs C W Thomas, Donna and Roger, Dr and Mrs A K Clarke, Dr and Mrs M E Wilson, Colin and Peggy Wilshire, Tony and Jill Radnor, Ian and Joan Blackwell, Barry Gibbs

DUNTISBOURNE ABBOTS
SO9709 MAP 4

Five Mile House 🍴 ◄

Off A417 at Duntisbourne Abbots exit sign; then, coming from Gloucester, pass filling station and keep on parallel to main road for 200 yards; coming from Cirencester, take Duntisbourne Abbots services sign, then immediate right and take underpass below main road, then turn right at T junction; avoid going into Duntisbourne Abbots village; pub is on the old main road; GL7 7JR

A lively landlord and a favourite with many for its good food, beer and atmosphere; plenty of original character, woodburning stove and newspapers; nice views from garden

Extremely popular with our readers, this cheerfully run, imposing stone pub is one where people tend to return on a regular basis for the good food, beer, and friendly welcome from both the licensees and their staff. There's plenty of original character and the front room has a companionable bare-boards drinking bar on the right (plenty of convivial banter from the locals), with wall seats around the big table in its bow window and just one other table. On the left is a flagstoned hallway tap room snug formed from two ancient high-backed settles by a woodburning stove in a tall carefully exposed old fireplace; newspapers to read. There's a small cellar bar, a back restaurant down steps and a family room on the far side; darts. Donningtons BB, Timothy Taylors Landlord and Wells & Youngs Bitter on handpump (the cellar is temperature-controlled) and an interesting wine list (strong on new world ones); service remains efficient even when really pushed. The gardens have nice country views; the country lane was once Ermine Street, the main Roman road from Wales to London.

🍴 **Cooked by the landlord, the very popular bar food includes sandwiches, soup, chicken liver pâté, deep-fried mild goats cheese with chilli jam, gammon with egg and pineapple, chicken breast stuffed with stilton, wrapped in bacon with a mushrooms and brandy cream sauce, local trout with prawn and caper butter, shoulder of lamb stuffed with redcurrant and mint with a redcurrant and port sauce, daily specials and puddings; there's also a good value two-course lunch option.** *Starters/Snacks: £3.95 to £5.95. Main Courses: £7.95 to £15.50. Puddings: £3.95 to £5.95*

Free house ~ Licensees Jo and Jon Carrier ~ Real ale ~ Bar food (12-2.30, 6-9.30; 12-2.30, 7-9 Sun) ~ Restaurant ~ (01285) 821432 ~ Children welcome if well behaved ~ Dogs allowed in bar ~ Open 12-3, 6-11; 12-3, 7-10.30 Sun

Recommended by Mr and Mrs J Brown, Guy Vowles, Gordon and Jay Smith, Neil and Anita Christopher, Bren and Val Speed, Mr and Mrs I and E Bell, Mark and Joanna, Nick and Meriel Cox, George and Maureen Roby, Keith and Sue Ward, David Morgan, Dr A J and Mrs Tompsett, E McCall, T McLean, D Irving, R Huggins, Giles and Annie Francis, Tom and Ruth Rees, Paul and Shirley White, W W Burke, Dennis Jenkin, the Didler, Julie and Bill Ryan, Carol Broadbent, Mrs Roxanne Chamberlain, J Crosby

DURSLEY
ST7598 MAP 4

Old Spot ◄ £

Hill Road; by bus station; GL11 4JQ

Unassuming and cheery town pub with up to ten real ales and regular beer festivals

With plenty of good-humoured locals and a splendid choice of real ales from all over the country, it's not surprising that this cheerful, unassuming pub is so popular. As well as four annual beer festivals, there might be Butcombe Bitter and Blonde and Uley Old Ric with changing guests such as Bath Ales Festivity, Broughton Merlins Ale, Caledonian Deuchars IPA, Cotswold Spring Olde English Rose, Everards Tiger, Otter Ale and Stroud Budding on handpump; quite a few malt whiskies too. The front door opens into a deep pink little room with stools on shiny quarry tiles along its pine boarded bar counter and old enamel beer advertisements on the walls and ceiling; there's a profusion of porcine paraphernalia. A small room on the left leading off from here has shove-ha'penny, cribbage and dominoes, and the little dark wood floored room to the right has a stone fireplace. A step takes you down to a cosy Victorian tiled snug and (to the right) the meeting room.

🍴 **Bar food includes toasted ciabattas, ploughman's, pork and apple burger with bacon, chicken fajitas, beery sausages with leeks and onion gravy, lamb and mint pie, home-cooked ham with parsley sauce, ratatouille bake, and puddings such as white chocolate cheesecake and jam and coconut sponge.** *Starters/Snacks: £2.95 to £5.75. Main Courses: £4.25 to £7.25. Puddings: £3.75*

Free house ~ Licensee Steve Herbert ~ Real ale ~ Bar food (12-8 Mon-Thurs; 12-3 Fri-Sun) ~ No credit cards ~ (01453) 542870 ~ Children in family room before 7pm ~ Dogs welcome ~ Various live artists Weds evenings ~ Open 11-11

Recommended by Clive and Valerie Alpe, Andy and Claire Barker, Clare Rosier, PL, Andrew Birkinshaw, Stuart Paulley, Rob and Jane Woodward, Carol Broadbent

EWEN

SU0097   MAP 4

Wild Duck ♀

Village signposted from A429 S of Cirencester; GL7 6BY

Bustling, civilised inn with open fires, a nice mix of furniture, and well liked food and drink; sheltered garden

This bustling 16th-c inn is actually more like an old manor house in part than a typical pub and is on the edge of a peaceful village, though handy for Cirencester. The high-beamed main bar has a nice mix of comfortable armchairs and other seats, paintings on the red walls, crimson drapes, a winter open fire, and maybe candles on tables. The residents' lounge, which overlooks the garden, has a handsome Elizabethan fireplace and antique furnishings. Besides Duckpond Bitter (brewed especially for the pub), you'll find Butcombe Bitter, Greene King Abbot, Theakstons Best and Old Peculier and Charles Wells Bombardier on handpump, 37 wines by the glass, several malts and local liqueurs; piped music and giant chess in the garden. There are wooden seats and tables under parasols and outdoor heaters in the neatly kept and enclosed courtyard garden. You will be asked to leave your credit card behind the bar. Very occasionally, things can go wrong. That can of course happen anywhere; perhaps the management here could be more sympathetic in the event.

🍴 **Interesting bar food includes soup, ploughman's, baked camembert wrapped in parma ham with chilli jam, duck liver parfait with onion marmalade and pickles, home-made burger with bacon, cheese and coleslaw, mediterranean vegetable and bean stew, seared scallops with basil mash, asparagus, parmesan and lemon dressing, roast lamb chump with rosemary and redcurrant sauce and onion chutney, rib-eye steak with tiger prawns and garlic butter, and daily specials.** *Starters/Snacks: £4.50 to £7.95. Main Courses: £8.50 to £19.95. Puddings: £4.50 to £6.95*

Free house ~ Licensees Tina and Dino Mussell ~ Real ale ~ Bar food (12-2, 6.45-10; all day weekends) ~ Restaurant ~ (01285) 770310 ~ Children welcome ~ Dogs allowed in bar and bedrooms ~ Open 11-11(midnight Sat); 12-11 Sun ~ Bedrooms: £70B/£95B

Recommended by Evelyn and Derek Walter, Mr and Mrs J Brown, E McCall, T McLean, D Irving, R Huggins, Guy Vowles, Richard and Sheila Fitton, Mrs Carolyn Dixon, Tom and Ruth Rees, Mrs M B Gregg, Julie and Bill Ryan, Ian and Joan Blackwell

FAIRFORD

SP1501   MAP 4

Bull 🛏

Market Place; GL7 4AA

Rather smart old hotel with beams, timbers and pubby furnishings in relaxed bar, residents' lounge, and reasonably priced bar food; charming village

Although this is a rather smart and civilised hotel, it does have a sizeable main bar with a bustling, chatty atmosphere and plenty of cheerful locals. It's nicely laid out with beams and timbers, comfortably old-fashioned pubby furnishings including dark pews and settles (try to sit at the big table in the bow window overlooking the little market square), and on its ochre walls, aircraft pictures and photographs of actors and actresses who have stayed here. The coal-effect gas fire is rather realistic. The long bar has Arkells 2B, 3B and Kingsdown on handpump, and service is friendly. Up a few stone steps a nice little residents' lounge has some attractive soft leather sofas and armchairs around its big stone fireplace, and fishing prints and plates. Disabled lavatories. The village is charming, and the church just along the street has Britain's only intact set of medieval stained-glass windows.

🍴 **Reasonably priced, traditional bar food includes lunchtime filled baguettes and baked potatoes, soup, chicken liver pâté, bacon and stilton mushrooms, cumberland sausage with onion gravy, home-baked ham with chips, creamy courgette and mushrooms with pasta, half a roast chicken, and puddings.** *Starters/Snacks: £2.95 to £4.50. Main Courses: £5.95 to £15.95. Puddings: £3.75*

Arkells ~ Tenants Judy and Mark Dudley ~ Real ale ~ Bar food (12-9.15; 12-2, 6.30-9 Sun) ~ Restaurant ~ (01285) 712535 ~ Children welcome ~ Dogs allowed in bar and bedrooms ~ Open 11-11; 12-10.30 Sun ~ Bedrooms: £39.50(£49.50B)/£79.50B
Recommended by Graham Oddey, Peter and Audrey Dowsett, Ian Phillips, Dr Ron Cox, E McCall, T McLean, D Irving, R Huggins

FORD
SP0829 MAP 4

Plough
B4077 Stow—Alderton; GL54 5RU

A good mix of customers in bustling, well run pub – gets packed on race days – and good food and beer

There's a really good friendly and chatty atmosphere here and quite a mix of customers – the pub is opposite a well known racehorse trainer's yard so many of the customers are stable hands and jockeys, though there are locals and visiting diners, too. It does get packed on race meeting evenings. The beamed and stripped-stone bar has racing prints and photos on the walls, old settles and benches around the big tables on its uneven flagstones, oak tables in a snug alcove, four welcoming fires (two are log-effect gas), and darts, games machine, TV (for the races), board games and piped music. Donnington BB and SBA and a summer guest beer on handpump; efficient service, even when busy. There are benches in the garden, pretty hanging baskets and a play area at the back. The Cotswold Farm Park is nearby.

🍴 **Enjoyable bar food includes lunchtime filled baguettes, baked ham and free-range eggs, liver and smoky bacon with onion gravy and steak and mushroom in ale pie with evening extras such as venison casserole, half a crispy duck with orange and Cointreau sauce and half a shoulder of lamb with mint and rosemary jus; they offer breakfasts for travellers on the way to the Gold Cup meeting at Cheltenham and have traditional asparagus feasts every April to June.** *Starters/Snacks: £4.00 to £6.50. Main Courses: £8.00 to £15.00. Puddings: £4.50*

Donnington ~ Tenant Craig Brown ~ Real ale ~ Bar food (all day in summer and all day all year Fri-Sun; 12-2, 6.30-9 winter Mon-Thurs) ~ Restaurant ~ (01386) 584215 ~ Children welcome ~ Dogs allowed in bar ~ Open 10am-2am; 11am-1am(midnight Sun) Sat ~ Bedrooms: £40S/£70S
Recommended by Andy and Claire Barker, R J Herd, Peter and Audrey Dowsett, Paul and Shirley White, John and Hazel Williams, Lawrence Pearse, Di and Mike Gillam, Guy Vowles, the Didler, Nigel and Sue Foster

FRAMPTON MANSELL
SO9201 MAP 4

White Horse
A419 Cirencester—Stroud; GL6 8HZ

Smart dining pub with contemporary décor, interesting modern food including fresh fish from seafood tank, and well chosen wine list; landscaped garden

Most customers come to this smart dining pub to enjoy the imaginative modern food though there is a small space for those who just pop in for a drink. It's tastefully decorated more in the style of a restaurant than a pub with mulberry, cream and chocolate paintwork, comfortable light beige chairs around clothed tables on the seagrass flooring and interesting pictures on the walls. The cosy bar area has a large sofa and comfortable chairs, and Uley Bitter and a guest such as Hook Norton Best on handpump, ten wines by the glass, plus house champagne, from a well chosen wine list (with helpful notes) and quite a few malt whiskies. The landscaped garden is a pleasant place for a meal or a drink.

⑪ **As well as a three-course fixed price menu (Monday-Thursday), the interesting food includes lunchtime snacks such as filled baguettes and paninis, pork and apple sausages with onion gravy, croque monsieur and home-glazed honey-roast ham and eggs, plus soup, warm salad of pigs cheeks, black pudding and glazed apple, seared cornish scallops, jerusalem artichoke mash with chilli and parsley oil, wild mushroom filled puff pastry case with red pepper coulis, fillets of red mullet with pak choi, anchovies, black olives and fennel butter, braised ham hock with a chorizo, flageolet and tomato broth, and puddings like steamed marmalade pudding with crème anglaise or chocolate and banana brownie with mascarpone; they also have a seawater tank to keep fresh cornish lobsters, crabs, native oysters, clams and mussels.** *Starters/Snacks: £3.95 to £8.50. Main Courses: £10.95 to £14.95. Puddings: £3.50 to £5.75*

Free house ~ Licensees Shaun and Emma Davis ~ Real ale ~ Bar food (12-2.30(3 Sun), 7-9.45; not Sun evening) ~ Restaurant ~ (01285) 760960 ~ Children welcome ~ Dogs welcome ~ Open 11-3, 6-11; 12-4 Sun; closed Sun evening, 25 and 26 Dec, 1 Jan and first four weekdays Jan

Recommended by Andy and Claire Barker, Richard and Sheila Fitton, Dr and Mrs C W Thomas, Tom and Ruth Rees, Di and Mike Gillam, J Crosby

FRAMPTON ON SEVERN   SO7408   MAP 4

Bell ◖

3 miles from M5 junction 13; from A419 left on to A38 then following village signpost right on to B4071; The Green; GL2 7EP

By large village cricket green and with plenty of outside seats and children's farm; a good choice of drinks, enjoyable food, and friendly service

In summer, you can watch – pint in hand – cricket being played opposite this handsome creeper-covered three-storey Georgian inn on what is said to be England's longest village green. Inside, the opened-up bars are attractively refurbished with some tub armchairs by the modern corner servery. There's a log fire and an extensive carpeted dining area with a mix of comfortable chairs around a variety of tables. Felinfoel Best Bitter, Otter Ale and Wickwar Cotswold Way on handpump, some local liqueurs and several wines by the glass; friendly staff and piped music, games machine, board games and dominoes. In front of the building are some picnic-sets under cocktail parasols with more in the garden with a good play area and what amounts to a kids' farm complete with dartmoor ponies, pigs, goats, sheep and ducks. The pub is a short walk away from the Sharpness Canal.

⑪ **Under the new licensee, bar food includes lunchtime filled baguettes and ploughman's, nachos with tomato and lime salsa and grilled cheese, soup, chicken liver parfait with red onion marmalade, ham and free-range eggs, chicken madras, steak in ale pie, beer-battered haddock, indian vegetable stew, lamb noisettes with garlic fennel and a red wine and mint jus; puddings such as lemon and champagne cheesecake or sticky toffee pudding; they also offer two- and three-course set lunches** *Starters/Snacks: £3.95 to £6.95. Main Courses: £7.95 to £17.95. Puddings: £3.50 to £5.50*

Enterprise ~ Lease Rob Cinnamond ~ Real ale ~ Bar food (12-9(9.30 Fri and Sat)) ~ Restaurant ~ (01452) 740346 ~ Children welcome ~ Open 11am-midnight(1am Sat); 12-11 Sun; closed 25 and 26 Dec ~ Bedrooms: £60B/£90B

Recommended by Lynn Elliott, Jo Rees, Michael Longman, Andy and Claire Barker, Ken Marshall, Mr and Mrs A J Hudson, Mr and Mrs J Brown, A and B D Craig, Pauline and Philip Darley

---

Please keep sending us reports. We rely on readers for news of new discoveries, and particularly for news of changes – however slight – at the fully described pubs. No stamp needed: The Good Pub Guide, FREEPOST TN1569, Wadhurst, E Sussex TN5 7BR or send your report through our website: www.goodguides.co.uk

GUITING POWER   SP0924 MAP 4

Hollow Bottom

Village signposted off B4068 SW of Stow-on-the-Wold (still called A436 on many maps); GL54 5UX

Popular old inn with lots of racing memorabilia and a good bustling atmosphere

---

Frequented by jockeys, owners and trainers, this 17th-c inn is a friendly place with plenty of atmosphere. The comfortable beamed bar has lots of racing memorabilia including racing silks, tunics and photographs and a winter log fire in an unusual pillar-supported stone fireplace. The public bar has flagstones and stripped stone masonry and racing on TV; newspapers to read, darts, board games and piped music. Caledonian Deuchars IPA, Fullers London Pride and a beer named for the pub (from Badger) on handpump, 15 malt whiskies, and nine wines and four champagnes by the glass; obliging service. From the pleasant garden behind the pub are views towards the peaceful sloping fields; decent nearby walks.

🍴 Bar food includes good filled baguettes and baked potatoes, soup, ham and eggs, cottage pie, sausages with mash and gravy, pork fillet in cider and cream, wild mushroom and spinach lasagne, slow-cooked lamb shoulder, and daily specials. *Starters/Snacks: £4.95 to £6.95. Main Courses: £7.95 to £16.95. Puddings: £2.80 to £4.95*

Free house ~ Licensees Hugh Kelly and Charles Pettigrew ~ Real ale ~ Bar food (all day) ~ Restaurant ~ (01451) 850392 ~ Children welcome ~ Dogs allowed in bar and bedrooms ~ Open 9am-midnight ~ Bedrooms: £45B/£70B

Recommended by Keith and Sue Ward, Michael Sargent, Mr and Mrs J Brown, Tim Barrett, Marian Higton, Roger Maskew, Michael and Jenny Back, C A Hall, Mike and Mary Carter, Jeff and Sue Evans, Martin and Pauline Jennings, Ralph Kenber, Jack and Sandra Clarfelt

HINTON DYRHAM   ST7376 MAP 2

Bull

2.4 miles from M4 junction 18; A46 towards Bath, then first right (opposite the Crown); SN14 8HG

16th-c stone pub in peaceful village with friendly atmosphere, enjoyable food, real ales and sizeable garden with children's play equipment

---

Handy for the M4, this is a pretty 16th-c pub with a chatty, friendly atmosphere. The main bar has two huge fireplaces, low beams, oak settles and pews on ancient flagstones and a nice window seat; there's also a stripped stone back area. Wadworths IPA, 6X and Summersault and a guest like Theakstons Black Bull on handpump, several malt whiskies and ten wines by the glass; piped music. Plenty of picnic-sets and play equipment in a sizeable sheltered upper garden with more seats on the sunny front balcony.

🍴 Interesting bar food includes sandwiches and ploughman's (not Friday or Saturday evenings), soup, sautéed chicken livers on garlic and herb toast, smoked salmon cheesecake with a lime and lemon dressing, ham and egg, daily changing sausages (made in the pub), stilton, leek and mushroom crumble, faggots with truffle and parsley mash, thai chicken stir fry, pork chop with a cider and stilton sauce and sage and onion mash, and puddings such as hazelnut and honey fool and banana bread and butter pudding; there's a good value lunch for two people on Tuesday-Thursday lunchtimes. *Starters/Snacks: £4.25 to £6.75. Main Courses: £8.95 to £17.25. Puddings: £4.25 to £5.25*

Wadworths ~ Tenants David and Elizabeth White ~ Real ale ~ Bar food (not Sun evening or Mon lunchtime) ~ Restaurant ~ (0117) 937 2332 ~ Children allowed in restaurant only until 7pm ~ Dogs allowed in bar ~ Open 12-3, 6-11; 12-11 Sat and Sun; 12-3, 6-11 Sat and 12-4, 7-11 Sun in winter; closed Monday lunchtime

Recommended by Peter Dewhurst, June and Robin Savage, Comus and Sarah Elliott, Michael Doswell, Meg and Colin Hamilton

---

We say if we know a pub has piped music.

KILKENNY

SP0018   MAP 4

Kilkeney Inn

On A436, 1 mile W of Andoversford, near Cheltenham – OS Sheet 163 map reference 007187; GL54 4LN

Reliable contemporary dining pub with popular food, real ales and very good, obliging service; seats outside with pleasant views

This is a spacious and reliable modernised dining pub with particularly quick, helpful and friendly staff. The extended, bright bar has neatly alternated stripped cotswold stone and white plasterwork, as well as gleaming dark wheelback chairs around the tables and an open fire. There's also a light and airy conservatory. St Austell Tribute, Wells & Youngs Bombardier and Youngs Waggledance on handpump, and a good choice of wines by the glass. From the seats and tables out on the terrace and lawn there are attractive Cotswold views.

🍴 As well as popular lunchtime bar food such as filled ciabattas, omelettes, sausage and mash and gammon and egg, there might be goats cheese with onion marmalade, filo prawns with chilli dip, chicken liver pâté, thai fishcakes, chicken with brie and pesto and a cranberry and red wine sauce, beef, onion and stilton pie, slow-roasted shoulder of lamb, baked bass with a fresh herb and white wine sauce, and puddings like fruit brûlée and chocolate fudge cake. *Starters/Snacks: £4.95 to £6.95. Main Courses: £8.95 to £17.95. Puddings: £5.75*

Charles Wells ~ Lease Nigel and Jean White ~ Real ale ~ Bar food ~ Restaurant ~ (01242) 820341 ~ Well behaved children allowed ~ Jazz monthly Sun lunchtime ~ Open 12-2.30, 6-11; 12-10.30 Sun ~ Bedrooms: /£95S

Recommended by Mr and Mrs C R Little, Russell Grimshaw, Kerry Purcell, Neil and Anita Christopher, M Thomas

LITTLE BARRINGTON

SP2012   MAP 4

Inn For All Seasons 🍴 ♀

On the A40 3 miles W of Burford; OX18 4TN

Fish specials as well as other interesting food in handsome old inn; super wines, big log fire, and pleasant garden; very busy during Cheltenham Gold Cup Week

The second generation of the Sharp family are now running this handsome old inn and there's a friendly, outgoing atmosphere. The attractively decorated, mellow lounge bar has low beams, stripped stone and flagstones, old prints, leather-upholstered wing armchairs and other comfortable seats, country magazines to read, and a big log fire. From a particularly good wine list, there are 20 wines by the glass (from a 120 bin list), 60 malt whiskies, and Sharps Own, Wadworths 6X and maybe a guest from Brakspears or Wye Valley on handpump; friendly, kind service. There's also a conservatory and restaurant. Cribbage, board games and piped music. The pleasant garden has tables, a play area, and aunt sally, and there are walks straight from the inn. It gets very busy during Cheltenham Gold Cup Week.

🍴 Using seasonal produce and with a fresh brixham fish board, the lunchtime food might include doorstep sandwiches with a mug of soup, grilled paninis, bubble and squeak with smoked bacon and fried egg, smoked salmon omelette with lemon butter sauce and welsh rarebit with evening choices like fillet of home-cured cod with potato and tarragon salad and grain mustard dressing, terrine of local game with caramelised vegetables and sweet and sour beetroot, flash-fried squid with lime, mushroom, cranberry and brie wrapped in pastry with a spinach cream sauce, whole cock crabs, light home-smoked and roasted gressingham duck with mixed bean cassoulet, river dart salmon with a vermouth, smoked bacon and spinach sauce, and puddings such as chocolate mousse and red gooseberry fool with sponge fingers. *Starters/Snacks: £4.50 to £7.50. Main Courses: £7.95 to £18.50. Puddings: £4.50 to £6.50*

Free house ~ Licensees Matthew and Heather Sharp ~ Real ale ~ Bar food (available during opening hours) ~ Restaurant ~ (01451) 844324 ~ Children welcome ~ Dogs allowed in bar and bedrooms ~ Open 10.30-2.30, 6-11; 12-2.30, 7-10.30 Sun ~ Bedrooms: £65B/£110B

Recommended by KN-R, Keith and Sue Ward, Dave Braisted, Graham Oddey, Richard Marjoram, Peter and Audrey Dowsett, David Glynne-Jones, Dennis Jenkin

LITTLETON-UPON-SEVERN
ST5989 MAP 2

White Hart 🍺

3½ miles from M48 junction 1; B4461 towards Thornbury, then village signposted; BS35 1NR

A good mix of customers and log fires in three main rooms, nice country furnishings, and good beer and food; nearby walks

This is a relaxing and friendly place to come for a pint or a bite to eat. It's a cosy 17th-c farmhouse and the three main rooms have log fires and fine furnishings such as long cushioned wooden settles, high-backed settles, oak and elm tables and a loveseat in the big low inglenook fireplace. There are flagstones in the front, huge tiles at the back, and smaller tiles on the left, plus some old pots and pans, a lovely old White Hart Inn Simonds Ale sign and hops on beams; by the black wooden staircase are some nice little alcove seats. Similarly furnished, a family room has some sentimental engravings, plates on a delft shelf and a couple of high chairs; a back snug has pokerwork seats. Youngs Bitter, Special and a seasonal beer plus a guest such as Charles Wells Bombardier on handpump and several wines by the glass. Outside, there are picnic-sets on the neat front lawn with interesting cottagey flowerbeds, and by the good big back car park are some attractive shrubs and teak furniture on a small brick terrace; boules. Several enjoyable walks from the pub.

🍴 **Good bar food includes lunchtime filled baguettes, ploughman's and a full breakfast, as well as home-cooked ham and free-range eggs, thai-style fishcakes with prawn crackers and sweet chilli sauce, home-made burger with mozzarella and tomato, tagliatelle with red pepper and tomato sauce, sausage of the day with beer and shallot gravy, beer-battered haddock with home-made mushy peas and chicken breast wrapped in bacon, roasted in thyme and rosemary and topped with smoked applewood cheddar with a cider and onion sauce.** *Main Courses: £7.95 to £13.95. Puddings: £3.95 to £4.95*

Youngs ~ Managers Greg Bailey and Claire Wells ~ Real ale ~ Bar food (12-2(2.30 Sat and Sun), 6.30(6 Sun)-9.30(9 Sun)) ~ (01454) 412275 ~ Children in family area and games room ~ Dogs welcome ~ Open 12-midnight

Recommended by Michael Doswell, Donna and Roger, Pete Devonish, Ian McIntyre, Dave Braisted, Will Stevens, Tom Evans, Bob and Angela Brooks, Mike and Mary Carter, A and B D Craig

LOWER ODDINGTON
SP2326 MAP 4

Fox 🍽 🍷 🛏

Signposted off A436 between Stow and Chipping Norton; GL56 0UR

Super inn with excellent food and wines, well kept beer, and particularly helpful staff

Extremely highly thought of by a great many of our readers, this is a very well run, smart and busy inn with a lovely atmosphere and particularly good service. Most people come to enjoy the delicious food or to stay overnight in the comfortable bedrooms but there is space at the bar and some bar stools for those just wanting a drink and a chat, and they do keep Greene King Abbot, Hook Norton Best, Wadworths 6X and a beer from Wickwar on handpump; a good few wines by the glass. The simply furnished rooms have fresh flowers and flagstones, hunting scene figures above the mantelpiece, a display cabinet with pewter mugs and stone bottles, daily newspapers and an inglenook fireplace. The terrace has a custom-built awning and outdoor heaters, and the cottagey garden is pretty. A good eight-mile walk starts from here (though a stroll around the pretty village might be less taxing).

🍴 **Served by neat, uniformed staff, the interesting modern food might include rough and smooth pâté with star anise and fig and port chutney, pear and roquefort tart, potted shrimps, home-baked ham with cumberland sauce, seared scallops with rocket and ginger dressing, steak and kidney pie, mozzarella, sun-dried tomato, artichoke and pesto lasagne, grilled spatchcocked quail with puy lentils and madeira, lamb shank braised with red wine and whole roast garlic, and puddings such as double-chocolate brownies and rice pudding with plum jam.** *Starters/Snacks: £3.95 to £7.50. Main Courses: £9.50 to £15.50. Puddings: £4.75 to £5.50*

Free house ~ Licensees James Cathcart and Ian MacKenzie ~ Real ale ~ Bar food (12-2(3.30 Sun), 6.30-10(7-9.30 Sun)) ~ Restaurant ~ (01451) 870555 ~ Children welcome ~ Dogs allowed in bar ~ Open 12-3, 6-11(midnight Sat); 12-4, 6.30-11 Sun; closed 25 Dec ~ Bedrooms: /£68S(£95B)

Recommended by Laurence and Kim Manning, Noel Grundy, MDN, Phil and Gill Wass, A Warren, Evelyn and Derek Walter, Bruce and Sharon Eden, Richard Greaves, Graham Oddey, Paul Boot, Keith and Sue Ward, Mr and Mrs J Brown, Rod Stoneman

NAILSWORTH

ST8499   MAP 4

Egypt Mill 🛏

Just off A46; heading N towards Stroud, first right after roundabout, then left; GL6 0AE

Stylishly converted mill with lovely summer terrace and interesting split-level bar

Perhaps edging towards becoming more of a restaurant than a pub, this is a stylish conversion of a three-floor stone-built mill still with working waterwheels and the millstream flowing through. The brick-and-stone-floored split-level bar gives good views of the wheels, and there are big pictures and lots of stripped beams in the comfortable carpeted lounge, along with some hefty yet elegant ironwork from the old mill machinery; piped music. Ideal for summer evenings, the floodlit terrace garden by the millpond is pretty, and there's a little bridge over from the car park. It can get quite crowded on fine weekends, but it's spacious enough to feel at its best when busy. Nailsworth Mayor's Bitter and The Town Crier on handpump, and ten wines by the glass. More reports please.

🍴 **Bar food includes sandwiches, soup, game terrine with port and juniper berry chutney, home-smoked chicken caesar salad, sweet potato and honey mustard pancakes with bean cassoulet and cajun crème fraîche, chicken and mushroom suet pudding, calves liver and bacon with red onion marmalade and horseradish cream, minted glazed lamb shank, bass with spaghetti vegetables and beetroot butter, and puddings such as banoffi pie and passion fruit and orange tart with champagne sorbet; Sunday roasts.** *Starters/Snacks: £3.95 to £7.50. Main Courses: £8.95 to £15.95. Puddings: £4.95 to £6.50*

Free house ~ Licensees Stephen Webb and Rob Aldridge ~ Real ale ~ Bar food (all day Sun) ~ Restaurant ~ (01453) 833449 ~ Children welcome with restrictions ~ Open 11-midnight; 12-midnight Sun ~ Bedrooms: £75B/£90B

Recommended by Ian Phillips, Dr and Mrs C W Thomas, Andy and Claire Barker, J Roy Smylie, J Crosby, Karen Eliot

Weighbridge 🍴 🍷

B4014 towards Tetbury; GL6 9AL

Super two-in-one pies served in cosy old-fashioned bar rooms, a fine choice of drinks, lots of black ironware hanging from beams, and sheltered landscaped garden

Readers very much enjoy their visits to this well run, bustling pub. It's a welcoming place with friendly, helpful staff and of course their two-in-one pies are extremely popular. The relaxed bar has three cosily old-fashioned rooms with stripped stone walls, antique settles and country chairs, window seats and open fires. The black beamed ceiling of the lounge bar is thickly festooned with black ironware – sheepshears, gin traps, lamps, and a large collection of keys, many from the old Longfords Mill opposite the pub. Upstairs is a raftered hayloft with an engaging mix of rustic tables. No noisy games machines or piped music. Uley Old Spot and Laurie Lee and Wadworths 6X on handpump, 16 wines (and champagne) by the glass, Weston's cider and ten malt whiskies. Behind the building is a sheltered landscaped garden with picnic-sets under umbrellas. Good disabled access and facilities.

🍴 **The two-in-one pies come in a large bowl, and half the bowl contains the filling of your choice whilst the other is full of home-made cauliflower cheese (or broccoli mornay or root vegetables), and topped with pastry: turkey and trimmings, salmon in a creamy sauce, steak and mushroom, roast root vegetables, pork, bacon and celery in stilton sauce or chicken, ham and leek in a cream and tarragon sauce; you can also have mini versions or straightforward pies, Other dishes include home-made soup, filled baguettes or filled**

baked potatoes, spinach and mushroom lasagne, salmon fishcakes, and puddings such as banana crumble or steamed chocolate pudding. *Starters/Snacks: £3.95 to £5.45. Main Courses: £6.95 to £14.95. Puddings: £3.45 to £4.75*

Free house ~ Licensee Howard Parker ~ Real ale ~ Bar food (12-9.30) ~ Restaurant ~ (01453) 832520 ~ Children allowed away from the bars until 9pm ~ Dogs welcome ~ Open 12-11; 12-10.30 Sun; closed 25 Dec and ten days in Jan

Recommended by Andy and Claire Barker, M G Hart, Norma and Noel Thomas, E McCall, T McLean, D Irving, R Huggins, James Read, Ginette Medland, Tom and Ruth Rees, Andrew Shore, Maria Williams, Dr and Mrs C W Thomas, PRT

NETHER WESTCOTE   SP2220 MAP 4

Westcote Inn 🍴 🍷 🛏

Pub signposted off A424 Burford—Stow; OX7 6SD

Beautifully refurbished, all very contemporary and stylish, with fine food and drink and a friendly atmosphere

After a complete refurbishment and with a new name (it was formerly the New Inn), this is now a stylish and friendly place with a fresh contemporary feel. It's all very light and airy and the main bar, the Tack Room, has stripped stone walls, beams, dark wooden tables and chairs and high bar stools on nice flagstones and lots of racing memorabilia such as Cheltenham Festival Tickets, passes, jockey colours and so forth; the pub even supports its own race horse, Westcote, which is syndicated by enthusiasts from the village and, as some of the best racehorse trainers live in the area, many of the customers are to do with the racing world. There's a smart Champagne Bar with comfortable leather seats on the wood-strip floor, an open fire and a high vaulted ceiling, a coffee lounge and a rather chic restaurant; a TV shows re-runs of horse races from all over the country. Hook Norton and a couple of changing guest beers and over 20 wines (including champagne) by the glass from a carefully chosen list; piped music, darts, badminton, croquet and football. There are seats on the terrace and in the garden and lovely views across the Evenlode Valley; spit-roasts and barbecues out here in summer.

🍴 **As well as lunchtime sandwiches, filled baked potatoes and a proper breakfast, the very good bar food might include soup, duck liver pâté with orange and thyme syrup, crab and salmon fishcake with lemon mayonnaise, baked peppers, ratatouille, wild mushrooms, rocket and parmesan salad, beer-battered cod with pea purée, gloucestershire old spot sausages with onion mash and thyme gravy, steak and kidney in ale pie, and puddings such as warm treacle tart with clotted cream and rhubarb crème brûlée.** *Starters/Snacks: £4.95 to £7.95. Main Courses: £7.95 to £14.95. Puddings: £4.95 to £5.95*

Free house ~ Licensee Julia Reed ~ Real ale ~ Bar food (12-2.30, 7-9.30; maybe all day summer Sun) ~ Restaurant ~ (01993) 830888 ~ Children welcome ~ Dogs allowed in bar and bedrooms ~ Live music two or three times a month ~ Open 11am-1am ~ Bedrooms: /£95B

Recommended by Richard Greaves, Noel Grundy, Myra Joyce, Julia Reed

NEWLAND   SO5509 MAP 4

Ostrich 🍷 🍺

Off B4228 in Coleford; or can be reached from the A466 in Redbrook, by the turning off at the England—Wales border – keep bearing right; GL16 8NP

Liked by walkers and their dogs with a friendly feel in the spacious bar; open fire and newspapers to read, and popular food

Parts of this friendly and relaxed old pub – in a charmingly relaxed village – date back to the 13th c. The low-ceilinged bar is spacious but cosily traditional, with creaky floors, uneven walls with miners' lamps, window shutters, candles in bottles on the tables, and comfortable furnishings such as cushioned window seats, wall settles and rod-backed country-kitchen chairs. There's a fine big fireplace, newspapers to read, perhaps quiet piped blues and board games. The pub dog is called Alfie. A marvellous choice of up to eight well kept real ales on handpump might include Adnams Broadside, Bath Ales Rare Hare, Fullers London Pride, Gales HSB, Greene King IPA, Sharps Doom Bar, Timothy Taylors Landlord and Wye Valley Butty Bach. There are seats in a walled garden behind and out in front; the church, known as the Cathedral of the Forest, is well worth a visit.

🍴 **Popular bar food includes soup, ploughman's with home-made chutney, sausages with onion gravy, salmon and spinach fishcakes with parsley sauce, pasta with fresh tomato and basil sauce, sizzling pork ribs, steak in ale pie and nice daily specials; you can also choose from the restaurant menu in the bar.** *Starters/Snacks: £5.50 to £6.00. Main Courses: £8.50 to £18.00. Puddings: £4.50*

Free house ~ Licensee Kathryn Horton ~ Real ale ~ Bar food (12-2.30, 6.30(6 Sat)-9.30) ~ Restaurant ~ (01594) 833260 ~ Children welcome ~ Dogs allowed in bar ~ Open 12-3, 6.30(6 Sat)-11; 12-4, 6.30-10.30 Sun

Recommended by John and Gloria Isaacs, Rob and Penny Wakefield, Revd Michael Vockins, Marcus Bristow, John and Tania Wood

NORTH CERNEY
SP0208 MAP 4

Bathurst Arms 🍴 ♍
A435 Cirencester—Cheltenham; GL7 7BZ
GLOUCESTERSHIRE DINING PUB OF THE YEAR

Well run by a convivial landlord with plenty of character in the beamed bar, a fine wine list, super food, and comfortable bedrooms; nearby walks

This very well run pub (freshly refurbished this year) manages to combine its dining side with a proper pubby bar and comfortable bedrooms. Not always easy to do, but the genuinely friendly landlord seems to have got the balance just right. The original beamed and panelled bar has a fireplace at each end (one quite huge and housing an open woodburner), a good mix of old tables and nicely faded chairs, and old-fashioned window seats. There are country tables in an oak-floored room off the bar, as well as winged high-backed settles forming a few booths around other tables; board games and piped music. A whole wall in the restaurant displays the extremely good, carefully chosen wine list (with around ten wines and champagnes by the glass), and they also keep Hook Norton Best, Wickwar Cotswold Way and a guest such as Whittington Cats Whiskers on handpump; local drinks, too. The pleasant riverside garden has picnic-sets sheltered by trees and shrubs, and there are plenty of surrounding walks.

🍴 **Excellent bar food includes sandwiches, pressed terrine of pheasant, foie gras and pistachios with grape salad, slow-cooked duck in a crispy spring roll with mango and pawpaw salsa and sweet chilli sauce, sweet potato, butternut squash and cashew nut in pastry with cauliflower sauce, beef in ale pie, salmon with sesame stir-fried noodles and a pea and white radish broth, roasted loin of gloucester old spot pork with redcurrant gravy, local lamb with anchovy crust and sherry vinegar sauce, and puddings such as ginger and syrup sponge or dark belgian chocolate mousse with amaretti biscuits and orange sauce.** *Starters/Snacks: £3.95 to £6.95. Main Courses: £9.95 to £16.95. Puddings: £4.95 to £6.95*

Free house ~ Licensee James Walker ~ Real ale ~ Bar food (12-2(2.30 Fri and Sat, 3 Sun), 6(7 Sun)-9(9.30 Fri and Sat)) ~ Restaurant ~ (01285) 831281 ~ Children welcome ~ Dogs allowed in bar and bedrooms ~ Open 12-3, 6-11; 12-4, 7-10.30 Sun ~ Bedrooms: £55B/£75B

Recommended by Guy Vowles, Howard and Lorna Lambert, Alan Bulley, V Brogden, G Dunstan, E McCall, T McLean, D Irving, R Huggins, Giles and Annie Francis, R Hebblethwaite, Jude Wright, Chris Flynn, Wendy Jones, Paul and Shirley White, John and Jackie Walsh

---

If a service charge is mentioned prominently on a menu or accommodation terms, you must pay it if service was satisfactory. If service is really bad, you are legally entitled to refuse to pay some or all of the service charge as compensation for not getting the service you might reasonably have expected.

NORTHLEACH   SP1114 MAP 4

Wheatsheaf 🛏

West End; the inn is on your left as you come in following the sign off the A429, just SW of its junction with the A40; GL54 3EZ

Smartly refurbished coaching inn run by three sisters with modern food, real ales and a relaxed atmosphere; lovely bedrooms

Reopened after a refurbishment, this handsome 17th-c stone coaching inn is run by the landlady's three friendly daughters. The big-windowed airy linked rooms have high ceilings, smart leather dining chairs around a mix of tables, flagstones in the central bar and wooden floors in the dining rooms, church candles and light modern paintwork and minimalist décor. Fullers London Pride and Hook Norton on handpump and quite a few wines by the glass. There are seats in the pretty back garden. Cheltenham race course is nearby. More reports on the changes please.

🍴 As well as lunchtime sandwiches, the good bar food includes soup, lightly spiced tiger prawns with pickled cucumber and herb sauce, chicken liver pâté, beefburger with a choice of toppings, thai green chicken curry, fresh cod in beer batter, a pie of the day, bass fillets with citrus crushed potatoes and a chive beurre blanc, roast rack of lamb with rosemary red wine jus, daily specials, and puddings. *Starters/Snacks: £4.50 to £9.95. Main Courses: £9.95 to £19.00. Puddings: £4.95*

Punch ~ Lease Jo Champion ~ Real ale ~ Bar food ~ Restaurant ~ (01451) 860244 ~ Children welcome but must be with an adult ~ Open 11-11; 12-10.30 Sun ~ Bedrooms: £65S/£85S

Recommended by Dennis Jenkin, Mike and Mary Carter, Paul Goldman, Ian and Joan Blackwell

OLDBURY-ON-SEVERN   ST6092 MAP 2

Anchor 🍷 🍺

Village signposted from B4061; BS35 1QA

Bustling country pub with well liked food, a fine choice of drinks; pretty garden and hanging baskets

Bustling and friendly, this is a well run and very popular country pub. The neatly kept lounge has an easy-going atmosphere, modern beams and stone, a mix of tables including an attractive oval oak gateleg, cushioned window seats, winged seats against the wall, oil paintings by a local artist and a big winter log fire. Diners can eat in the lounge or bar area or in the dining room at the back of the building (good for larger groups) and the menu is the same in all rooms. Well priced for the area and kept on handpump in very good condition, the real ales here might include Bass, Butcombe Bitter, Otter Bitter, Theakstons Old Peculier and a weekly guest; 15 wines by the glass and 75 malt whiskies. In summer, you can eat in the pretty garden and the hanging baskets and window boxes are lovely then; boules. They have wheelchair access and a disabled lavatory. Plenty of walks to the River Severn and along the many footpaths and bridleways, and St Arilda's church nearby is interesting, on its odd little knoll with wild flowers among the gravestones (the primroses and daffodils in spring are lovely).

🍴 Good, reasonably priced bar food such as ciabatta sandwiches, ploughman's, soup, twice-baked goats cheese soufflé, crab and scallops gratin, sausages with red onion gravy and marmalade, roasted aubergine and mushroom lasagne, steak and kidney pudding, chicken breast filled with spinach mousse, wrapped in parma ham with a white wine and leek sauce, partridge, pheasant and venison pie, a daily roast, and puddings such as dark and white chocolate mousse and treacle tart. *Starters/Snacks: £3.50 to £5.95. Main Courses: £7.25 to £12.75. Puddings: £3.25*

Free house ~ Licensees Michael Dowdeswell and Mark Sorrell ~ Real ale ~ Bar food (12-2(2.30 Sat, 3 Sun), 6-9(9.30 Fri and Sat)) ~ Restaurant ~ (01454) 413331 ~ Children in dining room only ~ Dogs allowed in bar ~ Open 11.30-3, 6(6.30 winter weekdays)-11; 11.30-11 Sat; 12-11 Sun

Our website is at: www.goodguides.co.uk

Recommended by Mr and Mrs J P Blake, Dr and Mrs M E Wilson, Tom Evans, Lawrence Pearse, Tom and Ruth Rees, Will Stevens, Dr and Mrs C W Thomas, Barry and Anne, C A Hall, Andrew Shore, Maria Williams, Pauline and Philip Darley, Bob and Angela Brooks, Colin and Peggy Wilshire, Donald Godden, James Morrell, Bernard Stradling, J and F Gowers

PAXFORD   SP1837   MAP 4

Churchill Arms 🍽 ♉ 🛏

B4479, SE of Chipping Campden; GL55 6XH

Particularly well run inn, super food and choice of drinks, first-class relaxed service and comfortable bedrooms

Run by professional, hands-on licensees who really care about their customers and their pub, this is – as they themselves put it – 'just the place to enjoy a drink and have some very good food.' They also have three well equipped and comfortable little rooms with lovely views, and offer particularly nice breakfasts. The simply furnished flagstoned bar has low ceilings, assorted old tables and chairs and a snug warmed by a good log fire in its big fireplace; there's also a dining extension. Arkells Moonlight, Hook Norton and a guest like Wye Valley Hereford Pale Ale on handpump, some european and american bottled beers and several wines by the glass (including sweet ones) from a thoughtfully chosen list; excellent service from bright waitresses, board games. There are some seats outside, aunt sally, and there are laminated local maps showing walks of varying lengths in the bar.

🍴 **Delicious, creative food includes good soup, duck confit pancake with leeks and cheese glaze, pressed pork, chicken and sweetbread terrine with roast beetroot and sour cream, peppered loin of tuna with horseradish, lemon and parsley, honey-roast ham with egg, supreme of organic salmon with saffron and parmesan risotto and courgette spaghetti, calves liver with bacon and flageolet beans, assiette of rabbit with madeira, breast of guinea fowl with spinach, chorizo and oven-dried tomato, and puddings such as triple-chocolate torte with raspberry parfait and soft almond meringue with saffron poached pear and apricot parfait. In the best of pub traditions, they don't take bookings, so you must get there early to be sure of a table.** Starters/Snacks: £4.00 to £8.00. Main Courses: £8.00 to £18.00. Puddings: £4.00 to £6.50

Free house ~ Licensees Sonya Kidney and Leo Brooke-Little ~ Real ale ~ Bar food ~ (01386) 594000 ~ Children welcome ~ Open 11.30-3, 6-11; 12-3, 7-10.30 Sun ~ Bedrooms: £40B/£70B

Recommended by Susan and Nigel Brookes, D C Leggatt, R J Herd, Noel Grundy, Laurence and Kim Manning, Heather and Dick Martin

POULTON   SP1001   MAP 4

Falcon

London Road (A417 Fairford—Cirencester); GL7 5HN

Stylishly decorated pub with a fair range of drinks and bar food

A new licensee has taken over this stylishly decorated pub. There's a carpeted bar area on the left (liked by locals), with mixed bar stools, nicely waxed tables, chapel chairs and other more interesting seats, a restrained selection of photographs on watery grey-green walls and maybe fresh flowers on the unobtrusively modern bar counter: Hook Norton Best and Wickwar BOB on handpump, several wines by the glass and local soft drinks. This bar opens through into a similarly furnished dining area with a log fire in the imposing stone fireplace and steps up to a further back dining room (and a view into the kitchen); piped music. More reports please.

🍴 **Bar food now includes sandwiches, chicken liver parfait with onion marmalade, torbay crab cake with home-made mayonnaise, fillet of salmon with carrot and courgette linguini and basil cream, wild mushroom risotto with truffle oil, beer-battered haddock, gloucester old spot chop with grain mustard mash and sage and apple jus, and puddings such as chocolate and hazelnut brownie with chocolate sauce and sticky toffee pudding** with clotted cream; there's also a good value two-course set lunch. *Starters/Snacks: £3.00 to £8.00. Main Courses: £8.00 to £20.00. Puddings: £5.00 to £8.00*

Free house ~ Licensee Steve Jenner ~ Real ale ~ Bar food (12-2.30, 5.30-9(10 Sat); not Sun evening or Mon) ~ Restaurant ~ (01285) 850844 ~ Children welcome ~ Dogs allowed in bar ~ Open 11-3, 5-11; 12-10.30 Sun; closed Sun evening, Mon; 26 Dec-1 Jan

Recommended by Guy Vowles, Richard and Sheila Fitton, Richard Atherton, Adrian White, Keith and Sue Ward, Bernard Stradling, Michael Dallas, J Crosby, Mr and Mrs A H Young

SAPPERTON
SO9403 MAP 4

Bell ⊕ ⚲ ◧

Village signposted from A419 Stroud—Cirencester; OS Sheet 163 map reference 948033; GL7 6LE

Super pub with beamed cosy rooms, a really good mix of customers, delicious food, local ales, and very pretty courtyard

We think the words of one of our respected readers rather sum things up here. 'I have no burning desire to own a pub, but if I did, this splendid place would fit the bill rather nicely.' The licensees put a lot of hard work and careful thought into how they run their pub and judging by how many enthusiastic reports we get, they've more than succeeded. There is quite an emphasis on the excellent food but there are plenty of local drinkers too and this year Harry's Bar has been refurbished with big cushion-strewn sofas, benches and armchairs where you can read the daily papers with a pint in front of the woodburning stove – or simply have a pre-dinner drink. The two other cosy rooms have stripped beams, a nice mix of wooden tables and chairs, country prints and modern art on stripped stone walls, one or two attractive rugs on the flagstones, fresh flowers and open fires. They support only local breweries and the four ales on handpump might be Bath Ales SPA, Butcombe Bitter, Uley Old Spot and a guest such as Stroud Budding or Wickwar Cotswold Way; over 20 wines by the glass from a large and diverse wine list with very helpful notes, Ashton Press cider, 20 malt whiskies, several armagnacs and cognacs and local soft drinks. Harry the springer spaniel is very sociable but must not be fed for health reasons; the gents' has schoolboy humour cartoons on the walls. There are tables out on a small front lawn and in a partly covered and very pretty courtyard, for eating outside. Horses have their own tethering rail (and bucket of water).

⊞ **Bar food is exceptionally good and imaginative.** New this year is the lighter lunch menu: sandwiches, 'grazing boards' of antipasti, risotto of crab with a free-range poached egg, very popular home-made burger with bacon and cheese topping and a daily main course such as deep-fried fish and chips, steak and kidney pudding or cottage pie; in the evening there's home-made tagliatelle with goats cheese, wilted spinach and pine kernels, seared scallops with a cauliflower purée and a bacon and chicory salad, gloucester old spot belly pork with parsnip mash and saffron and apple jelly, ginger and chilli pot-roasted free-range chicken breast, chump of lamb with rosemary and root vegetables, and puddings like caramel mousse with apple fritters and vanilla brûlée with a pineapple turnover; super complimentary home-made bread and olives, and they sell their own home-made chutneys and jellies. *Starters/Snacks: £4.50 to £7.95. Main Courses: £9.95 to £20.00. Puddings: £6.75*

Free house ~ Licensees Paul Davidson and Pat LeJeune ~ Real ale ~ Bar food ~ Restaurant ~ (01285) 760298 ~ Children allowed but must be over 10 in evenings ~ Dogs welcome ~ Open 11-3, 6.30-11; 12-3, 7-10.30 Sun; closed some winter Mons; 25 Dec

Recommended by Graham Oddey, Dr A J and Mrs Tompsett, Brenda and Stuart Naylor, David Morgan, David Gunn, John Morgan, Mr and Mrs J Brown, Carol Mills, Mrs L Aquilina, Adrian White, Richard and Jean Phillips, Mr and Mrs A J Hudson, E McCall, T McLean, D Irving, R Huggins, Philip and Jude Simmons, Julie and Bill Ryan, Michael Doswell, Simon and Sally Small, John Holroyd, Pauline and Philip Darley, J Crosby, R S Jalbot, Bernard Stradling, John Balfour

---

Post Office address codings confusingly give the impression that some pubs are in Gloucestershire, when they're really in Warwickshire (which is where we list them).

SOUTHROP   SP2003   MAP 4

Swan 🍴 🍷

Village signposted off A361 Lechlade—Burford; GL7 3NU

Creeper-covered pub with proper village bar, consistently imaginative food, a fine choice of drinks and enthusiastic landlord

The hard-working and enthusiastic licensee of this creeper-covered old place is very keen that, despite serving consistently good interesting food, this should remain a proper village pub that is actively involved in village life. The chatty public bar is very much for those wanting a pint and 'a good chin wag' and the skittle alley has been refurbished to accommodate their three skittle teams – though diners may use it when there are no matches. The charmingly refurbished low-ceilinged front dining rooms have flagstones, antiques and attractive pictures, well spaced tables, a log fire and a thriving upmarket atmosphere. Hook Norton, Wadworths 6X and a guest like St Austells Tribute on handpump, a large collection of malt whiskies and over 20 wines by the glass including champagne and sweet wines from an extensive list with helpful, detailed notes. There are tables in the sheltered back garden and the village is pretty, especially at daffodil time.

🍴 Using produce from their own kitchen garden and their own pork, the inventive – if not cheap – food might include lunchtime filled baguettes, ploughman's, smoked salmon and scrambled eggs, home-baked ham and eggs, and deep-fried pollack with tartare sauce with more elaborate choices such as interesting soups, pork and green peppercorn terrine with fig chutney, crab vinaigrette, confit tuna salad with fennel, cherry tomatoes, tapenade aïoli and a soft boiled egg, linguini with prosciutto cream, broad beans, peas and mint, fillet of bass with crushed jerusalem artichoke, pea and fresh black truffle vinaigrette, stir-fried pork with shi-itake mushrooms, mangetout, coriander and sticky jasmine rice, and puddings like vanilla bavarois with mixed berry compote and hot chocolate fondant with vanilla ice-cream; good value two- and three-course set lunch menus. *Starters/Snacks: £4.95 to £7.50. Main Courses: £8.50 to £18.50. Puddings: £5.00 to £6.50*

Free house ~ Licensee Graham Williams ~ Real ale ~ Bar food ~ Restaurant ~ (01367) 850205 ~ Children welcome ~ Dogs allowed in bar ~ Open 12-3(3.30 Sat and Sun), 6-11

Recommended by Richard Stancomb, Graham Oddey, Richard and Sheila Fitton, Noel Grundy, Paul and Shirley White, Keith and Sue Ward, E McCall, T McLean, D Irving, R Huggins, John Morgan

TETBURY   ST8494   MAP 4

Gumstool 🍴 🍷 🛏

At Calcot Manor Hotel; A4135 W; GL8 8YJ

Civilised bar with relaxed atmosphere (part of very smart Calcot Manor Hotel), super choice of drinks, and delicious food

Consistently reliable and civilised, this bar/brasserie is attached to the very smart Calcot Manor Hotel. It has an informal and relaxed atmosphere (and they are genuinely helpful and kind to children) and keeps Butcombe Bitter, Greene King IPA, Uley Best, and Wickwar Cotswold Way on handpump, a dozen interesting wines by the glass and lots of malt whiskies. The stylish layout is well divided to give a feeling of intimacy without losing the overall sense of contented bustle: flagstones, elegant wooden dining chairs and tables, well chosen pictures and drawings on mushroom-coloured walls, and leather armchairs in front of the big log fire; piped music and board games. Westonbirt Arboretum is not far away.

🍴 Imaginative bar food includes sandwiches, ham hock and bacon terrine with piccalilli, warm crab and leek tart with lemon dressing, portobello mushroom with toasted goats cheese, confit onion and dried tomato, chicken livers on toast with a garlic, shallot, tarragon and mustard cream, grilled halloumi cheese, polenta and wood-roasted mediterranean vegetables, crispy battered fresh cod, free-range pork and leek sausages with beer gravy, beef bourguignon, half a roasted pheasant with bacon and bread sauce, daily specials, and puddings such as marbled chocolate brownie with vanilla seed ice-cream and toffee crème brûlée. *Starters/Snacks: £6.25 to £9.20. Main Courses: £8.25 to £14.25. Puddings: £5.25 to £7.95*

Free house ~ Licensees Paul Sadler and Richard Ball ~ Real ale ~ Bar food (12-2(4 Sun), 5.30-9.30) ~ Restaurant ~ (01666) 890391 ~ Children welcome ~ Open 12-11(10.30 Sun) ~ Bedrooms: £180B/£205B

Recommended by Mrs L Aquilina, Bernard Stradling, KC, Dr and Mrs C W Thomas, Andy and Claire Barker, Tom and Ruth Rees, Guy Vowles

Snooty Fox ♀ 🛏

Market Place; small residents' car park, nearby pay & display; free car park some way down hill; GL8 8DD

Smart hotel with unstuffy bar, real ales, lots of wines by the glass, and popular food

There's a good mix of customers in the high-ceilinged main bar on the left here, and although part of a hotel, it does have a bustling unstuffy atmosphere and three real ales on handpump: Moles Best, Otter Bitter and Wickwar Cotswold Way. Also, 20 wines by the glass (including rosé champagne as well as 'ordinary'), a fine collection of armagnac, cognac, calvados, and port, and an espresso machine; good service from neat young staff and unobtrusive piped jazz. This front room – stripped stone, like much of the rest of the ground floor – has comfortable sturdy leather-armed chairs round the cast-iron tripod tables on its carpet, a big log fireplace flanked by an imposing pair of brass flambeaux, brass ceiling fans, and Ronald Searle pony-club cartoons; board games. Behind is a similar room, with a colourful rug on bare boards and a leather sofa among other seats. On the right a smaller quieter room now has church candles on the dining tables and subdued lighting. Outside, a sheltered entryway has teak tables and chairs facing the ancient central covered market. More reports please.

🍴 Well liked bar food includes sandwiches and filled baguettes, soup, corned beef hash with eggy bread, macaroni cheese, home-cooked ham and free-range eggs, gloucester old spot sausages with onion gravy, and all-day breakfast; you may also choose from the bistro menu which might have chicken liver parfait with tomato chutney, prawn and crab thermidor, pasta with wild mushroom, avocado, tarragon and cheese cream sauce, a pie of the day and a daily fish dish and slow-cooked aberdeen angus with cured ham dumplings. Puddings like banoffi stack with banana crème anglaise and steamed white chocolate pudding with chocolate Baileys cream. *Starters/Snacks: £3.75 to £9.50. Main Courses: £8.75 to £19.00. Puddings: £4.95*

Free house ~ Licensee Marc Gibbons ~ Real ale ~ Bar food (12-2(3 Sun), 6-9.30(9 Sun)) ~ Restaurant ~ (01666) 502436 ~ Children welcome ~ Dogs allowed in bar and bedrooms ~ Open 11-11; 12-10.30 Sun ~ Bedrooms: £79B/£95B

Recommended by Mrs Anne Callender, John Dwane, E McCall, T McLean, D Irving, R Huggins, Nick and Meriel Cox

Trouble House ♀

A433 towards Cirencester, near Cherington turn; GL8 8SG

Smart and friendly bars with customers to match, an ambitious menu, good drinks, and attentive service

Most customers come to this rather smart place – popular with the country set – for a special meal out. Furnishings are mainly close-set stripped pine or oak tables with chapel chairs, some wheelback chairs and the odd library chair, and there are attractive mainly modern country prints on the cream or butter-coloured walls. On the left is a parquet-floored room with a chesterfield by the big stone fireplace, a hop-girt mantelpiece and more hops hung from one of its two big black beams. In the small saggy-beamed middle room, you can commandeer one of the bar stools where they have Wadworths IPA and 6X on handpump, and a good wine list with helpful notes and 17 wines (including champagne) by the glass; piped music and attentive service. You can also sit out at picnic-sets on the gravel courtyard behind.

🍴 Up to now the food has included imaginative dishes from an interesting menu; as we went to press a new licensee took over – he is a chef but this is his first pub so any news would be most helpful. *Starters/Snacks: £6.50 to £12.00. Main Courses: £15.00 to £19.00. Puddings: £6.00 to £9.50*

Wadworths ~ Licensees Martin and Neringa Caws ~ Real ale ~ Bar food (not Sun evening or Mon) ~ Restaurant ~ (01666) 502206 ~ Children allowed away from bar area; must be over 10 in evening ~ Dogs welcome ~ Open 11.30-3, 6.30(7 winter)-11; 12-3 Sun; closed Sun evening, all day Mon; Christmas and New Year period

Recommended by BOB

TODENHAM   SP2436   MAP 4

Farriers Arms ♀

Between A3400 and A429 N of Moreton-in-Marsh; GL56 9PF

Fine views from well run country pub with interesting décor, popular food, and friendly licensees

This is a well run, unspoilt pub with a helpful and friendly landlady. The bar has nice wonky white plastered walls, hops on the beams, fine old polished flagstones by the stone bar counter and a woodburner in a huge inglenook fireplace. A tiny little room off to the side (full of old books and interesting old photographs) can seat parties of ten people. Hook Norton Best and Wye Valley Butty Bach on handpump, and ten wines by the glass; piped music, darts and board games. The pub has fine views over the surrounding countryside from the back garden and there are a couple of tables with views of the church on a small terrace by the quiet little road; there's an aunt sally pitch in the car park. Good surrounding walks.

🍴 Well thought of, nicely presented bar food includes sandwiches, soup, chicken liver parfait with cumberland sauce, pigeon breast, bacon and pine nut tossed salad, ham and eggs, beer-battered cod, roast vegetables and goats cheese cannelloni with pesto and parmesan cream, pork tenderloin wrapped in parma ham with grain mustard mash and thyme gravy, daily specials and Sunday roast beef. *Starters/Snacks: £4.00 to £6.00. Main Courses: £9.00 to £17.00. Puddings: £4.00 to £5.50*

Free house ~ Licensees Nigel and Louise Kirkwood ~ Real ale ~ Bar food (12-2(2.30 Sun), 7-9(9.30 Fri and Sat)) ~ Restaurant ~ (01608) 650901 ~ Children welcome ~ Dogs allowed in bar ~ Open 12-3, 6.30-11; 12-3, 7-10.30 Sun

Recommended by Martin and Pauline Jennings, Susan and John Douglas, Peter and Jean Hoare, Clive and Fran Dutson, Ian and Nita Cooper, Mike and Mary Carter, John Holroyd, H O Dickinson, Andy and Claire Barker, Alun Evans, Paul Goldman, C and R Bromage, Paul Butler

UPPER ODDINGTON   SP2225   MAP 4

Horse & Groom ♀

Village signposted from A436 E of Stow-on-the-Wold; GL56 0XH

Pretty cotswold stone inn with attractive garden and a good choice of local beers and other drinks

In fine weather you can sit on the terrace and in the pretty garden of this attractive cotswold stone inn where there are grape vines bounded by dry-stone walls and cottages. Inside, the bar has pale polished flagstones, a handsome antique oak box settle among other more modern seats, oak beams in the ochre ceiling, stripped stone walls, and an inglenook fireplace. Wickwar BOB and Wye Valley Best and Hereford Pale Ale on handpump, 30 wines by the glass (including english wines), farm cider and local soft drinks. More reports please.

🍴 Ambitious bar food includes lunchtime sandwiches, balsamic, red onion marmalade and marinated anchovy tart with salsa verde dressing, hot smoked potted salmon with pickled cucumber ribbons, organic blue cheese cheesecake with pickled walnuts, trio of gloucester old spot sausages with onion gravy, shank of lamb with parsnip purée, puy lentils, pancetta and thyme jus, seared bass fillets with dill and leek risotto, daily specials, and puddings such as iced banana parfait with butterscotch sauce and glazed lemon tart. *Starters/Snacks: £4.95 to £7.50. Main Courses: £10.95 to £19.95. Puddings: £5.75 to £7.95*

Free house ~ Licensees Simon and Sally Jackson ~ Real ale ~ Bar food (12-2, 6.30-9.30) ~ Restaurant ~ (01451) 830584 ~ Children welcome ~ Open 12-3, 5.30-11; 12-11 Sat; 12-3.30, 5.30-10.30 Sun; closed first two weeks Jan ~ Bedrooms: £73S/£83S(£93B)

Recommended by Keith and Sue Ward, Graham and Doreen Holden, Martin and Pauline Jennings, Bernard Stradling, Alun Evans, P Michelson, Dr and Mrs F Murgatroyd, Graham Oddey, Joan and Tony Walker

WOODCHESTER   SO8302   MAP 4

Ram ◖

High Street, South Woodchester; off A46 S of Stroud; GL5 5EL

Half a dozen interesting ales and spectacular views, a friendly landlord and fair-priced food in attractive country pub

The welcoming and obliging landlord of this attractive country pub keeps his six real ales on handpump particularly well. Changing regularly, these might include Archers Village, Butcombe Bitter, Cotswold Spring Olde English Rose, Otter Ale, Stroud Budding and Uley Old Spot. The relaxed L-shaped beamed bar has a nice mix of traditional furnishings (including several cushioned antique panelled settles) on bare boards, stripped stonework, and three open fires. There are seats outside on the terrace and spectacular valley views; in summer they hold various events out here – open air theatre, live music and so forth.

🍴 Good value, enjoyable bar food includes sandwiches, soup, king prawns in filo pastry, tomato and mozzarella bruschetta, spinach and ricotta cannelloni, old spot sausages with mash and onion gravy, steak in ale pie, cold poached salmon with lemon and dill dressing, chargrilled chicken breast with mango salsa, and puddings such as treacle sponge with custard or white chocolate and raspberry cheesecake; on Monday-Thursday they offer a £5 main course. *Starters/Snacks: £3.00 to £4.25. Main Courses: £5.00 to £12.95. Puddings: £3.50 to £3.95*

Free house ~ Licensee Tim Mullen ~ Real ale ~ Bar food ~ (01453) 873329 ~ Children welcome ~ Dogs allowed in bar ~ Open 11-11

Recommended by Andy and Claire Barker, Andrew Shore, Maria Williams, Dr A J and Mrs Tompsett, Guy Vowles, E McCall, T McLean, D Irving, R Huggins

LUCKY DIP

Besides the fully inspected pubs, you might like to try these Lucky Dips recommended to us and described by readers (if you do, please send us reports: www.goodguides.co.uk).

ALDERTON [SP9933]
Gardeners Arms GL20 8NL [Beckford Rd, off B4077 Tewkesbury—Stow]: Thatched Tudor pub with snug bars and informal restaurant, decent home-made food from filled baps and baked potatoes to bistro dishes, fresh fish and good Sun roast, well kept Greene King and guest beers, above-average wines, hospitable landlady and good service, log fire; may be piped music; dogs and children welcome, tables on sheltered terrace, good-sized well kept garden with boules *(B M Eldridge, LYM)*

ALDSWORTH [SP1510]
☆ *Sherborne Arms* GL54 3RB [B4425 Burford—Cirencester]: Cheerfully unpretentious, with good reasonably priced pubby food, four mainstream real ales, farm cider, quick service, beams, stripped stone, central log fire between smallish bar and big dining area, attractive conservatory, walking sticks for sale, games area with darts and lots of

board games; piped music, games machine; dogs welcomed kindly, disabled access and facilities, pleasant front garden *(Jonathan Martin, E McCall, T McLean, D Irving, R Huggins, David Gunn, BB, R S Jalbot)*

AMBERLEY [SO8401]
☆ *Black Horse* GL5 5AL [off A46 Stroud—Nailsworth; Littleworth]: Easy-going local with spectacular views from conservatory (foreground may be more workaday), Greene King IPA and Wells & Youngs Bombardier, open fire, flagstones and high-backed settles, lots of cheerful sporting pictures (and TV for big matches), large family area on left (huge food choice), games room; plenty of tables on pleasant back terrace with barbecue, more on secluded lawn *(LYM, R B Gardiner, Colin McKerrow, Dr A Y Drummond, E McCall, T McLean, D Irving, R Huggins, Lawrence Pearse, Gloria Bax, John Beeken, John Saville)*

ANDOVERSFORD [SP0219]

☆ *Royal Oak* GL54 4HR [signed just off A40; Gloucester Rd]: Cosy and attractive beamed village pub, lots of stripped stone, nice galleried raised dining room beyond big central open fire, good choice of real ales inc Hook Norton Best, good coffee, prompt friendly service; popular quiz night, tables in garden *(Mr and Mrs J Brown, Brian McBurnie, BB)*

APPERLEY [SO8528]

☆ *Coal House* GL19 4DN [village signed off B4213 S of Tewkesbury; Gabb Lane]: Light and airy pub in splendid riverside position, welcoming staff, Hook Norton Best and a couple of other interesting changing ales, plenty of blackboards for enjoyable inexpensive food from baguettes to steak sizzlers, two dining areas, walkers welcome; plenty of tables on front terrace and lawn with Severn views, play area, moorings *(Lawrence Pearse, BB, Neil and Anita Christopher)*

ARLINGHAM [SO7011]

☆ *Old Passage* GL2 7JR [Passage Rd]: Good interesting food esp fish and seafood in upmarket restaurant rather than pub (they do keep a real ale, but you can't really go just for a drink – the serving counter is in the restaurant area), friendly helpful staff, crisp décor; beautiful setting, french windows to pleasant terrace and big garden down to River Severn *(Mr and Mrs A J Hudson, BB, Dr A J and Mrs Tompsett)*

AUST [ST5788]

Boars Head BS35 4AX [½ mile from M48 junction 1, off Avonmouth rd]: Ivy-covered pub handy for the 'old' Severn bridge, with dark furniture in series of linked rooms and alcoves, beams and some stripped stone, huge log fire, quick friendly service, real ales such as Bath Gem, Courage Best and Otter, good house wines, wide food choice from baguettes to steak; piped music; children in eating area away from bar, dogs on lead in bar, pretty sheltered garden *(Mr and Mrs A J Hudson, Donald Godden, Ian Phillips, LYM, Colin Moore, Donna and Roger)*

AWRE [SO7008]

☆ *Red Hart* GL14 1EW [off A48 S of Newnham]: Unusually tall brick-built village inn with neat heavy-beamed and flagstoned bar, illuminated well and other interesting features, real ale, farm cider, good wines by the glass, cheerful service, friendly atmosphere, board games; piped music; children and dogs welcome, picnic-sets out in front, comfortable bedrooms, good breakfast, cl Sun evening and Mon/Tues lunchtimes in winter, open all day Sat *(David Ashton, Liz and Tony Colman, LYM, Bob Richardson, Bob and Margaret Holder, Rose Warwick, James Stephens, John and Alison Hamilton, J Crosby, Dr A J and Mrs Tompsett)*

BERRY HILL [SO5712]

Gamekeeper GL16 7QP [Glencarn Place, Five Acres (A4136, just W of B4432)]: Friendly pub with reasonably priced filling pubby food from sandwiches and baked potatoes up, well kept real ale; children welcome *(Mr and Mrs G Ives)*

BIBURY [SP1106]

☆ *Swan* GL7 5NW [B4425]: Hotel in lovely spot facing River Coln, good welcoming service and well kept Hook Norton Best in comfortable and attractive side bar used by locals, exemplary bar stools, blazing fire, nice modern adjoining brasserie with enjoyable up-to-date food, smart formal dining room; teak tables out on heated flagstoned terrace, pleasant waterside garden, luxurious bedrooms *(Keith and Sue Ward, V Brogden, BB, E McCall, T McLean, D Irving, R Huggins)*

BIRDLIP [SO9316]

Air Balloon GL4 8JY [A417/A436 roundabout]: Busy usefully placed chain dining pub, standard value food from sandwiches, baguettes and wraps up all day, changing ales such as Hook Norton Old Hooky, helpful service, many levels and alcoves inc separate restaurant and brasserie, pubbier front corner with open fire, beams and stripped stone; unobtrusive piped music; tables, some covered, on heated terrace and in garden with play area, open all day *(Ian and Joan Blackwell, Tony and Caroline Elwood, Adrian Johnson)*

BISHOP'S CLEEVE [SO9527]

Swallow GL52 8DR [Bishops Drive]: Large Chinese-run brick-built estate pub, straightforward main bar with Sharps Doom Bar, good value generous cantonese food in restaurant, takeaways too *(Guy Vowles)*

BISLEY [SO9006]

Stirrup Cup GL6 7BL [Cheltenham Rd]: Long rambling well furnished local with three well kept ales such as Wickwar Cotswold Way, good modestly priced food from sandwiches and good baguettes to generous Sunday roasts, prompt friendly service, decent wines, no piped music; dogs welcome *(Guy Vowles)*

BOURTON-ON-THE-WATER [SP1620]

Duke of Wellington GL54 2BY [Sherbourne St]: Large stone-built pub under friendly newish management, good value pubby food, well kept real ales, relaxing open-plan carpeted bar with leather sofas, back dining room, log fire; garden tables, bedrooms *(Ted George, Roger and Pauline Pearce)*

Old Manse GL54 2BX [Victoria St]: River Windrush view from front garden and one end of long turkey-carpeted beamed bar (over-21s only), good choice of enjoyable food from all-day doorstep sandwiches up, Greene King IPA and Abbot, friendly attentive staff, big log fire, attractive old prints, bookshelves, some stripped stone, pretty restaurant (children allowed here); TV, machines, piped music or juke box; good bedrooms, open all day *(George Atkinson, BB, K H Frostick, Keith and Sue Ward)*

BROAD CAMPDEN [SP1537]

☆ *Bakers Arms* GL55 6UR [off B4081]: Cheerful and respectable traditional pub with real ales such as Donnington BB, Salopian, Stanway Stanney, Timothy Taylors Landlord and Wells & Youngs Bombardier, welcoming licensees and prompt service, well priced and wholesome straightforward food (all day in summer) from lunchtime sandwiches and baguettes up, inglenook in snug beamed and stripped stone bar, beamed and stripped stone dining room, traditional games; no credit cards, no dogs; children in eating areas, tables out on terrace and garden behind with play area, open all day Fri-Sun and summer *(Keith and Sue Ward, Noel Grundy, Barry and Anne, LYM, Paul and Shirley White, Brian and Anita Randall, H O Dickinson, Theocsbrian, B M Eldridge, Paul Humphreys)*

BROADWELL [SP2027]

☆ *Fox* GL56 OUF [off A429 2 miles N of Stow-on-the-Wold]: Relaxing pub overlooking broad green in pleasant village, welcoming attentive service, good range of homely pub food (not Sun evening) from baguettes to popular Sun lunch, good fresh veg, low-priced Donnington BB and SBA, decent wines, good summer lemonade, nice coffee, stripped stone and flagstones, beams hung with jugs, log fire, darts, dominoes and chess, plain public bar with pool room extension, pleasant separate restaurant; may be piped music; tables out on gravel, good big back family-friendly garden with aunt sally, meadow behind for Caravan Club members *(Lawrence Pearse, BB, Keith and Sue Ward)*

BROCKHAMPTON [SP0322]

☆ *Craven Arms* GL54 5XQ [off A436 Andoversford—Naunton]: Attractive 17th-c inn nicely tucked away in hillside village with lovely views and walks, friendly and sociable licensees, good value food in biggish linked eating areas off smaller bar servery, well kept ales such as Sharps and Tetleys, low beams, thick roughly coursed stone walls, some tiled flooring, mainly pine funiture with some wall settles, tub chairs, shove-ha'penny; children welcome, sizeable garden, comfortable bedrooms, cl Sun evening *(LYM, Brian McBurnie, Keith and Sue Ward, Neil and Anita Christopher)*

BROCKWEIR [SO5301]

Brockweir Inn NP16 7NG [signed just off A466 Chepstow—Monmouth]: Proper country local well placed for Wye Valley walkers (but no muddy boots), beams and stripped stonework, quarry tiles, sturdy settles, woodburner, snugger carpeted alcoves, real ales such as Adnams Broadside, Butcombe and Hook Norton Best, Stowford Press cider, friendly landlord, upstairs restaurant, conservatory; pool, machines and piped music in public bar; dogs allowed, children in eating area, small garden with interesting covered terrace; open all day Sat, bedrooms *(LYM, Bob and Margaret Holder)*

CAMBRIDGE [SO7403]

George GL2 7AL [3 miles from M5 junction 13 – A38 towards Bristol]: Big, busy and welcoming, with two spacious dining areas, good value generous food from filled rolls and baked potatoes up inc bargain lunches, well kept Adnams and Wickwar BOB, helpful well organised service, log fire; garden with barbecues, fowl pen and play area, also pleasant small camp site, handy for Slimbridge wildfowl centre, open all day Sun *(Neil and Anita Christopher, Michael and Jenny Back, Mike and Mary Clark)*

CAMP [SO9111]

☆ *Fostons Ash* GL6 7ES [B4070 Birdlip—Stroud, junction with Calf Way]: Cotswold inn recently reopened by small local group after attractive reworking as open-plan dining pub, good food inc interesting lunchtime sandwiches and imaginative light dishes, Greene King IPA and Wickwar Cotswold Way and BOB, decent wines by the glass, friendly efficient young staff, log fire, one end with settees and easy chairs; tables in garden with heated terrace and play area, good walks *(David Morgan, Neil and Anita Christopher, Guy Vowles)*

CHARFIELD [ST7192]

Pear Tree GL12 8TP [Wotton Rd (B4058, but at W end of village; handy for M5 junction 14)]: Simple friendly two-bar village local with welcoming landlady, well kept ales such as Hook Norton, Hop Back and Wickwar, games room; open all day wknds *(Michael and Jenny Back)*

CHARLTON KINGS [SO9619]

Owl GL53 8EB [Cirencester Rd (A435)]: Friendly open-plan extended pub, recently refurbished as airy family dining pub, with Brakspears, Flowers and Fullers London Pride, low-priced simple food; children welcome *(BB, Jude Wright, Nick and Meriel Cox)*

CHELTENHAM [SO9421]

Bath Tavern GL53 7JT [Bath Rd]: Compact and welcoming bay-windowed local with well kept Bath Spa and Gem, good choice of wines by the glass, bargain generous pubby food *(Andy and Claire Barker)*

Jolly Brewmaster GL50 2EZ [Painswick Rd]: Open-plan linked areas around big semi-circular serving bar, good range of ales such as Archers, Caledonian Deuchars IPA, Donnington SBA and Hook Norton Best, growing number of farm ciders, perhaps a perry, friendly obliging young staff, log fires; dogs welcome, coachyard tables *(Guy Vowles)*

☆ *Plough* GL52 3BG [Mill St, Prestbury]: Well preserved thatched village pub opp church, cosy and comfortable front lounge, service from corner corridor hatch in locals' charming and basic flagstoned back tap room, grandfather clock and big log fire, consistently friendly service, Adnams Best and Broadside and Wells & Youngs Bombardier tapped from the cask, Stowford Press farm cider, ready-filled rolls, perhaps a simple hot dish; outstanding good-sized flower-filled back garden with immaculate boules pitch *(Guy Vowles, Donna and Roger, Jason Chess, M Thomas, B M Eldridge)*

Restoration GL50 1DX [High St]: Long rambling 16th-c pub, much restored and useful for the two main shopping arcades, with lots of beams and dim-lit bric-a-brac, some leather sofas as well as simpler wooden furniture, good bustling atmosphere, St Austell Tribute and Wychwood Hobgoblin, good coffee and wines by the glass, daily papers, raised dining area with decent food inc good baguettes, friendly young staff; piped music, TV *(Michael Dandy, Bruce and Sharon Eden)*

Sudeley Arms GL52 2PN [Prestbury Rd]: Chatty traditional pub with homely arch-divided lounge, proper public bar, real ales such as local Goffs Jouster, Timothy Taylors Landlord and two or three changing guests, darts, cards; open all day *(Pete Baker)*

Swan GL50 1DX [High St]: Friendly local with good value proper pub food, three well kept changing real ales *(Alun Beach)*

CHIPPING CAMPDEN [SP1539]

☆ **Kings Arms** GL55 6AW [High St]: Small recently refurbished hotel now calling itself just Kings, food from lunchtime sandwiches and pubby dishes to more elaborate evening choice, helpful and friendly young staff, Hook Norton beers, good choice of wines by the glass, good log fire, daily papers, charming fresh contemporary décor in bar/brasserie and separate restaurant; secluded back garden with picnic-sets and terrace tables, 12 comfortable bedrooms, open all day Sat *(Michael Dandy, LYM)*

☆ **Lygon Arms** GL55 6HB [High St]: Welcoming and obliging staff in appealing low-beamed bar with open fires, stripped stone and lots of horse pictures, wide choice of good value food till late evening from baked potatoes and good sandwiches to interesting more pricy dishes, real ales such as Hook Norton Old Hooky and Wye Valley HBA, small separate back restaurant; children welcome, tables in shady courtyard, comfortable well equipped beamed bedrooms, good breakfast, open all day wknds and summer *(Alain and Rose Foote, Barry and Anne, Michael Dandy, LYM, Derek and Sylvia Stephenson, Donna and Roger)*

Noel Arms GL55 6AT [High St]: Handsome old inn with two popular bars, polished oak settles, attractive old tables, armour, casks hanging from beams, antique prints, tools and traps on stripped stone walls, decent food from sandwiches to some interesting dishes, two Hook Norton ales and a guest such as Purity UBU, coal fire, good restaurant; children welcome, tables in enclosed courtyard, nice bedrooms, good breakfast *(LYM, Michael Dandy, Derek and Sylvia Stephenson)*

☆ **Red Lion** GL55 6AS [Lower High St]: Hop-hung beams, flagstones and stripped stone in several peaceful linked rooms, enjoyable fresh food reasonably priced for the area from baguettes up, friendly efficient service, Greene King IPA and Old Speckled Hen, decent wine choice, fine range of malt

whiskies, log fires, roomy eating area and upstairs dining room; may be quiet piped classical music, big-screen sports TV and pool in games bar; picnic-sets in sheltered back courtyard, five comfortable character bedrooms *(Michael Dandy, Paul Goldman, Neil and Anita Christopher)*

CIRENCESTER [SP0202]

☆ **Corinium** GL7 2DG [Dollar St/Gloucester St]: Civilised and comfortable, with big log fire, attractive antique coaching prints, good mix of tables, sofas and small armchairs, real ales inc strongish ones, decent wines, bar food from sandwiches, baguettes and baked potatoes up, nicely decorated restaurant; no piped music; entrance through charming courtyard with tables, attractive back garden, good bedrooms *(E McCall, T McLean, D Irving, R Huggins, BB)*

Drillmans Arms GL7 2JY [Gloucester Rd, Stratton]: Genuine and popular old two-room local, friendly and relaxing, with low beams, log fires, four real ales inc a guest beer, reasonable food, skittle alley doubling as eating area; tables out by small car park *(E McCall, T McLean, D Irving, R Huggins)*

Fleece GL7 2NZ [Market Pl]: Substantial old hotel, good choice of bar food from baguettes and baked potatoes up, helpful obliging staff, real ales such as Butcombe and Hook Norton Best, bay window looking up market place to parish church, substantial restaurant; terrace tables, bedrooms *(June and Robin Savage, BB)*

Plough GL7 2LB [Stratton]: Arkells pub with good service, real ales, good value food inc generous ham ploughman's and OAP bargain lunches, rustic pine tables in open-plan bar, separate dining room *(Guy Vowles, E McCall, T McLean, D Irving, R Huggins)*

☆ **Twelve Bells** GL7 1EA [Lewis Lane]: Cheery backstreet pub made distinctive by Bob the no-nonsense landlord, his son's cooking – bargain generous fresh food inc local produce and some unusual dishes lunchtime and early evening (may be goose around Christmas), and Abbey Bellringer and five quickly changing interesting guest beers all in fine condition; good coal fires in all three small old-fashioned low-ceilinged rooms, sturdy pine tables and rugs on quarry tiles in back dining area, pictures for sale, clay pipe collection; piped music may be loud; small sheltered unsmart back terrace *(Giles and Annie Francis, E McCall, T McLean, D Irving, R Huggins, Guy Vowles, Roger Fox, Mike Pugh, Pete Baker, Canon Michael Bourdeaux, BB)*

CLEARWELL [SO5708]

Butchers Arms GL16 8JS [High St]: Large and attractive old stone-built pub with well kept real ales, enjoyable reasonably priced food, friendly staff, subdued red upholstery, hops and fairy lights on dark low beams, big log fire, separate dining room; children welcome, tables in neat sheltered courtyard with pond and flowers *(David Knowles)*

CLIFFORD'S MESNE [SO6922]

☆ *Yew Tree* GL18 1JS [out of Newent, past Falconry Centre]: Large open-plan divided pub on slopes of May Hill (NT), relaxed atmosphere and genial staff, enjoyable home-made food (not Sun evening to Tues lunchtime) from good ciabattas up, two real ales, good house wines; children welcome, tables out on sunny terrace, play area *(Mike and Mary Carter, B M Eldridge)*

COATES [SO9600]

☆ *Tunnel House* GL7 6PW [follow Tarlton signs (right then left) from village, pub up rough track on right after rly bridge; OS Sheet 163 map ref 965005]: Rambling country pub, quite a favourite, with beams, flagstones and log fire in homely and idiosyncratic original bar, more conventional pastel-décor eating extension and back conservatory (fills quickly), four real ales such as Archers, Wickwar Cotswold Way and Wye Valley, Stowford Press cider, nice wines by the glass, enjoyable food from sandwiches to interesting blackboard dishes, quick friendly service, amiable ambling black labrador; can be overrun with Agriculture College students term-time wknd evenings; children and dogs welcome (play area and nice walled-in kids' lawn outside, too), impressive views from tables on pleasant terrace, big garden sloping down to former canal (under slow restoration) by its tunnel entrance, Sunday barbecues, good walks *(Brian and Anita Randall, E McCall, T McLean, D Irving, R Huggins, Michael Dallas, Andrew Shore, Maria Williams, David Morgan, Alan Bulley, Giles and Annie Francis, Guy Vowles, Tom and Ruth Rees, Julie and Bill Ryan, Meg and Colin Hamilton, LYM, V Brogden)*

CODRINGTON [ST7278]

Codrington Arms BS37 6RY [Wapley Rd; handy for M4 junction 18, via B4465]: Family dining pub dating partly from 15th c, several comfortable rooms, well spaced tables, wide choice of blackboard food, quick friendly service, well kept real ales, good house wines, big log fire; piped music; big garden with good views and play area *(MRSM)*

COLD ASTON [SP1219]

☆ *Plough* GL54 3BN [aka Aston Blank; off A436 (B4068) or A429 SW of Stow-on-the-Wold]: Small 17th-c pub nicely redecorated for new owners, friendly helpful manageress, affordable and enterprising country cooking (particularly well chosen meats), well kept Donnington BB, Hook Norton Best and North Cotswold Pig Brook, good choice of wines by the glass, log fire, low black beams and flagstones, old-fashioned simple furnishings – just a dozen or so tables; children welcome, picnic-sets under cocktail parasols on small side terraces, good walks *(LYM, Keith and Sue Ward)*

COLEFORD [SO5813]

☆ *Dog & Muffler* GL16 7AS [Joyford, best approached from Christchurch 5-ways junction B4432/B4428, by church – B4432

towards Broadwell, then follow signpost; also signposted from the Berry Hill post office cross-roads; beyond the hamlet itself, bear right and keep your eyes skinned]: Very prettily set 17th-c country pub, cosy original beamed bar with log-effect gas fire in big fireplace, beamed and flagstoned back part with bright conservatory restaurant and verandah, cheerful helpful staff, good food from sandwiches and baguettes up, Sam Smiths and local Freeminers Speculation; children welcome, well spaced picnic-sets in large attractive sheltered garden with lovely views and good segregated play area, nice walks, good value bedrooms *(Mr and Mrs M E Hawkins, LYM, John and Tania Wood)*

COLESBOURNE [SO9913]

Colesbourne Inn GL53 9NP [A435 Cirencester—Cheltenham]: Civilised 18th-c grey stone gabled coaching inn with wide changing choice of enjoyable food all home-made from the bread to some enterprising dishes (can take a while), Wadworths IPA and 6X, lots of wines by the glass, linked rooms with partly panelled dark red walls, log fires, soft lighting, comfortable mix of settles and softly padded seats, separate candlelit dining room; dogs welcome, views from attractive back garden and terrace, nine nice bedrooms in converted stable block *(Gary Roeder, LYM, Keith and Sue Ward, E McCall, T McLean, D Irving, R Huggins)*

COMPTON ABDALE [SP0717]

☆ *Puesdown Inn* GL54 4DN [A40 outside village]: Appealing and spacious series of stylish upmarket bar areas, wide choice of good enterprising food using local supplies and often unusual ingredients from sandwiches up, neat staff, Fullers London Pride and Hook Norton ales, good wines by the glass, good coffees, log fire and woodburner, leather or brightly upholstered sofas and armchairs, big art posters and other interesting pictures, bare boards, bright rugs and rafter-effect ceilings, cream and dark red walls, mainly stripped stone in extensive eating areas, well reproduced piped music, friendly chocolate labradors; nice garden behind, bedrooms *(BB, P and J Shapley)*

COOMBE HILL [SO8827]

Swan GL19 4BA [A38/A4019]: Light and airy pub popular for big helpings of good value fresh food from generous sandwiches up, several rooms, polished boards and panelling, red leather chesterfields, quick attentive service, Greene King Abbot, Uley Old Spot and a guest beer, decent house wine; piped music may obtrude *(Ralph Kenber)*

EASTLEACH TURVILLE [SP1905]

☆ *Victoria* GL7 3NQ [off A361 S of Burford]: Low-ceilinged open-plan rooms around central servery, attractive seats built in by log fire, unusual Queen Victoria pictures around the back, Arkells ales, several wines by glass, wide choice of straightforward pub food (not winter Sun evening) from good baguettes up, friendly service; piped music; children and dogs welcome, picnic-sets in pleasant front garden looking down over picturesque village *(Maurice Holt, Paul and Shirley White, C and R Bromage, P and J Shapley, Julie and Bill Ryan, Meg and Colin Hamilton, LYM)*

EBRINGTON [SP1839]

☆ *Ebrington Arms* GL55 6NH [off B4035 E of Chipping Campden or A429 N of Moreton-in-Marsh]: Proper relaxed country pub handy for Hidcote and Kiftsgate, good sensibly priced pubby food, friendly service, local Purity Pure UBU, Timothy Taylors Landlord and Wells & Youngs Bombardier, Thatcher's farm cider, lively low-beamed bar with stripped stone, flagstones and inglenooks, attractive dining room; no dogs at meal times; children welcome, picnic-sets on pleasant sheltered terrace, good play area, bedrooms *(LYM, Keith and Sue Ward, Clive and Fran Dutson, Guy Vowles, Michael Clatworthy, P J F Cooper)*

ELKSTONE [SO9610]

☆ *Highwayman* GL53 9PL [Beechpike; off northbound A417 6 miles N of Cirencester]: Interesting 16th-c building, a rambling and relaxing warren of low beams, stripped stone, cosy alcoves, antique settles, armchairs and sofa among more usual furnishings, good value very generous home-made food, full Arkells ale range, good house wines, friendly staff, good log fires, big back eating area; may be quiet piped music; disabled access, good family room, outside play area *(Paul and Shirley White, Brian McBurnie, the Didler, E McCall, T McLean, D Irving, R Huggins, LYM, G W Scarr)*

FOSSEBRIDGE [SP0711]

☆ *Fossebridge Inn* GL54 3JS [A429 Cirencester—Stow-on-the-Wold]: Handsome Georgian inn doing well under current father-and-daughter management, attractively refurbished much older two-room back bar with beams, arches, stripped stone and good log fire, pleasant more modern side area, tasty food from sandwiches to good straightforward main dishes here or in dining area, prompt friendly service, well kept Fullers London Pride, Greene King IPA, Hook Norton and St Austell Tribute; children welcome, tables out in attractive streamside garden with terrace, comfortable bedrooms *(LYM, Giles and Annie Francis, Guy Vowles, Keith and Sue Ward)*

FRAMPTON COTTERELL [ST6781]

Rising Sun BS36 2HN: Popular tucked-away village pub with good range of local ales in comfortable partly divided flagstoned bar, upper dining area and conservatory, skittle alley *(E McCall, T McLean, D Irving, R Huggins)*

GLASSHOUSE [SO7121]

Glasshouse Inn GL17 0NN [off A40 just W of A4136]: Homely beamed country pub with appealing and interesting old-fashioned and antique furnishings and décor, cavernous black hearth, flagstoned conservatory, well

kept ales inc Butcombe tapped from the cask, Stowford Press cider, decent very generous food inc thai dishes; piped music, no children inside, no bookings, and they may try to keep your credit card while you eat; good disabled access, neat garden with interesting topiary and lovely hanging baskets, nearby paths up wooded May Hill, cl Sun evening *(the Didler, Theocsbrian, LYM, M J Winterton, J E Shackleton, Colin Moore, Dr A J and Mrs Tompsett, Guy Vowles, Phil and Sally Gorton)*

GLOUCESTER [SO8218]

Dick Whittingtons House GL1 2PE [Westgate St]: Unusual in being listed Grade I, early Tudor behind its 18th-c façade, probably former guild hall and mansion house; comfortably updated inside, welcoming staff, good straightforward food choice, changing real ales, wide range of customers from shoppers to rugby supporters; attractive courtyard, open all day *(Theocsbrian, Klaus and Elizabeth Leist)*

Fountain GL1 2NW [Westgate St/Berkeley St]: Popular pub under new management, civilised L-shaped bar with good range of real ales and reasonably priced usual food, attractive prints, handsome stone fireplace (pub dates from 17th c), plush seats and built-in wall benches, log-effect gas fire; good disabled access, tables in pleasant courtyard, handy for cathedral, open all day *(BB, Colin and Ruth Munro, B M Eldridge)*

Royal Oak GL3 3TW [Hucclecote Rd, Hucclecote; quite handy for M5 junction 11A]: Bright modern open-plan pub, good value food inc bargain Sun roasts, pleasant landlord, real ales; plenty of picnic-sets on attractive terrace and lawns *(B M Eldridge)*

Tall Ship GL1 2EX [Southgate St]: Extended Victorian pub by entry to historic docks, raised dining area with wide food choice from paninis and seafood tapas to good fresh fish (can take a while at busy times), morning coffee and afternoon tea, Wadworths and a guest beer, cheerful young staff, landlady helpful on wine choice; pool table and juke box on left; tables on pretty terrace, seafood barbecues, open all day *(Mrs Hazel Rainer, Pat and Tony Martin, Susan and Nigel Brookes, B M Eldridge)*

GREAT BARRINGTON [SP2013]

Fox OX18 4TB [off A40 Burford—Northleach; pub towards Little Barrington]: 17th-c pub with stripped stone and simple country furnishings in low-ceilinged small bar, Donnington BB and SBA, farm cider and good apple juice, friendly staff, wide blackboard choice of quickly served food (all day Sun and summer Sat, not Mon night in winter) from sandwiches up, big river-view dining room in former skittle alley, traditional games; can get very busy, games machine, TV; children welcome, heated terrace by River Windrush (swans and private fishing), informal orchard with pond, open all day *(David Glynne-Jones, LYM, Stuart Turner, the Didler, Mr and Mrs*

John Taylor, Pete Baker, Mrs June Wilmers,
C and R Bromage, Brian and Rosalie Laverick)
GREAT RISSINGTON [SP1917]
☆ *Lamb* GL54 2LN [off A40 W of Burford, via Gt
Barrington]: Partly 17th-c, with warm, bright
and cosy low-beamed two-room bar, friendly
landlord, two well kept Hook Norton ales,
good wines by the glass, good value pubby
food inc wknd meal deals, open fire, darts,
dominoes, and cribbage, olde-worlde
candlelit restaurant; sports TV; children
welcome, new furniture in pretty and
sheltered hillside garden, bedrooms *(LYM,
David A Hammond, Mrs Frances Pennell,
Lawrence Pearse)*
GRETTON [SP0130]
Royal Oak GL54 5EP [off B4077 E of
Tewkesbury]: Civilised linked bare-boarded or
flagstoned rooms, beams hung with tankards
and chamber-pots, interesting old motor-
racing pictures, nice mixed bag of seats and
tables, stripped country furnishings in
dining conservatory, enjoyable food, well
kept Goffs and a guest ale, decent wines;
children and dogs welcome, fine views from
flower-filled terrace, big pleasant garden
with play area and tennis, GWR private
railway runs past, good nearby walks, open
all day summer wknds *(LYM, Giles and
Annie Francis)*
GUITING POWER [SP0924]
☆ *Farmers Arms* GL54 5TZ [Fosseway (A429)]:
Stripped stone, flagstones, particularly well
kept cheap Donnington BB and SBA, wide
blackboard range of unpretentious food from
sandwiches and good ham ploughman's up
inc children's dishes, prompt friendly service,
good coal or log fire, carpeted back dining
area, skittle alley, games area with darts,
dominoes, cribbage, pool, skittle alley; piped
music, games machine; children welcome,
garden with quoits, lovely village, good
walks, bedrooms *(LYM, Guy Vowles, Di and
Mike Gillam, the Didler)*
HANHAM [ST6470]
Old Lock & Weir BS15 3NU [Hanham Mills;
follow sign to Chequers pub down narrow
dead end]: Idyllic setting by River Avon,
plain but comfortable inside, cheerful
atmosphere, friendly attentive young staff,
good value food from baguettes up inc Sun
lunch, well kept real ales; children and dogs
welcome, extensive waterside gardens and
landing stage *(Jim Grant)*
HILLESLEY [ST7689]
Fleece GL12 7RD [Hawkesbury Rd/Chapel
Lane]: Attractive two-bar village pub with
simple traditional furnishings, hearty food
from good big rolls to interesting variations
on pubby favourites, prompt friendly service,
well kept ales, decent wines, upper dining
bar; pleasant garden tables, small village in
lovely countryside nr Cotswold Way, simple
bedrooms *(Guy Vowles, M G Hart)*
HORSLEY [ST8497]
☆ *Tipputs* GL6 0QE [Tiltups End; A46 2 miles S
of Nailsworth]: Enjoyable food all day from
wide range of sandwiches, light dishes and

pubby favourites to interesting evening
meals, attentive young staff, beams and
stripped stone in L-shaped bar with big log
fire and abstract art, comfortable leather
seats in anteroom to galleried barn
restaurant; nice chairs and tables in pretty
garden with raised deck, lovely setting,
open all day *(Tom and Ruth Rees, E McCall,
T McLean, D Irving, R Huggins)*
HYDE [SO8801]
Ragged Cot GL6 8PE [Burnt Ash; off A419 E
of Stroud, OS Sheet 162 map ref 886012]:
Nicely placed 17th-c pub with comfortably
padded seat right round beamed and
stripped stone bar, log fire, Uley Old Spot
and Wickwar Cotswold Way, decent choice of
wines, friendly hospitable service even when
busy, back dining extension; picnic-sets (and
interesting pavilion) in garden, comfortable
bedrooms in adjacent converted barn *(LYM,
Andy and Claire Barker, E McCall, T McLean,
D Irving, R Huggins)*
KEMBLE [ST9899]
Thames Head GL7 6NZ [A433 Cirencester—
Tetbury]: Stripped stone, timberwork, log
fire, intriguing little front alcove (perhaps
an ostler's lookout), softly lit cottagey back
area with pews and log-effect gas fire in big
fireplace, country-look dining room with
another big gas fire, good value wines,
Arkells 2B and 3B, decent bar food, pleasant
staff, skittle alley; TV; children welcome,
tables outside, good value four-poster
bedrooms, nice walk to nearby low-key
source of River Thames *(Stephen Woad, LYM,
E McCall, T McLean, D Irving, R Huggins)*
KEMPSFORD [SU1916]
George GL7 4EQ [High St]: Nicely
refurbished, with woodburner in roomy new
bare-boards dining area as well as in
carpeted bar, welcoming landlord, enjoyable
and sensibly priced freshly made food, well
kept Arkells ales; children welcome, big back
play area *(Sam Samuells)*
KILCOT [SO6925]
Kilcot Inn GL18 1NG [B4221, not far from
M50 junction 3]: Current chef doing good
range of food from good baguettes and local
cheeses to fresh fish and rare breed meats,
Bass and Greene King Old Speckled Hen,
good service, interesting modern yew chairs
among other wood furniture on bare boards
or flagstones, woodburner, stripped beams,
rustic bare brick and terracotta paintwork;
dogs welcome, garden picnic-sets *(Clive,
Alec and Joan Laurence, Theocsbrian,
Neil and Anita Christopher)*
KINETON [SP0926]
☆ *Halfway House* GL54 5UG [signed from
B4068 and B4077 W of Stow-on-the-Wold]:
Unpretentiously comfortable, with good
traditional food using local ingredients from
baguettes up, cheap Donnington BB and SBA
from nearby brewery kept well, decent wines,
farm cider, pub games, restaurant; children
welcome (lunchtime can get very busy in
school hols), attractive sheltered back
garden, tables on narrow front terrace too,

simple comfortable bedrooms, good walks (LYM, Theocsbrian, Keith and Sue Ward)

KINGSCOTE [ST8196]

☆ *Hunters Hall* GL8 8XZ [A4135 Dursley—Tetbury]: Tudor beams, stripped stone, big log fires and plenty of character in individually furnished linked rooms, some sofas and easy chairs, wide food choice from lunchtime sandwiches and good ham ploughman's up, Greene King IPA and Abbot and Uley Hogs Head, friendly and informal if not always speedy service, flagstoned back bar with darts, pool and TV; children and dogs welcome, garden with good play area, bedrooms, open all day (John Dwane, Guy Vowles, LYM, Simon Collett-Jones, Tom and Ruth Rees, Mr and Mrs A J Hudson, Donna and Roger)

LECHLADE [SU2199]

New Inn GL7 3AB [Market Sq (A361)]: Genial helpful licensees and good prompt service in roomy unpretentious front bar, wide choice of good value generous food from good filled baguettes up, huge log fire, changing real ales such as Archers Best, Greene King and Youngs Special, large pleasant back restaurant; quiet piped music, end games machine, projector TV for sports; tables and play area in big garden down to Thames, good walks, 29 comfortable bedrooms (Peter and Audrey Dowsett, M Joyner, Meg and Colin Hamilton, E McCall, T McLean, D Irving, R Huggins)

☆ *Trout* GL7 3HA [A417, a mile E]: Three-room pub dating from 15th c, olde-worlde décor with low beams, flagstones, stuffed fish and fishing prints, good log fire, pleasant landlord, real ales such as Courage Best and Sharps Doom Bar, good value wines, enjoyable generous food inc plenty of fish and vegetarian, local paintings for sale, small charity book stall, dining room; children in eating areas, board games and magazines, jazz Tues and Sun, fishing rights, early June steam rally; nice big Thames-side garden with boathouse bar, boules, aunt sally, bouncy castle and swings, camping, open all day summer Sat (Jennifer Banks, LYM, Paul and Shirley White, Kalman Kafetz)

LEIGHTERTON [ST8290]

Royal Oak GL8 8UN [off A46 S of Nailsworth]: Neatly kept old stone-built pub, beams, log fires and mullioned windows, good value pubby food from soup and sandwiches to roasts, good OAP wkdy lunches, Butcombe, Wickwar Cotswold Way and a weekly guest beer, prompt service, thoughtful and friendly; piped music; nice garden, quiet village, good walks, quite handy for Westonbirt Arboretum (Guy Vowles, J and F Gowers)

LITTLE WASHBOURNE [SO9933]

Hobnails GL20 8NQ [B4077 Tewkesbury—Stow-on-the-Wold]: Attractive traditional front core with 15th-c beams and log fire, comfortable and extensive eating areas around this, wide choie of enjoyable food, welcoming staff, good range of real ales,

decent wines; children welcome, disabled facilities, terrace tables, play area, bedroom extension (B M Eldridge, LYM)

LOWER SWELL [SP1725]

Golden Ball GL54 1LF [B4068 W of Stow-on-the-Wold]: Simple and spotless stone-built beamed local with well kept Donnington BB and SBA from the pretty nearby brewery, good range of ciders and perry, enjoyable plain food inc curry nights, friendly landlord, big log fire, games area behind sturdy chimneystack, small evening restaurant, conservatory; no dogs or children; small garden with occasional barbecues, aunt sally and quoits, three decent simple bedrooms, pretty village, good walks (LYM, Keith and Sue Ward)

LOWER WICK [ST7096]

Pepper Pot GL11 6DD [signed off A38 Bristol—Gloucester just N of Newport]: Under new ownership and refurbished in fresh contemporary style as dining pub, using entirely local supplies and fresh non-farm fish; still has a bar area (BB)

MARSHFIELD [ST7773]

☆ *Catherine Wheel* SN14 8LR [High St; signed off A420 Bristol—Chippenham]: Attractive traditional stripped stone pub with friendly staff, decent food inc good choice of Sun roasts, good range of real ales, farm cider, interesting wines by the glass, plates and prints, medley of settles, chairs and stripped tables, cottagey back family bar, charming Georgian dining room with open fire in impressive fireplace, darts, dominoes, no music or machines; flower-decked back yard, unspoilt village, bedrooms, open all day Sat (Dr and Mrs A K Clarke, LYM, Graham Rooth, Guy Vowles, Julie and Bill Ryan, Donna and Roger)

Lord Nelson SN14 8LP [A420 Bristol—Chippenham; High St]: Spacious range of sympathetically lightened up beamed rooms (inc former stables still with runnel down middle of flagstones), wide choice of quickly served inexpensive generous food, good choice of real ales, friendly obliging service, open fires, bistro restaurant, games bar with pool and machines; charming small courtyard, bedrooms in cottage annexe (Guy Vowles, Dr and Mrs A K Clarke)

MAYSHILL [ST6882]

☆ *New Inn* BS36 2NT [Badminton Rd (A432 Frampton Cotterell—Yate)]: Good food (all day Sun), friendly staff and well kept local Cotswold Spring and interesting changing ales in popular largely 17th-c coaching inn with two comfortably carpeted bar rooms leading to restaurant, log fire; children and dogs welcome, garden with play area (Charles Morrison, E McCall, T McLean, D Irving, R Huggins)

MEYSEY HAMPTON [SU1199]

☆ *Masons Arms* GL7 5JT [just off A417 Cirencester—Lechlade; High St]: 17th-c village pub under friendly new landlord, lively evening atmosphere, well kept ales such as Hook Norton, farm cider, enjoyable straightforward food, longish open-plan beamed bar with big inglenook log fire one end, restaurant; piped music; children and dogs welcome, tables out on green, pleasant compact bedrooms, good breakfast *(Russell Grimshaw, Kerry Purcell, LYM, Matthew Shackle, Sara Fulton, Roger Baker, E McCall, T McLean, D Irving, R Huggins)*

MICKLETON [SP1543]

☆ *Kings Arms* GL55 6RT [B4632 (ex A46)]: Civilised open-plan family lounge, wide choice of good locally sourced food from well filled sandwiches to unusual specials and good value OAP lunches, convivial atmosphere, Bass and Flowers, farm cider, nice mix of comfortable chairs, soft lighting, interesting homely décor, log fire, small welcoming locals' bar with darts, dominoes and cribbage; piped music may obtrude; tables outside, handy for Kiftsgate and Hidcote *(Keith and Sue Ward, BB, Martin and Pauline Jennings)*

MINCHINHAMPTON [SO8500]

Lodge GL6 9AQ [Nailsworth—Brimscombe – on common fork left at pub's sign; OS Sheet 162 map ref 853008]: Smartly reworked dining pub with civilised bistro feel and modern décor and furnishings, enjoyable and imaginative food inc lighter dishes, good pleasant service, Sharps Doom Bar, decent wines by the glass; children welcome, tables on neat lawn with attractive flower border, looking over common with grazing cows and horses *(LYM, Mr and Mrs A J Hudson, David Morgan)*

MISERDEN [SO9308]

Carpenters Arms GL6 7JA [off B4070 NE of Stroud]: Handy for Misarden Park visitors, two open-plan bar areas with low beams, old wooden tables on bare boards, stripped stone walls and two big log fires, small dining room, straightforward bar food, Caledonian Deuchars IPA, Greene King IPA and Wadworths 6X, friendly staff; children and dogs welcome, garden tables, open all day Sun *(Neil and Anita Christopher, Dave Braisted, Michael Dallas, E McCall, T McLean, D Irving, R Huggins, LYM)*

MORETON-IN-MARSH [SP2032]

Inn on the Marsh GL56 0DW [Stow Rd]: Wide range of reasonably priced food cooked to order (so allow plenty of time), may be some dutch dishes, baguettes too, Banks's, Marstons Pedigree and a guest beer, friendly service, cosy and unpretentious beamed bar with inglenook woodburner, comfortable armchairs and sofa, lots of pictures particularly ducks, smartly attractive modern dining conservatory; small back garden, bedrooms *(Tony and Wendy Hobden, George Atkinson, Nigel and Sue Foster)*

☆ *Redesdale Arms* GL56 0AW [High St]: Handsome old coaching inn with relaxed atmosphere, prettily lit alcoves and big stone fireplace in solidly furnished comfortable panelled bar on right, log fires, real ales, small but good wine list, cafetière coffee, interesting choice of good value

generous food, spacious back child-friendly restaurant and dining conservatory, darts in flagstoned public bar; piped music, fruit machine, TV; tables out on heated floodlit courtyard decking, comfortable well equipped bedrooms beyond *(BB, Peter and Jean Hoare, Pat and Clive Sherriff, Keith and Sue Ward, Dr and Mrs A K Clarke)*

NAILSWORTH [ST8499]

☆ *Britannia* GL6 0DG [Cossack Sq]: Large open-plan food pub very popular locally for wide range of good familiar bistro food (evening booking recommended), friendly efficient service even when busy, good choice of real ales and wines by the glass, thriving atmosphere, big log fire *(Tom and Ruth Rees, Ian Phillips, Colin Moore, Keith and Sue Ward)*

Village Inn GL6 0HH [Bath Rd]: Brewing its own good value Nailsworth ales, take-aways too (a cask works out at little more than £1 a pint), appealingly done series of rambling linked areas with steps down to back area for view of the process, woody décor with panelling, dividers and oak floors, pub food, no machines or juke box; open all day *(E McCall, T McLean, D Irving, R Huggins)*

NAUNTON [SP1123]

☆ *Black Horse* GL54 3AD [off B4068 W of Stow]: Unspoilt stripped-stone pub with friendly landlady, well priced Donnington BB and SBA, good simple fresh food from huge baguettes and baked potatoes to Sun roasts (veg may come from local allotments), plain tables on flagstones, black beams and log fire, darts, cribbage, dominoes, dining room; piped music, food can take a while; children and dogs welcome, some nice seating outside, bedrooms with own bathrooms, charming village, fine Cotswold walks *(Theocsbrian, Nick Lawless, Pete Baker, LYM, Patmos, Keith and Sue Ward)*

NEWPORT [ST6997]

Stagecoach GL13 9PY [A38]: Traditional roadside pub dating from 16th c, beams, horsebrasses and log fire in cosy bar's interesting fireplace, Butcombe, Courage Best and Greene King, wide food choice (all day Sun) from toasties, baguettes and light dishes up, good-sized comfortable eating area; children welcome, garden with terrace and boules pitch *(Alain and Rose Foote)*

NORTH NIBLEY [ST7495]

☆ *Black Horse* GL11 6DT [Barrs Lane]: Friendly pub on Cotswold Way with new licensees putting emphasis on enjoyable somewhat restauranty food, lunchtime/afternoon sandwiches too, Greene King IPA and Hop Back Summer Lightning, decent wines, nice décor inc fireside armchairs by good log fire in carpeted bar, neat restaurant; a few tables in pretty garden, good value cottagey bedrooms, good breakfast *(Jason Nabb, Matthew Shackle, LYM)*

☆ *New Inn* GL11 6EF [E of village itself; Waterley Bottom – OS Sheet 162 map ref 758963]: Peacefully tucked away, with well kept and interesting changing ales from antique beer engines, friendly service, bar food from good baguettes to venison and imaginative dishes, pleasantly pubby furnishings in partly stripped stone lounge bar, simple cosy public bar with traditional games (and TV); children and dogs welcome, lots of tables on tranquil lawn with neat new covered decking (pool table here), open all day wknds, has been cl Mon lunchtime *(Paul Humphreys, Theocsbrian, Neil and Lorna Mclaughlan, LYM, Rob and Jane Woodward, Alain and Rose Foote)*

NORTON [SO8524]

Kings Head GL2 9LR [just off A38; Old Tewkesbury Rd]: Useful stop, with decent efficiently served food, Greene King Old Speckled Hen and Goffs Jouster, spacious simply furnished divided bar; garden tables *(Dr A J and Mrs Tompsett)*

NYMPSFIELD [SO7900]

Rose & Crown GL10 3TU [The Cross; signed off B4066 Stroud—Dursley]: Stone-built pub popular for plentiful food (through Sun afternoon) from sandwiches, baguettes and baked potatoes up, efficient friendly service, Bath Gem, Otter and Uley, decent wines, local farm cider, wide choice of coffees and teas, daily papers, log fire, pine tables and bare boards in beamed front bar, pews and other seats in large back dining area; piped music; children and dogs welcome, picnic-sets in side yard and on sheltered lawn with good play area, bedrooms adjacent, handy for Cotswold walks and Woodchester mansion and park (NT) *(BB, Bruce and Sharon Eden, Tom and Ruth Rees, John and Gloria Isaacs, J and F Gowers, Paul Humphreys)*

OLD SODBURY [ST7681]

Cross Hands BS37 6RJ [junction of A46 with A432; 1½ miles from M4 junction 18]: Spacious pub/hotel, comfortable bar popular with passing travellers, Greene King IPA and Abbot, log-effect gas fires, bar food and restaurant; comfortable bedrooms *(LYM, Donna and Roger)*

☆ *Dog* BS37 6LZ [3 miles from M4 junction 18, via A46 and A432; The Hill (a busy road)]: Two-level bar with low beams and stripped stone, extremely wide choice of good value food from sandwiches and several soups up inc meal deals, quick friendly young staff, Wadworths 6X and other changing ales such as Hook Norton Old Hooky, Wickwar BOB and Worthington, quiz nights Sun/Mon; games machine, juke box; children welcome, big garden with barbecues and good play area, bedrooms, open all day *(Tom Evans, Dr and Mrs A K Clarke, Cathy Robinson, Ed Coombe, John and Gloria Isaacs, Richard Fendick, Roger Smith, Paul Humphreys, Dr and Mrs C W Thomas, Gary Marchant, Donna and Roger, Dave Braisted, LYM, J and F Gowers)*

PAINSWICK [SO8609]

Royal Oak GL6 6QG [St Mary's St]: Old-fashioned partly 16th-c three-room town local with appealing nooks and crannies, some attractive old or antique seats, plenty of prints, Black Sheep, Moles Best and Shepherd Neame Spitfire, decent wines, open

fire, small sun lounge; children in eating area, dogs welcome in public bar, suntrap pretty courtyard *(Giles and Annie Francis, Brian McBurnie, LYM)*

PARKEND [SO6107]

Fountain GL15 4JD [just off B4234]: Proper traditional 18th-c village inn by terminus of restored Lydney—Parkend railway, three well kept changing ales inc local Freeminer, wide choice of bargain fresh food inc good range of curries, welcoming efficient service, real fire, assorted chairs and settles in two linked rooms, old local tools and photographs; children and dogs welcome, wheelchair access *(Pete Baker, Guy Vowles, B M Eldridge)*

RUARDEAN [SO6117]

Malt Shovel GL17 9TW: Friendly new licensees in stripped stone local with sturdy traditional furnishings and good log fire in flagstoned bar, good choice of real ales, farm cider, enjoyable seasonal food, attractive dining room; appealing old-world bedrooms *(R Williams)*

RUSPIDGE [SO6511]

New Inn GL14 3AR: Traditional stone-built village pub with warm welcome, relaxed friendly atmosphere, home-made pubby food from sandwiches to steaks, special diets catered for, good range of real ales and other drinks; two comfortable bedrooms, cl lunchtime but open all day Sun and summer Sat *(B M Eldridge)*

SAPPERTON [SO9303]

Daneway Inn GL7 6LN [Daneway; off A419 Stroud—Cirencester]: Quiet local in charming wooded countryside, flagstones and bare boards, amazing floor-to-ceiling carved oak dutch fireplace, sporting prints, Wadworths ales, Weston's farm cider, reasonably priced generous simple food from filled baps up, friendly landlord and staff, small family room, traditional games in inglenook public bar; no dogs; camping possible, terrace tables and lovely sloping lawn, good walks by canal under restoration with tunnel to Coates *(E McCall, T McLean, D Irving, R Huggins, Len Clark, LYM)*

SHEEPSCOMBE [SO8910]

☆ *Butchers Arms* GL6 7RH [off B4070 NE of Stroud]: Busy 17th-c dining pub, current management doing decent food with good puddings range, well kept changing ales such as Hook Norton Best, roaring woodburner, seats in big bay windows, flowery-cushioned chairs and rustic benches, lots of bric-a-brac, restaurant, traditional games; children in eating areas, tables outside, terrific views *(LYM, Paul and Shirley White, Alain and Rose Foote, Andrew Shore, Maria Williams)*

SHIPTON MOYNE [ST8989]

☆ *Cat & Custard Pot* GL8 8PN [off B4040 Malmesbury—Bristol; The Street]: Well run pub with good choice of good value robust food from sandwiches and great ham and eggs to steaks and restaurant dishes (booking recommended even wkdy lunch), well kept Fullers London Pride, Wadworths 6X and a guest beer such as Timothy Taylors

Landlord, Thatcher's cider, good friendly service, several dining areas, hunting prints (even a pub racehorse), cosy back snug, no piped music; dogs welcome, picturesque village (*Richard Stancomb, Peter and Audrey Dowsett, Gordon and Jay Smith, Catherine Pitt, BB, D M and B K Moores*)

SHIPTON OLIFFE [SP0218]

Frogmill GL54 4HT [just off A40/A436 S of Andoversford]: Friendly 17th-c stone-built coaching inn with large flagstoned bar, enjoyable food, well kept Bass, attractive beamed restaurant; tables on streamside terrace with waterwheel, big play area, comfortable bedrooms (*M Thomas*)

SIDDINGTON [SU0399]

☆ *Greyhound* GL7 6HR [Ashton Rd; village signed from A419 roundabout at Tesco]: Two linked rooms each with a big log fire, enjoyable food from sandwiches to bargain lunchtime carvery and unusual fish dishes, Badger Tanglefoot, Wadworths IPA and seasonal beers, welcoming service, public bar with slate floor, darts and cribbage; piped music; garden tables, open all day (*LYM, Paul and Shirley White, E McCall, T McLean, D Irving, R Huggins*)

SLAD [SO8707]

Woolpack GL6 7QA [B4070 Stroud—Birdlip]: Friendly old hillside village local with lovely valley views, several linked rooms with Laurie Lee and other interesting photographs, some of his books for sale, log fire and nice tables, good value pubby food (not Sun evening) from sandwiches and baguettes up inc generous Sun roast, well kept Bass and Uley ales, local farm ciders and perry, decent wines by the glass, good young staff, games and cards; dogs welcome (*Bob and Angela Brooks, Alain and Rose Foote, Pete Baker, Tom and Ruth Rees*)

SLIMBRIDGE [SO7204]

☆ *Tudor Arms* GL2 7BP [Shepherds Patch; off A38 towards Wildfowl & Wetlands Trust]: Welcoming and obliging, with plentiful generous food all day wknds, half a dozen changing ales such as Bartrams, Goffs, Palmers, Uley, Wadworths and Wickwar, good wines by the glass, farm cider, linked areas with parquet floor, flagstones or carpet, some leather chairs and settles, conservatory, darts, pool and skittle alley; children and dogs welcome, disabled facilities, picnic-sets outside, handy for Wildfowl Trust and canal boat trips, bedrooms in small annexe, open all day (*Dr A J and Mrs Tompsett, Donna and Roger*)

SNOWSHILL [SP0933]

☆ *Snowshill Arms* WR12 7JU: Pleasantly airy and unpretentious country pub in honeypot village, quick friendly service even when busy, Donnington BB and SBA, reasonably priced simple food from sandwiches up, log fire, stripped stone, neat array of tables, local photographs; skittle alley, charming village views from bow windows and from big back garden with little stream and play area, friendly local-feel midweek winter and

evenings, can be very crowded other times – get there early for a table; children welcome if eating, handy for Snowshill Manor and walks on Cotswold Way (*LYM, Keith and Sue Ward, Guy Vowles, Martin and Karen Wake, Edna Jones*)

SOMERFORD KEYNES [SU0195]

☆ *Bakers Arms* GL7 6DN: Pretty stone-built pub popular for bistro-style food from baguettes and ciabattas up, real ales, good house wine, two log fires, lots of pine tables in two linked stripped-stone areas with soft lighting and burgundy walls, young staff; children very welcome, big garden with play area and good barbecues, lovely Cotswold village (*Mark and Ruth Brock, Guy Vowles, Julia Morris*)

SOUTH CERNEY [SU0496]

Royal Oak GL7 5UP [High St]: Thriving and sympathetically extended ancient local with cosy bars and small back dining area, welcoming landlord, Fullers London Pride and guest beers, food from good value sandwiches and baguettes up, woodburner; pleasant garden behind with big terrace and summer marquee (*E McCall, T McLean, D Irving, R Huggins, Dr A Y Drummond*)

ST BRIAVELS [SO5504]

George GL15 6TA [High Street]: Rambling linked black-beamed rooms with old-fashioned seating, toby jugs and antique bottles, big stone open fireplace, very wide choice of wholesome food inc popular OAP lunches, Freeminer Bitter, Fullers London Pride, RCH Pitchfork and a couple of guest beers, Stowford Press cider, restaurant; piped music; children and dogs welcome, flagstoned terrace over former moat of neighbouring Norman fortress, bedrooms (*Guy Vowles, Dr W J M Gissane, LYM, Denys Gueroult, Bob and Margaret Holder, John and Tania Wood*)

STANTON [SP0634]

☆ *Mount* WR12 7NE [off B4632 SW of Broadway; no through road up hill, bear left]: Proper country pub in great spot up steep lane from golden-stone village, views to welsh mountains, esp from large terrace (great on summer evenings); good friendly service, farm cider, decent bar food (not Sun evening) inc super ploughman's, Donnington BB and SBA, heavy beams, flagstones and big log fire in original core, horseracing pictures and trappings, roomy picture-window extensions, one with cricket memorabilia; well behaved children allowed, attractive garden with pets' corner, open all day Sat and summer Sun (*Martin and Pauline Jennings, Maureen and Keith Gimson, Paul J Robinshaw, LYM, Ian and Joan Blackwell, Edna Jones*)

STAUNTON [SO7829]

Swan GL19 3QA [Ledbury Rd (A417)]: Doing well under hard-working current licensees, good local atmosphere, enjoyable food from baguettes to good big steaks and fish, well kept Timothy Taylors Landlord and farm ciders; pretty gardens (*Sue and Dave Harris*)

STAVERTON [SO9022]

Pheasant GL51 0SS [Gloucester Rd (B4063 W of Cheltenham)]: Attractively fresh contemporary décor, wholesome bar and restaurant food, well kept real ale such as Fullers London Pride and Sharps Doom Bar *(Kieran Tingle)*

STONEHOUSE [SO8005]

Woolpack GL10 2NA [High St]: Roomy and unspoilt, with four well kept ales inc Uley Hogshead and Wadworths 6X, good value pubby food, low ceilings, lots of interesting prints *(Tom Evans)*

STOW-ON-THE-WOLD [SP1925]

☆ **Eagle & Child** GL54 1BN [attached to Royalist Hotel, Digbeth Street]: Smart little dining bar attached to handsome old hotel, woodburner, flagstones, low beams and dark pink walls, back conservatory, nice mix of tables (no bar as such), up-to-date food from baguettes up, Hook Norton ales, good if not cheap wine and malt whisky choice, friendly staff; may be piped music; children and dogs welcome, small back courtyard, good bedrooms, open all day *(Jude Wright, LYM, Michael Dandy, Keith and Sue Ward, George Atkinson)*

Grapevine GL54 1AU [Sheep St]: Substantial hotel with relaxing small front bar, food from generous sandwiches, baguettes and tapas to steak and bass, helpful service, Hook Norton Old Hooky and a guest beer such as Wells & Youngs, good choice of wines by the glass, good coffee, separate brasserie and restaurant with live vine; pavement tables, bedrooms, open all day *(Michael Dandy, David and Jean Hall)*

Kings Arms GL54 1AF [The Square]: Enjoyable food from good sandwiches to lots of fish, real food for children, good choice of wines by the glass, Greene King IPA and Abbot, good coffee (opens early for this), daily papers, some Mackintosh-style chairs on polished boards, bowed black beams, some panelling and stripped stone, log fire, charming upstairs dining room overlooking town; piped music; bedrooms, open all day *(Michael Dandy, BB, Jane Taylor, David Dutton)*

☆ **Queens Head** GL54 1AB [The Square]: Splendidly unpretentious for this upmarket town, well kept low-priced Donnington BB and SBA, good wines by the glass, good value sandwiches and basic pub meals (not Sun), good friendly service, lots of tables in bustling and chatty stripped stone front lounge, heavily beamed and flagstoned back bar with high-backed settles, big log-effect fire, horse prints, usual games; piped music; dogs and children positively welcome (pub dog lets herself in by opening back door), tables in attractive sunny back courtyard, occasional jazz Sun lunchtime *(LYM, Michael Dandy, the Didler, Tracey and Stephen Groves, Paul and Shirley White, Keith and Sue Ward, Lawrence Pearse)*

Unicorn GL54 1HQ [Sheep St (A429 edge of centre)]: Handsome hotel with comfortably

traditional low-beamed and flagstoned upmarket bar used by locals, Hook Norton ales, good range of food, restaurant; bedrooms *(W W Burke)*

STROUD [SO8404]

Clothiers Arms GL5 3JJ [Bath Rd]: Extended 18th-c pub with good choice of good value food, good prompt service, Wychwood Hobgoblin and other ales in busy bar with old Stroud Brewery decorations, pleasant airy dining room; garden tables *(Ralph Kenber, Dave Braisted)*

Lord John GL5 3AB [Russell St]: Airy split-level Wetherspoons in former PO sorting office, striking décor with something of a railway theme, tables in alcoves, their usual good value food and wide choice of sensibly priced ales inc interesting guest beers; disabled facilities, terrace tables *(Tony Hobden)*

Queen Victoria GL5 1QG [Gloucester St]: Welcoming open-plan local with four unusual changing real ales, end pool room supported by decorative steelwork; sports TV, live music; picnic-sets outside *(Tony Hobden)*

SWINEFORD [ST6969]

Swan BS30 6LN [A431, right on the Somerset border]: Smartly simple décor and furnishings in pub based originally on three cottages, well kept Bath ales and a guest such as Butcombe, good value enterprising food from good doorstep sandwiches up *(M G Hart)*

TETBURY [ST8893]

Priory GL8 8JJ [London Rd]: More good eating house than pub, with big central log fire in high-raftered stone-built former stables, and strong emphasis on local produce – not just the meat, veg and cheese, but beer, wine and sparkling wine too, even an enterprising local slant to their wood-fired pizzas; comfortable coffee lounge, live music Sun; children very welcome, terrace tables, 14 good bedrooms *(anon)*

TEWKESBURY [SO8832]

Bell GL20 5SA [Church St]: Interesting hotel bar with black oak beams and timbers, neat 17th-c oak panelling, medieval leaf-and-fruit frescoes, tapestries and armchairs, enjoyable bar food in roomy and comfortable eating area, attractive restaurant, real ales, decent house wines, good coffee, friendly service, big log fire; garden above Severn-side walk, nr abbey; bedrooms *(J and F Gowers, BB)*

Berkeley Arms GL20 5PA [Church St]: Pleasantly olde-worlde medieval timbered pub (most striking part down the side alley), with Wadworths and guest ales, friendly landlord and quick service, open fire, enjoyable generous pubby food (not Mon), separate basic front public bar, raftered ancient back barn restaurant; open all day Fri/Sat, bedrooms *(Theocsbrian, Dave Braisted, P Dawn)*

Gupshill Manor GL20 5SG [Gloucester Rd (off A38 S edge of town)]: Recently reopened after refurbishment, with good value food (all day Sun) inc interesting dishes, great range of wines by the glass, Greene King real ales; children welcome, disabled access, good-sized garden with heated terraces, open all day *(Andy and Claire Barker)*

Olde Black Bear GL20 5BJ [High St]: The county's oldest pub and well worth a look for its intricately rambling rooms with ancient tiles, heavy timbering and low beams; reasonably priced wines and real ales (nice glasses), open fires, well worn furnishings, basic food; piped music, and they may try to keep your credit card while you eat; children welcome, terrace and play area in riverside garden, open all day *(Roger and Anne Newbury, the Didler, S H Johnston, Maureen and Keith Gimson, LYM, Ann and Colin Hunt, P Dawn)*

THRUPP [SO8603]

Waggon & Horses GL5 2BL [London Rd]: Handsome roadside free house, well kept local Stroud beers, good atmosphere, motorcyclists welcome (landlord rides a Ducati) *(Giles and Annie Francis)*

TOCKINGTON [ST6086]

Swan BS32 4NJ [Tockington Green]: Roomy pub with well kept ale, helpful service, reasonably priced food, log fire, beams and standing timbers, bric-a-brac on stripped stone walls; may be piped music; tables in tree-shaded garden, quiet village *(Dr and Mrs A K Clarke)*

TODDINGTON [SP0432]

Pheasant GL54 5DT [A46 Broadway—Winchcombe, junction with A438 and B4077]: Attractive extended stone-built pub with emphasis on good choice of reasonably priced food, real ales, lots of railway prints – handy for nearby preserved Gloucestershire Warwickshire Railway station; no dogs while food served *(B M Eldridge)*

TOLLDOWN [ST7577]

☆ *Crown* SN14 8HZ [a mile from M4 junction 18 – A46 towards Bath]: Heavy-beamed dining pub with generous interesting food from good ciabattas up, helpful service, Wadworths ales, good house wines and still a welcome for people dropping in for just a drink, good log fire, simple furnishings and light fresh décor; good disabled access, children in eating area and restaurant, good garden with play area, comfortable bedrooms *(Dr and Mrs A K Clarke, Brian P White, LYM, Tom and Ruth Rees)*

TORMARTON [ST7678]

Compass GL9 1JB [handy for M4 junction 18]: Busy extended off-motorway hotel/conference centre with choice of rooms inc cosily old-fashioned beamed bar open all day for wide choice of food, pleasant conservatory, friendly quick service, Bass, Butcombe and Timothy Taylors Landlord, good wine choice, open fire, restaurant; children welcome, garden tables, comfortable bedrooms, open all day *(M J Winterton, LYM)*

TWYNING [SO8737]

☆ *Fleet* GL20 6FL [off westbound A38 slip rd from M50 junction 1]: Family holiday pub in

superb setting at end of quiet lane though just off motorway, good river views from roomy high-ceilinged bars, interesting boating-theme décor, wide choice of enjoyable fresh food inc good lunchtime baps and baguettes, five real ales, woodburner, airy back restaurant area, tearoom and tuck shop; games room with darts and bar billiards, piped music, machines, entertainment Fri/Sat; service, usually good, may occasionally falter; children welcome, disabled access, picnic-sets in big waterside garden with two floodlit terraces, rockery cascade and safe enclosed children's area with chipmunk corner; stop on Tewkesbury—Bredon summer boat run, bedrooms, open all day *(LYM, Carol Broadbent, Dr A J and Mrs Tompsett, Carol and David Havard)*

UPTON CHEYNEY [ST6969]

Upton Inn BS30 6LY [signed off A431 at Bitton]: Much-refurbished bar with good value interesting home-made food inc good fish choice, friendly helpful service, decent wines and real ale, smart unchanging restaurant with wall hangings, chandeliers and blackamoor statues; tables outside, picturesque spot *(Meg and Colin Hamilton, MRSM)*

WESTBURY-ON-SEVERN [SO7114]

☆ *Red Lion* GL14 1PA [A48, corner Bell Lane]: Substantial beamed and half-timbered traditional pub on busy road but by quiet church-side lane to river, welcoming atmosphere, genial landlord, generous interesting home cooking, well kept ales such as Fullers London Pride, decent wine, comfortable bar with button-back wall seats, velvet curtains, coal stove, big dining room with old pews; handy for Westbury Court gardens (NT) *(M J Winterton, BB, B M Eldridge)*

WESTONBIRT [ST8690]

Hare & Hounds GL8 8QL [A433 SW of Tetbury]: Substantial roadside hotel with separate entrance for cheerful turkey-carpeted pub end, high-backed settles, snacks and good more substantial meals, Wadworths 6X, central log-effect gas fire, sporting prints, games in public bar on left; small tweedy more central cocktail bar, pleasant gardens, good value bedrooms, handy for Arboretum *(Dr and Mrs C W Thomas, BB, Dr and Mrs A K Clarke)*

WHITMINSTER [SO7607]

☆ *Frombridge Mill* GL2 7PD [Frombridge Lane (A38 nr M5 junction 13)]: Mill-based dining pub with cosy and comfortable largely carpeted bar and dining areas, some tables overlooking river, decent reasonably priced food inc popular good value lunchtime carvery (you can have just a starter), attentive staff, well kept Greene King real ales; picnic-sets in good-sized garden with play area, lovely setting overlooking weir *(Dr and Mrs C W Thomas)*

Old Forge GL2 7NY [A38 1½ miles N of M5 junction 13]: Welcoming L-shaped beamed pub with small carpeted bar, games room, good generous inexpensive food (not Sun evening or Mon) from baguettes to Sun roast, well kept real ales such as Butcombe and Greene King, decent wines, happy staff, dining room with panelled dado; children welcome, dogs allowed in part of bar, garden tables *(Dennis Jenkin)*

WICK [ST7072]

☆ *Rose & Crown* BS30 5QH [High St (A420)]: Busy and roomy Chef & Brewer, no 'chain pub' feel and plenty of character in linked largely unspoilt 17th-c rooms with low beams, mixed furnishings and candlelight, coal fire in big stone fireplace, pleasant views, friendly helpful staff, Courage Best, Greene King Old Speckled Hen, Wells & Youngs Bombardier and an unusual guest beer, good wines by the glass, very wide food choice, daily papers; good disabled access, picnic-sets out on terrace, open all day *(Dr and Mrs A K Clarke, BB, B N F and M Parkin, Ian and Joan Blackwell)*

WINCHCOMBE [SP0228]

Old White Lion GL54 5PS [North St]: Olde-worlde refurbishment, light and pleasant, with friendly staff, interesting enjoyable food, real ale, small bar, separate restaurant; pleasant back garden, bedrooms *(Susan and Nigel Brookes)*

Plaisterers Arms GL54 5LL [Abbey Terr]: Unspoilt and interesting 18th-c pub with stripped stonework, beams, Hogarth prints, bric-a-brac and flame-effect fires, well kept Goffs Jouster and Greene King ales, enterprising food, two chatty front bars both with steps down to dim-lit lower back dining area with tables in stalls; dogs welcome, plenty of tables and good play area in charming secluded back garden, long and narrow, comfortable simple bedrooms with own bathrooms (tricky stairs), handy for Sudeley Castle *(BB, John Smart)*

WINTERBOURNE [ST6678]

Willy Wicket BS36 1DP [Wick Wick Close, handy for M4 junction 19 via M32, A4174 E]: Relaxing Vintage Inn family dining pub with all-day food, Butcombe and St Austell, two eating areas off big central bar, two log fires, stripped stone, picture windows; open all day *(Donna and Roger)*

WITHINGTON [SP0315]

Kings Head GL54 4BD [Kings Head Lane]: Back bar with thriving old-fashioned feel, Hook Norton and a changing Wickwar beer tapped from the cask, friendly landlady and dog, pickled eggs, darts, shove-ha'penny, table skittles and pool, neat partly stripped stone lounge area; pleasant garden behind *(E McCall, T McLean, D Irving, R Huggins, Giles and Annie Francis)*

WOODCHESTER [SO8403]

Old Fleece GL5 5NB [Rooksmoor; A46 a mile S of Stroud – not to be confused with Fleece at Lightpill a little closer in]: Emphasis on wide choice of interesting freshly made bar food from unusual lunchtime sandwiches up, children's helpings, informal bare-boards décor in open-plan line of three big-windowed room areas, friendly welcome, Bass and Greene King IPA from bar on right, good wines by the glass, local non-alcoholic drinks, big log fire, candles, daily papers, stripped stone or dark salmon pink walls; children welcome, two roadside terraces, one heated *(BB, Neil and Anita Christopher, Dave Irving, Andy and Claire Barker, E McCall, T McLean, D Irving, R Huggins)*

☆ *Royal Oak* GL5 5PQ [off A46; Church Road, N Woodchester]: Relaxing and comfortable low-beamed bar on right with oak tables, soft seats by big log fire in huge fireplace next to sprucely old-fashioned stripped stone dining area on left, good generous honest food (best to book for Sun roast), helpful welcoming service, real ales such as Adnams Broadside, Greene King IPA and Sharps Doom Bar, fresh flowers, nice views; big-screen TV for special events, piped music; children and dogs welcome, open all day *(Andy and Claire Barker, Mrs Rosemary Reeves, LYM, E McCall, T McLean, D Irving, R Huggins, Cherry Ann Knott)*

'Children welcome' means the pubs says it lets children inside without any special restriction; readers have found that some may impose an evening time limit – please tell us if you find this.

Hampshire

We've tracked down quite a few strong new entries here this year, confirming the trend of recent years which has seen Hampshire gaining a place among the best areas for good pubs. This year's finds are the welcoming Dog & Crook at Brambridge (good food), the pretty thatched Three Tuns at Bransgore, the relaxed and friendly Hampshire Bowman at Dundridge, the neatly updated Robin Hood at Durley, the riverside Boot at Houghton (another place for good food), the handsome waterfront Old Customs House in Portsmouth, the appealingly laid out Dukes Head just outside Romsey (fresh fish specialities), the warmly welcoming Rising Sun at Swanmore, the friendly old Brushmakers Arms at Upham (new licensees since it was last in the *Guide*), the cheerful and bustling Crown at Upton, and the streamside Willow Tree in Winchester (interesting food). Other pubs doing particularly well this year are the Fox at Bramdean (well heeled and civilised), the Chestnut Horse at Easton (flourishing under new management), the Shoe at Exton (the hard-working young couple here are doing very well indeed), the Royal Oak at Fritham (a much enjoyed New Forest pub), the Vine in Hambledon (interesting bric-a-brac and welcoming landlord), the Hawkley Inn at Hawkley (quite a few changes going down well here – as do those ten real ales), the Trooper near Petersfield (such a lovely landlord), the Falcon at Rotherwick (a nice country pub), the Plough at Sparsholt (a bustling well run dining pub), the Harrow at Steep (an unspoilt gem), and the Black Boy (marvellously eccentric décor) and Wykeham Arms (civilised and interesting), both in Winchester. Among these, especially good food can be found in the Fox, the Chestnut Horse, the Trooper, the Plough, and the Wykeham Arms. It is the Wykeham Arms in Winchester which takes the title of Hampshire Dining Pub of the Year. In general this is a rather pricy area for pub food, and drinks too tend to cost rather more than the national norm. The main local brewer is Ringwood (Gales, which used to be a Hampshire beer, is now part of Fullers and brewed by them up in London). Other smaller local brewers such as Itchen Valley and the new (good value) Bowman are well worth looking out for. In the Lucky Dip section at the end of the chapter, pubs showing particularly well are the Globe in Alresford, White Buck at Burley, Fox & Hounds at Crawley, Queens Head at Dogmersfield, Queen at Dummer, George at East Meon, Plough at Longparish, Trusty Servant at Minstead, White Horse near Petersfield, newly redesigned Still & West in Portsmouth, Rose & Thistle at Rockbourne, White Lion at Soberton, White Hart in Stockbridge, Cricketers Arms at Tangley, Thomas Lord at West Meon, Red House in Whitchurch and Eclipse in Winchester.

BANK

SU2806   MAP 2

Oak 🍺

Signposted just off A35 SW of Lyndhurst; SO43 7FD

Tucked-away New Forest pub with well liked food and interesting décor

Although a new licensee has taken over this New Forest pub and the place is now owned by Fullers, it remains extremely busy and well liked with five real ales and nice food. On either side of the door in the bay windows of the L-shaped bar are built-in green-cushioned seats, and on the right there are two or three little pine-panelled booths with small built-in tables and bench seats. The rest of the bar has more floor space with candles in individual brass holders on a line of stripped old and newer blond tables set against the wall on bare floorboards, with more seats at the back; some low beams and joists, fishing rods, spears, a boomerang and old ski poles on the ceiling and on the walls are brass platters, heavy knives, stuffed fish and guns. There's also a big fireplace, cushioned milk churns along the bar counter and little red lanterns among hop bines above the bar. Fullers London Pride and a seasonal beer like London Porter, Gales HSB and Ringwood Best and Fortyniner on handpump. The pleasant side garden has picnic-sets and long tables and benches by the big yew trees.

🍴 **Popular bar food includes lunchtime doorstep sandwiches, baked brie with almonds and honey, various cured meats with roasted red pepper and pickles, pork and herb sausages with rich onion gravy, a pie of the day, vegetarian lasagne, greek salad topped with feta cheese and olives, fresh cod in beer batter, daily specials, and puddings such as chocolate bread and butter pudding or raspberry roulade.** *Starters/Snacks: £3.95 to £5.95. Main Courses: £8.50 to £15.50. Puddings: £4.25*

Fullers ~ Manager Martin Sliva ~ Real ale ~ Bar food (12-2.30, 6-9.30(9 Sun)) ~ (023) 8028 2350 ~ Children welcome until 6pm ~ Dogs welcome ~ Open 11.30-11; 12-10.30 Sun; 11.30-3, 6-11 weekdays in winter

Recommended by Mayur Shah, Mike and Sue Loseby, Brian Root, Louise English, Pam and John Smith, George Atkinson, Philip and Susan Philcox, Simon Watkins, Sue Demont, Tim Barrow, C J Cox, A Monro, Peter Titcomb, Janet Whittaker, Tom and Jill Jones, Kevin Flack, Graham and Glenis Watkins, D P and M A Miles, A G Marx, P E Wareham, Dr D J R Martin, Bob and Margaret Holder, Roger and Kate Sweetapple, Ian Wilson

BENTLEY

SU8044   MAP 2

Bull

A31 Alton—Farnham dual carriageway, east of village itself; accessible from both carriageways, but tricky if westbound; GU10 5JH

Cosy old place with tasty food and four real ales – an unexpected trunk road respite

With a fair range of real ales and enjoyable food, this busy 15th-c inn makes a good break from the busy A31 trunk road. The main room on the right, restful despite some traffic noise, has soft lighting, witty sayings chalked on low black beams in its maroon ceiling, lots of local photographs on partly stripped brick walls and pub chairs around neat stripped pub tables. The back room on the left has a good log fire in a huge hearth, a cushioned pew by one long oak-planked table, and in a snug and narrow back alcove another pew built around a nice mahogany table; piped music. Courage Best, Fullers London Pride, Hogs Back TEA and Ringwood Best on handpump and eight wines (and champagne) by the glass. There are plenty of pretty summer flowering tubs and hanging baskets outside and picnic-sets and a teak table and chairs on the side terrace.

🍴 **Good changing blackboard food includes sandwiches, soup, ploughman's, popular lambs kidneys in mustard and honey on toast, a proper prawn cocktail laced with brandy, sausages and mash, noisettes of lamb with apricot and spinach stuffing and honey and mint jus, roasted vegetable and cheese wellington, beef stroganoff, magret of duck with poached pear and calvados sauce, various fish dishes, and puddings such as white chocolate and raspberry tart and citrus and passion fruit crunch.** *Starters/Snacks: £4.50 to £7.95. Main Courses: £9.95 to £18.95. Puddings: £4.50*

Enterprise ~ Lease Grant Edmead ~ Real ale ~ Bar food (12-2.30, 6.30-9.30; 12-3, 6-8.30 Sun) ~ Restaurant ~ (01420) 22156 ~ Children allowed but with restrictions ~ Dogs allowed in bar ~ Open 10.30-11; 12-10.30 Sun; closed 25 and 26 Dec

Recommended by Ian Phillips, John and Rosemary Haynes, Janet Whittaker, Steve Derbyshire

BENTWORTH
SU6640   MAP 2

Sun 🍺

Sun Hill; from the A339 coming from Alton the first turning takes you there direct; or in village follow Shalden 2¼, Alton 4¼ signpost; GU34 5JT

Marvellous choice of real ales and welcoming landlady in popular country pub; nearby walks

There's always a bustling atmosphere and plenty of customers in this charming 17th-c country pub run by a friendly, hands-on landlady. Many are drawn here for the eight real ales on handpump: Badger Hopping Hare, Flower Pots, Fullers London Pride, Hogs Back TEA, Ringwood Best and Old Thumper, Stonehenge Pigswill and Timothy Taylors Landlord on handpump; several malt whiskies. The two little traditional communicating rooms have high-backed antique settles, pews and schoolroom chairs, olde-worlde prints and blacksmith's tools on the walls, and bare boards and scrubbed deal tables on the left; big fireplaces (one with an open fire) and candles make it especially snug in winter; an arch leads to a brick-floored room with another open fire. There are seats out in front and in the back garden and pleasant nearby walks.

🍴 Well liked bar food includes sandwiches, soup, creamy garlic mushrooms, pork and leek sausages, liver and bacon, avocado and stilton bake, fresh tagliatelle with smoked salmon, lemon and dill cream sauce, steak and kidney pie, daily specials, and puddings.
Starters/Snacks: £3.95 to £4.75. Main Courses: £8.95 to £13.95. Puddings: £3.95

Free house ~ Licensee Mary Holmes ~ Real ale ~ Bar food (12-2, 7-9.30) ~ (01420) 562338 ~ Children welcome (with restrictions) ~ Dogs welcome ~ Open 12-3, 6-11; 12-10.30 Sun

Recommended by Ann and Colin Hunt, Tony and Jill Radnor, Simon Fox, Paul A Moore, S G N Bennett, the Didler, Phyl and Jack Street, R B Gardiner, Mr and Mrs R W Allan, Mr and Mrs H J Langley

BRAISHFIELD
SU3724   MAP 2

Wheatsheaf 🍷

Village signposted off A3090 on NW edge of Romsey, pub just S of village on Braishfield Road; SO51 0QE

Cheerful pub with interesting and unusual décor, five real ales, and food using their own produce; nearby walks

The atmosphere in this friendly pub is relaxed and cheerful and the rambling layout and idiosyncratic décor have been carefully thought out – and although it sounds a bit of a mish-mash, it does work well. There are all sorts of tables from elegant little oak ovals through handsome Regency-style drum tables to sturdy more rustic ones, with a similarly wide variety of chairs, and on the stripped brick or deep pink-painted walls a profusion of things to look at, from Spy caricatures and antique prints through staffordshire dogs and other decorative china to a leg in a fishnet stocking kicking out from the wall and a jokey 'Malteser grader' (a giant copper skimmer). Ringwood Best, Timothy Taylors Landlord and guest beers such as Caledonian Deuchars IPA, fff Moondance and Hampshire Pride of Romsey on handpump, 16 wines by the glass and speciality belgian beers; daily papers, several reference books; piped music and board games. Disabled access and facilities. Unusually, the chairs, tables and picnic-sets out on the terrace are painted in greek blue; pétanque. There are woodland walks nearby and the pub is handy for the Sir Harold Hillier Arboretum.

🍴 Using their own rare breed pigs for the pork dishes, their home-grown vegetables and fruit and their own eggs, the popular food here might include interesting soup, goats cheese and caramelised onion tart with beetroot and rocket, wild mushroom risotto, oak smoked haddock with tomato tarte tatin, crispy leeks and cream of seafood sauce, pork with stuffed english apple and black pudding, oxtail and lambs kidney suet pudding, local venison steak with a black cherry compote, and puddings like mixed berry and sultana cheesecake with pear and fudge yoghurt ice-cream and treacle tart with orange marmalade ice-cream; they also offer two-course set meals. *Starters/Snacks: £4.25 to £7.95. Main Courses: £9.95 to £17.95. Puddings: £4.95*

Enterprise ~ Lease Peter and Jenny Jones ~ Real ale ~ Bar food (12-3, 6.30-9.30; all day Sun) ~ Restaurant ~ (01794) 368372 ~ Children welcome away from bar ~ Dogs allowed in bar ~ Open 11am-11.30pm(midnight Sat)

Recommended by James Ponsford, Glen and Nola Armstrong, Tom and Jill Jones, Ann and Colin Hunt, Simon Watkins, Phyl and Jack Street, John and Bettye Reynolds, Lynn Sharpless, A and B D Craig

BRAMBRIDGE
SU4721   MAP 2

Dog & Crook ♀
Village signed off M3 junction 12 exit roundabout, via B3335; SO50 6HZ

A genuine warm welcome, attentive, kind staff and a super choice of good food – especially fish

The cheerful staff in this bustling pub really go out of their way to make their customers feel welcome and comfortable. And even though there is quite an emphasis on the good food, there's a nice area for those just wanting a chat and a pint, and the atmosphere feels properly pubby. There's a cosy dining room, and the bar has lots of neat tables under hop-hung beams, Fullers London Pride and HSB and Ringwood Best on handpump and 14 wines by the glass; piped music. The decking outside has alloy tables and chairs under a fairy-lit arbour and there's a grass area beyond that; Itchen Way walks nearby.

 As well as a fantastic, daily-changing fish board with choices such as home-made thai spiced fishcakes with sweet chilli dressing, a trio of fish with orange segments and a cognac marie-rose drizzle, supreme of nile perch with tiger prawns and cornish mackerel grilled with a cranberry and mustard marinade, the extremely popular food includes lunchtime filled baguettes and baked potatoes, steak in ale pie, local sausages with rich onion gravy and a curry of the day plus chicken liver parfait with home-made tomato chutney, a tartlet of red onion, wild mushroom and walnuts, herb-crusted lamb with port and rosemary jus and chicken stuffed with mozzarella cheese and pesto, wrapped in bacon with a light korma cream; super puddings. *Starters/Snacks: £3.25 to £6.25. Main Courses: £7.95 to £16.95. Puddings: £2.75 to £4.50*

Enterprise ~ Lease Kevin Dawkins ~ Real ale ~ Bar food (12-2.30, 5.30-9.30; Sat 12-9.30(8.30 Sun)) ~ Restaurant ~ (01962) 712129 ~ Children in restaurant ~ Dogs allowed in bar ~ Open 12-3, 5-11; 12-midnight(11pm Sun) Sat

Recommended by Phyl and Jack Street, A and B D Craig, Ann and Colin Hunt

BRAMDEAN
SU6127   MAP 2

Fox ⊗
A272 Winchester—Petersfield; SO24 0LP

Civilised dining pub with popular food and friendly staff; no children inside (though the spacious garden has play equipment)

The long-serving landlady and her staff continue to make both visitors and locals welcome in this rather smart, weatherboarded dining pub. The carefully modernised black beamed open-plan bar is civilised and grown up (no children inside), with tall stools with proper backrests around the L-shaped counter and comfortably cushioned wall pews and wheelback chairs – the fox motif shows in a big painting over the fireplace and on much of the decorative china. Greene King Ruddles County on handpump, decent wine by the glass, and piped music. At the back of the building is a walled-in terraced area and a neatly kept spacious lawn spreading among the fruit trees; a play area has a climbing frame and slide. Good surrounding walks.

🍴 Consistently good, if not cheap, the food includes lunchtime sandwiches, wild boar pâté, large portobello mushroom baked with dolcelatte, scallops with smoked bacon, chicken curry, fresh deep-fried fillet of cod in batter, chicken breast with parma ham in Boursin sauce, steak and kidney pie, roast confit of duck with an orange gravy, and puddings such as chocolate st emilion and treacle and orange tart with clotted cream. *Starters/Snacks: £4.95 to £7.95. Main Courses: £10.95 to £17.95. Puddings: £3.95 to £4.95*

Greene King ~ Tenants Ian and Jane Inder ~ Real ale ~ Bar food ~ (01962) 771363 ~ Open 11-3, 6(6.30 Mon and Tues)-11; 12-3.30, 7-10.30 Sun; closed Sun evenings Jan-March

Recommended by Glenwys and Alan Lawrence, W A Evershed, Phyl and Jack Street, Ann and Colin Hunt, Mr and Mrs R W Allan, Helen and Brian Edgeley, W W Burke, Janet Whittaker

BRANSGORE   SZ1997   MAP 2

Three Tuns 🍺

Village signposted off A35 and off B3347 N of Christchurch; Ringwood Road, opposite church; BH23 8JH

Enjoyable interesting food in pretty thatched pub with proper old-fashioned bar and good beers as well as civilised main dining area

The roomy low-ceilinged and carpeted main area has a fireside 'codgers' corner' as well as its good mix of comfortably cushioned low chairs around a variety of dining tables, and opens on to an attractive and extensive shrub-sheltered terrace with picnic-sets on its brick pavers; beyond here are more tables out on the grass, looking out over pony paddocks. On the right is a separate traditional regulars' bar that seems almost taller than it is wide, with an impressive log-effect stove in a stripped brick hearth, some shiny black panelling, and individualistic pubby furnishings. They have Caledonian Deuchars IPA, Hop Back Summer Lightning, Ringwood Best and Fortyniner and Timothy Taylors Landlord on handpump, and a good choice of wines by the glass and hot drinks; service is polite and efficient.

🍴 Besides usual bar food such as lunchtime sandwiches, fishcakes, curry and aberdeen angus burgers, they do several interesting soups, enterprising light dishes such as lime and dill marinated crab and bramley apple gateau or honey-roast quail, up-to-date main dishes such as thai monkfish, seared chicken breast with coriander butter or rare tuna with herb and lime crust, and nice variations on traditional puddings such as apple and lemon crumble; children's helpings of some dishes. *Starters/Snacks: £4.50 to £7.00. Main Courses: £6.50 to £17.00. Puddings: £4.50*

Enterprise ~ Licensee Peter Jenkins ~ Real ale ~ Bar food (all day Sun) ~ Restaurant ~ (01425) 672232 ~ Children in restaurant and lounge until 8pm ~ Dogs allowed in bar ~ Open 11.30-11; 12-10.30 Sun

Recommended by Rodger and Yvonne MacDonald, W A Evershed, Tony and Caroline Elwood, Phyl and Jack Street, John and Penelope Massey Stewart

CHERITON   SU5828   MAP 2

Flower Pots ★ 🍺 £

Pub just off B3046 (main village road) towards Beauworth and Winchester; OS Sheet 185 map reference 581282; SO24 0QQ

Own-brew beers in rustic pub with simple rooms and straightforward food

The two little rooms in this homely village local are rustic and simple, though the one on the left is a favourite, almost like someone's front room with country pictures on its striped wallpaper, bunches of flowers and some ornaments on the mantelpiece over a small log fire. Behind the servery is disused copper filtering equipment, and lots of hanging gin traps, drag-hooks, scaleyards and other ironwork. The neat extended plain public bar (where there's a covered well) has board games. Their own brewed beers (you can tour the brewery by arrangement) include Flower Pots Bitter, Goodens Gold and TBA on handpump. The pretty front and back lawns have some old-fashioned seats and there's a summer marquee; maybe summer morris dancers. The pub is near the site of one of the final battles of the Civil War, and it got its name through once belonging to the retired head gardener of nearby Avington Park. No children inside.

🍴 **Bar food from a fairly short straightforward menu includes sandwiches, toasties and baps, filled baked potatoes, ploughman's and various hotpots; on Wednesdays they serve only curries. The menu and serving times may be restricted at weekend lunchtimes if they're busy.** *Starters/Snacks: £3.00 to £6.60. Main Courses: £6.10 to £6.40*

Own brew ~ Licensees Jo and Patricia Bartlett ~ Real ale ~ Bar food (not Sun evening or bank hol evenings) ~ No credit cards ~ (01962) 771318 ~ Dogs welcome ~ Open 12-2.30, 6-11; 12-3, 7-10.30 Sun ~ Bedrooms: £40S/£65S

Recommended by Phyl and Jack Street, Ann and Colin Hunt, R G Trevis, Tony and Jill Radnor, Paul and Shirley White, the Didler, Val and Alan Green, R T and J C Moggridge, Peter and Liz Holmes, Lynn Sharpless, Bruce Bird, Janet Whittaker, Patrick Hall, Colin and Janet Roe, Mr and Mrs W D Borthwick, MLR, Phil and Sally Gorton

DUNDRIDGE   SU5718   MAP 2

Hampshire Bowman 🍺

Off B3035 towards Droxford, Swanmore, then right at Bishops W signpost; SO32 1GD

Friendly country pub with half a dozen quickly changing real ales, homely food and peaceful garden

Customers of all ages enjoy this individualistic country tavern that has been extended without losing its relaxed and friendly atmosphere; no mobile phones or noisy games machines or piped music. There's a smart new stable bar that sits comfortably alongside the cosy unassuming original bar, some colourful paintings and up to six quickly changing real ales tapped from the cask by the cheerful landlady: Bowman Swift One, Hop Back Crop Circle, Ringwood Fortyniner, Stonehenge Danish Dynamite and Suthwyk Bloomfields. Several wines by the glass and local cider (from April–October); board games, puzzles and Daisy the pub dog. There are picnic-sets on the attractive lawn and on the new terrace; lovely sunsets and peaceful downland walks.

🍴 **Well liked homely bar food includes good daily specials plus sandwiches, filled baguettes and baked potatoes, creamy vegetable pasta, gloucester old spot sausages, chilli con carne, gammon and egg, liver and bacon with onion gravy, thai chicken curry, and puddings such as cherry and apricot lattice pie and ginger sponge pudding.** *Starters/Snacks: £3.25 to £4.95. Main Courses: £6.50 to £12.95. Puddings: £3.95*

Free house ~ Licensee Heather Seymour ~ Bar food (12-2, 6.30-9; all day Fri-Sun) ~ (01489) 892940 ~ Children in stable bar only until 9pm ~ Dogs welcome ~ Open 12-3, 6-11; 12-11 Fri, Sat and Sun

Recommended by W A Evershed, Wendy Straker, Ann and Colin Hunt, the Didler, Christine Bridgwater

DURLEY   SU5217   MAP 2

Robin Hood

Durley Street, just off B2177 Bishops Waltham—Winchester – brown signs to pub; SO32 2AA

Carefully thought-out food in a neatly updated pub with go-ahead young licensees

Stripped down and opened up, this has dark bare boards, cream walls and ceiling, neat modern lighting and minimal decoration. On the left is a locals' area with a few big plain tables, lots of ancient team photographs, and darts; on the right, leather sofas around a splendidly rustic low table, a red-cushioned wall pew built around another big stripped table, and an open fire (the shelves of interesting-looking old books actually form a concealed door to the lavatories). This part merges into a light and airy restaurant part with contemporary multi-ply tables and smart comfortable metal-framed chairs on newish dark flagstones, and outside here are well spaced picnic-sets on a terrace, decking and grass. They have Greene King IPA, Morlands Original and Old Speckled Hen on handpump, with a guest such as Batemans XXXB, nicely served coffee and decent wines by the glass, and service is attentive and welcoming; the boston terrier is called Mylo. They have frequent events, from a quiz every other Monday to wine tastings and so forth; darts, board games and maybe faint piped music. The village has some interesting footpaths.

🍴 Cooked by the good young chef, the bar food at lunchtime might include sandwiches and pizzas, tempura of fish with sweet chilli dipping sauce, home-made pâté with toasted brioche, sausages with caramelised red onion jus, lightly battered fish and chips with parma ham and pea purée and free-range chicken caesar salad, with evening extras such as goats cheese and caramelised onion tart, home-made fishcake with poached egg, wild cod fillet with parsley velouté and thyme fondant potato, flash-roasted thyme and lemon marinated lamb rump with dauphinoise potatoes, spit-roasted whole poussin with chorizo jus, and puddings like raspberry and stem ginger parfait and spotted dick with crème anglaise. *Starters/Snacks: £4.95 to £7.95. Main Courses: £8.95 to £17.50. Puddings: £4.95 to £6.95*

Free house ~ Licensees Antony and Jo Robertson ~ Real ale ~ Bar food (12-2, 6.30-9.30; all day Fri and Sat and until 6pm Sun) ~ Restaurant ~ (01489) 860229 ~ Children welcome ~ Dogs allowed in bar ~ Open 12-3, 5-11; 12-midnight Fri and Sat; 12-10.30 Sun; closed Sun evening from 7pm

Recommended by Phyl and Jack Street

EASTON   SU5132   MAP 2

Chestnut Horse 🍴 ♟

3.6 miles from M3 junction 9: A33 towards Kings Worthy, then B3047 towards Itchen Abbas; Easton then signposted on right – bear left in village; SO21 1EG

Cosy dining pub with log fires, fresh flowers and candles, deservedly popular (if not cheap) food and friendly staff; Itchen Valley walks nearby

Although Badger now own this well run dining pub and there's a new licensee (who used to work for the previous people), readers have been quick to tell us how much they have enjoyed their recent visits. The open-plan interior manages to have a pleasantly rustic and intimate feel with a series of cosily separate areas and the snug décor takes in candles and fresh flowers on the tables, log fires in cottagey fireplaces and comfortable furnishings. The black beams and joists are hung with all sorts of jugs, mugs and chamber-pots and lots of attractive pictures of wildlife and the local area. Badger First Gold, a seasonal beer and a beer named for the pub on handpump; friendly, helpful service and piped music. There are good tables out on a smallish sheltered decked area with colourful flower tubs and baskets and plenty of walks in the Itchen Valley from here.

🍴 As well as lunchtime sandwiches, the good, restauranty food might include soup, tian of fresh crab and crayfish tails, confit duck terrine with spinach, orange and pink grapefruit salad, thai-style moules, red onion and celeriac galette with a wholegrain mustard and gruyère cream sauce, supreme of chicken with mushrooms and ham, fillets of bass with roasted fennel, orange and peppercorn beurre blanc, ostrich fillet with tomato and marjoram polenta and marsala jus, and puddings such as dark chocolate and orange steamed pudding and plum tarte tatin with butterscotch sauce. There's also a popular and much more reasonably priced two-course menu (not available weekend evenings or Sunday lunchtime). *Starters/Snacks: £4.95 to £7.95. Main Courses: £11.95 to £16.95. Puddings: £5.95 to £7.95*

Badger ~ Tenant Karen Wells ~ Real ale ~ Bar food (12-2.30, 6-9.30; 12-8.30(4 winter) Sun) ~ Restaurant ~ (01962) 779257 ~ Children welcome ~ Dogs allowed in bar ~ Open 11-3, 5.30-11.30; 11am-11.30pm Sat; 12-10.30 Sun; closed from 5.30pm Sun in winter

Recommended by Mrs S Barker-Ryder, Tom and Ruth Rees, David and Sue Smith, Lynn Sharpless, W A Evershed, Patrick Hall, Simon Fox, Phyl and Jack Street, Andy Reid, Dr D and Mrs B Woods, Ann and Colin Hunt, Mike and Jayne Bastin, GHC, Michael Dandy, Martin and Karen Wake, Susan and John Douglas, Mrs Ann Gray

---

Please tell us if the décor, atmosphere, food or drink at a pub is different from our description. We rely on readers' reports to keep us up to date. No stamp needed: The Good Pub Guide, FREEPOST TN1569, Wadhurst, E Sussex TN5 7BR.

EXTON   SU6120 MAP 2

Shoe

Village signposted from A32 NE of Bishop's Waltham – brown sign to pub into Beacon Hill Lane; SO32 3NT

Hard-working licensees in country pub by River Meon with comfortable linked rooms and nice food

As well as raised beds which produce some of the organic herbs and vegetables used in the popular cooking here, there is now a greenhouse for fruits, chillies, peppers and asparagus. This is a nicely located country pub and the three linked rooms have a friendly relaxed atmosphere, comfortable pub furnishings, cricket and country prints, and in the right-hand room (which is panelled) a log fire. Wadworths 6X, IPA and a seasonal guest on handpump and 14 wines by the glass; helpful, welcoming service. You can sit at picnic-sets and watch the ducks on the River Meon from beneath a floodlit sycamore across the road and there are seats under parasols at the front. There are now baby-changing facilities, a disabled lavatory and ramp access.

🍽 Cooked by the landlord, the imaginative food might include nice sandwiches and platters, crab and leek tart with cucumber and lime salad and parmesan crisp, chicken, mushroom and tarragon terrine with cranberry and red onion, pork and leek sausages with red wine gravy, bubble and squeak and french onion rings, baked portabello mushroom in filo pastry with spinach, blue cheese and honey-roast shallots, smoked haddock with poached egg and butter sauce, loin of pork with orange and sage crust, roast garlic mash and sage jus, moroccan lamb casserole, and puddings such as white chocolate and ginger terrine and apple and wild berry meringue tart. They make their own bread, pickles and chutneys. *Starters/Snacks: £4.00 to £7.00. Main Courses: £8.00 to £15.00. Puddings: £4.65*

Wadworths ~ Tenants Mark and Carole Broadbent ~ Real ale ~ Bar food (12-2, 6-9(8.30 Sun and Mon, 9.30 Fri and Sat)) ~ (01489) 877526 ~ Children welcome ~ Dogs allowed in bar ~ Open 11-3, 6-11

Recommended by Ann and Colin Hunt, Peter Meister, Glenwys and Alan Lawrence, W A Evershed, Michele Gunning, Tina and David Woods-Taylor, Matt and Cathy Fancett, Brian Robinson

FRITHAM   SU2314 MAP 2

Royal Oak 🍺

Village signed from exit roundabout, M27 junction 1; quickest via B3078, then left and straight through village; head for Eyeworth Pond; SO43 7HJ

Rural New Forest spot and part of a working farm; traditional rooms, log fires, seven real ales and simple lunchtime food

This typifies the very best of simple country pubs. There are plenty of chatty locals (almost invariably with a dog in tow), a genuinely warm welcome from the friendly staff and really enjoyable, good quality unfussy food. Three neatly kept black-beamed rooms are straightforward but full of proper traditional character, with prints and pictures involving local characters on the white walls, restored panelling, antique wheelback, spindleback and other old chairs and stools with colourful seats around solid tables on new oak flooring, and two roaring log fires. The back bar has quite a few books. A fine range of seven well kept ales is tapped from the cask: Hop Back Summer Lightning, Ringwood Best and Fortyniner and changing guests from brewers such as Bowan and Keysone. Also, a dozen wines by the glass (mulled wine in winter) and maybe a September beer festival; darts and board games. Summer barbecues are put on in the neatly kept big garden which has a marquee for poor weather. The pub is part of a working farm so there are ponies and pigs out on the green and plenty of livestock nearby.

🍽 Using eggs from their free-range hens and home-made cheeses, the much liked simple lunchtime food is limited to soups, ploughman's, pies and quiches, cumberland sausage ring and smoked chicken breast wrapped in bacon. *Starters/Snacks: £4.50. Main Courses: £6.00 to £7.50*

Free house ~ Licensees Neil and Pauline McCulloch ~ Real ale ~ Bar food (lunchtime only) ~ No credit cards ~ (023) 8081 2606 ~ Children welcome if well behaved ~ Dogs welcome ~ Open 11-3, 6-11; 11-11 Sat; 12-10.30 Sun; 11-3 weekdays in winter

Recommended by N R White, Kevin Flack, W W Burke, Peter Titcomb, Dr A J and Mrs Tompsett, Ann and Colin Hunt, the Didler, Mike and Linda Hudson, G Coates, Peter and Anne Hollindale, Pete Baker, Dick and Madeleine Brown

HAMBLEDON   SU6414   MAP 2

Vine

West Street, just off B2150; PO7 4RW

Interesting food, nice drinks, quite a bit of bric-a-brac and a good local feel

Run by welcoming and attentive licensees, this 400-year-old village pub is popular with both locals and visitors. There's plenty of bric-a-brac throughout the beamed rooms such as signed cricket bats, lots of old books, a well used piano, old sporting and country prints as well as some interesting watercolours of early 20th-c regimental badges and old pictures of HMS *Hambledon* on the walls, a boar's head, an old leather sofa and pewter tankards. Jennings Cocker Hoop, Marstons Bitter, Ringwood Bold Forester and a couple of guests on handpump, 11 wines by the glass and Thatcher's cider; cards, shove-ha'penny and cribbage and there's a 35ft well. There are seats and tables on decking in the back garden. The birthplace of the game of cricket is just outside the village on Broadhalfpenny Down.

🍴 **Reasonably priced and well liked bar food** includes sandwiches, ploughman's, soup, mustard and white bean pâté with garlic toasts, shredded crispy duck salad with spiced plum dressing, ham and eggs, sausages with herb mash and caramelised onion gravy, posh shepherd's pie, slow-roasted pork belly with grilled black pudding and grainy mustard mash, seafood risotto and fillet of turbot with braised butter bean and chorizo ragoût. *Starters/Snacks: £4.00 to £9.00. Main Courses: £6.95 to £16.50. Puddings: £4.00 to £5.50*

Marstons ~ Tenants Tom and Vicki Faulkner ~ Real ale ~ Bar food (not Sun evening) ~ Restaurant ~ (023) 9263 2419 ~ Children welcome but not late in the evening ~ Dogs allowed in bar ~ Live music once a month ~ Open 11.30-3, 6-11; 12-4, 7-10.30 Sun

Recommended by Ann and Colin Hunt, Bruce Bird, Mrs Maricar Jagger, Diana Brumfit, D and J Ashdown

HAWKLEY   SU7429   MAP 2

Hawkley Inn 🍺

Take first right turn off B3006, heading towards Liss ¼ mile from its junction with A3; then after nearly 2 miles take first left turn into Hawkley village – Pococks Lane; OS Sheet 186 map reference 746292; GU33 6NE

Ten real ales and good homely food in warmly friendly pub; comfortable new bedrooms

There have been quite a few changes here this year but readers have been quick to voice their approval. Five comfortable new ensuite bedrooms have been added and a new kitchen constructed and the back rooms have been knocked through, effectively creating a central bar so you can now walk all round the pub. These back rooms (hung with paintings by local artists) now look over the garden and new back terrace. But this remains a proper country pub with walking boots, wellies, horses, bikes – and of course a smashing range of ten real ales on handpump: Ballards Best, Bowman Ales Swift One, Dark Star Hophead, fff Moondance, Hop Back Summer Lightning and Moosedrool (brewed especially for the pub), RCH East Street Cream, Sharps Doom Bar and Suthwyk Skew Sunshine Ale and Bloomfields. A dozen malt whiskies and a local cider and perry on handpump; friendly service. The front rooms remain unchanged and there are open fires, board games and piped music. The pub is on the Hangers Way Path, and at weekends there are plenty of walkers (and it does tend to be crowded then).

Please let us know of any pubs where the wine is particularly good.

🍴 **Good bar food includes sandwiches, interesting soups, crab cakes with sweet chilli dip, bacon, brie and mushroom tart, faggots with onion gravy, nice sausages and mash, cottage pie, beef stew, grilled duck breast with peppercorn sauce, bass fillets with peppers and aubergine, and puddings such as spotted dick or super treacle tart.** *Starters/Snacks: £4.25 to £5.50. Main Courses: £7.50 to £13.50. Puddings: £2.50 to £4.50*

Free house ~ Licensee Nick Troth ~ Real ale ~ Bar food (12-2(2.30 Sat), 7-9.30; 12-3, 7-9 Sun) ~ (01730) 827205 ~ Children welcome until 8pm ~ Dogs allowed in bar ~ Live jazz and blues some winter Sat evenings ~ Open 12-3(4 Sat), 5.30-11; 12-4, 7-10.30 Sun; closed evening 25 Dec and on 26 Dec and 1 Jan ~ Bedrooms: £69B/£75S(£85B)

Recommended by W A Evershed, JMM, Simon Fox, P E Wareham, Martin and Karen Wake, R B Gardiner, Wendy Arnold, Ann and Colin Hunt, the Didler, Mrs Margo Finlay, Jörg Kasprowski, Derek and Sylvia Stephenson, Tony and Jill Radnor, Susan and John Douglas

HOUGHTON   SU3432   MAP 2
Boot
Village signposted off A30 in Stockbridge; SO20 6LH

Riverside pub with good generous food either in cheerful locals' bar or in roomy more decorous lounge/dining room

The long sheltered lawn behind here runs down to a lovely tranquil stretch of the River Test (quick-flowing, and unfenced here), where you may be able to arrange fishing with the pub – though one monster trout in the bar's generous assortment of stuffed creatures was actually taken on the Itchen. This nice country bar is bustling and pubby, with a good log fire, plenty of regulars both at the counter and around the various tables, and perhaps one or two dogs making themselves at home (visiting dogs may get a chew). Service is efficient and natural – treating people good-naturedly as individuals without being artificially over-friendly. They have Ringwood Best and Bold Forester on handpump; there may be faint piped music. On the left is a much more extensive part with attractive modern dining chairs around good solid tables. The Test Way cycle path is on the far side of the river.

🍴 **Huge helpings of good bar food run from popular piles of chunky cheesy chips through croque monsieur or massively filled baguettes or ciabattas with abundant fresh salad to home-grown asparagus spears with hollandaise, crab cake with wholegrain mustard, spring onion and chilli dip, chicken stuffed with brie and watercress, baked camembert with garlic and thyme, free-range pork loin slow-roasted with apple jus, fillet steak with wild mushroom sauce, and puddings such as chocolate fudge brownie with chocolate sauce or rhubarb crumble. They make a point of using well hung meat with real flavour.** *Starters/Snacks: £5.50. Main Courses: £9.50 to £16.00. Puddings: £5.00*

Free house ~ Licensees Richard and Tessa Affleck ~ Real ale ~ Bar food (not Sun or Mon evenings) ~ (01794) 388310 ~ Children welcome if well behaved ~ Dogs welcome ~ Open 11-3, 6-11; 12-3, 7-10.30 Sun; weekday evening opening 7pm in winter

Recommended by Edward Mirzoeff, Ann and Colin Hunt, Julia and Richard Tredgett, Helen and Brian Edgeley, Patrick Hall

LITTLETON   SU4532   MAP 2
Running Horse 🍴 ♟
Village signposted off B3049 just NW of Winchester; Main Road; SO22 6QS

Inventive food in stylish, elegant rooms, a fine choice of drinks, and nice terraces

It's a surprise to find this smart and stylish dining pub in such a rustic village setting. The bar has some deep leather chairs as well as ochre-cushioned metal and wicker ones around matching modern tables on its polished boards, up-to-date lighting, good colour photographs of hampshire landscapes and townscapes, a potted palm as well as a log fire and venetian blinds in its bow windows. The neat modern marble and hardwood bar counter (with swish leather, wood and brass bar stools) has Palmers IPA and Ringwood Best on handpump, 14 wines by the glass and good coffee. Linking openly from here, the back restaurant area has the same sort of elegant modern furniture on flagstones. Good disabled access and facilities and maybe piped pop music. There are green metal tables and chairs out on terraces front and back and picnic-sets on the back grass by a spreading sycamore.

🍴 Enjoyable food includes lunchtime sandwiches, ciabattas and ploughman's, soup, duck and apricot terrine with cumberland dressing, black pudding, poached egg and hollandaise, oriental vegetable parcels with sesame and soy dressing, game pudding, thai green chicken curry, calves liver with port and pancetta jus, bass fillets with anchovy, caper and lemon butter and duck breast with honey, lime and ginger glaze. *Starters/Snacks: £4.95 to £6.95. Main Courses: £10.95 to £17.50. Puddings: £3.75 to £6.50*

Free house ~ Licensee Kathryn Crawford ~ Real ale ~ Bar food (12-2, 6-9(8 Sun, 9.30 Fri and Sat)) ~ Restaurant ~ (01962) 880218 ~ Children welcome if well behaved ~ Dogs allowed in bar ~ Open 11-3, 5.30-11; 11-11 Sat; 12-3, 5.30-10.30 Sun ~ Bedrooms: £65B/£75B

Recommended by Phyl and Jack Street, John and Joan Calvert

LOWER WIELD   SU6339 MAP 2

Yew Tree ♀

Turn off A339 NW of Alton at Medstead, Bentworth 1 signpost, then follow village signposts; or off B3046 S of Basingstoke, signposted from Preston Candover; SO24 9RX

Relaxed atmosphere, super choice of wines and popular food in pleasant country pub; sizeable garden and nearby walks

The atmosphere in this tile-hung country pub is nicely informal and you can expect a warm welcome from the friendly and enthusiastic landlord. A small flagstoned bar area on the left has a few military prints above its stripped brick dado, a steadily ticking clock and a log fire. Around to the right of the serving counter – which has a couple of stylish wrought-iron bar chairs – it's carpeted, with a few attractive flower pictures; throughout there is a mix of tables, including some quite small ones for two, and miscellaneous chairs. A dozen or more wines by the glass from a well chosen list which may include Louis Jadot burgundies from a shipper based just along the lane and summer rosé. Bowman Ales Swift One and a beer from fff named after the pub on handpump. There are solid tables and chunky seats out on the front terrace, picnic-sets in a sizeable side garden, pleasant views, and a cricket field just across the quiet lane. Nearby walks include one around lovely Rushmoor Pond.

🍴 Tasty bar food includes chicken liver pâté with home-made spicy plum chutney, salmon and crab cake with home-made tartare sauce, sausages of the week with caramelised red onion gravy, spinach and ricotta cannelloni with cashew pesto, cream and cheese, tasty lamb and mint steamed pudding, steamed red snapper with fennel, leeks, dill and Pernod, and puddings such as apricot and white chocolate bread and butter pudding and cranberry, blackcurrant and apple crumble. *Starters/Snacks: £3.95 to £6.95. Main Courses: £7.50 to £17.95. Puddings: £4.50*

Free house ~ Licensee Tim Gray ~ Real ale ~ Bar food (12-2, 6.30-9(8.30 Sun) ~ (01256) 389224 ~ Children welcome ~ Dogs allowed in bar ~ Open 12-3, 6-11; 12-10.30 Sun; closed Mon; first two weeks Jan

Recommended by Roger Chacksfield, Richard Foskett, Stephanie Lang, Stephen Moss, Ann and Colin Hunt, R B Gardiner, Tony and Jill Radnor, Janet Whittaker, P E Wareham, Phyl and Jack Street, Peter and Andrea Jacobs, Martin and Karen Wake, Mr and Mrs W Mills, Shawn O'Rourke, Matt and Cathy Fancett, Simon Smith

---

Bedroom prices normally include full english breakfast, VAT and any inclusive service charge that we know of. Prices before the '/' are for single rooms, after for two people in double or twin (B includes a private bath, S a private shower). If there is no '/', the prices are only for twin or double rooms (as far as we know there are no singles). If there is no B or S, as far as we know no rooms have private facilities.

LYMINGTON   SZ3295 MAP 2

Kings Head 🍺

Quay Hill; pedestrian alley at bottom of High Street, can park down on quay and walk up from Quay Street; SO41 3AR

Rambling beamed and timbered pub with nice mix of old-fashioned seating, decent food and beer, and newspapers to read

This 17th-c pub rambles up and down steps and through timber dividers with tankards hanging from great rough beams. The mainly bare-boarded rooms contain a nice old-fashioned variety of seating at a great mix of tables from an elegant gateleg to a huge chunk of elm, and the local pictures include good classic yacht photographs. A cosy upper corner past the serving counter has a good log fire in a big fireplace, its mantelpiece a shrine to all sorts of drinking paraphernalia from beer tankards to port and champagne cases. Adnams Bitter, Gales HSB, Greene King Old Speckled Hen and a guest like Ringwood Bold Forester on handpump, and several wines by the glass; daily papers in a rack and piped pop music. More reports please.

🍽 **Bar food includes sandwiches, tiger prawns in tempura batter with sweet chilli dip, lasagne, lambs liver on mash, pasta with chicken and bacon in creamy parmesan sauce, steak and mushroom in ale pie, daily specials, and puddings such as apple crumble.** *Starters/Snacks: £4.95 to £6.95. Main Courses: £7.95 to £15.95. Puddings: £4.35*

Inn Partnership (Pubmaster) ~ Lease Paul Stratton ~ Real ale ~ Bar food (11-2.15(3 Fri-Sun), 6-10) ~ (01590) 672709 ~ Children welcome ~ Dogs welcome ~ Open 11-3, 6-midnight; 11-1am Fri and Sat; 12-11 Sun; closed 25 and 26 Dec

Recommended by Fr Robert Marsh, Michael Sargent, Di and Mike Gillam, Pam and John Smith, Diane Hibberd

OVINGTON   SU5631 MAP 2

Bush

Village signposted from A31 on Winchester side of Alresford; SO24 ORE

Cottagey pub with waterside back garden, several peaceful rooms, and high quality food

This is a delightful spot for lunch on a sunny day sitting at one of the picnic-sets by the River Itchen; this year they've built a sizeable barbecue. Inside it's charming and cottagey, with a marked absence of piped music, fruit machines or pool tables. A low-ceilinged bar is furnished with cushioned high-backed settles, elm tables with pews and kitchen chairs, masses of old pictures in heavy gilt frames on the walls, and a roaring fire on one side with an antique solid fuel stove opposite. Wadworths IPA, 6X, JCB and a seasonal ale and a guest like Jennings Mountain Man on handpump, 11 wines by the glass and quite a few country wines. Occasionally staff here don't quite meet the high standards of service which the licensees have maintained for so long. Look out for the sociable scottish springer spaniel, Paddy; board games. Please note that if you want to bring children it's best to book, as there are only a few tables set aside for families. Nice nearby walks.

🍽 **The food is of high quality and might include sandwiches, ploughman's, soup, organic smoked trout mousse, black pudding and chicory salad with mustard vinaigrette and poached egg, onion tart with goats cheese and olives, steak and mushroom pie, tiger prawn and rocket linguini in a chilli tomato sauce, slow-roasted belly pork with organic cider sauce, and puddings such as rhubarb crumble with lemon grass and stem ginger ice-cream and plum and port tart with custard.** *Starters/Snacks: £4.95 to £10.95. Main Courses: £9.50 to £14.95. Puddings: £4.80*

Wadworths ~ Managers Nick and Cathy Young ~ Real ale ~ Bar food (not Sun evening) ~ (01962) 732764 ~ Children allowed but only four tables for families ~ Dogs welcome ~ Open 11-3, 6-11(all day summer hols); 12-3, 7-10.30 Sun; closed 25 Dec

Recommended by Martin and Karen Wake, Ann and Colin Hunt, W A Evershed, W W Burke, N R White, GHC, Lynn Sharpless, R B Gardiner, Tony and Jill Radnor, Nick Lawless, Phyl and Jack Street, Matt and Cathy Fancett, Helen and Brian Edgeley, John and Tania Wood, Val andAlan Green, Tracey and Stephen Groves

PETERSFIELD

SU7227   MAP 2

Trooper 🍴 🍺 🛏️

From B2070 in Petersfield follow Steep signposts past station, but keep on up past Steep, on old coach road; OS Sheet 186 map reference 726273; GU32 1BD

Charming landlord, very popular food (must book in advance), decent drinks, and little persian knick-knacks and local artists' work; good bedrooms

Run by an exceptionally friendly landlord who makes his customers feel genuinely warmly welcomed, this country dining inn is a fine all-rounder with well kept beers, extremely good food and comfortable bedrooms. There's an island bar, blond chairs and a mix of tripod tables on bare boards or red tiles, tall stools by a broad ledge facing big windows that look across to rolling downland fields, old film star photos and paintings by local artists for sale, little persian knick-knacks here and there, quite a few ogival mirrors, lit candles all over the place, fresh flowers, and a well tended log fire in the stone fireplace; carefully chosen piped music, and newspapers and magazines to read. Adnams TEA, Ballards Best and Ringwood Best on handpump and several wines by the glass. The attractive raftered restaurant has french windows to a partly covered sunken terrace, and there are lots of picnic-sets on an upper lawn. The horse rail in the car park ('horses and camels only before 8pm') does get used, though probably not often by camels.

🍽️ **Really enjoyable bar food includes sandwiches, soup, confit duck with red onion marmalade, chicken satay, roquefort and chive tart topped with walnuts, garlic and parsley, sausages and mash in a giant yorkshire pudding with onion gravy, free-range chicken, smoked bacon and mushroom pie, organic salmon fillet with a lime, ginger and chilli dressing, slow-roasted half shoulder of lamb with rich honey and mint gravy and filo-wrapped venison fillet with madeira and cranberry sauce.** *Starters/Snacks: £5.00 to £7.00. Main Courses: £9.50 to £18.50. Puddings: £5.00 to £7.00.*

Free house ~ Licensee Hassan Matini ~ Real ale ~ Bar food (12-2(2.30 Sun), 6-9(9.30 Fri, Sat)) ~ Restaurant ~ (01730) 827293 ~ Children must be seated and supervised by an adult ~ Dogs allowed in bar ~ Open 12-3, 7-11; 12-4 Sun; closed Sun evening and all day Mon (but may open Mon evening in summer) ~ Bedrooms: £69B/£89B

Recommended by Ray J Carter, Tracey and Stephen Groves, Ann and Colin Hunt, Bruce and Penny Wilkie, Mike and Mary Carter, Bren and Val Speed, Tony and Jill Radnor, Brian and Janet Ainscough, Joan Thorpe, Keith and Chris O'Neill, Tina and David Woods-Taylor, Karen Eliot

PORTSMOUTH

SZ6399   MAP 2

Old Customs House

Vernon Buildings, Gunwharf Quays; follow brown signs to Gunwharf Quays car park – usually quickest to park on lower level, come up escalator, turn left towards waterside then left again; PO1 3TY

Handsome historic building well converted in prime waterfront development

This fine brick building was indeed the former Georgian customs house, then an administration building for HMS *Vernon*, the Royal Navy's mine clearance and diving school (it has some memorabilia of those days). Around it now are the spacious walkways of a bright and extensive modern waterside shopping centre, and just around the corner is the graceful new Spinnaker Tower, 165 metres (540 ft) tall, which gives staggering vistas from its viewing decks. The pub is well laid out, with several big-windowed high-ceilinged rooms off a long central spine which houses the serving bar and a separate food/coffee ordering counter – they have loads of good coffees and teas, as well as a good range of wines by the glass, and Fullers Chiswick, London Pride, ESB, Discovery and HSB. This floor, with good disabled access and facilities, has bare boards, nautical prints and photographs on pastel walls, coal-effect gas fires, nice unobtrusive lighting, and well padded chairs around sturdy tables in varying sizes; the sunny entrance area has leather sofas. Broad stairs take you up to a carpeted more restauranty floor, with similar décor. Staff are efficient, housekeeping is good, the piped music well reproduced, and the games machines silenced. Picnic-sets out in front are just yards from the water.

🍴 **A good range of wraps and organic baps includes crab, with light dishes such as creamed cheese and garlic mushrooms on toast, steamed mussels, four different types of nachos, pubby main dishes such as fishcakes, bangers and mash, shepherd's pie, liver and bacon, lamb shoulder in mint and honey, and puddings such as spotted dick or fruit crumble.** *Starters/Snacks: £3.75 to £5.25. Main Courses: £6.95 to £12.45. Puddings: £3.75 to £4.45*

Fullers ~ Manager David Hughes ~ Real ale ~ Bar food ~ Restaurant ~ (023) 9283 2333 ~ Children allowed until 8pm but must go to upstairs restaurant after that ~ Open 10am-midnight(1am Fri, 2am Sat); 10am-11pm Sun

Recommended by Dr and Mrs M E Wilson, Ann and Colin Hunt, Graham and Glenis Watkins, Tony and Wendy Hobden

ROMSEY   SU3523   MAP 2

Dukes Head

A3057 out towards Stockbridge; SO51 0HB

Excellent fresh fish and shellfish in attractive multi-room dining pub; seats in nice garden

This is an attractive 16th-c dining pub with keen and confident licensees. There's a picturesque series of small linked rooms each with its own distinct and interesting décor (one has portraits of dukes on the walls), a big log fire, and for those just wanting a drink, a few unlaid tables in the bar. Hop Back Summer Lightning and Ringwood Best on handpump and several wines by the glass. There are picnic-sets out in front and nicer tables on a sheltered back terrace in the pleasant garden.

🍴 **Changing twice daily and specialising in fresh brixham and lymington fish and shellfish, the popular food might include filled baguettes, breton-style fish soup with rouille, croûtons and gruyère, moules marinière, an assiette of shellfish with mussels, brown shrimp, scallops, clams and prawns, bass with saffron potatoes and spring vegetables, fillet of turbot with mornay sauce, whole crab and lobster and non-fishy dishes such as mediterranean vegetable salad topped with warm goats cheese, lamb shank and stir-fried duck, with puddings like panna cotta with raspberries and spotted dick with custard.** *Starters/Snacks: £4.50 to £7.50. Main Courses: £9.50 to £22.50. Puddings: £5.50*

Enterprise ~ Lease Suzie Russell ~ Real ale ~ Bar food ~ (01794) 514450 ~ Children welcome ~ Dogs allowed in bar ~ Live jazz/blues Sun lunchtime ~ Open 11.30-3.30, 5.30-11; 12-4.30 Sun; closed Sun evening

Recommended by J V Dadswell, Richard Atherton, David and Sheila Pearcey, Martin and Karen Wake

ROTHERWICK   SU7156   MAP 2

Falcon

4 miles from M3 junction 5; follow Newnham signpost from exit roundabout, then Rotherwick signpost, then turn right at Mattingley, Heckfield signpost; village also signposted from B3349 N of Hook, then brown signs to pub; RG27 9BL

Plenty of seating in various rooms, a relaxed country atmosphere, open fires, tasty food, and sizeable back garden

This is an enjoyable country pub with a pleasantly relaxed atmosphere in the open-plan rooms: quite a mixture of dining chairs gathered around an informal variety of tables on varnished floorboards, big bay windows with sunny window seats and minimal decoration on its deep red walls. There are flowers on the tables and perhaps a big vase of lilies on the terracotta-coloured central bar counter. A rather more formal back dining area is round to the right, and on the left are an overstuffed sofa and a couple of ornate easy chairs by one log fire. Brakspears Bitter and Fullers London Pride; piped music. You can sit out at tables and benches at the front and back of the building and the sizeable informal back garden looks into grazing pastures. Easy walks nearby.

🍴 **Well presented bar food at lunchtime includes sandwiches, filled baked potatoes and baguettes, ploughman's, honey-roast ham and eggs, spicy cajun stir fry, chicken caesar** salad, and home-made rump burger with evening choices such as moules marinière, chinese-style barbary duck pancakes, steak and mushroom in ale pie, roasted vegetable lasagne, calves liver and bacon, lamb shank with a redcurrant and mint gravy, and daily specials. *Starters/Snacks: £3.95 to £5.95. Main Courses: £9.95 to £14.95. Puddings: £4.50*

Unique (Enterprise) ~ Lease Andy Francis ~ Real ale ~ Bar food (12-2, 6.45-9.30; 12-3, 7-9 Sun (not Sun evenings in winter)) ~ Restaurant ~ (01256) 762586 ~ Children welcome (no high chairs) ~ Dogs allowed in bar ~ Open 11-2.30, 6-11; 12-10.30 Sun; 12-4, 7-10.30 Sun in winter

Recommended by Martin and Karen Wake, Brian Dawes, Mayur Shah, G Garvey, KC, Dr and Mrs Jackson, John Cook, Rob

ROWLAND'S CASTLE   SU7310   MAP 2

Castle Inn

Village signposted off B2148/B2149 N of Havant; Finchdean Road, by junction with Redhill Road and Woodberry Lane; PO9 6DA

A cheerful feel and generous food served by smart staff in bustling pub; largish garden

This is a smashing pub with friendly hands-on licensees who create a cheerful, welcoming atmosphere. There are two appealing little eating rooms on the left. The front one has rather nice simple mahogany chairs around sturdy scrubbed pine tables, rugs on flagstones, a big fireplace, and quite a lot of old local photographs on its ochre walls. The back one is similar, but with bare boards and local watercolour landscapes by Bob Payne for sale. There is a small separate public bar on the right with a good fire and Fullers London Pride, Gales Butser and HSB and a guest like Adnams Bitter on handpump. The publicans' own ponies are in view from the largish garden, which is equipped with picnic-sets and a couple of swings; disabled access and facilities are good.

🍴 Served by smartly dressed staff, the reasonably priced lunchtime menu includes filled baguettes, ploughman's, beef in ale pie, lasagne and chicken balti; dishes are a little pricier in the evening with choices such as deep-fried mushrooms in garlic butter, prawn and crabmeat cocktail, pork stroganoff and lamb shoulder braised in honey and mint; **Monday is curry night.** *Starters/Snacks: £4.25 to £7.50. Main Courses: £6.50 to £12.25. Puddings: £4.50*

Gales (Fullers) ~ Tenants Jan and Roger Burrell ~ Real ale ~ Bar food (12-9 Tues-Sat; 12-3, 6-9 Mon; 12-3 Sun; no food Sun evening) ~ Restaurant ~ (023) 9241 2494 ~ Children welcome until 9pm ~ Dogs allowed in bar ~ Open 11-midnight(1am Sat); 12-midnight Sun

Recommended by R M Corlett, Ian Phillips, Colin Chapman, Claire Hardcastle, Tony Hobden, Ann and Colin Hunt, Bruce Bird, Tony and Wendy Hobden

SOUTHSEA   SZ6499   MAP 2

Wine Vaults 🍺

Albert Road, opposite Kings Theatre; PO5 2SF

A fine range of real ales, reasonably priced food and a bustling atmosphere

There's a fine range of eight real ales on handpump in this busy pub: Fullers Chiswick, Discovery, London Pride and ESB and four changing guests. The straightforward bar has wood-panelled walls, pubby tables and chairs on the wooden floor and an easy-going, chatty feel; maybe newspapers to read, piped music. More reports please.

🍴 Handily served all day, the reasonably priced bar food might include sandwiches, deep-fried breaded brie with a port and cranberry jus, a shared antipasti plate, very popular nachos and other mexican dishes, corn-fed chicken breast stuffed with cheese and sun-dried tomatoes, beer-battered cod, and puddings such as apple and blackberry crumble. *Starters/Snacks: £3.25 to £5.95. Main Courses: £4.25 to £12.95. Puddings: £3.95*

Fullers ~ Manager Sean Cochrane ~ Real ale ~ Bar food (all day) ~ Restaurant ~ (023) 9286 4712 ~ Children welcome until 9pm ~ Dogs allowed in bar ~ Open 12-11 (12, Fri Sat; 10.30 Sun)

Recommended by Ian Phillips, Ann and Colin Hunt, the Didler

SPARSHOLT   SU4331   MAP 2

Plough 🍴 ♀

Village signposted off B3049 (Winchester—Stockbridge), a little W of Winchester; SO21 2NW

Neat, well run dining pub with interesting furnishings, an extensive wine list, and popular bar food; garden with children's play fort

Readers really enjoy their visits to this bustling, well run pub. Everything is neatly kept and the main bar has an interesting mix of wooden tables and chairs with farm tools, scythes and pitchforks attached to the ceiling. Wadworths IPA, 6X, JCB and a seasonal beer on handpump, and an extensive wine list with a good selection by the glass, including champagne and pudding wine; friendly, efficient service. Disabled access and facilities; there's a children's play fort, and plenty of seats on the terrace and lawn.

🍴 **Food is good and popular and includes sandwiches, ciabattas and ploughman's, soup, salmon and crab fishcake with saffron sauce, sautéed kidneys and smoked bacon with wild mushroom and port sauce, leek, mushroom and stilton pastry with orange and walnut salad, pork and chive sausages with red wine gravy, smoked haddock, salmon and prawn pie, lamb shank with carrot and swede mash and rosemary jus, duck breast with plum sauce, and puddings like chocolate brownie with banana ice-cream and crème brûlée.** *Starters/Snacks: £4.95 to £6.95. Main Courses: £9.95 to £19.95. Puddings: £5.50*

Wadworths ~ Tenants Richard and Kathryn Crawford ~ Real ale ~ Bar food (12-2, 6-9(8.30 Sun)) ~ (01962) 776353 ~ Children welcome except in main bar area ~ Dogs welcome ~ Open 10.30-3, 5.30-11; 12-3, 6-11 Sun

Recommended by Michael Lewis, M K Milner, C and H Greenly, GHC, Phyl and Jack Street, Mrs S Barker-Ryder, Mr and Mrs M Stratton, Val and Alan Green, John and Joan Calvert, Ann and Colin Hunt, Karen Eliot, N Vernon, Susan and John Douglas, R Lake

STEEP   SU7525   MAP 2

Harrow 🍺

Take Midhurst exit from Petersfield bypass, at exit roundabout first left towards Midhurst, then first turning on left opposite garage, and left again at Sheet church; follow over dual carriageway bridge to pub; GU32 2DA

Unchanging, simple place with long-serving landladies, beers tapped from cask, unfussy food, and big free-flowering garden; no children inside

This is a little gem and a firm favourite with those who love genuinely unspoilt and unpretentious places. It's a proper village pub – run by the same family for over 70 years – where you can find adverts for logs next to calendars of local views being sold in support of local charities, and you are bound to be drawn into light-hearted conversation by the chatty locals. The cosy public bar has hops and dried flowers hanging from the beams, built-in wall benches on the tiled floor, stripped pine wallboards, a good log fire in the big inglenook, and wild flowers on the scrubbed deal tables; board games. Ringwood Best, Suthwyk Bloomfields and maybe a guest like Palmers IPA are tapped straight from casks behind the counter, and they've local wine, and apple and pear juice; staff are polite and friendly, even when under pressure. The big garden is left free-flowering so that goldfinches can collect thistle seeds from the grass. The Petersfield bypass doesn't intrude on this idyll, though you will need to follow the directions above to find it. No children inside, and dogs must be on leads.

🍴 **Good helpings of unfussy bar food include sandwiches, home-made scotch eggs, hearty ham, split pea and vegetable soup, ploughman's, cottage pie, lasagne and quiches, and puddings such as super treacle tart or seasonal fruit pies.** *Starters/Snacks: £3.10 to £4.30. Main Courses: £7.75 to £11.00. Puddings: £3.70*

Free house ~ Licensees Claire and Denise McCutcheon ~ Real ale ~ Bar food (not Sun evening) ~ No credit cards ~ (01730) 262685 ~ Dogs welcome ~ Open 12-2.30, 6-11; 11-3, 6-11 Sat; 12-3, 7-10.30 Sun; closed winter Sun evenings

Recommended by Tracey and Stephen Groves, W A Evershed, the Didler, Jill Townsend, Tony and Jill Radnor, Mrs Rita Cox, Simon Fox, Phil and Sally Gorton, Ann and Colin Hunt, David Gunn

STOCKBRIDGE

SU3535 MAP 2

Grosvenor

High Street; SO20 6EU

Old-fashioned coaching inn with pubby bar, oak-panelled restaurant, and decent food and drinks

Old-fashioned and comfortable, this Georgian coaching inn has several well divided separate areas including a relaxing, high-ceilinged main bar with a good log fire. There are candles in bottles on a mix of pubby tables, cushioned captain's chairs and high-backed dining chairs in green and orange stripes on the patterned carpet and swagged curtains. Greene King IPA and Abbot on handpump, alongside a dozen wines by the glass, and decent coffee; piped music. The impressive oak-panelled restaurant has some hand-etched panels of horses done 200 years ago with a poker from the fire. A back conservatory has more tables. A couple of pavement tables stands out beside the imposing front portico, with more in the good-sized back garden, prettily laid out with attractive plantings. This is an appealing little town, with good antiques shops, the National Trust Common Marsh along the River Test, and downland walks all around.

🍴 **Bar food includes sandwiches or filled baguettes and baked potatoes, smoked mackerel mousse, chicken liver and mushroom pâté, local trout in light lemon butter (they will cook your own-caught trout, too), lasagne, spinach and ricotta tortellini, thai chilli chicken, gressingham duck with griottine cherries, and puddings such as lemon and lime cheesecake and banana and toffee crêpes.** *Starters/Snacks: £4.25 to £6.45. Main Courses: £5.95 to £14.95. Puddings: £4.25 to £6.95*

Greene King ~ Managers David and Margo Fyfe ~ Real ale ~ Bar food ~ Restaurant ~ (01264) 810606 ~ Children welcome away from bar ~ Dogs allowed in bar and bedrooms ~ Open 11-11(10.30 Sun) ~ Bedrooms: £85B/£99.50B

Recommended by Ann and Colin Hunt, Edward Mirzoeff, D Hillaby, N Vernon, Tom and Jill Jones, Ian Phillips, R B Gardiner

SWANMORE

SU5815 MAP 2

Rising Sun ♀ 🍺

Village signposted off A32 N of Wickham and B2177 S of Bishops Waltham; pub E of village centre, at Hillpound on the Droxford Road; SO32 2PS

Friendly licensees make this proper country pub a warmly welcoming all-rounder

The low-beamed carpeted bar in this 17th-c coaching inn has some easy chairs and a sofa by its good log fire, and a few tables with pubby seats. Beyond the fireplace on the right is a pleasant much roomier dining area, with similarly unpretentious furnishings, running back in an L past the bar; one part of this has stripped brick barrel vaulting. The sociable and quick-witted landlord is much in evidence, making for an easy-going and good-natured atmosphere. Besides well kept Marstons Pedigree and Ringwood Best or Fortyniner on handpump, they have two changing guest beers such as Greene King Old Speckled Hen and Hop Back Summer Lightning, and a good range of a dozen or so wines by the glass. There may be faint piped music. There are picnic-sets out on the side grass with a play area, and the Kings Way long distance path is close by – it's best to head west for pleasant walks.

🍴 **A nice choice of good value pubby food includes sandwiches, organic baguettes, baked potatoes, honey-baked ham and eggs, liver and bacon, cottage pie, vegetable and stilton bake, tarragon chicken and wild mushroom stroganoff; in the evening, there's also chicken liver pâté with cumberland sauce, devilled whitebait, field mushrooms filled with goats cheese, fillet of trout with caper butter, pork medallions with grain mustard and maple syrup sauce and grilled scottish steak with port and stilton.** *Starters/Snacks: £4.75 to £7.95. Main Courses: £13.50 to £16.95. Puddings: £4.25*

Pubs with outstanding views are listed at the back of the book.

Punch ~ Lease Mark and Sue Watts ~ Real ale ~ Bar food (12-2, 6-9) ~ Restaurant ~
(01489) 896663 ~ Children allowed but must be well behaved ~ Dogs allowed in bar ~
Open 11.30-3, 5.30-11; 12-3, 5.30-10.30 Sun

Recommended by Val and Alan Green, Ann and Colin Hunt, Phyl and Jack Street

TICHBORNE
SU5730   MAP 2

Tichborne Arms
Village signed off B3047; SO24 0NA

Traditional pub in rolling countryside and liked by walkers; big garden

A new licensee has taken over this attractive thatched pub but luckily has no plans for
any major changes. The comfortable square-panelled room on the right has wheelback
chairs and settles (one very long), a stone fireplace and latticed windows. On the left is
a larger, livelier, partly panelled room used for eating. Pictures and documents on the
walls recall the bizarre Tichborne Case, in which a mystery man from Australia claimed
fraudulently to be the heir to this estate. Hidden Pint, Hop Back Summer Lightning,
Ringwood Best and fff Stairway are tapped from the cask, alongside a decent choice of
wines by the glass, country wines and farm cider; sensibly placed darts, shove-ha'penny
and cribbage. The labrador is called Holly. There are picnic-sets in the big, neat garden.
The Wayfarers Walk and Itchen Way pass close by and the countryside around is
attractively rolling.

🍴 **Reasonably priced bar food includes a changing pâté, oriental crispy duck rolls, steak,
stilton and ale pie, chicken curry, vegetable pancake with cheese topping, fresh crab
salad, and puddings such as profiteroles with chocolate sauce.** *Starters/Snacks: £3.75 to
£7.25. Main Courses: £7.50 to £13.95. Puddings: £3.65 to £4.95*

Free house ~ Licensee Leonard Larden ~ Real ale ~ Bar food (12-2(3 Sat and Sun), 6.30-9.30) ~
(01962) 733760 ~ Children welcome ~ Dogs welcome ~ Open 11.30-3(4 Sat), 6.30-11(midnight
Sat); 12-4, 7-11 Sun; closed evenings of 25 and 26 Dec and 1 Jan

*Recommended by Ann and Colin Hunt, Dr D and Mrs B Woods, R B Gardiner, Susan and John Douglas, the Didler,
Sean A Smith, Lynn Sharpless, Matt and Cathy Fancett, Christine Bridgwater*

UPHAM
SU5320   MAP 2

Brushmakers Arms
Off Winchester—Bishops Waltham downs road; Shoe Lane; SO32 1JJ

Friendly old place with extensive displays of brushes, local beers; and nice unfussy food

The new licensee in this friendly old place was previously the head chef and plans to run
the pub as a proper village local. Picking up on the pub's name, the walls in the L-shaped
bar (divided in two by a central brick chimney with a woodburning stove) are hung with
quite a collection of old and new brushes. A few beams in the low ceiling add to the
cosiness, and there are comfortably cushioned settles and chairs and a variety of tables
including some in country-style stripped wood; there's also a little back snug with fruit
machine, dominoes and board games. Hampshire Ironside and Uncle Bob, Ringwood Best
and changing guests on handpump; the pub cats are called Gilbert and Kera and the
ghost is known as Mr Chickett. The big garden is well stocked with mature shrubs and
trees and there are picnic-sets on a sheltered back terrace amongst tubs of flowers, with
more on the tidy tree-sheltered lawn. It's best to park by the duck pond; good walks
nearby.

🍴 **Well liked, straightforward bar food includes sandwiches, soup, cheese and bacon skins,
baked brie with redcurrant sauce, vegetable lasagne, sausage and mash, cajun chicken,
battered cod, liver and bacon with onion gravy, cider-baked ham with grain mustard
cream, and puddings.** *Starters/Snacks: £4.50 to £6.00. Main Courses: £7.50 to £15.95.
Puddings: £4.50*

Free house ~ Licensee Keith Venton ~ Real ale ~ Bar food (12-2, 6(7 Sun)-9(9.30 Fri, Sat)) ~ (01489) 860231 ~ Children welcome ~ Dogs allowed in bar ~ Open 11-3, 5.45-11; 12-3, 7-10.30 Sun

Recommended by Jenny and Peter Lowater, Ann and Colin Hunt, Sean A Smith

UPTON   SU3555   MAP 2

Crown

N of Hurstbourne Tarrant, off A343; SP11 0JS

Cheerful village pub with well liked food and beer, friendly licensee, and good nearby walks

Once discovered, customers tend to come back to this friendly and attractive dining pub again and again. The linked cottagey rooms have a happy, bustling atmosphere, pine tables and chairs, a pleasant modicum of sporting prints, horse tack and so forth and good log fires; there's also a back conservatory extension. Fullers London Pride and Gales Butser Bitter on handpump and smiling service; piped music. There's a small garden and terrace and lovely nearby walks.

🍴 **Very reasonably priced bar food includes soup, ploughman's, bangers and lyonnaise mash, sweet chilli bean pot, omelettes, battered haddock, lasagne, pies like lamb in ale or steak and kidney, and chicken curry.** *Starters/Snacks: £3.95 to £5.95. Main Courses: £5.95 to £16.95. Puddings: £3.95*

Free house ~ Licensee Bill Evans ~ Real ale ~ Bar food (12-2, 6(7 Sun)-9) ~ Restaurant ~ (01264) 736265 ~ Children welcome ~ Dogs allowed in bar ~ Open 12-3, 6(7 Sun)-11

Recommended by J D G Isherwood, Michael Dallas, Ann and Colin Hunt, Mrs Pat Crabb

WHERWELL   SU3839   MAP 2

Mayfly

Testcombe (over by Fullerton, and not in Wherwell itself); A3057 SE of Andover, between B3420 turn-off and Leckford where road crosses River Test; OS Sheet 185 map reference 382390; SO20 6AX

Busy pub with decking and conservatory seats overlooking the River Test, half a dozen ales, and bar food usefully served all day

This busy pub's splendid setting makes it very popular in fine weather, so it's a good idea to arrive early if you want to bag one of the tables on the decking area beside the River Test (where you can watch the ducks and maybe plump trout). Inside, the spacious, beamed and carpeted bar has fishing pictures on the cream walls, rustic pub furnishings, and a woodburning stove; piped music. Efficient staff serve six real ales on handpump: Greene King Abbot, Ringwood Best, Wadworths 6X and Wychwood Hobgoblin together with a couple of guests such as Hop Back Summer Lightning and Ringwood Fortyniner. More reports please.

🍴 **Handily available all day, the bar food comes from a buffet-style servery: they do a choice of hot and cold meats, pies and quiches, salads and quite a great selection of cheeses. There's also a blackboard menu with vegetable stroganoff, sausage and mash, fish pie, baked trout and so forth, and puddings like fruit crumbles and bread and butter pudding.** *Starters/Snacks: £4.95 to £9.50. Main Courses: £8.00 to £15.95. Puddings: £4.50*

'Children welcome' means the pub says it lets children inside without any special restriction. If it allows them in, but to restricted areas such as an eating area or family room, we specify this. Places with separate restaurants often let children use them, hotels usually let them into public areas such as lounges.
Some pubs impose an evening time limit – let us know if you find this.

Enterprise ~ Manager Barry Lane ~ Real ale ~ Bar food (11.30-9) ~ (01264) 860283 ~ Children welcome if well behaved ~ Dogs welcome ~ Open 10am-11pm(10pm Sun-Weds)

Recommended by Mrs Pam Mattinson, R G Trevis, GHC, Kate Evans, Phyl and Jack Street, Lynn Sharpless, Bill and Jessica Ritson, Ann and Colin Hunt, Barry and Molly Norton, Sally and Tom Matson

White Lion

B3420, in village itself; SP11 7JF

Pleasant pub with long-serving licensees; plenty of seats outside

As well as being on the Test Way, this old-fashioned 17th-c pub has a nice walk leading over the River Test and meadows to Chilbolton; plenty of seats in the courtyard and on the terrace. The multi-level beamed bar has delft plates, sparkling brass, Bass and Ringwood Best on handpump, and 11 wines by the glass; friendly staff. The Village Bar has an open fire, and there are two dining rooms; piped music. The chocolate labrador is called Harley.

🍴 **Straightforward bar food includes filled baguettes, ploughman's, scampi, a pie and a curry of the day, spinach and red pepper lasagne, gammon and egg, daily specials, and puddings.** *Starters/Snacks: £4.95 to £6.95. Main Courses: £8.75 to £14.95. Puddings: £3.50 to £4.50*

Punch ~ Lease Adrian Stent and Pat Fairman ~ Real ale ~ Bar food ~ (01264) 860317 ~ Children in dining room only ~ Dogs welcome ~ Folk club first and third Thurs evening of month ~ Open 11-2.30(3 Sat), 6-10.30(11 Thurs-Sat); 12-3, 7-10.30 Sun; closed 25 Dec ~ Bedrooms: £42.50S/£54.50S

Recommended by Mike Turner, Ann and Colin Hunt, Barry and Sue Pladdys, Edward Mirzoeff, Phyl and Jack Street, Mike Gorton, B J Harding, Helen and Brian Edgeley, Dr D J and Mrs S C Walker, Mr and Mrs A H Young

WINCHESTER   SU4828   MAP 2

Black Boy 🍺

A mile from M3 junction 10 northbound; B3403 towards city then left into Wharf Hill; rather further and less easy from junction 9, and anyway beware no nearby daytime parking – 220 metres from car park on B3403 N, or nice longer walk from town via College Street and College Walk, or via towpath; SO23 9NQ

Busy town pub with several different areas crammed full of interesting knick-knacks, straightforward bar food and decent wines; no children

Certainly eccentric, this old-fashioned place is decorated with character and wit but is not for those seeking sophisticated surroundings. There are floor-to-ceiling books in some parts, lots of big clocks, mobiles made of wine bottles or strings of spectacles, some nice modern nature photographs in the lavatories and on the brightly stained walls on the way, and plenty of other things that you'll enjoy tracking down. Furnishings are similarly wide-ranging. Several different areas run from a bare-boards barn room with an open hayloft (an evening dining room) down to an orange-painted room with big oriental rugs on red-painted floorboards. The five well kept beers on handpump are more or less local: Flower Pots Bitter, Hop Back Summer Lightning and Ringwood Best alongside a couple of guests such as Archers Best Bitter and Itchen Valley Grim Reaper; decent wines, two log fires. Well chosen and reproduced piped music; table football, ring and hook, shove-ha'penny, board games, cribbage and dominoes; a couple of slate tables out in front, more tables on an attractive secluded terrace with barbecues. No children.

🍴 **Lunchtime bar food includes sandwiches, a pasta dish, shepherd's pie and beer-battered cod and chips; evening restaurant meals are more elaborate.** *Starters/Snacks: £4.50. Main Courses: £6.50 to £8.00. Puddings: £3.50 to £4.50*

Free house ~ Licensee David Nicholson ~ Real ale ~ Bar food (not Sun evening, Mon, or Tues lunchtime) ~ Restaurant ~ (01962) 861754 ~ Children must be well behaved and supervised ~ Dogs allowed in bar ~ Open 11-3, 5-11; 12-3, 7-10.30 Sun

Recommended by Peter Dandy, Sean A Smith, James Price, Ann and Colin Hunt, Simon Fox, Pete Baker, Phil Bryant

Willow Tree

Durngate Terrace; no adjacent weekday daytime parking, but Durngate Car Park is around corner in North Walls; a mile from M3 junction 9, by Easton Lane into city; SO23 8QX

Snug Victorian pub with landlord/chef using much local produce for enjoyable and interesting food; nice riverside garden

The carpeted lounge/dining bar on the right is comfortably relaxed, with wall banquettes below little topographical prints and photographs on its muted orange stripey wallpaper, low ceilings and soft lighting; two bays of good sturdy dining tables at the back have mainly Impressionist prints and quite a few books around them. There's a separate proper public bar, with tiled floor and traditional wall seats; piped music, TV, games machine, darts, chess, backgammon and pool. They have Greene King IPA and a guest such as Belhaven Six Nations on handpump, and decent wines. The young staff are cheerful and efficient. A narrow tree-shaded garden, partly paved and with plenty of heaters, stretches back between two branches of the River Itchen.

🍴 Good and generous proper cooking here with some innovative flavours might include sandwiches, paninis, omelettes, interesting soups (one consists of three different soups in one bowl – each a different colour), grilled goats cheese with beetroot, terrine of foie gras with madeira jelly, sausages of the day with onion gravy, salmon and haddock kedgeree, calves liver, onion and bacon, pork chops with apple and green peppercorns, and good puddings like pineapple tarte tatin and warm chocolate fondant; super summer barbecues. The landlord, looking every cosy inch a happy chef, gives Monday cookery classes. *Starters/Snacks: £3.50 to £6.50. Main Courses: £5.00 to £15.00. Puddings: £2.50 to £4.50*

Greene King ~ Tenant James Yeoman ~ Real ale ~ Bar food (12-3, 6-10.30; 12-6 Sun; not Sun evening) ~ Restaurant ~ (01962) 877255 ~ Children welcome ~ Dogs allowed in bar ~ Open 12-3, 5(6 in winter)-11.30; 12-midnight Fri and Sat; 12-10.30 Sun

Recommended by Diana Brumfit, Phil and Sally Gorton

Wykeham Arms ★

Kingsgate Street (Kingsgate Arch and College Street are now closed to traffic; there is access via Canon Street); SO23 9PE

HAMPSHIRE DINING PUB OF THE YEAR

Lovely pub with excellent service, imaginative food, super wines, and lots to look at; no children inside

'It's always a joy to come here' and 'what a treasure' are just two of the enthusiastic comments from readers about this civilised and very well run pub. A series of bustling rooms radiating from the central bar has 19th-c oak desks retired from nearby Winchester College, a redundant pew from the same source, kitchen chairs and candlelit deal tables, and the big windows have swagged paisley curtains; all sorts of interesting collections are dotted around. A snug room at the back, known as the Jameson Room (after the late landlord Graeme Jameson), is decorated with a set of Ronald Searle 'Winespeak' prints, a second one is panelled, and all of them have log fires. Fullers London Pride, Chiswick, Gales Butser Bitter and a couple of guests on handpump, and 19 wines by the glass (including champagne) from an extensive and interesting wine list. The neatly uniformed staff give first class service. There are tables on a covered back terrace (they will serve food at lunchtime only here), with more on a small but sheltered lawn. No children inside.

🍴 Extremely good and attractively presented, the lunchtime bar food might include sandwiches, spiced salmon and coconut fishcakes with coriander and lime yoghurt dressing, smoked salmon and smoked trout with apple and celeriac remoulade and grain mustard and dill dressing, spicy beef, lamb and coriander skewers with moroccan-style rice and spiced jus, baked bass fillet with couscous and red pepper coulis and smoked chicken and mango salad with honey and ginger dressing; evening choices such as smoked haddock, potato and cheddar tartlet with rocket pesto, wild mushroom and basil risotto, gressingham duck breast with pea purée and Cointreau sauce and local lamb with redcurrant and mint jus. Puddings like pear and almond brûlée and warm chocolate and cherry brownie, toasted almonds and pistachio anglaise. *Starters/Snacks: £4.25 to £6.95. Main Courses: £5.95 to £18.50. Puddings: £4.75*

Gales (Fullers) ~ Managers Peter and Kate Miller ~ Real ale ~ Bar food (12-2.30, 6.30-8.45; not Sun evenings) ~ Restaurant ~ (01962) 853834 ~ Dogs allowed in bar and bedrooms ~ Open 11-11; 12-10.30 Sun ~ Bedrooms: £62B/£100B

Recommended by GHC, Lynn Sharpless, John Oates, Denise Walton, Peter and Andrea Jacobs, Martin and Karen Wake, Simon Fox, John and Julie Moon, M K Milner, W A Evershed, David Dyson, Pam and John Smith, Ann and Colin Hunt, Chris Flynn, Wendy Jones, Andy Booth, Simon Rodway, Barry and Anne, Val and Alan Green, Peter Dandy, Richard Mason, the Didler, Bill and Jessica Ritson, James Price, I H Curtis, J and F Gowers, Peter and Liz Holmes

LUCKY DIP

Besides the fully inspected pubs, you might like to try these Lucky Dips recommended to us and described by readers (if you do, please send us reports: www.goodguides.co.uk).

ALRESFORD [SU5832]
☆ *Bell* SO24 9AT [West St]: Relaxing Georgian coaching inn with welcoming hands-on licensees, interesting good value food from sandwiches and light dishes up, good real ales, fairly priced wines, log fire, daily papers, good décor, smallish dining room; tables in attractive back courtyard, comfortable bedrooms, open all day *(Val and Alan Green, Ann and Colin Hunt, D and J Ashdown)*
Cricketers SO24 9LW [Jacklyns Lane]: Large friendly local with popular and appetising low-priced food inc special deals, book ahead for Sun, real ales, good service, cottagey eating area down steps; sizeable garden with covered terrace and good play area *(Phyl and Jack Street, Sheila and Robert Robinson, D and J Ashdown)*
☆ *Globe* SO24 9DB [bottom of Broad St (B3046) where parking is limited]: Comfortable dining pub with good atmosphere, enjoyable fresh food (all day summer wknds) from pricy lunchtime baguettes up, interesting range of ales inc Itchen Valley Godfathers and Wadworths 6X, good choice of wines by the glass, log fires each end, unusual pictures, restaurant allowing children; plenty of picnic-sets in garden with splendid outlook over historic Alresford Pond, open all day Sun and summer Sat *(W A Evershed, Jim and Janet Brown, Ann and Colin Hunt, LYM, Val and Alan Green, David Howe)*
Running Horse SO24 9BW [Pound Hill]: Comfortably updated family-run Georgian pub, father running the bar and son doing the enjoyable food, friendly staff, Greene King real ales inc XX Mild, reasonably priced wines, daily papers, exemplary ladies'; piped music; plenty of tables on pleasant back terrace, open all day, cl Sun evening *(Bill Watson)*
ALTON [SU7139]
Eight Bells GU34 2DA [Church St]: Straightforward old-fashioned local with several good changing ales such as Hogs Back TEA and Ringwood Best, rolls served most lunchtimes, helpful landlord; small back garden, open all day *(Simon Fox, Derek and Sylvia Stephenson)*
Railway Arms GU34 2RD [Anstey Rd, opp

station rd]: Town local owned by fff, with their good beers kept well, farm ciders, german beers, occasional guest beers; picnic-sets on front terrace, more out behind, open all day *(Simon Fox)*
AMPFIELD [SU4023]
White Horse SO51 9BQ [A31 Winchester—Romsey]: Much extended open-plan pub, plenty of room for both eaters and drinkers, friendly staff, well kept Ringwood and Wadworths, good choice of wines by the glass, decent coffee, blazing log fires, comfortable period-effect furniture, interesting décor, Victorian prints and advertising posters in dining room; tables outside, pub backs on to golf course and village cricket green; handy for Hillier arboretum, good walks in Ampfield Woods *(Ann and Colin Hunt, A and B D Craig, SJ)*
ARFORD [SU8236]
☆ *Crown* GU35 8BT [off B3002 W of Hindhead]: Welcoming low-beamed pub with coal and log fires in several areas from bustling bar to quiet candlelit upper dining room, enjoyable if not cheap food from sandwiches to game and splendid puddings, friendly efficient staff, Adnams, Fullers London Pride, Greene King Abbot and a guest beer, decent wines by the glass; piped music; children welcome in eating areas, picnic-sets out in peaceful dell by a tiny stream across the road *(LYM, Tony and Jill Radnor, R B Gardiner, Keith and Margaret Jackson)*
ASHMANSWORTH [SU4157]
Plough RG20 9SL: Friendly no-frills local in attractive village, two quarry-tiled rooms knocked together, well kept Archers Village, Best and Golden and a changing guest tapped from the cask, good basic lunchtime bar food, pleasant attentive service, log fire, no piped music; seats outside, good walks, handy for Highclere Castle, cl Mon *(R T and J C Moggridge, the Didler)*
AVON [SZ1498]
New Queen BH23 7BG [B3347 S of Ringwood]: Modern family dining pub with different areas and levels, flagstone floors, comfortable corners and low pitched ceiling, good value traditional pub food, Badger ales, good wines by the glass, helpful staff; tables out on spacious covered terrace and lawn with play area, bedrooms *(Mrs C Berry)*

AXFORD [SU6043]

Crown RG25 2DZ [B3046 S of Basingstoke]: Efficient young staff, thriving atmosphere, real ales, several wines by the glass, enjoyable food, three pleasantly refurbished linked rooms, small log fire; children welcome, suntrap terrace and sloping shrub-sheltered garden (LYM, Mr and Mrs D Renwick, John Cook)

BALL HILL [SU4263]

Furze Bush RG20 0NQ [leaving Newbury on A343 turn right towards East Woodhay]: Pews and pine tables, clean airy décor, wide choice of quickly served generous good value bar food, well kept real ales, decent wines, log fire, restaurant; children welcome, tables on terrace by good-sized sheltered lawn with fenced play area (Mr and Mrs H J Langley, LYM)

BARTON STACEY [SU4341]

Swan SO21 3RL [village signed off A30]: Former coaching inn with chesterfields in nice little lounge area between beamed front bar and dining area, back restaurant (not always open), pleasant staff, real ales inc Wadworths 6X, good choice of wines; tables on front lawn and in informal back garden (Colin Wood)

BASING [SU6653]

Millstone RG24 8AE [Bartons Lane, Old Basing (attached to Bartons Mill Restaurant)]: Converted mill in lovely spot by River Loddon, enjoyable food from baked potatoes to duck confit, well kept Wadworths ales and a guest beer tapped from the cask, good choice of wines by the glass, quick service even when busy; children welcome, big garden with terrace, handy for ruins of Basing House (K Sloan)

BAUGHURST [SU5860]

Wellington Arms RG26 5LP [Baughurst Rd]: Neatly kept country pub with great emphasis on traceable largely organic fresh ingredients in enjoyable food (not Sun evening, Mon or lunch Tues) inc their own rare-breed eggs, herbs and honey, cheerful service, interesting drinks choice, strong australian connections; picnic-sets in attractive garden (anon)

BEAUWORTH [SU5624]

Milbury's SO24 0PB [off A272 Winchester/Petersfield]: New landlord doing simple traditional bar meals such as hotpots, casseroles and pies in attractive ancient pub, beams, panelling and stripped stone, massive 17th-c treadmill for much older incredibly deep well, log fires in huge fireplaces, Greene King ales and a guest such as St Austell Tinners, reasonably priced wines by the glass; piped music; children in eating areas, garden with fine downland views, good walks, has been open all day wknds and summer (Ann and Colin Hunt, LYM, Martin and Karen Wake, Helen and Brian Edgeley, the Didler)

BIGHTON [SU6134]

Three Horseshoes SO24 9RE [off B3046 in Alresford just N of pond; or off A31 in Bishops Sutton]: Old-fashioned country local with very friendly licensees, Fullers/Gales ales, decent house wines, straightforward bar food, eggs and chutney for sale, Sun bar nibbles, woodburner in huge fireplace, dining room, darts and pool in bare-boards stripped-stone back public bar; may be piped music; children welcome, good walks nearby, cl Mon lunchtime (Ann and Colin Hunt, the Didler, W A Evershed)

BISHOP'S SUTTON [SU6031]

Ship SO24 0AQ [B3047, on Alton side of Alresford]: Relaxed and simple, with welcoming obliging landlord, Ringwood Best and a guest beer, short sensible food choice inc lovely puddings, good fire, attractive small back dining room; well behaved dogs and children welcome, tables in garden with a couple of thatched parasols, handy for Watercress Line, good walks (LYM, Ann and Colin Hunt)

BISHOP'S WALTHAM [SU5517]

☆ *Bunch of Grapes* SO32 1AD [St Peters St – just along from entrance to central car park]: Neat and civilised little pub in attractive quiet medieval street, smartly updated furnishings and décor yet keeping individuality and unspoilt feel (run by same family for a century), Courage Best and Greene King IPA tapped from the cask, good chatty landlord and regulars; charming back terrace garden with own serving bar (BB, Stephen and Jean Curtis, the Didler)

White Horse SO32 1FD [Beeches Hill, off B3035 NE]: Open-plan pub with central log fire, hop-hung beams and joists, fancy knotwork, candles in bottles, friendly licensees, Adnams, Ringwood Best and Shepherd Neame Spitfire, decent wines by the glass and country wines, good value food inc excellent vegetarian choice and bargain lunches, all freshly made so may be a wait; unobtrusive piped music; picnic-sets on front terrace, small menagerie of rescued domestic and farmyard animals, open all day (Val and Alan Green, BB, K Sloan)

BOLDRE [SZ3198]

☆ *Red Lion* SO41 8NE [off A337 N of Lymington]: Nice tables out among flower tubs and baskets in newly reworked garden, black-beamed rooms with entertaining collection of bygones, pews and other seats, log fires, pleasant landlady and staff, Ringwood Best and Fortyniner and a guest beer, great choice of wines by the glass, well liked bar food from generous sandwiches to plenty of fish; children and dogs allowed, open all day (Dr D J R Martin, Michael and Maggie Betton, Ann and Colin Hunt, Phyl and Jack Street, Nick Lawless, LYM)

BRAISHFIELD [SU3725]

Newport Inn SO51 0PL [Newport Lane – from centre follow Michelmersh, Timsbury signpost]: Plain two-bar brick local, hard-used elderly furnishings, simple huge cheap sandwiches and bargain ploughman's, well kept Fullers/Gales ales, down-to-earth veteran licensees, cribbage; piped music, wknd piano singsongs; informal and relaxing tree-shaded garden with old furniture, busy bird feeder, may be geese, ducks or chickens *(Lynn Sharpless, the Didler, BB)*

BROCKENHURST [SU3002]

Foresters Arms SO42 7RR [Brookley Rd]: Cheerful village pub, old beams and brickwork, carpeted lounge with enjoyable pubby food from sandwiches up, neat polite staff, Ringwood Best; TV in smaller bar; garden tables *(Ann and Colin Hunt, Peter Dandy)*

Snakecatcher SO42 7RL [Lyndhurst Rd]: Well run local with decent food from sandwiches to steaks cooked to order, interesting split-level bar and restaurant areas inc cosy part with log fire and easy chairs, real ales, nice choice of wines by the glass, good service; garden tables, good walks nearby *(Peter Dandy, Kevin Flack)*

BROOK [SU2713]

☆ *Green Dragon* SO43 7HE [B3078 NW of Cadnam, just off M27 junction 1]: Big open-plan New Forest dining pub dating from 15th c, neatly staffed, with wide choice of enjoyable fresh food inc plenty of seasonal game and fish as well as sensibly priced pubby favourites, Fullers London Pride, Gales HSB and Ringwood, several linked areas with stripped pine and other pubby furnishings; attractive small terrace and larger garden with paddocks beyond, picturesque village *(Dick and Madeleine Brown, BB)*

BROUGHTON [SU3032]

Tally Ho SO20 8AA [High St, opp church; signed off A30 Stockbridge—Salisbury]: Relaxed local atmosphere in open-plan largely tiled square bar, helpful welcoming landlady, good value home-made food from sandwiches up, two well kept Ringwood ales, good house wines in two glass sizes, two open fires, hunting prints, local landscapes for sale, darts, no piped music; children welcome, tables in charming secluded back garden, good walks; has been cl Tues *(BB, George Atkinson)*

BUCKLERS HARD [SU4000]

Master Builders House SO42 7XB: Original small yachtsman's bar with beams, flagstones and big log fire attractive when not too crowded, real ales such as Bass, Hook Norton Old Hooky and Ringwood Best, bar food (not cheap); part of a substantial Best Western hotel complex in charming carefully preserved waterside village (you have to pay to enter it), great views from picnic-sets, good bedrooms *(LYM, Steve Whalley)*

BURGATE [SU1515]

Tudor Rose SP6 1LX [A338 about a mile N of Fordingbridge]: Picturesque black and white thatched pub dating from 14th c, very low well padded beams (and they say a door-slamming ghost), wide choice of generous straightforward food all day, Ringwood beers, friendly attentive service, log-effect gas fire in big fireplace; children welcome, picnic-sets out in front, smallish back garden with

play area, Avon Valley footpath passes the door, fine pedestrian suspension bridge, open all day *(Dave Braisted, Phyl and Jack Street)*

BURGHCLERE [SU4660]

Carpenters Arms RG20 9JY [Harts Lane, off A34]: Pleasantly furnished small pub with cheerful helpful landlord gradually improving, big helpings of bar food from well presented sandwiches to some ambitious dishes, well kept Arkells, decent choice of wines by the glass, good country views from dining extension; unobtrusive piped music; garden tables, handy for Sandham Memorial Chapel (NT) *(Mr and Mrs H J Langley)*

BURLEY [SU2202]

☆ *White Buck* BH24 4AZ [Bisterne Close; ¼ mile E, OS Sheet 195 map ref 223028]: Long comfortable bar in 19th-c mock-Tudor hotel, vast choice of reasonably priced good generous food, Fullers/Gales ales and a guest such as Tom Woods, good wines by the glass and coffee, lots of worthwhile pictures, log fires each end, courteous attentive staff, thriving atmosphere, pleasant end dining room with tables out on decking (should book – but no bookings Sun lunchtime); may be quiet piped music; children and dogs welcome, pleasant front terrace and spacious lawn, lovely New Forest setting, well equipped bedrooms, superb walks towards Burley itself and over Mill Lawn *(BB, Tom and Jill Jones, John and Joan Calvert, George Atkinson, Colin Chapman, Claire Hardcastle, Peter Titcomb, Conor McGaughey)*

BURSLEDON [SU4809]

☆ *Fox & Hounds* SO31 8DE [Hungerford Bottom; two miles from M27 junction 8]: Rambling 16th-c Chef & Brewer of unusual character, ancient beams, flagstones and big log fires, linked by pleasant family conservatory area to ancient back barn with buoyant rustic atmosphere, lantern-lit side stalls, lots of interesting and authentic farm equipment; Courage Best and Fullers London Pride, lots of wines, wide choice of enjoyable reasonably priced food from sandwiches up, cheerful obliging staff, daily papers; children allowed, tables outside *(Ann and Colin Hunt, Philip Casey, Bruce and Penny Wilkie, LYM)*

☆ *Jolly Sailor* SO31 8DN [off A27 towards Bursledon Station, Lands End Rd; handy for M27 junction 8]: Busy efficiently laid out Badger dining pub, bright and fresh, in superb spot overlooking yachting inlet, good current management, their usual food, ales and good wine choice, log fires; open all day *(Ann and Colin Hunt, John and Bettye Reynolds, Peter Titcomb, Ian Phillips, LYM, the Didler, Stuart and Doreen Ritchie)*

CADNAM [SU3114]

Compass SO40 2HE [Winsor, off Totton—Cadnam rd at Bartley crossroads; OS Sheet 195 map ref 317143]: Popular and appealing 16th-c beamed local off the beaten track, some recent gentle refurbishments, helpful licensees, good range of real ales, pine tables for enjoyable simple food from good bacon doorsteps up, log fires; side garden with decorative arbour, open all day *(Phyl and Jack Street)*

☆ *Sir John Barleycorn* SO40 2NP [Old Romsey Rd; by M27, junction 1]: Wide choice of enjoyable up-to-date food in picturesque low-slung thatched pub extended from low-beamed and timbered medieval core on left, sensible prices, real ales inc Ringwood, reasonably priced wines, two good log fires, prompt and friendly young staff, modern décor and stripped wood flooring; dogs and children welcome, suntrap benches in front and out in colourful garden, open all day *(Phyl and Jack Street, LYM, Colin Wood)*

CANTERTON [SU2613]
Sir Walter Tyrell SO43 7HD [off A31 W of Cadnam, follow Rufus's Stone sign]: Large pretty pub by lovely New Forest clearing often with ponies, hard-working staff coping well with families and big groups, real ales inc Ringwood, popular food, long divided front bar, long back dining room; big play area, sheltered terrace, adjacent camp site, good base for walks *(N R White)*

CHALTON [SU7315]
☆ *Red Lion* PO8 0BG [off A3 Petersfield—Horndean]: Largely extended thatched all-day dining pub (its interesting 16th-c heart around an ancient inglenook fireplace is nowadays really rather lost in the much more standardised surrounding parts); they keep Fullers/Gales ales and lots of country wines, helpful and efficient good-humoured staff; children and dogs allowed, good disabled access and facilities, nice views from neat rows of picnic-sets on rectangular lawn by large car park, handy for Queen Elizabeth Country Park, open all day *(Ann and Colin Hunt, LYM, Tony and Wendy Hobden)*

CHARTER ALLEY [SU5957]
White Hart RG26 5QA [White Hart Lane, off A340 N of Basingstoke]: Handsome beamed village pub with good changing choice of real ales such as Otter and West Berkshire, continental beers, summer farm cider, decent wines, impressive collection of whisky bottles, comfortable lounge bar with woodburner in big fireplace, dining area, simple public bar with skittle alley; small garden with terrace tables *(J V Dadswell, Bruce Bird)*

CHAWTON [SU7037]
☆ *Greyfriar* GU34 1SB [off A31/A32 S of Altont; Winchester Rd]: Spick-and-span open-plan beamed dining pub opp Jane Austen's house, enjoyable food from sandwiches and baguettes up, Fullers London Pride, ESB and guest beer, decent wines by the glass, good coffees, relaxed atmosphere and quite a few older midweek lunchers, comfortable seating and sturdy pine tables in neat linked areas, open fire in restaurant end; piped music; tables on terrace in small garden; dogs in bar, children until 9pm, good nearby walks, open all day *(Tony and*

Jill Radnor, Meg and Colin Hamilton, Wendy Arnold, R B Gardiner, Tom and Jill Jones, Bruce Bird, David and Sue Smith, Ann and Colin Hunt, LYM)

CHILWORTH [SU4118]
Chilworth Arms SO16 7JZ [Chilworth Rd (A27 S'ton—Romsey)]: Former Clump reopened and renamed after fundamental reworking as smart dining pub, enjoyable food with contemporary touches, well kept Greene King ales, good choice of wines by the glass, friendly mainly antipodean service, part divided off with leather sofas and log fire; disabled facilities, large garden, open all day *(Phyl and Jack Street, Mrs C Osgood)*

COLDEN COMMON [SU4821]
☆ *Fishers Pond* SO50 7HG [Main Rd (B3354)]: Big busy well organised family pub in style of a converted water mill, newly refurbished with log fires and cosy old-world corners, vast choice of reasonably priced generous food all day inc children's, Marstons and related real ales, decent coffee, efficient service; tables on extended terrace by pretty woodside lake with ducks, handy for Marwell Zoo, open all day *(Phyl and Jack Street, Ann and Colin Hunt)*

Rising Sun SO21 1SB [Spring Lane]: Two welcoming bars, one with games area, pleasant dining room, cheerful cook doing sensibly priced food from sandwiches and baguettes to good hot dishes, real ales such as Fullers London Pride, Gales HSB and Ringwood Best; quiet piped music; big garden with play area *(Diana Brumfit, Val and Alan Green)*

CRAWLEY [SU4234]
☆ *Fox & Hounds* SO21 2PR [off A272 or B3420 NW of Winchester]: Striking almost swiss-looking building in picturesque village with duck pond, enjoyable mix of reasonably priced traditional and modern food with simple good value price structure, friendly efficient young staff, good choice of real ales and wines by the glass, mix of attractive wooden tables and chairs on polished floors in neat and attractive linked beamed rooms with three log fires and civilised atmosphere; garden tables, bedrooms in converted outbuildings *(Phyl and Jack Street, LYM, J Stickland, Diana Brumfit)*

CRONDALL [SU7948]
Hampshire Arms GU10 5QU [village signed off A287 S of Fleet; Pankridge St]: Smartly refurbished as more restaurant than pub, with enjoyable brasserie food lunchtime and wkdy evenings, interesting more elaborate restaurant menu, almost hotelish décor and furnishings for small bar, comfortable leather armchairs and sofa by splendid log fire, a dozen good wines by the glass, friendly French staff; children welcome, heated tables in back garden *(KC, BB)*

Plume of Feathers GU10 5NT [The Borough]: Attractive smallish 15th-c village pub popular for generous enjoyable food from interesting snacks up in bar and smarter restaurant end, friendly helpful antipodean staff, Greene King ales, decent wines by the glass, beams and dark wood, prints on cream walls, log fire in big brick fireplace; children welcome, two red telephone boxes in garden, picturesque village *(Betty Laker, Tony and Jill Radnor)*

CURDRIDGE [SU5314]

Cricketers SO32 2BH [Curdridge Lane, off B3035 just under a mile NE of A334 junction]: Open-plan low-ceilinged Victorian village local with banquettes in lounge area, traditional public area, rather smart dining part, friendly attentive licensees, wide choice of well presented generous food inc sandwiches and good value daily specials, Greene King ales; quiet piped music; tables on front lawn, pleasant footpaths *(Paul and Shirley White)*

DAMERHAM [SU1016]

☆ *Compasses* SP6 3HQ [signed off B3078 in Fordingbridge, or off A354 via Martin; East End]: Appealing country inn with up to five real ales such as Fullers London Pride and Hop Back Summer Lightning, good choice of wines by the glass, well over a hundred malt whiskies, good food from sandwiches up esp soups, shellfish and cheeses, friendly obliging staff, neatly refurbished small lounge bar divided by log fire from pleasant dining area with booth seating (children allowed here), pale wood tables and kitchen chairs, separate locals' bar with pool; long pretty garden by attractive village's cricket ground, high downland walks, nice bedrooms *(Noel Grundy, Mr and Mrs D Renwick)*

DIBDEN PURLIEU [SU4106]

Heath SO45 4PW [Beaulieu Rd; B3054/A326 roundabout]: Pleasantly refurbished Whitbreads pub with variety of linked areas, good range of food, efficient service, real ales such as Ringwood, Shepherd Neame Spitfire and Wadworths 6X; children welcome *(Phyl and Jack Street)*

DOGMERSFIELD [SU7852]

☆ *Queens Head* RG27 8SY [village signed off A287 and B3016 W of Fleet; Pilcot]: Great atmosphere and masses of menu boards with all tables set for eating in well divided dining bar, wide range of good value food from baguettes up, particularly good vegetarian choice, swift friendly service, two or three real ales, good choice of wines esp new world, dark pink walls, some stripped brickwork, a couple of low beams; well reproduced piped music, booking advised evenings (two sittings); tree-shaded picnic-sets on front grass, pretty setting, cl Mon *(Jennifer Banks, BB, Fred and Kate Portnell)*

DOWNTON [SZ2793]

Royal Oak SO41 0LA [A337 Lymington—New Milton]: Neat, bright and cheerful partly panelled family pub with good value food, well kept Gales HSB and Ringwood Best, good wine choice, efficient and pleasant young staff, nice touches such as good-sized napkins, small restaurant; unobtrusive piped music; huge well kept garden with good play

area *(Glenwys and Alan Lawrence, Mr and Mrs R W Allan, Brian Root)*

DROXFORD [SU6018]

White Horse SO32 3PB [A32; South Hill]: Quiet rambling pub with several small linked areas, low beams, bow windows, alcoves and log fires, two dining rooms, Greene King ales, wide food choice from good value ciabattas up, pleasant staff, roomy separate public bar with plenty of games, also TV and CD juke box; children and dogs welcome, tables out in sheltered flower-filled courtyard, open all day, rolling walking country *(LYM, Val and Alan Green, W A Evershed, Ann and Colin Hunt)*

DUMMER [SU5846]

☆ *Queen* RG25 2AD [½ mile from M3 junction 7; take Dummer slip road]: Comfortable beamed pub well divided with lots of softly lit alcoves, Courage Best, Fullers London Pride, John Smiths and a guest such as Hogs Back TEA, good choice of wines by the glass, popular food from lunchtime sandwiches and light dishes up, good friendly service even on busy Sun lunchtime, big log fire, Queen and steeplechase prints, no mobile phones, restaurant allowing children; games machine, well reproduced piped music; picnic-sets under cocktail parasols on terrace and in extended back garden, attractive village with ancient church *(Edward Mirzoeff, P E Wareham, Martin and Karen Wake, LYM, W W Burke, Ian Phillips, Mrs Ann Gray, Jennifer Banks)*

EAST BOLDRE [SU3700]

☆ *Turf Cutters Arms* SO42 7WL [Main Rd]: Small dim-lit New Forest country local, warmly welcoming and unpretentious, ponies wandering past, perhaps a regular arriving on horseback, lots of beams and pictures, nicely worn in furnishings on bare boards and flagstones, log fire, huge helpings of simple local food from sandwiches and basic dishes to quite a lot of game, three Ringwood ales and Wadworths 6X, several dozen malt whiskies, fish tanks, friendly dogs; children welcome, garden tables, good heathland walks, three big old-fashioned bedrooms, good breakfast *(BB, Val and Alan Green, Sue Demont, Tim Barrow, K H Frostick)*

EAST END [SZ3696]

East End Arms SO41 5SY [back road Lymington—Beaulieu, parallel to B3054]: Civilised and friendly New Forest country local, stylish and enterprising meals making a nice contrast with the simplicity of its plain bright bar, log fire, well kept Ringwood Best on handpump and other ales tapped from the cask, good choice of wines by the glass, helpful staff, longish neat candlelit dining lounge with nice pictures; tables in small pleasant garden, popular with families *(BB, Michael and Maggie Betton)*

EAST MEON [SU6822]

☆ *George* GU32 1NH [Church St; signed off A272 W of Petersfield, and off A32 in West Meon]: Relaxing heavy-beamed rustic pub with wide choice of generous good value bar and restaurant food from sandwiches up, helpful friendly service, inglenook log fires, cosy areas around central bar counter, Badger ales, good choice of wines; soft piped music; children welcome, nicely laid out back terrace, five comfortable bedrooms (book well ahead), good breakfast, pretty village with fine church, good walks *(V Brogden, Mr and Mrs A P Betts, LYM, W A Evershed, MLR, Ann and Colin Hunt, Phyl and Jack Street, William Ruxton)*

EAST TYTHERLEY [SU2927]

Star SO51 0LW [off B3084 N of Romsey]: Pretty country dining pub, bar with attractive log fires, leather sofas and tub chairs, Ringwood Best and Fortyniner and a couple of guest beers; children welcome, smartly furnished terrace and play area, bedrooms overlooking cricket pitch, good breakfast and nearby walks, cl Sun evening and Mon *(Christopher and Elise Way, Roger Price, LYM)*

EASTON [SU5132]

☆ *Cricketers* SO21 1EJ [off B3047]: Pleasantly smartened-up open-plan local with chatty and welcoming NZ landlord, Ringwood Best and two other real ales, reasonably priced wines, good value generous food from sandwiches to piping hot dishes inc good choice of OAP lunches, Sun bar nibbles, prompt service, pleasant mix of pub furnishings, darts and shove-ha'penny one end, small bright restaurant, good wine range; well cared for bedrooms, handy for Itchen Way walks *(BB, Ann and Colin Hunt, Tony and Jill Radnor)*

EMERY DOWN [SU2808]

☆ *New Forest* SO43 7DY [village signed off A35 just W of Lyndhurst]: Comfortable and spacious, in one of the best bits of the New Forest for walking, hard-working new licensee, enjoyable food from filled baguettes and innovative snacks up, welcoming staff, good choice of real ales inc Ringwood Best and of wines by the glass, proper coffee, attractive softly lit separate areas on varying levels, each with its own character, hunting prints, two log fires; children allowed, small pleasant three-level garden *(Ann and Colin Hunt, Revd Michael Vockins, LYM, George Murdoch, Brian Collins)*

EVERSLEY [SU7861]

Golden Pot RG27 0NB [B3272]: Enjoyable food from baguettes up in recently refurbished linked areas with nicely spaced tables, quick cheerful service, Greene King ales, good wines by the glass; piped music; dogs allowed in bar, picnic-sets outside with masses of colourful flowers, cl winter Sun evening *(Mrs Pam Mattinson, KC, LYM)*

EWSHOT [SU8150]

Windmill GU10 5BJ [Church Lane, off A287]: Small pub with quick friendly service, well kept ales such as Fullers London Pride and Wadworths 6X, usual food, cellar bar, snug and dining room, green plush seating; enormous garden with Sun lunchtime barbecues *(John Coatsworth)*

FACCOMBE [SU3958]

☆ *Jack Russell* SP11 0DS [signed from A343 Newbury—Andover]: Light and airy creeper-covered pub in village-green setting opp pond by flint church, decorous bar with a few forestry saws and the like, quick friendly service even on busy wknds, well kept Greene King IPA and Shepherd Neame Spitfire, good coffee, bar food (not Sun evening) from good snacks to Sun roasts, darts, sturdy oak tables in carpeted conservatory restaurant; disabled facilities, picnic-sets out on lawn by beech trees, bedrooms spotless and cheerful, good walks with rewarding views *(BB, Phyl and Jack Street, Michael Dallas, Angus and Rosemary Campbell, Sue Demont, Tim Barrow)*

FAIR OAK [SU4919]

Fox & Hounds SO50 7HB [Winchester Rd (A3051)]: Comfortable and attractive open-plan family dining pub with good value home-made food (all day wknds) inc OAP wkdy lunches, quick cheerful young staff, good wines by the glass, Greene King Abbot and Marstons Pedigree, exposed brickwork, beam-and-plank ceilings, soft lighting, conservatory; children welcome, disabled access, pretty hanging baskets, big garden with play area, path to nearby Bishopstoke woods, open all day *(Barry and Susanne Hurst)*

FAREHAM [SU5806]

Cob & Pen PO16 8SL [Wallington Shore Rd, not far from M27 junction 11]: Well kept Adnams Broadside, Ringwood Best and Timothy Taylors Landlord, fairly priced simple food, friendly staff, pleasant pine furnishings, flagstones and carpets, nice separate games room; large garden, handy for waterside walks *(Stephen and Jean Curtis, Val and Alan Green)*

FARRINGDON [SU7135]

Rose & Crown GU34 3ED [off A32 S of Alton; Crows Lane – follow Church, Selborne, Liss signpost]: Cheerful and attractive L-shaped bar mainly laid for the good choice of enjoyable food, warmly welcoming efficient service even when busy, real ales, decent wines and coffee, log fire, fresh flowers, candles and nice lighting, daily papers, spotless back dining room; wide views from big well kept back garden *(Peter Salmon, BB, Ann and Colin Hunt, Tony and Jill Radnor)*

FINCHDEAN [SU7312]

George PO8 0AU: Popular for good value food in lounge and neat public bar, Youngs real ale, cheerful smartly dressed staff; dogs welcome, good nearby walks, open all day Sun *(W A Evershed, Ann and Colin Hunt)*

FISHERS POND [SU4920]

Queens Head SO50 7HF [Portsmouth Rd]: Well modernised big dining pub with well spaced tables, reasonably priced traditional and some more unusual food all day from sandwiches up, pleasant atmosphere; children's play facilities, handy for Marwell Zoo *(Diana Brumfit)*

FLEET [SU8155]
Heron on the Lake GU51 2RY [Old Cove Rd]:
Welcoming Chef & Brewer by Fleet Pond,
done out with lots of beams, nooks and
corners, two log fires, Courage Directors,
Hogs Back TEA and two guest ales, decent
reasonably priced food, friendly attentive
service, good coffee; piped music; open all
day *(Paul Humphreys)*
FORDINGBRIDGE [SU1314]
Augustus John SP6 1DG [Station Rd]: Good
service without its being pushy, enjoyable
food (free puddings midweek), spotless
housekeeping, reasonably priced wines;
picnic-sets outside, four comfortable
bedrooms *(Pat and Robert Watt)*
George SP6 1AH [Bridge St]: Refreshing new
contemporary décor keeping a pleasant
degree of pubby cosiness, wide choice of
enjoyable food, Greene King Abbot and Old
Speckled Hen; lovely spot, terrace and
conservatory facing visibly trout-filled
River Avon *(George Murdoch)*
FREEFOLK [SU4848]
☆ *Watership Down* RG28 7NJ [Freefolk Priors,
N of B3400 Whitchurch—Overton; brown
sign to pub]: Engaging unpretentious
country pub, ancient brick flooring around
bar counter with five well kept changing ales
mainly from smallish local brewers,
welcoming prompt service and chatty
atmosphere, popular cheapish food from
sandwiches to good value Sun roasts, one
neat carpeted area with rabbit pictures and
well padded wall seating, another with darts,
table football, veteran one-arm bandit and
other games (TV too), comfortable dining
conservatory; picnic-sets in big sloping
informal garden with sturdy timber play
area, more under heaters beside pub,
pleasant walks *(BB, Tom Evans, Pete Baker)*
FROGHAM [SU1712]
☆ *Foresters Arms* SP6 2JA [Abbotswell Rd]:
Busy New Forest pub comfortably refurbished
in polished rustic style, chef/landlord doing
enjoyable blackboard food from sandwiches
to very popular Sun lunch (get there early or
book – the compact dining room fills
quickly), reasonable prices, attentive young
staff, Wadworths and guest ales, good wines
by the glass; children welcome, pleasant
garden with pretty front verandah and good
play area, small camp site adjacent, nearby
ponies and good walks; may be all too firmly
cl Tues lunchtime *(Phyl and Jack Street,
Kevin Flack, John and Joan Calvert, LYM)*
GOODWORTH CLATFORD [SU3642]
Royal Oak SP11 7QY: Smart and comfortable
L-shaped bar with friendly efficient service,
good food from pub staples to uncommon
dishes such as mutton, well kept local ale,
welcoming landlord; Weds quiz night;
sheltered and very pretty dell-like garden,
large and neatly kept, attractive Test
Valley village, good walks by River Anton
(Miss L Buxton)
GOSPORT [SU6100]
Clarence PO12 1BB [Clarence Rd/Mumby Rd

(A32)]: Partly 18th-c, incorporating former
chapel from the Isle of Wight, heavy
furnishings, old books, equestrian and other
prints, wide choice of food in bar and
upstairs restaurant, well kept Oakleaf beers
from over the road (and you can see their
own former microbrewery through glass
panels in bar and minstrel's gallery), log and
coal fires, relaxed atmosphere, Edwardian
dining room, some live music; may be piped
radio; dogs welcome, tables outside, open all
day *(Bruce Bird)*
Jolly Roger PO12 4LQ [Priory Rd, Hardway]:
Old beamed harbour-view pub with enjoyable
fairly priced food, good friendly service, four
real ales such as Greene King Abbot and
Youngs Special, decent house wines, attractive
eating area *(Mr and Mrs J Underwood)*
Queens PO12 1LG [Queens Rd]: Classic bare-
boards local whose long-serving landlady
keeps five interesting changing ales in top
condition, popular Oct beer festival, quick
service, Sun bar nibbles, perhaps huge filled
rolls and other simple food, three areas off
bar with good log fire in interesting carved
fireplace, sensibly placed darts, docile
pyrenean mountain dog; TV room – children
welcome here daytime; cl lunchtimes Mon-
Thurs, open all day Sat *(Ann and Colin Hunt,
Bruce Bird)*
GREYWELL [SU7151]
Fox & Goose RG29 1BY [nr M3 junction 5;
A287 towards Odiham then first right to
village]: Two-bar village pub with country-
kitchen furniture, friendly helpful service,
food from sandwiches up, changing real ales;
good-sized garden behind, attractive village,
handy for Basingstoke Canal walks *(Ann and
Colin Hunt)*
HAMBLE [SU4806]
Bugle SO31 4HA [3 miles from M27 junction
8]: Roomy waterside pub sprucely
refurbished with sturdy furniture, beams,
flagstones and bare boards, enjoyable food
(all day wknds) using local ingredients and
fresh fish, good choice of wines by the glass,
two or three real ales, log fires; terrace
tables, open all day *(LYM)*
King & Queen SO31 4HA [3 miles from M27
junction 8; High St]: Well run seaside-feel
pub with real ales such as Fullers London
Pride, good value food, pine tables on bare
boards; soft piped music; showers and
laundry room for dirty sailors, tables on
front gravel *(anon)*
Olde Whyte Harte SO31 4JF [High St;
3 miles from M27 junction 8]: Welcoming
Yorkshire landlord in cheery 16th-c bar,
cheeky graffiti on low beams, monkeys and
yachting memorabilia, big inglenook log fire,
well integrated flagstoned eating area
allowing children, generous fresh food all day
inc plenty of fish, Fullers and Gales ales, good
wines by the glass and country wines, decent
coffee; piped music; some tables in small
walled garden, handy for nature reserve, open
all day *(LYM, Bruce and Penny Wilkie,
Mayur Shah, Ann and Colin Hunt)*

HILL TOP [SU4003]

Royal Oak SO42 7YR [B3054 Beaulieu—Hythe]: Good-sized neatly kept pub looking out over New Forest, several well kept ales such as Adnams Broadside, good range of above-average food; tables and chairs in pleasant garden behind, handy for Exbury Gardens *(Dr Martin Owton)*

HOOK [SU7354]

Crooked Billet RG27 9EH [A30 about a mile towards London]: Comfortably extended and welcoming roadside pub with large dining area, wide choice of enjoyable food inc interesting specials and plenty of fish, swift helpful service, well kept Courage Best and Directors and a quickly changing guest beer, reasonably priced wines, good range of soft drinks, daily papers in sofa-and-log-fire area; soft piped music; children welcome, attractive smallish garden by stream with trout and ducks *(Sue and Mike Todd)*

HORSEBRIDGE [SU3430]

John o' Gaunt SO20 6PU [off A3057 Romsey—Andover, just SW of Kings Somborne]: Nice spot in River Test village, log fire in simple L-shaped bar, nice prints in small back dining area, young chef doing enjoyable food inc some interesting dishes, well kept Ringwood ales, friendly service; picnic-sets out on side arbour *(BB, Phyl and Jack Street, Ann and Colin Hunt, GHC)*

HURSLEY [SU4225]

Dolphin SO21 2JY [A3090 Winchester—Romsey]: Big country pub with reasonably priced food inc children's helpings, well kept real ales, attentive staff; attractive garden, animals for children to watch *(A and B D Craig)*

HURSTBOURNE TARRANT [SU3853]

George & Dragon SP11 0AA [A343]: Attractive whitewashed village pub with low beams and inglenook (log-effect gas fire), good value home-made food from baked potatoes up, real ales, friendly welcome, back locals' bar; small secluded terrace, bedrooms, pretty village in walking country, open all day Sun *(LYM, Ann and Colin Hunt)*

KEYHAVEN [SZ3091]

Gun SO41 0TP: Busy 17th-c pub looking over boatyard and sea to Isle of Wight, low-beamed bar with lots of nautical memorabilia and plenty of character (less in family rooms), good choice of generous food using local produce, real ales tapped from the cask such as Gales HSB, Greene King Old Speckled Hen, Ringwood and Wadworths 6X, well over a hundred malt whiskies, brisk service, bar billiards; back conservatory, garden with swings and fishpond *(A and B D Craig, Dr A J and Mrs Tompsett)*

KING'S SOMBORNE [SU3531]

Crown SO20 6PW [A3057]: Long low pub opp village church, newly reopened by pleasant young couple aiming to keep food simple, fresh and local, well kept real ales such as Bass, Flowers IPA and Ringwood, several linked brightly redecorated rooms; garden

behind, Test Way and Clarendon Way footpaths nearby *(Mr and Mrs H J Langley)*

LISS [SU7826]

Jolly Drover GU33 7QL [London Rd, Hill Brow]: Neatly run and comfortable old pub notable for its very friendly service (good with disabled people), good choice of pubby food from sandwiches to good fish, real ales such as Fullers London Pride, Ringwood Best and Timothy Taylors Landlord, good choice of wines by the glass; tables and chairs on sheltered terrace, six bedrooms, cl Sun evening *(Andy Willerton, Philip and Christine Kenny)*

LOCKS HEATH [SU5006]

☆ *Jolly Farmer* SO31 9JH [2½ miles from M27 junction 9; A27 towards Bursledon, left into Locks Rd, at end T junction right into Warsash Rd then left at hire shop into Fleet End Rd]: Wide choice of enjoyable food from filled baps to fresh fish, local meats and good value very popular two-sitting Sun lunch in appealing series of linked softly lit rooms, nice old scrubbed tables (quite close-set) and masses of interesting bric-a-brac and prints, good quick friendly service, interesting long-serving landlord, Fullers London Pride, Gales HSB and a guest beer, decent wines and country wines, coal-effect gas fires; two sheltered terraces (one with a play area and children's lavatories), nice bedrooms *(Ann and Colin Hunt, Matt Long, LYM)*

LONG SUTTON [SU7447]

☆ *Four Horseshoes* RG29 1TA [signed off B3349 S of Hook]: Unpretentious well kept open-plan black-beamed country local with long-serving landlord cooking good pubby food, very welcoming landlady, good range of changing real ales such as Gales, decent wines and country wine, two log fires, daily papers, no piped music, small glazed-in verandah; disabled access, picnic-sets on grass over road, boules pitch and play area, good value bedrooms *(Tony and Jill Radnor, BB)*

LONGPARISH [SU4243]

☆ *Plough* SP11 6PB [B3048, off A303 just E of Andover]: Comfortable open-plan pub refurbished as cosy dining pub under new licensees, good reasonably priced pleasant home cooking with larger evening menu, friendly efficient service, good choice of wines by the glass, Gales and Ringwood ales, log fire; children in eating areas, disabled access and facilities, tables on terrace and in nice garden, bedrooms *(Gareth Lewis, Dennis Jenkin, LYM, Mr and Mrs J R Shrimpton, John Balfour)*

LONGSTOCK [SU3537]

☆ *Peat Spade* SO20 6DR [off A30 on W edge of Stockbridge]: Airy and attractive dining pub with lots of close-set tables, doors to terrace from dining room, bistroish décor with quite a fishing and shooting theme, even a little fishing shop at the end of the garden, and they can arrange good fishing; attentive licensees and polite young staff, Ringwood

Best and a guest beer, quite a few wines by the glass, decent if not cheap food, upstairs lounge with board games; no under-10s; dogs welcome in bar, plenty of Test Way and water-meadow walks, bedrooms, open all day *(Simon and Mandy King, Mrs S Barker-Ryder, I H Curtis, LYM, Ann and Colin Hunt)*

LOWER FROYLE [SU7643]

Anchor GU34 4NA [signed N of A31 W of Bentley]: Beamed pub dating from 14th c, undergoing extensive refurbishment for reopening as dining pub in similar style to and under same management as Peat Spade in Longstock, work delayed by severe fire damage in early spring 2007; as we go to press, hopes for completion by autumn 2007, should be well worth investigation *(BB)*

LYMINGTON [SZ3294]

☆ *Fishermans* SO41 8FD [All Saints Rd, Woodside]: More restaurant than pub now (though locals still use the small bar between dining rooms), wide choice of good traditional and more interesting food inc very popular Sun lunch, friendly helpful staff, pleasant atmosphere, Ringwood ales, decent wines; wknd booking recommended *(Graham and Glenis Watkins, David Sizer)*

LYNDHURST [SU3007]

☆ *Crown Stirrup* SO43 7DE [Clay Hill; A337 ½ mile S]: Two friendly low-beamed rooms, 17th-c or older, with well kept ales, good simple choice of reasonably priced food from burgers to dover sole, good wine list and service, pine furniture, log fires, stripped brick in flagstoned dining room; children and dogs welcome, covered back terrace, picnic-sets in pleasant side garden with play area and gate to Forest *(Tony and Caroline Elwood, Prof and Mrs Tony Palmer)*

Waterloo Arms SO43 7AS [Pikes Hill, off A337 N]: Rambling thatched 17th-c New Forest pub with low beams, pleasant furnishings, log fire, interesting beers tapped from the cask, good wine list, generous food, comfortable bar, roomy separate back dining area; large attractive back garden with play area, guinea pigs and rabbits *(Ann and Colin Hunt, Alan M Pring)*

MEDSTEAD [SU6537]

Castle of Comfort GU34 5LU [signed off A31 at Four Marks; Castle St]: Leisurely village local, homely and traditional beamed lounge bar, several well kept good value ales, good basic bar lunches inc soup and sandwiches, toasties and ploughman's, friendly landlady and good service, plush chairs, big woodburner and small open fireplace, spartan public bar with darts etc; sunny front verandah, more tables in neat side garden with fairy lights and play tree, nice downland walks to the west *(BB, Roger Chacksfield, Christine Bridgwater)*

MEONSTOKE [SU6120]

Bucks Head SO32 3NA [village signed just off A32 N of Droxford]: Partly panelled L-shaped dining lounge looking over road to water meadows, enjoyable sensibly priced food inc popular Sun roasts, well kept Greene King IPA and Old Speckled Hen, decent wines, log fire, plush banquettes, rugs on bare boards, well spaced tables, unspoilt public bar with leather settee by another log fire, darts and juke box; tables and picnic-sets in small garden, lovely village setting with ducks on pretty little River Meon, good walks, open all day wknds *(Ann and Colin Hunt, BB, Tony Carter)*

MICHELDEVER [SU5138]

☆ *Half Moon & Spread Eagle* SO21 3DG [brown sign to pub off A33 N of Winchester]: Simply decorated village local reopened early summer 2007 under new tenants (too soon for us to rate it), leather armchairs, solid seats and a woodburner in appealing beamed bar, Greene King ales, good choice of wines by the glass, games area; up to now has been enjoyed for its food and atmosphere; sheltered back terrace and garden, pleasant walks nearby; reports please *(LYM)*

MINSTEAD [SU2810]

☆ *Trusty Servant* SO43 7FY [just off A31, not far from M27 junction 1]: Attractive 19th-c pub in pretty New Forest hamlet with interesting church, wandering cattle and ponies and plenty of easy walks, easy-going two-room bar and big airy separate dining room (children allowed here), informally friendly service, real ales inc Ringwood Best, decent house wines and country wines, enjoyable generous food all day from sandwiches, baguettes and baked potatoes to good game dishes, piano singalong Fri; dogs welcome in bar, front picnic-sets, big sloping area around behind, character bedrooms, open all day *(Ann and Colin Hunt, Claire Friend, David Adams, Brian Root, D P and M A Miles, Evelyn and Derek Walter, Richard May, Kevin Flack, Kath and Ted Warren, Charlie and Chris Barker, N R White, Bob and Angela Brooks, Don Manley, LYM, Conor McGaughey)*

MONXTON [SU3144]

Black Swan SP11 8AW [High St]: Rambling 17th-c pub with decent food from baguettes up, OAP lunch Mon-Thurs, children-free deals 6-7, real ales such as Ringwood Best and Timothy Taylors Landlord, good choice of wines by the glass, log fire, daily papers, young staff (service can slow when busy); piped music, car park some way down street; children and dogs welcome, picnic-sets in lovely sheltered garden by stream with ducks, open all day *(Mrs Joyce Robson, Edward Mirzoeff, Phyl and Jack Street, Alec and Joan Laurence, LYM, Michael and Jenny Back)*

NEW CHERITON [SU5827]

Hinton Arms SO24 0NH [A272 nr B3046 junction]: Clean, bright and neatly kept, with sensible choice of enjoyable very generous food, four real ales from Hampshire and Ringwood; terrace tables and big garden, very handy for Hinton Ampner House (NT) *(Val and Alan Green, BB, Christine Bridgwater)*

NEWNHAM [SU7054]
Old House At Home RG27 9AH [handy for M3 junction 5; A287 then keep on across A30]: Civilised and welcoming bay-windowed dining pub in secluded hamlet, good fresh food, not cheap but good value and changing daily, with tempting puddings and generous cafetière coffee, keeps a friendly pubby atmosphere too, with regulars at the bar, real ales and good fire; pleasant walks nearby (J J B Rowe)

NORTH WALTHAM [SU5645]
Fox RG25 2BE [signed off A30 SW of Basingstoke; handy for M3 junction 7]: Comfortable village pub with enjoyable food from sandwiches and baguettes to venison and Sun roasts, well kept Adnams Broadside and Ringwood Best, welcoming landlord and well trained staff, foxy décor, log fire in bright elongated dining area; children welcome, lovely outside with fine floral displays and farmland views, pleasant village in nice spot (walk to Jane Austen's church at Steventon) (J R Ringrose, S Crowe)
Wheatsheaf RG25 2BB [visible from M3 and handy for junction 7, via A30]: Former Georgian coaching inn with enjoyable bar food, quick service by particularly friendly staff, well kept ales, decent wines by the glass, daily papers, three log fires, beams and panelling, oak furniture; comfortable up-to-date bedroom wing (Stephen Allford)

OAKLEY [SU5851]
Fox RG23 7HH [Newfound (B3400 W of Basingstoke)]: Fullers pub with wide food choice from baguettes and baked potatoes up, sizeable back restaurant, skittle alley; pretty hanging baskets, garden (Michael Dandy)

ODIHAM [SU7450]
Bell RG29 1LY: Simple unspoilt two-bar local in pretty square opp church, friendly regulars and staff, real ale (Ann and Colin Hunt)
Water Witch RG29 1AL [Colt Hill – quiet no through rd signed off main st]: Olde-worlde décor in nicely kept Chef & Brewer nr picturesque stretch of Basingstoke Canal, big but cosily divided, with wide choice of reliable food yet pleasantly pubby atmosphere, good friendly landlady and staff, real ales; lovely hanging baskets, big garden with extensive children's facilities, very busy wknds (Jennifer Banks, Ann and Stephen Saunders, R T and J C Moggridge, Gordon Prince)

OTTERBOURNE [SU4623]
Old Forge SO21 2EE [Main Rd]: Reliable and popular chain pub, pleasantly refurbished with tables spread through linked rooms, friendly staff, good sensibly priced drinks range, usual food all day, log fires (Phyl and Jack Street)

OWSLEBURY [SU5123]
Ship SO21 1LT [off B2177 Fishers Pond—Lower Upham; Whites Hill]: Nice 17th-c building with black oak beams and timbers, log fire in big central fireplace, well kept real ales inc Greene King, good choice of wines by the glass, friendly service, pub games and skittle alley, comfortable dining area and restaurant; plenty of space outside with play area, toddler zone, pets corner and garden kitchen for family food (Paul and Shirley White, W A Evershed, LYM, Ann and Colin Hunt)

PARK GATE [SU5108]
Talisman SO31 7GD [Bridge Rd, Park Gate (A27, a mile from M27 junction 9)]: Large hospitable Badger dining pub, busy and always coping well, with their real ales kept well, good choice of wines, generous popular food, beams, oak panels, bare boards and carpets, flame-effect fire; quiet piped music; children welcome, large back garden with play area (Jenny and Peter Lowater, Bruce and Penny Wilkie)

PETERSFIELD [SU7423]
Good Intent GU31 4AF [College St]: Neat and tidy proper pub with five well kept Fullers/Gales ales, enjoyable freshly made pubby food strong on sausages, affable landlord, low oak beams and log fires in 16th-c core, well spaced good-sized pine tables with flowers, camera collection, cosy family area; live music Thurs and Sun (Val and Alan Green, W A Evershed, Andrew and Debbie Ettle)
Square Brewery GU32 3HJ [The Square]: Neatly kept Fullers pub with four of their ales, small and quite imaginative choice of sensibly priced pubby food, armchairs one end with TV and games machines (Val and Alan Green)
☆ *White Horse* GU32 1DA [up on old downs rd about halfway between Steep and East Tisted, nr Priors Dean – OS Sheet 186 or 197, map ref 715290]: Charming country pub high and isolated on the downs, two relaxed and idiosyncratically old-fashioned rustic parlours (candlelit at night), attractive family dining room, open fires throughout, good range of real ales, friendly helpful staff, food (not Sun evening) from generous ciabattas to smartly served restaurranty dishes; they may try to keep your credit card while you eat; children welcome, rustic tables out by floodlit pond, open all day wknds (W A Evershed, Tony and Jill Radnor, Martin and Karen Wake, Val and Alan Green, the Didler, LYM, Ann and Colin Hunt, N K Crace)

PILLEY [SZ3298]
☆ *Fleur de Lys* SO41 5QG [off A337 Brockenhurst—Lymington; Pilley St]: Upscale dining pub with pretty contemporary décor keeping old boards, heavy beams, and dining room's huge inglenook log fire, good food, Ringwood Best and Fortyniner, decent wines, friendly service; piped music turned off on request; fine forest and heathland walks nearby (LYM, Michael and Maggie Betton, Dr D J R Martin, Kevin Flack)

PORTSMOUTH [SZ6399]
Bridge Tavern PO1 2JJ [East St, Camber Dock]: Flagstones, bare boards and lots of dark wood, comfortable furnishings, good

water views, Fullers and Gales ales, country wines, smiling service, straightforward food from baguettes and baked potatoes up, maritime theme; waterside terrace, nice position *(Mrs Maricar Jagger, Paul and Shirley White, Ann and Colin Hunt)*

Sallyport PO1 2LU [High St, Old Portsmouth]: Interesting old hotel's comfortable bar with leather chesterfields, soft lighting, lots of naval prints, chamber pots hanging from beams, attractively priced usual bar food from sandwiches and baked potatoes up, several real ales inc Fullers London Pride and Gales HSB, decent coffee, upstairs restaurant; bedrooms, open all day *(Ann and Colin Hunt, Kevin Flack)*

☆ **Spice Island** PO1 2JL [Bath Sq]: Vast largely Georgian waterside pub with good friendly service under current management, Greene King ales, all-day food, big windows overlooking passing ships in roomy modernised bare-boards areas, part dark and panelled in galleon style, family area (one of the few in Portsmouth), bright upstairs restaurant; disabled access and facilities, tables out in harbourside square, open all day *(Barry and Anne, Michael and Alison Sandy, Mrs Maricar Jagger)*

☆ **Still & West** PO1 2JL [Bath Sq, Old Portsmouth]: Just reopened after costly refurbishment, oriental rugs on new dark oak boards, rich curtains, subtle up-to-date colour scheme, fireside sofas, super views of narrow harbour mouth and across to Isle of Wight, especially from new glazed-in panoramic dining area, sensibly priced interesting food (all day in summer), friendly and accommodating young staff, well kept Fullers HSB and London Pride, good choice of wines by the glass; piped music, nearby pay & display; children welcome, lots of picnic-sets on waterfront terrace, handy for the Historic Dockyard, open all day; initial reports on the redesign are very promising – more reports please *(LYM, Susan and John Douglas, Joan York, Colin Moore)*

RINGWOOD [SU1604]

Elm Tree BH24 3DY [Hightown]: Attractive and roomy thatched pub converted from 300-year-old farm, pleasant service, good value standard food inc locally popular 2-for-1 Thurs steak night, well kept Ringwood Best; tables out under cocktail parasols *(John and Penelope Massey Stewart)*

Fish BH24 2AA [off A31 W of town]: Large well divided pub with welcoming staff, wide choice of good value food, several real ales, log fire, eating area allowing children; piped music; tables on riverside lawn (traffic noise) with play area, open all day *(Mrs C Osgood, LYM, Colin Wood)*

ROCKBOURNE [SU1118]

☆ **Rose & Thistle** SP6 3NL [signed off B3078 Fordingbridge—Cranborne]: Attractive 16th-c thatched pub with good value interesting food, a couple of ales such as Fullers London Pride and Hampshire Strongs Best, good range of wines, efficient attentive staff,

civilised flagstoned bar with antique settles, old engravings and cricket prints, good coal fire, traditional games, log fires in two-room restaurant; may be piped classical music; children and dogs welcome, tables by thatched dovecot in neat front garden, charming tranquil spot in lovely village, good walks *(Keith and Jean Symons, Colin Chapman, Claire Hardcastle, W W Burke, LYM)*

ROMSEY [SU3521]

Old House At Home SO51 8DE [Love Lane]: Friendly and attractive 16th-c thatched pub surrounded by new development, appealingly individual and old-fashioned décor, good freshly made food from reasonably priced sandwiches up, good thoughtful service, well kept Fullers/Gales ales *(Peter and Liz Holmes, A and B D Craig)*

SARISBURY [SU5008]

Bold Forester SO31 7EL [handy for M27 junction 9; Bridge Rd (A27), Sarisbury Green]: Roomy and well run Victorian building, polite staff, Fullers London Pride, Gales HSB, Ringwood Fortyniner and Charles Wells Bombardier, very wide food choice from baguettes up, pictures of this increasingly built-up area in its strawberry-fields days; large nicely planted garden behind *(Bruce and Penny Wilkie, Val and Alan Green)*

SELBORNE [SU7433]

☆ **Selborne Arms** GU34 3JR [High St]: Character tables, pews and deep settles made from casks on antique boards in appealing bar, twinkly landlord and friendly staff, fine changing choice of largely local real ales, sensible range of good food from baguettes up, good choice of wines by the glass (three glass sizes), nice coffee, big log fire, daily papers, smart carpeted dining room with lots of local photographs; plenty of tables in garden with arbour, terrace, orchard and good play area, right by walks up Hanger, and handy for Gilbert White museum, open all day wknds *(Brian and Janet Ainscough, W A Evershed, Ann and Colin Hunt, Chantal Croneen, Michael and Judy Buckley, Gerald and Gabrielle Culliford, BB, Michael B Griffith, Val and Alan Green, Martin and Karen Wake)*

SETLEY [SU3000]

Filly SO42 7UF [Lymington Rd (A337 Brockenhurst—Lymington)]: Cheery pub very popular wknds for wide choice of generous enjoyable home-made food inc Sun carvery, real ales, decent wines, quick service, interesting beamed front bar with inglenook, nice dining area; some tables outside, New Forest walks, open all day *(Ann and Colin Hunt, LYM, Vince Eveleigh, John and Joan Calvert)*

SHAWFORD [SU4724]

Bridge Hotel SO21 2BP: Large beamed Chef & Brewer useful for good choice of promptly served food all day, efficient friendly staff, real ales inc an unusual guest beer, decent wines, several interesting rooms, smart décor, cosy nooks and corners; pleasant terrace and large garden with play area, downland and Itchen Way walks *(Phyl and Jack Street, Mrs Hilarie Taylor, Val and Alan Green)*

SHEDFIELD [SU5513]

Wheatsheaf SO32 2JG [A334 Wickham— Botley]: Busy and friendly no-fuss local with four reasonably priced ales such as Archers IPA and Goddards Best tapped from the cask, farm cider, short sensible choice of bargain bar lunches; dogs welcome, garden, handy for Wickham Vineyard, open all day *(Val and Alan Green)*

SHERFIELD ENGLISH [SU3022]

Hatchet SO51 6FP [Romsey rd]: Traditional beamed and panelled pub, good generous fairly priced food (best to book evenings), real ale, good wine choice, attentive staff, end woodburner, restaurant area; picnic-sets out in front, back play area *(Alan M Pring)*

SILCHESTER [SU6262]

Calleva Arms RG7 2PH [The Common]: Spacious cheerful bar on left with interestingly carved bench seats, smart dining areas on right, good value food from sandwiches and baguettes up, pleasant service, real ales inc Fullers/Gales, reasonably priced wines by the glass, family conservatory; handy for the Roman site, sizeable attractive garden *(J V Dadswell, Mrs J H S Lang)*

SOBERTON [SU6116]

☆ *White Lion* SO32 3PF [School Hill; signed off A32 S of Droxford]: Georgian-fronted 16th-c village pub under new licensees (she cooked here in the 1990s when it was a main entry), good food (not Sun/Mon evenings) from good value lunchtime bar snacks to wider and rather smarter evening menu, a real ale brewed for them by Hampshire and others from Bass, Palmers and Oakleaf, good house wines, comfortable dining lounge, rambling restaurant and unspoilt bare-boards low-ceilinged bar with built-in wooden wall seats and traditional games, golden labrador; children in eating areas, small sheltered pretty garden with suntrap fairy-lit terrace and covered tables, nice spot by green, good walks nearby, open all day Thurs-Sun *(LYM, Val and Alan Green, Ann and Colin Hunt, W A Evershed)*

SOPLEY [SZ1596]

☆ *Woolpack* BH23 7AX [B3347 N of Christchurch]: Pretty thatched pub with rambling open-plan low-beamed bar, rustic furniture, woodburner and little black kitchen range, welcoming helpful staff, very wide choice of enjoyable food from sandwiches and ploughman's to steaks and Sun roasts, Ringwood Best and Fortyniner and Wadworths 6X, good house wine, modern dining conservatory; piped music, bustling Fri/Sat night; children in eating areas, tables on terrace and in charming garden with weeping willows, duck stream and footbridges, open all day *(LYM, Mrs Pat Crabb, Brian Root, W W Burke, Phil Bryant)*

SOUTHAMPTON [SU4113]

Cowherds SO15 7NN [The Common (off A33)]: Big busy Vintage Inn dining pub in nice setting by common, welcoming atmosphere, low beams, cosy alcoves and tables in nice little bay windows, lots of Victorian photographs, carpets on polished boards, log fires, quick cheerful service, reasonably priced generous pub food inc fresh fish, real ales, good wine choice; very busy with young people Sun; tables outside with tie-ups and water for dogs *(Bob and Margaret Holder)*

Crown SO17 1QE [Highcrown St, Highfield]: Five well kept ales inc local Hampshire Strongs Best and Ringwood in bustling warmly relaxed local, substantial bargain lunchtime food from baked potatoes up, helpful staff, open fires; piped music, can be packed with students and academics from nearby Uni; dogs allowed in main bar (giving country feel in the suburbs), heated covered terrace, popular Sun quiz night, open all day *(Warwick Payne)*

☆ *Duke of Wellington* SO14 2AH [Bugle St (or walk along city wall from Bar Gate)]: Ancient timber-framed building on 13th-c foundations, bare boards, log fire, appealing enthusiastic landlord and really helpful service, full Wadworths ale range kept well, good choice of wines by the glass, good varied bar food (not Sun evening); piped music can be loud in cheery front bar, staider back area welcoming children; very handy for Tudor House Museum, open all day *(Val and Alan Green, Pam and John Smith)*

Richmond SO17 2FW [Portswood Rd]: Spotless local with well kept Greene King ales and a weekly guest beer, friendly staff, big brass till, liner pictures, may be fresh lunchtime rolls and sandwiches; juke box *(Peter and Liz Holmes)*

South Western Arms SO17 2HW [Adelaide Rd, by St Denys stn]: Ten or so well kept changing ales, good friendly staff, easy-going atmosphere, basic food and décor (bare boards and brickwork, toby jugs and stag's head on beams, lots of woodwork, ceiling beer mats), darts, pool and table football, upper gallery where children allowed; popular with students; terrace picnic-sets *(Warwick Payne)*

Standing Order SO14 2DF [High St]: Big busy Wetherspoons with half a dozen or so real ales, low-priced food, helpful efficient young staff, cosy corners (strange and interesting collection of books in one), civilised atmosphere; open all day *(Val and Alan Green)*

SOUTHSEA [SZ6498]

5th Hampshire Volunteer Arms PO5 2SL [Albert Rd]: Friendly two-bar backstreet local, Fullers/Gales ales and guests such as Greene King Abbot, old photographs of the regiment's members, good juke box; open all day *(the Didler, R M Corlett)*

Hole in the Wall PO5 3BY [Gt Southsea St]: Small friendly and relaxed local in old part of town, effectively tap for good Oakleaf ales brewed nearby (head brewer was landlord), also a couple of well kept guest beers such as Hogs Back TEA, three farm ciders, speciality sausages and substantial home-made pies with mash (not Sun evening), nicely old-fashioned dark décor, daily papers; cl till 5 exc Fri, open all day wknds *(Jonathan Martin, Mrs Maricar Jagger, R M Corlett)*

India Arms PO5 3BY [Gt Southsea St]: Reopened 2007 after comfortable refurbishment as interesting combination of large pub (three or four real ales such as Ballards and Gribble) and good indian tiffin room, may have indian bar nibbles some nights *(Mrs Maricar Jagger)*

King Street Tavern PO5 4EH [King St]: Friendly local in attractive Georgian area, spectacular 1870 tiled façade, good new licensees, well kept Wadworths, enjoyable genuinely home-made food, nice simple furnishings, bare boards and original fittings, bar billiards, shove-ha'penny and other traditional games, occasional live music; tables in courtyard, cl Mon, open all day Sun *(Phil and Sally Gorton)*

Red White & Blue PO4 0DW [Fawcett Rd]: Busy open-plan corner local, Fullers/Gales ales, food till 5 (not Sun); games nights, often live bands wknd and monthly jazz night; open all day *(Colin Moore, the Didler)*

STOCKBRIDGE [SU4036]

Leckford Hutt SO20 6DE [London Rd (A30 nearly 3 miles E)]: Now a restaurant (the Clos du Marquis), with newish chef/landlord doing good french food, interesting wines by the glass, cosy beamed dining rooms, easy chairs and settees in log-fire lounge; children and dogs welcome, tables and gazebo in secure garden behind, cl Sun evening and Mon *(anon)*

☆ *Three Cups* SO20 6HB [High St]: Distinctive coaching inn dating from 1500, cosy low-beamed bar, high-backed settles, various country paraphernalia such as fishing gear, guns and taxidermy, Fagins, Gales, Ringwood Best and a guest beer, good wines by the glass, food (often good) from baguettes to restaurant dishes; children and dogs welcome, verandah and charming cottage garden with streamside terrace, bedrooms, open all day *(LYM, Geoffrey Kemp, Dennis Jenkin, Dr and Mrs A K Clarke, Patrick Hall, John and Julie Moon, Brian Robinson, I H Curtis, Mr and Mrs A Curry, Edward Mirzoeff, John Coatsworth)*

☆ *White Hart* SO20 6HF [High St; A272/A3057 roundabout]: Roomy and welcoming divided beamed bar, attractive décor with antique prints, oak pews and other seats, attentive service, enjoyable generous fresh food from sandwiches and delicious crispy baguettes up, Fullers and Gales ales, good coffee, decent wines and country wines, reasonable prices, comfortable restaurant with blazing log fire (children allowed); disabled access and facilities, tables on terrace and in good garden, comfortable bedrooms, open all day *(Stephen and Jean Curtis, A and B D Craig, Diana Brumfit, Helen and Brian Edgeley, GHC, John and Joan Calvert, Mr and Mrs C Prentis, LYM, D Hillaby)*

SWANMORE [SU5816]

Hunters SO32 2PZ [Hillgrove]: Popular and comfortably worn-in dining pub, excellent for children, with big plain family room, winding garden with secluded tables (each with a buzzer for when your food's ready) and several substantial play areas for different age groups, plenty under cover and even one for babies; friendly and devoted long-serving landlord, well kept Gales HSB, Ringwood Best and Charles Wells Bombardier tapped from the cask, good house wine and country wines, attentive service, lots of boxer pictures, bank notes, carpentry and farm tools; piped music may be rather loud; very busy wknds, nice walks N of village *(Val and Alan Green)*

TANGLEY [SU3252]

☆ *Cricketers Arms* SP11 0SH [towards the Chutes]: Relaxed old-fashioned tucked-away country pub with good local ales tapped from the cask, good value food inc fresh baguettes and good generous pizzas, hospitable landlord and good staff massive inglenook log fire in small tiled-floor front bar, bar billiards, friendly black labradors (Pots and Harvey), bistroish back flagstoned extension with a one-table alcove off, some good cricketing prints; dogs welcome, tables on neat terrace, good Nordic-style back bedroom block, unspoilt countryside *(I A Herdman, Phil and Sally Gorton, John and Julie Moon, LYM)*

Fox SP11 0RU [crossroads S of village, towards Andover]: Welcoming little beamed and timbered pub with friendly newish tenants doing good value bar food, three real ales, big log fires, two pleasant family dining rooms *(J Stickland)*

TIMSBURY [SU3325]

☆ *Bear & Ragged Staff* SO51 0LB [A3057 towards Stockbridge; pub marked on OS Sheet 185 map ref 334254]: Reliable roadside dining pub with wide blackboard choice of reliable food all day, friendly efficient service, real ales such as Gales HSB, Ringwood Best and Timothy Taylors Landlord, lots of wines by the glass, log fire, good-sized beamed interior; children in eating area, tables in extended garden with good play area, handy for Mottisfont, good walks *(Phyl and Jack Street, Alec and Barbara Jones, LYM)*

TITCHFIELD [SU5305]

Queens Head PO14 4AQ [High St; off A27 nr Fareham]: Ancient pub with good value straightforward food esp fish cooked by friendly landlord, good fresh veg, four changing real ales, reasonable prices, interesting smallish 1930s-feel bar with old local pictures, window seats and central brick fireplace, small attractive dining room; picnic-sets in prettily planted small back yard, pleasant conservation village nr nature reserve and walks to coast, bedrooms *(A and B D Craig, Ann and Colin Hunt, Charles and Pauline Stride)*

Wheatsheaf PO14 4AD [East St; off A27 nr Fareham]: Welcoming new young licensees and good atmosphere, long bow-windowed front bar, separate back dining room, three well kept ales, log fires *(Ann and Colin Hunt)*

TURGIS GREEN [SU6959]

☆ *Jekyll & Hyde* RG27 0AX [A33 Reading—Basingstoke]: Bustling rambling pub with nice mix of furniture and village atmosphere in black-beamed and flagstoned bar, prompt cheerful service, four Badger ales, good coffee, blazing fire, daily papers, some interesting prints, larger stepped-up three-room dining area with sensibly priced pubby food from sandwiches up all day inc breakfast, children's helpings (they are welcome); piped music; disabled facilities, lots of picnic-sets in good sheltered garden (some traffic noise) with terrace, play area and various games, bedrooms, open all day *(LYM, Michael Dandy, Richard and Margaret, John and Fiona Merritt, KC)*

TWYFORD [SU4824]

Phoenix SO21 1RF [High St]: Cheerful open-plan local with lots of prints, bric-a-brac and big end inglenook log fire, friendly long-serving landlord (here throughout the *Guide*'s life) and attentive staff, Greene King ales, good coffee, decent wines, raised dining area, side skittle alley; unobtrusive piped music; children allowed at one end lunchtime, garden *(Lynn Sharpless, Ann and Colin Hunt)*

UPPER CLATFORD [SU3543]

Crook & Shears SP11 7QL [off A343 S of Andover, via Foundry Rd]: Cosy two-bar 17th-c thatched pub, several homely olde-worlde seating areas, bare boards and panelling, good changing ale range, decent food from doorstep sandwiches up, woodburner, small dining room, back skittle alley with own bar; pleasant secluded garden behind *(the Didler)*

WALHAMPTON [SZ3396]

Walhampton Arms SO41 5RE [B3054 NE of Lymington; aka Walhampton Inn]: Rambling Georgian-style roadhouse renamed under new licensees (was called Towles), emphasis on restaurany food inc reasonably priced carvery (wknds and Weds) in raftered former stables and two adjoining areas, pleasant lounge on right, Ringwood and other ales; attractive courtyard, good walks nearby inc Solent Way, open all day *(Phyl and Jack Street, David M Cundy)*

WALTHAM CHASE [SU5614]

Black Dog SO32 2LX [Winchester Rd]: Low-ceilinged two-bar pub covered with lovely hanging baskets, wide choice of enjoyable food, three well kept Greene King ales, decent wine, friendly licensees and good service, large log fire, back restaurant extension; tables in good-sized neatly kept garden *(Peter and Liz Holmes)*

Chase SO32 2LL [B2177]: Neat and friendly two-bar pub with changing ales such as Fullers ESB, Sharps Cornish Coaster and a Hampshire seasonal beer, bargain generous food from baguettes, paninis and focaccia up *(Val and Alan Green)*

WARSASH [SU4806]

Rising Sun SO31 9FT [Shore Rd; OS Sheet 196 map ref 489061]: Picture-window waterside pub with boating atmosphere, nautical charts and D-Day naval memorabilia, enjoyable food, good staff, Greene King and Ringwood ales, long bar part tiled-floor and part boards, fine Hamble estuary views esp from summer restaurant up spiral stairs; estuary walks, handy for Hook nature reserve *(A and B D Craig, Simon Marley)*

WELL [SU7646]

Chequers RG29 1TL [off A287 via Crondall, or A31 via Froyle and Lower Froyle]: Appealing low-beamed tavern with enjoyable food, welcoming service, well kept Badger Best, roaring log fire, panelled walls with 18th-c country-life prints and old sepia photographs, pews, brocaded stools and a few GWR carriage lamps; picnic-sets on vine-covered terrace and in spacious back garden *(LYM, J R Ringrose, Janet Whittaker)*

WEST END [SU4714]

Southampton Arms SO30 2HG [Moorgreen Rd, off B3035]: Sizeable city-edge pub firmly run by friendly landlady, Ringwood ales, enjoyable reasonably priced food, comfortable and cosy bar, attractive conservatory restaurant; good garden *(Phyl and Jack Street)*

WEST MEON [SU6424]

☆ *Thomas Lord* GU32 1LN [High St]: Welcoming and chatty newish landlords and lively warm-hearted atmosphere in thoroughly individual pub, enjoyable food (not Sun evening) showcasing local suppliers (some local foods available from deli counter), plenty of dining tables in fresh and airy main bar but also cosy library room with leather armchairs by one of the two log fires, several real ales tapped from the cask inc local fff, good farm ciders, wines and coffee in variety, cricket prints and memorabilia; children and dogs welcome (the pub dog's called Frank), picnic-sets in sheltered side garden, good walks W of village, cl Mon, open all day wknds *(Ann and Colin Hunt, BB, Prof and Mrs Tony Palmer, W A Evershed, Kevin Malam, Gerry Price, Christine Bridgwater)*

WHITCHURCH [SU4648]

Prince Regent RG28 7LT [London Rd]: Unpretentious L-shaped alehouse with Hop Back Summer Lightning, Otter and Stonehenge Pigswill, chatty locals, cards, piano, pool, valley view from back window; open all day *(Pete Baker)*

☆ *Red House* RG28 7LH [London St]: Neat and cheerful pub very popular for landlord/chef's good daily-changing choice of food from home-baked baguettes and hearty bar lunches to more stylish and individual dishes and beautiful puddings, chatty compact dining area up a step on right (big mirrored arches making it seem more extensive), sturdy tables on woodstrip flooring, a few big prints, friendly efficient service under hands-on landlady, Itchen Valley and guest beers, decent house wines, some very low beams, good log fire; separate traditional flagstoned public bar with juke box and TV; children welcome, tables on attractive back terraces with play area, own menu and hatch service (BB, Lynn Sharpless, Pete Baker, Diana Brumfit)

White Hart RG28 7DN [Newbury St]: Impressive former coaching inn now a busy and comfortably worn in pub with big public bar well away from dining areas, pleasant staff, good value food, well kept Arkells ales; bedrooms, open all day inc breakfast (Val and Alan Green)

WICKHAM [SU5711]

Kings Head PO17 5JN [The Square]: Pretty town pub with good service, reasonably priced usual food, Fullers/Gales ales, good coffee, log fire, big-windowed and solidly furnished open-plan bar, restaurant nicely secluded up some steps; tables out on square and in back garden (former coach yard) with play area, attractive village (BB, Peter and Anne Hollindale)

WINCHESTER [SU4728]

Bell SO23 9RE [St Cross Rd]: Unpretentious local welcoming visitors with enjoyable freshly made food inc good value paninis, friendly helpful landlord, Greene King ales, decent wines by the glass, liner pictures in comfortable sunny lounge, cosy public bar and sectioned-off dining area; big pleasant walled garden with swing and slide, handy for St Cross Hospital (ancient monument, not a hospital), lovely water-meadows walk from centre (Val and Alan Green, Lynn Sharpless, Phil and Sally Gorton)

Bishop on the Bridge SO23 9JX [High St]: Neatly kept pub with good varied food choice, efficient friendly staff; pleasant riverside terrace (N Vernon, Val and Alan Green)

☆ **Eclipse** SO23 9EX [The Square, between High St and cathedral]: Particularly welcoming licensees in picturesque and unaffected 14th-c local with massive beams and timbers in its two small rooms, cheerful atmosphere, four well kept ales inc Fullers London Pride and Ringwood, decent choice of wines by the glass, bargain simple lunchtime food from ciabattas to popular Sun roasts, oak settles; can get crowded; children in back area, seats outside, very handy for cathedral (Simon Fox, A and B D Craig, Val and Alan Green, LYM, Ann and Colin Hunt, June and Robin Savage, Canon Michael Bourdeaux)

Guildhall Tavern SO23 9LH [Colebrook St]: Once the Guild Hall's public reading room, recently refurbished to give a variety of seating areas, with Ringwood ales, straightforward bar food (Val and Alan Green)

Hyde Tavern SO23 7DY [A333, continuing out of Jewry St]: Quietly unassuming old-fashioned 15th-c two-bar local well cared for by welcoming landlady, now has good changing choice of ales such as Adnams, Ringwood and Wells & Youngs, two charming simply furnished bars with hardly a true right-angle, corner piano; lovely secluded garden (Pete Baker, Phil and Sally Gorton)

Old Gaol House SO23 8RZ [Jewry St]: Big Wetherspoons very popular for all-day food and good choice of local and other beers, low prices, decent coffee; children welcome (Ann and Colin Hunt, Craig Turnbull, Tim and Ann Newell)

Old Market SO23 9EX [The Square]: Rambling pleasantly refurbished corner pub, proper pizzas and pasta among wide choice of other dishes, Caledonian Deuchars IPA; right on Cathedral Close (LYM, Val and Alan Green)

Old Vine SO23 9HA [Great Minster St]: Light and airy brasserie-wine bar style refurbishment opp cathedral, well kept Adnams, Ringwood Best and Timothy Taylors Landlord, good tables and chairs on oak boards, restaurant food as well as contemporary and more familiar snacks from sandwiches up, quick service by brisk young staff; tables on sheltered terrace, partly covered and heated, charming and individual new bedrooms, open all day (Margaret McPhee, James Price, Tony and Jill Radnor)

Queen SO23 9PG [Kingsgate Rd]: Roomy pub in attractive setting opp college cricket ground, wide choice of mainstream food inc Sun lunch and children's dishes, well kept Greene King ales, decent wines, cheerful landlord and staff, low ceilings, cricketing and other prints on dark panelling, bric-a-brac on window sills, central fireplace, darts in public bar; piped music; disabled facilities, open all day, tables on front terrace and in large attractive garden (Val and Alan Green)

Royal Oak SO23 9AU [Royal Oak Passage, off upper end of pedestrian part of High St opp St Thomas St]: Otherwise standard pub with Greene King ales and decent food, notable for the intriguing cellar bar (not always open) whose massive 12th-c beams and Saxon wall give it some claim to be the country's oldest drinking spot; piped music, games machines, packed with young people Fri/Sat nights (the Didler, Ann and Colin Hunt, Ian and Nita Cooper, LYM)

WOLVERTON [SU5658]

George & Dragon RG26 5ST [Towns End; just N of A339 Newbury—Basingstoke]: Comfortably worn-in rambling open-plan pub with wide choice of enjoyable unpretentious food, good range of well kept beers, decent wines, helpful service, log fires, hops on beams, pleasant dining area, no piped music, skittle alley; no children in bar; large garden with small terrace, bedrooms (J V Dadswell, Mark and Ruth Brock)

WOODGREEN [SU1717]
☆ *Horse & Groom* SP6 2AS [off A338 N of Fordingbridge]: Nicely set New Forest pub with comfortably relaxed linked beamed rooms around servery, nature photographs, log fire in pretty Victorian fireplace, Badger ales, good choice of good value home-cooked food, friendly landlord; picnic-sets on front terrace and in spreading back garden *(Kevin Flack, LYM)*

Several well known guide books make establishments pay for entry, either directly or as a fee for inspection. These fees can run to many hundreds of pounds. We do not. Unlike other guides, we never take payment for entries. We never accept a free meal, free drink, or any other freebie from a pub. We do not accept any sponsorship – let alone from commercial schemes linked to the pub trade. All our entries depend solely on merit. And we are the only guide in which virtually all the main entries have been gained by a unique two-stage sifting process: first, a build-up of favourable reports from our thousands of reader-reporters, then anonymous vetting by one of our senior editorial staff.

Herefordshire

It's great here to find so many pubs offering local ciders, perries and apple juices too. Small local breweries make their mark here, as well – particularly Wye Valley, which supplies nearly half the county's best pubs with their best-priced beer. Perhaps because of this, drinks prices in the area tend to be rather lower than the national norm. Food has always been a strong point in Herefordshire pubs. A remarkably high proportion of them provide meals which put many restaurants to shame. The downside of this is that eating out in pubs here can be quite costly – not paying over the odds for something ordinary, but because you are tempted to splash out on something really good. Pubs offering particularly interesting dishes for a special meal out include the Riverside Inn at Aymestrey (a fine place to stay as well), the Roebuck at Brimfield (new French restaurateur owners have given the place a stylish refurbishment), the Feathers in Ledbury (the chatty locals' bar is as popular as ever, too), the Stagg at Titley (exceptional food), and the Three Crowns in Ullingswick (more and more of a dining pub nowadays). The Herefordshire Dining Pub of the Year title goes to the Stagg at Titley – the hard-working licensees have now been at this ground-breaking place for ten years, and we'd say it's better than ever. Several good new entries this year are the New Inn at St Owen's Cross (friendly, with enjoyable food and drinks), the Saracens Head in a very popular beauty spot on the Wye at Symonds Yat (waterside terraces, a fine range of drinks, and up-to-date food), the smartly reworked Mill Race at Walford, and the Bell in Yarpole (imaginative contemporary cooking in this well run village pub). In the Lucky Dip section at the end of the chapter, pubs for the notebook include the Green Dragon at Bishops Frome, Hostelrie at Goodrich, Olde Tavern in Kington, Crown & Anchor at Lugwardine, Salutation in Weobley and Live & Let Live at Whitbourne.

AYMESTREY

SO4265   MAP 6

Riverside Inn 🍴 ♀ 🛏

A4110, at N end of village, W of Leominster; HR6 9ST

Lovely spot with seats making most of the view, and river fishing for residents; cosy, rambling rooms, open fires, enjoyable food, and warm welcome

If a group of 18 picky country ladies could not fault their visit to this friendly half-timbered inn, who are we to disagree. The rambling beamed bar has several cosy areas and the décor is drawn from a pleasant mix of periods and styles, with fine antique oak tables and chairs, stripped pine country kitchen tables, fresh flowers, hops strung from a ceiling wagon-wheel, horse tack and nice pictures. Warm log fires in winter, while in summer big overflowing flower pots frame the entrances; fairly quiet piped pop music. Ludlow Gold and Wye Valley Hereford Pale Ale on handpump, two local farm ciders and more than 20 malt whiskies. The landlord likes to talk to his customers and service is good. Picnic-sets make the most of the attractive position by a double-arched bridge over the River Lugg and there are rustic tables and benches up above in a steep tree-sheltered garden. Residents can try fly-fishing.

🍴 Using local specialist producers and growing much of their own vegetables and fruit, the enjoyable lunchtime bar food includes filled baguettes, ploughman's, soup, baked field mushroom with cheese, toasted pine nuts and balsamic dressing, a trio of sausages with creamy mash, parmesan roulade stuffed with mediterranean vegetables, baked whole trout with caper and dill butter, good cod and chips, lambs liver and bacon with apple, bacon and onion gravy and rib-eye steak with peppercorn and herb butter; in the evening there might be rack of lamb with pea purée and mint jus and chicken wrapped in smoked bacon with an apricot and almond lightly spiced sauce, with puddings such as chocolate pecan brownie with cinnamon ice-cream and ginger wine trifle. *Starters/Snacks: £3.75 to £5.75. Main Courses: £7.95 to £19.95. Puddings: £4.75 to £5.50*

Free house ~ Licensees Richard and Liz Gresko ~ Real ale ~ Bar food (12-2.15, 7-9.15) ~ Restaurant ~ (01568) 708440 ~ Children welcome ~ Dogs allowed in bar and bedrooms ~ Open 11-3, 6-11; 12-3, 6.30-11 Sun; closed 26 Dec, early Jan ~ Bedrooms: £45B/£70B

Recommended by Ian Stafford, Simon Fox, Mike and Lynn Robinson, Noel Grundy, Rob Winstanley, Mike and Mary Carter, JHW, J Jennings, Tracey and Stephen Groves, Graham and Glenis Watkins, Tony and Sally Hope, Denys Gueroult

BODENHAM   SO5454   MAP 4

Englands Gate
Just off A417 at Bodenham turn-off, about 6 miles S of Leominster; HR1 3HU

Some fine original features in comfortable 16th-c inn, several character rooms, and pleasant garden

In an attractive area, this half-timbered 16th-c coaching inn has a rambling, open-plan interior that looks every year of its age. It has a vast central stone chimneypiece, heavy brown beams and joists in low ochre ceilings, well worn flagstones, sturdy timber props, one or two steps, and lantern-style lighting. One corner has a high-backed settle with scatter cushions, a cosy partly stripped-stone room has a long stripped table that would be just right for a party of eight and a lighter upper area with flowers on its tables has winged settles painted a cheery yellow or aquamarine. Woods Butty Bach and Shropshire Lad plus a guest beer on handpump; piped pop music and TV. There are tables out in the garden. More reports please.

🍴 Bar food at lunchtime includes open steak sandwich, deep-fried cod in beer batter, caramelised onion and goats cheese filo tart, chilli con carne and spicy cumberland sausage with onion gravy, with evening choices such as chicken liver parfait with spicy pear chutney, roast rack of lamb with garlic and herb crust and red wine jus, gressingham duck breast with ginger and Pernod sauce and chicken breast on parsnip purée with wild mushrooms and marsala cream sauce. *Starters/Snacks: £3.50 to £5.75. Main Courses: £6.95 to £18.95. Puddings: £3.95*

Free house ~ Licensee Evelyn McNeil ~ Real ale ~ Bar food (12-2.30, 6-9.30; 12-3 Sun; not Sun evening (from Sept-June)) ~ Restaurant ~ (01568) 797286 ~ Children welcome until 9pm ~ Dogs allowed in bar ~ Open 12-11(midnight Sat)

Recommended by Dr A J and Mrs Tompsett, Nigel Long, Dr and Mrs Michael Smith, Ken Millar, Carol Broadbent, Reg Fowle, Helen Rickwood

BRIMFIELD   SO5267   MAP 4

Roebuck Inn 🍴 ♀ 🛏
Village signposted just off A49 Shrewsbury—Leominster; SY8 4NE

Smartly refurbished dining pub with new French owners, bistro-style food and updated bedrooms

French restaurateurs have now taken over this smart dining pub and given it a stylish refurbishment. The front lounge bar has dark brown and orange club chairs, sofas and an open fire in the impressive inglenook fireplace. The middle bar area also has an open fire but has kept more of a pubby feel, and what was the dining room is now more of a bistro with chunky cord seating in brown and apricot around contemporary wooden tables and modern art on deep-coloured walls. The bedrooms were being given a total make-over as we went to press. Banks's and Marstons Pedigree on handpump and eight wines by the glass plus champagne and pudding wines; quite a few teas and coffees, and piped jazz. There are some seats outside on the heated and sheltered terrace. More reports on the changes here, please.

📖 **Fine, contemporary food now includes sandwiches, goats cheese and fennel tart with balsamic roasted cherry tomatoes, game terrine with cassis jelly, ravioli of scottish salmon with petit ratatouille and basil cream, coq au vin, fresh tuna with pesto and roasted peppers, venison, oyster and wild mushroom in ale pie, stuffed breast of lamb with aubergine gratin and rosemary jus, and puddings such as pecan cheesecake with Baileys ice-cream and apple tart with yoghurt sorbet; there's also a two-course lunch (not Sunday).** *Starters/Snacks: £3.50 to £5.50. Main Courses: £9.95 to £13.50. Puddings: £4.50 to £5.50*

Union Pub Company ~ Lease F Choblet ~ Real ale ~ Bar food ~ Restaurant ~ (01584) 711230 ~ Children welcome ~ Open 11.30-2.30, 6.30-11; 12-3 Sun; closed Sun evening ~ Bedrooms: £50B/£80B

Recommended by Elizabeth Carnie, Leo and Barbara Lionet, W H and E Thomas, Mr and Mrs C W Widdowson

CAREY   SO5631   MAP 4

Cottage of Content

Village signposted from good back road betweeen Ross-on-Wye and Hereford E of A49, through Hoarwithy; HR2 6NG

Country furnishings in rustic cottage and seats on terraces

As we went to press, we heard that this cottagey pub was up for sale. It's changed relatively little over the years with lots of beams, prints on the walls and country furnishings such as stripped pine kitchen chairs, long pews by one big table and various old-fashioned tables on flagstones or bare boards. Hook Norton Best and Wye Valley Butty Bach on handpump and summer farm cider; piped music. There are picnic-sets on the flower-filled front terrace with a couple more on a back terrace. We'd be grateful for news on any change of ownership.

📖 **Bar food has included filled baguettes and ciabattas, filled baked potatoes, ploughman's, chicken liver pâté with red onion jam, lasagne, cod in parsley beer batter, steak and kidney pie, chicken breast stuffed with brie and bacon, fried bass with saffron and garden herb risotto and fillet of herefordshire beef on celeriac remoulade.** *Starters/Snacks: £5.25 to £8.95. Main Courses: £9.50 to £16.00. Puddings: £4.95*

Free house ~ Licensee Svenia Wolf ~ Real ale ~ Bar food (12-1.45, 7-9) ~ Restaurant ~ (01432) 840242 ~ Children welcome ~ Dogs allowed in bar and bedrooms ~ Open 12-2.30, 6.30-11; 12-2.30 Sun; closed Sun evening and Mon ~ Bedrooms: £40B/£60B

Recommended by Alec and Joan Laurence, Norman and Sarah Keeping, Noel Grundy, Dr W J M Gissane, the Didler, Dr and Mrs Michael Smith, Mike and Mary Carter, Steve Bailey, Reg Fowle, Helen Rickwood, Barry and Patricia Wooding

DORSTONE   SO3141   MAP 6

Pandy

Pub signed off B4348 E of Hay-on-Wye; HR3 6AN

Ancient and pretty inn by village green with flagstones, timbers and vast open fireplace, decent food, and seats and play area in side garden

As this pretty half-timbered 12th-c pub is on the Herefordshire Trail, it is popular with walkers. The neatly kept homely main room (on the right as you go in) has heavy beams in the ochre ceiling, stout timbers, upright chairs on its broad worn flagstones and in its various alcoves, and a vast open fireplace with logs; a side extension has been kept more or less in character. Wye Valley Butty Bach and a changing guest on handpump, decent wines, summer farm cider and several malt whiskies; board games, quoits and piped music. The handsome red setter is called Apache, and the neat side garden has picnic-sets and a play area. More reports please.

🍴 Bar food includes filled baguettes, soup, lasagne, fish pie, hungarian goulash, lamb shank with redcurrant and red wine sauce, duck with honey, mustard and orange sauce, and puddings such as caribbean bread and butter pudding and chocolate truffle torte. *Starters/Snacks: £2.95 to £5.50. Main Courses: £7.95 to £16.50. Puddings: £4.25*

Free house ~ Licensees Bill and Magdalena Gannon ~ Real ale ~ Bar food ~ (01981) 550273 ~ Children welcome until 9pm ~ Dogs allowed in bar ~ Open 12-3, 6-11.30; 12-11.30 Sat; 12-3, 6.30-10.30 Sun; closed Mon lunchtime all year and all day Mon in winter

Recommended by Sue Demont, Tim Barrow, Ken Marshall, G W H Kerby, Mrs Phoebe A Kemp, Guy Vowles, the Didler

HEREFORD   SO5139   MAP 6

Victory 🍺 £

St Owen Street, opposite fire station; HR1 2QD

Extraordinary nautical décor in city pub with eight own-brewed beers plus guests, and straightforward bar food

The focus is very much on the eight well kept own-brew beers in this city pub: Spinning Dog Chase Your Tail, Herefordshire Cathedral, Light Ale, Organic Bitter and Owd Bull, Mutleys Dark, Mutleys Revenge, Mutts Nutts and Top Dog. Several ciders and a perry. The nautical décor is quite a surprise. The counter re-creates a miniature galleon complete with cannon poking out of its top, and down a companionway the long back room is well decked out as the inside of a man o' war: dark wood, rigging and netting everywhere, benches along sides that curve towards a front fo'c'sle, stanchions and ropes forming an upper crow's nest, and appropriate lamps. Service is friendly and informal (they'll show you around the brewery if they're not busy). Juke box (can be very loud), piped music, darts, games machine, TV, skittle alley, table skittles, board games and a back pool table. The garden has a pagoda, climbing plants and some seats.

🍴 Straightforward bar food (not available in winter) includes sandwiches, ploughman's, chilli con carne, chicken curry, and steak; curry night is Friday. *Starters/Snacks: £1.50 to £3.00. Main Courses: £3.50 to £6.00. Puddings: £2.00 to £3.50*

Own brew ~ Licensee James Kenyon ~ Real ale ~ Bar food (not in winter) ~ Restaurant (Sun only) ~ No credit cards ~ (01432) 342125 ~ Children welcome ~ Dogs welcome ~ Live band Sat ~ Open 12(11 Sat)-12; 3pm-midnight in winter; closed winter lunchtimes

Recommended by Reg Fowle, Helen Rickwood

HOARWITHY   SO5429   MAP 4

New Harp 🍷 🍺

Village signposted off A49 Hereford—Ross-on-Wye; HR2 6QH

Contemporary décor in busy country pub where walkers and dogs are welcome; plenty of outside seats, fair range of interesting drinks

Walkers (and their muddy boots and dogs) are made welcome at this bustling country pub which is on the Herefordshire Trail. The bars are decorated in a contemporary style with mainly crisp off-white paintwork, nicely lit modern artwork including cartoons and caricatures, brown leather tub armchairs in front of a woodburning stove, a mix of comfortable dining chairs around individual tables, stone floor tiling and some stripped masonry. The bar angles round to a cosy dining room and the atmosphere is relaxed throughout. Freeminer Fairplay, Hook Norton Hooky Bitter, St Austell Tribute and Spinning Dog Mutleys Revenge on handpump, a growing collection of unusual bottled beers, farm cider and a fair range of wines by the glass; you may be able to get bowls of nuts and other nibbles. The hungarian vizsla is called Foxy; piped music and board games. Bow windows look up the hill to a remarkable italianate Victorian church with a tall tower, and the little stream which runs through the pretty tree-sheltered garden soon meets the nearby River Wye. There are plenty of picnic-sets, some on decking in a sort of arbour, and in summer they have barbecues and erect a marquee.

🍴 **Each item on the menu is paired with a drink or two that will complement it:** **sandwiches, home-smoked fish with home-made chutney, thai fishcakes with lemon crème fraîche, wild mushroom, tarragon and pine nut cannelloni, lambs liver on spring onion and chorizo mash with mushroom and shallot gravy, sweet glazed bacon steak on bubble and squeak with black pudding fritter and cider and mustard sauce, daily specials, and puddings.** *Starters/Snacks: £4.00 to £6.00. Main Courses: £9.00 to £17.00. Puddings: £4.95*

Badger ~ Tenants Fleur and Andrew Cooper ~ Real ale ~ Bar food (12-2.30, 6-9.30) ~ (01432) 840900 ~ Children welcome ~ Dogs welcome ~ Open 12-11(10.30 Sun); 12-3, 6(5 Fri)-11 weekdays in winter

Recommended by Guy Vowles, Mike and Mary Carter, Andy and Claire Barker, Dr W J M Gissane, MLR

LEDBURY

SO7137   MAP 4

Feathers

High Street (A417); HR8 1DS

Chatty, relaxed bar in handsome timbered hotel, and more decorous lounges; good food, friendly staff and comfortable bedrooms

The Top Bar remains the heart of this very handsome black and white Tudor hotel. There are beams and restored brickwork, seats around oak tables on the oak flooring and plenty of chatty and cheerful locals enjoying a pint quite uninhibited by those enjoying the food and wines at the brasserie tables behind them. This room has beams and timbers, hop bines, some country antiques, 19th-c caricatures and fancy fowl prints on the stripped brick chimneybreast (lovely winter fire), copper jam pots and fresh flowers on the tables – some very snug and cosy, in side bays. The lounge is a civilised place for afternoon teas, with high-sided armchairs and sofas in front of a big log fire and newspapers to read. Fullers London Pride and Greene King Old Speckled Hen on handpump, 15 wines by the glass, 28 malt whiskies and friendly, helpful staff. In summer, the sheltered back terrace has abundant pots and hanging baskets.

🍴 **Good food at lunchtime includes wild boar and pistachio terrine with cumberland sauce, carpaccio of bass and pink grapefruit, smoked chicken caesar salad, organic salmon and chive fishcakes with parsley sauce and confit leg of duck with haricot bean cassoulet and confit garlic; evening dishes such as smoked salmon and leek mousse with horseradish mayonnaise, pigeon breast with smoked bacon and hazelnut dressing, pasta with creamed white wine and stilton sauce, roast loin of venison with wild mushrooms and chocolate sauce, and puddings like mango panna cotta with orange sorbet and dark chocolate tart with strawberry ice-cream; very nice breakfasts.** *Starters/Snacks: £4.25 to £6.95. Main Courses: £10.25 to £18.50. Puddings: £5.95*

Free house ~ Licensee David Elliston ~ Real ale ~ Bar food (12-2(2.30 Sat, Sun), 7-9.30(10 Fri, Sat)) ~ Restaurant ~ (01531) 635266 ~ Children welcome ~ Dogs allowed in bedrooms ~ Open 11-11; 12-10.30 Sun ~ Bedrooms: £79.50B/£115B

Recommended by Bernard Stradling, A S and M E Marriott, Rod Stoneman, Dr W J M Gissane, Mr and Mrs A J Hudson, J E Shackleton, Dr D J and Mrs S C Walker, J Crosby, Mike and Mary Carter

---

A very few pubs try to make you leave a credit card at the bar, as a sort of deposit if you order food. They are not entitled to do this. The credit card firms and banks which issue them warn you not to let them out of your sight. If someone behind the counter used your card fraudulently, the card company or bank could in theory hold you liable, because of your negligence in letting a stranger hang on to your card. Suggest instead that if they feel the need for security, they 'swipe' your card and give it back to you. And do name and shame the pub to us.

LITTLE COWARNE

SO6050   MAP 4

Three Horseshoes ♀ 🛏

Pub signposted off A465 SW of Bromyard; towards Ullingswick; HR7 4RQ

Long-serving licensees and welcoming staff in bustling country pub with well liked food using their own chutneys and pickles and home-grown summer salad

Now joined by their son as head chef, the long-serving licensees continue to run this friendly inn with considerable enthusiasm. The quarry tiled L-shaped middle bar has leather-seated bar stools, upholstered settles and dark brown kitchen chairs around sturdy old tables, old local photographs above the corner log fire, and hop-draped black beams in the dark peach ceiling. Opening off one side is a skylit sun room with wicker armchairs around more old tables; the other end has a games room with darts, pool, juke box and games machine; also cribbage. Greene King Old Speckled Hen, Marstons Pedigree and Wye Valley Bitter on handpump, farm ciders and perry and a dozen wines by the glass; obliging service, and disabled access. A roomy and attractive stripped-stone raftered restaurant extension has a Sunday lunchtime carvery. There are well sited tables on the terrace or on the neat prettily planted lawn.

🍽 **Using their own-grown produce (and that of their neighbours and family) and other carefully sought out local producers, the enjoyable food might include sandwiches, ploughman's, soup, pork and pheasant pâté with spiced damsons, thai-style fishcakes with dipping sauce, cod fillet wrapped in bacon with blue cheese sauce, steak in ale pie, butternut squash and spinach risotto, pork fillet and crispy pork belly with plum sauce, lamb curry, and puddings such as plum and almond crumble and damson gin crème brûlée; they make their own preserves to sell: marmalade, raspberry, strawberry and damson jams, spiced pears and plums, beetroot and horseradish relish, pickled walnuts and apple and ginger chutney.** *Starters/Snacks: £3.95 to £5.50. Main Courses: £9.25 to £14.95. Puddings: £3.95*

Free house ~ Licensees Norman and Janet Whittall ~ Real ale ~ Bar food (not winter Sun evening) ~ Restaurant ~ (01885) 400276 ~ No children in bar after 9pm ~ Open 11-3(3.30 Sat), 6.30-midnight; 12-4, 7-10.30 Sun; closed Sun evening in winter ~ Bedrooms: £35S/£60S

Recommended by Mike and Mary Carter, Theocsbrian, Carol Broadbent, Denys Gueroult, Michael Doswell, Martin and Pauline Jennings, J E Shackleton, Noel Grundy, Reg Fowle, Helen Rickwood

ORLETON

SO4967   MAP 6

Boot

Just off B4362 W of Woofferton; SY8 4HN

Nice little pub with welcoming bars, some original 16th-c features and decent food

Both locals and visitors feel at home in this little 400-year-old village local. The traditional-feeling bar has a mix of dining and cushioned carver chairs around a few old tables on the red tiles, one very high-backed settle, hops over the counter and a warming fire in the big fireplace with horsebrasses along its bressumer beam. The lounge bar is up a couple of steps, and has green plush banquettes right the way around the walls, mullioned windows, an exposed section of wattle and daub, standing timbers and heavy wall beams. There's a small restaurant on the left. Hobsons Best and Town Crier and a guest like Black Sheep on handpump; cribbage and dominoes. There are seats in the garden under a huge ash tree, a barbecue area, and a fenced-in children's play area. More reports please.

🍽 **Lunchtime bar food includes sandwiches, filled hot baguettes, ploughman's, stilton mushrooms, pâté, steak in ale pie, lambs liver, bacon and onion gravy and gammon and egg, with evening choices such as chicken and asparagus pie, duck breast with black cherry and port sauce, salmon with dill and mustard cream sauce and mixed grill; daily specials, and puddings.** *Starters/Snacks: £4.00 to £6.00. Main Courses: £5.50 to £9.00. Puddings: £3.50*

Free house ~ Licensees Philip and Jane Dawson ~ Real ale ~ Bar food ~ Restaurant ~ (01568) 780228 ~ Children welcome ~ Dogs allowed in bar ~ Open 12-3, 6-11

Recommended by Rob Winstanley, Carol Broadbent

SELLACK   SO5526   MAP 4

Lough Pool ★ ♀
Back road Hoarwithy—Ross-on-Wye; HR9 6LX

Unspoilt country pub with individual furnishings in beamed bars, a good choice of food and drinks, lots of seats outside

Set in countryside full of bridleways and walks, this attractive black and white timbered cottage has plenty of picnic-sets on the neat front lawned area and pretty hanging baskets. Inside, the beamed central room has kitchen chairs and cushioned window seats around wooden tables on the mainly flagstoned floor, sporting prints, bunches of dried flowers and fresh hop bines, and a log fire at one end with a woodburner at the other. Other rooms lead off, gently brightened up with attractive individual furnishings and nice touches like the dresser of patterned plates; newspapers are left out for customers. John Smiths and Wye Valley Bitter and Butty Bach and a couple of guests such as Greene King Old Speckled Hen and St George & The Dragon (brewed by Wadworths for Manns) on handpump, several malt whiskies, local farm ciders, perries and apple juices, and 14 wines by the glass from a thoughtful wine list.

🍴 Using home-grown herbs and rare breed meat, the menu might include lunchtime ploughman's, pork and apple sausages with onion gravy and beer-battered cod, plus goats cheese brûlée with tomato and chive salad, parfait of duck livers with a blackberry, onion and port compote, tian of spiced sweet potato and courgette with cream reduction topped with a couscous crust and a roast red pepper, shallot and garlic reduction, chicken breast glazed with honey and black pepper with caesar salad, trio of lamb cutlets with port jus, and puddings like coconut, toffee and banana brûlée with malibu espresso and pear and ginger pudding with cinnamon ice-cream and light toffee sauce. *Starters/Snacks: £4.95 to £8.95. Main Courses: £9.50 to £16.00. Puddings: £6.75*

Free house ~ Licensees David and Janice Birch ~ Real ale ~ Bar food ~ Restaurant ~ (01989) 730236 ~ Children welcome ~ Dogs allowed in bar ~ Themed live music on certain events ~ Open 11.30-11(midnight Sat); 12-10.30 Sun; closed Sun in Nov, Jan and Feb

Recommended by Jane McQuitty, Mike and Mary Carter, JMC, Mrs Hazel Rainer, Tom Evans, Bernard Stradling, Lucien Perring, Dr and Mrs A J Edwards, Noel Grundy, Bren and Val Speed, Alec and Barbara Jones, Bill and Jessica Ritson, K S Whittaker, J Crosby

ST OWEN'S CROSS   SO5424   MAP 4

New Inn
Junction A4137 and B4521, W of Ross-on-Wye; HR2 8LQ

Huge inglenooks, beams and timbers, a friendly welcome, enjoyable food and fine choice of drinks; lovely hanging baskets, big garden with views

Attractively refurbished by the friendly licensees, this black and white 16th-c timbered coaching inn is now open all day. The lounge bar and restaurant have huge inglenook fireplaces, dark beams and timbers, various nooks and crannies, old pews and a mix of tables and chairs and lots of watercolours on warm red walls. Marstons Pedigree plus guests such as Adnams Explorer, Hop Back Crop Circle and Jennings Cocker Hoop on handpump, ten ciders and perries, several malt whiskies and ten wines by the glass; piped music, darts, pool, dominoes, cribbage and board games. The hanging baskets are quite a sight and in summer, the big enclosed garden really comes into its own; fine views stretch across the countryside to the distant Black Mountains.

🍴 Enjoyable bar food includes filled bloomers, soup, chicken liver pâté with home-made chutney, creamy garlic mushrooms, steak, mushroom and ale pie, sweet and sour mixed bean hotpot, beer-battered cornish fish, pork and leek sausages with onion sauce, braised belly of pork on home-made black pudding with cider sauce, duck breast with honey and whisky sauce, and puddings like chocolate fudge brownie with chocolate sauce and summer pudding; morning coffee and afternoon tea. *Starters/Snacks: £4.05 to £6.25. Main Courses: £6.95 to £19.50. Puddings: £3.50 to £4.95*

Marstons ~ Lease Nigel Maud ~ Real ale ~ Bar food (12-9) ~ Restaurant ~ (01989) 730274 ~ Children welcome ~ Dogs allowed in bar ~ Open 11-11; 12-11 Sun ~ Bedrooms: £45B/£70S(£80B)

Recommended by Dr and Mrs Michael Smith, DFL, B M Eldridge, Tom Evans

STOCKTON CROSS   SO5161   MAP 4

Stockton Cross Inn

Kimbolton; A4112, off A49 just N of Leominster; HR6 0HD

Half-timbered pub with local ales and tasty food, huge log fire, seats in pretty garden

New licensees have taken over this attractive half-timbered pub and the real ales on handpump now include Hobsons Town Crier, Teme Valley This and Wye Valley Butty Bach. The long, heavily beamed bar has a handsome antique settle and old leather chairs and brocaded stools by the huge log fire in the broad stone fireplace. At the far end is a woodburning stove with heavy cast-iron-framed tables and sturdy dining chairs, and up a step, a small area has more tables. Old-time prints, a couple of épées on one beam and lots of copper and brass complete the picture; piped music. There are tables out in the pretty garden.

🍴 **Reasonably priced bar food includes sandwiches, thai crab cakes, mussels with white wine and garlic, local sausages, chicken caesar salad, leek, stilton and walnut tart with chive mash, spicy beef stir fry, salmon fillet with watercress sauce and crushed broad beans, roast rump of lamb with sweet potato mash, and puddings such as chocolate mousse with coffee ice-cream and vanilla panna cotta.** *Starters/Snacks: £3.95 to £6.50. Main Courses: £8.95 to £15.50. Puddings: £4.95*

Free house ~ Licensee Mike Betley ~ Real ale ~ Bar food ~ (01568) 612509 ~ Children welcome ~ Open 12-3, 7-11; closed Sun and Mon evenings

Recommended by W H and E Thomas, Mike and Mary Carter, UN, Dr and Mrs Michael Smith, Bernard Stradling, Carol Broadbent, Mr and Mrs F E Boxell

SYMONDS YAT   SO5616   MAP 4

Saracens Head 🛏

Symonds Yat E, by ferry, ie over on the Gloucs bank; HR9 6JL

Lovely riverside spot, contemporary food and a fine range of drinks in friendly inn; waterside terraces, comfortable bedrooms and plenty to do nearby

There's a little hand ferry (pulled by one of the staff) that crosses the River Wye in front of this 17th-c inn. It's a lovely spot and there are lots of picnic-sets out on a waterside terrace and plenty to do nearby. Inside, it's warm and relaxed with cheerful staff who make you feel at home. The busy, basic flagstoned public bar has Courage Directors, Greene King Old Speckled Hen, Theakstons Old Peculier and Wye Valley Butty Bach and Hereford Pale Ale on handpump, nine wines by the glass and three farm ciders; piped music, TV, games machine and pool. There's also a cosy lounge and a modernised bare-boards dining room. As well as bedrooms in the main building, there are two contemporary ones in the boathouse annexe. This is a nice place to stay out of season.

🍴 **As well as lunchtime sandwiches, filled baguettes, chargrilled bruschettas and ploughman's, the interesting modern food might include a plate of local cheeses with quince jelly, pressed terrine of wild rabbit and chicken with raisins and verjus syrup, open ravioli of seared scallops and broad beans with lemon grass and chervil foam, sunblush tomato, asparagus spears and wild rocket risotto with herb pesto, chargrilled old spot pork chop with roasted fennel and caper jus, rump of lamb with spring onion potato cake, roasted beetroot and mint pesto and roasted lemon sole with braised baby gem lettuce and a brown shrimp butter.** *Starters/Snacks: £4.25 to £7.25. Main Courses: £11.95 to £18.95. Puddings: £5.50*

Free house ~ Licensees P K and C J Rollinson ~ Real ale ~ Bar food ~ Restaurant ~ (01600) 890435 ~ Children welcome ~ Dogs allowed in bar ~ Open 11-11(10.30 Sun); closed 25 Dec ~ Bedrooms: £50B/£74B

Recommended by Lawrence Bacon, Jean Scott, John and Helen Rushton, Ian Phillips, Mike and Lynn Robinson, B M Eldridge, Dr D J and Mrs S C Walker

TITLEY   SO3359   MAP 6

Stagg ⊗ ⨀ ⇔

B4355 N of Kington; HR5 3RL

HEREFORDSHIRE DINING PUB OF THE YEAR

Fantastic food using tip-top ingredients served in extensive dining rooms, a fine choice of drinks, two-acre garden, comfortable bedrooms

Mr and Mrs Reynolds have now been running this impressive dining pub for ten years and our readers enjoy their visits hugely. Obviously the imaginative food is the main draw but it's a lovely place to stay either in bedrooms above the pub or in a Georgian vicarage four minutes away, and a lot of effort goes into creating an atmosphere that appeals to both visitors and locals. The bar, though comfortable and hospitable, is not large, and the atmosphere is civilised rather than lively. Hobsons Best and Town Crier on handpump, 13 wines by the glass including champagne and pudding wines from a carefully chosen wine list and local ciders, perry, apple juice and pressés. The two-acre garden has seats on the terrace and a croquet lawn.

⊞ **Exceptional food using their own-grown vegetables, pigs and free-range chickens includes a bar snack menu (not Saturday evenings or Sunday lunch) with filled baguettes, sausages and mash, three-cheese ploughman's with home-made pickle, smoked haddock risotto, cod goujons with home-made chips, devilled kidneys and scallops on parsnip purée with black pepper oil; more elaborate choices such as foie gras with apple jelly, butternut squash risotto, pigeon breast with smoked bacon and cabbage, chicken breast on pearl barley with roast root vegetables, saddle of venison with wild mushrooms and kümmel, duck breast with ginger, mustard and sweet wine sauce, and puddings like poached pear with chocolate sorbet and mousse and three crème brûlées of vanilla, cardamom and coffee. The british cheeseboard is fantastic with 23 different ones, mostly from Herefordshire and Wales.** *Starters/Snacks: £3.70 to £7.90. Main Courses: £8.50 to £16.50. Puddings: £5.30*

Free house ~ Licensees Steve and Nicola Reynolds ~ Real ale ~ Bar food (12-2, 6.30-9; not Sun evening or Mon) ~ Restaurant ~ (01544) 230221 ~ Children welcome ~ Dogs allowed in bar ~ Open 12-3, 6.30-11; 12-3 Sun; closed Sun evening and Mon, 1 and 2 Jan, first week Nov, first week Feb, 25-27 Dec ~ Bedrooms: £60B/£85B

Recommended by Bruce and Sharon Eden, Blaise Vyner, Chris Flynn, Wendy Jones, Rob Winstanley, J C Clark, Dr and Mrs Michael Smith, R Seifas, J Crosby, Mr and Mrs R S Ashford

ULLINGSWICK   SO5949   MAP 4

Three Crowns ⊗ ⨀

Village off A465 S of Bromyard (and just S of Stoke Lacy) and signposted off A417 N of A465 roundabout – keep straight on through village and past turn-off to church; pub at Bleak Acre, towards Little Cowarne; HR1 3JQ

Well presented food in busy dining pub with candlelight and proper napkins, and nice views from heated terrace

Very much a dining pub rather than somewhere to drop in for a casual drink, this attractive old country pub has open fires, hops strung along the low beams of its smallish bar, traditional settles, a mix of big old wooden tables with small round ornamental cast-iron-framed ones, and more usual seats; there are one or two gently sophisticated touches such as candles on tables and proper napkins. Hobsons Best, Timothy Taylors Landlord and Wye Valley Butty Bach on handpump, several wines by the glass and local cider and apple juice. Nice summer views from tables out on the attractively planted lawn, and outside heaters for chillier evenings.

⊞ **As well as a two- and three-course blackboard lunch menu (not Sunday), the interesting food includes cheese and spinach soufflé, stir-fried mussels with fermented** black beans, spring onion and ginger, home-smoked pollack with spinach, poached egg and hollandaise, slow-roasted belly of organic pork with black pudding and mustard mash, confit leg and roast breast of duck with cider brandy, apples and peppercorns, and puddings like crème caramel with armagnac prunes or warm chocolate fondant with black forest ice-cream. *Starters/Snacks: £6.50. Main Courses: £14.50. Puddings: £5.00*

Free house ~ Licensee Brent Castle ~ Real ale ~ Bar food (12-2.30, 7-9.30(9 Sun)) ~ Restaurant ~ (01432) 820279 ~ Children welcome ~ Open 12-3, 7-11; 12-2, 7-9 Sun; closed Mon and a few days in Dec (best to phone) ~ Bedrooms: /£95B

Recommended by Andy and Claire Barker, Chris Flynn, Wendy Jones, Denys Gueroult, Bernard Stradling, J E Shackleton, A J Ward, M Sackett, Mr and Mrs F E Boxell, Carol Broadbent

UPTON BISHOP   SO6326   MAP 4

Moody Cow

2 miles from M50 junction 3 westbound (or junction 4 eastbound), via B4221; continue on B4221 to rejoin at next junction; HR9 7TT

Enjoyable dining pub with interesting food, a friendly welcome, open fire and some cow-related ornaments

This is a really nice and rather smart dining pub with welcoming licensees, a relaxed atmosphere and super food; as we went to press we heard that it was up for sale but nothing had been finalised at that time. It's laid out in snug areas that angle in an L around the bar counter, with rough sandstone walls, new slate flooring, an open fire, and a parade of cow-related ornaments and pictures. On the far right is a biggish rustic and candlelit restaurant with rafters, and a fireside area with armchairs and sofas. The far left has a second smaller dining area, just five or six tables with antique pine-style tables and chairs. Hook Norton and Wye Valley Best on handpump.

🍴 Consistently good, the bar food includes sandwiches, soup, thai crab fishcakes, duck pâté with beetroot and horseradish chutney, fresh scallops with a light fish cream, breast of chicken in garlic, fresh herbs, chilli and saffron with spring onion mash, red onion and goats cheese tarte tatin, braised and glazed rolled belly pork with home-smoked bacon, chestnuts and bubble and squeak, seared salmon with red onion, garlic and rosemary lyonnaise potatoes, and puddings such as lovely sticky toffee pudding and raspberry crème brûlée. *Starters/Snacks: £4.50 to £7.95. Main Courses: £8.95 to £17.95. Puddings: £4.50 to £5.75*

Free house ~ Licensee James Lloyd ~ Real ale ~ Bar food ~ Restaurant ~ (01989) 780470 ~ Well behaved children welcome ~ Dogs allowed in bar ~ Open 12-2.30, 6.30-11; 12-3 Sun; closed Sun evening and Mon

Recommended by Mike and Mary Carter, Theocsbrian, Julian Cox, Bernard Stradling, Nigel Clifton, Mr and Mrs F E Boxell, Guy Vowles, Dr W J M Gissane, JCW, Carol Broadbent

WALFORD   SO5820   MAP 4

Mill Race ♀

B4234 Ross—Lydney; HR9 5QS

Contemporary furnishings in uncluttered rooms, a welcome for both diners and drinkers, and up-to-date daily specials served by attentive staff; terrace tables, nearby walks

Although there's some emphasis in this pink-washed pub on the interesting food, the new licensee welcomes drinkers too. The layout and décor are fresh and contemporary with a row of tall arched windows giving an airy feel in the main part, which has some comfortable leather armchairs and sofas on its flagstones, as well as stylish smaller chairs around broad pedestal tables. The granite-topped modern bar counter stretching back from here has Wye Valley Bitter and Butty Bach on handpump, Weston's farm cider, and a good choice of reasonably priced wines by the glass; opposite are a couple of tall nicely clean-cut tables with matching chairs. Service is friendly and attentive. The walls are mainly cream or dark pink, with just one or two carefully placed prints, and good unobtrusive lighting. One wall stripped back to the stonework has a woodburning stove, open also to the comfortable and compact dining area on the other side. There are stylish tables out on the terrace; a leaflet available at the pub details a pleasant round walk of an hour or so.

🍽 **They take pride in using named local suppliers for their careful mix of traditional dishes with up-to-date specialities: sandwiches, soup, roast aubergine pâté with olives and pickled cucumber, deep-fried goats cheese with a couscous and pine nut crust and apple and watercress salad, ham and egg, sausage and mash, asparagus, sweet potato and leek tortilla, honey-glazed duck with red chard and spinach leaves and a raspberry dressing, rare breed sirloin steak topped with flat mushrooms and stilton, and puddings such as lemon tart or chocolate fudge brownie with clotted cream; Wednesday is fish night.** *Starters/Snacks: £4.00 to £8.00. Main Courses: £8.00 to £22.00. Puddings: £5.00*

Free house ~ Licensee Rebecca Freeman ~ Real ale ~ Bar food ~ (01989) 562891 ~ Children welcome ~ Open 11-3, 5-11; 11-11 Sat; 12-11 Sun

Recommended by Tony and Glenys Dyer, Martin and Pauline Jennings, Dr W J M Gissane, R T and J C Moggridge

WALTERSTONE   SO3424   MAP 6
Carpenters Arms
Village signposted off A465 E of Abergavenny, beside Old Pandy Inn; follow village signs, and keep eyes skinned for sign to pub, off to right, by lane-side barn; HR2 ODX

Unchanging country tavern with traditional rooms, in same family for many years

You can be sure of a warm welcome from the friendly landlady in this stone tavern set on the edge of the Black Mountains. It has been in the same family for many years and little has changed. The traditional rooms have ancient settles against stripped stone walls, some pieces of carpet on broad polished flagstones, a roaring log fire in a gleaming black range (complete with pot-iron, hot-water tap, bread oven and salt cupboard), and pewter mugs hanging from beams. The snug main dining room has mahogany tables and oak corner cupboards and maybe a big vase of flowers on the dresser. Another little dining area has old oak tables and church pews on flagstones; piped music. Breconshire Golden Valley and Ramblers Ruin and Wadworths 6X are tapped from the cask. The outside lavatories are cold but in character.

🍽 **Straightforward food such as sandwiches and rolls, soup, ploughman's, beef in Guinness pie, lamb cutlets with redcurrant and rosemary sauce, a vegetarian choice, daily specials, and puddings.** *Starters/Snacks: £4.00. Main Courses: £8.00 to £11.00. Puddings: £4.00*

Free house ~ Licensee Vera Watkins ~ Real ale ~ Bar food (12-2.30, 7-9.30) ~ Restaurant ~ No credit cards ~ (01873) 890353 ~ Children welcome ~ Open 12-11

Recommended by M J Winterton

WELLINGTON   SO4948   MAP 6
Wellington 🍺
Village signposted off A49 N of Hereford; pub at far end; HR4 8AT

Welcoming pub with good food and real ales, warm winter log fire, and summer barbecues in pleasant garden

This is a well run pub with something for everyone. It looks a bit unassuming from outside, but the landlord has worked hard to create somewhere locals and diners alike feel comfortable and welcomed. The bar has big high-backed dark wooden settles, an open brick fireplace with a log fire in winter and fresh flowers in summer, and historical photographs of the village and antique farm and garden tools around the walls; the charming candlelit restaurant is in the former stables. Hobsons Best, Timothy Taylors Landlord, Wye Valley Butty Bach and a guest such as Greene King Old Speckled Hen on handpump; several wines by the glass, a dozen malt whiskies and good, attentive service. Darts, board games and piped music. At the back is a pleasant garden with tables where they may hold summer barbecues.

🍴 Good bar food includes sandwiches, soup, crab and ginger cake with wilted spinach and white wine and chive sauce, ham hock and parsley terrine with caramelised quince, devilled kidneys, wild mushroom and ricotta pancake galette with tomato and basil sauce, rump of lamb with aubergine, feta and rosemary gratin and redcurrant jus, grilled fillet of salmon with spring onion and roast red pepper risotto, and puddings such as champagne rhubarb and vanilla crème brûlée or warm chocolate fondant pudding with griottine cherries; their two- or three-course roast Sunday lunches are particularly good. *Starters/Snacks: £3.75 to £7.50. Main Courses: £8.50 to £17.50. Puddings: £4.75*

Free house ~ Licensees Ross and Philippa Williams ~ Real ale ~ Bar food (not Sun evening or Mon lunchtime) ~ Restaurant ~ (01432) 830367 ~ Children welcome ~ Dogs allowed in bar ~ Open 12-3, 6(7 Sun)-11; closed Mon lunchtime

Recommended by Ian Stafford, Mrs J Gowan, Nick and Meriel Cox, Ruth and Andrew Crowder, Dr A J and Mrs Tompsett

WHITNEY-ON-WYE   SO2447   MAP 6

Rhydspence 🛏

A438 Hereford—Brecon; HR3 6EU

Rambling, smart rooms in splendid old building with heavy beams and timbers, decent bar food and drinks, and nice views

Often called the first and last pub in England, this very picturesque ancient black and white country inn is right on the border with Wales which follows the line of the little stream in the garden; there are seats and tables out here and fine views over the Wye valley. Inside, the rambling, smartly kept rooms have heavy beams and timbers, attractive old-fashioned furnishings, and there's a log fire in the fine big stone fireplace in the central bar. Next to the bar is a bistro-type eating area which opens into the family room. Bass and Robinsons Best on handpump and local Dunkerton's cider.

🍴 Tasty bar food includes soup, chicken liver pâté, ploughman's, cajun chicken, tagine of spiced beans and vegetables, lasagne, steak and kidney pie, a hot curry and lamb shank with red wine gravy. *Starters/Snacks: £3.85 to £5.95. Main Courses: £7.50 to £17.50. Puddings: £4.50*

Free house ~ Licensee Peter Glover ~ Real ale ~ Bar food ~ Restaurant ~ (01497) 831262 ~ Children welcome ~ Open 11(12 Sun)-2.30, 7-11(10.30 Sun); closed two weeks in Oct ~ Bedrooms: £42.50S/£85B

Recommended by Chris Flynn, Wendy Jones, Mrs Ann Gray, Duncan Cameron, Rodney and Norma Stubington, John and Sylvia Harrop

WOOLHOPE   SO6135   MAP 4

Butchers Arms 🍺

Signposted from B4224 in Fownhope; carry straight on past Woolhope village; HR1 4RF

Pleasant country inn in peaceful setting with a fair choice of real ales

In a charming spot, this pleasant old pub keeps five real ales on handpump: Hook Norton Bitter, Shepherd Neame Spitfire, Wye Valley Butty Bach and a couple of guests such as Timothy Taylors Landlord and Whittington Nine Lives. One of the spacious bars has very low beams decorated with hops, old-fashioned well worn built-in seats with brocaded cushions, high-backed chairs and stools around wooden tables, and a brick fireplace. Broadly similar though with fewer beams, the other bar has a large built-in settle and another log fire; piped music and darts. The quiet garden has picnic-sets and flowering tubs and borders looking on to a willow-lined brook. To enjoy some of the best of the surroundings, turn left as you come out and take the tiny left-hand road at the end of the car park; this turns into a track and then into a path, and the view from the top of the hill is quite something.

If we know a pub has an outdoor play area for children, we mention it.

🍴 Bar food includes sandwiches, ploughman's, vegetable lasagne, quiche of the day, sausages with spring onion mash and poached salmon fillet. *Starters/Snacks: £3.95 to £5.95. Main Courses: £7.25 to £19.95. Puddings: £3.95 to £4.95*

Free house ~ Licensees Cheryl and Martin Baker ~ Real ale ~ Bar food (not winter Mon lunchtime) ~ Restaurant ~ (01432) 860281 ~ Children welcome ~ Dogs allowed in bedrooms ~ Open 12-3, 6.30-11(midnight Sat); 12-3, 7-10.30 Sun; closed Mon lunchtime in winter ~ Bedrooms: £35/£50

Recommended by Noel Grundy, W H and E Thomas

YARPOLE
SO4664   MAP 6

Bell 🍴
Just off B4361 N of Leominster; HR6 0BD

Modern cooking using home-grown vegetables in black and white village pub, particularly good service, real ales and extensive gardens

Doing very well as a dining pub with welcoming management, this is a picturesquely timbered ancient building extended into a former cider mill. There's a basic tap room, a comfortable beamed lounge bar with a log fire and a large, high-raftered restaurant featuring a cider press and mill wheel; a mix of traditional furniture on the red patterned carpet, some modern art on the walls and brass taps embedded into the stone bar counter. Hook Norton Hooky Bitter, Timothy Taylors Landlord and Wye Valley Hereford Pale Ale on handpump and a short but interesting wine list; efficient service even when busy. The golden labrador is called Marcus; piped music. There are picnic-sets under green parasols in the sunny flower-filled garden and the pub is very handy for Croft Castle.

🍴 Using all home-grown vegetables, the imaginative contemporary food includes sandwiches, smoked haddock and leek fishcake with crushed peas and pea velouté, a fricassee of local snails with garlic and parsley, pressed ham hock terrine with honey and mustard vinaigrette, free-range chicken kiev with creamed leeks, fish pie, warm pithiviers of field mushrooms, jersey royals and local asparagus, slow-roast leg of rabbit with pommes boulangère and mustard and basil sauce, roast fillet of black bream, piperade, poached egg and basil oil, and puddings such as raspberry and vanilla crème brulée and sherry trifle; good value two- and three-course set menus. *Starters/Snacks: £4.45 to £5.75. Main Courses: £7.50 to £14.50. Puddings: £4.95 to £5.50*

Enterprise ~ Tenant Claude Bosi ~ Real ale ~ Bar food (12-2.30(3 Sun), 6.30-9.30; not Mon) ~ Restaurant ~ (01568) 780359 ~ Children welcome ~ Dogs allowed in bar ~ Open 12-3, 6.30-11(10.30 Sun); closed Mon except for bank hols

Recommended by Alan and Eve Harding, Kevin Thorpe, Miss Jacquie Edwards, Don Beattie, J E Shackleton

LUCKY DIP

Besides the fully inspected pubs, you might like to try these Lucky Dips recommended to us and described by readers (if you do, please send us reports: www.goodguides.co.uk).

ABBEY DORE [SO3830]
Neville Arms HR2 0AA [B4347]:
Unpretentious country pub nr Norman abbey church, log fire in cosy bar, efficient welcoming staff, good simple food at fair prices, well kept real ales, comfortable separate beamed restaurant/steak bar; tables outside with covered terrace, charming Golden Valley views, three bedrooms in separate block *(BB, Peter Dingley)*
ALMELEY [SO3351]
Bell HR3 6LF [off A480, A4111 or A4112 S of Kington]: Welcoming little country local, well kept Wye Valley and a guest ale, small lounge with room for just a dozen or so

people eating (Thurs-Sat evening meals, and good value Sun roast), traditional games, no piped music; boules pitch *(MLR)*
ASTON CREWS [SO6723]
☆ *Penny Farthing* HR9 7LW: Good food and service under new landlord in roomy and relaxing partly 15th-c pub, Black Sheep, good value wines, log fires, easy chairs, lots of beams, horsebrasses, harness and farm tools, feature well in bar, two restaurant areas, one with pretty valley and Forest of Dean views; may be subdued piped music; tables in charming garden, bedrooms *(Mike and Mary Carter, Lucien Perring, BB)*

BISHOPS FROME [SO6648]

☆ **Green Dragon** WR6 5BP [just off B4214 Bromyard—Ledbury]: Attractive unspoilt flagstoned local with plenty of character, half a dozen interesting well kept changing ales such as Felinfoel Double Dragon and Timothy Taylors Landlord, farm ciders, friendly newish licensees, good value soup, sandwiches and baked potatoes, fine log fire; children welcome, tables outside, on Herefordshire Trail, open all day Sat *(LYM, Guy Vowles, Reg Fowle, Helen Rickwood)*

BOSBURY [SO6943]

☆ **Bell** HR8 1PX [B4220 N of Ledbury]: Wide range of very generous popular food, friendly attentive staff, attractively priced Hancocks HB and a guest beer, good choice of good value wines by the glass, tastefully decorated lounge with fresh flowers on tables, thriving public bar, restaurant; unobtrusive piped music *(Chris Flynn, Wendy Jones, J E Shackleton, Reg Fowle, Helen Rickwood)*

BROMYARD [SO6554]

☆ **Falcon** HR7 4BT [Broad St]: Attractive timbered inn, several well laid out rooms with fascinating bulging walls and ancient windows, informal atmosphere in beamed and panelled bar and small lounge with leather chairs and settees, good food from good sandwiches to some enterprising and inventive country cooking and popular Sun lunch, Brains Rev James and Wye Valley; comfortable bedrooms *(Kevin Jeavons, Alison Turner, Dick and Madeleine Brown)*

Rose & Lion HR7 4AJ [New Rd]: Cheery local tied to Wye Valley brewery, their full range in top condition from central island servery, delightful landlady, simple comfortable lounge and games-minded public bar with darts, cards etc; tables out in pleasant courtyard, open all day wknds *(Pete Baker, Lynne Carter)*

CANON PYON [SO4648]

Nags Head HR4 8NY [A4110]: Good value food in traditional flagstoned bar and long restaurant with well feature, welcoming atmosphere, real ales and decent wines by the glass, no piped music; children welcome, extensive garden with play area, charming sensibly priced bedrooms in attached converted brewhouse, open all day wknds *(BB, Mr and Mrs S J East)*

COLWALL [SO7542]

Colwall Park WR13 6QG [Walwyn Rd (B4218 W of Malvern)]: Unpretentiously comfortable hotel bar with good choice of real ales inc Wye Valley, nice wines by the glass, good food inc generous sandwiches using home-baked bread, friendly staff; dogs allowed, terrace tables, bedrooms *(Theocsbrian, John Lloyd, Dennis Jenkin, Carol Broadbent)*

Crown WR13 6QP [Walwyn Rd]: Welcoming and carefully refurbished, carpeted bar with step up to parquet-floor area with log fire, nice prints and lighting, reasonably priced good generous food cooked to order from

sandwiches and ploughman's to popular Sun lunch, friendly helpful service, three well kept real ales, decent wines, daily papers *(Ian and Denise Foster, BB)*

CRASWALL [SO2736]

Bulls Head HR2 0PN [Hay-on-Wye—Llanfihangel Crucorney Golden Valley rd]: Remote stone-built country pub under new management yet again, one or two well kept Wye Valley ales and several farm ciders and perry tapped from the cask, low beams and flagstones in unaffectedly basic rustic bar, log fire in old cast-iron stove, traditional games, steps up to smarter dining area (good, if not cheap); tables in good-sized enclosed garden with play area, peaceful walking area, simple bedrooms, cl Mon *(David and Margaret Clark, Guy Vowles, MLR, LYM)*

EARDISLEY [SO3149]

Tram HR3 6PG: Old beamed village local with friendly new licensees, chef/landlord doing sensible honest food, changing real ales such as Greene King IPA and Timothy Taylors Landlord, one bar with woodburner, another served by hatch with open fire and pool; boules pitch *(C E Clarke, MLR)*

FOWNHOPE [SO5734]

New Inn HR1 4PE: Welcoming pub popular at lunchtime for enjoyable food from sandwiches up (all freshly made so may be a wait), friendly local atmosphere and attentive staff, well kept ales such as Hobsons Choice, Woods Shropshire Lad and Wye Valley Butty Bach, small dining area; picturesque village nr unusual church and nice views *(Reg Fowle, Helen Rickwood)*

GOODRICH [SO5618]

Cross Keys HR9 6JB [just off A40 outside village]: Four real ales, good farm cider, generous food, barn restaurant *(Lucien Perring, Dr A J and Mrs Tompsett)*

☆ **Hostelrie** HR9 6HX: Appealing and unusual Victorian building with turreted gothic extension, traditional softly lit panelled bar and lounge, roomy and individual with beams and stripped stone, good value food cooked to order (so can take a while) inc local produce and imaginative dishes, good friendly service, two real ales and four ciders, good choice of wines, generous hot drinks, pretty dining room; TV; children welcome, attractive garden, bedrooms, pleasant village nr Goodrich Castle and Wye Valley Walk *(Tom and Ruth Rees, Lucien Perring, Martin and Pauline Jennings, Dr A J and Mrs Tompsett, Mike and Mary Carter, Denys Gueroult, John and Tania Wood)*

HAMPTON BISHOP [SO5538]

Bunch of Carrots HR1 4JR: Spaciously refurbished beamed country pub by River Wye, good helpful service, consistently good carvery and wide choice of other enjoyable food in bars and restaurant, well kept real ales, local farm cider, lovely log fires; children and dogs welcome, garden with play area *(Lucien Perring, Steff Clegg)*

HAREWOOD END [SO5227]
Harewood End Inn HR2 8JT [A49 Hereford—Ross]: Attractive and comfortable panelled dining lounge with wide food choice even Mon night, efficient staff, well kept ales such as Brains Rev James and Wye Valley Butty Bach, good value wines, magazines; nice garden and walks, good bedrooms with own bathrooms *(Tim and Sue Halstead, Dr and Mrs Michael Smith, Reg Fowle, Helen Rickwood)*
HEREFORD [SO5139]
Barrels HR1 2JQ [St Owen St]: Cheery two-bar local with excellent low-priced Wye Valley Hereford and Dorothy Goodbodys ales (formerly brewed here), barrel-built counter also serving guest beers, several farm ciders, friendly efficient staff, side pool room with games, juke box and big-screen sports TV, lots of modern stained glass; piped blues and rock, live music at beer festival end Aug; picnic-sets out on back cobbles, open all day *(the Didler, BB, MLR, Reg Fowle, Helen Rickwood)*
Bay Horse HR4 0SD [Kings Acre Rd]: Cheerful and relaxed, with enjoyable filling food inc speciality well garnished open sandwiches, real ales such as Flowers and Wye Valley Butty Bach, local farm cider, friendly staff, attractive upmarket décor in large two-level main room, smaller side room and new conservatory extension; piped music *(Reg Fowle, Helen Rickwood)*
Galanthus Gallery HR2 9DH: Interesting stop for walkers – tea room and art gallery, but they do serve bottled Wye Valley beers *(Reg Fowle, Helen Rickwood)*
Kings Fee HR1 2BP [Commercial Rd]: Nice fresh Wetherspoons, good coffee as well as their usual food and fine choice of good value well kept real ales inc useful three-glass tasters; open all day from breakfast time on *(Ann and Colin Hunt, Reg Fowle, Helen Rickwood)*
KENTCHURCH [SO4125]
Bridge Inn HR2 0BY [B4347 Pontrilas—Grosmont]: Ancient attractively refurbished rustic pub with friendly landlord, good choice of good value food (not Sun evening or Mon/Tues) from enterprising open sandwiches up, Hook Norton and Wye Valley ales, farm cider, welcoming service, big log fire, games area, two nice dogs (kept out when food served), small pretty back restaurant overlooking River Monnow (two miles of trout fishing); waterside tables, bedrooms, handy for Herefordshire Trail, cl Mon/Tues lunchtime *(Guy Vowles, Reg Fowle, Helen Rickwood)*
KINGTON [SO3056]
☆ *Olde Tavern* HR5 3BX [Victoria Rd, just off A44 opp B4355 – follow sign to Town Centre, Hospital, Cattle Mkt; pub on right opp Elizabeth Rd, no inn sign but Estd 1767 notice]: Splendidly old-fashioned, like stepping into an old sepia photograph of a pub (except for the strip lights – it's not at all twee), four good local Dunn Plowman ales at bargain prices, meals using fresh local produce in popular new back bistro (Fri-Sat evening and Sun lunch), hatch-served side room opening off small plain parlour and public bar, plenty of dark brown woodwork, big windows, old settles and other antique furniture on bare floors, gas fire, friendly dog called Fanny, china, pewter and curios, welcoming locals, no music or machines; children welcome, though not a family pub; cl wkdy lunchtimes, outside gents' *(Pete Baker, BB, the Didler, MLR, Reg Fowle, Helen Rickwood)*
Wine Vaults HR5 3BJ [High St]: Simple one-room town pub brewing its own good Arrow Bitter and Quiver *(MLR)*
LEDBURY [SO7137]
Horseshoe HR8 1BP [Homend]: Pretty timbered pub, cosy inside, with Marstons Pedigree, Timothy Taylors Landlord and a guest beer, enjoyable bar food, log fire; steps up to entrance; open all day *(BB, Simon Marley)*
Prince of Wales HR8 1DL [Church Lane; narrow passage from Town Hall]: Charmingly old-fashioned pub tucked nicely down charming narrow cobbled alley, well kept ales such as Banks's, Brains Rev James and Sharps Doom Bar, lots of foreign bottled beers, bargain simple home-made food, jovial landlord, low-beamed front bars, long back room; a couple of tables in yard crammed with lovely flower tubs and hanging baskets *(Simon Vernon, Simon Marley, Alan Bowker)*
LEINTWARDINE [SO4073]
Lion SY7 0JZ [High St]: Hotel in beautiful spot by packhorse bridge over River Teme, helpful efficient staff and friendly atmosphere, good bar food, popular two-room restaurant, well kept real ale; nice safely fenced riverside garden with play area, attractive bedrooms *(Mike and Lynn Robinson)*
LEOMINSTER [SO4959]
Bell HR6 8AE [Etnam St]: Well kept Wye Valley ales from central servery, good value simple lunchtime food from sandwiches up, friendly staff, thriving local atmosphere, log fire, beams and bare boards; tables out on good-sized back terrace, open all day *(Simon Vernon, MLR)*
Chequers HR6 8AE [Etnam St]: Attractive 15th-c beamed and timbered two-bar pub with friendly and enthusiastic newish licensees doing good value food from sandwiches up, three or four well kept interesting real ales, new back dining room; tables outside *(MLR)*
Grape Vaults HR6 8BS [Broad St]: Compact well preserved two-room pub, friendly and busy, with well kept Marstons and guest ales, Stowford Press cider, wide range of simple freshly cooked food, coal fire, panelling, etched windows, original dark high-backed settles, veteran tables, bottle collection, old local prints and posters, shelves of books in snug, no machines or music *(Guy Vowles)*

LONGTOWN [SO3228]

Crown HR2 OLT: Reopened under new landlady, with Wye Valley and another real ale, food lunchtime and evening from sandwiches to woodburner in front bar, small side room, large back room with darts and pool; garden, cl Weds/Thurs lunchtimes *(MLR)*

LUGWARDINE [SO5441]

☆ *Crown & Anchor* HR1 4AB [just off A438 E of Hereford; Cotts Lane]: Attractively cottagey timbered pub with good food inc plenty of lunchtime sandwiches, well kept Butcombe, Timothy Taylors Landlord and guest beers, several wines by the glass, several smallish rooms, some interesting furnishings and big log fire, no piped music or machines; one or two recent service setbacks, which we trust have been temporary; children welcome, pretty garden, open all day *(Brian Brooks, Noel Grundy, Dr and Mrs Michael Smith, Lucien Perring, Bernard Stradling, Denys Gueroult, Ken Millar, LYM)*

MORDIFORD [SO5737]

☆ *Moon* HR1 4LW [B4224 SE of Hereford]: Country pub in good spot by Wye tributary, black beams and roaring log fire, wide choice of home-made food inc fresh fish, well kept ales inc Wye Valley and Spinning Dog, local farm ciders, reasonably priced wines, welcoming helpful staff, back bar popular with young locals and students out from Hereford; children in eating areas, open all day wknds *(LYM, Trevor Williams)*

MUCH DEWCHURCH [SO4831]

Black Swan HR2 8DJ [B4348 Ross—Hay]: Roomy and attractive beamed and timbered pub, partly 14th-c, with warm local atmosphere and log fires in cosy bar and lounge with eating area, reasonably priced food, well kept ales such as Bass, Brains Rev James and Wye Valley, decent wines, star barmaid; no credit cards *(M J Winterton)*

PEMBRIDGE [SO3958]

Kings House HR6 9HB [East St]: Comfortable and tidy timber-framed inn with attentive staff, enjoyable food, Wye Valley real ale, log fire, interesting old cameras, framed ephemera and memorabilia, good book collection *(Reg Fowle, Helen Rickwood)*

New Inn HR6 9DZ [Market Sq (A44)]: Ancient inn overlooking small black-and-white town's church, unpretentious three-room bar with antique settles, beams, worn flagstones and substantial log fire, one room with sofas, pine furniture and books, Black Sheep and Fullers London Pride, traditional games, quiet little family dining room (not Sun evening); simple bedrooms *(David Eberlin, LYM)*

PETERSTOW [SO5524]

Red Lion HR9 6LH [A49 W of Ross]: Country pub with impressive range of enjoyable fresh food, small helpings available, good choice of real ales inc Timothy Taylors Landlord and Wye Valley, farm cider, friendly staff, log fires, open-plan bar with large dining area

and conservatory; busy wknds; children welcome, back play area *(Rob and Penny Wakefield, Anthony Double)*

PRESTON [SO3841]

Yew Tree HR2 9JT: Welcoming tucked-away pub handy for River Wye, generous 'camper's special' meals with an early sitting helpful for families, quickly changing real ales, pool, occasional blues or folk music; children welcome *(Reg Fowle, Helen Rickwood)*

ROSS-ON-WYE [SO5924]

Kings Head HR9 5HL [High St]: Comfortably old-fashioned beamed and panelled hotel bar, blazing log fire, lots of old pictures and some cosy armchairs, generous good value pubby food from good sandwiches and baked potatoes up, two Wye Valley beers perhaps with a guest beer, swift friendly service, airy newer dining extension; dogs welcome, bedrooms, open all day *(Tony and Wendy Hobden, Dr W J M Gissane, Derek and Sylvia Stephenson, Lucien Perring)*

Mail Rooms HR9 5BS [Gloucester Rd]: Light and airy Wetherspoons, open and modern, with their usual food (using local ingredients) and attractively priced beers and wines, silenced TV; children in family area till 7, pleasant terrace with tables under big parasols, open all day *(Reg Fowle, Helen Rickwood, Mike and Mary Carter)*

Riverside HR9 7BT [Wye St]: Attractive pub well refurbished by hospitable young licensees, comfortable leather sofas and sturdy tables and chairs on flagstone floors, interesting choice of good proper cooking using fresh local ingredients, well kept Freeminer and Iron Brew, local farm cider; big-screen sports TV in public bar; big round picnic-sets out on decking, superb spot by Wye-side public meadows, bedrooms *(Alan and Sue Forster)*

STAUNTON ON WYE [SO3645]

New Inn HR4 7LR: 16th-c two-bar village pub, pleasantly relaxed and old-fashioned, with well kept Wye Valley ale, good value generous home-made food lunchtimes and Fri/Sat evenings, friendly helpful young licensees, cosy alcoves; nice garden with quoits and boules *(Reg Fowle, Helen Rickwood, MLR)*

TARRINGTON [SO6140]

Tarrington Arms HR1 4HX [A438 E of Hereford]: Welcoming and cosy, with enjoyable varied food in bar and well run restaurant; bellringers may be in at 9 after Fri practice *(Mike and Mary Carter, Reg Fowle, Helen Rickwood)*

TILLINGTON [SO4645]

☆ *Bell* HR4 8LE: Family-run pub with warmly welcoming landlord, good home cooking in bar and restaurant inc nice baguettes and choice of generous speciality winter bowls, Wye Valley ales with a guest such as Spinning Dog, daily papers, comfortable pine furniture with banquettes in lounge extension; children welcome, steps up to good big garden with play area *(Reg Fowle, Helen Rickwood, Bruce Bird)*

UPPER COLWALL [SO7643]

Chase WR13 6DJ [Chase Rd, off B4218 Malvern—Colwall, 1st left after hilltop on bend going W]: Plenty of tables for wide range of enjoyable good value generous food from sandwiches to good Sun roast, friendly staff and buoyant atmosphere, good range of real ales and of wines by the glass, great views; dogs and walkers welcome, attractive garden, open all day *(Ian and Denise Foster)*

WEOBLEY [SO4051]

☆ *Salutation* HR4 8SJ [off A4112 SW of Leominster]: Beamed and timbered old inn at top of delightful village green, pleasant new licensees keeping same chef (he has good sources of local meat and other produce), real ales such as Goffs, Spinning Dog and Butty Bach, good range of wines by the glass, good log fires, relaxed lounge, conservatory restaurant, public bar; children welcome, tables with parasols on sheltered back terrace, bedrooms, open all day *(Norman and Penny Davies, the Didler, R T and J C Moggridge, Norman and Sarah Keeping, LYM)*

WHITBOURNE [SO7156]

☆ *Live & Let Live* WR6 5SP [off A44 Bromyard—Worcester at Wheatsheaf]: Spotlessly kept two-bar pub with quick welcoming service, three real ales from Hobsons and Wye Valley, enjoyable food using good local ingredients, good choice of wines by the glass, beams and big log fire, red plush seats and a couple of settees, darts, nice relaxed atmosphere in big-windowed restaurant; children welcome, picnic-sets in informal garden with swings

and country views *(Christopher Roberts, BB, M and GR)*

WHITCHURCH [SO5417]

Crown HR9 6DB [just off A40 Ross—Monmouth]: Dating from 16th c but greatly expanded, beams and stripped stone mixed with red and blue paintwork and modern art and furnishings in big wood-floored main bar, real ales inc Bass, good choice of food, log fire and settees, good-sized dining area; tables outside, bedrooms *(Neil and Anita Christopher)*

WOOLHOPE [SO6135]

☆ *Crown* HR1 4QP: Welcoming and hard-working hands-on licensees doing good range of good value food from sandwiches and baked potatoes up, Black Sheep and Wye Valley real ale, local farm cider, good hot drinks, open fire, comfortable neatly kept lounge bar divided by timbers from dining area; piped music, sports TV; children welcome, big garden with outdoor heaters and lighting, on Three Choirs Way, open all day Sat *(Guy Vowles, Martin and Pauline Jennings, LYM)*

WOONTON [SO3552]

☆ *Lion* HR3 6QN [A480 SE of Kington]: Congenial beautifully placed country pub with warmly welcoming affable landlord and informal atmosphere, landlady cooks enjoyable home-made food using local produce from hot beef and other sandwiches up, also dishes (and wines and beers) suitable for vegans, and gluten-free dishes, local real ale, spotless furnishings, separate restaurant, good views; monthly vintage sports car meeting second Tues; pleasant garden *(W H and E Thomas)*

Post Office address codings confusingly give the impression that some pubs are in Herefordshire when they're really in Gloucestershire or even in Wales (which is where we list them).

Hertfordshire

Since the Bricklayers Arms in Flaunden was last in the *Guide* as a main entry, quite a few years ago, new licensees and a French chef have really pulled it up in the world, transforming it into an extremely good dining pub with a wine list to match. This new entry gains both a Food Award and a Wine Award right away. Not only that: it's so enjoyable for a special meal out that it wins the title of Hertfordshire Dining Pub of the Year. The other great new entry in the county is the Fox at Willian (a pretty village enclave in Letchworth Garden City). Its great wine list also gains it a Wine Award, and it's firmly in the running for a Food Award too. The civilised yet thoroughly lively Alford Arms at Frithsden serves a very good seasonally changing menu with a thoughtful wine list, and the Greyhound at Aldbury is well liked too for its good food. The unspoilt Valiant Trooper in the same village is a great all-rounder – generally a little more down-to-earth with pubbier food and more real ales. The unassuming and cosy White Horse in Hertford with its great range of ten attractively priced real ales is also worth a stop for its very good value tasty food, as is the lovingly kept traditional Holly Bush at Potters Crouch. On the whole pub food prices tend to offer good value in Hertfordshire, being noticeably lower than in many places for equivalent quality. Drinks prices here, however, are rather higher than the national norm, with Fullers and Greene King between them dominating supplies to the better pubs. The main local beer is McMullens, which goes chiefly to pubs tied to that brewer; in other pubs, the local beer you are most likely to find is Tring. Pubs which currently stand out in the Lucky Dip section at the end of the chapter are the Horns near Datchworth, Beehive at Epping Green, Green Man at Great Offley, Old Cross Tavern in Hertford, Woodman at Nuthampstead, Boot at Sarratt, Six Bells in St Albans and George & Dragon at Watton-at-Stone.

ALDBURY   SP9612   MAP 4

Greyhound

Stocks Road; village signposted from A4251 Tring—Berkhamsted, and from B4506; HP23 5RT

Spacious and cosy old dining pub with traditional furnishing, popular food, and courtyard

Benches outside this handsome virginia creeper covered inn face a picturesque village green complete with stocks and a duck pond lively with wildfowl. The beamed interior shows some signs of considerable age (around the copper-hooded inglenook, for example), with plenty of tables in the two traditionally furnished rooms off either side of the drinks and food serving areas. In winter the lovely warm fire and subtle lighting make it feel really cosy. An airy oak floored restaurant at the back overlooks a suntrap gravel courtyard. Three beers on handpump are usually Badger Best and Tanglefoot and Harveys Sussex Best.

🍴 Food here does draw a crowd, but the friendly staff cope well and meals are served promptly. The short but sensible menu includes something for most tastes: soup, paninis, ploughman's, roast butternut squash, sage and pine nut risotto, gammon and eggs, cured meat platter with parmesan, smoked haddock on mash with poached egg and butter sauce, shepherd's pie, thai king prawn curry, lamb tagine with lemon and honey couscous, parsley and cheese crusted cod loin and fillet of beef with pink peppercorn sauce. *Starters/Snacks: £3.50 to £5.50. Main Courses: £9.00 to £14.50. Puddings: £3.95*

Badger ~ Tenant Tim O'Gorman ~ Real ale ~ Bar food (till 2.30 Sun; not Sun and Mon evenings) ~ (01442) 851228 ~ Children welcome ~ Dogs allowed in bar ~ Open 11.30-11; 12-10.30 Sun ~ Bedrooms: £65S/£75B

Recommended by John Baish, David and Ruth Shillitoe, Mrs Deborah Chalmers, Ross Balaam, Gill and Keith Croxton, Michael Dandy, Sheila Topham, John and Elisabeth Cox, Roy Hoing

Valiant Trooper 🍺
Trooper Road (towards Aldbury Common); off B4506 N of Berkhamsted; HP23 5RW

Cheery all-rounder with appealing interior, five interesting real ales, generous helpings of tasty food, garden

The first of the nicely unspoilt rooms at this engaging pub is beamed and tiled in red and black, and has built-in wall benches, a pew and small dining chairs around the attractive country tables, and an inglenook fireplace. Futher in, the middle bar has spindleback chairs around tables on a wooden floor, some exposed brickwork, and signs warning you to 'mind the step'. The far room has nice country kitchen chairs around individually chosen tables, and a woodburning stove, and the back barn has been converted to house a restaurant. On handpump, a jolly decent range of very well kept beers might include Archers Village, Brakspears, Oakham JHB and Tring Jack o' Legs, with around a dozen wines by the glass; dominoes, cribbage and bridge on Monday nights. The enclosed garden has a play house for children and the pub is nicely positioned for walks through the glorious beech woods of the National Trust's Ashridge Estate.

🍴 Quickly served bar food includes well filled baked potatoes, open sandwiches or ciabattas and ploughman's, with daily specials such as soup, creamy mushroom carbonara, roast chicken and steak and kidney pie, and puddings such as chocolate and brandy torte. *Starters/Snacks: £3.50 to £5.50. Main Courses: £9.00 to £14.50. Puddings: £3.95*

Free house ~ Licensee Tim O'Gorman ~ Real ale ~ Bar food (till 2.30 Sun; not Mon and Sun evenings) ~ Restaurant ~ (01442) 851203 ~ Children in first bar and restaurant till 8.30pm ~ Dogs allowed in bar ~ Open 12-11(10.30 Sun)

Recommended by Sheila Topham, Mrs Deborah Chalmers, Colin McKerrow, David and Ruth Shillitoe, Michael Dandy, Paul Humphreys, Brian Root, Klaus and Elizabeth Leist, Roy Hoing

ASHWELL   TL2739 MAP 5
Three Tuns
Off A505 NE of Baldock; High Street; SG7 5NL

Comfortable gently old-fashioned hotel with generous helpings of tasty food, and substantial garden

Wood panelling, relaxing chairs, big family tables, lots of pictures, stuffed pheasants and fish, piped light classical music and antiques lend an air of Victorian opulence to the cosy lounge at this flower bedecked 18th-c inn. The recently refurbished public bar is more modern, with leather sofas on reclaimed oak flooring, and pool, darts, cribbage, dominoes, a games machine and SkyTV. They stock a good choice of wines, as well as Greene King IPA, Abbot and a guest beer on handpump. A big terrace has metal tables and chairs, and you can play boules in the shaded garden which has picnic-sets under apple trees. The charming village is full of pleasant corners and is popular with walkers as the landscape around rolls enough to be rewarding.

We say if we know a pub allows dogs.

🍴 Nicely presented food might include soup, filled baguettes, chicken liver pâté, herring fillets in madeira, ploughman's, grilled vegetable kebabs on noodles with spicy red pepper dip, chicken and leek bake, grilled salmon fillet, 8oz fillet steak, with puddings such as raspberry and cream flan and profiteroles with rum and chocolate sauce. *Starters/Snacks: £4.50 to £6.25. Main Courses: £6.45 to £16.95. Puddings: £3.95 to £5.00*

Greene King ~ Tenants Claire and Darrell Stanley ~ Real ale ~ Bar food (12-2.30, 6-9.30; all day Fri-Sun and bank hols) ~ Restaurant ~ (01462) 742107 ~ Children welcome ~ Dogs allowed in bar ~ Open 11-11; 12-10.30 Sun ~ Bedrooms: £39/£49(£59S)(£69B)

Recommended by Mike Dean, Lis Wingate Gray, Michael Dandy, Peter and Margaret Glenister, Mrs Diane M Hall, Gordon Neighbour, Dave Braisted, Conor McGaughey

BATFORD
TL1415   MAP 5

Gibraltar Castle
Lower Luton Road; B653, S of B652 junction; AL5 5AH

Pleasantly traditional pub with interesting militaria displays, some emphasis on food (booking advised); terrace

This neatly kept little place is stashed with an impressive collection of military paraphernalia including rifles, swords, medals, uniforms and bullets (with plenty of captions to read). Pictures depict its namesake, and various moments in the Rock's history. The long carpeted bar has a pleasant old fireplace, comfortably cushioned wall benches, and a couple of snugly intimate window alcoves, one with a fine old clock. In one area the low beams give way to soaring rafters. Several board games are piled on top of the piano, and they've piped music. They stock a thoughtful choice of wines by the glass and a good range of malt whiskies, and serve three Fullers beers on handpump. Hanging baskets and tubs dotted around lend colour to a decked back terrace, and there are a few more tables and chairs in front by the road,

🍴 Quickly served tasty food includes a good range of lunchtime sandwiches, ploughman's, sausage and mash, cajun chicken, mushroom and mascarpone lasagne, fish and chips, smoked fish salad and fillet steak; booking is recommended for Sunday roast. *Starters/Snacks: £3.95 to £6.25. Main Courses: £8.95 to £16.95. Puddings: £3.95 to £5.25*

Fullers ~ Lease Hamish Miller ~ Real ale ~ Bar food (12-4, 7-9; till 4 on Sun, not Sun evening) ~ Restaurant ~ (01582) 460005 ~ Children welcome ~ Dogs allowed in bar ~ Live music Tues evenings from 9pm ~ Open 11.30-11; 12-10.30 Sun

Recommended by Angus and Carol Johnson, Mr and Mrs John Taylor, Grahame Brooks, David and Ruth Shillitoe, Michael Dandy, Derek Harvey-Piper

CHAPMORE END
TL3216   MAP 5

Woodman 🍺
Off B158 Wadesmill—Bengeo; 300 yards W of A602 roundabout keep eyes skinned for discreet green sign to pub pointing up otherwise unmarked narrow lane; OS Sheet 166 map reference 328164; SG12 OHF

Peaceful country local with down-to-earth interior, beers straight from the cask, lunchtime snacks (occasionally more), cheery staff, and garden with play area

Tucked away near the duck pond in a small hamlet, this welcoming early Victorian local wanders you pleasantly back through time. Two straightforward little linked rooms have plain seats around stripped pub tables, flooring tiles or broad bare boards, log fires in period fireplaces, cheerful pictures (for sale), lots of local notices, and darts on one side, with a piano (and a couple of squeeze boxes) on the other; boules, chess, backgammon, shove ha'penny and cribbage. They have well kept Greene King IPA, Abbot and usually a couple of guests such as Batemans XXXB and Belhaven Six Nations tapped from the cask, as well as several malt whiskies. There are picnic-sets out in front under a couple of walnut trees, and a bigger garden at the back has a good fenced play area. The car park has little room but there is usually plenty of on-street parking.

🍴 Served by cheerful staff, the very short lunchtime menu includes sandwiches, soup and ploughman's. On Thursday evening the very small kitchen conjures up a reasonably priced two-course meal such as loin of lamb with apricots and pine nuts, and baked vanilla and lemon cheesecake. In winter they serve a Sunday lunchtime roast and in summer they have regular barbecues and tasty hog roasts. *Starters/Snacks: £3 to £6*

Greene King ~ Tenant Dr Danny Davis ~ Real ale ~ Bar food (lunchtimes only and maybe Thurs evening) ~ No credit cards ~ (01920) 463143 ~ Children welcome in lounge bar till 8pm ~ Dogs welcome ~ Open acoustic second Mon of month ~ Open 12-2.30, 5.30-11; 12-11 Sat, Sun; closed Mon lunchtime

Recommended by Andy and Jill Kassube, Robert Turnham, Jeremy Hemming, Ian Arthur, Pat and Tony Martin

COTTERED
TL3229   MAP 5

Bull
A507 W of Buntingford; SG9 9QP

Neatly kept extended dining pub with polished antiques, good (though not cheap) food and big attractive garden

The airy low-beamed front lounge is well cared for, with good pieces of furniture on a stripped wood floor, a warming fire, Greene King IPA and Abbot and decent wines. A second bar has darts and a games machine; unobtrusive piped music. The pub is surrounded by trees and faces a row of pretty thatched cottages, and benches and tables in the attractive big garden make the best of the lovely setting.

🍴 Thoughtfully presented bar food includes lunchtime sandwiches, toasties and ploughman's. Other dishes include soup, fresh crab, steak and kidney pie, chicken fillet in cream, wine, garlic and mushroom sauce, bass on tomato and king prawn risotto, rack of lamb with port sauce and fillet steak; 5% service charge except if dining in the Hunt Bar. You can get tea here on summer Sunday afternoons (3-6). *Starters/Snacks: £3.25 to £8.00. Main Courses: £8.50 to £18.00. Puddings: £4.65 to £5.50*

Greene King ~ Tenant Darren Perkins ~ Real ale ~ Bar food (12-2, 6.30-9.30; 12-3.30, 6.30-9 Sun) ~ Restaurant ~ (01763) 281243 ~ No under-7s Mon-Sat, no prams ~ Open 12-3, 6.30-11; 12-10.30 Sun

Recommended by Jack and Sandra Clarfelt, Mrs Margo Finlay, Jörg Kasprowski, John Branston, Ian Phillips, Brian and Rosalie Laverick, Simon Watkins

FLAUNDEN
TL0101   MAP 5

Bricklayers Arms 🍴 ♟
Off A41; Hogpits Bottom; HP3 0PH
HERTFORDSHIRE DINING PUB OF THE YEAR

Cosy traditional country restaurant (drinkers welcome) with emphasis on beautifully prepared food (booking almost essential) and very good wine list

Originally two cottages and now covered with virginia creeper, this well refurbished, low brick and tiled 18th-c pub is tucked away down a winding country lane. The low-beamed bar is snug and comfortable, with roaring winter log fires and dark brown wooden wall seats. Stubs of knocked-through oak-timbered walls keep some feeling of intimacy in the three areas that used to be separate rooms. Although the emphasis is very much on the food, locals do still pop in for a drink. They've a very good wine list (with about 20 by the glass) as well as Fullers London Pride, Greene King IPA and Old Speckled Hen, Timothy Taylors and a guest such as Tring Jack o' Legs on handpump. This is a lovely peaceful spot in summer, when the old-fashioned garden with its foxgloves against sheltering hedges comes into its own. Just up the Belsize road there's a path on the left which goes through delightful woods to a forested area around Hollow Hedge.

🍴 On the whole, food is fairly elaborate and not cheap, but the French chef takes tremendous care over preparation and ingredients. Some of the herbs and vegetables come from the pub's garden, and they smoke their own meats and fish. The menu (a fusion of anglo and gallic styles) might include starters such as soup, smoked fish selection, crab with smoked salmon and buttermilk cream on blinis, fried foie gras with roasted apples and sherry jus, main courses such as battered cod, quail stuffed with mushrooms with balsamic sauce, saffron and grilled pepper risotto with parmesan tuile, fried bass with creamy wine, red pepper, shallot and basil sauce, beef fillet with green peppercorn, brandy and cream sauce, and puddings such as lemon tart with panna cotta ice-cream, raspberry mousse on a pistachio sponge and hot chocolate sponge pudding; **Sunday roast.** *Starters/Snacks: £4.95 to £12.95. Main Courses: £9.95 to £18.95. Puddings: £4.60 to £5.95*

Free house ~ Licensee Alvin Michaels ~ Real ale ~ Bar food (12-2.30(3.30 Sun); 6.30-9.30(8.30 Sun)) ~ Restaurant ~ (01442) 833322 ~ Children welcome lunchtimes only ~ Dogs allowed in bar ~ Open 12-midnight(11 Sun)

Recommended by C J Woodhead, Jarrod and Wendy Hopkinson, Tracey and Stephen Groves, Mike Turner, James Paterson

FRITHSDEN   TL0109   MAP 5

Alford Arms 🍴 ♀

From Berkhamsted take unmarked road towards Potten End, pass Potten End turn on right, then take next left towards Ashridge College; HP1 3DD

Attractively located thriving dining pub with stylish interior, good food from imaginative menu, and thoughtful wine list including many by the glass

It's worth booking to be sure of a table at this very popular place, and as parking can be a problem we suggest getting there early. The fashionably elegant but understated interior has simple prints on pale cream walls, with blocks picked out in rich Victorian green or dark red, and an appealing mix of good antique furniture (from Georgian chairs to old commode stands) on bare boards and patterned quarry tiles. It's all pulled together by luxurious opulently patterned curtains; piped jazz. Welcoming young staff are thoughtful and conscientious. A good wine list includes ten good pudding wines and 15 other wines by the glass, and they've Brakspears, Flowers Original, Marstons Pedigree and Rebellion IPA on handpump. The pub stands by a village green and is surrounded by lovely National Trust woodland. There are plenty of tables out in front.

🍴 The seasonally changing menu might include starters such as soup, seared king prawns and calamari on thai spiced couscous, fried pigeon breast with creamed savoy cabbage, bacon and blueberry reduction, main courses such as smoked haddock and crayfish pie with smoked cheese mash, moroccan bean tagine with tabbouleh and minted yoghurt, crispy skinned black bream on fennel and mooli slaw with tomato tapenade, carrot and ginger reduction and rib-eye steak with green peppercorn sauce. Puddings might be tarte tatin with apple and cinnamon ice-cream, apricot sticky toffee pudding and sorbets with raspberry sauce, and they've a british cheese plate; Sunday roast *Starters/Snacks: £3.75 to £7.00. Main Courses: £10.75 to £14.75. Puddings: £4.00 to £6.50*

Salisbury Pubs ~ Lease Richard Coletta ~ Real ale ~ Bar food (12-2.30(4 Sun), 7-10) ~ Restaurant ~ (01442) 864480 ~ Children welcome ~ Dogs allowed in bar ~ Open 11-11; 12-10.30 Sun

Recommended by John Picken, Ian Phillips, Maggie Atherton, Steven Page, Professors Alan and Ann Clarke, Neil Ingoe, Brian P White, John and Joyce Snell, Rosemary Smith, John Baish, Michael Dandy, Karen Eliot, James Paterson

---

Real ale to us means beer which has matured naturally in its cask – not pressurised or filtered. We name all real ales stocked. We usually name ales preserved under a light blanket of carbon dioxide too, though purists – pointing out that this stops the natural yeasts developing – would disagree (most people, including us, can't tell the difference!).

HERTFORD   TL3212   MAP 5

White Horse 🍺 £

Castle Street; SG14 1HH

Impressive range of real ales and very reasonably priced food at unpretentious homely town-centre pub

A great range of half a dozen thoughtfully sourced guest beers is on offer here, with the choice often changing from one day to the next. As well as their usuals (Fullers Chiswick, Discovery, ESB and London Pride), you might find guests from brewers such as Butcombe, Freeminer and RCH. During their May and August bank holiday beer festivals they keep even more. They also have around 20 country wines. Parts of the building date from the 14th c, and you can still see Tudor brickwork in the three quietly cosy upstairs rooms. Downstairs, the two main rooms are small and homely. The one on the left is more basic, with bare boards, some brewery memorabilia and a few rather well worn tables, stools and chairs. An open fire separates it from the more comfortable right-hand bar, which has a cosily tatty armchair, some old local photographs, beams and timbers, and a red-tiled floor. Service can be quite chatty; bar billiards, darts, shove-ha'penny, shut-the-box, cribbage and dominoes. The pub faces the castle, and there are two benches on the street outside.

🍽 **The very inexpensive home-made bar food includes sandwiches, soup, baguettes and ploughman's, and daily specials such as beef and vegetable pie, moroccan chicken, wild boar casserole, braised armenian lamb shanks and sausages and bubble and squeak with onion gravy. On Sunday they do a remarkably good value two-course and three-course lunch, and on Monday evenings they do one exotic dish such as a curry; they can do children's portions. Starters/Snacks: £2.40 to £4.50. Main Courses: £5.00 to £5.25**

Fullers ~ Lease Nigel Crofts ~ Real ale ~ Bar food (12-2(1-3 Sun)); 6-when sold out (Mon only)) ~ (01992) 501950 ~ Well supervised children in upstairs family room until 9pm ~ Dogs welcome ~ Open 12-2.30, 5.30-11; 12-11(10.30 Sun) Sat

Recommended by Andy and Jill Kassube, Pat and Tony Martin, Gordon Tong

POTTERS CROUCH   TL1105   MAP 5

Holly Bush 🍺 £

2¼ miles from M25 junction 21A: A405 towards St Albans, then first left, then after a mile turn left (ie away from Chiswell Green), then at T junction turn right into Blunts Lane; can also be reached fairly quickly, with a good map, from M1 exits 6 and 8 (and even M10); AL2 3NN

Lovingly kept cottage with gleaming furniture, fresh flowers, china, very well kept Fullers beers, good value traditional lunchtime snacks, and attractive garden

Everything at this much loved pretty wisteria-swamped white building is immaculate. Thoughtfully positioned fixtures create the illusion that there are lots of different rooms – some of which have the feel of a smart country house. In the evenings, neatly placed candles cast glimmering lights over the mix of darkly varnished tables, all of which have fresh flowers. There are quite a few antique dressers (several filled with plates), a number of comfortably cushioned settles, the odd plant, a fox's mask, some antlers, a fine old clock, carefully lit prints and pictures, daily papers, and on the left as you go in, a big fireplace. The long, stepped bar has particularly well kept Fullers Chiswick, ESB, London Pride and a Fullers seasonal beer on handpump, and the sort of reassuringly old-fashioned till you hardly ever see these days. Led by the impeccably dressed landlord, service is calm, friendly and efficient, even when they're busy. Behind the pub, the fenced-off garden has a nice lawn, handsome trees, and sturdy picnic-sets – it's a very pleasant place to sit in summer. Though the pub seems to stand alone on a quiet little road, it's only a few minutes' drive from the centre of St Albans (or a pleasant 45-minute walk). More reports please.

🍴 Straightforward, freshly prepared bar food, from a fairly short menu, includes sandwiches, burgers, baked potatoes, chilli or very good generously sized fish, cheese and meat platters, apple pie and chocolate fudge cake. *Starters/Snacks: £2.80 to £5.50. Main Courses: £6.10 to £8.80. Puddings: £3.10*

Fullers ~ Tenant R S Taylor ~ Real ale ~ Bar food (lunchtime only, not Sun) ~ (01727) 851792 ~ Open 11.30-2.30, 6-11; 12-2.30, 7-10.30 Sun

Recommended by John and Joyce Snell, Mr and Mrs John Taylor, Mr and Mrs Stevenson, John Picken, Professors Alan and Ann Clarke, Gordon Prince, Mr and Mrs Mike Pearson, Chris Edwards

PRESTON
TL1824 MAP 5

Red Lion 🍺

Village signposted off B656 S of Hitchin; The Green; SG4 7UD

Homely village local with changing beers and neatly kept colourful garden

Bought by villagers when Whitbreads threatened closure in 1982, this old village pub was the first in the country to be acquired by its community. The main room on the left has sturdy well varnished pub furnishings including padded country-kitchen chairs and cast-iron-framed tables on a patterned carpet, a log fire in a brick fireplace, and foxhunting prints. The somewhat smaller room on the right has steeplechasing prints, some varnished plank panelling, and brocaded bar stools on flagstones around the servery; dominoes. Fullers London Pride, Youngs and three guests from brewers such as Cairngorm, Red Squirrel and Tring are particularly well kept on handpump. They also tap farm cider from the cask, have several wines by the glass (including an english house wine), a perry, and mulled wine in winter. A few picnic-sets out on the front grass face across to lime trees on a peaceful village green. At the back, a pergola covered terrace gives way to many more picnic-sets (with some shade from a tall ash tree) in the good-sized sheltered garden beyond. It's all very neatly kept and there's a colourful herbaceous border.

🍴 As well as lunchtime sandwiches and ploughman's, the reasonably priced straightforward food includes soup, grilled goats cheese, pâté, quiche, chilli, creamy haddock tart, steak and kidney pie, and daily specials. *Starters/Snacks: £3.00 to £4.50. Main Courses: £4.95 to £9.00. Puddings: £3.50 to £4.00*

Free house ~ Licensee Tim Hunter ~ Real ale ~ Bar food (not Sun or Tues evenings) ~ No credit cards ~ (01462) 459585 ~ Children welcome away from bar ~ Dogs allowed in bar ~ Open 12-2.30, 5.30-11; 12-3, 5.30-12 Sat; 12-3, 7-10.30 Sun

Recommended by John Walker, John and Patricia White, John and Joyce Snell, Steve Nye, David and Ruth Shillitoe, R T and J C Moggridge, Eithne Dandy

ROYSTON
TL3540 MAP 5

Old Bull £

High Street, off central A10 one-way system – has own car park, or use central car park; SG8 9AW

Bow-fronted early Georgian coaching inn with pleasant spacious interior and good value food

In days of old, when up to 100 horses might have been stabled at this town hotel, the courtyard here would have been a bustling roar. Today it's a peaceful suntrap, equipped with outdoor heaters and modern tables and chairs. The roomy high-beamed ceilinged bar, with handsome fireplaces, exposed timbers, big pictures and rather fine flooring, has easy chairs, a leather sofa and a table of papers and magazines (and ready-to-pour coffee) at the entrance end with the bar counter. Further in, tables are set out for eating. They have well kept Greene King Abbot and IPA and a changing guest such as Hardys and Hansons Olde Trip on handpump, and several decent wines by the glass. The atmosphere is chatty and relaxed with fairly unobtrusive piped music; cribbage and dominoes.

🍴 Under new licensee, good-value bar food includes sandwiches, soup, ploughman's, filled yorkshire pudding, lasagne, thai red vegetable curry, battered cod, crispy duck pancakes, rib-eye steak, and puddings such as pecan pie or lemon meringue roulade. There is a separate more formal restaurant; carvery. *Starters/Snacks: £3.85 to £7.00. Main Courses: £5.95 to £10.00. Puddings: £4.50*

Greene King ~ Lease Peter Nightingale ~ Real ale ~ Bar food (12-2.30, 7-9; 12-9 Sat, 12-8 Sun) ~ Restaurant ~ (01763) 242003 ~ Children welcome with restrictions ~ Dogs allowed in bar ~ Open 11-11(midnight Thurs-Sat); 12-10.30 Sun ~ Bedrooms: £75S/£90S(£105B)

Recommended by Pat and Tony Martin, Kay and Alistair Butler, John Branston

SARRATT   TQ0498   MAP 5

Cock

Church End: a very pretty approach is via North Hill, a lane N off A404, just under a mile W of A405; WD3 6HH

Plush pub popular with older dining set at lunchtime; Badger beers, children's play area and summer bouncy castle

---

The latched front door to this nicely positioned cream-painted 17th-c country local opens into a homely carpeted snug with a vaulted ceiling, original bread oven, and a cluster of bar stools. Through an archway, the partly oak-panelled cream-walled lounge has a lovely log fire in an inglenook, pretty Liberty-style curtains, pink plush chairs at dark oak tables, and lots of interesting artefacts and several namesake pictures of cocks, and Badger Best, Sussex, Tanglefoot and a Badger guest on handpump; piped music, fruit machine and TV. The restaurant is in a nicely converted barn. Picnic-sets in front look out across a quiet lane towards the churchyard. The terrace at the back gives open country views, and a pretty, sheltered lawn has tables under parasols. There are also a children's play area and a bouncy castle during summer weekends.

Ⓜ **Bar food includes soup, sandwiches, battered cod, steak and ale pie and specials such as chilli, bass, swordfish and vegetable lasagne.** *Starters/Snacks: £3.95 to £5.95. Main Courses: £7.95 to £14.95. Puddings: £4.75*

Badger ~ Tenants John and Maggie Moir ~ Real ale ~ Bar food (12-2.30, 6-9; not Sun, Mon evening) ~ Restaurant ~ (01923) 282908 ~ Children over 5 welcome ~ Dogs welcome ~ Open 12-11(9 Sun)

Recommended by Ian Phillips, Peter and Margaret Glenister, Howard Dell, N R White, Maggie Atherton, Jarrod and Wendy Hopkinson, Mr and Mrs John Taylor, Roy Hoing

WILLIAN   TL2230   MAP 5

Fox ♀ ⬛

A mile from A1(M) junction 9; A6141 W towards Letchworth then first left; SG6 2AE

Good imaginative food and nice range of drinks in civilised and freshly decorated new dining pub

---

Anyone familiar with the White Horse at Brancaster Staithe on the north Norfolk coast (see our entry for that fine pub) will certainly spot the strong family resemblance in this new sister-pub. It has a long proper bar, carefully lit, with boxy contemporary bar stools around the modern counter, which has Adnams Best, Fullers London Pride, Woodfordes Wherry and a guest such as Potton Village Bike on handpump, a good wine list with about a dozen by the glass, and a nice range of spirits. There are comfortable light wood chairs and tables here, on stripped boards or big ceramic tiles, with a clean-cut décor and modern pictures on white or pastel walls; well reproduced piped music, relatively unobtrusive TV. You can have pubby snacks in this bar at lunchtime (except perhaps on Sundays), but the main food action is in the spreading eating areas, which have a similarly fresh and relaxed mood, with stylish modern dining chairs, tables and table settings, bigger artworks, and fresh flowers. The young staff, pleasant and attentive, look as if they really enjoy their work. A side terrace has smart tables under cocktail parasols, and there are picnic-sets in the good-sized garden behind, below the handsome tower of the 14th-c All Saints church. Across the road is a large pond.

🍴 The imaginative menu, well executed, might include sandwiches such as warm chinese chicken with lemon grass and herb mayonnaise, starters or light dishes such as broccoli, watercress and stilton soup, salmon niçoise salad, norfolk crab and oysters, main courses such as pea risotto with parmesan and truffle oil, battered cod with pea purée, seared bass with star anise and clove pickled apples, sausage and mash, beef and Guinness pie, and rib-eye steak, and puddings such as passion fruit brûlée with meringue fingers and glazed cinnamon rice pudding with red wine poached plums. *Starters/Snacks: £4.50 to £8.95. Main Courses: £8.95 to £15.50. Puddings: £4.95*

Free house ~ Licensee Cliff Nye ~ Real ale ~ Bar food (12-2(3 Sun), 6.45-9.15(6.30-9.30 Sat); not Sun evening) ~ Restaurant ~ (01462) 480233 ~ Children welcome ~ Dogs allowed in bar ~ Open 12-11(midnight Fri, Sat, 10.30 Sun)

Recommended by Richard Pettengell, Peter and Margaret Glenister, Scott McGinlay

LUCKY DIP

Besides the fully inspected pubs, you might like to try these Lucky Dips recommended to us and described by readers (if you do, please send us reports: www.goodguides.co.uk).

ALDENHAM [TQ1498]
Round Bush WD25 8BG [Roundbush Lane]: Friendly village local with plenty of atmosphere, enjoyable food, well kept Marstons Pedigree and good service *(Ross Balaam)*
AMWELL [TL1613]
Elephant & Castle AL4 8EA [signed SW from Wheathampstead]: Low-beamed 18th-c pub with good blackboard food choice (not Sun/Mon evenings), four real ales, friendly staff, two log fires (one in a great inglenook), panelling, quarry tiles and stripped brickwork, immensely deep covered well shaft in back room, no piped music; they may try to keep your credit card while you eat; children welcome, secluded and spacious floodlit garden *(LYM, JJW, CMW)*
AYOT GREEN [TL2213]
Waggoners AL6 9AA [off B197 S of Welwyn]: Pleasant and attentive newish licensees, beers inc Adnams and Greene King, enjoyable well served food inc good lunchtime deals and wider more expensive evening choice, cosy low-beamed bar, comfortable good-sized restaurant extension; attractive and spacious suntrap back garden with sheltered terrace and play area (some A1(M) noise), wooded walks nearby, open all day *(Peter and Margaret Glenister, BB)*
BARKWAY [TL3834]
Tally Ho SG8 8EX [London Rd (B1368)]: Smart cosy bar with three interesting changing ales from small breweries tapped from the cask, good choice of wines by the glass, current chef doing good food from good value sandwiches up, friendly staff, comfortable sofas, daily papers, log fire and a second in candlelit restaurant area, no music or machines; picnic-sets in good-sized garden *(M R D Foot, Shirley Sandilands)*
BENINGTON [TL3022]
Lordship Arms SG2 7BX [Whempstead Rd]: Comfortable and unpretentious, with eight good real ales inc interesting guest beers, September beer festival, good value simple

lunchtime food (can book Sun roast), welcoming attentive landlord, lots of telephone memorabilia; no credit cards *(Steve Nye, Gordon Neighbour)*
BERKHAMSTED [SP9907]
Boat HP4 2EF [Gravel Path]: Nicely renovated open-plan Fullers pub in attractive canalside setting, their ales kept well with a guest such as Adnams, wide choice of food (can take quite a while) from sandwiches up, good choice of wines by the glass, panelling and old photographs inc lots of Graham Greene; games machines, big-screen sports TV, piped music; children welcome, waterside verandah and terrace, pleasant walks, open all day, no under-21s Fri/Sat nights *(Michael Dandy, LYM)*
BOURNE END [TL0206]
Three Horseshoes HP1 2RZ [Winkwell; just off A4251 Hemel—Berkhamsted]: Friendly 16th-c family pub in charming setting by unusual swing bridge over Grand Union Canal, tables out by water, bay-windowed extension overlooking canal; cosy and homely low-beamed three-room core with inglenooks, one with an Aga, friendly landlord, well kept Adnams Broadside, Shepherd Neame Spitfire and a guest such as Greene King Old Speckled Hen, short choice of enjoyable food (not Sun evening); children welcome, open all day *(LYM, Ross Balaam)*
BOXMOOR [TL0406]
Fishery HP1 1NA [Fishery Rd]: Big-windowed roomy open-plan bar comfortably reworked as an Ember Inn, open fire, good value mainstream food inc bargain early suppers for two, eating area with fine view of canal and brightly painted barges, three real ales, lots of wines by the glass; tables out by water *(LYM, G Robinson)*
BRENT PELHAM [TL4331]
Black Horse SG9 0AP: Attractive, civilised and neatly kept, with beams and log fires, separate bars and restaurant, good reasonably priced fresh food, friendly helpful licensees, TV room for children; big garden

in peaceful village, bedrooms, open all day
(Mrs Margo Finlay, Jörg Kasprowski)

CHIPPERFIELD [TL0401]

Two Brewers WD4 9BS [The Common]:
Attractive country hotel housing popular
bow-windowed Chef & Brewer with roomy
linked areas, two log fires, pretty décor,
good if not cheap food all day from
sandwiches and baked potatoes up, good
choice of wines by the glass, pleasant staff,
real ales; provision for children, comfortable
bedrooms, nice spot on common *(N Vernon,
LYM)*

CHISWELL GREEN [TL1304]

Three Hammers AL2 3EA [just S of St
Albans; Watford Rd]: Neatly kept Ember Inn
with good changing real ale choice, good
value food inc a few unusual dishes, prompt
helpful service, several areas on different
levels around central bar, a few rather low
beams, abstracts and photographs of old
St Albans; no children inside; garden tables
(KC)

CHORLEYWOOD [TQ0395]

Black Horse WD3 5EG [Dog Kennel Lane, the
Common]: Popular and very welcoming to
families, walkers and even dogs (basket of
dog biscuits on mantelpiece), plenty of
good-sized tables under low dark beams in
attractively divided traditional room with
thick carpet, good value food (not Mon)
from sandwiches and baked potatoes to
steaks and popular Sun lunch, well kept
Adnams, Highgate Mild, Wadworths 6X and
Wells & Youngs Bitter and Bombardier,
decent wines (and tea and coffee), quick
friendly service, daily papers, coal-effect fire,
no music; family area, separate bar with
SkyTV; pretty setting, picnic-sets overlooking
common *(Ian Phillips, Roy Hoing)*

☆ *Gate* WD3 5SQ [Rickmansorth Rd]: Open-plan
dining pub with clean-cut and attractive
contemporary décor, wide range of enjoyable
up-to-date food inc pizzas, pastas and salads
(in same mould as Fox in Harpenden), Bass
and Timothy Taylors Landlord, sensibly
priced wines by the glass, genial and helpful
largely antipodean staff; plenty of garden
tables *(Michael Dandy, Mr and Mrs M Lindsay-
Bush, LYM, John Branston)*

Land of Liberty Peace & Plenty WD3 5BS
[Long Lane, Heronsgate; just off M25,
junction 17]: Comfortably old-fashioned
open-plan pub with half a dozen interesting
real ales, Weston's farm cider and perry, good
soft drinks choice, belgian bottled beers and
brewery memorabilia, enjoyable bar lunches,
seating inc cosy corner banquette, no music,
skittles; no children inside; dogs welcome,
tables in garden behind, open all day
(Tracey and Stephen Groves, Tony Hobden)

Stag WD3 5BT [Long Lane/Heronsgate Rd]:
Spacious open-plan Edwardian pub with
McMullens ales, decent wines and food,
reasonable prices, quiet relaxed atmosphere,
large L-shaped bar with eating area
extending into conservatory; tables on back
lawn, play area, open all day *(Howard Dell,*

Tracey and Stephen Groves, Tony Hobden)

White Horse WD3 5SD [A404 just off M25
junction 18]: Pleasantly decorated beamed
and carpeted pub with Greene King IPA and
Abbot, wide choice of decent pubby food
from sandwiches and baked potatoes up,
friendly landlady, daily papers, pub games,
fish tank; piped music, TV, Tues quiz night;
tables in neat back courtyard, open all day
(Michael Dandy)

COLEMAN GREEN [TL1912]

John Bunyan AL4 8ES: Quietly set beamed
country local with well kept McMullens ales,
good value unpretentious home cooking,
efficient helpful service, warm log fire,
simple furnishings, masses of decorative
plates, mugs, jugs and other china; big
garden with play area and front terrace,
good walks *(Ross Balaam)*

COLNEY HEATH [TL2006]

Crooked Billet AL4 0NP [High St]: Charming
weatherboarded pub with four interesting
and well kept changing ales, lots of unusual
bottled beers, friendly helpful staff, bargain
pubby food from baguettes and baked
potatoes up, series of small low-ceilinged
rooms with woodburner, seated alcoves and
traditional tiled bar, Arsenal FC photographs;
piped music, games; big garden with play
area, barbecues and partly covered terrace
(Michael Dandy, LYM)

☆ *Plough* AL4 0SE [handy for A1(M) junction 3;
A414 towards St Albans, doubling back at
first roundabout then turning off left]:
Pleasantly refurbished 18th-c low-beamed
thatched local, warm and cosy with big log
fire, chatty atmosphere, good value generous
standard food from sandwiches, baguettes
and ciabattas up (lunchtime Mon-Sat, and
Fri/Sat evening), well kept Greene King IPA
and Abbot and Fullers London Pride, friendly
efficient staff, small brighter back dining
area; white iron tables on pretty front
terrace, picnic-sets on sheltered back terrace
and lawn *(Ivan Ericsson, BB, John Picken,
Peter and Margaret Glenister, Brian and
Rosalie Laverick)*

DATCHWORTH [TL2717]

☆ *Horns* SG3 6RZ [Bramfield Rd]: Pretty flower-
decked Tudor pub facing small green, low
beams and big inglenook one end, high
rafters and rugs on patterned bricks the
other, attractive décor, wide choice of good
reasonably priced food from proper
sandwiches to splendid paella (best to book
Sun), quick friendly service, real ales inc one
brewed for the pub; picnic-sets on front
lawn *(LYM, Gordon Neighbour, Frazer and
Louise Smith, Anthony Lewis)*

EPPING GREEN [TL2906]

☆ *Beehive* SG13 8NB [back rd Cuffley—Little
Berkhamsted]: Cosy and popular, with wide
choice of good generous reasonably priced
food esp fish, impressive children's menu,
pleasant staff, good range of wines by the
glass and Adnams and Greene King IPA,
comfortable beamed dining area on left;
tables overlooking fields *(Kenneth and*

Mary Davies, J Marques, Gordon Neighbour, Geoff and Sylvia Donald, Professors Alan and Ann Clarke, Mrs E E Sanders)

GREAT AMWELL [TL3712]

George IV SG12 9SW: Pleasant pub in pretty spot by church and river, generous good value home-made food in bar and restaurant, friendly attentive staff, real ales *(Roger and Pauline Pearce)*

GREAT OFFLEY [TL1427]

Gloucester Arms SG5 3DG [Luton Rd (A505)]: Interesting part clapboarded building neatly refurbished as reasonably priced dining pub, sofas in small bar, main eating area with open kitchen doing good choice from paninis and baked potatoes up, lunchtime carvery Sun, Greene King ales, good choice of wines by the glass; piped music, no under-21s in bar; small front garden, open all day, cl Mon lunchtime *(Michael Dandy)*

☆ *Green Man* SG5 3AR [signed off A505 Luton—Hitchin; High St]: Roomy and comfortably olde-worlde Chef & Brewer with very wide choice of enjoyable generous food, well organised friendly staff, John Smiths or Wells & Youngs Bombardier and Theakstons Bitter and Old Peculier, good choice of wines by the glass, good coffee, blazing log fires, large flagstoned conservatory; may be unobtrusive piped classical music; children welcome, peaceful country views from picnic-sets in back garden with pleasant terrace, striking inn-sign, open all day *(Wendy Cox, Ross Balaam, Michael Dandy, LYM, Peter and Margaret Glenister)*

Red Lion SG5 3DZ [Kings Walden Rd]: Friendly unpretentious opened-up local, low beams, big inglenook log fire, three or four changing ales such as Thwaites and Wells & Youngs, good choice of wines by the glass, reasonably priced generous food from sandwiches up inc OAP wkdy lunches, small conservatory restaurant; piped music; picnic-sets in small sunny back garden, good walks from pub, simple bedrooms *(Peter and Margaret Glenister, Steve Nye, Conor McGaughey)*

HARPENDEN [TL1314]

Cross Keys AL5 2SD [High St]: Compact beamed pub with three real ales from metal-topped bar, log fire in public bar, simple lounge, basic lunchtime pub food (not Sun) from sandwiches up, young staff; informal garden *(M Thomas)*

Engineer AL5 1DJ [St Johns Rd]: Two-bar pub in residential area, Adnams, Greene King IPA and Shepherd Neame Spitfire, good choice of wines by the glass, reasonably priced pubby bar food from sandwiches up, welcoming helpful staff, conservatory restaurant with different menu inc Sun roasts; piped music, games, TV; pleasant garden with terrace and small fishpond *(Michael Dandy)*

Fox AL5 3QE [Luton Rd, Kinsbourne Green; 2¼ miles from M1 junction 10; A1081 (ex A6) towards town]: Refurbished as

contemporary dining pub, tiled floor, some leather armchairs and sofas, lots of modern dining tables, typical up-to-date food inc plenty of salads, pasta and pizzas, good service, interesting wines by the glass, Bass and Timothy Taylors Landlord, open fire; piped music; terrace tables *(Michael Dandy, Giles Barr, Eleanor Dandy)*

Old Bell AL5 3BN [Luton Rd (A1081)]: Compact Chef & Brewer with decent food, good choice of wines by the glass, Adnams, Courage Best and Wells & Youngs Bombardier, daily papers, pub games; large back tree-shaded garden *(Michael Dandy, Eithne Dandy)*

Rose & Crown AL5 1PS [Southdown Rd]: Enjoyable food from good baguettes up, Adnams and Greene King IPA, good coffee, quick service, daily papers, small bar area with a couple of settees, airy back conservatory restaurant, games; piped music; side terrace and back garden *(M Thomas, Michael Dandy)*

Silver Cup AL5 2JF [St Albans Rd (A1081)]: Friendly neatly refurbished pub with four real ales such as Marstons Pedigree, St Austell Tribute and Wells & Youngs Eagle and Bombardier, good choice of wines by the glass, wide choice of food from sandwiches, baguettes and pubby favourites to good pricier restaurant dishes, ample breakfast even for non-residents, attentive service, bare-boards bar and carpeted dining area, prints of old Harpenden; quiet piped music, TVs in bar; tables outside, four bedrooms, open all day from 7.30 *(Michael Dandy, Brian and Janet Ainscough, Ben Weedon, Ian Arthur)*

☆ *White Horse* AL5 2JP [Hatching Green]: Timbered building well refurbished as smart dining pub, attractive modern furniture and décor though keeping log fire and original fabric, good food with some unusual dishes, front bar with Fullers London Pride and Tring Brock, good helpful service, daily papers; piped music; terrace tables *(Michael Dandy, Mr and Mrs John Taylor, Mrs Anne Callender)*

HEMEL HEMPSTEAD [TL0411]

☆ *Crown & Sceptre* HP2 6EY [Bridens Camp; leaving on A4146, right at Flamstead/Markyate sign opp Red Lion]: Well kept Adnams Broadside, Greene King IPA and Abbot and a guest beer, enjoyable pubby food from wide range of sandwiches and baguettes up, welcoming licensees and cheerful atmosphere, log fires, rambling layout with unpretentious furnishings inc some venerable settles, darts and dominoes, books and magazines; TV; children and dogs welcome, garden with play area, wandering chickens, rabbits and scarecrow, heated front picnic-sets, good walks, open all day summer wknds *(Dennis Jones, LYM, Michael Dandy, Ross Balaam)*

Olde Chequers HP2 6HH [Gaddesden Row; N, towards Markyate]: Attractively refurbished brick-built pub with well kept Adnams Bitter and Broadside and Greene King Abbot, good range of wines by the glass, generous sensibly priced usual food from sandwiches up, helpful service, small bar, large back dining areas with a mix of furnishings on carpet, flagstones or bare boards, log fires; garden picnic-sets and play area *(Michael Dandy, Giles Barr, Eleanor Dandy)*

HERTFORD [TL3212]

☆ **Old Cross Tavern** SG14 1JA [St Andrew St]: Compact conversion from antiques shop, very popular for its seven or eight particularly well kept real ales inc interesting guest beers, farm cider and perry, good home-made lunchtime food, friendly olde-worlde feel with log fire, brass, china etc; dogs welcome, small heated back terrace, open all day *(Ian Arthur, Tony Hobden)*

HEXTON [TL1030]

Raven SG5 3JB [signed off B655]: Built in the style of this attractive mock-Tudor estate village, very popular for wide range of good value food from baguettes and baked potatoes to swordfish and steaks, two children's menus, friendly efficient service, real ales such as Badger K&B, Black Sheep, Everards Tiger and Greene King IPA, good choice of wines by the glass, open fire, plenty of dining tables in four linked areas, oil paintings (some for sale); piped music; big garden with heated terrace, barbecue, good play area *(Michael Dandy, Gordon Tong)*

HIGH WYCH [TL4614]

Rising Sun CM21 0HZ: Cosy old-fashioned local, serving hatch to carpeted lounge with coal or log fire, central area with Courage Best and good guest beers tapped from casks behind the counter, friendly landlord and locals, bar lunches, bare-boards games room (children allowed) with darts and woodburner, no mobile phones or music; tables in small garden *(Pete Baker, the Didler)*

HUNSDON [TL4114]

☆ **Fox & Hounds** SG12 8NJ [High St]: Welcoming bistro pub with good enterprising fresh food inc home-baked bread, three real ales, good choice of wines by the glass, friendly efficient service, log fires, door to lavatories disguised as bookcases, no piped music *(Kath Edwards, LYM, J Marques, Mrs Margo Finlay, Jörg Kasprowski, Ian Arthur)*

KIMPTON [TL1718]

White Horse SG4 8RJ [High St]: Welcoming refurbished pub, nice traditional feel despite the laminate floor and light décor, enjoyable pub food from baguettes and pizzas up, friendly helpful service, McMullens and a guest ale, good value small bottles of wine, log fire, airy and spotless dining area, darts in games area up a few steps; some tables out by road or car park *(David and Ruth Shillitoe, Mr and Mrs R A Buckler, Michael Dandy)*

KNEBWORTH [TL2320]

☆ **Lytton Arms** SG3 6QB [Park Lane, Old Knebworth]: Several spotless big-windowed rooms around large central servery, several

changing real ales, two farm ciders, good choice of wines, good value food from interesting choice of sandwiches, baguettes and baked potatoes up, friendly staff, good log fire, daily papers, conservatory; children and dogs welcome, picnic-sets on front terrace, back garden with play area, nice surroundings, open all day wknds *(Deborah Shearly, Gerry and Rosemary Dobson, LYM, David and Ruth Shillitoe)*

NEWGATE STREET [TL3005]

Crown SG13 8RP: Attractive and cosy flower-decked pub with friendly staff and landlord, good varied home-made food, Greene King IPA and Abbot, good house wine; small well behaved dogs welcome, colourful garden, handy for Northaw Great Wood walks *(Lucien Perring, J Marques)*

NUTHAMPSTEAD [TL4134]

☆ **Woodman** SG8 8NB [off B1368 S of Barkway]: Tucked-away thatched and weatherboarded village pub, welcoming and well run, sofa and other furnishings in comfortable unspoilt bar with worn tiled floor, nice inglenook log fire, another fire opposite and 17th-c low beams and timbers, old local photographs, enjoyable home-made food (not Sun evening) inc good home-baked bread, efficient friendly service, dining room, no music; interesting USAF memorabilia (nearby World War II airfield), inc a memorial outside; benches out overlooking tranquil lane, comfortable bedrooms, open all day Sat *(BB, M R D Foot, Margaret and Allen Marsden, Mrs P J Pearce)*

POTTEN END [TL0108]

Martins Pond HP4 2QQ [The Green]: Small friendly traditional pub with enjoyable food inc nice twists on pubby favourites, Fullers London Pride and Greene King IPA; small garden with picnic-sets, opp pretty green and pond *(Ian Phillips)*

REDBOURN [TL1111]

Chequers AL3 7AD [St Albans Rd (A5183), nr M1 junction 9]: Small rebuilt Chef & Brewer family dining pub with thatch, flagstones and dark wood, Adnams Broadside, Theakstons Coopers Butt and Wells & Youngs Bombardier, good choice of wines by the glass, friendly service; piped music, games; large back terrace and small pleasant garden *(Giles Barr, Eleanor Dandy, Michael Dandy)*

Hollybush AL3 7DU [Church End]: Picturesque old pub in pretty spot nr medieval church, enjoyable straightforward food, Adnams and Brakspears, friendly efficient staff, black-beamed lounge with big brick fireplace and heavy wooden doors, larger area with some built-in settles; tables in sunny garden (some M1 noise) *(Ross Balaam)*

REED [TL3636]

☆ **Cabinet** SG8 8AH [off A10; High St]: 16th-c weatherboarded building now a civilised and attractive restaurant rather than pub, good food much enjoyed by readers, friendly management, very small bar with pricy drinks inc fine choice of wines by the glass, Adnams, Greene King IPA and a seasonal beer, inglenook log fire; piped music; charming big garden with pond *(Adrian White, B N F and M Parkin, David and Ruth Shillitoe, LYM, Maggie Atherton)*

RICKMANSWORTH [TQ0592]

Rose & Crown WD3 1PP [Woodcock Hill/Harefield Rd, off A404 E of Rickmansworth at Batchworth]: Friendly low-beamed pub with warm coal fire, plenty of character, and real ales such as Caledonian Deuchars IPA and Timothy Taylors Landlord in traditional country bar, good up-to-date food choice from nice sandwiches up (cooked dishes can sometimes take a while), airy restaurant extension; large peaceful garden, wide views from big car park *(Mike Turner, Tracey and Stephen Groves)*

RUSHDEN [TL3031]

☆ *Moon & Stars* SG9 0TA [Mill End; off A507 about a mile W of Cottered]: Cottagey beamed country pub with friendly and hard-working young licensees, good freshly made food (not Sun/Mon evenings) in neatly kept relaxed and welcoming lounge bar and small dining room (worth booking), inglenook log fire, Greene King and guest ales; well behaved children welcome, pleasant garden with heated terrace and barbecues, peaceful country setting *(LYM)*

SARRATT [TQ0499]

☆ *Boot* WD3 6BL [The Green]: Attractive early 18th-c tiled pub on good form, with enjoyable pubby food inc some innovative sandwiches, good friendly service, well kept Greene King ales, cosily cheerful rambling bar with unusual inglenook fireplace, more modern dining room; garden, pleasant spot facing green, handy for Chess Valley walks *(LYM, KC, Brian P White, N R White, C Galloway)*

SOUTH MIMMS [TL2201]

Black Horse EN6 3PS [Blackhorse Lane; off B556]: Beamed village pub with welcoming staff, Greene King ales, reasonably priced food inc good value Sun roast and speciality sweet pancakes *(Tony Liles)*

ST ALBANS [TL1307]

Blue Anchor AL3 4RY [Fishpool St]: Popular dining lounge with good value sandwiches and other bar food (not Sun evening), McMullens ales, attractive prices, welcoming landlord, daily papers, small locals' bar with sensibly placed darts, real fire; sizeable garden, handy for Roman remains *(the Didler)*

Farmers Boy AL1 1PQ [London Rd]: Unpretentious bay-windowed pub brewing its own distinctive Verulam ales and lager, continental bottled beers, lots of old prints on softly lit ochre walls, imposing clock, log fire, back open kitchen serving straightforward food from sandwiches and baked potatoes up all day, helpful staff; SkyTV; open all day, suntrap back terrace with barbecues *(the Didler)*

Farriers Arms AL3 4PT [Lower Dagnall St]:

Plain friendly two-bar local in no-frills old part, McMullens inc Mild and guest beers, bar food wkdys, lots of old pictures of the pub (Campaign for Real Ale started here in the early 1970s) *(Andy and Jill Kassube, the Didler)*

Fighting Cocks AL3 4HE [Abbey Mill Lane; through abbey gateway – you can drive down]: Much modernised odd-shaped former abbey gatehouse with some original features inc sunken Stuart cockpit, some low and heavy beams, and big inglenook fires; well kept real ales, decent food, friendly helpful service; piped music; children welcome (good family room), attractive public park beyond garden, open all day *(LYM, John Roots)*

Garibaldi AL1 1RT [Albert St; left turn down Holywell Hill past White Hart – car park left at end]: Fullers local with their ales and guest beers, good wines by the glass, some unusual cooking as well as traditional dishes, cheerful staff; may be piped music; children welcome, open all day *(the Didler, Andy and Jill Kassube, LYM)*

Lower Red Lion AL3 4RX [Fishpool St]: Convivial beamed local dating from 17th c (right-hand bar has the most character), up to eight or so interesting and well kept changing ales, imported beers on tap and in bottle, May Day and Aug bank hol beer festivals, friendly staff, inexpensive lunchtime food inc sandwiches, speciality sausages and popular Sun roast, red plush seats and carpet, board games; no nearby parking; tables in good-sized back garden, pleasant bedrooms, open all day wknds *(the Didler, Andy and Jill Kassube, Pete Baker)*

☆ *Plough* AL4 0RW [Tyttenhanger Green, off A414 E]: Village pub long popular for its fine changing range of real ales, friendly efficient staff, good value straightforward lunchtime food, good log fire, interesting old beer bottles and mats, lovely longcase clock, back conservatory; big garden with play area *(the Didler, LYM, Nick and Clare)*

Portland Arms AL3 4RA [Portland St/Verulam Rd]: Relaxed local with good value home-made food esp good meat dishes, Fullers full beer range kept well, friendly licensees, big open fire *(Andy and Jill Kassube)*

Rose & Crown AL3 4SG [St Michaels St]: 16th-c beamed and timbered town pub with Adnams, Fullers London Pride and Greene King ales, welcoming service, speciality lunchtime sandwiches with a few hot dishes, big log fire; children welcome, lots of tables and benches outside, pretty floral and ivy-hung back yard *(LYM, Mike and Jennifer Marsh)*

☆ *Six Bells* AL3 4SH [St Michaels St]: Well kept rambling town pub with good fresh generous food from lunchtime ciabattas to interesting specials, nice relaxed atmosphere even when busy, cheerful helpful service, real ales such as Adnams, Fullers London Pride and Greene

King IPA and Abbot, low beams and timbers, log fire, quieter panelled dining room; children welcome, occasional barbecues in small back garden, very handy for Roman Verulam Museum, open all day Fri-Sun *(Mike and Jennifer Marsh, LYM, John Silverman, Professors Alan and Ann Clarke)*

White Hart Tap AL1 1QJ [Keyfield, round corner from Garibaldi]: Friendly neatly kept white-panelled Victorian pub with four changing ales, good value quickly served fresh lunchtime food; tables outside, open all day *(Andy and Jill Kassube)*

STAPLEFORD [TL3017]
Woodhall Arms SG14 3NW [High Rd]: Well kept Batemans and Great Easter beer, good food inc popular Sun lunch in good-sized restaurant; bedrooms *(Gordon Neighbour)*

TRING [SP9211]
☆ *Robin Hood* HP23 5ED [Brook St (B486)]: Décor lightened up by friendly new tenants, well kept Fullers and guest beers, wide choice of enjoyable food inc fresh fish, several comfortable smallish linked areas inc dining conservatory with woodburner, artworks for sale, minimal other decoration; children welcome now, tables on small pleasant back terrace, free public car park nearby *(John Branston, Roger E F Maxwell, BB, Laura Rolfe)*

WADESMILL [TL3517]
Sow & Pigs SG12 0ST [Cambridge Rd, Thundridge (A10 N of Ware)]: Cheerful recently refurbished dining pub, enjoyable generous food from sandwiches up, pleasant staff, changing real ales, good house wines, spacious beamed dining room off central bar with pig ornaments, log fire; no dogs, children in eating areas, tables outside, open all day *(Keith and Janet Morris, Adele Summers, Alan Black, LYM)*

WARE [TL3514]
Rose & Crown SG12 0AD [Watton Rd]: Unpretentious two-bar pub with McMullens ales from central servery, usual food, conservatory; garden behind, open all day Fri-Sun *(Tony Hobden)*

WATTON-AT-STONE [TL3019]
☆ *George & Dragon* SG14 3TA [High St

(B1001)]: Friendly and appealing country dining pub with generally good and imaginative food from sandwiches up, good warmly welcoming staff, Greene King IPA and Abbot and a guest beer, well chosen wines, interesting mix of antique and modern prints on partly timbered walls, big inglenook fireplace, daily papers; children welcome in eating areas, pretty shrub-screened garden with heaters and boules, open all day wknds *(Peter, LYM, Michael Lewis, Mrs E E Sanders, Peter Saville, David and Ruth Shillitoe)*

WESTMILL [TL3626]
☆ *Sword in Hand* SG9 9LQ [village signed off A10 S of Buntingford]: 14th-c colourwashed pub in pretty village, enjoyable food in bar and dining room inc good roast beef on Sun and imaginative puddings, welcoming service, Greene King IPA and a guest beer, beams, pine tables and bare boards or tiles, log fires, fire service memorabilia; children welcome till 8, tables on attractive terrace and in side garden, good play area, has been cl Sun evening and Mon *(Roderick Braithwaite, LYM)*

WESTON [TL2529]
Cricketers SG4 7DA [Damask Green Rd]: Enjoyable pubby food with particularly good chips, well kept ales such as Church End and Fullers London Pride, good friendly service *(Ross Balaam)*

WHEATHAMPSTEAD [TL1712]
Wicked Lady AL4 8EL [Nomansland Common; B651 ½ mile S]: Unpretentious modern chain dining pub, wide range of food inc some unusual dishes, well kept Timothy Taylors Landlord, good choice of wines by the glass, reasonable prices, good attentive young staff, plenty of tables, low beams, lots of stainless steel, conservatory; tables in large garden *(LYM, Lawrence Pearse)*

WILSTONE [SP9014]
Half Moon HP23 4PD [Tring Rd, off B489]: Low-roofed village pub with good value pubby food, well kept Adnams Broadside and a guest such as Jennings Cumberland, friendly efficient staff, big focal log fire, low beams, old local pictures and lots of brasses; handy for Grand Union Canal walks *(Ross Balaam)*

Post Office address codings confusingly give the impression that some pubs are in Hertfordshire, when they're really in Bedfordshire, Buckinghamshire or Cambridgeshire (which is where we list them).

Isle of Wight

Given equivalent quality, pub food prices on the island tend to be a little higher than in many mainland places. However, there are some real treats to be found here, if you know where to look. Fresh seafood, in particular, is a high point. One or two of the pubs on the island even seem to compete to serve the biggest and best crab and lobster salads. Most notable of these are the waterside Crab & Lobster at Bembridge, the thriving New Inn at Shalfleet, and the happy Spyglass in Ventnor – also by the sea. There's plenty of cheery holiday atmosphere to be found at pubs here – look out for entries that have great waterside locations (like the Crab & Lobster and Spyglass above, and the Sun mentioned below), where lovely sea views give you a real vacation feel. The Folly in Cowes, by the Medina Estuary, has a good-fun atmosphere that families find very welcoming. For a more sophisticated but equally relaxed atmosphere try the Seaview Hotel – we do like both its food and its good informal service. Indeed, not for the first time, the Seaview Hotel wins the title of Isle of Wight Dining Pub of the Year. Real ale is not neglected on the island, either, though, as with food, you have to reconcile yourself to paying prices that are rather above average. The constantly changing range served at the interesting Sun at Hulverstone means that last year they offered over 250 different beers. Goddards are the local beers that you are most likely to find in the better pubs here, often at lower prices than mainland beers, with Ventnor ales also quite widely available. In the Lucky Dip section at the end of the chapter, pubs you might like to note particularly are the Buddle at Niton, Horse & Groom at Ningwood and Fishermans Cottage down on Shanklin beach.

ARRETON   SZ5386   MAP 2

White Lion
A3056 Newport—Sandown; PO30 3AA

Pleasantly pubby local with basic food and three real ales

The beamed lounge bar at this welcoming white-painted village house has dark pink walls or stripped brick above stained pine dado, gleaming brass and horse tack, and lots of cushioned wheelback chairs on the patterned red carpet. There is very quiet piped music, and the public bar has a games machine and darts; Badger Best, Fullers London Pride and Timothy Taylors Landlord on handpump. There's also a restaurant, family room and stable room. The pleasant garden has a small play area. More reports please.

🍽 **Straightforward food includes sandwiches, baguettes, ploughman's, soup, chilli, lasagne, vegetable curry, haddock and chips, pie of the day, steaks, and a handful of specials.** *Starters/Snacks: £3.25 to £5.95. Main Courses: £5.95 to £15.95. Puddings: £3.50*

Enterprise ~ Lease Chris and Kate Cole ~ Real ale ~ Bar food (12-9) ~ (01983) 528479 ~ Children in family room ~ Dogs allowed in bar ~ Open 11(12 Sun)-11
Recommended by Lew and Dot Hood, Tony and Penny Burton, Neil and Anita Christopher

BEMBRIDGE

SZ6587   MAP 2

Crab & Lobster 🛏

Foreland Fields Road, off Howgate Road (which is off B3395 via Hillway Road); PO35 5TR

Prime seaside position draws crowds; seafood and other pubby dishes in big helpings, pleasant bedrooms

Picnic sets on the terrace outside this well positioned inn, which is perched on low cliffs within yards of the shore and prettily adorned with flower baskets in summer, take in great views over the Solent. The dining area and some of the bedrooms share the same view. Inside it's roomier than you might expect (just as well as it does get busy) and it's done out in an almost parlourish style, with lots of yachting memorabilia, old local photographs, and a blazing fire in winter months; darts, dominoes and cribbage. Flowers Original, Goddards Fuggle-Dee-Dum and Greene King IPA are on handpump, with decent house wines, about 20 malt whiskies, farm cider and good coffee; piped music (even in the lavatories).

🍴 Lots of fresh local seafood dishes take in crab cakes, spicy baked local crab, grilled salmon fillet, seafood tagliatelle, hot or cold crab and lobster platter for two, and a half or whole lobster. Other generously served dishes include sandwiches (including very good crab ones), soup, assorted pâtés, ploughman's, lasagne, vegetarian curry, mixed grill and steaks, with puddings such as treacle sponge. *Starters/Snacks: £3.50 to £7.95. Main Courses: £7.95 to £23.95. Puddings: £3.95*

Enterprise ~ Lease Richard, Adrian and Pauline Allan ~ Real ale ~ Bar food (12-2.30, 6-9.30) ~ Restaurant ~ (01983) 872244 ~ Children welcome ~ Dogs allowed in bar ~ Open 11-3, 6-11 (11-11 July, Aug); 12-3, 6-10.30(12-10.30 July, Aug) Sun ~ Bedrooms: £40B/£80B

Recommended by R G Trevis, Julie and Bill Ryan, Alan and Paula McCully, Derek and Sylvia Stephenson, Mr and Mrs H J Langley, Mrs Brenda Calver, Glenwys and Alan Lawrence, Pam and Alan Neale, Dr Alan and Mrs Sue Holder

BONCHURCH

SZ5778   MAP 2

Bonchurch Inn

Bonchurch Shute; from A3055 E of Ventnor turn down to Old Bonchurch opposite Leconfield Hotel; PO38 1NU

Unusual italian-owned establishment rambling around central courtyard; italian influence in menu and wines

The bar, restaurant, family room and kitchens at this curious little place are spread around a cosy cobbled courtyard, and the entire set-up is snuggled below a steep, rocky slope. On warm summer days, the courtyard, with its tables, fountain and pergola, has a slightly continental feel. The layout derives from its 1840s Victorian origins as the stables for the nearby manor house. The furniture-packed bar has a good chatty local atmosphere, and conjures up images of salvaged shipwrecks, with its floor of narrow-planked ship's decking, and seats like the ones that old-fashioned steamers used to have. A separate entrance leads to the fairly basic family room (a bit cut off from the congenial atmosphere of the public bar). As well as Scottish Courage Directors and Best tapped from the cask, there are italian wines by the glass and a few french wines; darts, shove-ha'penny, dominoes and cribbage. The pub owns a holiday flat for up to six people.

🍴 Tasty bar food includes italian dishes such as lasagne, tagliatelle carbonara, seafood risotto or spaghetti, as well as traditional dishes such as sandwiches, soup, grilled plaice, chicken cordon bleu and steak; there is a £1 charge for credit cards. *Starters/Snacks: £4.50 to £8.00. Main Courses: £6.95 to £14.95. Puddings: £3.00 to £5.00*

Free house ~ Licensees Ulisse and Gillian Besozzi ~ Real ale ~ Bar food ~ Restaurant ~ (01983) 852611 ~ Children in family room ~ Open 11(12 in winter)-3, 6.30-11; 12-3, 7-10.30 Sun ~ Bedrooms: /£80B

Recommended by W W Burke

If you know a pub's ever open all day, please tell us.

COWES   SZ5092 MAP 2

Folly

Folly Lane – which is signposted off A3021 just S of Whippingham; PO32 6NB

Glorious water views from a very popular place with cheery family holiday atmosphere and moorings; good range of food served from breakfast on

Rumour has it that this splendidly positioned building originated from a french sea-going barge that beached here during a smuggling run in the early 1700s. The laid-back timbered interior certainly gives the sense of a ship's below decks. Straightforward but atmospheric furnishings include wooden tables (ready to be danced on come Saturday night) and chairs, and stools on the bare boards. All in all this is a cheery lighthearted place, with happy staff – not surprisingly it gets very busy in summer. Greene King IPA and Old Speckled Hen and Goddards on handpump; pool and piped music. Idling away the time watching all the nautical activity on the wide Medina estuary from seats on a waterside terrace is a lovely way to spend a summer afternoon – big windows in the bar share the same views. If you're using the river, they have moorings, a water taxi and showers, they even keep an eye on weather forecasts and warnings, and they've long-term parking on the field. They set up a bouncy castle in the landscaped garden in summer. Watch out for the sleeping policemen along the lane if you come by car.

🍽 **Breakfast is served first thing, followed by the lunchtime and (more substantial) evening menus. Dishes are sensibly priced and include soup, sandwiches, cod and chips, beef and ale pie, brie, mushroom and cranberry wellington, chicken caesar salad, roast duck with morello cherry and kirsch sauce, 8oz sirloin steak, and good old favourite puddings such as rhubarb crumble and sticky toffee pudding.** *Starters/Snacks: £3.75 to £6.95. Main Courses: £7.25 to £14.00. Puddings: £3.75 to £4.95*

Greene King ~ Managers Andy and Cheryl Greenwood ~ Real ale ~ Bar food (9-9(10 Sat in summer)) ~ (01983) 297171 ~ Dogs welcome ~ Live music Sat evening and Thurs and Fri evenings in summer ~ Open 11-11(11.45 Sat, 11 Sat in winter); 12-10.30 Sun
Recommended by Mr and Mrs H J Langley, Mrs Linda Campbell, Ian Pickard

FRESHWATER   SZ3487 MAP 2

Red Lion ♀

Church Place; from A3055 at E end of village by Freshwater Garage mini-roundabout follow Yarmouth signpost, then take first real right turn signed to Parish Church; PO40 9BP

Good mix of locals and visiting diners, reasonable range of drinks, decent food and no children at understated tucked-away pub

The grown-up atmosphere here tends to be appreciated by visitors without smaller children. Though the food is a draw, chatting locals occupying stools along the counter keep a pubby feel. The not overdone but comfortably furnished open-plan bar has fires, low grey sofas and sturdy country-kitchen style furnishings on mainly flagstoned floors, and bare board flooring too. The well executed paintings hung round the walls (between photographs and china platters) are by the licensee's brother and are worth a look. Bass, Flowers Original, Wadworths 6X and a guest such as Goddards are kept under light blanket pressure, and the good choice of wines includes 16 by the glass. Fines on mobile phone users go to charity (they collect a lot for the RNLI); there's a games machine but no music. There are tables on a carefully tended grass and gravel area at the back (some under cover), beside which is the kitchen's herb garden, and a couple of picnic-sets in a quiet square at the front have pleasant views of the church. The pub is virtually on the Freshwater Way footpath that connects Yarmouth with the southern coast at Freshwater Bay.

🍽 **Food is listed on blackboards behind the bar and, as well as lunchtime filled baguettes and ploughman's, might include soup, whitebait, crab stuffed mushrooms, battered cod and mushy peas, halibut steak with lemon butter, mushroom stroganoff, venison medallions with port and redcurrant sauce, crab or lobster salad and rib-eye steak, with puddings such as apple crumble, black cherry trifle or bread and butter pudding.** *Starters/Snacks: £5.00 to £8.00. Main Courses: £9.00 to £17.00. Puddings: £5.50*

Enterprise ~ Lease Michael Mence ~ Real ale ~ Bar food (12-2, 6.30(7 Sun)-9) ~
(01983) 754925 ~ Children over 10 ~ Dogs welcome ~ Open 11.30-3, 5.30-11; 11.30-4, 6-11
Sat; 12-3, 7-11 Sun

*Recommended by Rob Winstanley, Minda and Stanley Alexander, Paul Boot, Peter Titcomb, Alan and Paula McCully,
Di and Mike Gillam, Derek and Sylvia Stephenson*

HULVERSTONE   SZ3984   MAP 2

Sun

B3399; PO30 4EH

**Lovely thatched building with terrific coastal views, down-to-earth old-world appeal and
four quickly changing real ales**

This thatched whitewashed country pub is in a captivating setting, with views from its
charming and secluded cottagey garden (which has a terrace and several picnic-sets)
down to a wild stretch of coast. It's very well positioned for some splendid walks along
the cliffs, and up Mottistone Down to the prehistoric Long Stone. The bar is full of
friendly chatter and is unpretentiously traditional and low-ceilinged, with a fire blazing
at one end (with horsebrasses and ironwork hung around the fireplace), a nice mix of old
furniture on flagstones and floorboards, and stripped brick stone and walls; piped music, darts and
board games. Leading off from one end is the traditionally decorated more modern dining
area, with large windows making the most of the view. The four quickly changing real ales
are quite a feature here. Last year they got through 264 different beers from brewers
such as Hampshire, Shepherd Neame, Wychwood and Youngs. Staff are helpful and
friendly.

🍴 **Bar food includes sandwiches, whitebait, ploughman's, sausage and mash, lasagne,
curry, pie of day and mixed grill. The specials board might include duck and hoi-sin spring
rolls, soup, griddled black pudding with cranberry dip, swordfish steak, whole trout and
8oz fillet steak. They also do an 'all you can eat' curry night on Thursdays, and Sunday
roasts.** *Starters/Snacks: £3.95 to £5.95. Main Courses: £5.95 to £14.95. Puddings: £3.50*

Enterprise ~ Lease Chris and Kate Cole ~ Real ale ~ Bar food (12-9) ~ (01983) 741124 ~
Children welcome ~ Dogs allowed in bar ~ Open 11-11; 12-10.30 Sun

Recommended by Alan and Paula McCully, Phil Merrin, J Hilary, Louise Locock

SEAVIEW   SZ6291   MAP 2

Seaview Hotel 🍽 ♟ 🛏

High Street; off B3330 Ryde—Bembridge; PO34 5EX

ISLE OF WIGHT DINING PUB OF THE YEAR

**Well run, small relaxed hotel with informal bar, delicious food, top-notch attentive
service, good wine list, and lovely bedrooms**

This very well run smashing 200-year-old hotel is civilised yet enjoyably relaxed, with a
bustling atmosphere, proper old-fashioned service, and reception rooms ranging from
pubby to formal dining. The bay-windowed bar at the front has an impressive array of
naval and merchant ship photographs, as well as Spy nautical cartoons for *Vanity Fair*,
original receipts for Cunard's shipyard payments for the *Queen Mary* and *Queen Elizabeth*,
and a line of close-set tables down each side on the turkey carpet. There's a much more
down-to-earth atmosphere in the simpler back bar, which has traditional wooden
furnishings on bare boards, lots of seafaring paraphernalia around its softly lit ochre
walls, and a log fire. Drinks include Goddards and a couple of guests such as Greene King
IPA and Shepherd Neame Bishops Finger on handpump, a good selection of malt whiskies,
a farm cider (in summer) and a good wine list (including a couple from local vineyards);
TV, darts and board games. Tables on little terraces on either side of the path to the front
door take in glimpses of the sea and coast, and some of the attractive bedrooms also
have a sea view. They may ask to keep your credit car behind the bar if you run a tab.

🍴 Very good well presented and generously served bar food includes soup, hot crab ramekin, filled baguettes, fish pie, venison and wild boar sausages and mash, creamed leek, mushroom and stilton gratin, sirloin steak, battered haddock and mushy peas, and puddings such as sticky toffee pudding and vanilla rice pudding with chocolate soup; Sunday roast. *Starters/Snacks: £4.50 to £7.25. Main Courses: £8.95 to £14.95. Puddings: £4.95 to £5.50*

Free house ~ Licensee Andrew Morgan ~ Real ale ~ Bar food (12-2.30, 7-9.30) ~ Restaurant ~ (01983) 612711 ~ No children under five in restaurant ~ Dogs welcome ~ Open 10-11(midnight Sat); 12-10.30 Sun ~ Bedrooms: £100B/£120B

Recommended by Michael Sargent, Derek and Sylvia Stephenson, Steve and Liz Tilley, David H T Dimock, B N F and M Parkin, Rob Winstanley, Peter Titcomb, David Glynne-Jones

SHALFLEET   SZ4089 MAP 2

New Inn 🍽 ☐ 🍺
A3054 Newport—Yarmouth; PO30 4NS

Cheerful old pub strong on fresh seafood, good beers and wines too

This popular 18th-c fisherman's haunt is just a short stroll from the marshy inlets of the yacht-studded Newtown estuary. Its strengths lie equally in its cheery welcome, good food and well kept beer. The partly panelled flagstone public bar has yachting photographs and pictures, a boarded ceiling, scrubbed pine tables, and a log fire in the big stone hearth. The carpeted beamed lounge bar has boating pictures and a coal fire, and the snug and gallery have slate floors, bric-a-brac and more scrubbed pine tables. Flowers Original, Goddards, Marstons Pedigree and Ventnor Golden are kept under a light blanket pressure, and they stock around 60 wines; piped music.

🍴 A big draw here is their famous seafood platter and crab and lobster salads, which are served alongside up to 12 different types of fresh fish – there might be crab and prawn cocktail, grilled grey mullet with mustard and horseradish sauce and grilled sole with lime, ginger and rocket. Other dishes on the changing menu could be soup, sausage with sage and mustard mash, lamb steak with moroccan-style bean salad and 8oz fillet steak with garlic tiger prawns. You will need to book, and there may be double sittings in summer. *Starters/Snacks: £4.00 to £7.00. Main Courses: £7.00 to £15.00. Puddings: £3.00 to £5.00*

Enterprise ~ Lease Mr Bullock and Mr McDonald ~ Real ale ~ Bar food (12-2.30, 6-9.30) ~ Restaurant ~ (01983) 531314 ~ Children welcome ~ Dogs allowed in bar ~ Open 12-3, 6-11

Recommended by Peter Titcomb, B N F and M Parkin, Steve Jones, Paul Boot, Julie and Bill Ryan, Minda and Stanley Alexander, Steve and Liz Tilley, Martin and Karen Wake, Andrew Stephenson

SHORWELL   SZ4582 MAP 2

Crown
B3323 SW of Newport; PO30 3JZ

Popular rambling pub with good choice of decent food, pretty stream-side garden with play area

In warmer months the tranquil tree-sheltered garden at this country pub draws quite a crowd of holidaymakers. Closely spaced picnic-sets and white garden chairs and tables are set out by a sweet little stream, that broadens out into a small trout-filled pool, and a decent children's play area is within easy view. Inside, four rooms spread pleasantly around a central bar, and the chatty regulars who gather here lend some local character. The beamed knocked-through lounge has blue and white china in an attractive carved dresser, old country prints on stripped stone walls, other individual furnishings, and a winter log fire with a fancy tile-work surround. Black pews form bays around tables in a stripped-stone room off to the left, with another log fire; piped music. Badger Tanglefoot, Flowers Original and Wadworths 6X are well kept alongside a guest such as Goddards, all on handpump.

🍴 Enjoyable bar food includes sandwiches, ploughman's, soup, pâté of the day, crab cocktail, ploughman's, lasagne, vegetable curry and fisherman's pie, with daily specials such as venison sausages on smoked bacon mash, lemon crusted mackerel, steak and kidney pie, lamb tagine, haddock kedgeree, pheasant with prune and port jus, and puddings such as treacle tart, fruit crumble and local ice-creams. *Starters/Snacks: £3.50 to £7.95. Main Courses: £4.95 to £14.95. Puddings: £2.50 to £3.95*

Enterprise ~ Lease Mike Grace ~ Real ale ~ Bar food ~ (01983) 740293 ~ Children welcome ~ Dogs welcome ~ Open 10.30-3, 6-10.30; 10.30(12 Sun)-10.30 Sat; 10.30-3, 6-10.30 every day in winter

Recommended by Mr and Mrs H J Langley, M and GR, Phil and Sally Gorton, Louise Locock

VENTNOR
SZ5677   MAP 2

Spyglass 🍺

Esplanade, SW end; road down very steep and twisty, and parking nearby can be difficult – best to use the pay-and-display (free in winter) about 100 yards up the road; PO38 1JX

Interesting waterside pub with appealing collection of seafaring bric-a-brac, half a dozen very well kept beers and enjoyable food

This cheerful place is in a super position, perched on the sea wall just above the beach – tables outside on a terrace have lovely views over the water. A fascinating jumble of seafaring memorabilia fills the snug quarry-tiled interior, with anything from wrecked rudders, ships' wheels, old local advertisements and rope-makers' tools to stuffed seagulls, an Admiral Benbow barometer and an old brass telescope; games machine and piped music. Half a dozen well kept hand-pulled real ales include Badger First Gold and Tanglefoot and Ventnor Gold, alongside three guests such as Badger Fursty Ferret, Goddards Fuggle-Dee-Dum and Ventnor Molly Downer. There are strolls westwards from here along the coast towards the Botanic Garden as well as heftier hikes up on to St Boniface Down and towards the eerie shell of Appuldurcombe House (muddy boots are not a problem here).

🍴 Generous helpings of very tasty bar food are promptly served and include sandwiches, soup, seafood chowder, ploughman's, crab tart, sausages and mash, steak and kidney or fisherman's pie, sirloin steak, and seafood stew, as well as several seasonal fish dishes and crab and lobster salad. *Starters/Snacks: £4.50 to £5.95. Main Courses: £6.95 to £18.95. Puddings: £4.50*

Free house ~ Licensees Neil and Stephanie Gibbs ~ Real ale ~ Bar food (12-9.30) ~ (01983) 855338 ~ Children welcome ~ Dogs allowed in bar ~ Live entertainment every night ~ Open 10.30-11 ~ Bedrooms: /£70B

Recommended by Colin Gooch, Tony and Penny Burton, Daniel and Lynda Friel, Mr and Mrs H J Langley, Steve and Liz Tilley, B N F and M Parkin, Andrew Stephenson, Neil and Anita Christopher

LUCKY DIP

Besides the fully inspected pubs, you might like to try these Lucky Dips recommended to us and described by readers (if you do, please send us reports: www.goodguides.co.uk).

ARRETON [SZ5484]
Fighting Cocks PO30 3AR [Hale Common, just S]: Large recently extended and refurbished dining pub with enjoyable usual food, friendly licensees and staff, real ales, good wines by the glass, adults' restaurant and separate flagstoned family room *(Helen Jukes, Neil and Anita Christopher)*
BRADING [SZ6087]
Smart Fox PO36 0DG [High St]: Stylishly reworked under newish licensees, with wall pews and comfortable modern dining chairs on bare boards, stripped stonework, low

beams and log fire, generous enjoyable food inc home-baked breads in relaxed bar and carpeted dining room, well kept real ales, decent wines by the glass, old well *(Helen Maynard)*
FISHBOURNE [SZ5592]
Fishbourne Inn PO33 4EU [from Portsmouth car ferry turn left into Fishbourne Lane no through road]: Spacious and neatly kept open-plan mock-Tudor pub peacefully placed nr ferry terminal and coast path, quick friendly service even when packed, good value food (all day Sun) from nice crab

sandwiches to grills and fresh fish, real ales such as Goddards and Wadworths 6X, comfortable modern repro furniture, open fire and bright and airy dining area; wheelchair access, tables in good-sized attractive front garden, open all day wknds *(Michael Tack, Lew and Dot Hood, John Coatsworth, BB, Liz and Brian Barnard, Derek and Sylvia Stephenson)*

NEWPORT [SZ4989]

Castle PO30 1BQ [High St]: Attractively and comfortably refurbished in traditional style with dark beamery, lattice-effect windows, log-effect gas fire and reproduction furniture, it is in fact genuinely ancient – as the flagstones and massive end stone wall show; real ales such as Badger, smiling service, fresh food all day (lunchtime only Sun/Mon), civilised bar and dining area; some live music, usually Fri/Sat; dogs welcome, disabled access, tables in heated and sheltered back courtyard, open all day *(anon)*

NINGWOOD [SZ3989]

☆ *Horse & Groom* PO30 4NW [A3054 Newport—Yarmouth, a mile W of Shalfleet]: Rambling old pub taken in hand and attractively refurbished by owners of New Inn at Shalfleet (see main entries), now a good roomy family dining pub with sensibly priced food all day inc Sun carvery, friendly helpful staff, real ales inc Goddards, comfortable fireside leather armchairs; plenty of tables outside, play area, open all day *(Guy and Caroline Howard)*

NITON [SZ5075]

☆ *Buddle* PO38 2NE [St Catherines Rd, Undercliff; off A3055 just S of village, towards St Catherines Point]: Plenty of character in prettily updated former smugglers' haunt, heavily varnished beams, big flagstones, broad stone fireplace, friendly relaxed service, Adnams and local island ales, wide food choice (can be very busy at lunchtime), amiable dogs, attractive bay-windowed games barn with bar billiards; clifftop views from well cared for sloping garden and terraces, good walk to lighthouse; open all day *(Rob Winstanley, Tony and Penny Burton, K Almond, Derek and Sylvia Stephenson, LYM, Steve Jones, Louise Locock)*

ROOKLEY [SZ5183]

Chequers PO38 3NZ [S of village, Chequers Inn Rd/Niton Rd]: Big family pub with mother-and-baby room, good children's games in plain and roomy family area as well as large safely fenced play area outside, downland views, usual food all day from sandwiches and baked potatoes up, puddings in display cabinet, real ales such as Goddards and Wadworths 6X, close-set tables in unpretentious dining lounge with log fire, flagstoned locals' bar with pool, darts and TV; children and dogs welcome, handy for Godshill, open all day *(LYM, Alan and Paula McCully, Wendy Cox)*

SANDOWN [SZ5984]

Clancys PO36 8LT [Beachfield Rd]: Friendly modern bar/restaurant, bright and spacious, strong on cocktails, fair choice of wines, reasonably priced food freshly made by antipodean licensees, from snacks and pizzas to evening meals – they do their best to meet special wishes; may be cl winter Sun/Mon evenings *(David Hunt)*

SHANKLIN [SZ5881]

☆ *Fishermans Cottage* PO37 6BN [bottom of Shanklin Chine]: Thatched shoreside cottage in terrific setting surrounded by beached boats, tucked into the cliffs, steep walk down beautiful chine, lovely seaside walk to Luccombe; flagstones and some stripped stone, repro furniture, nets slung from low beams, old local pictures and bric-a-brac, simple bar lunches from sandwiches and baked potatoes up, more enterprising evening choice, convivial atmosphere, helpful staff, well kept Goddards, frequent entertainment; piped music; wheelchair access, children welcome, tables out on terrace, open all day in summer when fine *(Michael Tack, BB)*

Village Pub PO37 6NS [High St, Old Village]: Pretty thatched building with good range of Goddards ales, enjoyable food inc good dressed crab, pleasant staff, cheerful L-shaped bar with dining area, large upstairs restaurant; small pleasant heated back terrace, open all day *(Paul Boot, Alan and Paula McCully)*

VENTNOR [SZ5677]

St Boniface Arms PO38 1LT [High St]: Refurbished and renamed by former long-serving licensees of the Crab & Lobster, welcoming traditional-style pub/restaurant with fine choice of wines by the glass, Bass and guest beers such as Black Sheep, family room; terrace tables *(Steve and Liz Tilley)*

☆ *Volunteer* PO38 1ES [Victoria St]: Chatty and unpretentious little two-room local, cheerful and warmly welcoming licensees, half a dozen or so well kept changing ales such as Butcombe, Courage, Greene King Abbot and Ventnor Gold, reasonable prices, coal fire, comfortable red plush banquettes, darts, the local game of rings, perhaps sandwiches or finger buffet if you order specially; quiet piped music; no children, quiz nights, open all day *(BB, David Ellerington, Andrew Stephenson)*

WHITWELL [SZ5277]

☆ *White Horse* PO38 2PY [High St]: Popular thatched pub with well kept Badger Best, Fullers London Pride, Greene King Abbot, Ventnor Golden and Wells & Youngs Best, wide range of good value generous food from pub staples to some more restauranty dishes and good Sun roasts, quick, helpful and friendly service, large cheery high-ceilinged family dining area with small beamed bar and second area (with darts) off; may be piped music; picnic-sets on pleasant lawn *(Betty Laker, W W Burke, BB)*

Kent

As this county is so close to home for us, we are glad that it now has so many thriving pubs! Those doing particularly well at the moment include the friendly Unicorn at Bekesbourne, the civilised and foody Three Chimneys near Biddenden, the interestingly furnished Wheatsheaf at Bough Beech, the unchanging and charming Gate Inn by the marshes at Boyden Gate, the distinctive old Woolpack, another marshside pub, down at Brookland, the easy-going Queens just outside Hawkhurst, the well run and welcoming Harrow on Ightham Common, the foody Mundy Bois at Pluckley, the rather smart Chaser at Shipbourne, the unspoilt Red Lion at Snargate, the well run and civilised Lord Raglan near Staplehurst (excellent value beer) and the friendly Pepper Box at Ulcombe. Added to these are five interesting new entries: the French-run Timber Batts at Bodsham, with good restaurant food and sensible bar snacks; the Royal Oak, a second entry for us in Brookland, a charming all-rounder; the Plough at Ivy Hatch, another place for good food – somewhat restauranty, but pleasantly informal; the Granville at Lower Hardres, stylish and up to date, with enjoyable food, yet friendly and warm-hearted; and the Coastguard at St Margaret's Bay, another welcoming all-rounder, with terrific sea views. In the country as a whole, it's getting much easier to find really good food in pubs. To some extent, Kent has been rather left behind by this trend, though its pub food prices are if anything higher than average. So, for a special meal out, you have to know exactly where to head for. Places we'd particularly recommend are the Timber Batts, the Three Chimneys near Biddenden, the Bottle House near Penshurst and Sankeys in Tunbridge Wells. Of these, Sankeys, with its good food, particularly seafood, in a buoyant pubby atmosphere is Kent Dining Pub of the Year. Drinks prices in the county are, like food, higher than average. The main local brewer is Shepherd Neame. Goachers is increasingly widely available in good pubs, often at an attractive price; another good local beer to look out for is Larkins, and the much newer Westerham is already making quite a name for itself locally. Finally, it's worth noting that the Lucky Dip section at the end of the chapter has a good few particularly appealing pubs, such as the Griffins Head at Chillenden, Fountain at Cowden, Kentish Rifleman at Dunks Green (recent fire damage being repaired as we go to press), Green Man at Hodsoll Street, Duke William at Ickham, Cock at Luddesdown, Rock and Spotted Dog both in or near Penshurst, Sportsman in Seasalter and Bell at Smarden.

Looking for a pub with a really special garden, or in lovely countryside, or with an outstanding view, or right by the water? They are listed separately, at the back of the book.

BEKESBOURNE

TR1856   MAP 3

Unicorn

Coming from Patrixbourne on A2, turn left up Bekesbourne Hill after passing railway line (and station); coming from Littlebourne on A257, pass Howletts Zoo – Bekesbourne Hill is then first turning on right; turning into pub car park is at bottom end of the little terrace of houses on the left (the pub is the far end of this terrace); CT4 5ED

Small, friendly pub, simply furnished bars and enjoyable food

New owners took over here just after we had gone to press last year and reports since then have been very enthusiastic. It's a smashing little pub with just a few scrubbed old pine tables and bentwood café chairs on worn floorboards, a canary ceiling and walls above a dark green dado, minimal décor, and a handful of bar stools against the neat counter. Adnams Broadside and Shepherd Neame Master Brew on handpump, with a carefully chosen wine list, local cider, apple and pear juice and a fair choice of coffees and teas. There's a piano in one corner, plenty of board games and piped music. A side terrace is prettily planted and there's a garden with benches and boules. Parking in front is tricky but there is a large car park at the back which you get to by the small track at the end of the adjacent terrace of cottages.

🍽 **Good enjoyable food now includes filled baguettes, soup, smoked mackerel pâté, avocado and seafood salad, cauliflower cheese topped with bacon, home-cooked ham and egg, lambs liver and bacon with a rich onion gravy, local cod in beer batter, popular steak in ale pie, interesting daily specials, and puddings such as rhubarb and apple crumble and lemon torte with honeycomb ice-cream.** *Starters/Snacks: £3.75 to £4.50. Main Courses: £7.50 to £9.95. Puddings: £3.95*

Free house ~ Licensees Mike and Monica Head ~ Real ale ~ Bar food (not Sun evening or Mon or Tues) ~ No credit cards ~ (01227) 830210 ~ Children welcome ~ Open 12-3, 6-11; 12-3 Sun; closed Sun evening, all day Mon and Tues

Recommended by Emma Ryan, Kevin Thorpe, Mr and Mrs G Wolstenhulme, Brian Munday, Basil Wynbergen

BIDDENDEN

TQ8238   MAP 3

Three Chimneys

A262, 1 mile W of village; TN27 8LW

Pubby beamed rooms of considerable individuality, log fires, imaginative food and pretty garden

This is just the place to head for after a visit to nearby Sissinghurst Gardens. It's a pretty, old-fashioned cottage with a series of low-beamed, very traditional little rooms with plain wooden furniture and old settles on flagstones and coir matting, some harness and sporting prints on the stripped brick walls and good log fires. Adnams Best, Wadworths 6X and a seasonal beer from Harveys tapped straight from casks racked behind the counter, several wines by the glass, local cider and apple juice and ten malt whiskies. The simple public bar has darts, dominoes and cribbage. French windows in the civilised candlelit bare-boards restaurant open on to the garden (ploughman's only out here) with picnic-sets in dappled shade, and the smart terrace area has tables and outdoor heaters.

🍽 **Extremely good – if not cheap – bar food includes soup, ploughman's, baked field mushrooms with caramelised red onions and grilled goats cheese, thai-style crab cakes, sun-dried tomato, roasted red pepper, basil and goats cheese risotto cake on wilted spinach and tomato sauce, seared king scallops with wine wine, bacon and parmesan sauce, lambs liver and bacon with port and red onion gravy and roast cod fillet in brown butter with capers, lemon and prawns.** *Starters/Snacks: £3.95 to £7.95. Main Courses: £11.95 to £18.95. Puddings: £3.95 to £6.50*

Free house ~ Licensee Craig Smith ~ Real ale ~ Bar food (12-2, 6.30-9; 12-2.30, 6-9 Sun) ~ Restaurant ~ (01580) 291472 ~ Children allowed but no provision for them ~ Dogs welcome ~ Open 11.30-3, 6-11; 12-3.30, 6.30-10.30 Sun; closed 25 and 31 Dec

Recommended by Mr and Mrs Mike Pearson, Glenwys and Alan Lawrence, the Didler, Alan and Anne Driver, John Evans, Michael and Anne Brown, Cathryn and Richard Hicks, N R White, Alan Cowell, B and M Kendall, J P Humphery, M G Hart

BODSHAM   TR1045   MAP 3

Timber Batts 🍴 🍷

Following Bodsham, Wye sign off B2068 keep right at unsigned fork after about 1½ miles; TN25 5JQ

Lovely french food (bar snacks too) and charming French owner in cottagey old country pub, good real ales, enjoyable wines and fine views

Originally a 15th-c farmhouse, this hilltop pub is tucked away in lovely country with fine wide-spreading valley views from straightforward seats and tables in the back garden. It's run by a personable and charming French landlord who is keen to keep a proper pubby feel and local drinkers in the public bar – despite a strong emphasis on the extremely good french food. The little heavy-beamed cottagey area to the right has a couple of comfortable armchairs and two wicker chairs each with a small table, an open fire in the brick fireplace with photographs of the pub above it, some hunting horns and a few high bar chairs; down a little step is more of a drinking part with a mix of cushioned dining chairs, a wall settle, two long tables and several bar stools. There are various froggy cushions and knick-knacks on the window sills (the pub is known locally as Froggies at the Timber Batts). To the left of the entrance is the large but informal beamed restaurant with a happy mix of attractive stripped pine tables and pews and all sorts of dark tables and dining chairs on the carpet, wine labels in a glass frame and wine box tops on the walls, a nice stripped pine cupboard in one corner, and a brick fireplace. Adnams Bitter, Fullers London Pride and Woodfordes Wherry on handpump and very good french wines by the glass (some from Mr Gross's cousin's vineyard). With such a pleasant, chatty feel, we felt on our inspection visit that the piped pop music was unnecessary.

🍴 **As well as proper pub food such as filled baguettes, croque monsieur omelettes, ham and egg and sausage and mash, the delicious french food using top local produce (cooked by the landlord's son) might include interesting soup, prawns in herbs and garlic with coquilles st jacques, stuffed mussels, pigeon supreme with ginger, duck confit salad, moules marinière with frites, rack of lamb with herbs, prime fillet of beef with roquefort sauce, and puddings such as tarte tatin and crème brûlée; lovely french cheeses.**
Starters/Snacks: £5.00 to £9.50. Main Courses: £6.00 to £19.00. Puddings: £5.50

Free house ~ Licensee Joel Gross ~ Real ale ~ Bar food (12-2.30, 7-9.30) ~ Restaurant ~ (01233) 750237 ~ Children welcome ~ Dogs welcome ~ Magic night usually first Tues of month ~ Open 12-2.30, 6.30-11; 12-3, 7-10.30 Sun; closed Mon

Recommended by John and Enid Morris, Stephen Allford, Derek Thomas

BOUGH BEECH   TQ4846   MAP 3

Wheatsheaf 🍷 🍺

B2027, S of reservoir; TN8 7NU

Ex-hunting lodge with lots to look at, fine range of local drinks, popular food and plenty of seats in appealing garden

This is a friendly pub with a warm welcome for all – and even when very busy, which it usually is – service manages to remain helpful and efficient. There's a lot of history and masses of interesting things to look at and the neat central bar and the long front bar (with an attractive old settle carved with wheatsheaves) have unusually high ceilings with lofty oak timbers, a screen of standing timbers and a revealed king post; dominoes and board games. Divided from the central bar by two more rows of standing timbers – one formerly an outside wall to the building – are the snug and another bar. Other similarly aged features include a piece of 1607 graffiti, 'Foxy Holamby', thought to have been a whimsical local squire. On the walls and above the massive stone fireplaces there are quite a few horns and heads as well as a sword from Fiji, crocodiles, stuffed birds, swordfish spears and a matapee. Thoughtful touches include piles of smart magazines, tasty nibbles and winter chestnuts to roast. Quite a choice of local drinks such as Harveys Best, Shepherd Neame Master Brew, and from a village just three miles away, Westerham Brewery Grasshopper Kentish Bitter and 1965 on handpump; three farm ciders, a decent wine list, several malt whiskies, summer Pimms and winter mulled wine. Outside is appealing too, with plenty of seats, flowerbeds and fruit trees in the sheltered side and back gardens. Shrubs help divide the garden into various areas, so it doesn't feel too crowded even when it's full.

🍴 **As well as light lunchtime dishes such as filled ciabattas, ploughman's, moules marinière with frites, smoked haddock and spring onion fishcakes and pie and mash, the popular food might include soup, duck and fig terrine with plum and apple chutney, local pork and herb sausages, vegetable curry, lambs liver, bacon and black pudding, wok-fried prawns, roasted guinea fowl with caramelised orange and ginger stuffing and Cointreau and red wine sauce, and puddings like chocolate and hazelnut meringue roulade or mango and coconut cheesecake.** *Starters/Snacks: £4.95 to £7.95. Main Courses: £8.95 to £14.95. Puddings: £3.95 to £4.50*

Enterprise ~ Lease Liz and David Currie ~ Real ale ~ Bar food (12-10) ~ (01732) 700254 ~ Children welcome in one part of bar only ~ Dogs welcome ~ Open 11am-11.30pm(midnight Sat)

Recommended by Mike and Sue Losebey, Will Watson, A J Ward, Bob and Margaret Holder, Mrs Jane Kingsbury, R and M Thomas, Mr and Mrs Mike Pearson, Andrew Wallace, Malcolm and Jane Levitt, Michael and Anne Brown, GHC, Tina and David Woods-Taylor, Debbie and Neil Hayter, B J Harding, Christopher Turner, Grahame Brooks

BOYDEN GATE   TR2265   MAP 3

Gate Inn ★ 🍺 £

Off A299 Herne Bay—Ramsgate – follow Chislet, Upstreet signpost opposite Roman Gallery; Chislet also signposted off A28 Canterbury—Margate at Upstreet – after turning right into Chislet main street keep right on to Boyden; the pub gives its address as Marshside, though Boyden Gate seems more usual on maps; CT3 4EB

Friendly, long-serving landlord in unchanging pub, well kept beers, simple food, and tame ducks and geese to feed

Known locally as Marshside, this is a fine example of an unspoilt and traditional village pub. It's been run by the same landlord for 33 years now and you can be quite sure of a genuinely warm welcome – whether you are a regular or a visitor. The comfortably worn interior is properly pubby with an inglenook log fire serving both the well worn quarry-tiled rooms, flowery-cushioned pews around tables of considerable character, hop bines hanging from the beams and attractively etched windows. Shepherd Neame Master Brew, Spitfire and a seasonal ale are tapped from the cask and you can also get interesting bottled beers, half a dozen wines by the glass, and country wines; board games. The sheltered hollyhock flowered garden is bounded by two streams with tame ducks and geese (they sell bags of food, 10p), and on fine summer evenings you can hear the contented quacking of a multitude of ducks and geese, coots and moorhens out on the marshes.

🍴 **Tasty bar food includes lots of different sandwiches and melts, soup, a big choice of baked potatoes and burgers, ploughman's, home-made vegetable flan, spicy hotpots and gammon and egg.** *Starters/Snacks: £3.00 to £4.90. Main Courses: £6.25. Puddings: £2.80*

Shepherd Neame ~ Tenant Christopher Smith ~ Real ale ~ Bar food ~ No credit cards ~ (01227) 860498 ~ Well behaved children in eating area of bar and family room ~ Dogs welcome ~ Open 11-3, 6-11; 10-4, 7-11 Sun

Recommended by Norman Fox, Bruce Eccles, Kevin Thorpe, David and Ruth Shillitoe

BROOKLAND   TQ9825   MAP 3

Royal Oak
High St; TN29 9QR

Sympathetic modern refurbishments to lovely old building with comfortable atmosphere, bar food and garden

Contemporary interior design works nicely with the ancient architectural features at this well proportioned cream-painted pub. The bar is light and airy with creamy walls, pale solid timbering and lovely big windows hung with forest green velvet curtains. Leather upholstered chairs around new oak tables and one nice old pew spread over a floor surface that runs from flagstones into oak boards then bricks; piped music and woodburner too. Locals pop in all evening to sit at the granite-topped counter (with Adnams and Harveys Sussex on handpump) on high cream leather backed bar stools and chat to the informative landlord (do ask him about the local area if you get a chance). His equestrian interests are manifest in a lovely set of racing watercolours and couple of signed photographs on the lime white wall panelling in the bar, and in a rather special set of Cecil Aldin prints displayed in the restaurant (with its well spaced tables and big inglenook fireplace). French windows from here open on to a terrace with metal chairs, and a narrow garden, which is laid out around the terrace (with picnic-sets), and there are quaint views of the ancient church and graveyard next door. There's a basketball hoop and some toys out here.

🍴 **Decent bar food from the menu or specials board might include starters such as rabbit and mushroom won tons, quail egg and bacon salad and poached salmon and smoked salmon with prawns and cream cheese and chive dressing, main courses such as battered cod and chips, roast pork belly on roast potatoes and parsnips, three types of sausage and mash, grilled lamb loin steak with black pudding and port and rosemary sauce, and puddings such as honeycomb crunch ice-cream and summer fruits in champagne jelly.** *Starters/Snacks: £4.50 to £6.50. Main Courses: £7.50 to £15.95. Puddings: £4.75 to £5.95*

Enterprise ~ Lease David Rhys Jones ~ Real ale ~ Bar food (12-2.30, 6.30-9.30) ~ Restaurant ~ (01797) 344215 ~ Children welcome ~ Dogs welcome ~ Open 12-3, 6-11; closed Sun evening ~ Bedrooms: /£60(£70B)

Recommended by M Coates

Woolpack

On A259 from Rye, about 1 mile before Brookland, take the first right turn signposted Midley where the main road bends sharp left, just after the expanse of Walland Marsh; OS Sheet 189 map reference 977244; TN29 9TJ

15th-c pub with simple furnishings, massive inglenook fireplace, big helpings of tasty straightforward food and large garden

A new barbecue area has been built in the big garden here and they are hoping to arrange summer Sunday evening hog roasts and so forth; plenty of picnic-sets under parasols, well developed shrubs and pretty hanging baskets, and it's all nicely lit up in the evenings. Inside this pretty 15th-c white pub there's plenty of marshland character and a good, friendly bustling atmosphere. The ancient entrance lobby has an uneven brick floor and black-painted pine-panelled walls, and to the right, the simple quarry-tiled main bar has basic cushioned plank seats in the massive inglenook fireplace (with a lovely log fire on chilly days), a painted wood-effect bar counter hung with lots of water jugs and some very early ships' timbers (maybe 12th c) in the low-beamed ceiling; a long elm table has shove-ha'penny carved into one end and there are other old and newer wall benches, chairs at mixed tables with flowers and candles and photographs of locals on the walls. To the left of the lobby is a sparsely furnished little room and an open-plan family room; piped music. Shepherd Neame Master Brew, Spitfire and a seasonal brew on handpump; look out for the two pub cats, Liquorice and Charlie Girl.

🍴 **Big helpings of good bar food include sandwiches, filled baguettes and baked potatoes, ploughman's, soup, garlic mushrooms, sausages, ham and egg, steak pie, vegetable curry, spaghetti bolognese, battered cod, partridge with bacon in a red wine and cream sauce, and puddings such as honey and cinnamon pudding or cherry pie.** *Starters/Snacks: £3.75 to £6.50. Main Courses: £4.75 to £14.95. Puddings: £3.75*

Shepherd Neame ~ Tenant Barry Morgan ~ Real ale ~ Bar food (12-2.30, 6-9; all day in summer and all day winter weekends) ~ (01797) 344321 ~ Children in family room ~ Dogs welcome ~ Open 11-3, 6-11; 11-11 Sat (and all July and August); 12-10.30 Sun

Recommended by MJVK, Stephen Harvey, Arthur Pickering, V Brogden, Peter Meister, Mike Gorton, Kevin Thorpe

---

Half pints: by law, a pub should not charge more for half a pint than half the price of a full pint, unless it shows that half-pint price on its price list.

CHIDDINGSTONE
TQ5045 MAP 3

Castle Inn ♀

Village signposted from B2027 Tonbridge—Edenbridge; TN8 7AH

Cosy old pub in pretty National Trust village with well liked food and beer and secluded garden

Records show there was a building called Waterslip House here in 1420, and this rambling old place's stone foundations probably go back as far as that – so it could be where Anne Boleyn found shelter when she was stranded in a terrible blizzard on her way to nearby Hever. The handsome, carefully modernised beamed bar has well made settles forming booths around the tables, cushioned sturdy wall benches, an attractive mullioned window seat in one small alcove, and latticed windows (a couple of areas are no smoking); darts and board games. Larkins Traditional and winter Porter (both brewed in the village) and Harveys Best on handpump, an impressive wine list and quite a few malt whiskies. There are tables in front of the building facing the church with more in the pretty secluded vine-hung garden. The licensees publish three circular walks from the village.

🍴 Priced in euros and sterling, there's a good value two- and three-course lunchtime bar menu with dishes such as soup, venison terrine, a vegetarian choice, local rabbit stew and breast of chicken marinated in thyme, with evening choices like marinated tiger prawns, goats cheese on chargrilled aubergine, pork tenderloin on spinach tagliatelle with mushroom sauce, mediterranean risotto and local rack of lamb with lightly minted gravy; puddings include mixed fruit crumble and crème brûlée. *Starters/Snacks: £3.95 to £5.35. Main Courses: £6.15 to £7.75. Puddings: £3.95*

Free house ~ Licensee Nigel Lucas ~ Real ale ~ Bar food (11(12 Sun)-6, 7-9.30) ~ Restaurant ~ (01892) 870247 ~ Children welcome away from public bar ~ Dogs allowed in bar ~ Open 11-11; 12-11 Sun

Recommended by Will Watson, Kevin Thorpe, Dr Danny Nicol, N R White, GHC

GROOMBRIDGE
TQ5337 MAP 3

Crown

B2110; TN3 9QH

Charming village pub with quite a bit of bric-a-brac in snug, low-beamed rooms, and enjoyable food and drink

Overlooking the steep village green, this tile-hung pub is part of a row of pretty cottages; there are picnic-sets out in front on a wonky but sunny brick terrace. Inside, the snug left-hand room has old tables on worn flagstones and a big brick inglenook with a cosy winter log fire – arrive early for a table in here. The other low-beamed rooms have roughly plastered walls, some squared panelling and timbering, and a quite a bit of bric-a-brac, from old teapots and pewter tankards to antique bottles. Walls are decorated with small topographical, game and sporting prints and there's a circular large-scale map with the pub at its centre. The end room (normally for eaters) has fairly close-spaced tables with a variety of good solid chairs, and a log-effect gas fire in a big fireplace. Greene King IPA, Larkins Traditional Ale and Harveys Best on handpump and up to ten wines by the glass. There's a back car park and pub garden. A public footpath across the road beside the small chapel leads through a field to Groombridge Place Gardens. More reports please.

🍴 Well liked bar food at lunchtime includes filled baguettes and baked potatoes, bruschetta with different toppings, pasta with tuna, oregano, chilli and tomatoes, cumberland sausage and onion gravy, beer-battered haddock and home-cooked ham and eggs with evening dishes such as grilled goats cheese on baby spinach with sunblush tomatoes and balsamic syrup, smoked duck breast with apple and celeriac remoulade and walnuts, rump of lamb with rosemary potatoes and red wine jus, chicken in pesto sauce with mushrooms, bacon and duck breast with an orange and Cointreau sauce. *Starters/Snacks: £3.50 to £5.50. Main Courses: £7.90 to £13.50. Puddings: £4.00 to £5.00*

Free house ~ Licensee Peter Kilshaw ~ Real ale ~ Bar food (12-3, 6.30-9.30; 12-4 Sun) ~
Restaurant ~ (01892) 864742 ~ Children welcome ~ Dogs allowed in bar ~ Open 11-3, 6-11;
11-11 Sat; 12-11 Sun; 12-5 Sun in winter; closed winter Sun evening ~ Bedrooms:
£40/£45(£60S)

Recommended by Peter Meister, B J Harding, B and M Kendall, Mrs Margo Finlay, Jörg Kasprowski

HAWKHURST   TQ7630   MAP 3

Queens
Rye Road (A268 E); TN18 4EY

**Attractively decorated spreading rooms in pleasant inn; usefully open all day for bar meals
plus breakfast and afternoon tea**

Although this wisteria-clad old place might look a bit like a hotel, the atmosphere inside
has a proper pubby feel and you can expect a warm welcome from the friendly staff. The
spreading interior is opened up and appealingly decorated in keeping with its age (it was
first recorded as an inn in the 16th c). There are comfortable fireside sofas at the front
and further in, terracotta, sand or pea-green colourwashes give an airy feel despite the
heavy low beams; also, a nice mix of old oak tables (candlelit at night) on bare boards
with plenty of scattered rugs. Around to the right, the piano bar is where they have the
live music and serve breakfast and teas (they may show DVDs at times); newspapers to
read and piped music. Fullers London Pride and Harveys Best on handpump. The tables on
decking at the front (more in a side courtyard) are pleasant to sit at. More reports please.

🍴 **Good, well liked bar food includes sandwiches or filled baguettes, ploughman's, soup,
an antipasti plate, wild mushroom risotto, ham and egg, sausages with onion gravy, steak
in Guinness pie, crispy beer-battered haddock, tasty coq au vin, duck with savoy cabbage,
bacon and rosemary jus, daily specials, and puddings such as warm chocolate brownies
with chocolate sauce and summer berry pavlova.** *Starters/Snacks: £4.95 to £7.95. Main
Courses: £7.95 to £15.95. Puddings: £4.95*

Enterprise ~ Tenant Janelle Tresidder ~ Real ale ~ Bar food (8.30am-9.30pm(till 10 Sat and
Sun)) ~ Restaurant ~ (01580) 753577 ~ Children welcome ~ Jazz Sun lunchtime ~ Open
11-midnight(1am Sat); 11-11 Sun ~ Bedrooms: £50S/£85S

*Recommended by Jason Caulkin, Louise English, Kevin Thorpe, Grahame Brooks, Peter Meister, Arthur Pickering,
Rod Stoneman, Mr and Mrs Mike Pearson, Laurence and Kim Manning, John Branston, Richard and
Emily Whitworth*

HOLLINGBOURNE   TQ8354   MAP 3

Windmill ♀
*A mile from M20 junction 8: A20 towards Ashford (away from Maidstone), then left into
B2163 – Eyhorne Street village; ME17 1TR*

Small pubby core but mainly set for dining; sunny little garden

Handy for the M20, this attractive pub has new licensees. The pubbiest part can be found
tucked away up steps towards the back with bar stools around the island serving bar:
Flowers IPA, Harveys Best and Shepherd Neame Masterbrew on handpump and several
wines by the glass. Under heavy low black beams, several small or smallish mainly
carpeted areas link together around this central core, sometimes partly separated by
glazed or stained-glass panels; the solid pub tables have padded country or library chairs.
Soft lighting, black timbers in ochre walls, shelves of books and the good log fire in the
huge inglenook fireplace add up to a pleasantly old-world feel. Piped music. A neatly
kept sunny little garden has picnic-sets under cocktail parasols and a play area. More
reports please.

You can send us reports through our website: www.goodguides.co.uk or directly to us
at The Good Pub Guide, FREEPOST TN1569, Wadhurst, E Sussex TN5 7BR.

⁅🍴⁆ Bar food at lunchtime now includes sandwiches, filled baguettes and filled baked potatoes, ploughman's, ham and eggs, and battered cod; also, chicken liver pâté, deep-fried brie wedges with raspberry coulis, burgers with different sauces, knuckle of ham with leek sauce, oriental wok-tossed vegetables, cajun chicken salad, a pie of the day, salmon fillet with parsley and cheese sauce, and daily specials. *Starters/Snacks: £4.25 to £6.95. Main Courses: £7.95 to £22.95. Puddings: £3.50 to £4.95*

Enterprise ~ Lease Lee and Jan Atkinson ~ Real ale ~ Bar food (12-2.30, 6-10; 12-10 Sat(till 9.30 Sun)) ~ Restaurant ~ (01622) 880280 ~ Children welcome ~ Dogs welcome ~ Open 11-3, 5-11; 11-11 Sat; 12-10.30 Sun; closed 25 Dec

Recommended by E D Bailey, Alan Cowell, Stephen Moss

IGHTHAM COMMON   TQ5855   MAP 3

Harrow ⚲

Signposted off A25 just W of Ightham; pub sign may be hard to spot; TN15 9EB

Emphasis on good food in friendly, smart dining pub, fresh flowers and candles and pretty back garden

With a friendly welcome from the landlord and his staff and very good food, it's not surprising that this civilised country inn is so well liked. Two attractively decorated rooms have fresh flowers and candles, smart dining chairs on the herringbone-patterned wood floor and a winter fire. The bigger room is painted a cheerful sunny yellow above the wood-panelled dado, there's a charming little antiquated conservatory and a more formal dining room. Greene King IPA and Abbot on handpump and several wines by the glass There are tables and chairs out on a pretty little pergola-enclosed back terrace and the pub is handy for Ightham Mote.

⁅🍴⁆ Very enjoyable, if not cheap, the bar food (which can be eaten anywhere except the dining room) might include interesting soups, coarse pork pâté with an apricot compote, goats cheese tart, popular salmon and chive fishcakes with citrus sauce, tagliatelle with wild mushrooms and spinach, sausage and mash, calves liver and bacon with shallots and red wine, duck with plum tarte tatin and bubble and squeak, and puddings such as poached pear with red wine jelly and vanilla ice-cream, and rhubarb crumble and custard. *Starters/Snacks: £5.00 to £7.50. Main Courses: £9.50 to £18.50. Puddings: £5.50*

Free house ~ Licensees John Elton and Claire Butler ~ Real ale ~ Bar food (12-2, 6-9; not Sun evening or Mon) ~ Restaurant ~ (01732) 885912 ~ Children in family room and dining room only ~ Open 12-3, 6-11; closed Sun evening and all day Mon; 25 and 26 Dec and 1 Jan

Recommended by Brian Root, Andrea Rampley, Mr and Mrs Mike Pearson, Heather and Dick Martin, Gordon Ormondroyd, Stuart and Doreen Ritchie, Derek Thomas, Michael and Anne Brown, Alistair Forsyth, Mrs A Green, E D Bailey, Catherine and Richard Preston, GHC, Dr L R Canning, N R White

IVY HATCH   TQ5854   MAP 3

Plough ⁅🍴⁆ ⚲

Village signposted off A227 N of Tonbridge; High Cross Road; TN15 0NL

Emphasis on interesting restaurant-style food (bar snacks too) in nicely laid out dining pub; quite a choice of drinks and helpful, friendly staff

Carefully refurbished, this tile-hung country dining pub is mainly popular for its particularly good food but drinkers are made very welcome, too. There's a pleasantly informal atmosphere, a cosy bar with an inglenook fireplace and Harveys Best and a couple of guests from Goachers, Larkins or Westerham Brewery on handpump, a thoughtful wine list, local fruit juices and a cocktail menu. There's a happy hour between 5.30 and 6.30 for some drinks; efficient service by attentive knowledgeable staff and piped jazz. The conservatory-style dining room with its plum-coloured walls is very attractive. They may keep your credit card while you eat outside.

If we know a pub does summer barbecues, we say so.

🍴 Letting the top quality local ingredients speak for themselves, the imaginative food includes lunchtime bar snacks such as sandwiches, ploughman's and salads like sweet chilli beef or goats cheese and toasted pine nuts, as well as soup, corn-fed chicken and cream cheese roulade, sweet potato and aubergine terrine, pork cutlet with cauliflower mash and dijon mustard sauce, cod fillet with braised fennel and tomato concasse, langoustines and white wine and herb sauce, barbary duck breast with buttered spinach on ribbons of yellow courgettes and puddings such as rich dark chocolate sponge with chocolate sauce and pistachio and cashew nut tart with vanilla ice-cream. *Starters/Snacks: £4.95 to £7.95. Main Courses: £10.95 to £22.95. Puddings: £4.75*

Free house ~ Licensee Michelle Booth ~ Real ale ~ Bar food (12-2.30(2 in restaurant), 5.30-7(7-10 in restaurant); 12-3 Sun (only a light menu Sun evening)) ~ Restaurant ~ (01732) 810100 ~ Children welcome ~ Dogs allowed in bar ~ Live music summer Sun evenings ~ Open 11-3, 5.30-11; 12-10.30 Sun

Recommended by Robert Gomme, Simon and Sally Small, Evelyn and Derek Walter, B and M Kendall, Darren Burrows, M Greening

LANGTON GREEN   TQ5439   MAP 3

Hare ♀

A264 W of Tunbridge Wells; TN3 0JA

Interestingly decorated Edwardian pub with a fine choice of drinks and popular food

The choice of drinks in this Edwardian roadside pub continues to impress readers: Greene King IPA, Abbot and Old Speckled Hen and a guest such as Ruddles County on handpump, over 100 whiskies, 20 vodkas, 18 wines by the glass and farm ciders. The front bar tends to be where drinkers gather and the knocked-through interior has big windows and high ceilings that give a spacious feel. Décor, more or less in period with the building, runs from dark-painted dados below light walls, 1930s oak furniture, and turkey carpets on stained wooden floors to old romantic pastels, and a huge collection of chamber-pots hanging from one beam. Interesting old books, pictures and two huge mahogany mirror-backed display cabinets crowd the walls of the big room at the back, which has lots of large tables (one big enough for at least a dozen) on a light brown carpet; from here french windows open on to picnic-sets on a big terrace, and nice views of the tree-ringed village green. Parking is limited. More reports please.

🍴 Bar food such as sandwiches, foie gras terrine with sauternes jelly, moules marinière, steakburger topped with cheese and tomato, home-cooked ham with free-range eggs, sweet potato and chilli tortellini with spinach and sunblush tomatoes, sausages and mash, smoked cod and bacon fishcakes, duck breast with hazelnut sauce and saffron mash, and puddings like banoffi pie with fruit coulis and apple and cinnamon crumble with custard. *Starters/Snacks: £4.50 to £7.00. Main Courses: £8.00 to £15.00. Puddings: £4.75 to £5.25*

Brunning & Price ~ Tenant Christopher Little ~ Real ale ~ Bar food (11-9.30(10 Fri and Sat); 12-9 Sun) ~ (01892) 862419 ~ Children in eating area till 7pm ~ Dogs allowed in bar ~ Open 11-11(midnight Fri and Sat); 11-10.30 Sun

Recommended by Colin and Janet Roe, Mrs Margo Finlay, Jörg Kasprowski, Derek Thomas

LOWER HARDRES   TR1453   MAP 3

Granville ♀

B2068 S of Canterbury; Faussett Hill, Street End; CT4 7AL

Surprisingly modern décor in several connected rooms, a fine choice of wines, good service and popular food; cosy little shady garden

Inside this much extended and, from outside, slightly unprepossessing building, it's quite a surprise to find such a light and airy pub with attractive contemporary furnishings. Several linked areas include comfortable squashy sofas, a nice mix of pale and dark tables with cushioned dining chairs, and – through shelves of large coloured church candles – a glimpse of the chefs hard at work in the kitchen. The appealing décor includes interesting modern photographs and animal lino cuts on pale yellow walls above a dark red dado, a couple of large modern candelabra-type ceiling lights, one area with the floor attractively patterned in wood and tiles, and an unusual central fire with a large conical hood. There's a shelf with daily papers and board games, and a proper public bar with settles, farmhouse chairs and a woodburning stove. Shepherd Neame Master Brew and a seasonal beer on handpump and good wines from a long handwritten blackboard list; very helpful, friendly bar ladies. French windows lead to the garden with rustic-style picnic-sets under a large spreading tree, and there are some more traditional picnic-sets on a small sunny terraced area.

🍴 Bar food comes with slices of freshly made herby bread and a little dish of olives: rock oysters, moules marinière, grilled baby dover sole, chicken liver parfait with caramelised onions, roast pork belly with apple sauce, crispy duck with smoked chilli salsa and sour cream, organic salmon with balsamic vinaigrette, chicken breast with truffle cream sauce, whole roast wild bass with garlic and rosemary, and puddings such as panettone bread and butter pudding and rhubarb sorbet with burnt cream. *Starters/Snacks: £4.95 to £7.50. Main Courses: £11.95 to £17.95. Puddings: £5.50*

Shepherd Neame ~ Tenant Gabrielle Harris ~ Real ale ~ Bar food (not Sun evening or Mon) ~ (01227) 700402 ~ Children welcome ~ Dogs allowed in bar ~ Open 12-3, 5.30-11; 12-11 Sat
Recommended by Colin McKerrow, R Goodenough

NEWNHAM   TQ9557   MAP 3

George

The Street; village signposted from A2 just W of Ospringe, outside Faversham; ME9 0LL

Old-world village pub with open-plan rooms, a fair choice of drinks and food, and seats in a spacious garden; pleasant walks nearby

Even if you haven't visited this friendly local for a while, a return trip will show no changes. A series of spreading open-plan rooms still has hop-strung beams, rugs on stripped, polished floorboards, stripped brickwork, gas-type chandeliers, open fires, candles and lamps on handsome tables and attractively upholstered mahogany settles. Shepherd Neame Master Brew, Spitfire, and a seasonal beer on handpump, a dozen wines by the glass; piped music. The spacious sheltered garden has some picnic-sets and there are pleasant nearby walks.

🍴 Generous helpings of nice bar food include lunchtime sandwiches, filled baguettes and baked potatoes, ploughman's, ham and eggs, bangers and mash, vegetable curry, steak and kidney pudding, daily specials, and puddings such as gypsy tart and banoffi pie. *Starters/Snacks: £4.95 to £7.95. Main Courses: £8.95 to £16.95. Puddings: £4.25 to £5.75*

Shepherd Neame ~ Tenants Chris and Marie Annand ~ Real ale ~ Bar food ~ Restaurant ~ (01795) 890237 ~ Children welcome ~ Open 11-3.30, 6.30-11; 12-4, 7-11 Sun
Recommended by B and M Kendall, Norman Fox, N R White

OARE   TR0163   MAP 3

Shipwrights Arms

S shore of Oare Creek, E of village; coming from Faversham on the Oare road, turn right into Ham Road opposite Davington School; or off A2 on B2045, go into Oare village, then turn right towards Faversham, and then left into Ham Road opposite Davington School; OS Sheet 178 map reference 016635; ME13 7TU

Remote pub with simple little bars; in marshland with lots of surrounding bird life

After enjoying one of the surrounding walks, this unspoilt old tavern – in the middle of marshland – is just the place for a restorative drink; there are seats in the large garden. Inside, the three simple little bars are dark, separated by standing timbers and wood partitions or narrow door arches. A medley of seats runs from tapestry cushioned stools and chairs to black wood-panelled built-in settles forming little booths, and there are pewter tankards over the bar counter, boating jumble and pictures, pottery boating figures, flags or boating pennants on the ceilings, several brick fireplaces and a good woodburning stove. Look out for the electronic wind gauge above the main door, which takes its reading from the chimney. A beer from Goachers and Whitstable and maybe a couple of guests tapped from the cask; piped local radio. Parking can be difficult at busy times.

🍴 **Standard bar food such as sandwiches, ploughman's and sausage and mash.** *Starters/Snacks: £3.95 to £4.95. Main Courses: £6.95 to £11.65. Puddings: £3.95 to £4.95*

Free house ~ Licensees Derek and Ruth Cole ~ Real ale ~ Bar food (not Sun evening or winter Mon) ~ (01795) 590088 ~ Children welcome away from bar area ~ Dogs allowed in bar ~ Open 11-3(4 Sat), 6-11; 12-4, 6-11 Sun; closed Mon Oct-Feb

Recommended by the Didler, R B Gardiner, N R White, Andrea Rampley, Colin Moore, Kevin Thorpe, Louise English, Gary Smith

PENSHURST

TQ5142   MAP 3

Bottle House 🍴

Coldharbour Lane, Smarts Hill; leaving Penshurst SW on B2188 turn right at Smarts Hill signpost, then bear right towards Chiddingstone and Cowden; keep straight on; TN11 8ET

Busy pub with low-beamed bar and cosy areas leading off, deservedly popular food, sunny terrace, nearby walks

Bustling and popular, this tile-hung country pub has now been run by the same family for 21 years. The low-beamed and neatly kept front bar has a well worn brick floor that extends behind the polished copper-topped bar counter and big windows that look on to a terrace with climbing plants, hanging baskets, and picnic-sets under cocktail parasols. The simply decorated red-carpeted main bar has massive hop-covered supporting beams, two large stone pillars with a small brick fireplace (with a stuffed turtle to one side), and old paintings and photographs on mainly plastered walls; quite a collection of china pot lids, with more in the low-ceilinged dining room. Several cosy little areas lead off the main bar – one is covered in sporting pictures right up to the ceiling and another has pictures of dogs. Harveys Bitter and Larkins Best on handpump and several wines by the glass; piped music. Good surrounding walks.

🍴 **Well liked bar food served by efficient staff might include club sandwiches and large filled baguettes, soup, goose liver and sauternes pâté, filo prawns with hoi sin sauce, deep-fried sesame coated brie with plum and apple chutney, chilli con carne, home-baked honey and mustard ham and eggs, vegetable lasagne, beer-battered cod, local sausages with onion gravy, cajun chicken, pheasant breast stuffed with wild boar and bacon en croûte, and puddings such as honey and cinnamon sponge with custard and warm chocolate fondant with white chocolate ice-cream.** *Starters/Snacks: £4.25 to £6.50. Main Courses: £7.95 to £16.95. Puddings: £4.95*

Free house ~ Licensees Gordon and Val Meer ~ Real ale ~ Bar food (12-9.30) ~ Restaurant ~ (01892) 870306 ~ Children welcome ~ Dogs allowed in bar ~ Open 11-11; 11-10.30 Sun; closed 25 Dec

Recommended by Cathryn and Richard Hicks, E D Bailey, Tony Brace, Tina and David Woods-Taylor, Howard and Margaret Buchanan, Louise English, Martin and Pauline Jennings, Mr and Mrs J Robertson, John Branston, B J Harding, Sharon and Alan Corper, Bob and Margaret Holder

---

Several well known guide books make establishments pay for entry, either directly or as a fee for inspection. These fees can run to many hundreds of pounds.
We do not. Unlike other guides, we never take payment for entries. We never accept a free meal, free drink, or any other freebie from a pub. We do not accept any sponsorship – let alone from commercial schemes linked to the pub trade.
All our entries depend solely on merit.

PLUCKLEY   TQ9243   MAP 3

Dering Arms ♀

Pluckley Station, which is signposted from B2077; or follow Station Road (left turn off Smarden Road in centre of Pluckley) for about 1.3 miles S, through Pluckley Thorne; TN27 0RR

Fine fish dishes plus other good food in striking building, stylish main bar, carefully chosen wines, and roaring log fire; refurbished bedrooms

The bedrooms in this striking old building have been refurbished this year and they are hoping to add new bedrooms in a converted stable block. The stylishly plain high-ceilinged main bar has a solid country feel with a variety of good wooden furniture on stone floors, a roaring log fire in the great fireplace, country prints and some fishing rods. The smaller half-panelled back bar has similar dark wood furnishings, and an extension to this area has a woodburning stove, comfortable armchairs and sofas and a grand piano; board games. Goachers Gold Star, Old Ale and a beer named for the pub on handpump, a good wine list, local cider and quite a few malt whiskies. Classic car meetings (the long-standing landlord has a couple) are held here on the second Sunday of the month.

🍽 Bar food, with quite an emphasis on fresh local fish, includes soup, soft herring roes with crispy smoked bacon, chicken livers with a brandy cream sauce, a pie of the day, skate wing with capers and beurre noisette, confit of duck with wild mushroom sauce, salmon fishcakes with sorrel sauce, fillet of bass with minted leeks and bacon and a red wine sauce, daily specials, and puddings such as lemon posset and tiramisu parfait with coffee sauce; the fruits de mer platter needs 24 hours' notice. *Starters/Snacks: £4.25 to £6.95. Main Courses: £9.45 to £21.95. Puddings: £4.25 to £6.95*

Free house ~ Licensee James Buss ~ Real ale ~ Bar food (not Sun evening, not Mon) ~ Restaurant ~ (01233) 840371 ~ Children in Club Room bar ~ Dogs allowed in bar ~ Open 11.30-3, 6-11; 12-3 Sun; closed Sun evening, all day Mon, 25-28 Dec ~ Bedrooms: £40(£60S)/£50(£75S)

Recommended by Derek Thomas, Grahame Brooks, Bruce Eccles, Peter Meister, Laurence Wynbergen, Ann and Colin Hunt, Philip and Cheryl Hill, Mr and Mrs Mike Pearson, M G Hart

Mundy Bois

Mundy Bois – spelled Monday Boys on some maps – off Smarden Road SW of village centre; TN27 0ST

Friendly country pub with relaxing bars, traditional bar food and more elaborate restaurant menu, and play area in nice garden

Run by friendly people, this quietly set pub is popular for its good food. The relaxed main bar with its massive inglenook fireplace (favourite spot of Ted the pub labrador) leads on to a little pool room; TV, darts and piped music. The small snug bar has chesterfield sofas beside a roaring log fire and seats on the oak flooring and is also used as a pre and post drinking area for the restaurant. Shepherd Neame Master Brew, Wadworths 6X and a guest beer on handpump and nine wines by the glass. There are seats in the pretty garden, which has a good children's play area, and you can eat on the terrace which looks over to the hillside beyond.

🍽 Carefully cooked bar food includes toasted sandwiches and filled baguettes, ploughman's, soup, venison pâté, half a dozen garlic snails, pasta with tomato and vegetable sauce, ham and eggs, four-egg omelettes, steak and kidney pie, chicken curry, aberdeen angus burger, honey-glazed duck breast with garlic potatoes, bass with vegetable spaghetti in white wine sauce, and puddings such as light coffee and vanilla crème brûlée and white and dark chocolate cake with vanilla ice-cream; you can also eat from the pricier and more elaborate restaurant menu in the bar. *Starters/Snacks: £3.95 to £6.50. Main Courses: £6.25 to £15.50. Puddings: £4.25*

Free house ~ Licensees Peter and Helen Teare ~ Real ale ~ Bar food ~ Restaurant ~ (01233) 840048 ~ Children welcome ~ Dogs allowed in bar ~ Open 11.30-3, 6-11; 11.30-11 Fri and Sat; 12-10.30 Sun; closed 25 Dec

Recommended by Lea Randolph, B and M Kendall, N R White, Philip and Cheryl Hill, Rod Stoneman, M G Hart

SELLING

TR0455   MAP 3

Rose & Crown

Signposted from exit roundabout of M2 junction 7: keep right on through village and follow Perry Wood signposts; or from A252 just W of junction with A28 at Chilham follow Shottenden signpost, then right turn signposted Selling, then right signposted Perry Wood; ME13 9RY

Nice summer garden, winter log fires, hop-covered beams and several real ales

In summer, the cottagey garden behind this country pub is pretty and charmingly planted with climbers, ramblers and colourful plants; plenty of picnic-sets, a children's play area and outdoor heaters. The flowering tubs and hanging baskets in front are pretty too. Inside, there are comfortably cushioned seats, winter log fires in two inglenook fireplaces, hop bines strung from the beams, and fresh flowers; steps lead down to another timbered area. Adnams Southwold, Goachers Mild, Harveys Sussex Best and Robinsons Unicorn on handpump; piped music, cribbage, dominoes, cards and shut-the-box. Good surrounding walks. More reports please.

🍴 **Standard bar food includes sandwiches, filled baked potatoes, ploughman's, soup, whitebait, steak and mushroom pudding, vegetarian pancake, fish pie, daily specials, and puddings.** *Starters/Snacks: £2.50 to £5.00. Main Courses: £6.95 to £9.95. Puddings: £4.00*

Free house ~ Licensees Tim Robinson and Vanessa Grove ~ Real ale ~ Bar food (not Mon evenings) ~ Restaurant ~ (01227) 752214 ~ Children welcome ~ Dogs allowed in bar ~ Open 11-3(3.30 in winter), 6.30-11; 11-11 Sat; 12-10.30 Sun; 12-3.30, 7-10.30 Sun in winter

Recommended by the Didler, E D Bailey, M and R Thomas, Gerry and Rosemary Dobson, N R White, Kevin Thorpe, Paul Jones

SHIPBOURNE

TQ5952   MAP 3

Chaser ♀

Stumble Hill (A227 N of Tonbridge); TN11 9PE

Comfortable, civilised country pub, log fires, popular food, quite a few wines by the glass, and covered and heated outside terrace

With friendly staff and a good bustling atmosphere, this rather smart pub is liked by those wanting just a drink as well as diners here to enjoy the popular food. There are several open-plan areas that meander into each other, all converging on a large central island bar counter: stripped wooden floors, frame-to-frame pictures on deepest red and cream walls, stripped pine wainscoting, an eclectic mix of solid old wood tables (with candles) and chairs, shelves of books, and open fires. A striking school chapel-like restaurant, right at the back, has dark wood panelling and a high timber vaulted ceiling. French windows open on to a covered and heated central courtyard with teak furniture and big green parasols, and a side garden, with the pretty church rising behind, is nicely enclosed by hedges and shrubs. Greene King IPA and Abbot and a couple of guest beers on handpump, quite a few wines by the glass and several malt whiskies; piped music and board games. There is a small car park at the back or you can park in the lane opposite by a delightful green; farmer's market on Thursday morning.

🍴 **Good bar food includes interesting sandwiches, ploughman's, soup, chicken liver parfait with red onion marmalade, fried scallops on cauliflower purée with black pudding and wild mushrooms, local bangers and mash with roasted onion gravy, tagliatelle with paprika chicken, mushrooms, peppers and coriander, honey-roast ham with two free-range eggs, salmon and haddock fishcakes with lemon mayonnaise, half shoulder of lamb with dijon mustard and brioche crumb and redcurrant, red wine and rosemary gravy, daily specials, and puddings such as apple and raspberry crumble and lemon zest cheesecake with ginger ice-cream.** *Starters/Snacks: £3.95 to £7.95. Main Courses: £6.95 to £15.95. Puddings: £4.25 to £4.95*

Whiting & Hammond ~ Lease Darren Somerton ~ Real ale ~ Bar food (12-9.30(9 Sun)) ~ (01732) 810360 ~ Children welcome ~ Dogs welcome ~ Open 11am-midnight; 12-11 Sun

Recommended by E D Bailey, Gerry and Rosemary Dobson, Gordon Ormondroyd, Jerry Green, Louise English, GHC, Tony Brace, Derek Thomas

SNARGATE
TQ9928   MAP 3

Red Lion ★ ◀

B2080 Appledore—Brenzett; TN29 9UQ

Unchanging, simple tavern, good chatty atmosphere and straightforward furnishings; no food

For 97 years this quite unspoilt village local has been run by the same family. Three simple little rooms still have their original cream tongue and groove wall panelling, a couple of heavy beams in a sagging ceiling, dark pine Victorian farmhouse chairs on bare boards, lots of old photographs and other memorabilia, and a coal fire; outdoor lavatories, of course. Lighting is dim but they do light candles at night. One small room, with a frosted glass wall through to the bar and a sash window looking out to a cottage garden, has only two dark pine pews beside two long tables, a couple more farmhouse chairs and an old piano stacked with books. Toad in the hole, darts, shove-ha'penny, cribbage, dominoes, nine men's morris and table skittles. Goachers Light and Mild, and a couple of guests from brewers such as Grand Union or Whitstable are tapped straight from casks on a low rack behind an unusual shop-like marble-topped counter (little marks it out as a bar other than a few glasses on two small shelves, some crisps and half a dozen spirits bottles); you can also get Double Vision cider from nearby Staplehurst and country wines.

🍴 **No food.**

Free house ~ Licensee Mrs Jemison ~ Real ale ~ No credit cards ~ (01797) 344648 ~ Children in games room ~ Dogs allowed in bar ~ Open 12-3, 7-11

Recommended by Pete Baker, Kevin Thorpe, the Didler, Phil and Sally Gorton, Louise English, MP

ST MARGARET'S BAY
TR3744   MAP 3

Coastguard ♀ ◀

Off A256 NE of Dover; keep on down through the village towards the bay, pub off on right; CT15 6DY

Bustling and friendly seaside place with terrific views, plenty of fish on menu, nautical décor, fine range of drinks, helpful uniformed staff

This is Britain's closest pub to France – so much so that when you enter the car park, your mobile phone thinks it actually is there and you are then paying more for your calls; the views across the sea to France are tremendous. It's a cheerful and lively place and the warm, carpeted, wood-clad bar has lots of shipping memorabilia, Cottage Great Bear, Grand Union Bitter and Northumberland Fog on the Tyne on handpump, interesting continental beers, 40 malt whiskies, Weston's cider and a carefully chosen wine list; good service even when busy. The restaurant has wooden dining chairs and tables on a wood-strip floor and more fine views; piped music. There are lots of tables out on a prettily planted balcony that look across the Straits of Dover and more down by the beach below the National Trust cliffs.

🍴 **Using only local, carefully sourced produce with quite an emphasis on fish, the enjoyable food includes sandwiches, pâté with tarragon and orange, marinated seafood salad, popular hot-devilled crab, roast mediterranean vegetables with couscous and goats cheese, beer-battered cod, free-range chicken with wild mushrooms and sage butter, fish pie, daily specials, and puddings such as dark chocolate and porter cake and Baileys crème brûlée; the cheeseboard is particularly good.** *Starters/Snacks: £4.00 to £5.50. Main Courses: £9.50 to £26.00. Puddings: £4.50 to £8.50*

Free house ~ Licensee Nigel Wydymus ~ Real ale ~ Bar food (12.30-2.45, 6.30-8.45) ~ Restaurant ~ (01304) 853176 ~ Children allowed away from bar ~ Dogs allowed in bar ~ Open 11-11(10.30 Sun); closed 25 Dec

Recommended by Chris Parkins, Arthur Pickering, Kevin Thorpe

Waterside pubs are listed at the back of the book.

STAPLEHURST   TQ7846   MAP 3

Lord Raglan

About 1½ miles from town centre towards Maidstone, turn right off A229 into Chart Hill
Road opposite Chart Cars; OS Sheet 188 map reference 785472; TN12 0DE

Simple and relaxed with chatty locals, beams and hops, good value bar snacks, and nice little terrace

Even when this friendly country pub is very busy – which it usually is – the licensees and their staff keep things running smoothly. There's an enjoyably cheerful feel and the interior is cosy but compact, with a narrow bar – you walk in almost on top of the counter and chatting locals – widening slightly at one end to a small area with a big log fire in winter. In the other direction it works its way round to an intimate area at the back, with lots of wine bottles lined up on a low shelf. Low beams are covered with masses of hops, and the mixed collection of comfortably worn dark wood furniture on quite well used dark brown carpet tiles and nice old parquet flooring is mostly 1930s. Goachers Light, Harveys Best, and a guest like Westerham Brewery Finchcocks on handpump, a good wine list, and local farm cider. Small french windows lead out to an enticing little high-hedged terraced area with green plastic tables and chairs, and there are wooden picnic-sets in the side orchard; reasonable wheelchair access.

🍽 **Popular bar food includes sandwiches, filled baguettes, ploughman's, garlic mushrooms, ham or sausage and egg, macaroni cheese, grilled lamb chops, poached salmon with lemon and herb sauce, stir-fried beef and peppers, swordfish steak with lime butter, and puddings.** *Starters/Snacks: £3.95 to £5.95. Main Courses: £7.95 to £19.50. Puddings: £4.50*

Free house ~ Licensees Andrew and Annie Hutchison ~ Real ale ~ Bar food (12-2.30, 7-10; not Sun) ~ (01622) 843747 ~ Children welcome ~ Dogs welcome ~ Open 12-3, 6.30(6 Sat)-11; closed Sun

Recommended by Mr and Mrs Mike Pearson, John and Joan Calvert, Sue Williams

STODMARSH   TR2160   MAP 3

Red Lion 🛏

High Street; off A257 just E of Canterbury; CT3 4BA

Super country pub with very cheerful landlord, lots to look at, super choice of food and drink and pretty garden with roaming ducks and chickens

This marvellous place is a cross between a proper country pub and an antiques shop and you could spend ages just looking at all the things on the shelves and walls. It's run by an exceptionally obliging if slightly eccentric and cheerful landlord who will go out of his way to be the perfect host. Full of character, several idiosyncratic rooms wrap themselves around the big island bar. You'll find hops all over the place, wine bottles (some empty and some full) crammed along mantelpieces and along one side of the bar, all manner of paintings and pictures, copper kettles and old cooking implements, well used cookery books, big stone bottles and milk churns, trugs and baskets, and old tennis racquets and straw hats; one part has a collection of brass instruments, sheet music all over the walls, and some jazz records, and a couple of little stall areas have hop sacks draped over the partitioning. There are green-painted, cushioned mate's chairs around a mix of nice pine tables, lit candles in unusual metal candleholders, a big log fire, and fresh flowers; piped jazz, and bat and trap. Greene King IPA and maybe a guest are tapped straight from the cask, and they've a good wine list with several by the glass, excellent summer Pimms and winter mulled wine, and cider. There are picnic-sets under umbrellas in the back garden, with pretty flowerbeds and roaming ducks and chickens; conservatory has been added this year. Please note that the bedrooms though much enjoyed by readers don't have their own bathrooms.

🍽 **Using allotment vegetables and home-reared meat, the good food might include filled baguettes (not Sunday lunch or Saturday evening), smoked haddock and salmon fishcakes with chilli sauce, baby leeks wrapped in parma ham with a light hollandaise sauce, stuffed portabello mushroom with vegetable ravioli, rack of local lamb stuffed with** rosemary and garlic, baked wild salmon fillet with a home-grown herb and almond sauce, beef and cider pie, duck breast with a summer fruit and vintage port sauce, and puddings such as banoffi pie and brandy bread and butter pudding. *Starters/Snacks: £4.95 to £6.95. Main Courses: £10.95 to £15.95. Puddings: £4.50*

Free house ~ Licensee Robert Whigham ~ Real ale ~ Bar food ~ Restaurant ~ (01227) 721339 ~ Children welcome ~ Dogs allowed in bar ~ Open 10.30am-11.30pm(11pm Sun) ~ Bedrooms: £45/£70

Recommended by Kevin Thorpe, Norman Fox, John Saville, B and M Kendall, M G Hart, Conor McGaughey

STOWTING
TR1241   MAP 3

Tiger

3.7 miles from M20 junction 11; B2068 N, then left at Stowting signpost, straight across crossroads, then fork left after ¼ mile and pub is on right; coming from N, follow Brabourne, Wye, Ashford signpost to right at fork, then turn left towards Posting and Lyminge at T junction; TN25 6BA

Peaceful country pub with friendly staff, interesting traditional furnishings and open fires; good walking country

After a stroll on the Wye Downs or while walking the North Downs Way, you'll find this 17th-c pub is a peaceful place to relax. It's traditionally furnished and decorated with plain chairs and dark pews built in against the walls, candles stuck into bottles, faded rugs on the dark floorboards, and some floor-to-ceiling plank panelling; there's an open fire at each end of the main bar, paintings for sale, and books meant to be opened, rather than left as shelf decoration. Fullers London Pride, Harveys Best, Shepherd Neame Master Brew and Spitfire and Theakstons Old Peculier on handpump, lots of malt whiskies, and local cider. There are seats out on the front terrace and an outside shelter for smokers with an open fire.

🍴 **Bar food includes filled baguettes, soup, deep-fried camembert with berry coulis, seared scallops and smoked salmon in creamy cheese sauce, steak in ale pie, risotto with toasted walnuts, roquefort and apple, seafood spaghetti and evening dishes like spicy chilli and ginger chicken, pork loin with apple compote and fillet steak and tiger prawn skewers; puddings such as banoffi pie and sticky toffee pudding.** *Starters/Snacks: £4.95 to £7.95. Main Courses: £8.95 to £18.50. Puddings: £3.95 to £4.95*

Free house ~ Licensees Emma Oliver and Benn Jarvis ~ Real ale ~ Bar food (all day) ~ Restaurant ~ (01303) 862130 ~ Children welcome ~ Dogs welcome ~ Jazz Mon evenings ~ Open 12-midnight(11pm Sun)

Recommended by Tina and David Woods-Taylor, Mr and Mrs Mike Pearson, Tony Brace, Norman Fox, Eddie Edwards

TUNBRIDGE WELLS
TQ5638   MAP 3

Beacon ♀ 🛏

Tea Garden Lane; leaving Tunbridge Wells westwards on A264, this is the left turn-off on Rusthall Common after Nevill Park; TN3 9JH

Pleasant spreading bar, good bar food and local beers and fine views from seats on wooden decking

Popular locally (especially at weekends), this airy Victorian pub has a good bustling atmosphere. The dining area and spreading bar run freely into each other with stripped panelling, wooden floors and ornately built wall units giving a solidly comfortable feel; the sofas by the fireside are sought after in colder weather. Harveys Best, Larkins Traditional Ale and Timothy Taylors Landlord on handpump, and decent wines. The seats under parasols on the raised wooden decked area at the back enjoy good sunsets and the grounds have footpaths between lakes and springs, as well as summer boules and (very rare for a pub these days) even rounders.

🍴 **Well liked bar food includes lunchtime sandwiches, soup, chicken, smoked bacon and thyme terrine, moules marinière, shepherd's pie with minted peas, sweet potato and red** onion tarte tatin with lemon, mint and spinach salad, pork loin on braised lentils with apple horseradish and chicory salad, natural smoked haddock in stilton cream on grain mustard mash, seared scallops and tiger prawns with chilli and egg noodles, daily specials, and puddings such as raspberry panna cotta and treacle tart with clotted cream. *Starters/Snacks: £4.25 to £7.50. Main Courses: £9.25 to £17.50. Puddings: £4.75*

Free house ~ Licensee John Cullen ~ Real ale ~ Bar food (12-2.30, 6.30-9.30(10 Fri); all day Sat; 12-5, 6.30-9 Sun) ~ Restaurant ~ (01892) 524252 ~ Children welcome ~ Dogs allowed in bar ~ Open 10.30am-11pm; 12-10.30 Sun ~ Bedrooms: £68.50B/£97B

Recommended by Chris and Sheila Smith, Colin and Janet Roe, V Brogden, M Greening, B and M Kendall, Derek Thomas

Sankeys

Mount Ephraim (A26 just N of junction with A267); TN4 8AA
KENT DINING PUB OF THE YEAR

Super fish dishes plus other good food in informal downstairs brasserie bar, pubby street-level bar, local beer and very good wine list

There's always a lively atmosphere in the downstairs flagstoned brasserie bar here, with plenty of animated, chatty customers. Big mirrors spread the light and there are stripped brick walls, pews or chairs around sturdy tables, and french windows that open on to a nice suntrap decked garden. Light and airy with big windows and high ceilings, the street level Town Bar tends to attract a younger crowd and has comfortably laid-out leather sofas round low tables, pews round pubby tables on bare boards, a beer oriented décor, and a big flat screen TV for sports (the landlord is a keen rugby fan, and runner). A fine collection of rare enamel signs, too. Larkins Traditional Ale and Porter and a guest beer on handpump, a very good wine list with several by the glass, and lots of fruit beers and exotic brews; piped music. More reports please.

⑪ With quite an emphasis on fish, the good bar food includes filled baguettes, shellfish soup, queenie scallops with garlic butter, moules marinière, trio of sausages, calves liver and bacon, fish pie, wild mushroom risotto, steamed monkfish with ginger and chilli and cornish cock crab salad. *Starters/Snacks: £5.00 to £7.00. Main Courses: £7.50 to £20.00. Puddings: £4.95*

Free house ~ Licensee Guy Sankey ~ Real ale ~ Bar food (12-3, 6-10; all day Sat; not Sun) ~ Restaurant ~ (01892) 511422 ~ Children welcome ~ Dogs allowed in bar ~ Live bands Sun evening ~ Open 11(12 Sun)-11(midnight Sat); closed 25 Dec, 1 Jan

Recommended by John A Barker

ULCOMBE   TQ8550   MAP 3

Pepper Box

Fairbourne Heath; signposted from A20 in Harrietsham, or follow Ulcombe signpost from A20, then turn left at crossroads with sign to pub, then right at next minor crossroads; ME17 1LP

Friendly country pub with homely bar, lovely log fire, consistently good food, fair choice of drinks and seats in pretty garden

Readers really enjoy their visits to this cosy and traditional country pub and you can be sure of a friendly welcome from the licensees and their polite, efficient staff. The homely bar has standing timbers and low beams hung with hops, copper kettles and pans on window sills, some very low-seated windsor chairs and two leather sofas by the splendid inglenook fireplace with its lovely log fire. A side area, more functionally furnished for eating, extends into the opened up dining room. Shepherd Neame Master Brew, Spitfire and a seasonal beer on handpump, local apple juice and several wines by the glass; piped music. The two cats are called Murphy and Jim. There's a hop-covered terrace and a garden with shrubs, flowerbeds and a small pond. The name of the pub refers to the pepperbox pistol – an early type of revolver with numerous barrels; the village church is worth a look. The Greensand Way footpath is nearby. No children inside.

🍴 Consistently good bar food includes sandwiches, soup, baked field mushroom topped with goats cheese, walnut and basil, tiger prawns with garlic butter, chilli and ginger, deep fried whitebait with tartare sauce, chargrilled peppered lamb fillet with beetroot, crème fraîche and mint with a watercress salad, aubergine stuffed with couscous and mediterranean vegetables, sea bream fillet with brown butter and capers with parsley mash, and puddings such as poached pears with toffee sauce and calvados ice-cream and chocolate and nut cake. *Starters/Snacks: £4.00 to £7.00. Main Courses: £7.50 to £17.00. Puddings: £4.00*

Shepherd Neame ~ Tenants Geoff and Sarah Pemble ~ Real ale ~ Bar food (12-2, 7-9.30; not Sun evening) ~ Restaurant ~ (01622) 842558 ~ Dogs allowed in bar ~ Open 11-3, 6.30-11; 12-4 Sun; closed Sun evening

Recommended by Philip and Cheryl Hill, N R White, P and D Carpenter, John and Jackie Walsh, Jan and Alan Summers, Mike Gorton

WEST PECKHAM   TQ6452   MAP 3

Swan on the Green 🍺

From A26/A228 heading N, bear left at roundabout on to B2016 (Seven Mile Lane), then second left; ME18 5JW

Attractive village green setting, own-brewed beers, well liked bar food and light and airy bars

The setting opposite the charming village green is quite a boon for this tucked away country pub. Their own-brewed real ales are a popular feature too. On handpump, there might be Bewick, Fuggles, Ginger Swan, Swan Mild and Trumpeter; Biddendens farm cider. The bar is light, airy and open-plan, with rush-seated dining chairs and cushioned church settles around an attractive mix of well spaced refectory and other pale oak tables on wood strip floors. Attractive decorations include big bunches of flowers (one placed in the knocked-through brick fireplace), hops on beams, some modern paintings at one end and black and white photographs of regulars at the other end; piped classical music and daily papers. The nearby church is partly Saxon.

🍴 Tasty but not cheap bar food includes lunchtime filled ciabattas or ploughman's, soup, king prawns in garlic and lemon butter, antipasti plate for two, smoked haddock on crushed new potatoes, roast pepper and wild mushroom risotto, chargrilled beef with onions, calves liver and bacon, and puddings such as lemon syllabub and Baileys crème brûlée. *Starters/Snacks: £5.20 to £7.95. Main Courses: £9.25 to £15.95. Puddings: £4.50*

Own brew ~ Licensee Gordon Milligan ~ Real ale ~ Bar food (not Sun or Mon evenings) ~ Restaurant ~ (01622) 812271 ~ Children welcome ~ Dogs welcome ~ Open 11-3(4 Sat), 6-11; 12-7 Sun; closed all Sun evening and Mon evening from 8.30

Recommended by Simon and Sally Small, Graham Burling, Philip and Cheryl Hill, Annette Tress, Gary Smith, Martin and Pauline Jennings, Mr and Mrs Mike Pearson, Gordon Ormondroyd, Ben and Helen Ingram, Malcolm and Jane Levitt, Dr Ron Cox, Sue Demont, Tim Barrow

LUCKY DIP

Besides the fully inspected pubs, you might like to try these Lucky Dips recommended to us and described by readers (if you do, please send us reports: www.goodguides.co.uk).

APPLEDORE [TQ9529]
Black Lion TN26 2BU [The Street]: Compact 1930s village pub with bustling atmosphere, very welcoming helpful staff, appetising range of generous food all day from simple cheese sandwiches to imaginative dishes, lamb from Romney Marsh and local fish, three or four well kept changing ales, Biddenden farm cider, log fire, partitioned back eating area; tables out on green, attractive village, good Military Canal walks

(Mrs C Lintott, Mrs Hazel Rainer, Mr and Mrs Mike Pearson, M G Hart)
BADLESMERE [TR0154]
Red Lion ME13 0NX [A251, S of M2 junction 6]: Attractive and spacious partly 16th-c country pub, Fullers London Pride, Greene King Abbot, Shepherd Neame and three changing guests from small breweries, Johnson's farm cider from Sheppey, enjoyable food (not Sun pm) using local produce, beams and stripped brickwork, pool

and pub games, Easter and Aug bank hol beer festivals; piped music, live Fri; large garden, open all day Fri/Sat, cl Mon lunchtime *(Kevin Thorpe)*

BENENDEN [TQ8032]
Bull TN17 4DE [The Street]: Well run proper traditional village inn, well kept Harveys, local farm cider, reasonably priced pubby food; stylish bedrooms *(R J H Taylor)*

BETHERSDEN [TQ9239]
Bull TN26 3LB [A28 E]: Welcoming refurbished pub opp village cricket ground, decent food from bar snacks to meals in popular open-style restaurant, Shepherd Neame ales and good choice of wines by the glass, friendly staff and cat called Alan, quick service even though busy *(Adrian Farrar, Elaine Edmondson)*

BOTOLPHS BRIDGE [TR1233]
Botolphs Bridge Inn CT21 4NL [W of Hythe]: Unpretentious Edwardian country pub notable for its wide choice of good generous home-made food at sensible prices inc Sun roasts, quick pleasant service, good value wines, Greene King real ales, two log fires, airy chatty open-plan bar with games area, small dining room one end (children allowed here); small garden *(Mrs Hazel Rainer, Grahame Brooks)*

BOUGHTON STREET [TR0659]
☆ *White Horse* ME13 9AX [nr M2 junction 7; The Street]: Comfortably refurbished former coaching inn, dark beams, tiles and bare boards, open fires and woodburner, friendly uniformed staff, well prepared food, well kept Shepherd Neame ale, good wine choice, daily papers; piped music; children welcome, tables in attractive garden, good value bedrooms, good breakfast, open all day *(LYM, Lisa Robertson)*

BRABOURNE LEES [TQ0740]
Blue Anchor TN25 6QQ [Bridge St]: Newish management putting emphasis on enjoyable reasonably priced food from tapas to restaurant meals, good lunch menu, friendly atmosphere; pretty garden *(Tom and Marie Heffernan)*

BRASTED [TQ4755]
White Hart TN16 1JE [High St (A25)]: Carefully preserved Battle of Britain bar with signatures and mementoes of Biggin Hill fighter pilots in roomy well run Vintage Inn, several other snug softly lit areas, beams and log fires, helpful and friendly landlady and staff, good choice of wine by the glass, Shepherd Neame Spitfire; children welcome, big neatly kept garden with well spaced tables and play area; pretty village with several antiques shops, open all day *(LYM, Christine and Neil Townend, N R White, B J Harding)*

BRENCHLEY [TQ6841]
Halfway House TN12 7AX [Horsmonden Rd]: Attractive olde-worlde mix of rustic and traditional furnishings on bare boards, two log fires, particularly friendly landlord, enjoyable pubby food and very popular Sun carvery, good changing choice of interesting

real ales tapped from the cask inc local brews, two eating areas; picnic-sets and play area in big garden, bedrooms *(Peter Meister)*

BRIDGE [TR1854]
Plough & Harrow CT4 5LA [High St]: Small popular local in 17th-c former maltings, friendly and unpretentious, with Shepherd Neame Bitter, Best and seasonal ales, good wine choice, coal fire and lots of sporting prints in open-plan brick-walled lounge, public bar with bar billiards and open fire, back games room with darts, TV and woodburner – pub is HQ of over 30 clubs and groups; no food; children and dogs welcome away from bar, disabled access, open all day Sat *(Kevin Thorpe)*

White Horse CT4 5LA [High St]: Imaginative food choice, on the pricy side but good, from bar lunches to more elaborate restaurant dishes using listed local suppliers, well kept ales such as Fullers London Pride and Shepherd Neame Master Brew and Spitfire on handpump, Biddenden farm cider, fine choice of wines by the glass and friendly efficient service; nice bar with relaxed atmosphere, large Elizabethan inglenook fireplace with some fine stone carving, lots of old photographs and pictures of the pub, a couple of homely worn armchairs in one corner, comfortable sofa and low table in front of the bar and larger parquet-floored area with wheelchairs around a mix of pubby tables; pleasant two-part restaurant with rust-coloured napkins in wine glasses, framed prints on the walls and woodburning stove in brick fireplace; unobtrusive piped music; dogs welcome, picnic-sets and barbecue area amongst established flower beds in back garden, attractive village *(Mr and Mrs Mike Pearson, N R White, BB)*

BROADSTAIRS [TR3866]
Brown Jug CT10 2EW [Ramsgate Rd]: Long-serving landlady in basic and unchanging old-style two-bar local, Greene King and guest beers, some tapped from the cask, board and quiz games; open all day wknds *(the Didler)*

Neptunes Hall CT10 1ET [Harbour St]: Chatty early 19th-c two-bar Shepherd Neame local with attractive bow windows and original shelving and panelling, carpeted back lounge with open fire, lunchtime snacks, real ales, friendly landlord, pub dog, military photographs; occasional live folk (daily during Aug folk festival); children and dogs welcome, enclosed terrace, open all day *(Kevin Thorpe, N R White, the Didler)*

Tartar Frigate CT10 1EU [Harbour St, by quay]: Appealing stone-built harbourside pub with interesting local photographs and fishing memorabilia, hanging pots and brasses, soft lighting, bare boards, tiles and plush seating, friendly service, real ales inc Greene King Abbot, generous local fish and seafood in busy upstairs restaurant (not Sun evening) with good view; piped music, locals' bar with pool, plastic glasses for outdoor drinkers *(Liz and John Soden, N R White)*

White Swan CT10 3AZ [Reading St, St Peters]: Much modernised 17th-c pub with armchairs, toby jugs and old village prints in comfortable lounge, Adnams and five unusual changing beers, simple bargain food (not Sun) such as sandwiches, toasties and pasta, pool and darts (and cheaper beer) in plain public bar; dogs welcome, open all day Sat *(Kevin Thorpe)*

CANTERBURY [TR1457]

Abode Hotel CT1 2RX [bar behind former County Hotel, High St]: Good food in attractive and comfortable contemporary beamed bar behind this substantial hotel, which now also includes a good Michael Caine restaurant; well redesigned bedrooms, open all day *(Keith and Chris O'Neill)*

Bat & Ball CT1 3NX [Old Dover Rd]: Cheery carpeted bar with attractive side-on pews, well kept Shepherd Neame and other ales inc a local guest beer, enjoyable food, bare-boards side room with pool and big-screen sports TV – cricket takes priority; suntrap terrace *(Tracey and Stephen Groves)*

Dolphin CT1 2AA [St Radigunds St]: Smart dining pub, civilised and friendly, with comfortable sofas, old and new pictures on warm red walls above stripped dado, books to read, board games, bric-a-brac on delft shelf, good choice of home-made blackboard food from baguettes to fish specials, real ales such as Fullers London Pride, Greene King and Timothy Taylors Landlord, country wines, flagstone conservatory with fine collection of advertising mirrors; popular Mon quiz night; disabled access, children welcome, good-sized garden behind, open all day *(Kevin Thorpe)*

Millers Arms CT1 2AA [St Radigunds St/Mill Lane]: Neat and tidy Shepherd Neame pub with their ales and perhaps a guest such as Hop Back Summer Lightning, good wine choice, bar food, several pleasantly refurbished rooms inc restaurant (good Sun lunch), interesting pictures and sayings; unobtrusive piped music; decent bedrooms, quiet street nr river and handy for Marlow Theatre *(N R White, Keith and Chris O'Neill)*

Old Brewery Tavern CT1 2RX [High St]: Plush and airy new bistro bar in former brewery, good if not cheap bar food from sandwiches up, two changing ales such as Hopdaemon and Shepherd Neame, pine flooring, comfy seats and polished dining tables, modern prints on pastel walls, plasma TVs and flame-effect fires, soft settees and more dining tables in adjoining high-ceilinged former warehouse, also smart restaurant and champagne bar *(Kevin Thorpe)*

Old Gate CT1 3EL [New Dover Rd (A2050 S)]: Big reliable Vintage Inn, several distinct areas, stripped brick and beams, two large open fires, bookshelves, big prints, old wooden table and chairs, reasonably priced food all day, wide range of wines by the glass, real ales such as Adnams, Greene King and Shepherd Neame, well organised staff, daily papers; some piped music; easy disabled access, bedrooms in adjacent Innkeeper's Lodge, picnic-sets in small back garden *(Kevin Thorpe, Michael Dandy)*

Phoenix CT1 3DB [Old Dover Rd]: Two friendly linked rooms in comfortably olde-worlde beamed tavern with hundreds of pump clips on ceiling and lots of prints, well kept Greene King Abbot, Wells & Youngs Bitter and Bombardier and three unusual guest beers, winter beer festival, cheap all-day pub food, daily papers, pub games, books for sale; small TV, limited parking; dogs welcome, bedrooms, open all day (Sun afternoon break) *(Kevin Thorpe, Tracey and Stephen Groves)*

Simple Simons CT1 2AG [Church Lane – the one off St Radigund St, 100 yds E of St Radigunds car park]: Step down into basic pub in 14th-c building, pleasantly chatty front bar with heavy beams, broad floorboards, flagstones and some stripped masonry, two woodburners, dim-lit upstairs banqueting hall, friendly young staff, well kept Bass and lots of guest beers, impressive pump clip collection, low-priced simple lunchtime food inc sandwiches and good home-made pies; may be piped classical music by day, more studenty evening, good jazz nights; dogs welcome, tables in brick-paved courtyard, open all day *(Kath Hunt, N R White, Kevin Thorpe, Mr and Mrs John Taylor)*

CHILHAM [TR0653]

White Horse CT4 8BY [The Square]: Pleasantly modernised two-room beamed bar with good log fire, well kept ales such as Rother Valley Level Best, decent wines, smiling service, back eating area with separate ordering counter for good value food from baguettes and baked potatoes up; piped music; a couple of tables out on the corner of Kent's prettiest village square *(LYM, M G Hart)*

CHILLENDEN [TR2653]

☆ **Griffins Head** CT3 1PS: Good-sized helpings of consistently appealing home-made food, Shepherd Neame real ales and good wines in attractive beamed, timbered and flagstoned 14th-c pub with two bar rooms and back flagstoned dining room, warm atmosphere, big log fire, local regulars; small children not welcome; pleasant garden surrounded by wild roses, super Sun barbecues, attractive countryside *(Janey, Philip and Cheryl Hill, Guy Vowles)*

CHIPSTEAD [TQ4956]

Bricklayers Arms TN13 2RZ [Chevening Rd]: Attractive pub overlooking lake and green, good value food (not Sun evening), full range of Harveys beers kept well and tapped from casks behind long counter, good atmosphere, heavily beamed bar with open fire and fine racehorse painting, unpretentious larger back restaurant *(B J Harding)*

COWDEN [TQ4640]

Fountain TN8 7JG [off A264 and B2026; High St]: New licensees for attractive tile-hung beamed country local in pretty village, steep steps to unpretentious dark-panelled corner bar with Harveys IPA, Best and a guest beer, decent wines, darts and good log fire, mix of tables in adjoining room, woodburner in small back dining room with one big table; piped music; walkers and dogs welcome, garden picnic-sets, has been cl Mon lunchtime (N R White, BB)

☆ *Queens Arms* TN8 5NP [Cowden Pound; junction B2026 with Markbeech rd]: Friendly two-room country pub like something from the 1930s, with splendid landlady, Adnams, coal fire, darts; dogs welcome, occasional folk music or morris dancers; may be cl wkdy lunchtimes but normally opens 10am (the Didler, Pete Baker)

DARGATE [TR0761]

Dove ME13 9HB [Village signposted from A299]: Tucked-away dining pub tied to Shepherd Neame, which has been very popular for good restaurant food, but faces a change of tenant around the time this edition is published; has had unspoilt rambling rooms, plenty of seats and stripped wood tables, log fire and attractive sheltered garden – reports on new regime, please (LYM)

DEAL [TR3752]

☆ *Bohemian* CT14 6HY [Beach St]: Relaxed chatty bar opp pier popular for its four well kept changing real ales and good range of continental beers, good choice of wines by the glass, friendly helpful service, leather sofas, open fire, wooden floors and abstract paintings on red walls, good seafront views from upstairs restaurant; easy wheelchair access, heated back terrace, open all day Fri-Sun and summer, cl Mon in winter (N R White)

Kings Head CT14 7AH [Beach St]: Handsome three-storey Georgian inn with lovely hanging baskets just across from promenade and sea, interesting maritime décor and cricket memorabilia in comfortable areas around central servery with Fullers London Pride, Harveys Best and Shepherd Neame Bitter and Spitfire, friendly service, flame-effect gas fires, usual food from cheap sandwiches up, darts; piped music, TV, popular with young locals wknd evenings; new front terrace area, bedrooms, open all day (Craig Turnbull, LYM, B J Harding, Rod Stoneman, N R White, Kevin Thorpe)

Ship CT14 6JZ [Middle St]: Neatly kept local, Caledonian Deuchars IPA, three ales from local Gadds and a guest beer, friendly landlord, lots of dark woodwork, stripped brick and local ship and wreck pictures, piano and woodburner in side bar, no piped music or machines; dogs welcome, small pretty walled garden, open all day (Kevin Thorpe, N R White)

DOVER [TR3241]

Blakes CT16 1PJ [Castle St]: Four or five interesting changing real ales, usually Kentish, in small flagstoned cellar bar, good lunchtime bar food (not Sun) inc good value sandwiches and home-smoked food, upstairs restaurant, farm cider and perry, good choice of malt whiskies and of wines by the glass, chatty licensees and locals, daily papers, partly panelled brick and flint walls, friendly pub cat; may be quiet piped music; well behaved children welcome, suntrap walled terrace, bedrooms, open all day (till 4 Sun) (Arthur Pickering, Kevin Thorpe)

DUNKS GREEN [TQ6152]

☆ *Kentish Rifleman* TN11 9RU [Dunks Green Rd]: Timbered Tudor pub closed by fire damage in spring 2007, so we hope it's rapidly back to normal – it had been on increasingly good form, with a particularly friendly helpful landlord, real ales such as Fullers London Pride, Greene King, Harveys and Westerham, good helpings of enjoyable homely food, cosy log fire, plenty of character, rifles on low beams, well divided dining lounge, old high-backed seats in small public bar; children welcome, tables in pretty garden behind, good walks (Simon and Sally Small, Bob and Margaret Holder, BB, Robert Gomme, Tina and David Woods-Taylor, GHC, N R White, Michelle Harris)

ELHAM [TR1743]

Kings Arms CT4 6TJ [St Marys Rd]: Friendly landlord in traditional pub with relaxing attractive lounge bar, good open fire, good value food, Flowers, Greene King and Harveys, unobtrusively attentive service, steps down to big dining area, public bar with games; opp church in square of charming village, attractive sheltered garden (Keith Wright, David Barnes)

ETCHINGHILL [TR1639]

New Inn CT18 8DE [Canterbury Rd (former B2065)]: Neatly kept bright and airy pub with wide range of enjoyable food (good with special diets), friendly efficient staff, real ales such as Fullers London Pride, Hydes Jekylls Gold and Shepherd Neame, good value wines by the glass, beams and flagstones, spacious dining room (Rod Stoneman)

EYNSFORD [TQ5365]

Malt Shovel DA4 0ER [Station Rd]: Traditional dark-panelled pub with black beams and copper kettles, well kept interesting changing ales, good choice of wine by the glass;, friendly attentive staff, wide range of pub food inc plenty of daily specials, popular Sun lunch, restaurant; car park across busy road; children welcome, handy for castles and Roman villa (N R White, GHC)

FAIRSEAT [TQ6361]

Vigo TN15 7JL [Gravesend Rd (A227)]: Unspoilt pub dating from 15th c, neat and simple, with well kept Harveys and Westerham, zealous engaging landlord, stripped stonework and open fire, no food, dadlums table; on North Downs Way, cl wkdy lunchtimes (Giles and Annie Francis)

FARNINGHAM [TQ5466]

Pied Bull DA4 0DG [High St]: Pub/restaurant with interesting choice of enjoyable food (can take a while) inc fresh seafood and home-made puddings, popular restaurant; pleasant small garden *(William Ruxton)*

FAVERSHAM [TR0161]

Albion ME13 7DH [Front Brents]: Light and airy waterside mexican bar with simple furnishings, modern pictures on terracotta walls, light bar food and some current emphasis on mexican/latino dishes, Shepherd Neame ales inc seasonal from the nearby brewery, genial staff, flowers and candles on tables; children welcome, disabled lavatories, picnic-sets out by riverside walkway (Saxon Shore long-distance path), open all day summer *(B J Harding, LYM, Kevin Thorpe, the Didler)*

Anchor ME13 7BP [Abbey St]: Two-bar pub with new licensees doing good value changing food and real Shepherd Neame ales, simple bare-boards bar with log fire, ancient beams, dark panelling, low lighting, frosted windows and boat pictures and models, small side room with pub games and books, new restaurant; piped radio; dogs welcome, tables in pretty enclosed garden with bat and trap, attractive 17th-c street nr historic quay, open all day *(Kevin Flack, Kevin Thorpe, the Didler, N R White)*

Bear ME13 7AG [Market Pl]: Late Victorian (back part dates from 16th c), locals' front bar, snug hung with chamber pots and back dining lounge off side corridor, friendly service, relaxed atmosphere, Shepherd Neame ales from the nearby brewery, basic good value lunchtime home cooking; tables outside, lively musical following, open all day Sat *(the Didler, N R White)*

Crown & Anchor ME13 8JN [The Mall]: Friendly and brightly lit open-plan local dating from 19th c, Shepherd Neame real ales, wkdy lunchtime food inc authentic goulash (long-serving Hungarian licensees), games area with darts and pool, no TV or music *(the Didler, N R White)*

Elephant ME13 8JN [The Mall]: Picturesque flower-decked terrace town pub under welcoming young landlady, five changing real ales, belgian beers on tap, local cider, central log fire, daily papers, modern prints on pastel walls, tables and chairs on bare boards, darts; juke box, games machine; children welcome, suntrap back terrace with fishpond, open from 3 wkdys, all day wknds *(BB, Kevin Thorpe, the Didler)*

Phoenix ME13 7BH [Abbey St]: Ancient two-bar pub with heavy beams and stripped stone, real ales such as Greene King K&B, Rother Valley and Shepherd Neame, bar food inc some authentic thai dishes and take-aways, central fireplace, smart candlelit oriental restaurant; fruit machine, juke box; open all day *(Kevin Thorpe)*

Railway Hotel ME13 8PE [Preston St]: Large handsomely refurbished Victorian station hotel, well kept Shepherd Neame from long highly polished bar with elaborate mirrored back, frosted glass and reinstalled partitions, period lamps and warm red décor, leather settees and open fire in further room, daily papers, darts corner, good value restaurant, no music or TV; seven bedrooms, open all day *(Kevin Thorpe)*

Sun ME13 7JE [West St]: Roomy and rambling old-world 15th-c weatherboarded town pub with good unpretentious atmosphere in small low-ceilinged partly panelled rooms, good value low-priced lunchtime food, Shepherd Neame beers inc seasonal one from nearby brewery, quick pleasant service, smart restaurant; unobtrusive piped music; wheelchair access possible (small step), tables in pleasant back courtyard, interesting street, nine bedrooms, open all day *(the Didler)*

FINGLESHAM [TR3353]

Crown CT14 0NA [just off A258 Sandwich—Deal; The Street]: Neatly kept low-beamed 16th-c country pub with good value food from usual pub dishes to interesting specials, five well kept ales such as Gadds, Hopdaemon and Shepherd Neame, Aug beer festival, good service, daily papers, log fire, split-level softly lit carpeted bar with stripped stone and inglenook log fire, tables here and in two other attractive dining rooms; children welcome, lovely big garden with play area and barbecues, field for caravans, open all day wknds *(Kevin Thorpe, N R White)*

FRITTENDEN [TQ8141]

Bell & Jorrocks TN17 2EJ: Traditional simple timber-framed village local with well kept ales such as Adnams Best, Harveys Best and Hop Back Summer Lightning, good basic home-made food, friendly landlord, nice atmosphere, open fire; Apr beer festival, adjoining post office *(Peter Meister)*

GOUDHURST [TQ7237]

Star & Eagle TN17 1AL [High St]: Striking medieval building, now a small hotel, with settles and Jacobean-style seats in heavily beamed open-plan areas, wide choice of good generous freshly made food from crusty ciabattas to full meals, log fires, well kept Adnams (the bar itself seems fairly modern), good coffee, interesting smuggling-days history, lovely views from roomy restaurant; children welcome, tables out behind with same views, attractive village, character bedrooms (some sharing bathroom), open all day *(Tina and David Woods-Taylor, LYM, Ann and Colin Hunt, Roy and Lindsey Fentiman)*

GRAVESEND [TQ6473]

Crown & Thistle DA12 2BJ [The Terrace]: Friendly and chatty old-fashioned local with five interesting changing beers from small breweries, bar nibbles, brewery pictures, no juke box or machines, can order in meals from nearby indian/chinese restaurant; no children, occasional live music; handy for historic riverside, open all day *(Richard Pitcher, the Didler)*

HARBLEDOWN [TR1358]

Old Coach & Horses CT2 9AB [Church Hill]: Enjoyable food, helpful friendly service, good beer and wines by the glass, cosy atmosphere; great views from garden with friendly cockerel, peaceful setting (Mrs Jennifer Hurst, Hetty Dean)

HAWKHURST [TQ7529]

Eight Bells TN18 4NX [The Moor]: Proper pub with reasonably priced food using good local ingredients, prompt service, Adnams, Greene King K&B and Marstons Fever Pitch; large garden (Ian Phillips)

HEADCORN [TQ8344]

George & Dragon TN27 9NL [High St]: Good atmosphere and service, welcoming landlady, wide range of enjoyable home-made food lunchtime and evening, good drinks, open fires, separate dining room (Jan and Alan Summers)

HERNE [TR1865]

☆ *Butchers Arms* CT6 7HL [Herne St (A291)]: Tiny newish sawdust-floor pub with five particularly well kept changing real ales tapped from the cask such as Dark Star, Fullers ESB, Goachers and Harveys Best, interesting bottled beers and Biddenden farm cider, just a couple of benches and butcher's-block chairs, some wines too but no food (you can bring your own) beyond fierce pickles, chess, no music or TV; dogs welcome, tables out under awning, cl Sun/Mon, short lunchtime opening (Kevin Thorpe)

HERNHILL [TR0660]

☆ *Red Lion* ME13 9JR [off A299 via Dargate, or A2 via Boughton Street and Staplestreet]: Pretty Tudor inn by church and attractive village green, densely beamed and flagstoned, log fires, pine tables, friendly helpful staff, enjoyable food inc huge salads, Fullers London Pride, Shepherd Neame and a guest beer, decent house wines, upstairs restaurant; children welcome, big garden with boules and good play area, bedrooms (LYM, N R White, Mary McSweeney)

HODSOLL STREET [TQ6263]

☆ *Green Man* TN15 7LE [off A227 S of Meopham]: Welcoming landlord and good staff in pretty pub by village green with Flowers, Fullers London Pride, Wells & Youngs and a guest beer, decent wines, good food from lunchtime sandwiches, wraps and baguettes to generous wholesome main dishes inc local game (best to book), neat tables in big airy and relaxed rooms around hop-draped central bar, interesting old local photographs and antique plates, log fire; piped music; children and dogs allowed, tables out on lawn, play area, North Downs walks, open all day Fri-Sun (Martin Smith, M Greening, Fiona McElhone, Annette Tress, Gary Smith, LYM, Simon Pyle, Gerry and Rosemary Dobson, GHC, Sherree Fagge)

HUCKING [TQ8458]

Hook & Hatchet ME17 1QT [village signed off A249; Church Rd]: Isolated country pub of great potential, in enviable spot by Woodland Trust's Hucking Estate, plenty of nearby interesting walks, three Shepherd Neame ales, usual food, open fire, mix and match functions on broad bare boards; piped music may be loud; children welcome, tables out on heated verandah, picnic-sets in neat garden, open all day (Dave Braisted, LYM, Lesley and Peter Barrett, Gerry and Rosemary Dobson)

ICKHAM [TR2258]

☆ *Duke William* CT3 1QP [off A257 E of Canterbury; The Street]: Attractively reworked by new licensees, interesting food, real ales such as Adnams, Harveys Best and Shepherd Neame Bitter and Spitfire from central servery, daily papers, open-plan beamed bar with log fire, polished boards and modern prints on pastel walls, local paintings in side dining room, new back conservatory; disabled facilities, large partly covered terrace with barbecue, neat garden, open all day (LYM, Kevin Thorpe)

IDE HILL [TQ4851]

Cock TN14 6JN [off B2042 SW of Sevenoaks]: Pretty village-green pub with warmly pubby atmosphere, quick effficient service, Greene King ales, wholesome food (not Sun evening) from sandwiches and ploughman's up, fine log fire, bar billiards; piped music, no children; some seats out in front, handy for Chartwell and nearby walks – so gets busy (LYM, N R White, GHC, Gwyn Jones)

Woodman TN14 6BU [Whitley Row, Goathurst Common; B2042 N]: Large well run former Chef & Brewer, wide blackboard choice of all-day food from hot baguettes to some south african specialities (landlord's from there), friendly well trained young staff, decent wine, real ales, woodburner; manicured lawns, good walks (Tina and David Woods-Taylor, N R White, Tony Brace)

IDEN GREEN [TQ8031]

Woodcock TN17 4HT [from village centre follow Standen Street signpost, then fork left down Woodcock Lane (this is not the Iden Green nr Goudhurst)]: Small unsmart country tavern tucked away outside village, flagstones and low beams, woodburner in big inglenook, several small nooks with homely furniture, well kept Greene King ales, straightforward bar food, partly panelled dining area; piped radio; seats and occasional barbecues in pretty side garden, open all day (Lisa Robertson, LYM, Andrea Rampley)

IGHTHAM [TQ5956]

George & Dragon TN15 9HH [A227]: Picturesque timbered dining pub, early 16th-c but much modernised, food from generous snacks (all day till 6.30, not Sun) up, Shepherd Neame ales inc seasonal, decent wines, good choice of fruit juices, sofas among other furnishings in long sociable main bar, heavy-beamed end room, woodburner and open fires, restaurant; children in family/restaurant areas, back terrace, open all day, handy for Ightham Mote (NT), good walks (GHC, LYM, Derek Thomas)

KILNDOWN [TQ7035]

☆ **Globe & Rainbow** TN17 2SG [signed off A21 S of Lamberhurst]: Small cheerful local bar with well kept Harveys and Fullers London Pride, simple bare-boards dining room with enjoyable fresh food inc hastings fish and local lamb, friendly helpful service, fair range of wines by the glass; pleasant country views from picnic-sets out on decking by village cricket pitch (V Brogden, Bob and Margaret Holder, BB)

KINGSDOWN [TR3748]

Kings Head CT14 8BJ [Upper St]: Chatty and unpretentious tucked-away local with Fullers London Pride, Greene King IPA and a guest beer, bar food (not Mon evening), four small split-level rooms, black timbers, faded cream walls, pubby decorations and open fires, darts; piped music, games machine; garden with skittle alley, open all day Sun, cl wkdy lunchtimes (Kevin Thorpe, N R White)

Rising Sun CT14 8AH [Cliffe Rd]: Attractive 17th-c clapboard pub by pebble beach, brasses, country prints, old brickwork and beams, a changing ale such as Fullers London Pride, log fire, pubby food from sandwiches up, darts and books for sale in back bar with maritime memorabilia and old local photographs; disabled access from back garden, picnic-sets on sunken front terrace, good walks (Kevin Thorpe)

KNOCKHOLT [TQ4658]

Crown TN14 7LS [Main Rd]: Cheerful old-fashioned village pub, unchanged for decades, with attractive dark ochre décor, friendly relaxed service from proper old-school licensees, good value home-made comfort food lunchtimes and Sat evening inc sandwiches and sensibly priced hot dishes, well kept ales such as Adnams and Fullers London Pride, walkers with muddy boots welcome in public bar; picnic-sets on lawn with fishpond, colourful flowers, path to North Downs Way (N R White, Robert Gomme)

LAMBERHURST [TQ6735]

Swan TN3 8EU [Lamberhurst Down]: Pretty dining pub by green (and vineyards), pleasant contemporary wine bar feel with comfortable sofas and chairs, flagstones or bare boards, modern art on mushroom walls, dark blinds and swagged beige curtains, good wines by the glass inc local english ones, well kept Harveys and Westerham ales, log fires, familiar service, ambitious food from open sandwiches up; children welcome, tables out on back terrace (Nigel and Jean Eames, Daniel Winfield, BB)

LEEDS [TQ8253]

George ME17 1RN [Lower St]: Nicely modernised village pub with pubby furnishings, lots of standing timbers, Shepherd Neame ales, bar food, darts; TV; children and dogs welcome, picnic-sets in good-sized garden (Conor McGaughey)

LEIGH [TQ5446]

Fleur de Lis TN11 8RL [High St]: Newly decorated country pub with some emphasis on good range of food from walkers' lunches to well prepared restaurant dishes using fresh ingredients, friendly welcome, Greene King ales, scrubbed tables on flagstones (Gwyn Jones, J Noble)

Plough TN11 9AJ [Powder Mill Lane/Leigh Rd, off B2027 NW of Tonbridge]: Attractive Tudor building opened up around big central hearth, food from generous baked potatoes and ciabattas up, real ales such as Badger, Harveys and Shepherd Neame, good wine range; pleasant walks (M G, BB, GHC)

LEYSDOWN-ON-SEA [TR0266]

Ferry House ME12 4BQ [Harty Ferry Rd, Sheerness]: At seaside end of long bumpy single-track road through salt marshes full of birds, friendly staff, sensibly short choice of enjoyable food inc fish and game, decent wines by the glass (keg beers), bare boards, panelled dado, cask stools, games room with pool, TV and machines, attractive newish barn-style high-raftered restaurant; they may try to keep your credit card while you eat; children welcome, disabled access, picnic-sets in large garden looking across to Kent mainland, play area, open all day Sat, cl Sun evening and Mon (Dave Braisted, Colin Moore, Kevin Thorpe)

LUDDESDOWN [TQ6667]

☆ **Cock** DA13 0XB [Henley Street, N of village – OS Sheet 177 map reference 664672; off A227 in Meopham, or A228 in Cuxton]: Distinctive tucked-away early 18th-c country pub, friendly long-serving landlord, half a dozen well kept changing ales inc Adnams Best and Broadside, Goachers Mild and Woodfordes Wherry, farm ciders, all-day pubby food (not Sun evening) from wide choice of sandwiches and toasties up, rugs on polished boards in pleasant bay-windowed lounge bar, quarry-tiled locals' bar, two woodburners, pews and other miscellaneous furnishings, aircraft pictures, masses of beer mats and bric-a-brac inc stuffed animals, model cars and beer can collections, traditional games inc bar billiards and three types of darts board, back dining conservatory; no children allowed in bar or heated back covered terrace; dogs welcome, big secure garden with boules, open all day (LYM, Dr Danny Nicol, Kevin Thorpe, N R White, LM)

LYNSTED [TQ9460]

Black Lion ME9 0RJ: 16th-c local extended in keeping with original core, well kept Goachers ales, good simple fresh home cooking inc popular Sun lunch (always fully booked), Pawley's local farm cider, good-natured forthright landlord and two friendly dogs, settles and old tables on bare boards, log fires, plenty of old advertisements and something of a 1950s/60s feel; well behaved children welcome, garden with play area (Annette Tress, Gary Smith)

MAIDSTONE [TQ7655]

Pilot ME15 6EU [Upper Stone St (A229)]: Busy old roadside pub, enjoyable low-priced simple home-made bar lunches (not Sun), well kept Harveys, good friendly landlord, whisky-water jugs hanging from ceiling, darts and pool; tables on back terrace (the Didler)

Rifle Volunteers ME14 1EU [Wyatt St/Church St]: Old-fashioned backstreet pub tied to local Goachers, three of their ales inc Mild, good value simple home-made food, chatty long-serving landlord, two gas fires, darts, no machines; tables outside (the Didler)

MARDEN THORN [TQ7643]

Wild Duck TN12 9LH [Pagehurst Lane; off A229 in Staplehurst or B2079 in Marden]: Unpretentious country pub with decent food inc Sun carvery, Adnams Broadside, good value wines by the glass, pleasant staff, good-sized dining room; garden with climbing frame and slide, cl Tues (Glenwys and Alan Lawrence, John and Joan Calvert, BB)

MARSHSIDE [TR2266]

Hog & Donkey CT3 4EH [North Stream]: This remote and idiosyncratic 18th-c pub has now closed, on the retirement of its very long-serving landlord (BOB)

MARTIN [TR3347]

Old Lantern CT15 5JL [off A258 Dover—Deal; The Street]: Pretty 17th-c cottage, low beams, stripped brick and cosy corners in small neat bar with dining tables, popular home-made food, welcoming attentive staff, Shepherd Neame, decent wines, open fire, soft lighting; quiet piped music; sizeable play area in good-sized pretty gardens, beautiful setting, cl winter Sun evenings (N R White, Janey, Kevin Thorpe)

MAYPOLE [TR2064]

Prince of Wales CT3 4LN [S of Herne Bay]: Compact front bar with pine tables, two open fires, china and old photographs, food all day in attractive and good-sized newly extended back dining room with modern prints on warm red walls, Shepherd Neame Bitter and a guest such as Black Sheep, good staff; very busy wknds, piped music, occasional live; children and dogs welcome, garden with terrace tables (and perhaps summer opera), open all day (Kevin Thorpe)

NEWNHAM [TQ9557]

Tapster ME9 0NA [Parsonage Farm, Seed Rd]: Good upmarket meals rather than snacks in long bistro/bar with reclaimed broad boards, beams and brickwork, real ales such as Archers, Greene King IPA and Wells & Youngs, freshly squeezed orange juice and good choice of wines by the glass inc champagne, friendly staff and three lively dogs, huge log fireplace, candles, flowers and white linen, big pot plants and ferns, bar end with leather settees and daily papers; piped jazz, live 1st Sun monthly; dogs and children welcome, picnic-sets in big garden with cider press, open all day (afternoon break Fri/Sat), cl Mon (Kevin Thorpe)

NORTHBOURNE [TR3352]

Hare & Hounds CT14 0LG [off A256 or A258 nr Dover; The Street]: Popular village pub under newish management, real ales such as

Adnams Best, Flowers IPA, Harveys Best and Shepherd Neame Spitfire (Aug beer festival), unusual spanish soft drinks, pubby food from sandwiches up, friendly efficient service, log fires each end, local paintings for sale; terrace tables, big play area (N R White, Pamela and Alan Neale, Kevin Thorpe, Mr and Mrs Mike Pearson)

OTFORD [TQ5259]

Bull TN14 5PG [High St]: Attractively laid out 15th-c Chef & Brewer, their usual huge food choice from sandwiches and baguettes up all day, good Sun lunch, friendly attentive staff, four changing ales, decent wines, several quietly spacious rooms, log fires in two enormous fireplaces, soft lighting and candles; nice garden behind (Alan M Pring, N R White)

Crown TN14 5PQ [High St, pond end]: 16th-c two-bar local opp village pond, pleasantly chatty lounge with sofas, Black Sheep real ale, cheerful friendly staff, reasonably priced lunchtime food inc good Sun roasts; walkers and dogs welcome, good walks nearby (N R White)

Horns TN14 5PH [High St]: 15th-c beams and timbers, big inglenook log fire, plush seats and wheelback chairs, neatly cottagey decorations, tables set for good rather than cheap food, Westerham real ale (Tony and Glenys Dyer)

PENSHURST [TQ4943]

☆ **Rock** TN8 7BS [Hoath Corner, Chiddingstone Hoath; OS Sheet 188 map ref 497431]: Two charmingly old-fashioned and simple little beamed rooms with farmers and dogs, stripped brick and timbers, wonky brick floors, woodburner in inglenook, well kept local Larkins, good choice of simple good value food (not Sun), good house wines, local farm cider, friendly staff, ring the bull (with a real bull's head), steps up to small dining room; children and dogs welcome, no mobile phones; front terrace, back garden, beautiful countryside nearby (handy for Eden Valley walk), cl Mon (Andrea Rampley, GHC, Gwyn Jones)

☆ **Spotted Dog** TN11 8EP [Smarts Hill, off B2188 S]: Quaint old tiled pub with good bar food changing daily, local Larkins and a guest beer, local farm cider, pleasant relaxed young staff, cosy inglenook log fire, heavy low beams and timbers, antique settles and more straightforward furnishings, rugs and tiles, attractive moulded panelling, restaurant (very popular for Sun lunch, must book), new side shop selling local produce; unobtrusive piped music; children welcome till 7pm, tables out in front and on attractive tiered back terrace, open all day summer Thurs-Sun (N R White, Simon Pyle, B J Harding, Nick Lawless, J B Young, Nigel and Jean Eames, LYM)

PETT BOTTOM [TR1652]

Duck CT4 5PB [off B2068 S of Canterbury, via Lower Hardres]: Long bare-boards pine-panelled room with two log fires, dining end with good blackboard food choice from light dishes up, popular Sun roasts, decent wines, welcoming attentive service, bar end with well kept Shepherd Neame Bitter and Spitfire and a guest such as Harveys, darts and TV; piped music, occasional live; children welcome, sizeable pretty garden with terrace and barbecues, attractive downland spot, camp site, open all day wknds *(LYM, Kevin Thorpe)*

PLAXTOL [TQ6054]

☆ *Golding Hop* TN15 0PT [Sheet Hill (½ mile S of Ightham, between A25 and A227)]: Secluded country local, small and simple dim-lit two-level bar with hands-on landlord who can be very welcoming, Adnams, Youngs and a couple of guest beers, four local farm ciders (sometimes even their own), basic good value fresh bar snacks (not Mon/Tues evenings), woodburner, bar billiards; portable TV for big sports events, game machine; suntrap streamside lawn and well fenced play area over lane, open all day Sat *(the Didler, Bob and Margaret Holder, N R White, LYM, Gwyn Jones)*

PLUCKLEY [TQ9245]

Black Horse TN27 0QS [The Street]: Attractive and interesting medieval pub behind Georgian façade, bare boards and flagstones, hops on beams, four log fires inc vast inglenook, plenty of old things to look at, cheery atmosphere, wide food choice from baguettes up (just roasts on Sun), real ales inc Adnams, roomy carpeted side and back dining areas; piped music, big-screen TV, games machine; children allowed if eating, picnic-sets in spacious informal garden by tall sycamores, good walks, open all day Fri-Sun *(Ann and Colin Hunt, BB, Louise English)*

PRATTS BOTTOM [TQ4762]

Bulls Head BR6 7NQ [Rushmore Hill]: Quaint interesting pub in nice spot opp village green, good value pubby food, Fullers London Pride and a guest beer, moody décor, beams and bare boards; well chosen piped music *(Mike Buckingham)*

RAMSGATE [TR3764]

Artillery Arms CT11 9JS [West Cliff Rd]: Chatty open-plan corner local with Wells & Youngs Bombardier and four esoteric changing beers, farm cider, cheap rolls all day, straightforward two-level bar with fire at top end, artillery prints and interesting stained-glass windows dating from Napoleonic wars; juke box can be loud; good wheelchair access, children and dogs welcome, open all day *(Kevin Thorpe)*

Churchill Tavern CT11 9JX [Paragon (seafront)]: Big clifftop pub rebuilt in the 1980s with old beams, bare bricks, stained glass, pews and farm tools, long bar with Dark Star and up to half a dozen or so other changing ales, friendly young staff, good value food in bar or popular back cottage restaurant, open fire, dim lighting, pool in games corner; subdued piped music; children and dogs welcome, harbour, marina and Channel views, open all day *(Kevin Thorpe, N R White)*

Montefiore Arms CT11 7HJ [Trinity Pl]: Chatty unpretentious little backstreet pub, simply furnished single room, bargain Archers and a guest beer, keen landlord; darts, TV and piped radio; children welcome away from bar, cl Weds lunchtime *(Kevin Thorpe)*

ROCHESTER [TQ7468]

Coopers Arms ME1 1TL [St Margarets St]: Jettied Tudor building behind cathedral, cosily unpretentious and quaint inside, bustling local atmosphere, friendly staff, two comfortable bars, generous cheap wkdy bar lunches, well kept Courage Best and Directors; tables in attractive courtyard *(Craig Turnbull, B J Harding)*

RODMERSHAM [TQ9161]

Fruiterers Arms ME9 0PP [Bottles Lane]: Traditional pub with well kept ales inc Shepherd Neame, good bar menu, restaurant with good value Sun roasts, tempting puddings; nice garden, surrounding orchards *(Tony Liles)*

SANDGATE [TR2035]

Ship CT20 3AH [High St]: Friendly traditional two-room pub with well kept ales inc local ones, farm cider, decent fairly priced wine, inexpensive pub food inc local fish, affable attentive landlord, unpretentious décor, barrel seats and tables, lots of nautical prints and posters; sea views from tables out behind *(BB, David Lowe)*

SANDWICH [TR3358]

George & Dragon CT13 9EJ [Fisher St]: 15th-c building attractively opened up and restored keeping old beams and feel of small original rooms, welcoming chatty landlady, friendly civilised atmosphere, enjoyable food inc wood-fired pizzas and unusual dishes from open-view kitchen, well kept ales such as Adnams, Harveys and Shepherd Neame, good choice of wines by the glass; children and dogs welcome, pretty back terrace *(N R White)*

SEASALTER [TR0864]

☆ *Sportsman* CT5 4BP [Faversham Rd, off B2040]: Good imaginative contemporary cooking (not Sun evening or Mon, best to book other times, and not cheap) using local supplies in restauranty dining pub in caravan land, just inside the sea wall; relaxed atmosphere and friendly service in two plain linked rooms and long conservatory, wooden floor, big film star photographs, pine tables, wheelback and basket-weave dining chairs, well kept Shepherd Neame ales, well chosen wines; under same management as Granville at Lower Hardres – see main entries; children welcome, open all day Sun *(Derek Thomas, Dr K P Tucker, LYM, Andrea Rampley, N R White, Gary Smith)*

SELLING [TR0356]

☆ *White Lion* ME13 9RQ [off A251 S of Faversham (or exit roundabout, M2 junction 7); The Street]: 17th-c pub with well kept Shepherd Neame ales from unusual semicircular bar counter, decent wines, friendly helpful staff, wide blackboard food choice, log fire in hop-hung main bar with paintings for sale, another fire in small lower lounge with comfortable settees, back restaurant; children welcome; picnic-sets in attractive garden, colourful hanging baskets *(LYM, Kevin Thorpe)*

SEVENOAKS [TQ5555]

Bucks Head TN15 0JJ [Godden Green, just E]: Flower-decked pub with picnic-sets out on front terrace overlooking informal green and duckpond, welcoming landlady and thoughtful service, good value blackboard food from sandwiches to lots of fish specials, well kept Shepherd Neame ales inc seasonal, log fires in splendid inglenooks, neatly kept bar and restaurant area, no piped music; no dogs or muddy boots; children welcome, tables on back lawn with mature trees, bird fountain, pergola and views over quiet country behind Knole *(Alison and Graham Hooper, Richard Pitcher)*

Chequers TN13 1LD [High St]: Friendly beamed and flagstoned pub, nice change from the town's teen bars, with enthusiastic new young licensees doing good practical range of food *(R Arnold, Gwyn Jones)*

SHATTERLING [TR2658]

Frog & Orange CT3 1JR: Welcoming and neatly kept, with lots of stripped pine and old maps and photographs on partly stripped brick walls, pubby food from sandwiches, light dishes and pasta to plenty of fish, popular Sun lunches and other restaurant dishes, a couple of changing real ales; children welcome *(Phil and Jane Hodson)*

SHEERNESS [TQ9175]

Red Lion ME12 1RW [High St, Bluetown]: Solitary blitz survivor opp dockyards, lovingly preserved Victorian interior with cobblestones and masses of nautical memorabilia, three well kept changing guest beers from far and wide, pleasant staff, open fire, may be Sun bar nibbles; piped music, games and TV in side bar; rooftop garden, tables outside, open all day *(Kevin Thorpe)*

Ship on Shore ME12 2BX [Marine Parade, towards Minster]: Well run civilised pub with good value food, Courage Directors and summer guest beers, games area with pool well separated from quieter bar/dining area; apparently built partly with solidified concrete from 19th-c shipwreck *(Colin Moore)*

SHORNE [TQ6971]

Copperfield DA12 3JW [Gravesend Rd (A226)]: Rambling pub with nice wooden furniture in several linked areas, enjoyable and plentiful pubby food, real ales such as Greene King Old Speckled Hen; large terrace with country views towards Thames estuary *(Gill and Keith Croxton)*

SMARDEN [TQ8642]

☆ *Bell* TN27 8PW [from Smarden follow lane between church and Chequers, then left at T junction; or from A274 take unsignposted turn E a mile N of B2077 to Smarden]: Pretty rose-covered 17th-c inn with friendly

atmosphere and friendly service, enjoyable bar food from ciabattas to steaks, Shepherd Neame and other ales, local cider, country wines, winter mulled wine, rambling low-beamed little rooms, dim-lit and snug, nicely creaky old furnishings on ancient brick and flagstones or quarry tiles, warm inglenooks, end games area; picnic-sets in attractive mature garden *(John Currie, the Didler, LYM, Ann and Colin Hunt)*

SOUTHBOROUGH [TQ5742]

Hand & Sceptre TN4 0QB [London Rd (A26)]: Well run revamped former Harvester facing green and cricket ground, more continental-feel bar/restaurant with nice lounge area and enjoyable food *(Derek Thomas)*

SPELDHURST [TQ5541]

George & Dragon TN3 0NN [signed from A264 W of T Wells]: Handsome partly 13th-c timbered building with emphasis on imaginative if not cheap food using local and organic supplies, panelling, massive beams and flagstones, log fires inc one in a huge inglenook, Harveys PA and Best and Larkins, lots of malt whiskies, attractive upstairs restaurant; provision for children, garden tables *(Mrs C Lintott, LYM, Derek Thomas)*

ST MARGARET'S AT CLIFFE [TR3544]

Smugglers CT15 6AU [High St]: Friendly Spanish landlord and wife doing very wide choice of enjoyable reasonably priced food from good value baguettes up inc good tapas, home-made pizzas and Sun lunch, well kept Greene King ales, compact cosy bar, attractive dining room (paintings for sale) and conservatory; imaginatively terraced partly covered garden *(Dr K P Tucker, M G Hart)*

ST NICHOLAS AT WADE [TR2666]

Bell CT7 0NT [just off A299; The Street]: Olde-worlde 16th-c beamed two-bar pub busy wknds for good value generous unfussy food from baguettes to fresh fish and sell-out Sun roasts, ancient stripped brickwork and big log fire in antique high grate, Adnams Broadside, Greene King IPA and a guest beer, friendly staff, restaurant, pool and games in big back room; children and dogs welcome, open all day wknds *(Kevin Thorpe, Conor McGaughey)*

STALISFIELD GREEN [TQ9552]

Plough ME13 0HY [off A252 in Charing]: New licensees in peaceful village-green pub with large old-fashioned tables and chairs in dining areas on either side of bar, enjoyable food inc some interesting dishes and nice puddings, Shepherd Neame real ales; tables in big pleasant garden, attractive setting, good view and walks *(Peter Meister, Robert Lloyd)*

STONE IN OXNEY [TQ9428]

Ferry TN30 7JY: Good atmosphere in former smugglers' haunt by what used to be the landing for the Oxney ferry, reasonably priced food, good service; big garden *(V Brogden)*

STONE STREET [TQ5755]
Padwell Arms TN15 0LQ [off A25 E of
Sevenoaks, on Seal—Plaxtol by-road; OS
Sheet 188 map ref 569551]: Orchard-view
country pub with quick pleasant service, good
changing choice of well kept ales such as
Larkins and Timothy Taylors Landlord, wide
choice of home-made food (served Sun
evening too) from baguettes up, nice wines
and good coffee, comfortable banquettes and
log fire, airy back dining area; pub dog
perhaps over-keen to be friendly; tables on
front terrace (lovely flowering baskets and
window boxes), more in pleasant back garden,
plenty of shade, good walks *(Malcolm Stapley,
E D Bailey, BB, GHC, the Didler)*
☆ *Snail* TN15 0LT: Smart well run pub-styled
restaurant, wide choice of good food at big
oak farmhouse tables, plenty of fish, good
wines, Harveys and a guest beer, ad lib
coffee, friendly staff and relaxed atmosphere,
pleasant brasserie layout with beams, oak
panelling and some stripped stone;
attractive rambling garden, handy for
Ightham Mote *(E D Bailey, BB,
Gordon Ormondroyd, John Marshall)*
SUNDRIDGE [TQ4855]
White Horse TN14 6EH [Main Rd]: Recently
refurbished and under friendly hands-on new
Australian landlady, with good interesting
range of all-day food from bar snacks to
restaurant meals, well kept Fullers London
Pride with guest such as Adnams Broadside
and Caledonian Deuchars IPA, log fires and
low beams; garden tables *(Mike Buckingham)*
TENTERDEN [TQ8833]
William Caxton TN30 6JR [West Cross; top
of High St]: 15th-c local, heavy beams and
bare boards, huge inglenook log fire,
woodburner in smaller back bar, wide
blackboard choice of enjoyable reasonably
priced food, Shepherd Neame real ales, good
service, darts, pleasant small dining room;
piped music; children and dogs welcome,
tables in attractive front area, open all day
(the Didler, V Brogden)
THURNHAM [TQ8057]
☆ *Black Horse* ME14 3LD [not far from M20
junction 7; off A249 at Detling]: Popular
rebuilt dining pub with huge choice of
enjoyable food all day, Fullers London Pride,
Swale Kentish Pride and a guest beer, farm
ciders and country wines, friendly staff, log
fires, dogs welcome, pleasant garden with
partly covered back terrace, water features
and nice views, by Pilgrims Way and handy
for North Downs, bedrooms, open all day
(M Greening, Bob Pike)
TONBRIDGE [TQ5945]
Vauxhall Inn TN11 0NA [Vauxhall
Lane/Pembury Rd]: Chef & Brewer with good
choice of food, two real ales, tea and coffee;
disabled parking, access and facilities, open
all day *(A Benson)*
TOYS HILL [TQ4752]
Fox & Hounds TN16 1QG [off A25 in Brasted,
via Brasted Chart and The Chart]: Emphasis
on good if pricy food (not Sun evening),

interesting blackboard choice, good neat
service, Greene King IPA and Abbot, smart
comfortable modern dining extension, nice
softly lit and tiled-floor original core by coal
fire; piped music, occasional live; disabled
access and facilities, pleasant tree-sheltered
garden, good walks nearby, open all day
summer, cl Mon *(Grahame Brooks, N R White,
William Ruxton, LYM, Simon Rodway,
Jenny and Brian Seller, Cathryn and
Richard Hicks, Alan Cowell)*
TUNBRIDGE WELLS [TQ5839]
Opera House TN1 1RT [Mount Pleasant Rd]:
Large Wetherspoons restoration of 1900s
opera house (had been a bingo hall later),
with original circle and stalls, stage lighting
and ornate ceiling; real ales inc more or less
local guest beers, usual cheap Wetherspoons
food, lower family area; can get crowded
wknd evenings *(Tony Hobden)*
UNDER RIVER [TQ5552]
☆ *White Rock* TN15 0SB [SE of Sevenoaks, off
B245]: Well run village pub, attractive and
relaxed, with enjoyable well priced food from
hot filled rolls to full meals, coffee and
cakes between times, Fullers London Pride,
Harveys and Westerham SPA, friendly service
and interesting mix of customers, beams,
bare boards and stripped brickwork in cosy
original part with adjacent dining area,
public bar with pool in modern extension;
quiet piped music; children welcome, pretty
front garden, back terrace and big back
lawn, handy for Knole Park and Greensand
Way (walkers asked to use side door), open
all day *(GHC, Tina and David Woods-Taylor,
N R White, John Tuck, R B Gardiner,
E D Bailey, DFL)*
WAREHORNE [TQ9832]
Woolpack TN26 2LL [off B2067 nr
Hamstreet]: Big neatly kept 16th-c dining
pub with good value generous food in
rambling bar and big candlelit restaurant,
popular carvery Weds evening (booking
essential), elaborate puddings, well kept
Harveys Best, decent wines, efficient service,
huge inglenook, heavy beams, plain games
room; picnic-sets out overlooking quiet lane
and meadow with lovely big beech trees, lots
of flower tubs and little fountain, not far
from the good Woodchurch rare breeds
centre *(Mr and Mrs Mike Pearson, BB)*
WESTWELL [TQ9847]
Wheel TN25 4LQ: Reopened under new
landlord with catering background, wide
choice of good food, efficient attentive
service *(Mr and Mrs Mike Pearson)*
WHITSTABLE [TR1167]
Continental CT5 2BP [Beach Walk]:
Unpretentious mix of 19th-c seafront hotel,
pub/café and brasserie restaurant, outlet for
Whitstable brewery (in fact over towards
Maidstone) under same ownership, friendly
service, relaxed atmosphere, large windows
looking over Thames estuary (on a clear day
you can see Southend); children welcome,
metal tables and chairs outside *(N R White,
Bob and Margaret Holder)*

Whitstable Brewery Bar CT5 2BP [East Quay]: New beach bar, five real ales and various lagers and fruit beers from the associated Whitstable brewery (near Maidstone), light, airy and simple with sea-view picture windows, functional span ceiling, flagstone floor with long tables and benches around the edge, leather settees in one corner, woodburner, Fri music night; July beer festival; picnic-sets out on the shingle, cl winter Mon-Weds, open all day *(Keith and Chris O'Neill)*

WICKHAMBREAUX [TR2258]

Rose CT3 1RQ [The Green]: Friendly helpful new licensees in attractive 16th-c or older pub, good value home-made food, Adnams Broadside, Greene King IPA and a guest beer, Addlestone's farm cider, small bare-boards beamed bar with log fire in big fireplace, dining area beyond standing timbers, panelling and stripped brick; no children or dogs (there is a pub dog); garden with barbecues, nice spot across green from church and watermill, open all day *(Kevin Thorpe, Mrs M Grimwood)*

WITTERSHAM [TQ8927]

Swan TN30 7PH [Swan St]: Large village pub dating from 17th c, well kept Harveys Best, Goachers Light and Mild and four changing microbrews, beer festivals, wide food choice from sandwiches up, back lounge bar with open fire, china and pictures, public with darts and pool; TV; garden with picnic-sets, open all day *(Kevin Thorpe)*

WORMSHILL [TQ8757]

Blacksmiths Arms ME9 0TU [handy for M20 junction 8]: Attractive 18th-c low-beamed pub with big log fire, candles, old prints and well worn tiles in small bar area, smarter furnishings in upper eating room, flame-effect fire in stripped brick carpeted restaurant, good range of changing real ales, Stowford Press cider, nice choice of chip-free food from baguettes to some quite expensive main dishes; no children, cl Sun evening and Mon (and may occasionally close for local events) *(Philip and Cheryl Hill)*

WORTH [TR3356]

☆ **St Crispin** CT14 0DF [signed off A258 S of Sandwich]: Dating from 16th c, with stripped brickwork, bare boards and low beams in comfortably refurbished bar, generous popular home-made food here and in restaurant and back conservatory from good baguettes to some imaginative dishes, welcoming attentive staff, changing real ales, some tapped from the cask, such as Harveys and Timothy Taylors Landlord, belgian beers, local farm cider, well chosen wines, central log fire; good bedrooms (inc some motel-style extension), charming big garden behind with terrace and barbecue, lovely village position *(Rona Murdoch, Mrs Frances Pennell, N R White)*

If a pub tries to make you leave a credit card behind the bar, be on your guard. The credit card firms and banks which issue them condemn this practice. After all, the publican who asks you to do this is in effect saying: 'I don't trust you'. Have you any more reason to trust his staff? If your card is used fraudulently while you have let it be kept out of your sight, the card company could say you've been negligent yourself – and refuse to make good your losses. So say that they can 'swipe' your card instead, but must hand it back to you. Please let us know if a pub does try to keep your card.

Lancashire
(with Greater Manchester and Merseyside)

This area's hefty roster of good pubs is boosted further this year with the addition of no fewer than six new main entries: the welcoming Cavendish Arms at Brindle has been freshened up by a new landlord, the tucked-away Plough at Eaves near Broughton has an appealing country atmosphere, at the Rams Head up at Denshaw the licensees' adjacent produce shop adds an extra dimension, the charming Devonshire Arms in Mellor is an enjoyable throwback to the traditional way of doing things, the handsomely reworked Highwayman at Nether Burrow shows the other end of the pub spectrum at its best, and the civilised Old Sparrow Hawk at Wheatley Lane is a very rewarding all-rounder. There really is something for everyone here – you can take your pick between stylish up-to-date places with great menus (quite a few here have been refurbished in a contemporary fashion), traditional pubs that serve great real ales, and those that manage to do both really well. The area also has more than its fair share of places deserving of our Place to Stay Award. What scores high points again and again is a genuinely warm welcome and real attention to what customers want. Great all-rounders include the civilised Eagle & Child at Bispham Green and the stylish Sun in Lancaster (with a new Place to Stay Award this year). The best real ale pubs are the Victorian Philharmonic Dining Rooms in Liverpool, the down-to-earth Taps in Lytham, a pair of engaging Manchester pubs, the Britons Protection and the Marble Arch, and the warmly welcoming Dressers Arms at Wheelton. Pub food tends to be very generous in the area, and taking quality into account tends to be somewhat cheaper than in most places. Some prime places for dining out are the Lunesdale Arms at Tunstall (which gains a new Food Award this year), the comfortably civilised Bay Horse at Bay Horse, the styishly upmarket Three Fishes at Great Mitton, the smartly enjoyable Spread Eagle at Sawley, and the beautiful Inn at Whitewell. It's the Inn at Whitewell, with its excellent food, good choice of wines and lovely interior, that gains the title of Lancashire Dining Pub of the Year. Drinks prices in the area are well below the national average, and it's still possible – though getting much harder – to find a pint of good beer for under £2. Low prices certainly don't mean low quality. The five pubs we found charging least for beer here all qualify for our Beer Award, showing that their beers are better than in many more expensive pubs. Quite a few pubs in the area brew their own beer, which almost always brings rewards in terms of value for money. Robinsons and Thwaites, the main regional brewers, both price their beers competitively, and a throng of good smaller brewers jostles for attention. Ones we found supplying the cheapest beers offered by at least some main entry pubs here were Hydes, who brew Boddingtons now, Thomas Hardy

(Burtonwood), who brew Websters, and Bowland, Lees, Cains and Lancaster. Pubs to look out for in the Lucky Dip section at the end of the chapter are the Fenwick Arms at Claughton, Crown in Croston, Hest Bank Hotel, Baltic Fleet in Liverpool, Mr Thomas Chop House in Manchester, Wheatsheaf at Raby, Fishermans Retreat at Ramsbottom, Freemasons Arms at Wiswell and Calfs Head at Worston.

BARNSTON   SJ2783   MAP 7

Fox & Hounds 🍺 £

3 miles from M53 junction 3: A552 towards Woodchurch, then left on A551; CH61 1BW

Tidy pub with unusual collections, very reasonably priced lunchtime food and good range of drinks including interesting guest beers

It's a good idea to arrive early if you want to sample the good-value lunchtime bar food at this well looked after pub. There's an impressive array of drinks too, with Theakstons Best and Old Peculier and Websters Yorkshire, along with three guests such as Brimstage Trappers Hat and Rhode Island Red and Greene King Abbot and on handpump; 60 whiskies and a dozen wines by the glass. Tucked away opposite the serving counter is a charming old quarry-tiled corner with an antique kitchen range, copper kettles, built-in pine kitchen cupboards, and lots of earthenware or enamelled food bins. With its own entrance at the other end of the pub, a small locals' bar is worth a peek for its highly traditional layout – as well as a collection of hundreds of metal ashtrays on its delft shelf; beside it is a snug where children are allowed. The main part of the roomy carpeted bay-windowed lounge bar has red plush button-back built-in banquettes and plush-cushioned captain's chairs around the solid tables, and plenty of old local prints on its cream walls below a delft shelf of china, with a collection of police and other headgear; darts and board games. There are some picnic-sets under cocktail parasols out in the yard behind, below a farm.

🍴 **Very traditional pubby food includes open sandwiches, soup, filled baked potatoes, quiche, various platters such as greek salad, ploughman's, mushroom stroganoff, lamb casserole and dumplings, hot pie of the day, fish and chips and roasts; Sunday roasts.** *Starters/Snacks: £1.95 to £4.25. Main Courses: £3.95 to £8.25. Puddings: £4.25*

Free house ~ Licensee Ralph Leech ~ Real ale ~ Bar food (12-2 (may stop earlier Sun)) ~ (0151) 648 1323 ~ Children in snug ~ Dogs allowed in bar ~ Open 11-11; 12-10.30 Sun

Recommended by Clive Watkin, Maurice and Gill McMahon, Dr R A Smye, Ann and Tony Bennett-Hughes, Chris Glasson, Paul Boot

---

BAY HORSE   SD4952   MAP 7

Bay Horse 🍽 🍷

1¼ miles from M6 junction 33: A6 southwards, then off on left; LA2 0HR

Comfortably stylish pub with emphasis on super thoughtfully prepared innovative food; good range of drinks, garden

Warm and cosy, the beamed red-walled bar at this popular dining pub is attractively decorated, with a good log fire, cushioned wall banquettes in bays, and gentle lighting, including table lamps on window sills – look out for the friendly cat. As well as a decent, fairly priced wine list (about a dozen wines by the glass, and fruit wines too), very helpful staff serve Black Sheep, Moorhouses Pendle Witches Brew and Thwaites Lancaster Bomber from handpumps, and 15 malt whiskies. There are usually fresh flowers on the counter, and maybe piped music. A series of small rambling dining areas has the feel of a civilised country restaurant, with red décor, another log fire, candle-flame-effect lights and nice tables, including one or two good-sized ones in intimate self-contained corners. The pub is in a peaceful location (though the railway is not far off), and there are tables out in the garden behind. Note they don't accept lunchtime bookings for parties of fewer than eight.

🍽 **A good deal of attention goes into the food here, with innovative use of carefully sourced ingredients, and though not cheap, helpings are generous. As well as imaginative lunchtime sandwiches, they have lunch and evening menus that might include starters such as smoked duck caesar salad, roast scallops and smoked salmon with saffron and truffle dressing, pickled herrings with beetroot relish and fennel and morecambe bay shrimps in herb butter. Main courses might be slow-cooked goosnargh duck with boozy prunes, mutton shank cooked in red wine and thyme with goats cheese mashed potato, and bass with orange and beetroot butter, with puddings such as treacle and walnut tart with nutmeg ice-cream and pears poached in white wine; british cheeseboard.** *Starters/Snacks: £4.25 to £7.95. Main Courses: £11.95 to £21.95. Puddings: £4.95 to £6.75*

Mitchells ~ Tenant Craig Wilkinson ~ Real ale ~ Bar food (12-1.45(2 Sat, 3 Sun), 7-9.15(6.30-8.30 Sun)) ~ (01524) 791204 ~ Children welcome ~ Open 12-3, 6.30-midnight; 12-midnight Sun; closed Mon, Tues ~ Bedrooms: /£79B

Recommended by K S Whittaker, Brian Wainwright, Sarah and Peter Gooderham, Michael Doswell, Rob and Catherine Dunster, Revd D Glover, Jane and Martin Bailey, Jo Lilley, Simon Calvert, Dr D J and Mrs S C Walker, J S Burn, Mrs A Green, Margaret Dickinson

BISPHAM GREEN   SD4813   MAP 7

Eagle & Child 🍽 🍷 ◖
Maltkiln Lane (Parbold—Croston road, off B5246); L40 3SG

Well liked friendly pub with antiques in stylishly simple interior, interesting range of beers, very well prepared food, and nice garden

Well divided by stubs of walls, the largely open-plan bar here is gently civilised. Attractively understated old furnishings include a mix of small oak chairs around tables in corners, an oak coffer, several handsomely carved antique oak settles (the finest apparently made partly from a 16th-c wedding bed-head), and old hunting prints and engravings. There's coir matting in the snug, and oriental rugs on flagstones in front of the fine old stone fireplaces. An interesting range of five changing beers might typically include Barngates K9, Moorhouses Blonde Witch, Phoenix Navvy, Southport Sandgrounder, Thwaites Original and Weetwood Cheshire Cat, and they also keep a changing farm cider, decent wines, some country wines and around 30 malt whiskies. They hold a popular beer festival over the first May bank holiday weekend. The handsome side barn was being converted into a deli, with an antiques shop above, and smokers can retreat to the cart shed. A nice wild garden has crested newts and nesting moorhens; the pub's dogs are called Harry and Doris. You can try your hand at bowls or croquet on the neat green outside this brick pub, but beware that the crowns deceive even the most experienced players.

🍽 **There's quite an emphasis on the well cooked food (you should book) which includes soup, imaginative sandwiches, chicken caesar salad, steak and ale pie, fish and chips, cumberland sausage and mash, and crayfish and lemon or mushroom and rosemary risotto, with specials such as roast red pepper and goats cheese tart, seared scallops with mango salad, roast suckling pig with cider and apple gravy, and roast monkfish with pancetta, white wine, cream and chives.** *Starters/Snacks: £3.75 to £7.00. Main Courses: £8.50 to £16.50. Puddings: £4.00 to £4.50*

Free house ~ Licensees Monica Evans and David Anderson ~ Real ale ~ Bar food (12-2, 5.30-8.30(9 Fri, Sat); 12-8.30 Sun) ~ (01257) 462297 ~ Children welcome in dining areas ~ Dogs allowed in bar ~ Open 12-3, 5.30-11; 12-10.30 Sun

Recommended by Steve Whalley, Geoff and Teresa Salt, Revd D Glover, Mark Lowe, Jo Lilley, Simon Calvert, Andrea Rampley, Mr and Mrs J N Graham, K S Whittaker, Dr Phil Putwain

BRINDLE   SD5924   MAP 7

Cavendish Arms

*3 miles from M6 junction 29; A6 towards Whittle-le-Woods then left on B5256
(Sandy Lane); PR6 8NG*

Freshened-up village pub with good value pubby food, and terrace

A warmly welcoming and energetic new landlord has brightened up and comfortably
refurbished this interesting place. It takes its name from William Cavendish, who in 1582
gained the village of Brindle when the previous owner forfeited his lands on going into
the Tower of London. Several cosy snugs have unusual stained-glass partitions, and you
can just make out the handsome stone church tower and churchyard through the stained-
glass latticed windows. Marstons Burton or Banks and a guest such as Wadworths
Summersault are served on handpump. A canopied terrace has picnic-sets, and a rockery
and water feature to one side.

🍽 **Sensibly priced food (from new kitchen) includes sandwiches, soup, caesar salad, thai
fishcakes, spare ribs, steak and ale pie, chilli, cheddar-stuffed chicken, battered cod,
mushroom and spinach risotto, steaks** *Starters/Snacks: £3.50 to £4.95. Main Courses: £6.75 to
£11.95. Puddings: £3.25 to £3.50*

Burtonwood (Marstons) ~ Lease Martin Cavanagh ~ Real ale ~ Bar food (12(4 Mon)-9) ~
Restaurant ~ (01254) 852912 ~ Children welcome ~ Open 12(4 Mon)-11(12 Fri, 10.30 Sun);
may close 3pm-5pm Tues-Fri Oct-Feb
Recommended by Graham Patterson, Dr D J and Mrs S C Walker, John and Eleanor Holdsworth

BROUGHTON   SD4838   MAP 7

Plough at Eaves

*A6 N through Broughton, first left into Station Lane just under a mile after traffic lights,
then bear left after another 1½ miles; PR4 0BJ*

Cosy old place in very peaceful spot; good value traditional food

Do persevere with finding this very tucked away unfussy old country pub, it's well worth
it for a peaceful moment sitting on metal and wood-slat seats at the cast-iron-framed
tables set out along the front of the building, by the quiet lane. Inside, the two homely
low-beamed lattice-windowed bars are neat and traditionally furnished with a mixture of
wooden chairs, tables and upholstered seats, and there are three aged guns over one
good copper-hooded open fire with a row of Royal Doulton figurines above another. The
restaurant is now extended into a conservatory and there's a further dining area in
another very comfy room. Thwaites Original and Lancaster Bomber on handpump, piped
music and games machine. There's a well equipped children's play area at the back.

🍽 **Bar food includes breaded camembert, sandwiches, stir fries, various filled pastas,
steak and kidney pie, poached salmon in lemon butter and peppered steak, with home-
made puddings including fresh fruit pavlova and chocolate fudge cake.** *Starters/Snacks:
£3.25 to £6.30. Main Courses: £6.25 to £14.95. Puddings: £3.95*

Thwaites ~ Tenants Doreen and Mike Dawson ~ Real ale ~ Bar food (12-2.15(3.15 Sat), 6(5.30
Sat)-9.15; 12-8 Sun) ~ Restaurant ~ (01772) 690233 ~ Children welcome away from bar ~ Open
12-3, 5.30-12; 12-12 Sat and Sun; closed Mon lunchtimes
Recommended by Robin and Janice Dewhurst, Margaret Dickinson

Bedroom prices normally include full English breakfast, VAT and any inclusive service
charge that we know of. Prices before the '/' are for single rooms, after for two people in
double or twin (B includes a private bath, S a private shower). If there is no '/', the
prices are only for twin or double rooms (as far as we know there are no singles).

BURY   SD8015   MAP 7

Lord Raglan ◀

2 miles off M66 northbound, junction 1; A56 S then left in Walmersley, up long cobbled lane to Mount Pleasant, Nangreaves; if coming from N, stay on A56 S instead of joining M66, and turn left in Walmersley as above; BL9 6SP

Individually run place with fabulous views and extensive range of own-brew beers

High on the moors above Bury, this neatly kept 18th-c pub produces a range of eight own-brew beers. Well kept on handpump (alongside an interesting seasonal guest) they are Leyden Balaclava, Black Pudding, Crowning Glory, Forever Bury, Light Brigade, Nanny Flyer, Raglan Sleeve and Sebastopol. They've also got 30 malt whiskies and interesting foreign bottled beers, and they hold a beer festival in June. All sorts of bric-a-brac is dotted around the snug beamed front bar, with lots of pewter, brass and interesting antique clocks, and there's a mix of spindleback chairs and old wooden settles. The back room has a huge open fire, china on a high delft shelf and welsh dresser, and windows giving a splendid view down the valley. A plainer but more spacious dining room on the left is panelled in light wood; TV, board games and piped music.

🍽 **Available in the bar or the restaurant, the menu includes open sandwiches, soup, smoked fish platter, ploughman's, steak and ale pie, prawn curry, red thai vegetable curry, chicken balti, poached salmon fillet, fried plaice, chicken chasseur and steaks. One or two readers have told us that food service stops very promptly, possibly even a bit early sometimes.** *Starters/Snacks: £2.70 to £4.85. Main Courses: £6.25 to £12.75. Puddings: £1.90 to £3.25*

Own brew ~ Licensee Brendan Leyden ~ Real ale ~ Bar food (12-2, 7(5 Fri)-9;12-9 Sat, Sun) ~ Restaurant ~ (0161) 764 6680 ~ Children welcome ~ Dogs allowed in bar ~ Open 12-2.30, 7(5 Fri)-11; 12-11(10.30 Sun) Sat
Recommended by Brian Wainwright, Mark and Diane Grist

CHIPPING   SD6141   MAP 7

Dog & Partridge

Hesketh Lane; crossroads Chipping—Longridge with Inglewhite—Clitheroe; PR3 2TH

Comfortable old-fashioned dining pub in grand countryside, with traditional food

Within walking distance of the dramatic high moors of the Forest of Bowland, this comfortable and much-extended dining pub dates back to 1515. The main lounge has small armchairs around fairly close-set low tables on a blue patterned carpet, brown-painted beams, a good winter log fire, and multicoloured lanterns; piped music. Tetleys Bitter and Mild with a weekly changing guest such as Black Sheep Bitter on handpump are served by friendly well trained staff. Smart casual dress is preferred in the stable restaurant. More reports please.

🍽 **Bar food includes soup, sandwiches, duck and orange pâté, leek and mushroom crumble, steak and kidney pie, roast chicken, roast duckling with apple sauce and stuffing, and grilled sirloin steak with mushrooms, with puddings (some home-made) such as fruit pie or raspberry shortcake.** *Starters/Snacks: £3.30 to £5.50. Main Courses: £9.00 to £14.00. Puddings: £4.10*

Free house ~ Licensee Peter Barr ~ Real ale ~ Bar food (12-1.45; 7(6.30 Sat)-9; 12-8.30 Sun) ~ Restaurant (7(6.30 Sat)-9 Mon-Sat; 12-8.30 Sun) ~ (01995) 61201 ~ Children welcome ~ Open 11.45-3, 6.45-11; 11.45-10.30 Sun; closed Mon
Recommended by Brian Wainwright, Dennis Jones

Post Office address codings confusingly give the impression that some pubs are in Lancashire when they're really in Cumbria or Yorkshire (which is where we list them).

DENSHAW

SD9711   MAP 7

Rams Head

2 miles from M62 junction 2; A672 towards Oldham, pub N of village; OL3 5UN

Roaring fires and tasty food in inviting old-world moorland pub with farm shop

This comfortable pub has fine views down the Tame Valley and over the moors, and is well placed for walks – up towards Brushes Clough reservoir, say. Its snug traditional interior has beam-and-plank ceilings and good log fires, and is furnished with oak settles, and benches built into the panelling of its four thick-walled little rooms; Black Sheep and Timothy Taylors on handpump; piped music. You can buy locally sourced meat and other produce, and have a coffee, in their adjacent shop.

🍴 **Bar food might include soup, pheasant terrine, king prawns fried in garlic and ginger, fried tuna with pepper crust on fried noodle salad, baked haddock on mash with asparagus and carrots and cheese sauce, roast partridge wrapped in maple-cured bacon on braised red cabbage with chocolate sauce, sirloin steak; Sunday roasts.** *Starters/Snacks: £3.95 to £6.95. Main Courses: £9.95 to £15.95. Puddings: £3.95 to £4.95*

Free house ~ Licensee Geoff Haigh ~ Real ale ~ Bar food ~ Restaurant ~ (01457) 874802 ~ Children welcome till 8pm (7pm Sat) ~ Open 12-2.30, 6-11; 12-10.30 Sun

Recommended by Jak Radice, John and Eleanor Holdsworth, K C and B Forman

FENCE

SD8237   MAP 7

Fence Gate ♀

2.6 miles from M65 junction 13; Wheatley Lane Road, just off A6068 W; BB12 9EE

Smartly refurbished pub and brasserie with great wine list, five real ales and popular tasty food

This big stylishly extended stone house is both bang up to date yet still determinedly pubby, cleverly blending its gently upmarket touches with more traditional features. There are often as many cosmopolitan groups sipping Pimms as there are locals downing pints, but somehow both seem completely at home. An almost bewildering array of blackboards above the bar counter shows off the good, comprehensive wine list (plenty by the glass), and they also have Caledonian Deuchars IPA, Courage Directors, Theakstons Best, two changing guests such as local Bowland Hen Harrier and Moorhouses Premier, and various teas and coffees. Plenty of polished panelling and timbers divide the carpeted bar into several distinct-feeling areas: there's an almost clubby corner with a small bookcase, a fish in a glass case, and a big fire, while just along from here is a part with sporting prints above the panelling, a number of stools, and a TV. Leading off the central section with its mix of wooden tables and chairs is a very comfortable area with red-patterned sofas and lots of cushions, and there's a more unusual bit with tables on a raised step beneath carved panelling; piped music; very good service. The imposing building dates from the 17th c and is said to be haunted by Horatio, the unfortunate victim of a shooting accident.

🍴 **Bar food is popular, particularly their award-wining home-made sausages – organic meats are combined with all sorts of different ingredients, anything from local cheese or their own black pudding to blueberries and calvados or sun-dried tomato and chilli. Other dishes include soup, sandwiches, vegetable lasagne, pies such as steak, ale and mushroom or local lamb and vegetable, good home-made burgers, cod and chips, daily specials, puddings such as apple and raspberry crème brûlée and lancashire cheese and apple tart, and they do a local cheese platter. The brasserie is very highly regarded.** *Starters/Snacks: £3.85 to £4.95. Main Courses: £5.35 to £9.50. Puddings: £4.95 to £7.75*

Free house ~ Licensee Kevin Berkins ~ Real ale ~ Bar food (12-2.30 (3 Sun), 6.30-9.30(8.30 Sun)) ~ Restaurant ~ (01282) 618101 ~ Children welcome ~ Open 12-11.30(1am Fri, Sat, 11 Sun)

Recommended by Steve Whalley, Margaret Dickinson

GOOSNARGH
SD5738   MAP 7

Horns ♀ 🛏

Pub signed from village, about 2 miles towards Chipping below Beacon Fell; PR3 2FJ

Traditional plush pub popular for dining; nice chintzy bedrooms

Although food is the main attraction at this mock-Tudor coaching inn, you can just sit and enjoy a drink. The quietly relaxing and neatly kept rooms have patterned carpets, traditional red plush upholstered chairs around pub tables, colourful flower displays, and winter log fires. Beyond the lobby, the pleasant front bar opens into attractively decorated middle rooms; piped music. They stock an extensive wine list with quite a few by the glass, a fine choice of malt whiskies, and have Black Sheep on handpump.

🍴 **Bar food includes sandwiches, ploughman's, soup, duck liver pâté, spicy southport shrimps, prawns and salad, steak and kidney pie, roast pheasant with cranberry sauce, and scampi, or you can eat a five-course meal from the elaborate restaurant menu.** *Starters/Snacks: £4.25 to £4.95. Main Courses: £8.95 to £12.95. Puddings: £4.95*

Free house ~ Licensee Mark Woods ~ Real ale ~ Bar food ~ Restaurant ~ (01772) 865230 ~ Children welcome ~ Open 11.30-3, 6.30-11; 12-3, 6.30-10.30 Sun; closed Mon lunchtime ~ Bedrooms: £59B/£85B

Recommended by Ray and Winifred Halliday, Ken Richards, Richard Endacott, W W Burke

GREAT MITTON
SD7139   MAP 7

Three Fishes

Mitton Road (B6246, off A59 NW of Whalley); BB7 9PQ

Stylish modern conversion, tremendous attention to detail, excellent food with a contemporary twist, interesting drinks

Smartly renovated by the people behind the renowned restaurant-with-rooms, Northcote Manor, this 16th-c dining pub is one of the county's stand-out places to eat, thanks to its very good regional cooking. They don't take bookings (except for groups of eight or more), but write your name on a blackboard when you arrive, and find you when a table becomes free – the system works surprisingly well, even at the busiest times. The interior stretches back much further than you'd initially expect. The areas closest to the bar are elegantly traditional with a couple of big stone fireplaces, rugs on polished floors, newly upholstered stools, and a good chatty feel; then there's a series of individually furnished and painted rooms with exposed stone walls and floors, careful spotlighting, and wooden slatted blinds, ending with another impressive fireplace. The long bar counter (with elaborate floral displays) serves Thwaites Original and Lancaster Bomber, a guest from Bowland, cocktails, a good choice of wines by the glass and unusual soft drinks. Overlooking the Ribble Valley, the garden has tables and perhaps its own menu in summer. They have facilities for the disabled.

🍴 **You order your meal at various food points dotted around, and the emphasis is on traditional lancastrian dishes with a modern twist. Products are carefully sourced from small local suppliers, many of whom are immortalised in black and white photographs on the walls, and located on a map on the back of the menu. Most dish descriptions indicate the origins of the main ingredient – the beef particularly is exclusive to here, coming from a unique herd of british whites. As well as imaginative lunchtime sandwiches, there might be shrimps with a toasted muffin, treacle-baked ribs with devilled black peas, cod fishcake with parsley sauce, house-cured meat or a seafood platter, fish pie, battered haddock, lancashire hotpot with pickled red cabbage, slow-baked pigs trotters with chicken and blackpudding stuffing, sausage and mash, 10oz sirloin steak, and puddings such as chocolate and orange pudding with clotted cream and curd tart with lemon ice-cream. You may need to order side dishes with some main courses.** *Starters/Snacks: £4.75 to £8.50. Main Courses: £8.75 to £13.90. Puddings: £4.50*

Pubs close to motorway junctions are listed at the back of the book.

Free house ~ Licensees Nigel Haworth, Andy Morris ~ Real ale ~ Bar food (12-2, 6(5.30 Sun)-9; 12-8.30 Sun) ~ (01254) 826888 ~ Children welcome ~ Dogs welcome ~ Open 12-11

Recommended by Mrs P J Carroll, Susan and Nigel Brookes, J F M and M West, Brian Wainwright, Paul Ribchester, Maurice and Gill McMahon, Jo Lilley, Simon Calvert, Rob Bowran, Mark O'Sullivan, John and Sylvia Harrop

LANCASTER

SD4761   MAP 7

Sun ♀ 🍺 🛏

Church Street; LA1 1ET

Contemporary updates to lovely old building, fantastic range of drinks including eight real ales, food served from breakfast on, comfortably modern bedrooms

Beautifully restored and extended over the last couple of years, this historic hotel in the heart of the city imaginatively blends its oldest features with some that are bang up to date. It's both warmly traditional and comfortably contemporary – and the food and drinks are impressive too. The beamed bar is atmospheric and characterful, with plenty of panelling, chunky modern tables on the part flagged and part wooden floors, a 300-year-old oak door (discovered during renovations), several fireplaces (the biggest filled with a huge oak cask), and subtly effective spotlighting. The size of the bar counter belies the range of drinks available: you'll generally find three real ales from the Lancaster Brewery (set up in 2005 by the company behind the pub's transformation), as well as five changing guests from brewers such as Elwoods, Jennings, Thwaites and Wadworths, some 80 belgian and bottled beers, 24 or so well chosen wines by the glass, lots of whiskies and spirits, and some unique teas and coffees from a local wholesaler. There's a discreet TV in a corner. A passageway leads to a long narrow room that's altogether cooler, still with exposed stone walls, but this time covered with changing art exhibitions; the furnishings in here are mostly soft and low, with lots of dark brown pouffes and stools. Some more substantial wooden tables and high-backed chairs lead into a conservatory; piped music, fruit machine.

🍽 **Bar food kicks off with an unusual breakfast menu (maybe devilled kidneys) where you pay for the number of components you pick. The lunchtime menu might typically include soup, ciabattas, ploughman's, cheese and onion pie with white wine and mustard gravy, steak and ale pie, sausage and mash, and changing specials such as goats cheese, tomato and spinach quiche, black pudding on mash with dijon mustard and smoked bacon sauce, fried sardines with greek salad, and seared tuna steaks with a red onion, tomato and basil sauce. There isn't a full evening menu, but the excellent cheese and pâté menu is served pretty much all day.** *Starters/Snacks: £3.50 to £6.50. Main Courses: £8.00 to £9.50. Puddings: £3.00 to £3.50*

Free house ~ Licensee Dominic Kiziuk ~ Real ale ~ Bar food (7.30(8 Sat, 8.30 Sun)-10.30(11 Sat, Sun); 12-9) ~ (01524) 66006 ~ Children welcome away from bar ~ Monthly bands ~ Open 10am-midnight (12.30 Fri, Sat); 10am-11.30pm Sun ~ Bedrooms: £60S/£60S(£70B)

Recommended by Mike Pugh, Jim and Maggie Cowell, Jo Lilley, Simon Calvert, John and Shirley North

LIVERPOOL

SJ3589   MAP 7

Philharmonic Dining Rooms ★ 🍺

36 Hope Street; corner of Hardman Street; L1 9BX

Beautifully preserved Victorian pub with superb period interior and ten real ales

A wonderful period piece, this spectacular marble-fronted Victorian pub attracts a pleasant mix of customers from theatre-goers to students, locals and tourists, and there's an impressive range of beer. The centrepiece is a mosaic-faced serving counter, from which heavily carved and polished mahogany partitions radiate under the intricate plasterwork high ceiling. The echoing main hall is decorated with stained glass including contemporary portraits of Boer War heroes Baden-Powell and Lord Roberts, rich panelling, a huge mosaic floor, and copper panels of musicians in an alcove above the fireplace. More stained glass in one of the little lounges declares 'Music is the universal language of mankind', and backs this up with illustrations of musical instruments. Two side rooms are called Brahms and Liszt, and there are two plushly comfortable sitting rooms. Don't miss the original 1890s Adamant gents' lavatory (all pink marble and glinting mosaics); ladies are allowed a look if they ask first. They have up to ten changing guest ales on handpump, with usually a Cains beer and unusual guests from brewers such as Orkney; quiz machine and mellow piped jazz or blues.

⑪ **Straightforward food (which can be eaten only in the table-service grand lounge dining room) could include soup, baked potatoes, sandwiches, ploughman's, steak pie, fish and chips and puddings (from £2.75). It's best to phone first to check if they're serving food in the evenings.** *Starters/Snacks: £2.95 to £3.95. Main Courses: £5.95 to £10.95. Puddings: £2.95*

Mitchells & Butlers ~ Manager Marie-Louise Wong ~ Real ale ~ Bar food (12-9) ~ Restaurant ~ (0151) 707 2837 ~ Dogs welcome ~ Open 12-12

Recommended by Tracey and Stephen Groves, David and Ros Hanley, Mark and Diane Grist, the Didler, Rob and Catherine Dunster, Clive Watkin, Dr Phil Putwain, P Dawn

LONGRIDGE   SD6038   MAP 7

Derby Arms ♀

Chipping Road, Thornley; 1½ miles N of Longridge on back road to Chipping; PR3 2NB

Convivial traditional country pub with hunting and fishing paraphernalia (and menu to match) and very decent wine list

Overlooking the Forest of Bowland, this nicely unchanged and unfailingly welcoming country pub has a hunting and fishing theme in its main bar. Old photographs commemorate notable catches, and there's some nicely mounted bait above the comfortable red plush seats, together with a stuffed pheasant that seems to be flying in through the wall. To the right is a smaller room with sporting trophies and mementoes, and a regimental tie collection; piped music and darts. The gents' has dozens of riddles on the wall – you can buy a sheet of them in the bar and the money goes to charity. Along with a good range of wines, including several half-bottles and a dozen or so by the glass (they're particularly strong on south african), you'll find Black Sheep and Marstons Pedigree on handpump. A few tables out in front, and another two behind the car park, have fine views across to the Forest of Bowland. Note that they sometimes close earlier than midnight during the week.

⑪ **As well as several fresh fish dishes such as potted shrimps, mussels, fresh dressed crab, oysters and monkfish, the enjoyable food might include sandwiches, soup, ploughman's, ham, egg and chips, spicy chicken satay, vegetarian hotpot, steak and kidney pudding, crisp roast goosnargh duckling and aberdeen angus fillet steak rossini. They also have pheasant, hare, rabbit, partridge, woodcock, rabbit and mallard in season; puddings such as home-baked fruit pies** *Starters/Snacks: £3.95 to £7.95. Main Courses: £8.95 to £19.95. Puddings: £3.50 to £4.95*

Punch ~ Lease Mrs G M Walne ~ Real ale ~ Bar food (12-2.15, 6-9.15(9.45 Fri, Sat); 12-9.15 Sun) ~ Restaurant ~ (01772) 782623 ~ Children welcome away from main bar ~ Open 12-3, 6(5.30 Sat)-12; 12-11 Sun

Recommended by Maurice and Gill McMahon, Margaret Dickinson, Dennis Jones, Peter Craske

---

> If a service charge is mentioned prominently on a menu or accommodation terms, you must pay it if service was satisfactory. If service is really bad, you are legally entitled to refuse to pay some or all of the service charge as compensation for not getting the service you might reasonably have expected.

LYDGATE   SD9704   MAP 7

White Hart ⊕ ♀ ⇔

Stockport Road; Lydgate not marked on some maps so not to be confused with the one near Todmorden; take A669 Oldham—Saddleworth, and after almost 2.5 miles turn right at brow of hill to A6050, Stockport Road; OL4 4JJ

Smart up-to-date dining pub (drinkers welcome too) with not cheap but excellent food, half a dozen beers, very good wine list, garden and comfortable bedrooms

Though this striking upmarket stone-built inn (overlooking Saddleworth Moor) can feel a little like a smart restaurant-with-rooms, it's very much a proper pub too, with a good few locals clustered round the bar, or in the two simpler rooms at the end. Many of the building's older features remain, but the overall style is fairly contemporary – beams and exposed stonework are blended skilfully with deep red or purple walls, punctuated with a mix of modern paintings, black and white photos, and stylised local scenes; most rooms have a fireplace and fresh flowers. The warmly elegant brasserie is the biggest of the main rooms and service from the smartly dressed staff is good. The wine list includes around 20 by the glass and beers are Black Sheep, Lees Bitter, Tetleys, Timothy Taylors Golden Best and Landlord and a changing guest from a brewer such as Pictish on handpump. There are picnic sets on the lawn behind. They put on plenty of special events based around themed menus, including wine and beer tastings, comedy acts and even a brass band contest. Bedrooms are comfortable, with free internet access. More reports please.

⊞ **The thoughtfully prepared meals are pricier than in most pubs around here, but the quality is consistently high. A typical menu might include open sandwiches, starters such as soup, oysters, duck rillette with mulled wild gooseberries and melba toast, baked terrine of potato and goats cheese with beetroot and cress salad, main courses such as sausages and a mash of your choice (maybe cheddar cheese and worcester), braised shoulder of lamb with rocket mint pesto, roast chicken breast coq au vin, vegetable cannelloni with asparagus and tomato compote, battered haddock with minted peas and caper beurre blanc, and rib-eye steak. They do a fish menu on Tuesday evenings.** *Starters/Snacks: £5.25 to £8.00. Main Courses: £11.50 to £21.00. Puddings: £4.95 to £6.00*

Free house ~ Licensee Charles Brierley ~ Real ale ~ Bar food (12-2.30, 6-9.30; 1-7.30 Sun) ~ Restaurant ~ (01457) 872566 ~ Children welcome ~ Open 12-11(midnight Sat) ~ Bedrooms: £90B/£120B

Recommended by Revd D Glover

LYTHAM   SD3627   MAP 7

Taps ◀ £

A584 S of Blackpool; Henry Street – in centre, one street in from West Beach; FY8 5LE

Thriving seaside pub with down-to-earth atmosphere, eight real ales and straightforward lunchtime snacks; open all day

This enthusiastically run pub can get full to capacity, but even then staff cope with admirable efficiency. With a good mix of customers, the Victorian-style bare-boarded bar has a sociable unassuming feel, plenty of stained-glass decoration in the windows, depictions of fish and gulls reflecting the pub's proximity to the beach (it's a couple of minutes' walk away), captain's chairs in bays around the sides, open fires, and a coal-effect gas fire between two built-in bookcases at one end. There's also an expanding collection of rugby memorabilia with old photographs and portraits of rugby stars on the walls; shove-ha'penny, dominoes, a quiz machine and a fruit machine. There are seat belts on the bar and headrests in the gents' to help keep you out of harm's way if you have one too many. Greene King IPA and Taps Best (brewed for the pub by Titanic) are kept on handpump alongside six ever-changing real ales from brewers such as Batemans, Hopback and Nethergate – you can see them all in the view-in cellar; also country wines and a farm cider. There are a few seats and a heated canopied area outside. Parking is difficult near the pub so it's probably best to park at the West Beach car park on the seafront (free on Sunday), and walk.

🍴 A handful of cheap bar snacks includes sandwiches, soup and a hot roast sandwich, filled baked potatoes, burgers, chilli and curry. *Starters/Snacks: £1.95 to £3.95. Puddings: £1.50*

Greene King ~ Manager Ian Rigg ~ Real ale ~ Bar food (12-2, not Sun) ~ No credit cards ~ (01253) 736226 ~ Children welcome away from the bar till 7pm ~ Open 11-11(midnight Fri, Sat)

Recommended by Pam and John Smith, Steve Whalley, Ken Richards, the Didler

MANCHESTER   SJ8397   MAP 7

Britons Protection ♀ £

Great Bridgewater Street, corner of Lower Mosley Street; M1 5LE

Lively city pub with unspoilt small rooms, huge range of whiskies, five real ales, inexpensive lunchtime snacks, and garden

Handy for Bridgewater Hall and well known to many orchestral musicians, this busy but welcoming city-centre pub is run with considerable gusto and service is helpful. The plush little front bar has a fine chequered tile floor, some glossy brown and russet wall tiles, solid woodwork and elaborate plastering. A tiled passage lined with battle murals depicting the Peterloo Massacre of 1819, which took place a few hundred yards away, leads to two cosy inner lounges, both served by hatch, with attractive brass and etched glass wall lamps, a mirror above the coal-effect gas fire in the simple art nouveau fireplace, and again good solidly comfortable furnishings. As something of a tribute to Manchester's notorious climate, the massive bar counter has a pair of heating pipes as its footrail. Although it's busy at lunchtime, it's usually quiet and relaxed in the evenings; piped music. As well as a terrific range of around 235 malt whiskies and bourbons, they have Jennings, Robinsons, Tetleys and two changing guests from brewers such as Coach House and Hydes on handpump, and good wines too. There are tables out on the garden behind. They host various evening events, including poetry readings, storytelling, silent film shows and acoustic gigs. Football supporters are excluded on match days.

🍴 Straightforward bar food includes soup, sandwiches, ploughman's, ham and egg or leek and mushroom crumble or various pies, and home-made daily specials. *Starters/Snacks: £1.85 to £4.95*

Punch ~ Lease Peter Barnett ~ Real ale ~ Bar food (11-2.30) ~ (0161) 236 5895 ~ Very well behaved children welcome ~ Film shows, music hall, storytelling nights and poetry readings first Fri; acoustic gigs third Fri and at other times ~ Open 11-11.30(11 Sun)

Recommended by Jo Lilley, Simon Calvert, Mark and Diane Grist, the Didler, John Fiander, Mrs Hazel Rainer, Pam and John Smith, GLD, Stephen and Jean Curtis, Dr and Mrs A K Clarke, Joe Green

Dukes 92 £

Castle Street, below the bottom end of Deansgate; M3 4LZ

Waterside pub with spacious interior, minimalist but comfortable modern and period furnishings and good value food till mid-afternoon

There's a tangibly upbeat feel nowadays to the revived area around the Rochdale Canal basin where this converted stable block stands by revamped warehouses – tables outside make the best of the view over the bottom lock of the canal. Inside, black wrought-iron work contrasts boldly with whitewashed bare plaster walls, the handsome bar is granite-topped, and an elegant spiral staircase leads to an upper room and balcony. Down in the main room the fine mix of well spaced furnishings is mainly Edwardian in mood, with one particularly massive table, elegantly comfortable chaises-longues and deep armchairs. There might be a real ale on handpump from a brewer such as Timothy Taylor (though some readers have found no real ale), and they've decent wines, a wide choice of malt whiskies, and the belgian wheat beer Hoegaarden on tap; piped jazz. A gallery has temporary exhibitions of local artwork.

🍴 They do an excellent range of over three dozen cheeses, and several pâtés with generous helpings of granary bread. Other good value bar food includes soup, sandwiches, pizzas, salads and specials such as fish and chips or chicken curry; puddings include chocolate fudge cake and sticky toffee pudding. *Starters/Snacks: £2.95. Main Courses: £6.50. Puddings: £3.95*

Free house ~ Licensee James Ramsbottom ~ Real ale ~ Bar food (12-3(4.30 Fri-Sun); snacks available outside these times) ~ (0161) 839 8646 ~ Children welcome until 8pm ~ Dogs allowed in bar ~ Sun afternoon in summer ~ Open 11.30-11(1 Fri, Sat); 12-10.30 Sun
Recommended by Mrs Hazel Rainer, G V Price, Joe Green

Marble Arch 🍺 £

Rochdale Road (A664), Ancoats; corner of Gould Street, just E of Victoria Station; M4 4HY

Cheery town pub with noteworthy Victorian interior, great range of real ales including own brews, very reasonably priced food, and small garden

This alehouse takes its name from the porphyry entrance pillars that hint at the admirably preserved Victorian splendours inside – certainly reason enough to visit in itself, but readers also enjoy it for its outstanding range of well kept real ales (including the pub's own brew), sensibly priced food and friendly atmosphere. The interior has a magnificently restored lightly barrel-vaulted high ceiling, and extensive marble and tiling – the frieze advertising various spirits, and the chimney breast above the carved wooden mantelpiece particularly stand out. Furniture is a cheerful mix of rustic tables and chairs, including a long communal table, and all the walls are stripped back to their original glazed brick; there's a collection of breweriana, and a display cabinet with pump clips, and look out for the sloping mosaic floor in the bar; TV, games machine, piped music and a juke box. From windows at the back, you can look out over the brewery (tours by arrangement) where they produce their distinctive Lagonda IPA, GSB, Manchester Bitter, Marble Best, Marble Ginger Ale and a seasonal brew. They also have four guest ales from brewers such as Phoenix, Pictish, Roosters and Salamander, as well as a farm cider. The Laurel and Hardy Preservation Society meet here on the third Wednesday of the month and show old films; little garden.

🍴 Good-value food includes soup, generously filled sandwiches, black pudding with new potatoes and poached egg, ploughman's, steak and ale or fish pie, chunky vegetable hotpot, sausage and mash, chicken pot-roasted in ginger beer with spring onion, mushroom and honey sauce, and puddings such as bread and butter pudding. *Starters/Snacks: £3.50 to £5.95. Main Courses: £6.95 to £8.00. Puddings: £2.50 to £3.50*

Own brew ~ Licensee Jan Rogers ~ Real ale ~ Bar food (11.30(12 Sat, Sun)-8(6 Sun)) ~ Restaurant ~ (0161) 832 5914 ~ Well behaved children until 8pm ~ Dogs allowed in bar ~ Open 11.30-11(midnight Fri, Sat); 12-11 Sun
Recommended by Pat and Tony Martin, Revd D Glover, Joe Green, the Didler, Mark and Diane Grist, Tony Hobden

MELLOR   SJ9888   MAP 7

Devonshire Arms

This is the Mellor nr Marple, S of Manchester; heading out of Marple on the A626 towards Glossop, Mellor is the next road after the B6102, signposted off on the right at Marple Bridge; Longhurst Lane; SK6 5PP

Charming little pub with wide choice of food, attractive gardens and play area

This well maintained unpretentious local has a delightfully welcoming atmosphere and something of a period flavour in its three little rooms. The cheerful little front bar has a warming winter fire in a sizeable Victorian fireplace with a deep-chiming clock above it, an unusual curved bar (with Robinsons Best and Mild and a Robinsons guest and sangria in summer), and a couple of old leather-seated settles among other seats. Both of the two small back rooms have Victorian fireplaces – the one on the right has an unusual lion couchant in place of a mantelpiece, and one room has french windows opening on to the extensive garden. Out here a waterfall plays into a well stocked fish pond, over which a chinese bridge leads to a covered terrace, and there's a children's play area tucked away in the small tree-sheltered lawn; more picnic-sets out in front; boules.

🍴 **The wide choice of good generous pubby food might typically include pea and ham soup, sandwiches, ploughman's, battered haddock or chicken and pies such as steak and kidney or chicken and ham.** *Starters/Snacks: £2.50 to £3.75. Main Courses: £9.25 to £16.95. Puddings: £3.75 to £4.25*

Robinsons ~ Tenants John and Liz Longworth ~ Real ale ~ Bar food (12-9 Sat, Sun) ~ (0161) 4272563 ~ Children welcome ~ Jazz second Tues ~ Open 11.45-3, 6-midnight; 11.45(12 Sun)-midnight summer holidays and Sat

Recommended by Hilary Forrest, Roger Yates, Dennis Jones, David Hoult

Oddfellows Arms

Keep on along Longhurst Lane for nearly 2 miles, and up into Moor End Road; SK6 5PT

Welcoming new licensees, lunchtime snacks, interesting more elaborate evening dishes

Warmed by open fires, the pleasant low-ceilinged flagstoned bar here is a nice civilised place for a meal. Five well kept changing beers might be Black Sheep, Deuchars IPA, Greene King Abbot, Jennings Cumberland and Timothy Taylors Landlord. There are a few tables out by the road. It can be tricky to secure a parking space when they're busy. More reports on the new regime please.

🍴 **As well as sandwiches and soup, a light lunchtime snack menu includes salads such as poached salmon in the summer, with heartier dishes such as beef stew in the winter. The more elaborate monthly changing evening menu might include black pudding with creamy wholegrain mustard sauce or confit of shredded duck salad, goats cheese on focaccia, roast lamb shank with garlic mash, fried bass with garlic and thyme, steaks, and puddings such as strawberry and champagne meringue roulade.** *Starters/Snacks: £3.95 to £5.95. Main Courses: £9.95 to £14.95. Puddings: £4.25*

Enterprise ~ Tenants Andy and Debbie Moore ~ Real ale ~ Bar food (12-2.30, 5.30-9.30; 12-5 Sun) ~ Restaurant ~ (0161) 449 7826 ~ Children welcome ~ Open 12-11(10.30 Sun); closed Mon

Recommended by Roger Yates, Jack Morley

NETHER BURROW   SD6175   MAP 7

Highwayman

A683 S of Kirkby Lonsdale; LA6 2RJ

Substantial old stone house with country interior serving carefully sourced and prepared food; lovely gardens

This 17th-c inn in the pretty Lune Valley has been reopened after a handsome reworking by the owners of the Three Fishes at Great Mitton. Although large, its flagstoned interior is nicely divided into nooks and corners, with a big log fire at one end; this, another smaller fire and the informal wooden furnishings give it a relaxed comfortable feel. Black and white wall prints (and placemats) show local farmers and producers from whom the pub sources its ingredients – clearly real characters, some of these, and this seems to work nicely through into their produce. Thwaites Lancaster Bomber and Original and a guest are served on handpump, alongside good wines by the glass and about a dozen malts – service is faultless. French windows open to a big terrace and lovely gardens.

🍴 **Traditional lancastrian recipes are tweaked to bring them up-to-date, and prepared using very carefully sourced products from small local suppliers (marked on a map on the back of the menu). As well as bar nibbles and imaginative sandwiches, there might be starters such as chicken liver pâté, warm shrimps with mace butter and toasted muffin, day-old lancashire curd with crumpet and beetroot and mustard cress salad, main courses such as fish pie, battered haddock, hotpot with pickled red cabbage, chicken breast with avocado, curd and salad, cheese and onion pie and steaks, and puddings such as chocolate and orange pudding, curd tart with lemon ice-cream and sticky toffee pudding.** *Starters/Snacks: £3.50 to £6.50. Main Courses: £9.50 to £16.50. Puddings: £4.50*

Free house ~ Licensee Andy Morris ~ Real ale ~ Bar food (12-2, 6(5.30 Sat)-9; 12-8.30 Sun) ~
(01254) 826888 ~ Children welcome ~ Dogs allowed in bar ~ Open 12-11(10 Sun)

Recommended by Maurice and Gill McMahon, Karen Eliot

RIBCHESTER   SD6535   MAP 7

White Bull 🛏

Church Street; turn off B6245 at sharp corner by Black Bull; PR3 3XP

Friendly 18th-c inn with unusual views from pleasant garden, and interesting bar food

The spacious main bar here is very traditional, with comfortable old settles, Victorian
advertisements and various prints on cream walls, and a stuffed fox in two halves that
looks as if it's jumping through the wall. Floors vary between stripped wood and carpets;
TV, games machine, pool and board games. Four real ales on handpump might be from
Black Sheep, Bowland, Charles Wells and Copper Dragon. In summer the big garden makes
a pleasant spot to sit and contemplate the ruins of the adjacent Roman bathhouse –
incidentally, look out for the tuscan pillars in the pub's porch. They came from a nearby
building and are also thought to be of Roman origin. New licensees have upgraded the
bedrooms.

🍴 **Most areas are laid out for dining. The menu and specials board might include starters
such as pea and mint risotto, smoked mackerel pâté with pickled cucumber, main courses
such as parmesan, asparagus and spinach tart, grilled lemon sole with parsley butter,
hotpot with braised red cabbage, and puddings such as sticky toffee pudding and toasted
banana bread with rum and raisin ice-cream.** *Starters/Snacks: £3.00 to £6.00. Main Courses:
£7.50 to £16.00. Puddings: £4.00*

Enterprise ~ Lease Chris Bell ~ Real ale ~ Bar food (12-2.30, 6-9.30; 12-8 Sun; not Mon) ~
Restaurant ~ (01254) 878303 ~ Children welcome ~ Open 11.30-12(11 Sun) ~ Bedrooms:
£55B/£70B

*Recommended by David Morgan, Brian and Janet Ainscough, Dennis Jones, Joan York, A Benson, Trevor and
Sylvia Millum*

RIMINGTON   SD8045   MAP 7

Black Bull

Off A59 NW of Clitheroe, at Chatburn; or off A682 S of Gisburn; BB7 4DS

**Comfortably civilised and rather unusual, with huge collection of transport models, and
imaginative food**

An astonishing collection of model trains, planes, cars, ships, and assorted railway
memorabilia fills the airy, rather elegant rooms here. They have a special night for rail
buffs on the last Thursday of each winter month (£3.50), with pie and peas, film shows
and soundtracks of vintage locos. The big traditional main bar has a model locomotive in a
glass case beside an attractively tiled fireplace, a plane hanging from the ceiling, various
platform signs on the walls, and comfortable banquettes and window seats; a central area
with leatherette chairs leads through to a quietly refined dining room, with an exhibition
of wildlife art on the walls; piped music. Timothy Taylors Landlord and a couple of guests
from brewers such as Copper Dragon and Theakstons are served on handpump.

🍴 **Very good bar food is listed on blackboards (it's best to avoid sitting at the tables
underneath them), and might include soup, bouillabaisse, sandwiches, grilled goats
cheese with apricot chutney, guinea fowl with tapenade, fried chicken breast in cranberry
sauce, and halibut with creamy cheese sauce; puddings might include raspberry pavlova
and apple crumble. High tea is served on Sundays.** *Starters/Snacks: £4.25 to £5.95. Main
Courses: £7.95 to £18.00. Puddings: £4.50*

Free house ~ Licensee Neil Buckley ~ Real ale ~ Bar food (12-2.30 (also 4-6 Sun); not Sun
evening) ~ Restaurant ~ (01200) 445220 ~ Children welcome until 8pm ~ Open 12-3,
6.30-midnight; 12-midnight Sat; 12-11 Sun; closed Mon in winter ~ Bedrooms: £39.95S/£75S

Recommended by Steve Whalley

SAWLEY
SD7746   MAP 7

Spread Eagle ⑪ ♀

Village signposted just off A59 NE of Clitheroe; BB7 4NH

Enjoyable classy dining pub with beautifully presented imaginative food from short lunchtime bar menu and in riverside restaurant; good wine list

The light and airy continental-feeling main bar at this smart but welcoming dining pub has comfortable banquette seating and is decorated with lots of paintings and prints and lovely photographs of local views; roaring winter coal fire and piped music. The Sawleys Drunken Duck here is brewed for the pub by local microbrewery Bowland and is served alongside Thwaites Lancaster Bomber, an impressive wine list of 150 bins (a dozen are offered by the glass), and around 60 whiskies. Smartly dressed knowledgeable staff offer swift attentive service. The pub is in a lovely location by the River Ribble and ruins of a 12th-c cistercian abbey, and is handy for the Forest of Bowland – an upland with terrific scope for exhilarating walks; two smoking porches.

⑪ **The short lunchtime bar menu might include soup, filled rolls, grilled black pudding medallion with black peas, mash and balsamic reduction, grilled goats cheese on stewed red onions and mustard seed pastry and warm ham salad with lancashire cheese. In the restaurant you can choose from a more extensive menu which includes dishes such as roasted vegetable plate, pea and broad bean risotto, knuckle of lamb cooked in lemon mint with gremolata, seared bass with sauce vierge, and grilled 8oz fillet; they also do good value set course menus and have various theme and gourmet evenings.** *Starters/Snacks: £3.00 to £6.95. Puddings: £3.50 to £5.50*

Free house ~ Licensees Nigel and Ysanne Williams ~ Real ale ~ Bar food (12-2 Tues-Sat only) ~ Restaurant ~ (01200) 441202 ~ Children welcome ~ Open 12-3, 6-11; closed first week in January winter; closed Sun evening, all day Mon

Recommended by Steve Whalley, Susan and Nigel Brookes, Paul Edwards, Margaret Dickinson, John and Hilary Penny, Norma and Noel Thomas, Ann and Tony Bennett-Hughes, Jim and Sheila Prideaux

STALYBRIDGE
SJ9598   MAP 7

Station Buffet ◼ £

The Station, Rassbottom Street; SK15 1RF

Victorian station buffet bar with eight quickly changing beers and a few cheap basic snacks

You'll find this enchantingly unpretentious rest stop on platform one of the Stalybridge station on the Manchester to Huddersfield line, and, as one reader says, it's 'well worth missing a few trains for'. Friendly staff serve a marvellous range of up to 20 interesting guest ales a week alongside house beers Bass, Boddingtons and Flowers, farm cider and belgian and other foreign bottled beers. The bar has a welcoming fire below an etched-glass mirror, old photographs of the station in its heyday, and other railway memorabilia; there's a little conservatory. An extension along the platform leads into what was the ladies' waiting room and part of the station-master's quarters. This has original ornate ceilings and a dining/function room with Victorian-style wallpaper; board games, cards, newspapers and magazines. On a sunny day you can sit out on the platform.

⑪ **They do cheap old-fashioned snacks such as tasty black peas and sandwiches, and three or four daily specials such as home-made pie with peas, bacon casserole and all day breakfast; freshly made coffee and tea by the pot.** *Starters/Snacks: £0.50 to £3.25*

Free house ~ Licensees John Hesketh and Sylvia Wood ~ Real ale ~ Bar food (12-9.30) ~ No credit cards ~ (0161) 303 0007 ~ Children welcome ~ Dogs welcome ~ Open 11-11; 12-10.30 Sun

Recommended by John Fiander, Len Beattie, Dennis Jones, the Didler

---

Smoking is not allowed inside any pub. Some pubs now have outdoor shelters, open on two sides and sometimes heated, where smoking is allowed.

TUNSTALL   SD6073   MAP 7

Lunesdale Arms ⓘ ⓨ

A683 S of Kirkby Lonsdale; LA6 2QN

Light and airy civilised pub with emphasis on good imaginative food, separate area with traditional games

There's a bright homely atmosphere at this nice dining pub in the Lune Valley (the pretty village has a church with Brontë associations), and bare boards create a lively acoustic. On one side of the central bar part, a white-walled area has a good mix of stripped and sealed solid dining tables, and blue sofas facing each other across a low table (with daily papers) by a woodburning stove with a stone mantelpiece. Another area has pews and armchairs (some of the big unframed oil paintings are for sale), and at the other end, an airy games section has pool, table football, board games and TV. A snugger little flagstoned back part has another woodburning stove. Besides Black Sheep and a guest from a brewer such as Dent on handpump they have half a dozen wines by the glass and 20 malts; piped music.

ⓘ **Food is prepared with admirable attention to detail – readers particularly praise the home-made bread and chips. The constantly changing menu might include vegetable broth, sandwiches, goats cheese en croûte with tomato and red pepper tapenade, sausage and mash, steak, Guinness and mushroom pie, roast leg of lamb with spinach rice and raita, slow-roast pork belly with haricot beans, smoked sausage, sage and tomato sauce, scallops in puff pastry with watercress sauce, and puddings such as damson crème brûlée and seville orange upside-down cake with crème fraîche. They do Sunday lunch and smaller helpings of some main courses.** *Starters/Snacks: £4.00 to £6.95. Main Courses: £8.50 to £14.95. Puddings: £4.25*

Free house ~ Licensee Emma Gillibrand ~ Real ale ~ Bar food ~ (01524) 274203 ~ Children welcome ~ Dogs allowed in bar ~ Live piano music most Thurs nights ~ Open 11(12 Sun)-3.30, 6-midnight(1 Sat); closed Mon

Recommended by John and Sylvia Harrop, Paul Boot, W K Wood, Michael Doswell, John Lane, Karen Eliot, Peter Burton, Alun and Stephanie Llewellyn, Jo Lilley, Simon Calvert, Glenwys and Alan Lawrence

UPPERMILL   SD0006   MAP 7

Church Inn ◀ £

From the main street (A607), look out for the sign for Saddleworth Church, and turn off up this steep narrow lane – keep on up! OL3 6LW

Lively good value community pub with own brews from big range, lots of pets, and good food; children very welcome

This highly individual pub, isolated up by the moors, is home to the range of eight to 12 very modestly priced Saddleworth beers (with prices from a staggeringly modest £1.40 a pint) that are brewed by the landlord here. Some of the seasonal ones (look out for Rubens, Ayrtons, Robins and Indya) are named after the licensee's children and appear around their birthdays. They also keep three constantly changing guests, maybe Holts, Millstone and Robinsons, and continental wheat beer and dark lager on tap too. On Wednesdays, local bellringers arrive to practise with a set of handbells that are kept here, while anyone is invited to join the morris dancers who meet here on Thursdays. Outside, there's a delightful assortment of pets roaming around in the garden or in view in the adjacent field – rabbits, chickens, dogs, ducks, geese, horses and a couple of peacocks, as well as an increasing army of rescued cats resident in an adjacent barn. Children and dogs are made to feel very welcome. The big unspoilt L-shaped main bar has high beams and some stripped stone; one window at the end of the bar counter looks down over the valley, and there's also a valley view from the quieter dining room; the conservatory opens on to a new terrace. Comfortable furnishings include settles and pews as well as a good individual mix of chairs, and there are lots of attractive prints, staffordshire and other china on a high delft shelf, jugs, brasses and so forth; TV (only when there's sport on) and unobtrusive piped music. The horse-collar on the wall is worn by the winner of their annual gurning (face-pulling) championship (part of the lively Rush Cart Festival, usually held over the August bank holiday).

🍴 Reasonably priced bar food includes soup, sandwiches, ploughman's, steak and ale pie, roast beef, jumbo cod, and puddings such as home-made cheesecake. *Starters/Snacks: £1.85 to £3.25. Main Courses: £5.95 to £11.75. Puddings: £2.50*

Own brew ~ Licensee Julian Taylor ~ Real ale ~ Bar food (12-2.30, 5.30-9; 12-9 Sat, Sun, bank hols) ~ Restaurant ~ (01457) 820902 ~ Children welcome ~ Dogs allowed in bar ~ Open 12-12(11 Sun)

Recommended by the Didler, Dennis Jones, Len Beattie, Bob Broadhurst, John Fiander

WHEATLEY LANE   SD8338   MAP 7

Old Sparrow Hawk

Wheatley Lane Road; towards E end of village road which runs N of and parallel to A6068; one way of reaching it is to follow Fence, Newchurch 1¾ signpost, then turn off at Barrowford ¾ signpost; BB12 9QG

Comfortably civilised, with very well prepared food and half a dozen real ales

This country dining pub is attractively laid out in several distinct areas, some with carpet and some with red tiles. Locals pop in for an early evening drink and there's a buoyant relaxed atmosphere. It's a characterful place, with interesting furnishings, dark oak panelling and timbers, stripped stonework, lots of snug corners including a nice area with a fire, and a sofa under a domed stained-glass skylight; daily papers, piped music, games machine, board games and TV. Fresh flowers cheer up the cushioned leatherette bar counter where lots of good wines by the glass, Bass, Moorhouses, Thwaites and three guests, and wheat beers on tap are served. Heavy wood tables out on a spacious and attractive front terrace (pretty flowerbeds and a water feature) have good views to the moors beyond Nelson and Colne.

🍴 Good fresh bar food includes interesting sandwiches, wraps and ciabattas, soup, caesar salad, lancashire cheese and leek tart, crispy duck salad, fish pie, sausage and mash, battered haddock, risotto of summer greens with pear and pine nut salad, lamb steak with garlic and rosemary potatoes, and puddings such as lemon tart or baked strawberry cheesecake. *Starters/Snacks: £4.25 to £6.25. Main Courses: £9.25 to £18.50. Puddings: £4.50 to £6.75*

Mitchells & Butlers ~ Tenant Stephen Turner ~ Real ale ~ Bar food (12-2.30, 5-9; 12-9.30 Sat; 12-8 Sun) ~ Restaurant ~ (01282) 603034 ~ Children welcome away from bar ~ Dogs welcome ~ Open 12-11(12 Sat, 10.30 Sun)

Recommended by Kevan Tucker, Andy Devanney, Steve Whalley, K C and B Forman

WHEELTON   SD6021   MAP 7

Dressers Arms 🍺 £

2.1 miles from M61 junction 8; Briers Brow, off A674 Blackburn road from Wheelton bypass (towards Brinscall); 3.6 miles from M65 junction 3, also via A674; PR6 8HD

Good choice of beer and big helpings of food at invitingly traditional pub run by warm friendly licensees

Much bigger than it looks from the outside, the low-beamed rooms at this enticingly snug place are nicely atmospheric and full of traditional features, including a handsome old woodburning stove in the flagstoned main bar. Candles on tables add to the welcoming feel, and there are newspapers and magazines; piped music, juke box, pool table, games machine and TV. They usually keep eight real ales, including their own Big Franks (now brewed off the site), Tetleys and Timothy Taylors Landlord, plus five guests from brewers such as Caledonian, Moorehouses, Phoenix and Thwaites; also around 20 malt whiskies, and some well chosen wines. There are lots of picnic-sets, a large umbrella with lighting and heaters on a terrace in front of the pub. Their big car park is across the road. The licensees are great pet-lovers and welcome dogs.

⑪ **Pubby bar food includes soup, breaded mushrooms, sandwiches, hot filled baguettes, vegetable curry, hotpot, steak pudding, paella, fish and chips and 12oz sirloin steak, and there's a cantonese restaurant on the first floor; Sunday carvery.** *Starters/Snacks: £3.00 to £6.00. Main Courses: £5.00 to £10.95. Puddings: £3.75*

Own brew ~ Licensees Steve and Trudie Turner ~ Real ale ~ Bar food (12-2.30, 5-9; 12-9 weekends and bank hols) ~ Restaurant ~ (01254) 830041 ~ Children welcome away from bar ~ Dogs welcome ~ Open 11-12.30am(1am Fri, Sat)

Recommended by Brian Wainwright, Ann and Tony Bennett-Hughes, Mike and Linda Hudson, Keith and Chris O'Neill, R T and J C Moggridge, Steve Whalley

WHITEWELL

SD6546 MAP 7

Inn at Whitewell ★★ ⑪ ♀ 🛏

Most easily reached by B6246 from Whalley; road through Dunsop Bridge from B6478 is also good; BB7 3AT

LANCASHIRE DINING PUB OF THE YEAR

Very civilised hotel with smartly pubby atmosphere, excellent food and luxury bedrooms

There are delightful views over the adjacent River Hodder and across towards the lovely high moors of the Forest of Bowland from the riverside bar and adjacent terrace at this elegant manor house hotel. It's a beautifully decorated place, with handsome furnishings standing out well against powder blue walls that are neatly hung with attractive prints. The old-fashioned pubby main bar has antique settles, oak gateleg tables, sonorous clocks, old cricketing and sporting prints, roaring log fires (the lounge has a very attractive stone fireplace), and heavy curtains on sturdy wooden rails; one area has a selection of newspapers and magazines, local maps and guide books, there's a piano for anyone who wants to play, and even an art gallery. In the early evening, there's a cheerful bustle but once the visitors have gone, the atmosphere is tranquil and relaxing. Their good wine list includes around 230 wines (there is a good wine shop in the reception area), and the three real ales on handpump might be from Bowland, Copper Dragon and Timothy Taylor. Staff are courteous and friendly. This is a relaxing place to stay, with plenty of fell walking. They own several miles of trout, salmon and sea trout fishing on the Hodder, and with notice they'll arrange shooting and will make up a picnic hamper.

⑪ **Besides lunchtime sandwiches, delicious, well presented food includes soup, warm crab cakes, smoked fillet of trout with beetroot salad, duck confit salad with sweet pickled carrot, ginger, coriander and sesame oil, fish pie, bangers and champ, roast duck breast with red wine jus, spring roll of butternut and caramelised onion with carrot and coriander salad and spicy tomato dressing. They also do daily specials such as fried pork belly on onion mash with honey-roast tomatoes, fried bass fillet with roast peppers and aubergines with olive tapenade and basil pesto. You can have coffee and cream teas all day, and they sell jars of home-made jam and marmalade.** *Starters/Snacks: £3.65 to £7.50. Main Courses: £7.25 to £13.75. Puddings: £3.50 to £4.50*

Free house ~ Licensee Charles Bowman ~ Real ale ~ Bar food (12-2, 7.30-9.30) ~ Restaurant ~ (01200) 448222 ~ Dogs welcome ~ Open 11am-midnight ~ Bedrooms: £70B/£96B

Recommended by Derek and Sylvia Stephenson, Revd D Glover, Karen Eliot, J F M and M West, Jo Lilley, Simon Calvert, Anthony Longden, Mrs P J Carroll, Brian Wainwright, Michael and Deirdre Ellis, K S Whittaker, Steve Whalley, David and Sue Smith, Noel Grundy, Dr K P Tucker, W W Burke

---

Stars after the name of a pub show exceptional character and appeal.
They don't mean extra comfort. And they are nothing to do with food quality, for which
there's a separate knife-and-fork symbol. Even quite a basic pub
can win stars, if it's individual enough.

YEALAND CONYERS
SD5074   MAP 7

New Inn

3 miles from M6 junction 35; village signposted off A6; LA5 9SJ

Good generous food all day and warm welcome at village pub near M6

This ivy-covered 17th-c village pub makes a relaxing break from the motorway. It's useful too if you're exploring the area's wonderfully varied walks up Warton Crag and through Leighton Moss RSPB reserve. Inside, the simply furnished little beamed bar on the left has a cosy village atmosphere, with its log fire in the big stone fireplace. On the right, two communicating shiny beamed dining rooms are filled with closely set dark blue furniture and an attractive kitchen range. Robinsons Hartleys XB and another of their beers are served on handpump alongside around 30 malt whiskies; piped music and very friendly service. A sheltered lawn at the side has picnic-sets among roses and flowering shrubs.

🍽 **Hearty helpings of bar food include sandwiches, baguettes and baked potatoes (all with interesting fillings), and soup, ploughman's, mussels with creamy garlic sauce, sausage with spinach mash, spicy mexican bean chilli tortilla, chicken in a basket and salmon fillet poached in white wine with prawn, cucumber and lemon reduction.** *Starters/Snacks: £3.65 to £5.95. Main Courses: £8.95 to £12.50. Puddings: £3.95 to £4.75*

Robinsons ~ Tenants Bill Tully and Charlotte Pinder ~ Real ale ~ Bar food (11.30(12 Sun)-9.30) ~ Restaurant ~ (01524) 732938 ~ Children welcome ~ Dogs allowed in bar ~ Open 11.30-11; 12-10.30 Sun

Recommended by Dr D J and Mrs S C Walker, Rhiannon Davies, Tony and Caroline Elwood, Ann and Tony Bennett-Hughes, Peter and Eleanor Kenyon, Bruce and Sharon Eden, Joan York, Michael Doswell, Andrew York, Richard Greaves, Steve Whalley

---

LUCKY DIP

Besides the fully inspected pubs, you might like to try these Lucky Dips recommended to us and described by readers (if you do, please send us reports: www.goodguides.co.uk).

ALTHAM [SD7732]
Walton Arms BB5 5UL [Burnley Rd (A678)]: Attractive and relaxed, with wide range of good reasonably priced food from filled rolls up, well kept Jennings, good value wines, friendly efficient service, oak furniture in flagstoned dining room *(Bob Broadhurst)*
APPLEY BRIDGE [SD5210]
Dicconson Arms WN6 9DY [B5375 (Appley Lane North)/A5209, handy for M6 junction 27]: Well run and civilised, with good value food inc generous lunches, fast friendly service *(Simon J Barber)*
Waters Edge [Mill Lane, off B5375; handy for M6 junction 27]: Fairly large single-storey open-plan pub by Leeds & Liverpool Canal, good choice of very reasonably priced pub food, Tetleys Bitter and Mild, pleasant newish young landlady; waterside picnic-sets, separate restaurant cruise boat based here *(Doug Christian)*
ARKHOLME [SD5872]
Bay Horse LA6 1AS [B6254 Carnforth—Kirkby Lonsdale]: Neatly kept and homely old three-room country pub with good value basic food from sandwiches up, one or two well kept changing ales such as Bass, Black Sheep or Everards Tiger, friendly landlord and prompt service, lovely inglenook, good atmosphere, pictures of long-lost London

pubs; own bowling green, handy for charming Lune Valley walks, cl Mon *(MLR)*
BARTON [SD5138]
Fox PR3 5AB [A6 N of Broughton]: Former beamed Vintage Inn under newish landlord, roomy quarry-tiled bar, comfortable settees and other seats and plenty of well spaced tables in linked areas off, decent food all day inc wkdy two-for-one deals, good choice of wines by the glass, helpful well trained young staff; games area with pool, Thurs quiz night; children welcome, wknd bouncy castle *(Ray and Winifred Halliday)*
BASHALL EAVES [SD6943]
Red Pump BB7 3DA [NW of Clitheroe, off B6478 or B6243]: Friendly country pub with good individual food from light dishes through well prepared pubby favourites to some interesting specials and good value Sun lunch, well kept Bowland and Moorhouses ales, two pleasantly up-to-date dining rooms, more traditional central bar with log fire and settles; two bedrooms, good breakfast, own fishing on River Hodder *(Alyson and Andrew Jackson, Steve Whalley)*
BEBINGTON [SJ3385]
Travellers Rest CH62 1BQ [B5151, not far from M53 junction 4; New Ferry Rd, Higher Bebington]: Friendly semi-rural corner pub

with several areas around central bar, good value popular bar lunches from good sandwiches to mixed grill (not Sun), up to eight real ales inc some from small breweries, efficient staff, alcoves, beams, brasses etc; no children, open all day *(MLR)*

BELMONT [SD6715]

☆ *Black Dog* BL7 8AB [Church St (A675)]: Nicely set Holts dining pub with their usual sensibly priced food (not Tues evening, all day Fri-Sun) and bargain beers, cheery small-roomed traditional core (may sometime have coal fires), friendly staff, picture-window extension; children welcome, seats outside giving moorland views above the village, good walks, decent bedrooms, open all day *(Tom and Jill Jones, Norma and Noel Thomas, Pam and John Smith, LYM, Pat and Tony Martin, the Didler)*

BELTHORN [SD7324]

Grey Mare BB1 2PG [Elton Rd/Grane Rd (A6177), handy for M65 junction 5]: Bargain traditional food lunchtime and evening in popular Thwaites pub high on Oswaldtwistle Moor, their ales inc Dark Mild, attractive new conservatory, fine views across to Blackburn, Preston and even Blackpool *(Brian Wainwright)*

BILSBORROW [SD5039]

☆ *Owd Nells* PR3 0RS [off A6 N of Preston; at S end of village take Myerscough Coll of Agriculture turn into St Michaels Rd]: Nice pastiche of old rustic pub in busy thatched tourist complex by Lancaster Canal, up to a dozen or more real ales, good choice of generous bar food, good value wines, tea and coffee, flagstones and low beams by central bar counter, high pitched rafters each end, plenty of games, adjacent restaurant, hotel, craft and teashops; children welcome, good play area outside (even cricket and bowls), comfortable bedrooms, open all day *(Stephen Hargreaves, Emma Critchley, Paul Ribchester)*

BIRKENHEAD [SJ3288]

Crown CH41 6JE [Conway St]: Friendly three-room pub popular for interesting changing ales inc Cains, Weston's farm cider, good value generous food all day till 6, good tilework; terrace tables, open all day *(the Didler)*

Dispensary CH41 5DQ [Chester St]: Comfortable Cains pub with guest beers too, good value lunchtime food, handsome glass ceiling; handy for ferry, open all day *(the Didler)*

Stork CH41 6JN [Price St]: Early 19th-c, four well restored civilised rooms around island bar, polished mosaic floor, old dock and ferry photographs, several real ales, bargain basic food wkdy lunchtime and early evening, tiled façade; open all day *(the Didler, C J Fletcher, MLR)*

BLACKO [SD8542]

Moorcock BB9 6NG [A682 towards Gisburn]: Beautifully placed moorland dining pub, roomy and comfortably old-fashioned, with

big picture windows for breathtaking views, tables set close for the huge range of popular and often enterprising food inc lamb from their own flock and excellent beef, very friendly helpful staff, decent wine, Thwaites Bitter and Mild under top pressure; tables in hillside garden with various animals, open all day for food Sun, children and dogs welcome, bedrooms *(Norma and Noel Thomas, LYM)*

BLACKSTONE EDGE [SD9617]

☆ *White House* OL15 0LG [A58 Ripponden—Littleborough, just W of B6138]: Beautifully placed moorland dining pub with remote views, emphasis on bargain hearty food from sandwiches up, prompt friendly service, Theakstons Best and changing guest ales, belgian bottled beers, cheerful atmosphere, carpeted main bar with hot coal fire, other areas off, one with small settees, though most tables used (and often booked, wknd evenings) for food; children welcome, open for food all day Sun *(Brian and Anna Marsden, LYM)*

BOLTON [SD7109]

Hen & Chickens BL1 1EX [Deansgate]: Smart open-plan corner pub handy for magistrates' court, popular hearty food inc good home-made pies, efficient friendly staff, three changing real ales, traditional décor; open all day, cl Sun lunchtime *(Andy Hazeldine, Joe Green)*

Howcroft BL1 2JU [Pool St]: Friendly local serving as tap for good Bank Top ales, also guest beers, bargain pubby lunches, lots of small screened-off rooms around central servery with fine glass and woodwork inc cosy snug with coal fire, bright and airy front room, conservatory, plenty of pub games, popular monthly poetry nights; crown bowling green, open all day *(Andy Hazeldine, the Didler, Joe Green)*

Olde Man & Scythe BL1 1HL [Churchgate]: Lively local in interesting timbered building (largely 17th-c with cellar dating from 12th c), low-beamed and flagstoned drinking area, two quieter bare-boards rooms, well kept Boddingtons, Holts and guest beers, Thatcher's farm cider, swift cheerful service, pubby lunchtime snacks (not Sun), low prices, darts and chess, sign language evenings; no children, piped music; delightful back terrace, handy for shopping area, open all day *(Pam and John Smith, Nick Holding)*

Spinning Mule BL1 1JT [Nelson Sq]: Typical Wetherspoons, good choice of real ales inc good value local ones, reasonably priced food all day, quick service; very busy with young people Sat night *(Ben Williams)*

Swan BL1 1HJ [Churchgate]: 19th-c (and partly 17th-c) hotel's small comfortable bar across cobbled alley, woody décor, fine real ale range inc Bank Top and Moorhouses, belgian beers on tap and in bottle, no music; courtyard tables, bedrooms, open till 1am Thurs-Sat *(Andy Hazeldine, Doug Christian)*

BURNLEY [SD8332]

Inn on the Wharf BB11 1JG [Manchester Rd (B6240)]: Well converted wharfside buildings by Leeds—Liverpool Canal, handy for centre, clean and spacious, with smart décor of beams, stripped stone and flagstones, polite efficient staff, good choice from sandwiches up at all-day food bar (busy lunchtime), well kept Greene King IPA, sensible prices; children welcome, waterside terrace, next to little Toll House Museum *(Margaret Dickinson, Len Beattie)*

Thornton Arms BB10 3JS [Brownside Rd]: Converted from old barn a few decades ago by the man whose name it bears, low-priced pubby food all day, well kept Thwaites; pleasant short walk down to Rowley Fishing Lodge, open all day *(Len Beattie)*

BURTON-IN-KENDAL [SD5376]

Kings Arms LA6 1LR [Main St]: Village pub with masses of old local memorabilia and advertisements in bar, wide range of good value substantial food inc local dishes here or in two knocked-through dining rooms, popular Mon steak night and Sun roasts, good atmosphere, five or six real ales, separate locals' area with pool and TV; comfortable bedrooms *(Bruce Braithwaite)*

BURY [SD8313]

Trackside BL9 0EY [East Lancs Railway Station, Bolton St]: Busy station bar by East Lancs steam railway, great range of real ales and bottled imports, farm cider, bargain wkdy lunches (from breakfast time till 5 wknds); open all day *(P Dawn, the Didler)*

CARNFORTH [SD4970]

County Hotel LA5 9LD [Lancaster Rd (A6)]: Comfortable hotel with main bar well used by locals, reliable traditional food from good sandwiches to full meals in neat well divided informal restaurant/café off, good service; bedrooms, handy for *Brief Encounter* visitor centre *(Margaret Dickinson, Mrs Hazel Rainer)*

CATFORTH [SD4735]

Running Pump PR4 0HH [Catforth Rd]: Roadside pub with chef/tenants doing good imaginative food (all day Sun, not Mon), freshly made so may be a wait, well kept Robinsons, log fire, thriving local atmosphere in bar, separate restaurant *(T Freaney)*

CATON [SD5364]

Ship LA2 9QJ [Lancaster Rd]: Roomy and reliable open-plan dining pub with good choice of reasonably priced food from sandwiches to generous fresh fish and Sun lunch, properly cooked veg, Thwaites ales and decent wines, efficient friendly staff, appealing nautical bric-a-brac, good fire in charming antique fireplace; subdued piped music; garden tables, handy for Lune Valley and Forest of Bowland *(Margaret Dickinson)*

CHEADLE HULME [SJ8787]

Micker Brook SK8 5NU [Councillor Lane]: Brewers Fayre family dining pub worth knowing for bargain carvery all week (cheapest before 5 Mon-Sat); children very welcome *(Caroline and Gavin Callow)*

CHIPPING [SD6243]

Tillotsons Arms PR3 2QE [Talbot St]: Comfortable traditional bar with padded chairs and wall banquettes, pleasant dining room, good choice of reasonably priced pubby food, well kept Tetleys inc Mild, nice wine by the glass, good service; cl Mon lunchtime, open all day Sun *(Alan and Eve Harding)*

CHORLEY [SD5817]

Hop Pocket PR7 3JQ [Carr Lane]: Clean and comfortable, with good service, good value pubby food from hot barm cakes up, Weds quiz night with bargain curry, good value house wines, well kept Thwaites, pool; big-screen sports TV, well reproduced piped music and music videos, Thurs blues night *(Andy Sinden, Louise Harrington)*

Yew Tree PR6 9HA [Dill Hall Brow, Heath Charnock – out past Limbrick towards the reservoirs]: Attractive tucked-away restauranty pub with good value enjoyable food from open kitchen, lunchtime sandwiches and paninis too, helpful friendly staff; children welcome, picnic-sets in sheltered garden, open all day Sun *(Gordon Tong)*

CHURCHTOWN [SD3618]

Bold Arms PR9 7NE [off A565 from Preston, taking B5244 in Southport; Botanic Rd]: Substantial coaching inn handy for the Botanic Gardens, lots of panelling and glazed partitions giving separate rooms (children allowed in one), good value simple food from sandwiches up, well kept ales inc interesting guest beers, competent staff, plenty of atmosphere; tables outside in picturesque surroundings *(MLR)*

CLAUGHTON [SD5666]

☆ *Fenwick Arms* LA2 9LA [A683 Kirkby Lonsdale—Lancaster]: Welcoming black and white pub recently featured on *Kitchen Nightmares*, enjoyable food inc fine yorkshire pudding, good licensees and cheerful staff, Black Sheep and Boddingtons, nice range of wines, log fires, armchairs and cosy traditional décor; piped music *(Jo Lilley, Simon Calvert, Karen Eliot)*

CLITHEROE [SD6642]

☆ *Craven Heifer* BB7 3LX [Chipping Rd out of Chaigley through Walker End, off B6243 about 4 miles W]: Attractively refurbished and civilised country dining pub with wide range of good food from bar favourites to smarter restaurant dishes, children's helpings, friendly service, interesting changing wine choice, real ales such as Moorhouses Premier, large dining room, bar area with comfortable armchairs, sofas and big log fire, fine views; tables outside, cl Mon/Tues *(Michael and Deirdre Ellis, Phillip Marchant)*

New Inn BB7 2JN [Parson Lane]: Spotless traditional four-room local with great range of real ales such as Black Sheep, Copper Dragon Orange Pippin, Goose Eye, Moorhouses and Timothy Taylors from central bar, friendly and obliging expert staff, log

fires in both front rooms; open all day
(Steve Whalley, Doug Christian)

COLNE [SD8738]

Golden Ball BB8 8LF [Burnley Rd (A56)]:
Pleasantly refurbished pub has good-sized
dining area with alcove tables and good
value food all day, good choice of Cains and
other ales from horseshoe bar; linked to
popular nearby Boundary Mill outlet store –
china, glass, designer clothes (Alan and
Eve Harding)

COMPSTALL [SJ9690]

Andrew Arms SK6 5JD [George St (B6104)]:
Enjoyable food inc bargain lunch Mon and
other good deals, Robinsons real ale,
enterprising choice of wines by the glass,
busy back dining room; handy for Etherow
Country Park (Dennis Jones)

CONDER GREEN [SD4556]

☆ *Stork* LA2 0AN [just off A588]: Fine spot
where River Conder joins the Lune Estuary
among bleak marshes, cheery bustle and two
blazing log fires in rambling dark-panelled
rooms, generous popular food inc all-day
sandwiches and light snacks, friendly
efficient young staff, three real ales such as
Black Sheep; pub games inc pool, juke box
or piped music; children welcome, handy for
Glasson Dock, comfortable bedrooms, open
all day (John Butterfield, Margaret Dickinson,
LYM)

COWAN BRIDGE [SD6277]

☆ *Whoop Hall* LA6 2HP [off A65 towards
Kirkby Lonsdale]: Spacious and comfortable
linked areas with wide choice of interesting
quick food all day from 8am from popular
buttery, pleasant neat staff, Black Sheep and
Greene King, decent wines, log fire, pool;
piped music; children welcome, garden well
off road with views from back terrace,
play area, comfortable bedrooms
(Margaret Dickinson, LYM, Pat and
Stewart Gordon)

CROSTON [SD4818]

☆ *Crown* PR26 9RN [Station Rd]: Popular
beamed village pub with good value food inc
daily roasts, OAP wkdy lunches, steak night
Mon, fish night Fri, hard-working young
licensees, Thwaites; children welcome, lots
of hanging baskets, picnic-sets and boules
out by back car park (John Cunningham, Jim
and Maggie Cowell, Mrs Y G Pearson)

☆ *Wheatsheaf* PR26 9RA [Town Rd]: Convivial,
relaxed and chatty, with generous interesting
food (usually all day) inc home-baked bread,
reasonable prices, good friendly service,
good changing range of well kept ales, good
choice of wines by the glass, stripped boards
and quarry tiles, 19th-c local photographs,
hops and fresh flowers, alcoves and candle
light; unobtrusive piped music; tables
out on sunny terrace, open all day
(John Cunningham, Hazel Auty, Jim and
Maggie Cowell, Tony and Caroline Elwood)

DARWEN [SD7222]

Old Rosins BB3 3QD [Pickup Bank,
Hoddlesden, off A6177 Haslingden—
Belthorn opp Grey Mare]: Large extended

open-plan moorland inn with comfortable
banquettes and good log fire, mugs; jugs
and chamber-pots hanging from beams,
picture-window views from dining end,
friendly staff, real ales such as John Smiths
and Timothy Taylors Landlord, plenty of malt
whiskies, new world wines, food from
sandwiches to steaks; fruit machine, piped
music; children welcome, picnic-sets on big
crazy-paved terrace, bedrooms, open all day
(Norma and Noel Thomas, LYM)

DOBCROSS [SD9906]

Swan OL3 5AA [The Square]: Low-beamed
pub with three interesting areas off small
central bar, partitioned settles, flagstones
and traditional settles, friendly atmosphere,
full Jennings ale range and a guest such as
Greene King Abbot; has been popular for
enjoyable varied well priced home-made food
and Thurs folk night, but on the market early
2007 – news please; children welcome,
tables outside, attractive village below
moors (John Fiander, Pete Baker)

DOLPHINHOLME [SD5153]

Fleece LA2 9AQ [back rds, a couple of miles
from M6 junction 33]: Friendly hotel with
tasty traditional food, helpful staff, well kept
ales, dining area off comfortable beamed
lounge, bar with darts and table skittles, log
fire; bedrooms (Mrs A Green)

DOWNHAM [SD7844]

☆ *Assheton Arms* BB7 4BJ [off A59 NE of
Clitheroe, via Chatburn]: Neatly kept pub
in lovely village location, good value food
from small open kitchen, quick service, lots
of wines by the glass, Marstons Bitter and
Pedigree, low-beamed L-shaped bar with
pews, big oak tables and massive stone
fireplace; piped music; children and dogs
welcome, picnic-sets outside, prime spot
in lovely village, open all day Sun
(Trevor and Sylvia Millum, LYM, Mr and
Mrs John Taylor)

ECCLES [SJ7798]

Albert Edward M30 0LS [Church St]: Cheery
pub with good range of beers, corridor to
popular back dining area; small sheltered
back terrace overlooking Ashton Canal, open
all day (the Didler)

Grapes M30 7HD [Liverpool Rd, Peel Green;
A57 ½ mile from M63 junction 2]: Handsome
brawny Edwardian local with superb etched
glass, wall tiling and mosaic floor, lots of
mahogany, eye-catching staircase, bargain
Holts Bitter and Mild with a good guest
beer, fairly quiet roomy lounge areas
(children welcome till 7pm), pool in classic
billiards room, vault with Manchester darts,
drinking corridor; tables outside, open all
day (Pete Baker, Pam and John Smith,
the Didler)

Lamb M30 0BP [Regent St (A57)]: Full-
blooded Edwardian three-room local,
splendid etched windows, fine woodwork and
furnishings, extravagantly tiled stairway,
admirable trophies in display case, bargain
Holts Bitter and Mild and lunchtime
sandwiches, full-size snooker table in

original billiards room; open all day
(the Didler, Pam and John Smith)

Royal Oak M30 0EN [Barton Lane]: Large old-fashioned Edwardian pub on busy corner, several rooms off corridor, handsome tilework and fittings, cheap Holts Bitter and Mild, good licensees, pool; children allowed daytime in former back billiards room (may be organ singalongs), open all day
(the Didler)

Stanley Arms M30 0QN [Eliza Ann St/Liverpool Rd (A57), Patricroft]: Lively mid-Victorian local with bargain Holts Bitter and Mild, lunchtime filled rolls, popular front bar, hatch serving lobby and corridor to small back rooms, one with cast-iron range
(Pam and John Smith, the Didler)

White Lion M30 0ND [Liverpool Rd, Patricroft, a mile from M63 junction 2]: Welcoming Edwardian traditional local, clean, tidy and popular with older people, with great value Holts Bitter and Mild, games in lively public bar, other rooms off tiled side drinking corridor *(the Didler, Pete Baker)*

ECCLESTON [SD5117]

☆ *Original Farmers Arms* PR7 5QS [Towngate (B5250, off A581 Chorley—Southport)]: Long low-beamed pub/restaurant, wide choice of consistently good competitively priced food all day from open sandwiches and wkdy daytime bargains to huge mixed grill, tempting puddings cabinets as you go in, cheery décor, good choice of real ales and of wines by the glass, pleasant smartly uniformed staff, darts; piped music and machines (can be noisy), parking can be tight when busy; good value bedrooms some with own bathroom, open all day *(Mike and Linda Hudson, BB, Ian and Sue Wells)*

EDGWORTH [SD7316]

Black Bull BL7 0AF [Bolton Rd, Turton]: Good value imaginative dishes from the brother and sister who now run the food side of this three-room pub, moor and reservoir views from attractive light and airy restaurant extension, friendly staff, five well kept changing ales, open fire; good walks *(Loraine and David Groom, Norma and Noel Thomas)*

White Horse BL7 0AY [Bury Rd/Blackheath Rd]: Big stone-built pub with friendly efficient staff, well kept ales such as Bank Top Flat Cap, Greene King Ruddles Best, Marstons Pedigree and Theakstons Best, open-plan bar with open fire, carved dark oak panelling and beams, old local photographs, end dining room; piped music may obtrude, big-screen TV, games machine; children welcome, tables outside, open all day at least in summer *(LYM, Steve Whalley)*

EGERTON [SD7015]

Cross Guns BL7 9TR [Blackburn Rd (A666)]: Friendly pub below moors (used by mountain rescue team), good choice of sensibly priced bar food inc enjoyable hot sandwiches, up to five real ales, bubbly staff, Sat live music;

children welcome in dining area
(Sammie Banks)

EUXTON [SD5319]

Plough PR7 6HB [Runshaw Moor; a mile from A49/B5252 junction]: Spotless black-beamed country dining pub with olde-worlde décor and antiques, good atmosphere, enjoyable food inc good value imaginative dishes (very popular wknds), well kept Jennings and Theakstons, sympathetic extension; piped music, big-screen TV; big sheltered back garden with heated terrace under awning, lawn tables and small play area
(Margaret Dickinson)

Railway PR7 6LA [The Ordnance, Wigan Rd]: Newly opened dining pub with enjoyable enterprising but unpretentious food (all day Sun) from sandwiches and light dishes up, leather sofas in comfortable lounge, civilised open-plan dining areas, Burtonwood ale; heated partly enclosed terrace
(Wendy Rogers)

FENCE [SD8237]

Forest BB12 9PA [Cuckstool Lane (B6248) off Barrowford Rd (A6068)]: Civilised Pennine-view dining pub (all day Sun) with enjoyable food in nicely lit open-plan bar and ornately panelled brasserie, some small helpings for children, well kept mainstream ales, good choice of wines by the glass, good coffee, friendly helpful service, lots of paintings, vases, plates and books, front conservatory; may be unobtrusive piped music; children welcome, open all day *(Bob Broadhurst, LYM)*

FLEETWOOD [SD3348]

☆ *North Euston* FY7 6BN [Esplanade, nr tram terminus]: Big architecturally interesting Victorian railway hotel dominating the seafront, extensive pubby bar giving great sea and hill views, friendly helpful staff, good changing real ale choice such as Greene King, Timothy Taylors and Theakstons, enjoyable lunchtime food from sandwiches up, lots of separate-seeming areas inc large family room, café-bar and two restaurants; live music Fri-Sun; seats outside, comfortable bedrooms, open all day (Sun afternoon break) *(David and Ruth Hollands, BB, Ian and Sue Wells, Margaret Dickinson)*

Wyre FY7 6HF [Marine Hall, Esplanade]: Part of exhibition/entertainment centre, quiet and comfortable, with banquettes and padded chairs in three linked domed areas, picture-window views across to Morecambe Bay, boats and ships; enthusiast landlord keeps half a dozen or more well priced ales in top condition, such as Courage Directors, Moorhouses Pendle Witches Brew and Phoenix Navvy, plenty of country wines and malt whiskies, hot drinks machine; children welcome, three picnic-sets outside (plastic glasses here) *(Steve Whalley)*

GARSTANG [SD4943]

Bradbeer Bar PR3 1YE [Garstang Country Hotel & Golf Club; B6430 S]: Relaxed and spacious bar overlooking golfing greens, good value imaginative food, helpful well trained staff, big log fire; tables outside, bedrooms *(Margaret Dickinson)*

Royal Oak PR3 1ZA [Market Pl]: Comfortable and roomy small-town inn dating from 16th c, attractive panelling, several eating areas inc charming snug, reliably enjoyable generous food (all day Sun) inc imaginative specials, small helpings for children or OAPs, Robinsons real ales, good value coffee, restaurant, spotless housekeeping; disabled access, comfortable bedrooms, open all day Fri-Sun *(Pam and John Smith)*

☆ **Th'Owd Tithebarn** PR3 1PA [off Church St]: Rustic barn with big flagstoned terrace overlooking Lancaster Canal marina, Victorian country life theme with very long refectory table, antique kitchen range, masses of farm tools, stuffed animals and birds, flagstones and high rafters, simple food all day from filled baguettes up, Flowers IPA and Tetleys, country wines, quieter parlour welcoming children; piped music in main bar may be loud; open all day summer *(Margaret Dickinson, LYM, A Benson)*

Wheatsheaf PR3 1EL [Park Hill Rd (one-way system northbound)]: Small and spotless low-beamed pub with gleaming copper and brass, good range of well priced freshly cooked good food, cheerful friendly service even when busy, decent malt whiskies *(Margaret Dickinson, BB)*

GREAT HARWOOD [SD7332]

Royal BB6 7BA [Station Rd]: Substantial Victorian pub with good changing range of real ales from small breweries inc ones from their nearby Red Rose brewery, good soft drinks choice inc their own sarsaparilla, simple traditional fittings, friendly atmosphere, pub games inc pool and darts; big-screen TV, live music Fri; terrace tables (partly covered), newly refurbished bedrooms, cl lunchtime Mon-Thurs, otherwise open all day *(the Didler)*

Victoria BB6 7EP [St Johns St]: Splendid beer range with Bowland Gold and half a dozen or more changing guests, friendly landlady and regulars, unspoilt traditional Edwardian layout with five rooms off central bar, one with darts, one with pool, two quiet snugs, some handsome tiling; tables out behind, opens 4.30 (3 Fri, all day wknds), cl wkdy lunchtimes *(Pete Baker, the Didler)*

GRIMSARGH [SD5934]

Plough PR2 5JR [Preston Rd (B6243 Preston—Longridge)]: Well kept changing ales, good choice of popular food from sandwiches up, friendly helpful staff, appealing country décor with plenty of variety from tiles, flagstones and bare boards to carpeting *(David and Ruth Hollands)*

HALTON [SD5064]

Greyhound LA2 6LZ [Low Rd]: Neatly kept traditional stone-built pub with attractively refurbished linked rooms, good freshly made unpretentious food (small helpings available), great log fire in cosy turkey-carpeted lounge, games end with pool; children welcome, disabled access and

facilities, picnic-sets outside, handy for River Lune and good cycle tracks, open all day *(Jenny Natusch)*

HAMBLETON [SD3741]

Shard Riverside FY6 9BT [off A588 towards Poulton; Old Bridge Lane]: Substantially extended pub on Wyre Estuary by former toll bridge, small smartly refurbished lounge with restaurant tables beyond, wide choice of reasonably priced fresh food from soup and ploughman's up, pleasant helpful staff, well kept real ales; nice outdoor tables overlooking water, 18 bedrooms, open all day *(Margaret Dickinson)*

Shovels Inn FY6 9AL [Green Meadow Lane]: Old-fashioned pub with proper food from sandwiches to restaurant dishes, mature attentive staff, real ales such as Black Sheep, Boddingtons and Fullers London Pride; disabled access *(A Benson)*

HAPTON [SD7930]

Hapton Inn BB11 5QL [Accrington Rd (A679); handy for M65 junction 8 or (eastbound only) 9, and Hapton stn]: Popular dining pub with good value food (all day wknds) in bar and beamed restaurant, three well kept ales such as Bowland and Timothy Taylors Landlord, farm cider, rustic bric-a-brac, play room; garden tables, good moorland walks, open all day wknds *(Len Beattie)*

HASKAYNE [SD3608]

Ship L39 7JP [Rosemary Lane, just off A567]: By Leeds & Liverpool Canal, well kept ales such as Black Sheep, Cains IPA and Shepherd Neame Spitfire, decent if not cheap food, two cosy rooms, two more airy, navigation lights, ship models etc; waterside garden with pergola terrace and play area *(Liz and Brian Barnard)*

HASLINGDEN [SD7823]

Griffin BB4 5AF [Hud Rake, off A680 at N end]: Friendly basic local brewing its own cheap Porters ales in the cellar, farm cider, L-shaped bar with views from comfortable lounge end, darts in public end; open all day *(Pete Baker)*

HAWKSHAW [SD7515]

☆ **Red Lion** BL8 4JS [Ramsbottom Rd]: Roomy, comfortable and attractive pub/hotel, friendly welcome and efficient cheerful service, good generous fresh local food in cosy bar and separate well run restaurant, good changing real ale range; comfortable if rather creaky bedrooms, quiet spot by River Irwell, open for food all day wknds *(John and Sylvia Harrop, Ben Williams, Phil and Helen Holt)*

HEST BANK [SD4766]

☆ **Hest Bank Hotel** LA2 6DN [Hest Bank Lane; off A6 just N of Lancaster]: Picturesque three-bar coaching inn in attractive setting close to Morecambe Bay, wide range of good fresh hearty food all day from sandwiches and local potted shrimps to mixed grill and fresh fish, bargain lunches, Black Sheep, Boddingtons, Caledonian Deuchars IPA, Timothy Taylors Landlord and an interesting guest beer, decent wines, friendly and helpful young staff, comfortably worn-in furnishings, separate restaurant area with pleasant conservatory; children welcome, plenty of tables out by Lancaster Canal, open all day; changed hands in early summer 2007, so may well change quite a bit now – news please *(Julian and Janet Dearden, Peter Forster, Karen Eliot, J M Daykin, BB, MLR)*

HEYSHAM [SD4161]

Royal LA3 2RN [Main St]: Four changing real ales, well priced wines and decent food inc early evening bargains in early 16th-c quaint and low-beamed two-bar pub; dogs allowed (not at meal times), tables out in front and good-sized sheltered garden, pretty village with great views from interesting church *(Tony and Maggie Harwood, A Benson)*

HOGHTON [SD6225]

Boatyard PR5 0SP [A675 Preston—Bolton, NW of A674 junction]: Country dining pub on mound by Leeds & Liverpool Canal with plenty of boats to watch, friendly staff, good value pubby food all day, Thwaites real ales, Victorian-style décor; tables outside, beached barge in grounds *(Ben Williams)*

HOLDEN [SD7749]

☆ *Copy Nook* BB7 4NL [the one up by Bolton by Bowland]: Roomy and attractive dining pub with friendly relaxing atmosphere, pleasant helpful staff, wide choice of generous popular food from sandwiches up in bar's two dining areas and restaurant, reasonable prices, well kept ales such as Marstons Pedigree, good wine choice, log fire; piped music; children welcome, good walking area, six comfortable bedrooms *(BB, Brian and Janet Ainscough, Mrs P Beardsworth, Dudley and Moira Cockroft)*

HOYLAKE [SJ2189]

Ship CH47 3BB [Market St]: Cosy and friendly refurbished pub dating from18th c, wide choice of well kept ales, enjoyable food inc popular Sun lunch, good service, maritime pictures and lots of ship models *(Dr D Hannam)*

HURST GREEN [SD6837]

Punch Bowl BB7 9QW [Longridge Rd (B6243 W), Dutton]: Hard-working licensees, good choice of enjoyable food from sandwiches and baked potatoes to full meals, Thwaites ales, nook-and-cranny eating area off pleasant bar, log fires, dark-panelled Jacobean dining room with minstrel gallery; children welcome, tables out on spacious lawn, good walks, five bedrooms, open all day from 10am *(Margaret Dickinson)*

☆ *Shireburn Arms* BB7 9QJ [Whalley Rd]: Quiet comfortable 17th-c hotel in idyllic setting with panoramic views from lovely neatly kept back garden and attractive terrace, friendly service, good reasonably priced food from sandwiches and snacks (9-5) through pubby favourites to restaurant dishes, half-price children's helpings, Thwaites and other ales, armchairs and log fire in beamed lounge bar,

light and airy restaurant, separate tea room; safe low-key play area, pretty Tolkien walk from here, appealing bedrooms, good breakfast *(Susan and Nigel Brookes, Margaret Dickinson)*

HYDE [SJ9495]

Cheshire Ring SK14 2BJ [Manchester Rd (A57, between M67 junctions 2 and 3)]: Welcoming pub tied to Cheshire's small Beartown brewery, their real ales at tempting prices, guest beers and imports on tap, farm cider, good house wines, good value sandwiches; open all day (has been cl till 2 Mon-Weds) *(Dennis Jones, the Didler)*

Hare & Hounds SK14 3AA [Werneth Low Rd]: Rambling and welcoming Chef & Brewer high in Werneth Low Country Park, their usual food, Boddingtons, Wells & Youngs Bombardier and two guest beers, good landlord, low-beamed traditional layout, great log fires; terrace with stunning views and telescope *(Stewart Rigby)*

Sportsman SK14 2NN [Mottram Rd]: Unpretentious Victorian local popular for its half a dozen or more real ales, good prices, welcoming licensees, open fires, memorabilia and plenty of atmosphere; children and dogs welcome *(the Didler)*

INGLEWHITE [SD5439]

Green Man PR3 2LP [Silk Mill Lane; 3 miles from A6 – turn off nr Owd Nells, Bilsborrow]: Old-fashioned red plush in polished bar and dining room, lots of pictures and bric-a-brac, good straightforward generous food served piping hot at attractive prices, good sandwiches, well kept beer, staff pleasant and attentive even when busy, big log fire; garden with unspoilt views nr Beacon Fell Country Park, camp site behind, bedrooms *(Margaret Dickinson)*

LANCASTER [SD4861]

Gregson LA1 3PY [Moorgate]: Well kept Thwaites and a guest ale, enjoyable food, friendly relaxed atmosphere, catering well for a wide range of age groups *(Andrew Paylor)*

☆ *Water Witch* LA1 1SU [parking in Aldcliffe Rd behind Royal Lancaster Infirmary, off A6]: Cheerful and attractive conversion of 18th-c canalside barge-horse stabling, flagstones, stripped stone, rafters and pitch-pine panelling, fine changing beer choice, lots of bottled beers, dozens of wines by the glass and good spirits range from mirrored bar, enjoyable stylishly cooked local food inc good cheeseboard, upstairs restaurant; children in eating areas, tables outside, open all day *(Jim and Maggie Cowell, Mrs Hazel Rainer, Jo Lilley, Simon Calvert, LYM)*

LATHOM [SD4511]

Ship L40 4BX [off A5209 E of Burscough; Wheat Lane]: Big pub tucked below embankment at junction of Leeds & Liverpool and Rufford Branch canals, several separate beamed rooms, some interesting canal memorabilia and naval pictures and crests, Cains and guest beers, some parts set for the reasonably priced unpretentious food from lunchtime sandwiches up (small helpings available), prompt service even when busy; games room with pool, big-screen sports TV, no dogs till after 9 – unusual local food rule; children welcome, lots of tables outside, open all day (*MLR, BB, J A Hooker, Mrs Dilys Unsworth, Nick Holding*)

LEIGH [SJ6599]

Waterside WN7 4DB [Twist Lane]: Civilised pub in tall converted 19th-c warehouses by Bridgewater Canal, handy for indoor and outdoor markets, wide choice of enjoyable reasonably priced food all day inc OAP and other deals, Greene King and related ales, good friendly service, chatty lunchtime atmosphere; live music or disco Thurs-Sat; children welcome, disabled access and facilities, plenty of waterside tables, ducks and swans, open all day (*GLD, Ben Williams, John Fiander*)

LITTLE ECCLESTON [SD4240]

Cartford PR3 0YP [Cartford Lane, off A586 Garstang—Blackpool, by toll bridge]: New French landlord giving a lift to the food at this pleasantly atmospheric farmhouse in scenic countryside by toll bridge on River Wyre; traditional rambling interior on four levels with oak beams, log fire, oak boards and flagstones, and rustic furnishings; Theakstons XB, Best and Old Peculier and a guest such as Hart (from the microbrewery located behind); children welcome, tables outside, bedrooms, open all day (*BOB*)

LITTLE LEVER [SD7407]

Jolly Carter BL3 1BW [Church St]: Bright and comfortable, with good value home-made food, Bank Top, Greene King Old Speckled Hen and Timothy Taylors Landlord, modern décor, friendly helpful long-serving licensees; handy for Bolton Branch of Manchester, Bolton & Bury Canal (*Ben Williams*)

LITTLEBOROUGH [SD9316]

Moor Cock OL15 0LD [Halifax Rd]: Friendly family-run pub with great views over Manchester area, wide choice of good value food from sandwiches up in bar and smart restaurant, well kept Timothy Taylors Landlord and two guest beers; bedrooms (*Tony Hobden*)

Summit OL15 9QX [Summit Ave/Todmorden Rd]: At the top of a tremendous flight of locks on the Rochdale Canal (take some five hours to ascend), open-plan linked areas with fires each end, well kept Thwaites, decent generous cheap food (not Sun-Tues evenings) inc Sun carvery; piped music, Thurs quiz night, some live music; children welcome, good-sized garden (*Tony Hobden*)

LIVERPOOL [SJ3489]

☆ *Baltic Fleet* L1 8DQ [Wapping, nr Albert Dock]: Beer taken seriously here, with its own Wapping brews as well as interesting guest ales, friendly service, short simple choice of bargain bar food, loads of nautical paraphernalia, big arched windows, prominent woodwork, unpretentious mix of furnishings, upstairs restaurant; piped music, TV; children welcome in eating areas, dogs in bar, back terrace, open all day (*LYM, Tracey and Stephen Groves, the Didler, C J Fletcher, Paul Davies, Mark and Diane Grist*)

☆ *Cains Brewery Tap* L8 5XJ [Stanhope St]: Well restored Victorian pub with Cains full beer range (inc their good Mild) at attractive prices, guest beers, friendly efficient staff, good well priced wkdy food till 6 (2 Sat), nicely understated décor, wooden floors, plush raised side snug, interesting old prints and breweriana, handsome bar, flame-effect gas fire, daily papers, cosy relaxing atmosphere; sports TV; good value brewery tour ending here with buffet and singing; open all day (*the Didler, C J Fletcher*)

Carnarvon Castle L1 1DS [Tarleton St]: Long, narrow and companionable, with compact bar and comfortable back lounge, Cains Bitter and Mild and a guest or two, breakfasts (from 10) and lunchtime bar snacks, cabinet of Dinky toys and other eclectic collections, no music; open all day, cl Sun evening, Mon/Tues lunchtime (opens 8pm then) (*the Didler*)

☆ *Cracke* L1 9BB [Rice St]: Friendly backstreet local, Cains, Phoenix and guest beers, farm cider, very cheap food till 6, bare boards and pews, unusual Beatles diorama in largest room, lots of posters for local events and pictures of local buildings; juke box and TV, popular mainly with young people; sizeable garden, open all day (*C J Fletcher, the Didler*)

Crown L1 1JQ [Lime St]: Well preserved art nouveau showpiece with fine tiled fireplace and copper bar front, plush banquettes, splendid ceiling in airy corner bar, smaller back room with another good fireplace, impressive staircase sweeping up under splendid cupola to handsome area with ornate windows, generous bargain food till early evening, well priced Cains and guest beers (*Joe Green, C J Fletcher, the Didler*)

☆ *Dispensary* L1 2SP [Renshaw St]: Small chatty central pub with Cains inc Mild and two guest beers, bottled imports, friendly staff, good value wkdy food 12-7, polished panelling, marvellous etched windows, bare boards, comfortable raised back bar, Victorian medicine bottles and instruments; open all day (*C J Fletcher, the Didler, Joe Green*)

☆ *Doctor Duncan* L1 1HF [St Johns Lane]: Neat and convivial Victorian pub with several rooms inc impressive back area with pillared and vaulted tiled ceiling, particularly attentive staff, full Cains range and up to four guest beers, belgian beers on tap, enjoyable food from sandwiches to economical main dishes till 7 (Tues curry night), pleasant helpful service, daily papers and magazines; may be piped music, can get lively evenings, busy wknds; family room, open all day (*C J Fletcher, the Didler*)

Fly in the Loaf L1 9AS [Hardman St]: Smart gleaming bar devoted to real ales, mostly local and Okells (from Isle of Man), popular home-made food, one long room, small snug with sofa; open all day *(Tracey and Stephen Groves)*

Globe L1 1HW [Cases St, opp station]: Chatty comfortably carpeted local, pleasant staff, Cains and guest beers, lunchtime filled cobs, cosy snug, tiny quiet sloping-floor back lounge, lots of prints of old Liverpool; may be piped music; open all day *(the Didler, Joe Green)*

Grapes L2 6RE [Mathew St]: Friendly open-plan local with Cains, Tetleys and guest beers, good value lunchtime bar food, cottagey décor with flagstones, old range, wall settles, mixed furnishings; open all day *(the Didler)*

Lion L2 2BP [Moorfields, off Tithebarn St]: Ornate Victorian tavern with great changing choice of over half a dozen real ales, friendly atmosphere and landlord interested in pub's history, lunchtime food inc splendid cheese and pie specialities, sparkling etched glass and serving hatches in central bar, unusual wallpaper, big mirrors, panelling and tilework, two small back lounges (one with fine glass dome), coal fire; open all day *(Paul Davies, MLR, C J Fletcher, Pete Baker, the Didler, Mark and Diane Grist)*

Ma Boyles L3 1LG [Tower Gardens, off Water St]: Backstreet pub with neat plain décor, good value bar food (all day Sat) from dim sum and pies to galway oysters, well kept Cains ales, quieter downstairs bar; big-screen TV; open all day, cl Sat night and Sun *(the Didler, Tracey and Stephen Groves)*

Midland L1 1JP [Ranelagh St]: Well kept Victorian local with original décor, ornate lounge, long corner bar, nice etched glass, mirrors and chandeliers; keg beers *(the Didler)*

Peter Kavanaghs L8 7LY [Egerton St, off Catherine St]: Rambling shuttered pub with interesting décor in several small rooms inc old-world murals, stained glass and lots of bric-a-brac inc bicycle hanging from ceiling, Cains, Greene King Abbot and a guest beer, friendly staff; open all day *(the Didler, C J Fletcher)*

Poste House L1 6BU [Cumberland St]: Small comfortably refurbished early 19th-c backstreet local surrounded by huge redevelopment, friendly licensees and chatty regulars, Cains Bitter and Mild and a guest beer, good wkdy lunches, daily papers and may be free bar nibbles, room upstairs; open all day *(the Didler, Jeremy King)*

Pump House L3 4AN [Albert Dock]: Multi-level dockside conversion, good Mersey views, lots of polished dark wood and bare bricks, tall chimney, mezzanine and upper gallery with exposed roof trusses, marble counter with beers such as Greene King Ruddles from bulbous beer engines (and brass rail supported by elephants' heads), food all day, friendly staff; waterside tables, boat trips in season; open all day *(Dave Braisted)*

Roscoe Head L1 2SX [Roscoe St]: Tastefully refurbished keeping appealing layout of three spotless little unspoilt rooms, warm, friendly and civilised, with changing ales such as Jennings Cumberland and Tetleys Mild and Bitter, good service, good value wkdy home-made lunches, interesting memorabilia; open all day *(Joe Green, David Martin, C J Fletcher, the Didler)*

Ship & Mitre L2 2JH [Dale St]: Friendly gaslit local popular with university people, up to a dozen changing unusual real ales, imported beers, two farm ciders, good-humoured service, good value basic food lunchtime and (not Mon-Weds) early evening, pool, weekly themed beer nights; piped music; open all day, cl Sun lunchtime *(the Didler, Mark and Diane Grist)*

Swan L1 4DQ [Wood St]: Busy bare-boards pub with Hydes, Phoenix, several guest beers, Weston's farm cider, good value cobs and home-cooked wkdy lunches, friendly staff, comfortable loft in second upstairs bar; good loud 1970s rock juke box; open all day *(the Didler)*

☆ *Thomas Rigbys* L2 2EZ [Dale St]: Spacious beamed and panelled pub with great range of beers inc imports from impressively long bar, steps up to main area, reasonably priced hearty home-made food (with accompanying beer recommendations) all day till 7; disabled access, tables and chairs outside, open all day *(Helen Slater, Jeremy King)*

Vines L1 1JQ [Lime St]: Comfortable and friendly, with Victorian mahogany and mosaic tilework, handsome high-ceilinged room on right with stained glass; can get very busy; open all day *(the Didler)*

LONGRIDGE [SD6137]

Corporation Arms PR3 2YJ [Lower Rd (B6243)]: Comfortably refurbished 18th-c pub with wide range of largely traditional food all day, small helpings available, three or four changing guest beers, lots of malt whiskies, good atmosphere in three small linked rooms and restaurant; bedrooms and breakfast good, open all day *(John and Alison Hamilton, Jim and Maggie Cowell)*

LONGTON [SD4825]

Rams Head PR4 5HA [Liverpool Rd; on A59 in centre of village]: Reopened after major refurbishment, good value food all day in comfortable bar/lounge and small restaurant, several real ales; children welcome, open all day *(Jim and Maggie Cowell)*

LOWER BARTLE [SD4832]

Sitting Goose PR4 0RT [off B5411 just NW of Preston; Lea Lane]: Olde-worlde country pub with pleasant décor, enjoyable food in bar and restaurant, good service, well kept Thwaites ales, log fire, conservatory; tables out overlooking trees and fields *(Margaret Dickinson)*

LYTHAM ST ANNES [SD3428]

Blossoms FY8 4EP [Woodlands Rd]: Brightly refurbished, with good value food and four changing ales inc Timothy Taylors *(Ben Williams)*

Fairhaven FY8 1AU [Marine Drive]: Neat modern pub with wide choice of generous fresh food from sandwiches and baguettes up, mainstream real ales, helpful staff; handy for beach and Fairhaven Lake *(Ken Richards)*

MANCHESTER [SJ8398]

☆ *Ape & Apple* M2 6HQ [John Dalton St]: Big friendly open-plan pub with bargain Holts and hearty bar food, comfortable seats in bare-boards bar with nice lighting and lots of old prints and posters, armchairs in upstairs lounge; piped music, TV area, games machines; unusual brick cube garden, bedrooms, open all day *(the Didler)*

Bar Fringe M4 5JN [Swan St]: Bare-boards café-bar specialising in beers from the low countries, also four changing real ales from local small breweries, farm cider, friendly staff, enjoyable food till 6 (4 Sat/Sun), daily papers, shelves of empty beer bottles, cartoons, posters and bank notes, polished motorcycle hung above door, games inc pinball, good music; tables out behind, open all day *(the Didler)*

Boundary M34 5HD [Audenshaw Rd (A6140/A6017, nr Guide Bridge stn – and M60 junction 23)]: Imposing pub extended over the years, long lounge with dining area and conservatory popular for wide range of good honest generous pub food all day, well kept changing ales from interesting small breweries, traditional vault with games; terraced garden overlooking Ashton Canal, open all day *(Dennis Jones)*

Castle M4 1LE [Oldham St, about 200 yards from Piccadilly, on right]: Simple traditional front bar, small snug, full Robinsons range from fine bank of handpumps, games in well used back room, nice tilework outside; no food, children allowed till 7, open all day (cl Sun afternoon) *(the Didler, Tony Hobden)*

Circus M1 4GX [Portland St]: Compact traditional pub with particularly well kept Tetleys from minute corridor bar (or may be table drinks service), friendly landlord, celebrity photographs, leatherette banquettes in panelled back room, no music or machines; often looks closed but normally open all day (you may have to knock) *(the Didler, Mark and Diane Grist)*

City Arms M2 4BQ [Kennedy St, off St Peters Sq]: Five or six quickly changing real ales, belgian bottled beers, occasional beer festivals, busy for bargain bar lunches inc sandwiches and baked potatoes, quick service, coal fires, bare boards and banquettes, prints, panelling and masses of pump clips, handsome tiled façade and corridor; good piped music, TV, games machine; wheelchair access but steps down to back lounge, open all day *(the Didler)*

Coach & Horses M45 6TB [Old Bury Rd, Whitefield; A665 nr Besses o' the Barn stn]: Early 19th-c, keeping several separate rooms, popular and friendly, with bargain Holts beers, table service, darts, cards; open all day *(the Didler)*

Crescent M5 4PF [Crescent (A6), Salford – opp Salford Uni]: Three areas off central servery with up to eight changing real ales, farm ciders and lots of foreign bottled beers, friendly staff, buoyant local atmosphere (popular with students and Uni staff), low-priced food, open fire, homely unsmart décor, pool room, juke box; small enclosed terrace, open all day *(the Didler)*

Crown & Kettle M4 5FF [Oldham Rd/Gt Ancoats St]: Comfortably refurbished and partly panelled three-room Victorian pub, up to eight mainly local real ales, farm cider, popular bar lunches inc daily roast, coal fire, ornate high ceilings with remarkably intricate plasterwork, decorative windows; open all day *(BB, the Didler)*

Didsbury M20 2SG [Wilmslow Rd, Didsbury]: Roomy and softly lit beamed pub popular for wide choice of enjoyable food (even Mon night) inc Sun lunch, no booking, friendly efficient service, log fire in stone fireplace, some quiet alcoves, mixed old oak and pine furniture, dark panelling; quiet piped music; tables outside, open all day *(J and F Gowers)*

Dutton Arms M3 1EU [Park St, Strangeways]: Welcoming old-fashioned backstreet local almost in shadows of prison, three rooms with Hydes beers from central servery, plenty of bric-a-brac; open all day *(the Didler)*

Eagle M3 7DW [Collier St, Salford (keep on Greengate after it leaves B6182)]: Old-fashioned basic backstreet pub popular with older regulars, bargain Holts Bitter and Mild, friendly service, cheap filled rolls, bar servery to tap and passage, old Salford pictures; sports TV; open all day *(the Didler)*

Egerton Arms M3 5FP [Gore St, Salford; A6 by stn]: Several rooms, chandeliers, art nouveau lamps, low-priced Holts Bitter and Mild and guest beers, friendly service; open all day *(the Didler)*

Grey Horse M1 4QX [Portland St, nr Piccadilly]: Small traditional one-bar Hydes local, their Bitter and Mild, some unusual malt whiskies, panelled servery with colourful glazed gantry, lots of prints, photographs and plates, no juke box or machines; can bring in good sandwiches from next door, open all day *(the Didler, Dennis Jones, Mark and Diane Grist)*

Hare & Hounds M4 4AA [Shudehill, behind Arndale]: Unpretentious 18th-c favourite of older locals, long narrow bar linking front snug and comfortable back lounge (with TV), notable tilework, panelling and stained glass, Holts and Tetleys, friendly staff; games and machine, piano singalongs Weds and Sun; open all day *(Joe Green, the Didler, Pete Baker, Mark and Diane Grist)*

Jolly Angler M1 2JW [Ducie St]: Plain backstreet local, long a favourite, small and friendly, with Hydes ales, coal or peat fire; darts, pool and sports TV, informal folk nights Thurs and Sun; open all day Sat *(P Dawn, Pete Baker, the Didler, BB)*

Kings Arms M3 6AN [Bloom St, Salford]: Plain tables, bare boards and flagstones contrasting with opulent maroon and purple décor and stained glass, good changing real ale range, lunchtime food (not Sat); juke box, music, poetry or theatre nights upstairs; open all day (cl Sun evening) *(the Didler)*

Metropolitan M20 2WS [Lapwing Lane, Didsbury]: Huge welcoming dining pub, smiling helpful service, enjoyable generous food from wholesome bar lunches to some interesting evening dishes, popular Sun lunch, well kept ales such as Burtonwood, Caledonian Deuchars IPA and Timothy Taylors Landlord, good coffee, impressive décor with separate areas and unspoilt airy feel, open fires, gabled roof; tables out on heated decking, outside summer bar *(Margaret and Jeff Graham)*

☆ *Mr Thomas Chop House* M2 7AR [Cross St]: Good plain traditional lunchtime food, friendly well informed staff who cope quickly however busy it is, good wines by the glass, well kept real ale, attractive city-pub Victorian décor, front bar with bare boards, panelling, original gas lamp fittings and stools at wall and window shelves, back tiled eating area, period features inc wrought-iron gates for wine racks; open all day *(Revd D Glover, GLD, Dennis Jones, the Didler, Roger Yates)*

New Oxford M3 6DB [Bexley Sq, Salford]: Doing well under friendly new Irish couple, eight well kept and interesting changing real ales inc Northern, good range of imported beers, light and airy décor in small front bar and back lounge, coal fire, plans for fresh food; open all day *(the Didler)*

Old Monkey M1 4GX [Portland St]: Holts showpiece recently built in traditional style, generous tasty food and their Bitter and Dark Mild, bargain prices, quick friendly service even when busy, etched glass and mosaic tiling, interesting memorabilia, upstairs lounge, wide mix of customers *(the Didler, Dr and Mrs A K Clarke)*

☆ *Peveril of the Peak* M1 5JQ [Gt Bridgewater St]: Vivid art nouveau green external tilework, interesting pictures, lots of mahogany, mirrors and stained or frosted glass, log fire, very welcoming family service, changing mainstream ales from central servery, cheap basic lunchtime food (not Sun), three sturdily furnished bare-boards rooms, busy lunchtime but friendly and homely evenings; TV; children welcome, pavement tables, cl wknd lunchtimes, open all day Fri *(Joe Green, the Didler, Mark and Diane Grist, Stephen and Jean Curtis, LYM)*

Plough M18 7FB [Hyde Rd (A57), Gorton]: Classic tiling, windows and gantry in unspoilt Robinsons bar, two quieter back lounges, wooden benches in large public bar, small pool room and lots of pub games; TV; open all day *(the Didler)*

☆ *Rain Bar* M1 5JG [Gt Bridgewater St]: Lots of woodwork and flagstones in former umbrella works, full range of Lees beers kept well, masses of wines by the glass, good value pubby food all day inc 9am wknd breakfast, welcoming efficient staff, relaxed atmosphere, daily papers, coal fire in small snug, large upstairs café-bar too; piped music may be loud; no under-21s or scruffs evenings, good back terrace overlooking spruced-up Rochdale Canal, handy for Bridgwater Hall, open all day *(Dennis Jones, the Didler, Dr and Mrs A K Clarke)*

Sams Chop House M2 1HN [Back Pool Fold, Chapel Walks]: Small pleasant dining pub, offshoot from Mr Thomas Chop House, with thriving atmosphere, good beers, huge helpings of good plain english food, good wine choice, formal waiters, original Victorian décor *(Revd D Glover, GLD)*

☆ *Sinclairs* M3 1SW [2 Cathedral Gates, off Exchange Sq]: Charming low-beamed and timbered 18th-c pub (rebuilt here in redevelopment), bargain Sam Smiths OB, good all-day menu highlighting oysters, brisk friendly service, great atmosphere, quieter upstairs bar with snugs and Jacobean fireplace; can take a while to get served when busy, plastic glasses for the tables out by modern Exchange Sq; open all day *(the Didler, Dennis Jones, LYM, Clive Flynn, Jeremy King)*

Smithfield M4 5JZ [Swan St]: Unpretentious open-plan local with interesting and well kept changing ales, some in jugs from the cellar, frequent beer festivals, bargain food from sandwiches up from open kitchen servery, daily papers, friendly landlady; pool on front dais, games machine, juke box, sports TV in back lounge/eating area; good value bedrooms in nearby building, open all day *(Joe Green, the Didler, BB)*

White Lion M3 4NQ [Liverpool Rd, Castlefield]: Lots of dark wood, tables for eating up one side of three-sided bar, home-made food all day inc good hot beef sandwiches and children's helpings, changing ales inc Phoenix and Timothy Taylors Landlord, decent house wine, good tea, friendly service, real fire, lots of prints and Man Utd pictures, shelves of bottles and jugs; big-screen sports TVs, nostalgic discos Fri-Sun; disabled access, children welcome, tables out among excavated foundations of Roman city overlooking fort gate, handy for Museum of Science and Industry and Royal Exchange Theatre, open all day *(the Didler, Dennis Jones)*

MARPLE [SJ9389]

Hare & Hounds SK6 7EJ [Dooley Lane (A627 W)]: Attractive old pub above River Goyt, modern layout and décor, triple row of matched tables in dining area, usual food (just sandwiches Mon-Weds), Hydes ales from stainless servery *(Dennis Jones, Len Beattie)*

MAWDESLEY [SD4914]

Red Lion L40 2QP [off B5246 N of Parbold]: Recently reopened after refurbishment, darkly traditional bars, enjoyable food in stylish and airy conservatory restaurant, friendly attentive service, well kept ales such as Caledonian Deuchars IPA and Timothy Taylors Landlord, decent wines by the glass; piped music; children in eating areas, tables in courtyard behind, more in front, walk to Harrock Hill for great views, open all day *(Norma and Noel Thomas, LYM)*

MORECAMBE [SD4464]

York LA4 5QH [Lancaster Rd]: Lively local atmosphere, real ales such as Black Sheep and Everards Beacon and Tiger, popular lunchtime food in neat and simple new dining room (not Mon/Tues), enthusiastic new football-fan landlord, pool; big-screen sports TV, bedrooms planned *(Dave Sainsbury)*

NEWTON [SD6950]

Parkers Arms BB7 3DY [B6478 7 miles N of Clitheroe]: Great position, with lovely views from restaurant and garden; plush banquettes, mixed chairs and tables, log fires, a real ale such as Copper Dragon or Flowers IPA, good range of malt whiskies, plain pubby food (all day wknds), darts and pool; piped music, TV; children welcome, bedrooms, open all day wknds *(Norma and Noel Thomas, Ann and Tony Bennett-Hughes, LYM, Dennis Jones)*

OAKENCLOUGH [SD5347]

Country Lodge PR3 1UL: More restaurant than pub, real ales and locals in small welcoming bar, reliable food cooked by landlady here and in immaculate dining room, reasonable prices; three recently refurbished bedrooms *(Graham and Doreen Holden)*

OSWALDTWISTLE [SD7226]

☆ *Britannia* BB5 3RJ [A677/B6231]: Convivial traditional core with log-burning ranges, cosy button-back banquettes, attractive décor, well kept Thwaites ales, friendly attentive bar service and character locals, dining area extended into adjoining barn, reasonably priced food (all day Sun), good Fri quiz night; children in family restaurant, suntrap back terrace with moorland views and play area, open all day *(BB, Steve Whalley)*

PENDLETON [SD7539]

☆ *Swan With Two Necks* BB7 1PT: Welcoming olde-worlde pub in attractive streamside village below Pendle Hill, simply furnished, warm and tidy, with good blackboard range of inexpensive generous home cooking (not Mon), friendly service, changing ales such as Moorhouses and Phoenix; large garden, open all day Sun, cl Tues *(LYM, Pete Baker)*

PRESTON [SD5329]

Black Horse PR1 2EJ [Friargate]: Friendly unspoilt pub in pedestrian street, full Robinsons ale range, inexpensive lunchtime food, unusual ornate curved and mosaic-tiled Victorian main bar, panelling, stained glass and old local photographs, two quiet cosy comfortable enclosed snugs off, mirrored back area, upstairs 1920s-style bar, good juke box; no children, open all day from 10.30, cl Sun evening *(the Didler, Nick Holding, Pete Baker, Pam and John Smith)*

Blue Bell PR1 3BS [Church St]: Oldest pub in town, large but cosy and chatty, with good lunchtime choice of bargain basic food from back servery, cheap well kept Sam Smiths from long bar, no piped music *(Jim and Maggie Cowell)*

New Britannia PR1 2XB [Heatley St, just off Friargate]: Half a dozen or more changing real ales, bargain simple lunches, lively friendly atmosphere *(Pam and John Smith)*

RABY [SJ3179]

☆ *Wheatsheaf* CH63 4JH [off A540 S of Heswall; Raby Mere Rd]: Attractive thatched and timbered pub with unspoilt homely furnishings in chatty rambling bar inc high-backed settles making a snug around fine old fireplace, splendid choice of mainstream ales and of malt whiskies, nice wines, polite attentive service even when busy, spacious barn restaurant (evenings not Sun/Mon, and good Sun lunch) with conservatory; children and dogs allowed, picnic-sets on terrace and in pleasant back garden, pretty village, open all day *(MLR, Dr Phil Putwain, Alan and Eve Harding, Keith and Sue Campbell, A and B D Craig, Mr and Mrs M Stratton, LYM, Malcolm Ravenscroft)*

RAMSBOTTOM [SD8017]

☆ *Fishermans Retreat* BL0 0HH [Twine Valley Park, Bye Rd; signed off A56 N of Bury at Shuttleworth]: Splendid remote spot tucked away among well stocked trout lakes, extraordinary choice of several hundred whiskies (whisky shop here too, and monthly winter tasting nights with the haggis piped in), good value interesting and generous food all day (not Mon) using properly hung prime meats from their own surrounding farm, well kept changing ales, welcoming family service, busy restaurant (no bookings); well behaved children welcome, open all day *(Mark and Diane Grist)*

RIBCHESTER [SD6535]

Ribchester Arms PR3 3ZP [B6245]: Very wide choice of enjoyable food from bar snacks to imaginative specials and tender Sun roasts, attentive management and young well trained staff, comfortable bar and two pleasant dining rooms; children welcome, bedrooms, tables outside with plenty of space *(Peter Fitton)*

RILEY GREEN [SD6225]

Royal Oak PR5 0SL [A675/A6061]: Cosy low-beamed three-room former coaching inn, good home cooking inc notable steaks, four well kept Thwaites ales from long back bar, friendly efficient service, ancient stripped stone, open fires, seats from high-backed settles to red plush armchairs, lots of nooks and crannies, turkey carpet, soft lighting, impressive woodwork, fresh flowers, interesting model steam engines and plenty of bric-a-brac, two comfortable dining rooms; can be packed Fri night and wknds; tables outside, short walk from Leeds & Liverpool Canal, footpath to Hoghton Tower, open all day Sun *(Richard and Karen Holt, BB)*

ROMILEY [SJ9390]

Duke of York SK6 3AN [Stockport Rd]: Old-fashioned real ale pub with good friendly atmosphere, lots of woodwork, bar area opening into two smaller rooms, one up steps with creaky floorboards and hatch service, back vaults bar, popular upstairs restaurant (not Suns in Advent) *(Dennis Jones)*

Foresters Arms SK6 4PU [Greave, towards Werneth Low]: Useful food pub under new licensees, good-value straightforward simple comfortable décor *(Dennis Jones)*

RUFFORD [SD4517]

Rufford Arms L40 1SQ [Liverpool Rd (A59)]: Spick and span, with enjoyable food, charming well trained staff; tables outside (busy road) *(Margaret Dickinson, Ian and Sue Wells)*

SALTERFORTH [SD8845]

Anchor BB18 5TT [Salterforth Lane]: Friendly local in nice spot by Leeds & Liverpool Canal, four well kept real ales, bargain generous home-made food, dining area, pool room off big public bar; garden with play area *(Richard and Karen Holt, Dr K P Tucker)*

SAMLESBURY [SD6229]

Nabs Head Hotel PR5 0UQ [Nabs Head Lane]: Neatly kept bay-windowed pub, light and airy, with good value straightforward home-made food inc popular Sun lunch, hard-working friendly staff, well kept Thwaites ales, charming décor; peaceful country hamlet, handy for Samlesbury Hall *(Stuart Paulley)*

SCOUTHEAD [SD9706]

Old Original OL4 3RX [Thurston Clough Rd, just off A62 Oldham—Huddersfield]: Homely and welcoming, open-plan but partitioned, spectacular Pennine and E Manchester views, eating area with reasonably priced food, real ales such as Timothy Taylors Landlord and Thwaites, decent wines, soft lighting; piped music *(John R Tonge)*

SLAIDBURN [SD7152]

☆ *Hark to Bounty* BB7 3EP [B6478 N of Clitheroe]: Pretty old stone-built inn in charming Forest of Bowland village, neat rather modern décor in line of linked rooms, wide choice of good value generous fresh food (lots of tables) inc light dishes and old-fashioned puddings, good hospitable service, three real ales, decent wines and whiskies, comfortable chairs by open fire, games room with darts, pool and machines one end, well appointed restaurant the other; pleasant garden behind, good walks, bedrooms, open all day *(Norma and Noel Thomas, LYM, Jeremy Whitehorn, Hilary Forrest)*

ST HELENS [SJ5393]

Sutton Oak WA9 4JG [Bold Rd]: Popular for well kept changing beers such as Boddingtons, Theakstons Mild and Websters, farm ciders, Aug bank hol beer festival; big-screen sports TV; children welcome, good-sized garden with terrace and play area, open all day Fri-Sun, cl other lunchtimes *(anon)*

Wheatsheaf WA9 4HN [Mill Lane]: Traditional timbered pub, neat and cosy, with gleaming brasses, welcoming local atmosphere, well kept beer, restaurant food; colourful garden, bowling green, bedrooms *(anon)*

STOCKPORT [SJ8990]

☆ *Arden Arms* SK1 2LX [Millgate St, behind Asda]: Welcoming pub with good interesting fresh lunchtime food, fast cheerful service, full Robinsons ales range, well preserved traditional horseshoe bar, old-fashioned tiny snug through servery, two coal fires, longcase clocks, well restored tiling and panelling; tables out in courtyard sheltered by the original stables, open all day *(Pete Baker, Dennis Jones, the Didler)*

Blossoms SK2 6LS [Buxton Rd (A6)]: Bustling main-road Victorian local with Robinsons Best, Hatters Mild and (from bar-top cask) Old Tom, good home-made pies and other lunchtime food, three rooms off corridor inc attractive back lounge with handsome fireplace, pool room; open all day wknds *(the Didler)*

Crown SK4 1AR [Heaton Lane, Heaton Norris]: Partly open-plan Victorian pub popular for huge real ale range inc Black Sheep and local Three Rivers, three cosy lounge areas off gaslit bar, stylish décor, good value lunches Thurs-Sat, farm cider, pool, darts; TV, frequent live music; tables in cobbled courtyard, vast viaduct above, open all day Fri/Sat *(the Didler)*

Navigation SK4 1TY [Manchester Rd (B6167, former A626)]: Recently refurbished, with friendly service, half a dozen or so local Beartown ales and a guest beer, farm ciders tapped from cellar casks, continental bottled beers; open all day *(the Didler)*

Nursery SK4 2NA [Green Lane, Heaton Norris; off A6]: Very popular for enjoyable straightforward lunchtime food from servery on right with visible kitchen, good Sun lunch, friendly efficient service, good value Hydes ales, big bays of banquettes in panelled front lounge, brocaded wall banquettes in back one; children welcome if eating, on narrow cobbled lane at E end of N part of Green Lane, immaculate bowling green behind, open all day wknds *(BB, the Didler, Pete Baker)*

Olde Woolpack SK3 0BY [Brinksway, just off M60 junction 1 – junction A560/A5145]: Well run three-room pub with Theakstons and interesting changing guest beers, good value home-made food, friendly landlord, traditional layout with drinking corridor; open all day wknds *(the Didler)*

Queens Head SK1 1JT [Little Underbank (can be reached by steps from St Petersgate)]: Splendid Victorian restoration, long and narrow, with charming separate snug and back dining area, rare brass cordials fountain, double bank of spirits taps and old spirit lamps, old posters and adverts, reasonably priced lunchtime snacks, bargain Sam Smiths, daily papers, good friendly bustle, bench seating and bare boards; famous tiny gents' upstairs, some live jazz; open all day *(Dennis Jones, the Didler)*

☆ *Railway* SK1 2BZ [Avenue St (just off M63 junction 13, via A560)]: Redevelopment looming over future of bright and airy L-shaped bar with its own Porters ales and wknd guest beers, lots of foreign beers, farm cider, masses of whiskies and country wines, decent straightforward home-made pub lunches (not Sun), bargain prices throughout, friendly staff, old Stockport prints and memorabilia, bar billiards, tables out behind; has been open all day, news please *(the Didler)*

☆ *Red Bull* SK1 3AY [Middle Hillgate]: Steps up to friendly well run local, impressive beamed and flagstoned bar with dark panelling, substantial settles and seats, open fires, lots of pictures, mirrors and brassware, traditional island servery with Robinsons ales from nearby brewery, good value home-cooked bar lunches (not Sun); quiet at lunchtime, can get crowded evening, open all day (cl Sun afternoon) *(the Didler, LYM)*

Swan With Two Necks SK1 1RY [Princes St]: Traditional local, comfortable panelled bar, back skylit dining corridor, Robinsons ales inc Old Tom, friendly efficient service, decent lunchtime food; handy for shops, open all day, cl Sun *(the Didler, Dennis Jones)*

TYLDESLEY [SD6902]

Mort Arms M29 8DG [Elliott St]: Bargain Holts Bitter and Mild in two-room 1930s pub, etched glass and polished panelling, comfortable lounge with old local photographs, friendly landlord and regulars, darts and dominoes, TV horseracing Sat; open all day *(the Didler)*

WADDINGTON [SD7243]

Lower Buck BB7 3HU [Edisford Rd]: Traditional moorland local with friendly new landlord, well kept local ales inc Mild, popular basic home cooking, coal fire, hatch-service lobby, front bar with built-in dresser, sympathetic décor inc lovely coloured leaded glass; pretty village *(BB, Noel Grundy)*

☆ *Waddington Arms* BB7 3HP [Clitheroe Rd]: Good food (all day wknds) using fresh local produce from sandwiches to regional dishes and more up-to-date things, good cheerful staff, four or more well kept ales, flagstones and bare boards, woodburner in big 17th-c inglenook, red-walled room off with leather sofa and motor-racing pictures, neat quarry-tiled dining extension; children welcome, six comfortable chintzy bedrooms – where the church bells either will or won't lull you to sleep *(Noel Grundy)*

WALMER BRIDGE [SD4723]

Fox Cub PR4 5JT [Liverpool New Rd]: Vintage Inn with appealing traditional layout, furnishings and décor, their usual all-day food, proficient service and fine choice of wines by the glass – lots of wine racks

and bottles around; tables outside, open all day *(Margaret Dickinson, Ray and Winifred Halliday)*

WEST BRADFORD [SD7444]

Three Millstones BB7 4SX [Waddington Rd]: Attractive old building recently reopened as more of a dining pub, with four comfortable linked areas, two real ales, friendly service, open fire *(John and Helen Rushton)*

WEST KIRBY [SJ2186]

White Lion CH48 4EE [Grange Rd (A540)]: Interesting 17th-c sandstone pub, several small beamed areas on different levels, Courage Directors, John Smiths, Theakstons and a guest beer, friendly staff, good value simple bar lunches inc wide choice of sandwiches, coal stove; no children even in attractive secluded back garden up steep stone steps, open all day *(MLR)*

WIGAN [SD5806]

Royal Oak WN1 1XL [Standishgate (A49)]: Good Mayflower ales brewed and kept well here, good range of other beers inc imports, food till 6 Weds-Sat; brewery tours can be arranged; tables out behind, open all day, cl lunchtime Mon/Tues *(Andy Hazeldine, Mark and Diane Grist)*

WISWELL [SD7437]

☆ *Freemasons Arms* BB9 9DF [Vicarage Fold; just NE of Whalley]: Good enterprising up-to-date meals freshly cooked to order in cosy, friendly and spotless tucked-away Victorian pub, big helpings, well kept changing local ales such as Bowland and Moorhouses, remarkable choice of wines at very fair prices, lots of malt whiskies, friendly efficient service, small simply furnished bar and upstairs restaurant (must book Fri/Sat evening), no piped music or TV; lovely village below Pendle Hill, cl Mon/Tues, open all day Sun *(K C and B Forman)*

WORSTON [SD7642]

☆ *Calfs Head* BB7 1QA: Large country hotel, well run and busy, with wide choice of enjoyable moderately priced food in bar and spacious conservatory looking out towards Pendle Hill, real ales such as Jennings Cumberland and Marstons Pedigree, restaurant with popular Sunday carvery; tables in large attractive garden with stream, ducks and geese, 11 comfortable bedrooms, open all day *(Brian Wainwright, John and Helen Rushton, Margaret Dickinson)*

WREA GREEN [SD3931]

☆ *Grapes* PR4 2PH [Station Rd]: Busy Chef & Brewer with good layout of cosy olde-worlde linked areas, helpful staff, enjoyable fresh food from good sandwiches to some imaginative specials, well kept ales inc Timothy Taylors Landlord, good choice of wines by the glass, open fire and candles; tables out overlooking village green, picturesque church *(Norma and Noel Thomas, Christine and Neil Townend)*

Villa PR4 2PE [Moss Side Lane (B5259)]: Lots of small seating areas in smart hotel's welcoming panelled bar, well kept Copper Dragon, enjoyable food, log fire, daily papers; good-sized garden, disabled access and facilities, bedrooms, open all day (the Didler)

WRIGHTINGTON [SD5011]

Rigbye Arms WN6 9QB [3 miles from M6 junction 27; off A5209 via Robin Hood Lane and left into High Moor Lane]: 16th-c inn in attractive moorland setting, good staff and nice relaxed atmosphere, good value generous food inc some interesting specials, good fresh veg, real ales inc Greene King Old Speckled Hen and Timothy Taylors Landlord, decent wines *(Mr and Mrs John Taylor, John and Sylvia Harrop)*

A very few pubs try to make you leave a credit card at the bar, as a sort of deposit if you order food. They are not entitled to do this. The credit card firms and banks which issue them warn you not to let them out of your sight. If someone behind the counter used your card fraudulently, the card company or bank could in theory hold you liable, because of your negligence in letting a stranger hang on to your card. Suggest instead that if they feel the need for security, they 'swipe' your card and give it back to you. And do name and shame the pub to us.

Leicestershire
and Rutland

Food prices in this area's pubs are pretty much in line with the national average, but the quality is often well above average. One in three of the main entries here serves food so good that they qualify for our Food Award symbol. This is a considerably higher ratio than in most other areas. So there are plenty of options for a really special meal out. This year, the top contenders here are the Three Horse Shoes at Breedon on the Hill, the Olive Branch at Clipsham, the Fox & Hounds at Exton, the Olde White Hart at Lyddington, the Red Lion in Stathern and the Kings Arms in Wing. It's interesting that, of these half-dozen excellent dining pubs, four are in Rutland and only two in Leicestershire, despite Rutland's being so very much smaller. And it is a Rutland pub which takes the top title of Leicestershire and Rutland Dining Pub of the Year: the Olive Branch at Clipsham, still top of the dining pub tree for food here despite the strong competition. Other pubs here doing particularly well these days are the friendly Sugar Loaf at Ab Kettleby, good all round, the interestingly furnished Cow & Plough at Oadby (very strong on the beer side), the Grainstore in Oakham (a nice all-round pub brewing its own splendid beers), the warmly welcoming and charmingly individual New Inn at Peggs Green, the bustling Griffin in Swithland, and a new entry, the Wheatsheaf on the edge of Woodhouse Eaves (enjoyable food in this appealing country pub). In general, drinks prices in the area are closely in line with the national average, but there's quite a range between the cheapest places and the most expensive. Reassuringly, most of the pubs here that have won our Beer Award for sheer quality also price their ales attractively, giving excellent value. It's also worth noting that the Grainstore's fine beers are quite widely available in other good pubs in the area. Indeed, we found they featured a Grainstore beer as their cheapest much more often than they did a beer from Everards, the big Leicester brewery. In the Lucky Dip section at the end of the chapter, pubs currently showing very well are the Sun at Cottesmore, Peacock at Croxton Kerrial, Bell at Gumley, Swan in the Rushes in Loughborough, Olde Red Lion in Market Bosworth, Nags Head at Saltby, and (too restauranty for the main entries now, but very good) the Bakers Arms at Thorpe Langton.

Post Office address codings confusingly give the impression that some pubs are in Leicestershire, when they're really in Cambridgeshire (which is where we list them).

AB KETTLEBY
SK7519   MAP 7

Sugar Loaf

Nottingham Road (A606 NW of Melton); LE14 3JB

Well run friendly pub, reasonably priced tasty bar food and well kept beers

This is a well run and busy pub and the sort of place our readers like to return to. The open-plan bar is comfortably modernised and warm, with big black and white photographs of Shipstones brewery dray horses and a variety of country prints on the ragged canary walls. A bare-boards end area with a coal-effect gas fire has darts, cribbage, dominoes and a quiet juke box. Good solid pale wood tables and chairs on the discreetly patterned carpet spread from here into a pleasant dining conservatory. The substantial carved bar counter, with well cushioned stools, has Bass, Fullers London Pride and guests like Black Sheep, Courage Directors and Timothy Taylors Landlord on handpump; friendly staff and piped music. There are a few picnic-sets out by the road and car park.

🍴 Consistently good, fairly straightforward bar food includes filled baguettes and baked potatoes, ploughman's, soup, stilton mushrooms, a trio of sausages with red wine gravy, lasagne, beef in ale pie, chicken breast with garlic mushrooms and smoked bacon sauce, a pasta of the day, brie and cranberry wellington and fillet of salmon with creamy prawn sauce. *Starters/Snacks: £3.95 to £6.45. Main Courses: £6.45 to £15.95. Puddings: £3.50*

Free house ~ Licensees Josephine and Dennis Donovan ~ Real ale ~ Bar food (12-9.30) ~ Restaurant ~ (01664) 822473 ~ Children in eating area of bar ~ Open 11-11.30(12.30 Fri); 12-10.30 Sun

Recommended by Ruth Jeanes, Rob Darlington, Andrea and Guy Bradley, P Dawn, Jeff and Wendy Williams, Phil and Jane Hodson, Derek and Sylvia Stephenson

BARROWDEN
SK9400   MAP 4

Exeter Arms 🍺

Main Street, just off A47 Uppingham—Peterborough; LE15 8EQ

Own-brew beers and decent food in quietly set old pub; plenty of seats outside

Well worth the detour, this peaceful and neatly kept 17th-c coaching inn is very well liked by our readers. One reason is the own-brew beers which are brewed in an old free-standing barn behind: Beach, Bevin, Hopgear and BEEC alongside a couple of guests on handpump. The long cheery yellow open-plan bar stretches away either side of a long central counter, and is quite straightforwardly furnished with wheelback chairs at tables at either end of the bar, on bare boards or blue patterned carpet. There's quite a collection of pump clips, beer mats and brewery posters; cribbage, dominoes, shove-ha'penny, piped music, and boules. There are picnic-sets on a narrow front terrace overlooking the pretty village green, and ducks on the pond, with broader views stretching away beyond, and more well spaced picnic-sets in a big informal grassy garden at the back. There are red kites in the nearby Fineshades woods – nice walks here too.

🍴 As well as lunchtime sandwiches and ploughman's, the food now includes soup, a changing pâté, mushrooms stuffed with stilton and walnuts, ham and egg, ricotta, spinach and potato layer bake, sausages with red wine gravy, steak in ale pie, chicken wrapped in bacon with a Boursin cheese sauce, and puddings such as chocolate sponge with hot chocolate sauce or treacle tart. *Starters/Snacks: £3.95 to £4.95. Main Courses: £7.95 to £11.95. Puddings: £4.25*

Own brew ~ Licensee Martin Allsopp ~ Real ale ~ Bar food (not Sun evening, Mon) ~ Restaurant ~ (01572) 747247 ~ Children welcome away from the bar ~ Dogs allowed in bar ~ Open 12-2.30, 6-11; 12-4, 7-10.30 Sun; 12-5 Sun in winter; closed Mon lunchtime, also Sun evening in winter ~ Bedrooms: £37.50S/£75S

Recommended by the Didler, Andy and Jill Kassube, Noel Grundy, John Wooll, Duncan Cloud, Jeff and Wendy Williams, O K Smyth, Barry Collett, Mike and Sue Loseby

BREEDON ON THE HILL

SK4022 MAP 7

Three Horse Shoes

Main Street (A453); DE73 1AN

Comfortable pub with super food and friendly licensees

Run by helpful and friendly people, this is a pleasant pub with particularly good food and it has been simply restored to reveal the attractive period heart of the building. Heavy worn flagstones, a log fire, pubby tables, a dark wood counter and sludgy green walls and ceilings give a timeless feel to the clean cut central bar: Greene King Old Speckled Hen and Marstons Pedigree on handpump, 30 malt whiskies and decent house wines. Beyond here on the left is a step up to a further eating room, with maroon walls, dark pews and cherry-stained tables. The two-room dining area on the right has a comfortably civilised chatty feel with big quite close-set antique tables on seagrass matting and colourful modern country prints and antique engravings on canary walls. Even at lunchtime there are lighted candles in elegant modern holders.

Ⓜ Enjoyable and interesting – if not cheap – food includes filled ciabattas and club sandwiches, soup, duck terrine with caramelised oranges, grilled asparagus with parmesan, pasta with salmon and dill cream sauce, aubergine, black olive and polenta layer with sun-dried tomato dressing, pheasant with whisky, halibut steak with garlic and prawn sauce, lamb shank with mustard mash, and puddings such as treacle oat tart and sticky toffee pudding; good Sunday lunch. *Starters/Snacks: £4.50 to £5.95. Main Courses: £5.95 to £9.95. Puddings: £4.95 to £5.95*

Free house ~ Licensees Ian Davison, Jennie Ison, Stuart Marson ~ Real ale ~ Bar food (12-2, 5.30-7(restaurant food till 9.15); not Sun) ~ Restaurant ~ (01332) 695129 ~ Children in restaurant ~ Dogs allowed in bar ~ Open 11.30-2.30, 5.30-11; 12-2.30 Sun; closed Sun evening, 25 and 26 Dec, 1 Jan

Recommended by Richard and Jean Green, P Dawn, Phil and Jane Hodson, Clive and Fran Dutson, Kay and Alistair Butler

CLIPSHAM

SK9716 MAP 8

Olive Branch ★

Take B668/Stretton exit off A1 N of Stamford; Clipsham signposted E from exit roundabout; LE15 7SH

LEICESTERSHIRE AND RUTLAND DINING PUB OF THE YEAR

A very special place for an exceptional meal in comfortable surroundings, fine choice of drinks and luxury bedrooms

This is a lovely, civilised place for a special meal out with superb food served by friendly and attentive staff and our readers have also very much enjoyed the stylish and beautifully decorated bedrooms, too. The various smallish attractive rambling rooms have dark joists and beams, country furniture, an interesting mix of pictures (some by local artists) and there's a cosy log fire in the stone inglenook fireplace. Many of the books were bought at antiques fairs by one of the partners, so it's worth asking if you see something you like, as much is for sale; piped music. A carefully chosen range of drinks includes Grainstore Olive Oil and a guest beer on handpump, an enticing wine list (with about 18 by the glass), a fine choice of malt whiskies, armagnacs and cognacs, and up to a dozen different british and continental bottled beers. Outside, there are tables, chairs and big plant pots on a pretty little terrace, with more on the neat lawn, sheltered in the L of its two low buildings.

Ⓜ Excellent food includes sandwiches, a good value two- and three-course set lunch, and inventive soups, brawn and apple terrine with home-made chutney, cod and parmesan fritters with horseradish mayonnaise, artichoke and beetroot risotto with beetroot crisps, sausages with english mustard mash, roast leg of local hare with mustard tagliatelle, monkfish wrapped in parma ham, pea and lemon grass broth, purple potatoes and vegetable samosa, stuffed leg of guinea fowl with sweet potato mash and confit shallot, and puddings such as chocolate fondant with pistachio ice-cream and caramelised lemon tart with raspberry sorbet; delicious breakfasts. *Starters/Snacks: £4.50 to £8.95. Main Courses: £10.50 to £19.50. Puddings: £4.50 to £6.50*

Free house ~ Licensees Sean Hope and Ben Jones ~ Real ale ~ Bar food (12-2(3 Sun),
7-9.30(9 Sun)) ~ Restaurant ~ (01780) 410355 ~ Children welcome ~ Dogs allowed in bar and
bedrooms ~ Open 12-3, 6-11; 12-11(10.30 Sun) Sat; closed 26 Dec, 1 Jan ~ Bedrooms:
£75S(£85B)/£85S(£95B)

*Recommended by Bruce and Sharon Eden, Mrs Sheila Stothard, Noel Grundy, Malcolm and Jane Levitt,
Lin Ounsworth, John and Bettye Reynolds, M and C Thompson, Barry Collett, Mrs Brenda Calver, W K Wood,
H Paulinski, Peter and Jean Hoare, Howard and Margaret Buchanan, P Dawn, A G Marx, Robert Naylor, Mike and
Sue Loseby, Di and Mike Gillam, Paul Humphreys*

EMPINGHAM   SK9908   MAP 4

White Horse

Main Street; A606 Stamford—Oakham; LE15 8PS

Usefully open all day, with decent food and drinks

As this sizeable old stone pub is open all day, it's very handy if you are visiting Rutland
Water. The bustling open-plan carpeted lounge bar has a big log fire below an unusual
free-standing chimney-funnel, fresh flowers and Adnams Bitter, Greene King Old Speckled
Hen and a guest like Grainstore Triple B on handpump, several wines by the glass and
quite a few malt whiskies; newspapers to read, TV and piped music. There are some rustic
tables and seats among urns of flowers outside. Bedrooms are in a converted stable block
and they have wheelchair access.

🍴 **Bar food includes sandwiches and filled baguettes, ploughman's, soup, chicken liver
parfait, pasta with tomato and mediterranean vegetable sauce, beef and mushroom in ale
pie, fishcakes of the day, lamb ragoût, chicken wrapped in bacon with a creamy cheese
sauce, daily specials, puddings and Sunday roast.** *Starters/Snacks: £3.45 to £5.45. Main
Courses: £8.85 to £14.95. Puddings: £3.95*

Enterprise ~ Lease Ian and Sarah Sharp ~ Real ale ~ Bar food (12-6(though hot food only till
2.15), 7-9.30; 12-9 Sun) ~ (01780) 460221 ~ Children welcome away from bar ~ Dogs allowed
in bedrooms ~ Open 11am-midnight; closed 25 Dec ~ Bedrooms: £50B/£65B

*Recommended by Howard and Margaret Buchanan, David Swift, Michael Dandy, Fred Chamberlain, Maurice and
Janet Thorpe, Arthur Pickering, Duncan Cloud*

EXTON   SK9211   MAP 7

Fox & Hounds

Signposted off A606 Stamford—Oakham; LE15 8AP

**Bustling and well run with italian emphasis on popular food, log fire in comfortable
lounge and quiet garden**

Facing the quiet village green, this handsome and busy old coaching inn owes its
grandeur largely to the fact that the quiet back road was once the main Oakham coach
route. The comfortable high-ceilinged lounge bar is traditionally civilised with some dark
red plush easy chairs, as well as wheelback seats around lots of pine tables, maps and
hunting prints on the walls, fresh flowers and a winter log fire in a large stone fireplace.
Archers Best Bitter, Grainstore Ten Fifty and Greene King IPA on handpump and a good
range of wines by the glass; helpful service, piped music and TV. The sheltered walled
garden has seats among large rose beds on the pleasant well kept back lawn that looks
out over paddocks.

🍴 **As the landlord is Italian, the menu includes quite a few italian dishes: filled ciabattas
and paninis, a vast selection of handmade pizzas in almost every combination you could
imagine (Monday-Saturday evenings only), risotto with fresh asparagus and sun-dried
tomatoes with parmesan shavings, linguini with jumbo prawns and scottish smoked
salmon in a garlic cream sauce and spaghetti bolognese; also, gammon and egg, lambs
liver and bacon, chicken stuffed with apricot and stilton in a light madeira and sage
sauce, chargrilled rack of lamb, rosemary and minted mash, and puddings like chocolate
brownie and crème brûlée.** *Starters/Snacks: £3.50 to £5.75. Main Courses: £8.25 to £14.95.
Puddings: £3.95 to £4.50*

Free house ~ Licensees Valter and Sandra Floris ~ Real ale ~ Bar food (not Sun evening or Mon) ~ Restaurant ~ (01572) 812403 ~ Children welcome ~ Dogs allowed in bar and bedrooms ~ Open 11-3, 6-11; 11-3, 8-11 Sun; closed Mon ~ Bedrooms: £45B/£60(£70B)

Recommended by P Dawn, A J W Smith, Val and Alan Green, Michael Sargent, Mike and Heather Watson, Jeff and Wendy Williams, Richard and Jean Green, A G Marx, Roy Bromell, Jim Farmer, Mrs Brenda Calver, Bruce and Penny Wilkie, Colin McKerrow, Lesley and Barbara Owen

LYDDINGTON   SP8796   MAP 4

Old White Hart 🍴

Village signposted off A6003 N of Corby; LE15 9LR

Well run, popular inn with welcoming staff, roaring fires, and very good food; pretty garden

Consistently enjoyable, this fine old place is run by friendly and attentive licensees. The softly lit front bar has a glass-shielded roaring log fire, low ceilings and heavy bowed beams, a relaxed local atmosphere and just four close-set tables. This room opens into an attractive restaurant, and on the other side is another tiled-floor room with rugs, lots of fine hunting prints, cushioned wall seats and mate's chairs and a woodburning stove. Fullers London Pride and Greene King IPA and Abbot on handpump and several wines by the glass; shove-ha'penny, cribbage and dominoes. The pretty walled garden (with eight floodlit boules pitches) is very pleasant and there are seats by outdoor heaters; if you sit out here on Thursday evening you may hear the church bell-ringers. The pub is handy for Bede House and there are good nearby walks.

🍴 From a sensibly short menu, the very well liked food includes filled baguettes, soup, duck liver parfait with fig and tomato chutney, warm mushroom, gruyère and rosemary tartlet, cod, brown shrimp and baby spinach topped with parmesan sauce, toad-in-the-hole, steak and mushroom suet pudding, rack of lamb with roast gravy, fresh fish and vegetarian choices, daily specials, and puddings such as dark chocolate, pear and cinnamon tart with pear sorbet and sticky toffee pudding with butterscotch sauce and vanilla pod ice-cream. *Starters/Snacks: £4.95 to £8.95. Main Courses: £9.95 to £17.95. Puddings: £5.95 to £6.25*

Free house ~ Licensees Stuart and Holly East ~ Real ale ~ Bar food (not winter Sun evening) ~ Restaurant ~ (01572) 821703 ~ Children welcome ~ Open 12-3, 6.30-11; 12-3, 7-10.30 Sun ~ Bedrooms: £60B/£85B

Recommended by Jeff and Wendy Williams, Ben and Helen Ingram, Jim Farmer, A G Marx, Noel Grundy, Tracey and Stephen Groves, Mr and Mrs G S Ayrton, Revd L and S Giller, Mike and Sue Loseby, John and Sylvia Harrop, John Wooll

MOWSLEY   SP6488   MAP 4

Staff of Life 🍷

Village signposted off A5199 S of Leicester; Main Street; LE17 6NT

Neat, high-gabled pub popular for a good meal out; seats in back garden

Locals do drop into this spotlessly kept high-gabled pub for a drink but most customers are here to enjoy the popular food. The roomy bar is quite traditional with a panelled ceiling, comfortable seating, including some high-backed settles on flagstones, Banks's Bitter and Jennings Cumberland on handpump and up to 20 wines (and champagne) by the glass. The restaurant is rather like a country barn; piped music. The back garden has a large pergola and teak furniture.

🍴 As well as lunchtime sandwiches, the good food might include soup, chicken liver, smoked bacon and foie gras terrine with roasted red onion jam, linguini with scallops, rocket and chilli, mushroom stroganoff, a pie and potato cakes of the day, chicken breast stuffed with porcini mushrooms with crisp pancetta and rich gravy, lamb cutlets with a redcurrant, blueberry and rosemary jus, sea bream with fennel, shallots, garlic and tomatoes, and puddings such as chocolate fondant and lemon and raspberry tart. *Starters/Snacks: £4.25 to £7.95. Main Courses: £9.95 to £16.95. Puddings: £4.95 to £5.95*

Free house ~ Licensee Spencer Farrell ~ Real ale ~ Bar food (12-2.30(3 Sun), 6.30-9.30(6-8.30 Mon); 12-3 Sun; not Sun evening or Mon lunchtime) ~ Restaurant ~ (0116) 240 2359 ~ Children welcome but not in back garden ~ Open 12-3, 6-11; 12-10.30 Sun; closed Mon lunchtime except bank hols

Recommended by David Field, Phil and Jane Hodson, Steph and Harry Short, Ian and Joan Blackwell, Duncan Cloud, Dennis and Gill Keen, Jeff and Wendy Williams, P Tailyour, Richard J Stanley, Ian Blackwell

NEWTON BURGOLAND   SK3709 MAP 4

Belper Arms

Village signposted off B4116 S of Ashby or B586 W of Ibstock; LE67 2SE

Plenty of nooks and seating areas with original features in ancient pub, well liked food, changing ales and seats in rambling garden

A new landlord has taken over this bustling, friendly pub but there are no plans for any major changes. The original building has been very opened up but there are lots of ancient interior features such as the heavy beams, changing floor levels and varying old floor and wall materials that break the place up into enjoyable little nooks and seating areas. Parts are said to date back to the 13th c and much of the exposed brickwork certainly looks at least three or four hundred years old. A big freestanding central chimney at the core of the building has a cottagey old black range on one side and open fire on the other, with chatty groups of nice old captain's chairs. There's plenty to look at, from a suit of old chain mail, to a collection of pewter teapots, some good antique furniture and, framed on the wall, the story of the pub ghost – Five to Four Fred. Bass, Black Sheep, Greene King IPA and a couple of guest beers on handpump and quite a few wines by the glass; piped music and dominoes. There are seats in the rambling garden and on the terrace.

🍴 **Good, reasonably priced bar food includes filled baguettes, soup, pâté with cumberland sauce, garlic mushrooms, tempura prawns with chilli, ham and eggs, vegetable lasagne, chicken and bacon pasta in a white wine sauce, lamb steak with onion gravy, butterfly pork with black pudding and a wholegrain mustard sauce, mixed seafood platter, and puddings such as chocolate fudge cake and apple crumble.** *Starters/Snacks: £3.95 to £6.00. Main Courses: £8.95 to £11.95. Puddings: £3.95*

Punch ~ Lease Nick Plews ~ Real ale ~ Bar food (12-2.30, 6.30-9 Mon-Thurs; 12-3, 6-9 Fri and Sat; 12-5 Sun; no food Sun evening) ~ Restaurant ~ (01530) 270530 ~ Children welcome ~ Dogs allowed in bar ~ Open 12-12

Recommended by Duncan Cloud, R T and J C Moggridge, C J Pratt, Andy Chapman, Ian and Jane Irving, Derek and Sylvia Stephenson, Dr and Mrs A K Clarke, Simon Fox, Michael Butler, the Didier, R M Chard, Robert F Smith

OADBY   SK6202 MAP 4

Cow & Plough 🍺

Gartree Road (B667 N of centre); LE2 2FB

Fantastic collection of brewery memorabilia, interesting real ales and good, interesting food

With plenty of character, the two dark back rooms known as the Vaults are the best part of this interesting old place. They contain an extraordinary and ever-expanding collection of brewery memorabilia and almost every piece has a story behind it: enamel signs and mirrors advertising long-forgotten brews, an aged brass cash register and furnishings and fittings salvaged from pubs and even churches (there's some splendid stained glass behind the counter). The pub first opened about 16 years ago with just these cosily individual rooms, but it soon tripled in size when an extensive long, light, flagstoned conservatory was added to the front; it too has its share of brewery signs and the like, as well as plenty of plants and fresh flowers, a piano, beams liberally covered with hops, and a real mix of traditionally pubby tables and chairs, with lots of green leatherette sofas, and small round cast-iron tables. One section has descriptions of all Leicester's pubs. Grainstore Skydiver and Steamin Billy Bitter on handpump alongside guests such as

Abbeydale Absolution, Black Sheep Bitter, Jennings Mild and Ossett Dazzler, a dozen country wines, several wines by the glass and up to six ciders; TV, darts, board games and shove-ha'penny. There are picnic-sets outside.

📶 **Using carefully chosen ingredients, the interesting bar food might include sandwiches, unusual soups, king scallops and capers with dijon aïoli, chargrilled black pudding on bubble and squeak with red wine and shallot gravy, pine nut and wild mushroom risotto, free-range pork chop with apple, cider and rhubarb compote, free-range chicken breast stuffed with a pumpkin seed and spinach mousse with a mustard cream sauce and puddings. Two- and three-course set Sunday lunches.** *Starters/Snacks: £4.90 to £9.90. Main Courses: £7.50 to £15.90. Puddings: £4.50 to £5.50*

Free house ~ Licensee Barry Lount ~ Real ale ~ Bar food (12-3, 6-9 (not Sun or Mon evenings); 12-5 Sun) ~ Restaurant ~ (0116) 272 0852 ~ Children allowed but not in front of bars ~ Dogs welcome ~ Jazz Weds lunchtime, blues Sun evening ~ Open 11(midday Sun)-11; 11-3, 5-11 weekdays in winter

Recommended by Jim Farmer, David Field, Janice and Phil Waller, the Didler, Chris Evans, Duncan Cloud, Barry Collett

OAKHAM   SK8509   MAP 4

Grainstore 🍺 £

Station Road, off A606; LE15 6RE

Super own-brewed beers in converted rail grain warehouse, friendly staff, cheerful customers and pubby food

The own-brewed beers in this converted three-storey Victorian grain warehouse are served both traditionally at the left end of the bar counter, and through swan necks with sparklers on the right: Grainstore Cooking Bitter, Gold, Rutland Panther, Steamin' Billy, Ten Fifty and Triple B. The friendly staff are happy to give you samples. Laid back or lively, depending on the time of day, with noises of the brewery workings above, the interior is plain and functional with wide well worn bare floorboards, bare ceiling boards above massive joists which are supported by red metal pillars, a long brick-built bar counter with cast-iron bar stools, tall cask tables and simple elm chairs. In summer they pull back the huge glass doors that open on to a terrace with picnic-sets, and often stacked with barrels; games machine, darts, board games, shove-ha'penny, giant Jenga and bottle-walking; disabled access. You can tour the brewery by arrangement, they do take-aways, and hold a real ale festival with over 65 real ales and lots of live music during the August bank holiday weekend.

📶 **Decent good value pubby food includes sandwiches, soup, baguettes, baked potatoes, burgers, sausage and mash, chilli, steak in ale pie and all day breakfast.** *Starters/Snacks: £3.50 to £5.00. Main Courses: £5.00 to £7.50*

Own brew ~ Licensee Tony Davis ~ Real ale ~ Bar food (11-3; not Sun) ~ (01572) 770065 ~ Children welcome till 8pm ~ Dogs allowed in bar ~ Live blues first Sun of month, jazz third and fourth Sun ~ Open 11-11(midnight Fri and Sat)

Recommended by Anthony Barnes, P Dawn, Barry Collett, Richard and Karen Holt, Mike and Sue Loseby, Arthur Pickering, the Didler, Jim Farmer

PEGGS GREEN   SK4117   MAP 7

New Inn £

Signposted off A512 Ashby—Shepshed at roundabout, then turn immediately left down Zion Hill towards Newbold; pub is 100 yards down on the right with car park on opposite side of road; LE67 8JE

Intriguing bric-a-brac in unspoilt pub, a friendly welcome, good value food and drinks; cottagey garden

Don't be put off by the slightly scuffy and unprepossessing look of this unspoilt little pub from the outside. Once inside, there's an instantly welcoming and almost cosseting atmosphere created by the friendly Irish licensees – and plenty of chatting locals. Its two cosy tiled front rooms have an incredible collection of old bric-a-brac (it'll keep you busy for ages) which covers almost every inch of the walls and ceilings. The little room on the left, a bit like a kitchen parlour (they call it the Cabin), has china on the mantelpiece, lots of prints and photographs and little collections of this and that, three old cast-iron tables, wooden stools and a small stripped kitchen table. The room to the right has nice stripped panelling, and masses more appealing bric-a-brac. The small back Best room, with a stripped wooden floor, has a touching display of old local photographs including some colliery ones. Bass, Caledonian Deuchars IPA and Marstons Pedigree on handpump; piped music, cribbage and dominoes. Plenty of seats in front of the pub with more in the peaceful back garden.

🍽 **As well as filled baps, the very good value, satisfying food includes ham and eggs, corned beef hash, steak in ale pie, faggots and peas, sausages in onion gravy and smoked haddock.** *Starters/Snacks: £1.50 to £2.75. Main Courses: £3.95 to £4.95. Puddings: £1.95 to £2.50*

Enterprise ~ Lease Maria Christina Kell ~ Real ale ~ Bar food (12-2; 6-8 Mon; not Tues-Sat evenings; not Sun) ~ No credit cards ~ (01530) 222293 ~ Well behaved children welcome ~ Dogs allowed in bar ~ Open 12-2.30, 5.30-11; 12-3, 6.30-11 Sat; 12-3, 7-10.30 Sun

Recommended by Phil and Jane Hodson, B and M Kendall, Peter and Jean Hoare, Ian and Joan Blackwell, OPUS, the Didler, Clive and Fran Dutson, David and Sue Atkinson, Susan and John Douglas

SOMERBY
SK7710   MAP 7

Stilton Cheese 🍺

High Street; off A606 Oakham—Melton Mowbray, via Cold Overton, or Leesthorpe and Pickwell; can also be reached direct from Oakham via Knossington; LE14 2QB

Bustling and cheerful with chatty staff, local real ales, and seats on heated terrace

The real ales remain quite a draw to this friendly village pub. Kept on handpump, there might be Grainstore Ten Fifty, Marstons Pedigree, Tetleys and guests like Burton Bridge XL Bitter and Slaters Original; over 25 malt whiskies plus a proper cider. The comfortable hop-strung beamed bar/lounge has dark carpets, lots of country prints on its stripped stone walls, a collection of copper pots, a stuffed badger and plenty of seats; shove-ha'penny, cribbage and dominoes. There are seats and outdoor heaters on the terrace.

🍽 **Bar food includes sandwiches, ploughman's, soup, deep-fried breaded mushrooms with garlic mayonnaise, lasagne, sausages and mash with onion gravy, macaroni cheese, battered cod and chilli con carne.** *Starters/Snacks: £3.25 to £5.25. Main Courses: £7.25 to £12.95. Puddings: £3.75*

Free house ~ Licensees Carol and Jeff Evans ~ Real ale ~ Bar food (12-2, 6(7 Sun)-9) ~ (01664) 454394 ~ Children welcome ~ Dogs allowed in bedrooms ~ Open 12-3, 6-11; 12-3, 7-10.30 Sun ~ Bedrooms: £30/£40

Recommended by Jim Farmer, Derek and Sylvia Stephenson, I J and S A Bufton, Robert Turnham, Anthony Barnes, M and GR

STATHERN
SK7731   MAP 7

Red Lion 🍴 ⛾ 🍺

Off A52 W of Grantham via the brown-signed Belvoir road (keep on towards Harby – Stathern signposted on left); or off A606 Nottingham—Melton Mowbray via Long Clawson and Harby; LE14 4HS

Splendid range of drinks and imaginative food in civilised dining pub, open fires, good garden with play area; own shop too

Although there's quite an emphasis on the particularly good food here, its heart remains very much a village pub with plenty of chatty locals and a fine range of drinks: Grainstore Olive Oil, Batemans XB and Fullers London Pride on handpump, alongside draught belgian beer and continental bottled beers, several ciders, a varied wine list with quite a number by the glass, winter mulled wine and summer home-made lemonade. There's a relaxed country pub feel to the yellow room on the right and the lounge bar has sofas, an open fire and a big table with books, newspapers and magazines; it leads off the smaller, more traditional flagstoned bar with terracotta walls, another fireplace with a pile of logs beside it, and lots of beams and hops. Dotted around are various oddities picked up by one of the licensees on visits to Newark Antiques Fair: some unusual lambing chairs for example and a collection of wooden spoons. A little room with tables set for eating leads to the long, narrow main dining room and out to a nicely arranged suntrap with good hardwood furnishings spread over its lawn and terrace; there's an unusually big play area behind the car park with swings, climbing frames and so on. This is under the same ownership as the Olive Branch in Clipsham.

🍴 **Using carefully sourced produce, the exceptional dishes might include sandwiches, toasties and ploughman's, soup, eggs benedict, chicken liver and foie gras parfait with chutney, tomato, red onion and blue goats cheese tart, smoked haddock with spring onion mash and grain mustard sauce, sausages with onion gravy, moroccan-style chicken with couscous and saffron dressing, evening extras like local hare wellington with red wine sauce and organic pork loin with sage and onion mash and glazed apples, and puddings such as crème brûlée with rhubarb compote and warm chocolate torte with pistachio ice-cream; plenty of interesting nibbles, good value two- and three-course lunches and their own home-made preserves, pickles and fully prepared dishes and hampers to buy.** *Starters/Snacks: £4.50 to £6.25. Main Courses: £10.50 to £17.50. Puddings: £5.75 to £6.50*

Free house ~ Licensees Sean Hope and Ben Jones ~ Real ale ~ Bar food (12-2(3 Sun; 5 some summer Sats), 7-9.30; not Sun evening or Mon) ~ Restaurant ~ (01949) 860868 ~ Children welcome ~ Dogs allowed in bar ~ Open 12-3, 6-11; 12-11 Fri and Sat; 12-6.30 Sun; closed Sun evening, all day Mon

Recommended by Philip and Susan Philcox, Chris Evans, David Glynne-Jones, MP, Richard, Phil and Jane Hodson, Bill and Marian de Bass, Peter and Jean Hoare, P Dawn, Andy and Jill Kassube, Derek and Sylvia Stephenson

STRETTON
SK9415   MAP 8

Jackson Stops

Rookery Lane; a mile or less off A1, at B668 (Oakham) exit; follow village sign, turning off Clipsham road into Manor Road, pub on left; LE15 7RA

Interesting former farmhouse with decent drinks and popular food

Under a new landlord, this is an appealing old farmhouse. The homely black-beamed country bar down on the left has some timbering in its ochre walls, a couple of bar stools, a cushioned stripped wall pew and an elderly settle on the worn tile and brick floor, with a coal fire in the corner. The smarter main room on the right is light and airy with linen napkins and lit candles in brass sticks on the nice mix of ancient and modern tables, dark blue carpeting, a couple of striking modern oils alongside a few tastefully disposed farm tools on the mainly canary coloured stone walls and another smokeless coal fire in a stone corner fireplace. Right along past the bar is a second dining room, older in style, with stripped stone walls, a tiled floor and an old open cooking range. The unobtrusive piped music in the main dining room doesn't disturb the chatty and relaxed atmosphere. Adnams Bitter and Broadside and Greene King IPA on handpump and several good wines by the glass. More reports please.

🍴 **Well liked bar food includes sandwiches, soup, chicken liver parfait with red onion marmalade, confit duck leg with orange segments, baked field mushroom with goats cheese, sweet peppers, chilli and tomato oil, rack of local lamb with sweet potato mash and redcurrant jus, pork tenderloin with black pudding and a stilton and cider cream and a fresh fish dish of the day; there's also a two-course weekday lunch menu.** *Starters/Snacks: £4.95 to £8.95. Main Courses: £8.95 to £18.95. Puddings: £5.95 to £7.95*

Free house ~ Licensee Richard Graham ~ Real ale ~ Bar food (12-2, 6-9(9.30 Sat); 11-2.30 Sun; not Sun evening or Mon) ~ Restaurant ~ (01780) 410237 ~ Children welcome but must leave restaurant by 8pm at weekends ~ Open 12-2.30, 6-11; 11-4 Sun; closed Mon and 25 Dec

Recommended by B and M Kendall, M and C Thompson, Arthur Pickering, Malcolm and Jane Levitt, Robert Naylor, Phil and Jane Hodson, Maurice and Janet Thorpe

Ram Jam Inn ♀ 🛏

Just off A1: heading N, look out for warning signs some 8 miles N of Stamford, turning off at big inn sign through service station close to B668; heading S, look out for B668 Oakham turn-off, inn well signed on left ¼ mile after roundabout; LE15 7QX

Popular and useful A1 stop-off, even for breakfasts, with good drinks and modern food in appealing linked areas; comfortable bedrooms

A new landlady has taken over this refurbished dining place, handily serving food all day. As you go in, the first part of the big open-plan bar/dining area now has bucket chairs around a mix of tables on the new carpet, three cosy sofas and daily newspapers and a couple of weekly changing beers such as Greene King IPA and Marstons Pedigree on handpump; good house wines with several by the glass and excellent coffee. This area spreads on back to two more rooms, one with an open fire.

🍴 **Good modern food includes sandwiches, smokies baked with double cream and cheese, salmon and prawn fishcake with red onion relish, cannelloni stuffed with chicken and mushrooms in a rich tomato sauce, braised beef in a rich brandy and pink peppercorn cream, tartlet of wild mushroom ragoût with sun-dried tomatoes and cheese, steak and chips, and puddings such as warm banoffi crumble with caramelised cream and brioche bread and butter pudding with vanilla custard.** *Starters/Snacks: £3.50 to £7.95. Main Courses: £7.95 to £12.95. Puddings: £2.95 to £4.75*

Oxford Hotels ~ Manager Sue Addnit ~ Real ale ~ Bar food (all day) ~ Restaurant ~ (01780) 410776 ~ Children welcome away from bar ~ Open 7am-11pm ~ Bedrooms: £55B/£65B

Recommended by Eithne Dandy, Paul and Ursula Randall, J F M and M West, Louise Gibbons, Comus and Sarah Elliott, B and M Kendall

SWITHLAND

SK5512   MAP 7

Griffin 🍺

Main Street; between A6 and B5330, between Loughborough and Leicester; LE12 8TJ

A good mix of cheerful customers, fair-priced food and half a dozen real ales in bustling atmosphere

This attractively converted stone-built pub is popular with locals and with visitors to Bradgate Country Park; there are walks in Swithland Woods. The beamed communicating rooms have some panelling, a nice mix of wooden tables and chairs and bar stools, and a friendly, bustling atmosphere. Adnams Bitter, Everards Beacon, Greene King Abbot and three changing guests on handpump, several malt whiskies and wines by the glass from a good wine list. Piped music, board games and skittle alley. The tidy garden, overlooking open fields, is by a stream.

🍴 **Sensibly priced bar food includes sandwiches, ploughman's, a proper pork pie, soup, pie of the day, a trio of local sausages with onion gravy, wild mushroom risotto, medallions of pork tenderloin with apple mash, daily specials, and puddings such as treacle sponge or double mint and chocolate terrine.** *Starters/Snacks: £2.95 to £6.95. Main Courses: £6.95 to £16.95. Puddings: £3.75 to £4.95*

Everards ~ Tenant John Cooledge ~ Real ale ~ Bar food (not Mon) ~ Restaurant ~ (01509) 890535 ~ Well supervised children welcome ~ Open 10am-11pm; 11-10.30 Sun

Recommended by Jim Farmer, Pete Baker, Chris Moore, Bob, Duncan Cloud, Derek and Sylvia Stephenson, Dr and Mrs A K Clarke

---

Bedroom prices normally include full english breakfast, VAT and any inclusive service charge that we know of. Prices before the '/' are for single rooms, after for two people in double or twin (B includes a private bath, S a private shower). If there is no '/', the prices are only for twin or double rooms (as far as we know there are no singles). If there is no B or S, as far as we know no rooms have private facilities.

WING   SK8902   MAP 4

Kings Arms 🍴 🍷 🛏

Village signposted off A6003 S of Oakham; Top Street; LE15 8SE

Nicely kept old pub, big log fires, super choice of wines by the glass and interesting modern cooking

Well run and rather civilised, this neat 17th-c inn is much enjoyed by our readers. The attractive bar has various nooks and crannies, nice old beams and stripped stone, two large log fires (one in a copper-canopied central hearth), and flagstoned or wood-strip floors. Friendly, helpful staff serve 28 wines by the glass, as well as Grainstore Cooking, Marstons Pedigree, Shepherd Neame Spitfire and Timothy Taylors Landlord on handpump and several ciders; piped music and board games. There are seats out in front, and more in the sunny yew-sheltered garden; the new car park has plenty of space. There's a medieval turf maze just up the road and we are told that the pub is just a couple of miles away from England's osprey hot-spot.

🍴 Carefully cooked and imaginative, the bar food includes sandwiches, warm herb, lentil and walnut salad with grilled goats cheese, a plate of tapas, sausages with yorkshire pudding and onion gravy, beef in ale stew with dumplings, oriental chicken stir fry, venison saddle with port and cranberry jus, tandoori halibut with spiced chickpea and tomato ragoût, and puddings such as vanilla waffles with chocolate or butterscotch sauce and white chocolate crème brûlée with cocoa tuiles and fresh berries. *Starters/Snacks: £3.50 to £7.00. Main Courses: £8.50 to £19.50. Puddings: £5.50 to £6.50*

Free house ~ Licensee David Goss ~ Real ale ~ Bar food (not Mon lunch and not winter Mon (except for residents)) ~ Restaurant ~ (01572) 737634 ~ Well supervised children welcome but not in restaurant after 7.30pm ~ Open 12–midnight; may close in afternoon if not busy; closed Mon lunchtime and all day Mon in winter (except for residents) ~ Bedrooms: £65B/£75B

Recommended by Michael Doswell, Ben and Helen Ingram, O K Smyth, Michael Sargent, J S Rutter, Phil and Jane Hodson, Jeff and Wendy Williams, Mrs Diane M Hall, Mark Farrington, Roy Bromell

WOODHOUSE EAVES   SK5313   MAP 7

Wheatsheaf 🛏

Brand Hill; beyond Main Street, off B591 S of Loughborough; LE12 8SS

Bustling and friendly country pub with charming licensees, interesting things to look at, good bistro-type food and fair choice of drinks; new, well equipped bedrooms

This rather smart country pub is run by a family who really care so you can be sure of a friendly welcome. It's open plan with beams, a log fire, motor-racing memorabilia and pictures and artefacts to do with winter sports, a chatty bustling atmosphere, and Adnams Broadside, Greene King IPA, Marstons Pedigree, Tetleys and Timothy Taylors Landlord on handpump with several wines including champagne by the glass from a thoughtful list. There's also a cosy new area called The Mess for more intimate dining which has an RAF Hurricane propeller and (upstairs) a newly refurbished light and airy cottagey restaurant. There are seats on the floodlit and heated terrace. No children.

🍴 As well as sandwiches, ciabattas, filled baguettes and ploughman's, the enjoyable bistro-style menu might include soup, chicken liver pâté, haddock smokies with wine, cream, tomatoes and cheese, rösti potato cakes with sweet chilli dressing, red pepper, mushroom and spinach lasagne, salmon and crab fishcakes with parsley sauce, minted lamb burger with beetroot and a fried egg, gammon with pineapple and welsh rarebit topping, tuna steak with coconut, lime, mango and noodles, and lamb noisettes with feta salad. *Starters/Snacks: £4.25 to £5.25. Main Courses: £9.95 to £17.95. Puddings: £4.50 to £4.95*

Free house ~ Licensees Richard and Bridget Dimblebee ~ Real ale ~ Bar food (not Sun evening) ~ Restaurant ~ (01509) 890320 ~ Children allowed if eating ~ Dogs allowed in bar ~ Open 12–2(2.30 Sat and Sun), 6–11(10.30 Sun) ~ Bedrooms: £55S/£65S

Recommended by Michael Brunning, Peter and Joyce Hewitt

LUCKY DIP

Besides the fully inspected pubs, you might like to try these Lucky Dips recommended to us and described by readers (if you do, please send us reports: www.goodguides.co.uk).

BELMESTHORPE [TF0410]
☆ **Blue Bell** PE9 4JG [Village signposted off A16 just E of Stamford]: Cottagey 17th-c pub taken in hand by welcoming and experienced new licensees, well kept Greene King Abbot, Oakham JHB and two guest beers, sensibly priced pubby food (all day Fri/Sat, not Sun/Mon evenings) from baguettes and baked potatoes up, linked beamed rooms with pews, settles, and huge stone inglenook; garden with plenty of picnic-sets, cl Mon lunchtime, open all day Fri-Sun (LYM)

BRAUNSTON [SK8306]
☆ **Old Plough** LE15 8QT [off A606 in Oakham; Church St]: Welcoming black-beamed pub, comfortably opened up, with log fire, well kept Grainstore and interesting guest ales, enjoyable food inc beer-based dishes, friendly staff, appealing back dining conservatory (children allowed); tables in sheltered garden, open all day (Jim Farmer, Duncan Cloud, LYM, Barry Collett)

BRUNTINGTHORPE [SP6089]
☆ **Joiners Arms** LE17 5QH [Church Walk/Cross St]: More bistro restaurant than pub, good imaginative up-to-date food and popular Sun lunches in three beamed areas of open-plan dining lounge, Greene King IPA from small bar counter, good value wines, good friendly service, lots of china and brasses; they don't serve tap water; cl Sun evening and Mon (Gerry and Rosemary Dobson, Jeff and Wendy Williams)

BURTON ON THE WOLDS [SK5921]
Greyhound LE12 5AG [Melton Rd (B676)]: Very popular since recent refurbishment, friendly chatty staff, enjoyable reasonably priced food in bar and restaurant, four real ales, interesting malt whiskies and brandies, games room with pool; terrace tables and picnic-sets in garden behind (Phil and Jane Hodson)

BURTON OVERY [SP6797]
☆ **Bell** LE8 9DL [Main St]: Interesting choice of consistently good if not cheap food using local produce in L-shaped open-plan bar and dining room, Adnams, Bass, Greene King Old Speckled Hen and Marstons Pedigree, good log fire, comfortable settees, darts and games machine round corner; children welcome, good garden, lovely village, open all day wknds (R L Borthwick, Mrs L Aquilina, David Crews)

CASTLE DONINGTON [SK4426]
☆ **Nags Head** DE74 2PS [Diseworth Rd/Hill Top; A453, S end]: Good low-beamed bistro pub with wide food choice (all day wknds, at least in summer) from baguettes and paninis up, Banks's and related beers, good range of wines by the glass, large airy dining area with open-view kitchen, quarry-tiled bar opening into smaller back dining room; may be piped music (Dave Braisted, LYM, Robert Garner)

CATTHORPE [SP5578]
Cherry Tree LE17 6DB [Main St, just off A5 S of M1/M6/A14 interchange]: Attractive country local with helpful enthusiastic landlord, well kept Adnams, a Mild brewed for the pub and a guest ale, good value pubby food (not Sun evening) from sandwiches up, quick service, dark panelling, lots of plates and pictures, woodburner, darts and hood skittles on right, dining on left; garden tables, open all day wknds (Rona Murdoch)

CHURCH LANGTON [SP7293]
Langton Arms LE16 7SY [B6047 about 3 miles N of Mkt Harborough; just off A6]: Civilised extended village pub with good choice of pubby food, friendly efficient service, Greene King IPA and Abbot or Ruddles County, decent wines, small side eating area, restaurant; piped music; garden with play area (Gerry and Rosemary Dobson, David Field)

COLEORTON [SK4016]
Angel LE67 8GB [The Moor]: Friendly modernised old inn with attractive oak beams, enjoyable home-made food inc unusual fish dishes, well kept Everards Beacon, Marstons Pedigree and Shepherd Neame Spitfire, coal fires, hospitable attentive staff; tables outside (L T McGrath)
Kings Arms LE67 8GD [The Moor (off A512)]: Relaxed two-bar village pub with up to four real ales, good choice of wines by the glass and of reasonably priced fresh food; picnic-sets under cocktail parasols in front garden (Mark Toussaint)

COPT OAK [SK4812]
Copt Oak LE67 9QB [Whitwick Rd, handy for M1 junction 22]: Comfortable family dining pub with good views over Charnwood Forest, wide choice of food (all day Sun), quick friendly service, Marstons Pedigree, woodburner; piped music, can be very busy wknds (George Atkinson)

COTTESMORE [SK9013]
☆ **Sun** LE15 7DH [B668 NE of Oakham]: 17th-c thatched and stone-built village pub with good atmosphere and pleasant staff, good choice of wines by the glass, Adnams Best, Everards Tiger and a guest beer, good coffee, very wide choice of reasonably priced bar food from lunchtime sandwiches up, stripped pine on flagstones, inglenook log fire, attractive décor with lots of pictures and ornaments, carpeted back restaurant; piped music; dogs and children welcome in bar, terrace tables, open all day wknds (Roy Bromell, Derek and Sylvia Stephenson, Mrs Hazel Rainer, Michael Dandy, LYM)

CROPSTON [SK5511]
Bradgate Arms LE7 7HG [Station Rd]: Much modernised extended village pub with good atmosphere, traditional snug, wide range of pub food, well kept Banks's and Marstons

Pedigree, attractive prices, lower family
dining area, skittle alley; games machines,
piped music; biggish garden with play area,
handy for Bradgate Park *(LYM, David Morgan)*
CROXTON KERRIAL [SK8329]
☆ *Peacock* NG32 1QR [A607 SW of Grantham]:
Much modernised 17th-c former coaching inn
with friendly attentive service, good value
straightforward food well made using good
ingredients, real ales such as Black Sheep,
Greene King IPA and Wells & Youngs, decent
wines, log fire in big open-plan bare boards
beamed bar with chunky stripped tables,
small simple dining room and garden room;
said to be haunted by former landlord (never
does anything that might upset customers);
well behaved children welcome, picnic-sets
in inner courtyard and pleasant sloping
garden with views, good bedroom block
*(Phil and Jane Hodson, Andy and
Jill Kassube, BB, Derek and
Sylvia Stephenson)*
DADLINGTON [SP4097]
☆ *Dog & Hedgehog* CV13 6JB [The Green]:
Much extended comfortable dining pub with
enjoyable interesting food early evening
bargains and huge grills, friendly landlord,
attentive staff, thriving atmosphere, well
kept ales such as Chapel End and Hook
Norton Old Hooky, great views over Ashby
Canal and Bosworth Field, attractive village;
may be piped music; children welcome
*(Mr and Mrs I Moules, C J Pratt, Rob and
Catherine Dunster, Charles and Pauline Stride)*
DISEWORTH [SK4524]
Bull & Swan DE74 2QD [handy for M1
junction 23A; first left off A453 after East
Midlands Airport main entrance]: Friendly
village pub with good choice of enjoyable
food and of real ales, homely atmosphere,
good log fire, beams and brasses; games
machine; open all day Sun *(Mike and
Jenny Beacon)*
DUNTON BASSETT [SP5490]
Dunton Bassett Arms LE17 5JJ [Bennetts
Hill]: New licensees in neatly kept pub with
thriving flagstoned bar and oriental touches
to décor of adjoining eating area, attentive
staff, quite separate (and separately run)
chinese restaurant; six comfortable bedrooms,
good breakfast, cl lunchtime Mon-Weds, open
all day Thurs-Sun *(Gordon Keightley)*
EAST LANGTON [SP7292]
Bell LE16 7TW [Off B6047; Main St]:
Appealing country pub under friendly new
licensees (second change in under a year),
Brewsters, Greene King IPA and Abbot and
local Langton ale, enjoyable if rather pricy
food, long low-ceilinged stripped-stone
beamed bar, woodburner, plain wooden
tables; tables out on sloping front lawn
(LYM, Gerry and Rosemary Dobson)
EDITH WESTON [SK9205]
Wheatsheaf LE15 8EZ [King Edwards Way]:
Handy for Rutland Water, generous bar food
from snacks to haunch of venison, Everards
ales; children welcome, terrace tables
(Duncan Cloud)

FOXTON [SP6989]
Foxton Locks LE16 7RA [Foxton Locks, off A6
3m NW of Market Harborough (park by bridge
60/62 and walk)]: Large comfortably
reworked L-shaped bar with further room off,
warm welcome, wide choice of usual food
from baguettes up, prompt efficient service,
half a dozen real ales such as Caledonian
Deuchars IPA, Fullers London Pride and
Theakstons; picnic-sets on large raised
terrace and decking with canvas awning,
steps down to more picnic-sets on safely
railed waterside lawn – nice setting at foot
of long flight of canal locks
(Gerry and Rosemary Dobson, M J Winterton)
GLOOSTON [SP7495]
Old Barn LE16 7ST [off B6047 in Tur
Langton]: Appealing and interesting 16th-c
village pub reopened under new licensees,
enjoyable food (good value wkdy lunches
popular with older people), good service,
beams, stripped kitchen tables, country
chairs and log fire; tables out in front,
bedrooms *(LYM, O K Smyth)*
GREETHAM [SK9314]
☆ *Wheatsheaf* LE15 7NP [B668 Stretton—
Cottesmore]: Linked L-shaped rooms with
wide choice of good value generous food
from long-serving chef, Greene King IPA and
John Smiths, friendly service, blazing open
stove; soft piped music, end games room
with darts, pool and big-screen sports TV;
dogs welcome, wheelchair access, tables out
on front lawn and on back terrace by pretty
little stream, boules, popular annexe
bedrooms, open all day Sat *(Michael and
Jenny Back, BB)*
GRIMSTON [SK6821]
☆ *Black Horse* LE14 3BZ [off A6006 W of
Melton Mowbray; Main St]: Popular village
pub with welcoming bar licensees, Adnams
and Marstons Pedigree, wide choice of good
value wholesome food inc pigeon, lamb and
hotpot, log fire, darts; attractive village with
stocks and 13th-c church *(LYM,
David Barnes, Duncan Cloud)*
GUMLEY [SP6890]
☆ *Bell* LE16 7RU [NW of Market Harboro; Main
St]: Cheerful neatly kept beamed village pub
with traditional country décor, good value
straightforward food (not Mon evening) from
sandwiches to steaks inc popular OAP
bargains and good Sun lunch, friendly
attentive staff, real ales such as Batemans
Hooker, Greene King IPA and Timothy Taylors
Landlord, good soft drinks choice, open fire,
darts and cribbage, small dining room
(children over 5 allowed here), interesting
cricket memorabilia in lobby; pretty terrace
garden (not for children or dogs) with aviary,
cl Sun evening *(P Tailyour, Barry Collett, LYM,
Jim Farmer, George Atkinson)*
HALLATON [SP7896]
☆ *Bewicke Arms* LE16 8UB [off B6047 or
B664]: Welcoming and attractive thatched
pub dating from 16th c, good value food
(not Sun evening) from sandwiches to steak
and restaurant dishes, Adnams, Fullers and

Archers or Grainstore, two bar dining areas, restaurant of small linked areas, log fires, scrubbed pine tables, some interesting memorabilia about the ancient local Easter Monday inter-village bottle-kicking match; darts, shove-ha'penny, piped music; children in eating areas, stables tearoom/gift shop across yard, big terrace overlooking paddock and lake, bedrooms, open all day Sun *(Duncan Cloud, Stuart and Alison Ballantyne, Phil and Jane Hodson, Jim Farmer, David Field, LYM, George Atkinson, Edmund Coan)*

HATHERN [SK5021]
Dew Drop LE12 5HY [Loughborough Rd (A6)]: Friendly traditional two-room beamed local with Greene King ales, plenty of malt whiskies, coal fire, darts and dominoes; tables outside, open all day wknds *(the Didler)*

HEMINGTON [SK4527]
Jolly Sailor DE74 2RB [Main St]: Cheerful and picturesque old village local with friendly long-serving landlord, enjoyable fresh bar food (not Sun), Bass, Greene King Abbot and several other changing ales inc a Mild, summer farm cider, decent wines by the glass, good range of malt whiskies and other spirits, good log fire each end, big country pictures, bric-a-brac on heavy beams and shelves, candlelit back restaurant Fri/Sat night, table skittles; quiet piped music, games machines; beautiful hanging baskets and picnic-sets out in front, open all day wknds *(the Didler)*

HINCKLEY [SP4092]
Lime Kilns LE10 3ED [Watling St (A5)]: Good choice of food, efficient service, Marstons Pedigree, reasonable prices, comfortable furnishings; big garden by tranquil Ashby Canal, some moorings *(anon)*

HOBY [SK6717]
Blue Bell LE14 3DT [Main St]: Attractive thatched pub with three airy linked rooms, good realistically priced food from lunchtime sandwiches and baguettes through pubby favourites to the welcoming French landlord/chef's evening specialities, good helpful service, well kept Everards, comfortable modern furniture, separate dining area; pleasant garden with play area *(Richard and Jean Green)*

HOSE [SK7329]
Black Horse LE14 4JE [Bolton Lane]: Down-to-earth beamed and quarry-tiled Tynemill pub with amiable landlord, interesting quickly served blackboard food (not Sun evening) in bar and panelled restaurant, well kept Castle Rock and several other ales, coal fire, darts; pretty village, nice countryside, has been cl Mon-Thurs lunchtimes *(the Didler, Eddie and Lynn Jarrett)*

HOUGHTON ON THE HILL [SK6703]
Old Black Horse LE7 9GD [Main St (just off A47 Leicester—Uppingham)]: Lively and comfortable, with above-average home-made food (no hot food Mon lunchtime), welcoming helpful staff, Everards and a

guest beer, good sensibly priced wines by the glass, bare-boards dining area with lots of panelling; piped music; big attractive garden *(Jim Farmer)*

HUNGARTON [SK6907]
Black Boy LE7 9JR [Main St]: Large partly divided open-plan bar with wide choice of enjoyable food cooked to order (Tues-Sat evenings; wknd booking advised), well kept Everards Tiger and a guest beer, friendly landlord and staff, minimal decoration, open fire *(Jim Farmer)*

ILLSTON ON THE HILL [SP7099]
☆ *Fox & Goose* LE7 9EG [Main St, off B6047 Mkt Harboro—Melton]: Welcoming and individual two-bar local, plain, comfortable and convivial, with interesting pictures and assorted oddments, Everards ales and a guest beer, table lamps, good coal fire, no food; cl Mon lunchtime *(LYM, the Didler)*

KEGWORTH [SK4826]
Britannia DE74 2EU [London Rd]: Friendly new management, bargain food inc all-day Sun roasts, Hardys & Hansons ales; no credit cards; tables outside *(M J Winterton)*
☆ *Cap & Stocking* DE74 2FF [handy for M1 junction 24, via A6; Borough St]: Old-fashioned three-room pub nicely pottering along in some previous century, brown paint, etched glass, coal fires, big cases of stuffed birds and locally caught fish, Bass (from the jug) and well kept guest beers such as Jennings and Wells & Youngs Bombardier, home-made food (not Weds evening) from fresh sandwiches to bargain Sun lunch, dominoes, back room opening to secluded garden with decking; piped music, no credit cards; children welcome *(Pete Baker, the Didler, LYM, Bill Strang, Stuart Pearson)*
Otter DE74 2EY [London Rd]: Large friendly Vintage Inn by River Soar, good choice of wines by the glass and of soft drinks, Marstons Pedigree, decent food all day from sandwiches up, assorted furnishings in several linked areas; quiet piped music; children welcome, waterside terraces, open all day *(JJW, CMW)*
Red Lion DE74 2DA [a mile from M1 junction 24, via A6 towards Loughborough; High St]: Half a dozen or more good changing real ales and good range of whiskies and vodkas in four brightly lit traditional rooms around small servery, limited choice of good wholesome food (not Sun), assorted furnishings, coal and flame-effect fires, delft shelf of beer bottles, daily papers, darts and cards, family room; picnic-sets in small back yard, garden with play area, well equipped bedrooms with own bathrooms, open all day *(the Didler, Pete Baker, BB)*

KIBWORTH BEAUCHAMP [SP6894]
☆ *Coach & Horses* LE8 0NN [A6 S of Leicester]: Snug and popular turkey-carpeted local with attentive efficient staff and friendly long-serving landlord, equally long-serving chef doing wide choice of good honest home-made food at very reasonable prices (mainly roasts on Sun), well kept Bass, Greene King

IPA and a guest such as Wadworths 6X or Wells & Youngs Special, good sicilian wines, china and pewter mugs on beams, relaxing candlelit restaurant, no piped music (*P Tailyour, Jim Farmer, BB, Duncan Cloud*)

KILBY [SP6295]

Dog & Gun LE18 3TD [Main St, off A5199 S of Leicester]: Welcoming much-extended pub locally popular for wide choice of enjoyable straightforward food from baguettes up, helpful service, Bass, Greene King Abbot, Marstons Pedigree and Websters (also the name of the lovely white cat), good wine choice, coal fire, attractive side restaurant with grandfather clock; disabled access, colourful back garden with terrace and pergola (*Duncan Cloud, Michael and Jenny Back*)

KIRBY MUXLOE [SK5104]

Royal Oak LE9 2AN [Main St]: Comfortable modernish pub with good value food from wide range of baguettes through usual bar dishes to fish specialities and Sun lunch, good friendly service, well kept Adnams and Everards, sizeable restaurant; handy for nearby 15th-c castle ruins (*Gerry and Rosemary Dobson*)

KNIPTON [SK8231]

☆ *Manners Arms* NG32 1RH [signed off A607 Grantham—Melton Mowbray; Croxton Rd]: Handsome Georgian hunting lodge beautifully renovated by Duke and Duchess of Rutland as upscale country inn, hunting prints and furniture from Belvoir Castle, log fire, light bar dishes, changing guest beers and good choice of wines by the glass, wide range of interesting food using local produce in sizeable stylish restaurant with attractive conservatory, impeccable service, sumptuous lounge; terrace with ornamental pool, lovely views over pretty village, ten comfortable individually furnished bedrooms, open all day (*P Dawn, Tom and Marie Heffernan, BB*)

KNOSSINGTON [SK8008]

Fox & Hounds LE15 8LY [off A606 W of Oakham; Somerby Rd]: The friendly couple whose good local food brought this handsome ivy-covered building into the main entries last year left in Jan and we found it closed subsequently, so we'd very much like further news; it's attractive inside, with a simply modernised knocked-through beamed bar, comfortable end dining area, and big back garden (*LYM*)

LANGHAM [SK8411]

☆ *Noel Arms* LE15 7HU [Bridge St]: This pleasant country pub, with low beams, flagstones, central log fire and enjoyable food, drinks and service was closed for thorough refurbishment as this edition went to press – news please; bedrooms (*LYM*)

LEICESTER [SK5804]

Ale Wagon LE1 1RE [Rutland St/Charles St]: Basic 1930s two-room local with great beer choice inc its own Hoskins ales, Weston's perry, coal fire, plenty of events such as comedy nights; handy for station, open all day (Sun afternoon break) (*the Didler*)

Barley Mow LE1 6FE [Granby St]: Large traditional open-plan Everards pub with lunchtime bar food, guest beers, pool, darts, upper coffee/ale bar; piped music, games machines; open all day (*Valerie Baker*)

Criterion LE1 5JN [Millstone Lane]: Modern building with good value pizzas (not Sun/Mon), cobs and tapas any time, Sun lunches, good changing choice of unusual real ales and great range of continental beers, decent wines by the glass, rather wine-bar-like carpeted main room with dark wood and burgundy décor, relaxed room on left with games, some live music; reasonable wheelchair access (small front step), picnic-sets outside (*Tony Kelly, the Didler*)

☆ *Globe* LE1 5EU [Silver St]: Lots of woodwork in old-fashioned partitioned areas off central bar, mirrors and wrought-iron gas lamps, charming more peaceful upstairs dining room, Everards and guest ales, friendly attentive staff, low-priced honest food 12-7 from snacks up; piped pop music (not in snug), very popular with young people wknd evenings; children allowed in some parts, open all day (*the Didler, David and Sue Smith, LYM, Dave Braisted*)

☆ *Out of the Vaults* LE1 6RL [King St/New Walk]: Great quickly changing range of interesting real ales from a dozen handpumps in long high-ceilinged bar, friendly chatty landlady, enthusiast landlord, wkdy lunchtime cobs, baguettes and curries, decent reasonably priced wines by the glass, simple seating and stripped tables on bare boards; open all day (*the Didler*)

Rutland & Derby Arms LE1 5JN [Millstone Lane]: Smartly renovated old pub with four Everards ales, Greene King IPA, Wells & Youngs Bombardier, very wide choice of lagers and impressive spotlit spirits range, interesting well priced food using local organic meat, home-baked sourdough bread, friendly service, clean-cut modern décor and subdued lighting; well reproduced piped music; terrace tables (*Kerry Law, Val and Alan Green*)

☆ *Swan & Rushes* LE1 5WR [Oxford St/Infirmary Sq]: Well kept Oakham and lots of changing guest beers, good choice of belgian beers, farm cider, thriving atmosphere in two rooms with big oak tables, enjoyable bar lunches (not Mon or Sat); live music Sat; open all day (*James Crouchman, the Didler, Valerie Baker*)

LONG CLAWSON [SK7227]

Crown & Plough LE14 4NG [off A606 NW of Melton Mowbray; East End]: 17th-c pub with low bowed beams, stripped masonry, inglenooks, a mix of seats around scrubbed pine tables, some comfortable sofas, real ales such as Adnams, Everards Tiger and Marstons Pedigree; children and dogs welcome, tables in sheltered courtyard, five new bedrooms, may cl Mon lunchtime (*Gwyn and Anne Wake, David Glynne-Jones, LYM*)

LOUGHBOROUGH [SK5320]

Albion LE11 1QA [canal bank, about ¼ mile from Loughborough Wharf]: Cheerful chatty local by Grand Union Canal, emphasis on at least three changing real ales inc one from local Wicked Hathern, friendly owners, cheap straightforward home-made food, coal fire, darts room; children welcome, occasional barbecues, budgerigar aviary in nice big courtyard (*Brian and Ruth Archer, P Dawn, the Didler, Gwyn and Anne Wake*)

☆ *Swan in the Rushes* LE11 5BE [A6]: Cheery bustling bare-boards town local with good value Castle Rock and wide range of other interesting changing real ales tapped from the cask, plenty of foreign bottled beers, farm cider, good value straightforward chip-free food (not Sat/Sun evenings), daily papers, traditional games, open fire, three smallish high-ceilinged rooms; good juke box; children in eating areas, tables outside, bedrooms, open all day (*P Dawn, Pete Baker, Richard and Karen Holt, the Didler, Mrs Hazel Rainer, LYM, BB, Sue Demont, Tim Barrow*)

Tap & Mallet LE11 1EU [Nottingham Rd]: Basic friendly pub noted for five or six changing microbrews, foreign beers on tap, farm cider and perry, coal fire, pool, occasional beer festivals; walled back garden with play area and pets corner, open all day wknds (*the Didler, P Dawn*)

LUTTERWORTH [SP5484]

Unicorn LE17 4AE [Church St, off A426; handy for M1 junction 20]: Welcoming town pub, banquettes in lounge and back restaurant, bargain lunchtime food from sandwiches up inc children's dishes and popular OAP deals, nice log fire, well kept Bass, Greene King IPA and Robinsons, more basic bar with traditional games inc food skittles; sports TV, no credit cards; open all day (*P Tailyour, Pete Baker*)

MARKET BOSWORTH [SK4003]

☆ *Olde Red Lion* CV13 0LL [Park St; from centre follow Leicester and Hinckley signs]: Cheerful and civilised black-beamed split-level pub with real ales such as Burton Bridge XL, Greene King Abbot and Marstons Pedigree, sensibly priced food (not Sun/Mon evenings) from sandwiches and baked potatoes up inc proper steak and kidney pie, prompt efficient service, plushly tidy L-shaped bar; may be piped music; children welcome, picnic-sets and play area in sheltered courtyard, attractive village, five comfortable bedrooms, open all day Fri-Sun (*LYM, Pete Baker, C J Fletcher, Derek and Sylvia Stephenson*)

MARKET HARBOROUGH [SP7387]

Angel LE16 7AF [High St]: Former coaching inn with decent food from sandwiches, paninis and other pubby lunchtime bar food to restaurant meals, friendly and efficient uniformed staff, Grainstore and Marstons Pedigree, good coffee, daily papers; bedrooms (*Michael Dandy, Gerry and Rosemary Dobson*)

Sugar Loaf LE16 7NJ [High St]: Popular Wetherspoons, smaller than many, with

pleasant atmosphere, half a dozen sensibly priced real ales, good value food all day; children allowed, open all day (*Gerry and Rosemary Dobson, Michael Dandy*)

☆ *Three Swans* LE16 7NJ [High St]: Handsome coaching inn now a Best Western conference hotel, beams and old local prints in plush and peaceful panelled front bar, flagstoned back dining lounge and fine courtyard conservatory (opened Weds-Fri evenings as good value bistro) in more modern part, friendly staff, wide range of good value bar lunches from sandwiches up, some bar food early evenings, Bass and Wells & Youngs Bombardier, decent wines, good coffee, more formal upstairs restaurant; piped music; attractive suntrap courtyard, good bedroom extension (*Anthony Barnes, Gerry and Rosemary Dobson, George Atkinson*)

MEDBOURNE [SP7992]

☆ *Nevill Arms* LE16 8EE [B664 Market Harborough—Uppingham]: The friendly licensees who ran this handsome streamside inn so well for 30 years sold it in spring 2007 (they now run the next-door cottages as B&Bs), and as we went to press the new people had not yet properly settled in, with only simple food while the kitchen was being rebuilt – so we'd like more reports; it's an attractive old place, with log fires, lofty dark joists and mullioned windows, and has had Adnams, Fullers London Pride, Greene King Abbot and guest beers, with seats out overlooking the village green (*LYM*)

NETHER BROUGHTON [SK6925]

☆ *Red House* LE14 3HB [A606 N of Melton Mowbray]: Substantial and elegant extended Georgian house, emphasis on good popular restaurant (best to book), also good sensibly priced bar food from sandwiches and local cheeses to steaks, comfortable lounge bar with red leather fireside settees and armchairs, bar on right with TV, changing real ales, fine range of spirits; garden picnic-sets, eight well equipped stylish bedrooms (*Phil and Jane Hodson, P Dawn, BB*)

NORTH LUFFENHAM [SK9303]

Horse & Panniers LE15 8JR [Church St]: Warmly welcoming village pub known locally as Nag 'n' Bags, dating from 1640 but largely 18th-c, enjoyable simple food, well kept ales such as Greene King IPA, Grainstore and Timothy Taylors Landlord, speciality cocktails; three good value bedrooms, bunkhouse, cl Tues lunchtime, open all day wknds (*Tom Morgan*)

OADBY [SP6399]

Grange LE2 4RH [Glen Rd (A6)]: Roomy Vintage Inn based on attractive early 19th-c farmhouse, wide range of standard food, friendly staff, good wine choice, real ales, log fires, old local photographs, daily papers, good mix of customers; picnic-sets out in front, open all day (*David Field, Lesley and Barbara Owen*)

OAKHAM [SK8508]

Admiral Hornblower LE15 6AS [High St]: Several differently decorated areas from panelling and tradition to fresher informality, warm and inviting with three log fires, interesting menu using their own herbs, extremely well organised service, well kept real ales, conservatory; garden tables, comfortable bedrooms (H Paulinski)

Horseshoe LE15 6LE [Braunston Rd]: 1960s pub with enjoyable fresh food inc two-for-one lunches Weds-Fri, Everards and guest beers, friendly service, pleasant open-plan lounge bar, smaller lounge leading to dining area; some picnic-sets out in front, garden behind (Barry Collett)

Wheatsheaf LE15 6QS [Northgate]: Attractive 17th-c local nr church, Adnams, Everards and guest ales, enjoyable lunchtime pub food inc particularly good puddings, friendly helpful service, open fire, plenty of bric-a-brac, cheerful bar, comfortable quieter lounge and conservatory (children welcome in it); pretty suntrap back courtyard with interesting and entertaining installation, nearby play park (Barry Collett, Fiona McElhone)

OAKTHORPE [SK3212]

Shoulder of Mutton DE12 7QT [Chapel St]: Friendly 18th-c black and white village pub with good range of real ales, good restaurant (no food Sun evenings or Mon); disabled facilities (B M Eldridge)

REDMILE [SK7836]

Peacock NG13 0GA [Main St]: Attractive stone-built dining pub with enjoyable food, good choice of wines by the glass, friendly management and staff, well kept ales, big log fires in set of spotless linked rooms, beams, country furniture and old prints, some stripped golden stone, spacious conservatory-style area; teak tables on terrace and back decking, peaceful setting nr Belvoir Castle, ten good bedrooms (Stephen Woad, MP, LYM)

Windmill NG13 0GA [off A52 Grantham—Nottingham; Main St]: Dining pub with wide choice of enjoyable home-made food from baguettes to steaks, wkdy meal deals and Sun roasts, Greene King Ruddles, good wines by the glass, good friendly service, up-to-date décor keeping original features inc log fire in bar's old fireplace; children welcome (Ellen Stephenson, N R White, Barry Collett)

ROTHLEY [SK5812]

Woodmans Stroke LE7 7PD [Church St]: Immaculate upscale pub with good value wkdy lunchtime bar food from sandwiches up, changing ales such as Bass and Greene King Abbot, good wines by the glass inc champagne (and they do a nice Pimms), friendly family service, beams and settles in front rooms, lots of rugby and cricket memorabilia; sports TV; cast-iron tables out in attractive garden with heaters and aviary, open all day (David Glynne-Jones, Rona Murdoch)

SADDINGTON [SP6591]

Queens Head LE8 0QH [S of Leicester between A5199 (ex A50) and A6; Main St]:

Reasonably priced tasty food (not Sun evening) from baguettes to steaks and a fair amount of fish, Everards and guest ales, decent wines, quick polite service, daily papers, lots of knick-knacks and plastic plants; no under-5s, steps from area to area; country and reservoir views from dining conservatory and tables in long sloping garden (Gerry and Rosemary Dobson, Dennis and Gill Keen, LYM)

SALTBY [SK8426]

☆ *Nags Head* LE14 4RN [Back St]: Small beamed and stone-built pub with good shortish blackboard choice of enjoyable home cooking, bargain OAP lunches Tues/Thurs, choice of Sun roasts, up to three changing ales such as Fullers London Pride (landlord won't stock more than he knows he can sell while still in top condition), decent wines by the glass, friendly licensees, relaxed chatty atmosphere in three traditional rooms each with own fireplace; soft piped music; dogs welcome, cl Sun evening, Mon lunchtime (Lesley and Barbara Owen, BB, Derek and Sylvia Stephenson)

SEATON [SP9098]

☆ *George & Dragon* LE15 9HU [Main St]: Good generous sensibly priced food from sandwiches and baguettes to hot dishes cooked to order, Fri steak nights, Sun roasts, welcoming licensees, quick service, real ales such as Adnams Broadside, Black Sheep, Grainstore Ten Fifty and Marstons Pedigree, good wine choice, daily papers, nice solid fuel stove, two cosy bars, one with wide variety of sports memorabilia; piped jazz; tables outside, unspoilt village, good views of famous viaduct (BB, Philip and Susan Philcox, M and C Thompson, Rona Murdoch, Barry Collett)

SHEARSBY [SP6290]

☆ *Chandlers Arms* LE17 6PL [Fenny Lane, off A50 Leicester—Northampton]: Friendly and attentive new licensees in comfortable village pub with good choice of well kept changing ales such as Black Sheep, Brains Rev James, Grainstore and Jennings, good choice of home-made bar lunches with more interesting evening menu and Sun roasts, warm atmosphere, brocaded wall seats, wheelback chairs, flowers on tables, house plants, swagged curtains; tables in secluded raised garden, attractive village (BB, Peter Cole)

SIBSON [SK3500]

Cock CV13 6LB [A444 N of Nuneaton; Twycross Rd]: Ancient picturesque black and white timbered and thatched building, Bass and Hook Norton Best, a dozen wines by the glass, low doorways, heavy black beams and genuine latticed windows, immense inglenook; piped music, games machine; children welcome, tables in courtyard and small garden, handy for Bosworth Field (Joan and Tony Walker, Ian and Jane Irving, LYM, Helen Rowett)

SILEBY [SK6015]

☆ **White Swan** LE12 7NW [Swan St]: Bright, cheerful and relaxed, with good choice of attractively priced home cooking (not Sun evening or Mon lunchtime, and may be a wait if busy) from home-baked rolls up, well kept Fullers London Pride, nice house wines, good friendly staff and chatty locals, comfortable and welcoming dining lounge, small tasteful book-lined restaurant (booking needed) (Jim Farmer, Dr Ann Henderson)

SOMERBY [SK7710]

☆ **Three Crowns** LE14 2PZ [off A606 Oakham—Melton Mowbray; High St]: Very low-beamed village pub with friendly landlord, big log fire, good local Parish Bitter as well as Bass and Greene King IPA, bargain simple food, quite a mix of old-fashioned chairs around dark oak tables, darts, May beer festival; piped music, TV, games machine; children and dogs welcome, tables in walled garden, newly refurbished bedrooms, open all day Sun (Ian Stafford, Barry Collett, Phil and Jane Hodson, LYM, O K Smyth, Gerry and Rosemary Dobson)

SOUTH LUFFENHAM [SK9401]

Coach House LE15 8NT [Stamford Rd (A6121)]: Chef/landlord doing enjoyable and interesting food from good range of sandwiches and snacks up, quick cheerful young staff, changing real ales such as Adnams, Greene King IPA and Oakham JHB, good choice of wines by the glass, pink walls, flagstones and much scrubbed pine furniture in good-sized comfortable bar, elegant restaurant; comfortable bedrooms, good breakfast (M and C Thompson, Michael Doswell, E Matthews, Russell Carter, R L Borthwick)

THORPE LANGTON [SP7492]

☆ **Bakers Arms** LE16 7TS [off B6047 N of Mkt Harboro]: Civilised restaurant rather than pub now, and very popular as that, doing good imaginative meals in cottagey beamed linked areas with stylishly simple country décor, but still has well kept local Langton ale as well as good choice of wines by the glass, friendly attentive staff; no under-12s; garden picnic-sets, cl wkdy lunchtimes, Sun evening and Mon (LYM, Gerry and Rosemary Dobson, Mike and Sue Loseby, Duncan Cloud, Lesley and Barbara Owen, P Tailyour)

TUGBY [SK7600]

Fox & Hounds LE7 9WB [A47 6 miles W of Uppingham]: Newish licensees have thoroughly refurbished this attractive village-green pub, enjoyable food inc midweek OAP bargains, fine range of well kept real ales, friendly service, Weston's farm cider, two-level layout with pleasant décor and relaxed atmosphere, open fire; tables in good-sized garden with terrace (Jim Farmer, R L Borthwick, Andrew Cross)

TUR LANGTON [SP7194]

Crown LE8 OPJ [off B6047; Main St (follow Kibworth signpost from centre)]: Attractive pub with decent food from basic dishes up,

friendly service, Caledonian Deuchars IPA, Courage Directors and Greene King IPA, flagstoned bar with central log fire, side room with pool, back restaurant with own bar; terrace tables (Jim Farmer, LYM)

UPPER HAMBLETON [SK8907]

☆ **Finches Arms** LE15 8TL [off A606]: Outstanding views over Rutland Water from suntrap back hillside terrace and picture-window modern restaurant at smart dining pub with stylish cane furniture on wooden floors, open fire in knocked-through front bar, imaginative food (not Sun evening), Greene King Abbot, Oakham JHB, Timothy Taylors Landlord and a guest beer; generally a top-notch place and quite a favourite with many, but food service – usually friendly foreigners, helpful and efficient – has been known to falter; piped music; bedrooms, open all day (LYM, Mrs M B Gregg, Fred Chamberlain, Christopher Turner, Anthony Barnes, Roy Bromell, Michael Dandy, Gerry and Rosemary Dobson, Mike and Sue Loseby, M C and S Jeanes, Mike and Heather Watson, Philip and Susan Philcox, Ian and Jane Irving)

UPPINGHAM [SP8699]

Falcon LE15 9PY [High St East/Market Sq]: Civilised and relaxing coaching inn with plenty of character in oak-panelled bar and comfortable lounge, light and airy, with skylights and big windows over market sq, pleasant light lunches inc sandwiches and rolls, afternoon teas, friendly attentive well trained staff, well kept Greene King IPA, Abbot and Old Speckled Hen, good coffee, nice open fire, daily papers and magazines; bedrooms, back barrier-exit car park (W W Burke)

WALTHAM ON THE WOLDS [SK8024]

Marquis of Granby LE14 4AH [High St]: Friendly new licensees in unpretentious stone-built country local with good value generous pubby food from baguettes up, quick service, well kept ales, reasonably priced wines by the glass, upper games area with pool, skittle alley (Phil and Jane Hodson)

☆ **Royal Horseshoes** LE14 4AJ [Melton Rd (A607)]: Attractive thatched stone-built inn, sturdily furnished and comfortable, with quick friendly service and spotless housekeeping, consistently enjoyable food (best to book evenings), Fullers London Pride and Greene King Abbot, good wines and fair range of malts, open fires in all three linked areas, aquarium in end dining area; subtle piped music; children welcome in eating area, tables outside, four bedrooms (Phil and Jane Hodson, LYM, Derek and Sylvia Stephenson)

WESTON BY WELLAND [SP7791]

Wheel & Compass LE16 8HZ [Valley Rd]: Recently enlarged dining pub with wide choice of enjoyable attractively priced food, Bass, Marstons Pedigree and three changing guest beers, friendly staff, comfortable bar, back dining area and separate restaurant;

open all day wknds *(Rona Murdoch, Guy and Caroline Howard)*

WHITWICK [SK4316]

Three Horseshoes LE67 5GN [Leicester Rd]: Friendly and utterly unpretentious local, bar and tiny snug, Bass and Marstons Pedigree, log fires, darts, dominoes and cards, no food; outdoor lavatories *(Pete Baker, the Didler)*

WIGSTON [SP6099]

William Wygston LE18 1DR [Leicester Rd]: Roomy Wetherspoons, bright and airy, with bargain food deals, well priced real ales, quick helpful service; accessible books – not exactly riveting except for specialists *(Veronica Brown)*

WOODHOUSE EAVES [SK5214]

Old Bulls Head LE12 8RZ [Main St]: Large open-plan pub with enjoyable food inc some interesting dishes, Marstons Pedigree and Timothy Taylors Landlord, beamery, books and bric-a-brac, games area *(Duncan Cloud)*

WYMESWOLD [SK6023]

Three Crowns LE12 6TZ [Far St (A6006)]: Snug and chatty 18th-c village local with

impressive service from friendly staff, good value food inc lots of specials, four or five real ales such as Adnams, Belvoir and Marstons, good soft drinks choice, attentive service, pleasant character furnishings in beamed bar and lounge, darts; picnic-sets out on decking *(Brian and Ruth Archer, the Didler, John and Sylvia Harrop)*

Windmill LE12 6TT [Brook St]: Village pub refurbished by new landlord, enjoyable food using local ingredients, good friendly service; children welcome *(Francoise Vero)*

WYMONDHAM [SK8518]

Berkeley Arms LE14 2AG [Main St]: Attractive old stone building with welcoming helpful staff, enjoyable generous fresh food inc imaginative dishes in good-sized main bar, dining lounge and elegant restaurant, changing ales such as Adnams, Greene King IPA, Hydes and Marstons Pedigree, Addlestone's cider, good coffee, appealingly pubby uncluttered décor with pine furniture; well spaced picnic-sets in pleasant garden, nice village, cl Mon lunchtime *(Louise Etherington, David Barnes)*

Ideas for a country day out? We list pubs in really attractive scenery at the back of the book – and there are separate lists for waterside pubs, ones with really good gardens, and ones with lovely views.

Lincolnshire

The elegant George of Stamford here is on top form, with exemplary service, delicious food, and a civilised but relaxed atmosphere. On a smaller scale and with a more bustling town feel, the café-style Wig & Mitre in Lincoln is another very civilised place – useful in opening from 8am, with food from breakfast till midnight; it gains a Food Award this year. The Chequers at Woolsthorpe also wins a Food Award this year: on really good form, serving well prepared food in a comfortably relaxed atmosphere. Of these three good food pubs, it's the George in Stamford that is, for the sixth year in a row, Lincolnshire Dining Pub of the Year. Other pubs doing well here include the family-run Wheatsheaf at Dry Doddington, a very warm-hearted all-rounder, and the friendly traditional Welby Arms at Allington. Pub food prices here are fairly close to the national average, but drinks prices tend to be slightly lower than the norm. Batemans is the county's classic brewery, with good value beers (and appealing tied pubs). It's also well worth looking out for ales from the newer local Tom Woods, though the beer which we found most often featuring as the lowest-priced in the county's better pubs was that welcome interloper from Yorkshire, Black Sheep. Though this year none of the pubs from the Lucky Dip section at the end of the chapter quite made promotion to the main entries, we do have our eye on some particularly promising prospects, notably the contrasting Angel & Royal and Blue Pig, both in Grantham, Reindeer in Long Bennington, Red Lion at Redbourne, White Swan in Scotter and Cross Keys at Stow. We'd be particularly grateful for your thoughts on these – and of course on any other Lucky Dip entries (a couple of dozen of these are quite new to the *Guide* this year).

ALLINGTON   SK8540   MAP 7

Welby Arms ♀ 🍺 🛏

The Green; off A1 N of Grantham, or A52 W of Grantham; NG32 2EA

Friendly inn near A1 with agreeable food, six real ales and pleasant bedrooms

The large traditionally furnished bar at this comfortably bustling pub is divided by a stone archway and has black beams and joists, log fires (one in an attractive arched brick fireplace), red velvet curtains, and comfortable burgundy button-back wall banquettes and stools. Half a dozen very well kept real ales (served through a sparkler) include Charles Wells Bombardier and Eagle, John Smiths, Timothy Taylors Landlord and a couple of guests such as Adnams Broadside and Badger Tanglefoot; also ten wines by the glass, and 20 malt whiskies; dominoes, cribbage, and piped music. The civilised back dining lounge (where they prefer you to eat) looks out on to tables in a sheltered walled courtyard with pretty summer hanging baskets, and there are more picnic-sets out on the front lawn.

🍽 Bar food is popular and might include soup, filled baguettes (including hot sirloin steak and stilton), chicken liver pâté, chicken pasta, steak and mushroom in ale pie and chargrilled steaks, and specials such as pork and black pudding sausage, fresh grimsby haddock with mushy peas, lambs liver and onions, lamb shank or poached plaice with prawn sauce. Best to book to be sure of a table. *Starters/Snacks: £3.75 to £5.50. Main Courses: £7.95 to £13.50. Puddings: £3.50 to £4.95*

Free house ~ Licensee Matt Rose ~ Real ale ~ Bar food (12-2, 6.30-9) ~ Restaurant ~ (01400) 281361 ~ Well behaved children welcome at lunchtime and early evening ~ Open 12-2.30(3 Sat), 6-11; 12-10.30 Sun ~ Bedrooms: £48S/£60S

Recommended by Michael and Jenny Back, Maurice and Janet Thorpe, Andy and Jill Kassube, Mrs Brenda Calver, W M Paton, Nigel and Sue Foster, Sally Anne and Peter Goodale, Roger and Pauline Pearce, Maurice Ricketts, Jill and Julian Tasker

BARNOLDBY LE BECK   TA2303   MAP 8

Ship ♀

Village signposted off A18 Louth—Grimsby; DN37 0BG

Tranquil dining pub with carefully collected bric-a-brac in plush Victorian interior, and good seafood

There's a sedately relaxed atmosphere at this neatly kept little cream painted pub, which houses a delightful collection of beautifully kept Edwardian and Victorian bric-a-brac. Charming items run from stand-up telephones and violins to a horn gramophone, as well as bowler and top hats, old racquets, crops, hockey sticks and a lace dress. Heavy dark-ringed drapes swathe the windows, with grandmotherly plants in ornate china bowls on the sills. Furnishings include comfortable dark green plush wall benches with lots of pretty propped-up cushions and heavily stuffed green plush Victorian-looking chairs on a green fleur de lys carpet. Many of the tables are booked for dining. Well kept Black Sheep and Timothy Taylors Landlord on handpump and a good wine list; piped music. A fenced-off sunny area behind has hanging baskets and a few picnic-sets under pink cocktail parasols.

🍴 Enjoyable food could include soup, sandwiches or filled baguettes, chicken liver and brandy pâté with redcurrant and mint jelly, salmon, prawn and white fish crêpe, spinach and ricotta filo parcel with red onion and rocket salad, beef in ale, fish pie, poached salmon with penne and lemon and watercress sauce and battered haddock, with quite a few fresh fish specials such as seared scallops, skate and turbot, and puddings such as hot chocolate and brandy fudge cake. *Starters/Snacks: £4.00 to £6.00. Main Courses: £8.50 to £18.00. Puddings: £4.25*

Inn Business ~ Tenant Michele Hancock ~ Real ale ~ Bar food ~ Restaurant ~ (01472) 822308 ~ Children welcome ~ Open 12-3, 6-12; 12-11 Sun

Recommended by Maurice and Janet Thorpe, James Browne, Lesley and Barbara Owen, Kay and Alistair Butler

BELCHFORD   TF2975   MAP 8

Blue Bell 🍽

Village signposted off A153 Horncastle—Louth (and can be reached by the good Bluestone Heath Road off A16 just under 1½ miles N of the A1104 roundabout); Main Road; LN9 6LQ

Emphasis on imaginative modern food at cottagey 18th-c dining pub

The cosy comfortable bar here has a relaxing pastel décor, some armchairs and settees, as well as more upright chairs around good solid tables, and well kept Black Sheep and a guest such as Adnams Explorer on handpump; friendly, prompt service. The neat terraced garden behind has picnic-sets. This is a good base for Wolds walks and the Viking Way, though hikers must take their boots off – particularly as they've recently put in new carpets.

🍴 From an inventive changing menu, there might be sandwiches, starters such as goats cheese cheesecake, ham hock terrine with honey and grain mustard, confit of duck leg on puy lentil roast tomato, thyme and chorizo sauce, main courses such as beef and Guinness pie, sausage on truffle mash, cod baked with pumpkin crust and white wine cream sauce, twice-baked cheddar soufflé on spinach with red pepper coulis, saddle of venison wrapped in pancetta with lincoln blue cheese on parsnip purée with redcurrant sauce and fillet steak with green pepper and Guinness sauce, and puddings such as summer fruit pudding and warm chocolate brownie with pistachio ice-cream. *Starters/Snacks: £3.25 to £6.95. Main Courses: £9.95 to £19.25. Puddings: £3.95 to £4.50*

Free house ~ Licensees Darren and Shona Jackson ~ Real ale ~ Bar food ~ Restaurant ~ (01507) 533602 ~ Children welcome ~ Open 11.30-2.30, 6.30-11; 12-4 Sun; closed Sun evening, Mon and second and third weeks in Jan

Recommended by Dr K A McLauchlan, Mrs R McLauchlan, Mr and Mrs J Brown, Mrs P Bishop, David Barnes, Malcolm Brown, Revd L and S Giller, Mrs Brenda Calver, Keith Wright

BILLINGBOROUGH   TF1134   MAP 8

Fortescue Arms

B1177, off A52 Grantham—Boston; NG34 0QB

Fresh flowers and good value food at welcoming low-beamed country pub; pretty gardens

Lots of old stonework, exposed brickwork, wood panelling, beams and big log fires in two cosy see-through fireplaces give plenty of character to this lovely old place. Its several turkey-carpeted rooms have bay window seats, pleasant mainly Victorian prints, fresh flowers and pot plants, brass and copper, a stuffed badger and pheasant, and various quiz books. Attractive dining rooms at each end have flagstones and another open fire. Unusually, a long red and black tiled corridor runs right the way along behind the serving bar, making it an island. Here you'll find well kept Fullers London Pride, Greene King IPA Timothy Taylors Landlord and a guest such as Greene King Abbot on handpump; piped music and TV. There are picnic-sets on a lawn under apple trees on one side, and on the other a sheltered courtyard with flowers planted in tubs and a manger.

🍴 Very generously served food includes sandwiches and baguettes, ploughman's, soup, crispy whitebait, smoked mackerel, several pies, thai curry, chicken breast in white wine and mushroom sauce, battered cod, goats cheese and red onion tart, roast duck in orange sauce and 16oz T-bone; Sunday roasts. *Starters/Snacks: £2.95 to £5.95. Main Courses: £6.95 to £15.95. Puddings: £3.50 to £5.95*

Churchill Taverns ~ Managers Terry and Nicola Williams ~ Real ale ~ Bar food (12-2, 6-9.30; 12-9.30 weekends) ~ Restaurant ~ (01529) 240228 ~ Children welcome ~ Open 12-3, 5.30-11; 12-midnight Sat; 12-11 Sun

Recommended by W M Paton, Sally Anne and Peter Goodale, Beryl and Bill Farmer

CONINGSBY   TF2458   MAP 8

Lea Gate Inn

Leagate Road (B1192 southwards, off A153 E); LN4 4RS

Cosy old-fashioned interior, decent food, attractive garden, play area

Before the fens were drained, a perilous track through the marshes ran past this traditional 16th-c inn. Outside by the door, you can still see the small iron gantry that used to hold a lamp to guide travellers safely through the mist. The interior still conjures up the atmosphere of highwaymen lurking in snugs and visitors tucking themelves away from the bad weather. Three dimly lit areas have heavy black beams supporting ochre ceiling boards and are attractively furnished with antique oak settles with hunting-print cushions. Two great high-backed settles make a snug around the biggest of the fireplaces, and another fireplace has an interesting cast-iron depiction of the Last Supper; Charles Wells Bombardier and Theakstons XB and a guest such as Timothy Taylors Landlord on handpump; piped music. The appealing garden has tables and an enclosed play area.

🍴 Quickly served (even when busy) bar food includes soup, lunchtime sandwiches, grilled goats cheese on a croûton, mushroom stroganoff, steak and kidney pie, chicken breast filled with fresh spinach with tangy lemon and cream sauce, honey-glazed duck breast with plum and fresh ginger sauce, fried salmon with lime and coriander dressing and beef

wellington, and puddings such as banoffi pie and Baileys and chocolate cheesecake.
Starters/Snacks: £3.25 to £5.95. Main Courses: £7.95 to £12.95. Puddings: £3.25

Free house ~ Licensee Mark Dennison ~ Real ale ~ Bar food (12-2, 6-9) ~ Restaurant ~
(01526) 342370 ~ Children welcome ~ Open 11(12 Sun)-3, 6-11 ~ Bedrooms: £60B/£80B
*Recommended by Bill and Sheila McLardy, Martin and Alison Stainsby, the Didler, Ron and Sheila Corbett,
W K Wood*

DRY DODDINGTON
SK8546   MAP 8

Wheatsheaf
1½ miles off A1 N of Grantham; Main Street; NG23 5HU

Happy bustling family-run pub with good food; handy for A1

The atmosphere at this spotlessly kept mainly 16th-c colourwashed village pub is
buoyantly friendly, and the cheery landlord seems to have time for a word with everyone.
The front bar is basically two rooms, with a log fire, a variety of settles and chairs, and
tables in the windows facing across to the green and the lovely 14th-c church with its
crooked tower. The serving bar on the right has well kept Caledonian Deuchars IPA,
Greene King Abbot, Timothy Taylors Landlord and Tom Woods Best on handpump, good
hot drinks, and a nice choice of wines by the glass. A slight slope takes you back down
to the comfortable thickly carpeted and recently extended dining room with its relaxing
red and cream décor. Once a cow byre, this part is even more ancient than the rest of the
building, perhaps dating from the 13th c. The front terrace has neat dark green tables
under cocktail parasols, among tubs of flowers; disabled access at the side.

🍴 **Good food might include soup, fried black pudding with onion bruschetta topped with
a poached egg, sweet chilli, prawn and cod fishcake with oyster and ginger sauce, steak
and ale pie, roast duck breast with morello cherry and brandy sauce, crispy cod with
tomato and cucumber salsa, and 12oz rib-eye.** *Starters/Snacks: £4.25 to £5.95. Main Courses:
£7.95 to £16.95. Puddings: £3.25 to £3.95*

Free house ~ Licensees Bob and Josie Dyer ~ Real ale ~ Bar food (12-2, 6-9.30; 12-8 Sun) ~
Restaurant ~ (01400) 281458 ~ Children welcome if dining ~ Open 12-2.30(3 Sat), 5(6 Sat)-11;
12-8 Sun; closed Sun evening, Mon, Tues morning
*Recommended by Michael and Jenny Back, Andy and Jill Kassube, Grahame Brooks, Di and Mike Gillam, Derek and
Sylvia Stephenson, Mrs Roxanne Chamberlain, Frank Gorman*

HOUGH-ON-THE-HILL
SK9246   MAP 8

Brownlow Arms
High Road; NG32 2AZ

Refined country house with beamed bar, imaginative food and graceful terrace

This smartly upmarket old stone inn is in a peaceful village and has a comfortably
civilised air. The beamed bar (drinkers are welcome) has plenty of panelling, some
exposed brickwork, local prints and scenes, a large mirror, and a pile of logs beside the
big fireplace. Seating is on mismatched, elegant armchairs, and the carefully arranged
furnishings give the impression of several separate and surprisingly cosy areas; piped
easy listening. Greene King IPA, Marstons Pedigree and Timothy Taylors Landlord and a
good choice of malt whiskies are served by friendly, impeccably polite staff. The well
equipped bedrooms are attractive, and breakfasts are hearty.

🍴 **Very good (though not cheap) food might include starters such as butternut and
parmesan soup, baked cheese soufflé with smoked haddock, leeks and cream, confit of
pork belly with parsnip and vanilla purée, main courses such as beef bourguignon, stilton
risotto with celeriac and leaf spinach, herb-crusted confit of lamb shoulder with crushed
winter vegetables and red wine rosemary jus, duck breast and creamed brussels sprouts
with chestnuts and bacon, and puddings such as warm chocolate brownie with honeycomb
ice-cream and vanilla panna cotta with plums poached in wine.** *Starters/Snacks: £4.75 to
£7.95. Main Courses: £12.50 to £15.95. Puddings: £5.50*

Free house ~ Licensee Paul L Willoughby ~ Real ale ~ Restaurant ~ (01400) 250234 ~
Open 6-11; 12-3 Sun; closed Mon, lunchtimes Tues-Sat, Sun evening, 1 week in September,
3 weeks in January ~ Bedrooms: £65B/£96B

Recommended by Andy and Jill Kassube, Keith Wright, Maurice and Janet Thorpe, Dr A G Gibson

INGHAM
SK9483   MAP 8

Inn on the Green
The Green; LN1 2XT

Nicely modernised place popular for good food; chatty atmosphere

It's quite likely that most of the tables at this welcoming pub will be occupied by diners
– no mean feat given that the beamed and timbered dining room is spread over two
floors. Though there's some emphasis on food, it feels like a proper pub, with a good
chatty atmosphere throughout, particularly in the locals' bar, with its inglenook fireplace.
There's lots of exposed brickwork, and a mix of brasses and copper, local prints and bric-
a-brac. The brick bar counter has home-made jams, marmalade and chutney for sale
alongside Black Sheep and a couple of guests such as Greene King IPA and Shepherd
Neame Spitfire; readers have particularly praised the wines here. Opposite is a
comfortably laid-back area with two red leather sofas; piped music, and service is good.

🍴 **Good food is all home made. As well as sandwiches, a typical menu might include
starters such as leek and potato soup, smoked haddock risotto, potted pork and guinea
fowl with pickled gherkins, main courses such as chicken breast with mushroom stuffing
baked in pastry, goats cheese and shallot tart, rabbit and mustard stew and rib-eye steak,
and puddings such as warm chocolate cheesecake and lemon tart with chocolate sorbet.**
Starters/Snacks: £3.50 to £4.85. Main Courses: £5.00 to £10.95. Puddings: £3.60 to £3.90

Free house ~ Licensees Andrew Cafferkey and Sarah Sharpe ~ Real ale ~ Bar food (12-2.15,
6.30-9.30; 12-6.30 Sun) ~ Restaurant ~ (01522) 730354 ~ Children welcome ~ Open 11.30-3,
6-11; 11-3, 6-midnight Sat; 12-10.30 Sun; closed Mon

Recommended by Derek and Sylvia Stephenson

LINCOLN
SK9771   MAP 8

Victoria 🍺 £
Union Road; LN1 3BJ

Simple and popular real-ale pub with nine beers and cheap lunchtime food

This down-to-earth early Victorian local (which isn't to everyone's taste), up a steep back
street behind the castle, is popular for its fine choice of up to nine real ales and good
value straightforward food. Along with Batemans XB and XXXB, Castle Rock Harvest Pale
and Timothy Taylors Landlord, friendly staff serve five or six guests from brewers such as
Hopback and Highwood, as well as foreign draught and bottled beers, around 20 country
wines, a farm cider on tap, and cheap soft drinks. They hold beer festivals in the last
week in June and the first week in December. The simply furnished little tiled front
lounge has a coal fire and pictures of Queen Victoria and attracts a nicely mixed
clientele; it gets especially busy at lunchtime and later on in the evening. There's a small
conservatory and a gravelled side garden, which has good views of the castle.

🍴 **Basic lunchtime food, from a short menu, includes filled cobs, all-day breakfast, beef
stew, chilli, curry and ploughman's; Sunday roast.** *Starters/Snacks: £1.95 to £3.75. Main
Courses: £4.95 to £5.25. Puddings: £1.95*

Batemans ~ Tenant Neil Renshaw ~ Real ale ~ Bar food (12(11 Sat)-2.30(2 Sun)) ~ (01522)
536048 ~ Well behaved children welcome ~ Open 11(12 Sun)-11(11.30 Sat)

Recommended by Andy and Jill Kassube, Joe Green, the Didler, P Dawn, Fred and Lorraine Gill, David Carr

Wig & Mitre ★ ⑪ ⚲

Steep Hill; just below cathedral; LN2 1LU

Civilised café-style dining pub with imaginative (though not cheap) food all day and chatty bustling atmosphere

Spreading over a couple of floors, this very popular place dates from the 14th c, and has plenty of period architectural features. The big-windowed beamed downstairs bar has exposed stone walls, pews and gothic furniture on oak floorboards, and comfortable sofas in a carpeted back area. Upstairs, the somewhat calmer dining room is light and airy, with views of the castle walls and cathedral, shelves of old books, and an open fire. Walls are hung with antique prints and caricatures of lawyers and clerics, and there are plenty of newspapers and periodicals lying about – even templates to tempt you to a game of noughts and crosses. They have nearly three dozen wines by the glass (from a good list), lots of liqueurs and spirits and well kept Batemans XB and Black Sheep on handpump. It can get busy at peak times so it's useful to know that you can pop in and get something to eat at almost any time of day.

⑪ As well as a full breakfast and a sandwich menu, seasonal dishes might include soup, iranian caviar, cheese, red onion and thyme soufflé, smoked salmon with shallots, capers and lemon, roast halibut bourguignon, fried pork fillet with black pudding and celeriac purée, spinach, pine nuts and tomatoes, and goats cheese wrapped in filo pastry with rosemary butter. Puddings might be apricot cheesecake with walnut shortbread and dark chocolate and orange crème brûlée. Some reader's have found the food a bit pricy, though most feel it's worth the money. *Starters/Snacks: £4.75 to £8.75. Main Courses: £10.95 to £22.95. Puddings: £4.95*

Free house ~ Licensee Toby Hope ~ Real ale ~ Bar food (8am-12pm) ~ Restaurant ~ (01522) 535190 ~ Children welcome ~ Open 8am-12pm

Recommended by Sarah and Peter Gooderham, Adrian Johnson, N R White, W M Lien, John and Bettye Reynolds, Richard, MDN, David and Ruth Hollands, Mike Vincent, Paul Boot, Peter and Eleanor Kenyon, David Glynne-Jones, Michael Butler, Kevin Blake, David Carr, Mrs R McLauchlan, Mr and Mrs Richard Osborne, Christopher Turner

ROTHWELL   TF1499   MAP 8

Blacksmiths Arms

Off B1225 S of Caistor; LN7 6AZ

Appealing beamed pub with decent food, five real ales and tables outside

The pleasant heavily beamed bar at this long white-painted pub is divided by a couple of arches and has a warm central coal fire, attractive wildlife prints, comfortable chairs and tables and a relaxed atmosphere; piped music, fruit machine, pool, darts and dominoes. Batemans Salem Porter, Black Sheep and Highwood Shepherds Delight are served on handpump alongside two guest beers and 15 malt whiskies. There are plenty of tables outside and the pub is handy for the Viking Way. Take care coming out of the car park as the pub is on a blind bend.

⑪ Fairly pubby food includes sandwiches, soup, smoked haddock and prawn risotto, burgers, salmon and prawn salad, lasagne, steak and ale pie, lamb shank in red wine sauce, battered haddock and steaks. They do a Sunday roast and an early evening special offer menu Monday to Friday. *Starters/Snacks: £2.75 to £5.75. Main Courses: £7.50 to £16.75. Puddings: £3.50*

Free house ~ Licensee Rachel Flello ~ Real ale ~ Bar food (12-2(3 Sun), 5(6 Sat, Sun)-9(9.30 Fri, Sat)) ~ Restaurant ~ (01472) 371300 ~ Open 12-3, 5-11.30; 12-11.30 Sat; 12-11 Sun
Recommended by Derek and Sylvia Stephenson

Post Office address codings confusingly give the impression that a few pubs are in Lincolnshire, when they're really in Cambridgeshire (which is where we list them).

SOUTH WITHAM

SK9219   MAP 8

Blue Cow 🍺

Village signposted just off A1 Stamford—Grantham (with brown sign for pub); NG33 5QB

Tap for its own Blue Cow real ales; traditional interior, pubby food, garden

This white-painted country pub has a relaxed pubby atmosphere in its two appealing rooms, which are completely separated by a big central open-plan counter, and have cottagey little windows. Décor is themed on a strong shade of blue – there are plush blue banquettes, blue flowery carpets and blue floral upholstered stools. Dark low beams and standing timbers are set off against a wealth of exposed stone-walls – this is actually a much older building than a first glance at its exterior might suggest. Some areas have shiny flagstones, and there are cottagey pictures and a mantelpiece above the fireplace in one bar; piped music, darts and TV. The attractive garden has tables on a pleasant terrace.

🍴 **Tasty quite straightforward food might include sandwiches, soup, baked potatoes, fish and chips, pies, duck in port sauce, curries and steaks.** *Starters/Snacks: £3.25 to £5.50. Main Courses: £5.50 to £12.75. Puddings: £2.00 to £3.25*

Own brew ~ Licensee Simon Crathorn ~ Real ale ~ Bar food (12-2.30, 6-9.30) ~ Restaurant ~ (01572) 768432 ~ Children welcome ~ Dogs welcome ~ Open 12-11 ~ Bedrooms: £45S/£55S

Recommended by the Didler, Andy and Jill Kassube, Comus and Sarah Elliott, B and M Kendall

STAMFORD

TF0306   MAP 8

George of Stamford ★ 🍽 ♓ 🛏

High Street, St Martins (B1081 S of centre, not the quite different central pedestrianised High Street); PE9 2LB

LINCOLNSHIRE DINING PUB OF THE YEAR

Handsome and historic coaching inn, relaxed and civilised, with very good food and wines, lovely courtyard, garden and bedrooms

This beautifully preserved grand old coaching inn was built in 1597 for Lord Burghley (though there are visible parts of a much older Norman pilgrims' hospice, and a crypt under the cocktail bar that may be 1,000 years old). During the 18th and 19th centuries it was the hub of 20 coach trips a day between London and York (two of the front rooms take their names from these destinations). Seating in the beautifully furnished rooms ranges through leather, cane and antique wicker to soft settees and easy chairs. The central lounge has sturdy timbers, broad flagstones, heavy beams, and massive stonework, and the York Bar (where you can get snacks) is surprisingly pubby. More elaborate meals are served in the oak-panelled restaurant (jacket and tie required) and less formal Garden Lounge restaurant (which has well spaced furniture on herringbone glazed bricks around a central tropical grove). The staff are professional, with waiter drinks service in the charming cobbled courtyard at the back, which has comfortable chairs and tables among attractive plant tubs and colourful hanging baskets on the ancient stone buildings. There's also a neatly kept walled garden, with a sunken lawn where croquet is often played. The very good range of drinks includes Adnams Broadside, Fullers London Pride and Greene King Ruddles County on handpump, an excellent choice of wines (many of which are italian and good value, with about 16 by the glass), freshly squeezed orange juice and malt whiskies.

🍴 **Snacks in the York Bar include soup, sandwiches, chicken liver pâté with cumberland sauce and ploughman's. Besides a generous cold buffet, the menu in the Garden Lounge takes in pasta strips with salmon and fresh peas in a saffron cream, oysters, dressed crab, caesar salad, smoked salmon fishcakes with spring onion and coriander and lamb shank with roast butternut squash and mint and chilli dressing; full afternoon tea.** *Starters/Snacks: £4.90 to £9.35. Main Courses: £9.95 to £22.00. Puddings: £5.75*

Pubs staying open all afternoon at least one day a week are listed at the back of the book.

Free house ~ Licensees Chris Pitman and Ivo Vannocci ~ Real ale ~ Bar food (11-11) ~
Restaurant ~ (01780) 750750 ~ Children welcome ~ Dogs allowed in bar and bedrooms ~ Open
11-11; 12-11 Sun ~ Bedrooms: £85B/£125B

*Recommended by Roy Bromell, Sally Anne and Peter Goodale, Michael Sargent, Derek Thomas, Les and Sandra
Brown, the Didler, Michael Dandy, David Carr, Kay and Alistair Butler, Mrs Margo Finlay, Jörg Kasprowski, Mike and
Sue Loseby, Fred Chamberlain, P Dawn, Mike Ridgway, Sarah Miles, David and Ruth Shillitoe, Di and Mike Gillam,
Mrs L Davies, Roy Hoing, Charles Gysin*

SURFLEET   TF2528   MAP 8
Mermaid
Just off A16 N of Spalding, on B1356 at bridge; PE11 4AB

Friendly old-fashioned pub with extensive waterside garden

The pretty terraced garden at this old-fashioned pub has lots of seats with thatched
parasols, and its own bar. The children's play area is safely walled from the River Glen
which runs beside the pub. Décor in the two very traditional high-ceilinged rooms is
largely 70s in style, with green patterned carpets and red Anaglypta dado, huge netted
sash windows, navigation lanterns, horse tack on cream textured walls and a mixture of
banquettes and stools; cribbage and dominoes. A small central glass-backed bar counter
(complete with what is surely quite collectable Babycham décor) serves Adnams
Broadside, Everards Original or Tiger and Greene King IPA on handpump, as well as quite
a few malt whiskies. Two steps down, the restaurant is decorated in a similar style; piped
music.

🍽 **Bar food includes filled ciabattas, soup, sausage and mash, ricotta and goats cheese
tart with mediterranean vegetables, lasagne, roast oxtail and mash, battered cod with
chips and mushy peas, roast duck and 10oz sirloin steak.** *Starters/Snacks: £3.95 to £5.75.
Main Courses: £7.00 to £14.95. Puddings: £3.50*

Free house ~ Licensee Chris Bustance ~ Real ale ~ Bar food (11.45-2, 6-9; 12-3, 6-9 Sun) ~
Restaurant ~ (01775) 680275 ~ Children welcome ~ Open 11.30-11; 12-10.30 Sun;
closed 3-5.30 in winter

*Recommended by Dr and Mrs R G J Telfer, Ian Stafford, Beryl and Bill Farmer, Michael and Jenny Back,
Ryta Lyndley*

WOOLSTHORPE   SK8334   MAP 8
Chequers 🍽 🍷
The one near Belvoir, signposted off A52 or A607 W of Grantham; NG32 1LU

**Interesting food at comfortably relaxed inn with good drinks; appealing castle views from
outside tables**

The heavy-beamed main bar at this 17th-c coaching inn has two big tables (one a
massive oak construction), a comfortable mix of seating including some handsome
leather chairs and leather banquettes, and a huge boar's head above a good log fire in
the big brick fireplace. Among cartoons on the wall are some of the illustrated claret
bottle labels from the series commissioned from famous artists, initiated by the late
Baron Philippe de Rothschild. The lounge on the right has a deep red colour scheme,
leather sofas, and big plasma TV, and on the left, there are more leather seats in a dining
area housed in what was once the village bakery. A corridor leads off to the light and airy
main restaurant which has contemporary pictures and a second bar; piped music. A good
range of drinks includes well kept Brewster's Marquis and a guest such as Black Sheep on
handpump, a selection of belgian beers, local fruit pressées, over 35 wines by the glass,
over 20 champagnes and 50 malt whiskies. There are good quality teak tables, chairs and
benches outside, and beyond some picnic-sets on the edge of the pub's cricket field, with
views of Belvoir Castle.

🍽 **Food ranges from pub classics to more imaginative dishes, but it's all pretty good.
There might be inventive sandwiches (such as red pepper, feta and olive), starters such as
cream of celeriac soup with stilton dumplings, ham hock and rabbit terrine, warm pigeon**

salad with lentil dressing, mushrooms and bacon lardons, main courses such as bass with braised fennel, brown shrimp and tomato butter sauce, gnocchi with blue cheese and herb cream cheese sauce, sausage and mash, roast saddle of venison with sweet potato purée and juniper and port jus, steaks, and puddings such as lemon tart and raspberry coulis; good value three-course weekday evening menu. *Starters/Snacks: £4.50 to £7.50. Main Courses: £11.00 to £19.00. Puddings: £5.50*

Free house ~ Licensee Justin Chad ~ Real ale ~ Bar food (12-2.30, 5.30-9.30; 12-4, 6-8.30) ~ Restaurant ~ (01476) 870701 ~ Children welcome ~ Dogs allowed in bar and bedrooms ~ Open 12-3, 5.30-11; 12-11 Sat; 12-10.30 Sun ~ Bedrooms: £49S(£55B)/£59B

Recommended by Barry Collett, Bruce and Sharon Eden, Derek and Sylvia Stephenson, Mrs E A Macdonald, Andy and Jill Kassube, MJB, Peter and Jo Smith, Ian Stafford

LUCKY DIP

Besides the fully inspected pubs, you might like to try these Lucky Dips recommended to us and described by readers (if you do, please send us reports: www.goodguides.co.uk).

ALFORD [TF4575]
☆ **Half Moon** LN13 9DG [West St (A1004)]: Well run pub/hotel with four real ales such as Bass, Everards Tiger and Greene King IPA, very wide food choice from sandwiches and baked potatoes to particularly good fish dishes, long-serving licensees and competent helpful staff, spacious L-shaped bar, attractive dining room, decorous lounge; children welcome (adaptable menu for them), nice fairy-lit back garden with barbecues, up-to-date bedrooms *(BB, Val and Alan Green, Richard and Jean Green)*
BARKSTON [SK9341]
Stag NG32 2NB [Church St]: Appealing beamed country pub with welcoming landlord, cheerful helpful staff, good home-made pubby food in left-hand dining bar with mixed tables and chairs, well kept Everards and a guest beer such as Tom Woods Highwood Bomber County, good wine choice, pool, darts and TV in second bar, small back conservatory; picnic-sets out in front and in back garden, pleasant village *(Andy and Jill Kassube)*
BOSTON [TF3444]
Coach & Horses PE21 6SY [Main Ridge]: Friendly traditional one-bar pub with well kept Batemans XB and XXB, good coal fire, pool and darts; cl wkdy lunchtimes *(the Didler)*
BRANDY WHARF [TF0196]
☆ **Cider Centre** DN21 4RU [B1205 SE of Scunthorpe (off A15 about 16 miles N of Lincoln)]: Up to 15 ciders on draught, eight tapped from casks, many more in bottles and other smallish containers, also country wines and meads; plain take-us-as-you-find-us bright main bar and dimmer lounge with lots of cider memorabilia and jokey bric-a-brac, reasonably priced straightforward food (all day Sun); piped music, and housekeeping could be perked up; children in eating area, simple glazed verandah, tables and play area in meadows or by river with moorings and slipway, may be cl Mon, open all day wknds *(the Didler, LYM)*

CASTLE BYTHAM [SK9818]
☆ **Castle Inn** NG33 4RZ [off A1 Stamford—Grantham, or B1176]: Comfortable black-beamed village pub with enjoyable straightforward food from baguettes and ciabattas up, Tues fish night, Fri steak night, helpful friendly staff, two quickly changing real ales, often local, good hot drinks, armchairs and huge log fire, pub dog called Skye, occasional beer festivals; disabled access, back terrace, cl Mon *(Michael and Jenny Back, LYM)*
CAYTHORPE [SK9348]
Red Lion NG32 3DN [signed just off A607 N of Grantham; High St]: Reopened early 2006 under new management, some emphasis on local supplies for the sensibly unpretentious food, Adnams and Everards ales, several small and simply decorated linked areas, beams and big inglenook, immaculate lavatories; back terrace by car park *(Phil and Jane Hodson, David and Gilly Wilkins, BB)*
Waggon & Horses NG32 3DR [High St]: Helpful pleasant staff, enjoyable if not cheap food freshly made to order, real ale *(MJB)*
CLEETHORPES [TA3009]
No 2 Refreshment Room DN35 8AX [Station Approach]: Well kept one-room platform bar with five changing ales from small breweries, friendly service, no food; tables out under heaters, open all day *(the Didler, P Dawn)*
☆ **Willys** DN35 8RQ [Highcliff Rd; south promenade]: Open-plan bistro-style seafront pub with panoramic Humber views, café tables, tiled floor and painted brick walls; visibly brews its own good beers, also Batemans and other changing ales, belgian beers, popular beer festival Nov, good value lunchtime home cooking (evening food too Mon/Tues and Thurs), friendly staff, nice mix of customers from young and trendy to weather-beaten fishermen; quiet juke box; a few tables out on the prom, open all day *(P Dawn, the Didler)*
CORBY GLEN [TF0024]
Coachman NG33 4NS [A151, between A1 and Bourne]: Pleasant atmosphere and staff,

wide choice of enterprising blackboard food, real ales, scrubbed pine tables and open fire *(Lesley and Barbara Owen, LYM)*

DYKE [TF1022]

Wishing Well PE10 0AF [village signed off A15 N of Bourne; Main St]: Long heavily beamed stripped stone front bar with huge fireplace, friendly helpful staff, Everards Tiger, Greene King Abbot and three guest beers, reasonably priced straightforward bar food from sandwiches to steaks, big restaurant, darts, pool, TV and so forth in public bar, small conservatory; children welcome, garden with tables and play area, bedrooms *(Barry Collett, LYM, Tony Brace)*

FULBECK [SK9450]

Hare & Hounds NG32 3JJ [The Green (A607 Leadenham—Grantham)]: Reopened after successful refurbishment, good variety of tables, chairs and sofas in linked areas, enjoyable bar food from sandwiches up, good range of ales and wines by the glass, attractive upstairs restaurant; nice village *(Michael and Maggie Betton)*

GAINSBOROUGH [SK8189]

Eight Jolly Brewers DN21 2DW [Ship Court, Silver St]: Small comfortable real ale pub with up to eight from small breweries inc its own Maypole, farm cider, simple lunchtime food (not Sun), friendly staff and locals, beams, bare bricks and brewery posters, quieter bar upstairs; folk club, open all day *(Michael and Maggie Betton, D A Bradford, the Didler)*

GEDNEY DYKE [TF4125]

Chequers PE12 0AJ [off A17 Holbeach—Kings Lynn]: Unpretentious and hospitable Fenland dining pub, food from sandwiches with home-baked bread to interesting main dishes, Adnams and Greene King Abbot, good coffee, simple bar with open fire, dining conservatory; piped music; children welcome, garden picnic-sets, cl Mon; late news as we went to press suggests this may have closed *(Ken Marshall, LYM, Ryta Lyndley, Eddie and Lynn Jarrett, John Wooll, Comus and Sarah Elliott, K E and B Billington, E J Sayer)*

GRANTHAM [SK9135]

☆ *Angel & Royal* NG31 6PN [High St]: Comfortable hotel with elaborate carved 14th-c stone façade, well restored ancient upstairs bars with formidable inglenook fireplaces and a charming little medieval oriel window seat jutting over the road, stylish downstairs bistro/bar with elegant modern tables, comfortable chairs on pale oak boards, up-to-date pastels and some stripped stonework, two real ales, wide choice of modern and traditional food, not cheap but worth the money, from good sandwiches up, grand-manner wknd restaurant; piped music, TV; children in eating areas, well equipped bedrooms in modern back extension alongside narrow flagstoned inner coachway, open all day *(LYM, David and Deirdre Renwick, Richard and Jean Green)*

Beehive NG31 6SE [Castlegate]: Hive of bees in the good-sized back garden's lime tree has been this simple brightly lit town pub's unique inn sign for a couple of centuries or more – same strain of bees all that time; real ales such as Everards and Newby Wyke, friendly service, coal fire; back games area with machines, juke box and TVs; children welcome till 7.30, open all day *(LYM, the Didler)*

☆ *Blue Pig* NG31 6RQ [Vine St]: Pretty jettied Tudor pub with half a dozen interesting changing ales, good generous basic pub lunches, reasonable prices, quick cheerful service, friendly unpretentious bustle, low beams, panelling, stripped stone and flagstones, open fire, daily papers, lots of pig ornaments, prints and bric-a-brac; piped music, juke box, games machines, no children or dogs; tables out behind, open all day *(BB, Nigel and Sue Foster, the Didler)*

Nobody Inn NG31 6NU [North St]: Friendly bare-boards open-plan local with five or six good ales mainly from local breweries such as Newby Wyke and Oldershaws; back games room with pool, table footer, SkyTV; open all day *(the Didler)*

Tollemache NG31 6PY [St Peters Hill/Catherine Rd]: Roomy and popular Wetherspoons in former Co-op (appropriate memorabilia), interesting choice of well kept ales, good coffee, prompt helpful service, good value food inc generous children's bargains, big lower-level family area, leather settee and armchairs by open fire, old books and local pictures; attractive big terrace with fountain and play area, open all day, handy for Belton House *(Andy and Jill Kassube)*

GREATFORD [TF0811]

Hare & Hounds PE9 4QA: Appealing dining pub with wide choice of enjoyable fresh food inc very popular bargain lunch (worth booking), pleasant staff, well kept ales such as Adnams Broadside, Oakham and Charles Wells Bombardier, large beamed bar, smaller dining room; picnic-sets in small back garden, attractive village *(LYM, Roy Bromell)*

HACONBY [TF1025]

Hare & Hounds PE10 0UZ [off A15 N of Bourne; West Rd]: Emphasis on enjoyable imaginative food at sensible prices in recently upgraded pub *(Tony Brace)*

HALTON HOLEGATE [TF4165]

☆ *Bell* PE23 5NY [B1195 E of Spilsby]: Pretty village local, simple but comfortable and consistently friendly, with Batemans XB, Highwood Tom Woods Bomber County and guest beers, Lancaster bomber pictures, pub games, low-priced generous food cooked by landlord; children in back eating area with tropical fish tank and restaurant *(LYM, the Didler)*

HARLAXTON [SK8833]

Gregory Arms NG32 1AD [A607 Grantham—Melton]: Attractively restored and opened-up dining pub under welcoming management (new 2006), good food with nice slants on traditional dishes, interesting reasonably priced wines, well kept ales inc Theakstons XB, informal area around bar linking to further eating areas, glass-covered well *(Michael and Maggie Betton)*

KIRKBY LA THORPE [TF0945]

Queens Head NG34 9NW [Boston Rd, backing on to A17]: Attractive and comfortable dining pub with large bar, small cosy restaurant and light and airy conservatory, good choice of enjoyable food from well filled sandwiches and baguettes (home-baked bread) to fresh fish, pleasant service, Batemans and Marstons Pedigree, decent house wine; easy disabled access, terrace tables *(Maurice and Janet Thorpe, Bill and Sheila McLardy)*

KIRKBY ON BAIN [TF2462]

Ebrington Arms LN10 6YT [Main St]: Generous good value food inc cheap Sun lunch, five or more well kept changing ales such as Black Sheep, prompt welcoming service, daily papers, low 16th-c beams, two open fires, nicely set out dining areas each side, copper-topped tables, wall banquettes, jet fighter and racing car pictures, games area with darts, restaurant, beer festivals Easter and Aug bank hols; may be piped music; wheelchair access, tables out in front, swings on side lawn, camp site behind, open all day *(Brian Wiles)*

LEADENHAM [SK9452]

Willoughby Arms LN5 0PP [High St; A17 Newark—Sleaford]: Good-looking pub with pleasant décor in comfortable bar, friendly hard-working staff, good food in two eating areas; comfortable bedrooms *(Beryl and Bill Farmer, Christopher Turner)*

LINCOLN [SK9772]

Duke William LN1 3AP [Bailgate]: Converted row of 18th-c oak-beamed cottages close to cathedral with friendly wkdy evening atmosphere (can be busier wknds), Greene King Abbot, lunchtime bar food, restaurant; 12 bedrooms, good breakfast *(Michael Butler)*

Golden Eagle LN5 8BD [High St]: Traditional two-bar Tynemill town pub, up to half a dozen or more good value changing ales such as Batemans, Castle Rock and Everards, good choice of country wines, cheap soft drinks, bargain lunchtime rolls, cheery back bar; tables in good-sized garden behind, open all day *(the Didler, Andy and Jill Kassube)*

Lion & Snake LN1 3AR [Bailgate]: Reputedly the city's oldest pub, thoughtful friendly service, well kept Marstons, simple food and unpretentious surroundings; tables outside *(MDN)*

Morning Star LN2 4AW [Greetwell Gate]: Friendly well scrubbed local handy for cathedral, enjoyable cheap lunches esp Fri specials, reasonably priced Bass, Greene King Abbot, Tetleys, Charles Wells Bombardier and guest beers, helpful service, coal fire, aircraft paintings, two bar areas and comfortable snug with sofas; enthusiastic singer/pianist Sat night; nice outside area, open all day

exc Sun *(Pete Baker, David and Ruth Hollands, the Didler, John Robertson)*

Pyewipe LN1 2BG [Saxilby Rd; off A57 just S of bypass]: Much extended and well worn in 18th-c waterside pub particularly popular for Sun lunch, wide range of other decent food inc good fish choice, friendly attentive staff, Boddingtons, Greene King Abbot, Timothy Taylors Landlord and Wells & Youngs Bombardier, great position by Roman Fossdyke Canal (nice two-mile walk out from centre); pleasant tables outside, comfortable reasonably priced bedroom block *(David and Ruth Hollands, Maurice and Janet Thorpe, M and C Thompson, Michael Butler)*

Sippers LN5 7HW [Melville St, opp bus stn]: Two-bar pub with good value lunchtime food inc good Sun lunch (can book evening meals too), Hop Back real ales with others such as John Smiths and Marstons Pedigree; open all day (Sun afternoon break) *(the Didler, Joe Green)*

☆ *Strugglers* LN1 3BG [Westgate]: Smartly simple character local with thriving atmosphere, particularly well kept ales such as Bass, Batemans, Black Sheep, Fullers London Pride and Timothy Taylors Landlord, good value above-average lunchtime food (not Sun/Mon), coal-effect fire in small back snug, interesting pictures, heaters and canopy for terrace tables (no under-18s inside), open all day *(David and Ruth Hollands, Kevin Blake, Michael Butler, the Didler)*

Swanholme LN6 3RX [Doddington Rd]: Large modern lakeside pub, comfortable and friendly, with real ale in pleasant bar, enjoyable food all day in big dining area with facilities for children; spacious back terrace overlooking water *(Mrs Brenda Calver)*

Tap & Spile LN1 1ES [Hungate]: Half a dozen well kept changing ales such as Caledonian Deuchars IPA, farm cider and country wines from central bar, small choice of reasonably priced pubby food, friendly staff and atmosphere, linked areas with bare boards and brickwork, stone floors, framed beer mats, prints and breweriana; live music Fri; open all day *(Joe Green, the Didler)*

Tower LN1 3BD [Westgate]: Three well kept real ales, good choice of wines and malt whiskies, comfortable conservatory bar, enjoyable light bistro food, evening restaurant; 14 comfortably updated bedrooms, cathedral views from stylish heated terrace, open all day *(John Duncan)*

Treaty of Commerce LN5 7AF [High St]: Warmly welcoming, lively and simple pub in beamed Tudor building with fine old stained glass, antique etchings and panelling, good value bar lunches (not Sun/Mon) from generous baguettes up, well kept Batemans and guest beers, darts; open all day *(the Didler, Andy and Jill Kassube)*

LITTLE BYTHAM [TF0117]

☆ *Willoughby Arms* NG33 4RA [Station Rd, S of village]: Good Newby Wyke beers from back microbrewery, interesting guest beers, Weston's farm cider, frequent beer festivals, reasonably priced substantial food from sandwiches up, friendly helpful staff, daily papers, simple bar with wall banquettes, stripped tables and coal fire, pleasant end dining room; piped music, airy games room with pool and sports TV; good disabled access, children welcome, picnic-sets in pleasant good-sized back garden with quiet country views, bedrooms, open all day wknds (BB, the Didler, Bill and Sheila McLardy)

LONG BENNINGTON [SK8344]

☆ **Reindeer** NG23 5DJ [just off A1 N of Grantham]: Thriving atmosphere in old inn with welcoming landlady, good choice of enjoyable home-made food from sandwiches up in bar and more formal dining lounge, cut-price small helpings, well kept real ales, good wines (Maurice and Janet Thorpe, Grahame Brooks)

LOUTH [TF3287]

Olde Whyte Swanne LN11 9NP [Eastgate]: Low 16th-c beams, coal or log fires in comfortable and relaxed front bar and dining room, good choice of enjoyable food all day using local produce, helpful friendly staff, real ales such as Black Sheep, Greene King and Theakstons; children welcome, open all day from 9.30, bedrooms (the Didler)

Wheatsheaf LN11 9YD [Westgate]: Cheerful early 17th-c low-beamed pub, coal fires in all three bars, changing real ales and a late May beer festival, decent lunchtime food (not Sun), old photographs; tables outside, open all day Sat (Maurice and Janet Thorpe, the Didler)

MARKET DEEPING [TF1309]

Deeping Stage PE6 8EA [Market Pl]: Enjoyable bar food from baguettes up, pleasant helpful staff, lounge bar with contemporary décor and comfortable leather easy chairs and settees, neat modern restaurant; picnic-sets on flagstoned terrace by River Welland, eight comfortable bedrooms, open all day from 10 (Richard Fox)

MESSINGHAM [SE8905]

Bird in the Barley DN17 3SQ [Northfield Rd (A159 S of Scunthorpe)]: Large U-shaped pub with central bar, welcoming staff, decent well presented food (not Sun evening or Mon), reasonable prices, farmland views; cl Mon lunchtime (Kay and Alistair Butler)

NETTLEHAM [TF0075]

Plough LN2 2NR [just off A46/A15; 1 The Green]: Good choice of enjoyable reasonably priced food in spotless proper village pub, well kept Batemans XXXB, obliging landlady (Ann Tyas, Alastair Robertson)

NEWTON [TF0436]

Red Lion NG34 0EE [off A52 E of Grantham]: Country pub of some character, old-fashioned seating, partly stripped stone walls with old farm tools and stuffed birds and animals, Batemans XB and Everards Old Original, straightforward bar food from sandwiches up inc carvery dishes; piped

music, games machine; tables in sheltered back garden with terrace (LYM, Maurice and Janet Thorpe, W W Burke)

NORTH KELSEY [TA0401]

Butchers Arms LN7 6EH [Middle St; off B1434 S of Brigg]: Busy village local with five well kept Tom Woods Highwood beers, low ceilings, flagstones, bare boards, dim lighting, good value cold lunches, enthusiastic cheerful service, log fire, pub games; garden picnic-sets, opens 4 wkdys, open all day wknds (the Didler)

OWSTON FERRY [SE8100]

White Hart DN9 1RT [North St]: Enjoyable home-made pubby food Thurs-Sun inc Thurs bargain suppers for two, John Smiths and a guest such as Adnams or Batemans; HD sports TV; barbecues in garden by River Trent (good spot to watch the Aegir tidal bore – Environment Agency website has timetable) (Rob Vevers)

REDBOURNE [SK9799]

☆ **Red Lion** DN21 4QR [Main Rd (B1206 SE of Scunthorpe)]: Welcoming and comfortable traditional coaching inn with thriving atmosphere, good value home-made food from lunchtime sandwiches and baguettes up inc some individual dishes and specials, and nice cheeses, helpful staff, three or four real ales such as Black Sheep, Tetleys and Wells & Youngs Bombardier, coal fire, flagstones, polished panelling and some duck ornamentation, darts end, garden room restaurant; dogs welcome, garden with terrace, attractive village, decent bedrooms and breakfast, open all day (Trevor and Sheila Sharman, BB, Michael Butler)

SAXILBY [SK8975]

Bridge LN1 2LX [Gainsborough Rd]: Large mock-Tudor canalside pub with good food range inc fresh fish, Greene King and Abbot, quick efficient service, roomy new back conservatory; neat and extensive waterside lawns (David and Ruth Hollands)

SCAMPTON [SK9579]

Dambusters LN1 2SD [High St]: Beams, hops and masses of interesting Dambusters and other World War II memorabilia, reasonably priced simple food (not Sun/Mon evenings) inc good Sun lunch served well into late afternoon, pleasant nostalgic atmosphere, Greene King and guest beers, log fire, adjoining post office; very near Red Arrows runway viewpoint (Mrs Carolyn Dixon, Kay and Alistair Butler)

SCOTTER [SE8800]

☆ **White Swan** DN21 3UD [The Green]: Comfortable well kept dining pub, varied well prepared generous food inc fish board and bargain three-course special, friendly landlady and good cheerful service, Black Sheep, John Smiths, Websters and interesting changing guest beers, several levels inc snug panelled area by one fireplace, big-windowed restaurant looking over lawn with picnic-table sets to duck-filled River Eau (best to book wknds); piped music, steps up to entrance; 14 comfortable bedrooms in modern extension, open all day Fri-Sun (BB, Keith Wright, Kay and Alistair Butler)

SKEGNESS [TF5661]

☆ **Vine** PE25 3DB [Vine Rd, off Drummond Rd, Seacroft]: Refurbished as Best Western hotel, based on late 18th-c country house, Batemans ales, good bar food using local produce, welcoming fire, imposing antique seats and grandfather clock in turkey-carpeted hall, inner oak-panelled room, restaurant; tables on big back sheltered lawn with swings, comfortable bedrooms, peaceful suburban setting not far from beach and bird-watching, open all day (P Dawn, BB, the Didler, John Tav)

SLEAFORD [TF0645]

Barge & Bottle NG34 7TR [Carre St]: Large busy open-plan pub handsomely done by local furniture-making family, impressive range of nine changing ales such as Batemans, Black Sheep, Greene King, Highwood, Springhead, Tetleys and Theakstons, wide range of usual food from baguettes to full meals and good value Sun carvery, also children's dishes, teas, bargain early breakfasts and plenty of special offers, back restaurant/conservatory; piped music; riverside terrace, children welcome, handy for arts centre, open all day (Andy and Jill Kassube, Tony and Wendy Hobden)

SOUTH ORMSBY [TF3675]

☆ **Massingberd Arms** LN11 8QS [off A16 S of Louth]: Small brick-built village pub, friendly and relaxed, with unusual arched windows, obliging landlord, Tom Woods and other changing ales, short choice of enjoyable fresh food inc game and good Sun lunch, restaurant; no credit cards; pleasant garden, good Wolds walks, cl Mon lunchtime (the Didler, Derek and Sylvia Stephenson)

SOUTH THORESBY [TF4076]

☆ **Vine** LN13 0AS [about a mile off A16 N of Ulceby Cross]: Two-room village inn with small local pub part – tiny passageway servery, steps up to three-table lounge, separate pool room; wide choice of quickly served food, prompt welcoming service, Batemans XB, good value wines, nicely panelled dining room; tables in pleasant big garden, bedrooms (the Didler)

STAMFORD [TF0306]

☆ **Bull & Swan** PE9 2LJ [High St, St Martins]: New licensees in traditional pub with three low-beamed connecting rooms, good log fires, gleaming copper and brass, has had friendly helpful staff, enjoyable food, real ales such as Adnams, Caledonian Deuchars IPA and Wychwood Hobgoblin; children welcome, tables out in former back coachyard, bedrooms, good breakfast; reports on new regime, please (LYM, Ray and Winifred Halliday, Kay and Alistair Butler, Mike Ridgway, Sarah Miles, P Dawn)

☆ **Crown** PE9 2AG [All Saints Pl]: Substantial stone-built hotel, long a popular meeting point, with emphasis on good seasonal country cooking using local produce from

light snacks up, very friendly staff, four good changing ales inc Ufford, decent wines, whiskies and coffee, distinctively updated spacious main bar, long leather-cushioned bar counter, substantial pillars, unusual lighting giving pinkish hue, step up to more traditional flagstoned area with stripped stone and and lots of leather sofas and armchairs, fresh flowers, civilised dining room; heated outdoor area for smokers, comfortable quiet bedrooms, open all day (Derek Thomas, BB, M and C Thompson, Andy and Jill Kassube)

Green Man PE9 2YQ [Scotgate]: Half a dozen or more changing ales inc Caledonian Deuchars IPA and Theakstons, belgian beers, farm ciders, friendly staff, good value lunchtime food, sturdy scrubbed pale wood tables on flagstones, log fire, steps up to back room with good bottle collection and TV; garden tables, comfortable bedrooms sharing bathroom, open all day (P Dawn, the Didler)

Jims Yard PE9 1PL [Ironmonger St]: New bar opened late summer 2006, pleasant staff, wide-ranging good food at value prices (Roy Bromell)

Periwig PE9 2AG [Red Lion Sq/All Saints Pl]: Good value food from baguettes and good cheeseboards up, half a dozen good real ales such as Milestone and Oakham, nice coffees, gallery above narrow split-level bar, bistro-style eating area, attractive façade; piped music, sports TV, can get busy with lively young people evenings; open all day (Andy and Jill Kassube, P Dawn)

STOW [SK8881]

☆ **Cross Keys** LN1 2DD [B1241 NW of Lincoln]: Reliable extended dining pub nr Saxon minster church, charming helpful service, prettily presented fresh food inc lots of interesting blackboard specials served piping hot, particularly good veg and good puddings, well kept Greene King, Highgate Tom Woods and Theakstons ales, good range of wines, quick friendly service, big woodburner in attractively modernised bar; may be piped music; cl Mon lunchtime (BB, Dr and Mrs J Temporal, Bill and Sheila McLardy, David and Ruth Hollands)

SURFLEET SEAS END [TF2729]

☆ **Ship** PE11 4DH [Reservoir Rd; off A16 N of Spalding]: Handsomely rebuilt riverside pub with river view from smart big-windowed upstairs restaurant and its balcony, broad steps up from flagstoned hall, woodburner and leather sofas in good-sized bar with well spaced old scrubbed tables in big open bays, young chef doing good food using local supplies, good staff, well kept ales; tables out on bank over road (Sally Anne and Peter Goodale)

SUSWORTH [SE8302]

☆ **Jenny Wren** DN17 3AS [East Ferry Rd]: Popular neatly kept country pub in nice setting with long partly divided bar/dining area overlooking River Trent, wide choice of good enterprising food at reasonable prices inc lots of fish and local produce, panelling, stripped brickwork, low beams and brasses, busy décor and plenty of tables, pleasant staff, real ales such as John Smiths and Tom Woods, good wines by the glass, two open fires; some picnic-sets on terrace and more across quiet road by water, monthly classic car rallies *(Emma Mitchell, Mr and Mrs G Sadie, BB)*

SWINDERBY [SK8862]

☆ *Dovecote* LN6 9HN [Halfway House, Newark Rd (A46, Lincoln-bound carriageeway)]: Attractive 18th-c building reopened 2005 after careful restoration, wide choice of generous food from doorstep sandwiches and good pubby standbys to imaginative dishes and even lobster, two real ales inc local Poachers Pride, rugs on flagstones, old auction notices lining walls, farm tools on ceiling, neatly kept separate dining room (not always open); children welcome *(James Browne, David and Ruth Hollands)*

TATTERSHALL THORPE [TF2159]

Blue Bell LN4 4PE [Thorpe Rd; B1192 Coningsby—Woodhall Spa]: Attractive very low-beamed pub said to date from 13th c and used by the Dambusters, RAF memorabilia and appropriate real ales such as Highgate Tom Woods Bomber County and Poachers Pathfinders, good choice of reasonably priced bar food inc bargain pie, log fires, small dining room; tables in garden, impressive lavatera bushes, bedrooms *(the Didler)*

TETFORD [TF3374]

☆ *White Hart* LN9 6QQ [East Rd, off A158 E of Horncastle]: Early 16th-c rustic pub with good value food inc good local beef, Adnams, Fullers London Pride and Greene King, farm cider, friendly staff, old-fashioned curved-back settles, slabby elm tables, red tiled floor and log fire in pleasant quiet inglenook bar, basic games room; tables on sheltered back lawn, simple bedrooms,

pretty countryside, cl Mon lunchtime *(LYM, the Didler)*

WAINFLEET [TF5058]

☆ *Batemans Brewery* PE24 4JE [Mill Lane, off A52 via B1195]: Circular bar in brewery's ivy-covered windmill tower with Batemans ales in top condition, czech and belgian beers on tap, ground-floor dining area with unpretentious lunchtime food such as local sausages and pork pies, games room with plenty of old pub games (more of these outside), lots of brewery memorabilia and plenty for families to enjoy; entertaining brewery tours at 2.30, brewery shop (helpful service), tables out on terrace and grass, opens 11.30-3.30 *(P Dawn, Andy and Jill Kassube, the Didler)*

WELTON HILL [TF0481]

☆ *Farmers Arms* LN2 3RD [Market Rasen Rd (A46 NE of Lincoln)]: Well run, comfortable and very spacious dining pub, hearty helpings of good fresh sensibly priced food from baguettes to popular Sun lunch, emphasis on top-notch local produce, lots of wine by the glass (wine-themed décor and events), changing ales such as Ringwood Bold Forester and local Tom Woods, prompt service from helpful friendly licensees and neat staff, panelling and some stripped brickwork, houseplants and fresh flowers; good disabled access *(BB, Mrs Brenda Calver, R Pearce)*

WOODHALL SPA [TF1962]

☆ *Abbey Lodge* LN10 6UH [B1192 towards Coningsby]: Family-run roadside inn with good reasonably priced food from sandwiches to substantial meals, affable staff, nice pubby feel mixing eating and drinking sides well, bustling discreetly decorated bar with good choice of beers and wines, Victorian and older furnishings, World War II RAF pictures, Marstons Pedigree; children over 10 in restaurant, may be piped music; cl Sun *(Mr and Mrs J Brown, John Branston, LYM)*

Norfolk

Pubs in this part of the country bustle with friendliness and are often full of cheerful customers. Of course many of these are visitors, particularly in the summer, but the locals seem to be out in force whatever the weather. Pubs on particularly good form currently include the Kings Head at Bawburgh (smiling service and really good food), the White Horse in Blakeney (a busy little hotel), the White Horse at Brancaster Staithe (a super all-rounder), the Hoste Arms in Burnham Market (stylish, smart and very well run), the Crown at Colkirk (new to this edition, an appealing and unpretentious all-rounder), the Walpole Arms at Itteringham (popular for its ambitious food), the Angel at Larling (friendly landlord and good beers), the busy Fat Cat in Norwich (up to 30 real ales at appealing prices), the Rose & Crown at Snettisham (always raising its game, with very wide appeal), the cheerful Ostrich at South Creake (good choice of food and drink), the Woolpack at Terrington St John (the bouncy landlady makes this special), the Old Ram at Tivetshall St Mary (smart coaching inn with over two dozen wines by the glass), the Three Horseshoes at Warham (for those who love unchanging pubs) and the Wheatsheaf at West Beckham (a friendly village local with a welcome for all). Pub food here can be extremely good, and it's often imaginative too. What's more, with abundant fresh shellfish and fish, large estates that provide good game, and plenty of fine meat and fresh produce, prices for this top quality are no higher than the national average. Places offering super meals are the Kings Head at Bawburgh, the White Horse at Brancaster Staithe, the Hoste Arms in Burnham Market, the Saracens Head near Erpingham, the Walpole Arms at Itteringham, the Gin Trap at Ringstead and the Rose & Crown at Snettisham. Our Norfolk Dining Pub of the Year is the Hoste Arms in Burnham Market. Pubs currently catching our eye in the Lucky Dip section at the end of the chapter are the Black Boys in Aylsham, Spread Eagle at Barton Bendish, Chequers at Binham, Buckinghamshire Arms at Blickling, George at Cley next the Sea, Kings Head at Coltishall, Three Pigs at Edgefield, restauranty Kings Head at Great Bircham, Windmill at Great Cressingham, Rose & Crown at Harpley, Recruiting Sergeant at Horstead, Jolly Farmers at North Creake and Stag at West Acre. Drinks prices in Norfolk tend to be perhaps a trifle higher than the national norm. It's particularly worth looking out for the local Woodfordes beer, not just because it's good, but because it's quite often the cheapest beer a pub sells.

BAWBURGH

TG1508   MAP 5

Kings Head 🍴 🍷

*Pub signposted down Harts Lane off B1108, which leads off A47 just W of Norwich;
NR9 3LS*

**A wide choice of super food and drinks, cheerful service and small rooms with plenty of
atmosphere**

In a nice spot opposite a small green, this bustling old pub is particularly popular for its
top quality food served with a smile. There are wooden floors, leather sofas and seats, a
mix of nice old wooden tables and wooden or leather dining chairs, low beams and some
standing timbers, a warming log fire in a large knocked-through canopied fireplace, and a
couple of woodburning stoves in the restaurant areas. Adnams Bitter and Broadside and
Woodfordes Wherry on handpump, 20 wines by the glass and quite a few malt whiskies;
piped music. Seats outside in the garden.

🍴 **Attractively presented and imaginative, the bar food includes lunchtime filled rolls and
ciabattas and ploughman's, interesting soups, smoked haddock and prawn kedgeree with a
soft free-range egg, chilli, coriander and crispy onions, saffron, pea and mint risotto with
wild mushrooms, rocket and parmesan, and steak and mushroom pudding with honey-
roasted carrots; more elaborate choices as well such as seared scallops with cauliflower
purée and crispy bacon, potted brown shrimps with mace butter, crispy beef stir fry with
oyster sauce and noodles and moroccan chicken with aubergine ragoût, lemon couscous,
spinach and crème fraîche; puddings like rich dark chocolate pot with chantilly cream and
griottine cherries and warm treacle tart with home-made vanilla ice-cream, and two- and
three-course set meals, too.** *Starters/Snacks: £5.00 to £8.50. Main Courses: £8.50 to £12.50.
Puddings: £5.50 to £7.50*

Free house ~ Licensee Anton Wimmer ~ Real ale ~ Bar food (12-2(2.30 Sun), 6-9; not Sun or
Mon evenings) ~ Restaurant ~ (01603) 744977 ~ Children welcome ~ Dogs allowed in bar ~
Open 11-11; 12-10.30 Sun; closed evenings 25, 26 Dec and 1 Jan
*Recommended by Margaret McPhee, Anthony Barnes, Mark, Amanda, Luke and Jake Sheard, Sally Anne and Peter
Goodale, Alan Cowell*

BLAKENEY

TG0243   MAP 8

Kings Arms 🍺

West Gate Street; NR25 7NQ

**A stroll from the harbour, friendly and chatty, with reasonably priced straightforward food;
walled garden**

Mr and Mrs Davies have now run this attractive white inn for over 30 years. It's just a
stroll from the harbour and the three simply furnished, knocked-through pubby rooms
have a good mix of locals and visitors, low ceilings, some interesting photographs of the
licensees' theatrical careers, other pictures including work by local artists, and what must
be the smallest cartoon gallery in England – in a former telephone kiosk. Look out for the
brass plaque on the wall that marks a flood level. There's an airy garden room, too; darts,
games machine, bar billiards and board games. Adnams, Greene King Old Speckled Hen,
Marstons Pedigree and Woodfordes Wherry on handpump, and quite a few wines by the
glass. Lots of tables and chairs in the large garden; good nearby walks.

🍴 **Fair-priced bar food includes sandwiches, soup, filled baked potatoes, rough pork pâté,
vegetable burgers, local mussels (winter only), a pie of the day, gammon and egg, and
puddings such as chocolate torte or lemon tart.** *Starters/Snacks: £3.95 to £7.50. Main
Courses: £6.50 to £13.00. Puddings: £3.95 to £5.95*

Free house ~ Licensees John Howard, Marjorie Davies and Nick Davies ~ Real ale ~ Bar food
(12-9.30(9 Sun)) ~ (01263) 740341 ~ Children welcome ~ Dogs welcome ~ Open 11-11;
12-10.30 Sun; closed evening 25 Dec ~ Bedrooms: £45S/£65S
*Recommended by MDN, Pat and Tony Martin, Geoff and Pat Bell, David Carr, Ann and Colin Hunt, Alan Cole, Kirstie
Bruce, Simon Cottrell, Dr and Mrs P Truelove, Roger Wain-Heapy, Christopher Turner, Joan York, Steve Whalley*

White Horse

Off A149 W of Sheringham; High Street; NR25 7AL

Cheerful small hotel with popular dining conservatory, enjoyable food and drinks and helpful staff

To be sure of a table, it's best to book in advance as this friendly and busy little hotel is very popular. The long main bar is predominantly green with a venetian red ceiling and restrained but attractive décor, including watercolours by a local artist. Many people, though, head for the big back dining conservatory. Adnams Bitter, Greene King Abbot and Woodfordes Wherry on handpump, and 30 wines by the glass. There are tables in a suntrap courtyard and a pleasant paved garden. The quayside is close by.

🍴 Generous helpings of bar food includes sandwiches, deep-fried local whitebait, country pâté with home-made chutney, caesar salad with crayfish tails, risotto of wild mushrooms with parmesan and truffle oil, lunchtime fish pie, confit shoulder of lamb with lentil gravy and boulangère potatoes, local mussels, venison casserole with thyme mash and puddings such as lemon tart with crème fraîche and banana and rum tarte tatin with rum and raisin ice-cream; good, proper breakfasts. *Starters/Snacks: £3.95 to £7.25. Main Courses: £8.95 to £17.95. Puddings: £4.75*

Free house ~ Licensees Dan Goff and Simon Scillitoe ~ Real ale ~ Bar food (12-2.15(2.30 Sat and Sun), 6-9(9.30 Fri and Sat)) ~ Restaurant ~ (01263) 740574 ~ Children in conservatory ~ Open 11-11 ~ Bedrooms: /£110S(£70B)

Recommended by Ann and Colin Hunt, Minda and Stanley Alexander, David Ebertin, MDN, John Wooll, Alan Cole, Kirstie Bruce, Colin Goddard, Mrs Brenda Calver, A J Avery

BRANCASTER STAITHE TF7944 MAP 8

Jolly Sailors

Main Road (A149); PE31 8BJ

Own-brewed beers and good food in cosy rooms and plenty of seats in sizeable garden; great for bird-watching nearby

Some gentle refurbishment here this year but nothing that changes the welcoming and relaxed atmosphere. It remains an unpretentious and simply furnished little pub with three cosy rooms, an open fire and a good mix of pubby seats and tables. From their on-site microbrewery they produce Brancaster Staithe Brewery Old Les and IPA and keep a guest like Woodfordes Mardlers on handpump. There's a sizeable garden and covered terrace with plenty of picnic-sets and there's a children's play area. This is prime bird-watching territory and the pub is set on the edge of thousands of acres of National Trust dunes and salt flats; walkers are welcome.

🍴 Enjoyable freshly prepared food includes filled baguettes, oysters and mussels from the harbour just across the road, crab salad, haddock in beer batter, locally smoked cod in lemon risotto, honey-glazed home-cooked ham and egg, local sausages made with beer, steak and kidney pie, and puddings. *Starters/Snacks: £4.50 to £5.95. Main Courses: £8.50 to £18.95. Puddings: £4.50 to £6.95*

Free house ~ Licensee Mr Boughton ~ Real ale ~ Bar food (12-9) ~ Restaurant ~ (01485) 210314 ~ Children welcome ~ Dogs allowed in bar ~ Open 11(12 Sun)-11

Recommended by John Wooll, Ann and Colin Hunt, David and Sue Smith, Eddie and Lynn Jarrett, Pete Baker, Pat and Clive Sherriff, Philip and Susan Philcox, P Dawn, Tracey and Stephen Groves, Roger Wain-Heapy

---

'Children welcome' means the pub says it lets children inside without any special restriction. If it allows them in, but to restricted areas such as an eating area or family room, we specify this. Places with separate restaurants often let children use them, hotels usually let them into public areas such as lounges. Some pubs impose an evening time limit – let us know if you find this.

White Horse

A149 E of Hunstanton; PE31 8BY

Excellent food in big airy dining conservatory looking over tidal bird marshes, proper bar too; comfortable bedrooms

There's something for everyone here. For those wanting a more informal bar meal or just a pint and a chat (and there are plenty of locals dropping in), the front bar is the place to head for and there are now plenty of seats outside, some under cover and with heaters, for casual dining. This bar has good local photographs on the left, with bar billiards and maybe piped music, and on the right is a quieter group of cushioned wicker armchairs and sofas by a table with daily papers and local landscapes for sale. This runs into the back dining area and adjoining conservatory restaurant with well spaced furnishings in unvarnished country-style wood and some light-hearted seasidey decorations; through the big glass windows you can look over the sun deck to the wide views of the tidal marshes and Scolt Head Island beyond. Adnams Bitter, Fullers London Pride, Woodfordes Wherry, and a guest like Timothy Taylors Landlord on handpump from the handsome counter, several malt whiskies and about a dozen wines by the glass from an extensive and thoughtful wine list; friendly service. The coast path runs along the bottom of the garden. Our readers really enjoy the comfortable bedrooms.

The food, using delicious local fish, is very good indeed. From the bar menu, there might be filled ciabattas, mussels in white wine, cream and parsley, tempura of tiger prawns with rock salt and lemon, deep-fried fillet of cod with pease pudding and home-made tartare sauce, corned beef hash on toasted muffin with buttered spinach and caper and garlic butter and roasted belly of local pork with caramelised apple. In the restaurant there's slow-braised saddle of hare with game jus and creamed polenta, galette of smoked haddock with curried cream sauce, fried rump of lamb with celeriac purée, crisp pancetta and red wine jus, slow-roast duck leg with pak choi and soy dressing and grilled fillet of lemon sole stuffed with salmon and fennel with spaghetti of cucumber; puddings such as lavender and ricotta torte with honey ice-cream and orange syrup and chocolate marquise with black cherry compote and clotted cream. *Starters/Snacks: £4.95 to £5.25. Main Courses: £8.95 to £11.95. Puddings: £3.95 to £4.95*

Free house ~ Licensees Cliff Nye and Kevin Nobes ~ Real ale ~ Bar food (12-2, 6.30-9; café open all day) ~ Restaurant ~ (01485) 210262 ~ Children welcome ~ Dogs allowed in bar and bedrooms ~ Open 11-11(10.30 Sun) ~ Bedrooms: £85B/£120B

Recommended by Michael Sargent, Adrian White, Mrs A J Robertson, Peter Rozée, Lesley and Barbara Owen, Mike and Sue Loseby, Mrs Brenda Calver, Ann and Colin Hunt, John Wooll, Derek and Sylvia Stephenson, Brian Root, Mrs E Tyrrell, Neil Ingoe, M and C Thompson, Simon Rodway, K Christensen, R M Chard, Steve Whalley, Tracey and Stephen Groves

BURNHAM MARKET

TF8342 MAP 8

Hoste Arms

The Green (B1155); PE31 8HD
NORFOLK DINING PUB OF THE YEAR

Civilised and stylish with first-rate food and drinks, very good staff, plenty of different rooms and big eating area in lovely garden; super bedrooms

Whatever your mood, this very smart, civilised and welcoming place has the room for you. The panelled proper bar on the right still retains the atmosphere of a village pub and there's a nice mix of chatty customers, a log fire and a series of watercolours showing scenes from local walks. A bow-windowed bar on the left has comfortable seats and there's a conservatory with leather armchairs and sofas and a lounge for afternoon tea; several restaurants, too. Adnams Bitter, Greene King Abbot, and Woodfordes Nelsons Revenge and Wherry on handpump, over 20 wines by the glass from a fantastic list and 25 malt whiskies; friendly, helpful staff. The lovely walled garden has plenty of seats and a big awning covers the sizeable eating area.

Excellent food includes sandwiches, soup, oriental-style spicy salmon fishcake with sweet chilli sauce, mackerel, chargrilled aubergine and courgette terrine with red pepper coulis, oysters (cold or hot), cromer crab salad with cucumber noodles and lemon grass dressing, steak and kidney pudding with spring onion mash, pad thai chicken stir-fry, roasted rack of lamb with sun-dried tomato and olive oil mash and tapenade jus, roasted fillet of cod with pea purée, roasted shallots, crispy parma ham and béarnaise sauce, and puddings such as praline and milk chocolate fondant with crushed hazelnuts and coconut ice-cream and banana tarte tatin with fresh passion fruit and liquorice ice-cream. *Starters/Snacks: £4.50 to £11.95. Main Courses: £9.95 to £23.50. Puddings: £5.95 to £9.25*

Free house ~ Licensees Paul Whittome and Emma Tagg ~ Real ale ~ Bar food ~ Restaurant ~ (01328) 738777 ~ Children welcome ~ Dogs allowed in bar and bedrooms ~ Open 11-11(10.30 Sun) ~ Bedrooms: £90S/£122B

Recommended by Walter and Susan Rinaldi-Butcher, John Winstanley, Jenny and Peter Lowater, Roger Wain-Heapy, D J Elliott, Adrian White, Michael and Maggie Betton, Sue Demont, Tim Barrow, Sally Anne and Peter Goodale, Louise English, Simon Rodway, W W Burke, Jack Shonfield, George Cowie, Minda and Stanley Alexander, Alan Cole, Kirstie Bruce, Mike and Sue Loseby, Roy Hoing

BURNHAM THORPE
TF8541 MAP 8

Lord Nelson ◀

Village signposted from B1155 and B1355, near Burnham Market; PE31 8HL

Interesting Nelson memorabilia, fine drinks including secret rum-based recipes, tasty food, and much character; play area in big garden

A friendly new landlord has taken over this 17th-c pub, and is keeping it a proper local (though welcoming to visitors, too) with spanish conversation and book clubs, Sunday evening quizzes and a music night on Thursdays. There's plenty of memorabilia and pictures of Nelson (who was born in this sleepy village) and the little bar has well waxed antique settles on the worn red flooring tiles and smoke ovens in the original fireplace. An eating room has flagstones, an open fire and more pictures of Nelson and there are a couple of other rooms as well. Greene King IPA and Abbot, Woodfordes Wherry and a couple of guest beers tapped from the cask, 14 wines by the glass and secret rum-based recipes called Nelson's Blood and Lady Hamilton's Nip; Nelson's Blood was first concocted in the 18th century and is passed down from landlord to landlord by word of mouth. There's a good-sized play area and pétanque in the very big garden.

🍴 As well as lunchtime open sandwiches, the good bar food includes soup, a plate of cured meats with roasted artichoke and shallots, parmesan croquettes, local mussels in white wine, garlic and cream, steak in ale pudding, sun-dried tomato, olive and goats cheese tart, braised lamb shank with rosemary sauce, fillet of bass with spinach, pine nuts and crustacean sauce, duck in lavender sauce and puddings such as passion fruit crème brûlée and belgian chocolate mousse. *Starters/Snacks: £4.50 to £7.50. Main Courses: £6.45 to £19.50. Puddings: £5.50*

Greene King ~ Lease Simon Alper ~ Real ale ~ Bar food (12-2(2.30 Sat), 7-9(9.30 Sat); not Sun evening or Mon) ~ Restaurant ~ (01328) 738241 ~ Children welcome but not in evening restaurant ~ Dogs allowed in bar ~ Live bands Thurs evenings ~ Open 12-3, 6-11; 12-10.30 Sun; closed Mon (though open throughout school hols)

Recommended by Jeremy and Jane Morrison, the Didler, Pete Baker, Tracey and Stephen Groves, Pat and Tony Martin, Sue Demont, Tim Barrow, Kerry Law, Jeff and Wendy Williams, Alan Cole, Kirstie Bruce, Brian Root, Mike Ridgway, Sarah Miles, Derek and Sylvia Stephenson, Barry Collett

COLKIRK
TF9226 MAP 8

Crown ♀

Village signposted off B1146 S of Fakenham, and off A1065; Crown Road; NR21 7AA

Neatly kept, bustling local with cheerful landlord, splendid wines, popular tasty food, and pleasant garden

Although this reliable pub has a strong local following, the attentive and friendly landlord takes great care to welcome visitors, too. The two bars are comfortable and cosy and kept spotless with solid country furniture on the rugs and flooring tiles, interesting things to look at and open fires. Greene King IPA, Abbot and a guest such as Greene King Ale Fresco on handpump and a splendid range of wines, many by the glass; quick service even when busy, pub games. There's also a sunny dining room. Outside are a suntrap terrace, a pleasant garden and plenty of picnic-sets.

🍴 Well priced, popular bar food includes filled baguettes, soup, anchovy and bacon salad, deep-fried mushrooms with sweet chilli dip, smoked duck with plum chutney, asparagus and sun-dried tomato flan, steak in ale pie, baked chicken with melted cheese and bacon, half a lobster and seafood salad, braised lamb shank in onion gravy, and puddings such as lemon and passion fruit cheesecake and chocolate brownie with chocolate and mint ice-cream. Starters/Snacks: £3.25 to £5.25. Main Courses: £7.95 to £13.95. Puddings: £4.25

Greene King ~ Tenant Roger Savell ~ Real ale ~ Bar food ~ Restaurant ~ (01328) 862172 ~ Children in eating area of bar and restaurant ~ Dogs allowed in bar ~ Open 11-2.30, 6-11; 12-3, 7-10.30 Sun

Recommended by Peter Rozée, R C Vincent, Mr and Mrs T B Staples, Mark, Amanda, Luke and Jake Sheard, George Atkinson, Comus and Sarah Elliott, Tracey and Stephen Groves

ERPINGHAM   TG1732   MAP 8

Saracens Head 🍴 ⟡ 🛏

At Wolterton – not shown on many maps; Erpingham signed off A140 N of Aylsham; keep on through Calthorpe, then where road bends right take the straight-ahead turn-off signposted Wolterton; NR11 7LZ

Charming long-serving landlord in simply furnished dining pub, gently civilised atmosphere, good food and well liked bedrooms

They do keep Adnams Bitter and Woodfordes Wherry on handpump but there's no doubt that this rather civilised place, run with some individuality by the convivial Mr Dawson-Smith for 18 years, is becoming more of a restaurant-with-rooms nowadays. The two-room bar is simple and stylish with high ceilings, terracotta walls, and red and white striped curtains at its tall windows – all lending a feeling of space, though it's not actually large. There's a mix of seats from built-in leather wall settles to wicker fireside chairs as well as log fires and flowers, and the windows look out on to a charming old-fashioned gravel stableyard with picnic-sets. A pretty six-table parlour on the right, in cheerful nursery colours, has another big log fire. There's an interesting wine list, local apple juice and decent malt whiskies; the atmosphere is enjoyably informal. The Shed next door (run by Mr Dawson-Smith's daughter Rachel) is a workshop and showcase for furniture and interior pieces. Lovely, comfortable bedrooms that our readers like very much.

🍴 Enjoyable food includes mussels with cider and cream, red onion and goats cheese tart, grilled halloumi on a lavender croûte with sunblush tomatoes and cream, baked avocado with sweet pear and mozzarella, baked cromer crab with apple and sherry, venison medallions with red fruit jus, local pheasant with calvados and cream, and puddings such as treacle tart and Baileys dark chocolate pot with orange jus; good value two-course lunch. Starters/Snacks: £3.95 to £7.25. Main Courses: £11.95 to £15.00. Puddings: £4.95

Free house ~ Licensee Robert Dawson-Smith ~ Real ale ~ Bar food (12.30-2, 7.30-9) ~ Restaurant ~ (01263) 768909 ~ Children welcome but must be well behaved ~ Dogs allowed in bedrooms ~ Open 11.30-3.30, 6-11; 12-3, 7-10.30 Sun; closed 25 Dec and evening 26 Dec ~ Bedrooms: £45B/£85B

Recommended by Anthony Barnes, Bill Strang, Stuart Pearson, Roddy and Kate Steen, DF, NF, John Winstanley, T Walker, Paul and Sue Dix, Brenda Crossley, Dr and Mrs P Truelove, Philip and Susan Philcox, Dennis and Gill Keen, Sue Demont, Tim Barrow, Pete Devonish, Ian McIntyre, John Wooll, Paul Humphreys, Peter and Jean Dowson

---

Cribbage is a card game using a block of wood with holes for matchsticks or special pins to score with; regulars in cribbage pubs are usually happy to teach strangers how to play.

HOLKHAM
TF8943   MAP 8

Victoria ♀ 🍴
A149 near Holkham Hall; NR23 1RG

Informal but smart and stylish, food using first-class produce, lovely bedrooms; huge beaches and nature-reserve salt marshes close by

Although this is quite obviously a small hotel rather than a pub, there are bars with an informal – if quite upmarket – feel and a relaxed, chatty atmosphere. Virtually the whole of the ground floor is opened up into linked but quite individual areas. The main bar room, decorated in cool shades of green, has an eclectic mix of furnishings including deep low sofas with a colourful scatter of cushions, a big log fire, a dozen or so fat lighted candles in heavy sticks and many more tea lights, and some decorations conjuring up India (such as the attractive rajasthan cotton blinds for a triple bow window). The island servery has a decent range of wines by the glass as well Adnams Bitter, Fullers London Pride and Woodfordes Nelsons Revenge on handpump; good coffees, hot chocolate, piped music. Two linked dining rooms continue the mood of faintly anglo-indian casual elegance. Several separate areas outside with plenty of tables and picnic-sets include a sheltered courtyard with a high retractable awning; there's also an orchard with a small play area. Just across the road is a walk down past nature-reserve salt marshes, alive with many thousands of geese and duck in winter, to seemingly endless broad beaches. The informal style of the place can occasionally mean that things don't run like clockwork – disconcerting perhaps given the expectations that come with the prices, but all part of the appeal to the inn's aficionados.

🍽 Using top-notch local produce, some from the owners' Holkham estate, there's a small bar menu (not always available, sadly) with sandwiches, soup, ploughman's, an antipasti plate and haddock and chips; more elaborate dishes also, such as terrine of pheasant and foie gras with quince jelly, mussels with cider, shallots and thyme cream, venison burger with mustard mayonnaise and root vegetable crisps, risotto of butternut squash, parmesan and sage, slow-braised hare with pappardelle and steamed beef in Guinness pudding with shallot purée and puddings such as hot chocolate fondant with peanut butter ice-cream and baked egg custard tart with nutmeg ice-cream. *Starters/Snacks: £5.00 to £9.00. Main Courses: £9.00 to £17.00. Puddings: £6.00*

Free house ~ Licensee Tom Coke ~ Real ale ~ Bar food ~ Restaurant ~ (01328) 711008 ~ Children welcome ~ Dogs allowed in bar ~ Open 11(12 Sun)-11 ~ Bedrooms: £110B/£135B
Recommended by J D Taylor, Tracey and Stephen Groves, Mike and Sue Loseby

ITTERINGHAM
TG1430   MAP 8

Walpole Arms ◀
Village signposted off B1354 NW of Aylsham; NR11 7AR

Ambitious food in popular dining pub, quietly chatty open-plan bar, decent drinks and good garden

Well run and certainly busy, this popular dining pub is run by a friendly landlord. The sizeable open-plan bar is rather civilised and has exposed beams, stripped brick walls, little windows, a mix of dining tables and quietly chatty atmosphere. Adnams Bitter and Broadside, Woodfordes Wherry and a beer named for the pub brewed for them by Wolf on handpump, 12 wines by the glass, Aspell's cider and some belgian beers. Behind the pub is a two-acre landscaped garden and there are seats on the vine-covered terrace. They plan to construct a proper booth outside for smokers.

🍽 As well as a snack menu with ploughman's, salmon, leek and dill potato cake and beef stovey with fried egg and piquant salad, the interesting food might include salad of Cashel Blue, chicory, toasted walnuts and pickled pear, spanish-style rillettes of pork with little gherkins, rock salt and crostini, risotto of wild and cultivated mushrooms, squash and tarragon with parmesan and truffle oil, local mussels steamed with cider, onion, bacon and thyme, saltimbocca of pheasant with herb polenta, and puddings such as chocolate parfait with citrus salad and quince tarte tatin with peach sorbet. *Starters/Snacks: £5.50 to £6.95. Main Courses: £9.50 to £14.50. Puddings: £4.75 to £5.75*

Free house ~ Licensee Richard Bryan ~ Real ale ~ Bar food (not Sun evening and not Mon or Tues evenings in Jan/early Feb) ~ Restaurant ~ (01263) 587258 ~ Children welcome ~ Dogs allowed in bar ~ Occasional live music ~ Open 12-3, 6-11; 12-3, 7-10.30 Sun; closed 25 Dec

Recommended by John Winstanley, Pete Devonish, Ian McIntyre, P Dawn, Mike and Shelley Woodroffe, Philip and Susan Philcox, John Evans, David Twitchett, Mrs Brenda Calver, Dennis and Gill Keen, Anthony Barnes, Robert Tapsfield

LARLING   TL9889   MAP 5

Angel 🍺 🛏

From A11 Thetford—Attleborough, take B1111 turn-off and follow pub signs; NR16 2QU

In same family since 1913, with good-natured chatty atmosphere, good beers and well liked food

Mr Stammers is an invariably friendly landlord who takes a real interest in his beers and our readers enjoy their visits here very much. It's been in the same family since 1913 and they still have the original visitors' books with guests from 1897 to 1909. The comfortable 1930s-style lounge on the right has cushioned wheelback chairs, a nice long cushioned and panelled corner settle, some good solid tables for eating and some lower ones, and squared panelling; also, a collection of whisky-water jugs on the delft shelf over the big brick fireplace, a woodburning stove, a couple of copper kettles, and some hunting prints. The atmosphere is chatty and relaxed and there's a good mix of customers. Adnams Bitter and four guests from breweries like Crouch Vale, Church End, Elgoods and Wolf on handpump and they hold an August beer festival with over 70 real ales and ciders, live music and barbecue food; also, around 100 malt whiskies and several wines by the glass. The quarry-tiled black-beamed public bar has a good local atmosphere, with darts, games machine, juke box (a rarity nowadays), board games and piped music. A neat grass area behind the car park has picnic-sets around a big fairy-lit apple tree, and a safely fenced play area. They also have a four-acre meadow and offer caravan and camping sites from March to October. Peter Beale's old-fashioned rose nursery is nearby.

🍴 **Good value straightforward bar food includes sandwiches, filled baked potatoes, creamy mushroom pot, whitebait, ham and egg, omelettes, burgers, stilton and mushroom bake, thai green chicken curry, smoked haddock mornay and mixed grill.** *Starters/Snacks: £2.25 to £5.25. Main Courses: £4.95 to £16.95. Puddings: £4.25*

Free house ~ Licensee Andrew Stammers ~ Real ale ~ Bar food (all day) ~ Restaurant ~ (01953) 717963 ~ Children welcome ~ Open 10-midnight ~ Bedrooms: £40B/£70B

Recommended by J F M and M West, Stuart and Alison Ballantyne, Julian and Janet Dearden, Edward Mirzoeff, George Atkinson, Alan Cowell, Mike and Shelley Woodroffe, A J Murray, John and Elisabeth Cox, Peter and Jean Dowson, Mike and Helen Rawsthorn, Mrs Jane Kingsbury

MORSTON   TG0043   MAP 8

Anchor

A149 Salthouse—Stiffkey; The Street; NR25 7AA

Quite a choice of rooms filled with bric-a-brac and prints, generous food and efficient service

You can book seal-spotting trips from this busy pub and the surrounding area is wonderful for bird-watching and walking. There's a contemporary airy extension on the left with groups of deep leather sofas around low tables, grey-painted country dining furniture, fresh flowers and fish pictures. On the right are three more traditional rooms with pubby seating and tables on shiny black floors, coal fires, local 1950s beach photographs and lots of prints and bric-a-brac. Greene King IPA, Old Speckled Hen and local Winters Gold on handpump, decent wines by the glass, oyster shots (a local oyster in vodka), and daily papers. Service is pleasant and efficient. There are tables and benches out in front, with more tables on a side lawn.

🍴 Freshly prepared enjoyable bar food includes sandwiches, soup, ham hock terrine with mustard and pickles, flash-fried whitebait with lemon mayonnaise, salmon and local crab cakes with pickled fennel salad, bangers and mash with caramelised onion gravy, slow-cooked free-range pork belly with creamed celeriac and apple chutney, loin of lamb with pea and mint purée, whole baked baby brill with tomato and caper butter, asparagus and confit potatoes, daily specials, and puddings. *Starters/Snacks: £4.50 to £7.95. Main Courses: £8.25 to £19.50. Puddings: £3.95 to £6.25*

Free house ~ Licensee Sam Handley ~ Real ale ~ Bar food (12-2.30, 6-9(9.30 Fri and Sat); 12-8 Sun) ~ Restaurant ~ (01263) 741392 ~ Children welcome ~ Dogs allowed in bar ~ Open 11-11

Recommended by Brian Root, Tracey and Stephen Groves, Adele Summers, Alan Black

NORWICH   TG2309   MAP 5

Adam & Eve £

Bishopgate; follow Palace Street from Tombland, N of cathedral; NR3 1RZ

Seats by fantastic array of hanging baskets and tubs, plenty of history in ancient pub

The award-winning colourful tubs and hanging baskets here are quite a sight in summer and it's nice to admire them from one of the many picnic-sets. The pub is thought to date back to at least 1249 (when it was used by workmen building the cathedral) and even has a Saxon well beneath the lower bar floor, though the striking dutch gables were added in the 14th and 15th centuries. The little old-fashioned bars have antique high-backed settles, cushioned benches built into partly panelled, and tiled or parquet floors. Adnams Bitter, Greene King IPA, Theakstons Old Peculier and Wells & Youngs Bombardier on handpump, over 50 malt whiskies, quite a few wines by the glass and Aspall's cider; piped music and board games. Ghost walks start and end here from June to September three evenings a week. More reports please.

🍴 Straightforward bar food such as sandwiches and filled baguettes, ploughman's, soup, chilli con carne, steak and mushroom pie, cheese and vegetable bake, ham and eggs and battered cod; daily specials. *Starters/Snacks: £3.85 to £4.95. Main Courses: £4.95 to £8.95. Puddings: £3.95*

Unique (Enterprise) ~ Lease Rita McCluskey ~ Real ale ~ Bar food (12-7; 12-2.30 Sun; not Sun evening) ~ (01603) 667423 ~ Children in snug until 9pm ~ Open 11-11; 12-10.30 Sun; closed 25-26 Dec, 1 Jan

Recommended by W W Burke, Pat and Clive Sherriff, the Didler, John Wooll, Revd R P Tickle, Ian Chisholm, David and Sue Smith, Christopher Turner, David and Sue Atkinson, Joan York, Dennis Jones

Fat Cat 🍺

West End Street; NR2 4NA

A place of pilgrimage for beer lovers, and open all day

This is a beer drinkers' haven with up to 30 quickly changing real ales on at any one time. As well as their own beers (brewed at their sister pub, The Shed) Fat Cat Bitter, Honey, Marmalade, Meow Mild and Top Cat, the fantastic choice (on handpump or tapped from the cask in a stillroom behind the bar – big windows reveal all) might include Adnams Bitter and Broadside, Burton Bridge Stairway to Heaven, Castle Rock Elsie Mo, Elgoods Black Dog Mild, Enville Ginger, Felinfoel Double Dragon, Fullers ESB and London Pride, Greene King Abbot, Kelham Island Pale Rider, Oakham JHB and Bishops Farewell, Orkeney The Red MacGregor, RCH Firebox, St Peters Grapefruit, Sinclair Skull Splitter, Shepherd Neame Spitfire, Stonehenge Danish Dynamite, Timothy Taylors Landlord, Winters Revenge and Woodfordes Wherry. You'll also find eight draught beers from belgium and germany and up to 16 bottled belgian beers, 15 country wines, and local farm cider. There's a lively bustling atmosphere at busy times, with maybe tranquil lulls in the middle of the afternoon, and a good mix of cheerful customers. The no-nonsense furnishings include plain scrubbed pine tables and simple solid seats, lots of brewery memorabilia, bric-a-brac and stained glass. There are tables outside.

🍴 Bar food consists of a dozen or so rolls and good pies at lunchtime (not Sunday). *Starters/Snacks: £0.60*

Free house ~ Licensee Colin Keatley ~ Real ale ~ Bar food (available until sold out; not Sun) ~ No credit cards ~ (01603) 624364 ~ Children allowed in conservatory ~ Open 12-11; 11(12 Fri)-midnight Sat; 12-10.30 Sun; closed evening 31 Dec

Recommended by Ben Taylor, Ian Phillips, the Didler, P Dawn, Roger Wain-Heapy, G Coates, Comus and Sarah Elliott, David and Sue Atkinson

OLD BUCKENHAM   TM0691   MAP 5
Gamekeeper
B1077 S of Attleborough; The Green; NR17 1RE

Appealing layout enjoyed by drinkers and diners, seasonal tasty food, friendly service and seats on heated terrace

Neatly kept and genuinely friendly, this is a civilised and pretty 16th-c pub. The beamed bar, with two main areas, has a big open woodburning stove in a capacious inglenook fireplace, a pleasant variety of seating and tables including a couple of sturdy slabs of elm and two unusual interior bow windows showing off rustic bygones including stuffed birds. The corner counter serves Adnams Bitter, Timothy Taylors Landlord and Wolf Golden Jackal on handpump, a good range of wines by the glass and winter mulled wine. Tiffanyesque lamps over this counter, church candles and dried hops help towards a cosy pub atmosphere. Besides the comfortable main back dining area, which includes some stripped high-backed settles, there is a small separate room with a crushed raspberry colour scheme and two long rustic tables. Piped music, a discreetly placed fruit machine, skittle alley, darts and board games; the friendly patterdale terrier is called Ollie. Tables out on the back terrace have heaters and there are picnic-sets on the grass beyond.

🍴 Tasty seasonal food includes sandwiches, filled baguettes and baked potatoes, soup, chicken liver pâté, omelettes, ham and eggs, red thai vegetable curry, local sausages with rich onion gravy, steak in ale pie and slow-braised shoulder of lamb; popular Sunday carvery. *Starters/Snacks: £4.00 to £6.50. Main Courses: £7.95 to £15.00. Puddings: £4.25*

Enterprise ~ Lease Keith and Val Starr ~ Real ale ~ Bar food (12-2.30, 6.30-9; 12-4 Sun; not Sun or Mon evenings) ~ Restaurant ~ (01953) 860397 ~ Children allowed away from bar ~ Dogs allowed in bar and bedrooms ~ Open 11.45-11; 12-10.30 Sun ~ Bedrooms: £35/£55

Recommended by Alan Cole, Kirstie Bruce, Ian Chisholm, Charles Gysin, John Wooll

RINGSTEAD   TF7040   MAP 8
Gin Trap 🍴
Village signposted off A149 near Hunstanton; OS Sheet 132 map reference 707403; PE36 5JU

Well run and attractive coaching inn with good interesting food and new dining conservatory

Much enjoyed by our readers, this attractive white-painted 17th-c coaching inn has friendly new licensees this year, who have built on a dining conservatory that overlooks the garden. The neat bar has beams, a woodburning stove, captain's chairs and cast-iron-framed tables. They have Adnams Bitter, Woodfordes Wherry and a guest beer on handpump, and seven wines by the glass; very good service, piped music. Outside, a handsome spreading chestnut tree shelters the car park and the neatly kept back garden has seats on the grass or small paved area, and pretty flowering tubs. The Peddar's Way is close by.

🍴 Appetising, well presented bar food inlcudes sandwiches, interesting soups, pressed corn-fed chicken, apricot and sage terrine with home-made piccalilli, dill-crusted home-cured scottish salmon, glazed clam and cockle tagliatelle with chive and caviar fish cream, wild mushroom and fresh herb risotto with cep sauce, crispy confit duck leg salad with roasted baby beetroot, shallot dressing and sour cream, maize-crusted baked chicken kiev with home-made noodles and seasonal asparagus and line-caught wild bass with pea mash, crispy onion rings and dill butter sauce; there are lighter lunchtime dishes, and **puddings, too.** *Starters/Snacks: £5.00 to £8.50. Main Courses: £8.50 to £17.00. Puddings: £5.50 to £6.00*

Free house ~ Licensee Cindy Cook ~ Real ale ~ Bar food (12-2(2.30 Sat and Sun), 6-9(9.30 Fri and Sat)) ~ Restaurant ~ (01485) 525264 ~ Children welcome ~ Dogs welcome ~ Open 11.30-11(midnight Fri and Sat); 11.30-3, 6-11 in winter ~ Bedrooms: /£100S(£120B)

Recommended by John Wooll, Ian Woodroffe, Mrs Mary Jacobs, Ann and Colin Hunt, Tracey and Stephen Groves, Sue Demont, Tim Barrow, Keith Eastelow, Roy Hoing

---

SNETTISHAM
TF6834   MAP 8

Rose & Crown ⓘ🍴 ♀ 🛏

Village signposted from A149 King's Lynn—Hunstanton just N of Sandringham; coming in on the B1440 from the roundabout just N of village, take first left turn into Old Church Road; PE31 7LX

Constantly improving old pub, log fires and interesting furnishings, thoughtful food, fine range of drinks and stylish seating on heated terrace; well equipped bedrooms

---

This particularly well run and pretty white cottage manages to appeal to a very wide mix of customers. It's popular locally so lots of people pop in for a pint and a chat which creates an informal and cheerful feel and visitors come from far and wide to enjoy the good, carefully presented food. Families too feel comfortable here with proper meals for children and the chance to burn it all off on the excellent wooden play fort in the garden. A new residents' lounge is to be created with armchairs, sofas and magazines and this will also be available as a private dining room. There are two bars, each with a separate character: an old-fashioned beamed front bar with black settles on its tiled floor and a big log fire, and a back bar with another large log fire and the landlord's sporting trophies and old sports equipment. The Garden Room has inviting wicker-based wooden chairs, careful lighting and a quote by Dr Johnson in old-fashioned rolling script on a huge wall board. Adnams Bitter, Bass, Fullers London Pride and Woodfordes Wherry on handpump, 20 wines by the glass, organic fruit juices and farm cider; very helpful, friendly service. In the garden, new retractable awnings and wall-mounted heat lamps are to be installed and there is to be a tucked-away area with a heater and overhead cover for smokers; stylish café-style blue chairs and tables under cream parasols on the terrace and colourful herbaceous borders. Two of the comfortable bedrooms are downstairs and there are disabled lavatories and wheelchair ramps.

🍴 Using as much local produce as possible, the imaginative food includes lunchtime sandwiches (not Sunday), nice soups, ham hock and smoked goose terrine with warm pea purée, seared scallops, crispy pork belly and cauliflower purée, salmon and butterfish brochettes with chilli sauce, pure beefburger with bacon, cheese, relish and fries, game pie, grilled mediterranean vegetables and goats cheese melt, moroccan pork curry with cucumber dip, braised lamb knuckle with white bean purée and butternut fritters, daily specials, and puddings like banana bread cake with clotted cream and plum compote and chocolate and panna cotta torte. *Starters/Snacks: £4.50 to £6.95. Main Courses: £7.25 to £14.75. Puddings: £4.95 to £5.95*

Free house ~ Licensee Anthony Goodrich ~ Real ale ~ Bar food (12-2(2.30 Sat and Sun), 6.30-9(9.30 Fri and Sat)) ~ Restaurant ~ (01485) 541382 ~ Children welcome ~ Dogs allowed in bar and bedrooms ~ Open 11-11; 12-10.30 Sun ~ Bedrooms: £60B/£85B

Recommended by John Wooll, Adrian White, A G Marx, Sue Demont, Tim Barrow, Paul Humphreys, Louise English, Mark, Amanda, Luke and Jake Sheard, Ron and Sheila Corbett, Tracey and Stephen Groves, Barry and Patricia Wooding, Jeff and Wendy Williams, David Eberlin, John Saville, Ann and Colin Hunt, Comus and Sarah Elliott, Margit Severa, DF, NF

Bedroom prices normally include full english breakfast, VAT and any inclusive service charge that we know of. Prices before the '/' are for single rooms, after for two people in double or twin (B includes a private bath, S a private shower).

SOUTH CREAKE
TF8635 MAP 8

Ostrich ⬛
B1355 Burnham Market—Fakenham; NR21 9PB

Hard-working, friendly owners keep everything tip-top here; all-Norfolk beer festival late summer, well liked food, cheerful atmosphere and smart, heated terrace

Run by friendly licensees, this bustling village pub has a cheerfully informal atmosphere and a good choice of food and drink. It's attractively laid out and the comfortable carpeted bar has modern landscape prints on the apricot walls, Greene King IPA and Abbot, Shepherd Neame Spitfire and Woodfordes Wherry on handpump and a good choice of wines; they do an all-Norfolk beer festival in late summer. There are colourful scatter cushions on the dark leather sofa and armchairs in an area off on the left, which has some interesting books, an oriental rug on its bare boards and a woodburning stove. Further areas include a maroon-walled dining room with white-painted tables and rush-seat chairs on very broad floorboards, and another spacious raftered dining room with similar décor. The two beagles are friendly; piped music and board games. The sheltered and heated back gravel terrace has stylish furnishings under big canvas parasols and there's a lively water feature.

🍽 **Well liked bar food includes sandwiches, chicken liver parfait, local seasonal mussels, scallops and tiger prawns, roast mediterranean vegetables with pesto and melted goats cheese, thai green chicken curry, beef in ale pie, pork chop with a honey and mustard glaze and mustard mash, foil-baked bass fillet with white wine and thyme, and puddings such as Baileys crème brûlée and sticky toffee pudding with butterscotch sauce; they still hold their steak night on Tuesdays.** *Starters/Snacks: £4.95 to £6.95. Main Courses: £7.95 to £16.95. Puddings: £5.25*

Free house ~ Licensees Simon and Emma Gardner ~ Real ale ~ Bar food ~ Restaurant ~ (01328) 823320 ~ Children welcome ~ Dogs allowed in bar ~ Open 12-11.30(midnight Sat); 12-3, 5-11.30 in winter ~ Bedrooms: /£50S
Recommended by Mike and Shelley Woodroffe, Tracey and Stephen Groves, R C Vincent

STANHOE
TF8037 MAP 8

Crown
B1155 towards Burnham Market; PE31 8QD

Interesting furnishings in unspoilt local, no-nonsense food and drink and ex-RAF landlord

Liked by those who prefer their pubs plain and simple, this little open-plan local is firmly run by a straight-talking ex-RAF landlord. The small connected rooms are clean and bright with a relaxed atmosphere, aircraft pictures on the white walls, upholstered wall seats and wheelback chairs around dark tables on the carpet and a central log fire. Beams and joists overhead – one beam densely studded with coins – and gas masks, guns and various military headgear behind the bar. Elgoods Cambridge and Greyhound on handpump and decent house wines and coffee; piped music. There are tables on a side lawn with a couple of apple trees, and a bigger lawn behind with room for caravans; fancy breeds of chicken may be running free.

🍽 **A sensibly short choice of no-nonsense bar food includes sandwiches, soup, garlic mussels, ham and egg, steak and kidney pie, a vegetarian dish, braised liver, and puddings.** *Starters/Snacks: £4.00 to £4.50. Main Courses: £7.00 to £7.80. Puddings: £4.00*

Elgoods ~ Tenants Page and Sarah Clowser ~ Bar food (not Sun evening) ~ No credit cards ~ (01485) 518330 ~ Children allowed but must be well behaved ~ Dogs allowed in bar ~ Open 12-3, 6(7 Sun)-midnight
Recommended by Sue Crees, Jeff and Wendy Williams, David Carr, R C Vincent, Tracey and Stephen Groves

STIFFKEY

TF9643 MAP 8

Red Lion

A149 Wells—Blakeney; NR23 1AJ

Bustling atmosphere and attractive layout in popular and well run all-rounder

Bustling and warmly friendly, this is a traditional pub with plenty of cheerful customers. The oldest parts of the simple bars have a few beams, aged flooring tiles or bare floorboards, and big open fires; there's also a mix of pews, small settles and a couple of stripped high-backed settles, a nice old long deal table among quite a few others and oil-type or lantern wall lamps. Woodfordes Nelsons Revenge and Wherry and guests like Front Street Priory Ale and Woodfordes Stewkey Brew on handpump, quite a few wines by the glass, over 30 malt whiskies; board games. A back gravel terrace has proper tables and seats, with more on grass further up beyond; there are some pleasant walks nearby. Bedrooms should be open by the time this edition is published.

🍴 **Bar food includes sandwiches, soup, grilled goats cheese with a salad of charred vegetables and pesto oil, sausages with red wine onion, honey-roast ham and eggs, a pie of the day, half a roast chicken and chips, and puddings.** *Starters/Snacks: £3.50 to £5.25. Main Courses: £6.50 to £13.95. Puddings: £2.95 to £4.95*

Free house ~ Licensee Andrew Waddison ~ Real ale ~ Bar food (all day Sun) ~ (01328) 830552 ~ Children welcome ~ Dogs welcome ~ Occasional live bands ~ Open 11-11; 12-3, 6-11 winter

Recommended by Pat and Clive Sherriff, Nigel and Sue Foster, Derek Field, Sue Demont, Tim Barrow, John Wooll, Keith Eastelow, Geoff and Pat Bell, Julia Mann, Tracey and Stephen Groves, John and Judith Jones, Graham and Rosemary Smith, Ann and Colin Hunt, Robert Tapsfield, the Didler

STOW BARDOLPH

TF6205 MAP 5

Hare Arms ♀

Just off A10 N of Downham Market; PE34 3HT

Long-serving licensees, a genuinely friendly atmosphere, tasty bar food and more elaborate restaurant menu; big back garden

The friendly licensees have now been running this neatly kept creeper-covered pub for 31 years. The bustling bar has a proper village pub feel, interesting bric-a-brac, old advertising signs, fresh flowers, plenty of tables around its central servery and a good log fire. This bar opens into a spacious heated and well planted conservatory. Greene King IPA, Abbot and Old Speckled Hen, and a guest like Batemans XXXB on handpump, a decent range of wines and quite a few malt whiskies. There are plenty of seats in the large garden behind with more in the pretty front garden, and chickens and peacocks roam freely. Church Farm Rare Breeds Centre is a two-minute walk away. More reports please.

🍴 **As well as lunchtime sandwiches, filled baked potatoes and ploughman's, the popular bar food might include a curry of the day, mushroom stroganoff, sausages on sweet potato mash with red onion gravy, steak and peppercorn pie, local pork steak with an apricot, ginger and breadcrumb topping, smoked haddock and crayfish tails with tomatoes in a cream and parmesan sauce, daily specials and puddings; there's also a more elaborate restaurant menu.** *Starters/Snacks: £3.50 to £7.75. Main Courses: £8.25 to £16.00. Puddings: £4.50*

Greene King ~ Tenants David and Trish McManus ~ Real ale ~ Bar food (12-2, 7-10) ~ Restaurant ~ (01366) 382229 ~ Children in conservatory and on Sundays in coach house ~ Open 11-2.30, 6-11; 12-2.30, 7-10.30 Sun; closed 25 and 26 Dec

Recommended by John Wooll, Brian Root, Ann and Colin Hunt, Tracey and Stephen Groves, Anthony Barnes

---

We mention bottled beers and spirits only if there is something unusual about them – imported belgian real ales, say, or dozens of malt whiskies; so do please let us know about them in your reports.

SWANTON MORLEY   TG0217   MAP 8

Darbys 🍺
B1147 NE of Dereham; NR20 4NY

Eight real ales in unspoilt country local, plenty of farming knick-knacks, tasty bar food, and play area

There's a fine choice of up to eight real ales on handpump in this creeper-covered local: Adnams Best and Broadside, Badger Tanglefoot, Fullers London Pride, Woodfordes Wherry and three changing guest beers. The long bare-boarded country-style bar has a comfortable lived-in feel, with big stripped pine tables and chairs, lots of gin traps and farming memorabilia, a good log fire (with the original bread oven alongside) and tractor seats with folded sacks lining the long, attractive serving counter. A step up through a little doorway by the fireplace takes you through to the dining room. The children's room has a toy box and a glassed-over well, floodlit from inside; piped music. The garden has a children's play area. Plenty to do locally (B&B is available in carefully converted farm buildings a few minutes away) as the family also own the adjoining 720-acre estate. More reports please.

🍴 *Bar food includes sandwiches, filled baked potatoes, garlic and stilton mushrooms, steak and mushroom in ale pot, stir-fried chicken with cashew nuts, spinach and potato madras, deep-fried beer-battered haddock, and puddings such as raspberry cheesecake and apple pie. Starters/Snacks: £3.50 to £5.75. Main Courses: £5.95 to £13.25. Puddings: £4.25*

Free house ~ Licensees John Carrick and Louise Battle ~ Real ale ~ Bar food (12-2.15, 6.30-9.45) ~ Restaurant ~ (01362) 637647 ~ Children welcome ~ Dogs allowed in bar ~ Open 11.30-3, 6-11; 11.30-11 Sat; 12-10.30 Sun

Recommended by R C Vincent, Ian Phillips, Mark, Amanda, Luke and Jake Sheard, Bruce Bird

TERRINGTON ST JOHN   TF5314   MAP 8

Woolpack
Village signposted off A47 W of King's Lynn; PE14 7RR

Exceptionally cheerful landlady and plenty of happy banter in busy roadside pub with popular food and beer and lots of local customers

You can be sure of a cheerful and friendly welcome from the boisterous landlady of this airy roadside pub and as it's very popular locally, there's plenty of chatty banter. The rooms are decorated with Mrs Carter's bright modern ceramics and contemporary prints, and the bar has red plush banquettes and matching or wheelback chairs around its dark pub tables, a patterned red carpet, and terracotta pink walls. The large back dining room (which looks out on to the garden) has comfortable green seating and an art deco décor punctuated by Mondrian prints. Greene King IPA, Highwood Best Bitter and a guest such as Shepherd Neame Spitfire or Wells & Youngs Bombardier on handpump; games machine and piped music; good disabled access. There are picnic-sets on neat grass by a herb garden and the car park (which has recycling bins including Planet Aid clothes and shoes).

🍴 *Reliably good value, popular food includes sandwiches, seasonal soup, chicken liver pâté with fruit coulis, stuffed nutty aubergine, tuna steak with red onion chutney and redcurrant reduction, lambs liver and smoked bacon with red wine gravy, steak and kidney pudding, a big mixed grill, daily specials, and the famous pudding trolley with all manner of home-made crumbles, pies, tarts, fresh fruit pavlovas and cheesecakes. Starters/Snacks: £2.95 to £3.95. Main Courses: £7.95 to £12.50. Puddings: £3.95*

Free house ~ Licensees Lucille and Barry Carter ~ Bar food ~ Restaurant ~ (01945) 881097 ~ Children in eating area of bar and restaurant ~ Open 11.30-2.30, 6.30-11; 12-2.30, 7-10.30 Sun; closed evenings 25 and 26 Dec

Recommended by Michael and Jenny Back, K Christensen, Bruce Bird, Sally Anne and Peter Goodale, Duncan Cloud, Mr and Mrs Bentley-Davies, Ian Stafford, Philip and Susan Philcox, Ryta Lyndley

THORNHAM

TF7343   MAP 8

Lifeboat 🛏

Turn off A149 by Kings Head, then take first left turn; PE36 6LT

Good mix of customers and lots of character in traditional inn, five open fires and super surrounding walks

There's plenty of character here and the main Smugglers bar has low settles, window seats, pews, carved oak tables and rugs on the tiles, and masses of guns, swords, black metal mattocks, reed-slashers and other antique farm tools; it's lit with antique paraffin lamps suspended among an array of traps and yokes on its great oak-beamed ceiling. A couple of little rooms leads off here, and all in all there are five open fires. No games machines or piped music, though they still play the ancient game of 'pennies' which was outlawed in the late 1700s, and dominoes. Up some steps from the conservatory is a sunny terrace with picnic-sets, and further back is a children's playground with fort and slide. Adnams Bitter, Greene King IPA and Abbot, Nethergate Barley Special and Woodfordes Wherry on handpump, several wines by the glass, farm cider and local apple juice. The inn faces half a mile of coastal sea flats, and there are lots of lovely surrounding walks. Most of the bedrooms have distant sea views.

🍴 **As well as filled baguettes and ploughman's, bar food includes chicken and duck liver pâté with redcurrant sauce, mussels in white wine, garlic, onions, cream and parsley, chilli spiced five-bean cassoulet, beer-battered cod with tartare sauce, lambs liver and bacon with a sticky onion and madeira gravy, local pheasant casserole, daily specials, and puddings such as chocolate and Guinness sponge and raspberry crème brûlée.** *Starters/Snacks: £3.95 to £6.90. Main Courses: £8.95 to £18.00. Puddings: £3.00 to £4.60*

Maypole Group ~ Manager Leon Mace ~ Real ale ~ Bar food (12-2.30, 6-9.30) ~ Restaurant ~ (01485) 512236 ~ Children welcome ~ Dogs allowed in bar and bedrooms ~ Open 11-11 ~ Bedrooms: £70B/£100B

Recommended by the Didler, Simon Rodway, Jeff and Wendy Williams, Mike and Sue Loseby, Tracey and Stephen Groves, Brian Root, Mark Farrington, Richard Siebert, Margit Severa, A G Marx, Mark, Amanda, Luke and Jake Sheard, Pat and Tony Martin, Eddie and Lynn Jarrett, John Wooll, Louise English, David Eberlin, Ann and Colin Hunt, Pat and Clive Sherriff, Adrian White, Giles and Annie Francis, K Christensen

TIVETSHALL ST MARY

TM1785   MAP 5

Old Ram 🍷 🛏

A140 15 miles S of Norwich, outside village; NR15 2DE

Stylish small hotel with a fine choice of food and drink, comfortable bars with open fires, and smart terrace with heaters; lovely bedrooms

A great deal of thought and care goes into the running of this smart, much extended 17th-c coaching inn. There is some emphasis on the lovely bedrooms and the good food but plenty of customers drop in to enjoy the Adnams Bitter, Woodfordes Wherry and guests like Fullers London Pride or Marstons Pedigree on handpump; 28 wines by the glass, fresh fruit juices, several malt whiskies and cornish ice-cream milkshakes. The spacious country-style main room has lots of stripped beams and standing timbers, antique craftsmen's tools on the ceiling, a huge log fire in the brick hearth, a turkey rug on rosy brick floors and a longcase clock. It's ringed by smaller side areas, and one dining room has striking navy walls and ceiling, swagged curtains and an open woodburning stove; this leads to a second comfortable dining room and gallery. Games machine, TV and piped music. The sheltered flower-filled terrace is very civilised with outdoor heaters and big green parasols.

🍴 **Served by friendly, attentive staff and using personally chosen produce, the popular bar food includes lunchtime sandwiches and a filled baked potato of the day, soup, roast baby pork ribs in barbecue sauce, tiger prawns in filo pastry with lemon grass mayonnaise and sweet chilli dressing, niçoise salad, vegetarian cannelloni, corn-fed chicken with crispy smoked bacon and mustard and tarragon sauce, steak and mushroom pie, grilled skate in black butter, daily specials and puddings like sticky toffee pudding and tiramisu; good value weekday two-course OAP menu (not evenings).** *Starters/Snacks: £4.50 to £6.95. Main Courses: £8.95 to £17.95. Puddings: £4.50 to £5.95.*

Free house ~ Licensee John Trafford ~ Real ale ~ Bar food (all day from 7.30am) ~ Restaurant ~ (01379) 676794 ~ Children allowed but must be over 7 after 8pm ~ Open 8am-midnight(1am Fri and Sat); closed 25 and 26 Dec ~ Bedrooms: £65.50B/£90B

Recommended by Trevor and Sylvia Millum, Bryan and Mary Blaxall, Beryl and Bill Farmer, Mrs Romey Heaton, Alan Cole, Kirstie Bruce, Liz and Brian Barnard, Ian and Nita Cooper, Chris and Marion Gardiner

WARHAM   TF9441   MAP 8

Three Horseshoes ★ 🍺 🛏

Warham All Saints; village signposted from A149 Wells-next-the-Sea—Blakeney, and from B1105 S of Wells; NR23 1NL

Old-fashioned pub with gas lighting in simple rooms, interesting furnishings and pubby food; gramophone museum

This is a place of great, unspoilt character – no tabs, no credit cards, no booking tables in advance and plenty of local customers. The simple interior with its gas lighting looks little changed since the 1920s and parts of the building date back to the 1720s. There are stripped deal or mahogany tables (one marked for shove-ha'penny) on a stone floor, red leatherette settles built around the partly panelled walls of the public bar, royalist photographs and open fires in Victorian fireplaces. An antique American Mills one-arm bandit is still in working order (it takes 5p pieces), there's a big longcase clock with a clear piping strike and a twister on the ceiling to point out who gets the next round; darts, cribbage and dominoes. Greene King IPA and Woodfordes Wherry on handpump, local cider and home-made lemonade; friendly service. One of the outbuildings houses a wind-up gramophone museum – opened on request. There's a courtyard garden with flower tubs and a well, and a garden.

🍴 **Large helpings of proper pub food such as beans on toast, filled baked potatoes, home-cooked gammon, cheese and vegetable pie, braised rabbit or pheasant, several pies and puddings like gold syrup sponge or a cheesecake.** *Starters/Snacks: £3.50 to £5.20. Main Courses: £7.50 to £8.90. Puddings: £3.25*

Free house ~ Licensee Iain Salmon ~ Real ale ~ Bar food (12-1.45, 6-8.30) ~ No credit cards ~ (01328) 710547 ~ Children welcome away from bar area ~ Dogs welcome ~ Open 11.30-2.30, 6-11; 12-2.30, 6-10.30 Sun ~ Bedrooms: £28/£56(£60S)

Recommended by Philip and Susan Philcox, M Mossman, John Beeken, Ben and Helen Ingram, Anthony Longden, the Didler, Roddy and Kate Steen, Pete Baker, Paul and Sue Dix, J D Taylor, Ann and Colin Hunt, Liz and Guy Marshlain, John Wooll, Tracey and Stephen Groves, Barry Collett

WELLS-NEXT-THE-SEA   TF9143   MAP 8

Crown 🍷 🛏

The Buttlands; NR23 1EX

Friendly, informal bar and sunny conservatory in smart coaching inn, local real ales and helpful staff

The beamed bar in this rather smart 16th-c coaching inn is a friendly place with an informal mix of furnishings on the stripped wooden floor, local photographs on the red walls, a good selection of newspapers to read in front of the open fire and Adnams Bitter, Woodfordes Wherry and a guest like Woodfordes Nelsons Revenge on handpump; 17 wines by the glass and quite a few whiskies and brandies. The sunny conservatory has wicker chairs on the tiled floor, beams and modern art and there's a pretty restaurant, too; piped music. There are seats outside on the sheltered sun deck.

People named as recommenders after the main entries have told us that the pub should be included. But they have not written the report – we have, after anonymous on-the-spot inspection.

🍴 Bar food includes sandwiches, soup, steamed local mussels with white wine, garlic and cream, deep-fried fishcakes with tartare sauce, goats cheese and rosemary brûlée with pickled tomato, marinated pork belly with stir-fried noodles and hot and sour sauce, beef burger with gruyère cheese, sweet onions and pepper relish, venison casserole, baked fillet of cod with saffron mash and celeriac remoulade, mozzarella and vegetable tart, and puddings like chocolate brownie or vanilla pod crème brûlée. *Starters/Snacks: £1.40 to £5.45. Main Courses: £8.95 to £13.95. Puddings: £4.85 to £6.25*

Free house ~ Licensees Chris and Jo Coubrough ~ Real ale ~ Bar food (12-2.30, 6.30-9.30) ~ Restaurant ~ (01328) 710209 ~ Children welcome ~ Dogs allowed in bar ~ Open 11-11 ~ Bedrooms: £110B/£120B

Recommended by Ian Chisholm, David and Sue Smith, John Wooll, Mr and Mrs L Haines, Tracey and Stephen Groves, D J Elliott, Graham and June Ward, Walter and Susan Rinaldi-Butcher, John Evans, Simon Cottrell, David Carr, Adele Summers, Alan Black

Globe
The Buttlands; NR23 1EU

Attractive contemporary layout, fair-priced food and drink, and nice back coachyard

This handsome Georgian inn overlooks a pretty, leafy square and is only a short walk from the quay. Inside has been carefully made over to give a relaxed contemporary feel, and the opened-up rooms spread spaciously back from the front bar. Three big bow windows look over to a green lined by tall lime trees, there are well spaced tables on oak boards, walls in grey, cream or mulberry have moody local landscape photoprints, and the modern lighting is well judged. Adnams Bitter, Fullers London Pride and Woodfordes Nelsons Revenge and Wherry on handpump, a good choice of wines and nice coffee; friendly staff, piped music and TV. A nicely updated (and heated) back coachyard has dark green cast-iron furniture on pale flagstones among trellis tubs with lavender, roses and jasmine.

🍴 Very good bar food includes sandwiches, various small sharing plates of marinated olive, chipolatas with mustard dip or hummus with pitta bread, pasta with field mushrooms, garlic cream sauce and parmesan, deep-fried haddock with mushy peas and home-made tartare sauce, popular pies, daily specials, and puddings such as white chocolate crème brûlée and warm rice pudding with plum compote; bargain steak night is Wednesday. *Starters/Snacks: £4.00 to £6.00. Main Courses: £8.00 to £14.00. Puddings: £5.00*

Free house ~ Licensee Steve Loakes ~ Real ale ~ Bar food ~ (01328) 710206 ~ Children welcome ~ Dogs allowed in bar ~ Open 11-11; 12-10.30 Sun ~ Bedrooms: £75B/£115B

Recommended by DF, NF, Steve Nye, Derek Field, Sarah Flynn, J D Taylor, Tracey and Stephen Groves, Vicky Trumper, Paul Humphreys

WEST BECKHAM   TG1439   MAP 8
Wheatsheaf 🍺
Off A148 Holt—Cromer; Church Road; NR25 6NX

Fine real ales and home-made food in nice, traditional pub with seats, swings and chickens in front garden

Chatty and relaxed, this flint-walled and pleasantly traditional pub is the most likely place to find many of the villagers on a dreary winter's day. There's a fine range of real ales tapped from the cask or on handpump that might include Greene King IPA, Woodfordes Nelsons Revenge and Wherry and guests like Batemans XXXB, Fullers London Pride and Greene King Abbot; Weston's cider and several wines by the glass. The bars have beams and cottagey doors, a roaring log fire in one part with a smaller coal one in another, comfortable chairs and banquettes and perhaps the enormous black cat. Games machine, piped music, dominoes and cards. Plenty of seats out in the partly terraced front garden and an area for children with swings, some elusive rabbits, and chickens. There is a purpose-built hut for smokers, with seats.

🍴 Popular bar food such as lunchtime filled baps, baguettes, ciabattas, baked potatoes and ploughman's as well as soup, chicken liver pâté with redcurrant sauce, ham and egg, liver and bacon with rosemary gravy, vegetable and mixed bean lasagne, beer-battered cod with mushy peas, venison and cranberry casserole, steak and kidney pudding, daily specials, and puddings like chocolate and Baileys crème brûlée and passion fruit cheesecake. *Starters/Snacks: £3.75 to £5.50. Main Courses: £7.50 to £12.95. Puddings: £4.25*

Free house ~ Licensees Clare and Daniel Mercer ~ Real ale ~ Bar food (not Sun evening) ~ Restaurant ~ (01263) 822110 ~ Children welcome away from bar ~ Dogs allowed in bar ~ Jazz days in July and August ~ Open 11.30(12 in winter)-3, 6.30-11; 12-3, 7-10.30 Sun in winter

Recommended by Derek Field, John Beeken, M Mossman, Philip and Susan Philcox, Ian Chisholm, MDN, Ryta Lyndley, Fred and Lorraine Gill, Tracey and Stephen Groves

WINTERTON-ON-SEA
TG4919   MAP 8

Fishermans Return 🍽 🛏

From B1159 turn into village at church on bend, then turn right into The Lane; NR29 4BN

Long-serving licensees in busy little local with a fair choice of real ales and warm log fire; sheltered garden, nearby sandy beach

Dogs – and their owners – are made welcome in this busy and attractive little pub and the sandy nearby beach is handy for a walk. The cosily white-painted lounge bar has a roaring log fire, neat brass-studded red leatherette seats and vases of fresh flowers. The panelled public bar has low ceilings and a glossily varnished nautical air (good fire in here too), and there's a family room, dining room, and small public bar. It's been well run by the same hospitable licensees for over 30 years who keep a good choice of real ales on handpump: Adnams Bitter, Broadside and a seasonal beer and Woodfordes Nelsons Revenge and Wherry. Several malt whiskies, Old Rosie cider, and wines by the glass. Darts, pool, juke box and piped music. In fine weather you can sit on the attractive wrought-iron and wooden benches on a pretty front terrace with lovely views or in the sheltered garden.

🍴 Bar food includes toasties, filled baked potatoes, ploughman's, burgers, vegetarian omelette, fish pie, chilli con carne, and puddings. *Starters/Snacks: £3.75 to £6.25. Main Courses: £6.25 to £11.75. Puddings: £3.75*

Free house ~ Licensees John and Kate Findlay ~ Real ale ~ Bar food ~ (01493) 393305 ~ Children welcome in family room, dining room and one bar ~ Dogs welcome ~ Open 11-2.30, 6-11; 11-11 Sat; 12.10.30 Sun ~ Bedrooms: £50B/£70B

Recommended by Alan Cole, Kirstie Bruce, John Saville, Mrs Romey Heaton, Pete and Sue Robbins, Ryta Lyndley, C Galloway

WOODBASTWICK
TG3214   MAP 8

Fur & Feather 🍽

Off B1140 E of Norwich; NR13 6HQ

Full range of first-class beers from next-door Woodfordes brewery, tasty food, friendly service and suprisingly modern décor

With the brewery next door, it's not surprising that the full range of Woodfordes beers in this converted thatched cottage is in tip-top condition. Tapped from the cask, they include Admirals Reserve, Headcracker, Mardlers, Nelsons Revenge, Norfolk Nog, Sundew and Wherry; fast, friendly service. You can also visit the brewery shop. The style and atmosphere are not what you'd expect of a brewery tap as it's set out more like a dining pub and the décor is modern. Ten wines by the glass; piped music. The pub forms part of a very attractive estate village and has tables out in a pleasant garden.

Smoking is not allowed inside any pub.

---

⑪ **Bar food includes sandwiches, filled baguettes and baked potatoes, soup, game pâté with redcurrant and port sauce, home-baked ham and eggs, five-bean enchilada, bangers and mash with beer gravy, steak in ale pie, lambs liver and bacon, seafood medley, and puddings such as crème brûlée and carrot and walnut cake.** *Starters/Snacks: £2.25 to £5.25. Main Courses: £8.00 to £13.50. Puddings: £4.25 to £4.75*

Woodfordes ~ Tenant Tim Ridley ~ Real ale ~ Bar food (12-2(3 Sun), 6-9) ~ Restaurant ~ (01603) 720003 ~ Well behaved children welcome until 9pm ~ Open 11.30-11; 12-10.30 Sun; 11.30-3, 6-11(10.30 Mon and Tues; still open all day Sun) in winter

Recommended by R C Vincent, Pat and Clive Sherriff, Kerry Law, Pete and Sue Robbins, Comus and Sarah Elliott, the Didler, Alan Cole, Kirstie Bruce, Fred and Lorraine Gill, Alastair Gibson, Gerry and Rosemary Dobson

LUCKY DIP

Besides the fully inspected pubs, you might like to try these Lucky Dips recommended to us and described by readers (if you do, please send us reports: www.goodguides.co.uk).

ACLE [TG4111]
Bridge Inn NR13 3AS [N on A1064]: Big riverside pub geared to holiday traffic, two rooms off central bar, Adnams and Woodfordes Wherry, good log fire, usual bar food from baguettes and baked potatoes up, good-sized vaulted-ceiling restaurant, several interconnecting rooms comfortably furnished with a variety of settles, chairs and tables *(Gerry and Rosemary Dobson)*
ATTLEBOROUGH [TM0495]
Griffin NR17 2AH [Church St]: Much modernised former coaching inn next to magnificent church, Greene King IPA and Abbot, local Wolf beers and a guest such as Spectrum Bezants, bargain food from sandwiches up, pleasant modern furnishings in longish bar, small restaurant area; games and piped music *(W W Burke)*
Mulberry Tree NR17 2AS [Station Rd]: Good imaginative upmarket food, well kept ales such as Adnams and Timothy Taylors Landlord, neat and stylish décor in bar and restaurant; tables out under cocktail parasols in garden with bowling green, comfortable bedrooms *(Alan Cole, Kirstie Bruce)*
AYLMERTON [TG1840]
Roman Camp NR11 8QD [Holt Rd (A148)]: Comfortable panelled bar with cosy armchair sitting room off, light and airy dining room with parlour palms, well kept Adnams, Timothy Taylors Landlord and Charles Wells Bombardier, helpful staff, reasonably priced food; picnic-sets in attractive sheltered garden behind *(Judith Salter)*
AYLSHAM [TG1926]
☆ *Black Boys* NR11 6EH [Market Pl]: Attractive 17th-c market-place inn with panelled bar and dining room, friendly helpful young staff, Adnams IPA, Greene King Abbot and IPA and a guest beer, good range of food from generous light dishes up; pavement tables, bedrooms *(David Edwards, Keith Reeve, Marie Hammond, John Wooll)*
BARFORD [TG1107]
☆ *Cock* NR9 4AS [B1108 7 miles W of Norwich]: Nicely restored traditional main-road pub brewing its own good attractively priced Blue Moon ales, good food (freshly made, so

may take a time) from large lunchtime sandwiches to interestingly cooked main dishes and plenty of fish, friendly helpful service and pleasantly relaxed atmosphere, good mix of candlelit tables, shove-ha'penny, smarter back restaurant extension; well chosen piped music, occasional jazz *(BB, Bruce Bird)*
BARTON BENDISH [TF7105]
☆ *Spread Eagle* PE33 9DP [off A1122 W of Swaffham; Church Rd]: Attractive dining pub with good fresh inventive food cooked by landlord inc light lunches and local game, service prompt and welcoming even when busy, decent wines inc champagne by the glass, real ales such as Adnams, scrubbed tables in two neat and rather elegant small front rooms, back evening restaurant; pleasant garden, quiet village, cl all Mon, Tues/Weds lunchtime, open all day Sun till 6 *(Sally Anne and Peter Goodale, Anthony Barnes, Mr and Mrs C Prentis, BB, Nicky Prentis)*
BINHAM [TF9839]
☆ *Chequers* NR21 0AL [B1388 SW of Blakeney]: Friendly and efficient staff in long low-beamed 17th-c pub with splendid coal fires each end, enjoyable changing home-made food from chatty chef using local produce (no booking), their own Front Street ales, quickly changing guest beers and fine choice of bottled imports, decent house wines, inglenook, sturdy plush seats, some nice old local prints; picnic-sets out in front and on grass behind, interesting village with huge priory church *(Steve Nye, Judith Salter, Pete Baker, Philip and Susan Philcox, BB, Ann and Colin Hunt, MDN, Tracey and Stephen Groves, Derek Field, Julia Mann, R C Vincent)*
BLAKENEY [TG0244]
Blakeney Hotel NR25 7NE [The Quay]: Well run hotel nicely set nr bird marshes, elegant harbour-view bar with good sensibly priced lunchtime sandwiches and other food, friendly attentive staff, good atmosphere, well kept Greene King IPA and Abbot, games room; dogs welcome, bedrooms very comfortable, swimming pool, well set up for family breaks *(MDN, W W Burke)*

BLICKLING [TG1728]

☆ *Buckinghamshire Arms* NR11 6NF [B1354 NW of Aylsham]: Handsome Jacobean inn by gates to Blickling Hall (NT), small and appealing proper unpretentious bar as well as more extensive eating areas, wide choice of enjoyable if not cheap food from baguettes and baked potatoes up, friendly helpful service, well kept Adnams Best and Broadside and Woodfordes Wherry, local cider, good range of wines; well behaved children in restaurant, lots of tables out on big lawn with summer food servery, bedrooms with own bathrooms, may open all day in summer (*Mrs Mahni Pannett, Terry Mizen, J F M and M West, Brian Root, Philip and Susan Philcox, Keith Reeve, Marie Hammond, LYM, Rob Winstanley*)

BRESSINGHAM [TM0781]

Chequers IP22 2AG [Low Rd]: Friendly and popular pub opp church, thriving atmosphere and enjoyable food in two dining areas; well behaved children welcome (*Bill and Marian de Bass*)

BROOKE [TM2899]

Kings Head NR15 1AB [Norwich Rd (B1332)]: Recently taken over by good Norwich restaurateurs, stripped wood and scrubbed pine tables in convivial bar with log fire and smart eating area up a step, good interesting food from lunchtime ciabattas up, splendid choice of wines by the glass (and of glass sizes), friendly efficient service, small back restaurant, picnic-sets in sheltered garden (*Roger and Lesley Everett*)

BURNHAM OVERY STAITHE [TF8444]

Hero PE31 8JE [A149]: Interesting and tasty up-to-date food, good range of wines by the glass, Adnams, contemporary décor with stripped wood or painted floors, comfortable bar with woodburner, two dining areas and pastel walls (*Roger and Lesley Everett*)

BURSTON [TM1383]

Crown IP22 5TW [Mill Rd]: Friendly two-bar country pub with good relaxed atmosphere, lots of old woodwork, simple fresh home cooking using local supplies, well kept ales, small restaurant (*Alan Cole, Kirstie Bruce*)

BUXTON [TG2322]

Old Crown NR10 5EN [Crown Rd]: Good choice of enjoyable sensibly priced food, well kept ales such as Adnams and Woodfordes Wherry, good housekeeping (*Brian and Jean Hepworth*)

CASTLE ACRE [TF8115]

Albert Victor PE32 2AE [Stocks Green]: Recently reopened after refurbishment, interesting choice of enjoyable food, pleasant staff, Greene King ales, good range of wines by the glass; large attractive back garden and pergola (*Anthony Barnes, Chris and Susie Cammack*)

CASTLE RISING [TF6624]

Black Horse PE31 6AG: Large comfortable dining pub with plenty of tables in two front areas and smarter back dining room, real ales such as Adnams, Elgoods, Marstons Pedigree and Woodfordes Wherry, decent

choice of wines by the glass, reasonably priced standard food all day from baguettes and baked potatoes to steak and Sun lunch, friendly landladies, good furnishings inc sofas; piped music, no dogs; children particularly welcome, close-set tables out under cocktail parasols, by church and almshouses in pleasant unspoilt village, open all day (*Mike Ridgway, Sarah Miles, John Wooll, Tracey and Stephen Groves, Ryta Lyndley*)

CAWSTON [TG1422]

☆ *Ratcatchers* NR10 4HA [off B1145; Eastgate, S of village]: Dining pub with L-shaped beamed bar, open fire, nice old chairs and fine mix of walnut, beech, elm and oak tables, quieter candlelit dining room on right, Adnams Bitter and Broadside and a beer from Woodfordes, quite a few malt whiskies, conservatory; piped music, no dogs; children welcome, heated terrace, open all day Sun (*J S and S Chadwick, Philip and Susan Philcox, Sheila and Brian Wilson, LYM, David Twitchett, Dr and Mrs R G J Telfer, Barry Collett, Roy Hoing*)

CHEDGRAVE [TM3699]

White Horse NR14 6ND [Norwich Rd]: Welcoming service, good food from home-baked bread sandwiches up using local produce (fresh cooking, so may be a wait), Adnams Bitter and Broadside, Flowers IPA and Timothy Taylors Landlord, good choice of wines by the glass and bottle, log fire, panelled tap room, restaurant; children welcome (*Roger and Lesley Everett, Richard and Margaret McPhee*)

CLEY NEXT THE SEA [TG0443]

☆ *George* NR25 7RN [High St, off A149 W of Sheringham]: Good atmosphere and smiling service in well run pub/hotel with pleasant contemporary décor, friendly staff, some emphasis on enjoyable and fairly priced food inc good fish, good choice of wines by the glass, well kept Greene King Abbot; sizeable garden over road, lovely walks, bedrooms (*Terry Mizen, Mrs Romey Heaton, Charles Gysin, LYM*)

Three Swallows NR25 7TT [off A149; Newgate Green]: Straightforward food (all day wknds) from sandwiches up, unpretentious take-us-as-you-find-us style, banquettes around long high leathered tables, log fire, steps up to another small family eating area, second log fire in further stripped pine dining room on left, Adnams and Greene King IPA and Abbot from unusual richly carved bar, decent wines, nice photographs, dominoes, cribbage; children and dogs welcome, big garden with budgerigar aviary, surprisingly grandiose fountain, wooden climbing frame; handy for the salt marshes, simple bedrooms, open all day wknds and summer (*Geoff and Pat Bell, R C Vincent, MDN, LYM, Pat and Tony Martin, Barry Collett, Derek Field, Roy Hoing*)

COLTISHALL [TG2719]

☆ *Kings Head* NR12 7EA [Wroxham Rd (B1354)]: Welcoming dining pub close to river, good imaginative food esp fish, generous bar snacks and good value lunch deals, thai menu too, Adnams, good wines, friendly helpful service, open fire, lots of fishing nets and several stuffed fish inc a 50lb pike (personable chef/landlord competes in international fishing contests); piped music; reasonably priced bedrooms, decent breakfast, moorings nearby *(BB, Andrew Gardner, J S and S Chadwick, M J Bourke)*

COLTON [TG1009]
Ugly Bug NR9 5DG [well signed once off A47]: New licensees yet again for comfortable country pub with plenty of beamery, plush banquettes and old enamel advertisements in extensive carpeted bar, good service, decent helpings of standard food from lunchtime sandwiches up in bar and restaurant, OAP deals, changing real ales such as Woodfordes Wherry, sensible choice of wines, conservatory; terrace and big garden with koi carp in pretty lake, bedrooms *(Bill and Sheila McLardy, BB)*

CROMER [TG2242]
Red Lion NR27 9HD [off A149; Tucker St]: Pubby carpeted bar in substantial Victorian seafront hotel with great sea views, stripped flint and William Morris wallpaper, old bottles and chamber-pots, lots of lifeboat pictures, Adnams and Woodfordes Wherry, friendly staff, pleasant old-fashioned atmosphere (rather like that of the town itself), wide choice of reasonably priced standard food, restaurant; tables in back courtyard, comfortable bedrooms *(MDN, Fred and Lorraine Gill, Edward Mirzoeff)*

DOCKING [TF7637]
Railway Inn PE31 8LY [Station Rd]: Unpretentious local with wide choice of good sensibly priced home cooking inc fresh fish and Thurs steak night, generous helpings, polite attentive service, two or three well kept ales such as local Buffys Bitter, good house wines, small chummy bar with woodburner, pool and TV in little lounge behind, panelled and carpeted dining room with lots of fresh flowers and some rail prints and posters; pleasant small side garden with marquee, open all day wknds *(Tracey and Stephen Groves, James Crouchman, George Atkinson, Derek and Sylvia Stephenson)*

EAST BARSHAM [TF9133]
White Horse NR21 0LH [B1105 3 miles N of Fakenham]: Extended pub with big log fire in long beamed main bar, steps to other areas, real ales such as Adnams Bitter and Broadside and Wells & Youngs Bombardier, decent wine, good coffee, pleasant staff, wide choice of straightforward food inc OAP lunches, two small attractive dining rooms; piped music, darts; children welcome, well priced bedrooms *(Philip and Susan Philcox, R C Vincent)*

EAST RUSTON [TG3428]
Butchers Arms NR12 9JG [back rd Horning—Happisburgh, N of Stalham]: Comfortable

village local, friendly and well run, with generous enjoyable food inc bargain lunchtime dish of the day, real ales, two dining rooms; attractive garden, pretty hanging baskets, handy for Old Vicarage garden *(Michael Sargent, Roy Hoing)*

EDGEFIELD [TG0934]
☆ *Three Pigs* NR24 2RL [Norwich Rd (B1149)]: Continuing refurbishment by new licensees, good cheerful service, already getting very popular for good distinctive food from open-view kitchen, from lunchtime sandwiches up inc pork specialities and several interesting dishes, good choice of local beers inc Yetmans, nice range of wines by the glass; children welcome, disabled access, work on new outdoor seating area as we go to press *(June and Ken Brooks, Derek Field, Tracey and Stephen Groves)*

FAKENHAM [TF9129]
Crown NR21 9BP [Market Pl]: Elizabethan inn completely refurbished in clean-cut contemporary style, modern wood tables, chrome and steel fittings, Adnams and Fullers London Pride, good choice of wines by the glass, sensibly priced tasty bar and restaurant food, friendly if not always speedy service, interesting former gallery staircase; courtyard tables, bedrooms, open all day from 10 *(LYM, John Wooll)*

GAYTON [TF7219]
Crown PE32 1PA [Lynn Rd (B1145/B1153)]: Low-beamed pub with plenty of character, unusual old features and charming snug as well as three main areas, good choice of sensibly priced food inc good value sandwiches, light dishes and lunchtime hot buffet, friendly service, Greene King ales, limited but good wine choice, efficient service, good log fire, games room; tables in sheltered and attractive garden *(Tracey and Stephen Groves, LYM, Hamish Breach)*

GELDESTON [TM3990]
☆ *Locks* NR34 0HW [off A143/A146 NW of Beccles; off Station Rd S of village, obscurely signed down long rough track]: Remote pub alone at the navigable head of the River Waveney, ancient tiled-floor core with beams, candles and big log fire, large extension for summer crowds, Green Jack and guest ales tapped from casks, enjoyable food, friendly informal service; wknd music nights, summer evening barbecues; riverside garden, open all day; cl Mon, Tues in winter *(LYM, Alan Cole, Kirstie Bruce, the Didler)*
Wherry NR34 0LB [The Street]: Enjoyable food from good ploughman's up, well kept Adnams; pleasant garden *(Alan Cole, Kirstie Bruce)*

GREAT BIRCHAM [TF7632]
☆ *Kings Head* PE31 6RJ [B1155, S end of village (called and signed Bircham locally)]: More hotel/restaurant than pub now, but still has plenty of regulars and interesting choice of local real ales in small attractively contemporary bar with log fire and comfortable sofas; good innovative food is

confined to the light and airy modern restaurant, much stainless steel, glass and plain dark wood, leather-walled back area, sumptuous lavatories; tables and chairs out front and back with rustic view, comfortable bedrooms, good breakfast *(LYM, Tracey and Stephen Groves)*

GREAT CRESSINGHAM [TF8401]

☆ *Windmill* IP25 6NN [village signed off A1065 S of Swaffham; Water End]: Masses of interesting pictures and bric-a-brac in well managed warren of rambling linked rooms with plenty of cosy corners, keenly priced fresh bar food from baguettes to steak (shame about those sauce sachets), three Sun roasts, log or coal fire, Adnams Bitter and Broadside, Greene King IPA, Windy Miller Quixote (brewed for the pub) and interesting guest beers, good coffee, decent wines, plenty of malt whiskies, cheery staff, well lit pool room, pub games; faint piped music, big sports TV in side snug; children and dogs welcome, picnic-sets and good play area in big garden, new bedroom extension *(LYM, MDN, Mike and Shelley Woodroffe, Simon and Mandy King, Minda and Stanley Alexander, Julian and Janet Dearden, Charles Gysin, Rita Scarratt, Gordon Neighbour, Mrs Shirley Hughes, Miss A G Drake)*

GREAT MASSINGHAM [TF7922]

Dabbling Duck PE32 2HN [Abbey Rd]: Former Rose & Crown, completely refurbished and reopened by small group of villagers after some years' closure; welcoming and attractive, with small and well thought out choice of good food (best to book), scrubbed kitchen tables, pale green décor, shelves of books and board games; by village green with big duck pond, bedrooms *(Sally Anne and Peter Goodale)*

GREAT YARMOUTH [TG5206]

Red Herring NR30 3HQ [Havelock Rd]: Welcoming unpretentious open-plan alehouse with Greene King and several changing ales at attractive prices inc a Mild, farm cider, rock collection, old local photographs, books to read, games area with pool; open all day Sun *(Mrs M Hatwell, the Didler)*

HARPLEY [TF7825]

☆ *Rose & Crown* PE31 6TW [off A148 Fakenham—Kings Lynn; Nethergate St]: Refreshing contemporary décor with local artwork and old wooden tables, reliable food inc some interesting dishes as well as the usual pubby things, well organised friendly young staff, good choice of wines by the glass, three well kept ales inc Greene King, big log fire, dining room on left; tables in attractive garden, cl Mon, Tues lunchtime *(John Wooll, R C Vincent, BB, Mark, Amanda, Luke and Jake Sheard)*

HEACHAM [TF6737]

Fox & Hounds PE31 7EX [Station Rd]: Unpretentious open-plan pub brewing its own good Fox Heacham Gold, also well kept guest beers and Saxon farm cider, friendly service, good generous food (not Sun

evening), nice mix of seating on the right, pine tables in spotless light and airy dining area; pool, games machine; small garden, open all day *(Tracey and Stephen Groves)*

HETHERSETT [TG1504]

Queens Head NR9 3DD [Norwich Rd (B1172)]: Large pub, very popular wknds, with enjoyable reasonably priced food inc good fish and (best to book) Sun carvery, welcoming efficient staff, Adnams Bitter and Broadside and Greene King IPA, good value wines, back family dining extension; nice garden with heaters and play area *(Maggie Cooper)*

HEVINGHAM [TG1720]

Marsham Arms NR10 5NP [B1149 N of Norwich]: Roomy modern-feeling roadside pub with cheerful and long-serving chef/landlord doing wide range of generous standard food and good specials, self-serve salad cart, children's helpings, well kept ales inc Adnams and Fullers London Pride, good wines and country wines, friendly helpful staff; double family room on right, good wheelchair access, tables in garden behind, well appointed roomy chalet bedrooms behind *(BB, Roger and Lesley Everett)*

HOLT [TG0738]

Feathers NR25 6BW [Market Pl]: Unpretentious town hotel with bustling locals' bar comfortably extended around original panelled area with open fire, attractive entrance/reception area with antiques, helpful friendly staff, good value promptly served generous food, Greene King IPA and Abbot, decent wines, good coffee, calm dining room; piped music, busy on Sat market day; dogs welcome *(J S and S Chadwick, W W Burke, BB, Derek Field)*

HONINGHAM [TG1011]

Olde Buck NR9 5BL [The Street, just off A47]: Picturesque 16th-c pub with linked beamed rooms, particularly helpful friendly service, wide-ranging well prepared food from good sandwiches up, well kept Adnams Broadside, good choice of soft drinks, reasonably priced wines *(John Saville, Richard and Jean Green)*

HORSTEAD [TG2619]

☆ *Recruiting Sergeant* NR12 7EE [B1150 just S of Coltishall]: Large, friendly and pleasantly refurbished, with good value generous food from fresh baguettes up inc good fish choice, splendid service even though busy, real ales inc one brewed for the pub, impressive choice of reasonably priced wines by the glass, big open fire, brasses and muskets, music-free smaller room; children welcome *(Leda Hayton, W M Lien, M J Bourke)*

INGHAM [TG3926]

Swan NR12 9AB: Ancient low-beamed thatched inn with interesting corners in compact dimly lit rambling rooms on two levels, scrubbed tables and fishing boat photographs, welcoming landlord, charming staff and jolly atmosphere, enormous helpings of good food from baguettes and standard pubby things to more elaborate dishes, five well kept ales inc Woodfordes Wherry and Nelsons Revenge, small family room; small enclosed garden and courtyard, five bedrooms in detached block *(Tracey and Stephen Groves, Mr and Mrs D S Price)*

KENNINGHALL [TM0386]

Red Lion NR16 2EP [B1113 S of Norwich; East Church St]: Stripped beams, old pictures and floor tiles, cosy panelled snug, open fires, back stable-style restaurant area with woodburner, enjoyable fresh food from good baguettes up, friendly helpful young staff, well kept Greene King, Woodfordes Wherry and guest beers; tables out by back bowling green, bedrooms in former stable block, open all day wknds *(Bruce Bird)*

KING'S LYNN [TF6119]

Bradleys PE30 5DT [South Quay]: Stylishly simple bar/restaurant with good sensibly priced food, good choice of wines by the glass, Adnams, beautiful curtains, ornate mirrors, plenty of flowers, local artwork, more expensive upstairs restaurant with lunch deals; quayside tables and small back garden, open all day *(John Wooll)*

Crown & Mitre PE30 1LJ [Ferry St]: Old-fashioned pub full of Naval and nautical memorabilia, generous sandwiches, baked potatoes and a hot dish lunchtimes, three or four constantly changing real ales, river views from back conservatory *(John Wooll)*

Dukes Head PE30 1JS [Tuesday Market Pl]: Imposing early 18th-c hotel with decent food from baguettes up in simple and informal front dining room (something of a well kept rum tea room in atmosphere), efficient friendly service, local pictures, sofas in inner lounge, sedate back bar and more formal restaurant; bedrooms *(John Wooll)*

Wenns PE30 5DQ [Saturday Market Pl]: Up-to-date town pub with Greene King ales, decent wines, wide choice of reasonably priced simple food from baguettes and baked potatoes up, efficient friendly service *(David Carr)*

LITTLE DUNHAM [TF8612]

Black Swan PE32 2DG [off A47 E of Swaffham]: Roomy pub with tables in front bar and in side restaurant areas, enjoyable fresh food, welcoming helpful service, well kept real ales, pleasant décor with old pictures *(Eric Bojku)*

LITTLE FRANSHAM [TF8911]

Canary & Linnet NR19 2JW [Maid Rd (A47 Swaffham—Dereham)]: Friendly 16th-c former blacksmith's cottage with good value food (not Sun evening) in beamed bar and back restaurant, good service, well kept Greene King IPA and guests such as Adnams Broadside and Woodfordes Wherry, decent wines, inglenook woodburner, pictures and brasses; charming cottage garden *(Sally Anne and Peter Goodale)*

LITTLE SNORING [TF9632]

Green Man NR21 0AY [Holt Rd]: Modern-style building with reasonably priced pubby food, Adnams and Youngs ales, decent wines

by the glass, pleasant service, front bar with children's/pool room on left and good-sized dining room on right; children welcome *(John Wooll)*

MUNDFORD [TL8093]

Crown IP26 5HQ [off A1065 Thetford—Swaffham; Crown Rd]: Friendly and unassuming heavily beamed olde-worlde pub with huge fireplace, interesting local memorabilia, good range of real ales, dozens of malt whiskies, sensibly priced down-to-earth food, spiral iron stairs to large restaurant with restaurant, games, TV and juke box in red-tiled locals' bar; children and dogs welcome, back terrace and garden with wishing well, bedrooms with own bathrooms, open all day *(LYM, Roy and Lindsey Fentiman, Will Watson)*

NEW BUCKENHAM [TM0890]

Kings Head NR16 2AN [Market Pl]: Homely 17th-c pub on green opp medieval market cross, Adnams and Cottage Gone With The Whippet, helpful friendly service, cheerful regulars, reasonably priced pubby food cooked to order from sandwiches up, comfortable and atmospheric back dining area *(Ian Phillips)*

NEWTON [TF8315]

George & Dragon PE32 2BX [A1065 4 miles N of Swaffham]: Useful roadside pub with several small dining areas popular with older people (good value meals for them), friendly new management, real ales; pleasant garden with play area, great views to Castle Acre Priory *(Mark, Amanda, Luke and Jake Sheard)*

NORTH CREAKE [TF8538]

☆ *Jolly Farmers* NR21 9JW [Burnham Rd]: Lurid yellow exterior hides low-beamed pub with attractive candlelit back dining room, chatty landlord striking good balance between proper old-fashioned pub atmosphere and the food side with its careful use of local produce, good log fire in one small bar, woodburner and pool in the other, well kept Adnams and Woodfordes, good wines by the glass, impressively sturdy country furnishings; children welcome in dining areas, tables in sheltered garden, charming village, cl Mon/Tues in winter *(BB, Terry Mizen, Peter Worsnop, Tracey and Stephen Groves, John and Elizabeth Leigh, R L Borthwick)*

NORTH WOOTTON [TF6424]

House on the Green PE30 3RE [Ling Common Rd]: Much changed under current landlord, tidy and roomy, with good range of food from basic garden menu through baguettes, baked potatoes and other light lunches to more elaborate dishes, friendly attentive staff, good choice of well kept beers; good welcome for families, lots of tables out on back terrace and lawn, bowling green and some play equipment *(R C Vincent)*

NORWICH [TG2408]

Coach & Horses NR1 1BA [Thorpe Rd]: Light and airy tap for Chalk Hill brewery, with their own good ales and guest beers, friendly service, good choice of generous home cooking 12-9 (8 Sun), also breakfast with limitless coffee; bare-boards L-shaped bar with open fire, lots of dark wood, posters and prints, pleasant back dining area; sports TV; disabled access possible (not to lavatories), picnic-sets on front terrace, may be summer barbecues, open all day *(the Didler)*

Compleat Angler NR1 1NS [Prince of Wales Rd, on bridge by stn]: Chain pub worth knowing for its position opp River Wensum boat station, terrace tables by colourful window boxes; Woodfordes Wherry and other real ales, usual bar lunches from sandwiches up; TV, games machines *(Dennis Jones)*

Ketts NR1 4EX [Ketts Hill]: Several separate areas inc smart conservatory/games room, good choice of changing ales such as Crouch Vale and Woodfordes, frequent beer festivals, friendly atmosphere, food using local organic meats inc evening curries and Sun roasts; tables in small garden behind, open all day *(James Crouchman)*

Kings Head NR3 1JE [Magdalen St]: Handsome Victorian-style renovation, up to 14 handpumps for fine range of well kept changing regional ales and a local farm cider, good choice of imported beers, enthusiastic landlord; open all day *(Bruce Bird)*

Rouen NR1 3JX [Farmers Ave]: Relaxed atmosphere, good value food, well kept Adnams and Greene King, quick and helpful friendly service, great Norwich views from upstairs dining room; big-screen TV *(Tony Middis)*

Take Five NR3 1HF [opp Cathedral gate]: Pleasant and relaxed cross between pub and studenty café, St Peters and Woodfordes Wherry, farm cider, impressive wine choice inc many organic by the glass, good value cheerful largely vegetarian and organic food inc generous fresh light dishes, helpful young staff *(Keith Reeve, Marie Hammond, Peter and Pat Frogley, John Wooll)*

Woolpack NR3 1DJ [Muspole St]: Small warmly friendly local with real ales and good value pubby food inc no-frills night Weds and bargain Sun roasts; pub cat called Monty *(Sarah Buttifant)*

OLD HUNSTANTON [TF6842]
Ancient Mariner PE36 6JJ [part of L'Estrange Arms Hotel, Golf Course Rd]: Relaxed and cheerful rambling barn conversion, dark low beams and timbers, bare bricks and flagstones, masses of maritime bric-a-brac, several little areas inc conservatory and upstairs family gallery, pleasant furnishings, well kept Adnams Bitter and Broadside, Woodfordes Wherry and a guest beer, good wines by the glass, courteous and efficient young staff, popular menu, open fires, papers and magazines; hotel in prime spot, terrace and long sea-view garden down to dunes, children welcome, play area, nice bedrooms, open all day Fri-Sun and summer *(Bruce Bird, Tracey and Stephen Groves)*

Neptune PE36 6HZ [Old Hunstanton Rd]: Friendly landlord and good service, log fire,

daily papers and magazines, local landscapes and Lloyd Loom chairs in small front bar with three real ales such as Greene King Abbot, good wines by the glass, short good value lunchtime food choice, equally appealing if more pricy evening menu, plenty of local fish, nice prints in stylish side dining room; small gravel terrace, seven bedrooms *(John Wooll, Tracey and Stephen Groves)*

REEPHAM [TG0922]
☆ *Kings Arms* NR10 4JJ [Market Pl]: Attractive 17th-c coaching inn with good range of ales inc Adnams and Woodfordes Wherry, wide choice of reasonably priced food from sandwiches up, decent wines by the glass, friendly efficient service, warm local atmosphere, pleasant décor in several linked areas, beams and stripped brickwork, three open fires, games area one end, steps to restaurant; tables out in sunny courtyard, bedrooms *(Ian Chisholm, Comus and Sarah Elliott)*

☆ *Old Brewery House* NR10 4JJ [Market Sq]: Georgian hotel with big log fire in high-ceilinged panelled bar overlooking old-fashioned town square, lots of farming and fishing bric-a-brac, Greene King and a guest such as Adnams, decent wines by the glass, attentive friendly staff, reasonably priced food from well filled sandwiches up, side lounge, dining area, public bar and restaurant; piped music; children and dogs welcome, tables in attractive courtyard with covered well and garden with pond and fountain, bedrooms, open all day *(MDN, the Didler, George Atkinson, LYM, John Wooll)*

ROCKLAND ST MARY [TG3204]
New Inn NR14 7HP [New Inn Hill]: Over rd from staithe, traditional local-feel core with coal fire, sofas, darts and real ales such as Adnams Broadside, more contemporary eating area opening into attractive barn-style restaurant extension with picture-window views, reasonably priced enjoyable pubby food, friendly service; children welcome, good disabled access, front terrace tables, back garden, good walks to Rockland Broad and bird hides *(Mark, Amanda, Luke and Jake Sheard)*

ROYDON [TF7022]
Three Horseshoes PE32 1AQ [the one nr Kings Lynn; Lynn Rd]: Two-bar pub with wide choice of good value food from familiar basics to real exotics, friendly attentive service, pleasant décor in bar and restaurant, Greene King and other ales; tables outside *(R C Vincent)*

SALTHOUSE [TG0743]
☆ *Dun Cow* NR25 7XA [A149 Blakeney—Sheringham]: Airy pub overlooking salt marshes, well used by holidaymakers, with generous unpretentious food all day from good fresh crab sandwiches and baked potatoes to local fish, pleasant staff, Adnams Broadside and Greene King IPA and Abbot, decent wines, open fires, stripped beams and cob walls in big barn-like main

bar, family bar and games room with pool; piped radio, blues nights; coast views from big attractive walled front garden, sheltered courtyard with figs and apples, separate family garden with play area, good walks and bird-watching, bedrooms and self-catering *(Roger Wain-Heapy, Ben and Helen Ingram, John Evans, BB, Derek Field, David Eberlin, Roy Hoing)*

SCULTHORPE [TF8930]

Sculthorpe Mill NR21 9QG [inn signed off A148 W of Fakenham, opp village]: Rebuilt 18th-c mill conversion notable for its appealing riverside setting, seats out under weeping willows and in attractive garden behind; mainly light, airy and functional inside, with sturdy new tables and big prints in two more conversational rooms on right, reasonably priced standard food from sandwiches and snack menu to full meals, well kept Greene King IPA and Old Speckled Hen, decent house wines, good service; piped music may be loud; children in eating areas, open all day wknds and summer, comfortable bedrooms, good breakfast *(John Evans, John Wooll, Tracey and Stephen Groves, LYM, Sue Crees)*

SEDGEFORD [TF7036]

☆ ***King William IV*** PE36 5LU [B1454, off A149 Kings Lynn—Hunstanton]: Friendly and popular, with hard-working obliging staff, good value mainly traditional food, Adnams and Woodfordes Wherry, well chosen wines, convivial panelled bar and two dining areas, warm woodburner; attractive terrace and garden, nice bedrooms, good breakfast *(Tracey and Stephen Groves, Scott Emery, Mr and Mrs A Hetherington)*

SHERINGHAM [TG1543]

Lobster NR26 8JP [High St]: Sizeable pub almost on seafront, seafaring décor in tidy panelled bar with old sewing-machine treadle tables and warm fire, Adnams, Greene King and interesting guest beers, farm cider, decent wines, good value quickly served generous bar meals (they are helpful with special dietary needs), restaurant with good seafood specials, public bar with games inc pool, no piped music; dogs on leads allowed, two courtyards with summer hog roasts and heated marquee, open all day *(David Carr, David and Sue Smith, Fred and Lorraine Gill)*

SMALLBURGH [TG3324]

☆ ***Crown*** NR12 9AD: 15th-c thatched and beamed village inn with friendly proper landlord, good pub atmosphere, well kept Adnams, Caledonian Deuchars IPA and Greene King IPA and Abbot, good choice of wines by the glass, straightforward home-made food in bar and upstairs dining room, prompt service, daily papers, darts; no dogs or children inside; picnic-sets in sheltered and pretty back garden, bedrooms, cl Mon lunchtime, Sun evening *(Philip and Susan Philcox, P B Morgan, BB)*

SOUTH WOOTTON [TF6622]

Farmers Arms PE30 3HQ [part of Knights Hill Hotel, Grimston Rd (off A148/A149)]: Olde-

worlde conversion of barn and stables, popular for speedily served food all day in bar and restaurant, real ales such as Adnams and Fullers, good wines, abundant coffee, polite efficient service, stripped brick and timbers, quiet snugs and corners; piped music may obtrude; children welcome, tables and play area outside, comfortable bedrooms, open all day *(R C Vincent, Tracey and Stephen Groves)*

SOUTHREPPS [TG2536]

Vernon Arms NR11 8NP [Church St]: Old-fashioned village pub with welcoming service, enjoyable food running up to steaks and well priced crab and lobster specials, real ales such as Adnams, Black Sheep, Timothy Taylors and Wells & Youngs, good choice of malt whiskies *(M J Winterton)*

SPOONER ROW [TM0997]

Three Boars NR18 9LL [just off A11 SW of Wymondham]: Olde-worlde two-bar village pub with good friendly staff, great atmosphere, well kept Adnams, good wine choice, good if not cheap food in restaurant *(Brenda Crossley)*

STOKE FERRY [TL7000]

Blue Bell PE33 9SW [Lynn Rd]: Current chef/landlord doing enjoyable food (not all menu may be available) in warmly welcoming village pub with attractive décor, good wines by the glass, two open fires *(Chris and Susie Cammack, Sally Anne and Peter Goodale)*

STOKE HOLY CROSS [TG2302]

Wildebeest NR14 8QJ [Norwich Rd]: Restauranty pub with emphasis on good interesting bistro-style food but provision for drinkers in attractive old bar, good beer and wine by the glass, good cheerfully welcoming service, some unusual decorations inc african wooden masks; shame about the piped music *(Sue Demont, Tim Barrow, Sheila and Brian Wilson)*

SUTTON [TG3823]

☆ ***Sutton Staithe*** NR12 9QS [signed off A149 S of Stalham]: In unspoilt part of the Broads, linked areas with cosy alcoves and some flagstones, welcoming service, well kept Adnams ales, good value simple lunchtime food and wider choice of home-made evening dishes, traditional puddings and children's dishes, bargain prices, river-view restaurant with popular Sun carvery, games area with pool; tables on pretty terrace and in good-sized garden with good play area, nearby moorings, ten comfortable bedrooms *(Philip and Susan Philcox, LYM)*

SWANTON ABBOT [TG2625]

Jolly Farmers NR10 5DW [off B1150 S of N Walsham]: Welcoming country local with three linked rooms, well kept ales such as Greene King, good helpings of reasonably priced traditional food *(Brian and Jean Hepworth)*

TACOLNESTON [TM1495]

Pelican NR16 1AL [Norwich Rd]: Spotless, with considerate service and enjoyable reasonably priced food *(Roy Moseley)*

WALCOTT [TG3532]
Lighthouse NR12 0PE [Coast Rd, nr church (B1159 S of village)]: Cheery rather than smart, with friendly helpful staff, wide range of generous fresh family food from toasties up, Adnams and other changing ales; children in dining room and family room with toys; tables on covered terrace, summer barbecues and evening entertainment marquee, good walks nearby *(Mr and Mrs D S Price)*

WALSINGHAM [TF9336]
Black Lion NR22 6DB [Friday Market Pl]: Dates from 14th c, comfortable and welcoming, with three panelled rooms, cast-iron stove in one, open fire in another, various alcoves and small restaurant; wide choice of good value bar food from lunchtime baguettes up, well kept Woodfordes, decent wines, prompt service; good bedrooms *(Julia Mann)*
Bull NR22 6BP [Common Place/Shire Hall Plain]: Cheery pub in centre of pilgrimage village, darkly ancient bar's walls covered with clerical visiting cards, welcoming landlord and good-humoured staff, nice lunchtime sandwiches and generous and interesting fresh hot dishes, well kept Adnams, Greene King and guests such as Black Sheep and Brains SA; picnic-sets out in courtyard and on attractive flowery terrace on busy village square *(Sue Demont, Tim Barrow, Julia Mann)*

WELLS-NEXT-THE-SEA [TF9143]
☆ *Bowling Green* NR23 1JB [Church St]: Attractively refurbished and welcoming L-shaped bar, hearty traditional food at raised dining end (freshly made so may be a wait), friendly helpful service, Greene King IPA and Abbot and Woodfordes Wherry and Nelsons Revenge, two woodburners, panelling, flagstone and brick floor, simple furnishings; tables out on back terrace, quiet spot on outskirts *(David Carr, Eddie and Lynn Jarrett, John Wooll)*
Edinburgh NR23 1AE [Station Rd/Church St]: Friendly traditional pub with good value pubby food from interesting filled rolls to lovely home-made puddings, well kept Hancocks and a guest such as Iceni Raspberry Wheat, sizeable restaurant, lots of local photographs for sale; piped music, no

credit cards; children treated well, small back terrace, three bedrooms *(Mike Ridgway, Sarah Miles, David Carr)*

WEST ACRE [TF7815]
☆ *Stag* PE32 1TR [Low Rd]: Appealing pub tucked away in attractive spot in very quiet village, limited choice of good value home cooking using local produce from good value baguettes up, particularly cheerful and welcoming service, good choice of changing real ales in small bar, occasional beer festivals, neat dining room; cl Mon *(BB, Colin McKerrow, Mark, Amanda, Luke and Jake Sheard)*

WEYBOURNE [TG1143]
Ship NR25 7SZ [The Street (A149 W of Sheringham)]: Wide choice of above-average food (not Sun evening) from plenty of sandwiches and baked potatoes to good puddings, friendly staff, real ales such as Adnams, decent wines by the glass, big comfortably straightforward bar and two dining rooms; unobtrusive piped music; garden tables and tearoom, cl Mon *(Tony Middis, Roger Wain-Heapy)*

WIVETON [TG0442]
Bell NR25 7TL [Blakeney Rd]: Open-plan dining pub refurbished by new owners and reopened Easter 2007 after some months' closure, minimalist décor, reasonably priced food, well kept beers inc local Yetmans, log fire, large conservatory; tables out on lawn and garden behind *(BB, Charles Gysin)*

WRETHAM [TL9290]
Dog & Partridge IP24 1QS [Watton Rd]: Welcoming local with hard-working licensees, above-average food, well kept Greene King IPA *(Hugh and Anne Pinnock)*

WYMONDHAM [TG1001]
☆ *Green Dragon* NR18 0PH [Church Street]: Picturesque heavily timbered jettied 14th-c inn, cosy unsmart beamed and timbered back bar, log fire under Tudor mantelpiece, interesting pictures, bigger dining area (children allowed), friendly and helpful if not always speedy service, Adnams Bitter and Broadside and a guest beer, food inc fresh fish and good veg; children and dogs welcome; modest bedrooms, nr glorious 12th-c abbey church *(LYM, the Didler, W W Burke, P M Newsome)*

Northamptonshire

Our new find here, the comfortably contemporary Samuel Pepys at Slipton, stocks half a dozen interesting real ales, and given that no pub in this county currently has a Food Award, we'll be watching keenly in the hopes that their very promising start on this front will earn them one by next year. New licensees at the Falcon at Fotheringhay mean that this good dining pub's Food Award is at least temporarily on hold, but first indications are most encouraging. The Royal Oak at Eydon and the George at Great Oxendon both have good food, too. Though we haven't felt 100% confident at naming any of these four Dining Pub of the Year here, we are confident that all four are rewarding choices for special meals out. There's plenty of enjoyable food in other pubs here too. And Northamptonshire boasts no fewer than six pubs with Beer Awards, including the Fox & Hounds at Great Brington (nine changing beers at this appealing all-rounder of considerable character), and the lovely old Queens Head in Bulwick, which gains its Award for the first time this year (great value here, too). Other pubs doing well here are the cosy Great Western Arms at Aynho, the enjoyable Red Lion in Crick and the lively Ship in Oundle. Some rising stars to look out for in the Lucky Dip section at the end of the chapter are the New Inn at Buckby Wharf, White Swan at Harringworth, Stags Head at Maidwell, Malt Shovel in Northampton, Red Lion at Sibbertoft and Three Conies at Thorpe Mandeville.

AYNHO   SP4932   MAP 4

Great Western Arms

Just off B4031 W, towards Deddington; Aynho Wharf, Station Road; OX17 3BP

Civilised pub with attractive old interior, interesting railway memorabilia, well liked food, and moorings

This much enjoyed inn is sandwiched rather unceremoniously between a railway and the Oxford Canal – but don't be deterred by its unassuming appearance. Its series of linked rambling rooms is divided enough to give a cosy intimate feel, and the golden stripped stone of some walling tones well with the warm cream and deep red plasterwork elsewhere. Attractive furnishings include good solid country tables and regional chairs on broad flagstones. A good log fire warms cosy seats in two of the areas and there are candles and fresh flowers throughout as well as daily papers and glossy magazines. Readers enjoy the extensive and interesting GWR collection which includes lots of steam locomotive photographs; the dining area on the right is rather elegant; piped music. They have well kept Hook Norton and a guest on handpump, and good wines by the glass; service is welcoming and attentive. Opening out of the main bar, the former stable courtyard behind has white cast-iron tables and chairs; there are moorings and a marina nearby. Please tell us about the bedrooms here.

Tipping is not normal for bar meals, and not usually expected.

Please use this card to tell us which pubs *you* think should or should not be included in the next edition of *The Good Pub Guide*. Just fill it in and return it to us — no stamp or envelope needed. Don't forget you can also use the report forms at the end of the *Guide*, or report through our web site: www.goodguides.co.uk

ALISDAIR AIRD

In returning this form I confirm my agreement that the information I provide may be used by The Random House Group Ltd, its assignees and/or licensees in any media or medium whatsoever.

YOUR NAME AND ADDRESS (BLOCK CAPITALS PLEASE)

☐ *Please tick this box if you would like extra report forms*

REPORT ON
(pub's name)

Pub's address

☐ **YES Main Entry** ☐ **YES Lucky Dip** ☐ **NO don't include**
Please tick one of these boxes to show your verdict, and give reasons and descriptive comments, prices etc

☐ Deserves FOOD award ☐ Deserves PLACE-TO-STAY award

REPORT ON
(pub's name)

Pub's address

☐ **YES Main Entry** ☐ **YES Lucky Dip** ☐ **NO don't include**
Please tick one of these boxes to show your verdict, and give reasons and descriptive comments, prices etc

☐ Deserves FOOD award ☐ Deserves PLACE-TO-STAY award

THE GOOD PUB GUIDE

The Good Pub Guide
FREEPOST TN1569
WADHURST
E. SUSSEX
TN5 7BR

🍴 Lots of seafood and fish dishes feature amongst the freshly made food, which might include fried sardines, whitebait, sausage and mash, various pasta dishes, vegetable risotto, steak and kidney pie, kedgeree, grilled tuna with vegetable salsa, bass with red pepper sauce and rack of lamb with honey and rosemary. *Starters/Snacks: £5.95 to £7.95. Main Courses: £7.95 to £19.95. Puddings: £3.95 to £4.95*

Hook Norton ~ Lease Frank Baldwin ~ Real ale ~ Bar food (12-2(3 Sun), 6.30-9) ~ Restaurant ~ (01869) 338288 ~ Children welcome with restrictions ~ Dogs allowed in bar ~ Open 12-3, 6-11; closed Sun evening ~ Bedrooms: £65B/£75B

Recommended by George Atkinson, P and J Shapley, D A Bradford, Susan and John Douglas, Charles and Pauline Stride, Stuart Turner, Sir Nigel Foulkes, Gwyn and Anne Wake, Michael Dandy, Trevor and Judith Pearson, Gerry and Rosemary Dobson

BADBY
SP5558   MAP 4

Windmill

Village signposted off A361 Daventry—Banbury; NN11 3AN

Homely thatched country dining pub with popular food and friendly service

Two beamed and flagstoned bars have a nice country feel with an unusual woodburning stove in an enormous tiled inglenook fireplace, simple country furnishings in good solid wood, and cricketing and rugby pictures. There's also a comfortably cosy lounge. Bass, Flowers Original, Hook Norton Old Hooky and Timothy Taylors Landlord are well kept on handpump, with good fairly priced wines by the bottle. The brightly lit carpeted restaurant is more modern; quiet piped music and TV. There's a pleasant terrace out by the green of this attractive ironstone village, and a nice path leads south through Badby Wood (carpeted with bluebells in spring) to a landscaped lake near Fawsley Hall.

🍴 It can get full here so it is worth booking. Dishes typically include soup, vegetable or beef lasagne, chilli, battered cod and pie of the day with daily specials such as smoked duck breast, fried scallops with chinese pork belly, spinach and ricotta tortellini with wild mushroom sauce, lemon sole with garlic prawns, lamb loin wrapped in bacon with rosemary, redcurrant and port sauce and 12oz rump steak. *Starters/Snacks: £3.50 to £6.50. Main Courses: £8.95 to £16.95. Puddings: £3.50*

Free house ~ Licensees John Freestone and Carol Sutton ~ Real ale ~ Bar food (12-2(2.30 Sun), 7-9.30(9 Sun)) ~ Restaurant ~ (01327) 702363 ~ Children welcome ~ Dogs allowed in bar and bedrooms ~ Open 11.30-3, 5.30-11; 11.30-11 Sat, Sun ~ Bedrooms: £59.50B/£72.50B

Recommended by Dr and Mrs T E Hothersall, Sally Anne and Peter Goodale, John and Joyce Snell, Oliver Richardson, George Atkinson, W W Burke, George Cowie, Trevor and Judith Pearson

BULWICK
SP9694   MAP 4

Queens Head 🍺

Just off A43 Kettering—Duddington; NN17 3DY

Ancient pub with cheery involved licensees, interesting beers, popular heartily flavoured food including game

Very friendly licensees inject a happy enthusiasm for country life, food and real ale into this lovely 600-year-old stone cottage row. Whilst its unaltered appearance and character remain those of a delightfully traditional village local (bellringers pop in after their Wednesday practice, and the darts and dominoes teams are very active), there's something extra here too. Thoughtfully sourced beers – well kept and served from a stone bar counter – include Shepherd Neame Spitfire, with three or four interesting guests from brewers such as Church End, Golcar and the very local Rockingham; a good wine list includes interesting bin-ends (nine by the glass) and they've over 20 malt whiskies. The timeless beamed bar has stone floors and a fire in a stone hearth at one end; darts, shove-ha'penny, dominoes and piped music. This is an attractive bypassed village in an area where you may be lucky enough to see red kites and there can be few more pleasant experiences than a summer evening on the garden terrace (with its own well) listening to swallows and martins, sheep in the adjacent field and bells ringing in the nearby church.

🍴 A big draw is the changing choice of robustly flavoured food, which is cooked fresh to order, using local produce where possible: lunchtime sandwiches, soup, pressed game terrine with cranberry and orange relish, sweet potato, basil and parmesan risotto, fettuccine with wild rabbit, tarragon and root vegetables in rabbit sauce, grilled pork cutlet marinated in lemon, garlic and sage, grilled aberdeenshire fillet steak, and puddings such as chocolate terrine with caramel sauce or lemon polenta cake with lemon and vanilla syrup. *Starters/Snacks: £4.95 to £9.95. Main Courses: £8.95 to £19.95. Puddings: £4.95 to £5.95*

Free house ~ Licensee Geoff Smith ~ Real ale ~ Bar food (12-2.30, 6-9.30; not Sun evening) ~ Restaurant ~ (01780) 450272 ~ Children welcome away from bar ~ Dogs allowed in bar ~ Open 12-3, 6-11.30(7-11 Sun); closed Mon

Recommended by Ian Stafford, Michael and Jenny Back, Val and Alan Green, Ian Judge, Mike and Sue Loseby, J C M Troughton

CRICK   SP5872   MAP 4

Red Lion 🍺 £

1 mile from M1 junction 18; in centre of village off A428; NN6 7TX

Nicely worn-in friendly pub off M1 with good value straightforward lunchtime food and pricier more elaborate evening menu

Readers really enjoy the welcoming atmosphere at this traditional old stone thatched pub. The cosy low-ceilinged bar is nice and traditional, with lots of comfortable seating, some rare old horsebrasses, pictures of the pub in the days before it was surrounded by industrial estates, and a tiny log stove in a big inglenook. Four well kept beers on handpump include Wells & Young Bombardier, Greene King Old Speckled Hen, Theakstons Best and a guest from a brewer such as Adnams Broadside. There are a few picnic-sets under cocktail parasols on grass by the car park, and in summer you can eat on the terrace in the old coachyard, which is sheltered by a Perspex roof; lots of pretty hanging baskets.

🍴 Homely bar food includes sandwiches and ploughman's, chicken and mushroom pie, leek and smoky bacon bake, plaice and vegetable pancake rolls. Prices go up a little in the evening when they offer a wider range of dishes that might include stuffed salmon fillet, lamb shank, half a roast duck and sirloin steak; puddings such as lemon meringue pie; bargain-price Sunday roast. *Starters/Snacks: £2.00 to £3.50. Main Courses: £4.50 to £13.50. Puddings: £2.10 to £2.75*

Wellington ~ Lease Tom and Paul Marks ~ Real ale ~ Bar food (not Sun evening) ~ (01788) 822342 ~ Children under 14 welcome lunchtimes only ~ Dogs welcome ~ Open 11-2.30, 6.15-11; 12-3, 7-10.30 Sun

Recommended by C J Pratt, Mike and Jayne Bastin, Brian P White, Edward Leetham, Andrew Gardner, Charles and Pauline Stride, Ted George, George Atkinson, Liz and Brian Barnard, Michael Dandy, Ian Stafford, Stephen Funnell, Denis Newton, Susan and John Douglas, Mr and Mrs Staples, Mrs M Wheatley, JJW, CMW

EAST HADDON   SP6668   MAP 4

Red Lion

High Street; village signposted off A428 (turn right in village) and off A50 N of Northampton; NN6 8BU

Injection of fresh energy from new licensees in appealing old hotel; modernised menu and very pleasant grounds

Gentle improvements to this rather smart substantially-built golden stone inn have in no way detracted from its appealingly traditional interior. A neat carpeted lounge bar has old prints, attractive white-painted panelling with recessed china cabinets, and a couple of beams; piped music. Well trained staff serve Adnams Broadside, Charles Wells Bombardier and Eagle, and a guest such as Youngs on handpump, and decent wines with about ten by the glass. The walled side garden is pretty, with lilac, fruit trees, roses and neat flowerbeds. It leads back to the bigger lawn, which has well spaced picnic-sets. A small side terrace has more tables under cocktail parasols, and a big copper beech shades the gravel car park. The attractive restaurant overlooks the garden.

🍴 Food is popular so you may need to book. As well as filled baguettes, dishes might include soup, crispy soft shell crab with mango and pineapple chutney, chicken liver parfait, steak and ale pie, fish and chips with mushy peas, duck breast with wilted cabbage and bacon and red wine sauce, grilled bass with stir-fried vegetables and soy and ginger, roast peppers with buffalo mozzarella and tomato and basil couscous, and puddings such as strawberry crème brûlée and raspberry pavlova. *Starters/Snacks: £3.95 to £8.95. Main Courses: £9.95 to £21.95. Puddings: £5.00*

Charles Wells ~ Lease Nick Bonner ~ Real ale ~ Bar food (12-2, 7-9.30, not Sun evening) ~ Restaurant ~ (01604) 770223 ~ Children welcome in eating areas ~ Open 12-2.30, 6-11; 12-10.30 Sat, Sun ~ Bedrooms: £60S/£75S

Recommended by Gerry and Rosemary Dobson, Michael Dandy, Mrs E A Macdonald, George Atkinson

EYDON   SP5450   MAP 7

Royal Oak

Lime Avenue; village signed off A361 Daventry—Banbury, and from B4525; NN11 3PG

Enjoyable low-beamed old place with good lunchtime snacks and imaginative evening menu

The room on the right at this stone village pub has cushioned wooden benches built into alcoves, seats in a bow window, some cottagey pictures, flagstones, and an open fire in an inglenook fireplace. The bar counter, with bar stools, runs down a long central flagstoned corridor room and links several other small idiosyncratic rooms. An attractive covered terrace with hardwood furniture is a lovely place for a meal in fine weather. Friendy staff serve well kept Fullers London Pride, Greene King IPA, Timothy Taylors Landlord and a guest such as Archers on handpump; piped music and table skittles. More reports please.

🍴 The lunchtime menu is fairy pubby, with maybe baguettes, smoked salmon plate, fishcakes and steak. More elaborate evening items might be starters such as smoked salmon filled with crab, crayfish, lemon and dill and butternut, ricotta and sage ravioli with garlic and sage butter, main courses such as maple syrup and sesame seed glazed roast duck breast on parsnip saffron mash with caramelised pears and rhubarb, roast plum tomato, mozzarella and basil tarte tartin, and grilled bream fillet on seafood risotto with lemon and herb dressing, with puddings such as cappuccino mousse with ginger biscuit or meringue nest filled with fruit. *Starters/Snacks: £4.50 to £6.00. Main Courses: £8.00 to £14.50. Puddings: £4.50*

Free house ~ Licensee Justin Lefevre ~ Real ale ~ Bar food (12-2, 7-9; not Mon) ~ Restaurant ~ (01327) 263167 ~ Well behaved children welcome away from the bar ~ Dogs allowed in bar ~ Open 12-2.30, 6-11; 12-3, 7-10.30 Sun

Recommended by John Baish, Ruth Kitching, Mick Furn

FARTHINGSTONE   SP6155   MAP 4

Kings Arms ◀

Off A5 SE of Daventry; village signposted from Litchborough on former B4525 (now declassified); NN12 8EZ

Individual place with carefully sourced regional foods, cosy traditional interior and lovely gardens; note limited opening times

The timelessly intimate flagstoned bar at this quirky gargoyle-embellished stone 18th-c country pub has a huge log fire, comfortable homely sofas and armchairs near the entrance, whisky-water jugs hanging from oak beams, and lots of pictures and decorative plates on the walls. A games room at the far end has darts, dominoes, cribbage, table skittles and board games. Thwaites Original and Wells & Youngs are well kept on handpump alongside a guest such as St Austell Tribute, the short wine list is quite decent, and they have a few country wines. Look out for the interesting newspaper-influenced décor in the outside gents'. The tranquil terrace is charmingly decorated with hanging baskets, flower and herb pots and plant-filled painted tractor tyres. They grow their own salad vegetables and there's a cosy little terrace by the herb garden. The list of retail food produce on sale makes very tempting reading indeed. Products (including cheeses, cured and fresh meat and cured and fresh fish) are sourced for their originality of style, methods of rearing and smoking or organic farming methods. This is a picturesque village, and there are good walks including the Knightley Way. It's worth ringing ahead to check the opening and food serving times as the friendly licensees are sometimes away unexpectedly.

⏹ **Bar food might include soup, good filled baguettes, ploughman's, loch fyne fish platter and a british cheese platter, with a couple of main courses such as yorkshire pudding filled with steak and kidney or game casserole and cumbrian wild boar sausage and mash.** *Starters/Snacks: £3.95 to £5.95. Main Courses: £5.95 to £8.50. Puddings: £3.90*

Free house ~ Licensees Paul and Denise Egerton ~ Real ale ~ Bar food (12-2 Sat, Sun only) ~ No credit cards ~ (01327) 361604 ~ Children welcome in main bar if supervised ~ Dogs welcome ~ Open 7(6.30 Fri)-11; 12-3.30, 7(9 Sun)-11 Sat; closed weekday lunchtimes and Mon, Weds evenings

Recommended by George Atkinson, Pete Baker, Derek and Sylvia Stephenson

FOTHERINGHAY   TL0593   MAP 5

Falcon ♀

Village signposted off A605 on Peterborough side of Oundle; PE8 5HZ

Upmarket dining pub in new hands, good food from snacks up, good range of drinks and attractive garden

The buzz of contented conversation fills the neatly kept little bar at this civilised pub. It's sedately furnished with cushioned slatback armchairs and bucket chairs, good winter log fires in a stone fireplace, and fresh flower arrangements. The conservatory restaurant is pretty, and if the weather's nice the attractively planted garden is particularly enjoyable. Though the main draw is dining, there is a thriving little locals' tap bar (and darts team) if you do just want a drink. The very good range of beverages includes changing beers such as Adnams, Digfield Shacklebush and Potton Village Bike on handpump, good wines (20 by the glass), organic cordials and fresh orange juice. The vast church behind is worth a visit, and the ruins of Fotheringhay Castle, where Mary Queen of Scots was executed, are not far away. Please do tell us about the new regime – we're keeping our fingers crossed the food continues to be as good under the new people.

⏹ **Imaginative (if not cheap) bar food includes whitebait, sandwiches, battered fish and chips, ploughman's, mezze and sausage and mash from a snack menu, and there's a specials menu that might include crab bruschetta with fennel and dandelion salad, mushroom soup, chicken liver pâté with red onion jam, saffron, red pepper and mozzarella risotto, roast pork loin, grilled beef with wild garlic, and puddings such as peaches poached in vanilla and raspberry and sticky toffee pudding, and a local cheese platter.** *Starters/Snacks: £4.50 to £6.50. Main Courses: £7.50 to £10.50. Puddings: £5.50*

Free house ~ Licensees Sally Facer and Jim Jeffries ~ Real ale ~ Bar food (12-2.15, 6.15-9.15(8.30 Sun)) ~ Restaurant ~ (01832) 226254 ~ Children welcome ~ Dogs allowed in bar ~ Open 12-3, 6-11(10.30 Sun)

Recommended by Mike and Sue Loseby

Real ale to us means beer which has matured naturally in its cask – not pressurised or filtered. We name all real ales stocked. We usually name ales preserved under a light blanket of carbon dioxide too, though purists – pointing out that this stops the natural yeasts developing – would disagree (most people, including us, can't tell the difference!).

GREAT BRINGTON   SP6664   MAP 4

Fox & Hounds/Althorp
Coaching Inn ◀

Off A428 NW of Northampton, nr Althorp Hall; NN7 4JA

Friendly and cosy golden stone thatched building with great choice of real ales, tasty food, sheltered courtyard and play area

The ancient bar at this old coaching inn has a lovely relaxed atmosphere with lots of old beams and saggy joists, an attractive mix of country chairs and tables (maybe with fresh flowers) on its broad flagstones and bare boards, plenty of snug alcoves, nooks and crannies, some stripped pine shutters and panelling, two fine log fires, and an eclectic medley of bric-a-brac from farming implements to an old typewriter and country pictures. An impressive range of nine real ales includes Greene King IPA, Abbot and Old Speckled Hen and Fullers London Pride, with up to five guests from a thoughtfully sourced range of brewers such as Archers, Hoggleys (local to them), Scatter Rock and Stonehenge, and they've about a dozen wines by the glass and a dozen malt whiskies. Service is friendly and good; piped music. A cellarish games room down some steps has a view of the casks in the cellar. The coach entry from the road opens into a lovely little paved courtyard with sheltered tables and tubs of flowers, and there is more seating, with a play area, in the side garden.

🍽 **Very tasty bar food includes sandwiches and baguettes, soup, oriental chicken strips, grilled goats cheese, leek and cheese macaroni, beef and Guinness casserole, halloumi stuffed chicken breast with tomato sauce, cod with tarragon béarnaise sauce, and sirloin steak, with puddings such as apple bread and butter pudding and lemon and lime cheesecake.** *Starters/Snacks: £4.25 to £7.95. Main Courses: £7.95 to £9.95. Puddings: £3.95 to £6.95*

Free house ~ Licensee Jacqui Ellard ~ Real ale ~ Bar food (12-2.30, 6.30-9.30) ~ Restaurant ~ (01604) 770164 ~ Children welcome ~ Dogs allowed in bar ~ Jazz, folk, R&B Tues evening ~ Open 11-11; 12-10.30 Sun

Recommended by Alain and Rose Foote, Trevor and Judith Pearson, Michael Dandy, George Atkinson, Sue and Keith Campbell, David and Sue Atkinson

GREAT OXENDON   SP7383   MAP 4

George 🍷 🛏

A508 S of Market Harborough; LE16 8NA

Elegant 16th-c pub with emphasis on dining (you may need to book); garden and comfortable bedrooms

The clubby bar here has been thoughtfully put together with rather luxurious dark wallpaper showing off the panelled dark brown dado, green leatherette bucket chairs around little tables, daily papers on poles, and a big log fire; the turkey-carpeted conservatory overlooks a shrub-sheltered garden. There may be piped easy-listening music. The entrance lobby has easy chairs and a former inn-sign, while the lavatories are entertainingly decked out with rather stylish naughty pictures. Well kept Adnams, Youngs Special and a guest ale on handpump, 15 wines by the glass and around 15 malts.

🍽 **Good bar food includes soup, cold platters such as italian meats, cheese or fish, filled baguettes, mushrooms stuffed with spinach and pine nuts and topped with stilton, pork and leek sausages and chive mash, honey-roast lamb shank, battered cod, chips and mushy peas, roast lamb shank with garlic mash and rosemary gravy, and puddings such as apple and blackberry pie or bread and butter pudding; two-course Sunday lunch.** *Starters/Snacks: £4.95 to £7.95. Main Courses: £8.95 to £17.95. Puddings: £4.75 to £5.75*

Free house ~ Licensee David Dudley ~ Real ale ~ Bar food ~ Restaurant ~ (01858) 465205 ~ Children welcome ~ Dogs allowed in bedrooms ~ Open 11.30-3, 5.30-11.30; 12-3 Sun; closed Sun and bank holiday evenings ~ Bedrooms: £57.50B/£65.50B

Recommended by Richard Atherton, Mrs M B Gregg, Jeff and Wendy Williams, W W Burke, Steve Nye, Duncan Cloud, Anthony Barnes, Alan Sutton, Julian Saunders, Derek Stafford, Gerry and Rosemary Dobson

KILSBY   SP5671   MAP 4

George

2½ miles from M1 junction 18: A428 towards Daventry, left on to A5 – look out for pub off on right at roundabout; CV23 8YE

Handy for M1; warm welcome, good local atmosphere, proper public bar, old-fashioned décor and tasty wholesome food

The very cheery landlady keeps a good balance between the popular dining aspect and the traditional public bar – this is just one of a handful of main entries that still has a pool table – at this nice village pub. The high-ceilinged wood panelled lounge on the right, with plush banquettes, a coal-effect gas stove and a big bay window, opens on the left into a smarter but relaxed attractive area with solidly comfortable furnishings. The long brightly decorated back public bar has a juke box, darts, that good pool table, a fruit machine and TV. Fullers London Pride, Greene King IPA and Abbot and a guest such as Newmans Wolvers will be kept on handpump, and they've a splendid range of malt whiskies, served in generous measures. There are wood picnic-sets out in the back garden, by the car park.

🍴 **The pubby lunch menu includes sandwiches, soup, breaded brie with cranberry sauce, prawn cocktail, sausage, egg and chips, baguettes, ploughman's and beef or vegetable lasagne, while the evening menu typically features chicken liver pâté, steak, salmon fillet, penne with cream and mushroom sauce, beef and ale pie and lamb shank; readers recommend the children's menu here. It's best to book if you go for Sunday lunch.** *Starters/Snacks: £4.90 to £7.90. Main Courses: £8.90 to £15.90. Puddings: £2.90 to £4.90*

Punch ~ Lease Maggie Chandler ~ Real ale ~ Bar food (12-2(4 Sun), 6-9; 12-4 Sun; not Sun evening) ~ Restaurant ~ (01788) 822229 ~ Well supervised children in restaurant and lounge ~ Open 11.30-3, 5.30-11; 12-5, 7.30-11 Sun; closed Mon lunchtime ~ Bedrooms: £38/£56

Recommended by George Atkinson, Ted George, Keith and Chris O'Neill, P Dawn, Rob and Catherine Dunster, David and Pam Wilcox, Michael and Alison Sandy, Denis Newton, Michael and Maggie Betton, Michael Dandy, Simon and Amanda Baer, Richard and Linda Ely, Bruce and Sharon Eden

NETHER HEYFORD   SP6658   MAP 4

Olde Sun 🍺 £

1¼ miles from M1 junction 16: village signposted left off A45 westbound – Middle Street; NN7 3LL

Unpretentious place with diverting bric-a-brac, very reasonably priced food, garden with play area

Nooks and crannies in the several small linked rooms at this 18th-c golden stone pub are packed with all sorts of curios, from gleaming brassware (one fireplace is a grotto of large brass animals) to colourful relief plates, 1930s cigarette cards, railway memorabilia and advertising signs, World War II posters and rope fancywork. Furnishings are mostly properly pubby, with the odd easy chair. There are beams and low ceilings (one painted with a fine sunburst), partly glazed dividing panels, steps between some areas, rugs on parquet, red tiles or flagstones, a big inglenook log fire – and up on the left a room with full-sized hood skittles, a games machine, darts, TV, cribbage, dominoes and sports TV; piped music. Well kept Banks's, Greene King Ruddles, Marstons Pedigree and a guest such as Skinners are served on handpump from two counters by friendly efficent staff – the old cash till on one is stuck at one and a ha'penny. The enjoyable collections of bygones and bric-a-brac continue in the garden, with blue-painted grain kibblers and other antiquated hand-operated farm machines, some with plants in their hoppers, beside a fairy-lit front terrace with picnic-sets.

🍴 **A short choice of snacky meals includes sandwiches, soup, scampi and chips, potato baked with bacon, onions and cream cheese, lasagne and coq au vin. There may be a few more dishes in the evening.** *Starters/Snacks: £3.25 to £3.75. Main Courses: £4.95 to £5.75. Puddings: £1.50 to £5.25*

Free house ~ Licensees P Yates and A Ford ~ Real ale ~ Bar food (not Sun evenings) ~ Restaurant ~ (01327) 340164 ~ Children welcome ~ Open 12-2.30, 5-11; 12-midnight Fri, Sat; 12-11 Sun

Recommended by Peter and Jean Hoare, Michael Dandy, Mr and Mrs G Hughes, W W Burke, Sam and Christine Kilburn, Ian Stafford, David and Karen Cuckney, Margaret McPhee, JJW, CMW, Joan York

OUNDLE
TL0388 MAP 5

Ship 🍺
West Street; PE8 4EF

Bustling down-to-earth town pub with a couple of interesting beers and good value pubby food

Hearty chatter fills the air at this enjoyable local, though it doesn't seem to bother Midnight, the companionable black and white pub cat. The heavily beamed lounge bar (watch your head if you are tall) is made up of three areas that lead off the central corridor. Up by the street there's a mix of leather and other seats, with sturdy tables and a warming log fire in a stone inglenook, and down one end a charming little panelled snug has button-back leather seats built in around it. The wood-floored public side has a TV, games machine, a juke box and board games; piped music. Digfield Barnwell and Fools Nook are served alongside an interesting guest or two such as Hampshire Heaven Can Wait, and they've a good range of malt whiskies. The wooden tables and chairs out on the series of small sunny sheltered terraces are lit at night.

🍴 **Enjoyable bar food served in generous helpings might include soup, vegetarian or beef lasagne, haddock, chicken breast with mushroom sauce, pork curry and rib-eye steak; Sunday roast.** *Starters/Snacks: £2.00 to £5.50. Main Courses: £7.50 to £9.50. Puddings: £3.95 to £4.50*

Free house ~ Licensees Andrew and Robert Langridge ~ Real ale ~ Bar food (12-3, 6-9; 12-9 Sat, Sun) ~ (01832) 273918 ~ Open 11-11.30; 11-12 Sat; 12-11 Sun ~ Bedrooms: £30(£35S)/£60(£60S)(£70B)

Recommended by Keith and Margaret Kettell, Ryta Lyndley, Howard and Margaret Buchanan, the Didler, Di and Mike Gillam, Barry Collett

SLIPTON
SP9579 MAP 4

Samuel Pepys ♀ 🍺
Off A6116 at first roundabout N of A14 junction, towards Twywell and Slipton, bearing right to Slipton; the pub (in Slipton Lane) is well signed locally; NN14 3AR

Exemplary dining pub with prompt friendly service, good beers, nice surroundings and garden

This smartly reworked and spotlessly kept stone-built pub is very popular for its food side, but still keeps a properly pubby feel in its long back bar. This has some very heavy low beams, a good log fire in the stone chimneybreast's big raised hearth, and chapel chairs and other simple seating on its carpet, making for an informal eating area with some snug corners and good lighting. The bar counter has some comfortable bar chairs, and more importantly a good range of half a dozen real ales on handpump or tapped straight from the cask, including Greene King IPA, Hop Back Summer Lightning, John Smiths, Oakham JHB and Potbelly Aisling (from Kettering) and interesting changing guest beers such as Brewsters Hop a Doodle Doo and Great Oakley Wots Occurring. They have a good interesting choice of wines by the glass and by the bottle, at reasonable prices. At one side, beyond a great central pillar that looks as if it was once part of a ship's mast, is an area with squashy leather seats around low tables. Beyond here is the main dining room, which has comfortably modern chairs around neatly set tables, and which extends into a fresh and roomy conservatory, with pleasant country views; piped music. Service is friendly and helpful, and there is wheelchair access throughout. The sheltered garden has picnic-sets under cocktail parasols, and a terrace with heaters.

⟨❢⟩ **Bar food includes sandwiches, soup, smoked salmon with sweetcorn fritters, thai watermelon, goats cheese and mango salad, fish broth, cod and chips, grilled gammon with pineapple and black bean stir fry and grilled rib-eye steak, and puddings such as lemon and brandy syllabub and sticky toffee pudding.** *Starters/Snacks: £4.30 to £5.90. Main Courses: £7.70 to £19.90. Puddings: £5.10*

Mercury Inns ~ Manager Frazer Williams ~ Real ale ~ Bar food (12-2.15, 7-9.30(9 Sun)) ~ Restaurant ~ (01832) 731739 ~ Children welcome ~ Dogs allowed in bar ~ Open 13-3, 6-11; 12-11(10.30 Sun) Sat

Recommended by Michael and Jenny Back, Howard and Margaret Buchanan, Andy Chapman, Dave and Jen Harley, Michael Sargent

SULGRAVE
SP5545   MAP 4

Star 🛏

E of Banbury, signposted off B4525; Manor Road; OX17 2SA

Distinctive country pub with decent food, nice gardens and good bedrooms

The peaceful bar at this fine old 17th-c creeper-covered farmhouse is unpretentiously furnished with small pews, cushioned window seats and wall benches, kitchen chairs and cast-iron-framed tables. There are polished flagstones in an area by the big inglenook fireplace, with red carpet elsewhere. Look out for the stuffed back end of a fox as it seems to leap into the wall. Framed newspaper front pages record historic events such as Kennedy's assassination and the death of Churchill; Hook Norton Hooky and Old Hooky and a guest such as Bath Wild Hare on handpump. In summer you can eat outside under a vine-covered trellis, and there are benches at the front and in the back garden. The pub is a short walk from Sulgrave Manor, the ancestral home of George Washington, and is handy for Silverstone.

⟨❢⟩ **Bar food includes soup, smoked trout pâté, sausage and mash, thai chicken curry, salmon steak with watercress sauce, and puddings such as lemon tart or chocolate brandy cream.** *Starters/Snacks: £4.50 to £7.00. Main Courses: £8.00 to £22.00. Puddings: £4.00 to £4.95*

Hook Norton ~ Tenant Andron Ingle ~ Real ale ~ Bar food (12-2(2.30 Sun), 6-9.30(8.30 Sun)) ~ Restaurant ~ (01295) 760389 ~ Children in restaurant ~ Dogs allowed in bar ~ Open 12-3, 6-11; 12-10.30 Sun ~ Bedrooms: £50S/£80S

Recommended by Mr and Mrs R A Buckler, Alan Sutton, Trevor and Judith Pearson, Tom Evans, Michael Sargent

WADENHOE
TL0183   MAP 5

Kings Head

Church Street; village signposted (in small print) off A605 S of Oundle; PE8 5ST

Country pub in idyllic riverside spot; decent range of beers, pubby food

This stone-built 16th-c inn is by a big wooded meadow next to the River Nene, with views of the church, and if you're arriving by boat there's no charge for a mooring if you are using the pub. Picnic-sets among the willows and aspens on the sloping grass make pleasant vantage points. This is a pretty village of up-and-down lanes and thatched stone cottages and because of the pub's lovely setting it does get very busy on summer days. There's an uncluttered simplicity to the very welcoming partly stripped-stone main bar, which has pleasant old worn quarry-tiles, solid pale pine furniture with a couple of cushioned wall seats, and a leather-upholstered chair by the woodburning stove in the fine inglenook. The bare-boarded public bar has similar furnishings and another fire; steps lead up to a games room with dominoes and table skittles, and there's yet more of the pale pine furniture in an attractive little beamed dining room. As well as Digfield Barnwell and Kings Head and Oakham JHB a couple of guest beers might be from brewers such as Crouch Vale and Nethergate, and they've belgian fruit beers and a dozen wines by the glass.

🍴 Pubby bar food might include filled lunchtime rolls, soup, ham, egg and chips, fish and chips, pea and mint risotto, sausage and mash, penne with three-cheese sauce, chicken breast with creamed leeks and grain mustard and 8oz rib-eye, with puddings such as sticky toffee pudding, chocolate orange cheesecake and steamed chocolate pudding. *Starters/Snacks: £3.95 to £5.00. Main Courses: £6.50 to £13.95. Puddings: £4.95*

Free house ~ Licensee Peter Hall ~ Real ale ~ Bar food (12-2.15(2.30 Sun), 6.30-9.15; not Sun evening) ~ Restaurant ~ (01832) 720024 ~ Children welcome ~ Dogs allowed in bar ~ Open 11-11; 12-10.30 Sun

Recommended by Ryta Lyndley, Michael Tack

WOODNEWTON
TL0394 MAP 5

White Swan

Main Street; back roads N of Oundle, easily reached from A1/A47 (via Nassington) and A605 (via Fotheringhay); PE8 5EB

Nicely unpretentious village pub with good straightforward food, and garden

Pretty with hanging baskets, this stone-built house keeps the emphasis on its pubby atmosphere. The interior is fairly traditional, with dark wood tables and wheelback chairs on carpets and old local photographs on cream walls. Adnams, Black Sheep and Green King IPA are served on electric pump alongside a guest such as Timothy Taylors Landlord, and a draught cider; piped music, darts and board games. The attractive back garden has flower borders round a lawn with tables and a boules pitch (league matches Tuesday evenings). More reports please.

🍴 Enjoyable bar food might include soup, filled baguettes and potatoes, chilli, curries, casseroles and steaks; Sunday roast. *Starters/Snacks: £2.95 to £6.25. Main Courses: £6.50 to £14.95. Puddings: £2.50 to £4.50*

Punch ~ Lease Steve Anker ~ Real ale ~ Bar food (12.30-2.30, 6-9; 9-11am then 12.30-9 Sat, Sun) ~ Restaurant ~ (01780) 470381 ~ Children in restaurant ~ Dogs allowed in bar ~ Open 12-3, 6-11; 12-midnight Sat, Sun; closed Mon lunchtime

Recommended by John Branston

LUCKY DIP

Besides the fully inspected pubs, you might like to try these Lucky Dips recommended to us and described by readers (if you do, please send us reports: www.goodguides.co.uk).

ABTHORPE [SP6446]
New Inn NN12 8QR [signed from A43 at 1st roundabout S of A5; Silver St]: Tucked-away partly thatched real country local, rambling dim-lit bars, beams, stripped stone, inglenook log fire, masses of pictures and old family photographs, cheerful staff, Hook Norton, good choice of soft drinks, bar food from sandwiches to Sun lunch, daily papers, darts, shove-ha'penny and hood skittles, two pub dogs; nice big garden, quiet village *(Val and Alan Green, BB, JJW, CMW)*
APETHORPE [TL0295]
Kings Head PE8 5DG [Kings Cliffe Rd]: Roomy and attractive stone-built pub in conservation village, comfortable and welcoming lounge with log fire, cosy bar with pool, changing real ales, good coffee, obliging licensees and staff, arch to big dining area with wide choice of good value food inc fish, separate bar food menu (not Mon); children welcome, picnic-sets in small sheltered courtyard *(R L Borthwick)*

BARNWELL [TL0584]
☆ *Montagu Arms* PE8 5PH [off A605 S of Oundle, then fork right at Thurning, Hemington sign]: Attractive stone-built pub, good range of food from baguettes with enterprising fillings to good interesting meals, sensible prices, changing ales such as Adnams and Castle Rock, decent wines, helpful cheerful staff, log fire, low beams, flagstones or tile and brick floors, neat back dining room; games room off yard, big garden with good well equipped play area, pleasant streamside village with good walks, open all day wknds *(John Saul, BB, George Atkinson)*
BRACKLEY HATCH [SP6441]
☆ *Green Man* NN13 5TX [A43 NE of Brackley (tricky exit)]: Much extended Chef & Brewer dining pub on busy dual carriageway nr Silverstone, comfortable old-look beamed lounge area, conservatory overlooking road, big family restaurant, wide range of all-day food, relaxed atmosphere, quick, friendly and

helpful service, Theakstons Best and Wells & Youngs Bombardier, good wines and coffee, daily papers, log fire; unobtrusive piped music, games; tables on lawn, bedrooms in Premier Lodge behind, open all day *(Michael Dandy, BB, George Atkinson)*

BRAFIELD-ON-THE-GREEN [SP8258]

☆ *Red Lion* NN7 1BP [A428 5 miles from Northampton towards Bedford]: Smart comfortably modern bistro-style dining pub with upscale food from good glorified sandwiches and ciabattas up in two main rooms, small drinking area with a couple of settees, good choice of wines by the glass, friendly attentive service, Fullers London Pride, Greene King Old Speckled Hen and Wells & Youngs Bombardier; picnic-sets front and back, open all day *(Michael Dandy, Bruce and Sharon Eden, Mike Ridgway, Sarah Miles, Alan Sutton)*

BRAUNSTON [SP5465]

Admiral Nelson NN11 7HJ [Dark Lane, Little Braunston, overlooking Lock 3 just N of Grand Union Canal tunnel]: 18th-c ex-farmhouse in peaceful setting by Grand Union Canal Lock 3 and hump bridge, good value food with interesting as well as basic dishes, well kept ales such as Black Sheep and Timothy Taylors Landlord, good choice of wines by the glass, good landlady and cheery service, cosy tiled-floor part by bar, longer dining end and back restaurant, lively games area with pool and table skittles; lots of picnic-sets in pleasant waterside garden over bridge, towpath walks *(Rob and Catherine Dunster)*

BRAYBROOKE [SP7684]

Swan LE16 8LH [Griffin Rd]: Nicely laid out thatched pub with well kept Everards ales, enjoyable pub food from baguettes and light lunches up, friendly service, reasonably priced wines *(S Holder, Gerry and Rosemary Dobson)*

BROUGHTON [SP8375]

Red Lion NN14 1NF [High St]: Large village pub with up to nine real ales, farm cider and good choice of wines by the glass from central bar, enjoyable food (freshly made so may be a wait) inc lunchtime and early evening bargains, comfortable lounge and dining room, plainer public bar with games; piped music; small pleasant garden with water feature, open all day wknds *(JJW, CMW)*

BUCKBY WHARF [SP6066]

☆ *New Inn* NN6 7PW [A5 N of Weedon]: Nicely spruced up by cheerful and attentive new Irish landlord, good range of enjoyable quickly served pubby food, well kept mainly local real ales, good short choice of wines, several rooms radiating from central servery inc small dining room with nice fire, games area with table skittles and TV; picnic-sets out on pleasant terrace by busy Grand Union Canal lock *(Rob and Catherine Dunster, LYM, George Atkinson)*

BUGBROOKE [SP6756]

Wharf Inn NN7 3QB [The Wharf; off A5 S of Weedon]: Super spot by canal, plenty of

tables on big lawn with moorings and summer boat trips; emphasis on big water-view restaurant, also bar and lounge with pleasant informal small raised eating area on either side, lots of stripped brickwork, wide choice of generous food from baguettes up, real ales such as Batemans Rosey Nosey, Frog Island Best, Greene King IPA and St Austell Tinners, farm cider, lots of wines by the glass, nice fire; may be piped radio; children very welcome *(George Atkinson, JJW, CMW, BB)*

CHACOMBE [SP4943]

☆ *George & Dragon* OX17 2JR [handy for M40 junction 11, via A361; Silver St]: Beams, flagstones, panelling, clock collection, log fire in massive fireplace and even an old well, enjoyable food, good choice of wines by the glass, Everards real ales, restaurant, darts and dominoes; TV, piped music; children and dogs welcome, two bedrooms, pretty village with interesting church, open all day *(Chris Glasson, Oliver Richardson, BB, William Ruxton, Mark and Diane Grist)*

CHAPEL BRAMPTON [SP7366]

☆ *Brampton Halt* NN6 8BA [Pitsford Rd, off A5199 N of Northampton]: Former stationmaster's house on Northampton & Lamport Railway (which is open wknds), recently well remodelled with large restaurant, railway memorabilia and train theme throughout (some furnishings like railway carriages), popular generous food from sandwiches up, Everards Tiger and Original and Fullers London Pride, efficient attentive service, games and TV in bar; piped music; children welcome, lots of tables in garden with awnings and heaters, pretty views over small lake, Nene Valley Way walks *(Gerry and Rosemary Dobson, JJW, CMW, Mike and Margaret Banks, Eithne Dandy, George Atkinson)*

Spencer Arms NN6 8AE [Northampton Rd]: Beamed Chef & Brewer family dining pub, table service throughout, plenty of stripped tables in long timber-divided L-shaped bar, decent sensibly priced food, Adnams and Theakstons Old Peculier, two log fires, daily papers; piped music; tables outside *(Gerry and Rosemary Dobson, Eithne Dandy, George Atkinson)*

Windhover NN6 8AF [Welford Road (A5199)/Pitsford Rd]: Roomy well done Vintage Inn dining pub with good choice of wines and soft drinks, changing real ales, food all day inc lunchtime sandwiches, feature log fire; piped music; disabled access and facilities, picnic-sets in good-sized front garden with terrace, pleasant Brampton Valley Way walks *(Eithne Dandy, Michael Tack)*

CHARLTON [SP5235]

Rose & Crown OX17 3DP [Main St]: Thatched pub with beams, stripped stone and inglenook fireplaces, well spaced pale wood tables and chairs, enjoyable food from bar snacks up; picnic-sets out in front and in garden with wisteria arbour, appealing small village *(Tony Mason, LYM)*

CRICK [SP5872]

Old Royal Oak [handy for M1 junction 18, via A428; Church St]: Pleasant old beamed village pub, cosy log fires in two rooms, good choice of well kept real ales, filled rolls, darts, pool and hood skittles in games room, back chinese restaurant; piped music, games machine; open from early afternoon wkdys, open all day wknds *(JJW, CMW, the Didler)*

EASTCOTE [SP6853]

Eastcote Arms NN12 8NG [off A5 N of Towcester]: Traditional furnishings and cottagey décor, friendly attentive service, well kept ales such as Adnams, Black Sheep, Fullers London Pride and Greene King IPA, decent wines and malt whiskies, food from baguettes to restaurant dishes, two flame-effect gas fires, hood skittles in small back bar; good-sized neat back garden with picnic-sets and other tables, peaceful village, cl Mon lunchtime, open all day Fri *(Gerry and Rosemary Dobson, LYM, JJW, CMW)*

EASTON ON THE HILL [TF0104]

Blue Bell PE9 3LR [High St]: Recently refurbished stone-built village pub, strong italian influence in menu and staff, good food (not Mon), real ales, pleasant atmosphere, pool and TV in neat games area, restaurant; children welcome, picnic-sets in good-sized sheltered garden behind, cl Mon lunchtime *(Roy Bromell)*

EVENLEY [SP5834]

☆ *Red Lion* NN13 5SH [The Green]: Small local under new management, Banks's, Marstons Pedigree and a related guest beer, decent coffee and choice of wines, particularly good value sandwiches and wide choice of other food, relaxed atmosphere, inglenook, beams and some flagstones; piped music; tables out in neatly kept garden, one or two seats out in front opp broad village green *(Michael Dandy, George Atkinson)*

GAYTON [SP7054]

Queen Victoria NN7 3HD [High St]: Four comfortable areas off central bar, Wells & Youngs Eagle and Bombardier, good wine choice, attentive friendly staff, wide choice of enjoyable food (not Sun evening) from baguettes up, light panelling, beams, lots of pictures, books and shelves of china, inglenook woodburner, pool; piped music, games machines, Tues quiz night; bedrooms, cl Mon *(LYM, JJW, CMW)*

GREAT BILLING [SP8162]

Elwes Arms NN3 9DT [High St]: Thatched stone-built 16th-c village pub, two bars (steps between rooms), wide choice of good value food (all day Fri-Sun), three or four real ales, good choice of other drinks, pleasant dining room (children allowed), darts; piped music, TV, Sun quiz night, no dogs; tables and chairs in garden with covered terrace and play area *(JJW, CMW)*

GREAT DODDINGTON [SP8864]

Stags Head NN29 7QT [High St (B573 S of Wellingborough)]: Old stone-built local with pleasant bar and split-level lounge/dining room, Black Sheep and Wadworths 6X, good choice of soft drinks, cheery service, good value hearty pub food from reasonably priced sandwiches up, also separate barn restaurant extension, public bar with pool and games; piped music; picnic-sets out in front and in garden *(Mr and Mrs Bentley-Davies, Michael E Bridgstock, Michael Dandy)*

GREAT HOUGHTON [SP7959]

Old Cherry Tree NN4 7AT [Cherry Tree Lane; a No Through Road off A428 just before the White Hart]: Thatched village pub with low beams, open fires, stripped stone and panelling, decent freshly made food from lunchtime baguettes up with wider evening choice, real ales such as Badger and Wells & Youngs, good wine choice, steps up to restaurant; quiet piped music; garden tables *(JJW, CMW, Gerry and Rosemary Dobson, Michael Dandy)*

GREENS NORTON [SP6649]

Butchers Arms NN12 8BA [High St]: Large comfortably refurbished lounge, four well kept changing ales, wide choice of good value food from sandwiches up inc popular pizzas, friendly staff, separate bar and games room with darts and pool; piped music, TV, games machines; disabled access, picnic-sets out in front, pretty village nr Grafton Way walks *(Thomas Brigstocke)*

GRETTON [SP8994]

Hatton Arms NN17 3DN [Arnhill Rd]: Pretty thatched and stone-built two-bar country pub dating from 14th c, heavy beams and flagstones, well kept changing ales inc Great Oakley (from just the other side of Corby) and Marstons Pedigree, good wines by the glass, friendly efficient service, good fresh food, open fire, sofa and other mixed furnishings, relaxed and attractive back dining room; terrace picnic-sets with Welland Valley views, cl Mon, open all day Sun *(anon)*

HACKLETON [SP8054]

White Hart NN7 2AD [B526 SE of Northampton]: Comfortably traditional 18th-c country pub with wide choice of generous food from sandwiches and baked potatoes up inc early evening bargains, Fullers London Pride, Greene King IPA and a guest beer, decent choice of other drinks, good coffee, dining area up steps, stripped stone, beamery and brickwork, illuminated well, brasses and artefacts, split-level flagstone bar with flame-effect fire, pool and hood skittles; children welcome (not in bar after 5), garden with picnic-sets and goal posts, open all day *(Michael Dandy, JJW, CMW)*

HARRINGWORTH [SP9197]

☆ *White Swan* NN17 3AF [SE of Uppingham; Seaton Rd]: Friendly new management in striking stone-built Tudor inn with imposing central gable, enjoyable food (not Sun evening) inc popular Sun lunch, changing real ales such as Batemans XB, good wines by the glass, solid tables and elaborate hand-crafted oak counter in central bar, open fire dividing bar from roomy dining area with cottagey décor, interesting documentation on magnificent nearby viaduct, traditional games; may be piped music; terrace tables, six good bedrooms (LYM, Barry Collett)

HOLCOT [SP7969]

White Swan NN6 9SP [Main St; nr Pitsford Water, N of Northampton]: Good new landlord refurbishing attractive partly thatched village pub, hospitable series of rooms with bar on right and dining rooms on left, well kept ales such as Batemans, Black Sheep and Caledonian, good straightforward food, good value Sun lunch all afternoon, pleasant service; open all day Sun and summer, children welcome (S Holder, Gerry and Rosemary Dobson)

KETTERING [SP8778]

Alexandra Arms NN16 0BU [Victoria St]: Real ale pub, with ten changing quickly, hundreds each year, amazing collection of pump clips in front lounge, also their own Nobbys ale, may be sandwiches, back games bar with hood skittles; tables on back terrace, open all day (from 2 wkdys) (Mick Furn, the Didler)

KINGS SUTTON [SP4936]

Butchers Arms OX17 3RD [Whittall St]: Well run village pub with full Hook Norton range kept well, good value food, helpful service, conservatory dining extension; TV; tables outside with aunt sally, in neat sandstone village easily spotted by spire (Roy and Lindsey Fentiman)

LITTLE ADDINGTON [SP9573]

Bell NN14 4BD [signed off A6 NW of Rushden; High St]: Much-extended stone-built village pub with popular restaurant especially for its midweek bargains, sofas in solidly furnished bar, Greene King IPA, Marstons Pedigree and a guest beer, pool; tables out under sturdy arbour on front terrace by big orderly car park (BB, Michael Tack)

LITTLE BRINGTON [SP6663]

☆ *Old Saracens Head* NN7 4HS [4½ miles from M1 junction 16, first right off A45 to Daventry; also signed off A428; Main St]: Pleasant old pub under new management, enjoyable food from interesting baguettes and wraps up, real ales such as Adnams Broadside, Greene King IPA, Shepherd Neame Spitfire and Timothy Taylors Landlord, roomy U-shaped lounge with good log fire, flagstones, chesterfields and lots of old prints, book-lined dining room; plenty of tables in neat back garden, handy for Althorp House and Holdenby House (Gerry and Rosemary Dobson, BB, George Atkinson)

LODDINGTON [SP8178]

Hare NN14 1LA [Main St]: Welcoming 17th-c stone-built dining pub, carpeted throughout, with wide choice of enjoyable good value food (not Sun evening or Mon) from generous baguettes to fish and game specialities in two eating areas, good-sized helpings, tablecloths and fresh flowers, Adnams and continental lagers in small bar, good wine and soft drinks choice, good coffee, pleasant helpful service; piped music; picnic-sets on front lawn (Alan Vann, Michael Dandy)

LOWICK [SP9780]

☆ *Snooty Fox* NN14 3BH [off A6116 Corby—Raunds]: Attractively reworked and spacious 16th-c pub with leather sofas and chairs, beams and stripped stonework, log fire in huge stone fireplace, open kitchen doing bar food from sandwiches up inc steak counter, Greene King IPA and two guest beers such as Batemans and Highgate, board games; piped music, games machine; dogs and children welcome, picnic-sets on front grass, open all day (Mrs Phoebe A Kemp, Ryta Lyndley, Howard Dell, B N F and M Parkin, Trevor and Sylvia Millum, LYM, Ben and Helen Ingram)

MAIDWELL [SP7477]

☆ *Stags Head* NN6 9JA [Harborough Rd (A508 N of Northampton)]: Good value fresh food from baguettes to seasonal game in three linked areas, attractively light and airy, off small, spotless and comfortable beamed front bar with log fire and well chosen pictures, interesting local guest beers, good choice of wines and soft drinks, friendly staff, log fire; quiet piped music; disabled facilities, tables on terrace (dogs on leads allowed here) by neat back lawn with paddock beyond, bedrooms, not far from splendid Palladian Kelmarsh Hall in its parkland (Michael Dandy, George Atkinson, Gerry and Rosemary Dobson, JJW, CMW)

MILTON MALSOR [SP7355]

Greyhound NN7 3AP [2¼ miles from M1 junction 15, via A508; Towcester Rd]: Big busy Chef & Brewer, well refurbished in olde-worlde mode, lots of cosy alcoves, hops on 15th-c beams, old pictures and china, pewter-filled dresser, candlelit pine tables, good log fire, well kept Greene King IPA, Wells & Youngs Bombardier and a guest beer, good range of wines, wide choice of food all day (they try out some new dishes for the chain here), prompt cheerful service; piped jazz or classical music; well behaved seated children welcome, spreading front lawn with duck/fish pond, open all day (Ryta Lyndley, LYM, George Atkinson)

NASSINGTON [TL0696]

Queens Head PE8 6QB [Station Rd]: Recently smartly refurbished with stylish bar/bistro and separate restaurant, wide choice of enjoyable food from sandwiches, ploughman's and home-made burgers to restaurant dishes inc good value lunches, pleasant staff, fair choice of wines by the glass, changing real ales, good coffee; pretty garden by River Nene, delightful village, nine chalet bedrooms (Roy Bromell)

NORTHAMPTON [SP7759]

Britannia NN4 7AA [3¾ miles from M1 junction 15; Old Bedford Rd (off A428)]: Big modernised Chef & Brewer with massive beams, mix of flagstones and carpet, 18th-c 'kitchen', Courage Best, Marstons Pedigree, Ringwood Fortyniner and Wells & Youngs Bombardier, good choice of wines by the glass, their usual food all day from sandwiches up, conservatory; piped music, no dogs; children welcome, picnic-sets by River Nene, open all day *(JJW, CMW, Michael Dandy, LYM)*

Fox & Hounds NN2 8DJ [Harborough Rd, Kingsthorpe (A508)]: Spacious pub useful for wide range of all-day food from sandwiches up, friendly service, Greene King IPA and Abbot and a guest beer such as Potbelly; big-screen TV, games machine; open all day *(Gerry and Rosemary Dobson)*

☆ *Malt Shovel* NN1 1QF [Bridge St (approach rd from M1 junction 15); best parking in Morrisons opp back entrance]: Full Great Oakley beer range and up to ten or so changing and often recherché real ales, also Rich's farm cider, belgian bottled beers, over 50 malt whiskies, country wines, good soft drinks choice, occasional beer festivals, daily papers, breweriana inc some from Carlsberg Brewery opposite, open fire, darts, cheap pubby lunchtime food (not Sun); blues bands Weds; children and dogs welcome, disabled facilities, picnic-sets on small back terrace *(JJW, CMW, Diane Hibberd, Mick Furn, the Didler, Bruce Bird, George Atkinson)*

ORLINGBURY [SP8672]

Queens Arms NN14 1JD [off A43 Northampton—Kettering, A509 Wellingborough—Kettering; Isham Rd]: 18th-c stone-built village pub with armchairs and sofas in large airy lounge, neat décor and beamery, half a dozen changing ales, wide choice of enjoyable food from sandwiches up in bar and evening/wknd restaurant, bargains Tues-Thurs; children welcome, nice garden with play area, open all day wknds *(JJW, CMW)*

PITSFORD [SP7567]

Griffin NN6 9AD [off A508 N of Northampton]: Neat beamed bar, back lounge with steps up to small eating area and pleasant restaurant extension, with interesting pictures, old advertisements and so forth, some tables outside, in pretty village nr Pitsford Water/Brixworth Country Park; has been popular for reasonably priced very generous food from lunchtime baguettes and bar dishes to wider restaurant choice, well kept Greene King IPA and Abbot, Fullers London Pride or Timothy Taylors Landlord and Wells & Youngs Special, and good value wines, but may be changing hands late summer 2007; news please *(Michael Dandy, George Atkinson, Alan Sutton, Gerry and Rosemary Dobson, Revd R P Tickle)*

POTTERSPURY [SP7543]

Cock NN12 7PQ [High St; off A5]: Unassuming traditional pub with inglenook log fire, four real ales, usual food (not Sun evening) inc OAP deals Mon-Thurs, friendly staff, games room with pool and darts, dining room; piped music, some live;

children welcome, terrace tables and small garden with picnic-sets *(JJW, CMW)*

RAVENSTHORPE [SP6670]

☆ *Chequers* NN6 8ER [Chequers Lane]: Extended local with wide range of reliable generous food from baguettes and baked potatoes to steaks, Greene King IPA, Fullers London Pride and interesting changing guest beers, good soft drinks choice, friendly attentive staff, open fire, lots of bric-a-brac hung from beams and stripped stone walls, dining room, games room; TV, games machine; children welcome, small secluded back terrace and play area, open all day Sat *(JJW, CMW, Gerry and Rosemary Dobson, Michael Dandy, George Atkinson)*

RUSHDEN [SP9566]

Station Bar NN10 0AW [Station Approach]: Not a pub, but part of station HQ of Rushden Historical Transport Society (non-members can sign in), restored in 1940s/60s style, with Fullers London Pride and interesting guest beers, tea and coffee, friendly staff, filled rolls (perhaps hot dishes too, occasional barbecues), gas lighting, enamelled advertisements, old-fangled furnishings; authentic waiting room with piano, also museum and summer trains and steam-ups; cl wkdy lunchtimes *(the Didler, P Dawn)*

RUSHTON [SP8483]

Thornhill Arms NN14 1RL [Station Rd]: Pleasantly furnished rambling dining pub prettily set opp attractive village's cricket green, wide choice of good value food from sandwiches up inc OAP bargain lunches in several neatly laid out dining areas inc smart high-beamed back restaurant, well kept Greene King Abbot and Wells & Youngs Bombardier, relaxed comfortable atmosphere, open fire; bedrooms *(Alan Weedon)*

SIBBERTOFT [SP6782]

☆ *Red Lion* LE16 9UD [off A4303 or A508 SW of Mkt Harboro; Welland Rise]: Good food cooked by landlord for comfortable partly panelled bar, interestingly old-fashioned, or contrasting light and airy bistro-style dining room with modern tables on tiles, splendid wine list (they do tastings), Bass and Youngs, sociable landlady and good service; covered terrace tables, large garden, two quiet well equipped bedrooms with kitchens for do-it-yourself breakfast, cl Sun evening and Mon/Tues lunchtimes *(Jeff and Wendy Williams, E J Webster, Dr S Edwards, John Wooll, Richard Pick, George Atkinson)*

STOKE BRUERNE [SP7449]

Navigation NN12 7SY: Large canalside pub, several levels and cosy corners, sturdy wood furniture, reasonably priced generous usual food from sandwiches up inc Sun lunch till 5, Marstons Pedigree and Hop Back Summer Lightning, good choice of wines by the glass, pleasant helpful young staff, separate family room, pub games; piped music; plenty of tables out overlooking water, big play area, open all day *(Michael Dandy, Simon Jones)*

SUDBOROUGH [SP9682]

Vane Arms NN14 3BX [off A6116; Main St]: Traditional thatched village pub with low beams, stripped stonework, cosy plush lounge, inglenook fires, enjoyable home-made food from lunchtime sandwiches up, well kept Everards ales, good choice of wines, pleasant staff, upstairs restaurant; bedrooms in purpose-built block, pretty village, cl Mon *(Dave and Jen Harley, LYM)*

THORPE MANDEVILLE [SP5344]

☆ *Three Conies* OX17 2EX [off B4525 E of Banbury]: Attractive 17th-c pub doing well under current attentive young licensees, wide choice of enterprising food from good value sandwiches up (prices rise 1p a minute between 6 and 9, so go early for bargains), well kept Hook Norton ales, beamed bar with some stripped stone, flagstones and bare boards, two or three good log fires, mix of old dining tables, large family dining room; piped music; tables out in front and on lawn *(LYM, Mick Furn, Brian Englefield, Tom Evans, C J Pratt, E A and D C T Frewer)*

TOWCESTER [SP6654]

☆ *Red Lion* NN12 8LB [Foster's Booth (A5 3m N)]: Attractive 16th-c former posting inn, relaxed and unpretentious, with cheery hard-working landlord, Fullers London Pride, Timothy Taylors Landlord and a guest beer, good value food cooked by landlady from good sandwiches and bargain light dishes up, daily papers, dark wood furniture in carpeted lounge bar/dining area with big inglenook fireplace, beams and bric-a-brac, copper and brass, another fire in chatty quarry-tiled public bar with hood skittles and darts in carpeted games room; quiet piped music, TV; children welcome, garden picnic-sets *(JJW, CMW, George Atkinson, Michael Dandy)*

Saracens Head NN12 6BX [Watling St W]: Substantially modernised coaching inn with interesting *Pickwick Papers* connections (especially in the kitchen Dickens described, now a meeting room), open fire in long comfortable three-level lounge with lively bar and dining area, Greene King IPA and Old Speckled Hen, neat efficient staff, good value pub food inc sizzler specialities; piped music, TV; children welcome, small attractive back courtyard, well equipped bedrooms *(Michael Dandy, LYM, Pete Coxon)*

WALGRAVE [SP8072]

Royal Oak NN6 9PN [Zion Hill, off A43 Northampton—Kettering]: Friendly old stone-built local with up to five changing real ales, good value food (not Sun evening) from sandwiches and baked potatoes through fish and chips to wild boar, quick pleasant service, long three-part carpeted beamed bar with small lounge and restaurant extension behind; children welcome, small garden, play area, open all day Sun *(JJW, CMW, Michael Dandy, Val and Alan Green)*

WEEDON [SP6359]

Crossroads NN7 4PX [3 miles from M1 junction 16; A45 towards Daventry; High St,

on A5 junction]: Plush and spacious Chef & Brewer with well divided beamed bar and dining area, friendly staff, real ales such as Timothy Taylors Landlord, good coffee, decent food, log fires; piped jazz or classical music; picnic-sets in attractive gardens down to river, comfortable Premier Lodge bedroom block *(George Atkinson, LYM)*

☆ *Narrow Boat* NN7 4RZ [Stowe Hill (A5 S)]: Spacious terrace and big garden sloping down to canal (very popular in summer), small L-shaped bar with canal prints, sofa, easy chairs and low tables, high-raftered back restaurant extension with canal views, wide food choice from generous baguettes and baked potatoes to good value Sun lunch (all afternoon), worth the wait when it's busy, Wells & Youngs ales, some good value wines, open fire; games machine, skittles, quiet piped music; bedrooms in back motel extension, narrowboat hire next door *(Jeanette McFadden, Gerry and Rosemary Dobson, LYM, George Atkinson)*

WELLINGBOROUGH [SP9069]

Locomotive NN8 4AL [Finedon Rd (A5128)]: Old-fashioned two-bar pub with up to half a dozen interesting changing real ales, big lunchtime baguettes, friendly landlord, lots of train memorabilia inc toy locomotive running above bar, log fire, daily papers, games room with pool, pin table and hood skittles; may be quiet piped music; dogs welcome, picnic-sets in small front garden, open all day (Sun afternoon break) *(JJW, CMW, the Didler)*

WELTON [SP5866]

☆ *White Horse* NN11 2JP [off A361/B4036 N of Daventry; behind church, High St]: Two-bar beamed village pub with decent reasonably priced food, several changing real ales and nice house wines, welcoming service, cosy dining areas, big open fire, public bar with woodburner, darts, table skittles and pool room; attractively lit garden with play area, terrace and barbecue *(Andrew Gardner, J V Dadswell)*

WILBY [SP8666]

Horseshoe NN8 2UE [Main Rd]: Five real ales, good soft drinks choice, good value food (not Sun/Mon evenings) in friendly old stone-built village pub with horseshoe bar, games area with darts and hood skittles, no piped music; jazz Mon, quiz Tues, no credit cards; picnic-sets out in front, garden with play area *(JJW, CMW)*

WOODFORD [SP9677]

Dukes Arms NN14 4HE [High St]: Simple village-green pub with several real ales, enjoyable food (not Sun evening) inc some less common dishes, large bar and beamed dining lounge, woodburner, games room with hood skittles and pool, friendly pub dogs, May beer festival; piped music, TV, games machines; children welcome, pleasant garden with small play area, walks nearby *(JJW, CMW)*

YARDLEY HASTINGS [SP8656]

☆ *Red Lion* NN7 1ER [High St, just off A428 Bedford—Northampton]: Pretty thatched stone-built pub with good value food (not Sun/Mon evenings) from sandwiches up, wider evening choice, friendly landlord and relaxed atmosphere, Wells & Youngs Eagle and Winter Warmer, good range of soft drinks, linked rooms with beams and stripped stone, lots of pictures, plates and interesting brass and copper, separate small annexe with hood skittles; quiet piped music, TV, no dogs; children welcome, picnic-sets in nicely planted sloping garden, and in front, open all day wknds *(George Atkinson, Michael Dandy, Mike Ridgway, Sarah Miles, BB)*

Real ale may be served from handpumps, electric pumps (not just the on-off switches used for keg beer) or – common in Scotland – tall taps called founts (pronounced 'fonts') where a separate pump pushes the beer up under air pressure.

Northumbria
(County Durham, Northumberland and Tyneside)

Quite a number of the pubs in this county have earned our Stay Award, and readers have much enjoyed their comfortable and often very well equipped bedrooms and super breakfasts. These places include the Lord Crewe Arms at Blanchland (full of history and worth a visit for that alone), the Manor House Inn at Carterway Heads (close to moorland pastures and with nice views), the Fox & Hounds in Cotherstone (newly redecorated this year), the Victoria in Durham (good value rooms in the city centre), the Keelman in Newburn (home of the Big Lamp Brewery and again, good value bedrooms), the Cook & Barker Arms at Newton-on-the-Moor (interesting food), the Masons Arms at Rennington (A1 break or good base for the coast), the Rose & Crown in Romaldkirk (imaginative food, charming village location), the Olde Ship in Seahouses (full of fascinating seafaring memorabilia), the Battlesteads at Wark (really welcoming and with good food), and the Anglers Arms at Weldon Bridge (a large fishing hotel with quite an emphasis on the restaurant side). Real ales play a strong part here too, with lots of interesting local beers being represented, and often quite a fine choice too: the Rat in Anick (six fine ales, plenty of knick-knacks), the Dipton Mill Inn at Diptonmill (own brew beers and good value meals), the Victoria in Durham (up to half a dozen good ales, interesting memorabilia fitting its name), the Queens Head at Great Whittington (the new licensee has made it more of a village pub now), the Feathers at Hedley on the Hill (another new licensee here, using little local breweries), the Keelman in Newburn (its on-site Big Lamp Brewery is very good), the Crown Posada in Newcastle (an old-fashioned gem with six good beers), the interesting Cluny also in Newcastle (seven ales and a huge range of other drinks, too), the very nautical Olde Ship in Seahouses (in the same family for over a century) and the welcoming Battlesteads at Wark (more well kept beers). There's a lot of fine local fish, local meat and game and organic produce in this area, and those making the best of it are the County in Aycliffe, the Feathers at Hedley on the Hill, the Cook & Barker Arms at Newton-on-the-Moor and the Rose & Crown at Romaldkirk. Our choice for Northumbria Dining Pub of the Year is the Feathers at Hedley on the Hill, its keen new young owners making an immediate good impact. Although pub food's not generally cheap in this area, there are bargains to be found, particularly in the cities. And drinks prices are well below the national average, with the Keelman's own brews standing out as exceptional value. These Big Lamp beers are quite widely available at other good pubs – often as the cheapest on sale there. Other local brews which we found at least some of our main entries featuring as their best-priced beers are Camerons, Hadrian & Border, Mordue and Matfen, and there are well over a dozen more small local breweries in the area.

ANICK   NY9565   MAP 10

Rat 🍺

Village signposted NE of A69/A695 Hexham junction; NE46 4LN

Views over North Tyne Valley from terrace and garden, lots of interesting knick-knacks and six real ales

---

There are charming views of the North Tyne Valley in the area around Hexham from tables out on the terrace here; the charming garden has a dovecote, statues and attractive flowers. Inside, this pleasantly relaxed country pub has lots of interesting knick-knacks: antique floral chamber-pots hanging from the beams, china and glassware, maps and posters, and framed sets of cigarette cards. A coal fire blazes invitingly in the blackened kitchen range and lighting is soft and gentle. Furnishings keep up the cosily traditional mood with brocaded chairs around old-fashioned pub tables; piped music, daily papers and magazines. The conservatory has pleasant valley views. Half a dozen changing real ales on handpump always include Caledonian Deuchars and Marstons Pedigree with guests from Hadrian & Border and Mordue. Parking is limited.

🍴 **Standard bar food includes open sandwiches, soup, ploughman's, 'rat burger', lasagne, daily specials, and puddings such as banoffi pie.** *Starters/Snacks: £2.90 to £5.50. Main Courses: £6.95 to £14.95. Puddings: £3.25 to £4.25*

Free house ~ Licensee Anthony Hunter ~ Real ale ~ Bar food ~ (01434) 602814 ~ Children welcome ~ Open 11.30-3, 6-11; 11.30-11 Sat; 12-10 Sun; 11.30-3, 6-11 Sat and Sun in winter

Recommended by Pat and Stewart Gordon, Mart Lawton

AYCLIFFE   NZ2822   MAP 10

County 🍴 🍷 🍺

The Green, Aycliffe village; just off A1(M) junction 59, by A167; DL5 6LX

Exceptional cooking by chef/landlord in renowned dining pub, welcoming and civilised atmosphere, light modern furnishings, good wines by the glass

---

Although most customers do come to this renowned dining pub to enjoy the excellent food, the licensees stress that non-diners are always welcome and there is a bar area for those just wanting a relaxing drink. The minimalist décor and blond wood floors in the extended bar and bistro are light and modern, the atmosphere is civilised but welcoming and the service good and attentive. As well as a good choice of wines by the glass, they've Wells & Youngs Bombardier on handpump alongside a couple of guests such as Greene King Ruddles County and Highgate Fury; piped music. The green opposite is pretty. More reports please.

🍴 **Delicious bar food includes sandwiches, nice soups, pasta of the day, sausages and mash with onion gravy, lambs liver and bacon, beer-battered cod with mushy peas and home-made tartare sauce and salmon fillet wrapped in pancetta with herby lentils; with more elaborate choices such as smoked haddock with poached egg, spinach, champ and hollandaise, breast of duckling with port sauce, figs, prunes and apples and confit belly pork, brazed pig cheeks, garlic sausage cassoulet and mash; puddings like warm spiced banana cake with butterscotch sauce and white chocolate and lemon mousse with marinated cherries.** *Starters/Snacks: £4.95 to £5.95. Main Courses: £9.95 to £10.50. Puddings: £5.00*

Pubs brewing their own beers are listed at the back of the book.

Free house ~ Licensee Andrew Brown ~ Real ale ~ Bar food (not Sun evening) ~ Restaurant ~ (01325) 312273 ~ Children welcome (with restrictions) ~ Open 12-3, 5.30(6.30 Sat)-11; 12-3.30 Sun; closed Sun evening; 25 and 26 Dec

Recommended by Mart Lawton, Michael Doswell, M A Borthwick, Louise Gibbons, Comus and Sarah Elliott

BLANCHLAND   NY9650   MAP 10

Lord Crewe Arms 🛏️

B6306 S of Hexham; DH8 9SP

Ancient, historic building with some unusual features and straightforward food

The history and tremendous age of this fine old hotel are reason enough to come here. It dates back to the 13th c when the Premonstratensians built this remote village robustly enough to resist most border raiding parties and it is still separated from the rest of the world by several miles of moors, rabbits and sheep. An ancient-feeling bar is housed in an unusual long and narrow stone barrel-vaulted crypt, its curving walls being up to eight feet thick in some places. Plush stools are lined along the bar counter on ancient flagstones and next to a narrow drinks shelf down the opposite wall; TV. Upstairs, the Derwent Room has low beams, old settles, and sepia photographs on its walls, and the Hilyard Room has a massive 13th-c fireplace once used as a hiding place by the Jacobite Tom Forster (part of the family who had owned the building before it was sold in 1704 to the formidable Lord Crewe, Bishop of Durham). Black Sheep and Wylam Gold Tankard on handpump. The lovely walled garden was formerly the cloisters.

🍴 **Straightforward bar food includes soup, filled rolls, ploughman's, cumberland sausage with black pudding, and daily specials.** *Starters/Snacks: £2.75 to £3.60. Main Courses: £7.00 to £9.50. Puddings: £3.50*

Free house ~ Licensees A Todd, Peter Gingell and Ian Press, Lindsey Sands ~ Real ale ~ Bar food ~ Restaurant ~ (01434) 675251 ~ Children welcome ~ Dogs welcome ~ Open 11-11; 11-3, 6-11 Mon in winter ~ Bedrooms: £80B/£120B

Recommended by Tony and Maggie Harwood, M J Winterton, Mike Vincent, Chris and Sue Bax, P and J Shapley, Ann and Tony Bennett-Hughes

CARTERWAY HEADS   NZ0452   MAP 10

Manor House Inn 🍷 🍺 🛏️

A68 just N of B6278, near Derwent Reservoir; DH8 9LX

Popular inn with a good choice of drinks, nice views and comfortable bedrooms

Picture windows in the comfortable lounge bar (with a woodburning stove) and in the restaurant of this bustling slate-roofed stone house give views over moorland pastures towards the Derwent Valley and reservoir; rustic tables in the garden have the same views. The locals' bar has an original boarded ceiling, pine tables, chairs and stools, old oak pews, and a mahogany counter. Courage Directors, Theakstons Best, Wells & Youngs Bombardier and a guest from Caledonian, Mordue or Wylam on handpump, 70 malt whiskies and a dozen wines by the glass; darts, board games and piped music (only in the bar). More reports please.

🍴 **Bar food includes sandwiches, soup, fried scallops with chilli jam, local trout, pheasant breast with black pudding, haggis and swede, chicken supreme with asparagus tips and cheese sauce, game casserole, baked salmon with braised fennel and puddings such as sticky toffee pudding. Though the food here is certainly up to award quality at its best, there have been occasional signs this last year or so that it hasn't been as unfailingly consistent as we are used to from this team; we trust these have been temporary hitches. You can buy local produce, as well as chutneys, puddings and ice-cream made in the kitchens from their own little deli.** *Starters/Snacks: £3.50 to £7.95. Main Courses: £7.25 to £17.50. Puddings: £3.75 to £4.50*

Free house ~ Licensees Moira and Chris Brown ~ Real ale ~ Bar food (12-9.30(9 Sun)) ~ Restaurant ~ (01207) 255268 ~ Well behaved children welcome away from bar ~ Dogs welcome ~ Open 11-11; 12-10.30 Sun ~ Bedrooms: £43S/£65S

Recommended by Tony and Maggie Harwood, Arthur Pickering, Mr and Mrs John Taylor, John Foord, M J Winterton, Susan and John Douglas, J F M and M West, Michael Butler, John Robertson, Bruce and Sharon Eden, Liz and Brian Barnard, Will and Kay Adie, Alex and Claire Pearse, D Hillaby, Andy and Jill Kassube, Adrian Johnson

CORBRIDGE
NY9868   MAP 10

Errington Arms
About 3 miles N of town; B6318, on A68 roundabout; NE45 5QB

Reopened after a fire, keeping its good father-and-son team; relaxed and friendly with enjoyable food

This 18th-c stone-built inn has been very nicely restored after a severe fire which kept it closed for much of 2006. The father and son who run it are on fine form, helping to give it a good relaxed atmosphere. It has oak beams, a nice mix of candlelit tables on the light wooden floor, some pine planking and stripped stonework, burgundy paintwork, ornamental plaques, a large heavy mirror, and a log fire; there is still a modicum of bric-a-brac, on window sills and so forth. Black Sheep Bitter and Jennings Cumberland on handpump; piped music. Out on the front terrace are some sturdy metal and teak tables under canvas parasols.

🍴 **As well as sandwiches, ploughman's and salads, the enjoyable food includes soup, duck and port mousse with redcurrant, orange and mint coulis, fried king prawns with bean sprout salad and a chilli soy broth, mushroom and spinach omelette, lamb and beef stew with orange and rosemary, breadcrumbed chicken topped with mozzarella, basil and tomato, wild boar and pheasant pie and seared duck breast with a chive and mushroom risotto and blueberry and red wine jus.** *Starters/Snacks: £3.95 to £4.95. Main Courses: £6.50 to £14.50. Puddings: £4.95*

Punch ~ Lease Nicholas Shotton ~ Real ale ~ Bar food (12-2.30(3 Sun), 6.50-9.30) ~ Restaurant ~ (01434) 672250 ~ Children welcome ~ Open 11-3, 6-11; 12-3 Sun; closed Sun evening, Mon (exc bank hols)

Recommended by Susan and John Douglas, Michael Doswell, Andy and Jill Kassube

COTHERSTONE
NZ0119   MAP 10

Fox & Hounds 🛏
B6277 – incidentally a good quiet route to Scotland, through interesting scenery; DL12 9PF

Redecorated 18th-c inn with cheerful beamed bar, homely bar food and quite a few wines by the glass

This newly redecorated 18th-c country inn is next to the West Green and to a fine stretch of the River Tees. The simple but cheery beamed bar has a partly wooden floor (elsewhere is carpeted), a good winter log fire, thickly cushioned wall seats and local photographs and country pictures on the walls in its various alcoves and recesses. Black Sheep Best and Ale and Village Brewer White Boar (brewed for them by Hambleton) on handpump, 11 wines by the glass and several malt whiskies from smaller distilleries; efficient service from the friendly staff. Don't be surprised by the unusual lavatory attendant – an african grey parrot called Reva. Seats outside on the new terrace and quoits. More reports please.

🍴 **Bar food includes lunchtime sandwiches, soup, pork, sage and apple pie, warm bacon, wensleydale cheese, cranberry and fresh apple salad, beer-battered haddock with minted peas, ratatouille filled pancake with white wensleydale cheese, salmon, prawn and mackerel fishcake with home-made tartare sauce and pheasant on bubble and squeak mash with rich roast gravy.** *Starters/Snacks: £3.50 to £6.00. Main Courses: £7.50 to £15.00. Puddings: £3.95 to £4.50*

Free house ~ Licensees Nichola and Ian Swinburn ~ Real ale ~ Bar food ~ Restaurant ~ (01833) 650241 ~ Children allowed but not in bar unless eating ~ Dogs allowed in bedrooms ~ Open 12-3, 6-11; 12-3, 6.30-10.30 Sun; they close half an hour earlier lunchtime in winter ~ Bedrooms: £47.50B/£75B

Recommended by I A Herdman, Sarah and Peter Gooderham, M J Winterton, David and Katharine Cooke, Brian and Rosalie Laverick

DIPTONMILL
NY9261 MAP 10

Dipton Mill Inn ♀ 🍺 £

Just S of Hexham; off B6306 at Slaley, Blanchland and Dye House, Whitley Chapel signposts (and HGV route sign); not to be confused with the Dipton in Durham; NE46 1YA

Own-brew beers, tasty good value bar food and garden with terrace and aviary

The cheery landlord here is a brewer in the family-owned Hexhamshire Brewery and their Hexhamshire Devils Water, Devils Elbow, Old Humbug, Shire Bitter and Whapweasel are all well kept on handpump; 17 wines by the glass, 25 malt whiskies, and Weston's Old Rosie cider. The neatly kept, snug bar has dark ply panelling, low ceilings, red furnishings, a dark red carpet and two welcoming open fires. In fine weather it's pleasant to sit out on the sunken crazy-paved terrace by the restored mill stream, or in the attractively planted garden with its aviary. There's a nice walk through the woods along the little valley and Hexham race course is not far away.

🍴 As well as a fine range of northumbrian cheeses, the good value food might include sandwiches, ploughman's, good soups, mince and dumplings, tagliatelle with creamy basil sauce and parmesan, chicken in sherry sauce, lamb steak in wine and mustard sauce, and puddings such as apple and pear crumble and chocolate rum truffle tart. *Starters/Snacks: £2.25. Main Courses: £5.25 to £7.50. Puddings: £2.00 to £2.50*

Own brew ~ Licensee Geoff Brooker ~ Real ale ~ Bar food (12-2, 6.30-8.30; not Sun evening) ~ No credit cards ~ (01434) 606577 ~ Children welcome ~ Open 12-2.30, 6-11; 12-3 Sun; closed Sun evening

Recommended by Michael Doswell, Bruce and Sharon Eden, Alex and Claire Pearse, Neil Whitehead, Victoria Anderson, Mart Lawton, Bob Richardson, the Didler, Andy and Jill Kassube

DURHAM
NZ2742 MAP 10

Victoria 🍺 🛏

Hallgarth Street (A177, near Dunelm House); DH1 3AS

Unchanging and neatly kept Victorian pub with royal memorabilia, cheerful locals and well kept real ales; good value bedrooms

With a friendly landlord and cheerful locals, this immaculately kept city pub has changed little since it was built in the closing years of Queen Victoria's reign. The very traditional layout means three little rooms lead off a central bar with typically Victorian décor: mahogany, etched and cut glass and mirrors, colourful William Morris wallpaper over a high panelled dado, some maroon plush seats in little booths, leatherette wall seats, long narrow drinkers' tables, handsome iron and tile fireplaces for the coal fires, a piano, and some photographs and articles showing a very proper pride in the pub; there are also lots of period prints and engravings of Queen Victoria and staffordshire figurines of her and the Prince Consort. Big Lamp Bitter, Darwin Ghost, Durham Magus, Hexhamshire Devils Elbow and Mordue Five Bridge Bitter on handpump; also cheap house wines, around 80 malts and a great collection of 40 irish whiskeys. Dominoes. The good value bedrooms are simple but pleasant; a hearty breakfast (good vegetarian one too) is served in the upstairs dining room.

🍴 They only do lunchtime toasties.

Free house ~ Licensee Michael Webster ~ Real ale ~ (0191) 386 5269 ~ Children welcome ~ Dogs welcome ~ Open 11.45-3, 6-11; 12-2.30, 7-10.30 Sun ~ Bedrooms: £46B/£60B

Recommended by Blaise Vyner, C Sale, the Didler, Sue and Derek Irvine, Pete Baker, Tracey and Stephen Groves, Dr and Mrs P Truelove

GREAT WHITTINGTON   NZ0070   MAP 10

Queens Head 🍺

Village signposted off A68 and B6018 just N of Corbridge; NE19 2HP

Relaxed and civilised inn with new licensees, log fires, good food and seats outside

New licensees have taken over this simple but civilised stone inn and it's now more like a proper village pub with a relaxed atmosphere and locals dropping in for a drink. Modern furnishings alongside some handsome carved oak settles and two roaring log fires give the two fairly simple beamed rooms an elegantly comfortable feel. Two beers from the local Matfen Brewery on handpump, quite a few malt whiskies and several wines by the glass. There are seats on the small front lawn and this attractive old building is in a smart stone-built village surrounded by partly wooded countryside.

🍴 **Well liked bar food at lunchtime now includes sandwiches, soup with home-made bread, fishcake with cucumber and spring onion salad and chilli dip, creamed button mushrooms topped with black pudding fritters, local cod in beer batter with home-made tartare sauce, sunblush tomato and roasted red pepper risotto and steak in ale suet pudding; evening choices like venison terrine with pickled plums, local hot smoked salmon and crab tian with an avocado salsa and tomato dressing, honey-roasted breast of local duck, halibut fillet with toasted herb crust, roasted fennel and horseradish cream, and puddings such as pecan banana sticky toffee pudding with butterscotch sauce and chocolate orange crème brûlée.** *Starters/Snacks: £3.95 to £5.50. Main Courses: £6.95 to £17.50. Puddings: £4.75 to £5.50*

Free house ~ Licensee Gill Jackman ~ Real ale ~ Bar food (12-2.30, 6-9; 12-8 Sun) ~ Restaurant ~ (01434) 672267 ~ Children welcome ~ Dogs allowed in bar ~ Open 12-2.30, 6-11; 12-11(10.30 Sun) Sat
Recommended by Nigel Cummings, Lawrence Pearse, Gerry Miller, Mart Lawton, M A Borthwick, Michael Doswell

GRETA BRIDGE   NZ0813   MAP 10

Morritt Arms ☕ 🛏️

Hotel signposted off A66 W of Scotch Corner; DL12 9SE

Country house hotel with nice pubby bar, fantastic mural, interesting food, attractive garden and play area, nice bedrooms

Dating back to the 17th c, this is a former coaching inn built on the ruins of a Roman settlement. There's a nicely pubby bar around which runs a remarkable mural painted in 1946 by J T Y Gilroy – better known for his old Guinness advertisements – of Dickensian characters. Big windsor armchairs and sturdy oak settles cluster around traditional cast-iron-framed tables, large windows look out on the extensive lawn, and there are nice open fires. A new conservatory corridor leads from here through french windows to the function room. Black Sheep and Timothy Taylors Landlord on handpump, quite a few malt whiskies and an extensive wine list. The attractively laid out garden has some seats with teak tables in a pretty side area looking along to the graceful old bridge by the stately gates to Rokeby Park; there's a play area for children. This is a lovely spot and in 1839 Charles Dickens visited one of the inns at Greta Bridge whilst researching for *Nicholas Nickleby*. At the end of the 18th and beginning of the 19th centuries, painters such as Turner and Cotman painted many of the beauty spots in and around this area.

🍴 **Good modern bar food includes sandwiches, soup, goats cheese and spring onion tart with cherry tomato salsa, pressed ham, potato and parsley terrine, braised ham with a fried egg and mustard butter sauce, prawn linguini with sweet chilli jam, seared calves liver with garlic mash, free-range chicken supreme with rocket pesto and sunblush tomato risotto, bass with scallion mash and beetroot purée, and puddings such as warm chocolate fondant with clotted cream and banana tarte tatin with caramel ice-cream; generous breakfasts.** *Starters/Snacks: £4.00 to £7.00. Main Courses: £9.00 to £20.00. Puddings: £5.00 to £6.00*

Free house ~ Licensees Peter Phillips and Barbara Johnson ~ Real ale ~ Bar food (12-3, 6-9.30) ~ Restaurant ~ (01833) 627232 ~ Children welcome ~ Dogs allowed in bar and bedrooms ~ Open 11-11; 12-10.30 Sun ~ Bedrooms: £85B/£105B

Recommended by Helen Clarke, Dr and Mrs R G J Telfer, Janet and Peter Race, Danny Savage, J V Dadswell, David and Ruth Hollands, David Hall, David and Jean Hall, Tom and Jill Jones, Arthur Pickering, Barry Collett, J Crosby, Dr and Mrs P Truelove, Roger A Bellingham

HALTWHISTLE
NY7166 MAP 10

Milecastle Inn

Military Road; B6318 NE – OS Sheet 86 map reference 715660; NE49 9NN

Close to Hadrian's Wall and some wild scenery, with cosy little rooms, winter log fires and generous bar food; fine views and walled garden

Despite the remote situation – on a moorland road running alongside Hadrian's Wall – this little 17th-c pub does get very busy at peak times. The snug little rooms of the beamed bar are decorated with brasses, horsey and local landscape prints and attractive fresh flowers, and have two winter log fires; at lunchtime the small comfortable restaurant is used as an overflow. Friendly hard-working staff serve Big Lamp Bitter and Prince Bishop and Marstons Pedigree from handpump and they have a fair collection of malt whiskies and a good wine list; piped music. The tables and benches out in a pleasantly sheltered big walled garden with a dovecote and rather stunning views are popular in summer, and there's a large car park.

🍴 Generously served bar food includes sandwiches, soup, game pâté, hot and spicy chicken wings, omelettes, vegetable lasagne, battered cod, chicken tikka, cumberland sausage, steak and kidney pie, daily specials and puddings. *Starters/Snacks: £3.00 to £5.25. Main Courses: £7.25 to £12.95. Puddings: £3.95*

Free house ~ Licensees Clare and Kevin Hind ~ Real ale ~ Bar food (12-9; 12-2.45, 6-9 in winter) ~ Restaurant ~ (01434) 321372 ~ Children welcome ~ Open 12-11; 12-3, 6-9.30 in winter; closed 26 Dec

Recommended by Tony and Maggie Harwood, Michael and Jean Hockings, Michael Dandy, Mark and Ruth Brock, Louise English, Edward Leetham, Tom and Jill Jones, Neil Whitehead, Victoria Anderson

HEDLEY ON THE HILL
NZ0759 MAP 10

Feathers

Village signposted from New Ridley, which is signposted from B6309 N of Consett; OS Sheet 88 map reference 078592; NE43 7SW

NORTHUMBRIA DINING PUB OF THE YEAR

Interesting beers from small breweries, imaginative food and a friendly welcome in quaint tavern

New licensees have taken over this quaint stone-built inn – now open all day – and should have opened bedrooms by the time this edition is published. It's a friendly place with a comfortable pubby atmosphere and a good mix of locals and visitors. Three neat bars have beams, open fires, stripped stonework, solid furniture and old black and white photographs of local places and farm and country workers. Small-scale breweries are well represented and might feature Mordue Workie Ticket on handpump with three guests from Big Lamp, Orkney and Wylam; ten wines by the glass, farm cider and quite a choice of soft drinks. They hold a beer festival at Easter with over two dozen real ales (and a barrel race on Easter Monday). Picnic-sets in front are a nice place to sit and watch the world drift by.

🍴 Details of their carefully chosen suppliers are listed on the menu, and the appealing choice of food at lunchtime might include sandwiches, ploughman's, soup, corn-fed chicken liver parfait with pickles, cumberland sausage with beer gravy, chicken caesar salad with pickled anchovies, local cheese and dry-cured bacon and grilled mackerel with pink fir apple potatoes and a grain mustard butter, with evening choices such as lamb hotpot with pickled red cabbage, root vegetable gratin with poached duck egg, local mussels with cider, wild garlic, parsley and home-baked bread, and puddings like marmalade bakewell tart and chocolate brownie with jersey ice-cream. *Starters/Snacks: £3.95 to £6.95. Main Courses: £6.95 to £16.95. Puddings: £2.95 to £5.95*

Free house ~ Licensees Rhian Cradock and Helen Greer ~ Real ale ~ Bar food (not Mon evening) ~ (01661) 843607 ~ Children welcome ~ Dogs welcome ~ Live music Mon evenings ~ Open 11-11; 12-10.30 Sun ~ Bedrooms: /£65S

Recommended by Lawrence Pearse, Chris and Sue Bax, Alex and Claire Pearse, M A Borthwick, Keith Cohen, Andy and Jill Kassube, Maddie Maughan, Gail Squires

LANGLEY ON TYNE
NY8160 MAP 10

Carts Bog Inn
A686 S, junction B6305; NE47 5NW

Remote moorland pub with blazing log fire and well liked food in neat beamed rambling bar

This is a very pleasant proper pub by the moors and dry-stone walled pastures above the Tyne Valley; tables in the garden make the most of the view. The neatly kept main black-beamed bar has a blazing log fire in the central stone fireplace, local photographs and horsebrasses, and windsor chairs and comfortably cushioned wall settles around the tables. It rambles about with flagstones here, carpet there, and mainly white walls with some stripped stone. A restaurant (once a cow byre) with more wall banquettes has pool, piped music, darts and quoits. Mordue Five Bridge and a couple of guests such as Derwent Wintergold and Wylam Magic on handpump, several malt whiskies and a big choice of soft drinks; quick, friendly service.

🍴 **Reasonably priced bar food includes sandwiches, soup, deep-fried haggis in light beer batter, chicken in white wine, tarragon, garlic and cream, steak in ale casserole, vegetable moussaka, pork stroganoff, pheasant with honey and prunes, and puddings such as baked orange and vanilla cheesecake and sticky toffee pudding with butterscotch sauce.** *Starters/Snacks: £4.00 to £5.75. Main Courses: £7.50 to £18.50. Puddings: £4.50*

Free house ~ Licensee Kelly Norman ~ Real ale ~ Bar food (12-2, 6.30-9; not Mon lunchtime) ~ (01434) 684338 ~ Children welcome ~ Dogs allowed in bar ~ Live folk second Thurs evening of month ~ Open 12-2.30, 5-11; 12-11(10.30 Sun) Sat; closed Mon lunchtime

Recommended by Comus and Sarah Elliott, Di and Mike Gillam, Dr Graham Thorpe, Mart Lawton, Dr and Mrs R G J Telfer, Michael Dandy, Brian Brooks

NEW YORK
NZ3269 MAP 10

Shiremoor Farm
Middle Engine Lane/Norham Road, off A191 bypass; NE29 8DZ

Cleverly transformed farm buildings with interesting furnishings and décor, popular food all day, decent drinks, and covered and heated terrace

Don't be too put off by the uninspiring surroundings as these former farm buildings house a very busy, large dining pub. The spacious interior is furnished with a mix of interesting and comfortable furniture and there's a big kelim on the broad flagstones, warmly colourful farmhouse paintwork on the bar counter and several other tables, conical rafters of the former gin-gan, a few farm tools and evocative country pictures. Gentle lighting in several well divided spacious areas cleverly picks up the surface modelling of the pale stone and beam ends. Mordue Workie Ticket, Timothy Taylors Landlord and two guests like Crouch Vale Brewers Gold and Jennings Cumberland on handpump and decent wines by the glass. The granary extension is pleasant for families. There are seats outside on the covered, heated terrace.

🍴 **Popular food served all day might include sandwiches, warm chorizo and potato salad, chargrilled vegetable ravioli, king prawn and pepper kebabs with fresh lime zest, chilli con carne, steak in ale casserole, sizzling chicken strips in black bean sauce, pork loin medallions with a brandy, mushroom and mustard sauce, and puddings such as gooseberry, apple and blackberry crumble and dark chocolate, coffee and caramel cheesecake.** *Starters/Snacks: £4.95 to £5.95. Main Courses: £5.95 to £10.95. Puddings: £3.95*

Free house ~ Licensee C W Kerridge ~ Real ale ~ Bar food (all day) ~ (0191) 2576302 ~ Children welcome away from main bar ~ Open 11-11

Recommended by Comus and Sarah Elliott, Mrs Carolyn Dixon, J R Ringrose, Mart Lawton

NEWBURN   NZ1665   MAP 10

Keelman 🍺 £ 🛏

Grange Road: follow Riverside Country Park brown signs off A6085 (the riverside road off A1 on Newcastle's W fringes); NE15 8ND

Impressive range of own-brewed beers in converted pumping station, easy-going atmosphere, excellent service, straightforward food, bedroom block

This unusual and rather distinguished-looking granite pub is the tap for Big Lamp Brewery, on the same site. The bar counter's impressive array of eight handpumps usually dispenses the full range of their beers, obviously kept in tip-top condition and very reasonably priced. If you're confused about which one to go for, the neatly dressed staff will happily let you sample a couple first: Big Lamp Bitter, Double M, Summerhill Stout, Prince Bishop Ale, Premium, Embers and Blackout. There's an easy-going atmosphere and a good mix of customers in the high-ceilinged bar which has lofty arched windows, making it light and airy, and well spaced tables and chairs. There are more tables in an upper gallery and the modern all-glass conservatory dining area (pleasant at sunset) contrasts stylishly with the original old building. Service is first-class, the hands-on landlord is quick to help out when needed and the whole place is kept spick and span; piped music. There are plenty of picnic-sets, tables and benches out on the terraces, among flower tubs and beds of shrubs. This is a great base for walks along the Tyne, with six up-to-date bedrooms in an adjoining block.

🍴 **Reasonably priced and served in generous helpings, the straightforward food includes sandwiches, soup, filled baked potatoes, beef in ale pie, large fish and chips, grilled trout and a big mixed grill; they do an early evening special on weekdays from 5pm till 7pm.** *Starters/Snacks: £1.40 to £4.45. Main Courses: £5.50 to £10.45. Puddings: £1.99 to £3.40*

Own brew ~ Licensee George Story ~ Real ale ~ Bar food (12-9) ~ Restaurant ~ (0191) 267 0772 ~ Children welcome until 9pm ~ Open 11-11; 12-10.30 Sun ~ Bedrooms: £45.50S/£65S

Recommended by Mart Lawton, Mike and Lynn Robinson, Graham Oddey, T Stone, Celia Minoughan, John Foord, Mr and Mrs Maurice Thompson, Liz and Brian Barnard, Prof and Mrs Tony Palmer, Arthur Pickering, Andy and Jill Kassube

NEWCASTLE UPON TYNE   NZ2464   MAP 10

Cluny 🍺 £

Lime Street (which runs between A193 and A186 E of centre); NE1 2PQ

Carefully converted whisky-bottling plant doubling as art gallery and studio; sparsely decorated bar, super ales from local breweries and simple bar food

A new licensee has taken over this interesting place which doubles as an art gallery and studio for local artists and craftspeople and has live music every night. It's an imaginatively converted whisky-bottling plant and the back area has changing exhibitions of paintings, sculptures and pottery. The friendly L-shaped bar is trendy and gently bohemian-feeling despite its minimalist décor, with slightly scuffed bare boards, some chrome seating and overhead spotlights. A fine range of real ales on handpump such as Black Sheep Bitter, Camerons Roaring Lion, Durham Magus, Jarrow Bitter, Mordue Five Bridge Bitter and Saltaire Winter; three farm ciders, rotating continental and american beers on tap, lots of bottled world beers, a good range of soft drinks and a fine row of rums, malt whiskies and vodkas and banana smoothies. A raised area looking down on the river has comfortable seating including settees and there are daily papers and local arts magazines. A separate room has a stage for live bands; disabled access and facilities, fruit machine and well reproduced piped music. To get here – opposite the Ship

on Lime Street look out for a cobbled bank leading down to the Ouseburn, by the Byker
city farm, and stretching down here, the pub is below the clutch of bridges.

🍴 **Simple bar food, served by cheerful staff, includes soup, sandwiches or toasties,
ploughman's, burgers, spinach, chickpea and mushroom chilli, daily specials, and puddings
such as fudge cake.** *Starters/Snacks: £2.50 to £3.50. Main Courses: £4.50 to £7.00. Puddings:
£1.00 to £3.00*

Head of Steam ~ Licensee Julian Ive ~ Real ale ~ Bar food (12-9 daily) ~ (0191) 230 4474 ~
Children welcome until 7pm ~ Live bands every night ~ Open 11.30-11(till 1am Fri and Sat);
12-10.30 Sun; closed 25 Dec, 1 Jan

Recommended by Mike and Lynn Robinson, Eric Larkham, Blaise Vyner, Graham Oddey

Crown Posada 🍺

*The Side; off Dean Street, between and below the two high central bridges (A6125 and
A6127); NE1 3JE*

**Busy city-centre pub with grand architecture, lots of locals in long narrow bar, tip-top
beers and a warm welcome; almost no food**

It might be best to visit this old-fashioned and friendly little gem during the week when
regulars sit reading papers in the front snug – it is usually packed at weekends. It's the
city's second oldest pub and the architecture alone makes it worth the trip. A golden
crown and magnificent pre-Raphaelite stained-glass windows add grandeur to an already
imposing carved stone façade, while inside highlights include the elaborate coffered
ceiling, stained glass in the counter screens, a line of gilt mirrors each with a tulip lamp
on a curly brass mount matching the great ceiling candelabra. Fat low-level heating pipes
make a popular footrest when the east wind brings the rain off the North Sea. It's a very
long and narrow room, making quite a bottleneck by the serving counter; beyond that, a
long soft green built-in leather wall seat is flanked by narrow tables. There's a fruit
machine, and an old record player in a wooden cabinet provides mellow background music
when the place is quiet; dominoes. From half a dozen handpumps and kept in fine
condition, the real ales might include house beers like Hadrian Gladiator, Jarrow Bitter
and Timothy Taylors Landlord with guests such as Durham Golden Sceptre, Rudgate Viking
and Wylam Whistle Stop. It's only a few minutes' stroll to the castle.

🍴 **They may offer lunchtime sandwiches but nothing else.**

Sir John Fitzgerald ~ Licensee Derek Raisbeck ~ Real ale ~ No credit cards ~ (0191) 232 1269 ~
Open 11-11; 7-10.30 Sun; closed Sun lunchtime

*Recommended by Peter Smith, Judith Brown, Eric Larkham, Joe Green, P Dawn, Mark and Diane Grist,
Arthur Pickering, Pete Baker, the Didler, Mike and Lynn Robinson, Celia Minoughan, Di and Mike Gillam, Andy and
Jill Kassube*

NEWTON-BY-THE-SEA   NU2424   MAP 10

Ship

*Village signposted off B1339 N of Alnwick; Low Newton – paid parking 200 metres up road
on right, just before village (none in village); NE66 3EL*

**In charming square of fishermen's cottages by green sloping to sandy beach, good simple
food, fine spread of drinks; best to check winter opening times**

As one reader put it 'this is one of those places which feels just right the moment you
open the door'. It has an enchanting coastal setting in a row of converted fishermen's
cottages and looking across a sloping village green to a sandy beach just beyond. The
plainly furnished bare-boards bar on the right has nautical charts on its dark pink walls,
beams and hop bines. Another simple room on the left has some bright modern pictures
on stripped-stone walls, and a woodburning stove in its stone fireplace; darts, dominoes.
It can get very busy indeed at lunchtimes (quieter at night and during the winter) and
service does slow down then, especially when queues build up. Hadrian & Border Farne
Island Pale Ale, Gladiator and Magic Kingdom, Matfen Brewery Magic and Wylam Summer
Magic on handpump (in the winter they may have just two ales); also decent wines, farm

cider, an espresso machine (colourful coffee cups, good hot chocolate), several malt whiskies and good soft drinks. Darts and board games. Out in the corner of the square are some tables among pots of flowers, with picnic-sets over on the grass. There's no nearby parking, but there's a car park up the hill.

🍴 Using local free-range and organic produce, the well liked food at lunchtime includes **toasties, stotties and ciabattas, ploughman's, fishcakes and kipper pâté, with evening choices such as grilled goats cheese with tomato and basil, silver anchovies on wild rocket salad, hot mexican beans in a tortilla wrap with wild rice, cheese and sour cream, gammon with mustard mash, smoked haddock fillet on spring onion and parsley mash, and puddings like apple crumble and speciality ice-creams.** *Starters/Snacks: £3.50 to £6.75. Main Courses: £7.00 to £14.95. Puddings: £3.50 to £5.50*

Free house ~ Licensee Christine Forsyth ~ Real ale ~ Bar food (12-2.30 Mon-Sat (not winter evenings except Fri and Sat 7-8) but 12-2.30, 7-8 summer) ~ No credit cards ~ (01665) 576262 ~ Children welcome ~ Dogs welcome ~ Live folk/blues/jazz; phone for details ~ Open 11-11; 12-10.30 Sun; 11-4 Mon-Weds; 11-4, 8-11 Thurs; 11-4, 6-11 Fri; all day Sat; 12-5 Sun in winter; closed Mon-Weds evenings in winter

Recommended by Comus and Sarah Elliott, Graham Oddey, Di and Mike Gillam, Mike and Sue Loseby, Paul and Ursula Randall, Ian Thurman, the Didler, P Dawn, Will and Kay Adie, Susan Hart, Dr D J and Mrs S C Walker, Michael Butler, Tony and Jill Radnor

NEWTON-ON-THE-MOOR
NU1705 MAP 10

Cook & Barker Arms 🍴 🛏
Village signposted from A1 Alnwick—Felton; NE65 9JY

Emphasis on generous food but with a pubby-feeling beamed bar and quite a range of drinks; comfortable bedrooms

---

You'd never know you were so close to the A1 – readers have found it quiet in the garden and in the bedrooms (which are very comfortable). It's a friendly stone-built inn with most customers here to enjoy the good food. The relaxed and unfussy long beamed bar feels distinctly pubby though, with stripped stone and partly panelled walls, brocade-seated settles around oak-topped tables, brasses, a highly polished oak servery, and a lovely fire at one end with a coal-effect gas fire at the other. An eating area has oak-topped tables with comfortable leather chairs and french windows leading on to the terrace; piped music. Black Sheep, Courage Directors, Theakstons XB and Timothy Taylors Landlord on handpump, a dozen wines by the glass from an extensive list and quite a few malt whiskies; helpful service.

🍴 The licensees have bought a farm and plan to grow organic vegetables and raise organic **cattle, sheep and rare breed pigs for use in the pub. Popular, interesting bar food includes sandwiches, interesting soups, poached free-range egg with smoked salmon on a toasted muffin, terrine of wild boar with caramelised apple wrapped in cured ham with red onion marmalade, tagliatelle with tomatoes, olives, spinach and basil, crab cakes with spinach, butter sauce and pommes frites, stir-fried beef with noodles and spring onions, chicken with leeks, stilton and bacon, and puddings; a more elaborate à la carte menu and a good value three-course evening menu, too.** *Starters/Snacks: £3.25 to £6.00. Main Courses: £6.95 to £14.50. Puddings: £4.50*

Free house ~ Licensee Phil Farmer ~ Real ale ~ Bar food (12-2, 6-9) ~ Restaurant (12-2, 7-9) ~ (01665) 575234 ~ Children welcome ~ Open 11-11; 12-10.30 Sun ~ Bedrooms: £47B/£75B

Recommended by MJVK, Philip and Susan Philcox, Walter and Susan Rinaldi-Butcher, M A Borthwick, Arthur Pickering, Mrs Jennifer Hurst, Glenys and John Roberts, Dr Peter D Smart, Mart Lawton, John and Sylvia Harrop, P and J Shapley, Christine and Phil Young, K S Whittaker, Comus and Sarah Elliott, Mr and Mrs M Porter, R M Corlett, Mike and Sue Loseby, Charles and Pauline Stride

---

Stars after the name of a pub show exceptional quality. One star means most people (after reading the report to see just why the star has been won) would think a special trip worth while. Two stars mean that the pub is really outstanding – for its particular qualities it could hardly be bettered.

RENNINGTON   NU2118   MAP 10

Masons Arms 🛏

Stamford Cott; B1340 NE of Alnwick; NE66 3RX

Comfortable bedrooms make this a good base for nearby coast; very neatly kept pub, local beers and seats outside

Run by helpful, friendly people, this spotlessly kept pub remains a popular place to stay when exploring the nearby coast. The neat and well equipped bedrooms are in an adjacent stable block and annexe and the proper breakfasts are good. The beamed lounge bar is pleasantly modernised and comfortable, with wheelback and mate's chairs around solid wood tables on a patterned carpet, plush bar stools, and plenty of pictures (some may be for sale), photographs and brass. The dining rooms have pine panelling and wrought-iron wall lights; piped classical music. Hadrian & Border Secret Kingdom and guests like Hadrian & Border Farne Island Pale Ale and Northumberland St Patrick's Special on handpump. There are sturdy rustic tables on the little front lavender-surrounded terrace, and picnic-sets at the back.

🍴 Straightforward bar food includes soup, craster kipper pâté, curry of the day, vegetarian moussaka, lemon sole stuffed with prawns, roast duck with orange sauce, and puddings like passion fruit gateau and lemon meringue pie. *Starters/Snacks: £3.50 to £5.50. Main Courses: £6.95 to £13.95. Puddings: £3.75 to £5.50*

Free house ~ Licensees Bob and Alison Culverwell ~ Real ale ~ Bar food (12-2, 6.30-9) ~ Restaurant ~ (01665) 577275 ~ Children welcome ~ Dogs allowed in bedrooms ~ Open 12-11(10.30 Sun) ~ Bedrooms: £55B/£80S(£75B)

Recommended by P and J Shapley, Stuart Paulley, Michael Butler, Bill Strang, Stuart Pearson, Robert Stephenson, Dr D J and Mrs S C Walker

ROMALDKIRK   NY9922   MAP 10

Rose & Crown ★ 🍴 🍷 🛏

Just off B6277; DL12 9EB

Good base for the area with accomplished cooking, civilised comfort and attentive service; lovely bedrooms

This civilised 18th-c country inn is an extremely comfortable place to stay with very well equipped bedrooms and bathrooms; they also provide their own in-house guide to tried and tested days out and about in the area and a *Walking in Teesdale* book. The traditional cosy beamed bar has old-fashioned seats facing a warming log fire, a Jacobean oak settle, lots of brass and copper, a grandfather clock, and gin traps, old farm tools, and black and white pictures of Romaldkirk on the walls. Black Sheep Best Bitter and Emmerdale and Theakstons Best are on handpump alongside 14 wines by the glass, organic fruit juices and pressed vegetable juices. The smart brasserie-style Crown Room (bar food is served in here) has large cartoons of French waiters on dark red walls, a grey carpet and smart high-back chairs. The hall has farm tools, wine maps and other interesting prints, along with a photograph (taken by a customer) of the Hale Bopp comet over Romaldkirk church. There's also an oak-panelled restaurant. Lovely in summer, tables outside look out over the village green, still with its original stocks and water pump. The village is close to the excellent Bowes Museum and the High Force waterfall, and has an interesting old church.

🍴 The imaginative food (only the frites and ice-cream are bought in and they make their own chutneys, jams, marmalades and bread) in the bar at lunchtime might include filled baguettes, stotties and ciabattas, ploughman's, soup, chicken liver pâté with port and orange sauce, cheddar and spinach soufflé with a light chive cream, pork sausage with black pudding mustard mash and shallot gravy, potato gnocchi with blue wensleydale cheese, steak, kidney and mushroom in ale pie and smoked haddock risotto with prawns, mascarpone cheese and chives; evening choices such as seared tuna with french bean and tomato salad and honey vinaigrette, smoked salmon soufflé with Noilly Prat chive cream, baked halibut with cotherstone cheese and red onion marmalade, confit duck leg with puy lentils, smoked bacon and red wine and chargrilled rump of venison with button mushrooms, olorosso sherry and cream; puddings like calvados and apple cobbler with vanilla ice-cream and chocolate and orange torte. You do need to book to be sure of a table. *Starters/Snacks: £4.25 to £6.75. Main Courses: £9.50 to £14.75. Puddings: £4.25*

Free house ~ Licensees Christopher and Alison Davy ~ Real ale ~ Bar food (12-1.45, 6.30-9.30) ~ Restaurant ~ (01833) 650213 ~ Children welcome but must be over 6 in restaurant ~ Dogs allowed in bar and bedrooms ~ Open 11-3, 5.30-11; 12-3, 7-10.30 Sun; closed 24-26 Dec ~ Bedrooms: £80B/£130B

Recommended by Alex and Claire Pearse, Pat and Tony Martin, J C Clark, Mrs Sheila Stothard, Pat and Stewart Gordon, Margaret and Roy Randle, Mrs Roxanne Chamberlain, Brian Brooks, Arthur Pickering, Mike and Sue Loseby, Rodney and Norma Stubington, J Crosby

SEAHOUSES
NU2232   MAP 10

Olde Ship ★ 🍺 🛏
Just off B1340, towards harbour; NE68 7RD

Lots of atmosphere, fine choice of ales and maritime memorabilia in bustling little hotel; views across harbour to Farne Islands

Lively and friendly and full of customers, this popular hotel (overlooking the little village's harbour) has been in the same family for a century. The bar remains a tribute to the sea and seafarers and even the floor is scrubbed ship's decking – and, if it's working, an anemometer takes wind speed readings from the top of the chimney. Besides lots of other shiny brass fittings, ship's instruments and equipment, and a knotted anchor made by local fishermen, there are sea pictures and model ships, including fine ones of the North Sunderland lifeboat, and Seahouses' lifeboat the *Grace Darling*. There's also a model of the *Forfarshire*, the paddle steamer Grace Darling went to rescue in 1838 (you can read more of the story in the pub), and even the ship's nameboard. One clear glass window looks out across the harbour to the Farne Islands, and as dusk falls you can watch the Longstones lighthouse shine across the fading evening sky. The bar is gently lit by stained-glass sea picture windows, there are new lantern lights and a winter open fire; piped music and dominoes. A fine choice of seven real ales on handpump might include Bass, Black Sheep Best Bitter and Hadrian & Border Farne Island Pale Ale with guests like Courage Directors, Greene King Old Speckled Hen and Ruddles County and Theakstons Best; also, a new wine list and quite a few malt whiskies. The pub is not really suitable for children though there is a little family room, and along with walkers, they are welcome on the battlemented side terrace (you'll find fishing memorabilia even out here). This and a sun lounge look out on the harbour. You can book boat trips to the Farne Islands Bird Sanctuary at the harbour, and there are bracing coastal walks, particularly to Bamburgh, Grace Darling's birthplace.

🍽 Standard bar food includes sandwiches, ploughman's, chicken liver pâté, soup, spicy lamb stew, steak in Guinness pie, chilli bean hotpot, and puddings like apple crumble and coffee and walnut sponge; nice breakfasts. *Starters/Snacks: £4.00 to £5.25. Main Courses: £9.00 to £10.75. Puddings: £4.00 to £5.75*

Free house ~ Licensees Alan and Jean Glen ~ Real ale ~ Bar food (no evening food mid-Dec to mid-Jan) ~ Restaurant ~ (01665) 720200 ~ Children in small back lounge ~ Open 11(12 Sun)-11 ~ Bedrooms: £55S/£110B

Recommended by Mr and Mrs Staples, Bruce and Sharon Eden, John Robertson, Christopher Turner, DFL, Mr and Mrs L Haines, Ian Thurman, Comus and Sarah Elliott, Will and Kay Adie, Di and Mike Gillam, P Dawn, Ian and Jane Irving, Sue and Dave Harris, Alan and Paula McCully, Paul and Ursula Randall, Dr D J and Mrs S C Walker, Louise English, N R White, Richard Tosswill, Tony and Maggie Harwood, Mike and Sue Loseby, Graham Findley, Andy and Jill Kassube, the Didler

---

Bedroom prices normally include full english breakfast, VAT and any inclusive service charge that we know of. Prices before the '/' are for single rooms, after for two people in double or twin (B includes a private bath, S a private shower). If there is no '/', the prices are only for twin or double rooms (as far as we know there are no singles).

STANNERSBURN

NY7286 MAP 10

Pheasant

Kielder Water road signposted off B6320 in Bellingham; NE48 1DD

Warmly friendly village local close to Kielder Water with quite a mix of customers and nice homely bar food; seats in streamside garden

Readers enjoy their visits to this spotlessly kept and friendly village inn and many of them choose to stay overnight; the bedrooms are to be refurbished in early 2008. The low-beamed comfortable traditional lounge has ranks of old local photographs on stripped stone and panelling, red patterned carpets and upholstered stools ranged along the counter. A separate public bar is similar but simpler and opens into a further cosy seating area with beams and panelling. The evening sees a good mix of visitors and locals, when the small dining room can get quite crowded. Marstons Pedigree, Timothy Taylors Landlord and Wylam Gold on handpump (only one real ale during the winter), over 30 malt whiskies, and a decent reasonably priced wine list; courteous staff, piped music. The pub is in a peaceful valley surrounded by quiet forests and is handy for Kielder Water; there are picnic-sets in the streamside garden and a pony paddock behind. Dogs may be allowed in some bedrooms by arrangement.

🍴 **Very good bar food includes lunchtime sandwiches, soup, smoked salmon pâté, caramelised red onion and goats cheese tartlet, chicken casserole, mushroom and spinach lasagne, baked bass with lemon and parsley sauce, roast lamb with redcurrant and rosemary jus, confit duck breast with port and raspberry sauce, and puddings such as apple and orange crumble and lemon and lime cheesecake.** *Starters/Snacks: £3.25 to £5.25. Main Courses: £8.25 to £10.25. Puddings: £4.25*

Free house ~ Licensees Walter and Robin Kershaw ~ Real ale ~ Bar food (12-2.30(2 Sun), 7-9) ~ Restaurant ~ (01434) 240382 ~ Children welcome ~ Dogs allowed in bedrooms ~ Open 11-3, 6.30-11.30; 12-3, 7-11 Sun; closed Mon, Tues Nov-Mar ~ Bedrooms: £50S/£85S

Recommended by Pat and Stewart Gordon, Dennis Jones, Mark and Ruth Brock, Mr and Mrs L Haines, Michael Dandy, David Cosham, Les and Sandra Brown, Dr Peter D Smart, Sara Fulton, Roger Baker, Alex and Claire Pearse, Arthur Pickering, Lawrence Pearse, David and Pauline Hambley, Dr Peter Crawshaw

STANNINGTON

NZ2179 MAP 10

Ridley Arms

Village signposted just off A1 S of Morpeth; NE61 6EL

Several differing linked rooms in well run pub with half a dozen real ales, generous food, terrace tables

Handy for the A1, this efficiently run pub still manages to keep a nice pubby feel despite the emphasis on food – which is usefully served all day. It's arranged into several separate areas, each slightly different in mood and style from its neighbours. The front is a proper bar area with darts and a fruit machine and stools along the counter. The beamed dining areas lead back from here, with a second bar counter, comfortable armchairs and upright chairs around shiny dark wood tables on polished boards or carpet, portraits and cartoons on cream, panelled or stripped stone walls, careful lighting and some horsey statuettes. Black Sheep Best Bitter, Timothy Taylors Landlord and guests like Hadrian & Border Secret Kingdom, Jennings Cumberland, Mordue Geordie Pride and York Yorkshire Terrier on handpump, 14 wines by the glass; good, brisk service and piped music, games machine, darts, board games and good disabled access. There are tables outside on a terrace.

🍴 **Quite a choice of good, generously served bar food includes sandwiches, soup, crispy duck and watercress salad, leek and wild mushroom tart, sticky spare ribs with an orange and chilli glaze, seared lambs liver with red wine and onions, locally caught seafood pie, harissa chicken with herby couscous, aberdeen angus casserole with lentils, shallots and whisky, daily specials, and puddings such as caramelised rice pudding with apricot compote and toasted almonds and iced hazelnut parfait with praline toffee wafers.** *Starters/Snacks: £3.50 to £5.50. Main Courses: £6.50 to £15.00. Puddings: £4.50 to £4.75*

Sir John Fitzgerald ~ Managers Lynn and Gary Reilly ~ Real ale ~ Bar food (12-9.30(9 Sun)) ~ (01670) 789216 ~ Children under 10 must leave by 8pm ~ Open 11.30-11; 12-10.30 Sun

Recommended by P Price, Celia Minoughan, Dr Peter D Smart, Comus and Sarah Elliott, Derek and Sylvia Stephenson, Keith Cohen, Jan Moore

WARK

NY8676 MAP 10

Battlesteads 🍺 🛏️

B6320 N of Hexham; NE48 3LS

A fine stop on a scenic route with good local ales, fair value tasty food and relaxed atmosphere; comfortable bedrooms, good walks

Converted from an 18th-c farmstead, this family-run inn is a particularly friendly place. The nicely restored carpeted bar has a log fire, horsebrasses around the fireplace and on the low beams, comfortable seats including some dark blue wall banquettes, old *Punch* country life cartoons on the off-white walls above its dark dado, and double doors to a panelled inner snug. There's a relaxed unhurried atmosphere and good changing local ales such as Black Sheep Best Bitter, Durham Magus and Wylam Gold Tankard from handpumps on the heavily carved dark oak bar counter; good coffee, cheerful service. Some of the bedrooms are on the ground floor (with disabled access). There are picnic-sets on a terrace in the walled garden, and fine walks nearby.

🍽️ **Good value food includes lunchtime snacks such as sandwiches, filled baked potatoes, ploughman's and soup as well as grilled goats cheese with a grape salsa, devilled kidneys on hot buttered toast, chicken, king prawn or vegetable fajitas with salsa, sour cream and salad, lamb with leek, rosemary and redcurrant jus, gammon and egg, cajun chicken, daily specials, and puddings like sticky toffee pudding with warm toffee sauce and whisky and marmalade bread and butter pudding.** *Starters/Snacks: £3.25 to £4.95. Main Courses: £8.50 to £17.50. Puddings: £3.75 to £4.75*

Free house ~ Licensees Richard and Dee Slade ~ Real ale ~ Bar food (12-3, 7-10) ~ Restaurant ~ (01434) 230209 ~ Children welcome ~ Dogs allowed in bar and bedrooms ~ Open 10(11 Sun)-11; 12-3, 6-11 in winter ~ Bedrooms: £45S/£80B

Recommended by Comus and Sarah Elliott, BOB, Michael Doswell, Andy and Jill Kassube

WELDON BRIDGE

NZ1398 MAP 10

Anglers Arms 🛏️

B6344, just off A697; village signposted with Rothbury off A1 N of Morpeth; NE65 8AX

Large helpings of straightforward food in appealing and interesting bar or converted railway dining car, comfortable bedrooms, fishing on River Coquet

This bustling hotel is run more or less as a restaurant but you can still happily just have a drink around the bar, too. Nicely lit and comfortable, the traditional turkey-carpeted bar is divided into two parts: cream walls on the right, and oak panelling and some shiny black beams hung with copper pans on the left, with a grandfather clock and sofa by the coal fire, staffordshire cats and other antique ornaments on its mantelpiece, old fishing and other country prints, some in heavy gilt frames, a profusion of other fishing memorabilia, and some taxidermy. Some of the tables are lower than you'd expect for eating, but their chairs have short legs to match – different, and rather engaging. Batemans XXXB, Theakstons Best, Timothy Taylors Landlord and Youngs & Wells Bombardier on handpump and decent wines; piped music. The restaurant is in a former railway dining car with crisp white linen and a pink carpet. There are tables in the attractive garden with a good play area that includes an assault course; they have rights to fishing on a mile of the River Coquet just across the road.

🍽️ **Generous helpings of food include sandwiches, home-made chicken liver pâté, prawn and smoked salmon salad, cod and chips, mince and dumplings, sausage casserole, steak in ale pie, mixed grill, and puddings.** *Starters/Snacks: £3.95 to £6.25. Main Courses: £6.95 to £22.50. Puddings: £4.95*

Free house ~ Licensee John Young ~ Real ale ~ Bar food (12-9.30) ~ Restaurant ~
(01665) 570271 ~ Children welcome ~ Dogs allowed in bedrooms ~ Open 11-11; 12-11 Sun ~
Bedrooms: £39.50S/£70S

*Recommended by Richard C Morgan, Di and Mike Gillam, Dr Peter D Smart, Dr and Mrs R G J Telfer, GSB,
Comus and Sarah Elliott, Graham Oddey, David and Sue Smith, Mart Lawton, Michael Doswell*

LUCKY DIP

Besides the fully inspected pubs, you might like to try these Lucky Dips recommended to us and
described by readers (if you do, please send us reports: www.goodguides.co.uk).

ACOMB [NY9366]
Miners Arms NE46 4PW [Main St]: Charming
small 18th-c country pub with real ales such
as Black Sheep and Yates, good value simple
home cooking by landlady (not wkdy
lunchtimes) from sandwiches to good value
Sun lunch, comfortable settles in carpeted
bar, huge fire in stone fireplace, friendly cat;
children in small back dining room, tables
out in front and back courtyard, has been
open all day Sun and summer
(Michael Dandy)
ALLENHEADS [NY8545]
☆ *Allenheads Inn* NE47 9HJ [just off B6295]:
Country local splendidly placed high in wild
former lead-mining country (and on the C2C
Sustrans cycle route), four well kept ales
such as Black Sheep and Jarrow, decent
wine, still some of the bric-a-brac which it
used to be famous for, usual food from cheap
toasties up, country dining room, games
room with darts and pool; piped music, TV;
children welcome, tables out beside some
agricultural machinery, good value bedrooms,
open all day *(Dennis Jones, LYM, Ann and
Tony Bennett-Hughes)*
ALNMOUTH [NU2410]
☆ *Red Lion* NE66 2RJ [Northumberland St]:
Attractive 16th-c inn, relaxed and
unpretentious, with cheerful staff, good
modestly priced pubby food (not winter Mon
evening) inc great fish and seafood and
winter game casserole, real ales such as
Black Sheep and local Barefoot Mellow
Yellow, good choice of mainly new world
wines by the glass, front bistro-style
restaurant, log fire in cosy old-fashioned
panelled back locals' bar full of theatre bills
and memorabilia; may be piped music;
children and dogs welcome, neat garden by
alley with raised deck looking over Aln
Estuary, comfortable bedrooms, super
breakfast, open all day wknds *(Derek and
Sylvia Stephenson, Celia Minoughan,
N R White, Comus and Sarah Elliott,
Dr Roger Smith, Judy Nicholson, Alan and
Paula McCully)*
ALNWICK [NU1813]
John Bull NE66 1UY [Howick St]: Friendly
real ale pub, essentially front room of a
terraced house, with great changing range,
also bottled imports and dozens of malt
whiskies; cl wkdy lunchtime, open all
day wknds *(Ian Humphreys,
the Didler)*

BAMBURGH [NU1834]
☆ *Victoria* NE69 7BP [Front St]: Substantial
hotel with lots of mirrors and pictures in
comfortable two-part panelled bar, peaceful,
light and airy, smart more upmarket brasserie
beyond, good quickly prepared food all day
from sandwiches up, two rotating real ales
from Black Sheep and/or Mordue, good wines
by the glass, friendly young staff, young
children's playroom; comfortable bedrooms
(popular with coach parties), lovely setting,
open all day *(Comus and Sarah Elliott,
Michael Doswell)*
BARNARD CASTLE [NZ0516]
Old Well DL12 8PH [The Bank]:
Interesting Tudor coaching inn with two
busy bars and dining areas inc pleasant
conservatory, generous enjoyable food from
sandwiches and baked potatoes up, friendly
helpful staff, well kept ales inc Black Sheep
and Theakstons Best, decent wines;
secluded terrace over town walls, good
value refurbished bedrooms – a good base
for Bowes Museum *(Andrew and
Christine Gagg)*
BARRASFORD [NY9173]
☆ *Barrasford Arms* NE48 4AA [off A6079 north
of Hexham]: Amiable new chef/landlord
winning plaudits for good interesting
country cooking (not Sun evening) inc good
value light lunch dishes, friendly attentive
young staff, real ales, good value wines by
the glass, log fire and warm pubby
atmosphere in compact traditional bar, two
smallish dining rooms nicely blending
contemporary and traditional, lovely views;
good walks, 11 bedrooms, cl Mon lunchtime,
open all day wknds *(Michael Doswell,
Margaret and Mike Iley)*
BEAMISH [NZ2153]
☆ *Beamish Mary* DH9 0QH [off A693 signed No
Place and Cooperative Villas, S of museum]:
Friendly down-to-earth former pit village pub
with up to ten well kept mainly local ales,
two farm ciders, wide choice of good value
generous food inc massive mixed grill and
popular Sun lunch, efficient helpful staff,
coal fires, two bars with 1960s-feel mix of
furnishings, bric-a-brac, 1920s/30s
memorabilia and Aga, Durham NUM banner
in games room; piped music, live music most
nights in converted stables concert room,
annual beer festival; children allowed until
evening, bedrooms *(Arthur Pickering,
Peter Smith, Judith Brown, Mr and Mrs*

Maurice Thompson, Dr Roger Smith, Judy Nicholson)

Sun DH9 0RG [far side of Beamish Open Air Museum – paid entry]: Turn-of-the-century pub moved from Bishop Auckland as part of the lively and excellent museum; authentic décor and very basic real period feel at quieter times, with costumed bar staff, well kept Theakstons Old Peculier and Wensleydale ales, good sandwiches and pork pies, big coal fires *(LYM, Peter Smith, Judith Brown, Dennis Jones, Michael Doswell)*

BELSAY [NZ1277]

Highlander NE20 0DN [A696 S of village]: Roomy country dining pub, reasonably priced food from good lunchtime baguettes up, comfortable raised side area with nice plain wood tables and high-backed banquettes, plenty of nooks and corners for character, Black Sheep and Timothy Taylors Landlord, good log fires, plainer locals' bar; unobtrusive piped music; open all day, handy for Belsay Hall and Gardens *(Dr Peter D Smart, Michael Doswell)*

BERWICK-UPON-TWEED [NT9952]

☆ **Barrels** TD15 1ES [Bridge St]: Convivial pub with thorough-going nautical décor in bar, car memorabilia and other bric-a-brac, Beatles pictures and eccentric furniture in lounge; good choice of real ales and malt whiskies, lunchtime filled rolls and imaginative evening food (perhaps not winter) from snacks and tapas to main dishes, friendly accommodating staff; live music downstairs, good juke box; open all day, cl midweek lunchtimes in winter *(Mike and Lynn Robinson, the Didler)*

☆ **Foxtons** TD15 1AB [Hide Hill]: More chatty and comfortable two-level wine bar than pub, with wide choice of good imaginative food, prompt friendly service, good range of wines, whiskies and coffees, real ales such as Caledonian and Timothy Taylors, lively side bistro; busy, so worth booking evenings, open all day, cl Sun *(John and Sylvia Harrop, Ian and Nita Cooper)*

Pilot TD15 1LZ [Low Greens]: Small beamed and panelled backstreet local with changing real ales from the region, old nautical photographs and knick-knacks, comfortable back lounge, Hadrian & Border and a guest beer (they may let you taste), darts and quoits; fiddle music Thurs; garden tables, bedrooms, open all day Fri-Sun and summer *(Comus and Sarah Elliott, the Didler)*

Rob Roy TD15 2BE [Dock View Rd/Dock Rd, Spittal (Tweedmouth)]: Quiet and cosy seaview restaurant (rather than pub, though they do bar meals too) with good fresh local fish and outstanding speciality fish soup, dark fishing-theme rustic bar with roaring fire and polished wood floor, pleasant dining room; keg beers but decent wines and good fresh coffee; may be cl wkdy lunchtimes out of season *(Alan Cole, Kirstie Bruce)*

BIRTLEY [NZ2856]

Mill House DH3 1RE [Blackfell; handy for A1

southbound, just S of Angel, A1231 Sunderland/Washington slip rd]: Popular and busy extended dining pub with enjoyable food all day, compact bar area, changing real ale, decent house wines, dining room with olde-barn décor, alcoved eating areas and conservatory *(Gerry and Rosemary Dobson)*

BOWES [NY9913]

☆ **Ancient Unicorn** DL12 9HL: Substantial stone inn with some 17th-c parts and interesting *Nicholas Nickleby* connection, warmly welcoming licensees, well kept ales such as Black Sheep, Fullers London Pride and Jennings Cumberland (spring beer festival), good value generous fresh food from sandwiches and well filled baked potatoes to steak, pleasant atmosphere in spacious and comfortable open-plan bar with small but hot open fire, coffee shop; new split-level terrace, well refurbished bedrooms in converted stables block around big cobbled courtyard *(G Deacon, Hilary Forrest, Philip and Sally Tavener, Sarah and Peter Gooderham, LYM)*

CAUSEY PARK BRIDGE [NZ1894]

Oak NE61 3EL [off A1 5 miles N of Morpeth]: Family-friendly country pub/restaurant with nice atmosphere, enjoyable food inc interesting dishes and good value Sun lunch, courteous efficient staff; garden *(Guy Howard)*

CHATTON [NU0528]

☆ **Percy Arms** NE66 5PS [B6348 E of Wooller]: Comfortable stone-built country inn with real ales, plenty of malt whiskies, cheerful efficient staff, popular pubby food in bar and attractive panelled dining room from lunchtime sandwiches up, lounge bar extending through arch, public bar with games; piped music; children in good family area and dining room, picnic-sets on small front lawn, bedrooms (12 miles of private fishing) *(Bob and Louise Craft, Di and Mike Gillam, Paul and Ursula Randall, LYM, Comus and Sarah Elliott)*

CONSETT [NZ1151]

Grey Horse DH8 6NE [Sherburn Terr]: Well run two-bar beamed 19th-c pub brewing its own Consett ales such as Red Dust and Steel Town in former back stables, also a guest such as Daleside, dozens of malt whiskies, occasional beer festivals, very friendly licensees, two coal fires, good range of customers, pool; pavement tables, open all day *(Andy and Jill Kassube)*

CORBRIDGE [NY9964]

Angel NE45 5LA [Main St]: Small 17th-c hotel with good fresh food (not cheap by northern standards) from sandwiches to stylish restaurant meals, up to half a dozen real ales such as Black Sheep, Marstons Pedigree, Mordue and Wylam Gold, good wines and coffees, large plain modern bar and adjoining plush panelled lounge; big-screen TV; children welcome, pleasant bedrooms, nr lovely bridge over River Tyne *(Susan and John Douglas, Blaise Vyner, Michael Butler, Comus and Sarah Elliott,*

Michael Doswell, LYM, Andy and Jill Kassube, Peter and Eleanor Kenyon)

☆ **Black Bull** NE45 5AT [Middle St]: Neatly kept traditional pub spreading through rambling linked rooms, reasonably priced food all day from sandwiches and light lunches up, good friendly service, four changing ales inc Black Sheep and Greene King IPA, good attractively priced wine choice, roaring fire, comfortable mix of seating inc traditional settles in stone-floored low-ceilinged core; open all day *(Comus and Sarah Elliott, Tony and Maggie Harwood, John Foord, Michael Butler, Monica Shelley)*

Dyvels NE45 5AY [Station Rd]: Refurbished under new owners, with simple and unusual well priced bar food, five well kept ales such as Black Sheep, Caledonian Deuchars IPA and Wadworths 6X; children welcome, garden with terrace tables, decent bedrooms, open all day *(Andy and Jill Kassube)*

CORNSAY [NZ1443]

Black Horse DH7 9EL: Usually three or four well kept changing local and regional ales, Easter beer festival, good range of malt whiskies, cheerful staff, well presented straightforward food Tues-Sat evenings; hilltop hamlet with great views; cl lunchtime exc Sun *(Alasdair Sutherland)*

COTHERSTONE [NZ0119]

Red Lion DL12 9QE: Traditional beamed 18th-c village pub with good value food (not Mon-Thurs) in bar and restaurant from sandwiches through familiar things to some interesting dishes, Jennings and a guest beer, log fire, snug; children, boots and dogs welcome, garden tables, bedrooms *(Lesley and Peter Barrett)*

CRAMLINGTON [NZ2373]

Snowy Owl NE23 8AU [just off A1/A19 junction via A1068; Blagdon Lane]: Large Vintage Inn, relaxed and comfortable, with reasonable prices, good choice of wines, reliable all-day food inc popular Sun lunch, friendly efficient service, Bass and Black Sheep, beams, flagstones, hop bines, stripped stone and terracotta paintwork, soft lighting and an interesting mix of furnishings and decorations, daily papers; may be piped music; bedrooms in adjoining Innkeepers Lodge, open all day *(Michael Doswell, Dr Peter D Smart, Comus and Sarah Elliott)*

CRASTER [NU2519]

Jolly Fisherman NE66 3TR [off B1339, NE of Alnwick]: Simple friendly take-us-as-you-find-us local in great spot, with picture window and picnic-sets on grass behind giving sea views over harbour and towards Dunstanburgh Castle (lovely clifftop walk); real ales such as Black Sheep and Greene King Old Speckled Hen, crab sandwiches, crab soup, seafood from smokery opp, games area with pool and juke box; children and dogs welcome, open all day in summer *(Elspeth Borthwick, Arthur Pickering, Derek and Sylvia Stephenson, Dr D J and Mrs S C Walker, LYM, the Didler)*

CROOKHAM [NT9138]

Blue Bell TD12 4SH [Pallinsburn; A697 Wooler—Cornhill]: Small traditional bar, separate lounge and smart comfortably carpeted L-shaped dining area with wide choice of enjoyable home-made food, welcoming landlord, friendly unpretentious atmosphere, Marstons Pedigree and Theakstons; bedrooms, handy for Flodden Field *(Comus and Sarah Elliott, N R White)*

CULLERCOATS [NZ3671]

Queens Head NE30 4QB [Front St]: Cheerful local with good value food, well kept Bass, friendly efficient staff *(Mike and Lynn Robinson)*

DARLINGTON [NZ2814]

No 22 DL3 7RG [Coniscliffe Rd]: Friendly and quite smart, with its own Village ales (brewed by Hambleton) and others such as Daleside and Highgate, belgian beers, enthusiastic landlord, wide range of good lunchtime food, good service, daily papers, bistro feel in two linked rooms, unusual vaulted wood ceiling; open all day, cl Sun *(Andrew York)*

DUNSTAN [NU2419]

Cottage NE66 3SZ [off B1339 Alnmouth—Embleton]: Big well worn in pub with low beams and lots of dark wood, some stripped brickwork, banquettes and dimpled copper tables, basic bar food, 1970ish restaurant, well kept Belhaven, Wylam and a guest beer, young staff who do their best, conservatory, games area; children welcome, tables out on terrace and lawn, adventure play area *(Dr Peter D Smart, LYM)*

DURHAM [NZ2742]

Court Inn DH1 3AW [Court Lane]: Unpretentious traditional town pub with good hearty home-made food all day from sandwiches to steaks and late-evening bargains, real ales such as Bass, Marstons Pedigree and Mordue, extensive stripped brick eating area, no mobile phones; bustling in term-time with students and teachers, piped pop music; seats outside, open all day *(BB, Mr and Ursula Randall, Pete Baker, Mr and Mrs Maurice Thompson)*

☆ **Dun Cow** DH1 3HN [Old Elvet]: Unspoilt traditional town pub in pretty 16th-c black and white timbered cottage, cheerful licensees, tiny chatty front bar with wall benches and greedy pub dog, corridor to long narrow back lounge with banquettes, machines etc (can be packed with students), particularly well kept Castle Eden and other ales such as Black Sheep and Caledonian Deuchars IPA, good value basic lunchtime snacks, decent coffee; piped music; children welcome, open all day Mon-Sat, Sun too in summer *(Pete Baker, LYM, N R White, C Sale, the Didler, Paul and Ursula Randall, Barry and Anne)*

Market Tavern DH1 3NJ [Market Pl]: Recently refurbished olde-worlde pub with two or three well kept real ales, useful at lunchtime for good value freshly made food *(Tony and Maggie Harwood)*

Stonebridge Inn DH1 3RX [Stonebridge
(A690 SW)]: Welcoming rustic pub with
conservatory, attentive staff, changing ales
such as Banks's and Hop Back Summer
Lightning, food inc Sun lunch (Mr and Mrs
Maurice Thompson)

Swan & Three Cygnets DH1 3AG [Elvet
Bridge]: Comfortably refurbished Victorian
pub in good bridge-end spot high above
river, city views from big windows and
picnic-sets out on terrace, friendly service,
bargain lunchtime food from hot filled
baguettes up, cheap well kept Sam Smiths
OB; open all day (BB, MDN)

EAST ORD [NT9851]
Salmon TD15 2NS: Small and friendly, with
well kept real ale and enjoyable food;
children welcome, tables outside (Alan Cole,
Kirstie Bruce)

EBCHESTER [NZ1054]
☆ **Derwent Walk** DH8 0SX [Ebchester Hill
(B6309 outside)]: Interesting pub by the
Gateshead—Consett walk for which it's
named, wide range of consistently good
value home-made food from unusual hot
sandwiches through interesting dishes of the
day to steaks, great choice of wines by the
glass at reasonable prices, full Jennings
range kept well and a guest beer, friendly
staff, good log fire and appealing old
photographs, conservatory with fine Derwent
Valley views; walkers welcome, pleasant
heated terrace (Arthur Pickering, Andy and
Jill Kassube, Prof and Mrs Tony Palmer,
Bruce and Sharon Eden)

EDMUNDBYERS [NZ0150]
Punch Bowl DH8 9NL: Unpretentious recently
refurbished local, welcoming landlord and
helpful staff, Black Sheep, good reasonably
priced simple food, big L-shaped bar with
huge leather settee, pleasant conservatory
restaurant, pool room popular with young
people (their music may be loud), lots of
events inc big-screen movie night; bedrooms
with own bathrooms, open all day
(John Foord, Tony and Maggie Harwood)

EGGLESTON [NY9923]
Three Tuns DL12 0AH [Church Bank]:
Attractive pub by broad sloping Teesdale
village green, log fire and some interesting
furniture in relaxing traditional lounge bar,
welcoming landlady and locals, generous
popular food (not Sun evening) in big-
windowed back room, well kept changing
ales such as York Battleaxe; children
welcome, tables on terrace and in garden
(LYM, Rona Murdoch)

EGLINGHAM [NU1019]
Tankerville Arms NE66 2TX [B6346
Alnwick—Wooler]: Traditional pub with coal
fire each end of carpeted bar, plush
banquettes, black joists, some stripped
stone, real ales such as Black Sheep and
Hadrian & Border, decent wines and malt
whiskies, restaurant; piped music; children
welcome, nice views from garden picnic-sets,
attractive village; the chef/landlord who won
a place in the main entries here for his good

value enterprising food has now left (LYM)

ELLINGHAM [NU1625]
☆ **Pack Horse** NE67 5HA [signed off A1 N of
Alnwick]: Compact stone-built country pub,
recently refurbished, with fresh flowers in
former games room extended as light and
airy new dining room, good choice of fresh
food using local produce from baguettes and
substantial sandwiches up, wider evening
choice, Black Sheep, good coffee, quick
friendly attentive service, feature fireplace in
beamed bar with a forest of jugs, small
comfortable lounge; enclosed garden, good
value bedrooms, peaceful village (David and
Jane Hill, Comus and Sarah Elliott,
Michael Doswell)

ELWICK [NZ4532]
McOrville TS27 3EF [¼ mile off A19 W of
Hartlepool]: Open-plan dining pub with good
blackboard food, Black Sheep and a
changing ale such as Caledonian Deuchars
IPA, Shepherd Neame Spitfire or Timothy
Taylors Landlord, carved panelling, slippers
provided for walkers (Arthur Pickering, JHBS)

EMBLETON [NU2322]
Sportsman NE66 3XF: Large plain bar/bistro
in pub/hotel with nearby beach and
stunning views to Dunstanburgh Castle,
impressive food using prime local produce,
fish and game at reasonable prices, good
small interesting wine list, real ales such as
Mordue Workie Ticket and Timothy Taylors
Landlord, friendly cheerful service; frequent
wknd live music; lots of tables on heated
terrace, coast-view bedrooms, may cl in
winter (Paul and Ursula Randall,
Mrs E E Sanders)

ETAL [NT9239]
☆ **Black Bull** TD12 4TL [off B6354 SW of
Berwick]: Thatched cottage in pretty village
nr castle ruins and light railway, spacious
unpretentious open-plan beamed lounge bar
popular for decent food from good value
baguettes to good fish, steaks and good
vegetarian choice, well kept ales such as
Black Sheep, Marstons Pedigree and
Theakstons, lots of malt whiskies, farm cider,
quick friendly service, interesting witch-
theme décor; games room with darts,
dominoes, pool, TV, juke box and piped
music; children in eating area, picnic-sets
outside, open all day Sat (Comus and
Sarah Elliott, Alan Cole, Kirstie Bruce, Val and
Alan Green, LYM, Mrs E E Sanders)

FELTON [NU1800]
☆ **Northumberland Arms** NE65 9EE [village
signed off A1 N of Morpeth]: Attractive old
inn with beams, stripped stone and good
coal fires in roomy and comfortable open-
plan bar, nice mix of furnishings inc big blue
settees, elegant small end restaurant; good
range of food, well kept Bass and Black
Sheep Best, good coffee and wines, pleasant
atmosphere, laid-back service; well
reproduced piped music, esp in conservatory
pool room; five bedrooms, steps down to
bench by River Coquet, open all day
(Comus and Sarah Elliott, BB)

FROSTERLEY [NZ0236]
☆ *Black Bull* DL13 2SL [just off A689 W of centre]: Doing particularly well under newish licensees, three interesting traditional beamed and flagstoned rooms with two coal fires, fine photographs, four well kept unusual real ales, farm cider and perry, carefully chosen wines and malt whiskies, good food using local and organic ingredients inc good choice of light lunchtime dishes and (not Sun/Mon) short and interesting evening menu, coffee and tempting pastries all day; live music Tues, occasional art shows; attractive no smoking terrace with old railway furnishings (opp steam station), open all day, cl Mon lunchtime *(Joan Kureczka, Geoff and Angela Jacques)*

GAINFORD [NZ1716]
Lord Nelson DL2 3DY [Main Rd (A67)]: Big airy bar with Black Sheep and Wells & Youngs Bombardier, enjoyable sensibly priced food (just roast for Sun lunch), obliging flexible staff *(Richard Tosswill)*

GATESHEAD [NZ3061]
Green NE10 8YB [White Mare Pool, Wardley; W of roundabout at end of A194(M)]: Large refurbished pub, light and airy, half a dozen or more reasonably priced ales inc local Mordue, good range of wines, good value freshly prepared bar/bistro food, friendly helpful staff, picture-window outlook on golf course; light piped music, very busy wknds *(Gerry and Rosemary Dobson)*
Lambton Arms NE9 7XR [Rockcliffe Way, Eighton Banks]: Comfortably updated pub with good range of straightforward food in bar and restaurant (should book wknds), Greene King IPA, Abbot and Old Speckled Hen, good wine choice, cafetière coffee, reasonable prices, pleasant friendly service; children welcome, open all day *(Gerry and Rosemary Dobson)*

GREAT LUMLEY [NZ2949]
Old England DH3 4JB [Front St]: Popular village local, friendly helpful staff, enjoyable reasonably priced bar food inc popular bargain Sun lunch, two or three changing real ales, large comfortable lounge, bar partitioned off *(Mr and Mrs Maurice Thompson)*

HALTWHISTLE [NY7064]
☆ *Black Bull* NE49 0BL [just off Market Sq, behind indian restaurant]: Particularly well kept Big Lamp Price Bishop, Jennings Cumberland and four quickly changing local guest ales, enterprising food all day (not till 7 Mon) inc seafood, game and bargain winter lunches, lively local atmosphere and friendly landlord, brasses on low beams, stripped stone with shelves of bric-a-brac, log fires, corridor to small dining room, darts and monthly quiz night; limited disabled access, dogs welcome in flagstoned part, attractive garden, open all day wknds and summer, cl Mon lunchtime *(Tony and Maggie Harwood, Edward Leetham, Helen Clarke)*

HARTBURN [NZ1185]
Dyke Neuk NE61 3SL [B6343 W of Morpeth, and 2 miles E of village]: Real ale, good value food in beamed bar and restaurant, lots of pictures; pleasant garden *(Mike and Lynn Robinson)*

HAWTHORN [NZ4145]
Stapylton Arms SR7 8SD [off B1432 S of A19 Murton exit]: Chatty carpeted bar with lots of old local photographs, a well kept ale such as Black Sheep, enjoyable food made by landlady from sandwiches to steaks and Sun roasts, friendly family service; dogs on leads allowed, may be open all day on busy wknds, nice wooded walk to sea (joins Durham Coastal Path) *(JHBS)*

HAYDON BRIDGE [NY8364]
☆ *General Havelock* NE47 6ER [A69]: Civilised and individually furnished dining pub, open kitchen doing sensibly short choice of particularly good interesting food using local ingredients from baguettes and reasonably priced lunchtime dishes to more upmarket evening set menus and super puddings, changing local real ales, good wines by the glass and coffee, relaxing leisurely atmosphere, open fires, smart and tranquil Tyne-view stripped stone back restaurant; children welcome, tables on lovely riverside terrace *(Dr Peter D Smart, Tony and Maggie Harwood, Marcus Byron, LYM, Mr and Mrs A Blofield)*
Railway NE47 6JG [Church St]: Friendly and obliging licensees, wide range of well kept ales such as Caledonian Deuchars IPA, reasonably priced home-made meals (breakfast room serves as café for locals); low-priced bedrooms *(David Godfrey, Comus and Sarah Elliott)*

HEDDON-ON-THE-WALL [NZ1366]
Swan NE15 0DR: Big open-plan stone-built pub, welcoming atmosphere, good value food with separate sandwich menu, Theakstons Best, beamed area with farm tools and bric-a-brac, comfortable corners elsewhere with built-in banquettes; picnic-sets in large informal garden with Tyne Valley views *(Monica Shelley)*

HEIGHINGTON [NZ2422]
Bay Horse DL5 6PE [West Green]: 17th-c village-green pub with good value home-made pubby bar food, real ales such as Jennings Cumberland and John Smiths, restaurant *(Andy and Jill Kassube)*
George & Dragon DL5 6PP [East Green]: Two-bar pub behind church, new owners working hard on the food side, doing small set menu and lots of good sensibly priced specials for lounge and conservatory restaurant, good range of well kept real ales; children welcome, cl Mon lunchtime, open all day Fri-Sun *(Andy and Jill Kassube)*

HEXHAM [NY9363]
Tap & Spile NE46 1BH [Battle Hill/Eastgate]: Comfortably worn-in open-plan bare-boards pub with well kept Caledonian Deuchars IPA, Greene King Abbot and quickly changing guest beers from

central bar, country wines, good filling low-priced food, warm coal-effect fire, pleasant polite staff, some live music; no dogs; children welcome, open all day *(John Foord)*

HIGH HESLEDEN [NZ4538]

Ship TS27 4QD [off A19 via B1281]: Half a dozen good changing ales from the region at appealing prices, log fire, lots of sailing ship models inc big one hanging from bar ceiling, enjoyable bar food and some interesting restaurant dishes; yacht and shipping views from car park, six bedrooms in new block, cl Mon *(JHBS)*

HOLWICK [NY9126]

Strathmore Arms DL12 0NJ [back rd up Teesdale from Middleton]: Quiet and unassuming country pub in beautiful scenery just off Pennine Way, good real ales, welcoming landlord, good home cooking at attractive prices, log fire, darts, piano; bedrooms and camp site, open all day *(Arthur Pickering, Sarah and Peter Gooderham)*

HOLY ISLAND [NU1241]

☆ *Crown & Anchor* TD15 2RX [causeway passable only at low tide, check times (01289) 330733]: Comfortable and unpretentious pub/restaurant with compact bar and roomy and spotless modern back dining room, Black Sheep and Caledonian Deuchars IPA, enjoyable simple lunchtime food from a good sandwich range inc crab ciabattas to a few pubby main dishes, wider evening choice running up to duck, salmon etc, pleasantly simple pink and beige décor with interesting rope fancy-work; attractive site, garden picnic-sets looking across to castle, three bedrooms, good breakfast *(Michael Doswell, Dr A McCormick, P Dawn)*

Ship TD15 2SJ [Marygate]: Nicely set pub (very busy in tourist season), renovated bar with big stove, maritime/fishing memorabilia and pictures, bare-boards eating area, pubby food from rather pricy sandwiches up, a Hadrian & Border ale brewed for the pub in summer, good choice of whiskies; no dogs, even in sheltered garden; three comfortable Victorian-décor bedrooms, usually closes for three wks midwinter *(P Dawn, N R White, Comus and Sarah Elliott, Keith and Chris O'Neill)*

HUMSHAUGH [NY9171]

Crown NE46 4AG: Old pub in attractive village with very popular Weds bargain lunch, dauntingly big helpings, organic real ale, efficient friendly staff, decent wines, cheerful bar, comfortable separate dining room; dogs allowed exc at busy times, bedrooms *(Bill and Sheila McLardy, Michael Doswell, Brian and Rosalie Laverick)*

KENTON BANKFOOT [NZ2068]

Twin Farms NE13 8AB [Main Road]: Good Fitzgerald pub in elegant period rustic style, recycled stone, timbers etc, several pleasant areas off central bar, decent food from good value sandwiches up, wide range of well kept changing ales inc local ones, well chosen wines, real fire, quick friendly service, well

run restaurant; piped music, machines; children welcome, disabled facilities, open all day *(Peter and Eleanor Kenyon)*

LAMESLEY [NZ2557]

Ravensworth Arms NE11 0ER [minor rd S of Gateshead western bypass, A1, Team Valley junction]: Popular stone-built Chef & Brewer, stripped brick and recycled timber dividers, reasonably priced fresh food from sandwiches to steak, fish and game, cheerful helpful staff, good wine choice, three or four real ales; piped music; children welcome, play area and picnic-table sets outside, 13 bedrooms, open all day *(Christine and Phil Young)*

LANGDON BECK [NY8531]

Langdon Beck Hotel DL12 0XP [B6277 Middleton—Alston]: Unpretentious isolated pub well placed for walks and Pennine Way, good choice of bar food, helpful friendly staff, five real ales, wonderful views from dining room; bedrooms *(Mr and Mrs Maurice Thompson, Sarah and Peter Gooderham)*

LESBURY [NU2311]

☆ *Coach* NE66 3PP: Nicely furnished cosy bar, armchairs and settees in lounge, cheerful licensees, wide choice of enjoyable food from sandwiches to some interesting dishes and restaurant meals, happy to meet special requests, Black Sheep, good choice of wines, good coffee and tea (free refills), may be Sun bar nibbles; children welcome till 7.30, pretty outside, with masses of flowers *(Comus and Sarah Elliott, Gail and Simon Rowlands)*

LOWICK [NU0139]

☆ *Black Bull* TD15 2UA [Main St (B6353, off A1 S of Berwick-upon-Tweed)]: Nicely decorated village pub, bright and cheerful, with good plentiful modestly priced food using local produce from soup and sandwiches up (take-aways too), Belhaven 60/- and 70/- and Theakstons (just one real ale at quiet seasons), quick friendly service even when busy, comfortable main bar, small back bar, spotless big back dining room; children welcome, three attractive bedrooms, on edge of small pretty village *(John Foord, Comus and Sarah Elliott, Alan and Gill Bridgman)*

LUCKER [NU1530]

Apple NE70 7JH [off A1 N of Morpeth]: Civilised bar area with restful colour-scheme and some massive blocks of stripped stone, woodburner in large fireplace, roomy big-windowed side dining area, darts, dominoes and board games; has been a popular main entry for the previous tenants' enjoyable fresh food, good friendly service and short well chosen wine list (no real ales), but changed hands summer 2007 – reports please *(LYM)*

MARSDEN [NZ3964]

Marsden Grotto NE34 7BS [Coast Rd; passage to lift in A183 car park, just before Marsden from Whitburn]: Pub/restaurant uniquely built into seaside cliff caverns, with

10p lift (or dozens of steps) down to two floors – upper pink plush, lower brown varnish; Black Sheep and another real ale, enjoyable food in bar and restaurant with good fish choice, summer barbecue lunches, good sea views, step straight out on to beach *(John Coatsworth)*

MILBOURNE [NZ1275]

Waggon NE20 0DH [Higham Dykes; A696 NW of Ponteland]: Popular comfortably refurbished open-plan bar with soft lighting, beams, stripped stone and panelling, huge fire each end, wide choice of reasonably priced food from lunchtime sandwiches to restaurant dishes (small helpings available), friendly attentive staff, well kept ales *(Bill and Sheila McLardy)*

MILFIELD [NT9333]

Red Lion NE71 6JD [Main Rd (A697 Wooler—Cornhill)]: Cosy and welcoming inside, with new chef/landlord doing enjoyable sensibly priced food, good service *(J A Groves)*

NETHERTON [NT9807]

Star NE65 7HD [off B6341 at Thropton, or A697 via Whittingham]: Neat simple local in superb remote countryside, many original features, Castle Eden tapped from cellar casks and served from hatch in small entrance lobby, large high-ceilinged room with panelled wall benches, charming service and welcoming regulars; no food, music or children; unfortunately rarely open – Weds, Fri and Sun evenings are the best bet *(Mike and Lynn Robinson, the Didler)*

NEWBIGGIN-BY-THE-SEA [NZ3188]

Cresswell Arms NE64 6DR [High St]: Friendly local worth knowing for limited choice of bargain bar lunches, good cheap beers *(Tony and Maggie Harwood)*

Queens Head NE64 6AT [High St]: Friendly talkative landlord an ambassador for real ales, massed pump clips are testament to the many hundreds he's had here inc bargain-price house beer, several high-ceilinged rooms, plenty of character and thriving atmosphere; dogs welcome (not in sitting room), open all day from 10 *(the Didler, Tony and Maggie Harwood)*

NEWCASTLE UPON TYNE [NZ2565]

☆ *As You Like It* NE2 1DB [Archbold Terrace, Jesmond]: Simply cooked interesting food using northumbrian produce in unusual new dining pub in modern block, runs like clockwork with friendly staff, good wines by the glass, continental beers, Big Lamp Prince Bishop and Jarrow Rivet Catcher and good soft drinks choice, long bar with intriguing mix of furnishings from banquettes and french fauteuils to pine and sturdy rustic tables, restful lighting, exuberant eclectic décor inc huge carved tusks and other exotica, indoor play area, late night wknd live music, downstairs delicatessen; children welcome and well catered for, attractive covered terrace, open all day *(Michael Doswell)*

☆ *Bacchus* NE1 6BX [High Bridge East, between Pilgrim St and Grey St]: Rebuilt just up the road from its former site, elegant and comfortable, with relaxed atmosphere, good modern lunchtime food (not Sun) from interesting doorstep sandwiches and ciabattas through unusual light dishes to more substantial things all at keen prices, half a dozen changing real ales and plenty of bottled imports, good photographs of the region's former industries; open all day but cl Sun lunchtime *(Joe Green, Eric Larkham)*

Bob Trollopes NE1 3JF [Sandhill]: Enjoyable entirely vegetarian food, vegan too if you want, in interesting rambling 17th-c quayside building; appealing prices, changing ales, friendly staff *(Joe Green)*

Bodega NE1 4AG [Westgate Rd]: Majestic Edwardian drinking hall next to Tyne Theatre, colourful walls and ceiling, snug front cubicles, spacious tiled back area with a handsome rug under two magnificent stained-glass cupolas; Big Lamp Prince Bishop, Durham Magus, Mordue Geordie Pride (sold here as No 9) and three quickly changing interesting guest beers, farm cider, friendly service, lunchtime food, table football; juke box or piped music, machines, big-screen TV, busy evenings; open all day *(the Didler, P Dawn, Eric Larkham, Andy and Jill Kassube)*

☆ *Bridge Hotel* NE1 1RQ [Castle Sq, next to high level bridge]: Big cheery high-ceilinged room divided into several areas leaving plenty of space by the bar with replica slatted snob screens, particularly well kept Black Sheep, Caledonian Deuchars IPA, Durham, Mordue Workie Ticket and up to three or four guest beers, friendly staff, bargain lunchtime food and Sun afternoon teas, magnificent fireplace, great views of river and bridges from raised back area; sports TV, piped music, games machines, very long-standing Mon folk club upstairs; tables on flagstoned back terrace overlooking section of old town wall, open all day *(the Didler, P Dawn, Mike and Lynn Robinson, LYM, John Foord, Eric Larkham, Brian and Rosalie Laverick)*

Cumberland Arms NE6 1LD [Byker Buildings]: Friendly traditional local with four particularly well kept changing local ales (tapped straight from the cask if you wish), farm cider, good value toasties, obliging staff; live music or other events most nights, tables outside overlooking Ouseburn Valley, cl wkdy lunchtimes, open all day wknds *(Mike and Lynn Robinson, Eric Larkham)*

Falcons Nest NE3 5EH [Rotary Way, Gosforth – handy for racecourse]: Roomy Vintage Inn in their comfortably relaxing traditional style of olde-worlde linked rooms, good choice of food from interesting sandwiches and light dishes up, good choice of wines by the glass, well kept Black Sheep and Timothy Taylors Landlord, friendly service; open all day, bedrooms in adjacent Innkeepers Lodge block *(Michael Doswell)*

Tilleys NE1 4AW [Corner Westgate Rd and Thornton St]: Large bar next to Tyne Theatre and nr performing arts college and live music centre, so interesting mix of customers, good range of well kept ales such as Jarrow Westoe IPA, farm cider, good choice of bottled beers, generous home-made lunchtime food, artworks for sale; open all day *(Eric Larkham, Andy and Jill Kassube)*

NEWTON UNDER ROSEBERRY [NZ5613]
Kings Head TS9 6QR: Recently converted cottage row in attractive village below Roseberry Topping, emphasis on wide choice of enjoyable generous food in large restaurant area; stylish modern bedrooms, good breakfast *(Michael Butler)*

NORTH SHIELDS [NZ3568]
☆ *Magnesia Bank* NE30 1NH [Camden St]: Lively and well run, half a dozen or more well kept ales inc Black Sheep, Durham, Jarrow and Mordue in lined glasses, good wines and coffee, vast choice of cheerful home-made lunchtime food from cheap toasties to local lamb and fish, super puddings, good value all-day breakfast from 8.30am, attentive friendly uniformed staff and approachable chef, intriguing mix of customers, open fire in roomy bar with raised eating areas, side restaurant (same menu); quiet piped pop music, TV, machines, upstairs comedy nights, live music Fri/Sat; children welcome, tables outside, open all day *(P Dawn, Mike and Lynn Robinson, J R Ringrose, Pat Woodward)*
☆ *Wooden Doll* NE30 1JS [Hudson St]: Bare-boards pub with high view of fish quay and outer harbour from picture-window extension, enjoyable food from good sandwiches to fresh local fish, full Jennings range kept well, good service, informal mix of furnishings; disabled facilities, children welcome till 8, some live music, open all day Sat *(Mike and Lynn Robinson, LYM, Christine A Murphy)*

PONTELAND [NZ1771]
Badger NE20 9BT [Street Houses; A696 SE, by garden centre]: Well done Vintage Inn, more character than most pubs in the area, enjoyable food all day, real ales, good range of wines by the glass and good hot drinks, friendly attentive uniformed staff, good log fire, relaxing rooms and alcoves, old furnishings and olde-worlde décor; talk of planned reworking as more of a table-service bistro/brasserie – so may all change; children welcome, open all day *(GSB, Peter and Eleanor Kenyon, Alan Cole, Kirstie Bruce, Mrs E E Sanders, Dr Peter D Smart, BB)*

RENNINGTON [NU2118]
☆ *Horseshoes* NE66 3RS [B1340]: Comfortable flagstoned pub with friendly landlord, real ales such as Hadrian & Border and John Smiths, generous popular food inc two-course lunch deals and good meat and smoked fish, decent wines by the glass, good local feel (may be horses in car park), simple neat bar with lots of horsebrasses, spotless

compact restaurant with blue and white china; children welcome, tables outside, attractive quiet village nr coast *(Michael Butler, Comus and Sarah Elliott)*

RIDING MILL [NZ0161]
☆ *Wellington* NE44 6DQ [A695 just W of A68 roundabout]: Reliable and popular 17th-c Chef & Brewer, vast good value blackboard food choice from hot ciabatta sandwiches to nice puddings, good friendly service, Courage Directors and Theakstons Bitter and Black Bull, good choice of wines by the glass, beams and candlelight, two big log fires and mix of tables and chairs, some upholstered, some not; piped classical music, can get busy; disabled access, children welcome, play area and picnic-sets outside, pretty village with nearby walks and river *(Mrs E E Sanders, Dr Peter D Smart, Louise Gibbons, Andy and Jill Kassube)*

ROOKHOPE [NY9342]
Rookhope Inn DL13 2BG [off A689 W of Stanhope]: Friendly local on coast-to-coast bike route, three or four real ales such as Jennings Fish King and Timothy Taylors Landlord, simple home-made food from fresh sandwiches to good Sun roast, open fire, small dining room; some live music; seats outside, bedrooms *(Joan Kureczka, Ann and Tony Bennett-Hughes)*

SHINCLIFFE [NZ2940]
☆ *Seven Stars* DH1 2NU [High St N (A177 S of Durham)]: 18th-c village pub back on form under welcoming new licensees, enjoyable gently upmarket food at sensible prices, well kept ales inc Black Sheep, quick pleasant service, coal fire and plenty of atmosphere in lounge bar, candlelit dining room; children in eating areas, some picnic-sets outside, eight bedrooms, open all day *(LYM, Andy and Alice Jordan)*

SLALEY [NY9658]
☆ *Travellers Rest* NE46 1TT [B6306 S of Hexham (and N of village)]: Attractive and busy stone-built country pub, spaciously opened up inside, with farmhouse-style décor, beams, flagstones and polished wood floors, huge fireplace, comfortable high-backed settles forming discrete areas, attentive staff, popular generous food from simple low-priced hot dishes (12-5) to wider but still relatively cheap mealtime choice (not Sun evening) in bar and appealingly up-to-date dining room, good children's menu, basic sandwiches, friendly staff, five real ales such as Black Sheep, Greene King, Mordue and Wylam, limited wines by the glass; dogs welcome, tables outside with well equipped adventure play area on grass behind, three good value bedrooms, open all day *(Andy and Jill Kassube, Michael and Jean Hockings, Peter and Jane Burton, Mart Lawton)*

SOUTH SHIELDS [NZ3567]
Alum Ale House NE33 1JR [Ferry St (B1344)]: Relaxed 18th-c pub handy for ferry, big bars with polished boards, coal fire in old inglenook range, pictures and

newspaper cuttings, Marstons-related ales, hot drinks, good value basic lunchtime bar food; piped music, machines, some live music, good beer festivals; children welcome, open all day *(the Didler, Mike and Lynn Robinson)*

Beacon NE33 2AQ [Greens Pl]: Open-plan pub overlooking river mouth, Adnams, Caledonian Deuchars IPA and Marstons Pedigree from central bar, good value lunchtime food, obliging service, stove in back room, two raised eating areas, sepia photographs and bric-a-brac, darts and dominoes; games machine, quiet piped music; open all day *(the Didler)*

Littlehaven Hotel NE33 1LH [River Dr]: Hotel rather than pub, but does bar meals in sea-view conservatory, splendid beach-edge location at the mouth of the Tyne; bedrooms *(John Coatsworth)*

Steamboat NE33 1EQ [Mill Dam/Coronation St]: Masses of interesting nautical bric-a-brac esp in split-level back room, friendly landlord, Black Sheep, Caledonian Deuchars IPA, Greene King and local guest beers, bargain stotties, pool in central area; usually open all day, nr river and market place *(the Didler, Mike and Lynn Robinson)*

STOCKTON-ON-TEES [NZ4419]

Sun TS18 1SU [Knowles St]: Friendly town local specialising in Bass at tempting price, quick service even when busy; folk night Mon, open all day *(the Didler)*

SUNDERLAND [NZ3956]

Fitzgeralds SR1 3PZ [Green Terr]: Bustling two-bar city pub popular for up to ten real ales inc several from local Darwin, helpful staff, friendly atmosphere, generous cheap food from toasties, baguettes and ciabattas to basic hot dishes; children welcome lunchtime *(Mr and Mrs Maurice Thompson)*

Kings Arms SR4 6BU [Beach St, Deptford]: Chatty early 19th-c pub with several traditional panelled areas around central high-backed bar, well kept Timothy Taylors Landlord and half a dozen changing ales from small breweries, two coal fires, easy chairs and lots of dark wood, food Weds-Sun evenings *(Mr and Mrs Maurice Thompson)*

THROPTON [NU0202]

☆ *Three Wheat Heads* NE65 7LR [B6341]: 300-year-old village inn favoured by older people for its sedate dining atmosphere, good coal fires (one in a fine tall stone fireplace), straightforward bar food inc daily roasts, Black Sheep and Theakstons, pleasant hill-view dining area, darts and pool; piped music; children welcome, garden with play area and lovely views to Simonside Hills, decent bedrooms, open all day wknds *(Comus and Sarah Elliott, Dr Peter D Smart, LYM, Alan and Paula McCully, Richard C Morgan, DFL)*

TYNEMOUTH [NZ3668]

Tynemouth Lodge NE30 4AA [Tynemouth Rd (A193), ½ mile W of Tynemouth Metro stn]: Genuine-feeling little Victorian-style local (actually older), very popular for particularly

well kept Bass, Belhaven 80/-, Caledonian Deuchars IPA and a guest beer at sound prices, farm cider, decent wines, coal fire; no dogs or children; tables in back garden, open all day *(LYM, J R Ringrose)*

WARDEN [NY9166]

Boatside NE46 4SQ [½ mile N of A69]: Cheerful pleasantly modernised dining pub with good service, enjoyable fresh food inc good sandwiches, pubby lunch popular with older people, well kept Black Sheep, Mordue Five Bridge and Wylam Gold Tankard, pine dining room; children welcome, small neat enclosed garden, attractive spot by Tyne bridge *(Gerry Miller, Michael Doswell, Bill and Sheila McLardy)*

WASHINGTON [NZ3054]

Courtyard NE38 8AB [Arts Centre Washington, Biddick Lane]: Relaxed open-plan bar with four or five changing real ales, farm cider and perry, occasional beer festivals, bar food inc good value Sun lunch; live music Mon; tables outside, open all day *(Mr and Mrs Maurice Thompson)*

WEST BOLDON [NZ3561]

Black Horse NE36 0QQ [Rectory Bank, just off A184]: Mix of old and modern furnishings from pews and Victorian tables to comfortable sofas, lots of bric-a-brac, contemporary photographs and artworks, good choice of tasty food, real ales such as Bass, John Smiths, Tetleys and Timothy Taylors Landlord, restaurant; some monumental outside seating *(Michael Butler)*

WHITFIELD [NY7857]

Elks Head NE47 8HD [off A686 SW of Haydon Bridge]: Open-plan pub, light and spacious, with friendly new management, pleasant carpeted bar, good value food from generous sandwiches up, real ale, games area with pool; occasional live entertainment; children welcome, picnic-sets in small pretty front garden with quoits, three bedrooms sharing bathrooms, scenic area *(anon)*

WHITLEY BAY [NZ3473]

Briardene NE26 1UE [The Links]: Spotless brightly decorated and very well furnished two-room seaside pub with up to eight interesting changing ales, good value hearty food, friendly efficient staff; seats outside with play area, open all day *(J R Ringrose)*

WIDDRINGTON [NZ2596]

Widdrington Inn NE61 5DY [off A1068 S of Amble]: Comfortably carpeted open-plan pub popular for bargain food all day from baguettes and baked potatoes to main dishes in two sizes of helping, thoughtful children's dishes, good friendly staff, Marstons Pedigree, reasonably priced wines by the glass; open all day *(Michael Doswell, Comus and Sarah Elliott)*

WOLSINGHAM [NZ0737]

Mill Race DL13 3AP: Unpretentious pub with enthusiastic licensees, Black Sheep and two or three other real ales, good home cooking in bar and restaurant; bedrooms, good generous breakfast *(Joan Kureczka)*

WOOLER [NT9928]

Red Lion NE71 6LD [High St]: Good changing choice of enjoyable unpretentious food in bar and small dining room inc super puddings, two real ales and several malt whiskies, quick friendly service, darts and pool; TV *(C A Hall)*

WYLAM [NZ1164]

☆ *Boathouse* NE41 8HR [Station Rd, handy for Newcastle—Carlisle rail line; across Tyne from village (and Stephenson's birthplace)]: Thriving convivial riverside pub with good range of northern ales inc three local Wylam ones, keen prices, good choice of malt whiskies, good cheap simple wknd bar lunches inc delicious baps and bargain Sun lunch, polite helpful young staff, bright low-beamed bar with cheery open stove, separate dining room; loud band nights; children and dogs welcome, seats outside, open all day *(Michael and Jean Hockings, the Didler, Mike and Lynn Robinson, Arthur Pickering, Eric Larkham, Andy and Jill Kassube, Comus and Sarah Elliott)*

Fox & Hounds NE41 8DL [Main Rd]: Immaculate cosily refurbished local, roomy, bright and rather homely, friendly helpful licensees, enjoyable food inc some unusual dishes (chef prepared to try almost anything, given notice), Black Sheep and Jennings Cumberland, good coffee; nr River Tyne, and George Stephenson's cottage is a short walk along the old railway track *(John Foord, Michael Doswell)*

Several well known guide books make establishments pay for entry, either directly or as a fee for inspection. These fees can run to many hundreds of pounds. We do not. Unlike other guides, we never take payment for entries. We never accept a free meal, free drink, or any other freebie from a pub. We do not accept any sponsorship – let alone from commercial schemes linked to the pub trade. All our entries depend solely on merit.

Nottinghamshire

Happily, the two new main entries in this county take in opposite ends of the spectrum – the Martins Arms at Colston Bassett is a smart dining pub with imaginative food and fine furnishings, while the Keans Head in Nottingham is yet another offering in the very successful group of down-to-earth real ale pubs belonging to Tynemill. The Lincolnshire Poacher in Nottingham is another in this same group, also doing very well this year, as is the Vat & Fiddle – the company really does have a winning formula with their good range of real ales, good value food that's simple and tasty, and plain but genuine interiors. Indeed, add the two own brew pubs in this county to the mix (the Black Horse at Caythorpe and Fellows Morton & Clayton in Nottingham), and it becomes clear that this is a great place for real ale. And that's without even mentioning the very pubby Bell and the intriguing Olde Trip to Jerusalem in Nottingham, and the happy Victoria at Beeston – all with great ranges of real ales, and really fairly priced food. Drinks prices in the county's pubs tend to be comfortably below the national average, and for enjoyable pub meals this is one of the very cheapest parts of the country. If you are looking for a smarter dining experience, then it's worth trying the Cock & Hoop in Nottingham (a real contrast to the other entries in this big university town), or the lovely Caunton Beck at Caunton, which – remarkably, for a pub without bedrooms – serves food continuously from 8am till 11pm. The imaginative food here, along with its very welcoming atmosphere, earns it the title of Nottinghamshire Dining Pub of the Year. In the Lucky Dip section at the end of the chapter, pubs we've got our eyes on include the Horse & Plough in Bingham, Rancliffe Arms at Bunny, Marquis of Granby at Granby, Beehive at Maplebeck, Fox & Crown in Newark, Red Lion at Thurgarton and Stratford Haven in West Bridgford. Now that the Hardys & Hansons brewery has been closed (the beers now come from Suffolk-based Greene King, who took it over), it's Tynemill's house brewery Castle Rock which has to count as the main local brewer. There are plenty of other small breweries here which you may come across, such as Nottingham, Caythorpe, Springhead, Mallard, Alcazar and Milestone.

BEESTON   SK5336   MAP 7

Victoria

Dovecote Lane, backing on to railway station; NG9 1JG

Welcoming down-to-earth converted railway inn with impressive choice of drinks (including up to 12 real ales) and enjoyable fairly priced food

---

The chatty lounge and bar here back on to the railway station, and a covered heated area outside has tables overlooking the platform, with trains passing just a few feet away. Its three interesting rooms have kept their original long narrow layout and are nicely unpretentious, with unfussy décor, simple solid traditional furnishings, fires, stained-glass windows and stripped woodwork and floorboards (woodblock in some rooms); newspapers, dominoes, cribbage and board games. A nice varied crowd gathers here, and even at busy times service is helpful and efficient. Their extraordinary range of drinks starts with Batemans, Castle Rock Harvest Pale and Everards Tiger, which are well kept alongside up to nine guest ales. Running through as many as 500 widely sourced beers each year these might be from brewers as far flung as Adnams, Copper Dragon, Elgoods, Harviestoun, Holt, Howard Town, Hydes, Isle of Skye and Oldershaw. They've also continental draught beers, farm ciders, over 100 malt whiskies, 20 irish whiskeys, and over two dozen wines by the glass. A lively time to visit is during their two-week beer and music festival at the end of July. Parking is limited and readers have warned us about active parking wardens in the area.

🍴 **Tasty good value bar food is listed on a blackboard, and might include leek and potato soup, sausage and mash, mushroom and sweet pepper stroganoff, salmon with dill mustard mayonnaise and braised beef in red wine and stilton, with puddings such as apple crumble and dark chocolate fudge cake** *Starters/Snacks: £3.95 to £4.55. Main Courses: £6.95 to £11.95. Puddings: £3.50 to £4.50*

Free house ~ Licensees Neil Kelso and Graham Smith ~ Real ale ~ Bar food (12-8.45(7.45 Sun)) ~ (0115) 925 4049 ~ Children welcome till 8pm ~ Dogs allowed in bar ~ Live music Sun evenings and jazz Mon evenings Sept-May ~ Open 11(12 Sun)-11

Recommended by Rona Murdoch, P T Sewell, David Eberlin, MP, Andrew Beardsley, Alison Lawrence, Ian Stafford, P Dawn, Peter and Jean Hoare, Simon Pyle, the Didler, C J Fletcher, G D K Fraser

CAUNTON   SK7459   MAP 7

Caunton Beck 🍴 🍷
Newark Road; NG23 6AE
NOTTINGHAMSHIRE DINING PUB OF THE YEAR

Civilised dining pub with very good food all day from breakfasts first thing, good wine list, nice terrace

Surprisingly, this lovely building is almost new, but as it was reconstructed using original timbers and reclaimed oak, around the skeleton of the old Hole Arms, it seems old. Scrubbed pine tables, clever lighting, an open fire and country-kitchen chairs, low beams and rag-finished paintwork in a spacious interior create a comfortably relaxed atmosphere. Warmly welcoming service also contributes to making this a memorable place. Over two dozen of the wines on the very good wine list are available by the glass, and they've well kept Bateman Valiant, Marstons Pedigree and Websters Yorkshire on handpump; also espresso coffee; daily papers and magazines, no music. With lots of flowers and plants in summer, the terrace is very pleasant when the weather is fine.

🍴 **You can get something to eat at most times of the day, starting with a hearty english breakfast which is served until midday (11.30 weekends and bank holidays), then delicious sandwiches and a fairly elaborate quarterly changing menu later on. Dishes might include starters such as leek and potato soup, warm salad of black pudding with bacon mushrooms stuffed with tomato and basil with goats cheese, main courses such as sausage and mash, roast chicken breast wrapped in parma ham with stilton and sage potatoes, roast salmon fillet with crab and coriander tartare, fillet steak with wild mushroom and roquefort tartlet, and puddings such as honeycomb and white chocolate and raspberry crème brûlée and banoffi cheesecake.** *Starters/Snacks: £4.75 to £8.50. Main Courses: £9.95 to £19.95. Puddings: £4.95*

Free house ~ Licensee Julie Allwood ~ Real ale ~ Bar food (8am-11pm) ~ Restaurant ~ (01636) 636793 ~ Children welcome ~ Dogs allowed in bar ~ Open 8am-11pm

Recommended by Ray and Winifred Halliday, Gerry and Rosemary Dobson, J R Ringrose, Derek and Sylvia Stephenson, Maurice and Janet Thorpe, Adrian White, Eithne Dandy, K Bennett, D A Bradford, Gordon Ormonroyd, Richard, Louise Gibbons, Richard Marjoram, Blaise Vyner

---

The 🍺 symbol shows pubs which keep their beer unusually well, have a particularly good range or brew their own.

CAYTHORPE   SK6845   MAP 7

Black Horse 🍺

Turn off A6097 ¼ mile SE of roundabout junction with A612, NE of Nottingham; into Gunthorpe Road, then right into Caythorpe Road and keep on; NG14 7ED

Quaintly old-fashioned little pub brewing its own beer, simple interior and homely enjoyable food; no children or credit cards

This 300-year-old country local has been run by the same family for nearly 40 years. The timelessly uncluttered carpeted bar has just five tables, with brocaded wall banquettes and settles, a few bar stools (for the cheerful evening regulars), a warm woodburning stove, decorative plates on a delft shelf and a few horsebrasses on the ceiling joists. Off the front corridor is a partly panelled inner room with a wall bench running right the way around three unusual long copper-topped tables, and quite a few old local photographs; down on the left an end room has just one huge round table; darts and dominoes. The very tasty Caythorpe Dover Beck is brewed in outbuildings here and is well kept alongside two changing guests such as Black Sheep and Greene King Abbot. There are some plastic tables outside, and the River Trent is fairly close, for waterside walks.

🍽 **Simple, but very enjoyable reasonably priced food from a shortish menu includes soup, prawn cocktail or cod roe on toast, king prawns in chilli sauce, good fried cod, haddock or plaice, seafood salad, fillet steak, and puddings such as egg custard with soft fruit and treacle sponge with custard. Booking is essential.** *Starters/Snacks: £2.00 to £5.50. Main Courses: £4.50 to £14.00. Puddings: £2.75 to £4.50*

Own brew ~ Licensee Sharron Andrews ~ Real ale ~ Bar food (12-1.45, 7-8.30; not Sat evening, or Sun) ~ Restaurant ~ No credit cards ~ (0115) 966 3520 ~ Dogs allowed in bar ~ Open 12-2.30, 6-11; 12-5, 8-11 Sun; closed Mon (except bank hols)

Recommended by P T Sewell, Peter and Jean Hoare, Des and Jen Clarke, J R Ringrose, the Didler, Derek and Sylvia Stephenson

COLSTON BASSETT   SK6933   MAP 7

Martins Arms 🍷 🍺

Village signposted off A46 E of Nottingham; School Lane, near market cross in village centre; NG12 3FD

Smart country dining pub with imaginative food (if pricy), good range of drinks including eight real ales, and lovely grounds

Antique furnishings, hunting prints and warm log fires in the Jacobean fireplaces give an upmarket air to the comfortable bar here, and there's a proper snug. Service from neatly uniformed staff is fairly formal, and if you choose to eat in the elegant restaurant (smartly decorated with period fabrics and colourings) you really are getting into serious dining. Eight well kept real ales on handpump include Bass, Greene King IPA, Marstons Pedigree and Timothy Taylors Landlord, and guests from brewers such as Batemans, Black Dog, Black Sheep and Woodfordes, and they've a good range of malt whiskies and cognacs and an interesting wine list; cribbage and dominoes. The sizeable attractive lawned garden backs on to estate parkland (you might be asked to leave your credit card behind the bar if you want to eat out here). You can play croquet in summer, and they've converted the stables into an antiques shop. Readers recommend visiting the church opposite, and Colston Bassett Dairy just outside the village, which sells its own stilton cheese.

🍽 **The very good food is not cheap, but readers feel it's worth the price: lunchtime sandwiches and filled ciabattas, ploughman's, starters such as soup, fried chicken livers with shallots, mushrooms and bacon in puff pastry, confit duck and orange salad and fried scallops with citrus dressing and crispy pancetta, main courses such as rump of lamb with rosemary and garlic with redcurrant jus, roasted mediterranean vegetable tartlet with mozzarella, fried salmon with asparagus and champ mash and grilled rib-eye with stilton sauce, and puddings such as banana mousse with dark chocolate sorbet and white chocolate sauce or poached pear and amaretto tart.** *Starters/Snacks: £4.95 to £8.00. Main Courses: £10.00 to £21.50. Puddings: £6.50*

Free house ~ Licensees Lynne Strafford Bryan and Salvatore Inguanta ~ Real ale ~ Bar food (12-2, 6-10; not Sun evenings) ~ Restaurant ~ (01949) 81361 ~ Children welcome in snug and dining room ~ Open 12-3, 6-11
Recommended by Peter and Jo Smith, David Morgan, the Didler, P Dawn, Brian and Jean Hepworth

HALAM   SK6754   MAP 7

Waggon & Horses ⓨ
Off A612 in Southwell centre, via Halam Road; NG22 8AE

Civilised heavily oak-beamed dining pub with inventive seasonally changing menu

The spotlessly kept open-plan interior here has a pleasant brightly congenial dining atmosphere (though drinkers are welcome), and is nicely divided into smallish sections – an appealing black iron screen dividing off one part is made up of tiny african-style figures of people and animals. Good sturdy high-back rush-seat dining chairs are set around a mix of solid mainly stripped tables, there are various wall seats, smaller chairs and the odd stout settle. Pictures range from kitten prints to Spy cricketer caricatures on walls painted cream, brick red and coffee; candles throughout give a pleasant night-time glow. Three Thwaites beers are well kept on handpump; piped music. Out past a piano and grandfather clock in the lobby are a few roadside picnic-sets by pretty window boxes.

Ⓨ **Imaginative food might include pea and watercress soup with mint crème fraîche, seared scallops with cauliflower purée and parma ham, main courses such as warm mushroom and brie tartlet with provençale vegetables, grilled pork fillet with creamed leeks and baked apples, baked cod fillet with roast fennel and truffle cream, and fried rib-eye with stilton and port sauce, and puddings such as baked pecan and chocolate tart with marinated oranges, and lime and mascarpone cheesecake with sweet wine and mint syrup. They also do a good value two-course menu (lunchtimes (not Sun) and 6pm to 7pm Monday-Thursday).** *Starters/Snacks: £4.00 to £8.00. Main Courses: £9.00 to £17.00. Puddings: £4.00 to £6.00*

Thwaites ~ Tenant Roy Wood ~ Real ale ~ Bar food (11.30-2.30(3 Sun), 5.30-9; not Sun evening) ~ Restaurant ~ (01636) 813109 ~ Children welcome ~ Open 11.30-3, 5.30-11.30; 11.30-11.30 Sat; 11.30-10.30 Sun

Recommended by Derek and Sylvia Stephenson, Peter and Jean Hoare, JJW, CMW, Michael Doswell, David Glynne-Jones, Colin Fisher, R and M Tait, Mike and Mary Carter

LAXTON   SK7266   MAP 7

Dovecote
Signposted off A6075 E of Ollerton; NG22 0NU

Friendly new licensees in traditional pub near A1; bar food and garden

New people taking over at this red-brick free house just as we went to press seem set to keep its good pubby atmosphere, and we're hoping that food continues to be as good as it has been in the past (you may need to book). The central lounge has dark wheelback chairs and tables on wooden floors, and a coal-effect gas fire. This opens through a small bay (the former entrance) into a carpeted dining area. Around the other side, another little lounge leads through to a pool room with darts, fruit machine and dominoes; piped music. Three changing beers on handpump might be Fullers London Pride, one from Hydes and Wells & Youngs Bombardier, and they've around eight wines by the glass. There are wooden tables and chairs on a small front terrace by a sloping garden, which has a disused white dovecote. The pub is handy for the A1, and they have a site and facilities for six caravans. Laxton is home to three famous huge medieval open fields – it's one of the few places in the country still farmed using the traditional open field system. Every year in the third week of June the grass is auctioned for haymaking, and anyone who lives in the parish is entitled to a bid – and a drink. You can get more information about it all from the visitor centre behind the pub.

🍽 Served by friendly courteous staff, fairly priced dishes come in big helpings and might include soup, sandwiches, grilled goats cheese salad, garlic prawns, steak and kidney pudding, mushroom stroganoff and scampi, with specials such as chicken and mushroom cream pie, battered cod, and pork medallions in mushroom and brandy cream. The puddings (maybe cheesecake) are made by Aunty Mary who lives in the village. *Starters/Snacks: £3.50 to £5.95. Main Courses: £7.25 to £16.00. Puddings: £3.95*

Free house ~ Licensees David and Linda Brown ~ Real ale ~ Bar food (12-2, 6.30(6 Sat, 7 Sun)-9) ~ Restaurant ~ (01777) 871586 ~ Children welcome ~ Dogs allowed in bar ~ Open 11.30-3, 6.30(6 Sat)-11; 12-3, 7-10.30 Sun

Recommended by Peter and Jean Hoare, J R Ringrose, Richard Cole, Gerry and Rosemary Dobson, Mrs Hazel Rainer, David and Ruth Hollands, Mike and Linda Hudson, Ray and Winifred Halliday, Nick and Meriel Cox

MORTON
SK7251 MAP 7

Full Moon

Pub and village signposted off Bleasby—Fiskerton back road, SE of Southwell; NG25 0UT

Sensibly priced decent food at friendly village pub with traditional plush décor, and play area in nice garden

This cosy dining pub is tucked away in a remote hamlet not far from the River Trent. L-shaped and beamed, the main part is traditionally decorated with pink plush seats and cushioned black settles around a variety of pub tables, and wheelback chairs in the side dining area, and a couple of fireplaces. Fresh flowers and the very long run of Christmas plates on the walls add a spot of colour; look out for the two sociable pub cats. Charles Wells Bombardier, Greene King Ruddles and a changing guest or two such as Caythorpe Dover Beck and Theakstons are well kept on handpump; piped music, games machines and board games. Lots of effort has gone into the garden which comprises a peaceful shady back terrace with picnic-sets, with more on a sizeable lawn, and some sturdy play equipment.

🍽 As well as daily specials, enjoyable food includes soup, sandwiches (even on Sundays), grilled goats cheese on a cinnamon and fruit croûton, sausage and mash, battered cod, steak and kidney pie, chicken and bacon salad, parsnip and chestnut bake, lamb shank in minted gravy, and steaks. They do a good value early evening two-course menu 6-7pm; **Sunday roast.** *Starters/Snacks: £2.75 to £6.75. Main Courses: £5.25 to £15.50. Puddings: £2.75 to £3.95*

Free house ~ Licensees Clive and Kim Wisdom ~ Real ale ~ Bar food (12-2, 6-9.30(6.30-10 Fri, Sat); 12-2.30, 7-9.30 Sun) ~ Restaurant ~ (01636) 830251 ~ Children welcome ~ Open 11-3, 6-11(midnight Sat); 12-3, 7-11 Sun

Recommended by J R Ringrose, the Didler, Michael Doswell, Maurice and Janet Thorpe, Phil and Jane Hodson, Gordon Prince, Richard Greenwood, Keith Wright, Derek and Sylvia Stephenson, Simon Pyle, P Dawn, Paul Humphreys, Dean Rose

NOTTINGHAM
SK5739 MAP 7

Bell 🍺 £

Angel Row, off Market Square; NG1 6HL

Great range of real ales from remarkable cellars in historic yet pubby place with regular live music and simple food

A little dwarfed by the office tower next door, this ancient 500-year-old building is reputed to have formed part of a Carmelite friary. Its venerable age is clearly evident throughout – some of the original timbers have been uncovered, and in the front Tudor bar you can see patches of 300-year-old wallpaper (protected by glass). With quite a café feel in summer, this room is perhaps the brightest, with french windows opening to tables on the pavement, and bright blue walls. The room with the most aged feel is the very pubby low-beamed Elizabethan Bar, with its half-panelled walls, maple parquet floor and comfortable high-backed armchairs. Upstairs, at the back of the heavily panelled

Belfry (usually open only at lunchtime), you can see the rafters of the 15th-c crown post roof, and you can look down on the busy street at the front; TV, fruit machine and piped music. The labyrinthine cellars (tours 7.30pm Tues) are about ten metres down in the sandstone rock, and the efforts of the hardworking Norman monks who are said to have dug them is still much appreciated as they keep an extensive range of ten real ales down here. These include Greene King Abbot, IPA and Old Speckled Hen, alongside six or seven guests from thoughtfully sourced local and far-flung brewers such as Black Sheep, Mordue, Nottingham, Timothy Taylor and Wyre Piddle. The friendly welcoming staff and landlord, also serve ten wines by the glass, quite a few malt whiskies and a farm cider.

🍴 **Reasonably priced straightforward bar food includes soup, burgers, ploughman's, beef pie, battered cod, vegetable risotto, apple pie and rhubarb crumble.** *Starters/Snacks: £3.15 to £3.85. Main Courses: £6.35 to £8.35. Puddings: £3.35*

Greene King ~ Manager Brian Rigby ~ Real ale ~ Bar food (12-8) ~ Restaurant ~ (0115) 947 5241 ~ Children in restaurant ~ Dogs allowed in bar ~ Live jazz Sun lunchtime and Mon, Tues evenings, commercial rock Weds, covers band Sat ~ Open 10-11(midnight Weds, Thurs, 12.30 Fri, Sat); 11-midnight Sun

Recommended by the Didler, David Carr, P Dawn, Bruce Bird, C J Fletcher, Rona Murdoch, Dr and Mrs A K Clarke

Cock & Hoop 🛏

Lace Market Hotel, High Pavement; NG1 1HF

Civilised pub with emphasis on imaginative food and good service; smart bedrooms in linked hotel

This carefully restored place is in the heart of the Lace Market, opposite the former courthouse and jail, and is a welcome alternative to the somewhat louder bars that at weekends characterise this area of town. It's part of Nottingham's nicest hotel, but feels quite separate, with its own entrance, leading into a tiny front bar. There are a few tables and comfortable armchairs in here, as well as a small pewter-topped counter serving Caledonian Deuchars IPA, Fullers London Pride, Nottingham Cock & Hoop, Timothy Taylors Landlord and a guest such as Black Sheep from handpump. A corridor and stairs lead off to the most distinctive part of the pub – the big downstairs cellar bar, a long, windowless flagstoned room with partly panelled stripped brick walls, leatherette sofas and upholstered chairs and stools, and, on one side, several tiny alcoves each with a single table squeezed in; piped music, TV. It can get busy at lunchtimes. Bedrooms are comfortably upmarket (the ones overlooking the street can be noisy at weekends) and breakfasts are good.

🍴 **Good bar food (only some readers feel it's pricy) includes starters and snacks such as caesar salad, open prawn sandwich on grilled garlic bread, trio of smoked salmon and trout and mackerel mousse with horseradish cream, main courses such as ploughman's, chilli lamb burger, poached salmon with avocado and potato salad, pork fillet marinated in honey, sage and garlic with dijon mash, and puddings such as minted red berry jelly with clotted cream, chocolate terrine with passion fruit sorbet and champagne poached rhubarb panna cotta; Sunday roasts.** *Starters/Snacks: £4.95 to £7.95. Main Courses: £8.95 to £12.95. Puddings: £4.50 to £6.50*

Free house ~ Licensee Andrew Hunt ~ Real ale ~ Bar food (12-10) ~ Restaurant ~ (0115) 852 3231 ~ Children welcome with restrictions ~ Dogs allowed in bedrooms ~ Open 12-11 (1am Fri, Sat); 12-10.30 Sun ~ Bedrooms: £79.95S/£118.90B

Recommended by P Dawn, Andy and Jill Kassube, Alan Taylor, the Didler, Simon J Barber, Michael Dandy, Jeremy King

Fellows Morton & Clayton 🍺 £

Canal Street (part of inner ring road); NG1 7EH

Lively town pub with canalside terrace, good value food and own brew beers

A lively atmosphere fills the spreading interior of this former canal warehouse, which is popular with local workers at lunchtime, and a younger set in the evening. The softly lit downstairs bar has dark red plush seats built into alcoves on shiny blond wood floors, lots of exposed brickwork, a glossy dark green high ceiling, more tables on a raised carpeted area, and a rack of daily newspapers; piped pop music, games machines and big TVs. From a big window in the glassed-in area at the back you can see the little brewery where they make the tasty Samuel Fellows and Matthew Claytons Original served here. These are well kept alongside Deuchars IPA, Fullers London Pride, Timothy Taylors Landlord and a guest such as Black Sheep. A large decked terrace at the back overlooks the canal and is a great place for a summer evening drink; service is prompt and friendly and a reader tells us there is disabled access, and there is parking at the back.

🍴 **Popular, quite pubby food, might include soup, pâté, sandwiches and wraps, haddock and chips, niçoise salad, beefburger in ciabatta, sausage and mash, steak and kidney pie and 8oz sirloin; breakfast 10-11.30am Saturday and Sunday.** *Starters/Snacks: £2.85 to £4.75. Main Courses: £5.25 to £10.50. Puddings: £3.50*

Own brew ~ Licensees Les Howard and Keely Willans ~ Real ale ~ Bar food (not Sun evening) ~ Restaurant ~ (0115) 950 6795 ~ Children in restaurant ~ Live music Friday ~ Open 11-11(1 Fri, Sat); 10-11 Sun

Recommended by G Coates, Veronica Brown, Andrew Beardsley, Alison Lawrence, David Carr, Bruce Bird, the Didler, Michael Dandy, P Dawn, C J Fletcher

Keans Head ♀ 🍺 £
St Mary's Gate; NG1 1QA

Bustling and friendly central pub, usefully serving good value food all day, wide choice of drinks, smiling service and informal chatty atmosphere

Just two minutes from the city centre, this is an unpretentious and cheery Tynemill pub that at first glance looks a bit like a café. It's in the attractive Lace Market area and usefully offers enjoyable food all day. There's some exposed brickwork and red tiling, simple wooden furnishings on the wood-boarded floor, a low sofa by a big window overlooking the street, various pieces of artwork and beer advertisements on the walls, and a small fireplace. Friendly staff serve Batemans XB and Castle Rock Harvest Pale and Elsie Mo with three well kept guests such as Abbeydale Moonshine, Atlas Latitude and Newby Wyke White Squall on handpump, draught belgian beers, interesting bottled beers and soft drinks, around two dozen wines by the glass, and lots of coffees and teas; daily newspapers to read and piped music. Students often drop in for breakfast. St Mary's Church next door is worth a look.

🍴 **Popular, good value bar food includes snacks such as pork pie and scotch egg as well as sandwiches, soup, a daily pasta dish and a daily pie, sausage and mash, home-made pizzas, mozzarella and risotto balls, spicy meatballs, corned beef hash with home-made baked beans, and various cakes like chocolate or lemon drizzle.** *Starters/Snacks: £2.25 to £4.25. Main Courses: £5.25 to £7.95. Puddings: £2.25*

Tynemill ~ Manager Charlotte Blomley ~ Bar food (12-9) ~ (0115) 947 4052 ~ Children allowed until 5pm (6pm weekends) ~ Open 10.30am-11pm; 10am-12.30am Sat; 12am-10.30pm Sun

Recommended by Simon J Barber, the Didler, Andy and Ali, MP, Michael Dandy, Val and Alan Green, Andy and Jill Kassube, Gary Rollings, Debbie Porter

Lincolnshire Poacher 🍺 £
Mansfield Road; up hill from Victoria Centre; NG1 3FR

Chatty down-to-earth pub with great range of drinks (11 real ales), good value food, and terrace

The traditional big wood-floored front bar at this relaxing place has a cheerful atmosphere, wall settles, plain wooden tables and breweriana. It opens on to a plain but lively room on the left, with a corridor that takes you down to the chatty panelled no smoking back snug, with newspapers, cribbage, dominoes, cards and backgammon. A conservatory overlooks tables on a large heated terrace behind. Their impressive range of drinks includes 11 real ales (Batemans XB and Valiant and the local Castle Rock Harvest Pale, which are well kept alongside guests from a good variety of brewers such as Caledonian, Clarks, Everards, Isle of Skye, Timothy Taylor and Ossett), seven continental draught beers, around 20 continental bottled beers, good farm cider, around 70 malt whiskies and ten irish ones, and very good value soft drinks. It can get very busy in the evening, when it's popular with a younger crowd.

🍴 Very good value tasty bar food from a changing blackboard menu might include haggis, neeps and tatties, cottage pie, leek and goats cheese pie, butternut squash thai curry, beef braised in beer with mash, and chicken breast with leeks and apples in a creamy cider sauce. *Starters/Snacks: £2.50 to £4.50. Main Courses: £5.00 to £6.95. Puddings: £2.50 to £3.50*

Tynemill ~ Manager Karen Williams ~ Real ale ~ Bar food (12(10 Sat)-8(5 Sat, Sun)) ~ (0115) 941 1584 ~ Children welcome away from bar ~ Dogs allowed in bar ~ Live music Sun evening from 8.30 ~ Open 11-11(midnight Thurs, Fri); 10-midnight Sat; 12-11 Sun

Recommended by Richard, the Didler, Derek and Sylvia Stephenson, David Carr, P Dawn, Des and Jen Clarke, MP

Olde Trip to Jerusalem ★ 🍺 £

Brewhouse Yard; from inner ring road follow The North, A6005 Long Eaton signpost until you are in Castle Boulevard, then almost at once turn right into Castle Road; pub is up on the left; NG1 6AD

Ancient pub partly built into sandstone caves, good range of real ales, reasonably priced pubby food

It is indeed old – largely 17th-c – though you should take with a big pinch of salt suggestions that it's of any greater antiquity. It's certainly quite unlike any other you'll visit. Its name refers to the 12th-c crusaders who used to meet nearby on their way to the Holy Land – pub collectors of today still make their own crusades to come here. Some of its rambling rooms are burrowed into the sandstone rock below the castle, and the siting of the current building is attributed to the days when a brewhouse was established here to supply the needs of the castle above. The panelled walls of the unusual upstairs bar (which may have served as cellarage for that earlier medieval brewhouse) soar narrowly into a dark cleft above. Also mainly carved from the rock, the downstairs bar has leatherette-cushioned settles built into dark panelling, tables on flagstones, and snug banquettes built into low-ceilinged rock alcoves. If you prefer not to visit with the crowds, it's best to go early evening or on a winter lunchtime, but staff do cope efficiently with the busy mix of tourists, conversational locals and students. They keep their real eight or nine ales in top condition, including a Greene King stable alongside a couple of changing guests from brewers such as Burton Bridge and Oakham on handpump. They've ring the bull and a rather out of place games machine. There are some seats in a snug courtyard. The museum next door is interesting.

🍴 Attractively priced straightforward bar food includes soup, burgers, baguettes, tortilla wraps, steak and kidney pudding, lasagne, red pepper and mushroom lasagne and rump steak. *Starters/Snacks: £2.20 to £5.99. Main Courses: £4.65 to £8.85. Puddings: £2.40 to £3.99*

Greene King ~ Manager Allen Watson ~ Real ale ~ Bar food (12-8) ~ (0115) 9473171 ~ Children allowed until 7pm ~ Storyteller last Thurs ~ Open 10.30-11(midnight Sat); 11-11 Sun

Recommended by Colin Gooch, the Didler, Michael Dandy, A P Seymour, Bruce Bird, Derek and Sylvia Stephenson, Andrew Beardsley, Alison Lawrence, Phil and Jane Hodson, Kevin Blake

Vat & Fiddle 🍺 £

Queens Bridge Road, alongside Sheriffs Way (near multi-storey car park); NG2 1NB

Ten real ales at very welcoming down-to-earth pub next to the Castle Rock brewery

This well loved plain little brick pub is chatty and relaxed, relying more on genuine character perhaps than other Nottingham main entries. The fairly functional open-plan interior has a strong unspoilt 1930s feel, with cream and navy walls and ceiling, varnished pine tables and bentwood stools and chairs on parquet and terrazzo flooring, patterned blue curtains, and some brewery memorabilia. An interesting display of photographs depicts demolished pubs in a nearby area. Also magazines and newspapers to read, piped music some of the time, a fruit machine, and Kipper the cat. As well as four Castle Rock beers (the pub is right next door to the brewery and you'll probably see some comings and goings), they serve half a dozen interesting guests from brewers such as Archers, Burton Bridge, Black Sheep, Hop Back, Newby Wyke and Oakham. They also have around 70 malt whiskies, a changing farm cider, a good range of continental bottled beers, several polish vodkas and good value soft drinks, and have occasional beer festivals too. There are picnic-sets in front by the road.

🍴 **Two or three specials such as chilli or curry are served at lunchtime and rolls are available until they run out of stock.** *Starters/Snacks: £1.80 to £2.50. Main Courses: £4.95 to £5.50*

Tynemill ~ Manager Sarah Houghton ~ Real ale ~ Bar food (12-2.30 Mon-Fri; rolls all day) ~ (0115) 985 0611 ~ Children welcome away from bar ~ Dogs allowed in bar ~ Open 11-11(midnight Fri, Sat); 12-11 Sun

Recommended by P Dawn, the Didler, Bruce Bird, Des and Jen Clarke, C J Fletcher, Rona Murdoch

RANBY   SK6580   MAP 7

Chequers

Ranby signposted off A620 Retford—Worksop, just E of A1; DN22 8HT

Neatly kept waterside pub with plush décor and reasonably priced food

This extensive open-plan place is right next to the Chesterfield Canal, and has tables on a small terrace behind – if you're lucky you may be able to watch a colourful narrowboat being moored; there is some noise out here from the A1 traffic beyond. Inside, the main neatly kept area opens into three more or less self-contained uniformly decorated carpeted side bays. The front one on the right has an appealingly homely feel – it's laid out like a pleasantly kitsch parlour with deeply cushioned sofa and wing armchairs, dolls, nice lamps and coal-effect fire in an attractive panelled surround. Other furnishings are more orthodox, good and solid in a pleasant variety of styles, and the walls are coloured and textured. They have well kept Black Sheep and Marstons Pedigree on handpump; there may be piped music.

🍴 **Generous attractively priced food includes soup, duck and cranberry terrine, battered onions and dips, lobster soup, prawn cocktail, lunchtime sandwiches, sausage and mash, lamb in cinnamon and apricot sauce, poached salmon with hollandaise, cherry tomato and red onion tart, chicken curry, scampi and 5oz rib-eye steak; Sunday roast.** *Starters/Snacks: £3.95 to £4.95. Main Courses: £6.95 to £13.95. Puddings: £3.95*

Enterprise ~ Lease Christopher Jessop ~ Real ale ~ Bar food (12-2, 6-9; 12-9.30 Sat, 12-8 Sun) ~ Restaurant ~ (01777) 703329 ~ Children welcome away from bar ~ Open 12-3, 5.30-10.30; 12-11 Sat, Sun; closed Mon except bank hols

Recommended by Mr and Mrs I Templeton, Stephen Woad, R T and J C Moggridge, A D Lealan, Mr and Mrs P Eastwood, Richard Cole

LUCKY DIP

Besides the fully inspected pubs, you might like to try these Lucky Dips recommended to us and described by readers (if you do, please send us reports: www.goodguides.co.uk).

AWSWORTH [SK4844]
Gate NG16 2RN [Main St, via A6096 off A610 Nuthall—Eastwood bypass]: Friendly old traditional local nr site of once-famous railway viaduct (photographs in passage), well kept Greene King ales inc Hardys & Hansons Mild, coal fire in quiet comfortable lounge, small pool room; tables out in front, skittles pitch, open all day *(the Didler)*
BAGTHORPE [SK4751]
Dixies Arms NG16 5HF [2 miles from M1 junction 27; A608 towards Eastwood, then first right on to B600 via Sandhill Rd, then first left into School Rd; Lower Bagthorpe]:

Reliably well kept ales such as Adnams, Greene King Abbot and Theakstons Best in unspoilt 18th-c beamed and tiled-floor local, good fire in small part-panelled parlour's fine fireplace, entrance bar with tiny snug, longer narrow room with toby jugs, darts and dominoes, Sat folk music, Sun quiz night; good big garden with play area and football pitch, own pigeon, gun and morris dancing clubs; open 2-11, all day wknds *(the Didler, Andy and Jill Kassube, Kevin Blake, Derek and Sylvia Stephenson)*
Shepherds Rest NG16 5HF [2 miles from M1 junction 27, via A608 towards Eastwood,

then off B600; Lower Bagthorpe]:
Extensively refurbished old pub with
pleasant staff, changing ales such as Brains
Gold, Greene King Abbot and Wells & Youngs
Bombardier, enjoyable food (not Sun or Mon
evening) inc good fish and good value Thurs
steak night; piped music; children welcome,
garden with play area, pretty surroundings,
open all day *(JJW, CMW, Derek and
Sylvia Stephenson)*

BARNBY IN THE WILLOWS [SK8552]
Willow Tree NG24 2SA [Front St; off A17 E of
Newark]: Extended 18th-c village pub with
original features in open-plan L-shaped
beamed bar, friendly service, reasonably
priced fresh food evenings and wknds in bar
and restaurant, three real ales, good soft
drinks choice, log fires throughout, games
room; piped music; children welcome,
courtyard tables, seven bedrooms
(Maurice and Janet Thorpe)

BATHLEY [SK7758]
Crown NG23 6DA [Main St]: Cheerful family-
run village local with three well kept
Marstons-related ales such as Mansfield
Riding, wide choice of enjoyable low-priced
food inc Sun roasts, log fire, piano and pub
games; small garden with barbecue, open all
day Fri-Sun *(JJW, CMW)*

BEESTON [SK5236]
Crown NG9 1FY [Church St]: Beamed
traditional local with Greene King ales inc
Hardys & Hansons, small bar with high-
backed settles, settles and darts in larger
panelled room, comfortable lounge; terrace
tables, open all day *(the Didler, Dr and Mrs
A K Clarke)*
Hop Pole NG9 4AE [High Rd, Chilwell]: Two-
bar pub reopened and under enthusiastic
young landlord, well kept Black Sheep,
Castle Rock Elsie Mo and Harvest Pale and a
guest beer, efficient informal service, limited
sensibly priced traditional food; children and
dogs welcome, sheltered outside area, small
secure garden *(MP)*

BINGHAM [SK7039]
☆ *Horse & Plough* NG13 8AF [off A52; Long
Acre]: Low beams, flagstones and stripped
brick, prints and old brewery memorabilia,
comfortable open-plan seating inc pews,
Bass, Caledonian Deuchars IPA, Wells &
Youngs Bombardier and several guest beers
(may offer tasters), good wine choice,
generous wkdy lunchtime sandwiches and
normally three or four hot bar dishes,
popular upstairs evening grill room (Tues-
Sat, and Sun lunch) with polished boards,
hand-painted murals and open kitchen;
piped music; open all day *(the Didler,
P Dawn, David Glynne-Jones, BB)*

BLEASBY [SK7149]
Waggon & Horses NG14 7GG [Gypsy Lane]:
Comfortable banquettes in country pub's
carpeted lounge, coal fire in character bar
with pub games, pleasant chatty landlord,
wife makes good value fresh lunchtime food
from snacks up, Marstons-related ales inc
Mansfield, back lobby with play area and

comfortable chairs to watch over it; piped
music; tables outside, small camping area
behind *(the Didler, J R Ringrose)*

BRAMCOTE [SK5037]
White Lion NG9 3HH [just off A52 W of
Nottingham; Town St]: Small neat open-plan
pub with friendly locals, well kept Greene
King Hardys & Hansons from bar serving two
split-level adjoining rooms, darts and
dominoes; tables in garden behind
(the Didler, Alan Bowker, MP)

BUNNY [SK5829]
☆ *Rancliffe Arms* NG11 6QT [Loughborough Rd
(A60 S of Nottingham)]: Substantial early
18th-c former coaching inn reopened as
dining pub after extensive refurbishment,
emphasis on extensive bistro-style dining
area with upscale food inc adventurous
dishes, popular Sun carvery, friendly efficient
service, sofas and armchairs in comfortable
bar with real ales such as Brains St Davids,
Jennings Cumberland and Sneck Lifter and
Wrangler Station Master *(John and
Sylvia Harrop, Gwyn and Anne Wake, P Dawn,
Gerry and Rosemary Dobson)*

CAR COLSTON [SK7242]
Royal Oak NG13 8JE [The Green, off Tenman
Lane (off A46 not far from A6097 junction)]:
Largeish 18th-c pub opp one of England's
biggest village greens, woodburner in main
room, Adnams, Jennings and other ales,
enjoyable unpretentious pub food, keen
young licensees, unusual vaulted brick
ceiling in second room; picnic-sets on roomy
back lawn, open all day wknds, cl Mon
lunchtime *(Richard and Jean Green)*

COLLINGHAM [SK8361]
Kings Head NG23 7LA [High St]: Gently
upscale modern pub behind unpretentious
Georgian façade, changing ales such as
Timothy Taylors Landlord from long steel bar,
courteous young staff, bar sandwiches, good
restaurant dishes with unusual touches,
takeaways too, ad lib coffee, pine furniture,
abstracts on light and airy dining area's
colour-washed walls; garden tables, open all
day, cl Sun evening *(Kevin Thorpe, David and
Ruth Hollands)*
Royal Oak NG23 7RA [Station Rd]: Two-bar
village pub with well kept Marstons Pedigree
and local Springhead, traditional food with
some interesting dishes and good fish,
considerate service, restaurant; children
welcome, garden *(Barbara Carver)*

COTGRAVE [SK6435]
Rose & Crown NG12 3HQ [Main Rd, off
A46 SE of Nottingham]: Comfortable and
well kept village pub, consistently good
value food all day inc mid-week and early
evening bargains, also more elaborate
evening/wknd dishes, young helpful staff,
friendly atmosphere, four changing ales
such as Caledonian Deuchars IPA, good
soft drinks choice, log fires, back eating
area with fresh flowers and candles;
children welcome, garden picnic-sets
*(Richard and Jean Green, Sally and
Dave Bates, P Dawn)*

EAST MARKHAM [SK7373]

Crown NG22 0QJ [High St (off A57)]: Reworked as dining pub, with carefully sourced food cooked in open kitchen, friendly service (Ken Jones)

EASTWOOD [SK4846]

Foresters Arms NG16 2DN [Main St, Newthorpe]: Friendly local with Greene King Hardys & Hansons, darts, dominoes and table skittles, open fire, old local photographs, lounge with wknd organ singalong; TV; nice garden, occasional barbecues (the Didler)

ELKESLEY [SK6875]

☆ *Robin Hood* DN22 8AJ [just off A1 Newark—Blyth; High St]: Neatly kept dining pub handy for A1; dark furnishings on patterned carpets, yellow walls, Marstons Pedigree, pool and board games; piped music, TV; children and dogs welcome, picnic-sets and play area, cl Sun evening, Mon lunchtime (Alan Cole, Kirstie Bruce, Gordon Ormondroyd, N R White, Jill and Julian Tasker, Christopher Turner, A J Bowen)

EVERTON [SK6991]

Blacksmiths Arms DN10 5BQ [Church St]: L-shaped bar in 18th-c pub with dining area down step opening into well heated conservatory, wide choice of enjoyable food, good range of real ales such as Barnsley, Beartown and Theakstons Old Peculier, friendly chatty staff, pool in games room; children and dogs welcome, smallish garden with play area, comfortable bedrooms, open all day (Mrs Hazel Rainer, Derek and Sylvia Stephenson, JJW, CMW)

FARNSFIELD [SK6257]

White Post NG22 8HN [A617/A614 roundabout]: Roomy Marstons dining pub nicely laid out and cosily divided by standing timbers, good value food, three real ales, good choice of wines by the glass, good service; children welcome, tables outside, play area (Phil and Jane Hodson)

GRANBY [SK7436]

☆ *Marquis of Granby* NG13 9PN [off A52 E of Nottingham; Dragon St]: 18th-c pub in attractive Vale of Belvoir village, now friendly tap for Brewsters (just over near Plungar) and nicely refurbished by them, with their ales and guest beers from chunky yew bar counter, two small rooms with broad flagstones, some low beams and stripped stone, comfortable new seating around the tables, log fire; live music Sat; wheelchair access (and a welcome for dogs), cl wkdy lunchtimes, open all day Fri-Sun (BB, the Didler, Gary Rollings, Debbie Porter)

GRINGLEY ON THE HILL [SK7390]

Blue Bell DN10 4RF [High St, just off A361 Bawtry—Gainsboro]: Friendly village local on several levels, well kept ales such as Adnams, Caledonian Deuchars IPA and Wells & Youngs Bombardier, reasonably priced blackboard food, small pleasant dining room, neatly tucked away games room with pool and TV; children and dogs welcome, open all day wknds, cl wkdy lunchtimes (Derek and Sylvia Stephenson)

GUNTHORPE [SK6843]

Unicorn NG14 7FB [Trentside]: Picturesque riverside setting, several family-oriented rooms inc smart panelled restaurant, well kept ales, wide range of good value food; busy with summer river trade; bedrooms (Mrs Hazel Rainer)

HOVERINGHAM [SK6946]

Marquis of Granby NG14 7JR [Main St (off A612)]: Simple but attractive bar, friendly local atmosphere, welcoming and accommodating family service, four real ales such as Bass and Black Sheep, decent wines by the glass, good value interesting meals, stylish restaurant (David Tindal)

☆ *Reindeer* NG14 7JR [Main St]: Unpretentious low-beamed Tynemill pub with particularly friendly staff, four or five good changing ales such as Black Sheep, Castle Rock and Fullers London Pride, good wines by the glass, good short choice of enjoyable food, fair value if not cheap, from pubby things to enterprising dishes, coal fires in bar and back dining lounge, daily papers; children welcome, picnic-sets outside, cl Sun evening, Tues lunchtime and Mon, open all day Sat, and Sun till 5 (Phil and Jane Hodson, the Didler, J R Ringrose, JJW, CMW)

KIMBERLEY [SK4944]

☆ *Nelson & Railway* NG16 2NR [Station Rd; handy for M1 junction 26 via A610]: Cheery and chatty beamed Victorian pub expanding its dining side into adjoining building, well kept Greene King ales inc Hardys & Hansons, efficient service, mix of Edwardian-looking furniture, brewery prints and railway signs, traditional games inc alley and table skittles; piped music, games machine; dogs allowed in bar, children in restaurant, tables and swings in good-sized cottagey garden, good value bedrooms, open all day (LYM, the Didler, Karen Eliot, Pete Baker, Derek and Sylvia Stephenson)

Stag NG16 2NB [Nottingham Rd]: Friendly 16th-c traditional local kept spotless by devoted landlady, two cosy rooms, small central counter and corridor, low beams, dark panelling and settles, good range of real ales, vintage working penny slot machines and Shipstones brewery photographs; attractive back garden with play area, cl wkdy lunchtime (opens 5; 1.30 Sat, 12 Sun) (the Didler, P Dawn)

LINBY [SK5351]

Horse & Groom NG15 8AE [Main St]: Picturesque and unpretentious, with three rooms and pleasant colour scheme, wide choice of decent straightforward food (not Sun-Thurs evenings), three or four changing ales such as Theakstons and Wells & Youngs Bombardier, friendly staff, inglenook log fire, conservatory, no mobile phones; quiet piped music, big-screen TV, games machine in lobby; tables outside, big play area, attractive village nr Newstead Abbey, open all day (the Didler, Richard Greenwood, JJW, CMW)

LOWDHAM [SK6646]
Worlds End NG14 7AT [Plough Lane]: Small
village pub with reasonably priced food inc
popular OAP wkdy lunches and other deals,
three real ales, good choice of other drinks,
log fire in pubby beamed bar, restaurant;
piped music; children welcome, picnic-sets,
some under awning, in garden *(JJW, CMW,
Richard)*
MANSFIELD [SK5260]
Nell Gwynne NG18 5EX [Sutton Rd (A38 W of
centre)]: Former gentlemen's club with the
look of a private house, Greene King Abbot
and a guest such as Cottage, easy mix of age
groups, homely lounge with log-effect gas
fire, old colliery plates and mementos of
old Mansfield pubs, games room; sports TV,
piped music, nearby parking can be difficult;
has been cl Mon-Thurs lunchtimes
(Derek and Sylvia Stephenson, the Didler)
Railway Inn NG19 8AD [Station St; best
approached by viaduct from nr market pl]:
Friendly traditional pub with long-serving
landlady, attractively priced Batemans XB
and a seasonal beer, bargain home-made
lunches, divided main bar and separate
room; handy for Robin Hood Line stn,
normally open all day, cl Sun evening
(P Dawn, Pete Baker, the Didler)
MANSFIELD WOODHOUSE [SK5463]
Greyhound NG19 8BD [High St]: Popular
village local with Greene King IPA, Marstons
Mansfield, Theakstons Mild, Websters and
one or two guest beers, cosy lounge, darts,
dominoes and pool in busy bar; quiz nights
Mon and Weds; open all day *(the Didler,
P Dawn)*
MAPLEBECK [SK7160]
☆ *Beehive* NG22 0BS [signed down pretty
country lanes from A616 Newark—Ollerton
and from A617 Newark—Mansfield]:
Relaxing and unspoiled beamed country tavern in nice
spot, chatty landlady, tiny front bar, slightly
bigger side room, traditional furnishings, coal
or log fire, free antique juke box, changing
real ales such as local Milestone; tables on
small terrace with flower tubs and grassy
bank running down to little stream, play area
with swings, barbecues; no food, may be cl
wkdy winter lunchtimes, very busy wknds and
bank hols *(LYM, the Didler, J R Ringrose)*
NEWARK [SK7953]
Castle NG24 1BE [Castle Gate]: Good range
of up-to-date lunchtime snacks from
baguettes up, five or so real ales and several
wines by the glass in bare-boards front
room, long panelled and carpeted back
room, old wooden furniture, lots of mirrors
and prints on colourful walls; piped music
(Andy and Jill Kassube)
Castle & Falcon NG24 1TW [London Rd]:
Former coaching inn now a friendly bustling
local, John Smiths and guest beers,
comfortable back lounge and family
conservatory; lively games bar with darts,
dominoes, pool and TV, skittle alley; small
terrace, evening opening 7, cl lunchtime
Tues-Thurs *(the Didler)*

☆ *Fox & Crown* NG24 1JY [Appleton Gate]:
Convivial bare-boards open-plan Tynemill
pub, chatty and relaxed, with good bargain
simple food from filled rolls, baguettes,
paninis and baked potatoes up, Castle Rock
ales and several interesting guest beers from
central servery, Stowford Press cider, lots of
whiskies, vodkas and other spirits, good tea,
coffee and decent wines by the glass,
friendly obliging staff, several side areas;
piped pop music may be loudish; children
welcome, good wheelchair access, open all
day *(David and Ruth Hollands,
Mrs Hazel Rainer, P Dawn, the Didler,
Barbara Carver, Andy Booth, David Carr,
Gwyn and Anne Wake, BB)*
Mail Coach NG24 1TN [London Rd, nr
Beaumond Cross]: Friendly open-plan
Georgian pub, three candlelit separate areas
with old-world décor, lots of chicken
pictures, hot coal fires and comfortable
chairs, Flowers IPA and Original and two or
more local guest beers, pleasant staff,
lunchtime food (not Mon), pub games;
upstairs ladies'; tables on back terrace
(the Didler, P Dawn, Kevin Blake)
Old Malt Shovel NG24 1HD [North Gate]:
Welcoming and comfortably opened-up, with
enjoyable food from doorstep sandwiches to
restaurant dishes, several good changing
ales such as Timothy Taylors Landlord and
Wells & Youngs Bombardier, choice of teas,
open fire, lots of books and bottles on
shelves, cheerfully laid-back atmosphere and
service, pub games, skittle alley; wheelchair
access, terrace tables, open all day Weds-Sun
(P Dawn, the Didler, David Carr)
NEWSTEAD [SK5252]
Station Hotel NG15 0BZ [Station Rd]: Busy
basic red-brick village local opp station on
Robin Hood rail line, Barnsley Bitter and
Robinsons Old Tom Mild, fine old railway
photographs, pub games; juke box, TV
(the Didler)
NORMANTON ON TRENT [SK7969]
☆ *Square & Compass* NG23 6RN [signed off
B1164 S of Tuxford; East Gate]: Low-beamed
village pub with good sensibly priced food
inc Sun lunch, good choice of beers; children
welcome in eating areas, small play area out
behind, motel-style bedrooms, open all day
(Andy and Jill Kassube, LYM, J V Dadswell)
NOTTINGHAM [SK5739]
☆ *Canal House* NG1 7EH [Canal St]: Big
conversion of wharf building, bridge over
indoors canal spur complete with
narrowboat, lots of bare brick and varnished
wood, huge joists on studded steel beams,
long bar with good choice of house wines
(two glass sizes), Castle Rock and changing
guest beers, lively efficient staff, sensibly
priced pubby food, lots of standing room;
good upstairs restaurant and second bar,
masses of solid tables out on attractive
waterside terrace; piped music (live Sun),
popular with young people at night; open all
day *(Bruce Bird, Michael Dandy, P Dawn,
the Didler, BB, David Carr)*

Coopers Arms NG3 6JH [Porchester Rd, Thornywood]: Solid Victorian local with three unspoilt rooms, Black Sheep, Theakstons and guest ales, small family room in skittle alley; cl Weds lunchtime *(the Didler)*

Fox & Crown NG6 0GA [Church St/Lincoln St, Old Basford]: Good range of Alcazar beers brewed at back of unpretentious open-plan pub (window shows the brewery, tours Sat, next-door beer shop), also guest beers, good continental bottle choice, enjoyable fresh food inc thai and wide choice of early evening home-made pizzas, helpful staff; pub itself may possibly change hands as landlord wants to concentrate on the brewery – news please; good piped music, games machines, big-screen sports TV; disabled access, tables out behind, open all day *(the Didler, Kevin Blake, P Dawn)*

Gladstone NG5 2AW [Loscoe Rd, Carrington]: Welcoming local with well kept ales such as Adnams Broadside, Caledonian Deuchars IPA, Castle Rock Harvest Pale, Fullers London Pride, Greene King Abbot and Timothy Taylors Landlord, great range of malt whiskies, helpful landlord and friendly staff, cosy comfortable lounge with reading matter, basic bar with old sports equipment and darts; piped music may be loud, big-screen sports TV; upstairs folk club Weds, quiz Thurs; tables in yard with lots of hanging baskets, cl wkdy lunchtimes, open all day wknds (from 3 Fri) *(the Didler, Richard, P Dawn, MP, Jeremy King)*

Globe NG2 3BQ [London Rd]: Light and airy roadside pub with six well kept ales mainly from local breweries, coal fire; handy for cricket or football matches, open all day *(the Didler, Des and Jen Clarke, P Dawn)*

Horse & Groom NG7 7EA [Radford Rd, New Basford]: Unpretentious and well run partly open-plan pub by former Shipstones brewery, still with their name and other memorabilia, friendly atmosphere, eight good changing ales, good value fresh straightforward food from sandwiches to Sun lunches, daily papers, nice snug, wknd live music; open all day *(the Didler, Kevin Blake, P Dawn)*

☆ **Lion** NG7 7FQ [Lower Mosley St, New Basford]: Three or four Batemans ales and half a dozen interesting changing guest beers from one of city's deepest cellars (glass viewing panel – and can be visited at quiet times), farm ciders, ten wines by the glass, wide choice of good value wholesome home-made food all day inc doorstep sandwiches, children's helpings and summer barbecues; open plan but the feel of separate areas, bare bricks and polished dark oak boards, coal or log fires, daily papers; live music Fri/Sat, jazz Sun lunchtimes; well behaved children welcome, pleasant terrace, open all day *(the Didler, P Dawn, Kevin Blake)*

News House NG1 7HB [Canal St]: Friendly two-room Tynemill pub with half a dozen or more well kept changing ales inc bargain Castle Rock, belgian and czech imports on tap, farm cider, good wine and hot drinks choice, decent fresh lunchtime food inc good value Sun lunch, mix of bare boards and carpet, one room filled with local newspaper front pages spanning years of events and personalities, bar billiards, attractive blue exterior tiling; big-screen sports TV; open all day *(the Didler, P Dawn, Andy and Jill Kassube, David Carr)*

Old Moot Hall NG3 2DG [Carlton Rd, Sneinton]: Since being tied to Tom Woods Highwood, has gained attractive décor, with comfortable seating and plenty of tables on polished boards, coal-effect gas fire; up to eight changing ales, good choice of wines by the glass, friendly staff, enjoyable simple food; upstairs bar with pool and big-screen sports TV; open all day *(the Didler, P Dawn, A and P Lancashire)*

Pit & Pendulum NG1 2EW [Victoria Street]: Dark gothick theme bar with ghoulish carving and creeping ivy lit by heavy chandeliers and (electronically) flaring torches, all sorts of other more or less cinematic horror allusions in the décor, standard fairly priced all-day bar food, well reproduced piped music; keg beers; good wheelchair access, open all day *(Michael Dandy, David Carr, LYM, Jeremy King)*

☆ **Plough** NG7 3EN [St Peters St, Radford]: Unpretentious two-room 19th-c pub brewing its own good value Nottingham ales, also a guest beer and farm cider, bargain food inc fresh rolls, popular Sun lunch (live jazz then) and Tues curry night, two coal fires, nice windows, new seating and lighting, bar billiards and other traditional games, Thurs irish music night (may be free chilli); Sun barbecues, open all day Fri-Sun *(P Dawn, the Didler)*

☆ **Salutation** NG1 7AA [Hounds Gate/Maid Marion Way]: Proper pub, with low beams, flagstones, ochre walls and cosy corners inc two small quiet rooms in ancient lower back part, plusher modern front lounge, good real ales such as Burton Bridge Porter, Timothy Taylors Landlord and Wentworth Bumble Beer, enjoyable plain quickly served food till 7, helpful staff; piped music; open all day *(Val and Alan Green, Michael Dandy, BB, David Carr)*

Sir John Borlase Warren NG7 3GD [Ilkeston Rd/Canning Circus (A52 towards Derby)]: Good atmosphere in several recently refurbished linked rooms with interesting Victorian decorations, enjoyable limited food, friendly staff, several real ales; children welcome (not Fri/Sat evenings), tables in nicely lit back garden *(BB, Peter and Jean Hoare, David Carr)*

ORSTON [SK7741]

Durham Ox NG13 9NS [Church St]: New local landlady for comfortable split-level open-plan village pub opp church, Fullers London Pride, Greene King IPA, Marstons Pedigree and local guest beers, hot coal fire, interesting RAF/USAF memorabilia; terrace tables, nice garden, pleasant countryside, open all day Sat (the Didler)

OXTON [SK6250]

Olde Bridge NG25 0SE [Nottingham Rd (B6386, just off A6097)]: Large well kept 19th-c pub, partly panelled, with pleasant atmosphere, full Everards range, good soft drinks choice, hard-working staff, daily papers, restaurant area; piped music, games machines; disabled facilities, children welcome, large garden, cl Mon, open all day Sat (N R White, JJW, CMW, J R Ringrose)

PLUNGAR [SK7634]

Anchor NG13 0JJ [Granby Lane]: Traditional well run Vale of Belvoir pub dating from late 18th c, changing choice of enjoyable fresh food, friendly helpful landlord, three real ales, open-plan layout, restaurant (not Mon) (S and J McGarry)

RADCLIFFE ON TRENT [SK6439]

Black Lion NG12 2FD [Main Rd (A52)]: Courage Directors, Greene King IPA, Timothy Taylors Landlord and quickly changing guest beers, all-day food, big comfortable lounge with games machine and coal fire, cheery bar with pool and big-screen sports TV; new landlord having some discos and karaoke; big enclosed garden behind, barbecues and play area, open all day (the Didler, Mrs Hazel Rainer)

Horse Chestnut NG12 2BE [Main Rd]: Handsomely reworked by owners of Horse & Groom in Nottingham, Batemans XB, Caledonian Deuchars IPA, Fullers London Pride and several guest beers, enjoyable food, friendly efficient staff, two-level main bar and library room, panelling, parquet and polished brass and woodwork, impressive lights; disabled access, attractive new terrace (the Didler)

Trent NG12 1AE [Shelford Rd]: Well run and comfortable, with wide food choice inc wkdy lunchtime OAP bargains, good range of changing ales, well chosen wines, friendly efficient service; extensive decking with colourful flowers (David Glynne-Jones, P Dawn)

SELSTON [SK4553]

Horse & Jockey NG16 6FB [handy for M1 junctions 27/28; Church Lane]: Dating from 17th c, recently refurbished keeping its atmosphere, different levels, low beams and flagstones, several real ales such as Bass, Brains Rev James, Greene King Abbot and Timothy Taylors Landlord, some tapped from the cask, bargain cobs wkdys, friendly staff, coal fire in cast-iron range, top games area with darts and pool (R T and J C Moggridge, the Didler, Derek and Sylvia Stephenson)

SOUTH LEVERTON [SK7881]

Plough DN22 0BT [Town St]: Tiny local doubling as morning post office, basic trestle tables, benches and pews, real fire, Greene King Ruddles County and a guest beer, traditional games; tables outside, open all day (from early afternoon wkdys) (the Didler)

STRELLEY [SK5141]

Broad Oak NG8 6PD [Main St, off A6002 nr M1 junction 26]: Notable for its position in extraordinary preserved village enclave on edge of Nottingham, with picnic-sets out under huge ancient oak; well kept Hardys & Hansons ales, decent food, lots of partitioned areas, comfortable banquettes, no piped music; play area in back garden (Mark O'Sullivan)

THURGARTON [SK6949]

☆ *Red Lion* NG14 7GP [Southwell Rd (A612)]: Cheery 16th-c pub with good fresh food (all day wknds and bank hols) inc fresh fish and some adventurous dishes in brightly decorated split-level beamed bars and restaurant, prompt friendly service even though busy, well kept ales such as Black Sheep, Caledonian Deuchars IPA and Marstons Mansfield, comfortable banquettes and other seating, flame-effect fire, lots of nooks and crannies, big windows to attractive good-sized two-level back garden with well spaced picnic-sets (dogs on leads allowed here); unobtrusive games machine, steepish walk back up to car park; children welcome (David Glynne-Jones, BB, J R Ringrose, Derek and Sylvia Stephenson, Dean Rose)

UNDERWOOD [SK4751]

☆ *Red Lion* NG16 5HD [off A608/B600, nr M1 junction 27; Church Lane]: Reliable sensibly priced family food inc OAP lunches, other bargains and good fresh fish (best to book) in welcoming 17th-c split-level beamed village pub, Caledonian Deuchars IPA, Marstons Pedigree and interesting guest beers, good service, open-plan quarry-tiled bar with slightly enlarged dining area, open fire, some cushioned settles, pictures and plates on dressers, no piped music; children welcome, picnic-sets and large adventure playground in big garden with terrace and barbecues, attractive setting, open all day Fri-Sun (the Didler, Kevin Blake, Derek and Sylvia Stephenson, Andy and Jill Kassube)

WATNALL CHAWORTH [SK5046]

☆ *Queens Head* NG16 1HT [3 miles from M1 junction 26: A610 towards Nottingham, left on B600, then keep right; Main Rd]: Great fish and chips and wide range of other good value food (all day summer) in tastefully extended low-beamed pub with well kept ales such as Adnams, Everards, Greene King IPA and Wells & Youngs Bombardier, efficient friendly service, beams and stripped pine, coal fire, intimate snug, dining area; piped music; picnic-sets on spacious and attractive back lawn with big play area, open all day (the Didler, Derek and Sylvia Stephenson)

Royal Oak NG16 1HS [Main Rd; B600 N of Kimberley]: Friendly beamed village local with interesting plates and pictures, Greene King IPA, Abbot and Hardys & Hansons, fresh cobs, woodburner, back games room and pool room, upstairs lounge open Fri-Sun; sports TV, some live music; tables outside, open all day (the Didler)

WELLOW [SK6766]
Durham Ox NG22 0EA [Newark Rd]:
Comfortable, warm and friendly, several small
linked rooms, beams and log fire, bargain
food all day, well kept ales such as Greene
King Ruddles County and Jennings Robin
Redbreast; handy for Rufford Country Park,
open all day *(Gordon Ormondroyd)*

WEST BRIDGFORD [SK5838]
Southbank NG2 5GJ [Trent Bridge]: Bright
well run sports bar with good real ale choice
inc Caledonian, Fullers, Mallard and Timothy
Taylors, wide range of other drinks, polished
wood floors, sofas, good all-day food choice
from baguettes and light dishes to mixed
grills, friendly efficient staff; several big
screens and lots of other sports TVs, some
live music; big garden overlooking river,
handy for cricket ground and Notts Forest FC,
open all day *(the Didler, P Dawn)*
☆ *Stratford Haven* NG2 6BA [Stratford Rd,
Trent Bridge]: One of Tynemill's best pubs,
bare-boards front bar leading to linked areas
inc airy skylit and carpeted yellow-walled
back part with relaxed local atmosphere,
Castle Rock and good changing guest beers,
exotic bottled beers, farm ciders, ample
whiskies and wines, good value simple
home-made food all day, daily papers; some
live music (nothing too noisy), can get
crowded; handy for cricket ground and
Nottingham Forest FC, tables outside, open
all day *(the Didler, MP, P Dawn, Des and
Jen Clarke, Kevin Blake, BB, Derek and
Sylvia Stephenson)*

WEST MARKHAM [SK7273]
☆ *Mussel & Crab* NG22 0PJ [Sibthorpe Hill;
B1164 nr A1/A57/A638 roundabout N of

Tuxford]: Pub/restaurant specialising in good
fish and seafood fresh daily from Brixham,
other enjoyable dishes on vast array of
blackboards, interesting open-plan bar and
roomy dining areas (beams and stripped
stone, or more flamboyant pastel murals
with fishy theme), prompt friendly service,
good wines by the glass (wine racks around
the room), Tetleys, good coffee; good
disabled access, picnic-sets on terrace, play
area, views over wheatfields *(M and
C Thompson, Mrs Brenda Calver)*

WINTHORPE [SK8156]
Lord Nelson NG24 2NN [Gainsborough Rd]:
Friendly pub by former mill race, wide choice
of enjoyable food, three real ales, sofas and
easy chairs as well as usual seats and tables,
woodburner and fresh flowers, dining room;
picnic-sets in good-sized garden, open all
day wknds *(JJW, CMW)*

WORKSOP [SK5879]
Regency S80 1PS [Carlton Rd]: Changing ales
such as Batemans XXXB and John Smiths
Magnet, very friendly staff, generous
straightforward food at bargain prices,
armchairs in civilised bar, comfortable dining
room; bedrooms *(Tony and Wendy Hobden)*

WYSALL [SK6027]
Plough NG12 5QQ [Keyworth Rd; off A60 at
Costock, or A6006 at Wymeswold]:
Welcoming and attractive 17th-c beamed
village pub, changing real ales, generous
enjoyable food inc popular Sun lunch, two
rooms on either side of central bar with nice
mix of furnishings, soft lighting, big log fire;
french doors to pretty terrace with flower
tubs and baskets *(P Dawn, Gwyn and
Anne Wake)*

Post Office address codings confusingly give the impression that a few pubs are in
Nottinghamshire, when they're really in Derbyshire (which is where we list them).

Oxfordshire

Pubs here are on great form these days. As a result we have a big influx of new main entries this year. These are the smart and civilised Saye & Sele Arms at Broughton (nice food), the Half Moon in Cuxham (young friendly chef/patron cooking super food), the handsome old Woodman in Fernham (plenty to look at, and a good range of beers), the Greyhound on Gallowstree Common (a celebrity chef's pub), the Rose & Crown at Shilton (a charming village pub, nice all round), the Swan at Swinbrook (enterprising cooking in this carefully refurbished pub, with its lovely oak garden room), and the Kings Arms in Woodstock (stylishly reworked, with rewarding food and good bedrooms). The Chequers at Churchill is also back where it belongs in the main entries this year, now that its exceptional licensees have decided to stay on. Other pubs doing especially well here include the unpretentious Reindeer in Banbury (well worth a good look around), the timeless Black Horse at Checkendon, the family-run Merrymouth at Fifield (a good all-rounder), the historic and particularly interesting White Hart at Fyfield (enterprising cooking here), the well run Gate Hangs High nicely set near Hook Norton (deservedly popular for meals out), the small and civilised Bell at Langford (another fine all-rounder), the bustling Blue Boar not far from the Thames in Longworth, the buoyant Rose & Crown and ancient Turf Tavern, both in Oxford, the happy unspoilt Royal Oak at Ramsden (great choice of wines by the glass to go with their surprisingly good food), the nice little Red Lion at Steeple Aston, the Masons Arms at Swerford (good contemporary cooking in this relaxed dining pub), and the successfully refurbished Trout by the Thames at Tadpole Bridge (good food here too). It has to be said that this is not a cheap area for pub meals. Prices do tend to be higher than average, which puts special emphasis on the importance of looking for value. Fortunately, there is plenty of real quality to be found. As well as the pubs already picked out for their cooking, good food plays a strong part in the appeal of the Chequers at Aston Tirrold, the Radnor Arms in Coleshill and the Baskerville Arms at Shiplake. So the county now has at least a dozen pubs which really shine for a special meal out. Our top choice as Oxfordshire Dining Pub of the Year is the Trout at Tadpole Bridge. And a special mention too for the Royal Oak at Ramsden, keeping such a nice modest pubby character as well as serving such good food. Other good thoroughly unpretentious pubs here are the Black Horse at Checkendon and the Falkland Arms at Great Tew. In the Lucky Dip section at the end of the chapter, pubs showing particularly well are the Abingdon Arms at Beckley, Joiners Arms at Bloxham, Crown at Church Enstone, Plough at Finstock, Anchor in Henley, Pear Tree in Hook Norton, Navy Oak at Leafield, Nut Tree at Murcott, Crown at Nuffield, Bear and Eagle & Child in Oxford, Lamb at Satwell, Bell at Shenington, Wykham Arms at Sibford Gower, restaurant-y Cherry Tree and Crooked Billet, both at Stoke Row, Plough at West Hanney and smart Bear in Woodstock. Drinks prices in the county, like food prices, tend to be appreciably above the national norm. As so often, pubs with the best beer often charge relatively low prices for it. And here, the local Hook Norton beers are significantly cheaper than their competitors. Other local beers to look out for, though these tend to be more expensive, include White Horse, Burford, Brakspears and Loddon.

ALVESCOT
SP2704 MAP 4

Plough
B4020 Carterton—Clanfield, SW of Witney; OX18 2PU

Useful for wide choice of straightforward food all day, bric-a-brac and aircraft prints in neat pubby bar; colourful hanging baskets

This busy pub is now open all day and serves food throughout that time too. The neatly kept bar has a good pubby atmosphere, a collection of aircraft prints and a large poster of Concorde's last flight, as well as plenty of cottagey pictures, china ornaments and house plants, a big antique case of stuffed birds of prey, sundry bric-a-brac, and a log fire. Comfortable seating includes cushioned settles, a nice armchair, and of course the bar stools bagged by cheerful regulars in the early evening. Wadworths IPA and 6X on handpump. There's a proper public bar with TV and darts; piped music and skittle alley. There are picnic-sets on the back terrace and a couple out in front below particularly colourful hanging baskets by the quiet village road; aunt sally. More reports please.

🍴 From a sizeable menu, bar food might include filled rolls, soup, deep-fried baby camembert with cranberry sauce, cheesy garlic mushrooms, combination starters for two, battered cod, chicken kiev, mozzarella and sun-dried tomato quiche, liver and bacon casserole, steak and kidney pudding, half a lamb shoulder in minted gravy, daily specials, and puddings. *Starters/Snacks: £4.25 to £8.25. Main Courses: £7.50 to £13.95. Puddings: £3.60 to £3.75*

Wadworths ~ Tenant Kevin Robert Keeling ~ Real ale ~ Bar food (all day) ~ (01993) 842281 ~ Children allowed until 8.30pm ~ Dogs allowed in bar ~ Open 11.30-11; 12-10.30 Sun
Recommended by KN-R, Pat and Roger Davies

ASTON TIRROLD
SU5586 MAP 2

Chequers 🍴 ☐
Village signposted off A417 Streatley—Wantage; Fullers Road; OX11 9EN

Atmosphere and food of a rustic french restaurant in pubby surroundings, nice french wines, restrained décor and stylish service; charming cottagey garden

Cleverly, this charming place (which formally calls itself the Sweet Olive at the Chequers) has the shape and atmosphere of a welcoming village pub combined with the heart and soul of a rustic french restaurant. The pubby and chatty main room has a proper bar counter, complete with sturdy bar stools (and people using them), and Caledonian Deuchars IPA and Hook Norton Hooky on handpump, as well as good coffees and a nice range of french wines by the glass, including a pudding wine; attentive service. It has grass matting over its quarry tiles, six or seven sturdy stripped tables with mate's chairs and cushioned high-backed settles against the walls, a small fireplace, and plain white walls. There are two or three wine cartoons, and wine box-ends, mainly claret and sauternes, panel the back of the servery. A second rather smaller room, set more formally as a restaurant, has a similarly restrained décor of pale grey dado, white-panelled ceiling and red and black flooring tiles. There may be soft piped music. A charming small cottagey garden, well sheltered by flowering shrubs, angles around the pub, with picnic-sets under cocktail parasols and a play tree; aunt sally.

⑪ **The very good food comes with a slate of olives and good breads as well as a handsomely ringed linen napkin: filled baguettes, crispy duck salad, warm goats cheese salad with roasted red peppers, scallops with lime butter sauce, slow-cooked moroccan lamb with couscous, breast of chicken with wild mushroom sauce and fresh pasta, onglet of beef with shallots and white wine, panache of fish with champagne and saffron sauce and lemon rice, and puddings such as treacle sponge with custard and chocolate délice with espresso ice-cream.** *Starters/Snacks: £4.50 to £9.95. Main Courses: £9.95 to £15.50. Puddings: £4.95 to £5.95*

Enterprise ~ Lease Olivier Bouet and Stephane Brun ~ Real ale ~ Bar food (not winter Sun evening; not Weds; not Feb) ~ Restaurant ~ (01235) 851272 ~ Children welcome ~ Dogs allowed in bar ~ Open 12-3, 6-midnight(11.30 Sun); closed Weds; Sun evening Oct-Apr; all Feb

Recommended by I H G Busby, Hunter and Christine Wright, Roderick Braithwaite, Dr D Scott, J V Dadswell, Susan and John Douglas

BANBURY   SP4540   MAP 4

Reindeer ⬛ £
Parsons Street, off Market Place; OX16 5NA

Plenty of shoppers and regulars in interesting town pub, fine real ales, simple food and roaring log fires; no under-21s

There are always plenty of chatty customers in this well run and unpretentious town pub and the atmosphere is relaxed and friendly. Readers like the warmly welcoming front bar with its heavy 16th-c beams, very broad polished oak floorboards, magnificent carved overmantel for one of the two roaring log fires, and traditional solid furnishings. It's worth looking at the handsomely proportioned Globe Room used by Cromwell as his base during the Battle of Edgehill in 1642. Quite a sight, it still has some wonderfully carved 17th-c dark oak panelling. Well kept Hook Norton Best Bitter, Old Hooky, Hooky Dark and a couple of changing guest beers on handpump, country wines, several whiskies and winter mulled wines; piped music, skittle alley. The little back courtyard has tables and benches under parasols, aunt sally and pretty flowering baskets. No under-21s (but see below).

⑪ **Served only at lunchtime, straightforward bar food in generous helpings might include sandwiches, soup, omelettes, good filled baked potatoes, all day breakfast, and daily specials.** *Starters/Snacks: £2.50 to £3.50. Main Courses: £4.50 to £8.00. Puddings: £1.80 to £2.95*

Hook Norton ~ Tenants Tony and Dot Puddifoot ~ Real ale ~ Bar food (11-2.30) ~ (01295) 264031 ~ Children allowed away from main bar area ~ Dogs allowed in bar ~ Open 11-11; 12-3 Sun; closed Sun evening

Recommended by the Didier, Ted George, Keith and Sue Ward, Derek and Sylvia Stephenson, Mark and Diane Grist, Nick and Meriel Cox

BROUGHTON   SP4238   MAP 4

Saye & Sele Arms
B4035 SW of Banbury; OX15 5ED

Smartly refurbished 16th-c house with good generously served food, particularly attentive service

Very handy for Broughton Castle, this attractive old stone house is a comfortable spot for a good meal, and the service is particularly welcoming and attentive: when we arrived we were immediately shown to a table in the bar, and didn't have to move again until it was time to leave. Food is very much at the heart of things, but locals do pop in for a drink, and there's a good range of beers, with Adnams Best joined by three changing guests like Exmoor Hound Dog and Fullers Chiswick and London Pride. Though essentially one long room, the refurbished bar has three distinct areas – a dining room at one end, with dozens of tankards and cups hanging from the beams, and neatly folded napkins on the tables, then a tiled area beside the bar counter, with cushioned window seats, a few brasses, and dark wooden furnishings, and finally a carpeted room with red walls and a mirror above the big fireplace. On our visit there were a good few people happily eating – although oddly, most of them were doing it in virtual silence, so the atmosphere was rather subdued. A pleasant terrace with picnic-sets leads to a nice lawn with plastic tables, and aunt sally. The pub takes its name from the residents of Broughton Castle, open on Sunday and Wednesday afternoons in season (and Thursday afternoons in summer).

🍴 **Generously served and tasty, with well filled sandwiches and ciabattas, butternut squash, red onion and nut crumble, chicken, avocado and bacon salad, upside-down tart with caramelised onion, sautéed courgette and field mushroom topped with a fondue of basil, mozzarella and tomato, a pie of the day (served in a proper, deep-filled slice), rack of lamb on minted mash with redcurrant jus, lobster fricassee or thermidor, and good puddings; our vegetables were particularly good. They have a choice of roasts and fresh fish on Sundays.** *Starters/Snacks: £3.85 to £6.25. Main Courses: £3.95 to £17.50. Puddings: £4.95*

Free house ~ Licensees Danny and Liz McGeehan ~ Bar food (12-2(3 weekends), 7-9.30 (not Sun evenings)) ~ (01295) 263348 ~ Children welcome till 9pm ~ Open 11.30-2.30(3 Sat), 7-11; 11.30-5 Sun; closed Sun evenings, 25 Dec, and maybe evening 26 Dec

Recommended by George and Maureen Roby, P and J Shapley, K H Frostick, Paul Humphreys

CAULCOTT

SP5024   MAP 4

Horse & Groom 🍺
Lower Heyford Road (B4030); OX25 4ND

Bustling and friendly cottage with obliging new licensees (he is also the chef) and great changing beer choice

Hard-working and friendly new licensees have taken over this partly thatched cottage and Mr Prigent is also the chef. It's not a huge place: an L-shaped red-carpeted room angles around the servery, with plush-cushioned settles, chairs and stools around a few dark tables at the low-ceilinged bar end and a blazing fire in the big inglenook, with brassware under its long bressumer beam; shove-ha'penny and board games. The far end, up a shallow step, is set for dining with lots of decorative jugs hanging on black joists, and some decorative plates; also, some lovely watercolours and original drawings dotted around. The friendly staffordshire bull terrier is called Minnie. Hook Norton Best and three changing guests on handpump and decent house wines. There is a small side sun lounge and picnic-sets under cocktail parasols on a neat lawn.

🍴 **Bar food includes lunchtime sandwiches, croque monsieur, various pâtés, nice sausages, fillets of fresh cod and duck breast both with changing sauces, lamb shank with crushed potatoes, and puddings such as sticky toffee pudding with butterscotch sauce.** *Starters/Snacks: £3.95 to £5.50. Main Courses: £8.50 to £16.00. Puddings: £4.25 to £5.25*

Free house ~ Licensees Anne Gallacher and Jerome Prigent ~ Real ale ~ Bar food (not Sun evening) ~ Restaurant ~ (01869) 343257 ~ Children must be over 10 in dining room (not allowed in bar) ~ Open 12-3, 6-11; 12-3, 7-10.30 Sun

Recommended by Dave Lowe, Guy Vowles, D P and M A Miles, Ken and Barbara Turner, Dick and Madeleine Brown

CHECKENDON

SU6684   MAP 2

Black Horse
Village signposted off A4074 Reading—Wallingford; coming from that direction, go straight through village towards Stoke Row, then turn left (the second turn left after the village church); OS Sheet 175 map reference 666841; RG8 OTE

Simple place liked by walkers and cyclists for a pint and snack

The same family have been running this unpretentious, simple country local for 101 years now. The back still room where three changing West Berkshire beers are tapped from the cask has a relaxed, unchanging feel and the room with the bar counter has some tent pegs ranged above the fireplace, a reminder that they used to be made here. A homely side room has some splendidly unfashionable 1950s-look armchairs and there's another room beyond that. There are seats out on a verandah and in the garden. The surrounding countryside is very attractive and enjoyed by walkers and cyclists.

🍴 **They offer only filled rolls and pickled eggs.**

Free house ~ Licensees Margaret and Martin Morgan ~ Real ale ~ No credit cards ~ (01491) 680418 ~ Children allowed but must be very well behaved ~ Open 12-2(2.30 Sat), 7-11; 12-3, 7-10.30 Sun; closed evening 25 Dec

Recommended by Pete Baker, Torrens Lyster, the Didler, Susan and John Douglas

CHIPPING NORTON   SP3127   MAP 4

Chequers ★ ♀ ◖

Goddards Lane; OX7 5NP

Bustling and friendly town pub open all day, with cheerful mix of customers and simple bars

Although a new licensee has taken over here, readers are happy to report that very little has changed and it is still a busy and friendly pub with a good mix of customers. The three softly lit beamed rooms have no frills, but are clean and comfortable with low ochre ceilings, plenty of character, and blazing log fires. Efficient staff serve very well kept Fullers Chiswick, London Pride, ESB and seasonal brews on handpump and they have good house wines, all available by the glass. The conservatory restaurant is light and airy and used for more formal dining. The town's theatre is next door.

🍴 **Seasonally changing bar food includes lunchtime sandwiches, ploughman's with home-made chutneys, game pâté, rabbit and fish pies, jerusalem artichoke, rocket and parmesan risotto, lancashire hotpot, and puddings.** *Starters/Snacks: £4.50 to £7.95. Main Courses: £7.95 to £11.95. Puddings: £3.95 to £4.50*

Fullers ~ Lease John Cooper ~ Real ale ~ Bar food (12-2.30, 6-9.30; 12-5 Sun; not Sun evening) ~ Restaurant ~ (01608) 644717 ~ Children allowed but no facilities for them ~ Dogs allowed in bar ~ Open 11-11; 12-10.30 Sun; closed 25 Dec

Recommended by Miss A G Drake, Robert Gomme, Sean A Smith, Michael Dandy, Richard Greaves, Keith and Sue Ward, M Joyner, the Didler, Chris Glasson, R C Vincent, Peter and Anne Hollindale, Simon D H Robarts Briggs, Mike and Mary Carter, P and J Shapley, Paul Goldman, Barry Collett, Nick and Meriel Cox, George Atkinson

CHURCHILL   SP2824   MAP 4

Chequers

B4450 Chipping Norton—Stow (and village signposted off A361 Chipping Norton—Burford); Church Road; OX7 6NJ

Exceptionally welcoming licensees in busy village pub with plenty of space and popular food

Happily, the delightfully friendly licensees of this 18th-c village pub have decided not to move on for the moment, which comes as a great relief to all their customers. Even after just one visit, Mrs Golding will remember your name and you will be genuinely welcomed back as an old friend. The front bar has a light stone flagstoned floor, a couple of old timbers, modern oak furnishings, some exposed stone walls around a big inglenook (with a good winter log fire) and country prints on the pale yellow walls; newspapers are laid out on a table. At the back is a big extension that's a bit like a church with soaring rafters and there's a cosy but easily missed area upstairs. Hook Norton Hooky Bitter and a couple of changing guest beers on handpump and a good wine list. The pub's outside is cotswold stone at its most golden, and the village church opposite is impressive.

🍴 **Well presented, popular bar food includes lunchtime sandwiches, soup, duck liver terrine with mango chutney, smoked bacon and leek tartlet with mascarpone cheese, brie and broccoli puff pastry pie with chive white wine sauce, breast of guinea fowl wrapped in bacon with butternut squash and wild mushrooms, salmon with mustard and herb crust, spinach and tomatoes, Thursday night crispy duck with cheese mash and red wine sauce,** and puddings such as toffee and caramel charlotte with butterscotch sauce and passion fruit bavarois; Sunday roasts. *Starters/Snacks: £4.00 to £6.75. Main Courses: £11.00 to £16.50. Puddings: £5.00*

Free house ~ Licensees Peter and Assumpta Golding ~ Real ale ~ Bar food ~ Restaurant ~ (01608) 659393 ~ Children welcome ~ Open 12-11

Recommended by Stuart Turner, Mr and Mrs I and E Bell, Richard Greaves, David Glynne-Jones, Mr and Mrs Hignell, Noel Grundy, Colin McKerrow, Richard Wyld, Graham Oddey, Sean A Smith, Tom Evans, Richard Atherton, Bernard Stradling, Sir Nigel Foulkes

CLIFTON
SP4931   MAP 4

Duke of Cumberlands Head ♀
B4031 Deddington—Aynho; OX15 0PE

Homely touches and big log fire in low-beamed bar, tasty food, and short walk to canal

The hospitable landlord has a warm welcome for all his customers in this popular thatched and golden stone pub. The low-beamed turkey-carpeted lounge has a good log fire in a vast stone fireplace, attractive paintings by the landlord's mother of lilies and rhododendrons grown by her on the west coast of Scotland, and mainly sturdy kitchen tables, with a few more through in the little dining room, which has some stripped stone; none of the walls or ceilings is straight. Black Sheep, Hook Norton Best and maybe Archers Village or Adnams Bitter on handpump, plenty of wines to choose from (the landlord was in the wine trade for many years) and 30 malt whiskies. Picnic-sets out on the grass behind. The canal is a short walk away.

🍴 **Enjoyable bar food includes sandwiches, soup, chicken liver pâté, herrings marinated in dill and madeira, deep-fried fillet of haddock, calves liver in a grain and mustard sauce, lancashire hotpot, chicken supreme in tarragon sauce, braised lamb shank, and puddings such as honey stem-ginger cheesecake and summer pudding.** *Starters/Snacks: £3.50 to £6.00. Main Courses: £9.00 to £16.00. Puddings: £4.00*

Free house ~ Licensee Nick Huntington ~ Real ale ~ Bar food (not winter Sun evening or Mon lunchtime all year) ~ (01869) 338534 ~ Children welcome ~ Dogs allowed in bar and bedrooms ~ Open 12-3, 6.30-11; 12-3, 6.30-10.30 Sun; closed winter Sun evening and Mon lunchtime all year ~ Bedrooms: £60B/£75B

Recommended by John and Heather Phipps, Simon Collett-Jones, Pam and John Smith, Sean A Smith, Richard Marjoram, K H Frostick, A G Marx, Andrew Shore, Maria Williams, Sir Nigel Foulkes, Simon Jones, George Atkinson, J and F Gowers, Mr and Mrs John Taylor

COLESHILL
SU2393   MAP 4

Radnor Arms 🍴 ♀ ◧
B4019 Faringdon—Highworth; village signposted off A417 in Faringdon and A361 in Highworth; SN6 7PR

National Trust pub with imaginative food, good choice of drinks and friendly service; small back garden and good nearby walks

Despite the fine quality of the food, this friendly place remains very much a pub in atmosphere. The small welcoming carpeted bar has White Horse Bitter and Wells & Youngs Bitter tapped from casks behind the counter, which like as not has a couple of locals chatting over their pints; a good range of wines by the glass, a few malt whiskies and summer Pimms and elderflower pressé. This room has a couple of cushioned settles as well as its comfortable plush carver chairs, and a woodburning stove; a back alcove has a few more tables. Steps take you down into the main dining area, once a blacksmith's forge: with a lofty beamed ceiling, this has kept its brick chimney stack angling up (with a log fire now) and its canary walls are decorated with dozens of forged tools and smith's gear. A small garden up behind, with a big yew tree, has picnic-sets under cocktail parasols; plenty of good walking nearby. The pub, like the attractive village itself, is owned by the National Trust.

Ⓜ️ **Very good, interesting bar food includes lunchtime sandwiches, soup, crab, chilli and ginger linguini with parsley and olive oil, fried pigeon breast on a celeriac potato cake with apple purée and sherry raisins, tagine of roasted vegetables with coriander couscous, daube of beef with glazed carrots and parsnips, guinea fowl on roasted squash and pancetta risotto with caramelised button onions, roasted chump of lamb with lentil and bacon casserole, and puddings such as crème brûlée or chocolate pot.** *Starters/Snacks: £3.95 to £7.95. Main Courses: £8.25 to £15.25. Puddings: £4.95*

Free house ~ Licensees Chris Green and Shelley Crowhurst ~ Real ale ~ Bar food (no food Sun evening) ~ Restaurant ~ (01793) 861575 ~ Children welcome ~ Dogs allowed in bar ~ Open 11.30-3, 6-11; 12-3, 7-10.30 Sun; closed Mon

Recommended by D R Ellis, Peter and Audrey Dowsett, William Goodhart, Derek Allpass

CROWELL   SU7499   MAP 4

Shepherds Crook 🍺

B4009, 2 miles from M40 junction 6; OX39 4RR

Village pub with straight-talking landlord, quite a choice of often local beers and well liked food (plenty of fish)

This is a traditional village pub with plenty of locals and a straight-talking landlord who is not afraid to have opinions. The bar is unpretentious and chattily pubby with beams and exposed brickwork, stone-flagged floors, books on shelves and in a case, and an open fire in a brick fireplace; standing timbers divide it from a dining area with high wooden rafters, sporting prints and chunky tables. Black Sheep, Chiltern Beechwood Bitter, Hop Back Summer Lightning and a couple of guest beers on handpump and wines that come from small producers (like the Lebanon); farm cider. The golden retriever is called Compton and the labrador, Sobers. No music or machines; dominoes, cribbage. There are a few tables in front on the green, and decent walks nearby.

Ⓜ️ **As well as growing his own vegetables, the landlord used to be a fish merchant and the fish is delivered overnight from the west country: lunchtime sandwiches and smoked salmon with scrambled eggs, soup, anchovies on toast, king prawns with garlic and chilli, smoked fish platter with a glass of aquavit, sausages with mustard mash and onion gravy, steak and kidney pie, chunky hake steak in a garlic and parsley broth, pork steak with creamy mustard and mushroom sauce, fillet of bass with spring onion, ginger and garlic, and puddings such as banoffi pie and chocolate and ginger tart; four or five choices of fish and chips on Friday evenings.** *Starters/Snacks: £4.95 to £7.50. Main Courses: £8.95 to £15.00. Puddings: £4.50 to £6.00*

Free house ~ Licensees Steve and Elizabeth Scowen ~ Real ale ~ Bar food (12-2.30, 7-9.30; 12-3, 7-9 Sun) ~ Restaurant ~ (01844) 351431 ~ Children allowed away from bar but must be well behaved ~ Dogs welcome ~ Open 11.30-3, 5-11; 11.30-11 Sat; 12-11 Sun

Recommended by John Holroyd, Mr and Mrs John Taylor, Torrens Lyster, Tracey and Stephen Groves, David Lamb

CUXHAM   SU6695   MAP 4

Half Moon 🍽️

4 miles from M40 junction 6; S on B4009, then right on to B480 at Watlington; OX49 5NF

Lovely 16th-c country pub with relaxed atmosphere and super food cooked by friendly chef/landlord

Run by an enthusiastic young chef/owner, this beautiful 16th-c thatched house is in a sleepy hamlet surrounded by lovely countryside. There's a genuinely friendly welcome and a relaxed atmosphere and although much emphasis is placed on the delicious food, there's a pubby atmosphere where drinkers are made to feel equally at home. The small red and black tiled bar has a brick fireplace and two main eating areas have old beams, Edwardian tables and chairs and Brakspears on handpump and several wines by the glass including prosecco and pink champagne. There are wooden-slatted and metal chairs and tables in the good-sized garden and attractive window boxes.

⌘ Using home-grown vegetables and produce from their own cold smokehouse, the excellent food might include nibbles like home-made crisps with chilli jam, goose salami and olives and tapenade palmiers and parmesan cream, as well as soup, pork pie with piccalilli, deep-fried sprats with garlic mayonnaise, potted crab, smoked haddock and salmon fishcakes with tartare sauce, pork belly with scallops, black pudding and apples, steak in Guinness pie with cheddar and suet crust, crispy duck with red cabbage, seared beef medallions with wild mushroom risotto, seasonal game, and puddings such as champagne and orange jelly and sticky toffee pudding with vanilla ice-cream; Friday breakfast and Saturday brunch too. *Starters/Snacks: £3.50 to £6.00. Main Courses: £9.50 to £18.50. Puddings: £4.50*

Brakspears ~ Tenant Andrew Hill ~ Real ale ~ Bar food (12-2, 6-9 plus 9-11 Fri breakfast; 10-2, 6-9 Sat; 12-3 Sun; no food Sun evening) ~ Restaurant ~ (01491) 614151 ~ Children welcome but must be dining with parents after 7pm ~ Dogs welcome ~ Open 12-2.30, 5.30-11; 12-10 Sun

Recommended by Mrs E A Macdonald, Tim and Gill Bullivant, I H G Busby, Dennis and Doreen Haward, Richard Endacott, Jeremy Hebblethwaite, R K Phillips

EAST HENDRED   SU4588   MAP 2
Eyston Arms
Village signposted off A417 E of Wantage; High Street; OX12 8JY

Attractive bar areas with low beams, flagstones, log fires and candles, imaginative food and helpful service

With a good welcome from the cheerful staff, this neatly kept dining pub is furnished in a modern country style. The several separate-seeming areas have a pleasant atmosphere, nice tables and chairs on the flagstones and carpet, some cushioned wall-seats, stripped timbers, particularly low ceilings and beams, and a piano; an attractive inglenook has a winter log fire. The bar counter has olives to pick at and even on a sunny day the candles may be lit. Hook Norton and Wadworths 6X on handpump, good wines, piped easy-listening music, cribbage, chess and dominoes. Picnic-sets outside overlook the pretty village lane.

⌘ The food can be very good indeed and at lunchtime might include filled ciabatta sandwiches, soup, hot chicken and crispy pancetta salad, salt-crusted king prawns with aïoli, an antipasti plate for two and ham and eggs; in the evening, there might be warm scallop and monkfish terrine, beef carpaccio, venison burger with balsamic onion chutney, melted dolcelatte and chilli jam, vegetable risotto, seafood linguini, cod on creamy saffron and crab mashed potatoes with a bouillabaisse sauce, rack of lamb with roasted garlic and tarragon sauce, crushed potatoes, caramelised onions and spinach, and puddings such as panna cotta with berries and poached pear in cranberry and vodka with crème fraîche. *Starters/Snacks: £5.00 to £9.75. Main Courses: £12.50 to £17.50. Puddings: £5.00*

Free house ~ Licensee George Dailey ~ Real ale ~ Bar food (12-2, 7-9; 12-3.30, 7-9 Sun) ~ Restaurant ~ (01235) 833320 ~ Children must be well behaved and sitting at tables ~ Dogs allowed in bar ~ Open 11-11; 12-10.30 Sun; closed Sun evening in winter

Recommended by Bob and Margaret Holder, Sir John Palmer, Franklyn Roberts, Terry Miller, Peter and Jan Humphreys, Dr D Scott, C R Crofton, Peter Titcomb, Trevor and Sylvia Millum

FERNHAM   SU2991   MAP 4
Woodman ⌘
A420 SW of Oxford, then left into B4508 after about 11 miles; village a further 6 miles on; SN7 7NX

Half a dozen real ales and generous food in charming old-world country pub

With friendly, attentive staff and consistently good food, it's not surprising that this country pub is so popular. The heavily beamed rooms are full of an amazing assortment of old objects like clay pipes, milkmaids' yokes, leather tack, coach horns, an old screw press, some original oil paintings and good black and white photographs of horses. Comfortable seating includes cushioned benches, pews and windsor chairs, and the candlelit tables are simply made from old casks; big wood fire. Half a dozen real ales from breweries like Butts, Greene King, Moles, Sharps, Wadworths, White Horse and Wychwood tapped from the cask, several wines by the glass and malt whiskies and farm cider in summer; they hold a three-day beer festival in September. Piped music and TV. There are seats outside on the terrace. Disabled lavatories.

🍴 Generous helpings of reasonably priced bar food include sandwiches, filled baguettes and ploughman's, soup, chicken liver pâté with spiced apricot chutney, garlic mushrooms in a cream sauce topped with crispy pancetta, smoked haddock fishcakes with braised fennel and vanilla balsamic dressing, vegetable and cashew nut stir fry, sausage and champ with cider and red onion gravy, cod in beer batter, free-range chicken breast stuffed with smoked mozzarella on roasted pineapple with sweet chilli and coconut sauce, daily specials, and puddings. *Starters/Snacks: £4.50 to £6.95. Main Courses: £8.50 to £15.00. Puddings: £4.95*

Free house ~ Licensee Steven Whiting ~ Real ale ~ Bar food (12-2, 6.30-9.30) ~ Restaurant ~ (01367) 820643 ~ Children welcome ~ Dogs allowed in bar ~ Open 11-11; 12-10.30 Sun

Recommended by Tony and Tracy Constance, Peter and Audrey Dowsett, Mary Rayner, Dick and Madeleine Brown, Mark and Ruth Brock

FIFIELD   SP2318   MAP 4

Merrymouth
A424 Burford—Stow; OX7 6HR

Family-run 13th-c inn with simple beamed bar, popular food and drink, and comfortable bedrooms

Dating back to the 13th c, this popular inn is run by pleasant, sociable licensees. The simple but comfortably furnished L-shaped bar has nice bay-window seats, flagstones, horsebrasses and antique bottles hanging from low beams, some walls stripped back to the old masonry and an open fire in winter. Burford Brewery Bitter and Wychwood Hobgoblin on handpump and decent wines; piped classical music. There are tables on a terrace and in the back garden (there may be a little noise from fast traffic on the road). Readers continue to enjoy staying in the quaint, well cared for bedrooms. The pub's name comes from the Murimuth family who once owned the village.

🍴 As well as light lunches such as filled baguettes, pork sausages with onion gravy, smoked haddock with welsh rarebit topping and a tomato salsa and stilton, leek and bacon pie, the reasonably priced, well liked bar food might include soup, pork and black pudding patties, prawn provençale, ham and eggs, butternut squash and sweet potato bake, creamy pork with cider, sage and cream, chicken with bacon, mushrooms, cheese and cream, rack of lamb with rosemary, port and redcurrant jus, daily specials, and puddings like raspberry marshmallow meringue and chocolate and almond torte. *Starters/Snacks: £3.95 to £5.95. Main Courses: £7.95 to £14.95. Puddings: £4.50*

Free house ~ Licensees Andrew and Timothy Flaherty ~ Real ale ~ Bar food (12-2.30, 6.30(7 Sun)-9) ~ Restaurant ~ (01993) 831652 ~ Children welcome ~ Dogs welcome ~ Open 11-3, 6-11; 11-3, 7-10 Sun; closed Sun evening in winter ~ Bedrooms: £45S/£65B

Recommended by Dennis Jones, Noel Grundy, Lesley and Barbara Owen, Mr and Mrs F E Boxell, Andrew Shore, Maria Williams

---

A very few pubs try to make you leave a credit card at the bar, as a sort of deposit if you order food. They are not entitled to do this. The credit card firms and banks which issue them warn you not to let them out of your sight. If someone behind the counter used your card fraudulently, the card company or bank could in theory hold you liable, because of your negligence in letting a stranger hang on to your card. Suggest instead that if they feel the need for security, they 'swipe' your card and give it back to you. And do name and shame the pub to us.

FYFIELD   SU4298   MAP 4

White Hart ⊕ ⊈ ◀

In village, off A420 8 miles SW of Oxford; OX13 5LW

Impressive place with grand main hall, minstrel's gallery and interesting side rooms, imaginative modern food, fine choice of drinks, and elegant seating on very big terrace

The friendly and hands-on young licensees at this former medieval chantry house work extremely hard to please both diners and those dropping in for just a chat and a pint. It's an impressive and civilised place with many original features and is well worth wandering around. The bustling main restaurant is a grand hall with soaring eaves, beams, huge stone-flanked window embrasures and flagstoned floors and is overlooked by a minstrel's gallery on one side and several other charming and characterful side rooms on the other. In contrast, the side bar is cosy with a large inglenook fireplace at its centre and a low beamed ceiling; there are flowers all around and evening candles. Clark's Classic Blonde, Hampshire Ironside, Hook Norton Old Hooky, St Austells Tribute and White Horse Village Idiot on handpump, around 14 wines by the glass including champagne and pudding wines and several malt whiskies; they hold beer festivals on May and August bank holiday weekends. Piped music and board games. There are elegant metal seats around tables under smart umbrellas on the really big terrace, and flower-edged lawns. Plenty to see nearby and the Thames-side walks are well worth taking.

🍴 Cooked by the licensee (who makes his own bread and pasta and grows some of his own herbs, fruit and vegetables), the particularly good food includes interesting soups, beetroot, feta and hazelnut roulade with citrus dressing, chicken and duck liver parfait with spiced apricot chutney, hot smoked salmon fishcake with poached egg and chive beurre blanc, sharing antipasti, mezze or fish boards, gnocchi with chilli-roasted pumpkin, nutmeg and sage butter, toad in the hole with colcannon and sweet onion and madeira gravy, cape-style seafood curry with turmeric rice, slow-roasted pork belly with roasted garlic and shallot mash and apple sauce, and puddings such as raspberry panna cotta with raspberry coulis and sticky toffee and date pudding with poached date purée and clotted cream; they also offer two- and three-course set lunch menus. *Starters/Snacks: £5.50 to £10.00. Main Courses: £9.95 to £17.95. Puddings: £4.95 to £5.95*

Free house ~ Licensee Mark Chandler ~ Real ale ~ Bar food (12-2.30, 7-9.30; 12-4 Sun; not Sun evening) ~ Restaurant ~ (01865) 390585 ~ Children welcome ~ Live jazz during May and August bank hol beer festivals ~ Open 11.30-3.30, 6-11; 11.30-11 Sat; 12-10.30 Sun

Recommended by E A and D C T Frewer, Dick and Madeleine Brown, Andrea and Guy Bradley, David and Cathrine Whiting, Ken and Barbara Turner, Keith and Margaret Kettell, David and Elaine Shaw, Mark and Ruth Brock, Colin and Janet Roe, William Goodhart, Shirley Sandilands, J Crosby

GALLOWSTREE COMMON   SU7081   MAP 2

Greyhound

Gallowstree Road, Shiplake Bottom (though heading E from Gallowstree Common it's past the sign for Rotherfield Peppard); off B481 at N end of Sonning Common; RG9 5HT

Attractive restauranty country pub (Antony Worrall Thompson's), very good food, local beers and a pretty garden

The more obviously restauranty of Antony Worrall Thompson's two pubs, this is nevertheless a comfortable and extraordinarily popular place for a civilised meal – and it has three well chosen real ales. The food's not what you'd call cheap, but the prices aren't dissimilar to plenty of other Oxfordshire dining pubs, and the quality is consistently good. There's no escaping who the owner is: the water and some of the condiments are his own brand (and indeed some of the meats come from his own farms), but for many of the people who flock here every night, that celebrity link is a big part of the appeal. Just don't expect the man himself to be cooking your meal, or even be around – though he does occasionally pop in. Most of the tables throughout are set for eating, with wine glasses; the nicest and certainly the cosiest part is what they call the bottom restaurant, to the left of the door; it has more of the feel of an upmarket country pub, with beams and timbers, comfortable and plentiful cushions on wall benches beside chunky wooden tables, and smart curtains around the small windows. The main restaurant is at the other end and is much busier, with rafters from the high ceiling, lots of packed-together tables, plenty more cushions, and some stuffed animal heads; both rooms are candlelit at night. In between is the bar, which has Fullers London Pride, Loddon Hoppit, and Rebellion IPA on handpump; there's a good wine list. Though not at all individual, service is polite and generally efficient; piped music. There are tables on a back terrace, and plenty more in the attractive front garden, with a pond. Booking is recommended (and essential at weekends). The ubiquitous chef's other pub, the Lamb, is a few minutes away at Satwell; the food there is all under ten pounds, but it doesn't take bookings, so you'll need to get there early, or be prepared for a wait.

Ⓘ There's a strong emphasis on the steaks and burgers, all using 35-day hung prime aberdeen angus beef, but the main menu also has devilled kidneys in baked field mushrooms, herring roes on toast, white suckling pig with apple chilli jelly, beef stroganoff, free-range chicken on grilled vegetables, calves liver, bacon and mash, and daily specials (including a vegetarian dish). They have had good value set lunches. Starters/Snacks: £4.50 to £7.95. Main Courses: £10.95 to £29.95. Puddings: £5.95

Free house ~ Real ale ~ Bar food (12-3(4 Sat), 6-9.30 (10.30 Fri, Sat); 12-9 Sun) ~ Restaurant ~ (0118) 9722 227 ~ Children welcome ~ Dogs allowed in bar ~ Open 12-3, 5.30-11; 12-11 Sat; 12-10.30 Sun; closed evening 25 Dec

Recommended by Rob Winstanley

GODSTOW   SP4809   MAP 4

Trout
Off A34 Oxford bypass northbound, via Wytham, or A40/A44 roundabout via Wolvercote; OX2 8PN

Major refurbishment blending original features with modern touches in medieval pub; good food, relaxed atmosphere and delightful waterside terrace

Reopened a few months ago after a big refurbishment, this pretty medieval pub now combines many original old features with new contemporary furnishings. It's been opened up inside and there are four different areas: what was the old bar is now a Wine Room, there's an Alice in Wonderland room, the Morse Room (still with the framed book covers) and the older section of the restaurant. It's all very attractively done, and there are beams, flagstones, bare floorboards and log fires alongside a mix of high-backed plush or leather dining chairs (and some extraordinarily high-backed chairs in the Alice in Wonderland room), church chairs, a mix of wooden tables and plenty of prints; piped music. Timothy Taylors Landlord on handpump and quite a few wines by the glass. Outside, the large terrace with plenty of seats and tables under large parasols has also had a makeover. This is a lovely riverside spot with a bridge across to the island (where they hope to be able to offer table service); wandering peacocks, too. More reports on the changes, please.

Ⓘ Good modern food includes various sharing plates and fired pizzas, soup, smoked trout pâté with horseradish remoulade, stilton, onion and watercress tart, sausages of the day, steakburger topped with cheese, onion and mustard mayonnaise, coconut chicken with mango chutney, duck confit with champ and plum chutney, moroccan lamb chops with saffron potatoes, chorizo, peas and onions, wild mushroom lasagne, daily specials, and puddings such as chocolate fondant and apple crumble. Starters/Snacks: £4.00 to £8.00. Main Courses: £7.00 to £17.50. Puddings: £5.00

Mitchells & Butlers ~ Manager Bernard Smith ~ Real ale ~ Bar food ~ Restaurant ~ (01865) 302071 ~ Well behaved children allowed ~ Open 11-11

Recommended by P and J Shapley

GREAT TEW   SP3929   MAP 4

Falkland Arms

Off B4022 about 5 miles E of Chipping Norton; The Green; OX7 4DB

Idyllic golden-stone cottage in lovely village with plenty of character in unspoilt bars and fine choice of ales

Taking its name from associations with the Falkland family (the 5th Viscount Falkland became treasurer to the navy in 1690 and gave his name to the Falkland Islands), this busy pub is just one of the untouched golden-stone buildings in this idyllic village. The unspoilt and partly panelled bar has high-backed settles and a diversity of stools around plain stripped tables on flagstones and bare boards, one, two and three-handled mugs hanging from the beam-and-board ceiling, dim converted oil lamps, shutters for the stone-mullioned latticed windows, and a fine inglenook fireplace with a blazing fire in winter. Wadworths IPA, 6X and a seasonal ale plus guests such as Oakham JHB, Smiles Heritage and Timothy Taylors Best. The counter is decorated with tobacco jars and different varieties of snuff which you can buy, and you'll also find 40 malt whiskies, 16 country wines, and farm cider; darts and board games. You have to go out into the lane and then back in again to use the lavatories; and they may try to keep your credit card while you eat. There are tables out in front of the pub and picnic-sets under cocktail parasols in the garden behind. Dogs must be on a lead. Small good value bedrooms (no under-16s). No mobile phones.

🍴 Lunchtime bar food includes filled baguettes, ploughman's, soup, beef in ale pie and mushroom stroganoff, with evening bar snacks that are limited to their hand-raised pork pies – though you can eat more sophisticated food in the restaurant then (best to book in advance). *Starters/Snacks: £4.50 to £6.26. Main Courses: £9.25 to £16.95. Puddings: £4.75*

Wadworths ~ Managers Paul Barlow-Heal and S J Courage ~ Real ale ~ Bar food (12-2, 7-8; not Sun evening) ~ Restaurant ~ (01608) 683653 ~ Children in restaurant lunchtimes only ~ Dogs allowed in bar ~ Live folk Sun evening ~ Open 11.30-2.30(3 winter Sat), 6-11; 11.30-11 Sat; 12-10.30 Sun; 12-3, 7-10.30 Sun in winter ~ Bedrooms: £50S/£80S(£110B)

Recommended by Graham and Doreen Holden, Nick Lawless, K H Frostick, Trevor and Judith Pearson, Rona Murdoch, Mr and Mrs G Hughes, the Didler, Mr and Mrs W D Borthwick, John Saville, R L Borthwick, Dave Lowe, M J Winterton, Barry Collett

HIGHMOOR   SU6984   MAP 2

Rising Sun

Witheridge Hill, signposted off B481; OS Sheet 175 map reference 697841; RG9 5PF

Thoughtfully run and pretty pub with a mix of diners and drinkers; interesting daily specials

Although most of this pretty black and cream pub is laid out for dining, the two front rooms are for those just wanting a drink. On the right by the bar, there are wooden tables and chairs and a sofa on the stripped wooden floors, cream and terracotta walls and an open fire in the big brick inglenook fireplace. The main area spreading back from here has shiny bare boards and a swathe of carpeting with well spaced tables and attractive pictures on the walls. Brakspears Bitter and a seasonal beer on handpump; piped music and board games. Seats and tables in the back garden; boules.

🍴 As well as sandwiches, bar food includes soup, venison and chilli pâté, wild mushrooms in a creamy garlic and white wine sauce, thick sliced honey-roasted ham with eggs, quorn bolognese, smoked paprika chicken with roasted red pepper, butternut squash and coriander couscous and mint and cucumber yoghurt, pork schnitzel with pear and spiced fruit chutney, and puddings such as hot date cake with toffee sauce or rice pudding with home-made strawberry jam. *Starters/Snacks: £2.50 to £7.25. Main Courses: £7.50 to £13.50. Puddings: £3.95 to £6.50*

Brakspears ~ Tenant Judith Bishop ~ Real ale ~ Bar food (12-2.30, 7-9.30; 12-3, 6.30-9; no food winter Sun evening) ~ Restaurant ~ (01491) 640856 ~ Children allowed if eating and must be strictly supervised by parents ~ Dogs allowed in bar ~ Open 12-3, 6-11; 12-11 Sat; 12-10.30 Sun

Recommended by P Price, Ron Deighton, John Roots, Bob and Margaret Holder, Susan and John Douglas

HOOK NORTON

SP3534   MAP 4

Gate Hangs High 🍴 ♟ 🍺

Banbury Road; a mile N of village towards Sibford, at Banbury—Rollright crossroads; OX15 5DF

Refurbished bar and popular food and beer in friendly country pub; nice place to stay and pretty courtyard garden

You can be sure of a genuinely friendly welcome in this tucked-away country pub. There's been some refurbishment to the bar this year but there are still the joists in the long, low ceiling, assorted chairs and stools around traditional tables, a gleaming copper hood over the hearth in the inglenook fireplace and Hook Norton Best and Old Hooky with a guest such as St Austells Tribute on handpump, bottled beers and decent wines. You'll need to book for Saturday evening and Sunday lunch in the slightly chintzy side dining extension; piped music and dominoes. There's a pretty courtyard garden and seats on a broad lawn behind the building with holly and apple trees and fine views; the flower tubs and wall baskets are very colourful. Readers continue to enjoy staying in the barn bedrooms here and the breakfasts are very good.

🍴 **Well liked bar food includes especially nice sandwiches, black pudding rösti with poached egg and bacon, lambs kidneys with onion, braised rabbit with mustard and cider, half duck with orange marmalade sauce and rack of lamb with mint and pear; there are also set weekday menus.** *Starters/Snacks: £3.75 to £6.95. Main Courses: £6.95 to £17.95. Puddings: £4.50 to £6.00*

Hook Norton ~ Tenant Stephen Coots-Williams ~ Real ale ~ Bar food (12-2.30, 6-10; all day Sat and Sun) ~ Restaurant ~ (01608) 737387 ~ Children welcome ~ Dogs allowed in bar and bedrooms ~ Open 12-3, 6-11.30; 12-11.30(10.30 Sun) Sat ~ Bedrooms: £45B/£60B

Recommended by Keith and Sue Ward, Mrs Pam Mattinson, Chester Armstrong, Stuart Turner, G T Cannon, Andrew Shore, Maria Williams, M and GR, Mary McSweeney, R C Vincent, Sir Nigel Foulkes, A G Marx, Paul Humphreys, J Crosby

KINGSTON BLOUNT

SU7399   MAP 4

Cherry Tree

1.9 miles from M40, junction 6: B4009 towards Chinnor; Park Lane; OX39 4SL

Interesting up-to-date décor, ambitious food and a decent choice of wines in bustling pub

Handy for the M40, this smart and uncluttered pub has a surprisingly contemporary interior – given the unassuming brick façade. The long single-room bar has light school chairs around chunky tables on its stripped wood floor, with soft leather sofas facing each other beside a small brick fireplace at one end. The cool décor of cream and olive-beige, set off by fresh flowers, big modern abstracts and modern lighting, makes for a light and airy feel. This relaxed chatty atmosphere continues into the good-sized popular back dining room. Brakspears Bitter, Special and a seasonal beer on handpump and a fair choice of wines by the glass; staff take their cue well from the friendly young licensees. Piped music.

🍴 **Bar food includes sandwiches, soup, coarse duck pâté with pear chutney, field mushrooms with bacon and dolcelatte, steak, kidney and ale pie, baked cod with basil crust and provençale sauce, spinach and goats cheese pancakes, chicken wrapped in bacon with mushroom stuffing and tarragon cream sauce, pork wellington with mustard sauce, daily specials, and puddings.** *Starters/Snacks: £3.50 to £6.50. Main Courses: £8.75 to £14.50. Puddings: £4.95*

Brakspears ~ Tenant Sharon Dallacosta ~ Real ale ~ Bar food (12-2.30, 7-9.30; 12-8.30 Sun) ~ Restaurant ~ (01844) 352273 ~ Children in restaurant (not on Fridays or Saturdays) ~ Open 12-11(10.30 Sun); closed 25 and 26 Dec, 1 Jan ~ Bedrooms: £70B/£80B

Recommended by Gerry and Rosemary Dobson, Torrens Lyster, Tracey and Stephen Groves

---

Waterside pubs are listed at the back of the book.

LANGFORD   SP2402   MAP 4

Bell ♀ ◖

Village signposted off A361 N of Lechlade, then pub signed; GL7 3LF

Beams, flagstones, a good log fire, well chosen wines and beer and enjoyable bar food in civilised pub

Although the food in this popular little dining pub is unquestionably the main thing, they do keep Hook Norton Hooky Bitter, Timothy Taylors Landlord and Wells & Youngs Bombardier on handpump, farm cider and ten wines by the glass. The simple low-key furnishings and décor add to the appeal: the main bar has just five sanded and sealed mixed tables on grass matting, a variety of chairs, three nice cushioned window seats, am attractive carved oak settle, polished broad flagstones by a big stone inglenook fireplace with a good log fire, low beams and butter-coloured walls with two or three antique engravings. A second even smaller room on the right is similar in character; daily papers on a little corner table. Service is friendly and efficient and the new bearded collie is called Madison; piped music. Therë are two or three picnic-sets out in a small garden with a play house. They are still hoping to add bedrooms; dogs must be on a lead. This is a quiet and charming village.

⌽ As well as filled rolls and ciabattas, the good food includes soup, crayfish salad with lime and coriander dressing, a choice of italian meats with sunblush tomato, olive and pesto salad, warm tartlet of mediterranean vegetables with halloumi, steak and kidney pie, gammon steak with eggs, thai green chicken curry, duck breast with honey-roasted root vegetables, herb roast potatoes and red wine jus, grilled halibut with lightly curried vegetables and green-lip mussels, and puddings such as hot chocolate fondant with coffee ice-cream and steamed treacle sponge with warm crème anglaise. *Starters/Snacks: £3.95 to £7.95. Main Courses: £7.95 to £15.95. Puddings: £4.75*

Free house ~ Licensees Paul and Jackie Wynne ~ Real ale ~ Bar food (not Sun evening or Mon) ~ Restaurant ~ (01367) 860249 ~ Children welcome but under-3s must leave by 7pm ~ Dogs allowed in bar ~ Open 12-3, 7-11(midnight Fri, 11.30 Sat); 12-3.30 Sun; closed Sun evening, all day Mon, first week Jan

Recommended by Noel Grundy, Graham Oddey, Tony and Jill Radnor

LEWKNOR   SU7197   MAP 4

Olde Leathern Bottel

Under a mile from M40 junction 6; just off B4009 towards Watlington; OX49 5TH

Unchanging bustling country local with decent food and beer and seats in sizeable garden

As this pleasant country pub is so close to the M40 it does get busy at lunchtime, so it's best to arrive early to be sure of a table. There are heavy beams and low ceilings in the two bar rooms as well as rustic furnishings, open fires, and an understated décor of old beer taps and the like; the family room is separated only by standing timbers, so you won't feel segregated from the rest of the pub. Brakspears Bitter and Special and a monthly guest beer on handpump, and all their wines are available by the glass. The attractive sizeable garden has plenty of picnic-sets under parasols and a children's play area.

⌽ Bar food includes lunchtime filled baguettes or ploughman's with chips and salad, soup, thai crab cakes, ham and eggs, beef curry, spinach and red pepper lasagne, chicken stir fry, line-caught bass with minted potatoes, roasted duck breast with plum sauce, and puddings such as chocolate mousse or raspberry cheesecake. *Starters/Snacks: £4.95. Main Courses: £6.95 to £14.95. Puddings: £4.50*

Brakspears ~ Tenant L S Gordon ~ Real ale ~ Bar food (12-2, 7-9.30) ~ (01844) 351482 ~ Children in restaurant and family room ~ Dogs allowed in bar ~ Open 10.30-2.30(3 Sat), 6-11; 12-3, 7-10.30 Sun

Recommended by Howard Dell, John and Jill Perkins, Chris Smith, Dr D J and Mrs S C Walker, Ian Phillips, D Hillaby, Mark and Ruth Brock, William Goodhart

LONGWORTH

SU3899   MAP 4

Blue Boar

Off A420/A415; Tucks Lane; OX13 5ET

Smashing old pub with a friendly welcome for all, good wines and beer and fairly priced good food; Thames-side walks nearby

Readers very much enjoy their visits to this welcoming 17th-c thatched stone pub and there are usually plenty of chatty locals enjoying a pint – always a good sign. The three low-beamed, characterful little rooms are warmly traditional with well worn fixtures and furnishings, and two blazing log fires, one beside a fine old settle. Brasses, hops and assorted knick-knacks like skis and an old clocking-in machine line the ceilings and walls, there are fresh flowers on the bar and scrubbed wooden tables, and faded rugs on the tiled floor; benches are firmly wooden rather than upholstered. The main eating area is the red-painted room at the end and there's a newer restaurant extension, too. Brakspears, Greene King Old Speckled Hen and Timothy Taylors Landlord on handpump, 30 malt whiskies, and a wide choice of wines, several by the glass. The licensee has been here for 29 years, though his friendly young team are generally more in evidence. There are tables in front and on the back terrace, and the Thames is a short walk away.

⑪ There's quite a range of reasonably priced and well liked bar food such as good lunchtime sandwiches, soup, antipasti, burger, steak in Guinness and creamy fish pies, several vegetarian dishes and more interesting changing weekend specials; meals are promptly served, in good-sized helpings. They hold a pig roast day on the bank holiday at the end of May. *Starters/Snacks: £4.50 to £5.95. Main Courses: £7.50 to £15.95. Puddings: £4.25 to £5.95*

Free house ~ Licensee Paul Dailey ~ Real ale ~ Bar food (12-2(2.30 Sat, 3 Sun), 7-10(9 Sun)) ~ Restaurant ~ (01865) 820494 ~ Children welcome ~ Dogs allowed in bar ~ Open 12-11(midnight Sat); closed 25 Dec, 1 Jan

Recommended by Peter and Audrey Dowsett, BOB, Barry and Anne, George Atkinson, Dick and Madeleine Brown, William Goodhart

OXFORD

SP5107   MAP 4

Rose & Crown

North Parade Avenue; very narrow, so best to park in a nearby street; OX2 6LX

Long-serving licensees in lively friendly local, a good mix of customers, fine choice of drinks and proper home cooking

In a smart narrow street, this rather straightforward but friendly pub is run by long-serving licensees and the sharp-witted Mr Hall makes all his customers, locals and visitors, very welcome. The front door opens into little more than a passage by the bar counter. The panelled back room, with traditional pub furnishings, is slightly bigger, and you'll find reference books for crossword buffs; no mobile phones, piped music or noisy games machines but they do have board games. Adnams Bitter and Broadside and Hook Norton Old Hooky on handpump, around 30 malt whiskies and a large choice of wines. The pleasant walled and heated back yard can be completely covered with a huge awning; at the far end is a 12-seater dining/meeting room. The lavatories are pretty basic.

⑪ Traditional but enjoyable food at honest prices includes a good choice of interesting sandwiches and baguettes, various dips with pitta bread, filled baked potatoes, omelettes, sausage or ham with egg, chips and beans, and a hot dish of the day such as turkish meatballs with couscous, beef stew with mustard dumplings and chilli con carne; popular Sunday roast. *Starters/Snacks: £4.95 to £5.25. Main Courses: £7.00 to £8.45. Puddings: £2.95 to £3.45*

Punch ~ Tenants Andrew and Debbie Hall ~ Real ale ~ Bar food (12-2.15(3.15 Sun), 6-9) ~ No credit cards ~ (01865) 510551 ~ Well behaved children welcome at weekends until 5pm ~ Open 10-midnight(1am Sat); closed 25 Dec

Recommended by the Didler, Torrens Lyster, Chris Glasson

Turf Tavern ◢

Tavern Bath Place; via St Helen's Passage, between Holywell Street and New College Lane; OX1 3SU

Interesting pub hidden away behind high walls with a dozen ales, regular beer festivals, nice food, and knowledgeable staff

Much the same as when Hardy described it in *Jude the Obscure*, this popular pub is secluded from the modern bustle of the city down little passages and alleyways – and not easy to find. There's quite a mix of customers in the two dark-beamed and low ceilinged small bars – students usually play a major part – though there are many more who, whatever the time of year, prefer to sit outside in the three attractive walled-in flagstoned or gravelled courtyards (one has its own bar); in winter, they have coal braziers so you can roast chestnuts or toast marshmallows and there are canopies with lights and heaters. Up to a dozen real ales on handpump: Bath Gem, B&T Black Dragon Mild, Caledonian Deuchars IPA, Greene King Ruddles Best, Lees Dragons Fire, Tom Wood Hop & Glory, Wentworth Needles Eye and three from the White Horse Brewery (including one named for the pub). Regular beer festivals, Weston's Old Rosie cider and winter mulled wine. Service is generally bright and knowledgeable, but can be stretched when busy (which it often is).

🍴 **Reasonably priced bar food includes sandwiches, filled baked potatoes, soup, chicken liver and mushroom pâté, vegetable balti, steak in ale pie, cumberland sausages and mash, lasagne, smoked haddock and spring onion fishcakes, shoulder of lamb with rich minted gravy, and puddings such as sticky toffee pudding with toffee sauce or rhubarb crumble.** *Starters/Snacks: £3.35 to £3.65. Main Courses: £5.65 to £8.95. Puddings: £3.35*

Greene King ~ Manager Darren Kent ~ Real ale ~ Bar food (12-7.30(7 Sun)) ~ (01865) 243235 ~ Dogs welcome ~ Live music Thurs evening ~ Open 11-11; 12-10.30 Sun

Recommended by the Didler, B J Harding, Tracey and Stephen Groves, E McCall, T McLean, D Irving, R Huggins, Jeremy Whitehorn, LM, Tim and Ann Newell, Dave Lowe, Michael Dandy, Mrs Margo Finlay, Jörg Kasprowski, Veronica Brown, Peter Dandy, Roger Shipperley

RAMSDEN
SP3515   MAP 4

Royal Oak 🍴 ⏷ ◢

Village signposted off B4022 Witney—Charlbury; OX7 3AU

Chatty, unpretentious pub with friendly licensees, 30 wines by the glass, very good food and heated back terrace

'A very happy place' is how one reader described this well run and unpretentious village inn. It seems to appeal to all ages from grandchildren through to grandparents and the staff remain friendly and helpful no matter how busy they are. The basic furnishings are comfortable, with fresh flowers, bookcases with old and new copies of *Country Life* and, when the weather gets cold, a cheerful log fire; no piped music or games machines – just a relaxed and chatty atmosphere. Butts Barbus Barbus, Hook Norton Best and Wells & Youngs Bombardier on handpump, a splendid choice of 30 wines by the glass, farm cider and several armagnacs. There are tables and chairs out in front and on the heated terrace behind the restaurant (folding back doors give easy access). The bedrooms are in separate cottages.

🍴 **Generous helpings of highly enjoyable bar food include lunchtime sandwiches, ploughman's, sausages with onion gravy and smoked scotch salmon with scrambled egg, as well as soup, real burgers with bacon and cheese or mushroom and soured cream, a pie of the week, fresh pasta with wild mushroom truffle sauce, fresh crab and smoked salmon fishcakes with a piquant tomato and sweet pepper sauce, daily specials, and puddings; they also offer a Thursday evening steak, pudding and glass of wine deal.** *Starters/Snacks: £3.95 to £7.50. Main Courses: £8.50 to £16.00. Puddings: £4.95*

Real ale to us means beer which has matured naturally in its cask – not pressurised or filtered.

Free house ~ Licensee Jon Oldham ~ Real ale ~ Bar food (12-2, 7-10) ~ Restaurant ~ (01993) 868213 ~ Children in dining room with parents ~ Dogs allowed in bar ~ Open 11.30-3, 6.30-11; 12-3, 7-10.30 Sun; closed 25 and 26 Dec ~ Bedrooms: £40S/£60S

Recommended by Rainer Zimmer, Chris Glasson, Simon Cottrell, Matthew Shackle, Brian T Smith, William Bakersville, Graham Oddey, Michael and Wendy Howl, Mr and Mrs Billy Rideout, P and J Shapley, Franklyn Roberts, Richard Marjoram, John Cook, Richard Atherton, Mrs D Rawlings, Mr and Mrs P Dolan

ROKE   SU6293   MAP 2

Home Sweet Home
Village signposted off B4009 Benson—Watlington; OX10 6JD

New licensees doing imaginative food in rather smart yet relaxed country pub

Now owned by Wadworths and with a new licensee, this is a rather smart and tiled old house in a quiet hamlet. As we went to press, the new people were finding their feet so things décor-wise may change. The two smallish bar rooms have a relaxed and informal atmosphere and there are heavy stripped beams, a particularly striking big log fire and traditional furniture; the carpet room on the right leads through to the restaurant area (the only place with piped music). Wadworths IPA, 6X, JCB and a guest beer on handpump, and eight wines by the glass. They plan to get the well working again and to have a water feature running over the home-grown herbs; nice tables and chairs in the low-walled front garden and plenty of flowers; more reports on the new regime, please.

▥ **Interesting bar food includes lunchtime sandwiches, crab spring rolls with an asparagus salad and white truffle dressing, grilled mackerel with a rhubarb sauce, goats cheese on a herb salad with a parmesan crisp, tomato compote and balsamic syrup, spinach and ricotta tartlet with roast vine tomatoes and basil, grilled cod fillet with artichokes, olives and tomatoes, roast confit leg of guinea fowl with green lentils, watercress and cherry vinaigrette, lamb chump with garlic, roast peppers and salsa verde, and puddings like chilled chocolate fondant with pistachio ice-cream and a chocolate biscuit and strawberry semi-freddo with shortbread and custard; super cheeseboard, too.** *Starters/Snacks: £3.95 to £5.75. Main Courses: £9.50 to £15.25. Puddings: £4.25 to £5.25*

Wadworths ~ Tenant Paul McCrystal ~ Real ale ~ Bar food (12-2, 6-9; not Sun evening (though that may change)) ~ Restaurant ~ (01491) 838249 ~ Well behaved children allowed but no facilities for them ~ Dogs allowed in bar ~ Open 12-3, 6-11; 12-11(10.30 Sun) Sat

Recommended by Richard Marjoram, Julia and Richard Tredgett, Steve and Liz Tilley, T R and B C Jenkins, John Baish, Susan and John Douglas, Piotr Chodzko-Zajko

SHILTON   SP2608   MAP 4

Rose & Crown
Just off B4020 SE of Burford; OX18 4AB

Simple and appealing little village pub, with relaxed civilised atmosphere, good locally sourced food

There's a lovely, unspoilt feel to this mellow 17th-c stone-built village pub. It's simple and unfussy, in a subtly upmarket way, and though on our evening visit the tables were being snapped up fast (the good food is making it a popular place to eat), the atmosphere remained relaxed and unhurried. We spotted quite a few signs of the improvements the newish landlord has made – in particular restoring the ceiling, and undoing some of the previous changes he felt had disguised a few of the building's original features. It's all very understated: the small front bar has proper wooden beams and timbers, exposed stone walls, and a stove in a big fireplace, with half a dozen or so wonky tables on the red tiled floor, and a few locals at the planked counter. It opens into a similar, bigger room used mainly for eating, with flowers on the tables, and another fireplace. Hook Norton Old Hooky, Youngs, and a seasonal guest on handpump. At the side, an attractive garden has picnic sets. In time, the landlord hopes to add bedrooms.

▥ **With an emphasis on seasonal local produce, the sensibly short menu might include lunchtime ciabattas, soups like beetroot, duck terrine with apricot, feuilleté of asparagus,** seven or so main courses such as smoked haddock, salmon and prawn pie, belly of pork braised with flageolet beans, or chicken sautéed with tomato, mushroom and balsamic sauce and wild rice, and puddings like pear and chocolate frangipane pudding or rhubarb fool. Dishes may be cheaper at lunchtime than in the evening. *Starters/Snacks: £4.40 to £6.00. Main Courses: £6.00 to £14.50. Puddings: £4.00 to £5.50*

Free house ~ Licensee Martin Coldicott ~ Bar food ~ (01993) 842280 ~ Well behaved children allowed ~ Dogs allowed in bar ~ Open 12-3, 6-11; 12-12 Fri, Sat; 12-10.30 Sun; closed 25 Dec

Recommended by Mrs Angela Brown, Pete Baker, David Lamb

SHIPLAKE   SU7779 MAP 2

Baskerville Arms ⅋ ♀

Station Road, Lower Shiplake (off A4155 just S of Henley); RG9 3NY

Mainly laid out for the imaginative food though proper public bar too, real ales and several wines by the glass, interesting sporting memorabilia and pretty garden

There is a public bar in this neat brick house with blue armchairs, darts and piles of magazines where locals gather for a chat and a pint of Fullers London Pride, Loddon Hoppit, and Timothy Taylors Landlord on handpump – but mostly, it's laid out for eating; 30 malt whiskies and ten wines by the glass. Apart from the wooden flooring around the light, modern bar counter, it's all carpeted and there are a few beams, pale wooden furnishings (lit candles on all the tables), plush red banquettes around the windows, and a brick fireplace with plenty of logs next to it. A fair amount of sporting memorabilia and pictures, especially old rowing photos (the pub is very close to Henley) and signed rugby shirts and photographs (the pub runs its own rugby club), plus some maps of the Thames are hung on the red walls, and there are flowers and large houseplants dotted about. It all feels quite homely, but in a smart way, with some chintzy touches such as a shelf of china dogs. The pretty garden has a proper covered barbecue area and smart teak furniture under huge parasols.

🍴 **Good, interesting food at lunchtime includes open sandwiches using home-made bread, soup, grilled bacon and melted cambozola with cranberry dressing, tortilla with free-range eggs, vegetables, soured cream and parmesan, popular tuna burger and steak and kidney pie with evening choices such as home-cured gravadlax on beetroot salad, english asparagus and pea risotto, home-smoked fillet of beef with smoked paprika and sesame crust, stuffed pigs trotter with saffron and garlic mayonnaise, chargrilled local pork with mustard and sage mash and fig and tomato chutney, fillet of bass on a saffron and prawn chowder, and puddings like lemon tart with raspberry coulis and chocolate brownie with vanilla ice-cream; on Tuesdays, the landlord cooks a set menu called Graham's Kitchen Nightmares.** *Starters/Snacks: £5.95 to £7.00. Main Courses: £9.95 to £18.50. Puddings: £4.95*

Enterprise ~ Lease Graham and Mary Cromack ~ Real ale ~ Bar food ~ Restaurant ~ (0118) 940 3332 ~ Children welcome but no babies in evening restaurant ~ Dogs allowed in bar ~ Open 11.30-2.30, 6-11; 12-4, 7-10.30 Sun ~ Bedrooms: £45S/£75S

Recommended by Paul Humphreys, Mark and Diane Grist

STANTON ST JOHN   SP5709 MAP 4

Star

Pub signposted off B4027, in Middle Lane; village is signposted off A40 heading E of Oxford (heading W, you have to go to the Oxford ring-road roundabout and take unclassified road signposted to Stanton St John, Forest Hill etc); OX33 1EX

Friendly landlord in nice village pub with interesting rooms and Wadworths beers

Tucked away at the end of the village, this is a pleasant old place that's popular locally. It is appealingly arranged over two levels and the oldest parts are two characterful little low-beamed rooms – one with ancient brick flooring tiles and the other with quite close-set tables. Up some stairs is an attractive extension on a level with the car park with old-fashioned dining chairs, an interesting mix of dark oak and elm tables, rugs on flagstones, bookshelves on each side of an attractive inglenook fireplace (good blazing fires in winter), shelves of good pewter, terracotta-coloured walls with a portrait in oils, and a stuffed ermine. Wadworths IPA, 6X and JCB on handpump and nine wines by the glass. There's a family room and conservatory, too; piped music, games machine, shove-ha'penny and board games. The walled garden has seats among the flower beds; children's play equipment.

🍴 **Bar food includes sandwiches, ploughman's, filled baked potatoes, soup, beef in ale pie, bulgar wheat and walnut casserole, lasagne, battered haddock, chicken kiev and lamb shank in redcurrant and rosemary.** *Starters/Snacks: £4.95 to £5.95. Main Courses: £8.50 to £13.25. Puddings: £4.25*

Wadworths ~ Tenant Michael Urwin ~ Real ale ~ Bar food ~ (01865) 351277 ~ Children in family room ~ Dogs allowed in bar ~ Open 11-2.30, 6.30-11; 12-2.30, 7-10.30 Sun

Recommended by Douglas and Ann Hare, Ian Phillips, Paul Humphreys, Simon and Sally Small, Robert Gomme, Roy Hoing

STEEPLE ASTON SP4725 MAP 4

Red Lion
Off A4260 12 miles N of Oxford; OX25 4RY

Friendly village pub with beamed bar, nice straightforward food, local beers, and suntrap terrace

A friendly, hard-working landlord runs this little stone village pub. The comfortable partly panelled bar is welcoming and relaxed with beams, an antique settle and other good furnishings, Hook Norton Hooky Bitter, Old Hooky and a seasonal beer on handpump and several wines by the glass; good service. There's a back conservatory-style dining extension, too. The suntrap front terrace has lovely flowers and shrubs.

🍴 **At lunchtime, the pubby bar food choice might include filled baguettes, soup, local sausages with beans, cheese and onion omelette, corned beef hash and beef in ale pie, with evening dishes such as creamy garlic mushrooms, baby camembert melted in its box with toast fingers, steamed mussels in white wine and shallots, gammon and eggs, free-range chicken breast wrapped in smoked bacon and topped with stilton sauce, and puddings like warm chocolate fudge cake and apple strudel tart.** *Starters/Snacks: £3.50 to £6.50. Main Courses: £5.00 to £15.00. Puddings: £3.00 to £5.00*

Hook Norton ~ Tenant Melvin Phipps ~ Real ale ~ Bar food (12-2(4 Sun), 7-9) ~ Restaurant ~ (01869) 340225 ~ Children welcome ~ Dogs allowed in bar ~ Open 12-3, 5-11; 12-11 Sat

Recommended by John and Heather Phipps, J and M Taylor, Craig Turnbull, BOB, Paul Humphreys, Nigel and Jean Eames

SWERFORD SP3830 MAP 4

Masons Arms 🍴
A361 Banbury—Chipping Norton; OX7 4AP

Attractive dining pub with modern cooking by chef/landlord, airy dining extension, civilised and relaxed atmosphere, country views from outside tables

Although most emphasis in this very popular dining pub is, not surprisingly, on the particularly good food cooked by the chef/patron Mr Leadbeater, there is a friendly, relaxed and bustling atmosphere that prevents it becoming an out-and-out restaurant. The dining extension is light and airy and the bar has pale wooden floors with rugs, a carefully illuminated stone fireplace, thoughtful spotlighting, and beige and red armchairs around big round tables in light wood. Doors open on to a small terrace with a couple of stylish tables, while steps lead down into a cream-painted room with chunky tables and contemporary pictures. Round the other side of the bar is another roomy dining room with great views by day, candles at night, and a civilised feel. Brakspears Special and Hook Norton Best on handpump and several wines by the glass. Behind is a neat square lawn with picnic-sets and views over the Oxfordshire countryside.

🍴 Using rare breed and traceable meat, the enjoyable food at lunchtime includes sandwiches, ploughman's, pork terrine with chutney, greek salad, home-baked ham with free-range eggs, a vegetarian pasta dish of the day, chicken korma and roast salmon with mustard beetroots and new potatoes; there's also soft roes on toast with capers and parsley, finnan haddock and cream cheese pâté, grilled pigeon breast with hazelnut mash and red wine jus, chickpea and mushroom jalfrezi, slow-roasted belly of gloucester old spot with pear mayonnaise and celeriac coleslaw, braised shoulder of lamb with honey and rosemary jus and wing of skate with brown shrimp butter; in the evening they offer a good value two- and three-course set menu. *Starters/Snacks: £4.50 to £6.50. Main Courses: £5.50 to £9.95. Puddings: £5.50*

Free house ~ Licensee Bill Leadbeater ~ Real ale ~ Bar food ~ Restaurant ~ (01608) 683212 ~ Children welcome ~ Open 10-4, 6-11; 10-10.30 Sun; 10-3, 6-11 and 10-4, 7-10.30 Sun in winter

Recommended by Nigel and Sue Draper, Richard Marjoram, Dr Nigel Bowles, Chris Glasson, Hugh Spottiswoode, M and GR, David Glynne-Jones, Robert Gomme, Michael Dandy, P and J Shapley, Paul Butler

SWINBROOK   SP2812   MAP 4

Swan 🍴 �

Back road a mile N of A40, 2 miles E of Burford; OX18 4DY

Civilised 17th-c pub with handsome new oak garden room, nicely smartened-up bars, local beers and contemporary food

A lovely new green oak garden room, with high-backed beige and green dining chairs around pale wood tables and views over the garden and orchard, has been added on to the back of this 17th-c country pub – all very smart and civilised. The small dining room to the right of the entrance now opens into the bar and the extension beyond. No longer dimly lit, this little bar has retained its simple antique furnishings, settles and benches and open fire, and locals still drop in for a pint and a chat; there's a stuffed swan in an alcove. As the pub is owned by the Duchess of Devonshire – the last of the Mitford sisters who grew up in the village – there are lots of old Mitford family photographs blown up on the walls; the licensees here also run the Kings Head at Bledington in Gloucestershire. Hook Norton, Wadworths 6X and a local guest beer on handpump, 13 wines by the glass, a proper bloody mary and local apple juice; piped music. This is a lovely spot by a bridge over the River Windrush and seats by the fuchsia hedge make the best of the view. As we went to press, work was beginning on new bedrooms.

🍴 Good modern bar food now includes lunchtime sandwiches, sautéed chicken livers with garlic, tarragon, white wine and cream in a filo basket, potted shrimps, roast butternut squash tarte tatin, bass on aubergine purée with a fennel and tomato salsa, venison and aberdeen angus pie, roast smoked duck breast on baby spinach with rösti potato and redcurrant wine jus, and puddings such as caramelised rice pudding with plum compote and baked vanilla cheesecake laced with dark chocolate. *Starters/Snacks: £5.95 to £6.55. Main Courses: £11.50 to £18.50. Puddings: £5.95*

Free house ~ Licensees Archie and Nicola Orr-Ewing ~ Real ale ~ Bar food (not Sun evening) ~ Restaurant ~ (01993) 823339 ~ Well behaved children welcome away from bar ~ Dogs allowed in bar ~ Open 11-3, 6-11; 11(12 Sun)-11 Sat; 11-3, 6-11 Sat in winter; closed 25 Dec

Recommended by Malcolm and Jo Hart, David Handforth, E A and D C T Frewer, Richard Greaves, A G Marx, Mr and Mrs C Prentis, Klaus and Elizabeth Leist

---

'Children welcome' means the pub says it lets children inside without any special restriction. If it allows them in, but to restricted areas such as an eating area or family room, we specify this. Some pubs may impose an evening time limit. We do not mention limits after 9pm as we assume children are home by then.

TADPOLE BRIDGE SP3200 MAP 4

Trout ⑪ ♆ 🛏

Back road Bampton—Buckland, 4 miles NE of Faringdon; SN7 8RF

OXFORDSHIRE DINING PUB OF THE YEAR

Carefully refurbished country inn with River Thames moorings, fine choice of drinks, particularly good restaurant-style food, lovely summer garden; super bedrooms

Completely refurbished throughout, this is a civilised and comfortable place in a peaceful spot by the Thames. The L-shaped bar has attractive pink and cream checked chairs around a mix of nice wooden tables, some rugs on the flagstones, a modern wooden bar counter with terracotta paintwork behind, fresh flowers, a woodburning stove and a large stuffed trout. The airy restaurant is appealingly candlelit in the evenings. Butts Barbus Barbus, Ramsbury Bitter, Windrush Burford Ale and Wells & Youngs Bitter on handpump, ten wines by the glass from a carefully chosen list, some fine sherries and several malt whiskies; the hard-working licensees positively welcome locals who pop in for a pint and have a strong regular following. There are good quality teak chairs and tables under blue parasols in the lovely garden and six moorings for visiting boats; if you are arriving by boat, it's best to get here early in summer. The bedrooms are exceptionally well equipped and extremely attractive.

⑪ As well as lunchtime filled baguettes (not Sunday), the carefully sourced food includes terrine of ham hock, ox tongue and foie gras wrapped in prosciutto, smoked haddock fishcake with a lightly poached egg, hollandaise sauce and crispy pancetta, roasted flat mushrooms marinated with chilli, garlic and herbs with a red pepper dressing, ratatouille feuilleté with a fresh tomato confit and basil sauce, roast rump of lamb with lentils and gratin potatoes and red wine jus, whole split hen crab, chilli, ginger and cream sauce, roast leg of partridge with braised red cabbage and potato and butter bean cake, and puddings like crème brûlée with roasted bananas and rich dark chocolate tart with mango sorbet. *Starters/Snacks: £5.95 to £9.95. Main Courses: £11.25 to £17.95. Puddings: £5.95*

Free house ~ Licensees Gareth and Helen Pugh ~ Real ale ~ Bar food (not winter Sun evening) ~ Restaurant ~ (01367) 870382 ~ Children welcome ~ Dogs welcome ~ Open 11.30-3(3.30 Sat), 6-11; 12-4, 6.30-10.30 Sun; closed Sun evening in winter; 24 and 25 Dec ~ Bedrooms: £70B/£100B

Recommended by David and Cathrine Whiting, Jonathan Aquilina, Mr and Mrs D S Price, Di and Mike Gillam, Derek Thomas, Simon Collett-Jones, Mr and Mrs G S Ayrton, Bob and Margaret Holder, Charles Artley, Jane Skerrett, Mr and Mrs J C Cetti, M S Pizer, Jeff and Wendy Williams, Peter Titcomb, Dave Braisted

WOODSTOCK SP4416 MAP 4

Kings Arms 🛏

Market Street/Park Lane (A44); OX20 1SU

Stylishly refurbished hotel in centre of attractive town, good creative food, enjoyable atmosphere, comfortable bedrooms

Of all the pubs in this smart and attractive old town it's this well refurbished hotel right in the heart of things that readers currently enjoy the most. It's stylish and contemporary, but also laid-back and friendly, and locals and visitors alike find it a relaxing place for a meal, snack, or just a coffee. The licensees (who've been in these pages before when they ran the Bat & Ball at Cuddesdon) have spent the last decade gradually improving the place; their aim has been to make everything traditional with a modern twist, and it works rather well. The bar is simple and unfussy, yet still comfortable and characterful, with brown leather furnishings, smart blinds and black and white photos throughout, and at the front an old wooden settle and interesting little woodburner. There's a stylish marble bar counter, and, in the room leading to the brasserie-style dining room, an unusual stained-glass structure used for newspapers and magazines; the restaurant is attractive, with its hanging baskets and fine old fireplace. Marstons Pedigree and Theakstons Best on handpump, good coffees and afternoon tea, freshly squeezed orange juice, and a dozen or so malt whiskies; efficient service from smartly uniformed staff, piped music. When we last called in, the atmosphere was gently humming, with a nice mix of ages. Readers have enjoyed staying here, and particularly praised the breakfasts (available from 7.30-noon for non-residents too). There are a couple of tables on the street outside.

🕮 Much enjoyed by readers, with rustic rolls (lunchtime only), soup, asparagus, parmesan and smoked ham tart with hollandaise sauce, home-made burgers with organic beef, corn fed chicken breast with leek, bacon and mushroom crumble, lemon grass and parmesan risotto cake on spiced sweet potato and spinach, pot roast brisket of beef with bubble and squeak, roast shallots and red wine sauce, and specials like lamb rump with dauphinoise potatoes and aubergine purée or pan-fried tiger scallops and tiger prawns with clams and white crab meat. Some dishes are cheaper at lunchtime. You can usually get something to eat outside the main meal times, and they do afternoon teas. *Starters/Snacks: £4.75 to £8.25. Main Courses: £7.50 to £13.75. Puddings: £4.75 to £6.75*

Free house ~ Licensees David and Sara Sykes ~ Bar food (12-2.30, 6.30-9.30) ~ Restaurant ~ (01993) 813636 ~ Children welcome in bar and restaurant but no under-12s in bedrooms ~ Open 11-11; closed evening 25 Dec ~ Bedrooms: £75S/£140S

Recommended by David Glynne-Jones, Guy Vowles, J and M Taylor, Michael Dandy

LUCKY DIP

Besides the fully inspected pubs, you might like to try these Lucky Dips recommended to us and described by readers (if you do, please send us reports: www.goodguides.co.uk).

ADDERBURY [SP4735]
Plough OX17 3NL [Aynho Rd]: Attractively furnished medieval thatched pub, welcoming cottagey atmosphere and log fire in small L-shaped bar, enjoyable bar lunches from wide choice of sandwiches and baguettes to half a dozen bargain home-made hot dishes, helpful staff, Charles Wells Eagle and Bombardier and a guest beer, good choice of wines by the glass, larger separate restaurant with broad menu; piped music, TV, games; tables outside *(Michael Dandy, E A and D C T Frewer, Helen Rowett)*
☆ *Red Lion* OX17 3NG [The Green; off A4260 S of Banbury]: Attractive and congenial, with three linked bar rooms, big inglenook log fire, panelling, high stripped beams and stonework, old books and Victorian and Edwardian pictures, Greene King ales, good wine range and coffee, helpful friendly staff, daily papers, popular pubby food (all day wknds) from baguettes, ciabattas and baked potatoes to steak, games area on left; piped music; children in eating area, picnic-sets out on new roadside terrace, 12 comfortable bedrooms, open all day summer *(George Atkinson, E A and D C T Frewer, Michael Dandy, Fred Chamberlain, LYM)*
ASHBURY [SU2685]
Rose & Crown SN6 8NA [B4507/B4000; High St]: Relaxing, roomy and comfortable open-plan beamed bistro bar with helpful newish licensees, good sensibly priced food, Arkells 2B and 3B, good range of wines by the glass, highly polished woodwork, traditional pictures, chesterfields, deep armchairs and pews, raised section with further oak tables and chairs, charming roomy restaurant; tables out in front, lovely view down pretty village street of thatched cottages, 11 bedrooms – handy for Ridgeway *(BB, Tony and Tracy Constance, Mike and Mary Wakefield)*

ASTHALL [SP2811]
Maytime OX18 4HW [off A40 at W end of Witney bypass, then 1st left]: Genteel dining pub with good food from sandwiches and snacks up (just set lunch on Sun), good welcoming and helpful service, good wine range, small proper bar with two changing real ales, flagstones and log fire, ironically interesting pictures, slightly raised plush dining lounge neatly set with tables, airy conservatory restaurant with family area; piped music; in tiny hamlet, nice views of Asthall Manor and watermeadows from garden, attractive walks, quiet comfortable bedrooms around pretty courtyard garden *(David Handforth, BB, Stuart Turner)*
BANBURY [SP4540]
Exchange OX16 5LA [High St]: Popular neatly kept Wetherspoons with helpful staff, their usual value-oriented food and beer, family eating area well away from bar; open all day *(Craig Turnbull, Ted George)*
BARNARD GATE [SP4010]
☆ *Boot* OX29 6XE [off A40 E of Witney]: Welcoming and attractive stone-tiled dining pub with enjoyable food from sandwiches up, Brakspears and Hook Norton Best, decent wines, stout standing timbers and stub walls with latticed glass, huge log fire, solid country tables and chairs on bare boards, masses of celebrity footwear, piano; children welcome, tables out in front, open all day wknds *(Bruce and Penny Wilkie, Graham Oddey, LYM)*
BECKLEY [SP5611]
☆ *Abingdon Arms* OX3 9UU [signed off B4027; High St]: Interesting old pub in unspoilt village with good food from sandwiches to nicely presented main dishes inc some imaginative things, friendly bustling staff, Brakspears, good value wines, bare boards, lots of beams and stripped stone, two real fires, a variety of seating inc pews, board

games, separate dining room; extensive pretty garden dropping away from floodlit terrace to orchard with superb views over RSPB Otmoor reserve – good walks *(Brian Root, Peter and Anne Hollindale, David Morgan, LYM, Colin McKerrow)*

BINFIELD HEATH [SU7479]

☆ *Bottle & Glass* RG9 4JT [off A4155 at Shiplake; between village and Harpsden]: Chocolate-box thatched black and white timbered Tudor cottage with emphasis on good value food from sandwiches up, bleached pine tables, low beams and flagstones, fine fireplace, black squared panelling, Brakspears and Wychwood, good choice of wines by the glass, shove-ha'penny, dominoes; no children or dogs inside; lovely big garden with tables under little thatched roofs *(the Didler, Rebecca Knight, LYM)*

BLADON [SP4414]

White House OX20 1RW [Park St (A4095)]: Relaxed and cheerful pub opp church where Churchill is buried, good value traditional home-made food all day inc low-priced Sun roast, Greene King ales, good young lively staff, endearing mix of old tables and chairs in long bar with individual old-fashioned décor and ceiling bric-a-brac, rocking chair by good log fire; darts, weekly quiz, occasional live music; tables outside (those round the side are quieter), aunt sally, handy for back gate of Blenheim Park (beautiful right-of-way walk) *(E A and D C T Frewer)*

BLEWBURY [SU5385]

Red Lion OX11 9PQ [Nottingham Fee – narrow turning N from A417]: Attractive downland village pub under welcoming landlords, enjoyable honest food, well kept Brakspears and a guest beer, beams, tiled floor and big log fire, cribbage, dominoes, no piped music or machines, restaurant (children allowed); terrace tables in quiet back garden, pretty surroundings *(Ray J Carter, LYM, C Harris, William Goodhart)*

BLOXHAM [SP4235]

☆ *Joiners Arms* OX15 4LY [off A361; Old Bridge Rd]: Good relaxed pubby feel in series of rambling, attractively refurbished rooms, mix of traditional and more unusual light furnishings, big stone fireplace, careful spotlighting, exposed well in floor of high-raftered back room (with TV), above-average all-day food inc interesting blackboard specials, good fish and bargain Tues night steaks in bar or restaurant (on several levels), good welcoming service, Brakspears and Theakstons Best, various coffees, good choice of wines; fire-door disabled access from car park, several appealing outside areas – the nicest down some steps by a stream, with picnic-sets and heater, open all day *(BB, Keith and Sue Ward)*

Red Lion OX15 0SJ [High St (A361)]: Comfortable beamed pub under new ownership, good choice of reasonably priced food in bar and dining area, friendly

efficient service, good range of wines by the glass, open fire; children welcome, picnic-sets in attractive garden *(Mr and Mrs A G Terry)*

BOARS HILL [SP4901]

Fox OX1 5DR [between A34 and B4017; Fox Lane]: Well run and attractive Chef & Brewer in pretty wooded countryside, comfortable and spacious, with interesting rambling rooms on different levels, huge log fireplaces, prompt service, wide choice of generous reasonably priced food, well kept ales, decent wine, polite service, day's paper framed in gents'; may be soft piped classical music or jazz; children welcome, pleasant raised verandah, charming big sloping garden with play area, open all day *(anon)*

BODICOTE [SP4637]

Plough OX15 4BZ [Goose Lane/High St; off A4260 S of Banbury]: Pleasantly refurbished 14th-c pub with low heavy beams, stripped stone and small open fire, well kept Wadworths ales, good value simple lunches, good service and friendly locals; darts, TV and games machine in public bar *(J R Ringrose, BB, the Didler)*

BRIGHTWELL BALDWIN [SU6594]

Lord Nelson OX49 5NP [off B480 Chalgrove—Watlington, or B4009 Benson—Watlington]: Civilised dining pub with wide range of enjoyable and generous if not cheap food esp duck and game, stylish décor, careful lighting, dining chairs around invitingly big candlelit tables, nice silverware, pleasant staff, real ales and decent house wines, good log fires, snug armchair area, plenty of Nelson memorabilia; service may slow on busy Sundays; children and dogs welcome, front verandah, charming back garden *(Di and Mike Gillam, LYM, Peter and Giff Bennett)*

BUCKLAND [SU3497]

Lamb SN7 8QN [off A420 NE of Faringdon]: Smart 18th-c stone-built dining pub with popular food (not Mon) from lunchtime special deals to grander and more expensive evening menus, Hook Norton Best, good choice of wines by the glass, lamb motif everywhere, formal restaurant; piped music, service can sometimes slow; children welcome, pleasant tree-shaded garden, good walks nearby, comfortable bedrooms, cl Sun evening and over Christmas/New Year *(Pat and Roger Davies, Sue Demont, Tim Barrow, Philip and June Caunt, Hon Richard Godber, LYM, Alan and Carolin Tidbury, the Didler)*

BUCKNELL [SP5525]

☆ *Trigger Pond* OX27 7NE [handy for M40 junction 10; Bicester Rd]: Neatly kept stone-built pub opp the pond, good range of enjoyable sensibly priced food from sandwiches up (must book Sun lunch), welcoming atmosphere, particularly helpful staff and friendly young licensee happy to try 'off menu' requests, full Wadworths beer range, good value wines, restaurant; colourful terrace and garden *(John and*

Joyce Snell, E A and D C T Frewer, Trevor and Judith Pearson)

BURCOT [SU5695]

Chequers OX14 3DP [A415 Dorchester—Abingdon]: Attractive thatched pub thoroughly reworked by new owners as neat dining pub with contemporary black and white décor, leather sofas around big log fire, welcoming service, enjoyable food from lunchtime sandwiches and other pubby dishes up, good wine range; children welcome, wheelchair access, tables out on floodlit terrace and on lawn among flowers and fruit trees *(LYM, Paul Jacobs)*

BURFORD [SP2512]

Angel OX18 4SN [Witney St]: New landlord for long heavy-beamed dining pub in attractive ancient building, good brasserie food; three comfortable bedrooms *(LYM, Mr and Mrs M Pattinson)*

Cotswold Arms OX18 4QF [High St]: Cosy bar and larger back dining area, wide choice of enjoyable pubby food from baguettes and ploughman's to steak, Courage Best and Theakstons XB, pleasant staff, beautiful stonework, two flame-effect stoves; tables out in front and in back garden *(Michael Dandy, K Turner, Ian Phillips)*

Golden Pheasant OX18 4QA [High St]: Small early 18th-c hotel under new management, settees, armchairs, well spaced tables and warm woodburner in flagstoned split-level bar, reasonably priced food from sandwiches up, well kept Greene King ales, good house wines, pleasant if not always speedy service, back dining room down some steps; children welcome, pleasant back terrace, open all day *(Rona Murdoch, C and R Bromage, Sue Hiscock, Maureen and Keith Gimson, E McCall, T McLean, D Irving, R Huggins, Guy Vowles, BB, Ian Phillips, Michael Dandy, Peter and Jan Humphreys)*

Lamb OX18 4LR [Sheep St (B4425)]: 16th-c stone-built inn well worth a visit for its broad flagstones, polished oak boards and fine log fireplace – one of the nicest pub buildings around, with a lovely suntrap garden, too; but no longer a consistently top value choice for food, drinks or service; children welcome, open all day *(the Didler, R Halsey, LYM, Carol Mills, Susan and Nigel Wilson, Penny Sheppard, E McCall, T McLean, D Irving, R Huggins, Michael Dandy, Ian Phillips, P R Waights, Paul and Shirley White, David Glynne-Jones, Mr and Mrs M Pattinson, Nick and Meriel Cox)*

Mermaid OX18 4QF [High St]: Handsome jettied Tudor dining pub with beams, flagstones, panelling and stripped stone, good log fire, well kept if not cheap Greene King ales, lots of wines by the glass, nice winter mulled wine, enjoyable sensibly priced food from lunchtime baguettes up, good fresh veg, prompt service, bay seating around row of close-set tables on the left, further airy back dining room and upstairs restaurant; piped music, games machine; children in eating areas, picnic-sets under

cocktail parasols outside, open all day *(Mike and Mary Carter, K Turner, LYM, Stuart Turner, Guy Vowles, Dr Phil Putwain)*

Old Bull OX18 4RG [High St]: Handsome building well reconstructed in the 1980s with beams, panelling and big fireplaces, then smartly refurbished in wine bar/bistro style, comfortable seating and open fire, steps down to further eating area, restaurant behind, good friendly service, Greene King ales, decent wines, wide choice of usual food from sandwiches up; piped music; children welcome, open all day, tables out in front or back through old coach entry, comfortable bedrooms *(Michael Dandy, C and R Bromage, LYM)*

☆ *Royal Oak* OX18 4SN [Witney St]: Relaxed and homely 17th-c stripped stone local, an oasis in this smart village, with long-serving friendly landlord, Wadworths from central servery, good range of generous good value food using local produce from filled rolls up, good service, over a thousand beer mugs and steins hanging from beams, antlers over big log fire (underfloor heating too), some comfortable sofas as well as pine tables, chairs and benches on flagstones, more in carpeted back room with bar billiards; terrace tables, sensibly priced bedrooms off garden behind *(Pete Baker, Stuart Turner, Michael Dandy, Revd R P Tickle, Ian Phillips, Ted George)*

CHADLINGTON [SP3222]

☆ *Tite* OX7 3NY [off A361 S of Chipping Norton, and B4437 W of Charlbury; Mill End, slightly out of village – at garage turn towards Churchill, then left at playground]: Lovely traditional local with big log fire in huge fireplace, settles, wooden chairs, prints, rack of guide books, daily papers, small vine-covered back restaurant, superb garden full of shrubs, some quite unusual, with stream running under pub, good walks nearby. Has been popular under its cheerful long-serving licensees for good home-made food, great choice of real ales, good house wines and farm cider, but they were retiring and selling as we went to press – news please *(BB)*

CHARLBURY [SP3519]

☆ *Bell* OX7 3PP [Church St]: Attractive civilised two-room bar in small olde-worlde 17th-c hotel, welcoming and relaxed, flagstones, stripped stonework and huge inglenook log fire, good bar lunches (not Sun) from sandwiches to short choice of imaginative dishes, friendly attentive service, Greene King and a guest ale, good value wines, wide choice of malt whiskies, pleasant restaurant; children welcome in eating area, dogs in bar, pleasant garden tables, comfortable quiet bedrooms, good breakfast *(Diana Campbell, E A and D C T Frewer, LYM, Sue Hiscock, George Atkinson)*

CHESTERTON [SP5521]

Red Cow OX26 1UU [The Green]: Comfortably updated softly lit traditional local with beams, brasses, old photographs, two log fires, lunchtime food from baguettes and ciabattas to good value hot dishes, Greene King ales, good coffee, small dining area; picnic-sets out under cocktail parasols *(E A and D C T Frewer)*

CHIPPING NORTON [SP3127]

Blue Boar OX7 5NP [High St/Goddards Lane]: Spacious and cheerful two-bar stone-built pub divided by arches and pillars, wide choice of sensibly priced food at separate servery from sandwiches and baked potatoes to generous Sun roasts, Greene King IPA and Ruddles and Hook Norton, beamed back restaurant by long light and airy flagstoned dining conservatory; piped pop music, games machines; children welcome, open all day Sat *(Michael Dandy, Keith and Sue Ward)*

Crown & Cushion OX7 5AD [High St]: Attractive and relaxed compact bar at the back of handsome old-fashioned 16th-c hotel, log fire, beams, some stripped stone and flagstones, Greene King IPA and Ruddles County and Hook Norton Old Hooky, good coffee, wide choice of bar food, flower-decked conservatory; children welcome, tables in sheltered suntrap courtyard, good bedrooms *(LYM, Michael Dandy)*

Fox OX7 5DD [Market Pl]: Well placed unpretentious pub with lots of pictures and open fire in quiet lounge, well kept Hook Norton ales, good coffee, simple inexpensive bar food, welcoming landlord, upstairs dining room; children and dogs welcome, good value bedrooms *(LYM, Chris Glasson)*

CHISLEHAMPTON [SU5998]

Coach & Horses OX44 7UX [B480 Oxford—Watlington, opp B4015 to Abingdon]: Extended former 16th-c coaching inn with two beamed bars, homely and civilised, and sizeable restaurant (polished oak tables and wall banquettes); good choice of well prepared food from baguettes and good ploughman's to game specials, friendly obliging service, well kept ales inc Flowers and Hook Norton, big log fire; piped music; neat terraced gardens overlooking fields by River Thame, some tables out in front, motel-style bedrooms in separate block in back courtyard *(BB, Roy Hoing)*

CHOLSEY [SU5985]

Morning Star OX10 9QL [Papist Way]: Neatly kept 20th-c brick-built local with welcoming new landlord and family, wide choice of reasonably priced pubby food, back conservatory; picnic-sets under cocktail parasols on sheltered back terrace *(Rob)*

CHRISTMAS COMMON [SU7193]

Fox & Hounds OX49 5HL [off B480/B481]: Upmarket Chilterns pub in lovely countryside, emphasis on airy and spacious front barn restaurant and conservatory with interesting food from open kitchen (no food, not even crisps, for 'walk-ins' if they're busy with restaurant bookings), Brakspears and Wychwood, proper coffee, two compact beamed rooms simply but comfortably furnished, bow windows, red and black tiles

and big inglenook, snug little back room; children and dogs welcome, rustic benches and tables outside, open all day wknds *(Dr and Mrs R E S Tanner, the Didler, LYM, Fred and Kate Portnell)*

CHURCH ENSTONE [SP3725]

☆ *Crown* OX7 4NN [Mill Lane; from A44 take B4030 turn off at Enstone]: Popular and attractive old pub, smart and uncluttered, with congenial bar, good enterprising fresh food (not Mon night) from tasty lunchtime baguettes to good Sun lunch, friendly staff, Hook Norton Best, Shepherd Neame Spitfire and Wychwood Hobgoblin, decent wines by the glass, log fire in brass-fitted stone fireplace, beams, stripped stone and sisal matting, good-sized light modern dining area and roomy conservatory; may be piped music, may be cl Mon lunchtime; garden tables *(Stuart Turner, Dave Lowe, Pam Adsley, Mrs M B Gregg, Richard Marjoram, Guy Vowles, LYM)*

CHURCH HANBOROUGH [SP4212]

Hand & Shears OX29 8AB [opp church; signed off A4095 at Long Hanborough, or off A40 at Eynsham roundabout]: Open-feeling bistro-style pub with long gleaming bar, sofa one end, steps down into roomy back eating area, another small dining room, good value generous fresh food from plenty of sandwiches and light dishes up, Hook Norton ales, open fires *(E A and D C T Frewer, BB)*

CRAWLEY [SP3412]

☆ *Lamb* OX29 9TW [Steep Hill; just NW of Witney]: Comfortably extended 17th-c stone-built pub with unspoilt old beamed bar with lovely fireplace and cricket bats above counter, steps to candlelit dining room, wide choice of well liked food from baguettes and usual dishes to interesting specials, good choice of wines by the glass, well kept ales such as Brakspears and Wychwood Hobgoblin, quick and very helpful, friendly service; views from tables on terraced lawn behind, pretty village, good walks – on new Palladian Way *(Guy Vowles, Brenda and Stuart Naylor, Richard Atherton, Richard Marjoram, BB)*

CRAYS POND [SU6380]

White Lion RG8 7SH [B471 nr junction with B4526, about 3 miles E of Goring]: Welcoming low-ceilinged pub popular for enjoyable food from fresh baguettes to restaurant dishes esp fish, good value wknd lunches, well kept beer, good wine choice, relaxed casual atmosphere with proper front bar, hands-on licensees and friendly attentive service, open fire, attractive conservatory; big garden with play area, lovely countryside *(Paul Suter, Rob Winstanley, I H G Busby)*

CROPREDY [SP4646]

Red Lion OX17 1PB [off A423 N of Banbury]: Rambling old thatched stone-built pub charmingly placed opp pretty village's churchyard, enjoyable food from sandwiches and baguettes to good value Sun lunch (two rooms set for eating), low beams, inglenook log fire, high-backed settles, brass, plates and pictures, friendly staff, changing ales such as Greene King IPA, Marstons Pedigree, Oxfordshire Marshmellow and Shepherd Neame Spitfire, games room; piped music, limited parking; children allowed in dining part, picnic-sets under cocktail parasols on back terrace by car park (*George Atkinson, Simon Jones, LYM, Mr and Mrs B A R Frost, Bob and Laura Brock, Charles and Pauline Stride*)

CUDDESDON [SP5902]

Bat & Ball OX44 9HJ [S of Wheatley; High St]: Civilised pub full of all sorts of interesting cricketing memorabilia, low beams, some flagstones, Banks's LBW, Marstons Pedigree and a guest beer, decent wines, friendly attentive young staff, big dining extension; cribbage, dominoes, piped music; children welcome, pleasant back terrace with good views, aunt sally, comfortable annexe bedrooms (some small), open all day (*Paul Humphreys, LYM, Brian Root, Roy Hoing*)

CUMNOR [SP4604]

Vine OX2 9QN [Abingdon Rd]: Cosy and welcoming beamed pub with wide choice of good value unpretentious food from baguettes and light dishes up, real ales such as Hook Norton Old Hooky and Wells & Youngs Bombardier, back dining area and conservatory, games room with darts and pool; occasional live music; well behaved children and dogs welcome, picnic-sets in attractive back garden with aunt sally, open all day (*David Howe, Robert Garner*)

DEDDINGTON [SP4631]

☆ *Deddington Arms* OX15 0SH [off A4260 (B4031) Banbury—Oxford; Horse Fair]: Beamed and timbered hotel with emphasis on sizeable back eating area, contemporary furniture on stripped wood and much ochre paintwork, friendly attentive young staff, pleasant bar with mullioned windows, good log fire, real ales such as Jennings Cumberland and Tetleys, good choice of wines by the glass; unobtrusive piped music; open all day, comfortable chalet bedrooms around courtyard, good breakfast, attractive village with lots of antiques shops and good farmers' market 4th Sat (*Mr and Mrs John Taylor, Trevor and Judith Pearson, LYM, Michael Dandy, Hugh Spottiswoode, P and J Shapley, George Atkinson*)

☆ *Unicorn* OX15 0SE [Market Pl]: Cheerful 17th-c inn run by helpful mother and daughter, good value generous food (not Sun evening) from sandwiches and baked potatoes to plenty of fish in L-shaped bar and beamed dining areas off, Hook Norton and Fullers London Pride, good choice of wines by the glass, proper coffee, daily papers, inglenook fireplace, pub games; dogs welcome in bar, cobbled courtyard leading to lovely walled back garden, open all day (from 9 for good 4th Sat farmers' market), good bedrooms (*Michael Dandy, BB, Trevor and Judith Pearson*)

DIDCOT [SU5290]

Broadways OX11 8RG [Broadway]: Town local worth knowing by day for good value pubby food all day inc OAP and early evening bargains, Fullers London Pride and John Smiths, friendly staff, daily papers; can get more lively evenings, karaoke or DJs Thurs-Sat (*Roy Sanders*)

DORCHESTER [SU5794]

Fleur de Lys OX10 7HH [High St]: Former coaching inn opp abbey, dating from 16th c, traditional two-level interior, wide choice of food inc imaginative dishes, well kept Greene King ales, interesting old photographs of the pub; children welcome, picnic-sets on front terrace and in back garden (*Alan and Carolin Tidbury, I H G Busby*)

DUCKLINGTON [SP3507]

☆ *Bell* OX29 7UP [off A415, a mile SE of Witney; Standlake Rd]: Pretty thatched local with wide choice of generous good value home-made food (not Sun eve) inc particularly good sandwiches, Greene King ales, good house wines, friendly service; big stripped stone and flagstoned bar with scrubbed tables, log fires, glass-covered well, old local photographs, farm tools, hatch-served public bar, roomy and attractive well laid out back restaurant, its beams festooned with bells; cards and dominoes, no piped music; small garden behind with play area, colourful hanging baskets, nine bedrooms (*BB, Pete Baker*)

EAST HENDRED [SU4588]

Plough OX12 8JW [off A417 E of Wantage; Orchard Lane]: Big beamed village pub with friendly helpful staff, wide blackboard range of enjoyable food, well kept Greene King ale, usual public bar and airy and lofty-raftered main room, interesting farming and wartime memorabilia; piped music, big-screen TV; pleasant garden with good play area, attractive village (*Harvey Smith, BB*)

Wheatsheaf OX12 8JN [signed off A417; Chapel Sq]: Attractive 16th-c black and white timbered village pub with big inglenook log fire in quarry-tiled bar, other cosy rooms off, well kept ales, enjoyable interesting food, restaurant; tables in colourful back garden, open all day wknds (*LYM, Mark and Ruth Brock*)

ENSLOW [SP4818]

Rock of Gibraltar OX5 3AY [A4095 about 1½ miles SW of Kirtlington]: Tall friendly pub with fresh tasty reasonably priced food, good service, three real ales such as Hook Norton, beams, stripped stone, bright narrowboat paintwork, modern dining extension overlooking Oxford Canal, upper conservatory with even better view; popular Thurs folk night; dogs welcome, lots of picnic-sets under cocktail parasols in pretty waterside garden (*Pete Baker, Chris Glasson, R S Jalbot*)

EWELME [SU6491]

Shepherds Hut OX10 6HQ [off B4009 about 6 miles SW of M40 junction 6; High St]: New management doing good choice of fair-priced generous food in cheery unpretentious country local, Greene King and guest ales, decent coffee, small restaurant; big-screen sports TV; children welcome, small pleasant garden with terrace and barbecues, open all day *(Geoff and Teresa Salt, BB, David Glynne-Jones, David Lamb)*

EYNSHAM [SP4309]

Queens Head OX29 4HH [Queen St]: Nice old two-bar village pub with good friendly service, simple food inc splendid basic hot lunchtime sandwiches, well kept beer inc regular guests *(David Handforth)*

FEWCOTT [SP5327]

White Lion OX27 7NZ [a mile from M40 junction 10, via B430 then 1st right; Fritwell Rd]: Cosy village local with four changing real ales from small breweries; children welcome, open all day wknds, cl wkdy lunchtimes and Sun evening *(Roger Shipperley)*

FILKINS [SP2304]

Five Alls GL7 3JQ [signed off A361 Lechlade—Burford]: Big 18th-c cotswold stone pub doing well under current friendly licensees, relaxed local atmosphere, enjoyable home-made traditional food, well kept Brakspears and a guest beer, decent house wines, beams, flagstones, stripped stone and good log fire, settees, armchairs and rugs on polished boards, good-sized eating areas; quiz and theme nights; plenty of tables on terrace and neat lawns, five good bedrooms, nice village *(BB, Graham Oddey)*

FINSTOCK [SP3616]

☆ *Plough* OX7 3BY [just off B4022 N of Witney; High St]: Rambling thatched and low-beamed village pub gently smartened up, long divided bar with welcoming log fire in massive stone inglenook, good food brought out by chef, well kept ales such as Adnams, Brakspears and Hook Norton, small sensibly priced choice of decent wines, pleasant service, stripped-stone dining room; children welcome, sizeable garden with old-fashioned roses and aunt sally, good walks *(S Crowe, Mr and Mrs J C Cetti, Chris Glasson, LYM, Stuart Turner)*

FREELAND [SP4112]

Oxfordshire Yeoman OX29 8AQ [Wroslyn Rd]: Friendly and cosy village local with reasonably priced home-made food, real ale, open fire and low ceilings; pleasant small garden *(Helene Grygar)*

FRINGFORD [SP6028]

Butchers Arms OX27 8EB [off A421 N of Bicester]: Picturesque and comfortably furnished rambling village pub with good service, wide choice of generous pubby food from sandwiches and ciabattas up, Adnams Broadside, Caledonian Deuchars IPA and Marstons Pedigree, good soft drinks choice, darts and TV in L-shaped bar, separate smaller dining room; tables out under parasols facing village green *(E A and D C T Frewer, Michael Dandy)*

FRITWELL [SP5229]

Kings Head OX27 7QF [quite handy for M40

junction 10; East St]: Well run pub in small village, welcoming landlord, good beer range, generous food in bar and attractive dining room, darts and pool; children welcome *(David Campbell, Vicki McLean)*

GORING [SU5980]

☆ *Catherine Wheel* RG8 9HB [Station Rd]: Smart and well run, with friendly landlord and good informal atmosphere in two neat and cosily traditional bar areas, especially the more individual lower room with its low beams and big inglenook log fireplace; well priced and generous straightforward home-made food inc Tues steak night, Brakspears, Hook Norton and Wychwood ales, Stowford Press cider, decent wine, good coffee; back restaurant (children welcome here), notable door to gents'; nice courtyard and garden behind, handy for Thames Path, attractive village, open all day *(the Didler, Paul Humphreys, Rob Winstanley, BB)*

GOZZARD'S FORD [SU4698]

Black Horse OX13 6JH [off B4017 NW of Abingdon; N of A415 by Marcham—Cothill rd]: Well kept beer, good generous food esp fish and seafood, decent wines, real ales such as Batemans, Caledonian Deuchars IPA and Wells & Youngs Bombardier, cheerful family service, ancient traditional pub in tiny hamlet; nice garden *(William Goodhart)*

GREAT HASELEY [SP6301]

Old Plough OX44 7JQ [handy for M40 junction 7; Rectory Rd]: Small friendly thatched and beamed pub very popular for good inventive food from bar snacks and business lunches to leisurely evening meals (they bake their own bread, too), good wines by the glass, Shepherd Neame Spitfire, friendly helpful staff, buoyant pubby atmosphere with thriving darts and cribbage teams; attractive garden with aunt sally, quiet area *(Tim Lumb)*

HAILEY [SU6485]

☆ *King William IV* OX10 6AD [the Hailey nr Ipsden, off A4074 or A4130 SE of Wallingford]: Outstanding views from attractive 16th-c pub in charming peaceful countryside, some concentration on wide choice of good generous mainly traditional food, friendly landlord and helpful staff, thriving atmosphere, Brakspears and Wychwood ales, beams, bare bricks and tiled floor (carpet in middle room), big inglenook log fire, neat décor and traditional furnishings, extended dining room; tables on front terrace *(the Didler, LYM)*

☆ *Lamb & Flag* OX29 9UB [B4022 a mile N of Witney; Middletown]: Rambling beamed and stone-built 17th-c village pub with plenty of character, some ancient flagstones, woodburner in inglenook fireplace, friendly attentive staff, affordable fresh home cooking, well kept Greene King ales, good choice of wines by the glass and well served coffee, bright lighting, darts; good big well kept family-friendly garden *(E A and D C T Frewer, BB, Keith and Sue Ward)*

HARWELL [SU4988]
Kingswell OX11 0LZ [A417; Reading Rd]:
Substantial hotel with good imaginative bar
food as well as restaurant meals, helpful
staff; comfortable bedrooms
(Henry Midwinter)
HEADINGTON [SP5506]
Masons Arms OX3 8LH [Quarry School Pl]:
Well run open-plan local with Caledonian
Deuchars IPA, St Austell Tribute, two guest
beers and its own Old Bog brews, darts, Sat
quiz night; children welcome, heated outside
seating, aunt sally, cl wkdy lunchtimes, open
all day Sat *(Roger Shipperley)*
HENLEY [SU7682]
☆ *Anchor* RG9 1AH [Friday St]: Not one for
people who like everything just so, but an
individualistic favourite of many others: old-
fashioned, homely and informally run, two
slightly cluttered and nicely lived-in front
rooms, hearty food (not Sun/Mon evenings)
from lunchtime open sandwiches up, well
kept Brakspears ales, good range of malt
whiskies and new world wines by the glass,
friendly chocolate labrador called Ruger,
straight-talking landlady, simple back dining
room (well behaved children allowed here);
charming back terrace, open all day
*(the Didler, Tracey and Stephen Groves,
Anthony Longden, Tim and Ann Newell,
Peter Smith, Judith Brown, Tony and
Tracy Constance, Ian Phillips, Geoff Simms,
Brian P White, LYM)*
Angel on the Bridge RG9 1BH [Thames-side,
by the bridge]: Worth knowing for prime spot
by Thames, with nice waterside deck (plastic
glasses for this), small front bar with open
fire, back bar and adjacent bistro restaurant
with settles, good choice of wines by the
glass, food from sandwiches and usual pubby
lunchtime dishes to midweek meal deals and
more elaborate evening menu, Brakspears
beer; open all day at least in summer
(Michael Dandy, Paul Humphreys)
HIGHMOOR [SU7084]
☆ *Dog & Duck* RG9 5DL [B481]: Appealing
country pub settling down well under new
landlord, helpful friendly staff, good log fires
in small beamed bar and not much larger
flagstoned dining room with old prints and
pictures, family room leading off, careful
choice of good value traditional food,
Brakspears ales, good choice of wines by the
glass, welcoming service; children and dogs
welcome, attractive long garden with some
play equipment and small sheep paddock,
plenty of surrounding walks *(Mrs M Phythian,
LYM, the Didler)*
HOOK NORTON [SP3533]
Pear Tree OX15 5NU [Scotland End]: Well
worn in village pub with full Hook Norton
beer range kept well from nearby brewery,
country wines, usual bar food (not Sun
evening) from doorstep sandwiches and baked
potatoes up, knocked-together bar area with
country-kitchen furniture, good log fire, daily
papers and magazines; TV; children and dogs
welcome, sizeable attractive garden with

outdoor chess, wendy house and play area,
bedrooms, open all day *(Chris Glasson, P Rose,
LYM, Dennis Jenkin, K H Frostick, Tom Evans,
Tracey and Stephen Groves)*
☆ *Sun* OX15 5NH [High Street]: Beamed front
bar with huge log fire and flagstones, cosy
carpeted back room leading into attractive
dining room, Hook Norton ales and several
wines by the glass, food from bar snacks
through pubby choices to restaurant meals,
darts and dominoes; young foreign staff, TV;
children and dogs welcome, disabled
facilities, tables out in front and on back
terrace, well equipped bedrooms *(Pete Baker,
Michael Clatworthy, K H Frostick,
Richard Greaves, LYM)*
KELMSCOTT [SU2499]
☆ *Plough* GL7 3HG [NW of Faringdon, off B4449
between A417 and A4095]: Pretty pub in
lovely spot nr upper Thames (good moorings
a few mins' walk away), beams, ancient
flagstones, stripped stone and log fire,
friendly relaxed atmosphere, food (all day
wknds) from sandwiches to often delicious
main dishes, Archers Best, Hook Norton Best,
Timothy Taylors Landlord, and Wychwood
Hobgoblin, Black Rat farm cider, solid
wooden seats in dining room, chocolate
labrador appropriately called Hope; they may
try to keep your credit card while you eat,
and some variation in standards this last
year; children, dogs and booted walkers
welcome, garden with aunt sally, picnic-sets
under cocktail parasols out in front too,
eight good bedrooms, open all day *(LYM,
Dr Paull Khan, Canon Michael Bourdeaux,
David Handforth, Charles and Pauline Stride,
Ian Phillips, Gordon and Jay Smith,
Richard and Sheila Fitton, Ian and
Nita Cooper, Peter and Audrey Dowsett,
Colin Piper, Angus and Rosemary Campbell,
Dr and Mrs M E Wilson)*
KIDLINGTON [SP4914]
Dogwood OX5 1EA [Oxford Rd (A4260)]:
Former Squire Bassett, completely freshened
up in nicely restrained style, decent pubby
food from baguettes and wraps up inc
bargain deals for couples and families, smart
back garden room; children welcome, good-
sized garden with terrace *(David Campbell,
Vicki McLean)*
Kings Arms OX5 2AJ [The Moors, off High St
(not the Harvester out on the Bicester Rd)]:
Friendly local with enjoyable wkdy lunchtime
food from sandwiches up, Greene King IPA
and a couple of other changing ales, homely
lounge, games in proper public bar; children
welcome, courtyard tables with occasional
barbecues, open all day wknds *(Pete Baker)*
KINGHAM [SP2624]
Plough OX7 6YD [The Green]: Prettily set
village-green inn reopened summer 2007
after refurbishment as dining pub by new
young owners, promising plans for bar and
restaurant food using very local supplies
(she's a well schooled chef), even some local
wines; seven bedrooms; more reports please
(anon)

☆ **Tollgate** OX7 6YA [Church St]: Civilised beamed and flagstoned former farmhouse just right for this attractive village, with good choice of well cooked food (not Sun evening or Mon) from lunchtime baguettes and light dishes to restaurant meals inc good if not cheap Sun lunch, Hook Norton and unusual local Cotswold Lager, good wines by the glass, friendly landlord and prompt service, inglenook fires; teak garden tables, nine comfortable bedrooms (Keith and Sue Ward, Guy Vowles)

KIRTLINGTON [SP4919]

Dashwood OX5 3HJ [South Green]: Former Dashwood Arms village pub carefully remodelled and upgraded as contemporary restaurant-with-rooms, clean, cool and bright, with enjoyable food (not Sun evening); 12 comfortable and stylish bedrooms (Richard Marjoram)

Oxford Arms OX5 3HA [Troy Lane]: Oak-beamed pub popular for enjoyable generous if not cheap food from proper sandwiches and imaginative starters to traditional english main dishes, charming young staff, good reasonably priced wines by the large glass, Hook Norton Best and two other ales from congenial central bar with small standing area, leather settees and open fire one end, separate dining room; small sunny back garden (Colin and Ruth Munro, E A and D C T Frewer)

LEAFIELD [SP3215]

☆ **Navy Oak** OX29 9QQ [Lower End]: Roomy and elegant dining areas with sight of enthusiastic chef/landlord preparing short choice of good food, stylish relaxing bar with grandfather clock, exposed stonework, dark wooden tables, magazines to read, and brown leather sofas around big fireplace, good service by friendly landlady and staff, well kept Hook Norton beers, good choice of wines; piped easy listening music; children welcome away from bar (BB, Brenda and Stuart Naylor, Richard Greaves, David and Susan Hancock)

LONG HANBOROUGH [SP4214]

George & Dragon OX29 8JX [Main Rd (A4095 Bladon—Witney)]: Enjoyable generous food, friendly efficient staff, three real ales, modern thatched dining extension to 18th-c or older core (originally a low-beamed farm building); children welcome (Tim Venn)

LONG WITTENHAM [SU5493]

Plough OX14 4QH [High St]: Friendly refurbished pub with well kept Greene King ales, good value wines by the glass and coffee, good service, decent food (all day wknds, OAP bargains Mon-Thurs lunchtimes), low beams and lots of brass, inglenook log fires, dining room, games in public bar; dogs welcome, Thames moorings at bottom of long spacious garden with aunt sally, bedrooms (Chris Glasson, Lynne Carter)

LOWER HEYFORD [SP4824]

☆ **Bell** OX25 5NY [Market Sq]: Good range of generous enjoyable food freshly cooked to order inc popular specials and several elaborate ice-cream concoctions (it's welcoming to children), in pleasantly refurbished rooms around central beamed bar; charming creeper-clad building in small village square of thatched cottages, cheerful helpful staff, real ales such as Adnams and Wells & Youngs, good coffees inc flavoured lattes; disabled facilities, nice long lawned garden with aunt sally, nearby Oxford Canal walks (Trevor and Judith Pearson, Meg and Colin Hamilton, K H Frostick, BB)

MIDDLETON STONEY [SP5323]

☆ **Jersey Arms** OX25 4AD [Ardley Rd (B430/B4030)]: Small 19th-c stone-built hotel with nicely countrified bow-windowed bar, beams, oak flooring and some stripped stone, attractive tables, sofa and daily papers, good inglenook log fire, home-made fresh food from well filled baguettes up (sandwiches too if you ask), friendly owner and staff, good range of wines and spirits, good coffee, Bass or Wadworths 6X, attractive two-level dining room; piped music, TV, car park across road; tables in courtyard and garden, comfortable bedrooms (BB, Cathryn and Richard Hicks, E A and D C T Frewer, Michael Dandy, Barry Steele-Perkins)

MILCOMBE [SP4034]

Horse & Groom OX15 4RS [off A361 SW of Banbury]: Cheerful and hard-working new landlord doing reasonably priced generous fresh food with real ales such as Hook Norton, Wychwood Hobgoblin and Wells & Youngs, settee and inglenook woodburner in appealing low-beamed and flagstoned bar, back restaurant; children welcome, lots of picnic-sets out in front, bedrooms, handy for Wigginton Heath waterfowl and animal centre (Keith and Sue Ward, BB, George Atkinson)

MILTON [SP4535]

☆ **Black Boy** OX15 4HH [off Bloxham Rd; the one nr Adderbury]: Neatly refurbished dining pub with good comfortable furnishings, but still plenty of oak beams, exposed stonework, flagstones, and a lovely big inglenook; most tables set for the enjoyable and affordable home-made food, friendly licensees, good service, Greene King Ruddles, daily papers, some cricket memorabilia, candlelit restaurant; piped music; dogs welcome in bar, tables in garden beyond car park, with plenty of space (some traffic noise), heaters and aunt sally (Chris Glasson, BB)

MINSTER LOVELL [SP3111]

New Inn OX29 0RZ [Burford Rd]: Handsomely rebuilt and extended as rewarding pub/restaurant with enjoyable food from antipasti, lunchtime sandwiches and light dishes to major meals, good choice of wines by the glass, Hook Norton and Wadworths 6X, friendly efficient service, tremendous views over pretty Windrush Valley; children welcome, tables on big heated terrace, lovely setting (Sarah and Peter Gooderham, David Glynne-Jones, Mrs Ann Gray)

MURCOTT [SP5815]

☆ **Nut Tree** OX5 2RE [off B4027 NE of Oxford]: Charming open-plan beamed and thatched medieval building brightened up inside by gifted new chef/landlord, a real boost to the food side with some exciting choices, good deep flavours and interesting veg (they now keep their own pigs on a nearby farm), still a nice pubby feel with log fire, real ales inc Hook Norton, good reasonably priced wines by the glass, neat friendly young staff, small back conservatory-style restaurant; pretty garden with terrace, pond and aunt sally, bedrooms (Dr R H Wilkinson, Mrs Jane-Ann Jones, Chris Smith, LYM, E A and D C T Frewer, Mr and Mrs J C Cetti, Jenny and Peter Lowater)

NEWBRIDGE [SP4001]

☆ **Rose Revived** OX29 7QD [A415 7 miles S of Witney]: Roomy and well reworked pub with comfortable settees, attractive prints and photographs, central log-effect fire between two dining areas, beamed side areas, reliably enjoyable food from good soup and sandwiches up all day (can take a while if they're busy), cheerful and patient young staff, Greene King ales, good coffee; some live music; children welcome, lovely big lawn by the upper Thames, prettily lit at night (good overnight mooring free), unobtrusive play area, comfortable bedrooms (Dick and Madeleine Brown, Meg and Colin Hamilton, Peter Smith, Judith Brown, Charles and Pauline Stride, LYM, David Handforth, George Atkinson)

NORTH HINKSEY [SP4905]

Fishes OX2 0NA [off A420 just E of A34 ring road; N Hinksey Lane, then pass church into cul de sac signed to Rugby club]: Comfortable Victorian-style open-plan lounge and pleasant family conservatory, good choice of good value food (not Sun evening) inc some imaginative dishes and innovative picnic baskets, friendly staff, well kept ales, decent house wines, traditional games; piped music; big streamside garden with good play area and two aunt sally pitches (Henry Midwinter)

NORTH NEWINGTON [SP4139]

Blinking Owl OX15 6AE [Main St]: Relaxing ivy-covered stone-built village local, well kept Bass and Hook Norton, cheery helpful landlord, good choice of food (not Mon) freshly made by landlady inc good value sandwiches, beams, sturdy tables and some sofas in long beamed bar, log fire usually through till June, small family dining area; piped music; back garden, two bedrooms (Paul Humphreys)

NUFFIELD [SU6787]

☆ **Crown** RG9 5SJ [A4130/B481]: Attractive small country pub with enjoyable unpretentious but interesting food from sandwiches up, reasonable prices, cheerful helpful staff, well kept Brakspears, good house wines, simple country furniture and inglenook log fire in beamed lounge bar; walkers welcome (good walks nearby),

children in small family room, pleasant garden with tables outside front and back (John Roots, Howard Dell, LYM, Bruce Horne, David Lamb, Roy Hoing)

OXFORD [SP5007]

Anchor OX2 6TT [Hayfield Rd]: New licensees putting a lot of thought into their interesting reasonably priced food using local supplies, friendly efficient service, good value house wine, period furnishings, log fire, separate dining area (Vivien Lewsey)

☆ **Bear** OX1 4EH [Alfred St/Wheatsheaf Alley]: Two charming little low-ceilinged and partly panelled 16th-c rooms, not over-smart and often packed with students, thousands of vintage ties on walls and beams, simple reasonably priced lunchtime food most days inc sandwiches, four well kept changing real ales from centenarian handpumps on pewter bar counter, no games machines; upstairs ladies'; tables outside, open all day summer (LYM, Tim and Ann Newell, Tracey and Stephen Groves, E McCall, T McLean, D Irving, R Huggins, the Didler, Sapna Thottathil, Michael Dandy)

Bookbinders Arms OX2 6BT [Victor St]: Mellow little local, friendly and unpretentious, with good range of well kept ales, reasonably priced simple food, free peanuts, masses of interesting bric-a-brac, darts, cards and shove ha'penny (Gwyn Jones, Len Beattie)

☆ **Eagle & Child** OX1 3LU [St Giles]: Attractive panelled front bar, compact mid-bars full of actors' and Tolkien/C S Lewis memorabilia, tasteful stripped-brick modern back dining extension with conservatory, friendly service, bargain range of pubby food from sandwiches up, Brakspears, Caledonian Deuchars IPA, Fullers London Pride and Hook Norton, good choice of wines by the glass, newspapers, events posters; piped music, busy at lunchtime, no dogs; open all day (the Didler, BB, Michael Dandy, Revd R P Tickle, Dick and Madeleine Brown, Roger Shipperley, Sapna Thottathil, Chris Glasson)

Gardeners Arms OX2 6JE [1st left after Horse & Jockey going N up Woodstock Rd]: Relaxed local and University atmosphere and nice mix of furnishings in chatty open-plan panelled bar, good filling home-made vegetarian food at appealing prices (appealing tastes too, even for carnivores), friendly staff, several well kept changing ales such as Hook Norton and Timothy Taylors Landlord, farm cider; children welcome in back room, tables outside (LYM, Sapna Thottathil)

Harcourt Arms OX2 6DG [Cranham Terr]: Friendly local with proper landlord and some character, pillars dividing it, good value snacks, Fullers ales, two log fires, good choice of board games, well reproduced piped jazz (P S Hoyle, Sapna Thottathil)

Head of the River OX1 4LB [Folly Bridge; between St Aldates and Christchurch Meadow]: Civilised well renovated pub by river, boats for hire and nearby walks; split-level downstairs bar with dividing brick arches, flagstones and bare boards, Fullers ales inc HSB, good choice of wines by the glass, popular pubby food from sandwiches up inc some contemporary dishes, daily papers; piped music, games machines; tables on big heated waterside terrace, bedrooms *(Michael Dandy)*

☆ *Kings Arms* OX1 3SP [Holywell St]: Bustling 16th-c pub with Wells & Youngs and guest beers such as Everards, fine choice of wines by the glass, cosy comfortably worn in partly panelled side and back rooms, daily papers, relaxed atmosphere; children in all-day eating area with counter servery doing usual food (all day wknds) from sandwiches up, a few tables outside, open all day *(Peter Dandy, LYM, the Didler, P S Hoyle, Simon Jones, Pat and Tony Martin, Dave Lowe, Michael Dandy)*

Lamb & Flag OX1 3JS [St Giles/Banbury Rd]: Old pub owned by nearby college, modern airy front room with big windows over street, more atmosphere in back rooms with exposed stonework and low panelled ceilings, changing ales such as Palmers Best and a beer they brew for the pub (L&F Gols), Shepherd Neame Spitfire, Skinners Betty Stogs and Theakstons Old Peculier, good value well served lunchtime food from baguettes and baked potatoes to choice of suet puddings, cheerful service; can be a pain at night *(Michael Dandy, David Campbell, Vicki McLean, Roger Shipperley, Sapna Thottathil)*

Perch OX2 0NG [narrow lane on right just before MFI, leaving city on A420]: This beautifully set nice pub suffered a bad fire in May 2007; we look forward to its rebuilding, which will be a long and complex job, and in the mean time hope that its summer bar for the dozens of outside tables (and good robust play area) may function through the summer; news please *(LYM)*

Royal Oak OX2 6HT [Woodstock Rd, opp Radcliffe Infirmary]: Maze of little rooms meandering around central bar, low beams, simple furnishings, wide and interesting range of beers on tap and in bottle inc belgian imports, lunchtime food bar, daily papers, open fire, prints and bric-a-brac, games room with darts, pool etc; piped music; small back terrace, open all day *(Sapna Thottathil)*

☆ *Watermans Arms* OX2 0BE [South St, Osney (off A420 Botley Rd via Bridge St)]: Tidy and unpretentious riverside local tucked away nr Osney Lock, welcoming landlord, Greene King ales, good generous home cooking; tables outside, open all day *(Mr and Mrs B A R Frost, Pat and Roger Davies, Anthony Ellis)*

☆ *White Horse* OX1 3BB [Broad St]: Bustling and studenty, squeezed between bits of Blackwells bookshop, small narrow bar with snug one-table raised back alcove, low beams and timbers, ochre ceiling, beautiful view of the Clarendon building and Sheldonian, friendly staff, good value lunchtime food (the few tables reserved for this) from sandwiches up, several changing real ales, Addlestone's cider *(E McCall, T McLean, D Irving, R Huggins, Dave Lowe, the Didler, Giles and Annie Francis, Mike Vincent, Michael Dandy, BB)*

PISHILL [SU7190]

☆ *Crown* RG9 6HH [B480 Nettlebed—Watlington]: Popular dining pub in wisteria-covered ancient building, black beams and timbers, good log fires and candlelight, wholesome home-made food from good baguettes up inc carefully chosen ingredients and local venison, good service, Brakspears and Wychwood; children welcome in restaurant, picnic-sets on attractive side lawn, pleasant bedroom in separate cottage, pretty country setting – lots of walks *(the Didler, LYM, Howard Dell, Susan and John Douglas)*

RADCOT [SU2899]

Swan OX18 2SX [A4095 2½ miles N of Faringdon]: Cheerful Thames-side pub with friendly efficient staff, log fire, Greene King ales, lots of stuffed fish, food from baguettes up (the hearty Sun roast is popular); piped music; children in eating area, pleasant waterside garden, summer boat trips (lift to bring wheelchairs aboard), four good value bedrooms *(LYM, Tim Venn, Peter Smith, Judith Brown)*

ROTHERFIELD GREYS [SU7282]

Maltsters Arms RG9 4QD: Welcoming old country local with friendly landlord, reasonably priced enjoyable food from rolls and paninis to piping hot specials and good Sun lunch (best to book wknds), Brakspears Bitter and Best, good wines by the glass, lots of cricket memorabilia; small garden, not far from Greys Court (NT), lovely country views *(Philip and June Caunt, Fred and Kate Portnell, Roy Hoing)*

SANDFORD-ON-THAMES [SP5301]

Fox OX4 4YN [off A4074 S of Oxford; Henley Rd]: Friendly unspoilt two-room local, darts, cards and dominoes in simple front bar, smaller basic back lounge, well kept ales such as Bath Spa, Black Sheep and Jennings Cumberland, coal fire; TV *(Pete Baker)*

SATWELL [SU7083]

☆ *Lamb* RG9 4QZ [2 miles S of Nettlebed; follow Shepherds Green signpost]: Cosy and attractive 16th-c low-beamed cottagey dining pub in same ownership as Greyhound on Gallowstree Common (see main entries), unspoilt olde-worlde décor with big log fireplace and tiled floors, good wholesome country food at appealing prices, pleasant efficient staff, Brakspears ale, good mix of ages inc plenty of young people; tables out in prettily reworked garden, nice spot *(LYM, Dick and Madeleine Brown, P M Newsome, Fred and Kate Portnell)*

SHENINGTON [SP3742]

☆ *Bell* OX15 6NQ [off A422 NW of Banbury]: Consistently good reasonably priced real home cooking in hospitable 17th-c two-room pub, good sandwiches too, low-priced Hook Norton Best, good wine choice, friendly informal service and long-serving licensees, relaxed atmosphere, heavy beams, some flagstones, stripped stone and pine panelling, coal fire, friendly dogs, cribbage, dominoes; children in eating areas, nice tables out in front, small attractive back garden, charming quiet village, good surrounding walks, bedrooms, cl Mon (and perhaps other wkdy) lunchtimes *(Sir Nigel Foulkes, LYM, K H Frostick, Graham and Nicky Westwood, Paul Humphreys)*

SHIPLAKE [SU7678]

Plowden Arms RG9 4BX [Reading Rd (A4155)]: Neat and friendly, with three linked rooms and side dining room, hard-working landlord and friendly staff, good range of home-made food from well filled baguettes up, Brakspears, good coffee, log fire; handy for Thames walk *(Paul Humphreys, Roy Hoing)*

SHIPTON-UNDER-WYCHWOOD [SP2717]

☆ *Lamb* OX7 6DQ [off A361 to Burford; High St]: New licensees who think of this as a restaurant-with-rooms and a bit too good for the Guide, but it is a nice place – pleasant atmosphere in cosy and comfortable bar with some stripped stone and log fire (they can be a bit sniffy if you want just a drink), very good food with some emphasis on fish, Greene King ales, good value wines, sophisticated restaurant area in fascinating Elizabethan core; children welcome, tables outside, five attractive bedrooms (some over bar) *(Michael Kirby, Brenda and Stuart Naylor, LYM, Christopher White)*

SHRIVENHAM [SU2488]

☆ *Prince of Wales* SN6 8AF [High St; off A420 or B4000 NE of Swindon]: Warmly friendly 17th-c stone-built local with thriving atmosphere, hearty food (not Sun evening) from enterprising sandwiches to Sun roasts, well kept Wadworths, good soft drinks choice, spotless low-beamed lounge, pictures, lots of brasses, log fire and candles, small dining area, side bar with darts, board games and machines; may be quiet piped music, no dogs; children welcome, picnic-sets and heaters in secluded back garden *(R T and J C Moggridge, Gordon and Jay Smith)*

SIBFORD GOWER [SP3537]

☆ *Wykham Arms* OX15 5RX [signed off B4035 Banbury—Shipston on Stour; Temple Mill Rd]: Pretty and cottagey thatched and flagstoned restauranty dining pub doing good meals inc good value set lunch, nice snacks and bar meals too, friendly attentive staff, Fullers London Pride and Hook Norton Best, good wines by the glass and coffee, comfortable open-plan low-beamed stripped-stone lounge, pleasant pictures, table made from glass-topped well, inglenook tap room; children welcome; country views from big well planted garden, lovely manor house

opp; has been cl Mon lunchtime *(Guy Vowles, Simon Jones, Keith and Sue Ward, LYM, Steve and Liz Tilley)*

SOULDERN [SP5231]

Fox OX27 7JW [off B4100; Fox Lane]: Pretty village pub with enjoyable fresh food from good baguettes to local beef, Brakspears and good choice of wines by the glass, proper coffee, comfortable open-plan beamed layout, big log fire, settles and chairs around oak tables, oriental prints, no piped music; delightful village, garden and terrace tables, four good value bedrooms, open all day Fri-Sun *(E A and D C T Frewer)*

SOUTH NEWINGTON [SP4033]

☆ *Duck on the Pond* OX15 4JE: Thriving dining pub with tidy modern-rustic décor in small flagstoned bar and linked carpeted eating areas up a step with fresh flowers and lit candles, interesting choice of generous enjoyable food from wraps, melts and other light dishes to steak and mixed grill, changing ales such as Archers Golden and Farnham Desert Rat, accommodating landlord and neat and friendly young staff, woodburner; piped music; lots of tables out on deck and lawn, pretty pond with geese, open all day *(Chris Glasson, BB, Keith and Sue Ward, Michael Dandy, Ted George, George Atkinson)*

STANFORD IN THE VALE [SU3393]

Horse & Jockey SN7 8NN [Faringdon Rd]: Popular old local in racehorse country, low ceilings, flagstones and woodburner in big fireplace, good drawings and paintings of horses and jockeys, friendly landlord, Batemans XXB and Greene King ales, bar food and charming restaurant; dogs welcome, play area *(Peter and Audrey Dowsett)*

STANTON ST JOHN [SP5709]

☆ *Talk House* OX33 1EX [Middle Rd/Wheatley Rd (B4027 just outside)]: Peacefully placed 17th-c pub with enjoyable food, Hook Norton Best, Wadworths 6X and a guest beer, helpful service, Oxford academia prints on partly stripped stone walls, lots of oak beams, flagstones and tiles, simple and solid rustic furnishings, pleasant area by log fire; children welcome in restaurant, tables in sheltered courtyard, comfortable bedrooms, has been open all day in summer *(Sue Demont, Tim Barrow, Graham Oddey, LYM)*

STEVENTON [SU4691]

North Star OX13 6SG [Stocks Lane, The Causeway, central westward turn off B4017]: Carefully restored old-fangled village pub with tiled entrance corridor, main area with ancient high-backed settles around central table, Greene King ales from pump set tucked away in side tap room, hatch service to another room with plain seating, a couple of tables and good coal fire, simple lunchtime food, young friendly staff; piped music, sports TV, games machine; tables on side grass, front gateway through living yew tree *(the Didler, Pete Baker, LYM, Alan and Carolin Tidbury)*

STOKE LYNE [SP5628]

Peyton Arms OX27 8SD [from minor road off B4110 N of Bicester fork left into village]: Largely unspoilt stone-built pub under new landlord, Hook Norton beers from casks behind small corner bar in sparsely decorated front snug, filled rolls, tiled floor, inglenook log fire, games room with darts and pool; no children or dogs; pleasant garden with aunt sally, open all day Sat, cl Sun evening and Mon *(Pete Baker, the Didler, Mick Furn, Roger Shipperley)*

STOKE ROW [SU6884]

☆ *Cherry Tree* RG9 5QA [off B481 at Highmoor]: Contemporary dining pub with particularly good if not cheap food (freshly made so can take a while at busy times), Brakspears ales, good choice of wines by the glass, enthusiastic young staff, minimalist décor and solid country furniture in four linked rooms with stripped wood, heavy low beams and some flagstones; TV in bar; good seating in attractive garden, nice nearby walks, five bedrooms in new block *(Howard Dell, Richard Endacott, Susan and John Douglas, I H G Busby, Mrs Pam Mattinson, Rob Winstanley, BB)*

☆ *Crooked Billet* RG9 5PU [Nottwood Lane, off B491 N of Reading – OS Sheet 175 map ref 684844]: Very nice place, but restaurant not pub (so not eligible for the main entries – you can't have just a drink); charming rustic pub layout though, with heavy beams, flagstones, antique pubby furnishings and great inglenook log fire as well as crimsonly Victorian dining room; wide choice of well cooked interesting meals using local produce inc good value lunch (you can have just a starter), particularly helpful and knowledgeable friendly staff, Brakspears tapped from the cask (no bar counter), good wines, relaxed homely atmosphere – like a french country restaurant; children truly welcome, occasional live music, big garden by Chilterns beechwoods *(Bob and Judy Smitherman, LYM, Tim Venn, the Didler, Rob Winstanley)*

SUNNINGWELL [SP4900]

☆ *Flowing Well* OX13 6RB [just N of Abingdon]: Attractive timbered pub with good enterprising home-made food from baguettes to restaurant dishes, welcoming staff, well kept Greene King and Wadworths ales, good wine choice inc many organic ones, plus organic coffees and juices, remarkable collection of rare rums, pool, cheerful relaxed atmosphere, unpretentious furnishings and warm décor; TV, may be piped jazz (live some nights); they may try to keep your credit card while you eat; garden with small well and picnic-sets under cocktail parasols *(BB, Derek Goldrei)*

SUTTON COURTENAY [SU5094]

Swan OX14 4AE [The Green]: Restaurant pub with smiling speedy service even when busy, pleasant atmosphere, well kept beers, decent fresh food (all day wknds); garden tables *(John and Helen Rushton)*

SWALCLIFFE [SP3737]

Stags Head OX15 5EJ [The Green, just off B4035]: Welcoming new licensees in easy-going low-beamed bar with big woodburner, high-backed wooden pews and cushioned seats, local paintings for sale, lighter room with lots more tables, well kept real ale, Weston's farm cider, enjoyable home-made food; children and dogs welcome, neatly terraced hillside gardens, has been cl Sun evening, Mon lunchtime *(Mr and Mrs G Hughes, LYM, M and GR, Alun Evans)*

TETSWORTH [SP6801]

Red Lion OX9 7AS [A40, between M40 junctions 6 and 7]: Neat and attractive bistro-feel pub overlooking big village green, several spacious areas around central bar counter with pale wood floors, Greene King Abbot and a guest beer, bar food and library/conservatory restaurant (children welcome, though this bit has not always been cl Sun), board games; open all day *(Graham and Elizabeth Hargreaves, LYM, Mr and Mrs J P Blake)*

THAME [SP7105]

Falcon OX9 3JA [Thame Park Rd]: Open-plan pub much improved under new ownership, Hook Norton ales, friendly service, decent food; inn sign looks more like kite than falcon – perhaps a name change is in the offing; open all day *(Roger Shipperley)*

Rising Sun OX9 2BZ [High St]: Three linked rooms with flagstones and bare boards, something of a wine bar/brasserie atmosphere, good management, Brakspears real ales inc a seasonal one, lots of good wines by the glass, dark courtyard now glassed over as thai restaurant (leaving just a small terrace now), pubbier lunchtime snacks like baguettes and burgers too; open all day *(Tim and Ann Newell)*

Swan OX9 3ER [Upper High St]: Heavily beamed 16th-c former coaching inn with changing real ales such as Brakspears, Hydes and Skinners, largely thai food in bars and upstairs evening restaurant with medieval ceiling, all-day sandwiches, friendly informal service, individual furnishings and bric-a-brac, big log fire; big-screen sports TV in main bar, two more in back bars, some live music; children and dogs welcome, open all day, bedrooms *(Tim and Ann Newell, LYM, Derek and Sylvia Stephenson)*

THRUPP [SP4815]

☆ *Boat* OX5 1JY [off A4260 just N of Kidlington]: Stone-built pub in good spot near though not beside Oxford Canal, so gets busy in summer (when service can be affected), good surprisingly upscale meals, friendly landlord, Greene King ales, decent wine, coal fire, old canal pictures and artefacts, bare boards and stripped pine, restaurant, no piped music; nice safely fenced garden behind with plenty of tables, some in shade *(Sue Demont, Tim Barrow, D A Bradford, Meg and Colin Hamilton, Pete Baker, A Darroch Harkness, Bob and Laura Brock)*

WANTAGE [SU3987]
King Alfreds Head OX12 8AH [Market Pl]:
Interestingly refurbished linked areas with
enjoyable fresh food from doorstep
sandwiches to some unusual bistro dishes,
well kept real ales, good choice of wines by
the glass; unusual garden and barn area
(Lois Chell)
☆ ***Royal Oak*** OX12 8DF [Newbury St]:
Welcoming two-bar local with lots of ship
photographs and naval hatbands, friendly
landlord very careful with his ales such as
Bass or Marstons Pedigree, Wadworths 6X
and two beers brewed for him by West
Berkshire; table football, darts, cribbage;
cl wkdy lunchtimes, bedrooms *(BB,
the Didler)*
Shoulder of Mutton OX12 8AX [Wallingford
St]: Friendly and chatty local, coal fire and
racing TV in bar, passage to two small snug
back rooms, changing well kept ales; tables
on back terrace, open all day *(the Didler,
Pete Baker)*
WARBOROUGH [SU5993]
Cricketers Arms OX10 7DD [Thame Rd (off
A329)]: New licensees doing good choice of
sensibly priced food in neat and pleasantly
decorated pub, Greene King IPA and Abbot,
proper bar and dining area; tables outside
(David Lamb)
WARDINGTON [SP4946]
Hare & Hounds OX17 1SH [A361 Banbury—
Daventry]: Roomy and comfortable
traditional village local with well kept Hook
Norton ales, friendly welcome, games room
with darts and pool; piped music, games
machine; largish garden with play area
(Mark and Diane Grist)
WATLINGTON [SU6894]
Chequers OX49 5RA [3 miles from M40,
junction 6, via B4009; Love Lane]: Attractive
rambling bar with very wide choice of good
value food from sandwiches to steaks and
popular Sun lunch, well kept Brakspears ales
inc seasonal, good atmosphere, character
seating and a few good antique oak tables,
low beams and candles, steps down to
further eating area, vine-hung conservatory
(children allowed here); picnic-sets in pretty
garden, nice walks nearby *(Graham Oddey,
LYM)*
WEST HANNEY [SU4092]
☆ ***Plough*** OX12 0LN [Church St]: Unspoilt and
pretty 16th-c thatched family local with
attractive timbered upper storey, original
timbers and uneven low ceilings, homely
lounge with good log fire in stone fireplace,
genial landlord, pubby atmosphere, popular
sensibly priced food from sandwiches and
baguettes up, well kept ales such as
Brakspears, Butts, Greene King Abbot and
Timothy Taylors Landlord, interesting
whiskies, good coffee, small dining room,
darts in public bar, friendly cat; children and
dogs welcome, tables on back terrace, play
area, good walks *(Helene Grygar, Dick and
Madeleine Brown, Dr Williams, Alan and
Carolin Tidbury, BB)*

WESTON-ON-THE-GREEN [SP5318]
Ben Jonson OX25 3RA [B430 nr M40
junction 9]: Ancient thatched and stone-
built country pub recently refurbished under
new management, oak furniture in beamed
bar with pastel décor and interesting
sculpture, well kept Hook Norton, enjoyable
if not cheap food, two dining rooms
(E A and D C T Frewer)
Chequers OX25 3QH [handy for M40 junction
9, via A34; Northampton Rd (B430)]:
Extended thatched pub with three
refurbished sitting areas off large semi-
circular raftered bar, Fullers and a guest
beer, good value wines by the glass,
welcoming service, good value food; tables
under cocktail parasols in attractive garden
with animals *(Miss E Ackrill)*
WHITCHURCH [SU6377]
Ferry Boat RG8 7DB [High St]: Enjoyable
home-made food at reasonable prices,
friendly efficient staff, smart contemporary
décor, real ale such as Timothy Taylors
Landlord *(Mr and Mrs C Crichton)*
WITNEY [SP3509]
Angel OX28 6AL [Market Sq]: Wide choice of
bargain food from good sandwiches up inc
OAP specials in comfortably bustling 17th-c
town local, real ales such as Courage Best,
Hook Norton Best and Wells & Youngs
Bombardier, daily papers, welcoming
unpretentious surroundings and hot coal fire,
quick friendly service even when packed;
piped music, big-screen sports TV, pool
room, coffee bar, bingo nights; parking
nearby can be difficult, smokers' shelter
behind *(MDN, Peter and Audrey Dowsett)*
Royal Oak OX28 6HW [High St]: Small cosy
lounge and larger bar, good choice of
generous lunchtime food, Brakspears and
Wychwood ales, cheery staff
(Richard Marjoram, Pete Baker)
WOODSTOCK [SP4416]
☆ ***Bear*** OX20 1SZ [Park St]: Small heavy-
beamed bar at front of smart and attractive
ancient hotel, cosy alcoves, immaculate and
tastefully casual mix of antique oak,
mahogany and leather furniture, paintings
and sporting trophies, blazing inglenook log
fire, good fresh sandwiches and hot bar
lunches (not cheap), quick friendly service,
good choice of wines by the glass, Stones
ale, restaurant; no dogs; tables in back
courtyard, good bedrooms, open all day
*(DFL, Chris Glasson, BB, Michael Dandy,
Conor McGaughey)*
Crown OX20 1TE [High St (A44)]: Large
comfortable L-shaped bar with Greene King
IPA and Abbot, daily papers, log fire,
baguettes, salads, pizzas and pastas in
roomy restaurant with conservatory, popular
prices; piped music, sports TV one end;
bedrooms, open all day *(Michael Dandy,
Derek and Sylvia Stephenson)*
Feathers OX20 1SX [Market St]: Not a pub
but a formal Cotswold hotel with attractive
period furnishings, and does have enjoyable
though pricy bar food, good wines by the

glass and daily papers in small comfortable back bar with nice log fire, opening on to charming sunny courtyard garden with heaters; piped music; children welcome, good bedrooms *(LYM, Michael Dandy)*

Woodstock Arms OX20 1SX [Market St]: 16th-c heavy-beamed stripped-stone pub, lively and stylishly modernised, with above-average food showing real care in preparation, prompt welcoming service by helpful young staff, Greene King IPA and Old Speckled Hen, good wine choice, daily papers, log-effect gas fire in splendid stone fireplace, long narrow bar, end eating area; piped music; dogs welcome, tables out in attractive yard, bedrooms, open all day *(Michael Dandy, Chris Glasson, John Holroyd, Paul Goldman, Conor McGaughey)*

WOOTTON [SP4320]

Killingworth Castle OX20 1EJ [Glympton Rd; B4027 N of Woodstock]: Striking three-storey 17th-c coaching inn with cheerful hard-working landlord and lively local atmosphere, Greene King ales, decent house wines, wide choice of generous if not cheap food, long narrow main bar with pine furnishings, parquet floor, candles, lots of brasses and log fire with books above it, daily papers, bar billiards, darts and shove ha'penny in smaller games end, attractive garden; soft piped music, frequent live music nights; bedrooms *(Craig Adams, Felicity Davies, Pete Baker, BB)*

YARNTON [SP4711]

Red Lion OX5 1QD [Cassington Rd]: Refurbished as country dining pub by current newish licensees, reasonably priced food from sandwiches to fresh locally sourced meat and fish, Greene King ales, tiled floors, red walls and nice medley of furnishings, inc unusual Lloyd Loom-style bucket chairs in bar; large quiet garden *(Tim Venn)*

Turnpike OX5 1PJ [A44 N of Oxford]: Large Vintage Inn pub/restaurant with good atmosphere in spacious low-ceilinged bar areas, prompt pleasant service, reliable food all day, log fire *(Chris Glasson, David Green)*

Shropshire

This is not a particularly cheap area for eating out in pubs, but there is plenty of real value to be found. Doing very well this year for food are the Fox at Chetwynd Aston, the stylish Inn at Grinshill (a very comfortable place to stay in), and the Armoury at Shrewsbury, where new staff are moving things from strength to strength (and the drinks are good, too); the Fox and the Armoury are both part of the excellent small Brunning & Price group. From this shortlist, the Armoury in Shrewsbury earns the accolade of Shropshire Dining Pub of the Year; it's very unusual to find such a good relaxed dining pub of real character in a city. Bishop's Castle is a remarkable stronghold of good pubs, with the appealing Castle Hotel at the top of the town, and two other good pubs which both brew their own beers. Good all-rounders that are currently scoring high points with readers include the Church Inn nicely placed right at the heart of things in Ludlow (comfortable bedrooms, and an impressive beer selection), the warm-hearted Talbot in Much Wenlock (back in these pages after a break – our only new main entry in the county this year), the friendly Sun out at Norbury (another nice place to stay in, with consistently commendable food), and the Bottle & Glass at Picklescott, run with tremendous flair and enthusiasm. The Horseshoe at Bridges, the Royal Oak at Cardington and the Ragleth at Little Stretton are in great countryside, particularly well placed for walkers. In the Lucky Dip section at the end of the chapter, pubs to note include the Railwaymans Arms in Bridgnorth, White Horse at Clun, Sun at Corfton, Riverside at Cressage, Crown at Hopton Wafers, Pound at Leebotwood, Navigation at Maesbury Marsh, and Stiperstones Inn. Drinks prices in the county tend to be rather lower than the norm, with the two own-brew pubs in Bishop's Castle setting a good price example. Hobsons, from a fairly young brewery just outside Cleobury Mortimer, is the most widely available local beer, and is often the cheapest beer on offer in good pubs here. Other good local brews to look out for include Hanby and Woods.

BISHOP'S CASTLE   SO3288   MAP 6
Castle Hotel 🛏
Market Square, just off B4385; SY9 5BN

Friendly old coaching inn with bags of charm

Up at the top of the town, this substantial, welcoming and pleasantly old-fashioned inn dates from 1719. Neatly kept and attractively furnished, the clubby little beamed and panelled bar, glazed off from the entrance, has a good coal fire, old hunting prints and sturdy leather chairs on its muted carpet. It opens into a much bigger room, with maroon plush wall seats and stools, big Victorian engravings, and another coal fire in an attractive cast-iron fireplace. The lighting in both rooms is gentle and relaxing, and the pub tables have unusually elaborate cast-iron frames; bar billiards and board games.

Hobsons Best and Town Crier, and local Six Bells Big Nevs are on handpump, they've decent wines, and over 30 malt whiskies. The handsome panelled dining room is open in the evening and on Sunday lunchtime. The bedrooms are spacious and full of period character, and the breakfasts are good. It is especially lovely in summer, when the pub is festooned with pretty hanging baskets, and the back garden has terraces with blue chairs on either side of a large formal raised fish pond, pergolas and climbing plants, and stone walls; it looks out over the town rooftops to the surrounding gentle countryside. A new extension links the garden to the bars, with access for the disabled, via a lower courtyard.

🍴 **Served in the bar or dining area, enjoyable bar food is made with good quality ingredients. At lunchtime the menu includes filled baguettes and vegetarian flan, and perhaps steak and kidney pie or chicken curry. The evening menu has a short choice, with for instance soup, lamb samosas with sweet chilli dip, game pie, fried duck breast with orange and redcurrant gravy, rump or fillet steak, and a few specials like pheasant breasts or braised venison steaks.** *Starters/Snacks: £3.95 to £5.95. Main Courses: £6.25 to £14.95. Puddings: £4.25*

Free house ~ Licensees David and Nicky Simpson ~ Real ale ~ Bar food (12-1.45, 6.30(7 Sun)-8.45) ~ (01588) 638403 ~ Children welcome ~ Dogs welcome ~ Open 12-2.30, 6-11; 12-11.30 Sat; 12-11 Sun; 12-2.30, 6-11 winter ~ Bedrooms: £45B/£80S

Recommended by Bruce Purvis, Kevin Thorpe, J C Clark, P Dawn, Ian Phillips, the Didler, Tracey and Stephen Groves

Six Bells 🍺
Church Street; SY9 5AA

Deservedly popular own-brew pub

Well liked for its chatty atmosphere, this former coaching inn has excellent beers brewed on the premises. Big Nevs is most people's favourite, and you'll also find Cloud Nine and Goldings Best plus a seasonal brew like Marathon Ale, and they also keep a wide range of country wines. You can arrange a tour of the brewery, and they have a beer festival on the second full weekend in July. The no-frills bar is really quite small, with an assortment of well worn furniture and old local photographs and prints. The second, bigger room has bare boards, some stripped stone, a roaring woodburner in the inglenook, plenty of sociable locals on the benches around plain tables, and lots of board games (you may find people absorbed in Scrabble or darts). The service is very friendly. It can be packed here at the weekend.

🍴 **Good value tasty bar food includes lunchtime soup, sandwiches and ploughman's, and in the evening there could be sausages and mash, salmon fillet or pork tenderloin with mustard and cider sauce.** *Starters/Snacks: £3.50 to £4.00. Main Courses: £8.00 to £13.00. Puddings: £4.00*

Own brew ~ Licensee Neville Richards ~ Real ale ~ Bar food (12-1.45, 6.30-8.45; not Sun evening or Mon) ~ No credit cards ~ (01588) 630144 ~ Children welcome if well behaved ~ Dogs allowed in bar ~ Open 12-2.30, 5-11; 12-11 Sat; 12-3.30, 7-10.30 Sun; closed Mon lunchtime

Recommended by the Didler, Kevin Thorpe, Bruce Bird, P Dawn, MLR, Ian Phillips, D Hillaby, Paul Davies, Rona Murdoch, Andrew Stephenson, Tracey and Stephen Groves

Three Tuns 🍺
Salop Street; SY9 5BW

Unpretentious own-brew pub scoring well for food as well as beer from its unique four-storey Victorian brewhouse

You might chance upon morris dancers, a brass band playing in the garden or the local rugby club enjoying a drink at this markedly ungimmicky and individual pub. It serves the excellent beers that are brewed in the Victorian John Roberts brewhouse across the yard: John Roberts XXX, Castle Steamer, Clerics Cure, Qu'Offas and 3 Eight are served from old-fashioned handpumps. They always have a farm cider or perry on too; several wines by the glass. They do carry-out kegs, and the brewery (which is a separate business) sells beer by the barrel; a popular annual beer festival takes place in July. Full of friendly conversation and undisturbed by piped music, the beamed rooms are very simply furnished with low-backed settles and heavy walnut tables, with newspapers left out for customers to read, and a good range of board games.

🍴 **Tasty, and in generous portions, bar food includes sandwiches, soup, satay king prawns, fish and chips, braised beef and wild mushrooms cooked in beer, red bean and lentil chilli, and sausages and mash.** *Starters/Snacks: £3.50 to £7.00. Main Courses: £8.50 to £14.95. Puddings: £3.75*

Free house ~ Tenant Tim Curtis-Evans ~ Real ale ~ Bar food (12-3, 7-9; not Sun evening) ~ Restaurant ~ (01588) 638797 ~ Children welcome in dining areas ~ Dogs allowed in bar ~ Live music most Fri and Sat evenings ~ Open 12-11(10.30 Sun)

Recommended by Mike and Lynn Robinson, Tracey and Stephen Groves, Pat and Tony Martin, JMM, Ian Phillips, Kevin Thorpe, Paul Davies, the Didler, P Dawn, Kerry Law, Andrew Stephenson

BRIDGES   SO3996   MAP 6

Horseshoe 🍺
Near Ratlinghope, below the W flank of the Long Mynd; SY5 0ST

Lively rural pub out in the Shropshire hills, friendly staff who cope well under pressure

There's plenty of live music going on at this out-of-the-way pub in a scenic spot looking over the Long Mynd, and they now offer accommodation too. The interior has light oak beams, log burners and lots of rustic bygones, and the down-to-earth yet comfortable bar has interesting windows, lots of farm implements, pub mirrors and musical instruments, and they tend to have three local real ales, such as Six Bells Big Nev and Coud Nine, and Wood Quaff on handpump. A small dining room leads off from here; sometimes there may be discreet piped music. Tables are placed out by the little River Onny, and they're planning a covered shelter for smokers. Breakfasts include organic cereals, fresh fruit and organic bread; we would welcome reports from readers who stay here.

🍴 **Served by efficient staff, bar food includes sandwiches, soup, sausage and mash, fresh fish dishes such as cod and chips, steak and irish stout pie and vegetarian lasagne. On Wednesday evenings they have a 'feast for a fiver', with two courses for just £5.** *Starters/Snacks: £2.25 to £6.25. Main Courses: £6.75 to £12.50. Puddings: £3.95*

Free house ~ Licensees Bob and Maureen Macauley ~ Real ale ~ Bar food (12-2.45, 6-8.45; 12-8.45 Sat; 12-4 Sun) ~ No credit cards ~ (01588) 650260 ~ Children welcome till 8.30pm if supervised ~ Dogs welcome ~ Live music Mon, Wed, Fri and Sat evenings ~ Open 12(6 Mon)-12; closed Sun evenings if quiet in winter ~ Bedrooms: £35S/£70S

Recommended by Gerry and Rosemary Dobson, Chris Flynn, Wendy Jones, Des and Ursula Weston, Richard, J S Burn

BROMFIELD   SO4877   MAP 6

Clive/Cookhouse ♀ 🛏
A49 2 miles NW of Ludlow; SY8 2JR

Elegant minimalist dining pub with similarly stylish bedrooms

There's a crisp, contemporary look to this sophisticated dining pub (known in full as the Clive Bar Restaurant with Rooms), within a neatly kept Georgian brick house, named after former resident Clive of India. Both the front and rear sections are in a brightly minimalist city style. During the day the focus is on the dining room, with modern light wood tables, and a big open kitchen behind the end stainless steel counter. A door leads through into the bar, sparse but neat and welcoming, with round glass tables and metal chairs running down to a sleek, space-age bar counter with fresh flowers, newspapers and spotlights. Then it's down a step to the Clive Arms Bar, where traditional features like the huge brick fireplace (with woodburning stove), exposed stonework, and soaring beams and rafters are appealingly juxtaposed with wicker chairs, well worn sofas and new glass tables; piped jazz. The good wine list includes several by the glass, and Hobsons Best is on handpump; they also have a range of coffees and teas. An attractive secluded terrace has tables under cocktail parasols and a fish pond. They have 15 stylishly modern, good-sized bedrooms, and breakfast is excellent. No children inside.

🍴 Besides baguettes, good bar food includes soup, roasted peppers and aubergine with wrekin white cheddar and dressed leaves, and main courses with thick cut chips such as battered cod, sirloin of shropshire beef, and roasted vegetable pizza. The separate lunch and dinner menus could include starters like roasted garlic, endive and oyster mushroom in tarragon cream with rigatoni pasta, and main courses such as roast pork fillet and hereford apples with butter mash, or polenta with fricassee of oyster mushrooms and grilled asparagus; the puddings feature hot chocolate brownie and warm carrot and walnut cake with lemon frosting and honey ginger ice-cream. One reader found service was rather rushed on a Saturday evening. *Starters/Snacks: £4.75 to £7.95. Main Courses: £6.95 to £15.95. Puddings: £4.95 to £5.95*

Free house ~ Licensee Paul Brooks ~ Real ale ~ Bar food (12-3, 6.30-9.30; 12-9.30 Sat, Sun) ~ (01584) 856565 ~ Open 11-11; 12-10.30 Sun; closed 25, 26 Dec ~ Bedrooms: £50B/£75B

Recommended by Liz and Tony Colman, Michael Sargent, Ian Phillips, Des and Ursula Weston, Mr and Mrs M Stratton, L and D Webster, Richard, P J and R D Greaves

CARDINGTON   SO5095   MAP 4

Royal Oak

Village signposted off B4371 Church Stretton—Much Wenlock, pub behind church; also reached via narrow lanes from A49; SY6 7JZ

Wonderful rural position, heaps of character inside too

In glorious countryside – the summit of Caer Caradoc is a couple of miles to the west – this is the oldest pub in Shropshire. Not much has changed inside over the centuries: the rambling, low-beamed bar has a roaring winter log fire, cauldron, black kettle and pewter jugs in its vast inglenook fireplace, the old standing timbers of a knocked-through wall, and red and green tapestry seats solidly capped in elm; darts and dominoes. A comfortable dining area has exposed old beams and studwork. Hobsons, Wye Valley Butty Bach and a couple of guests such as Three Tuns XXX and Woods Parish are on handpump. Tables in the front courtyard make the most of the setting. Note that they allow dogs in the bar area, but only outside food service times.

🍴 Using seasonal produce such as game and local specialities, bar food from the menu and specials board might include soup, baguettes, ploughman's, wenlock edge cottage herb sausages in giant yorkshire pudding, leek and shropshire blue tartlets, steak and bass in lemon butter or venison steak with honey and mustard sauce; Sunday roasts. *Starters/Snacks: £2.95 to £8.50. Main Courses: £7.95 to £15.95. Puddings: £2.50 to £3.95*

Free house ~ Licensees Steve Oldham and Eira Williams ~ Real ale ~ Bar food (not Sun evening) ~ Restaurant ~ (01694) 771266 ~ Children welcome ~ Open 12-2.30(3.30 Sun), 7-12(1 Fri, Sat); closed Mon except bank hols

Recommended by TOH, C and R Bromage, MLR, Des and Ursula Weston, D Hillaby, David Edwards, Carol and Colin Broadbent, Tracey and Stephen Groves

CHETWYND ASTON   SJ7517   MAP 7

Fox

Village signposted off A41 and A518 just S of Newport; TF10 9LQ

Civilised 1920s dining pub with generous food and interesting ales served by ever-attentive staff

A new entry in the last edition of this *Guide*, this dining pub has gone from strength to strength, with readers enthusing about its delicious food and good range of ales, and friendly staff who keep a high level of service even at busy times. This roomy extended 1920s building (formerly called the Three Fishes) has been handsomely done up by the small Brunning & Price group that now runs it. As usual, they've used good materials, and the style will be familiar to anyone who has tried their other pubs, though in a good way – not at all mass-produced. A series of linked semi-separate areas, one with a broad arched ceiling, has plenty of tables in all shapes and sizes, some quite elegant, and a vaguely matching diversity of comfortable chairs, all laid out in a way that's fine for eating but serves equally well for just drinking and chatting. There are masses of attractive prints, three open fires, a few oriental rugs on polished parquet or boards, some attractive floor tiling; big windows and careful lighting help towards the relaxed and effortless atmosphere (though no doubt the easy-going nature of people in from the nearby agricultural college and the Lilleshall Sport England centre helps too). The handsome bar counter, with a decent complement of bar stools, serves an excellent changing range of about a dozen wines by the glass; Thwaites Original, Timothy Taylors Landlord, Woods Shropshire Lad and three guests from brewers such as Hop Back, Holdens or Slaters are well kept on handpump. The staff, mainly young, are well trained, cheerful and attentive. Disabled access and facilities are good (no push chairs or baby buggies, though); there is a selection of board games. There are picnic-sets out in a good-sized garden with quiet country views from the sunny terrace, or shade from some mature trees.

🍴 Served in generous portions, well liked food from a changing menu could include soup, ploughman's, sandwiches, goats cheese tart, black pudding and chorizo in sherry butter, roast pheasant, butternut squash and sage tortellini, buttercross rare breed roast pork with apple sauce and stuffing, and puddings such as rhubarb parfait with raspberry sauce or warm chocolate brownie with chocolate fudge sauce. *Starters/Snacks: £4.50 to £6.95. Main Courses: £7.95 to £15.95. Puddings: £4.25 to £4.95*

Brunning & Price ~ Manager Sam Cornwall-Jones ~ Real ale ~ Bar food (12-10(9.30 Sun)) ~ (01952) 815940 ~ Children welcome till 7pm ~ Dogs allowed in bar ~ Open 12-11(10.30 Sun)

Recommended by J S Burn, Alan and Eve Harding, R T and J C Moggridge, Steve Whalley, John Whitehead, D Weston, Mrs Philippa Wilson, Kevin Thomas, Nina Randall, Gary Rollings, Debbie Porter, Bruce and Sharon Eden

GRINSHILL   SJ5223   MAP 7

Inn at Grinshill 🛏

Off A49 N of Shrewsbury; SY4 3BL

Looks after its customers admirably: a civilised place to stay or dine

Formerly the Elephant and Castle, this elegantly refurbished early Georgian country inn enjoys a growing reputation for its excellent food and welcoming staff. Greene King Ruddles, Hanbys Drawell and Theakston XB, plus a guest from a brewer such as Wells & Youngs are on handpump, and they have 13 wines by the glass. The comfortable 19th-c bar has an open log fire, while the spacious contemporary styled main restaurant has a view straight into the kitchen, and doors into the rear garden, which is laid out with tables and chairs; TV, piped music, dominoes, and an evening pianist on Friday. Beautifully decorated bedrooms have wide-screen TV and broadband access. Though not at all high, the nearby hill of Grinshill has an astonishingly far-ranging view.

🍴 Prepared with care, the very good food might include sandwiches, soup, mussels, guinea fowl with tomato mousseline and wild mushrooms, roasted pork fillet or carpaccio of tuna with bean sprout salad, and lunchtime specials like sausage and mash or cod and chips. At lunchtime (not Sunday) and before 7.30 during Thursday and Friday (all evening on other weekdays) you can take advantage of the three-course 'lunchtime and early bird menu'. *Starters/Snacks: £4.95 to £10.00. Main Courses: £13.00 to £25.00. Puddings: £4.50 to £7.50*

Free house ~ Licensees Kevin and Victoria Brazier ~ Real ale ~ Bar food (12-2.30, 6.30-9.30; not Sun evening) ~ Restaurant ~ (01939) 220410 ~ Children welcome ~ Dogs allowed in bar ~ Open 11-3, 6-11; 11-11 Sat; 12-4.30 Sun; closed Mon in winter; closed Sun and bank hol evenings ~ Bedrooms: £60S/£120B

Recommended by Poppy Laight, Alan and Eve Harding, Derek and Sylvia Stephenson, M Thomas, Noel Grundy, J S Burn, A J Bowen, Tom and Jill Jones

---

If we know a pub has an outdoor play area for children, we mention it.

IRONBRIDGE   SJ6603   MAP 6

Malthouse ♀ ⇌

The Wharfage (bottom road alongside Severn); TF8 7NH

Right in the heart of the historic gorge, with pleasantly airy décor and tasty bar food

This imaginatively converted malthouse is useful if you're exploring the fascinating industrial history of Ironbridge Gorge, and the bedrooms are nicely done. The spacious bar is broken up by white-painted iron pillars that support the heavy pine beams. A mix of scrubbed light wooden tables with candles, cream-painted banquettes and bright pictures keeps it light and airy; piped music. Greene King IPA, Scottish Courage Directors and a guest such as Black Sheep are on handpump, and they've a wide choice of wines including several by the glass. The atmosphere is quite different in the restaurant, which has a much more elaborate menu. There are a few tables outside in front by the car park; heaters and as we went to press there were plans to erect a covered area for smokers. Note that they may retain your credit card if you eat in the bar. More reports please.

🍴 **Appropriately informal, the bar menu includes dishes such as soup, focaccias, burgers, fishcakes, smoked bacon and seafood chowder, and goats cheese and pear filo; there's also a children's menu. The restaurant menu (also usually available in the bar, except on busy Saturdays) could include tomato, ricotta and mascarpone lasagne, fried chicken breast with goats cheese and basil, or baked fillet of salmon with crab and spring onion mash.** *Starters/Snacks: £4.00 to £7.95. Main Courses: £7.95 to £17.95. Puddings: £1.50 to £5.50*

Malthouse Pubs Ironbridge Ltd ~ Lease Alex and Andrea Nicoll ~ Real ale ~ Bar food (12-2.30, 6-9.30, Sat 12-9.30, Sun 12-8.30) ~ Restaurant ~ (01952) 433712 ~ Children welcome ~ Dogs allowed in bar ~ Live music Weds, Thurs evenings ~ Open 11-11(12 Sat) ~ Bedrooms: /£67B

Recommended by R T and J C Moggridge

LITTLE STRETTON   SO4492   MAP 6

Ragleth

Village signposted off A49 S of Church Stretton; Ludlow Road; SY6 6RB

Prettily placed family-friendly pub, tastefully renovated; fine hill walks nearby

Beneath the steep slopes of the Long Mynd, this 17th-c brick-built pub makes a particularly inviting place to sit outside on a fine summer's day, with tables on a lawn shaded by a tulip tree looking across to a thatched and timbered church, and there's a good play area. Inside it has been nicely opened up and refurbished. The bay-windowed front bar, with a warming fire in winter, is light and airy with fresh plaster and an eclectic mix of light wood old tables and chairs, and some of the original wall brick and timber work has been exposed. The heavily beamed brick-and-tile-floored public bar has a huge inglenook; darts, board games and piped music. Hobsons Best, Scottish Courage Directors and a guest such as Banks's Fine Fettle or Theakstons Old Peculier are on handpump.

🍴 **Served by friendly young staff, the good reasonably priced bar food might include baguettes, soup, ploughman's, a choice of fresh fish specials, Sunday roasts, crispy half duckling with orange and Grand Marnier sauce, lamb cutlets with rosemary and redcurrant gravy, roasted mediterranean vegetable lasagne, and steak and ale pie.** *Starters/Snacks: £3.95 to £5.95. Main Courses: £7.95 to £13.95. Puddings: £3.50 to £4.50*

Free house ~ Licensees Chris and Wendy Davis ~ Real ale ~ Bar food (12-2.30, 6.30-9(9.30 Fri, Sat)) ~ Restaurant ~ (01694) 722711 ~ Children welcome ~ Dogs allowed in bar ~ Open 12-3, 6.30-11; 12-11 Sat; 12-10.30 Sun; closed Sat and Sun afternoons in winter; closed 25 Dec

Recommended by C and R Bromage, Stephen and Tina Haynes, TOH

> Post Office address codings confusingly give the impression that some pubs are in Shropshire, when they're really in Cheshire (which is where we list them).

LUDLOW   SO5174   MAP 4

Church Inn 🍺
Church Street, behind Butter Cross; SY8 1AW

Town-centre inn with impressive range of real ales from all over, pubby food

Right in the centre of this conspicuously handsome country town and behind the ancient
Butter Cross, this bustling inn generates a welcoming atmosphere. They serve a great
choice of eight well kept real ales from Hobsons, Ludlow, Weetwood and Wye Valley, as
well as guests from breweries all over Britain – such as Kelham Island, Orkney and
Thornbridge; also several malt whiskies and country wines. Appealingly decorated, with
comfortable banquettes in cosy alcoves off the island bar, and pews and stripped
stonework from the church (part of the bar is a pulpit), the interior is divided into three
areas; hops hang from the heavy beams; daily papers and piped music. There are displays
of old photographic equipment, plants on window sills, and church prints in the side room;
a long central area with a fine stone fireplace (good winter fires) leads to lavatories. The
more basic side bar has old black and white photos of the town. The civilised upstairs
lounge has vaulted ceilings and long windows overlooking the church, display cases of
glass, china and old bottles, and musical instruments on the walls, along with a mix of
new and old pictures. In summer you can get three different types of Pimms, while in
winter there's mulled wine and hot toddy, and they do a roaring trade in tea and coffee
too. The bedrooms are simple but comfortable; good breakfasts. Car parking is some way
off. The owners have recently acquired the Charlton Arms, down the hill on Ludford Bridge.

🍽 **Straightforward pubby food includes sandwiches, ludlow sausage baguette, soup,
sausage and mash, cod in beer batter, sirloin steak, shropshire pork pies and a changing
choice of vegetarian dishes such as quiche.** *Starters/Snacks: £3.70 to £4.50. Main Courses:
£7.95 to £10.45. Puddings: £3.95*

Free house ~ Licensee Graham Willson-Lloyd ~ Real ale ~ Bar food (12-2.30(3.30 Sat), 6.30-9;
12-3, 6-8.30 Sun) ~ Restaurant ~ (01584) 872174 ~ Children welcome ~ Dogs welcome ~ Open
11-11; 12-11 Sun ~ Bedrooms: £35B/£60B

*Recommended by JMM, Kevin Thorpe, P Dawn, Rob and Catherine Dunster, Tracey and Stephen Groves, Roger and
Anne Newbury, Joe Green, Richard, Mike and Lynn Robinson, Des and Ursula Weston, Joan York, N R White,
Gwyn and Anne Wake*

MUCH WENLOCK   SO6299   MAP 4

George & Dragon 🍺
High Street (A458); TF13 6AA

Bustling, cosily atmospheric, plenty to look at and usefully open all day

Under a new licensee since the last edition of the *Guide*, this town-centre local has a
fascinating stash of memorabilia. There are old brewery and cigarette advertisements,
bottle labels and beer trays, and George-and-the-Dragon pictures, as well as around 500
jugs hanging from the beams. Furnishings such as antique settles are among more
conventional seats, and there are a couple of attractive Victorian fireplaces (with coal-
effect gas fires). At the back is the restaurant. Black Sheep, Greene King Abbot, Hobsons
Town Crier, Timothy Taylors Landlord and a couple of guests are on handpump, and they
also have country wines; piped music and occasional TV for major events. More reports on
the new regime please.

🍽 **Available in the restaurant or the bar, food includes lunchtime sandwiches, soup, fish
and chips, faggots and peas and evening dishes such as black pudding with caramelised
red cabbage, rack of lamb, thai chicken curry and vegetable lasagne.** *Starters/Snacks: £3.95
to £5.50. Main Courses: £5.50 to £12.95. Puddings: £3.95*

Punch ~ Lease Angela Gray ~ Real ale ~ Bar food (12-2, 6-9 (not Weds or Sun evenings)) ~
(01952) 727312 ~ No children after 6pm except in restaurant ~ Dogs allowed in bar ~
Occasional live music on Sun afternoons ~ Open 12-11(12 Fri, 10.30 Sun)

*Recommended by Steve Whalley, Pat and Tony Martin, Pete Baker, Alan and Eve Harding, Paul and Margaret Baker,
Maurice and Gill McMahon, Jenny and Peter Lowater*

Talbot 🛏

High Street (A458); TF13 6AA

Ancient building with friendly welcome, tasty food, pretty courtyard, and bedrooms

Dating back to 1360, this inn was once part of Wenlock Abbey, the ruins of which still stand nearby. The several neatly kept areas have low ceilings, and comfortable red tapestry button-back wall banquettes around their tables. The walls are decorated with local pictures and cottagey plates, and there are art deco-style lamps and gleaming brasses. Bass and a guest such as Shepherd Neame Spitfire are served on handpump, and they've several malt whiskies, and nine wines by the glass; quiet piped music. It also has a little courtyard with green metal and wood garden furniture and pretty flower tubs. There's a cheap car park close by.

🍽 **The lunchtime menu is fairly pubby with soup, sandwiches, baguettes, filled baked potatoes, lasagne, sirloin steak and specials such as fish and lamb and leek pie, and there is a more elaborate (and not as cheap) evening menu with dishes such as salmon in cream, champagne and pink peppercorn sauce, duck with black pudding, redcurrant and port juice, pork calvados and steaks.** *Starters/Snacks: £4.50 to £5.75. Main Courses: £7.95 to £11.95. Puddings: £3.95*

Free house ~ Licensees Mark and Maggie Tennant ~ Real ale ~ Bar food (12-2.30, 6-9(8 Sun)) ~ Restaurant ~ (01952) 727077 ~ Children welcome ~ Open 11-3, 6-2am; 11-2am Fri, Sat; 12-4, 6-2am Sun ~ Bedrooms: £40B/£80B

Recommended by Brian Goodson, MDN, Jennifer Banks, John Wooll, Steve Whalley, John Oates, Denise Walton, Alan and Eve Harding

MUNSLOW   SO5287   MAP 2

Crown 🍺

B4368 Much Wenlock—Craven Arms; SY7 9ET

Cosy, ancient village inn with local ales and cider

Although it looks Georgian from outside, this former court house in Corve Dale feels much more ancient as soon as you step inside, and it's full of comfortable corners. The split-level lounge bar has a pleasantly old-fashioned mix of furnishings on its broad flagstones, a collection of old bottles, country pictures, and a bread oven by its good log fire. There are more seats in a traditional snug with its own fire, and the eating area has tables around a central oven chimney, stripped stone walls, and more beams and flagstones; piped music. The three or four beers on handpump are Holdens Black Country, Golden Glow, Mild and John Roberts XXX, alongside a local farm cider and several malt whiskies. Look out for Jenna, the boxer who usually makes her rounds at the end of the evening. More reports please.

🍽 **The imaginative food is produced with thought. As well as lunchtime sandwiches, the changing menu might include soup, breast of shropshire farm chicken with fondant potato and cream sauce of pink peppercorns and rosemary, fillet or sirloin steak, mushroom risotto, confit of duck leg with warmed apple chutney, glazed shallots and port wine syrup, and puddings such as spiced ginger parkin with rhubarb compote; also a selection of english and welsh cheeses.** *Starters/Snacks: £4.75 to £7.95. Main Courses: £11.50 to £16.95. Puddings: £4.95*

Free house ~ Licensees Richard and Jane Arnold ~ Real ale ~ Bar food (12-2, 6.45-8.45; 6.30-8 Sun) ~ Restaurant ~ (01584) 841205 ~ Children welcome in restaurant and seated in bar early evening ~ Open 12-3, 6.30-11(6.15-10.30 Sun); closed Mon ~ Bedrooms: £50S/£70S(£75B)

Recommended by Alan and Eve Harding, Joan York, R A P Cross, Colin Wood

---

A few pubs try to make you leave a credit card at the bar, as a sort of deposit if you order food. This is a bad practice, and the banks and credit card firms warn you not to let your card go like this.

NORBURY

SO3692 MAP 6

Sun 🛏

Off A488 or A489 NE of Bishop's Castle; OS Sheet 137 map reference 363928; SY9 5DX

Civilised dining pub with bedrooms, in prime hill-walking country not far from the Stiperstones

In a charmingly sleepy village beneath the southern flank of Norbury Hill, this dining pub has a delightful garden and pond. A proper tiled-floor bar has settees and Victorian tables and chairs, cushioned stone seats along the wall by the gas stove, and a few mysterious implements (the kind that it's fun to guess about) on its neat white walls. The restaurant side has a charming lounge with button-back leather wing chairs, easy chairs and a chesterfield on its deep-pile green carpet, as well as a welcoming log fire, nice lighting, willow-pattern china on a dark oak dresser, fresh flowers, candles and magazines; service is friendly. Wye Valley Bitter and maybe a guest in summer are kept on handpump under a light blanket pressure, and they have several malts and decent house wines. Note the unusual opening times.

🍽 The bar menu is fairly short, with baguettes, ploughman's, cumberland sausage and chips, shropshire rump steak, smoked trout and scampi. The elegantly furnished dining room has a different menu for evening meals and Sunday lunch (booking required). *Starters/Snacks: £3.75 to £4.95. Main Courses: £8.75 to £11.75. Puddings: £3.75 to £4.95*

Free house ~ Licensee Carol Cahan ~ Real ale ~ Bar food (7-9.30; 12-2 Sun only) ~ Restaurant ~ (01588) 650680 ~ Children welcome Sunday lunchtime only; no children in bedrooms ~ Open 7-11; 12-3, 7-10.30 Sun; closed lunchtimes (except Sun) and all day Mon, Tues ~ Bedrooms: /£90S

Recommended by Brian and Jacky Wilson, Jan and Alan Summers, Paul Davies, Susan Batten

PICKLESCOTT

SO4399 MAP 6

Bottle & Glass

Village signposted off A49 N of Church Stretton; SY6 6NR

Remote village pub with a charismatic and hospitable landlord who gets all the details right

It's well worth the pilgrimage along tortuous country lanes to this remote but surprisingly busy 16th-c pub, where a charismatic, bow-tied landlord makes things tick along with great aplomb. He works hard to make sure everyone is happy, easily running the bar and striking up conversations with customers – ask him to tell you about the antics of the resident ghost of the former landlord, Victor. Much to the delight surely of the two resident cats, Hello and Cookie, the fire rarely goes out in the small low-beamed and quarry-tiled cosy candlelit bar. The lounge, dining area and library area (for dining or sitting in) have open fires. Beers brewed by Hobsons, Three Tuns and Woods are on handpump; unobtrusive piped classical music. There are picnic-sets in front and the pub has a lovely position 1,000 feet above sea level and near the Long Mynd.

🍽 Very good home-made bar food (promptly served, in hearty helpings) might include filled baps, soup, ploughman's, roquefort stuffed pear with green mayonnaise, steak, kidney and Guinness pie, fish pie, game and red wine casserole, sausages and mash, vegetarian dishes like greek filo feta and spinach pie, and rosemary and garlic-crusted rack of lamb with red wine, honey and redcurrant sauce; very tasty puddings such as sticky toffee pudding or chocolate mint roulade. *Starters/Snacks: £3.50 to £6.50. Main Courses: £8.50 to £16.50. Puddings: £4.50 to £4.95*

Free house ~ Licensees Paul and Jo Stretton-Downes ~ Real ale ~ Bar food ~ (01694) 751345 ~ Children welcome in dining areas until 9pm ~ Dogs allowed in bar ~ Open 12-3.30, 6-11.30; closed Sun evening, Mon

Recommended by Phil and Jane Hodson, Angus and Carol Johnson, J C Brittain-Long, George and Maureen Roby, TOH, Phil Merrin, Ken Marshall, Carol and Colin Broadbent

SHREWSBURY   SJ4812   MAP 6

Armoury 🍽 ⏚ 🍺
Victoria Quay, Victoria Avenue; SY1 1HH
SHROPSHIRE DINING PUB OF THE YEAR

Smart pub in interestingly converted riverside warehouse, run by friendly and enthusiastic young staff, good food all day

'I wish there were many more places like this in our towns,' enthuses one reader of this large, airy town pub where the food and beer both come in for high praise. The spacious open-plan interior, with its long runs of big arched windows with views across the broad river, at this 18th-c former warehouse can make quite an impression when you first arrive. It's light and fresh, but the eclectic décor, furniture layout and lively bustle give a personal feel. Mixed wood tables and chairs are grouped on expanses of stripped wood floors, a display of floor-to-ceiling books dominates two huge walls, there's a grand stone fireplace at one end, and masses of old prints mounted edge to edge on the stripped brick walls. Colonial-style fans whirr away on the ceilings, which are supported by occasional green-painted standing timbers, and glass cabinets display collections of explosives and shells. The long bar counter has a terrific choice of drinks with up to eight real ales from brewers such as Hanby, Thwaites, Three Tuns and Woods well kept on handpump, a great wine list (with 16 by the glass), around 50 malt whiskies, a dozen different gins, lots of rums and vodkas, a variety of brandies, and some unusual liqueurs. Tables at one end are laid out for eating. The massive uniform red brick exteriors are interspersed with hanging baskets and smart coach lights at the front, and there may be queues at the weekend. The pub doesn't have its own parking, but there are plenty of places nearby.

🍽 Superbly cooked bar food, from an interesting daily changing menu, could include sandwiches, ploughman's, roast pepper and tomato soup, smoked haddock and salmon fishcake with tomato and onion salad, shepherd's pie, braised lamb shank with celeriac mash, salmon and king prawn risotto, orange and rosemary roasted belly pork, penne pasta with roast shallots, wild mushrooms, spinach and gruyère, and steak and oxtail casserole with horseradish dumplings; puddings might feature apple and raspberry crumble, or chocolate pancakes with orange and chestnut cream. *Starters/Snacks: £4.25 to £6.95. Main Courses: £7.95 to £17.95. Puddings: £4.95 to £5.25*

Brunning & Price ~ Manager Angharad Williams ~ Real ale ~ Bar food (12-9.30(9 Sun)) ~ (01743) 340525 ~ Children welcome till 7pm ~ Dogs allowed in bar ~ Open 12-11.30(11 Sun); closed 25, 26 Dec

Recommended by Richard C Morgan, Steve Whalley, Mrs Suzy Miller, Des and Ursula Weston, Mrs Hazel Rainer, Martin and Karen Wake, Kerry Law, Dave Webster, Sue Holland, P Dawn, Gerry and Rosemary Dobson

---

LUCKY DIP

Besides the fully inspected pubs, you might like to try these Lucky Dips recommended to us and described by readers (if you do, please send us reports: www.goodguides.co.uk).

ALL STRETTON [SO4595]
Yew Tree SY6 6HG [Shrewsbury Rd (B4370)]: Appealing old pub with enjoyable food (not Mon, and may take a while at busy times), small helpings available, Fullers London Pride, Hobsons Best and a changing Wye Valley ale, pleasant service, good log fire, houseplants and lots of interesting watercolours, bookable dining room (not always open), lively nicely worn in bar with darts, two big dogs; no credit cards; children welcome, small village handy for Long Mynd, cl Tues *(TOH, A N Bance, MDN, Sarah and Peter Gooderham, Alan and Eve Harding, Margaret Dickinson)*

ANCHOR [SO1785]
Anchor SY7 8PR [B4368 W of Clun]: Cosy unspoilt country tavern (the 'Mermaid's Rest', 'clean and romantic in the afternoon sun', in Mary Webb's 1922 *Seven for a Secret*), friendly owners, three woodburners, landlady cooks good meals to order with a day or two's notice, well kept Hobsons and Six Bells *(Mr and Mrs Draper)*

ASTON MUNSLOW [SO5187]
Swan SY7 9ER: Ancient pub with several rambling linked areas in varying styles, attentive efficient service, good choice of food inc good value set lunches, real ales such as Hobsons, fairly priced wines, log

fires; garden with shady areas *(Alan and Eve Harding)*

ASTON ON CLUN [SO3981]

Kangaroo SY7 8EW [Clun Rd]: Open-plan country pub with good food from notable ploughman's to interesting evening dishes, real ales inc one brewed for them by Six Bells, friendly service, central fireplace in main bar, front public bar with railway memorabilia inc large model train over fireplace, little side dining room; tables in large back garden, interesting village among poplars below Hopesay Hill, open all day Fri-Sun *(Robert W Buckle)*

ATCHAM [SJ5409]

☆ *Mytton & Mermaid* SY5 6QG: Comfortable hotel rather than pub, but with really nice friendly atmosphere, big log fire and sofas in relaxed bar, good food from paninis to guinea fowl here or in large bustling restaurant, keen young staff, real ales such as Salopian Shropshire Gold, good wine choice, some theme nights; pleasant Severn-view bedrooms, nice setting opp entrance to Attingham Park (NT) *(Des and Ursula Weston, Glen and Nola Armstrong, Mrs Suzy Miller, Tom and Jill Jones, Bruce and Sharon Eden)*

BRIDGNORTH [SO6890]

Down WV16 6UA [The Down, Ludlow Rd, 3 miles S]: Attractive old stone-built pub overlooking rolling countryside, enjoyable reasonably priced food inc good carvery and vegetarian choice, real ales inc one brewed for the pub, good cheerful service even when busy *(Jennifer Banks, Mr and Mrs F E Boxell)*

Friars WV16 4DW [St Marys St, Central Ct (down passage from High St)]: Peaceful town pub in quaint location in sheltered courtyard of half-timbered buildings, well kept ales such as Holdens and Wye Valley, cheerful service, reasonably priced simple food, good coffee; piped music; bedrooms, open all day wknds and summer *(George Atkinson)*

☆ *Railwaymans Arms* WV16 5DT [Severn Valley Stn, Hollybush Rd (off A458 towards Stourbridge)]: Bathams, Hobsons and other good value local ales in chatty old-fashioned converted waiting-room at Severn Valley steam railway terminus, bustling on summer days, with coal fire, station nameplates, superb mirror over fireplace, may be simple summer snacks; children welcome, wheelchair access, tables out on platform – the train to Kidderminster (another bar there) has an all-day bar and bookable Sun lunches *(Ian and Liz Rispin, Joe Green, the Didler, LYM, Ian Stafford)*

BROOME [SO4081]

Engine & Tender SY7 0NT: Homely bar with one or two well kept local ales from art deco servery, railway memorabilia and other bric-a-brac, cosy corners with tables for eating, also quite extensive restaurant with interesting collection of pottery inc teapots and shelves of jugs, good pubby food (not Mon) inc generous Sun roast and good

puddings, good value wines, cheerful helpful unhurried service, lushly planted conservatory, games room with pool and glassed-over well; caravan site with hook-up points and showers, nice countryside *(MLR)*

BUCKNELL [SO3574]

Baron of Beef SY7 0AH [Chapel Lawn Rd; just off B4367 Knighton Rd]: Smartly decorated dining pub in fine countryside, good bar food inc enterprising dishes, largish upstairs restaurant with own bar and popular wknd carvery, friendly staff, well kept Greene King IPA, Hobsons and Woods, farm cider, decent house wines, big log fire in front bar, back lounge with fresh flowers, interesting prints, rustic memorabilia inc grindstone and cider press; wknd live music; well behaved children and dogs welcome, lovely views, big garden with skittles and play area, camping field *(anon)*

BURLTON [SJ4526]

Burlton Inn SY4 5TB [A528 Shrewsbury—Ellesmere, nr B4397 junction]: The Beans who made this attractively refurbished old pub so popular for their good imaginative food and thoughtful service have sold it to Robinsons; sporting prints, log fires, comfortable snug, restaurant with garden dining room opening to pleasant terrace, more tables on lawn; has welcomed children and dogs, disabled facilities, good bedrooms; more reports on new regime, please *(LYM)*

BURWARTON [SO6185]

☆ *Boyne Arms* WV16 6QH [B4364 Bridgnorth—Ludlow]: Imposing Georgian coaching inn with charming new licensees, enjoyable generous food inc Mon/Tues OAP lunches, changing well kept ales such as Bathams Best, Greene King IPA, Woods Shropshire Lad and Wychwood Hobgoblin, cheerful atmosphere, restaurant, public bar with pool and other games; tables in large garden with good timber adventure playground *(Carol and Colin Broadbent, Mr and Mrs F E Boxell)*

CALVERHALL [SJ6037]

Old Jack SY13 4PA [New St Lane]: Neatly kept beamed bar with log fire and button-back banquettes, enjoyable home-made food (best to book wknds) inc pies to take away, smiling service, arches to separate dining area opening on to terrace *(Susan and Nigel Brookes, Rachel Grounds, John Waddington)*

CLEE HILL [SO5975]

Kremlin SY8 3NB [track up hill off A4117 Bewdley—Cleobury, by Victoria Inn]: Shropshire's highest pub, with splendid view S from garden and terrace, enjoyable bar food, real ales such as Hobsons, John Smiths and Tetleys, farm cider *(Mike and Lynn Robinson, Dave Braisted)*

CLEOBURY MORTIMER [SO6775]

Royal Fountain DY14 8BS [Church St]: Friendly pub with real ale, home-made food inc enterprising specials, sensibly short wine list; garden tables *(Joe Green)*

CLUN [SO3080]

Sun SY7 8JB [High St]: Another change of management in beamed and timbered Tudor pub with some sturdy antique furnishings, modern paintings and older prints, enormous open fire in flagstoned public bar with darts, cards and dominoes, larger carpeted lounge bar, food from sandwiches up, Banks's Bitter and Best with a guest such as Jennings; children allowed in eating area, terrace tables in back garden, lovely village, nice bedrooms, open all day *(Pat and Tony Martin, BB, Kevin Thorpe, the Didler, Rona Murdoch)*

☆ *White Horse* SY7 8JA [Market Sq]: Well run low-beamed open-plan local dating from 18th c, helpful friendly landlord and staff, good value food from lunchtime cheese-on-toast specialities to particularly good Sun lunch, half a dozen well priced changing ales such as Hobsons, Salopian, Six Bells and Wye Valley, Weston's farm cider, good coffee, daily papers, inglenook and open woodburner, country bric-a-brac, pool and juke box in panelled games end; children welcome, pavement tables in front, small back garden, open all day *(Theocsbrian, Alan and Eve Harding, MLR, Bruce Bird)*

COALBROOKDALE [SJ6604]

☆ *Coalbrookdale Inn* TF8 7DX [Wellington Rd, opp Museum of Iron]: Handsome dark brick 18th-c pub with half a dozen quickly changing real ales from square counter in simple convivial tiled-floor bar, good sensibly priced food cooked to order using local meats, cheeses etc here or in quieter refurbished dining room, farm ciders, country wines, good log fire, local pictures, piano, naughty beach murals in lavatories; long flight of steps to entrance; dogs welcome, a few tables outside, comfortable well equipped bedrooms *(Warren Marsh, DC, the Didler, BB)*

COALPORT [SJ6902]

☆ *Boat* TF8 7LS [Ferry Rd, Jackfield; nr Mawes Craft Centre]: Long but cosy 18th-c quarry-tiled bar, coal fire in lovely range, reasonably priced fresh food inc good value Sun lunch, welcoming service, Marstons-related ales, Weston's farm cider, darts; summer barbecues on big tree-shaded lawn, in delightful if floodable part of Severn Gorge, footbridge making it handy for Coalport China Museum, may be cl wkday lunchtimes *(BB, the Didler, Martin and Karen Wake)*

COCKSHUTT [SJ4329]

☆ *Leaking Tap* SY12 0JQ [A528 Ellesmere—Shrewsbury]: Comfortable and attractive, with good varied food (Sun lunch very popular), reasonable prices, friendly licensees, good beer and wines by the glass *(Jill Sparrow)*

CORFTON [SO4985]

☆ *Sun* SY7 9DF [B4368 Much Wenlock—Craven Arms]: Very welcoming chatty landlord (if he's not busy in the back brewery) in unsmart two-bar country local with its own good unfined Corvedale ales and a guest beer, lots of breweriana, public bar with internet access as well as darts and pool, good value pubby food from generous baguettes to bargain Sun lunch (service can slow if busy), dining room with covered well, tourist information; piped music; particularly good disabled access throughout, tables on terrace and in good-sized garden with good play area *(MLR, BB, Gwyn and Anne Wake, Carol and Colin Broadbent)*

CRESSAGE [SJ5704]

☆ *Riverside* SY5 6AF [A458 NW, nr Cound]: Spacious pub/hotel, light and airy, with pleasant mix of furnishings, limited choice of enjoyable food changing monthly inc lunchtime baguettes (and their own free-range eggs), reasonable prices, unrushed service, good value wines by the glass, well kept changing ales such as Salopian Shropshire Gold, lovely Severn views from roomy conservatory; french windows to big terraced garden with wandering rare-breed chickens, comfortable bedrooms, good breakfast, open all day wknds *(Neil and Brenda Skidmore, D Hillaby, LYM, Mr and Mrs M Sykes)*

CROSS HOUSES [SJ5307]

Bell SY5 6JJ: Pleasantly simple traditional two-bar pub, good value straightforward food, well kept local Salopian ales; attractive side beer garden, back camp site, bedrooms *(Robert W Buckle)*

CRUCKTON [SJ4311]

Hare & Hounds SY5 8PW [B4386]: Friendly efficient service, good reasonably priced home-made food inc plenty of fresh fish, pleasant lounge/dining area *(Alan and Eve Harding)*

EDGERLEY [SJ3517]

☆ *Royal Hill* SY10 8ES [off A5 following MoD Nesscliff Trg Camp signs, then Melverley signs]: Nicely unspoilt 17th-c beamed country local tucked away in quiet spot, worn tiled corridor behind tall settles forming snug around coal fire, little parlour with settee, easy chair, rocking chair and TV, back bar with two Salopian beers, occasional plain food; children welcome, long old-fashioned benches out in front, picnic-sets over lane on banks of River Severn, pleasant caravan/camp site, cl winter wkdy lunchtimes, open all day wknds *(BB, Noel Grundy, the Didler)*

ELLESMERE [SJ3934]

☆ *Black Lion* SY12 0EG [Scotland St; back car park on A495]: Good simple substantial food at bargain prices, helpful staff, relaxed beamed bar with interesting décor and some nice unusual features such as the traditional wood-and-glass screen along its tiled entrance corridor, quiet and comfortable roomy dining room; piped music; bedrooms, handy car park, not far from canal wharf *(Adrian Johnson, Rita and Keith Pollard, BB, D Hillaby, A Darroch Harkness)*

White Hart SY12 0ET [Birch Rd]: Attractive little black and white pub, one of the oldest in Shrops, with well kept changing real ales, friendly landlord, good Sun lunch (no wkdy food); not far from canal *(Simon Vernon)*

FORD [SJ4113]

Pavement Gates SY5 9LE [Welshpool Rd (A458 W of Shrewsbury)]: Relaxing dining pub under newish licensees, appealing contemporary refurbishment, comfortable lounge with daily papers and board games, smart restaurant, enjoyable food all day from enterprising light dishes up, good service, sensibly priced wines; open all day *(anon)*

HAMPTON LOADE [SO7486]

River & Rail WV16 6BN: Welcoming modern pub handy for River Severn and steam railway (Apr-Oct ferry from station), wide choice of enjoyable and substantial fresh food from sandwiches to tempting puddings, efficient service, real ale and country wines; big attractive garden with plenty of under-cover seating *(Caroline and Michael Abbey, John and Gloria Isaacs, Carol and Colin Broadbent)*

HODNET [SJ6128]

☆ *Bear* TF9 3NH [Drayton Rd (A53)]: Small beamed quarry-tiled bar with log fire, broad arch to rambling open-plan carpeted main area with blond seats and tables set for the good range of reasonably priced food from sandwiches up, friendly helpful staff, good wines by the glass, three real ales, snug end alcoves with heavy 16th-c beams and timbers; children welcome (high chairs and child-size cutlery), six good value bedrooms, opp Hodnet Hall gardens and handy for Hawkstone Park, open all day *(BB, Jill Sparrow, Bob and Margaret Holder)*

HOPTON WAFERS [SO6376]

☆ *Crown* DY14 0NB [A4117]: Attractive 16th-c beamed and creeper-covered inn with relaxed atmosphere and friendly service, enjoyable food (all day Sun) from baguettes to good puddings, big inglenook, light and comfortable décor and furnishings, four well kept ales such as Hobsons Best, Timothy Taylors Landlord and Woods Shropshire Lad, good choice of wines; children welcome, dogs welcome in bar and pretty bedrooms, inviting garden with duck pond, stream and terraces, open all day *(Lynda and Trevor Smith, K S Whittaker, Ian and Jane Irving, Mrs A J Evans, Alan and Eve Harding, Andy Sinden, Louise Harrington, Carol and Colin Broadbent, Martin and Pauline Jennings, LYM, Walter and Susan Rinaldi-Butcher, Mike and Lynn Robinson, Julian Saunders)*

IRONBRIDGE [SJ6703]

It's All About Me TF8 7AD [High St]: Comfortable and relaxing wine bar/restaurant with real ale and good soft drinks as well as the drinks you'd expect, interesting food from tapas up; children and dogs welcome, sun terrace with Gorge views, play area, cl Mon, open all day *(Adrian Woolcott)*

Swan TF8 7NH [Wharfage]: Friendly ex-warehouse with dark woodwork and lots of alcoves, good range of decent food from baguettes to some interesting dishes, friendly efficient service, real ales and a continental beer on tap, separate candlelit red-décor dining area; tables outside *(Martin and Karen Wake, M Joyner)*

Tontine TF8 7AL [Tontine Hill]: Friendly 18th-c hotel, not in best area but with good atmosphere in both bars, nice mix of leather armchairs and sofas with more pubby furniture, attractive fireplaces, lots of pictures, Banks's, Enville and Greene King Abbot, good choice of food from sandwiches and baked potatoes up, brisk friendly service; reasonably priced bedrooms *(Dennis Jones)*

White Hart TF8 7AW [Wharfage]: Under same management as nearby Malthouse, fresh and airy contemporary décor, enjoyable bistro-style food (all day Sun), quiet at lunchtime, special deals Mon-Thurs evenings; picnic-sets out facing river over road, four comfortable bedrooms, open all day *(M Joyner)*

LEEBOTWOOD [SO4798]

☆ *Pound* SY6 6ND [A49 Church Stretton—Shrewsbury]: Smart dining pub in thatched 16th-c building, promptly served good food inc interesting even quite complex dishes as well as ham and eggs and so forth, pleasant newish licensees and staff, Fullers London Pride and Greene King IPA or Abbot, decent wines by the glass; garden tables *(TOH, BB, Tom and Jill Jones, Carol and Colin Broadbent)*

LLANFAIR WATERDINE [SO2376]

Waterdine LD7 1TU [signed from B4355; turn left after bridge]: Spotless old inn nicely set nr good stretch of Offa's Dyke Path, emphasis on good if not cheap food (must book) inc inventive recipes in rambling series of heavy-beamed rooms with cosy alcoves, woodburner and some flagstones, small back conservatory looking down to River Teme (the Wales border); picnic-sets in lovely garden *(LYM, Rodney and Norma Stubington)*

LUDLOW [SO5174]

Charlton Arms SY8 1PJ [Ludford Bridge]: Former coaching inn in great spot overlooking River Teme and the town, attractive refurbishment of both bars now complete, with comfortable seating and good real ales, but work on kitchen still under way as we went to press – may well be finished by the time this edition is in the shops (news please); waterside garden and terrace, bedrooms (may be traffic noise), open all day *(Joe Green)*

Old Bull Ring Tavern SY8 1AB [Bull Ring]: Striking timbered building now run well by friendly family, home-made food inc great pies and roasts, good sandwiches too, pleasant friendly service, real ales; children welcome, terrace tables *(Joe Green)*

Rose & Crown SY8 1AP [Church St, behind Buttercross]: Small unpretentious pub useful for decent reasonably priced home-made food all day, real ales such as Adnams and Tetleys, attractively laid dining room, interesting artwork; picnic-sets behind, pretty spot *(Mike and Lynn Robinson)*

Unicorn SY8 1DU [Corve St, bottom end]: Attractive small 17th-c coaching inn with opened-up low-beamed and partly panelled bar of great potential, real ales such as Bass, Black Sheep and Wye Valley, simple food; children and dogs welcome, terrace among willows by river, open all day wknds *(LYM)*

MADELEY [SJ69034]

All Nations TF7 5DP [Coalport Rd]: Simple 18th-c pub up steps from road, refurbished but unspoilt, with distinctive Worfield Dableys, Coalport Dodger, Gold and a seasonal ale from back brewery, bargain hefty filled rolls and pork pies, coal fires each end, old photographs; picnic-sets on heated terrace, handy for Blists Hill (you may find actor/staff from there, in full Victorian costume), open all day Fri-Sun *(Martin and Karen Wake, Kevin Thorpe)*

MAESBURY MARSH [SJ3125]

☆ **Navigation** SY10 8JB: Pub bistro and restaurant in great location towards the limit of navigation on partially restored Montgomery Canal, three changing real ales and farm cider in character bar area with beams, stripped brickwork and choir stalls complete with misericords, good food (not Tues or Sat evenings) inc home-baked breads and some really enterprising recipes, friendly helpful service, summer bank hol beer festival; waterside terrace, two bedrooms, cl Mon, Tues lunchtime, Sun evening *(Bob and Laura Brock, Jane and Martin Headley)*

MARTON [SJ2802]

☆ **Sun** SY21 8JP [B4386 NE of Chirbury]: Welcoming licensees keeping good balance between genuine village pub part with locals playing dominoes, Banks's and Worthington, and enjoyable pubby bar food; and separate restaurant with up-to-date décor, good serious cooking, and good choice of reasonably priced wines by the glass – best to book evenings *(Alan and Eve Harding, William Ruxton)*

MUCH WENLOCK [SO6299]

Gaskell Arms TF13 6AQ [High St (A458)]: Two comfortable areas divided by brass-canopied log fire, friendly attentive service, enjoyable straightforward bar food at sensible prices, real ales such as John Smiths and Wells & Youngs, brasses, prints and banknotes, civilised old-fashioned restaurant; subdued piped music, games machine in lobby; roomy neat garden, bedrooms *(Alan and Eve Harding)*

NEWCASTLE [SO2482]

☆ **Crown** SY7 8QL [B4368 Clun—Newtown]: Pretty village pub, warm and friendly, with good choice of reasonably priced beers such as Hobsons and Timothy Taylors Landlord, settees and woodburner in smart stripped stone lounge with some well spaced tables in two dining areas, good coffee, attractively priced standard food from sandwiches to steak, rustic locals' bar and games room;

piped music; tables outside, charming well equipped bedrooms above bar, attractive views and walks, open all day Sat *(Rona Murdoch, A N Bance, LYM)*

NEWPORT [SJ7419]

Bridge Inn TF10 7JB [Bridge Terrace, Chetwynd End]: Comfortable and neatly kept 17th-c black and white local with three real ales, good choice of other drinks, reasonably priced bar food and small separate dining room; tight car park entry; good-sized garden, bedrooms *(John Tav)*

NORTON [SJ7200]

☆ **Hundred House** TF11 9EE [A442 Telford—Bridgnorth]: Lovely garden with old-fashioned roses, herbaceous plants and big working herb garden; neatly kept bar with appealing gothic décor, Highgate Davenports, a Bitter and Mild brewed for the pub and a guest beer, good wine choice, enjoyable food, log fires (not always lit) in handsome old fireplaces or working coalbrookdale ranges, generally good service; piped music; comfortable bedrooms *(David and Ruth Hollands, Martin and Karen Wake, Mr and Mrs M Stratton, JMC, Des and Ursula Weston, A and B D Craig, David Edwards, Maurice and Gill McMahon, Alan and Eve Harding, LYM, Tracey and Stephen Groves)*

QUEENS HEAD [SJ3326]

☆ **Queens Head** SY11 4EB [just off A5 SE of Oswestry, towards Nesscliffe]: Emphasis on wide choice of generous good value food (all day Fri and wknds) from speciality sandwiches and other snacks to lots of fish and steaks, Theakstons Best and Old Peculier and two guest beers, good wines by the glass, pleasant helpful staff, two well refurbished dining areas with hot coal fires, nice roomy conservatory overlooking restored section of Montgomery Canal; picnic-sets under cocktail parasols in suntrap waterside garden, country walks *(Alex and Claire Pearse, UN)*

SHIFNAL [SJ74508]

White Hart TF11 8BH [High St]: Half a dozen or more interesting changing ales inc local ones in friendly timbered 17th-c pub, quaint and old-fashioned, separate bar and lounge, comfortable without pretension, wide range of sandwiches and promptly served good value home-made hot dishes, good choice of wines by the glass, welcoming staff; couple of steep steps at front door *(the Didler)*

SHREWSBURY [SO4912]

Coach & Horses SY1 1NF [Swan Hill/Cross Hill]: Friendly old-fashioned Victorian local, panelled throughout, with main bar, cosy little side room and back dining room, good value fresh food inc daily roast and some unusual dishes, Bass, Goodalls Gold (brewed for pub by Salopian) and a guest beer, relaxed atmosphere, prompt helpful service even when busy, interesting prints; pretty flower boxes outside, open all day *(Pete Baker, Dave Webster, Sue Holland, John Tav, the Didler, P Dawn)*

Golden Cross SY1 1LP [Princess St]:
Attractive partly Tudor hotel with restaurant
and quiet bar, welcoming attentive service,
short choice of good interesting food inc
home-baked bread, good range of wines by
the glass, well kept ales such as Banks's and
Salopian, pleasant helpful staff; four good
value bedrooms (Alan and Eve Harding)

☆ **Loggerheads** SY1 1UG [Church St]: Friendly
and gossipy old-fashioned local, panelled
back room with flagstones, scrubbed-top
tables, high-backed settles and coal fire,
three other rooms with lots of prints,
flagstones and bare boards, quaint linking
corridor and hatch service of Banks's Bitter
and Mild and other Marstons-related ales,
exemplary bar staff, bargain lunchtime food
(not Sun) inc doorstep sandwiches, baked
potatoes and good steak pie with great
chips; darts, dominoes, poetry society,
occasional live music; open all day
(Dave Webster, Sue Holland, the Didler,
Pete Baker, P Dawn)

☆ **Three Fishes** SY1 1UR [Fish St]: Well run
timbered and heavily beamed 16th-c pub
with well kept Caledonian Deuchars IPA,
Fullers London Pride, Salopian, Timothy
Taylors Landlord and interesting guest beers,
good value wines, good friendly service even
when busy, old pictures, no mobiles;
normally have good value hearty bar food
(not Sun evening); open all day Fri/Sat
(LYM, Theo, Anne and Jane Gaskin,
Tracey and Stephen Groves, the Didler,
Dr John Worthington, Helen McLagan,
Andy and Alice Jordan, Dave Webster,
Sue Holland, Derek and Sylvia Stephenson,
Dr B and Mrs P B Baker, John Coatsworth)

Wheatsheaf SY1 1ST [High St]: Comfortable
open-plan beamed lounge, tasty home
cooking, well kept Banks's, good choice of
wines by the glass, pleasant helpful staff;
open all day (D E Lowe)

STIPERSTONES [SJ3600]

☆ **Stiperstones Inn** SY5 0LZ [signed off A488
S of Minsterley; OS Sheet 126 map ref
364005]: Simple bargain fresh food all day in
warm-hearted walkers' pub (they sell maps)
with Six Bells or Woods Parish, small
modernised lounge bar, comfortable
leatherette wall banquettes, lots of brassware
on ply-panelled walls, decent wine, real fire,
darts in plainer public bar, restaurant; may be
unobtrusive piped music; tables outside,
cheap bedrooms (small dogs welcome), good
breakfast (Roy Payne, BB, Jeff Davies)

STREET DINAS [SJ3338]

Greyhound SY11 3HD [B5069 St Martin's—
Oswestry]: Comfortable bar profusely
decorated with pictures, interesting
memorabilia from nearby Ifton colliery,
hundreds of whisky miniatures and beer
bottles, masses of chamber-pots hanging
from beams, Banks's Best and Greene King
Abbot, welcoming landlady, good value food
from good baguettes up, dining room, back
games room and end TV; tables in
individualistic garden with water features,

Reliant Robin as a sort of sculpture
(Michael and Jenny Back)

UPTON MAGNA [SJ5512]

Corbet Arms SY4 4TZ: Big L-shaped dining
lounge, busy wknds, with panelling, pictures
and a modicum of bric-a-brac, popular food
(not Mon), three well kept Marstons-related
ales, decent house wines, armchairs by log
fire, spotless housekeeping, darts in smaller
public bar; great view to the Wrekin from
tables in attractive garden, handy for
Haughmond Hill walks and Attingham Park
(NT), neat bedrooms (Phil and Jane Hodson)

WELLINGTON [SJ6410]

Wickets TF1 2EB [Holyhead Rd]: Light
modern refurbishment but keeping some
interesting memorabilia dating from World
War I, Greene King Old Speckled Hen and
Wells & Youngs Bombardier, wide choice of
popular food from snacks up, substantial
helpings and sensible prices, good seating in
tiled bar, dining area (Gill and Keith Croxton)

WENTNOR [SO3892]

☆ **Crown** SY9 5EE [off A489]: Popular dining
pub dating from 16th c, real ales such as
Greene King Old Speckled Hen, Hobsons
Best, John Roberts XXX and Woods
Shropshire Lad, decent wines, good choice of
malt whiskies, good log fires, daily papers,
dominoes and cribbage, big restaurant;
terrace tables, bedrooms, open all day wknds
(TOH, LYM, Steve Whalley, Phil and
Jane Hodson, Jan and Alan Summers)

WHITCHURCH [SJ5441]

Horse & Jockey SY13 1LB [Church St]: Three
or four cosy and comfortable dining areas
with good value food, friendly attentive
service (Alan and Eve Harding)

White Bear SY13 1AR [High St]: Busy
friendly pub with enjoyable bar meals, real
ales, quick service; tables in small courtyard
(Mrs Hazel Rainer)

☆ **Willey Moor Lock** SY13 4HF [Tarporley Rd;
signed off A49 just under 2m N]: Large pub
in picturesque spot by Llangollen Canal,
linked rooms with low beams, countless
teapots, two log fires, cheerful chatty
atmosphere, half a dozen changing ales from
small breweries, around 30 malt whiskies,
good value quickly served simple food from
sandwiches and baked potatoes up; piped
music, games machine, several dogs and
cats, various 'rule' notices; children welcome
away from bar, terrace tables, secure garden
with big play area (LYM, Anthony Pike, MLR,
A Darroch Harkness)

WHITTINGTON [SJ3231]

White Lion SY11 4DF [Castle St]: Sizeable
nicely refurbished pub just below castle, well
kept beer, enjoyable food, good wines by the
glass, some soft leather sofas, small dining
room, conservatory; plenty of tables in good
outdoor area (Jill Sparrow)

WISTANSTOW [SO4385]

Plough SY7 8DG [off A49 and A489 N of
Craven Arms]: Plain high-raftered pub,
informally welcoming tap for Woods brewery
and well worth knowing for their good beers

at low prices; quick friendly service, straightforward food, interesting collection of royal wedding commemorative beers, games area with darts, dominoes and pool, small bar and larger simple dining room; piped music; children and dogs welcome, cl Mon evening in winter *(Tracey and Stephen Groves, Mrs Phoebe A Kemp, J C Clark, Pauline and Philip Darley, Pat and Tony Martin, Tony and Dot Mariner)*

WORFIELD [SO7595]

☆ *Dog* WV15 5LF [off A454 W of Bridgnorth; Main St]: Pretty pub in beautiful unspoilt stone-built village, three sprucely decorated areas with emphasis on food from good

value baguettes to plenty of wknd seafood, well kept changing ales inc local brews, good house wines, log fire; children welcome *(Carol and Colin Broadbent, Mrs E A O'Byrne)*

YORTON [SJ5023]

Railway SY4 3EP: Same family for some 70 years, friendly and chatty mother and daughter, unchanging atmosphere, plain tiled bar with hot coal fire, old settles and a modicum of railway memorabilia, big back lounge (not always open) with fishing trophies, Woods and other mainly local real ales, farm ciders, darts and dominoes – no piped music or machines; seats out in yard *(the Didler)*

We checked prices with the pubs as we went to press in summer 2007. They should hold until around spring 2008 – when our experience suggests that you can expect an increase of around 10p in the £.

Somerset

In this chapter we include Bristol, as well as Bath. There's a great deal of real, solid down-to-earth character in many of the pubs here – and while our chosen pubs are, of course, welcoming to visitors, the local following seems stronger than in many other counties. There are unspoilt favourites and smarter places too, but all now seem keen to support the bountiful local produce – local beers and ciders as well as food. Three new entries reflect this brightly: the George in Croscombe (good cooking by landlady, relaxed atmosphere fuelled by hands-on landlord); the stylish and civilised old Lord Poulett Arms at Hinton St George (good all round, with nice bedrooms); and the Exmoor Forest Inn at Simonsbath (another fine all-rounder, very welcoming). In recent months readers have also been particularly enthusiastic about the Globe in Appley (unchanging and appealing country pub), the Square & Compass just above Ashill (run with real enthusiasm with licensees who love their live music), the Red Lion at Babcary (friendly young landlord and super food), the Three Horseshoes at Batcombe (the new bedrooms are a particular success, as is the elaborate food), in Bath two pubs, the King William (quite quirky, with interesting meals) and the Old Green Tree (a favourite with many), the Cat Head at Chiselborough (a surprising find, so handy for the A303), the Crown at Churchill (unspoilt and friendly, with ten real ales), the Black Horse at Clapton-in-Gordano (very popular for its old-fashioned charm, and an M5 escape), the Queens Arms at Corton Denham (informally smart with imaginative food), the Strode Arms at Cranmore (good proper pub food and very attractive bars), Woods in Dulverton (fantastic wines, lovely food and smart but informal feel), the very well run Helyar Arms at East Coker (30 wines by the glass), the Tuckers Grave at Faulkland (an unspoilt gem), the Rose & Crown at Huish Episcopi (a splendid whiff of yesteryear), the Kings Arms at Litton (bar snacks plus up-to-date meals in really nice surroundings), the Pilgrims at Lovington (smart dining pub with good food cooked by the landlord), the Royal Oak at Luxborough (marvellous place to stay, in lovely countryside), the Notley Arms at Monksilver (well run by friendly licensees, with enjoyable food), the Halfway House at Pitney (cheerful village pub with ten real ales), the civilised Carpenters Arms at Stanton Wick (very popular for its imaginative food), the Rose & Crown in Stoke St Gregory (long-serving family boosting its buoyant atmosphere) and the Tarr Farm at Tarr (such a fine setting, and good food). As you can see from this long list, good food, often imaginative, features strongly at many of these pubs. Woods in Dulverton, with good interesting food, fine wines and beers to go with it, and a warm pubby atmosphere in its compact bar and eating area, is Somerset Dining Pub of the Year. Good pub food in the county is generally priced close to the national average. Drinks prices too are not far off the norm – perhaps a little lower. Butcombe and Exmoor are the local beers we found most often in good pubs here, and are also often the cheapest offered by a pub. Other good value local beers well worth looking out for, and fairly widely available, are RCH, Cotleigh, Abbey, Bath, Taunton, Masters, Blindmans, Cottage and Milk Street. The Lucky Dip section at the end of the chapter is particularly rich in good pubs. To help you pick your way through it, we'd specially mention the Ring o' Bells in Ashcott, Coeur de Lion and George in Bath, Adam & Eve and Kings Head in Bristol, Bell at Buckland Dinham, Farmers Arms at Combe Florey, Luttrell Arms in Dunster, Rose & Crown at East Lambrook, Faulkland Inn, Hope & Anchor at Midford, Fleur de Lys at Norton St Philip, Ship at Porlock Weir, Pack Horse at South Stoke, Lowtrow Cross Inn at Upton, Vobster Inn, Cotley Inn at Wambrook, Slab House at West Horrington and Royal Oak at Withypool.

APPLEY   ST0721   MAP 1

Globe ⊕

Hamlet signposted from the network of back roads between A361 and A38, W of B3187 and W of Milverton and Wellington; OS Sheet 181 map reference 072215; TA21 0HJ

Consistently enjoyable country pub with well liked bar food, real ales and local juices, and seats in garden

Reliably well run, this 15th-c pub has a relaxed, welcoming atmosphere and a good mix of both locals and visitors. The simple beamed front room has a built-in settle and bare wood tables on the brick floor, and another room has a GWR bench and 1930s railway posters; there's a further room with easy chairs and other more traditional ones, open fires, and a collection of model cars, art deco items and *Titanic* pictures; skittle alley. A brick entry corridor leads to a serving hatch with a beer brewed for them by the new Masters brewery a couple of miles S of here, and a guest like Exmoor Fox or Sharps Doom Bar on handpump; also local cider, cordials and fruit juices. Seats, climbing frame and swings outside in the garden; the path opposite leads eventually to the River Tone.

⊞ As well as lunchtime snacks such as filled baguettes, ploughman's, home-cooked ham and egg and burgers, the generous helpings of tasty bar food include soup, chicken liver pâté with caramelised red onion chutney, seafood pancake, red onion and goats cheese tart, chicken breast on fresh linguini with a wild mushroom, white wine and cream sauce topped with crispy grilled parma ham, moroccan lamb casserole, venison pie, half a roast duckling with madeira sauce, and puddings such as sunken chocolate cake with warm chocolate sauce and sticky toffee pudding. *Starters/Snacks: £3.50 to £8.95. Main Courses: £8.95 to £14.95. Puddings: £3.50 to £5.50*

Free house ~ Licensees Andrew and Liz Burt ~ Real ale ~ Bar food ~ Restaurant ~
(01823) 672327 ~ Children welcome ~ Open 11-3, 6.30-midnight; 12-3, 7-11 Sun; closed Mon except bank hols

Recommended by John and Fiona McIlwain, Bob and Margaret Holder, MB, the Didler

---

ASHILL   ST3116   MAP 1

Square & Compass

Windmill Hill; off A358 between Ilminster and Taunton; up Wood Road for 1 mile behind Stewley Cross service station; OS Sheet 193 map reference 310166; TA19 9NX

Friendly simple pub with local ales, tasty food and good regular live music in sound-proofed barn

A large glass-covered walled terrace is to be built on to the front of this traditional pub and a new kitchen installed. But it remains an appealing place with welcoming licensees and friendly, chatty customers. The sweeping views over the rolling pastures around

Neroche Forest can be enjoyed from the upholstered window seats in the little bar and there are other seats, an open winter fire – and perhaps the pub cats Daisy and Lilly. Exmoor Ale and Gold, Otter Bitter and a guest beer on handpump and good house wines by the glass. The piped music is often classical. There's a garden with picnic-sets, and good regular live music in their sound-proofed Barn.

🍽 **Generously served bar food includes sandwiches, filled baguettes and baked potatoes, ploughman's, soup, hot garlic king prawns, fried brie, local sausages with onion gravy, ham and egg, mushroom stroganoff, sweet and sour pork, chicken curry, lambs kidneys braised with sherry and dijon mustard, mixed grill, and puddings such as banoffi pie or chocolate fudge cake; on Sundays there may be only a roast.** *Starters/Snacks: £3.50 to £5.00. Main Courses: £5.00 to £15.00. Puddings: £3.50 to £5.00*

Free house ~ Licensees Chris, Janet and Beth Slow ~ Real ale ~ Bar food (not Tues, Weds or Thurs lunchtimes) ~ Restaurant ~ (01823) 480467 ~ Children welcome ~ Dogs welcome ~ Monthly live music in separate barn ~ Open 12-2.30, 6.30-11; 12-2.30, 7-10.30 Sun; closed Tues, Weds and Thurs lunchtimes

Recommended by M Jav, Pat and Tony Martin, Mr and Mrs Colin Roberts, B J Harding

AXBRIDGE
ST4354   MAP 1

Lamb
The Square; off A371 Cheddar—Winscombe; BS26 2AP

Bustling pub on market square with rambling bar, local beers and fairly priced food

As this ancient pub is right on the market square, there's usually quite a bustle of shoppers and locals. The big rambling bar is full of heavy beams and timbers, cushioned wall seats and small settles and there's an open fire in one great stone fireplace and a collection of tools and utensils including an unusual foot-operated grinder in another. Bath Ales Gem, Butcombe Bitter and Gold and a changing guest on handpump from a bar counter built largely of bottles, and local cider; shove-ha'penny, cribbage, dominoes, table skittles and skittle alley. Although the sheltered back garden is not big, it's prettily planted with rock plants, shrubs and trees. The National Trust's medieval King John's Hunting Lodge is opposite.

🍽 **Good value bar food includes lunchtime sandwiches and filled baguettes, filled baked potatoes, ploughman's, soup, chicken liver pâté with fruit chutney, whitebait with tartare sauce, popular beef in ale pie, a curry of the day, home-cooked ham and eggs, roasted mediterranean vegetable pancake, battered cod, chicken topped with cheese and parma ham, daily specials, and puddings.** *Starters/Snacks: £2.95 to £5.25. Main Courses: £6.75 to £12.25. Puddings: £3.35 to £3.95*

Butcombe ~ Manager Alan Currie ~ Real ale ~ Bar food (12-2.30, 6.30-9(9.30 Sat); not Sun evening) ~ (01934) 732253 ~ Children in dining area only ~ Dogs allowed in bar ~ Open 11.30-3, 6-11; 11.30-11.30 Thurs, Fri and Sat; 12-10.30 Sun

Recommended by Andrea Rampley, Matthew Shackle, Len Clark, B and M Kendall, Peter Mack Wilkins, Mr and Mrs B Hobden, Peter Craske

BABCARY
ST5628   MAP 2

Red Lion 🍴 ♀
Off A37 south of Shepton Mallett; 2 miles or so north of roundabout where A37 meets A303 and A372; TA11 7ED

Relaxed, friendly thatched pub with interesting food, local beers and comfortable rambling rooms

Deservedly popular, this well run golden stone thatched pub is much enjoyed by our readers – and despite the emphasis on the good food, the atmosphere and feel of the place remains properly pubby. Several distinct areas work their way around the carefully refurbished bar. To the left of the entrance is a longish room with dark pink walls, a squashy leather sofa and two housekeeper's chairs around a low table by the woodburning stove and a few well spaced tables and captain's chairs including a big one in a bay window with built-in seats. There are elegant rustic wall lights, some clay pipes in a cabinet, and local papers to read; board games and gardening magazines too. Leading off here with lovely dark flagstones is a more dimly lit public bar area with a panelled dado, a high-backed old settle and other more straightforward chairs; darts, board games and bar billiards. The good-sized smart dining room has a large stone lion's head on a plinth above the open fire (with a huge stack of logs to one side), a big rug on polished boards, and properly set tables. Three real ales on handpump often from Bath Ales, Otter and Teignworthy, ten wines by the glass, a few malt whiskies and fruit smoothies. There's a long informal garden with picnic tables and a play area with slide for children.

🍴 **Promptly served, interesting bar food includes snacks such as doorstep sandwiches, ploughman's, sausage and mash with onion jus, home-made burger and ham and eggs as well as soup, game terrine with grape confit, scallop and crab pastry with a tomato and chive salsa, udon noodles with julienne vegetables and coconut sauce, vine tomato, goats cheese and courgette tart, teriyaki salmon with pak choi and rice noodles, ginger, coriander and lime-marinated poussin with sweet roast potato, butterflied lamb rump with winter vegetables and dauphinoise potatoes, daily specials, and puddings like strawberry brûlée with almond biscuit and warm apple and blackberry pie with crème anglaise.** *Starters/Snacks: £3.95 to £6.50. Main Courses: £8.50 to £17.50. Puddings: £4.00 to £6.00*

Free house ~ Licensee Charles Garrard ~ Real ale ~ Bar food (12-3(2.30 in winter), 7-9(10 Fri and Sat)) ~ Restaurant ~ (01458) 223230 ~ Children welcome ~ Dogs allowed in bar ~ Live jazz Sun ~ Open 12-3(2.30 in winter), 6-midnight; 12-4(2.30 in winter) Sun; closed Sun evening

Recommended by Bob and Margaret Holder, Guy Vowles, Ian Phillips, Tom Evans, Brian and Bett Cox, Mr and Mrs A R Maden, Michael Doswell, Edward Mirzoeff, Di and Mike Gillam, Paul and Annette Hallett

BATCOMBE   ST6839   MAP 2

Three Horseshoes 🍴 ♀ 🛏

Village signposted off A359 Bruton—Frome; BA4 6HE

Well run, attractive dining pub with smart rooms, friendly staff, elaborate food and quite a choice of drinks; comfortable bedrooms

This is a civilised and neatly kept honey-coloured stone dining pub with welcoming, convivial staff. The long and rather narrow main room is smartly traditional with beams, local pictures on the lightly ragged dark pink walls, built-in cushioned window seats and solid chairs around a nice mix of old tables and a woodburning stove at one end with a big open fire at the other. At the back on the left, the snug has dark panelled walls, tiled floors and old pictures and there's also a pretty stripped stone dining room (no mobile phones); best to book to be sure of a table, especially at weekends. Adnams Broadside and Butcombe Bitter and Bats in the Belfry (brewed for the pub) on handpump, and eight wines by the glass. There are picnic-sets on the heated back terrace with more on the grass and a pond with koi carp. The pub is on a quiet village lane by the church which has a very striking tower. The bedrooms are comfortable and the breakfasts are good.

🍴 **Very popular food using home-grown vegetables includes brasserie-style light lunches such as filled paninis, soup, pork terrine, home-made burger with melted blue cheese, field mushrooms and cornichons, chilli and lime crab cakes with ginger syrup and beer-battered scottish halibut goujons as well as haggis on toast with morels and a shot of whisky, warm salad of home-smoked free-range chicken with lardons of home-cured crispy bacon and tarragon olive oil, moules marinière, puff pastry case filled with ricotta, leeks and celeriac in a tomato sauce with parsnip crisps, slow-braised lamb shoulder with shallot and red wine gravy, sautéed guinea fowl on savoy cabbage and baby vegetables braised in roast chicken stock, daily specials, and puddings.** *Starters/Snacks: £4.25 to £10.50. Main Courses: £7.50 to £19.50. Puddings: £4.75*

> If we don't specify bar meal times for a main entry, these are normally
> 12-2 and 7-9; we do show times if they are markedly different.

Free house ~ Licensees Bob Wood and Shirley Greaves ~ Real ale ~ Bar food (not Sun evening or Mon) ~ Restaurant ~ (01749) 850359 ~ Children in eating areas but must be 13 in evening ~ Dogs allowed in bar and bedrooms ~ Occasional live music ~ Open 11-3, 6.30-11; 12-3, 7.30-10.30 Sun; closed Mon ~ Bedrooms: £50B/£75B

Recommended by Paul and Annette Hallett, Mrs Sandie H Robbins, Michael Doswell, Mrs P Nurcombe, Mark Flynn, Elizabeth Johnson, Ann Brock, Mr Galais, S Haines, Dennis and Gill Keen, Mr and Mrs Steele

BATH

ST7565   MAP 2

King William ♀

Thomas Street, corner with A4 London Road – may be no nearby parking; BA1 5NN

Simple bars in small corner pub with informally friendly service, interesting food and drink; upstairs dining room

Customers are certainly comfortable dropping into this little corner pub for a drink and a chat but the individual food can be very good. The two plain, un-smart rooms have simple seating and just three chunky old tables each on dark bare boards and big windows looking out on the busy street; at night heavy curtains can keep out the lights of the traffic. Blindmans Golden Spring, Otter and Palmers Copper on handpump and a fine choice of good wines by the glass including sherries and ports. Helpful informal service by nice young staff, daily papers, a few lighted church candles, and perhaps a big bunch of lilies on the counter. Steep stairs go up to a simple and attractive dining room, used mainly on Wednesday to Saturday evenings, decorated with Jane Grigson *British Cooking* prints.

🍽 Interesting food might include sandwiches, soup, ham hock terrine with gherkin and egg dressing, cheddar fritters with kale and beetroot and green sauce, artichoke, lentil and leek gratin with nuts, oats and cheese, mutton stew with liver dumpling, skate, cockle and bass stew, roast beef with horseradish cream, and puddings such as hot chocolate pot and mulled wine poached plums with vanilla sauce; there's also a two- and three-course set menu. *Starters/Snacks: £5.50 to £7.50. Main Courses: £10.00 to £15.50. Puddings: £5.00*

Free house ~ Licensees Charlie and Amanda Digney ~ Real ale ~ Bar food (12-2, 6-11 (restaurant until midnight Thurs-Sat); not Sun evening) ~ Restaurant ~ (01225) 428096 ~ Children welcome ~ Dogs allowed in bar ~ Open 12-3, 6-11.30(5-midnight Fri); 12-midnight Sat; 12-11 Sun; 12-3, 5-midnight Mon-Fri in winter; closed 25 and 26 Dec

Recommended by Richard and Lynn Seers, Trevor and Sylvia Millum

Old Green Tree 🍺

12 Green Street; BA1 2JZ

Super little pub with fine choice of real ales, enjoyable traditional food, lots of cheerful customers and friendly service

Much loved by our readers, this appealing and traditional little pub is always busy (and sometimes packed) so to get a table, you must arrive before midday. They still keep a fine choice of six real ales on handpump including Green Tree brewed for them by Blindman's Brewery, as well as RCH Pitchfork, Wickwar Brand Oak and Mr Perretts Traditional Stout and two changing guests. Also, ten wines by the glass from a nice little list with helpful notes, 35 malt whiskies, winter hot toddies and a proper Pimms. It's laid-back and cosy rather than particularly smart – though there has been some redecoration this year – and the three small oak-panelled and low wood-and-plaster ceilinged rooms include a comfortable lounge on the left as you go in, its walls decorated with wartime aircraft pictures in winter and local artists' work during spring and summer, and a back bar; the big skylight lightens things up attractively. No music or machines; chess, cribbage, dominoes, backgammon, shut-the-box, Jenga. The gents' is down steep steps. No children.

🍽 Generous helpings of popular lunchtime bar food include soup and sandwiches, ploughman's, bangers and mash with cider or beer and onion sauce, beef in ale pie, lamb tagine, and daily specials such as mushroom and leek risotto, curry of the day, and smoked trout and asparagus. *Starters/Snacks: £5.50. Main Courses: £7.50 to £10.00*

Free house ~ Licensees Nick Luke and Tim Bethune ~ Real ale ~ Bar food (lunchtime until 3) ~ No credit cards ~ Dogs allowed in bar ~ Open 11-11; 12-10.30 Sun; closed 25 and 26 Dec

Recommended by Dr and Mrs M E Wilson, Clare Rosier, Donna and Roger, W W Burke, Edward Mirzoeff, Susan and Nigel Wilson, Dennis Jones, Ian Phillips, Peter Craske, the Didler, John Saville, Bill and Jessica Ritson, Tom and Ruth Rees, Pete Baker, Colin and Peggy Wilshire, Alain and Rose Foote, Mike Pugh, Dr and Mrs A K Clarke, Derek and Sylvia Stephenson, Michael Dandy, Bruce and Penny Wilkie, Tony and Jill Radnor, Malcolm Ward

Star ◀

Vineyards; The Paragon (A4), junction with Guinea Lane; BA1 5NA

Quietly chatty and unchanging old town local, brewery tap for Abbey Ales; filled rolls only

The historic interior of this honest old town pub has not changed for years and there's a quiet, chatty atmosphere not spoilt by noisy fruit machines or music. It's the brewery tap for Abbey Ales, so among the five real ales you'll always find Abbey Bellringer – and Bass tapped straight from the cask. Not smart, the four (well, more like three and a half) small linked rooms are served from a single bar, separated by sombre panelling with glass inserts. They are furnished with traditional leatherette wall benches and the like – even one hard bench that the regulars call Death Row – and the lighting's dim, and not rudely interrupted by too much daylight. Friendly staff and customers; it does get busy at weekends.

🍴 **Filled rolls only though they may have rather unusual bar nibbles Sunday lunchtime and Thursday evening.** *Starters/Snacks: 1.80*

Punch ~ Lease Paul Waters and Alan Morgan ~ Real ale ~ Bar food (see text) ~ (01225) 425072 ~ Dogs allowed in bar ~ Open 12-2.30, 5.30-midnight; 12-midnight Sat and Sun

Recommended by Pete Baker, Donna and Roger, the Didler, Dr and Mrs A K Clarke, Ian Phillips

BLEADON   ST3457   MAP 1

Queens Arms ◀

Village signed just off A370 S of Weston; Celtic Way; BS24 0NF

Busy, cheerful pub with some interesting décor in linked rooms, real ales tapped from the cask, good home cooking and seats on pretty terrace

The carefully divided areas in this well run 16th-c pub have a cheerfully chatty and convivial atmosphere. Plenty of distinctive touches include the dark flagstones of the terracotta-walled restaurant and back bar area, candles on sturdy tables flanked by winged settles, old hunting prints, a frieze of quaint sayings in Old English print, and above all, the focal servery where the real ales are tapped from the cask: Bath Ale Gem Bitter, Butcombe Bitter and Gold and a changing guest such as Wadworths 6X. Several wines by the glass. There is a big solid fuel stove in the main bar and a woodburning stove in the stripped-stone back tap bar; games machine and darts. The pretty, heated terrace has picnic-sets on flagstones, a pergola, shrubs and flowers.

🍴 **Good bar food includes lunchtime filled baguettes and ciabattas, ploughman's, ham and eggs and omelettes, as well as soup, whitebait, garlic mushrooms, mozzarella wrapped in parma ham, chicken in a wild mushroom sauce, steak in ale pie, pork in cider sauce, mushroom and stilton tagliatelle, a daily changing fish dish, and puddings such as crème brûlée and sticky toffee pudding.** *Starters/Snacks: £3.95 to £5.50. Main Courses: £6.95 to £14.95. Puddings: £4.00*

Butcombe ~ Manager Andrew Pearson ~ Real ale ~ Bar food (12-6 Sun) ~ Restaurant ~ (01934) 812080 ~ Children welcome away from bar ~ Dogs allowed in bar ~ Open 11.30-11; 12-10.30 Sun

Recommended by Dr Martin Owton, Peter Mack Wilkins, Brian Root, Comus and Sarah Elliott, P and J Shapley, Bob and Margaret Holder

---

By law pubs must show a price list of their drinks. Let us know if you are inconvenienced by any breach of this law.

CHEW MAGNA   ST5763   MAP 2

Bear & Swan 🍴 ♀

B3130 (South Parade), off A37 S of Bristol; BS40 8SL

Successfully ambitious food in relaxed and civilised linked rooms, good range of drinks

Given that this is quite an austere-looking building, it's quite a surprise to find the
open-plan rooms splendidly mix the traditional with the modern. The left-hand end,
beyond a piano, is an L-shaped dining room, with stripped stone walls, dark dining
tables, a woodburning stove, bare boards and an oriental rug. The other half, also bare
boards with the odd oriental rug, has various sizes of pine tables, pews and raffia-seat
dining chairs. In this part a relaxed and civilised mix of customers runs from young men
chatting on the bar stools through smart lunching mums sipping champagne to older
people reading the racing form; there may also be a friendly golden labrador. Décor is
minimal, really just plants in the windows with their heavy dark blue curtains and some
china above the huge bressumer beam over a splendid log fire; a wide-screen TV may be
on with its sound turned down; cribbage. The long bar counter has Butcombe Bitter,
Courage Best and a guest beer on handpump and around 20 wines by the glass. The car
park is small, and street parking needs care (and patience).

🍽 **As well as bar food such as filled baguettes, fish pie, omelettes and gammon and egg,
there are more elaborate choices like soup, goats cheese and red onion tartlet with prune
sauce, chicken liver parfait with plum syrup, mussel and salmon fishcake with sweet chilli
and ginger, spinach and ricotta tortellini with red pepper coulis, medallions of pork with
paprika sauce, pancetta and caramelised apples, duck with hoi sin sauce, lamb rump with
tomatoes, aubergine and pesto, tuna with artichoke, tomato, feta and caper salad, and
puddings such as crème brûlée or chocolate tart.** *Starters/Snacks: £4.00 to £7.00. Main
Courses: £6.00 to £10.00. Puddings: £5.00*

Free house ~ Licensees Nigel and Caroline Pushman ~ Real ale ~ Bar food (12-2(3 Sun), 7-10;
not Sun evening) ~ Restaurant ~ (01275) 331100 ~ Well behaved children welcome ~ Dogs
allowed in bar ~ Open 11-11(midnight Sat); 11-7 Sun; closed Sun evening ~ Bedrooms:
£50S/£80S

*Recommended by M G Hart, Bob, Gaynor Gregory, Dr and Mrs C W Thomas, John Urquhart, Angus and
Rosemary Campbell, Dr and Mrs A K Clarke*

CHISELBOROUGH   ST4614   MAP 1

Cat Head

Take the slip road off A303 at Crewkerne A356 junction; TA14 6TT

**Handy for the A303 with consistently warm welcome, neat attractive bars, enjoyable food
and thoughtful choice of drinks; pretty garden**

Lots of customers drop in here at both lunchtime and in the evening for a welcome break
from the busy A303. It's an old sandstone pub in a peaceful village with genuinely
friendly licensees, enjoyable food and a pleasant, relaxed atmosphere. The spotless,
traditional flagstoned rooms have light wooden tables and chairs, some high-backed
cushioned settles, flowers and plants, a woodburning stove and curtains around the small
mullioned windows. Butcombe Bitter, Otter Bitter and St Austells Tribute on handpump, a
good wine list and Thatcher's cider; piped music, darts, alley skittles and board games.
There are seats on the terrace and in the attractive garden where there are plenty of
colourful plants; nice views over the village, too.

🍽 **Well presented and popular, the bar food at lunchtime includes filled ciabattas,
ploughman's, soup, peppered smoked mackerel pâté with oatcakes, baked smoked haddock
and prawn mornay, steak and kidney pie, wild rabbit in mustard and thyme and roast lamb
shank with red onion gravy with evening choices such as a plate of tapas for two people,
field mushrooms topped with garlic and stilton, salmon and prawn fishcake with coriander
mayonnaise, pork tenderloin with calvados cream and apple, grilled whole bass with
fennel, half a crispy duck with scrumpy sauce, and puddings like chocolate and pecan pie
or lemon brioche pudding.** *Starters/Snacks: £3.90 to £6.10. Main Courses: £11.40 to £14.80.
Puddings: £4.30 to £4.95*

Enterprise ~ Lease Duncan and Avril Gordon ~ Real ale ~ Bar food ~ Restaurant ~
(01935) 881231 ~ Children welcome ~ Open 12-3, 6-11(midnight Sat; 10.30 Sun); closed
evening 25 Dec

Recommended by Patricia Jones, Charles Gysin, Mrs S J Frost, Frank Willy, Revd D E and Mrs J A Shapland,
Mrs A Macartney, Richard Endacott, Theo, Anne and Jane Gaskin, Ian and Nita Cooper, Jill Healing, Kate and
Ian Hodge, Mike Gorton, Peter Craske

CHURCHILL   ST4459   MAP 1

Crown 🍺 £

The Batch; in village, turn off A368 into Skinners Lane at Nelson Arms, then bear right;
BS25 5PP

Unspoilt and unchanging small cottage with friendly customers and staff, super range of
real ales and homely lunchtime food

Filled with the chat of friendly contented customers, this simple and unpretentious little
cottage is a firm favourite with many of our readers. Little has changed over many years
and the small and rather local-feeling stone-floored and cross-beamed room on the right
has a wooden window seat, an unusually sturdy settle, and built-in wall benches; the
left-hand room has a slate floor, and some steps past the big log fire in a big stone
fireplace lead to more sitting space. No noise from music or games (except perhaps
dominoes) and a fine range of up to ten real ales tapped from the cask: Bass, Butcombe
Bitter, Cotleigh Batch, Palmers IPA, RCH Hewish, East Street Cream and PG Steam,
St Austells Tribute and a guest or two. Farm ciders, too. Outside lavatories. There are
garden tables at the front, a smallish back lawn and hill views; the Mendip Morris Men
come in summer. Good walks nearby.

🍴 **Straightforward lunchtime bar food includes sandwiches, good soup, filled baked**
potatoes, ploughman's, chilli con carne, beef casserole, broccoli and stilton bake, and
puddings like hot chocolate fudge cake and treacle pudding. *Starters/Snacks: £3.95 to*
£6.25. Main Courses: £4.95 to £7.95. Puddings: £3.90

Free house ~ Licensee Tim Rogers ~ Real ale ~ Bar food (12-2.30; not evenings) ~ No credit
cards ~ (01934) 852995 ~ Children welcome away from bar ~ Dogs welcome ~ Open 11-11;
12-10.30 Sun

Recommended by Tom Evans, Michael Doswell, John Urquhart, the Didler, R T and J C Moggridge, Rod and
Chris Pring, Bob and Margaret Holder, Joan and Tony Walker, Peter Mack Wilkins, Andrea Rampley, John and
Gloria Isaacs

CLAPTON-IN-GORDANO   ST4773   MAP 1

Black Horse

4 miles from M5 junction 19; A369 towards Portishead, then B3124 towards Clevedon; in N
Weston opposite school turn left signposted Clapton, then in village take second right,
maybe signed Clevedon, Clapton Wick; BS20 7RH

Ancient pub with lots of cheerful customers, friendly service, real ales and cider and
straightforward bar food; pretty garden

Always busy and run by friendly people, this unspoilt old pub makes a good lunchtime
break from the M5. The partly flagstoned and partly red-tiled main room has winged
settles and built-in wall benches around narrow, dark wooden tables, window seats, a big
log fire with stirrups and bits on the mantelbeam and amusing cartoons and photographs
of the pub. A window in an inner snug is still barred from the days when this room was
the petty-sessions gaol; high-backed settles – one a marvellous carved and canopied
creature, another with an art nouveau copper insert reading East, West, Hame's Best –
lots of mugs hanging from its black beams, and plenty of little prints and photographs.
There's also a simply furnished room which is the only place families are allowed; piped
music, darts, TV and board games. Butcombe Bitter, Courage Best, Shepherd Neame
Spitfire, Wadworths 6X and Websters Green Label on handpump or tapped from the cask;
also farm ciders, eight wines by the glass and efficient service. There are some old rustic

tables and benches in the garden, with more to one side of the car park, and the summer flowers are really quite a sight. Paths from the pub lead up Naish Hill or along to Cadbury Camp.

🍴 Straightforward lunchtime bar food includes filled baguettes, ploughman's and a few hot dishes like soup, lamb hotpot, cottage pie, moussaka and chilli. *Starters/Snacks: £2.95 to £6.75. Main Courses: £5.75 to £6.75*

Inntrepreneur ~ Tenant Nicholas Evans ~ Real ale ~ Bar food (not evenings, not Sun) ~ No credit cards ~ (01275) 842105 ~ Children in very plain family room only ~ Dogs welcome ~ Live music Mon evening ~ Open 11-11; 12-10.30 Sun

Recommended by Will Stevens, Gaynor Gregory, Peter Mack Wilkins, Dave Braisted, the Didler, Philip and Jude Simmons, Rona Murdoch, Tom Evans, J and F Gowers, Dr and Mrs A K Clarke

COMPTON MARTIN   ST5457   MAP 2
Ring o' Bells 🍺
A368 Bath—Weston; BS40 6JE

Country pub with new licensee, traditional bars, real ales, local cider and standard bar food

---

A new licensee has taken over this bustling country pub. It's in an attractive spot overlooked by the Mendip Hills and the big garden has plenty of seats, swings, a slide and a climbing frame. Inside, the cosy, traditional front part of the bar has rugs on the flagstones and inglenook seats right by the log fire, and up a step is a spacious carpeted back part with largely stripped stone walls and pine tables. Butcombe Bitter, IPA and Gold and a guest like Fullers London Pride on handpump and local ciders; piped music. Blagdon Lake and Chew Valley Lake are not far away. More reports please.

🍴 Bar food includes sandwiches, filled baked potatoes, soup, ham and eggs, omelettes, ploughman's, broccoli, mushroom and almond tagliatelle, beef in ale pie, lasagne and steaks. *Starters/Snacks: £3.00 to £5.00. Main Courses: £4.50 to £12.00. Puddings: £2.50 to £4.50*

Butcombe ~ Manager Brian Clarke ~ Real ale ~ Bar food (12-2.45, 6-8.45(6.30-8.30 Sun)) ~ Restaurant ~ (01761) 221284 ~ Children allowed until 8.30pm ~ Dogs allowed in bar ~ Open 11.30-3, 5.30-11; 11-11 Sat; 12-10.30 Sun

Recommended by Meg and Colin Hamilton, Tom Evans, Bob and Angela Brooks, Peter Mack Wilkins

CORTON DENHAM   ST6322   MAP 2
Queens Arms 🛏
Village signposted off B3145 N of Sherborne; DT9 4LR

Informally smart, honey-coloured stone inn, super choice of drinks, imaginative food and friendly staff

---

Rather smart in an informal and relaxed way, this Georgian honey-coloured stone inn is popular with customers of all ages. The plain high-beamed bar has a woodburning stove in the inglenook at one end with rugs on flagstones in front of the raised fireplace at the other end, some old pews, barrel seats and a sofa, church candles and maybe a big bowl of lilies; a little room off here has just one big table – nice for a party of eight or so. Expect nice touches like pistachios, good marinated olives and hand-raised pork pies on the bar counter. The young staff go out of their way to be helpful. On the left the comfortable dining room, dark pink with crisp white paintwork, has good oak tables and a log fire. They have an extraordinary range of good bottled beers from around the world, Butcombe Bitter, Timothy Taylors Landlord and guests like Otter Bitter and Roosters Body Warmer on handpump, 14 wines by the glass including pudding wine, 40 malt whiskies, and three farm ciders. A south-facing back terrace has teak tables and chairs under cocktail parasols (or heaters if it's cool), with colourful flower tubs. The village lane has some parking nearby, though not a great deal.

🍴 As well as having their own pigs and hens (which of course supply the pub), the produce used here is sourced very locally. Food is imaginative and includes lunchtime sandwiches, interesting soup, pheasant, cep and foie gras terrine with cranberry chutney, lightly curried lambs kidneys on granary toast, an all-day breakfast, roasted courgettes and garlic tagliatelle with a creamy white wine sauce, grilled chicken breast on chorizo and cannelloni bean cassoulet, honey-glazed confit of pork belly with cider jus, and puddings such as honey plum pavlova with mascarpone cream and bitter chocolate torte with orange syrup. *Starters/Snacks: £4.25 to £5.75. Main Courses: £7.60 to £14.50. Puddings: £4.50 to £5.25*

Free house ~ Licensees Rupert and Victoria Reeves ~ Real ale ~ Bar food (12-3, 6-10; 12-4, 6-9.30 Sun) ~ Restaurant ~ (01963) 220317 ~ Children welcome ~ Dogs allowed in bar ~ Open 11-3, 6-11; 11-11 Sat; 11-10.30 Sun ~ Bedrooms: £60S(£70B)/£75S(£90B)

Recommended by Clare West, Christine Cox, B and F A Hannam, Robert and Christina Jones, Mark Flynn, OPUS

CRANMORE   ST6643   MAP 2

Strode Arms 🍴 ♀

West Cranmore; signposted with pub off A361 Frome—Shepton Mallet; BA4 4QJ

Imaginative food and wide choice of drinks in pretty country pub with attractive, comfortable bars; pretty outside

This pretty former farmhouse is an attractive sight in summer with its neat stonework, cartwheels on the walls, colourful tubs and hanging baskets, and seats under umbrellas on the front terrace, looking across to the village pond; there are more seats in the back garden. Inside, the rooms have charming country furnishings, fresh flowers, pot plants, a grandfather clock on the flagstones, remarkable old locomotive engineering drawings and big black and white steam train murals in a central lobby, newspapers to read, and lovely log fires in handsome fireplaces. Wadworths 6X, IPA and seasonal brews on handpump, eight wines by the glass from an interesting list, several malt whiskies and quite a few liqueurs and ports; friendly, attentive service. The East Somerset Light Railway is nearby and there may be a vintage sports car meeting on the first Tuesday of each month.

🍴 Well presented and particularly good, the bar food includes filled baguettes, ploughman's, soup, toad in the hole with rich onion gravy, ravioli in cream, garlic and pea purée, smoked salmon and crayfish risotto with rocket and parmesan, ham and egg, and steak and kidney pie, with more elaborate choices such as roast duck breast with fresh fig, smoked bacon, chestnut and port sauce, free-range chicken, leek and brie lattice with white wine and cream and wild mushroom and asparagus lasagne, and puddings like white chocolate and vanilla seed cheesecake with cherry compote and marmalade and whisky sponge pudding with lavender honey ice-cream. *Starters/Snacks: £3.95 to £6.26. Main Courses: £6.75 to £14.95. Puddings: £4.35 to £4.50*

Wadworths ~ Tenants Tim and Ann-Marie Gould ~ Real ale ~ Bar food (not Sun evening) ~ Restaurant ~ (01749) 880450 ~ Children in restaurant until 7.30pm ~ Dogs allowed in bar ~ Open 11.30-3, 6-11; 12-3, 7-10.30 Sun

Recommended by Gaynor Gregory, Mrs Pat Crabb, Geoffrey Kemp, John Urquhart, Richard Fendick, Sylvia and Tony Birbeck, Pat and Robert Watt, M G Hart

CROSCOMBE   ST5844   MAP 2

George 🍺

Long Street (A371 Wells—Shepton Mallet); BA5 3QH

Carefully renovated old coaching inn, cheerful Canadian landlord, enjoyable food cooked by landlady, good local beers, attractive garden

This 17th-c coaching inn is doing particularly well under its warmly friendly Canadian landlord. A lot of hard work has gone into the renovations: the former tack room and stables are now part of the framework and the old coach house has been converted into a self-contained flat; they hope to open more bedrooms soon. The main bar has some stripped stone, a winter log fire in the inglenook fireplace, dark wooden tables and chairs and more comfortable seats and the family grandfather clock. The attractive dining room has more stripped stone, local artwork and photographs on the dark orange walls, and high-backed cushioned dining chairs around a mix of tables. King George the Thirst is brewed exclusively for them by Blindmans and they also keep Butcombe Bitter and a couple of guests like Cheddar Potholer and Newmans Bite IPA on handpump; local farm ciders and a short choice of sensibly priced wines. Darts, table skittles, shove-ha'penny, dominoes and a canadian wooden table game called crokinole; occasional piped music. The friendly pub dog is called Tessa. The attractive, sizeable garden has seats on the heated and covered terrace; children's area and boules.

Ⓜ **Cooked by the landlady, the very good bar food includes sandwiches, chicken liver pâté, crab cakes with a sweet chilli dip, scallops fried with chorizo in a light wine sauce, sausage and mash, steak in ale pie, goujons of monkfish with tamarind and spring onions, pork tenderloin with apricot and ginger, free-range duck breast glazed with damson sauce, and lovely puddings such as summer pudding, treacle tart, crème brûlée and their own ice-creams; their Sunday roasts are popular.** *Starters/Snacks: £2.25 to £4.85. Main Courses: £6.95 to £15.95. Puddings: £4.35*

Free house ~ Licensees Peter and Veryan Graham ~ Real ale ~ Bar food ~ Restaurant ~ (01749) 342306 ~ Children welcome ~ Dogs welcome ~ Open 12-2.30, 7(6 Fri)-11.30 ~ Bedrooms: /£70B

Recommended by Hugh Roberts, Len Clark, Barbara Close, Peter Dearing, Terry Buckland

DULVERTON
SS9127 MAP 1

Woods ★
Bank Square; TA22 9BU
SOMERSET DINING PUB OF THE YEAR

Happily mixing diners and drinkers in smartly informal place with exceptional wines and delicious food

This is a smashing place with an excellent atmosphere mixing lots of diners with cheerful drinkers at the bar. It's comfortably relaxed, mildly upmarket in a country way, and very Exmoor – plenty of good sporting prints on the salmon pink walls, some antlers, other hunting trophies and stuffed birds and a couple of salmon rods. There are bare boards on the left by the bar counter, which has well kept Exmoor Ale, O'Hanlons Royal Oak, Otter Head and St Austells Woods Own Ale (brewed especially for them) tapped from the cask, a farm cider and a range of organic soft drinks. You can order any of the 400 or so wines from the amazing wine list by the glass, and the landlord also keeps an unlisted collection of about 500 well aged new world wines which he will happily chat about; they have daily papers. Its tables partly separated by stable-style timbering and masonry dividers, the bit on the right is carpeted and has a woodburning stove in the big fireplace set into its end wall, which has varnished plank panelling. There may be unobjectionable piped music. Big windows keep you in touch with what's going on out in the quiet town centre (or you can sit out on the pavement at a couple of metal tables). A small suntrap back courtyard has a few picnic-sets.

Ⓜ **Delicious food at lunchtime might include filled baguettes and warm topped bruschetta, interesting soup, croque monsieur, super chicken liver parfait with red onion marmalade with port reduction and melba toast, tagliatelle of wild mushrooms with truffle cream and baby cress salad, braised beef with calves liver, roasted root vegetables and celeriac purée and fillet of pollack on buttered spinach with puy lentils, pancetta, capers and red wine sauce, with evening choices such as twice-baked roquefort soufflé on chicory salad with pear chutney and walnut dressing, ballotine of guinea fowl with braised gem lettuce, dauphinoise potatoes and poultry juices, fillet of turbot with seared langoustines with beer sauce and herby jersey royals, and puddings such as raspberry délice with lemon posset, blueberry and cherries in kirsch and rich chocolate tart with banana gelato and mocha sauce.** *Starters/Snacks: £5.50 to £7.00. Main Courses: £9.95 to £17.00. Puddings: £5.00 to £5.50*

Free house ~ Licensee Patrick Groves ~ Real ale ~ Bar food ~ Restaurant ~ (01398) 324007 ~ Children welcome ~ Dogs welcome ~ Open 11-3, 6-midnight(1am Sat); 12-3, 7-11 Sun

Recommended by James Crouchman, Mr and Mrs A R Maden, Jeremy Whitehorn, Len Clark, Lyn Dixon, Peter Craske

EAST COKER

ST5412 MAP 2

Helyar Arms ♀ 🛏

Village signposted off A37 or A30 SW of Yeovil; Moor Lane; BA22 9JR

Well run pub, professional staff, comfortable big bar, inventive food and an especially good wine list

In an attractive village, this is a neatly kept heavy-beamed pub with friendly, professional staff. There's a spacious and comfortable turkey-carpeted bar carefully laid out to give a degree of intimacy to its various candlelit tables, helped by soft lighting, a couple of high-backed settles, and squashy leather sofas at each end. There are lots of hunting and other country pictures, brass and copper ware and a log fire. Steps lead up to a good-sized back high-raftered dining room with well spaced tables. Butcombe Bitter, Flowers Original and Greene King IPA on handpump, local farm cider, reasonably priced wines (30 by the glass), and daily papers; piped music and board games. There are a few picnic-sets out on a neat lawn, and they have a skittle alley.

🍴 **Good fresh imaginative food uses local produce from named suppliers and they have home-pickled eggs (plain or balsamic), and do a weekday lunchtime deal where you buy a main course and get your starter or pudding for half price: lunchtime sandwiches, ploughman's, hand-raised pork pie with home-made chutney, sautéed lambs kidneys with roasted red onion and deep-fried sage leaves, home-baked ham with free-range eggs, beer-battered brixham haddock with home-made tartare sauce, linguini with wild mushrooms, cream and parsley, thai red chicken curry and chargrilled lamb chops with rosemary potatoes and madeira jus; puddings such as profiteroles with chantilly cream and warm chocolate sauce and blossom honey cheesecake.** *Starters/Snacks: £5.00 to £8.00. Main Courses: £8.00 to £15.00. Puddings: £5.00 to £6.00*

Punch ~ Tenant Ian McKerracher ~ Real ale ~ Bar food (12-2.30, 6.30-9.30(9 Sun)) ~ Restaurant ~ (01935) 862332 ~ Children welcome ~ Dogs welcome ~ Open 11-3, 6-11; 11-11 Sat; 12-10.30 Sun ~ Bedrooms: £59S/£79S

Recommended by Theo, Anne and Jane Gaskin, Charles Gysin, Christina Dowsett, Paul and Annette Hallett, Gill Elston, John A Barker, Mrs Angela Graham, Roland and Wendy Chalu

EXFORD

SS8538 MAP 1

White Horse 🛏

B3224; TA24 7PY

Bustling inn, popular locally, with decent standard food, good choice of malt whiskies and well liked bedrooms

The River Exe runs past this biggish, three-storey creepered place with its half-timbered top storey and the attractive village is particularly pretty in summer; tables outside enjoy the view. The more or less open-plan bar has windsor and other country kitchen chairs, a high-backed antique settle, scrubbed deal tables, hunting prints, photographs above the stripped pine dado, and a good winter log fire; it can get very busy. Exmoor Ale, Dunkery Ale and Gold and Sharps Doom Bar on handpump, over 100 malt whiskies and Thatcher's cider. They run daily Landrover 'safaris' to explore Exmoor's wildlife. The village green with children's play equipment is next to the pub.

🍴 **Straightforward but very good value bar food includes sandwiches, filled baguettes and baked potatoes, ploughman's, soup, breaded haddock, ham and egg, steak in ale pie, daily specials and puddings; on Sundays they may offer only a three-course set meal; cream teas.** *Starters/Snacks: £3.95 to £7.15. Main Courses: £6.00 to £18.00. Puddings: £4.25*

Free house ~ Licensees Peter and Linda Hendrie ~ Real ale ~ Bar food (12-2.30, 6-9.30) ~ Restaurant ~ (01643) 831229 ~ Children welcome ~ Dogs allowed in bar and bedrooms ~ Open 11-11(midnight Sat) ~ Bedrooms: £65B/£130B

Recommended by Peter and Jean Hoare, Howard and Lorna Lambert, A S and M E Marriott, George Atkinson, Martin and Pauline Jennings, Lynda and Trevor Smith, Stan and Hazel Allen, Nick Lawless, J L Wedel

---

Pubs in outstandingly attractive surroundings are listed at the back of the book.

FAULKLAND · ST7555 · MAP 2

Tuckers Grave ★ £
A366 E of village; BA3 5XF

Quite unspoilt and unchanging little cider house with friendly locals and charming licensees

At its best when you can chat to the friendly locals and charming licensees, this little gem remains much loved by many of our readers. It still claims the title of Smallest Pub in the *Guide* and nothing has changed for many years: the flagstoned entry opens into a teeny unspoilt room with casks of Bass and Butcombe Bitter on tap and Thatcher's Cheddar Valley cider in an alcove on the left. Two old cream-painted high-backed settles face each other across a single table on the right and a side room has shove-ha'penny. There are winter fires and maybe newspapers to read; also a skittle alley and lots of tables and chairs on an attractive back lawn with good views.

🍴 **There may be lunchtime sandwiches.**

Free house ~ Licensees Ivan and Glenda Swift ~ Real ale ~ No credit cards ~ (01373) 834230 ~ Children allowed but with restrictions ~ Open 11.30-3, 6-11; 12-3, 7-10.30 Sun; closed 25 Dec and evening 26 Dec

Recommended by Dr and Mrs M E Wilson, MLR, Ian Phillips, Dr and Mrs A K Clarke, Pete Baker, Ann and Colin Hunt, E McCall, T McLean, D Irving, R Huggins, the Didler

---

HINTON ST GEORGE · ST4212 · MAP 1

Lord Poulett Arms 🍴 🍷 🛏
Off A30 W of Crewkerne, and off Merriott road (declassified – former A356, off B3165) N of Crewkerne; TA17 8SE

Attractive old stone inn with friendly licensees, charming antique-filled rooms, imaginative food, good choice of drinks, pretty garden; nice old-fashioned bedrooms

Run by friendly, helpful people, this substantial 17th-c thatched pub is in a charming stone village and nearby walks. It's extremely attractive inside with several cosy linked areas: rugs on bare boards or flagstones, open fires – one in an inglenook and one is a raised fireplace that separates two rooms – walls of honey-coloured stone or painted in bold Farrow & Ball colours, hops on beams, antique brass candelabra, fresh flowers and candles and some lovely old farmhouse, windsor and ladderback chairs around fine oak or elm tables. The atmosphere is civilised and relaxed with plenty of locals dropping in for a drink. Branscombe Branoc with a couple of guests like Branscombe BVB Own Label and Otter Ale on handpump, several wines by the glass, home-made sloe gin and mulled wine and in summer, scrumpy cider by the jug. The cat is called Honey. Outside, under a wisteria-clad pergola, there are white metalwork tables and chairs in a mediterranean-style lavender-edged gravelled area, a couple of boules pistes (two keen pub teams) and picnic-sets in a wild flower meadow. The bedrooms are pretty with some proper character and the breakfasts are good.

🍴 **Using home-made bread and home-grown herbs, the most enjoyable food might include a filled baguette of the day, interesting soups (the bouillabaisse using local fish is popular), house-cured organic trout, beef carpaccio, sake and maple-marinated scallops, mozzarella, peach and beetroot salad with crème fraîche dressing, mixed mushroom and wild rocket tagliatelle, sweet soy glazed bacon loin, faggot and champ, lamb chump with puy lentils and crumbled feta, braised hare in port, and puddings such as fennel and orange custard filo pastry stack and baked lemon and chocolate tart; the chef is Japanese.** Starters/Snacks: £4.50 to £6.00. Main Courses: £10.00 to £15.00. Puddings: £5.00

Free house ~ Licensees Steve Hill and Michelle Paynton ~ Real ale ~ Bar food ~ Restaurant ~ (01460) 73149 ~ Children welcome ~ Dogs allowed in bar ~ Regular events with live music ~ Open 12-3, 6.30-11 ~ Bedrooms: /£88B

Recommended by Bob and Margaret Holder, OPUS, MLR, Steven and Nic, Glen and Nola Armstrong, Ian Malone

HUISH EPISCOPI
ST4326   MAP 1

Rose & Crown £
Off A372 E of Langport; TA10 9QT

In the same family for over 140 years and a real throwback; local ciders and beers, simple food and friendly welcome

Very much a family-run affair – Mrs Pittard keeps an eye on her customers and tells them stories of the past as she was actually born in the pub – this thatched tavern remains completely unspoilt and determinedly unpretentious. There's no bar as such – to get a drink, you just walk into the central flagstoned still room and choose from the casks of Teignworthy Reel Ale and guests such as Glastonbury Mystery Tor, Hopback Crop Circle and Summer Lightning and Palmers 200; farm cider, too. This servery is the only thoroughfare between the casual little front parlours with their unusual pointed-arch windows and genuinely friendly locals; good helpful service. Shove-ha'penny, dominoes and cribbage, and a much more orthodox big back extension family room has pool, darts, games machine and juke box; skittle alley and popular quiz nights. There are tables in a garden and a second enclosed garden has a children's play area. Summer morris men, fine nearby walks and the site of the Battle of Langport (1645) is close by.

ꆛ **Using some home-grown fruit and vegetables, the simple, cheap food includes generously filled sandwiches, filled baked potatoes, ploughman's, pork, apple and cider cobbler, steak in ale pie, stilton and broccoli tart, chicken breast in tarragon sauce, and puddings such as chocolate torte with chocolate sauce and lemon sponge pudding with lemon cream.** *Starters/Snacks: £2.30 to £4.70. Main Courses: £6.50 to £6.95. Puddings: £3.50*

Free house ~ Licensee Mrs Eileen Pittard ~ Real ale ~ Bar food (12-2, 6-7.30; not Sun evening) ~ No credit cards ~ (01458) 250494 ~ Children welcome ~ Dogs welcome ~ Folk singers every third Sat (not June-Aug) and irish night last Thurs in month ~ Open 11.30-2.30, 5.30-11; 11.30-11 Fri and Sat; 12-10.30 Sun

Recommended by Dr and Mrs M E Wilson, MLR, the Didler, Pete Baker, Donna and Roger, Neil and Anita Christopher

KINGSDON
ST5126   MAP 2

Kingsdon Inn
At Podimore roundabout junction of A303, A372 and A37 take A372, then turn right on to B3151, right into village, and right again opposite post office; TA11 7LG

Charming old cottage with low-ceilinged rooms, local cider, west country beers and nice food

New licensees again for this very pretty old thatched cottage. There are four charmingly decorated, low-ceilinged rooms. On the right are some very nice old stripped pine tables with attractive cushioned farmhouse chairs, more seats in what was a small inglenook fireplace, a few low sagging beams, fresh flowers and newspapers, and an open woodburning stove. Down three steps through balustrading is a light, airy room with cushions on stripped pine built-in wall seats, more stripped pine tables and a winter open fire, while a similarly decorated room has more tables and another fireplace. Butcombe Bitter, Otter Bitter and a guest like Cheddar Ales Potholer on handpump, local cider, and up to a dozen wines by the glass. They take bookings only for groups of six or more so it's worth arriving early for a table. There are some picnic-sets on the grass in front and the pub is handy for Lytes Cary (National Trust) and the Fleet Air Arm Museum.

ꆛ **Good bar food at lunchtime now includes ciabatta sandwiches, ploughman's, soup, whitebait, duck liver pâté, poached salmon with parsley sauce, steak and kidney or walnut, leek and stilton pie and chicken in cider, mushrooms and cream, with evening dishes such as fishcakes with chilli mayonnaise, lambs kidneys in madeira sauce, pork fillet with toasted almonds and cream, seared fillet of bass in a fennel and cream sauce, roast rack of lamb in a port and redcurrant sauce and venison casserole; Sunday roast set menu.** *Starters/Snacks: £3.80 to £5.90. Main Courses: £7.95 to £16.50. Puddings: £4.20 to £4.90*

Game Bird Inns ~ Managers Linda Woods and Martin Brelsford ~ Real ale ~ Bar food (12-2, 6.30-9.30(9 Sun)) ~ Restaurant ~ (01935) 840543 ~ Children welcome ~ Dogs welcome ~ Open 12-3, 5.30-11; 12-11 Sat; 12-10.30 Sun ~ Bedrooms: £45S/£70S

Recommended by Colin and Peggy Wilshire, Mike Gorton, Brian P White, Brian and Bett Cox, Michael Doswell, Gareth Lewis, Edward Mirzoeff, KC, Clare West, R G Trevis, Mike and Heather Watson, Ian Phillips, Pat and Robert Watt, J D O Carter, Andrew Shore, Maria Williams, John and Enid Morris

LITTON

ST5954 MAP 2

Kings Arms ⊕

B3114, NW of Chewton Mendip on A39 Bath—Wells; BA3 4PW

Super food and fine choice of drinks in well run, interesting and friendly pub; riverside terrace, bedrooms

Although there is quite an emphasis on the very good food in this partly 15th-c place, the hard-working licensees say that the Kings Arms is, and will always be, a proper pub. There's a big entrance hall with polished flagstones, and bars lead off to the left with low heavy beams and more flagstones; a nice bit on the right beyond the huge fireplace has a big old-fashioned settle and a mix of other settles and wheelback chairs. Throughout there are paintings, four open fires, and a full suit of armour in one alcove; the rooms are divided up into areas by standing timbers. Greene King IPA, Abbot and Ruddles County and a guest on handpump, ciders, several malt whiskies, summer Pimms and an extensive wine list; friendly, attentive service. The terrace overlooking the River Chew has plenty of wooden tables and chairs and there are good quality picnic-sets on the lawn; pétanque.

⊞ As well as some pubby lunchtime food such as ploughman's, filled baked potatoes, lamb and beefburgers, ham and egg and sausage and mash, there are more elaborate choices like baked garlic and rosemary studded camembert, scallops with balsamic reduction and basil, sweet pepper risotto with rocket and parsley oil, free-range pork loin with apple mash and apple, sage and brandy cream with a sage crisp, cajun-style chicken caesar salad, thai beef curry with jasmine rice, crayfish tails and blue swimming crab with a fennel and chicory salad and dill and sushi ginger oil, and puddings such as chocolate torte with vanilla ice-cream and lavender panna cotta, strawberry and rose petal syrup. *Starters/Snacks: £3.50 to £5.95. Main Courses: £9.50 to £19.95. Puddings: £3.95 to £5.95*

Greene King ~ Lease Will and Mary Nicholls ~ Real ale ~ Bar food (12-2, 7-9, though in summer they serve snacks in the garden all day) ~ Restaurant ~ (01761) 241301 ~ Children welcome ~ Dogs welcome ~ Jazz Sun evening, folk Weds evening ~ Open 11.30-11; 12-10.30 Sun; 12-3, 6-11 in winter ~ Bedrooms: /£69S

Recommended by Liz and Tony Colman, Rod and Chris Pring, Richard Fendick, Dr and Mrs A K Clarke

LOVINGTON

ST5831 MAP 2

Pilgrims ⊕ ♟

B3153 Castle Cary—Keinton Mandeville; BA7 7PT

Rather smart but relaxed dining pub with particularly good food cooked by landlord, local beer and cider, and decked terrace; bedrooms

Describing themselves as 'the pub that thinks it's a restaurant' and now called The Pilgrims, this is civilised and rather upmarket – though not in a stuffy way. The chatty and relaxed bar has a few stools by a corner counter, a rack of daily papers, 16 wines by the glass, local cider and cider brandy and Cottage Champflower on handpump from the nearby brewery. A cosy little dark green inner area has sunny modern country and city prints, a couple of shelves of books and china, a cushioned pew, some settees and an old leather easy chair by the big fireplace. With flagstones throughout, this runs into the compact eating area, with candles on tables and some stripped stone; piped music. There's also a separate, more formal carpeted dining room. The landlady's service is efficient and friendly. The enclosed garden has tables, chairs and umbrellas on a decked terrace. The car park exit has its own traffic lights – on your way out line your car up carefully or you may wait for ever for them to change.

🏠 Cooked by the landord and using locally sourced produce, the lunchtime menu might include open sandwiches, soup, mussels in cider with leeks and garlic, hot potted smoked haddock in a cheese sauce with piquant tomato sauce, vegetarian paella, bangers and mustard mash with onion gravy, beer-battered cod and chicken and bacon pilau, with evening choices such as pheasant pâté with home-made granary bread, teriyaki beef, goats cheese baked in filo pasty with sunblush tomato salsa, monkfish and scallops with smoked bacon, wild mushrooms and crème fraîche, rack of lamb with a redcurrant and rosemary gravy and red mullet fillets on mediterranean vegetables; puddings like sticky toffee pudding and lemon posset and local cheeses. They will prepare smaller helpings if required. *Starters/Snacks: £4.00 to £8.00. Main Courses: £7.00 to £23.00. Puddings: £5.00 to £6.00*

Free house ~ Licensees Sally and Jools Mitchison ~ Real ale ~ Bar food ~ Restaurant ~ (01963) 240597 ~ Children welcome ~ Dogs allowed in bar ~ Open 12-3, 7-11(10 Sun); closed two weeks in Oct ~ Bedrooms: /£90B

Recommended by A Warren, Ian and Nita Cooper, Paul and Annette Hallett, Roger White, Michael Doswell, Mrs J H S Lang

LUXBOROUGH
SS9837 MAP 1

Royal Oak 🍽 🛏

Kingsbridge; S of Dunster on minor roads into Brendon Hills – OS Sheet 181 map reference 983378; TA23 0SH

Smashing place to stay in wonderful countryside, imaginative food, local beers and ciders, especially attentive staff

Readers enjoy staying here very much as the staff are particularly helpful and friendly, the breakfasts are really good and there are memorable walks in wonderful surrounding countryside; people do take their dogs, too. The bar rooms date back to the 14th century and have beams and inglenooks, good log fires, flagstones in the front public bar, a fishing theme in one room, and a real medley of furniture. Cotleigh Tawny and Snowy, Exmoor Gold and Palmers IPA on handpump, local farm ciders, several wines by the glass and a good range of malt whiskies. No music or machines; cribbage, dominoes and board games. There are tables out in the charming back courtyard.

🏠 Carefully sourced imaginative food includes sandwiches, mussels steamed with a tomato, orange and cardamom broth, mixed game terrine with spicy quince compote, beetroot cured salmon with deep-fried vegetable crisps and shallot crème fraîche, enoki and oyster mushroom risotto with aubergine tempura, cod fillet wrapped in parma ham with sweet potato mash and olive oil, roast rack of exmoor lamb with puy lentils and parsley jus, pork tenderloin with sautéed apples and dates, green chilli and cinnamon, daily specials, and puddings. Best to book a table as there are often walking and shooting parties in. They do good breakfasts if you stay. *Starters/Snacks: £4.95 to £7.25. Main Courses: £9.95 to £16.25. Puddings: £3.75 to £4.75*

Free house ~ Licensees James and Sian Waller and Sue Hinds ~ Real ale ~ Bar food ~ Restaurant ~ (01984) 640319 ~ Children must be over 10 in evening and in bedrooms ~ Dogs allowed in bar and bedrooms ~ Folk music second Fri of month ~ Open 12-2.30, 6-11; closed 25 Dec ~ Bedrooms: £55B/£65B

Recommended by A S and M E Marriott, J Roy Smylie, Jean Sole, David Crook, R G Stollery, Mr and Mrs Peter Larkman, Paul and Sue Dix, John and Alison Hamilton, Lynda and Trevor Smith, Gaynor Gregory, Kirsteen Margetson, Bill and Cindy Clarke, Len and June Hayle, Catherine Langley, Dave Braisted, the Didler, Bob and Margaret Holder, C J Pratt, John and Gloria Isaacs, John Urquhart, Helen Sharpe, Andrew and Debbie Ettle, J L Wedel, Martin Hatcher, Sue Demont, Tim Barrow, Andrew Shore, Maria Williams, Paul and Karen Coen Cornock

MELLS
ST7249   MAP 2

Talbot 🛏

W of Frome; off A362 W of Buckland Dinham, or A361 via Nunney and Whatley; BA11 3PN

Interesting bar rooms in carefully restored old inn with attractive furnishings, friendly service and well liked food

The public bar in this interesting old inn is in a carefully restored tithe barn with old beams under the high ceiling, agricultural artefacts on the stone walls and a big mural behind the counter. Butcombe, and in summer Fullers London Pride are tapped from the cask; piped music, TV and darts. Back in the main building, the attractive dining room has stripped pews, mate's and wheelback chairs, fresh flowers and candles in bottles on the mix of tables, and sporting and riding pictures on the walls, which are partly stripped above a broad panelled dado, and partly rough terracotta-colour. A small corridor leads to a nice little reception with an open fire and on to restaurant rooms with solid oak tables, high-backed settles and wheelback chairs on a rough pine floor. Friendly service from hard-working staff. There are seats in a very pleasant cobbled courtyard with a vine-covered pergola.The village was purchased by the Horner family of the 'Little Jack Horner' nursery rhyme and the direct descendants still live in the manor house next door. Dogs are allowed only in the public bar.

🍴 Popular bar food includes sandwiches, soup, duck liver, pork and pistachio nut pâté with spiced apple chutney, warm crab and asparagus tart with watercress salad and lemon dressing, calves liver with horseradish mash, smoked bacon and red wine onion gravy, tagliatelle with asparagus and smoked salmon in a creamy herb sauce, rabbit, pork and cider pie and roasted cod fillet with saffron mash, wild mushrooms and lemon chive sauce. *Starters/Snacks: £4.75 to £7.50. Main Courses: £12.50 to £17.95. Puddings: £5.50*

Free house ~ Licensee Roger Stanley Elliott ~ Real ale ~ Bar food (12-2, 6.30-9) ~ Restaurant ~ (01373) 812254 ~ Children welcome but not in bar after 7.30pm ~ Dogs allowed in bar ~ Open 12-2.30, 6.30-11; 12-3, 7-10.30 Sun ~ Bedrooms: £75B/£95B

Recommended by Kath and Ted Warren, Martin Hatcher, Ian Phillips, Anthony Barnes, Simon Marshall, Clive and Geraldine Barber, Richard and Lynn Seers, Ann and Colin Hunt, Andrew and Debbie Ettle, Clare Rosier, Graham Holden, Julie Lee

MONKSILVER
ST0737   MAP 1

Notley Arms

B3188; TA4 4JB

Friendly, busy pub in lovely village with beamed rooms, a fair choice of drinks and enjoyable food; neat streamside garden

What had been the family room in this bustling pub is now the Tack Room and is decorated with horse tack (saddles, bridles and so forth) but still has some toys. The beamed and L-shaped bar has small settles and kitchen chairs around the plain country wooden and candlelit tables, original paintings on the ochre-coloured walls, fresh flowers and a couple of woodburning stoves. Bath Ales Gem, Exmoor Ale and Wadworths 6X on handpump, farm ciders and eight wines by the glass; dominoes, board games and a skittle alley. Good service from the friendly staff and attentive landlord. The immaculate garden has plenty of tables and runs down to a swift clear stream. This is a lovely village.

🍴 They use home-grown herbs and local produce, and list their suppliers by name on the menu; the popular food includes lunchtime filled paninis, ploughman's and ham and egg as well as hot stuffed pitta breads, soup, faggots with dijon mustard mash and onion gravy, home-made lamb burgers with sweet chilli and mint salsa, beer-battered cod fillet, pasta with a spicy tomato, caper, black olive and chilli sauce, ostrich steak with a mushroom or black pepper sauce, daily specials, and puddings like triple chocolate brownies with ice-cream and treacle tart. *Starters/Snacks: £3.95 to £6.95. Main Courses: £7.95 to £13.95. Puddings: £3.95 to £5.95*

Unique (Enterprise) ~ Lease Russell and Jane Deary ~ Real ale ~ Bar food (not Mon lunchtime or winter Mon) ~ (01984) 656217 ~ Children allowed if well behaved ~ Dogs welcome ~ Open 12-2.30, 6.30-10.30(11 Sat); 12-2.30, 7-10.30 Sun; closed Mon lunchtime (all day Mon in winter)

NORTH CURRY
ST3125 MAP 1

Bird in Hand

Queens Square; off A378 (or A358) E of Taunton; TA3 6LT

Village pub with beams and timbers, cricketing memorabilia, friendly staff and decent food and drink

The bustling but cosy main bar in this friendly, well run village pub has some nice old pews, settles, benches, and old yew tables on the flagstones, original beams and timbers, some locally woven willow work, and a cheerful atmosphere; cricketing memorabilia, and a log fire in the inglenook fireplace. Otter Bitter and a couple of guests like Cheddar Ales Potholer and Cotleigh Barn Owl on handpump, Rich's farm cider, and eight wines by the glass. Piped music.

🍽 **Bar food includes sandwiches, ploughman's, moules marinière, mediterranean vegetable kebabs with tomato and basil sauce, pork fillet medallions with grain mustard sauce, rack of lamb with mint and red wine, venison steak in a port, orange and redcurrant sauce; daily specials, puddings and Sunday roasts.** *Starters/Snacks: £3.95 to £8.95. Main Courses: £10.95 to £15.95. Puddings: £4.50*

Free house ~ Licensee James Mogg ~ Real ale ~ Bar food ~ Restaurant ~ (01823) 490248 ~ Children welcome ~ Dogs allowed in bar ~ Open 12-3, 6-11.30; 12-4, 6-midnight Sat; 12-3, 7-11.30 Sun; closed evenings 25 and 26 Dec

NORTON ST PHILIP
ST7755 MAP 2

George 🛏

A366; BA2 7LH

Wonderful ancient building full of history and interest, with popular food, pleasant service and fine spacious bedrooms

It's worth visiting this exceptional building to take in the fine surroundings of a place that has been offering hospitality to locals and travellers for 600 years. The central Norton Room, which was the original bar, has really heavy beams, an oak panelled settle and solid dining chairs on the narrow strip wooden floor, a variety of 18th-c pictures, an open fire in the handsome stone fireplace, and a low wooden bar counter. Wadworths IPA and 6X and a guest beer on handpump and pleasant service. As you enter the building, there's a room on the right with high dark beams, squared dark half-panelling, a broad carved stone fireplace with an old iron fireback and pewter plates on the mantelpiece, a big mullioned window with leaded lights, and a round oak 17th-c table reputed to have been used by the Duke of Monmouth who stayed here before the Battle of Sedgemoor – after their defeat, his men were imprisoned in what is now the Monmouth Bar. The Charterhouse Bar is mostly used by those enjoying a drink before a meal: a wonderful pitched ceiling with trusses and timbering, heraldic shields and standards, jousting lances, and swords on the walls, a fine old stone fireplace, high-backed cushioned heraldic-fabric dining chairs on the big rug over the wood plank floor, and an oak dresser with some pewter. The dining room (a restored barn with original oak ceiling beams, a pleasant if haphazard mix of early 19th-c portraits and hunting prints, and the same mix of vaguely old-looking furnishings) has a good relaxing, chatty atmosphere. The bedrooms are very atmospheric and comfortable – some reached by an external Norman stone stair-turret, and some across the cobbled and flagstoned courtyard and up into a fine half-timbered upper gallery (where there's a lovely 18th-c carved oak settle). A stroll over the meadow behind the pub (past the picnic-sets on the narrow grass pub garden) leads to an attractive churchyard around the medieval church whose bells struck Pepys (here on 12 June 1668) as 'mighty tuneable'.

🍴 **Well liked bar food includes sandwiches, various platters, mushroom and leek gratin, cottage pie, ham and egg, and chicken curry with more elaborate choices such as game terrine with chutney, goats cheese and caramelised red onion tartlet, fillet of local trout with a lemon and caper glaze, nut roast with red lentils and cider, lamb tagine, steak and mushroom in ale pie and venison with a port and onion sauce.** *Starters/Snacks: £4.95 to £5.95. Main Courses: £7.50 to £15.95. Puddings: £4.50 to £4.95*

Wadworths ~ Managers David and Tania Satchell ~ Real ale ~ Bar food (12-2, 7-9; all day in summer) ~ Restaurant ~ (01373) 834224 ~ Well behaved children welcome ~ Dogs allowed in bar and bedrooms ~ Open 11-2.30, 5.30-11; 11-11(10.30 Sun) Sat ~ Bedrooms: £60B/£80B

Recommended by Ian Phillips, E McCall, T McLean, D Irving, R Huggins, J Stickland, the Didler, Warren Marsh, Donna and Roger, Ann and Colin Hunt, Rod and Chris Pring, Alain and Rose Foote, Simon Collett-Jones, Dr and Mrs A K Clarke

OAKE
ST1526 MAP 1

Royal Oak 🍺

Hillcommon, N; B3227 W of Taunton; if coming from Taunton, ignore signpost on left for Oake and go 200 yards, pub is on left directly off B3227; TA4 1DS

Decent real ales and summer beer festival in neat pub under new landlord

As well as holding a real ale festival with live jazz in July, the new licensee of this neat country pub keeps Downton Chimera IPA, RCH Pitchfork, Sharps Doom Bar and Taunton Brewing Company Taunton Ale on handpump; quite a few malt whiskies. The spacious bar has several separate-seeming areas around the central servery; on the left is a little tiled fireplace, with a big woodburning stove on the other side. The windows have smart curtains, there are plenty of fresh flowers and lots of brasses on the beams and walls. At the back is a long dining area which leads out to a pleasant sheltered garden. Skittle alley in winter and piped music. More reports please.

🍴 **Lunchtime bar food includes sandwiches, filled baked potatoes, soup, thai crab cakes with sweet chilli, cod in beer batter, lambs liver and bacon with white onion gravy, home-baked ham with free-range eggs and a daily carvery; in the evening, there might be mussels in cider and cream, garlic mushrooms, chargrilled aubergine and courgette bake, chicken in barbecue sauce topped with bacon and cheese, crispy belly pork with cider and apple gravy and braised lamb shank.** *Starters/Snacks: £3.95 to £6.95. Main Courses: £5.95 to £15.95. Puddings: £4.50 to £5.95*

Free house ~ Licensee Richard Bolwell ~ Real ale ~ Bar food (12-2, 6.30-9.30) ~ Restaurant ~ (01823) 400295 ~ Children welcome ~ Open 12-3, 6-11.30(midnight Sat)

Recommended by Andy and Jill Smith, J L Wedel, Theo, Anne and Jane Gaskin, Christine and Neil Townend

PITNEY
ST4527 MAP 1

Halfway House 🍺

Just off B3153 W of Somerton; TA10 9AB

Up to ten real ales, local ciders and continental bottled beers in bustling friendly local; good simple food

Of course the fine range of up to ten real ales tapped from the cask in this traditional village local draws in many customers, but our readers also enjoy the genuinely friendly welcome and atmosphere. Changing regularly, the beers might include Adnams Broadside, Bath Ales Festivity, Branscombe BVB Own Label, Butcombe Bitter, Hop Back Summer Lightning, Otter Bright and Bitter, RCH Pitchfork and Teignworthy Reel Ale. They also have 20 or so continental bottled beers, Hecks's and Wilkins's farm ciders and 15 malt whiskies; cribbage, dominoes and board games. There's a good mix of people chatting at communal tables in the three old-fashioned rooms, all with roaring log fires and a homely feel underlined by a profusion of books, maps and newspapers. There are tables outside.

🍴 **Good simple filling food includes hot smoked foods from their own garden smokery as well as sandwiches, soup, filled baked potatoes, ploughman's with home-made pickle,**

lamb stew with dumplings and fish pie; in the evening they do about half a dozen home-made curries. *Starters/Snacks: £3.95 to £5.95. Main Courses: £5.95 to £9.95. Puddings: £2.00 to £3.50*

Free house ~ Licensee Julian Lichfield ~ Real ale ~ Bar food (12-2.30, 6.30-9.30; not Sun) ~ (01458) 252513 ~ Children welcome with restrictions ~ Dogs welcome ~ Open 11.30-3, 5.30-11(midnight Sat); 12-3, 7-11 Sun

Recommended by Guy Vowles, Peter Meister, the Didier, Andrea Rampley, Mrs M B Gregg, Theo, Anne and Jane Gaskin, John and Gloria Isaacs

PORTISHEAD
ST4777   MAP 1

Windmill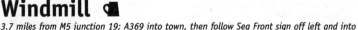

3.7 miles from M5 junction 19; A369 into town, then follow Sea Front sign off left and into Nore Road; BS20 6JZ

Large and efficient family dining pub in lovely spot with quite a few real ales and decent food

This is by no means a traditional pub and is very different to many of the other places in this *Guide*. It's a busy three-level family dining pub and an efficient mealtime stop from the motorway – but it does have a marvellous view in fine weather from the wall of picture windows on the top and bottom floors, looking out over the Bristol Channel to Newport and Cardiff (with the bridges on the right). The bottom floor is a simple easy-going family area, the top one a shade more elegant with its turkey carpet, muted green and cream wallpaper and dark panelled dado. The middle floor, set back from here, is quieter and (with its black-painted ceiling boards) more softly lit. Unexpectedly, they have up to six quickly changing real ales on handpump such as Bass, Butcombe Gold, Courage Best, RCH Pitchfork and two guest beers such as Exmoor Beast and Stag. Out on the seaward side are picnic-sets on three tiers of lantern-lit terrace.

▥ **To eat, you find a numbered table, present yourself at the order desk (by a slimline pudding show-cabinet), pay for your order, and return to the table with a tin (well, stainless steel) tray of cutlery, condiments and sauce packets. It works well: sandwiches, filled baked potatoes, ploughman's, soup, spinach and sweetcorn bake, steak and mushroom in ale pie, faggots, lambs liver, a curry and lamb shank; dishes for smaller appetites, too.** *Starters/Snacks: £3.25 to £4.75. Main Courses: £6.95 to £10.95. Puddings: £1.50 to £3.95*

Free house ~ Licensee J S Churchill ~ Real ale ~ Bar food (all day) ~ (01275) 843677 ~ Children in family area ~ Dogs allowed in bar ~ Open 11-11; 12-10.30 Sun

Recommended by Ian Legge, Tom Evans, Dave Braisted, Andrea and Guy Bradley, P and J Shapley

SHEPTON MONTAGUE
ST6731   MAP 2

Montague Inn ♀
Village signposted just off A359 Bruton—Castle Cary; BA9 8JW

Friendly licensees in busy country pub with real ales, fresh bar food and pretty heated terrace

From the good quality seats and tables on the heated, pretty terrace behind this busy little country pub there are pleasant views; more seats in the gardens, too. Inside, the rooms are simply but tastefully furnished with stripped wooden tables and kitchen chairs, and there's a log fire in the attractive inglenook fireplace. French windows in the restaurant lead to the terrace. Bath Ales Gem and Butcombe Bitter with perhaps a couple of guests like Greene King Abbot and Otter Ale tapped from the cask; local cider and several wines, including champagne, by the glass, and smiling, helpful service.

▥ **As they don't have a freezer, the bar food is extremely fresh and quickly changing: lunchtime sandwiches and ploughman's, as well as soup, good seared scallops with avocado and bacon salad, fish or cottage pie, confit of duck, rump steak, daily specials, and puddings.** *Starters/Snacks: £3.95 to £8.50. Main Courses: £13.50 to £21.95. Puddings: £6.50*

Free house ~ Licensee Sean O'Callaghan ~ Bar food (12-2(3 Sun and bank hols), 7-9; not Sun evening or Mon) ~ Restaurant ~ (01749) 813213 ~ Children welcome ~ Dogs allowed in bar ~ Open 12-3, 6-11; closed Sun evening and all day Mon (except bank hols)

Recommended by H G H Stafford, Mrs J H S Lang, Derek and Heather Manning, Clare West, Dennis and Gill Keen, Colin and Janet Roe, Mrs Christa Sansom, Paul and Annette Hallett

SIMONSBATH   SS7739   MAP 1

Exmoor Forest Inn 🛏

B3223/B3358; TA24 7SH

In lovely surroundings with plenty of fine walks, comfortable inn with enjoyable food, good range of drinks and friendly licensees

The hard-working licensees here are no strangers to this *Guide* – they used to run the Merrie Harriers in Clayhidon (in Devon) a couple of years back. They've spent 18 months renovating both this inn and its outbuildings to create a comfortable and warmly welcoming place. It's in lovely surroundings and perfectly positioned for a first or last night's stay on the Two Moors Walk linking Exmoor to Dartmoor; they provide dog beds, bowls and towels. The bar has a few red plush stools around little circular tables by the bar counter and steps up to a larger area with joists in the ceiling, cushioned settles, upholstered stools and mate's chairs around a mix of dark tables, a woodburning stove with two shelves of stone flagons to one side and hunting prints, trophies and antlers on the walls. The walls of the Tack Room are covered in all sorts of horse tack – saddles, bridles, stirrups, horseshoes and so forth with similar tables and chairs as well as one nice long table for a bigger party. Cotleigh Tawny and Exmoor Gold plus a couple of summer guests such as Otter Bitter and St Austells Tribute on handpump, local cider and local juices, 30 malt whiskies and several wines by the glass; friendly service. There's a cosy little residents' lounge and an airy dining room. Picnic-sets and wooden and metal benches around tables under parasols in the front garden. Annie the beer-drinking dog has come with them from their last pub and they also have Billy the lurcher and Noddy the collie.

🍴 Good enjoyable bar food includes lunchtime filled rolls and filled large baked potatoes, soup, chicken liver pâté with hawthorn jelly, goats cheese baked with hazelnuts with cranberry sauce, ham and free-range eggs, sausages with mustard mash and onion gravy, sweet potato and cashew nut korma, free-range caribbean-style chicken with a mandarin sauce, confit of duck on onion marmalade, lovely scallops with thyme and garlic butter, and puddings such as dark chocolate and black cherry mousse cake and glazed lemon tart with raspberry coulis; west country cheeseboard. *Starters/Snacks: £3.95 to £6.95. Main Courses: £7.50 to £16.50. Puddings: £4.25 to £5.50*

Free house ~ Licensees Chris and Barry Kift ~ Real ale ~ Bar food ~ Restaurant ~ (01643) 831341 ~ Children welcome ~ Dogs allowed in bar and bedrooms ~ Open 12-3, 6.30-11(10.30 Sun) ~ Bedrooms: £45S/£80S

Recommended by Michael David Doyle, Mrs D Wilford, Lynda and Trevor Smith, Rona Murdoch, Gordon and Jay Smith, Mark Okunie Wski

STANTON WICK   ST6162   MAP 2

Carpenters Arms 🍴 ♇ 🛏

Village signposted off A368, just W of junction with A37 S of Bristol; BS39 4BX

Bustling warm-hearted dining pub in nice country setting with imaginative food, friendly staff and good drinks

This is a civilised and neatly kept dining pub with plenty of loyal customers from quite a wide area. The Coopers Parlour on the right has one or two beams, seats around heavy tables and attractive curtains and plants in the windows; on the angle between here and the bar area there's a fat woodburning stove in an opened-through corner fireplace. The bar has wood-backed built-in wall seats and some leather fabric-cushioned stools, stripped stone walls and a big log fire. There's also a snug inner room (lightened by mirrors in arched 'windows') and a restaurant with leather sofas and easy chairs in a comfortable lounge area. Butcombe Bitter, Courage Best and Wadworths 6X on handpump, ten wines by the glass and a dozen malt whiskies; games machine and TV. They may ask you to leave your credit card behind the bar. This is a lovely rural setting and there are picnic-sets on the front terrace; pretty flowerbeds and attractive hanging baskets and tubs.

🍴 **As well as light lunchtime choices such as sandwiches, mussels in a light curry and coriander cream sauce, beefburger on toasted focaccia with tomato and mozzarella, spaghetti tossed with cherry tomato, black olives, red onion, basil and garlic, thai-style chicken skewers with sweet chilli mayonnaise and fish pie, the enjoyable food might also include smoked haddock and dill fishcake with a light horseradish cream, baked field mushrooms with garlic butter gratinated stilton and herb crumb, leek, brie and walnut tart, game casserole, honey and mustard-glazed pork chop on apple and black pudding with a sage and red wine sauce, fillet of cod on braised spring cabbage and bacon with parsley sauce, and puddings such as sticky toffee slice with vanilla ice-cream and glazed lemon tart with raspberry sorbet.** Starters/Snacks: £3.95 to £8.95. Main Courses: £11.95 to £16.95. Puddings: £4.95

Buccaneer Holdings ~ Manager Simon Pledge ~ Real ale ~ Bar food (12-2, 7-10; 12-2.30, 7-9.30 Sun) ~ Restaurant ~ (01761) 490202 ~ Children welcome ~ Dogs allowed in bar ~ Open 11-11; 12-10.30 Sun; closed evenings 25 and 26 Dec ~ Bedrooms: £67B/£95B

Recommended by Angus and Rosemary Campbell, Dr and Mrs C W Thomas, Pat and Tony Martin, John and Bettye Reynolds, Andrew Shore, Maria Williams, Dr and Mrs A K Clarke, Bob and Angela Brooks, John Urquhart, Steve and Liz Tilley, Donna and Roger, B N F and M Parkin, MRSM

STOKE ST GREGORY   ST3527   MAP 1

Rose & Crown 🍴 ♀

Woodhill; follow North Curry signpost off A378 by junction with A358 – keep on to Stoke, bearing right in centre, passing church and follow lane for ½ mile; TA3 6EW

Friendly and cheerful family-run pub with snug eating areas, good bar food and west country beers

For nearly 30 years, this cheerful and characterful country pub has been run by the same friendly family. The cosy bar is decorated in a pleasant stable theme: dark wooden loose-box partitions for some of the interestingly angled nooks and alcoves, lots of brasses and bits on the low beams and joists, stripped stonework, a wonky floor, and appropriate pictures including a highland pony carrying a stag. Many of the wildlife paintings on the walls are the work of the landlady, and there's an 18th-c glass-covered well in one corner. The two rooms of the dining area lead off here with lots of country prints and paintings of hunting scenes, animals, and birds on the walls, more horsebrasses, jugs and mugs hanging from the ceiling joists, and candles in bottles on all tables. Butcombe Bitter, Exmoor Ale and Otter Ale on handpump and decent wines; piped music. Under cocktail parasols by an apple tree on the sheltered front terrace are some new picnic-sets. The pub is in an interesting Somerset Levels village with willow beds still supplying the two basket works.

🍴 **Good, popular bar food at lunchtime includes interesting sandwiches using their own home-made granary bread, ploughman's, soup, home-cooked ham and eggs, beer-battered haddock with mushy peas, sausages made from their own pigs and grilled lambs liver and bacon; evening choices such as goats cheese and pecan salad with honey and mustard vinaigrette, moules marinière, stilton and mushroom vol-au-vent, red snapper fillet with a spicy cream and lemon sauce, tandoori chicken, rack of lamb with a herb and garlic crust with red wine jus, daily specials, and puddings.** Starters/Snacks: £3.75 to £8.50. Main Courses: £8.50 to £16.50. Puddings: £3.75 to £5.50

Free house ~ Licensees Stephen, Sally, Richard and Leonie Browning ~ Real ale ~ Bar food ~ Restaurant ~ (01823) 490296 ~ Children welcome ~ Dogs allowed in bar ~ Open 11-3, 6.30-11; 12-3, 7-10.30 Sun ~ Bedrooms: £36.50(£46.50B)/£53(£73B)

Recommended by Revd D E and Mrs J A Shapland, Peter Mack Wilkins, Donna and Roger, Bob and Margaret Holder, M G Hart, Duncan Cloud, Sara Fulton, Roger Baker, Edward Delling-Williams

---

Pubs with attractive or unusually big gardens are listed at the back of the book.

TARR   SS8632   MAP 1

Tarr Farm ⓘ 🛏

Tarr Steps – rather narrow road off B3223 N of Dulverton, very little nearby parking (paying car park quarter-mile up road); OS Sheet 181 map reference 868322 – as the inn is on the E bank, don't be tempted to approach by car from the W unless you can cope with a deep ford; TA22 9PY

Lovely Exmoor setting looking over Tarr Steps and lots to do nearby; super food, a fine range of drinks, friendly staff and bedrooms

Given the glorious setting, this inn does get very busy – even out of season – but the friendly staff work hard to keep their customers happy. It's set on an Exmoor hillside looking down on Tarr Steps just below – that much-photographed clapper bridge of massive granite slabs for medieval packhorses crossing the River Barle as it winds through this lightly wooded combe. The pub part consists of a line of compact and unpretentious rooms, with plenty of good views, slabby rustic tables, stall seating, wall seats and pub chairs, a woodburning stove at one end, salmon pink walls, nice game bird pictures and a pair of stuffed pheasants. The serving bar up a step or two has Exmoor Ale and Gold on handpump, eight wines by the glass and a good choice of other drinks. The residents' end has a smart little evening restaurant (you can eat from this menu in the bar), and a pleasant log-fire lounge with dark leather armchairs and sofas. Outside, lots of chaffinches hop around between slate-topped stone tables above the steep lawn.

🍽 Good bar food includes sandwiches, soup, duck liver parfait with apple chutney, warm venison salad with crispy parsnips and cherry tomatoes, mild chicken curry, toulouse sausages with onion gravy, honey-roast ham with free-range eggs and pasta with porcini mushrooms and thyme in a tomato and mascarpone sauce; from the evening menu there might be smoked eel and trout risotto with vermouth, watercress and parsley, steamed scallops and tiger prawns with black bean, sesame, ginger and spring onion, saddle of local lamb stuffed with black olive and garlic tapenade, parsnip dauphinoise and sunblush tomato juice and roasted veal rump with sweetbreads, tomato tarte tatin and provençale sauce; puddings such as Baileys bread and butter pudding with crème anglaise and sticky toffee pudding with butterscotch sauce. *Starters/Snacks: £3.95 to £7.95. Main Courses: £7.95 to £18.95. Puddings: £4.95 to £6.95*

Free house ~ Licensees Richard Benn and Judy Carless ~ Real ale ~ Bar food (12-3, 6.30-9.30) ~ Restaurant ~ (01643) 851507 ~ Children allowed lunchtimes only ~ Dogs allowed in bar and bedrooms ~ Open 11-11; closed 1-9 Feb ~ Bedrooms: £90B/£150B

Recommended by Dr Ian S Morley, John and Jackie Chalcraft, Stan and Hazel Allen, Martin and Pauline Jennings, Gavin and Helen Griggs, John and Jackie Walsh, Tony and Tracy Constance

TRISCOMBE   ST1535   MAP 1

Blue Ball ⓘ 🍷

Village signposted off A358 Crowcombe—Bagborough; turn off opposite sign to youth hostel; OS Sheet 181 map reference 155355; TA4 3HE

Fine old building with enjoyable food and drink and seats on decking making the most of the views; bedrooms

Very popular locally, this 15th-c thatched stone-built inn places much emphasis on its very good food – most tables are given over to eating – but the licensees are still happy for customers to drop in for a drink and a chat. On the first floor of the original stables, it's a smart place, sloping down gently on three levels, each with its own fire, and cleverly divided into seating by hand-cut beech partitions. Cotleigh Tawny, and a couple of guests like Exmoor Gold and St Austells HSD on handpump and eight wines by the glass; piped music. The decking at the top of the woodside, terraced garden makes the most of the views. There is a chair lift to the bar/restaurant area for the disabled.

🍽 Good food at lunchtime includes filled rolls, ploughman's, soup, beer-battered king prawns with sweet chilli sauce, confit duck leg terrine with grain mustard dressing, steak and mushroom or fish pie, vegetable curry, cajun chicken casserole and calves liver and bacon, with evening extras such as crayfish risotto and pesto-dressed salad leaves, baked aubergine filled with couscous and mediterranean vegetables topped with goats cheese, free-range duck breast with black cherry sauce and fondant potatoes and baked bream with garlic, coriander and lime butter; puddings like dark chocolate marquise with raspberry sorbet and toffee tart with banana ice-cream. *Starters/Snacks: £2.25 to £6.95. Main Courses: £7.95 to £17.95. Puddings: £4.95 to £8.95*

Punch ~ Lease Sue and Gerald Rogers ~ Real ale ~ Bar food (12-2.30, 7-9.30) ~ Restaurant ~ (01984) 618242 ~ Well behaved children welcome ~ Dogs allowed in bar ~ Open 12-4, 6-11(10.30 Sun); closed evenings 25 and 26 Dec and 1 Jan ~ Bedrooms: £40B/£60B

Recommended by Bob and Margaret Holder, Mr and Mrs C R Little, P Dawn, John A Barker, Mrs P Bishop, Michael and Catherine Mills, Rod and Chris Pring, Gordon and Jay Smith, Mr and Mrs D Scott, Mike and Sue Loseby

WELLS
ST5445 MAP 2

City Arms 🍺
High Street; BA5 2AG

Busy town centre pub with seven real ales, fine choice of whiskies and wines and food served all day from 8am

There's a fine choice of seven real ales on handpump in this busy 16th-c place: Badger Tanglefoot, Butcombe Bitter, Cheddar Ales Potholer, Greene King Abbot, IPA and Old Speckled Hen and Sharps Doom Bar. They also keep 35 malt whiskies and 16 wines by the glass. The main bar operates as a café bar-patisserie during the day and a bistro at night and they have two kitchens to cope with demand. There's also a first floor terrace in the cobbled courtyard. Board games and piped music. The building was originally a jail, and you can still see a couple of small, barred windows in the courtyard.

🍴 Bar food includes sandwiches, soup, chicken liver pâté, grilled goats cheese with chargrilled aubergine and balsamic dresing, fish pie, lambs liver with smoked bacon, chargrilled cajun chicken, steak in ale pie, aberdeen angus steaks and evening extras like pork loin with apple and cider cream sauce and monkfish medallions in prawn and ginger sauce; good breakfasts. *Starters/Snacks: £3.50 to £5.50. Main Courses: £5.95 to £8.75. Puddings: £3.50 to £3.95*

Free house ~ Licensee Jim Hardy ~ Real ale ~ Bar food (all day till 10pm) ~ Restaurant ~ (01749) 673916 ~ Children welcome ~ Dogs allowed in bar ~ Open 8am-1130pm (midnight Sat)

Recommended by Terry Buckland, Ann and Colin Hunt, John and Alison Hamilton, J Roy Smylie

Crown 🛏
Market Place; BA5 2RF

Handy for the centre with bustling bars, a large choice of bar and bistro food and decent drinks; bedrooms

A large group of bell ringers who stayed for a couple of nights at this brightly modernised former coaching inn tell us they enjoyed their visit very much. It's in a fine spot in the Market Place overlooked by the cathedral and William Penn is said to have preached from a window here in 1685. The walls in the various bustling bar areas are painted white or blue, there's light wooden flooring, and plenty of matching chairs and cushioned wall benches; up a step is a comfortable area with a sofa and newspapers. A sunny back room (where children tend to go) has an exposed stone fireplace, GWR prints, and a couple of games machines and TV; it opens on to a small courtyard with a few tables. Archers Best Bitter, Butcombe Bitter, Moles Best Bitter and Sharps Doom Bar on handpump and 11 wines by the glass; piped music.

🍴 Reliable bar food at lunchtime includes sandwiches and paninis, ploughman's, soup, ham and egg, sausages with onion cider gravy, burgers and beef stew with evening dishes such as chicken and wild mushroom pâté, vegetable, chestnut and tomato crumble, faggots in onion gravy, creamy fish pie and chicken stuffed with wild mushrooms and pancetta with madeira jus; puddings like blackberry crème brûlée and baked rum and chocolate cheesecake with orange sauce. *Starters/Snacks: £3.75 to £5.50. Main Courses: £4.95 to £6.50. Puddings: £4.25*

Free house ~ Licensee Adrian Lawrence ~ Real ale ~ Bar food (12-9.30; 12-2(2.30 Weds and Sun), 6-9.30 in winter) ~ Restaurant ~ (01749) 673457 ~ Children welcome until 8pm ~ Dogs allowed in bedrooms ~ Open 10am-11.30pm(midnight Fri and Sat, 11pm Sun); closed 25 Dec ~ Bedrooms: £60S/£90S

Recommended by John Coatsworth, M G Hart, B J Harding, Colin and Janet Roe, Anthony Barnes, Steve and Liz Tilley

WOOKEY   ST5245   MAP 2

Burcott

B3139 W of Wells; BA5 1NJ

Unspoilt, friendly roadside pub with neat bars, west country beers, reliable food and new bedrooms

They've now opened bedrooms in the converted stables next to this neat roadside pub. The two simply furnished and old-fashioned small front bar rooms have exposed flagstoned floors, lantern-style lights on the walls and a woodburning stove. The lounge has a square corner bar counter, fresh flowers at either end of the mantelpiece above the tiny stone fireplace, Parker-Knollish brocaded chairs around a couple of tables and high bar stools; the other bar has beams (some willow pattern plates on one), a solid settle by the window and a high backed old pine settle by one wall, cushioned mate's chairs and fresh flowers on the mix of nice old pine tables and a hunting horn on the bressumer above the fireplace. Darts, shove-ha'penny, cribbage and dominoes and built-in wall seats and little framed advertisements in a small right-hand room; piped music. Branscombe Vale Branoc, Hop Back Summer Lightning, RCH Pitchfork and Teignworthy Old Moggie on handpump, and several wines by the glass. The window boxes and tubs in front of the building are pretty in summer and a sizeable garden has picnic-sets, plenty of small trees and shrubs and views of the Mendip Hills.

Well liked food using traceable meats includes lunchtime sandwiches, filled baguettes and baked potatoes and ploughman's as well as garlic mushrooms, salmon and dill fishcakes, vegetable and cashew nut bake, steak in ale pie, honey-roast ham and eggs, chicken in an apricot and stilton cream sauce, slow-roasted lamb rump in honey and balsamic jus, daily specials and puddings. *Starters/Snacks: £4.50 to £5.75. Main Courses: £7.50 to £16.50. Puddings: £3.95*

Free house ~ Licensees Ian and Anne Stead ~ Real ale ~ Bar food (not Sun or Mon evenings) ~ Restaurant ~ (01749) 673874 ~ Well behaved children in restaurant only ~ Open 11.30-2.30, 6-11; 12-3, 6-11 Sat; 12-3, 7-10.30 Sun; closed 25 and 26 Dec, 1 Jan ~ Bedrooms: /£60S

Recommended by Tom Evans, Peter Mack Wilkins, Anthony Barnes, Mr and Mrs R Duys, Alan and Paula McCully

LUCKY DIP

Besides the fully inspected pubs, you might like to try these Lucky Dips recommended to us and described by readers (if you do, please send us reports: www.goodguides.co.uk).

ASHCOTT [ST4436]
Pipers TA7 9QL [A39/A361, SE of village]: Cheerful welcome and consistently good home cooking (sandwiches too) in dining pub with large beamed lounge, good range of mainstream and other ales, Addlestone's cider, good choice of wines by the glass, prompt helpful service, woodburner, leather armchairs, pictures for sale and potted plants, prettily set beamed dining area; unobtrusive piped music; pleasant roadside garden *(Dr and Mrs C W Thomas)*
☆ *Ring o' Bells* TA7 9PZ [High St; pub well signed off A39 W of Street]: Wide choice of good value wholesome home-made food from fresh sandwiches and rolls to serious meals

in friendly and neatly kept local, quickly changing real ales, Wilkins's farm cider, steps up and down making snug comfortably modernised areas, separate stripy pink dining room, decent wines, helpful service, inglenook woodburner; piped music, games machines, skittle alley; attractively planted back garden with play area and shaded terrace, camping *(Liz and Tony Colman, Meg and Colin Hamilton, Dr A J and Mrs Tompsett, Christine and Neil Townend, Peter Mack Wilkins, BB, Andy and Jill Smith)*
BARRINGTON [ST3918]
☆ *Royal Oak* TA19 0JB: Roomy updated stone-built dining pub with good if not cheap food with a fresh modern twist from enterprising

sandwiches to steaks and speciality fish (veg may come from nearby Barrington Court), friendly efficient service, real ales inc Bass and Butcombe, solid modern furnishings in light and airy lounge bar (children welcome here), no piped music; large outdoor area, opp church in beautiful village (*Dr and Mrs R G J Telfer, Anneliese Cooke, Revd L J and Mrs Melliss*)

BATH [ST7564]

Ale House BA1 1NG [York St]: Quiet and unassuming city-centre local with big windows to street, helpful friendly landlord, Courage Best, Fullers London Pride and a guest beer, flame-effect fire, Bath RFC memorabilia, bargain lunchtime food from baked potatoes up in rambling cellar bar, more seating upstairs; unobtrusive corner TV (*Dr and Mrs M E Wilson, Ian Phillips, Colin and Peggy Wilshire, Michael Dandy, Susan and Nigel Wilson*)

Bell BA1 5BW [Walcot St]: Eight regular real ales, interesting guest beers and farm cider in long narrow split-level dark-ceilinged pub with lots of pump clips and gig notices, good value baguettes, bar billiards; calm at lunchtime, packed and lively with loud piped music evenings, frequent live music; canopied garden (*Dr and Mrs A K Clarke, Pete Baker, Clare Rosier, Donna and Roger*)

Boathouse BA1 3NB [Newbridge Rd]: Large, light and airy family-friendly pub in nice riverside spot nr Kennet & Avon marina, good value food from filled ciabattas to steaks and restaurant dishes, efficient courteous service, Brains ales, decent house wines, rugs on wooden floor, wicker furniture and potted plants in conservatory on lower level, apple-theme and waterside decorations; children very welcome, picnic-sets out in neat garden with steps up to boat-view balcony (*Dr and Mrs A K Clarke*)

☆ *Coeur de Lion* BA1 5AR [Northumberland Pl; off High St by W H Smith]: Tiny single-room pub, perhaps Bath's prettiest, simple, cosy and friendly, with Abbey ales and a guest such as Wells & Youngs Bombardier, candles and log-effect gas fire, good mulled wine at Christmas, lunchtime filled rolls in summer; may be piped music, stairs to lavatories; tables out in charming flower-filled flagstoned pedestrian alley, open all day (*LYM, Michael Dandy, Dr and Mrs A K Clarke, the Didler, Dr and Mrs M E Wilson*)

Cross Keys BA2 5RZ [Midford Rd (B3110)]: New licensees in pleasant dining lounge with smarter end restaurant, good value enjoyable food perhaps moving gently up market, real ales such as Courage, Wadworths and Wells & Youngs Bombardier; big garden with aviary (*Meg and Colin Hamilton, Dr and Mrs A K Clarke, Nigel Long*)

Crystal Palace BA1 1NW [Abbey Green]: Cheerfully busy two-room pub with something of a winebar feel, dark panelling and tiled floors, freshly prepared straightforward food (not Sun evening) inc lunchtime snacks, speedy friendly service,

well kept ales such as Abbey Bellringer and O'Hanlons, log fire, family room and conservatory; piped music, they may try to keep your credit card while you eat; sheltered heated courtyard with lovely hanging baskets (*Dr and Mrs M E Wilson, Tom and Jill Jones, LYM, Dr and Mrs A K Clarke*)

Forester & Flower BA2 5BZ [Bradford Rd, Combe Down]: Newly reopened as good value dining pub, good Sun roast beef, a couple of well kept ales (*Mark O'Sullivan*)

Garricks Head BA1 1ET [Theatre Royal, St Johns Pl]: Well run and civilised traditional pub, open fire in both rooms, good food (that bit different without being affected), friendly helpful service, good choice of wines by the glass and of Milk Street and guest ales such as Palmers, quickly served food even when busy; handy for theatre (*Steve and Liz Tilley, W W Burke*)

Gascoyne Place BA1 1EY [Sawclose]: Stylish and comfortable new pub in 18th-c building, good choice of drinks, bar food all day, front bar with gallery, boarded ceiling and stripped masonry in long back bar, upstairs restaurant; Sun jazz night; open all day (*anon*)

☆ *George* BA2 6TR [Bathampton, E of Bath centre, off A36 or (via toll bridge) off A4; Mill Lane]: Popular and comfortably extended Chef & Brewer dining pub in nice canalside spot, good-sized bar opening through arches into rambling beamed rooms with soft lighting, candles on nice mix of tables, rugs on polished boards, dark panelling, period portraits and plates, three log fires, wide blackboard food choice all day at good range of prices from baguettes to duck and fresh fish (can be long delays when it's busy), good range of real ales and wines by the glass, plenty of well organised young uniformed staff; may be quiet piped music; children welcome, picnic-sets on enclosed suntrap terrace and out on grass (shorter menu for outside) (*Dr and Mrs M E Wilson, Meg and Colin Hamilton, Dr and Mrs A K Clarke, Norman and Sarah Keeping, Alain and Rose Foote, Richard Fendick*)

Hare & Hounds BA1 5TJ [Lansdown Rd, Lansdown Hill]: Elegant stone building with superb views over Charlcombe and the Swainswick Valley from big garden and terrace, attractive and comfortably furnished long well divided bar, Abbey Bellringer and Courage, enjoyable food, friendly staff, leaded lights in mullioned windows, lots of woodwork, hanging bird cages and shelves of bric-a-brac, roomy eating area and conservatory (*Dr and Mrs M E Wilson, Dr and Mrs A K Clarke*)

☆ *Hop Pole* BA1 3AR [Albion Buildings, Upper Bristol Rd]: Bustling Bath Ales pub, also farm cider, decent wines by the glass and good soft drinks, good if pricy food Tues-Sun lunchtimes from sandwiches through modern recipes using good fresh ingredients to juicy steak in bar and former skittle alley restaurant, traditional settles and other pub furniture on bare boards in four tastefully reworked linked areas, lots of black woodwork and ochre walls, no juke box or pool; children welcome while food served, attractive two-level back courtyard with boules, terrace tables, fairy-lit vine arbour and summer houses with heaters, opp Victoria Park with its great play area, open all day Fri-Sun (Colin and Peggy Wilshire, Dr and Mrs M E Wilson, BB)

Marlborough BA1 2LY [Marlborough Buildings]: Sensibly priced fresh bar food inc interesting dishes, welcoming mix of ages; courtyard garden (Mary Docherty)

Olde Farmhouse BA1 5EE [Lansdown Rd]: Nicely cleaned up under new management, with increased interest in the food side, well kept real ales inc Abbey Bellringer from neighbouring microbrewery, log fire, L-shaped parquet-floor bar with wall seats, panelling, stained-glass lamps and bar gantry, big jazz pictures; jazz some evenings, open all day (the Didler, Dr and Mrs A K Clarke)

Pig & Fiddle BA1 5BR [Saracen St]: Lively pub with several good sensibly priced ales such as Abbey, Bath and Butcombe, two big open fires, clocks set to different time zones, bare boards and cheery red and yellow walls and ceiling, good value prompt straightforward food inc takeaways lunchtime till early evening, steps up to darker bustling servery and little dining area, games area and several TVs; lots of students at night, good piped trendy pop music then; picnic-sets on big heated front terrace, open all day (Dr and Mrs A K Clarke, Derek and Sylvia Stephenson, Dr and Mrs M E Wilson, BB, Donna and Roger, the Didler)

Pulteney Arms BA2 6ND [Daniel St/Sutton St]: Refurbished under current friendly landlord to keep its cosy cheerful character, with Bath Gem, Fullers London Pride, Wadworths 6X, Wells & Youngs and a guest beer, enjoyable fresh pubby food inc good big baps, daily papers, lots of Bath RFC memorabilia, traditional furniture on wooden floors, gas lamps and two gas fires, new upstairs dining room; unobtrusive piped music, TV; pavement tables (Dr and Mrs M E Wilson, Ian Phillips, Colin and Peggy Wilshire, Pete Baker, Dr and Mrs A K Clarke)

Raven BA1 1HE [Queen St]: Small friendly pub with four changing mainly west country ales, particularly good lunchtime pies, sausages and savoury mash, cheerful helpful staff, open fire, charity bookshelves, some stripped stone, upstairs dining room (Meg and Colin Hamilton, Dr and Mrs A K Clarke, Andrew and Debbie Ettle)

Richmond Arms BA1 5PZ [Richmond Pl, off Lansdown Rd]: Small 18th-c house nicely refurbished under friendly new licensees, good imaginative food, good wine choice, Bass and Butcombe, bare boards, pine tables and chairs, attractive décor, unusual quiet setting off the tourist track; children welcome, tables in enclosed pretty front garden (Dr and Mrs A K Clarke, Trevor and Sylvia Millum)

Salamander BA1 2JL [John St]: Busy city local tied to Bath Ales, their full range and guest beers kept well, bare boards, black woodwork and dark ochre walls, popular simple bar lunches from sandwiches up (get there early for a table), two rooms downstairs, open-kitchen upstairs restaurant, decent wines, daily papers, open all day (BB, Derek and Sylvia Stephenson, Steve and Liz Tilley, Dr and Mrs M E Wilson, Dr and Mrs A K Clarke, Colin and Peggy Wilshire)

White Hart BA2 6AA [Widcombe Hill]: Pleasantly refurbished bare-boards bistro-style pub popular for its food (best to book), Butcombe from attractive panelled bar, farm cider, helpful staff, fresh flowers; pretty garden (Donna and Roger)

BECKINGTON [ST8051]

☆ *Woolpack* BA11 6SP [Warminster Rd, off A36 bypass]: Well refurbished and civilised old inn with charming helpful staff, unusual and well prepared if not cheap food from well filled ciabattas up, well kept Greene King, decent wines, big log fire and chunky candlelit tables in flagstoned bar, attractive smarter oak-panelled dining room and conservatory; children welcome, comfortable period bedrooms with own bathrooms (but avoid the attic), open all day (LYM, Dr and Mrs M E Wilson, Dr and Mrs A K Clarke)

BISHOP'S WOOD [ST2512]

Candlelight TA20 3RS [off A303/B3170 S of Taunton]: Under new management, roomy yet cosy, with real ales such as Butcombe, log fire, pleasant dining room; nice side water garden and fish ponds by back terrace (Dr and Mrs M E Wilson)

BLACKFORD [ST4147]

Sexeys Arms BS28 4NT [B3139 W of Wedmore]: The young French chef/landlord and his friendly wife who made this pretty roadside Tudor pub so popular for its food have now left (LYM)

BLAGDON [ST5058]

☆ *New Inn* BS40 7SB [off A368; Park Lane]: Good new landlord in nicely set pub with tables outside looking down to Blagdon Lake and beyond, old-fashioned beamed bar with some comfortable antique settles among more modern furnishings, two inglenook log fires, well kept real ales, good wines by the glass, decent food, quick friendly service (Bob and Angela Brooks, LYM, Angus and Rosemary Campbell, M G Hart, Hugh Roberts, Steve Pocock, Paul Booth)

BLAGDON HILL [ST2118]

Blagdon Inn TA3 7SG [4 miles S of Taunton]: Former White Lion refurbished, opened up and newly furnished in contemporary style under current owners, enjoyable reasonably priced blackboard food, well kept beers, good choice of wines, lively friendly service, log fire; terrace tables (I H G Busby, MB)

BRADFORD-ON-TONE [ST1722]

☆ *White Horse* TA4 1HF [fairly nr M5 junction 26, off A38 towards Taunton]: Neat and comfortable 17th-c stone-built local in quiet village, wide choice of good reasonably priced standard food in straightforward bar eating area and cheerfully decorated dining room, big helpings, welcoming licensees and staff, Badger Tanglefoot and Cotleigh Tawny, decent wines, malt whiskies, armchairs by ornate woodburner, hunting cartoons, bar billiards, skittle alley; piped music; pretty back garden with fairy-lit arbour and picnic-sets on lawn, skittle alley *(Christine and Neil Townend, Brian and Bett Cox, Geoff and Sylvia Donald, BB, Charles, Bob and Margaret Holder)*

Worlds End TA4 1ET [S of village, towards Silver Street; on A38 NE of Wellington]: Former Heatherton Grange Inn renamed and reopened under new owners, a welcoming stop *(Christine and Neil Townend)*

BRENDON HILLS [ST0334]

Raleghs Cross TA23 0LN [junction B3190/B3224]: Busy family-friendly upland inn, huge comfortably modernised bar with rows of plush banquettes, back restaurant, wide choice of popular generous food, good puddings, Cotleigh, Exmoor and Sharps Doom Bar, efficient service; children in restaurant and family room, no dogs; plenty of tables outside with play area, views to Wales on clear days, good walking country, 17 comfortable bedrooms, open all day summer *(Nigel Long, Bob and Angela Brooks, Stan and Hazel Allen, LYM, B M Eldridge)*

BRISTOL [ST5672]

☆ *Adam & Eve* BS8 4ND [Hope Chapel Hill, Hotwells]: Quietly tucked away pub, recently refurbished under new management, dark bare boards and clean cheerful décor, several real ales, cider and perry, belgian beers, good organic wines and juices, good inexpensive creative food changing daily, interesting recipes and organic ingredients, friendly staff, relaxed country-pub atmosphere, log fire, pleasant nooks and corners, café chairs and wall settles; not much parking nearby *(Gaynor Gregory, Mark O'Sullivan, BB, Lil Sheeley)*

Albion BS8 4AA [Boyce's Avenue, Clifton]: Recently refurbished as more of a dining pub, enjoyable food and good range of real ales; tables out in appealing flagstoned courtyard off cobbled alley; open all day, cl Mon lunchtime *(Philip and Jude Simmons, LYM)*

Bag o' Nails BS1 5UW [St Georges Rd, by B4466/A4 Hotwells roundabout]: Proudly old-fashioned real ale tavern popular for its half a dozen or so changing brews and lots of bottled beers, with a Nov beer festival; piped music; open all day Fri-Sun *(the Didler)*

Bridge Inn BS2 0JF [Passage St]: Neat little one-bar city pub nr floating harbour, good friendly service, lots of film stills and posters, Bath and guest ales, lunchtime sandwiches and limited hot food, padded wall seats; well reproduced piped music; tables outside, open all day *(the Didler, Donna and Roger)*

☆ *Commercial Rooms* BS1 1HT [Corn St]: Spacious Wetherspoons with lofty domed ceiling and snug cubicles along one side, gas lighting, comfortable quieter room with ornate balcony; wide changing choice of good real ales, their sensibly priced food all day, friendly chatty bustle, wind indicator, and surprising ladies' rest room with chesterfields and open fire; good location, very busy wknd evenings, side wheelchair access *(Gordon Tong, the Didler, Donna and Roger, Dr and Mrs A K Clarke)*

☆ *Cornubia* BS1 6EN [Temple St]: Small 18th-c backstreet real ale tavern freshened up under good new licensees, good Hidden ales and several recherché guest beers, interesting bottled beers and farm cider, small woody seating areas; can be crowded evenings; picnic-sets on cobbles outside, open all day, has been cl Sun *(the Didler, Alan Pratt-Walters)*

Greyhound BS8 4BZ [Princess Victoria St, Clifton]: Locals' front bar, corridor to back room with leather sofas and low tables as well as normal ones, good helpings of straightforward pub food, recent simple refurbishment, pool; sports TV, unobtrusive piped music; dogs welcome *(Donna and Roger)*

Hatchet BS1 5NA [Frogmore St]: Lively lunchtime atmosphere with well priced simple food from sandwiches up, well kept Butcombe *(Steve and Liz Tilley)*

Highbury Vaults BS2 8DE [St Michaels Hill, Cotham]: Small partly dark-panelled rooms with old-fashioned furniture and prints, well kept Bath, St Austell and Wells & Youngs, cheap bar food (not Sat/Sun evenings), bar billiards, dominoes, cribbage; busy with Univ students and teachers, steep steps to lavatories; children welcome, attractive and relaxed back terrace with lots of seating and heated arbour, open all day *(the Didler, Donna and Roger, LYM, LM)*

Hope & Anchor BS8 1DR [Jacobs Wells Rd, Clifton]: Pleasant atmosphere in bare-boards 18th-c pub with real ales such as Caledonian Deuchars IPA and 80/- and two from Cotleigh from central bar, large shared pine tables, good service, good value substantial food inc lots of sandwiches, interesting dishes and sumptuous ploughman's – very popular lunchtime; piped music, occasional live, can get crowded late evening; disabled access, summer evening barbecues in good-sized tiered back garden with interesting niches *(Bob and Margaret Holder, Len Clark, Jeremy King)*

Kensington Arms BS6 6NP [Stanley Rd]: New dining pub with good atmosphere in bar, short choice of good food in upstairs restaurant *(Gaynor Gregory)*

☆ *Kings Head* BS1 6DE [Victoria St]: Friendly relaxed 17th-c pub with big front window and splendid mirrored bar back, corridor to cosy panelled back snug with serving hatch, Bass and Courage Best, toby jugs on joists, old-fashioned local prints and photographs, interesting gas pressure gauge, generous reasonably priced food wkdy lunchtimes (get there early if you want a seat); no credit cards; pavement tables, cl Sat lunchtime, open all day Weds-Fri *(Pete Baker, Gordon Tong, the Didler, BB, Pete Walker, Di and Mike Gillam)*

Lamplighters BS11 9XA [Station Rd, Shirehampton]: Decent sensibly priced straightforward food, good range of beers, efficient friendly service *(John and Gloria Isaacs)*

Llandoger Trow BS1 4ER [off King St/Welsh Back]: By docks, interesting as the last timber-framed building built here, impressive flower-decked façade, reasonably priced bar food inc daytime bargains (not Sun), upstairs restaurant, Greene King IPA and Old Speckled Hen, friendly staff, some small alcoves and rooms with original fireplaces and carvings around central servery, wide mix from students to tourists; piped music; picnic-sets out by cobbled pedestrianised street, bedrooms in adjacent Premier Lodge *(Neil and Anita Christopher, Jeremy King)*

Mall BS8 4JG [The Mall, Clifton]: Basic downstairs bar with well kept Archers, Bath Gem, Timothy Taylors Landlord, interesting continental beers and lots of wines by the glass, tall windows and ornate ceiling upstairs with leather sofas; small garden behind *(Andy and Claire Barker, Donna and Roger)*

Nova Scotia BS1 6XJ [Baltic Wharf, Cumberland Basin]: Unspoilt old pub on S side of Floating Harbour, views to Clifton and Avon Gorge, Bass, Courage Best, Wickwar Tom and a guest beer, Thatcher's farm cider, good value blackboard food from filling baguettes to fresh fish and moroccan dishes, wooden seats in four linked areas, nautical charts as wallpaper; plenty of tables out by water, bedrooms *(Hywel Bevan, Dr and Mrs A K Clarke)*

Old Fish Market BS1 1QZ [Baldwin St]: Imposing red and cream brick building converted to roomy pub, good mural showing it in 1790s along one wall, green décor, lots of dark wood inc handsome counter, parquet floor, relaxed friendly atmosphere, good value mainly thai food all day, four well kept Fullers ales and a guest such as Butcombe, good coffee, daily papers; quiet piped music, unobtrusive sports TV, games machines; open all day *(Pete Walker, Dr and Mrs M E Wilson, Jeremy King)*

Penny Farthing BS8 2PB [Whiteladies Rd, Clifton]: Bright panelled ex-bank with Bath Gem and full Wadworths range racked behind bar, late Victorian bric-a-brac inc penny-farthing (and photographs of them), armchairs opp bar, lots of table seating, very reasonably priced home-made food lunchtime and evening, friendly helpful staff; big-

screen TV, can get very busy evenings, with doorman; pavement tables *(the Didler, Donna and Roger)*

Robin Hoods Retreat BS7 8BG [Gloucester Rd, Bishopston]: Smartly refurbished horseshoe bar with eight well kept ales, good wines by the glass, good food, cheerful staff, daily papers, small dining area just off bar (which can be noisy Fri night) *(Matthew Shackle, Gaynor Gregory, Dr and Mrs A K Clarke)*

Rose of Denmark BS8 4QL [Dowry Pl]: Friendly pubby atmosphere, good value home-made food, restaurant *(John and Gloria Isaacs)*

Royal Oak BS8 4JG [The Mall, Clifton]: Simple open-plan pub with well kept Butcombe, Courage Best, Fullers London Pride, Otter and Sharps Doom Bar, stripped stone, bare boards and hops on beams, Aga in front bar, open fire and settles in upper back part; open all day, cl Sun evening *(Donna and Roger)*

Wellington BS7 8UR [Gloucester Rd, Horfield (A38)]: Lively and roomy 1920s pub done up in traditional unpretentious style by Bath Ales, their beers served by friendly knowledgeable staff, enjoyable simple fresh food inc generous Sun roasts, comfortable seating, large horseshoe bar; jazz and blues nights, very busy on home match days for Bristol RFC or Bristol Rovers; small terrace, open all day Sun, and Fri/Sat in summer *(Dr and Mrs A K Clarke, Matthew Shackle, Len Clark)*

White Lion BS9 3HN [Passage Rd, Westbury-on-Trym]: Popular Ember Inn well divided into cosy and attractive carpeted areas with open fires and easy chairs as well as dining tables, Bass, Butcombe and Worthington ales, good choice of wines by the glass, pleasant staff and atmosphere, usual food; plenty of tables in nice garden *(Dr and Mrs C W Thomas)*

White Lion BS8 4LD [Princes Buildings, Clifton]: Worth knowing for its terrace bar overlooking Clifton Bridge; simple inside, with high tables and stools, leather sofas and chairs, pricy Butcombe and blackboard bar food from baguettes up *(Donna and Roger)*

Windmill BS3 4LU [Windmill Hill]: Recently well refurbished with bare boards and pleasant décor, buoyant casual relaxed atmosphere, Bristol Beer Factory ales, wholesome soups, pies and tapas; tables out on small deck *(Gaynor Gregory, Dr M E Williams)*

Yeoman BS14 9HX [Wells Rd (A37)]: Modern pub recently refurbished in minimalist style as part of Sizzling Pub chain, enjoyable restaurant food, good choice of wines by the glass, Bass and a guest beer; children welcome *(Gaynor Gregory)*

BROADWAY [ST3215]

Bell TA19 9RG [Broadway Lane]: Flagstoned village pub with enjoyable bargain food, Wells & Youngs Bombardier, big open fire, small restaurant area *(Jenny and Brian Seller)*

BROMPTON REGIS [SS9531]

☆ *George* TA22 9NL: 17th-c ex-farmhouse in quiet remote village, warmly welcoming and accommodating chef/landlord, wide choice of reasonably priced home-made food inc local trout, imaginative dishes and good Sun roast, well kept Cotleigh Tawny and/or Barn Owl and Exmoor, organic wines, woodburners, no juke box or machines, skittle alley; may be quiet piped music; children and dogs welcome, Exmoor views from pleasant garden by churchyard, good walks, cl Mon *(Jeremy Whitehorn, John and Christine Cross)*

BRUTON [ST6834]

Sun BA10 0AH [High St]: Quaint old two-bar local with warm welcome, Greene King real ales and huge english mastiff *(Robert Hilton, Meg and Colin Hamilton)*

BUCKLAND DINHAM [ST7551]

☆ *Bell* BA11 2QT [High St (A362 Frome—Radstock)]: 16th-c pub with helpful friendly landlady, great atmosphere and interesting décor in narrow beamed main bar, pine furnishings inc booth settles, woodburner in huge inglenook; generous good value food inc local speciality sausages and pies, Butcombe, Fullers London Pride and Wychwood Hobgoblin, quite a few malt whiskies, two-level dining room (children allowed), cribbage, dominoes; piped music; dogs welcome, sheltered garden with side terraces *(Dave Braisted, LYM, Andrew and Debbie Ettle, Ian Phillips)*

BURTLE [ST4042]

Burtle Inn TA7 8NG [Catcott Rd]: Friendly and obliging service in country local with good value food inc good sandwiches and special offers, real ales inc Bass and Boddingtons, log fire, two dining rooms, neat staff; children welcome *(Rod and Chris Pring, Peter Mack Wilkins, Steve Ballinger)*

BUTLEIGH [ST5133]

Rose & Portcullis BA6 8TQ: Newish licensees in unpretentious country pub, good choice of enjoyable popular food inc carvery, real ales inc Butcombe, nice dining room; terrace tables, pretty back garden with play area *(Revd John Hibberd)*

CATCOTT [ST3939]

☆ *Crown* TA7 9HQ [off A39 W of Street; Nidon Lane, via Brook Lane]: Quietly set and roomy country dining pub popular with well heeled locals, meals rather than snacks, with cheerful landlord, real ales such as Butcombe and Fullers London Pride, farm cider brought from the cellar, decent wines by the glass, cheddar bar nibbles, leather armchairs in one area, skittle alley; may be piped music; children welcome, picnic-sets and play area out behind, bedrooms *(LYM, Mr and Mrs A R Maden, Philip Lane, Dr and Mrs A K Clarke, Peter Meister, Michael and Wendy Staples, Terry Buckland)*

CHARLTON ADAM [ST5328]

Fox & Hounds TA11 7AU [Broadway Rd, just off A37 about 3 m N of Ilchester]: Big friendly and neatly kept pub with prompt pleasant service, enjoyable home-made food *(Richard Marjoram)*

CHEDDAR [ST4553]

Gardeners Arms BS27 3LE [Silver St]: Comfortably modernised pub tucked quietly away in the old part of the town, well kept Adnams, Butcombe and Courage Best, cheery log fires, food from pubby dishes to wild boar and kangaroo, attractive two-room beamed dining area, interesting old photographs; children and dogs welcome, picnic-sets with playthings and a wendy house in quiet back garden, open all day *(Dr and Mrs A K Clarke, Comus and Sarah Elliott, Rod and Chris Pring, LYM, Richard Fendick)*

White Hart BS27 3QN [The Bays]: Good choice of pub food from sandwiches up, good service, Butcombe, Greene King Old Speckled Hen and Wadworths 6X, log fire; quiet back garden with high fence and steep narrow sheep pasture above *(Mr and Mrs D Phillips)*

CHEW MAGNA [ST5861]

Pony & Trap BS40 8TQ [Knowle Hill, New Town; back rd to Bishop Sutton]: Enjoyable food, good relaxing atmosphere and pleasant service under new licensees in small gently refurbished tucked-away pub with comfortable layout, flagstones, antiques and candles, Butcombe and Courage ales, good coffee, downstairs restaurant – great views at the back; good walks, delightfully rural hillside setting near Chew Valley Lake *(Gaynor Gregory, Nigel Long)*

CHILCOMPTON [ST6451]

Somerset Wagon BA3 4JW [B3139; Broadway]: Cosy and friendly, with enjoyable food inc good range of home-made pies, reasonable prices, helpful and flexible staff, well kept Butcombe and Wadworths 6X, pleasant olde-worlde areas off central bar, lots of settles, log fire; small front garden *(Mark Flynn)*

CLEVEDON [ST4071]

☆ *Old Inn* BS21 6AE [Walton Rd (B3124 on outskirts)]: Friendly mix of regulars and visitors, young and old, in neatly extended beamed pub with good solid furniture on its carpets, good value food (all day Sat), real ales such as East Street, Otter, Theakstons and Wychwood; bedrooms, open all day *(Tom Evans, Will Stevens, Tim and Rosemary Wells)*

Salthouse BS21 7TR [Salthouse Rd, above Marine Lake]: Large nautical-theme bar in enviable position giving stunning sea and pier views, simple furnishings, good choice of beers, enjoyable reasonably priced food inc some interesting dishes, fish and seafood, proficient service, dining room; piped music may obtrude; picnic-sets on large front terrace, open all day *(Tom and Ruth Rees, Mr and Mrs G Ives)*

COLEFORD [ST6848]

Kings Head BA3 5LU [Underhill]: Popular extended village pub with local Blindmans Buff, RCH Steaming and a local farm cider in big bar with woodburner, bar food, separate pool room; large lawn, plenty of walks (Ian Phillips)

COMBE FLOREY [ST1531]

☆ *Farmers Arms* TA4 3HZ [off A358 Taunton—Williton, just N of main village turn-off]: Neatly kept thatched and beamed pub well reorganised internally for dining, enjoyable food using prime local produce, real ales such as Exmoor and Otter, local farm cider, comfortable drinking area with log fire (not always lit); may be piped music; plenty of tables in attractive garden, by summer steam line (Bob and Margaret Holder, David and Pauline Brenner, Geoff and Sylvia Donald, David Barnes, BB, E V Lee, Mr and Mrs Tucker, Dr and Mrs P Humphrey)

COMBE HAY [ST7359]

☆ *Wheatsheaf* BA2 7EG [off A367 or B3110 S of Bath]: Good interesting food from sandwiches and tasty home-baked breads through short changing choice of up-to-date starters and main dishes to tempting puddings, Butcombe beers, local farm cider, good wine choice, quick friendly service, plush fireside sofas and big fresh and airy dining area with stylish light modern furnishings (though not everyone will like the radical contemporary winebar-style makeover of a pub dating from 1576); tables in attractive terraced garden overlooking church and steep valley, dovecotes built into the walls, plenty of good nearby walks, comfortable bedrooms in outbuildings, cl Mon (J and J Palmer, Adele Barton, LYM, Dr and Mrs A K Clarke)

COMPTON DUNDON [ST4832]

Castlebrook Inn TA11 6PR [Castlebrook]: Cheerful two-bar village local, warm and friendly, with super flagstone floors, blazing log fire, Sharps Doom Bar, quick service, good value enjoyable straightforward food inc Sun carvery in big back simple family restaurant; tables on big lawn behind with play area (Edward Mirzoeff, R J Townson)

CONGRESBURY [ST4363]

Plough BS49 5JA [High St (B3133)]: Old-fashioned flagstoned local full of life, well kept changing ales inc Butcombe and RCH, quick smiling service, basic bar lunches inc sandwiches and faggots, three cosy areas off main bar, two log fires, old prints, farm tools and sporting memorabilia, darts, table skittles, shove ha'penny and cards; small garden with boules and aviary, occasional barbecues, open all day Sat (Philip and Jude Simmons, Steve and Liz Tilley)

☆ *White Hart* BS49 5AR [Wrington Rd, off A370 Bristol—Weston]: Pleasant heavy-beamed main bar with country-kitchen furniture and big stone inglenooks, two areas off and big bright conservatory, usual bar food, Badger Gold, Tanglefoot and a guest beer, board games, family room; may

be piped music; dogs welcome, picnic-sets under back terrace arbour and in big garden (Richard Fendick, Bob and Margaret Holder, Brian Root, Bob and Angela Brooks, LYM)

CORSTON [ST7065]

Globe BA2 9BB [A4/A36 roundabout]: Large rambling chain pub with enjoyable food all day in several linked dining areas, prompt friendly service; pleasant back terrace (Guy Vowles)

CROSS [ST4254]

New Inn BS26 2EE [A38 Bristol—Bridgwater, junction A371]: Friendly straightforward roadside pub with good atmosphere, interesting food in pleasant dining area, good choice of weekly-changing ales, reasonable prices, fine views, upstairs games room (Hugh Roberts, Peter Mack Wilkins)

CROWCOMBE [ST1336]

☆ *Carew Arms* TA4 4AD [Village (and pub) signposted just off A358 Taunton—Minehead]: New licensees in interesting 17th-c beamed inn with hunting trophies and inglenook woodburner in appealingly old-fashioned front public bar, well kept Exmoor ales, Lane's strong farm cider and good choice of wines by the glass, traditional games and skittle alley, smarter dining room (where children allowed); wandering jack russells, and service may be slow; picnic-sets out in informal garden with good play things, open all day summer wknds (LYM, Mike and Sue Loseby, the Didler, Bob and Margaret Holder)

DOULTING [ST6444]

Poachers Pocket BA4 4PY [Chelynch Rd, off A361]: Popular modernised local, flagstones with some carpet, plentiful good value food from sandwiches through good specials to Sun roasts, quick service, well kept ales inc Butcombe, local farm cider (a spring cider festival, as well as an autumn beer one), well spaced tables, pub games and piano, log fire in stripped-stone end wall, dining conservatory; children in eating area and large family room/skittle alley, back garden with country views (B and K Hypher, LYM, Susan and Nigel Wilson)

☆ *Waggon & Horses* BA4 4LA [Doulting Beacon, 2 miles N of Doulting]: Nicely set rambling pub with homely mix of tables inc antiques, Butcombe, Greene King IPA and Wadworths 6X, quite a few wines by the glass, reasonably priced food (more reports on this, please), beamed upper gallery; quiet children and dogs allowed, big attractive walled garden with wildlife pond and climber (LYM, Richard Fendick, Susan and Nigel Wilson)

DUNSTER [SS9943]

☆ *Luttrell Arms* TA24 6SG [High St; A396]: Small hotel in 15th-c timber-framed abbey building, unpretentious high-beamed back bar hung with bottles, clogs and horseshoes, stag's head and rifles on walls above old settles and more modern furniture, big log fires, good if not cheap bar food inc substantial sandwiches with home-baked bread, small helpings available, friendly attentive staff, Cotleigh Tawny and Exmoor Fox, good wines in three glass sizes; dogs welcome in bar, ancient glazed partition dividing off small galleried and flagstoned courtyard, upstairs access to quiet attractive garden with Civil War cannon emplacements and great views, comfortable bedrooms (have to stay two nights wknds) *(John and Gloria Isaacs, Mrs M Ainley, Peter Titcomb, BB, Tom and Ruth Rees, Peter and Margaret Glenister, D W Stokes, H O Dickinson, Sue Demont, Tim Barrow)*

Stags Head TA24 6SN [West St]: Olde-worlde 15th-c inn on flintstone pavement below castle, friendly staff, good bustling atmosphere, enjoyable food from traditional pub dishes to eastern exotics, brisk service by attentive entertaining staff, Archers, Cotleigh and Exmoor ales, beams, timbers and inglenooks; dogs welcome, bedrooms *(Peter and Jean Hoare, Andrew and Debbie Ettle, Paul and Karen Cornock)*

EAST LAMBROOK [ST4218]

☆ *Rose & Crown* TA13 5HF: Neatly kept attractive stone-built pub sympathetically extended from compact 17th-c core with inglenook log fire, friendly atmosphere and welcoming helpful staff, good inexpensive food freshly made using local supplies from baguettes and bar snacks up inc fish specialities, full Palmers real ale range, farm cider, decent wines by the glass, restaurant extension showing old well through central glass floor panel; opp East Lambrook Manor Garden *(A S and M E Marriott, Evelyn and Derek Walter, R Gutteridge, Meg and Colin Hamilton)*

EAST LYNG [ST3328]

Rose & Crown TA3 5AU [A361 about 4 miles W of Othery]: Attractive coaching inn under new tenants, decent food, real ales, log fire and some nice features inc unusual bow window seat in open-plan beamed lounge, skittle alley; lovely rural views from plenty of tables in pretty back garden *(Derek and Heather Manning, Bob and Margaret Holder, LYM)*

EAST WOODLANDS [ST7944]

☆ *Horse & Groom* BA11 5LY [off A361/B3092 junction]: Small pub tucked away down country lanes, thoughtful choice of enjoyable well priced fresh food worth waiting for (not Sun evening), friendly service, Archers Golden, Branscombe Vale Branoc and Butcombe tapped from the cask, choice of wine glass sizes, pews and settles in flagstoned bar, woodburner in comfortable lounge, big dining conservatory, traditional games; dogs welcome away from restaurant, children in eating areas, disabled access, picnic-sets in nice front garden with more seats behind, handy for Longleat *(LYM, Gaynor Gregory, N F C Phillips, Richard Fendick, the Didler)*

EASTON-IN-GORDANO [ST5175]

Rudgleigh Inn BS20 0QD [A369 a mile from M5 junction 19]: Two-bar refurbished

roadside pub popular for enjoyable promptly served food at sensible prices from baguettes up, Bath and Courage ales, extension restaurant suiting families, welcoming service; piped music; big well tended enclosed garden with willows, tamarisks, play area and cricket-field view, open all day wkdys *(Donald Godden, LYM, Tom Evans)*

EMBOROUGH [ST6251]

Old Down BA3 4SA: Ancient pub with particularly well kept local ales and farm cider, helpful landlady, enjoyable inexpensive food; bedrooms *(John Coatsworth)*

ENMORE [ST2635]

Enmore Inn TA5 2AH [Enmore Rd]: Good value Sun carvery using good local meat, real ales *(Brian and Genie Smart)*

Tynte Arms TA5 2DP: Open-plan pub with west country real ales from long bar, wide choice of good generous food cooked by landlady inc lots of fish, good puddings and good value set menus, plenty of dining tables, attractive décor and low beams; car park over road, good walking country *(Bob and Margaret Holder, Richard Wyld, B M Eldridge)*

EXFORD [SS8538]

Crown TA24 7PP [The Green (B3224)]: Attractive Exmoor inn under new management, relaxed two-room bar with hunting décor, old local photographs and big stone fireplace, Exmoor Ale and Gold and a guest beer, Thatcher's farm cider, good value bar food inc some interesting dishes, restaurant; piped music, TV; dogs and children welcome, charming waterside garden behind, smaller terraced side garden overlooking village and green, bedrooms, has been open all day wknds *(George Atkinson, LYM, John and Jackie Walsh, B M Eldridge)*

FAILAND [ST5171]

Failand Inn BS8 3TU [B3128 Bristol—Clevedon]: Simply furnished old coaching inn with tasty reasonably priced popular food, cheerful efficient service, real ales, good wines by the glass, comfortable dining extension; may be piped music *(Mr and Mrs John Taylor, John and Gloria Isaacs)*

FARMBOROUGH [ST6660]

Butchers Arms BA2 0AE [Timsbury Rd]: Comfortable two-bar village local with friendly staff and atmosphere, three real ales, varied restauranty food inc bargain Sun lunch; children and dogs welcome *(Dr and Mrs A K Clarke)*

New Inn BA2 0BY [Bath Rd (A39)]: Roomy roadside pub/restaurant with Greene King ales, friendly staff, generous traditional food *(Dr and Mrs A K Clarke)*

FAULKLAND [ST7354]

☆ *Faulkland Inn* BA3 5UH: L-shaped country pub well refurbished by friendly newish tenants, buoyant cheerful atmosphere, enjoyable food using good local meats, fish and veg, from interesting hot or cold filled sandwiches up, good staff, Butcombe Bitter and Gold, decent wines, daily papers, contemporary colours alongside beams, flagstones and some stripped stone, dining area on left, games area in public end, restored skittle alley; TV; children welcome, picnic-sets on small back lawn, four good value bedrooms, pretty village *(Dr and Mrs A K Clarke, Andrew and Debbie Ettle, BB, Ian Phillips)*

FIVEHEAD [ST3522]

Crown TA3 6PQ: Dating from 16th c, with traditional décor, enjoyable home-made food, small helpings for children and others, four real ales *(anon)*

FRESHFORD [ST7960]

☆ *Inn at Freshford* BA2 7WG [off A36 or B3108]: Roomy beamed stone-built dining pub, comfortable and traditional, very busy for Tues OAP lunch, Butcombe, Courage Best, Wadworths 6X and a guest beer, usual pub food from sandwiches, baguettes and filled baked potatoes up, friendly staff; piped music; children and dogs welcome, picnic-sets in pretty garden, attractive spot by river *(Ann and Colin Hunt, MRSM, Tony and Wendy Hobden, LYM, Jason Caulkin, Dr and Mrs A K Clarke, Dr and Mrs M E Wilson, Andrew Shore, Maria Williams)*

GLASTONBURY [ST4938]

George & Pilgrims BA6 9DP [High St]: Comfortable 15th-c inn with magnificent carved stone façade and some interesting features – handsome stone fireplace (flame-effect gas fire), oak panelling and traceried stained-glass bay window (rest of pub more ordinary); well kept Butcombe Gold, St Austell Tribute and a house beer, local country wine, decent food; children in buffet and upstairs restaurant, bedrooms *(LYM, Joan and Michel Hooper-Immins)*

King Arthur BA6 9NB [Benedict St]: Great atmosphere in friendly recently refurbished pub with fine range of real ales at good prices, farm ciders, good live music Fri – can get packed; tables in nice outside area *(D M Paterson)*

☆ *Who'd A Thought It* BA6 9JJ [Northload St]: Interesting and attractive, with high-backed curved settle, coal fire, pine panelling, stripped brick, beams and flagstones, and nicely quirky oddments, well kept Palmers ales, good choice of wines by the glass, good value usual food from toasties to good steaks, daily papers; children and dogs welcome, pleasant garden, comfortably refurbished bedrooms, open all day *(Terry Buckland, LYM, Bob and Angela Brooks, Fred and Lorraine Gill)*

HALLATROW [ST6357]

Old Station BS39 6EN [A39 S of Bristol]: Reliable bar food and well kept ales such as Bass and Butcombe in unusual bar full of zany interest with a forest of cluttered bric-a-brac, also italian dishes in railcar restaurant; piped music may be loud; children in eating areas, garden with well equipped play area, bedrooms *(LYM, John and Fiona McIlwain)*

HALSE [ST1428]

New Inn TA4 3AF [off B3227 Taunton—Bampton]: Traditional 17th-c stone-built inn with its own Taunton Vale ales and guest beers, local farm ciders, decent generous food, friendly if not always speedy service, woodburner in big inglenook, oak beams, dining room, separate games area and skittle alley; tables in garden, lovely village *(MLR, I H G Busby, Peter Mack Wilkins)*

HARDWAY [ST7234]

☆ *Bull* BA10 0LN [off B3081 Bruton—Wincanton at brown sign for Stourhead and King Alfred's Tower; Hardway]: Charming beamed country dining pub popular locally, esp with older people wkdy lunchtimes, for fine choice of reliably good and generous if not cheap food in comfortable bar and character dining rooms, pleasant long-serving licensees, quick friendly obliging service, well kept Butcombe, good wines by the glass, farm cider, log fire; unobtrusive piped music; tables and barbecues in new garden behind, more in rose garden over road, bedrooms *(Colin and Janet Roe, Sylvia and Tony Birbeck)*

HILLFARRANCE [ST1624]

Anchor TA4 1AW: Comfortable pub with dining area off attractive two-part bar extended by new owners, good choice of enjoyable food, pleasant atmosphere, Butcombe and Exmoor, family room; garden with play area, bedrooms, caravan site, holiday apartments *(Bob and Margaret Holder)*

HINTON CHARTERHOUSE [ST7758]

Rose & Crown BA2 7SN [B3110 about 4 miles S of Bath]: Proper pub freshened and smartened up by affable new licensees, good choice of good value generous home-made food inc plenty of fish and good puddings, big log fire in ornate fireplace, Bass, Butcombe and two or three other ales tapped from casks, reasonably priced wines, roomy linked areas, nice panelling and candles on tables, restaurant, skittle alley; children welcome, small terrace, bedrooms, open all day Sat *(Dr and Mrs M E Wilson, BB, Meg and Colin Hamilton, Ian Phillips)*

☆ *Stag* BA2 7SW [B3110 S of Bath; High St]: Attractively furnished ancient pub very popular for good sensibly priced straightforward food from sandwiches up in cosy bar and two pleasant stripped-stone dining areas, real ales such as Butcombe, friendly helpful service, coal-effect gas fire, no piped music; provision for children, tables outside, has been open all day *(Dr and Mrs M E Wilson, Bryan Pearson, Ann and Colin Hunt, LYM)*

HOLCOMBE [ST6649]

☆ *Ring o' Roses* BA3 5EB [Village signposted off A367 by War Memorial in Stratton-on-the-Fosse, S of Radstock]: Extensively modernised quietly placed country pub with Otter ales, local cider and several wines by the glass, pleasant layout with several linked areas inc pubby tables on flagstones, sofas, easy chairs, panelling and carpet elsewhere, woodburners, good-sized dining area – the food, not cheap, can be very good indeed (there have been one or two disappointments this last year); piped music; children and dogs welcome, picnic-sets outside, peaceful farmland views, bedrooms, open all day wkdys *(Brian England, S G N Bennett, M G Hart, Mike Dean, Lis Wingate Gray, Mrs Lorna Bloodworth, Vince Lewington, JCW, Ian Phillips, LYM)*

HOLFORD [ST1541]

Plough TA5 1RY [A39]: Welcoming newish tenants doing enterprising good value fresh filling food from doorstep sandwiches up in unassuming village pub with well kept ales such as Butcombe, Otter and South Hams Devon Pride, decent wines by the glass, good service, log fire in snug; wonderful Quantocks walks *(David Barnes, Dennis Jenkin, Claire Hayman)*

HOLYWELL LAKE [ST1020]

Holywell Inn TA21 0EJ [off A38]: Comfortable pub doing well under new licensees, good value food inc remarkable vegetarian range with their Sunday carvery, Cotleigh and Wadworths 6X, quiet relaxed atmosphere *(Peter Barnes)*

HORFIELD [ST5977]

Inn on the Green BS7 0PA [Filton Rd]: Civilised two-bar real ale pub with changing choice of up to a dozen or more and several farm ciders, tasters offered, sensibly priced fresh baguettes and a few hot dishes, friendly service, games area inc pool tables in former skittle alley, big-screen sports TVs *(M G Hart, Len Clark)*

ILCHESTER [ST5222]

Ilchester Arms BA22 8LN [Church St]: Friendly hotel with Butcombe in small peaceful pine-panelled bar on right, bistro with reasonably priced mediterranean-leaning food inc light lunches, restaurant; comfortable bedrooms *(B and F A Hannam, Michael Doswell)*

KELSTON [ST7067]

Old Crown BA1 9AQ [Bitton Rd; A431 W of Bath]: Four small convivial traditional rooms with beams and polished flagstones, carved settles and cask tables, logs burning in ancient open range, two more coal-effect fires, well kept ales such as Bath Gem, Butcombe Gold and Blonde and Wadworths 6X tapped from the cask, Thatcher's cider, well priced wines, friendly staff, cheap wholesome bar food (not Sun or Mon evenings) inc good salads, small restaurant (not Sun), no machines or music; dogs welcome, children in eating areas, picnic-sets under apple trees in sunny sheltered back garden, open all day wknds *(Andrew and Debbie Ettle, LYM)*

KENN [ST4169]

Drum & Monkey BS21 6TJ [B3133 Yatton—Clevedon]: Neatly kept village pub, good value food inc good theme nights Mon, good friendly service, well kept real ales, thriving local atmosphere, open fires, brasses and copper-topped tables *(anon)*

KEYNSHAM [ST6669]

☆ *Lock-Keeper* BS31 2DD [Keynsham Rd (A4175)]: Bustling and popular, in lovely spot on Avon island with lots of picnic-sets out under glazed canopy, big heated deck and shady garden by lock, marina and weir; well kept Wells & Youngs ales, appealing well priced food served promptly from sandwiches, paninis and baked potatoes to more upmarket dishes, friendly helpful young staff, small room by bar, arches to unpretentious main divided room with rust and dark blue décor, black beams and bare boards, barrel-vaulted lower area; boules *(M G Hart, Bob, Matthew Shackle, Andrew and Debbie Ettle, Dr and Mrs M E Wilson, Dr and Mrs A K Clarke)*

KILMERSDON [ST6952]

Jolliffe Arms BA3 5TD: Large attractive stone-built Georgian pub overlooking pretty churchyard, Butcombe and Fullers London Pride, good wines by the glass, reasonably priced home-made pub food, friendly service, linked areas reminiscent of old-fashioned farmhouse parlour, some huge black flagstones; picnic-sets out in front *(Ian Phillips)*

LANGFORD BUDVILLE [ST1122]

Martlet TA21 0QZ [off B3187 NW of Wellington]: Cosy and comfortably refurbished pub with good value food, friendly staff, well kept Cotleigh ales, open fires, inglenook, beams and flagstones, central woodburner, steps up to carpeted lounge with another woodburner; skittle alley *(Heather Coulson, Neil Cross)*

LANGLEY MARSH [ST0729]

Three Horseshoes TA4 2UL [Village signposted off B3227 from Wiveliscombe]: The long-serving licensees have now left this traditional red sandstone pub, and much has changed; back bar has low modern settles and polished wooden tables, a local stone fireplace, Otter and St Austell Tribute tapped from the cask, decent food in bar and dining area; piped music; seats on verandah and in sloping back garden; more reports on new regime *(LYM, Bob and Margaret Holder)*

LONG ASHTON [ST5570]

Dovecote BS41 9LX: Former Smyth Arms, now a large Vintage Inn with their usual food and reasonably priced drinks inc good choice of wines by the glass, attentive young staff; open all day *(MB)*

MARK [ST3747]

Pack Horse TA9 4NF [B3139 Wedmore—Highbridge; Church St]: Attractive family-run 16th-c village pub by church, very popular wknds for its wide food choice inc good Sun roast, daily brixham fish and delicious puddings, Butcombe and Fullers London Pride, good friendly service *(Terry Buckland)*

MIDFORD [ST7660]

☆ *Hope & Anchor* BA2 7DD [Bath Rd (B3110)]: Good attractively presented interesting food from light dishes to mouthwatering more elaborate things and imaginative puddings in civilised bar, heavy-beamed and flagstoned restaurant end, and new back conservatory, real ales such as Bath Gem, Butcombe Gold and Sharps Doom Bar, good house wines, proper coffee, relaxed atmosphere, log fire; tables on newly reworked sheltered back terrace with upper tier beyond, pleasant walks on disused Somerset & Dorset railway track *(Gaynor Gregory, Chris and Ann Coy, M G Hart, BB, Roger Wain-Heapy, Bryan Pearson)*

MIDSOMER NORTON [ST6654]

White Hart BA3 2HQ [The Island]: Chatty and individualistic Victorian local with several rooms, Bass and Butcombe tapped from the cask, old local coal-mining photographs and memorabilia, enjoyable bar snacks; bedrooms, open all day *(Dr and Mrs A K Clarke, the Didler)*

MILBORNE PORT [ST6718]

Queens Head DT9 5DQ [A30 E of Sherborne]: Under newish management, with enjoyable food inc plenty of sandwiches, well kept Butcombe, good wines by the glass, good coffee, quick friendly service, neat beamed lounge, restaurant and conservatory, games in public bar, skittle alley; provision for children and quiet dogs, reasonable disabled access, tables in sheltered courtyard and garden with play area, three cosy good value bedrooms *(LYM, Dennis Jenkin)*

MINEHEAD [SS9746]

Hairy Dog TA24 5AZ [The Avenue]: Huge modern family pub with wide choice of generous fresh food from baguettes to steaks and carvery, good choice of beers, friendly young staff giving prompt attentive service even when busy, conservatory, big-screen sports TVs, games machines; good disabled access and facilities, terrace, big play area *(Colin Gooch)*

MONKTON COMBE [ST7761]

Wheelwrights Arms BA2 7HB [just off A36 S of Bath; Church Cottages]: Modern dining bar décor, four ales inc Bath and Butcombe from new high modern counter, rather pricy food (plus 10% discretionary service charge); big-screen music videos; attractively expanded garden with valley view, eight well equipped bedrooms in separate block *(LYM, Dr and Mrs M E Wilson)*

MONTACUTE [ST4916]

☆ *Phelips Arms* TA15 6XB [The Borough; off A3088 W of Yeovil]: Roomy and airy open-plan bar and smart yet relaxed restaurant, friendly helpful service even when busy, simple choice of enjoyable fresh food inc several fish dishes, Palmers ales, good choice of wines by the glass, farm cider, good coffee, nice fireplace and old-fashioned décor; children and dogs welcome, skittle alley, tables in attractive walled garden behind, comfortable bedrooms, pretty square next to Montacute House *(Chris Wall, BB, David Miles-Dinham, Bob and Margaret Holder)*

NAILSEA [ST4469]

Blue Flame BS48 4DE [West End]: Small, decidedly unsmart and very well worn 19th-c farmers' local, two rooms with mixed furnishings, Butcombe, RCH East St Cream, Thatcher's farm cider, filled rolls (may be pie deliveries Thurs), coal fire, pub games; plain-speaking landlord, outside lavatories inc roofless gents', and what little parking there is may be filled with Land Rovers and tractors; children's room, sizeable informal garden with barbecue, open all day summer wknds *(the Didler, Philip and Jude Simmons, Catherine Pitt)*

Moorend Spout BS48 4BB [Union St]: Low-priced straightforward food (not Sun evening) and real ales such as Butcombe and Ushers in neatly kept early 18th-c beamed local with friendly helpful family service; may be piped music; picnic-sets on terrace and sheltered lawn *(Richard Fendick)*

Sawyers Arms BS48 1BT [High St]: Friendly town local with Courage Best and a guest beer, lunchtime food, darts; unobtrusive sports TV *(Steve and Liz Tilley)*

NETHER STOWEY [ST1939]

Rose & Crown TA5 1LJ [St Mary St]: Buoyant local atmosphere in former 16th-c posting inn, three real ales inc Cotleigh and local Stowey, Thatcher's farm cider, good value fresh filling food (not Sun evening), friendly landlord, separate public bar off narrow courtyard, restaurant (not Mon/Tues); dogs and children welcome, garden tables, bedrooms, open all day *(Gavin Robinson, R M Corlett)*

NEWTON ST LOE [ST7065]

☆ *Globe* BA2 9BB: Roomy and popular, nicely refurbished with pleasant décor and dark wood partitions, pillars and timbers giving secluded feel, accent on enjoyable food all day, well kept beer, friendly helpful service from well trained young staff, good atmosphere *(Dr and Mrs A K Clarke, J and F Gowers, Dr and Mrs M E Wilson)*

NORTH PETHERTON [ST2933]

Walnut Tree TA6 6QA [Fore St; A38; handy for M5 junction 24]: Best Western hotel's plush bar used by locals and popular for moderately priced wkdy bar lunches, helpful well trained staff, well kept Exmoor ale, decent wines by the glass, also cheerfully decorated bistro and more formal restaurant; bedrooms spacious and well equipped *(Paul and Ursula Randall)*

NORTON FITZWARREN [ST2026]

Cross Keys TA2 6NR [A358 roundabout NW of Taunton]: Good Chef & Brewer in extended 19th-c stone building, friendly cheerful staff, their usual sensibly priced menu, real ales such as Fullers London Pride, Gales HSB, Holts Touch Wood and a Youngs seasonal beer, good wine choice, generous coffee, log fire in big hearth; open all day *(Ian Phillips)*

NORTON ST PHILIP [ST7755]

☆ *Fleur de Lys* BA2 7LG [High St]: Chatty local in 13th-c stone cottages stitched together centuries ago, friendly landlord, Wadworths

beers, good value home-made food from
baguettes through sausages and mash etc to
steak, good log fire in huge fireplace, steps
and pillars giving cosy feel of separate
rooms in beamed and flagstoned areas
around central servery; children very
welcome, skittle alley (the Didler, Dr and Mrs
A K Clarke, Dr and Mrs M E Wilson, Donna and
Roger, BB, R K Phillips, Ann and Colin Hunt)

ODCOMBE [ST5015]
Masons Arms BA22 8TX [41 Lower
Odcombe]: Enjoyable food, good range of
reasonably priced beers, helpful management
and staff, efficient service even on busy Sat
night (Dr D Parsons, Dr H Stephenson)

PENSFORD [ST6263]
George & Dragon BS39 4BH [High St]:
Friendly local with enjoyable pubby food inc
OAP bargains, Butcombe Bitter; nice
courtyard for smokers and dogs (Geoff and
Brigid Smithers)

PITMINSTER [ST2219]
Queens Arms TA3 7AZ [off B3170 S of
Taunton (or reached direct); nr church]:
Village pub with good chef using local
produce for his enjoyable food from homely
staples to good fish choice and upmarket
bistro dishes (can take a while at busy
times), real ales inc Cotleigh and Otter,
interesting reasonably priced wines by the
glass, log fires, simple wooden bar furniture,
pleasant dining room; bedrooms with own
bathrooms (Bob and Margaret Holder,
Alyson Hartley, Sarah Abbot)

PORLOCK [SS8846]
☆ *Ship* TA24 8QD [High St]: Enthusiastic new
landlord working hard in picturesque family
pub, thatch, beams, flagstones and big
inglenook log fires, quick friendly staff,
enjoyable food from sandwiches up inc local
lamb, venison and fish, Cotleigh and guest
beers, back dining room, small locals' front
bar with games; children welcome, attractive
split-level sunny garden with decking,
nearby nature trail to Dunkery Beacon,
bedrooms (LYM, John Urquhart,
Edward Leetham)

PORLOCK WEIR [SS8846]
☆ *Ship* TA24 8QD [separate from but run in
tandem with neighbouring Anchor Hotel]:
Unpretentious old-world thatched bar in
wonderful spot by peaceful harbour (so can
get packed), dark low beams, flagstones and
stripped stone, big log fire, simple pub
furniture, four ales inc Cotleigh Barn Owl
and Exmoor, Inch's cider, good whisky and
soft drinks choice, friendly young staff, usual
generous food from thick sandwiches up,
plainer overflow rooms across small back
yard; piped music, big-screen TV, little free
parking but pay & display opposite; children
and dogs welcome, sturdy picnic-sets on side
terraces, good coast walks, decent bedrooms
(David Crook, D W Stokes, Cathy Robinson,
Ed Coombe, Dr Peter Crawshaw,
George Atkinson, Tracey and Stephen Groves,
Edward Leetham, Ian and Joan Blackwell,
Stan and Hazel Allen, BB)

PORTBURY [ST4975]
☆ *Priory* BS20 7TN [Station Rd, ½ mile from
A369 (just S of M5 junction 19)]: Reliable
and very popular well extended Vintage Inn
dining pub/hotel, several beamed rooms
with nice mix of solid furnishings in alcoves,
log fire, plenty of friendly attentive staff,
well kept Bass, good range of house wines,
wide choice of promptly served and
reasonably priced usual food all day till 10;
piped music; picnic-sets out on back lawn,
bedrooms, open all day (Dr A J and Mrs
Tompsett, JCW, Richard Fendick, Dr and Mrs
C W Thomas, MB, Bob and Margaret Holder)

PORTISHEAD [ST4676]
Poacher BS20 6AJ [High St]: Large pub
popular with older lunchers for wide range of
freshly cooked low-priced food with real veg,
changing well kept ales such as Butcombe
Blond (a proper part for village beer-
drinkers, with a big fireplace), friendly staff;
quiz nights, cl Sun pm (Tom Evans)

PRIDDY [ST5450]
Hunters Lodge BA5 3AR [from Wells on A39
pass hill with TV mast on left, then next
left]: Welcoming and unchanging walkers'
and potholers' pub above ice-age cavern',
in
same family for generations, Butcombe and
Exmoor tapped from casks behind the bar,
Weston's farm cider, wholesome cheap snacks
such as fresh rolls and local cheeses, log
fire, flagstones; garden picnic-sets,
bedrooms (Jon Barnfield, Gaynor Gregory,
LYM)
☆ *Queen Victoria* BA5 3BA [village signed off
B3135; Pelting Drove]: Relaxed character
country local with friendly service, Butcombe
Bitter and Gold and Wadworths 6X tapped
from the cask, three good log fires (one
open on two sides), organic beers, farm
ciders and perries, good coffee, good value
basic wholesome food, stripped stone and
flagstones, interesting bric-a-brac, collected
furnishings inc miscellaneous tables and old
pews; good garden for children over road,
great walks, cl lunchtime Oct-Apr exc hols,
open all day wknds and high season
(John Hillman, J and F Gowers)

RODE [ST8053]
☆ *Bell* BA11 6PW [Frome Rd (A361)]:
Comfortably well worn and spotless, with
friendly licensees and quick obliging service,
good atmosphere, nice choice of enjoyable
generous food from good hot-filled
sandwiches up, Courage Best and three
Butcombe beers, roomy sparely decorated
bar on left with a couple of armchairs as
well as pleasantly practical furnishings, step
up to good-sized pool room, smaller lounge
bar on right leading to busy attractively set
restaurant; dogs welcome, plenty of tables
on spreading lawn (John and Joan Nash, Ted
George, Dr and Mrs A K Clarke)
Mill BA11 6AG: Popular family pub in
beautifully set former watermill, smart
restauranty layout and up-to-date décor and
artwork, children's room with impressive
games; live music Fri may be loud; garden

and decks overlooking river, big play area
(Dr and Mrs M E Wilson, Marjorie Hayter,
Andrew and Debbie Ettle, Angus and
Rosemary Campbell)

ROWBERROW [ST4458]

Swan BS25 1QL [off A38 S of A368
junction]: New management in spacious and
neatly laid out dining pub opp pond, olde-
worlde beamery and so forth (most
atmosphere in nicely unsophisticated old bar
part), popular food from substantial
lunchtime sandwiches, baguettes and baked
potatoes up, Bass and Butcombe Bitter,
Blond and Gold, good choice of wines by the
glass, Thatcher's cider, good log fires (LYM,
Tom Evans, Bob and Angela Brooks,
Ian Legge, Philip Kingsbury)

RUMWELL [ST1923]

Rumwell Inn TA4 1EL [A38 Taunton—
Wellington, just past Stonegallows]: Good
comfortable atmosphere, old beams and cosy
corners, lots of tables in several areas,
enjoyable well served restaurantry food inc
good Sun roasts, changing real ales, good
coffee, roaring log fire, family room; tables
in nice garden, handy for Sheppy's Cider
(R G Humphreys, Heather Coulson, Neil Cross)

SALTFORD [ST6867]

Bird in Hand BS31 3EJ [High St]:
Comfortable and friendly, with lively front
bar, good range of beers such as Abbey
Bellringer, Butcombe and Courage, farm
cider, attractive back conservatory dining
area popular locally for good value fresh
food from mini-ploughman's to daily roast,
huge omelettes and whitby fish, quick
service even when quite a queue for food,
lots of bird pictures, small family area; live
entertainment; picnic-sets down towards
river, handy for Bristol—Bath railway path
(Andrew and Debbie Ettle, Dr and Mrs
A K Clarke)

Jolly Sailor BS31 3ER [Mead Lane]: Great
spot by lock and weir on River Avon, with
dozens of picnic-sets and own island
between lock and pub; enjoyable standard
food from baked potatoes and lunchtime
baguettes to several fish dishes, friendly
service, well kept Butcombe, Courage Best
and guest beers, log fires, conservatory
restaurant; children welcome (W J Simpson,
Roger Edward-Jones)

SIDCOT [ST4256]

Sidcot Hotel BS25 1NN [Bridgwater Rd (A38)]:
Clean, bright and friendly chain pub, lovely
views, Wadworths 6X, decent choice of wines,
good staff, promptly served food all day;
disabled access (Comus and Sarah Elliott)

SOMERTON [ST4928]

Globe TA11 7LX [Market Pl]: Chatty old
stone-built local with good interesting
reasonably priced home-made bar food,
attentive friendly staff, well kept Butcombe
and Dartmoor, good choice of wine, two
spacious bars, log fire, flagstone or board
floors, dining conservatory, back games
room, no music; skittle alley, garden tables
(Dave Braisted)

SOUTH CHERITON [ST6924]

White Horse BA8 0BL [A357 Wincanton—
Blandford]: Doing well under friendly and
enthusiastic new young owners, well kept
real ale, small choice of well cooked nicely
served food at reasonable prices, small
individual dining areas, family room with
games; garden tables (Mark Flynn,
Elaine Pert)

SOUTH STOKE [ST7461]

☆ *Pack Horse* BA2 7DU [off B3110, S edge of
Bath]: Intriguing and unspoilt medieval pub,
a former priory (central passageway still a
public right of way to the church), with
heavy beams, handsome inglenook log fire,
antique settles and scrubbed tables on
flagstones, good choice of real ales such as
Butcombe and Wadworths 6X, plenty of farm
cider, willing staff, good choice of robust
good value food, shove-ha'penny tables;
children welcome, lots of tables in spacious
back garden, open all day wknds (Jane and
Graham Rooth, E McCall, T McLean, D Irving,
R Huggins, Dr and Mrs A K Clarke, LYM,
Guy Vowles, David Hoult)

SPARKFORD [ST6026]

Sparkford Inn BA22 7JH [just W of
Wincanton; High St]: Big softly lit low-
beamed rambling pub, a popular stop-off for
its variety of pubby food and lunchtime
carvery, pleasant mix of furnishings, real ale
and decent wines by the glass; children and
dogs welcome, outside tables and play area,
well equipped bedrooms, open all day (LYM,
J Stickland, Brian P White, Steve Jones)

STANTON DREW [ST5963]

Druids Arms BS39 4EJ [off B3130]: Pleasant
proper pub, cheap snacks; good garden with
ancient stones (Gaynor Gregory)

STAPLE FITZPAINE [ST2618]

☆ *Greyhound* TA3 5SP [off A358 or B3170 S of
Taunton]: Rambling country pub increasingly
popular for good choice of enjoyable food
and of changing real ales, good wines by the
glass, welcoming atmosphere and friendly
service, flagstones, inglenooks, pleasant mix
of settles and chairs, log fires throughout,
olde-worlde pictures, farm tools and so
forth; children welcome, good bedrooms in
modern extension (Bob and Margaret Holder,
Brian and Bett Cox, LYM)

STOKE GIFFORD [ST6178]

Fox Den BS34 8TJ [New Rd]: Old-look pub,
inside and out, recently built as part of
Holiday Inn Express, useful for reasonably
priced standard food, with friendly efficient
service and well kept real ale (Mike and
Mary Carter)

STOKE ST MARY [ST2622]

Half Moon TA3 5BY [from M5 junction 25
take A358 towards Ilminster, 1st right, right
in Henlade]: Much-modernised village pub
very popular lunchtime for wide choice of
hearty good value food from sandwiches to
steaks, pleasant staff, Butcombe,
Boddingtons, Fullers London Pride and
Greene King Abbot, nice coffee, quite a few
malt whiskies, thriving local atmosphere in

several comfortable open-plan areas inc restaurant; children welcome, picnic-sets in well tended garden *(LYM, Bob and Margaret Holder, Brian and Genie Smart)*

TAUNTON [ST2525]

☆ *Hankridge Arms* TA1 2LR [Hankridge Way, Deane Gate (nr Sainsbury); just off M5 junction 25 – A358 towards city, then right at roundabout, right at next roundabout]: 16th-c former farm reworked as well appointed old-style Badger dining pub, splendid contrast to the modern shopping complex around it, buoyant atmosphere and quick friendly service, generous enjoyable food from interesting soups, sandwiches and baguettes through sensibly priced pubby things to restaurant dishes, Badger ales, decent wines, big log fire; piped music; dogs welcome, plenty of tables in pleasant outside area *(Chris Glasson, Dr and Mrs A K Clarke)*

Malt & Hops TA1 1SP [Tancred St]: Roomy bars with pleasant mildly continental atmosphere, good local beer and wines by the glass, imaginative food (cooked to order so can take a while), tapas at the bar, attentive staff; piped music may be loud; courtyard garden *(JT, C J Baker)*

Vivary Arms TA1 3JR [Wilton St; across Vivary Park from centre]: Quiet and pretty local dating from 18th c, good value distinctive fresh food from good soup and baked potatoes to plenty of fish, in snug plush lounge and small dining room, prompt helpful young staff, relaxed atmosphere, well kept ales inc Wells & Youngs, decent wines, interesting collection of drinking-related items; bedrooms in Georgian house next door *(Bob and Margaret Holder)*

TIMBERSCOMBE [SS9542]

Lion TA24 7TP [Church St]: Thoroughly refurbished Exmoor-edge former coaching inn dating from 15th c, thriving village-pub atmosphere in comfortable flagstoned main bar and three rooms off, wide choice of enjoyable honest pub food from good fresh baguettes up, friendly service, Exmoor Gold and St Austell Tribute tapped from the cask, reasonable prices, good log fire; dogs welcome, bedrooms *(Brian and Anita Randall, Sue Demont, Tim Barrow)*

TINTINHULL [ST5019]

Crown & Victoria BA22 8PZ [Farm St, village signed off A303]: Roomy, light and airy main bar, pleasant conservatory, attractive choice of generous fairly priced food cooked to order, Butcombe and Wadworths, wine in big glasses; disabled facilities, well kept big garden with play area, bedrooms, handy for Tintinhull House (NT) *(LYM, Dave Braisted, Neil and Anita Christopher)*

TRULL [ST2122]

Winchester Arms TA3 7LG [Church Rd]: Cosy streamside village pub with good choice of fresh food inc good value set menu and lots of puddings, Exmoor ales, friendly attentive staff, small dining room, skittle alley; garden tables, bedrooms *(Bob and Margaret Holder, David and Teresa Frost)*

TYTHERINGTON [ST7645]

Fox & Hounds BA11 5BN: 17th-c, with roomy and tidy L-shaped stripped-stone bar, generous interesting food (not Mon) inc unusual curries and Sun roasts, Bass, Butcombe and a guest beer tapped from the cask, farm ciders, welcoming landlord and atmosphere, small dining area; tables outside, comfortable bedrooms, good breakfast *(MRSM)*

UPTON [ST0129]

☆ *Lowtrow Cross Inn* TA4 2DB: Good fresh home-made food in character low-beamed bar and more straightforward back restaurant, plenty of atmosphere, relaxed and pubby, Badger, Bass and Cotleigh, friendly landlord and staff, efficient service, nice rugs on bare boards or flagstones, enormous inglenook; no dogs; children welcome, attractive surroundings, bedrooms *(Jeremy Whitehorn, Richard and Anne Ansell, LYM, John Hopkins)*

VOBSTER [ST7049]

☆ *Vobster Inn* BA3 5RJ [Lower Vobster]: New Spanish chef/landlord in relaxed and roomy old stone-built dining pub, enjoyable reasonably priced food inc good local cheese plate, some spanish dishes and fish fresh daily from Cornwall, friendly helpful staff, Butcombe, good wines by the glass, three comfortable open-plan areas with antique furniture inc plenty of room for just a drink; tables on side lawn with colourful bantams, peaceful views, boules, adventure playground behind *(Gaynor Gregory, Liz and Tony Colman, Sylvia and Tony Birbeck, Ian Phillips, BB)*

WAMBROOK [ST2907]

☆ *Cotley Inn* TA20 3EN [off A30 W of Chard; don't follow the small signs to Cotley itself]: Well run stone-built pub, smartly unpretentious, with good one-price blackboard food cooked to order, may be lunchtime sandwiches and light dishes too, welcoming efficient staff, two well kept Otter ales, good choice of wines, nice ambiance, simple flagstoned entrance bar opening on one side into small plush bar, several open fires, popular two-room dining area (best to book, children allowed here); piped music, skittle alley; lovely view from terrace tables, play area in nice garden below, good bedrooms, quiet spot with plenty of surrounding walks *(Mike Gorton, Phil and Sally Gorton, LYM, Bob and Margaret Holder, Mr and Mrs W Mills, Stephen and Jean Curtis)*

WANSTROW [ST7141]

☆ *Pub* BA4 4SZ [Station Rd (A359 Nunney— Bruton)]: Attractive, individual and civilised, with friendly owners, good fresh food cooked by landlady, five or six well kept changing ales inc local Blindmans, interesting wines by the glass, comfortable traditional furniture on flagstone floor, log fire, case of interesting books, separate dining room, darts, bar billiards, skittle alley; tables in charming little floral courtyard, cl Mon lunchtime *(Mark O'Sullivan, Philip and Jude Simmons, Susan and Nigel Wilson)*

WATERROW [ST0525]

☆ *Rock* TA4 2AX [A361 Wiveliscombe—Bampton]: Good food inc some elaborate dishes and fresh brixham fish, well kept ales such as Cotleigh Tawny and Exmoor Gold, friendly family service, log fire (not always lit) in neat bar exposing the rock it's built on, couple of steps up to dining room; good well equipped bedrooms, charming setting in small valley village *(Bob and Margaret Holder, John and Fiona McIlwain)*

WEDMORE [ST4347]

New Inn BS28 4DU [Combe Batch]: Traditional pub with friendly staff, good range of local beers, local farm cider, good wines by the glass, sensibly priced usual food (not Sun) *(Rod and Chris Pring)*

WELLS [ST5546]

☆ *Fountain* BA5 2UU [St Thomas St]: Comfortable and very friendly big-windowed dining pub, largely laid for eating in the downstairs bar (which has a good log fire), and steep stairs up to the original dining room; enthusiastic staff, popular sensibly priced food from filled baguettes to good value meals inc fresh fish, interesting dishes and a good Sun lunch, well kept Butcombe and Courage Best, good choice of wines, good coffee, daily papers; can be fully booked even wkdys, may be piped music; children welcome, right by cathedral and moated Bishop's Palace *(Peter Mack Wilkins, Gaynor Gregory, John Coatsworth, Terry Buckland, BB)*

Globe BA5 2PY [Priest Row]: Rooms either side of ancient flagstoned corridor, lively mix of young and old, real ales such as Butcombe and Shepherd Neame Spitfire, good value food, friendly service; big-screen TV, games area *(Stuart Graham, BB)*

Kings Head BA5 2SG [High St]: Interesting ancient building, beams and galleries at various levels in high-ceilinged back hall house, deal tables in flagstoned front bar, enjoyable lunchtime food from sandwiches up, East Street and Otter ales; attracts young people in evening, with loud live music then; dogs welcome *(Ian Phillips)*

WEST CAMEL [ST5724]

Walnut Tree BA22 7QW [off A303 W of Wincanton; Fore St]: Extended upmarket dining pub/hotel, comfortable grey plush banquettes and red plush cushioned wicker chairs, good choice of enjoyable home-made brasserie and restaurant food (not Sun evening or Mon lunchtime), friendly efficient uniformed staff, well kept Bass and Butcombe; neatly kept garden, pretty village, good bedrooms *(anon)*

WEST HATCH [ST2719]

Farmers TA3 5RS [W of village, at Slough Green; from A358 head for RSPCA centre and keep past]: Spacious and friendly 16th-c beamed dining pub with French chefs doing good food, Otter ales tapped from the cask, good service, open fires, bleached wood

furniture, stylishly simple modern décor, quiet cosy bar off restaurant; children and dogs welcome, garden with nice herb garden, small terrace and play area, comfortable bedrooms *(Bob and Margaret Holder, Simon and Amanda Holder)*

WEST HORRINGTON [ST5948]

☆ *Slab House* BA5 3EQ [B3139 Wells—Emborough, NE of village]: Pretty open-plan country dining pub, smallish partly flagstoned bar area with cosy corners, old engravings, lots of cottagey bric-a-brac and quite a clock collection, roaring log fires, wide choice of good generous food from sandwiches to imaginative dishes, quick friendly service, nice relaxed atmosphere, well kept ales such as Bass, Boddingtons and Greene King IPA, good-sized comfortable restaurant; discreet piped music; spotless lavatories, tables out on floodlit nicely planted sunken terrace and on big neat lawns, play area *(BB, Dr and Mrs C W Thomas)*

WEST HUNTSPILL [ST3145]

Crossways TA9 3RA [A38 (between M5 exits 22 and 23)]: Friendly proper pub with several seating areas inc a family room, interesting decorations, beams and log fires, good value food, well kept ales such as Exmoor Gold, local farm cider, decent wines, quick attentive service, no piped music; skittle alley and pub games, picnic-sets among fruit trees in sizeable informal garden *(LYM, Tom Evans)*

WEST MONKTON [ST2628]

Monkton TA2 8NP: Comfortable and roomy country bar/restaurant doing well under hard-working landlord, several linked areas; lots of tables in streamside meadow, peaceful spot *(Bob and Margaret Holder)*

WESTON-SUPER-MARE [ST3161]

Regency BS23 2AG [Lower Church Rd]: Comfortable and civilised, with bargain home-made lunchtime pubby food from sandwiches and baguettes up, good real ales, particularly local ones; no close parking; seats out in front *(Peter Mack Wilkins, Frank Willy)*

Woolpack BS22 7XE [St Georges, just off M5, junction 21]: Olde-worlde 17th-c coaching inn under new management, friendly atmosphere, bargain bar lunches, Bath Gem and several Butcombe ales, pleasant window seats and library-theme area, small but attractive restaurant, conservatory, skittle alley; they may try to keep your credit card while you eat *(Comus and Sarah Elliott)*

WHATLEY [ST7347]

Sun BA11 3LA: Well run, with enjoyable generous food inc proper pies, changing daily and using only fresh local produce, local real ales, good choice of wines by the glass, pleasant décor; spectacular views from hilltop terrace *(D P and M A Miles)*

WHEDDON CROSS [SS9238]

Rest & Be Thankful TA24 7DR [A396/B3224, S of Minehead]: Friendly new owners doing good choice of food inc Sun carvery lunch, Exmoor and guest ales, comfortably modern two-room bar with two log fires, huge jug collection, games area with darts and pool, restaurant, skittle alley; juke box or piped music; tables out in back courtyard adjoining Exmoor public car park (with lavatory for the disabled), four good bedrooms and breakfast, good walking country (LYM, Tim and Rosemary Wells, B M Eldridge)

WIDCOMBE [ST2216]

☆ *Holman Clavel* TA3 7EA [Culmhead, by ridge rd W of B3170 2 miles S of Corfe]: Charmingly unspoilt deep-country local dating from 14th c and named after the massive holly chimney-beam over its huge log fire, comfortable dining area, good sensibly priced home cooking strong on fish and seafood, friendly informal staff, Butcombe Bitter and Gold and Fullers London Pride, colourful wine list, nice atmosphere with fresh local produce for sale, original skittle alley; dogs welcome, small garden, handy for Blackdown Hills, open all day (I H G Busby, BB, David and Helen Sawyer, Anthony Double)

WINCANTON [ST7128]

Red Lion BA9 9LD [Market Pl]: Unpretentious, comfortable and relaxed open-plan pub with helpful licensees, enjoyable food inc pizzas and fish fresh, well kept Wadworths real ales, good wines by the glass, woodburner in big inglenook (Natalie)

WINSCOMBE [ST4257]

Woodborough BS25 1HD [Sandford Rd]: Big beamed dining pub, smart, comfortable and busy, with good range of above-average food inc local produce and good veg, helpful friendly staff, good wine choice, separate drinking areas (Ken Flawn, Hugh Roberts)

WINSFORD [SS9034]

☆ *Royal Oak* TA24 7JE [off A396 about 10 miles S of Dunster]: Prettily placed thatched and beamed Exmoor inn, Brakspears and Butcombe tapped from the cask, good wines by the glass, thriving chatty atmosphere in attractively furnished lounge bar with big stone fireplace and big bay-window seat looking across towards village green and foot and packhorse bridges over River Winn, more eating space in second bar, several pretty and comfortable lounges, nice pub labrador; children and dogs welcome, good bedrooms (Mr and Mrs W Mills, George Atkinson, Dr Peter Crawshaw, LYM, GSB, Philip and Jude Simmons, Gordon and Jay Smith, A S and M E Marriott, B M Eldridge)

WITHAM FRIARY [ST7440]

☆ *Seymour Arms* BA11 5HF [signed from B3092 S of Frome]: Well worn-in rustic flagstoned local, two simple rooms off hatch-service corridor, one with darts, the other with central table skittles; Bass and Cottage, Rich's local farm cider, open fire, cards and dominoes – no juke box or machines; good-sized attractive garden by main rail line (Pete Baker, MLR, the Didler)

WITHYPOOL [SS8435]

☆ *Royal Oak* TA24 7QP [off B3233]: Character inn now taken in hand (after some ups and downs) by promising new manageress, steps between two beamed bars with lovely log fire and some nice old oak tables, Exmoor Ale and a guest beer, several wines by the glass, friendly helpful service, food from familiar bar food to more expensive restaurant dishes; children and dogs welcome, terrace seating, pretty riverside village tucked below some of Exmoor's finest parts, nicely redecorated bedrooms, good breakfast, open all day (LYM, John and Jackie Walsh, Mike and Nicky Pleass)

WIVELISCOMBE [ST0827]

Bear TA4 2JY [North St]: Good range of well priced home-cooked food from burgers and good sandwiches up, well kept local Cotleigh and other west country ales, farm ciders, attentive friendly landlord, games area; garden with play area, good value bedrooms, open all day (Dr A J and Mrs Tompsett)

WRAXALL [ST4971]

New Battleaxes BS48 1LQ [Bristol Rd]: Large neatly kept rambling pub with daily bargain carvery, real ale; handy for Tyntesfield (NT) (Mr and Mrs A J Hudson)

Old Barn BS48 1LQ [just off Bristol Rd (B3130)]: Rustic gabled barn conversion with scrubbed tables, school benches and soft sofas under oak rafters, stripped boards, flagstones and festoons of dried flowers; welcoming atmosphere and friendly service, several real ales inc Butcombe, St Austell and Timothy Taylors tapped from the cask, good wines by the glass; two TV screens, Sun quiz night; garden with good play area and barbecues (can bring your own meat) on cobbled terrace (Steve and Liz Tilley, Philip Lane, the Didler)

YEOVIL [ST5416]

Plucknett BA20 2EE [Preston Rd]: Enjoyable food with some emphasis on so-called healthy eating, friendly helpful service, good beer (anon)

Though we don't usually mention it in the text, most pubs will now make coffee or tea – always worth asking.

Staffordshire

Staffordshire has some splendidly timeless pubs, solidly old-fashioned with a cheery welcome and lots of genuine character. The epitome is the Yew Tree at Cauldon, one of our all-time favourites. Like many of the best pubs it's far from smart, but packed with interest, utterly genuine, run by a devoted and friendly landlord, and with prices that – like the place itself – are decidedly behind the times. One of our two new entries here this year shows off the other end of the pub scale: the Hand & Trumpet at Wrinehill has been handsomely reworked as a civilised new dining pub, with a fine range of drinks alongside its up-to-date all-day food. Our other new entry, the Queens Head in Lichfield, has a great choice of real ales and great value simple food. Other pubs on fine form here are the unaffected Burton Bridge Inn in Burton upon Trent (with its own good Burton Bridge ales), the ancient Cat at Enville (the distinctively flavoured beers brewed in the village go down well with their hearty sausage and mash menu), the pubby old Goats Head in Abbots Bromley (good hearty food here), and the nicely located George at Alstonefield (its new menu hits the mark). Pub food in the county generally scores on value rather than finesse; prices for typical pub meals are well down on the national average. For more of a special meal in attractive surroundings, our choice as Staffordshire Dining Pub of the Year is the newcomer, the Hand & Trumpet at Wrinehill. Drinks prices too are well below the national norm (the area's main brewer is Marstons, based in Burton). In the Lucky Dip section at the end of the chapter, pubs to watch include the Burnt Gate at Anslow, Boat near Lichfield (good dining pub) and Olde Dog & Partridge in Tutbury. It's worth mentioning that this year the section includes a higher proportion than usual of pubs which have never before crossed our radar – a sign, we think, of rapidly rising standards in the area's pubs.

ABBOTS BROMLEY
SK0824 MAP 7

Goats Head
Market Place; WS15 3BP

Well run old-world pub with tasty food, attractive location

This charming old black and white timbered pub overlooks the centre of an unspoilt village, which is famous for its annual traditional horn dance. The opened-up cream painted interior has attractive oak floors, with furniture running from the odd traditional oak settle to comfy leather sofas, and a big inglenook has a warm fire. Served by attentive staff, the Black Sheep, Marstons Pedigree and two guests such as Brimstage Scarecrow and Greene King Abbot are well kept on handpump, and you can have any of the wines on their good wine list by the glass; piped music, TV. Picnic-sets and teak tables out on a neat sheltered lawn look up to the church tower behind.

🍴 Generously served enjoyable and reasonably priced bar food (with good chips, salad or vegetables) includes sandwiches, soup, thai fishcakes, cottage pie, pizzas, salmon fillet with hollandaise, 16oz rump steak, daily specials such as bacon-wrapped chicken breast with pesto, grilled sardines and halibut steak with prawns, and puddings such as lemon pie or plum crumble. Steaks are discounted on Monday evening. *Starters/Snacks: £4.50 to £5.25. Main Courses: £6.95 to £15.95. Puddings: £3.95*

Punch ~ Lease Dawn Skelton ~ Real ale ~ Bar food (12-2.30, 6-9; 12-9(8 Sun) Sat) ~ Restaurant ~ (01283) 840254 ~ Children welcome in restaurant ~ Dogs allowed in bar ~ Open 12-11 ~ Bedrooms: /£40

Recommended by R T and J C Moggridge, Matthew Hegarty, Derek and Sylvia Stephenson, J A Hooker, Tony and Wendy Hobden, Neil and Brenda Skidmore, Bob, Roger and Anne Newbury, C J Fletcher, Richard and Jean Green, David J Austin

ALSTONEFIELD   SK1355 MAP 7

George
Village signposted from A515 Ashbourne—Buxton; DE6 2FX

Nice old pub with good range of fairly priced food, a Peak District classic

A good variety of customers, including cyclists and walkers (though no muddy boots) enjoys the charming local atmosphere at this stone-built Peak District pub. It's by the green in a peaceful farming hamlet – it's a real pleasure to sit out beneath the inn-sign and watch the world go by, or in the big sheltered stableyard behind the pub. The unchanging straightforward low-beamed bar has a copper-topped counter with well kept Marstons Pedigree, Burtonwood and a guest such as Highwood Bomber County on handpump, a collection of old Peak District photographs and pictures, and a roaring coal fire on chilly days; dominoes.

🍴 New licensees have upgraded the menu since the last edition of the *Guide*. As well as sandwiches, the lunchtime menu might include parsnip soup, chicken and apricot terrine wrapped in bacon, caramelised onion tart, spinach and ricotta cannelloni, lemonade battered haddock and beef and Guinness pie. In the evening a handful of additional dishes might be confit of duck leg on puy lentil and winter vegetable stew and braised pork belly with garlic mash, with puddings such as sticky toffee pudding, mango and white chocolate mousse with Cointreau ice-cream. You order food from the friendly staff at the kitchen door. *Starters/Snacks: £4.00 to £5.00. Main Courses: £7.50 to £14.95. Puddings: £4.00*

Marstons ~ Lease Emily and Ben Hammond ~ Real ale ~ Bar food (12-2.30, 7-9; not Sun evening) ~ (01335) 310205 ~ Children welcome ~ Dogs welcome ~ Open 11-3, 6-11; 11-11 Sat; 12-11 Sun

Recommended by Susan and Nigel Brookes, Andy and Claire Barker, Paul J Robinshaw, Theocsbrian, John Saul, the Didler, I J and S A Bufton, Dr David Clegg, Richard, John Tav, Roderick Braithwaite, J and E Dakin, Maurice and Gill McMahon

BURTON UPON TRENT   SK2523 MAP 7

Burton Bridge Inn 🍴 £
Bridge Street (A50); DE14 1SY

Straightforward cheery tap for the Burton Bridge Brewery; lunchtime snacks only

This genuinely friendly down-to-earth old brick local showcases the beers (Bitter, Festival, Golden Delicious, Porter and XL) that are brewed by Burton Bridge Brewery across the long old-fashioned yard at the back. These are well kept and served on handpump alongside a guest such as RCH Pitchfork or Timothy Taylors Landlord, alongside around 20 whiskies and over a dozen country wines. The simple little front area leads into an adjacent bar, separated from an oak beamed and panelled lounge by the serving counter. The bar has wooden pews, plain walls hung with notices, awards and brewery memorabilia, and the lounge has oak beams, a flame-effect fire and old oak tables and chairs; skittle alley. The panelled upstairs dining room is open only at lunchtime. A blue-brick terrace overlooks the brewery.

🍴 **Simple but hearty bar snacks (lunchtime only) take in filled cobs (including roast beef and pork), filled yorkshire pudding and ploughman's.** *Starters/Snacks: £2.20 to £4.00*

Own brew ~ Licensees Kevin and Jan McDonald ~ Real ale ~ Bar food (lunchtime only, not Sun) ~ No credit cards ~ (01283) 536596 ~ Dogs welcome ~ Open 11.30-2.15, 5-11; 12-2, 7-10.30 Sun; closed bank hol Mon lunchtime

Recommended by P Dawn, Theo, Anne and Jane Gaskin, C J Fletcher, the Didler, Pete Baker, David Carr, R T and J C Moggridge

CAULDON

SK0749 MAP 7

Yew Tree ★★ £

Village signposted from A523 and A52 about 8 miles W of Ashbourne; ST10 3EJ

Treasure-trove of fascinating antiques and dusty bric-a-brac, very idiosyncratic

One reader makes a pilgrimage to this timelessly idiosyncratic place with plenty of 2p pieces to play the working polyphons, and another affectionately describes it as a junk shop with a bar. Over the years, the charming landlord has amassed a museum's-worth of curiosities, and for most readers the dust and wear and tear just add to the atmosphere. The most impressive pieces are perhaps the working polyphons and symphonions – 19th-c developments of the musical box, often taller than a person, each with quite a repertoire of tunes and elaborate sound-effects. But there are also two pairs of Queen Victoria's stockings, ancient guns and pistols, several penny-farthings, an old sit-and-stride boneshaker, a rocking horse, swordfish blades, a little 800 BC greek vase, and even a fine marquetry cabinet crammed with notable early staffordshire pottery. Soggily sprung sofas mingle with 18th-c settles, plenty of little wooden tables and a four-person oak church choir seat with carved heads which came from St Mary's church in Stafford; above the bar is an odd iron dog-carrier. As well as all this there's an expanding choir of fine tuneful longcase clocks in the gallery just above the entrance, a collection of six pianolas (one of which is played most nights) with an excellent repertoire of piano rolls, a working vintage valve radio set, a crank-handle telephone, a sinuous medieval wind instrument made of leather, and a Jacobean four-poster which was once owned by Josiah Wedgwood and still has his original wig hook on the headboard. Clearly it would be almost an overwhelming task to keep all that sprucely clean. The drinks here are very reasonably priced (so no wonder it's popular with locals), and you'll find well kept Bass, Burton Bridge and Grays Dark Mild on handpump or tapped from the cask, along with about a dozen interesting malt whiskies; piped music (probably Radio 2), darts, shove-ha'penny, table skittles, dominoes and cribbage. When you arrive don't be put off by the plain exterior, or the fact that the pub is tucked unpromisingly between enormous cement works and quarries and almost hidden by a towering yew tree.

🍴 **Simple good value tasty snacks include pork, meat and potato, chicken and mushroom and steak pies, hot big filled baps and sandwiches, quiche, smoked mackerel or ham salad, and home-made puddings.** *Starters/Snacks: £0.70 to £3.50*

Free house ~ Licensee Alan East ~ Real ale ~ Bar food ~ No credit cards ~ (01538) 308348 ~ Children in polyphon room ~ Dogs welcome ~ Folk music first Tues in month ~ Open 10-2.30 (3 Sat), 6-1am; 12-3, 7-1am Sun

Recommended by N R White, Simon Fox, Mark Flynn, the Didler, Andy and Claire Barker, John and Fiona McIlwain, Susan and Nigel Brookes, P Dawn, Richard, John and Enid Morris

ENVILLE

Cat ◀

A458 W of Stourbridge (Bridgnorth Road); DY7 5HA

Aged beamed pub with locally brewed beers, interesting guests, mix-and-match range of sausage, mash and gravies, and pretty courtyard

The nicest part of this welcoming country pub is the bar closest to the road, where its 17th-c origins seem clearest. Here, two linked carpeted rooms, with a slight step between, have heavy black beams, ancient wall timbers, a log fire in a small brick fireplace, cast-iron framed and other pub tables, and brocaded wall seats with comfortable matching oak carver chairs – the tabby cat may have its eye on one, but the quiet collie wouldn't dare. The Enville real ales served here are brewed on the other side of the estate, using honey to add to their distinctive tastes: typically Ale, White, Ginger or Phoenix on handpump; also has three or four guests from brewers such as Highgate, Kinver and Wye Valley; the landlord can help with your choice. He does mulled wine in winter, and keeps a range of country wines; darts and piped music. A comfortable back family area has plush wall banquettes and dark tables, and there is a restaurant upstairs. You come into the pub through a splendidly old-fashioned paved yard alongside the monumentally tall and massive estate wall, and back here there are picnic-sets on a gravel terrace. The estate has attractive lakeside grounds, and the pub is also on the Staffordshire Way, so is popular with walkers.

🍴 **A speciality here is the sausage mix and match menu. The sausages are made for the pub by a local butcher. You choose from a list of ten, and from a list of eight mashes and eight gravies, putting them together in any combination you want – you might go for olde english sausages with bacon and leek mash and Guinness and mushroom gravy or tomato and garlic sausages with pesto mash and balsamic reduction gravy. Other generous helpings of quickly served bar food include sandwiches, hot baguettes, vegetarian pasta of the day, battered cod, steak and ale pie, and daily specials such as butternut and baby corn tartlet and tuna steak with olives and citrus fruits.** *Starters/Snacks: £3.00 to £3.50. Main Courses: £6.50 to £8.50. Puddings: £3.50*

Free house ~ Licensee Guy Ayres ~ Real ale ~ Bar food (12-2(2.30 Sat, 3 Sun), 7-9.30) ~ Restaurant ~ (01384) 872209 ~ Children in family room and main lounge ~ Dogs allowed in bar ~ Open 12-2.30(3 Sat), 6.30-11; 12-5.30 Sun; closed Sun evening, Mon
Recommended by the Didler, John and Helen Rushton, Guy Vowles, Lynda and Trevor Smith

HOAR CROSS

Meynell Ingram Arms

Abbots Bromley Road, off A515 Yoxall—Sudbury; DE13 8RB

Interesting choice of thoughtfully prepared food in cheery traditional bar and smarter dining areas; courtyard and garden

Well regarded for its very good, carefully sourced food, this is an attractive, bustling place, with an enjoyably buoyant feel. It appeals to drinkers as much as diners, and the big car park fills up fast, as do the several neat little rooms that ramble round the central bar counter. It's been carefully extended in recent years, with the smartest area being the brightly painted room leading to the dining room, with its elegant red curtains and coal effect fire. Elsewhere there's a traditional red-tiled room with a brick fireplace, hunting pictures and a bespectacled fox's head, comfortably upholstered seats, a few beams and brasses, and yellow walls displaying local notices and certificates praising the food. Marstons Pedigree, Timothy Taylors Landlord and a changing guest such as Greene King Old Speckled Hen on handpump and good wines; helpful young staff. There are tables in a courtyard behind, and some on the grass in front; it's a pretty spot in summer. More reports please.

🍴 **The wide choice of food includes lunchtime sandwiches and hot filled cobs, soup, fish and saffron soup with parmesan pastry, ploughman's, mushroom and parmesan risotto with caramelised baby onions and roast courgettes, pork and apple sausages with mustard mash, cider and sultanas, roast chicken breast with mushroom and tarragon risotto and** madeira sauce, beer-battered haddock with mushy peas, roast bass fillet with lemon crushed potatoes and pistou vegetable broth, braised shin of beef with horseradish potatoes, caramelised onions and beer sauce, steak, and puddings such as spotted dick and warm chocolate brownie with pecan nut ice-cream. *Starters/Snacks: £3.25 to £6.55. Main Courses: £8.15 to £16.95. Puddings: £4.50 to £5.50*

Free house ~ Licensees Jane and Mike Chappell ~ Real ale ~ Bar food (not Sun evening) ~ Restaurant ~ (01283) 575202 ~ Children welcome ~ Dogs welcome ~ Open 12-11(12 Fri, Sat); 12-10.30 Sun

Recommended by Pete Baker, David Martin, C J Fletcher

KIDSGROVE
SJ8354 MAP 7

Blue Bell ◀

25 Hardings Wood; off A50 NW edge of town; ST7 1EG

Astonishing tally of thoughtfully sourced real ales on six constantly changing pumps at simple little beer pub

The constantly changing real ales at this converted double cottage at the junction of the Trent & Mersey and Macclesfield canals is carefully selected from smaller, often unusual brewers, such as Acorn, Castle Rock, Crouch Vale, Oakham, Townhouse and Whim. More than 2300 brews have passed through the pumps over the last nine years. Lagers are restricted to czech or belgian brews, there's also usually a draught continental beer, at least one farm cider, a good range of bottled beers, and various coffees and soft drinks. Service is friendly and knowledgeable. The four small, carpeted rooms are unfussy and straightforward, with only a few tables in each, and blue upholstered benches running around white-painted walls; there's a gas effect coal fire, and maybe soft piped music. There are tables in front, and more on a little back lawn. Note the limited opening hours.

🍴 **Food is limited to filled rolls at the weekend.**

Free house ~ Licensees Dave and Kay Washbrook ~ Real ale ~ No credit cards ~ (01782) 774052 ~ Quiet well behaved children welcome ~ Dogs welcome ~ Impromptu acoustic Sun evening ~ Open 7.30-11; 1-4, 7-11 Sat; 12-10.30 Sun; closed lunchtime and Mon

Recommended by Dave Webster, Sue Holland, the Didler

LICHFIELD
SK1109 MAP 4

Queens Head ◀ £

Queen Street; public car park just round corner in Swan Road, off A51 roundabout; WS13 6QD

Great cheese counter, bargain lunchtime hot dishes, fine range of real ales

A few minutes' walk from the graceful cathedral and other attractions in the city's attractive largely pedestrianised centre, this handsome Georgian brick building is done up inside as an old-fashioned alehouse. It has Marstons Pedigree and Timothy Taylors Landlord on handpump, and three changing guest beers such as Adnams Broadside, Blythe Staffie (from nearby Rugeley) and Jennings Cocker Hoop, all well kept. The single long room has a mix of comfortable aged furniture on bare boards, some stripped brick, Lichfield and other pictures on the ochre walls above a panelled dado, and big sash windows. The atmosphere is comfortable, grown-up and relaxed, and the staff are friendly and helpful; terrestrial TV for sports events. There's a small garden.

🍴 **The highlight is the cabinet of cheeses on the left of the bar, including some interesting local ones such as Dovedale Blue. Throughout the day (unless it gets too busy) you can make up your own very generous ploughman's, perhaps with some pâté too, with a basket of their good crusty granary bread, home-made pickles, onions and gherkins. At lunchtime (not Sunday) they also have a good range of over two dozen enjoyable pubby hot dishes at amazingly low prices, such as their pedi pie (steak pie made with Marstons Pedigree).** *Starters/Snacks: £2.50 to £4.50*

Marstons ~ Lease Denise Harvey ~ Real ale ~ Bar food (12-2.15 (cheese all day if not too busy)) ~ No credit cards ~ (01543) 410932 ~ Dogs allowed in bar ~ Open 12-11(11.30 Fri, Sat); 12-3, 7-11 Sun

Recommended by Simon Fox, Nicola Ridding, Richard Green

STOURTON   SO8485 MAP 4

Fox

A458 W of junction with A449, towards Enville; DY7 5BL

Cosy series of rooms at welcoming country pub, nice bar food and garden

Standing alone in woodland surroundings (with well spaced picnic-sets on a terrace and big stretch of sloping grass), this neatly kept roadside pub is well placed for Kinver Country Park walks, and the Staffordshire Way. Inside, several cosily small areas ramble back from the small serving bar by the entrance, with its well kept Bathams Best and a guest such as Bass on handpump (and a noticeboard of hand-written travel offers). Tables are mostly sturdy and varnished, with pews, settles and comfortable library or dining chairs on green or dark blue carpet and bare boards. A good positive colour scheme picked up nicely by the curtains, and some framed exotic menus and well chosen prints (jazz and golf both feature). The woodburning stoves may be opened to give a cheery blaze on cold days. They put out big bunches of flowers, and the lighting (mainly low voltage spots) has been done very carefully, giving an intimate bistro feel in the areas round on the right, but the warm atmosphere is largely down to the welcoming family who've been running it for over 30 years. Dining areas include a smart conservatory which has neat bentwood furniture and proper tablecloths; piped music.

🍴 Bar food includes lunchtime sandwiches, as well as soup, tomato and basil pasta, mediterranean risotto, battered cod, fish or steak and stout pie and 8oz sirloin steak; it's a good idea to book if you want to go to one of their fortnightly fish evenings. *Starters/Snacks: £3.00 to £4.00. Main Courses: £4.00 to £7.95. Puddings: £2.95 to £3.95*

Free house ~ Licensee Stefan Caron ~ Real ale ~ Bar food (12-2, 7-9.30; 12-5 Sun) ~ (01384) 872614 ~ Children welcome lunchtimes ~ Open 11-3, 4.30-11; 11-11 Sat; 12-10.30(11-9 in winter) Sun

Recommended by Chris Glasson, Theo, Anne and Jane Gaskin, R T and J C Moggridge

WETTON   SK1055 MAP 7

Olde Royal Oak £

Village signposted off Hulme End—Alstonefield road, between B5054 and A515; DE6 2AF

Friendly traditional pub in lovely location; good value straightforward food

Nestling as it does in the heart of lovely National Trust countryside, with Wetton Mill and the Manifold Valley nearby, and a croft behind the pub for caravans and tents, it's not surprising that this aged white-painted and shuttered stone-built village house is popular with walkers (boot covers at both doors). There's a good convivial atmosphere in the bar, which has black beams with white ceiling boards above, small dining chairs around rustic tables, an oak corner cupboard, and a coal fire in the stone fireplace. The bar extends into a more modern-feeling area, which in turn leads to a carpeted sun lounge looking out over the small garden; piped music, darts, TV, shove-ha'penny, cribbage and dominoes. You can choose from more than 30 whiskies, and they've well kept Greene King Abbot, Theakstons Best and a guest, usually from Belvoir, on handpump.

🍴 Reasonably priced bar food includes filled baps, soup, breaded mushrooms, spicy chicken dippers, battered cod, a vegetarian dish of the day, gammon with pineapple and egg, chicken tikka and steaks, and puddings such as treacle sponge or strawberry ice-cream sundae. *Starters/Snacks: £2.95 to £3.35. Main Courses: £4.95 to £10.95. Puddings: £2.95*

Pubs staying open all afternoon at least one day a week are listed at the back of the book.

Free house ~ Licensees Brian and Janet Morley ~ Real ale ~ Bar food ~ (01335) 310287 ~
Children in sun lounge ~ Dogs allowed in bar ~ Open 12-2.30(3 Sat, Sun), 7-11; closed Mon,
Tues lunchtime, and all day Mon in winter ~ Bedrooms: /£40S

Recommended by the Didler, Paul J Robinshaw, Richard, Andy and Claire Barker

WRINEHILL   SJ7547 MAP 7

Hand & Trumpet ⊕ ♟ ◧

A531 Newcastle—Nantwich; CW3 9BJ

STAFFORDSHIRE DINING PUB OF THE YEAR

**Civilised and attractive, with good food all day, nice range of real ales and wines; pleasant
garden**

This large roadside pub was attractively made over in 2006 by the Brunning & Price team,
as an eastwards extension of their small Cheshire-based group. The focal point is the
handsome solidly built bar counter, with half a dozen handpumps dispensing well kept
real ales such as Caledonian Deuchars IPA, Thwaites Original and Timothy Taylors
Landlord, a couple of guests from brewers such as Northern and Titanic and possibly a
perry. They also keep a fine range of about 21 wines by the glass and have about 85
whiskies. Around this are linked open-plan areas with a good mix of dining chairs and
varying-sized tables on polished tiles or stripped oak boards, and several big oriental
rugs that soften the acoustics as well as the appearance. There are lots of nicely lit prints
on cream walls above the mainly dark dado, a good coal fire in the attractive tiled
fireplace on the left, one or two houseplants, and plenty of daylight from bow windows
and in one area a big skylight. Service is relaxed and friendly; good disabled access and
facilities. French windows open on to a stylish balustraded deck with teak tables and
chairs looking down on ducks swimming on a big pond in the sizeable garden, which has
plenty of trees.

🍴 **Imaginative bar food includes interesting sandwiches, starters such as fresh crumpet
with smoked salmon, poached egg and caper dressing, seared scallops with bacon and
pumpkin purée, coarse wild boar and black pudding pâté with rhubarb chutney, main
courses such as burger and chips, smoked haddock and salmon fishcake with tomato
salad, butternut squash stuffed with roast pepper, feta and mint and roast pork belly with
parsnip and apple mash, and puddings such as sticky toffee pudding and toffee bananas
on french toast with coconut ice-cream, and a good cheeseboard.** *Starters/Snacks: £4.95 to
£8.00. Main Courses: £8.75 to £15.00. Puddings: £4.95*

Brunning & Price ~ Manager John Unsworth ~ Real ale ~ Bar food (12-10(9.30 Sun)) ~
(01270) 820048 ~ Children welcome till 7pm ~ Dogs allowed in bar ~ Open 11.30-11(10.30 Sun)

Recommended by Gary Rollings, Debbie Porter, Sue Leighton

LUCKY DIP

Besides the fully inspected pubs, you might like to try these Lucky Dips recommended to us and
described by readers (if you do, please send us reports: www.goodguides.co.uk).

ALREWAS [SK1715]
Crown DE13 7BS [Just off A38; Post Office
Rd]: Friendly and cosy local with welcoming
helpful staff, three real ales such as Bass
and Wells & Youngs Bombardier, enjoyable
pub food inc OAP deals and good value Sun
carvery lunch, decent wines, small
comfortable dining room; tables out in front
and in pleasant back garden *(Brian and
Jacky Wilson, Joan and Tony Walker,
John Tav)*
☆ *George & Dragon* DE13 7AE [off A38; Main
St]: Three friendly low-beamed linked rooms
with good value generous honest food,

Marstons-related ales, efficient staff eager to
please, attractive paintings; piped music;
children welcome in eating area, pleasant
partly covered garden with good play area,
opens 5 wkdys *(John and Yvonne Davies,
John Tav, LYM)*
ALSTONEFIELD [SK1255]
☆ *Watts Russell Arms* DE6 2GD [Hopedale]:
Cheerful light and airy beamed pub handy
for Dovedale and the Manifold (can get
busy wknds), well kept Black Sheep,
Timothy Taylors Landlord and an occasional
guest beer, decent range of soft drinks,
food from sandwiches, wraps and tortillas

up, traditional games; children welcome, picnic-sets under parasols on sheltered tiered terrace and in garden, cl Mon and winter Sun evening (LYM, the Didler, John Tav)

ANSLOW [SK2125]

Bell DE13 9QD [Main Rd]: Warm friendly atmosphere, good choice of real ales, good wines by the glass; restaurant cl Mon, Sun evening (B M Eldridge)

☆ *Burnt Gate* DE13 9PY [Hopley Rd]: Comfortable country dining pub with good fresh food inc some imaginative dishes and speciality kebabs, friendly efficient staff, good choice of wines by the glass, Bass and Marstons Pedigree, proper bar with coal fire as well as restaurant (Paul Humphreys, C J Fletcher)

ARMITAGE [SK0716]

☆ *Plum Pudding* WS15 4AZ [Rugeley Rd (A513)]: Canalside pub and brasserie with modern warm colour scheme, good contemporary food inc good value set menu, sandwiches and light dishes, Greene King Old Speckled Hen, Marstons Pedigree and Bass or Tetleys, decent wines (choice of large or giant glasses), friendly service; no dogs, loud live music Fri; tables on waterside terrace and narrow canal bank (moorings available), bedrooms in neighbouring cottage (Bren and Val Speed, BB)

BIDDULPH [SJ8959]

Talbot ST8 7RY [Grange Rd (N, right off A527)]: Pleasant Vintage Inn family dining pub, handy for Biddulph Grange gardens (Paul J Robinshaw)

BISHOP'S WOOD [SJ8309]

Royal Oak ST19 9AE [Ivetsey Bank Rd]: Refurbished under good new licensees, three real ales, well packed food from sandwiches to steaks (Robert Garner)

BLITHBURY [SK0819]

Bull & Spectacles WS15 3HY [Uttoxeter Rd (B5014 S of Abbots Bromley)]: Obliging friendly service, wide choice of homely food inc bargain lunchtime Hot Table – half a dozen or so generous main dishes with help-yourself veg, and some puddings (David Green, Helen Rowett)

BLYTHE BRIDGE [SJ9640]

Black Cock ST11 9NT [Uttoxeter Rd (A521)]: Roadside local with welcoming helpful staff, some tables set aside for the enjoyable fresh food, real ales such as Caledonian Deuchars IPA, Greene King Abbot, Shepherd Neame Spitfire and Wells & Youngs Bombardier, good wine choice, great 50s and Beatles memorabilia (Tony and Maggie Harwood, the Didler)

BRADLEY [SJ8717]

Red Lion ST18 9DZ [off A518 W of Stafford; Smithy Lane]: Small friendly old-world 16th-c village pub, Bass and good guest beers, honest straightforward food from sandwiches to good Sun lunch, OAP midweek bargains, decent wine choice, dining room (Donald and Maureen Barber, Neil and Brenda Skidmore)

BRAMSHALL [SK0633]

Old Bramshall Inn ST14 5BG: Attractive welcoming country pub, light and fresh, with quick friendly service, four real ales inc Bass, reasonably priced food with ample veg (John Tav)

BRANSTON [SK2221]

Bridge Inn DE14 3EZ [off A5121 just SW of Burton; Tatenhill Lane, by Trent & Mersey Canal Bridge 34]: Cosy low-beamed canalside pub very popular at wknds for Italian landlord's good reasonably priced pizzas and pastas (so may be a wait for a table – hang in there for his rather special tiramisu), friendly staff and atmosphere, Marstons Pedigree, warm log fire; tables in waterside garden, good moorings, basic supplies for boaters and caravanners (C J Fletcher)

BURTON UPON TRENT [SK2423]

☆ *Coopers Tavern* DE14 1EG [Cross St]: Traditional pub with friendly new family settling in well, coal fire in homely front parlour, Hop Back Summer Lightning, Tower and other well kept changing ales from casks in back room with cask tables, lunchtime food (Pete Baker, David Carr, LYM, C J Fletcher, the Didler)

Derby Inn DE14 1RU [Derby Rd]: Unspoilt and well worn-in friendly local with particularly good Marstons Pedigree, long-serving landlord (but he's starting to talk of retirement – so go while you can), local produce for sale wknd, brewery glasses collection in cosy panelled lounge, lots of steam railway memorabilia in long narrow bar; sports TV; dogs welcome, open all day Fri/Sat (the Didler, C J Fletcher)

Devonshire Arms DE14 1BT [Station St]: Two-bar pub with good range of Burton Bridge ales and continental bottled beers, also country wines, decent food (all day Fri/Sat, not Sun), lots of snug corners; pleasant back terrace with water feature, open all day Fri/Sat (the Didler, C J Fletcher)

Old Cottage Tavern DE14 2EG [Rangemoor St/Byrkley St]: Tied to local small brewery Old Cottage, their tasty beers and guest ales, good value food (not Sun evening) inc bargain specials and good Sun lunch, solid fuel stove, four rooms inc games room and cosy back restaurant; open all day (C J Fletcher, the Didler)

Wetmore Whistle DE14 1SH [Wetmore Rd]: Tastefully renovated Tynemill pub, plenty of individual touches, two unpretentiously comfortable linked areas and back café, good value simple nourishing food all day inc good breakfast from 8am, Castle Rock Harvest Pale, Marstons Pedigree and two or more guest beers tapped from the cask, continental beers on tap or by bottle, farm ciders, good choice of wines by the glass, good landlady and staff; open all day (the Didler, C J Fletcher)

BUTTERTON [SK0756]

Black Lion ST13 7SP [off B5053]: Traditional 18th-c low-beamed stone-built inn in Peak District conservation village, logs blazing in inner room's kitchen range, some banquette seating, good-humoured efficient service even when busy, enjoyable bar food from filled rolls up, half a dozen well kept ales, reasonable prices, traditional games and pool room; piped music; children in eating areas, terrace tables, tidy bedrooms, cl Mon and Tues lunchtimes *(DC, LYM, the Didler)*

CANNOCK [SJ9710]

Linford Arms WS11 1BN [High Green]: Wetherspoons in 18th-c building, eight well kept ales and their usual attractively priced food, good house wine, friendly fast service and hands-on manager, quiet family area upstairs; can get noisy at night; tables outside, open all day *(John Tav)*

Shoal Hill WS11 1RF [Sandy Lane]: Smart pub popular with walkers for low-priced bar food from baguettes and baked potatoes up, friendly helpful staff, Greene King ales, large light restaurant *(Neil and Brenda Skidmore, Robert Garner)*

CAULDON LOWE [SK0748]

Cross ST10 3EX [Waterhouses, A52 Stoke—Ashbourne]: Welcoming neatly kept country pub with well kept Wadworths, wide choice of reasonably priced food, extended beamed restaurant; pleasant bedrooms, scenic setting *(John Tav)*

CLIFTON CAMPVILLE [SK2511]

Green Man B79 0AX [Main St]: Low-beamed 15th-c village pub with inglenook and chubby armchair in public bar, airy modernised dining lounge, welcoming efficient service, Bass, Marstons Pedigree and a changing guest beer, good range of food from huge hot baguettes to substantial good value Sun roast, games area with pool; children in back family room, garden with play area *(Geoff Ziola, LYM)*

CODSALL [SJ8603]

Codsall Station WV8 1BY [Chapel Lane/Station Rd]: Pub in simply restored listed waiting room and ticket office (station still used by trains) with added conservatory, good range of Holdens beers inc one brewed for the pub, good value basic food(not Sun/Mon) from sandwiches and baked potatoes to wknd specials; terrace tables, open all day wknds *(Robert Garner, the Didler)*

CONSALL [SK0049]

☆ *Black Lion* ST9 0AJ [Consall Forge, OS Sheet 118 map ref 000491; best approach from Nature Park, off A522, using car park ½ mile past Nature Centre]: Traditional take-us-as-you-find-us tavern tucked away in rustic old-fashioned canalside settlement by restored steam railway station, enjoyable generous unpretentious food freshly made by landlord from huge baguettes to good fish choice, good coal fire, Marstons Best and Pedigree; piped music, no muddy boots; busy wknd lunchtimes, good walking area *(Bob and Laura Brock, LYM, the Didler)*

CRESSWELL [SJ9739]

☆ *Izaak Walton* ST11 9RE [off A50 Stoke—Uttoxeter via Draycott in the Moors;

Cresswell Lane]: Well refurbished country dining pub with wide food choice all day from sandwiches and light dishes to steaks and mixed grill, friendly efficient staff, real ales such as Adnams Best, Bass and Fullers London Pride, good wines by the glass, prints and panelling, several small rooms and larger upstairs area; well behaved children welcome, disabled facilities (but some steps), attractive back garden, open all day *(Joan and Tony Walker, LYM, Susan and Nigel Brookes)*

ETRURIA [SJ8747]

Plough ST1 5NS [Etruria Rd (off A53 opp Festival site)]: Small two-room pub devoted entirely to food in the evenings (drinkers then confined to small back yard), huge choice of good value food served till late esp steaks, fine sandwich range popular too at lunchtime, very friendly licensees and staff, five well kept Robinsons/Wards real ales, nice atmosphere and décor *(R T and J C Moggridge)*

FOUR ASHES [SJ9108]

Four Ashes WV10 7BU [Station Drive (off A449)]: Marstons ales, bar food from sandwiches to steaks inc carvery all day Thurs *(Robert Garner)*

FRADLEY [SK1414]

White Swan DE13 7DN [Fradley Junction]: Perfect canalside location at Trent & Mersey and Coventry junction, very popular summer wknds, with cheery traditional public bar, quieter plusher lounge and lower vaulted back bar (where children allowed), real fire, cribbage, dominoes Marstons Pedigree, usual food from sandwiches to Sun carvery; waterside tables, good canal walks *(LYM, Paul J Robinshaw)*

GAILEY [SJ8810]

Bell ST19 9LN [A5 a mile S]: Former coaching inn with well kept ales inc Banks's, popular reasonably priced food esp ham and eggs, pleasant service; nice garden by ornamental pond *(John Tav)*

HANLEY [SJ8847]

Coachmakers Arms ST1 3EA [Lichfield St]: Friendly traditional town pub, three small rooms and drinking corridor, Bass and good range of guest beers, darts, cards and dominoes, original seating and local tilework; children welcome, open all day, cl lunchtime Sun *(the Didler)*

HARTSHILL [SJ8645]

Jolly Potters ST4 7NH [Hartshill Rd (A52)]: Traditional local with changing real ales from central servery, corridor to public bar (with TV) and three small homely lounges; open all day *(the Didler, Pete Baker)*

HAUGHTON [SJ8620]

Shropshire ST18 9HB [A518 Stafford—Newport]: Converted barn at one end of long narrow lounge, plenty of tables for wide choice of attractively priced food from baguettes up, well kept Adnams Broadside, Greene King Old Speckled Hen and Marstons Pedigree; nice shady garden overlooking quiet pastures *(Bren and Val Speed)*

HIGH OFFLEY [SJ7725]

Anchor ST20 0NG [off A519 Eccleshall—Newport; towards High Lea, by Shrops Union Canal, Bridge 42; Peggs Lane]: Real boaters' pub on Shrops Union Canal, little changed in the century or more this family have run it, two small simple front rooms, Marstons Pedigree and Wadworths 6X in jugs from cellar, Weston's farm cider, may be lunchtime toasties, owners' sitting room behind bar, occasional wknd singalongs; outbuilding with small shop and semi-open lavatories, lovely garden with great hanging baskets and notable topiary anchor, caravan/ camp site, cl Mon-Thurs winter *(Angus and Carol Johnson, the Didler, Andrew Gardner)*

HILDERSTONE [SJ9434]

Roebuck ST15 8SF [Sandon Rd (B5066)]: Four well kept real ales, quick friendly service, open fire, bar snacks evenings (not Mon) and wknd lunchtimes, games area; open from mid-afternoon, all day Fri-Sun *(John Tav)*

Spotgate ST15 8RP [Spot Acre; B5066 N]: Friendly efficient service, Marstons Pedigree, reasonably priced wines, enjoyable bar food, also very wide food choice for two opulent 1930/40s Pullman dining coaches behind *(Susan and Nigel Brookes, Terry Gurd)*

HIMLEY [SO8990]

☆ *Crooked House* DY3 4DA [signed down rather grim lane from B4176 Gornalwood—Himley, OS Sheet 139 map ref 896908]: Extraordinary sight, building thrown wildly out of kilter (mining subsidence), with slopes so weird things look as if they roll up not down them; otherwise a basic well worn low-priced pub with Banks's Bitter and Mild and guest beers, Weston's Old Rosie cider, cheery staff, straightforward food (all day in summer), some local antiques in level more modern extension, conservatory; children in eating areas, big outside terrace, open all day wknds and summer *(the Didler, R T and J C Moggridge, Ian Phillips, LYM)*

HOPWAS [SK1704]

Tame Otter B78 3AT [Hints Rd (A51 Tamworth—Lichfield)]: Cosy Vintage Inn with usual beams, nooks and alcoves, three log fires, easy chairs, settles, dining chairs, old photographs and canalia, friendly well trained staff, reasonably priced food all day, good choice of wines, real ale *(W M Lien, Derek and Heather Manning, Colin Gooch)*

HUDDLESFORD [SK1509]

Plough WS13 8PY [off A38 2 miles E of Lichfield, by Coventry Canal]: Waterside dining pub extended from 17th-c cottage, enjoyable and interesting food from sandwiches up in four neat and pleasant eating areas, cheerful attentive staff, well kept ales such as Greene King Old Speckled Hen and Marstons Pedigree, good range of wines; attractive hanging baskets, canalside tables, hitching posts *(Lesley and Barbara Owen)*

HULME END [SK1059]

Manifold Inn SK17 0EX [B5054 Warslow—Hartington]: Attractive 18th-c country pub nr river, real ales such as Bass, Marstons Pedigree and Whim Hartington (check that you're paying the locals' rate), wide choice of generous good value food using local produce, higher evening prices, cosy soft seating in neat lounge bar, log-effect gas fires and some stripped stone, separate light and airy dining room and conservatory; children and cyclists welcome, disabled facilities, tables outside, camp site, bedrooms in converted stone smithy off secluded back courtyard *(John Beeken, Greta and Christopher Wells, BB, I J and S A Bufton, Paul and Margaret Baker)*

KING'S BROMLEY [SK1216]

Royal Oak DE13 7HZ [Manor Rd (A515)]: Pleasant family-run country local with good value food inc interesting dishes using good local ingredients, three real ales *(Leo and Barbara Lionet)*

KINVER [SO8483]

Constitutional Social Club DY7 6HL [High St]: A club, but ring the bell and speak to the steward to be signed in, fine changing choice of bargain real ales, friendly staff and members, pool, restaurant; open evenings and wknds *(the Didler)*

Plough & Harrow DY7 6HD [High St (village signed off A449 or A458 W of Stourbridge); aka the Steps]: Friendly old split-level Bathams local with their Best, Mild and XXX on top form, good choice of ciders and malt whiskies, plain bar food (filled rolls even Sun lunchtime), low prices, film star pictures; proper public bar with darts, dominoes etc, lounge with nostalgic juke box, sports TV and games machine; children allowed in some parts, tables in back courtyard, open all day wknds *(Pete Baker, the Didler, Helen Maynard)*

KNIGHTON [SJ7240]

White Lion TF9 4HJ [B5415 Woore—Mkt Drayton]: Friendly unpretentious local, three log or coal fires, three good changing ales, nice choice of generous home-made food (not Mon), cosy dining area, conservatory and restaurant; large adventure playground *(Susan and Nigel Brookes)*

LEEK [SJ9856]

Den Engel ST13 5HG [Stanley St]: Neatly kept belgian-style bar in high-ceilinged former bank, many dozens of belgian beers inc lots on tap, three dozen genevers, three or four changing real ales; piped classical music; tables on back terrace, open all day Weds-Sun, cl Mon/Tues lunchtimes *(the Didler)*

Quiet Woman ST13 5DN [St Edward St]: Several real ales, good value bar food and friendly fast service in quiet traditional old timbered pub's comfortable lounge area *(John Tav)*

☆ *Wilkes Head* ST13 5DS [St Edward St]: Convivial three-room local dating from 18th c (still has back coaching stables), tied to Whim with their ales and interesting guest beers, good choice of whiskies, farm cider, friendly chatty landlord, welcoming regulars and dogs, filled rolls, pub games, gas fire, lots of pumpclips; juke box in back room, Mon music night; children allowed in one room (but not really a family pub), fair disabled access, tables outside, open all day exc Mon lunchtime (the Didler, Pete Baker)

LICHFIELD [SK0705]

☆ *Boat* WS14 0BU [A461 Walsall Rd, off A5 at Muckley Corner; handy for M6 Toll (but pay again when you rejoin it)]: Immaculately kept modern bistro pub with good imaginative food (all day Sun) on huge floor-to-ceiling blackboard, open kitchen and nice layout inc cheery café part and more conventionally comfortable areas, three changing real ales from brewers such as Blythe and Wells & Youngs, good choice of wines by the glass; faint piped music; children welcome, good disabled access, decking tables, open all day Sun (Clifford Blakemore, Phil and Jane Hodson, Ian and Jane Irving, Karen Eliot, N R White, R T and J C Moggridge, John and Yvonne Davies, John and Hazel Williams, Mrs Ann Gray, Colin Fisher, Trevor and Sheila Sharman, Glenwys and Alan Lawrence, Brian and Jacky Wilson)

Horse & Jockey WS14 9JE [Tamworth Rd (A51 Lichfield—Tamworth)]: Dining pub with friendly helpful service, enjoyable generous food, cosy atmosphere in four linked softly lit rooms with some panelling, settles, sepia photographs, books, plates and so forth, Black Sheep, Marstons, Timothy Taylors Landlord and guest beers (S P Watkin, P A Taylor)

LONGDON [SK0814]

Swan With Two Necks WS15 4PN [off A51 Lichfield—Rugeley; Brook Lane]: Long low-beamed quarry-tiled bar and two-room carpeted restaurant, five hot coal fires, wide food choice from lunchtime sandwiches up inc generous popular cod and chips, Adnams, Caledonian Deuchars IPA, Timothy Taylors Landlord and a guest beer; piped music, no children; picnic-sets and swings in garden with summer servery (LYM, John Tav)

LONGNOR [SK0965]

Olde Cheshire Cheese SK17 0NS: 14th-c building, a pub for 250 years, Robinsons real ales, friendly service, tasty nourishing food, plenty of bric-a-brac and pictures in traditional main bar and two attractive dining rooms with their own separate bar; hikers welcome, bedrooms (John Dwane)

MEERBROOK [SJ9960]

Lazy Trout ST13 8SN: Wide choice of good value food from traditional bar dishes to restaurant meals, good quick friendly service, three well kept changing ales, decent wines, cosily old-fashioned bar on left, comfortable room on right with log fire and dining area; no dogs, games machines; plenty of tables in pleasant garden behind, attractive setting, good walks (John Rushton, Brian and Jean Hepworth, Dr D J and Mrs S C Walker)

MILWICH [SJ9533]

Red Lion ST15 8RU [Dayhills; B5027 towards Stone]: Old-fashioned bar at end of working farmhouse, old settles, tiled floor, inglenook log or coal fire, Bass and one or two guest beers tapped from the cask, friendly welcome, darts, dominoes and cribbage; cl lunchtimes exc Sun, cl Sun evening (the Didler)

NEWBOROUGH [SK1325]

Red Lion DE13 8SH [Duffield Lane]: Old pub facing church in quiet village, comfortable bar with leather armchairs and open fire, Marstons Pedigree and good choice of other drinks, enjoyable fair-priced food (inc take-aways) from mid-afternoon Weds-Fri, all day wknds (B M Eldridge, LYM)

NEWCASTLE-UNDER-LYME [SJ8443]

Seabridge ST5 3HA [Seabridge Lane]: Neatly kept and unpretentious, with several well kept ales inc Bass, quick friendly service, food inc bargain Sun roast (John Tav)

PENKRIDGE [SJ9214]

Littleton Arms ST19 5AL [St Michaels Sq/A449 — M6 detour between junctions 12 and 13]: Former Vintage Inn now made over (like some others in this chain) in more of a brasserie style aiming a little upscale with its food, good choice of wines by the glass, well kept real ales, quick helpful service from friendly young staff; children welcome, open all day (John and Alison Hamilton)

☆ *Star* ST19 5DJ [Market Pl]: Charming open-plan local with new landlord restarting good value food service, lots of low black beams and button-back red plush, Marstons-related ales, friendly service, open fires; piped music, sports TV; open all day, terrace tables (Robert Garner, Colin Gooch, BB, Dr and Mrs A K Clarke)

RUSHTON SPENCER [SJ9362]

Rushton Inn SK11 0SE [A523]: Handy for Rudyard Lake and the Reaches, decent fresh food, Flowers real ale; two bedrooms (Derek and Sylvia Stephenson)

SALT [SJ9527]

☆ *Holly Bush* ST18 0BX [off A51 S of Stone]: Charming thatched, timbered and heavily beamed medieval pub very popular for its generous mainly traditional all-day food (you may have to queue for a table), with well kept Adnams, Marstons Pedigree and a guest beer, cheerful staff, coal fire in fine inglenook; though most readers are full of enthusiasm one or two disappointments have cropped up this last year – we hope this has been a temporary blip; children welcome, attractive garden with wood-fired oven for pizzas and so forth, open all day (Simon and Sally Small, Roger and Anne Newbury, Michael and Jenny Back, Dr and Mrs A K Clarke, Pat and Tony Martin, LYM, M and GR, Richard Endacott, Dave Webster, Sue Holland, R T and J C Moggridge, R M Chard, Trevor and Sheila Sharman, John and Yvonne Davies, Maurice and Gill McMahon)

SAVERLEY GREEN [SJ9638]
Greyhound ST11 9QX: Large country pub with good range of real ales, spreading bar areas, reasonably priced food; garden tables *(John Tav)*

SLITTING MILL [SK0217]
Horns WS15 2UW [Slitting Mill Rd]: Good choice of food with more elaborate evening menu, five or six real ales inc Bass, Caledonian, Marstons and Timothy Taylors Landlord *(Robert Garner)*

STAFFORD [SJ9223]
Greyhound ST16 2PU [County Rd]: Unpretentious two-bar town pub with surprisingly large range of well kept ales from all over, landlord may offer a taster; sports TVs and usual games in lively public bar *(Pete Baker)*
Lamb ST16 2QB [Broad Eye]: Neatly kept town pub with well kept Banks's and Marstons Pedigree, attractively priced food; open all day *(John Tav)*
Picture House ST16 2HL [Bridge St/Lichfield St]: Art deco cinema well converted by Wetherspoons keeping ornate ceiling plasterwork and stained-glass name sign, bar on stage with up to five real ales at competitive prices, farm cider, friendly service, seating in stalls, circle and upper circle, popular food all day, lively atmosphere, film posters, Peter Cushing mannequin in preserved ticket box; good disabled facilities, spacious terrace overlooking river, open all day *(John Tav, R T and J C Moggridge)*
Shrewsbury Arms ST16 2NG [Eastgate St]: Compact friendly local with several rooms, well kept Greene King Abbot, bargain basic pub food *(R T and J C Moggridge)*
Spittal Brook ST17 4LP [Lichfield Rd, just off A34]: Friendly two-bar local with five well kept real ales, farm cider, popular pubby food (not Sun evening), good log fire, darts, board games; Tues folk nights, lively quiz Weds; dogs welcome, garden fenced off from main railway line, open all day Sat *(John Tav)*
Star & Garter ST17 4AW [Wolverhampton Rd (A449)]: Busy town local with good choice of reasonably priced real ales, friendly licensees; some live music; garden facing road *(John Tav, Mark Hannan)*
Vine ST16 2JU [Salter St]: Large traditional hotel with roomy and neatly kept well divided bar, quick friendly service, wide food choice inc bargains for two, well kept Bass, restaurant; children welcome, 27 bedrooms *(John Tav)*

STOKE-ON-TRENT [SJ8649]
Bulls Head ST6 3AJ [St Johns Sq, Burslem]: Amazing choice of belgian beers as well as good Titanic and guest beers in two-room town pub with good service even when busy, coal fire, bar billiards; good juke box; cl till 3 wkdys, open all day Fri-Sun *(the Didler, P Dawn, R T and J C Moggridge)*
Malt 'n' Hops ST4 3EJ [King St, Fenton]: Lively open-plan pub popular for its well

kept changing real ales inc ones from Tower, imports too; sports TV *(the Didler)*
Potter ST4 3DB [King St, Fenton]: Unpretentious three-room local with several changing ales such as Coach House and Greene King; sports TV; open all day *(the Didler)*

STONE [SJ9034]
Langtrys ST15 8EB [Oulton St]: Four real ales, good wines by the glass, enjoyable food, quick friendly service *(John Tav)*
Swan ST15 8QW [Stafford St (A520)]: Converted warehouse by Trent & Mersey Canal, up to ten well kept ales inc several from small local brewers, log fires, buoyant atmosphere, good service even when crowded, bar lunches (not Sun/Mon); frequent live music nights; terrace tables, open all day *(John Tav)*
Wayfarer ST15 0NB [A34 outside]: Good daily carvery using local supplies, well kept Marstons Pedigree; children welcome, disabled facilities, open all day wknds *(Steve Walters)*

SWYNNERTON [SJ8535]
Fitzherbert Arms ST15 0RA [village signposted off A51 Stone—Nantwich]: Olde-worlde beamed pub with young helpful staff, enjoyable straightforward food inc special deals for two *(Susan and Nigel Brookes)*

TAMWORTH [SK2004]
Market Vaults B79 7LU [Market St]: Splendidly unpretentious little two-bar pub in pedestrian street, lots of brass, dark oak, original fireplaces and even tales of lost secret tunnel, hard-working welcoming landlord, well kept Banks's Original and Bitter and a guest beer, bargain lunchtime food – pounce quickly for a table in the small back dining area *(Pete Baker)*
Tweeddale Arms B79 7JS [Albert Rd/Victoria Rd]: Substantial building with modern airy atmosphere, daily papers, pleasant spacious restaurant with reasonably priced food inc good steaks, attentive service, Marstons Pedigree; games machines; bedrooms *(Colin Gooch, John and Yvonne Davies)*

TATENHILL [SK2021]
☆ *Horseshoe* DE13 9SD [off A38 W of Burton; Main St]: Friendly pub with reliable reasonably priced food (all day Sat) from sandwiches to steaks inc proper children's food, tiled-floor bar, cosy side snug with woodburner, two-level restaurant and back family area, Marstons ales, good wine range, quick polite service; pleasant garden, good play area with pets corner *(C J Fletcher, LYM, Brian and Jacky Wilson)*

THORNCLIFFE [SK0158]
Red Lion ST13 7LP: Comfortable and attractively homely 17th-c pub with good value fresh food from sandwiches up, Thurs steak night, all-day Sun roasts, prompt service, good atmosphere, log fires, wide range of wines and beers, dining room, games area with pool; children welcome *(Mr and Mrs B Jones, Brian and Jean Hepworth)*

TRYSULL [SO8594]
Bell WV5 7JB [Bell Rd]: Extended red brick village local, softly lit lounge with lots of table lamps, big grandfather clock, inglenook fire and good chatty atmosphere, cosy bar with brasses and locomotive number-plates, Holdens Bitter, Special and Golden Glow, Bathams Best and a guest beer, interesting bar food from sandwiches up at fair prices, evening restaurant Weds-Sat; open all day wknds *(the Didler)*

TUTBURY [SK2128]
☆ **Olde Dog & Partridge** DE13 9LS [High St; off A50 N of Burton]: Good Chef & Brewer in handsome Tudor inn, rambling extensively back with heavy beams, timbers, various small rooms, nooks and corners, their usual food all day inc generous snacks, several real ales such as Everards, Greene King and Marstons Pedigree, attentive cheerful staff, good log fire; comfortable well equipped bedrooms, open all day *(Derek and Sylvia Stephenson, Paul and Margaret Baker, LYM, Colin Fisher)*

WALL [SK0906]
Trooper WS14 0AN [Watling St, off A5]: Small refurbished pub under greek/italian ownership, wide choice of fairly priced food from bar dishes to lots of seafood, pleasant efficient service, Marstons Pedigree and Tetleys, separate restaurant; interesting spot just above Letocetum Roman site, terrace tables, good-sized garden, open all day wknds *(Steve Jennings)*

YARLET [SJ9129]
Greyhound ST18 9SD: Busy food pub with friendly efficient service, reasonably priced food inc plenty of fish, large dining conservatory *(Susan and Nigel Brookes)*

Post Office address codings confusingly give the impression that some pubs are in Staffordshire, when they're really in Cheshire or Derbyshire (which is where we list them).

Suffolk

Many of our main entries here are genuinely friendly and rather civilised places, often in lovely old buildings – and several are by water, giving them an added bonus for visitors. Food plays a big part in this county, with chefs tending to let the top-quality local produce speak for itself – while the cooking is modern and imaginative, it's not in any way pretentious. It's not cheap, though; prices tend to be on the high side of average. So this is an area where it particularly pays to know the places to head for. Pubs doing specially well for fine food include the Crown at Buxhall (there's still a tiny pubby part, but most emphasis now is on dining), the Beehive at Horringer (the long-serving licensees are most welcoming), the Angel in Lavenham (extremely popular and civilised), the Anchor at Nayland (their adjacent farm produces eggs, meat and vegetables using traditional farming methods), the Plough at Rede (robustly flavoured dishes and lots of seasonal game), the Ravenwood Hall at Rougham (a lovely place where they smoke their own meat and fish), the Crown in Snape (handy for the Maltings), the Crown in Southwold (super wines, too), the Crown at Stoke-by-Nayland (delicious modern dishes), the Anchor in Walberswick (contemporary dishes, well cooked, and carefully integrated with their good beers), and the Crown at Westleton (making a very welcome return to the *Guide*, under a new team, after several years' break). It's the Crown at Westleton that wins the title Suffolk Dining Pub of the Year for its imaginative food, thoroughly home-made all the way from their bread and light snacks through good country main dishes to unusual ice-creams. Other places doing very well this year are the Butt & Oyster at Chelmondiston (lovely spot with interesting river views), the Dog at Grundisburgh (run by two brothers), the Five Bells in Hessett (bustling and homely), the Fat Cat in Ipswich (another new entry, with a fantastic range of ales), St Peters Brewery at South Elmham (a wonderful old building and with very good own brews, too), the Lord Nelson in Southwold (a particularly well run and enjoyable local), the smartly reworked Fountain at Tuddenham (yet another new entry, a very promising dining pub), and the Bell at Walberswick (always busy and close to a nice beach). Our pick from the Lucky Dip section at the end of the chapter includes the Sorrel Horse at Barham, Cock at Brent Eleigh, Bull in Cavendish, Froize at Chillesford (more restaurant than pub), Eels Foot at Eastbridge, Swan at Hoxne, Ship at Levington, Ramsholt Arms at Ramsholt, Golden Key in Snape, Duke of Marlborough at Somersham, Waggon & Horses in Sudbury, Dolphin at Thorpeness and De La Pole Arms at Wingfield. As with food, drinks prices here tend to be rather higher than the national norm. Adnams is the main local beer to look out for, showing as the cheapest beer on offer in a very high proportion of the county's good pubs – Adnams also supply particularly good wines.

BRAMFIELD   TM3973 MAP 5

Queens Head
The Street; A144 S of Halesworth; IP19 9HT

Popular pub with pretty garden, organic produce for bar food and decent choice of drinks

The best place to sit in this bustling pub is in the high-raftered lounge bar with its scrubbed pine tables, good log fire in the impressive fireplace and a sprinkling of farm tools on the walls; a separate side bar has light wood furnishings. Adnams Bitter and Broadside, a decent wine list with seven by the glass, local apple juice and home-made elderflower cordial. Cheerful blue-painted picnic-sets under blue and white umbrellas in the pretty garden and there's a dome-shaped bower made of willow. The church next door is rather lovely.

🍴 Here they use produce from small organic local farms and make their own preserves and bread; the bar food includes filled baguettes, soup, mushrooms with cream, garlic and cheese, grilled polenta with roast marinated peppers, lamb and rosemary crumble, ratatouille pancake topped with cheese, large mackerel with orange sauce, pork chop braised in cider and apples with mustard mash, steak and kidney in ale pie, and puddings such as rich chocolate and brandy pot and warm apricot frangipane tart. *Starters/Snacks: £3.95 to £7.95. Main Courses: £7.95 to £14.95. Puddings: £3.25 to £4.35*

Adnams ~ Tenants Mark and Amanda Corcoran ~ Real ale ~ Bar food (till 10pm Sat) ~ (01986) 784214 ~ Children welcome away from main bar area ~ Dogs welcome ~ Open 11.45-2.30, 6.30-11; 12-3, 7-10.30 Sun; closed 26 Dec

Recommended by Charles and Pauline Stride, John and Bettye Reynolds, J F M and M West, Philip and Susan Philcox, Simon Cottrell, Comus and Sarah Elliott, Tina and David Woods-Taylor, Rosemary Smith, Pat and Tony Hinkins, V Brogden, Mrs L Pratt, John Wooll, Bryan and Mary Blaxall, Jim and Sheila Prideaux

BURY ST EDMUNDS   TL8564 MAP 5

Nutshell
The Traverse, central pedestrian link off Abbeygate Street; IP33 1BJ

Teeny, simple local with lots of interest on the walls and a couple of real ales

This cheerful, quaint and friendly bare-boards local is absolutely tiny – just half a dozen customers make it seem pretty full. The timeless interior contains a short wooden bench along its shop-front corner windows, one cut-down sewing-machine table, an elbow rest running along its rather battered counter, and Greene King IPA and Abbot on handpump served by the chatty landlord. A mummified cat, which was found walled up here (something our ancestors did quite commonly to ward off evil spirits) hangs from the dark brown ceiling (and also seems to have a companion rat), along with stacks of other bric-a-brac, from bits of a skeleton through vintage bank notes, cigarette packets and military and other badges to spears and a great metal halberd; piped music, chess and dominoes. The stairs up to the lavatories are very steep and narrow. The modern curved inn sign is appealing. No children.

🍴 No food at all.

Greene King ~ Lease Martin Baylis ~ Real ale ~ No credit cards ~ (01284) 764867 ~ Dogs welcome ~ Open 11(12 in winter)-11; 12-10.30 Sun; closed 1 Jan

Recommended by David and Sue Smith, David Carr, R T and J C Moggridge, the Didler, Joe Green

> Post Office address codings confusingly give the impression that some pubs are in
> Suffolk, when they're really in Cambridgeshire, Essex or Norfolk
> (which is where we list them).

Old Cannon 🍺

Cannon Street, just off A134/A1101 roundabout N end of town; IP33 1JR

New licensees for busy own-brew town pub with guest beers, farm cider and pubby lunchtime food

New licensees have taken over this busy pub but happily, not much has changed. It looks more like a stylish private town house than a pub and the bar has miscellaneous chairs around a few tables on dark bare boards, dark red or ochre walls (one with a big mirror), and plenty of standing space. The main feature of the bar is the two huge, gleaming stainless steel brewing vessels (in use each Monday) which produce the pub's own Old Cannon Best, Gunner's Daughter, Blonde Bombshell and other seasonal ales. A couple of guests from brewers such as Adnams and Nethergate on handpump, a farm cider, continental beers and seven wines by the glass. Piped music. Behind, through the old side coach arch, is a good-sized cobbled courtyard neatly set with planters and hanging baskets, with rather stylish metal tables and chairs. The old brewhouse across the courtyard has been converted into bedrooms. No children and no dogs.

🍽 Bar food at lunchtime includes good sandwiches, soup, home-cooked sugar-baked ham and egg, wild mushroom and tagliatelle in a white wine and garlic cream sauce, toad in the hole, beef and mushrooms braised in ale, and chicken korma with coconut rice; the menu for the smarter evening restaurant is more elaborate. *Starters/Snacks: £4.25 to £5.95. Main Courses: £7.95 to £16.95. Puddings: £4.25*

Free house ~ Licensees Mike and Judith Shallow ~ Real ale ~ Bar food (not Sun evening or all day Mon) ~ Restaurant ~ (01284) 768769 ~ Open 12-3, 5-11; 12-3, 7.30-10.30 Sun; closed Mon lunchtime, 25 and 26 Dec ~ Bedrooms: £55S/£69S

Recommended by Keith Reeve, Marie Hammond, John Robertson, Joe Green, John and Patricia White, Julia Mann, Ryta Lyndley

BUXHALL   TM9957 MAP 5

Crown 🍴 🍷

Village signposted off B1115 W of Stowmarket; fork right by post office at Gt Finborough, turn left at Buxhall village sign, then second right into Mill Road, then right at T junction; IP14 3DW

Emphasis on interesting food in 17th-c rural pub, lots of wines by the glass, quite a few malt whiskies, pretty garden

There is a cosy little bar on the left in this tucked-away country pub with an open fire in a big inglenook, a couple of small round tables on a tiled floor and low hop-hung beams, but the emphasis really is on the food. Standing timbers separate this bar from another area with pews and candles and flowers on beech tables with leather chairs, and there's a further light and airy room which they call the Mill Restaurant. As well as Cox & Holbrook Old Mill (brewed just two minutes away), they have Greene King IPA and Woodfordes Wherry on handpump, 30 wines by the glass and 30 whiskies. Plenty of seats and solid wood tables under parasols on the heated terrace and they've a pretty garden, with nice views over gently rolling countryside. A large enclosed side garden has wooden decking and raised flowerbeds.

🍽 Good bar food includes sandwiches, soup, pea risotto with basil and parmesan pesto, grilled king prawns with garlic butter and lime, venison casserole with herb dumplings, plaice fillets stuffed with prawns served with spinach, asparagus and a light cream sauce, chicken breast stuffed with sage and cheese and wrapped in parma ham, pork medallions with calvados-soaked prunes, tagliatelle and a mustard sauce and slow-roasted lamb hearts stuffed with sausage meat, apricots and fresh herbs. *Starters/Snacks: £4.95 to £7.50. Main Courses: £9.50 to £15.95. Puddings: £4.95 to £6.95*

Greene King ~ Lease Trevor Golton ~ Real ale ~ Bar food (not Sun evening or Mon) ~ Restaurant ~ (01449) 736521 ~ Children welcome if well behaved ~ Dogs allowed in bar ~ Open 12-3, 6.30-11.30; 12-3 Sun; closed Sun evening, Mon, 25 and 26 Dec

Recommended by Pamela Goodwyn, Tina Humphrey, Mrs Sheila Stothard, George Cowie, Tina and David Woods-Taylor, Bill Strang, Stuart Pearson, J F M and M West, Derek Field, Mike and Shelley Woodroffe

CHELMONDISTON   TM2037 MAP 5

Butt & Oyster

Pin Mill – signposted from B1456 SE of Ipswich; IP9 1JW

Chatty old pub above River Orwell with nice views, decent food and drink, and seats on the terrace

Try to get to this simple old bargeman's pub early and bag one of the window seats. Through the bay windows there's a fine view of the ships coming down the River Orwell from Ipswich and of the long lines of moored black sailing barges; the suntrap terrace shares the same view. The half-panelled timeless little smoke room is pleasantly worn and unfussy and has model sailing ships around the walls and high-backed and other old-fashioned settles on the tiled floor; ferocious beady-eyed fish made by a local artist stare at you from the walls. Adnams Best and Broadside and Greene King IPA with summer guests such as Greene King Old Speckled Hen and Wychwood Hobgoblin on handpump or tapped from the cask and several wines by the glass; board games, dominoes and bar skittles. The annual Thames Barge Race (end June/beginning July) is fun.

🍽 **Tasty bar food includes sandwiches, soup, smoked trout and bacon terrine, sausages with caramelised onion gravy, pistachio, cranberry and date roulade, suet pudding of the day, fish pie, smoked meat platter.** *Starters/Snacks: £3.95 to £8.95. Main Courses: £6.95 to £14.95. Puddings: £3.25 to £4.75*

Punch ~ Lease Steve Lomas ~ Real ale ~ Bar food (12-2.30, 6.30-9.30; all day weekends) ~ (01473) 780764 ~ Children in dining rooms only ~ Dogs allowed in bar ~ Acoustic jam session every second Sun ~ Open 11-11; 12-10.30 Sun
Recommended by the Didler, Pamela Goodwyn, Ken Millar, David Carr, Mrs Romey Heaton, JDM, KM

COTTON   TM0667 MAP 5

Trowel & Hammer ♀

Mill Road; take B1113 N of Stowmarket, then turn right into Blacksmiths Lane just N of Bacton; IP14 4QL

Pleasant thatched pub with seats in pretty back garden, some sort of food served all day and real ales

The spreading series of quiet areas in this civilised thatched pub has lots of beamery and timber baulks, plenty of wheelbacks and one or two older chairs and settles around a variety of tables and a big log fire. Adnams Broadside and Greene King IPA and Old Speckled Hen on handpump, and decent wines. Piped music, pool, games machine and juke box. The back garden is pretty with colourful flowers, there are seats and tables under thatched umbrellas and some large ornamental elephants; swimming pool and croquet.

🍽 **As well as tapas served all day, there's quite a choice of food: sandwiches and filled paninis, soup, filled baked potatoes, burgers, nachos with various toppings, steak in ale hotpot, mushrooms stroganoff, gammon and egg, cajun chicken, crayfish and salmon chilli pasta, daily specials, and puddings such as belgian chocolate bombe and lemon meringue pie.** *Starters/Snacks: £2.25 to £7.95. Main Courses: £7.95 to £18.95. Puddings: £3.25 to £5.95*

Free house ~ Licensee Sally Burrows ~ Real ale ~ Bar food (12-3, 6-9(9.30 Fri and Sat); tapas served all day; 12-9 Sun) ~ Restaurant ~ (01449) 781234 ~ Children welcome but must be well behaved ~ Live music Sat evening ~ Open 12-11(1am Fri and Sat)
Recommended by Stephen P Edwards, Alan Jefferson, Bill Strang, Stuart Pearson

---

Bedroom prices are for high summer. Even then you may get reductions for more than one night, or (outside tourist areas) weekends. Winter special rates are common, and many inns cut bedroom prices if you have a full evening meal.

DENNINGTON

TM2867 MAP 5

Queens Head

A1120; IP13 8AB

Fine Tudor building next to the church with refurbished bars, pleasant service and plenty of seats outside in attractive garden

As well as some seats on a side lawn that is attractively planted with flowers and sheltered by some noble lime trees, there's a pond at the back with ducks, koi carp and goldfish and more seating; the pub backs on to Dennington Park which has swings and so forth for children and is by the church. It's a fine Tudor building and the arched rafters in the steeply roofed part of the bar are reminiscent of a chapel – in fact, it was owned for centuries by a church charity. With some refurbishment this year, the main neatly kept L-shaped room has comfortable padded wall seats on the partly carpeted and partly tiled floor, stripped wall timbers and beams and a handsomely carved bressumer beam. Adnams Bitter and maybe a guest such as Archers Village on handpump and local cider; piped music.

🍴 **Bar food includes lunchtime sandwiches, filled baked potatoes and ploughman's plus soup, pork pâté with plums and brandy, smoked haddock and spring onion fishcakes, vegetable bake, battered cod, sweet and sour pork, duck with port and raspberry sauce, trout with ginger butter, and puddings such as chocolate truffle torte and knickerbocker glory.** *Starters/Snacks: £3.50 to £5.50. Main Courses: £7.50 to £13.95. Puddings: £3.50 to £3.95*

Free house ~ Licensees Hilary Cowie, Peter Mills ~ Real ale ~ Bar food ~ Restaurant ~ (01728) 638241 ~ Children in family room ~ Open 11-2.30, 6-11; 12-2.30, 6-10.30 Sun; 11-2.30, 6.30-10.30 in winter; closed 25 and 26 Dec

Recommended by Michael Clatworthy, Keith Berrett, Julia Mann

EARL SOHAM

TM2263 MAP 5

Victoria 🍺 £

A1120 Yoxford—Stowmarket; IP13 7RL

Nice beers from brewery across the road in friendly and relaxed little pub, and well liked reasonably priced food

Run by a friendly, efficient landlord, this is an unpretentious pub with an easy-going local atmosphere. And the beers are certainly well kept as the Earl Soham brewery is right across the road: Albert, Victoria and Gold on handpump. Farm cider too. The well worn bar is fairly basic and sparsely furnished with stripped panelling, kitchen chairs and pews, plank-topped trestle sewing-machine tables and other simple scrubbed pine country tables, tiled or board floors, an interesting range of pictures of Queen Victoria and her reign, and open fires. There are seats on the raised back lawn, with more out in front. The pub is quite close to a wild fritillary meadow at Framlingham, and a working windmill at Saxtead.

🍴 **Good proper pub food includes sandwiches, ploughman's, soup, corned beef hash, vegetarian pasta dishes, a changing curry, and puddings.** *Starters/Snacks: £4.00 to £5.00. Main Courses: £6.50 to £11.50. Puddings: £3.95*

Free house ~ Licensee Paul Hooper ~ Real ale ~ Bar food (12-2, 7-10) ~ (01728) 685758 ~ Children welcome ~ Dogs allowed in bar ~ Open 11.30-3, 6-11; 12-3, 7-10.30 Sun

Recommended by Comus and Sarah Elliott, Pete Baker, Mike and Sue Loseby, Stephen P Edwards

---

The letters and figures after the name of each town are its Ordnance Survey map reference. 'Using the *Guide*' at the beginning of the book explains how it helps you find a pub, in road atlases or on large-scale maps as well as in our own maps.

ERWARTON   TM2134 MAP 5

Queens Head ♀ ◖

Village signposted off B1456 Ipswich—Shotley Gate; pub beyond the attractive church and the manor with its unusual gatehouse (like an upturned salt-cellar); IP9 1LN

Pleasant old pub with a relaxed atmosphere, decent drinks, well liked bar food (especially the daily specials) and seats outside

The friendly bar in this relaxed 16th-c pub has bowed black oak beams in its shiny low yellowing ceiling, comfortable furnishings, several sea paintings and photographs and a cosy coal fire. If they trim the foliage, you should get a view across fields to the Stour estuary. Adnams Bitter, Broadside and maybe a seasonal guest and Greene King IPA on handpump, a decent wine list, local cider and several malt whiskies. There's a pleasant conservatory dining area; darts, bar billiards, shove-ha'penny, board games and piped music. The gents' has quite a collection of navigational charts. There are picnic-sets under summer hanging baskets in front.

🍴 Tasty bar food includes sandwiches, ploughman's, sausage and mash, ham and eggs, pork with apricot stuffing with a brandy and madeira sauce, partridge or pheasant casserole, battered fresh cod fillet, vegetable curry, steak and kidney pudding, daily specials, and puddings. *Starters/Snacks: £3.95 to £4.75. Main Courses: £7.95 to £9.50. Puddings: £3.75 to £4.25*

Free house ~ Licensees Julia Crisp and G M Buckle ~ Real ale ~ Bar food ~ Restaurant ~ (01473) 787550 ~ Children allowed away from bar areas ~ Open 11-3, 6.30-11

Recommended by Mrs Carolyn Dixon, Pamela Goodwyn, A J Murray, Judi Bell, Tom Gondris

GREAT GLEMHAM   TM3461 MAP 5

Crown ◖

Between A12 Wickham Market—Saxmundham and B1119 Saxmundham—Framlingham; IP17 2DA

Neat pub in pretty village with friendly landlord, log fires and fresh flowers, decent real ales and enjoyable food

In a particularly pretty village, this neat pub is run by a friendly landlord. There's a big entrance hall with sofas on rush matting and an open-plan beamed lounge with wooden pews and captain's chairs around stripped and waxed kitchen tables, and local photographs and interesting paintings on cream walls; fresh flowers, some brass ornaments and log fires in two big fireplaces. Adnams Bitter and Earl Soham Victoria with a guest such as Brandon Rusty Bucket and St Austells Tribute are served from old brass handpumps and they've six wines by the glass, Aspall's cider and several malt whiskies. A tidy flower-ringed lawn, raised above the corner of the quiet village lane by a retaining wall, has some seats and tables under cocktail parasols; disabled access.

🍴 Enjoyable bar food includes sandwiches, ploughman's, soup, rollmop herring with potato salad, ham and free-range eggs, roasted mediterranean vegetable pasta topped with goats cheese, loin of pork stuffed with chestnuts and apricots with rosemary gravy, beer-battered cod, chicken with crispy pancetta and broad bean and thyme risotto, and puddings such as lemon-scented shortbread with chantilly cream and strawberries or passion fruit cheesecake. *Starters/Snacks: £4.25 to £4.95. Main Courses: £6.25 to £12.50. Puddings: £4.95*

Free house ~ Licensee Dave Cottle ~ Real ale ~ Bar food (11.30-3, 6.30-9; 12-4, 7-9 Sun) ~ (01728) 663693 ~ Children welcome ~ Dogs welcome ~ Open 11.30-3, 6.30-11; 12-4, 7-10.30 Sun; closed Mon except bank hols

Recommended by Simon Cottrell, Ian and Nita Cooper, George Atkinson, Simon Rodway, Pete and Sue Robbins, Comus and Sarah Elliott, Roger White, Charles and Pauline Stride, Neil Powell, Peter and Pat Frogley, Pamela Goodwyn, Derek and Maggie Washington

GRUNDISBURGH

TM2250 MAP 5

Dog ♀

Off A12 via B1079 from Woodbridge bypass; The Green – village signposted; IP13 6TA

Civilised, friendly pub run by two brothers with enjoyable food, nice choice of drinks and log fire; garden with play area

You can be sure of a friendly welcome in this pink-washed pub attractively placed near the village green. It's run by two brothers who have refurbished the public bar on the left which now has oak settles and dark wooden carvers around a mix of tables on the tiles and an open log fire – no more games machines or piped music. The softly lit and relaxing carpeted lounge bar on the left remains unchanged: comfortable seating around dark oak tables, antique engravings on its crushed raspberry walls and unusual flowers in the windows. It links with a similar bare-boards dining room, with some attractive antique oak settles. Adnams Bitter and Broadside and a guest like Timothy Taylors Landlord on handpump, half a dozen wines by the glass and good espresso coffee; the atmosphere is civilised and relaxed. The jack russell is called Poppy. There are quite a few picnic-sets out in front by flowering tubs and the fenced back garden has a play area.

🍴 Cooked by one of the landlords using seasonal produce and plenty of local game, the bar food includes sandwiches, marinated white anchovies or hummus with bread sticks, smooth chicken liver pâté with melba toast and apple chutney, smoked haddock fishcake with tomato and basil sauce, goats cheese with red onion, toasted pepper and basil tart, slow-cooked american-style beef short ribs, braised shoulder of lamb, game casserole, gressingham duck confit in garlic and red wine with truffle mash, and puddings such as banana and bacardi crème brûlée and hazelnut, Amaretto and chocolate loaf with chantilly cream. *Starters/Snacks: £2.50 to £5.25. Main Courses: £8.00 to £12.00. Puddings: £3.25 to £4.25*

Punch ~ Lease Charles and James Rogers ~ Real ale ~ Bar food (12-2(3 Sun), 6-9) ~ Restaurant ~ (01473) 735267 ~ Children welcome away from bar area ~ Dogs allowed in bar ~ Open 12-3, 5.30-11 Mon and Tues; all day the rest of the week

Recommended by J B and M E Benson, J F M and M West, John Saul, Charles and Pauline Stride, Wendy and Fred Cole, Pamela Goodwyn

HESSETT

TL9361 MAP 5

Five Bells

Off A14 E of Bury; The Street; IP30 9AX

Bustling pub with a good mix of customers, interesting food and relaxed atmosphere in the several interconnected rooms

This is a pleasantly relaxed place – a pub for at least 250 years – that is liked by both locals and visitors. It's more or less open plan with one or two black beams in its rather low shiny ochre ceiling, a good log fire in the carpeted area on the left, and big rugs on red flooring tiles over on the right. There's a nice mix of tables and country prints above the panelled dado. Greene King IPA and Abbot with a guest such as Hardys & Hansons Olde Trip on handpump, piped music, darts and cribbage. The sheltered back garden has a boules pitch. The pub is just a little way down the road from a spectacular square-towered flint-built Norman church.

🍴 Enjoyable food cooked by Mrs Muir includes sandwiches or filled baguettes and ploughman's, toasted brie with olives and sun-dried tomatoes, goats cheese and strawberry salad, smoked salmon and prawn tart, three curries and three vegetarian dishes that change daily, steak and kidney pie, lamb and mint suet pudding, battered cod and chips, thai-style duck with saffron rice, and puddings such as bakewell tart or lemon crème brûlée. *Starters/Snacks: £3.50 to £5.75. Main Courses: £7.95 to £13.50. Puddings: £3.75 to £4.25*

Greene King ~ Tenant John Muir ~ Real ale ~ Bar food (12-2, 6.30-9.30; not Sun evening, not Mon) ~ Restaurant ~ (01359) 270350 ~ Children welcome ~ Dogs allowed in bar ~ Open 12-3, 5(6 Sat)-11; 12-4, 7-10.30 Sun; closed Mon lunchtime, evenings 25 and 26 Dec

Recommended by Mrs Kay Dewsbury, Derek Field, J F M and M West, Chilvers

HORRINGER

TL8261 MAP 5

Beehive 🍴 ♀
A143; IP29 5SN

Imaginative food in civilised pub with long-serving licensees and nice little rambling rooms; attractive back terrace

The friendly licensees have now been at this civilised pub for 22 years and many of their customers have been with them all that time – though they are always happy to welcome new ones. The rambling series of little rooms is furnished with good quality old country furniture on the sage green carpet or flagstones and there's a cottagey feel, largely because they've refrained from pulling walls down to create an open-plan layout favoured by many places nowadays. Despite some very low beams, stripped panelling and brickwork, good chalky heritage wall colours keep it fairly light and airy. Greene King IPA, Abbot and maybe Old Speckled Hen on handpump, and several wines by the glass. An attractively planted back terrace has picnic-sets and more seats on a raised lawn. Their friendly (and now rather elderly) dog Muffin remains a great hit with readers and Skye the westie is learning the ropes quickly.

🍴 **Changing daily, the interesting food might include soup, potted pork and foie gras pâté, avocado stuffed with smoked eel and horseradish mousse, home-made pork and paprika sausages with creamy mash and gravy, smoked haddock florentine, warm mushroom and blue cheese tart, confit of duck with red cabbage, sole with chive butter, and puddings such as steamed lemon sponge with sweet lemon sauce and vanilla panna cotta with espresso syrup.** *Starters/Snacks: £1.20 to £6.95. Main Courses: £8.95 to £15.95. Puddings: £4.95*

Greene King ~ Tenants Gary and Dianne Kingshott ~ Real ale ~ Bar food (not Sun evening) ~ (01284) 735260 ~ Children welcome ~ Open 12-2.30, 7-11; closed Sun evening, 25 and 26 Dec
Recommended by Jeremy Whitehorn, G D Baker, Simon Cottrell, Eamonn and Natasha Skyrme, Mrs Carolyn Dixon, John Saville

IPSWICH

TM1844 MAP 5

Fat Cat 🍺
Spring Road, opposite junction with Nelson Road (best bet for parking up there); IP4 5NL

Fantastic range of changing real ales in well run town pub; garden

They keep a fantastic range of 20 real ales in this friendly and very busy town pub. On handpump or tapped from the cask in the tap room, these might include Adnams Bitter, Arundel Sussex Gold, Coach House Gunpowder Mild, Crouch Vale Brewers Gold, Dark Star Original and Hophead, Fat Cat Top Cat and Honey Cat, Fullers London Pride, Grainstore 1050, Moles Barley Mole, Oakham White Dwarf and JHB, St Peters Golden and Mild, Woodfordes Wherry and many more. Also, quite a few belgian bottled beers, farm cider and fruit wines. The bare-boarded bars have a mix of café and bar stools, unpadded wall benches and cushioned seats around cast-iron and wooden pub tables, and lots of enamel brewery signs of varying ages on the canary yellow walls; no noisy machines or music to spoil the cheerful and chatty atmosphere. The pub cat is called Dave and the sausage dog, Stanley. There's also a spacious and useful back conservatory, and several picnic-sets on the terrace and lawn. Very little nearby parking. No children or dogs.

🍴 **They do only scotch eggs, pasties and filled baguettes.** *Starters/Snacks: £2.50*

Free house ~ Licensees John and Ann Keatley ~ Real ale ~ Bar food ~ (01473) 726524 ~ Open 12-11; 11am-midnight Sat
Recommended by G Coates, Kerry Law, Ian and Nita Cooper, the Didler, Danny Savage

---

We say if we know a pub allows dogs.

LAVENHAM

Angel ★ ⑪ � ⬛ 🛏

Market Place; CO10 9QZ

Fine range of drinks and interesting food in handsome and civilised Tudor inn; comfortable bedrooms and sizeable back garden

The bedrooms in this attractive Tudor inn have been refurbished this year and have digital TVs and wireless broadband; do note though that at weekends they take only two-night bookings. The light and airy long bar area has plenty of polished dark tables, a big inglenook log fire under a heavy mantelbeam, and some attractive 16th-c ceiling plasterwork – even more elaborate pargeting in the residents' sitting room upstairs. Round towards the back on the right of the central servery is a further dining area with heavy stripped pine country furnishings. They have shelves of books, dominoes and lots of board games. Adnams Bitter and Broadside, Greene King IPA and Nethergate Suffolk County on handpump, local cider, ten wines by the glass and 23 malt whiskies. Picnic-sets out in front overlook the former market square and there are tables under parasols in a sizeable sheltered back garden; it's worth asking if they've time to show you the interesting Tudor cellar.

Ⅲ Using local, traceable produce, the interesting high-quality bar food includes some lunchtime choices such as sandwiches, braised duck leg with garlic mash, home-cooked free-range gammon salad and tomato, mozzarella and basil tart as well as soup, chicken, pork, apricot and basil terrine, sweet-cured herrings marinated in honey, mustard and dill, steak in ale pie, spinach, sweet potato and mushroom lasagne, grilled fillets of whiting and cod with curly kale and seafood bisque, medallions of pork fillet with crispy bacon, red pepper and sage sauce, chicken breast with parsnip purée, and puddings like lemon meringue roulade and crème brûlée; they also have a good value two-course midweek evening menu. *Starters/Snacks: £3.95 to £7.25. Main Courses: £9.25 to £14.95. Puddings: £4.50*

Free house ~ Licensees Roy Whitworth and John Barry ~ Real ale ~ Bar food (12-2.15, 6.45-9.15) ~ Restaurant ~ (01787) 247388 ~ Children welcome ~ Dogs allowed in bar and bedrooms ~ Classical piano (played by Roy for 17 years) Fri evenings ~ Open 10am-11pm; 12-10.30 Sun; closed 25 and 26 Dec ~ Bedrooms: £60B/£80B

Recommended by MDN, MJB, Pamela Goodwyn, the Didler, Walter and Susan Rinaldi-Butcher, David Carr, Mrs Carolyn Dixon, N R White, DFL, Tina and David Woods-Taylor, I A Herdman, Tina Humphrey, Mike Gorton, Paul and Margaret Baker, David Twitchett, Jim and Sheila Prideaux

LAXFIELD

Kings Head ★ ⬛

Behind church, off road toward Banyards Green; IP13 8DW

Unspoilt old pub of real character, helpful staff, appealing bar food and several real ales; self-contained flat to rent

Although there's another new licensee for this unspoilt 15th-c pub, there's a tremendously informal atmosphere and the charmingly old-fashioned rooms have plenty of character. Lots of people like the front room best, with a high-backed built-in settle on the tiled floor and an open fire. Two other equally unspoilt rooms – the card and tap rooms – have pews, old seats, scrubbed deal tables and some interesting wall prints. There's no bar – instead, the genial and helpful staff potter in and out of a cellar tap room to pour pints of Adnams Bitter, Broadside, Explorer and seasonal ales and maybe Fullers London Pride or Timothy Taylors Landlord straight from the cask; several wines by the glass, piped music, cards and board games. Outside, the garden has plenty of benches and tables, there's an arbour covered by a grape and hop vine, and a small pavilion for cooler evenings. They have a self-contained flat to rent.

The details at the end of each main entry start by saying whether the pub is a free house, or if it's tied to a brewery or pub group (which we name).

🍴 Interesting bar food includes sandwiches, soup, duck and pork terrine with apple cider relish, grilled chicken livers wrapped in bacon with raspberry vinaigrette, roasted ratatouille en croûte on a tomato and red onion salsa, steak in ale pie, lamb cutlets with redcurrant gravy, roasted bass on a timbale of steamed vegetables with a Noilly Prat sauce, medallions of fillet steak with creamy madeira sauce, and puddings such as pistachio rose petal cheesecake and fruit crumble. *Starters/Snacks: £3.95 to £6.95. Main Courses: £5.95 to £9.95. Puddings: £4.50*

Adnams ~ Tenant Mike Blackmore ~ Real ale ~ Bar food (not Sun evening) ~ Restaurant ~ (01986) 798395 ~ Younger children in card room and older ones allowed in restaurant ~ Dogs allowed in bar ~ Open 12-3, 6-11; 12-11 Sat and Sun; 12-3, 6-11 weekends in winter

Recommended by Tracey and Stephen Groves, the Didler, Alan Cole, Kirstie Bruce, Michael Clatworthy, Pete Baker, Comus and Sarah Elliott

LIDGATE   TL7257 MAP 5

Star ♀

B1063 SE of Newmarket; CB8 9PP

Attentive service, spanish and english food, a warm welcome and seats out in front and in back garden

---

Run by friendly and competent people, this village dining pub places much emphasis on the wide choice of food. The main room has handsomely moulded heavy beams, a good big log fire, candles in iron candelabra on good polished oak or stripped pine tables and some antique catalan plates over the bar; darts, ring the bull and piped music. Besides a second similar room on the right, there's a cosy little dining room on the left. Greene King IPA, Abbot and Ruddles County on handpump and decent house wines. There are some tables out on the raised lawn in front and in a pretty little rustic back garden. Dogs may be allowed with permission from the landlady.

🍴 The main course prices are pretty top whack for a pub but the food is good and interesting mixing both english and spanish dishes (the landlady is Spanish): gazpacho, pâté, catalan salad, boquerones (fresh anchovies floured and fried), piquillo peppers and cod brandade, lasagne, daube of beef, cod in garlic mousseline, lamb steaks in blackcurrant, spanish roast lamb, pig cheeks, venison steaks in port, and puddings such as chocolate roulade and strawberry cream tart. *Starters/Snacks: £5.50 to £5.90. Main Courses: £10.50 to £18.50. Puddings: £4.95 to £5.50*

Greene King ~ Lease Maria Teresa Axon ~ Real ale ~ Bar food (12-2.30(3 Sun), 7-10; not Sun evening) ~ Restaurant ~ (01638) 500275 ~ Children welcome ~ Open 12-3, 6-midnight; 12-3.30, 7-11 Sun; closed 25 and 26 Dec, 1 Jan

Recommended by John Saville, Michael Sargent, M and GR, Jim and Sheila Prideaux

LONG MELFORD   TL8646 MAP 5

Black Lion ♀ 🛏

Church Walk; CO10 9DN

Civilised hotel with relaxed and comfortable bar, a couple of real ales, modern bar food, attentive uniformed staff; lovely bedrooms

---

Customers do happily drop in for just a drink but there's no doubt that this is a civilised and comfortable hotel with prices to match. One side of the oak serving counter is decorated in ochre and has bar stools, deeply cushioned sofas, leather wing armchairs and antique fireside settles, while the other side, decorated in shades of terracotta, has leather dining chairs around handsome tables set for the good modern food; open fires in both rooms. Big windows with swagged-back curtains have a pleasant outlook over the village green and there are large portraits of racehorses and of people. Service by neatly uniformed staff is friendly and efficient. Adnams Best and Broadside tapped from the cask, 13 wines by the glass and several malt whiskies. There are seats and tables under terracotta parasols on the terrace and more in the appealing Victorian walled garden.

🍽 Attractively presented – if not cheap – the good food might include filled huffers (a type of roll), scallops wrapped in bacon on buttered spinach with cheese sauce, mussels with shredded fennel in a Pernod cream sauce, marinated potted gressingham duck with home-made walnut bread, sausage and mash with caramelised onion and red wine gravy, coq au vin, fresh battered haddock, basil ravioli with wild mushrooms and goats cheese on tomato and red pepper stew, lambs liver and onion steamed suet pudding, and puddings such as dark chocolate tart with orange salad and rhubarb and ginger crumble. *Starters/Snacks: £5.50 to £9.50. Main Courses: £8.95 to £18.95. Puddings: £4.95 to £7.25*

Ravenwood Group ~ Manager Yvonne Howland ~ Real ale ~ Bar food (12-2.30, 7-9.30(10 Sat)) ~ Restaurant ~ (01787) 312356 ~ Children welcome ~ Dogs allowed in bar and bedrooms ~ Open 11-10(10.30 Sat) ~ Bedrooms: £97.50B/£150B

Recommended by Comus and Sarah Elliott, John Saville, Derek and Sylvia Stephenson, Jim and Sheila Prideaux

NAYLAND

TL9734 MAP 5

Anchor 🍽 ☒

Court Street; just off A134 – turn off S of signposted B1087 main village turn; CO6 4JL

Friendly well run pub with interesting food using own farm and smokehouse produce, real ales, wines from own vineyard, and riverside terrace

In warm weather you can sit at picnic-sets on the back terrace here looking across to the peaceful River Stour and its quacking ducks and enjoying a drink or a meal. Inside, the pub is light and sunny with interesting old photographs of pipe-smoking customers and village characters on its pale yellow walls, farmhouse chairs around a mix of tables, and coal and log fires at each end. Another room behind has similar furniture and an open fire and leads into a small carpeted sun room. Up some quite steep stairs is the stylish restaurant. Adnams Bitter, Greene King IPA, Pitfield East Kent Goldings and a guest beer on handpump and several wines by the glass (some from their own vineyard). The bare-boards front bar is liked by regulars who gather for a pint and a chat; piped music. Their farmland next door is being worked by suffolk punch horses using traditional farming methods. The suffolk punch is a seriously endangered species and visitors are welcome to watch these magnificent animals or maybe try their hands at the reins – which our readers have enjoyed very much.

🍽 From their Heritage Farm next door they produce free-range eggs, vegetables and home-reared lambs, pigs, beef, game, trout and venison; they also have their own smokehouse. As well as lunchtime sandwiches and bar nibbles, the imaginative food might include interesting soups, seared scallop and pancetta on pea purée with mint oil, a smoked platter of fish, meat and cheeses, mushroom and truffle risotto, spicy meatballs with home-made spaghetti, beer-battered haddock, steak in Guinness pudding, baked local pheasant breast wrapped in pork and herb sausage meat with red wine jus, and puddings such as sticky toffee pudding with butterscotch sauce and vanilla crème brûlée with fresh lychees. *Starters/Snacks: £3.50 to £6.50. Main Courses: £7.70 to £14.70. Puddings: £4.00 to £5.00*

Free house ~ Licensee Daniel Bunting ~ Real ale ~ Bar food (12-2(3 Sat), 6.30-9(9.30 Fri and Sat); 10-3, 5-8.30 Sun) ~ Restaurant ~ No credit cards ~ (01206) 262313 ~ Children welcome ~ Open 11-3, 5-11; 11-11 Sat; 10am-10.30pm Sun

Recommended by Bryan and Mary Blaxall, Robert Turnham, Rosemary Smith, Derek Thomas, Ray J Carter, Bernard Phelvin, Adele Summers, Alan Black, Richard Siebert, Mrs P Lang

NEWBOURNE

TM2743 MAP 5

Fox

Off A12 at roundabout 1.7 miles N of A14 junction; The Street; IP12 4NY

Friendly, relaxed pub with good generous food in attractive rooms; nice garden

The atmosphere here is relaxed and pubby, even though food has pride of place. As you come in, there's an eye-catching array of some two or three dozen little black hanging panels that shows, in white writing, one dish to each, what's on offer. Also, a few shiny black beams in the low rather bowed ceiling, slabby elm and other dark tables on the bar's tiled floor, a stuffed fox sitting among other decorations in an inglenook, and a warm décor in orange and crushed raspberry. A comfortable carpeted dining room with a large modern artwork and several antique mirrors on its warm yellow walls opens off on the left and overlooks the courtyard. Adnams Bitter and Greene King IPA and Abbot on handpump, decent wines by the glass and prompt, friendly service; piped music. There are picnic-sets out in front, with more in an attractive garden with a pond; it's a quiet spot.

🍴 **As well as good generous lunchtime baps, the quickly served food might include soup, chicken liver and juniper berry pâté, tempura-battered king prawns with teriyaki sauce, stilton and vegetable crumble, seafood gratin, sticky lamb with honey and rosemary, cajun chicken, pork in a creamy apple sauce, venison and green peppercorn cobbler, and daily specials.** *Starters/Snacks: £3.75 to £5.45. Main Courses: £7.95 to £15.95. Puddings: £3.45 to £4.95*

Punch ~ Lease Steve and Louise Lomas ~ Real ale ~ Bar food (12-2.30, 6.30-9.30; all day weekends) ~ Restaurant ~ (01473) 736307 ~ Children welcome ~ Dogs allowed in bar ~ Open 11-11

Recommended by Comus and Sarah Elliott, Pamela Goodwyn, Alan Payne, Mrs Hilarie Taylor

REDE   TL8055 MAP 5

Plough 🍴 ♟

Village signposted off A143 Bury St Edmunds—Haverhill; IP29 4BE

Promptly served, reliably good food in 16th-c pub, several wines by the glass and friendly service

This white-painted thatched old pub is very neat and pretty and a reliable place to come for an enjoyable meal. As it's so popular, it's best to book a table, especially at weekends. The traditional bar has low black beams, comfortable seating and a solid-fuel stove in its brick fireplace. Fullers London Pride, Greene King IPA and a guest beer kept under light blanket pressure and quite a few wines by the glass; piped music. There are picnic-sets in front and a sheltered cottagey garden at the back. More reports please.

🍴 **Well cooked and constantly changing, the good food includes goats cheese melt, venison pâté with onion and mustard chutney, mixed seafood salad, stuffed pigeon on mixed lentils, lamb, olive and artichoke stew, steak and kidney pudding, grilled tuna with an italian herb sauce, basil and tomato chicken and lamb shank.** *Starters/Snacks: £3.95 to £6.95. Main Courses: £9.95 to £18.95. Puddings: £4.25*

Greene King ~ Lease Brian Desborough ~ Real ale ~ Bar food (not Sun evening) ~ Restaurant ~ (01284) 789208 ~ Children welcome at lunchtime but must be over 10 in evening ~ Open 11-3, 6.30-11.30; 12-3, 7-11 Sun

Recommended by Helen and Christopher Roberts, Judi Bell, John and Bettye Reynolds

ROUGHAM   TL9063 MAP 5

Ravenwood Hall 🍴 ♟ 🛏

Just off A14 E of Bury St Edmunds; IP30 9JA

Welcoming and civilised all-day bar in comfortable country house hotel, peaceful A14 break; real ales, fine wines, imaginative food and good service; lovely grounds

This year, a Garden Room with a high ceiling, large fireplace and views over the swimming pool and grounds has been added to this civilised and peaceful country house hotel. The bedrooms in the main house have been refurbished, too. It's the thoroughly welcoming all-day bar, though, that earns it a place in this particular guidebook. Basically two fairly compact rooms, this has tall ceilings, gently patterned wallpaper, and heavily draped curtains for big windows overlooking a sweeping lawn with a stately cedar. The part by the back serving counter is set for food, its nice furnishings including well upholstered settles and dining chairs, sporting prints and a log fire. Adnams Bitter and Broadside on handpump, good wines by the glass, mulled wine around Christmas, and freshly squeezed orange juice; neat unobtrusive staff give good service. The other end of the bar has horse pictures, several sofas and armchairs with lots of plump cushions, one or two attractively moulded beams, and a good-sized fragment of early Tudor wall decoration above its big inglenook log fire; piped music and board games. They have a more formal quite separate restaurant. Outside, teak tables and chairs, some under a summer house, stand around a swimming pool, and out in the wooded grounds big enclosures by the car park hold geese and pygmy goats; croquet.

⍟ Interesting, attractively presented bar food might include soup, terrine of confit duck, foie gras, sauternes jelly and toasted brioche, super coquille st jacques, moules marinière, sausages with caramelised onions and rich gravy, beer-battered haddock, ham hock pot-roasted in cider with pink fir potatoes, butternut squash and celeriac roly-poly with white onion sauce, chicken wrapped in parma ham with sage stuffing and a rich jus, and puddings such as rich chocolate mocha tart with vanilla crème fraîche and cherry and almond clafoutis with a cinnamon cream. They smoke their own meats and fish, make their own preserves, and use as much local produce as possible. *Starters/Snacks: £5.50 to £7.50. Main Courses: £11.95 to £18.95. Puddings: £5.25 to £7.50*

Free house ~ Licensee Craig Jarvis ~ Real ale ~ Bar food (12-2.30, 7-9.30(10 Fri and Sat)) ~ Restaurant ~ (01359) 270345 ~ Children welcome ~ Dogs allowed in bar and bedrooms ~ Open 11-10.30 ~ Bedrooms: £97.50B/£135B

Recommended by Comus and Sarah Elliott, Alan Cole, Kirstie Bruce, J F M and M West, Derek Field

SNAPE   TM3958 MAP 5

Crown ⍟ ⚲
B1069; IP17 1SL

Busy pub – handy for the Maltings – with efficient, friendly staff, good food, a thoughtful wine list and attractive bar; bedrooms

Even when this well run pub is very busy, the hard-working staff remain friendly and efficient. The attractive bar is furnished with striking horseshoe-shaped high-backed settles around a big brick inglenook with a log fire, spindleback and country kitchen chairs, and nice old tables on some old brick flooring; an exposed panel shows how the ancient walls were constructed, and there are lots of beams in the various small side rooms. The wine list is thoughtful, with 15 wines by the glass (including champagne and pudding wine), and they've Adnams Bitter, Broadside and a seasonal ale on handpump. The bedrooms are up very steep stairs and the beams and sloping floors and doorways you may have to stoop under are not for everyone. Seats and tables in pretty roadside garden. No children.

⍟ Enjoyable bar food includes soup, goats cheese cheesecake, coarse pork and pigeon terrine, seared jumbo scallops, steak and kidney suet pudding, lamb tagine, salmon and horseradish fishcake, calves liver on creamy mash, griddled tuna on stir-fried noodles with soy and sesame dressing, and puddings such as sticky toffee pudding and chocolate soufflé torte with pistachio ice-cream. *Starters/Snacks: £4.25 to £8.95. Main Courses: £9.90 to £15.95. Puddings: £3.95 to £4.95*

Adnams ~ Tenant Diane Maylot ~ Real ale ~ Bar food (12-2.30, 7-9.30) ~ (01728) 688324 ~ Open 12-3, 6(7 Sun)-11; closed evening 26 Dec ~ Bedrooms: £70B/£80B

Recommended by Comus and Sarah Elliott, Vanessa Young, Steve Barnes, Ali Henderson, Simon Rodway, Pamela Goodwyn, John and Enid Morris, Edward Mirzoeff, W K Wood, Michael Dandy, Mike and Heather Watson, David Twitchett, W W Burke, Mrs Carolyn Dixon, Ryta Lyndley, Mr and Mrs L Haines, Roger and Lesley Everett, Ray J Carter, Peter and Pat Frogley, Rob and Catherine Dunster, Charles and Pauline Stride, MDN, George Atkinson, J F M and M West, Jim and Sheila Prideaux

---

If a service charge is mentioned prominently on a menu or accommodation terms, you must pay it if service was satisfactory. If service is really bad, you are legally entitled to refuse to pay some or all of the service charge as compensation for not getting the service you might reasonably have expected.

SOUTH ELMHAM   TM3385 MAP 5

St Peters Brewery
St Peter S Elmham; off B1062 SW of Bungay; NR35 1NQ

Lovely manor dating back to 13th century with genuinely old furnishings, own brew beers, decent food and friendly staff

This medieval manor is a lovely and rather special place with the added attraction that it brews its own beers. St Peter's Hall, to which the brewery is attached, itself dates back to the late 13th century but was much extended in 1539 using materials from the recently dissoved Flixton Priory. Genuinely old tapestries and furnishings make having a drink in the small main bar feel more like a trip to a historic home than a typical pub outing, but the atmosphere is relaxed and welcoming, with candles and fresh flowers on the dark wooden tables, and comfortable seats – from cushioned pews and settles to a 16th-c French bishop's throne. Their beers are made using water from a 100-metre (300-ft) bore hole, in brewery buildings laid out around a courtyard; gift shop, too. On handpump and served by warmly friendly staff, the three real ales might include St Peters Best Bitter, Organic Ale and Golden Ale and the others are available by bottle. There's a particularly dramatic high-ceilinged dining hall with elaborate woodwork, a big flagstoned floor and an imposing chandelier, as well as a couple of other appealing old rooms reached up some steepish stairs. Outside, tables overlook the original moat where there are friendly black swans.

🍴 **Under the new licensee, the bar food – which can take a while – includes filled baguettes, soup, chicken liver parfait with chutney, thai chilli crab cakes, pork and leek sausages on creamy whole grain mustard mash, ham and eggs, wild mushroom risotto, steak in ale pie, slow-braised lamb shank, daily specials, and puddings such as sticky toffee pudding with vanilla ice-cream and spiced apple crumble.** *Starters/Snacks: £4.95 to £5.95. Main Courses: £8.50 to £17.95. Puddings: £5.50 to £5.95*

Own brew ~ Licensee Nigel Hindle ~ Real ale ~ Bar food (12-2(4 Sun), 7-9) ~ Restaurant ~ (01986) 782288 ~ Children welcome ~ Dogs allowed in bar ~ Open 11-3, 6-11; 11-11 Sat; 12-10.30 Sun

Recommended by Mrs M Hatwell, Adele Summers, Alan Black, M and GR, Jonathan Brown, John Saville, Ian and Nita Cooper, Charles and Pauline Stride, Richard and Margaret McPhee, Peter and Pat Frogley, the Didler, Mike Gorton, Simon and Mandy King, Ken Millar, Marion and Bill Cross, Richard Pitcher

SOUTHWOLD   TM5076 MAP 5

Crown
High Street; IP18 6DP

Civilised and smart old hotel with relaxed bars, a fine choice of drinks, papers to read, interesting food and seats outside; bedrooms

Our readers are rather keen on the smaller back oak-panelled locals' bar in this smart old hotel as it has more of a traditional pubby atmosphere with red leatherette wall benches and a red carpet. The extended elegant beamed main bar has a relaxed atmosphere and a good mix of customers, a stripped curved high-backed settle and other dark varnished settles, kitchen chairs and some bar stools, pretty flowers on the tables and a carefully restored and rather fine carved wooden fireplace; maybe newspapers to read. Adnams Bitter, Broadside, Explorer and maybe Old Ale on handpump, a splendid wine list with a monthly changing choice of 20 interesting varieties by the glass or bottle, quite a few malt whiskies and local cider. The tables out in a sunny sheltered corner are very pleasant.

🍴 **Good bar food uses local, organic produce and might include sandwiches, nice soup, braised lamb sweetbreads with lentils and sherry, pheasant and wild duck terrine with beer chutney, cod and salmon fishcake with chive beurre blanc, onion, pumpkin, wild mushroom and parmesan tart topped with a free-range egg, herb-crusted gurnard with butter bean, chorizo and clam casserole and aïoli, braised lamb shank with pease pudding and root vegetables, roast partridge with colcannon and caramelised pears, daily specials, and puddings such as white and dark chocolate mousse with milk chocolate ice-cream and blackberry délice with apple sorbet.** *Starters/Snacks: £4.95 to £11.95. Main Courses: £11.95 to £19.95. Puddings: £5.00 to £6.50*

Adnams ~ Manager Francis Guildea ~ Real ale ~ Bar food (12-3, 5.30-9.30 in summer; 12-2, 6.30-9 in winter) ~ Restaurant ~ (01502) 722275 ~ Children in bars if with adult ~ Dogs allowed in bar ~ Open 11-11 ~ Bedrooms: £90B/£140B

Recommended by Rob and Catherine Dunster, Simon Rodway, Andrea Rampley, Comus and Sarah Elliott, Mike and Sue Loseby, Mike Gorton, Michael Dandy, Ray J Carter, Gerald and Gabrielle Culliford, MJVK, Tina and David Woods-Taylor, John and Elisabeth Cox, M and GR, John and Enid Morris, Tracey and Stephen Groves, David and Sue Atkinson, Robert and Susan Phillips, David Carr, Stephanie Sanders, W K Wood, Richard Pitcher

Harbour Inn 🍺

Blackshore, by the boats; from A1095, turn right at the Kings Head, and keep on past the golf course and water tower; IP18 6TA

Bustling waterside pub with lots of outside seats, interesting nautical décor, plenty of fish, and real ales

It's a good idea to get to this busy pub early so you can bag one of the seats in front of the building and watch all the activity on the Blyth Estuary quay; there are also lots of tables and a little terrace with fine views across the marshy fields towards the town and lighthouse. As the friendly licensee is a lifeboatman, the nautical character here is pretty genuine. The back bar has a wind speed indicator, model ships, a lot of local ship and boat photographs, smoked dried fish hanging from a line on a beam, a lifeboat line launcher and brass shellcases on the mantelpiece over a stove; also, rustic stools and cushioned wooden benches built into its stripped panelling. The tiny, low-beamed, tiled and panelled front bar has antique settles and there's a dining extension with a raised deck in front of it. Adnams Bitter, Broadside and Explorer on handpump and several wines by the glass; piped music. Look out for the 1953 flood level marked on the outside of the pub.

🍽 **Popular bar food includes filled baguettes, soup, moules marinière, cod and salmon fishcakes with dill mayonnaise, roasted cherry tomato, spinach and brie tart, chicken caesar salad with crispy smoked bacon, beer-battered cod, haddock and plaice (served wrapped in paper on Friday evenings), daily specials, and puddings such as cherry crumble and chocolate and hazelnut brownie.** *Starters/Snacks: £4.25 to £5.75. Main Courses: £8.95 to £11.95. Puddings: £4.65 to £4.95*

Adnams ~ Tenant Colin Fraser ~ Real ale ~ Bar food (12-2.30, 6-9) ~ Restaurant ~ (01502) 722381 ~ Children in bottom bar and restaurant ~ Dogs allowed in bar ~ Open 11-11; 11-10.30 Sun

Recommended by Mike Gorton, Pete Baker, Fiona McElhone, John and Jackie Walsh, the Didler, Philip and Susan Philcox, Mike and Sue Loseby, Michael Dandy, Peter and Pat Frogley, Eddie and Lynn Jarrett, Andrea Rampley, Richard Pitcher, Steve Whalley

Lord Nelson 🍺

East Street, off High Street (A1095); IP18 6EJ

Smashing town pub with lots of locals and visitors, cheerful and chatty, excellent service, home-made pubby food and good choice of drinks; seats outside

Mr Illston's daughter and new husband are now helping with the running of this smashing town pub. It's a chatty, friendly and lively place with lots of locals and visitors coming and going – but even when really busy, the good-natured service remains quick and attentive. The partly panelled bar and its two small side rooms are kept spotless, with good lighting, a small but extremely hot coal fire, light wood furniture on the tiled floor, lamps in nice nooks and corners and some interesting Nelson memorabilia, including attractive nautical prints and a fine model of HMS *Victory*. Adnams Bitter, Broadside, Explorer and maybe Oyster Stout on handpump and good wines (and champagne) by the glass. Daily papers but no piped music or games machines. There are nice seats out in front with a sidelong view down to the sea and more in a sheltered (and heated) back garden, with the brewery in sight (and often the appetising fragrance of brewing in progress). The seafront is just moments away. Disabled access is not perfect but is possible, and they help.

🍴 Tasty home-made bar food includes sandwiches, ploughman's, soup, cornish pasty, cheese and bacon quiche, chicken curry, lots of salads, cod in beer batter, ham and chips, a couple of daily specials, and generous puddings such as sticky toffee pudding. *Starters/Snacks: £2.75 to £5.95. Main Courses: £6.50 to £11.50. Puddings: £3.50*

Adnams ~ Tenant John Illston ~ Real ale ~ Bar food ~ No credit cards ~ (01502) 722079 ~ Children in areas to side of bar until 9pm ~ Dogs welcome ~ Open 10.30am-11pm; 12-10.30 Sun

Recommended by the Didler, N R White, Pete Baker, Comus and Sarah Elliott, Andrea Rampley, Mike and Sue Loseby, Derek Field, David Carr, Charles and Pauline Stride, Michael Dandy, Blaise Vyner, Mike Gorton, Keith and Janet Morris, Richard Pitcher, Jeff Davies, Alan and Eve Harding

STOKE-BY-NAYLAND   TL9836 MAP 5

Angel ♀

B1068 Sudbury—East Bergholt; also signposted via Nayland off A134 Colchester—Sudbury; CO6 4SA

Elegant, comfortable inn with attractive bars, modern cooking, decent choice of drinks and neat uniformed staff; bedrooms

A new licensee has taken over this elegant inn but doesn't plan any big changes. The comfortable main bar area has handsome Elizabethan beams, some stripped brickwork and timbers, a mixture of furnishings including wooden bar stools, leather sofas, wing armchairs and a mix of dining chairs, local watercolours, modern paintings and older prints and a huge log fire. Round the corner is a little tiled-floor stand-and-chat bar. Neatly uniformed staff serve Adnams Bitter and Broadside and Greene King IPA on handpump and several wines by the glass. Another room has a low sofa and wing armchairs around its woodburning stove and mustard-coloured walls and the restaurant has a 52ft well. There are seats and tables on a sheltered terrace.

🍴 Appetising bar food now includes sandwiches, soup, smoked duck, wild mushroom and baby leek terrine with truffle dressing, polenta and mediterranean vegetable tower with tomato and basil sauce, steak and kidney pie, pork satay with peanut sauce and coconut rice, lemon, thyme and honey poussin, salt and pepper calamari with chilli dip, griddled liver and bacon on bubble and squeak mash with a rich madeira sauce and roast rack of lamb with herb crust and a garlic and rosemary sauce. *Starters/Snacks: £3.50 to £7.25. Main Courses: £7.75 to £19.95. Puddings: £4.25 to £5.50*

Horizon Inns ~ Manager Ron Straalen ~ Real ale ~ Bar food (12-2, 6-9.30; all day Sun) ~ Restaurant ~ (01206) 263245 ~ Children in lounge and restaurant ~ Dogs allowed in bar ~ Open 11-11(10.30 Sun) ~ Bedrooms: £70B/£85B

Recommended by David Twitchett, MDN, W K Wood, N R White, M and GR, Norman Fox, Michael Hasslacher, Mrs P Lang, Pamela Goodwyn

Crown ★ ♀

Park Street (B1068); CO6 4SE

Smart dining pub with attractive modern furnishings, bistro-style food, fantastic wine choice and new bedrooms

Most of this smart dining pub is open to the three-sided bar servery, yet it's well divided, and with two or three more tucked-away areas too. The main part, with a big woodburning stove, has quite a lot of fairly closely spaced tables in a variety of shapes, styles and sizes; elsewhere, several smaller areas have just three or four tables each. Seating varies from deep armchairs and sofas to elegant dining chairs and comfortable high-backed woven rush seats – and there are plenty of bar stools. This all gives a good choice between conviviality and varying degrees of cosiness and privacy. There are cheerful wildlife and landscape paintings on the pale walls, quite a lot of attractive table lamps, low ceilings (some with a good deal of stripped old beams), and floors varying from old tiles through broad boards or dark new flagstones to beige carpet; daily papers. Adnams Bitter, Greene King IPA and a couple of guest beers on handpump and a fantastic choice of 28 wines by the glass from a list of around 200 kept in an unusual glass-walled wine 'cellar' in one corner. A sheltered (and heated) back terrace, with cushioned teak chairs and tables under big canvas parasols, looks out over a neat lawn to a landscaped shrubbery that includes a small romantic ruined-abbey folly. There are many more picnic-sets out on the front terrace. Disabled access is good and the car park is big; more reports please.

⑪ Imaginative modern food includes soup, smoked eel, potato pancakes, rocket and horseradish crème fraîche, rabbit and prune terrine with spiced apple chutney, linguini with wild mushrooms, spring greens, lemon and parmesan, sausages with onion gravy and mash, seville orange braised beef with roast shallots and dauphinoise potatoes, grilled cornish mackerel fillets with french beans, rocket and a soft boiled egg, lamb rump with butter beans, caramelised red onions, chorizo and minted aïoli, and puddings such as plum crumble or chocolate truffle brioche with clotted cream. *Starters/Snacks: £4.25 to £7.95. Main Courses: £8.95 to £17.50. Puddings: £4.25 to £5.95*

Free house ~ Licensee Richard Sunderland ~ Real ale ~ Bar food (12-2.30, 6-9.30 (10 Fri, Sat); 12-9 Sun) ~ (01206) 262001 ~ Children allowed away from bar ~ Dogs allowed in bar ~ Open 11-11; 12-10.30 Sun; closed 25 and 26 Dec ~ Bedrooms: £80B/£100B

Recommended by Derek Thomas, MDN, J F M and M West, Pamela Goodwyn, Ken Millar, Will Watson, David Twitchett, N R White, Mrs P Lang, Marion and Bill Cross

SWILLAND   TM1852 MAP 5

Moon & Mushroom ♀ ◖

Village signposted off B1078 Needham Market—Wickham Market, and off B1077; IP6 9LR

Half a dozen real ales and tasty food in friendly pub with homely interior; seats on terraces

On a warm summer day with its archway of grapevines and roses, terraces with awnings and lots of flowers, this has the feel of a continental tarverna. But inside there's a homely, pubby feel with quarry tiles, log fires, old tables and other antique furniture and a fine choice of at least six real ales tapped from casks racked up behind the long counter: Crouch Vale Brewers Gold, Nethergate Umbel Ale, Wolf Bitter and Golden Jackal, and Woodfordes Norfolk Nog and Wherry. Quite a few wines by the glass.

⑪ Bar food includes ploughman's, soup, mackerel pâté, vegetable lasagne, beef in ale with dumplings, wild rabbit pie, pigeon and black pudding casserole, mexican chicken, pork in cider, and puddings such as bread and butter pudding or crème brûlée; they also offer two- and three-course lunches. *Starters/Snacks: £3.95 to £4.25. Main Courses: £8.95 to £9.95. Puddings: £4.25*

Free house ~ Licensees Nikki Gavin and Martin Burgess ~ Real ale ~ Bar food (12-2.30, 7-8.30; not Mon) ~ Restaurant ~ (01473) 785320 ~ Children allowed with some restrictions ~ Dogs allowed in bar ~ Folk music every other Sun in summer ~ Open 11.30-2.30, 6-11; 12-3, 7-10.30 Sun; closed Mon lunchtime

Recommended by Jonathan Brown, Charles and Pauline Stride, the Didler, Pam and David Bailey, Peter Comeau, Adele Summers, Alan Black, Mrs Carolyn Dixon, N R White, Ian and Nita Cooper

TUDDENHAM   TM1948 MAP 5

Fountain ♀

Village signposted off B1077 N of Ipswich; The Street; IP6 9BT

17th-c village pub recently renovated as a dining pub with light wooden furnishings and original beams and timbering and well thought-of contemporary cooking; plenty of outside seating

In a pretty village on the outskirts of Ipswich, this is a recently renovated 17th-c dining pub. There is a nod to drinkers (who do still pop in) with space in the bar and Adnams Bitter on handpump, but there's no doubt that most emphasis is on the modern cooking. The several linked café-style rooms have original heavy beams and timbering, stripped wooden floors, a mix of wooden dining chairs around a medley of light wood tables, an open fire and a few prints (including some Giles ones) on the white walls – but décor is minimal. Several wines by the glass and piped music. Outside on the covered and heated terrace are wicker and metal chairs and wooden tables and lots of picnic-sets on a sizeable lawn.

🍽 As well as a two- and three-course set menu, the contemporary food might include filled baguettes, sunblush tomato, basil and pine nut pâté, sweet pickled herring and beetroot salad, duck samosas with pepper, pineapple and coriander salsa, hot scottish smoked salmon niçoise salad, confit duck with cherry and red wine sauce, roast vegetable lasagne, grilled organic salmon with brown shrimps and lemon butter sauce, thai green chicken curry, mediterranean lamb sausages with onion and red wine gravy, and puddings like Baileys crème brûlée and chocolate brownie with Grand Marnier and toffee sauce. *Starters/Snacks: £4.60 to £5.50. Main Courses: £7.90 to £13.90. Puddings: £4.25*

Punch ~ Lease Charles Lewis and Scott Davidson ~ Real ale ~ Bar food (12-2(3 Sun), 6-9(9.30 Sat); not Sun evening) ~ Restaurant ~ (01473) 785377 ~ Children welcome ~ Open 12-3, 6-12; closed Sun evening

Recommended by Mrs Hilarie Taylor, Tom Gondris, J F M and M West, Pamela Goodwyn

WALBERSWICK
TM4974 MAP 5

Anchor 🍽 ♟ 🍺
Village signposted off A12; The Street (B1387); IP18 6UA

Good mix of locals and visitors in well run, attractively furnished inn, fine range of drinks, appetising modern cooking and good service; bedrooms

A new flagstoned terrace has been added to this well run pub, and on summer weekends it often has a fruits de mer stand and perhaps a fish barbecue. Inside, there's a genuine mix of both locals and visitors and the big-windowed comfortable front bar has heavy stripped tables on its dark blue carpet, sturdy built-in wall seats cushioned in green leather and nicely framed black and white photographs of local fishermen and their boats on the varnished plank panelling. Log fires in the chimneybreast divide this room into two snug halves. They have loads of bottled beers from all over the world, 23 interesting wines by the glass including champagne and a pudding one, Adnams Bitter, Broadside and winter Tally Ho on handpump and good coffee; particularly good service, daily papers, darts and board games. They held their first mini beer festival in August. Quite an extensive dining area stretching back from a more modern-feeling small lounge on the left is furnished much like the bar – though perhaps a bit more minimalist – and looks out on a good-sized sheltered and nicely planted garden. The pub is right by the coast path, and there's a pleasant walk across to Southwold – in season you can also cross by a pedestrian ferry.

🍽 From a well chosen menu, the carefully cooked food (with a beer or wine to match each dish) might include soup, smoked duck breast with warm, spiced puy lentils, twice-baked soufflé with caramelised onions, seared scallops with jerusalem artichoke purée and bacon, bubble and squeak with free-range poached eggs and a mushroom and stilton sauce, beer-battered local cod with jalapeno tartare sauce, slow-braised lamb shoulder on a pearl barley risotto, oxtail braised in ale with horseradish mash, and puddings such as hot chocolate pudding with ice-cream and vanilla and rosemary panna cotta with raspberry coulis. *Starters/Snacks: £4.95 to £7.75. Main Courses: £9.00 to £14.50. Puddings: £3.50 to £4.95*

Adnams ~ Lease Mark and Sophie Dorber ~ Real ale ~ Bar food (12-3, 6-9; all day Sat and Sun during half term and school hols) ~ Restaurant ~ (01502) 722112 ~ Children in dining room and family room ~ Dogs allowed in bar ~ Open 11-11; 11-4, 6-11 in winter ~ Bedrooms: £75B/£90B

Recommended by Comus and Sarah Elliott, Charles and Pauline Stride, Evelyn and Derek Walter, Roger and Pauline Pearce, Dr and Mrs M E Wilson, Tracey and Stephen Groves, Richard Pitcher, W K Wood, Roger and Lesley Everett, Mike and Sue Loseby, Jim and Sheila Prideaux, Maurice Ricketts, Bob and Margaret Holder, Michael and Ann Cole, J F M and M West

Bell ♀ 🛏

Just off B1387; IP18 6TN

Busy well run inn close to beach (bedrooms overlook sea or river) with nice original features, fine choice of drinks and well liked food

A couple of readers were surprised to find that even on a blustery mid-winter Monday this efficiently run pub was extremely busy; there are often queues at peak times. The bars have brick floors, well worn uneven flagstones and wonky steps and oak beams that were here 400 years ago when the sleepy little village was a flourishing port. The rambling traditional main bar has curved high-backed settles, tankards hanging from oars above the counter and a woodburning stove in the big fireplace; a second bar has a very large open fire. Adnams Bitter, Broadside, Explorer and a seasonal ale on handpump, 20 wines by the glass, local cider, mulled wine and hot spiced ginger in winter and several malt whiskies; darts and board games. The landlady's daughter runs a ceramics business from a shed in the garden. This is a great setting close to the beach (most of the well appointed bedrooms look over the sea or river) and tables on the sizeable lawn are sheltered from the worst of the winds by a well placed hedge; boules.

🍴 **Popular bar food includes lunchtime sandwiches, soup, potted shrimps, smokies in creamy cheese sauce, spicy chilli with rice and sour cream, cumberland sausage with free-range egg, blue cheese, red onion and mushroom tartlets, beer-battered haddock, cajun chicken, confit of duck leg with red onion marmalade, daily specials, and puddings such as steamed syrup pudding or pecan pie.** *Starters/Snacks: £3.95 to £7.50. Main Courses: £7.50 to £13.95. Puddings: £3.50 to £4.50*

Adnams ~ Tenant Sue Ireland Cutting ~ Real ale ~ Bar food ~ Restaurant ~ (01502) 723109 ~ Children welcome except in one bar ~ Dogs allowed in bar and bedrooms ~ Open 11-3, 6-11; all day during school summer hols; 11am-midnight(10.30 Sun) Sat; 12-10.30 Sun ~ Bedrooms: £70S/£90S(£100B)

Recommended by Charles and Pauline Stride, John and Enid Morris, Michael Dandy, Simon Rodway, the Didler, Stephanie Sanders, Mike and Sue Loseby, Blaise Vyner, Comus and Sarah Elliott, Evelyn and Derek Walter, John Saul, Ryta Lyndley, E Rankin, Bob and Margaret Holder

WALDRINGFIELD   TM2844 MAP 5

Maybush

Off A12 S of Martlesham; The Quay, Cliff Road; IP12 4QL

Busy pub in lovely riverside position with plenty of tables making the most of the view, lots of room inside, nautical décor and fair choice of drinks and bar food

To be sure of bagging a table on the heated verandah in front of this busy family pub overlooking the River Deben, you must get here pretty promptly. Inside, the spacious bar has quite a nautical theme with lots of old lanterns, pistols and so forth, as well as aerial photographs, an original Twister board and fresh flowers. Alhough it's all been knocked through, it's divided into separate areas by fireplaces or steps; piped music. A glass case has an elaborate ship's model and there are a few more in a lighter, high-ceilinged extension. Adnams Bitter and Broadside and Greene King IPA on handpump and a fair choice of wines by the glass. There are river cruises available nearby but you have to pre-book them.

🍴 **Well liked, straightforward bar food includes sandwiches, soup, deep-fried garlic mushrooms with mayonnaise dip, breaded brie wedges with plum sauce, burgers, cumberland sausage and mash with onion gravy, vegetable lasagne, steak and kidney pudding, chicken dijon, and daily specials.** *Starters/Snacks: £3.95 to £5.45. Main Courses: £7.95 to £15.95. Puddings: £3.45 to £4.75*

Punch ~ Lease Steve and Louise Lomas ~ Real ale ~ Bar food (all day) ~ (01473) 736215 ~ Children welcome ~ Dogs allowed in bar ~ Open 11-11

Recommended by Michael Clatworthy, Peter Meister, David Carr, Mrs A J Robertson, Mrs Romey Heaton, J F M and M West, Pamela Goodwyn

WESTLETON

TM4469 MAP 5

Crown ⓦ ♟ 🍺 🛏️

B1125 Blythburgh—Leiston; IP17 3AD

SUFFOLK DINING PUB OF THE YEAR

Lovely old coaching inn with stylish, refurbished bedrooms, cosy chatty bar, plenty of dining areas, carefully chosen drinks and delicious food

This carefully refurbished old coaching inn is a particularly enjoyable place to stay with stylish, cosseting bedrooms and good breakfasts – and there's plenty to do nearby. The bar area is really cosy and attractive with a lovely log fire, plenty of original features, Adnams Bitter and guests from local breweries such as Blackfriars, Green Jack, Earl Soham and St Peter's Brewery on handpump, local cider, around a dozen wines including champagne and sweet wine by the glass from a thoughtfully chosen list, and quite a few malt whiskies; attentive, helpful and friendly service, piped music, board games, dominoes and cribbage. There's also a parlour, dining room and a conservatory. The charming terraced gardens have plenty of seats.

🍽 **Extremely good bar food – they make their own bread, chutneys and ice-creams – includes nice sandwiches, soup, a plate of tapas, crab and sweetcorn spring rolls with citrus salsa, terrine of pork tenderloin and confit rabbit leg with cherry tomato relish, beef and mushroom steamed suet pudding, creamy butternut squash and caramelised baby onion risotto, seared salmon with an olive tapenade and herb crust and warm sorrel and potato salad, chicken breast with bashed neeps, fried ceps and a madeira sauce, gressingham duck with plum tart and rich kirsch jus, daily specials, and puddings such as caramelised vanilla crème brûlée with rhubarb compote, and chocolate bread and butter pudding with stem ginger ice-cream; there's also a seafood salad menu.** *Starters/Snacks: £3.95 to £8.50. Main Courses: £9.50 to £22.00. Puddings: £4.50 to £5.50*

Free house ~ Licensee Matthew Goodwin ~ Real ale ~ Bar food (12-2.30, 7-9.30) ~ Restaurant ~ (01728) 648777 ~ Children welcome ~ Dogs allowed in bar and bedrooms ~ Occasional live piano ~ Open 11-11; closed 25 Dec ~ Bedrooms: £85S/£110B

Recommended by Tracey and Stephen Groves, Comus and Sarah Elliott, Giles and Annie Francis, Michael and Ann Cole

LUCKY DIP

Besides the fully inspected pubs, you might like to try these Lucky Dips recommended to us and described by readers (if you do, please send us reports: www.goodguides.co.uk).

ALDEBURGH [TM4656]
☆ *Cross Keys* IP15 5BN [Crabbe St]: Well worn-in 16th-c pub extended from low-beamed core with antique settles, Victorian prints, woodburners, Adnams ales (the full range), good wines by the glass, friendly and obliging landlord and staff, simple food (out of season may be only wknds) inc fresh fish, Sunday papers; can be crowded, games machine; open all day July/Aug, children in eating areas, picnic-sets in sheltered back yard by promenade – one of very few Suffolk places where you can eat outside by the beach; elegant bedrooms *(Ryta Lyndley, Comus and Sarah Elliott, LYM, Simon Cottrell, MDN, Michael Dandy)*
Mill IP15 5BJ [Market Cross Pl, opp Moot Hall]: Friendly 1920s seaside pub with cheerful chatty licensees and regulars, good value fresh food (not Sun evening) from sandwiches and baguettes to very local fish and crabs, hard-working staff, well kept Adnams ales, decent coffee, three smallish rooms inc back dining room, RNLI and

military memorabilia, cushioned wall seats and padded stools, cosy beamed dining room with *Gypsy Queen* model, cream teas July/Aug; games machine; dogs welcome, bedrooms, open all day *(Peter and Pat Frogley, Edward Mirzoeff, the Didler, Terry Buckland, Steve Whalley, Michael Dandy)*
Wentworth IP15 5BB [Wentworth Rd]: Old-fashioned hotel not pub, useful for good value bar lunches in a choice of welcoming areas, well kept Adnams and a good choice of wines by the glass, pleasant long-serving staff; conservatory, colourful seafront flagstoned terrace and new suntrap sunken garden, bedrooms *(Terry Mizen, Mr and Mrs T B Staples, Simon Rodway, Steve Whalley, Pamela Goodwyn)*
ALDRINGHAM [TM4461]
Parrot & Punchbowl IP16 4PY [B1122/B1353 S of Leiston]: Attractive beamed pub under new licensees, good fairly priced food inc local fish, good wine choice, well kept Adnams and Greene King IPA, decent coffee, two-level restaurant; children

welcome; nice sheltered garden, also family garden with adventure play area *(BB, Simon Rodway)*

BARHAM [TM1251]

☆ *Sorrel Horse* IP6 0PG [Old Norwich Rd]: Thriving open-plan country local with good log fire in central chimneybreast, black beams and timbers, Adnams, Shepherd Neame Spitfire and Theakstons Best, friendly helpful landlord and staff, ample wholesome home cooking, two dining areas off; piped local radio; well behaved children allowed, picnic-sets on side grass with big play area, eight comfortable bedrooms in converted barn, open all day Weds-Sun *(David Miles-Dinham, J F M and M West, BB, David Eberlin)*

BARNBY [TM4789]

Swan NR34 7QF [off A146 Beccles—Lowestoft; Swan Lane]: Plush beamed dining pub with Lowestoft connections giving excellent choice of good fresh fish, good welcoming service, Adnams ales and good house wines, pleasant good-sized dining room, fishing décor *(Martin and Pauline Jennings)*

BEYTON [TL9363]

White Horse IP30 9AB [signed off A14 and A1088; Bury Rd]: Village-green pub very popular with older lunchers, helpful landlady and staff, substantial home-made pubby food, well kept Greene King IPA, decent wines by the glass, no music *(J F M and M West)*

BILDESTON [TL9949]

☆ *Crown* IP7 7EB [B1115 SW of Stowmarket]: Picturesque and impressively refurbished 15th-c timbered country inn, smart beamed main bar with inglenook log fire, good if not cheap upmarket food, Adnams ales, good choice of wines by the glass, kind relaxed service, dining room; children welcome, nice tables out in courtyard, more in large attractive garden, quiet comfortable bedrooms *(LYM, MDN, Hunter and Christine Wright, Pamela Goodwyn)*

BLYTHBURGH [TM4575]

☆ *White Hart* IP19 9LQ [A12]: Open-plan family dining pub with fine ancient beams, woodwork and staircase, full Adnams ale range and good range of wines in two glass sizes, good coffee, friendly efficient service, sensibly priced blackboard food; children in eating areas, spacious lawns looking down on tidal marshes (barbecues), magnificent church over road, bedrooms, open all day *(B J Harding, Comus and Sarah Elliott, LYM)*

BOXFORD [TL9640]

White Hart CO10 5DX [Broad St]: Newly reopened under new management after costly refurbishment as upscale dining pub, priced to match (pushing towards £3 for a shandy), enjoyable enterprising food, Greene King ales *(PL)*

BRANTHAM [TM1234]

Bull CO11 1PN [E, junction A137/B1080]: Recently refurbished country pub with cheerful new big-windowed restaurant

extension, views to Stour Estuary; children welcome, good-sized garden with terrace picnic-sets and play area *(Pamela Goodwyn)*

BRENT ELEIGH [TL9348]

☆ *Cock* CO10 9PB [A1141 SE of Lavenham]: Relaxed and unspoilt thatched country local with piano in clean and cosy snug, benches, table and darts in second small room, antique flooring tiles, lovely coal fire, ochre walls with old photographs of local villages (the village church is well worth a look), Adnams and Greene King IPA and Abbot, organic farm cider, no food beyond crisps and pickled eggs; picnic-sets up on side grass with summer hatch service, attractive inn-sign, bedrooms *(the Didler, BB, Giles and Annie Francis)*

BROMESWELL [TM3050]

☆ *Cherry Tree* IP12 2PU [Orford Rd, Bromeswell Heath]: Neat beamed pub with rambling dining area and central bar, good choice of enjoyable wide-ranging food, pleasant service, Adnams, open fire; tables outside, big adventure playground, charming inn-sign *(Lew and Dot Hood, BB, C and R Bromage)*

BUNGAY [TM3389]

Castles NR35 1AF [Earsham St]: Dining pub with good reasonably priced choice in black-beamed front restaurant area, open fire and welcoming informal atmosphere, Greene King IPA, friendly efficient staff, small pubby back bar with french windows to pretty garden; four comfortable bedrooms *(KC, Julia Mann)*

Chequers NR35 1HD [Bridge St]: Old low-ceilinged two-room local in pretty street nr river, friendly staff, bargain simple lunchtime food from toasties and baguettes up, well kept Adnams, Fullers and interesting guest beers; piped music *(Ron and Val Broom)*

BURES [TL9033]

Eight Bells CO8 5AE [Colchester Rd]: Pleasant old-fashioned local with good value lunchtime food in attractive simple bar, several real ales inc a guest *(Marianne and Peter Stevens)*

BURY ST EDMUNDS [TL8564]

Angel IP33 1LT [Angel Hill]: Thriving long-established country-town hotel with good food from bar snacks to beautifully presented meals in elegant Regency restaurant and terrace rooms, helpful friendly service, Adnams in rather plush bar, cellar grill room; comfortable bedrooms *(David Carr, John Wooll)*

Dog & Partridge IP33 1QU [Crown St]: Rambling town pub with lots of plain wood in several areas – old, very old and new linked together; Greene King from nearby brewery, decent usual food, pleasant efficient service, lively young evening/wknd atmosphere *(John Wooll)*

Flying Fortress IP31 2QU [Mount Rd, Gt Barton (out towards Thurston, parallel to A143)]: Much enlarged former HQ of USAF support group, on edge of housing estate now covering Rougham ex-airfield – the original for the classic war film *Twelve o'Clock High*, with World War II bomber models and evocative black and white pictures; comfortable modern lounge area, well kept Adnams and Greene King IPA from long bar, quick friendly service, good value food inc warm baguettes from carvery (big echoic restaurant area); tables outside, old fire-engine for children to play on (J F M and M West)

☆ *Fox* IP33 1XX [Eastgate St]: Tidily kept ancient beamed pub with informal atmosphere, sensibly short choice of enjoyable and imaginative food using fresh local supplies, well kept beers, good wines, staff welcoming even at busy Sat lunchtime (Stuart and Alison Ballantyne, Alan Cole, Kirstie Bruce, M and GR, Paul J Davies)

☆ *Rose & Crown* IP33 1NP [Whiting St]: Unassuming black-beamed town local with affable helpful landlord, bargain simple lunchtime home cooking (not Sun), particularly well kept Greene King ales inc Mild and a guest beer such as St Austell, pleasant lounge with lots of piggy pictures and bric-a-brac, good games-oriented public bar with darts, cards and dominoes, rare separate off-sales counter; nice little back courtyard, open all day wkdys (Pete Baker, Julia Mann, Tony and Jill Radnor, Ryta Lyndley)

CAMPSEA ASHE [TM3356]
Dog & Duck IP13 0PT [Station Rd]: Attractive family-friendly pub, good range of enjoyable food, welcoming helpful licensees and staff, Adnams and Woodfordes Wherry tapped from the cask, pleasant dining room; tables out in front, nice garden with good play area, five bedrooms with own bathrooms (Simon Cottrell, C and R Bromage, Pamela Goodwyn, J F M and M West)

CAPEL ST MARY [TM0938]
White Horse IP9 2JR [London Rd (A12)]: Useful stop for popular food inc carvery, real ale, friendly welcome (S Cook)

CAVENDISH [TL8046]
☆ *Bull* CO10 8AX [A1092 Long Melford—Clare]: New licensees as we went to press, who we hope will keep up its fine recent record for good sensibly priced food, welcoming service, well kept Adnams ales and good value wines by the glass and coffees; heavy beams and timbers, fine fireplaces; children in eating areas, tables in garden, summer barbecues, car park (useful in this honeypot village) (Marianne and Peter Stevens, Paul Humphreys, LYM, PL, Marion and Bill Cross)

CHELSWORTH [TL9848]
☆ *Peacock* IP7 7HU [B1115 Sudbury—Needham Mkt]: Attractive and prettily set old dining pub with good food, friendly helpful service, well spaced comfortable tables, lots of Tudor brickwork and exposed beams, well kept Greene King Old Speckled Hen and Woodfordes Wherry in immaculately kept separate pubby bar with big inglenook log fire; nice small garden, pretty village (Ian Wilson, Margaret McPhee, LYM, MDN, Pamela Goodwyn)

CHILLESFORD [TM3852]
☆ *Froize* IP12 3PU [B1084 E of Woodbridge]: Restaurant rather than pub (open only when they serve food, ie not Mon, nor Sun-Weds evenings), particularly good cooking in pleasantly decorated bar and restaurant, warmly welcoming service, good value two-course buffet-style or carvery lunch, wide choice of more elaborate evening meals, local fish, pork, game and venison, original puddings, Adnams, good wines by the glass; may be cl Feb for hols (Simon Rodway, LYM, C and R Bromage, Mr and Mrs A Curry, Gordon Neighbour)

CLARE [TL7645]
Bell CO10 8NN [Market Hill]: Large timbered inn with comfortably rambling beamed lounge, splendidly carved black beams, old panelling and woodwork, Greene King ales and decent wines, food from sandwiches up, dining room with feature fireplace, conservatory opening on to terrace, darts and pool in public bar; games machine and TV, service may deteriorate when busy; nice bedrooms off back courtyard (special village, lovely church), open all day Sun (Michael Dandy, LYM, Dave Braisted)

☆ *Swan* CO10 8NY [High St]: Busy village local with good value food from sandwiches and baked potatoes up, friendly service, Greene King ales, good choice of wines by the glass, lots of copper and brass and huge log fire in main room, public bar with World War II memorabilia (dogs allowed here), dining room; big-screen sports TV; good tables on back terrace among lovely flower tubs (Michael Dandy, BB, Tony and Jill Radnor)

DEBENHAM [TM1763]
Angel IP14 6QL [High St]: Friendly obliging staff, enjoyable food in bar and dining room with pine tables on tiled floor, plenty of local produce, good choice for Sun carvery, real ales inc Earl Soham, farm cider; picnic-sets in small tidy garden, three comfortable bedrooms (Adele Summers, Alan Black)

DUNWICH [TM4770]
☆ *Ship* IP17 3DT [St James St]: Handy halt in charming seaside village (coastal erosion has submerged most of it), woodburner and lots of sea prints and nauticalia in traditional tiled bar, Adnams Bitter and Broadside and a Mauldons ale from antique handpumps, popular fish and chips, evening restaurant, simple conservatory; children and dogs welcome, large pleasant garden, bedrooms, open all day (Edward Mirzoeff, LYM, Giles and Annie Francis, Dave Braisted, Evelyn and Derek Walter, Tracey and Stephen Groves, Tina and David Woods-Taylor, Julia Mann, Mike and Sue Loseby, Roy Hoing, Simon Cottrell, Simon Rodway, Michael and Ann Cole)

EAST BERGHOLT [TM0734]
☆ *Kings Head* CO7 6TL [Burnt Oak, towards Flatford Mill]: Attractively extended, good value food inc unusual dishes, Greene King and guest ales, decent wines and coffee, friendly staff and atmosphere, well kept

beamed lounge with comfortable sofas, interesting decorations; piped classical music; lots of room in pretty garden, flower-decked haywain, baskets and tubs of flowers in front *(Mrs Carolyn Dixon, Mike and Mary Carter, Edward Leetham)*

EASTBRIDGE [TM4566]

☆ *Eels Foot* IP16 4SN [off B1122 N of Leiston]: Cheerful beamed country local, friendly helpful landlord, well kept Adnams ales, good local cider, light modern furnishings, wide choice of food from good value hot-filled rolls to fresh fish, obliging service, log fire, darts in side area, neat back dining room; famously long-running sing-song Thurs; walkers, children and dogs welcome, attractive garden with picnic-sets and swings, pretty village handy for Minsmere bird reserve (nice 2½-mile walk from sluice), particularly good new bedrooms, open all day in summer *(Charles and Pauline Stride, LYM, Simon Rodway, S P Watkin, P A Taylor, John Beeken, Joan York, Julia Mann, A G Marx)*

EASTON [TM2858]

White Horse IP13 0ED [N of Wickham Market on back rd to Earl Soham and Framlingham]: Neatly kept pink-washed two-bar country pub, bigger than it looks, with wide choice of popular food in bar and dining room, Adnams, welcoming staff, open fires; children in eating area, nice garden *(Gordon Neighbour, LYM, Pamela Goodwyn)*

EDWARDSTONE [TL9542]

White Horse CO10 5PX [Mill Green]: Under new management and now something of an eco-pub (wind turbine out behind), up to half a dozen well kept changing ales inc a Mild (dark beer festivals every few months), strong local farm cider, hearty food (not Mon), rustic décor; nice big garden, camp site, has been cl lunchtimes on Mon, Tues and Thurs *(Giles and Annie Francis)*

EYKE [TM3151]

Elephant & Castle IP12 2QG [The Street]: Well kept Adnams and Fullers London Pride from central bar with public area and games room one side, small simple dining area the other, enjoyable food, friendly service; bedrooms *(C and R Bromage)*

FELIXSTOWE FERRY [TM3237]

☆ *Ferry Boat* IP11 9RZ: Relaxed and cottagey extended and much modernised 17th-c family pub tucked between golf links and dunes nr harbour, Martello tower and summer rowing-boat ferry, good value food from snacks to fresh fish, Adnams Best and Greene King IPA and Old Speckled Hen, welcoming helpful service, good log fire; piped music; dogs welcome, tables out in front, on green opposite, and in securely fenced garden, busy summer wknds, good coast walks *(Peter Meister, Comus and Sarah Elliott, LYM, Charles and Pauline Stride)*

☆ *Victoria* IP11 9RZ: Child-friendly riverside pub, good value generous no-nonsense food inc local fish, cheerful efficient staff, Adnams and Greene King ales, tempting

liqueur coffees, good log fire in snug, sea views from upstairs dining area *(Mike and Mary Carter, Ryta Lyndley, Pamela Goodwyn)*

FORWARD GREEN [TM0959]

☆ *Shepherd & Dog* IP14 5HN: Good modern dining-pub refurbishment with attractive décor, good interesting bar and restaurant food, well kept Greene King IPA, good wines by the glass and coffee, further renovations under way *(Alan Cole, Kirstie Bruce, Richard Siebert, J F M and M West)*

FRAMLINGHAM [TM2862]

☆ *Station Hotel* IP13 9EE [Station Rd (B1116 S)]: High-ceilinged big-windowed bar with pine tables and chairs on stripped boards, good value food, imaginative and generous inc good fish (an emphasis on smoked), four Earl Soham ales and a guest beer, good choice of house wines, welcoming service, informal relaxed atmosphere, plenty of train pictures, small tiled-floor back snug; children welcome, picnic-sets in good-sized pleasant garden *(MLR, BB, Tom Gondris, Pete Baker, Gordon Neighbour)*

HALESWORTH [TM3979]

Triple Plea IP19 8QW [Broadway (A144 N)]: Popular dining pub doing well under current licensees, sensibly short choice of enjoyable home-made food, leather sofas and open fire in relaxed lounge, pleasant restaurant/conservatory *(N Murphy, Julie Gilbert)*

HARTEST [TL8352]

☆ *Crown* IP29 4DH [B1066 S of Bury St Edmunds]: Pink-washed pub by church behind pretty village green, smartly minimalist décor with quality tables and chairs on tiled floor, good log fire in impressive fireplace, wide choice of enjoyable food from baguettes up, Greene King ales, quick friendly service, two dining rooms and conservatory; piped music; children and dogs welcome, tables on big back lawn and in sheltered side courtyard, good play area *(Adele Summers, Alan Black, LYM, Clive Flynn)*

HENLEY [TM1552]

Cross Keys IP6 0QP [Main Rd]: Refurbished under new and enthusiastic young couple, well kept beer, good wines by the glass, good value home-made food all day; children welcome *(J F M and M West)*

HINTLESHAM [TM0843]

George IP8 3NH [George St]: Modern stripped-down décor, comfortable eating area with roomy conservatory restaurant, flagstoned bar, good value food from big filled baguettes up inc OAP bargain lunches; garden tables *(J F M and M West)*

HOLBROOK [TM1636]

Compasses IP9 2QR [Ipswich Rd]: Roomy and tidy, with nice range of good value food from good baguettes up, prompt cheerful service, Adnams and Greene King ales, big log fire, restaurant; garden with play area, good spot on Shotley Peninsula *(Keith Berrett, Pamela Goodwyn, Charles and Pauline Stride)*

HOXNE [TM1877]

☆ *Swan* IP21 5AS [off B1118, signed off A140 S of Diss; Low St]: Striking late 15th-c building, broad oak floorboards, handsomely carved timbering in colourwashed walls, armchairs by deep-set inglenook log fire, another huge log fire in dining room, Adnams Bitter and Broadside and good guest beers tapped from the cask, bank hol beer festivals, enjoyable bar food from baguettes and light dishes up, friendly landlord, hard-working cheerful staff, lighted candles; children welcome, sizeable attractive garden behind, summer barbecues *(Alan Cole, Kirstie Bruce, LYM, Michael Clatworthy)*

ICKLINGHAM [TL7872]

Red Lion IP28 6PS [A1101 Mildenhall—Bury St Edmunds]: Civilised 16th-c thatched dining pub with enjoyable food from baguettes up, beamed open-plan bar with cavernous inglenook fireplace and attractive furnishings, Greene King ales; picnic-sets out on front lawn and back terrace overlooking fields *(LYM, John and Bettye Reynolds, Dan Graham)*

IPSWICH [TM1545]

Emperor IP1 4BP [Norwich Rd]: Chatty local atmosphere in well worn in traditional bar, well kept Ansells Mild, Wells & Youngs and two guest beers, real fire, small range of bar snacks served all day; easy disabled access (no special lavatory), good value basic bedrooms sharing bathroom, open all day *(G Coates)*

Greyhound IP1 3SE [Henley Rd/Anglesea Rd]: Comfortable Victorian décor, well kept Adnams and guest ales, good substantial home cooking (even the burgers are good, and plenty for vegetarians), quick service, young staff helpful even when it's crowded; children welcome, quiet back terrace *(the Didler)*

Lord Nelson IP4 1JZ [Fore St]: Ancient local with bare boards, timbering, huge fireplace and barrels, friendly prompt service, generous pub food (not Sun evening) inc good fresh specials, well kept Adnams ales tapped from the cask; handy for waterfront, bedrooms *(G Coates)*

Milestone IP4 2EA [Woodbridge Rd]: Open-plan mock-Tudor pub with Adnams, Fullers, Greene King and up to a dozen or so guest beers, farm ciders, several dozen whiskies, home-made food lunchtime and Mon-Weds evening, real fire; big-screen sports TV, live bands; disabled access, large front terrace, open all day wknds *(G Coates, the Didler)*

Salutation IP4 1HB [Carr St]: Welcoming pub in pedestrian area, good service, Bass, good value inexpensive food, dining area *(Alan and Eve Harding)*

IXWORTH [TL9370]

Greyhound IP31 2HJ [High St]: Comfortable local with Greene King IPA and Abbot, occasional guest beers, simple well cooked food *(George Cowie)*

LAVENHAM [TL9148]

Cock CO10 9SA [Church St]: Comfortable thatched village pub with friendly attentive service, Adnams and Greene King ales, good wine choice, generous food inc popular Sun roasts, separate family dining room, plush lounge, basic bar; no dogs; seats out in front and back garden, nice view of church *(the Didler, P and D Carpenter, Adele Summers, Alan Black, MLR, Clive Flynn)*

LAYHAM [TM0340]

☆ *Marquis of Cornwallis* IP7 5JZ [Upper St (B1070 E of Hadleigh)]: Tidy and restauranty beamed 16th-c pub popular for enjoyable carefully prepared food (two evening sittings), quick attentive service, buoyant evening atmosphere, pleasant pine furniture, warm coal fire, proper bar with Greene King and Woodfordes, good wines and coffee; valley views, picnic-sets in lovely riverside garden, open all day Sat in summer, cl Sun evening *(MDN, Judi Bell, N R White)*

LEVINGTON [TM2339]

☆ *Ship* IP10 0LQ [Gun Hill/Church Lane]: Charming old pub with good food inc fair-priced fresh fish and seafood (no bookings), good choice of wines by the glass, Adnams Best and Broadside, welcoming helpful service, old-fashioned wooden furnishings on flagstone floor, nautical décor and pictures; no children inside, front picnic-sets with a bit of an estuary view, more out behind, attractive surroundings, good walks, cl Sun evening *(Peter Meister, Rosemary Smith, Pamela Goodwyn, LYM, George Cowie, Andrew Shore, Maria Williams)*

LONG MELFORD [TL8645]

☆ *Bull* CO10 9JG [Hall St (B1064)]: Lovely medieval great hall, now a hotel, with beautifully carved beams in old-fashioned timbered front lounge, antique furnishings, log fire in huge fireplace, visitors' more spacious back bar with sporting prints, well kept Greene King IPA and Abbot, good range of bar food from good filled huffers to one-price hot dishes inc imaginative salads and fresh fish, friendly helpful staff, daily papers, restaurant; children welcome, courtyard tables, comfortable bedrooms, open all day Sat/Sun *(C and R Bromage, Derek and Sylvia Stephenson, LYM)*

George & Dragon CO10 9JA [Hall St]: Clean and airy pubby bar and dining room, reasonably priced food, roaring log fires, Greene King real ales, decent wines, good polite service; sheltered garden and courtyard, five comfortable bedrooms, open all day *(MDN)*

MARKET WESTON [TL9777]

☆ *Mill* IP22 2PD [Bury Rd (B1111)]: Opened-up pub with attractively priced lunches using local produce, OAP discounts, thoughtful evening menu, Adnams, Greene King IPA, Woodfordes Wherry and an Old Chimneys beer from the village brewery, local farm cider, enthusiastic effective service, two log fires, dominoes; children welcome, small well kept garden *(Derek Field)*

MARTLESHAM [TM2446]

☆ *Black Tiles* IP12 4SP [off A12 Woodbridge—Ipswich; Black Tiles Lane]: Spotless and spacious family dining pub, comfortable contemporary bistro-style restaurant with garden room (children allowed here), big woodburner in appealing bar, wide choice of good inexpensive generous home-made food using local produce served quickly by smart helpful staff, daily roast, Adnams Bitter and Broadside and a guest beer, good choice of wines by the glass; attractive garden with heated terrace tables, open all day *(Charles and Pauline Stride, LYM, Pamela Goodwyn)*

MELTON [TM2850]

Wilford Bridge IP12 2PA [Wilford Bridge Rd]: Light, roomy and well organised, with emphasis on good value food from good sandwiches to local fish in two spacious bars and restaurant, steak nights Mon/Tues, takeaways, Adnams and Greene King Old Speckled Hen, good wines by the glass, prompt friendly service; nearby river walks *(Pamela Goodwyn)*

MONKS ELEIGH [TL9647]

Swan IP7 7AU [B1115 Sudbury—Stowmarket]: Proper pub with chef/landlord doing good freshly made rather restauranty food (and recipe books), real ales inc Adnams and Greene King, good value wines, welcoming efficient service, comfortably modernised lounge bar, open fire, two separate dining areas; bedrooms *(Mrs Carolyn Dixon, Clive Flynn)*

ORFORD [TM4249]

Crown & Castle IP12 2LJ: Restaurant with rooms rather than pub, small smartly minimalist bar (used largely for pre-meal drinks) with well kept Adnams and good wines by the glass, helpful efficient service, good individual food from light lunches up, wider evening choice; tables outside, residents' garden, 18 good chalet bedrooms *(Michael Dandy, A J Murray, Tom Gondris, C and R Bromage)*

☆ *Jolly Sailor* IP12 2NU [Quay Street]: Sadly the charming long-serving Attwoods have left this unspoilt 17th-c pub after 25 years as a main entry – we await reports on their successors, and any changes to these snugly traditional rooms served from counters and hatches in an old-fashioned central cubicle; we can't imagine them losing the good Adnams beers and wines, and you can of course rely on the lovely surrounding coastal walks – picnic-sets on the back grass have views over the marshes *(LYM, Michael Dandy)*

☆ *Kings Head* IP12 2LW [Front St]: Now under same ownership as nearby Crown & Castle, compact bar and adjacent airy dining room with ancient bare boards and stripped brickwork, Adnams ales, good wines and coffee, good reasonably priced traditional food, friendly efficient staff; seats outside and nearby pub garden, attractive character bedrooms with own bathrooms *(LYM, Michael Dandy, A J Murray)*

OTLEY [TM1852]

White Hart IP6 9NS [Helmingham Rd (B1079)]: Attractively refurbished pub increasingly popular locally for its enjoyable home-made food and good Earl Soham beers, good wines by the glass too; sizeable pretty garden, handy for Helmingham Hall gardens *(J F M and M West)*

RAMSHOLT [TM3041]

☆ *Ramsholt Arms* IP12 3AB [signed off B1083; Dock Rd]: Lovely isolated spot overlooking River Deben, recently redecorated open-plan nautical bar busy on summer wknds and handy for bird walks and Sutton Hoo; quickly served wholesome food esp good value seafood and seasonal game, two sittings for Sun lunch, Adnams ales and a guest such as Woodfordes, decent wines by the glass, winter mulled wine, good log fire, easy-going contented atmosphere (one of the dogs can let himself in); children very welcome, plenty of tables outside with summer afternoon terrace bar (not Sun), roomy bedrooms with stunning view, open all day *(LYM, Pamela Goodwyn, J F M and M West, Peter Meister, Comus and Sarah Elliott)*

RENDHAM [TM3564]

White Horse IP17 2AF [B1119 Framlingham—Saxmundham]: Partly divided open-plan pub with good simple traditional home cooking inc Sun lunch, generous helpings and named local sources, welcoming atmosphere, Earl Soham Bitter, Timothy Taylors Landlord, Woodfordes Wherry and a guest beer, two open fires, interesting books and local walks leaflet; garden tables, lovely spot opp 14th-c church *(Mr Biagioni, John Beeken, C and R Bromage, Charles and Pauline Stride, Derek and Maggie Washington)*

SAXTEAD GREEN [TM2564]

Old Mill House IP13 9QE [B1119; The Green]: Roomy dining pub across green from windmill, beamed carpeted bar, neat country-look flagstoned restaurant extension, wooden tables and chairs, pretty curtains, friendly service, popular fresh food from generous starters to good puddings, well kept Adnams, decent wines; discreet piped music; children very welcome, attractive and sizeable garden with terrace and good play area *(J F M and M West, LYM)*

SHOTTISHAM [TM3244]

Sorrel Horse IP12 3HD [Hollesley Rd]: Charming two-bar thatched Tudor local, attentive helpful landlord, Greene King ales tapped from the cask, limited tasty home-made food from granary baguettes up, good log fire in tiled-floor bar with games area, attractive dining room; tables out on green of tucked-away village *(the Didler, C and R Bromage)*

SNAPE [TM4058]

☆ *Golden Key* IP17 1SA [Priory Lane]: Another change of management for appealing old pub, scrupulous housekeeping, good home cooking using all fresh produce, attentive staff, well kept Adnams ales from highly polished handpumps, good wines by the glass, extensive low-beamed restaurant; children welcome, good disabled access, tables on front terrace, sheltered flower-filled garden, comfortable bedrooms *(Terry and Jackie Devine, LYM)*

☆ *Plough & Sail* IP17 1SR [the Maltings]: Pleasant layout with bright and airy eating areas, quieter original core enjoyed by regulars with sofas, settles and log fires, enjoyable up-to-date food from generous sandwiches and baguettes to interesting main dishes, genial barman and fast professional food service, well kept Adnams ales, good wines by the glass; children welcome, teak tables out in big enclosed flower-filled courtyard, lovely surroundings with good walks, open all day in summer *(C and R Bromage, Comus and Sarah Elliott, LYM, A J Murray, Terry and Jackie Devine, Keith and Janet Morris, Tracey and Stephen Groves, Andy Lickfold, Pamela Goodwyn, Dr and Mrs M E Wilson)*

SOMERLEYTON [TM4797]

Dukes Head NR32 5QR [Slugs Lane (B1074)]: Surprisingly stylish inside, with thriving stripped-stone pubby bar, Adnams ales and occasional beer festivals, enjoyable seasonal food (can take a while) using local produce, family dining extension; regular live music; tables out on grass, country views, a stiff walk up from River Waveney *(Kate Abbot, Dr and Mrs M E Wilson)*

SOMERSHAM [TM0848]

☆ *Duke of Marlborough* IP8 4QA [off A14 just N of Ipswich; Main Rd]: Pub/restaurant with good service and atmosphere, good fresh food from lunchtime baguettes and baked potatoes to some interesting hot dishes, Greene King IPA and Old Speckled Hen, decent wines and coffee, pleasant efficient young staff, sturdy pine tables on stripped boards in big open room, attractive country prints and 17th-c inglenook, light and airy turkey-carpeted dining room *(Pamela Goodwyn, BB, Adele Summers, Alan Black)*

SOUTH COVE [TM4982]

Five Bells NR34 7JF [B1127 Southwold—Wrentham]: Friendly, well run and spacious creeper-covered pub with stripped pine, three Adnams ales, local Aspall's farm cider, good value meals in bar and restaurant inc generous Sun lunch, good service; tables out in front, play area, caravan site in back paddock, bedrooms *(Charles and Pauline Stride)*

SOUTHWOLD [TM5076]

☆ *Red Lion* IP18 6ET [South Green]: Good atmosphere, warm friendly service, reasonably priced wholesome pubby food from sandwiches up inc good fish and chips, well kept Adnams ales, big windows looking over green to sea, pale panelling, ship pictures, lots of brassware and copper, pub games, separate dining room; children and dogs welcome, lots of tables outside, right by the Adnams retail shop; bedrooms small

but comfortable *(BB, Mike Gorton, Michael Dandy, Trevor and Sylvia Millum)*

Sole Bay IP18 6JN [East Green]: Café-bar with bright décor and lighting, full Adnams ale range and good wine choice, cheerful and efficient smartly dressed staff, good simple food from impressive doorstep sandwiches up, mix of furnishings from pale wood to settles, conservatory; live music Fri; tables on side terrace, moments from sea and lighthouse *(Michael Dandy, LYM, David Carr, Comus and Sarah Elliott)*

☆ *Swan* IP18 6EG [Market Pl]: Relaxed and comfortable back bar in smart hotel, full range of Adnams ales and bottled beers, fine wines and malt whiskies, good bar lunches (not cheap, but worth it) from enormous baguettes and ciabattas to ten or so main dishes, pleasant staff, pricy coffee and teas in luxurious chintzy front lounge, restaurant; good bedrooms inc garden rooms where (by arrangement) dogs can stay too *(Michael Dandy, LYM, Mike and Heather Watson)*

STONHAM ASPAL [TM1359]

Ten Bells IP14 6AF [The Street]: Extensively modernised early 17th-c timbered village pub with inglenook in extended beamed main bar, small lounge bar with dining area beyond, enjoyable home-made food, well kept real ales, cheerful relaxed atmosphere; disabled facilities, terrace and garden tables, open all day wknds *(Adele Summers, Alan Black)*

STOWUPLAND [TM0759]

Crown IP14 4BQ [Church Rd (A1120 just E of Stowmarket)]: Traditional local with enjoyable pubby food inc imaginative curries and meats from good local butcher, well kept Greene King, brasses and farm tools, lively back bar with darts, pool and big-screen sports TV *(Stephen P Edwards, J F M and M West)*

STUTTON [TM1434]

Gardeners Arms IP9 2TG [Manningtree Rd, Upper Street (B1080)]: Adnams, Greene King and a guest beer, friendly landlord, generous and enjoyable fresh straightforward food inc good value Sun lunch in separate dining room; garden tables, open all day *(Tony and Shirley Albert, Edward Leetham)*

SUDBURY [TL8741]

☆ *Waggon & Horses* CO10 1HJ [Church Walk]: Appealing bar, interesting and comfortable, with good choice of reasonably priced fresh food inc good sandwiches, proper pies and good value OAP deals, good beers and house wines, friendly helpful staff, log fire; very busy wkdy lunchtimes, get there early or book; pleasant walled garden with picnic-sets, handy for Gainsborough House *(Peter and Jean Hoare, David Miles-Dinham, George Cowie, Alan and Eve Harding)*

White Horse CO10 1RF [North St]: Bustling town pub with several linked bare-boards areas, good value lunchtime food from sandwiches to steaks, well kept Greene King IPA, Abbot and a seasonal beer, helpful friendly staff *(MLR)*

THORNDON [TM1469]
Black Horse IP23 7JR [off A140 or B1077,
S of Eye; The Street]: Ancient country pub,
friendly and individual, with several well
kept ales, beams, lots of timbering, stripped
brick, big fireplaces, ancient floor tiles in
small bar areas, roomy dining areas; well
behaved children in eating areas, tables on
spacious lawn with country views (LYM,
David Twitchett)

THORPENESS [TM4759]
☆ *Dolphin* IP16 4NB: Attractive almost
scandinavian décor, light and bright, very
busy lunchtime for enjoyable food from
sandwiches up, Adnams, good wine range,
welcoming landlord and relaxed helpful
service, interesting photographs of this
quaint purpose-built seaside holiday village
with its boating lake; children and dogs
welcome, large attractive garden with
summer bar and barbecue, three
comfortable and appealingly decorated
bedrooms (Tracey and Stephen Groves,
Mrs Romey Heaton, W K Wood,
Pamela Goodwyn)

THURSTON [TL9165]
Fox & Hounds IP31 3QT [Barton Rd]:
Quite an imposing building, welcoming
inside, with well kept Adnams, Greene King
and guest ales, pubby furnishings in neatly
kept carpeted lounge, pool in public bar,
usual food (not Sun evening or Mon);
picnic-sets in garden and on small side
terrace, open all day Fri-Sun
(M R D Foot)

WINGFIELD [TM2276]
☆ *De La Pole Arms* IP21 5RA [off B1118 N of
Stradbroke; Church Rd]: Timbered 16th-c pub
reopened under friendly new owners, good
range of well kept beers and wines, short
choice of enjoyable country cooking using
prime local ingredients, freshly decorated
quarry-tiled bar areas with log fires in big
inglenooks, restaurant; unobtrusive piped
music; children and dogs welcome, good
disabled access, interesting small village
(Mr and Mrs A Campbell, LYM, Jane
Greenwood, David Barnes)

WOODBRIDGE [TM2648]
Cherry Tree IP12 4AG [opp Notcutts Nursery,
off A12; Cumberland St]: Comfortably worn-
in open-plan pub, Adnams and guest ales
helpfully described (June beer festival),
good wines by the glass, welcoming helpful
staff, substantial pubby food at sensible
prices (breakfast too), beams and two log
fires, pine furniture, old local photographs
and aircraft prints; children welcome, garden
with play area, three good bedrooms in
adjoining barn conversion, open all day
wknds (Simon Cottrell, Tony and
Shirley Albert, Russell and Alison Hunt,
Danny Savage, Jenny and Brian Seller)
Olde Bell & Steelyard IP12 1DZ [New St, off
Market Sq]: Ancient pub, unpretentious and
well worn-in, friendly mix of drinking and
eating in bar, Greene King IPA and Abbot,
short choice of usual food from bargain soup
and sandwich to local fish, steelyard still
overhanging the street; back terrace
(W W Burke, David Carr, Alan and
Eve Harding)
Seckford Hall IP13 6NU [signed off A12
bypass, N of town; Seckford Hall Rd, Great
Bealings]: Civilised Tudor country-house
hotel not pub, but its dark and friendly
comfortable bar makes a good coffee break,
and has good bar snacks, Adnams and good
wines inc lots of half bottles, also good
value though not cheap fixed-priced
restaurant meals, sunny conservatory; terrace
tables, extensive grounds with lake, leisure
centre and swimming pool, good bedrooms
(J F M and M West, Pamela Goodwyn,
George Atkinson)

YOXFORD [TM3969]
☆ *Griffin* IP17 3EP [High St]: Happy 14th-c
village pub with log fire and nice corner sofa
in appealing main bar, good value generous
food using local supplies, well kept Adnams
and changing guest beers, decent reasonably
priced wines, friendly helpful staff, charming
log-fire restaurant; good value beamed
bedrooms, good breakfast (Stephen and Jean
Curtis, Comus and Sarah Elliott, Keith and
Janet Morris)

Anyone claiming to arrange or prevent inclusion of a pub in the *Guide* is a fraud.
Pubs are included only if recommended by genuine readers and if our own anonymous
inspection confirms that they are suitable.

Surrey

Surrey's pubs have been setting increasingly high standards recently. As a result there's been quite an influx of exciting new main entries over the last few years, with a corresponding shift of quite a few old stagers to the Lucky Dip section at the end of the chapter. This isn't necessarily to say that those have got worse, it's just that their competitors have been setting an even stiffer pace. An example is another new entry this year, the Three Horseshoes at Thursley, a pub recently rescued by a consortium of villagers from the pub fate worse than death (transformation into a private house – as one reader says, a special place in hell may be reserved for those who perpetrate this). It's now a charming mildly upscale country pub. One of the most successful enduring places here is the welcoming Seven Stars in Leigh, its enthusiastic licensees ensuring this is a really enjoyable place to visit. The Withies at Compton is also doing well – to many its lovely old pubby bar is just what the better class of english pub should be. Liked just as much by readers, but for rather different reasons, is the interestingly decorated Hare & Hounds in Lingfield. It's somewhere a bit more individual and quirky, with jolly good food from a menu that is just a little out of the ordinary too. The two contenders for the county Dining Pub Award are the Parrot in Forest Green and the Inn at West End. The Inn at West End's enthusiastic licensees inject that extra something that makes it special – they put on all sorts of events, import wines themselves, grow some of their own produce. All this care results in some memorable meals. The Parrot's licensees, who managed the remarkable feat of bringing a real breath of the countryside into good pubs they ran previously in London, are doing tremendously well now that they are working with the real thing – not just the attractive country pub itself, but also their own farm's meat on the imaginative menu, and a lovely little farm shop attached to the pub. This year it gains not just a Food Award but also a Star; and the Parrot at Forest Green is our choice as Surrey Dining Pub of the Year. Pubs we'd note from the Lucky Dip section at the end of the chapter are the Jolly Farmers at Buckland, Ramblers Rest near Chipstead, White Horse at Hascombe, Hautboy at Ockham, Kings Arms and Old School House in Ockley, Good Intent at Puttenham, White Horse in Shere and Onslow Arms at West Clandon. The local beer you are most likely to come across here is Hogs Back, and it's also worth looking out for Leith Hill and Surrey Hills. Drinks prices tend to be very high indeed in Surrey pubs – well above the national norm. Pub food prices here are however not nearly so out of line, though they do tend to be a touch above average.

CHARLESHILL

SU8844 MAP 2

Donkey

B3001 Milford—Farnham near Tilford; coming from Elstead, turn left as soon as you see pub sign; GU10 2AU

Cottagey dining pub with attractive garden and good local walks

The bright saloon at this beamed 18th-c place has lots of tables for dining, polished stirrups, lamps and watering cans on the walls, and prettily cushioned built-in wall benches, while the lounge has a fine high-backed settle, highly polished horsebrasses, and swords on the walls and beams. All their wines (including champagne) are available by the glass, and you'll also find Greene King IPA, Abbot and Old Speckled Hen on handpump; piped music. The attractive garden also has a terrace and plenty of seats and there's a wendy house. On the edge of woodlands, it has been a pub since 1850 and takes its name from donkeys that were once kept to transport loads up the hill opposite: even today you might meet two friendly donkeys here, called Pip and Dusty. Attractive local walking areas through heathlands include Crooksbury Common, and there are paths into the woods around the pub. More reports please.

🍽 **Friendly staff serve lunchtime sandwiches, soup, chicken liver and brandy pâté, scallops with crispy bacon, garlic and herb butter, battered prawns, scampi, venison and red wine sausages, mango stuffed chicken breast with mild curry sauce, steaks, roast gressingham duck with black cherry and port sauce, and daily specials that take in quite a few fish dishes such as dover sole, cod mornay, salmon with wilted spinach, crab or lobster; Sunday roast.** *Starters/Snacks: £3.75 to £8.95. Main Courses: £9.95 to £22.95. Puddings: £4.95*

Greene King ~ Lease Lee and Helen Francis ~ Real ale ~ Bar food (12-2.30(4 Sun), 6-9.30(8.30 Sun)) ~ Restaurant ~ (01252) 702124 ~ Children welcome ~ Dogs allowed in bar ~ Open 11-3, 6-11; 12-4, 6-10.30 Sun

Recommended by Mr and Mrs A Curry, Tom and Ruth Rees

COBHAM

TQ1059 MAP 3

Plough ♀

3.2 miles from M25 junction 10; A3, then right on A245 at roundabout; in Cobham, right at Downside signpost into Downside Bridge Road; Plough Lane; KT11 3LT

Civilised and welcoming country local with reasonably priced lunchtime snacks, more elaborate pricier evening menu, and garden

The cheerful low-beamed bar at this pretty brick house has a relaxed atmosphere, with Courage Best, Fullers London Pride, Hogs Back TEA and a guest such as Adnams Explorer on handpump, a fine choice of wines by the glass including champagne, and good coffee – served with hot milk. Round to the right, a cosy parquet-floored snug has cushioned seats built into nice stripped pine panelling, and horse-racing prints. The main part is carpeted, with a mix of pubby furnishings, and past some standing timbers a few softly padded banquettes around good-sized tables by a log fire in the ancient stone fireplace. The restaurant part (with pews, bare boards and white table linen) rambles around behind this; piped music and TV. A terrace has picnic-sets sheltering beside a very high garden wall. Service is swift and good-natured and there are disabled access and facilities.

🍽 **You order your meal from a separate servery. The lunchtime bar menu includes sandwiches, baguettes, game terrine, soup, garlic snails, fish and chips, pastry filled with vegetables in pesto and steak. The evening menu includes fish soup, warm salmon mousseline with anchovy sauce, red mullet with ratatouille and vanilla butter sauce, roast duck breast with juniper berries and cider and honey sauce, and pork belly with orange sauce, with puddings such as fruit crumble or iced nougat with candied fruits.** *Starters/Snacks: £4.95 to £7.95. Main Courses: £5.95 to £16.95. Puddings: £3.95 to £6.95*

Free house ~ Licensee Joe Worley ~ Real ale ~ Bar food (12-2.30(3 Fri, Sat), 7-9.30; 12-6 Sun; not Fri, Sat evening) ~ Restaurant ~ (01932) 589790 ~ Children welcome ~ Dogs allowed in bar ~ Occasional jazz bands ~ Open 11-11; 12-10.30 Sun

Recommended by C and R Bromage, Shirley Mackenzie, David Twitchett, Ian Phillips, Geoffrey Kemp, Tom and Ruth Rees, Phil Bryant, Piotr Chodzko-Zajko

COLDHARBOUR
TQ1544 MAP 3

Plough ◀

Village signposted in the network of small roads around Leith Hill; RH5 6HD

Good walkers' lunch stop with own brew beers

This scenically placed inn is in a peaceful hamlet so high in the Surrey hills you might find yourself in the clouds. There's some of the best walking in the county around here, with paths up to the tower and viewpoint on Leith Hill and further afield to Friday Street and Abinger Common. The pub has its own brewery (Leith Hill) which produces the excellent Crooked Furrow, Hoppily Ever After and Tallywhacker which are served here on handpump, alongside a couple of guests such as Ringwood Old Thumper and Shepherd Neame Spitfire; also Biddenden farm cider and several wines by the glass. Two bars (each with a lovely open fire) have stripped light beams and timbering in warm-coloured dark ochre walls, with quite unusual little chairs around the tables in the snug red-carpeted games room on the left (with darts, board games and cards), and little decorative plates on the walls; the one on the right leads through to the candlelit restaurant; at busy times it may be hard to find somewhere to sit if you're not dining. The front and the terraced back gardens have picnic-sets, tubs of flowers and a fishpond full of water-lilies.

🍴 **Bar food includes soup, seared squid or king prawns in garlic butter, pork and leek sausage, baked stuffed red peppers with herb and garlic potatoes, baked trout with celery and walnut stuffing, confit of duck with orange and burgundy jus, and puddings such as chocolate and cherry trifle, apple and cinnamon crumble and fresh fruit crème brûlée.** *Starters/Snacks: £4.95 to £7.95. Main Courses: £6.95 to £13.95. Puddings: £3.95 to £4.95*

Own brew ~ Licensees Richard and Anna Abrehart ~ Real ale ~ Bar food (12-2.30, 6-9.30(9 Sun)) ~ Restaurant ~ (01306) 711793 ~ Children welcome with restrictions ~ Dogs allowed in bar ~ Open 11.30-11.30(midnight Sat); 12-10.30 Sun ~ Bedrooms: £59.50S/£69.50S(£95B)

Recommended by Pete Baker, Norma and Noel Thomas, T S Meakin, Brian and Janet Ainscough, Mike Buckingham, Paul Humphreys, Phil and Sally Gorton, A J Longshaw, Andy Booth, Kevin Thorpe, Tony and Jill Radnor, Susan and John Douglas

COMPTON
SU9646 MAP 2

Withies

Withies Lane; pub signposted from B3000; GU3 1JA

Smart and very civilised, with attractive pubby bar, up-market restaurant; pretty garden

Smart yet atmospheric and welcoming, with emphasis on the restaurant side, this civilised 16th-c pub preserves a genuinely pubby low-beamed bar. It has some fine 17th-c carved panels between the windows, and a splendid art nouveau settle among the old sewing-machine tables; you'll find a good log fire in a massive inglenook fireplace. Badger K&B, Greene King IPA and Hogs Back TEA are on handpump; piped music. Even when it's busy, the pleasant uniformed staff remain helpful and efficient. A mass of flowers borders the neat lawn in front, and weeping willows overhang the immaculate garden, where there are plenty of dining tables under an arbour of creeper-hung trellises, more on a crazy-paved terrace and others under old apple trees. Polsted Manor and Loseley Park are a pleasant walk up the lane from here.

🍴 **They do good straightforward bar food such as soup, sandwiches or filled baked potatoes, 6oz sirloin steak sandwich, quiche, smoked salmon pâté, ploughman's, cumberland sausages with mash and onion gravy and seafood platter. The restaurant is more formal and is very popular with a well heeled local set.** *Starters/Snacks: £4.00 to £11.50. Puddings: £5.75*

Free house ~ Licensees Brian and Hugh Thomas ~ Real ale ~ Bar food (12-2.30, 7-9.30) ~ Restaurant ~ (01483) 421158 ~ Children welcome ~ Open 11-3, 6-11; 12-4 Sun; closed Sun evening

EASHING   SU9543 MAP 2

Stag ♀

Lower Eashing; Eashing signposted off A3 southbound, S of Hurtmore turn-off; or pub signposted off A283 just SE of exit roundabout at N end of A3 Milford bypass; GU7 2QG

Gentle improvements by new licensees to lovely old riverside pub with good seasonal menu

A small new management group, who run just four pubs, have freshened up this cosy old place. It's older than its Georgian brick faÁade suggests, dating back in part to the 15th century. The attractively opened-up interior includes a charming old-fashioned locals' bar on the right with red and black quarry tiles by the counter. They serve Hogs Back TEA and a couple of guests such as Fullers London Pride and Shepherd Neame Spitfire on handpump, and about 14 wines by the glass. A cosy gently lit snug beyond has a low white plank ceiling, a big stag print and stag's head on dark green walls, books on shelves by the log fire, and sturdy cushioned housekeeper's chairs grouped around dark tables on the brick floor. An extensive blue-carpeted area rambles around on the left, with similar comfortable dark furniture, some smaller country prints and decorative plates on red, brown or cream walls, and round towards the back a big woodburning stove in a capacious fireplace under a long mantelbeam; piped music and daily papers. The river room looks out on to mature trees by a millstream, and there are picnic-sets and tables under cocktail parasols set out on a terrace and in a lantern-lit arbour.

🍽 As well as ploughman's, hot ciabattas and steaks, the seasonally changing blackboard menu might include beef carpaccio and rocket, baked mushrooms topped with chorizo and mushrooms, baked lemon sole with caper sauce, beef, stilton and ale pie, roast duck with morello cherry sauce, and puddings such as raspberry pavlova and warm chocolate brownie. *Starters/Snacks: £4.50 to £7.50. Main Courses: £7.50 to £16.00. Puddings: £4.50 to £5.00*

Punch ~ Lease Mark Robson ~ Real ale ~ Bar food (12-3, 6-9(9.30 Fri, Sat); 12-4, 6-8.30 Sun) ~ Restaurant ~ (01483) 421568 ~ Children welcome away from bar ~ Dogs allowed in bar ~ Open 12-3, 5-11, 12-11 Fri, Sat; 12-10.30 Sun

ELSTEAD   SU9044 MAP 2

Mill at Elstead ♀ 🍺

Farnham Road (B3001 just W of village, which is itself between Farnham and Milford); GU8 6LE

Fascinating and beautifully located watermill conversion with river running right underneath, great service, big attractive waterside garden, Fullers beers, bar food

The long cobbled drive, crossing a bridge and then winding between tall trees and a spreading meadow, makes clear that you are heading for something out of the ordinary. And there it is ahead: a stately four-storey brick-built watermill, largely 18th-c, straddling the River Wey. Inside, you are greeted by a great internal waterwheel, and the gentle rush of the stream turning below your feet. The building has been converted most sympathetically, making for a good rambling series of linked bar areas on the ground floor, and further seating including a restaurant area upstairs. There are so many different spaces that you can pick an area to suit almost any mood: brown leather armchairs and antique engravings by a longcase clock; neat modern tables and dining chairs on pale woodstrip flooring; big country tables and rustic prints on broad ceramic tiles; dark boards and beams, iron pillars and stripped masonry; a log fire in a huge inglenook, or a trendy finned stove with a fat black stovepipe. Throughout, big windows make the most of the charming surroundings – broad millpond, swans, weeping willows. Service is commendably helpful, friendly and personal. They have Fullers Discovery, London Pride, ESB and a seasonal beer on handpump and a good range of wines by the glass; piped music and games machine. There are plenty of picnic-sets in a variety of appealing waterside seating areas outside, with flares and good floodlighting at night.

🕮 **Quite pubby bar food includes soup, baked camembert and chutney, prawn cocktail, tortilla and dips, battered hake and chips, steakburger, tuna steak salad, and steak and stilton pie, with a carvery on winter Sundays.** *Starters/Snacks: £3.95 to £6.00. Main Courses: £9.95 to £17.95. Puddings: £5.25*

Fullers ~ Managers Carol and Brian Jewell ~ Real ale ~ Bar food (12-9.30(10 Fri, Sat; 8 Sun)) ~ (01252) 703333 ~ Children welcome ~ Open 11-11; 11.30-10.30 Sun

Recommended by R Lake, Susan and John Douglas

ESHER   TQ1566 MAP 3

Marneys ♀

Alma Road (one way only), Weston Green; heading N on A309 from A307 roundabout, after Lamb & Star pub turn left into Lime Tree Avenue (signposted to All Saints Parish Church), then left at T junction into Chestnut Avenue; KT10 8JN

Cottagey little pub with nordic influence (particularly in the menu), and attractive garden

The family who own this quaint little place are Norwegian, and proudly display their country's flags and national anthem. The chatty low-beamed and black and white plank-panelled bar (it's worth arriving early as it does get full) has shelves of hens and ducks and other ornaments, small blue-curtained windows, and perhaps horse racing on the unobtrusive corner TV; piped music. On the left, past a little cast-iron woodburning stove, a dining area (somewhat roomier but still small) has big pine tables, pews and pale country kitchen chairs, with attractive goose pictures. Drinks include Courage Best, Fullers London Pride and a guest such as Wells & Youngs Bombardier on handpump, 16 wines and pink champagne by the glass, enterprising soft drinks, norwegian schnapps and good coffee. Service by friendly uniformed staff is quick and efficient; and they have daily papers on sticks. The pleasantly planted sheltered garden has a decked area, bar, black picnic-sets and tables under green and blue canvas parasols, and occasionally a Spanish guitarist playing under the willow tree; the front terrace has dark blue cast-iron tables and chairs under matching parasols, with some more black tables too, with table lighting and views over the nicely rural-feeling common and duck pond.

🕮 **The sensibly small choice of well liked food includes some scandinavian dishes: baguettes, scandinavian meatballs and red cabbage, chilli, good soused herring fillets, frikadeller (danish meatcakes), and home-made puddings such as apple crumble; they usually have around nine specials such as mediterranean penne pasta, cod fishcakes and calves liver; they are happy to provide children's portions.** *Starters/Snacks: £4.50 to £5.00. Main Courses: £8.50 to £10.50. Puddings: £3.00 to £4.95*

Free house ~ Licensee Henrik Platou ~ Real ale ~ Bar food (12-2.15(12.30-3 Sun); not evenings) ~ (020) 8398 4444 ~ Children welcome until 6pm ~ Dogs welcome ~ Open 11-11; 12-10.30 Sun

Recommended by Ian Phillips, Ellen Weld, David London, Ron and Sheila Corbett, John Millwood, Jennie George

---

If a pub tries to make you leave a credit card behind the bar, be on your guard. The credit card firms and banks which issue them condemn this practice. After all, the publican who asks you to do this is in effect saying: 'I don't trust you'. Have you any more reason to trust his staff? If your card is used fraudulently while you have let it be kept out of your sight, the card company could say you've been negligent yourself – and refuse to make good your losses. So say that they can 'swipe' your card instead, but must hand it back to you. Please let us know if a pub does try to keep your card.

FOREST GREEN   TQ1241 MAP 3

Parrot ★ ⑪ ♀ ◀

B2127 just W of junction with B2126, SW of Dorking; RH5 5RZ

SURREY DINING PUB OF THE YEAR

Top notch beamed pub with produce from the owners' farm on the menu and in attached shop, excellent food, good range of drinks, and lovely garden

Comfortably civilised, this enjoyably relaxed pub has a particularly attractive bar, with its profusion of heavy beams, timbers and flagstones, and huge inglenook fireplace. There's plenty of space, with a couple of cosy rambling areas hidden away behind the fireplace, and some more spread out tables opposite the long brick bar counter, which has a few unusual wooden chairs in front. Ringwood Best and Wells & Youngs are served alongside three guests such Adnams Broadside, Nethergate Augustinian and Ringwood Old Thumper on handpump, freshly squeezed orange juice, local apple juice and 14 wines by the glass; newspapers, piped music and TV. Tables outside in front face the village cricket field and there are more among several attractive gardens, one with apple trees and rose beds. The owners have their own farm not far away at Coldharbour and you can buy their meats, as well as cheese, bread and preserves in their farm shop at the pub.

⑪ **With the pork and lamb on the frequently changing menu coming from their own farm, beautifully prepared dishes might include soup, pork, pheasant and port terrine, whiskey cured gravadlax, goats cheese parcel with red berry chutney, steak and onion pie, smoked haddock and scallops with parsley sauce, beefburger, roast butternut squash stuffed with ratatouille and goats cheese with apricot and coriander couscous, poached shoulder of lamb with caper berry sauce and sirloin steak with horseradish butter, puddings such as apple and raisin crumble and lemon tart with lemon sorbet, and a good cheese platter; they do a choice of good, popular Sunday roasts.** *Starters/Snacks: £4.75 to £6.00. Main Courses: £9.25 to £16.00. Puddings: £4.50*

Free house ~ Licensee Charles Gotto ~ Real ale ~ Bar food (12-3(4 Sun), 6-10 (9 Sun)) ~ Restaurant ~ (01306) 621339 ~ Children welcome until 7pm ~ Dogs allowed in bar ~ Open 11(12 Sun)-11; 12-10.30 Sun

Recommended by Gordon Stevenson, John Branston, Susan and John Douglas, Mike and Lynn Robinson, C and R Bromage, Guy Vowles, Ian and Barbara Rankin, Fr Robert Marsh, Pamela and Alan Neale, R Lake, Tony and Jill Radnor, Pam and Alan Neale, Mr and Mrs A H Young

LEIGH   TQ2147 MAP 3

Seven Stars ♀

Dawes Green, S of A25 Dorking—Reigate; RH2 8NP

Popular welcoming dining pub with really enjoyable food and good wines

An ancient sign painted on the wall inside this tile-hung country pub reads '...you are Wellcome to sit down for your ease, pay what you call for and drink what you please': today the licensees and enthusiastic staff are just as welcoming as it seems the licensees were when the place opened in 1637. The comfortable saloon bar has a 1633 inglenook fireback with the royal coat of arms, and there's a plainer public bar. The sympathetically done restaurant extension at the side incorporates 17th-c floor timbers imported from a granary. Greene King Old Speckled Hen, Fullers London Pride and Wells & Youngs Bitter are served from handpump, alongside decent wines with ten by the glass. Outside, there's plenty of room in the beer garden at the front, on the terrace and in the side garden.

⑪ **From the different lunchtime and evening menus very good bar food includes soup, chicken and liver fois gras parfait, crispy whitebait with caper and lemon mayonnaise, salmon and crab cake with dill and cucumber salsa, confit of duck leg with parmesan mustard onion mash and thyme jus, curry, tempura scampi, battered fish, game burger with tomato-onion-port relish and steak, and puddings such as chocolate and praline cheesecake and lemon posset with plum and cinnamon compote. On Tuesday evenings they have a tapas menu and they do two sittings for Sunday lunch. It's advisable to book at all times.** *Starters/Snacks: £2.25 to £6.95. Main Courses: £7.95 to £13.95. Puddings: £3.95 to £4.95*

Punch ~ Lease David and Rebecca Pellen ~ Real ale ~ Bar food (12-2.30(3 Sat, 4 Sun), 6-9(6.30-9.30 Fri, Sat); not Sun evening) ~ Restaurant ~ (01306) 611254 ~ Dogs allowed in bar ~ Open 12-11(9 Sun)

Recommended by Jenny and Brian Seller, DWAJ, C and R Bromage, Mike and Heather Watson, Colin McKerrow, Ian Macro

LINGFIELD   TQ3844 MAP 3

Hare & Hounds 🍴 🍺

Turn off B2029 N at the Crowhurst/Edenbridge signpost, into Lingfield Common Road (coming from the A22 towards Lingfield on B2029, this is the second road on your left); RH7 6BZ

Excellent bar food at easy-going pub, interestingly decorated and more sophisticated than it looks; garden

There's a nicely genuine and unsmartened tone to this eclectically furnished place. The smallish open-plan bar is light and airy by day, with soft lighting and nightlights burning on a good mix of different-sized tables at night – when it's full of the chatter of happy customers, some drinking, some eating, all mixing comfortably. Partly bare boards and partly flagstones, it has a variety of well worn scatter-cushioned dining chairs and other seats from pews to a button-back leather chesterfield, and black and white pictures of jazz musicians on brown tongue-and-groove panelling; perhaps piped music. The bar opens into a quieter dining area with big abstract-expressionist paintings. Fullers London Pride, Greene King Abbot and Wells & Youngs Bitter are on handpump, and eight of their decent wines are available by the glass. Tables are set out in a pleasant split-level garden, with some on decking. This is good walking country near Haxted Mill – walkers can leave their boots in the porch. They hold Irish theme and cabaret nights around every two months and quiz nights every Monday.

🍴 They make their own soda bread, ice-cream and pasta, and the well presented, daily changing bar food (booking advised) might include starters such as soup, warm dill, lemon and vodka marinated salmon with honey and mustard crème fraîche, seared scallops with pea purée, orange and vanilla sauce and risotto primavera, with main courses such as roast veal chop with spinach and sage gnocchi, parma ham and roast garlic jus, venison fillet with sweet sherry onions and smoked chilli jam and swordfish with truffle mash, pak choi and cannellini bean relish, and puddings such as brown bread ice-cream with coconut cookie. *Starters/Snacks: £4.95 to £8.50. Main Courses: £8.95 to £17.50. Puddings: £5.25 to £5.50*

Punch ~ Lease Fergus Greer ~ Real ale ~ Bar food (12-2.30(3.30 Sun), 7-9.30(10 Sat)) ~ (01342) 832351 ~ Children welcome ~ Dogs allowed in bar ~ Open 11.30-11(12 Sat); 12-8 Sun; closed Sun evening

Recommended by Sharon and Alan Corper, Derek Thomas, Paul A Moore, Jill Franklin, Ian Wilson, Neil Hardwick, Grahame Brooks, Annette Tress, Gary Smith

MICKLEHAM   TQ1753 MAP 3

Running Horses 🍴 🍷 🛏

Old London Road (B2209); RH5 6DU

Upmarket pub with elegant restaurant and comfortable bar, sandwiches through to very imaginative dishes

You will feel perfectly at ease if you just want to enjoy a drink at this rather smart place. It has two calmly relaxing bar rooms, neatly kept and spaciously open-plan, with fresh flowers or a fire in an inglenook at one end, lots of race tickets hanging from a beam, some really good racing cartoons, hunting pictures and Hogarth prints, dark carpets, cushioned wall settles and other dining chairs around straightforward pubby tables and bar stools. Adnams, Fullers London Pride, Greene King Abbot and Wells & Youngs Bitter are on handpump alongside good wines by the glass, from a serious list; piped music. The extensive restaurant leads straight out of the bar and, although it is set out quite formally with crisp white cloths and candles on each table, it shares the thriving atmosphere of the bar. There are picnic-sets on a terrace in front by lovely flowering tubs and hanging baskets, with a peaceful view of the old church with its strange stubby steeple.

🍴 **There is a tempting choice of food (you can eat from the restaurant menu in the bar) including soup, well filled lunchtime chunky sandwiches, lobster and shellfish chowder, carpaccio of ostrich with balsamic caramelised tomatoes and parmesan, devilled kidneys in puff pastry, salmon and crab fishcakes, bubble and squeak, spinach, mushroom and cherry risotto, lamb shank braised with balsamic and burgundy, and steaks, with puddings such as vanilla panna cotta with melon coulis, chocolate pudding and warmed berries in Drambuie syrup with lemon sorbet and brandy snap.** *Starters/Snacks: £4.75 to £6.95. Main Courses: £11.50 to £18.25. Puddings: £5.50 to £6.25*

Punch ~ Lease Steve and Josie Slayford ~ Real ale ~ Bar food (12-2(3 Sun), 7(6.30 Sun)-9) ~ Restaurant ~ (01372) 372279 ~ Dogs allowed in bar ~ Open 11.30-11; 12-10.30 Sun ~ Bedrooms: £85(£85S)(£95B)/£95(£95S)(£130B)

Recommended by Gordon Stevenson, S Topham, Susan and John Douglas, Paul Humphreys, Sheila Topham, Pam and Alan Neale, Conor McGaughey

NEWDIGATE   TQ2043 MAP 3
Surrey Oaks 🍺
Off A24 S of Dorking, via Beare Green; Parkgate Road; RH5 5DZ

Interesting real ales at traditional pub with straightforward bar food and enjoyable garden for children

The welcoming landlord at this cottagey 16th-c country pub is a real ale enthusiast and holds beer festivals over the May Whitsun and August bank holiday weekends. He serves five well kept real ales on handpump, with Harveys Best and Surrey Hills Ranmore alongside constantly rotating guests such as Grand Union One Hop and Ossett Silver King; there are also belgian bottled beers, several wines by the glass and a farm cider. The pubby interior is interestingly divided into four areas; in the older part locals gather by a coal-effect gas fire in a snug little beamed room, and a standing area with unusually large flagstones has a woodburning stove in an inglenook fireplace. Rustic tables are dotted around the light and airy main lounge to the left, and there's a pool table in the separate games room; fruit machine and piped classical music. The garden is nicely complicated, with a terrace, and a rockery with pools and a waterfall, and a play area and two goats to keep children amused.

🍴 **Bar food includes filled baguettes, ploughman's, ham, eggs and chips, battered fish, with specials such as sausage and mash, fish pie, steak and ale pie and calves liver, bacon and onion gravy.** *Starters/Snacks: £4.00 to £5.00. Main Courses: £6.50 to £7.50. Puddings: £2.50 to £3.50*

Admiral Taverns ~ Licensee Ken Proctor ~ Real ale ~ Bar food (12-2(2.50 Sat, Sun), 6.30-9(9.30 Sat); not Sun, Mon evening) ~ (01306) 631200 ~ Children welcome ~ Dogs allowed in bar ~ Open 11.30-2.30, 5.30-11; 11.30-3, 6-11 Sat; 12-10.30 Sun

Recommended by C and R Bromage, Norma and Noel Thomas, Conor McGaughey

OTTERSHAW   TQ0263 MAP 3
Castle 🍺
2.6 miles from M25 junction 11; heading S on A320, after A319 roundabout pass church on right, then after another 350 yards or so take sharp left turn into Brox Road; KT16 0LW

Basic pub with half a dozen real ales, relaxed atmosphere, and garden

The two unpretentious bars (maybe too simple for some) at this early Victorian local have log fires, paraphernalia on black ceiling joists and walls hung with horse tack. There are small pictures and some stripped brickwork (including little stub walls making two or three snugly cushioned side booths); the bar on the right opens into a dining area and a long narrow side conservatory with tables down one side. Under quite an armoury of guns, the servery between the two separate bars has half a dozen ales on handpump – probably Adnams, Fullers London Pride, Greene King Abbot, Harveys Best, Hop Back Summer Lightning and Timothy Taylors Landlord, as well as Addlestone's cider and eight wines by the glass. In the left-hand bar a low table made from an old smith's bellows has a good collection of upmarket magazines; piped music. There are tables on grass by the car park, and the front terrace is set well back from the fairly quiet road.

🍴 **Pubby bar food includes lunchtime sandwiches and paninis, and soup, ploughman's, curry, chilli, fish or steak and ale pie and puddings such as apple crumble; Sunday roast.** *Starters/Snacks: £3.75 to £5.50. Main Courses: £7.50 to £12.95. Puddings: £4.95 to £7.95*

Punch ~ Lease John Olorenshaw ~ Real ale ~ Bar food (12-2, 6.30-9; 12-4 Sun; not Sun evening) ~ (01932) 872373 ~ Children (not babies) in conservatory ~ Dogs allowed in bar ~ Open 11-2.30, 5.30-11; 11-11 Sat; 12-10.30 Sun

Recommended by JMM, Simon Collett-Jones, Ian Phillips, Phil Bryant

THURSLEY   SU9039 MAP 2
Three Horseshoes
Dye House Road, just off A3 SW of Godalming; GU8 6QD

Appealing and civilised cottagey country pub with good restaurant food as well as bar snacks

This charming partly 16th-c country pub was reopened fairly recently by a group of locals (including a former Lord Mayor of London), who rescued it from the threat of being turned into a private house, after its closure a few years ago. Registered as a beer house since 1841, the tile-hung cottagey building dates partly from the 16th c, with Georgian and Victorian alterations. And it's now been reworked as a nice combination of mildly upmarket country local and attractive restaurant. The congenial beamed front bar has well kept Fullers London Pride, Hogs Back TEA and a guest such as Sharps Doom Bar on handpump, a winter log fire, and warmly welcoming service; piped music. There's some emphasis on the attractive restaurant area behind, with beamery and paintings of local scenes. The attractive two-acre garden has picnic-sets and a big play fort, and there are smarter comfortable chairs around terrace tables; pleasant views over the green. The village church is worth a visit, and this is an appealing area, though hundreds of acres of nearby heathland were destroyed in 2006 by Surrey's worst heath fire of recent years.

🍴 **Bar food includes chicken liver parfait, guinea fowl, venison and mushroom terrine, goats cheese crème brûlée with chilli jam, roast veal fillet with cep jus, rabbit stew with leek dumplings, asparagus risotto with smoked cherry tomato salad, steak and kidney pie, globe artichoke with wild rocket, poached duck egg hollandaise with grilled asparagus, blackberry jelly with blackberry sorbet and butterscotch tart; Sunday roast.** *Starters/Snacks: £4.50 to £12.00. Main Courses: £8.00 to £14.00. Puddings: £4.50 to £6.50*

Free house ~ Licensees David Alders and Sandra Proni ~ Real ale ~ Bar food (12.30-2.15(3 Sun), 7-9.15; not Sun evening) ~ Restaurant ~ (01252) 703268 ~ Children welcome ~ Dogs allowed in bar ~ Open 12-3, 5.30-11; 12-11 Sat

Recommended by Richard Freeman, Phil and Sally Gorton, Christopher and Elise Way, Michael B Griffith, Mr and Mrs Gordon Turner, Ian Phillips

WEST END   SU9461 MAP 2
Inn at West End 🍴 🍷
Just under 2½ miles from M3 junction 3; A322 S, on right; GU24 9PW

Enjoyable fresh-feeling dining pub with excellent food, good wines, and terrace.

The enthusiastic and very welcoming licensee couple at this appealingly up-to-date pub ensure that all aspects of the business are on top form. The interior is open-plan, with bare boards, attractive modern prints on canary yellow walls above a red dado, and a line of dining tables with crisp white linen over pale yellow tablecloths on the left. The bar counter (Fullers London Pride and a guest such as Hogs Back TEA on handpump), straight ahead as you come in, is quite a focus, with chatting regulars on the comfortable bar stools. The very good food here is well complemented by the knowledgeably chosen house wines (ten by the glass), several sherries and dessert wines, and as the landlord is a wine merchant they can supply by the case. The area on the right has a pleasant relaxed atmosphere, with blue-cushioned wall benches and dining chairs around solid pale wood tables, broadsheet daily papers, magazines and a row of reference books on the brick chimneybreast above a woodburning stove. This opens into a garden room, which in turn leads to a pergola-covered (with grapevine and clematis) terrace.

🍴 **Carefully prepared using thoughtfully sourced ingredients (some of the herbs and vegetables are grown here, and they pluck their own game), bar food might include soup, sandwiches, chicken liver salad with black pudding, pine nuts and garlic croûtons, kedgeree, salmon and dill fishcakes, sausage and mash, mushroom, walnut, cheese and spinach wellington with garlic and herb sauce, roast pork belly with black pudding and honey and thyme jus, sirloin steak, and puddings such as caramelised bread and butter pudding or crème brûlée with chocolate chip cookie.** *Starters/Snacks: £5.25 to £8.95. Main Courses: £10.75 to £19.95. Puddings: £5.25 to £6.95*

Enterprise ~ Lease Gerry and Ann Price ~ Real ale ~ Bar food (12-2.30, 6.30-9.30; 12-3, 6-9 Sun) ~ Restaurant ~ (01276) 858652 ~ Well behaved children over 5 welcome in restaurant if dining ~ Dogs allowed in bar ~ Open 12-3, 5-11; 12-11 Sat; 12-10.30 Sun

Recommended by A Warren, David and Sue Smith, Philip and Jude Simmons, Edward Mirzoeff, John and Rosemary Haynes, David and Ruth Shillitoe, Guy Consterdine, Miss A E Dare, Ian Phillips, P Waterman

WEST HORSLEY   TQ0853 MAP 3

Barley Mow

Off A246 Leatherhead—Guildford at Bell & Colvill garage roundabout; The Street; KT24 6HR

Nice country pub with lunchtime snacks and more in the evening; garden

Tucked behind a handsome horse chestnut tree, this attractive place is distinguished by particularly attentive and good-humoured service, under a charming black-waistcoated Colombian manager. The low-beamed bar has Fullers London Pride, Greene King IPA, Shepherd Neame Spitfire and Wells & Youngs Bitter on handpump, about ten wines by the glass and decent spirits; daily papers, unobtrusive piped music and small TV. The flagstoned part on the right probably dates from the 16th c, and with its big log fire under an unusual domed smoke canopy is quite a magnet for dogs and their owners at weekends. The left-hand side is carpeted, with comfortable library chairs, flowers on its pubby tables (two of them copper-topped and framed with cast iron), cottagey lantern lighting, and another fireplace. The vintage and classic racing-car prints in a less ancient front extension are a sign of the pub's popularity with motor enthusiasts – when they meet here you might find all sorts of treasures in the car park. On the left, the comfortable and softly lit restaurant, with white tablecloths and more fresh flowers, includes what looks like a former barn, with pitched rafters. The good-sized garden, sheltered, well planted and neatly kept, has picnic-sets

🍴 **Lunchtime bar food includes soup, sausage and mash, ham, egg and chips and fish and chips. They've a very short tapas menu, which runs for both sessions, and a more elaborate evening menu which might include norwegian fish soup, baked figs stuffed with blue cheese, baked bass, stuffed aubergine, calves liver on mustard mash with raspberry and brandy sauce, and puddings such as berry cheesecake or chocolate and raspberry roulade; Sunday roast.** *Starters/Snacks: £3.95 to £5.95. Main Courses: £6.00 to £9.95. Puddings: £4.50*

Punch ~ Lease John and Juliette Andon ~ Real ale ~ Bar food (12-2.30, 6-9(9.30 Fri, Sat); 12-4.30 Sun, not Sun evening) ~ Restaurant ~ (01483) 282693 ~ Children welcome away from bar ~ Dogs allowed in bar ~ Open 11-11; 12-10.30 Sun

Recommended by Colin Christie, Dr D J and Mrs S C Walker, Ian Phillips, DWAJ, Susan and John Douglas

---

If we know a pub does summer barbecues, we say so.

WORPLESDON   SU9854 MAP 3

Jolly Farmer

Burdenshott Road, off A320 Guildford—Woking, not in village – heading N from Guildford on the A320, turn left after Jacobs Well roundabout towards Worplesdon Station; OS Sheet 186 map reference 987542; GU3 3RN

Traditional place with pubby food and attractive sheltered garden

This white-painted village pub has dark beams and pub furniture and slate flooring. The bar retains a pubby feel, with Fullers Discovery, London Pride and HSB on handpump, plus a guest such as Titanic Steerage, and a large wine list with about 14 by the glass. You can eat here, or in a dining extension with stripped brickwork, rugs on bare boards and well spaced tables. The back garden has grape vines and fruit trees, and picnic-sets under cocktail parasols; piped music. The car park is shared with Whitmore Common, and there are walks from here into the surrounding woods.

🍴 Bar food includes sandwiches, soup, garlic chilli tiger prawns, salmon soufflé, grapefruit, rocket and pine nut salad, sausage with bubble and squeak, cod and chips, fish pie, sirloin steak, daily specials such as beef wellington, pork fillet with sage and onion stuffing and stuffed baked bass, and puddings such as fruit crumble, sticky toffee pudding and chocolate soufflé. *Starters/Snacks: £3.50 to £6.50. Main Courses: £9.95 to £17.95. Puddings: £5.00*

Fullers ~ Managers Tara and Owen Bossert ~ Real ale ~ Bar food (12-3, 6-9.30 (sandwiches 3-6 Fri, Sat); 12-9 Sun) ~ Restaurant ~ (01483) 234658 ~ Children welcome ~ Open 12-11(10.30 Sun)

Recommended by Mayur Shah, Ian Phillips, Phil Bryant, Gerry and Rosemary Dobson

LUCKY DIP

Besides the fully inspected pubs, you might like to try these Lucky Dips recommended to us and described by readers (if you do, please send us reports: www.goodguides.co.uk).

ABINGER COMMON [TQ1146]
☆ *Abinger Hatch* RH5 6HZ [off A25 W of Dorking, towards Abinger Hammer]: Eager to please staff, friendly and attentive, in beautifully placed woodland dining pub, popular food (not Sun evening) from interesting light dishes up, Fullers London Pride and Ringwood Best and Fortyniner, heavy beams and flagstones, log fires, pews forming booths around oak tables in carpeted side area, plenty of space (it gets very busy wknds); piped music, plain family extension; dogs welcome, tables and friendly ducks in nice garden, nr pretty church and pond, summer barbecues, open all day *(Edward Mirzoeff, LYM, P Waterman, Mike and Lynn Robinson, Sue and Mike Todd)*

ADDLESTONE [TQ0464]
Waggon & Horses KT15 1QH [Simplemarsh Rd]: Pretty and very welcoming suburban mock-Tudor local kept spotless, with genial licensees, real ales such as Greene King Abbot, Flowers Original and Hancocks HB, rows of cups and trophies; flowers and picnic-sets on small front terrace, back terrace and garden *(Ian Phillips)*

ASH VALE [SU8952]
Swan GU12 5HA [Hutton Rd, off Ash Vale Rd (A321) via Heathvale Bridge Rd]: Big friendly three-room Chef & Brewer on the workaday Basingstoke Canal, huge

blackboard choice of decent food all day (can take a while when very busy), good sandwiches, Courage Directors, Wells & Youngs and a guest beer, good reasonably priced wines by the glass, good cheerful staff inc chefs in tall white hats, large log fire; piped classical music; children welcome, attractive garden, well kept heated terraces and window boxes, open all day *(Philip and June Caunt, KC, Mrs Pam Mattinson)*

BATTS CORNER [SU8140]
Blue Bell GU10 4EX: Quietly set country pub recently reopened by father-and-son team after long closure and substantial reworking inc new flooring and servery, pleasant chatty atmosphere, freshly made bar food from baguettes to bass (father is chef), well kept fff Moondance, a beer brewed by them for the pub and Hogs Back TEA, half a dozen wines by the glass, log fire, restaurant; dogs and muddy boots welcome (numerous good walks nearby), picnic-sets in big garden with rolling views, new terrace and plans for play area, handy for Alice Holt Forest *(BB, Phil and Sally Gorton, N R White)*

BETCHWORTH [TQ1950]
Arkle Manor RH3 7HB [Reigate Rd]: Smart recent upgrade for rambling chain dining pub, enjoyable gently upscale food, attractive layout with easy chairs and so

forth, real ales, thriving atmosphere
(Mike and Heather Watson)

☆ **Dolphin** RH3 7DW [off A25 W of Reigate; The Street]: 16th-c village pub on Greensand Way with plain tables on ancient flagstones in neat and homely front bar, smaller bar, panelled restaurant bar with blazing fire and chiming grandfather clock, nice old local photographs, Wells & Youngs ales perhaps inc a seasonal guest; children and dogs welcome, seats in small front courtyard, picnic-sets in back garden, open all day (LM, B and M Kendall, Tina and David Woods-Taylor, the Didler, LYM)

BLACKBROOK [TQ1846]

☆ **Plough** RH5 4DS [just S of Dorking]: Chris and Robin Squire, friendly licensees at this neatly kept white-fronted Badger pub (nicely placed by oak woods) for every edition of this Guide, have now hung up their beer mugs; reports on the new regime please. (LYM)

BLETCHINGLEY [TQ3250]

Red Lion RH1 4NU [Castle St (A25), Redhill side]: Tudor dining pub recently refurbished with chunky tables and fresh modern style alongside its old oak beams, enjoyable generous food, friendly staff, Greene King IPA, good choice of wines by the glass, feature wine vault (Grahame Brooks)

Whyte Harte RH1 4PB [2½ miles from M25 junction 6, via A22 then A25 towards Redhill]: Low-beamed Tudor pub with old prints and big inglenook log fire in extensive open-plan bar, pleasant staff, enjoyable food, Wells & Youngs Bombardier, reasonably priced wines; seats outside, attractive village street (shame about the traffic), comfortable bedrooms (Roger White, LYM, Geoffrey Kemp)

BROOK [SU9238]

Dog & Pheasant GU8 5UJ [Haslemere Rd (A286)]: Big busy low-beamed roadside pub in attractive spot opp cricket green nr Witley Common, enjoyable food from tapas and lunchtime sandwiches up inc interesting dishes, well kept Fullers London Pride, Greene King Old Speckled Hen, Ringwood Best and Youngs, good choice of wines, log fire, pleasant atmosphere and comfortably traditional décor, shove-ha'penny, small restaurant, family eating area; picnic-sets in pretty garden and on small front terrace (R B Gardiner)

BUCKLAND [TQ2250]

☆ **Jolly Farmers** RH3 7BG [Reigate Rd (A25)]: Convivial tastefully modernised dining pub with good if not cheap food from a few lunchtime sandwiches and familiar favourites using good ingredients to wider evening choice, thriving atmosphere, cheerful expert staff, real ale such as Hop Back Summer Lightning or Timothy Taylors Landlord, enterprising choice of soft drinks, integral farm shop (John Branston, Mike and Heather Watson, Conor McGaughey)

BURROWHILL [SU9763]

Four Horseshoes GU24 8QP [B383 N of Chobham]: Old-fashioned cottagey local,

dark and cool inside on hot days, log fires in both rooms winter, well kept Brakspears and Courage Best, simple yet imaginative bar food from tapas up at sensible prices, dining room; lots of picnic-sets out overlooking green (some under ancient yew) (Ian Phillips)

BYFLEET [TQ0661]

Plough KT14 7QT [High Rd]: Interesting changing ales such as Archers Blackjack Porter, Fullers London Pride, Greene King IPA, Shepherd Neame Kent Best, Whitstable Oyster Stout and Wychwood Hobgoblin, comfortably relaxed atmosphere, good value food from sandwiches and baguettes up, two log fires, medley of furnishings, lots of farm tools, brass and copper, dominoes; picnic-sets in pleasant back garden (Ian Phillips)

CAMBERLEY [SU8760]

Claude du Vall GU15 3RB [High St]: Roomy modern Wetherspoons with fine range of real ales, their usual food, good coffee, and prices setting an excellent example for Surrey; small side terrace, open all day (Ian Phillips)

CATERHAM [TQ3355]

Olde King & Queen CR3 5UA [High St]: Thriving 16th-c Fullers local with ochre walls, flagstoned bar, room off with open fire, books and brass ornaments, small partly panelled eating area with very low boarded ceiling, good beers, friendly young landlord, quick service even when busy, small menu of good value basic food (not Sun) from sandwiches up; terrace tables, open all day (Tony Hobden, Conor McGaughey)

CHARLTON [TQ0868]

Harrow TW17 0RJ [Charlton Rd, Ashford Common; off B376 Laleham—Shepperton]: Popular thatched 17th-c pub with well kept Greene King ales, generous good value pubby food from baguettes up, good indian dishes too (friendly Asian landlord); sports TV; picnic-sets out on small front lawn (Mayur Shah, Ian Phillips)

CHERTSEY [TQ0566]

Boathouse KT16 8JZ [Bridge Rd]: Roomy and locally popular modern family pub in good Thames-side spot, reasonably priced food from sandwiches and baked potatoes up, Courage Best, Greene King Abbot and Wells & Youngs Special, buttercup colour scheme; picnic-sets on attractive waterside terrace, moorings, comfortable bedrooms in adjoining Bridge Lodge (Ian Phillips)

Crown KT16 8AP [London St (B375)]: Traditional Youngs pub with button-back banquettes in spreading high-ceilinged bar, sonorous longcase clock, pubby food all day from sandwiches and ciabattas up, decent wines by the glass, Wells & Youngs Bitter, Bombardier and Ramrod, neatly placed darts, restaurant; big-screen sports TV each end, fruit machines; children and dogs welcome, garden bar with conservatory, tables in courtyard and garden with pond; smart 30-bedroom annexe (Geoffrey Kemp, Ian Phillips, JJW, CMW)

Kingfisher KT16 8LF [Chertsey Bridge Rd (Shepperton side of river)]: Big Vintage Inn particularly liked by older people for its delightful spot by Thames lock, repro period décor and furnishings in spreading series of small intimate areas, Fullers London Pride, Greene King Old Speckled Hen and Marstons Pedigree, good wine choice, reasonably priced food, friendly attentive staff, good log fires, daily papers, large-scale map for walkers, interesting old photographs and prints; soft piped music; familes welcome if eating (otherwise no under-21s), riverside garden by road, open all day *(Simon Collett-Jones, Ron and Sheila Corbett, Ian Phillips)*

CHIDDINGFOLD [SU94323]

☆ *Mulberry* GU8 4SS [Petworth Rd (A283 S)]: Relaxed country inn (owned by DJ Chris Evans) with welcoming fire in huge inglenook, stylish pictures in attractive rambling panelled bar, couple of steps down to appealing carpeted dining area, sofas by second back log fire with plenty of reading, enjoyable if not cheap food from sandwiches and baguettes up, well kept Greene King IPA and Hogs Back TEA, good choice of wines by the glass, friendly attentive staff; tables on covered verandah, picnic-sets among fruit trees on neat lawn with wendy house and play area, well equipped bedrooms in separate block, open all day wknds *(BB, Andy and Claire Barker, Nathan Tough)*

☆ *Swan* GU8 4TY [Petworth Rd (A283 S)]: Attractive dining pub, comfortable and smartly up to date, with good choice of food from tempting if not cheap sandwich range up in light and airy dining bar and restaurant, several real ales, thoughtful wine choice, friendly relaxed service; pleasant back terrace with big sunshades, good bedrooms *(Christopher and Elise Way, John and Rosemary Haynes, LYM, Martin and Karen Wake, Gerry and Rosemary Dobson)*

CHIPSTEAD [TQ2757]

☆ *Ramblers Rest* CR5 3NP [Outwood Lane (B2032)]: Picturesque aggregation of partly 14th-c former farm buildings, recently well modernised, airy and spacious, with good up-to-date food inc interesting dishes (best to book for Sun lunch), friendly efficient service even when busy, Fullers London Pride and Pilgrim, good wines by the glass, panelling, flagstones, low beams, log fires and daily papers; children and dogs welcome, big pleasant garden with terrace, attractive views, good walks nearby, open all day *(BB, N R White, Melanie Eskenazi, Grahame Brooks, C and R Bromage, Sheila Topham)*

Well House CR5 3SQ [Chipstead signed with Mugswell off A217, N of M25 junction 8]: Partly 14th-c, cottagey and comfortable, with lots of atmosphere, huge helpings of plainly served food (not Sun evening) from hefty sandwiches and baguettes to some interesting blackboard specials, efficient staff, log fires in all three rooms, real ales such as Adnams, Everards Tiger, Fullers

London Pride, Hogs Back Hair of the Hog and Wadworths 6X; dogs allowed; large attractive hillside garden with well reputed to be mentioned in Domesday Book, delightful setting *(N R White, LYM, Conor McGaughey, John Coatsworth)*

CHURT [SU8538]

Crossways GU10 2JE: Great choice of up to seven or eight interesting changing ales at reasonable prices, good value home-made pub lunches (not Sun) from good sandwiches up, two distinct down-to-earth bar areas, friendly atmosphere; garden, open all day Fri/Sat *(Mr and Mrs A Curry, R B Gardiner)*

CLAYGATE [TQ1563]

Foley Arms KT10 0LZ [Hare Lane]: Victorian two-bar local with amiable landlord, real fires, popular reasonably priced lunches from proper sandwiches up, Wells & Youngs ales; good folk club Fri; open all day, attractive garden with play area *(Conor McGaughey)*

COBHAM [TQ1058]

Cricketers KT11 3NX [Downside Common, S of town past Cobham Park]: Village-green pub popular for its position and olde-worlde character, low beams, standing timbers, blazing log fire, horsebrasses and unsmart furnishings, Fullers London Pride, Gales and Greene King Old Speckled Hen served very cool, basic pub food, separate restaurant; they may try to keep your credit card while you eat; children welcome, neat garden with heated terrace, open all day *(Ian Phillips, Roy and Lindsey Fentiman, Evelyn and Derek Walter, LYM, Dr Ron Cox)*

Running Mare KT11 3EZ [Tilt Rd]: Attractive old pub overlooking green, popular for its good food (very busy Sun lunchtime), good service, two timbered bars and restaurant; children very welcome (can be noisy with them) *(Shirley Mackenzie)*

DORKING [TQ1649]

☆ *Kings Arms* RH4 1BU [West St]: Rambling 16th-c pub in antiques area, masses of timbers and low beams, nice lived-in furniture in olde-worlde part-panelled lounge, warm relaxed atmosphere, mainstream and interesting guest ales, friendly efficient service, reliable low-priced home-made food from sandwiches and baked potatoes to roasts and a good pie of the day, prompt polite service, attractive old-fashioned back dining area; piped music; open all day *(Edna Jones, Fr Robert Marsh, Conor McGaughey)*

DORMANSLAND [TQ4042]

Old House At Home RH7 6QP [West St]: Warmly friendly comfortable country local with well kept Shepherd Neame ales, wide choice of enjoyable generous food using fresh produce, good Sun lunch (booking recommended), good-natured proper landlord *(Tony Carter)*

EAST CLANDON [TQ0551]

☆ *Queens Head* GU4 7RY [just off A246 Guildford—Leatherhead; The Street]: Rambling dining pub, part of small Surrey group, with enjoyable reasonably priced food from baguettes and light dishes to popular Sun roasts, good friendly service under keen manager, real ales such as Shepherd Neame from fine old elm bar counter, small, comfortable and spotless connecting rooms, big inglenook log-effect fire; children welcome, picnic-sets on pretty front terrace and in quiet side garden, handy for two NT properties, cl Sun evening *(LYM, John Evans, Ian Phillips, Mike and Heather Watson, KC)*

EAST HORSLEY [TQ0952]

Duke of Wellington [A246 Guildford—Leatherhead]: Prominent former early 19th-c coaching inn, Courage Best, Caledonian Deuchars IPA and Fullers London Pride, pubby food inc pizzas, dining areas on left, games room on right (with pool, machines and sports TV); picnic-sets outside, seven bedrooms in new annexe *(Ian Phillips)*

EFFINGHAM [TQ1153]

Sir Douglas Haig KT24 5LU [off A246 Leatherhead—Guildford]: Large open-plan beamed pub, new management keeping up its reputation for enjoyable standard food, good-sized helpings and sensible prices, real ales inc Fullers London Pride, good choice of coffees; piped music; children in eating area, tables on attractive terrace and back lawn, decent bedrooms, open all day *(LYM, DWAJ)*

ELSTEAD [SU9043]

Woolpack GU8 6HD [B3001 Milford—Farnham]: Welcoming pub with enjoyable generous food (can take a long while), well kept Brakspears and Greene King ales tapped from the cask, good choice of wines by the glass, high-backed settles in long airy main bar, open fires each end, country décor, darts in back room; children allowed, garden with picnic-sets, open all day wknds *(LYM, Derek and Sylvia Stephenson)*

ENGLEFIELD GREEN [SU9872]

☆ *Fox & Hounds* TW20 0XU [Bishopsgate Rd, off A328 N of Egham]: Welcoming 17th-c bare-boards pub by Windsor Park and a very short stroll from Savill Garden, enterprising if not cheap bar food (can take a while), Brakspears, Hogs Back TEA and guest beers, fine choice of wines and malt whiskies, cheerful log fire, attractive candlelit back restaurant; may be piped music; children welcome, tables on pretty front lawn and back terrace, open all day (afternoon break Jan-Easter) *(Ian Phillips, Derek and Sylvia Stephenson, LYM)*

Happy Man TW20 0QS [Harvest Rd]: Friendly and unpretentious two-bar late Victorian backstreet local with inexpensive pubby food, four well kept changing ales mainly from smaller breweries, darts area; open all day *(Pete Baker)*

Sun TW20 0UF [Wick Lane, Bishopsgate]: Well used beamed local, nothing too fancy, prompt pleasant service, well kept Adnams, Courage Best and Greene King Abbot, good blackboard wine choice, enjoyable food from good sandwiches and baked potatoes to Sun lunch, reasonable prices, daily papers, lovely log fire in back conservatory, biscuit and water for dogs, interesting beer bottle and bank note collections, conservatory; soft piped music; quiet garden with aviary, handy for Savill Garden and Windsor Park *(Ian Phillips, LM, Simon Collett-Jones)*

EPSOM [TQ2059]

Amato KT18 7AS: Traditional L-shaped carpeted bar, Fullers London Pride, Harveys and Wells & Youngs, decent pubby food (not Sun/Mon nights) from sandwiches up, racing décor; big-screen sports TV; pleasant garden, rural spot nr Epsom Downs *(Phil Bryant)*

☆ *Derby Arms* KT18 5LE [Downs Rd, Epsom Downs]: Comfortable Vintage Inn traditional dining pub very popular with older people and families for wide choice of reasonably priced food from good sandwich range up, efficient welcoming service even when busy, good choice of wines by the glass, Fullers London Pride, log fires; open all day Sun, nice tables outside, good views – opp racecourse grandstand (yet surprisingly little racing memorabilia) *(DWAJ, N R White, C and R Bromage)*

Rubbing House KT18 5LJ [Epsom Downs]: Spacious dining pub with attractive modern décor, good value promptly served food, pleasant efficient service even when busy, Fullers London Pride, serious wine list, racecourse views, upper balcony; tables outside *(Sue and Mike Todd, DWAJ, Mike and Sue Richardson, C and R Bromage)*

White Horse KT18 7JU [Dorking Rd]: Recently refurbished as comfortably unpretentious family dining pub, enjoyable home-made food (all day wknds) from ciabattas and light lunchtime dishes to some enterprising meals, small helpings for children as well as proper cooking for them, smiling service, Fullers London Pride and a guest such as Greene King Abbot, various bargain offers; jazz Sun lunchtime and Tues; children welcome, disabled facilities, picnic-sets outside with covered deck, Sat barbecues and play area *(anon)*

ESHER [TQ1264]

☆ *Prince of Wales* KT10 8LA [West End Lane; off A244 towards Hersham, by Princess Alice Hospice]: Warm and homely Chef & Brewer dining pub, particularly welcoming and well run, with wide choice of reasonably priced food from sandwiches up, calm corners, turkey carpets, old furniture, prints and photographs, real ales such as Greene King Old Speckled Hen and Wells & Youngs Bombardier, good wine choice, daily papers; car park exit needs care; big shady garden, lovely village setting nr green and pond *(Ian Phillips, LM, Ron and Sheila Corbett)*

FARNHAM [SU8448]

Lobster Pot GU9 0NS [Upper Hale Rd]: Thriving atmosphere and wide choice of enjoyable food (not Sun evening) from baguettes, good value popular lunchtime dishes and enterprising proper children's food to daily fresh fish, ingredients all from named suppliers, friendly helpful smartly dressed staff, good wines by the glass, real ales; open all day *(Mr and Mrs A Curry)*

Shepherd & Flock GU9 9JB [Moor Park Lane, on A31/A324/A325 roundabout]: Flower-decked pub with good atmosphere, friendly staff, changing ales such as fff Alton Pride, Hogs Back Hair of the Hog, Ringwood Old Thumper and Sharps Atlantic, enjoyable simple pub lunches, simple up-to-date décor; picnic-sets out in front and in pleasant enclosed back garden with barbecue, nicely tucked away from the traffic, open all day wknds *(Ian Phillips)*

Spotted Cow GU10 3QT [Bourne Grove, Lower Bourne (towards Tilford)]: Simple country pub with helpful and attentive youngish licensees, well kept changing ales, straightforward food from sandwiches and baked potatoes up; jazz nights; play area in big attractive garden, nice surroundings, open all day Fri-Sun *(Liz and Brian Barnard)*

FRIDAY STREET [TQ1245]

Stephan Langton RH5 6JR [off B2126]: New licensees in prettily placed pub, bar and restaurant food (not Sun evening or Mon, and no longer the sort of thing which made it Surrey's top dining pub of 2007), Fullers London Pride, Hogs Back TEA and Surrey Hills Ranmore, farm cider; piped music, only a few parking spaces at the pub; children and dogs welcome, tables outside, good nearby walks inc Leith Hill, open all day *(LYM)*

FRIMLEY GREEN [SU8856]

Old Wheatsheaf GU16 6LA [Frimley Green Rd (B3411, was A321)]: Quick friendly service, Greene King ales, enjoyable bar food inc sandwiches, baguettes and generous daily specials, comfortable banquettes and country prints in opened-up bar, evening restaurant; terrace tables *(Mr and Mrs P A Stevens, R T and J C Moggridge)*

GOMSHALL [TQ0847]

Compasses GU5 9LA [A25]: Plain bar (open all day) and much bigger neat and comfortable dining area, very popular for good value generous food from sandwiches and baked potatoes to steak, good service, real ales and decent wines by the glass; may be piped music, very busy in summer; children welcome, pretty garden sloping down to roadside mill stream, open all day *(Gordon Prince, DWAJ, LYM)*

GUILDFORD [SU9949]

Kings Head GU1 3XQ [Quarry St]: Neatly kept pub with lots of beams and stripped brickwork, inglenook fire, cosy corners with armchairs, well kept Courage Best and Directors and Wychwood Hobgoblin, decent wines, reasonably priced standard food from baguettes up, polite service; games machines, big-screen sports TV, no dogs; picnic-sets in pleasant back courtyard with roof terrace giving castle views *(Ian Phillips)*

Olde Ship GU2 4EB [Portsmouth Rd (St Catherine's, A3100 S)]: Three cosy areas around central bar, ancient beams, bare boards and flagstones, good log fire in big

fireplace, woodburner the other end, comfortable mix of furniture, good wood-fired pizzas and good range of interesting but unpretentious and fairly priced bistro-style food, well kept Greene King and a guest beer such as Black Sheep, decent wines, quick, friendly and helpful service; no music (unless you count the occasional morris men) *(Phil and Sally Gorton)*

HAMBLEDON [SU9639]

☆ **Merry Harriers** GU8 4DR [off A283; just N of village]: Charmingly old-fashioned and homely country local popular with walkers, huge inglenook log fire, dark wood with cream and terracotta paintwork, pine tables, impressive collection of chamber-pots hanging from beams, Greene King IPA and Abbot, Hogs Back TEA and Hop Back Crop Circle, farm cider, decent wines and coffee, attentive staff, reasonably priced fresh simple food from sandwiches up, daily papers and classic motorcycle magazines, pool room; big back garden in attractive walking countryside near Greensand Way, picnic-sets in front and over road – caravan parking *(Phil and Sally Gorton, Susan and John Douglas)*

HASCOMBE [TQ0039]

☆ **White Horse** GU8 4JA [B2130 S of Godalming]: Picturesque old rose-draped pub with attractively simple beamed public bar, traditional games and quiet small-windowed alcoves, more restauranty dining bar (children allowed), good bar food from sandwiches, baguettes and interesting light dishes up, Adnams and Harveys, good wines by the glass, prompt service, log fires or woodburners; small front terrace, spacious sloping back lawn, pretty village with good walks from the pub, open all day wknds *(Jenny and Brian Seller, LYM, Gerry and Rosemary Dobson, Martin and Karen Wake, Mr and Mrs A H Young)*

HOLMBURY ST MARY [TQ1144]

☆ **Kings Head** RH5 6NP: Relaxed bare-boards pub in popular walking country (leave muddy boots in porch), sensibly short choice of good fresh food using local supplies, friendly helpful young licensees, well kept ales such as Kings and Surrey Hills Shere Drop, good wines by the glass, two-way log fire, small traditional back restaurant (fish recommended), public bar with darts, TV and games machine; pretty spot with seats out facing village green, more in big sloping back garden, open all day at least wknds and summer *(Tom and Ruth Rees, Barry Steele-Perkins, Kevin Flack, Susan and Erik Falck-Therkelsen)*

Royal Oak RH5 6PF: Low-beamed 17th-c coaching inn with current landlady cooking some interesting dishes, tasty food from baguettes up, well kept ales such as Everards, decent wines by the glass, fresh flowers, log fire; tables on front lawn, pleasant spot by green and church, good walks, bedrooms *(Mike and Heather Watson, C and R Bromage, Kevin Flack)*

HORSELL [SU9859]
Cricketers GU21 4XB [Horsell Birch]: Warm and friendly local little changed under new licensees, long neatly kept bar, quietly comfortable end sections, extended back eating area, carpet and shiny boards, good straightforward food (all day Sun and bank hols), Adnams Broadside, Courage Best and Fullers London Pride, cheerful service, children well catered for; picnic-sets out in front and in big well kept garden, wide views over Horsell Common *(Phil Bryant, Ian Phillips)*
Crown GU21 4ST [Church Hill/High St]: Thriving atmosphere in appealing pub noted for real ales such as Fullers London Pride, Marstons Fever Pitch, Sharps Doom Bar and Wells & Youngs Bombardier; garden with weeping willows *(Ian Phillips)*
Plough GU21 4JL [off South Rd; Cheapside]: Small friendly pub overlooking wooded heath, relaxed atmosphere, well kept changing ales such as Cains IPA, Greene King IPA and Old Speckled Hen and St Austell Dartmoor Best, good choice of wines by the glass and of malt whiskies, good value fresh pubby food (all day Sat, not Sun evening) from sandwiches up, quiet dining area one side of L, games machines and TV the other; children and dogs welcome (and hay for visiting horses), garden tables, play area, open all day *(Ian Phillips)*
Red Lion GU21 4SS [High St]: Large comfortable pub with good food from sandwiches up, Courage Best, Fullers London Pride and Greene King IPA, decent wines, friendly staff, picture-filled barn restaurant where children allowed; ivy-clad passage to garden with picnic-sets under cocktail parasols and comfortable chairs on terrace, good walks nearby *(Ian Phillips, N R White)*
HORSELL COMMON [TQ0160]
☆ *Bleak House* GU21 5NL [Chertsey Rd; The Anthonys; A320 Woking—Ottershaw]: Smart gastropub aka Sands at Bleak House, grey split sandstone for floor and face of bar counter, tasteful mushroom and white décor with black tables, sofas and stools, good food from baguettes to aberdeen angus steak, Hogs Back TEA and Hop Garden Gold and Wells & Youngs Bombardier, lots of friendly uniformed staff; piped music, lively acoustics; tables in pleasant back garden merging into woods with good shortish walks to sandpits which inspired H G Wells's War of the Worlds, bedrooms *(Ian Phillips, Guy Consterdine)*
HURTMORE [SU9445]
Squirrel GU7 2RN [just off A3 nr Godalming, via Priorsfield Rd]: Comfortable, fresh and airy bar with two fff ales, Fullers London Pride and quickly changing guest beers, decent wines, good choice of enjoyable bar food, friendly service, cosy corners with sofas, bar billiards, informal back restaurant and conservatory; piped music, sports TV; disabled facilities, sizeable pleasant garden with heated terrace and play area,

comfortable bedrooms, good breakfast, open all day *(BB, Phil Bryant)*
IRONS BOTTOM [TQ2546]
Three Horseshoes RH2 8PT [Sidlow Bridge, off A217]: Down-to-earth country local with short choice of good value carefully made food from hot baguettes up, Fullers London Pride and guest beers, darts; tables outside, summer barbecues *(Mike and Heather Watson, John Branston)*
KINGSWOOD [TQ2456]
☆ *Kingswood Arms* KT20 6EB [Waterhouse Lane]: Attractive old roadhouse, big and busy, with good atmosphere in rambling bar, enjoyable generous food from good sandwiches up, helpful friendly staff, real ales such as Adnams, Fullers London Pride and Wells & Youngs, hanging plants in pleasant light and airy conservatory dining extension; spacious rolling garden with play area *(Gordon Neighbour, Mike and Heather Watson)*
KNAPHILL [SU9557]
Hunters Lodge GU21 2RP [Bagshot Rd]: Attractive and comfortable Vintage Inn with linked beamed rooms, good log fires, reasonably priced bar food from sandwiches up, good choice of wines by the glass, Fullers London Pride and Greene King Old Speckled Hen; daily papers; disabled facilities, tables in pleasant well established garden *(Ian Phillips)*
LALEHAM [TQ0470]
☆ *Anglers Retreat* TW18 2RT [B376 (Staines Rd)]: 1930s pub, thriving and comfortable, with French chef doing wide food choice (all day wknds) inc lots of fresh fish, pale panelling, big tropical aquarium set into wall, even larger one in smart restaurant area extended into conservatory, two bright coal fires, Brakspears and a guest beer, decent wines; unobtrusive piped music, fruit machine, no dogs; children welcome, seats out in front, play area in back garden, open all day *(Geoffrey Kemp, Mayur Shah, LYM)*
☆ *Three Horseshoes* TW18 1SE [Shepperton Rd (B376)]: Light and airy beamed and flagstoned bar with contemporary décor, comfortable sofas, daily papers, log fire, two restaurant areas and conservatory, bar food (all day wknds), Courage Best, Fullers London Pride, Wells & Youngs Special and a couple of guest beers, lots of wines by the glass; piped music (may be obtrusive), big-screen TV, can get busy, and they may try to keep your credit card if you eat; children welcome, garden and pavement tables, nr pleasant stretch of the Thames, open all day *(JMM, John Robertson, LYM, Ian Phillips)*
LYNE [TQ0166]
Royal Marine KT16 0AN [Lyne Lane]: Friendly and cosy little pub, neat as a new pin, real ales such as Archers King George V, Hogs Back TEA and Wells & Youngs Bombardier, simple reasonably priced pub food, lots of nautical bric-a-brac and fine collection of pewter mugs; some picnic-sets out in front, attractive small back garden,

cl Sun evening, early Sat evening too
(Ian Phillips, Hunter and Christine Wright)
MARTYRS GREEN [TQ0857]

☆ *Black Swan* KT11 1NG [handy for M25
junction 10; off A3 S-bound, but return N of
junction]: Reopened as large upscale dining
pub after extensive makeover (utterly
changed from its days as the 'Slaughtered
Lamb' in *An American Werewolf in London*),
mix of seating and spacious contemporary
décor in open-plan linked areas, friendly
service, grand choice of wines inc several
champagnes, wide choice of enjoyable food
inc afternoon bar dishes, not so much a
place for the casual drinker but does have
Adnams, Bass, Hogs Back TEA and Surrey
Hills Shere Drop as well as bar stools and
quiet corners with soft settees; children
welcome, stylish black slate furniture out on
extensively landscaped terrace, open all day
*(P and J Shapley, Ian Phillips,
Conor McGaughey)*
MICKLEHAM [TQ1753]

☆ *King William IV* RH5 6EL [just off A24
Leatherhead—Dorking; Byttom Hill]: Chris
and Jenny Grist who were so popular in their
15 years here have now retired; a nice spot,
with pleasant outlook from snug plank-
panelled front bar and plenty of tables
(some in extended open-sided heated
shelter) in lovely terraced garden, traditional
interior, Adnams Best, Badger Best, Hogs
Back TEA and a guest beer, pubby and more
elaborate food; piped music, no under-12s;
cl Sun and Mon evening *(LYM, Tom and
Rosemary Hall, Cathryn and Richard Hicks,
N R White)*
NUTFIELD [TQ3050]

Queens Head RH1 4HH [A25 E of Redhill]:
Congenial atmosphere, good fresh
unpretentious food from good value rare
beef sandwiches up, cheerful efficient staff,
helpful even when busy, three or four well
kept ales inc Shepherd Neame Spitfire,
simple bare wood décor in tiled bar,
carpeted restaurant, no piped music
(John Branston, Hamish and Gillian Turner)
OCKHAM [TQ0756]

☆ *Hautboy* GU23 6NP [Ockham Lane – towards
Cobham]: Remarkable red stone Gothick
folly, emphasis on upstairs brasserie bar like
a 19th-c arts & crafts chapel, darkly panelled
and high-vaulted, with medieval-style murals
and minstrels' gallery, imaginative choice of
good food from sandwiches, ciabattas and
baked potatoes up inc bargain two-course
lunch, Ringwood Best and Fortyniner, Hogs
Back TEA and Surrey Hills Shere Drop,
Thatcher's farm cider, friendly helpful young
staff; children welcome, tables on cricket-
view terrace and in secluded orchard garden
with play area, bedrooms *(LYM, Ian Phillips,
Ian and Barbara Rankin)*
OCKLEY [TQ1439]

☆ *Kings Arms* RH5 5TS [Stane St (A29)]:
Attractive 17th-c country inn now part of a
small group of upscale dining pubs (though
you can have just a drink – several well kept

mainstream ales, good choice of wines by
the glass, attentive friendly staff, starched
napkins and pretty tablecloths, comfortable
olde-worlde décor inc masses of antique
prints, good inglenook log fire, heavy beams
and timbers, low lighting; children welcome,
discreetly placed picnic-sets in immaculate
big back garden, good bedrooms *(LYM,
Gordon Ormondroyd, Mike and
Heather Watson, Ian and Barbara Rankin,
Gerald and Gabrielle Culliford)*

☆ *Old School House* RH5 5TH [Stane St]:
Primarily a restaurant with fish emphasis,
but has thriving pubby eating area around
small bar counter with well kept Fullers ales,
good wines by the glass inc champagne,
wonderful log fire, buoyant atmosphere,
prompt attentive young staff, good bar food
from sandwiches up and good value two-
course lunch; picnic-sets under cocktail
parasols on sunny terrace with flowers
around car park *(John Evans, Gerald and
Gabrielle Culliford, Mike and Heather Watson,
BB, Michael Sargent)*
OUTWOOD [TQ3246]

Bell RH1 5PN [Outwood Common, just E of
village; off A23 S of Redhill]: Attractive
extended and neatly kept 17th-c country
pub/restaurant, mildly upscale food in softly
lit smartly rustic beamed bar and sparser
restaurant area, Fullers ales and a guest such
as Harveys, good wines by the glass, log
fires; children and dogs welcome, piped
music; summer barbecues and cream teas,
picnic-sets in pretty fairy-lit garden with
country views, handy for windmill *(LYM,
Geoffrey Kemp, N R White)*
OXTED [TQ3852]

Crown RH8 9LN [High St, Old Oxted; off A25
not far from M25 junction 6]: Handsome
Elizabethan pub with four ales, good value
food, cosy traditional décor, classic Victorian
panelling in upper dining bar *(Quentin and
Carol Williamson)*

☆ *George* RH8 9LP [High St, Old Oxted]: Smart
dining pub with butcher-block tables,
attractive prints and cream and beige décor,
two chatty front areas and more formal
bistro area, enjoyable home-made food,
good choice of wines by the glass, Badger
ales, open fire; back decking with arbour
(Derek Thomas, LYM, Ian Phillips)
PIRBRIGHT [SU9455]

Cricketers GU24 0JT [The Green]: Chatty
local overlooking green and duck pond, well
kept Cains, Fullers London Pride and Surrey
Hills Shere Drop and Gilt Complex, bargain
basic pubby food, plain extension with pool
and games machines *(Shirley Mackenzie,
Phil Bryant)*

☆ *Royal Oak* GU24 0DQ [Aldershot Rd; A324S
of village]: Relaxed and cottagey old Tudor
pub, well kept Greene King IPA, Abbot and
Ruddles County, Hogs Back TEA and perhaps
guest ales, good range of wines by the glass,
sensibly priced pubby food, three log fires,
heavily beamed and timbered rambling side
alcoves, ancient stripped brickwork, family

room; disabled facilities, extensive colourful fairy-lit gardens, good walks, open all day *(LYM, Gordon Prince, Ian Phillips)*

White Hart GU24 0LP [The Green]: Modern dining-pub refurbishment and back to its proper name after a spell as the Moorhen, sturdy pale wood furniture on black and white tartan carpet, some original flagstones and log fires in restored fireplaces, three well kept ales inc Hogs Back TEA, daily papers, food from usual bar dishes to more interesting restaurant meals – dining area up steps popular with ladies who lunch; soft piped music; good tables and chairs in pleasant fenced front garden, play area behind *(Steve Nye, Ian Phillips)*

PUTTENHAM [SU9347]

☆ *Good Intent* GU3 1AR [signed off B3000 just S of A31 junction; The Street/Seale Lane]: Unspoilt beamed village local thriving under friendly and energetic new licensees, four well kept changing ales such as Courage Best, Fullers HSB, Ringwood Best and Hogs Back TEA, good range of good value fresh food (not Sun/Mon evenings) from sandwiches and baked potatoes up inc popular Weds fish night, pre-ordering for muddy walkers available, farm cider, decent wine choice, handsome log fire in cosy front bar with alcove seating, pool, old photographs of the pub, simple dining area; children and dogs welcome, picnic-sets in small sunny garden, good walks, open all day wknds *(Phil and Sally Gorton, Phil Hanson, BB, N R White)*

PYRFORD LOCK [TQ0559]

Anchor GU23 6QW [3 miles from M25 junction 10 – S on A3, then take Wisley slip rd and go on past RHS Garden]: Now a Badger family dining pub, reopened early summer 2007 after extensive redevelopment, wide choice of pubby food all day, sandwiches and baguettes too, gently folksy décor inc narrow-boat memorabilia; children welcome, dogs allowed in part of bar, splendid terrace with dozens of tables in lovely spot by bridge and locks on River Wey Navigation (very handy for RHS Wisley), fenced-off play area, open all day *(Ian Phillips, W W Burke, LYM)*

REIGATE HEATH [TQ2349]

☆ *Skimmington Castle* RH2 8RL [off A25 Reigate—Dorking via Flanchford Rd and Bonny's Rd]: Fine views from lots of seating outside quaint country pub popular with walkers and riders, dark-panelled beamed cosy rooms with miscellany of furniture, big log fireplace, Adnams, Harveys Best and a guest ale such as Hop Back Summer Lightning, lots of wines by the glass, Addlestone's farm cider, ring-the-bull; piped music; children welcome, open all day Sun *(George Davidson, LM, N R White, P and J Shapley, Martin and Karen Wake, Conor McGaughey, LYM)*

RIPLEY [TQ0556]

Anchor GU23 6AE [High St]: Former 16th-c almshouse, interesting cool dark low-beamed connecting areas served by single bar, daily papers, Fullers London Pride and Greene King IPA, nautical memorabilia and photographs of Ripley's cycling heyday, coal-effect stove, pubby food inc thai dishes; disabled facilities, tables in coachyard *(C and R Bromage, Ian Phillips, BB, Terry Buckland)*

Jovial Sailor GU23 6EZ [Portsmouth Rd]: Large popular Chef & Brewer, cheerful helpful staff, well kept changing ales such as Black Sheep, Greene King Old Speckled Hen and Hop Garden Gold, good wine choice, their usual food all day, wide appeal esp to young lady lunchers, log fire, standing timbers, beams, stripped brickwork and country bric-a-brac; piped music; garden tables *(Ian Phillips, Phil Bryant)*

Seven Stars GU23 6DL [Newark Lane (B367)]: Neat traditional 1930s pub popular lunchtimes for good value generous food from sandwiches and baked potatoes to plenty of seafood, lots of blackboards, good Sun lunches, well kept Fullers London Pride, Greene King Abbot, Shepherd Neame Spitfire and Wells & Youngs Special, decent wines, friendly service; piped music; picnic-sets in large tidy garden behind *(Ian Phillips)*

Talbot GU23 6BB [High St]: Impressive beamed coaching inn with good big log fireplaces in both roomy and traditional front bars, welcoming helpful staff, enjoyable if not cheap food from generous baguettes up, Fullers London Pride, Greene King IPA, Hogs Back TEA and Shere Drop, decent wine, daily papers, nice atmosphere, minimalist back brasserie; bedrooms, tables in back courtyard, antiques centre in outbuildings *(Ian Phillips, Conor McGaughey)*

SENDMARSH [TQ0455]

Saddlers Arms GU23 6JQ [Send Marsh Rd]: Friendly new licensees in unpretentious low-beamed local with creeper-covered porch, Fullers London Pride, Marstons Pedigree, Shepherd Neame Spitfire and Wells & Youngs Bitter, enjoyable home-made pub food from sandwiches up, open fire, toby jugs, brassware etc; picnic-sets out front and back *(Ian Phillips, Shirley Mackenzie)*

SHACKLEFORD [SU9345]

☆ *Cyder House* GU8 6AN [Peper Harow Lane]: Interesting blackboard choice of enjoyable food from ciabattas up in civilised country pub, small helpings available, chatty friendly staff, well kept Badger ales and Hogs Back TEA, decent house wines, log or coal fires, light and airy roomy layout rambling around central servery, lots of mellow pine, children's room; fruit machine and sports TV in side room, may be piped music; picnic-sets on terrace and back lawn, play area, nice leafy village setting, cl Sun evening *(BB, George and Maureen Roby)*

SHAMLEY GREEN [TQ0343]

Red Lion GU5 0UB [The Green]: Welcoming dining pub with smart décor, dark polished furniture, rows of books, open fires, local cricketing photographs, reliable food all day from good well filled sandwiches with chips to steaks, children's helpings and unusual puddings, well kept Adnams Broadside and Wells & Youngs, farm cider, good choice of wines, cafetière coffee, restaurant; open all day, children welcome, sturdy tables in nice garden, bedrooms *(S and N McLean, LYM)*

SHEPPERTON [TQ0765]

Thames Court TW17 9LJ [Shepperton Lock, Ferry Lane; turn left off B375 towards Chertsey, 100yds from Square]: Huge Vintage Inn well placed by Thames, heaters on attractive tree-shaded terrace extended to make the most of it, good choice of wines by the glass, real ales, usual food from snacks up all day, galleried central atrium with separate attractive panelled areas up and down stairs, two good log fires, daily papers; children welcome, open all day *(Mayur Shah)*

SHERE [TQ0747]

☆ *White Horse* GU5 9HF [signed off A25 3 miles E of Guildford; Middle St]: Well run Chef & Brewer, popular with families and a lovely place to take foreign visitors – uneven floors, massive beams and timbers, Tudor stonework, olde-worlde décor with oak wall seats and two log fires, one in a huge inglenook, several rooms off small busy bar, good choice of reasonably priced food all day from sandwiches and baguettes up, friendly efficient staff and warm atmosphere, real ales such as Courage, Hogs Back TEA and Greene King Old Speckled Hen, lots of sensibly priced wines by the glass; dogs welcome, picnic-sets in big back garden, beautiful fir-set village, open all day *(R B Gardiner, Ian Phillips, LYM, John Branston, Mark Percy, Lesley Mayoh, Kevin Flack)*

SOUTH GODSTONE [TQ3549]

Fox & Hounds RH9 8LY [Tilburstow Hill Rd/Harts Lane, off A22]: Pleasant country pub with racing prints and woodburner in low-beamed bar, welcoming staff, enjoyable food from pubby staples with proper chips to good seafood, nice puddings, well kept Greene King ales from tiny bar counter, evening restaurant (not Sun/Mon evenings); may be piped music; children in eating area, small attractive garden *(LYM, Geoffrey Kemp)*

SUNBURY [TQ1068]

Admiral Hawke TW16 6RD [Green St]: Cheerful, warm and comfortable, with reasonably priced pubby food inc Sun roasts, hospitable staff, real ales inc Adnams and Courage, back dining conservatory; TV *(Gerry and Rosemary Dobson)*

Flower Pot TW16 6AA [Thames St, Lower Sunbury; handy for M3 junction 1, via Green St off exit roundabout]: Comfortable 18th-c inn with friendly local feel, good home-made food from reasonably priced sandwiches and bar snacks to restaurant dishes with emphasis on fish, Fullers London Pride, Greene King Abbot and Wells & Youngs Bombardier, good choice of wines by the glass, helpful cheerful young staff; five recently updated bedrooms *(Ian Barker, Ian Phillips, Gerry and Rosemary Dobson)*

SUTTON GREEN [TQ0054]

Olive Tree GU4 7QD [Sutton Green Rd]: Welcoming modern dining pub with good honest food inc fish and seafood, cheaper bar menu inc sandwiches, Fullers London Pride, Harveys and Timothy Taylors Landlord, good choice of wines by the glass, friendly staff, relaxing dining room with minimalist décor *(R Lake, C A Hall, Barry Steele-Perkins, Phil Bryant)*

TANDRIDGE [TQ3750]

Barley Mow RH8 9NJ [Tandridge Lane, off A25 W of Oxted]: Doing well under new licensees, enjoyable food in several eating areas, proper bar too, well kept Badger K&B, good wines by the glass, friendly service *(Evelyn and Derek Walter, Grahame Brooks)*

THAMES DITTON [TQ1567]

Albany KT7 0QY [Queens Rd, signed off Summer Rd]: Thames-side chain pub included for its lovely position, nice balconies and lots of tables on terrace and lawn with great views across river; thoroughly modern inside, teak furniture on woodblock floors (lively acoustics), up-to-date lighting, some leather sofas, usual food served piping hot, good choice of wines by the glass, log fire, daily papers, river pictures, waitress-service restaurant; moorings, open all day *(R Lake, Tom and Ruth Rees, Jennie George, Dr Ron Cox)*

Crown KT7 0QQ [Summer Rd]: Enjoyable food, good choice of wines by the glass, friendly young staff *(Tom and Ruth Rees)*

☆ *Olde Swan* KT7 0QQ [Summer Rd]: Large well managed riverside pub (one of very few to be Grade I listed) with helpful service, consistently good reasonably priced food (all day wknds, inc Sun carvery), well kept Greene King ales and a guest beer, good choice of wines by the glass, cosy Victorian-style décor, log fires, one long bar with three good-sized areas inc civilised black-panelled upper bar overlooking quiet Thames backwater, restaurant; provision for children and dogs, moorings and plenty of waterside tables, open all day *(BB, Tom and Ruth Rees)*

THE SANDS [SU8846]

Barley Mow GU10 1NE [Littleworth Rd, Seale; E of Farnham]: Comfortable village pub with polished pine tables and simple chairs on polished boards, a step or two down to small dining area, well kept Hogs Back TEA, Fullers London Pride and Hook Norton Old Hooky, good if pricy home-made food, pleasant service, log fire; picnic-sets in secluded attractive garden with terrace, well placed for woodland walks *(Liz and Brian Barnard, N R White)*

TILFORD [SU8743]

☆ *Barley Mow* GU10 2BU [The Green, off B3001 SE of Farnham; also signed off A287]: Opposite pretty cricket green, with woodburner in snug little low-ceilinged traditional bar, nice scrubbed tables in two small rooms set for food on left, interesting cricketing prints and old photographs, pubby food inc late Sun lunch (bar snacks earlier till 2 that day), wknd afternoon teas, charming friendly service, well kept Courage Best, Fullers London Pride and Greene King Abbot, imaginative wine list; darts, table skittles, no children except in back coach house; pretty setting opposite cricket green, picnic-sets in plain back garden fenced off from small stream *(Ian Phillips, BB)*

Duke of Cambridge GU10 2DD [Tilford Rd]: Civilised pub under newish licensees, enjoyable food inc good fish, efficient service; piped music; garden tables, good play area *(R B Gardiner)*

VIRGINIA WATER [SU9968]

Rose & Olive Branch GU25 4LH [Callow Hill]: Small unpretentious pub, relaxed and congenial, with friendly helpful service, wide choice of good home-made food from good lunchtime sandwich range to lots of fish and speciality pies (busy lunchtime and wknds, best to book then), Greene King ales, decent wines, matchbox collection; quiet piped music; children allowed lunchtime, tables on front terrace and in garden behind, good walks *(Phil Bryant)*

WARLINGHAM [TQ3955]

Botley Hill Farmhouse CR6 9QH [Limpsfield Rd (B269)]: Busy more or less open-plan dining pub, low-ceilinged linked rooms up and down steps, soft lighting, spreading carpet, quite close-set tables, big log fireplace in one attractive flagstoned room, restaurant with overhead fishing net and seashells, hard-working friendly staff, well kept ales such as Fullers London Pride, Greene King IPA, Abbot and Old Speckled Hen and Kings Horsham, good house wines, food from lunchtime snacks to plenty of fish and popular Sun lunch; loud live music some nights; children welcome away from bar, cream teas, wknd entertainments, courtyard tables, neat garden with play area and toddlers' park, ducks and aviary *(N R White, BB, Ian Phillips)*

WEST CLANDON [TQ0451]

☆ *Bulls Head* GU4 7ST [A247 SE of Woking]: Friendly and comfortably modernised, based on 1540s timbered hall house, very popular esp with older people lunchtime for reliable hearty food from sandwiches, ploughman's and baked potatoes through home-made proper pies to steak, prices very reasonable by Surrey standards, small lantern-lit beamed front bar with open fire and some stripped brick, contemporary artwork for sale, older local prints and bric-a-brac, steps up to simple raised back inglenook dining area, helpful staff, Courage Best, Greene King Old Speckled Hen and Wadworths 6X, good coffee, no piped music, games room with darts and pool; no credit cards; children and dogs on leads welcome, tables and good play area in pleasant garden, convenient for Clandon Park, good walking country *(R Lake, DWAJ, Ian Phillips, C J Roebuck, Mike and Heather Watson)*

☆ *Onslow Arms* GU4 7TE [A247 SE of Woking]: Popular partly 17th-c country pub in same

smallish Auberge group as Plough, Cobham (see main entries), mix of stylish french brasserie with traditional bar's dark nooks and corners, heavy beams and flagstones, warm seats by inglenook log fires, welcoming staff, good value food (not Sun evening) from baguettes up inc imaginative twists on pubby favourites, Courage Best and Directors, Greene King Old Speckled Hen and Ringwood Fortyniner, decent wines; piped music may be a tad loud; children welcome (and dogs in bar), great well lit garden, open all day *(Mike and Heather Watson, Geoffrey Kemp, LYM, Barry Steele-Perkins, Phil Bryant)*

WEST HORSLEY [TQ0752]

King William IV KT24 6BG [The Street]: Comfortable early 19th-c pub with very low-beamed open-plan rambling bar, reasonably priced proper food from sandwiches up here and in updated conservatory restaurant, good choice of wines by the glass, well kept ales such as Courage and Surrey Hills Shere Drop, good coffee, log fire, board games; children and dogs very welcome, good disabled access, small garden and terrace with gorgeous hanging baskets *(Shirley Mackenzie, Ian Phillips)*

WESTHUMBLE [TQ1751]

Stepping Stones RH5 6BS [just off A24 below Box Hill]: Comfortable dining pub with consistently good sensibly priced straightforward lunchtime food and more elaborate evening menu, good friendly service even when busy, circular bar with Fullers London Pride, Greene King Abbot and a guest beer (drinks brought to table), clean uncluttered décor, open fire, no music; can get packed Sun; children and walkers welcome, terrace and garden with summer barbecue and play area *(DWAJ, Sue and Mike Todd)*

WEYBRIDGE [TQ0765]

Minnow KT13 8NG [Thames St/Walton Lane]: Attractive dining pub with variety of areas, contemporary pastel décor and unusual decorative panels, chunky tables and chairs with some sofas and armchairs, buoyant atmosphere with good mix of ages, helpful staff, enjoyable fresh food inc pizzas, pasta and traditional dishes, good range of real ales such as Timothy Taylors Landlord, good wines by the glass, open fire in raised hearth; picnic-sets in large front garden with heaters and awning *(Phil Bryant, Minda and Stanley Alexander)*

☆ *Old Crown* KT13 8LP [Thames St]: Friendly and comfortably old-fashioned three-bar pub dating from 16th c, very popular lunchtime for good value traditional food from sandwiches and baked potatoes up esp fresh grimsby fish, Courage Best and Directors, Hepworths Pullman and Wells & Youngs Bitter, service good even when busy, family lounge and conservatory, coal-effect gas fire; may be sports TV in back bar with Lions RFC photographs; children welcome, suntrap streamside garden *(DWAJ, JMM, Ian Phillips,*

Mark Percy, Lesley Mayoh)

☆ *Prince of Wales* KT13 9NX [Cross Rd/Anderson Rd off Oatlands Drive]: Congenial and attractively restored, reasonably priced generous blackboard food inc interesting dishes and Sun lunch with three roasts, real ales such as Adnams, Boddingtons, Fullers London Pride, Tetleys and Wadworths 6X, ten wines by the glass, relaxed lunchtime atmosphere, friendly service, log fire, daily papers, stripped pine dining room down a couple of steps; big-screen TVs for major sports events; well behaved children welcome *(Minda and Stanley Alexander)*

WINDLESHAM [SU9264]
Bee GU20 6PD [School Rd]: Compact local popular for its three or four well kept real ales, friendly staff, usual food, coal-effect gas fire, dining area; may be discreet piped music; small garden with play area *(Dr Martin Owton)*

☆ *Half Moon* GU20 6BN [Church Rd]: Popular much extended family pub with reliable food inc Sun lunch, real ales such as Fullers London Pride, Sharps Doom Bar, Theakstons Old Peculier and Timothy Taylors Landlord, Weston's farm cider, decent wines, good range of children's drinks, cheerful efficient staff, log fires, World War II pictures, modern furnishings, attractive barn restaurant out along covered flagstoned walkway; piped music, silenced fruit machine; children welcome, huge tidy garden with two terraces and well used play area *(Ian Phillips, R Lake)*

WOKING [TQ0058]
Wetherspoons GU21 5AJ [Chertsey Rd]: Large and busy with shoppers yet with lots of intimate areas and cosy side snugs, good range of food all day, half a dozen or more interesting well kept real ales, good choice of coffees, fair prices, friendly helpful staff, daily papers, interesting old local pictures, no music; open all day from 9 *(Tony Hobden, Ian Phillips)*

WONERSH [TQ0145]
Grantley Arms GU5 0PE [The Street]: Extended 16th-c pub with pews and other assorted country furnishings in rambling beamed bar, up to half a dozen quickly changing ales such as Greene King Abbot, Highgate Lonewolf, Kings Horsham Best and

Shepherd Neame Spitfire, wide-ranging menu (all day Sun) from pubby basics and reasonably priced light lunchtime dishes to more sophisticated specials, cheerful helpful staff; no dogs; children welcome, terrace tables *(Phil Bryant)*

WOOD STREET [SU9550]
Royal Oak GU3 3DA [Oak Hill]: Brightly lit popular pub, comfortably unpretentious, with good changing ales such as Hogs Back TEA, Lloyds Mild, Oakham JHB and Shere Drop, friendly staff, good low-priced plain cooking with lots of fresh veg and nice puddings *(Phil Bryant, Liz and Brian Barnard, Ian Phillips)*

WOODHAM [TQ0361]
Victoria KT15 3QE [Woodham Lane]: Reopened under new management after bright minimalist refurbishment as bar and smart evening restaurant, limited yet varied choice of enjoyable lunchtime bar food, Caledonian Deuchars IPA, Greene King IPA, Timothy Taylors Landlord and Wells & Youngs Bombardier, friendly outgoing Australian landlord; subdued piped music *(Ian Phillips, Phil Bryant)*

WORPLESDON [SU9654]
Fox GU3 3PP [Fox Corner]: Modernised pub/restaurant with wicker chairs and pine tables, Courage Best and Greene King IPA, good if not cheap food, good service, proper bar area too; watch out for the low step across the bar; big pretty garden with picnic-sets under dark green parasols, heated terrace *(Ian Phillips)*

WRECCLESHAM [SU8344]
☆ *Bat & Ball* GU10 4SA [Bat & Ball Lane, South Farnham; approach from Sandrock Hill and Upper Bourne Lane then narrow steep lane to pub]: Neatly refurbished pub tucked away in hidden valley known locally as Boundstone, wide range of above-average pubby and more upmarket food (small helpings available) inc good puddings, up to half a dozen or more changing ales such as one brewed for them by Itchen Valley, good choice of wines by the glass, friendly staff; they may try to keep your credit card while you eat, sports TV; disabled facilities, dogs welcome, provision for children, tables out on attractive heated terrace and in garden with substantial play fort, open all day *(BB, R Lake)*

Post Office address codings confusingly give the impression that some pubs are in Surrey when they're really in Hampshire or London (which is where we list them). And there's further confusion from the way the Post Office still talks about Middlesex – which disappeared in 1965 local government reorganisation.

Sussex

For a wealthy county, it's heartening that there are still so many genuinely unspoilt cottagey pubs here – often with long-serving landlords and landladies. Examples currently on fine form include the firmly run Rose Cottage at Alciston, the charming Cricketers Arms at Berwick, the bustling Basketmakers Arms in Brighton, the lively Six Bells at Chiddingly, the unchanging Royal Oak at Chilgrove and the ancient Royal Oak at Wineham. Less simple than these places but also on top form this year are the Stag at Balls Cross (consistently well run and enjoyable), the Greys in Brighton (good live music and interesting food), the Fox Goes Free at Charlton (handy for Goodwood and always busy), the Jolly Sportsman at East Chiltington (first-class imaginative food – at a price), the Star & Garter at East Dean (a super all-rounder), the Three Horseshoes at Elsted (a smashing pub and quietly civilised), the Griffin at Fletching (particularly well run and gently upmarket), the Queens Head at Icklesham (very good licensees keeping everything running smoothly), and the Giants Rest in Wilmington (extremely well liked, again partly because of its friendly licensees). Our three new entries here are the stylish yet relaxed Royal Oak at East Lavant (rewarding restauranty food), the interesting Huntsman at Eridge Station (good country cooking in this unaffected pub), and the Half Moon at Warninglid (another properly unpretentious country pub with surprisingly interesting food). Apart from these three, foody places to head for are the Blackboys Inn, the Curlew near Bodiam, the Greys in Brighton, the White Horse at Chilgrove, the Jolly Sportsman at East Chiltington, the Star & Garter at East Dean, the Three Horseshoes at Elsted and the Griffin at Fletching. For a special meal out the Sussex Dining Pub of the Year is the Griffin at Fletching. This is one of the country's most expensive areas for eating out in pubs, and Sussex drinks prices are also markedly higher than the national norm. Harveys of Lewes often provide local pubs with their cheapest beer, and smaller local breweries to look out for include Ballards, Arundel, Dark Star, Kings, Weltons, Rother Valley, Hammerpot and Whites. In the Lucky Dip section at the end of the chapter, strongly supported pubs include the Anchor Bleu in Bosham, Old House At Home at Chidham, Swan near Dallington, Tiger at East Dean (normally a main entry, new landlord too recently arrived for us to form a firm view yet), White Dog at Ewhurst Green, Bulls Head in Fishbourne, Trevor Arms at Glynde, Woodmans Arms at Hammerpot, Lewes Arms in Lewes, Mark Cross Inn, Badgers near Petworth, Plough at Plumpton Green, Plough at Udimore, Brewers Arms at Vines Cross and Cat at West Hoathly.

ALCISTON   TQ5005 MAP 3

Rose Cottage

Village signposted off A27 Polegate—Lewes; BN26 6UW

Old-fashioned cottage with fresh local food, cosy fires and country bric-a-brac, a good little wine list and local beers

In the same family for more than 40 years, this is an old-fashioned little cottage with a good mix of locals and visitors. There are cosy winter log fires, half a dozen tables with cushioned pews under quite a forest of harness, traps, a thatcher's blade and lots of other black ironware, and more bric-a-brac on the shelves above the stripped pine dado or in the etched-glass windows; in the mornings you may also find Jasper the parrot (he gets too noisy in the evenings and is moved upstairs). There's a lunchtime overflow into the restaurant area as they don't take bookings in the bar then. Harveys Best and a guest from Kings on handpump, a good little wine list with fair value house wines and a few nice bin ends, and two local farm ciders; the landlord is quite a plain-speaking character. Piped music, darts and board games. There are heaters outside for cooler evenings and the small paddock in the garden has ducks and chickens; boules. Nearby fishing and shooting. The charming little village (and local church) are certainly worth a look. They take bedroom bookings for a minimum of two nights.

🍴 Using fresh local and often organic produce, the bar food includes ploughman's, soup, coarse pâté, pork sausages with chips and tomato chutney, honey-roast ham with poached egg, various salads, scampi, popular fish pie and steak and kidney pudding, daily specials, and puddings such as apple pie or cheesecake with raspberry sauce; their Friday night mussels are usually a sell-out. *Starters/Snacks: £3.25 to £5.95. Main Courses: £7.75 to £17.50. Puddings: £4.00*

Free house ~ Licensee Ian Lewis ~ Real ale ~ Bar food ~ Restaurant ~ (01323) 870377 ~ Children allowed if over 10 ~ Dogs allowed in bar ~ Open 11.30-3, 6.30-11; 12-3, 6.30-10.30 Sun; closed 25 and 26 Dec and evening 1 Jan ~ Bedrooms: /£50S

Recommended by PL, the Didler, Michael Hasslacher, Jenny and Peter Lowater, John and Jill Perkins, R and S Bentley, Jude Wright, P and J Shapley, N R White, Alan Cowell

ALFRISTON   TQ5203 MAP 3

George

High Street; BN26 5SY

Venerable inn in lovely village with comfortable, heavily beamed bars, good wines and well liked food; fine nearby walks

The long bar in this 14th-c timbered inn has massive low beams hung with hops, appropriately soft lighting and a log fire (or summer flower arrangement) in a huge stone inglenook fireplace that dominates the room, with lots of copper and brass around it. There are settles and chairs around sturdy stripped tables, Greene King IPA, Abbot, Old Speckled Hen and perhaps a guest beer on handpump, decent wines including champagne by the glass, board games and piped music. The restaurant is cosy and candlelit – or you can sit out in the charming flint-walled garden behind. Two long-distance paths, the South Downs Way and Vanguard Way cross here and Cuckmere Haven is close by. This is a lovely village and popular with tourists.

🍴 Bar food includes sandwiches, soup, aubergine, tomato and goats cheese stack, sautéed crevettes and chorizo in chilli oil, chicken, spinach and red pepper terrine with lime pickle, baked haddock with welsh rarebit topping on spring onion mash, sweet potato, pea and broad bean risotto with parmesan, steak tartare, rack of lamb with tomato and olive sauce, and puddings such as crème brûlée (a different flavour each day) and banana and Baileys bread and butter pudding; helpings are not vast. *Starters/Snacks: £4.00 to £6.50. Main Courses: £8.00 to £16.50. Puddings: £4.25*

Greene King ~ Lease Roland and Cate Couch ~ Real ale ~ Bar food (12-2.30, 7-9(10 Fri and Sat)) ~ Restaurant ~ (01323) 870319 ~ Children welcome ~ Dogs allowed in bar and bedrooms ~ Open 11-11(midnight Fri and Sat); closed 25 and 26 Dec ~ Bedrooms: £60S/£110B

Recommended by David and Karen Cuckney, Catherine and Richard Preston, Glenwys and Alan Lawrence, Guy Vowles, W A Evershed, Ann and Colin Hunt

ARLINGTON
TQ5507 MAP 3

Old Oak

Caneheath, off A22 or A27 NW of Polegate; BN26 6SJ

Beamed comfortable rooms in pleasant country pub, straightforward pubby food, real ales and quiet garden

After a walk in the nearby Abbot's Wood nature reserve, the seats in the peaceful garden of this 18th-c former set of almshouses are a nice place to relax with a pint. Inside, the L-shaped bar is open-plan with heavy beams, well spaced tables and comfortable seating, log fires, and Badger Best, Harveys Best, and a changing guest such as Adnams Broadside tapped from the cask; several malt whiskies, piped music, darts, toad in the hole (a Sussex coin game) and dominoes.

🍴 **Straightforward bar food with some daily specials includes filled baguettes, ploughman's, soup, duck and orange pâté, ham and eggs, vegetable lasagne, curry, home-made steak and mushroom in ale pie and a roast of the day.** *Starters/Snacks: £3.95 to £4.95. Main Courses: £5.95 to £9.95. Puddings: £4.25*

Free house ~ Licensees Mr J Boots and Mr B Slattery ~ Real ale ~ Bar food (12-2.30, 6.30-9.30; all day weekends) ~ Restaurant ~ (01323) 482072 ~ Children welcome ~ Dogs allowed in bar ~ Open 11-11

Recommended by Jenny and Peter Lowater, Fr Robert Marsh

BALLS CROSS
SU9826 MAP 2

Stag 🍺

Village signposted off A283 at N edge of Petworth, brown sign to pub there too; GU28 9JP

Smashing little pub with a friendly landlord, well kept beer, nice traditional food and seats in sizeable garden

Our readers find this unspoilt little 16th-c pub consistently enjoyable. The tiny flagstoned bar has a winter log fire in its huge inglenook fireplace, just a couple of tables, a window seat, and a few chairs and leather-seated bar stools. On the right, a second room with a rug on its bare boards has space for just a single table. Beyond is an appealing old-fashioned dining room with quite a few horsey pictures. There are yellowing cream walls and low shiny ochre ceilings throughout, with soft lighting from little fringed wall lamps, and fishing rods and country knick-knacks hanging from the ceilings. On the left a separate carpeted room with a couple of big Victorian prints has table skittles, darts and board games. Badger Best, K&B and seasonal guest on handpump, decent wines by the glass, summer cider and some nice malt whiskies. The good-sized garden behind, divided by a shrubbery, has teak or cast-iron tables and chairs, picnic-sets, and in summer a couple of canvas awnings; there are more picnic-sets out under green canvas parasols in front, and the hitching rail does get used. The veteran gents' (and ladies') are outside.

🍴 **Traditional bar food (using game bagged by the landlord) includes lunchtime filled baguettes and baked potatoes, soup, fried garlic mushrooms, cumberland sausage and chips, home-baked ham and eggs, chilli con carne, battered cod with mushy peas, macaroni cheese, steak and kidney pudding and slow-cooked venison casserole.** *Starters/Snacks: £4.50 to £7.00. Main Courses: £7.50 to £18.00. Puddings: £4.00 to £4.50*

Badger ~ Tenant Hamish Barrie Hiddleston ~ Real ale ~ Bar food (not Sun evening) ~ Restaurant ~ (01403) 820241 ~ Children in dining area or games room but must be well behaved ~ Dogs allowed in bar and bedrooms ~ Open 11-3, 6-11; 12-3, 7-10.30 Sun ~ Bedrooms: £30/£60

Recommended by Jude Wright, Susan and John Douglas, R B Gardiner, David Cosham, Jeremy Whitehorn, Phil and Sally Gorton

BERWICK   TQ5105 MAP 3

Cricketers Arms
Lower Road, S of A27; BN26 6SP

Cottagey and unchanging in a quiet setting with welcoming little bars, nice staff, traditional food (all day weekends); charming garden

There's a happy atmosphere here – both in front of and behind the bar. The three small cottagey rooms are all similarly furnished with simple benches against the half-panelled walls, a pleasant mix of old country tables and chairs, a few bar stools and some country prints; quarry tiles on the floors (nice worn ones in the middle room), two log fires in little brick fireplaces, a huge black supporting beam in each of the low ochre ceilings, and (in the end room) some attractive cricketing pastels; some of the beams are hung with cricket bats. Harveys Best and two seasonal ales tapped from the cask and decent wine; cribbage, dominoes and an old Sussex coin game called toad in the hole. The front garden is delightful and old-fashioned with seats amidst small brick paths and mature flowering shrubs and plants; there are more seats behind the building. The wall paintings in the nearby church done by the Bloomsbury Group during WWII are worth a look.

🍽 **Good straightforward bar food includes home-made soup, garlic mushrooms, country pâté, local sausages, filled baked potatoes, ploughman's, gammon and egg, chicken, bacon and mushroom warm salad, steaks, and daily specials.** *Starters/Snacks: £4.50 to £6.75. Main Courses: £6.95 to £15.95. Puddings: £4.50*

Harveys ~ Lease Peter Brown ~ Real ale ~ Bar food (12-2.15, 6.30-9; all day weekends and in summer) ~ (01323) 870469 ~ Children in family room until 9pm ~ Dogs welcome ~ Open 11-11; 12-10.30 Sun; 11-3, 6-11 weekdays in winter; closed 25 Dec

Recommended by Simon and Mandy King, Kevin Thorpe, the Didler, Jenny and Peter Lowater, M and R Thomas, Richard Pitcher, Mike Gorton, Mrs Mahni Pannett, Alan Cowell, Michael Sargent

BLACKBOYS   TQ5220 MAP 3

Blackboys Inn 🍽
B2192, S edge of village; TN22 5LG

A welcome for both diners and drinkers in pretty 14th-c pub, interesting food, good choice of drinks and plenty of seats in nice garden

Although there's quite an emphasis on the imaginative food in this pretty 14th-c pub, drinkers are still made very welcome. The bustling locals' bar has a good, chatty atmosphere and the other little rooms have dark oak beams, bare boards or parquet, antique prints, and usually, a good log fire in the inglenook fireplace. Harveys Best, Dark Mild and a couple of seasonal guests on handpump and several wines by the glass; piped music. The garden has plenty of rustic tables overlooking the pond, with more under the chestnut trees. The Vanguard Way passes the pub, the Wealdway goes close by, and there's the Woodland Trust opposite. More reports please.

🍽 **Quite a wide choice of interesting bar food includes ploughman's, home-made burgers, soup, chilli squid, guinea fowl terrine with wild mushroom chutney, potted mackerel, chicken in muscat wine with tarragon and black pudding, scallops with smoked salmon, cream and parmesan, fresh asparagus risotto, pork cassoulet, and puddings such as chocolate almond torte and raspberry brûlée.** *Starters/Snacks: £4.50 to £7.50. Main Courses: £7.50 to £16.00. Puddings: £4.95*

Harveys ~ Tenant Paul James ~ Real ale ~ Bar food (all day) ~ Restaurant ~ (01825) 890283 ~ Children welcome ~ Dogs allowed in bar ~ Open 11am-midnight

Recommended by Steve Godfrey, Ann and Colin Hunt, Jude Wright, Tom and Jill Jones

---

People named as recommenders after the main entries have told us that the pub should be included. But they have not written the report – we have, after anonymous on-the-spot inspection.

BODIAM   TQ7626 MAP 3

Curlew ⑪

B2244 S of Hawkhurst, outside village at crossroads with turn-off to Castle; TN32 5UY

Popular dining pub with relaxed atmosphere, a fine wine list, real ales, friendly service and enjoyable food

Drinkers do drop into this popular dining pub – especially in the early evening – but most customers are here to enjoy the good food. Badger Best and Everards Tiger on handpump. The main bar has timbered walls and ceilings and a woodburning stove, and off to the right is a smaller room with more timbering in the red walls and neat napkinned tables. Badgers Gold and Timothy Taylors Landlord on handpump and several wines by the glass from a fine, large list and local cider; friendly, helpful service. The back restaurant is more formal though still keeping a relaxed atmosphere. The terraced garden is pretty in summer and there are lots of flowering baskets and troughs.

⑪ **Attractively presented food includes light lunches such as filled baguettes, calves liver and bacon with garlic mash and caramelised onion gravy, smoked haddock risotto with poached egg and hollandaise sauce and chicken curry with coconut cream rice as well as ham hock and parsley terrine with home-made piccalilli, a plate of spanish and italian meats, wild mushroom and broad bean pasta with truffle cream, rump of lamb with horseradish polenta, braised root vegetables and beetroot jus, fish and shellfish with baby vegetables and ramen noodles, and puddings such as crème brûlée and toffee bread and butter pudding with crème anglaise; they also offer a two- and three-course set menu.** *Starters/Snacks: £5.95 to £11.95. Main Courses: £7.95 to £19.50. Puddings: £4.95*

Free house ~ Licensee Simon Lazenby ~ Bar food (not Sun evening) ~ Restaurant ~ (01580) 861394 ~ Children welcome ~ Dogs allowed in bar ~ Open 11.30-11; 12-5 Sun; 11.30-3, 6-11 in winter; closed Sun evening

Recommended by Dave Braisted, Mrs J Ekins-Daukes, Mr and Mrs Hale, John Bell, Steve Godfrey, Jane Jeffcoate, Laurence and Kim Manning, Peter Meister, Louise English, Richard Mason, JMC, M G Hart

BRIGHTON   TQ3104 MAP 3

Basketmakers Arms £

Gloucester Road – the E end, near Cheltenham Place; off Marlborough Place (A23) via Gloucester Street; BN1 4AD

Bustling backstreet pub with friendly landlord, plenty of chatty customers, great drinks range, enjoyable food

The friendly and enthusiastic Mr Dowd has now been running this thriving local for 20 years. There's always a good mix of customers and a chatty, bustling atmosphere in the two small low-ceilinged rooms as well as brocaded wall benches and stools on the stripped wood floor, lots of interesting old tins all over the walls, cigarette cards on one beam with whisky labels on another, beermats, and some old advertisements, photographs and posters; piped music. Fullers London Pride, ESB, Butser and HSB and guests like Adnams Broadside and Butcombe on handpump, good wines (house wines come in three different glass sizes), at least 90 malt whiskies, 15 bourbons, ten irish whiskeys and good coffees; they do a splendid Pimms, and staff are helpful and cheerful. There are three metal tables out on the pavement.

⑪ **Good value enjoyable bar food using local, organic produce includes lots of sandwiches, filled baked potatoes, ploughman's, particularly good home-made meaty and vegetarian burgers, mexican chilli beef, tuna steak with salad, daily specials, and puddings such as sticky toffee pudding and chocolate pudding with custard or cream; popular Sunday roasts.** *Starters/Snacks: £2.75 to £3.95. Main Courses: £3.95 to £6.95. Puddings: £3.25*

Gales (Fullers) ~ Lease P and K Dowd, A Mawer, J Archdeacon ~ Real ale ~ Bar food (12-8.30(5 Sun, 6 Sat)) ~ (01273) 689006 ~ Children welcome until 8pm ~ Dogs allowed in bar ~ Open 11-11(midnight Thurs-Sat); 12-11 Sun; closed 26 Dec

Recommended by MLR, the Didler, Mayur Shah, Jude Wright, Ann and Colin Hunt, Janet Whittaker, Torrens Lyster, Bruce Bird, Richard Harris

Greys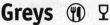

Southover Street, off A270 Lewes Road opposite The Level (public park); BN2 9UA

A good mix of drinkers and diners in friendly, bustling and interesting local, thoughtful choice of drinks, popular food; live music Monday evenings

This is an interesting place with a friendly welcome and a relaxed, informal mix of drinkers and diners. It's basically a good little restaurant sharing one small L-shaped room with an unabashed pubby local. Furnishings are basic, with simple wall seats and stools around mixed pub tables on bare boards and flagstones, ochre walls, and some varnished plank panelling around a flame-effect stove below a big metal canopy; piped music is at a reasonable level. The serving bar is on the right, with Harveys Best and Timothy Taylors Landlord on handpump, Leffe Blond on tap, a considerable range of belgian bottled beers, and a cheery local crowd on the bar stools and at the nearby tables; service by smiling, efficient staff. The five or six tables on the left, each with a little vase of flowers and lighted tea lamp, are the food bit – one corner table is snugged in by a high-backed settle, and another at the back is tucked into a quiet corner. The stair wall is papered with posters and flyers from bands, singers and poets who have performed here. The house wines, from Burgundy, are excellent value. There is not much daytime parking on this steep lane or the nearby streets. No children inside.

🍴 **From a shortish menu, the good food might include soup, toulouse sausages with onion gravy, seafood salad, game stew, lamb cutlets with fresh tarragon sauce, vegetable korma, fish pie, sirloin steak with a burgundy and shallot sauce, and puddings such as dark and white chocolate terrine with strawberry sauce and bread and butter pudding; they also offer good value two- and three-course set meals.** *Starters/Snacks: £4.50 to £5.00. Main Courses: £9.50 to £12.50. Puddings: £4.00 to £4.50*

Free house ~ Licensees Chris Taylor and Gill Perkins ~ Real ale ~ Bar food (12-2, 6-9; not Mon, or Tues all day, not Weds or Thurs lunchtimes or Sun evenings) ~ Restaurant ~ (01273) 680734 ~ Live music Mon evening ~ Open 4-11; 12-midnight Fri and Sat; 12am-11pm Sun; closed lunchtimes Mon-Thurs

Recommended by Guy Vowles, Tony and Wendy Hobden, MLR, Ann and Colin Hunt, Sue Demont, Tim Barrow

BURPHAM   TQ0308 MAP 3

George & Dragon 🍖

Warningcamp turn off A27 outside Arundel: follow road up and up; BN18 9RR

Popular dining pub in hilltop village with efficient service, appealing food, well kept ales and relaxed atmosphere

Even when busy – which this popular dining pub usually is – service manages to remain friendly and efficient. The front part is a restaurant with a wooden floor and a woodburning stove in a big inglenook on the right and a carpeted area has an old wireless set, nice scrubbed trestle tables and bar stools along the counter serving Arundel Gold, Kings Red River and Wells & Youngs Special from handpump. There's a couple of tables in a small light flagstoned middle area and a conservatory extension that looks over the garden. The back part of the pub, angling right round behind the bar servery, with a further extension beyond one set of internal windows, has solid pale country-kitchen furniture on neat bare boards and a fresh and airy décor with a little bleached pine panelling and long white curtains. The garden has picnic-sets under cocktail parasols. The lane up to this remote hill village is long and winding and the pub is at the end of the village between the partly Norman church (which has some unusual decoration) and cricket ground.

🍴 **Inventive food includes lunchtime ciabatta, ploughman's and small salads as well as smoked chicken and duck terrine with orange chutney, deep-fried herb crusted brie with a cranberry, redcurrant and port confit, walnut-crusted cod loin with parsnip purée, leek, smoked cheddar and butternut squash risotto, duck breast with redcurrant and black cherry sauce, lamb shank with mint and apricot glaze, and puddings such as lime and cassis panna cotta and chocolate and hazelnut terrine.** *Starters/Snacks: £5.50 to £6.45. Main Courses: £11.95 to £20.95. Puddings: £5.25*

Free house ~ Licensees Alastair and Angela Thackeray ~ Real ale ~ Bar food ~ Restaurant ~ (01903) 883131 ~ Children welcome ~ Dogs allowed in bar ~ Open 11-11; 12-10 Sun

Recommended by Miss J F Reay, Karen Eliot, Ian and Jane Irving, Elizabeth, Barry King, R T and J C Moggridge, Howard Dell, Cathryn and Richard Hicks, Martin and Karen Wake, Emma Ryan, Marianne and Peter Stevens, Ann and Colin Hunt, Sue Demont, Tim Barrow, Joan York, Tony and Wendy Hobden

BYWORTH   SU9821 MAP 2

Black Horse 🍺

Off A283; GU28 0HL

Usefully serving food all day, open fires, papers to read, several real ales; nice garden

Open all day and handily serving food all day as well, this rural pub has a quietly chatty atmosphere. There are large open fires and the simply furnished though smart bar has pews and scrubbed wooden tables on its bare floorboards, pictures and old photographs on the walls and newspapers to read. The back dining room has lots of nooks and crannies and upstairs is a games room with pool, bar billiards, darts, a juke box, games machine and board games; lovely views of the downs. Arundel Sussex Gold, Fullers London Pride, Timothy Taylors Landlord and Wells & Youngs Bitter on handpump. The particularly attractive garden has tables on a steep series of grassy terraces sheltered by banks of flowering shrubs that look across a drowsy valley to swelling woodland. More reports please.

🍴 As well as sandwiches, filled baked potatoes and ploughman's (served until 6pm), the bar food includes soup, thai fishcakes with sweet chilli sauce, lots of home-made pizzas, a pie of the day, home-cooked ham and two free-range eggs, cheese-topped cottage pie, beer-battered haddock and slow-roasted lamb shoulder in mint gravy. *Starters/Snacks: £3.25 to £6.95. Main Courses: £7.95 to £14.95. Puddings: £3.25 to £4.95*

Free house ~ Licensee Mark Robinson ~ Real ale ~ Bar food (all day) ~ Restaurant ~ (01798) 342424 ~ Children welcome ~ Dogs allowed in bar ~ Open 11.30-11; 12-10.30 Sun

Recommended by Kevin Thorpe, R B Gardiner, Dave Lowe, John Beeken, Jude Wright, Rosemary and Tom Hall, Bruce Bird, Mr and Mrs G Hughes

CHARLTON   SU8812 MAP 2

Fox Goes Free

Village signposted off A286 Chichester—Midhurst in Singleton, also from Chichester—Petworth via East Dean; PO18 0HU

Comfortable old pub with well organised staff, popular food and drink; nice surrounding walks

As there are some fine surrounding walks you are quite likely to find several walkers and their dogs at the bar in this busy pub, giving the place an informal and relaxed atmosphere. It's handy for Goodwood (and does get crowded on race days) and for the Weald and Downland Open Air Museum. Throughout, there are old irish settles, tables and chapel chairs, and the first of the dark and cosy series of separate rooms is a small bar with an open fireplace. Standing timbers divide a larger beamed bar which has a huge brick fireplace with a woodburning stove and old local photographs on the walls. A dining area with hunting prints looks over the garden and the South Downs beyond. The family extension is a clever conversion from horse boxes and the stables where the 1926 Goodwood winner was housed; darts and fruit machine. Archers Golden, Ballards Best, Harveys Best and a beer named for the pub on handpump, and eight wines by the glass. The attractive garden has plenty of picnic-sets among fruit trees and the terrace has fine downland views. It's a shame they insist on keeping your credit card behind the bar (one reader still had to do this even though he was paying with cash).

🍴 Well presented bar food includes filled baguettes, soup, chicken liver parfait with apple chutney, baked goats cheese with red pepper coulis, sausage and mash with onion gravy, honey-roast ham and egg, a curry of the day, red snapper on fennel and rocket salad with a citrus dressing, chicken breast wrapped in parma ham with creamed leeks, confit of organic pork with bubble and squeak, and puddings such as Baileys crème brûlée with honeycomb ice-cream and vanilla rice pudding. *Starters/Snacks: £4.95 to £7.95. Main Courses: £8.50 to £16.95. Puddings: £5.50*

Free house ~ Licensee David Coxon ~ Real ale ~ Bar food (12-2.30, 6.30-10; all day weekends) ~ (01243) 811461 ~ Children welcome ~ Dogs allowed in bar ~ Live music Weds evenings ~ Open 11-11(midnight Sat); 12-10.30 Sun ~ Bedrooms: £50S/£80S

Recommended by Mrs S Gardner, Paul and Shirley White, Tony and Wendy Hobden, W A Evershed, Tony and Jill Radnor, Ann and Colin Hunt, Ian Wilson, Bruce Bird, R G Trevis, MLR, John Evans, Tom and Jill Jones

CHIDDINGLY   TQ5414 MAP 3

Six Bells ★ £
Village signed off A22 Uckfield—Hailsham; BN8 6HE

Lively, unpretentious village local with good weekend live music, extremely good value bar food and friendly long-serving landlord

Happily, nothing changes at this unspoilt and old-fashioned pub. It's well run by the long-serving landlord, the atmosphere remains cheerful and friendly and the live music at weekends is as popular as ever. The bars have log fires as well as solid old wood furnishings such as pews and antique seats, lots of fusty artefacts and interesting bric-a-brac, and plenty of local pictures and posters. A sensitive extension provides some much needed family space; dominoes and cribbage. Courage Directors, Harveys Best and a guest beer on handpump. Outside at the back, there are some tables beyond a big raised goldfish pond and a boules pitch; the church opposite has an interesting Jefferay monument. Vintage and Kit car meetings outside the pub every month. This is a pleasant area for walks.

🍴 **The tasty but traditional bar food is exceptionally good value: french onion soup, filled baked potatoes, ploughman's, lentil, leek and mushroom loaf, chicken curry, steak and kidney pie, spare ribs in barbecue sauce and hock of ham.** *Starters/Snacks: £2.50 to £6.20. Main Courses: £4.75 to £7.50. Puddings: £3.50*

Free house ~ Licensees Paul Newman and Emma Bannister ~ Real ale ~ Bar food (12-2.30, 6-9.30; all day Fri-Sun) ~ (01825) 872227 ~ Children in family room ~ Dogs allowed in bar ~ Live music Fri, Sat and Sun evenings and Sun lunchtime ~ Open 11-3, 6-11; 11am-midnight Sat; 12-10.30 Sun

Recommended by Jenny and Peter Lowater, Mayur Shah, N R White, John Beeken, Kevin Thorpe

CHILGROVE   SU8116 MAP 2

Royal Oak
Off B2141 Petersfield—Chichester, signed Hooksway down steep single track; PO18 9JZ

Unchanging and peaceful country pub with welcoming landlord, decent traditional bar food and big pretty garden

What our readers like so much about this tucked away downland cottage is that it remains consistently enjoyable and unchanging. It's simply furnished with plain country-kitchen tables and chairs and there are huge log fires in the two cosy rooms of the partly brick-floored beamed bar. There's also a cottagey dining room and plainer family room. Arundel Castle and ASB, Hammerpot Red Hunter and a changing guest beer on handpump; piped music, cribbage and shut-the-box. There are plenty of picnic-sets under parasols on the grass of the big, pretty garden. The South Downs Way is close by.

🍴 **Sensibly priced traditional bar food includes ploughman's, filled baked potatoes, tuna pasta bake, sausage or chicken with chips, pies such as venison or steak and kidney, more elaborate choices such as salmon fillet with a creamy red thai sauce, half shoulder of lamb with red wine and rosemary and slow-cooked pork hock with apple and cider sauce, and puddings.** *Starters/Snacks: £4.50. Main Courses: £5.75 to £12.45. Puddings: £3.95*

Free house ~ Licensee Dave Jeffery ~ Real ale ~ Bar food (not Sun evening or Mon) ~ Restaurant ~ (01243) 535257 ~ Children in family room until 8pm ~ Dogs allowed in bar ~ Live music second Fri evening of the month ~ Open 11.30-2.30, 6-11; 12-3 Sun; closed Sun evening and all day Mon

Recommended by Marianne and Peter Stevens, Torrens Lyster, R B Gardiner, W A Eversherd, Ann and Colin Hunt, Prof and Mrs S Barnett

White Horse ⓦ 🍷 🛏

B2141 Petersfield—Chichester; PO18 9HX

Fantastic choice of wines and super food in quietly upmarket inn; comfortable bedrooms

The attentive landlord in this civilised and quietly upmarket dining inn tells us he is happy to welcome walkers, cyclists and dogs but is keen that we should mention that they do not sell drinks on their own and that some food (whether that is a bowl of soup, a baguette or full meal) must be taken, too. There are dark brown deco leather armchairs and a sofa grouped on dark boards near the bar counter, and on either side are three or four well spaced good-sized sturdy tables with good pale spindleback side and elbow chairs on lighter newer boards. The light and airy feeling is helped by uncluttered cream walls, clear lighting and a big bow window. The bar counter is made up from claret, burgundy and other mainly french wooden wine cases – and fine wines play an important part here with 600 wines on their exceptional list; on the restaurant menu they recommend a wine to go with every dish. Ballards on handpump and well reproduced piped music. The bar has a woodburner on one side and a log fire on the other. Past here, it opens into a restaurant with comfortable modern seats and attractively laid tables – as in the bar, generously spaced out. Outside, one neat lawn has teak tables and chairs under an old yew tree; the pond has been restored this year. Comfortable bedrooms in separate annexe and super continental breakfasts brought to your room in a wicker hamper.

🍴 Using organic, local produce the appetising food includes bar snacks such as filled baked potatoes and filled baguettes as well as more elaborate choices from the restaurant menu (eaten in the bar, too) like soup, warm salad of black pudding with scallops and orange sauce, smoked haddock tart topped with a poached free-range egg and hollandaise, calves liver and bacon with shallot gravy, chargrilled aubergine and courgette stack with butter bean purée, lamb hotpot, baked crab thermidor, fillet of beef with green peppercorn sauce, and puddings such as warm chocolate tart with orange ice-cream and raspberry soufflé; they also have a dining club where they design menus and wine around a theme. *Starters/Snacks: £5.95 to £9.50. Main Courses: £14.95 to £22.50. Puddings: £6.95 to £8.95*

Free house ~ Licensee Charles Burton ~ Real ale ~ Bar food (12-2, 7-10; not Sun evening or all day Mon) ~ Restaurant ~ (01243) 535219 ~ Children welcome ~ Dogs allowed in bar and bedrooms ~ Piano Sat evening in restaurant and some Suns ~ Open 11-3, 6-11; 12-3 Sun; closed Sun evening ~ Bedrooms: £95B/£120B

Recommended by John Evans, Ann and Colin Hunt, Miss A E Dare

COOLHAM   TQ1423 MAP 3

George & Dragon

Dragons Green, Dragons Lane; pub signed just off A272, about 1½ m E of village; RH13 8GE

Pleasant little country cottage with beamed bars, decent food and drink and friendly service

This tile-hung cottage is handy for Shipley Windmill, the former home of Hilaire Belloc. The cosy bar has heavily timbered walls, a partly woodblock and partly polished-tile floor, unusually low and massive black beams (see if you can decide whether the date cut into one is 1677 or 1577), simple chairs and rustic stools, some brass, and a big inglenook fireplace with an early 17th-c grate. There's also a smaller back bar and restaurant. Badger K&B and a seasonal ale on handpump; pleasant, helpful service and a relaxed atmosphere. The sizeable orchard garden which is neatly kept with pretty flowers and shrubs has quite a few picnic-sets; the little front garden has a sad 19th-c memorial to the son of a previous innkeeper. The pub changed hands as we went to press – news please.

🍴 Well liked bar food includes lunchtime sandwiches, filled baked potatoes and ploughman's as well as soup (always vegetarian), salmon and crab thai fishcakes with dipping sauce, chicken liver pâté, ham and eggs, field mushrooms stuffed with goats cheese and herbs, breaded chicken breast with herb and garlic butter, steak, stilton and mushroom pie, and puddings such as Baileys crème brûlée and chocolate slice. *Starters/Snacks: £3.95 to £6.50. Main Courses: £7.75 to £12.50. Puddings: £3.95*

Badger ~ Real ale ~ Bar food (12-2(3 Sun), 6.30-9) ~ Restaurant ~ (01403) 741320 ~ Children welcome ~ Dogs allowed in bar ~ Open 12-3, 6-11; 12-11(10.30 Sun) Sat
Recommended by John Beeken, Terry Buckland, Katharine Cowherd, Philip and Cheryl Hill, David Coleman

COWBEECH   TQ6114 MAP 3
Merrie Harriers
Village signposted from A271; BN27 4JQ

New landlord for village inn with beams and log fire in pleasant bar and plenty of fish on menu; seats in terraced garden

A new licensee took over this white clapboarded village inn just as we went to press, but has no plans to change too much. The beamed and panelled bar has a log fire in the brick inglenook, quite a mix of tables and Harveys Best and Timothy Taylors Landlord on handpump; several wines by the glass. There's also a brick-walled and oak-ceilinged back restaurant; piped music. The terraced garden – with country views – has rustic seats amongst colourful shrubs and pots. More reports on the new regime, please.

🍴 Bar food now includes lunchtime sandwiches, whitebait, ham and eggs, lasagne, grilled trout and tuna steak, and from the à la carte menu there might be king prawns in garlic and brandy, caramelised scallops with crispy parma ham and tangerine salad, steak and kidney pie, walnut and gorgonzola ravioli with a tomato, mozzarella and basil sauce, smoked duck breast with their own fig jam, calves liver and bacon, whole bass stuffed with herbs and lemon, and puddings such as individual banoffi pavlova and sticky toffee pudding with butterscotch sauce. *Starters/Snacks: £4.25 to £6.95. Main Courses: £9.95 to £16.95. Puddings: £4.95*

Free house ~ Licensee Duncan Smart ~ Real ale ~ Bar food ~ Restaurant ~ (01323) 833108 ~ Children welcome ~ Dogs allowed in bar ~ Open 11.30-3(4 Sat), 6-11; 12-4, 6-10.30 Sun
Recommended by Mike Gorton

DITCHLING   TQ3215 MAP 3
Bull ♀
High Street (B2112); BN6 8TA

Handsome old building with cosy atmosphere in rambling traditional bars, good choice of drinks, quite an emphasis on food; nearby walks

This 16th-c inn is said to get its name from the Papal Bull designating it as a safe house for pilgrims and travellers to the great monastery at Lewes. The invitingly cosy main bar on the right is quite large, rambling and pleasantly traditional with well worn old wooden furniture, beams and floorboards and a blazing winter fire. To the left, the nicely furnished rooms have a calm, restrained mellow décor and candles, and beyond that there's a snug area with chesterfields around a low table; piped music. Harveys Best and Timothy Taylors Landlord with a couple of guests such as Goddards Fuggle-Dee-Dum and Weltons Old Cocky on handpump and 14 wines by the glass. Picnic-sets in the good-sized pretty downland garden which is gently lit at night look up towards Ditchling Beacon and there are more tables on a suntrap back terrace; good wheelchair access. The charming old village is a popular base for the South Downs Way and other walks. More reports please.

🍴 Well liked bar food includes sandwiches, soup, tuna tartare with quail egg, rocket and toast, chicken, smoked bacon and gherkin terrine with onion jam, pure scotch beefburger with monterey jack cheese and coleslaw, beer-battered haddock, local sausages with bubble and squeak mash and onion gravy, roasted red onion, goats cheese and thyme tarte tatin, sautéed chicken breast stuffed with mozzarella and smoked bacon, veal, ham and mushroom pie, and puddings such as chocolate and hazelnut brownie and caramelised orange and toffee bread and butter pudding. *Starters/Snacks: £4.00 to £7.00. Main Courses: £9.50 to £17.00. Puddings: £5.50 to £6.50*

Free house ~ Licensee Dominic Worrall ~ Real ale ~ Bar food (12-2.30, 7-9.30; 12-6 Sun; not Sun evening) ~ (01273) 843147 ~ Children welcome ~ Dogs allowed in bar ~ Open 11-11; 12-10.30 Sun ~ Bedrooms: /£80B
Recommended by Andy and Claire Barker

DONNINGTON   SU8501 MAP 2

Blacksmiths Arms

Turn off A27 on to A286 signposted Selsey, then almost immediately left on to B2201; PO20 7PR

Big garden with quite a few animals, attractive bar rooms with lots to look at

This is a small white roadside cottage with a big garden that is popular with families: play area with swingboats, a climbing frame, a rabbit called Barnham, three miniature schnauzers (Tess, Cleo, and Alfie), a cat (Amber), four tortoises (only allowed in the garden on special occasions), and plenty of picnic-sets. Inside, the small low-ceilinged rooms are attractively decorated and have Victorian prints on the walls, solid, comfortable furnishings, and a relaxed atmosphere. There's a back restaurant. Fullers London Pride, Greene King Abbot and Oakleaf Bitter on handpump.

🍴 Bar food (not cheap) includes lunchtime sandwiches and filled baguettes, ploughman's, soup, home-cooked ham and egg, a pie of the day, roasted goats cheese and vegetable wellington, beer-battered cod, beef curry, duck breast with home-made orange marmalade, selsey crab salad, and puddings. *Starters/Snacks: £4.95 to £7.95. Main Courses: £9.95 to £16.95. Puddings: £4.95*

Punch ~ Lease George and Lesley Ward ~ Real ale ~ Bar food (12-2.30, 6.30-8.30) ~ Restaurant ~ (01243) 783999 ~ Children welcome ~ Dogs allowed in bar ~ Open 11-3, 5.30-11(10 winter Mon and Tues); 11-3, 6-midnight Sat; 12-10 Sun
Recommended by Lawrence Pearse, Bob and Margaret Holder, Susan and John Douglas, Joan York

EAST ASHLING   SU8207 MAP 2

Horse & Groom ♀ 🍺

B2178 NW of Chichester; PO18 9AX

Busy country pub with real ales in unchanging front drinkers' bar, plenty of dining space and decent food

If you're heading for the Portsmouth ferries, this bustling country pub is a useful place to stop – it's also handy for Kingly Vale Nature Reserve. But if it's just a drink you're after, many customers head for the front part with its old pale flagstones and a woodburning stove in a big inglenook on the right or the carpeted area with its old wireless set, nice scrubbed trestle tables and bar stools lining the counter. Dark Star Hophead, Harveys Bitter, Hop Back Summer Lightning and Wells & Youngs on handpump and several wines by the glass; board games. There's also a small light flagstoned middle area with a couple of tables. The back part of the pub, angling right round behind the bar servery, with a further extension beyond one set of internal windows, has solid pale country-kitchen furniture on neat bare boards, and a fresh and airy décor, with a little bleached pine panelling and long white curtains. French windows lead out to a garden with picnic-sets under cocktail parasols. It does get extremely busy on Goodwood race days.

🍽 As well as sandwiches and filled baguettes, the bar food might include filled baked potatoes, ploughman's, home-cooked ham and eggs, cajun chicken, steak in ale pie, lamb cutlets with rosemary jus, whole baked plaice with lemon butter, and puddings. *Starters/Snacks: £5.95 to £7.95. Main Courses: £9.95 to £15.95. Puddings: £3.95 to £4.95*

Free house ~ Licensee Michael Martell ~ Real ale ~ Bar food (12-2.15(2 Sat, 2.30 Sun), 6.30-9.15) ~ Restaurant ~ (01243) 575339 ~ Children welcome ~ Dogs allowed in bar and bedrooms ~ Open 12-3, 6-11; 12-6 Sun; closed Sun evening ~ Bedrooms: £40.50B/£65B

Recommended by Paul and Shirley White, Bruce Bird, Ann and Colin Hunt, Tony and Wendy Hobden, Malcolm Pellatt, Gordon Neighbour, David Coleman, Ian and Joan Blackwell

EAST CHILTINGTON

TQ3715 MAP 3

Jolly Sportsman 🍽 ♀

2 miles N of B2116; Chapel Lane – follow sign to 13th-c church; BN7 3BA

Excellent modern food in civilised, rather smart place, small bar for drinkers, contemporary furnishings, fine wine list and huge range of malt whiskies; nice garden

Although most people come to this professionally run, civilised place for the imaginative modern cooking, there are a couple of chairs in the chatty little bar by the winter log fire set aside for drinkers and a mix of furniture on the stripped wood floors. Dark Star Hophead and Mighty Oak Simply the Best tapped from the cask, a remarkably good wine list with nine by the glass, over 100 malt whiskies and quite a few cognacs and armagnacs. The larger restaurant is smart but informal with contemporary light wood furniture and modern landscapes on coffee-coloured walls. There are rustic tables and benches under gnarled trees in a pretty cottagey front garden with more on the terrace and the front bricked area, and the large back lawn with a children's play area looks out towards the South Downs; good walks nearby.

🍽 As well as a two- and three-course set lunch menu, the first class – if not cheap – food might include snail and parsley risotto, chilli salt squid salad, duck liver parfait with onion marmalade, seared mackerel fillet and scallop with tomato and onion reduction, crispy duck confit with plum and ginger compote, local lamb with aubergine, spinach and pepper stew, poached skate wing with lemon, caper and chive butter sauce, and puddings such as panna cotta with poached quince and pear purée and apricot, walnut and ginger toffee pudding. *Starters/Snacks: £4.85 to £8.50. Main Courses: £8.75 to £18.50. Puddings: £4.75 to £5.95*

Free house ~ Licensee Bruce Wass ~ Real ale ~ Bar food (12-2.15(3 Sun), 7-9(10 Fri and Sat); not Sun evening or Mon) ~ Restaurant ~ (01273) 890400 ~ Children welcome ~ Dogs welcome ~ Open 12-2.30, 6-11; 12-11 Sat; 12-4 Sun; closed Sun evening, all day Mon, three days Christmas

Recommended by David Cumberland, Barry and Victoria Lister, June Pullen, Susan and John Douglas, Sue Demont, Tim Barrow

EAST DEAN

SU9012 MAP 2

Star & Garter 🍽 ♀

Village signposted with Charlton off A286 in Singleton; also signposted off A285; note that there are two East Deans in Sussex (this one is N of Chichester) – OS Sheet 197 map reference 904129; PO18 0JG

Attractively furnished bar rooms in light and airy well run pub, relaxed atmosphere, helpful owners and enjoyable food and drink

'A good all-rounder' is how several readers have described this consistently enjoyable brick and flint pub. It is more or less one roomy square area, with sturdy and individual mainly stripped and scrubbed tables in various sizes and an interesting variety of seating from country-kitchen chairs through chunky modern dining chairs to cushioned pews and some handsome 17th-c or 18th-c carved oak seats; broad stripped boards, a few stripped beams, and some stripped panelling and masonry. The high ceiling, big windows and uncluttered walls give a light and airy feel, and tables over on the right-hand side can be booked; helpful, welcoming owners, an easy-going atmosphere, a rack of daily papers by the entrance, and piped music. The bar counter (with a few bar stools, often used for those reading menus) is over on the left, with a dozen or so well chosen wines by the glass, Arundel Gauntlet and Ballards Best and Nyewood Gold tapped from casks in a back stillroom, a couple of farm ciders such as Weston's and Whitehead's, a dozen malt whiskies, and an espresso machine. The sheltered terrace behind has teak tables and chairs with big canvas parasols and heaters; steps go up to a walled lawn with picnic-sets (there are also a few steps up to the front door). The pub is on the South Downs Way.

🍴 As well as plenty of seafood and a daily specials board, there's a shortish menu that includes lunchtime filled baguettes, grilled goats cheese with baby beetroot and beetroot dressing, salt duck on marinated fennel, celery and radish, pasta in wild mushroom sauce, steak and kidney pudding, chicken breast in creamy tarragon sauce, slow-cooked shank of lamb with red onions in a port and rosemary sauce, and puddings such as chocolate and ginger baked cheesecake and Baileys bread and butter pudding with custard; they also offer a good value, early evening main course option. *Starters/Snacks: £4.00 to £8.50. Main Courses: £8.50 to £17.00. Puddings: £5.00 to £5.75*

Free house ~ Licensee Oliver Ligertwood ~ Real ale ~ Bar food (12-2.30, 6.30-10; all day weekends) ~ Restaurant ~ (01243) 811318 ~ Children welcome ~ Dogs allowed in bar ~ Open 11-3, 6-11; 11am-midnight Fri and Sat; 12-10.30 Sun; 11-3, 6-11 Fri in winter; closed evenings 25 and 26 Dec ~ Bedrooms: £60S(£80B)/£80S(£100B)

Recommended by Janet Whittaker, Tony and Wendy Hobden, Ann and Colin Hunt, M and GR, Cathy Robinson, Ed Coombe, OPUS, Mr and Mrs Gordon Turner, Bruce and Penny Wilkie, R B Gardiner, W A Evershed, Mrs Jennifer Hurst, William Goodhart

EAST LAVANT   SU8608 MAP 2

Royal Oak 🍴 ♀ 🛏

Village signposted off A286 N of Chichester; Pook Lane; PO18 0AX

Bustling and friendly dining pub with cheerful landlord, proper drinking area, excellent food, extensive wine list and real ales; super bedrooms

Handy for Goodwood and Chichester, this pretty little white house has cushioned seats and tables under green parasols on the flagstoned front terrace and far-reaching views to the Downs; rambling around the side and back are terraced, brick and grass areas with more seats and attractive tubs and baskets. Inside, it's open plan with a decent, well used drinking area at the front with wall seats and sofas, good lighting, Badger K&B and Stinger and Ballards Best tapped from the cask, 14 wines by the glass from an extensive wine list, and friendly, attentive service; there's real attention to detail. The attached seating area is focused on dining and sensitively furnished with brown suede and leather dining chairs around scrubbed pine tables and pictures of local scenes and of motor sport on the yellow walls; the atmosphere throughout is informal and relaxed, there are winter log fires, church candles, low beams and exposed brickwork. The bedrooms are stylish and well equipped and they also have self-catering cottages. The car park is across the road; good walks.

🍴 First-class food includes soup, terrine of ham hock and foie gras, red cabbage and celeriac salad, oriental crispy duck with watercress and bean shoot salad, soy, honey and ginger, wild mushroom and artichoke risotto with truffle oil, salmon fishcakes (kiln-smoked), buttered spinach and parsley and caper sauce, scottish beefburger with roasted cherry tomato salsa, confit of duck leg, savoy cabbage and boulangère potatoes with a red wine and puy lentil sauce, calves liver and bacon with celeriac mash, fried kale and red wine sauce, daily specials, and puddings such as sticky toffee and apple pudding with cinnamon ice-cream or chocolate and pistachio slice with elderflower ice-cream. *Starters/Snacks: £5.50 to £9.00. Main Courses: £11.50 to £19.00. Puddings: £5.50*

Free house ~ Licensee Nick Sutherland ~ Real ale ~ Bar food ~ (01243) 527434 ~ Children welcome ~ Dogs allowed in bar ~ Open 11-11 ~ Bedrooms: £75B/£90B

Recommended by David M Godfrey, Tracey and Stephen Groves, Lionel and Sylvia Kopelowitz, Ian and Joan Blackwell

ELSTED

SU8119 MAP 2

Three Horseshoes 🍴 🍺

Village signposted from B2141 Chichester—Petersfield; also reached easily from A272 about 2 miles W of Midhurst, turning left heading W; GU29 0JY

Bustling, friendly and well run country pub, congenial little beamed rooms, proper food, good drinks; wonderful views from flower-filled garden

A favourite with many, this 16th-c pub manages – as one of our readers put it – to appeal 'to both the real ale and champagne crowd'. It's very well run and the snug little rooms have a friendly, chatty atmosphere, ancient beams and flooring, antique furnishings, log fires and candlelight, fresh flowers on the tables and attractive prints and photographs; it's best to book to be sure of a table. Racked on a stillage behind the bar counter, the real ales include a changing beer from Bowman, Ballards Best, Fullers London Pride, Harveys Best and Flowerpots Bitter; summer cider; dominoes. The garden in summer is lovely with plenty of tables, pretty flowers (and two new rose beds) and stunning views; maybe free-roaming bantams, too.

🍴 **Particularly good food includes soup, a generous ploughman's with a good choice of cheeses, smoked duck, roasted pepper and bacon salad, venison either as a fillet with a port and redcurrant sauce or in a winter stew, cottage pie, butternut squash and brie lasagne, lamb with apples and apricots, fish pie, seasonal crab and lobster, and puddings such as treacle tart or various cheesecakes.** *Starters/Snacks: £4.50 to £7.95. Main Courses: £8.50 to £15.95. Puddings: £4.95*

Free house ~ Licensee Sue Beavis ~ Real ale ~ Bar food ~ (01730) 825746 ~ Well behaved children allowed ~ Dogs allowed in bar ~ Open 11-2.30, 6-11; 12-3, 7-10.30 Sun

Recommended by Michael B Griffith, R B Gardiner, Nick Lawless, W A Evershed, John Evans, Paul and Shirley White, Adrian Wilkes, Miss A E Dare, Jeff Davies, Miss J F Reay, Ian and Joan Blackwell, Tony and Jill Radnor

ERIDGE STATION

TQ5434 MAP 3

Huntsman 🍷 🍺

Signposted off A26 S of Eridge Green; Eridge Road; TN3 9LE

Refurbished little country local with friendly landlord, interesting bar food (lots of seasonal game), excellent wines and seats in sizeable garden

This small and unpretentious country local has been refurbished this year. The two rooms have been partially opened up to create more space, wooden floorboards have been installed throughout and new dark wooden dining chairs and a nice mix of matching tables have been added. There are plenty of amusing pictures of hunting scenes. The quietly friendly landlord has considerable wine expertise (they offer a fantastic choice of over two dozen wines by the glass) and Badger Best, First Gold and Tanglefoot are particularly well kept on handpump; farm cider, good coffee. A new decked area with outdoor heaters and picnic-sets has been built, and there's now an outside bar; more picnic-sets on the lawn among weeping willows and other trees. They organise quite a few events, such as summer barbecues. Motorcyclists meet here on Tuesday nights, and usually on the first Sunday in August stage a highly polished bike show in the garden. The building started life around the middle of the last century as an Abergavenny estate hotel for the station, and still has the Abergavenny arms above the main door. It's virtually alone here apart from the station itself – which on weekdays is responsible for filling the hamlet's roadside verges with commuters' cars. Plenty of space at weekends, though.

🍴 **As well as sandwiches, the interesting bar food might include soup, smoked haddock fishcake with tomato and basil sauce, red onion and goats tart with fig sauce, couscous and cheddar loaf with spiced winter vegetables, home-cooked ham and eggs, pigeon burger with cranberry and red onion relish served on a large mushroom, steak and Guinness sausages with colcannon mash and onion gravy, and puddings such as date and walnut pudding with toffee sauce and chocolate, sweet chestnut and Cointreau torte.** *Starters/Snacks: £4.50 to £7.00. Main Courses: £8.00 to £18.00. Puddings: £4.00 to £5.50*

Badger ~ Tenants Simon Wood and Nicola Tester ~ Real ale ~ Bar food (11.30-2(2.30 Sat, 3 Sun), 6-9(9.30 Fri and Sat); not Sun evening or Mon) ~ (01892) 864258 ~ Children allowed but with restrictions ~ Dogs allowed in bar ~ Open 11.30-3(2.30 winter weekdays), 5.30-11; 11.30-11 Sat; 12-11 Sun; 12-4, 7-10.30 Sun in winter; closed Mon (except bank hols when open 12-4); first two weeks Jan

Recommended by Ian Phillips, Paul A Moore, Pete Walker, Bill and Pauline Harvey, Robert A Dean

FITTLEWORTH   TQ0118 MAP 2

Swan 🛏

Lower Street (B2138, off A283 W of Pulborough); RH20 1EL

Pretty tile-hung inn with comfortable beamed bar and plenty of seats in big back garden; comfortable bedrooms

As we went to press, there was a possibility of some change in management at this pretty tile-hung inn. The beamed main bar is comfortable and relaxed with windsor armchairs and bar stools on the part-stripped wood and part-carpeted floor, there are wooden truncheons over the big inglenook fireplace (which has good winter log fires), and Fullers London Pride and Youngs on handpump; piped music. There's a big back lawn with plenty of well spaced tables and flowering shrubs and benches in front by the village lane; good nearby walks in beech woods. More reports on any changes, please.

🍴 **Bar food has included lunchtime sandwiches and ploughman's, soup, pâté, smoked haddock with a rarebit topping on bubble and squeak topped with a poached egg, bangers and mash, cajun chicken, home-made vegetable samosas and steaks.** *Starters/Snacks: £5.00 to £7.00. Main Courses: £10.95 to £18.95. Puddings: £4.95 to £6.75*

Enterprise ~ Real ale ~ Bar food ~ Restaurant ~ (01798) 865429 ~ Children allowed until 9pm ~ Dogs allowed in bar ~ Open 10-3, 5-11(10.30 in winter); 12-4, 7-10.30 Sun ~ Bedrooms: £55B/£85B

Recommended by R B Gardiner, BOB, Karen Eliot, Jude Wright

FLETCHING   TQ4223 MAP 3

Griffin ★ 🍴 ♟ 🛏

Village signposted off A272 W of Uckfield; TN22 3SS

SUSSEX DINING PUB OF THE YEAR

Busy, gently upmarket inn with good service, excellent interesting food, a fine wine list, real ales and comfortable bedrooms; big garden with far views

Both the licensees and their young, friendly staff are sure to make you welcome in this civilised old inn. It does get extremely busy (particularly at weekends) but service remains efficient with a light touch and plenty of humour. There are beamed and quaintly panelled bar rooms with blazing log fires, old photographs and hunting prints, straightforward close-set furniture including some captain's chairs, and china on a delft shelf. There's a small bare-boarded serving area off to one side and a snug separate bar with sofas and TV. Badger Tanglefoot, Harveys Best and Kings Horsham Best on handpump and a fine wine list with 13 (including champagne and sweet wine) by the glass. The two acres of garden behind the pub look across fine rolling countryside towards Sheffield Park and there are plenty of seats here and on the sandstone terrace with its woodburning oven. The bedrooms, particularly the newish ones in the next door building, are very comfortable.

'Children welcome' means the pub says it lets children inside without any special restriction. If it allows them in, but to restricted areas such as an eating area or family room, we specify this. Some pubs may impose an evening time limit. We do not mention limits after 9pm as we assume children are home by then.

🍴 First class food using their own vegetables includes hot ciabatta sandwiches, interesting soups, scallops with crispy pancetta and a tomato and coriander salsa, chicken, pigeon and venison terrine with pear chutney, green thai vegetable curry with butternut squash, spinach and coconut, beer-battered cod, wild boar sausages on chorizo and chickpea stew, moules with frites and aïoli, honey-glazed confit of duck with puy lentils, coriander, sweet potato and spinach, and puddings such as white chocolate brioche bread and butter pudding and vanilla and grappa panna cotta with a spiced apricot and almond compote. *Starters/Snacks: £5.50 to £8.50. Main Courses: £9.50 to £15.95. Puddings: £5.50*

Free house ~ Licensees J Pullan, T Erlam, M W Wright ~ Real ale ~ Bar food (12-2.30, 7-9.30) ~ Restaurant ~ (01825) 722890 ~ Children welcome if supervised ~ Dogs allowed in bar ~ Live jazz Fri evening and Sun lunchtime ~ Open 12-midnight(11 Sun); 12-3, 6-11 in winter; closed 25 Dec and evening 26 Dec and 1 Jan ~ Bedrooms: £60B/£80S(£95B)

Recommended by Andy Booth, Edward Faridany, Kenneth Gervase-Williams, Tom and Ruth Rees, Alan Clark, John Ralph, Gerry and Rosemary Dobson, R B Gardiner, John and Jackie Chalcraft, Mike and Mary Carter, Mike Gorton, Ann and Colin Hunt, Andrea Rampley, Simon Rodway, Grahame Brooks, David Cosham, Martin and Karen Wake, Ian and Sue Hiscock, Susan and John Douglas, P Waterman, Peter Meister, Alan Cowell, Richard Harris

HEATHFIELD

TQ5920 MAP 3

Star 🍺

Old Heathfield – head E out of Heathfield itself on A265, then fork right on to B2096; turn right at signpost to Heathfield Church then keep bearing right; pub on left immediately after church; TN21 9AH

Pleasant old pub with bustling, friendly atmosphere, good mix of locals and visitors, well liked food and decent choice of drinks; pretty garden

As we went to press the kitchens were closed for refurbishment and a new licensee had just taken over this nice old pub. There is always a good mix of locals and visitors and the L-shaped beamed bar has a roaring winter log fire in the inglenook fireplace, panelling, built-in wall settles and window seats, and just four or five tables; a doorway leads into a similarly furnished room. The tables are candlelit at night and it's all spotlessly kept. Harveys Best, Shepherd Neame Best and a guest beer on handpump, and half a dozen good wines by the glass; piped music. The garden is very prettily planted, there's rustic furniture under smart umbrellas, and lovely views of rolling oak-lined sheep pastures. Turner thought it fine enough to paint. More reports please.

🍴 Chalked up on boards, the well liked food might include lunchtime sandwiches, marinated anchovies with roast tomatoes and rocket, crayfish and avocado salad, salmon fillet with red pepper and tomato salsa, steak and mushroom pie, local fish and chips, oyster mushroom risotto, half shoulder of lamb in rosemary, garlic and redcurrant, honey-roast pork with apple compote, and puddings such as hot chocolate fondant with vanilla ice-cream. *Starters/Snacks: £4.50 to £8.50. Main Courses: £8.50 to £19.50. Puddings: £5.50*

Free house ~ Licensee Sarah Percival ~ Real ale ~ Bar food (12-2.15, 7-9.30) ~ Restaurant ~ (01435) 863570 ~ Children in eating area of bar ~ Dogs welcome ~ Open 11.30-3, 5.30-11; 12-4, 7-10.30 Sun

Recommended by Susan and John Douglas, Kevin Thorpe, Dr Nigel Bowles, Mr and Mrs Hale

HORSHAM

TQ1730 MAP 3

Black Jug 🍷

North Street; RH12 1RJ

Bustling town pub with wide choice of drinks, efficient staff, well liked food

A new licensee has taken over here but has not made any big changes. There's an airy, open-plan, turn-of-the-century-style room with a large central bar, a nice collection of sizeable dark wood tables and comfortable chairs on a stripped wood floor and interesting old prints and photographs above a dark wood panelled dado on the cream walls. A spacious conservatory has similar furniture and lots of hanging baskets. Adnams Broadside, Greene King IPA, Hop Back Crop Circle, St Austell Tribute and Weltons Old Cocky on handpump, around 60 malt whiskies, lots of gins, vodkas and rums and 20 wines by the glass. The pretty flower-filled back terrace has plenty of garden furniture by outside heaters. The small car park is for staff and deliveries only but you can park next door in the council car park.

🍴 Bar food includes sandwiches, ploughman's, potted salmon with pickled cucumber, warm salad of bacon, black pudding, poached egg and mustard dressing, baked ham and free-range eggs, roasted vegetable hotpot, rump of lamb with garlic mash and spinach and rosemary sauce, roast breast of duck with juniper sauce, beef and stilton pie, and puddings such as dark chocolate torte with cinnamon custard and treacle sponge pudding. *Starters/Snacks: £4.25 to £7.25. Main Courses: £8.95 to £14.25. Puddings: £4.95*

Brunning & Price ~ Manager Neil Gander ~ Real ale ~ Bar food (all day) ~ (01403) 253526 ~ Children over 10 with adults, daytime only ~ Dogs allowed in bar ~ Open 12-11(midnight Fri and Sat); 12-10.30 Sun; closed 25 Dec, 1 Jan
Recommended by Dave Lowe, Jude Wright, Ian Phillips, Tony and Wendy Hobden

ICKLESHAM   TQ8716 MAP 3

Queens Head ♀ ⊲

Just off A259 Rye—Hastings; TN36 4BL

Friendly, well run country pub, extremely popular with locals and visitors, with a good range of beers, proper home cooking and seats in garden with fine views

This is a really enjoyable, consistently well run pub that people come back to again and again. The long-serving landlord and his staff are friendly and efficient, there's always a good, bustling atmosphere, and a pleasing range of real ales. The open-plan areas work round a very big serving counter which stands under a vaulted beamed roof, the high beamed walls and ceiling of the easy-going bar are lined with shelves of bottles and covered with farming implements and animal traps, and there are well used pub tables and old pews on the brown patterned carpet. Other areas have big inglenook fireplaces and the back room is decorated with old bicycle and motorbike prints and has some old bikes hanging from the ceiling. Courage Directors and Greene King IPA and Abbot with guests such as Gales HSB, Harveys Best, Hogs Back Hair Of The Hog and Rother Valley Level Best on handpump, Biddenden cider, and a dozen wines by the glass. Piped jazz or blues and darts. Picnic-sets look out over the vast, gently sloping plain of the Brede Valley from the little garden, there's a children's play area, and boules. Good local walks.

🍴 The reasonably priced, well liked bar food includes sandwiches, filled baked potatoes, ploughman's, soup, chicken liver pâté, ham and egg, a curry of the day, leek, brie and bacon pasta, steak and mushroom in ale pie, leek and smoked haddock mornay, a mixed grill, daily specials, and puddings such as apple pie and profiteroles with chocolate sauce. *Starters/Snacks: £4.00 to £5.95. Main Courses: £7.25 to £14.95. Puddings: £3.50 to £3.95*

Free house ~ Licensee Ian Mitchell ~ Real ale ~ Bar food (12-2.30, 6-9.30; all day Sat, Sun and bank hols; not 25 or 26 Dec) ~ (01424) 814552 ~ Well behaved children in eating area of bar until 8.30pm ~ Dogs allowed in bar ~ Live music Sun 4-6pm ~ Open 11-11; 12-10.30 Sun; closed evenings 25 and 26 Dec
Recommended by Kevin Thorpe, Stephen Harvey, Peter Meister, Christopher Turner, N R White, Lucien Perring, Chris Maynard, E D Bailey, Tina and David Woods-Taylor, Steve Godfrey, Mike Gorton, Danielle Glann, Gene and Tony Freemantle

---

Please keep sending us reports. We rely on readers for news of new discoveries, and particularly for news of changes – however slight – at the fully described pubs. No stamp needed: The Good Pub Guide, FREEPOST TN1569, Wadhurst, E Sussex TN5 7BR or send your report through our website: www.goodguides.co.uk

LODSWORTH   SU9321 MAP 2

Halfway Bridge Inn ♀ 🛏

Just before village, on A272 Midhurst—Petworth; GU28 9BP

Smart, contemporary décor in several dining areas, log fires, real ales, quite a few wines by the glass, modern food; lovely bedrooms

Smart and civilised, this 17th-c inn is perhaps more restaurant than pub but those wanting just a drink do still drop in and are made welcome. The three or four bar rooms are carefully furnished with good oak chairs and an individual mix of tables, and down some steps is the restaurant area; one of the log fires is contained in a well polished kitchen range. Ballards Best, Ringwood Best, and Skinners Betty Stogs on handpump and 14 wines by the glass; piped music. At the back there are seats on a small terrace. The bedrooms in the former stable yard are extremely stylish and comfortable.

🍴 **Interesting food includes lunchtime sandwiches, soup, herb-crusted sardines with home-made garlic focaccia croûte, sautéed pigeon breasts in a demerara and balsamic sauce, tagliatelle with roasted peppers and pesto and a basil and sunblush tomato salad, steak and kidney suet pudding, trout fillets with a parsnip and horseradish purée and fried garlicky cherry tomatoes, rack of local lamb with redcurrant mint jus, daily specials, and puddings such as strawberry and raspberry millefeuilles with a blueberry coulis and warm chocolate fondant with home-made chocolate and thyme ice-cream.** *Starters/Snacks: £4.50 to £8.95. Main Courses: £10.00 to £14.95. Puddings: £4.95 to £6.95*

Free house ~ Licensee Paul Carter ~ Real ale ~ Bar food (12-2.30, 6.30-9.15(8.30 Sun)) ~ Restaurant ~ (01798) 861281 ~ Children welcome ~ Dogs allowed in bar ~ Open 11-11; 12-10.30 Sun ~ Bedrooms: £65B/£110B

Recommended by Ann and Colin Hunt, Mrs L Aquilina, Derek Thomas

OVING   SU9005 MAP 2

Gribble Inn

Between A27 and A259 just E of Chichester, then should be signposted just off village road; OS Sheet 197 map reference 900050; PO20 2BP

Own-brewed beers in bustling thatched pub with beamed and timbered linked rooms, traditional bar food and pretty garden

The own brews in this 16th-c thatched pub remain popular and include Gribble Ale, Pigs Ear, Pukka Mild, Reg's Tipple, and winter Wobbler, and they also keep Badger First Gold on handpump (the pub's owned by Badger). The chatty bar has lots of heavy beams and timbering, old country-kitchen furnishings and pews and the several linked rooms have a cottagey feel and huge winter log fires. Decent wine and farm cider. Board games, table football and a separate skittle alley. Seats outside under a covered area and more chairs in the pretty garden with apple and pear trees; at the end of the garden are some rabbits.

🍴 **Bar food at lunchtime includes doorstep sandwiches, filled baked potatoes, ploughman's, soup, mushrooms in garlic, steak and kidney pudding, beery sausages with gravy, a daily vegetarian pasta dish, lambs liver and bacon, beer-battered fish with mushy peas, and home-cooked ham and egg; in the evening, there are quite a few daily specials.** *Starters/Snacks: £5.25 to £6.95. Main Courses: £8.95 to £15.95. Puddings: £4.25 to £4.95*

Own brew ~ Tenants Dave and Linda Stone ~ Real ale ~ Bar food (12-2.30, 6-9.30) ~ Restaurant ~ (01243) 786893 ~ Children under 9 in family room; if older, can go in restaurant ~ Dogs allowed in bar ~ Jazz first Tues of month, live bands last Fri of month ~ Open 11-3, 5.30-11; 11-11.30 Fri and Sat; 12-10.30 Sun; 11-3, 5.30-11 Fri in winter

Recommended by PL, Peter Titcomb, R G Trevis, R B Gardiner, Paul and Shirley White, David H T Dimock, Mike and Lynn Robinson, Susan and John Douglas, Ann and Colin Hunt, Tony and Wendy Hobden

PETWORTH   SU9921 MAP 2

Welldiggers Arms

Low Heath; A283 towards Pulborough; GU28 OHG

Country pub with long-serving landlord, unassuming rooms and home-cooked bar food

The smallish L-shaped bar in this country pub, with its unassuming style and appearance, has low beams, a few pictures (Churchill and gun dogs are prominent) on shiny ochre walls above a panelled dado, a couple of very long rustic settles with tables to match, and some other stripped tables (many are laid for eating); a second rather lower side room has a somewhat lighter décor. No music or machines. Wells & Youngs Bitter on handpump, and decent wines by the glass. Outside, screened from the road by a thick high hedge, are plenty of tables and chairs on pleasant lawns and a terrace, looking back over rolling fields and woodland. More reports please.

🍴 **Bar food includes sandwiches, ploughman's, soup, grilled king prawns in garlic, smooth duck pâté, half a dozen oysters, steak, Guinness and stilton pie, home-cooked ham and eggs, braised oxtail with dumplings, smoked haddock on spinach with chive butter sauce, half a roast duck with apple sauce, and daily specials.** *Starters/Snacks: £5.95 to £9.50. Main Courses: £6.50 to £19.50. Puddings: £5.95*

Free house ~ Licensee Ted Whitcomb ~ Real ale ~ Bar food (12-2, 6-9 but also see opening hours) ~ Restaurant ~ (01798) 342287 ~ Children allowed in saloon bar ~ Dogs welcome ~ Open 11-3.30, 6-11.30; 12-4 Sun; closed Mon; closed Tues, Weds and Sun evenings
Recommended by Mrs D W Privett, Terry Buckland, R B Gardiner, James Marchant

RINGMER   TQ4313 MAP 3

Cock

Uckfield Road – blocked-off section of road off A26 N of village turn-off; BN8 5RX

Popular food in 16th-c pub, log fire in heavily beamed bar, a fine choice of drinks, garden with wide views – nice sunsets

To be sure of a table at the weekend in this white-painted weatherboarded ex-coaching house, it's best to book – especially for Sunday lunch. The unspoilt, heavily beamed bar has traditional pubby furniture on flagstones, a log fire in the inglenook fireplace (lit from October to May), and Harveys Best and winter Old with a guest like Fullers London Pride on handpump; farm cider, a dozen wines by the glass and a dozen malt whiskies and winter mulled wine. The ruby king charles cavalier is called Fred; piped music. There are lots of picnic-sets on the terrace and in the garden and views across open fields to the South Downs; dogs are offered a bowl of water and a chew.

🍴 **Well liked bar food includes sandwiches, egg and prawn mayonnaise, deep-fried camembert with cranberry sauce, honey-roast ham with free-range eggs, steak and kidney pudding, vegetarian curry, venison sausages and mustard mash, chicken breast with a cheese and spinach sauce, griddled tuna steak with a tomato, basil and olive sauce, and puddings such as white and dark chocolate terrine and rhubarb crumble.** *Starters/Snacks: £3.95 to £5.25. Main Courses: £5.95 to £18.75. Puddings: £4.25 to £5.25*

Free house ~ Licensees Ian and Matt Ridley ~ Real ale ~ Bar food (12-2, 6-9.30; all day Sun) ~ Restaurant ~ (01273) 812040 ~ Children allowed in restaurant areas ~ Dogs allowed in bar ~ Open 11-3, 6-11.30; 11am-11.30pm Sun
Recommended by John Beeken, Ann and Colin Hunt, Tony and Wendy Hobden, Steve Godfrey, John Branston

---

Bedroom prices normally include full english breakfast, VAT and any inclusive service charge that we know of. Prices before the '/' are for single rooms, after for two people in double or twin (B includes a private bath, S a private shower). If there is no '/', the prices are only for twin or double rooms (as far as we know there are no singles).

RYE   TQ9220 MAP 3

Mermaid ♀ ⇘
Mermaid Street; TN31 7EY

Lovely old timbered inn on famous cobbled street with civilised, antiques-filled bar and other rooms, good wine list, short choice of decent bar food; smart restaurant and bedrooms

The beautiful black and white timbered façade, with its distinctive sign hanging over the steeply cobbled street, has barely altered since this hotel was built in the 15th and 16th centuries; the cellars are two or three centuries older than that. It's extremely civilised with prices to match, and the little bar is where those in search of a light lunch and a drink tend to head for: quite a mix of quaint, closely set furnishings such as Victorian gothic carved oak chairs, older but plainer oak seats, and a massive deeply polished bressumer beam across one wall for the huge inglenook fireplace. Three antique but not ancient wall paintings show old english scenes. Courage Best and Greene King Old Speckled Hen on handpump and a good wine list; piped music (bar only), dominoes and cribbage. Seats on a small back terrace overlook the car park where – on bank holiday weekends – there are morris dancers.

🍴 **A short choice of bar food includes sandwiches, goats cheese and spinach omelette, moules marinière, smoked haddock and salmon fishcakes, steak and kidney pudding, minute steak with a blue cheese salad, and puddings. The smart restaurant offers two- and three-course set lunches.** *Starters/Snacks: £6.50 to £8.75. Main Courses: £8.00 to £15.50. Puddings: £6.00*

Free house ~ Licensees Robert Pinwill and Mrs J Blincow ~ Real ale ~ Bar food (12-2.30, 6.30-9.30) ~ Restaurant ~ (01797) 223065 ~ Children welcome away from main bar ~ Open 11-11; 12-10.30 Sun ~ Bedrooms: £90B/£180B
Recommended by Mrs Hazel Rainer, the Didler, N R White, Adrian Johnson

SALEHURST   TQ7424 MAP 3

Salehurst Halt
Village signposted from Robertsbridge bypass on A21 Tunbridge Wells—Battle; Church Lane; TN32 5PH

Friendly little local in quiet hamlet, chatty atmosphere, home-cooked food and real ales; nice little back garden

With a relaxed, chatty atmosphere, this little pub is in a quiet hamlet close to the church. To the right of the door there's an area with a big squishy black sofa, a sizeable cushioned wooden settle and just one small table on the stone floor, a TV and an open fire. To the left it's set up for dining with a mix of wheelback and other wooden dining chairs around light wooden tables on the bare-boarded floor and country prints on the walls; maybe piped local radio and board games. Harveys Best and Old Ale and a changing guest on handpump and Biddenden cider; decent wines and friendly service. There's a back terrace with metal chairs and tiled tables and a charming little garden.

🍴 **Well liked bar food includes filled baguettes, soup, tasty fishcakes with hollandaise sauce, popular burgers with various toppings, home-made pizzas, jerk chicken with mango salsa, local cod in beer batter, home-glazed ham and eggs, and puddings.** *Starters/Snacks: £4.00 to £5.00. Main Courses: £6.00 to £12.00. Puddings: £3.50 to £4.50*

Free house ~ Licensee Andrew Augarde ~ Real ale ~ Bar food (12-3, 7-9.30; not Mon, not evenings Tues, Weds and Sun) ~ Restaurant ~ (01580) 880620 ~ Children welcome ~ Dogs allowed in bar ~ Open 12-3, 6-11(10.30 Sun); 12-11 Sat; closed Mon; first two weeks Jan
Recommended by Mrs Hazel Rainer, Pamela and Douglas Cooper, Brian Root

SINGLETON
SU8713 MAP 2

Partridge

Just off A286 Midhurst—Chichester; heading S into the village, the main road bends sharp right – keep straight ahead instead; if you miss this turn, take the Charlton road, then first left; PO18 0EY

Well run, friendly village pub with daily papers and log fires, real ales, enjoyable food and pretty walled garden

Neatly kept and with friendly service from smartly dressed staff, this well run and pretty black and cream pub dates from the 16th c. There are polished wooden floors, flagstones and daily papers, some small rooms with red settles, a woodburning stove and winter log fires, and a roomy back bar extension. Fullers London Pride, Kings Horsham Best and Ringwood Best on handpump, and decent wines by the glass; piped music. There's a terrace and a big walled garden with colourful flowerbeds and fruit trees. The Weald & Downland Open Air Museum is just down the road, and Goodwood Racecourse is not far away.

⊞ **As well as sandwiches, the enjoyable bar food includes soup, scallop and bacon salad with a honey mustard dressing, pâté, oriental vegetable stir fry, chicken breast with smoky bacon in a hickory sauce topped with melted cheese, salmon and crab cakes with hollandaise sauce, steak in ale pie, lamb shank in red wine, garlic and rosemary, and seafood salad.** *Starters/Snacks: £5.50 to £7.50. Main Courses: £9.95 to £17.50. Puddings: £4.50*

Enterprise ~ Lease Tony Simpson ~ Real ale ~ Bar food (all day weekends) ~ Restaurant ~ (01243) 811251 ~ Children welcome away from bar area ~ Dogs allowed in bar ~ Open 11.30-3, 6-11; 11.30-11 Sat and Sun

Recommended by Lionel and Sylvia Kopelowitz, W A Evershed, Dick and Madeleine Brown, Cathy Robinson, Ed Coombe, Sue and Mike Todd, Ann and Colin Hunt, Bruce Bird, Prof and Mrs S Barnett

TROTTON
SU8322 MAP 2

Keepers Arms

A272 Midhurst—Petersfield; pub tucked up above road, on S side; GU31 5ER

Very different furnishings under new licensee, beams, open fires and nice old furniture, decent real ales, modern food and seats on sunny terrace

Under its new landlord (who also runs the Hawkley Inn, a main entry in Hampshire), this is now a very different pub. Gone are all the ethnic artefacts and furnishings and often unusual piped music. There's now a new cosy little dining room with a bench seat around all four walls and a large central table that is proving popular with regular customers. The beamed L-shaped bar has timbered walls and some standing timbers, comfortable sofas and winged-back old leather armchairs around the big log fire, and simple rustic tables on the oak flooring. Elsewhere, there are a couple of unusual adult high chairs at an oak refectory table, two huge Georgian leather high-backed chairs around another table and, in the dining room, elegant oak tables, comfortable dining chairs and a woodburning stove. Ballards Best, Bowman Quiver and Swift One, Dark Star Hophead and Hop Back Summer Lightning on handpump and good wines. There are tables and seats on the south-facing terrace. More reports on the changes, please.

⊞ **Contemporary bar food – helpings are not huge – includes sandwiches, gazpacho with selsey crab mayonnaise, parma ham with celeriac remoulade, parmesan, salad and truffle oil, pigeon and prune terrine with vinaigrette of puy lentils, risotto of broad beans, peas, asparagus and truffles, fried black bream with herb couscous, green beans and sauce vierge, corn-fed chicken breast with tarragon jus, honey-roasted gressingham duck breast with bubble and squeak, pak choi and spiced duck sauce, and puddings such as chocolate délice, tropical fruit salad and mango sorbet and lemon parfait with raspberries.** *Starters/Snacks: £5.00 to £10.00. Main Courses: £10.00 to £19.00. Puddings: £5.00 to £6.50*

Free house ~ Licensee Nick Troth ~ Real ale ~ Bar food (till 10pm Sat) ~ Restaurant ~ (01730) 813724 ~ Children welcome ~ Dogs allowed in bar ~ Open 12-3, 5.45-11; 12-4, 7-10.30 Sun; closed 25 Dec

Recommended by BOB

WARNINGLID
TQ2425 MAP 3

Half Moon ⍢

*B2115 off A23 S of Handcross, or off B2110 Handcross—Lower Beeding – village is
signposted; The Street; RH17 5TR*

**Good modern cooking in simply furnished village local, informal chatty atmosphere,
friendly service, real ales and decent wines, and seats in sizeable garden; no children**

It's quite a surprise to find such inventive food in a traditional village local, but the hard-
working, friendly young licensees offer just that – and on our mid-week evening
inspection visit, the place was packed. This is no straightforward dining pub – there's a
lively locals' bar too, reached from the car park through the garden. Down a couple of
steps to the main bar, which again is pretty unpretentious, with an informal chatty feel:
plank panelling and bare brick, built-in cushioned wall settles, a mix of tables (all with
candles and fresh flowers) on bare boards, a step down to a smaller carpeted area with big
paintings. It's all spotless. Black Sheep Bitter, Greene King Old Speckled Hen and Harveys
Best on handpump, and several decent wines by the glass; friendly service. There are quite
a few picnic-sets outside on the lawn in the sheltered, sizeable garden. No children inside.

🍴 **Extremely good and served in generous helpings, the food at lunchtime includes filled
ciabattas, ploughman's, ham and egg, chicken caesar salad, calves liver and smoked
bacon, and beer-battered halloumi cheese with pea purée and tomato fondue; in the
evening, there's a sharing plate of ciabatta with delicious basil pesto, hummus and olive
tapenade, beef, field mushroom and ale pie, beer-battered fish with pea purée, roquefort
cheese with rocket, pear and confit onion salad, bass fillets with shrimp bisque, rösti
potato and mangetout stir fry, and daily specials; super puddings such as almond brittle
parfait with an espresso shot and summer pudding with vanilla bean ice-cream.** *Main
Courses: £9.00 to £15.50. Puddings: £4.95*

Free house ~ Licensees John Lea and James Amico ~ Real ale ~ Bar food (12-2, 6-9.30; not Sun
evening) ~ (01444) 461227 ~ Dogs allowed in bar ~ Open 11.30-2.30, 5.30-11; 12-10.30 Sun

Recommended by Don Scarff, Terry Buckland, Chris Wall, Liz and Brian Barnard

WARTLING
TQ6509 MAP 3

Lamb ⍨

Village signposted with Herstmonceux Castle off A271 Herstmonceux—Battle; BN27 1RY

**Bustling, friendly pub with log fires in several areas, cheerful atmosphere and enjoyable
food; pretty back terrace**

As this pub does get extremely busy at weekends, our readers tend to prefer it during the
week. It's a friendly, cheerful place with several log fires and you can sit in the little bar,
the beamed and timbered snug (mind your head on the low entrance beam), the
comfortable lounge with its sofas and armchairs and the main restaurant. Doors lead up
steps to a back terrace with seats on the pretty, flower-filled terrace. Harveys Best, Kings
Horsham Best and a guest beer on handpump, ten wines by the glass (including
champagne), and helpful staff. It's best to book to be sure of a table.

🍴 **Good food includes bar snacks like filled baps, ploughman's, steakburger and various
caesar salads as well as soup, chicken liver and mushroom pâté with cumberland sauce,
king scallops with basil pesto and parmesan crumbs, a pie and a risotto of the day,
vegetarian wellington, venison medallions with red wine gravy and dauphinoise potatoes,
chicken breast on a bacon, cabbage and stilton potato cake with a wild mushroom and
madeira jus, and puddings such as banana pavlova with butterscotch sauce and chocolate
and praline bread and butter pudding.** *Starters/Snacks: £4.25 to £7.95. Main Courses: £8.95
to £18.95. Puddings: £4.95*

Free house ~ Licensees Robert and Alison Farncombe ~ Real ale ~ Bar food (11.45-2.15, 6.45-9;
12-2.30 Sun; not Sun evening) ~ Restaurant ~ (01323) 832116 ~ Children in eating areas ~
Dogs allowed in bar ~ Open 11-3, 6-11; 12-3 Sun; closed Sun evening

*Recommended by Sue Demont, Tim Barrow, Geoff and Marion Cooper, Jenny and Peter Lowater, V Brogden,
Barry and Victoria Lister, P and J Shapley*

WILMINGTON

TQ5404 MAP 3

Giants Rest

Just off A27; BN26 5SQ

Cheerful landlord with a friendly welcome for all in busy country pub; informal atmosphere, pub games on each table, popular country cooking and new bedrooms

You can be sure of a genuinely warm welcome from the friendly landlord and his staff in this busy country pub. It's a popular place with South Downs walkers and the majestic chalk-carved figure of the Long Man of Wilmington is nearby. The long wood-floored bar and adjacent open areas have simple chairs and tables, wooden table games, Beryl Cook paintings, candles on tables, an open fire and a nice informal atmosphere. Harveys Best, Hop Back Summer Lightning and Timothy Taylors Landlord on handpump; piped music. Plenty of seats in the front garden, and Elizabeth David the famous cookery writer is buried in the churchyard at nearby Folkington; her headstone is beautifully carved and features mediterranean vegetables and a casserole. You must book to be sure of a table, especially for Sunday lunch. They now have letting bedrooms.

🍴 **Good, reasonably priced country cooking might include filled baked potatoes, ploughman's, soup, baked field mushroom with garlic, goats cheese and pesto, venison sausages or home-cooked ham with bubble and squeak and home-made chutney, african spinach, peanut and sweet potato stew, hake, coriander, spring onion and chilli fishcakes, rabbit and bacon pie, beef in Guinness with rosemary dumplings, daily specials, and puddings such as sticky date and walnut pudding and warm chocolate fudge brownie.** *Starters/Snacks: £3.50 to £6.00. Main Courses: £8.50 to £15.00. Puddings: £4.50 to £6.50*

Free house ~ Licensees Adrian and Rebecca Hillman ~ Real ale ~ Bar food (12-2(2.30 Sun), 7-9) ~ Restaurant ~ (01323) 870207 ~ Children welcome if well behaved ~ Dogs allowed in bar ~ Open 11.30-3, 6-11; 11.30-11 Sat; 12-10.30 Sun ~ Bedrooms: /£60

Recommended by John and Bettye Reynolds, Barry and Victoria Lister, PL, Jenny and Peter Lowater, N R White, Kevin Thorpe

WINEHAM

TQ2320 MAP 3

Royal Oak £

Village signposted from A272 and B2116; BN5 9AY

Splendidly old-fashioned local with long-serving landlord, interesting bric-a-brac in simple rooms, real ales and limited snacks

In the same family for over 50 years, this remains a welcoming and unchanging old-fashioned local with no fruit machines, piped music or even beer pumps. Logs burn in an enormous inglenook fireplace with a cast-iron Royal Oak fireback, and there's a collection of cigarette cards showing old english pubs, a stuffed stoat and crocodile, a collection of jugs, ancient corkscrews decorating the very low beams above the serving counter, and racing plates, tools and a coach horn on the walls; maybe a nice tabby cat, and views of quiet countryside from the back parlour. Harveys Best with a guest such as Wadworths 6X tapped from the cask in a stillroom; darts and board games. There are some picnic-sets outside – picturesque if you are facing the pub. More reports please.

🍴 **Limited bar snacks only – winter soup, sandwiches and ploughman's.** *Starters/Snacks: £2.50 to £5.00*

Punch ~ Tenant Tim Peacock ~ Real ale ~ Bar food (served during opening hours) ~ No credit cards ~ (01444) 881252 ~ Children allowed away from main bar ~ Dogs allowed in bar ~ Open 11-2.30, 5.30(6 Sat)-11; 12-3, 7-10.30 Sun

Recommended by Terry Buckland, Mrs Mahni Pannett, Barry and Sue Pladdys, Jude Wright, N R White

---

Looking for a pub with a really special garden, or in lovely countryside, or with an outstanding view, or right by the water? They are listed separately, at the back of the book.

LUCKY DIP

Besides the fully inspected pubs, you might like to try these Lucky Dips recommended to us and described by readers (if you do, please send us reports: www.goodguides.co.uk).

ALFRISTON [TQ5203]

☆ *Star* BN26 5TA [High St]: Fascinating fine painted medieval carvings outside, heavy-beamed old-fashioned bar (busy lunchtime, quiet evenings) with some interesting features inc medieval sanctuary post, antique furnishings and big log fire in Tudor fireplace, easy chairs in comfortable lounge, Bass, Fullers London Pride and Harveys Best, decent wines by the glass, good coffee and service, daily papers and magazines, more space behind for eating, food from sandwiches and baked potatoes to restaurant dishes; good modern bedrooms in up-to-date part behind, open all day summer *(the Didler, LYM, Ann and Colin Hunt)*

AMBERLEY [S00313]

☆ *Black Horse* BN18 9NL [off B2139]: Pretty pub with quiet garden, main bar with plenty of pictures, high-backed settles on flagstones, beams over serving counter festooned with sheep bells and shepherds' tools, lounge with many antiques and artefacts, log fires in both bars and restaurant, straightforward bar food (all day Sun), Greene King IPA and Wells & Youngs Bombardier; piped music, children must be well behaved, dogs in bar, open all day *(Mayur Shah, David H T Dimock, LYM, Barry Collett)*

Bridge BN18 9LR [B2139]: Popular open-plan dining pub, comfortable and relaxed even when busy, with pleasant bar and separate two-room dining area, decent range of reasonably priced food from sandwiches up, well kept Harveys and other ales; children and dogs welcome, seats out in front, more tables in side garden, open all day *(Lawrence Pearse, LYM)*

☆ *Sportsmans* BN18 9NR [Crossgates; Rackham Rd, off B2139]: Great views over Amberley Wild Brooks from pretty little back conservatory and tables outside (good walks too), friendly enthusiastic landlord and helpful staff, well kept Fullers London Pride, Harveys Best and two interesting guest beers, lots of wines by the glass, food from sandwiches up, three bars inc brick-floored games room; quiet piped music; children welcome, bedrooms *(LYM, Richard May, Jason Caulkin, C and R Bromage, Tony and Wendy Hobden, Bruce Bird, Martin and Karen Wake)*

ANGMERING [TQ0704]

☆ *Spotted Cow* BN16 4AW [High St]: Good interesting generous food (very popular wkdy lunchtimes with older people) from sandwiches up, friendly and enthusiastic chef/landlord, real ales such as Greene King IPA and Old Speckled Hen, Harveys Best, Ringwood Boondoggle and Timothy Taylors Landlord, good choice of wines by the glass, smallish bar on left, long dining extension with large conservatory on right, two log

fires, smuggling history, sporting caricatures, no piped music; children welcome, big garden with boules and play area; open all day Sun, afternoon jazz sometimes then, lovely walk to Highdown hill fort *(Derek and Heather Manning, Bruce Bird, Tony and Wendy Hobden, N R White)*

ARDINGLY [TQ3430]

☆ *Gardeners Arms* RH17 6TJ [B2028 2 miles N]: Reliable reasonably priced pub food in olde-worlde linked rooms, Badger beers, pleasant efficient service, daily papers, standing timbers and inglenooks, scrubbed pine furniture on flagstones and broad boards, lots of old local photographs, mural in back part; attractive wooden furniture on pretty terrace, lots of picnic-sets in side garden, opp S of England show ground and handy for Borde Hill and Wakehurst Place, open all day at least wknds *(BB, Harvey Smith, Susan and John Douglas, Tony and Wendy Hobden)*

Oak RH17 6UA [Street Lane]: Beamed 14th-c dining pub with Harveys Best, Kings Red River and a guest beer, good range of wines by the glass, wide choice of reasonably priced food, olde-worlde décor with lots of brass, bric-a-brac and lace curtains, magnificent old fireplace, simple bright restaurant extension; tables in pleasant garden, handy for show ground and reservoir walks *(Terry Buckland, Bruce Bird)*

ARLINGTON [TQ5407]

Yew Tree BN26 6RX [off A22 nr Hailsham, or A27 W of Polegate]: Neatly modernised two-bar Victorian village pub popular for generous food (can ask for smaller helpings) from hot filled rolls and small range of starters to much wider choice of main dishes, Harveys Best and decent wines, log fires, prompt service even when busy, thriving local atmosphere, darts, conservatory; children welcome, good big garden with play area by paddock with farm animals, good walks *(BB, Fr Robert Marsh, Stuart and Diana Hughes)*

ARUNDEL [TQ0208]

☆ *Black Rabbit* BN18 9PB [Mill Rd, Offham; keep on and don't give up!]: Long nicely refurbished riverside pub well organised for families, lovely spot nr wildfowl reserve, lots of tables outside, timeless views of water-meadows and castle; enjoyable range of all-day food, Badger real ales, good choice of decent wines by the glass, friendly service, log fires; shame about the piped music; doubles as summer tea shop, with summer boat trips, good walks, open all day *(Susan and John Douglas, Gene and Kitty Rankin, LYM, Val and Alan Green)*

☆ *Swan* BN18 9AG [High St]: Smart but relaxed open-plan L-shaped bar with attractive woodwork and matching fittings, friendly efficient young staff, Fullers ales, good tea and coffee, good value food from baguettes and baked potatoes to restaurant meals, sporting bric-a-brac and old photographs, beaten brass former inn-sign on wall, restaurant; good bedrooms, open all day *(LYM, Sue and Mike Todd, Bruce Bird, Paul Rampton, Ann and Colin Hunt)*

ASHURST [TQ1816]

☆ *Fountain* BN44 3AP [B2135 S of Partridge Green]: Attractive and well run 16th-c country local with fine old flagstones, friendly rustic tap room on right with some antique polished trestle tables and housekeeper's chairs by inglenook log fire, second inglenook in opened-up heavy-beamed snug, attentive young staff, interesting blackboard food as well as pub staples, Fullers London Pride, Harveys and Kings Horsham; dogs welcome, no under-10s, prettily planted garden with duck pond *(Pete Walker, PL, David Field, Terry Buckland, LYM, Karen Eliot)*

BATTLE [TQ7515]

Chequers TN33 0AT [Lower Lake (A2100 SE)]: Attractive stone-built pub, partly medieval and roomy inside, with several linked beamed areas, enjoyable pubby food from sandwiches up, well kept Fullers London Pride, Harveys and a guest beer, open fires, friendly staff, pool; back terrace tables, bedrooms (one said to be haunted by a dog), open all day *(Phil and Jane Hodson)*

BECKLEY [TQ8423]

Rose & Crown TN31 6SE [Northiam Rd (B2088)]: Recently refurbished village pub with good friendly service, good value generous standard food from sandwiches, baguettes and baked potatoes up, well kept changing beers such as Harveys Best, Rother Valley and Timothy Taylors Landlord from hop-draped bar, cosy lower eating area with log fire and model boat; children welcome, views from pleasant garden *(Bruce Bird)*

BEPTON [SU8620]

Country Inn GU29 0LR [Severals Rd]: Old-fashioned local with well kept Ballards Mild and Fullers London Pride, good value pubby food, log fire, darts-playing regulars, heavy beams and stripped brickwork; picnic-sets and play area outside, quiet spot *(John Beeken)*

BERWICK [TQ5206]

Berwick Inn BN26 6SZ [by station]: Genial hands-on landlord in roomy and rambling pub with cheery family emphasis, good choice of decent food all day, Harveys Best, obliging service, log fire, pool in upper front games room, conservatory; piped music; large garden behind with good playground and attractive Perspex-roofed garden bar *(Paul A Moore, LYM, Ann and Colin Hunt)*

BEXHILL [TQ7208]

Denbigh TN39 4JE [Little Common Rd (A259 towards Polegate)]: Doing well under new licensees, enjoyable food from bar meals to restaurant dishes inc good cold buffet and good value OAP lunch, thriving atmosphere,

neat service, three real ales, interesting wines and spirits *(Simon D H Robarts Briggs, C and R Bromage)*

BILLINGSHURST [TQ0830]

☆ *Blue Ship* RH14 9BS [The Haven; hamlet signposted off A29 just N of junction with A264, then follow signpost left towards Garlands and Okehurst]: Unpretentious pub in quiet country spot, beamed and brick-floored front bar with blazing inglenook log fire, scrubbed tables and wall benches, Badger ales served from hatch, limited home-made food, two small carpeted back rooms, darts, bar billiards, shove-ha'penny, cribbage, dominoes, reasonably priced traditional bar food (not Sun or Mon evenings), no mobile phones; no credit cards; children in one back room, seats by trees or tangle of honeysuckle around front door *(the Didler, LYM)*

BOARSHEAD [TQ5332]

Boars Head TN6 3HD [Eridge Rd, off A26 bypass]: Attractive old unspoilt pub with good friendly service, good value fresh homely food, Adnams, Fullers London Pride and Harveys Best, separate restaurant; nice grounds, picturesquely ageing outbuildings *(Ian Phillips, Mrs Stella Knight)*

BOGNOR REGIS [SZ9298]

Navigator PO21 2QA [Marine Drive West]: Enjoyable well priced food in comfortable carpeted bar and picture-window seafront restaurant, good staff; comfortable bedrooms, some with sea view *(Diana King)*

BOSHAM [SU8003]

☆ *Anchor Bleu* PO18 8LS [High St]: Beautifully placed waterside pub with pleasantly served and reasonably priced straightforward food inc seafood and steak, helpful friendly licensees, well kept Timothy Taylors Landlord and three changing guest beers, two nicely simple period rooms with lots of nautical bric-a-brac; little terrace outside massive wheel-operated bulkhead door to ward off high tides (cars parked on seaward side often submerged), sea and boat views, charming village, open all day *(Michael B Griffith, W W Burke, LYM, George and Elizabeth Storton, Bruce Bird, Judy Bow, Arnold Rose, OPUS, Ian Phillips)*

Berkeley Arms PO18 8HG [just outside old village]: Cheery local with competitively priced food inc speciality sausages, fresh fish and Sun roast, well kept Fullers, lounge with eating area, public bar; front terrace tables *(Nigel and Kath Thompson)*

BRIGHTON [TQ3104]

Black Lion BN1 1ND [Black Lion St]: Big open-plan pub with stripped pine tables and some leather sofas on wooden floor, prints and soft lighting, Greene King IPA, good choice of wines by the glass; piped music, TV, games machine; tables outside *(Michael Dandy)*

☆ *Cricketers* BN1 1ND [Black Lion St]: Cheerful and genuine town pub, friendly bustle at busy times such as trades union conference, good relaxed atmosphere when quieter, cosy and darkly Victorian with loads of interesting bric-a-brac – even a stuffed bear; attentive quick service, Adnams Broadside, Greene King Old Speckled Hen, Harveys and Wells & Youngs Bombardier tapped from the cask, good coffee, well priced pubby lunchtime food from sandwiches and baked potatoes up in covered ex-stables courtyard and upstairs bar, restaurant (where children allowed); piped music; open all day (LYM, *Michael Dandy, Mayur Shah, Bruce Bird, Keith and Chris O'Neill, Sue Demont, Tim Barrow)*

☆ *Evening Star* BN1 3PB [Surrey St]: Chatty pub with several good Dark Star beers (originally brewed here) and lots of changing beers from other small breweries, interesting bottled belgian beers too, enthusiastic landlord (may let you sample before you buy), farm ciders and perries, lots of country wines, good lunchtime baguettes (rolls Sun), simple pale wood furniture on bare boards, good mix of customers; unobtrusive piped music, some live; pavement tables, open all day (*Bruce Bird, MLR, BB, Sue Demont, Tim Barrow*)

Lord Nelson BN1 4ED [Trafalgar St]: Four-room town pub with well kept Harveys ales inc seasonal and Mild, good value lunchtime food from sandwiches to interesting specials and Sun roasts, pleasant young staff, log fire, daily papers, old football photographs and theatre and cinema posters, back conservatory; pub games, sports TV; open all day (*MLR, Bruce Bird*)

Prince Arthur BN1 3EG [Dean St]: New couple putting some emphasis on good value home cooking in small one-room traditional pub with friendly staff, back conservatory; children and dogs welcome, pavement picnic-sets, more out behind, has been cl Mon (*Anne Grigg*)

West Quay BN2 5UT [Brighton Marina]: Wetherspoons Lloyds No 1, large and popular, with big windows and terraces around two sides overlooking the water; their usual food (*Keith and Chris O'Neill*)

BROWNBREAD STREET [TQ6714]

☆ *Ash Tree* TN33 9NX [off A271 (was B2204) W of Battle; 1st northward rd W of Ashburnham Pl, then 1st fork left, then bear right into Brownbread Street]: Tranquil country local tucked away in isolated hamlet, cosy beamed bars with nice old settles and chairs, stripped brickwork, two inglenook fireplaces, well kept ales inc Harveys, wide choice of wines, cheerful service, tasty food, interesting dining areas with timbered dividers; children in eating area, pretty garden with picnic-sets, open all day (*LYM, Jeremy Billingham*)

BURGESS HILL [TQ3019]

Woolpack RH15 8TS [Howard Ave]: Useful family pub in big 1930s-look roadhouse, several eating areas, wide choice of reasonably priced pubby food from snacks up, Courage Best, Wadworths 6X and three guest beers changing weekly; piped music

may obtrude; plenty of tables outside (*Tony and Wendy Hobden*)

BURY [TQ0013]

Squire & Horse RH20 1NS [Bury Common; A29 Fontwell—Pulborough]: Sizeable beamed roadside pub with wide range of popular generous home-made food inc good fish (worth booking as can get very busy), attentive service, well kept Fullers London Pride and Harveys Best and Old, good choice of wines, Sun bar nibbles, several neat and attractive partly divided areas, pink plush wall seats, hunting prints and ornaments, flame-effect stoves and fresh flowers; pleasant garden with pretty terrace (some road noise) (*Lawrence Pearse, BB, Tony and Wendy Hobden, David Coleman*)

CATSFIELD [TQ7213]

White Hart TN33 9DJ [A269]: Welcoming staff, enjoyable honest food from good value lunchtime snacks up, well kept Harveys, warm log fire; good walking country (*Christopher Turner*)

CHICHESTER [SU8605]

Bell PO19 6AT [Broyle Rd]: Spotless and comfortable, with good interesting changing real ales and wines, generous reasonably priced food from separate counter inc good puddings, pleasant staff coping well when busy, daily papers, bric-a-brac on high beams; children welcome, pleasant partly covered back terrace, handy for Festival Theatre (*Tony Hobden, Craig Turnbull, Bruce Bird, David Carr*)

Dolphin & Anchor PO19 1QD [West St]: Well run Wetherspoons in former hotel opp cathedral, good value food from 9am breakfast on, six low-priced real ales; small family area till 7 (not wknds), very busy with young people Sat night, doorman and queues to get in; disabled access, pleasant back terrace, open all day (*Tony Hobden, David Carr*)

Fountain PO19 1ES [Southgate]: Attractive front bar with bric-a-brac, small dining room behind, wide choice of enjoyable food, friendly efficient staff, Badger beers; open all day (*Gordon Prince*)

Four Chestnuts PO19 7EJ [Oving Rd]: Roomy and friendly open-plan pub, family-run, with good generous basic lunchtime food (not Mon/Tues), well kept Caledonian Deuchars IPA, Tetleys Dark Mild and a local guest beer, helpful service, daily papers, games room, skittle alley, some live music; open all day (*Tony Hobden, Bruce Bird*)

George & Dragon PO19 1NQ [North St]: Bustling simply refurbished bare-boards bar with good range of beers and wines, wholesome plentiful food at attractive prices, pleasant service, conservatory; tables out on quiet back terrace, good value bedrooms (*David Carr, David H T Dimock, J A Snell*)

CHIDHAM [SU7804]

☆ *Old House At Home* PO18 8SU [off A259 at Barleycorn pub in Nutbourne; Cot Lane]: Cottagey old pub doing well under current management, cheerful and welcoming, with enjoyable food esp good local fish, Adnams Broadside, Fullers London Pride, Ringwood Best and Wells & Youngs, log fire, low beams and timbering, windsor chairs and long wall seats, restaurant area, no piped music or machines; children in eating areas, tables outside, remote unspoilt farm-hamlet location, nearby walks by Chichester Harbour, open all day wknds *(Ann and Colin Hunt, LYM, Mrs Stephanie Carson, R G Trevis, William Ruxton)*

CLAPHAM [TQ1105]

Coach & Horses BN13 3UA [Arundel Rd (A27 Worthing—Arundel)]: Recently reopened under new management after refurbishment as brightly modern uncluttered restaurantly dining pub, informally smart, with well cooked food, Flowers and Greene King Abbot, friendly young staff; new outside seating area *(Tony and Wendy Hobden, Val and Alan Green)*

CLIMPING [TQ0001]

Black Horse BN17 5RL [Climping St]: Attractive olde-worlde dining pub with wide choice of good value food from good interesting sandwiches up, very popular Sun lunch (best to book), friendly attentive service, Courage Best and Directors, good choice of wines by the glass, pleasant dining rooms, country views from the back; tables out behind, walk to beach *(B S Gill, MDN, M and R Thomas)*

COLGATE [TQ2232]

Dragon RH12 4SY [Forest Rd]: Small work-a-day two-bar pub with well kept Badger ales, good value home-made food from interesting sandwiches to local game, log fire, good service, dining area; big garden, pleasant and secluded – good for children *(Ivan Turner, Terry Buckland)*

COMPTON [SU7714]

☆ *Coach & Horses* PO18 9HA [B2146 S of Petersfield]: 17th-c two-bar local in pleasant village not far from Uppark (NT), open fire, pine shutters and panelling, decent bar food from baguettes up, Ballards Best and Dark Star Hop Head and Pale Ale, bar billiards; games machine; children and dogs welcome, tables out by village square *(W A Evershed, Tracey and Stephen Groves, LYM)*

COOKSBRIDGE [TQ4014]

Rainbow BN8 4SS [junction A275 with Cooksbridge and Newick rd]: Dining pub with good interesting restaurant food, friendly attentive service, fine choice of wines, small bar well used by locals *(Brad Featherman and Marion Hunt)*

COOLHAM [TQ1223]

Selsey Arms RH13 8QJ [A272/B2139]: Welcoming three-room local with Fullers London Pride, Flowers and Harveys Best, enjoyable blackboard food from sandwiches and baked potatoes up, two linked areas with plates, prints and blazing log fires; garden fenced off from road in front, another behind with lots of trees *(Tony and Wendy Hobden, Bruce Bird, Stephen Harvey)*

COUSLEY WOOD [TQ6533]

☆ *Old Vine* TN5 6ER [B2100 Wadhurst—Lamberhurst]: Popular and attractive dining pub with lots of old timbers and beams, wide range of generous enjoyable food inc good fish, good house wines, Greene King IPA and Harveys, rustic pretty restaurant on right, pubbier bare-boards or brick-floored area with woodburner by bar, good friendly service; dogs welcome, a few tables out behind *(Ian Phillips, BB)*

COWFOLD [TQ2122]

Coach House RH13 8BT [Horsham Rd]: Smart, comfortable and welcoming, with enjoyable food, Fullers London Pride, good coffee and service, attractive traditional main bar, settees by log fire, roomy neatly laid restaurant area, locals' bar (no children in this bit) with darts and pool; large garden with corner play area, open all day *(David H T Dimock, Ann and Colin Hunt)*

CUCKFIELD [TQ3025]

Rose & Crown RH17 5BS [London Rd]: Low beams and panelling, Badger ales, good choice of wines by the glass, open fire in dining area, pool and games in public bar; piped music; tables out in front and in back garden, lots of nice tubs and hanging baskets, open all day *(Michael Dandy)*

White Harte RH17 5LB [South St; off A272 W of Haywards Heath]: Pretty partly medieval pub, food servery (thai take-aways too now) in comfortable and relaxing beamed and timbered lounge, well kept Badger Best, K&B and Tanglefoot, sturdily furnished chatty public bar with inglenook log fire and darts; piped music, TV; children and dogs welcome, tables in back yard *(Terry Buckland, W A Evershed, Michael Dandy, LYM)*

DALLINGTON [TQ6619]

☆ *Swan* TN21 9LB [Woods Corner, B2096 E]: New licensees summer 2007 (just too late for this edition) in low-beamed country pub with softly lit bare-boards beamed bar with a couple of sofas and warm log fire, small comfortable back dining room with far views to Beachy Head, and steps down to smallish garden; it's been open all day, and popular for enjoyable food from lunchtime sandwiches to interesting dishes and local fish, Harveys Best, Shepherd Neame and a guest beer, good wines by the glass and coffee, and a welcome for children and dogs – reports on the new regime please *(BB)*

DANEHILL [TQ4128]

☆ *Coach & Horses* RH17 7JF [off A275, via School Lane towards Chelwood Common]: Well run dining pub in attractive countryside, good if not cheap restauranty food (not Sun evening) served with style – and linen napkins, Harveys Best and Wychwood Shires, good wines by generous glass, little hatch-served public bar with simple furniture on highly polished boards and small woodburner, main bar on the left with big Victorian prints and mix of chairs around attractive old tables on fine brick floor, dining extension, darts; may try to keep your credit card while you eat outside; children and dogs welcome, plenty of tables in big attractive garden with terrace under huge maple *(Mr and Mrs R A Bradbrook, Pamela Goodwyn, John and Patricia Deller, R M Yard, LYM, Pete Walker)*

DELL QUAY [SU8302]

Crown & Anchor PO20 7EE [off A286 S of Chichester – look out for small sign]: Modernised 15th-c pub in splendid spot on site of Roman quay overlooking Chichester Harbour – best at high tide and quiet times, can be packed on sunny days; comfortable bow-windowed lounge bar, panelled public bar (dogs welcome), two log fires and lots of beams, Wells & Youngs ales, wide choice of wines by the glass, all-day servery doing popular food from good crab sandwiches up; terrace picnic-sets, nice walks *(Derek and Heather Manning, Mrs Romey Heaton, BB, David Carr, OPUS, W A Evershed)*

DENTON [TQ4502]

☆ *Flying Fish* BN9 0QB [Denton Rd]: French chef/landlord doing good well priced food from interesting baguettes up inc seasonal food esp game and fresh fish from nearby Newhaven, in attractive 17th-c flint village pub by South Downs Way, tiled floors throughout, comfortable high-ceilinged dining room with bric-a-brac, two smaller rooms off bar, Shepherd Neame ales, friendly prompt service under welsh landlady; attractive sloping garden behind, more tables on long deck and out in front, bedrooms *(John Beeken, the Didler)*

DIAL POST [TQ1519]

Crown RH13 8NH [Worthing Rd (off A24 S of Horsham)]: Friendly and enthusiastic new licensees, well kept Harveys Best, Kings Horsham Best and a seasonal ale, good wines, enjoyable food using local sources inc tapas and lunchtime sandwiches, two log fires, lots of beams, country bric-a-brac, front sun lounge, back dining room with extension down steps; garden *(Bruce Bird, Tony and Wendy Hobden)*

DITCHLING [TQ3215]

White Horse BN6 8TS [West St]: Thriving village pub nr church, well kept Harveys Best and two or three guests such as Bath Gem, Dark Star Nut Brown and Rugby Tom Browns Porter, lots of wines by the glass, unpretentious food from sandwiches up, quick friendly helpful service, log fire and chunky tables in L-shaped bar with games area; unobtrusive piped music; pretty courtyard, open all day *(MLR, John Beeken, John Coatsworth)*

DUNCTON [SU9517]

Cricketers GU28 0LB [set back from A285]: Newly renovated country pub under aunt, uncle and nephew, enjoyable food from sandwiches up, local real ales, decent wines by the glass, inglenook fireplace, cricketing pictures and bats on walls, shove-ha'penny, cribbage and dominoes; piped music; children and dogs welcome, picnic-sets in

charming garden behind with creeper-covered bower and proper barbecue, open all day (till 8 Sun) *(David Cosham, LYM, Jude Wright)*

EARTHAM [SU9309]

☆ *George* PO18 0LT [signed off A285 Chichester—Petworth, from Fontwell off A27, from Slindon off A29]: Well kept pub with genial landlord, helpful staff, well kept Greene King Ruddles Best and Weltons Best, wide range of good value blackboard food inc tapas, well listed wines, log fire, light wood furnishings in comfortable lounge, attractive public bar with games, old farm tools and photographs, darts, backgammon, restaurant; piped music; easy disabled access, children welcome in eating areas, large pretty garden, attractive surroundings, open all day summer wknds *(Nicholas and Dorothy Stephens, John Beeken, LYM, David Carr, W A Evershed)*

EASEBOURNE [SU8922]

☆ *White Horse* GU29 0AL [off A272 just NE of Midhurst]: Relaxing beamed village pub, comfortably worn fireside armchairs in well divided mainly bare-boards bar with small dining area, convivial landlord, efficient friendly service, good value traditional food from baked potatoes up (worth booking wknds), Greene King ales, two open fires, no piped music; children and dogs welcome (nice pub dog), tables on bare grass and in sunny courtyard *(Jeremy Whitehorn, LYM, Prof H G Allen)*

EAST DEAN [TV5597]

Tiger BN20 0DA [Pub (with village centre) signposted – not vividly – off A259 Eastbourne—Seaford; not to be confused with the East Dean near Chichester]: A new licensee for this long, low tiled pub overlooking delightful cottage-lined green and with pretty window boxes and flowering climbers; just a very few tables in two smallish rooms so best to arrive early; low beams hung with pewter and china, polished rustic tables and distinctive antique settles, old prints and so forth; Harveys Best and a couple of guests, several wines by glass; bar food has been imaginative; popular with walkers; no children inside *(V Brogden, Ann and Colin Hunt, Pete Walker, Kevin Thorpe, Mr and Mrs John Taylor, LYM)*

EAST GRINSTEAD [TQ3936]

☆ *Old Mill* RH19 4AT [Dunnings Rd, S towards Saint Hill]: Low-ceilinged 16th-c former mill cottage built right over stream, attractively reworked as good informal dining pub, with good choice of wines by the glass, Harveys ales, friendly service; children welcome, tables in pretty garden, handy for Standen (NT) *(LYM, Mrs Stella Knight)*

EAST HOATHLY [TQ5116]

☆ *Foresters Arms* BN8 6DS [off A22 Hailsham—Uckfield; South St]: Village pub with opened-up bar, quiet at lunchtime, with good value traditional food (not Sun evening or Mon), Harveys Best and Old and perhaps a seasonal ale, several wines by the glass, darts, board games; piped music, TV, games machine; provision for children and dogs, disabled facilities, tables out under parasols, open all day wknds, cl Mon lunchtime (Neil Hardwick, Grahame Brooks, Tony and Wendy Hobden, LYM, Kevin Thorpe)

☆ Kings Head BN6 6DR [High St]: 1648 ales brewed here inc Original and a seasonal beer, also Harveys Best, in long friendly and comfortably worn-in open-plan bar with some dark panelling and old local photographs, wide choice of enjoyable sensibly priced food, helpful service, log fire, daily papers, restaurant; TV; tables in garden up steps behind (John Beeken, Roger and Lesley Everett, Kevin Thorpe)

EAST PRESTON [TQ0701]
Sea View BN16 1PD [Sea Rd]: Comfortable seaside pub with neat, friendly and efficient staff, well kept Arundel Castle, Fullers London Pride and Greene King IPA, good value home-made food (not Sun/Mon evenings), OAP lunches Mon/Tues; nice garden (Bruce Bird)

EAST WITTERING [SZ7997]
Royal Oak PO20 8BS [Stocks Lane]: Simple pub with warm welcome and enjoyable pubby food from baked potatoes to Sun roasts; big garden (Klaus and Elizabeth Leist)
Thatched Tavern PO20 8PU [Church Rd]: Low-ceilinged thatched pub with reasonably priced food, Greene King Old Speckled Hen and Wells & Youngs, friendly staff; dogs welcome, tables outside with play area, masses of flowers, not far from Chichester Harbour (J A Snell)

EASTBOURNE [TV6198]
Buccaneer BN21 4BW [Compton St, by Winter Gardens]: Popular open-plan bar shaped like a galleon, Bass, Greene King Abbot, Tetleys and guest beers, bar food, theatre memorabilia; open all day (the Didler)

☆ Lamb BN21 1HH [High St]: Two main heavily beamed traditional bars off pretty and well run Tudor pub's central servery, spotless antique furnishings (but not too smart), good inglenook log fire, Harveys ales, generous reasonably priced food, thriving atmosphere, upstairs dining room (Sun lunch); by ornate church away from seafront, popular with students evenings (Michael and Ann Cole)
Ship BN20 7RH [Meads St]: Friendly tastefully refurbished pub with big leather sofas, enjoyable food inc fresh local fish, relaxed atmosphere, real ales such as Bass, Fullers London Pride and Harveys Best; disabled access, nicely planted garden with huge decked area and barbecue (David Burston, Michael and Ann Cole)
Terminus BN21 3NS [Terminus Rd]: Recently refurbished with interesting railway photographs (even section of ancient track, found in renovations), efficient and polite young staff, full Harveys ale range kept well, enjoyable generous home-made lunches inc

OAP deals, exotic plants in small sun lounge (Bruce Bird)

ELSTED [SU8320]
Elsted Inn GU29 0JT [Elsted Marsh]: This attractive two-bar country pub with its lovely enclosed downs-view garden and well appointed adjacent bedroom block had an unexpected change of licensees in 2007; reports on new regime please (LYM)

EWHURST GREEN [TQ7924]
☆ White Dog TN32 5TD: Extensive and attractive partly 17th-c pub/restaurant in fine spot above Bodiam Castle (and quite handy for Great Dixter), wide choice of good value food, friendly attentive staff, well kept Harveys and Youngs, log fire and polished flagstones, cheerful unpretentious atmosphere, evening restaurant; walkers and children welcome, bedrooms, tables in big garden making the most of the view (Philip and Cheryl Hill, M Greening, LYM, Pierre Richterich, M Joyner)

FAIRWARP [TQ4626]
Foresters Arms TN22 3BP [B2026]: Chatty Ashdown Forest local handy for Vanguard Way and Weald Way, comfortable lounge bar, wide food choice from baguettes and light dishes to steak and Sunday lunch, friendly staff cope well even when busy, Badger ales, farm cider, woodburner; piped music; children and dogs welcome, tables out on terrace and in garden, play area on small village green opp, has been open all day summer (Neil Hardwick, Mrs Stella Knight, LYM, N R White)

FALMER [TQ3508]
Swan BN1 9PD [Middle St (just off A27 bypass)]: In same family for last century, good choice of beers inc two german ones on tap, ciders too, simple food, Mercedes memorabilia, model railway (M Greening)

FERNHURST [SU9028]
Red Lion GU27 3HY [3m S of Haslemere; The Green, off A286 via Church Lane]: Wisteria-covered 15th-c pub tucked quietly away by green and cricket pitch nr church, heavy beams, attractive layout and furnishings, good value food from interesting sandwiches and snacks to fresh fish, Fullers ales, good wines, polite efficient staff, restaurant; children welcome, pretty gardens front and back (BB, Tony and Wendy Hobden)

FERRING [TQ0903]
Henty Arms BN12 6QY [Ferring Lane]: Lounge and dining area recently opened together, well kept Caledonian Deuchars IPA, Fullers London Pride, Wells & Youngs Bitter and other changing ales, beer festival late July, attractively priced food even Sun evening, friendly neatly dressed staff, log fire, separate public bar with games and TV; garden tables (Tony and Wendy Hobden, Bruce Bird)

FIRLE [TQ4607]
☆ Ram BN8 6NS [village signed off A27 Lewes—Polegate]: 17th-c village pub with chatty local atmosphere, pleasant décor with

pictures on carefully contrasting coloured walls, good mix of unassuming furnishings inc some big comfortable armchairs, log fires, well kept reasonably priced Harveys Best and seasonal Old, food from sandwiches and some interesting light dishes up; children and dogs welcome, tables in big walled garden behind, open all day *(BB, Kevin Thorpe)*

FISHBOURNE [SU8304]

☆ *Bulls Head* PO19 3JP [Fishbourne Rd (A259 Chichester—Emsworth)]: Relaxing and comfortable beamed village pub with pretty window boxes, fair-sized main bar, Fullers ales, neat staff, good log fire, daily papers, popular quickly served food (not Sun evening), children's area, restaurant area, outstanding lavatories; skittle alley, terrace picnic-sets, bedrooms *(David H T Dimock, Klaus and Elizabeth Leist, Bruce Bird, Ann and Colin Hunt, Ian Phillips, Dr Alan and Mrs Sue Holder)*

FOREST ROW [TQ4235]

Brambletye RH18 5EZ [A22]: Long bar at side of hotel with Fullers and Gales ales kept well, good value food, friendly staff, open fire; children welcome, tables in colourful courtyard with fountain and bedrooms off *(Dave Braisted)*

FULKING [TQ2411]

Shepherd & Dog BN5 9LU [off A281 N of Brighton, via Poynings]: Bow-windowed Badger dining pub with olde-worlde feel despite modern tables and chairs, painted panelling and new granite bar counter, wide food choice (all day wknds), their real ales, good wine choice, log fire; beautiful spot below downs, pretty streamside garden with decking and upper play lawn, open all day *(LYM, Jude Wright)*

GLYNDE [TQ4508]

☆ *Trevor Arms* BN8 6SS: Well kept Harveys ales and bargain food from ploughman's and baked potatoes to good Sun roasts, jovial landlord and friendly staff, good range of spirits, small bar with corridor to impressive dining room, Glyndebourne posters and photographs; tables in large garden with downland backdrop, Glyndebourne musicians may play out here on summer Suns *(Tony and Wendy Hobden, John Beeken, Oliver Wright, G H Wagstaff, John Tav)*

GOLDEN CROSS [TQ5312]

Golden Cross Inn BN27 4AW [A22 NW of Hailsham]: Well kept Harveys and good traditional pub food (not Sun evening) inc lots of different fresh veg, separate public bar, welcoming courteous service *(Martin and Alison Stainsby)*

GORING-BY-SEA [TQ1004]

Swallows Return BN12 6NZ [Titnore Lane, off A259/A2032 Northbrook College roundabout]: Vintage Inns barn conversion, their usual food all day inc sandwiches till 5, Bass and Harveys Best, good choice of wines by the glass, good coffee, log fire as well as central heating, upper gallery; open all day *(Malcolm Pellatt)*

GRAFFHAM [SU9217]

Foresters Arms GU28 0QA: Friendly smallish two-room 17th-c pub kept spotless and doing well under current regime, changing local ales such as Ballards, Kings and Weltons, good wine choice, enjoyable home-made meals using local produce, pleasant young staff, big log fire in fine old fireplace, heavy timbering and stripped brick, country sports pictures, old pulpit as feature of small pretty restaurant (can be fully booked); tables in big pleasant garden, bedrooms, good walks *(John Beeken, Bruce Bird)*

White Horse GU28 0NT: Spotless family pub with good food from familiar favourites to upscale dishes, well kept ales such as Ballards, Goddards and Hampshire, attentive friendly licensees, log fires, walkers welcome (good area), small dining room and conservatory restaurant with good South Downs views; terrace, big garden with sheltered summer marquee, open all day Sun in summer *(Bruce Bird)*

HAILSHAM [TQ5809]

Grenadier BN27 1AS [High St (N end)]: Striking early 19th-c pub with warm welcome, traditional games in nice panelled locals' bar, comfortable lounge bar, simple lunchtime meals, full Harveys ale range; children welcome in lounge, dogs in public bar *(Pete Baker)*

HALNAKER [SU9008]

☆ *Anglesey Arms* PO18 0NQ [A285 Chichester—Petworth]: Nicely unpretentious bar with Adnams Best, Wells & Youngs and a guest such as Caledonian Deuchars IPA, decent wines, good generous imaginative food inc local organic produce and selsey fish, friendly helpful service, simple but smart L-shaped dining room with woodburners, stripped pine and some flagstones (children allowed), traditional games; tables in large tree-lined garden *(Ewart McKie, Nicholas and Dorothy Stephens, R B Gardiner, Bruce Bird, LYM, Tony and Wendy Hobden)*

HAMMERPOT [TQ0605]

☆ *Woodmans Arms* BN16 4EU: Pretty thatched pub comfortably rebuilt after 2004 fire, beams and timbers, enjoyable pubby food from sandwiches and baked potatoes up, Fullers ales, Sun bar nibbles, quick service by neat polite staff, log fire in big fireplace; piped music; tables outside with summer marquee, open all day Fri/Sat and summer Sun, may be cl Sun evening *(Ann and Colin Hunt, Val and Alan Green, Tony and Wendy Hobden, John Beeken, Brad Featherman and Marion Hunt, Mark Weber, LYM)*

HANDCROSS [TQ2529]

☆ *Royal Oak* RH17 6DJ [Horsham Rd (A279, off A23)]: Good interesting food from light dishes to seasonal game, generous helpings, friendly atmosphere and good prompt service, well kept Fullers London Pride, Harveys and a guest such as Timothy Taylors Landlord, winter mulled wine, old photographs and curios; comfortable tables on terrace with pleasant arbour overlooking fields and woods, handy for Nymans (*C and R Bromage, Brian Root, Jack and Sandra Clarfelt*)

HARTFIELD [TQ4735]

Anchor TN7 4AG [Church St]: Popular 15th-c local with good-natured atmosphere, friendly landlady, Adnams, Bass, Flowers IPA, Fullers ESB and Harveys Best, generous usual bar food, heavy beams and flagstones, little country pictures and houseplants, inglenook log fire and a woodburner, comfortable dining area, darts in lower room; piped music; children welcome, seats out on front verandah, garden with play area, open all day (*LYM, Pamela and Douglas Cooper, N R White*)

☆ *Haywaggon* TN7 4AB [High St (A264)]: Friendly and busy, with two big log fires, pews and lots of large tables in spacious low-beamed bar, wide range of blackboard bar food and good value former bakehouse restaurant, well kept Harveys and a guest such as Westerham, cheerful service, good choice of wines by the glass, nice dog; picnic-sets outside, comfortable new bedrooms in former stable block (*Pamela and Douglas Cooper, Mike Gorton*)

HASTINGS [TQ8209]

First In Last Out TN34 3EY [High St, Old Town]: Congenial and chatty beer-drinkers' local brewing its own good value FILO beers, a guest ale too, monthly beer and music festivals, farm cider, central raised log fire, simple lunchtime food (not Sun/Mon) inc decent sandwiches, open-plan bar with dark wood booths, posts and character cat presiding in central armchair, no machines or piped music; gents' down a few steps, parking nearby difficult; small covered back terrace, open all day (*Kevin Thorpe*)

HENFIELD [TQ2016]

Old Railway Tavern BN5 9PJ [Upper Station Rd]: Recently refurbished under friendly new licensees, now doing thai as well as local english food, restaurant, takeaways too (*L Woodward*)

White Hart BN5 9HP [High St (A281)]: Friendly 16th-c village pub with interesting tiled roof, cheery landlord, good service, Badger beers, farm cider, large civilised dining area with enjoyable food inc interesting up-to-date dishes and tempting puddings, decent wines with choice of glass sizes, comfortable L-shaped lounge, log fire, lots of panelling, tools hanging from low beams, horsebrasses, paintings, prints, photographs and fresh flowers; children welcome, small pleasant courtyard garden with play things (*Terry Buckland, William Ruxton*)

HERMITAGE [SU7505]

☆ *Sussex Brewery* PO10 8AU [A259 just W of Emsworth]: Bustling and interesting, with small bare-boards bar, good winter fire in huge brick fireplace, simple furniture, little flagstoned snug, Wells & Youngs ales and a

guest beer, several wines by the glass, straightforward food inc wide choice of speciality sausages, two dining rooms, one overlooking garden; children and dogs welcome, picnic-sets in small back courtyard, open all day (*Ian Phillips, M and R Thomas, LYM*)

HEYSHOTT [SU8918]

☆ *Unicorn* GU29 0DL [well signed off A286 S of Midhurst]: Welcoming village-green pub, well kept ales inc local Ballards, good if not cheap food from lunchtime sandwiches and baguettes up, cheerful service even when busy, thriving atmosphere, comfortably cushioned bar, attractive dining area; children allowed, reasonable disabled access, pretty garden with barbecue, charming downland setting handy for South Downs Way (*Paul Booth*)

HOLTYE [TQ4538]

White Horse TN8 7ED [Holtye Common; A264 East Grinstead—Tunbridge Wells]: Ancient gently refurbished village inn with welcoming atmosphere, enjoyable pubby food from sandwiches and baked potatoes up inc OAP Tues lunch, well kept ales inc Harveys, good service, log fire, illuminated aquarium set into floor; good disabled facilities, marvellous view from back lawn, bedrooms (*anon*)

HOUGHTON [TQ0111]

George & Dragon BN18 9LW [B2139 W of Storrington]: Elizabethan beams and timbers, attractive old-world bar rambling up and down steps (so not good for disabled people), great views from back extension, reasonably priced food freshly made to order under new chef, real ales such as Harveys Best, decent wines; children welcome, relaxing Arun Valley views too from terraces of charming well organised sloping garden, good walks, open for food all day wknds (*LYM, Tony and Wendy Hobden, David Coleman*)

HURSTPIERPOINT [TQ2816]

☆ *New Inn* BN6 9RQ [High St]: Ancient pub dating from 1450 and now thoroughly reworked under new management (in same small local group as Bull in Ditchling – see main entries), comfortable and appealing, with real ales inc Adnams Broadside and Harveys Best, good wines by the glass, enjoyable food, several softly lit linked beamed areas; garden tables, open all day (*LYM, James and Ginette Read*)

ICKLESHAM [TQ8716]

Robin Hood TN36 4BD [Main Rd]: Friendly down-to-earth local with cheerful staff, enjoyable unpretentious food, Fullers London Pride and other beers, log fire, games area with pool on left, back dining extension; fortnightly summer Sun car boot sale, picnic-sets in garden with Brede Valley views (*Tom and Jill Jones, Peter Meister*)

ISFIELD [TQ4516]

Halfway House TN22 5UG [Rose Hill (A26)]: Tastefully extended rambling pub with enjoyable good value home cooking inc Sun lunch and local game in season, cheerful young landlord, well kept Harveys ales inc a seasonal beer, low beams and timbers, dark pub furniture inc a couple of high-backed settles on turkey carpet, busy restaurant; they may try to keep your credit card while you eat; children and dogs welcome, picnic-sets in small back garden with play area *(BB, John Beeken)*

Laughing Fish TN22 5XB: Recently opened up Victorian local with good value pubby food, several Greene King ales, friendly staff, traditional games, immaculate new lavatories; entertaining beer race Easter bank hol Mon; children welcome, picnic-sets in small pleasantly shaded walled garden with enclosed play area, right by Lavender Line *(Mrs Hazel Rainer, John Beeken, BB, Ron Gentry)*

KEYMER [TQ3115]

Greyhound BN6 8QT [Keymer Rd (B2116)]: Rambling partly Elizabethan pub with low beams and panelling, enjoyable simple bar food from sandwiches up at attractive prices, more elaborate restaurant menu inc Italian chef's pasta, welcoming attentive service (newish management), Fullers London Pride and HSB and Harveys Best, log-effect inglenook fire in carpeted bar, pool; picnic-sets on terrace in garden behind *(Barry and Victoria Lister, Tony Hobden, John Beeken)*

KINGSFOLD [TQ1635]

Wise Old Owl RH12 3SA [A24 Dorking—Horsham, nr A29 junction]: 1930s former Vintage Inn reworked as interesting combination of deli (local meats, bread, jams etc) and pub, with decent food from sandwiches up, Harveys Best and Hogs Back TEA, log fires *(Ian Phillips)*

KINGSTON NEAR LEWES [TQ3908]

Juggs BN7 3NT [village signed off A27 by roundabout W of Lewes]: Ancient rose-covered pub with heavy 15th-c beams and very low front door, lots of neatly stripped masonry, sturdy wooden furniture on bare boards and stone slabs, smaller eating areas inc family room, well kept Shepherd Neame ales, good coffee and wine list, log fires, dominoes and shove-ha'penny; piped music; nice seating areas outside, compact well equipped play area *(Ian Phillips, Fr Robert Marsh, LYM)*

KIRDFORD [TQ0126]

Foresters Arms RH14 0ND: Well run beamed pub set back from green, reasonably priced blackboard food from sandwiches and baked potatoes up, Badger ales, log fires, pale wood dining furniture; picnic-sets in front, pretty garden behind, boules pitch *(Ian Phillips)*

☆ *Half Moon* RH14 0LT [opp church, off A272 Petworth—Billingshurst]: 17th-c tile-hung upmarket bar/restaurant, picturesque and charmingly set, with enjoyable food at linen-set tables in immaculate roomy and rambling low-beamed dining area, good wines by the glass, kind professional service, Fullers London Pride from curved counter in

attractive partly quarry-tiled bar with log fire; tables in pretty back garden and out in front *(LYM, Clare Thornton-Wood, Derek and Maggie Washington)*

LAMBS GREEN [TQ2136]

Lamb RH12 4RG: Comfortable well divided old beamed pub with four Kings ales kept well, Biddenden farm cider, wide range of enjoyable pubby blackboard food, good helpings, friendly helpful young staff, flagstones and nice log fire in main bar, some horse tack and so forth, conservatory restaurant; quiet piped music; terrace tables, pleasant walks *(Shaun O'Dell, Tony Hobden, BB, Bruce Bird)*

LANCING [TQ1704]

Crabtree BN15 9NQ [Crabtree Lane]: Friendly pub with good landlord and staff, changing independent ales such as Ballards, Goddards, Sharps and local Hammerpot, games area in large public bar, comfortable Spitfire lounge with unusual 30s ceiling, art deco lights, model planes and old photographs, food inc evening thai buffets, Sun roast and hot counter; garden with downs views and play area *(Bruce Bird)*

LEWES [TQ4109]

Brewers Arms BN7 1XN [High St]: Straightforward local with Harveys Best and interesting guest ales, local photographs and clay pipe collection in front bar, quiet lounge, back room with pool and pub games, low-priced food all day till 6.45; sports TV; open all day *(Tony Hobden, Mrs Hazel Rainer, Bruce Bird, the Didler, Kevin Thorpe)*

Elephant & Castle BN7 2DJ [White Hill]: Friendly bare-boards local popular for its big-screen sports TV, enthusiastic chatty landlord, well kept Black Sheep, Caledonian Deuchars IPA and Harveys Best, farm cider, food inc burgers made from organic sussex beef, interesting mix of bric-a-brac, large main room and side room with pool and some settles *(Bruce Bird, Tony Hobden, BB)*

Gardeners Arms BN7 2AN [Cliffe High St]: Traditional small local opp brewery, light, airy and quiet, with Harveys and interesting changing ales and farm ciders, good value rolls, baguettes and pasties all day, good friendly service (with helpful opinions on the beers), plain scrubbed tables on bare boards around three narrow sides of bar, daily papers and magazines, Sun bar nibbles; open all day *(Anne and Tim Locke, Kevin Thorpe, BB)*

John Harvey BN7 2AN [Bear Yard, just off Cliffe High St]: Tap for nearby Harveys brewery (with separate good brewery shop), all their beers inc seasonal kept perfectly, some tapped from the cask, generous decent value food from lunchtime sandwiches, baked potatoes and ciabattas up, friendly efficient young staff, basic dark flagstoned bar with one great vat halved to make two towering 'snugs' for several people, lighter room on left; piped music and machines; a few tables outside, open all day, breakfast from 10am (Mrs Hazel Rainer, BB, Anne and Tim Locke, David Swift)

Kings Head BN7 1HS [Southover High St]: Popular straightforward corner local with Bass and Harveys Best from central bar, reasonably priced usual food from sandwiches and baked potatoes up, cheerful helpful staff, raised eating area with flame-effect fire, sofa in side alcove, monarch portraits and collections of cup and cheese dishes, board games; back garden, bedrooms (John Beeken, Mrs Hazel Rainer)

☆ **Lewes Arms** BN7 1YH [Castle Ditch Lane/Mount Pl – tucked behind castle ruins]: Unpretentious corner local built into castle ramparts, chatty and friendly, small front bar and hatchway, larger lounge with eating area off, Harveys Best back on handpump (after vigorous local protests to Greene King regional management who control the pub and had destocked it) with a Greene King ale and guest such as Hop Back Summer Lightning, good wines by the glass, farm cider, bargain simple food from good baguettes and tapas up 12-6, daily papers, local pictures, lots of traditional games and special events, no music or mobiles; small heated terrace, open all day (Geoff and Carol Thorp, Sue Demont, Tim Barrow, Tony Hobden, BB, John Beeken, Conor McGaughey, Kevin Thorpe)

Snowdrop BN7 2BU [South St]: Two spacious well worn-in bar areas with the cliffs as a backdrop and a maritime décor with figureheads, ship lamps etc, fairly straightforward bar food, Adnams Broadside, Harveys Best and perhaps a guest beer, dominoes, spiral stairs up to more seats and pool; piped music, nearby parking if pub's small space full; local bands Sat evening, children and dogs welcome, open all day (Ann and Colin Hunt, LYM, Sue Demont, Tim Barrow, Kevin Thorpe)

LICKFOLD [SU9226]

☆ **Lickfold Inn** GU28 9EY [NE of Midhurst, between A286 and A283]: Attractive dining pub with Tudor beams, ancient flooring bricks and big log fire in huge inglenook, simple pale wooden furnishings in bar and back dining room, smarter restaurant (tablecloths, sofas and rugs on bare boards) upstairs, good wines by the glass, imaginative food, welcoming efficient staff; sleek terrace tables under big parasols, picnic-sets in interesting garden (John Evans, Tom and Jill Jones, LYM)

LINDFIELD [TQ3425]

Stand Up RH16 2HN [High St]: Recently refurbished traditional pub now tied to Dark Star with their ales and guest beers, two welcoming and knowledgeable landladies, enjoyable evening pub food (Andrew and Susan Kerry-Bedell)

LITTLEHAMPTON [TQ0202]

☆ **Arun View** BN17 5DD [Wharf Rd; W towards Chichester]: Roomy and comfortable 18th-c pub in lovely spot right on harbour with river directly below windows, worth booking

for its interesting food with good fresh fish (very popular lunchtime with older people, a younger crowd evenings), sandwiches too, Ringwood Best and Old Thumper and Youngs Special, good wine list, good cheerful service even when busy, lots of drawings, caricatures and nautical collectables, flagstoned and panelled back public bar, large conservatory and flower-filled terrace both overlooking busy waterway and pedestrian bridge; disabled facilities, summer barbecues evenings and wknds, winter live music, bright and modest good value bedrooms (Ian and Jane Irving, Bruce Bird, Craig Turnbull, Tony and Wendy Hobden)

LITTLEWORTH [TQ1921]

Windmill RH13 8EJ [pub sign on B2135; village signed off A272 southbound, W of Cowfold]: Small spotless local, most hospitable, with log fires in panelled flagstoned public bar and compact cosy beamed lounge/eating area, enjoyable sensibly priced generous food (take-away fish and chips Fri night), well kept Badger beers, bric-a-brac large and small inside and out, darts, dominoes, cards and bar billiards, two easy-going pub dogs, no music; children welcome, peaceful and attractive side garden (Bruce Bird)

LODSWORTH [SU9223]

☆ **Hollist Arms** GU28 9BZ [off A272 Midhurst—Petworth]: Cheerful and civilised village pub overlooking small green, Kings Horsham Best, Timothy Taylors Landlord and Wells & Youngs, good wines by the glass and coffee, good range of generous enjoyable bar food inc fresh fish and shellfish, popular Sun lunch, relaxed atmosphere, lively landlord and prompt charming service, interesting books and magazines, country prints, sofas by log fire; must book Sat night, outside lavatories; may be piped classical music; children welcome, nice tree-lined back garden, good walks (R B Gardiner, Ron Gentry)

LOWFIELD HEATH [TQ2539]

Flight RH11 0QA [Charlwood Rd]: Pictures and models of aircraft, friendly helpful staff, nice range of food, well kept beers; caters well for children in conservatory with view of planes taking off from Gatwick, tables outside too (R C Vincent)

LOXWOOD [TQ0331]

Onslow Arms RH14 0RD [B2133 NW of Billingshurst]: Comfortable, relaxing and popular, with enjoyable food inc light dishes and smaller helpings, friendly informal service, Badger ales, good house wines, plenty of coffees and teas, lovely old log fireplaces, daily papers; dogs welcome, picnic-sets in good-sized pleasant garden sloping to river and nearby newly restored Wey & Arun Canal, good walks and boat trips (Lucien Perring, Mike and Lynn Robinson, Peter and Anne Hollindale)

LURGASHALL [SU9327]

Noahs Ark GU28 9ET [off A283 N of Petworth]: Relaxed 16th-c country pub perfectly placed overlooking churchyard and cricket green, two neat beamed bars with log fires, one in a capacious inglenook, pastel walls with small windows, new tenants moving the food upmarket (Sun lunch very popular though not cheap), good wines by the glass, Greene King ales; may be soft piped music; children welcome, picnic-sets on front grass, more in back garden, has been cl winter Sun evening; reports on new regime please (LYM, Michael B Griffith, R B Gardiner, Gerry and Rosemary Dobson)

MAPLEHURST [TQ1924]
White Horse RH13 6LL [Park Lane]: Friendly long-serving licensees in peaceful beamed country local, four seating areas inc homely cosy corners and sun lounge with redundant church furniture and lots of plants, log fire, well kept ales such as Archers, Harveys and Weltons, farm cider, decent wines, bargain coffee, good value sandwiches, toasties, baked potatoes and one or two simple hot dishes, good service, lots of traditional games, no music or machines; children welcome, pleasant outlook from back garden with play area, beautiful wisteria in front, car enthusiasts' evenings (Bruce Bird, Martin and Karen Wake)

MAREHILL [TQ0618]
White Horse RH20 2DY [Mare Hill Rd (A283 E of Pulborough)]: Several linked areas with plenty of individuality, pubby menu and some more imaginative specials, well kept Fullers ales, decent coffee, friendly staff, two open fires; dogs welcome, garden tables, handy for RSPB Pulborough Brooks Reserve, open all day wknds (Tony and Wendy Hobden, John Beeken)

MARESFIELD [TQ4422]
Piltdown Man TN22 3XL [A272 Newick Rd]: Newish management, enjoyable food, pleasant staff and décor (not very pubby), a named goldfish on each table (Mrs Stella Knight)

MARK CROSS [TQ5831]
☆ *Mark Cross Inn* TN6 3NP [A267 N of Mayfield]: Now under same management as Chaser at Shipbourne (Kent main entry), spreading linked areas on varying levels, brisk and friendly informal service, real ales inc Harveys Best and Timothy Taylors Landlord, good wines by the glass, nice coffee, huge helpings of hearty somewhat pricy food, real mix of dark wood tables and cushioned dining chairs, walls crowded with prints, old photographs and postcards, church candles, houseplants; doors out to decking with nice teak furniture, picnic-sets out on grass, broad Weald views (Colin McKerrow, BB, Peter Meister)

MIDDLETON-ON-SEA [SU9800]
Elmer PO22 6HD [Elmer Rd]: Comfortable central bar with front games room and back restaurant, full food range from baguettes up, friendly efficient service, Fullers ales; bedrooms (Tony and Wendy Hobden)

MIDHURST [SU8821]
Bricklayers Arms GU29 9BX [Wool Lane/West St]: Two cosily welcoming olde-worlde bars, good local atmosphere, enjoyable generous home-made food inc Sun roast, Greene King IPA and Abbot, friendly efficient service, sturdy old oak furniture, 17th-c beams, old photographs and bric-a-brac; courtyard tables out under cocktail parasols (Craig Turnbull)
Wheatsheaf GU29 9BX [Wool Lane/A272]: Dating from 16th c, its cosy low-beamed and timbered bars recently tastefully refurbished with regency-style furniture, interesting menu, Badger ales; open all day (Christine A Murphy)

MILLAND [SU8328]
Rising Sun GU30 7NA [Iping Rd junction with main rd through village]: Latest change of licensees – now two enthusiastic young couples – giving good value food in light and airy main bar, friendly service, Fullers ales, bar billiards; children welcome (very popular with families wknds), picnic-sets in good-sized neatly kept garden, good walking area (Mike Friend, Mike Edwards, BB, Michael B Griffith)

MILTON STREET [TQ5304]
☆ *Sussex Ox* BN26 5RL [off A27 just E of Alfriston – brown sign to pub]: Attractive and friendly country pub with magnificent downs views, smallish beamed and brick-floored bar with roaring woodburner, enjoyable food, well kept Dark Star, Harveys and an interesting guest beer, enthusiastic young licensees and quick service even when busy, good family dining area (book well ahead in summer) with nice prints; piped music; big lawn and terrace, lots of good walks (LYM, Michael B Griffith, Bruce Bird)

NETHERFIELD [TQ7118]
Netherfield Arms TN33 9QD [just off B2096 Heathfield—Battle]: Unpretentious low-ceilinged country pub with wide choice of enjoyable home-made food inc good specials, friendly attentive service, Fullers London Pride, decent wines, inglenook log fire, cosy restaurant, no music; lovely back garden (Paul and Bryony Walker, BB)

NORMANS BAY [TQ6806]
Star BN24 6QG [signed off A259 E of Pevensey, or off B2182 W out of Bexhill]: Modernised family dining pub massively extended from lower 16th-c core, often very busy indeed, with wide choice of generous food, Greene King Old Speckled Hen and Harveys Best, friendly service; piped music; garden with tables under trees, good big play area and pool with waterfowl, good walks inland away from the caravan sites, open all day (LYM, Tony and Wendy Hobden)

NORTHCHAPEL [SU9529]
Half Moon GU28 9HP [A285 Guildford—Petworth]: Warm-hearted beamed pub, partly 15th-c, with masses of bric-a-brac (more in the nice garden), welcoming service, enjoyable generous straightforward food with

good veg, several real ales *(Klaus and Elizabeth Leist)*

NORTHIAM [TQ8224]

Hayes Arms TN31 6NN [Church Lane]: Civilised Georgian-fronted hotel, enjoyable sensibly priced food in comfortable and extensive brasserie-style bar, friendly helpful staff, heavy Tudor beams, log fire in big brick inglenook, small back restaurant; bedrooms *(Ian Phillips)*

NUTBOURNE [TQ0718]

Rising Sun RH20 2HE [off A283 E of Pulborough; The Street]: Unspoilt creeper-covered village pub dating partly from 16th c, beams, bare boards and scrubbed tables, friendly young landlord and staff, well kept changing ales such as Adnams, Fullers London Pride and Harveys Best, enjoyable food from pubby favourites to ostrich steak, big log fire, daily papers, enamel advertising signs and 1920s fashion and dance posters, chess and cosy games room, attractive beamed back restaurant; children and dogs allowed, two garden areas with small back terrace under apple tree, handy for Nutbourne Vineyard *(Bruce Bird, John Beeken, Tony and Wendy Hobden)*

OFFHAM [TQ3912]

☆ *Blacksmiths Arms* BN7 3QD [A275 N of Lewes]: Civilised open-plan dining pub, open sandwiches, baked potatoes, ploughman's and usual pubby things as well as good fresh fish and other specials, Harveys Best and a seasonal beer, good friendly uniformed staff, huge end inglenook fireplace; french windows to terrace with picnic-sets, four bedrooms *(LYM, Tony and Wendy Hobden)*

Chalk Pit BN7 3QF [A275 N of Lewes]: Bright and pleasant, with friendly licensees, Harveys Best and Old, decent wines by the glass, good value standard food all day inc good Sun roasts, neat restaurant; dogs welcome in bar, bedrooms, open all day *(Tony and Wendy Hobden, Terry Buckland)*

PAGHAM [SZ8998]

Lamb PO21 4NJ [Pagham Rd]: Rambling flower-decked pub with generous enjoyable food, Fullers London Pride, Greene King Abbot and Wells & Youngs Bitter and Special, prompt service even when busy, restaurant, lots of beams, timbers and paintings; unobtrusive piped music; garden tables *(Bruce Bird)*

Lion PO21 3JX [Nyetimber Lane]: Civilised low-beamed two-bar pub with good value food inc good Sun roasts, well kept beers, small restaurant; big suntrap terrace *(Mrs Brenda Calver)*

PATCHING [TQ0705]

Fox BN13 3UJ [Arundel Rd; signed off A27 eastbound just W of Worthing]: Under same friendly efficient management as Spotted Cow in Angmering, popular for generous good value fresh food from imaginative sandwiches, baguettes and baked potatoes up, popular Sun roasts (book ahead for these), well kept Harveys Best, Shepherd

Neame Spitfire and a guest beer, good wine choice, daily papers, large dining area off roomy panelled bar, hunting pictures; quiet piped music, nice big tree-shaded garden with play area, small caravan site, open all day wknds *(Cathryn and Richard Hicks, Bruce Bird, Tony and Wendy Hobden)*

PETT [TQ8713]

Royal Oak TN35 4HG [Pett Rd]: Particularly generous enjoyable food from sandwiches up inc OAP lunches and very popular Sun lunch in well run friendly local, roomy main bar with big log fireplace, quick service, Harveys Best, Timothy Taylors Landlord and a guest such as Kings, attractive dining areas *(Pamela and Douglas Cooper, Peter Meister, Lucien Perring)*

PETWORTH [SU9719]

☆ *Badgers* GU28 0JF [Station Rd (A285 1½ miles S)]: Smart restauranty dining pub with up-to-date rather upmarket food served generously at well spaced tables mixing old mahogany and waxed stripped pine, charming wrought-iron lamps, log fires, friendly staff, Badger Best and K&B (there is a small drinking area by the entrance), good range of wines; children in eating area of bar if over 5, stylish tables and seats out on terrace by water lily pool, bedrooms, cl winter Sun evenings *(Gerald and Gabrielle Culliford, LYM, Peter Mueller, Pat Woodward)*

PLUMPTON [TQ3613]

Half Moon BN7 3AF [Ditchling Rd (B2116)]: Welcoming bustle in long beamed and timbered bar, Harveys Best and Weltons, good value pubby food from baked potatoes and baguettes up, good log fire with unusual flint chimneybreast, jug collection and painting of regulars, games area, small dining area; children welcome, tables in wisteria front courtyard and big back downs-view garden with big play area, good walks *(Tony and Jill Radnor, John Beeken)*

PLUMPTON GREEN [TQ3617]

☆ *Plough* BN7 3DF: Two-bar pub with enjoyable food from filled bagels up (they list many of their suppliers), notably friendly attentive service, Harveys ales inc seasonal (they may offer tasters), striking Spitfire and Hurricane pictures as well as books and bric-a-brac; tables on covered terrace and in large attractive downs-view garden with play area, open all day *(Bruce Bird, Terry Buckland, John Beeken)*

Winning Post BN7 3DR [Station Rd]: Roomy plush lounge, well kept Harveys Best and Timothy Taylors Landlord, good variety of reasonably priced pub food, bare-boards public bar with darts and bar billiards; tables under cocktail parasols on small terrace, more in enclosed raised garden *(John Beeken)*

PORTSLADE [TQ2505]

Stanley Arms BN41 1SS [Wolseley Rd]: Homely backstreet pub, friendly and welcoming, with well kept changing ales such as Bath, Dark Star and Kings; open all day wknds, but note they are only open from 2 wkdys *(Tony Hobden)*

POUNDGATE [TQ4928]

Crow & Gate TN6 3TA [A26 Crowborough—Uckfield]: Old pub extended as beamed Vintage Inn, nice mix of furniture, good log fire, their usual food, Harveys Best, lots of wines by the glass, good value coffee, efficient service; piped music, games; good disabled access, children welcome, tables outside, play area *(Michael Dandy)*

POYNINGS [TQ2611]

☆ *Royal Oak* BN45 7AQ [The Street]: Large darkly beamed chatty bar with wide choice of enjoyable food (can book tables), good service even when very busy, Courage Directors, Greene King Old Speckled Hen and Harveys from three-sided servery, woodburner, no piped music; big attractive garden with barbecue, climbing frame and country/downs views *(Mrs Mahni Pannett, N R White, William Goodhart)*

PUNNETTS TOWN [TQ6320]

☆ *Three Cups* TN21 9LR [B2096 towards Battle]: Low-beamed country pub bought and refurbished 2007 by small group of locals, new emphasis on the food side, real ales, log fire in companionable bar's big fireplace, compact back dining room, traditional games; children and dogs welcome, tables outside, great walks, has been open all day wknds *(Kevin Thorpe, LYM)*

RAKE [SU8027]

Sun GU33 7PQ [London Rd (A3 S of Liphook)]: Comfortable dining pub with two roomy brasserie dining areas, wide choice of real food inc seafood, steaks cut to order and small helpings for children, Greene King IPA and Abbot, decent wines by the glass, good friendly service, a couple of leather armchairs and woodburner in bar; piped music may obtrude; tables on back canopied terrace with lovely valley views *(anon)*

RINGMER [TQ4415]

Old Ship BN8 5RP [Uckfield Rd (A26 Lewes—Uckfield, outside village S of Isfield turnoff)]: Sizeable low-beamed pub with comfortable areas each side of servery, wide choice of enjoyable home-made fresh food from sandwiches, baguettes and baked potatoes to steaks, friendly speedy service, real ales such as Courage Directors and Harveys Best, farm cider, nautical pictures and memorabilia; good-sized attractive garden with play area *(Iain Forbes, Lionel and Sylvia Kopelowitz, Michael Dandy, Ben Burdass)*

ROBERTSBRIDGE [TQ7323]

☆ *George* TN32 5AW [High St]: Armchairs and sofa by inglenook log fire on right, attractive contemporary dining area on left, friendly helpful licensees, Adnams Explorer, Badger and Harveys, good wines by the glass, good choice of enjoyable reasonably priced food, bustling, chatty atmosphere; piped pop music, live lunchtime last Sun of

month; children and dogs welcome, tables in garden behind *(BB, Nigel and Jean Eames, K M Sharp)*

Ostrich TN32 5DG [Station Rd]: Cheerful open-plan former station hotel, enjoyable food from filled rolls up, Adnams, Harveys Best and a guest beer, coal fire, eye-catching artworks, games room; tables in attractive garden, bedrooms, open all day *(the Didler)*

ROGATE [SU8023]

☆ *White Horse* GU31 5EA [East St; A272 Midhurst—Petersfield]: Rambling heavy-beamed local in front of village cricket field, civilised and friendly, with Harveys full range kept particularly well, relaxed atmosphere, flagstones, stripped stone, timbers and big log fire, attractive candlelit sunken dining area, good generous reasonably priced food (not Sun eve or Mon), friendly staff, traditional games (and quite a collection of trophy cups), no music or machines; quiz and folk nights; some tables on back terrace, open all day Sun *(Michael B Griffith, Bruce Bird, LYM, J Stickland)*

ROTTINGDEAN [TQ3702]

Coach House BN2 7HR [High St, St Margarets]: Seaside pub with friendly staff, generous pubby food from sandwiches and baked potatoes up; handy for Undercliff Walk *(Jude Wright)*

RUNCTON [SU8900]

Royal Oak PO20 1LN [Pagham Rd, S]: Very popular for its sizzling steaks, friendly staff, Gales HSB *(A and B D Craig)*

RUSHLAKE GREEN [TQ6218]

☆ *Horse & Groom* TN21 9QE [off B2096 Heathfield—Battle]: Friendly new landlady in cheerful village-green local, little L-shaped low-beamed bar with small brick fireplace and local pictures, small room down a step with horsey décor, simple beamed restaurant, food (not cheap) inc local fish and game, Shepherd Neame Bitter and Spitfire, decent wines by the glass; children and dogs welcome, cottagey garden with plenty of seats and pretty country views, nice walks *(John Bell, David Barnes, William Ruxton, LYM)*

RUSPER [TQ2037]

Star RH12 4RA [off A264 S of Crawley]: Several linked rooms in rambling beamed coaching inn, friendly helpful staff, cosy atmosphere, Fullers London Pride, Greene King Abbot, Harveys Best and Shepherd Neame Spitfire, wide choice of decent food from sandwiches and light meals up, open fires; picnic-sets on small back terrace *(Ian Phillips)*

RYE [TQ9220]

George TN31 7JT [High St]: Sizeable hotel given contemporary refurbishment under new owners, lively up-to-date feel in bar and adjoining dining area, Adnams, Harveys Best and Greene King Old Speckled Hen, a couple of continental beers on tap, enjoyable food, some French staff; good bedrooms *(Peter Meister)*

Globe TN31 7NX [Military Rd]: Under new management, with pleasant homely décor, well kept real ale, good reasonably priced home-made food inc fresh local seafood (V Brogden)

Ypres Castle TN31 7HH [Gun Garden; steps up from A259, or down past Ypres Tower]: Nicely placed, with informal and unpretentious traditional bars, lots of artworks (though it's not a smart place), log fire, Adnams Broadside, Harveys Best and Wells & Youngs Bombardier, good choice of wines by the glass, food inc good local fish, comfortable restaurant area; children welcome lunchtime, dogs in bar, tables outside, open all day summer Sats, cl Tues in winter and Sun evening (LYM, Sarah Hapgood, Mrs Hazel Rainer, Louise English, Gwyn Jones, Tim Maddison, Peter Meister)

RYE HARBOUR [TQ9419]
William the Conqueror TN31 7TU: Welcoming harbourside pub with fair-priced food, friendly staff, good range of Shepherd Neame ales, lively local atmosphere, big beamed lounge, games in separate public bar (BB, Clive Flynn)

SCAYNES HILL [TQ3824]
Sloop RH17 7NP [Freshfield Lock]: Promptly served blackboard food (all day Sun), Greene King and guest ales, decent wines, bar billiards and traditional games, interesting photographs in pleasantly furnished linked areas; children in eating areas, lots of tables in sheltered garden (LYM, Mrs Hazel Rainer)

SEAFORD [TV4799]
White Lion BN25 2BJ [Claremont Rd]: Well run by genial Irish landlord, good food range from sandwiches and baked potatoes to local fish and Sun roasts, children's helpings, real ales such as Fullers, Harveys and Shepherd Neams, conservatory; bedrooms, open all day (Paul A Moore, Fr Robert Marsh)

SELHAM [SU9320]
Three Moles GU28 0PN [village signed off A272 Petworth—Midhurst]: Small simple old-fashioned pub tucked away in woodland village, quietly relaxing atmosphere, friendly enthusiastic landlady, Skinners Betty Stogs and unusual guest beers collected direct from small breweries (one always a Mild, others often west country), farm cider, daily papers, darts, bar billiards, plenty of board games, very mixed furniture, a few oil lamps and pictures, no mobile phones – but has internet link; steep steps up to bar, no food or children, monthly singsongs, June beer festival; garden tables, nice walks, open all day wknds (Kevin Thorpe, Bruce Bird, Phil and Sally Gorton)

SELMESTON [TQ5006]
Barley Mow BN26 6UE [A27 Eastbourne—Lewes]: Open-plan pub doing well since refurbishment, wide blackboard choice of reasonably priced pubby food all day inc children's dishes, well kept Adnams Broadside and Harveys Best, well trained young staff, eating areas on both sides of

central bar area; unobtrusive piped music; large garden with decking and sturdy timber play area, open all day (BB, Kevin Thorpe)

SELSEY [SZ8692]
Lifeboat PO20 0DJ [Albion Rd, nr seafront]: Congenial unpretentious pub (dogs allowed) with dining extension, wide choice of low-priced food from sandwiches up, well kept Arundel ASB and Fullers London Pride, friendly helpful staff; tables out on big verandah (Tony and Wendy Hobden, David H T Dimock)

Seal PO20 0JX [Hillfield Rd]: Lively refurbished local with enjoyable food inc local fish, friendly staff, real ales such as Badger and Hop Back, good choice of wines by the glass; quiz nights (anon)

SHIPLEY [TQ1321]
☆ *Countryman* RH13 8PZ [SW of village, off A272 E of Coolham]: Nicely updated early 19th-c pub popular for wide choice of good food from warm baguettes and baked potatoes through tapas to game and fresh seafood, real ales such as Bass, Kings Horsham Best and Youngs Special, friendly uniformed staff, large neatly laid dining area, welcoming timbered and flagstoned bar with inglenook log fire, comfortable lounge with big leather sofas; evening opening not till 6.30; picnic-sets and play equipment in pretty garden, horse park, handy for Shipley windmill and D-Day Airfield at Coolham (Richard Allen, Mrs Jennifer Hurst, James Anderson, Terry Buckland)

SHOREHAM-BY-SEA [TQ2105]
Buckingham Arms BN43 5WA [Brunswick Rd, by stn]: Big open-plan pub with good choice of real ales, good value lunchtime food from sandwiches up; small garden behind (Tony Hobden)

Fly Inn BN43 5FF [signed off A27, A259]: Not a pub, but this small bar is worth knowing for its interesting 1930s art deco airport building and uninterrupted downs views with plenty of light aircraft action; well kept changing real ales, promptly served simple food, cheerful staff; piped music; children welcome, terrace tables, small airport museum (John Saville)

Red Lion BN43 5TE [Upper Shoreham Rd, opp church]: Modest dim-lit low-beamed and timbered 16th-c pub with settles in snug alcoves, good value generous pubby food inc good Sun lunch, well kept changing ales such as Badger, Grand Union, Harveys, Ringwood and Shepherd Neame, post-Easter beer festival, decent wines, farm cider, lively landlord and friendly efficient staff, log fire in unusual fireplace, another open fire in dining room, further bar with covered terrace; may be piped music; pretty sheltered garden behind, good downs views and walks (Tony and Wendy Hobden, Ian Phillips, Jestyn Phillips)

SHORTBRIDGE [TQ4521]
Peacock TN22 3XA [Piltdown; OS Sheet 198 map ref 450215]: Neatly rebuilt beamed and timbered bar, comfortable and welcoming,

with big inglenook, enjoyable generous food inc good fish, well kept Fullers London Pride and Harveys, restaurant; piped music; children welcome, good-sized garden *(BB, Mrs Stella Knight)*

SLAUGHAM [TQ2528]

Chequers RH17 6AQ [off A23 S of Handcross]: Newly reopened as dining pub (after spell as a restaurant), rustic wooden furniture and comfortable sofas, wide choice of home-made food from simple things to smart seafood, two changing real ales, good wines by the glass, helpful young staff, open fire, no music; pretty village, lakeside walks *(Terry Buckland)*

SMALL DOLE [TQ2112]

Fox & Hounds BN5 9XE [Henfield Rd]: Open-plan village local with good choice of usual food from sandwiches and baked potatoes up, Harveys Best and Wells & Youngs Bombardier, raised dining areas; piped music; terrace tables, handy for downland walks *(Mrs Mahni Pannett)*

ST LEONARDS [TQ7608]

Bull TN38 8AY [Bexhill Rd (A259)]: Well run local, cheerful and unpretentious, with Shepherd Neame ales, good wine list, usual pub food from sandwiches to Sun roasts, prompt polite service, good-sized dining room; friendly pub cat, terrace tables and play area *(Stephen Harvey, Valerie Baker)*

Comet TN38 8BU [Harley Shute Rd]: Bar food and Sun lunches in open-plan Shepherd Neame pub, pool; no children; good-sized garden front and back, handy for holiday park opp *(Valerie Baker)*

STAPLEFIELD [TQ2728]

Jolly Tanners RH17 6EF [Handcross Rd, just off A23]: Neatly kept two-level local with two good log fires, lots of china, brasses and old photographs, well kept Hop Back Summer Lightning, Timothy Taylors Landlord, a Mild and Addlestone's cider, good May beer festival, friendly landlord and chatty atmosphere; piped music, jazz Sun evening, fortnightly quiz Thurs; children and dogs welcome, attractive nicely kept garden with lots of space for children, terrace tables under cocktail parasols and picnic-sets on grass, by cricket green, quite handy for Nymans (NT) *(C and R Bromage, Tony and Wendy Hobden, Bruce Bird, N R White, Mike Anderson)*

Victory RH17 6EU [Warninglid Rd]: Nicely placed dining pub overlooking cricket green, friendly new licensees doing wide choice of enjoyable food inc good if not cheap fish and seafood, good atmosphere, Harveys Best, decent wines, woodburner, traditional décor with old prints; children welcome, picnic-sets and play area in garden *(N R White, Mike Anderson)*

STEYNING [TQ1711]

Chequer BN44 3RE [High St]: Recently refurbished timber-framed Tudor pub with Fullers London Pride and HSB, Kings Horsham Best and Timothy Taylors Landlord, good choice of wines, usual food from

sandwiches and snacks up, friendly service, log fire, antique snooker table; bedrooms *(anon)*

STOPHAM [TQ0318]

☆ *White Hart* RH20 1DS [off A283 E of village, W of Pulborough]: Interesting and well worn-in old pub, heavy beams, timbers and panelling, log fire and sofas in one of its three snug rooms, changing ales such as Arundel Gold and Hogs Back TEA, wide food choice from baguettes and baked potatoes through pubby staples to venison, friendly young staff, paintings for sale; piped music; children welcome, play area over road, tables (some under cover) out by River Arun *(John Beeken, Bruce Bird, R B Gardiner, LYM)*

STOUGHTON [SU8011]

Hare & Hounds PO18 9JQ [signed off B2146 Petersfield—Emsworth]: Airy pine-clad country dining pub with simple contemporary décor, enjoyable reasonably priced food inc good Sun roast, four well kept ales inc Harveys, bright cheerful service, big open fires; children in eating areas, tables on pretty front terrace and in back garden, lovely setting nr Saxon church, good walks nearby *(LYM, R and M Thomas, W A Evershed, Ann and Colin Hunt, Tony Warren)*

TICEHURST [TQ6831]

Bull TN5 7HH [Three Legged Cross; off B2099 towards Wadhurst]: Attractive 14th-c hall house with friendly service, enjoyable food, well kept Harveys, two big log fires in very heavy-beamed old-fashioned simple two-room bar, contemporary furnishings and flooring in light and airy dining extension; charming front garden with fish pond, bigger back one with play area *(BB, John Williams)*

TILLINGTON [SU9621]

☆ *Horse Guards* GU28 9AF [off A272 Midhurst—Petworth]: Prettily set 18th-c dining pub with good enterprising food using local produce, enthusiastic young licensees, real ales such as Fullers, Greene King and Wells & Youngs, good choice of wines by the glass, log fire and country furniture in neat beamed front bar, lovely views from bow window, dining room; may be piped music; terrace tables and sheltered garden behind, attractive ancient church opposite, bedrooms in pub and adjoining cottage *(LYM, David Collison, Kevin Thorpe, Mrs L Aquilina, Grahame Brooks)*

UCKFIELD [TQ4723]

Firemans Arms TN22 3AN [Five Ash Down, off A26 N – not to be confused with Five Ashes, towards Mayfield]: Recently refurbished Victorian pub, two bars and dining room, lots of steam railway memorabilia (it's that sort of fireman), wide choice of sensibly priced chippy food, Harveys Best and a guest beer; garden behind, open all day Fri-Sun *(Tony and Wendy Hobden)*

UDIMORE [TQ8519]

Kings Head TN31 6BG: Proper traditional chatty village pub with consistently well kept Harveys, Wells & Youngs and Timothy Taylors Landlord or Best from long bar, good-sized helpings of low-priced pubby food inc popular Sun lunch in dining area, long-serving licensees, open fires, low beams, plain tables and chairs on bare boards *(Peter Meister, PL)*

☆ *Plough* TN31 6AL [Cock Marling (B2089 W of Rye)]: Civilised and popular, with good fresh home-made food from soup and nice lamb sandwiches up, Greene King IPA, Ringwood Fortyniner and a guest beer, reasonably priced wines, relaxed friendly service, basic front bar with brass bric-a-brac and woodburner, open fire and farming prints in small pleasant carpeted dining area, books for sale; dogs welcome, tables on good-sized suntrap back terrace, open all day *(Kevin Thorpe, Mrs Hazel Rainer, Peter Meister)*

VINES CROSS [TQ5917]

☆ *Brewers Arms* TN21 9EN [a mile E of Horam]: Nice small four-room Victorian pub well run by two brothers, one the friendly chef doing enjoyable fresh food from good freshly baked rolls, ciabattas and pubby country hot dishes to some rather smarter things, real ales, decent wines by the glass, pleasantly informal décor and church candles; plenty of locals in public bar; picnic-sets out in front, pretty flower tubs *(BB)*

WADHURST [TQ6131]

Best Beech TN5 6JH [Mayfield Lane (B2100 a mile W)]: Pleasant dining pub with enjoyable food using some local produce in cosy eating area with lots of pictures, bar on left with wall seats, plenty of comfortable sofas, coal fire, well kept Adnams, Harveys and Wells & Youngs, good choice of wines by the glass, quick pleasant service; may be piped music; back restaurant, tables outside, good value bedrooms, good breakfast *(BB, Mrs Stella Knight)*

WALDERTON [SU7910]

☆ *Barley Mow* PO18 9ED [Stoughton rd, just off B2146 Chichester—Petersfield]: Attractive flagstoned country pub popular for good choice of good value generous food from baguettes up, real ales such as Fullers, Ringwood and Wells & Youngs, friendly efficient service even on busy wknds, two log fires and rustic bric-a-brac in U-shaped bar with roomy dining areas, no music; children welcome, skittle alley, nice furniture in big pleasant streamside back garden with fish pond, aviary and swings, good walks, handy for Stansted House *(M and R Thomas, R B Gardiner, W A Evershed)*

WARBLETON [TQ6018]

Warbil in Tun TN21 9BD [S of B2096 SE of Heathfield]: Pretty dining pub with good choice of good value food esp meat, nice puddings, well kept reasonably priced Harveys Best, good coffee, welcoming and cosily civilised atmosphere, beams and red plush, huge log fireplace; tables on roadside green, attractive tucked-away village *(Michael and Ann Cole)*

WARNHAM [TQ1533]

Greets RH12 3QY [Friday St]: Beamed 15th-c pub with good value food, good choice of real ales, decent wines, attentive staff, appealing simple décor with stripped pine tables on uneven flagstones, inglenook log fire, lots of nooks and corners, convivial locals' side bar; garden tables *(Malcolm Pellatt)*

Sussex Oak RH12 3QW [just off A24 Horsham—Dorking; Church St]: Cheerful country pub with big inglenook log fireplace, mix of flagstones, tiles, wood and carpeting, heavy beams and timbers, comfortable sofas, Adnams, Fullers London Pride, Timothy Taylors Landlord, Wells & Youngs and a guest beer from carved servery, Weston's farm cider, plenty of wines by the glass, food (all day wknds, not Mon evenings) from sandwiches and baked potatoes to steaks, high-raftered restaurant, bar billiards; piped music; children and dogs welcome, disabled facilities, picnic-sets in large pleasant garden, open all day *(Brian Mathers, LYM, Kevin Thorpe)*

WASHINGTON [TQ1213]

Frankland Arms RH20 4AL [just off A24 Horsham—Worthing]: Wide choice of unpretentious food all day from warm baguettes to good puddings, take-away pizzas too, Flowers IPA, Fullers London Pride and a guest beer such as Arundel, good value wines by the glass, log fires, pleasant service, sizeable restaurant, public bar with pool and TV in games area; disabled facilities, Post Office in outbuilding, walkers welcome, tables in neat garden below Chanctonbury Ring *(Des and Jen Clarke, Tony and Wendy Hobden, N R White)*

WEST ASHLING [SU8007]

Richmond Arms PO18 8EA [just off B2146; Mill Rd]: Friendly unpretentious village local in quiet pretty setting nr big mill pond with ducks and geese, welcoming licensees, well kept Greene King and guest ales, good value basic generous food from sandwiches and baked potatoes up, bare boards and flagstones, two open fires, darts, pool and a skittle alley; children allowed, picnic-sets out by pergola, has been open all day Sun and summer Sat *(John Beeken, LYM, Ann and Colin Hunt)*

WEST CHILTINGTON [TQ0917]

Five Bells RH20 2QX [Smock Alley, off B2139 SE]: Large open-plan beamed and panelled bar with old photographs, unusual brass bric-a-brac, real ales inc Arundel Dark Mild, Harveys and guests from small breweries, farm cider, pubby food (not Sun evening or Mon) inc good ploughman's, friendly enthusiastic landlord, log fire, daily papers, big pleasant conservatory dining room, no piped music; peaceful garden with terrace, bedrooms *(Tony and Wendy Hobden, Bruce Bird)*

WEST DEAN [SU8512]

Selsey Arms PO18 0QX [A286 Midhurst—Chichester]: Large welcoming late 18th-c pub with comfortable dining bar (becomes thai restaurant at night), plentiful enjoyable food, Fullers London Pride, Ringwood Best and Wadworths 6X, decent wines and coffee, efficient friendly service, log fire, smart traditional public bar with good home-made crisps and Sun bar nibbles *(Ann and Colin Hunt, R B Gardiner, Tony and Wendy Hobden, R Lake)*

WEST HOATHLY [TQ3632]

☆ *Cat* RH19 4PP [signed from A22 and B2028 S of E Grinstead; North Lane]: Attractive country dining pub with several seating areas, beams, panelling, fresh flowers and inglenook log fires, well kept Harveys and perhaps other ales such as Black Sheep, decent wines, enjoyable food from sandwiches to interesting main dishes, attentive landlord and cheerfully efficient service even when they're busy; tables out on newish terrace, quiet view of church *(JMM, Bruce Bird, Terry Buckland, LYM, Don Scarff)*

Intrepid Fox RH19 4QG [Hammingden Lane/North Lane, towards Sharpthorne]: Comfortably up-to-date former Vinols Cross Inn, genial landlord welcoming to all inc booted walkers, good generous food inc restauranty dishes, good wines by the glass, Harveys and guest beers, cosy log fire *(Mrs Tester, C and R Bromage)*

WEST MARDEN [SU7713]

Victoria PO18 9EN [B2146 2 miles S of Uppark]: Light fresh décor, short choice of good food in bar and small back candlelit restaurant, three real ales such as Harveys, Ringwood and Timothy Taylors Landlord, good choice of reasonably priced wines, old royal wedding photographs, pleasant end alcove with old-fashioned sofa by log fire, friendly attentive staff, no piped music; attractive garden, good walks nearby, bedrooms *(Bruce Bird, Ann and Colin Hunt, Jon and Penny Barnes)*

WEST WITTERING [SZ8099]

Lamb PO20 8QA [Chichester Rd; B2179/A286 towards Birdham]: Several rooms neatly knocked through in 18th-c country pub, immaculate furnishings, rugs on tiles, blazing fire, Badger ales, decent wines, reasonably priced food from separate servery inc full bar menu on Sun lunchtime, friendly staff; dogs on leads allowed, lots of tables out in front and in small sheltered back garden with terrace - good for children; busy in summer - handy for beach *(David H T Dimock, Klaus and Elizabeth Leist, BB, E J Seddon, Ian and Joan Blackwell)*

WHATLINGTON [TQ7619]

☆ *Royal Oak* TN33 0NJ [A21 N of village]: Welcoming service in beamed pub dating from 14th c, reasonably priced food, well kept Badger and Harveys Best, big log fire, decent wines, end dining area with stripped pine tables and chairs, well worn bar furniture, some character, separate restaurant for busy times; tables in back garden *(Brian Root, Pamela and*

Douglas Cooper, BB, David Barnes, M and R Thomas, Mike Gorton)

WINCHELSEA [TQ9017]

☆ *New Inn* TN36 4EN [German St; just off A259]: New licensee in attractive dining pub with good sandwiches as well as enjoyable main dishes inc local fish and good value Sun lunch, several Greene King ales, decent wines, friendly service, log fire, Georgian décor with turkey carpet and some slate flagstones, little-used back public bar with darts, pool and machines; piped music, plans for jazz or blues nights; children in eating area, pleasant walled garden, six pretty bedrooms (some sharing bathrooms), delightful setting opp church - Spike Milligan buried in graveyard *(Peter Meister, Grahame Brooks, LYM, Lucien Perring, Adrian Johnson)*

WISBOROUGH GREEN [TQ0526]

Cricketers Arms RH14 0DG [Loxwood Rd, just off A272 Billinghurst—Petworth]: Attractive old pub, open-plan and popular for its food, with five or six real ales, cheerful staff, two big woodburners, pleasant mix of country furniture, stripped brick dining area on left; live music nights; tables out on terrace and across lane from green *(Mike and Lynn Robinson, Alec and Joan Laurence, Tom and Jill Jones, LYM)*

Three Crowns RH14 0DX [Billinghurst Rd (A272)]: Long neat pub with real ales such as Badger, Ballards and Kings from end bar, standard food from sandwiches and baguettes up (can sometimes take a while), heavy beams and stripped brick in dining area, good coffee; disabled facilities, sizeable tree-shaded back garden *(Mike and Lynn Robinson, John Beeken)*

WITHYHAM [TQ4935]

☆ *Dorset Arms* TN7 4BD [B2110]: Pleasantly unpretentious 16th-c pub handy for Forest Way walks (not to mention nearby Ferrari garage), good friendly service, Harveys full beer range kept well, decent wines inc local ones, enjoyable traditional food from filled rolls to seasonal game, reasonable prices, good log fire in Tudor fireplace, sturdy tables and simple country seats on wide oak boards (sometimes a bit uneven - beware of wobbles), darts, dominoes, shove-ha'penny, cribbage, pretty dining area; piped music may obtrude; dogs welcome, white tables on brick terrace by small green *(Geoffrey Kemp, Michael and Ann Cole, LYM, N R White)*

WORTHING [TQ1404]

Cricketers BN14 9DE [Broadwater St W, Broadwater Green (A24)]: Extended panelled local with welcoming staff, well kept Bass, Fullers London Pride, Harveys, Wells & Youngs Special and guest beer, log fires, reasonably priced popular food, friendly staff, steps down to small lounge with dining room beyond, no music or machines; good-sized garden with bouncy castle *(Jude Wright, A Walker)*

Selden Arms BN11 2DB [Lyndhurst Rd, between Safeway and hospital]: Friendly local with up to half a dozen good real ales inc Dark Star Hophead and Ringwood Fortyniner, farm cider, welcoming Lancashire landlady and locals, bargain lunchtime food inc popular doorstep sandwiches, log fire, lots of old pub photographs; open all day *(P Dawn, Bruce Bird)*

YAPTON [SU9704]

Maypole BN18 0DP [signed off B2132

Arundel rd; Maypole Lane]: Chatty landlord and regulars in old-fashioned quiet local with bargain bar food inc Sun roasts, well kept Ringwood Best, Skinners Betty Stogs and several changing guests inc a local Mild, log fire in cosy lounge, skittle alley, spring and autumn beer festivals, occasional live music; seats outside, open all day *(Bruce Bird)*

Several well known guide books make establishments pay for entry, either directly or as a fee for inspection. These fees can run to many hundreds of pounds. We do not. Unlike other guides, we never take payment for entries. We never accept a free meal, free drink, or any other freebie from a pub. We do not accept any sponsorship – let alone from commercial schemes linked to the pub trade. All our entries depend solely on merit. And we are the only guide in which virtually all the main entries have been gained by a unique two-stage sifting process: first, a build-up of favourable reports from our thousands of reader-reporters, then anonymous vetting by one of our senior editorial staff.

Warwickshire
(with Birmingham and West Midlands)

Pub traditionalists revel in this area, which has a good many classic unspoilt inns, keeping their original interior and character largely intact over the years. One of the best is the Beacon in Sedgley (as a bonus it's also home to the Sarah Hughes brewery), where locals gather in the hallway by a tiny serving booth. The chatty multi-roomed Old Swan in Netherton also brews its own beers, and tucked away in the country, the unpretentious Griffin at Shustoke has a great choice of around ten real ales. The down-to-earth Turf in Bloxwich has been in the same family for over 130 years, while the Case is Altered at Five Ways has been licensed to sell beer for over three centuries – we keep a picture of its interior on our office wall, to remind us of what good pubs are all about. It can't be coincidence that every one of these simple and genuine pubs has a Beer Award, including the thriving Vine in Brierley Hill, which continues to amaze with its incredibly good value food. Only three of these places serve food, and it isn't just their interiors that haven't changed over the years – neither have their prices. Each one of the three has a Bargain Award for its hearty good value food, and pubs in the West Midlands conurbations generally are among the cheapest in the country both for pub food and for their drinks. At the other end of the spectrum, there's a good representation of fine dining establishments out in the countryside. The best of these are the gently civilised Kings Head at Aston Cantlow, the stylishly simple Howard Arms in Ilmington and the very enjoyable Bell in Welford-on-Avon. All three of these pubs are in lovely old buildings with a comfortably relaxed atmosphere, and it's the Kings Head at Aston Cantlow, with its thoughtfully put together menu, that is Warwickshire Dining Pub of the Year. Aside from the good clutch of free houses in this county, we've noticed a healthy range of pub ties to fairly local good-value brewers such as Bathams, Holdens and Donnington, but perhaps the most interesting tie is the magnificent Old Joint Stock in Birmingham, the most northerly pub owned by Fullers of south London. Other local beers to look out for include Purity, Slaughterhouse, Atomic and Beowulf. Pubs to note in the Lucky Dip section at the end of the chapter include the Bartons Arms in Birmingham, Malt Shovel at Gaydon, Herons Nest in Knowle, Bell at Monks Kirby, restaurany Butchers Arms at Priors Hardwick, Plough at Warmington and Great Western in Wolverhampton.

ARMSCOTE

SP2444 MAP 4

Fox & Goose ⊗ 🍸 🛏

Off A3400 Stratford—Shipston; CV37 8DD

Lively dining pub with locals' bar, imaginative food, good wines, and terrace

Enjoyable and very busy, this stylishly simple blacksmith's forge is an interesting mix of dining pub and local. The small flagstoned bar has red-painted walls, bright crushed velvet cushions plumped up on wooden pews, a big gilt mirror over a log fire, polished floorboards, and black and white etchings. In a quirky tableau above the dining room's woodburning stove a stuffed fox stalks a big goose. Hook Norton Old Hooky and Shepherd Neame Spitfire are served on handpump, alongside well chosen wines, and perhaps winter mulled wine and summer Pimms; helpful service from charming young staff; piped music. Outside, the garden has a vine-covered deck overlooking a lawn with tables, benches and fruit trees. Bedrooms, which are named after characters in Cluedo, are painted in strong colours after their namesakes, and are mildly quirky.

🍴 Under the new licensee, bar food is listed on a daily changing blackboard. As well as sandwiches, there might be goats cheese parcel, green bean and shallot salad, cod and pea linguini with caviar cream, rump of lamb, fillet steak with foie gras, and puddings such as eccles cake. *Starters/Snacks: £4.50 to £7.25. Main Courses: £9.00 to £18.50. Puddings: £4.50 to £6.95*

Free house ~ Licensee Paul Stevens ~ Real ale ~ Bar food ~ Restaurant ~ (01608) 682293 ~ Children welcome ~ Dogs allowed in bar and bedrooms ~ Open 12-3, 6-11.30(11 Sun) ~ Bedrooms: £60B/£100B

Recommended by Rob and Catherine Dunster, Keith and Sue Ward, A Warren, Samina Altaf, Susan and John Douglas, Margaret and Allen Marsden, George Atkinson, J Crosby, Carol and Colin Broadbent, Dr and Mrs A K Clarke

ASTON CANTLOW

SP1360 MAP 4

Kings Head ⊗ 🍸

Village signposted just off A3400 NW of Stratford; B95 6HY

WARWICKSHIRE DINING PUB OF THE YEAR

Gently civilised Tudor pub with nice old interior, good imaginative food, and pleasant garden

This well liked old black and white timbered pub is in the middle of a very pretty village – Shakespeare's parents are said to have married in the church next door. The beautifully kept bar on the right is a successful mix of rustic surroundings (flagstones, low beams, and old-fashioned settles around its massive inglenook log fireplace) with a subtly upmarket atmosphere. The chatty quarry-tiled main room has attractive window seats and oak tables. Charming staff serve Greene King Abbot, M&B Brew XI and a guest such as Purity Pure Gold on handpump, and decent wines; piped jazz. The garden is lovely, with a big chestnut tree, and the pub looks really pretty in summer with its colourful hanging baskets and wisteria.

🍴 The thoughtfully constructed menu might include sandwiches, soup, mushrooms stuffed with goats cheese, red pepper and basil, fried pigeon breast with wild mushroom salad, seared tiger prawns with chilli, garlic and sweet pepper sauce, duck on beetroot and lentil ragoût with port wine, smoked salmon and lemon grass fishcake, venison casserole with calvados sauce and salsify purée, tomato risotto, saddle of rabbit with braised cabbage and juniper berry sauce, and puddings such as warm chocolate torte with Amaretto ice-cream and cinnamon crème brûlée. *Starters/Snacks: £3.95 to £6.50. Main Courses: £10.25 to £15.50. Puddings: £4.95*

Enterprise ~ Lease Peter and Louise Sadler ~ Real ale ~ Bar food (12-2.30(3 Sun), 6.30-9.30; not Sun evening) ~ Restaurant ~ (01789) 488242 ~ Children welcome ~ Dogs allowed in bar ~ Open 11-3, 5.30-11; 11-11 Sat; 12-10.30(8.30 in winter) Sun

Recommended by Mrs Philippa Wilson, Stephen Wood, Des and Jen Clarke, David J Cooke, Dr D Scott, Caroline Shaw, Ian and Jane Irving, Rob and Catherine Dunster, Simon Fox, P Dawn, Cedric Robertshaw, Di and Mike Gillam, Joyce and Maurice Cottrell, Trevor and Sylvia Millum, John and Jackie Walsh

BIRMINGHAM

SP0686 MAP 4

Old Joint Stock ◀

Temple Row West; B2 5NY

Big bustling city pub with impressive Victorian façade and interior, Fullers beers and simple bar food all day; small back terrace

This is a well run cheery city centre pub opposite the cathedral. It does get busy, particularly with local office workers, but effortlessly absorbs what seem like huge numbers of people. The interior is quite a surprise: chandeliers hang from the soaring pink and gilt ceiling, gently illuminated busts line the top of the ornately plastered walls, and there's a splendid, if well worn, cupola above the centre of the room. Drinks are served from a handsome dark wood island bar counter, and big portraits and smart long curtains create an air of unexpected elegance. Around the walls are plenty of tables and chairs, some in cosy corners, with more on a big balcony overlooking the bar, reached by a very grand wide staircase. A separate room with panelling and a fireplace has a more intimate, clubby feel. This is the only pub we know of north of Bristol to be owned by the London-based brewer Fullers; it stocks their Chiswick, Discovery, ESB and London Pride, which are well kept alongside a guest from local Beowulf, and they have a decent range of about a dozen wines by the glass; helpful friendly service, teas, coffees, daily papers, TV, games machine and piped music. A small back terrace has some cast-iron tables and chairs.

🍴 **Very reasonably priced bar food includes soup, sandwiches, sausage of the week, lots of pies such as steak in ale or chicken and mushroom, and fish and chips.** *Starters/Snacks: £3.75. Main Courses: £4.25 to £7.95. Puddings: £3.75*

Fullers ~ Manager Alison Turner ~ Real ale ~ Bar food (12-8.30) ~ (0121) 200 1892 ~ Open 11-11; closed Sun

Recommended by Tim and Ann Newell, Colin Gooch, Simon Fox, Graham and Glenis Watkins, Barry Collett

BLOXWICH

SJ9902 MAP 4

Turf ◀

Wolverhampton Road, off A34 just S of A4124, N fringes of Walsall; aka Tinky's; WS3 2EZ

Simple eccentric family-run pub, utterly uncontrived

From the outside you could be forgiven for thinking that this quite unspoilt and old-fashioned local – in the same family for over 130 years – is no longer in business, as it appears to be a rather run-down terraced house. Once through the front door it still doesn't immediately look like a pub, but more like the hall of a 1930s home. The public bar is through a door on the right, and, reminiscent of a waiting room, it has wooden slatted benches running around the walls, with a big heating pipe clearly visible underneath; there's a tiled floor, three small tables, and William Morris curtains and wallpaper around the simple fireplace. What's particularly nice is that even though the unspoilt rooms are Grade II listed, it's far more than just a museum piece. It's alive and chatty with friendly locals happy to tell you the history of the place, and the particularly impressive changing beers, always very well kept, draw in a wider range of customers than you might expect. Four changing real ales are from brewers such as Bathams, Beowulf, Holdens, RCH and Titanic. There's hatch service (friendly and chatty) out to the hall, on the other side of the old smoking room, slightly more comfortable, with unusual padded wall settles with armrests. There's also a tiny back parlour with chairs around a tiled fireplace. The pub's basic charms won't appeal to those who like their creature comforts; the no-frills lavatories are outside, at the end of a simple but pleasant garden, and they don't do food – it almost goes without saying that there's no music or machines. The licensees didn't provide us with any up-to-date information so please check opening times before you visit.

🍴 **No food at all.**

Free house ~ Licensees Doris and Zena Hiscott-Wilkes ~ Real ale ~ No credit cards ~
(01922) 407745 ~ Open 12-3, 7-11(10.30 Sun)

Recommended by Ian and Liz Rispin, Pete Baker, R T and J C Moggridge, the Didler, Simon and Mandy King

BRIERLEY HILL   SO9286 MAP 4

Vine 🍴 £

B4172 between A461 and (nearer) A4100; straight after the turn into Delph Road; DY5 2TN

**Incredibly good value, very friendly classic down-to-earth Bathams tap; tables in back yard
and lunchtime snacks**

The cheery down-to-earth landlord and staff at this no-nonsense Black Country pub are
friendly and welcoming and the place is usually very busy. It's known locally as the Bull
& Bladder in reference to the good stained-glass bull's heads and very approximate
bunches of grapes in the front bow windows. The plainer front bar has wall benches and
simple leatherette-topped oak stools, and the comfortable extended snug on the left has
solidly built red plush seats. The tartan decorated larger back bar has brass chandeliers –
as well as darts, dominoes and a big-screen TV. A couple of tables and games machines
stand in a corridor. Some of the memorabilia you'll see, including one huge pair of horns
over a mantelpiece, relates to the Royal Ancient Order of Buffalos, who meet in a room
here. The very cheap Bitter and Mild (and perhaps Delph Strong in winter) are kept in top
condition and come from the next-door Bathams brewery. There are tables in a back yard,
and the car park is opposite.

🍴 **A couple of simple but tasty fresh lunchtime snacks (sandwiches, baguettes, steak and
mushroom pie and faggots, chips and peas) are sold at prices that prove a landlord can
make money (yes, we asked) and offer his customers fantastic value for money at the
same time.** *Starters/Snacks: £1.00 to £2.50*

Bathams ~ Manager Melvyn Wood ~ Real ale ~ Bar food (12-2 Mon-Fri) ~ No credit cards ~
(01384) 78293 ~ Children in family room ~ Dogs allowed in bar ~ Open 12-11(10.30 Sun)

Recommended by the Didler, Theo, Anne and Jane Gaskin, P Dawn

EASENHALL   SP4679 MAP 4

Golden Lion 🛏

*Village signposted from B4112 Newbold—Pailton, and from B4455 at Brinklow; Main
Street; CV23 0JA*

Comfortable hotel with traditional bar, good food and large garden

At the heart of this extended modern hotel are a welcoming 17th-c pub and restaurant.
The spotlessly kept tiled and flagstoned bar still has many of its original features,
including low beams, timbers and a fine carved settle. Yellow walls have occasional
stencilled lion motifs or Latin phrases, while a slightly raised area has a comfortable
little alcove with padding overhead; the lower level has a brick fireplace. Interesting
beers on handpump might be from Atomic (a local brewer) and perhaps Whites, alongside
several wines by the glass; piped music. There are tables at the side, and a good few
picnic-sets on a spacious lawn.

🍴 **As well as hot help-yourself buffet dishes (Monday-Saturday lunchtimes), bar food
includes good sandwiches, soup, continental meat platter, creamed garlic and stilton
mushrooms, red thai chicken curry, liver and mash, steak casserole, pasta with ratatouille,
and guinea fowl cooked in red wine, bacon and mushrooms.** *Starters/Snacks: £3.70 to £6.00.
Main Courses: £8.95 to £19.50. Puddings: £2.80 to £6.00*

Free house ~ Licensee James Austin ~ Real ale ~ Bar food ~ Restaurant ~ (01788) 832265 ~
Children welcome with restrictions ~ Open 10-11 ~ Bedrooms: £50S(£52B)/£72.50B

*Recommended by Martin and Pauline Jennings, Stuart and Alison Ballantyne, Ian Phillips, Gerry and
Rosemary Dobson, Rob and Catherine Dunster, Alan Johnson, Michael and Maggie Betton, George Atkinson,
Trevor and Sheila Sharman, Dr and Mrs A K Clarke*

EDGE HILL
SP3747 MAP 4

Castle
Off A422; OX15 6DJ

Curious gothic folly above historic battlefield, full of interest

---

This crenellated octagon tower (also known as the Round Tower or Radway Tower) is a folly that was built in 1749 by a gothic revival enthusiast to mark the spot where Charles I raised his standard at the start of the Battle of Edge Hill. It's said that after closing time you can hear ghostly battle sounds – a phantom cavalry officer has even been seen galloping by in search of his severed hand. And if you look down from the big attractive garden and terrace, you may be able to convince yourself that you can glimpse the battlefield, down beyond the trees; the views are outstanding when the leaves are gone in winter. The museum-like (and fairly well worn) interior has arched doorways, and the walls of the lounge bar, which has the same eight sides as the rest of the main tower, are decorated with maps, swords, pistols, photographs of re-enactments and a collection of Civil War memorabilia. They have Hook Norton Best Bitter, Old Hooky and Hooky Dark plus a monthly guest on handpump, and around 25 malt whiskies; piped music, games machine, TV, darts, pool, juke box, board games and aunt sally. Upton House is nearby on the A422, and Compton Wynyates, one of the most beautiful houses in this part of England, is not far beyond.

🍴 **Fairly basic bar food includes lunchtime soup, sandwiches and ploughman's, as well as sausage and egg, cottage pie, battered cod, steak in ale pie and rack of pork ribs in barbecue sauce.** *Starters/Snacks: £3.95 to £6.95. Main Courses: £4.95 to £13.95. Puddings: £3.75*

Hook Norton ~ Tenants Tony, Susan and Rory Sheen ~ Real ale ~ Bar food ~ (01295) 670255 ~ Children welcome ~ Dogs allowed in bar ~ Open 12-3(2.30 in winter), 6-midnight; 12-midnight Sat, Sun ~ Bedrooms: /£60S(£60B)

Recommended by John Dwane, G Coates, Barry and Susanne Hurst, Tracey and Stephen Groves, Susan and John Douglas, N R White

FIVE WAYS
SP2270 MAP 4

Case is Altered 🍺
Follow Rowington signposts at junction roundabout off A4177/A4141 N of Warwick, then right into Case Lane; CV35 7JD

Unspoilt convivial local serving well kept beers, including a couple of interesting guests

---

The servery at this tiled white-painted brick cottage has been licensed to sell beer for over three centuries – these days you'll find Greene King IPA, Hook Norton Old Hooky and a couple of guests such as Sharps Doom Bar and Slaughterhouse Saddleback, all served by a rare type of handpump mounted on the casks that are stilled behind the counter. You can be sure of a warm welcome from the friendly landlady and the old-fashioned rooms are filled with the sound of happy conversation and undisturbed by noisy games machines, music or children. A door at the back of the building leads into a modest small room with a rug on its tiled floor, and an antique bar billiards table protected by an ancient leather cover (it takes pre-decimal sixpences). From here, the simple little main bar has a fine old poster showing the old Lucas Blackwell & Arkwright brewery (now flats) and a clock with its hours spelling out Thornleys Ale – another defunct brewery; there are just a few sturdy old-fashioned tables, with a couple of stout leather-covered settles facing each other over the spotless tiles. Behind a wrought-iron gate is a little brick-paved courtyard with a stone table. Full disabled access.

🍴 **No food at all.**

Free house ~ Licensee Jackie Willacy ~ Real ale ~ No credit cards ~ (01926) 484206 ~ Open 12-2.30, 6-11; 12-2, 7-10.30 Sun

Recommended by Kerry Law, the Didier, Steve and Liz Tilley, Pete Baker

Fox & Hounds

Village signposted on right on A3400 3 miles S of Shipston-on-Stour; CV36 5NQ

Imaginative food with home-made breads and so forth at cosy old family-run inn

The unpretentious aged bar at this handsome 16th-c stone inn has hops strung from its low beams, an appealing collection of chairs and old candlelit tables on spotless flagstones, antique hunting prints, and a roaring log fire in the inglenook fireplace with its fine old bread oven. An old-fashioned little tap room serves Hook Norton Hooky, Purity Pure UBU and a guest from a brewer such as Cottage on handpump, and around 60 malt whiskies; piped music. A terrace has solid wood furniture and a well.

🍽 **The chef here is careful about sourcing ingredients, and makes the breads (with local organic flour) and chutneys that appear on the fairly elaborate bar and restaurant menus: sandwiches, ham hock and parsley terrine with pickled quail eggs and peach chutney, grilled mackerel fillet with watercress sauce and horseradish, seared scallops with fennel and apple salad, ploughman's with home-made bread and local ham, beef and cheese, broad bean risotto with rocket salad, sausages with tomato and bean ragoût, steaks, bream with lemon, herbs and olive oil, shin of beef braised in ale with horseradish mash, and puddings such as lemon and lime posset with strawberries and shortbread and sticky toffee pudding with butterscotch sauce.** *Starters/Snacks: £4.50 to £6.00. Main Courses: £10.00 to £16.00. Puddings: £5.50*

Free house ~ Licensee Gillian Tarbox ~ Real ale ~ Bar food (not Sun evening) ~ Restaurant ~ (01608) 674220 ~ Children welcome ~ Dogs allowed in bar ~ Open 12-3, 6-midnight(7-11 Sun); closed Mon ~ Bedrooms: £50B/£80B

Recommended by H O Dickinson, Ted George, Susan and John Douglas, Clive and Fran Dutson, Mrs Philippa Wilson, Keith and Sue Ward

Howard Arms

Village signposted with Wimpstone off A3400 S of Stratford; CV36 4LT

Emphasis on imaginative food and good wine list in lovely mellow-toned interior

The stylishly simple interior at this golden-stone inn is light, airy and gently traditional, with a few good prints on warm golden walls, rugs on broad polished flagstones, and a nice mix of furniture from hardwood pews to old church seats. The cosy log fire in a huge stone inglenook seems to be alight most of the year. They keep Everards Tiger, Hook Norton Old Hooky and a guest from a local brewer such as Purity on handpump, organic soft drinks and cider and 18 wines by the glass. The garden is lovely with fruit trees sheltering the lawn, a colourful herbaceous border, and a handful of tables on a neat york stone terrace; the chocolate-spotted dalmatian is called Loulou, and her wire haired german pointer companion is Nola. Readers very much enjoy staying in the comfortable bedrooms – the breakfasts are particularly good. The pub is nicely set beside the village green, and there are lovely walks on the nearby hills (as well as strolls around the village outskirts). The business was on the market as we went to press but as the current manager is likely to stay we're hoping that little will change if it is sold.

🍽 **Bar food ingredients are thoughtfully sourced, often from local suppliers and the imaginative menu (carefully written up on boards above the fire) changes two or three times a week. Dishes might include soup, chicken liver parfait with onion marmalade, parsnip, leek and sage risotto cake with mustard sauce, smoked salmon with warm potato cake, sour cream and chives, main courses such as beef, ale and mustard pie, braised oxtail, roast pheasant with cider, apples, cream and calvados, moroccan spiced vegetables and couscous in puff pastry with mint and coriander raita, fried bream with cannellini beans and gremolata and grilled rib-eye with peppercorn and brandy sauce, and puddings such as gingered panna cotta with spiced rhubarb and shortbread, chocolate pecan pie with bourbon ice-cream and spiced apple and sultana flapjack crumble, and organic ice-creams.** *Starters/Snacks: £3.75 to £7.50. Main Courses: £10.00 to £15.50. Puddings: £4.50 to £6.00*

Free house ~ Licensees Rob Greenstock and Martin Devereux ~ Real ale ~ Bar food (12-2, 7-9(9.30 Sat); 12-2.30, 6.30-8.30 Sun) ~ (01608) 682226 ~ Children under 8 welcome till 7.30pm ~ Open 11-2.30, 6-11; 12-3.30, 6-10.30 Sun ~ Bedrooms: £87.50B/£120B

Recommended by Mary McSweeney, Mr and Mrs G S Ayrton, Ian and Jane Haslock, Jonathan Aquilina, Bernard Stradling, Revd L and S Giller, David Handforth, Paul Humphreys, Alec and Barbara Jones, Clive and Fran Dutson, Hugh Bower, Rob, W M Lien, K H Frostick, David and Ruth Shillitoe, Chris Glasson, Andrea Rampley, David and Jean Hall, Martin and Pauline Jennings, Mrs Philippa Wilson, Noel Grundy, Donna and Roger, Mr and Mrs A H Young

LITTLE COMPTON
SP2530 MAP 4

Red Lion
Off A44 Moreton-in-Marsh—Chipping Norton; GL56 ORT

Comfortably unpretentious country pub serving generous tasty food; nice garden

This friendly 16th-c cotswold stone local makes a handy base for exploring the area. The simple traditionally decorated lounge is low-beamed, with pews and settles in snug alcoves and a couple of little tables by the log fire; service is friendly. The plainer public bar has another log fire, Donnington BB and SBA on handpump, several wines by the glass and farm cider; darts, pool, games machine, TV and juke box. The garden is well enclosed and rather pretty; aunt sally. More reports please.

🍴 **Bar food is served in generous helpings and includes lunchtime sandwiches, filled baguettes, filled baked potatoes and ploughman's, as well as soup, brie and bacon parcels with cumberland sauce, scampi, battered cod, seafood ragoût, shank of lamb with rosemary mash, mushroom risotto and vegetables baked in pastry, thai chicken curry, and puddings such as brioche bread and butter pudding and sticky toffee pudding.** *Starters/Snacks: £4.00 to £6.00. Main Courses: £8.75 to £17.00. Puddings: £4.00 to £5.50*

Donnington ~ Tenants Ian and Jacqui Sergeant ~ Real ale ~ Bar food ~ Restaurant ~ (01608) 674397 ~ Children welcome with restrictions ~ Dogs allowed in bar ~ Open 12-3, 6(7 Sun)-11 ~ Bedrooms: £55S/£65S

Recommended by Paul Goldman, Keith and Sue Ward

LONG ITCHINGTON
SP4165 MAP 4

Duck on the Pond
Just off A423 Coventry-Southam; The Green; CV47 9QJ

Well laid out relaxed dining pub serving good food

The surprisingly eclectic interior of this welcoming place is vaguely reminiscent of a 1970s french bistro. The central bar has dark wooden floorboards with a few scattered rugs, dark pine ceiling planks, royal blue banquettes, some barrel tables, bacchanalian carvings around its coal fire and some big brass wading birds. Wicker panels provide an unusual frontage to the bar counter, which has Wells & Youngs Bombardier and another beer such as their Winter Warmer on handpump, and several wines by the glass. Service is friendly and attentive. On each side of the bar, inviting dining areas have pine furniture (some tables painted in light red chequers), a wall of wine bottles, big Edwardian prints on sienna red walls, a crystal chandelier and a grandfather clock. Well produced piped pop or jazzy soul music. Tables and chairs in front look down on a pond, which does indeed have ducks; the main road is quite busy.

🍴 **Tasty bar food includes soup, sambuca and lemon grass home-cured salmon with citrus potato salad, chicken liver pâté with red onion marmalade, bacon and brie on orange salad, roast mediterranean vegetable pasta, sausage of the week with onion gravy, pork fillet stuffed with nettles on apple mash with cider cream sauce, spiced marinated tuna loin on couscous with coconut chutney, and steaks with mushrooms and béarnaise or peppercorn sauce.** *Starters/Snacks: £3.95 to £6.95. Main Courses: £8.95 to £16.95. Puddings: £4.95 to £5.95*

Charles Wells ~ Lease Andrew and Wendy Parry ~ Real ale ~ Bar food (12-2, 6.30-9.30; 12-10 Sat, 12-8.30 Sun) ~ Restaurant ~ (01926) 815876 ~ No children after 7pm Fri and Sat ~

Open 12-2.30, 5-11; 12-11(10.30 Sun) Sat; closed Mon except bank hols

Recommended by Nigel and Sue Foster, Lesley and Barbara Owen, Suzanne Miles, John Cook, George Atkinson, Keith Moss, Dr and Mrs A K Clarke

NETHERTON

SO9488 MAP 4

Old Swan 🍺 £

Halesowen Road (A459 just S of centre); DY2 9PY

Traditional unspoilt friendly local serving own-brew beers and limited bar food

Readers really enjoy the good own-brewed ales and chatty welcome from friendly regulars at this characterful local. Well kept alongside a seasonal guest, their beers are Old Swan Original, Dark Swan, Entire, and Bumble Hole. The unchanged multi-roomed layout should appeal to readers who are keen on original interiors. The front public bar is traditionally furnished, with mirrors behind the bar engraved with a swan design, an old-fashioned cylinder stove with its chimney angling away to the wall, and a lovely patterned ceiling with a big swan centrepiece. The cosy back snug is fitted out very much in keeping with the rest of the building, using recycled bricks and woodwork, and even matching etched window panels. Parking in front is difficult but there's a good car park at the back.

🍴 Lunchtime bar food is restricted to filled cobs and soup. The evening restaurant menu includes daily fresh fish dishes as well as home-made steak and kidney pie or gammon and egg. *Starters/Snacks: £2.25 to £3.85. Main Courses: £7.85 to £13.50. Puddings: £1.75 to £2.85*

Punch ~ Tenant Tim Newey ~ Real ale ~ Bar food (12-2, 6.30-9; 12-4 Sun, not Sun evening) ~ Restaurant ~ (01384) 253075 ~ Dogs allowed in bar ~ Open 11-11; 12-4, 7-10.30 Sun

Recommended by Ian and Liz Rispin, Pete Baker, Kerry Law, the Didler, Helen Maynard, P Dawn, R T and J C Moggridge, Mark and Diane Grist, Dr and Mrs A K Clarke

PRESTON BAGOT

SP1765 MAP 4

Crabmill

B4095 Henley-in-Arden—Warwick; B95 5EE

Contemporary mill conversion with comfortable modern décor, relaxed atmosphere, and smart bar food

A very stylish transformation of an old cider mill, this rambling place has a smart two-level lounge area with a good relaxed feel, soft leather settees and easy chairs, low tables, big table lamps and one or two rugs on bare boards. There's also an elegant and roomy low-beamed dining area, with candles and fresh flowers, and a beamed and flagstoned bar area with some stripped pine country tables and chairs, snug corners and a gleaming metal bar serving Greene King Abbot, Tetleys and Wadworths 6X on handpump. Piped music is well chosen and well reproduced. There are lots of tables, some of them under cover, out in a large attractive decked garden. Booking is advised, especially Sunday lunchtime when it's popular with families.

🍴 Under the new licensee, imaginative bar food includes crab and prawn cocktail, squid with asian vegetables and sechuan sauce, serrano ham, melon and manchego salad, swordfish steak with greek salad, sweet potato, spinach and goats cheese lasagne, fillet steak with bourguignon sauce, and puddings such as summer fruit jelly, orange and treacle tart and baked raspberry cheesecake. A couple of readers have felt that helpings could be more generous. *Starters/Snacks: £3.95 to £7.95. Main Courses: £10.00 to £18.00. Puddings: £5.25*

Enterprise ~ Lease Sally Coll ~ Real ale ~ Bar food (12-2.30(3.30 Sun), 6.30-9.30) ~ Restaurant ~ (01926) 843342 ~ Children welcome ~ Dogs allowed in bar ~ Open 11-11; 12-6 Sun; closed Sun evening

Recommended by P and J Shapley, Andy and Claire Barker, David Morgan, Dr Ron Cox, Andrew Stephenson, Karen Eliot

SEDGLEY
SO9293 MAP 4

Beacon ★ ◀

*Bilston Street (no pub sign on our visit, but by Beacon Lane); A463, off A4123
Wolverhampton—Dudley; DY3 1JE*

**Good unusual own-brew beers and interesting guests at beautifully preserved down-to-
earth Victorian pub**

The front door of this plain-looking old brick pub opens into a simple quarry-tiled drinking
corridor where you may find a couple of cheery locals leaning up against the walls going up
the stairs, chatting to the waistcoated barman propped in the doorway of his little central
serving booth. Go through the door into the little snug on your left and you can easily
imagine a 19th-c traveller tucked up on one of the wall settles, next to the imposing green-
tiled marble fireplace with its big misty mirror, the door closed for privacy and warmth and a
drink handed through the glazed hatch. The dark woodwork, turkey carpet, velvet and net
curtains, heavy mahogany tables, old piano and little landscape prints all seem unchanged
since those times. A sparsely decorated snug on the right has a black kettle and embroidered
mantel over a blackened range, and a stripped wooden wall bench. The corridor then runs
round the serving booth, past the stairs and into a big well proportioned dark-panelled old
smoking room with impressively sturdy red leather wall settles down the length of each side,
gilt-based cast-iron tables, a big blue carpet on the lino, and dramatic old sea prints. Round
a corner (where you would have come in from the car park) the conservatory is densely filled
with plants, and has no seats. Named after a former landlady, the well kept Sarah Hughes
beers brewed and served here include Dark Ruby, Pale Amber and Surprise Bitter – you can
arrange to look around the traditional Victorian brewery at the back. They also keep a couple
of guests such as Oakham Bishops Farewell and Thornbridge Jaipur. A children's play area in
the garden has a slide, climbing frame and roundabout.

🍴 **The only food served is cheese and onion cobs.**

Own brew ~ Licensee John Hughes ~ Real ale ~ No credit cards ~ (01902) 883380 ~ Children
allowed in the verandah ~ Dogs welcome ~ Open 12-2.30, 5.30-11; 12-3, 6-11 Sat; 12-3,
7-10.30 Sun

Recommended by Pete Baker, Mark and Diane Grist, Ian and Liz Rispin, the Didler, Kerry Law

SHUSTOKE
SP2290 MAP 4

Griffin ◀ £

*5 miles from M6 junction 4; A446 towards Tamworth, then right on to B4114 and go
straight through Coleshill; pub is at Church End, a mile E of village; B46 2LB*

**Ten real ales and simple good value lunchtime snacks at unpretentious country local;
garden and play area**

The smashing choice of real ales here is well kept on handpump and dispensed from a
servery under a very low heavy beam. They come from an enterprising range of brewers
such as Banks's, Bathams, Holdens, Hook Norton, RCH, St Austell and Theakstons; also
lots of english wines, farm cider, and mulled wine in winter. Usually busy with a cheery
crowd, the low-beamed L-shaped bar has log fires in two stone fireplaces (one's a big
inglenook). Besides one nice old-fashioned settle the décor is fairly simple, from
cushioned café seats (some quite closely spaced) to sturdily elm-topped sewing trestles,
lots of old jugs on the beams, beer mats on the ceiling and a games machine. Outside,
there are old-fashioned seats and tables outside on the back grass, a play area and a
large terrace with plants in raised beds.

🍴 **Straightforward but tasty bar food includes sandwiches, ploughman's, cheese and
broccoli bake, scampi, steak and ale pie, mixed grill and 10oz sirloin steak.**
Starters/Snacks: £2.50 to £4.00. Main Courses: £5.50 to £8.50

Free house ~ Licensee Michael Pugh ~ Real ale ~ Bar food (12-2; not Sun or evenings) ~
No credit cards ~ (01675) 481205 ~ Children in conservatory with parents ~ Dogs welcome ~
Open 12-2.30, 7-11; 12-3, 7-10.30 Sun

Recommended by John Saville, R T and J C Moggridge, Brian and Jacky Wilson, Carol and Colin Broadbent

WELFORD-ON-AVON

SP1452 MAP 4

Bell 🍴 ♈ ☕

Off B439 W of Stratford; High Street; CV37 8EB

Enjoyably civilised pub with appealing ancient interior, good food and great range of drinks including five real ales; terrace

Although most people visit this charming 17th-c place to dine (readers are very complimentary about the knowledgeable efficient staff), it still retains a relaxed and informal pubby atmosphere. The attractive interior (full of signs of the building's great age) is divided into five comfortable areas, each with its own character, from the cosy terracotta-painted bar to the light and airy gallery room with its antique wood panelling, solid oak floor and contemporary Lloyd Loom chairs. Flagstone floors, stripped or well polished antique or period-style furniture, and three good fires (one in an inglenook) give a feeling of warmth and cosiness. Flowers Original, Hobsons, Hook Norton Old Hooky, Purity Pure Gold and Pure UBU are well kept on handpump, and they've 15 wines including champagne and local wines by the glass; piped music. In summer the creeper-covered exterior is hung with lots of colourful baskets, and there are tables and chairs on a vine-covered dining terrace. The riverside village has an appealing church and pretty thatched black and white cottages.

🍴 Using local suppliers – which they list on the menu – food is gently imaginative and fairly priced: soup, sandwiches, hot steak and horseradish crème fraîche ciabatta, fried brie with a ginger and apricot compote, ploughman's, lasagne, gammon and eggs, beer-battered cod, minty lamb curry, specials such as bacon and blue cheese rarebit bruschetta, mexican salmon fillet on pea guacamole, roast vegetable and dolcelatte quiche, red thai beef curry, spicy chicken breast with fruity couscous, and puddings such as chocolate pot or coconut rice pudding with pineapple. *Starters/Snacks: £4.75 to £10.25. Main Courses: £9.75 to £16.95. Puddings: £5.25 to £5.95*

Laurel (Enterprise) ~ Lease Colin and Teresa Ombler ~ Real ale ~ Bar food (11.45-2.30(3 Sat), 6.45-9.30(6.15(6 Sat)-10 Fri); 12-9.30 Sun) ~ Restaurant ~ (01789) 750353 ~ Children welcome ~ Open 11.30-3, 6(6.30 weekdays in winter)-11; 11.30-11.30 Sat; 12-10.30 Sun

Recommended by Glenwys and Alan Lawrence, Keith and Sue Ward, Malcolm Brown, K H Frostick, Gerry and Rosemary Dobson, Lesley and Barbara Owen, Oliver Richardson, K S Whittaker, John Wooll, Di and Mike Gillam, Muriel and John Hobbs

LUCKY DIP

Besides the fully inspected pubs, you might like to try these Lucky Dips recommended to us and described by readers (if you do, please send us reports: www.goodguides.co.uk).

. **ALCESTER** [SP0957]
☆ *Holly Bush* B49 5QX [Henley St]: Warren of unpretentious 17th-c panelled rooms inc nice dining room off darkish central bar, good easy-going atmosphere, hard-working landlady and pleasant staff, enjoyable fair-priced food (not Mon) from good sandwiches and simple dishes to some interesting blackboard items, enterprising changing range of real ales such as Cannon Royall, Uley and local Purity, farm cider, dozens of whiskies, June and Oct beer festivals, no piped music; disabled access, attractive sheltered back garden, open all day *(Derek and Sylvia Stephenson, Des and Jen Clarke, Martin and Pauline Jennings, Pete Baker)*
ALDERMINSTER [SP2348]
☆ *Bell* CV37 8NY [A3400 Oxford—Stratford]: Neatly kept open-plan Georgian inn with emphasis on very good imaginative food, flagstones or polished wood floors,

inglenook stove, modern prints on green walls, Greene King IPA and Old Speckled Hen, great range of wines by the glass, conservatory with Stour Valley views; children and dogs welcome, terrace and garden, bedrooms; has been easily main entry standard and much enjoyed by readers, but on the market as we went to press – news please *(LYM)*
ALVESTON [SP2355]
Baraset Barn CV37 7RJ [Pimlico Lane]: Comfortable sofas and bucket seats in stylish lounge area with open fire, pleasantly cool dining area with enjoyable food from enterprising sharing platters up, good choice of wines by the glass inc champagne; terrace tables, open all day, cl Sun evening *(Helen Rowett)*
AMBLECOTE [SO9085]
Robin Hood DY8 4EQ [Collis St]: Small informal open-plan local, friendly and relaxed, with well kept Bathams and other

ales such as Naylors, Salopian and Skinners, farm ciders, good value food in dining area; children welcome if eating, comfortable bedrooms *(David Edwards)*

ARDENS GRAFTON [SP1153]

☆ *Golden Cross* B50 4LG [off A46 or B439 W of Stratford, OS Sheet 150 map ref 114538; Wixford rd]: Neat open-plan stone-built dining pub with good generous food from lunchtime sandwiches up, alert attentive staff, real ales such as local Purity Pure Gold, Wells & Youngs Bombardier and Special, decent wines, comfortable light wood furniture on flagstones, log fire, attractive décor and good lighting; piped music; wheelchair access, tables in charming garden, nice views *(Neil and Brenda Skidmore, Des and Jen Clarke, Stephen Wood, Mr and Mrs F E Boxell, George Atkinson, Carol and Colin Broadbent)*

AVON DASSETT [SP4049]

Avon CV47 2AS [off B4100 Banbury—Warwick]: Pleasant décor, relaxing atmosphere, good value hearty fresh food from sandwiches up inc great variety of sausages and mash, Courage, Hook Norton and a guest beer, several wines by the glass, interesting Civil War memorabilia, nice restaurant with plenty of fish, friendly service (may slow a bit when busy); wet and muddy walkers welcome – bar's flagstones cope well; tables out in front and at side, attractive small village on edge of country park *(Gill and Keith Croxton)*

BAGINTON [SP3375]

☆ *Old Mill* CV8 3AH [Mill Hill]: Olde-worlde Chef & Brewer conversion of old watermill nr airport (and Lunt Roman fort), heavy beams, timbers and candlelight, warm rustic-theme bar, linked dining areas on left, good wine choice, Courage Best and Directors, Greene King Old Speckled Hen and Theakstons Old Peculier, neat and friendly uniformed staff; lovely terraced gardens leading down to River Sower, 28 bedrooms *(Richard Tosswill, LYM, Rob and Catherine Dunster, Susan and John Douglas)*

BARFORD [SP2660]

Granville Arms CV35 8DS [Wellesbourne Rd (A429 S of Warwick)]: Pleasantly refurbished beamed dining pub, seasonal food with plenty of fresh fish, Hook Norton and changing guest beers, open fire in dining lounge, some leather armchairs and settees, separate bar and restaurant; children welcome, tables in good-sized garden with terrace *(Trevor and Sheila Sharman, Dr and Mrs A K Clarke)*

BARNT GREEN [SP0074]

☆ *Barnt Green* B45 8PZ [Kendal End Rd]: Large civilised Elizabethan pub with comfortable and eclectic contemporary décor, clubby seating in panelled front bar, large brasserie area, good innovative food from breads with dipping oils through wood-fired pizzas to rotisserie, real ales such as Black Sheep and Greene King Old Speckled Hen, relaxed atmosphere, prompt service by friendly

young staff; tables outside, handy for Lickey Hills walks *(D Halle, Caroline and Michael Abbey, Mike and Mary Carter, Nigel and Sue Foster)*

BARSTON [SP2078]

☆ *Bulls Head* B92 0JU [from M42 junction 5, A4141 towards Warwick, first left, then signed down Barston Lane]: Unassuming and genuine partly Tudor village pub, friendly landlord and efficient service, well kept ales such as Adnams, Hook Norton, Hydes and Timothy Taylors Landlord, enjoyable traditional food from sandwiches to good fresh fish and Sun lunch, log fires, comfortable lounge with pictures and plates, oak-beamed bar with a little Buddy Holly memorabilia, separate dining room; good-sized secluded garden alongside, hay barn behind, open all day wknds *(P Dawn, Clive and Fran Dutson, Pete Baker, Chris Evans)*

Malt Shovel B92 0JP [Barston Lane]: Attractive dining pub, light and airy, with good generous brasserie-style food (they're happy for you to have just an interesting starter), three well kept changing ales, good choice of wines, helpful young staff, stylish country-modern décor, converted barn restaurant; pleasant garden *(Mrs Philippa Wilson, R T and J C Moggridge)*

BILSTON [SO9496]

Trumpet WV14 0EP [High St]: Holdens and a guest beer, good free nightly jazz bands (quiet early evening before they start), trumpets and other instruments hang from ceiling, lots of musical memorabilia and photographs, back conservatory *(the Didler)*

BIRMINGHAM [SP0788]

☆ *Bartons Arms* B6 4UP [High St, Aston (A34)]: Magnificent Edwardian landmark, a trouble-free oasis in rather a daunting area, impressive linked richly decorated rooms from the palatial to the snug, original tilework murals, stained glass and mahogany, decorative fireplaces, sweeping stairs to handsome rooms upstairs, well kept Oakham and guest beers from ornate island bar with snob screens in one section, interesting imported bottled beers and frequent mini beer festivals, good choice of well priced thai food (not Mon), good young Australian staff; open all day *(BB, the Didler, Ian and Liz Rispin, Kerry Law, R T and J C Moggridge)*

Bennetts B2 5RS [Bennetts Hill]: Opulent bank conversion with egyptian/french theme, big mural, high carved domed ceiling, snugger side areas with lots of old pictures, ironwork and wood, relaxed atmosphere, comfortable seats inc armchair and leather settee, well kept ales inc Banks's and Marstons Pedigree, decent house wines, good coffee, friendly staff, dining area; piped music; good wheelchair access, but parking restrictions *(Mrs Hazel Rainer, Dr and Mrs A K Clarke)*

Brasshouse B1 2HP [Broad St]: Handsome and comfortable bank conversion with lots of dark oak and brass, enjoyable reasonably priced food, real ales such as Greene King Old Speckled Hen, unusual collection of builders' hard hats, attractive dining area; very handy for National Sea Life Centre and convention centre *(Colin Gooch, Dr and Mrs A K Clarke)*

Briar Rose B2 5RE [Bennetts Hill]: Civilised open-plan Wetherspoons with usual comfortable décor, menu and drinks offers inc four well kept changing guest beers, friendly staff, children allowed in separate back family dining room; lavatories down stairs, can get busy lunchtime and late evening; reasonably priced bedrooms, open all day *(Joe Green)*

Lord Clifden B18 6AA [Gt Hampton St]: Good value food from sandwiches to steaks and generous Sun roasts, real ales such as Timothy Taylors Landlord, prompt friendly service, contemporary artwork and sporting memorabilia, dominoes in locals' front bar; nostalgic juke box, Thurs quiz night, live music Sat; plenty of tables on attractive back terrace *(Samina Altaf)*

Old Fox B5 4TD [Hurst St (follow Hippodrome signs)]: Traditional two-room pub with splendid early 19th-c façade, changing ales such as Greene King Old Speckled Hen, Marstons Pedigree and Tetleys from island bar, bargain simple lunchtime food, friendly staff, interesting old photographs and posters; pavement tables *(Tony and Wendy Hobden, Giles and Annie Francis)*

Prince of Wales B1 2NP [Cambridge St]: Traditional pub surviving behind national indoor arena and rep theatre amidst the concrete newcomers, L-shaped bar with friendly mix of customers, half a dozen or more real ales such as Everards, Timothy Taylors and Wells & Youngs, bargain straightforward lunchtime food; may be piped music; popular with Grand Union Canal users in summer *(Pete Baker, Dr and Mrs A K Clarke)*

Tap & Spile B1 2JT [Gas St]: Well used pub with picnic-sets out by Gas Street canal basin, back-to-basics décor, three levels, bustling atmosphere, low-priced lunchtime bar food from baguettes up, several real ales, darts and dominoes; piped music, games machine, no children (faced a one-month licence suspension early 2007 for serving under-age customers); open all day *(LYM, Colin Gooch, Nigel and Sue Foster, Dr and Mrs A K Clarke)*

Villa Tavern B7 5PD [Nechells Park Rd]: Two-bar Victorian local with well kept ales inc a Mild, popular wkdy lunchtime food, darts, dominoes and pool; open all day Fri-Sun *(the Didler)*

Wellington B2 5SN [Bennetts Hill]: Tremendous range of changing real ales all from small breweries, also farm ciders, in roomy old-fashioned high-ceilinged pub, friendly staff, lots of prints; no food, but plates and cutlery if you bring your own – on cheese nights people bring different ones which are all pooled; tables out behind, open all day *(Dr and Mrs A K Clarke)*

White Swan B15 3TT [Harborne Rd/Richmond Hill Rd, Edgbaston]: Good choice of enjoyable bar and restaurant food in linked areas with modern décor, well kept Timothy Taylors Landlord, friendly quick service; handy for University *(John Saville)*

BODYMOOR HEATH [SP1996]

Dog & Doublet B76 9JD [Dog Lane]: Right by Birmingham & Fazeley Canal lock, three storeys but cosy, with friendly helpful service, wide choice of reasonably priced usual bar food from sandwiches up inc generous good value Sun lunch, well kept real ales, dark-panelled rooms both sides of bar, beams, brasses, bargees' painted ware, several open fires, tables in pleasant garden; bedrooms, nr Kingsbury Water Park *(Paul J Robinshaw)*

CHADWICK END [SP2073]

Orange Tree B93 0BN [A41]: Appealing dining pub with comfortably up-to-date layout, décor and atmosphere, enjoyable food with italian slant from enterprising light dishes up, good service *(Helen Rowett)*

CHURCHOVER [SP5180]

Haywaggon CV23 0EP [handy for M6 junction 1, off A426; The Green]: Neapolitan landlord does good if not cheap italian food (must book Sun lunch), attentive friendly landlady, changing ales such as Fullers London Pride and Shepherd Neame Spitfire, good coffee and wines by the glass, two snug eating areas, lots of beams, standing timbers, brasses, nooks and crannies; may be piped music; tables outside with play area, on edge of quiet village, beautiful views over Swift Valley *(BB, Rob and Catherine Dunster)*

COVENTRY [SP3279]

Old Windmill CV1 3BA [Spon Street]: Well worn timber-framed 15th-c pub with lots of tiny old rooms, exposed beams in uneven ceilings, carved oak seats on flagstones, inglenook woodburner, half a dozen real ales, basic lunchtime bar food (not Mon) served from the kitchen door, restaurant; popular with students and busy at wknds, fruit machine and juke box, no credit cards; open all day *(P Dawn, the Didler, LYM, Susan and John Douglas)*

DUDLEY [SO9487]

Park DY2 9PN [George St/Chapel St]: Tap for adjacent Holdens brewery, their beers kept well, good straightforward lunchtime food inc hot roast meat sandwiches, attractive prices, conservatory, small games room; sports TV *(the Didler)*

DUNCHURCH [SP4871]

☆ *Dun Cow* CV22 6NJ [a mile from M45 junction 1: A45/A426]: Handsomely beamed Vintage Inn with massive log fires and other traditional features, reasonably priced standard food all day, prompt pleasant service, good range of wines by the glass, real ales such as Bass and Everards Tiger from small bar counter; piped music; children welcome, tables out in attractive former coachyard and on sheltered side lawn, bedrooms in adjacent Innkeepers Lodge, open all day (P M Newsome, Suzanne Miles, Michael and Alison Sandy, David Green, LYM, John Cook, George Atkinson, Donna and Roger)

EATHORPE [SP3968]

☆ **Plough** CV33 9DQ [car park off B4455 NW of Leamington Spa]: Big helpings of good value pub food cooked by landlord inc generous wkdy bargain lunches in long neat split-level dining room, attentive landlady and speedy jolly service, good wine choice and coffee, Caledonian Deuchars IPA and Greene King Abbot, decent wines by the glass, open fire in small bar (Carol and David Havard, Keith and Sue Ward, Joan and Tony Walker, Rob and Catherine Dunster)

ETTINGTON [SP2550]

Houndshill House CV37 7NS [A422 towards Stratford; aka Mucky Mongrel]: Light and airy dining pub, very popular with families and OAPs, with friendly owners and staff, stripped-stone and beams, good choice of wines, well kept Hook Norton and Shepherd Neame Spitfire, standard food; children welcome, picnic-sets in big attractive garden with play area, good views from front, good well equipped bedrooms, camp site (George Atkinson)

FARNBOROUGH [SP4349]

☆ **Inn at Farnborough** OX17 1DZ [off A423 N of Banbury]: Best thought of now as upmarket restaurant rather than pub, priced way beyond pub levels, but enjoyed by many for its good food and modern minimalist décor blending attractively with flagstones, mullioned windows and thatched roof; cl Mon lunchtime (Simon Jones, LYM, Nicky McNeill, Mrs Philippa Wilson, M and C Thompson, George Atkinson, J Crosby)

GAYDON [SP3654]

☆ **Malt Shovel** CV35 0ET [very handy for M40 junction 12; Church Rd]: Very useful motorway break, with nice mix of relaxed pubby bar (which has sofas in cosy upper snug) and rather smart dining room – very popular with older people for Sun lunch; real ales such as Adnams, Fullers London Pride, Greene King IPA, Hook Norton and Shepherd Neame Spitfire, decent wines by the glass, log fire; service normally friendly; they may try to keep your credit card while you eat; smokers' shelter outside, open all day Fri-Sun (George Atkinson, Michael and Judy Buckley, Karen Eliot, Neil Ingoe, LYM, Liz and Brian Barnard, Tina and David Woods-Taylor, Mr Tarpey, David and Katharine Cooke, Tom and Jill Jones, Craig Turnbull, Mark and Ruth Brock, Rob and Catherine Dunster, Ian Phillips, Piotr Chodzko-Zajko, J V Dadswell, Anne Mallard, Gordon Prince, Val and Alan Green, N R White, Dr and Mrs A K Clarke)

GRANDBOROUGH [SP4966]

Shoulder of Mutton CV23 8DN [off A45 E of Dunchurch; Sawbridge Rd]: Well refurbished creeper-covered dining pub with friendly

helpful new licensees, short choice of modestly priced enjoyable food in L-shaped front bar, well kept Fullers London Pride and Greene King IPA and Abbot, attractive pine furnishings, beams and panelling, relaxed atmosphere, back locals' bar; garden with play area, has been cl Mon (Rob and Catherine Dunster)

HALESOWEN [SO9683]

Hawne Tavern B63 3UG [Attwood St]: Up to nine interesting real ales from sidestreet local's rough-cut central servery, bar with cushioned pews, darts and pool in games area, lounge with leatherette-backed wall banquettes, good value cheap food inc big baguettes, good staff; small terrace, cl till 4.30 wkdys, open all day wknds (G Coates, the Didler)

Somers Club B62 0JH [The Grange, Grange Hill (B4551 S)]: Early Georgian mansion, now a friendly sports and social club – visitors can sign in; comfortable bar with up to a dozen changing real ales from long counter inc Banks's, Bathams and Old Swan, simple snacks; bowling green in grounds behind (the Didler)

Waggon & Horses B63 3TU [Stourbridge Rd]: Bathams and up to a dozen or so interesting changing ales from small brewers in chatty bare-boards bar and more spacious lounge, country wines and belgian brews, good snacks, brewery memorabilia; TV, Tues music night; open all day (the Didler)

HALFORD [SP2645]

Halford Bridge CV36 5BN [Fosse Way (A429)]: Stone-built inn reopened under new ownership after extensive contemporary upscale refurbishment, good range of food from lunchtime baguettes and pubby favourites to more interesting dishes, good choice of wines by the glass, well kept Hook Norton and Wells & Youngs Bombardier, neat attentive staff; 12 bedrooms, open all day (Keith and Sue Ward)

HAMPTON IN ARDEN [SP2080]

White Lion B92 0AA [High St; handy for M42 junction 6]: Bustling traditional beamed pub with open fires, brasses and local memorabilia in carpeted bar, good straightforward food and friendly service, real ales such as Black Sheep and Hook Norton, back restaurant; seven bedrooms, attractive village, handy for NEC (LYM, P M Newsome, Trevor and Sylvia Millum)

HAMPTON LUCY [SP2557]

Boars Head CV35 8BE [Church St, E of Stratford]: Good new landlady in low-beamed two-bar local next to lovely church, five quickly changing real ales, generous reasonably priced lunchtime baguettes and other food from light meals up, good choice of wines by the glass, log fire; picnic-sets in neat and attractive secluded back garden, pretty village nr Charlcote House (Joan and Tony Walker)

HARBOROUGH MAGNA [SP4779]

Old Lion CV23 0HL [3 miles from M6 junction 1; B4122]: Busy village pub with welcoming staff, Greene King ales, decent wines by the glass, good helpings of food from sandwiches, baguettes and baked potatoes to some interesting dishes, popular OAP lunches, pool room, friendly side restaurant; children welcome, family events, open all day wknds *(John Wooll, Alan Johnson)*

HARBURY [SP3760]

Crown CV33 9HE [Crown St, just off B4452]: Attractive old stone-built pub, good value food from sandwiches up, main dishes cooked to order, up to half a dozen real ales, friendly locals and staff, small simple front bar, back lounge with sofas, dining room; children welcome, picnic-sets on back terrace *(Joan and Tony Walker)*

HAWKESBURY [SP3684]

Greyhound CV6 6DF [Sutton Stop, off Black Horse Rd/Grange Rd; jnctn Coventry and N Oxford canals]: Cosy unpretentious pub brimming with bric-a-brac, well kept ales inc Highgate Dark Mild, reasonably priced food, attentive staff, coal-fired stove, unusual tiny snug; children and dogs welcome, tables on attractive waterside terrace, wonderful spot if you don't mind pylons – like a prime piece of the Black Country transported 20 miles to Coventry suburbs *(Bob and Laura Brock)*

HENLEY-IN-ARDEN [SP1566]

Blue Bell B95 5AT [High St]: Impressive beamed and timber-framed building with fine coach entrance, flagstoned bar with good log fire and two dining areas, limited range of good interesting home-made food, well kept ales such as Black Sheep, Hook Norton and Timothy Taylors Landlord, good wines by the glass, bright cheerful service; dogs welcome, some courtyard tables *(Pippa and Clive, Marcus Pennycook, Cedric Robertshaw)*

KENILWORTH [SP2872]

Clarendon Arms CV8 1NB [Castle Hill]: Busy traditional pub opp castle, huge helpings of good value food in several rooms off long partly flagstoned bustling bar, largish peaceful upstairs dining room, good friendly staff, plenty of atmosphere, several real ales; best to book wknds, daytime car park fee deducted from bill *(Alan Johnson, John and Yvonne Davies, Martin Kane)*

☆ *Clarendon House* CV8 1LZ [High St]: Interesting choice of enjoyable snacks (all day) and meals in ancient timber building with leather armchairs and sofas in large redecorated front lounge with contemporary prints and china, Greene King ales and decent wines from long serving counter, daily papers, back dining room; piped music; comfortable bedrooms, open all day *(Andy and Jill Kassube, LYM, Joan and Tony Walker)*

Cross CV8 2EZ [New St]: Smart dining pub with good enterprising food from paninis up inc fixed menus, small bar with emphasis on lagers, wines and spirits; pleasant heated terrace and small garden, open all day *(Martin and Karen Wake, Cedric Robertshaw)*

Old Bakery CV8 1LZ [High St, nr A429/A452 junction]: Pleasant small hotel with charming two-room bar, well kept Hook Norton, Timothy Taylors Landlord and two changing guest beers, good choice of wines by the glass, no music or machines – can get very busy Thurs-Sat evenings; terrace tables, comfortable bedrooms, cl lunchtimes exc Sun *(Clive and Fran Dutson, John Joseph Smith, Andy and Jill Kassube)*

KNOWLE [SP1875]

☆ *Herons Nest* B93 0EE [Warwick Rd S]: Vintage Inn dining pub in former hotel, several individual rooms inc big dining room overlooking Grand Union Canal, some flagstones and high-backed settles, hops on beams, interesting décor, open fires, sensibly priced traditional food all day inc children's helpings, well organised service, plenty of good value wines by the glass, real ales; lots of tables out by water, moorings, Innkeepers Lodge bedrooms, open all day *(R T and J C Moggridge, David Green, Carol and Colin Broadbent, Hugh Bower, Martin Kane)*

LAPWORTH [SP1970]

☆ *Navigation* B94 6NA [Old Warwick Rd (B4439 S)]: Busy well worn in two-bar beamed pub by Grand Union Canal, high-backed winged settles on flagstones, built-in window seats, warm coal fire and some bright canal ware, modern back dining room, straightforward bar food, Bass, M&B Brew XI and a guest, around 30 malt whiskies; TV, and they may try to keep your credit card while you eat; children and dogs welcome, hatch service to waterside terrace (the ducks hoping for food can be too pushy), open all day *(Richard Endacott, Charles and Pauline Stride, Dr D J and Mrs S C Walker, Jean Barnett, David Lewis, P Price, LYM, David and Pam Wilcox, Martin and Karen Wake, Mark and Ruth Brock)*

LEAMINGTON SPA [SP3165]

Benjamin Satchwell CV32 4AQ [The Parade]: Well laid out Wetherspoons, tidy and airy, with their usual food all day, quick service, good choice of low-priced beers, two levels, some cosy seating, cheerful relaxed atmosphere, back family area; disabled access and facilities, open all day *(Ted George, Steve and Liz Tilley, Tim and Ann Newell)*

Cask & Bottle CV32 4SY [Kennedy Sq/Lansdowne St]: Bustling local with lots of bare wood and metal (makes the friendly L-shaped bar rather loud when busy), well kept Greene King Abbot, Wadworths 6X and a quickly changing guest beer, cheap cheerful food inc bargain wkdy sandwiches and popular Sun lunch, some side alcoves, huge table for groups one end; big-screen sports TV *(Steve and Liz Tilley)*

Somerville Arms CV32 4SX [Campion Terr]: Neat and cosy local with tiny unspoilt Victorian back lounge, well kept Adnams Broadside, Fullers London Pride and Greene King IPA and Old Speckled Hen, friendly staff, darts; quiz and music nights; tables out on wide pavement and in small courtyard, cl lunchtime *(Steve and Liz Tilley)*

LONG COMPTON [SP2832]

☆ *Red Lion* CV36 5JS [A3400 S of Shipston-on-Stour]: Relaxing layout and atmosphere, with old-fashioned built-in settles among other pleasantly assorted seats and tables, stripped stone, bare beams, panelling, flagstones, old prints and team photographs, good value substantial food from good sandwiches up in bar and restaurant, children's helpings, real ales such as Adnams Broadside and Hook Norton, good wines by the glass, welcoming landlady (second landlady in charge of the kitchen), log fires and woodburners, simple public bar with pool; unobtrusive piped music; dogs and children welcome, big back garden with picnic-sets and climber, comfortable bedrooms *(George Atkinson, LYM, Mike and Mary Carter, Chris Glasson, K H Frostick)*

LONG ITCHINGTON [SP4165]

Blue Lias CV47 8LD [Stockton Rd, off A423]: Fine setting on Grand Union Canal, good choice of ales inc Adnams Broadside, Greene King Old Speckled Hen and Wychwood Hobgoblin, quick pleasant service, snug booth seating in eating area; they may try to keep your credit card while you eat; plenty of tables in waterside grounds, also a separate outbuilding bar with tables under a dome *(Rob and Catherine Dunster, Charles and Pauline Stride, Nigel and Sue Foster)*

LOWER GORNAL [SO9291]

Black Bear DY3 2AE [Deepdale Lane]: Simple local based on former 18th-c farmhouse, Shepherd Neame and three or four changing beers, good choice of whiskies; open all day wknds, cl wkdy lunchtimes *(the Didler)*

Fountain DY3 2PE [Temple St]: Lively two-room local with helpful landlord and staff, well kept Enville, RCH and up to six changing ales (beer festivals Easter and Oct), two farm ciders, country wines and imported beers, enjoyable inexpensive food all day (not Sun evening), back dining area, pigs-and-pen skittles; piped music; open all day *(the Didler)*

Old Bulls Head DY3 2NU [Redhall Rd]: Busy Victorian local with its own Black Country ales from back microbrewery, may be good filled cobs, back games room; some live music; open all day wknds (from 4 wkdys) *(the Didler)*

LOWSONFORD [SP1868]

Fleur de Lys B95 5HJ [off B4439 Hockley Heath—Warwick; Lapworth St]: Prettily placed by Warwickshire Canal, simple décor in varying-sized linked beamed rooms, log fires, good seating inc sofas, friendly helpful service, Greene King ales, good choice of wines by the glass, lots of lollies and ice-creams as well as usual food from sandwiches up (can take a long while when busy); children welcome, large waterside garden with adventure play area, open all day *(LYM, Charles and Pauline Stride, Paul and Margaret Baker, Fiona McElhone)*

LOXLEY [SP2552]

☆ *Fox* CV35 9JS [signed off A422 Stratford—Banbury]: Neatly refurbished, cheerful and welcoming, very popular even midweek lunchtimes for good value inventive generous food from sandwiches to fish specialities, real ales inc Hook Norton, prompt service and friendly landlord, panelling and a few pictures, pleasant dining area; piped music; tables in good-sized garden behind, sleepy village handy for Stratford *(Keith and Sue Ward, Nigel and Sue Foster, R J Herd, Trevor and Sheila Sharman)*

LYE [SO9284]

Windsor Castle DY9 7DG [Stourbridge Rd, Lye]: Contemporary minimalist décor and furnishings, good value Sadlers ales brewed next door, guest beers too, friendly helpful staff, good range of enjoyable reasonably priced food inc some imaginative dishes often using ale in the recipe (snacks all day, no evening meals Sun), bright lighting and lively acoustics, some brewing memorabilia; open all day *(Nigel Espley, Liane Purnell)*

MAPPLEBOROUGH GREEN [SP0765]

Boot B80 7BJ [Birmingham Rd (A435)]: Recently refurbished, with relaxing atmosphere, tub chairs, comfortable table seating, enjoyable if not cheap food, good friendly service, good wines by the glass *(Mrs B H Adams)*

MONKS KIRBY [SP4682]

☆ *Bell* CV23 0QY [just off B4027 W of Pailton]: Hospitable long-serving Spanish landlord and his two sweet dogs enlivening this dimly lit pub, dark beams, timber dividers, flagstones and cobbles, very wide choice of good largely spanish food inc starters doubling as tapas, fine range of spanish wines and of brandies and malt whiskies, relaxed informal service, Bass and Flowers Original, plenty of brandies and malt whiskies, enjoyably appropriate piped music; children and dogs welcome, streamside back terrace with country view, may be cl Mon *(Jill and Julian Tasker, LYM, Jane Davies, Roger Braithwaite, Susan and John Douglas)*

☆ *Denbigh Arms* CV23 0QX [Main St]: New landlord in small friendly 17th-c beamed pub opp church, good unusual indian food, Greene King Abbot, Timothy Taylors Landlord and Theakstons XB, good wine choice, old photographs and interesting 18th-c pew seating, family room; play area *(June and Ken Brooks, Alan Johnson, Nigel Clifton)*

NAPTON [SP4560]

Folly CV47 8NZ [off A425 towards Priors Hardwick; Folly Lane, by locks]: Simple beamed boaters' pub in lovely spot by Napton locks on Oxford Canal, three bars on different levels, mix of furnishings inc huge farmhouse table in homely front bar, two big log fires, home-made pies, friendly staff, real ales inc one brewed for the pub, pool in back games room; very busy wknds; children welcome, big lawn with play area, wishing well and fine views (also all-day summer shop), cl wkdy lunchtimes in winter *(Mike and Mary Carter)*

NEWBOLD ON STOUR [SP2446]

☆ *Bird in Hand* CV37 8TR [Stratford Rd (A3400 S of Stratford)]: Neat L-shaped bar with comfortable well spaced dining tables, bow windows, charming friendly service, enjoyable food inc low-priced basic and snack menu and interesting more elaborate one, Hook Norton and guest beers, good tea and coffee, log fire, pool in side public bar *(BB, Colin Fisher, Pete Baker)*

NORTHEND [SP3952]

Red Lion CV47 2TJ [off B4100 Warwick— Banbury; Bottom St]: Bright and neat open-plan pub with good range of beers inc Marstons and Timothy Taylors Landlord, good coffee and choice of wines by the glass, enjoyable blackboard food, reasonable prices, friendly service, restaurant area; quite handy for National Herb Centre *(BB, K H Frostick)*

NUNEATON [SP3790]

Attleborough Arms CV11 4PL [Highfield Rd, Attleborough]: Large fairly recently rebuilt pub, attractively open, modern and comfortable, with enjoyable cheap lunchtime food, real ales, helpful service, exemplary lavatories; good disabled access *(Ian and Joan Blackwell)*

Felix Holt CV11 5BS [Stratford St]: Big Wetherspoons pub with good service even when very busy, wide range of very reasonably priced beers, nice décor, usual food all day; good disabled facilities *(Ted George, David M Smith)*

OFFCHURCH [SP3565]

Stags Head CV33 9AQ [Welsh Rd, off A425 at Radford Semele]: Low-beamed olde-worlde thatched village pub with popular usual food in neatly kept bar and spacious dining area with conservatory, friendly efficient service, John Smiths and a guest beer such as Hawkshead Lakeland Gold; quiet piped music; good-sized garden with play area *(Keith and Sue Ward)*

OLD HILL [SO9686]

Waterfall B64 6RG [Waterfall Lane]: Good value unpretentious two-room local, friendly staff, well kept Holdens, good value plain home-made food from hot filled baguettes with chips to Sun lunch, tankards and jugs hanging from boarded ceiling; piped music; children welcome, back garden with play area, open all day wknds *(the Didler)*

OLDBURY [SO9989]

Waggon & Horses B69 3AD [Church St, nr Savacentre]: Copper ceiling, original etched windows, open fire and Black Country memorabilia in busy town pub with Enville and two or three guest beers, wide choice of generous lunchtime food (not Sun) from sandwiches and baguettes up inc lots of puddings, decent wines, friendly efficient service even when busy, ornate Victorian tiles in corridor to lively comfortable back lounge with tie collection, side room with

high-backed settles and big old tables, bookable upstairs bistro Weds-Fri night; open all day *(Pete Baker, the Didler)*

OXHILL [SP3149]

Peacock CV35 0QU [off A422 Stratford— Banbury]: Refurbished under new licensees, cosy bar with real ales such as Greene King Abbot and Timothy Taylors Golden Best, traditional food in dining room; pretty village, open all day wknds, cl Mon *(anon)*

PATHLOW [SP1858]

Dun Cow CV37 0RQ [A3400 N of Stratford]: New management in pleasant country pub with good value home cooking, beams, flagstones and inglenook log fire, well kept local ales *(John Croxford)*

PRINCETHORPE [SP4070]

Three Horseshoes CV23 9PR [High Town; junction A423/B4453]: Friendly old beamed village pub under obliging new manager, Marstons Pedigree and Wells & Youngs Bombardier, enjoyable food, open fire, decorative plates, pictures, comfortable settles and chairs; TV one end; pleasant big garden with terrace and play area, bedrooms *(Rob and Catherine Dunster)*

PRIORS HARDWICK [SP4756]

☆ *Butchers Arms* CV47 7SN [off A423 via Wormleighton or A425 via Boddington, N of Banbury; Church End]: Upmarket old-fashioned restaurant in pleasantly reworked 14th-c building, oak beams, flagstones, panelling, antiques and soft lighting, huge choice of good if pricy food inc fixed price lunches, friendly Portuguese landlord, punctilious formal service, distinguished wine list (the beer is keg), small bar with inglenook log fire used mainly by people waiting for a table, also simple public bar; country garden *(BB, K H Frostick)*

PRIORS MARSTON [SP4857]

☆ *Holly Bush* CV47 7RW [off A361 S of Daventry; Holly Bush Lane]: New management in attractive extended golden stone inn with beams, flagstones and lots of stripped stone in rambling linked rooms, sturdy tables, some squashy leather sofas, Greene King IPA and Abbot and Hook Norton Old Hooky, usual food, big log fire and woodburners (not always lit), games area with bar billiards, pool and board games; piped music, TV, juke box, games machine; children and dogs welcome, sheltered garden, open all day wknds; more reports on new regime please *(LYM)*

RATLEY [SP3847]

☆ *Rose & Crown* OX15 6DS [off A422 NW of Banbury]: Cosy and charming ancient golden stone beamed pub, well kept Wells & Youngs Eagle, Bombardier and Winter Warmer and guests such as Greene King Abbot and St Austell Tribute, well made simple food from good sandwiches up, friendly helpful service, daily papers, woodburner in flagstoned area on left, big log fireplace in carpeted area on right, back restaurant; dogs and children welcome, tables in small gravel garden, nr lovely church in small sleepy village (Clive and Fran Dutson, BB)

ROWINGTON [SP1969]

☆ **Tom o' the Wood** CV35 7DH [off B4439 N of Rowington, following Lowsonford sign; Finwood Rd]: Comfortably furnished canalside pub/restaurant with new licensees using local produce for good home-made food from unusual sandwiches up, civilised lounge opening into conservatory, central bar, handsome Elizabethan ceiling in upstairs restaurant; tables on terrace and neat side lawn (LYM, Mr and Mrs D Heacock)

SHIPSTON-ON-STOUR [SP2540]

☆ **Black Horse** CV36 4BT [Station Rd (off A3400)]: 16th-c thatched pub with low-beamed bars off central entrance passage, good inglenook log fire, welcoming landlord, real ales such as Adnams and Greene King, enjoyable home-made food (not Sun evening) inc wkdy OAP bargain lunches, good choice of wines by the glass, interesting bric-a-brac, darts, dominoes and cribbage, small dining room; back garden with terrace, barbecue and aunt sally, comfortable bedrooms, good breakfast, open all day Sun (JHBS, K H Frostick, Kevin and Jane O'Mahoney)

George CV36 4AJ [High St]: Splendid early Georgian façade, carefully refurbished inside under new landlady, several linked areas inc one with deep leather armchairs and log fire, enjoyable mildly upmarket blackboard food, three real ales such as Fullers London Pride from central marble-topped counter; well modernised bedrooms, open all day (JHBS)

☆ **White Bear** CV36 4AJ [High Street]: Lively old town local with long narrow front bar's straightforward – even worn – furnishings contrasting with starched white tablecloths on dining tables, two log fires, Adnams, Bass, Hook Norton Old Hooky and a guest such as Newmans Wolvers, good wines by the glass, gently imaginative food (not Sun evening), darts; piped music, games machine, juke box, TV; children and dogs welcome, pavement tables, simple bedrooms, open all day (JHBS, P Dawn, LYM, W M Paton, Dr and Mrs A K Clarke)

SHREWLEY [SP2167]

Durham Ox CV35 7AY [off B4439 Hockley Heath—Warwick]: Spacious bistro-style country dining pub with warmly welcoming and cheerful young Australian staff, generally good if pricy food (and they add an 'optional' service charge) from interesting sandwiches to enterprising main dishes, real ales such as Greene King IPA; shame about the piped music and TV; pleasant garden, open all day (BB, Jason Caulkin, R L Borthwick)

SOLIHULL [SP1780]

Boat B91 2TJ [Hampton Lane, Catherine de Barnes (B4102, handy for M42 junctions 5 and 6)]: Recently converted Chef & Brewer by Grand Union Canal, their usual food, quick efficient service, real ales such as Greene King IPA (Alun Howells, Chris Evans)

STOURBRIDGE [SO9083]

Shrubbery Cottage DY8 1RQ [Heath Lane, Old Swinford (B4186 S)]: Welcoming L-shaped local with full Holdens ale range kept well, basic cobs, darts one end, people playing cards and dominoes the other; central wide-screen sports TV; open all day (Pete Baker, R T and J C Moggridge)

STRATFORD-UPON-AVON [SP2054]

Dirty Duck CV37 6BA [Waterside]: Bustling 16th-c chain pub nr Memorial Theatre, lots of signed RSC photographs, open fire, Flowers Original and Greene King IPA, good choice of wines by the glass, food all day, modern conservatory restaurant (best to book wknds); children allowed in dining area, attractive small terrace looking over riverside public gardens which tend to act as summer overflow, open all day (LYM, Mrs Hazel Rainer, Michael and Alison Sandy, Michael Dandy, Bob, Peter Dandy, Martin Kane)

☆ **Garrick** CV37 6AU [High St]: Bustling ancient pub with heavy beams and timbers, odd-shaped rooms and simple furnishings on bare boards, good-natured efficient staff, Greene King ales and perhaps a guest beer, decent wines by the glass, food from sandwiches and light dishes up all day, small air-conditioned back restaurant; piped music, TV, games machine; children welcome, open all day (Peter Dandy, Liz and Brian Barnard, LYM, Ted George, Val and Alan Green, Michael Dandy, Giles Barr, Eleanor Dandy, John Millwood, Neil and Anita Christopher, Derek and Sylvia Stephenson)

Pen & Parchment CV37 6YY [Bridgefoot, by canal basin]: Shakespeare theme and pleasant pubby atmosphere in L-shaped split-level lounge and snug, rustic-style beams, balusters, bare boards and tiles or flagstones, small alcoves, big open fire in old fireplace, prompt helpful service, good wine choice, Greene King IPA and Abbot and Timothy Taylors Landlord, wide choice of good value usual food; tables out among shrubs and ivy, pretty hanging baskets, good canal basin views (busy road), open all day (Mrs Hazel Rainer, Charles and Pauline Stride, Derek and Sylvia Stephenson, Roger and Anne Newbury, Meg and Colin Hamilton, Dave Braisted, Tim and Ann Newell)

☆ **West End** CV37 6DT [Bull St]: Attractively modernised and neatly kept old pub, a rare exception to Greene King's domination here, with well kept changing ales such as Adnams Broadside, Fullers London Pride, Hook Norton, Timothy Taylors Landlord and Uley Old Spot, friendly young staff, thriving atmosphere in nice lounge and several eating areas, shortish choice of good value seasonal food, good wine choice and interesting soft drinks range inc plenty of coffees, film star photographs; well chosen piped music; appealing terrace (PL, Derek and Sylvia Stephenson, Val and Alan Green, Dave Webster, Sue Holland)

Windmill CV37 6HB [Church St]: Ancient pub beyond the attractive Guild Chapel, with town's oldest licence and very low black beams; typical old-fashioned town local, complete with piped music, sports TV, games machines, given visitor appeal by its friendly efficient staff, wide choice of attractively priced food (till 7 wkdys) from sandwiches to substantial Sun lunch and some unusual main dishes, and big log fire; sensibly priced Flowers Original, Greene King IPA and wines by the glass; tables outside, open all day from noon *(David Coleman, Ted George, John and Yvonne Davies, Edward Mirzoeff)*

SUTTON COLDFIELD [SP1296]
Three Tuns B72 1XS [High St]: Cleverly refurbished to incorporate former coach entry as link between two cosy bars, great old-world atmosphere, Thwaites real ales; back courtyard *(Clifford Blakemore)*

TANWORTH-IN-ARDEN [SP1170]
☆ *Bell* B94 5AL [The Green]: Smart pub in pretty village, well kept ales such as Black Sheep and Timothy Taylors Landlord, good choice of wines by the glass, enjoyable food from light lunchtime dishes to full meals, comfortable modern furniture and good graphics, friendly staff; also houses deli and back post office; children in eating areas, outlook on peaceful green and lovely 14th-c church, back terrace with alloy planters, stylish modern bedrooms – good base for walks *(Rosanna Luke, Matt Curzon, LYM)*

TEMPLE GRAFTON [SP1355]
Blue Boar B49 6NR [a mile E, towards Binton; off A422 W of Stratford]: Extended country dining pub under newish management, above-average generous food from imaginative sandwiches up, four well kept changing ales, good coffee and wine choice, beams, stripped stonework and log fires, dining room with attractive farmhouse-kitchen mural; big-screen TVs; children and dogs welcome, picnic-sets outside, pretty flower plantings, comfortable well equipped bedrooms, open all day summer wknds *(LYM, Joan and Tony Walker)*

TIPTON [SO9792]
Rising Sun DY4 7NH [Horseley Rd (B4517, off A461)]: Friendly Victorian pub with well kept Banks's, Oakham JHB and guest beers in lined glasses, farm ciders, back lounge with coal fires, alcoves and original bare boards and tiles, lunchtime food; tables outside, open all day Fri/Sat *(the Didler)*

UFTON [SP3762]
White Hart CV33 9PJ [just off A425 Daventry—Leamington, towards Bascote]: Friendly old pub redecorated under new landlord, big unpretentious L-shaped beamed bar, several steps down to back dining part, stripped stone walls, good value food inc bargain OAP wkdy lunches, Greene King IPA and Old Speckled Hen; piped music; hatch service to hilltop garden with panoramic views *(DC, George Atkinson)*

ULLENHALL [SP1267]
Winged Spur B95 5PA: Traditional pub with good value unpretentious food from sandwiches up, well kept beer; picnic-sets in garden *(Pippa and Clive, Pat and Robert Watt)*

UPPER GORNAL [SO9292]
☆ *Britannia* DY3 1UX [Kent St (A459)]: 19th-c local popular for its old-fashioned character and particularly well kept Bathams Best and Mild (bargain prices), tiled floors, coal fires in front bar and time-trapped back room down corridor; nice flower-filled back yard, cl lunchtimes Mon-Thurs, open all day Fri/Sat *(Kerry Law, the Didler)*

Jolly Crispin DY3 1UL [Clarence St (A459)]: Friendly well run 18th-c local with up to ten or so interesting quickly changing ales, two farm ciders or perry, compact front bar, wall seats and mixed tables and chairs on tiled floor, lots of aircraft pictures in larger back room, beer festivals; open all day Fri/Sat, cl lunchtime Mon-Thurs *(Ian and Liz Rispin, the Didler)*

WALSALL [SP0198]
Arbor Lights WS1 1SY [Lichfield St]: Modern open-plan brasserie-style bar and restaurant, relaxed and friendly, with wide choice of wines, real ales, freshly made food all day from sandwiches and unusual starter/light dishes to good fish choice, good service *(anon)*

WARMINGTON [SP4147]
☆ *Plough* OX17 1BX [just off B4100 N of Banbury]: Attractive and unpretentious pub in delightful village with interesting church, well kept changing ales such as Adnams, Highgate Davenports, Hop Back GFB, Jennings Cumberland, Shepherd Neame Spitfire and St Austell Tribute, friendly enterprising landlord, efficient staff, log fire in big fireplace, ancient settle, nice chairs, Victorian prints, jugs, mugs and beermats on low heavy beams, good value popular food (not Sun evening), extended dining room; children and dogs welcome, tables on back terrace *(MLR, John Beeken, LYM, John Coatsworth, John Dwane, George Atkinson)*

WARWICK [SP2764]
Old Fourpenny Shop CV34 6HJ [Crompton St, nr racecourse]: Cosy and comfortable split-level pub with up to five well kept changing beers, welcoming licensees, good value food in bar and heavily beamed restaurant, cheerful service, no piped music; pleasant reasonably priced bedrooms *(Steve and Liz Tilley)*

☆ *Rose & Crown* CV34 4SH [Market Pl]: Up-to-date uncluttered refurbishment with big leather sofas and low tables by open fire in front, red-walled dining area behind on left with large modern photographs, interesting food all day at sensible prices from sandwiches and self-choice deli platters up, relaxed atmosphere, two well kept ales such as Wells & Youngs Bombardier and plenty of fancy keg dispensers, good wines by the glass, good strong coffee, friendly efficient service; tables out under parasols, comfortable good-sized bedrooms *(Martin and Karen Wake, LYM)*

☆ *Saxon Mill* CV34 5YN [Guy's Cliffe, A429 just N]: Good new management for pleasantly refurbished converted mill in lovely setting, wheel turning slowly behind glass, mill race under glass floor-panel, contemporary chairs and tables on polished boards and flagstones below the beams, cosy corners with leather armchairs and big rugs, smiling service, enjoyable food in bar and upstairs restaurant, a real ale; teak tables out on terraces by broad willow-flanked river, bridge to more tables on far side, delightful views across to Grade I ruins of Guy's Cliffe House, open all day *(Andy and Jill Kassube, Roy Bromell, Andy and Alice Jordan, LYM, Susan and John Douglas)*

☆ *Zetland Arms* CV34 4AB [Church St]: Cosy town pub with good sensibly priced traditional food (not wknd evenings) inc good sandwich choice, friendly quick service even when busy, Marstons Pedigree and Tetleys, decent wines in generous glasses, neat but relaxing small panelled front bar with toby jug collection, comfortable larger L-shaped back eating area with small conservatory; sports TV; children welcome, interestingly planted sheltered garden, bedrooms sharing bathroom *(LYM, Peter and Jean Hoare, Martin Kane)*

WELFORD-ON-AVON [SP1452]

Four Alls CV37 8PW [Binton Rd]: Attractive if unpubby light modern décor and furnishings in large L-shaped dining area, wide choice of reasonably priced food inc unusual light dishes, Shepherd Neame Spitfire and Wadworths 6X, good wines by the glass, cheerful antipodean service; pleasant terrace with heaters, fine spot by River Avon *(Andrew Richardson, W W Burke, Chris Glasson, Keith and Sue Ward)*

WELLESBOURNE [SP2755]

Kings Head CV35 9LT: Vintage Inn dining pub with contemporary furnishings in high-ceilinged lounge bar, log fire and smaller areas leading off, lively public bar with games, wide choice of wines by the glass, well kept beers, good value food from sandwiches up, friendly staff; piped music, no dogs; proper tables and chairs on small front terrace, more in prettily placed back garden facing church, bedrooms (handy for Stratford but cheaper), open all day *(Gordon Prince, LYM, Tom and Jill Jones)*

Stags Head CV35 9RD [old centre, Bridge St/ Walton Way]: Picturesque 17th-c thatched and timbered pub with good atmosphere in small simply furnished beamed lounge bar, flagstoned passage to larger stone-floored public bar, friendly licensees, good service even when busy, good value enjoyable usual food, well kept ales such as Badger Best, Bass, Fullers London Pride, Greene King Abbot, Marstons Pedigree and Timothy Taylors Landlord, lots of local history and photographs; picnic-sets in garden and out

in front, bedrooms, lovely setting in group of Elizabethan cottages *(Andy and Alice Jordan, BB)*

WHARF [SP4352]

Wharf Inn CV47 2FE [A423 Banbury— Southam, nr Fenny Compton]: Open-plan pub by Bridge 136 on South Oxford Canal, own moorings, good contemporary layout and furnishings, small central flagstoned bar, Hook Norton ales, limited menu; piped music, games machine; dogs welcome in bar, children away from bar, disabled access and facilities, waterside garden with picnic-sets and playhouse, open all day *(Simon Jones, LYM, Bob and Laura Brock)*

WHICHFORD [SP3134]

☆ *Norman Knight* CV36 5PE: Helpful new young couple in friendly and unpretentious two-room pub with good interesting changing beers, inc some from Wizard (though perhaps not in future when the brewery, formerly here, is re-established down in Devon), reasonably priced food from appealing sandwiches to good Sun roasts, decent wines, prompt service, darts and dominoes, flagstones and stone walls; some live music; dogs welcome, tables out in front by attractive village green, aunt sally, small back campsite, cl Mon lunchtime *(Guy Vowles, Pete Baker, JHBS, David Campbell, Vicki McLean)*

WHITACRE HEATH [SP2192]

Swan B46 2JA [off B4114 at Blyth End E of Coleshill]: Cheerful family pub with bargain food, real ales such as Courage Directors, Greene King Abbot and Old Speckled Hen, Marstons Pedigree, Shepherd Neame Spitfire and Wells & Youngs Bombardier; children very welcome, good play area *(Dick and Madeleine Brown)*

WILLOUGHBY [SP5267]

Rose CV23 8BH [just off A45 E of Dunchurch; Main St]: Partly thatched beamed pub with interesting food under current lively and flamboyant landlord (a rumour he may be moving on – news please), pleasant layout and décor, well kept Greene King Abbot, Hook Norton Best and Timothy Taylors Landlord; lots of outside seating at front and in garden with play area, flowers everywhere *(David M Smith)*

WISHAW [SP1694]

Cock B76 9QL [Bulls Lane]: Partly Tudor country pub, good seasonal range of appetising well presented food, prompt cheerful service, good choice of wines by the glass; children welcome *(Helen Rowett)*

WIXFORD [SP0854]

Fish B49 6DA [B4085 Alcester—Bidford]: Enjoyable reasonably priced food inc lots of chargrills and bargain roasts for two, cheerful helpful staff, good choice of changing ales, roomy L-shaped bar and snug, beams, polished panelling, carpets over flagstones, log fire, interesting bric-a-brac, stuffed fish, and quite an art gallery in corridor to lavatories; piped music; lovely riverside setting, nice on a summer's evening

(Carol and Colin Broadbent, Des and Jen Clarke, Mr and Mrs F E Boxell)

Three Horseshoes B49 6DG [B4085 off A46 S of Redditch, via A422/A435 Alcester roundabout, or B439 at Bidford]: Roomy, neat and friendly L-shaped pub with wide choice of generous affordable pubby food, Adnams, Church End, Marstons Pedigree and Timothy Taylors, helpful service, bric-a-brac from blowtorches to garden gnomes; pleasant seating areas outside *(Des and Jen Clarke, Keith and Sue Ward)*

WOLLASTON [SO8884]

Unicorn DY8 3NX [Bridgnorth Rd (A458)]: Cosy and friendly traditional local with well kept low-priced Bathams Bitter and Mild, unpretentious L-shaped bar and unspoilt back parlour, lots of brasses and knick-knacks, good lunchtime sandwiches; tables outside, open all day, Sun afternoon break *(the Didler)*

WOLVERHAMPTON [SO9098]

Combermere Arms WV3 0TY [Chapel Ash (A41 Tettenhall rd)]: Cosy old-fashioned three-room local with friendly service, well kept Banks's and guest beers, decent wines, lunchtime food from bargain sandwiches up, bare boards and quaint touches, Wolves photographs, bar billiards; tree growing in gents', courtyard and secluded garden, open all day wknds *(Ian and Liz Rispin, R T and J C Moggridge)*

☆ **Great Western** WV10 0DG [Corn Hill/Sun St, behind BR station]: Cheerful and down to earth, tucked interestingly away by cobbled lane down from main line station to GWR low-level one, with friendly very prompt service, particularly well kept Bathams and several Holdens ales at bargain prices, winter mulled wine (no tea or coffee), cheap hearty home-made lunchtime food (not Sun) from good filled cobs up, interesting railway and more recent motorcycle photographs, traditional front bar, other rooms inc neat dining conservatory; SkyTV; picnic-sets in yard with good barbecues, open all day (Sun afternoon break) *(Ian and Liz Rispin, BB, P Dawn, R T and J C Moggridge, Pete Baker, John Tav, the Didler, Robert Garner)*

Moseley Park WV10 6TA [Greenfield Lane; handy for M54 junction 2, first left off A449 S]: Large and comfortable modern dining pub, well laid out to give private-feeling spaces with neutral décor, sofas, soft lighting and log fire, contemporary food, smiling service, Banks's Original and Marstons Pedigree; bedrooms in adjoining Premier Travel Inn *(Ian Phillips, Jonathon Sheppard)*

WOOTTON WAWEN [SP1563]

☆ **Bulls Head** B95 6BD [just off A3400 Birmingham—Stratford]: New management in attractive black and white dining pub with low Elizabethan beams and timbers, leather sofas, armchairs and log fire in bar with three Marstons and related ales, enjoyable food served quickly by friendly staff, comfortable low-beamed dining room with rich colours, brocaded seats and tapestries; children welcome, garden tables, handy for one of England's finest churches and Stratford Canal walks *(Carol and Colin Broadbent, LYM, Mr and Mrs F E Boxell)*

A very few pubs try to make you leave a credit card at the bar, as a sort of deposit if you order food. They are not entitled to do this. The credit card firms and banks which issue them warn you not to let them out of your sight. If someone behind the counter used your card fraudulently, the card company or bank could in theory hold you liable, because of your negligence in letting a stranger hang on to your card. Suggest instead that if they feel the need for security, they 'swipe' your card and give it back to you. And do name and shame the pub to us.

Wiltshire

From unassuming country pubs to more foody places with really imaginative meals, Wiltshire has somewhere to delight most tastes, and we've added quite a few new finds this year. These are the distinctive old Blue Boar in Aldbourne, the nicely unpretentious Bakers Arms at Badbury, the stylish and interesting Castle Inn at Castle Combe (good to stay in), the friendly rambling Seymour Arms at East Knoyle, the Wheatsheaf at Oaksey (particularly good food), the Cross Keys at Upper Chute (a rewarding all-rounder), and the civilised White Horse at Winterbourne Bassett. Of our more established pubs here, a handful particularly stand out, with readers this year especially enjoying the Red Lion at Axford (very good upmarket food, strong on fish, and a good welcome too), the unpretentious Quarrymans Arms at Box (well liked for its welcoming, cheery atmosphere and no-frills style), the Compasses at Chicksgrove (an excellent all-rounder, praised for its food, welcome and bedrooms – it's a nice play to stay), the Fox & Hounds at East Knoyle (a beautiful thatched pub in a lovely spot, with good food cooked by the landlord), the busy and interesting George at Lacock (probably the best-loved of our three main entries here), the Malet Arms at Newton Tony (where much of the very good food has been bagged by the landlord), the Vine Tree at Norton (a favourite for its excellent food, with carefully sourced ingredients), and the wonderfully old-fashioned Haunch of Venison in Salisbury, with lots of history, and its famous mummified hand. Several of these are contenders for Wiltshire Dining Pub of the Year though, for the sheer enthusiasm expressed by readers over the last few months, that title goes to the Compasses at Chicksgrove (with the Red Lion and the Malet Arms not far behind, and one or two of the newcomers looking very promising). Other places for a reliable meal include the Three Crowns in Brinkworth, the Linnet at Great Hinton, the Bath Arms at Crockerton, the George & Dragon at Rowde (which now has bedrooms too), the Lamb at Semington (back in the *Guide* after a break, with very good meals), the Bridge at West Lavington, and the Pear Tree at Whitley. Quite a few Wiltshire pubs now do some main courses in a choice of sizes at lunchtime – which many readers really appreciate. And you can count on finding lamb on the menu: lots of landlords here told us it was by far their most popular dish now. Another re-entry is the Bell at Wylye, a cosy village pub revitalised by the local Hidden Brewery, whose beers feature increasingly in other pubs in the area. The main local brewer is Wadworths, often the cheapest beer offered by pubs here; it supplies good wines, too. Archers and Arkells are also significant players in the local pub scene, and smaller brewers to look out for include Hop Back, Stonehenge, Moles and Ramsbury. Perhaps because of the healthily competitive local brewing scene here, drinks prices tend to be a little lower than in most southern counties; pub food prices are not far off the average. In the Lucky Dip section at the end of the chapter, pubs to note include the Waggon

& Horses at Beckhampton, Kings Head at Chitterne, Royal Oak at Great Wishford, Angel in Hindon, Calley Arms at Hodson, Toll Gate in Holt, Hit or Miss in Kington Langley, Wheatsheaf at Lower Woodford, New Inn in Salisbury, Pembroke Arms in Wilton and Poplars at Wingfield.

ALDBOURNE   SU2675 MAP 2
Blue Boar
The Green (off B4192 in centre); SN8 2EN

Bags of character in friendly low-beamed traditional pub with enjoyable food and drink

Plenty of local regulars congregate here for bar lunches in the homely and relaxed left-hand bar, partly bare boards, partly faded carpet, with pubby seats around heavily rustic tables, lots of low black beams in the ochre ceiling, a boar's head above the bigger of the two fireplaces, a stuffed pine marten over one table, darts, and a corner cupboard of village trophies. Lots of unusual bottled beers line the rail above the dark pine dado. They have Wadworths IPA and 6X and maybe a guest like Everards Sunchaser on handpump, and a good choice of wines and soft drinks; service is friendly even when it's packed. A separate bare-boards dining bar on the right, stretching back further, has more table space, and is rather more modern in style, with its country pictures on cream or dark pink walls, but has a similar nicely pubby atmosphere. Picnic-sets and a couple of tall hogshead tables under big green canvas parasols out in front face the village green (and its parked cars); it's the sort of place where visiting riders may share their pints with their mounts (and indeed a manger at the back is now listed).

🍴 **Generous is too mean a word for the helpings here: even keen walkers who usually tell us about course after course have had to pass on puddings. Expect well filled baguettes, and things like minted shoulder of lamb, wild boar with apple cream and horseradish, popular steak and kidney pie, venison cooked with blackberries, and apple pie; Sunday roasts.** *Starters/Snacks: £3.50 to £4.95. Main Courses: £7.85 to £17.95. Puddings: £3.95*

Wadworths ~ Licensees Jaz and Mandy Hill ~ Real ale ~ Bar food (12-2, 7-9) ~ (01672) 540237 ~ Children welcome ~ Dogs welcome ~ Open 11.30-3, 5.30-11; 11.30-11 Sat; 12-10.30 Sun
Recommended by Dr and Mrs Ellison, Mary Rayner, John Downham, Guy Vowles

AXFORD   SU2470 MAP 2
Red Lion ♀
Off A4 E of Marlborough; on back road Mildenhall—Ramsbury; SN8 2HA

Pretty pub with emphasis on very good, upmarket food (lots of fish), with careful service from friendly staff, and locally brewed beers

Though it's the imaginative, home-cooked food that's the centre of attention at this flint-and-brick pub, readers have this year also highlighted the good service and friendly welcome, with one saying the landlord is never too busy to chat. It's not all top-end meals: they do bar snacks too, and keep Ramsbury Gold and Axford Ale from the little brewery on the edge of the village, along with a guest like Cottage Plunge; also, 15 wines by the glass and 20 malt whiskies. The beamed and pine-panelled bar has a big inglenook fireplace, and a pleasant mix of comfortable sofas, cask seats and other solid chairs on the parquet floor; the pictures by local artists are for sale. There are lovely views over a valley from good hardwood tables and chairs on the terrace, and you get the same views from picture windows in the restaurant and lounge. The sheltered garden has picnic-sets under parasols overlooking the river.

Smoking is not allowed inside any pub.

🍴 Carefully prepared food runs from lunchtime filled rolls and bar snacks like beef and Guinness casserole or gorgonzola, walnut and apple filo parcels (not Saturday evening or Sunday lunch), to the more restauranty menu with seared sliced goose breast, spring onion and watercress salad with damson and rosemary dressing, ham hock terrine with marinated vegetables, half a roasted guinea fowl with apricot, almond, sage and brandy jus, spiced chickpea cakes with coriander yoghurt, a separate fish menu offering chargrilled marlin steak with tropical fruit salsa or grilled fillet of brill with sorrel and cream sauce, and puddings like lime and coconut cheesecake. *Starters/Snacks: £4.95 to £7.50. Main Courses: £13.25 to £21.50. Puddings: £5.00*

Free house ~ Licensee Seamus Lecky ~ Real ale ~ Bar food (12-2, 7-9(but see text); not 25 Dec) ~ Restaurant ~ (01672) 520271 ~ Children welcome ~ Dogs allowed in bar ~ Open 12-2.30, 6.30-11; 12-2.30, 7-10.30 Sun

Recommended by Graham Cooper, Pat and Robert Watt, Bernard Stradling, Mike Vincent, Alan and Paula McCully, A J Andrews, Mr and Mrs Mike Pearson, Mrs Jill Wyatt, Mary Rayner, Peter Titcomb, Guy Vowles

BADBURY
SU1980 MAP 2

Bakers Arms
A mile from M4 junction 15; first left off A346 S, then bear left; SN4 0EU

Comfortably old-fashioned atmosphere in true village pub, a nice motorway escape

An idealised look back to the 1960s in these three smallish red-carpeted areas – house plants and red velvet curtains in the bow window, scatter cushions on grey leatherette seating, old clippings and photographs of the pub on cream-painted plank panelling, a hot coal or log fire, a proper pool and darts area (with a silenced games machine), friendly old-fashioned licensees, perhaps even piped Frank Sinatra. They have well kept Arkells 2B and 3B on handpump, and picnic-sets in a prettily tended garden (with a heated area for smokers).

🍴 Good value food runs from speciality sandwiches (their club sandwich defies completion) through a good choice of pubby favourites like ploughman's, steak and kidney pie and fish and chips, to specials such as lamb shank, liver, bacon and onions and broccoli, or leek and stilton bake. *Starters/Snacks: £2.40 to £6.30. Main Courses: £4.15 to £15.70. Puddings: £4.15 to £5.00*

Arkells ~ Tenant Dennis Fairal ~ Real ale ~ Bar food (12.30-2.30, 6.30-9 Mon-Thurs, 7-9.30 Fri/Sat; no food Sun evening) ~ Children over 10 in dining area ~ Open 12-3, 5.30-11; 12-4, 7-12 Sat; 12-4, 7-10.30 Sun

Recommended by Peter and Audrey Dowsett, Bill Leckey

BERWICK ST JAMES
SU0739 MAP 2

Boot
B3083, between A36 and A303 NW of Salisbury; SP3 4TN

Busy country pub in handy location not far from Stonehenge

Well known locally for its annual pumpkin competition – when growers from a surprisingly wide area battle it out to see who's produced the heaviest – this busy flint and stone pub is a popular lunchtime stop, with a good mix of customers. The partly carpeted and flagstoned bar has a huge winter log fire in the inglenook fireplace at one end, sporting prints over a small brick fireplace at the other, and houseplants on its wide window sills. A small back dining room has a nice mix of dining chairs around four tables, and pale gold walls with an attractively mounted collection of celebrity boots. Wadworths IPA and 6X and maybe a guest such as Archers Best on handpump; piped jazz. The neat sheltered side lawn has pretty flowerbeds and some well spaced picnic-sets.

🍴 Using vegetables from the big garden, the enjoyable home-cooked bar food might include well liked lunchtime baguettes and ploughman's, soup, baked goats cheese with date compote, chilli con carne, roast shoulder of lamb, trout supreme on pak choi with ginger and soy sauce, good winter game dishes, and steaks. *Starters/Snacks: £5.50 to £6.95. Main Courses: £8.50 to £16.95. Puddings: £4.95*

Wadworths ~ Tenant Kathie Duval ~ Real ale ~ Bar food (12-2.30, 6.30-9.30; not Sun evening or Mon) ~ (01722) 790243 ~ Children welcome ~ Dogs welcome ~ Open 12-3, 6-11.30; 12-3, 7-11 Sun; closed Mon lunchtime, and winter Sun evening

Recommended by Gwyn and Anne Wake, Mrs Joanna Jensen, D P and M A Miles, Roger and Pauline Pearce, Dr and Mrs Michael Smith, Amanda De Montjoie, John Saul

BERWICK ST JOHN   ST9422   MAP 2

Talbot

Village signposted from A30 E of Shaftesbury; SP7 0HA

Unspoilt and friendly pub in pretty village, with simple furnishings and tasty, reasonably priced food

Surrounded by thatched old houses, this nicely traditional Ebble Valley pub has a characterful, heavily beamed bar. It's simply furnished with cushioned solid wall and window seats, spindleback chairs, a high-backed built-in settle at one end, and a huge inglenook fireplace with a good iron fireback and bread ovens (much enjoyed by readers visiting in the winter). Bass, Ringwood Best, Wadworths 6X and a guest such as Keystone Large One on handpump; darts and cribbage. There are seats outside. More reports please.

🍽 **Good, reasonably priced bar food at lunchtime includes home-made soup, sandwiches, filled baguettes, and ploughman's, along with sausage and mash with onion gravy, salmon and broccoli mornay, vegetable pasta stir fry, and specials like chicken breast in a cider and spinach cream sauce, or red mullet fillets with parsnip mash drizzled with honey cream; Sunday roasts.** *Starters/Snacks: £4.50 to £6.00. Main Courses: £6.50 to £13.50. Puddings: £3.50 to £4.00*

Free house ~ Licensees Pete and Marilyn Hawkins ~ Real ale ~ Bar food (not Sun evening) ~ (01747) 828222 ~ Children in eating area of bar ~ Dogs allowed in bar ~ Open 12-2.30, 6.30-11; 12-4 Sun; closed Sun evening, all day Mon

Recommended by D and J Ashdown

BOX   ST8369   MAP 2

Quarrymans Arms

Box Hill; coming from Bath on A4 turn right into Bargates 50 yards before railway bridge, then at T junction turn left up Quarry Hill, turning left again near the top at grassy triangle; from Corsham, turn left after Rudloe Park Hotel into Beech Road, then third left on to Barnetts Hill, and finally right at the top of the hill; OS Sheet 173 map reference 834694; SN13 8HN

Cheerful and unpretentious, with great views, welcoming atmosphere, and good value food

Once the local of the Bath stone miners, this very friendly and easy-going place boasts beautiful sweeping views from the big windows of its dining room. The welcoming licensees run interesting guided trips down the mine itself, and there are plenty of mining-related photographs and memorabilia dotted around the interior. It's atmospheric and comfortable rather than overly smart (some parts have an air of mild untidiness), and one modernised room with an open fire is entirely set aside for drinking, with well kept Butcombe Best, Moles Best, Wadworths 6X and one or two local guests like Cheddar Potholer on handpump, as well as good wines and up to 60 malt whiskies. The pub is ideally placed for cavers, potholers and walkers; piped music, games machine and board games. An attractive outside terrace has picnic-sets; boules.

🍽 **Good value and cheerfully served, home-made bar food includes sandwiches, soup, macaroni cheese, ham, egg and chips, moules marinière, spaghetti carbonara, a popular steak and ale pie, daily specials such as liver and bacon, and a delicious bread and butter pudding.** *Starters/Snacks: £2.95 to £6.50. Main Courses: £4.95 to £16.00. Puddings: £2.50 to £5.00*

Free house ~ Licensees John and Ginny Arundel ~ Real ale ~ Bar food (11-3, 6-10 (but you must make bookings after 9pm)) ~ Restaurant ~ (01225) 743569 ~ Children welcome ~ Dogs

allowed in bar ~ Open 11-3, 6-12 Mon-Thurs; 11-midnight Fri, Sat and Sun ~ Bedrooms:
£25(£35S)(£35B)/£50(£65S)(£65B)

Recommended by Dr and Mrs M E Wilson, Clare Rosier, Amanda De Montjoie, Colin and Peggy Wilshire, Dr and Mrs A K Clarke, Gene and Kitty Rankin, Richard and Judy Winn, Jeff Davies, Guy Vowles

BRADFORD-ON-AVON
ST8261 MAP 2

Dandy Lion
35 Market Street; BA15 1LL

Lightly refurbished town centre pub with wide range of food – some served in choice of sizes

Refurbished under its newish licensees, and now open all day, this town pub has something of the feel of a continental café-bar rather than a typical local. Big windows on either side of the door look out on to the street, each with a table and cushioned wooden armchair, while further in, the pleasantly relaxed long main bar has nice high-backed farmhouse chairs, old-fashioned dining chairs, a long brocade-cushioned settle on the stripped wooden floor, a couple of rugs, and sentimental pictures on the panelled walls. Up a few steps at the back, a snug little bare-boarded room has a lovely high-backed settle and other small ones around sturdy tables, and a big mirror on a mulberry wall. The upstairs restaurant is candlelit at night. Butcombe Bitter, Wadworths IPA, 6X and seasonal beers on handpump, a dozen wines by the glass, and good coffees. More reports on the new regime, please.

🍽 **A broad choice of food (available all day at weekends) includes plenty of sandwiches, flatbreads and salads, crab cakes, grilled goats cheese and red onion marmalade on bruschetta with balsamic glaze, ham, egg and chips, steaks (served in small or large helpings), poached chicken supreme on bubble and squeak with bacon and leek sauce, slow-roasted duck leg with spiced plum sauce and dauphinoise potatoes, and puddings like chocolate and orange brioche pudding or apple custard and honey tart.**
Starters/Snacks: £4.25 to £7.95. Main Courses: £4.50 to £13.95. Puddings: £3.95 to £4.95

Wadworths ~ Real ale ~ Bar food (12-9.30(8.30 Sun)) ~ Restaurant ~ (01225) 863433 ~ Children allowed but away from bar ~ Open 10.30-11; 11.30-11 Sun

Recommended by Simon Collett-Jones, Douglas and Ann Hare

BREMHILL
ST9772 MAP 2

Dumb Post
Off A4/A3102 just NW of Calne; Hazeland, just SW of village itself, OS Sheet 173 map reference 976727; SN11 9LJ

Quirky and unspoilt, a proper country local with no frills, but lots of genuine character

Hidden amidst good walking country, this isn't for those with fussier tastes, but is run by and for people who like their pubs unpretentious and brimming with character. The main lounge is a glorious mix of mismatched, faded furnishings, vivid patterned wallpaper, and stuffed animal heads, its two big windows boasting an unexpectedly fine view down over the surrounding countryside. Not huge (it has a half dozen or so tables), it has something of the air of a once-grand but now rather faded hunting lodge. There's a big woodburner in a brick fireplace (not always lit), a log fire on the opposite side of the room, comfortably-worn armchairs and plush banquettes, a standard lamp, mugs, bread and a sombrero hanging from the beams, and a scaled-down model house between the windows; in a cage is an occasionally vocal parrot, Oscar. The narrow bar leading to the lounge is more dimly lit, but has a few more tables, exposed stonework, and quite a collection of toby jugs around the counter; there's a plainer third room with a pool table, darts, games machine, and piped music. Archers Best, Wadworths 6X and a guest on handpump; friendly service. There are a couple of picnic-sets outside, and some wooden play equipment. Note the limited lunchtime opening times.

🍽 **Bar food (served lunchtimes only) is simple, hearty and well liked by locals: toasted sandwich, sausage, egg and chips, ploughman's, steak and kidney pudding, and fish and chips; Sunday roasts.** *Starters/Snacks: £2.00 to £4.00. Main Courses: £4.00 to £6.50*

Free house ~ Licensee Mr Pitt ~ Real ale ~ Bar food (12-2) ~ No credit cards ~ (01249) 813192 ~ Children in eating area of bar ~ Dogs allowed in bar ~ Open 12-2 (not Mon-Thurs), 7-11 (12 Sat); 12-3, 7-11 Sun; closed Mon-Thurs lunchtimes

Recommended by Kevin Thorpe, Phil and Sally Gorton, Guy Vowles, JJW, CMW

BRINKWORTH   SU0184   MAP 2

Three Crowns ♀

The Street; B4042 Wootton Bassett—Malmesbury; SN15 5AF

Excellent (if sometimes pricy) food deservedly takes centre stage here, but this is still a pub, with five good beers and a carefully chosen wine list

The impressive food is the main draw here – it's not exactly cheap, particularly in the evenings, but can be ideal for a memorable treat. And it's the sort of place where you'll still be made welcome if all you want is a drink: they have Camerons Castle Eden Bitter, Fullers London Pride, Wadworths 6X and two guests like Archers Best and Greene King IPA on handpump, a carefully chosen wine list with 25 by the glass, around 20 malt whiskies, and home-grown apple juice. The bar part of the building is the most traditional, with big landscape prints and other pictures, some horsebrasses on dark beams, a log fire, a dresser with a collection of old bottles, big tapestry-upholstered pews, a stripped deal table, and a couple more made from gigantic forge bellows. Sensibly placed darts, shove-ha'penny, dominoes, cribbage, board games, games machine, and piped music. Most people choose to eat in the conservatory or the light and airy garden room. There's a refurbished terrace with outdoor heating to the side of the conservatory. The garden stretches around the side and back, with well spaced tables and a climbing frame, and looks over a side lane to the church, and out over rolling prosperous farmland. There's a smoking shelter.

🍽 **Changing every day, the elaborate menu covers an entire wall; at lunchtimes, as well as filled rolls, baked potatoes, and ploughman's, they might have crispy belly pork with fresh sage mash and onion gravy, home-made curry, and seafood pancake, while the main (and more expensive) menu has things like veal and mushroom or lamb and mint pie, wild boar with a shallot, stilton and sun-dried apricot sauce, baked local veal filled with seven-pepper cheese on a bed of thyme mash, slices of salmon and monkfish with scampi, prawns and mussels in a white wine and cream sauce, various steaks, and home-made puddings like chocolate and toffee sponge or white chocolate and raspberry brûlée.** *Starters/Snacks: £4.95 to £7.95. Main Courses: £8.95 to £19.95. Puddings: up to £6.45*

Enterprise ~ Lease Anthony Windle ~ Real ale ~ Bar food (12-2(3 Sun), 6-9.30 (8.30 Sun); not 25 or 26 Dec) ~ Restaurant ~ (01666) 510366 ~ Well behaved children in eating area; after 6pm by prior arrangement only ~ Dogs allowed in bar ~ Open 11-3, 6-11; 11-4, 6-12 Sat; 12-4, 6-10.30 Sun; closed 25 and 26 Dec

Recommended by Andrew Shore, Maria Williams, Dr and Mrs A K Clarke, John Baish, Tom and Ruth Rees, Richard and Sheila Fitton, June and Peter Shamash

CASTLE COMBE   ST8477   MAP 2

Castle Inn ♀ 🛏

Off A420; SN14 7HN

Appealing very well run combination of friendly all-day pubby bar and stylish small hotel, in perhaps the most lovely English village

The beamed bar has all the things you might expect in this timeless village – some stripped stone, a big inglenook log fire, comfortably padded bar stools as well as a handsome old oak settle and other good seats around the sturdy tables, hunting and vintage motor racing pictures, and the easy-going relaxed atmosphere generated by the exemplary landlord and his friendly and obliging staff. They have a fine collection of spirits and good wines (and ports) by the glass as well as Butcombe and Shepherd Neame Spitfire on handpump, and do good coffees. On either side are two snug old-world sitting rooms with comfortable settees and easy chairs, and besides the smart and attractive high-ceilinged formal dining room there is a big light-hearted upstairs eating room with a very effective sunblind system for its conservatory-style roof. This opens on to a charming small roof terrace with good cast-iron furniture, and there are more tables out in front, looking down this idyllic village street. The medieval church clock is fascinating. Very limited parking (if you're staying and have mobility problems they do try to help).

🍴 They do cream teas as well as a good choice of sensible bar food from soup, baguettes and ploughman's to tempura king prawns, ham and egg, sausage and mash, marinated chicken kebabs and steak and kidney pie with proper shortcrust pastry. The nicely served restaurant food is enjoyable, too (the slow-roasted lamb shank with a red wine sauce and spring onion mash is a favourite), and breakfasts are excellent. *Starters/Snacks: £3.95 to £9.95. Main Courses: £10.95 to £17.95. Puddings: £4.95 to £5.50*

Free house ~ Licensees Ann and Bill Cross ~ Real ale ~ Bar food (11.30-3, 6-9.30 (9 Sun, 10 Sat)) ~ Restaurant ~ (01249) 783030 ~ Children welcome ~ Dogs allowed in bar ~ Open 9.30am-11pm; closed 25 Dec ~ Bedrooms: £65S(£85B)/£110S(£110B)

Recommended by Mrs Ann Gray, J Roy Smylie, Ian Phillips, Cathy Robinson, Ed Coombe

CHICKSGROVE   ST9729   MAP 2

Compasses ★ 🍴 ♟ 🛏

From A30 5½ miles W of B3089 junction, take lane on N side signposted Sutton Mandeville, Sutton Row, then first left fork (small signs point the way to the pub, in Lower Chicksgrove; look out for the car park); SP3 6NB

WILTSHIRE DINING PUB OF THE YEAR

Delightfully unchanging ancient thatched house with top-notch innovative food, genuine welcome, and splendid bedrooms – an excellent all-rounder

'A cracking pub,' says one reader this year, and who could disagree? It manages to exceed the expectations raised by the beautiful exterior, and stands out for its warm welcome, excellent food, and sparkling bedrooms, all refurbished this year. The bar has old bottles and jugs hanging from beams above the roughly timbered counter, farm tools and traps on the partly stripped stone walls, and high-backed wooden settles forming snug booths around tables on the mainly flagstoned floor. Bass, Chicksgrove Churl (brewed for the pub by Wadworths), Wadworths 6X and a guest like Hidden Potential on handpump, several wines by the glass, and nine malt whiskies. The landlord and his family are very friendly, and they're happy to see children and dogs too. The quiet garden, terraces and flagstoned farm courtyard are very pleasant places to sit, and this really is a smashing place to stay, with lovely surrounding walks and plenty to do in the area.

🍴 Super bar food might include lunchtime filled loaves and ploughman's, scallops on a crab risotto with saffron sauce, duck, pheasant and pigeon terrine with port and onion chutney, slow-roasted shoulder of lamb with red wine and mint jus, goose breast on roasted baby vegetables with grape compote, roasted vegetable wellington, brill fillet with scallops and chive sauce, and puddings such as cranberry and lime panna cotta or pecan and treacle pie with clotted cream. *Starters/Snacks: £5.00 to £7.00. Main Courses: £8.00 to £18.00. Puddings: £4.50 to £6.00*

Free house ~ Licensee Alan Stoneham ~ Real ale ~ Bar food (not Sun evenings or Mon exc bank hols) ~ (01722) 714318 ~ Children welcome ~ Dogs welcome ~ Open 12-3, 6-11; 12-3, 7-10.30 Sun; closed 25 and 26 Dec ~ Bedrooms: £65S(£65B)/£85S(£90B)

Recommended by Mike Dean, Lis Wingate Gray, Bill and Jessica Ritson, Helen and Brian Edgeley, Andrew Hollingshead, Mr and Mrs Draper, Bob and Margaret Holder, Richard May, Mrs J H S Lang, Tony and Jill Radnor, Nick Lawless, Mr and Mrs A J Hudson, Frogeye, John Robertson, Ingrid Baxter, Mike and Linda Hudson, Andy and Claire Barker, Colin and Janet Roe

---

Our website www.goodguides.co.uk now includes a click-through to a little map for each pub.

CORSHAM   ST8770 MAP 2

Flemish Weaver
High Street; SN13 0EZ

Smart but friendly pub in heart of town, with emphasis on locally sourced food, and a nicely laid-back atmosphere

Opposite Corsham Court, this attractive and civilised mellow-stone pub was built in the early 17th c to house drovers in the wool trade. It's been sensitively modernised, but the three main areas – mostly set for eating – still have many original features, as well as patterned blue banquettes and matching chairs on slate floors, flowers on the tables, and tealights in the fireplaces; old black and white photographs on the walls. The three or four weekly changing beers might include some from the Bath Brewery and Hopback GFB on handpump or tapped from the cask, and they also do Thatcher's cider, several malt whiskies, eight wines by the glass from a carefully chosen list, and various organic juices; piped music. Service is friendly – but may slow down at busy times. They have a parsons terrier and a doberman. There are tables in the back courtyard.

🍽 **Relying on local produce and organic or free-range meat, the well liked bar food includes lunchtime baguettes, soup, salads and ploughman's, grilled mackerel fillets with gooseberry sauce, cauliflower and broccoli cheese bake, wild boar slow cooked in cider with prunes and pears, pheasant breast with bacon and leeks cooked in cider, plaice with chestnut mushrooms and a parmesan crust, and puddings like blackberry and almond tart or blueberry and white chocolate cheesecake.** *Starters/Snacks: £3.95 to £5.25. Main Courses: £8.50 to £15.50. Puddings: £4.50*

Enterprise ~ Lease Nathalie Bellamy and Jeremy Edwards ~ Real ale ~ Bar food (12-2.30 (3 Sun), 7-9.30; not Sun evening) ~ Restaurant ~ (01249) 701929 ~ Children welcome away from bar ~ Dogs allowed in bar ~ Open 10.30-3, 5.30-11; 12-3, 7-10.30 Sun

Recommended by Jean and Douglas Troup, Mr and Mrs P R Thomas, Michael Doswell, D P and M A Miles, Paul A Moore

Two Pigs 🍺
A4, Pickwick; SN13 0HY

Wonderfully eccentric pub for fans of beer and music, open evenings only, and at its best on Monday nights

One of those delightfully unusual places that you can't help thinking is more of a hobby than a business, this friendly little beer lover's pub is at its liveliest on Monday nights, when live blues draws a big crowd into the narrow and dimly lit flagstoned bar. The cheerfully eccentric feel owes much to the individualistic landlord, and there's a zany collection of bric-a-brac including enamel advertising signs on the wood-clad walls, pig-theme ornaments, and old radios. A good mix of customers gathers around the long dark wood tables and benches, and friendly staff serve well kept Hop Back Summer Lightning and Stonehenge Pigswill, along with a couple of changing guests such as Butcomb Blond and Cotswold Spring Codger; piped blues. A covered yard outside is called the Sty. Beware of their opening times – the pub is closed every lunchtime, except on Sunday; no food (except crisps) or under-21s.

🍽 **No food.**

Free house ~ Licensees Dickie and Ann Doyle ~ Real ale ~ No credit cards ~ (01249) 712515 ~ Live blues/rock Mon evening ~ Open 7-11; 12-2.30, 7-10.30 Sun

Recommended by Catherine Pitt, Dr and Mrs A K Clarke, Kevin Thorpe

---

Real ale may be served from handpumps, electric pumps (not just the on-off switches used for keg beer) or – common in Scotland – tall taps called founts (pronounced 'fonts') where a separate pump pushes the beer up under air pressure.

CROCKERTON   ST8642   MAP 2

Bath Arms

Just off A350 Warminster—Blandford; BA12 8AJ

Excellent food cooked by chef/landlord at attractively modernised dining pub, with pretty gardens, relaxed atmosphere, and two very stylish bedrooms

The landlord of this attractive old dining pub has quite a catering pedigree, but while the food and service are definitely, as one reader puts it, 'a cut above', he runs the place very much as a pub, not a restaurant. The building is very appealing from outside with plenty of picnic-sets in various garden areas. Inside, it's warmly welcoming with a thriving informal atmosphere, lots of well spaced tables on the parquet floor in the long, stylishly modernised two-roomed bar, beams in the whitewashed ceiling, and brasses. There's a restaurant at one end and a log fire in a stone fireplace at the other. Sharps Cornish Coaster, Wessex Crockerton Classic, and a couple of guest beers on handpump and quite a few wines by the glass; piped music. We've yet to hear from anyone who's stayed in the two splendidly stylish bedrooms, but imagine they would merit one of our stay awards – they're what you might expect to find in a chic boutique hotel rather than a country pub. Longleat is very close by.

🍴 **Cooked by the landlord using local produce, the good, attractively presented food might include baguettes, creamed onion soup with herb croûtons, duck sausage with pine nut and apple salad, eggs benedict, fillet of cod with saffron, fennel and red pepper, loin of pork chop with black pudding and parsnip purée, sticky beef with braised red cabbage, courgette and ruby chard gnocchi, and puddings like pecan tart or raspberry trifle; good children's menu.** *Starters/Snacks: £4.00 to £6.95. Main Courses: £9.95 to £15.95. Puddings: £4.50 to £5.95*

Wellington ~ Lease Dean Carr ~ Real ale ~ Bar food (12-2, 6.30-9) ~ Restaurant ~ (01985) 212262 ~ Children in restaurant ~ Dogs allowed in bar ~ Open 11-11; 11-11 Sat; 12-10.30 Sun ~ Bedrooms: /£75S

Recommended by J Stickland, Ian Phillips, Richard Fendick, Bob Monger, Edward Mirzoeff, Dr and Mrs J Temporal

DEVIZES   SU0061   MAP 2

Bear ♀ ◧

Market Place; SN10 1HS

Comfortable and individual coaching inn, with plenty of history, beers fresh from the local brewery, pleasant terrace, and unpretentious food

Guests as diverse as George II and Dr Johnson have stayed at this pleasant old coaching inn, a stone's throw from Wadworth's brewery. It's a properly characterful place, dating from 1559, and though it's been sympathetically upgraded over the years, there are plenty of reminders of its past. The big main carpeted bar has log fires, black winged wall settles and muted cloth-upholstered bucket armchairs around oak tripod tables; the classic bar counter has shiny black woodwork and small panes of glass. Separated from here by some steps, a room named after the portrait painter Thomas Lawrence (his father ran the establishment in the 1770s) has dark oak-panelled walls, a parquet floor, a big open fireplace, shining copper pans, and plates around the walls. Well kept Wadworths IPA, 6X and a seasonal guest on handpump, as well as a good choice of wines (including 16 by the glass), and quite a few malt whiskies. A mediterranean-style courtyard with olive trees, hibiscus and bougainvillea has some outside tables. One reader was impressed to find baby-changing facilities in the gents'. The brewery is just 150 yards away – you can buy beer in splendid old-fashioned half-gallon earthenware jars.

🍴 **Decent, straightforward bar food includes sandwiches and baguettes, soup, ham and egg, ploughman's, all-day breakfast, beer-battered fish, and warm chicken breast with mexican salad; children's menu. There are buffet meals in the Lawrence Room (you can eat these in the bar too), and they do pizzas Thurs-Sat evenings.** *Starters/Snacks: £3.25 to £5.50. Main Courses: £5.00 to £13.00. Puddings: £2.95 to £4.75*

Wadworths ~ Tenants Andrew and Angela Maclachlan ~ Real ale ~ Bar food (12.30-2.30, 7-9.30 Mon-Sat; 12-2, 7-8.45 Sun) ~ Restaurant ~ (01380) 722444 ~ Children welcome ~ Dogs allowed in bar ~ Live jazz/blues Fri and Sat in cellar bar ~ Open 9.30am-11pm; 10.30-10.30 Sun; closed 25 and 26 Dec ~ Bedrooms: £75S/£100B

Recommended by Dr and Mrs A K Clarke, Mike and Lynn Robinson, the Didler, Bill and Jessica Ritson, Blaise Vyner, Ann and Colin Hunt

DONHEAD ST ANDREW ST9124 MAP 2

Forester ♀

Village signposted off A30 E of Shaftesbury, just E of Ludwell; Lower Street; SP7 9EE

Attractive old thatched pub in charming village, good food – especially fish – and fine views from very pleasant big terrace

Under new management since our last edition, this 14th-c thatched pub is in a charming village, and has fine country views from a good-sized terrace with plenty of seats. Inside, the appealing bar has a welcoming atmosphere, stripped tables on wooden floors, a log fire in its big inglenook fireplace, and usually a few locals chatting around the servery: Butcombe, Ringwood Best, and a guest like Keystone Large One on handpump, and 18 wines (including champagne) by the glass. The comfortable main dining room has country-kitchen tables in varying sizes, nicely laid out with linen napkins, and attractive wrought-iron candlesticks – they sell these, if you like the design; there's also a second smaller and cosier dining room. No machines or piped music. Good walks nearby, for example to the old and 'new' Wardour castles. The neighbouring cottage used to be the pub's coach house. More reports on the new regime please.

Ⅲ **The changing menu has quite an emphasis on good, fresh fish from Cornwall – shellfish soup, salt and pepper squid, pan-seared scallops with garlic and hazelnut butter and pancetta, crab and chilli omelette, and an italian fish stew; they also do sandwiches, and things like chicken liver and foie gras parfait, poached ox tongue with creamed spinach, parsley potatoes and madeira jus, puddings such as blackcurrant délice with spiced plums, and some good local cheeses.** *Starters/Snacks: £4.00 to £9.00. Main Courses: £8.00 to £19.00. Puddings: £4.00 to £7.00*

Free house ~ Licensee Chris Matthew ~ Real ale ~ Bar food ~ Restaurant ~ (01747) 828038 ~ Children welcome ~ Dogs allowed in bar ~ Open 12-3, 6.30-11.30; closed winter Sun evening

Recommended by Keith and Jean Symons, John Robertson, Roger White, Sue Demont, Tim Barrow, Dennis and Gill Keen, J D O Carter, Paul Goldman, Michael Doswell, Liz and Tony Colman, Mrs J H S Lang

EAST KNOYLE ST8731 MAP 2

Fox & Hounds ♀

Village signposted off A350 S of A303; The Green (named on some road atlases), a mile NW at OS Sheet 183 map reference 872313; or follow signpost off B3089, about ½ E of A303 junction near Little Chef; SP3 6BN

Beautiful thatched village pub with splendid views, warmly welcoming service, good beers, and excellent food cooked by the landlord

Some readers are delighted this lovely, well run place is now signed from the main road, as the narrow lanes that lead to it can be a little confusing. It's well worth the effort though – tables facing the green in front of the ancient thatched building boast remarkable views right over into Somerset and Dorset. Inside there's the warmly welcoming feel of a proper long-established pub (rather than a more formal pub/restaurant), and the New Zealand licensees are particularly friendly. Around the central horseshoe-shaped servery are three linked areas on different levels, with big log fires, plentiful oak woodwork and flagstones, comfortably padded dining chairs around big scrubbed tables with vases of flowers, and a couple of leather settees; the furnishings are all very individual and uncluttered. There's a small light-painted conservatory restaurant. Service is prompt, smiling and helpful, and they have four real ales such as Butcombe, Hidden Potential, Keystone Large One, and Wessex Merrie Mink on handpump; also, farm cider, and a good choice of wines by the glass, quite a few from New Zealand. The nearby woods are good for a stroll.

🍴 **The landlord's often imaginative cooking is a big draw here: clay oven pizzas (not Sun lunch), lunchtime ploughman's and ciabatta melts (not Sun), steamed steak and kidney pudding, specials like mussels in a red thai curry sauce, pork rillettes with onion marmalade and pickles on toasted brioche, halibut on braised baby leeks and olives, lamb shank braised in red wine, and caramelised onion and leek tart, and puddings like apple and caramel pancake or pavlova with passion fruit coulis; children's menu.** *Starters/Snacks: £4.00 to £8.50. Main Courses: £8.50 to £16.00. Puddings: £4.75*

Free house ~ Licensees Murray and Pam Seator ~ Real ale ~ Bar food (12-2.30, 6-9) ~ (01747) 830573 ~ Well-behaved children welcome ~ Dogs welcome ~ Open 12-3, 6-11 (10.30 Sun); closed 25 Dec

Recommended by Dr and Mrs M E Wilson, W W Burke, David Stranack, Nick and Elaine Cadogan, Edward Mirzoeff, J Philip Geary, Roy Hoing

Seymour Arms

The Street; just off A350 S of Warminster; SP3 6AJ

Neatly kept and friendly, quite handy for A303, with reasonably priced, well liked food, rambling seating areas, real ales, and garden; bedrooms

Run by enthusiastic, hard-working and friendly licensees, this creeper-covered stone-built pub is a popular place for a drink or meal. The rambling L-shaped bar is attractively divided into separate snug seating areas though perhaps the cosiest beamed part is where there's a high-backed settle by the log fire, and a built-in window settle and farmhouse chairs by a nice little table; some brass bits and bobs dotted about, Wadworths IPA, 6X and JCB on handpump, and several wines by the glass. There are tables in the garden. Sir Christopher Wren was born in the village in 1632 – his father was rector of the church. The bedrooms are said to be good.

🍴 **Cooked by the landlord, the wide choice of good value food at lunchtime includes sandwiches, soup, garlic mushrooms, home-baked ham and egg, mushroom stroganoff, steak and mushroom in Guinness pie, beer-battered cod, and cajun chicken; evening choices such as duck and fig terrine with cumberland sauce, scallops with a raspberry and ginger dressing, halibut steak in lime and basil butter sauce, veal with wild mushrooms in a creamy marsala sauce and peppered tagliatelle, and chicken breast with red peppers in a creamy whisky sauce.** *Starters/Snacks: £3.50 to £5.95. Main Courses: £6.50 to £15.95*

Wadworths ~ Tenants Bruno and Terena Burgess ~ Real ale ~ Bar food (not Sun evening) ~ (01747) 830374 ~ Children welcome ~ Dogs allowed in bar ~ Open 12-3, 7-11; closed Mon ~ Bedrooms: £30S/£50S

Recommended by Mrs J Cooper, Roger and Pauline Pearce, Chris and Ann Coy, David Sizer

EBBESBOURNE WAKE

ST9924 MAP 2

Horseshoe ★

On A354 S of Salisbury, right at signpost at Coombe Bissett; village is around 8 miles further on; SP5 5JF

Restful, unspoilt country pub with a good welcome, beers tapped from the cask, popular home-made food, and views from pretty garden

Tucked away in fine downland, this enduring favourite is a charmingly unspoilt old country pub, very comfortable and particularly welcoming. The neatly kept bar has fresh home-grown flowers on the tables, lanterns, a large collection of farm tools and other bric-a-brac crowded along its beams, and an open fire; a conservatory extension seats ten people. Five real ales such as Goddards Bitter, Keystone Large One, Otter Best and Ringwood Best and Old Thumper are tapped from the cask, and they also do farm cider, and several malt whiskies. Booking is advisable for the small restaurant, especially at weekends when it can fill quite quickly. There are pleasant views over the steep sleepy valley of the River Ebble from seats in its pretty little garden, two goats in a paddock at the bottom of the garden, and two jack russells; good nearby walks. Morris dancers may call some evenings in summer.

🍴 **Well liked bar food includes lunchtime sausages, ploughman's, ham and eggs, watercress and mushroom lasagne, venison and mushroom pie, half a roast duck with a choice of sauces, and home-made puddings like treacle tart.** *Starters/Snacks: £4.50 to £6.95. Main Courses: £8.25 to £15.00. Puddings: £3.95 to £4.25*

Free house ~ Licensees Tony and Pat Bath ~ Real ale ~ Bar food (not Sun evening or Mon) ~ Restaurant ~ (01722) 780474 ~ Children welcome but not in main bar ~ Open 12-3, 6.30-11; 12-4 Sun; closed Sun evening and Mon lunchtime; all day 26 Dec ~ Bedrooms: /£70S(£70B)

Recommended by Noel Grundy, John Robertson, Mike and Linda Hudson, Douglas and Ann Hare, the Didler, Mr and Mrs Draper, Sue Demont, Tim Barrow, Pat and Robert Watt

FONTHILL GIFFORD   ST9231 MAP 2

Beckford Arms

Off B3089 W of Wilton at Fonthill Bishop; SP3 6PX

Civilised 18th-c country inn with smartly informal feel, and good food, especially in the evening

Its garden recently attractively landscaped (and with a new boules pitch added), this civilised country house is on the edge of a fine parkland estate with a lake and sweeping vistas. The rooms are smartly informal, big, light and airy, with stripped bare wood, a parquet floor and a pleasant mix of chunky tables with church candles. In winter, a big log fire burns in the lounge bar, which leads into a light garden room with a high pitched plank ceiling and picture windows looking on to a terrace. Locals tend to gather in the straightforward games room: darts, games machine, pool, board games, and piped music. They always have a couple of beers from the local Hidden and Keystone breweries, and one or two guests like Fullers London Pride or Greene King Abbot; also several wines by the glass. Though dogs are welcome, they should be on a lead. As we went to press they were adding more bedrooms – and planning a timely upgrade for the older ones. Service is generally warmly welcoming – though was less so for one reader who queried an unusually long wait for his family's food.

🍴 **Good, interesting food, using mostly organic meat, such as lunchtime home-cooked ham, egg and chips, and home-made burgers and sausages, and evening dishes like home-cured gravadlax, seared scallops with celeriac remoulade, a roasted aubergine, courgette and pepper bake with brie, stilton and parmesan, oven-roasted lamb rump on a bed of spring onion mash with home-made redcurrant jus, slow-roasted pork belly with braised red cabbage and baby sweetcorn, fish specials like bass with fennel confit and cherry tomato salad, and puddings such as home-made chocolate brownie.** *Starters/Snacks: £4.95 to £7.00. Main Courses: £8.00 to £17.50. Puddings: £5.50 to £5.95*

Free house ~ Licensee Alan Swann ~ Real ale ~ Bar food (not 25 Dec or 1 Jan) ~ (01747) 870385 ~ Well behaved children welcome ~ Dogs welcome ~ Open 12-11; 12-10.30 Sun; closed 25 Dec, evening 1 Jan ~ Bedrooms: £50S/£90B

Recommended by Pat and Robert Watt, Mr Walker, Peter Preston, Andy and Claire Barker, Dr and Mrs M E Wilson, MDN, Colin and Janet Roe

GREAT BEDWYN   SU2764 MAP 2

Three Tuns

Village signposted off A338 S of Hungerford, or off A4 W of Hungerford via Little Bedwyn; High Street; SN8 3NU

Thriving village pub with very good food, obliging hard-working staff, and eclectic décor

Packed at weekends, when it's a good idea to book, this cheery place has a genuinely pubby atmosphere despite the emphasis on good food, and you won't feel out of place if you just want a pint. Run by friendly, hard-working licensees (whose lovely dogs can be much in evidence), it has a traditional décor which is lifted out of the ordinary by some quirky touches, such as life-size models of the Blues Brothers at separate tables in the beamed, bare-boards front bar, and a similarly incongruous female mannequin in the back restaurant. Almost every inch of the walls and ceiling is covered by either the usual brasses, jugs, hops and agricultural implements, or more unusual collections such as ribbons from ships' hats, showbiz photos, and yellowing cuttings about the royal family, all of which reflect stages of the landlord's career. There's a profusion of chalked-up quotes and pithy comments, as well as an inglenook fireplace, and lighted candles in the evenings. Black Sheep, Flowers IPA, Fullers London Pride and Wadworths 6X on handpump (the cellar was once the village morgue), ten wines by the glass, 40 malt whiskies, and a good bloody mary; helpful service, piped music, and board games. The whitewashed building has quite a few plants in front, and a raised garden behind (with a heated smoking area). On Sunday lunchtimes, locals gather for the weekly meat raffle.

🍽 **Enjoyable bar food includes home-made soup, pan-fried scallops with chorizo and bacon, goats cheese salad with roasted peppers and balsamic, honey and walnut dressing, chicken, ham and leek pie, vegetable stew with pearl barley and dumpling, oxtail braised with tomatoes, onions, beer and celery, fillet of black bream with beansprout salad and ginger, lime and coconut sauce, and puddings; good Sunday roasts (with duck fat roasted maris pipers), and they also do a take-away menu.** *Starters/Snacks: £3.95 to £9.95. Main Courses: £7.95 to £15.95. Puddings: £3.95 to £4.95*

Punch ~ Lease Alan and Janet Carr ~ Real ale ~ Bar food (not Sun evening) ~ Restaurant ~ (01672) 870280 ~ Well behaved children welcome fom bar servery ~ Dogs allowed in bar ~ Open 11.30-3, 6-11; 12-6 Sun; closed Sun evening

Recommended by Mary Rayner, Geoff and Sylvia Donald, Mark Farrington

GREAT HINTON   ST9059   MAP 2

Linnet 🍽

3½ miles E of Trowbridge, village signposted off A361 opposite Lamb at Semington; BA14 6BU

Attractive dining pub, very much a place to come for a good meal rather than just a drink, with everything on the menu home made; worth booking in advance

All the food at this pretty brick pub is home made, from the bread, through the sausages, to the ice-cream. It's become perhaps a little restauranty in some ways, and such is its reputation that to be sure of a table, you may have to book even a few weeks in advance. The bar to the right of the door has a cream carpet and lots of photographs of the pub and the brewery, and there are bookshelves in a snug end part. The restaurant is candlelit at night. Wadworths 6X on electric pump, around two dozen malt whiskies, and several wines by the glass; piped music. In summer, the flowering tubs and window boxes with seats dotted among them are quite a sight.

🍽 **Prepared to a high standard, and served by attentive staff, dishes include focaccia or salads (lunchtimes only), curried chicken and pork terrine with brioche and apple chutney, duck and artichoke risotto with truffle oil, smoked haddock kedgeree fishcakes with lemon horseradish cream, braised beef and kidney pie in mustard pastry with celeriac mash, their speciality baked tenderloin of pork filled with prunes and spinach wrapped in smoked bacon on a wild mushroom sauce, pan fried bass fillets with smoked salmon and cream cheese dumplings, and puddings like steamed stem ginger pudding with clotted cream or cherry bread and butter pudding. They do a good value three-course lunch for £14.25, with a nice choice.** *Starters/Snacks: £4.95 to £6.95. Main Courses: £13.95 to £19.95. Puddings: £4.50 to £6.95*

Wadworths ~ Tenant Jonathan Furby ~ Real ale ~ Bar food (not Mon) ~ Restaurant ~ (01380) 870354 ~ Children welcome ~ Dogs allowed in bar ~ Open 11-3, 6-11; 12-3.30, 7-10.30 Sun; closed Mon; 25 and 26 Dec, 1 Jan

Recommended by Mr and Mrs A Curry, Dennis and Gill Keen

If we know a pub does sandwiches we always say so – if they're not mentioned, you'll have to assume you can't get one.

GRITTLETON

ST8680 MAP 2

Neeld Arms ♀ ◀ 🛏

Off A350 NW of Chippenham; The Street; SN14 6AP

Good, chatty atmosphere in cheery beamed village pub, with friendly locals, popular food, and comfortable bedrooms

Readers enjoy the convivial, chatty atmosphere at this cheerful 17th-c black-beamed pub – it's not at all unusual to strike up a conversation with – or even be served by – one of the friendly locals. It's largely open plan, with some stripped stone, a log fire in the big inglenook on the right and a smaller coal-effect fire on the left, flowers on tables, and a pleasant mix of seating from windsor chairs through scatter-cushioned window seats to some nice arts and crafts chairs and a traditional settle. The parquet-floored back dining area has yet another inglenook, with a big woodburning stove; even back here, you still feel thoroughly part of the action. Wadworths IPA and 6X and guests like Box Steam Brewery Reverend Awdry or Cotswold Spring Codger on handpump from the substantial central bar counter, and a good choice of reasonably priced wines by the glass; piped music, board games, cribbage and dominoes. There's an outdoor terrace, with pergola. The golden retriever is called Soaky. The pleasant bedrooms have all been refurbished.

🍽 **Well liked bar food includes lunchtime ciabattas, soup, ploughman's, steak and kidney pie, goats cheese and roasted vegetable parcels, mixed grill, daily changing specials such as local venison steak with red cabbage and juniper berries, slow-cooked pork loin with apple and fennel, or baked lemon sole, Sunday roasts, and puddings like bakewell tart or banoffi pie.** *Starters/Snacks: £3.95 to £5.50. Main Courses: £7.50 to £16.95. Puddings: £4.25*

Free house ~ Licensees Charlie and Boo West ~ Real ale ~ Bar food ~ Restaurant ~ (01249) 782470 ~ Children welcome ~ Dogs welcome ~ Open 12-3(3.30 Sat), 5.30(5 Fri)-12; 12-3.30, 7-11 Sun ~ Bedrooms: £55S(£55B)/£75S(£75B)

Recommended by Richard Stancomb, Ian Phillips, Dr and Mrs A K Clarke, David Collison, K Turner, Michael Doswell, John and Bettye Reynolds, Peter and Audrey Dowsett

HINDON

ST9132 MAP 2

Lamb

B3089 Wilton—Mere; SP3 6DP

Attractive old building with lots of character in smart, roomy bar

In the heart of the village, with a window seat at one end overlooking the church, this civilised hotel has a big welcoming log fire in its very appealing long, roomy bar. The two flagstoned lower sections have a very long polished table with wall benches and chairs, blacksmith's tools set behind a big inglenook fireplace, and high-backed pews and settles; deep red walls add to the comfortable, relaxed feel. Up some steps a third, bigger area has lots more tables and chairs – though it can fill up fast and at busy times you may not be able to find a seat. From the polished dark wooden counter, attentive staff serve Wells & Youngs Bitter, Special and a seasonal brew, and maybe Hop Back Summer Lightning on handpump, and a good choice of wines by the glass; the extensive range of whiskies includes all the malts from the Isle of Islay, and they have a wide choice of havana cigars. There are picnic-sets across the road (which is a good alternative to the main routes west); parking is limited.

🍽 **Blackboards list the enjoyable bar food, which might include soup, baguettes, a huge ploughman's, beer-battered fish with minted peas, a pie of the day, smoked haddock with black pudding, Guinness and mustard seed dressing, free-range chicken wrapped in parma ham with a wild mushroom and herb risotto and salsa verde, 21-day matured local steaks, local game, and puddings such as iced chocolate parfait with white chocolate sauce; you may be able to get cream teas throughout the afternoon.** *Starters/Snacks: £4.50 to £9.00. Main Courses: £9.00 to £17.00. Puddings: £4.95 to £5.50*

We say if we know a pub has piped music.

Free house ~ Licensee Nick James ~ Real ale ~ Bar food (12-2.30, 6.30(7 Sun)-9.30(9 Sun)) ~ Restaurant ~ (01747) 820573 ~ Children welcome ~ Dogs allowed in bar and bedrooms ~ Open 11(12 Sun)-11 ~ Bedrooms: £70B/£99B

Recommended by Dr and Mrs M E Wilson, Mike Gorton, E V Lee, W W Burke, Bernard Stradling, Colin and Janet Roe, Chris Bell, Mrs J H S Lang, JCW

HORTON   SU0363   MAP 2

Bridge Inn ◀

Signposted off A361 Beckhampton road just inside the Devizes limit; Horton Road; SN10 2JS

Well run and distinctive canalside pub, with good traditional pub food, and pleasant garden with aviary

Reliable and well organised, this neatly kept canalside pub has a safely-fenced garden area with picnic-sets and an aviary, with two or three dozen white fantail doves. Inside, there are black and white photos of bargee families and their steam barges among other old photographs and country pictures on the red walls above a high panelled dado. In the carpeted area on the left all the sturdy pale pine tables are set for food, and there's a log fire at the front; the right of the bar is a pubbier bit with similar country-kitchen furniture on reconstituted flagstones, and some stripped brickwork. Helpful staff serve superbly kept Wadworths IPA, 6X and a seasonal ale straight from the cask, as well as eight decent wines by the glass. Disabled lavatories, piped music. In 1810, the building was extended to include a flour mill and bakery using flour transported along the Kennet & Avon Canal; the pub now has its own moorings. It's handy for walks on the downs.

🍴 **The wide range of enjoyable pub food includes staples such as filled rolls and baguettes, ploughman's, breaded garlic mushrooms, large battered cod, and ham, egg and chips (not Sundays), along with minted lamb pudding and cod and prawn crumble, and more interesting specials like home-made crab cakes, sausage, bacon and bean casserole with tagliatelle, and tenderloin of pork stuffed with prunes and wilted spinach in a mushroom and cream sauce.** *Starters/Snacks: £2.10 to £5.65. Main Courses: £7.50 to £14.55. Puddings: £1.95 to £4.25*

Wadworths ~ Tenants Sue Jacobs and Kevin Maul ~ Real ale ~ Bar food (12-2.15, 7-9.15) ~ Restaurant ~ (01380) 860273 ~ Children under parental guidance all the time and away from bar ~ Dogs allowed in bar ~ Open 11.30-3(2.30 in winter), 6.30-11; 12-3, 6.30-10.30 Sun

Recommended by David Barnes, Michael Doswell, Paul A Moore, Dr and Mrs M E Wilson, Sarah and Peter Gooderham, Sheila and Robert Robinson

KILMINGTON   ST7835   MAP 2

Red Lion £ 🛏

B3092 Mere—Frome, 2½ miles S of Maiden Bradley; 3 miles from A303 Mere turn-off; BA12 6RP

Atmospheric, down-to-earth country inn owned by the National Trust, with good value no-nonsense lunches, and attractive garden

Popular with both locals and visitors, this down-to-earth ivy-covered country inn is owned by the National Trust, and has a good convivial atmosphere in its snug low-ceilinged bar. Pleasant furnishings such as a curved high-backed settle and red leatherette wall and window seats on the flagstones, photographs of locals pinned up on the black beams, and a couple of big fireplaces (one with a fine old iron fireback) with log fires in winter. A newer big-windowed eating area is decorated with brasses, a large leather horse collar, and hanging plates. Darts, shove-ha'penny and board games. Well kept Butcombe, Butts Jester, and a guest on handpump, Thatcher's Cheddar Valley cider and several wines by the glass; helpful service. There are picnic-sets in the big attractive garden (look out for Kim the labrador). A gate gives on to the lane which leads to White Sheet Hill, where there is riding, hang gliding and radio-controlled gliders, and Stourhead

Gardens are only a mile away. Though dogs are generally welcome, they're not allowed during lunchtime. There's a smokers' shelter in a corner of the car park.

🍽 **Served only at lunchtime, the straightforward bar menu includes soup, sandwiches, ploughman's, pasties, several pies like steak and kidney, fish or game, meat or vegetable lasagne, apple strudel, and a couple of daily specials such as a good chicken casserole.** *Starters/Snacks: £1.50 to £2.50. Main Courses: £5.40 to £7.50. Puddings: £4.50*

Free house ~ Licensee Chris Gibbs ~ Real ale ~ Bar food (12-1.50; not 25 and 26 Dec, or 1 Jan) ~ No credit cards ~ (01985) 844263 ~ Children welcome in eating area of bar till 8.30pm ~ Dogs allowed in bar ~ Open 11.30-2.30, 6.30-11; 12-3, 7-11 Sun; closed evening 25 Dec

Recommended by Peter Titcomb, Gloria Bax, Geoff and Carol Thorp, Edward Mirzoeff, Jenny and Peter Lowater

LACOCK   ST9168   MAP 2

George
West Street; SN15 2LH

Perhaps Lacock's best – unspoilt and homely, with bags of character, efficient, friendly staff, and popular bar food; a good bet for families, with superior children's menu, and a play area in the appealing back garden

Very much enjoyed by readers, this cosy pub is one of the oldest buildings in a particularly lovely village, dating back to 1361. It gets very busy indeed, but the long-standing landlord and his staff remain cheerful and efficient, and even at its most crowded it's rare to have to wait too long for your food. The low-beamed bar has upright timbers in the place of knocked-through walls making cosy rambling corners, candles on close-set tables (even at lunchtime), armchairs and windsor chairs, seats in the stone-mullioned windows, and flagstones just by the counter; piped music. The treadwheel set into the outer breast of the original great central fireplace is a talking point – worked by a dog, it was used to turn a spit for roasting. Wadworths IPA and 6X on handpump. Outside, there are picnic-sets with umbrellas in the attractive back garden and a good children's play area. It's worth arriving early – or booking ahead.

🍽 **Popular bar food includes lunchtime sandwiches, baguettes and ploughman's, as well as soup, breaded cheese of the day, a good value daily pasta dish, chicken breast stuffed with brie and wrapped in bacon with a redcurrant and merlot sauce, spinach and blue cheese crumble, rack of lamb with redcurrant and mint sauce, salmon fillet with a pesto crust, and puddings such as bread and butter pudding or apple and raspberry crumble; better than average children's menu.** *Starters/Snacks: £3.75 to £4.95. Main Courses: £4.75 to £14.50. Puddings: £4.25 to £4.50*

Wadworths ~ Manager John Glass ~ Real ale ~ Bar food (12-2.15, 6-9.15) ~ Restaurant ~ (01249) 730263 ~ Children in eating area of bar ~ Open 9am(10 Sun)-11pm

Recommended by Paul and Shirley White, Donna and Roger, John and Joan Nash, Mr and Mrs A J Hudson, Dr and Mrs M E Wilson, Colin and Janet Roe, Tom and Ruth Rees, Phil and Sally Gorton, Michael Doswell, Keith and Sue Ward, Dr and Mrs Ewing, Rod and Chris Pring, Kevin Thorpe, Anne Morris, B J Harding, Alastair Stevenson, Shirley Sandilands, Andrew Shore, Maria Williams

Red Lion
High Street; village signposted off A350 S of Chippenham; SN15 2LQ

Nicely pubby Georgian inn, with interesting bar, cosy snug, and popular home-made casseroles and pies

Handy for Lacock Abbey and the Fox Talbot Museum, this imposing National-Trust-owned Georgian inn had new managers again this year. Often busy, the long, airy pink-painted bar has a nice pubby atmosphere, as well as heavy dark wood tables and tapestried chairs, turkey rugs on the partly flagstoned floor, a fine old log fire at one end, aged-looking paintings, and branding irons hanging from the ceiling. The cosy snug has comfortable leather armchairs. Wadworths IPA, 6X and a seasonal beer on handpump, country wines, and several malt whiskies; games machines and piped music. In fine weather, seats outside are a pleasant place for a drink. The bedrooms are slightly more expensive at weekends. Dogs are allowed in the bar, but not the bedrooms.

🍽 Lunchtime bar food has been much enjoyed by readers, especially the home-made casseroles and pies; they also do sandwiches, baguettes, home-cooked ham and egg, and home-battered cod, with evening meals like bangers and mash, breast of chicken in a stilton sauce, fresh fish, and rib-eye steak. *Starters/Snacks: £5.50. Main Courses: £8.50 to £13.95. Puddings: £4.50*

Wadworths ~ Managers John Whitfield, John Warmington ~ Real ale ~ Bar food (12-2.30, 6-9) ~ (01249) 730456 ~ Children welcome ~ Dogs allowed in bar ~ Open 11.30-11; 11.30-11 Sat; 12-10.30 Sun ~ Bedrooms: £65B/£80B

Recommended by Ian Phillips, Mr and Mrs John Taylor, Gwyn Pickering, John and Joan Nash, JCW

Rising Sun 🍺

Bewley Common, Bowden Hill – out towards Sandy Lane, up hill past Abbey; OS Sheet 173 map reference 935679; SN15 2PP

Unassuming stone pub with welcoming atmosphere and great views from garden

The views – and sunsets – from the garden of this unpretentious stone-built pub are delightful, on a clear day extending up to 25 miles over the Avon Valley. There's a big two-level terrace with plenty of seats. Inside, the three welcoming little rooms are knocked together to form one simply furnished area, with a mix of old chairs and basic kitchen tables on stone floors, country pictures, and open fires. Welcoming staff serve Moles Best Bitter, Tap, Rucking Mole, Capture and a seasonal guest on handpump; darts, piped music. In winter, the conservatory is a better bet for the views. Like the other pubs in town, this can get busy. Their live music on Wednesdays is popular.

🍽 Bar food includes good, big filled baguettes, potato boats filled with mushrooms, bacon and stilton, smoked chicken salad with honey and mustard dressing, home-made broccoli and cheese lasagne or beef in ale pie, daily specials, and puddings such as apple and blackberry flapjack. *Starters/Snacks: £4.50 to £5.50. Main Courses: £7.50 to £16.95. Puddings: £4.50*

Moles ~ Managers Patricia and Tom Russell ~ Real ale ~ Bar food (12-2, 6-9) ~ Restaurant ~ (01249) 730363 ~ Children welcome ~ Dogs allowed in bar ~ Live entertainment every Weds evening ~ Open 12-3, 6-11(midnight Weds-Sat); 12-11 Sun

Recommended by Theocsbrian, Dr and Mrs M E Wilson, Paul and Shirley White, A P Seymour, Kevin Thorpe, Jeff Davies, Dr and Mrs A K Clarke, Simon Rodway

LOWER CHUTE   SU3153   MAP 2

Hatchet

The Chutes well signposted via Appleshaw off A342, 2½ miles W of Andover; SP11 9DX

Very pretty thatched country pub with restful atmosphere

One of the county's most attractive pubs, this is a neat and friendly thatched 16th-c house which some readers really enjoy going back to. The very low-beamed bar has a splendid 17th-c fireback in the huge fireplace (and a roaring winter log fire), a mix of captain's chairs and cushioned wheelbacks around oak tables, and a peaceful local feel. Greene King Old Speckled Hen, Matthews Brass Knocker, and Timothy Taylors Landlord on handpump; cards, chess, board games, and piped music. There are seats out on a terrace by the front car park, or on the side grass, as well as a smokers' hut, and a children's sandpit.

🍽 Thursday night is curry night, when you can eat as much as you like for £7.95. Other bar food includes lunchtime baguettes, ploughman's, liver and bacon, smoked haddock florentine, mushroom tortellini with sun-dried tomatoes and pesto, and daily specials such as lamb shank. *Starters/Snacks: £5.25 to £6.25. Main Courses: £7.95 to £16.95. Puddings: £3.75*

Free house ~ Licensee Jeremy McKay ~ Real ale ~ Bar food (12-2.15, 6.45-9.45) ~ Restaurant ~ (01264) 730229 ~ Children in restaurant and side bar only ~ Dogs allowed in bar ~ Open 11-3, 6-11; 12-3, 7-10.30 Sun ~ Bedrooms: £60S/£70S

LUCKINGTON

ST8384 MAP 2

Old Royal Ship

Off B4040 SW of Malmesbury; SN14 6PA

Friendly village pub by green, with good choice of drinks, generous bar food, and good play area in garden

Especially busy during the Badminton horse trials, this bustling, partly 17th-c pub has been pleasantly opened up, making in effect one long bar divided into three areas. The central servery has Archers Village, Bass, Wadworths 6X and a changing guest on handpump, and ten decent wines by the glass. On the right are neat tables, spindleback chairs and small cushioned settles on dark bare boards, with a small open fireplace and some stripped masonry. On the left, past an area with corks packed into its ceiling, there is more of a mix of tables and chairs, and a small step up to a carpeted section partly divided by rubber plants and dracaenas; in here, a trompe l'oeil stone staircase disappears up into a fictitious turret. Flowers on the tables, some rather lively yellow paintwork, and bright curtains add quite a touch of colour. Service is efficient and helpful; skittle alley and piped music. The garden beyond the car park has boules, a play area with a big wooden climbing frame, and plenty of seats on the terrace or grass. More reports please.

🍴 Bar food includes sandwiches, deep-fried whitebait, deep-fried chicken goujons with chilli dip, breaded plaice, steak and mushroom pie, chicken caesar salad, and specials like salmon fishcakes in a prawn sauce, spinach and brie tart, or braised lamb shank in a red wine, rosemary and garlic sauce; children's menu. *Starters/Snacks: £2.95 to £6.50. Main Courses: £5.50 to £17.75. Puddings: £2.50 to £4.25*

Free house ~ Licensee Helen Johnson-Greening ~ Real ale ~ Bar food (12-2.30, 6(7 Sun)-9.30) ~ Restaurant ~ (01666) 840222 ~ Children allowed away from bar area until 9.30pm ~ Jazz second Weds of month March-Nov ~ Open 11.30-3, 6-11; 11.30-11 Sat; 12-4, 7-10.30 Sun; closed evening 25 Dec

NEWTON TONY

SU2140 MAP 2

Malet Arms

Village signposted off A338 Swindon—Salisbury; SP4 0HF

Much-loved village pub with no pretensions but lots of genuine character, plus a good choice of local beers, and tasty home-made food, with some emphasis on seasonal game

The landlord of this proper village pub – a real favourite with some readers – is not only mad about cricket (he coaches the local school children), but keen on sourcing ingredients with zero 'food miles'. To that end, he's taken up the deer management on a local estate, so expect fresh venison to feature heavily on the menu in season; it's even utilised as the filling in their home-made pasties. He's keen on real ales too, so there's always a good mix of well kept brews, typically from Archers, Butcombe, Butts, Ramsbury, Stonehenge and Triple FFF, with guests like Coach Vale Brewers Gold; also farm cider, and round 15 malt whiskies. The two low-beamed interconnecting rooms have nice furnishings including a mix of different-sized tables with high winged wall settles, carved pews, chapel and carver chairs, and lots of pictures, mainly from imperial days. The main front windows are said to have come from the stern of a ship, and there's a log and coal fire in a huge fireplace. At the back is a homely dining room. The small front terrace has old-fashioned garden seats and some picnic-sets on the grass, and there are more tables in the back garden, along with a wendy house. There's also a little aviary, and a horse paddock behind. Getting to the pub takes you through a ford and it may be best to use an alternative route in winter, as it can be quite deep. The landlord no longer lives above the pub, and his pets, including the parrot, have moved down the road with him.

🍽 Chalked up on a blackboard, the very good, changing range of home-made food might include soup, olives and antipasti with hot ciabatta, lemon breaded sardine fillets with saffron mayonnaise, fettuccine with mushrooms, white wine, cream and parmesan, wild boar and apple sausages, wild rabbit in cider, mustard and cream, large grilled gammon steak with free-range eggs, good burgers, supreme of chicken braised in white wine with celery, garlic and shallots, and super puddings made by the landlady such as Mars Bar cheesecake, or sticky toffee pudding with walnut butterscotch and custard. *Starters/Snacks: £4.95 to £5.95. Main Courses: £8.25 to £15.00. Puddings: £4.50*

Free house ~ Licensee Noel Cardew ~ Real ale ~ Bar food (12-2.30, 6.30-10 (7-9.30 Sun)) ~ (01980) 629279 ~ Children allowed but not in bar area ~ Dogs allowed in bar ~ Open 11-3, 6-11; 12-3, 7-10.30 Sun; closed 25 and 26 Dec, 1 Jan

Recommended by Keith and Jean Symons, Howard and Margaret Buchanan, Michael Rigby, Dave Braisted, Pat and Tony Martin, M B Manser, Bren and Val Speed, John Driver

NORTON
ST8884 MAP 2

Vine Tree 🍽 ♟

4 miles from M4 junction 17; A429 towards Malmesbury, then left at Hullavington, Sherston signpost, then follow Norton signposts; in village turn right at Foxley signpost, which takes you into Honey Lane; SN16 0JP

Civilised dining pub where the good food makes excellent use of carefully sourced ingredients, but drinkers welcome too, and there can be lots going on

Converted from a 19th-c mill house that served drinks from its front window to passing carriages, this well run, civilised place is popular for its inventive and well sourced food – but you'll still find locals popping in for a drink and a chat. Three neatly kept little rooms open together, with old beams, some old settles and unvarnished wooden tables on the flagstone and oak floors, big cream church altar candles, a woodburning stove at one end of the restaurant and a large open fireplace in the central bar, and limited edition and sporting prints; look out for Clementine, the friendly and docile black labrador. Butcombe Bitter and a guest like Bath Spa or St Austell Tinners on handpump, around 35 wines by the glass from an impressive list (they do monthly tutored tastings), and quite a choice of malt whiskies and armagnacs; helpful, attentive staff. It's best to book if you want to eat here, especially at weekends; service is pleasant and sometimes charming. There are picnic-sets and a children's play area in a two-acre garden plus a pretty suntrap terrace with teak furniture under big cream umbrellas, a lion fountain, lots of lavender and box hedging. They have a busy calendar of events, with outdoor music in summer, vintage car rallies and lots going on during the Badminton horse trials. It's not the easiest place to find, and can feel more remote than its proximity to the motorway would suggest.

🍽 Relying on fresh, seasonal ingredients (the beef comes from the farm next door, and they get fresh scallops and mussels every day), the regularly changing menu might include filled ciabattas, soups such as mussel and saffron or white bean and thyme with truffle oil, creamy parfait of foie gras and chicken livers with grape and sauternes jelly, a rich brûlée of cornish beer crab marinière, pumpkin ravioli with walnut sauce, roast saddle and leg of wild rabbit, corn-fed chicken stuffed with mixed seafood with a mild red thai curry cream, chargrilled fillet of beef with vichy carrot purée, wild bass fillet with a scallop, leek and herb risotto and vanilla bean jus, and good puddings such as pink champagne and strawberry jelly with a sabayon of white peach, or blueberry crème brûlée; super cheeses with home-made apricot and ginger chutney, celery sticks and savoury biscuits, Sunday roasts, and proper children's meals. *Starters/Snacks: £4.95 to £6.95. Main Courses: £11.90 to £16.95. Puddings: £5.25 to £5.45*

Free house ~ Licensees Charles Walker and Tiggi Wood ~ Real ale ~ Bar food (12-2(2.30 Sat, 3.30 Sun), 7-9.30(10 Fri/Sat)) ~ Restaurant ~ (01666) 837654 ~ Children welcome ~ Dogs welcome ~ Live jazz and blues once a month, but every Sun during summer ~ Open 12-3(3.30 Sat), 6-midnight; 12-midnight Sun; closed 25 Dec

Recommended by Deborah Weston, Andrea and Guy Bradley, John and Gloria Isaacs, Mrs Ann Gray, Mike and Helen Rawsthorn, Matthew Shackle, Richard Stancomb, David Parker, Emma Smith, Andy and Claire Barker, Mr and Mrs J Brown, Rob Winstanley, Philip and Jude Simmons, Richard and Sheila Fitton, Rod Stoneman, Mary Rayner, J Crosby, Susan and Nigel Wilson

OAKSEY   ST9993 MAP 4

Wheatsheaf ⊕ ◀

Village signposted off A429 SW of Cirencester; turn left after church into Wheatsheaf Lane; SN16 9TB

Notable food showing flair in even simple things, in unpretentious tucked-away village pub – good beer, too

Besides the soft leather armchair by the log fire in its big stone hearth (with a 17th-c coffin lid above), the smallish parquet-floored bar has stylishly modern padded chairs and matching bar stools, latticed windows in stripped-stone walls, a few black beams in its low ochre ceiling, and darts over on the right. The part on the left, with a second log fire in a raised contemporary hearth, is set for eating, and a slope takes you up to a carpeted back area, also fairly compact, with more comfortably modern dining furniture around bookable tables. They have Hook Norton, and a couple of changing guest ales such as Bath Gem, Cotswold Spring English Rose or Wickwar Cotswold Way on handpump, and a good choice of wines by the glass; there may be local artwork for sale. The piped music is not obtrusive. There are picnic-sets out on the quiet front terrace, and they plan to rework the garden, perhaps with a play area.

⊕ **Popular cheesy chips, good sandwiches with home-baked bread, a short choice of bar meals beautifully made from good ingredients (the burgers use tasty rump steak, the sausages are gloucester old spot, and the mash may be delicious bubble and squeak), good puddings, home-made ice-creams and flavourful unchilled cheeses, interesting bar nibbles such as olives, home-pickled onions or eggs, and mixed chillies, and more elaborate restaurant dishes such as ham hock and potato terrine with apple and cinnamon purée, exmoor jersey blue tagliatelle with spinach and pine nuts, braised shoulder of lamb with mint dauphinoise potatoes, duck breast with duck boulangère, red cabbage and redcurrants, and puddings such as baked hot chocolate fondant with cookie dough ice-cream.** *Starters/Snacks: £3.95 to £6.50. Main Courses: £5.00 to £9.50. Puddings: £3.95 to £6.00*

Free house ~ Licensee Tony Robson-Burrell ~ Real ale ~ Bar food (12-2(3 Sun), 6.30-9; no food Mon) ~ Restaurant ~ (01666) 577348 ~ Children welcome ~ Dogs allowed in bar ~ Open 11.30-2.30, 6-11; 11.30-3, 6-12 Sat; 12-10 Sun; closed Mon lunch

Recommended by Michael Dallas, KC, Holly Brand

PITTON   SU2131 MAP 2

Silver Plough ♀

Village signposted from A30 E of Salisbury (follow brown tourist signs); SP5 1DU

Bustling country dining pub that feels instantly welcoming, the good food sometimes in a choice of sizes

Readers have enjoyed coming here this year, one saying he felt at home as soon as he walked in, and others praising the way some dishes are offered in two sizes. The comfortable front bar has plenty to look at, as the black beams are strung with hundreds of antique boot-warmers and stretchers, pewter and china tankards, copper kettles, toby jugs, earthenware and glass rolling pins, painted clogs, glass net-floats, and coach horns and so forth. Seats include half a dozen cushioned antique oak settles (one elaborately carved, beside a very fine reproduction of an Elizabethan oak table), and the timbered white walls are hung with Thorburn and other game bird prints, and a big naval battle glass-painting. There's a nicely bustling atmosphere and a wide mix of customers. The back bar is simpler, but still has a big winged high-backed settle, cased antique guns, substantial pictures, and – like the front room – flowers on its tables. There's a skittle alley next to the snug bar; piped music. Badger Gold, Sussex Bitter, Tanglefoot and a seasonal brew on handpump kept under light blanket pressure, quite a few country wines, and nine wines by the glass. A quiet lawn has picnic-sets and other tables under cocktail parasols; a patio has a heated area for smokers. The pub is well placed for good downland and woodland walks.

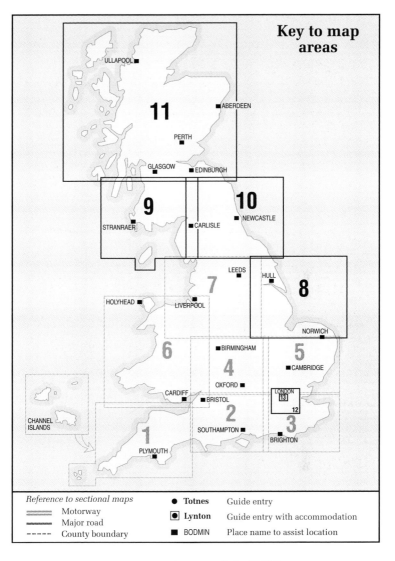

Key to map areas

11
ULLAPOOL
ABERDEEN
PERTH
GLASGOW
EDINBURGH

9
STRANRAER
CARLISLE

10
NEWCASTLE

7
LEEDS
HOLYHEAD
LIVERPOOL

8
HULL
NORWICH

6
BIRMINGHAM
4
OXFORD
CARDIFF
BRISTOL
2

5
CAMBRIDGE
LONDON 13
12

CHANNEL ISLANDS

1
PLYMOUTH
SOUTHAMPTON

3
BRIGHTON

Reference to sectional maps

≡≡≡ Motorway
━━━ Major road
---- County boundary

● **Totnes** Guide entry
◉ **Lynton** Guide entry with accommodation
■ **BODMIN** Place name to assist location

MAPS IN THIS SECTION

For Maps 1 – 7 see earlier colour section

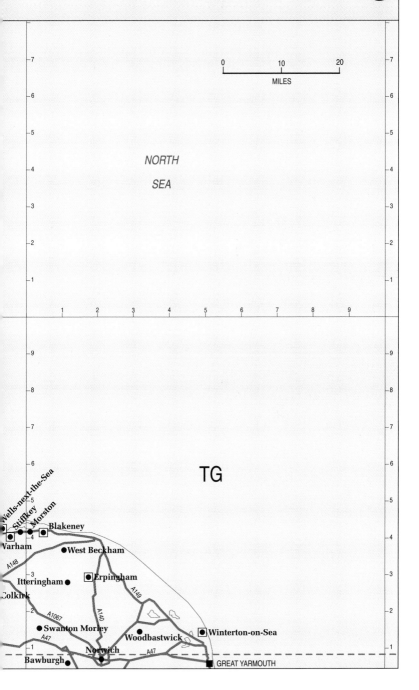

NORTH

SEA

0   10   20
MILES

1   2   3   4   5   6   7   8   9

TG

Wells-next-the-Sea

Stiffkey

Morston

Blakeney

West Beckham

Varham

A148

Erpingham

Itteringham

A149

Colkirk

A1067

A140

Swanton Morley

Woodbastwick

Winterton-on-Sea

A47

Norwich

A47

Bawburgh

GREAT YARMOUTH

9

GIGHA

A83

A841

ARRAN

BRODICK

A841

NR

CAMPBELTOWN

FIRTH OF CLYDE

A78

11

ARDROSSAN

KILMARNOCK

A78

AYR

A70

A77

—5

—4

—3

—2

—1

4   5   6   7   8   9

1   2   3   4

GIRVAN

A77

SOUTH AYRSHIRE

A714

NEWTON STEWART

NW

STRANRAER

A75

A747

—9

—8

—7

—6

—5

—4

—3

—2

—1

4   5   6   7   8   9

1   2   3   4

—9

—8

0   10   20
MILES

SOUTH
LANARKSHIRE

BORDERS

M74

GALASHIELS

Innerleithen

Melrose

NS

NT

EAST
AYRSHIRE

HAWICK

MOFFAT

DUMFRIES & GALLOWAY

M74

10

DUMFRIES

NX

Kingholm Quay

Gatehouse of Fleet

CARLISLE

NY

Armathwaite

SOLWAY
FIRTH

Hesket
Newmarket

Great
Salkeld

M6

Isle of Whithorn

Bassenthwaite

Cockermouth

Mungrisdale

PENRITH

WORKINGTON

Bassenthwaite
Lake

Scales

Yanwath

Keswick

Threlkeld

Loweswater

Askham

Buttermere

CUMBRIA

WHITEHAVEN

Stonethwaite

Chapel Stile

Ambleside

Langdale

Troutbeck

Santon Bridge

Elterwater

Little
Langdale

Staveley

Hawkshead

Ings

Crosthwaite

Seathwaite

Near Sawrey

Broughton
Mills

Cartmel Fell

KENDAL

Bouth

Levens

7

SD

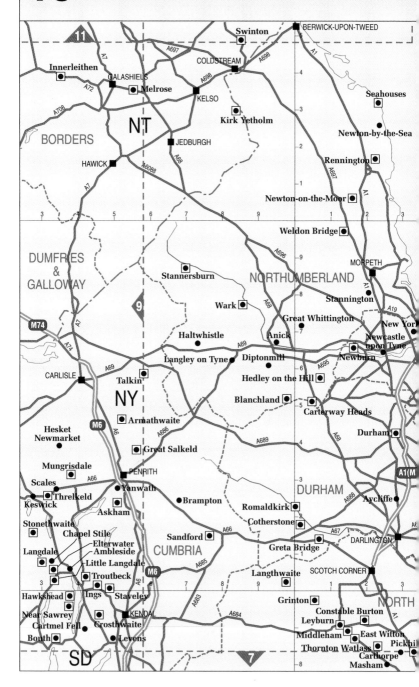

11

Innerleithen

GALASHIELS
Melrose

Swinton

BERWICK-UPON-TWEED

COLDSTREAM

KELSO

Kirk Yetholm

Seahouses

Newton-by-the-Sea

Rennington

BORDERS

NT

JEDBURGH

HAWICK

Newton-on-the-Moor

Weldon Bridge

DUMFRIES
&
GALLOWAY

Stannersburn

NORTHUMBERLAND

MORPETH

9

Wark

Great Whittington

Stannington

M74

Haltwhistle

Anick

New Yor

Newcastle
upon Tyne

Langley on Tyne

Diptonmill

Newburn

CARLISLE

Talkin

Hedley on the Hill

NY

Blanchland

Carterway Heads

Hesket
Newmarket

Armathwaite

Durham

Mungrisdale

Great Salkeld

A1(M

Scales
Threlkeld
Keswick

PENRITH

Yanwath

Brampton

DURHAM

Aycliffe

Stonethwaite

Askham

Romaldkirk

Chapel Stile
Elterwater
Ambleside

Sandford

Cotherstone

DARLINGTON

Langdale

Little Langdale

Greta Bridge

CUMBRIA

M6

Hawkshead

Troutbeck

Ings
Staveley

Langthwaite

SCOTCH CORNER

Near Sawrey
Cartmel Fell
Bouth

KENDAL

Crosthwaite

Levens

Grinton

Constable Burton
Leyburn

NORTH

Middleham
Thornton Watlass

East Witton

Pickhi

SD

Carthorpe
Masham

7

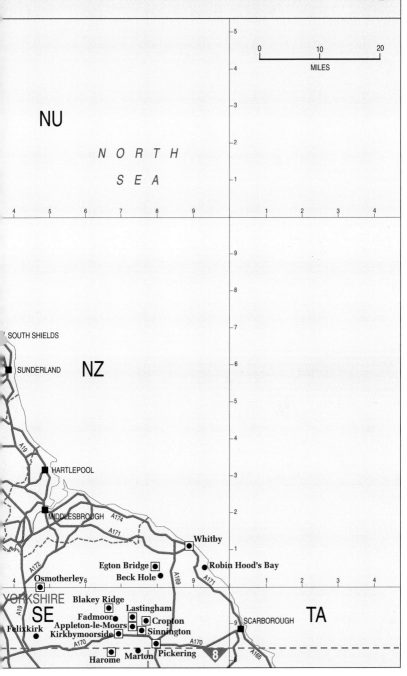

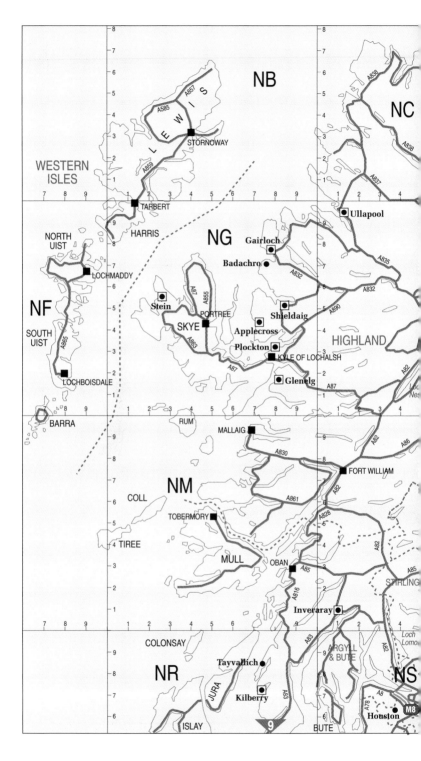

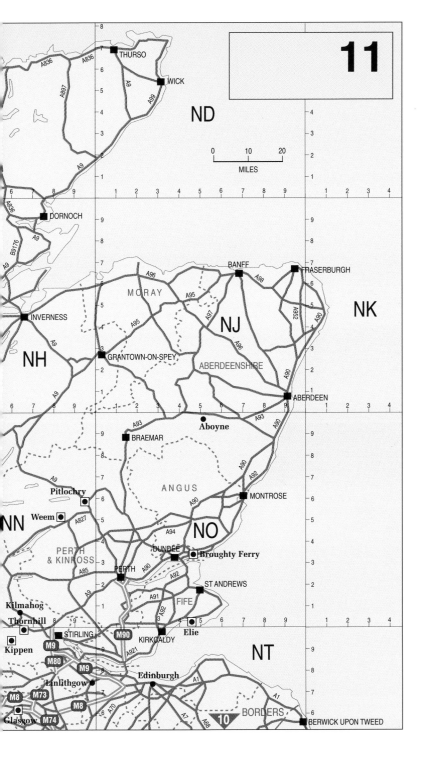

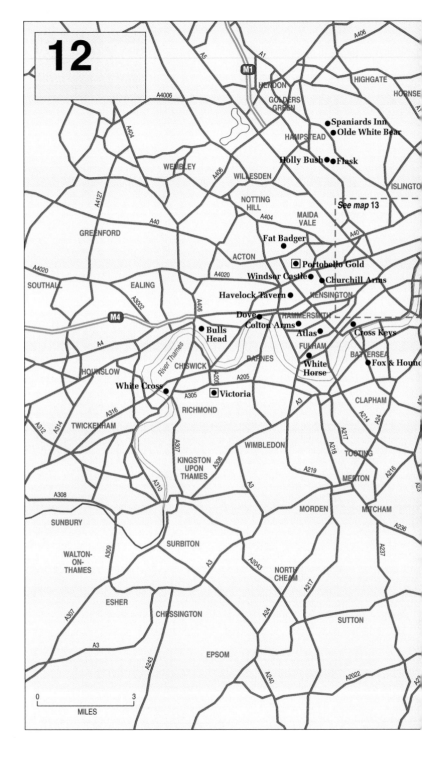

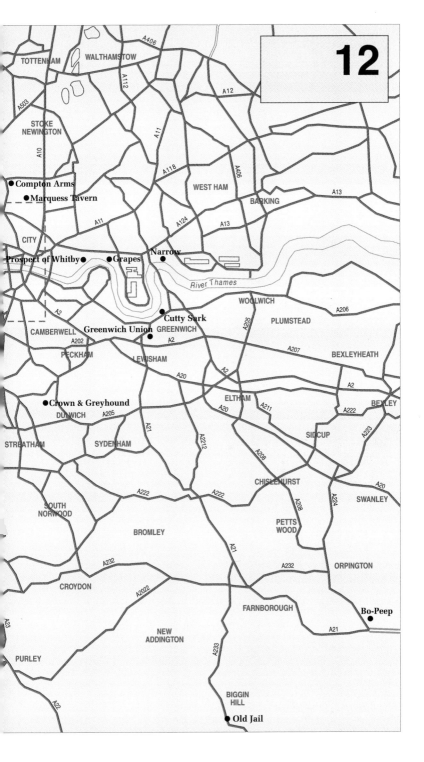

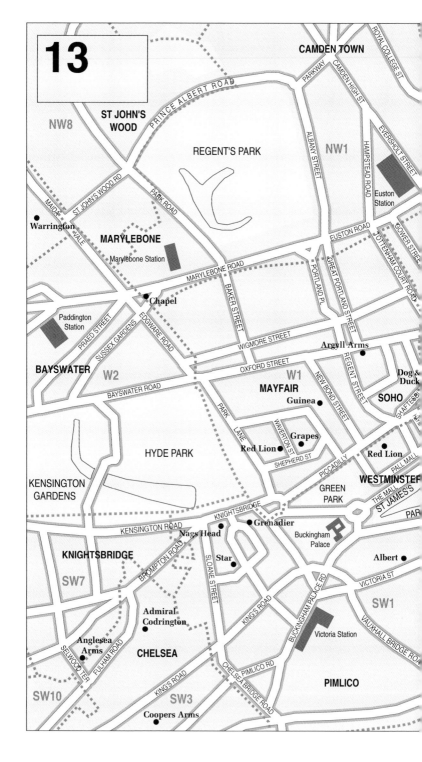

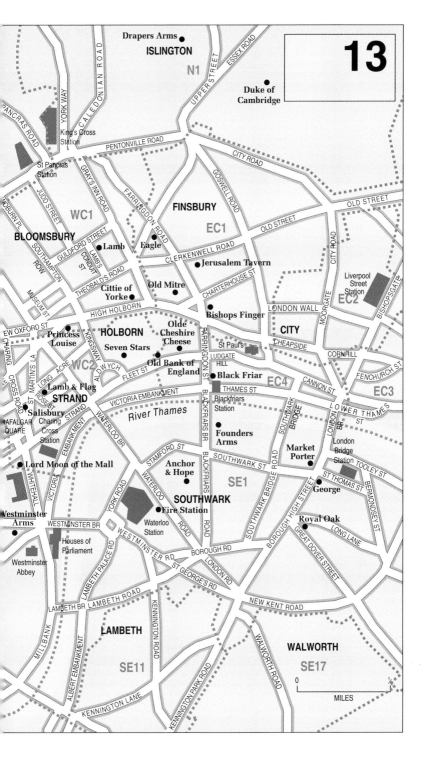

13

Drapers Arms ●
ISLINGTON

N1

Duke of ●
Cambridge

King's Cross
Station

PENTONVILLE ROAD

CITY ROAD

St Pancras
Station

OLD STREET

WC1

FINSBURY

OLD STREET

BLOOMSBURY

EC1

● Lamb Eagle ●

● Jerusalem Tavern

Liverpool
Street
Station

CLERKENWELL ROAD

Cittie of
Yorke ● Old Mitre ●

EC2

HIGH HOLBORN

● Bishops Finger

LONDON WALL

Princess ●
Louise

Olde
Cheshire
Cheese

CITY

HOLBORN

St Paul's ●

Seven Stars ●

CHEAPSIDE

WC2

Old Bank of
England ●

LUDGATE
HILL

CORNHILL

FLEET ST

EC4

● Black Friar

Lamb & Flag ●

THAMES ST

EC3

STRAND

VICTORIA EMBANKMENT

Blackfriars
Station

Salisbury ●

River Thames

Charing
Cross
Station

● Founders
Arms

Market
Porter ●

● Lord Moon of the Mall

Anchor
& Hope ●

London
Bridge
Station

● George

SOUTHWARK

Westminster
Arms ●

● Fire Station

Waterloo
Station

● Royal Oak

WESTMINSTER BR

Houses of
Parliament

BOROUGH RD

LONDON RD

Westminster
Abbey

ST GEORGE'S RD

NEW KENT ROAD

LAMBETH RD LAMBETH ROAD

LAMBETH

WALWORTH

SE11

SE17

0   1

MILES

KENNINGTON LANE

'Since I've discovered *The Good Pub Guide* I haven't had to suffer a bad pub again'
Simon Heptinstall, Mail on Sunday

'Easily the best'
Time Out

'The definitive guide to boozing'
The Times

* Since it was first published 26 years ago, *The Good Pub Guide* has received many fabulous recommendations because, unlike other guide books, it is totally independent. We never take payment for entries.

* Pubs are inspected anonymously by the editorial team, and we rely on reports from readers to tell us whether pubs deserve to be in the next edition.

* Don't forget to report to us on any pubs you visit over the coming year. You can use the card in the middle of the book, the forms at the back, or you can send reports via our website: www.goodguides.co.uk

Write and tell us about your favourite pub!

We'll send you more forms (free) if you wish.
You don't need a stamp in the UK.
Simply write to us at:

**The Good Pub Guide,
FREEPOST TN1569, WADHURST,
East Sussex TN5 7BR**

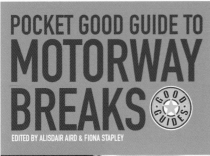

OVER 650 PLACES TO EAT, VISIT AND STAY
EASILY ACCESSIBLE FROM THE UK's MAIN ROADS

'Superb...contains hundreds of restaurants, cafés and places to stay that are in easy driving distance of the motorway'
Daily Express

'Saved my sanity... with a charming little eaterie just off the main drag'
Mail on Sunday

* Over 650 easy-to-reach, value-for-money places to eat, drink and visit

* Organised by major motorways and A-roads, with maps to show you how to get there

A brilliantly useful guide to good places to eat, drink, stay and visit – all easily accessible from motorways and main A-roads. Make life easier. Make life better. Buy your car a copy of the *Pocket Good Guide to Motorway Breaks*.

If you would like to order a copy of
Pocket Good Guide to Motorway Breaks (£5.99 each)
direct from Ebury Press (p&p free), please call our credit-card hotline on
01206 255 800
or send a cheque/postal order made payable to Ebury Press to
Cash Sales Department, TBS Direct,
Frating Distribution Centre, Colchester Road,
Frating Green, Essex CO7 7DW
or to order online visit **www.rbooks.co.uk**

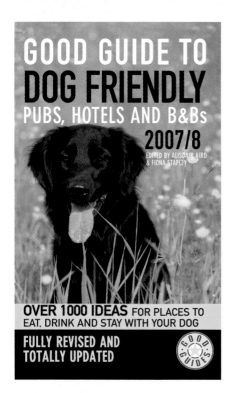

GOOD GUIDE TO DOG FRIENDLY PUBS, HOTELS AND B&Bs 2007/8

EDITED BY ALISDAIR AIRD & FIONA STAPLEY

OVER 1000 IDEAS FOR PLACES TO EAT, DRINK AND STAY WITH YOUR DOG

FULLY REVISED AND TOTALLY UPDATED

* Over 1000 places to eat, drink and stay with your dog

* Compiled by the editors of *The Good Pub Guide* with the same commitment to accuracy and independence

* Includes vital information on opening hours, prices and facilities

'[An] invaluable guide...smart and indispensable'
Daily Telegraph

'Invaluable' *Country Magazine*

'A great book for all dog lovers' *Scottish Sunday Post*

From the editors of *The Good Pub Guide* comes the latest edition of the *Good Guide to Dog Friendly Pubs, Hotels and B&Bs* – the definitive guide for dog owners.

If you would like to order a copy of the *Good Guide to Dog Friendly Pubs, Hotels and B&Bs 2007/2008* (£9.99) direct from Ebury Press (p&p free), please call our credit-card hotline on **01206 255 800** or send a cheque/postal order made payable to Ebury Press to **Cash Sales Department, TBS Direct, Frating Distribution Centre, Colchester Road, Frating Green, Essex CO7 7DW** or to order online visit **www.rbooks.co.uk**

🍴 Well liked bar food includes lunchtime baguettes, ploughman's and various salads like smoked chicken caesar (they do two sizes), home-made vegetable lasagne or steak and kidney pie (again, with a choice of size), and what they call their gastro menu with grilled goats cheese and caramelised onion tartlet, pan-fried scallops with pancetta salad, calves liver with mustard mash and juniper sauce, roast half shoulder of lamb with port and rosemary sauce, and bass fillets on crushed cherry tomato and olive potato with pesto sauce; good generously served puddings like Baileys cheesecake; children's menu. On Sunday they do a choice of roasts, and the menu is more limited. *Starters/Snacks: £3.95 to £6.95. Main Courses: £8.95 to £15.95. Puddings: £4.95*

Badger ~ Tenants Hughen and Joyce Riley ~ Real ale ~ Bar food (12-2, 6-9; 12-2.15, 6.30-8.30 Sun) ~ Restaurant ~ (01722) 712266 ~ Small children allowed in snug bar, but not restaurant or in front of main bar ~ Dogs allowed in bar ~ Open 11-3, 6-11(11.30 Sat); 12-4, 6.30-11 Sun; closed 25 Dec ~ Bedrooms: /£50S

Recommended by Phyl and Jack Street, Peter Neate, Patrick Hall, N R White, Clifford Blakemore, Edward Mirzoeff, John Robertson, Helen and Brian Edgeley, Noel Grundy, Richard Fendick

POULSHOT
ST9760   MAP 2

Raven 🍺
Village signposted off A361 Devizes—Seend; SN10 1RW

Reliable food and service in pretty setting

Just across from the village green, this is an attractively set pub with dependable home-made food. The two cosy black-beamed rooms are well furnished with sturdy tables and chairs and comfortable banquettes. Wadworths IPA, 6X and maybe a seasonal ale are tapped straight from the cask; obliging service. The gents' is outside. More reports please.

🍴 Bar food includes devilled whitebait or creamy garlic mushrooms, filled ciabattas, ham and eggs, vegetable curry, battered cod, steak and kidney pie, specials like grilled pork steak with leek, apple, cider and fresh herb sauce, liver and bacon and salmon fishcakes with chilli sauce, and puddings such as crème brûlée or morello cherry cheesecake. *Starters/Snacks: £3.50 to £6.95. Main Courses: £8.20 to £14.25. Puddings: £2.95 to £4.45*

Wadworths ~ Tenants Philip and Susan Henshaw ~ Real ale ~ Bar food (not Mon) ~ Restaurant ~ (01380) 828271 ~ Children allowed but must be accompanied by an adult at all times ~ Dogs allowed in bar ~ Open 11-2.30, 6.30-11; 12-3, 7-10.30 Sun; closed Mon; 25 Dec and evenings 26 and 31 Dec, and 1 Jan

Recommended by Mr and Mrs J Brown, Dr and Mrs A K Clarke

RAMSBURY
SU2771   MAP 2

Bell
Signed off B4192 NW of Hungerford, or A4 W; SN8 2PB

Smart, friendly pub refurbished after fire and once again selling food

This neatly kept dining pub suffered terrible fire damage last year and was unable to offer food for a while, but the kitchen has now reopened after a smart refurbishment. The airy bar has exposed beams, cream-washed walls, two woodburning stoves, and a chatty, relaxed atmosphere. Victorian stained-glass panels in one of the two sunny bay windows look out on to the quiet village street. The friendly landlord and staff serve local Ramsbury Gold and a beer named for the pub, along with a guest such as Moles Mole Catcher; there's a good choice of malt whiskies. There are picnic-sets on the raised lawn; roads lead from this quiet village into the downland on all sides. More reports please.

🍴 Bar food might include lunchtime sandwiches, soup, scallops with crab coleslaw and orange and sesame dressing, several meals in a choice of sizes like moules marinière or potato gnocchi with wild mushroom and truffle sauce, beef and ale pie, whole baked plaice with caper and brown shrimp butter, and seared fillet of beef with potato rösti, pickled shi-itake mushrooms and foie gras butter. On Thursdays they do a two-course lunch for £10, and on Tuesdays have a range of local sausages served with a glass of house wine. *Starters/Snacks: £4.95 to £9.50. Main Courses: £7.95 to £18.95. Puddings: £4.95 to £5.50*

Free house ~ Licensee Jeremy Parke ~ Real ale ~ Bar food (12-2.30(3 Sun), 7-.9.30; not Sun evening) ~ Restaurant ~ (01672) 520230 ~ Children welcome ~ Dogs allowed in bar ~ Open 11-3, 5.30-11; 11-11 Sat; 11-5 Sun; closed Sun evening

Recommended by Alan and Paula McCully, Mark and Ruth Brock

ROWDE

ST9762   MAP 2

George & Dragon 🍴 ♀

A342 Devizes—Chippenham; SN10 2PN

Gently upmarket coaching inn with good, varied food and nice atmosphere

Now with three smart, contemporary bedrooms, this attractive 17th-c coaching inn has two low-ceilinged rooms with plenty of wood, beams, and open fireplaces. There are large wooden tables, antique rugs, and walls covered with old pictures and portraits; the atmosphere is pleasantly chatty. Butcombe Bitter and a changing guest on handpump and an extensive wine list, with nine by the glass; board games. A pretty garden at the back has tables and chairs; they have barbecues in summer, and occasional events like wine and cheese tasting. The Kennet & Avon Canal is nearby. More reports please (we'd be interested to hear from people who've stayed here).

🍴 **As well as fish and seafood delivered daily from Cornwall, the menu might include roast tomato, onion and basil soup, caesar salad with fresh anchovies and garlic croûtons, wild mushroom, parmesan and black truffle oil risotto, devilled lambs kidneys with grainy mustard cream sauce, roast rack of lamb with spring onion and new potato compote, bass with pesto mash and crispy bacon, and puddings like apple and blueberry crumble or crème brûlée. They do a well liked three-course Sunday lunch for £15.50.** *Starters/Snacks: £5.00 to £8.50. Main Courses: £8.50 to £32.00. Puddings: £5.50 to £7.00*

Free house ~ Licensees Philip and Michelle Hale, Christopher Day ~ Real ale ~ Bar food (12-3, 7-10 Tues-Fri; 12-4, 6.30-10 Sat; 12-4 Sun; not Sun evening, or Mon) ~ Restaurant ~ (01380) 723053 ~ Children in restaurant ~ Dogs allowed in bar ~ Open 12-3(4 Sat and Sun), 7(6.30 Sat)-11; closed Sun evening, all day Mon, and first week Jan ~ Bedrooms: /£85S

Recommended by Mrs Joanna Jensen, Oliver Richardson, Dr and Mrs A K Clarke, Mr and Mrs A H Young, Andrew Shore, Maria Williams

SALISBURY

SU1429   MAP 2

Haunch of Venison

Minster Street, opposite Market Cross; SP1 1TB

Ancient pub oozing history, with tiny beamed rooms, unique fittings, and famous mummified hand; lovely atmosphere, decent snacks, and well kept beers

A must if you're visiting the city, this splendidly characterful place dates back to 1320, when it was used to house the craftsmen working on the cathedral's spire. The two tiny downstairs rooms are quite spit-and-sawdust in spirit, with massive beams in the white ceiling, stout oak benches built into the timbered walls, black and white floor tiles, and an open fire. A tiny snug (popular with locals, but historically said to be where the ladies drank) opens off the entrance lobby. Well kept Courage Best, Greene King IPA, and a guest such as Hop Back Summer Lightning on handpump from a unique pewter bar counter, and there's a rare set of antique taps for gravity-fed spirits and liqueurs. They've also 60 malt whiskies, decent wines (ten by the glass), herbal teas, and a range of brandies. Halfway up the stairs is a panelled room they call the House of Lords, which has a small-paned window looking down on to the main bar, and a splendid fireplace that dates back to the building's early years; behind glass in a small wall slit is the smoke-preserved mummified hand of an 18th-c card sharp still clutching his cards.

Food details, prices, timing etc refer to bar food (if that's separate and different from any restaurant there).

🍴 A short range of lunchtime bar snacks takes in baguettes, ploughman's, chicken liver parfait with red onion marmalade, sausages with grilled bread and tarragon aïoli, and scampi and chips; they do a three-course menu in the upstairs restaurant (£9.90) with dishes such as mustard and brown sugar baked ham with bubble and squeak, venison sausages, and vanilla and sloe gin panna cotta; decent children's menu. **Choice of Sunday roasts.** *Starters/Snacks: £3.50 to £6.90. Main Courses: £6.90 to £15.90. Puddings: £3.50 to £7.50*

Scottish Courage ~ Lease Anthony Leroy ~ Real ale ~ Bar food (12-2.30, 6-9.30(10 Sat)) ~ Restaurant ~ (01722) 411313 ~ Children allowed in bar with parents ~ Dogs allowed in bar ~ Open 11am-11.30pm; 12-10.30 Sun

Recommended by N R White, Bill and Jessica Ritson, Ann and Colin Hunt, Colin and Peggy Wilshire, Pete Walker, Mike and Lynn Robinson, Donna and Roger, the Didler, Ken and Joyce Hollis, Andy and Claire Barker

SEEND   ST9361   MAP 2

Barge
Seend Cleeve; signposted off A361 Devizes—Trowbridge, between Seend village and signpost to Seend Head; SN12 6QB

Popular canalside pub, refurbished this year but still with its quirky seating; nice garden to watch the boats, and pubby food

With new managers since February (they previously managed one of our Lacock main entries), this busy waterside pub has been refurbished since our last edition – nothing drastic, but opening it up to give a lighter, brighter feel. The neatly kept garden is an excellent place to watch the bustle of boats on the Kennet & Avon Canal – old streetlamps let you linger there after dark, and moorings by the humpy bridge are very useful for thirsty bargees. The bar has an unusual barge-theme décor, and intricately painted Victorian flowers cover the ceilings and run in a waist-high band above the lower walls. A medley of eye-catching seats includes milk churns, unusual high-backed chairs (made from old boat-parts), a seat made from an upturned canoe, and the occasional small oak settle among the rugs on the parquet floor; there's a well stocked aquarium, and a pretty Victorian fireplace. Wadworths IPA, 6X and seasonal brews on handpump, quite a few malt whiskies, and a good choice of wines by the glass.

🍴 Perhaps more obviously pubby than it was, bar food includes baguettes (often through the afternoon too), fish and chips, steak and ale pie, wild boar and apple sausages, and specials including fresh fish dishes such as tandoori-seared halibut. *Starters/Snacks: £3.50 to £6.95. Main Courses: £7.95 to £11.95*

Wadworths ~ Managers Paul and Sarah Haynes ~ Real ale ~ Bar food (12-3, 6-10 (some snacks 3-5)) ~ Restaurant ~ (01380) 828230 ~ Children welcome ~ Dogs allowed in bar ~ Open 11-11; 12-10.30 Sun

Recommended by R T and J C Moggridge, Tom and Jill Jones, Richard and Liz Dilnot, Richard and Jean Green, Paul and Shirley White, Helen and Brian Edgeley, Christine and Neil Townend, Mike and Lynn Robinson, Peter Titcomb, Dr and Mrs A K Clarke

SEMINGTON   ST9259   MAP 2

Lamb 🍽 ♉
The Strand; A361 Devizes—Trowbridge; BA14 6LL

Very good food in busy, ivy-covered dining pub, with wide range of wines and spirits, reliable service, and attractive garden

Readers who've been coming to this civilised creeper-covered eatery for 20 years say it goes from strength to strength. The standard of food is very high, but there seems to be that extra bit of attention with the service and welcome too. Though most people come here for a meal, they won't discourage you if you just want a pint, so while you can reserve a table in the dining areas, tables in the bar are kept on a first-come, first-serve basis. That said, they're snapped up rather quickly, particularly on Saturday evening or

Sunday lunchtime. A series of corridors and attractively decorated separate rooms radiates from the serving counter, with antique settles, a woodburning stove, and a log fire. Well kept Butcombe, O'Hanlons Yellowhammer, and Ringwood Best on handpump, a good wine list (with 13 by the glass), and an interesting range of armagnacs, cognacs and rums. There is a pleasant colourfully planted walled garden with tables, and views towards the Bowood Estate.

🍴 From a changing menu, the food might include sandwiches, home-made soup, grilled fig and chorizo salad with shaved parmesan, prawns in filo pastry with chilli dip, sausages of the day with bubble and squeak, smoked haddock with welsh rarebit, warm salad of locally smoked chicken and avocado, steak and mushroom pie, and specials like slow-roast belly of pork on braised vegetables. *Starters/Snacks: £3.95 to £4.95. Main Courses: £8.25 to £15.50. Puddings: £4.95*

Free house ~ Licensees Philip Roose-Francis and Sue and Tom Smith ~ Real ale ~ Bar food (not Sun evening) ~ (01380) 870263 ~ Children welcome ~ Dogs allowed in bar ~ Open 11.30-3, 6.30-11; 12-3 Sun; closed Sun evening, 25 and 26 Dec, 1 Jan

Recommended by Dr and Mrs M E Wilson, Mr and Mrs A Curry, Alan and Audrey Moulds, Dr and Mrs A K Clarke, Andrew Shore, Maria Williams

STOURTON
ST7733   MAP 2

Spread Eagle 🛏

Church Lawn; follow Stourhead brown signs off B3092, N of junction with A303 just W of Mere; BA12 6QE

Comfortably civilised country inn by National Trust gardens, with popular food, much of it from the estate; busy at lunchtimes, quieter later on

A handsome brick house set among elegant stone buildings at the head of Stourhead lake (all – including the pub – are owned by the National Trust), this civilised place has a very pleasant bonus if you stay: you can wander freely around the gardens outside their normal opening times – a nice way of enjoying them away from the crowds. The interior has an old-fashioned feel with antique panel-back settles, a mix of new and old solid tables and chairs, handsome fireplaces with good winter log fires, smoky old sporting prints, prints of Stourhead, and standard lamps or brass swan's-neck wall lamps. One room by the entrance has armchairs, a longcase clock and a corner china cupboard. Butcombe, Wessex Kilmington Best and a guest like Cheddar Valley Best on handpump, farm ciders and seven wines by the glass. There are benches in the courtyard behind. Though service is generally prompt and reliable, one reader this year experienced quite the opposite.

🍴 Bar food – not always cheap but consistently well liked – at lunchtime includes baguettes and soup (available in the afternoon as well), ham, free-range egg and chips, beef and ale casserole with thyme-roasted root vegetables and bubble and squeak mash, and wild mushroom and asparagus pie, with evening dishes like salmon fillet with crab and chive mash and hollandaise sauce, lamb shank with pickled red cabbage, and venison casserole with juniper, red wine, rosemary and shallot dumplings; puddings such as rum and orange bread and butter pudding or dark chocolate and brandy pot. *Starters/Snacks: £4.50 to £8.00. Main Courses: £7.50 to £16.00. Puddings: £4.50 to £6.00*

Free house ~ Licensees Stephen Ross, Jason Lindley ~ Real ale ~ Bar food (12-10) ~ Restaurant (evening) ~ (01747) 840587 ~ Children welcome ~ Open 10am-11pm; closed 25 Dec ~ Bedrooms: £80B/£110B

Recommended by Jenny and Brian Seller, Sheila Topham, John Robertson, Mayur Shah, Edward Mirzoeff, B J Harding, J L and C J Hamilton, Tracey and Stephen Groves, Colin and Janet Roe, Ian Phillips, Sue Demont, Tim Barrow

---

If a service charge is mentioned prominently on a menu or accommodation terms, you must pay it if service was satisfactory. If service is really bad, you are legally entitled to refuse to pay some or all of the service charge as compensation for not getting the service you might reasonably have expected.

UPPER CHUTE
SU2953   MAP 2

Cross Keys ♀ ◖

Tucked-away village N of Andover, best reached off A343 via Tangley, or off A342 in Weyhill via Clanville; SP11 9ER

Peacefully set true country pub, welcoming and relaxed, with enjoyable food and good beer and wines

Reopened in 2006 by a new young landlord with a background in farming and crop technology, this has a comfortably relaxed village atmosphere – in fact when the builders were finished local volunteers helped with the paintwork and bringing the garden back under control. It's open plan, with early 18th-c beams in the maroon ceiling, nice blue sofas and a cushioned pew built around the window by the good log fire in the big hearth on the left, pubby tables and a couple of leather armchairs by the woodburning stove on the right; darts are sensibly placed in an alcove over here. They have well kept Fullers London Pride, Discovery and Butser on handpump with changing guest beers such as Hop Back Entire Stout, and good wines by the glass; service is welcoming and helpful, and Pepper and Pudding, the charming black bulldogs, are quite soppy. Picnic-sets out under flowering cherries on the front south-facing terrace give far views over rolling wooded uplands; this is an interesting area for walking, and we look forward to hearing from readers who have stayed overnight.

〔☰〕 **Good and deliberately unpretentious, relying on careful individual preparation of really fresh local seasonal ingredients: potted mackerel with melba toast, prosciutto and goats cheese tart, salmon steak crusted with cajun seasoning, lamb steak with minted gravy, jerked red mullet, and puddings like apricot sponge or grand marnier crème brûlée. They do sandwiches, and have a Thursday curry night and Friday fish night.** *Starters/Snacks: £3.75 to £6.00. Main Courses: £6.95 to £11.95. Puddings: £4.25 to £4.75*

Free house ~ Licensees George and Sonia Humphrey ~ Bar food (12-2(2.30 Sun), 6-9; not Mon lunch) ~ Restaurant ~ (01264) 730295 ~ Accompanied children welcome till 9pm ~ Dogs allowed in bar and bedrooms ~ Open 11-2.30, 5-11; 11-midnight Sat; 12-11 Sun; closed Mon lunch ~ Bedrooms: £50S/£60S

Recommended by Ian Thomasson, K Louden

WEST LAVINGTON
SU0052   MAP 2

Bridge Inn 〔☰〕

A360 S of Devizes; Church Street; SN10 4LD

Welcoming village pub with good, french-influenced food and a light, comfortable bar

This comfortable and quietly civilised village pub is much enjoyed by readers for its efficient hospitality and very good food. The light, spacious bar comfortably mixes contemporary features such as spotlights in the ceiling with firmly traditional fixtures like the enormous brick inglenook that may be filled with big logs and candles; at the opposite end is a smaller modern fireplace, in an area set mostly for eating. Pictures on the cream-painted or exposed brick walls are for sale, as are local jams, and there are plenty of fresh flowers on the tables and bar; timbers and the occasional step divide the various areas. Greene King IPA and Old Speckled Hen and Hobgoblin IPA on handpump, and 11 wines by the glass; piped music in the evenings. At the back is a nice raised lawn area with several tables under a big tree; boules.

〔☰〕 **Attractively presented, and with the roots of the chef much in evidence, the menu includes lunchtime baguettes and ham and eggs, fish soup, leek and emmenthal tartlet, rabbit terrine, snails in their shell with garlic and herb butter, corn-fed-chicken casserole, bubble and squeak with free-range scrambled egg, haddock in beer batter, sautéed pheasant breast marinated with brandy and wild mushroom in a filo pastry basket, cheddar, sun-dried tomato and onion soufflé, baked pigeon confit with sauerkraut, smoked bacon and garlic sausage, and puddings like Pimms trifle and chocolate and hazelnut crème brûlée (they sometimes have a sampler dish with four mini puddings).** *Starters/Snacks: £4.15 to £6.25. Main Courses: £8.25 to £16.95. Puddings: £5.10 to £6.50*

Enterprise ~ Lease Cyrille and Paula Portier ~ Real ale ~ Bar food (12-2, 6.30-9; not Sun evening or Mon) ~ Restaurant ~ (01380) 813213 ~ Well behaved children welcome ~ Open 12-3, 6.30-11; 12-3 Sun; closed Sun evening and all day Mon; two weeks Feb

Recommended by Bill and Jessica Ritson, Trevor Swindells, L and D Webster, B and F A Hannam, Mr and Mrs A Curry, Jo and Mark Wadman

WHITLEY   ST8866   MAP 2

Pear Tree 🍴 ♀ 🛏

Off B3353 S of Corsham, at Atworth 1½, Purlpit 1 signpost; or from A350 Chippenham—Melksham in Beanacre turn off on Westlands Lane at Whitley 1 signpost, then left and right at B3353; SN12 8QX

Superior food in attractive, upmarket old farmhouse, not cheap, but worth the extra for some very inventive cooking; readers very much enjoy the set lunch

The sophisticated food is why most people come to this honey-coloured stone farmhouse, but it also appeals to those just wanting a drink, and is a fine place to stay – the bedrooms are very comfortable, and the breakfasts are excellent. The charming front bar has quite a pubby feel, with cushioned window seats, some stripped shutters, a mix of dining chairs around good solid tables, a variety of country pictures and a Wiltshire Regiment sampler on the walls, a little fireplace on the left, and a lovely old stripped stone one on the right. Candlelit at night, the popular big back restaurant (best to book) has green dining chairs, quite a mix of tables, and a pitched ceiling at one end with a quirky farmyard theme – wrought-iron cockerels and white scythe sculpture. Moles Best, Hidden Brewery Hidden Potential, and Wadworths 6X on handpump, and ten wines by the glass. A bright spacious garden room opens on to a terrace with good teak furniture and views over the carefully maintained gardens, which are prettily lit at night to show features like the ruined pigsty; more seats on the terrace, and boules. A couple of readers have this year experienced slight dips in the normally excellent service.

🍴 From an imaginative menu, the modern, carefully sourced food might include lunchtime sandwiches (some toasted), pumpkin soup with goats cheese and balsamic, pork and wild rabbit terrine with apricots, cashew nuts and chutney, home-made pork and herb sausages with colcannon, black cabbage and apple sauce, boneless wing of skate with creamed mash and sprouting broccoli, jerusalem artichoke risotto with chive butter, parmesan and truffle oil, baked rump of lamb with braised shoulder and devilled kidney, aged local steak with watercress and béarnaise, and puddings like dark chocolate tart with almond and sea salt ice-cream or vanilla cheesecake with mulled wine sorbet. They do a well liked set lunch, £15.50 for two courses, £18 for three. *Starters/Snacks: £4.95 to £6.95. Main Courses: £11.95 to £19.50. Puddings: £5.50*

Free house ~ Licensees Martin and Debbie Still ~ Real ale ~ Bar food (12-2.30, 6.30-9.30(10 Fri and Sat); 12-3, 7-9.30 Sun) ~ Restaurant ~ (01225) 709131 ~ Children in eating area of bar and restaurant ~ Dogs allowed in bar ~ Open 11(12 Sun)-11; closed 25 and 26 Dec, 1 Jan ~ Bedrooms: £75B/£105B

Recommended by Craig Adams, Felicity Davies, Pete Devonish, Ian McIntyre, P and J Shapley, Dr and Mrs M E Wilson, David Parker, Emma Smith, Amanda De Montjoie, Mr and Mrs A J Hudson, John Robertson, Bill and Jessica Ritson, M G Hart, W W Burke, Dr and Mrs T E Hothersall, A P Seymour, Kay and Alistair Butler, Alun Jones, Dr and Mrs A K Clarke, Mr and Mrs A H Young

WINTERBOURNE BASSETT   SU1075   MAP 2

White Horse

Off A4361 S of Swindon; SN4 9QB

Neat, civilised dining pub, friendly licensees, wide choice of enjoyable food, thoughtful choice of drinks, and sizeable garden

In a pleasant setting, this is a well run dining pub with cheerfully helpful licensees. The neat big-windowed bar is attractively extended and has traditional tables and chairs on the waxed wooden floors, old prints and paintings on the walls, plants dotted about, and

a little brick fireplace. There's a comfortable dining room and warm conservatory, too.
Wadworths 6X and IPA and a seasonal guest on handpump, 15 wines by the glass, winter
mulled wine and summer Pimms by the jug; piped music, darts and board games. There
are tables outside on a good-sized lawn and lovely hanging baskets.

🍴 **Quite a wide choice of well liked food includes filled baguettes, ploughman's, thai-
spiced fishcake, chicken liver pâté, almond and nut roast with cranberry and orange sauce,
beef in ale pie, fillet of cod in a creamy cheddar and leek sauce, and braised lamb shank
with red wine gravy – as well as more elaborate dishes such as crab and ginger ravioli
with a sweet chilli and mango sauce, roast tandoori salmon, pork tenderloin stuffed with
rosemary scented prunes, wrapped with bacon and served with a port and red wine jus,
and gressingham duck breast with a red berry sauce and red onion and tomato chutney;
puddings like dark chocolate torte and fruit crumble, a good value, two-course lunch and
an early-bird evening set menu.** *Starters/Snacks: £3.95 to £5.65. Main Courses: £6.25 to
£17.95. Puddings: £4.65 to £5.75*

Wadworths ~ Tenants Chris and Kathy Stone ~ Real ale ~ Bar food (12-2.30(4 Sun), 6-9.30) ~
Restaurant ~ (01793) 731257 ~ Children welcome ~ Open 11.30-3, 6-midnight; 12-3, 7-11 Sun

*Recommended by William Booth-Davey, Dr M Yates, J Collie, Baden and Sandy Waller, JJW, CMW, Tony Baldwin,
Mrs Jill Wyatt, M J Winterton, Mr and Mrs I Pillinger, P A Pillinger, Mrs B S Clarke*

WYLYE   SU0037   MAP 4

Bell 🍺

Just off A303/A36; High Street; BA12 0QP

**Cosy old village pub revitalised by local brewery, with good beers, pretty garden, and
popular food**

Prettily set in a peaceful village, this cosy partly 14th-c country pub is doing rather well
since it was taken over by the nearby Hidden Brewery, and though it's been spruced up
with a lick of paint and new carpets, it still has all its old charms. With a civilised
unhurried atmosphere, the neatly kept, black-beamed front bar has a log fire, and sturdy
rustic furnishings that go well with the stripped stonework and neat timbered
herringbone brickwork. Friendly staff serve well kept Hidden Passion, Pint, Pleasure and
Quest, all much enjoyed by readers. There are seats outside on a pleasant walled terrace
and in a back garden, which is attractively flanked by the church's clipped yews. The pub
has fine downland walks nearby, and is about 15 minutes' drive from Stonehenge. As we
went to press, their rather jolly website (www.thebellatwylye.com) had a coupon offering
a free drink with every pre-booked meal.

🍴 **Lunchtime bar food includes baguettes, ploughman's, soup, and steak and ale pie; in
the evenings they have things like pan-seared scallops with prawns and honey and
mustard dressing, tomato, avocado and mozzarella crostini, breast of lamb stuffed with
sage, onion and basil, with parsley mash, mint jelly and red wine gravy, pork belly pan-
fried in balsamic and chilli syrup, and chicken and pea risotto; children's menu.**
Starters/Snacks: £3.95 to £6.95. Main Courses: £6.50 to £14.00. Puddings: £4.25

Hidden ~ Lease Elizabeth Perry ~ Real ale ~ Bar food (12-2, 6-9(9.30 Fri/Sat); 12-2.30,
7-9 Sun) ~ Restaurant ~ (01985) 248338 ~ Children welcome ~ Dogs allowed in bar and
bedrooms ~ Monthly quiz in summer ~ Open 11.30-3, 6-11; 12-3, 6-10.30 Sun ~
Bedrooms: £50S(£50B)/£50S(£65B)

*Recommended by Richard J Mullarkey, Douglas and Ann Hare, David Morgan, John Coatsworth, Dr and Mrs
M E Wilson, Roy Hoing*

Real ale to us means beer which has matured naturally in its cask – not pressurised or
filtered. We name all real ales stocked. We usually name ales preserved under a light
blanket of carbon dioxide too, though purists – pointing out that this stops
the natural yeasts developing – would disagree (most people, including us,
can't tell the difference!).

LUCKY DIP

Besides the fully inspected pubs, you might like to try these Lucky Dips recommended to us and described by readers (if you do, please send us reports: www.goodguides.co.uk).

ALDBOURNE [SU2675]
Crown SN8 2DU [The Square]: Friendly new landlord in local prettily facing village green with pond and Early English church, well kept Greene King IPA and Wadworths 6X, enjoyable food, good service, comfortable two-part beamed lounge, oak bar furnishings, log fire in unusual huge inglenook linking to public bar, small nicely laid out dining room; tables under cocktail parasols in neat courtyard *(Jeff Davies)*

ALL CANNINGS [SU0761]
Kings Arms SN10 3PA [The Street]: Charming Victorian village pub with warm welcome, good choice of reasonably priced food from sandwiches up inc good curry range, well kept Wadworths IPA, 6X and a guest beer, good wine range; children welcome, large garden, not far from Kennet & Avon Canal moorings *(Anne and Alan Fleming)*

ALVEDISTON [ST9723]
Crown SP5 5JY [off A30 W of Salisbury]: 15th-c thatched inn with three cosy very low-beamed partly panelled rooms, deep pink paintwork, two inglenook fireplaces, enjoyable freshly made food, Ringwood Best and guest beers, good wines by the glass, darts, cribbage, dominoes; children welcome, pretty views from neatly kept attractive garden, good bedrooms *(Dr D Smith, J S Phillips, LYM, Pat and Robert Watt)*

AMESBURY [SU1541]
Antrobus Arms SP4 7EU [Church St]: Quiet, comfortable and relaxed with good food, no piped music, kind helpful staff, changing real ales, log fires in warmly welcoming smart yet pubby bar and communicating lounge overlooking beautiful walled garden, two dining rooms; children and dogs welcome, 17 bedrooms, open all day *(Gwyneth and Salvo Spadaro-Dutturi)*

AVEBURY [SU1069]
Red Lion SN8 1RF [High St (A361)]: Much-modernised and substantially extended from pretty thatched front part, in the heart of the stone circles – so gets plenty of customers; real ales such as Greene King, open fires, restaurant extension, popular summer motorcycle barbecue Weds nights; may be piped music; children welcome, open all day from breakfast on *(LYM, Rosanna Luke, Matt Curzon, Bob and Angela Brooks, John and Gloria Isaacs)*

BADBURY [SU1980]
Plough SN4 0EP [A346 (Marlborough Rd) just S of M4 junction 15]: Large rambling bar area, Arkells 2B, 3B and Kingsdown, decent wines, cheerful efficient staff and thriving atmosphere, simple good value food inc afternoon snacks and all-day Sun roasts in light and airy dining room (children allowed) looking over road to Vale of the White Horse with pianola and papers to read, darts; piped music; children welcome, play area in sunny

garden above, handy for Great Western Hospital, open all day *(Dr and Mrs A K Clarke, Alistair Forsyth, R T and J C Moggridge, Brian and Maggie Woodford, Richard and Judy Winn, Mrs Pat Crabb)*

BECKHAMPTON [SU0868]
☆ *Waggon & Horses* SN8 1QJ [A4 Marlborough—Calne]: Handsome old stone-and-thatch pub handy for Avebury, old-fashioned settles and comfortably cushioned wall benches in open-plan beamed bar with what some might call the patina of ages, friendly staff, dining area, sensible food (not Sun evening), well kept Wadworths ales and a guest beer, pool and pub games; piped music turned down on request; children in restaurant, pleasant raised garden with good play area, open all day, bedrooms *(Mike and Lynn Robinson, LYM, Sheila and Robert Robinson, Dr and Mrs A K Clarke, David Barnes, T R and B C Jenkins, Susan and John Douglas, Conor McGaughey, Martin and Sarah)*

BOX [ST8268]
Bear SN13 8NJ [High St (A4)]: 18th-c, with real ales such as Wadworths 6X and Wickwar Cotswold Way, welcoming staff, log fires, lively locals' bar with cards and dominoes, quiet lounge set for enjoyable reasonably priced food; bedrooms, backs on to cricket ground *(Dr and Mrs A K Clarke)*
Northey Arms SN13 8AE [A4, Bath side]: Stone-built dining pub reworked with simple contemporary décor and lighting, chunky modern furniture on pale hardwood floor, food from tapas and satisfying bar lunches to more ambitious evening menu, Wadworths ales, decent wines by the glass; children welcome, garden tables *(Michael Doswell)*
Queens Head SN13 8NH [High St]: Civilised open-plan local with old-world dark wood décor, prompt friendly service, three real ales, bargain food from snacks and light dishes such as baked potatoes up, valley views *(Dr and Mrs A K Clarke)*

BRADFORD LEIGH [ST8362]
Plough BA15 2RW [B2109 N of Bradford]: Emphasis on meals in extended and smartened up dining area (no baps or sandwiches), friendly efficient service, Moles and Wadworths 6X, log fires; darts and pool; children welcome, big garden with play area *(MRSM, Dr and Mrs A K Clarke)*

BRADFORD-ON-AVON [ST8260]
Barge BA15 2EA [Frome Rd]: Enthusiastic current landlord specialising in quickly changing well kept real ales, pleasant atmosphere, leather sofas in window, café area too; soft piped music; children welcome, steps up to waterside tables and more on own barge, softly coloured lamps out here *(Dr and Mrs A K Clarke, Dr and Mrs M E Wilson, Richard and Nicola Tranter)*
Beehive BA15 1UA [A363 out towards

Trowbridge]: Friendly local atmosphere in old-fashioned L-shaped pub nr canal on outskirts, good choice of changing ales, reasonably priced pubby food, good range of wines, helpful service, cosy log fires, candlelit tables, 19th-c playbills, cricketing prints and cigarette cards, darts; children and dogs welcome; attractive good-sized back garden, play area, barbecues *(BB, Mike Gorton, Dr and Mrs A K Clarke, Pete Baker)*

Bunch of Grapes BA15 1JY [Silver St]: Dim-lit wine-bar style décor, cask seats and rugs on bare boards in small front room, bigger tables on composition floor of roomier main bar, good real ales, range of wines and malt whiskies, good choice of interesting reasonably priced food in bar and upstairs eating area; a few tables on back terrace *(Dr and Mrs A K Clarke, BB, M and GR, Susan and Nigel Wilson)*

Castle BA15 1SJ [Mount Pleasant/Masons Lane]: Refurbished and reopened summer 2007, promising initial reports – cheerful atmosphere, enjoyable up-to-date food, good décor blending old materials with relaxed contemporary feel; children welcome, nice garden, nice spot above town, bedrooms planned, open all day *(Dr and Mrs M E Wilson, Keith Burnell)*

Cross Guns BA15 2HB [Avoncliff, outside town]: Almost a fairground atmosphere on busy summer days, hard-working friendly staff generally coping pretty well with swarms of people in floodlit partly concreted areas steeply terraced above the bridges, aqueducts and river (dogs allowed out here); appealingly quaint at quieter times, with friendly stripped-stone low-beamed bar, real ales such as Butcombe, Blind House, Box Steam and Theakstons Old Peculier, lots of malt whiskies and country wines, 16th-c inglenook, upstairs river-view restaurant; children welcome, open all day *(John and Gloria Isaacs, Dr and Mrs A K Clarke, Angus and Carol Johnson, LYM, Meg and Colin Hamilton, Wendy Straker, D P and M A Miles, Ian Phillips)*

Three Horseshoes BA15 1LA [Frome Rd, by station car park entrance]: Popular and unpretentious old pub recently freshened up, some tall tables and chairs in bar, plenty of nooks and corners, quickly served enjoyable if not cheap food, Butcombe and Wadworths 6X, friendly service, small restaurant; big-screen TV; tables on terrace with big barbecue *(Dr and Mrs A K Clarke, Dr and Mrs M E Wilson)*

BRATTON [ST9152]

Duke BA13 4RW [B3098 E of Westbury]: Comfortable, neat and civilised open-plan pub with restaurant area off traditional bar, very good generous food (freshly made, so may take a while) inc lunchtime bargains, well kept Moles real ale, quick pleasant service, exemplary lavatories; darts and fruit machine in public area, piped music; ancient whalebone arch to enclosed side garden,

nearby walks, bedrooms *(Geoff and Brigid Smithers, BB, David Morgan)*

BROAD HINTON [SU1176]

Bell SN4 9PF [A4361 Swindon—Devizes]: Old pub refurbished and reopened (had been closed for some time), nicely furnished open-plan L-shaped room already popular locally for enjoyable reasonably priced pubby food, well kept Greene King and Wadworths ales, decent wines by the glass, prompt friendly service; pleasant garden *(Keith and Jean Symons, Tony Baldwin)*

BROKENBOROUGH [ST9189]

Rose & Crown SN16 0HZ: Open-plan bar, lower back part mainly a restaurant area, good value food from baguettes to good steaks (best to book Fri/Sat night), welcoming owners, two well kept Uley ales *(Guy Vowles)*

BROKERSWOOD [ST8352]

Kicking Donkey BA13 4EG: Good value pubby food from baguettes up, well kept changing ales such as Bath Gem, Butcombe, Sharps Doom Bar and Wadworths 6X, good service, log fire, several linked areas and various nooks, beams and flagstones; children welcome, picnic-sets and good play area in pretty garden opp, lovely rural setting with woodland walks *(MRSM)*

BROUGHTON GIFFORD [ST8764]

Bell on the Common SN12 8LX [The Common]: Imposing rose-draped stone-built pub on huge informal village green, traditional furnishings, long-serving landlord and friendly staff, Wadworths from handpumps on back wall, big coal fire, enjoyable homely food, dining lounge full of copper and old country prints, rustic bar with local photographs old and new, small pool room with darts; juke box, popular quiz night; children welcome, charming flower-filled crazy-paved garden (occasional pig roasts and live music), bowls club next door *(Dr and Mrs A K Clarke, Dr and Mrs M E Wilson)*

Fox & Hounds SN12 8PN [The Street]: Go-ahead chef/landlord putting plenty of flavour into his reasonably priced locally sourced food (cooked to order, so can take a while), welcoming helpful service, fresh décor alongside traditional timbers, real ales such as Greene King, armchairs and sofa by entrance; big well kept garden behind *(MRSM, Catherine Pitt, Dr and Mrs M E Wilson)*

BURCOMBE [SU0631]

Ship SP2 0EJ [Burcombe Lane]: Cosy two-level dining pub with unpretentious bistro atmosphere, low beams, panelling and window seats, two log fires, pleasant décor, candles and soft lighting, young chef/landlord doing good choice of good value fresh food inc enterprising dishes, friendly efficient staff, Wadworths 6X, decent wines; unobtrusive piped music; children welcome, tables on front terrace and in peaceful riverside garden, pretty village *(John Coatsworth, Pat and Robert Watt, Colin and Janet Roe)*

CASTLE COMBE [ST8379]
Salutation SN14 7LH [The Gibb; B4039
Acton Turville—Chippenham, nr Nettleton]:
Roomy old pub with plenty of beamery,
choice of seating areas inc comfortable
lounge and locals' bar, huge handsome
fireplace, prompt welcoming service, friendly
staff, real ales such as Greene King IPA,
Wickwar Cotswold Way and Wychwood
Hobgoblin, good choice of wines, enjoyable
food from big baguettes up, separate
raftered thatched and timbered barn
restaurant, no piped music; children
welcome, pretty garden with pergola, open
all day (Dr and Mrs A K Clarke, Peter and
Audrey Dowsett, MRSM, Andrew Shore,
Maria Williams)
☆ *White Hart* SN14 7HS [signed off B4039
Chippenham—Chipping Sodbury]: Attractive
ancient stone-built pub with beams,
panelling, flagstones, seats in stone-
mullioned window, lots of old local
photographs, Wadworths ales, prompt
friendly service, log fires, wide choice of
enjoyable food from good value big
sandwiches and light dishes up, smart
modern restaurant on left; walkers welcome
(handy for Macmillan Way and new Palladian
Way), tables on pavement and in sheltered
courtyard; in centre of this honeypot village,
so can be very busy; open all day
(Ian Phillips, Phyl and Jack Street,
Guy Vowles, LYM, Lawrence Pearse)

CHILMARK [ST9732]
Black Dog SP3 5AH [B3089 Salisbury—
Hindon]: Appealing and fairly priced inc good
local steaks in 15th-c beamed village pub
with log fires in its various smallish rooms,
warm welcome and attentive polite service,
thriving atmosphere, Wadworths ales, good
value house wines, thriving local atmosphere;
rows of picnic-sets in good-sized roadside
garden with terrace (Mrs J H S Lang, Basil
and Sylvia Walden, Dr and Mrs M E Wilson,
Colin and Janet Roe, LYM)

CHILTON FOLIAT [SU3270]
Wheatsheaf RG17 0TE [B4192]: Well worn-in
beamed village local with welcoming and
chatty licensees, cheerful prompt service,
two smallish rooms, well kept Greene King
ales, good wines by the glass, low-priced
pubby food from doorstep sandwiches up,
open fire; dogs welcome, pool room, very
quiet piped music; big garden (Geoff and
Sylvia Donald, Alain and Rose Foote)

CHIPPENHAM [ST9073]
Kingfisher SN14 0JL [Hungerdown Lane]:
Welcoming local with Wadworths 6X,
interesting malt whiskies and brandies, good
lunchtime sandwiches and salads, antique
prints, board games; soft piped music,
frequent music and good quiz nights; tables
outside (Dr and Mrs A K Clarke)
Old Road Tavern SN15 1JA [Old Rd, by N
side of station]: Thriving town pub, very
friendly, with games-oriented public bar,
two-part lounge, Courage Best, Fullers
London Pride, Greene King Old Speckled Hen

and a guest beer, cheap lunchtime food from
sandwiches up; frequent wknd live music;
pleasant secluded little back garden (Dr and
Mrs A K Clarke, Pete Baker)

CHIRTON [SU0757]
Wiltshire Yeoman SN10 3QN [Andover Rd
(A342)]: New licensees doing good value
food inc bargain lunches and some
imaginative dishes without losing the local
atmosphere, good beer choice (I H G Busby,
Anthony Bowes)

CHISELDON [SU1879]
Patriots Arms SN4 0LU [New Rd (B4005, off
A346 just S of M4 junction 15)]: Big two-bar
pub with family room and restaurant, decent
food choice (not Sun evening), real ales,
daily papers; games machine; garden with
shelter and good play area, open all day
wknds, cl Mon (JJW, CMW)

CHITTERNE [ST9843]
☆ *Kings Head* BA12 0LJ [B390 Heytesbury—
Shrewton]: Welcoming local, relaxed and
understated, despite out-of-the-way setting
well liked for food from short choice of good
bar lunches to inventive evening meals inc
good fish; Butcombe and Wadworths 6X,
friendly tenants, good log fire, simple
traditional décor with wooden floors,
panelled dado and chunky old pine tables
with lighted candles; may be piped music;
lovely hanging baskets, tables on back
terrace, pretty village, good Salisbury Plain
walks (Terry Buckland, Ian Phillips, John and
Elisabeth Cox, BB)

CLYFFE PYPARD [SU0776]
Goddard Arms SN4 7PY: Cheery 16th-c local
with log fire and raised dining area in split-
level main bar, small sitting room with
another fire and two old armchairs, down-to-
earth chatty and welcoming licensees,
Wadworths 6X and guest beers like local
Ramsbury, farm cider, good value
straightforward fresh food, daily papers,
artwork for sale, pool room with darts,
cribbage etc; sports TV, no credit cards;
picnic-sets in back courtyard, bedrooms, also
Youth Hostel accommodation in former
skittle alley, tiny pretty thatched village in
lovely countryside, open all day wknds
(Pete Baker, Guy Vowles, BB)

CODFORD [ST9639]
George BA12 0NG [just off A36 W of A303
intersection; High St]: Old inn with knocked-
through L-shaped bar, stripped brickwork,
well spaced tables, big house plants,
contemporary art and lighting, log fire,
Timothy Taylors Landlord, nice baguettes and
some good cooking; piped music, disabled
access due for improvement; well behaved
children welcome, tables on narrow front
terrace overlooking road, bedrooms, has
been cl Sun evening and Tues (Gerry and
Rosemary Dobson, John A Barker,
J Stickland, Julia and Richard Tredgett,
Richard J Mullarkey, LYM)

COLLINGBOURNE DUCIS [SU2453]
Shears SN8 3ED [Cadley Rd]: Stylishly simple
thatched pub under new licensees, friendly

atmosphere, enjoyable food in bar and comfortable restaurant, real ales inc Brakspears, good wine choice; attractive courtyard garden, six nice bedrooms *(Michael Rigby, David Barnes)*

COLLINGBOURNE KINGSTON [SU2355]
Barleycorn SN8 3SD [A338]: Neat village pub with several well kept ales such as Hook Norton Old Hooky, Wadworths and Charles Wells Bombardier, wide blackboard choice of enjoyable bar food (can take quite a while – attractive restaurant may take priority), decent wines, friendly new owners, pool room, exemplary lavatories; piped music; tables in small garden *(Robin and Tricia Walker)*

CORSHAM [ST8670]
Hare & Hounds SN13 0HY [Pickwick (A4 E)]: Traditional local with fine changing choice of well kept ales such as Bath Gem, Hop Back Summer Lightning and Moles, annual beer festival, cheerful welcoming landlord, enjoyable straightforward food up to steaks, several rooms inc comfortable and attractive panelled lounge with log fire; unobtrusive piped music and sports TV in busy main bar, another room with alcove seating and pool; open all day Fri-Sun (and lunchtimes when the Two Pigs is not) *(David Parker, Emma Smith)*

CORTON [ST9340]
☆ *Dove* BA12 0SZ [off A36 at Upton Lovell, SE of Warminster]: Cottagey country pub in lovely valley, cheerful helpful landlord and staff, quietly tasteful yet unpretentious partly flagstoned main bar with huge central log fire and good pictures, enterprising range of good food at all price levels from baguettes to fresh fish and steaks, well kept ales such as Archers, Hop Back, Sharps Doom Bar or Shepherd Neame Spitfire, good wines by the glass, daily papers, conservatory; piped music; children welcome, tables on neat back lawn, comfortable wheelchair-friendly bedrooms, good fishing available *(Edward Mirzoeff, LYM, Dr and Mrs M E Wilson, Mr and Mrs Draper, David Morgan)*

CRICKLADE [SU1093]
Red Lion SN6 6DD [off A419 Swindon—Cirencester; High St]: Fine old 16th-c former coaching inn with great range of good real ales – Moles Best, Wadworths 6X and several guests such as Ramsbury, two farm ciders, good choice of malt whiskies, friendly landlord and helpful staff, sandwiches and simple hot dishes (not Mon/Tues), generous Sun carvery, log fire, interesting signs and bric-a-brac in large yet cosy bar, local artwork for sale, no music or mobile phones; neat garden, bedrooms, open all day *(E McCall, T McLean, D Irving, R Huggins, MLR, Pete Baker, Martin and Karen Wake)*

White Lion SN6 6DA [High St]: Two-bar pub with good service, good value generous food (limited lunchtime menu, more elaborate evening choice), three real ales such as Wychwood, good choice of soft drinks, pleasantly relaxed restaurant, games room;

tables out under cocktail parasols behind *(Alan and Eve Harding)*

DERRY HILL [ST9570]
Lansdowne Arms SN11 9NS [Church Rd]: Stately stone-built pub opposite one of Bowood's grand gatehouses, roomy, airy and civilised, with relaxed period flavour, hearty log fire and candles in bottles, Wadworths ales, good value wines by the glass, prompt attentive cheerful service, wide food choice from good range of huge sandwiches with chips up in bar and restaurant; faint piped music; fine views, picnic-sets in neat side garden, good play area *(Meg and Colin Hamilton, BB, Matthew Shackle, Dr and Mrs A K Clarke)*

DEVIZES [SU0061]
Black Swan SN10 1JQ [Market Pl]: Comfortably old-fashioned two-room hotel bar with friendly atmosphere, local and military memorabilia, wide choice of good value food in bar and upstairs restaurant, well kept Wadworths; good bedrooms, open all day *(Ann and Colin Hunt)*

Fox & Hounds SN10 3HJ [Nursteed (A342 S)]: Attractive thatched pub very popular locally for its enjoyable food inc prime steaks, well kept Wadworths IPA and 6X *(Mr and Mrs A Curry)*

DOWNTON [SU1721]
Wooden Spoon SP5 3PG [High St (A338 S of Salisbury)]: Convivial family-run pub with welcoming attentive service, good sensibly priced food from sandwiches and baguettes to wide choice of hot dishes using local produce, inc some interesting dishes, good steaks and popular Sun lunch, John Smiths, Ringwood and a guest beer, good value wines, public bar on left; children welcome *(Glen and Nola Armstrong, W W Burke, A and B D Craig)*

EASTON ROYAL [SU1961]
Bruce Arms SN9 5LR [Easton Rd]: 19th-c local with benches by two long scrubbed antique pine tables on bar's brick floor, homely carpeted and curtained parlour with easy chairs, old pictures, flowers and piano, Wadworths IPA and 6X, Pewsey organic cider, good filled rolls only, darts, extension with pool and TV; camping field, open all day Sun *(the Didler, Kevin Thorpe)*

EDINGTON [ST9353]
☆ *Lamb* BA13 4PG [Westbury Rd (B3098)]: Open-plan traditional beamed village pub with assorted pine furniture on bare boards, friendly atmosphere and cheerful helpful licensees, log fire, real ales such as Butcombe, Otter and Wadworths 6X, above-average food from good generous paninis up, dining room; pleasant garden tables (access to pretty village's play area beyond), great views, good walks *(Dr and Mrs M E Wilson)*

ERLESTOKE [ST9653]
George & Dragon SN10 5TX [High St (B3098 Westbury—Upavon)]: Attractive and unpretentious Elizabethan timbered two-bar local with low beams, Hidden Bitter and Shepherd Neame Spitfire, woodburner,

friendly dog, end games room; new bedroom extension *(Dr and Mrs M E Wilson)*

FARLEIGH WICK [ST8063]

Fox & Hounds BA15 2PU [A363 Bathford—Bradford, 2½ miles NW of Bradford]: Well extended low-beamed rambling pub doing well under current friendly efficient landlord, changing choice of enjoyable food inc some interesting dishes, real ales such as Bath Gem and Bass, large bare-boards dining area; attractive garden *(Dr and Mrs M E Wilson, MRSM)*

FORD [ST8474]

☆ *White Hart* SN14 8RP [off A420 Chippenham—Bristol]: Comfortable old-world stone-built country inn in attractive stream-side grounds, heavy black beams and a good log fire in its ancient fireplace, wide choice of food (all day Sun) from bar food and tapas to full meals, good choice of wines by the glass, real ales such as Abbey Bellringer, Courage and Wadworths 6X, friendly attentive service; piped music; children in restaurant, tables outside, pleasant bedrooms, good breakfast, open all day wknds *(Dr and Mrs A K Clarke, Dr and Mrs M E Wilson, Hugh Roberts, LYM, John and Gloria Isaacs, Julie and Bill Ryan)*

FROXFIELD [SU2968]

Pelican SN8 3JY [A4]: Extended former coaching inn with good value food, several real ales, relaxed atmosphere, pleasant clean décor in bars and dining area; attractive streamside garden with dovecot and duck pond, Kennet & Avon Canal walks *(Geoff and Sylvia Donald, Gavin Oclee Brown, Mark Farrington)*

GREAT CHEVERELL [ST9854]

Bell SN10 5TH [off B3098 Westbury—Mkt Lavington]: Cheerful mother and daughter in friendly dining pub with fresh light décor in bar and minimalist beamed restaurant, good value food from familiar favourites to more inventive dishes, Wadworths IPA and 6X and a guest beer, good choice of wines by the glass, log fire, comfortable chairs and settles, cosy little alcoves; garden picnic-sets, attractive village *(Mrs C D West, Mike and Lynn Robinson, Richard and Nicola Tranter)*

GREAT DURNFORD [SU1337]

☆ *Black Horse* SP4 6AY [follow Woodfords sign from A345 High Post traffic lights]: Cheery and homely, with some nice alcoves, one room with ship pictures, models and huge ensigns, another with a large inglenook woodburner, masses of bric-a-brac, Fullers London Pride, Ringwood and other ales, genial staff, food from baguettes up, darts, shove-ha'penny, table skittles, pinball, cribbage, dominoes and ring the bull; piped blues and jazz; children and dogs welcome, picnic-sets in big informal riverside garden with play area and barbecues, decent bedrooms, cl Sun evening and Mon in winter *(LYM, Ian Phillips)*

GREAT WISHFORD [SU0735]

☆ *Royal Oak* SP2 0PD [off A36 NW of Salisbury]: Emphasis on enjoyable food in appealing two-bar pub with big family dining area and restaurant, prompt service by friendly helpful young staff, three well kept changing ales such as Blindmans Mine, Keystone Gold and Ringwood Best (useful tasting notes), decent wines, pleasant décor with beams, panelling, rugs on bare boards and log fires; pretty village *(LYM, Simon Jones, Mr and Mrs Draper, Ian Phillips)*

HEDDINGTON [ST9966]

☆ *Ivy* SN11 0PL [off A3102 S of Calne]: Picturesque thatched 15th-c village pub with good inglenook log fire in take-us-as-you-find-us old-fashioned L-shaped bar, heavy low beams, timbered walls, assorted furnishings on parquet floor, brass and copper, Wadworths IPA, 6X and a seasonal beer tapped from the cask, good plain fresh home-made food (not Sun-Weds evenings, and may take a time if many locals in) from great lunchtime club sandwiches up, back family eating room, sensibly placed darts, piano, dog and cat; may be piped music; disabled access, open all day wknds, picnic-sets in front garden, attractively set hamlet *(Gordon and Jay Smith, George Atkinson, LYM, the Didler, Pete Baker)*

HEYTESBURY [ST9242]

☆ *Angel* BA12 0ED [just off A36 E of Warminster; High St]: Upmarket dining pub in quiet village just below Salisbury Plain, new chef doing enjoyable if pricy food inc notable steaks, prompt service by friendly young local staff, comfortable lounge opening into pleasant restaurant with courtyard garden, left-hand beamed dining bar with log fire, daily papers, straightforward furnishings and some attractive prints and old photographs, Greene King ales; piped music; children welcome, bedrooms due for refurbishment, open all day *(Jeremy Whitehorn, D P and M A Miles, Ian Malone, Ian Phillips, LYM, Brian Dean, Edward Mirzoeff, Stephen P Edwards)*

HIGHWORTH [SU2092]

☆ *Saracens Head* SN6 7AG [High St]: Civilised and relaxed rambling bar, wide choice of reasonably priced blackboard food, several real ales inc Arkells 2B and 3B tapped from casks in bar area, good soft drinks choice, comfortably cushioned pews in several interesting areas around great four-way central log fireplace, timbers and panelling, no mobile phones; quiet piped music; children in eating area, tables in smart partly covered courtyard with heaters, comfortable bedrooms, open all day wkdys *(LYM, Peter and Audrey Dowsett)*

HINDON [ST9032]

☆ *Angel* SP3 6DJ [B3089 Wilton—Mere]: Good varied choice of reasonably priced food from lunchtime snacks inc good baguettes up in 18th-c flagstoned coaching inn, hard-working staff, real ales such as Archers from chrome bar counter, decent wines, big fireplace, long cream dining room with huge window showing kitchen; piped music; children in eating areas, tables outside, seven comfortable bedrooms, good breakfast, open all day in summer *(Dr and Mrs M W A Haward, Pat and Robert Watt, John Evans, Colin and Janet Roe, Helen and Brian Edgeley, LYM, MDN)*

HODSON [SU1780]

☆ *Calley Arms* SN4 0QG [not far from M4 junction 15, via Chiseldon; off B4005 S of Swindon]: Neat and friendly open-plan pub with enterprising young licensees doing wide range of enjoyable fresh food, both traditional and more interesting dishes, quick cheerful service, Wadworths ales with a guest such as Everards Tiger, good choice of other drinks, open fire in nicely laid out main area, woodburner and darts in bare-boards part; may be faint piped music; children welcome, picnic-sets on sheltered back grass (hear the larks singing), pleasant placarded walk from the pub *(Mary Rayner, Sheila and Robert Robinson, Nick Duffy, BB)*

HOLT [ST8561]

☆ *Toll Gate* BA14 6PX [Ham Green; B3107 W of Melksham]: Appealing individual décor and furnishings and thriving atmosphere in comfortable bar, friendly helpful service, five good interesting changing ales, good choice of wines by the glass, farm cider and good coffee, generally very good food, daily papers, log fire, another in more sedate high-raftered ex-chapel restaurant up steps; piped music may obtrude; dogs welcome, no under-12s, picnic-sets out on back terrace, compact bedrooms, cl Sun evening, Mon *(Mrs Jill Wyatt, Dr and Mrs M E Wilson, W F C Phillips, Bryan Pearson, Mr and Mrs A Curry, Mr and Mrs P R Thomas, David and Jean Hall, LYM, Mr and Mrs A H Young, Ian Phillips)*

HOOK [SU0785]

Bolingbroke Arms SN4 8DZ [B4041, off A420 just W of M4 junction 16]: Well spaced tables in informal airy bare-boards bar with lots of light pine, armchair lounge, pleasantly decorated restaurant popular with older lunchers, Arkells ales, good soft drinks choice, good-sized helpings of food from sandwiches and baked potatoes up; quiet piped music; children welcome, picnic-sets in garden with pond and fountain, bedrooms, cl Sun evening *(JJW, CMW)*

KINGSDOWN [ST8167]

Swan SN13 8BP: Perched on steep hillside with great views, well kept beer, food inc good steaks, three small rooms, stripped stone walls *(Meg and Colin Hamilton)*

KINGTON LANGLEY [ST9277]

☆ *Hit or Miss* SN15 5NS [handy for M4 junction 17, off A350 S; Days Lane]: Cottagey and friendly, with delightfully chatty landlady, welcoming landlord and efficient service, small rather plush low-beamed cricket-theme bar, emphasis on left-hand restaurant with good log fire, good food from baguettes (not Sun) through familiar pub dishes and popular Sun lunch to game and fish, Adnams

and Timothy Taylors Landlord, good choice of wines by the glass, darts and pool in room off; tables out in front *(BB, Dr and Mrs M E Wilson, John and Gloria Isaacs, Michael Doswell)*

LANDFORD [SU2520]

Landford Poacher SP5 2EE [Southampton Rd (off A36)]: Edge of New Forest, new licensees settling in well, enjoyable food (all day wknds) inc interesting dishes, welcoming atmosphere, real ales such as Butcombe and Ringwood Best, restaurant; children and dogs welcome, disabled facilities, picnic-sets in good-sized garden, open all day, cl Mon lunchtime *(anon)*

LIDDINGTON [SU2081]

Village Inn SN4 0HE [handy for M4 junction 15, via A419 and B4192]: Comfortable, warm and welcoming, some emphasis on huge choice of good value food inc popular Sun roasts, linked bar areas and stripped stone and raftered back dining extension, Arkells ales, log fire, conservatory, no piped music; disabled access and facilities, terrace tables *(KC)*

LIMPLEY STOKE [ST7861]

☆ *Hop Pole* BA2 7FS [off A36 and B3108 S of Bath]: Largely panelled 16th-c stone-built two-bar pub with well kept ales such as Butcombe, Marstons Pedigree and Okells, wide choice of fairly priced enjoyable food (may be fully booked wknds), prompt cheerful service, log fire, traditional games; TV; children in eating areas, nice enclosed garden behind *(LYM, Dr and Mrs M E Wilson, John and Gloria Isaacs, Angus and Carol Johnson, Barry Gibbs, Peter and Audrey Dowsett, Dr and Mrs A K Clarke)*

LITTLE CHEVERELL [ST9953]

Owl SN10 4JS [just off B3098 Westbury—Upavon; Low Rd]: Compact two-room bar with cheerful landlady, real ales such as Brakspears and Ringwood, straightforward food, beams and mixed furnishings, back dining area; nice deck with heaters and canopy looking over tree-sheltered bird-filled garden dropping steeply to brook, fields beyond *(LYM, Mike and Lynn Robinson, Dr and Mrs M E Wilson)*

LOCKERIDGE [SU1467]

☆ *Who'd A Thought It* SN8 4EL [signed just off A4 Marlborough—Calne just W of Fyfield]: Friendly pub with two linked rooms set for good plentiful food from good value baguettes up, evening meals with fish emphasis, reasonable prices, small side drinking area, well kept Wadworths and a guest beer, good choice of wines by the glass, coal or log fire, interesting collection of cooperage tools, family room; unobtrusive piped music; pleasant back garden with play area, delightful quiet scenery, lovely walks *(Jenny and Brian Seller, Robert W Buckle, Angus and Rosemary Campbell, BB)*

LONGBRIDGE DEVERILL [ST8640]

George BA12 7DG [A350/B3095]: Extended village pub, spacious and relaxed even when busy, with pleasant efficient service, good reasonably priced food inc popular Sun carvery, well kept Fullers ales, restaurant *(B and F A Hannam)*

LOWER WOODFORD [SU1235]

☆ *Wheatsheaf* SP4 6NQ [signed off A360 just N of Salisbury]: Prettily set 18th-c dining pub, large, warm and friendly, with big helpings of enjoyable reasonably priced food, efficient service, well kept Badger ales, good wines, log fire, comfortable furnishings on oak floor with miniature footbridge over indoor goldfish pool; piped music; children welcome, good disabled access, baby-changing, good big tree-lined garden with play area *(LYM, Mr and Mrs A Curry)*

LUDWELL [ST9022]

Grove Arms SP7 9ND [A30 E of Shaftesbury]: Bright and roomy bar and linked dining areas in thatched hotel dating from 16th c, welcoming licensees and friendly well trained staff, good varied food from generous lunchtime sandwiches and other snacks to attractively priced main meals, Badger ales, good choice of wines by the glass, spotless housekeeping, restaurant; children welcome, good value bedrooms *(Colin and Janet Roe, Pat and Robert Watt)*

MALMESBURY [ST9287]

☆ *Smoking Dog* SN16 9AT [High St]: Twin-fronted mid-terrace town with two cosy flagstoned front bars, good choice of wines by the glass, Archers, Brains and guest beers, log fire, generally enjoyable modern food in back bistro with big stripped pine tables on bare boards, cheerful service, spring bank hol sausage and beer festival; children and dogs welcome, small quiet colourful garden up steep steps, bedrooms, open all day *(Paul A Moore, LYM, Guy Vowles, Baden and Sandy Waller, Tom and Ruth Rees, Amanda De Montjoie, Christine and Neil Townend, Klaus and Elizabeth Leist)*

Whole Hog SN16 9AS [Market Cross]: Homely basic furnishings on bare boards, market cross view from bar stools at window counter, piggy theme, quick friendly service, real ales such as Archers, Butts Golden Brown, St Georges seasonal, Wadworths 6X and Youngs, enjoyable reasonably priced pub food using good ingredients, daily papers, peaceful separate dining room (not Sun evening); games machines, bar can get noisy and crowded with young people evenings; open all day *(Robert Gomme)*

MARDEN [SU0857]

☆ *Millstream* SN10 3RH [off A342]: Pleasantly refurbished and extended open-plan upmarket bar/restaurant with newish chef doing good food inc his own bread and ice-creams, fresh local organic ingredients, Wadworths real ales and great wine choice inc champagne by the glass, beams, flagstones, log fires and woodburners, friendly attentive service, maps and guides as well as daily papers; children and well behaved dogs welcome, pleasant garden with neat terrace, cl Mon *(Bill and Jessica Ritson, Michael Doswell)*

MARSTON MEYSEY [SU1297]

Old Spotted Cow SN6 6LQ [off A419 Swindon—Cirencester]: L-shaped cotswold stone pub with welcoming licensees, real ales such as Milk Street, Wadworths and Youngs, decent wines, bar lunches and (not Sun) enjoyable evening meals, two open fires, light wood furniture on bare boards, plants and cow pictures, parquet-floored dining room, no piped music; spacious garden with picnic-sets and play area, open all day wknds *(J E Hutchinson, E McCall, T McLean, D Irving, R Huggins)*

MILDENHALL [SU2169]

☆ *Horseshoe* SN8 2LR: Relaxed and neatly kept traditional 17th-c thatched pub with good value food from sandwiches up, quick friendly service even when busy, well kept ales such as Archers and Wadworths, good value wines, three attractive partly partitioned beamed rooms; bedrooms, picnic-sets out on grass, pleasant village setting, good Kennet Valley and Savernake Forest walks *(Angus and Rosemary Campbell, Geoff and Sylvia Donald, Mark and Ruth Brock, Sue Demont, Tim Barrow)*

MONKTON FARLEIGH [ST8065]

Kings Arms BA15 2QH [signed off A363 Bradford—Bath]: Imposing 17th-c building recently brightened up inside, sofas, open fire and dining tables in one bar, huge inglenook and more dining tables in L-shaped beamed lounge, Bass, Butcombe and Wadworths 6X, good wine and whisky choice, enjoyable somewhat pricy food (all day wknds) inc popular family Sun lunch; piped music, unobtrusive big-screen TV; front partly flagstoned courtyard, well tended two-level back garden, lovely village, has been open all day wknds *(Dr and Mrs M E Wilson, Frank and Bridget Crowe)*

NETHERHAMPTON [SU1129]

☆ *Victoria & Albert* SP2 8PU [just off A3094 W of Salisbury]: Cosy black-beamed bar in simple thatched cottage with welcoming licensees and staff, good generous food from nicely presented sandwiches up, sensible prices and local supplies, changing ales such as Fullers London Pride and Palmers, farm cider, decent house wine, nicely cushioned old-fashioned wall settles on ancient floor tiles, restaurant; children welcome, hatch service for sizeable garden behind, handy for Wilton House and Nadder Valley walks *(Colin and Janet Roe, Ian and Sandra Thornton, Tony Orman, James Blood, LYM)*

NOMANSLAND [SU2517]

Lamb SP5 2BP [signed off B3078 and B3079]: Lovely New Forest village-green setting with friendly donkeys and ponies for unpretentious pub with wide range of bargain fresh food inc lots of pasta and fish, children's menu, Fullers London Pride and HSB and Ringwood Best and Fortyniner, short sensible wine list, friendly informal service, log fire in lounge bar, small dining room; pool and TV in public bar; tables out on terrace, green and garden behind, good walks, open all day *(Sally and Tom Matson, BB)*

NORTH WROUGHTON [SU1482]

Check Inn SN4 9AA [Woodland View (cul de sac off A4361 just S of Swindon)]: Extended real ale pub with interesting changing choice of up to ten, lots of bottled imports, farm cider, good soft drinks choice, helpful friendly service even when crowded, generous usual bar food, log fire, glossy pine furniture, various comfortable areas inc hatch-served side part, darts; games machine; children and dogs welcome, disabled access, heated front terrace, garden bar, boules, bedrooms, open all day Fri-Sun *(Tim and Rosemary Wells, JJW, CMW, Jeremy King)*

ODSTOCK [SU1426]

Yew Tree SP5 4JE [off A338 S of Salisbury; Whitsbury Rd]: Pretty thatched and low-beamed country dining pub with big blackboard choice of reasonably priced home-made food inc tapas, friendly staff, Ringwood and changing guest beers, decent wines, log fire, raised seating area at one end; pleasant garden, good walks *(Geoff and Molly Betteridge)*

PEWSEY [SU1561]

French Horn SN9 5NT [A345 towards Marlborough; Pewsey Wharf]: Cheery two-part back bar divided by log fire open to both sides, steps down to pleasant rather smarter flagstoned front dining area (children allowed here), enjoyable food, Wadworths ales, good choice of wines by the glass; piped music; picnic-sets on back terrace, walks by Kennet & Avon Canal below *(Meg and Colin Hamilton, BB, Neil and Anita Christopher, David Barnes)*

REDLYNCH [SU2021]

Kings Head SP5 2JT [off A338 via B3080; The Row]: Charming low-ceilinged cottagey 16th-c pub on edge of New Forest, friendly licensees and staff, real ales such as Hop Back Salisbury and Summer Lightning, Ringwood Best and Wadworths 6X, good house wines and coffee, interesting blackboard choice of good value food, log fire and woodburner, two carpeted bays, one a pleasant small conservatory, off beamed main bar, nice mix of furnishings and ornaments; dogs welcome, picnic-sets in side garden, nice Pepper Box Hill walks nearby, bedrooms *(BB, D B S Frost)*

SALISBURY [SU1430]

☆ ***Avon Brewery*** SP1 3SP [Castle St]: Long and narrow city bar, busy and friendly, with dark mahogany, frosted and engraved bow windows, friezes and attractive pictures, two open fires, sensibly priced food (not Sun evening) from sandwiches up, mainstream real ales, decent wines; piped music; long sheltered courtyard garden overlooking river, open all day *(LYM, Colin and Janet Roe, Craig Turnbull)*

Cornmarket Inn SP1 1TL [Market Pl]: Comfortable and handy for shops, with good value bar food inc generous sandwiches, well

kept Wadworths 6X, good friendly service, pictures *(Craig Turnbull)*

Kings Head SP1 2ND [Bridge St]: Wetherspoons Lloyds No 1 in nice spot by river (site of former hotel), variety of seating in large bar with separate TV area (and piped music), upstairs gallery, their usual low-priced menu inc breakfast; bedrooms, open all day from early *(Ann and Colin Hunt)*

☆ ***New Inn*** SP1 2PH [New St]: Ancient pub, recently comfortably refurbished while keeping its inglenook log fire, massive beams and timbers, quiet cosy alcoves, Badger beers, decent house wines, good cheerful service, enjoyable food from sandwiches to grills, separate children's area; walled garden with striking view of nearby cathedral spire, open all day summer wknds *(Ann and Colin Hunt, Sue and Mike Todd, John and Julie Moon, Colin and Peggy Wilshire, LYM, N R White)*

☆ ***Old Mill*** SP2 8EU [Town Path, W Harnham]: Charming 17th-c pub/hotel in glorious tranquil out-of-centre setting, unpretentious beamed bars with prized window tables, enjoyable reasonably priced bar food from sandwiches up, helpful staff, real ales, good wines and malt whiskies, good value lunch in attractive restaurant showing mill race; children welcome, picnic-sets in small floodlit garden by duck-filled millpond, delightful stroll across water meadows from cathedral (classic view of it from bridge beyond garden), bedrooms *(Tony and Jill Radnor, Tony and Wendy Hobden, LYM)*

☆ ***Wig & Quill*** SP1 2PH [New St]: Welcoming 16th-c former shop with low beams, soft lighting, rugs, sofa, worn leather armchairs, stuffed birds and low arches to linked rooms, friendly service, well kept Wadworths and guest beers tapped from the cask, decent wines and interesting summer drinks, daily papers, good value standard food (not winter evenings) from sandwiches up, tiled back eating room; dogs welcome, sunny sheltered courtyard behind with cathedral views, open all day *(Ann and Colin Hunt, Tony and Jill Radnor, Edward Mirzoeff, Tom and Jill Jones, Chris Glasson)*

Wyndham Arms SP1 3AS [Estcourt Rd]: Friendly modern corner local with Hop Back beers (originally brewed here, now from Downton), country wines, simple bar food, small front room, longer main bar; children welcome in front room, open all day wknds, cl lunchtime other days *(the Didler)*

SANDY LANE [ST9668]

George SN15 2PX [A342 Devizes—Chippenham]: Wide choice of enjoyable sensibly priced food, decent wines, good service, real ales inc Wadworths, interesting décor, back bar-restaurant; tables on front terrace, more in back garden with play area *(LYM, Mr and Mrs G Ives)*

SEMINGTON [ST8960]

Somerset Arms BA14 6JR [off A350 bypass 2 miles S of Melksham]: Cosy 16th-c coaching inn, heavy-beamed long bar, real and flame-effect fires, high-backed settles, plenty of tables, lots of prints and brassware, wide range of reasonably priced food in bar and restaurant from sandwiches and chips to some imaginative dishes, good atmosphere, cheerful service, Badger beers, good coffee; piped music; pleasant garden behind, short walk from Kennet & Avon Canal, open all day summer wknds *(Matthew Shackle, Dr and Mrs A K Clarke)*

SHAW [ST8765]

Golden Fleece SN12 8HB [Folly Lane (A365 towards Atworth)]: Attractive former coaching inn with good atmosphere in bright and clean low-ceilinged L-shaped bar and long sympathetic front dining extension, good range of food inc generous bargain lunches – very popular with older people, good welcoming service, real ales such as Bass, Fullers London Pride and Moles, farm cider, flame-effect fires; garden tables *(Dr and Mrs M E Wilson, Dr and Mrs A K Clarke)*

SHERSTON [ST8586]

Carpenters Arms SN16 0LS [Easton (B4040)]: Small-roomed low-beamed pub with friendly helpful staff, log fire, real ales, decent wines, reasonably priced food, settles and shiny tables, attractive modern conservatory and dining rooms, no piped music; TV in locals' bar; tables in pleasant garden with play area *(Richard Stancomb)*

☆ **Rattlebone** SN16 0LR [Church St (B4040 Malmesbury—Chipping Sodbury)]: Rambling beamed and stone-walled 17th-c village pub with welcoming licensees and good atmosphere, popular food from baguettes up, Wells & Youngs real ales, decent wines inc interesting bin-ends, log fire, cosy corners with pews, settles and country-kitchen chairs; children in restaurant, skittle alley, picnic-sets in back garden, has been open all day *(Paul and Shirley White, Bernard Stradling, Richard Stancomb, Donna and Roger, Bob and Angela Brooks, Guy Vowles, LYM, Jane and Graham Rooth)*

SHREWTON [SU0644]

Plume of Feathers SP3 4BZ [High St]: Long low friendly pub with Fullers ales, food in bar and restaurant; dogs welcome, picnic-sets in garden with terrace *(Gwyneth and Salvo Spadaro-Dutturi)*

SHRIVENHAM [SU2388]

Fat Dog SN6 8JL [Station Rd]: Contemporary refurbishment, with reasonably priced food at well spaced good-sized tables; piped music *(Mary Rayner)*

STAVERTON [ST8560]

Old Bear BA14 6PB [B3105 Trowbridge—Bradford-on-Avon]: Smart friendly staff, wide choice of reasonably priced good food inc fish and upmarket dishes from huge ciabattas up in neatly kept long bar divided into four sections, real ales such as Bass, Sharps Doom Bar and Wadworths 6X, nice mix of seats inc some high-backed settles, stone fireplaces (biggest in end dining area),

back restaurant (booking recommended Sun lunchtime) *(BB, Dr and Mrs M E Wilson)*

STEEPLE LANGFORD [SU0437]

☆ **Rainbow on the Lake** SP3 4LZ [just off A36 E of A303 junction; Salisbury Rd]: Attractive and popular family dining pub much extended from original narrow bar with sofas and so forth, great mix of tables in large comfortable dining area, interesting choice of enjoyable fresh food inc bargain wkdy lunches, friendly licensees, staff and dog, three changing real ales inc local brews, games room with darts and pool; nice lake and Wylye Valley views from sunny conservatory and verandah/terrace, picnic-sets on lawn, bedrooms *(Dr and Mrs M E Wilson, Richard Fendick)*

STIBB GREEN [SU2262]

☆ **Three Horseshoes** SN8 3AE [just N of Burbage]: Friendly old-world local with landlady's good honest home cooking (not Sun evening or Mon), speciality pies, competitive prices, quick service, Wadworths IPA and 6X, farm cider, inglenook log fire in comfortable beamed front bar, railway memorabilia and pictures (welcoming and attentive landlord is an enthusiast), small dining room; beautifully kept garden, cl Mon *(R T and J C Moggridge, Alan and Audrey Moulds, Pete Baker)*

STRATTON ST MARGARET [SU1787]

Rat Trap SN3 4TF [off A419; Highworth Rd]: Neat and comfortable dining pub with wide choice of inexpensive food, Arkells ales, decent wines, friendly service; piped music may obtrude *(Peter and Audrey Dowsett)*

SWINDON [SU1484]

Fletchers SN1 1RA [Fleet St]: Welcoming café-bar with good value pubby food from lunchtime baguettes up *(Mark and Ruth Brock)*

Glue Pot SN1 5BP [Emlyn Sq]: No-frills alehouse in Brunel's Railway Village, eight or so well kept beers, honest pub food, prompt welcoming service, pub games and high-backed settles around pine tables; sports TV, can get very busy; terrace tables, open all day *(M Joyner)*

UPTON SCUDAMORE [ST8647]

☆ **Angel** BA12 0AG [off A350 N of Warminster]: Stylish and roomy contemporary dining pub with airy bustling upper part, a few steps down to sofas and armchairs by more traditionally furnished lower dining area, good interesting food from open kitchen, Butcombe, Wadworths 6X and a guest beer, good changing wine choice, courteous and caring young staff, artwork for sale, daily papers, pub games; piped music, TV; sheltered flagstoned back terrace with big barbecue, bedrooms in house across car park *(LYM, Dr and Mrs M E Wilson, Geoffrey Kemp, Mr and Mrs A H Young)*

WANBOROUGH [SU2182]

Black Horse SN4 0DQ [2 miles from M4 junction 15; Callas Hill (former B4507 towards Bishopstone)]: Particularly helpful and friendly landlord in open-plan pub with wholesome lunchtime food from sandwiches to good value Sun roast, Arkells ales, good generous coffee, no piped music, some carefully exposed original panelling; picnic-sets in informal elevated garden with play area, caravan parking in adjoining field, lovely downland views *(Mrs L M Beard)*

Cross Keys SN4 0AP [Burycroft, Lower Wanborough]: Welcoming traditional village pub, much extended, with solid wood floor, alcoves and individual décor inc lots of bric-a-brac, well kept Wadworths, good choice of food (even Sun evening) inc succulent local ham, quick friendly service, back conservatory restaurant; quiet piped music *(Tim and Rosemary Wells)*

Plough SN4 0AE [High St, Lower Wanborough]: Thriving local atmosphere in long low thatched stone-built pub with three old-world rooms, interesting memorabilia, huge centrepiece inglenook log fire, good value nicely served home-made food, well kept ales such as Archers Village, Caledonian Deuchars IPA and Wadworths 6X, quick friendly service; open all day Sat *(R T and J C Moggridge)*

WEST LAVINGTON [SU0053]
Stage Post SN10 4HQ [High St (A360)]: Comfortable and welcoming roadside stop with big L-shaped bar and glazed front dining area, enjoyable food from baguettes and baked potatoes to steaks, decent drinks range inc good wine choice; reasonably priced bedrooms with own bathrooms *(Peter and Jean Hoare)*

WESTWOOD [ST8159]
New Inn BA15 2AE [off B3109 S of Bradford-on-Avon]: Traditional country pub, busy wknds but quiet midweek, with several linked rooms, beams and stripped stone, scrubbed tables on slate floor, generous popular food in bar and restaurant, Wadworths IPA and 6X; a few tables out behind, lovely hanging baskets, walks nearby, pretty village, has been cl Sun evening and Mon *(Meg and Colin Hamilton, BB)*

WILTON [SU0931]
☆ *Pembroke Arms* SP2 0BH [Minster St (A30)]: Elegant Georgian hotel handy for Wilton House, bar not cheap but roomy and comfortable, with excellent licensees and friendly service, tasty fresh lunchtime ciabattas, Badger real ale, good coffee and wines by the glass, open fire, plenty of daily papers and magazines, fresh flowers and candles, good restaurant; some outside tables, attractive bedrooms with marble bathrooms *(Edward Mirzoeff, BB, A D Lealan, John Robertson)*

WINGFIELD [ST8256]
☆ *Poplars* BA14 9LN [B3109 S of Bradford-on-Avon (Shop Lane)]: Attractive country pub very popular for good sensibly priced interesting food, especially with older people at lunchtime, Wadworths real ales, friendly fast service even when busy, warm atmosphere, no juke box or machines, light and airy family dining extension; tables out by own cricket pitch *(Dr and Mrs M E Wilson, LYM)*

WINSLEY [ST7960]
Seven Stars BA15 2LQ [off B3108 bypass W of Bradford-on-Avon (pub just over Wilts border)]: Roomy linked areas, welcoming and relaxed, with candles and dim lighting, low beams, some flagstones and stripped stone, snug alcoves, log-effect gas fires, Butcombe and Wadworths 6X, good wine choice, enjoyable food (worth booking) inc interesting specials and good vegetarian choice, pleasant staff; may be discreet piped music; picnic-sets out on neat terrace, adjacent bowling green, attractive village *(BB, Nigel Long, Dr and Mrs M E Wilson, MRSM)*

WOODBOROUGH [SU1159]
Seven Stars SN9 6LW [off A345 S of Marlborough; Bottlesford]: Some good meals and a friendly family at this pretty thatched pub, with Fullers London Pride, Wadworths 6X and a changing guest beer, good choice of wines, hunting prints, attractively moulded panelling, hot coal fire in the old range at one end, big log fire the other, nice mix of antique settles and country furniture, cosy nooks; piped music turned off on request; children and dogs welcome, extensive riverside gardens, open all day Sun *(Mr and Mrs A Curry, Mary Rayner, LYM, Bill and Jessica Ritson)*

WOOTTON BASSETT [SU0682]
Five Bells SN4 7BD [Wood St]: Friendly and rather enterprising town local with great atmosphere, well kept Fullers London Pride and four changing guest beers, farm cider, food a decided cut above the usual pub style, with good value substantial sandwiches, log fire, and some interesting notions like their Weds sausage night (may also be special menus during major sports matches), board games, darts; TV; tables in good recently done shaded courtyard, open all day Fri-Sun *(BB, Pete Baker)*

WOOTTON RIVERS [SU1963]
Royal Oak SN8 4NQ [off A346, A345 or B3087]: Attractive 16th-c beamed and thatched pub, wide range of reliable if not cheap food from lunchtime sandwiches, ciabattas and baguettes up, L-shaped dining lounge with woodburner, timbered bar with small games area, Fullers London Pride, Wadworths 6X and perhaps a guest beer, good wine list; children and dogs welcome, tables out in yard, pleasant village, bedrooms in adjoining house *(Neil and Anita Christopher, LYM, Gwyneth and Salvo Spadaro-Dutturi, Mrs J H S Lang, Peter Titcomb)*

Worcestershire

As it's so easy to drive out for a meal here from big cities like Birmingham, quite a few Worcestershire pubs are rather upmarket in character. However there are some delightful oddities too, such as the marvellously simple Monkey House at Defford (selling farm cider and virtually nothing else), and the thoroughly enjoyable King & Castle on the platform of the Severn Valley Railway in Kidderminster, where beer and food come at bargain prices. Also doing well are the memorabilia-packed Little Pack Horse in Bewdley, the heirloom-filled Fleece at Bretforton (now happily back on its feet after a fire closed it down not long ago), the welcoming and interesting Bell & Cross at Holy Cross (where the food deserves a special mention), the Walter de Cantelupe in Kempsey (also liked for its food and its garden; its rooms are each in a different character), the ever-friendly and chatty Nags Head in Malvern (with an impressive range of real ales; one couple said it sets the standard by which they judge all other pubs) and the prettily rustic Bell at Pensax. Places in particularly attractive old buildings or fine surroundings are the Farmers Arms at Birtsmorton (inexpensive and reassuringly unchanged), the Fox & Hounds at Bredon (in a charming thatched building), the Fountain at Clent (a civilised dining pub by the Clent Hills, with several interesting beers on offer), the Swan at Hanley Swan (very nicely refurbished and in an enticing setting by the village green) and the Talbot at Knightwick (a good place to enjoy a beer by the river – its own brews are very good value). Our choice as Worcestershire Dining Pub of the Year is the Bell & Cross at Holy Cross – the appealingly decorated small rooms add a good deal of atmosphere to an enjoyable meal out here. In the Lucky Dip section at the end of the chapter, pubs to look out for include the Admiral Rodney at Berrow Green (new licensees joined this previously popular main entry too late for us to rate it for this edition), Plough & Harrow at Drakes Broughton, Boot at Flyford Flavell, Royal Oak at Leigh Sinton and Pembroke House in Tenbury Wells. Generally speaking, pub food prices in the county are broadly in line with the national average. Drinks prices, however, are rather lower than average: small local brewers that we found supplying the cheapest beer in at least some of the main entries were Cannon Royall and Wyre Piddle.

BAUGHTON   SO8742   MAP 4

Jockey ♀

4 miles from M50 junction 1; A38 northwards, then right on to A4104 Upton—Pershore; WR8 9DQ

Thoughtfully run dining pub with an appealing layout

The welcoming licensees here serve Courage Directors and Theakstons alongside a changing guest from breweries such as Malvern Hills, and they've farm cider and a rewarding choice of wines, with ten by the glass. The layout is open plan but partly divided by stripped brick and timbering, with a mix of good-sized tables, a few horse-racing pictures on the butter-coloured walls, and a cream Rayburn in one brick inglenook; piped music. There are picnic-sets out in front, with an array of flowers (out here, but not inside, you might hear the motorway in the distance if there's an east wind).

🍴 As well as lunchtime sandwiches, baguettes and baked potatoes (not available on Sundays), bar food includes starters like whitebait or smoked duck breast, and main courses like poached salmon fillet with oyster mushroom white wine sauce, steak and kidney pie, sirloin or fillet steak, and specials that could include loin of lamb or poached scallops in creamy light curry sauce. *Starters/Snacks: £3.95 to £6.95. Main Courses: £8.95 to £17.95. Puddings: £2.95 to £4.25*

Free house ~ Licensee Colin Clarke ~ Real ale ~ Bar food (12-2(2.30 Sat, Sun), 6(7 Sun)-9) ~ Restaurant ~ (01684) 592153 ~ Children welcome, but with restrictions ~ Open 11.30-3(4 Sat), 6-11; 12-4, 7-10.30 Sun; closed Sun evenings in winter ~ Bedrooms: £40B/£60B

Recommended by John and Sarah Webb, J E Shackleton, Ken Marshall, Joyce and Maurice Cottrell, Carol and Colin Broadbent

BEWDLEY   SO7875   MAP 4

Little Pack Horse 🍺

High Street; no nearby parking – best to park in main car park, cross A4117 Cleobury road, and keep walking on down narrowing High Street; DY12 2DH

Timber-framed town pub full of interesting paraphernalia, and with a rewarding selection of beers

In a quiet back street in a very attractive riverside town, this is an enjoyable spot for a drink or a bar meal. Warmed by a woodburning stove, the interior has reclaimed oak panelling and floorboards, as well as an eye-catching array of old advertisements, photos and other memorabilia; there are plans to extend the restaurant upstairs. Alongside Black Sheep or Theakstons they have a guest such as Exmoor Gold or Shepherd Neame Spitfire, and a selection of bottled ciders and belgian and bavarian bottled beers; piped music and TV. There is an outside covered area with heaters, which is available for smokers. It's best to leave your car in the public car park near the river in the town, and walk up.

🍴 Food is reasonably priced, and lots of dishes are available in two sizes: sandwiches, sausage and mash, cod and chips, various savoury pies such as minted lamb and tattie, fresh fish, steaks and vegetable curry. *Starters/Snacks: £2.95 to £6.95. Main Courses: £5.25 to £15.95. Puddings: £3.20 to £4.50*

Punch ~ Lease Mark Payne ~ Real ale ~ Bar food (12-2.45, 6-9.30; 12-4, 5.30-9.45 Sat; 12-8 Sun) ~ Restaurant ~ (01299) 403762 ~ Children welcome until 7.30pm ~ Dogs allowed in bar ~ Open 12-3, 6-11; 12-12 Fri, Sat; 12-10.30 Sun

Recommended by Ian and Jane Irving, Richard, Alan and Eve Harding, Martin and Pauline Jennings, N R White

BIRTSMORTON   SO7936   MAP 4

Farmers Arms 🍺 £

Birts Street, off B4208 W; WR13 6AP

Unrushed half-timbered village local with plenty of character

Chatty locals gather at the bar of this unchanging half-timbered village pub, for Hook Norton Hooky and Old Hooky, which are on handpump alongside a changing guest from a brewer such as Wye Valley. Quietly free of piped music or games machines, the neatly kept big room on the right rambles away under very low dark beams, with some standing timbers, and flowery-panelled cushioned settles as well as spindleback chairs; on the left an even lower-beamed room seems even cosier, and in both the white walls have black timbering; the local cribbage and darts teams play here, and you can also play shove-ha'penny or dominoes. You'll find seats out on the large lawn, and the pub is surrounded by plenty of walks. More reports please.

🍴 **Unhurried staff serve very inexpensive simple bar food, which typically includes sandwiches, soup, ploughman's, cauliflower cheese, steak and kidney pie and burgers.** *Starters/Snacks: £1.95 to £5.95. Main Courses: £4.25 to £6.55. Puddings: £1.55 to £2.70*

Free house ~ Licensees Jill and Julie Moore ~ Real ale ~ Bar food (12-2, 6.30(7 Sun)-9) ~ No credit cards ~ (01684) 833308 ~ Children welcome ~ Dogs welcome ~ Open 11-4, 6-11; 12-4, 7-10.30 Sun

Recommended by Alec and Joan Laurence, the Didler, Steve Bailey, Ian and Nita Cooper

BRANSFORD

SO8052   MAP 4

Bear & Ragged Staff ♀

Off A4103 SW of Worcester; Station Road; WR6 5JH

Cheerfully run dining pub with pleasant places to sit both inside and outside

Run by friendly and enthusiastic staff, this pub focuses mostly on food. In fine weather, the garden and terrace are enjoyable places to sit, with a pleasant backdrop of rolling country. The interconnecting rooms give fine views too, and in winter you'll find an open fire; piped music. There are proper tablecloths, linen napkins and fresh flowers on the tables in the restaurant, which has a more expensive menu. They've a good range of wines to choose from, with about ten by the glass, lots of malt whiskies, quite a few brandies and liqueurs, and St Georges Best and Shepherd Neame Spitfire are on handpump. Good disabled access and facilities.

🍴 **Bar food includes lunchtime sandwiches, trio of sausages with parsnip-flavoured mash, steak and kidney pudding, curry of the day, ham, eggs and chips, and Sunday roasts; they also have a more expensive restaurant menu.** *Starters/Snacks: £4.50 to £7.50. Main Courses: £8.50 to £12.50. Puddings: £4.75*

Free house ~ Licensees Lynda Williams and Andy Kane ~ Real ale ~ Bar food ~ Restaurant ~ (01886) 833399 ~ Children welcome ~ Open 11.30-2.30, 6.30-11; 12-3, 7-10.30 Sun

Recommended by JCW, Chris Flynn, Wendy Jones, Denys Gueroult, Michael and Maggie Betton, Roger Braithwaite, Ann and Colin Hunt, Ken Millar

BREDON

SO9236   MAP 4

Fox & Hounds

4½ miles from M5 junction 9; A438 to Northway, left at B4079, then in Bredon follow signpost to church and river on right; GL20 7LA

An appealingly old-fashioned 15th-c pub not far off the motorway

A particularly handy place to know about if you're driving along the nearby M5, this delightful stone and timber thatched building stands by the church in a village beside the River Avon, and close to a magnificent barn owned by the National Trust. The open-plan carpeted bar has low beams, stone pillars and stripped timbers, a central woodburning stove, upholstered settles, a variety of wheelback, tub and kitchen chairs around handsome mahogany and cast-iron-framed tables, dried grasses and flowers and elegant wall lamps. There's a smaller side bar. Friendly efficient staff serve Banks's Bitter and Greene King Old Speckled Hen along with a guest such as Charles Wells Bombardier on handpump and eight wines by the glass; piped music. The exterior is especially pretty in summer, when it's decked with brightly coloured hanging baskets; some of the picnic-sets are under Perspex. More reports please.

🍴 **A fairly short lunchtime snack menu includes sandwiches, salads, ploughman's, sausages and mash, smoked haddock on cream onion mash and mushroom risotto, and there's a separate menu with starters such as grilled tiger prawn and confit duck terrine, with mains such as pork medallions in calvados, vegetable stir fry and chargrilled chicken supreme; also Sunday roasts, a fish board and two specials boards.** *Starters/Snacks: £3.95 to £8.50. Main Courses: £7.95 to £18.00. Puddings: £4.50*

Enterprise ~ Lease Cilla and Christopher Lamb ~ Real ale ~ Bar food ~ Restaurant ~ (01684) 772377 ~ Children welcome ~ Dogs allowed in bar ~ Open 12-3, 6(6.30 winter)-11

Recommended by Dr A J and Mrs Tompsett, Simon Jones, W H and E Thomas, J S Burn, John and Hazel Williams, Mrs Hazel Rainer, A G Marx, Andy and Claire Barker, Gerry and Rosemary Dobson, Tom and Jill Jones

BRETFORTON   SP0943   MAP 4

Fleece ★ £

B4035 E of Evesham: turn S off this road into village; pub is in centre square by church; there's a sizeable car park at one side of the church; WR11 7JE

Marvellously unspoilt and deservedly popular medieval pub owned by the National Trust

It's worth making a special trip to just to see inside this wonderfully evocative old former farmhouse and its contents. Before becoming a pub in 1848 the building was owned by the same family for nearly 500 years, and eventually left to the National Trust in 1977. Many of the furnishings, such as the great oak dresser that holds a priceless 48-piece set of Stuart pewter, are heirlooms passed down through that family for many generations, and now back in place. Plenty of oddities include a great cheese-press and set of cheese moulds, and a rare dough-proving table; a leaflet details the more bizarre items, and look out for the photographs of the terrible fire that struck this place a few years ago. The rooms have massive beams and exposed timbers, and marks scored on the worn and crazed flagstones were to keep out demons. There are two fine grandfather clocks, ancient kitchen chairs, curved high-backed settles, a rocking chair, and a rack of heavy pointed iron shafts, probably for spit roasting (though there have been all sorts of esoteric guesses), in one of the huge inglenook fireplaces, and two more log fires. A great choice of beers includes well kept Hook Norton Best, Purity Pure UBU and Uley Pigs Ear, with around a couple of guests from breweries such as Burton Bridge on handpump, along with farm cider, local apple juices, german wheat bear, and fruit wines. They have darts and various board games, but no piped music or fruit machines. They hold the annual asparagus auctions and Vale of Evesham Asparagus Festival (end of May) and village fête (August bank holiday Monday); there's sometimes morris dancing, and the village silver band plays here regularly too. The lawn around the beautifully restored thatched and timbered barn is a lovely place to sit, among the fruit trees, and at the front by the stone pump-trough; there are more picnic-sets in the front courtyard and a covered area for smokers. The pub gets very busy in summer, and parking can be difficult.

⑪ A shortish choice of very fairly priced bar food includes sandwiches, soup, baked camembert with cranberry sauce, deep-fried corn fritters with sweet chilli and soured cream, sausages or faggots and mash, steak and mushroom casserole with suet dumplings, fish dish of the day and beefburger. *Starters/Snacks: £3.50 to £5.50. Main Courses: £6.25 to £12.95. Puddings: £3.50 to £4.95*

Free house ~ Licensee Nigel Smith ~ Real ale ~ Bar food (12-2.30(4 Sun) 6.30-9; not Sun evening) ~ (01386) 831173 ~ Children welcome ~ Folk session, poetry and prose Thurs evening ~ Open 11-midnight; 11-3, 6-11 Mon-Fri; 11-11 Sat; 12-11 Sun in winter; closed weekdays 3-6 end Sept-end June ~ Bedrooms: /£85S

Recommended by Dave Braisted, Carol and Colin Broadbent, Michael and Alison Sandy, George Atkinson, Bob Broadhurst, Andy and Claire Barker, Noel Grundy, Ted George, W W Burke, Andrea Rampley, Pat and Tony Martin, Eithne Dandy, John Wooll, Steve Whalley, David A Hammond, Ann and Colin Hunt, Di and Mike Gillam, Susan and John Douglas, MLR

CHILDSWICKHAM   SP0738 MAP 4

Childswickham Inn ♀

Village signposted off A44 just NW of Broadway; WR12 7HP

Dining pub with plenty of pleasant corners amid contemporary furnishings

Run by attentive staff, this dining pub is a civilised place for a drink or a meal. The main area focuses on dining, with a mix of chairs around kitchen tables, big rugs on boards or broad terracotta tiles, more or less abstract contemporary prints on walls painted cream and pale violet or mauve, candlesticks in great variety, a woodburning stove and a piano; piped music. Off to the right is a modern-style lounge-like bar (snacks only, such as baguettes, in here), light and airy, with Hook Norton Hooky and Marstons Pedigree on handpump (from a counter that seems made from old doors), a good choice of over 50 french, italian and other wines (with ten sold by the glass), and good coffee in elegant cups; service is friendly and attentive. This small carefully lit room has a similarly modern colour-scheme with paintings by local artists, leather armchairs and sofas, and bamboo furniture. The entrance lobby has the biggest doormat we have ever seen – wall to wall – with good disabled access and facilities. A large sunny deck outside has tables, and the garden is nicely cottagey, with a lawn and borders. More reports please.

⊞ **Typical items from a weekly changing menu are lunchtime baguettes, soup, curries, pies and a fish of the day, and an evening menu that might include sea mussels in lightly curried sauce, crispy duck in kumquat sauce, grilled bass and a risotto of the day.** *Starters/Snacks: £6.95 to £9.95. Main Courses: £8.95 to £17.95. Puddings: £4.95*

Punch ~ Tenant Carol Marshall ~ Real ale ~ Bar food ~ Restaurant (not Sun evening or Mon lunch) ~ (01386) 852461 ~ Children welcome ~ Dogs allowed in bar ~ Open 12-3, 5.30-11 (12 Sat); 12-3 Sun; closed Sun evening, Mon
Recommended by Mike and Mary Carter, Edna Jones

CLENT   SO9279 MAP 4

Fountain

Off A491 at Holy Cross/Clent exit roundabout, via Violet Lane, then turn right at T junction; Adams Hill/Odnall Lane; DY9 9PU

Often packed to overflowing, a restaurany pub popular with the well heeled set

After eating at this hugely popular, upmarket dining pub, you can work off your food with a hike in the nearby Clent Hills. Although drinkers are welcome to stand at the bar, or sit if there is a table free, you may feel in the minority. With a buoyant atmosphere, the long carpeted dining bar – four knocked-together areas – is filled mainly by sturdy pine tables and country-kitchen or mate's chairs, with some comfortably cushioned brocaded wall seats. There are nicely framed local photographs on the ragged pinkish walls above a dark panelled dado, pretty wall lights, and candles on the tables. Three or four changing real ales might be from brewers such as Highwood, Jennings and Mansfield, and they've decent wines served in cut glass, and ten malts; also a choice of speciality teas and good coffees, and freshly squeezed orange juice; alley skittles; one reader found the piped music excessively loud and the tables packed uncomfortably close together. There are a few picnic-sets out in front. Note that they may close in the evening on winter Sundays. Booking is advisable.

⊞ **As well as lunchtime sandwiches, the menu and specials board might include soup, chicken liver pâté, fried plaice and chips, duck in red wine, mixed bean chilli and rather tasty-sounding puddings; service by uniformed staff is courteous, friendly and efficient.** *Starters/Snacks: £1.95 to £5.95. Main Courses: £11.95 to £17.95. Puddings: £4.95 to £5.95*

Union Pub Company ~ Lease Richard and Jacque Macey ~ Real ale ~ Bar food (12-2.15(4.30 Sun), 6-9(9.30 Fri, Sat); sandwiches only, Sun evening) ~ Restaurant ~ (01562) 883286 ~ Children welcome ~ Open 11-11; 12-10.30 Sun
Recommended by Theo, Anne and Jane Gaskin, Ian Phillips, Miss Glynis Hume, Lynda and Trevor Smith, Susan and John Douglas, Dr and Mrs A K Clarke

DEFFORD SO9042 MAP 4

Monkey House

A4104 towards Upton – immediately after passing Oak public house on right, there's a small group of cottages, of which this is the last; WR8 9BW

Astonishingly unspoilt time-warp survival with farm cider and a menagerie of animals

A real curio, this simple black and white thatched cider house has no inn sign outside, and drinks are limited to very inexpensive Bulmer's Medium or Special Dry cider tapped from barrels, poured by jug into pottery mugs (some locals have their own) and then served from a hatch beside the door. It has been in the same family for some 150 years and at first sight hardly resembles a pub at all. In the summer you could find yourself sharing the garden with the hens and cockerels that wander in from an adjacent collection of caravans and sheds; there's also a pony called Mandy, Tapper the jack russell, and Marie the rottweiler. Alternatively you can retreat to a small and spartan side outbuilding with a couple of plain tables, a settle and an open fire. The pub's name comes from the story of a drunken customer who, some years ago, fell into bramble bushes and swore that he was attacked by monkeys. Please note the limited opening times below.

🍴 Apart from crisps and nuts they don't do food, but you can bring your own.

Free house ~ Licensee Graham Collins ~ No credit cards ~ (01386) 750234 ~ Open 11-2.30, 6-10; 12-3.30 Sun; closed Tues, evenings Sun-Mon, lunchtimes Weds-Thurs
Recommended by Pete Baker, the Didler, R T and J C Moggridge

HANLEY SWAN SO8142 MAP 4

Swan 🍺 🛏

B4209 Malvern—Upton; WR8 0EA

Cheerful staff, stylish décor, and an appealing rural setting

Very attractively refurbished with a bright, contemporary country look, this nicely placed pub not far from the Malvern show ground is set well back from the road in lovely countryside, and faces a classic green complete with duck pond and massive oak tree. It has cream paintwork, some attractive new oak panelling contrasting with older rough timbering, well chosen prints, some stripped masonry and bare boards, a log fire, and stylishly rustic lamps. The layout comprises two main areas, the extended back part set for dining, with french windows looking out over the picnic-sets on the good-sized side lawn and its play area, and the front part more of a conventional bar; each area has its own servery. Good sturdy dining tables have comfortably high-backed chairs, and one part of the bar has dark leather bucket armchairs and sofas brightened up by scatter cushions; piped music, TV. On handpump are Adnams, Shepherd Neame Spitfire and a guest such as Charles Wells Bombardier. The young staff are attentive and helpful; disabled access and facilities. There are five newish bedrooms. Note that dogs are allowed in the bedrooms only.

🍴 As well as a good choice of sandwiches and a help yourself baked potato counter, the food includes items such as soup, skewer of tandoori spiced chicken fillet, battered cod and chips, braised lamb shank, celery, pepper and mushroom stroganoff, steaks and seafood stew. On Sundays virtually the whole pub is devoted to their popular Sunday lunch. *Starters/Snacks: £3.95 to £5.95. Main Courses: £7.50 to £12.95. Puddings: £3.95*

Punch ~ Lease Michelle Steggles and Adrian Bowden ~ Real ale ~ Bar food (12-2.30, 6.30-9) ~ Restaurant ~ (01684) 311870 ~ Children welcome except in bar area ~ Dogs allowed in bedrooms ~ Open 12-3, 6-11.30 ~ Bedrooms: £50B/£65B
Recommended by Chris Flynn, Wendy Jones, Pat and Graham Williamson, M Joyner, Dr A J and Mrs Tompsett, P Dawn, Mrs Ann Gray

---

Pubs close to motorway junctions are listed at the back of the book.

HOLY CROSS

S09278 MAP 4

Bell & Cross 🍽 ♟

4 miles from M5 junction 4: A491 towards Stourbridge, then follow Clent signpost off on left; DY9 9QL

WORCESTERSHIRE DINING PUB OF THE YEAR

Super food, staff with a can-do attitude, a pretty garden and small rooms with individual character

Continuing its winning ways, this charming place draws praise from readers for its food and ever-helpful staff, who are extremely welcoming if you are just popping in for a drink. With a classic unspoilt early 19th-c layout, the five small rooms and kitchen open off a central corridor with a black and white tiled floor: they give a choice of carpet, bare boards, lino or nice old quarry tiles, a variety of moods from snug and chatty to bright and airy, and an individual décor in each – theatrical engravings on red walls here, nice sporting prints on pale green walls there, racing and gundog pictures above the black panelled dado in another room. Two of the rooms have small serving bars, with Timothy Taylors Landlord, Wadworths 6X and maybe a guest such as Enville on handpump. You'll find over 50 wines (with 14 sold by the glass), a variety of coffees, daily papers, coal fires in most rooms, perhaps regulars playing cards in one of the two front ones, and piped music. You get pleasant views from the garden terrace.

🍽 **Delicious dishes, from a changing seasonal menu, include lunchtime snacks (not Sunday) such as sandwiches and paninis, very tasty fishcakes with white wine, prawn and chive sauce, smooth chicken liver parfait with caramelised plums, white onion and cider soup, roasted cod with mash and bacon, slow-cooked collar of pork with fondant potato, grilled calves liver with black pudding, vegetarian shepherd's pie, and specials. On Sunday lunchtime they do Sunday roasts only.** *Starters/Snacks: £4.50 to £7.00. Main Courses: £10.45 to £13.75. Puddings: £4.95 to £5.00*

Enterprise ~ Lease Roger and Jo Narbett ~ Real ale ~ Bar food (12-2(2.30 Sun),7-9(9.15 Fri, Sat)) ~ (01562) 730319 ~ Children welcome ~ Dogs allowed in bar ~ Open 12-3, 6-11; 12-4, 7-10.30 Sun

Recommended by Paul and Bryony Walker, Ian Phillips, Pete Baker, Mike and Linda Hudson, John Street, W H and E Thomas, David and Pauline, Karen Eliot, Margaret and Allen Marsden, Roy and Lindsey Fentiman, Clifford Blakemore, Susan and John Douglas, Dr and Mrs A K Clarke

KEMPSEY

S08548 MAP 4

Walter de Cantelupe ♟

A38, handy for M5 junction 7 via A44 and A4440; WR5 3NA

A warmly welcoming and unpretentious roadside inn, with enjoyable food and interesting drinks

They've redecorated the bar area of this friendly pub, but it still has an informal and well worn-in mix of furniture, an old wind-up HMV gramophone and a good big fireplace. Real ales are well kept on handpump and include Cannon Royall Kings Shilling, Timothy Taylors Landlord and Wye Valley Golden Ale together with a guest such as Three Tuns XXX. For non-beer drinkers they have locally grown and pressed apple juices, wines from a local vineyard, several wines by the glass, and in summer they also have a farm cider. Decorated in neutral colours, the dining area has various plush or yellow leather dining chairs, an old settle, a sonorous clock, and candles and flowers on the tables; piped music in the evenings, and board games. You can buy jars of home-made chutney and marmalade; cribbage, dominoes and table skittles. It has to be said that the informal and personal style of the service and food operation here, part of the charm when things are going well, can get a bit overwhelmed if more people than expected turn up. There's a pretty suntrap walled garden at the back, and a sheltered area for smokers. There are plans to add more bedrooms.

🍽 **Cooked by the friendly landlord (so expect a wait if it's busy), good value enjoyable bar food includes lunchtime sandwiches, soup, very good ploughman's, sausages and** mash, beef and ale pie, leek and mushroom risotto, sirloin steak and roast gressingham duck breast, as well as specials. *Starters/Snacks: £3.25 to £5.50. Main Courses: £6.85 to £14.00. Puddings: £3.50 to £4.95*

Free house ~ Licensee Martin Lloyd Morris ~ Real ale ~ Bar food (12-2(2.30 Sat), 6-9.30; 11.30-8 Sun) ~ Restaurant ~ (01905) 820572 ~ Children in dining area until 8.15pm ~ Dogs allowed in bar ~ Live folk music second Sun evening of month ~ Open 12(11.30 Sat)-2.30, 6-11; 11.30-10.30 Sun; closed Mon ~ Bedrooms: £44.50S(£49.50B)/£55S(£77B)

Recommended by Andy and Jill Kassube, P Dawn, David Morgan, Dr A J and Mrs Tompsett, Ken Marshall, Dr W J M Gissane, Mr and Mrs W D Borthwick, Hywel and Marilyn Roberts, M G Hart, Rhiannon Davies, Pat and Tony Martin, Dr and Mrs A K Clarke

KIDDERMINSTER
SO8376   MAP 4

King & Castle ⚫ £

Railway Station, Comberton Hill; DY10 1QX

Railway refreshment room within earshot of steam locos, and with one of the cheapest pints around

A splendidly evocative place at the terminus of the Severn Valley Railway, this painstaking re-creation of an Edwardian station refreshment room is right by the platform, so you can take your drink out on to the platform and watch steam trains coming in. The atmosphere is lively and sometimes noisily good-humoured, with a fine mix of customers. Furnishings are solid and in character, and there's the railway memorabilia that you'd expect. Bathams and remarkably low priced Wyre Piddle Royal Piddle (just £1.20 a pint) are superbly kept alongside a couple of changing guests from brewers such as Enville, Hobsons, Titanic and Wye Valley on handpump, and they've several malt whiskies. The cheerful landlady and friendly staff cope well with the bank holiday and railway gala day crowds, though you'll be lucky to find a seat then. You can use a Rover ticket to shuttle between here and the Railwaymans Arms in Bridgnorth (see Shropshire chapter); as we went to press the line had been damaged by major flooding, and the repairs may take some time.

⫿ The very reasonably priced straightforward menu includes toasted sandwiches, ploughman's, soup, hamburger in bap with chips, vegetable or chicken kiev, battered cod and all-day breakfast; they also do children's meals, and sometimes Sunday lunch. *Starters/Snacks: £1.95 to £3.25. Main Courses: £3.95 to £7.95. Puddings: £2.50*

Free house ~ Licensee Rosemary Hyde ~ Real ale ~ Bar food (9(9.30 Sun, 10 Sat)-5) ~ No credit cards ~ (01562) 747505 ~ Children welcome until 9pm if seated ~ Dogs welcome ~ Open 9-3, 5-11.30; 10am-11pm Sat; 9.30am-10.30pm Sun

Recommended by P Dawn, Joe Green, Dennis Jones

KNIGHTWICK
SO7355   MAP 4

Talbot ♀ ⚫ 🛏

Knightsford Bridge; B4197 just off A44 Worcester—Bromyard; WR6 5PH

Interesting old coaching inn with good beer from its own brewery

This friendly 15th-c coaching inn has a lovely patch of lawn across the lane by the River Teme (they serve out here too), or you can sit out in front on old-fashioned seats; smokers may use an outside shelter. Well kept on handpump and reasonably priced, This, That, T'other and seasonal ales are brewed in their own microbrewery from locally grown hops. They also have a guest such as Hobsons Bitter, as well as several different wines by the glass and a number of malt whiskies. With a good log fire in winter, the heavily beamed and extended carpeted lounge bar opens on to a terrace and an arbour with roses and clematis in summer. There is a variety of traditional seats from small carved or leatherette armchairs to the winged settles by the tall bow windows, and a vast stove squats in the big central stone hearth. The well furnished back public bar has pool on a raised side area, fruit machine and juke box; cribbage. A farmers' market takes place here on the second Sunday in the month.

🍴 **Straightforward bar food includes sandwiches, ploughman's and game pie, and there is a more expensive restaurant menu.** *Starters/Snacks: £6.50 to £10.00. Main Courses: £8.50 to £16.00. Puddings: £5.00 to £8.00*

Own brew ~ Licensee Annie Clift ~ Real ale ~ Bar food ~ Restaurant ~ (01886) 821235 ~ Children welcome ~ Dogs allowed in bar and bedrooms ~ Open 11-midnight(11 Sun) ~ Bedrooms: £50S/£84B

Recommended by Cathryn and Richard Hicks, Carol and Colin Broadbent, Ann and Colin Hunt, MP, P Dawn, Pat and Tony Martin, Noel Grundy, Kevin Thorpe, Howard Dell, Andy and Claire Barker

MALVERN   SO7845   MAP 4

Nags Head 🍺

Bottom end of Bank Street, steep turn down off A449; WR14 2JG

A terrific range of real ales, appealing layout and décor, and warmly welcoming atmosphere

---

Readers continue to be unanimous in their praise for this splendidly individual old pub, where the emphasis is strongly on the excellent beer, but the bar food is well liked too. They will happily give you a taste of their 16 real ales, very well kept on handpump. Along with Banks's, Bathams, Marstons Pedigree, St Georges Charger, Dragon Blood, Maidens Saviour, and Woods Shropshire Lad, you'll find changing guests (last year they got through over 1,000) from a wide geographical spread of brewers. They also keep a fine range of malt whiskies, belgian beers and decent wines by the glass, as well as Barbourne farm cider. The pub attracts a good mix of customers (with plenty of locals), and the mood is chatty and easy-going, with friendly young staff. There's a good variety of places to sit: a series of snug individually decorated rooms with one or two steps between, all sorts of chairs including leather armchairs, pews sometimes arranged as booths, a mix of tables with sturdy ones stained different colours, bare boards here, flagstones there, carpet elsewhere, and plenty of interesting pictures and homely touches such as house plants and shelves of well thumbed books; there's a coal fire opposite the central servery; broadsheet newspapers and a good juke box; piped music, shove-ha'penny, cribbage and dominoes. Outside are picnic-sets and rustic tables and benches on the front terrace and in a garden, there are heaters and umbrellas, and smokers can use a covered area.

🍴 **Tasty lunchtime bar food includes good sandwiches, ploughman's, soup, an antipasti board and traditional fish and chips. In the evenings they do meals (more expensive) only in the extension barn dining room.** *Starters/Snacks: £4.25 to £7.95. Main Courses: £3.50 to £9.50. Puddings: £4.00*

Free house ~ Licensee Nicola Abrams ~ Real ale ~ Bar food (12-2) ~ Restaurant ~ (01684) 574373 ~ Children welcome ~ Dogs allowed in bar ~ Open 11am-11.15pm(11.30 Sat); 12-11 Sun

Recommended by Dave Braisted, Dr and Mrs Jackson, Chris Flynn, Wendy Jones, Alistair Forsyth, Mike and Mary Clark, Mike Pugh, R T and J C Moggridge, David and Sue Smith, Richard, Theocsbrian, Ian and Nita Cooper, Ray and Winifred Halliday, Brian Banks, P Dawn, Barry Collett, Paul J Robinshaw

PENSAX   SO7368   MAP 4

Bell 🍺 £

B4202 Abberley—Clows Top, SE of the Snead Common part of the village; WR6 6AE

Admirably welcoming all-rounder, good fire and tasty, reasonably priced food

---

This mock-Tudor pub has received very enthusiastic reports, particularly for its food and the friendly welcome from its staff. As well as Hobsons, four well kept changing real ales on handpump might be from brewers such as Cannon Royall, Oakham, Three Tuns and Timothy Taylors, and they've three local ciders and a local perry on handpump as well as organic fruit juices; over the last weekend of June they hold a beer festival. The

L-shaped main bar has a restrained traditional décor, with long cushioned pews on its bare boards, good solid pub tables, and a woodburning stove. Beyond a small area on the left with a couple more tables is a more airy dining room, with french windows opening on to a wooden deck; the pub has a log fire for our more usual weather. Picnic-sets in the back garden look out over rolling fields and copses to the Wyre Forest.

🍴 Besides sandwiches and good value lunchtime weekday specials such as steak and ale pie, vegetable stir fry and sausage and mash, hearty enjoyable evening specials could include steaks, faggots and pork chop with black pudding; Sunday roast and children's menu. *Starters/Snacks: £3.50 to £4.75. Main Courses: £6.95 to £15.95. Puddings: £3.50*

Free house ~ Licensees John and Trudy Greaves ~ Real ale ~ Bar food (12-2(3 Sun), 7-9; not Sun evening or Mon lunchtime) ~ (01299) 896677 ~ Children welcome away from the bar ~ Dogs allowed in bar ~ Open 12-2.30, 5-11; closed Mon lunch except bank hols

Recommended by Lynda and Trevor Smith, Phil and Sally Gorton, Dave Braisted, MLR, Chris and Maggie Kent, Jean Stidwell

LUCKY DIP

Besides the fully inspected pubs, you might like to try these Lucky Dips recommended to us and described by readers (if you do, please send us reports: www.goodguides.co.uk).

ABBERLEY [SO7567]
Manor Arms WR6 6BN: Comfortable country inn nicely tucked away in quiet village backwater, façade emblazoned with coats of arms, warm welcome, quick friendly service, good generous plain cooking, Timothy Taylors Landlord and Wye Valley HPA, two bars and restaurant, interesting collection of toby jugs; ten reasonably priced bedrooms *(Alec and Susan Hamilton, Carol and Colin Broadbent)*
ALVECHURCH [SP0272]
Red Lion B48 7LG [in village, handy for M42 junction 2]: Beamed Vintage Inn with side snugs that nicely conceal its size, big log fires, soft lighting, good value food all day, good service, good choice of wines by the glass and hot drinks, real ales; quiet piped music; back garden, open all day *(Ann Griffiths)*
ASTWOOD BANK [SP0461]
Why Not B96 6LU [A441 towards Cook Hill]: Small neat pub with good value usual food, John Smiths; views from nice garden *(Dave Braisted)*
BECKFORD [SO9835]
☆ *Beckford Hotel* GL20 7AN [A435]: Attractive up-to-date furnishings and décor along with beams, log fires and some stripped stone, real ales such as Fullers London Pride, Purity and Theakstons XB, good range of wines by the glass, good service, some emphasis on wide choice of good value food from sandwiches up; large well kept garden with terrace tables, eight comfortable bedrooms *(Joyce and Maurice Cottrell, Mrs Pauline Wakeman, Bob Richardson, Martin and Pauline Jennings)*
BELBROUGHTON [SO9477]
Bell DY9 9XU [handy for M5 junction 4 via A491]: Handsome and interesting old building, popular neatly kept dining pub, with reasonably priced food inc some children's helpings, efficient service,

comfortable bar with striking stone inglenook, fine split-level barn of a restaurant with central log fire *(Gill and Keith Croxton, LYM, Mrs S Hayden)*
☆ *Queens* DY9 0DU [Queens Hill (B4188 E of Kidderminster)]: 18th-c pub by Belne Brook, several linked areas with nice mix of comfortable seating, 19th-c oak and other tables in varying sizes, enjoyable food inc interesting puddings, Banks's, Marstons Pedigree and good guest beers, good choice of wines by the glass, friendly efficient service, fresh flowers; children welcome, picnic-sets on small roadside terrace, pleasant village *(Clifford Blakemore, Paul and Bryony Walker, David Green)*
BERROW GREEN [SO7458]
☆ *Admiral Rodney* WR6 6PL [B4197, off A44 W of Worcester]: New licensees summer 2007 in pleasantly light and roomy high-beamed dining pub which has been a very popular main entry, big stripped kitchen tables and woodburner, Wye Valley Bitter and a couple of guest ales, charming end restaurant in rebuilt barn; children and dogs welcome, tables outside with pretty view and heated covered terrace, good walks, three good bedrooms, has been open all day wknds, cl Mon; reports on new regime please *(LYM)*
BOURNHEATH [SO9474]
☆ *Gate* B61 9JR [handy for M5 junction 4, via A491 and B4091; Dodford Rd]: Country dining pub with long-serving licensees, wide choice of attractively priced good fresh food from lunchtime and early evening bargains to all sorts of exotic dishes, good value Sun lunch, friendly staff helpful with special diets, quick service even though busy, real ales in cosy partitioned-off bar, attractive open dining area inc conservatory; nice garden *(David Edwards, Isabel York, Kevin Connor, Carol and Colin Broadbent)*

BRANSFORD [SO8053]

Fox WR6 5JL [A4103 Worcester—Hereford]: Attractive and spacious Chef & Brewer well divided to give cosy areas, friendly staff, Greene King Abbot and Hobsons, wide range of well priced food all day *(A J N Johnston)*

BROADWAS-ON-TEME [SO7555]

Royal Oak WR6 5NE: Unexpected interior, including comfortable sofas in relaxed main lounge bar and pubby dining area, vast lofty-raftered medieval-style dining hall, and separate public bar with pool (and juke box); food (all day wknds) from generous lunchtime sandwiches up quickly served by polite staff at refrigerated displays, choose your own meat or fish, or order from regular menu; Marstons Pedigree, decent wines by the glass; children welcome, open all day wknds *(David and Sue Smith)*

BROADWAY [SP0937]

☆ *Crown & Trumpet* WR12 7AE [Church St]: Cheerful 17th-c golden stone beamed local just behind green, friendly staff, Greene King Old Speckled Hen, Hook Norton Best or Old Hooky, local Stanway and Timothy Taylors Landlord, enjoyable bar food inc savoury pies, log fires, several traditional pub games; they may try to keep your credit card while you eat, piped music, live Sat; children welcome, tables on front terrace, bedrooms, open all day wknds and summer *(Donna and Roger, Peter Walker, W W Burke, Robert Ager, Malcolm Pellatt, Roger and Pauline Pearce, Pam Adsley, LYM)*

CALLOW HILL [SO7473]

Royal Forester DY14 9XW [nr Wyre Forest visitors' centre]: Dining pub dating in part from 15th c, good landlord, modern leather settees and bucket armchairs in lounge bar with well kept Fullers London Pride and local guest beers, emphasis on linked dining areas, food from inventive if not cheap lunchtime sandwiches to full meals; children welcome, seven stylish contemporary bedrooms *(Chris and Maggie Kent)*

CHADDESLEY CORBETT [SO8973]

Fox DY10 4QN [A448 Bromsgrove— Kidderminster]: Several eating and drinking areas, very popular for bargain OAP lunches (need to book), succulent carvery, four real ales inc Enville and Hobsons, young willing licensees, pleasant attentive service *(W H and E Thomas, V Wood, Mr and Mrs B Thomas)*

CHARLTON [SP0145]

Gardeners Arms WR10 3LJ [the one nr Pershore; Strand]: Friendly basic local on green of pretty thatched village, usual pub food inc lunchtime bargains (not Sun/Mon) esp for OAPs, well kept Marstons Pedigree, Tetleys and Wadworths 6X, limited wines, roomy dining area inc raised parlour-like part, inglenook woodburner, plain public bar with darts and pool room; children welcome, tables outside *(Martin and Pauline Jennings, Carol and Colin Broadbent)*

CLENT [SO9179]

French Hen DY9 9PY [Bromsgrove Rd]: Enjoyable food (all day wknds) from

baguettes up, friendly staff, real ales, comfortable back area with settees, dining room; handy for Clent Hills walks, open all day wknds *(Lynda and Trevor Smith)*

Hill Tavern DY9 9PS [Adams Hill]: At foot of Clent Hills (right by the car park), with new licensees doing enjoyable food, real ale, skittle alley; pleasant terrace *(L Davies)*

CONDERTON [SO9637]

Yew Tree GL20 7PP: Attractive local on S slope of Bredon Hill, well kept Goffs Jouster and Wadworths IPA and 6X, good value simple food, pleasant service, log fire, beams, flagstones and stripped stone; no cards; well kept pretty garden, good walks *(Di and Mike Gillam, Neil and Anita Christopher)*

CROPTHORNE [SO9944]

New Inn WR10 3NE [B4084 (former A44) Evesham—Pershore]: Popular welcoming food pub, good choice (all day wknds) using local produce from ciabattas up, well kept changing ales such as Black Sheep and Hook Norton, paintings for sale; piped music may obtrude, fires may not be lit; children welcome, large garden, open all day wknds *(Tony and Wendy Hobden, Steve and Liz Tilley, Phyllis McCombie, K H Frostick)*

CROWLE [SO9256]

☆ *Old Chequers* WR7 4AA [Crowle Green, not far from M5 junction 6]: New licensees in much modernised comfortable dining pub, still a useful motorway stop, with decent food (not Sun evening), St Austell Tribute, Timothy Taylors Landlord and a couple of guest beers from island bar, good wines by the glass, efficient service; children and dogs welcome, disabled access, picnic-sets in garden behind, open all day summer *(Andy and Claire Barker, Dr D J and Mrs S C Walker, LYM, David Green)*

CUTNALL GREEN [SO8868]

Chequers WR9 0PJ [Kidderminster Rd]: Comfortably and stylishly refurbished beamed country dining pub with enjoyable food inc some good italian dishes and pretty little puddings, pleasant atmosphere, good wine choice, real ales *(W H and E Thomas, R J Herd)*

DRAKES BROUGHTON [SO9248]

☆ *Plough & Harrow* WR10 2AG [A44 NW of Pershore]: Well run dining pub with good-sized restaurant area, comfortable and attractive rambling lounge, friendly courteous staff, two or three well kept ales changing weekly, sensible prices and bargain helpings for the elderly, log fire; may be two sittings on busy days; good disabled access, pleasant terrace, big orchard-side garden with play area, open all day *(Chris Flynn, Wendy Jones, Mr and Mrs F E Boxell, W H and E Thomas)*

DROITWICH [SO9063]

Hop Pole WR9 8ED [Friar St]: Traditional beamed 16th-c local with bargain home-made lunches inc Sun roasts, half a dozen or more real ales such as Malvern Hills and Wye Valley, friendly staff, dominoes, pool; loud music Thurs-Sat evenings, otherwise quiet; wicker furniture in partly canopied back garden, open all day *(Dr B and Mrs P B Baker)*

DUNHAMPSTEAD [SO9160]

☆ *Fir Trees* WR9 7JX [just SE of Droitwich, towards Sale Green – OS Sheet 150 map ref 919600]: Pretty and attractively refurbished country dining pub doing well under newish licensees, Hook Norton and guest beers, comfortable conservatory; tables in nicely upgraded garden with flower-filled terrace, nice spot not far from canal – good walks *(Dave Braisted, Lynda and Trevor Smith, LYM, Mr and Mrs F E Boxell)*

EARLS CROOME [SO8642]

Yorkshire Grey WR8 9DA [A38, N of M50 junction 1]: Stylish contemporary décor, friendly bustle, fair-priced enjoyable food inc some enterprising dishes, prompt service, Greene King Old Speckled Hen, sensibly priced wines, log fire, candlelit restaurant; disabled access, garden tables *(Denys Gueroult, Paul and Bryony Walker)*

ECKINGTON [SO9241]

Bell WR10 3AN [Church St (B4080)]: Attractive village pub popular with younger people, central servery for pleasant bar and big dining area, cool dining conservatory, enjoyable food, nice staff, Bass and Greene King Ruddles, pool table *(Mr and Mrs F E Boxell)*

ELDERSFIELD [SO8131]

☆ *Greyhound* GL19 4NX [signed from B4211; Lime St (don't go into Eldersfield itself), OS Sheet 150 map ref 815314]: Unspoilt country local with welcoming young licensees, good inexpensive country cooking (not Mon) by landlord, real ales such as Butcombe and Woods Parish tapped from the cask, big woodburner in appealing black-beamed ochre-walled public bar, horse-racing pictures in candlelit carpeted side room, lively skittle alley, strikingly modern lavatories with interesting mosaic in gents'; picnic-sets in small front garden, swings and dovecote out behind *(the Didler, BB)*

EVESHAM [SP0343]

Old Swanne WR11 4HG [High St]: Bustling Wetherspoons in well restored 16th-c building, popular for low-priced food all day from 9, several real ales, farm cider, cheerful mix of ages (family area); tables outside, open all day *(Edna Jones)*

FLADBURY [SO9946]

Chequers WR10 2PZ [Chequers Lane]: Attractive upmarket dining pub dating from 14th c, huge old-fashioned range with log fire at end of long bar, lots of local prints, short but nicely varied choice of good generous food from sandwiches inc Sun carvery, Black Sheep, Hook Norton and other ales, hard-working staff, charming beamed back restaurant with conservatory; children welcome, large pleasant garden with play area, peaceful pretty village, comfortable well equipped bedroom extension *(Martin and Pauline Jennings)*

FLYFORD FLAVELL [SO9754]

☆ *Boot* WR7 4BS [off A422 Worcester—Alcester; Radford Rd]: Good value generous food from lunchtime sandwiches to hearty and interesting country dishes, friendly staff, Greene King IPA, Marstons Pedigree and guest beers (quite a few in summer), log fire in ancient heavily beamed and timbered back core now mainly for dining, comfortable modern conservatory, little old-world beamed front bar with small inglenook log fire, cards and pool; piped music, games machine; children welcome, pretty garden with heaters and lighting, comfortable bedrooms, open all day Sun *(Mike and Mary Carter, Dave Braisted, Mr and Mrs H J Langley, Mike Dean, Lis Wingate Gray, Theo, Anne and Jane Gaskin, David Collison, LYM, Reg Fowle, Helen Rickwood, Ian and Joan Blackwell)*

FORHILL [SP0575]

☆ *Peacock* B38 0EH [handy for M42, junctions 2 and 3; pub at junction Lea End Lane and Icknield St]: Attractive, quietly placed and well run Chef & Brewer with wide range of generous enjoyable food, plenty of tables in comfortably fitted knocked-through beamed rooms, woodburner in big inglenook, Enville, Hobsons Best, Theakstons Old Peculier and two changing ales, friendly prompt helpful service; piped classical music; children welcome, picnic-sets on back terrace and front grass, open all day *(R T and J C Moggridge, John Beeken, LYM, Stan and Hazel Allen, Dennis and Gill Keen, Nigel and Sue Foster)*

GREAT WITLEY [SO7566]

Hundred House WR6 6HS [Worcester Rd]: Busy much-modernised hotel (former coaching inn and magistrates' court), friendly quick service, Banks's real ales, good choice of moderately priced food from sandwiches up inc good Sun lunch, pleasant restaurant; no dogs; bedrooms, handy for ruined Witley Court and remarkable church *(Alan and Eve Harding)*

GUARLFORD [SO8245]

Plough & Harrow WR13 6NY [B4211 W of Malvern]: Charmingly refurbished timbered country pub, cottagey and friendly, with helpful young staff, good if not cheap food inc their own veg, herbs and fruit, fresh mildly contemporary décor in comfortable bar and beamed dining room, well kept real ale; good-sized garden, nice spot on open common, cl Sun evening and Mon *(W H and E Thomas)*

HALLOW [SO8258]

Royal Oak WR2 6LD [Main Rd (A443 N of Worcester)]: Newly refurbished, with well kept changing ales such as Boddingtons, Flowers, Sadlers Worcester Sorcery and Wye Valley Hallow, good choice of food inc several curries and OAP wkdy discounts, cheerful helpful service, nice house wines, some hunting photographs; good-sized garden *(Dave Braisted)*

HANLEY CASTLE [SO8342]

☆ **Three Kings** WR8 0BL [Church End, off B4211 N of Upton upon Severn]: By no means smart, even a little unkempt, and all the more loved by those who put unspoilt character and individuality first; friendly and homely, with huge inglenook and hatch service in little tiled-floor tap room, consistently well kept Butcombe, Hobsons Best and two or three changing beers from small breweries usually inc a Mild, Nov beer festival, farm cider, dozens of malt whiskies, two other larger rooms, one with fire in open range, low-priced food (not Sun evening – singer then; be prepared for a possibly longish wait other times), seats of a sort outside; family room, bedroom (the Didler, P Dawn, Mrs M B Gregg, Carol and Colin Broadbent, Pete Baker, LYM)

HOLT HEATH [SO8063]

Red Lion WR6 6LX [Witley Rd (A443/A4133)]: Spacious neatly refurbished pubby bar with wide choice of enjoyable food (all day wknds), efficient service, sporting photographs and memorabilia, comfortable newly refurbished raftered restaurant; sports TV; picnic-sets in good-sized garden, open all day (Mr and Mrs F E Boxell)

KEMPSEY [SO8548]

Talbot WR5 3JA [Main Rd (A38)]: Bargain lunches in tall pub's open-plan restaurant, Marstons-related ales (Dave Braisted)

KIDDERMINSTER [SO8679]

Old Waggon & Horses DY10 3NX [Ismere (A451 towards Stourbridge)]: Good range of well kept local beers, good value food and friendly service in solid former carriers' pub with etched windows and hatch-style servery in quarry-tiled public bar, cosy L-shaped lounge and dining room with knick-knacks (Mr and Mrs F E Boxell)

LEIGH SINTON [SO7850]

☆ **Royal Oak** WR13 5DZ [Malvern Rd, junction with A4103 SW of Worcester]: Well run dining pub with reliably enjoyable and remarkably cheap pubby food very popular with older customers for its amazing value, notable Sun lunch and bargain Mon buffet, friendly staff and regulars, efficient service, Marstons-related ales, short choice of reasonably priced wines, coal fire, cheerful cartoons and polished bric-a-brac in carpeted beamed bar, attractive restaurant; charming flower-filled garden behind with cushioned seats in sheltered alcoves (Denys Gueroult, Chris Flynn, Wendy Jones, JCW)

LONGDON [SO8434]

☆ **Hunters Inn** GL20 6AR [B4211 S, towards Tewkesbury]: Attractive décor with beams, flagstones, timbers, some stripped brick and log fires, welcoming staff, imaginative food inc fresh fish and exotic dishes, real ales such as Malvern Hills and Wells & Youngs Bombardier, good choice of wines by the glass, raftered dining area, good views; extensive well tended garden (Carol and Colin Broadbent, Mr and Mrs F E Boxell, LYM)

LONGLEY GREEN [SO7250]

Nelson WR6 5EF: Good-sized pub with comfortable lounge bar, good friendly staff, good range of reliable home-made food inc generous fish and chips, real ales such as Adnams and Banks's, local farm cider; tables outside, good walks nearby (Jason Caulkin, Mark Farrington)

LULSLEY [SO7354]

Fox & Hounds WR6 5QT [signed a mile off A44 Worcester—Bromyard]: Pleasant tucked-away country pub with enjoyable reasonably priced food from sandwiches and baguettes to Sun lunch, well kept real ale, nice wines, smallish parquet-floored bar stepping down into neat dining lounge, open fire, pretty little restaurant on left, attractive conservatory; dogs welcome, quiet and colourful enclosed side rose garden, nice walks (BB, Lynda and Trevor Smith)

MALVERN [SO7640]

☆ **Malvern Hills Hotel** WR13 6DW [opp British Camp car park, Wynds Point; junction A449/B4232 S]: Red plush banquettes, turkey carpet and open fire in extensive dark-panelled lounge bar, very popular wknds (friendly staff cope unflappably), decent bar food, well kept changing ales such as Black Sheep, Ludlow Gold, Greene King IPA and Wye Valley Butty Bach, quite a few malt whiskies, good coffee, downstairs pool room, smart more expensive restaurant; well reproduced piped music; dogs welcome, great views from terrace picnic-sets, bedrooms small but comfortable, open all day – fine position high in the hills (BB, Guy Vowles, P Dawn, Mark Farrington)

MALVERN WELLS [SO7742]

Railway Inn WR14 4PA [Wells Rd (A449 towards Ledbury)]: Tidy nicely placed Malvern Hills pub with wide choice of enjoyable food inc Sun evening, friendly staff, Marstons-related ales, restaurant, separate skittle alley and pool table; terrace tables, fine views (Maureen and Keith Gimson)

MAMBLE [SO6971]

Sun & Slipper DY14 9JL [just off A456 Bewdley—Tenbury Wells]: Attractively decorated two-room 16th-c village pub, welcoming chatty atmosphere, well kept Banks's, Hobsons Best and a guest beer, enjoyable fairly priced food, log fires, two friendly dogs, darts, dominoes and pool; picnic-sets outside, cl Mon (BB, Dave Braisted, Pete Baker)

OMBERSLEY [SO8463]

☆ **Cross Keys** WR9 0DS [just off A449; Main Rd (A4133, Kidderminster end)]: Nicely decorated beamed front bar with cosy areas inc armchairs and sofa in small curtained-off room, Enville and Hook Norton ales, good value wines by the glass, good-humoured helpful and efficient service, good if not cheap food from generous sandwiches and light bar meals to (not Sun) the smart conservatory restaurant's fish specialities (Dr and Mrs Jackson, Colin Fisher)

Crown & Sandys WR9 0EW [A4133]: Big popular open-plan bistro pub with imaginative if not cheap food from lunchtime sandwiches up (discount for early meals), fine choice of wines by the glass inc champagnes, friendly young uniformed staff, airy modern décor but keeping beams, settles and nice log fire in old fireplace, limestone-floor conservatory leading to terrace with fountain and sizeable garden beyond; loud acoustics, with flagstones or wooden flooring and piped music; children welcome, bedrooms, open all day wknds (LYM, Grahame Brooks, W H and E Thomas)

☆ **Kings Arms** WR9 0EW [A4133]: Imposing black-beamed and timbered Tudor pub with friendly staff, well kept Marstons-related ales, good coffee, generous enjoyable food, four open fires, comfortable rambling rooms, cosy wood-floored nooks and crannies with rustic bric-a-brac, one room with Charles II's coat of arms decorating its ceiling; children welcome, good disabled access, colourful tree-sheltered courtyard, open all day Sun (W M Lien, Mike and Mary Carter, LYM, M and C Thompson, Nigel and Sue Foster)

PEOPLETON [SO9350]
Crown WR10 2EE: Peaceful village pub, pretty and cosy, beamed bar with big inglenook fireplace, good choice of food, good wines by the glass and coffee, friendly efficient service; flower-filled back garden (Caroline and Michael Abbey)

PERSHORE [SO9545]
☆ **Brandy Cask** WR10 1AJ [Bridge St]: Plain high-ceilinged bow-windowed bar, back courtyard brewery producing their own attractively priced real ales, guest beers too, Aug beer festival, quick friendly helpful service, coal fire, food from sandwiches to steaks, quaintly decorated dining room; well behaved children allowed; long attractive garden down to river (keep a careful eye on the children), with terrace, vine arbour and koi pond (BB, John Street, the Didler)

SEDGEBERROW [SP0238]
Queens Head WR11 7UE [Main St (B4078, just off A46 S of Evesham)]: Welcoming village pub with enjoyable traditional pub food, Hook Norton and one or two guest beers, farm cider, dining end allowing children, central area where the locals congregate, far end with piano, darts and comfortable settees among more usual pub furnishings, collection of old 3-D relief advertisements; open all day wknds (Pete Baker)

SEVERN STOKE [SO8544]
Rose & Crown WR8 9JQ [A38 S of Worcester]: Attractive 16th-c black and white pub, low beams, knick-knacks and good fire in character front bar, Marstons-related ales, decent choice of wines by the glass, good value home-made food from generous hot-filled baguettes with chips up, friendly staff, back dining room allowing children; nice big garden with picnic-sets and play area (Carol and Colin Broadbent,

R T and J C Moggridge, Dr A J and Mrs Tompsett)

SHATTERFORD [SO7981]
☆ **Bellmans Cross** DY12 1RN [Bridgnorth Rd (A442)]: French-mood dining pub with good interesting food from sandwiches up inc good Sun lunch, smart tasteful restaurant, French chefs and bar staff, pleasant deft service, neat timber-effect bar with Bass, Greene King Old Speckled Hen and a guest beer, good choice of wines by the glass inc champagne, teas and coffees; picnic-sets outside, handy for Severn Woods walks, open all day wknds (BB, Lynda and Trevor Smith, Theo, Anne and Jane Gaskin, Richard Tosswill)

STOKE POUND [SO9667]
☆ **Queens** B60 3AU [Sugarbrook Lane, by Bridge 48, Worcester & Birmingham Canal]: Newly reworked and reopened waterside dining pub with good promptly served food, generous if not cheap, inc popular Sun lunch, friendly staff, attractive minimalist contemporary décor, exemplary lavatories; nice garden with play area, large covered waterside terrace, moorings, good walk up the 36 locks of the Tardebigge Steps, quite handy for Avoncroft buildings museum (Mike and Mary Carter, Mrs B H Adams, Bob Dudley)

STOKE WHARF [SO9468]
Navigation B60 4LB [Hanbury Rd (B4091), by Worcester & Birmingham Canal]: Friendly good value pub with popular food and well kept changing ales, comfortably refurbished lounge (Dave Braisted, Paul J Robinshaw)

TENBURY WELLS [SO5966]
Fountain WR15 8TB [Oldwood, A4112 S]: Wide-ranging choice of quickly served enjoyable food in attractively restored 17th-c timbered pub, open-plan black-beamed lounge bar with huge aquarium, stuffed fish and other bric-a-brac, coal-effect gas fires in handsome fireplaces, big dining room beyond, five well kept changing ales, decent wines by the glass, good whisky choice, friendly service; children welcome, disabled facilities (also braille menus and staff trained in sign language), picnic-sets on big side lawn with boules, play barn and lots of play equipment, open all day (BB, Mr and Mrs F E Boxall)

Peacock WR15 8LL [Worcester Rd, Newnham Bridge (A456 about 1½ miles E – so inn actually in Shrops)]: Attractive 14th-c dining pub with attentive friendly service, good choice of wines by the glass, well kept ales such as Black Sheep, Greene King Abbot and Tetleys, several separate rooms, heavy black beams, big log fire in panelled front lounge, comfortable kitchen chairs and ex-pew settles, back family room, pleasant dining room; terrace picnic-sets, lovely setting by River Teme, six good bedrooms (W H and E Thomas, Chris Flynn, Wendy Jones, LYM)

☆ **Pembroke House** WR15 8EQ [Cross St]: Striking timbered building, oldest in town, combining friendly and appealing pub side (lots to look at in well divided open-plan beamed bars) with upmarket dining side, well above average reasonably priced fresh food (not Sun evening or Mon) from sandwiches up, generous helpings with lots of veg, more elaborate evening meals (booking recommended then), helpful staff, Hobsons and a guest beer such as Bathams, woodburner; open all day wknds *(MLR, Mr and Mrs J L Hall, Ann and Colin Hunt)*

Ship WR15 8AE [Teme St]: Bright dining room with enjoyable if not cheap food from sandwiches to fish and Sun lunch, thoughtful and genuine smiling service, easy mix of customers, fresh flowers, well kept Fullers London Pride and Hobsons Best, decent wines, good coffee, small L-shaped bar with lots of dark wood inc fine Elizabethan beams, little hunting prints and other pictures; piped music, parking not easy if you have mobility problems; picnic-sets in coach yard and on neat sheltered back lawn, comfortable bedrooms *(W H and E Thomas, BB, Alan and Eve Harding)*

TIBBERTON [SO9057]

Bridge Inn WR9 7NQ [Plough Rd]: By Worcester & Birmingham Canal, with enjoyable food (all day wknds) from good sandwiches to some interesting main dishes, Banks's and a guest beer, friendly young staff, two comfortably updated dining sections with central feature fireplace; separate public bar with sports TV and machines; picnic-sets by canal, separate play area *(Carol and Colin Broadbent)*

UPHAMPTON [SO8464]

Fruiterers Arms WR9 0JW [off A449 N of Ombersley]: Homely country local (looks like a private house with a porch) brewing its own good Cannon Royall ales, also farm cider, inexpensive fresh lunchtime sandwiches, simple rustic Jacobean panelled bar and lounge with comfortable armchairs, beamery, log fire, lots of photographs and local memorabilia, no music, plain pool room; garden, some seats out in front *(Pete Baker)*

UPTON UPON SEVERN [SO8540]

Swan WR8 0JD [Waterside]: Well refurbished under new ownership, well kept Marstons-related ales, enjoyable food and log fires in low-beamed main bar; attractive waterside garden, work on bedrooms still under way as we went to press *(BB, Brian and Anita Randall)*

White Lion WR8 0HJ [High St]: Good value well presented food and local changing real ales in family-run hotel's pleasant relaxed bar, helpful staff, comfortable lounge and restaurant, sofas, stag's head and old prints; covered courtyard, bedrooms *(Lynne Carter, BB, P Dawn)*

WEATHEROAK HILL [SP0574]

☆ *Coach & Horses* B48 7EA [Icknield St – coming S on A435 from Wythall roundabout, filter right off dual carriageway a mile S, then in village turn left towards Alvechurch; not far from M42 junction 3]: Roomy and cheery country pub brewing its own good

Weatheroak beers, also good choice of others from small breweries, farm ciders, plush-seated low-ceilinged two-level dining bar, tiled-floor proper public bar, bargain lunches, also modern restaurant with well spaced tables; piped music; children allowed in eating area, plenty of seats out on lawns and upper terrace, open all day wknds *(Dave Braisted, David Green, LYM, W H and E Thomas, the Didler)*

WELLAND [SO8039]

Anchor WR13 6LN [Drake St (A4104 just over ½ mile E of B4208 crossroads)]: Pretty flower-covered Tudor building with charming garden, spreading dining area with fine views, five or six real ales, all wines available by the glass (large measures for wine and spirits), shove-ha'penny, dominoes, chess, Jenga; may be unobtrusive piped music; children in restaurant, field for tents or caravans, appealingly furnished bedrooms (normally no access outside opening hours), cl Sun evening *(Canon George Farran, LYM, Dennis and Gill Keen, Julia and Richard Tredgett, David and Ruth Shillitoe, Sara Fulton, Roger Baker)*

WHITTINGTON [SO8752]

Swan WR5 2RL [just off M5 junction 7]: Country-style bar with lots of pews, changing imaginative food from interesting snacks up, friendly hard-working young staff coping well with the bustle, well kept Banks's and Marstons Pedigree, good choice of wines, log fire; children welcome, garden with play area *(Martin and Pauline Jennings)*

WOLVERLEY [SO8379]

Lock DY10 3RN [Wolverley Rd (B4189 N of Kidderminster, by Staffs & Worcs Canal)]: Cottagey-looking pub with bay window overlooking a lock on the quaint canal as it negotiates the red sandstone bluff into which the pub is set; pleasant and comfortable, with good value generous straightforward food, Marstons and guest ales, farm cider; lovely spot handy for Kingsford Country Park, some waterside tables *(Ian and Jane Irving)*

WORCESTER [SO8455]

Dragon WR1 1JT [The Tything]: Lively simply furnished open-plan alehouse with half a dozen or so well described and well kept unusual changing microbrews inc a Mild and Porter, local Saxon farm cider, friendly helpful staff, bargain wkdy lunchtime food; piped pop music; folksy live bands, partly covered back terrace, open all day Sat *(Joe Green)*

Old Rectifying House WR1 3NN [North Parade]: Interesting flagstoned building overlooking River Severn, enjoyable up-to-date food in downstairs brasserie from light dishes to good fish choice, reasonable prices, cheerful staff, well kept Greene King Old Speckled Hen, decent wines; piped music, jazz Sun afternoon and alternate Weds; open all day *(Joe Green)*

Plough WR1 2HN [Fish St]: Cosy pub with two rooms off entrance lobby, good simple wkdy food 12-5.30 (not Sun/Mon) using local produce, home-baked bread for sandwiches, particularly good vegetarian choice, four good changing real ales, farm cider; tables out on decking in pleasant back courtyard, open all day *(Dr B and Mrs P B Baker, Sarah Ling, Pete Baker)*

Swan With Two Nicks WR1 2DP [New St/Friar St]: Rambling town pub dating from 16th c, plenty of character in bare-boards front rooms, well kept Batemans, Hobsons and Woods, simple lunchtime food (can take a while); other areas for live music or discos;

open all day (not Sun lunchtime) *(Lawrence Pearse)*

WYRE PIDDLE [SO9647]
Anchor WR10 2JB [off A4538 WNW of Evesham]: Worth knowing for its position by River Avon, with moorings, covered back decking, floodlit lawn and view from big airy back bar; neat little lounge with leather sofas and armchairs, usual food (not Sun evening) from baguettes up, real ales; games machine; children and dogs welcome, open all day *(Dennis Jenkin, R T and J C Moggridge, Ken Marshall)*

Post Office address codings confusingly give the impression that some pubs are in Worcestershire, when they're really in Gloucestershire, Herefordshire, Shropshire or Warwickshire (which is where we list them).

Yorkshire

What always strikes us on our inspection visits to this vast county is how genuinely friendly and helpful the licensees are. This shows up too while we are editing. There are more main entries here than in any other county in this *Guide*, and virtually every single one helpfully sent back our fact checking sheet – it certainly puts the Home Counties to shame! Food features strongly in many Yorkshire pubs, from simple, hearty fare for walkers, right through the spectrum to stylish and imaginative meals in civilised dining pubs and restaurants-with-rooms. All this is helped of course by the bountiful local produce – plenty of fresh fish, game from the moors and fine beef and lamb. Prices vary widely, depending on quality, but a general rule of thumb in Yorkshire is that, for the same money, you'll get more on your plate than elsewhere. Pubs on top form for food include the Crab & Lobster at Asenby (smart dining rooms and an interesting bar), the Malt Shovel at Brearton (refurbished under new young licensees and with some swiss influence), the Fox & Hounds at Carthorpe (ambitious restaurant-style meals rather than bar food), the Wyvill Arms at Constable Burton (very well run and putting their big herb garden to good use), the Blue Lion at East Witton (civilised and smart, and nice to stay in), the Plough at Fadmoor (extremely enjoyable, with delicious food), the General Tarleton at Ferrensby (interesting meals and some refurbishment), the Star at Harome (inventive food using tip-top local produce cooked by their young chef/landlord), the Stone Trough at Kirkham (a new Food Award this year – doing very well), the Charles Bathurst at Langthwaite (bustling and friendly, with super food), the Appletree at Marton (run by people who really care, and use their own-grown produce), the Millbank at Mill Bank (an arty place with appealing food), the White Swan in Pickering (a civilised small hotel with relaxed bar), the Nags Head at Pickhill (busy dining pub with fine choice of drinks too), the Boars Head at Ripley (a bustling little bar in a smart hotel), the Three Acres at Shelley (a smashing all-rounder), the Fox & Hounds at Sinnington (very well run and enjoyable), the Pipe & Glass at South Dalton (good modern food in this stylish place), the St Vincent Arms at Sutton upon Derwent (well liked food plus nine real ales), the Sportsmans Arms at Wath in Nidderdale (lovely food and a special place to stay) and the Blacksmiths at Westow (some gentle redecoration by new licensee). From this huge list, we choose the Appletree at Marton as Yorkshire Dining Pub of the Year. There may be strong future competition from one of our new entries: the Gray Ox at Hartshead, with nice views, has a buoyant atmosphere and rewarding modern cooking. Another is the Narrow Boat in Skipton, a cheerful place with good local beers and decent proper home cooking. We also welcome back to the *Guide* the Abbey Inn at Byland Abbey, doing very well all round under its new owners, English Heritage. Other pubs doing especially well this year where perhaps the top priority is not the food include the unique Birch Hall at Beck Hole, the bustling Strines Inn at Bradfield, the reliable White Lion at Cray, the well run Durham Ox at Crayke, the friendly Bridge Inn at Grinton, the old-fashioned Kings Arms at Heath, the interesting Queens Head at Kettlesing, the lively Blacksmiths Arms at Lastingham, the highly enjoyable Golden Lion in Osmotherley, the smashing Wombwell Arms at Wass and the cheerful Maltings in York. With such beautiful scenery and marvellous walks, many inns and pubs make a fine base from which to enjoy them: the Lion at Blakey Ridge, the Strines Inn at Bradfield, the White Lion at Cray, the Blue Lion at East Witton, the General Tarleton at Ferrensby, the Bridge Inn at Grinton, the Star at Harome, the Charles Bathurst at Langthwaite, the Maypole at Long Preston, the Three Acres at Shelley, the Buck at Thornton Watlass, the Wombwell Arms at Wass and the Sportsmans Arms at Wath in Nidderdale. We have added over a hundred new entries to the Lucky Dip section at the end of the chapter this year. The choice there is now terrific. To help narrow it down, we'd pick out particularly, in East Yorkshire, the Seabirds in Flamborough, Wolds Inn at Huggate, Ferguson-Fawsitt Arms in Walkington; in North Yorkshire, the Falcon at Arncliffe, Kings Arms at Askrigg, Game Cock at Austwick, Hare & Hounds at Burton Leonard, Foresters Arms at Carlton, Olde Sun at Colton, Coverbridge Inn at East Witton, Tempest Arms at Elslack, Moorcock at Garsdale Head, Fairfax Arms at Gilling East, Old Bell in Harrogate, Blue Bell and Racehorses in Kettlewell, Blind Jacks in Knaresborough, Red Lion at Langthwaite, Ship in Saltburn-by-the-Sea, Anvil at Sawdon, Hare at Scawton, and Black Swan and Blue Bell in York; in South Yorkshire, the Devonshire Cat in Sheffield; and in West Yorkshire the Fleece at Addingham, Black Bull at Birstall, Kaye Arms at Grange Moor and Old Bore at Rishworth. Drinks prices are comfortably below the national average. Two national brands, Tetleys and John Smiths, are brewed here, and there is a host of worthwhile smaller breweries such as Sam Smiths (which almost guarantees low prices), Black Sheep (very frequently found as the lowest-priced beer offered in pubs here), Timothy Taylors, Theakstons, Clarks, York, Brown Cow, Saltaire, Wold Top and Copper Dragon. All of these turned up at least in some of our main entries as their cheapest beer offering.

ALNE

SE4965   MAP 7

Blue Bell
Off A19 NW of York; Main Street; YO61 1RR

Restauranty place open evenings only (apart from Sunday lunch), attractive furnishings and layouts, appealing food, real ales and friendly service

Although only open in the evening (apart from Sunday lunchtime), this rather restauranty place does get busy then. There are two linked front areas with neatly set tables, a coal fire on the left and a coal-fired stove on the right, old engravings on cream walls, and stripped joists in the dark red ceiling. The furnishings are an appealing mix of styles and periods; on the left there's a splendid big bow-window seat around one good-sized round table. Behind is a small sun lounge with a sofa, and beyond that, forming an L, what looks an older part of the building, with dark tables on quarry tiles; a little dickensian bow window opens on to a sort of external corridor around the angle of this L. John Smiths, Timothy Taylors Landlord and a guest from Black Sheep on handpump, and friendly, helpful service. A neat garden behind has metal tables and chairs on a small terrace, and some pretty arbour seats. More reports please.

🍴 Good, interesting food includes soup, haddock and salmon fishcakes with a sweet chilli dip, wensleydale mushrooms with cream and sage, beef daube with mustard mash and Guinness and red wine sauce, chicken florentine, lamb strudel with a red wine and redcurrant sauce, pork fillet with leeks and bacon, mushroom and cashew nut stroganoff, and puddings such as Malteser and Crunchie cheesecake and bread and butter pudding with custard; they still offer an early bird menu (Tuesday-Friday between 6 and 7pm). *Starters/Snacks: £3.95 to £6.95. Main Courses: £8.95 to £17.95. Puddings: £4.50 to £6.95*

Free house ~ Licensee Michael Anson ~ Real ale ~ Bar food (6-9; 12-8 Sun; not lunchtimes except Sun) ~ Restaurant ~ (01347) 838331 ~ Children welcome ~ Open 6-11; 12-10 Sun; closed lunchtimes except Sun

Recommended by Pat and Graham Williamson, Mr and Mrs P M Jennings, J R Ringrose, Jon and Siobhan Brier

APPLETON-LE-MOORS   SE7388   MAP 10

Moors 🛏

Village N of A170 just under 1½ miles E of Kirkby Moorside; YO62 6TF

Neat and unfussy pub with a good choice of drinks, proper country cooking using own-grown produce, plenty of nearby walks; comfortable bedrooms

This little stone-built pub is all strikingly neat and surprisingly bare of the usual bric-a-brac. Sparse decorations include just a few copper pans and earthenware mugs in a little alcove, a couple of plates, one or two pieces of country ironwork, and a delft shelf with miniature whiskies; the whiteness of walls and ceiling is underlined by the black beams and joists, and the bristly grey carpet. Perfect for a cold winter evening, there's a nice built-in high-backed stripped settle next to an old kitchen fireplace, and other seating includes an unusual rustic seat for two cleverly made out of stripped cartwheels; plenty of standing space. To the left of the bar, you'll probably find a few regulars chatting on the backed padded stools: Black Sheep and Courage Best on handpump, over 50 malt whiskies and a reasonably priced wine list. Darts and board games. There are tables in the walled garden with quiet country views and walks straight from here to Rosedale Abbey or Hartoft End, as well as paths to Hutton-le-Hole, Cropton and Sinnington. More reports please.

🍴 Using own-grown vegetables and salads and local organic produce, the well liked food might include partridge, hare, pheasant and venison plus soup, chicken liver pâté, fish pie, chicken in lemon and saffron sauce, lamb shoulder with apricot stuffing, baked gammon with pear and ginger sauce, celeriac and blue cheese pie, half a roast duck with orange sauce, and puddings such as apple and blackberry pie and Baileys chocolate fondue with fresh fruit. *Starters/Snacks: £2.95 to £4.95. Main Courses: £8.50 to £12.95. Puddings: £3.95*

Free house ~ Licensee Janet Frank ~ Real ale ~ Bar food (see opening hours; not Mon) ~ Restaurant ~ No credit cards ~ (01751) 417435 ~ Children welcome ~ Dogs allowed in bar and bedrooms ~ Open 7-11; 12-2, 7-11(10.30 Sun) Sat; closed Mon; closed Tues-Fri lunchtimes ~ Bedrooms: £40B/£60B

Recommended by Colin and Dot Savill, Roger Hobson, Lynda Lloyd

ASENBY   SE3975   MAP 7

Crab & Lobster 🍴🏮 ☕ 🛏

Village signposted off A168 – handy for A1; YO7 3QL

Interesting furnishings and décor in rambling bar, ambitious and enjoyable restauranty food, good drinks choice, attractive terrace; smart bedrooms

Although this interesting place is more of a dining than drinking pub it does keep Copper Dragon Golden Pippin and 1816, Theakstons XB and a guest on handpump. The rambling, L-shaped bar has an interesting jumble of seats from antique high-backed and other settles through settees and wing armchairs heaped with cushions, to tall and rather theatrical corner seats; the tables are almost as much of a mix, and the walls and available surfaces are quite a jungle of bric-a-brac, with standard and table lamps and candles keeping even the lighting pleasantly informal. There's also a dining pavilion with big tropical plants, nautical bits and pieces, and Edwardian sofas. Quite a few wines by the glass and maybe piped music. The gardens have bamboo and palm trees lining the paths, there's a gazebo at the end of the walkways, and seats on a mediterranean-style terrace. The opulent bedrooms (based on famous hotels around the world) are in the surrounding house which has seven acres of mature gardens, and 180-metre golf hole with full practice facilities.

🍴 **Imaginative – if not cheap – food includes a lunchtime fish club sandwich, pressed terrine of ham hock, duck confit and foie gras with a pear, sage and saffron chutney, twice-baked cheese and leek soufflé with a wild mushroom velouté, barbecue pork spare ribs with orange, ginger, treacle and Jack Daniels, chicken breast with ricotta and cherry tomatoes wrapped in pancetta with sage pasta and chicken cream, natural cured haddock with cheese and spring onion potatoes, poached egg and wholegrain mustard, honey and five-spice breast of goosnargh duck with spring onion drop scone and chinese vegetables, and puddings such as roast pineapple kebab with coconut fancies, rum and raisin panna cotta and banana fritters and warm chocolate and pecan brownie with summer berry compote and double vanilla ice-cream.** *Starters/Snacks: £5.50 to £9.50. Main Courses: £9.50 to £22.50. Puddings: £6.30 to £9.50*

Vimac Leisure ~ Licensee Mark Spenceley ~ Real ale ~ Bar food (12-2, 6.30-9.30) ~ Restaurant ~ (01845) 577286 ~ Well behaved children allowed ~ Open 11.30-11 ~ Bedrooms: £120B/£150B

Recommended by Peter and Lesley Yeoward, W K Wood, Michael Doswell, Ian and Jane Haslock, Gordon Ormondroyd, Gerry and Rosemary Dobson, Dr and Mrs R G J Telfer

BECK HOLE   NZ8202   MAP 10

Birch Hall

Signed off A169 SW of Whitby, from top of Sleights Moor; YO22 5LE

Extraordinary pub-cum-village-shop in lovely valley with friendly landlady, real ales and simple snacks, seats outside and wonderful surrounding walks

'A gem' and 'a place to be cherished' are just two descriptions readers have used to sum up this unique pub-cum-village-shop. There are two rooms with the shop selling postcards, sweeties and ice-creams in between, and hatch service to both sides. Furnishings are simple – built-in cushioned wall seats and wooden tables (spot the one with 136 pennies, all heads up, embedded in the top) and chairs on the floor (flagstones in one room, composition in the other), some strange items such as french breakfast cereal boxes and a tube of Macleans toothpaste priced 1/3d, and Black Sheep Bitter, Durham White Herald and maybe a guest beer on handpump; several malt whiskies. Friendly, welcoming staff, dominoes and quoits. Outside, an ancient oil painting of the view up the steeply wooded river valley hangs on the pub wall, there are benches out in front, and steps up to a little steeply terraced side garden. They have a self-catering cottage attached to the pub. It's in a beautiful steep valley and surrounded by marvellous walks; you can walk along the disused railway line from Goathland – part of the path from Beck Hole to Grosmont is surfaced with mussel shells.

🍴 **Bar snacks such as locally made pies, butties and home-made scones and cakes that include their lovely beer cake.** *Starters/Snacks: £0.90 to £2.20*

Free house ~ Licensee Glenys Crampton ~ Real ale ~ Bar food (available during all opening hours) ~ No credit cards ~ (01947) 896245 ~ Children in small family room ~ Dogs welcome ~ Open 11-11; 12-10.30 Sun; 11-3, 7.30-11 Weds-Sun in winter; closed winter Mon evening, all day Tues Nov-March

Recommended by Pat and Tony Martin, Peter and Jo Smith, John Fiander, the Didler, Arthur Pickering, Pete Baker, P Dawn, Sue Demont, Tim Barrow, Amanda Russell, Malcolm and Jane Levitt, Phil Bryant

---

Cribbage is a card game using a block of wood with holes for matchsticks or special pins to score with; regulars in cribbage pubs are usually happy to teach strangers how to play.

BEVERLEY   TA0339   MAP 8

White Horse £

Hengate, close to the imposing Church of St Mary's; runs off North Bar; HU17 8BN

Unspoilt Victorian pub with basic little rooms, simple furnishings, open fires, and traditional bar food

There's a carefully preserved Victorian feel in this determinedly traditional and quite-without-frills pub. The basic but very atmospheric little rooms are huddled together around the central bar: brown leatherette seats (high-backed settles in one little snug) and basic wooden chairs and benches on bare floorboards, antique cartoons and sentimental engravings on the nicotine-stained walls, a gaslit pulley-controlled chandelier, a deeply reverberating chiming clock, and open fires – one with an attractively tiled old fireplace. A framed history of the pub now hangs on the wall. Very cheap Sam Smiths OB on handpump; a separate games room has pool and there's a skittle alley. Upstairs is a large area with a sideboard full of children's toys and an open fire. John Wesley preached in the back yard in the mid-18th c.

⑪ **Simple food includes sandwiches, bangers and mash, steak in ale pie, lasagne, somerset pork, and puddings like spotted dick and custard.** *Starters/Snacks: £2.00 to £3.95. Main Courses: £3.50 to £5.50. Puddings: £2.00 to £3.00*

Sam Smiths ~ Manager Anna ~ Real ale ~ Bar food (10.30-2.45 Mon-Sat; no food Sun) ~ No credit cards ~ (01482) 861973 ~ Children welcome away from bar and adjacent lounge area until 8pm ~ Dogs allowed in bar ~ Open 11-11; 12-10.30 Sun

Recommended by David Carr, Pete Baker, Len Beattie, John Wooll, the Didler

BLAKEY RIDGE   SE6799   MAP 10

Lion 🍺 🛏

From A171 Guisborough—Whitby follow Castleton, Hutton le Hole signposts; from A170 Kirkby Moorside—Pickering follow Keldholm, Hutton le Hole, Castleton signposts; OS Sheet 100 map reference 679996; YO62 7LQ

Extended pub in great spot, usefully open for food all day; bedrooms

This is the highest point of the North York Moors National Park and as this extended pub is open all day it does make a useful stop for thirsty walkers. There are plenty of surrounding hikes (and the Coast to Coast Footpath is close by) and stunning views. If you are thinking of staying you must book well in advance. The beamed and rambling bars have warm open fires, a few big high-backed rustic settles around cast-iron-framed tables, lots of small dining chairs, a nice leather settee, and stone walls hung with some old engravings and photographs of the pub under snow (it can easily get cut off in winter). Greene King Old Speckled Hen, John Smiths, and Theakstons Best, Old Peculier, Black Bull and XB on handpump; piped music and games machine. It is popular with coach parties.

⑪ **Generous helpings of good basic bar food include lunchtime sandwiches and filled baked potatoes as well as soup, giant yorkshire pudding with gravy, home-cooked ham and egg, lasagne, chicken kiev, beef curry, battered cod, nut roast, daily specials, and puddings like sticky toffee sponge with custard and jam roly-poly.** *Starters/Snacks: £2.75 to £3.95. Main Courses: £8.50 to £15.95. Puddings: £3.75*

Free house ~ Licensee Barry Crossland ~ Real ale ~ Bar food (12-10) ~ Restaurant ~ (01751) 417320 ~ Children welcome ~ Dogs allowed in bar and bedrooms ~ Open 10am-11pm ~ Bedrooms: £20(£41.50B)/£54(£68B)

Recommended by R M Jones, Dr D J and Mrs S C Walker, Mark and Ruth Brock, Sylvia and Tony Birbeck, Sarah and Peter Gooderham, Sean A Smith, Tony and Penny Burton, Cathryn and Richard Hicks, Dr and Mrs Jackson, WW, John and Helen Rushton

---

If you know a pub's ever open all day, please tell us.

BOROUGHBRIDGE   SE3966   MAP 7

Black Bull ♀

St James Square; B6265, just off A1(M); YO51 9AR

Bustling old town pub, handy for A1, with reliable food, real ales and several wines by the glass

Much of this attractive old town pub has been redecorated this year and some of the furniture upholstered too. The main bar area has a big stone fireplace and comfortable seats and is served through an old-fashioned hatch; there's also a cosy snug with traditional wall settles, a tap room, lounge bar and restaurant. John Smiths, Timothy Taylors Landlord and a guest such as Roosters Yankee on handpump, ten wines by the glass and 19 malt whiskies; dominoes and chess. The two borzoi dogs are called Charlie and Sadie, and the cat Mimi; the local mummers perform here on the first Sunday of every month. The hanging baskets are lovely.

🍴 **As well as lots of sandwiches, the enjoyable bar food includes deep-fried mushrooms in a blue cheese dressing, a pie of the day, pork and chive sausages with onion gravy, beef curry, thai beef strips with stir-fried vegetables, noodles and a hot and sour sauce, gammon and egg, daily specials, and puddings such as banana and toffee roulade and apple pie.** *Starters/Snacks: £3.25 to £5.50. Main Courses: £5.95 to £9.25. Puddings: £3.75*

Free house ~ Licensees Anthony and Jillian Burgess ~ Real ale ~ Bar food (12-2(2.30 Sun), 6-9(9.30 Fri and Sat)) ~ Restaurant ~ (01423) 322413 ~ Children welcome ~ Dogs allowed in bar and bedrooms ~ Open 11-11(midnight Sat); 12-10.30 Sun ~ Bedrooms: £40S/£60S

Recommended by Janet and Peter Race, J R Ringrose, the Didler, J V Dadswell, Pete Baker

BRADFIELD   SK2290   MAP 7

Strines Inn 🛏

From A57 heading E of junction with A6013 (Ladybower Reservoir) take first left turn (signposted with Bradfield) then bear left; with a map can also be reached more circuitously from Strines signpost on A616 at head of Underbank Reservoir, W of Stocksbridge; S6 6JE

Friendly, bustling inn with fine surrounding scenery, good mix of customers, well liked food, changing ales and good bedrooms

This is a well run and enjoyable moorland inn and a nice place to stay overnight, too; the bedrooms have four-poster beds (one has an open fire) and a dining table as the good breakfasts are served in your room – and the front one overlooks the reservoir. The main bar has a welcoming atmosphere and a good mix of customers, black beams liberally decked with copper kettles and so forth, quite a menagerie of stuffed animals, homely red-plush-cushioned traditional wooden wall benches and small chairs, and a coal fire in the rather grand stone fireplace. A room off on the right has another coal fire, hunting photographs and prints, and lots of brass and china, and on the left is another similarly furnished room. Bradfield Farmers Pale Ale, Mansfield Bitter and Marstons Pedigree on handpump and several malt whiskies; piped music. Fine views from the picnic-sets, a safely fenced-in children's playground, and wandering peacocks. The surrounding walks and scenery are superb.

🍴 **Good bar food includes sandwiches and paninis, filled baked potatoes, soup, garlic mushrooms, filled giant yorkshire puddings, liver and onions, mushroom tagliatelle, a pie of the day, cajun chicken, meatballs and spaghetti, daily specials, and puddings such as bread and butter pudding and chocolate roulade.** *Starters/Snacks: £2.95 to £4.10. Main Courses: £6.45 to £13.60. Puddings: £2.80 to £3.40*

Free house ~ Licensee Bruce Howarth ~ Real ale ~ Bar food (12-2.30, 6-9 winter weekdays; all day weekends and summer weekdays) ~ (0114) 285 1247 ~ Children welcome ~ Dogs welcome ~ Open 10.30am-11pm; 10.30-3, 6-11 in winter; closed 25 Dec ~ Bedrooms: £55B/£75B

Recommended by Trevor and Judith Pearson, JJW, CMW, John and Joan Calvert, Mrs Jane Kingsbury, Dr and Mrs R G J Telfer, Peter F Marshall, the Didler, Gerry Miller, David and Ruth Hollands, Susan and John Douglas

BREARTON

SE3260 MAP 7

Malt Shovel ⑪ ♟ ◖

Village signposted off A61 N of Harrogate; HG3 3BX

Careful refurbishment of 16th-c village pub under young new licensees, welcoming atmosphere, imaginative food, real ales and fine wine list

New friendly young licensees – both professional opera singers – have taken over this 16th-c village pub and refurbished it throughout. Heavily beamed rooms radiate from the attractive linenfold oak bar counter with painted walls and light blue skirting, an attractive mix of wooden dining chairs and tables on wood or slate floors, and some partitioning that separates several candlelit dining areas; they are hoping to add a back conservatory. It's all very relaxed and welcoming with quite an emphasis on the imaginative food. Black Sheep Bitter and guests like Daleside Blonde and Timothy Taylors Landlord and an excellent wine list with 13 by the glass. There are seats on a heated outside terrace.

⑪ **With some swiss influence, the excellent food might at lunchtime include sandwiches using home-made bread, ploughman's, soup, a changing pâté with chutney, devilled kidneys, fish pie, calves liver and bacon, home-made pork sausages, and steak haché, plus more elaborate choices such as lamb sweetbreads in a light mustard sauce, seared scallops on black pudding with warm geranium jelly, crevettes in garlic butter, spinach pancake with gruyère, wiener schnitzel, goujons of monkfish with raspberry and chilli dip, half a crispy gressingham duck with brandy and orange sauce, slow-cooked pigs cheek on black pudding, and puddings such as crumbly, spicy apple tart with wensleydale and chocolate truffle cake with caramelised orange.** *Starters/Snacks: £4.50 to £8.00. Main Courses: £12.95 to £24.00. Puddings: £5.50*

Free house ~ Licensee Jurg Bleiker ~ Real ale ~ Bar food (not Sun evening) ~ Restaurant ~ (01423) 862929 ~ Children welcome ~ Open 12-3, 6-11; closed Sun evening

Recommended by Peter Burton, Blaise Vyner, Rona Murdoch, Keith Wright, Paul Boot, Yana Pocklington, Patricia Owlett, Tony and Penny Burton, G Dobson, Pierre Richterich, Dr Ian S Morley, Peter and Anne-Marie O'Malley, David Coleman

BURN

SE5928 MAP 7

Wheatsheaf ◖ £

A19 Selby—Doncaster; Main Road; YO8 8LJ

Plenty to look at and a friendly welcome, half a dozen real ales and good value straightforward food

You can be sure of a warm welcome from the landlord and his neat young staff in this mock-Tudor roadside pub. There's masses to look at inside: gleaming copper kettles, black dagging shears, polished buffalo horns and the like around its good log and coal fire (and a drying rack with bunches of herbs above it), decorative mugs above one bow-window seat, and cases of model vans and lorries on the cream walls. The highly polished pub tables in the partly divided open-plan bar have comfortable seats around them and John Smiths and Timothy Taylors Landlord and guests such as Brown Cow Silver Hammer, E & S Elland Yorkshireman, Rudgate Ruby Mild and Woldsway Pale Ale on handpump at attractive prices and over 50 malt whiskies. A pool table is out of the way on the left, cribbage, dominoes, games machine, TV, and there may be unobtrusive piped music. A small garden behind has picnic-sets on a heated terrace. More reports please.

⑪ **Good value, straightforward food might include sandwiches or burgers, ploughman's, lamb rogan josh, lasagne, chilli con carne, notable fish and chips, and daily specials.** *Main Courses: £2.95 to £8.95. Puddings: £2.00*

Free house ~ Licensee Andrew Howdall ~ Real ale ~ Bar food (12-2 daily, 6.30-8.30 Thurs, Fri and Sat; no food Sun-Weds evenings) ~ (01757) 270614 ~ Children welcome ~ Dogs welcome ~ Open 12-midnight(11 Sun)

Recommended by DC

BYLAND ABBEY   SE5478   MAP 7

Abbey Inn ☥ 🛏

The Abbey has a brown tourist-attraction signpost off the A170 Thirsk—Helmsley;
YO61 4BD

Antique furnishings in historic pub by abbey ruins, imaginative food, garden

Based around an ancient monastic core, this Victorian farmhouse, bought recently by
English Heritage, is located next to an abbey that was once the largest ecclesiastical
building in Europe, but which under the instructions of Henry VIII, was closed and
eventually fell into ruins. The two characterful front rooms have big fireplaces and are
finely furnished with oak and stripped deal tables, settees, carved oak seats, and
Jacobean-style dining chairs on the polished boards and flagstones; there are various
stuffed birds, little etchings, and china cabinets, and some discreet stripping back of
plaster to show signs of its venerable past. The Library has lots of bookshelves and a
large single oak table, and the big back room has lots of rustic bygones; piped music.
Well kept Black Sheep Bitter and locally brewed Byland Abbey on handpump, and an
interesting wine list with 20 (plus champagne) by the glass. Plenty of room outside on
the terrace and in the garden.

🍴 Imaginative food might include soup with ciabatta croûtons, chicken liver and wild
mushroom pâté with plum and apple chutney, antipasti, roast pepper stuffed with
mushroom risotto with tomato and garlic sauce, lancashire hotpot, cod loin on minted pea
purée, sliced halibut with a timbale of fresh crab and celeriac remoulade, chicken on
sunblush and black olive salad with basil couscous, griddled rack of venison with port and
thyme sauce, and puddings such as summer berry iced parfait, crème brûlée and sticky
toffee pudding. *Starters/Snacks: £4.00 to £7.50. Main Courses: £8.00 to £18.00. Puddings:*
£4.95 to £5.95

Free house ~ Licensee Deborah Whitwell ~ Real ale ~ Bar food (12-2(3 Sun), 6.30-9) ~
Restaurant ~ (01347) 868204 ~ Children welcome if eating ~ Open 12-3, 6-11; 12-4 Sun;
closed Sun evening, Mon lunchtime ~ Bedrooms: /£95B

Recommended by Dr and Mrs Jackson, Dr Peter Crawshaw, Peter Burton, Greta and Christopher Wells, Malcolm and
Jane Levitt

CARTHORPE   SE3083   MAP 10

Fox & Hounds 🍽 ☥

Village signposted from A1 N of Ripon, via B6285; DL8 2LG

Emphasis on ambitious food in friendly dining pub but drinkers welcome too; real ales and
extensive wine list

There's a good mix of both drinkers and diners in this neatly kept extended pub – but to
be sure of a table, it's best to book ahead. The cosy L-shaped bar has quite a few mistily
evocative Victorian photographs of Whitby, a couple of nice seats by the larger of its two
log fires, plush button-back built-in wall banquettes and chairs, plates on stripped
beams, and some limed panelling; piped light classical music. There is some theatrical
memorabilia in the corridors and an attractive high-raftered restaurant with lots of neatly
black-painted farm and smithy tools. Black Sheep and Worthingtons on handpump and an
extensive wine list; friendly, helpful service. More reports please.

🍴 Listing their local producers on the menu, the popular restaurant-style food includes
sandwiches, soup, honey-roasted ham hock terrine with home-made piccalilli, caramelised
onion and goats cheese tart, roast rack of lamb on a blackcurrant croûton with redcurrant
gravy, salmon fillet on spinach with a white wine and parsley sauce, chicken breast filled
with blue cheese and leeks in a creamy sauce, half a gressingham duckling with orange
sauce and parsley and thyme stuffing, daily specials, and puddings such as sticky ginger
pudding with toffee sauce, honeycomb ice-cream and sugared nuts and poached pear,
rhubarb ice-cream in a tuile basket with rich chocolate sauce; they also offer a Tuesday-
Thursday two- and three-course menu. *Starters/Snacks: £3.55 to £6.50. Main Courses: £9.95*
to £25.95. Puddings: £4.95 to £9.95

Free house ~ Licensees Vince and Helen Taylor ~ Real ale ~ Bar food (not Mon) ~ Restaurant ~ (01845) 567433 ~ Children welcome ~ Open 12-3, 7-11(10.30 Sun); closed Mon and first week Jan

Recommended by Jill and Julian Tasker, Janet and Peter Race, Jill Angold-Stevens

CHAPEL LE DALE
SD7477 MAP 7

Hill Inn 🍺

B5655 Ingleton—Hawes, 3 miles N of Ingleton; LA6 3AR

Friendly inn with grand surrounding walks, appealing food cooked by the licensees, a fair choice of real ales and comfortable bedrooms

With fine views to Ingleborough and Whernside, this warmly friendly inn is surrounded by wonderful remote walks. There are old pine tables and benches on the stripped wooden floors, nice pictures on the walls, stripped-stone recesses, a warm log fire, and Black Sheep Best and Yorkshire Square Ale, Dent Aviator and Theakstons Best on handpump; several wines by the glass. There's a dining room and a well worn-in sun lounge. It is essential you phone and check their opening hours before setting out. More reports please.

🍽 **Cooked by the licensees, the enjoyable food might include sandwiches, soup, chicken in a white wine, cream and tarragon sauce, pork with cider, apples and mushrooms, beef in ale casserole, duck breast with a prune, orange, redcurrant and port jus, and puddings such as warm chocolate pudding with a white chocolate sauce and home-made vanilla ice-cream and crème brûlée with an orange salad with home-made orange and yoghurt ice-cream.** *Starters/Snacks: £5.95 to £10.00. Main Courses: £9.95 to £18.00. Puddings: £5.65 to £6.25*

Free house ~ Licensee Sabena Martin ~ Real ale ~ Bar food (not Mon (but also see opening hours)) ~ Restaurant ~ (015242) 41256 ~ Children in dining areas if eating ~ Dogs allowed in bar ~ Open 6.30-11(but you must ring to check these times); 12-11 Sat; 12-11 (but will shut 3.30 if quiet, open 6.30) Sun; closed all Mon (except bank holidays) and maybe Tues-Fri lunchtimes ~ Bedrooms: /£70S

Recommended by Paul and Anita Holmes, S Gainsley

CONSTABLE BURTON
SE1690 MAP 10

Wyvill Arms 🍴 🍷 🍺

A684 E of Leyburn; DL8 5LH

Well run and friendly dining pub with excellent food, a dozen wines by the glass, real ales and efficient helpful service; bedrooms

With first class food and friendly, efficient service, it's not surprising that this well run dining pub is so popular. For drinkers, there is a small bar area with a mix of seating, a finely worked plaster ceiling with the Wyvill family's coat of arms, and an elaborate stone fireplace. The second bar, where food is served (though they also have a sizeable restaurant), has upholstered alcoves, hunting prints, and old oak tables; the reception area of this room includes a huge chesterfield which can seat up to eight people, another carved stone fireplace, and an old leaded church stained-glass window partition. Both rooms are hung with pictures of local scenes. Black Sheep, Theakstons Best, and a guest like Marstons Pedigree on handpump and a dozen wines by the glass; board games. Several large wooden benches under large white parasols for outdoor dining. Constable Burton Gardens are opposite and worth a visit.

🍽 **Using seasonal produce, herbs from their own big garden and game from the estate across the road, the particularly good food includes sandwiches, soup, terrine of smoked ham, wensleydale cheese and duck mousse with pear and apple chutney, salmon fishcakes on tomato carpaccio with spring onion and chilli jam, thai risotto with asian greens, steak and onion pie, breaded chicken supreme stuffed with mozzarella and smoked bacon on creamed leeks with stilton sauce, lamb fillet with a herb crust, sweet parsnip purée and lamb jus, and a daily fresh fish dish.** *Starters/Snacks: £2.95 to £7.50. Main Courses: £9.25 to £17.95. Puddings: £5.00 to £5.75*

Free house ~ Licensee Nigel Stevens ~ Real ale ~ Bar food (11.30-2.15, 5.30-11) ~ Restaurant ~ (01677) 450581 ~ Children welcome but must be well supervised ~ Dogs allowed in bar and bedrooms ~ Open 11-3, 5-11 ~ Bedrooms: £50B/£75B

Recommended by Ben and Helen Ingram, P and J Shapley, B and M Kendall, Janet and Peter Race, G Dobson, Mike and Jayne Bastin, John and Sylvia Harrop, Stephen Woad, M and GR, Dr and Mrs R G J Telfer

CRAY
SD9479   MAP 7

White Lion 🍺 🛏

B6160, Upper Wharfedale N of Kettlewell; BD23 5JB

Reliable, welcoming pub in fine countryside, plenty of walks, simply furnished rooms, good choice of drinks and food, and bedrooms

This former drovers' hostlery, the highest pub in Wharfedale and surrounded by superb countryside, is a reliably friendly place for walkers with their well behaved dogs; the landlord can also advise about other walks in the area. The simply furnished bar has an open fire, seats around tables on the flagstone floor, shelves of china, iron tools, old painted metal adverts for animal feed and so forth, and a high dark beam-and-plank ceiling; there's also a back room. Moorhouses Bitter, Timothy Taylors Golden Best and maybe Copper Dragon Golden Pippin and 1816 on handpump, nine wines by the glass, and around 20 malt whiskies; board games, ring the bull, and giant Jenga. In fine weather, you can sit at picnic benches above the very quiet steep lane or on the great flat limestone slabs in the shallow stream which tumbles down opposite.

🍴 **As well as lunchtime filled yorkshire puddings, filled baguettes and ploughman's, the bar food might include soup, chicken liver pâté, steak and mushroom or game casserole, baked goats cheese pie, pork fillet in a honey and spiced mustard cream, lambs liver and onions with mustard mash, and puddings such as lemon meringue pie; best to book to be sure of a table in the bar. If you eat between 5.45 and 6.15pm you get a 20% discount on a few items.** *Starters/Snacks: £3.95 to £4.50. Main Courses: £8.50 to £13.95. Puddings: £3.75*

Free house ~ Licensees Kevin and Debbie Roe ~ Real ale ~ Bar food ~ (01756) 760262 ~ Children welcome ~ Dogs welcome ~ Open 11-11 ~ Bedrooms: £50S/£65S

Recommended by W K Wood, Bruce and Sharon Eden, Tony and Betty Parker, Richard, Lawrence Pearse, Peter Smith, Judith Brown, Walter and Susan Rinaldi-Butcher, Peter F Marshall, the Didler, Dr and Mrs M E Wilson, G Dobson, Len Beattie, Blaise Vyner, Paul and Anita Holmes, Terry Mizen, Greta and Christopher Wells, Lynda and Trevor Smith, Richard Tosswill, Dr D and Mrs B Woods

CRAYKE
SE5670   MAP 7

Durham Ox

Off B1363 at Brandsby, towards Easingwold; West Way; YO61 4TE

Friendly country inn, interesting décor in old-fashioned, relaxing rooms, fine drinks and enjoyable bar food; bedrooms, lovely views

You can be sure of a friendly welcome in this bustling country pub. The old-fashioned lounge bar has an enormous inglenook fireplace, pictures and photographs on the dark red walls, interesting satirical carvings in its panelling (Victorian copies of medieval pew ends), polished copper and brass, and venerable tables and antique seats and settles on the flagstones. In the bottom bar is a framed illustrated account of the local history (some of it gruesome) dating back to the 12th c, and a large framed print of the original famous Durham Ox which weighed 171 stones. Theakstons Best, Timothy Taylors Landlord and a guest from Black Sheep or Hambleton on handpump, 12 wines by the glass, several malt whiskies and organic juices; piped music. There are seats outside on a terrace and in the covered courtyard and fantastic views over the Vale of York on three sides; on the fourth side there's a charming view up the hill to the medieval church. The comfortable bedrooms are in converted farm buildings. The tale is that this is the hill up which the Grand Old Duke of York marched his men.

ⅲ Good bar food includes open sandwiches (not Saturday evening), soup, welsh or yorkshire rarebit, eggs benedict, game terrine with date and squash chutney, bangers and mash, free-range chicken breast with mushrooms and tomatoes, ricotta and spinach roulade, fish and shellfish pie, lamb shank with red wine and rosemary reduction, and puddings such as chocolate and hazelnut brownie with chocolate sauce and ice-cream and vanilla pod crème brûlée. *Starters/Snacks: £3.95 to £6.95. Main Courses: £8.95 to £16.95. Puddings: £4.95 to £6.95*

Free house ~ Licensee Michael Ibbotson ~ Real ale ~ Bar food (12-2.30(3 Sun), 6-9.30(10 Sat; 8.30 Sun); not 25 Dec) ~ Restaurant ~ (01347) 821506 ~ Children welcome but must be well behaved ~ Dogs allowed in bedrooms ~ Open 12-3, 6-11; 12-midnight Sat; 12-11 Sun ~ Bedrooms: £60B/£80B

Recommended by Andy and Jill Kassube, S and N McLean, Brian and Pat Wardrobe, Gordon Ormondroyd, Dr Peter Crawshaw

CROPTON   SE7588   MAP 10

New Inn 🍺 🛏
Village signposted off A170 W of Pickering; YO18 8HH

Own-brew beers in friendly modernised village inn, traditional rooms, and home cooking; brewery tours, bedrooms

Six out of the ten own-brewed beers are kept on handpump in this friendly and comfortably modernised village inn: Cropton Endeavour Ale, Honey Gold, King Billy, Monkmans Slaughter, Two Pints and Yorkshire Moors Bitter. They also have a guest such as Theakstons Best and several malt whiskies and wines by the glass. The traditional village bar has wooden panelling, terracotta and plush seats, lots of brass, and a small fire. A local artist has designed historical posters all around the downstairs conservatory that doubles as a visitor centre during busy times. The elegant restaurant has locally made furniture and paintings by local artists. Darts, pool, games machine, juke box, TV and piped music. There's a neat terrace, a garden with a pond, and a brewery shop. Brewery Tours April-September 11.30-2.30, £3.50 per person.

ⅲ Bar food includes lunchtime sandwiches or ciabatta rolls, ploughman's, soup, salmon fishcakes with caper and lemon mayonnaise, broccoli and stilton quiche, beef and root vegetable or fish pie, and pork medallions in a calvados cream sauce. *Starters/Snacks: £3.95 to £6.95. Main Courses: £7.95 to £17.95. Puddings: £3.75*

Own brew ~ Licensee Philip Lee ~ Real ale ~ Bar food (12-2, 6-9) ~ Restaurant ~ (01751) 417330 ~ Children in family room, conservatory, lounge, restaurant and pool room ~ Dogs allowed in bar and bedrooms ~ Open 11-midnight; 12-11 Sun ~ Bedrooms: £45B/£80B

Recommended by Rosanna Luke, Matt Curzon, Sylvia and Tony Birbeck, Ann and Tony Bennett-Hughes, Pete Coxon, Mrs Roxanne Chamberlain, D Weston, Christopher Turner

EAST WITTON   SE1486   MAP 10

Blue Lion 🍽 🍷 🛏
A6108 Leyburn—Ripon; DL8 4SN

Civilised dining pub with interesting rooms, daily papers and real ales, inventive food and comfortable bedrooms; pretty garden

As well as being a comfortable place to stay, this is a smart and civilised dining pub with excellent food. The big squarish bar has high-backed antique settles and old windsor chairs on the turkey rugs and flagstones, ham-hooks in the high ceiling decorated with dried wheat, teazles and so forth, a delft shelf filled with appropriate bric-a-brac, several prints, sporting caricatures and other pictures on the walls, a log fire, and daily papers; the friendly labrador is called Archie. Black Sheep Riggwelter, Theakstons Best and John Smiths on handpump and an impressive wine list with quite a few (plus champagne) by the glass; courteous, attentive service. Picnic-sets on the gravel outside look beyond the stone houses on the far side of the village green to Witton Fell and there's a big, pretty back garden.

🍴 Imaginative, if not cheap, food might include sandwiches, game bird terrine with toasted brioche, sautéed king scallops with lemon and spring onion risotto, home-made tagliatelle with dry cured bacon, wild mushrooms and cream sauce, beef and onion suet pudding with dark onion sauce, poached fillet of smoked haddock on new potatoes topped with poached egg, leek and mushroom sauce and gruyère, slow-braised masala mutton with cumin sweet potato, peppered breast of duck with blackberry sauce, and puddings such as raspberry sorbet with orange salad and steamed chocolate sponge with dark chocolate sauce and pistachio ice-cream. *Starters/Snacks: £5.85 to £7.95. Main Courses: £9.80 to £19.50. Puddings: £4.95 to £5.95*

Free house ~ Licensee Paul Klein ~ Real ale ~ Bar food ~ Restaurant ~ (01969) 624273 ~ Children welcome ~ Dogs allowed in bar and bedrooms ~ Open 11-11 ~ Bedrooms: £59.50S/£79S(£89B)

Recommended by the Didler, Neil and Angela Huxter, Terry Mizen, Stephen Woad, Jon Forster, Blaise Vyner, Dr Peter Crawshaw, Lynda and Trevor Smith, David Hall, Comus and Sarah Elliott, I A Herdman, Peter Hacker, Anthony Longden, Jane Taylor, David Dutton, J and S Grabiner, Simon Rodway

EGTON BRIDGE
NZ8005 MAP 10

Horseshoe

Village signposted from A171 W of Whitby; via Grosmont from A169 S of Whitby; YO21 1XE

New licensees for charmingly placed inn, several beers, straightforward food and seats in attractive gardens

There are plenty of customers in this bustling inn drawn by the charming position. It's a peaceful spot and the attractive gardens have pretty roses and mature redwoods and there are seats on a quiet terrace and lawn. Inside, the bar has old oak tables, high-backed built-in winged settles, wall seats and spindleback chairs, a big stuffed trout (caught near here in 1913), pictures on the walls, and a warm log fire. Black Sheep Bitter, Tetleys and a couple of guest beers on handpump and quite a few malt whiskies. Darts, board games, and piped music. The bedrooms are comfortable if fairly basic and breakfasts are generous and good. A different way to reach the pub is to park by the Roman Catholic church, walk through the village and cross the River Esk by stepping stones. Not to be confused with a similarly named pub up at Egton. More reports on the new regime, please.

🍴 New licensees took over just as we went to press but had not changed the bar food: lunchtime sandwiches and filled baguettes, ploughman's, soup, chicken liver pâté, fish pie, lasagne, bacon chops with peach sauce, and daily specials. *Starters/Snacks: £3.70 to £7.00. Main Courses: £8.20 to £14.00. Puddings: £4.00 to £5.50*

Free house ~ Licensee Alison Underwood ~ Real ale ~ Bar food ~ Restaurant ~ (01947) 895245 ~ Children in restaurant and small back room ~ Dogs allowed in bar ~ Open 11.30-3, 6.30-11; 11.30-11 Fri and Sat; 12-10.30 Sun ~ Bedrooms: /£50(£60S)

Recommended by Peter and Jo Smith, Pete Baker, Dr and Mrs R G J Telfer, R Pearce, Phil and Jane Hodson, Sean A Smith

FADMOOR
SE6789 MAP 10

Plough

Village signposted off A170 in or just W of Kirkbymoorside; YO62 7HY

Particularly well run and enjoyable dining pub with a friendly welcome, civilised little rooms, excellent food and fine wines

A firm favourite with many of our readers – young and old – this remains a spotlessly kept and genuinely friendly dining pub. The elegantly simple little rooms have cushioned settles and a range of armed wheelbacks and other wooden dining chairs on seagrass floors (some fine rugs too), horse tack attached to beams, all sorts of prints and pictures on the yellow walls, and lots of wine bottles on display. Black Sheep Bitter and Tetleys on handpump, and an extensive wine list; piped music. There are seats on the terrace.

⑪ Delicious bar food includes sandwiches, interesting soups, seafood paella, seared king scallops with a fricassee of crushed garlic, spring onions and smoked bacon with lemon flavoured cream, whisky marinated smoked salmon with a pot of dijon and dill mayonnaise, chicken breast with a stilton and Guinness cream sauce, pork tenderloin with a wild mushroom, red chilli and spring onion sauce, slow-roasted boneless half gressingham duck with an orange, mandarin and brandy sauce, smoked haddock florentine topped with a warm poached egg, daily specials, and puddings such as smooth dark chocolate and Malibu terrine with a berry compote and raspberry crème brûlée with lemon and elderberry ice-cream; they also offer a good value two-course set menu (not Saturday evening or Sunday lunchtime). *Starters/Snacks: £4.95 to £7.95. Main Courses: £8.95 to £17.95. Puddings: £4.95 to £6.95*

Holf Leisure Ltd ~ Licensee Neil Nicholson ~ Real ale ~ Bar food (12-1.45, 6.30-8.45; 12-1.45, 7-8.30 Sun) ~ Restaurant ~ (01751) 431515 ~ Children allowed but must eat early in evening ~ Open 12-3, 6.30-11; 12-4, 7-10.30 Sun; closed 25 and 26 Dec, 1 Jan

Recommended by Sylvia and Tony Birbeck, Stephen Woad, WW, Ann and Tony Bennett-Hughes, Walter and Susan Rinaldi-Butcher, R Pearce, Greta and Christopher Wells, David and Jane Hill, Jean and Douglas Troup, Pauline and Derek Hodgkiss, Terry and Linda Moseley, Christopher Turner, Margaret Dickinson, John and Verna Aspinall

FELIXKIRK   SE4684   MAP 10

Carpenters Arms ⑪ ♀

Village signposted off A170 E of Thirsk; YO7 2DP

Busy family-run dining pub with pubby choices and more interesting dishes, good wine list, and several real ales

A mother and daughter run this busy bistro-like pub on the outskirts of Thirsk. There are three or four cosy areas that ramble around the bar counter (made partly from three huge casks), with dark beams and joists hung with carpentry tools and other bric-a-brac, comfortable seats around tables with check tablecloths and little lighted oil burners, and a couple of huge japanese fans by the stone fireplace. Black Sheep Bitter, John Smiths, Timothy Taylors Landlord and a guest beer on handpump, a good wine list and lots of coffees; piped music and board games. The two dalmatians are called Lola and Lloyd. The church is prettily floodlit at night and this is an attractive village.

⑪ As well as sandwiches and pubby dishes like steak and mushroom in ale pie, burger with bacon and cheese and local bangers and mash with onion gravy, the popular, interesting food includes crispy mississippi chicken with sweetcorn and cherry tomato relish, baked queen scallops with lemon, garlic and gruyère, goats cheese, sun-dried tomato and roasted red pepper risotto, chicken and mushroom wellington with mushroom and bacon sauce, spicy roast duck with oriental vegetable stir fry and plum and ginger dressing, cajun salmon with lime dressing, venison with sweet peppercorn sauce, and puddings like sherry trifle and dark chocolate tart with espresso ice-cream. *Starters/Snacks: £4.95 to £7.95. Main Courses: £8.95 to £17.25. Puddings: £4.50*

Free house ~ Licensee Karen Bumby ~ Real ale ~ Bar food (not Sun evening or Mon) ~ Restaurant ~ (01845) 537369 ~ Children welcome ~ Open 11.30-3, 6.30-11; 12-3 Sun; closed Sun evening, Mon and 25 Dec

Recommended by WW, Dr Ian S Morley, Michael Butler, Derek and Sylvia Stephenson, Peter Burton, J Crosby, M and GR

> 'Children welcome' means the pub says it lets children inside without any special restriction. If it allows them in, but to restricted areas such as an eating area or family room, we specify this. Places with separate restaurants often let children use them, hotels usually let them into public areas such as lounges.
> Some pubs impose an evening time limit – let us know if you find this.

FERRENSBY   SE3660   MAP 7

General Tarleton 🍴 ⟨ 🍺 ⟩ 🛏

A655 N of Knaresborough; HG5 OPZ

Civilised coaching inn with interesting food, lots of wines by the glass, friendly service and relaxed atmosphere; refurbished bedrooms

There has been some refurbishment to the beamed bar/brasserie in this civilised and rather smart old coaching inn with new carpets, paintwork and lighting but there are still brick pillars dividing up the several different areas to create the occasional cosy alcove, some exposed stonework, and neatly framed pictures of staff on the cream walls. Dark brown leather chairs are grouped around wooden tables, there's a big open fire, a friendly, relaxed atmosphere and a door leading out to a pleasant tree-lined garden – seats here as well as in a covered courtyard. If you reserve a table, they put your name on it rather than just the word 'reserved' which readers feel adds a nice personal touch. Black Sheep Bitter and Timothy Taylors Landlord on handpump, 17 good wines by the glass, and quite a few coffees. The bedrooms (some are still being renovated) are comfortable.

🍴 **Interesting, enjoyable food includes lunchtime open sandwiches, terrine of ham knuckle and foie gras with fig and balsamic marmalade, queenie scallops with gruyère and cheddar cheese, garlic, chilli, lemon and pine nuts, warm shredded duck salad with chorizo, pancetta and croûtons, pasta with mushrooms, artichokes, spinach, pine nuts and parmesan, beer-battered cod fillet with minted mushy peas, steak in ale pudding, confit of lamb with garlic and thyme jus, corn-fed chicken with baby leeks and wild mushroom sauce, daily specials, and puddings such as rhubarb crumble, brûlée and compote with home-made vanilla ice-cream and warm Valrhona chocolate fondant.** *Starters/Snacks: £4.95 to £7.50. Main Courses: £8.50 to £17.50. Puddings: £4.95 to £6.75*

Free house ~ Licensee John Topham ~ Real ale ~ Bar food (12-2, 6-9.15(9 Sun)) ~ Restaurant ~ (01423) 340284 ~ Children welcome ~ Dogs allowed in bedrooms ~ Open 12-3, 6-11 ~ Bedrooms: £85B/£97B

Recommended by Janet and Peter Race, Brian and Janet Ainscough, Graham and Doreen Holden, Blaise Vyner, June and Ken Brooks, Comus and Sarah Elliott, WW, Michael Butler, Dr Ian S Morley

GOOSE EYE   SE0240   MAP 7

Turkey 🍺

Just S of Laycock on road to Oakworth and Haworth, W of Keighley; OS Sheet 104 map reference 028406; BD22 0PD

Own-brew beer and roaring log fires in pleasant, friendly local

After a cold walk you will be welcomed into this pleasant pub by a friendly landlord and a roaring log fire. There are various cosy and snug alcoves, brocaded upholstery, walls covered with pictures of surrounding areas, and of course their own-brewed beers. Turkey Bitter and guests like Greene King Abbot, Jennings Cumberland and Tetleys on handpump. You can visit their microbrewery – they ask for a donation for Upper Wharfedale Fell Rescue. Over 40 whiskies, piped music, and a separate games area with pool, darts, and games machine.

🍴 **Generous helpings of decent, straightforward bar food include sandwiches, soup, a pie of the day, daily specials, and puddings.** *Starters/Snacks: £3.20 to £5.50. Main Courses: £7.60 to £11.00. Puddings: £2.90*

Own brew ~ Licensee Harry Brisland ~ Real ale ~ Bar food (12-2, 6-9; all day Sun; not Mon or Tues lunchtimes) ~ Restaurant ~ (01535) 681339 ~ Children welcome until 9pm ~ Dogs allowed in bar ~ Open 12-3, 5.30-11; 12-11 Fri and Sat; 12-10.30 Sun; closed Mon and Tues lunchtimes

Recommended by Greta and Christopher Wells, Matt Waite

GRINTON

SE0498 MAP 10

Bridge Inn 🍺 🛏️

B6270 W of Richmond; DL11 6HH

Enjoyable pub with most welcoming landlord, comfortable bars, log fires, a fine choice of drinks and often inventive food; neat bedrooms

This is a particularly well run country pub with a friendly, helpful landlord who welcomes wet walkers with their muddy boots and their dogs; this pretty Swaledale village is surrounded by good walks. The cheerful, gently lit red-carpeted bar has bow window seats and a pair of stripped traditional settles among more usual pub seats, all well cushioned, a good log fire, Jennings Cumberland and Cocker Hoop, and a guests such as Camerons Strongarm and a seasonal beer from Lees on handpump, nice wines by the glass, and a good collection of malt whiskies. On the right a few steps take you down into a dark red room with darts, board games, a well lit pool table and piped music. Friendly, helpful service. On the left, past leather armchairs and a sofa by a second log fire (and a glass chess set), is an extensive two-part dining room. The décor is in mint green and shades of brown, with a modicum of fishing memorabilia. There are picnic-sets outside, and the inn is right opposite a lovely church known as the Cathedral of the Dales. The bedrooms are neat and simple, with a good breakfast.

🍴 Using their own herbs, beef and lamb from a farm a few hundred yards away and game from the moor, the often interesting food includes bar snacks such as filled baguettes and baked potatoes as well as soup, baked black pudding with goats cheese and apple with cider, mustard and lime-dressed leaves, chicken liver pâté with spicy red onion marmalade and melba toast, pork fillet filled with chopped wild mushrooms and braised in tomato and sage sauce on dauphinoise potatoes, chinese gingered duck breast, gammon and egg, swordfish steak with herb croûtons and a light avocado, lime and white wine sauce, daily specials and puddings such as three-chocolate brownie with chocolate sauce and ginger sponge with sticky toffee sauce and vanilla ice-cream. *Starters/Snacks: £3.25 to £5.25. Main Courses: £7.25 to £15.95. Puddings: £4.25*

Jennings (Marstons) ~ Lease Andrew Atkin ~ Real ale ~ Bar food (all day) ~ Restaurant ~ (01748) 884224 ~ Children welcome ~ Dogs allowed in bar and bedrooms ~ weekly acoustic music Thurs evening ~ Open 12-midnight(1am Sat) ~ Bedrooms: £42S(£44B)/£68B

Recommended by Lucien Perring, Stephen Woad, David Hall, David and Karen Cuckney, Arthur Pickering, Tony and Betty Parker, Lynda and Trevor Smith, Blaise Vyner, David and Jean Hall, M and GR, Jill and Julian Tasker

HALIFAX

SE1027 MAP 7

Shibden Mill 🍷

Off A58 into Kell Lane at Stump Cross Inn, near A6036 junction; keep on, pub signposted from Kell Lane on left; HX3 7UL

Tucked-away restored mill with cosy rambling bar, five real ales, and good choice of wines by the glass

At the bottom of a peaceful valley stands this tucked-away, restored mill. The rambling bar has cosy side areas with banquettes heaped with cushions and rugs, there are well spaced tables and chairs, and the candles in elegant iron holders give a feeling of real intimacy; also, old hunting prints, country landscapes and so forth, and a couple of big log fireplaces. John Smiths, Theakstons XB, a beer brewed for them by Moorhouses, and a couple of guest beers on handpump, and a dozen wines by the glass. There's an upstairs restaurant; piped music. Out on an attractive heated terrace are plenty of seats and chairs; the building is prettily floodlit at night. More reports please.

🍴 Bar food includes sandwiches, ploughman's, tomato and goats cheese tart with balsamic ice-cream, fishcakes with thai spiced mayonnaise, lamb casserole, roast artichoke caponata, chicken pie, stuffed leg of wild rabbit, and puddings like strawberry shortcake with caramel ice-cream and banana and toffee bavarois with rosemary biscuits. *Starters/Snacks: £4.95 to £6.25. Main Courses: £8.95 to £17.50. Puddings: £4.95 to £5.75*

Free house ~ Licensee Glen Pearson ~ Real ale ~ Bar food (12-2, 6-9.30; all day Sun) ~ Restaurant ~ (01422) 365840 ~ Children welcome ~ Dogs allowed in bar ~ Open 12-2.30, 5.30-11; 12-11 Fri and Sat; 12-10.30 Sun; closed evenings of 25 and 26 Dec and 1 Jan ~ Bedrooms: £75B/£90B

Recommended by Revd D Glover, MDN, Gordon Ormondroyd, Alan Bowker, Clive Flynn, Simon Marley, Greta and Christopher Wells, Jane and Alan Bush

HAROME   SE6482   MAP 10

Star ★ ⊕ ♀ ◀ ⇔
Village signposted S of A170, E of Helmsley; YO62 5JE

Imaginative modern cooking by young landlord in pretty thatched pub, proper bar with real ales and first-class wines, garden with terrace, stylish bedrooms

It's the inventive modern food cooked by the young chef/patron that draws most customers to this pretty, thatched 14th-c inn. But the bar still has a proper pubby atmosphere, a dark bowed beam-and-plank ceiling, plenty of bric-a-brac, interesting furniture (this was the first pub that 'Mousey Thompson' ever populated with his famous dark wood furniture), a fine log fire, a well polished tiled kitchen range, and daily papers and magazines; as they don't take bar reservations, it's best to arrive early to get a seat. There's also a private dining room and a popular coffee loft in the eaves, and a separate restaurant. Black Sheep and a couple of guests from Hambleton and Theakstons on handpump, 17 wines by the glass, home-made fruit liqueurs, and coffees, teas and hot chocolate with marshmallows, all with home-made chocolates; piped music and board games. There are some seats and tables on a sheltered front terrace with more in the garden with fruit trees. Eight stylish bedrooms in converted farm buildings plus three suites in a thatched cottage, and there's a private dining room, too; you may have to book the bedrooms a very long way ahead. They run a café in the Walled Garden at Scampston Hall and also own a traditional butcher in the Market Place in Helmsley which specialises in home-made terrines, british cheeses, cooked meats and so forth. They also have a village cricket team.

🍽 **Using their own herbs and vegetables and produce from village farms and nearby estates, the contemporary, if a little complicated-sounding and certainly not cheap, food might include sandwiches, ploughman's, soup, terrine of pressed ham knuckle with grain mustard, quail egg and spiced pineapple pickle, grilled black pudding with fried foie gras, watercress, apple and vanilla chutney and scrumpy reduction, roast vegetable and braised chestnut bake with bay leaf cream and winter truffle mash, roast loin of hare with a haunch stew, parsnip purée and poached quince juices, calves liver with bubble and squeak rösti, crispy bacon, onions and thyme juices, lamb with pearl barley and rosemary juices, and puddings such as dark chocolate and orange tart with clementine sorbet and bramble sauce and baked banana tarte tatin with pontefract cake ice-cream and stewed raisin syrup; an excellent cheeseboard and a bakery/delicatessen that sells take-away meals and snacks as well as all manner of delicious goodies.** *Starters/Snacks: £7.95 to £11.95. Main Courses: £12.50 to £21.50. Puddings: £7.95 to £9.95*

Free house ~ Licensees Andrew and Jacquie Pern ~ Real ale ~ Bar food (11.30-2, 6.15-9.30; 12-6 Sun; not Mon) ~ Restaurant ~ (01439) 770397 ~ Children welcome ~ Open 11.30-3, 6.15-11; 7.30-11 Mon; 12-11 Sun; closed Mon lunchtime ~ Bedrooms: /£140B

Recommended by M and C Thompson, Ian and Jane Haslock, David Thornton, Phil and Jane Hodson, John Lane, Adrian White, Oliver Richardson, W K Wood, Neil Ingoe, Cathryn and Richard Hicks, J Crosby

---

Stars after the name of a pub show exceptional quality. One star means most people (after reading the report to see just why the star has been won) would think a special trip worth while. Two stars mean that the pub is really outstanding – for its particular qualities it could hardly be bettered.

HARTSHEAD

SE1822   MAP 7

Gray Ox ⑪

3.5 miles from M62 junction 25; A644 towards Dewsbury, left on to A62, next left on to B6119, then second left on to Hartshead Lane (past Hartshead Hall Lane); pub on right; WF15 8AL

Fine views from attractive dining pub, cosy beamed bars and comfortable dining areas, well liked modern cooking, real ales and wines by the glass

Alone on a moorland road, this attractive stone-built dining pub has fine views through its latticed windows across the Calder Valley to the distant outskirts of Huddersfield – the lights are pretty at night. The bars have beams and flagstones, a cosy décor, bentwood chairs and stripped pine tables, roaring log fires and a buoyant atmosphere; comfortable carpeted dining areas with bold paintwork and leather dining chairs around polished tables lead off. Jennings Cumberland and Cocker Hoop with guests like Black Sheep Ennerdale and Camerons Castle Eden on handpump, several wines by the glass, and helpful, chatty staff; piped music. There are picnic-sets outside.

⑪ **Quite a choice of good, modern food might include sandwiches, soup, chicken liver pâté with melba toast and chutney, king scallops wrapped in pancetta with mustard dressing, chicken breast stuffed with goats cheese with pesto dressing, beer-battered haddock, a proper brunch, sausages on wholegrain mustard mash with scrumpy marmalade, steak in ale pie, mushrooms stuffed with sage and onion with a rarebit topping on a potato rösti, steamed bass with udon noodles, wilted greens, soy, ginger and chilli, pot-roasted goosnargh duck with plum and grape chutney and cassis sauce, and puddings such as vanilla panna cotta with hot fudge sauce and strawberries with Pimms jelly.** *Starters/Snacks: £3.95 to £8.50. Main Courses: £8.95 to £20.00. Puddings: £4.95*

Banks's (Marstons) ~ Lease Ian Minto and Bernadette McCarron ~ Real ale ~ Bar food (12-3, 6-9; 12-7 Sun, not Sun evening) ~ Restaurant ~ (01274) 872845 ~ Children welcome ~ Dogs allowed in bar ~ Open 12-3, 6-11; 12-11 Sat; 12-10.30 Sun

Recommended by Andy and Jill Kassube, Michael Jones, AP, Gordon Ormondroyd

HEATH

SE3520   MAP 7

Kings Arms

Village signposted from A655 Wakefield—Normanton – or, more directly, turn off to the left opposite Horse & Groom; WF1 5SL

Old-fashioned gaslit pub in interesting location with dark-panelled original bar, real ales and decent straightforward bar food; seats outside

The gas lighting in this old-fashioned village pub adds a lot to the atmosphere and the original bar has a fire burning in the old black range (with a long row of smoothing irons on the mantelpiece), plain elm stools and oak settles built into the walls, and dark panelling. A more comfortable extension has carefully preserved the original style, down to good wood-pegged oak panelling (two embossed with royal arms), and a high shelf of plates; there are also two other small flagstoned rooms and the conservatory opens on to the garden. Clarks Classic Blonde and Westgate Gold and maybe a guest beer on handpump. Sunny benches outside face the village green that is surrounded by 19th-c stone merchants' houses and there are also picnic-sets on a side lawn and a nice walled flower-filled garden. The landlord tells us that with four exits to the pub, customers do leave without paying, so they ask for ID – though most people prefer to leave their credit card in the till.

⑪ **Good value, straightforward bar food includes sandwiches, ploughman's, soup, yorkshire pudding and onion gravy, omelettes, vegetable curry, steak in ale pie, beer-battered haddock, a full english breakfast, daily specials, and puddings like sponge pudding or apple pie and custard.** *Starters/Snacks: £2.85 to £4.25. Main Courses: £6.85 to £10.25. Puddings: £2.95*

Please let us know of any pubs where the wine is particularly good.

Clarks ~ Manager Alan Tate ~ Real ale ~ Bar food (all day Sun) ~ Restaurant ~ (01924) 377527 ~ Children allowed away from bar areas ~ Open 11.30-11(midnight Sat); 12-11 Sun; 11.30-3, 5.30-11 weekdays in winter
Recommended by Greta and Christopher Wells, Dave Braisted, the Didler

HETTON
SD9658 MAP 7

Angel ♀
Just off B6265 Skipton—Grassington; BD23 6LT

Dining pub with rambling timbered rooms, lots of wines by the glass, real ales and interesting food; heated terrace

Of the four timbered and panelled rambling rooms in this dining pub, perhaps the one with the most pubby atmosphere is the main bar with a Victorian farmhouse range in the big stone fireplace. There are lots of cosy alcoves, comfortable country-kitchen chairs or button-back green plush seats, Ronald Searle wine snob cartoons and older engravings and photographs, and log fires. Black Sheep Bitter and Timothy Taylors Landlord on handpump, around 25 wines by the glass including champagne and quite a few malt whiskies. Outside on a decked area with canopies and outdoor heaters there are lots of seats; more reports please.

🍴 **Bar food is often interesting: seafood baked in crispy pastry with lobster sauce, game terrine with foie gras butter and pear and saffron chutney, roast parsnip, butternut squash and bean cassoulet with a feta herb crust, roast breast and leg coq au vin of pheasant with salsify and lentil jus, venison with apple polenta, beetroot fondant, crispy brussels sprouts and red wine sauce, warm oak-smoked organic salmon with celeriac remoulade and bois boudran sauce, daily specials, and puddings such as chocolate and pecan tart with chocolate sauce and sticky toffee pudding with butterscotch sauce and chantilly cream.** *Starters/Snacks: £5.25 to £8.55. Main Courses: £8.95 to £15.50. Puddings: £4.75 to £6.75*

Free house ~ Licensee Bruce Elsworth ~ Real ale ~ Bar food (12-2.15(2.30 Sun), 6-9(10 Sat)) ~ Restaurant ~ (01756) 730263 ~ Children welcome ~ Dogs allowed in bedrooms ~ Open 12-3, 6-11(10 Sun); 12-2.30, 6-10.30(11 Sat) in winter; closed 25 Dec, 1 Jan, one week Jan ~ Bedrooms: /£130B
Recommended by Margaret and Jeff Graham, Mr and Mrs A Curry, Adrian White, Karen Eliot, Pierre Richterich, Yana Pocklington, Patricia Owlett, Roger Thornington

HULL
TA0928 MAP 8

Minerva 🍺
Park at top of pedestrianised area at top of Queen's Street and walk over Nelson Street or turn off Queen's Street into Wellington Street, right into Pier Street and pub is at top; no parking restrictions weekends, 2-hour stay Mon-Fri; HU1 1XE

Busy pub in restored waterfront spot, rambling rooms with interesting photographs, up to six real ales and decent standard bar food

There are seats out in front of this busy pub from which you can watch the passing boats – this is the heart of the attractively restored waterfront and bustling marina. Inside, several rooms ramble all the way round a central servery with comfortable seats, quite a few interesting photographs and pictures of old Hull and a big chart of the Humber. A tiny snug has room for just three people, and a back room (which looks out to the marina basin) houses a profusion of varnished woodwork; two coal fires in winter. Hartleys XB, Holt Bitter, Old Mill Bitter, Timothy Taylors Landlord and maybe a couple of guests on handpump. Games machine, TV, darts, board games and piped music. More reports please.

🍴 **Bar food includes sandwiches, filled baked potatoes, burger, ham and eggs, vegetarian pasta, beef in ale pie, chicken with barbecue sauce and bacon, minted lamb shoulder, and puddings.** *Starters/Snacks: £2.95 to £3.95. Main Courses: £6.45 to £11.95. Puddings: £2.95 to £3.45*

Spirit Group ~ Manager Adam Brailsford ~ Real ale ~ Bar food (12-2.30, 5-7.45; 12-7.45 Fri, Sat and Sun) ~ Restaurant ~ (01482) 326909 ~ Children in restaurant if eating ~ Jazz first Tues evening of month ~ Open 11-11; 12-10.30 Sun

Recommended by J R Ringrose, Paul and Ursula Randall, John Robertson, David Carr, the Didler, Pam and John Smith

Olde White Harte ★ £

Off 25 Silver Street, a continuation of Whitefriargate; pub is up narrow passage, and should not be confused with the much more modern White Hart nearby; HU1 1JG

Some fine original features in busy old pub, lots of malt whiskies, several real ales, cheap bar food and seats in heated courtyard

The three bars in this often busy, historic old place have some fine features. The downstairs one has attractive stained-glass windows that look out above the bow window seat, carved heavy beams support black ceiling boards, and there are two big brick inglenooks with a frieze of delft tiles. There's a new upstairs restaurant. The curved copper-topped counter serves Caledonian Deuchars IPA, McEwans 80/-, Theakstons Old Peculier and a guest like Wells & Youngs Bombardier on handpump and over 60 malt whiskies. It was in the heavily panelled room up the oak staircase that in 1642 the town's governor Sir John Hotham made the fateful decision to lock the nearby gate against Charles I, depriving him of Hull's arsenal; it didn't do him much good, as in the Civil War that followed, Hotham, like the king, was executed by the parliamentarians. There are seats in the heated courtyard.

Ⓜ **Good value bar food includes ciabatta sandwiches or filled baguettes, soup, steak and mushroom in ale pie, mushroom stroganoff, battered haddock with mushy peas and pork and leek sausages with onion gravy.** *Starters/Snacks: £1.95 to £3.95. Main Courses: £5.25 to £5.95. Puddings: £3.25 to £3.95*

Scottish Courage ~ Lease Bernard Copley ~ Real ale ~ Bar food (11.30-3.30; 12-5 Sun; evening food restaurant only (Weds-Sat); no food Mon or Tues evenings) ~ Restaurant ~ (01482) 326363 ~ Children in restaurant only ~ Dogs allowed in bar ~ Open 11am-midnight(1am Sat); 12-midnight Sun

Recommended by the Didler, W W Burke, David Carr, Paul and Ursula Randall, Pam and John Smith

KETTLESING   SE2257   MAP 7

Queens Head 🍺

Village signposted off A59 W of Harrogate; HG3 2LB

Lots to look at in friendly stone pub with open fires, chatty atmosphere, real ales and decent food; bedrooms

There's plenty to look at in this friendly stone-built pub. The L-shaped, carpeted main bar is decorated with Victorian song sheet covers, lithographs of Queen Victoria, little heraldic shields, and a delft shelf of blue and white china. There's also a quietly chatty atmosphere and lots of quite close-set elm and other tables around its walls, with cushioned country seats. Coal or log fires at each end and maybe unobtrusive piped radio. A smaller bar on the left, with built-in red banquettes, has cricketing prints and cigarette cards, coins and banknotes, and in the lobby there's a life-size portrait of Elizabeth I. Black Sheep Bitter, Roosters Hooligan and a guest on handpump; good service. Seats in the neatly kept suntrap back garden, and benches in front by the lane.

Ⓜ **Enjoyable bar food at lunchtime includes sandwiches, soup, filled yorkshire puddings, home-made burger, salads, omelettes, and a brunch, with evening choices such as chicken liver pâté, garlic mushrooms, wensleydale and bacon salad with croûtons, gammon with egg or pineapple, steak in ale pie, jumbo battered haddock, mixed grill, daily specials, and puddings.** *Starters/Snacks: £3.50 to £4.95. Main Courses: £5.96 to £15.95. Puddings: £3.95*

Smoking is not allowed inside any pub.

Free house ~ Licensees Louise and Glen Garbutt ~ Real ale ~ Bar food ~ (01423) 770263 ~ Children welcome ~ Open 11-2.30, 6-11; 12-11 Sun ~ Bedrooms: £73.50S(£55B)/£88S(£65B)

Recommended by Peter Burton, B and M Kendall, Walter and Susan Rinaldi-Butcher, G Dobson, Mr and Mrs Staples, L and D Webster, M E Hutchinson, Peter Hacker, Brian Wainwright

KIRK DEIGHTON   SE3950   MAP 7

Bay Horse ♀
B6164 N of Wetherby; Main Street; LS22 4DZ

Attractive dining pub with flagstoned entrance bar, candlelit tables in dining area, friendly service, decent wines and well liked bar food

As we went to press, we heard that this attractive dining pub was up for sale. There's a small flagstoned bar by the entrance if you want just a drink, with changing real ales on handpump such as Black Sheep Bitter, Copper Dragon Best Bitter, John Smiths and Timothy Taylors Landlord. Also, ten wines by the glass and good coffees from a solid mahogany bar counter with proper brass foot and elbow rails. The main dark terracotta dining area is not large, with perhaps a dozen or so candlelit tables, comfortable banquettes and other seats, rugs on flagstones, beams and pictures, and a relaxed atmosphere. It's worth booking quite well ahead, especially for evenings or weekends. Service is friendly and efficient; piped music and games machine. More reports please.

🍴 Good bar food at lunchtime includes sandwiches, ploughman's, soup, thai salmon fishcakes with dipping sauce, risotto with white onions, parmesan and truffle oil, beer-battered haddock, pork and sage sausages with beans and mash, and steak in ale pie; evening choices such as chicken liver parfait with red onion marmalade, queenie scallops with garlic, gruyère and breadcrumbs, goats cheese, pumpkin and potato fritatta, cod wrapped and baked in pancetta over slow-roasted tomato salad, corn-fed chicken with bacon, green beans and a light grainy mustard jus, and venison loin with buttered pears and red wine jus; there's also a set lunch menu. *Starters/Snacks: £2.95 to £6.50. Main Courses: £7.95 to £14.50. Puddings: £4.50*

Enterprise ~ Lease Karl and Amanda Maney ~ Real ale ~ Bar food (12-2.15, 6-9.15; not Sun evening, not Mon lunchtime) ~ Restaurant ~ (01937) 580058 ~ Children welcome away from bar ~ Dogs allowed in bar ~ Open 12-3, 5-11; 12-10.30 Sun; closed Mon lunchtime

Recommended by Alyson and Andrew Jackson, Michael and Maggie Betton, OPUS, Michael Doswell, Danny Savage, Howard and Margaret Buchanan, Derek and Sylvia Stephenson, Brian and Janet Ainscough

KIRKBYMOORSIDE   SE6986   MAP 10

George & Dragon 🛏

Market Place; YO62 6AA

Newly refurbished 17th-c coaching inn with convivial front bar, snug and bistro, good wines, real ales and comfortable bedrooms; new terraces

The new licensees of this handsome 17th-c coaching inn have made quite a few changes. There are new carpets and solid oak flooring, new furniture in the bar and bistro and a hand-made ash bar counter has been installed; a new snug area, too. The convivial front bar still has beams and panelling, an open log fire, Black Sheep Bitter, Copper Dragon Best Bitter, Tetleys and a guest beer on handpump and ten wines by the glass; piped music. A new front terrace has been created as have back terrace areas with outdoor heaters and giant parasols; plenty of seats. This is a pretty little town and market day is on Wednesdays. More reports please.

🍴 Bar food now includes sandwiches, sun-dried tomato and chicken liver pâté with chutney, haggis and black pudding gateau with a whisky and grain mustard sauce, yorkshire rarebit, steak in ale pie, fresh beer-battered haddock, slow-braised lamb shank with madeira jus, griddled halibut with sweet pepper and garlic butter, and puddings such as sponges, parfaits and crème brûlée. *Starters/Snacks: £4.00 to £6.50. Main Courses: £6.50 to £13.50. Puddings: £4.00 to £4.50*

Free house ~ Licensees David and Alison Nicholas ~ Real ale ~ Bar food (all day Easter-Oct) ~ Restaurant ~ (01751) 433334 ~ Children welcome ~ Dogs allowed in bar and bedrooms ~ Open 10.30am-11pm; 12-10.30 Sun ~ Bedrooms: £60B/£90B

Recommended by Pat and Tony Martin, Sue Demont, Tim Barrow, Ann and Tony Bennett-Hughes, Mark and Ruth Brock, Sarah and Peter Gooderham

KIRKHAM   SE7365   MAP 7

Stone Trough ⭐🍴 ♀ 🍺
Kirkham Abbey; YO60 7JS

Beamed, cosy rooms in well run country pub, interesting bar food, five real ales, quite a few wines by the glass and lovely valley views

From seats outside this bustling and enjoyable country inn, there are lovely views down the valley, and it's handy for Kirkham Abbey and Castle Howard. Inside, the several beamed and cosy rooms have warm log fires, Black Sheep Bitter, Tetleys, Timothy Taylors Landlord, and a couple of guests such as Suddabys Golden Chance and Theakstons Old Peculier on handpump and 11 wines by the glass; good, friendly service. There's also a snug, a new lounge area for drinkers and diners (which was the games room) and a restaurant; piped music, TV and board games.

🍴 Generous helpings of appealing bar food include lunchtime sandwiches, soup, potted brown shrimps and whitby crab with home-made tartare sauce, carpaccio of local beef fillet with smoked applewood cheddar salad and beetroot pesto dressing, wild boar sausages on rosemary mash with haricot bean and tomato gravy, grilled pork chop with garlic and honey-roasted parsnips and pink peppercorn sauce, roast mediterranean vegetable risotto with spinach and gruyère, baked scottish salmon fillet with pea and saffron risotto and spring onion sauce, daily specials, and puddings such as white chocolate and rum crème brûlée and banana fritters with vanilla ice-cream and raisin syrup. *Starters/Snacks: £4.50 to £7.95. Main Courses: £7.95 to £14.95. Puddings: £4.75*

Free house ~ Licensees Sarah and Adam Richardson ~ Real ale ~ Bar food (12-2, 6.30-8.30; not Mon) ~ Restaurant ~ (01653) 618713 ~ Well behaved children welcome ~ Open 12-2.30, 6-11; 12-11 Sat; 11.45-10.30 Sun; 12-2.30, 6-11 Sat in winter; closed Mon, 3-5 Jan

Recommended by Colin and Dot Savill, Mike Dean, Lis Wingate Gray, Eileen McCall, WW, Michael Dandy, R L Graham, Christopher Turner, Jeff and Wendy Williams, DC, S P Watkin, P A Taylor, J Crosby

LANGTHWAITE   NY9902   MAP 10

Charles Bathurst ⭐🍴 🍺 🛏
Arkengarthdale, a mile N towards Tan Hill; generally known as the CB Inn; DL11 6EN

Friendly country pub with bustling atmosphere, good mix of customers, thoughtful wine list, decent real ales and interesting bar food; comfortable bedrooms, lots of walks

This is a particularly well run inn with a good mix of both locals and visitors – and no matter how busy they are (and the place is often packed), the staff manage to remain helpful and friendly. The long bar has light pine scrubbed tables, country chairs and benches on stripped floors, plenty of snug alcoves, and a roaring fire. There's also a wooden floored dining room with views of Scar House, a shooting lodge owned by the Duke of Norfolk; other dining areas as well. The island bar counter has bar stools, Black Sheep Bitter and Riggwelter, John Smiths and Theakstons Best on handpump and nine wines by the glass from a sensibly laid-out list with helpful notes. Piped music, darts, pool, TV, dominoes, board games and quoits. The bedrooms are pretty and comfortable. This is a lovely spot with fine views over Langthwaite village and Arkengarthdale; fine surrounding walks.

🍴 Cooked with real flair, the very good food includes filled baguettes, crab and avocado in a filo basket with lime and coriander dressing, home-made rabbit sausage with apple compote and yorkshire pudding, goats cheese, tomato and red onion tartlet with rocket and pesto, seared halibut fillet with smoked salmon and prawn risotto, rump of lamb with spicy ratatouille, couscous and lamb jus, supreme of corn-fed chicken with button

mushroom gnocchi and blue cheese butter, and puddings such as espresso coffee crème brûlée with home-made shortbread biscuit and banana-filled crêpes with banoffi sauce and vanilla ice-cream. *Starters/Snacks: £5.50 to £6.95. Main Courses: £8.95 to £19.95. Puddings: £4.25 to £5.00*

Free house ~ Licensees Charles and Stacy Cody ~ Real ale ~ Bar food ~ (01748) 884567 ~ Children welcome ~ Dogs allowed in bedrooms ~ Open 11am–midnight; closed 25 Dec ~ Bedrooms: /£92.50B

Recommended by Jill and Julian Tasker, K S Whittaker, Richard, Mark and Ruth Brock, Dr Alan and Mrs Sue Holder, Dr and Mrs M E Wilson, Bruce and Sharon Eden, John Coatsworth, Ben and Helen Ingram, Anthony Barnes, Professors Alan and Ann Clarke, David Hall, David Thornton, Peter J and Avril Hanson, Lynda and Trevor Smith, Pat and Robert Watt, Helen Clarke, Arthur Pickering, David and Jean Hall, J Crosby

LASTINGHAM
SE7290   MAP 10

Blacksmiths Arms 🍺

Off A170 W of Pickering at Wrelton, forking off Rosedale road N of Cropton; or via Appleton or Hutton-le-Hole; YO62 6TL

Friendly village pub liked by walkers, with lively atmosphere, good service, traditional bars, quite a choice of drinks and decent food; bedrooms

There are always plenty of walkers and cyclists in this comfortable and neatly kept stone inn as it is in the National Park at the foot of the moors. The cosily old-fashioned beamed bar has a convivial atmosphere, friendly staff, a log fire in an open range, traditional furnishings, Theakstons Best and a couple of changing guests like Wold Top Mars Magic and a beer named for them from Moorhouses on handpump, ten wines by the glass, Cropton cider (brewed a couple of miles away), winter mulled wine and summer Pimms. Piped music, darts, dominoes and board games. There are seats in the back garden and the village is very pretty. It's worth a visit to the church as it has a unique Saxon crypt built as a shrine to St Cedd.

🍴 **Reasonably priced, well liked bar food at lunchtime includes hot toasted paninis (not Sunday lunchtime but they will offer a sandwich then), soup, steak in ale pie, tomato and lentil lasagne, beer-battered cod and yorkshire hotpot, with evening dishes such as crispy garlic mushrooms, yorkshire pudding with onion gravy, slow-roast lamb shank, fish pie, and puddings.** *Starters/Snacks: £2.95 to £5.50. Main Courses: £7.95 to £15.95. Puddings: £3.65*

Free house ~ Licensee Peter Trafford ~ Real ale ~ Bar food (not winter Tues lunchtime) ~ Restaurant ~ (01751) 417247 ~ Children welcome ~ Jamming session second Sun of month ~ Open 12-11.30; 12-2.30, 6-11.30 Mon-Thurs in winter; closed winter Tues lunchtime ~ Bedrooms: £50B/£70B

Recommended by Janet and Peter Race, Mike Dean, Lis Wingate Gray, Ann and Tony Bennett-Hughes, Sarah and Peter Gooderham, Jane Taylor, David Dutton, WW, David Barnes

LEDSHAM
SE4529   MAP 7

Chequers 🍺

1.5 miles from A1(M) junction 42: follow Leeds signs, then Ledsham signposted; also some 4 miles N of junction M62; Claypit Lane; LS25 5LP

Ambitious restaurant food – some bar snacks too – in friendly village pub, log fires in several beamed rooms, and real ales; pretty back terrace

The old-fashioned little central panelled-in servery in this friendly stone-built village pub has several small, individually decorated rooms leading off with low beams, lots of cosy alcoves, a number of toby jugs, and log fires. Brown Cow Bitter, John Smiths, Theakstons Best, Timothy Taylors Landlord and a guest beer on handpump. A sheltered two-level terrace behind the house has tables among roses and the hanging baskets and flowers are very pretty.

🍴 **There are some bar snacks such as sandwiches and filled baguettes, sausage and mash with gravy and steak and mushroom pie, but the emphasis is on the elaborately** described, restaurant-style food – at a price: chorizo sausage, chicken strips and bacon lardons in garlic oil, timbale of cajun chicken with sliced button mushrooms and balsamic syrup, hotpot of mediterranean vegetables on sun-dried tomato risotto, roasted salmon fillet on herby creamed cabbage, venison cutlets on braised red cabbage with juniper and blueberry syrup, cassoulet on a chunky bread croûte, daily specials, and puddings such as chocolate mousse cake and crème brulée topped with crunchy toffee. *Starters/Snacks: £4.65 to £7.95. Main Courses: £9.85 to £16.95. Puddings: £4.95 to £5.25*

Free house ~ Licensee Chris Wraith ~ Real ale ~ Bar food (12-9 Mon-Sat; not Sun) ~ Restaurant ~ (01977) 683135 ~ Well behaved children allowed ~ Dogs allowed in bar ~ Open 11-11; closed Sun

Recommended by Bob Broadhurst, Bill and Marian de Bass, Roger and Pauline Pearce, David and Pam Wilcox, Louise Gibbons, the Didler, Peter and Jean Hoare, Kevin Thorpe, Simon Jones, Peter Hacker, Paul and Ursula Randall, R M Corlett, Mike Dean, Lis Wingate Gray, OPUS, Andy and Jill Kassube

LEYBURN   SE1190   MAP 10

Sandpiper 🍽 🍷
Just off Market Place; DL8 5AT

Emphasis on appealing food though cosy bar for drinkers in 17th-c cottage, real ales, amazing choice of whiskies; bedrooms

Most customers come to this 17th-c cottage to enjoy the very good food, though there is a small cosy bar used by locals and Black Sheep Bitter and Special and a guest from Copper Dragon on handpump. This little bar has a couple of black beams in the low ceiling, antlers, brass jugs, and a few tables and chairs, and the back room up three steps has attractive Dales photographs; get here early to be sure of a seat. Down by the nice linenfold panelled bar counter there are stuffed sandpipers, more photographs and a woodburning stove in the stone fireplace; to the left is the restaurant. They keep over 100 malt whiskies and a decent wine list with eight by the glass; piped music. There are tables on the front terrace amidst the lovely hanging baskets and flowering climbers.

🍽 **Cooked by the landlord's son, the interesting food (listed on boards or recited by staff) includes lunchtime sandwiches, soup, pressed ham hock and chicken terrine, lamb kofta with mint and coriander yoghurt, omelette Arnold Bennett, beer-battered fish, moroccan spiced chicken with couscous, vegetable risotto, sausages with mash and onion gravy, slow-cooked beef with wild mushrooms, crispy duck leg with plum and orange sauce, daily specials, and puddings.** *Starters/Snacks: £4.50 to £7.50. Main Courses: £9.95 to £18.75. Puddings: £5.00 to £6.00*

Free house ~ Licensees Jonathan and Michael Harrison ~ Real ale ~ Bar food (12-2.30(2 Sun), 6.30-9(9.30 Fri and Sat); not Mon) ~ Restaurant ~ (01969) 622206 ~ Children welcome but with restrictions ~ Dogs allowed in bar ~ Open 11.30-3, 6.30-11; 12-3, 6.30-10.30 Sun; closed Mon; closed Tues in Jan ~ Bedrooms: £65S(£70B)/£75S(£80B)

Recommended by Karen Eliot, Barbara and Peter Kelly, Michael Butler, Terry and Linda Moseley, C and H Greenly, Alun Jones, W W Burke, Malcolm and Lynne Jessop, B and M Kendall, Stephen Woad, Ian and Celia Abbott, J Crosby, Stuart Paulley

LINTHWAITE   SE1014   MAP 7

Sair 🍺
Hoyle Ing, off A62; 3½ miles after Huddersfield look out for two water storage tanks (painted with a shepherd scene) on your right – the street is on your left, burrowing very steeply up between works buildings; OS Sheet 110 map reference 101143; HD7 5SG

A fine choice of own-brew beers in old-fashioned pub; open fires, simple furnishings, fine view from outside seats; no food

The fine choice of up to ten own-brewed beers on handpump continues to draw plenty of customers to this unspoilt and old-fashioned pub. On handpump, they include Linfit Bitter, Dark Mild, Special, Swift, Gold Medal, Autumn Gold, Old Eli, English Guineas Stout and Leadboiler; Weston's farm cider and a few malt whiskies. The four rooms are furnished with pews or smaller chairs on the rough flagstones or wooden floors and there are open fires in three rooms; the room to the left of the entrance has dominoes, a juke box, shove-ha'penny and cribbage. In summer, there are plenty of seats and tables in front of the pub that have a striking view across the Colne Valley. The Huddersfield Narrow Canal is restored through to Ashton; in the 3½ miles from Linthwaite to the highest, deepest and longest tunnel in Britain, there are 25 working locks and some lovely countryside.

🍴 **No food at all.**

Own brew ~ Licensee Ron Crabtree ~ Real ale ~ No credit cards ~ (01484) 842370 ~ Children welcome until 8pm ~ Dogs welcome ~ Open 5-11; 12-11 Sat; 12-10.30 Sun; closed weekday lunchtimes
Recommended by J R Ringrose, the Didler

LINTON   SE3846   MAP 7
Windmill
Leaving Wetherby W on A661, fork left just before hospital and bear left; also signposted from A659, leaving Collingham towards Harewood; LS22 4HT

Small beamed rooms, chatty civilised atmosphere, real ales, lunchtime snacks and more elaborate evening food; sunny terrace and sheltered garden

There's a good, relaxed atmosphere in this pleasant pub, helped by locals dropping in for a drink. The small beamed rooms have walls stripped back to bare stone, polished antique oak settles around copper-topped cast-iron tables, pots hanging from the oak beams, a high shelf of plates, and log fires. There's also a sizeable restaurant. John Smiths, Theakstons Best and a couple of guests like Jennings Cumberland Ale and Old Mill Bitter on handpump and several wines by the glass; piped music. The pear tree outside was raised from seed brought back from the Napoleonic Wars, and there are seats in the sheltered garden and on the sunny terrace at the back of the building.

🍴 **Reasonably priced lunchtime bar food includes quite a range of sandwiches, filled baked potatoes, chicken liver parfait with plum and apple chutney, chicken caesar salad and lemon-battered scampi; more elaborate evening dishes such as artichoke and whitby white crab with pepper and sunblush tomato salsa, confit duck, walnut, grape and chicory salad, caramelised red onion and goats cheese tart, moroccan lamb with chorizo, black olives and herb couscous, chicken breast on garlic roast peppers and butternut squash with tomato and chilli sauce, and bass fillet on wild mushroom and black truffle risotto.** *Starters/Snacks: £5.95 to £6.50. Main Courses: £6.95 to £10.50. Puddings: £3.95*

Scottish Courage ~ Lease Janet Rowley and John Littler ~ Real ale ~ Bar food (12-2, 5.30-9; 12-6.30 Sun; not Sun evening) ~ Restaurant ~ (01937) 582209 ~ Children allowed in dining room or if eating ~ Dogs allowed in bar ~ Live music monthly Sun; best to phone ~ Open 11-3, 5-11; 11-11 Sat; 12-10.30 Sun; closed 1 Jan
Recommended by OPUS, Jeremy King, Ray and Winifred Halliday, GSB, A S and M E Marriott, Tony and Penny Burton, Di and Mike Gillam, Mrs F Brooker

LINTON IN CRAVEN   SD9962   MAP 7
Fountaine
Just off B6265 Skipton—Grassington; BD23 5HJ

Neatly kept pub in charming village, attractive furnishings, open fires, five real ales, decent wines and interesting bar food; seats on terrace

Surrounded by lovely Dales countryside where there are fine walks, this neatly kept traditional-looking pub is in a delightful hamlet of charming stone cottages. There's a welcoming, bustling atmosphere, beams and white-painted joists in the low ceilings, log fires (one in a beautifully carved heavy wooden fireplace), attractive built-in cushioned wall benches and stools around a mix of copper-topped tables, little wall lamps and quite a few prints on the pale walls. Black Sheep Bitter, John Smiths, Tetleys and guests like

Copper Dragon 1816 and Golden Pippin on handpump and several wines by the glass; piped music. Outside on the terrace there are teak benches and tables under green parasols and pretty hanging baskets.

🍴 As well as hearty sandwiches in different breads, the attractively presented food might include tiger prawns in tomato, garlic and chilli, duck liver pâté with spicy fruit chutney, smoked deep-fried brie with a compote of sliced berries, fresh haddock in crispy batter with home-made tartare sauce and seed mustard dips, steak caesar salad, cumberland sausage with roasting juices, chicken in coriander, ginger and green chilli marinade with tomato and red onion salad, and tuna loin in thai spices with citrus aïoli; they also offer good value early evening weekday main courses. *Starters/Snacks: £2.25 to £5.95. Main Courses: £7.95 to £16.95. Puddings: £4.20*

Individual Inns ~ Manager Christopher Gregson ~ Real ale ~ Bar food (all day) ~ Restaurant ~ (01756) 752210 ~ Children welcome ~ Dogs allowed in bar ~ Open 11-11; 12-10.30 Sun

Recommended by WW, Lynda and Trevor Smith, Richard, Alyson and Andrew Jackson, Fred and Lorraine Gill, B and M Kendall, G Dobson, Paul Humphreys, Tony and Penny Burton, Simon and Mandy King

LITTON   SD9074 MAP 7

Queens Arms 🍺

From B6160 N of Grassington, after Kilnsey take second left fork; can also be reached off B6479 at Stainforth N of Settle, via Halton Gill; BD23 5QJ

Friendly pub in fantastic walking area, own-brew beers, good homely food and simply furnished bars; bedrooms including a walkers' room

In stunning countryside with lovely views, this friendly pub has plenty of local charm. The main bar on the right has a good coal fire, stripped rough stone walls, a brown beam-and-plank ceiling, stools around cast-iron-framed tables on the stone and concrete floor, a seat built into the stone-mullioned window, and signed cricket bats. The left-hand room is an eating area with old photographs of the Dales around the walls. As well as Litton Ale, they also offer one other – Dark Star, Potts Beck Ale or Litton Light on handpump from their own microbrewery. Darts, board games and piped music. There's a safe area for children in the two-level garden and plenty of surrounding walks – a track behind the inn leads over Ackerley Moor to Buckden, and the quiet lane through the valley leads on to Pen-y-ghent. Walkers enjoy staying here very much – and there is a walkers' room (price on request).

🍴 Enjoyable bar food includes sandwiches, filled baked potatoes, soup, rabbit pie, blue cheese, onion, mushrooms and olive tart, local leg of lamb, gammon and egg, daily specials, and puddings like rhubarb crumble and bread and butter pudding. *Starters/Snacks: £3.60 to £6.20. Main Courses: £8.10 to £16.00. Puddings: £4.10*

Own brew ~ Licensees Tanya and Neil Thompson ~ Real ale ~ Bar food (not Mon or Jan) ~ (01756) 770208 ~ Children welcome away from bar ~ Dogs allowed in bar and bedrooms ~ Open 12-3, 6.30-11; closed Mon (except bank hols) and all Jan ~ Bedrooms: /£75S

Recommended by Greta and Christopher Wells, Alyson and Andrew Jackson, Comus and Sarah Elliott, D W Stokes, B and M Kendall, Andy and Jill Kassube, Tony and Penny Burton, Dr D and Mrs B Woods

LONG PRESTON   SD8358 MAP 7

Maypole 🍺 🛏

A65 Settle—Skipton; BD23 4PH

A good base for walkers with friendly staff, bustling atmosphere, well liked pubby food and fair choice of real ales

There's a good mix of locals and visitors in this busy pub and the friendly staff make sure you get a warm welcome. It's also a good base for walking in the Dales and the bedrooms do get booked up quite a way ahead. The carpeted two-room bar has sporting prints and local photographs and a list of landlords dating back to 1695 on its butter-coloured walls, a delft shelf with whisky-water jugs and decorative plates, a couple of stags' heads, and good solid pub furnishings – heavy carved wall settles and the like, and heavy cast-iron framed pub tables with unusual inset leather tops. There is a separate country dining room. Moorhouses Premier Bitter, Timothy Taylors Landlord and two changing ales such as Copper Dragon Scotts 1816 and Wharfedale Folly Ale on handpump, ten wines by the glass, Weston's cider and several malt whiskies. There's a piano in the room on the left, darts, board games, dominoes and TV for important sporting events. Out behind is a terrace with a couple of picnic-sets under an ornamental cherry tree and another picnic-set on grass under a sycamore. If you're staying, they do a good breakfast.

🍴 **Tasty, reasonably priced bar food includes sandwiches, ploughman's, soup, chicken liver pâté, chestnut and fennel casserole, ham or sausage and eggs, steak in ale pie, fresh poached salmon salad, lasagne, trout with tarragon and lemon butter, braised shoulder of lamb in rosemary, daily specials, and puddings.** *Starters/Snacks: £3.50 to £5.95. Main Courses: £6.50 to £13.75. Puddings: £3.50 to £3.75*

Enterprise ~ Lease Robert Palmer ~ Real ale ~ Bar food (12-2, 6.30-9(9.30 Fri); 12-9.30 Sat; 12-9 Sun) ~ Restaurant ~ (01729) 840219 ~ Children welcome but not in bars after 9pm ~ Dogs allowed in bar and bedrooms ~ Open 12-2.30, 6-midnight; 12-midnight(11 Sun) Sat ~ Bedrooms: £29S/£55B

Recommended by Michael Butler, Len Beattie, Brian and Janet Ainscough, Dudley and Moira Cockroft, Adam F Padel, Pete Yearsley, Andy and Jill Kassube

LOW CATTON   SE7053   MAP 7

Gold Cup

Village signposted with High Catton off A166 in Stamford Bridge or A1079 at Kexby Bridge; YO41 1EA

Enjoyable food and a friendly welcome in pleasant, bustling pub; real ales, seats in garden and ponies in paddock

This is a spacious, pleasant pub with comfortable, communicating rooms and a warm welcome from staff. There's a fire at one end, plush wall seats and stools around good solid tables, some decorative plates and brasswork on the walls, and a relaxed atmosphere. The back bar has a woodburning stove in a brick fireplace and the restaurant has solid wooden pews and tables (said to be made from a single oak tree), and pleasant views of the surrounding fields. Black Sheep and John Smiths on handpump; piped music, pool, TV, dominoes and board games. The garden has a grassed area for children and the back paddock houses Candy the horse and Polly the shetland pony. They also own Boris the retired greyhound and have fishing rights on the adjoining River Derwent.

🍴 **Using local farm meat and summer produce from local allotments, the good bar food includes sandwiches, soup, crunchy crab cakes with spicy salsa, pear, stilton and crispy bacon salad, mushroom and ricotta crêpes topped with gruyère, chicken breast wrapped in bacon with creamy leek and stilton sauce, salmon and prawn pie, beef in beer topped with a mustard croûte, roast rack of lamb with mash and redcurrant gravy, and daily specials; they also offer two- and three-course set evening meals.** *Starters/Snacks: £3.00 to £4.50. Main Courses: £6.50 to £14.00. Puddings: £3.50*

Free house ~ Licensees Pat and Ray Hales ~ Real ale ~ Bar food (12-2.30, 6-9.30; all day weekends; not Mon lunchtime) ~ No credit cards ~ (01759) 371354 ~ Children welcome ~ Dogs allowed in bar ~ Open 12-2.30, 6-11; 12-11 Sat and Sun; closed Mon lunchtime

Recommended by Mr and Mrs P M Jennings, Pat and Tony Martin, Roger A Bellingham, David Carr, R T and J C Moggridge, Kay and Alistair Butler, Peter and Anne Hollindale

---

Several well known guide books make establishments pay for entry, either directly or as a fee for inspection. These fees can run to many hundreds of pounds. We do not. Unlike other guides, we never take payment for entries. We never accept a free meal, free drink, or any other freebie from a pub. We do not accept any sponsorship – let alone from commercial schemes linked to the pub trade. All our entries depend solely on merit.

LUND SE9748 MAP 8

Wellington 🍴 🍷

Off B1248 SW of Driffield; YO25 9TE

Good mix of diners and drinkers in smart, busy pub, plenty of space in several rooms, real ales and helpfully noted wine list, and interesting changing food

The most atmospheric part in this smart pub is the cosy Farmers Bar – a small heavily beamed room with an interesting fireplace and some old agricultural equipment. The neatly kept main bar is much brighter with a brick fireplace and bar counter, well polished wooden banquettes and square tables, dried flowers, and local prints on the textured cream-painted walls. Off to one side is a plainer flagstoned room, while at the other a york-stoned walkway leads to a room with a display case showing off the village's Britain in Bloom awards. The restaurant is supported by a back dining area where you cannot reserve a table – this seems to work well and the main bar in the evening remains a haven for drinkers only. Black Sheep Bitter, John Smiths, Timothy Taylors Landlord and a guest such as Naylors Pale Ale on handpump, a good wine list with a helpfully labelled choice by the glass, and 30 malt whiskies. Piped music, darts, pool, TV, games machine and board games. A small courtyard beside the car park has a couple of benches.

🍴 Good bar food at lunchtime includes sandwiches, soup, smoked haddock fishcakes with a mild curried apple sauce, chicken liver parfait with redcurrant and orange sauce, beer-battered local haddock, calves liver and bacon and breast of chicken on warm potato, rocket and parmesan salad; evening choices such as devilled lambs kidney and mushroom hotpot, king scallops with smoked bacon and garlic risotto, lamb and apricot suet pudding, monkfish poached in a vegetable and vermouth cream ragoût, and puddings like warm chocolate and pear frangipane tart with vanilla bean ice-cream and rum and raisin crème caramel. *Starters/Snacks: £3.95 to £6.95. Main Courses: £10.95 to £14.95. Puddings: £4.95 to £5.50*

Free house ~ Licensees Russell Jeffery and Sarah Jeffery ~ Real ale ~ Bar food (not Sun evening) ~ Restaurant (Tues-Sat evenings) ~ (01377) 217294 ~ Children welcome but must be over 12 in evening ~ Open 12-3, 6.30-11

Recommended by Colin McKerrow, June and Ken Brooks, Fred and Lorraine Gill, David Field, Pat and Tony Martin, J Crosby

MARTON SE7383 MAP 10

Appletree

Village signposted off A170 W of Pickering; YO62 6RD
YORKSHIRE DINING PUB OF THE YEAR

Carefully run and civilised pub with relaxed rooms, friendly welcome, super range of drinks and excellent food using the best (usually local) produce available

This civilised and neatly kept pub is run by people who really care and the landlady and her staff are genuinely helpful and friendly. The relaxed beamed lounge has comfortable settees in red or cream around polished low tables, an open fire in the stone fireplace and a modicum of carefully placed decorations on the red walls. There's also a small bar with Moorhouses TJs Tipple (named for the pub), Suddabys Windfall (brewed specially for them) and a guest such as Elgoods Thin Ice on handpump, 14 wines by the glass plus two champagnes and five sweet wines from an extensive list with helpful notes, home-made sloe gin and vodka and home-made rhubarb and ginger vodka and quite a collection of teas and coffees. Many customers head for the red-walled dining room which has well spaced farmhouse tables, fresh flowers, and masses of evening candles; piped music. There are cast-iron tables and chairs out on a sheltered flagstoned courtyard behind.

🍴 They grow much of their own vegetables, herbs and fruit, swap pints of beer with locals for other produce, use individual farmers to rear beef and geese for them and a local gamekeeper who reserves the best of the bag. Cooked by the landlord, the high quality food includes summer sandwiches, interesting soup, whitby crab cakes with sweet chilli and crème fraîche, caramelised shallot tarte tatin with pesto cream cheese and home-dried tomatoes, crispy duck and bacon salad with honey and mustard dressing, smoked haddock with lemon and pea risotto, rump of lamb with rosemary-crushed potatoes and redcurrant sauce, braised beef with red onion marmalade and horseradish cream, and puddings such as treacle tart with lemon curd ice-cream and steamed orange, apricot and nut pudding with custard; Sunday evening posh pie and pea supper. *Starters/Snacks: £4.00 to £7.00. Main Courses: £10.00 to £16.00. Puddings: £3.00 to £7.00*

Free house ~ Licensees Melanie and T J Drew ~ Bar food (12-2, 6(6.30 Sun)-9.30(9 Sun); not Mon or Tues) ~ Restaurant ~ (01751) 431457 ~ Children welcome away from bar ~ Dogs allowed in bar ~ Open 12-2.30, 6-11; 12-3, 6.30-10.30 Sun; closed Mon and Tues, two weeks Jan

Recommended by Brian and Pat Wardrobe, Gordon Ormondroyd, Richard and Mary Bailey, Michael and Anne McDonald, Jane Johnston, David Varley

MASHAM   SE2281   MAP 10

Black Sheep Brewery 🍺

Crosshills; HG4 4EN

Lively place with friendly staff, quite a mix of customers, unusual décor in big warehouse room, well kept beers (brewery tours and shop) and interesting food

This is more of a bistro than a pub but it's well run and lively and has a thriving mix of customers of all ages. A huge upper warehouse room has a bar serving well kept Black Sheep Best, Emmerdale Ale, Riggwelter and Special on handpump, several wines by the glass, and a fair choice of soft drinks. Most of the good-sized tables have cheery american-cloth patterned tablecloths and brightly cushioned green café chairs but there are some modern pubbier tables near the bar. There's a good deal of bare woodwork, with some rough stonework painted dark red or dark green, and green-painted steel girders and pillars. This big area is partly divided up by free-standing partitions and some big plants; piped music and friendly service. Interesting brewery tours and a shop selling beers and more or less beer-related items from pub games and T-shirts to pottery and fudge. A glass wall lets you see into the brewing exhibition centre. Picnic-sets out on the grass.

🍽 Well liked lunchtime food includes sandwiches, filled baked potatoes, soup, fishcakes, hot crispy duck, black pudding and bacon salad, omelettes, pork and ale sausages and steak in ale pie; evening dishes such as chicken supreme with wensleydale cheese wrapped in bacon and topped with a tomato and sage sauce, lemon sole with prawns and a lime and chive butter and braised lamb shank in ale. They also offer cream teas plus cakes and tray bakes, milk shakes, lots of coffees and hot chocolates, and an ice-cream menu. *Starters/Snacks: £4.25 to £6.75. Main Courses: £7.95 to £15.95. Puddings: £4.25*

Free house ~ Licensee Paul Theakston ~ Real ale ~ Bar food (12-2.30(3 Sun; they do evening food only Thurs-Sat) ~ Restaurant ~ (01765) 680100 ~ Children welcome ~ Open 10-5 Mon-Weds; 11-11 Thurs, Fri and Sat; 11-5 Sun; 10.30-3.30 Mon-Weds in winter; closed 25 and 26 Dec, 1 Jan

Recommended by Mr and Mrs Maurice Thompson, WW, Tony and Penny Burton, Janet and Peter Race, M and GR, Adrian Johnson

MIDDLEHAM   SE1287   MAP 10

Black Swan 🍺

Market Place; DL8 4NP

Handsome old inn in racing village with appropriate memorabilia, heavy-beamed bar, several dining areas, real ales and decent wines, straightforward bar food

If you are interested in racing, this 17th-c stone inn makes a good base as the village is famous for its racing industry – every morning strings of racehorses pass through on their way to the local gallops on the moor; there are nine racecourses within the vicinity. The immaculately kept heavy-beamed bar has high-backed settles built in by the big stone fireplace (where there's an open log fire), racing memorabilia on the stripped stone walls, horsebrasses and pewter mugs, and John Smiths, Theakstons Best, Black Bull and Old

Peculier and a guest like Yorkshire Dales Herriot Country Ale on handpump; a decent little wine list with several by the glass, and piped music, TV and board games. There are tables on the cobbles outside and in the sheltered back garden which has been landscaped this year; it overlooks the castle where Richard III spent his early years. Good walking country.

🍴 **Bar food includes lunchtime sandwiches and filled baguettes and baked potatoes, as well as beef in ale casserole, chicken curry, bangers and mash, battered haddock, mushroom and spinach lasagne, evening gammon and egg and mixed grill, daily specials, and puddings.** *Starters/Snacks: £3.95 to £6.95. Main Courses: £6.95 to £17.95. Puddings: £3.95 to £5.50*

Free house ~ Licensees John and James Verbeken ~ Real ale ~ Bar food ~ Restaurant ~ (01969) 622221 ~ Children allowed away from bar but must be supervised ~ Dogs allowed in bar ~ Open 11–midnight; 11–1am Fri and Sat; 12–11.30 Sun ~ Bedrooms: £40S/£70S(£80B)

Recommended by W W Burke, Stephen R Holman, DC, Greta and Christopher Wells, Jon Forster, John Unsworth, Catherine Smith

White Swan 🍷 🛏
Market Place; DL8 4PE

Quite a few changes to this extended inn over the last couple of years but it still has a proper pubby bar and real ales, well liked food and comfortable bedrooms

Overlooking the market square, this extended inn has a beamed and flagstoned entrance bar with a proper pubby atmosphere, a long dark pew built into a big window, a mix of chairs around a handful of biggish tables and an open woodburning stove. Black Sheep Bitter and Ale, John Smiths and Theakstons Best on handpump from the curved counter, 12 wines by the glass, 20 malt whiskies and quite a few teas and coffees. The dining room is light, spacious and modern with some popular window tables, a large fireplace, and in an area opposite the bar, some contemporary leather chairs and a sofa. The back room has now been converted into part of this dining room; piped music. The new bedrooms are comfortable and well appointed.

🍴 **Bar food includes sandwiches, soup, onion bhaji with mint and coriander, quite a few pizzas, steak in ale pie, chicken breast stuffed with wensleydale and served with a smoked bacon and parmesan risotto, vegetable curry, duck leg confit with bubble and squeak and red wine sauce, and puddings such as white chocolate and raspberry trifle and iced liquorice terrine with caramel sauce; they also offer a dish of the day and an early bird menu (Sunday-Friday 6.30-7.30).** *Starters/Snacks: £3.50 to £6.95. Main Courses: £7.25 to £13.95. Puddings: £4.25*

Free house ~ Licensees Andrew McCourt and Paul Klein ~ Real ale ~ Bar food (12–2.15, 6.30–9.15) ~ Restaurant ~ (01969) 622093 ~ Children welcome ~ Dogs allowed in bar ~ Open 11–midnight(11.30 Sun) ~ Bedrooms: £55B/£69B

Recommended by John Unsworth, Catherine Smith, Peter Burton, Richard, Michael Butler, Janet and Peter Race, WW, Bruce and Sharon Eden

MILL BANK   SE0321 MAP 7
Millbank 🍽 🍷
Mill Bank Road, off A58 SW of Sowerby Bridge; HX6 3DY

Imaginative food in cottagey-looking dining pub, real ales, fine wines and specialist gin list, friendly staff and interesting garden sculptures; walks nearby and good views

This is a notable dining pub with friendly staff, and it draws people in from far around. It looks cottagey and traditional from the outside but once inside, there's a clean-cut minimalist modern décor and local photographs for sale. The interior is divided into the tap room, bar and restaurant, with Tetleys and Timothy Taylors Landlord on handpump, and 20 wines by the glass including champagne, port and pudding wines; also, a specialised gin list. Outside, the terrace has a glass roof and fold-away windows that make the most of the glorious setting overlooking an old textile mill. Below this is a garden adorned with metal sculptures made from old farm equipment. The Calderdale Way is easily accessible from the pub.

🍴 **As well as sandwiches (served until 7pm), the inventive food might include unusual soups, crab cake with orange hollandaise and herb salad, sautéed foie gras with caramelised pear, duck leg and lentil stew, beef braised in Guinness with horseradish mash, spinach and onion rings, artichoke and chestnut pithiviers, roast suckling pig, black pudding hash browns, oriental sauce and roast carrot, smoked chicken and asparagus pie and halibut fillet with bubble and squeak, roast parsnip sauce and smoked eel fritters, and pheasant and pancetta hotpot; also, a two-course set menu (not Saturday evening or Sunday).** *Starters/Snacks: £4.95 to £9.95. Main Courses: £10.95 to £18.95. Puddings: £3.50 to £6.50*

Free house ~ Licensee Joe McNally ~ Real ale ~ Bar food (12-2.30, 6-9.30; 12-4.30, 6-8 Sun; not Mon lunchtime) ~ Restaurant ~ (01422) 825588 ~ Children welcome ~ Dogs allowed in bar ~ Open 12-2.30, 6-11; 12-10.30 Sun; closed Mon lunchtime, first two weeks Oct, first week Jan

Recommended by Dr K P Tucker, Gordon Ormondroyd, Walter and Susan Rinaldi-Butcher, David and Cathrine Whiting

NUNNINGTON   SE6679   MAP 7

Royal Oak 🍴

Church Street; at back of village, which is signposted from A170 and B1257; YO62 5US

Friendly staff and good food in reliable, neat pub, lots to look at in beamed bar, open fires and real ales

Efficient and friendly staff are sure to make you welcome at this neatly kept and attractive little pub. The bar has high black beams strung with earthenware flagons, copper jugs and lots of antique keys, one of the walls is stripped back to the bare stone to display a fine collection of antique farm tools, and there are open fires; carefully chosen furniture such as kitchen and country dining chairs or a long pew around the sturdy tables on the turkey carpet, and a lectern in one corner. Tetleys, Theakstons Old Peculier and Wold Top Wolds Way on handpump and several wines by the glass; piped music. Nunnington Hall (National Trust) is nearby. More reports please.

🍴 **Good bar food includes sandwiches, garlic mushrooms stuffed with stilton pâté, seafood hors d'oeuvres, blue cheese, wild mushroom and spinach cannelloni, chicken breast in orange and tarragon sauce, ham and mushroom tagliatelle, steak pie, pork fillet in barbecue sauce, sweet and sour prawns, and daily specials.** *Starters/Snacks: £4.50 to £7.00. Main Courses: £8.95 to £17.50. Puddings: £4.25*

Free house ~ Licensee Anthony Simpson ~ Real ale ~ Bar food (not Mon) ~ (01439) 748271 ~ Children welcome ~ Open 12-2.30, 6.30-11; 12-2.30, 7-10.30 Sun; closed Mon

Recommended by Mike Dean, Lis Wingate Gray, Peter Burton, Miss J E Edwards

OSMOTHERLEY   SE4597   MAP 10

Golden Lion 🍺

The Green, West End; off A19 N of Thirsk; DL6 3AA

Welcoming, bustling pub with simply furnished rooms, lots of malt whiskies, real ales, interesting bar food and fine surrounding walks

Bustling and warmly friendly, this attractive old stone pub is much enjoyed by our readers. The roomy beamed bar on the left, simply furnished with old pews and just a few decorations on its white walls, has a pleasantly lively atmosphere, candles on tables, John Smiths, Timothy Taylors Landlord and a guest from Daleside on handpump and over 50 malt whiskies. On the right, there's a similarly unpretentious and well worn-in eating area; best to book to be sure of a table as it does get pretty packed. There's also a separate dining room, mainly open at weekends, and a covered courtyard; piped music. Benches out in front look across the village green to the market cross. As the inn is the start of the 44-mile Lyke Wakes Walk on the Cleveland Way and quite handy for the Coast to Coast Walk, it is naturally popular with walkers.

🍴 Interesting bar food includes sandwiches, soup, deep-fried soft shell crab with lime mayonnaise, rough pâté with onion and apricot relish, spicy pork ribs, salmon fillet with creamy basil sauce, home-made lamb burger with mint jelly and balsamic dip, spinach, ricotta and pine nut lasagne, pork and parma ham with sage and marsala sauce, steak and kidney pie, charcoal-grilled poussin with rosemary and garlic, daily specials, and puddings such as middle eastern orange cake with marmalade cream and raspberry ripple cheesecake with raspberry coulis. *Starters/Snacks: £3.95 to £7.95. Main Courses: £6.50 to £16.95. Puddings: £4.50*

Free house ~ Licensee Christie Connelly ~ Real ale ~ Bar food (12-2.30, 6-9) ~ Restaurant ~ (01609) 883526 ~ Children welcome if eating ~ Dogs allowed in bar ~ Open 12-3, 6-11; 12-11(10.30 Sun) Sat; closed 25 Dec ~ Bedrooms: £60S/£90D

Recommended by Arthur Pickering, Martin and Alison Stainsby, Sylvia and Tony Birbeck, Dr and Mrs R G J Telfer, Neil and Anita Christopher, David Carr, Blaise Vyner, Roger Noyes, Stuart Paulley, Dr and Mrs P Truelove, Christopher Turner

PICKERING

SE7984   MAP 10

White Swan 🍴 ☉ 🛏

Market Place, just off A170; YO18 7AA

Relaxed little bar in civilised coaching inn, several smart refurbished lounges, attractive restaurant, real ales and excellent wine list, first-class food and luxurious bedrooms

This year, the bar, lounge and private dining room have been refurbished in this smart old coaching inn, a new residents' lounge has been converted from a beamed barn, and some new bedrooms added. But despite all this and the fact that the food is more restaurant in style than pub, there is a small bar with a relaxed atmosphere, panelling, a log fire, sofas and just four tables, and Black Sheep Bitter and Timothy Taylors Landlord on handpump, good house wines including pudding wines and a superb list of old St Emilions, and several malt whiskies. Opposite, a bare-boards room with a few more tables has another fire in a handsome art nouveau iron fireplace, a big bow window, and pear prints on its plum-coloured walls. The restaurant has flagstones, a fine open fire, rich tweed soft furnishings, comfortable settles and gothic screens. The old coach entry to the car park is very narrow.

🍴 At lunchtime, you can enjoy the excellent food in both the bar and restaurant but in the evening you may eat only in the restaurant: lunchtime sandwiches, interesting soups, whitby fishcakes, brown shrimp salad and tartare sauce, pressed ham knuckle terrine, quail egg salad and truffle oil, carpaccio of rare breed beef fillet with rocket and parmesan, rare breed pig sausage with mash and onion gravy, porcini and thyme risotto, posh fish and chips with mushy peas, braised oxtail with thyme roast onions, parsley carrots and creamed potatoes, duck breast with celeriac rösti, roast garlic and red wine onions, daily specials, and puddings such as crème caramel with rum-soaked raisins and apple crisps and chocolate pine nut tart with clotted cream; also, a good value two- and three-course set lunch menu and proper, reasonably priced children's menu. *Starters/Snacks: £4.25 to £10.25. Main Courses: £10.95 to £16.95. Puddings: £2.70 to £5.50*

Free house ~ Licensees Marion and Victor Buchanan ~ Real ale ~ Bar food ~ Restaurant ~ (01751) 472288 ~ Children welcome ~ Dogs allowed in bar and bedrooms ~ Open 10am-11pm; 12-3, 7-10.30 Sun; 10-3, 6-11 weekdays in winter ~ Bedrooms: £95B/£130B

Recommended by Paul Humphreys, Arthur Pickering, David Carr, Sylvia and Tony Birbeck, Michael Dandy, Pat and Graham Williamson, J Crosby, Phil Bryant

---

Bedroom prices normally include full english breakfast, VAT and any inclusive service charge that we know of. Prices before the '/' are for single rooms, after for two people in double or twin (B includes a private bath, S a private shower). If there is no '/', the prices are only for twin or double rooms (as far as we know there are no singles). If there is no B or S, as far as we know no rooms have private facilities.

PICKHILL   SE3483   MAP 10

Nags Head ⚐ ☗ 🛏

Take the Masham turn-off from A1 both N and S, and village signposted off B6267 in
Ainderby Quernhow; YO7 4JG

Busy dining pub with excellent food, a fine choice of carefully chosen drinks, a tap room
and smarter lounge, and friendly service

Most of the tables in this popular dining pub are laid for eating so if it is just a drink
you're after, head for the bustling tap room on the left: beams hung with jugs, coach
horns, ale-yards and so forth, and masses of ties hanging as a frieze from a rail around
the red ceiling. The smarter lounge bar has deep green plush banquettes on the matching
carpet, pictures for sale on its neat cream walls, and an open fire. There's also a library-
themed restaurant; piped music. Black Sheep, Hambleton Bitter, Theakstons Best and a
guest beer on handpump, a good choice of malt whiskies, vintage armagnacs, and a
carefully chosen wine list with several by the glass; friendly, obliging service. One table is
inset with a chessboard and they also have board games. There's a front verandah, a
boules and quoits pitch, and nine-hole putting green.

🍴 **Good, interesting food includes sandwiches, soup, fresh queenie scallops, herb butter and**
gruyère glaze, caramelised onion and butternut squash tart, confit shallots and tomato
dressing, potted prawns with five spice and lime herb croûton, home-made burger with
relish, bangers and mash with onion gravy, wild rocket and toasted pine nut risotto with
blue buffalo cheese, large deep-fried haddock with mushy peas, local game casserole, slow-
roast lamb shoulder on roasted root vegetables with rosemary juice, crispy half roast
gressingham duck with elderberry sauce, and puddings such as chocolate brioche bread and
butter pudding with crème anglaise and vanilla panna cotta with wild berry compote and
orange shortbread. *Starters/Snacks: £3.95 to £8.95. Main Courses: £8.95 to £19.75. Puddings: £4.95*

Free house ~ Licensee Edward Boynton ~ Real ale ~ Bar food (12-2, 6-9.30; 12-2, 6-9 Sun) ~
Restaurant ~ (01845) 567391 ~ Children in bistro bar and dining room until 7.30pm ~ Dogs
allowed in bedrooms ~ Open 11-11; 12-11 Sun ~ Bedrooms: £50S(£55B)/£80B

Recommended by Peter and Anne Hollindale, Ginny Barbour, Phil and Helen Holt, J A West, Barry and Anne,
Mr and Mrs Maurice Thompson, J F M and M West, Gordon Ormonroyd, Robert Stephenson, Tony and
Tracy Constance, Jill and Julian Tasker, Val and Alan Green, Michael Doswell

RIPLEY   SE2860   MAP 7

Boars Head ⚐ ☗ 🍺 🛏

Off A61 Harrogate—Ripon; HG3 3AY

Friendly bar liked by locals in smart hotel, real ales, excellent wine list and malt whiskies,
good food and helpful service; comfortable bedrooms

Although part of a smart and comfortable hotel, the relaxed and friendly bar here is still
very much used by locals and has an informal atmosphere and Black Sheep Bitter,
Theakstons Old Peculier, Timothy Taylors Landlord and a couple of changing guests on
handpump; an excellent wine list (with ten or so by the glass), around 20 malt whiskies
and lots of teas and coffees. It's a long flagstoned room with green checked tablecloths
and olive oil on all the tables, most of which are arranged to form individual booths. The
warm yellow walls have jolly little drawings of cricketers or huntsmen running along the
bottom, as well as a boar's head (part of the family coat of arms), an interesting
religious carving, and a couple of cricket bats; efficient staff even when very busy. Some
of the furnishings in the hotel came from the attic of next door Ripley Castle, where the
Ingilbys have lived for over 650 years. A pleasant little garden has plenty of tables.

🍴 **From a menu that changes every two weeks, the good food includes sandwiches, soup,**
fish terrine with citrus dressing, warm salad of chorizo and wild mushrooms, baked haddock
with a herb crust on fennel salad, pork and leek sausage with sunblush tomato mash, wild
mushroom stroganoff with fresh pasta, lambs liver with mint-crushed potatoes and bacon
and grape casserole, fillet of beef topped with sweet and sour onions and field mushroom,
and puddings such as millefeuilles of chocolate mousses and banoffi tart with toffee ice-
cream. *Starters/Snacks: £3.75 to £5.95. Main Courses: £9.95 to £16.50. Puddings: £4.50 to £5.50*

Free house ~ Licensee Sir Thomas Ingilby ~ Real ale ~ Bar food ~ Restaurant ~ (01423) 771888 ~ Children welcome ~ Dogs allowed in bedrooms ~ Open 11-11; 11-3, 5-11 in winter ~ Bedrooms: £105B/£125B

Recommended by Dr and Mrs Jackson, Comus and Sarah Elliott, Michael Butler, Keith Wright, Geoff and Teresa Salt, the Didler, Stephen R Holman, G Dobson, Martin and Pauline Jennings, Jack Morley, David Coleman

RIPPONDEN   SE0419 MAP 7

Old Bridge ⏛ 🍴

From A58, best approach is Elland Road (opposite Golden Lion), park opposite the church in pub's car park and walk back over ancient hump-back bridge; HX6 4DF

Pleasant old pub by medieval bridge with relaxed communicating rooms, half a dozen real ales, quite a few wines by the glass, lots of whiskies, and well liked food

'There's nothing nicer than escaping the M62 and coming to this old place with its honest welcome,' says one of our readers. It's a 15th-c pub with three communicating rooms, each on a slightly different level. There's a relaxed atmosphere, oak settles built into the window recesses of the thick stone walls, antique oak tables, rush-seated chairs, a few well chosen pictures and prints, and a big woodburning stove. Timothy Taylors Best, Golden Best and Landlord and three changing guests on handpump, a dozen wines by the glass, 30 malt whiskies, and a good choice of foreign bottled beers. This is a pleasant spot by the medieval pack-horse bridge over the little River Ryburn and there's a garden overlooking the water.

🍴 On weekday lunchtimes, bar food is only sandwiches and soup or the popular help-yourself carvery and salad buffet; at weekends and in the evening, there might be dolcelatte cheesecake with pickled pear, country-style terrine with apricot chutney, meat and potato pie, smoked haddock and spinach pancakes, gressingham duck on oriental noodles, slow-roast shoulder of lamb with rosemary, red wine and garlic, and puddings. *Starters/Snacks: £3.50 to £5.00. Main Courses: £4.95 to £12.95. Puddings: £3.50*

Free house ~ Licensees Tim and Lindsay Eaton Walker ~ Real ale ~ Bar food (12-2, 6.30-9.30; not Sat or Sun evening) ~ (01422) 822595 ~ Children in eating area of bar until 8pm but must be well behaved ~ Open 12-3, 5.30-11; 12-11(10.30 Sun) Sat

Recommended by Mrs Yvette Bateman, Greta and Christopher Wells

ROBIN HOOD'S BAY   NZ9505 MAP 10

Laurel

Village signposted off A171 S of Whitby; YO22 4SE

Charming little pub in unspoilt fishing village, neat friendly bar, one or more real ales and perhaps winter Saturday sandwiches – no other food

At the bottom of a row of fishermen's cottages, at the heart of one of the prettiest and most unspoilt fishing villages on the north-east coast, is this charming little pub. The beamed and welcoming main bar is neatly kept and is decorated with old local photographs, Victorian prints and brasses, and lager bottles from all over the world. There's an open fire and Caledonian Deuchars IPA and maybe Theakstons Best and Old Peculier on handpump; darts, board games, TV and piped music. In summer, the hanging baskets and window boxes are lovely. They have a self-contained apartment for two people.

🍴 Straightforward sandwiches winter Sat lunchtime only.

Free house ~ Licensee Brian Catling ~ Real ale ~ Bar food (see text) ~ No credit cards ~ (01947) 880400 ~ Children in snug bar only ~ Dogs welcome ~ Open 12-11(10.30 Sun); 12-10.30 Sun; opening time 3pm Mon-Thurs in winter and 2pm Fri in winter

Recommended by Peter and Jo Smith, Amanda Russell

SAWLEY   SE2467   MAP 7

Sawley Arms ♀
Village signposted off B6265 W of Ripon; HG4 3EQ

Old-fashioned dining pub with good restauranty food, decent house wines, and comfortable furnishings in small carpeted rooms; pretty garden

This spotlessly kept dining pub is particularly popular with older customers and is ultra-civilised in an old-fashioned, decorous sort of way; Mrs Hawes has been at the helm for 38 years now. The small turkey-carpeted rooms have log fires and comfortable furniture ranging from small softly cushioned armed dining chairs and settees, to the wing armchairs down a couple of steps in a side snug; maybe daily papers and magazines to read, piped music. There's also a conservatory; good house wines. In fine weather you can sit in the pretty garden where the flowering tubs and baskets are lovely; two stone cottages in the grounds for rent. Fountains Abbey (the most extensive of the great monastic remains – floodlit on late summer Friday and Saturday evenings, with a live choir on the Saturday) – is not far away.

🍴 **Restauranty food includes lunchtime sandwiches, soup with croûtons, salmon mousse, plaice mornay, steak pie, corn-fed chicken breast in a mushroom and herb sauce, and daily specials.** *Starters/Snacks: £4.00 to £6.50. Main Courses: £9.50 to £10.50. Puddings: £4.00 to £5.00.*

Free house ~ Licensee Mrs June Hawes ~ Bar food (not Mon evening or winter Sun evening) ~ Restaurant ~ (01765) 620642 ~ Open 11.30-3, 6.30-10.30; 12-3, 6-10.30 Sun; closed Sun and Mon evenings in winter
Recommended by G Dobson, WW, Brian Wainwright, Bryan and Mary Blaxall, David Coleman

SHEFFIELD   SK3687   MAP 7

Fat Cat 🍺 £
23 Alma Street; S3 8SA

Super own-brewed beers and guests in friendly, bustling town local, plenty of bottled beers too, remarkably cheap tasty food; brewery visits

Of course the fine own-brewed beers draw in the customers to this busy local but there's a friendly welcome too, and good, amazingly cheap food. The two small downstairs rooms have brewery-related prints on the walls, coal fires, simple wooden tables and cushioned seats around the walls, and jugs, bottles and some advertising mirrors; cards and dominoes and maybe the pub cat wandering around. The upstairs room has a TV for sport. As well as their own Kelham Island Bitter and Pale Rider and Timothy Taylors Landlord, there are seven changing guests all well kept on handpump. Also, foreign bottled beers, two belgian draught beers, fruit gin, country wines and farm cider. The Brewery Visitor Centre (you can book brewery trips (0114) 249 4804) has framed beer mats, pump clips and prints on the walls. There are picnic-sets in a fairy-lit back courtyard.

🍴 **Incredibly cheap, enjoyable bar food includes sandwiches, soup, ploughman's, cheese and cauliflower hotpot or spicy beef casserole, aubergine and tomato or steak pie, puddings like spotted dick or apple crumble and Sunday roast.** *Starters/Snacks: £3.00 to £3.50. Main Courses: £4.20 to £4.50. Puddings: £1.75.*

Own brew ~ Licensee Stephen Fearn ~ Real ale ~ Bar food (12-8; 12-3 Sun; not Sun evening or 25 and 26 Dec and 1 Jan) ~ No credit cards ~ (0114) 249 4801 ~ Children welcome away from main bar ~ Dogs welcome ~ Open 12-12; closed 25 Dec
Recommended by Pete Baker, Mark and Diane Grist, David Carr, the Didler, Kevin Blake, Brian and Anna Marsden, B and M Kendall

---

Planning a day in the country? We list pubs in really attractive scenery at the back of the book.

New Barrack 🍺 £

601 Penistone Road, Hillsborough; S6 2GA

Lively, popular and friendly, with 11 real ales and fine range of other drinks, good value food and lots going on

With up to 11 real ales, regular live music and a Wednesday evening quiz, this really friendly, sizeable pub has a lively atmosphere and plenty of customers; it gets even busier on match days. As well as regular beers such as Abbeydale Moonshine, Acorn Barnsley Bitter, Batemans Valiant and Castle Rock Elsie Mo and Harvest Pale, there are six constantly changing guests; also, real cider, a range of bottled belgian beers, and 28 malt whiskies. The comfortable front lounge has soft upholstered seats, old pine floors, a woodburning stove and collections of decorative plates, and there are two smaller rooms behind – one with high ceilings and benches, stools and tables around the edges, and a third room that is more set up for eating. TV, darts, dominoes, cars, cribbage, board games and piped music. Daily papers and magazines to read. There's a small walled back garden. Local parking is not easy.

🍽 **Tasty bar food includes sandwiches and filled baguettes, burgers, all day breakfast, pie and peas, pizzas, spicy vegetable gumbo, chicken piri-piri, chilli, and mixed grill.** *Starters/Snacks: £1.90 to £3.95. Main Courses: £4.35 to £9.95. Puddings: £1.50 to £3.50*

Tynemill ~ Manager Kevin Woods ~ Real ale ~ Bar food (11-3, 5-9; 12-3, 7-9 Sun) ~ (0114) 234 9148 ~ Children welcome until 9pm ~ Dogs welcome ~ Live music Sat, alternate Fri evenings and monthly Sun ~ Open 11-11; 11am-midnight Fri and Sat; 12-11 Sun

Recommended by B and M Kendall, David Carr, Mark and Diane Grist, the Didler, Andy and Jill Kassube

SHELLEY   SE2112   MAP 7

Three Acres 🍴 🍷 🍺 🛏

Roydhouse (not signposted); from B6116 heading for Skelmanthorpe, turn left in Shelley (signposted Flockton, Elmley, Elmley Moor) and go up lane for 2 miles towards radio mast; HD8 8LR

Delicious food and friendly service in busy, smart dining pub, several real ales and super choice of other drinks, and relaxed atmosphere; fine views, good bedrooms

You can be sure of a friendly welcome from the attentive, hard-working staff in this civilised former coaching inn – even when they are really busy. Most customers are here to enjoy the stylish food but they do keep Black Sheep, Tetleys and Timothy Taylors Landlord on handpump, over 40 whiskies and a fantastic (if not cheap) choice of wines with at least 17 by the glass. The roomy lounge bar has a relaxed, informal atmosphere, tankards hanging from the main beam, button-back leather sofas and old prints and so forth. To be sure of a table you must book quite a way ahead – try to get a place with a view; piped music. There are fine views across to Emley Moor. More reports please.

🍽 **Food is excellent (though pricy) from a sizeable menu: super open sandwiches on home-made bread, game soup with game forcemeat, potted shrimps with lemon and toasted soldiers, mini venison steak with béarnaise sauce, chicken liver parfait and rillettes of duck with pickled cherries and citrus onion marmalade, steak, kidney and mushroom in ale pie, cannelloni of baked aubergine and ratatouille with tomato butter sauce and melted manchego, beer-battered cod with beef dripping chips, mushy peas with ham hock and lemon and tartare sauce, chicken curry with peshwari naan, slow-roasted dry cured five spice and honey-glazed belly pork with crackling and broad beans in parsley sauce, crispy half duck with apple, sage and onion tarte tatin, and puddings such as marmalade sponge pudding with Drambuie and orange custard and brown bread ice-cream, brandysnap roll and chocolate and toffee sauce.** *Starters/Snacks: £4.95 to £9.95. Main Courses: £11.95 to £24.95. Puddings: £6.75*

Free house ~ Licensees Neil Truelove and Brian Orme ~ Real ale ~ Bar food ~ Restaurant ~ (01484) 602606 ~ Children welcome ~ Open 12-3, 6-11; closed 25 and 26 Dec, evening 31 Dec, 1 Jan ~ Bedrooms: £70B/£100B

Recommended by Simon Fox, Michael and Maggie Betton, Gordon Ormondroyd, J R Ringrose, Derek and Sylvia Stephenson, Trevor and Judith Pearson, W K Wood, Geoff and Teresa Salt, Michael Jones, K S Whittaker, Hunter and Christine Wright, Cedric Robertshaw, Dr and Mrs MW A Haward

SINNINGTON   SE7485   MAP 10

Fox & Hounds 🍴 🍷 🛏️

Just off A170 W of Pickering; YO62 6SQ

Proficiently run coaching inn with welcoming staff, fine choice of drinks, imaginative food and comfortable beamed bar

In a quiet and charming village, this is a well run and friendly 18th-c coaching inn and much enjoyed by our readers. The beamed bar has various pictures and old artefacts, a woodburning stove and comfortable wall seats and carver chairs around the tables on its carpet. The curved corner bar counter has Black Sheep Special and John Smiths on handpump, several wines by the glass and some rare malt whiskies. There's a lounge and separate restaurant, too; piped music and dominoes. In front of the building are some picnic-sets, with more in the garden.

🍽 As well as lunchtime sandwiches and hot ciabattas, the first class food might include soup, confit of duck leg with pak choi, mango, cashews and roast peppers, twice-baked stilton, dried tomato and cheddar soufflé with black grape compote, tiger prawns and scallop skewers marinated with rosemary, pear and star anise, daube of beef with celeriac dauphinoise, savoury choux pastry ring filled with tomato, pepper and basil fondue with mozzarella, roast red onion and rocket, pot-roast chicken breast with mushrooms, leeks, new potatoes and parmesan, beer-battered haddock with mushy peas and home-made tartare sauce, roast belly pork, creamed leeks, caramelised apple and cider jus, lamb with honey-roast swede, onions, thyme and black pudding mash, and daily specials; they may offer only full roasts on Sundays. *Starters/Snacks: £4.75 to £6.95. Main Courses: £8.75 to £18.95. Puddings: £4.25 to £4.65*

Free house ~ Licensees Andrew and Catherine Stephens ~ Real ale ~ Bar food ~ Restaurant (evening) ~ (01751) 431577 ~ Children welcome away from bar ~ Dogs allowed in bar and bedrooms ~ Open 12-2, 6-midnight; 12-2, 6.30-11 Sun; closed 25 and 26 Dec ~ Bedrooms: £59S(£69B)/£90S(£100B)

Recommended by Derek and Sylvia Stephenson, Ann and Tony Bennett-Hughes, Sarah and Peter Gooderham, Matthew Shackle, Jill and Julian Tasker, Cathryn and Richard Hicks, Michael Butler, Pat and Stewart Gordon, Janet and Peter Race, I D Barnett, Christopher Turner

SKIPTON   SD9851   MAP 7

Narrow Boat 🍺

Victoria Street; pub signed down alley off Coach Street; BD23 1JE

Lively, extended pub near canal with eight real ales, proper home cooking, friendly staff and good mix of customers

This is the first pub belonging to Market Town Taverns – a small local group – which we have added to the main entries. Others in the group share a similar style, and we would not be surprised if more joined the Narrow Boat in future editions. Several are included in the small print section at the end of the chapter. The bustling bar has a buoyant atmosphere, a good mix of both locals and visitors, old brewery posters and nice mirrors decorated with framed beer advertisements on the walls, church pews, dining chairs and stools around wooden tables, and an upstairs gallery area with an interesting canal mural. A fine range of up to eight real ales on handpump includes Black Sheep Bitter, Caledonian Deuchars IPA, a changing beer from Copper Dragon, Timothy Taylors Landlord and four guests from breweries such as Ossett, Salamander, Saltaire and Thwaites; some belgian beers, decent wines, and friendly efficient service. The pub is down a cobbled alley, with picnic-sets under a front colonnade, and the Leeds & Liverpool Canal is nearby.

🍽 Popular bar food at lunchtime includes sandwiches, soup, shepherd's pie, sausage and mash, irish stew and tuscan bean and vegetable casserole, with evening dishes like spicy meatballs in garlic and tomatoes, steak in ale or chicken and mushroom pie, pork loin with black pudding and cider sauce, slow-roast minted lamb shoulder, salmon with parsley and lemon sauce, chicken with tomatoes, peppers and chilli, and puddings such as cherry pie and chocolate brownie. *Starters/Snacks: £3.95 to £4.95. Main Courses: £5.95 to £10.30. Puddings: £3.50*

Market Town Taverns ~ Manager Ian Reid ~ Real ale ~ Bar food (12-2, 5.30-8; not Sun or Mon evenings) ~ (01756) 797922 ~ Children welcome if dining ~ Dogs allowed in bar ~ Monthly Folk, jazz or blues; best to phone for times ~ Open 12-11

Recommended by Alan and Eve Harding, Richard and Karen Holt, Alyson and Andrew Jackson, Phil and Carol Jones, Mr and Mrs Maurice Thompson, Bruce Bird, the Didler

SOUTH DALTON
SE9645   MAP 8

Pipe & Glass

West End; brown sign to pub off B1248 NW of Beverley; HU17 7PN

Interesting modern cooking by young chef/landlord in attractively refurbished dining pub, proper bar area with real ales, good service, garden and front terrace

Although there's much emphasis on the particularly good, interesting food in this attractive white-washed dining pub, there is a proper bar area where they don't take bookings. This area is beamed and bow-windowed, with a log fire, some old prints, plush stools and traditional pubby chairs around a mix of tables and even high-backed settles. Beyond that, all is airy and comfortably contemporary, angling around past some soft modern dark leather chesterfields into a light restaurant area overlooking Dalton Park, with high-backed stylish dining chairs around well spaced country tables on bare boards. The decorations – a row of serious cookery books, and framed big-name restaurant menus – show how high the young chef/landlord aims. John Smiths and guest beers like Copper Dragon Challenger IPA and Wold Top Falling Stone on handpump, ten wines by the glass, and Old Rosie cider. Service is friendly and prompt by bright and attentive young staff; disabled access, piped music. There are tables out on the garden's peaceful lawn beside the park and picnic-sets on the front terrace; people say the yew tree is some 500 years old. The village is charming, and its elegant Victorian church spire, 62 metres (204 ft) tall, is visible for miles around. They are hoping to open bedrooms some time during 2008.

🍴 Imaginative modern food includes sandwiches, cold pressed terrine of hare, ham hock and foie gras with cranberry and satsuma relish, sage-roast butternut squash and black pudding salad with poached egg, crispy bacon and roasted walnut dressing, sausages with bubble and squeak and onion gravy, hay-baked chicken with creamed leeks, parsnip dauphinoise and parsnip and smoky bacon fritters, three-onion quiche with parmesan and rocket salad and creamy onion sauce, braised lamb with champ potato and a pot of mutton and kidney casserole, grilled halibut fillet with cauliflower champ and crab and cockle stew, and puddings such as warm dark chocolate and chestnut pudding with hazelnut and whisky ice-cream and ginger burnt cream with stewed rhubarb.
Starters/Snacks: £4.95 to £6.95. Main Courses: £8.95 to £16.95. Puddings: £4.95 to £5.95

Free house ~ Licensees James Mackenzie and Kate Boroughs ~ Real ale ~ Bar food (12-3, 6.30-9.30; 12-4 Sun; no food Sun evening or Mon) ~ Restaurant ~ (01430) 810246 ~ Children welcome ~ Open 12-3, 6.30-11; 12-10.30 Sun; closed Mon except bank holidays, two weeks Jan

Recommended by Jonathan Laverack, Pat and Graham Williamson, John Saul, Walter and Susan Rinaldi-Butcher, J Crosby

SUTTON UPON DERWENT
SE7047   MAP 7

St Vincent Arms

B1228 SE of York; YO41 4BN

Consistently cheerful, with nine real ales plus other drinks, well liked bar food and more elaborate menu, friendly service

With a fine choice of up to nine real ales and a happy, bustling atmosphere, it's not surprising that this unchanging pub is so well liked. The parlour-style panelled front bar has traditional high-backed settles, a cushioned bow-window seat, windsor chairs and a gas-effect coal fire; another lounge and separate dining room open off. To be sure of a seat, it's best to get here early. On handpump, the beers might include Fullers London Pride, ESB and seasonal ales, Gales Festival Mild, Old Mill Bitter, John Smiths, Timothy Taylors Landlord and Golden Best, York Yorkshire Terrier and Wells & Youngs Bombardier;

nine wines by the glass, and several malt whiskies. There are seats in the garden. The pub is named after the admiral who was granted the village and lands by the nation as thanks for his successful commands – and for coping with Nelson's infatuation with Lady Hamilton. Handy for the Yorkshire Air Museum. More reports please.

🍴 **At lunchtime, the tasty bar food might include sandwiches and hot ciabattas, soup, baked mushrooms with goats cheese and pesto dressing, steak, mushroom and ale pie, lasagne and haddock and chips, with more elaborate choices such as chicken liver pâté with white onion jam, confit of duck on garlic mash with red wine reduction, vegetable stir fry, thai chicken, rack of lamb with herb crust and garlic and rosemary jus, beef stroganoff, and puddings such as treacle tart and tiramisu.** *Starters/Snacks: £3.50 to £6.50. Main Courses: £8.50 to £22.00. Puddings: £3.50 to £5.50*

Free house ~ Licensees Phil, Simon and Adrian Hopwood ~ Real ale ~ Bar food ~ Restaurant ~ (01904) 608349 ~ Children welcome ~ Open 11.30-3, 6-11; 12-3, 7-10.30 Sun

Recommended by Derek and Sylvia Stephenson, David Carr, Paul and Ursula Randall, Brian P White, Roger A Bellingham, J Crosby

SUTTON-ON-THE-FOREST
SE5864   MAP 7

Rose & Crown ♀
B1363 N of York; YO61 1DP

New landlord for neat pub, small beamed bar and larger dining room, pleasant staff and seats on terrace and in garden

A new licensee has taken over this neat, beamed pub. There's a small bar on the right with parquet-flooring, old engravings on cream and red walls, old-fashioned pub seating around a couple of dimpled copper tables, and some bric-a-brac on the mantelpiece. Black Sheep and Timothy Taylors Landlord on handpump from an intricately carved counter and 14 wines by the glass. The L-shaped dining room on the left is bigger with dining chairs and tables on its polished boards, more etchings on its cream walls, and a former inglenook; there's also a conservatory. Plenty of seats on a large decked terrace and in the garden and there's a sizeable heated thatched gazebo. More reports please.

🍴 **Bar food now includes sandwiches, duck liver pâté with onion marmalade, salmon rillettes with cucumber pickle and peppered crème fraîche, wild mushroom risotto, fillet of bass with cherry tomato confit, roast lamb rump with wilted spinach, monkfish wrapped in parma ham with scallops on pesto mash, and puddings such as crème brûlée or sticky toffee pudding.** *Starters/Snacks: £4.25 to £7.95. Main Courses: £9.95 to £18.95. Puddings: £4.25 to £6.50*

Free house ~ Licensee Ben Williams ~ Real ale ~ Bar food (12-2(3 Sun), 6-9; not Sun evening or Mon) ~ Restaurant ~ (01347) 811333 ~ Children welcome ~ Open 12-2, 6-11; 12-11 Sat; 12-3 Sun; closed Sun evening, all day Mon, first two weeks Jan

Recommended by Mr and Mrs P M Jennings, Judith and Edward Pearson, Michael Doswell

THORNTON IN LONSDALE
SD6873   MAP 7

Marton Arms ◀
Off A65 just NW of Ingleton (or can be reached direct from Ingleton); LA6 3PB

Fantastic choice of whiskies and real ales in beamed bars, open fires, seats on front terrace; good walking country

This is just the place for a drink as they keep around 361 malt whiskies and up to 15 real ales on handpump from breweries such as Black Sheep, Cairngorm, Caledonian, Copper Dragon, Dent, Jennings, Lancaster, Moorhouses, Theakstons, Timothy Taylors, Wharfedale and Wye Valley; Stoford Press cider and several wines by the glass. The beamed bar has stools on black boards by the long counter, lots of stripped pine tables, pews and built-in wall seats in the light and airy main part and biggish black and white local photographs; some train memorabilia. A curtained-off flagstoned public bar has darts and piped music – and both seating areas have open log fires. There are picnic-sets out on the front terrace, with more behind. This is great walking country; the 13th-c church opposite is where Sir Arthur Conan Doyle was married. More reports, particularly on the food please.

🍴 **Bar food includes sandwiches, soup, pâté, all-day breakfast, steak and kidney pudding, vegetarian cannelloni, burgers, battered haddock, pizzas, and daily specials.** *Starters/Snacks: £2.50 to £5.50. Main Courses: £7.95 to £17.95. Puddings: £3.85 to £4.85*

Enterprise ~ Lease Graham Wright ~ Real ale ~ Bar food (not Mon-Thurs lunchtimes in winter) ~ (0152 42) 41281 ~ Children allowed until 9pm ~ Open 12-2.30, 5.30-11; 12-11 Fri and Sat; 12-10.30 Sun; closed Mon-Thurs lunchtimes in winter ~ Bedrooms: £46S/£72S

Recommended by Rob Razzell, Alex and Claire Pearse, Mr and Mrs Maurice Thompson, David and Sue Smith, Andy and Jill Kassube

THORNTON WATLASS   SE2385   MAP 10

Buck 🍺 🛏️

Village signposted off B6268 Bedale—Masham; HG4 4AH

Friendly village pub with five real ales, traditional bars, well liked food, and popular Sunday jazz

This is a good, honest village pub with long-serving licensees (who have now been here 21 years) and a friendly atmosphere. The pleasantly traditional right-hand bar has upholstered old-fashioned wall settles on the carpet, a fine mahogany bar counter, a high shelf packed with ancient bottles, several mounted fox masks and brushes, and a brick fireplace. The Long Room (which overlooks the cricket green and has been redecorated this year) has large prints of old Thornton Watlass cricket teams, signed bats, and cricket balls and so forth. Black Sheep Bitter, John Smiths and Theakstons Bitter with guests like Barngates Pride of Westmoreland and Rudgate Battleaxe on handpump, over 40 interesting malt whiskies, and seven wines by the glass; darts, cribbage and dominoes. The sheltered garden has an equipped children's play area and summer barbecues, and they have their own cricket team; quoits.

🍴 **Good traditional bar food includes sandwiches, soup, rarebit with pear chutney, prawn and potted shrimp platter, omelettes, lasagne, steak and kidney pie, beer-battered cod, gammon and egg, and daily specials; there's also a more elaborate menu with thai-style fishcakes and chilli dipping sauce, aubergine and courgette layers with a rich tomato sauce topped with mozzarella, lamb shank with rich vegetable broth, and venison fillet glazed with a juniper and redcurrant sauce.** *Starters/Snacks: £3.75 to £6.50. Main Courses: £6.95 to £12.50. Puddings: £3.25 to £4.50*

Free house ~ Licensees Michael and Margaret Fox ~ Real ale ~ Bar food (12-2(3 Sun), 6.30-9.30) ~ Restaurant ~ (01677) 422461 ~ Children welcome ~ Dogs allowed in bedrooms ~ Jazz alternate Sun lunchtimes ~ Open 11am-midnight; closed evening 25 Dec ~ Bedrooms: £55S/£65(£75B)

Recommended by John Unsworth, Catherine Smith, Bill and Sheila McLardy, Adrian Barker, J R Ringrose, Michael Butler, Jill and Julian Tasker

WASS   SE5579   MAP 7

Wombwell Arms 🛏️

Back road W of Ampleforth; or follow brown tourist-attraction sign for Byland Abbey off A170 Thirsk—Helmsley; YO61 4BE

Consistently enjoyable village pub, friendly, bustling atmosphere, good mix of locals and visitors, appealing bar food and real ales

There's a good mix of both locals and visitors in this warmly friendly village pub. It's an attractive place with a bustling atmosphere, well kept ales and popular food and there are two cosy and neatly kept bars with plenty of simple character and log fires. The two restaurants are incorporated into a 17th-c former granary. Black Sheep Bitter and Special and Timothy Taylors Landlord on handpump, several malt whiskies, and seven wines by the glass; darts and board games.

⦿ Enjoyable bar food includes sandwiches, soup, twice-baked cheese soufflé with red onion marmalade, mussels in a lightly spiced creamy sauce, game casserole, seafood linguini, aubergine and goats cheese stack, baked cod on a warm green bean and chorizo salad, steak in Guinness pie, thai chicken curry, pork fillet cooked in mustard sauce with spring onion pancakes, and gressingham duck in a green peppercorn sauce. *Starters/Snacks: £3.95 to £7.50. Main Courses: £9.25 to £16.25. Puddings: £4.50*

Free house ~ Licensees Steve and Mary Wykes ~ Real ale ~ Bar food ~ Restaurant ~ (01347) 868280 ~ Children welcome ~ Dogs allowed in bar ~ Open 12-2.30(4 Sat and Sun), 6.15-11; closed Sun evening and all day Mon ~ Bedrooms: £42S/£70S

Recommended by I H G Busby, W K Wood, WW, D Mills, Alyson and Andrew Jackson, Dr and Mrs P Truelove, Dr and Mrs R G J Telfer, Patricia and Brian Copley, Jill Angold-Stevens, Mr Knarlson, P and J Shapley, Pat and Tony Martin, Comus and Sarah Elliott, Jeff and Wendy Williams, Michael Doswell, Dr Peter Crawshaw

WATH IN NIDDERDALE   SE1467   MAP 7

Sportsmans Arms ⦿ ♟ 🛏

Nidderdale road off B6265 in Pateley Bridge; village and pub signposted over hump-back bridge on right after a couple of miles; HG3 5PP

Beautifully placed restaurant-with-rooms plus welcoming bar, real ales and super choice of other drinks, imaginative food; comfortable bedrooms

This 17th-c sandstone place is more of a restaurant-with-rooms than a traditional inn, but it does have a welcoming bar with an open fire, Black Sheep Bitter and Wharfedale Folly Ale on handpump and locals who do still pop in – though most customers are here to enjoy the particularly good food. It remains civilised and friendly and has been run by the charming Mr Carter for 30 years. There's a very sensible and extensive wine list with 15 by the glass (including champagne), over 30 malt whiskies and several russian vodkas; quiet piped music. Benches and tables outside and seats in the pretty garden. As well as their own fishing on the River Nidd, this is an ideal spot for walkers, hikers and ornithologists, and there are plenty of country houses, gardens and cities to explore.

⦿ From an imaginative menu, the food in the bar includes lunchtime filled rolls and sandwiches, terrine of local game with rhubarb chutney, warm salad of chicken livers and black pudding, chicken breast stuffed with banana, pilau rice and curry sauce, sausages with red onion and chickpea gravy, salmon with ginger and spring onion, rib-eye steak with fries and aïoli, and puddings such as summer or winter pudding and double-chocolate roulade with chocolate ice-cream; more elaborate choices also such as seared king scallops with roasted pine nuts, parmesan and pancetta, best end of loin lamb on wilted spinach with roast garlic and vine tomatoes, venison with oyster mushrooms and a gin and juniper sauce, and fillet of haddock baked with warm rarebit on tomatoes with a basil and caper jus. *Starters/Snacks: £4.00 to £8.90. Main Courses: £8.50 to £17.00. Puddings: £4.50 to £6.50*

Free house ~ Licensee Ray Carter ~ Real ale ~ Bar food ~ Restaurant ~ (01423) 711306 ~ Children allowed until 9pm ~ Dogs allowed in bar ~ Open 12-2.30, 6.30-11; closed 25 Dec ~ Bedrooms: £70B/£120B

Recommended by Lynda and Trevor Smith, Mr and Mrs D J Nash, Edward Mirzoeff, Janet and Peter Race, Hunter and Christine Wright, Bill and Sheila McLardy, Stephen Woad, Terry and Linda Moseley, Peter and Lesley Yeoward, Pat and Tony Hinkins

WESTOW   SE7565   MAP 7

Blacksmiths ⦿

Off A64 York—Malton; Main Street; YO60 7NE

Some redecoration by new licensee in bustling dining pub, now more space for drinkers, imaginative food and real ales

A new licensee again for this busy dining pub who has given the place some gentle redecoration. There's now more space for drinkers and tables in the bar can only be booked before 7pm. This beamed area has traditional high-backed settles around sturdy stripped tables, each with a fat candle, a big open woodburning stove in the capacious brick inglenook, and a few small engravings (farm animals, scenes from Mr Sponge's Sporting Tour and the like) on the cream walls. Jennings Bitter and Cumberland and a guest such as Camerons Castle Eden on handpump and several wines by the glass; piped music. The main dining area is basically two linked smallish rooms with a medley of comfortable dining chairs including some distinctive antiques around candlelit stripped dining tables on the new wooden floor. There are picnic-sets on a side terrace.

🏵 **Imaginative and very good, the food might include sandwiches, whitby crab and lemon balm fishcakes with a celeriac and grain mustard rémoulade, millefeuilles of asparagus with wild mushrooms, a poached egg and parmesan cream, goats cheese and red onion marmalade ravioli with a sauté of mushrooms and aged balsamic, roast duck with vanilla pod mash, chilli roasted figs and red wine jus, sesame-encrusted monkfish with braised pak choi, summer vegetables and a tomato and basil liqueur, rack of lamb with ratatouille chutney, and puddings such as white chocolate and vanilla panna cotta with strawberry and basil consommé and iced nougatine and passion fruit parfait; there's also a set, good value two- and three-course bar menu.** Starters/Snacks: £3.95 to £6.25. Main Courses: £12.25 to £15.95. Puddings: £5.25

Free house ~ Licensee Jonathan Cliff ~ Bar food (12-2, 5.30-9; 12-4 Sun; not Sun evening, Mon, or Tues lunchtime) ~ Restaurant ~ (01653) 618365 ~ Children welcome ~ Dogs allowed in bar ~ Open 12-2, 5.30-11; 12-11(10.30 Sun) Sat; closed Mon all day, Tues lunchtime

Recommended by R L Graham, David and Cathrine Whiting, David and Lyndsay Lewitt, Christopher Turner, John H Smith, Dr Ian S Morley

WHITBY
NZ9011   MAP 10

Duke of York
124 Church Street, Harbour East Side; YO22 4DE

Fine harbourside position, window seats and bedrooms enjoy the view, several real ales and standard bar food

The position here is certainly worth a visit – try to arrive early to bag a table by the window and enjoy the view over the harbour entrance and the western cliff. The comfortable beamed lounge bar has fishing memorabilia (including the pennant numbers of local trawlers chalked on the beams) and Black Sheep, Caledonian Deuchars IPA, Courage Directors, John Smiths and Timothy Taylors Landlord on handpump; decent wines by the glass and quite a few malt whiskies, piped music (which a number of customers feel is unnecessary), TV, darts and games machine. All the bedrooms (apart from one) overlook the water. The pub is close to the famous 199 Steps that lead up to the abbey. There is no nearby parking.

🏵 **Straightforward bar food includes sandwiches, steak in ale or fish pie and large local cod or haddock in batter.** Starters/Snacks: £3.50 to £5.00. Main Courses: £6.50 to £8.50. Puddings: £3.50

Enterprise ~ Lease Lawrence Bradley ~ Real ale ~ Bar food (all day) ~ (01947) 600324 ~ Children allowed until 9.30pm ~ Live music Mon ~ Open 11-11; 12-11 Sun ~ Bedrooms: /£60B

Recommended by Ann and Tony Bennett-Hughes, David Carr, Ben Williams, Richard, the Didler, Amanda Russell, Pat and Graham Williamson, Patrick Wiegand, Michael Dandy, Christine and Neil Townend, Steve Whalley, Paul Humphreys

---

'Children welcome' means the pub says it lets children inside without any special restriction. If it allows them in, but to restricted areas such as an eating area or family room, we specify this. Places with separate restaurants often let children use them, hotels usually let them into public areas such as lounges.
Some pubs impose an evening time limit – let us know if you find this.

WIDDOP   SD9531   MAP 7

Pack Horse 🍺

The Ridge; from A646 on W side of Hebden Bridge, turn off at Heptonstall signpost (as it's a sharp turn, coming out of Hebden Bridge road signs direct you around a turning circle), then follow Slack and Widdop signposts; can also be reached from Nelson and Colne, on high, pretty road; OS Sheet 103 map reference 952317; HX7 7AT

Friendly pub high up on the moors and liked by walkers for generous, tasty food, five real ales and lots of malt whiskies; bedrooms

After a wet moorland walk, this isolated, traditional pub is a cosy haven. There's a warm welcome from the friendly staff and the bar has warm winter fires, window seats cut into the partly panelled stripped stone walls that take in the moorland view, sturdy furnishings, horsey mementoes, and Black Sheep Bitter, Greene King Old Speckled Hen, Thwaites Bitter, and a couple of guests such as Black Sheep Special and Thwaites Lancaster Bomber on handpump, around 130 single malt whiskies and some irish ones as well, and eight wines by the glass. The restaurant is open only on Saturday evenings. The friendly golden retriever is called Murphy and there's another dog called Holly. Seats outside and pretty summer hanging baskets. Leave your boots and backpacks in the porch.

🍽 **Well liked bar food at fair prices includes sandwiches, ploughman's, soup, pâté, garlic mushrooms, large burgers, steak and kidney pie, lasagne, vegetable bake, gammon and eggs, seafood thermidor, and daily specials. They do stop food service promptly.** *Starters/Snacks: £3.95 to £5.95. Main Courses: £5.95 to £15.95. Puddings: £3.50*

Free house ~ Licensee Andrew Hollinrake ~ Real ale ~ Bar food (not Mon or weekday winter lunchtimes) ~ (01422) 842803 ~ Children in eating area of bar until 8pm ~ Dogs allowed in bar ~ Open 12-3, 7-11; 12-11 Sun; closed weekday lunchtimes in winter; closed Mon ~ Bedrooms: £43S/£48B

Recommended by Brian Wainwright, Greta and Christopher Wells, Ann and Tony Bennett-Hughes, Len Beattie, Dr K P Tucker

YORK   SE5951   MAP 7

Maltings 🍺 £

Tanners Moat/Wellington Row, below Lendal Bridge; YO1 6HU

Bustling, friendly city pub with cheerful landlord, interesting real ales and other drinks, and good value food

Happily unchanging and much enjoyed by our readers, this lively and friendly city pub has a really good mix of customers, a fine range of quickly changing, interesting beers and good value food. The tricksy décor is entirely contrived and strong on salvaged somewhat quirky junk: old doors for the bar front and much of the ceiling, enamel advertising signs for the rest of it, what looks like a suburban front door for the entrance to the ladies', partly stripped orange brick walls, even a lavatory pan in one corner. As well as Black Sheep Bitter, the jovial landlord keeps five guest ales on handpump from breweries like Fat Cat, Hydes, Milestone, Roosters, Shardlow and York and holds frequent special events. He also has two or three continental beers on tap, up to four farm ciders, a dozen or so country wines, and more irish whiskeys than you normally see. Get there early to be sure of a seat; games machine. The day's papers are framed in the gents'. Nearby parking is difficult; the pub is very handy for the Rail Museum and the Yorkshire Eye.

🍽 **Generous helpings of tasty bar food include sandwiches, extremely good, truly home-made chips with chilli or curry, filled baked potatoes, haddock, beef in ale pie and stilton and leek bake.** *Main Courses: £3.50 to £5.25*

Free house ~ Licensee Shaun Collinge ~ Real ale ~ Bar food (12-2 weekdays, 12-4 weekends; not evenings) ~ No credit cards ~ (01904) 655387 ~ Children allowed after food service and must be well behaved ~ Dogs welcome ~ Blues Mon, folk Tues ~ Open 11-11; 12-10.30 Sun; closed 25 Dec

Recommended by Neil Whitehead, Victoria Anderson, Eric Larkham, Brian Wainwright, D L Parkhurst, Andy and Jill Kassube, David Carr, Pete Coxon, David Hoult, Mrs Hazel Rainer, the Didler, Mark and Diane Grist

LUCKY DIP

Besides the fully inspected pubs, you might like to try these Lucky Dips recommended to us and described by readers (if you do, please send us reports: www.goodguides.co.uk).

ADDINGHAM [SE0749]

☆ *Fleece* LS29 0LY [Main St]: Large well run pub with good value home-made food from hearty sandwiches using their own baked bread to generous blackboard meals using fresh local meat, whitby fish and smoked fish, popular Sun roasts (all day then) and some unusual dishes, quick friendly service, well kept Black Sheep and Timothy Taylors Landlord, good choice of wines by the glass, low ceilings, flagstones, candles and log fire, tap room with darts and dominoes; very busy wknds; children welcome, lots of picnic-sets on terrace, open all day *(Richard Crabtree, Gerry Miller, Mrs R A Cartwright, Tina and David Woods-Taylor, David Crook, Lucie Ware)*

ALDBOROUGH [SE4166]

Ship YO51 9ER [off B6265 just S of Boroughbridge, close to A1]: Attractive creeper-clad 14th-c village pub with heavy beams, some old-fashioned seats around cast-iron framed tables, lots of copper and brass, coal fire in stone inglenook, welcoming staff, John Smiths, Theakstons and Timothy Taylors Landlord, bar food; piped music; children welcome, tables on front terrace, handy for Roman remains and museum, comfortable bedrooms, open all day wknds *(Graham and Doreen Holden, LYM, Tony and Penny Burton, Malcolm and Jane Levitt)*

ALLERTHORPE [SE7847]

Plough YO42 4RW [Main St]: Airy two-room lounge bar with wide daily-changing choice of good sensibly priced food inc local game and nice puddings, friendly welcome, well kept Greene King Old Speckled Hen, Marstons Pedigree, Theakstons Best and Tetleys, decent house wines, well served coffee, snug alcoves, hunting prints, World War II RAF and RCAF photographs, open fires, restaurant, games extension with pool; piped music; tables out in pleasant garden, handy for Burnby Hall *(LYM, C A Hall)*

AMPLEFORTH [SE5878]

☆ *White Swan* YO62 4DA [off A170 W of Helmsley; East End]: Relaxed civilised atmosphere in three separate interestingly furnished and decorated rooms, good generous food from sandwiches up in bar and candlelit restaurant, nice home-made puddings, friendly efficient staff, Black Sheep and Timothy Taylors Landlord, good wines by the glass, blazing log fires, comfortable squashy seating, sporting prints, public bar with darts and dominoes; children welcome, attractive back terrace *(LYM, Walter and Susan Rinaldi-Butcher, Dr and Mrs R G J Telfer, Lily Hornsby Clark, WW, Martin and Alison Stainsby)*

APPLETREEWICK [SE0560]

☆ *Craven Arms* BD23 6DA [off B6160 Burnsall—Bolton Abbey]: Attractively placed creeper-covered 17th-c beamed pub with comfortably down-to-earth settles and rugs on flagstones, brown-painted ply panelling, coal fire in old range, good friendly service, three real ales such as Black Sheep and Wharfedale, good choice of wines by the glass, enjoyable reasonably priced home-made food from good sandwiches up, small dining room and interesting new very traditionally built barn extension with gallery; dogs and walking boots welcome (plenty of surrounding walks), nice views from front picnic-sets, more seats in back garden *(Greta and Christopher Wells, Mr and Mrs T Stone, LYM, Fred and Lorraine Gill, Lucien Perring, WW)*

ARNCLIFFE [SD9371]

☆ *Falcon* BD23 5QE [off B6160 N of Grassington]: A favourite basic country tavern, same family for generations (current landlord has nice dry sense of humour), lovely setting on moorland village green, no frills, coal fire in small bar with elderly furnishings, Timothy Taylors Landlord tapped from cask to stoneware jugs in central hatch-style servery, good plain generous lunchtime and early evening sandwiches and snacks from old family kitchen with range, attractive watercolours, sepia photographs and humorous sporting prints, simple back sunroom (children allowed here lunchtime) looking on to pleasant garden; no credit cards, cl winter Thurs evenings; two plain bedrooms (not all year), miles of trout fishing, good breakfast and evening meal *(the Didler, Neil and Angela Huxter, Clare Rosier, WW, Sarah Watkinson, Ann and Tony Bennett-Hughes, Comus and Sarah Elliott, Karen Eliot, Gerry Miller, LYM)*

ARTHINGTON [SE2644]

Wharfedale LS21 1NL [A659 E of Otley (Arthington Lane)]: Good value food from sandwiches and pub staples to restaurant dishes, Black Sheep, Timothy Taylors Landlord and Tetleys, several wines by the glass, efficient friendly service, roomy and comfortably old-fashioned open-plan bar, intimate alcoves, soft lighting, half-panelling and Yorkshire landscapes, separate more modern restaurant; disabled access and facilities, three new bedrooms *(Ray and Winifred Halliday, Tony and Penny Burton)*

ASKRIGG [SD9491]

☆ *Crown* DL8 3HQ [Main St]: Thriving open-plan local in popular and attractive James Herriot village, basic and cosy, with three areas off main bar, blazing fires inc old-fashioned range, relaxed atmosphere, simple home-made food inc cut-price small helpings, good value Sun lunch and good puddings choice, helpful cheerful staff, Black Sheep and Theakstons XB; children, dogs and walkers welcome, tables outside *(Lawrence Pearse, Dudley and Moira Cockroft, D W Stokes, M Greening, David and Karen Cuckney)*

☆ **Kings Arms** DL8 3HQ [signed from A684 Leyburn—Sedbergh in Bainbridge]: Early 19th-c coaching inn, great atmosphere in flagstoned main bar, relaxed and casual, with roaring log fire, attractive traditional furnishings and décor, small snug well used by locals, real ales such as Black Sheep, John Smiths, Theakstons Best and Old Peculier, decent wines by the glass, good choice of malt whiskies, good interesting food choice from nice sandwiches up, quick friendly service, another log fire in dining room, pool in barrel-vaulted former beer cellar; dogs welcome, tables out in pleasant courtyard, bedrooms run separately as part of Holiday Property Bond complex behind *(Greta and Christopher Wells, M Greening, G D Baker, Mrs E M Richards, Lawrence Pearse, LYM, Terry and Linda Moseley, Alvin Morris, John and Joan Calvert, Pat and Robert Watt, John and Enid Morris, Ian and Celia Abbott)*

ASKWITH [SD1648]
Black Horse LS21 2JQ [back rd Otley—Ilkley]: Biggish comfortable open-plan family pub in lovely spot with superb Wharfedale views from dining conservatory and good terrace, huge choice of usual food cooked well at sensible prices (best to book Sun lunch), well kept Timothy Taylors Landlord, courteous helpful staff, open fire *(Dudley and Moira Cockroft)*

AUCKLEY [SE6401]
Eagle & Child DN9 3HS [Main St]: Two-room village pub of some character, popular for its good value food from sandwiches up, real ales such as Anglo Dutch Ghost on the Rim, Black Sheep, John Smiths and Theakstons from island servery, good soft drinks choice, pleasant staff, separate dining area; children welcome *(JJW, CMW, W W Burke)*

AUSTWICK [SD7668]
☆ **Game Cock** LA2 8BB [just off A65 Settle—Kirkby Lonsdale]: Prettily placed below the Three Peaks, friendly barman and good log fire in homely old-fashioned beamed bare-boards back bar, Thwaites ales, nice coffee, most space devoted to the food side, with good fairly priced choice from sandwiches up inc good game pie, two dining rooms and modern front conservatory-type extension; dogs welcome, tables out in front with good play area, five neat bedrooms, good walks all round, open all day Sun *(BB, Michael Butler, Margaret Dickinson, Len Beattie, Mr and Mrs P Eastwood, Lucien Perring)*

BAILDON [SE1538]
Junction BD17 6AB [Baildon Rd]: Traditional welcoming alehouse with great range from Fullers to Oakham to local Yorkshire brews, basic food served till 7pm, popular Tues curry night *(Andy and Jill Kassube)*

BAINBRIDGE [SD9390]
☆ **Rose & Crown** DL8 3EE: Comfortable hotel with friendly and pubbily old-fashioned front bar overlooking moorland village green, beams, oak panelling, old settles and big log fire, welcoming service, Black Sheep and Theakstons, good coffee, reasonably priced wines by the glass, spacious back restaurant popular with families; children welcome, 11 bedrooms, open all day *(Michael and Maggie Betton, LYM, W W Burke, Kay and Alistair Butler)*

BEVERLEY [TA0339]
Dog & Duck HU17 8BH [Ladygate]: Cheerfully busy two-bar local handy for playhouse and Sat market, cheap home-made usual lunchtime food using local produce from sandwiches to bargain Sun lunch, well kept Greene King Abbot, John Smiths and an interesting guest beer, good value wines and good range of malt whiskies, helpful friendly staff, coal fires; piped music, games machine; good value bedrooms up outside iron staircase in courtyard – secure parking *(David Carr)*
Durham Ox HU17 9HJ [Norwood]: Proper pub with John Smiths, Tetleys and two guest beers, good value standard home-made food; open all day *(C A Hall)*
Molescroft Inn HU17 7EG [Molescroft Rd (A164/B1248 NW)]: Comfortable pub with friendly fast service, changing ales such as Jennings and Marstons Pedigree from central bar, good value pubby food from sandwiches and baked potatoes up inc popular Sun lunch, separate dining room *(Carole Jones)*

BILBROUGH [SE5346]
☆ **Three Hares** YO23 3PH [off A64 York—Tadcaster]: Smart village dining pub which has been popular for imaginative good food from sandwiches up, good choice of wines by the glass, Black Sheep and Timothy Taylors Landlord, and relaxing atmosphere, with sofas and log fire; new licensees summer 2007, too late for us to gauge – reports please *(BB)*

BILTON [SE4750]
Chequers YO26 7NN [B1224]: Reopened after refurbishment, friendly staff, well kept Black Sheep, Caledonian Deuchars IPA and guest beers such as Greene King Old Speckled Hen and Marstons Pedigree, enjoyable food in comfortable and polished linked bar areas and part-panelled dining room, sensibly priced wines; piped music *(Les and Sandra Brown)*

BINGLEY [SE1242]
Dick Hudsons BD16 3BA [Otley Rd, High Eldwick]: Comfortable old-world Vintage Inn, popular food, a couple of real ales, good choice of wines by the glass, quick service; tables out by cricket field, tremendous views and good walks, open all day *(Neil Whitehead, Victoria Anderson, Pat and Graham Williamson, R M Chard)*
Fisherman BD16 1TS [Wagon Lane, by Leeds & Liverpool Canal]: Straightforward waterside pub in nice spot by bridge and near locks, wide choice of food from sandwiches to full meals inc a daily-changing school pudding and quite enterprising specials, Black Sheep and Tetleys, cheerful helpful staff; children welcome *(Pat and Graham Williamson)*
Old White Horse BD16 2RH [Old Main St/Millgate (A650)]: Character 16th-c pub with well kept Black Sheep, Tetleys and

Worthington, simple food inc bargain baguettes, carpeted areas off flagstoned bar, pool room; riverside terrace *(Michael Butler)*

BIRSTALL [SE2126]

☆ *Black Bull* WF17 9HE [Kirkgate, off A652; head down hill towards church]: Medieval stone-built pub opp part-Saxon church, dark panelling and low beams in long row of five small linked rooms, traditional décor complete with stag's head and lace curtains, lively local atmosphere, good cheap home-made food inc bargain early meals and good value Sun lunch, good service, Boddingtons, Ossett Silver King and Worthington, upstairs former courtroom (now a function room, but they may give you a guided tour), popular quiz night Mon; children welcome *(Michael Butler, BB)*

BISHOP THORNTON [SE2663]

Chequers HG3 3JN: Busy traditional pub with good choice of good value reliable food inc bargain roasts, good choice of wines by the glass, efficient service; keg beers; bedrooms, cl Mon/Tues lunchtime *(Dudley and Moira Cockroft)*

BLACKTOFT [SE8424]

Hope & Anchor DN14 7YW: Super setting and views, four well kept ales inc Mild, enjoyable food, clean bright pub; picnic-sets nr river, great for bird-watchers as by RSPB reserve *(C A Hall)*

BOROUGHBRIDGE [SE3966]

Crown YO51 9LB [Bridge St]: Charming 18th-c hotel (former Great North Road coaching inn), pubby beamed front bar with stripped floor and wooden booths, comfortable lounge, well kept Black Sheep Bitter and Special, good if not cheap food from sandwiches to steaks; good bedrooms *(Mark O'Sullivan)*

BRADFORD [SE1528]

Chapel House BD12 0HP [Chapel House Buildings, Low Moor]: Busy pub in pretty setting opp church, plenty of atmosphere in L-shaped bar, well kept Greene King, usual food *(Gordon Ormondroyd)*

Cock & Bottle BD3 9AA [Barkerend Rd, up Church Bank from centre]: Carefully restored Victorian décor, deep-cut and etched windows and mirrors enriched with silver and gold leaves, stained glass, enamel intaglios, heavily carved woodwork and traditional furniture, coal fire; currently a Copper Dragon pub, with their real ales and guest beers; Thurs folk night, open all day *(BB, the Didler)*

Fighting Cock BD7 1JE [Preston St (off B6145)]: Busy bare-boards alehouse by industrial estate, a dozen well kept changing real ales inc Theakstons and Timothy Taylors, foreign bottled beers, farm ciders, good lively atmosphere, all-day doorstep sandwiches and simple lunchtime hot dishes (not Sun), low prices, coal fires; open all day *(the Didler, Andy and Jill Kassube, Gordon Ormondroyd)*

Haigys BD8 7QU [Lumb Lane]: Friendly, lively and distinctive local with cosy lounge

area, fine changing range of beers inc Ossett, Phoenix and Rooster, revolving pool table, music area; cl lunchtimes *(the Didler)*

New Beehive BD1 3AA [Westgate]: Robustly old-fashioned Edwardian inn with several rooms inc good pool room, huge range of beers, gas lighting, candles and coal fires; basement music nights; nice back courtyard, bedrooms, open all day (till 2am Fri/Sat) *(the Didler)*

BRAMHAM [SE4242]

Swan LS23 6QA [just off A1 2 miles N of A64]: Unspoilt and civilised three-room country local with engaging long-serving landlady, super mix of customers, John Smiths and Theakstons, no food, machines or music *(Les and Sandra Brown)*

BRIDGE HEWICK [SE3370]

Black-a-moor HG4 5AA [Boroughbridge Rd (B6265 E of Ripon)]: Roomy dining pub locally very popular for its appetising food using prime local produce, well kept Black Sheep, well chosen wines by the glass, friendly and willing young staff, good coffee, sofas in bar area; bedrooms *(Roger Noyes, I D Barnett, Roy Bromell, Michael Doswell)*

BRIGHOUSE [SE1323]

Red Rooster HD6 2QR [Brookfoot; A6025 towards Elland]: Flagstoned pub popular for real ales such as Caledonian Deuchars IPA, Moorhouses, Ossett, Roosters Yankee, Salamander, Timothy Taylors Landlord and new or esoteric guest beers, country wines, coffee, open fire, separate areas inc one with pin table, brewery memorabilia; small terrace, open all day Fri-Sun (cl till mid-afternoon other days) *(J R Ringrose, the Didler, Andy and Jill Kassube)*

BROUGH [SE9326]

Buccaneer HU15 1DZ [Station Rd]: Good value pubby lunchtime food, impressive service, three or four real ales such as Black Sheep and Tetleys; former Railway Tavern, renamed in the 1960s for the Blackburn (Hawker Siddeley) Buccaneer fighter/bomber produced nearby *(Pam and John Smith)*

BROUGHTON [SD9450]

☆ *Bull* BD23 3AE: Neatly modernised and well run old-fashioned pub very popular for good wholesome food – all home-made, even the chutneys – in bar and restaurant, cheerfully friendly staff, thriving atmosphere, polished brass and china, Black Sheep, Tetleys and a beer brewed for the pub, good wines by the glass *(LYM, Graham and Doreen Holden, Mr and Mrs A Silver, John and Sylvia Harrop)*

BURLEY IN WHARFEDALE [SE1646]

Queens Head LS29 7BU [Main St]: Locally very popular under newish landlord for enjoyable home-made food esp steaks (best to book wknds) *(Hendrik Le Roux)*

BURNT YATES [SE2561]

New Inn HG3 3EG [Pateley Bridge Rd]: Appealing pub redecorated by friendly new licensees, well kept Tetleys and York ales, good wines by the glass, short blackboard choice of good value country cooking, lots of interesting bric-a-brac, nicely panelled back restaurant; new terrace for smokers, chalet bedrooms (Comus and Sarah Elliott, Tony and Penny Burton, Tim and Ann Newell)

BURTON LEONARD [SE3263]

☆ **Hare & Hounds** HG3 3SG [off A61 Ripon—Harrogate, handy for A1(M) exit 48]: Hands-on new licensee in well organised country pub with enjoyable reasonably priced food from sandwiches and baked potatoes up, well kept Black Sheep from long counter, several wines by the glass and good choice of other drinks, pleasant service, large carpeted main area divided by log fire, traditional furnishings, bright little side room with sofa and easy chairs; children in eating areas, pretty back garden, has been cl Tues (Mrs Mahni Pannett, Jo Lilley, Simon Calvert, LYM, John and Jill Milton)

BURYTHORPE [SE7964]

Bay Horse YO17 9LJ [5 miles S of Malton]: Welcoming local atmosphere in recently refurbished linked rooms with pictures, books and armchairs, large civilised dining area, good value generous food (not Sun/Mon evenings), good range of real ales such as Timothy Taylors; nice Wolds-edge village (David Barnes, Christopher Turner)

CARLTON [SE0684]

☆ **Foresters Arms** DL8 4BB [off A684 W of Leyburn]: Welcoming pub with good food inc local game and venison, their own-brewed Wensleydale ale and several others such as Black Sheep, decent wines by the glass, very good service, log fire, low beams and flagstones; children welcome, picnic-sets out among tubs of flowers, pretty village at the heart of the Yorkshire Dales National Park, comfortable bedrooms, lovely views (LYM, Gerry Miller, Mr and Mrs Maurice Thompson, the Didler, Terry Mizen, Dr and Mrs R G J Telfer)

CARLTON-IN-CLEVELAND [NZ5203]

Lord Stones TS9 7JH: Looks ancient but recently built from reclaimed stone and timber, remote moorland pub handy for Cleveland Way walkers, very welcoming, with useful blackboard menu and Theakstons Old Peculier; open all day 9-5, plus summer evenings (JHBS)

CAWOOD [SE5737]

Castle YO8 3SH [Wistowgate]: Comfortable pub with friendly efficient service, wide range of home-made pubby food inc children's and smaller-appetite helpings, sandwiches too, Black Sheep, John Smiths and a weekly guest beer, good choice of sensibly priced wines by the glass, log fire, air-conditioned dining areas; back caravan standing (John and Sheila Coggrave)

CHAPELTOWN [SK3596]

Commercial S35 2XF [Station Rd]: Friendly three-room tap for Wentworth ales, quickly changing guest beers too, lots of pump clips in small snug, good choice of good value generous food all day (not Sun evening) inc good roasts and hot meat sandwiches on Sun, pictures and fans in lounge/dining room, games room with pool off L-shaped

bar; no music or dogs, picnic-sets in small garden, open all day Fri-Sun (the Didler)

CHERRY BURTON [SE9842]

Bay Horse HU17 7RF [off B1248 NW of Beverley]: 17th-c modernised Marstons pub, their related beers kept well, generous good value food inc particularly good meat and bargain high teas, roomy lounge, restaurant and games area (C A Hall)

CLAPHAM [SD7469]

New Inn LA2 8HH [off A65 N of Settle]: Welcoming riverside inn in famously pretty village, log fires, landlady's tapestries and caving and other cartoons in small comfortable lounge, changing well kept ales such as Black Sheep, Copper Dragon, Thwaites and Timothy Taylors, obliging staff, good honest food in bars and restaurant, public bar with pool in games area; dogs welcome, tables outside, handy for round walk to Ingleborough Cavern and more adventurous hikes, 20 comfortable bedrooms (Roy and Lindsey Fentiman, Adam F Padel, Mr and Mrs Maurice Thompson)

CLIFTON [SE1622]

☆ **Black Horse** HD6 4HJ [Westgate/Coalpit Lane; signed off Brighouse rd from M62 junction 25]: 17th-c pub/hotel with pleasant décor featuring racing, golf, football and former star performers at Batley Variety Club, front dining rooms with popular generous food from interesting ciabattas and other good lunchtime snacks to full meals, imaginative puddings and good value set dinners, smaller back area by bar counter mainly just standing room, beam and plank ceiling, open fire, well kept ales such as Black Sheep and Timothy Taylors Landlord, decent wines; 23 comfortable bedrooms, pleasant village (Michael Butler, Pat and Tony Martin, BB)

CLOUGHTON [SE9798]

☆ **Falcon** YO13 0DY [pub signed just off A171 out towards Whitby]: Big dependable open-plan pub, neatly kept and well divided, light and airy, with comfortable banquettes and other seats on turkey carpet, good value honest fresh food in quantity inc whopping steaks (no booking, but worth the wait for a table), John Smiths and Theakstons XB, attentive friendly family service, log fire in big stone fireplace, cheerful regulars, distant sea view from end windows; no dogs, piped music; picnic-sets on walled lawn, good bedrooms (BB, Sue and Dave Harris, Danny Savage)

COLTON [SE5444]

☆ **Olde Sun** LS24 8EP [off A64 York—Tadcaster]: Immaculate 17th-c beamed dining pub with young couple doing wide choice of good upscale food (must book Sun lunch), good welcoming service, well kept ales such as Black Sheep and Greene King, good choice of wines by the glass, several linked low-ceilinged rooms with nice collection of old chairs inc an antique settle around good solid tables, log fires, back delicatessen specialising in local produce;

picnic-sets on quiet front terrace and new decking, cl Mon *(Michael Swallow, BB, Les and Sandra Brown, Tom and Jill Jones, Tony and Penny Burton, Paul Dickinson, Matt Waite)*

CONEYTHORPE [SE3958]

Tiger HG5 0RY [E of Knaresborough]: New landlord in pretty dining pub on green of charming village, fresh open-plan refurbishment with linked areas around bar and adjoining dining room, comfortable feel, wholesome food sourced locally with emphasis on good value pricing, John Smiths and Theakstons Best *(WW)*

CONONLEY [SD9846]

New Inn BD20 8NR [Main St/Station Rd]: Compact busy village pub with good value generous home-made food, well kept Timothy Taylors ales, good service, pig pictures, smart games room; unobtrusive piped music *(Dudley and Moira Cockroft, Bruce Bird)*

COXWOLD [SE5377]

☆ *Fauconberg Arms* YO61 4AD [off A170 Thirsk—Helmsley]: Picturesque old pub recently reopened under new ownership after long closure, attractive décor in both friendly bars and upscale dining room, Farrow & Ball colours, beams, flagstones, log fire and candles, welcoming landlady and staff, relaxed atmosphere, enjoyable food, well kept Theakstons and Thwaites; children welcome, delightful unchanging village, four newly refurbished bedrooms, open all day in summer *(Karen Powell, LYM, Nigel Long)*

CRATHORNE [NZ4407]

Crathorne Arms TS15 0BA: Large dining pub with good range of enjoyable generous food inc some interesting recipes and splendid Sun lunch (very popular then), Black Sheep and Timothy Taylors, friendly obliging staff, thriving atmosphere; pleasant village *(Alyson and Andrew Jackson)*

CRIGGLESTONE [SE3217]

Red Kite WF4 3BB [Denby Dale Rd, Durkar (A636, by M1 junction 39)]: Vintage Inn dining pub done like a Georgian house adjoining a cottage row, pleasant atmosphere and décor, their usual good value food and wide range of wines by the glass, good service, Timothy Taylors Landlord and Tetleys, log fire, daily papers; lots of tables outside, bedrooms in adjacent Holiday Inn Express *(Michael Butler, Derek and Sylvia Stephenson)*

CROSS HILLS [SE0045]

Old White Bear BD20 7RN [Keighley Rd]: Enterprising local brewing its own good Naylors ales, quick friendly service, wide choice of popular home cooking, five welcoming rooms off central bar, beams and open fires, pub games; piped music, games machine, TV *(Len Beattie)*

DACRE BANKS [SE1961]

☆ *Royal Oak* HG3 4EN [B6451 S of Pateley Bridge]: Solid and comfortable stone-built pub with Nidderdale views, good value often enterprising food from sandwiches up, staff

helpful over special diets, Rudgate ales and Tetleys, good wine choice, good log fire in dining area, interesting old photographs, pool, dominoes, cribbage; TV and piped music; children in eating areas, terrace tables and informal back garden, three good value character bedrooms (bar below can stay lively till late), good breakfast *(LYM, Mrs M Tippett, Pat and Tony Martin)*

DALEHOUSE [NZ7717]

Fox & Hounds TS13 5DT [Dalehouse Bank, off A174 at Staithes]: Cosy and spotless country pub with friendly attentive staff, good usual home-made food from generous sandwiches through kippers and fresh fish to steaks, two or three real ales, fox and hounds theme; good walks *(Ben Williams)*

DEWSBURY [SE2622]

Huntsman WF12 7SW [Walker Cottages, Chidswell Lane, Shaw Cross – pub signed]: Cosy low-beamed converted cottages alongside urban-fringe farm, lots of agricultural bric-a-brac, friendly locals, Black Sheep, Timothy Taylors Landlord and Chidswell (brewed for them by Tom Woods), hot log fire, small front extension; no food evening or Sun/Mon lunchtime, busy evenings *(Michael Butler)*

Leggers WF12 9BD [Robinsons Boat Yard, Savile Town Wharf, Mill St E (SE of B6409)]: Friendly if basic wharfside hayloft conversion by marina, low-beamed upstairs bar with Everards Tiger, several sensibly priced guest and bottled belgian beers, farm cider, pies and sandwiches or filled rolls all day, real fire, helpful staff, daily papers, lots of old brewery and pub memorabilia, pool; picnic-sets outside, Calder boat trips, open all day *(Michael Butler, J R Ringrose, the Didler)*

Shepherds Boy WF13 2RP [Huddersfield Rd, Ravensthorpe]: Bargain generous basic lunchtime food, four Ossett ales and interesting guest beers, good range of foreign lagers and good choice of bottled beers *(Andy and Jill Kassube)*

☆ *West Riding Licensed Refreshment Rooms* WF13 1HF [Station, Wellington Rd]: Busy three-room early Victorian station bar on southbound platform, particularly well kept Anglo Dutch (from the related local brewery), Black Sheep, Timothy Taylors and other changing ales, farm ciders, bargain wkdy lunchtime food on scrubbed tables, popular pie night Tues and curry night Weds, daily papers, friendly staff, coal fire, lots of steam memorabilia inc paintings by local artists, jazz nights; disabled access, open all day *(Andy and Jill Kassube, the Didler)*

DONCASTER [SE5702]

Corner Pin DN1 3AH [St Sepulchre Gate W, Cleveland St]: Plushly refurbished beamed lounge with old local pub prints, welsh dresser and china, John Smiths and interesting guest beers, good value traditional food from fine hot sandwiches to cheap Sun roast, friendly landlady and locals, cheery bar with darts, games machine and TV; open all day *(the Didler)*

Hare & Tortoise DN4 7PB [Parrots Corner, Bawtry Rd, Bessacarr (A638)]: Useful Vintage Inn dining pub, varying-sized antique tables in eight small rooms off bar, sensibly priced food all day from sandwiches up, friendly efficient young staff, choice of real ales and good range of wines by the glass, log fire *(Mrs Hazel Rainer, W W Burke, Stephen Woad)*

Leopard DN1 3AA [West St]: Lively and friendly, with superb tiled façade, John Smiths, local Glentworth and guest beers, cheap basic lunchtime food, lounge with lots of bric-a-brac and children's games, basic bar area with pool and darts; nostalgic juke box, TV, games machine, good live music upstairs, can get very busy; disabled access, open all day *(the Didler)*

Plough DN1 1SF [W Laith Gate, by Frenchgate shopping centre]: Old-fashioned small local with low-priced ales such as Bass and Blackpool, old town maps, friendly long-serving licensees and chatty regulars, bustling front room with darts and dominoes (and sports TV), quieter back lounge; tiny central courtyard, open all day (Sun afternoon break) *(the Didler, Pete Baker)*

DORE [SK3081]
Dore Moor Inn S17 3AB [A625 Sheffield—Castleton]: Busy extended Vintage Inn on edge of Peak District, popular for early evening family meals; good value ample food, fine choice of wines by the glass, good coffee with refills, real ales, hard-working friendly staff, superb central log fires, lots of stripped pine, nice flower arrangements; tables outside, views over Sheffield *(Pete Coxon, Revd John Hibberd)*

DRIFFIELD [TA0257]
Bell YO25 6AN [Market Pl]: Elegant and well run 18th-c coaching hotel, friendly and relaxed, with long spaciously comfortable red plush bar, well kept ales such as Hambleton Stallion and Tom Woods Shepherds Delight and Bomber Command, flexible eating arrangements from bistro-style stripped-brick former Corn Exchange with lots of leafy-looking hanging baskets to delightful old-fashioned restaurant; children welcome, comfortable bedrooms, open all day (Sun afternoon break) *(Paul and Ursula Randall, John Robertson)*

EASINGWOLD [SE5270]
☆ *George* YO61 3AD [Market Pl]: Neat, bright and airy market town hotel popular with older people, pleasant bustle though quiet corners even when busy, carefully presented food inc generous sandwiches, good service by cheerful staff, Black Sheep, Moorhouses, Timothy Taylors Landlord and guest beers, warm log fires, interesting bric-a-brac; comfortable bedrooms, good breakfast *(David Greene, Janet and Peter Race, Roger A Bellingham, Derek and Sylvia Stephenson, Andy and Jill Kassube, Pete Coxon, Margaret Dickinson)*

EAST MARTON [SD9050]
Cross Keys BD23 3LP [A59 Gisburn—Skipton]: Roomy and civilised, attractively set back behind small green nr Leeds & Liverpool Canal (and Pennine Way), abstract prints on pastel walls contrasting with heavy beams, antique oak furniture and big log or coal fire, good range of generous food from enterprising sandwiches up, well kept ales such as Black Sheep, Copper Dragon, Timothy Taylors Landlord and Theakstons, decent ales, quick friendly helpful service, more restauranty dining room; quiet piped music; tables outside *(LYM, Len Beattie)*

EAST WITTON [SE1487]
☆ *Coverbridge Inn* DL8 4SQ [A6108 out towards Middleham]: Homely and welcoming unspoilt 16th-c country local with small character bar and larger eating areas off, good home-made food from tasty sandwiches to massive meals and prime local steak, lots of changing well kept mainly northern real ales, cheap wines by the glass, coal fire in old range; pleasant garden tables, bedrooms, open all day *(Mr and Mrs Maurice Thompson, David and Karen Cuckney, the Didler, LYM)*

EASTOFT [SE8016]
River Don DN17 4PQ [Sampson St]: Traditional village pub with two or three well kept changing ales from local breweries, June beer festival, enjoyable restaurant evenings Weds-Sat and all day Sun inc skillet meals and gargantuan mixed grill; orchard tables *(Rob Vevers)*

ECCUP [SE2842]
New Inn LS16 8AU [off A660 N of Leeds]: Attractive country pub in open country on Dales Way and nr Harewood Park, log fire in big comfortable lounge, good value food from sandwiches and bar meals to steaks and more enterprising dishes in dining area, well kept Timothy Taylors and Tetleys, friendly efficient service; tables and play area behind *(Andy and Jill Kassube)*

ELLAND [SE1021]
☆ *Barge & Barrel* HX5 9HP [quite handy for M62 junction 24; Park Rd (A6025, via A629 and B6114)]: Large welcoming pub, several good changing ales inc Black Sheep and local E&S cider, farm cider, pleasant staff, limited but generous low-priced tasty lunchtime food (not Mon), real fire, family room (with air hockey); piped radio, some live music; seats by Calder & Hebble Canal, limited parking, open all day *(J R Ringrose, the Didler, Stuart Paulley)*

ELSLACK [SD9249]
☆ *Tempest Arms* BD23 3AY [just off A56 Earby—Skipton]: Has been a real favourite for its atmosphere, good food and thorough reliability, but recently one or two disappointments have put a question mark over this record – we hope a temporary blip, perhaps related to the opening of their new bedroom wing; normally we'd expect good modern cooking, Black Sheep Bitter, Copper Dragon Golden Pippin, Timothy Taylors Landlord, Theakstons Best and a couple of guest beers, fine range of wines by the glass, three log fires in comfortable linked areas with quite a bit of stripped stonework, and

perhaps Molly the friendly black labrador; piped music; children allowed, tables outside, open all day *(Dr K P Tucker, Steve Whalley, Fred and Lorraine Gill, Geoffrey and Brenda Wilson, Karen Eliot, Dudley and Moira Cockroft, Mr and Mrs P Eastwood, G Dobson, Mrs R A Cartwright, Pat and Stewart Gordon, Trevor and Sylvia Millum, Jill and Julian Tasker, Brian Wainwright, LYM, John and Alison Hamilton, Mrs Sheila Stothard, Andrew and Christine Gagg)*

ELVINGTON [SE6947]

Grey Horse YO41 4AG [Main St (B1228 SE of York)]: Bustling village local with warmly friendly staff, wide choice of enjoyable food, well kept changing ales such as Black Sheep, John Smiths and Timothy Taylors Landlord, woodburners and comfortable restaurant extension; tables outside, bedrooms, open all day wknds *(David Carr)*

EMBSAY [SE0053]

Cavendish Arms BD23 6QT [Skipton Rd]: Pleasant pub next to steam railway station, with good value pubby food from sandwiches up, warmly welcoming landlady, Black Sheep, John Smiths and Theakstons *(M S Catling, Dudley and Moira Cockroft)*

Elm Tree BD23 6RB [Elm Tree Sq]: Popular well refurbished open-plan eating and drinking pub, good hearty home-made food lunchtime and from 5.30 inc good-sized children's helpings, modest prices, pleasant young staff, well kept ales inc Black Sheep, settles and old-fashioned prints, log-effect gas fire, dining room, games area; busy wknds esp evenings; comfortable good value bedrooms, handy for steam railway *(Mr and Mrs D J Nash)*

FILEY [TA1180]

Bonhommes YO14 9JH [The Crescent]: Friendly bar with several well kept ales such as Copper Dragon, Fullers, Wychwood and York; open all day till late *(Brian Daley)*

FINGHALL [SE1889]

☆ *Queens Head* DL8 5ND [off A684 E of Leyburn]: Warm and comfortable, with good log fires each end, some panelling, low black beams and lit candles, settles making stalls around big tables, friendly helpful young licensees, generous reasonably priced food, Black Sheep and Daleside, interesting well priced wines, good soft drinks, much extended back Wensleydale-view dining area, cards and dominoes; no dogs; children welcome, disabled facilities, garden tables sharing view, open all day *(J R Ringrose, BB, Julie Woffendin, Blaise Vyner)*

FLAMBOROUGH [TA2270]

North Star YO15 1BL [N Marine Rd]: Sizeable hotel with comfortable and pleasantly pubby bar and eating area, decent choice of enjoyable bar food inc game and fresh fish, restaurant; garden tables, comfortable bedrooms, huge breakfast *(Patricia and Brian Copley, Keith and Chris O'Neill)*

☆ *Seabirds* YO15 1PD [Tower St (B1255/B1229)]: Friendly recently redecorated village pub with shipping-theme

bar, woodburner and local pictures in comfortable lounge, wholesome food from sandwiches up, bargain lunches, fresh fish, good cheerful service, well kept Wold Top ale, decent wine list, smart light and airy dining extension; piped music; children and dogs welcome, tables in sizeable garden *(Carol and Dono Leaman, John and Sylvia Harrop, Patricia and Brian Copley, Susan and Nigel Brookes, LYM)*

FLAXTON [SE6762]

Blacksmiths Arms YO60 7RJ [off A64]: Small welcoming traditional pub on attractive village green, enjoyable food, well kept Black Sheep and Timothy Taylors ales, two cosy bars and simple dining room, no music *(Jane Taylor, David Dutton, Tim and Rosemary Wells)*

GARSDALE HEAD [SD7992]

☆ *Moorcock* LA10 5PU [junction A684/B6259; marked on many maps, nr Garsdale stn on Settle—Carlisle line]: Isolated stone-built inn with Black Sheep and its own Moorcock ale brewed down in Hawes, good value food all day from overstuffed sandwiches up, good choice of wines by the glass, welcoming landlord and helpful staff, pleasantly informal décor with non-matching furniture, log fire in small flagstoned bar, cosy corners in lounge bar; occasional live music such as classical guitar, tables outside with views of viaduct and Settle—Carlisle railway, bedrooms, open all day *(Mr and Mrs Maurice Thompson, Pat and Robert Watt, David and Karen Cuckney, Len Beattie, Bruce and Sharon Eden)*

GIGGLESWICK [SD8164]

☆ *Black Horse* BD24 0BE [Church St]: Quaint 17th-c village pub crammed between churchyard and pretty row of cottages, spotless cosy bar with horsey bric-a-brac and gleaming brasses, good simple reasonably priced food from sandwiches and baked potatoes up in bar or intimate dining room, nice home-made puddings, Tetleys and Timothy Taylors, friendly hands-on landlord and son, coal fire; three comfortable bedrooms *(Neil Whitehead, Victoria Anderson, Keith and Margaret Kettell, Martin and Alison Stainsby, Michael Butler)*

Harts Head BD24 0BA [Belle Hill]: Cheerful and quietly convivial family-run inn, real ales such as Barngates, Copper Dragon and Wells & Youngs, enjoyable food in bar and restaurant, good choice of wines by the glass; dogs welcome in public bar, bedrooms *(Mr and Mrs Maurice Thompson, Adam F Padel)*

GILLAMOOR [SE6890]

☆ *Royal Oak* YO62 7HX [off A170 in Kirkbymoorside]: Stone-built dining pub with good young staff under friendly hands-on landlady, Black Sheep Bitter and Riggwelter, John Smiths and Tetleys, good coffee and reasonably priced wines, roomy turkey-carpeted bar, heavy dark beams, log fires in two tall stone fireplaces (one with a great old-fashioned iron kitchen range), flowers and candles throughout, no music; comfortable modern bedrooms, good breakfast, attractive village handy for Barnsdale Moor walks, cl wkdy lunchtimes *(C A Hall, H O Dickinson, WW, David and Jane Hill, BB)*

GILLING EAST [SE6176]

☆ *Fairfax Arms* YO62 4JH [Main St (B1363)]: Attractive stone-built country inn, civilised and and comfortable, with cheerful quietly efficient staff, good appealingly presented food in bar and restaurant, big helpings, real ales such as Black Sheep and Jennings, good wine choice, beams and log fires; picnic-sets on streamside front lawn, pleasant village with castle and miniature steam railway, ten good bedrooms *(WW, Mr and Mrs P M Jennings, Michael and Anne McDonald, Michael Sargent, John and Verna Aspinall)*

GILLING WEST [NZ1805]

White Swan DL10 5JG [High St (B6274 just N of Richmond)]: 18th-c inn with well kept Black Sheep, log fire, enjoyable food in bar and dining room (bargain suppers Mon/Tues), pleasant accommodating staff, good local atmosphere, darts; attractive village *(J R Ringrose)*

GLAISDALE [NZ7805]

Arncliffe Arms YO21 2QL: Stone-built pub with traditional beamed bar, attractive contemporary dining room with good value food, real ales such as Black Sheep, Cropton Beggars Bridge and Timothy Taylors Landlord, takeaway fish and chips Thurs; five bedrooms *(Phil and Jane Hodson)*

GRANGE MOOR [SE2215]

☆ *Kaye Arms* WF4 4BG [A642 Huddersfield—Wakefield]: Very good firmly run dining rooms and bar, civilised, friendly and busy, enterprising proper food, sandwiches too (they bake and sell their own good bread), efficient staff, exceptional value house wines from imaginative list, hundreds of malt whiskies, log fire; keg beers; handy for Yorkshire Mining Museum, cl Mon lunchtime *(Stanley and Annie Matthews, Gordon Ormondroyd, Dr Rob Watson, LYM)*

GRASSINGTON [SE0064]

☆ *Black Horse* BD23 5AT [Garrs Lane]: Comfortably modern open-plan pub, very popular in summer, with cheerful entertaining service, good value food from good sandwiches and snacks up inc children's, well kept Black Sheep Bitter and Special, Tetleys and Theakstons Best and Old Peculier, open fires, darts in back room, small attractive restaurant; sheltered terrace, bedrooms comfortable, well equipped and good value, open all day *(Len Beattie, BB, B and M Kendall)*

☆ *Devonshire* BD23 5AD [The Square]: Handsome small hotel with good window seats and tables outside overlooking sloping village square, good range of generous food from well filled sandwiches and hot snacks to bargain two-course lunches in big popular restaurant, interesting pictures and ornaments, beams and open fires, pleasant

family room, good service from cheerful uniformed staff even though it's busy, buoyant mix of locals and visitors, real ales such as Black Sheep, Cains and Timothy Taylors Landlord, decent wines, top-up coffee; comfortable bedrooms, open all day Sun *(LYM, Alan Thwaite, Tony and Penny Burton, Paul Humphreys)*

Foresters Arms BD23 5AA [Main St]: Cheerful opened-up old coaching inn with friendly efficient staff, good value straightforward food, five changing ales such as Black Sheep and Wharfedale Folly, log fire, dining room off on right; pool and sports TV on left; children welcome, reasonably priced bedrooms, open all day *(B and M Kendall, the Didler, Fred and Lorraine Gill, Richard, Edna Jones, Rita and Keith Pollard)*

GREWELTHORPE [SE2376]

☆ *Crown* HG4 3BS [back rd NW of Ripon]: Comfortable two-room Dales bar with good value enterprising and generous food (not Mon lunchtime but all day Fri-Sun), friendly staff, Jennings real ales, log fires, separate back dining room; some good live music; children welcome, picnic-sets out in front, pleasant small village, good walks nearby *(Mrs M Granville-Edge, Tony and Jill Radnor)*

GUISELEY [SE1941]

Coopers LS20 8AH [Otley Rd]: Impressive café-bar with food from good lunchtime sandwiches through pastas and pies to evening steaks, local ales such as Abbeydale and Rudgate, jazz and comedy nights *(Andy and Jill Kassube)*

HALIFAX [SE0924]

Barum Top HX1 1NH [Rawson St]: Wetherspoons handy for cheap food all day, good range of beers and wines by the glass, balcony and family mezzanine; open all day *(John Wooll)*

☆ *Shears* HX3 9EZ [Paris Gates, Boys Lane; OS Sheet 104 map ref 097241]: Down steep cobbled lanes among tall working textile mill buildings, roomy locals' bar with bays of plush banquettes and plenty of standing space, Copper Dragon and Timothy Taylors ales, competent cheerful staff, good cheap generous lunchtime food from hefty hot-filled sandwiches up, local sports photographs; big-screen sports TV; seats out above the Hebble Brook *(BB, Sam and Christine Kilburn, the Didler, J R Ringrose)*

Three Pigeons HX1 2LX [Sun Fold, South Parade; off Church St]: Carefully restored 1930s pub with art deco fittings, ceiling painting in octagonal main area, original flooring, panelling and tiled fireplaces with log fires, well kept Ossett and local guest ales, friendly chatty staff, inexpensive popular wkdy lunchtime food, corridors and several rooms off; tables outside, handy for Eureka! Museum, open all day Weds-Sun *(Bruce Bird)*

HARDROW [SD8691]

☆ *Green Dragon* DL8 3LZ: Traditional Dales pub full of character, stripped stone, antique settles on flagstones, lots of bric-a-brac, low-beamed snug with log fire in old iron range, another in big main bar, well kept ales such as Black Sheep and Timothy Taylors Landlord, decent food from baguettes up, small neat restaurant; gives access (for a small fee) to Britain's highest single-drop waterfall; children welcome, bedrooms *(LYM, Peter Bloodworth, Susan Knight, Tom and Ruth Rees, David and Karen Cuckney)*

HAREWOOD [SE3245]
Harewood Arms LS17 9LH [A61 opp Harewood House]: Two comfortable rooms off busy hotel's spacious L-shaped lounge bar, good value food from sandwiches up (also breakfast and bacon and sausage sandwiches served till 11.30, and afternoon teas), friendly courteous staff, cheap Sam Smiths OB, decent house wines, good coffee, attractive dark green décor with Harewood family memorabilia, leisurely old-fashioned restaurant; back disabled access, bedrooms *(Stuart Paulley)*

HARMBY [SE1289]
Pheasant DL8 5PA [A684 about 1½ m E of Leyburn]: Small comfortable cheery two-bar local, welcoming licensees, well kept Black Sheep and Theakstons, lots of character, racing photographs, no food *(Stephen Woad)*

HARPHAM [TA0961]
St Quintin Arms YO25 4QY [Main St]: Comfortable and well run old white-painted village pub, friendly licensees and staff, wide choice of enjoyable good value food (not Tues lunchtime or Mon), well kept Courage Directors, John Smiths and Wold Top Mars Magic, moderately priced wines, some panelling, plates and photographs, spotless housekeeping, small dining room; piped music; attractive sheltered garden with new pond, three good value bedrooms *(Paul and Ursula Randall)*

HARROGATE [SE3155]
Coach & Horses HG1 1BJ [West Park]: Friendly bustling pub with local ales such as Daleside, Timothy Taylors and Tetleys, reasonably priced bar food, no piped music; open all day *(the Didler)*
Gardeners Arms HG1 4DH [Bilton Lane (off A59 either in Bilton itself or on outskirts towards Harrogate – via Bilton Hall Dr)]: Small stone-built house converted into friendly old-fashioned local, tiny bar and three small rooms, flagstone floors, panelling, old prints and little else; very cheap Sam Smiths OB, decent bar lunches (not Weds), big log or coal fire in stone fireplace, dominoes; children welcome, tables and play area in good-sized garden surrounding streamside garden, lovely peaceful setting near Nidd Gorge *(Michael Butler, the Didler)*
☆ *Old Bell* HG1 2SZ [Royal Parade]: Two-bar Market Town Taverns pub with handsome bar counter and friendly knowledgeable staff helpful choosing from their eight real ales such as Black Sheep, Copper Dragon Golden Pippin, Daleside, Roosters Yankee and Timothy Taylors Landlord, lots of continental

bottled beers, impressive choice of wines by the glass, good sandwiches with interesting choice of breads, good value hot dishes and quiet upstairs evening restaurant, no music or machines; no children; open all day *(Mr and Mrs P Eastwood, Dr Andy Wilkinson, Mr Tarpey, A S Maxted, Jo Lilley, Simon Calvert, Mrs J King, the Didler)*
Tap & Spile HG1 1HS [Tower St]: Friendly bare-boards local, central bar with two pleasant rooms off, up to ten changing ales inc local microbrews, helpful staff, good value basic lunchtime food, daily papers, old photographs, stripped stone and panelling; open all day *(the Didler)*

HARTOFT END [SE7493]
☆ *Blacksmiths* YO18 8EN [Pickering—Rosedale Abbey rd]: Good enterprising food inc fresh fish and veg and wider evening choice in civilised and relaxing 16th-c moorland pub, originally a farmhouse and gradually extended, three linked rooms with lots of original stonework, brasses, cosy nooks and crannies, John Smiths and Theakstons, good wines, friendly staff, open fires, attractive restaurant with cane furnishings; sports TV; children welcome, comfortable bedrooms *(S P Watkin, P A Taylor, R M Corlett)*

HAWES [SD8789]
Crown DL8 3RD [Market Pl]: Convivial traditional market town local with good range of good value quickly served substantial bar food, well kept Theakstons Best, XB and Old Peculier, good wines by the glass, quick service, coal fire each end; walkers welcome, children allowed away from bar, seats out on cobbled front forecourt *(Tom and Ruth Rees)*
☆ *White Hart* DL8 3QL [Main St]: Old-fashioned convivial local bustling wknds and Tues market day, quieter on left, wide choice of good value generous food from sandwiches to some interesting hot dishes in beamed bar and dining room, hot fire, Black Sheep, decent carafe wines, cheerful helpful staff, brisk service, daily papers, darts and dominoes; juke box; occasional craft fairs upstairs, good value bedrooms, good breakfast *(BB, Michael Tack, Tom and Ruth Rees, Lawrence Pearse)*

HAWNBY [SE5489]
Hawnby Hotel YO62 5QS [off B1257 NW of Helmsley]: Attractive pub with good choice of consistently enjoyable generous food inc imaginative up-to-date dishes in spotless inn, real ales inc Black Sheep and John Smiths, helpful welcoming service, owl theme in lounge, darts in tap room; views from pleasant garden tables, lovely village in picturesque remote walking country *(Arthur Pickering, Sarah and Peter Gooderham)*

HAWORTH [SE0336]
Haworth Old Hall BD22 8BP [Sun St]: Friendly open-plan 17th-c beamed and panelled building with valley views, three eating areas off long bar, log fire, stripped stonework, appropriately plain furnishings,

Marstons and Jennings ales, generous food from good sandwiches up, quick service by well trained cheerful staff; piped music; plenty of tables out in front, bedrooms, good breakfast, open all day *(the Didler)*

Old White Lion BD22 8DU [West Lane]: Wide choice of good value home-made food (all day Sun), Tetleys and Theakstons Best, friendly attentive staff, warm comfortable carpeted lounge with plush banquettes, soft lighting, beamed dining area; TV; children welcome, very handy for museum, spotless comfortable bedrooms, open all day *(Geoffrey and Brenda Wilson, George Atkinson)*

HEBDEN [SE0263]

☆ ***Clarendon*** BD23 5DE: Simple neatly kept country inn notable for consistently good enterprising changing food (not Mon) using quality local ingredients, splendid sandwiches too, well kept Black Sheep Bitter and Emmerdale, Timothy Taylors Landlord and/or Tetleys, good well described wines, friendly local licensees and good service, two-part bar and smallish restaurant, bric-a-brac and darts; three bedrooms with own bathrooms, close to good walks *(D W Stokes, Gordon Ormondroyd)*

HEBDEN BRIDGE [SD9827]

Fox & Goose HX7 6AZ [Heptonstall Rd]: Basic pub featuring quickly changing real ales, their house beer Slightly Foxed brewed by E&S Elland, several small rooms, occasional live music *(Tony Hobden)*

Hare & Hounds HX7 8TN [Billy Lane/Lands End Lane, Wadsworth – above E end of town]: Friendly helpful staff in well worn in traditional pub with enjoyable generous pub food inc Sun roasts, Timothy Taylors ales, roaring fire, playful boxer caller George, local artwork for sale; tables on terrace with lovely views, plenty of good walks (not to mention the walk up from the town), good bedrooms, cl wkdy lunchtimes, open all day wknds *(Bruce Bird)*

Stubbings Wharf HX7 6LU [a mile W]: Warm and friendly under new licensees, in good spot by Rochdale Canal with adjacent moorings, decent usual food (all day wknds), wide range of real ales inc local microbrews; open all day *(Tony Hobden)*

☆ ***White Lion*** HX7 8EX [Bridge Gate]: Solid stone-built inn with busy comfortable bar and country-furnished bare-boards back area with coal fire, good choice of sound reasonably priced home cooking all day (just lunchtime Sun), fish specialities, well kept Timothy Taylors Landlord and a guest beer, friendly service; disabled access and facilities, attractive secluded riverside garden, comfortable bedrooms *(V Brogden, David and Sue Smith)*

HECKMONDWIKE [SE2223]

☆ ***Old Hall*** WF16 9DP [New North Rd (B6117)]: Interesting largely 15th-c building, once home of Joseph Priestley, with lots of beams and timbers, mullioned windows, stripped masonry, snug low-ceilinged alcoves and

upper gallery room, cheap well kept Sam Smiths OB, enjoyable inexpensive food (not Sun evening, nothing hot Mon-Weds, darts, dominoes; fruit machine, piped music, TV; children welcome, open all day *(LYM, Gordon Ormondroyd)*

HELMSLEY [SE6183]

☆ ***Crown*** YO62 5BJ [Market Pl]: Welcoming and pleasantly furnished beamed front bar opening into bigger unpretentious central dining bar, separate dining room with conservatory area, good value decent food from sandwiches up, real ales, good wines by the glass, efficient staff, roaring fires; tables in sheltered garden behind, pleasant bedrooms *(Sarah and Peter Gooderham, BB, Margaret Dickinson)*

Feathers YO62 5BH [Market Pl]: Substantial stone inn with sensibly priced generous all-day bar food from sandwiches up, popular Sun lunch, well kept Black Sheep and Tetleys, good service, several rooms with comfortable seats, oak and walnut tables, flagstones or tartan carpet, nice prints, huge inglenook log fire, heavy medieval beams, panelled corridors; children in eating area, tables in attractive back garden, bedrooms, open all day *(LYM, Margaret Dickinson)*

☆ ***Royal Oak*** YO62 5BL [Market Pl]: Neatly updated two-bar inn with Marstons-related ales from impressive central servery, good value simple substantial food from sandwiches to Sun lunch, different evening menu, helpful chatty landlord, quick service even though busy, plenty of breweriana, pool in bare-boards back games area; piped music, TV; picnic-sets out behind, open all day, good bedrooms, big breakfast *(R N Lovelock, Margaret Dickinson)*

HELWITH BRIDGE [SD8169]

Helwith Bridge Inn BD24 0EH [off B6479 N of Stainforth]: Warm and cosy village inn, up to eight real ales in flagstoned bar, friendly regulars and walkers; by Settle—Carlisle railway *(Mr and Mrs Maurice Thompson)*

HIPPERHOLME [SE1224]

☆ ***Cock O' The North*** HX3 8EF [Southedge Works, Brighouse Rd (A644)]: Surprising find in portacabin on industrial estate: new tap for adjacent Halifax Steam brewery, and actually comfortable and thoroughly pubby inside, with half a dozen or more of their own frequently changing ales, a guest beer, good cordials, Burts crisps, discreet corner TV, and that's virtually it – pizzas can be delivered wknd evenings, may be bargain curry Weds; open all day wknds, cl wkdy lunchtimes *(Pat and Tony Martin)*

HOLME [SE1005]

☆ ***Fleece*** HD9 2QG [A6024 SW of Holmfirth]: Cosy pleasant L-shaped bar, Adnams Broadside and Marstons Pedigree, good coffee, good fresh pub food inc imaginative specials, OAP bargains and some special nights (best to book), warmly welcoming jovial landlord, pleasant staff, real fire, conservatory with nice flowers, pool/darts room; quiet piped music, Thurs quiz night;

tables out in front, attractive village setting just off Pennine Way below Holme Moss TV mast, great walks (they have plenty of leaflets, even walking socks and gloves for sale) *(Christine and Neil Townend, Barry and Yvonne Cox, Michael Butler, Gordon Ormonroyd)*

HOLMFIRTH [SD1405]

Bay Horse HD9 2JG [Penistone Rd, Hade Edge; B6106]: Simple welcoming local with enjoyable no-nonsense food *(Piotr Chodzko-Zajko)*

Rose & Crown HD9 2DN [aka The Nook; Victoria Sq]: Family-run stone-built local, friendly and basic, with several rooms, low beams, tiled floor, well kept real ales with plans for its own microbrewery, coal fire, pool room; occasional folk nights, tables outside, open all day *(the Didler)*

HORBURY [SE2918]

Boons WF4 6LP [Queen St]: Lively, chatty and comfortably unpretentious flagstoned local, Clarks, John Smiths, Timothy Taylors Landlord and three or four quickly changing guest beers, bare walls, Rugby League memorabilia, back tap room with pool; TV, can get crowded, no children; courtyard tables *(Michael Butler)*

Bulls Head WF4 5AR [Southfield Lane]: Large relaxed well divided pub, consistently good food inc tempting puddings and popular Sun lunch, attentive smartly dressed staff, Black Sheep and Cains, lots of wines by the glass, panelling and wood floors, linked rooms inc library, snug and restaurant; picnic-sets out in front *(Michael Butler, Mr and Mrs Ian King)*

HORTON IN RIBBLESDALE [SD8072]

Crown BD24 0HF [B6479 N of Settle]: Pretty pub by river, well placed for walkers (Pennine Way goes through car park, short walk from Settle—Carlisle line station), dark woodwork and lots of brass in low-ceilinged locals' bar and larger lounge, good fire in both, cheap and cheerful home cooking, well kept Black Sheep and Theakstons, nice wines by the glass, friendly helpful staff, restaurant, no music or machines; big attractive garden behind, good value comfortable bedrooms *(David and Karen Cuckney)*

HUBBERHOLME [SD9278]

☆ **George** BD23 5JE: Beautifully placed ancient Dales inn with River Wharfe fishing rights, heavy beams, flagstones and stripped stone, simple bar food from good value sandwiches to steak and local lamb, well kept Black Sheep Special and Copper Dragon Golden Pippin, good log fire, dominoes; no dogs, outside lavatories; children allowed in second room, tables outside, bedrooms, cl Mon *(LYM, Dr and Mrs Jackson, Richard Tosswill, Michael and Maggie Betton, Ben and Helen Ingram, Robert Wivell, Ann and Tony Bennett-Hughes, Terry Mizen, Blaise Vyner)*

HUDDERSFIELD [SE1416]

Albert HD1 2QF [Victoria Lane]: Well preserved high Victorian pub with well kept changing ales inc Acorn, Black Sheep, Caledonian Deuchars IPA and Timothy Taylors Landlord, handsome mahogany, marble, mirrors, etched glass and chandeliers, traditional red leather wall seats, steps up to compact lounge and good value dining room; bedrooms, open all day *(the Didler)*

☆ **Head of Steam** HD1 1JF [Station, St Georges Sq]: Railway memorabilia, model trains, cars, buses and planes for sale, friendly staff, long bar with up to eight changing ales such as Caledonian Deuchars IPA, Copper Dragon, Cottage and Phoenix Wobbly Bob, lots of bottled beers, farm ciders and perry, fruit wines, pies, ciabattas, baked potatoes and bargain Sun roasts, four rooms inc comfortable eating area by platform, hot coal fire, front room with breweriana; jazz Sun lunchtime, can be very busy; open all day *(Mrs Jane Kingsbury, J R Ringrose, Peter Smith, Judith Brown, Pat and Tony Martin, C J Fletcher, the Didler)*

Rat & Ratchet HD1 3EB [Chapel Hill]: Flagstoned local with several well kept Ossett ales and lots of guest beers, cheap lunchtime food (not Sun-Tues), friendly staff, more comfortable seating up steps, brewery memorabilia and music posters; open all day *(the Didler)*

Royal & Ancient HD5 0RE [Colne Bridge; B6118 just off A62 NE]: Roadside pub with well kept Marstons and related ales, log fires, food from sandwiches up inc popular Sun lunch, reasonable prices, attractive golfing theme bar with extended dining area; 200 yds from Huddersfield Broad Canal *(Gordon Ormondroyd)*

Shoulder of Mutton HD1 3TN [Neale Rd, Lockwood (off A616/B6108)]: Walnut-panelled four-room pub with well kept Timothy Taylors Landlord and guest beers, soft lighting; good juke box, big-screen TV *(the Didler)*

Spring Grove HD1 4BP [Spring Grove St]: Two-room pub reopened after careful refurbishment, great range of changing ales inc a Mild and a strong ale from ten handpumps, good range of vodkas and other drinks; back terrace, open all day *(the Didler)*

Star HD1 3PJ [Albert St, Lockwood]: Unpretentious local with seven changing ales particularly well kept by enthusiastic landlady, continental beers, farm cider, well organised beer festivals, bric-a-brac and customers' paintings, no juke box, pool or machines; cl Mon, and lunchtime Tues-Thurs, open all day wknds *(Andy and Jill Kassube, J R Ringrose, Gordon Ormondroyd, the Didler)*

Station Tavern HD1 1JF [St Georges Sq]: Open-plan bar by platform in station building, eight changing real ales, plans for café refreshments too, pool in one room; TV, live music Sat pm; open all day *(the Didler)*

White Cross HD2 1XD [Bradley Rd, Colne Bridge (A62/A6107)]: Six particularly well kept changing ales and nicely cooked bargain food in small simple two-room pub, popular Feb beer festival; open all day (Gordon Ormondroyd)

HUGGATE [SE8855]

☆ **Wolds Inn** YO42 1YH [Driffield Rd]: Traditional 16th-c village pub cheerfully blending locals' bar and games room with civilised and comfortable panelled lounge and decorous dining room, wide range of good generous food (meats especially well chosen), friendly family service, Greene King Old Speckled Hen, Timothy Taylors Landlord and Tetleys, pool and darts; benches out in front and pleasant garden behind with delightful views; may be cl lunchtime Mon-Thurs, bedrooms compact but clean and nicely appointed – lovely village, good easy walks, handy for Wolds Way (Mr and Mrs P M Jennings, WW)

HULL [TA1029]

Bay Horse HU2 8AH [Wincolmlee]: Popular unassuming corner local tied to Batemans, their beers kept well, good value basic food inc good home-made pies, pleasant licensees, big log fire, raftered extension lounge/dining room, interesting brewery memorabilia; open all day (the Didler)

George HU1 2EA [Land of Green Ginger]: Handsomely preserved traditional long Victorian bar, lots of oak, mahogany and copper, bargain lunchtime food inc good fish, well kept Bass and guest beers, good service; quiet piped music, games machines, can get very busy – get there early; children allowed in plush upstairs dining room, disabled access, open all day (LYM, Paul Crosskill)

Olde Black Boy HU1 1PS [High St, Old Town]: Appealing little black-panelled low-ceilinged front room with carved fireplace, lofty 18th-c back vaults bar with leather seating, interesting Wilberforce-related posters etc, good value food lunchtime (not Sun) and late afternoon (not wknds), also Sun breakfast, friendly service, several changing real ales such as Caledonian Deuchars IPA, country wines, old jugs and bottles, upstairs pool room and overflow wknd bar; darts, piano Thurs, games machine; children allowed, open all day (BB, the Didler)

HUNTON [SE1892]

Countrymans DL8 1PY: Welcoming and comfortable village inn, beams and panelling, interesting and enjoyable food, four real ales mainly from Masham, reasonably priced wines, dining room; seven bedrooms (Blaise Vyner, Ian Vipond)

HUTTON-LE-HOLE [SE7089]

Crown YO62 6UA [The Green]: Spotless bustling pub overlooking pretty village green with wandering sheep in classic coach-trip country, opened-up bar with adjoining dining area, good sandwiches and huge helpings of no-fuss food (all day Sun), efficient friendly service, well kept Black Sheep, lots of varnished woodwork and whisky-water jugs; children and dogs welcome, near Folk Museum and handy for

Farndale walks (Phil and Jane Hodson, Dr and Mrs R G J Telfer, Edward and Deanna Pearce, Sarah and Peter Gooderham)

ILKLEY [SE1147]

Ilkley Moor Vaults LS29 9HD [Stockeld Rd/Stourton Rd, off A65 Leeds—Skipton]: Under new management, with enjoyable food – not Sun evening – using local seasonal produce (they now bake their own bread), relaxing atmosphere, flagstones, log fires in both upstairs and downstairs bars, well kept Caledonian Deuchars IPA, Timothy Taylors Landlord and Theakstons Best, decent wines by the glass; open all day (Katherine Mawer)

INGBIRCHWORTH [SE2106]

Fountain S36 7GJ [off A629 Shepley—Penistone; Welthorne Lane]: Comfortable beamed country dining pub with enjoyable home-made food, real ales such as Black Sheep, John Smiths and Tetleys, good value coffee, log fires, roomy red plush lounge, cosy front bar and family room; well reproduced piped music; tables in sizeable garden overlooking reservoir with pretty walks, good bedrooms (Nigel and Sue Foster, BB, Phil and Helen Holt, Roger A Bellingham)

KEIGHLEY [SE0641]

Boltmakers Arms BD21 5HX [East Parade]: Split-level open-plan local with well kept Timothy Taylors Landlord, Best, Golden Best and guest beers, good value basic food all day, friendly landlord and staff, coal fire, nice brewing pictures; sports TV; short walk from Worth Valley Railway, open all day (the Didler)

Brown Cow BD21 2LQ [Cross Leeds St]: Friendly extensively refurbished local with particularly well kept Timothy Taylors ales and guest beers; open all day wknds (the Didler)

Cricketers Arms BD21 5JE [Coney Ln]: Popular for changing real ales, also farm cider and good value bottled beers; sports TV; open all day (the Didler)

Globe BD21 4QR [Parkwood St]: Comfortable friendly local by Worth Valley steam railway track, wkdy lunches, Timothy Taylors and a guest beer, farm cider, coal fire; tables out behind, open all day (the Didler)

KETTLEWELL [SD9672]

☆ **Blue Bell** BD23 5QX [Middle Lane]: Roomy knocked-through 17th-c pub thriving since takeover by Copper Dragon, their ales kept well, good food from sandwiches to lots of fresh fish, enthusiastic friendly service, good wine choice, snug simple furnishings, log fire, low beams and flagstones, old country photographs, attractive restaurant, daily papers; pool room; children welcome, picnic-sets out on cobbles facing Wharfe bridge, more on good-sized back terrace, decent bedrooms mainly in annexe, good breakfast (JJW, CMW, LYM, Len Beattie, Dr A McCormick, Bruce Bird, DA)

☆ **Racehorses** BD23 5QZ [B6160 N of Skipton]: Comfortable, civilised and friendly, with generous good value food from substantial lunchtime rolls and baguettes to local game, early evening bargains Sun-Thurs, well kept Timothy Taylors ales, good reasonably priced wines, efficient helpful staff, good log fire; dogs welcome in front bar, picnic-sets on attractive terrace, well placed for Wharfedale walks, good bedrooms with own bathrooms, open all day *(Sam and Christine Kilburn, BB, Len Beattie, B and M Kendall, DC, Dr D and Mrs B Woods)*

KILBURN [SE5179]

☆ **Forresters Arms** YO61 4AH [between A170 and A19 SW of Thirsk]: Next to Thompson furniture workshops (visitor centre opp) in pleasant village, with furniture from them, big log fire, good home-made food from good value baguettes to enterprising specials, welcoming father-and-son licensees, real ales such as Hambleton, John Smiths and Tetleys, side eating area, bar with pool room, restaurant; TV; well behaved children welcome, suntrap seats out in front, good value cheerful bedrooms, open all day *(LYM, Mrs Mahni Pannett, Andy and Jill Kassube, Margaret Dickinson)*

KILNSEA [TA4016]

Crown & Anchor HU12 0UB [Kilnsea Rd]: Unpretentious building typical of the area, in great remote location overlooking eroding Spurn Point bird reserve and Humber Estuary, single bar opening into two beamed lounges and linen-set restaurant, prints and bric-a-brac, well kept Timothy Taylors Landlord and Tetleys, low-priced wines, enjoyable reasonably priced straightforward food inc good fresh fish; piped music; picnic-sets in back garden and out in front facing Humber Estuary, four bedrooms, open all day *(John Robertson, Derek and Sylvia Stephenson, DC, Paul and Ursula Randall)*

KIRKBY MALZEARD [SE2374]

Henry Jenkins HG4 3RY [NW of Fountains Abbey]: Spotless pub with thriving local atmosphere, decent generous bar food at reasonable prices in small comfortable lounge bar with beams and brasses, real ales, attractive restaurant; Mr Jenkins is said to have lived in this appealing village from 1500 right through to 1670 *(Bill and Sheila McLardy, Tony and Jill Radnor)*

KNARESBOROUGH [SE3556]

☆ **Blind Jacks** HG5 8AL [Market Pl]: Charming and friendly multi-floor traditional tavern in 18th-c building, simple but attractive furnishings, brewery posters etc, particularly well kept Black Sheep, Timothy Taylors (inc their great Dark Mild) and other changing ales such as Copper Dragon, farm cider and foreign bottled beers, staff helpful in guiding your choice, bubbly atmosphere downstairs, quieter up; well behaved children allowed away from bar, open all day wknds, cl Mon till 5.30; Beer Ritz two doors away sells all sorts of rare bottled beers *(the Didler, Rona Murdoch, J R Ringrose, LYM)*

LANGSETT [SE2100]

Wagon & Horses S36 4GY [A616 Stocksbridge—Huddersfield]: Welcoming and comfortable main-road moors pub, blazing log fire, stripped stone and woodwork, enjoyable food inc good value Sun lunch, Theakstons, magazines to read *(Trevor and Judith Pearson, James A Waller)*

LANGTHWAITE [NZ0002]

☆ **Red Lion** DL11 6RE [just off Reeth—Brough Arkengarthdale rd]: Classic proper pub dating from 17th c, a favourite, homely and relaxing, in charming Dales village with ancient bridge; cheap nourishing lunchtime sandwiches, pasties and sausage rolls, well kept Black Sheep ales, Thatcher's farm cider, country wines, tea and coffee, character firm-viewed landlady; well behaved children allowed lunchtime in very low-ceilinged side snug; the ladies' is a genuine bathroom; seats outside, good walks all around, inc organised circular ones from the pub – maps and guides for sale *(Dr and Mrs M E Wilson, Ann and Tony Bennett-Hughes, LYM, Anthony Barnes, Arthur Pickering, David Thornton, David and Karen Cuckney, David and Jean Hall)*

LEAVENING [SE7863]

Jolly Farmers YO17 9SA [Main St]: Welcoming unpretentious village local, good choice of changing ales such as Timothy Taylors Landlord, good value pubby food (not Sun evening or Mon/Tues), lots of fresh veg, friendly licensees, smallish front bar with eating area behind and separate dining room, games room with pool; TV; cl Mon evening *(David Barnes, Christopher Turner)*

LEEDS [SE2932]

Cross Keys LS11 5WD [Water Lane]: Designer bar with polished wood floors, stripped brick, metal and timbers, four well kept ales such as Black Sheep, Copper Dragon, Marble Chocolate Stout and Roosters, good choice of imported bottled beers, enjoyable food (not Sun evening) with an up-to-date take on local tradition; tables under big canvas parasols in sheltered courtyard, open all day *(Andy and Jill Kassube)*

Duck & Drake LS2 7DR [Kirkgate, between indoor market and Parish Church]: Basic two-room proper pub with a dozen or more interesting reasonably priced real ales from central servery, farm cider, pleasant hard-working staff, good coal fires, bare boards, beer posters and mirrors, low-priced wkdy lunchtime bar snacks, games room with Yorkshire doubles dartboard as well as pool etc; juke box, big-screen TV, games machines; open all day *(Pete Baker, the Didler, Joe Green)*

Garden Gate LS10 2QB [Whitfield Pl, Hunslet]: Basic well used local interesting for its untouched flagstoned Victorian layout and intricate glass, ceramics and woodwork, with various rooms off central drinking corridor, Tetleys Bitter and Mild, farm cider, no food; open all day *(BB, the Didler)*

Grove LS11 5PL [Back Row, Holbeck]: Unspoilt 1930s-feel local, three or four rooms off drinking corridor, up to eight changing ales inc Adnams and Caledonian Deuchars IPA, farm cider; open all day

(the Didler, Mark and Diane Grist)

Palace LS2 7DJ [Kirkgate]: Pleasantly uncityfied, with stripped boards and polished panelling, unusual lighting from electric candelabra to mock street lamps, lots of old prints, friendly helpful staff, good value lunchtime food till 7 from sandwiches up inc two-for-one bargains and popular Sun roasts in dining area, fine changing choice of real ales, may be bargain wine offers; games end with pool, TV, good piped music; tables out in front and in small heated back courtyard, open all day *(the Didler, David Hoult)*

Scarborough LS1 5DY [Bishopgate St, opp stn]: Ornate art nouveau tiled curved façade, bare boards, barrel tables, lots of wood and stone, shelves of Victoriana, showy fireplace, half a dozen or more interesting changing real ales, farm cider, wide choice of cheap wkdy lunchtime food inc occasional special offers, friendly helpful staff, music-hall posters; very busy lunchtime and early evening, machines, big-screen sports TV; open all day *(the Didler)*

Viaduct LS1 3DL [Lower Briggate]: Pleasantly furnished long narrow bar, lots of wood, Tetleys and guest ales, popular lunchtime food, friendly helpful staff; actively caters for disabled customers, attractive back garden, open all day exc Sun afternoon *(the Didler)*

☆ **Victoria** LS1 3DL [Gt George St, just behind Town Hall]: Opulent bustling early Victorian pub with grand cut and etched mirrors, impressive globe lamps extending from the majestic bar, imposing carved beams, booths with working snob-screens in lounge, smaller rooms off, changing ales such as Black Sheep and Timothy Taylors, friendly efficient service by smart bar staff, reasonably priced food 12-6 from sandwiches and light dishes up in luncheon room with end serving hatch; open all day *(the Didler)*

☆ **Whitelocks** LS1 6HB [Turks Head Yard, off Briggate]: Classic Victorian survivor with long narrow old-fashioned bar, tiled counter, stained glass, grand mirrors, heavy copper-topped tables and red plush, with Caledonian Deuchars IPA, John Smiths, Theakstons Best and Old Peculier and six guest beers, and tables out in the narrow courtyard; has long been a favourite, but some recent lapses – we hope temporary – take it out of the very top rank; children in restaurant and top bar, live music Fri, open all day *(David Carr, Neil Whitehead, Victoria Anderson, the Didler, LYM)*

LELLEY [TA2032]
Stags Head HU12 8SN [Main St; NE of Preston]: Stylishly refurbished pub well run by long-serving landlady, enjoyable enterprising fresh food, Marstons Pedigree and John Smiths, decent wines by the glass, cheerful well turned out staff, sofas and a couple of high-stool tables, dining area one side and comfortable restaurant the other; TV *(Paul and Ursula Randall)*

LEYBURN [SE1190]
Black Swan DL8 5AS [Market Pl]: Attractive creeper-covered old hotel with chatty locals in cheerful open-plan bar, entertaining landlord, decent range of food inc popular Sun carvery, prompt helpful service, well kept ales such as Black Sheep, Marstons Pedigree, John Smiths and Timothy Taylors Landlord, good wines by the glass; no credit cards; children and dogs welcome, good disabled access, tables on cobbled terrace, nine bedrooms, open all day *(David and Karen Cuckney, B and M Kendall, Michael Tack, the Didler)*

LOCKTON [SE8488]
☆ **Fox & Rabbit** YO18 7NQ [just off A169 N of Pickering]: Smart and neatly kept by young brothers, one cooks enjoyable imaginative food, good sandwiches too, friendly efficient service, Black Sheep, plush banquettes, brasses, real fires, busy locals' bar with two pool tables, good views from comfortable dining area; tables outside and in sun lounge, nice spot on moors edge *(Michael Dandy, John H Smith, Sarah and Peter Gooderham, Colin and Dot Savill, Richard, LYM, Brian and Pat Wardrobe)*

LOFTHOUSE [SE1073]
Crown HG3 5RZ [the one in Nidderdale]: Prettily placed Dales pub, friendly and relaxed, with hearty simple bar food from good proper sandwiches up, well kept Black Sheep Bitter and Ossett Silver King, good coffee, small public bar, eating extension where children allowed, darts; bedrooms *(B and M Kendall)*

LOW BENTHAM [SD6469]
Punch Bowl LA2 7DD: New owners early 2007 quickly gaining support for their food, friendly efficient service, welcoming atmosphere, log fire, four real ales such as Black Sheep, Everards and Tetleys Mild, dining room *(Pat and Stewart Gordon, Karen Eliot)*

LOW ROW [SD9898]
☆ **Punch Bowl** DL11 6PF [B6270 Reeth—Muker]: Reopened after refurbishment by owners of the Charles Bathurst at Langthwaite (see main entries), fresh and light, with friendly staff, good food from lunchtime ciabattas up, a dozen good wines by the glass, well kept Black Sheep, log fire, leather armchairs, sturdy tables and chairs, minimal décor; great Swaledale views from terrace, 11 spacious stylish bedrooms, open all day in summer *(Bruce and Sharon Eden)*

MANFIELD [NZ2213]
Crown DL2 2RF [Vicars Lane]: Old-fashioned village local with enjoyable simple food such as baguettes and a few hot dishes, warmly welcoming regulars, Village Premium and a guest beer such as Mordue Workie Ticket, pool *(Andy and Jill Kassube)*

MANKINHOLES [SD9523]
Top Brink Inn OL14 6JB [Lumbutts]: Busy moorland village pub very popular for its good value well cooked straightforward food inc good steaks, several eating areas,

efficient friendly young staff, Boddingtons, Camerons Castle Eden, Timothy Taylors Landlord and a weekly guest beer; children welcome, fine views from conservatory and terrace tables, quite close to Pennine Way and nice walks to nearby monument on Stoodley Pike *(Tony Hobden)*

MARSDEN [SE0412]
Railway Hotel HD7 6DH [Station Rd]: Welcoming unpretentious tavern with four well kept ales, enjoyable reasonably priced home-made food from baguettes and filled baked potatoes to steak, good carvery Sun lunch, bargain wkdy early suppers, friendly young landlord; wheelchair access *(Stuart Paulley)*

☆ *Riverhead* HD7 6BR [Peel St, next to Co-op; just off A62 Huddersfield—Oldham]: Busy basic pub in converted grocer's, Ossett real ales, pubby food, perhaps also beers from the pub's own microbrewery down spiral stairs; unobtrusive piped music; wheelchair access, streamside tables, handy for Huddersfield Broad Canal and moorland walks, open all day wknds, has been cl till mid-afternoon wkdys *(J R Ringrose, the Didler)*

MARTON CUM GRAFTON [SE4263]
Olde Punch Bowl YO51 9QY [signed off A1 3 miles N of A59]: Comfortable and attractive, with well kept Black Sheep and Timothy Taylors Landlord, decent wines, cheerful staff, good food from imaginative sandwiches up inc ambitious evening menu, roomy heavy-beamed open-plan bar, open fires, brasses, framed old advertisements and photographs, restaurant, no piped music; children welcome, good play area and picnic-sets in pleasant garden *(Greta and Christopher Wells, LYM)*

MASHAM [SE2280]
Kings Head HG4 4EF [Market Pl]: Handsome stone inn in good position, two much modernised linked rooms with imposing fireplace and clock, well kept Theakstons ales and up to 20 wines by the glass, bar food (all day wknds), restaurant; piped music, games machine, TV; children in eating areas, good bedrooms in back courtyard area (some for disabled), open all day *(Mike and Jayne Bastin, Janet and Peter Race, Dr and Mrs Jackson, LYM, Angus Lyon, Pat and Tony Martin)*

☆ *White Bear* HG4 4EN [Wellgarth, Crosshills; signed off A6108 opp turn into town]: Bright and cheerful beamed and stone-built pub, small lino-floor public bar with darts, comfortable larger bare-boards lounge with coal fire, Caledonian Deuchars IPA, Theakstons and a changing guest beer, decent wines by the glass, good fairly priced food choice (not Sun evening) from sandwiches up, neat efficient staff; piped radio; metal tables and chairs out on terrace, open all day *(the Didler, Stuart Paulley)*

MEXBOROUGH [SK4799]
Concertina Band Club S64 9AZ [Dolcliffe Rd]: Friendly pubby club happy to sign in visitors and brewing its own good changing ales (may allow brewery tour at quiet times), also guest beers; large bar with stage and small games area with pool, other games and sports TV; cl Sun lunchtime *(the Didler)*

MILL BANK [SE0221]
Alma HX6 4NS [1½ miles off A58 at Triangle pub; Four Lane Ends]: Two cosy front bar rooms with pine furniture and country/fishing décor, home-made bar food inc pizzas, Timothy Taylors real ales, restaurant dishes in bright and airy bare-boards extension with fine Pennine views; bedrooms *(Andy and Jill Kassube)*

MIRFIELD [SE2019]
Navigation WF14 8NL [Station Rd]: By Calder & Hebble Navigation canal, interesting food using local ingredients in back restaurant, good Sun lunch and early evening bargains, good sandwiches in bar, well kept Theakstons *(Andy and Jill Kassube)*

MOULTON [NZ2303]
☆ *Black Bull* DL10 6QJ [just off A1 nr Scotch Corner]: New owner running this civilised and enjoyable dining pub much as before, good wines and spirits, individual furnishings, big log fire, dark-panelled side seafood bar with high seats at marble-topped counter, polished conservatory restaurant and even a Brighton Belle dining car; courtyard tables under trees *(Jill and Julian Tasker, LYM, Greta and Christopher Wells)*

MUKER [SD9097]
☆ *Farmers Arms* DL11 6QG [B6270 W of Reeth]: Plain walkers' pub in beautiful valley village, warm open fire, friendly staff and locals, Black Sheep and Theakstons, wines, teas and coffees, enjoyable straightforward food from sandwiches to generous pies, casseroles and so forth, simple modern pine furniture, flagstones and panelling, darts and dominoes; children welcome, hill views from terrace tables, self-catering studio flat *(the Didler, Arthur Pickering, LYM, J P Humphery, David Hall, Ben and Helen Ingram, David and Karen Cuckney, David and Jean Hall)*

MYTHOLMROYD [SE0125]
Shoulder of Mutton HX7 5DZ [New Rd, just across river bridge (B6138)]: Comfortable and friendly local, emphasis on bargain-price generous home cooking (not Tues) inc a couple of carvery joints, fish, good range of puddings, OAP lunches and children's helpings, family dining areas and cosy child- and food-free areas, well kept Black Sheep Best, Timothy Taylors Landlord and guests such as Copper Dragon, nice display of toby jugs and other china; streamside terrace *(Bruce Bird, Pete Baker)*

NORLAND [SE0622]
Blue Ball HX6 3RQ: Enjoyable food from sandwiches, baguettes and baked potatoes to Sun roasts, good puddings, Black Sheep and Timothy Taylors Landlord; plenty of tables outside, good views *(Pat and Tony Martin)*

NORTH DALTON [SE9352]

☆ *Star* YO25 9UX [B1246 Pocklington—
Driffield]: As we went to press, this
picturesque 18th-c inn was closed, waiting
for a new licensee; has been a nice spot,
with comfortable main right-hand eating
area, coal fire in pubby bar, Black Sheep,
John Smiths and Timothy Taylors Landlord,
several wines by the glass, some interesting
modern dishes in both bar and restaurant,
allowing children, and with bedrooms; news
please *(LYM)*

NORTH GRIMSTON [SE8467]

Middleton Arms YO17 8AX: Comfortable
dining pub, good value simple food from
sandwiches and baked potatoes up, well kept
Stones and Tetleys, homely dining area;
garden tables, nice Wolds-edge spot *(WW)*

NORTH STAINLEY [SE2876]

Staveley Arms HG4 3HT [A6108 Ripon—
Masham]: Neatly kept old country pub with
warmly welcoming helpful service, well kept
Marstons Pedigree and Theakstons, wide
blackboard choice of decent generous bar
food inc good carvery Thurs-Sat evening and
Sun lunch, sensibly priced wines by the
glass, high beams and flagstones, separate
dining area, some rustic bric-a-brac; handy
for Lightwater Valley, good value bedrooms
(Peter Adye)

NORTHALLERTON [SE3794]

Tithe Bar DL6 1DP [Friarage St]: Half a
dozen quickly changing real ales such as
Black Sheep, Caledonian Deuchars IPA and
Timothy Taylors, masses of continental
bottled beers, friendly staff, tasty food
lunchtime and early evening, traditional
settle and armchairs in one area, two rooms
with tables and chairs on bare boards (not
unlike a belgian bar), upstairs evening
brasserie; a Market Town Tavern, open all
day *(Mr and Mrs Maurice Thompson)*

NORWOOD GREEN [SE1326]

☆ *Old White Beare* HX3 8QG [signed off A641 in
Wyke, or off A58 Halifax—Leeds just W of
Wyke; Village St]: Large 17th-c building well
renovated and extended, small character
snug, lounge with beams and panelling,
friendly attentive staff, well kept ales such as
Timothy Taylors, good service, good choice of
sensibly priced food from sandwiches to meals
inc popular Sun lunch in imposing flagstoned
barn restaurant with gallery; picnic-sets on
front terrace and in back garden with
barbecue, Calderdale Way and Brontë Way
pass the door *(Gordon Ormondroyd,
Clive Flynn, Michael Butler)*

NOSTERFIELD [SE2780]

☆ *Freemasons Arms* DL8 2QP [B6267]: Busy
pub with lots to look at, flagstones, pews
and settles, low black beams hung with bric-
a-brac, big Queen Victoria prints, many old
enamel advertisements, hot coal fires, well
liked homely bar food, Black Sheep,
Theakstons Best, Timothy Taylors Landlord
and a guest beer, several wines by the glass,
dominoes; piped music; well behaved
children and dogs welcome, picnic-sets out

in front with pretty flower tubs and baskets,
self-catering flat, open all day Sun, cl Mon
(Pete Baker, LYM)

OAKWORTH [SE0138]

☆ *Grouse* BD22 0RX [Harehills, Oldfield;
2 miles towards Colne]: Comfortable old
Timothy Taylors pub well altered and
extended, their ales kept well, wide range of
enjoyable generous food all day, good
service, lots of bric-a-brac, gleaming copper
and china, prints, cartoons and caricatures,
charming evening restaurant; undisturbed
hamlet in fine moorland surroundings,
Pennine views, open all day *(Andy and
Jill Kassube, Geoffrey and Brenda Wilson,
Margaret Dickinson)*

OLDSTEAD [SE5380]

Black Swan YO61 4BL [Main St]: Refurbished
by new owners putting more emphasis on
the food side, good disabled access to the
comfortable back dining areas, not so easy
to the simple beamed and flagstoned bar
with pretty valley views from two big bay
windows, log fire, real ales such as Black
Sheep; children welcome, picnic-sets outside,
bedrooms in modern back extension,
beautiful surroundings *(WW, BB)*

OSMOTHERLEY [SE4597]

Queen Catherine DL6 3AG [West End]:
Welcoming family pub, friendly and
unpretentious, with old local prints and
simple modern décor, Tetleys and a guest
beer such as Hambleton, hearty helpings of
popular food all day, log fire, separate
dining area; children welcome, simple
comfortable bedrooms, good breakfast
*(Mrs Mahni Pannett, David Carr,
Michael Butler, Danny Savage, WW)*

☆ *Three Tuns* DL6 3BN [South End, off A19 N
of Thirsk]: Now small restaurant-with-rooms
rather than pub, reasonably priced stylish
and individual upmarket food (they warn
you it will take a while) in a bistro
atmosphere and setting, faux Rennie
Mackintosh décor mixing local sandstone
with pale oak panelling and furniture, no
real ales; children welcome, comfortable
and tasteful bedrooms, open all day,
good nearby walks *(LYM, Hunter and
Christine Wright)*

OSSETT [SE2719]

☆ *Brewers Pride* WF5 8ND [Low Mill Rd/Healey
Lane (long cul-de-sac by railway sidings, off
B6128)]: Friendly basic local with Rooster,
Timothy Taylors and its own Ossett beers
(now brewed nearby – the pub may still brew
occasional ales itself), cosy front room and
bar both with open fires, brewery
memorabilia and flagstones, small games
room, enjoyable lunchtime food (not Sun);
big back garden with local entertainment
summer wknds, nr Calder & Hebble Canal,
open all day wknds *(the Didler)*

OSWALDKIRK [SE6278]

Malt Shovel YO62 5XT [signed off
B1363/B1257 S of Helmsley]: Attractive
former small 17th-c manor house with
enjoyable food, well kept Sam Smiths OB,

friendly service, huge log fires, heavy beams and flagstones, fine staircase, simple traditional furnishings, two cosy bars, interestingly decorated dining room; views from good unusual garden *(LYM, Margaret Dickinson)*

OTLEY [SE2045]

Summer Cross LS21 1HN [East Busk Lane/Pool Rd]: Attractive up-to-date décor, well kept ales inc Black Sheep, enjoyable home-made food using local supplies, friendly atmosphere; views of Cheviots from big enclosed garden *(T Mills)*

OVERTON [SE2516]

Black Swan WF4 4RF [off A642 Wakefield—Huddersfield; Green Lane]: Traditional local, two knocked-together low-beamed rooms with lots of brasses and bric-a-brac, well kept John Smiths, popular Thurs quiz night (may be free food) *(Michael Butler)*

OXENHOPE [SE0434]

Dog & Gun BD22 9SG [Long Causeway; off B6141 towards Denholme]: Beautifully placed roomy moorland pub, bright and airy, with enthusiastic landlord and friendly regulars, good varied generous home cooking from sandwiches to lots of fish and Sun roasts (worth booking then), smart helpful waitress service, full Timothy Taylors beer range kept well, beamery, copper, brasses and delft shelves of plates and jugs, big log fire each end, padded settles and stools, a couple of smaller rooms, new restaurant extension, nice views *(Gordon Ormondroyd)*

PATRINGTON [TA3022]

Station Hotel HU12 0NE [Station Rd]: Light airy décor in sizeable main bar and conservatory restaurant, good range of above-average food from baguettes up all day, Tetleys and a couple of interesting guest beers, reasonably priced wines by the glass, courteous service; open all day *(C A Hall, Paul and Ursula Randall)*

POOL [SE2445]

White Hart LS21 1LH [just off A658 S of Harrogate, A659 E of Otley]: Former Vintage Inn now reworked in new more upmarket format of stylishly simple bistro eating areas and separate drinking part with armchairs and sofas, well kept Greene King Old Speckled Hen and Timothy Taylors Landlord, good choice of wines by the glass, enjoyable if rather pricy food inc sharing plates, friendly quick service *(Pat and Graham Williamson, Michael Butler, LYM)*

POTTO [NZ4703]

Dog & Gun DL6 3HQ [Cooper Lane]: Roomy tucked-away village pub with open fire in plush L-shaped bar with alcove seating, two dining areas, wide choice of bar food, friendly family service; bedrooms *(Neil and Anita Christopher)*

PUDSEY [SE2135]

Village Bar & Bistro LS28 5LD [Town St, Farsley]: Enjoyable food, good range of foreign beers, well priced cocktails *(Andy and Jill Kassube)*

RASTRICK [SE1421]

Globe HD6 3EL [Rastrick Common]: High above Brighouse, with bright fresh décor, friendly young staff, well kept Black Sheep and Tetleys, enjoyable food (all afternoon Sun), large attractive back dining conservatory *(Gordon Ormondroyd)*

RAWCLIFFE [SE6823]

Rose & Crown DN14 8RN [Riverside]: Thriving civilised local with well kept Timothy Taylors Landlord and three guest beers, some snacks; open all day wknds, cl wkdy lunchtimes *(Ben Pindar)*

REDMIRE [SE0491]

Bolton Arms DL8 4EA: Spotless traditional village pub with good plentiful home cooking from landlady's kitchen, popular Sun lunch, well kept Black Sheep, John Smiths, Theakstons and a seasonal beer, friendly helpful landlord, small neat bar and newly extended dining room, exemplary lavatories; popular with walkers, handy for Bolton Castle *(Mr and Mrs Ian King)*

REETH [SE0499]

Buck DL11 6SW: Friendly efficient staff, good value food in comfortable bar and restaurant, Black Sheep Bitter, Best and Special and Theakstons Old Peculier; annual jazz festival; very popular with hikers, with a few tables out in front, bedrooms, good breakfast *(Jill and Julian Tasker, M and GR)*

RICHMOND [NZ1700]

Castle Tavern DL10 4HU [Market Pl]: Small pub with Flowers IPA and Tetleys, generous bargain food (not Sun), some leather armchairs in part-panelled bar, steps down to dining room with panelling and stripped stone walls, lots of pictures and a stuffed carp *(Michael and Alison Sandy)*

RIPPONDEN [SE0319]

Beehive HX6 4NX [Hob Lane, off Cross Wells Rd]: Well run and welcoming small open-plan hillside pub with well kept Timothy Taylors ales and guests such as Moorhouses Pride of Pendle, flagstones and open fires, three steps up to dining area, good modestly priced food from bar snacks and early evening light dishes to fresh fish and other restaurant meals, quiet dog *(Simon Marley)*

RISHWORTH [SE0316]

☆ *Old Bore* HX6 4QU [Oldham Rd (A672)]: Comfortable and stylish dining pub with good food naming farm suppliers (best to book wknds), enthusiastic young staff, good choice of wines by the glass, Tetleys, Timothy Taylors and guest ales, plenty of bric-a-brac, old prints on individualistic wallpaper, flagstones and mixed furnishings; cl Mon *(Michael Jones, Rosemary Cladingbowl, David and Cathrine Whiting, Gordon Ormondroyd, John Proud)*

ROBIN HOOD'S BAY [NZ9504]

Bay Hotel YO22 4SJ [The Dock, Bay Town]: Friendly old village inn with fine sea views from cosy picture-window upstairs bar (downstairs open only at busy times), three real ales, log fires, good value generous home-made food in bar and separate dining area; tables outside, cosy bedrooms, open all day *(Amanda Russell, Arthur Pickering, Ian and Sue Wells)*

Olde Dolphin YO22 4SH [King St, Bay Town]: Snug 18th-c inn stepped up above sea front in attractive little town, convivial basic bar with friendly service, well kept ales inc Caledonian Deuchars IPA, good open fire, good value generous plain food inc local seafood, popular back games room allowing children, Fri folk club; piped music, can get crowded wknds, long walk back up to village car park; well behaved dogs welcome, cheap simple bedrooms *(Dr and Mrs Jackson)*

ROECLIFFE [SE3765]

☆ **Crown** YO51 9LY [W of Boroughbridge]: Nicely placed country inn with front seats overlooking quaint village green, and has been popular with readers, with an appealing flagstoned bar, comfortable lounge, spacious dining room, and bedrooms – scheduled to reopen in autumn 2007 after purchase by licensees of the Bay Horse at Kirk Deighton (see main entries), so should be a promising one to watch *(Michael Williamson, Michael Doswell, DC)*

ROTHERHAM [SK4490]

Hind S60 4EP [East Bawtry Rd]: Large neatly kept pub with decent food, friendly helpful staff *(Jayne Griffiths)*

SALTBURN-BY-THE-SEA [NZ6621]

☆ **Ship** TS12 1HF [A174 towards Whitby]: Beautiful setting among beached fishing boats, sea views from smart nautical-style black-beamed bars and big summer dining lounge with handsome ship model, wide range of inexpensive food inc fresh fish, well kept Tetleys, quick friendly helpful service, evening restaurant (not Sun), children's room; busy at holiday times; tables outside, smuggling exhibition next door *(Dr and Mrs R G J Telfer, LYM, Rona Murdoch, Michael Butler)*

SAWDON [TA9484]

☆ **Anvil** YO13 9DY [Main St]: Pretty high-raftered former smithy with friendly staff, enjoyable home-made food (not Sun evening), well kept Black Sheep and guest ales, immaculate housekeeping, feature smith's hearth and woodburner, lower-ceilinged second bar leading through to neat dining room, turkey carpet throughout; comfortable warm bedrooms *(Keith and Margaret Kettell, BB)*

SCARBOROUGH [TA0487]

Highlander YO11 2AF [Esplanade]: Clean, bright and comfortable, with magnificent collection of whiskies (tartan curtains and carpet too), well kept Tetleys and changing ales such as Fullers London Pride, good value pub food from generous sandwiches and toasties up, friendly obliging service, civilised atmosphere, sea views from front bar; front courtyard tables, bedrooms, handy for South Bay beach *(Margaret and Roy Randle)*

Leeds Arms YO11 1QW [St Marys St]: Proper traditional pub, interesting and friendly,

with lots of fishing and RNLI memorabilia, great atmosphere, no food or music *(Margaret and Roy Randle)*

Lord Rosebery YO11 1JW [Westborough]: Recently refurbished Wetherspoons in former Co-op (and once the local Liberal HQ), very busy and lively evenings, in traffic-free central shopping area; galleried upper bar, good beer range, enjoyable quickly served food inc Sun roast, obliging staff, local prints; disabled facilities, open all day *(MDN, David Carr)*

Scarborough Arms YO11 1HU [North Terr]: Comfortably unpretentious mock-Tudor pub, walls decorated with weaponry, good value filling meals (not Sun evening), Marstons, John Smiths Bitter and Magnet and a guest beer, helpful landlady, friendly staff, warm open range, darts, pool; children welcome, good outside seating, open all day *(Gordon Ormondroyd, David Carr)*

SCAWTON [SE5483]

☆ **Hare** YO7 2HG [off A170 Thirsk—Helmsley]: Warmly welcoming new owners doing good carefully cooked food, not cheap but rewarding, in attractive dining pub with well spaced stripped pine tables, heavy beams and some flagstones, old-fashioned range and woodburner, appealing prints, good wines by the glass, real ales; children welcome, open all day summer, cl Mon *(LYM, Michael and Anne McDonald, John Lane, WW, Peter and Anne-Marie O'Malley)*

SCHOLES [SK3895]

Bay Horse S61 2RQ [E of M1 junction 35 via A629]: Friendly and chatty village pub with real ales such as Timothy Taylors Landlord, food inc popular Sun roast; piped pop music; children welcome, disabled facilities, picnic-sets and play area in garden, open all day wknds, cl wkdy lunchtimes *(JJW, CMW)*

SEAMER [TA0183]

Copper Horse YO12 4RF [just S of Scarboro; Main St]: Good choice of generous tasty usual food in friendly dining areas off main bar, bright and clean with beams, brasses, stripped stone, good wood-floored and part carpeted, eager-to-please staff, John Smiths and Theakstons; pretty village *(Keith and Margaret Kettell)*

SETTLE [SD8163]

☆ **Golden Lion** BD24 9DU [B6480 (main rd through town), off A65 bypass]: Thriving atmosphere in well run market town inn with surprisingly grand staircase sweeping down into old-fashioned baronial-style high-beamed hall bar, lovely log fire, comfortable settles, plush seats, brass, prints and chinese plates on dark panelling; local and guest ales, decent wines by the glass, well priced food (all day wknds) inc popular pizzas and interesting specials, splendid dining room; public bar with darts, pool, games machines and TV; children in eating area, 12 good-sized comfortable bedrooms, hearty breakfast, open all day *(Michael Butler, Michael and Maggie Betton, LYM, John and Helen Rushton, Gerry Miller)*

☆ **Royal Oak** BD24 9ED [Market Pl (B6480, off A65 bypass)]: Large market-town inn with lots of highly waxed ornate oak panelling in spotless roomy and congenial open-plan bar, friendly staff, well kept mainly local ales, comfortable seats around brass-topped tables, restaurant, corner pool area; live music Sat; children welcome, comfortable bedrooms, good breakfast, open all day *(Michael Butler, LYM)*

SHEFFIELD [SK3687]

Bankers Draft S1 2GH [Market Pl]: Wetherspoons bank conversion, clean, tidy and very popular, bars on two roomy floors, standard food all day, good range of real ales, decent wines, friendly staff, lots of old prints; good disabled facilities, open all day from 10.30 *(Mrs Hazel Rainer)*

Bath S3 7QL [Victoria St, off Glossop Rd]: Two small colourfully restored bare-boards rooms with friendly staff, well kept changing mainly more or less local real ales from central servery, lunchtime bar food (not Sat), nice woodwork, tiles and glass; open all day, cl Sun lunchtime *(C J Fletcher, Pete Baker, Mrs Hazel Rainer, the Didler)*

☆ **Cask & Cutler** S3 7EQ [Henry St; Shalesmoor tram stop right outside]: Unpretentious and relaxed real ale pub continuing much as before under new landlord, some redecoration but same staff and fine changing range of up to ten real ales, dutch and belgian bottled beers, farm ciders and perry, coal fire in lounge on left, daily papers, pub games, good Nov beer festival; wheelchair access, tables in nice back garden, open all day Fri/Sat, has been cl Mon lunchtime *(David Carr, the Didler, Pete Baker)*

Cocked Hat S9 3TG [just off Attercliffe Common (A6178)]: Largely open-plan, tasteful dark colours, brewery memorabilia, well kept Marstons Pedigree, good value lunchtime food, welcoming landlord; quiet evenings *(Mrs Hazel Rainer, David Carr)*

Corner Pin S4 7QN [Carlisle St East]: Former 1860s tavern reopened after restoration, changing real ales such as Abbeydale, Acorn, Bradfield and Ossett, bar food changing daily, basic locals' bar, former dram shop now serving as quiet lounge; cl 8.30 Mon-Thurs, open all day Fri/Sat, cl Sun *(the Didler)*

☆ **Devonshire Cat** S1 4HG [Wellington St (some local parking)]: Bright and airy contemporary bar with plenty of room, polished light wood, some parquet, big modern prints, friendly staff knowledgeable about the dozen mainly Yorkshire real ales inc Abbeydale and Kelham Island, some tapped from the cask, eight foreign beers on tap, masses of bottled beers in glass-walled cool room, two farm ciders, tea and coffee, good value food more interesting than usual from end servery, plenty of board games; well reproduced piped music, wide-screen TV, silenced games machine, ATM, live music Weds, quiz night Mon; good disabled access and facilities, open all day *(BB, Mrs Hazel Rainer, C J Fletcher, the Didler, Brian and Anna Marsden)*

Gardeners Rest S3 8AT [Neepsend Lane]: Welcoming beer-enthusiast landlord now selling his own good Sheffield ales as well as several changing guest beers tapped from the cask, farm cider, continental beers on tap and in bottle, old brewery memorabilia, lunchtime food, daily papers, games inc bar billiards, changing local artwork; Thurs folk night, poetry/story-telling nights, Oct beer festival; disabled access and facilities, back conservatory and tables out overlooking River Don, open all day Fri-Sun, may not open till mid-afternoon other days *(the Didler, Pete Baker)*

Harlequin S3 8GG [Nursery St]: Comfortable open-plan pub with well kept Kelham Island and lots of guest beers, imports too, bargain fresh food, good landlady and staff; some live music; open all day *(the Didler)*

☆ **Hillsborough** S6 2UB [Langsett Rd/Wood St; by Primrose View tram stop]: Pub-in-hotel under friendly new young owners, eight quickly changing guest beers some from their own downstairs microbrewery, bare-boards bar, lounge, open fire, decent basic home-made food, daily papers, views to ski slope from attractive back conservatory and terrace tables; TV; good value simple bedrooms, covered parking, open all day *(the Didler)*

☆ **Kelham Island Tavern** S3 8RY [Kelham Island]: Very popular backstreet local, friendly and comfortable, with ten or so interesting well kept changing beers from small brewers, continental imports, farm cider, nice artwork, filled cobs and other lunchtime food (not Sun/Mon), Sun folk night; disabled facilities, attractive sheltered back terrace, open all day (Sun afternoon break) *(Mrs Hazel Rainer, Kevin Blake, the Didler, David Carr, Mark and Diane Grist)*

Milestone S3 8SE [Green Lane]: Compact pub reopened after long closure, enjoyable fresh food in bar and impressive upstairs restaurant, Kelham Island, Sheffield and Thornbridge ales, good range of foreign bottled beers, friendly staff, polished boards and appealing colour scheme *(the Didler)*

Red Deer S1 4DD [Pitt St]: Thriving backstreet local among Uni buildings, plenty of real ales from central bar, wide choice of good value simple wkdy lunchtime food, extended lounge with attractive raised back area; open all day, cl Sun lunchtime *(Bob, Mrs Hazel Rainer, the Didler)*

Red Lion S1 2ND [Charles St, nr stn]: Traditional local, comfortable rooms off welcoming central bar, ornate fireplaces and coal fires, attractive panelling and etched glass, good simple lunchtime food, small back dining room, pleasant conservatory *(Kevin Flack, Pete Baker, the Didler)*

Rising Sun S10 3QA [Fulwood Rd]: Great choice of Abbeydale and other ales and bottled beers, large pleasant lounge with games and reference books *(David and Ruth Hollands)*

Rose & Crown S6 4BN [Stour Lane, Wadsley]: Friendly 19th-c stone-built pub on several levels, four real ales, inexpensive generous wkdy food; no credit cards; terrace picnic-sets, views, open all day Sat (JJW, CMW)

Wadsley Jack S6 4BJ [Rural Lane]: Friendly early 19th-c pub with wide choice of enjoyable inexpensive food (not Sun evening) inc wkdy OAP bargain lunch, one or two real ales, good choice of wines by the glass, woodburner, teapot collection; piped music may be loud, games machine (JJW, CMW)

Walkley Cottage S6 5DD [Bole Hill Rd]: Warm-hearted 1930s pub, a surprise for the area and popular for half a dozen or more real ales and limited range of decent well priced food (not Sun evening) inc bargain OAP lunch Mon-Thurs and good Sun roasts, some take-aways, farm cider, good coffee and other drinks choice, daily papers, games room; piped music; children and dogs welcome, views from picnic-sets in small back garden with play area, lovely hanging baskets, open all day (Bob, JJW, CMW)

Woodseats Palace S8 0SD [Chesterfield Rd]: Wetherspoons cinema conversion, up to half a dozen or so well kept ales, friendly service, good value food all day, family area; TV, games machines; open all day (JJW, CMW)

SHERIFF HUTTON [SE6566]
Castle Inn YO60 6ST [village green]: Well kept cheap Sam Smiths OB, wholesome reasonably priced straightforward food from sandwiches and baked potatoes up (Pat and Tony Martin)

Highwayman YO60 6QZ [The Square]: Friendly old coaching inn nr Castle Howard, welcoming landlord, good value standard food from good sandwiches to delicious puddings and popular Sun lunch, John Smiths and Tetleys, decent house wines, log fires, oak beams in lounge and dining room, homely snug bar; good wheelchair access, big garden, attractive village with castle ruins and 12th-c church (Michael Butler, Martin and Alison Stainsby)

SHIPLEY [SE1437]
Fannys Ale & Cider House BD18 3JN [Saltaire Rd]: Interesting gaslit two-room roadside local with up to nine changing ales inc Timothy Taylors, foreign beers on tap and in bottle, farm cider; open all day, cl Mon lunchtime (the Didler)

Old Tramshed BD18 4DH [Bingley Rd]: Smart and roomy open-plan conversion with real ales such as Black Sheep and Timothy Taylors Landlord from curved counter, friendly service, good food choice inc set meal deals, steps down to part with sofas, armchairs and grand piano, more up in carpeted galleries; children welcome, open all day, cl Mon (Andy and Jill Kassube, Karen Eliot, Gordon Ormondroyd)

SICKLINGHALL [SE3648]
Scotts Arms LS22 4BD [Main St]: Hospitable and interesting olde-worlde pub with long blackboard menus of good generous food,

nice rambling layout, low beams, old timbers, log fire in double-sided fireplace, good service, well kept Timothy Taylors Landlord and Theakstons Old Peculier, good coffee and wine range, daily papers; big garden with play area (J R Ringrose, LYM, WW)

SKIPTON [SD9851]
Cock & Bottle BD23 1RD [Swadford St]: Old-fashioned open-plan local in former coaching inn, real ales, simple enjoyable food, welcoming licensees, beams and bare boards; small play area out behind (the Didler)

☆ **Royal Shepherd** BD23 1LB [Canal St; from Water St (A65) turn into Coach St, then left after bridge over Leeds & Liverpool Canal]: Convivial old-fashioned local with big bustling bar, snug and dining room, open fires, local Copper Dragon ales, decent wine, unusual sensibly priced whiskies, cheery landlord and brisk service, low-priced standard food from sandwiches and baked potatoes up, photographs of Yorks CCC in its golden days; games and piped music; children welcome in side room, tables out in pretty spot by canal (the Didler, John and Alison Hamilton, Stephen R Holman)

☆ **Woolly Sheep** BD23 1HY [Sheep St]: Big bustling pub with full range of Timothy Taylors ales, prompt friendly enthusiastic service, daily papers, two beamed bars off flagstoned passage, exposed brickwork, stone fireplace, lots of sheep prints and bric-a-brac, roomy comfortable lunchtime dining area, usual cheap generous food (plenty for children); unobtrusive piped music; spacious pretty garden, six good value bedrooms, good breakfast (Clive Flynn, Dr and Mrs M E Wilson, J R Ringrose)

SLAITHWAITE [SE0712]
White House HD7 5TY [Chain Rd (B6107 Meltham—Marsden)]: Attractive moorland inn with huge helpings of enjoyable home-made food, real ales such as Timothy Taylors Landlord, good choice of wines by the glass, good service, small bar with log fire, comfortable lounge on right, pleasant restaurant area on left; children welcome, tables out on front flagstones (Dr and Mrs Michael Smith, J R Ringrose)

SLEDMERE [SE9364]
Triton YO25 3XQ [junction B1252/B1253 NW of Gt Driffield]: Newly refurbished 18th-c inn in attractive spot, good log fire in comfortable carpeted lounge bar, good choice of food (all day Sun), well kept Greene King Old Speckled Hen and Wold Top, games room with darts, dominoes and pool; children welcome, five neat bedrooms, open all day Sun, cl Mon lunchtime (LYM, Roger A Bellingham)

SNAINTON [TA9182]
Coachman YO13 9PL [Pickering Rd W (A170)]: Interesting choice of good food at a price in beautiful dining room (they like you to book), Black Sheep in quiet bar (Peter Burton)

SNAPE [SE2684]

☆ *Castle Arms* DL8 2TB [off B6268 Masham—Bedale]: Comfortably updated low-ceilinged pub with good fresh enterprising food from interesting sandwiches up, well kept Marstons-related ales, helpful service, decent wines, good coffee, relaxed happy atmosphere, flagstoned bar with big inglenook coal fire, second flagstoned room and attractive rather smart small carpeted dining room, sporting prints; unobtrusive piped music; children and dogs welcome, tables in charming courtyard, pretty village very handy for Thorp Perrow, comfortable bedrooms (*Michael Swallow, BB*)

SOUTH CAVE [SE9231]

☆ *Fox & Coney* HU15 2AT [Market Pl (A1034)]: Pleasant pub with generous enjoyable standard food from baguettes to steaks, friendly efficient staff, real ales such as Caledonian Deuchars IPA and Timothy Taylors Landlord from central servery, coal fire, bright and comfortable warmly Victorian open-plan main bar and dining areas; bedrooms in adjoining hotel (*DC, Dr D J and Mrs S C Walker, Kay and Alistair Butler*)

SOWERBY BRIDGE [SE0523]

Puzzle Hall HX6 2QG [Hollins Mill Lane, off A58]: Welcoming nicely old-fashioned two-room bareboards pub in converted joinery workshop, seating from pews to comfortable sofas, at least eight real ales, lunchtime food planned, poetry readings, live music in back yard (covered in inclement weather); open all day (*Tony Hobden*)

Rams Head HX6 2AZ [Wakefield Rd]: Brews its own good well priced Ryburn ales, open fire in well divided stripped stone lounge bar, good value home-made food in L-shaped dining area (*Pete Baker*)

Shepherds Rest HX6 2BD [Bolton Brow]: Two-room pub with full Ossett ale range; suntrap terrace, open all day wknds, cl wkdy lunchtimes (*Pat and Tony Martin*)

SPROTBROUGH [SE5301]

☆ *Boat* DN5 7NB [3½ miles from M18 junction 2, less from A1(M) junction 36 via A630 and Mill Lane; Nursery Lane]: Roomy stone-built Vintage Inn dining pub, sensibly priced food from sandwiches and crusty buns to steak all day till 10, several snug flagstoned areas, log fires in big stone fireplaces, latticed windows, dark beams, well kept Black Sheep, John Smiths and Tetleys, plenty of wines by the glass, prompt friendly uniformed service; unobtrusive piped music, games machine, no dogs; tables in big sheltered prettily lit courtyard, River Don walks, open all day (*GSB, Mr and Mrs Gerry Price, Derek and Sylvia Stephenson, DC, LYM, Trevor and Judith Pearson, Stephen Woad*)

Ivanhoe DN5 7NS [quite handy for A1(M)]: Large mock-Tudor Sam Smiths pub, friendly and chatty, with their OB at an appealing price, bargain pubby food (not Sun evening) from hot servery inc popular Sun carvery, three linked rooms with conservatory extension overlooking cricket ground,

uniformed waitresses, no piped music, games bar with pool; games machines; children in eating areas, tables out on flagstoned terrace with play area, open all day (*Mr and Mrs Gerry Price, JJW, CMW, JHBS*)

STAINFORTH [SD8267]

Craven Heifer BD24 9PB [B6479 Settle—Horton-in-Ribblesdale]: Friendly Dales village local, small, cosy and clean, with Thwaites Bitter and Lancaster Bomber, log fire, reasonably priced bar food; good walks (*Mr and Mrs Maurice Thompson*)

STAITHES [NZ7818]

Captain Cook TS13 5AD [Staithes Lane/Top of Bank]: Ruggedly old-fashioned and unpretentious local with changing real ales such as bargain-price Rudgate Viking, dining room (food Fri-Sun evenings and Sun lunchtime), back family games room with pool, live music most wknds; open all day (*Pete Baker*)

STAMFORD BRIDGE [SE7055]

☆ *Three Cups* YO41 1AX [A166 W of town]: Spacious Vintage Inn family dining pub in timbered country style, relaxed atmosphere, reliable food all day, good range of wines by the glass, real ales, good welcoming staff, glass-topped 20-metre well; good disabled access, children welcome, good play area behind, bedrooms, open all day (*LYM, David Carr*)

STARBOTTON [SD9574]

Fox & Hounds BD23 5HY [B6160]: Small Dales inn in pretty village, friendly landlord, big log fire in attractively traditional beamed and flagstoned bar, compact dining room, Black Sheep and guest beers, usual bar food (gets busy, so there may be quite a wait for a meal); may be piped music, dogs allowed in bar; children welcome, cl Mon (*LYM, Len Beattie, the Didler*)

STILLINGTON [SE5867]

White Bear YO61 1JU [Main St]: Warm and friendly olde-worlde village pub, enjoyable pub food (not Sun evening), Black Sheep, good choice of reasonably priced wines by the glass; cl Mon (*Mr and Mrs D J Nash*)

STOCKTON ON THE FOREST [SE6556]

Fox YO32 9UW [off A64 just NE of York]: Attractive village pub with good welcoming service, enjoyable food, well kept Black Sheep, good choice of wines by the glass, good value coffee, three cosy and comfortable linked rooms and separate dining room; tables outside with lots of hanging baskets (*Roger A Bellingham, Jane Taylor, David Dutton*)

STOKESLEY [NZ5208]

☆ *White Swan* TS9 5BL [West End]: Good Captain Cook ales brewed in attractive and neatly kept pub, also Camerons Castle Eden, friendly young staff, may be good value baguettes in summer, three relaxing seating areas in L-shaped bar, log fire, lots of brass on elegant dark panelling, lovely bar counter carving, hat display, unusual clock, no music or machines; cl Tues lunchtime (*Blaise Vyner, Michael Butler, the Didler, Pete Baker*)

STUTTON [SE4841]

☆ **Hare & Hounds** LS24 9BR [Manor Rd]: Attractive stone-built pub with cosy low-ceilinged rooms, wide choice of enjoyable food (not Sun evening) from sandwiches up, quick pleasant service even though busy (helpful with wheelchairs), well kept cheap Sam Smiths OB, decent wine, well behaved children in restaurant; tables, some under cover, in long prettily planted sloping garden, has been cl Mon (Mrs P J Pearce, LYM)

SUTTON-ON-THE-FOREST [SE5864]

Blackwell Ox YO61 1DT [Huby Rd]: Spotless beamed and flagstoned bar with log fire, two smart dining rooms with sofas and armchairs by another fire, helpful hands-on landlady, good food from bar snacks to enterprising restaurant meals; comfortable bedrooms (Graham and Doreen Holden)

TAN HILL [NY8906]

Tan Hill Inn DL11 6ED [Arkengarthdale rd Reeth—Brough, at junction Keld/W Stonesdale rd]: Basic old stone pub included for its wonderful remote setting on Pennine Way – Britain's highest pub, full of bric-a-brac and pictures inc interesting old photographs, simple sturdy furniture, flagstones, ever-burning big log fire (with prized stone side seats); chatty atmosphere, Black Sheep and Theakstons ales (in winter the cellar does chill down – whisky with hot water's good then), help-yourself coffee, cheap food, pool in family room; may be piped radio, often snowbound, can get overcrowded; swaledale sheep show here last Thurs in May; children and dogs welcome, bedrooms, inc some in extension with own bathrooms, open all day (N R White, LYM, Tim and Ann Newell)

THIXENDALE [SE8461]

Cross Keys YO17 9TG [off A166 3 miles N of Fridaythorpe]: Unspoilt welcoming country pub in deep valley below the rolling Wolds, cosy L-shaped bar with fitted wall seats, relaxed atmosphere, Jennings, Tetleys and a guest beer, sensible home-made blackboard food; large pleasant garden behind, popular with walkers, handy for Wharram Percy earthworks, comfortable bedrooms, good breakfast (the Didler, Peter Smith, Judith Brown)

THORALBY [SE9986]

George DL8 3SU: Prettily set Dales village pub, two smallish cosy linked areas with four well kept ales inc Black Sheep, sensibly priced bar food from sandwiches to steaks, interesting bric-a-brac and woodburner, darts and dominoes; walkers welcome, terrace tables, two bedrooms (R N Lovelock)

THORNE [SE6713]

John Bull DN8 4JQ [Waterside, just off M18 junction 6]: Enjoyable reasonably priced food inc generous bargain carvery all week (not Mon), real ales such as Timothy Taylors Landlord, decent wine by the glass, bar (dogs welcome) with chatting locals, dining area (Miss J E Edwards, Sue and Neil Dickinson, Kay and Alistair Butler)

Punch Bowl DN8 4BE [under a mile from M18 junction 6; A614 S]: Neatly kept and nicely furnished, with reasonably priced food, Old Mill ales, good lavatories (Ian and Joan Blackwell)

THORNTON DALE [SE8383]

New Inn YO18 7LF [The Square]: Early 18th-c old-world beamed coaching inn with well kept Black Sheep and Theakstons, good home-made food using local ingredients; courtyard tables, attractive roomy bedrooms, good breakfast, pretty village in walking area (Colin McKerrow)

THRESHFIELD [SD9863]

Old Hall Inn BD23 5HB [B6160/B6265 just outside Grassington]: Olde-worlde atmosphere in three knocked-together rooms, high beam-and-plank ceiling, cushioned wall pews, tall well blacked kitchen range, log fires, enjoyable sensibly priced food in bar and restaurant, well kept Timothy Taylors ales; children in eating area, neat garden (Janet and Peter Race, V Brogden, LYM)

THUNDER BRIDGE [SE1811]

Woodman HD8 0PX [off A629 Huddersfield—Sheffield]: Two roomy and spotless bars with fresh décor and light woodwork, welcoming service, good value food, well kept Timothy Taylors Landlord and Tetleys, upstairs restaurant; 12 good bedrooms in adjoining cottages (Gordon Ormondroyd)

THWING [TA0570]

☆ **Falling Stone** YO25 3DS [off B1253 W of Bridlington; Main St]: New licensees in comfortable pub with Wold Top Gold and Falling Stone brewed (originally just for the pub) on farm a few miles away, steps up to pleasant back pool room, decent food, extensive dining area – part conservatory; children in eating area, has been closed Mon/Tues, also lunchtimes Weds-Fri (Dr Ian S Morley, LYM)

TOCKWITH [SE4652]

Spotted Ox YO26 7PY [Westfield Rd, off B1224]: Welcoming traditional beamed village local, three areas open off central bar with well kept Black Sheep, Tetleys and Timothy Taylors Landlord, good choice of sensibly priced home-made food inc OAP bargains, attentive staff, relaxed atmosphere, interesting local history; open all day Fri-Sun (Les and Sandra Brown)

TODMORDEN [SD9223]

Masons Arms OL14 7PN [A681/A6033, S of centre]: Welcoming traditional local with particularly well kept Copper Dragon ales and one or two interesting guest beers, enthusiastic landlord, decent food till 6, pump clips on beams and interesting photographs and cuttings in two knocked-together rooms with darts, cards and pool in popular games end (Bruce Bird)

TOPCLIFFE [SE4076]

Angel YO7 3RW [off A1, take A168 to Thirsk, after 3 miles follow signs for Topcliffe; Long St]: Big bustling place with friendly helpful service, well kept ales inc John Smiths,

Timothy Taylors Landlord and Theakstons, wide choice of reasonably priced enjoyable food from good sandwiches up, decent wines, separately themed areas inc attractive and softly lit stripped-stone faux-irish bar, also billiards room and two dining rooms; unobtrusive piped music; tables outside, bedrooms, good breakfast *(Gerry and Rosemary Dobson)*

TOTLEY [SK3080]

Crown S17 3AX [Hillfoot Rd]: Old-fashioned country pub with two rooms off central bar, friendly landlord and good staff, four or five real ales and good choice of other drinks, short choice of good plain home-cooked food (not Sun/Mon evenings); TV; dogs welcome, picnic-sets outside *(JJW, CMW, James A Waller)*

UPPER HOPTON [SE1918]

Travellers Rest WF14 8EJ [Hopton Lane]: Imposing hillside pub with popular bargain carvery lunchtime Tues-Fri, Fri/Sat evenings and all day Sun, well kept Black Sheep and Tetleys, beams and stripped stonework; children welcome *(Gordon Ormonroyd)*

WAKEFIELD [SE3320]

Fernandes Brewery Tap WF1 1UA [Avison Yard, Kirkgate]: Upper floor of 19th-c malt store, Fernandes ales brewed here and interesting guest beers, farm cider, unusual breweriana, friendly atmosphere, bare boards and rafters; cl Mon-Thurs lunchtime, open all day Fri-Sun with lunchtime soup and sandwiches then, brewery shop *(the Didler)*

Henry Boons WF2 9SR [Westgate]: Well kept Clarks from next-door brewery, also Black Sheep, Timothy Taylors and Tetleys, in two-room bare-boards local, friendly staff, barrel tables and breweriana, side pool area; gets busy late on with young people, juke box, machines, live bands; open all day *(the Didler)*

Redoubt WF2 8TS [Horbury Rd, Westgate]: Busy and friendly traditional pub, four compact rooms off long corridor, changing ales inc Timothy Taylors Landlord, Rugby League photographs and memorabilia, pub games; family room till 8, open all day *(the Didler)*

Talbot & Falcon WF1 3AP [Northgate]: Smart town pub with friendly long bar, panelling and lots of prints, back lounge, Black Sheep and Tetleys, foreign bottled beers, popular reasonably priced lunchtime food, quick service; TV, games machines; bedrooms, open all day *(Mrs Hazel Rainer)*

Wakefield Labour Club WF1 1QX [Vicarage St]: Red wooden shed rather like a works canteen inside, small and chatty – it is a club, but you can just sign in; changing keenly priced real ales usually inc Acorn, Bobs and Ossett, belgian beers, may be fresh allotment veg; picnic-sets outside, cl lunchtime Mon-Thurs and Sun evening *(the Didler)*

WALES [SK4782]

Duke of Leeds S26 5LQ [Church St]: Comfortable 18th-c stone-faced village pub with good value fresh food (all day Fri-Sun,

at least in summer), early evening and wkdy OAP bargains, John Smiths, Theakstons and two or three guest beers, good wine and soft drinks choice, quick friendly service, long dining lounge, lots of photographs, brass and copper, flame-effect gas fire; piped music, TV, may be cl Sat lunchtime for private functions; children welcome, new tables outside, nearby walks *(JJW, CMW)*

WALKINGTON [SE9937]

☆ *Ferguson-Fawsitt Arms* HU17 8RX [East End; B1230 W of Beverley]: Wide choice of enjoyable food inc good value carvery in airy flagstone-floored food bar, good friendly service, real ale, decent wine, interesting mock-Tudor bars; tables out on terrace, delightful village *(Michael J Caley, June and Ken Brooks, LYM)*

WALSDEN [SD9420]

Bird i' th' Hand OL14 6UH [A6033 S of Todmorden]: More café than pub, but has proper bar with Tetleys, wide range of food ordered at kitchen door, three rooms, quiz nights; children welcome *(Tony Hobden)*

Cross Keys OL14 6SX [Rochdale Rd, S of Todmorden]: Friendly local with Timothy Taylors Landlord and a guest beer, food (all day Sun) in lounge extending into conservatory overlooking restored Rochdale Canal, public bar with pool and big-screen TV; terrace tables, moorings, lots of good walks (nr Pennine Way), bedrooms, open all day *(Tony Hobden)*

WELL [SE2682]

Milbank Arms DL8 2PX [Bedale Rd]: Sympathetically restored beamed bar, amiable landlord, consistently good interesting food inc small-appetite lunchtime menu, well kept Black Sheep and Viking, log fire *(Michael Doswell, Ian Vipond)*

WENSLEY [SE0989]

Three Horseshoes DL8 4HJ: Three smartly simple flagstoned rooms refurbished under welcoming new licensees, Wensleydale and guest ales such as Black Sheep and John Smiths (they may offer tasters), straightforward food (not Sun evening); outside lavatories; tables outside, open all day *(Ben and Helen Ingram)*

WENTWORTH [SK3898]

Rockingham Arms S62 7TL [3 miles from M1 junction 36; B6090, signed off A6135; Main St]: Welcoming chain pub with comfortable traditional furnishings, open fires, stripped stone, rooms off inc dining/family room, good food choice all day (freshly made so can take a while), Theakstons ales and two local Wentworth ones, good choice of wines by the glass; quiet piped music, TV; dogs allowed in part, tables in attractive garden with own bowling green, bedrooms, open all day *(Mrs Hazel Rainer, BB)*

WEST BURTON [SE0186]

Fox & Hounds DL8 4JY [on green, off B6160 Bishopdale—Wharfedale]: Welcoming local on long green of idyllic Dales village, friendly service, Black Sheep and Copper Dragon, long low-beamed bar, pleasant dining room; piped music may obtrude, nearby caravan park; children and dogs welcome, good modern bedrooms, lovely walks and waterfalls nearby *(Brian and Janet Ainscough, Mr and Mrs Maurice Thompson, Martin and Alison Stainsby, David and Karen Cuckney, Stuart Paulley)*

WEST TANFIELD [SE2678]

Bruce Arms HG4 5JJ [A6108 N of Ripon]: Good rather upmarket food inc interesting dishes in intimate log-fire bar or smallish dining room (often fully booked at night), friendly service; bedrooms *(LYM, Steve Clarke)*

WEST WITTON [SE0588]

☆ *Wensleydale Heifer* DL8 4LS [A684 W of Leyburn]: Stylish restaurant-with-rooms rather than pub, good food with emphasis on local meat and fresh fish and seafood, cosy informal upmarket food bar as well as extensive main formal restaurant, daily papers and showcased malt whiskies; nice comfortable bedrooms (back ones quietest), good big breakfast *(Dr Alan and Mrs Sue Holder, Brian Young, BB, M S Catling)*

WETHERBY [SE4048]

Muse Café LS22 6NQ [Bank St]: Very popular small bar with enjoyable reasonably priced fresh food, four real ales sucvh as Caledonian Deuchars IPA and Timothy Taylors, continental lagers, good coffee, young friendly helpful staff, restaurant on right; open all day *(Danny Savage, Andy and Jill Kassube, Stuart Paulley)*

Swan & Talbot LS22 6NN [handy for A1; North St]: Traditional well decorated town pub, linked rooms each side of main bar, Caledonian Deuchars IPA, Fullers London Pride and John Smiths, good choice of reasonably priced tasty food esp fish and grills, Weds night bargains, pleasant chatty staff *(Tim and Ann Newell)*

WHISTON [SK4489]

☆ *Golden Ball* S60 4HY [nr M1 junction 33, via A618; Turner Lane, off High St]: Good atmosphere in charming extended Ember Inn, decent food, real ales such as Adnams, Caledonian Deuchars IPA, John Smiths, Stones and Timothy Taylors Landlord, several wines by the glass, good soft drinks choice, daily papers, log fire; quiet piped music, machines, quiz nights, no children inside; picnic-sets outside, open all day *(Derek and Sylvia Stephenson, Nigel and Sue Foster)*

WHITBY [NZ9010]

Middle Earth Tavern YO22 4AE [Church St]: Well used pub in quiet spot facing river and harbour, Black Sheep and Tetleys, bar food; tables outside *(David Carr)*

Station Inn YO21 1DH [New Quay Rd]: Three-room bare-boards pub under friendly and enthusiastic new licensees, eight well kept changing ales, farm cider, proper lunchtime home cooking inc local fish, good choice of wines by the glass, thriving atmosphere, traditional games; piped music, live Weds; open all day *(anon)*

White Horse & Griffin YO22 4BH [Church St]: Restaurant rather than pub (you can't have just a drink), but worth knowing for good value lunches esp local seafood – they do breakfasts for non-residents too, and more expensive evening meals; nice atmosphere, well kept Black Dog Whitby Abbey ale, very tall narrow front part, low-ceilinged open back area with big fireplace, corner bar, some long tables and cosy candlelit ambiance; bedrooms *(Sean A Smith)*

WHIXLEY [SE4457]

Anchor YO26 8AG [New Rd, E of village (1st left turn heading N from Green Hamerton on B6265)]: Family-friendly pub with traditional generous food inc bargain lunchtime carvery particularly popular with OAPs, friendly young staff, John Smiths and Tetleys, straightforward main eating extension, original core with some character and coal fire in small lounge *(Kay and Alistair Butler)*

YORK [SE5951]

☆ *Ackhorne* YO1 6LN [St Martins Lane, Micklegate]: Not over-modernised, with friendly landlord and family, helpful service, changing real ales from small brewers, up to four farm ciders, perry, country wines, foreign bottled beers, bargain basic food, not Sun, from good choice of sandwiches up (fresh chillies in the chilli), open fire, beams and bare boards, leather wall seats, Civil War prints, bottles and jugs, carpeted snug one end, daily papers, traditional games; silenced games machine, Sun quiz night; suntrap back terrace (steps a bit steep), open all day *(the Didler, Pat and Tony Martin, Roger A Bellingham, Mark and Diane Grist)*

☆ *Black Swan* YO1 7PR [Peaseholme Green (inner ring road)]: Striking timbered and jettied Tudor building, compact panelled front bar, crooked-floored central hall with fine period staircase, black-beamed back bar with vast inglenook, great atmosphere, real ales such as Fullers London Pride, Greene King Abbot, John Smiths and York Yorkshire Terrier, cheerful service, basic low-priced food from baked potatoes and baguettes up, decent wines; piped music, jazz and folk nights; useful car park *(Heidi Rowe, the Didler, LYM, Pete Coxon, Kevin Blake, Pete Baker)*

☆ *Blue Bell* YO1 9TF [Fossgate]: Delightfully old-fashioned Edwardian pub with super friendly atmosphere, chatty locals and landlady, real ales such as Adnams, Caledonian Deuchars IPA, Jennings Cumberland, Ossett Silver King and Timothy Taylors Landlord, good value sandwiches and tapas all day till 5 (not Sun), daily papers, tiny tiled-floor front bar with roaring fire, panelled ceiling, stained glass, bar pots and decanters, corridor to back room not much bigger, hatch service to middle bar, lamps and flickering candles, pub games; may be piped music; open all day *(Michael Dandy, the Didler, Kerry Law, David Carr, Pete Baker, WW, Pete Coxon, Mark and Diane Grist)*

Brigantes YO1 6JX [Micklegate]: Market Town Taverns bar/bistro, eight real ales and good range of bottled beers, farm cider, good wines and coffee, enjoyable unpretentious brasserie food from sandwiches up, courteous helpful staff, simple pleasant décor, no music – and no hen parties; open all day *(Fred and Lorraine Gill, WW, Andy and Jill Kassube, Mark and Diane Grist)*

Dormouse YO30 5PA [Shipton Rd, Clifton Park]: Purpose-built Vintage Inn, well designed and given plenty of character and atmosphere, with friendly efficient staff, their usual reasonably priced food, wide choice of good value wines, real ales; good disabled access *(Pat and Tony Martin)*

Gillygate YO31 7EQ [Gillygate]: Hearty helpings of decent food, friendly staff, good beer; reasonably priced bedrooms *(Steve Jennings)*

Golden Ball YO1 6DU [Cromwell Rd/Bishophill]: Unspoilt and buoyant 1950s local feel in friendly and well preserved four-room Edwardian pub, enjoyable straightforward wkdy lunchtime food, changing ales such as Caledonian Deuchars IPA, Marstons Pedigree and John Smiths, Sept beer festival, bar billiards, cards and dominoes; TV, can be lively evenings, live music Thurs; lovely small walled garden, open all day Thurs-Sun *(Pete Baker, Fred and Lorraine Gill, David Carr, the Didler)*

Golden Fleece YO1 9UP [Pavement]: Black Sheep, Greene King IPA and Timothy Taylors Landlord, good value usual food from sandwiches up all afternoon, long corridor from bar to comfortable back lounge (beware the sloping floors – it dates from 1503), interesting décor with quite a library, lots of pictures and ghost stories, pub games; piped music; children welcome, bedrooms *(David Carr, Michael Dandy, Michael and Alison Sandy, Kevin Blake, Pete Coxon)*

Golden Lion YO1 8BG [Church St]: Big comfortable open-plan pub done up in bare-boards Edwardian style (in fact first licensed 1771), beams, plenty of lamps, old photographs and brewery signs, John Smiths, Theakstons and half a dozen interesting changing ales, wide choice of sensible food all day from good sandwiches up, good range of wines by the glass, pleasant young staff; piped music; open all day *(Pat and Tony Martin, Kevin Blake, Pete Coxon)*

Golden Slipper YO1 7LG [Goodramgate]: Dating from 15th c, welcoming unpretentious bar and three comfortably old-fashioned small rooms, one lined with books, good cheap plain lunchtime food from sandwiches, baguettes and baked potatoes to tender Sun roast beef, well kept Caledonian Deuchars IPA, Greene King IPA and Old Speckled Hen and John Smiths, cheerful staff; TV; tables in back courtyard *(Paul and Ursula Randall, Pat and Graham Williamson, Pete Coxon)*

☆ *Last Drop* YO1 8BN [Colliergate]: Basic traditional York Brewery pub with several of their own beers and one or two well kept guests, decent wines and country wines, friendly helpful young staff, big windows overlooking pavement, bare boards, barrel tables and comfortable seats (some up a few steps), no music, machines or children, nice simple fresh food 12-4 inc sandwiches, paninis and good salads; piped music, no children, can get very busy lunchtime, attic lavatories; tables out behind, open all day *(David Carr, WW, Dr and Mrs P Truelove, Michael Dandy, Mark and Diane Grist)*

☆ *Lendal Cellars* YO1 8AA [Lendal]: Bustling split-level ale house down steps in broad-vaulted 17th-c cellars carefully spotlit to show up the stripped brickwork, stone floor, interconnected rooms and alcoves, good choice of fairly priced changing real ales, farm cider, decent coffee, good range of wines by the glass, foreign bottled beers, daily papers, cheerful staff, good plain food 11.30-7(5 Fri/Sat); good piped music, can get packed; children allowed if eating, open all day *(Dave Webster, Sue Holland, the Didler, Mrs Hazel Rainer, Dr D J and Mrs S C Walker, LYM)*

Masons Arms YO10 4AB [Fishergate]: 1930s local, two fires in panelled front bar with blow lamps and pig ornaments, attractive fireplaces, good range of beers inc guests, generous interesting home-made food, friendly service; comfortable bedroom block (no breakfast), tables out in front and on back riverside terrace *(Kevin Blake, Mrs Hazel Rainer)*

Minster Inn YO30 7BH [Marygate]: Modest Edwardian local, three chatty rooms off central corridor, bric-a-brac and dark old tables and settles, fires and woodburners, friendly landlord, well kept Marstons ales, sandwiches, traditional table games; piped music; tables out behind *(David Carr)*

Olde Starre YO1 8AS [Stonegate]: City's oldest licensed pub, a big tourist draw, with 'gallows' sign across town's prettiest street, original panelling and prints, green plush wall seats, several other little carpeted rooms off porch-like lobby, changing real ales such as Fullers and Theakstons Best from swing counter, cheerful young staff, low-priced food, daily papers; piped music, games machines; children welcome away from bar, flower-filled back garden and front courtyard with Minster glimpsed across the rooftops, open all day *(Michael Dandy, David Carr, Pete Coxon, LYM)*

Punch Bowl YO1 8AN [Stonegate]: Bustling family-run local with masses of hanging baskets, friendly helpful service, wide range of bargain generous food (12-2 and 3-6.45) from sandwiches up, small panelled rooms off corridor, TV in interesting beamed one on left of food servery, well kept York Yorkshire Terrier; unobtrusive piped music, games machines; open all day *(Edna Jones)*

Red Lion YO1 9TU [Merchantgate, between Fossgate and Piccadilly]: Low-beamed rambling rooms with plenty of atmosphere, some stripped Tudor brickwork, relaxed old-fashioned furnishings, well kept Black Sheep and John Smiths, reasonably priced bar lunches, good attentive staff; piped music; children welcome to eat at lunchtime, picnic-sets outside *(Pete Coxon, David Carr, LYM)*

Rook & Gaskill YO10 3WP [Lawrence St]: Now a Tynemill pub, up to a dozen ales inc Castle Rock and York Terrier, enjoyable food (not Sun), traditional décor, dark wood tables, banquettes, chairs and high stools, back conservatory; open all day *(David Carr, Pete Coxon, the Didler)*

☆ *Royal Oak* YO1 7LG [Goodramgate]: Comfortably worn in three-room black-beamed 16th-c pub simply remodelled in Tudor style 1934, blazing log fire in front room, prints, swords, busts and old guns, bargain generous pubby dishes (limited Sun evening) 11.30-8, sandwiches with home-baked bread after 3, speedy service from cheerful bustling young staff, Caledonian Deuchars IPA and Greene King Abbot, decent wines, good coffee, family room, games; piped music, can get crowded, outside gents'; handy for Minster, open all day *(Michael Dandy, David Carr, Pete Coxon, Kevin Blake, Pat and Tony Martin, BB)*

Snickleway YO1 7LS [Goodramgate]: Interesting little open-plan pub behind big shop-front window, cosy and comfortable, lots of antiques, copper and brass, good coal or log fire, Black Sheep, Greene King Old Speckled Hen and John Smiths, good value fresh well filled doorstep sandwiches, baked potatoes and a coupe of hot dishes lunchtimes, cheerful landlord, prompt service, splendid cartoons in gents', exemplary ladies'; unobtrusive piped music *(Pete Coxon, Michael Dandy, Kevin Blake, Paul and Ursula Randall)*

Swan YO23 1JH [Bishopgate St, Clementhorpe]: Unspoilt 1950s feel, friendly and chatty, hatch service to lobby for two small rooms off main bar, great staff, several changing ales inc Caledonian Deuchars IPA and Timothy Taylors Landlord; busy with young people wknds; small pleasant walled garden, nr city walls, open all day wknds *(Fred and Lorraine Gill, the Didler, Pete Baker)*

☆ *Tap & Spile* YO31 7PB [Monkgate]: Friendly open-plan late Victorian pub with Roosters and other interesting changing real ales, farm cider and country wines, decent wines by the glass, bookshelves, games in raised back area, cheap straightforward lunchtime bar food (not Mon); children in eating area,

tables on heated terrace and in garden, open all day *(Paul and Ursula Randall, LYM, Pete Coxon, the Didler)*

☆ *Three Legged Mare* YO1 7EN [High Petergate]: Bustling open-plan light and airy modern café-bar with York Brewery's full beer range kept well, good range of belgian Trappist beers, quick cheerful service (staff know about beers), generous interesting sandwiches and one or two basic lunchtime hot dishes, some comfortable sofas, back conservatory; no children; disabled facilities (other lavatories down spiral stairs), tables in back garden with replica of the original three-legged mare – a local gallows used for multiple executions *(Pete Coxon, WW, Pat and Tony Martin, Michael Dandy)*

☆ *York Arms* YO1 7EH [High Petergate]: Cheerful Sam Smiths pub by Minster, quick helpful service, good value sandwiches and simple hot dishes lunchtime to early evening (not Sun-Tues), snug little basic panelled bar (beware the sliding door), big modern back lounge, cosier partly panelled parlour full of old bric-a-brac, prints, brown-cushioned wall settles, dimpled copper tables and open fire, pub games, no piped music; open all day *(Michael Dandy, BB, Kevin Blake, David Carr)*

☆ *York Brewery Tap* YO1 6JT [Toft Green, Micklegate]: Peaceful upstairs lounge at York Brewery, their own full cask range in top condition at bargain price, also bottled beers, nice clubby atmosphere with friendly staff happy to talk about the beers, lots of breweriana and view of brewing plant, comfortable settees and armchairs, magazines and daily papers; no food, brewery tours by arrangement, shop; children allowed, open 11.30-7, cl Sun, annual membership fee £3 unless you live in York or go on the tour *(the Didler, David Carr, Peter F Marshall)*

☆ *Yorkshire Terrier* YO1 8AS [Stonegate]: York Brewery pub hiding behind traditional shop front (look for the brewery memorabilia in the window), their full beer range from smallish bar behind front brewery shop, tasting trays of four one-third pints, interesting bottled beers too, winter mulled wine, pleasant enthusiastic staff, dining room with soup, sandwiches and limited range of other good value food noon till 4 inc Sun, another room upstairs (where the lavatories are – there's a lift), small light and airy conservatory; open all day *(Andy and Jill Kassube, David Carr, Pat and Tony Martin, WW, Mrs Roxanne Chamberlain, Fred and Lorraine Gill, Paul and Ursula Randall, Dave Webster, Sue Holland, Matt Waite, Mark and Diane Grist)*

If we know a pub has an outdoor play area for children, we mention it.

London
Scotland
Wales
Channel Islands

London

It's been an exciting few months for London pubs, with several high-profile openings and well received new ventures; most hyped has been Gordon Ramsay's first foray into the field, the Narrow at Limehouse in East London, an appealingly refurbished harbourmaster's house by the river, with excellent classic British food in the smart dining room. It's one of a bumper crop of new entries to the *Guide* this year, of which two more also display a refreshing move away from the overly fancy food that's tripped up many a gastropub: both the Fat Badger in West London and the Marquess Tavern in North London put their energies into sourcing top-quality ingredients that are cooked simply and well, to tried and tested recipes. And in addition to their full menus, all three of these foody pubs have entirely separate but no less inspired bar menus, between them offering pork pies, sprats, quail eggs and even pigs trotters if you just want a snack. The other new entries have very different draws: best-known is the well run Salisbury right in the heart of town, a famously preserved Victorian pub full of glass and mirrors, with a good range of drinks and a bustling atmosphere. The Bishops Finger near Smithfield Market returns to the main entries after a break, and we've added two pubs in South London: the Greenwich Union (the only pub belonging to the small Meantime Brewery, whose drinks you'll often find in supermarkets, but here are all on draught) and the Bo-Peep in Chelsfield, out near the fringes of Kent (an unassuming country pub that's a remarkably handy lunch-stop from the M25). Of our established entries it's the ones in Central London that perhaps unsurprisingly have proved especially popular with readers this year, with current favourites including the Argyll Arms (enjoyably individual in an area where most pubs decidedly are not), the Black Friar (extraordinary décor, and good guest beers and decent all day food too), the Dog & Duck, the Eagle (still excellent food, and a buoyantly pubby feel), the Jerusalem Tavern (a firm favourite, once again receiving more praise from readers than any other London pub), the unspoilt Lamb, the busy Lamb & Flag, and the Seven Stars (quirky and atmospheric, with particularly good food). Standing out in South London is the Market Porter, with its extraordinary range of real ales, while West London stars are the Atlas (consistently good mediterranean-influenced meals, and a nice atmosphere too), and the well run Churchill Arms, enjoyed for its bustling local feel and bargain thai food. Some pubs have had big changes: the Fire Station at Waterloo has had a timely revamp, there are new licensees at the Grapes in Shepherd Market and the White Horse in Parsons Green, and as we went to press two of the city's best-preserved Victorian pubs were undergoing careful and very costly refurbishments – the Princess Louise, and the Warrington, with the latter about to reopen as Gordon Ramsay's second pub. London pub food can be fairly uniform these days – you can generally count on finding sausage and mash, fish and chips and the ubiquitous caesar salad – but we've noticed quite a few places now offer a number of sharing plates or platters, a nicely civilised way of snacking after work. Although London restaurants are notoriously expensive, where London pubs do score is on value. Given comparable quality, you can expect to pay less for a pub meal here than in most parts of the country. And of course we highlight a good few pubs where the meals are as good as any restaurant; of these, it's the Anchor & Hope that we've chosen as this year's London Dining Pub of the Year; it's busy, noisy, and you may have to wait for a table, but its distinctive food has proved hugely influential, inspiring a number of the foodier pubs that have opened this year. As ever, the bad news in London is the price of a pint: we found some Central London pubs charging as much as £3.20 for their cheapest real ale this year. Drinks prices in most London pubs are far higher than the national norm. Sam Smiths, even though based up in Yorkshire, are now virtually alone in keeping the price of a pint well below £2 in their London pubs. In quite a few pubs, the cheapest beer on offer is Adnams (from Suffolk), and Harveys (from Sussex) is a growing presence, also now on offer as the cheapest beer in several of our main entries. Now that Youngs have closed their London brewery (the Wells & Youngs beers come from Bedford), Fullers is the only sizeable London-based brewer; besides good beers, their pubs generally have good wines by the glass, too. The Lucky Dip section at the end of the chapter is divided into Central, East, North, South and West (with the pubs grouped by postal district). Outer London suburbs come last, by name, after the numbered postal districts. In this section, Central London pubs currently showing particularly well include the Banker (EC4), Buckingham Arms (SW1) and Chandos, Porterhouse and Welsh Harp (WC2); in East London, we'd pick out the Gun (E14); in North London, the Flask (N6); in South London, the Angel (SE16), Boathouse and Dukes Head (SW15) and Cats Back (SW18); in West London, the Anglesea Arms and Black Lion (W6); and in the outer districts, the Kings Arms in Hampton Court. We have inspected virtually all of these; they are firm recommendations.

CENTRAL LONDON

MAP 13

Admiral Codrington ♀

Mossop Street; ⊖ South Kensington; SW3 2LY

Bustling in the evenings, a smartly transformed Chelsea pub with very good food in back dining room

Elegantly reworked by Nina Campbell, this popular pub can be heaving in the evenings – but is generally much quieter (and perhaps less atmospheric) during the day. The chief draw remains the sunny back dining room, mainly because of the excellently prepared food, but also because of its design – particularly impressive in fine weather when the retractable glass roof slides open. The more pubby bar is an effective mix of traditional and chic, with comfortable sofas and cushioned wall seats, neatly polished floorboards and panelling, spotlights in the ceiling and lamps on elegant wooden tables, a handsome central counter, sporting prints on the yellow walls, and houseplants around the big bow windows. There's a model ship in a case just above the entrance to the dining room. Greene King IPA and Wells & Youngs Bombardier on handpump (not cheap, even for round here), and an excellent wine list, with nearly all available by the glass; various coffees, a range of havana cigars, and friendly service from smartly uniformed young staff. There may be piped pop or jazz – though in the evenings it will be drowned out by the sound of animated conversation; the dining room is quieter. At the side is a nice little terrace with tables, benches and heaters. They now have a bridge club upstairs. The pub is right in the heart of Chelsea, and though it's the kind of place where half the customers arrive by taxi, the clientele can be rather more varied than you might expect.

⏃ With particularly good fish, the main menu in the dining room might include spiced duck and jasmine tea broth, diver-caught scallops with pumpkin purée and shellfish vinaigrette, risotto of goats cheese, vine tomato and fresh basil, salmon and smoked haddock fishcakes, cod baked with tomatoes and mushrooms in a soft herb crust, slow-roast belly of pork with chorizo, canellini beans and rosemary jus, slow-braised oxtail with cauliflower risotto and parsley, and good puddings like pistachio and vanilla millefeuilles or chocolate and banana doughnuts; good farmhouse cheeses. It's worth booking, particularly at weekends. A separate, shorter lunchtime bar menu has things like cumberland sausage roll, a pint of prawns with lemon mayonnaise, home-made cottage pie, and good caesar salads. *Starters/Snacks: £5.00 to £8.00. Main Courses: £9.00 to £18.00. Puddings: £5.00 to £6.00*

Punch ~ Lease Langlands Pearse ~ Real ale ~ Bar food (12-2.30(3.30 Sat), 6.30-11; 12-4, 7-10 Sun ~ Restaurant ~ (020) 7581 0005 ~ Children in eating area of bar and restaurant ~ Open 11.30am-midnight; 12-10.30 Sun; closed 25 and 26 Dec

Recommended by Heather McQuillan, N R White

Albert
Victoria Street; ⊖ *St James's Park; SW1H 0NP*

Imposing old building with some interesting original features, good value food all day, popular upstairs carvery

Spruced up with a refurbishment not long before we went to press, this bustling 19th-c pub still has some of its original Victorian fixtures and fittings – notably the heavily cut and etched windows which run along three sides of the open-plan bar, giving the place a surprisingly airy feel. Always busy – especially on weekday lunchtimes and after work – it also has some gleaming mahogany, an ornate ceiling, and good solid comfortable furnishings. A wonderfully diverse mix of customers takes in tourists, civil servants and even the occasional MP: the Division Bell is rung to remind them when it's time to get back to Westminster. Service from the big island counter is efficient, friendly, and particularly obliging to people from overseas. Fullers London Pride, Greene King IPA and Wells & Youngs Bombardier on handpump, along with a couple of guests such as Caledonian Deuchars IPA; they do a good choice of wines by the glass. The handsome staircase that leads up to it is lined with portraits of prime ministers; piped music, fruit machine. Handily placed between Victoria and Westminster, the pub was one of the few buildings in this part of Victoria to escape the Blitz, and is one of the area's most striking sights (though it's now rather dwarfed by the surrounding faceless cliffs of dark modern glass).

⏃ Usefully served all day, the promptly served bar food includes soup, sandwiches, burgers, sausage and mash, fish and chips, changing hot specials like turkey casserole or sweet and sour chicken, while upstairs there's a better than average carvery (all day inc Sunday, £16.50 for three courses and coffee, £12.65 for two; it may be worth booking ahead). *Starters/Snacks: £3.65 to £4.95. Main Courses: £6.95 to £12.50. Puddings: £3.99*

Spirit Group ~ Manager Declan Clancy ~ Real ale ~ Bar food (11-10) ~ Restaurant ~ (020) 7222 5577 ~ Children in eating area of bar till 9.30pm ~ Open 11-12(11 Sun, and every day in winter); closed 25 Dec

Recommended by GHC, Kevin Blake, Ian Phillips, Michael Dandy, John Branston, Mike and Sue Loseby

Argyll Arms ◀

Argyll Street; ✚ Oxford Circus, opposite tube side exit; W1F 7TP

Unexpectedly individual pub just off Oxford Street, with interesting little front rooms, appealing range of beers, and good value straightforward food all day

More than just a useful escape from the Oxford Street crowds, this bustling Victorian pub – very much enjoyed by readers – is a genuinely characterful and rather distinctive place, with consistently reliable service (even at its busiest), and a good range of beers. Particularly unusual are the three atmospheric and secluded little cubicle rooms at the front, essentially unchanged since they were built in the 1860s. All oddly angular, they're made by wooden partitions with remarkable frosted and engraved glass, with hops trailing above. A long mirrored corridor leads to the spacious back room; newspapers to read, two fruit machines, piped music. The half dozen real ales on handpump typically include Black Sheep, Fullers London Pride, Timothy Taylors Landlord, Wells & Youngs, and guests like Marstons Pedigree and Shepherd Neame Spitfire; also several malt whiskies. The quieter upstairs bar overlooks the pedestrianised street – and the Palladium theatre if you can see through the impressive foliage outside the window; divided into several snugs with comfortable plush easy chairs, it has swan's-neck lamps, and lots of small theatrical prints along the top of the walls. The pub can get very crowded (and can seem less individual on busier evenings), but there's space for drinking outside.

🍽 **Decent value straightforward bar food is served almost all the hours they're open, kicking off with a well priced breakfast, then later with doorstep sandwiches, and traditional meals like fish and chips (served in a choice of helpings, normal or large), and beef and ale pie.** *Starters/Snacks: £3.00 to £5.00. Main Courses: £5.25 to £9.95. Puddings: £3.50*

Mitchells & Butlers ~ Manager Ransford Thomas ~ Real ale ~ Bar food (8am-10pm) ~ (020) 7734 6117 ~ Children in upstairs bar till 9pm ~ Open 8am-11(12 Fri, Sat); 12-10.30 Sun; closed 25 Dec

Recommended by Mrs Hazel Rainer, Michael Dandy, Derek Thomas, N R White, Mike Gorton, Ian Phillips, Tracey and Stephen Groves, the Didler, Mike and Sue Loseby, Peter Dandy, Barry Collett, Dr and Mrs A K Clarke

Bishops Finger ♀

West Smithfield, opposite Bart's; ✚ ⇌ Farringdon; EC1A 9JR

Nicely civilised little pub with particularly welcoming atmosphere, and good beers

In a verdant square beside Smithfield Market, this swish little pub has the full range of Shephed Neame beers in good condition, and a very nice, welcoming atmosphere. Comfortable and smartly civilised, the well laid-out room has cream walls, big windows, elegant tables with fresh flowers on the polished bare boards, a few pillars, and cushioned chairs under one wall lined with framed prints of the market. It can be busy after work, but rather relaxed and peaceful during the day. Shepherd Neame Master Brew, Spitfire, Bishops Finger and seasonal brews on handpump, with a wide choice of wines (eight by the glass), ten malt whiskies, and several ports and champagnes; friendly, efficient service. There are a couple of tables outside.

🍽 **Most people go for one of the ten or so varieties of sausage from a speciality shop nearby, all served with mash, but they also do soup, burgers, steaks, and specials like gammon, or beer-battered cod.** *Starters/Snacks: £3.50. Main Courses: £6.50 to £9.95*

Shepherd Neame ~ Manager Paul Potts ~ Real ale ~ Bar food (12-3, 6-9 (not Fri, or weekends)) ~ (020) 7248 2341 ~ Children welcome ~ Open 11-11; closed weekends and bank hols

Recommended by N R White, Michael Dandy, Peter Dandy, Ian Phillips, David Hall

---

Anyone claiming to arrange or prevent inclusion of a pub in the *Guide* is a fraud.
Pubs are included only if recommended by genuine readers and if our own anonymous
inspection confirms that they are suitable.

Black Friar

Queen Victoria Street; ⊖ ⇌ *Blackfriars; EC4V 4EG*

Remarkable art nouveau décor, also good choice of beers (with interesting guests), friendly atmosphere, and decent food all day

Though this old favourite has good – and sometimes unusual – beers, what makes it a must-see is its unique and quite extraordinary décor, which includes some of the best Edwardian bronze and marble art nouveau work to be found anywhere. The inner back room has big bas-relief friezes of jolly monks set into richly coloured florentine marble walls, an opulent marble-pillared inglenook fireplace, a low vaulted mosaic ceiling, gleaming mirrors, seats built into rich golden marble recesses, and tongue-in-cheek verbal embellishments such as Silence is Golden and Finery is Foolish. See if you can spot the opium-smoking hints modelled into the fireplace of the front room. The Adnams, Fullers London Pride and Timothy Taylors Landlord are joined by a couple of guests such as Black Sheep and Hook Norton Old Hooky, and there's a decent range of wines by the glass; fruit machine, prompt, friendly service. The pub does get busy, and in the evenings lots of people spill out on to the wide forecourt, near the approach to Blackfriars Bridge; there's some smart furniture out here (and in spring some rather impressive tulips). If you're coming by Tube, choose your exit carefully – it's all too easy to emerge from the network of passageways and find yourself on the wrong side of the street, or marooned on a traffic island.

🍴 **Specialising in pies such as chicken and asparagus, steak and stilton, or spinach, brie and redcurrant; other traditional meals, served all day, include sausages and mash, a vegetarian dish of the day, and fish and chips, some in a choice of sizes.** *Starters/Snacks: £2.95 to £5.95. Main Courses: £6.95 to £9.95. Puddings: £3.50*

Mitchells & Butlers ~ Manager Cecilia Soderholm ~ Real ale ~ Bar food (12-9) ~ (020) 7236 5474 ~ Open 11-11(11.30 Thurs, Fri); 12-11 Sat; 12-10.30 Sun; 11.30-11 winter

Recommended by N R White, Darren Le Poidevin, Peter Dandy, Ian Phillips, Donna and Roger, Eithne Dandy, the Didler, B and M Kendall, Susan and John Douglas, Barry Collett, C J Fletcher, Tom McLean, Ewan McCall, Dr and Mrs A K Clarke

Cittie of Yorke 🍺

High Holborn – find it by looking out for its big black and gold clock; ⊖ *Chancery Lane; WC1V 6BN*

Bustling old pub where the splendid back bar with its old-fashioned cubicles rarely fails to impress – and the beer is refreshingly low-priced

Another pub where the building itself is the main attraction, this unique place has an impressive back bar rather like a baronial hall, with its extraordinarily extended bar counter stretching off into the distance. A favourite with lawyers and City types, it has thousand-gallon wine vats resting above the gantry, big, bulbous lights hanging from the soaring high-raftered roof, and a nice glow from the fire. It can get busy in the evenings, but there's plenty of space to absorb the crowds – and indeed it's at the busiest times that the pub is at its most magnificent (it never feels quite right when it's quiet). Most people tend to congregate in the middle, so you should still be able to bag one of the intimate, old-fashioned and ornately carved booths that run along both sides. As it's a Sam Smiths pub, a bonus is the refreshingly cheap real ale, with the OB on handpump around a pound less than a typical London pint. The triangular Waterloo fireplace, with grates on all three sides and a figure of Peace among laurels, used to stand in the Hall of Grays Inn Common Room until less obtrusive heating was introduced. A smaller, comfortable panelled room has lots of little prints of York and attractive brass lights, while the ceiling of the entrance hall has medieval-style painted panels and plaster York roses. As in other Sam Smiths pubs, readers have noted unusual brands of spirits rather than the more familiar names. Smart, helpful staff; fruit machine. A pub has stood on this site since 1430, though the current building owes more to the 1695 coffee house erected here behind a garden; it was reconstructed in Victorian times, using 17th-c materials and parts.

⊞ Served from buffet counters in the main hall and cellar bar, bar food (not perhaps the pub's finest feature) includes sandwiches, soup, and half a dozen daily-changing hot dishes such as roasted vegetable lasagne, chilli, and fish and chips. *Starters/Snacks: £3.00 to £5.00. Main Courses: £5.00 to £6.50. Puddings: £3.50*

Sam Smiths ~ Manager Stuart Browning ~ Real ale ~ Bar food (12-3, 5-9; all day Sat) ~ (020) 7242 7670 ~ Children in eating area of bar ~ Open 11.30(12 Sat)-11; closed Sun, bank hols, 25 and 26 Dec

Recommended by the Didler, David and Sue Smith, Pete Coxon, Tracey and Stephen Groves, Ian Phillips, Keith and Chris O'Neill, Bruce Bird, Pete Walker, Donna and Roger, N R White, Dr and Mrs M E Wilson, Ewan McCall, C J Fletcher, Tom McLean, Barry Collett, Phil and Sally Gorton, Dr and Mrs A K Clarke

Coopers Arms

Flood Street; ⊖ *Sloane Square, but quite a walk; SW3 5TB*

Well positioned and properly pubby, a useful bolthole for Kings Road shoppers

Now with its own courtyard garden, this spacious open-plan pub is a useful retreat fom the bustle of the Kings Road. Relaxed and properly pubby (especially in the evenings), the bar has interesting furnishings such as kitchen chairs and some dark brown plush chairs on the floorboards, a mix of nice old good-sized tables, and a pre-war sideboard and dresser; also, LNER posters and maps of Chelsea and the Thames on the walls, an enormous railway clock, a fireplace with dried flowers, and tea-shop chandeliers – all watched over by the heads of a moose and a tusky boar. Wells & Youngs Bitter, Bombardier and Special on handpump, with 14 wines by the glass.

⊞ Home-made bar food might include soup, sandwiches, steak and kidney pie, burgers, fish and chips, and sharing plates of antipasti or baked camembert. *Starters/Snacks: £4.50 to £6.95. Main Courses: £8.95 to £16.95. Puddings: £4.50*

Youngs ~ Manager Colin Ryan ~ Real ale ~ Bar food (11-10(9 Sun)) ~ (020) 7376 3120 ~ Children in eating area of bar ~ Dogs allowed in bar ~ Open 11-11; 12-10.30 Sun

Recommended by BOB

Cross Keys

Lawrence Street; ⊖ *Sloane Square, but some distance away; SW3 5NB*

Civilised and warmly convivial, unusual style and décor; very short choice of bar food, and good (though not cheap) inventive meals in conservatory

Though this bustling pub dates back to 1765, it feels rather contemporary thanks to the distinctive décor by designer Rudy Weller, best known for his Horses of Helios in Piccadilly Circus. You can tell he had fun with this: there's an unusual array of brassware hanging from the rafters, including trumpets and a diver's helmet, as well as animal-skin prints on the furnishings, and quite a mix of sculptures, paintings and objects. The roomy high-ceilinged flagstoned bar also has an island servery, a roaring fire, lots of atmosphere, and a good range of customers; there's a light and airy conservatory-style back restaurant, with an ironic twist to its appealing gardening décor. Courage Best and Directors on handpump (not cheap, even for this area), and a good choice of wines by the glass. Attentive young staff; piped music. Like most pubs in the area, this can be busy and lively on Saturday evenings. More reports please.

⊞ The very short bar menu has things like ciabattas and wraps, toulouse sausages with mash and lentil jus, mature cheddar soufflé with anchovies, and caesar salad, while the main menu in the conservatory (served weekends too) might include dressed crab with caper berries, shallots and herb salsa, roasted emperor bream with minted peas and white and green beans, and pan roasted lamb fillet and braised tongue with polenta, roast figs, and salsa verde. They may do a two-course menu for £10.50 (£14.50 Sun). *Starters/Snacks: £4.50 to £9.00. Main Courses: £13.90 to £17.95. Puddings: £5.50*

Free house ~ Licensee Michael Bertorelli ~ Bar food (12-3, 6-8 (not weekends)) ~ Restaurant ~ (020) 7349 9111 ~ Dogs allowed in bar ~ Open 12-12; 12-11 Sun; closed bank hols

Recommended by Derek Thomas

Dog & Duck 🍺

Bateman Street, on corner with Frith Street; ⊖ *Tottenham Court Road, Leicester Square;*
W1D 3AJ

Tiny Soho pub squeezing in bags of character, with unusual old tiles and mosaics, good beers, and warmly welcoming atmosphere

---

All the letters we've had about this pint-sized corner house this year have highlighted the enjoyable atmosphere and friendly service. A Soho landmark, it hasn't really changed in the last 40 years. In the evenings it can be very busy indeed, packing a lot of atmosphere into a small space, so afternoons are probably the best time to fully appreciate the décor, which has some interesting detail and individual touches. On the floor near the door is an engaging mosaic showing a dog with its tongue out in hot pursuit of a duck; the same theme is embossed on some of the shiny tiles that frame the heavy old advertising mirrors. There are some high stools by the ledge along the back wall, further seats in a slightly roomier area at one end, and a fire in winter; the piped music is usually drowned out by the good-natured chatter. Well kept Fullers London Pride, Timothy Taylors Landlord and two changing guests like Adnams and Black Sheep on handpump from the unusual little bar counter; also Addlestone's cider, and decent wines by the glass. In good weather especially, most people tend to spill on to the bustling street, though even when the pub is at its busiest you may find plenty of space in the rather cosy upstairs bar. The pub is said to be where George Orwell celebrated when the American Book of the Month Club chose *Animal Farm* as its monthly selection. Ronnie Scott's jazz club is near by.

🍴 Served all day, good value bar snacks include quite a range of sausages, from cumberland to venison, juniper berry and gin, as well as summer salads, and fish and chips. *Starters/Snacks: £2.95 to £4.95. Main Courses: £5.95 to £7.95. Puddings: £3.50*

Mitchells & Butlers ~ Manager Natalie Hubbard ~ Real ale ~ Bar food (12-9.30) ~
(020) 7494 0697 ~ Open 11-11; 12-10.30 Sun; closed 25 Dec

Recommended by Tim Maddison, B and M Kendall, Donna and Roger, Mike Gorton, LM, the Didler, Ewan McCall, Tom McLean

Eagle 🍽 🍷

Farringdon Road; opposite Bowling Green Lane car park; ⊖ ⇌ *Farringdon, Old Street;*
EC1R 3AL

Still exceptional for food, London's original gastropub is busy, noisy, and 'shabby-chic', with really excellent meals from the open kitchen

---

One of the things readers like most about this still outstanding place – London's first gastropub – is that because the single room is dominated by the open kitchen, you can not only watch the efficient staff prepare your meal, but enjoy the aromas of the cooking. It's lost none of its assured touch: some say the mediterranean, almost rustic cooking is among the very best food you'll find in a pub. That said, it's busy, noisy, ever so slightly scruffy for some tastes, and you'll be lucky to bag an empty table without a wait, but it always feels chatty and pubby, with a buzzing informality that belies the quality of the food. On weekday lunchtimes especially (when staff from the *Guardian* offices next door can be a major part of the mix), dishes from the blackboard menu can run out or change fairly quickly, so it really is worth getting here as early as you possibly can if you're hoping to eat. Furnishings are basic and well worn – school chairs, a random assortment of tables, a couple of sofas on bare boards, and modern paintings on the walls (there's an art gallery upstairs, with direct access from the bar). Wells & Youngs Eagle and Bombardier on handpump, good wines including around 14 by the glass, and decent coffee; piped music (sometimes loud). Not the ideal choice for a quiet dinner, or a smart night out, the pub is generally quieter at weekends.

🍴 Very much enjoyed by readers this year, the short menu choice might include a very good, proper minestrone soup, crab, coriander and lemon linguini, their delicious and substantial marinated rump steak sandwich, bruschetta with grilled asparagus and poached organic egg, lamb chops with cracked wheat, broad beans, mint, lemon, cucumber and yoghurt, roast pollack with purple sprouting broccoli, anchovy, chilli and aïoli, gloucester old spot with cockles, paprika, parsley and potatoes, and a handful of tapas dishes like prawns 'pil pil' or pimentos piquillos; they always have a well chosen cheese, and portuguese custard tarts. *Starters/Snacks: £5.00. Main Courses: £6.50 to £14.50. Puddings: £1.20 (just tarts)*

Free house ~ Licensee Michael Belben ~ Real ale ~ Bar food (12.30-3(3.30 weekends), 6.30-10.30 (not Sun)) ~ (020) 7837 1353 ~ Children welcome ~ Dogs allowed in bar ~ Open 12-11(5 Sun); closed Sun evening, bank hols and a week at Christmas

Recommended by John and Gloria Isaacs, Tony and Jill Radnor, Simon and Mandy King, Andy and Claire Barker, Barry Collett, Conor McGaughey

Grapes

Shepherd Market; ⊖ Green Park; W1J 7QQ

Genuinely old-fashioned and individual, always packed in the evenings; new licensees have added thai food, and guest beers you'll rarely find in this area

New licensees have arrived at this engagingly old-fashioned pub, making quite a few changes: not to the look of the place (save a lick of paint, all is as it's been for quite some time), but they've started selling food again, and made the beers rather more interesting. You'll always find six on offer (as in most Mayfair pubs, not always cheap), with Adnams and Sharps Doom Bar and Special the house beers, joined by often rather unusual guests like Arundel Castle, Cains IPA, and Thwaites Lancaster Bomber. Genuinely atmospheric, the bar is enjoyable at lunchtime when you can more easily take in its traditional charms, but is perhaps at its best when it's so very busy in the evenings, and the cheery bustle rather adds to the allure. The dimly lit bar has plenty of well worn plush red furnishings, stuffed birds and fish in glass display cases, wooden floors and panelling, a welcoming coal fire, and a snug little alcove at the back; fruit machine. You'll generally see smart-suited drinkers spilling on to the square outside. The pub is in the heart of Shepherd Market, one of central London's best-kept secrets.

Thai – cooked by a Thai chef; also maybe baguettes and other traditional dishes like a pie or a roast. *Starters/Snacks: £3.00 to £4.50. Main Courses: £5.95 to £6.95*

Free house ~ Licensees John Shannon, Leigh Kelly ~ Real ale ~ Bar food ~ (020) 7493 4216 ~ Dogs allowed in bar ~ Open 11(12 Sat)-11; 12-10.30 Sun

Recommended by the Didler, N R White, Darren Le Poidevin, GHC, Peter Dandy, Michael Dandy, Jeremy Whitehorn, Dr and Mrs A K Clarke, Conor McGaughey

Grenadier

Wilton Row; the turning off Wilton Crescent looks prohibitive, but the barrier and watchman are there to keep out cars; walk straight past – the pub is just around the corner; ⊖ Knightsbridge; SW1X 7NR

Atmospheric old pub with lots of character and military history – though not much space; famous for its ghost, and its bloody marys

It doesn't take many people to fill up this snugly characterful pub, said to be London's most haunted. It's patriotically painted in red, white and blue, a reminder of the days when it was the mess for the officers of the Duke of Wellington. His portrait hangs above the fireplace, alongside neat prints of guardsmen through the ages, and there's a sentry box out in front. Even at the busiest of times the atmosphere is good-natured and smartly civilised, and you should generally be able to plonk yourself on one of the stools or wooden benches in the simple, unfussy bar. Adnams, Fullers London Pride, Timothy Taylors Landlord, Shepherd Neame Spitfire and Wells & Youngs Bombardier from handpumps at the rare pewter-topped bar counter, though on Sundays especially you'll find several of the customers here to sample their famous bloody marys, made to a unique recipe. At the back is an intimate restaurant. There's a single table outside in the attractive mews – surprisingly peaceful given the proximity to Knightsbridge and Hyde Park Corner. They may be closed to all but ticket holders on events such as the anniversary of the Battle of Waterloo, or Wellington's birthday.

⑪ **Straightforward bar food such as sandwiches, burgers, pies and fish and chips, with various sharing plates, and snacks like sausages on sticks.** *Main Courses: £4.25 to £9.95*

Spirit Group ~ Manager Cynthia Weston ~ Real ale ~ Bar food (12-3, 5.30-9.30; all day Sat, Sun (except break 5-6)) ~ Restaurant ~ (020) 7235 3074 ~ Open 11-11; 11-10.30 Sun

Recommended by Paul and Marion Watts, Ian Phillips, Kevin Blake, Andrea Rampley, GHC, N R White

Guinea

Bruton Place; ⊖ Bond Street, Green Park, Piccadilly, Oxford Circus; W1J 6NL

Prize-winning steak and kidney pie in tiny old-fashioned pub with friendly staff, and bustling atmosphere after work – when customers spill on to the street

There's been a pub on the site of this old-fashioned little place for centuries, though it was originally called the Pound, after the nearby cattle and hogpound; the name was changed in 1663 when the first golden guinea was struck. The main draw is their steak and kidney pie, served on weekday lunchtimes, though readers have this year also very much enjoyed the beer, and the friendly after-work atmosphere, when a mix of suited workers, tourists, and diners for the upmarket restaurant spill out on to the little mews in front, even in winter. Inside, it's almost standing room only, and the look of the place is appealingly simple: bare boards, yellow walls, old-fashioned prints, and a red-planked ceiling with raj fans. Three cushioned wooden seats and tables are tucked to the left of the entrance to the bar, with a couple more in a snug area at the back, underneath a big old clock; most people tend to prop themselves against a little shelf running along the side of the small room. Pleasant, cheery staff serve Wells & Youngs Bitter, Special, and seasonal brews from the striking bar counter, which has some nice wrought-iron work above it. Take care to pick the right entrance – it's all too easy to walk into the upscale Guinea Grill which takes up much of the same building; uniformed doormen will politely redirect you if you've picked the door to that by mistake.

⑪ **Served lunchtimes only, the steak and kidney pies are still the thing here – beyond these, the bar menu is limited to a few elaborate grilled ciabattas (these have won awards too), such as chicken siciliano, or a good one with steak and anchovy; there's a vegetarian one too. The adjacent restaurant also serves the pies, albeit more expensively.** *Starters/Snacks: £5.50 to £16.25. Main Courses: £8.50 to £34.00. Puddings: £3.95 to £5.95*

Youngs ~ Manager Carl Smith ~ Real ale ~ Bar food (12.30-2.30 Mon-Fri only) ~ Restaurant ~ (020) 7409 1728 ~ Open 11-11; 6-11 Sat; closed Sat lunchtime, all day Sun, bank hols

Recommended by Peter Dandy, Darren Le Poidevin, Barry and Anne, the Didler, N R White, Derek Thomas, Sue Demont, Tim Barrow

Jerusalem Tavern ★ ◀

Britton Street; ⊖ ⇌ Farringdon; EC1M 5UQ

A London favourite, delightfully atmospheric, even at its busiest, with full range of splendid St Peters beers, good lunchtime food, and helpful staff

As ever, much enjoyed by readers this year – even when it's been very crowded indeed – this carefully restored old coffee house is the only place to stock the whole range of brews from the Suffolk-based St Peters other than the brewery itself, with half a dozen tapped from casks behind the little bar counter, and the rest available in their elegant, distinctively shaped bottles. Depending on the season you'll find St Peters Best, Fruit Beer, Golden Ale, Grapefruit, Lemon & Ginger (a favourite with some regular visitors), Strong, Porter, Wheat Beer, Winter, and Spiced Ales, and you can buy them to take away too. Particularly inviting when it's candlelit on a cold winter's evening, the pub is a vivid re-creation of a dark 18th-c tavern, seeming so genuinely old that you'd hardly guess the work was done only a few years ago. The current building was developed around 1720, originally as a merchant's house, then becoming a clock and watchmaker's. It still has the shop front added in 1810, immediately behind which is a light little room with a couple of wooden tables and benches, a stack of *Country Life* magazines, and some remarkable old tiles on the walls at either side. This leads to the tiny dimly lit bar, which has a couple of unpretentious tables on the bare boards, and another up some stairs on a discreetly precarious-feeling though perfectly secure balcony – a prized vantage point. A plainer back room has a few more tables, a fireplace, and a stuffed fox in a case. There's a relaxed, chatty feel in the evenings, although these days it's getting harder to bag a seat here then. Staff are friendly and enthusiastic. There may be a couple of tables outside. Note the pub is closed at weekends. The brewery's headquarters in South Elmham is a main entry in our Suffolk chapter.

🍴 **Blackboards list the simple but well liked lunchtime food, the choice depending on what the staff have picked up from the local markets that day: good big doorstep sandwiches, and a couple of changing hot dishes such as chicken, bacon and asparagus pie, sausage and mash, stuffed aubergines, or pan-fried lamb with celeriac purée and mixed vegetables.** *Starters/Snacks: £3.00 to £7.00. Main Courses: £7.50 to £10.00*

St Peters ~ Manager Cheryl Jacob ~ Real ale ~ Bar food (12-3) ~ (020) 7490 4281 ~ Children allowed till 6pm ~ Dogs welcome ~ Open 11-11; closed weekends, bank hols, and maybe some days between Christmas and New Year

Recommended by Mike Gorton, N R White, Tracey and Stephen Groves, Giles and Annie Francis, Ian Phillips, Sue Demont, Tim Barrow, Gordon Prince, Bruce Bird, the Didler, Darren Le Poidevin, Ewan McCall, Susan and John Douglas, Donna and Roger

Lamb ★ 🍺
Lamb's Conduit Street; ⊖ Holborn; WC1N 3LZ

Famously unspoilt Victorian pub, full of character, with unique fittings and atmosphere

One reader regards a visit to this old favourite as his treat to himself whenever he visits London. It stands out for its unique Victorian fittings and atmosphere, with the highlight the bank of cut-glass swivelling snob-screens all the way around the U-shaped bar counter. Sepia photographs of 1890s actresses on the ochre panelled walls, and traditional cast-iron-framed tables with neat brass rails around the rim add to the overall effect. It can get busy in the evenings, but there's a very peaceful, relaxed atmosphere at quieter times (particularly the afternoons), when this can be a lovely place to unwind. Well kept Wells & Youngs Bitter, Bombardier, Special and seasonal brews like St Georges or Waggle Dance on handpump, and a good choice of malt whiskies. No machines or music. There's a snug little room at the back, slatted wooden seats out in front, and more in a little courtyard beyond. Like the street, the pub is named for the kentish clothmaker William Lamb who brought fresh water to Holborn in 1577. Note they don't allow children.

🍴 **Bar food includes soups like roasted pumpkin and sesame seed, their popular hot ham rolls, well liked traditional dishes like fish and chips, burgers, sausage and mash, and beef and ale pie, and puddings like peanut butter and chocolate chip cake; Sunday roasts.** *Starters/Snacks: £3.95 to £5.95. Main Courses: £7.50 to £10.00. Puddings: £3.50 to £3.95*

Youngs ~ Manager Suzanne Simpson ~ Real ale ~ Bar food (12-9) ~ (020) 7405 0713 ~ Open 11-midnight; 12-10.30 Sun

Recommended by B and M Kendall, Bruce Bird, Tracey and Stephen Groves, the Didler, GHC, David and Sue Smith, P Dawn, Sue Demont, Tim Barrow, James A Waller, Derek Thomas, Roy Hoing, Dr and Mrs A K Clarke

Lamb & Flag 🍺 £
Rose Street, off Garrick Street; ⊖ Leicester Square; WC2E 9EB

Historic yet unpretentious, full of character and atmosphere; busy in the evenings, it's this area's most interesting pub

Easily the most characterful pub around Covent Garden (meaning you'll rarely have it to yourself), this unspoilt and in places rather basic old tavern buzzes with atmosphere, especially in the evenings, when it's enormously popular with after-work drinkers and visitors. It can be empty at 5pm and cheerfully heaving by 6, and always has an overflow of people chatting in the little alleyways outside, even in winter. The more spartan front room leads into a snugly atmospheric low-ceilinged back bar, with high-backed black settles and an open fire; in Regency times this was known as the Bucket of Blood thanks to the bare-knuckle prize-fights held here. Half a dozen well kept real ales typically include Adnams, Courage Best and Directors, Greene King IPA, and Wells & Youngs Bitter and Special; also, a good few malt whiskies. The upstairs Dryden Room is often less crowded, and has more seats (though fewer beers); there's jazz up here every Sunday evening. The pub has a lively and well documented history: Dryden was nearly beaten to death by hired thugs outside, and Dickens made fun of the Middle Temple lawyers who frequented it when he was working in nearby Catherine Street.

🍴 **A short choice of simple food is served upstairs, lunchtimes only: soup, baked potatoes, a few daily changing specials like cottage pie, cauliflower cheese or fish and chips, and a choice of roasts.** *Starters/Snacks: £3.50. Main Courses: £5.50 to £7.50. Puddings: £3.50*

Free house ~ Licensees Terry Archer and Adrian and Sandra Zimmerman ~ Real ale ~ Bar food (12-3(5 Sat, Sun)) ~ (020) 7497 9504 ~ Children in upstairs dining room 11am-5pm only ~ Jazz Sun evenings ~ Open 11-11(11.30 Fri, Sat); 12-10.30 Sun; closed 25 and 26 Dec, 1 Jan
Recommended by the Didler, Donna and Roger, N R White, LM, Derek Thomas, Tom McLean, Ewan McCall, Mike and Sue Loseby

Lord Moon of the Mall 🍺 £

Whitehall; ⊖ ≋ *Charing Cross; SW1A 2DY*

Superior Wetherspoons pub with excellent value food and drink in perfect location close to all the sights; up to nine real ales, often unusual

More individual than many Wetherspoons pubs, this well run and nicely converted former bank is a very useful pit-stop for families and visitors touring the nearby sights, not least because the all-day food is far cheaper than you'll find anywhere else in the area. It's also excellent for beer drinkers: not only are the real ales quite substantially cheaper than at most pubs nearby, but the range is better too, with some particularly unusual (and rapidly changing) guests. You might find Springhead Charlie's Angel, Loddon Flight of Fancy, Wychwood Dogs Bollocks and a May Bock from Belgium alongside the regular Fullers London Pride, Greene King Abbot, Marstons Pedigree and Shepherd Neame Spitfire; prices for all of these are well below the London norm. They have occasional beer festivals, and also keep Weston's cider. The impressive main room has a splendid high ceiling and quite an elegant feel, with old prints, big arched windows looking out over Whitehall, and a huge painting that seems to show a well-to-do 18th-c gentleman; in fact it's Tim Martin, founder of the Wetherspoons chain. Once through an arch the style is more recognisably Wetherspoons, with a couple of neatly tiled areas and bookshelves opposite the long bar; silenced fruit machines, trivia, and a cash machine. Service can slow down at lunchtimes, when it does get busy. The back doors (now only an emergency exit) were apparently built as a secret entrance for the bank's account holders living in Buckingham Palace (Edward VII had an account here from the age of three). As you come out, Nelson's Column is immediately to the left, and Big Ben a walk of ten minutes or so to the right.

🍴 **The wide choice of bar food is from the standard Wetherspoons menu: sandwiches, bangers and mash, five-bean chilli, aberdeen angus steak pie, a big italian platter for sharing, and children's meals; after 2pm (and all day weekends) they usually have a two-for-one meal offer. The terms of the licence rule out fried food.** *Starters/Snacks: £2.50 to £5.00. Main Courses: £5.00 to £7.00. Puddings: £1.49 to £3.19*

Wetherspoons ~ Manager Mathew Gold ~ Real ale ~ Bar food (9am-11pm) ~ (020) 7839 7701 ~ Children welcome till 7pm if eating ~ Open 9am-11.30pm (12 Fri and Sat; 11 Sun)
Recommended by Pete Walker, Dr and Mrs A K Clarke, Stuart and Alison Ballantyne, Peter Dandy, Keith and Chris O'Neill, Michael Dandy, Darren Le Poidevin, Ian Phillips

---

'Children welcome' means the pub says it lets children inside without any special restriction. If it allows them in, but to restricted areas such as an eating area or family room, we specify this. Some pubs may impose an evening time limit. We do not mention limits after 9pm as we assume children are home by then.

Nags Head 🍺

Kinnerton Street; ⊖ Knightsbridge; SW1X 8ED

Genuinely unspoilt and very un-London, its distinctive bar filled with theatrical mementoes and friendly locals

This idiosyncratic little gem feels so much like an old-fashioned local in a sleepy village that you can scarcely believe you're only minutes from Harrods and the hordes of Knightsbridge. It's one of London's most unspoilt pubs (and indeed one of our own favourites), hidden away in an attractive and peaceful mews, and rarely getting too busy or crowded. There's a snugly relaxed, cosy feel in the small, panelled and low-ceilinged front room, where friendly regulars sit chatting around the unusual sunken bar counter. There's a log-effect gas fire in an old cooking range (seats by here are generally snapped up pretty quickly), then a narrow passage leads down steps to an even smaller back bar with stools and a mix of comfortable seats. Adnams Best and Broadside are pulled on attractive 19th-c china, pewter and brass handpumps, while other interesting old features include a 1930s what-the-butler-saw machine and a one-armed bandit that takes old pennies. The piped music is rather individual: often jazz, folk or 1920s-40s show tunes, and around the walls are drawings of actors and fading programmes from variety performances. There are a few seats and sometimes a couple of tables outside. Most readers are delighted by the forthright landlord's fairly hard-line policy on mobile phone use.

🍽 **Bar food (once again felt by readers to be rather less impressive than the rest of the pub) includes sandwiches, ploughman's, salads, sausage, mash and beans, chilli con carne, daily specials, and a choice of roasts; there's usually a £1.50 surcharge added to all dishes in the evenings, and at weekends.** *Starters/Snacks: £4.00. Main Courses: £6.00 to £7.00. Puddings: £3.00*

Free house ~ Licensee Kevin Moran ~ Real ale ~ Bar food (11-9.30 (12-8.30 Sun)) ~ No credit cards ~ (020) 7235 1135 ~ Open 11-11; 12-10.30 Sun

Recommended by Pete Baker, Kevin Thomas, Nina Randall, R T and J C Moggridge, the Didler, John and Gloria Isaacs, GHC, Sue Demont, Tim Barrow, B and M Kendall, Giles and Annie Francis, Kevin Blake, Barry and Anne

Old Bank of England 🍷

Fleet Street; ⊖ Temple; EC4A 2LT

Dramatically converted former bank building, with gleaming chandeliers in impressive, soaring bar, well kept Fullers beers, and good pies

You wouldn't immediately guess this rather austere Italianate building was a pub – in winter the clue is the Olympic-style torches blazing outside. It's a splendid conversion of a former branch of the Bank of England, and the opulent décor can take your breath away when seen for the first time. You can better appreciate the work that went into its transformation at quieter times – it's no less impressive at its busiest (usually straight after work), but the noise and bustle can sometimes leave as deep an impression then. The soaring, spacious bar has three gleaming chandeliers hanging from the exquisitely plastered ceiling, high above an unusually tall island bar counter, crowned with a clock. The end wall has big paintings and murals that look like 18th-c depictions of Justice, but in fact feature members of the Fuller, Smith and Turner families, who run the brewery the pub belongs to. There are well polished dark wooden furnishings, plenty of framed prints, and, despite the grandeur, some surprisingly cosy corners, with screens between some of the tables creating an unexpectedly intimate feel which readers really enjoy. Tables in a quieter galleried section upstairs offer a bird's-eye view of the action, and some smaller rooms (used mainly for functions) open off. Well kept Fullers Chiswick, Discovery, ESB, London Pride and seasonal brews on handpump, a good choice of malt whiskies, and a dozen wines by the glass. At lunchtimes the piped music is generally classical or easy listening; it's louder and livelier in the evenings. Note they don't allow children, and are closed at weekends. Pies have a long if rather dubious pedigree in this area; it was in the vaults and tunnels below the Old Bank and the surrounding buildings that Sweeney Todd butchered the clients destined to provide the fillings in his mistress Mrs Lovett's nearby pie shop.

🍴 Available all day, the good bar food has an emphasis on well liked home-made pies such as sweet potato and goats cheese, chicken, broccoli or gammon, leek and wholegrain mustard, but also includes sandwiches, soup, welsh rarebit, ploughman's, sausages and mash, lemon chicken and courgette salad, and fish and chips. They may do afternoon teas. *Starters/Snacks: £4.50 to £5.75. Main Courses: £7.95 to £10.95. Puddings: £3.95 to £4.95*

Fullers ~ Manager James Carman ~ Real ale ~ Bar food (12-9) ~ (020) 7430 2255 ~ Open 11-11; closed weekends, bank hols

Recommended by Barry Collett, Bruce Bird, Ian Phillips, Darren Le Poidevin, Dr and Mrs M E Wilson, Tracey and Stephen Groves, the Didler, Stuart and Alison Ballantyne, Peter Dandy, Dr and Mrs A K Clarke, David and Sue Smith

Olde Cheshire Cheese

Wine Office Court, off 145 Fleet Street; ⊖ ⇌ *Blackfriars; EC4A 2BU*

Much bigger than it looks, soaked in history, with lots of warmly old-fashioned rooms, cheap Sam Smiths beer, and convivial atmosphere

One of the London pubs we've had most reports about this year – all warmly positive – this atmospheric 17th-c former chop house has an enjoyable warren of dark, historic rooms. Over the years Congreve, Pope, Voltaire, Thackeray, Dickens, Conan Doyle, Yeats and perhaps Dr Johnson have called in, and many parts appear hardly to have changed since. It can get busy with tourists, but there are plenty of hidden corners to absorb the crowds. The unpretentious rooms have bare wooden benches built in to the walls, bare boards, and, on the ground floor, high beams, crackly old black varnish, Victorian paintings on the dark brown walls, and big open fires in winter. A particularly snug room is the tiny one on the right as you enter, but the most rewarding bit is the Cellar Bar, down steep narrow stone steps that look as if they're only going to lead to the loo, but in fact take you out an unexpected series of cosy areas with stone walls and ceilings, and some secluded alcoves. Sam Smiths OB on handpump, as usual for this brewery, extraordinarily well priced (over £1 less than the beer in some of our other London main entries). Service from smartly dressed staff is helpful, though sometimes less quick for food than it is for drinks. It's much quieter at weekends than during the week. In the early 20th century the pub was well known for its famous parrot that for over 40 years entertained princes, ambassadors, and other distinguished guests; she's still around today, stuffed and silent, in the restaurant on the ground floor.

🍴 With some choices available all day, bar food includes a good value lunchtime pie and mash buffet served in the cellar bar (12-2 only, £6.95), as well as sandwiches or paninis, and main dishes like steak and kidney pudding or fish and chips. *Main Courses: £6.95 to £9.95*

Sam Smiths ~ Manager Gordon Garrity ~ Real ale ~ Bar food (12-10 Mon-Fri; 12-8.30 Sat; not Sun (though restaurant open then)) ~ Restaurant ~ (020) 7353 6170 ~ Children in eating area of bar and restaurant ~ Open 11-11; 12-5 Sun; closed Sun evening

Recommended by LM, Eithne Dandy, Tracey and Stephen Groves, Richard Marjoram, Roy and Lindsey Fentiman, N R White, Barry Collett, Phil and Sally Gorton, Darren Le Poidevin, the Didler, Donna and Roger, C J Fletcher, Peter Dandy

Olde Mitre 🍺 £

Ely Place; the easiest way to find it is from the narrow passageway beside 8 Hatton Garden; ⊖ *Chancery Lane; EC1N 6SJ*

Hard to find but well worth it – an unspoilt old pub with lovely atmosphere, unusual guest beers, and bargain toasted sandwiches

Warmly praised this year by the readers who've managed to find it (it can be a real hidden treasure), this splendidly atmospheric old tavern is a wonderful refuge from the modern city nearby. Unspoilt and cosy, the small rooms have lots of dark panelling, as well as antique settles and – particularly in the popular back room, where there are more seats – old local pictures and so forth. It gets good-naturedly packed between 12.30 and 2.15, filling up again in the early evening, but in the early afternoons and by around 9pm becomes a good deal more tranquil. An upstairs room, mainly used for functions, may double as an overflow at peak periods. Adnams Bitter and Broadside, Caledonian Deuchars IPA, and one or two very carefully chosen guests like Orkney Dark Isle or Roosters Yankee on handpump; friendly service from the convivial landlord and obliging staff. No music, TV or machines – the only games here are darts, cribbage and dominoes. There's some space for outside drinking with some pot plants and jasmine in the narrow yard between the pub and St Ethelreda's church. Note the pub doesn't open weekends. The iron gates that guard one entrance to Ely Place are a reminder of the days when the law in this district was administered by the Bishops of Ely. The best approach is from Hatton Garden, walking up the right-hand side away from Chancery Lane; an easily missed sign on a lamppost points the way down a narrow alley.

🍴 **Served all day, bar snacks are limited to scotch eggs, pork pies and sausage rolls, and really good value toasted sandwiches with cheese, ham, pickle or tomato.** *Starters/Snacks: £1.25 to £1.50*

Punch ~ Managers Eamon and Kathy Scott ~ Real ale ~ Bar food (11.30-9.30) ~ (020) 7405 4751 ~ Open 11-11; closed weekends, bank hols

Recommended by N R White, Phil and Sally Gorton, Dr and Mrs M E Wilson, Steve Kirby, the Didler, Tom McLean, Ewan McCall, Sue Demont, Tim Barrow, Tracey and Stephen Groves

Princess Louise
High Holborn; ⊖ Holborn; WC1V 7EP

Expected to reopen December 2007 after meticulous refurbishment, an intact Victorian gin-palace with fabulously extravagant décor

This splendid Victorian gin-palace is currently closed for a major refurbishment, expected to be complete by December. Sam Smiths are known for their very careful restoration of old pubs, and they're certainly doing this one thoroughly: by the time it reopens, the pub will have been closed for around nine months. Regular visitors eagerly await the results: some of the furnishings had been starting to look a litle tired, and it should be quite a treat to see the décor restored to its magnificent best. Created by the finest craftsmen of the day and surviving essentially intact, the gloriously opulent main bar includes splendid etched and gilt mirrors, brightly coloured and fruity-shaped tiles, and slender portland stone columns soaring towards the lofty and deeply moulded crimson and gold plaster ceiling. Its architectural appeal is unique (even the gents' has its own preservation order) but the pub has also won praise for its friendly, bustling atmosphere, and of course its very nicely priced Sam Smiths OB on handpump from the long main bar counter. It's generally quite crowded on early weekday evenings (for some, adding to the appeal), but is usually quieter later on. It's worth checking the pub's reopened before making a special journey: if the number below doesn't work, you'll know they're still closed.

🍴 **Food has been served upstairs, with traditional things like home-made lasagne, pies, hotpot and breaded plaice, but details of the new menu hadn't been finalised as we went to press.**

Sam Smiths ~ Real ale ~ Bar food ~ (020) 7405 8816 ~ Open 11-11; 12-11 Sat; 12-10.30 Sun; closed 25 and 26 Dec, 1 Jan

Recommended by Donna and Roger, Bruce Bird, Mike Gorton, the Didler, Simon Collett-Jones, Ian Phillips, Ewan McCall, Barry Collett, Tom McLean

Red Lion 🍺
Duke of York Street; ⊖ Piccadilly Circus; SW1Y 6JP

Remarkably preserved Victorian pub, all gleaming mirrors and polished mahogany, though right in the heart of town, so does get busy

Filling up fast thanks to its busy location in the heart of the West End, this is one of London's best remaining examples of a proper Victorian pub, and is quite remarkably well preserved. When it was built its profusion of mirrors was said to enable the landlord to keep a watchful eye on local prostitutes, but the gleaming glasswork isn't the only feature of note: the series of small rooms also has a good deal of polished mahogany, as well as crystal chandeliers and cut and etched windows, and a striking ornamental plaster ceiling. Fullers London Pride, Timothy Taylors Landlord and a couple of changing guests like Hook Norton Old Hooky and Marstons Pedigree on handpump. Diners have priority on a few of the front tables, and there's a minuscule upstairs eating area. It can be very crowded at lunchtime and early evening (try inching through to the back room where there's sometimes more space); many customers spill out on to the pavement, in front of a mass of foliage and flowers cascading down the wall. The piped music can be loud at times, and the atmosphere is generally bustling; come at opening time to appreciate its period charms more peacefully. No children inside.

🍽 **Now served all day, simple dishes like sandwiches, salads, pies, and fish and chips.** *Starters/Snacks: £2.95. Main Courses: £5.95 to £9.95. Puddings: £4.50*

Mitchells & Butlers ~ Real ale ~ Bar food (12-10) ~ Restaurant ~ (020) 7321 0782 ~ Open 11-11; closed Sun, bank hols

Recommended by Mike Gorton, Michael Dandy, N R White, Darren Le Poidevin, the Didler, LM, Barry and Anne, Dr and Mrs M E Wilson, Andrew Wallace, Sue Demont, Tim Barrow, Dr and Mrs A K Clarke

Red Lion 🍺
Waverton Street; ⊖ Green Park; W1J 5QN

Civilised Mayfair pub with the feel of a village local, particularly welcoming service, and enjoyably cosy atmosphere; good beers and food too

Readers are particularly impressed by the service at this comfortably civilised pub, particularly from the landlord. As one says: 'It is an almost extinct habit to shout "thanks" when a customer leaves the pub, but he never failed to do so during our visit.' In one of Mayfair's quietest and prettiest corners, it feels like a rather smart village local, and on warm evenings you'll generally find plenty of drinkers chatting outside. It can get very busy indeed after work, but always keeps its warmly cosy feel. The main L-shaped bar has small winged settles on the partly carpeted scrubbed floorboards, and carefully framed London prints below the high shelf of china on the well polished, dark-panelled walls. Adnams, Fullers London Pride, Greene King IPA, and Wells & Youngs Ordinary and Bombardier on handpump, and they do rather good bloody marys (with a Very Spicy option); also a dozen malt whiskies, and around 14 wines by the glass; friendly, smiling service. The gents' usually has a copy of *The Times* at eye level. On Saturday evenings they generally have a pianist.

🍽 **Good, honest bar food (served from a corner at the front) includes sandwiches (they do good toasties), soup, ploughman's, cumberland sausage and mash, battered haddock, scampi, steak and stilton pie, and daily specials.** *Starters/Snacks: £2.95 to £4.00. Main Courses: £7.00 to £8.50. Puddings: £4.00*

Punch ~ Manager Greg Peck ~ Real ale ~ Bar food (12-3 (not weekends), 6-9.30) ~ Restaurant ~ (020) 7499 1307 ~ Children in restaurant ~ Dogs welcome ~ Open 12-11; 6-11 Sat; 6-10.30 Sun; closed Sat and Sun am, all day 25 and 26 Dec, 1 Jan

Recommended by Michael Dandy, Barry Collett, Barry and Anne, N R White, B and M Kendall, Revd R P Tickle, Sue Demont, Tim Barrow

Salisbury 🍷 🍺
St Martins Lane; ⊖ Leicester Square; WC2N 4AP

Gleaming Victorian pub surviving unchanged in the heart of the West End, good atmosphere, wide choice of drinks; it does get crowded

On fine form these days, this famous Victorian pub has survived intact from when it opened in 1892. A wealth of cut glass and mahogany, it was initially a restaurant called the Salisbury Stores (which explains the SS motif on the windows), before shortly afterwards becoming a pub, named for the three-times Prime Minister whose family owned the freehold. Not too much has changed since, and the atmospheric and busily pubby main bar is a delight at quieter periods (like mid-afternoon on a weekday) – it can be rather packed in the evenings. A curved upholstered wall seat creates the impression of several distinct areas, framed by wonderfully ornate bronze light fittings shaped like ethereal nymphs each holding stems of flowers; there are only four of these, but mirrors all around make it seem as though there are more, and that the room extends much further than it does. A back room popular for eating has plenty more glasswork, and there's a separate little side room with its own entrance. On the walls are old photographs and prints, and, tucked behind the main door, a well known picture of Marianne Faithfull taken here in 1964. Every inch of the walls and ceiling around the stairs down to the lavatories is coated with theatre posters (the pub is right in the heart of the West End). Cheerful staff serve six well kept beers such as Caledonian Deuchars IPA, Wadworths 6X, Wells & Youngs Bitter and Bombardier, and guests like Adnams Explorer and Jennings Cumberland, as well as almost 20 wines by the glass, coffees, Pimms in summer, and even fruit smoothies. Signs boast it's a sports free pub, with no TV or games machines, although, somewhat incongruously, there is a cash machine on one side of the big, panelled bar counter; piped music. There are some fine details on the exterior of the building too, and tables in a pedestrianised side alley.

🍴 **A mostly standard menu includes soup, sandwiches, chicken liver and heather honey pâté, bacon and free-range eggs, fish and chips, mushroom risotto, roast beef, and specials that always include at least one pie and type of sausage.** *Starters/Snacks: £3.29 to £4.49. Main Courses: £5.79 to £8.79. Puddings: £2.99 to £3.19*

Spirit ~ Manager Jas Teensa ~ Bar food (12-9) ~ (020) 7836 5863 ~ Children allowed in inside bar only till 5pm ~ Open 11-11(12 Fri); 12-12 Sat; 12-10.30 Sun; closed 25 Dec
Recommended by the Didler, David M Smith, Joe Green, Mike Gorton, Michael Dandy, Pete Coxon

Seven Stars

Carey Street; ⊖ Holborn (just as handy from Temple or Chancery Lane, but the walk through Lincoln's Inn Fields can be rather pleasant); WC2A 2JB

Quirky and very atmospheric pub with excellent service, distinctive food, and well chosen beers – not forgetting the boss cat

Facing the back of the Law Courts, this cosy little pub is run with a light touch and a healthy dose of eccentricity. Long a favourite with lawyers and reporters covering notable trials nearby, it has plenty of caricatures of barristers and judges on the red-painted walls of the two main rooms, along with posters of legal-themed British films, big ceiling fans, and a particularly relaxed, intimate atmosphere, much enjoyed by readers; checked table cloths add a quirky, almost continental touch. A third area is in what was formerly a legal wig shop next door – it still retains the original frontage, with a neat display of wigs in the window. Despite the extra space, the pub can fill up very quickly, with lots of the tables snapped up by people here for the excellent, individual food. The landlady has presented a BBC food series, and is quite an authority. Adnams, Crouch Vale Brewers Gold, Harveys Best, and a guest like Dark Star Best on handpump; they'll also mix a proper martini. Service is prompt and very friendly – one reader described it as 'outstanding hospitality'. On busy evenings there's an overflow of customers on to the quiet road in front; things generally quieten down after 8pm, and there can be a nice, sleepy atmosphere some afternoons. The Elizabethan stairs up to the lavatories are rather steep, but there's a good strong handrail. Tom Paine, the large and somewhat po-faced pub cat, remains very much a centre of attention: blackboards outside often recount his latest news, and indeed we've had as many reports about his moods over the last few months as we have about the pub's food (some find him a little grumpy – especially if you move the newspaper he likes to sleep on – but he took quite a shine to one correspondent). The licensees have a second pub, the Bountiful Cow, on Eagle Street near Holborn, which specialises in beef.

🍴 **Thoroughly honest rather than trendily fanciful, the changing blackboard menu might include things like welsh rarebit, corned beef hash with fried egg, oysters, roast guinea fowl in lemony jus, napoli sausages with mash, plenty of seasonal game, specials such as portuguese pork with clams or chargrilled bream, and various cheeses; at times you may also find vintage port with fruit cake.** *Starters/Snacks: £5.00 to £8.00. Main Courses: £8.00 to £16.50. Puddings: £4.00 to £7.00*

Free house ~ Licensee Roxy Beaujolais ~ Real ale ~ Bar food (12-3, 5-9 weekdays, 1-4, 6-9 weekends) ~ (020) 7242 8521 ~ Open 11-11; 12-11.30 Sat; 12-10.30 Sun; closed some bank hols (usually inc Christmas)

Recommended by Dr and Mrs M E Wilson, Ian Phillips, Tracey and Stephen Groves, N R White, Bruce Bird, Humphry and Angela Crum Ewing, the Didler, Sue Demont, Tim Barrow, Ewan McCall, Tom McLean, Phil and Sally Gorton, Dr and Mrs A K Clarke, Pete Coxon, David and Sue Smith

Star 🍺

Belgrave Mews West, behind the German Embassy, off Belgrave Square; ⊖ *Knightsbridge; SW1X 8HT*

Festooned with colourful hanging baskets, with a comfortably old-fashioned local feel inside

A lovely sight in summer with its astonishing array of hanging baskets and flowering tubs, this timeless pub was about to have a refurbishment as we went to press, with the aim of restoring some of its earlier character. Wooden floors will replace the carpets, and the friendly licensees were hoping they'd get planning permission to put back the original sash windows. With a restful local feel outside peak times (when it can be busy), the small bar has stools by the counter and tall windows, and an arch leading to the main seating area, with well polished wooden tables and chairs, heavy upholstered settles, globe lighting, and a raj fan. Fullers Chiswick, Discovery, ESB and London Pride on handpump; efficient service. The pub is said to be where the Great Train Robbery was planned. More reports please.

🍴 **Changing seasonally, the lunchtime bar menu might include bacon, asparagus, fine bean and poached egg salad, or ESB braised beef and kidney pudding, with evening dishes such as wild gammon with broad beans, broccoli and parsley buttered new potatoes, pan-fried calves liver and bacon with red wine and sage gravy, and 28-day hung rib-eye steak.** *Starters/Snacks: £3.95 to £6.25. Main Courses: £7.95 to £15.95. Puddings: £3.95 to £7.50*

Fullers ~ Managers Jason and Karen Tinklin ~ Real ale ~ Bar food (12-2.30, 6-9.30; no food weekends) ~ (020) 7235 3019 ~ Dogs allowed in bar ~ Open 11-11; 12-10.30 Sun; closed 25 and 26 Dec, 1 Jan

Recommended by the Didler, GHC, Dr Martin Owton, N R White, Sue Demont, Tim Barrow, Ian Phillips

Westminster Arms 🍺

Storey's Gate; ⊖ *Westminster; SW1P 3AT*

Bustling and unpretentious Westminter local, with good choice of beers and generous straightforward food

The nearest pub to both Westminster Abbey and the Houses of Parliament, this friendly and unpretentious local has a good mix of regulars, and can be packed after work with government staff and researchers, and even the occasional MP (if you hear something a bit like a telephone bell, it's the Division Bell, reminding them to go back across the road to vote). A good range of eight real ales takes in Adnams Best and Broadside, Brakspears, Fullers London Pride, Greene King Abbot, Thwaites Lancaster Bomber, Wells & Youngs and a guest like Hogs Back TEA; they also do decent wines, and several malt whiskies. The plain main bar has simple old-fashioned furnishings, with proper tables on the wooden floors, a good deal of panelling, and a fruit machine; there's not a lot of room, so come early for a seat. Bar food is served in the downstairs wine bar – a good retreat from the ground-floor bustle, with some of the tables in cosy booths; piped music (but not generally in the main bar). There are a couple of tables by the street outside. More reports please.

🍴 **Straightforward but well liked and generously served: filled baguettes, various salads or ploughman's, steak and kidney pie, fish and chips, and daily specials; you can get most of the same dishes in the more formal upstairs restaurant, but they may be slightly more expensive.** *Starters/Snacks: £3.00 to £4.50. Main Courses: £6.50 to £8.95. Puddings: £3.95*

Free house ~ Licensees Gerry and Marie Dolan ~ Real ale ~ Bar food (12-8 weekdays, 12-4 Sat, Sun) ~ Restaurant (weekday lunchtimes (not Weds)) ~ (020) 7222 8520 ~ Children in eating area of bar and restaurant ~ Open 11-11; 11-6 Sat; 12-5 Sun; closed 25 Dec

Recommended by Ian Phillips, Peter Dandy, the Didler, Dr Ron Cox, Dr and Mrs A K Clarke, N R White

EAST LONDON   MAP 12

Grapes

Narrow Street; ⊖ *Shadwell (some distance away) or Westferry on the Docklands Light Railway; the Limehouse link has made it hard to find by car – turn off Commercial Road at signs for Rotherhithe tunnel, then from the Tunnel Approach slip road, fork left leading into Branch Road, turn left and then left again into Narrow Street; E14 8BP*

Relaxed waterside pub, unchanged since Dickens knew it, with particularly appealing cosy back room, helpful friendly staff, and good Sunday roasts

This warmly welcoming 16th-c tavern is one of London's most engaging Thames-side pubs, tucked away well off the tourist route. Many readers will be delighted to learn the characterful landlady has bought the lease, ensuring all continues in its relaxed, timeless way. Charles Dickens used it as the basis of his Six Jolly Fellowship Porters in *Our Mutual Friend*, describing it as a place that 'softened your heart', and presciently predicting it would 'outlast many a better-trimmed building, many a sprucer public house'. It remains almost exactly as he would have known it – all the more remarkable considering the ultra-modern buildings that surround it. The back part is the oldest (and in winter when the fire is lit perhaps the cosiest), with the small back balcony a fine place for a sheltered waterside drink (smokers are welcome here); steps lead down to the foreshore. The chatty, partly panelled bar has lots of prints, mainly of actors, and old local maps, as well as some elaborately etched windows, plates along a shelf, and newspapers to read; shove-ha'penny, table skittles, cribbage, dominoes, chess, backgammon, and maybe piped classical or jazz. Well kept Adnams, Marstons Pedigree and Timothy Taylors Landlord on handpump, a choice of malt whiskies, and a good wine list; efficient, friendly service. The upstairs fish restauarant is very good, with fine views of the river. The pub was a favourite with Rex Whistler, who used it as the viewpoint for his rather special river paintings.

🍽 **Good bar food includes soup, sandwiches, ploughman's, a pint of shell-on prawns, bangers and mash, home-made fishcakes with caper sauce, dressed crab, and a highly regarded, generous Sunday roast (no other meals then, when it can be busy, particularly in season).** *Starters/Snacks: £3.25 to £8.95. Main Courses: £12.95 to £24.95. Puddings: £3.75 to £6.50*

Free house ~ Licensee Barbara Haigh ~ Real ale ~ Bar food (12-2(2.30 Sat, 3.30 Sun), 7-9(not Sun)) ~ (020) 7987 4396 ~ Dogs allowed in bar ~ Open 12-3, 5.30-11; 12-11 Sat; 12-10.30 Sun; closed 25-26 Dec, 1 Jan

Recommended by N R White, Andy and Jill Kassube, David Hall, Mike Gorton, Kurt Hollesen, Edward Leetham, LM

Narrow 🍽 🍷

Narrow Street; ⊖ ⇌ *Limehouse; E14 8DQ*

Superior interpretations of classic meals, all good value and well presented – but you'll probably need to book

The critics flocked to Gordon Ramsay's first pub when it opened this spring, and some clearly couldn't wait to knock it – undeservedly in our view. Trouble is, if you're a world-famous chef attaching your name to a pub then people are going to expect the most extraordinary meal they've ever had, and that's not what this place is about. Leave your preconceptions at the door and what you'll get is superior but essentially traditional pub grub, given a nice spin, cooked and served rather well, and sold at similar prices to what you'll often pay elsewhere for something much less enjoyable. The main snag is that as the menu is served only in the small, sunny dining room (with only limited tables), to be sure of eating, especially in the evening, you'll need to book, sometimes well in advance – though they do generally hold a couple of tables back (and indeed on a summer Monday lunchtime we arrived early and got a table without a reservation, with the stipulation we finish by 1.30). If you're unlucky, there is a separate bar menu too. The bar itself – nicely lightened up, and still very much a pub – is simple and smart, with white-painted walls and ceilings, and dark blue doors and woodwork. There are a couple of mosaic-tiled fireplaces, each with a mirror above, a couple of hat stands, and the odd colourfully striped armchair; piped music. Caledonian Deuchars IPA, Fullers London Pride and perhaps a guest on handpump at the long bar counter, which also has a good range of bottled beers, a varied wine list, and a draught wheat beer from the Meantime Brewery. The dining room is white too, with a glass skylight and big windows; it feels bright even on a dull day. The floors in here are polished wood, and the furnishings simple, matching, and dark; on the walls are maps and prints of the area, and a couple of oars. Service from some staff is briskly efficient – others go out of their way to chat and be friendly. As we went to press they were about to extend the restaurant on to part of the sizeable terrace. There are plenty of riverside tables for drinkers out here, beneath the handsome building (it's a former harbourmaster's house), with views around a breezy bend of the Thames.

🍴 There are a few surprises (pig's cheeks and neeps aren't yet a staple in most pubs), but the seasonally changing menu has a firm emphasis on modern interpretations of classic British dishes, so starters like soft herring roes on toast or pork pie and home-made piccalilli, and main courses such as haddock and chips with marrowfat peas, cock-a-leekie pie and mash (a bit too much pastry, but then it's some of the best pastry we've tasted), whole rainbow trout with samphire and peas, pea, leek and morel flan with poached egg, and hereford sirloin steak with portabello mushroom and anchovy butter. Puddings are particularly good: strawberry and sherry trifle, baked egg custard with goosnargh cakes or lemon posset with cherries. It's good value, and all dishes come with bread. The bar menu has a pint of prawns, potted shrimps with toast, ploughman's, and a mug of soup with bread. *Starters/Snacks: £4.00 to £7.00. Main Courses: £9.00 to £14.50. Puddings: £4.00 to £7.00*

Free house ~ Licensee Justin Whitehead ~ Real ale ~ Bar food (11.30-3, 6-10.30 weekdays, 12-10 Sat, 12-9 Sun) ~ Restaurant ~ 0207 592 7950 ~ Children in restaurant only ~ Open 10-11; 12-10.30 Sun

Recommended by N R White

Prospect of Whitby
Wapping Wall; ⊖ *Wapping; E1W 3SH*

Waterside pub with colourful history and good river views – welcoming to visitors and families

Claiming to be the oldest pub on the Thames (dating back to 1543), this cheery place rather plays upon its unspoilt old fittings and colourful history – and that's all part of the fun. Pepys and Dickens both regularly popped in, Turner came for weeks at a time to study the scene, and in the 17th century the notorious Hanging Judge Jeffreys was able to combine two of his interests by enjoying a drink at the back while looking down over the grisly goings-on in Execution Dock. It's an established favourite on evening coach tours thanks to the building and setting (readers don't always consider the food and drinks as much of a draw), and the tourists who flock here lap up the tales of Merrie Olde London. Plenty of bare beams, bare boards, panelling and flagstones in the L-shaped bar (where the long pewter counter is over 400 years old), and an unbeatable river view towards Docklands from tables in the waterfront courtyard. They have had Fullers London Pride, Greene King Old Speckled Hen and Wells & Youngs Bombardier on handpump (some may run out at times). Families are made very welcome. For a long while the pub was better known as the Devil's Tavern, thanks to its popularity with smugglers and other ne'er-do-wells.

🍴 A big range of the usual dishes is available all day – sandwiches, burgers, sausage and mash, and fish and chips; Sunday roasts. *Starters/Snacks: £4.00 to £9.00. Main Courses: £7.00 to £12.00. Puddings: £4.00*

Spirit Group ~ Manager Paul Davies ~ Real ale ~ Bar food (12-9) ~ Restaurant ~ (020) 7481 1095 ~ Children welcome till 9.30pm ~ Dogs welcome ~ Open 12-11(12 Fri, Sat); 12-10.30 Sun

Recommended by Stuart and Alison Ballantyne, Jeremy Whitehorn, N R White, the Didler, Derek Thomas

---

We include some hotels which have a good bar that offers facilities comparable to those of a pub.

NORTH LONDON   MAP 13

Chapel 🍴 🍷
Chapel Street; ⊖ Edgware Road; NW1 5DP

Very good food in bustling modern gastropub; it does get busy and sometimes noisy – all part of the atmosphere; good service

It's the good, well presented food that consistently earns this much-modernised child-friendly gastropub its entry. It does get busy, particularly in the evenings when it can be a little noisy, but service remains smiling and efficient, and the staff really know their stuff. The atmosphere is always cosmopolitan – perhaps more relaxed and civilised at lunchtime, when it's a favourite with chic local office workers, then altogether busier and louder in the evenings. Light and spacious, the cream-painted rooms are dominated by the open kitchen; furnishings are smart but simple, with plenty of plain wooden tables around the bar, a couple of comfortable sofas at the lounge end, and a big fireplace. You may have to wait for a table during busier periods. A real bonus is the spacious and rather calming outside terrace; they're adding canopies and heaters for smokers. Well kept Adnams and Greene King IPA on handpump, a decent choice of wines by the glass, cappuccino and espresso, fresh orange juice, and a choice of tisanes such as peppermint or strawberry and vanilla. In the evening, trade is more evenly split between diners and drinkers, and the music is more noticeable then, especially at weekends. More reports please.

🍴 Changing every day, the choice might include soups such as savoy cabbage, ham, potato and carrot, baked goats cheese with rosemary and honey, moules marinière, fusilli pasta with slow-cooked ham, paris mushroom and parsley cream sauce, portabello mushroom with buttered spinach, ricotta and almonds in puff pastry, pan-roasted duck breast glazed in thyme honey with parmesan polenta, turnips and carrots, springbok wellington with truffle oil mash, and pan-fried bass with crispy soft shell crab, saffron potato, steamed leek and coriander, and coconut coulis. *Starters/Snacks: £4.00 to £5.50. Main Courses: £8.50 to £15.00. Puddings: £4.00 to £5.00*

Punch ~ Lease Lakis Hondrogiannis ~ Real ale ~ Bar food (12-2.30(12.30-3 Sun), 7-10) ~ (020) 7402 9220 ~ Children welcome ~ Dogs welcome ~ Open 12-11; closed 25 and 26 Dec, Easter

Recommended by Sue Demont, Tim Barrow, Heather McQuillan, Dr and Mrs M E Wilson

Compton Arms £
Compton Avenue, off Canonbury Road; ⊖ ⇌ Highbury & Islington; N1 2XD

Tiny, well run pub with particularly good value food, and very pleasant garden

Hidden away in a peaceful mews, this is a tiny, well run pub rather like an appealing village local, where readers have enjoyed the service, drinks and food. An unexpected bonus is the very pleasant back terrace, with tables among flowers under a big sycamore tree; there may be heaters in winter, and barbecues in summer. The unpretentious low-ceilinged rooms are simply furnished with wooden settles and assorted stools and chairs, with local pictures on the walls; there's a TV for sport, but the only games are things like chess, Jenga and battleships. Well kept Greene King Abbot and IPA and a couple of changing guests like Batemans on handpump, and a choice of malt whiskies. The pub is deep in Arsenal country, so can get busy on match days. More reports please.

🍴 Decent, very good value bar food such as baguettes, filled baked potatoes, various burgers, fish and chips, steak and ale pie, eight different types of sausage with mashed potato and home-made red onion gravy, and particularly well liked daily specials. Their well priced Sunday roasts come in two sizes. *Starters/Snacks: £2.50 to £3.50. Main Courses: £5.75 to £6.95*

Greene King ~ Managers Scott Plomer and Eileen Shelock ~ Real ale ~ Bar food (12-2.30, 6-8.30 weekdays; 12-4 Sat and Sun) ~ (020) 7359 6883 ~ Children welcome in back room ~ Open 12-11(10.30 Sun); closed evening 25 Dec

Recommended by Joe Green

Drapers Arms ⊕ ♀

Far west end of Barnsbury Street; ⊖ ⇄ Highbury & Islington; N1 1ER

Hard to find but well worth it – a top-notch gastropub with especially memorable meals, and excellent range of wines

In a quiet residential street away from Islington's main drag, this striking Georgian townhouse is a top-notch gastropub – not exactly cheap, but very rewarding for a special night out. Colourful bunches of flowers, inset shelves of paperbacks and board games, and a couple of groups of sofas and armchairs offset what might otherwise seem rather a severe open-plan layout and décor, with high-backed dining chairs or booths on dark bare boards, high ceilings, a few big drapery prints on dusky pink walls, and a pair of large fireplaces and mirrors precisely facing each other across the front area; the overall effect is not unlike a bright, elegant wine bar. The choice of wines by the glass (including champagne) is excellent, and they have Courage Best and Greene King Old Speckled Hen on handpump, with a guest like Palmers IPA, and a dozen malt whiskies; there may be piped jazz and swing. Service is helpful and unobtrusive. More reports please.

🍴 With fresh carefully judged flavours and tempting presentation, the choice might include lunchtime sandwiches, fish soup with rouille, gruyère and croûtons, salt and pepper squid with thai spiced salad and chilli mayonnaise, smoked duck and beetroot salad with poached egg and parma ham, pappardelle with wild mushroom, rocket and parmesan, lemon and herb risotto with crab, prawns and grilled fennel, grilled scallops with montpellier butter, slow-roasted lamb with pea and lettuce stew and mint aïoli, herb crusted salmon with french beans and beurre blanc, aged rib-eye steak with red onion and chilli confit, and puddings like chocolate and poached pear cheesecake or a first-rate sticky toffee. *Starters/Snacks: £5.00 to £8.00. Main Courses: £11.50 to £17.00. Puddings: £5.50*

Free house ~ Licensees Mark Emberton and Paul McElhinney ~ Real ale ~ Bar food (12-3, 7-10 (6.30-9.30 Sun)) ~ Restaurant ~ (020) 7619 0348 ~ No children after 7pm unless family eating a full meal ~ Dogs allowed in bar ~ Open 12-11; 12-10.30 Sun; closed 24-27 Dec

Recommended by Maggie Atherton, Dr and Mrs M E Wilson

Duke of Cambridge ⊕ ♀ ◀

St Peter's Street; ⊖ Angel, though some distance away; N1 8JT

Trail-blazing organic pub with very good, carefully sourced food, and excellent range of unusual drinks; nice, chatty atmosphere too, with the feel of a comfortably upmarket local

The impeccably sourced drinks and food are still the main draw at this trailblazing cornerhouse – it was London's first organic pub, and though a meal here may cost slightly more than you'd pay elsewhere for a non-organic meal, it's worth the extra to enjoy choices and flavours you won't find anywhere else. They make all their own bread, pickles, ice-cream and so on, and everything else is sourced from smaller, independent suppliers. On handpump are four organic real ales such as East Kent Goldings Light Ale, SB and Shoreditch Stout from London's small Pitfield Brewery, and St Peters Best, and they also have organic draught lagers and cider, organic spirits, and a very wide range of good, organic wines, many of which are available by the glass. The full range of drinks is chalked on a blackboard, and also includes good coffees and teas, and a spicy ginger ale. The atmosphere is warmly inviting, and it's the kind of place that somehow encourages conversation, with a steady stream of civilised chat from the varied customers. The big, busy main room is simply decorated and furnished, with lots of chunky wooden tables, pews and benches on bare boards, a couple of big metal vases with colourful flowers, daily papers, and carefully positioned soft lighting around the otherwise bare walls. A corridor leads off past a few tables and an open kitchen to a couple of smaller candlelit rooms, more formally set for eating, and a conservatory. It's worth arriving early to eat, as they can get very busy.

🍴 Changing twice a day, the blackboard menu might include soups like lentil and pancetta, sardines on toast with lemon, tomato and olive paste, chicken liver, shallot and red wine parfait with beetroot relish and toast, braised sticky beef chuck with sweet potato mash, game pie (with venison, pigeon and partridge) and braised red cabbage, sautéed rosemary courgettes with gorgonzola, polenta, tomato sauce and dressed leaves, red kidney and root vegetable curry with naan bread and coconut and mint raita, haddock with curried peas, yellowed potatoes and beurre blanc, and puddings like quince crumble or warm chocolate and coconut fondant; children's helpings. *Starters/Snacks: £4.00 to £10.00. Main Courses: £9.50 to £16.00. Puddings: £6.00*

Free house ~ Licensee Geetie Singh ~ Real ale ~ Bar food (12.30-3(3.30 Sat and Sun), 6.30-10.30(10 Sun)) ~ Restaurant ~ (020) 7359 3066 ~ Children welcome ~ Dogs allowed in bar ~ Open 12-11(10.30 Sun); closed 24, 25 and 26 Dec

Recommended by Tony and Jill Radnor, Tracey and Stephen Groves, P Dawn

Flask ♀
Flask Walk; ⊖ Hampstead; NW3 1HE

Properly old-fashioned and villagey local, well liked by Hampstead characters; about to be refurbished as we went to press

This peaceful old local was expected to undergo a major refurbishment as we went to press, but the work should be finished by the time this edition hits the shops. It's the restaurant and eating areas that we're told will change the most (they'll probably be made bigger) – but the bar area is likely to stay pretty much the same and no wonder: its unassuming, properly old-fashioned and rather villagey feel is vey much key to the pub's appeal. A popular haunt of Hampstead artists, actors, and characters, its snuggest and most individual part is the cosy lounge at the front, with plush green seats and banquettes curving round the panelled walls, a unique Victorian screen dividing it from the public bar, and an attractive fireplace. A comfortable orange-lit room with period prints and a few further tables leads into the dining conservatory which has had lots of artificial plants. A couple of white iron tables are squeezed into the tiny back yard. Wells & Youngs Bitter, Special and seasonal brews on handpump, and around 16 wines by the glass. The plainer public bar (which you can get into only from the street) has leatherette seating, cribbage, backgammon, lots of space for darts, fruit machines, trivia, and big-screen SkyTV. There are quite a few tables out in the alley. Small dogs are allowed in the front bar only. The pub's name is a reminder of the days when it distributed mineral water from Hampstead's springs.

🍽 **Bar food has included sandwiches, soup, daily specials like chicken casserole or lamb curry, and good fish and chips, but it wasn't clear as we went to press what will be on the menu after the refurbishment.**

Youngs ~ Manager Simon Allen ~ Real ale ~ Bar food (12-8.30) ~ Restaurant ~ (020) 7435 4580 ~ Children welcome till 6pm ~ Dogs allowed in bar ~ Open 11-11(12 Fri and Sat); 12-10.30 Sun

Recommended by P Dawn, Darren Le Poidevin, Tim Maddison, Ian Phillips, the Didler, Barry Collett, Sue Demont, Tim Barrow

Holly Bush ♀ 🍺
Holly Mount; ⊖ Hampstead; NW3 6SG

Distinctive and convivial village local, with good food and drinks, and lovely unspoilt feel

The unique mood of this timeless favourite is really special, particularly in the evenings, when the old-fashioned and individual front bar has a distinctive gloom that's welcoming even in the height of summer, and there's a bustling mix of chatty locals and visitors. Under the dark sagging ceiling are brown and cream panelled walls (decorated with old advertisements and a few hanging plates), open fires, bare boards, and cosy bays formed by partly glazed partitions. Slightly more intimate, the back room, named after the painter George Romney, has an embossed red ceiling, panelled and etched glass alcoves, and ochre-painted brick walls covered with small prints; piped music, and lots of board and card games. Well kept Adnams Bitter and Broadside, Fullers London Pride, and Harveys Sussex on handpump (one of these is frequently replaced by a more unusual guest), plenty of whiskies, and a good, seasonally changing wine list. The upstairs dining room has table service Tuesday-Sunday – as does the rest of the pub on Sunday. There are tables on the pavement outside. Originally the stable block of a nearby house, the pub is reached by a delightful stroll along some of Hampstead's most villagey streets.

📖 **Now served all day, they generally have a half pint of prawns, welsh rarebit, various sausages with cheddar mash and gravy, pies like chicken, mushroom and London Pride or beef and Harveys, roast chicken in beer and paprika sauce, slow-roast lamb shank, puddings like chocolate, blood orange marmalade and malt whisky fondant, and some good cheeses. Some of their meat is organic.** *Starters/Snacks: £4.00 to £8.00. Main Courses: £8.00 to £15.00. Puddings: £5.00*

Punch ~ Lease Nicolai Outzen ~ Real ale ~ Bar food (12-10(9 Sun)) ~ Restaurant ~ (020) 7435 2892 ~ Children in eating area of bar and restaurant ~ Dogs allowed in bar ~ Open 12-11(10.30 Sun); closed 1 Jan

Recommended by Tim Maddison, the Didler, Tracey and Stephen Groves, Derek Thomas, Ian Phillips, Russell and Alison Hunt, Barry Collett, David M Smith

Marquess Tavern ♀

Canonbury Street/Marquess Road; ⊖ ⇌ Highbury & Islington, Angel; N1 2TB

Gastropub with honest seasonal british food, a very good range of drinks, and the feel of a proper local at the front

In a nice villagey corner of Islington, this imposing Victorian place is now a well regarded gastropub, particularly good for meat, but it has the feel of a relaxed, chatty local too, with quite a few regulars coming for just a drink. The bar is reassuringly traditional and fairly plain, with bare boards and a mix of candlelit wooden tables arranged around a big, horseshoe servery; there's a fireplace either side, one topped by a very tall mirror, as well as an old leather sofa, faded old pictures, and bar billiards in the corner (they have darts, cribbage and other games too, as well as piped music and a generally switched off TV). You can eat either in the bar or in the slightly stiffer back dining room, feeling much brighter with its white paint and skylight; it has an impressive brass chandelier. Real care has been taken selecting the drinks: in addition to up to six real ales from Wells & Youngs, they have a cask-conditioned cider or perry, a very good range of unusual bottled beers, well chosen wines (including several british) and 50 malt whiskies. Service is cheerful and friendly – though there can be a slightly longer than expected wait for food, and on busier days some dishes can run out. There are some peaceful picnic-sets in front. Note they don't open weekday lunchtimes.

📖 **The emphasis is on seasonal unfussy british food: starters like soft boiled duck egg and asparagus, chicken livers with girolles or leek and potato soup, and main courses such as whole gilthead bream with burnt butter and pink fir apple potatoes, gloucester old spot chop with creamed leeks and beer sauce, braised beef with Guinness and colcannon, or lamb with minted greens, barley, and jersey royals, with puddings like rice pudding with blood orange compote or apple and blackberry crumble. Particularly unusual is their acclaimed roast beef, sold by weight, in fairly susbstantial (and pricy) chunks (a blackboard lists what's available). They also have bar snacks like sprats, cornish pasty, and pork pie and piccalilli.** *Starters: £5 to £7.50; Main Courses: £11 to £22.50 (for the beef); Puddings: £5 to £5.50*

Youngs ~ Lease Will Beckett ~ Real ale ~ Bar food (6.30-10, plus 12-5 weekends only) ~ Restaurant ~ (020) 7354 2975 ~ Children welcome ~ Dogs allowed in bar ~ Open 5-11; 12-12 Sat; 12-11 Sun; closed weekday lunchtimes

Recommended by BOB

Olde White Bear

Well Road; ⊖ Hampstead; NW3 1LJ

Particularly friendly and atmospheric, with a wonderfully varied mix of customers; good range of beers, and sensibly priced food all day

Still attracting a wonderfully diverse mix of customers, this neo-Victorian pub is reckoned by many to be Hampstead's friendliest. The dimly lit knocked-through bar is smart but relaxed, with elegant panelling, wooden venetian blinds, and three separate-seeming areas: the biggest has lots of Victorian prints and cartoons on the walls, as well as wooden stools, cushioned chairs, a couple of big tasselled armchairs, a flowery sofa, a handsome fireplace and an ornate Edwardian sideboard. A brighter section at the end has elaborate brocaded pews, while a central area has dried flower arrangements and signed photographs of actors and playwrights. A good range of beers on handpump usually takes in Fullers London Pride, Shepherd Neame Spitfire and Wells & Youngs, with guests like Bath Barnstormer and Highgate Fury; also a decent range of whiskies. There are a few tables in front, and more in a courtyard behind. Regular visitors feel the piped music is louder in the evenings these days – perhaps reflecting its popularity then with a younger crowd (though the cheery, helpful staff are very proud of the eclectic range); cards, chess, TV, and excellent Thursday quiz nights. Parking nearby is mostly permits only (there are no restrictions on Sundays), but the pub sells visitors permits for up to two hours. The Heath is close by.

🍴 **Bar food is served all day, from a range including soup, sandwiches and ciabattas, various salads, feta and buckwheat stuffed peppers, spicy meatballs in tomato sauce with fusilli pasta, home-made beef and lamb burgers, haddock in beer batter, sausages and mash, beef in Guinness pie, and puddings like apple crumble and spotted dick; their choice of roasts on Sundays is very popular.** *Starters/Snacks: £4.00 to £6.50. Main Courses: £6.00 to £10.95. Puddings: £4.00*

Punch ~ Lease Christopher Ely ~ Real ale ~ Bar food (12-9) ~ (020) 7435 3758 ~ Children welcome ~ Dogs allowed in bar ~ Thurs quiz night (starts 9pm) ~ Open 11-11(11.30 Thurs, Fri, Sat); 12-11 Sun

Recommended by Tracey and Stephen Groves, Tim Maddison, Darren Le Poidevin, the Didler, Ian Phillips, N R White

Spaniards Inn 🍺

Spaniards Lane; ⊖ Hampstead, but some distance away, or from Golders Green station take 220 bus; NW3 7JJ

Very popular old pub with lots of character and history, delightful big garden, and wide range of drinks and good food

On good form at the moment, this busy and historic former toll house has a very large and quite charming garden, well liked by people with children and dogs, and nicely arranged in a series of areas separated by judicious planting of shrubs. A crazy paved terrace with slatted wooden tables and chairs opens on to a flagstoned walk around a small raised area with roses and a side arbour of wisteria, clematis and hops; you may need to move fast to bag a table. There's an outside bar, regular summer barbecues, and a new area for smokers. Dating back to 1585, the pub is well known for its tales of hauntings and highwaymen (some of which are best taken with a very large pinch of salt), and the low-ceilinged oak-panelled rooms are attractive and full of character, with open fires, genuinely antique winged settles, candle-shaped lamps in shades, and snug little alcoves. The atmosphere is friendly and chatty, and there's an impressive range of drinks, with between five and eight real ales typically including Adnams, Caledonian Deuchars IPA, Fullers London Pride, Harveys Sussex, and guests like Marstons Old Empire and Roosters Leg Horn; they have occasional themed beer festivals – the most recent showcased beers with dog-related names. They also have some unusual continental draught lagers, and 22 wines by the glass – though in summer you might find the most popular drink is their big jug of Pimms. The pub is believed to have been named after the Spanish ambassador to the court of James I, who had a private residence here. It's fairly handy for Kenwood. The car park fills up fast, and other parking nearby is difficult.

🍴 **Served all day, the well liked bar food might include soup, lunchtime sandwiches, caesar salad, a vegetarian pasta dish like baked sweet potato and goats cheese lasagne, very popular beer-battered fish and chips, welsh lamb with mustard mash, a fish of the day, and – particularly on Sundays, but often on other days too – some hearty dishes to share such as shoulder of lamb or prime rib of beef.** *Starters/Snacks: £3.80 to £5.75. Main Courses: £6.90 to £15.00. Puddings: £4.00*

Mitchells & Butlers ~ Manager David Nichol ~ Real ale ~ Bar food (11.30-10) ~ (020) 8731 6571 ~ Children welcome ~ Dogs welcome ~ Open 11-11(open from 10 at weekends)

Recommended by Ian Phillips, John Saville, Jo Lilley, Simon Calvert, N R White

SOUTH LONDON
MAP 13

Anchor & Hope ❶ ♀

*The Cut (B300, turning E off A301 Waterloo Road, S of Waterloo Station); ↔ ⇄ Waterloo,
Waterloo East; SE1 8LP*

LONDON DINING PUB OF THE YEAR

**Currently London's finest pub for eating, with really excellent, distinctive food, and a
buoyant informal atmosphere**

You wouldn't guess if you stumbled upon it by chance, but this vibrant bare-boards
gastropub is one of London's most fashionable places to eat, with decidedly unusual
meals thoughtfully prepared using excellent seasonal ingredients. A bit scruffy from the
outside, and with an atmosphere that's determinedly informal, it's very much of the Eagle
school: open kitchen and absolutely no booking – even well known faces have been made
to wait. It perhaps appeals to the same sort of people, but here there's a separate dining
room, and on arrival you can add your name to the list to be seated there. Alternatively
you can join the throng in the bar, which shares the same menu, but the dining room
tables are better for an unhurried meal; those in the bar are rather low and small. There's
a piano in one corner, and a big mirror behind the counter, but otherwise the bar is fairly
plain, with dark red-painted walls and big windows that open up in summer. On the other
side of a big curtain, the dining room is similar, but with contemporary paintings on the
walls. Well kept Wells & Youngs Bitter and Bombardier and a guest like St Austell Tinners
on handpump; there's a good wine list, served in tumblers and carafes rather than smart
glasses, but a popular choice before dinner is one of their sherries. It's all rather relaxed
and unstuffy, and the kind of place where strangers cheerfully ask what you're eating;
service is welcoming. There are a few metal tables in front on the street. They recently
opened a restaurant-with-rooms in the heart of the Livradois-Forez in France.

Ⓜ **Highly thought of in foody circles, the meals are listed on a blackboard that changes
twice a day: it might include soups like cabbage, white bean and preserved pork, unusual
starters such as beetroot, goats curd and mint, warm snail and bacon salad, or potted
bloater and pickled cucumber, main courses like haggis, swede stovey and a fried egg,
chicory tart and cep sauce, octopus salad, rabbit with fennel and olives, braised veal and
saffron risotto, roast pigeon with savoy cabbage, bacon and chestnuts, dishes to share
such as pot roast duck with faggots, bacon, turnips and peas or rib of beef, and puddings
like damson bakewell tart or blood orange and rhubarb trifle** *Starters/Snacks: £4.00 to
£9.00. Main Courses: £10.80 to £19.50. Puddings: £5.00*

Charles Wells ~ Lease Robert Shaw ~ Real ale ~ Bar food (12-2.30 (not Mon), 6-10.30; 2pm
sitting only on Sun) ~ Restaurant ~ (020) 7928 9898 ~ Children welcome ~ Dogs welcome ~
Open 11-12(closed till 5 Mon); 12.30-5 Sun; closed Mon lunch, Sun evening, last two weeks of
August, and Christmas and New year

*Recommended by Dr and Mrs M E Wilson, Tony and Jill Radnor, John Watson, Mayur Shah, Mike and Sue Loseby,
Ian Phillips*

Bo-Peep

*Chelsfield; 1.7 miles from M25 junction 4; Hewitts Road, which is last road off exit
roundabout; BR6 7QL*

**A very handy meal-stop from the motorway, with good fish and other meals popular with
older diners at lunchtime**

Doing well under its current owners, this is a proper little country pub, very handy from
the M25. The food is particularly popular with older people at lunchtimes, and indeed
there's a nice, genuinely old-fashioned air throughout. The attractive tile-hung house is
said to date from the 16th c, and the main bar – about to have a new stone floor as we
went to press – still has very low old beams, and an enormous inglenook, as well as
flowers on the tables, and a board with local notices. Two cosy little rooms for eating
open off, one with smart cushions and a wooden floor, and there's a light side room
looking over the country lane. The pub is candlelit at night. Courage Best, Greene King
Old Speckled Hen and Harveys Sussex on handpump; efficient service from cheery, helpful
staff, piped easy listening. A new terrace behind has lots of picnic-sets.

🍴 **The landlord is a fishmonger, so the fresh fish (typically salmon, bass, and sometimes monkfish and skate wing) are particularly well liked. As well as ploughman's and sandwiches (served all through the afternoon on Saturdays), other reliable home-made dishes might include steak and ale pie, scampi, bangers and mash in a giant yorkshire pudding, and specials like ham and egg, liver and bacon, or ham, pea and mint risotto.** *Starters/Snacks: £4.25 to £6.95. Main Courses: £8.95 to £15.95. Puddings: £4.25*

Free house ~ Licensees Kate Mansfield, Graham Buckley ~ Real ale ~ Bar food (12-2 (5.30 Sun), 6.30-9.30) ~ Restaurant ~ (01959) 534457 ~ Open 12-11(10.30 Sun); usually closed 3.30-5 in winter

Recommended by Anna Prior, B and M Kendall, N R White, GHC, Derek Thomas

Crown & Greyhound
Dulwich Village; ⇌ North Dulwich; SE21 7BJ

Comfortable Victorian pub with big back garden (barbecues in summer), good beers, and popular Sunday carvery

Ever so slightly smartened up with a minor facelift over the last year, this big, relaxed Victorian pub boasts a very pleasant back garden, with smart new tables shaded by a chestnut tree, and barbecues on summer weekends. The fence has murals painted by local schoolchildren, and they've french boules, and over-sized versions of games like Connect Four and dominoes. A big back dining room and conservatory open on to here, leading from the pleasantly furnished roomy main bar at the front. Refurbished but retaining many of its original features, this has some quite ornate plasterwork and lamps over on the right, and a variety of nicely distinct seating areas, some with traditional upholstered and panelled settles, others with stripped kitchen tables on stripped boards; there's a coal-effect gas fire and some old prints. As well as Fullers London Pride, Harveys Bitter and Wells & Youngs, they have a guest like Highgate Honey, and organise beer festivals at Easter and perhaps some other bank holidays. Known locally as the Dog, it was built at the turn of the century to replace two inns that had stood here previously, hence the unusual name. Busy in the evenings, but quieter during the day, it's handy for walks through the park, and for the Dulwich Picture Gallery. More reports please.

🍴 **Served all day, with sandwiches, various types of sausage, well liked home-made burgers (including vegetarian), and specials like beef wellington or 21-day hung rib-eye steak. Best to arrive early for their very popular Sunday carvery, as they don't take bookings; the pub can be popular with families then.** *Starters/Snacks: £3.90 to £6.00. Main Courses: £6.90 to £15.50. Puddings: £3.50*

Mitchells & Butlers ~ Manager Duncan Moore ~ Real ale ~ Bar food (12-10(9 Sun)) ~ (020) 8299 4976 ~ Children in restaurant ~ Dogs welcome ~ Open 11-11(12 Thurs,Fri,Sat); 12-10.30 Sun

Recommended by Dave W Holliday

Cutty Sark
Ballast Quay, off Lassell Street; ⇌ Maze Hill, from London Bridge; or from the river front walk past the Yacht in Crane Street and Trinity Hospital; SE10 9PD

Interesting old tavern with genuinely unspoilt bar, great Thames views, organic wines, and wide range of popular food

The unspoilt, dark flagstoned bar of this white-painted house has a genuinely old-fashioned feel, with rough brick walls, wooden settles, barrel tables, open fires, low lighting and narrow openings to tiny side snugs; you can almost imagine smugglers and blackguards with patches over their eyes. An elaborate central staircase leads to an upstairs room with a big bow window jutting out over the pavement – and splendid views of the Thames and Millennium Dome. Adnams Broadside, Fullers London Pride, St Austell Tribute and guests like Fullers Discovery and Greene King Old Speckled Hen on handpump, with a good choice of malt whiskies, and a range of organic wines; fruit machine, juke box. The pub is alive with young people on Friday and Saturday evenings, but can be surprisingly quiet some weekday lunchtimes. There's a busy riverside terrace across the narrow cobbled lane; morris dancers occasionally drop by. Parking is limited nearby – though, unusually for London, if you can bag a space it's free.

🍴 **A wide range of well cooked, promptly served meals, with fresh fish and vegetables delivered daily: well liked sandwiches, bangers and mash, specials such as chilli salmon on a bed of noodles or garlic peppered rib-eye steak, and Tuesday fish and chips night, with two helpings of battered haddock for £10.** *Starters/Snacks: £3.95 to £4.95. Main Courses: £5.00 to £12.95. Puddings: £3.95 to £4.95*

Free house ~ Licensee Paul Martin ~ Real ale ~ Bar food (12-9(10 Sat)) ~ (020) 8858 3146 ~ Children welcome till 9pm ~ Dogs allowed in bar ~ Open 11-11; 12-10.30 Sun

Recommended by John Saville, Simon and Mandy King, B and M Kendall, GHC, Jo Lilley, Simon Calvert, the Didler, N R White, Mike Gorton

Fire Station ♀

Waterloo Road; ⊖ ⇌ Waterloo, Waterloo East; SE1 8SB

Refreshed and smartened up, a conversion of a former fire station, with lively after-work atmosphere (it does get crowded then), and good food – particularly in back dining room

This busy conversion of the former LCC central fire station has had something of a facelift since our last edition: it's smarter than it was, and more obviously comfortable, with new furnishings throughout, and an attractive new bar counter. One thing that hasn't changed is its bustling atmosphere: even by 5pm it can be standing room only, with a nice chatty buzz and a varied mix of customers (some of them having business meetings here). Less like a warehouse than before, the bar has two knocked-through rooms, with lots of new wooden tables and a mix of chairs, a couple of pews and worn leather armchairs, some sizeable plants, and distinctive box-shaped floral lampshades hanging from the high ceilings; the back wall has three back-lit mirrored panels, and some red fire buckets on a shelf. Some of the walls – and the bar counter – have nice black, brick-shaped tiles. The back dining room has been slightly perked up too, with smarter chairs and tables. Fullers London Pride, Marstons Pedigree and a guest like Adnams Broadside on handpump, an excellent choice of wines, and now an increased range of spirits and cocktails. There are tables in front, and picnic sets in a scruffy side alley. It can get quite crowded after work, with loud chat and music combining in a cheery cacophony that most readers thoroughly enjoy, but some find a little overpowering. It's calmer at lunchtimes, and at weekends; two TVs. It's very handy for the Old Vic and Waterloo Station.

🍴 **They do breakfasts from 9pm, and now have an all-day bar menu with baguettes, interesting burgers (lamb and rosemary, or olive and sun-dried tomato), sausage and mash with savoy cabbage, and daily specials such as roast belly of pork, new forest lamb, and moroccan seafood stew, while the dining room menu has things like gilt-head bream and lemon butter with red chard and sweet potato mash, roast fillet of beef with watercress purée and wholegrain mustard mash, pan-fried haddock fillet with lightly spiced chickpea and pepper salad, and 28-day hung rib-eye steak.** *Starters/Snacks: £3.50 to £7.00. Main Courses: £6.95 to £20.00. Puddings: £5.00 to £7.00*

Marstons ~ Manager Tom Alabaster ~ Real ale ~ Bar food (11-11.30; 12-10 Sun) ~ Restaurant ~ (020) 7620 2226 ~ Children welcome till 10pm ~ Open 11-midnight; 12-10.30 Sun; closed 25 and 26 Dec

Recommended by Sue Demont, Tim Barrow, Mrs Hazel Rainer, Ian Phillips, Darren Le Poidevin, GHC, Susan and John Douglas

Founders Arms

Hopton Street (Bankside); ⊖ ⇌ Blackfriars, and cross Blackfriars Bridge; SE1 9JH

Superb location, with outstanding views along the Thames, and handy for Tate Modern and Shakespeare's Globe; decent efficiently served food from early till late

It's worth occasionally taking your eye off the views along the Thames to glance at the menu of this big modern pub: along the bottom it very handily identifies the main buildings you can see from the waterside terrace, with information on when they were built. Taking in St Paul's, the Millennium Bridge, and even the Tower of London way off in the distance, it's probably the best view you'll find at any pub along the river, particularly in the City, so it's no wonder most visitors here sit outside; there are plenty of picnic-sets for Thames-gazers. Rather like a huge conservatory, this is the handiest pub for Tate Modern, and Shakespeare's Globe is a short stroll away. If you're inside, the lighting is nice and unobtrusive so that you can still see out across the river at night. It can get busy, particularly on weekday evenings, when it's popular with young City types for an after-work drink. Wells & Youngs Bitter and Bombardier and seasonal brews from the modern bar counter angling along one side; there's a good range of other drinks too, including well over a dozen wines by the glass, and various coffees, tea and hot chocolate. Efficient, cheerful service; piped music, fruit machine. There's a new heated and covered area for smokers.

🕪 **Available all day (starting at 9pm for breakfast), and served without fuss or too much waiting around, bar food is useful rather than outstanding, with things like baguettes and paninis, soup, various pasta dishes, stilton and parsnip flan, sausages and mash, fish and chips, steak and ale pie, and moroccan lamb tagine; children's meals, and Sunday roasts.** *Starters/Snacks: £4.45 to £5.45. Main Courses: £7.45 to £11.95. Puddings: £3.95*

Youngs ~ Manager Paul Raynor ~ Real ale ~ Bar food (brunch 10-12; full menu 12-10) ~ (020) 7928 1899 ~ Children welcome away from bar ~ Open 10am(9 Sat, Sun)-11(midnight Fri, Sat)

Recommended by N R White, Meg and Colin Hamilton, the Didler, Eithne Dandy, Ian Phillips, Susan and John Douglas, Dr Ron Cox, Mike and Sue Loseby

Fox & Hounds 🕪 ♀
Latchmere Road; ⇌ Clapham Junction; SW11 2JU

Victorian local standing out for its excellent mediterranean cooking; mostly just evenings, but some lunchtimes too

Worth a detour for the excellent mediterranean cooking, this otherwise unremarkable big Victorian local is run by the two brothers who transformed the Atlas (see West London, below), and has a very similar style and menu. The pub can fill quickly, so you may have to move fast to grab a table. The spacious, straightforward bar has bare boards, mismatched tables and chairs, two narrow pillars supporting the dark red ceiling, photographs on the walls, and big windows overlooking the street (the view partially obscured by colourful window boxes). There are fresh flowers and daily papers on the bar, and a view of the kitchen behind. Two rooms lead off, one more cosy with its two red leatherette sofas. Caledonian Deuchars IPA, Fullers London Pride and Harveys on handpump; the carefully chosen wine list (which includes over a dozen by the glass) is written out on a blackboard. It's still very much the kind of place where locals happily come to drink – and they're a more diverse bunch than you might find filling the Atlas; the varied piped music fits in rather well. The refurbished garden has big parasols and heaters for winter. The same team have another two similarly organised pubs: the Cumberland Arms near Olympia, and the Swan in Chiswick. More reports please.

🕪 **Changing every day (though note they don't do food weekday lunchtimes), a typical choice might include portuguese chicken soup with mint, lemon, garlic, onion and rice, various antipasti, goats cheese salad with roast butternut squash, slow-roast tomatoes and pesto, chicken and pea risotto with mint and parmesan, pan-roast salmon fillet with braised puy lentils, grilled swordfish steak with sweet potato salad, red onion and mangetout, tuscan chicken casserole with celeriac and parsnip gratin, grilled lamb steak with cumin and black pepper, puddings like dark chocolate and almond cake or apple and date crumble, and unusual cheeses with apple and grilled bread.** *Starters/Snacks: £4.50 to £7.50. Main Courses: £8.50 to £14.00. Puddings: £4.50 to £5.50*

Free house ~ Licensees Richard and George Manners ~ Real ale ~ Bar food (7-10.30(10 Sun), plus 12.30-3 Fri, Sat, and 12.30-4 Sun (no lunch Mon-Thurs) ~ (020) 7924 5483 ~ Children welcome in eating area till 7pm ~ Dogs allowed in bar ~ Open 12-3(not Mon), 5-11 Mon-Thurs; 12-11 Fri, Sat; 12-10.30 Sun; closed Mon lunchtime, 23 Dec-1 Jan, Easter Sat and Sun

Recommended by BOB

> Prices of main dishes sometimes now don't include vegetables – if in doubt ask.

George ★

Off 77 Borough High Street; ⊖ ⇌ *Borough or London Bridge; SE1 1NH*

Beautifully preserved 16th-c coaching inn, with lots of tables in bustling courtyard to take in the galleried exterior; some cosy areas inside too, and good value lunchtime food

The splendidly preserved building is the main attraction here (it's perhaps the country's best example of a historic coaching inn), and whatever the season, readers enjoy sitting at one of the tables in the bustling cobbled courtyard looking up at the tiers of open galleries and soaking up the atmosphere. There may be morris men and even Shakespeare out here in summer, and heaters in winter. Owned by the National Trust, the building dates from the 16th c, but was rebuilt to the original plan after the great Southwark Fire of 1676. Inside, the row of no-frills ground-floor rooms and bars have square-latticed windows, black beams, bare floorboards, some panelling, plain oak or elm tables and old-fashioned built-in settles, along with a 1797 'Act of Parliament' clock, dimpled glass lantern-lamps and so forth. The best seats indoors are in a snug room nearest the street, where there's an ancient beer engine that looks like a cash register. In summer they open a bar with direct service into the courtyard (staff cope well with the crowds, though readers have found when it's busy it may be quicker to order your drinks inside). Greene King Abbot, IPA, Old Speckled Hen and a beer brewed by them for the pub, with perhaps a changing guest on handpump; mulled wine in winter, tea and coffee. An impressive central staircase goes up to a series of dining rooms and to a gaslit balcony; darts, trivia. What survives today is only a third of the original building; it was 'mercilessly reduced' as E V Lucas put it, during the period when it was owned by the Great Northern Railway Company. Unless you know where you're going (or you're in one of the many tourist groups that flock here in summer) you may well miss it, as apart from the great gates and sign there's little to indicate that such a gem still exists behind the less auspicious-looking buildings on the busy high street.

🍴 **Good value lunchtime bar food includes baguettes and wraps, soup, filled baked potatoes, ham, egg and chips, primavera risotto, scampi, sausage and mash, fish and chips, and puddings like black forest gateau or apple crumble; they do a Sunday carvery. In the evenings they do meals only in the balcony restaurant.** *Starters/Snacks: £2.55 to £4.95. Main Courses: £5.95 to £7.25. Puddings: £2.95 to £3.95*

Greene King ~ Manager Scott Masterson ~ Real ale ~ Bar food (12-5) ~ Restaurant (5-10 (not Sun)) ~ (020) 7407 2056 ~ Children in eating area of bar ~ Open 11-11; 12-10.30 Sun

Recommended by David and Sue Smith, the Didler, N R White, Ian Phillips, Derek and Sylvia Stephenson, W W Burke, Tracey and Stephen Groves, Roy and Lindsey Fentiman, Tom McLean, Ewan McCall, Mike and Sue Loseby

Greenwich Union 🍺

Royal Hill; ⊖ ⇌ *Greenwich; SE10 8RT*

Enterprising refurbished pub with distinctive beers from small local Meantime Brewery, plus other unusual drinks, and good, popular food

Slightly removed from Greenwich's many attractions, this enterprising and nicely renovated pub is tied to the small Meantime Brewery in nearby Charlton, and is the only place with all their distinctive unpasteurised beers on draught. They had seven of these when we last called in, including a traditional pale ale (served cool, under pressure) and a mix of proper pilsners, lagers and wheat beers, one a deliciously refreshing raspberry flavour. The helpful, knowledgeable staff will generally offer small tasters while you choose which one to drink. They also have Adnams on handpump, and a draught cider, as well as an expanding collection of unusual bottled beers, some their own, but others from Belgium, America and Australia. The rest of the drinks can be unfamiliar too, as they try to avoid the more common brands. The long, narrow stoneflagged room has several different parts: a simple area at the front with a few wooden chairs and tables, a stove and newspapers, then, past the bar counter with its headings recalling the branding of the brewery's first beers, several brown leather cushioned pews and armchairs under framed editions of *Picture Post* on the yellow walls; piped music. Beyond here a much lighter, more modern-feeling conservatory has comfortable brown leather wallbenches, a few original pictures and paintings, a TV in the corner, and white fairy lights under the glass roof; it leads out to an appealing back terrace with green picnic-sets and a couple of old-fashioned lampposts. The fence at the end is painted to resemble a poppy field, and the one at the side to represent wheat growing. Though there are plenty of tables out here, it can get busy in summer (as can the whole pub on weekday evenings). In front are a couple of tables overlooking the street. The brewery and pub were set up by Alastair Hook, who also founded the Freedom Brewery and the microbrew restaurant Mash; the beers can increasingly be found in pubs around the South East, or, in bottled form, in some supermarkets. There's a particularly good traditional cheese shop as you walk towards the pub.

🍽 Good and popular, from a seasonally changing menu that might include lunchtime sandwiches, a soup of the day such as red pepper with pesto, and seven or eight main courses like warm shredded duck salad with bacon and black pudding, home-made tagliatelle with toasted pine nuts, tomato and rocket, pea and spinach risotto, pan-seared baby squid with warm chorizo and chickpea salad, and slow-cooked free-range pork belly with coconut rice and pak choi; puddings such as rhubarab and pear crumble. Helpings are slightly smaller (and cheaper) at lunchtime. They do brunch on Saturdays, and a choice of roasts on Sunday. *Starters/Snacks: £3.00 to £6.00. Main Courses: £7.00 to £13.00. Puddings: £3.00 to £5.00*

Free house ~ Licensee Andrew Ward ~ Real ale ~ Bar food (12-4, 5.30-10 weekdays, 12-9 Sat, 12-10 Sun) ~ (020) 8692 6258 ~ Children welcome till 9pm ~ Dogs welcome ~ Open 12-11; 11-11 Sat; 11.30-10.30 Sun

Recommended by Andrew Wallace, N R White, the Didler

Market Porter 🍺

Stoney Street; ⊖ ⇄ London Bridge; SE1 9AA

Extraordinary range of up to a dozen unusual real ales in very popular, properly pubby place opening at 6am for workers at neighbouring market

This busily pubby place still has one of the biggest and most interesting ranges of real ales you're likely to come across, with many of the dozen or so carefully chosen and perfectly kept beers generally brews you've never heard of, let alone tried. The selection changes every day (they get through around 60 different ones a week), but when we last called they had Arundel Bullseye and Sussex Gold, Broughton Clipper IPA, Clarks Classic Blonde and Rams Revenge, Hogs Back TEA, Hook Norton Old Hooky, Real Ale Company Wallop, Sharps Eden, and a scrumpy alongside the regular Harveys. The pub opens between 6 and 8.30 on weekday mornings to serve the workers and porters from Borough Market (they do breakfasts then), but it's later in the day when things can get busy; you may not be able to read the names on all the beer pumps at lunchtimes and after work, when it can get crowded and noisy with good-natured chatter; most readers feel that's all part of the atmosphere. Service is particularly helpful and friendly, and it's usually quieter in the afternoons (or in the upstairs restaurant, looking over the market). The main part of the bar has rough wooden ceiling beams with beer barrels balanced on them, a heavy wooden bar counter with a beamed gantry, cushioned bar stools, an open fire, and 1920s-style wall lamps – it gets more old-fashioned the further you venture in; darts, fruit machine, TV, and piped music. The company that owns the pub has various others around London; ones with similarly unusual beers (if not quite so many) can be found in Stamford Street and Seymour Place.

🍽 Usually served in the upstairs restaurant (but everywhere on Sun), well liked sensibly priced lunchtime bar food includes sandwiches, paninis, caesar salad, sausages and mash, a changing home-made pie, fish and chips, and daily specials; good Sunday roasts. *Starters/Snacks: £3.00 to £5.00. Main Courses: £4.00 to £9.00*

Free house ~ Licensee Sarah Nixon ~ Real ale ~ Bar food (12-3(5 Sun)) ~ Restaurant ~ (020) 7407 2495 ~ Children in restaurant ~ Open 6-8.30am weekdays, then 11-11; 12-11 Sat; 12-10.30 Sun

Recommended by Darren Le Poidevin, Andrew Wallace, Pete Walker, Ian Phillips, Tracey and Stephen Groves, N R White, Susan and John Douglas, Derek Thomas, the Didler, Joe Green, P Dawn, GHC, Ian and Julia Beard, Bruce Bird, Rob Razzell, B and M Kendall, Sue Demont, Tim Barrow, Mike and Sue Loseby, Tom McLean, Ewan McCall, Mike Gorton

Old Jail

Jail Lane, Biggin Hill (first turn E off A233 S of airport and industrial estate, towards Berry's Hill and Cudham); no station near; TN16 3AX

Country pub close to the city, with big garden (popular with families at weekends), interesting traditional bars with RAF memorabilia, and good daily specials

On a narrow leafy lane and feeling very much in the countryside, you'll find it's easy to forget this good all-rounder is only ten minutes or so from the bustle of Croydon and Bromley. Formerly a mainstay of RAF pilots based at nearby Biggin Hill, it has a lovely big garden, with well spaced picnic-sets on the grass, several substantial trees, and a nicely maintained play area; it's a popular spot for families on fine weekends. Inside, several traditional beamed and low-ceilinged rooms ramble around a central servery, with the nicest parts the two cosy little areas to the right of the front entrance; divided by dark timbers, one has a very big inglenook fireplace with lots of logs and brasses, and the other has a cabinet of Battle of Britain plates. Other parts have wartime prints and plates too, especially around the edge of the dining room, up a step beyond a second, smaller fireplace. There's also a plainer, flagstoned room; discreet fruit machine, low piped music. Harveys, Shepherd Neame Spitfire and a guest like Greene King IPA on handpump; friendly, efficient service. With nice hanging baskets in front, the attractive building wasn't itself part of any jail, but was a beef shop until becoming a pub in 1869. More reports please.

🍴 There's a standard menu with things like sandwiches, soup, baked potatoes, and ploughman's, but the food to go for is the wide choice of good, blackboard specials, which might include local sausages with mash and red onion gravy, chicken tarragon with bacon and onion potato cake, slow-cooked beef with new potatoes and swede mash, roast spiced duck with parmentier potatoes and lemon grass jus, and rib-eye steak; they do a choice of roasts on Sundays. *Starters/Snacks: £3.25 to £4.95. Main Courses: £6.85 to £15.25. Puddings: £1.95 to £4.25*

Punch ~ Lease Richard Hards ~ Real ale ~ Bar food (12-2.30(3 Sat, Sun), 7-9.30(not Sun evening)) ~ (01959) 572979 ~ Children welcome ~ Dogs allowed in bar ~ Open 11.30-3, 6-11.30(all day Fri in summer); 12-11 Sat; 12-10.30 Sun

Recommended by GHC, N R White, Debbie and Neil Hayter, Rob Liddiard

Royal Oak 🍺

Tabard Street; ⊖ ⇄ Borough; SE1 4JU

Old-fashioned corner house owned by Sussex brewer Harveys, with all their beers excellently kept; good, honest food too

Slightly off the beaten track (and in rather unprepossessing surroundings), this old-fashioned corner house is the only London pub belonging to Sussex brewer Harveys, so you'll find the full range of their beers, impeccably kept. Best-loved among these is perhaps their Sussex Best, but you'll also find their stronger Armada, as well as Mild, Pale Ale, and changing seasonal brews. The brewery transformed the pub when they took over, and painstakingly re-created the look and feel of a traditional London alehouse – you'd never imagine it wasn't like this all along. Two busy little L-shaped rooms meander around the central wooden servery, which has a fine old clock in the middle. They're done out in a cosy, traditional style: patterned rugs on the wooden floors, plates running along a delft shelf, black and white scenes or period sheet music on the red-painted walls, and an assortment of wooden tables and chairs. It almost goes without saying, but there's no music or machines. Even on busier evenings there's usually a relaxed, chatty atmosphere – although a couple of readers have this year been disappointed by the service, and particularly by the way a member of staff told their group to quieten down.

🍴 Well liked by readers, honest bar food includes impressive doorstep sandwiches, and generously served daily specials like fillets of bass, or pies such as vegetable and stilton, lamb and apricot, or game; Sunday roasts. *Starters/Snacks: £3.50. Main Courses: £5.95 to £8.95. Puddings: £3.50*

Waterside pubs are listed at the back of the book.

Harveys ~ Tenants John Porteous, Frank Taylor ~ Real ale ~ Bar food (12-2.45 (not Sat), 5-9.15; 12-4.45 Sun) ~ (020) 7357 7173 ~ Dogs allowed in bar ~ Open 11-11; 6-11 Sat; 12-6 Sun; closed bank hols

Recommended by B and M Kendall, Mike and Sue Loseby, Derek and Sylvia Stephenson, N R White, Susan and John Douglas, Pete Walker, the Didler, Sue Demont, Tim Barrow, Mike Gorton

Victoria 🍽 ⏛ 🛏
West Temple Sheen; ⇌ Mortlake; SW14 7RT

Sophisticated reworked local with excellent food and wines, and smart contemporary style; good for families, superior summer barbecues, comfortable bedrooms

Well regarded for its superior food and as a peaceful place to stay, this once-incongruous local is these days a stylish gastropub with rooms just a short stroll from Richmond Park's Sheen Gate. The management's pedigree in some of London's most famous kitchens quickly becomes obvious (and indeed they call themselves a restaurant and bar), but that doesn't make it at all stuffy or self-important – in fact quite the opposite: though firmly upmarket, it still has the air of a favourite neighbourhood drop-in eating place. At lunchtimes it's popular with families, when children can enjoy the sheltered play area in the back garden while parents supervise from the charming back conservatory, but it's evenings here that we've enjoyed the most. It's particularly civilised and sophisticated then, and the huge glass room at the back seems especially stunning. Leading into that is essentially one big thoughtfully designed room, with wooden floors and armchairs, and separate-seeming areas with a fireplace, and plenty of contemporary touches. The wine list is very good, with plenty by the glass (including champagne), and they have various unusual sherries and malts; also Greene King Old Speckled Hen on handpump (not cheap). The garden has been renovated this year, with new paving and furniture; in summer, they have excellent barbecues on sunny weekends and Friday evenings. Bedrooms (in a secluded annexe) are simple and smart; it's 20 minutes by train to central London.

🍴 **The changing menu might include soups like pea and asparagus with creamed goats cheese and pea shoots, purple sprouting broccoli with gorgonzola polenta and romesco sauce, snails, bacon and laver bread on toast 'buttered' with a little duck fat, roast pumpkin and ricotta gnocchi with tomato and sage, wild boar and apple sausages with mash and onion gravy, steak and ale pie with celery leaf mash, steamed sea trout with braised fennel and artichokes and sauce vierge, and evening dishes like rabbit, planchada bean and chorizo estofado or roast spring lamb rump with salad, rösti and garlic sauce; puddings such as warm chocolate mousse with griottine cherries and shortbread or spotted dick. They do a two-course weekday lunch for £14.95, and good tapas in the bar every evening. The kitchen doesn't really close, serving morning coffee and tea and cake in between meals.** *Starters/Snacks: £4.95 to £9.95. Main Courses: £9.95 to £21.95. Puddings: £3.95 to £6.95*

Enterprise ~ Lease Mark Chester ~ Real ale ~ Bar food (12-3, 7-10; 12-4, 7-9 Sun) ~ Restaurant ~ (020) 8876 4238 ~ Children welcome ~ Open 11-11; 12-10.30 Sun; closed four days over Christmas ~ Bedrooms: £108.50S/£108.50S

Recommended by Pat Woodward, Maggie Atherton

White Cross ⏛
Water Lane; ⊖, ⇌ Richmond; TW9 1TH

Splendidly set Thames-side pub, with busy paved garden overlooking the river; busy in fine weather, but comfortable in winter too – though watch out for the tides

With a new licensee since our last edition, and repainted to restore a bit of its sparkle, this is a perfectly set Thames-side pub with a very pleasant paved garden in front to enjoy the river views. It gets quite busy out here in summer, when it can feel rather like a cosmopolitan seaside resort, and there's an outside bar to make the most of the sunshine (they may use plastic glasses for outside drinking). Inside, the two chatty main rooms have something of the air of the hotel this once was, with local prints and photographs, an old-fashioned wooden island servery, and a good mix of variously aged customers. Two of the three log fires have mirrors above them – unusually, the third is below a window. A bright and airy upstairs room has lots more tables, with a pretty cast-iron balcony opening off, a splendid view down to the water, and a couple more tables and chairs. Wells & Youngs Bitter, Special and seasonal beers on handpump, and a dozen or so carefully chosen wines by the glass; welcoming service, fruit machine, dominoes. The Thames here can rise quite rapidly, so it pays to check the tide times, especially if you're leaving your car by the river; you might return to find it marooned in a rapidly swelling pool of water. It's not unknown for the water to reach right up the steps into the bar, and this year readers who'd enjoyed a lunchtime visit and tried to return in the evening found access impossible until the tide receded. Boats leave from immediately outside for Kingston and Hampton Court.

🍴 **Served all day, bar food includes sandwiches, salads, sausage and mash, fish and chips, home-made pies, and daily roasts.** *Starters/Snacks: £3.00 to £6.00. Main Courses: £7.45 to £8.95. Puddings: £3.50*

Youngs ~ Manager Alex Gibson ~ Real ale ~ Bar food (12-9.30) ~ (020) 8940 6844 ~ Children in garden area only ~ Dogs welcome ~ Open 11-11; 12-10.30 Sun; closed 25 Dec (except open 12-2)

Recommended by Bruce Bird, Derek Thomas, the Didler, Alan and Carolin Tidbury

WEST LONDON   MAP 13

Anglesea Arms 🍺
Selwood Terrace; ⊖ *South Kensington; SW7 3QG*

Busy old local with good range of beers, and an enjoyably chatty atmosphere in the evenings (when it can get packed)

Often very busy indeed, the characterful bar of this bustling pub has something of a feel of a late-Victorian local. With an enjoyably chatty atmosphere, it has a mix of cast-iron tables on the bare wood-strip floor, panelling, and big windows with attractive swagged curtains; at one end several booths have partly glazed screens have worn cushioned pews and spindleback chairs. If there weren't so many people, there might be an air of rather faded grandeur, heightened by some heavy portraits, prints of London, and large brass chandeliers; perhaps incongruously, there's a TV too. On particularly busy days – when well heeled young locals are very much part of the mix – you'll need to move fast to grab a seat, but most people seem happy leaning on the central elbow tables. A good choice of six real ales takes in Adnams Bitter and Broadside, Brakspears Special, Fullers London Pride, and guests like Hogs Back TEA and Sharps Doom Bar; also a few bottled belgian beers, around 15 whiskies, and a varied wine list, with everything available by the glass. Down some steps is a dining room with a fireplace and table service – and generally a bit more space if you're eating; service is friendly and helpful. In summer the place to be is the leafy front terrace, with outside heaters for chillier evenings (and smokers).

🍴 **Changing every day, the menu might include one or two lunchtime sandwiches, soups like cauliflower and parmesan, a pint of prawns with mayonnaise, caesar salad with soft boiled egg and anchovies, cumberland sausage with champ, onion gravy and cabbage, battered haddock with chips, fettuccine with pesto, spinach, pine nuts and parmesan, and evening extras like lamb, white bean and bacon stew or chargrilled veal chop with roasted mediterranean vegetables and salsa verde; puddings like apple and peach crumble or dark chocolate mousse with toasted hazelnuts. It's worth booking for their good all-day Sunday roasts.** *Starters/Snacks: £4.50 to £8.00. Main Courses: £9.00 to £17.00. Puddings: £3.00 to £5.00*

Free house ~ Licensee Jenny Podmore ~ Real ale ~ Bar food (12-3, 6.30-10 weekdays; 12-5, 6-10(9.30 Sun) weekends) ~ Restaurant ~ (020) 7373 7960 ~ Children welcome in eating area till 8pm ~ Dogs allowed in bar ~ Open 11-11; 12-10.30 Sun; closed 25 and 26 Dec

Recommended by P Dawn, Brian and Janet Ainscough, Revd R P Tickle, the Didler

---

'Children welcome' means the pubs says it lets children inside without any special restriction; readers have found that some may impose an evening time limit – please tell us if you find this.

Atlas ♈ ♉

Seagrave Road; ● West Brompton; SW6 1RX

Spruced-up local with consistently excellent mediterranean cooking, very popular, especially in the evenings, when tables are highly prized

It's business as usual at this souped-up local, meaning a constantly changing choice of innovative, varied food, and a good, bustling feel in the evenings; some readers enjoy coming here again and again. The creative combination of flavours results in a very satisfying, enjoyable meal, and if there's a downside it's simply the place's popularity; tables are highly prized, so if you're planning a meal, arrive early, or swoop quickly. The long, simple knocked-together bar has been well renovated without removing the original features; there's plenty of panelling and dark wooden wall benches, a couple of brick fireplaces, a mix of school chairs, and well spaced tables. Smart young people figure prominently in the mix, but there are plenty of locals too, as well as visitors to the Exhibition Centre at Earls Court (one of the biggest car parks is next door). Well kept Caledonian Deuchars IPA, Fullers London Pride and a guest like Hop Back Summer Lightning on handpump, and a very good, carefully chosen wine list, with plenty by the glass; big mugs of coffee; friendly service. The piped music is unusual – on various visits we've come across everything from salsa and jazz to vintage TV themes; it can be loud at times, and with all the chat too, this isn't the place to come for a quiet dinner. Down at the end, by a hatch to the kitchen, is a TV (though big sports events are shown in a room upstairs). Outside is an attractively planted narrow side terrace, with an overhead awning; heaters make it comfortable even in winter. This was the first of a small group of pubs set up by two brothers; another, the Fox & Hounds, is a main entry in the South London section.

🍴 **Influenced by recipes from North Africa, Turkey and Italy, the menu changes twice a day but might include things like italian fish soup with tomatoes, mussels, prawns and basil, various antipasti, sautéed chorizo bruschetta with roast field mushrooms, cherry vine tomatoes and aïoli, smoked mackerel and pea risotto with lemon, mint and parsley, pan-roasted whole bream with spring onion and chilli salsa, grilled pork chop with fennel and black pepper and roast garlic mashed potatoes, braised lamb shank with tomato, coriander, courgette and fennel, and grilled rib-eye steak with celeriac and parsnip gratin; their delicious chocolate and almond cake is a mainstay, and they have unusual cheeses, served with apple and grilled bread.** *Starters/Snacks: £4.50 to £8.00. Main Courses: £8.00 to £14.00. Puddings: £4.50 to £5.00*

Free house ~ Licensees Toby Ellis, Richard and George Manners ~ Real ale ~ Bar food (12.30-3, 7-10.30 Mon-Sat; 12.30-4, 7-10 Sun) ~ (020) 7385 9129 ~ Children welcome till 7pm ~ Dogs welcome ~ Open 12-11(10.30 Sun); closed 24 Dec-1 Jan

Recommended by Robert Lester, Tim Maddison, Derek Thomas, Alistair Forsyth

Bulls Head

Strand-on-the-Green; ⇌ Kew Bridge; W4 3PQ

Cosy old Thames-side pub with tables by river, and atmospheric little rooms inside

Cosy and atmospheric with its dark, beamed rooms, this busy Chef & Brewer pub enjoys a delightful Thames-side setting, with a few tables in front by the river. On cooler days, if you get here early enough you should be able to bag one of the highly prized tables by the little windows, with nice views of the river past the attractively planted hanging flower baskets. The series of comfortably refurbished rooms rambles up and down steps, with plenty of polished dark wood and beams, and old-fashioned benches built into the simple panelling. The black-panelled alcoves make useful cubby-holes (especially snug on chilly autumn days), and there are lots of empty wine bottles dotted around. Up to six real ales on handpump such as Adnams, Bass, Greene King Old Speckled Hen, Hop Back Summer Lightning, Shepherd Neame Spitfire and Wells & Youngs Bombardier; good service from friendly uniformed staff. The pub can fill up fast. They do pitchers of Pimms in summer, and newspapers are laid out for customers. The original building served as Cromwell's HQ several times during the Civil War. More reports please.

🏵 Served all day, the big menu takes in everything from good sandwiches and filled baguettes, through fish and chips and beef and ale pie, to plenty of fresh fish, delivered daily; popular Sunday roasts. *Starters/Snacks: £3.49 to £4.99. Main Courses: £7.00 to £11.00. Puddings: £4.49*

Spirit Group ~ Manager Julie Whittingham ~ Real ale ~ Bar food (12-10) ~ (020) 8994 1204 ~ Children welcome ~ Open 11-11; 12-10.30 Sun

Recommended by Darren Le Poidevin, John Saville, N R White, Mayur Shah, Sue Demont, Tim Barrow, Susan and John Douglas

Churchill Arms 🍺

Kensington Church Street; ⊖ Notting Hill Gate, Kensington High Street; W8 7LN

Bustling old favourite that's like a friendly local, with very well kept beers, excellent thai food, and cheery Irish landlord; even at its most crowded, it stays relaxed and welcoming

It's only a few years since the genial Irish landlord here started planting flowers outside for the simple reason that there is no back garden, and it quickly became something of an obsession (indeed the façade is fast disappearing behind the rapidly expanding foliage); this year his efforts were rewarded when the pub's 85 window boxes and 42 hanging baskets won the Chelsea Flower Show's first-ever Boozers in Bloom competition. The pub's wonderfully cheery atmosphere owes a lot to his enthusiasm and commitment, and he's very much in evidence, delightedly mixing with customers as he threads his way through the evening crowds. It feels like a friendly local, and even when it's very busy (which it usually is on weekdays after work), you can quickly feel at home. One of the landlord's hobbies is collecting butterflies, so you'll see a variety of prints and books on the subject dotted around the bar. There are also countless lamps, miners' lights, horse tack, bedpans and brasses hanging from the ceiling, a couple of interesting carved figures and statuettes behind the central bar counter, prints of american presidents, and lots of Churchill memorabilia. Very well kept Fullers Chiswick, ESB, London Pride, and seasonal beers on handpump (this year they've had a guest like Thwaites Lancaster Bomber too), and a good choice of wines. The spacious and rather smart plant-filled dining conservatory may be used for hatching butterflies, but is better known for its big choice of excellent thai food. Fruit machine, TV; they have their own cricket and football teams. There can be quite an overspill on to the street, where there are some chrome tables and chairs. Look out for special events and decorations around Christmas, Hallowe'en, St Patrick's Day, St George's Day, and Churchill's birthday (30 November) – along with more people than you'd ever imagine could feasibly fit inside.

🏵 Good quality and splendid value, the conservatory has authentic thai food such as a very good proper thai curry, and various rice, noodle or stir-fried dishes. At lunchtimes they usually also have a very few traditional dishes like fish and chips or sausage and chips, and they do a good value Sunday roast. *Main Courses: £4.00 to £6.00*

Fullers ~ Manager Jerry O'Brien ~ Real ale ~ Bar food (12-10(9.30 Sun)) ~ Restaurant ~ (020) 7727 4242 ~ Children in restaurant ~ Dogs allowed in bar ~ Open 11-11(12 Thurs, Fri and Sat); 12-10.30 Sun; closed evening 25 Dec

Recommended by the Didler, LM, John Saville, Mrs Hazel Rainer, Pete Walker, Ian Phillips, Tracey and Stephen Groves, P Dawn, David M Smith

Colton Arms

Greyhound Road; ⊖ Barons Court; W14 9SD

Unspoilt little pub kept unchanged thanks to its dedicated landlord; it's peaceful and genuinely old-fashioned, with well kept beer

That such an unspoilt little gem has survived intact is down to the friendly, dedicated landlord, who has kept this peaceful, unassuming place exactly the same for the last 40 years. As he says, 'A pub like this is a little strange in London nowadays, but most people seem to like it'. Like an old-fashioned country pub in town, the main U-shaped front bar has a log fire blazing in winter, highly polished brasses, a fox's mask, hunting crops and plates decorated with hunting scenes on the walls, and a remarkable collection of handsomely carved 17th-c oak furniture. That room is small enough, but the two back rooms are tiny; each has its own little serving counter, with a bell to ring for service. Well kept Fullers London Pride and Timothy Taylors Landlord on handpump, with, in summer, Caledonian Deuchars IPA, and in winter, Greene King Old Speckled Hen. When you pay, note the old-fashioned brass-bound till. Pull the curtain aside for the door out to a charming back terrace with a neat rose arbour. The pub is next to the Queens Club tennis courts and gardens. More reports please.

🍴 **Just sandwiches, weekday lunchtimes only (from £3).**

Enterprise ~ Tenants N J and J A Nunn ~ Real ale ~ Bar food (12-2.30 weekday lunchtimes only) ~ No credit cards ~ (020) 7385 6956 ~ Children welcome in garden in summer ~ Dogs allowed in bar ~ Open 12-3, 5.30-11.30; 12-3.30, 7-11.30 Sat; 12-4, 7-11 Sun; closed some bank hols, including 25 and 26 Dec

Recommended by Ian Phillips, Darren Le Poidevin, Tracey and Stephen Groves, Susan and John Douglas

Dove
Upper Mall; ⊖ *Ravenscourt Park; W6 9TA*

Famous old pub with lovely back terrace overlooking river, and cosily traditional front bar; interesting history, and sometimes unusual specials

One of London's best known riverside pubs, this is said to be where 'Rule Britannia' was composed, and it was a favourite with Turner, who painted the view of the Thames from the delightful back terrace. In fact so many writers, actors and artists have passed through its doors over the years that there's a framed list of them all on a wall. By the entrance from the quiet alley, the front bar (said to be Britain's smallest) is cosy and traditional, with black panelling, and red leatherette cushioned built-in wall settles and stools around dimpled copper tables; it leads to a bigger, similarly furnished room, with old framed advertisements and photographs of the pub. That opens on to the terrace, where the main flagstoned area, down some steps, has a verandah and some highly prized tables looking over the low river wall to the Thames Reach just above Hammersmith Bridge. There's a tiny exclusive area up a spiral staircase, a prime spot for watching the rowing crews out on the water. They stock the full range of Fullers beers, with Chiswick, Discovery, ESB, London Pride and seasonal beers on handpump: no games machines or piped music. The pub isn't quite as crowded at lunchtimes as it is in the evenings. A plaque marks the level of the highest-ever tide in 1928. More reports please.

🍴 **Well liked bar food typically includes lunchtime sandwiches, vegetable moussaka, sausage and mash, salads, fish and chips, a proper ploughman's, popular platters for sharing, and perhaps some more unexpected specials like poussin, or game.** *Starters/Snacks: £4.25 to £4.95. Main Courses: £7.95 to £16.95. Puddings: £4.25*

Fullers ~ Manager Nick Kiley ~ Real ale ~ Bar food (12-3, 6-9 weekdays; 12-9 Sat; 12-5 Sun) ~ (020) 8748 9474 ~ Dogs allowed in bar ~ Open 11-11; 12-10.30 Sun

Recommended by Darren Le Poidevin, Tracey and Stephen Groves, N R White, Ian Phillips, the Didler

Fat Badger 🍴 🍷
Portobello Road; ⊖ *Ladbroke Grove, Westbourne Park (though perhaps the nicest walk is the long one from Notting Hill Gate); W10 5TA*

Relaxed and comfortably trendy gastropub with enjoyable, individual food – not overly fancy, but good quality and properly cooked; a laid-back pubby feel too

The team behind this reworked old local have a pedigree at some of London's best known eating places, so we wondered if it was going to be a little too full of itself, or rather self-consciously fashionable, but in fact when we called in, the opposite was true. We found it to be a relaxed and comfortably trendy place to eat, more welcoming and pubby than we'd expected, and with good quality, properly cooked food. The chef is influenced by the slow-food movement, so he sources well reared animals and birds and cooks them in honest, traditional ways. It's not fancy, and some will think it expensive, but the meats in particular are full of flavour, and it's all a refreshing and unusual change from most London gastropubs. At the end of the Portobello Road fewer people seem to get to, it can be pleasantly uncrowded some evenings, though tends to be busier Fridays and weekends (when service may slow down). The downstairs bar – quite spacious – has the expected polished bare boards and worn furnishings (some of the comfortable armchairs and leather sofas very much so), with scrubbed wooden tables, a mix of benches and pews, and a big mirror propped against one wall; a ledge beneath one of the big windows has plenty of board games, and above a door there's a stuffed badger in a glass case. More unusual is the pink toile de jouy wallpaper, at first glance the sort you might find in a country house, but look more closely and these aren't tranquil rural scenes – they're fiercely contemporary vignettes of urban life, replete with hoodies and even muggings. The good wine list is on a clipboard on the bar, where you'll also find two changing beers such as Adnams and Hop Back Summer Lightning. Upstairs, the dining room has simple wooden furnishings and standard lamps; a small scruffy roof terrace opens off. They may have an oyster counter in summer.

🍴 **Snacks on the bar menu can be rather unusual, typically including quail eggs with celery salt, haddock fritters or épigrammes of lamb, while the main menu – changing every meal time – might have particularly distinctive starters such as crubeens (pig's trotters) with sauce gribiche and watercress, smoked eel with leeks and lovage, and baked globe artichoke with goats cheese and herb crumb, main dishes like middlewhite pork, broccoli, fennel and anchovy sauce, grilled spatchcock poussin with chilli, garlic and rosemary oil, poached tronçon of turbot with marsh grasses and butter sauce, and marinated bavette with girolles, parsley and garlic, and puddings such as sticky toffee or lemon and elderflower cake.** *Starters/Snacks: £5.50 to £8.00. Main Courses: £10.50 to £17.00. Puddings: £5.00 to £7.50*

Free house ~ Licensees Rupert Walsh and Joad Hall ~ Real ale ~ Bar food (12-4, 6-10) ~ Restaurant ~ (020) 8969 4500 ~ Children welcome till 8pm ~ Dogs welcome ~ Open 12-11 (12 Fri, Sat)

Recommended by BOB

Havelock Tavern 🍴 ♀

Masbro Road; ⊖ ⇄ Kensington(Olympia); W14 0LS

Popular gastropub with friendly, often vibrant, atmosphere, very good food, and well chosen wines

Classy food is the focus here, particularly in the evenings, but by that we don't mean it's overly fancy: this is good, well conceived and executed cooking that readers really enjoy. It looks rather ordinary from the outside, and until 1932 the blue-tiled building was two separate shops (one was a wine merchant, but no one can remember much about the other), and it still has huge shop-front windows along both street-facing walls. Lighter and more airy than it was before a recent fire, the L-shaped bar is welcoming but plain and unfussy: bare boards, long wooden tables (you may end up sharing at busy times), a mix of chairs and stools, a few soft spotlights, and a fireplace. A second little room with pews leads to a small paved terrace, with benches, a tree, and wall climbers. Friendly staff serve Flowers Original, Fullers London Pride and Marstons Pedigree from handpumps at the elegant modern bar counter (they're not cheap), as well as a good range of well chosen wines, with around a dozen by the glass; mulled wine in winter, and in May and June perhaps home-made elderflower soda. No music or machines, but backgammon, chess, Scrabble and other board games. Plenty of chat from the mostly smart customers – at busy times it can seem really quite noisy. You may have to wait for a table in the evenings (when some dishes can run out quite quickly), but it can be quieter at lunchtimes, and in the afternoons can have something of the feel of a civilised private club. On weekdays, nearby parking is metered, though restrictions stop at 5pm.

🍴 **Well cooked and full of flavour, the choice changes every day but might include things like courgette, fennel and chilli soup, warm leek, spinach and goats cheese tart, fillets of red mullet wrapped in parma ham with baby spinach, green beans and salsa verde, thai red beef curry, chargrilled whole poussin with parsley and garlic butter, pan-fried bass with chickpeas, tomato, fennel and white wine, grilled leg of lamb with spinach, roast potatoes, peppers, aubergine, fennel and tzatziki, puddings like chocolate brownie or summer berry trifle, and some unusual cheeses served with apple chutney; you can't book tables (and they don't take credit cards).** *Starters/Snacks: £4.50 to £8.00. Main Courses: £8.50 to £15.00. Puddings: £4.00 to £6.50*

Free house ~ Licensees Peter Richnell, Jonny Haughton ~ Real ale ~ Bar food (12.30-2.30(3 Sun),
7-10(9.30 Sun)) ~ No credit cards ~ (020) 7603 5374 ~ Children welcome ~ Dogs welcome ~
Open 11-11; 12-10.30 Sun; closed Easter Sun
Recommended by Martin and Karen Wake, Derek Thomas

Portobello Gold ♀

Portobello Road; ➌ Notting Hill Gate; W11 2QB

**Enterprising Notting Hill stalwart, with relaxed atmosphere, wide choice of enjoyable food
(especially in attractive dining room), excellent range of drinks, and good value bedrooms**

An engaging combination of pub, hotel, restaurant and even Internet café, this unique
Notting Hill stalwart always seems to have something new; a typical week might find the
enterprising licensees organising live music sessions, revamping the bewildering array of
menus, or changing the art or photographs on the walls. Our favourite part is the rather
exotic-seeming back dining room, with big tropical plants, an impressive wall-to-wall
mirror, comfortable wicker chairs, stained wooden tables, and a cage of vocal canaries
adding to the outdoor effect. In the old days – when we remember this being a Hells
Angels hangout – this was the pub garden, and in summer they still open up the sliding
roof. The smaller front bar has a nice old fireplace, cushioned banquettes, daily papers,
and, more unusually, several Internet terminals (which disappear in the evening). The
atmosphere is cheerful and relaxed (at times almost bohemian), though they do often get
busy in the evenings. The Gold was the first place in the UK to serve oyster shooters (a
shot glass with an oyster, parmesan, horseradish, crushed chillies, Tabasco and lime), and
the good bar food still has something of an emphasis on oysters and seafood. Opening at
10am for coffee and fresh pastries, the bar has Fullers London Pride and a changing guest
like Hogs Back TEA, as well as several draught belgian beers, Thatcher's farm cider, a
good selection of bottled beers from around the world, and a wide range of interesting
tequilas and other well sourced spirits; the wine list is particularly good (the landlady
has written books on matching wine with food). They also have a cigar menu and various
coffees. Polite, helpful young staff; piped music, TV, chess, backgammon. There are one
or two tables and chairs on the pretty street outside, which, like the pub, is named in
recognition of the 1769 battle of Portobello, fought over control of the lucrative gold
route to Panama. A lively stall is set up outside during the Notting Hill Carnival. Parking
nearby is metered; it's not always easy to bag a space. The price we quote for bedrooms
is for the cheapest; some are small, but they're all particularly good value for the area
(and they have free Internet access); there's a spacious apartment with rooftop terrace
(and putting green).

🍴 **A wide choice, from various menus: bar food includes soup, toasted sandwiches, cajun
jumbo shrimp, various salads, half a dozen irish rock oysters, steamed mussels,
cumberland sausage on parsley mash with red onion gravy, chicken fajitas, fish and chips,
and puddings like chocolate and amaretti torte, while the seasonally changing restaurant
menu might have sautéed duck livers with shallots, pancetta and lambs lettuce, risotto
nuggets in herby tomato sauce and parmesan, slow-grilled salmon marinated in caribbean
blackened seasoning, rib-eye steak, and a big seafood platter. There's a choice of Sunday
roasts, and at lunchtime they usually do a good value set menu; also children's helpings,
and cream teas.** *Starters/Snacks: £2.75 to £7.75. Main Courses: £6.00 to £14.00. Puddings:
£2.80 to £6.50*

Enterprise ~ Lease Michael Bell and Linda Johnson-Bell ~ Real ale ~ Bar food (11am-11.15pm;
10.30-9.30 Sun) ~ Restaurant ~ (020) 7460 4910 ~ Children welcome but not in bar in evening
~ Dogs allowed in bar ~ Live music Sun from 6.30pm ~ Open 10am(9 Sat)-midnight(1.30 Sat);
10am-10.30pm Sun; closed 25-31 Dec ~ Bedrooms: £60S/£70S
Recommended by Brian and Janet Ainscough, John Saville, Ian Phillips

---

Please keep sending us reports. We rely on readers for news of new discoveries, and
particularly for news of changes – however slight – at the fully described pubs. No stamp
needed: The Good Pub Guide, FREEPOST TN1569, Wadhurst, E Sussex TN5 7BR or send
your report through our website: www.goodguides.co.uk

Warrington

Warrington Crescent; ● *Maida Vale; W9 1EH*

Reopening this autumn as Gordon Ramsay's second London pub, a Victorian gin palace with extaordinary décor – and now an upstairs restaurant with classic british food

Gordon Ramsay is said to have spent more than £6 million restoring and transforming this extraordinary late Victorian gin palace, expected to reopen around October. The combination of his brand and such a remarkable building should be potent, and they promise the bar will be restored to its original dazzling best. Until now the opulent art nouveau décor has been the highlight here, and particularly the splendid marble and mahogany bar counter, topped by an extraordinary structure that's rather like a cross between a carousel and a ship's hull, with cherubs thrown in for good measure. The drawings of nubile young women here and above a row of mirrors on the opposite wall are later additions, very much in keeping with the overall style, and hinting at the days when the building's trade was rather less respectable than it is today. Throughout are elaborately patterned tiles, ceilings and stained glass, and a remarkable number of big lamps and original light fittings; there's a small coal fire, and two exquisitely tiled pillars. It's always had a real bustling, local feel so it will be interesting to see if that remains. The main dining room will be upstairs (where the thai restaurant used to be) – as at Ramsay's company's first pub, the Narrow (see our East London main entries), you'll need to book, though they'll have a separate bar menu if you prefer to be spontaneous. Expect three real ales, and a good range of bottled beers and other drinks, with a fine choice of wines.

🍽 As at the Narrow, likely to be top-notch versions of classic favourites, with ploughman's, soup and other snacks on the bar menu, and upstairs seasonally changing things like haddock and chips, braised lamb neck and turnip pie with mash, whole rainbow trout with samphire and peas, and pea, leek and morel flan with poached egg. *Starters/Snacks: £4.00 to £7.00. Main Courses: £9.00 to £14.50. Puddings: £4.00 to £7.00*

Free house ~ Real ale ~ Bar food ~ (020) 7286 2929 ~ Children in restaurant ~ Open 11-11; 12-10.30 Sun
Recommended by BOB

White Horse ♀ ◧

Parsons Green; ● *Parsons Green; SW6 4UL*

Smart but relaxed local with new licensees this year – still the same emphasis on the excellent range of carefully sourced drinks, and superior food

The long-time licensee here moved on not long before we went to press, and the new people have a hard act to follow – but early signs are they're keeping things just the same, and in particular continuing to source a really impressive range of drinks. They have six well kept real ales on handpump, with things like Dark Star Hobhead, Fullers ESB, Harveys Sussex, Oakham GHB and Roosters Hooligan, along with half a dozen well chosen draught beers from overseas (usually belgian and german but occasionally from further afield), as well as 15 trappist beers, around 100 other foreign bottled beers, ten or so malt whiskies, and a constantly expanding range of good, interesting and reasonably priced wines. Looking very smart these days, the stylishly modernised U-shaped bar has plenty of sofas, wooden tables, and huge windows with slatted wooden blinds, and winter coal and log fires, one in an elegant marble fireplace. The pub is usually busy (and can feel crowded at times), but there are enough smiling, helpful staff behind the solid panelled central servery to ensure you'll rarely have to wait too long to be served. On summer evenings the front terrace overlooking the green has something of a continental feel, with crowds of people drinking al fresco; there are barbecues out here most sunny evenings then, when the pub's appeal to smart young people is more apparent than ever. They have quarterly beer festivals, often spotlighting regional breweries.

🍽 Changing bar food might include butternut squash and watercress risotto, ricotta and aubergine ravioli, slow-braised pork belly, beer-battered haddock, sausage and mash, and specials like lemon sole with pea mash, or seafood linguini. They still have a weekend brunch menu, and a popular Sunday lunch. *Starters/Snacks: £6.25 to £9.25. Main Courses: £9.75 to £14.75. Puddings: £4.50*

Mitchells & Butlers ~ Managers Sonia Harris, Dan Fox ~ Real ale ~ Bar food (12(11 Sat, Sun)10.30) ~ Restaurant ~ (020) 7736 2115 ~ Children welcome ~ Dogs allowed in bar ~ Open 11-midnight(12.30 Sat); 11-11 Sun

Recommended by LM, the Didler, Sue Demont, Tim Barrow

Windsor Castle

Campden Hill Road; ⊖ Holland Park, Notting Hill Gate; W8 7AR

Genuinely unspoilt, with lots of atmosphere in the tiny, dark rooms, and a bustling summer garden; good beers, and reliable food

With its wealth of dark oak furnishings and time-smoked ceilings, this warmly characterful Victorian pub oozes genuine atmosphere. Each of the tiny unspoilt rooms has its own entrance from the street, but it's much more fun trying to navigate through the minuscule doors between them inside. Finding people you've arranged to meet can be quite a challenge; more often than not they'll be hidden behind the high backs of the sturdy built-in elm benches. A cosy pre-war-style dining room opens off, and soft lighting and a coal-effect fire add to the old-fashioned charm. It's especially cosy in winter, but the pub's appeal is just as strong in summer, thanks to the big, tree-shaped garden behind, easily one of the best pub gardens in London. It's always busy out here when the sun's shining, but there's quite a secluded feel thanks to the high ivy-covered sheltering walls. The garden has its own bar in summer, as well as heaters for cooler days, and lots of tables and chairs on the flagstones. Well kept Adnams Broadside, Fullers London Pride, Timothy Taylors Landlord and a weekly changing guest on handpump, decent house wines, various malt whiskies, jugs of Pimms in summer, and perhaps mulled wine in winter; they have occasional beer festivals. No fruit machines or piped music. Usually fairly quiet at lunchtime, the pub is packed most evenings, and you'll need to move fast to bag a table. Service – though generally friendly – can vary at busier times. The bones of Thomas Paine are said to be buried in the cellar, after his son sold them to the landlord to settle a beer debt.

🍴 Bar food includes various sausages with mash, ciabattas, steamed mussels in white wine and cream, chicken caesar salad, beefburger with home-cut chips and red onion relish, fish and chips, and specials like roast bass with spicy couscous; they do a choice of roasts on Sunday (£9.95), when the range of other dishes may be more limited. *Starters/Snacks: £2.50 to £5.00. Main Courses: £5.50 to £11.00. Puddings: £3.50 to £3.90*

Mitchells & Butlers ~ Manager Richard Bell ~ Real ale ~ Bar food (12-3, 5-10 weekdays, 12-10 Sat, 12-9 Sun) ~ (020) 7243 9551 ~ Dogs welcome ~ Open 12-11(10.30 Sun)

Recommended by Gwyn and Anne Wake, the Didler, David and Sue Smith, Mark Percy, Lesley Mayoh, Ian Phillips, Giles and Annie Francis, N R White

LUCKY DIP

Besides the fully inspected pubs, you might like to try these Lucky Dips recommended to us and described by readers (if you do, please send us reports: www.goodguides.co.uk).

CENTRAL LONDON

EC1

Butchers Hook & Cleaver EC1A 9DY [W Smithfield]: Attractive Fullers bank conversion with their full ale range, decent pub food from nibbles and baguettes up, wkdy breakfast from 7.30am, friendly staff, daily papers, relaxed atmosphere, nice mix of chairs inc some button-back leather armchairs, wrought-iron spiral stairs to pleasant mezzanine with waitress service; big-screen sports TV; open all day *(Michael Dandy, Peter Dandy, BB)*

☆ *Hand & Shears* EC1A 7JA [Middle St]: Traditional panelled Smithfield pub dating from 16th c, three brightly lit rooms and small snug off central servery, bustling at lunchtime, quiet evenings, Courage and a guest ale, quick friendly service, interesting bric-a-brac and old photographs, reasonably priced food from filled rolls and baked potatoes up – evening too; open all day but cl weekends *(N R White, Michael Dandy, LYM)*

Sekforde Arms EC1R 0HA [Sekforde St]: Small and comfortably simple corner local with friendly licensees, Wells & Youngs ales, simple good value standard food, nice pictures inc Spy caricatures, upstairs restaurant (not always open), darts, cards and board games; pavement tables *(the Didler, Dr Ron Cox)*

EC2

☆ **Dirty Dicks** EC2M 4NR [Bishopsgate]: Busy re-creation of traditional City tavern with booths and barrel tables in bare-boards bar, interesting old prints inc one of Nathaniel Bentley the weird original Dirty Dick, Wells & Youngs ales, enjoyable food inc open sandwiches, baguettes and reasonably priced hot dishes, pleasant service, cellar wine bar with wine racks overhead in brick barrel-vaulted ceiling, further upstairs area too; games machines and TV, but otherwise loads of character – fun for foreign visitors; cl wknds (LYM, Tracey and Stephen Groves, Ian Phillips, the Didler)

EC3

East India Arms EC3M 4BR [Fenchurch St]: Archetypal Victorian City pub, Shepherd Neame ales, good service even with the lunchtime crowds, bar stools and standing room (Ian Phillips)

☆ **Lamb** EC3V 1LR [Grand Ave, Leadenhall Mkt]: Well run traditional stand-up bar, bustling atmosphere (can get very busy with sharp City lads), Wells & Youngs ales, friendly service, engraved glass, plenty of ledges and shelves, spiral stairs up to tables and seating in small light and airy carpeted gallery overlooking market's central crossing, corner servery doing good hot carvery baguettes; also basement bar with shiny wall tiling and own entrance (Ian Phillips, Derek Thomas, N R White)

Pitcher & Piano EC3V 3ND [Cornhill]: Booths down side of big bank-look main bar, downstairs restaurant, decent food and service, fair prices (John Evans)

Red Lion EC3V 9BJ [Lombard St – approach via Plough Court]: Cheerfully busy bar and downstairs lounge, Fullers London Pride, Greene King IPA and Wells & Youngs Bombardier, decent sandwiches, ploughman's and basic bar food (Ian Phillips)

Ship EC3V 0BP [Talbot Ct, off Eastcheap]: Quaint and interesting bare-boards courtyard pub full of City types downstairs, quieter upstairs with soft lighting, candles, old prints and dark décor, several well kept ales, simple low-priced lunchtime food; open all day, cl wknds (N R White)

Swan EC3V 1LY [Ship Tavern Passage, off Gracechurch St]: Bustling narrow flagstoned bar, particularly well kept Fullers ales, chatty landlord and friendly attentive service, generous lunchtime sandwiches, neatly kept Victorian panelled décor, larger carpeted upstairs room; silent corner TV, can get packed early wkdy evenings; usually cl at 9pm, cl wknds (N R White)

Wine Lodge EC3M 6BL [Fenchurch St]: Somewhat misleading name, as it's a typical City pub, with wide choice of pubby food from sandwiches up, Wells & Youngs ales, good staff, ground floor bar and another larger one in basement, roomy and light (Ian Phillips)

EC4

☆ **Banker** EC4R 3TE [Cousin Lane, by Cannon St Stn]: Attractive and bustling multi-level pub just below Cannon St railway bridge, stripped brick, mirrors and big chandelier in high-ceilinged bar, then steps up to two small rooms (one very cosy, with leather sofas – you can hear the trains rumbling overhead), linking to long, narrow glass-fronted room with thrilling Thames views shared by small outdoor deck; good range of Fullers ales and of wines by the glass, enjoyable food inc sharing plates (some nice cheeses), may be spit-roasts, smart attentive staff, relaxed chatty atmosphere, framed banknotes and railway posters; open all day (Derek Thomas, BB)

Centre Page EC4V 5BH [aka the Horn; Knightrider St]: Modernised old pub with row of window booths or 'traps' in narrow entrance room, more space beyond, traditional style with panelling and subdued lighting, chatty atmosphere, can be quieter than others in area, with mix of after-work drinkers and tourists having cappuccino; pleasant efficient staff, simple appetising bar menu (from breakfast at 9am), downstairs dining room, well kept Fullers beers, good tea, various coffees; may be piped music; tables outside have good view of St Paul's (N R White, BB)

Old Bell EC4Y 1DH [Fleet St, nr Ludgate Circus]: Bustling 17th-c tavern backing on to St Bride's the wedding-cake church, heavy black beams, brass-topped tables, dim lighting, stained-glass bow window, good changing choice of real ales from island servery, friendly efficient service, good value standard food, coal fire, cheerful atmosphere, tables tucked away at the back – a bit more relaxed (the Didler, BB, N R White, Tracey and Stephen Groves)

Olde Watling EC4M 9BR [Watling St]: Heavy-beamed and timbered post-Blitz replica of pub built by Wren in 1668 as site commissariat for his new St Paul's Cathedral, well kept ales such as Adnams, Fullers London Pride and Greene King IPA, good service, good wines by the glass, lunchtime bar food and upstairs restaurant; piped music; open all day (LYM, N R White)

Samuel Pepys EC4V 3PT [Brooks Wharf; Stew St, off Upper Thames St]: Enjoyable food in stylishly refurbished two-level pub with interesting views over Thames to Globe Theatre and Tate Modern, especially from its two breezy balconies, well kept ales such as Caledonian Deuchars IPA and Timothy Taylors Landlord, friendly helpful staff (BB, Christine Brown, Dr and Mrs A K Clarke)

Tipperary EC4Y 1HT [Fleet St]: Tiny downstairs bar with counter seating, Greene King ales, more room upstairs (Tracey and Stephen Groves)

SW1

☆ *Buckingham Arms* SW1H 9EU [Petty France]:
Well run 18th-c local, relaxed and chatty,
with Wells & Youngs ales from long bar, good
wines by the glass, friendly efficient service,
popular straightforward food (evenings too)
from back open kitchen, elegant mirrors and
woodwork, unusual long side corridor fitted
out with elbow ledge for drinkers, friendly
pub dog; two TVs; dogs welcome, handy for
Buckingham Palace, Westminster Abbey and
St James's Park, open all day *(LYM,
N R White, the Didler, Michael Dandy, Dr and
Mrs A K Clarke)*

Cask & Glass SW1E 5HN [Palace St]: Inviting
panelled room overflowing into street in
summer – colourful flowers then; good range
of Shepherd Neame ales, friendly licensees
and chatty local atmosphere, good value
lunchtime sandwiches, old prints and shiny
black panelling; quiet corner TV; handy for
Queen's Gallery *(N R White)*

☆ *Fox & Hounds* SW1W 8HR [Passmore
St/Graham Terr]: Small cosy bar with real
ales such as Adnams, Bass, Greene King IPA
and Harveys, bar food, friendly staff, wall
benches, big hunting prints, old sepia
photographs of pubs and customers, some
toby jugs, hanging plants under attractive
skylight in back room, coal-effect gas fire
and organ; can be very busy Fri night,
quieter wkdy lunchtimes *(the Didler,
Sue Demont, Tim Barrow)*

Gallery SW1V 3AS [Lupus St, opp Pimlico
tube station]: Light and airy atrium one end
with stairs up to gallery, attractive prints
and bric-a-brac, Bass, Courage Best, Greene
King Abbot and Shepherd Neame Spitfire,
reliable varied food; disabled access and
lavatories (conventional ones down stairs)
*(Dr and Mrs M E Wilson, Sue Demont,
Tim Barrow)*

☆ *Grouse & Claret* SW1X 7AP [Little Chester
St]: Well done pastiche of discreetly old-
fashioned mews tavern just off Belgrave Sq,
smart, welcoming and very well run, two
bars off central servery, attractive
furnishings inc plush little booths, Badger
ales, good choice of wines by the glass,
separate dining floors; open all day wkdys
(BB, John A Barker)

Jugged Hare SW1V 1DX [Vauxhall Bridge
Rd/Rochester Row]: Popular Fullers Ale & Pie
pub in impressive former colonnaded bank
with balustraded balcony, chandelier, prints
and busts; their real ales, friendly efficient
service, reasonably priced traditional food
from sandwiches up; games machine,
unobtrusive piped music; open all day
(the Didler, BB)

Marquis of Westminster SW1V 1RY [Warwick
Way]: Well kept Fullers London Pride, nicely
presented food, pleasant service, good local
atmosphere *(R T and J C Moggridge)*

☆ *Morpeth Arms* SW1P 4RW [Millbank]: Roomy
and comfortable nicely preserved Victorian
pub facing MI6 HQ across River Thames,
some etched and cut glass, old books and

prints, photographs, earthenware jars and
bottles, well kept Wells & Youngs ales, good
choice of wines and of good value food all
day from sandwiches up, welcoming landlord
and staff, good service even at busy
lunchtimes, upstairs dining room; games
machine; seats outside (a lot of traffic),
handy for Tate Britain *(BB, Mark Doughty,
Dr and Mrs M E Wilson, the Didler,
Mrs Margaret Ball, JJW, CMW, Dr Ron Cox)*

☆ *Red Lion* SW1Y 6PP [Crown Passage, behind
St James's St]: Buoyant early Victorian local
tucked down narrow passage nr St James's
Palace, dark oak panelling, settles and
leaded lights, well kept ales inc Adnams,
busy lunchtime (good bargain sandwiches),
room upstairs *(Dr and Mrs M E Wilson, John
and Gloria Isaacs, BB)*

Speaker SW1P 2HA [Great Peter St]: Pleasant
chatty atmosphere in unpretentious corner
pub, friendly helpful efficient licensees, good
choice of well kept ales inc guests, bar food,
political cartoons and prints *(N R White)*

Two Chairmen SW1Y 5AT [Warwick House
St]: Pleasant tucked-away pub with Courage
Best and Fullers London Pride, daily papers,
pubby food upstairs *(Kevin Flack)*

Wetherspoons SW1V 1JT [Victoria Station]:
Modern pub on mezzanine with glass wall
overlooking main concourse and platform
indicators, cheap changing ales inc
interesting guest beers, good choice of
wines by the glass, wide choice of
reasonably priced food all day, prompt
friendly service; some tables outside
(Michael Dandy, Sue Demont, Tim Barrow)

White Swan SW1V 2SA [Vauxhall Bridge Rd]:
Roomy recently refurbished pub handy for
the Tate, lots of dark dining tables on three
levels in long room, good value pubby food
from sandwiches up, Fullers London Pride,
Greene King and Wells & Youngs Bitter, lots
of wines by the glass, quick helpful
uniformed staff; quiet piped music; open all
day *(Mark Doughty, BB, JJW, CMW,
John Wooll)*

SW3

Cadogan Arms SW3 5UG [Kings Rd]:
Convivial place with well kept Fullers ales,
friendly atmosphere, pink walls, soft
lighting, lively young atmosphere, with pool
room, piped music, big-screen TVs and
games machines; open all day *(BB, Giles and
Annie Francis)*

Hour Glass SW3 2DY [Brompton Rd]: Small
well run pub handy for V&A and other nearby
museums, well kept Fullers London Pride and
a guest such as St Austell Tribute, freshly
squeezed fruit juice, good value pubby food
(not Sun), welcoming landlady and quick
young staff; sports TV; pavement picnic-sets
(LM)

Surprise SW3 4AJ [Christchurch Terr]:
Friendly, eclectic and enjoyably unassuming
late Victorian pub with well kept ales inc
Fullers London Pride, decent food, and
cheerful broad-spectrum mix of locals; often

surprisingly quiet evenings (this is a hidden corner of Chelsea), cosy and warm; not overly done up considering location, attractive stained-glass lanterns, 1970s mural around top of bar, leaded lights; well behaved dogs on leads, some tables outside *(anon)*

W1

Barley Mow W1U 6QW [Dorset St]: Chatty 18th-c pub, its small basic front bar made unusual by the three swiftly-bagged 19th-c cubicles opening on to serving counter (where poor farmers pawned their watches to the landlord in privacy); Adnams Broadside, Greene King IPA, Marstons Pedigree and Wells & Youngs Bombardier, all-day paninis, lunchtime two-for-one deals, wooden floors and panelled walls, old pictures, tiny back parlour; piped music, TV; open all day *(the Didler, Tracey and Stephen Groves, BB)*
Blue Posts W1B 5PX [Kingly St]: Compact pub with Greene King ales, upstairs dining area; attractive hanging baskets, a few pavement tables *(Michael Dandy)*
Clachan W1B 5QH [Kingly St]: Ornate plaster ceiling supported by two large fluted and decorated pillars, comfortable screened leather banquettes, smaller drinking alcove up three or four steps, Fullers London Pride, Greene King IPA, Wadworths 6X and Wells & Youngs Bombardier from handsome counter, food from sandwiches up; can get busy, but very relaxed in afternoons *(BB, Sue Demont, Tim Barrow, Michael Dandy)*
Cock W1W 8QE [Great Portland St]: Big corner local with enormous lamps over picnic-sets outside, florid Victorian/ Edwardian décor with handsome wood and plasterwork, some cut and etched glass, high tiled ceiling and mosaic floor, velvet curtains, coal-effect gas fire, cheap Sam Smiths OB from all four handpumps, popular food (not Fri-Sun evenings) in upstairs lounge with two more coal-effect gas fires, ploughman's downstairs too 12-6, friendly efficient service; open all day *(the Didler, Peter Dandy)*
French House W1D 5BG [Dean St]: Theatre memorabilia, good wines by the glass (keg beers but plenty of bottled ones) and lively chatty atmosphere – mainly standing room, windows keeping good eye on passers-by; can get very busy, open all day *(Mike Gorton)*
Jack Horner W1T 7QN [Tottenham Ct Rd]: Recently refurbished Fullers bank conversion with full range of their ales from island bar counter, good service, good choice of food, neat tables in quiet areas *(Peter Dandy)*
King & Queen W1W 6DL [Foley St]: Small friendly corner pub, real ales such as Adnams, St Austell Tribute and Wells & Youngs Bombardier, decent wines and enthusiast's spirits range, enjoyable wkdy lunchtime food inc fresh sandwiches and pubby hot dishes, reasonable prices; open all day *(Tony Galcius, Sue Demont, Tim Barrow)*

Kings Arms W1J 7QA [Shepherd Market]: Minimalist décor in old low-ceilinged pub with good value standard bar food from sandwiches and baked potatoes up, Fullers London Pride, Greene King IPA and Wells & Youngs Bombardier, upper dining gallery *(Michael Dandy, LYM)*
Pontefract Castle W1U 1QA [Wigmore St/St Christopher Pl]: Pleasantly traditional décor and civilised atmosphere, helpful staff, Fullers ales, enjoyable food esp home-made sausages in variety and bargain fishcakes *(Robert Gomme)*
Red Lion W1B 5PR [Kingly St]: Dark panelling, narrow front bar with deep leather banquettes, back bar with darts, bargain simple lunchtime food from sandwiches and baked potatoes up in comfortable upstairs lounge; we hope they'll bring back the well kept Sam Smiths OB *(Michael Dandy, BB, Peter Dandy)*

W2

Mad Bishop & Bear W2 1HB [Paddington Stn]: Up escalators from concourse, full Fullers ale range from long counter, good wine choice, good value if not always promptly served food from breakfast (7.30am on) and sandwiches to Sun roasts, cheery staff, ornate plasterwork, etched mirrors and fancy lamps inc big brass chandeliers, parquet, tiles and carpet, booths with leather banquettes, lots of wood and prints, train departures screen; TV, piped music, games machine; open all day, tables out overlooking concourse *(Dr and Mrs M E Wilson, Dr and Mrs A K Clarke, BB, Michael Dandy, Pete Walker)*
☆ *Victoria* W2 2NH [Strathearn Pl]: Interesting and well preserved corner local, lots of Victorian pictures and memorabilia, cast-iron fireplaces, wonderful gilded mirrors and mahogany panelling, brass mock-gas lamps above attractive horseshoe bar, bare boards and banquettes, relaxed atmosphere, friendly attentive service, full Fullers ale range, good choice of wines by the glass, well priced food counter; upstairs has leather club chairs in small library/snug (and, mostly used for private functions now, replica of Gaiety Theatre bar, all gilt and red plush); quiet piped music, TV (off unless people ask); pavement picnic-sets, open all day *(Sue Demont, Tim Barrow, LYM)*

WC1

Calthorpe Arms WC1X 8JR [Grays Inn Rd]: Relaxed and civilised corner pub with plush wall seats, Wells & Youngs ales, big helpings of popular food upstairs lunchtime and evening, good staff under friendly long-serving landlord; nice pavement tables, open all day *(the Didler)*
Dolphin WC1R 4PF [Red Lion St]: Small and cottagey, high stools and wide shelves around the walls, old photographs, horsebrasses, hanging copper pots and pans and so forth inside, simple wkdy lunchtime

food, several real ales; seats and flower-filled window boxes outside, open all day wkdys, plus Sat lunchtime *(the Didler)*

Mabels WC1H 9AZ [just off Euston Rd]: Neat and cosy open-plan pub with reasonably priced food from sandwiches and baguettes up, Shepherd Neame ales, good wine choice, friendly staff, bright carpeting, two levels; pavement tables, open all day *(Tracey and Stephen Groves, C J Fletcher)*

Penderels Oak WC1V 7HJ [High Holborn]: Vast Wetherspoons pub with their usual well priced food, but otherwise quite distinctive, with attractive décor and woodwork, lots of books, pew seating around central tables, huge choice of good value real ales, charming staff; open all day *(John Coatsworth, Tracey and Stephen Groves)*

Rugby WC1N 3ES [Great James St]: Sizeable corner pub with Shepherd Neame ales inc their seasonal beer from central servery, decent usual food, good service, darts, appropriate photographs; tables on pleasant terrace *(the Didler)*

Swintons WC1X 9NT [Swinton St]: Modern wkdy dining pub, comfortable and spacious, with efficient friendly service, real ales such as Black Sheep, extensive wine list, impressive choice of reasonably priced food from contemporary snacks up; no TVs or machines *(Joe Green)*

Union WC1X 9AA [Lloyd Baker St]: Victorian pub converted to bar/restaurant without losing attractive period décor and furnishings, sensibly short choice of good food even Sun evening, friendly service, good choice of beers such as Fullers London Pride and of wines *(John Knighton)*

WC2

☆ **Chandos** WC2N 4ER [St Martins Lane]: Busy downstairs bare-boards bar with snug cubicles, lots of theatre memorabilia on stairs up to more comfortable lounge with opera photographs, low wooden tables, panelling, leather sofas, coloured windows; cheap Sam Smiths OB, prompt cheerful service, generous reasonably priced food from sandwiches to Sun roasts, air conditioning, darts and pinball; can get packed early evening, piped music and games machines; note the automaton on the roof (working 10-2 and 4-9); children upstairs till 6pm, open all day from 9am (for breakfast) *(Michael Dandy, Susan and Nigel Wilson, LYM, GHC)*

Coal Hole WC2R 0DW [Strand]: Pleasant and comfortable, softly lit and relaxed downstairs dining bar with wall reliefs, mock-baronial high ceiling and raised back balcony, chatty front bar, good range of beers, decent house wine, well priced sandwiches, baked potatoes, good sausages and mash etc *(N R White, BB, GHC, Pete Coxon)*

☆ **Cross Keys** WC2H 9EB [Endell St/Betterton St]: Relaxed and chatty retreat, masses of photographs and posters inc Beatles

memorabilia, brassware and tasteful bric-a-brac on dark walls, bargain food inc impressive range of lunchtime sandwiches and a few hot dishes, Courage Best and Wells & Youngs ales, decent wines by the glass, quick friendly service even at busy times; games machine; gents' down stairs; sheltered picnic-sets out on cobbles, pretty flower tubs and hanging baskets, open all day *(the Didler, LYM)*

Devereux WC2R 3JJ [Devereux Ct, Essex St]: Comfortable softly lit L-shaped bar with lively décor, mainstream ales such as Courage and Greene King IPA, obliging service, lunchtime bar food *(Tracey and Stephen Groves)*

Edgar Wallace WC2R 3JE [Essex St]: Simple spacious open-plan pub, cosy and relaxing despite the bright lighting, enthusiastic landlord and friendly young staff, well kept Adnams, a beer brewed for them by Nethergate and several unusual guest beers (tasters offered), decent all-day food, interesting maps and prints of old London, stairs to room of Edgar Wallace memorabilia; open all day, cl wknds *(Tracey and Stephen Groves, Bruce Bird)*

Freemasons Arms WC2E 9NG [Long Acre]: Roomy and relaxed two-level pub with ornate woodwork and cupola ceiling, big windows, pleasing semicircular bar, interesting prints (and FA inaugurated here), small tables and lots of wood, well kept Shepherd Neame ales, attentive staff, sensibly priced food, quiz machine, big-screen TV; open all day *(BB, Tracey and Stephen Groves, Bruce Bird)*

Knights Templar WC2A 1DT [Chancery Lane]: Wetherspoons in big-windowed former bank, marble pillars, handsome fittings and plasterwork, good bustling atmosphere on two levels, some interesting real ales at bargain price, good wine choice, all-day food, friendly staff; remarkably handsome lavatories; open all day inc Sun *(Dr and Mrs M E Wilson, Tracey and Stephen Groves, Dr and Mrs A K Clarke)*

Lowlander WC2B 5RR [Drury Lane]: Smart well run brussels-style bar with major beers on tap, some from smaller low-country brewers, interesting bottled beers, waiter service, tall chairs at neat long rows of tables (one just for drinking), soothing leather banquettes at the back *(Tracey and Stephen Groves)*

Lyceum WC2R 0HS [Strand]: Panelling and pleasantly simple furnishings downstairs, with several small discreet booths, steps up to a bigger alcove with darts, food in much bigger upstairs panelled lounge with deep button-back leather settees and armchairs, low-priced Sam Smiths beer, generous straightforward food, civilised atmosphere *(Tracey and Stephen Groves)*

Marquis of Granby WC2N 4HS [Chandos Pl]: Long narrow pub with high window stools overlooking street, Adnams, Fullers London Pride and Greene King IPA, reasonably priced

pub food, daily papers; open all day
(the Didler)

☆ **Porterhouse** WC2E 7NA [Maiden Lane]: Good
daytime pub (can be crammed evenings),
London outpost of Dublin's Porterhouse
microbrewery, their interesting if pricy
unpasteurised draught beers inc Porter and
two Stouts (comprehensive tasting tray),
also their TSB real ale and a guest, lots of
bottled imports, good choice of wines by the
glass, reasonably priced food from soup and
open sandwiches up with some emphasis on
rock oysters, shiny three-level labyrinth of
stairs (lifts for disabled), galleries and
copper ducting and piping, some nice design
touches, sonorous openwork clock, neatly
cased bottled beer displays; piped music,
irish live music, big-screen sports TV
(relayed to gents'); tables on front terrace,
open all day (G Coates, Tracey and
Stephen Groves, BB)

Savoy Tup WC2R 0BA [Savoy St]: Typical
small city drinking pub opp small churchyard
behind Savoy Theatre, obliging service
(Christopher Turner)

Ship WC2A 3HP [Gate St]: Interesting bare-
boards corner pub in narrow alley with pews
and high-backed settles, leaded lights,
painted plaster relief ceiling and upstairs
overflow, changing real ales, decent pubby
food, friendly service; piped music may
obtrude (Tracey and Stephen Groves)

☆ **Ship & Shovell** WC2N 5PH [Craven Passage,
off Craven St]: Four well kept Badger ales
from hop-hung bar, decent reasonably priced
food from wide range of baguettes, bloomers
and ciabattas up, good friendly staff, bright
lighting, pleasant décor inc interesting
prints, mainly naval (to support a fanciful
connection between this former coalheavers' pub properly called Ship & Shovel
with Sir Cloudesley Shovell the early 18th-c
admiral), open fire, compact back section,
separate partitioned bar on opposite side of
alley – you can now also drink out under the
arch; TV; open all day (N R White, the Didler,
Sue Demont, Tim Barrow, John and
Gloria Isaacs, Ian Phillips, John A Barker)

☆ **Welsh Harp** WC2N 4HS [Chandos Pl]:
Unpretentious, friendly and well run, with
well kept Black Sheep, Harveys, Timothy
Taylors Landlord and three rotating ales such
as Adnams Regatta, Hop Back Summer
Lightning and York Yorkshire Terrier, New
Forest farm cider, good collection of
whiskeys and whiskies, helpful service, good
lunchtime baps with several types of
sausage, nice high benches around back
tables and along wall counter, some seats at
unusual counter facing pavement across fully
opening windows, red walls with some
interesting if not always well executed star
portraits, lovely front stained glass, good-
sized room upstairs; open all day (Tracey and
Stephen Groves, BB, Joe Green, Jarrod and
Wendy Hopkinson, John Branston)

EAST LONDON

E1

☆ **Dickens Inn** E1W 1UH [Marble Quay,
St Katharines Way]: Outstanding position
looking over smart docklands marina to
Tower Bridge, bare boards, baulks and
timbers, wide choice of enjoyable food from
separate servery (or pizza/pasta upstairs,
and smarter restaurant above that), friendly
helpful staff, real ales such as Adnams,
Greene King Old Speckled Hen and Wells &
Youngs Bombardier, decent wines by the
glass; piped music, machines; popular with
overseas visitors, attractive flower-filled
façade, tables outside (John Saville,
N R White, the Didler, LYM, GHC)

Oasis E1 4AA [Mile End Rd]: Enjoyable food
all day, real ales such as Adnams tapped
from the cask, mixed chairs and sturdy
tables on stripped boards, fresh
contemporary décor, upstairs overflow dining
room; open all day (anon)

Pride of Spitalfields E1 5LJ [Heneage St]:
Convivial East End local with Fullers London
Pride and interesting changing guest beers
from central servery, bar food, friendly staff
and chatty regulars, nice lighting,
interesting prints and comfortable
banquettes in lounge (Tracey and
Stephen Groves, David Hoult)

Princess of Prussia E1 8AZ [Prescot St]: Neat
and friendly, with well kept Shepherd Neame
ales, enjoyable seasonal cooking by mother,
welcoming daughter runs the bar; large
secluded back terrace (Gary Hodson)

Spitz E1 6BG [Commercial St]: Trendy
warehouse-style bar with fine selection of
continental beers, frequent live music; some
seats out in Spitalfields Market (Tracey and
Stephen Groves)

Ten Bells E1 6LY [Commercial St]: Perimeter
seating, old wooden flooring and wall tiles,
Wells & Youngs Bombardier from handsome
tall bar; opposite Hawksmoor's stunning
Church of St Mary (Tracey and
Stephen Groves)

E4

Harvester E4 9EY [New Rd]: New Harvester
built on site of former swimming pool,
friendly and popular (Robert Lester)

Royal Forest E4 7QH [Rangers Rd (A1069)]:
Large timbered Brewers Fayre backing on to
Epping Forest and dating partly from 17th c,
friendly helpful staff, Fullers London Pride,
good value restaurant; play area
(Robert Lester)

E8

LMNT E8 3NH [Queensbridge Rd, Hackney]:
Opera-theme bar dominated by huge 3D
sphinx head, eccentric table arrangements
(one above the bar, one in a giant urn, one
rather like being on board ship), good
service and good value food inc three-course
deals (cheapest at lunchtime); open all day
(Pat and Tony Martin)

E11

Duke of Edinburgh E11 2EY [Nightingale Lane]: Two-bar mock-Tudor local, warm and friendly, with bargain generous home cooking from hot sandwiches up lunchtime (not Sun) and all afternoon, Adnams and Wells & Youngs, decent wine, cheerful helpful landlady, lots of prints and plates, darts, cards and shove-ha'penny; big-screen sports TV; garden tables, open all day *(Pete Baker)*

George E11 2RL [High St Wanstead]: Large 18th-c coaching inn, now a Wetherspoons, real ales such as Shepherd Neame Spitfire, their usual reasonably priced food all day, friendly atmosphere, plenty of books to read, pictures of famous Georges down the ages *(Robert Lester)*

Nightingale E11 2EY [Nightingale Lane]: Popular all-rounder with wide choice of food from sandwiches up, half a dozen mainly mainstream ales from island bar serving several linked areas *(Pete Baker)*

E14

☆ **Gun** E14 9NS [Cold Harbour, Canary Wharf]: Well restored early 19th-c building, dark wood, white walls, bottles stacked to the ceiling, two back Thames-view bar rooms with good log fires, comfortable leather armchairs and chesterfields, settles and naval battle painting, Adnams Broadside, good choice of wines by the glass inc champagne, good coffees, interesting bar food, small romantic if expensive restaurant; attractive riverside terrace with good tables and chairs and fascinating views, open all day *(Maggie Atherton, Susan and John Douglas)*

E15

King Edward VII E15 4BQ [Broadway]: New licensees working hard to source prime ingredients for their bar and restaurant food, four changing real ales, pews, dark woodwork and etched glass screens in traditional bar, sofas in small lounge area, pleasant back dining area with well lit prints above panelled dado; well reproduced piped music, live music on Thurs *(anon)*

E17

Celsius E17 4QH [Hoe St]: Neatly kept pub with contemporary décor inc settees and leather cubes, reasonably priced food, speciality wheat beers *(Ron Deighton)*

NORTH LONDON

N1

Scolt Head N1 4HT [Culford Rd]: Former Sussex Arms, renamed and reworked, with a couple of real ales such as Caledonian Deuchars IPA in pleasant candlelit front bar, good choice of wines by the glass, enjoyable food in separate dining room, big back games room with pool and big-screen sports TV; occasional live music, plans for films and theatre; covered heated terrace *(Harry Davies)*

Wenlock Arms N1 7TA [Wenlock Rd]: Popular open-plan carpeted local in a bleak bit of London, warmly welcoming service, half a dozen or more well kept changing small-brewery ales from central servery, always inc a Mild, also farm cider and perry, foreign bottled beers, doorstep sandwiches inc good salt beef, alcove seating, piano in pride of place, coal fires, darts, back pool table; piped music, live jazz Tues and Fri, piano Sun lunch, open all day *(the Didler)*

N2

Bald Face Stag N2 8AB [High Rd]: Newly refurbished, with fresh décor and stripped boards (they got rid of four pool tables and a dozen TVs), enjoyable traditional and more contemporary food using rare-breed meats, friendly staff, good choice of wines by the glass, real ales; children welcome, tables in courtyard garden, open all day *(anon)*

N4

Faltering Fullback N4 3HB [Perth Rd/Ennis Rd]: Comfortable small corner pub, two softly lit bars, friendly staff and locals, Fullers London Pride, good value thai food in back room; may be quiet piped music, silenced sports TV; nice outside area *(Darren Le Poidevin, Giles and Annie Francis)*

Garden Ladder N4 1AL [Green Lanes]: Former tandoori restaurant comfortably reworked as bar/restaurant, well kept Courage Directors and a changing guest beer, decent wines by the glass, reasonably priced food all day inc Sun carvery, friendly staff; piped music; open all day *(anon)*

Oakdale Arms N4 1NP [Hermitage Rd]: Tucked-away oasis with up to eight real ales, food inc bargain curries Fri, relaxing open atmosphere *(Gavin Robinson)*

N6

Angel N6 5JT [Highgate High St]: Long neat L-shaped bar with well kept ales such as Caledonian Deuchars IPA, decent wines by the glass, up-to-date food from sandwiches up for most of the day, friendly management and efficient staff, tables round the sides, dim lighting; open all day *(Tracey and Stephen Groves, John Wooll)*

☆ **Flask** N6 6BU [Highgate West Hill]: Comfortable Georgian pub, intriguing up-and-down layout, sash-windowed bar hatch, panelling and high-backed carved settle in snug lower area with nice log fire, quick friendly service, Adnams Broadside and Timothy Taylors Landlord, several continental beers on tap, enjoyable changing all-day food (limited Sun) inc contemporary light dishes; very busy Sat lunchtime; well behaved children allowed, close-set picnic-sets out in attractive heated front courtyard with barbecues, handy for strolls around Highgate village or Hampstead Heath *(LYM,*

Ian Phillips, Russell Lewin, Tracey and
Stephen Groves, Jeremy King)
Wrestlers N6 4AA [North Rd]: L-shaped bar
with 1920s panelling, cosy corners,
comfortable sofa, well kept Fullers and
Youngs, games *(Tracey and Stephen Groves)*

N14
Old Cherry Tree N14 6EN [The Green]: Roomy
beamed Vintage Inn with wide choice of
wines by the glass, reasonably priced real
ales, good value food all day from breakfast
on, swift service, mix of big tables, some
leather chesterfields; children welcome,
bedrooms in adjacent Innkeepers Lodge,
open all day *(Colin Moore)*

N20
Orange Tree N20 8NX [Totteridge]: Attractive
low building by pond, former Vintage Inn,
now more contemporary, with emphasis on
family food such as pasta, pizzas and steaks,
spit-roasts too, some comfortable tub chairs,
inglenook log fire, good choice of wines by
the glass, several continental lagers and a
real ale; welcoming to children (and walkers,
who leave boots in porch), tables out in
pleasant surroundings – still a village feel,
open all day *(LYM, Kalman Kafetz)*

NW1
Crown & Goose NW1 7HP [corner of
Arlington Rd/Delancey St]: Good food (get
there early for this), Fullers London Pride
from horseshoe bar, candles at night
(Jeremy King)
☆ **Doric Arch** NW1 2DN [Eversholt St]: Renamed
former Head of Steam, virtually part of
Euston Station, up stairs from bus terminus
with raised back part overlooking it, a
Fullers pub but with great range of other
beers inc seasonal, friendly helpful staff,
good value food lunchtime and from 4.30
wkdys, extended lunchtime wknds),
pleasantly nostalgic atmosphere, intriguing
train and other transport memorabilia,
downstairs restaurant; discreet sports TV;
open all day *(BB, N R White, C J Fletcher,
Simon Marley)*
Euston Flyer NW1 2RA [Euston Rd, opp
British Library]: Spacious and comfortable
open-plan pub opp British Library, full
Fullers beer range, good value food all day
from big well filled fresh sandwiches up,
relaxed lunchtime atmosphere, plenty of
light wood, tile and wood floors, smaller
more private raised areas, big doors open to
street in warm weather; piped music, big-
screen TVs, games machines, can get packed
early evening, then again later; open all day,
cl 8.30pm Sun *(Stephen and Jean Curtis,
Simon Marley)*
Metropolitan NW1 5LA [Baker St Stn,
Marylebone Rd]: Wetherspoons in ornate
Victorian hall, large and rarely crowded, lots
of tables on one side, very long bar the
other, their usual good beer choice and
prices, efficient staff, good coffee,

inexpensive food; open all day *(Stephen and
Jean Curtis, Ian Phillips, Pete Walker)*
O'Neils NW1 2QS [Euston Rd]: Part of an
Irish-theme chain, this one worth knowing
for its good service, low-priced food and well
kept beers *(David Morgan)*

NW3
Duke of Hamilton NW3 1JD [New End]:
Attractive Fullers local with proper hands-on
landlord, good range of seating, tall
Edwardian central servery, interesting prints,
bric-a-brac and signed cricket bats, farm
cider and malt whiskies; raised back suntrap
terrace, next to New End Theatre, open all
day *(N R White, the Didler, Tracey and
Stephen Groves)*
Roebuck NW3 2PN [Pond St]: Plush and
individual, with well kept Adnams Broadside,
nice sofa, attractive variety of tables,
parquet flooring, lovely bead curtain
(Tracey and Stephen Groves)

NW8
Lords Tavern NW8 8QP [St Johns Wood Rd]:
Next to Lord's Cricket Ground, light and airy
with lots of glass and modern bare-boards
décor, Fullers London Pride, good wine
choice, decent if not cheap food from
sandwiches up (breakfast available some
match days), friendly service; tables out on
decking *(BB, Michael Dandy)*

SOUTH LONDON

E14
Cat & Canary E14 4DH [Fishermans Walk]:
Very good choice of wines by the glass,
Fullers and guest ales, decent bar food inc
speciality burgers, traditional décor; tables
out by dockside with heating and lights, nice
spot *(Colin Moore)*

SE1
☆ **Anchor** SE1 9EF [Bankside]: Much
refurbished pub in great spot nr Thames,
river views from outside tables and upper
floors inc timbered restaurant, beams and
stripped brickwork in biggish two-level open
bar, Courage Best and Wells & Youngs
Bombardier, a dozen wines by the glass,
various teas and coffees, simple low-priced
bar food all day, good atmosphere; piped
music may obtrude; summer barbecues,
children in top restaurant and family room,
bedrooms in friendly quiet Premier Travel Inn
behind, open all day *(B and M Kendall, GHC,
the Didler, LYM, N R White, John Beeken)*
Barrow Boy & Banker SE1 9QQ [Borough
High St, by London Bridge station]: Smart
and civilised bank conversion with biggish
upper gallery, full Fullers beer range kept
well, decent wines, good young manageress
and staff, competitively priced food from
sandwiches up, music-free; right by
Southwark Cathedral *(Charles Gysin,
Ian Phillips)*

Bridge House SE1 2UP [Tower Bridge Rd]: Relaxed Adnams bar with modern décor and sofas, their full ale range and good wine choice, good value generous food, friendly efficient service, downstairs dining area (Richard Siebert, N R White)

Hole in the Wall SE1 8SQ [Mepham St]: Quirky and decidely unsmart no-frills hideaway in railway arch virtually underneath Waterloo, rumbles and shakes with the trains, Adnams Bitter and Broadside, Battersea Bitter, Fullers London Pride and Wells & Youngs Bitter and Special, bargain basic food all day, small front bar, well worn mix of tables set well back from long bar in bigger back room; open all day, cl wknd afternoons (Ian Phillips, LYM, Sue Demont, Tim Barrow)

Kings Arms SE1 8TB [Roupell St]: Proper corner local, bustling and friendly, traditional bar and lounge, both distinctive and curved, Adnams, Fullers London Pride and Greene King IPA, good friendly service, flame-effect fires, food from thai dishes to good Sun roast, back extension with conservatory/courtyard dining area, long central table and high side tables, attractive local prints and eccentric bric-a-brac; open all day (Sue Demont, Tim Barrow, Andrew Wallace, Giles and Annie Francis, Ian Phillips)

Leather Exchange SE1 3HN [Leathermarket St]: Compact Fullers pub very popular lunchtime for good value generous food, their real ales, good wines, helpful friendly staff (Valerie Baker)

☆ **Lord Clyde** SE1 1ER [Clennam St]: neatly kept panelled L-shaped local in same family for 50 years, well kept Adnams Best, Fullers London Pride, Greene King IPA, Shepherd Neame Spitfire and Wells & Youngs Special, good value simple home-made food from good salt beef sandwiches up wkdy lunchtimes and early evenings, welcoming staff, darts in small thatch-service back public bar; striking tiled façade, open all day (Sat early evening break, cl 7pm Sun) (Pete Baker, Mike and Sue Loseby)

Ship SE1 1DX [Borough Rd]: Good choice of good value pubby food under popular newish landlord in attractive Fullers pub, long and narrow, with lots of wood, a local for the RPO; back terrace (Valerie Baker)

Studio Six SE1 9PP [Gabriel's Wharf, Upper Ground]: Bustling South Bank bar/bistro in two linked timber-framed buildings, glazed all round, picnic-sets on two terraces (one heated), good well priced modern food all day inc mezze and lots of fish, good choice of belgian beers on tap, decent wines, efficient service; soft piped music inside, beer may come in plastic mug outside; children welcome, great location, open all day (Sue Demont, Tim Barrow, BB)

Wheatsheaf SE1 9AA [Stoney St]: Simple bare-boards Borough Market local, well kept Wells & Youngs ales from central servery,

decent wine choice, lunchtime food, friendly staff, some brown panelling; piped music, sports TV in one bar, games machine; tables on small back terrace and out by market, open all day, cl Sun (the Didler)

SE3

Hare & Billet SE3 0QJ [Eliot Cottages, Hare & Billet Rd]: Pleasant and chatty open-plan traditional pub dating from 16th c, panelling, bare boards, good solid furniture and open fire, raised middle section, good value food inc interesting dishes and (till 7pm) Sun lunch, real ales such as Flowers and Greene King, good choice of wines, friendly landlady and staff, Blackheath views; open all day (N R White, BB)

SE10

Ashburnham Arms SE10 8UH [Ashburnham Grove]: Friendly Shepherd Neame local with good pasta and other food (not Mon); pleasant garden with barbecues (the Didler)

Plume of Feathers SE10 9LZ [Park Vista]: Low-ceilinged Georgian local with good value food from sandwiches and well filled baked potatoes up, Adnams and Fullers London Pride from central bar, good coffee, cheerful service, flame-effect fire in large attractive fireplace, lots of pictures and plates on ochre walls, back dining area; SkyTV sports; children welcome, play room across walled back garden (Greenwich Park playground nearby too), handy for Maritime Museum (LM, Pete Baker)

☆ **Richard I** SE10 8RT [Royal Hill]: Old-fashioned pubby atmosphere in friendly traditional two-bar local with Wells & Youngs ales, food inc notable sausages, good staff, no piped music, bare boards, panelling; children welcome, picnic-sets out in front, lots more in pleasant paved back garden with wknd barbecues – busy summer wknds and evenings (the Didler, N R White)

☆ **Trafalgar** SE10 9NW [Park Row]: Substantial 18th-c building with splendid river views from big windows directly above water in four still quite elegant if slightly worn rooms inc end dining room, all with oak panelling and good maritime and local prints; three ales inc Chatham Lord Nelson, popular food all day from standard menu (more interesting in dining room), good house wines, helpful young staff, good atmosphere, though spacious bars can get packed Fri/Sat evenings, piped music can be unusual; tables out by Nelson statue, handy for Maritime Museum (S Topham, N R White, BB)

SE12

Crown SE12 0AJ [Burnt Ash Hill]: Typical civilised suburban Youngs pub, cheerful staff and relaxed atmosphere, some seats in cosy alcoves, good range of bar food, Wells & Youngs ales; pleasant garden (Clive Flynn)

SE16

☆ **Angel** SE16 4NB [Bermondsey Wall E]: Handsomely refurbished Thames-side pub, appealing and civilised, with superb views to Tower Bridge and the City upstream, and the Pool of London downstream, from back lounge, upstairs restaurant, balcony supported above water by great timber piles, and from picnic-sets in garden alongside; softly lit front bars with two public areas on either side of snug, low-backed settles, old local photographs and memorabilia, etched glass and glossy varnish; food from baguettes to impressive main meals and good Sun roast, cheap Sam Smiths, kind friendly service; interesting walks round Surrey Quays (LYM, N R White)

☆ **Mayflower** SE16 4NF [Rotherhithe St]: Cosy old riverside pub with surprisingly wide choice of enjoyable generous food all day from sandwiches up inc good chips; black beams, panelling, nautical bric-a-brac, high-backed settles and coal fires, good Thames views from upstairs restaurant (cl Sat lunchtime), Greene King IPA, Abbot and Old Speckled Hen, good coffee and good value wines; piped music; children welcome, tables out on nice jetty/terrace over water, open all day, in unusual street with lovely Wren church (LYM, the Didler, Jeremy King)

SE22

Herne Tavern SE22 0RR [Forest Hill Rd]: Smart welcoming panelled pub with well kept ales such as Greene King Ruddles, Otter and Shepherd Neame Spitfire, enjoyable food in separate dining area; big garden with play area (Daniel Watson)

SE24

Commercial SE24 0JT [Railton Rd (opp Herne Hill Station)]: Roomy and comfortable, with sofas and easy chairs, decent beer such as Black Sheep, daily papers, lively young atmosphere; SkyTV (Giles and Annie Francis)

SW4

Abbeville SW4 9JW [Abbeville Rd]: Dining pub with sturdy furnishings, rugs on dark boards, warm décor, fresh waitress-served food inc mediterranean specials and wknd brunches, Fullers ales and a guest beer (Paul Magnusson)

SW11

Eagle SW11 6HG [Chatham Rd]: Attractive old backstreet local, real ales such as Flowers IPA, Fullers London Pride and Timothy Taylors Landlord, friendly helpful service, leather sofas in fireside corner of L-shaped bar; big-screen sports TV; back terrace with marquee, small front terrace too (Sue Demont, Tim Barrow)

Falcon SW11 1RU [St Johns Hill]: Edwardian pub with remarkably long light oak bar snaking back from lively front bar, period partitions, cut glass and mirrors, friendly service, well kept Fullers London Pride, bargain pub food such as pie and mash,

quieter back dining area, daily papers; big-screen TV (Dr Ron Cox)

SW12

☆ **Nightingale** SW12 8NX [Nightingale Lane]: Cosy and civilised early Victorian local, small woody front bar opening into larger back area and attractive family conservatory, well kept Wells & Youngs ales, enjoyable bar food, sensible prices, friendly staff; small secluded back garden (Sue Demont, Tim Barrow, BB)

SW13

Brown Dog SW13 0AP [Cross Str]: Well renovated former Rose of Denmark, enjoyable food, good choice of wines, friendly helpful staff, subtle lighting and open fires (Sandy Taylor)

SW14

Ship SW14 7QR [Thames Bank]: Comfortable pub with good Thames views, prompt friendly service, good range of reasonably priced generous pubby food from sandwiches up, Fullers London Pride, Greene King IPA and Wells & Youngs Bombardier, conservatory; terrace tables, not on river side (John Wooll)

SW15

☆ **Boathouse** SW15 2JX [Brewhouse Lane, Putney Wharf; [U] Putney Bridge, then cross the Thames – from the bridge you can see the pub on your left]: Busy Thames-side pub in new development, Wells & Youngs ales from long bar in tall glazed extension from former Victorian vinegar factory, low modern seating, young chatty atmosphere (popular with South Africans and antipodeans – the style of this clever conversion surely reminds them of places back home), quieter panelled room on another level behind, cosy upstairs panelled restaurant with another pubby bar; piped pop music; children in eating areas, glass-sided balcony and attractive riverside terrace, open all day (Peter Rozée, Michael Tack, Peter Dandy, John and Elisabeth Cox, LYM, Tracey and Stephen Groves)

Bricklayers Arms SW15 1DD [down cul-de-sac off Lower Richmond Rd nr Putney Bridge]: Gently freshened up keeping its properly pubby character, well kept ales such as Timothy Taylors Landlord, friendly young bar staff (Steve Derbyshire)

☆ **Dukes Head** SW15 1JN [Lower Richmond Rd]: Smartly modernised and expanded Victorian pub – much improved, with comfortable new furnishings in knocked-together front bars and trendy new downstairs cocktail bar in long disused skittle alley (hugely popular with young people wknds; some distinctive drinks); civilised light and airy dining room, good range of well presented pubby food all day, lots of sharing platters and snacks as well as full meals, ceiling fans, tables by window with great Thames view; Wells & Youngs ales, lots of wines by the glass; plastic glasses for outside terrace or riverside pavement across the road (on summer evenings rather like a seaside promenade); children welcome (high chairs and smaller helpings), open all day *(Peter Dandy, BB)*

☆ **Jolly Gardeners** SW15 1NT [Lacy Rd]: Stylishly cool bar with two changing real ales, quite a range of draught belgian beers, good choice of wines, herbal teas and smoothies, interesting enjoyable food changing weekly, plenty vegetarian, very friendly accommodating service, lots of sofas, trendy artwork, chill-out music, traditional board games; nice tables out on front terrace, one at the back *(Jude Wright, BB)*

Telegraph SW15 3TU [Telegraph Rd]: Recent cool refurbishment, enjoyable fresh food from sandwiches up, well kept Adnams Broadside and a couple of changing guest beers, friendly cheerful staff; attractive garden, nice spot opp cricket pitch *(Peter Dandy)*

SW18

Alma SW18 1TF [York Road; [U] Wandsworth Town]: Wells & Youngs ales and good choice of wines from island bar, bright and airy décor with mosaic plaques and birds in mirrors, sofas as well as informal mix of tables and chairs, well trained staff; pleasant garden *(Joe Green, LYM)*

Brewers SW18 2QB [East Hill]: Large two-bar Youngs pub nr their former brewery, good value food inc Sun lunches, separate restaurant; TV; bedrooms *(Peter Dandy)*

☆ **Cats Back** SW18 1NN [Point Pleasant]: Distinctive and well worn backstreet haven with motley furnishings from pews and scrubbed pine tables to pensioned-off chairs and sofas, loads of sundry bric-a-brac, pictures on red walls, dimmed chandeliers and lit candelabra, customers in keeping with the eccentric décor, well kept Adnams and Wells & Youngs ales, good choice of wines by the glass, good sandwiches and a couple of well priced hot dishes served till late, good service, blazing fire in small fireplace; well chosen piped music; pavement tables and diverse chairs, open all day *(LM, BB)*

Earl Spencer SW18 5JL [Merton Rd]: Some emphasis on the food side (reasonable prices), good choice of wines by the glass *(Peter Dandy)*

Pig & Whistle SW18 5LD [Merton Rd (A218)]: Well maintained Youngs pub, Wells & Youngs ales, enjoyable food inc good roasts, smart bar staff, pleasant décor *(Peter Dandy)*

SW19

Alexandra SW19 7NE [Wimbledon Hill Rd]: Large busy Youngs pub with Wells & Youngs ales and good choice of wines by the glass from central bar, enjoyable food from

sandwiches and toasted paninis up, helpful service, comfortably up-to-date décor in three linked areas inc bare-boards back dining areas; TV; attractive roof terrace, tables also out in mews *(Peter Dandy, Michael Dandy)*

Princess of Wales SW19 3BP [Morden Rd]: Traditional carpeted cream and brown pub with Wells & Youngs ales, friendly service, pub food from sandwiches up, back dining area, Diana Princess of Wales photographs above the panelled dado; steps down to back terrace tables *(Derek and Heather Manning)*

WEST LONDON

SW6

Duke on the Green SW6 4XG [New Kings Rd, Parsons Green]: Huge Edwardian pub, properly the Duke of Cumberland, revamped in brasserie style with well laid out high tables and chairs, a few settles in front part, enjoyable back restaurant (and come evening they pretty much expect you to eat), Wells & Youngs ale, uniformed staff; chrome tables out by pavement *(BB, the Didler)*

Farm SW6 1PP [Farm Lane]: Pleasant pub with good value food in bar and restaurant *(Robert Lester)*

SW10

Lots Road Pub & Dining Rooms SW10 0RJ [Lots Rd, opp entrance to Chelsea Harbour]: Unusually curved corner house with big windows and plenty of space, Fullers ales, good choice of wines, enjoyable food (all day Fri-Sun) from open kitchen counter – they do nice teas; open all day *(LYM, Giles and Annie Francis)*

W4

Bell & Crown W4 3PF [Strand on the Green]: Well run Fullers local, big and busy, with their ales, friendly service, sensibly priced food, cosy log fire, great Thames views from back bar and conservatory; piped music may obtrude; picnic-sets on terrace out by towpath, good walks, open all day *(N R White, Susan and John Douglas)*

City Barge W4 3PH [Strand on the Green]: Small panelled riverside bars with some nice original features in picturesque front part (reserved for diners lunchtime), airy newer back part done out with maritime signs and bird prints, bar food (not Sun, and may take quite a while) from sandwiches up, real ales, back conservatory, winter fires; waterside picnic-sets – nice spot to watch sun set over Kew Bridge *(N R White, LYM, Darren Le Poidevin, Mayur Shah)*

Devonshire House W4 2JJ [Devonshire Rd]: Spacious made-over contemporary dining pub with comfortable dining chairs and banquettes on bare boards, good interesting up-to-date food, friendly atmosphere and attentive service; cl Mon, open all day *(Simon Rodway)*

Duke W4 5LF [South Parade]: Imposing building, light and airy, with booth setting by large windows, interesting if not cheap changing ales; shaded outside seating *(G Coates)*

George IV W4 2DR [Chiswick High Rd]: Victorian pub with good choice of Fullers ales, decent food, good friendly atmosphere, mixed furnishings; Sat comedy club *(Peter Dandy)*

Roebuck W4 1PU [Chiswick High Rd]: Friendly and relaxing dining pub with comfortable leather seats in front bar, roomy and attractive back dining area opening into sheltered paved garden with hanging baskets, enjoyable reasonably priced food all day from open kitchen, good choice of wines by the glass, real ales such as Wells & Youngs; dogs welcome, open all day *(Simon Rodway)*

Swan W4 5HH [Evershed Walk, Acton Lane]: Enjoyable standard food, informal style, friendly overseas staff, good range of wines by the glass, three real ales; they may try to keep your credit card while you eat *(Simon Rodway)*

Tabard W4 1LW [Bath Rd]: No music, wide range of customers, helpful friendly staff, Adnams Broadside, Greene King IPA and Abbot and Marstons Pedigree, wide choice of wines, good imaginative food choice, lots of nooks and corners inc sunken medieval-style seating area, high frieze of William de Morgan tiles, William Morris wallpaper and carpets; fringe theatre upstairs; well behaved children welcome, disabled access, terrace tables, open all day *(G Coates)*

W5

Ealing Park Tavern W5 4RL [South Ealing Rd]: Sensibly short blackboard choice of particularly good daily-changing modern dishes from end kitchen in large open-plan dining room (booking virtually essential evenings), large bar too, Wells & Youngs ales, impressive wine list, good service *(K Drane, Dr Douglas Coombs, Simon Rodway)*

W6

☆ *Anglesea Arms* W6 0UR [Wingate Rd; [U] Ravenscourt Park]: Good interesting food inc wkdy set lunches in lively and bustling gastropub, most enjoyable, with good choice of wines by the glass and of real ales, close-set tables in dining room facing kitchen, roaring fire in simply decorated panelled bar; children welcome, tables out by quiet street, open all day *(LYM, the Didler, Martin and Karen Wake)*

☆ *Black Lion* W6 9TJ [South Black Lion Lane]: Welcoming and civilised cottagey pub kept spotless, helpful landlord and friendly staff, well kept ales such as Caledonian Deuchars IPA and Fullers London Pride, good choice of wines by the glass, modest choice of decent generous food from baguettes and baked potatoes up, comfortable mix of furnishings inc some high-backed settles, nicely

varnished woodwork, candles at night, dining area behind big log-effect gas fire, no TV or music but Mon film night; large pleasant heated terrace on quiet corner *(BB, Howard Dell, N R White)*

Stonemasons Arms W6 0LA [Cambridge Grove]: Good changing food from open kitchen in relaxed Hammersmith gastropub, fair prices, good service, plain décor, basic furnishings, lots of modern art, ceiling fans, mostly young customers evenings; piped music *(BB, Simon Rodway)*

W8

☆ *Scarsdale* W8 6HE [Edwardes Sq]: Busy Georgian pub in lovely leafy square, stripped wooden floors, two or three fireplaces with good coal-effect gas fires, lots of knick-knacks, ornate bar counter, interesting choice of enjoyable blackboard food from ciabattas to chargrilled steaks, plenty of light dishes, charming welcoming service, good range of real ales and of wines by the glass; tree-shaded front courtyard with impressive flower tubs and baskets, open all day *(LYM, Gloria Bax, John and Gloria Isaacs)*

☆ *Uxbridge Arms* W8 7TQ [Uxbridge St]: Small friendly backstreet local with three linked areas, changing real ales inc Fullers, good choice of bottled beers, china, prints and photographs; sports TV; open all day *(the Didler)*

W9

Waterway W9 2JU [Formosa St]: Bookable picnic-sets out on terrace by Grand Union Canal, enjoyable food inc fish and chargrills from open kitchen, well kept beer, good wines by the glass, happy staff, settees in bar area, restaurant *(Sally Anne and Peter Goodale)*

W14

Radnor Arms W14 8PX: Classic pub architecture and interesting windows, convivial and properly pubby inside, interesting regional ales inc Everards, friendly staff who are real ale enthusiasts, good choice of whiskies, plenty of small tables in both rooms, pub games; open all day *(the Didler, Tracey and Stephen Groves)*

Warwick Arms W14 8PS [Warwick Rd]: Early 19th-c, with lots of woodwork, comfortable atmosphere, friendly regulars (some playing darts or bridge), good service, Fullers ales from elegant Wedgwood handpumps, limited tasty food (not Sun evening), sensible prices; tables outside, handy for Earls Court and Olympia, open all day *(the Didler)*

OUTER LONDON

BARNET [TQ2497]

White Lion EN5 4LA [St Albans Rd]: Fullers inc Chiswick kept particularly well by Irish landlady, good value lunchtime baguettes and fish *(Jestyn Phillips)*

BECKENHAM [TQ3769]

Jolly Woodman BR3 6NR [Chancery Lane]: Small friendly old-fashioned local popular for good changing real ale choice inc Caledonian Deuchars IPA, Harveys and Timothy Taylors Landlord, welcoming service, good value changing lunchtime food; can get crowded evenings; picnic-sets out in flower-filled back yard and tiny street, cl Mon *(N R White, Gwyn Berry)*

BOTANY BAY [TQ2999]

Robin Hood EN2 8AP [2 miles from M25 junction 24; Ridgeway (A1005 Enfield rd)]: Useful open-plan 1930s McMullens extended roadhouse, clean and polished, wide choice of enjoyable food all day inc exceptional range of puddings, friendly uniformed staff, three or four well kept ales, decent wines; nice good-sized garden with roses and weeping willow, open all day *(Colin Moore)*

BRENTFORD [TQ1777]

Brewery Tap TW8 8BD [Catherine Wheel Rd]: Small friendly panelled Fullers local with their full ale range, three linked rooms, good value wkdy lunchtime blackboard specials, pool room; steps up from street; a picnic-set on small terrace, for boatyards at Grand Union Canal Thames lock, open all day *(Joe Green)*

BROMLEY [TQ4069]

Red Lion BR1 3LG [North Rd]: Chatty traditional backstreet local, soft lighting, shelves of books and heavy green velvet curtains, well kept Greene King, Harveys and guest beers, good service; picnic-sets on front terrace *(N R White)*

Two Doves BR2 8HD [Oakley Rd (A233)]: Popular unpretentious Youngs pub notable for its neatly kept pretty garden with terrace tables; pleasant local atmosphere inside, with friendly service, Wells & Youngs and occasional guest ales, modern back conservatory *(LM, N R White)*

CHISLEHURST [TQ4369]

Ramblers Rest BR7 5ND [Mill Place; just off Bickley Park Rd and Old Hill, by Summer Hill (A222)]: White weatherboarded local in picturesque hillside setting on edge of Chislehurst Common, particularly well kept Adnams Broadside, Brakspears and Fullers London Pride, good choice of good value food, friendly staff, pleasant unpretentious grown-up atmosphere, upper and lower bars; garden behind, grassy slope out in front (plastic glasses for there), handy for Chislehurst Caves *(Tony and Glenys Dyer, N R White, John Saville)*

Sydney Arms BR7 5PJ [Old Perry St]: Friendly atmosphere, brisk service even when busy, good range of inexpensive basic food even on Sun, well kept real ales, big conservatory; pleasant garden good for children, almost opp entrance to Scadbury Park, country walks *(GHC, B J Harding)*

Tigers Head BR7 5PJ [Watts Lane/Manor Park Rd (B264 S of common, opp St Nicholas's Church)]: Pleasantly airy Chef & Brewer overlooking church and common,

dating from 18th c and pleasantly divided into cosy low-beamed areas, friendly attentive staff, wide food choice inc variety of fish and Sun lunch, good wine list, real ales; smart casual dress code, no under-21s; side terrace tables, good walks nearby *(N R White)*

CROYDON [TQ3265]

George CR0 1LA [George St]: Relatively compact Wetherspoons with interesting real ales, usual food all day, smaller bar for back family area *(Tony Hobden)*

Ship CR0 1QD [High St]: Wide choice of good value food swiftly served in good-sized helpings, panelling and stained glass, very varied customers – even ghosts, they say; sports TV *(Ian and Julia Beard)*

Spread Eagle CR0 1NX [Katharine St]: Large Edwardian Fullers Ale & Pie pub with several of their real ales, friendly staff, high ceilings and panelling; sports TVs *(Sue and Mike Todd)*

CUDHAM [TQ4459]

Blacksmiths Arms TN14 7QB [Cudham Lane S]: Popular and chatty low-ceilinged local with friendly staff, real ales inc Adnams, enjoyable food, plenty of tables in eating area, blazing log fires, views over wooded valley; big garden, pretty window boxes, good 7-mile circular walk from here *(N R White)*

DOWNE [TQ4361]

Queens Head BR6 7US [High St]: Civilised and comfortable, with green and cream décor, latticed windows, lanterns and hops, Darwin texts and splendid log fire in lounge, good value food from sandwiches to popular Sun roasts, Adnams Bitter and Broadside, friendly staff, plush dining room; big-screen TV in public bar, well equipped children's room; picnic-sets on pavement, more in small pleasant back courtyard, handy for Darwin's Down House, good walks, open all day *(N R White)*

ENFIELD [TQ3198]

Fallow Buck EN2 9JD [Clay Hill]: Beamed green belt pub with wide choice of reliable food inc popular Sun lunch, a couple of real ales such as Adnams Broadside, good-sized eating area, tables outside, nice walks *(Colin Moore)*

HAMPTON COURT [TQ1668]

☆ *Kings Arms* KT8 9DD [Hampton Court Rd, by Lion Gate]: Recently well restored pub by Hampton Court itself, with comfortable furnishings inc sofas in back area, attractive Farrow & Ball colours, good open fires, oak panelling, beams and some stained glass, Badger beers, good choice of wines by the glass, sensibly priced pubby food from sandwiches up, pleasant efficient service; piped music; children and dogs welcome, picnic-sets on roadside front terrace, charming new bedrooms, open all day *(LYM, Ian Phillips, Susan and John Douglas)*

HAREFIELD [TQ0590]

Coy Carp UB9 6HZ [Copperhill Lane]: 1905 hotel expansively done out in olde-worlde

Vintage Inn style, with recycled beams, alcoves, log fire, their usual wide choice of well cooked food all day, young friendly staff, good range of wines, real ales such as Wells & Youngs Bombardier; garden tables, lovely spot by Grand Union Canal lock *(N R White)*

Kings Arms UB9 6BJ [Park Lane]: Wide choice of good value thai food and well kept beers in busy and otherwise straightforward town pub *(Stan Edwards)*

ICKENHAM [TQ0886]

Coach & Horses UB10 8LJ [High Rd]: Civilised and cosy Ember Inn with well kept real ales, decent food; no children *(Kevin Thomas, Nina Randall)*

ILFORD [TQ4589]

Dick Turpin IG2 7TD [Aldborough Rd N, off A12 Newbury Park]: Good value food in bar and restaurant, friendly efficient service, real ale; play area in large garden behind *(Robert Lester)*

Red House IG4 5BG [Redbridge Lane E; just off A12, handy for M11 via A406]: Popular multi-level Beefeater with friendly service, good value food; bedrooms in adjoining Premier Travelodge *(Robert Lester)*

ISLEWORTH [TQ1675]

London Apprentice TW7 6BG [Church St]: Large Thames-side pub furnished with character, wide choice of bar food from good sandwiches up (light flashes on your table when it's ready to collect), well kept Adnams Broadside, Courage Best and Fullers London Pride, good coffee, log fire, friendly young staff, upstairs river-view restaurant (open all Sun afternoon); may be piped music; children welcome, attractive waterside terrace, small riverside lawn, open all day *(LYM, N R White)*

KESTON [TQ4164]

Fox BR2 6BQ [Heathfield Rd]: Roomy and up-to-date open-plan local with well kept Adnams and Fullers London Pride, popular traditional food from sandwiches and baguettes up, friendly and helpful young staff, red décor; garden behind with decking, terrace and piped music *(anon)*

KEW [TQ1977]

Coach & Horses TW9 3BH [Kew Green]: Open-plan pub with Wells & Youngs ales and good coffees, standard bar food from sandwiches up, young friendly staff, restaurant; sports TV; teak tables on front terrace, nice setting handy for Kew Gardens *(Jeremy King, Alan and Carolin Tidbury)*

KINGSTON [TQ1869]

Boaters KT2 5AU [Canbury Gardens (park in Lower Ham Rd if you can)]: Family-friendly pub by Thames, half a dozen real ales, good choice of good value food inc Sun lunch, efficient staff, comfortable banquettes in quiet charming bar; in small park, ideal for children in summer *(Peter Smith, Judith Brown)*

Canbury Arms KT2 6LQ [Canbury Pk Rd]: Open-plan Victorian local with wooden bar furnishings, good ale range such as Badger

K&B, Gales, Hook Norton Old Hooky and Timothy Taylors Landlord, good value contemporary food (evenings too), friendly staff; well behaved children allowed till early evening, large side conservatory *(LM)*

MALDEN RUSHETT [TQ1763]

☆ *Star* KT22 0DP [Kingston Rd (A243 just N of M25 junction 9)]: Reliable family dining pub on Surrey border, good helpings of reasonably priced food from baguettes and baked potatoes to a good range of hot dishes, friendly service and atmosphere, nice log fire; quiet piped music *(DWAJ)*

OSTERLEY [TQ1578]

☆ *Hare & Hounds* TW7 5PR [Windmill Lane (B454, off A4 – called Syon Lane at that point)]: Spacious suburban Fullers dining pub, wide choice of enjoyable food from sandwiches to hearty reasonably priced main dishes, prompt friendly service, pleasant dining extension; spacious terrace and big floodlit mature garden, nice setting opp beautiful Osterley Park *(Roy and Lindsey Fentiman)*

RICHMOND [TQ1774]

Old Ship TW9 1ND [King St]: Three bustling linked bars, fine panelling upstairs, stained glass, old photographs, model ships and nauticalia, hands-on landlord and helpful staff, well kept Wells & Youngs ales, enjoyable bar food inc good Sun roast; parking almost impossible; open all day *(Bruce Bird)*

Racing Page TW9 1HP [Duke St]: Open-plan pub with modern furniture on bare boards, wide choice of good value generous thai food, decent wines; piped music, big-screen SkyTV sports; nice spot nr theatre and green *(Chris Evans)*

Lass o' Richmond Hill TW10 6JJ [Queens Rd, Richmond Hill – junction with Stafford Mews]: Rambling Chef & Brewer with decent food (very busy Sun lunchtime), good range of wines by the glass, three real ales inc Fullers London Pride, various areas on several levels; children welcome, small terrace *(Sue and Mike Todd)*

New Inn TW10 7DB [Petersham Rd (A307, Ham Common)]: Attractive and comfortable Georgian pub in good spot on Ham Common, comfortable banquettes and stools, brown décor, Adnams Broadside, Fullers London Pride and Wells & Youngs Bitter, food from ciabattas and other snacks to steaks and interesting specials, pleasant dining area, quick service, big log fire one side, coal the other; disabled facilities, picnic-sets out among flowers front and back *(Chris Evans)*

ROMFORD [TQ4889]

Moby Dick RM6 6QU [A1112/A12 (Whalebone Lane N)]: Large main-road pub/restaurant with good value carvery, games in public bar *(Robert Lester)*

TEDDINGTON [TQ1770]

Lion TW11 9DN [Wick Rd]: Backstreet pub with five or more particularly well kept interesting changing real ales, good value traditional pubby food inc popular Sun lunch, go-ahead licensees and friendly young staff; wknd live entertainment; attractive garden *(P Briggs, Andy Booth, Stephen Funnell)*

Tide End Cottage TW11 9NN [Broom Rd/Ferry Rd, nr bridge at Teddington Lock]: Friendly low-ceilinged pub in Victorian cottage terrace, lots of river, fishing and rowing memorabilia and photographs in two rooms united by big log-effect gas fire, well kept Greene King IPA, decent reasonably priced bar food to numbered tables from sandwiches up, back dining extension; sports TV in front bar, minimal parking; children welcome till 7.30pm, circular picnic-sets on front terrace *(LM, Rob Keenan, Chris Evans)*

TWICKENHAM [TQ1673]

Bear TW1 3LJ [York St]: Large civilised pub with lots of settees, up-to-date food from sandwiches and ciabattas up, familiar favourites too, decent range of beers, quick service *(Mayur Shah)*

Popes Grotto TW1 4RB [Cross Deep]: Huge relaxing suburban local with plenty of dark wood, comfortably spaced tables in eating area, efficient service, Wells & Youngs ales

from U-shaped central servery, good value lunchtime bar food from sandwiches through decent hot dishes to Sun roasts; children in eating area, tables in own garden, and pleasant public garden over rd sloping down to Thames (cl at night), modern bedroom wing *(BB, Mayur Shah)*

UXBRIDGE [TQ0582]

Load of Hay UB8 2PU [Villier St, off Cleveland Rd opp Brunel University]: Cheap food inc good steak and kidney pudding and popular Sun roast in rambling low-key local with mixed bag of furniture, four rotating real ales, impressive fireplace in back part; flower-filled back garden, pergola with vine *(John and Glenys Wheeler, Anthony Longden)*

Malt Shovel UB8 2JE [Iver Lane]: Good beer range, interesting sensibly priced food all day (not Sun) inc sustaining fresh sandwiches from 5pm *(Geoff and Sylvia Donald)*

WOODFORD GREEN [TQ4092]

Cocked Hat IG8 8LG [Southend Rd (A1400), just off M11 terminal roundabout]: Popular main-road Harvester with good value food, friendly service, pleasant atmosphere, Bass, separate proper bar area *(Robert Lester)*

Please tell us if any Lucky Dips deserve to be upgraded
to a main entry – and why. No stamp needed:
The Good Pub Guide, FREEPOST TN1569, Wadhurst, E Sussex TN5 7BR.

Scotland

Though it's the city pubs here that, perhaps unsurprisingly, readers generally write to us about the most, it's usually the splendidly remote coastal pubs that leave the fondest impression. The best stand out for their wonderful fresh seafood, of course, but the journey can sometimes be as much of a draw as the pubs themselves, with glorious views from single-track roads winding through mountains or along the coast; readers approaching one this year revelled in driving through the clouds. Two of these places are particularly impressive: the Applecross Inn at Applecross, where it's hard to tell whether it's the food or the lovely welcome that makes people so keen to return, and the Plockton Hotel at Plockton, about which we've received more letters this year than anywhere else in Scotland – full of superlatives and praise. Sadly, it was on the market as we went to press, so we're keeping our fingers crossed that nothing will change. Plenty of other main entries have this year changed hands or were about to – most recently the Glenelg Inn up towards Skye, where the new landlord told us he'll keep things much the same, though uniquely promised the addition of a helipad. Hotels and comfortable inns are a big part of the mix here: other favourites include the Old Inn at Gairloch, the Four Marys in Linlithgow, and the Stein Inn on Skye – all warmly enjoyed as places to stay, but where the food and service consistently please, too. The bedrooms at the Border at Kirk Yeltholm have been restored after their disastrous fire, and another nice old inn, the Traquair Arms at Innerleithen, returns to the *Guide* this year after several well received improvements. Back in the cities, there are several splendidly unspoilt places that combine gleaming old fittings with a wide choice of beers: by far the most popular are the Café Royal and Guildford Arms, both in Edinburgh. As we noticed last year, several pubs have perhaps broadened their appeal following the ban on smoking (which happened a year earlier here than in England); a good few pubs that we used to note could get smoky now feel completely different. Aside from some of the places already highlighted, particularly popular places for food include the Badachro Inn (good for fresh fish), the Masonic Arms in Gatehouse of Fleet (some really excellent, unusual meals), the Steam Packet in Isle of Whithorn (the inventive specials are the highlight), and the Lion & Unicorn at Thornhill in the Trossachs (well liked for its hearty, home-made meals). But it's the Applecross Inn that is this year's Scotland Dining Pub of the Year, thanks to its really good use of fresh local ingredients – and not just seafood: the well sourced venison and steak are much enjoyed too. Scotland is in general very good value for eating out in pubs. For the same sort of quality, you can now expect to pay considerably less than for a comparable meal in an English pub. And though drinks prices up here tend to be slightly higher than the overall UK average, nowadays Scottish pubs can be a treat for real ale drinkers. Almost all our main entries now stock at least one real ale, and in all but four the cheapest beer they stocked was one brewed north of the border. Most commonly, this was

Caledonian, and you'll find a number of beers from smaller breweries that you'll rarely find in pubs south of the border. The Isle of Skye brewery's beers are becoming quite widespread, but look out too for brews from Fyne, Harviestoun, Inveralmond, Broughton, An Teallach, Orkney and the Houston brewery, based at one of our main entries, the Fox & Hounds in Houston. Another brewpub, the Lade at Kilmahog, now has not only its own organic beers, but a shop selling a good range of bottled ones from other Scottish brewers. Belhaven, widely available, is now part of the Greene King brewing empire. In the Lucky Dip section at the end of the chapter, pubs and inns currently attracting notice include, in Argyll, the Bridge of Orchy Hotel, Clachaig in Glencoe and Oban Inn; in Berwickshire, the Black Bull in Lauder; in Dumfries-shire, the Cavens Arms in Dumfries; in Caithness, the Portland Arms in Lybster; in East Lothian, the Old Clubhouse in Gullane; in Inverness-shire, the Clachnaharry Inn in Inverness; in Kirkcudbrightshire, the Anchor in Kippford; in Midlothian, Bennets and the Kenilworth in Edinburgh; in Peebles-shire, the restauranty Horseshoe at Eddleston and the Gordon Arms at West Linton; in Perthshire, the Meikleour Hotel; in Ross-shire, the Rockvilla at Lochcarron; and on the Islands, the Port Charlotte Hotel on Islay.

ABOYNE

NO5298   MAP 11

Boat 🍺

Charlestown Road (B968, just off A93); AB34 5EL

Welcoming waterside pub with good food – some meals offered in smaller sizes; now open all day

New licensees arrived at this pleasantly pubby waterside inn not long before we went to press (coincidentally, the landlord has the same first name as his predecessor) – but the only thing they're really doing differently is to open all day. Inside, you are greeted by a model train, often chugging around just below the ceiling, making appropriate noises. The partly carpeted bar – with a counter running along through the narrower linking section – also has scottish pictures and brasses, a woodburning stove in a stone fireplace, and games in the public-bar end; piped music, TV. Spiral stairs take you up to a roomy additional dining area. Bass and a couple of real ales from scottish brewers such as Caledonian, Harviestoun, and Isle of Skye on handpump; also 40 malt whiskies. The pub – right by the River Dee – used to serve the ferry that it's named for; outside there are tables, and they have a self-catering flat, sleeping four people, at £55 a night. Reports on the new regime please.

🍽 Using plenty of fresh local produce, lunchtime bar food includes soup, sandwiches, traditional meals like very good fresh battered haddock, beefsteak pie and lasagne (all served in a choice of sizes), several vegetarian dishes, grilled fillet of bass with sweet cucumber salsa, pan-fried lemon and chilli chicken breast, daily specials (maybe including turbot, venison and salmon), and puddings like rhubarb and gingerbread fool or sticky toffee. *Starters/Snacks: £2.75 to £4.95. Main Courses: £6.95 to £17.90. Puddings: £3.75 to £4.95*

Free house ~ Licensees Wilson and Jacqui Clark ~ Real ale ~ Bar food (12-9 (only snacks between 2.30 and 6)) ~ Restaurant ~ (01339) 886137 ~ Children in lounge restaurant ~ Dogs allowed in bar ~ Open 11-11(12 Fri); 11-midnight Sat; 11-11 Sun

Recommended by J A West, Susan and John Douglas, Jean and Douglas Troup, Lucien Perring, J F M and M West

---

We say if we know a pub has piped music.

APPLECROSS   NG7144   MAP 11

Applecross Inn ★ ⑪ ⇌

Off A896 S of Shieldaig; IV54 8ND

SCOTLAND DINING PUB OF THE YEAR

Wonderfully remote pub reached by extraordinarily scenic drive; particularly friendly welcome, and excellent sensibly priced fresh seafood

This splendidly remote waterside pub is much loved for its individual welcome and faultless food, but getting here can be half the fun: it's reached by what's undoubtedly one of Britain's greatest scenic drives, over the Pass of the Cattle (Beallach na Ba). The alternative route, along the single-track lane winding round the coast from just south of Shieldaig, has equally glorious sea loch and then sea views nearly all the way; some readers like to go one way, then back the other. Tables in the nice shoreside garden enjoy magnificent views across to the Cuillin Hills on Skye. With a friendly mix of locals and visitors, the no-nonsense bar has a woodburning stove, exposed stone walls, and upholstered pine furnishings on the stone floor; Isle of Skye Blaven and Red Cuillin, and over 50 malt whiskies. There are lavatories for the disabled and baby changing facilities; pool (winter only), board games and juke box (musicians may take over instead). Bedrooms may have fruity and mineral water as well as the usual tea, coffee and shortbread.

⑪ **Most ingredients are local, with the keenly priced fresh seafood a real draw; chalked up on boards, the menu might include home-made soup or chowder, ploughman's, half a dozen local oysters, venison sausage with onion gravy and bubble and squeak, generous portions of haddock in a light batter, dressed crab salad, king scallops with garlic and crispy bacon on wild rice, specials like curried monkfish on mussels or beef fillet with braised oxtail, dumplings, celeriac gratin and mediterranean vegetables, and home-made puddings such as raspberry cranachan or caramel and chocolate baked cheesecake; they also do very good sandwiches.** *Starters/Snacks: £1.50 to £6.95. Main Courses: £7.95 to £16.95. Puddings: £3.95 to £5.95*

Free house ~ Licensee Judith Fish ~ Real ale ~ Bar food (12-9) ~ (01520) 744262 ~ Children welcome until 8.30pm ~ Dogs allowed in bar and bedrooms ~ Live music Thurs evenings May-Sept ~ Open 11am-11.30pm; 12.30-11 Sun; closed 25 Dec, 1 Jan ~ Bedrooms: £30/£60(£90S)(£90B)

Recommended by Edna Jones, G D Brooks, W Holborow, Barry Collett, Jarrod and Wendy Hopkinson, Bill Strang, Stuart Pearson, Chris Evans, Kay and Alistair Butler, Mrs A J Robertson, Mr and Mrs G D Brooks, Karen Eliot, Peter Meister, Richard and Emily Whitworth

BADACHRO   NG7873   MAP 11

Badachro Inn ⑪

2½ miles S of Gairloch village turn off A832 on to B8056, then after another 3¼ miles turn right in Badachro to the quay and inn; IV21 2AA

Convivial waterside pub with chatty local atmosphere, great views, and excellent fresh fish

Gently eavesdropping in the chatty bar of this white-painted house suggests that some of the yachtsmen have been calling in here annually for decades – the talk is still very much of fishing and boats. Making the most of its lovely setting on the southern shore of Loch Gairloch, it's a very friendly, welcoming place, busy in summer, with an appealing local atmosphere. There are some interesting photographs and collages on the walls, and they put out the Sunday newspapers. The quieter dining area on the left has big tables by a huge log fire, and there's a dining conservatory overlooking the bay. Friendly staff serve a couple of beers from the An Teallach, Caledonian or Isle of Skye breweries on handpump, and they've over 50 malt whiskies, and a good changing wine list, with several by the glass. Look out for the sociable pub spaniel Casper. Outside are heaters on decking, done in a nautical style with sail and rigging; there's a covered area for smokers. The pub is in a tiny village, and the quiet road comes to a dead end a few miles further on at the lovely Redpoint beach. The bay is very sheltered, virtually landlocked by Eilean Horrisdale just opposite; you may see seals in the water, and occasionally even otters. There are three pub moorings (free for visitors), and showers are available at a small charge. Usefully, there's Internet access.

🍴 **Enjoyable food – with the good fresh fish earning the place its food award – includes snacks such as sandwiches, soups like sweet potato and turnip, locally smoked mussels with cucumber and coriander dip, roast venison salad, creel-caught prawns, haggis, neeps and tatties, ploughman's, chicken with stir-fried paprika vegetables, beef and spring onion burger, changing specials like locally smoked haddock topped with welsh rarebit and locally caught langoustines or monkfish kebab, and home-made puddings such as chocolate marquise.** *Starters/Snacks: £3.25 to £6.95. Main Courses: £9.95 to £10.95. Puddings: £1.75 to £4.95*

Free house ~ Licensee Martyn Pearson ~ Real ale ~ Bar food (12-3, 6-9) ~ (01445) 741255 ~ Children welcome ~ Dogs allowed in bar ~ Occasional live music ~ Open 12-12; 12.30-11 Sun; closed weekdays till 4.30 and Sun evening in winter; closed 25 Dec

Recommended by R M Jones, Walter and Susan Rinaldi-Butcher, Mrs A J Robertson, Bill Strang, Stuart Pearson, Mr and Mrs G D Brooks, Peter Meister

BROUGHTY FERRY   NO4630   MAP 11

Fishermans Tavern 🍷 🍺

Fort Street; turning off shore road; DD5 2AD

Welcoming waterfront pub with good choice of beers changing daily, wide range of other drinks, enjoyable food with fish specials and barbecues

A pub since 1827 (when it was converted from a row of fishermen's cottages), this is a pleasant waterfront place for enjoying an interesting range of beers. The half dozen brews on handpump change almost every day, but you might typically find Caledonian Deuchars IPA, Glencoe Stout, Helburn Red Smiddy, and guests from brewers such as Fullers and Greene King. They also have some local country fruit wines, draught wheat beer, 26 wines by the glass, and a good range of malt whiskies. There's an enjoyable atmosphere, and the staff and locals are friendly. A little carpeted snug on the right has nautical tables, light pink soft fabric seating, basket-weave wall panels and beige lamps, and is the more lively bar; on the left is a secluded lounge area with an open coal fire. The carpeted back bar (popular with diners) has a Victorian fireplace; dominoes, TV and fruit machine, and a coal fire. On summer evenings there are tables on the front pavement, and they might have barbecues in the secluded walled garden (where they hold an annual beer festival on the last weekend in May). They have disabled lavatories, and baby changing facilities. Modern and comfortably equipped, the bedrooms extend into the neighbouring cottages; the residents' lounge has a sea view (the bay is just around the corner). The landlord has another pub nearby, and also runs the well preserved Speedwell Bar in Dundee. More reports please.

🍴 **As well as toasties, the enjoyable bar food might include soup, sandwiches, quorn chilli, venison casseroled in red wine, seafood crêpes with parmesan, lemon sole stuffed with prawns in mornay sauce, plenty of fresh fish specials (not Mon), a good seafood platter, and puddings like apple pie (£3.75). They do a two-course lunch for £10.55; children's menu.** *Starters/Snacks: £2.50 to £6.50. Main Courses: £7.55 to £11.45. Puddings: £1.90 to £3.80*

Free house ~ Licensee Jonathan Stewart ~ Real ale ~ Bar food (12-2.30 (12.30-3 weekends), 5-7.30) ~ Restaurant ~ (01382) 775941 ~ Children allowed in lounge during meal times ~ Dogs allowed in bar ~ Scots fiddle music Thurs night from 10 ~ Open 11am-12pm(1am Thurs-Sat); 12.30-12 Sun ~ Bedrooms: £44B/£69B

Recommended by BOB

Looking for a pub with a really special garden, or in lovely countryside, or with an outstanding view, or right by the water? They are listed separately, at the back of the book.

EDINBURGH   NT2574 MAP 11

Abbotsford ◀

Rose Street; E end, beside South St David Street; EH2 2PR

Bustling well preserved Victorian pub with constantly changing beers and good value food

Recently refurbished to better show off some of the original features, this nicely traditional city-centre pub offers five changing real ales from brewers like Atlas, Broughton, Fyne and Orkney, served from a set of air pressure tall founts, along with nearly 60 malt whiskies. The lively and welcoming single bar has dark wooden half-panelled walls, an impressive highly polished Victorian island bar counter, long wooden tables and leatherette benches, and a welcoming log-effect gas fire. There are prints on the walls, and a rather handsome plaster-moulded high ceiling; TV. Quick, helpful service.

🍴 **Reliable and good value, lunchtime bar food includes good ciabattas, soup, a pie of the day, a daily roast or haggis, neeps and tatties, and good home-made puddings; in the evenings they have a more elaborate menu for the restaurant only.** *Starters/Snacks: £3.50 to £5.95. Main Courses: £7.95 to £12.95. Puddings: £4.50*

Free house ~ Licensee Paul Tilsley ~ Real ale ~ Bar food (12-3) ~ Restaurant (12-2.15, 5.30-9.30) ~ (0131) 225 5276 ~ Children in restaurant only till 8pm ~ Dogs allowed in bar ~ Open 11am-12pm(1am Sat); 12-11 Sun; closed 25 Dec, 1 Jan

Recommended by Janet and Peter Race, Michael Dandy, the Didler, Ian and Nita Cooper, Doug Christian, Joe Green, Dr and Mrs A K Clarke

Bow Bar ★ ◀

West Bow; EH1 2HH

Eight splendidly kept beers – and lots of malts – in well run and friendly alehouse of considerable character

One of the city's finest pubs, this handsome, character-laden alehouse is tucked away below the castle. Busy and friendly with a good welcoming atmosphere, the simple, neatly kept rectangular bar retains its tall founts dating from the 1920s made by Aitkens, Mackie & Carnegie as well as an impressive carved mahogany gantry housing over 160 malts, including cask strength whiskies. There's a fine collection of appropriate enamel advertising signs and handsome antique trade mirrors, sturdy leatherette wall seats and heavy narrow tables on its wooden floor, and café-style bar seats. Eight superbly kept beers include Belhaven 80/-, Caledonian Deuchars IPA, Timothy Taylors Landlord and various changing guests like Dent Kamikaze, Fyne Maverick, Highland Scapa Special, Prestonpans 80/- and Stewarts Pentland IPA. There's a good choice of rums and gins too.

🍴 **Limited to tasty pies (from £1.45) and toasties (from £1.65).**

Free house ~ Licensee Helen McLoughlin ~ Real ale ~ Bar food (see text) ~ (0131) 226 7667 ~ No children ~ Dogs allowed in bar ~ Open 12-11.30; 12.30-11 Sun; closed 25-26 Dec, 1-2 Jan

Recommended by Pam and John Smith, Tracey and Stephen Groves, Doug Christian, Joe Green, Colin and Ruth Munro, the Didler, Dr and Mrs A K Clarke

Café Royal

West Register Street; EH2 2AA

Worth a visit just to see the gleaming, listed interior, but the food (especially the seafood) and the range of drinks are rewarding too

Wherever you sit in this dazzlingly ornate Victorian building you'll be rewarded with a splendid view of the wonderfully preserved listed interior, recently given a renewed sparkle. Built with what at the time were state-of-the art plumbing and gas fittings, its floor and stairway are laid with marble, chandeliers hang from the magnificent ceilings, and the big island bar is graced by a carefully re-created gantry. The high-ceilinged café rooms have a particularly impressive series of highly detailed Doulton tilework portraits of historical innovators Watt, Faraday, Stephenson, Caxton, Benjamin Franklin and Robert

Peel (forget police – his importance here is as the introducer of calico printing). There are some fine original fittings in the downstairs gents', and the stained-glass well in the restaurant is well worth a look. Alongside a decent choice of wines, with a dozen by the glass, they've 15 malt whiskies, and Caledonian Deuchars IPA and 80/- on handpump, with perhaps a couple of scottish guests like Arran Blonde and Isle of Skye Red Kullen; there's a TV (for major sports events) and piped music. It can get very busy at lunchtimes, so if you're keen to fully take in the look of the place, try to visit on a quieter afternoon.

🍽 **The restaurant specialises in seafood, so the bar menu has plenty of that too; you might find mussels (half a kilo, or a kilo – that's a lot of mussels), fine oysters with lovely bread, and specials like seared swordfish steak or tuna steak, as well as sandwiches, good sausage and mash, steak and ale pie, and puddings such as chocolate tart with raspberry sorbet.** *Starters/Snacks: £4.00 to £6.00. Main Courses: £7.00 to £10.00. Puddings: £4.00 to £5.00.*

Spirit ~ Manager Valerie Graham ~ Real ale ~ Bar food (11(12.30 Sun)-10) ~ Restaurant ~ (0131) 556 1884 ~ Children in restaurant ~ Open 11(12.30 Sun)-11(12 Thurs; 1 Fri and Sat)

Recommended by Tracey and Stephen Groves, Janet and Peter Race, Joe Green, Kay and Alistair Butler, Bruce and Penny Wilkie, P and D Carpenter, Comus and Sarah Elliott, Geoff and Pat Bell, Pam and John Smith, Christine and Neil Townend, P Dawn, Doug Christian, the Didler, Dr and Mrs A K Clarke

Guildford Arms 🍺

West Register Street; EH2 2AA

Busy and friendly, with sumptuous Victorian décor, and an extraordinary range of real ales

You'll rarely get to study the sumptuous interior of this enjoyable Victorian pub by yourself, but it's easy to see why so many people are drawn in: the main part is resplendent with painted plasterwork, mahogany fittings, original advertising mirrors and heavy swagged velvet curtains at the arched windows. The snug little upstairs gallery restaurant gives a dress-circle view of the main bar (notice the lovely old mirror decorated with two tigers on the way up). Another key part of the appeal is the extraordinary range of ten very well kept beers – typically Caledonian Deuchars IPA and XPA, Harviestoun Bitter & Twisted, Orkney Dark Island, Stewarts Pentland IPA, and Timothy Taylors Landlord, and a rapidly changing range of guests like Atlas Latitude, Broughton Greenmantle, Fyne Highlander, and Kelburn Red Smiddy; the helpful, friendly staff may offer a taste before you buy. Also, 18 wines by the glass, and a good choice of malt whiskies; board games, TV, fruit machine, piped music. They may have occasional mini beer festivals. This is the flagship of a small regional group of pubs and bars.

🍽 **The menu includes sandwiches, soup, haggis with whisky and warm oatcakes, thai green chicken curry, lamb chops with port gravy and mint, steak and ale pie, breaded haddock, various steaks, and specials such as a fish of the day; in the evenings food from the same menu is served only in the gallery restaurant.** *Starters/Snacks: £3.00 to £7.85. Main Courses: £6.90 to £14.95. Puddings: £3.60 to £4.95*

Free house ~ Licensee Scott Wilkinson ~ Real ale ~ Bar food (12-2.30(3 Sun), 6-9.30(10 Fri), 12-10 Sat) ~ Restaurant (12(12.30 Sun)-2.30, 6-9.30(10 Fri and Sat)) ~ (0131) 556 4312 ~ No children or dogs ~ Live music during Fringe Festival ~ Open 11(12.30 Sun)-11(midnight Fri and Sat); closed 25-26 Dec, 1-2 Jan

Recommended by the Didler, Pam and John Smith, P Dawn, Geoff and Pat Bell, Nick Holding, Comus and Sarah Elliott, Joe Green, Michael Dandy, Janet and Peter Race, Dr and Mrs A K Clarke

Kays Bar 🍺 £

Jamaica Street W; off India Street; EH3 6HF

Unpretentious and cosy backstreet pub with excellent choice of well kept beers, and the feel of a friendly local

It's the choice of beers that makes this welcoming backstreet pub worth a detour, but it has a very enjoyable local feel too, and though it gets busy (with an eclectic and sometimes lively mix of customers), it's not at all touristy. The eight superbly kept real ales on handpump might include Belhaven 80/-, Caledonian Deuchars IPA, Theakstons

Best and guests like Bass, Caledonian 80/-, Exmoor Gold, Greene King IPA, and Harviestoun Bitter and Twisted. The choice of whiskies is impressive too, with more than 50 malts between eight and 50 years old, and ten blended whiskies. The interior is decked out with various casks and vats, old wine and spirits merchant notices, gas-type lamps, well worn red plush wall banquettes and stools around cast-iron tables, and red pillars supporting a red ceiling. A quiet panelled back room leads off, with a narrow plank-panelled pitched ceiling and a collection of books ranging from dictionaries to ancient steam-train books for boys; lovely warming coal fire in winter. In days past, the pub was owned by John Kay, a whisky and wine merchant; wine barrels were hoisted up to the first floor and dispensed through pipes attached to nipples which can still be seen around the light rose. Service is friendly, obliging, and occasionally idiosyncratic; TV, dominoes and cribbage, Scrabble and backgammon.

🍴 **Straightforward but good value lunchtime bar food includes soup, sandwiches, haggis and neeps, mince and tatties, steak pie, beefburger and chips, and chicken balti.** *Starters/Snacks: £1.25. Main Courses: £2.50 to £4.95. Puddings: £2.50*

Free house ~ Licensee David Mackenzie ~ Real ale ~ Bar food (12(12.30 Sun)-2.30; not on rugby international days) ~ (0131) 225 1858 ~ Children allowed in back room until 6pm ~ Dogs welcome ~ Open 11am-12pm(1 Fri, Sat); 12.30-11 Sun

Recommended by the Didler, Peter F Marshall, Nick Holding, Doug Christian, R T and J C Moggridge, Dr and Mrs A K Clarke

Starbank 🍷 🍺 £

Laverockbank Road, off Starbank Road, just off A901 Granton—Leith; EH5 3BZ

Eight real ales and great views over the Firth of Forth in this cheery well run pub with nice feel to it

The impressive range of beers and waterside views are what really make this pub stand out, but it's a friendly, comfortably elegant place too – and all their wines are served by the glass. The long, light and airy bare-boarded bar looks out over the Firth of Forth, and has eight real ales, with Belhaven 80/- and Sandy Hunters, Caledonian Deuchars IPA, and Timothy Taylors Landlord alongside guests from breweries all over Britain such as Everards, Greene King, Harviestoun and Robinsons. There's a good selection of malt whiskies. You can eat in the conservatory restaurant, and there's a sheltered back terrace; TV. Dogs must be on a lead. Parking is on the adjacent hilly street.

🍴 **Good-value bar food includes soup, herring rollmop salad, a daily vegetarian dish, ploughman's, steak and ale pie, smoked haddock with poached egg, poached salmon, and minute steak.** *Starters/Snacks: £2.50 to £3.75. Main Courses: £5.25 to £7.50. Puddings: £3.75*

Free house ~ Licensee Valerie West ~ Real ale ~ Bar food (12-2.30, 6-9; 12(12.30 Sun)-9 weekends) ~ Restaurant ~ (0131) 552 4141 ~ Children allowed till 8.30pm ~ Dogs allowed in bar ~ Live music first Sat evening of month, and jazz second Sun afternoon of month ~ Open 11-11(12 Thurs-Sat); 12.30-11 Sun

Recommended by Ken Richards, Ian and Nita Cooper, Dr and Mrs A K Clarke

ELIE   NO4999   MAP 11

Ship 🛏

The Toft, off A917 (High Street) towards harbour; KY9 1DT

Friendly seaside inn with views over broad sandy bay, unspoilt bar and good seafood

Summer seems the perfect season to call at this welcoming harbourside pub, but some readers this year particularly enjoyed visiting on a fresh, windy day in December. Oystercatchers and gulls are very much in earshot from the terrace, which looks over a wide sandy bay enclosed by headlands. The unspoilt, villagey beamed bar has a buoyantly nautical feel, with friendly locals and staff, warming winter coal fires, and partly panelled walls studded with old prints and maps. There's also a simple carpeted back room; cards, dominoes and shut-the-box. On summer Sundays you can watch the progress of their cricket team (they have regular barbecues then too). Caledonian Deuchars IPA, several wines by the glass, and half a dozen malt whiskies. The comfortable bedrooms are in a guesthouse next door.

🍴 **Well presented bar food includes lunchtime sandwiches, good soup, roast pepper and gruyère tart, a daily mussels dish, smoked mackerel pâté, haddock and chips, steak and Guinness pie, and daily specials, including plenty of fresh fish. They do a good Sunday lunch, and in summer, weather permitting, serve lunches in the garden; children's meals.** *Starters/Snacks: £3.00 to £5.00. Main Courses: £8.00 to £15.00. Puddings: £4.00*

Free house ~ Licensees Richard and Jill Philip ~ Real ale ~ Bar food (12-2.30(12.30-3 Sun), 6-9(9.30 Fri, Sat); not 25 Dec, 1 Jan) ~ Restaurant ~ (01333) 330246 ~ No children under 14 in front bar ~ Dogs allowed in bar ~ Open 11-12(1 Fri, Sat); 12.30-12 Sun; closed 25 Dec ~ Bedrooms: £55B/£80B

Recommended by A P Ross, Comus and Sarah Elliott, Joyce and Maurice Cottrell, Michael Butler

GAIRLOCH
NG8075   MAP 11

Old Inn 🍴 🍷 🍺 🛏
Just off A832/B8021; IV21 2BD

Delightful old pub with wonderful fish and seafood straight from neighbouring harbour; good beers too, especially in summer

Fresh seafood is a speciality at this delightfully set 18th-c inn – it's just steps away from a little fishing harbour, and the chef sometimes visits the adjacent pier at midnight to see what's being landed. Picnic-sets are prettily placed outside by the trees that line the stream as it flows past under the old stone bridge; you might spot eagles over the crags above. The changing beers are a big draw – these days they have up to eight in summer, and three in winter: a typical selection might include Adnams, Black Sheep, Dundonnell An Teallach, Isle of Skye Blind Piper (a blend of Isle of Skye ales made for the pub and named after a famed 17th-c local piper) and Orkney Dark Island. They have a lot of fairly priced wines by the glass, a decent collection of 30 malt whiskies, and you can get speciality coffees. The landlady makes her own chutneys and preserves – and grows many of the herbs they use (they also track down organic vegetables). Credit (but not debit) cards incur a surcharge of £1.75. It's nicely decorated with paintings and murals on exposed stone walls, and the cheerfully relaxed public bar has chatty locals; darts, TV, fruit machine, pool and juke box. Good service from friendly staff. Nicely tucked away from the main shoreside road, the pub is well placed for strolls up Flowerdale valley to a waterfall.

🍴 **Bouillabaisse, seared scallops and langoustines are commonly on the board, and mussels, crabs, lobster, skate, haddock and hake often crop up too. They have a separate seafood menu with cod and monkfish bake and a grilled seafood platter, while the regular menu includes cullen skink, home-made game pâté with oatcakes, pheasant and venison casserole, fish pie, venison sausages or steak, 12oz sirloin steak, and puddings like clootie dumpling and custard or raspberry cranachan; they do children's meals, and lunchtime open sandwiches.** *Starters/Snacks: £3.45 to £5.25. Main Courses: £7.95 to £16.50. Puddings: £3.50 to £5.50*

Free house ~ Licensees Alastair and Ute Pearson ~ Real ale ~ Bar food (all day till 9.30 in summer) ~ Restaurant ~ (01445) 712006 ~ Children allowed in some rooms ~ Dogs allowed in bedrooms ~ Live music summer weekends ~ Open 11-1(12 Sat); 11-11.45 Sun; open only 4-12 weekdays in winter ~ Bedrooms: £40B/£75B

Recommended by Peter Meister, Mr and Mrs G D Brooks, Kay and Alistair Butler, Carol and Phil Byng, Edna Jones, Di and Mike Gillam, Barry Collett

---

Bedroom prices normally include full english breakfast, VAT and any inclusive service charge that we know of. Prices before the '/' are for single rooms, after for two people in double or twin (B includes a private bath, S a private shower). If there is no '/', the prices are only for twin or double rooms (as far as we know there are no singles).

GATEHOUSE OF FLEET
NX6056 MAP 9

Masonic Arms

Ann Street, off B727; DG7 2HU

Nicely transformed pub with really excellent, very popular food, and relaxed traditional bar

Such is the reputation of the food here that even on a midweek lunchtime it can be worth booking – or at least arriving early – to avoid a wait. It has a new licensee this year, but the head chef who's made the meals so popular has stayed. The comfortable two-room beamed bar is indeed a proper bar, with Caledonian Deuchars IPA and a guest like Caledonian Top Banana or Houston Peters Well on handpump, and a good choice of whiskies and wines by the glass, traditional seating, pictures on its lightly timbered walls, and blue and white plates on a delft shelf. Service is friendly and efficient, and there is a relaxed warm-hearted atmosphere. The bar opens into an attractive and spacious conservatory, with stylish and comfortable cane bucket chairs around good tables on its terracotta tiles, pot plants, and colourful pictures on one wall; it's airy even in bright sunlight (good blinds and ventilation). The conservatory also opens through into a smart contemporary restaurant, with high-backed thickly padded chairs around modern tables on bare boards. There are picnic-sets under cocktail parasols out in the neatly kept sheltered garden, and seats out in front of the flower-decked black and white building; this is an appealing small town, between the Solway Firth and the Galloway Forest Park.

🍴 Good generous interesting food includes lunchtime baguettes, home-made soup, smooth pâté of chicken livers with apricot, pan-fried crab cakes with wild garlic, king scallop tempura on fresh linguini with sweet chilli sauce, fillet of pork wrapped in serrano ham, grilled spring lamb cutlets with champ and herb and green peppercorn crust, risotto of spring vegetable with saffron and parmesan, local fish specials such as fresh lobster or fillet of bass with pesto and sauce vierge, and puddings like basked alaska or pistachio nut parfait with brandy snaps. Starters/Snacks: £3.10 to £7.00. Main Courses: £9.50 to £20.00. Puddings: £4.25 to £5.00

Free house ~ Licensee Paul Shepherd ~ Real ale ~ Bar food (12-2 and 6-9) ~ Restaurant ~ (01557) 814335 ~ Children welcome ~ Dogs allowed in bar ~ Open 11.30-2.30, 5.30-11.30; may be closed Mon and Tues in winter

Recommended by Dr and Mrs R G J Telfer, Stan and Hazel Allen, Nick Holding, Christine and Phil Young, Chris Smith, Mrs Pat Crabb

GLASGOW
NS5965 MAP 11

Babbity Bowster 🍴 🍷

Blackfriars Street; G1 1PE

Now a Glasgow institution, friendly, comfortable and sometimes lively – nice mix of traditional and modern, with almost continental feel, and good food

Enjoyed by readers for its genuinely welcoming and often lively atmosphere, this fine city-centre pub is a sprightly blend of both scottish and continental, and traditional and modern. A big ceramic of a kilted dancer and piper in the bar illustrates the mildly cheeky 18th-c lowland wedding tune (Bab at the Bowster) from which the pub takes its name – the friendly landlord or his staff will be happy to explain further. The simply decorated light interior has fine tall windows, well lit photographs and big pen-and-wash drawings of the city, its people and musicians, dark grey stools and wall seats around dark grey tables on the stripped wooden boards, and a peat fire. The bar opens on to a pleasant terrace with tables under cocktail parasols, trellised vines and shrubs; they may have barbecues out here in summer. You'll find Caledonian Deuchars IPA and a couple of sometimes rather unusual guests like Hampshire Mayhem and Houston Peters Well on air pressure tall fount, and a remarkably sound collection of wines, malt whiskies, and farm cider; good tea and coffee too. On Saturday evenings they have live traditional scottish music, while at other times you may find games of boules in progress outside. Note the bedroom price is for the room only.

🍴 A short but interesting bar menu includes scottish and french items such as hearty home-made soup, cullen skink, potted rabbit, croques monsieur, haggis, neeps and tatties (they also do a vegetarian version), stovies, mussels, cauliflower and mung bean moussaka, platter of scottish smoked salmon, roast leg of duck on a bed of haricot beans and sautéed potatoes, and a daily special. The airy upstairs restaurant has more elaborate meals. *Starters/Snacks: £3.50 to £5.95. Main Courses: £4.95 to £11.75. Puddings: £3.25 to £5.95*

Free house ~ Licensee Fraser Laurie ~ Real ale ~ Bar food (12-10) ~ Restaurant ~ (0141) 552 5055 ~ Children welcome ~ Live traditional music on Sat ~ Open 11(12.30 Sun)-12; closed 25 Dec ~ Bedrooms: £45S/£60S

Recommended by Nick Holding, Andy and Claire Barker, Barry Collett

Bon Accord 🍺 £
North Street; G3 7DA

One of Glasgow's best for real ale, with a choice of ten often uncommon brews; a good welcome too, and bargain food

Every year, six or seven hundred real ales pass through the pumps of this welcoming pub, arguably the city's best for beer drinkers. Carefully sourced from smaller breweries around Britain, the choice of ten might typically take in brews from Brakspears, Broughton, Caledonian, Durham, Hop Back, Fullers, Harviestoun, Houston, Kelham Island and Marstons. Whisky drinkers have lots to keep them happy too, with over 160 malts to choose from, and all 13 of their wines are available by the glass. With a good spread of customers (women find it comfortable here), the interior is neatly kept; partly polished bare-boards and partly carpeted, with a mix of tables and chairs, terracotta walls, and pot plants throughout; TV, fruit machine, cribbage, chess and piped music. It's open mike night on Tuesday, there's a quiz on Wednesday and a band on Saturday. More reports please.

🍴 Reasonably priced bar food includes baguettes, baked potatoes, lasagne, scampi and steak; they do a bargain two-course lunch. *Starters/Snacks: £1.80 to £2.95. Main Courses: £4.85 to £7.95. Puddings: £1.40 to £1.95*

Scottish Courage ~ Tenant Paul McDonagh ~ Real ale ~ Bar food (12(12.30 Sun)-8) ~ (0141) 248 4427 ~ Children allowed till 8pm ~ Live entertainment Tues and Sat ~ Open 11-12; 12.30-11 Sun

Recommended by BOB

Counting House 🍺 £
St Vincent Place/George Square; G1 2DH

Imaginative conversion of former bank, worth a look for décor alone, but also a great range of mostly scottish beers, and food all day

One of the more impressive Wetherspoons pubs, this gloriously converted former bank stays civilised and efficient even when it's crowded. The imposing interior is stunning, rising into a lofty, richly decorated coffered ceiling which culminates in a great central dome, with well lit nubile caryatids doing a fine supporting job in the corners. You'll also find the sort of decorative glasswork that nowadays seems more appropriate to a landmark pub than to a bank, as well as wall-safes, plenty of prints and local history, and big windows overlooking George Square. Away from the bar, several areas have solidly comfortable seating, while a series of smaller rooms – once the managers' offices – lead around the perimeter of the building. Some of these are surprisingly cosy, one is like a well stocked library, and a few are themed with pictures and prints of historical characters such as Walter Scott or Mary, Queen of Scots. The central island servery has a splendid choice of up to ten real ales on handpump – some very keenly priced: you might find Cairngorms Wildcat, Caledonian 80/- and Deuchars IPA, and Greene King Abbot, along with guests such as Harviestoun Ptarmigan, Orkney Dark Island, and Shepherd Neame Bishops Finger. They also do a good choice of bottled beers and malt whiskies, and a dozen wines by the glass; fruit machines. Friendly efficient staff. This is a handy place to wait if catching a train from Queen Street station.

🍴 **Served all day, by friendly staff, the usual wide choice of straightforward Wetherspoons food: baguettes and wraps, haggis, neeps and tatties, chilli con carne, liver and bacon casserole, breaded scampi, pasta, sausages and mash, Sunday roasts, and children's meals. They have a limited range of two meals for £6.99, and beer and a burger for £3.99. Tuesday is steak night, and Thursday curry night.** *Starters/Snacks: £2.29 to £5.00. Main Courses: £3.99 to £8.99. Puddings: £1.49 to £2.69*

Wetherspoons ~ Manager Stuart Coxshall ~ Real ale ~ Bar food (9am-11pm) ~ (0141) 225 0160 ~ Children in eating area of bar till 7pm if whole group eating ~ Open 9am-12pm; closed 25 Dec

Recommended by Andrew York, Barry Collett

GLENELG NG8119 MAP 11

Glenelg Inn 🍴
Unmarked road from Shiel Bridge (A87) towards Skye; IV40 8JR

Outstanding Skye views from charming inn reached by dramatic drive; enjoyably pubby in bar (under new licensee and open all day), good fresh local food

Glenelg is the closest place on the mainland to Skye, so this delightfully placed inn has lovely views across the water to the island. It's memorably reached by a single-track road climbing dramatically past heather-blanketed slopes and mountains with spectacular views to the lochs below. A new licensee took over just as we went to press, and is making some changes: for a start he plans to open all day (from 9am for coffees – he's introducing a full range), and the bar will be extended – though he says without any change to its character or atmosphere. He's also introducing a second real ale to go alongside the current one fom the Isle of Skye Brewery, and expanding the choice of bottled real ales and malt whiskies. Feeling a bit like a mountain cabin (and still decidedly pubby given the smartness of the rest of the place), the unpretentious green-carpeted bar gives an overwhelming impression of dark wood, with lots of logs dotted about, a big fireplace, and only a very few tables and well worn cushioned wall benches; when necessary crates and fish boxes may be pressed into service as extra seating. Black and white photographs line the walls at the far end around the pool table, and there are various joky articles and local information elsewhere; winter pool and maybe piped music (usually scottish). The locals are welcoming, and the friendly staff can organise local activities; there are plenty of enjoyable walks nearby. The beautifully kept garden has plenty of tables; a helipad is planned. Some of the bedrooms have great views, and in summer, there's a little car ferry across to Skye.

🍴 **With a renewed emphasis on fresh, local ingredients (particularly seafood), bar food might include soup, huge filled granary rolls, salads, haddock and chips, venison casserole, free-range chicken curry, and puddings such as home-made cranachan; Sunday roasts. They also do a very good four-course evening meal in the dining room (£29, perhaps less during the week).** *Starters/Snacks: £3.50. Main Courses: £7.00 to £15.00. Puddings: £3.00*

Free house ~ Licensee David Macleod ~ Real ale ~ Bar food (12-2, 6-9) ~ Restaurant ~ (01599) 522273 ~ Children welcome ~ Dogs welcome ~ Occasional live scottish music ~ Open 9am(for coffee)-12(11 Sun, 12.30 Sat, 1 Fri) ~ Bedrooms: /£120B

Recommended by Kay and Alistair Butler, Edna Jones, G D Brooks, W Holborow, Mike and Sue Loseby

---

Real ale to us means beer which has matured naturally in its cask – not pressurised or filtered. We name all real ales stocked. We usually name ales preserved under a light blanket of carbon dioxide too, though purists – pointing out that this stops the natural yeasts developing – would disagree (most people, including us, can't tell the difference!).

HOUSTON

Fox & Hounds 🍺

South Street at junction with Main Street (B789, off B790 at Langbank signpost E of Bridge of Weir); PA6 7EN

Welcoming village pub best known for the award-winning beers from their own Houston Brewery

The same family has run this welcoming village pub for 30 years, over the last few winning national acclaim for the tasty beers they produce in what was once a disused cellar. A window in the bar looks into the little brewery, which now sends its award-winning cask and bottled beers throughout the UK. You'll find their Killellan, St Peters Well, Texas and Warlock Stout kept in top condition, served by handpump alongside a seasonal brew such as Cheeky Wee Beastie and a guest like Batemans Hooker; they also have 12 wines by the glass, around 100 malt whiskies and freshly squeezed orange juice. The clean plush hunting-theme lounge has comfortable seats by a fire and polished brass and copper; piped music. Popular with a younger crowd, the lively downstairs bar has a large-screen TV, pool, juke box and fruit machines; board games, piped music. They have a quiz on Tuesdays. At the back is a covered and heated area with decking (where you can smoke). More reports please.

🍽 **Served upstairs (downstairs they do only substantial sandwiches), a good choice of enjoyable bar food might include soup, crayfish and avocado salad with lime mayonnaise, cod or scampi in their own beer batter, chargrilled venison sausages, grilled scallops with smoked bacon mash and mushroom cream, specials like charred baby spatchcock chicken or beef stroganoff laced with cognac, and puddings such as baked apple pie or warm fudge sundae.** *Starters/Snacks: £2.95 to £6.95. Main Courses: £6.50 to £19.95. Puddings: £2.95 to £5.00*

Own brew ~ Licensee Jonathan Wengel ~ Real ale ~ Bar food (12-10) ~ Restaurant ~ (01505) 612448 ~ Children in lounge and restaurant till 8pm ~ Dogs allowed in bar ~ Regular live music; quiz on Tues ~ Open 11-12(1am Fri, Sat); 12-12 Sun

Recommended by BOB

INNERLEITHEN

Traquair Arms 🛏

B709, just off A72 Peebles—Galashiels; follow signs for Traquair House; EH44 6PD

Comfortably refurbished village inn, popular with families, with friendly welcome and nice food (great puddings); a good bet if exploring the Borders

Doing well under its current licensees, who've done a fair amount of reburbishment and improvements since it last appeared in the *Guide*, this is an attractively modernised inn in a pretty village, very hospitable, with an easy mix of locals and visitors around the warm open fire in the main bar. Another room has something of the feel of a relaxed bistro, and has another fire, and high chairs for children; piped music. Served by pleasant staff, they have Caledonian Deuchars IPA and 80/-, and one of the tasty beers from nearby Traquair House on handpump; also several malt whiskies and draught cider. The garden at the back has been reopened, with picnic sets and a big tree on a neatly kept lawn. Bedrooms are comfortable, clean and fresh.

🍽 **Well liked bar food includes sandwiches, traditional cullen skink served with warm bread, grilled goats cheese salad, roast cherry tomatoes and beetroot salsa, beef, Traquair ale and oxtail stew with crisp buttered pastry, chive mash and buttered peas, pan-fried salmon with creamed leeks, new potatoes and lemon butter sauce, and good obviously home-made puddings like crème brûlée with almond shortbread.** *Starters/Snacks: £3.95 to £4.75. Main Courses: £6.95 to £14.00. Puddings: £3.95*

Free house ~ Licensee Dave Rogers ~ Real ale ~ Bar food (12-2, 5-9; 12-9 Sat, Sun) ~ Restaurant ~ (01896) 830229 ~ Children welcome ~ Dogs welcome ~ Open 11(12 Sun)-11(12 Sat); closed 25-26 Dec, 1-2 Jan ~ Bedrooms: £60S/£80S(£80B)

Recommended by Angus Lyon, Nick Holding, Tom and Jill Jones, R T and J C Moggridge, R M Corlett

INVERARAY

George £ 🛏

Main Street E; PA32 8TT

Well placed and attractive, with atmospheric old bar, enjoyable food and pleasant garden; comfortable bedrooms

---

For many the nicest place to stay in this handsome little Georgian town, this comfortably modernised inn has a bustling dark bar that oozes character from its bare stone walls, and shows plenty of age in its exposed joists, old tiles and big flagstones. Run by the same family since 1860, it has antique settles, cushioned stone slabs along the walls, carved wooden benches, nicely grained wooden-topped cast-iron tables, lots of curling club and ships' badges, and four cosy log fires in winter. There's a conservatory restaurant, and tables in a very pleasant, well laid-out garden. Two beers include one from Fyne or Houston, along with Caledonian Deuchars IPA on handpump, and they've over 60 malt whiskies; darts, bar games in summer. This is a civilised place to stay, the individually decorated bedrooms (reached by a grand wooden staircase) with jacuzzis or four-poster beds. It's near Inveraray Castle, and the shore of Loch Fyne (where you may glimpse seals or even a basking shark or whale), and well placed for the great Argyll woodland gardens, best for their rhododendrons in May and early June. One reader felt some out of reach surfaces and ledges can be a bit dusty. More reports please.

🍴 Swiftly served by friendly staff (you order at the table), generously served enjoyable bar food includes soup, ploughman's, haggis, neeps and tatties, steak pie, spaghetti bolognese, and evening dishes like crispy duck pancakes, a vegetarian dish of the day, haddock and chips, and lamb fillet with kale mash, pea purée and red wine sauce, with home-made puddings such as crumble or warm chocolate cake; proper children's meals. *Starters/Snacks: £2.95 to £7.95. Main Courses: £5.95 to £14.95. Puddings: £3.75*

Free house ~ Licensee Donald Clark ~ Real ale ~ Bar food (12-9) ~ Restaurant ~ (01499) 302111 ~ Children welcome ~ Dogs welcome ~ Live entertainment Fri and Sat ~ Open 11(12 Sun)-12.30 ~ Bedrooms: £35B/£70B

Recommended by Bob, Les and Sandra Brown, Peter Craske

ISLE OF WHITHORN

Steam Packet 🍽 ♀ 🛏

Harbour Row; DG8 8LL

Unfussy family-run inn with splendid views of working harbour from bar and some bedrooms, and good food – especially the inventive specials

---

From the big picture windows of this welcoming modernised inn you look out on to a restful scene of an attractive working harbour, with a crowd of yachts and fishing boats. Relaxed and unfussy, and run by the same family for over 20 years, it's an appealing place to stay or just pop in for a drink, and there's no piped music or fruit machines. The comfortable low-ceilinged bar is split into two: on the right, plush button-back banquettes and boat pictures, and on the left, green leatherette stools around cast-iron-framed tables on big stone tiles, and a woodburning stove in the bare stone wall. Bar food can be served in the lower-beamed dining room, which has excellent colour wildlife photographs, rugs on its wooden floor, and a solid fuel stove, and there's also a small eating area off the lounge bar, as well as a conservatory. They now have two guests like Houston Peters Well and Timothy Taylors Golden Best alongside the Theakstons XB on handpump, and they've two dozen malt whiskies, and a good wine list; TV, pool and board games. There are white tables and chairs in the garden. Several of the recently refurbished bedrooms have good views of the harbour. You can walk up to the remains of St Ninian's Kirk, on a headland behind the village.

If you have to cancel a reservation for a bedroom or restaurant, please telephone or write to warn them. You may lose your deposit if you've paid one.

🍽 All home made, the changing specials are the highlight: soups such as artichoke and wild cep, mature cheddar soufflé, seared king scallops seasoned with cumin with black pudding salad, venison rump steak with honey-roasted apple and bitter chocolate game jus, and breast of duck on charred pineapple with aromatic spiced rum reduction. They also do lunchtime ciabattas and open sandwiches, beer-battered haddock, navarin of lamb, steaks, and children's meals. *Starters/Snacks: £2.95 to £6.50. Main Courses: £5.95 to £17.00. Puddings: £1.25 to £3.50*

Free house ~ Licensee John Scoular ~ Real ale ~ Bar food (12-2, 6.30-9) ~ Restaurant ~ (01988) 500334 ~ Children welcome except in bar ~ Dogs allowed in bar and bedrooms ~ Open 11-11(12 Sat); 12-11 Sun; closed 2.30-6 Tues-Thurs in winter; closed 25 Dec ~ Bedrooms: £30B/£60B

Recommended by Stan and Hazel Allen, Mark O'Sullivan, Karen Eliot, Andrew Wallace, Nick Holding, Mrs Pat Crabb

KILBERRY   NR7164   MAP 11

Kilberry Inn 🛏

B8024; PA29 6YD

A stylish place to stay in wonderfully remote setting; no real ale but pubby feel to bar, and excellent, locally sourced food

Wonderfully remote, and reached by a splendid single-track drive offering stunning views of the coast, this is a very comfortable, gently upmarket place to stay, with excellent, locally sourced food (as they say, the cattle you saw on the way here may later make it on to the menu). The small beamed dining bar, tastefully and simply furnished, is relaxed and warmly sociable, with a good log fire; piped music. There's no real ale, but they do Fyne bottled beers and have a selection of malt whiskies (with quite a few local ones). The bedrooms are stylishly attractive. You'll know you've arrived when you spot the old-fashioned red telephone box outside the low red tin-roofed building. More reports please.

🍽 The lunchtime or evening menus might include soups such as roasted red pepper with basil and crumbled feta cheese, potted crab with lemon and toasted sourdough bread, green pea and smoked bacon tart, warm salad of monkfish and king scallops with a honey, orange and grain mustard dressing, haunch of wild venison cooked in red wine with wild mushrooms, pancetta and juniper berries, rack of lamb with roasted winter vegetables, and puddings like walnut, almond and amaretto cake with chocolate sauce or honey and mascarpone crème brûlée. *Starters/Snacks: £4.25 to £7.95. Main Courses: £9.95 to £13.95. Puddings: £4.95 to £5.25*

Free house ~ Licensees Clare Johnson and David Wilson ~ Bar food (12.30-2.30, 6.30-9) ~ Restaurant ~ (01880) 770223 ~ Children in family room but not main bar; only over-12s staying ~ Dogs allowed in bedrooms ~ Open 12.30-2.30, 6.30-11; closed Mon, plus Tues-Thurs in Nov and Dec, and also closed all Jan to mid-Mar ~ Bedrooms: /£90S

Recommended by J D G Isherwood

KILMAHOG   NN6008   MAP 11

Lade 🍷 🍺

A84 just NW of Callander, by A821 junction; FK17 8HD

Lively and pubby, with their own organic beers, and now a shop specialising in scottish brews; traditional scottish music at weekends, and good home-made food

One of the family that runs this lively, pubby inn is a real ale ethusiast, which explains not just their own excellent organic beers, but also the scottish real ale shop they opened here this year, with over 100 bottled brews from 26 microbreweries around Scotland. In the bar they always have their own WayLade, LadeBack and LadeOut on handpump, along with a guest such as Broughton Clipper, eight wines by the glass and about 25 malts. Several small beamed areas are cosy with red walls, panelling and stripped stone, and decorated with highland prints and works by local artists; piped music. A conservatory restaurant (with more ambitious dishes) opens on to a terrace and a pleasant garden with three fish ponds.

▥ Using local ingredients, food includes soup, sandwiches, ploughman's, battered haggis balls, fresh battered haddock, steak and ale pie, spinach gnocchi with sun-dried tomato, aubergine, courgette and peppers, whole pan-fried local trout, good burgers, and puddings like raspberry cranachan and iced peach and brandy-snap cheesecake. *Starters/Snacks: £3.75 to £8.00. Main Courses: £7.50 to £16.00. Puddings: £4.00 to £6.00*

Own brew ~ Licensees Frank and Rita Park ~ Real ale ~ Bar food (12(12.30 Sun)-9) ~ Restaurant ~ (01877) 330152 ~ Children welcome till 8pm ~ Dogs allowed in bar ~ Ceilidhs Fri and Sat evenings ~ Open 12-11(1am Fri, Sat); 12.30-10.30 Sun

Recommended by Darren and Jane Staniforth

KINGHOLM QUAY
NX9773   MAP 9

Swan
B726 just S of Dumfries; or signposted off B725; DG1 4SU

Useful on a sunny day, with tables in garden pleasant at the end of a walk, or bike ride from Dumfries

Handy for the Caerlaverock Nature Reserve with its multitude of geese, this can be a useful pub to know about on a fine day, when the tables in the garden are a pleasant place to sit, and there's an enjoyable two-mile walk or cycle ride from Dumfries along the River Nith using the tarmacked cycle path. It can be very busy in the evenings, and on Sundays, when it's popular with families. Inside, the well ordered lounge has a little coal fire, and there's Timothy Taylors Landlord on handpump in the neat and nicely furnished public bar, along with good house wines; TV and quiet piped music.

▥ A short selection of standard pub food: soup, haggis with melted cheese, steak pie, chicken with leeks and white wine, evening specials such as rack of ribs, steaks, and seafood risotto, and puddings like sticky toffee. Some dishes can be served in half helpings. Service, though generally efficient, can slow right down at busy times, and readers have found they can stick quite rigidly to their food service times. *Starters/Snacks: £3.00 to £4.10. Main Courses: £4.75 to £7.50. Puddings: £1.95 to £3.95*

Free house ~ Licensees Billy Houliston, Tracy Rogan and Alan Austin ~ Real ale ~ Bar food (5-8.45(9 Fri,Sat); 11.45-12.15, 4.45-8.45 Sun) ~ (01387) 253756 ~ Children welcome ~ Open 11.30-2.30, 5-10(11 Thurs-Sat); 11.30-11 Sun

Recommended by Mr and Mrs P R Thomas, Joe Green, Mark O'Sullivan

KIPPEN
NS6594   MAP 11

Cross Keys 🛏
Main Street; village signposted off A811 W of Stirling; FK8 3DN

Cosy and unpretentious village inn, popular with locals and visitors; changing hands as we went to press

As we went to press the licensees of this unpretentious village inn told us it was about to change hands – though they were confident that the new people were keen to keep things mostly unchanged. Its timeless atmosphere has been a large part of the appeal, and it's both warmly welcoming to visitors and has a strong local following. There's dark panelling and subdued lighting in the cosy bar, a straightforward lounge with a good log fire, and a coal fire in the attractive family dining room. Harviestoun Bitter & Twisted on handpump, and they've more than 30 malt whiskies; cards, dominoes, TV, and maybe a radio in the separate public bar; they hold a quiz night on the last Sunday of the month. Tables in the garden have good views towards the Trossachs; there's a canopy and heater for smokers. Reports on the new regime please.

▥ Enjoyable bar food has included things like sandwiches, soup, home-made lasagne, steak pie, fish pie, and lamb casserole – but obviously the choice and prices are likely to change under the new licensees. *Starters/Snacks: £3.45 to £4.95. Main Courses: £6.55 to £8.95. Puddings: £3.75 to £4.95*

Free house ~ Licensees Mr and Mrs Scott ~ Real ale ~ Bar food (12-2, 5.30-9; 12.30-8 Sun; not 25 Dec, 1 Jan, and winter Mons) ~ Restaurant ~ (01786) 870293 ~ Children welcome ~ Dogs allowed in bar and bedrooms ~ Open 12-2.30, 5.30-11(12 Fri); 12-12 Sat; 12.30-11 Sun ~ Bedrooms: /£70S

Recommended by Mr and Mrs M Stratton, Pat and Stewart Gordon

KIRK YETHOLM

NT8328   MAP 10

Border ⇐

Village signposted off B6352/B6401 crossroads, SE of Kelso; The Green; TD5 8PQ

Welcoming and comfortable hotel with good inventive food; repairs after last year's fire were almost complete as we went to press

Alfred Wainwright began the tradition that if you had walked the entire 256 miles of the Pennine Way National Trail you would get a free drink at this warmly friendly and comfortable hotel. He left some money here to pay for walkers claiming half a pint, but that's long since run out, and the pub has generally footed the bill of providing a pint for anyone who's completed it all and has with them a copy of the guide to the walk written and drawn by Wainwright. This year the Broughton Brewery has helped them out, and produced for the pub an exclusive beer, Pennine Way; they usually have another Scottish beer on handpump too, such as Atlas Three Sisters. This isn't just a pub for walkers though: it has good, interesting food, and comfortable bedrooms. The kitchen and bedrooms were particularly damaged by a fire last year, but their restoration was almost complete as we went to press (the refurbished bedrooms were set to open in July). Gently freshened up, the cheerfully unpretentious bar has beams, flagstones, and a log fire, as well as snug side rooms, a signed photograph of Wainwright and other souvenirs of the Pennine Way, and appropriate borders scenery etchings and murals. Decent wines by the glass, a good range of malt whiskies, and a water bowl for dogs; service is cheery and efficient. There's a roomy pink-walled dining room, a comfortably refurbished lounge with a second log fire, and a neat conservatory; TV, darts, pool, board games, and children's games and books. A sheltered back terrace has more picnic-sets, and the colourful window boxes and floral tubs make a very attractive display outside.

⑪ **Under its friendly chef/landlord and his wife, the food is careful and inventive without being at all pretentious; they've been using a temporary kitchen since the fire, and say that's limited what they can do, but they're still serving things like pan-fried fresh trout in oatmeal with home-made red onion marmalade, beef in Guinness, pork tenderloin medallions in a cream and brandy sauce with caramelised apple slices, lamb shoulder with minted gravy, wild mushroom risotto, chicken breast with cream, mustard, mushroom and whisky sauce, and specials with plenty of game such as marinated local pheasant breasts or venison. Also open sandwiches and baguettes, and proper children's meals.**
Starters/Snacks: £2.95 to £5.95. Main Courses: £7.95 to £10.95. Puddings: £3.95 to £4.95

Free house ~ Licensees Philip and Margaret Blackburn ~ Real ale ~ Bar food (12-2, 6-9, unless booked for weddings) ~ Restaurant ~ (01573) 420237 ~ Children welcome away from public bar ~ Dogs allowed in bar and bedrooms ~ Open 11(12 Sun)-11(12 Sat); closed 25 Dec ~ Bedrooms: £45B/£80B

Recommended by Mr D J Crawford, Prof and Mrs S Lockley, Joe Green, Julie Wilson, Carolyn Reid, John Evans, Mairi Reynolds

LINLITHGOW

NS0077   MAP 11

Four Marys ◼ £

High Street; 2 miles from M9 junction 3 (and little further from junction 4) – town signposted; EH49 7ED

Very popular old pub with mementoes of Mary, Queen of Scots, excellent range of beers, and good food and service

Highly thought of by readers again this year, this bustling place dates from the 16th c and takes its name from the four ladies-in-waiting of Mary, Queen of Scots, born at nearby Linlithgow Palace in 1542. Accordingly the pub is stashed with mementoes of the ill-fated queen, such as pictures and written records, a piece of bed curtain said to be hers, part of a 16th-c cloth and swansdown vest of the type she's likely to have worn, and a facsimile of her death-mask. Eight real ales are kept on handpump, with changing guests such as Cairngorm Tradewinds, Ossetts Silver King and Robinsons XB joining the regular Belhaven 80/- and St Andrews, Caledonian Deuchars IPA, and Greene King IPA; they also have a good range of malt whiskies (including a malt of the month) and several wines by the glass. During their May and October beer festivals they have 20 real ale pumps and live entertainment. Spotlessly kept, the L-shaped bar has mahogany dining chairs around stripped period and antique tables, a couple of attractive antique corner cupboards, and an elaborate Victorian dresser serving as a bar gantry. The walls are mainly stripped stone, including some remarkable masonry in the inner area; piped music. Service is charming. There's an outdoor smoking area with heaters, and tables and chairs. Parking can be difficult, but the pub is handy for the station. In earlier times the building was an apothecary's shop, where David Waldie experimented with chloroform – its first use as an anaesthetic.

🍴 **Readers enjoy the haggis, neeps and tatties, while other generously served good value bar food includes thick-cut sandwiches, baked potatoes, good cullen skink, home-made lasagne or steak pie, lamb shank, and specials such as pork fillet medallions with green pepper and brandy sauce, chicken fillets with black pudding and wholegrain mustard sauce, and salmon fillet on lemon mash with butter and tarragon sauce; children's menu.** *Starters/Snacks: £2.35 to £4.50. Main Courses: £5.50 to £15.95. Puddings: £3.50 to £3.95*

Belhaven (Greene King) ~ Managers Eve and Ian Forrest ~ Real ale ~ Bar food (12-3, 5-9 weekdays, 12-9 Sat, 12.30-8.30 Sun) ~ Restaurant ~ (01506) 842171 ~ Children welcome if eating, until 8pm ~ Open 11(12.30 Sun)-11(12 Thurs-Sat)

Recommended by P Price, A Darroch Harkness, Peter F Marshall, PL

MELROSE

NT5433   MAP 9

Burts Hotel 🍴 ⇌

B6374, Market Square; TD6 9PL

Reliable and comfortably bustling old inn with inviting bar, lots of whiskies, and very good food

An ideal place to stay and discover the area's charms, this comfortable 200-year-old inn is at the heart of this conspicuously attractive border town, in the market square, a few steps away from the abbey ruins. Pleasantly informal and inviting, the lounge bar has lots of cushioned wall seats and windsor armchairs, and scottish prints on the walls. There are 90 malt whiskies to choose from, and Caledonian Deuchars IPA and 80/- and a guest such as Timothy Taylors Landlord are kept on handpump; there's a good wine list too, with eight by the glass, though space for those just wanting a drink is fairly limited. In summer you can sit out in the well tended garden.

🍴 **Very good, and served by polite, smartly uniformed staff: soup, chicken liver parfait with home-made chutney, pan-seared scallops with boudin noir, pancetta and balsamic syrup, salads, aubergine gateau with goats cheese and spinach and red pepper dressing, grilled whole lemon sole, chicken breast with haggis and bacon, lambs liver with bubble and squeak, roast shallots and red onion gravy, rump of lamb with honey and mustard marinade and black pudding mash, pan-fried fillet of bass with king prawn risotto and asparagus, and puddings such as chocolate bread and butter pudding with bourbon ice cream or banana tarte tatin.** *Starters/Snacks: £5.50 to £9.50. Main Courses: £7.50 to £16.50. Puddings: £5.50 to £5.95*

Free house ~ Licensees Graham and Anne Henderson ~ Real ale ~ Bar food (12-2, 6-9.30; not 26 Dec, 2-3 Jan) ~ Restaurant ~ (01896) 822285 ~ Children welcome till 8pm ~ Dogs allowed in bar and bedrooms ~ Open 11-2.30, 5-11; 12-2.30, 6-11 Sun; closed 26 Dec, 2-3 Jan ~ Bedrooms: £60S(£60B)/£112S(£112B)

Recommended by Ian and Jane Irving, Lucien Perring, Mrs J H S Lang, John Evans, Nick Holding

There are report forms at the back of the book.

PITLOCHRY

Moulin

Kirkmichael Road, Moulin; A924 NE of Pitlochry centre; PH16 5EH

Attractive old inn with excellent own-brewed beers, nicely pubby bar, well presented tasty food all day; comfortable bedrooms

Though the excellent home-brewed beers are still the main draw for some, readers very much enjoy staying at this flower-bedecked 17th-c inn, which has a relaxed and comfortably traditional atmosphere. The beers are produced in the little stables across the street, so their Ale of Atholl, Braveheart, Moulin Light and the stronger Old Remedial are superbly kept on handpump; they also have around 40 malt whiskies, a good choice of wines by the glass, and carafes of house wine available by the litre and half litre. Although it has been much extended over the years, the bar, in the oldest part of the building, still seems an entity in itself, nicely pubby, with plenty of character. Above the fireplace in the smaller room is an interesting painting of the village before the road was built (Moulin used to be a bustling market town, far busier than upstart Pitlochry), while the bigger carpeted area has a good few tables and cushioned banquettes in little booths divided by stained-glass country scenes, another big fireplace, some exposed stonework, fresh flowers, and golf clubs and local and sporting prints around the walls; games include bar billiards and board games. Service is friendly; the landlord is a historic motor rallying fan. Surrounded by tubs of flowers, picnic-sets outside look across to the village kirk. The rooms are comfortable and breakfasts are good; they offer good value three-night breaks out of season. There are excellent walks nearby.

📶 The extensive bar menu includes baked potatoes and sandwiches served right through the afternoon, as well as soup, deep-fried haggis with piquant sauce, a platter of local smoked meats with oatcakes and rowan sauce, fish, chips and peas, grilled salmon steak with lemon and herb butter sauce, haggis, neeps and tatties, stuffed peppers, steak and ale pie, game casserole, pan-fried strips of venison with mushrooms and their own beer, 6oz minute steak stuffed with haggis, and puddings like bread and butter pudding or apple pie; children's meals. *Starters/Snacks: £2.95 to £6.25. Main Courses: £6.00 to £11.50. Puddings: £2.25 to £4.00*

Own brew ~ Licensee Heather Reeves ~ Real ale ~ Bar food (12-9.30; not 25 Dec) ~ Restaurant ~ (01796) 472196 ~ Children welcome away from bar ~ Dogs allowed in bar ~ Open 11(12 Sat, Sun)-11(11.45 Sat) ~ Bedrooms: £55S(£55B)/£70S(£70B)

Recommended by Paul and Ursula Randall, Joan York, Barry Collett, Charles and Pauline Stride

PLOCKTON

Plockton Hotel ★ 🍴 🛏

Village signposted from A87 near Kyle of Lochalsh; IV52 8TN

Welcoming loch-side hotel with wonderful views, excellent food, and particularly friendly staff – a real favourite with many readers

We know of families who make what they call an 'annual pilgrimage' to this much-loved hotel every year, thanks to the welcome, the seafood and the delightful location. Forming part of a long, low terrace of stone-built houses, it's set in a lovely National Trust for Scotland village. Tables in the front garden look out past the village's trademark palm trees and colourfully flowering shrub-lined shore, and across the sheltered anchorage to the rugged mountainous surrounds of Loch Carron; a stream runs down the hill into a pond in the landscaped back garden. With a buoyant, bustling atmosphere, the welcoming comfortably furnished lounge bar has window seats looking out to the boats on the water, as well as antiqued dark red leather seating around neat Regency-style tables on a tartan carpet, three model ships set into the woodwork, and partly panelled stone walls. The separate public bar has darts, pool, board games, TV and piped music, and on Wednesday evenings they have live traditional folk music. It's a good idea to book at busy times (when service can slow down). Caledonian Deuchars IPA and Isle of Skye Hebridean Gold on handpump, and bottled beers from the Isle of Skye brewery, along with a good collection of malt whiskies, and a short wine list. Most of the comfortable bedrooms are in the adjacent building – one has a balcony and woodburning stove, and they now have a few superior rooms, including one with a four-poster; half of them have extraordinary views over the loch ('ridiculously pretty', says one reader), and you can expect good breakfasts. A hotel nearby changed its name a few years ago to the Plockton Inn, so don't get the two confused. As we went to press, we heard that the family who have run the hotel so well for 20 years had put it on the market; fingers crossed any buyer doesn't change a thing.

🍴 **Especially good for fresh, local seafood, and with healthy eating choices marked on the menu: lunchtime sandwiches, soup (with home-made bread), haggis starter with a tot of whisky, smoked salmon platter, smokies, home-made lasagne, herring in oatmeal, grilled whole trout in lemon juice with toasted almonds, poached smoked fillet of haddock, venison casserole, supreme of chicken stuffed with argyle smoked ham and cheese in sun-dried tomato, garlic and basil sauce, good steaks, and fish specials such as chargrilled prawns with sun-dried tomato and garlic butter; children's meals.** *Starters/Snacks: £2.50 to £8.95. Main Courses: £7.50 to £19.50. Puddings: £2.95 to £4.50*

Free house ~ Licensee Tom Pearson ~ Real ale ~ Bar food (12(12.30 Sun)-2.15, 6-9) ~
Restaurant ~ (01599) 544274 ~ Children welcome ~ Traditional folk music Weds evenings ~
Open 11am-12pm(11.30 Sat); 12.30-11 Sun; closed 25 Dec, 1 Jan ~ Bedrooms: £60B/£100B

Recommended by Joan York, Joan and Tony Walker, Mr and Mrs G D Brooks, W Holborow, Kay and Alistair Butler, Brian McBurnie, Les and Sandra Brown, R M Jones, Edna Jones, J D Taylor, Di and Mike Gillam, Barry Collett, Mike and Sue Losely, Richard and Emily Whitworth

SHIELDAIG   NG8153   MAP 11

Tigh an Eilean Hotel 🛏

Village signposted just off A896 Lochcarron—Gairloch; IV54 8XN

Particularly fine views, good beers, and well liked food in simple bar of civilised, peaceful hotel

Separate from the civilised little hotel itself, this village bar at first seems quite basic, but has very good food indeed – especially the seafood and puddings. It enjoys fine views too, with tables outside in a sheltered little courtyard well placed to enjoy the gorgeous position at the head of Loch Shieldaig (which merges into Loch Torridon), beneath some of the most dramatic of all the highland peaks, and looking out to Shieldaig Island – a sanctuary for a stand of ancient caledonian pines. Isle of Skye Black Cuillin and Red Cuillin on handpump, along with maybe Plockton ales or a summer guest from the Black Isle brewery, as well as up to ten wines by the glass, and several malt whiskies; winter darts. Next door, the main building's bedrooms are comfortable and peaceful. The Beinn Eighe nature reserve isn't too far away. The courtyard has a covered area for smokers. There's still no sign of the hotel's much-vaunted bar extension (they suggest it may happen in 2008), but in the meantime they've added more comfortable tables, and a wooden floor. More reports please.

🍴 **Fresh fish and seafood, all hand-dived or creel-caught by local fishermen, feature heavily on the menu, and particularly among the daily specials, which might take in whole local langoustines with a lemon grass, chilli and coriander dipping sauce, potted crab, a battered fish of the day, grilled lemon sole, shallot and goats cheese tart, steak and kidney pie, and their popular seafood stew; other dishes include soup with home-made bread, sandwiches, home-made burgers, venison sausages and mash, haggis, neeps and tatties, and puddings like almond and quince flan; children's menu.** *Starters/Snacks: £3.50 to £5.90. Main Courses: £6.25 to £14.50. Puddings: £3.00 to £5.00*

Free house ~ Licensee Cathryn Field ~ Real ale ~ Bar food (12-8.30 (winter 12-2.30, 6-8.30)) ~
(01520) 755251 ~ Children welcome in restaurant and eating areas of bar till 9pm ~ Dogs
allowed in bedrooms ~ Traditional live folk music at some weekends and holidays ~ Open 11-11;
12-10 Sun; 12-10 (11 Fri, Sat) in winter ~ Bedrooms: £70B/£150B

Recommended by Bill Strang, Stuart Pearson, Peter Meister

Pubs with outstanding views are listed at the back of the book.

STEIN NG2656 MAP 11

Stein Inn 🛏

End of B886 N of Dunvegan in Waternish, off A850 Dunvegan—Portree; OS Sheet 23 map reference 263564; IV55 8GA

Lovely setting on northern corner of Skye, especially welcoming inn with good, simple food, and lots of whiskies; rewarding place to stay

Much enjoyed by readers who've stayed here this year (one says it was his nicest ever stay in a pub), this welcoming 18th-c inn has an extremely restful location by the water's edge on a far-flung northern corner of Skye. The tables outside are an ideal place to sit with a malt whisky (they've over 100 to choose from), and watch the sunset. Inside, the unpretentious original public bar has great character, with its sturdy country furnishings, flagstone floor, beam and plank ceiling, partly panelled stripped-stone walls and peat fire in a grate between the two rooms. The atmosphere can be surprisingly buzzing, and there's a good welcome from the owners and the evening crowd of local regulars (where do they all appear from?). Good service from the smartly uniformed staff. There's a games area with pool table, dominoes and cribbage, and maybe piped music. Caledonian Deuchars IPA and Isle of Skye Reeling Deck (specially brewed for the pub) are kept on handpump, along with a guest like Cairngorm Trade Winds; in summer they have several wines by the glass. There's a lively children's inside play area, and showers for yachtsmen. All the bedrooms have sea views, and breakfasts are good – it's well worth pre-ordering the tasty smoked kippers if you stay here. Useful campsites nearby.

🍽 **Using local fish and highland meat, the short choice of good, simple food includes good value sandwiches, various salads, battered haddock, and 8oz sirloin steak, with specials such as home-made soup, mussels, venison casserole, lamb chops with cranberry sauce, chicken supreme stuffed with haggis, and fresh langoustines; local cheeses, and puddings like eve's pudding.** *Starters: from £2.40 to £6.30; Main Courses: £5.95 to £12.95; Puddings: from £2.95 to £4.95*

Free house ~ Licensees Angus and Teresa Mcghie ~ Real ale ~ Bar food (12(12.30 Sun)-4, 6-9.30(9 Sun); not winter weekdays) ~ Restaurant ~ (01470) 592362 ~ Children welcome until 8pm if dining ~ Dogs allowed in bar and bedrooms ~ Open 11-12; 11.30-11 Sun; but 4-11 weekdays, 12-12 Sat, and 12.30-11 Sun in winter; closed 25 Dec, 1 Jan, winter weekday lunchtimes ~ Bedrooms: £26S/£52S(£74B)

Recommended by Ann O'Sullivan-Hollingnorth, Ian and Barbara Rankin, Joan and Tony Walker, John Robertson, Mike and Sue Loseby

SWINTON NT8347 MAP 10

Wheatsheaf 🍽 ☐ 🛏

A6112 N of Coldstream; TD11 3JJ

Civilised, upmarket inn with imaginative, elaborate food – not cheap, but rewarding; well chosen wines, comfortable bedrooms

A civilised base for exploring the River Tweed, the emphasis at this friendly restaurant is very much on dining – it's increasingly a restaurant-with-rooms, and you may find you'll only get a drink if you're eating or staying here. The carefully thought-out main bar area has an attractive long oak settle and comfortable armchairs, with sporting prints and plates on the bottle-green wall covering; a small lower-ceilinged part by the counter has pubbier furnishings, and small agricultural prints on the walls, especially sheep. A further lounge area has a fishing-theme décor (with a detailed fishing map of the River Tweed). The front conservatory has a vaulted pine ceiling and walls of local stone. Caledonian Deuchars IPA and Broughton Reiver on handpump, around 40 malt whiskies, and a fine choice of 150 wines (with ten by the glass). Breakfasts are good, with freshly squeezed orange juice.

🍽 **Skilfully prepared with fresh local ingredients, lunchtime food might include soup, sautéed paris brown mushrooms with bacon in a filo pastry case with glazed tobermory cheddar, pheasant, pork, chestnut and raisin terrine with a mulled apple sauce, confit of duck on braised red cabbage, and main courses like roast breast of pheasant wrapped in** parma ham on bacon braised barley with whisky cream sauce, seared salmon with gruyère and herb crust on savoury spinach, and braised shank of lamb with root vegetables and rosemary; in the evening they do the same starters, but more expensive main courses such as chargrilled loin of venison with butternut squash mash and chocolate sauce, or fillet of beef on an oyster mushroom, shallot and white truffle oil sauce; puddings like sticky ginger and pear pudding with fudge sauce or iced poppyseed and cinnamon parfait. Booking is recommended, particularly from Thursday to Saturday evening.

Starters/Snacks: £3.50 to £9.75. Main Courses: £8.50 to £19.75. Puddings: £5.00 to £6.50

Free house ~ Licensees Chris and Jan Winson ~ Real ale ~ Bar food (12-2, 6-9) ~ Restaurant ~ (01890) 860257 ~ Children under 6 in dining room until 7pm ~ Open 11-3, 6-11; 11-3, 6-10.30 Sun; closed Sun evening in Dec-Feb; 25-27 Dec ~ Bedrooms: £69S(£69B)/£104S(£104B)

Recommended by Les and Sheila Gee, Dr Peter D Smart, Alan Cole, Kirstie Bruce, Mrs Ellen Wort, John and Sylvia Harrop, John Evans, Carol and Colin Broadbent

TAYVALLICH
NR7487 MAP 11

Tayvallich Inn 🍴

B8025, off A816 1 mile S of Kilmartin; or take B841 turn-off from A816 2 miles N of Lochgilphead; PA31 8PL

Simple place specialising in seafood fresh from the loch across the lane, and good for families

---

Once the village bus station, these days this dining pub is worth a stop for its fresh seafood, caught by the boats out on Loch Steen across the lane. A pleasant place to make for on a sunny day, it has sliding glass doors opening on to a terrace with decking and awning, with lovely views over the yacht anchorage. Service is friendly, and people with children are made to feel welcome. Inside are exposed ceiling joists, pale pine chairs, benches and tables on the quarry-tiled floors, and local nautical charts on the cream walls; piped music. Malt whiskies include a full range of Islay malts, and they have Loch Fyne Maverick and Pipers Gold on handpump. More reports please.

🍴 Depending very much on what they've landed, the specials might include seared scallops on pea purée and black pudding, mussels, and langoustines grilled with cayenne pepper and olive oil; they also do things like roast red peppers stuffed with goats cheese, fish and chips, and 12oz scottish sirloin; children's meals (and fresh milk shakes).

Starters/Snacks: £3.95 to £7.95. Main Courses: £7.25 to £18.95. Puddings: £4.50 to £4.95

Free house ~ Licensee Roddy Anderson ~ Real ale ~ Bar food (12-2, 6-9) ~ Restaurant ~ (01546) 870282 ~ Children welcome till 8pm ~ Dogs allowed in bar ~ Live music two Sats a month ~ Open 12-12(1 Sat); 12-12 Sun; closed Mon and Tues in winter

Recommended by BOB

THORNHILL
NS6699 MAP 11

Lion & Unicorn

A873; FK8 3PJ

Busy and interesting pub with some emphasis on its good home-made food, well liked locally

---

Dating back in part to 1635, this characterful pub is very popular for its properly home-made food (around meal times most tables may be set for eating), but that's not the only draw: readers who briefly popped in to the cosy bar on a dreary winter's day say their spirits were immediately lifted by the beer and the blazing log fires. The carpeted front room has old walls, a beamed ceiling, and comfortable seating, while one dining room – with its own entrance – still has its original massive fireplace, almost big enough to drive a car into. Friendly obliging staff serve a couple of real ales on handpump such as Caledonian Deuchars IPA and a guest like Caledonian Six Nations or Harviestoun Bitter and Twisted (it's cheaper in the public bar than it is in the lounge), and they have a good choice of malt whiskies. A games room has a juke box, pool, fruit machine, TV, darts, and board games; quiz nights and piped music. There's a play area in the garden.

⑪ Served all day, bar food includes soup, starters such as haggis won tons or mussel stew, baked potatoes, steak pie, battered haddock, scampi, four vegetarian dishes such as stir-fried vegetables, lamb shank with apricot and rosemary, venison steak with claret and cranberry glaze, and puddings such as apple and cinnamon crumble; speciality coffees. *Starters/Snacks: £2.95 to £4.95. Main Courses: £6.95 to £17.95. Puddings: £3.95 to £4.95*

Free house ~ Licensees Fiona and Bobby Stevenson ~ Real ale ~ Bar food (12-9) ~ Restaurant ~ (01786) 850204 ~ Children in eating area of bar ~ Occasional live music ~ Open 11(12.30 Sun)-12(1 Sat); closed 1 Jan ~ Bedrooms: £55B/£75B
Recommended by Michael Butler, John Urquhart, John and Joan Nash, Tom and Rosemary Hall

ULLAPOOL

NH1294   MAP 11

Ferry Boat 🍺

Shore Street; coming from the S, keep straight ahead when main A835 turns right into Mill Street; IV26 2UJ

Unassuming, old-fashioned inn with nice loch views, and well priced home-made food

Straightforward and unassuming, the friendly, pubby bar of this nicely chatty 18th-c inn has big windows with good views over Loch Broom. With a ceilidh band on Thursday nights, the bar has yellow walls, brocade-cushioned seats around plain wooden tables, quarry tiles by the corner serving counter and patterned carpet elsewhere, a stained-glass door hanging from the ceiling, and a fruit machine; cribbage, dominoes, board games and piped music. A smaller more peaceful room has a coal fire, and a delft shelf of copper measures and willow-pattern plates. Dogs are allowed in the bar outside food serving times. There are up to three changing real ales from breweries such as An Teallach, Belhaven and Greene King on handpump. In summer you can sit on the wall across the road and take in the fine views to the tall hills beyond the attractive fishing port, with its bustle of yachts, ferry boats, fishing boats and tour boats for the Summer Isles. Take binoculars and you might even spot seals. More reports please.

⑪ Hearty, reasonably priced bar food might include sandwiches, home-made fishcakes, home-made steak pie, vegetarian nut roast, local haddock topped with tomato, cheese and herb crust, chicken stuffed with haggis with creamy white wine sauce, and puddings like chocolate sponge. *Starters/Snacks: £2.50 to £4.95. Main Courses: £6.00 to £11.00. Puddings: £3.00*

Punch ~ Tenant Terry Flower ~ Real ale ~ Bar food (12-7) ~ (01854) 612366 ~ Children in eating area of bar and restaurant till 8pm ~ Dogs allowed in bar ~ Ceilidh band Thurs nights ~ Open 11-11(10.30 Sun) ~ Bedrooms: £40S/£80B
Recommended by Peter Meister, N R White, Joan York, David and Sue Smith

WEEM

NN8449   MAP 11

Ailean Chraggan 🍽 🍷 🛏

B846; PH15 2LD

Changing range of well sourced creative food in friendly family-run hotel – a particularly nice place to stay

The views from the two terraces of this small and friendly family-run hotel look to the mountains beyond the Tay, and up to Ben Lawers – the highest peak in this part of Scotland. It's a lovely place to stay, with well liked food (worth booking at busy times) and a couple of beers from the local Inveralmond Brewery, usually Lia Fail, Independence, Ossian or Thrappledouser on handpump. You're likely to find chatty locals in the bar; winter darts and board games. There's also a very good wine list, with several wines by the glass, and you can choose from around 100 malt whiskies. The owners can arrange fishing nearby. More reports please.

⑪ As well as sandwiches, good changing dishes, served in either the comfortably carpeted modern lounge or the dining room, might include butternut squash and parsnip soup, salmon and scallop terrine with tomato, fennel and potato, moules marinière, courgette, goats cheese and vegetable quiche, fresh fillet of haddock, seared scallops with capsicum risotto and pesto, bouillabaisse with parmesan croûton and grilled oyster, medallion of local venison with baked apple, local cheese and cranberry and port jus, beef fillet mignons with herb crust and port jus, and puddings like praline semi-freddo with berry compote or yoghurt and lime mousse; they do children's meals too. *Starters/Snacks: £2.95 to £5.50. Main Courses: £8.75 to £16.95. Puddings: £2.50 to £5.50*

Free house ~ Licensee Alastair Gillespie ~ Real ale ~ Bar food ~ Restaurant ~ (01887) 820346 ~ Children welcome ~ Dogs allowed in bar and bedrooms ~ Open 11-11; closed 1-2 Jan, 25-26 Dec ~ Bedrooms: £57.50B/£95B

Recommended by Paul and Ursula Randall

LUCKY DIP

Besides the fully inspected pubs, you might like to try these Lucky Dips recommended to us and described by readers (if you do, please send us reports: www.goodguides.co.uk).

ABERDEENSHIRE

ABERDEEN [NJ9305]
Grill AB11 6BA [Union St]: Old-fashioned traditional local with real ales such as Caledonian 80/-, Courage and Isle of Skye Red Cuillin, enormous range of malt whiskies, polished dark panelling, ironic match-strike metal strip under bar counter, basic snacks; open all day *(the Didler, Graham Watson)*
☆ *Prince of Wales* AB10 1HF [St Nicholas Lane]: Individual old tavern worth knowing for its good range of well kept real ales from very long bar counter, flagstones, pews and screened booths, smarter lounge, bargain food; children welcome in eating area at lunchtime, open all day *(the Didler, LYM, Pete Walker)*
BALLATER [NO3795]
Alexandra AB35 5QJ [Bridge Sq]: Enjoyable food from sandwiches and interesting light dishes up, good drinks *(J F M and M West)*
CRATHIE [NO2293]
Inver AB35 5XN [A93 Balmoral—Braemar]: Sensitively refurbished 18th-c inn by River Dee, civilised and comfortable bar areas with log fires, some stripped stone and good solid furnishings inc leather settees, sensible choice of enjoyable fresh home-made food, decent wine by the glass, lots of whiskies; bedrooms *(J F M and M West)*
GARDENSTOWN [NJ7964]
Garden Arms AB45 3YP [Main St]: Simple pub with new licensees doing bargain pub lunches, Belhaven and Courage beer; pretty fishing village, beautiful coast *(David and Katharine Cooke)*
GLENKINDIE [NJ4413]
Glenkindie Arms AB33 8SX [A97]: Settling in well under hard-working newish licensees, wide choice of fresh fish, a changing real ale such as Belhaven; bedrooms, cl winter wkdy lunchtimes *(David and Betty Gittins)*
HUNTLY [NJ5239]
Gordon Arms AB54 8AF [The Square]: Good value bar lunches in neatly kept recently refurbished lounge *(David and Betty Gittins)*

MUIR OF FOWLIS [NJ5612]
Muggarthaugh AB33 8HX [Tough, just off A980]: Above-average food, good ingredients freshly cooked (so may be a wait), good friendly service, small neat bar with coal fire, TV and games room off, simple restaurant, Caledonian Deuchars IPA and a guest from Cairngorm or Tomintoul, nice wine choice; bedrooms, open for most of day at least in summer, handy for Craigievar (which has no catering), cl Mon *(David and Betty Gittins, Lucien Perring)*
OLDMELDRUM [NJ8127]
☆ *Redgarth* AB51 0DJ [Kirk Brae]: Good-sized comfortable lounge, traditional décor and subdued lighting, Caledonian Deuchars IPA, Timothy Taylors Landlord and a guest such as Shardlow Golden Hop, good range of malt whiskies, enjoyable bargain food, cheerful and attentive landlord and staff, restaurant; gorgeous views to Bennachie, immaculate bedrooms *(David and Betty Gittins)*

ARGYLL

BRIDGE OF ORCHY [NN2939]
☆ *Bridge of Orchy Hotel* PA36 4AB [A82 Tyndrum—Glencoe]: Comfortable and lively bar with nice views, wide choice of good fairly priced food in bar and restaurant, friendly young staff, well kept Caledonian 80/- and Fyne Maverick, dozens of malt whiskies, good choice of house wines, interesting mountain photographs; lovely bedrooms, good value bunkhouse, spectacular spot on West Highland Way (and if it's on time the sleeper from London gets you here just in time for breakfast) *(Michael and Maggie Betton)*
CAIRNBAAN [NR8390]
Cairnbaan Hotel PA31 8SQ [B841, off A816 N of Lochgilphead]: Charming spot overlooking busy canal lock and swing bridge, with walk to four central locks; cheerful small bar, warm and welcoming, with bare boards, bookshelves and immaculate restful décor, Fyne real ale, good food, carpeted conservatory and attractive restaurant; tables on flagstoned terrace,

attractive and comfortable bedrooms, good breakfast (useful too for canal users moored nearby), open all day *(Richard J Holloway)*

CAIRNDOW [NN1811]

Cairndow Stagecoach Inn PA26 8BN: Wonderful scenery, friendly locals, open all day for good bar food; dogs welcome, lovely peaceful garden right on shore of Loch Fyne, comfortable bedrooms *(Richard and Emily Whitworth)*

CONNEL [NM9034]

☆ *Oyster* PA37 1PJ: Cosy 18th-c inn opp former ferry slipway, lovely view across the water (esp at sunset), attractive bar and restaurant, good thriving highland atmosphere, enjoyable well prepared standard food, helpful friendly service even when busy, keg beers but good range of wines by the glass and of malt whiskies; comfortable bedrooms inc some new ones *(Topher Nairn, Ian Fleming, Charles and Pauline Stride)*

GLENCOE [NN1058]

☆ *Clachaig* PH49 4HX [old Glencoe rd, behind NTS Visitor Centre]: Lively extended inn doubling as mountain rescue post and cheerfully crowded with outdoors people in season, with mountain photographs in basic flagstoned walkers' bar (two woodburners and pool), quieter pine-panelled snug and big modern-feeling dining lounge – service can be better in here, with hot plates for the hearty all-day bar food, wider evening choice, great real ale fridge inc four brewed locally, unusual bottled beers, over 120 malt whiskies, annual beer festival, children in restaurant; live music Sat; good simple bedrooms, spectacular setting surrounded by soaring mountains *(LYM, Mr and Mrs Maurice Thompson, Dr Peter Crawshaw, Andy and Cath Pearson, Jarrod and Wendy Hopkinson, R M Jones)*

KILFINAN [NR9378]

Kilfinan Hotel PA21 2EP [B8000, Cowal Peninsula]: Warmly welcoming new owners in sporting hotel halfway down Cowal Peninsula, nr Loch Fyne shore, small public bar (used by locals) with communicating lounge, enjoyable food using local produce here and in restaurant, range of whiskies; comfortable bedrooms, quiet scenic spot *(Nina Randall, Kevin Thomas)*

LOCH ECK [NS1491]

Coylet PA23 8SG [S end – A815]: Attractive inn above the loch, between Benmore and Whistlefield, good reasonably priced local food in cosy bar or pleasant restaurant, helpful staff, well kept real ales such as Caledonian Deuchars IPA, good range of malt whiskies, friendly atmosphere; quite handy for Younger Botanic Gardens, boat hire available, charming bedrooms (spiral stair could be awkward for some) *(Richard and Emily Whitworth)*

Whistlefield PA23 8SG [from A815 turn into Ardentinny lane by loch]: Charmingly isolated 17th-c inn above loch, good atmosphere in low-ceilinged partly stripped-stone bar, enjoyable pubby food, good choice of malt whiskies, log fire, pictures and bric-a-brac, carpeted lounge bar, picture-window restaurant, frequent wknd folk nights; play area outside, eight comfortably updated bedrooms, bunkhouse *(LYM, Richard and Emily Whitworth)*

OBAN [NM8530]

☆ *Oban Inn* PA34 5NJ [Stafford St, nr North Pier]: Cheery 18th-c harbour-town local with pubby beamed and slate-floored downstairs bar, Caledonian Deuchars IPA and Theakstons Best, several dozen malt whiskies, partly panelled upstairs dining bar (good value food all day – may be a wait for a table) with button-back banquettes around cast-iron-framed tables, coffered woodwork ceiling, little stained-glass false windows and family area; fruit machine, juke box, piped music; dogs allowed in bar, open all day *(LYM, C J Fletcher, Mr and Mrs Maurice Thompson, N R White, Susan and John Douglas)*

TARBERT [NR8768]

Columba PA29 6UF [Pier Rd]: Civilised newly refurbished 1900s pub named for the then daily ferry from Glasgow, attractive and congenial bar, enjoyable food using local fish and fresh produce here, small room off, charming restaurant; seven comfortable bedrooms *(Richard J Holloway, A and B D Craig)*

AYRSHIRE

SORN [NS5526]

Sorn Inn KA5 6HU [Main St]: Unexpectedly smart restaurant-with-rooms in tiny conservation village, good bar food in chop house, imaginative cooking in upmarket restaurant, reasonable prices; comfortable bedrooms *(Roy Bromell, Mrs A J Robertson)*

BERWICKSHIRE

EYEMOUTH [NT9464]

Ship TD14 5HT [Harbour Road]: Old inn recently comfortably refurbished keeping some original features, friendly bar well liked by locals, enjoyable food inc scottish dishes and lots of fresh seafood, local real ales, plans for redesigning restaurant; six well equipped bedrooms, good breakfast, nice spot on quay of pretty fishing village *(Dr A McCormick)*

LAUDER [NT5347]

☆ *Black Bull* TD2 6SR [Market Pl]: Thriving atmosphere in comfortably refurbished 17th-c inn with chef/landlord doing good range of interesting food served in three linked areas, good choice of beers and good house wine, pleasant attentive staff; children welcome, comfortable bedrooms, open all day *(Pat and Stewart Gordon, LYM, David and Jane Hill)*

PAXTON [NT9352]

Cross TD15 1TE: Smart village pub with above-average modestly priced food inc good seafood, good service and enterprising landlady, good value house wines, real ales such as Mordue or Wylam, farm cider; cl Mon *(Stanley and Annie Matthews, Comus and Sarah Elliott, Dr John Lunn)*

RESTON [NT8762]

☆ *Red Lion* TD14 5JP [Main St (B6438)]: Neatly kept family-run pub, smallish choice of enjoyable food cooked to order, wider evening choice, Broughton and a guest beer, modestly priced wines, cheery bar with blazing log fire and collection of old cameras, attractive dining room; children welcome, tables under cocktail parasols in pretty back garden, cl Mon, also wkdy lunchtimes out of season, open all day summer wknds *(Comus and Sarah Elliott, Catherine Ferguson)*

CAITHNESS

HALKIRK [ND1359]

Commercial KW12 6XY [Bridge St]: Smartly upholstered lounge bar with old local photographs and paintings, friendly efficient service, limited but adventurous food range (not Mon/Tues) *(Sarah and Peter Gooderham)*

Ulbster Arms KW12 6XY [Bridge St]: Comfortable bar with wide range of food and lots of angling pictures *(Sarah and Peter Gooderham)*

LYBSTER [ND2436]

☆ *Portland Arms* KW3 6BS [A9 S of Wick]: Welcoming civilised 19th-c hotel, part attractively laid out as cosy country kitchen with Aga, pine furnishings and farmhouse crockery, smart bar-bistro with easy chairs on tartan carpet and cosy fire, straightforward sensibly priced bar food (all day Sun and summer), good selection of malt whiskies (keg beers), board games, restaurant; piped music; children welcome away from bar area, comfortable bedrooms, good spot nr spectacular cliffs and stacks, open all day wknds and summer *(Mr and Mrs G D Brooks, Bill Strang, Stuart Pearson, LYM, Alan Wilcock, Christine Davidson)*

DUMFRIES-SHIRE

AULDGIRTH [NX9186]

Auldgirth Inn DG2 0XG [just E of A76, about 8 miles N of Dumfries]: Ancient whitewashed stone-built inn with newish licensees settling in well, comfortable bar in side annexe with brasses, plates, pictures and a good log fire, above-average food from simple bar meals to more elaborate dishes, Houston real ales, separate dining room; tables outside, three bedrooms *(Stuart Turner)*

DUMFRIES [NX9776]

☆ *Cavens Arms* DG1 2AH [Buccleuch St]: Increasing emphasis on good food (all day Sat, not Mon) using Buccleuch beef and other prime ingredients from pubby standards to imaginative dishes, well kept Caledonian Deuchars IPA, Greene King Abbot, Phoenix Arizona and up to half a dozen changing guest beers, Stowford Press farm cider and perhaps a perry, fine choice of malt whiskies, friendly landlord and staff, civilised front part with lots of wood, bar stools and a few comfortable tables for drinkers at the back; can get very busy (but efficient table-queueing system), unobtrusive TV, no children or dogs; open all day *(Nick Holding, Joe Green)*

Coach & Horses DG1 2RS [Whitesands]: Small and congenial, simple furnishings on flagstones, good value inventive food from upstairs bistro, quick attentive service, more elaborate evening menu; sports TVs *(Kevin Jeavons, Alison Turner)*

GLENCAPLE [NX9968]

Nith DG1 4RE: Hotel with basic public bar (hatch service to sunny corner room), more comfortable lounge, picture-window dining room looking over river towards Criffel's hoary top, quickly served food, keg beer; spacious bedrooms, good breakfast *(Joe Green)*

GRETNA [NY3267]

Crossways DG16 5DN [Annan Rd]: Big pub opp the Retail Park, good value food from good sandwiches up, children's dishes; lots of flower baskets and tubs out in front *(Keith and Chris O'Neill)*

MOFFAT [NT0805]

☆ *Black Bull* DG10 9EG [Churchgate]: Attractive and well kept small hotel, plush dimly lit bar with Burns memorabilia, good value unpretentious food from sandwiches and light dishes up using local meats, helpful staff, Caledonian Deuchars IPA, McEwans 80/- and Theakstons XB, several dozen malt whiskies, friendly public bar across courtyard with railway memorabilia and good open fire, simply furnished tiled-floor dining room; piped music, side games bar with juke box, big-screen TV for golf; children welcome, tables in courtyard, 12 comfortable good value bedrooms, open all day *(Pat and Stewart Gordon, Ray and Winifred Halliday, Dave Braisted, LYM, Bill Strang, Stuart Pearson, Stephen R Holman)*

NEW ABBEY [NX9666]

Abbey Arms DG2 8BX [The Square]: Enjoyable pubby food from generous baguettes up, friendly attentive staff, a changing real ale such as Black Sheep, decent wines by the glass, small spotless parlour and fair-sized dark pink back dining room; dogs welcome, large front terrace, attractive village *(John Foord, Stan and Hazel Allen, Mrs Pat Crabb)*

EAST LOTHIAN

ABERLADY [NT4679]

Kilspindie House EH32 0RE [Main St]: Sizeable hotel with bar food (all day wknds) making good use of local produce, esp fish inc superb trout, high teas too, nice range of malt whiskies, real ale, good evening restaurant; 26 bedrooms *(W K Wood)*

EAST LINTON [NT5977]

☆ *Crown* EH40 3AG [Bridge St]: Appealing choice of good food, friendly staff, real ales such as Adnams Broadside, Caledonian Deuchars IPA and Wells & Youngs Waggle Dance *(Tom Riddell, Meg Robbins)*

☆ *Drovers* EH40 3AG [Bridge St (B1407), just off A1 Haddington—Dunbar]: Cosy 18th-c pub under new management, good pubby feel in recently refurbished bar with stripped woodwork, comfortable wall benches, quite a few pictures, real ales such as Caledonian Deuchars IPA and Greene King Abbot, good choice of coffees, pubby bar food, woodburner and daily papers, restaurant; piped music; children and dogs welcome, open all day Fri-Sun and summer *(Comus and Sarah Elliott, Michael Butler, Joan York)*

GIFFORD [NT5368]

Goblin Ha' EH41 4QH [Main St]: Contemporary décor and colour scheme in roomy and civilised front dining lounge, lively stripped-stone public bar with games area, varied food from simple bar lunches to more elaborate things, quick friendly service, real ales such as Caledonian Deuchars IPA, Marstons Pedigree and Timothy Taylors Landlord, airy back conservatory; children welcome in lounge and conservatory, tables and chairs in good big garden with small play area, bedrooms, open all day Fri-Sun *(C and H Greenly, Mrs K J Betts, Ken Richards)*

Tweeddale Arms EH41 4QU [S of Haddington; High St (B6355)]: Old-fashioned hotel in peaceful setting overlooking attractive village green, simple lounge bar with several malt whiskies and interesting modestly priced wines (keg beers), decent bar food from sandwiches up, public bar with games machine and darts, comfortably chintzy hotel lounge with antique tables and paintings, good restaurant meals; children welcome, bedrooms, open all day *(LYM, Dr A McCormick, Archie and Margaret Mackenzie, Angus Lyon)*

GULLANE [NT4882]

☆ *Old Clubhouse* EH31 2AF [East Links Rd]: Two spotless bars with Victorian pictures and cartoons, pre-war sheet music and other memorabilia, stuffed birds, open fires, wide range of enjoyable generous bar food, fast friendly service, McEwans 80/- and guest beers, views over golf links to Lammermuirs; children welcome, open all day *(C and H Greenly)*

HADDINGTON [NT5173]

Waterside EH41 4AT [Waterside; just off A6093, over pedestrian bridge at E end of Town]: Attractively set riverside dining pub with long cushioned benches and big tables in room off nicely worn in plush bar, stripped-stone dining conservatory, inexpensive quickly served tasty food, Belhaven, Caledonian Deuchars IPA, Courage

Directors and Theakstons, decent wines; children welcome, no dogs, tables out overlooking the water, open all day wknds *(LYM, Comus and Sarah Elliott)*

FIFE

CRAIL [NO6107]

Golf KY10 3TD [High St S]: Good service, hearty standard food from bargain sandwiches up, small traditional beamed locals' bar (with flat-screen TV), good range of malt whiskies, a real ale such as Caledonian Deuchars IPA, coal fire, airily refurbished dining room (they do high teas); simple comfortable bedrooms, good breakfast *(Comus and Sarah Elliott)*

ELIE [NO4900]

Station Buffet KY9 1BZ [High St]: Real ales such as Caledonian Deuchars IPA or Tetleys, bar snacks inc good home-made soup *(A Bowman)*

LOWER LARGO [NO4102]

Railway Inn KY8 6BU [Station Wynd]: Friendly pub nr harbour, good range of changing real ales, lots of railway and golf memorabilia, hot pies *(John Joseph Smith)*

INVERNESS-SHIRE

ARISAIG [NM6586]

Arisaig Hotel PH39 4NH: Magnificent view over harbour (with boat trips) and the Small Isles, cosy and welcoming lounge bar, enjoyable reasonably priced food esp fish, several dozen malt whiskies, old-fashioned juke box in public bar; bedrooms *(Dave Braisted)*

AVIEMORE [NH8612]

Cairngorm PH22 1PE [Grampian Rd (A9)]: Large flagstoned bar, lively and friendly, with wide choice of good value bar food using local produce, a real ale and good choice of other drinks, informal restaurant; sports TV; children welcome, comfortable bedrooms *(Michael and Maggie Betton)*

CARRBRIDGE [NH9022]

Dalrachney Lodge PH23 3AT [nr junction A9/A95 S of Inverness]: Traditional shooting-lodge-type hotel in lovely spot, enjoyable food in bar/bistro, friendly helpful staff, comfortable lounge with log fire in ornate inglenook, plenty of malt whiskies; children welcome, most bedrooms with mountain and river views *(Maurice and Gill McMahon)*

FORT WILLIAM [NN1073]

Ben Nevis Bar PH33 6DG [High St]: Roomy well converted raftered barn by path up to Ben Nevis, good value mainly straightforward food, Isle of Skye Hebridean Gold ale, prompt cheery service, harbour views from restaurant; TV, games, live music nights; bunk house below *(Michael and Maggie Betton, Sarah and Peter Gooderham)*

Nevis Bank PH33 6BY [off A82 bypass, N end of town]: Hotel bar popular with locals and walkers, decent bar food, friendly, prompt and tolerant service, wide range of whiskies; bedrooms *(Sarah and Peter Gooderham)*

GLEN SHIEL [NH0711]

☆ *Cluanie Inn* IV63 7YW [A87 Invergarry—Kyle of Lochalsh, on Loch Cluanie]: Welcoming inn in lovely isolated setting by Loch Cluanie (good walks), big helpings of good fresh bar food inc some interesting dishes in three knocked-together rooms with dining chairs around polished tables, overspill into restaurant, good local beer, fine range of malt whiskies, friendly efficient staff, warm log fire; children welcome, big comfortable modern bedrooms nicely furnished in pine, stunning views – great breakfasts for non-residents too *(Mrs J Main, R M Jones)*

INVERNESS [NH6446]

☆ *Clachnaharry Inn* IV3 8RB [High St, Clachnaharry (A862 NW of city)]: Congenial and cosily dim beamed real ale bar little changed since recent sale to Belhaven/Greene King, seven or eight kept well, warm chatty atmosphere, bargain freshly made food all day from big baked potatoes up, good staff, great log fire as well as gas stove, bottom lounge with picture windows looking over Beauly Firth; children welcome, tables out overlooking railway, lovely walks by big flight of Caledonian Canal locks, open all day *(Joe Green, Graham MacDonald)*

Hootanannay IV1 1ES [Church St]: Basic studenty music pub (so not exactly spick and span), dark walls, candlelight and Scottish musicians sitting around playing – truly atmospheric and great fun; Black Isle real ale, thai food *(R M Jones, Graham MacDonald)*

Phoenix IV1 1LX [Academy St]: Several changing real ales in bare-boards 1890s bar with much dark brown varnish and granite trough at foot of island servery, neat adjoining dining room with some booth seating; sports TVs *(Joe Green, Graham MacDonald)*

Snow Goose IV2 7PA [Stoneyfield, about ¼ mile E of A9/A96 roundabout]: Useful Vintage Inn dining pub, the most northerly of this chain, newly extended and well laid out with country-feel room areas, beams and flagstones, several log fires, soft lighting, interesting décor, their standard food (inc huge sandwiches till 5) and decent wines by the glass; comfortable bedrooms in adjacent Travelodge *(J F M and M West, Walter and Susan Rinaldi-Butcher)*

KIRKHILL [NH5644]

Old North IV5 7PX [Inchmore (A862 Inverness—Beauly)]: Traditional public bar with two real ales and good choice of malt whiskies, welcoming service, good straightforward home-made food using top local suppliers, log fire, cheery regulars, unpretentious pubby furnishings, beamery and pastel walls, another log fire in comfortable lounge *(Graham MacDonald, Sally and Tom Matson)*

ONICH [NN0361]

Onich Hotel PH33 6RY: Usual range of bar food in hotel's comfortable open lounge, pleasant prompt service, grand views over wonderful garden to Loch Linnhe; bedrooms *(Sarah and Peter Gooderham)*

KINCARDINESHIRE

CATERLINE [NO8678]

☆ *Creel* AB39 2UL: Good generous imaginative food esp soups and memorable local fish and seafood in big plain but comfortable lounge with woodburner, plenty of tables, several real ales such as Caledonian Deuchars IPA and Maclays 70/-, welcoming service, small second bar, compact seaview restaurant (same menu, booking advised); bedrooms, nice clifftop position in old fishing village, has been cl Tues, open all day Sun *(Brian McBurnie, R F Masters)*

KINROSS-SHIRE

KINNESSWOOD [NO1702]

Lomond KY13 9HN [A911 Glenrothes—Milnathort, not far from M90 junctions 7/8]: Enjoyable fresh food from sandwiches up in small bar and restaurant of well appointed and friendly small inn with lovely sunset views over Loch Leven, well kept real ales, decent wines, cheerful helpful staff, log fire; well placed decking, 12 comfortable bedrooms *(Dave Cuthbert)*

KIRKCUDBRIGHTSHIRE

HAUGH OF URR [NX8066]

Laurie Arms DG7 3YA [B794 N of Dalbeattie; Main St]: Comfortable village pub with incredibly wide choice of both basic and more elaborate dishes from sandwiches up, a couple of well kept changing ales such as Wadworths 6X, decent wines, log fires in both friendly bars, attractive décor with various knick-knacks, Bamforth comic postcards in the gents'; tables out on new terrace *(Nick Holding, Joe Green, J M Renshaw, Chris Smith, Mark O'Sullivan)*

KIPPFORD [NX8355]

☆ *Anchor* DG5 4LN [off A710 S of Dalbeattie]: Popular waterfront inn in lovely spot overlooking big natural harbour and peaceful hills, efficient uniformed staff, wide choice of good food from sandwiches to local fish and seafood, three local Sulwath ales, lots of malt whiskies, coal fire in neatly traditional back bar (dogs allowed in one area here), lounge bar (may be cl out of season), simple and roomy bright new dining room; piped music, TV and machines; children welcome, tables on front terrace, good walks and bird-watching, open all day in summer *(John Found, LYM)*

KIRKCUDBRIGHT [NX6850]

☆ *Selkirk Arms* DG6 4JG [High St]: 18th-c Best Western hotel with good food inc plenty of fresh local fish in comfortable partly panelled lounge bar and restaurant, local Sulwath ales, affable landlord and friendly efficient service, nice atmosphere, quiet modern décor; children welcome, tables in garden with 15th-c font, good value bedrooms *(BB, Nick Holding)*

NEW GALLOWAY [NX6478]

Ken Bridge Hotel DG7 3PR [A712, just off A713 N of Castle Douglas]: Good atmosphere in bar of small riverside hotel (own fishing), friendly owners and staff, Caledonian Deuchars IPA and Greene King, good choice of wines by the glass, enjoyable home-made food; tables out overlooking water, camp site, ten bedrooms *(Pat and Stewart Gordon)*

LANARKSHIRE

BIGGAR [NT0437]

Crown ML12 6DL [High St (A702)]: Two real ales and above-average food all day (children eat free in family parties), friendly atmosphere, coal fire in front bar, old-fashioned panelled lounge with old local pictures, recent restaurant extension; open all day *(J V Dadswell)*

GLASGOW [NS5865]

☆ *Horseshoe* G2 5AE [Drury St, nr Central Stn]: Classic high-ceilinged standing-room pub with enormous island bar, gleaming mahogany and mirrors, snob screens, other high Victorian features and interesting music-hall era memorabilia and musical intruments; friendly jovial staff and atmosphere, well kept ales inc Caledonian Deuchars IPA and 80/-, lots of malt whiskies, simple food served speedily in plainer upstairs bar and restaurant (where children allowed), inc long-served McGhees hot pies, reprieved in 2007 after devotees petitioned the chain which owns the pub to restore them to a mildly smartened-up new menu; games machine, piped music; open all day *(LYM, Pat and Bill Chalmers, Joe Green)*

Ingram G1 3BX [Queen St]: Civilised and well run Greene King (Belhaven) pub with well kept guest beers such as Caledonian Deuchars IPA and Orkney Dark Island, enterprising sandwiches and bargain generous home-made hot dishes *(Joe Green)*

Republic Bier Halle G1 3PL [Gordon St]: Dim-lit basement with bare masonry not unlike a continental beer hall, over 70 beers from around the world, friendly staff who know about them, popular food inc special deals; popular with young people, piped music can be loud at night *(Andrew York)*

State G2 4NG [Holland St]: High-ceilinged bar with marble pillars, lots of carved wood inc handsome oak island servery, half a dozen or so well kept changing ales inc southerners, bargain basic lunchtime food from sandwiches up, good atmosphere, friendly staff, armchair among other comfortable seats, coal-effect gas fire in big wooden fireplace, old prints and theatrical posters; piped music, games machine, wknd live music *(James Crouchman)*

NEILSTON [NS4857]

Travellers Rest G78 3NT [Neilston Rd]: Refurbished under newish owners, sensibly short choice of well above average food in bar and dining room; pleasant setting nr top of village, good views, bedrooms *(Pat and Bill Chalmers)*

MIDLOTHIAN

BALERNO [NT1566]

Johnsburn House EH14 7BB [Johnsburn Rd]: Handsome old-fashioned beamed bar in former 18th-c mansion with masterpiece 1911 ceiling by Robert Lorimer; Caledonian Deuchars IPA and interesting changing ales, coal fire, panelled dining lounge with good food inc shellfish and game, more formal evening dining rooms; children and dogs welcome, open all day wknds, cl Mon *(the Didler)*

CARLOPS [NT1656]

☆ *Allan Ramsay* EH26 9NF [A702]: Charming late 18th-c country inn, several interconnecting beamed rooms, eating areas each end (wide choice of good generous food all day), friendly helpful staff, well kept Caledonian Deuchars IPA and Inveralmond, good coffee, log fire, fresh flowers, witches' sabbath mural recalling local legend which the eponymous poet versified, lots of interesting Ramsay memorabilia in restaurant; piped music, games machine and TV; children welcome, small comfortable bedrooms, open all day *(Angus Lyon)*

CRAMOND [NT1877]

Cramond Inn EH4 6NU [Cramond Glebe Rd (off A90 W of Edinburgh)]: Softly lit smallish rooms done up traditionally, low-priced Sam Smiths beers inc a wheat beer, popular pubby food inc some local dishes such as haggis and bashed neeps, good friendly service and atmosphere, two coal and log fires; picturesque Firth of Forth village at mouth of River Almond, delightful views from tables out on grass by car park *(LYM, R T and J C Moggridge)*

EDINBURGH [NT2574]

☆ *Bennets* EH3 9LG [Leven St]: Ornate Victorian bar with original glass, mirrors, arcades, fine panelling and tiles, friendly service, real ales inc Caledonian Deuchars IPA from tall founts, over a hundred malt whiskies, bar snacks and bargain homely lunchtime hot dishes (not Sun; children allowed in eating area), second bar with counter salvaged from old ship; open all day *(Nick Holding, LYM, the Didler)*

Cloisters EH3 9JH [Brougham St]: Friendly and interesting ex-parsonage alehouse with Caledonian Deuchars and 80/- and half a dozen or so interesting guest beers, 70 malt whiskies, several wines by the glass, decent food till 3 (4 Sat) from toasties to Sun roasts, plenty for vegetarians, breakfast too, pews and bar gantry recycled from redundant church, bare boards and lots of brewery mirrors; lavatories down spiral stairs, folk music Fri/Sat; dogs welcome, open all day *(the Didler, UN)*

Deacon Brodies EH1 2NT [Lawnmarket]: Entertainingly commemorating the notorious highwayman town councillor who was eventually hanged on the scaffold he'd designed; ornately high-ceilinged city bar, Caledonian Deuchars IPA from long counter, comfortable upstairs waitress-service dining lounge, good value food from baguettes up, breakfast from 10am; games, piped music, TV; pavement seating *(Michael Dandy, BB)*

Dirty Dicks EH2 4LS [Rose St]: Small pub packed with eccentric bric-a-brac and decorations inc clock in floor, friendly attentive staff, good range of real ale, decent food, interesting ceiling in ladies' (so they say); tables outside *(Doug Christian)*

Dome EH2 2PF [St Georges Sq/George St]: Opulent italianate former bank, not cheap but worth it, huge main bar with magnificent dome, elaborate plasterwork and stained glass; central servery, pillars, lots of greenery, mix of wood and cushioned wicker chairs, Caledonian Deuchars IPA and 80/-, interesting food from generous sandwiches up, friendly efficient service, smart dining area; smaller and quieter art deco Frasers bar (may be cl some afternoons and evenings early in week) has atmospheric period feel, striking woodwork, unusual lights, red curtains, lots of good period advertisements, piped jazz, daily papers, same beers – also wines and cocktails; complex includes hotel bedrooms *(BB, Doug Christian)*

Doric EH1 1DE [Market St]: Plenty of atmosphere, simple furnishings and nice wood frontage in small bar, good range of beers inc Edinburgh EPA (brewed by Belhaven), decent wines, friendly young staff, good upstairs bistro with attractive lunchtime prices; TV *(Janet and Peter Race, Michael Dandy)*

Ensign Ewart EH1 2PE [Lawnmarket, Royal Mile; last pub on right before Castle]: Charming old-world pub handy for Castle (so can get very full), huge painting of Ewart at Waterloo capturing the french banner (it's on show in the castle), friendly efficient staff, well kept real ales, wide range of whiskies, usual food lunchtime and some summer evenings; games machine, traditional music most nights; open all day *(Peter F Marshall)*

☆ **Halfway House** EH1 1BX [Fleshmarket Cl (steps between Cockburn St and Market St, opp Waverley Stn)]: Tiny single-room pub off steep steps, very friendly and welcoming, lots of railway memorabilia, four well kept changing real ales often from a single brewer, good range of malt whiskies, enterprising food at bargain prices using top-quality carefully sourced supplies (can take a while at busy times); open all day, dogs and children welcome *(Joe Green)*

☆ **Jolly Judge** EH1 2PB [James Court, by 495 Lawnmarket]: Interesting and comfortable basement of 16th-c tenement with traditional fruit-and-flower-painted wooden

ceiling, relaxed atmosphere, friendly service, Caledonian 80/- and a guest beer, changing malt whiskies, hot drinks, lovely fire, quickly served lunchtime bar meals (children allowed then) and afternoon snacks; piped music; open all day, cl Sun lunchtime *(Doug Christian, LYM)*

☆ **Kenilworth** EH2 3JD [Rose St]: Edwardian pub with ornate high ceiling, carved woodwork and tiles, huge etched brewery mirrors and windows, red leather seating around tiled wall; central bar with well kept Caledonian Deuchars IPA and guest beers such as Cairngorm Wildcat and Harviestoun Bitter & Twisted, good choice of wines by the glass, quick friendly attentive service, good reasonably priced food from sandwiches up lunchtime and evening, back family room; piped music, discreetly placed games machines, TV; pavement tables, open all day *(P Dawn, Michael Dandy, Janet and Peter Race, BB, the Didler, Richard Tingle)*

Leslies EH9 1SU [Ratcliffe Terrace]: Handsome Victorian bar with snob screens and ornate decorative touches, good changing ale range, basic bar snacks *(Colin and Ruth Munro)*

Malt Shovel EH1 1BP [Cockburn St]: Three levels, lots of panelling, stained glass and mirrors, soft leather sofas in top room, changing real ales such as Caledonian Deuchars IPA and 80/- from long serving bar, friendly young staff, reasonably priced home-made pubby food from sandwiches to steaks; piped music, games; seats outside, open all day *(Michael Dandy)*

Milnes EH2 2PJ [Rose St/Hanover St]: Well reworked traditional city pub rambling down to several areas below street level, old-fashioned bare-boards feel, dark wood furnishings and panelling, cask tables, lots of old photographs and mementoes of poets who used the 'Little Kremlin' room here, usually several real ales (esp in the upper part entered from Rose St), good choice of wines by the glass, good value coffees, open fire, reasonably priced bar food all day, breakfast from 10am; piped music, games; pavement seats, open all day *(Nick Holding, the Didler, Michael Dandy, BB, Doug Christian)*

Oxford EH2 4JB [Young St]: Friendly no-frills pub with two built-in wall settles and unchanging welcoming regulars in tiny bustling front bar, quieter back room with dominoes, lino floor, well kept Caledonian Deuchars IPA and Belhaven 80/-, good range of whiskies, cheap filled cobs; lavatories up a few steps *(Peter F Marshall, Joe Green)*

☆ **Peacock** EH6 4TZ [Lindsay Rd, Newhaven]: Good honest food all day inc outstanding fresh fish in massive helpings in neat plushly comfortable pub with several linked areas inc conservatory-style back room leading to garden, McEwans 80/- and a guest such as Orkney Dark Island, efficient service; very popular, best to book evenings and Sun lunchtime; children welcome, open all day *(Mr and Mrs M Shirley, LYM)*

Sandy Bells EH1 2QH [Forrest Rd]: Small unpretentious neatly kept local with friendly regulars, live folk music most nights – gets crowded then, quieter during the day *(Sapna Thottathil)*

St Vincent EH3 6SW [St Vincent St]: Boasts one of city's longest continuous licences, dating back to 1830s; well kept real ales, chatty friendly staff, enjoyable food, low beams, 19th-c bar mirror; open all day Thurs-Sat *(Alex Thompson)*

☆ *Standing Order* EH2 2JP [George St]: Grand Wetherspoons conversion of former bank in three elegant Georgian houses, imposing columns, enormous main room with elaborate colourful high ceiling, lots of tables, smaller side booths, other rooms inc two with floor-to-ceiling bookshelves, comfortable green sofa and chairs, Adam fireplace and portraits; civilised atmosphere, friendly helpful staff, good value food (inc Sun evening), coffee and pastries, real ales inc interesting guest beers from very long counter; wknd live music, extremely popular Sat night; disabled facilities, open all day *(Doug Christian, Joe Green, BB)*

White Hart EH1 2JU [Grassmarket]: One of Edinburgh's oldest pubs, small, basic and easy-going, very popular with summer visitors; relaxed atmosphere, good friendly young staff, Caledonian Deuchars IPA and other ales, enjoyable food all day; piped music, live on wkdy nights and Sun afternoon; pavement tables a hit with smokers, open all day *(Nick Holding, Bruce and Penny Wilkie)*

MUSSELBURGH [NT3372]

Volunteer Arms EH21 6JE [N High St; aka Staggs]: Same family since 1858, unspoilt busy bar, dark panelling, old brewery mirrors, great gantry with ancient casks, Caledonian Deuchars IPA and 80/- and a quickly changing guest beer; dogs welcome, open all day *(Joe Green, the Didler)*

PEEBLES-SHIRE

EDDLESTON [NT2447]

☆ *Horseshoe* EH45 8QP [A703 Peebles—Penicuik]: Civilised old beamed pub/restaurant, French chef/landlord doing good imaginative mix of french and scottish cooking for bar and upmarket restaurant, charming helpful staff, attractive décor, soft lighting, comfortable seats, Bass and good choice of wines and whiskies, exemplary lavatories; eight well equipped annexe bedrooms, may be cl for a week or so Jan and Oct *(LYM, Archie and Margaret Mackenzie, Pat and Stewart Gordon)*

WEST LINTON [NT1451]

☆ *Gordon Arms* EH46 7DR [Dolphinton Rd (A702 S of Edinburgh)]: Unpretentious L-shaped stripped stone bar with a couple of leather chesterfields and more usual pub furniture, friendly local atmosphere, log fire, decent food (all day wknds) in bar and clean-cut more contemporary restaurant from

massive open sandwiches to good local lamb, good service, Caledonian Deuchars IPA and a guest beer; children welcome, dogs on leads too (biscuits for them), tables outside, bedrooms *(Nick Holding, Angus Lyon, BB, Ian Mcfarlane)*

PERTHSHIRE

AMULREE [NN9036]

Amulree Hotel PH8 0EF [A822]: In peaceful open country on River Braan, well appointed restaurant and bar, friendly staff; keg beer; comfortable bedrooms, good base for walking *(Paul and Ursula Randall)*

BALQUHIDDER [NN5420]

Kings House FK19 8NY: Cosy Rob Roy bar attached to hotel dating from 15th c, enjoyable bar food, open fire, tartan décor; bedrooms, attractive setting *(T H Little)*

DUNKELD [NO0242]

Taybank PH8 0AQ [Tay Terr]: Good value food, real ale, view over Tay and Georgian bridge; popular live music nights *(Dave Cuthbert)*

DUNNING [NO0114]

Kirkstyle PH2 0RR [B9141, off A9 S of Perth; Kirkstyle Sq]: Unpretentious olde-worlde streamside pub with chatty landlady and regulars, log fire, good choice of beers and whiskies, good service, enjoyable home-made food inc interesting dishes (must book in season), charming back restaurant with flagstones and stripped stone *(Susan and John Douglas, Charles and Pauline Stride)*

KENMORE [NN7745]

Mains of Taymouth Courtyard PH15 2HN [A827 just W]: Holiday village's welcoming contemporary bistro bar and restaurant, enjoyable food inc indoor barbecue, real ales, good friendly service; neat modern tables out on decking *(P and M A Hinchcliffe, Andy Cole)*

KILLIN [NN5733]

Coach House FK21 8TN: Welcoming to both diners and drinkers, Fyne Highlander and a seasonal ale, helpful staff, some live music *(Mr and Mrs Maurice Thompson)*

LOCH TUMMEL [NN8160]

Loch Tummel Inn PH16 5RP [B8019 4 miles E of Tummel Bridge]: Lochside former coaching inn with great views over water to Schiehallion, lots of walks and local wildlife, big woodburner in cosy partly stripped stone dining bar, good bar food inc game and home-smoked salmon lunchtime and early evening, changing real ale such as Greene King Old Speckled Hen, good choice of wines and whiskies, residents' converted hayloft restaurant, no music or machines; prompt bar closing time; attractive loch-view bedrooms with log fires, even an open fire in one bathroom, good breakfast, fishing free for residents; cl winter *(Paul and Ursula Randall, LYM)*

MEIKLEOUR [NO1539]

☆ *Meikleour Hotel* PH2 6EB [A984 W of Coupar Angus]: Good reasonably priced bar food inc fine sandwiches, friendly efficient service, three well kept ales such as Fyne and Inveralmond, local bottled water, and warm and enjoyable atmosphere in two quietly well furnished lounges, one with stripped stone and flagstones, another more chintzy, both with open fires, and back public bar; understated pretty building, picnic-sets in pleasant garden with tall pines and distant highland view, comfortable bedrooms, good breakfast, open all day wknds *(Susan and John Douglas, G Dobson, David and Katharine Cooke)*

ROSS-SHIRE

ALTANDHU [NB9812]
Fuaran IV26 2YR [15 miles off A835 N of Ullapool]: Splendidly remote, in gorgeous coastal scenery, all-day food inc good value toasties and take-aways, good wine by the glass *(J F M and M West)*

CROMARTY [NH7867]
☆ *Royal* IV11 8YN [Marine Terrace]: Pleasant old-fashioned harbourside hotel with cheerful helpful management, reasonably priced food esp fish, lots of malt whiskies (keg beers), sleepy sea views across Cromarty Firth to Ben Wyvis from covered front verandah, games etc in separate locals' bar; children and dogs welcome, comfortable bedrooms (not all have the view), good breakfast, open all day *(LYM, N R White, Charles and Pauline Stride)*

EDDERTON [NH7085]
Edderton Inn IV19 1LB [Station Rd]: Good value home-made food, a changing real ale such as Greene King Old Speckled Hen and plenty of local malt whiskies, in quiet and appealing small hotel recently refurbished by newish owners; six neat modern bedrooms *(Chris Evans)*

EVANTON [NH6066]
Balconie IV16 9UN [Balconie St]: Well kept village pub, good Black Isle real ales, usual malt whiskies, pleasant owners, friendly service, good bar food (plans for restaurant too) *(Mr and Mrs G D Brooks)*

KYLE OF LOCHALSH [NG7627]
Lochalsh Hotel IV40 8AF [Ferry Rd]: Large friendly hotel's lounge bar with civilised armchairs and sofas around low tables, plainer eating area, good simple bar food from generous inexpensive double sandwiches to dishes of the day, pleasant Skye Bridge views, quick friendly helpful service, good coffee; picnic-sets on spreading front lawns, bedrooms *(George Atkinson, Joan and Tony Walker)*

LOCHCARRON [NG9039]
☆ *Rockvilla* IV54 8YB: Small hotel doing well under current helpful owners, good reasonably priced food from sandwiches to local seafood and venison, quick service, up to three rotating local real ales, over 50 malt whiskies, light and comfortable bar with loch view, separate restaurant; comfortable bedrooms *(Jane and David Hill, Mr and Mrs G D Brooks, David and Jane Hill)*

PLOCKTON [NG8033]
☆ *Plockton Inn* IV52 8TW [Innes St; unconnected to Plockton Hotel]: Fresh substantial well cooked food at appealing prices inc good fish, congenial bustling atmosphere even in winter, friendly efficient service, real ales, good range of malt whiskies; lively separate bar for the younger element, some live traditional music; comfortable bedrooms *(Andrew Birkinshaw, Joan York)*

ROSEMARKIE [NH7357]
Plough IV10 8UF [High St]: Old-fashioned 17th-c pub with tasty food from wkdy lunchtime standards to interesting blackboard dishes, fresh local ingredients inc home-grown potatoes, three well kept scottish ales, good range of malt whiskies, log fire in small panelled locals' bar, cheerful helpful landlord, restaurant with linking lounge; small garden, open all day *(Chris Evans)*

ULLAPOOL [NH1293]
☆ *Ceilidh Place* IV26 2TY [West Argyle St]: Arty celtic café/bar with art gallery, bookshop and coffee shop, regular jazz, folk and classical music and other events, informal mix of furnishings, woodburner, wide choice of wholesome food from side servery, conservatory restaurant with some emphasis on fish; children welcome in eating areas, terrace tables, comfortable bedrooms, open all day *(R M Jones, Kevin Flack)*
Seaforth IV26 2UE [Quay St]: Roomy open-plan harbour-view bar with Hebridean and Isle of Skye ales, good range of malt whiskies, wide choice of appetising local seafood from end food counter, friendly chatty efficient staff, simple décor, upstairs evening restaurant; open till late *(Joan and Tony Walker)*

ROXBURGHSHIRE

ANCRUM [NT6224]
Cross Keys TD8 6XH [off A68 Jedburgh—Edinburgh]: Pleasant village green setting, locals' bar and three linked lounge/dining areas, friendly helpful staff, well kept Caledonian Deuchars IPA and 80/-, enjoyable sensibly priced food with some imaginative dishes and fresh local produce inc aberdeen angus steaks; nice back garden *(Jim Coghill)*

BONCHESTER BRIDGE [NT5812]
Horse & Hound TD9 8JN: Welcoming new owners, well kept changing ales such as Caledonian Deuchars IPA, good choice of reasonably priced food, low beams and log fire, evening restaurant; tables outside, bedrooms *(Pat and Stewart Gordon)*

KELSO [NT7234]
Cobbles TD5 7JH [Bowmont St]: Small ornate dining pub with modestly priced home-made food inc lots of fish, wall banquettes, some panelling, cheerful log-effect fire, end bar with decent wines and malt whiskies; keg beer; children welcome, disabled facilities *(Comus and Sarah Elliott)*

NEWCASTLETON [NY4887]
Grapes TD9 0QD [B6357 N of Canonbie; Douglas Sq]: Small hotel with central glass atrium for simple main bar, booth tables stretching back, friendly staff helpful in modifying menu for special diets etc, gabled and timbered upstairs restaurant extension, morning coffee and afternoon teas as well as usual food; keg beers; bedrooms *(Louise English)*

SELKIRKSHIRE

TUSHIELAW [NT3018]
☆ *Tushielaw Inn* TD7 5HT [Ettrick Valley, B709/B7009 Lockerbie—Selkirk]: Former coaching inn in lovely spot by River Ettrick, unpretentiously comfortable little bar attracting an interesting mix of customers, open fire, local prints and photographs, home-made bar food inc good aberdeen angus steaks, friendly family service, decent house wines, a good few malt whiskies, darts, cribbage, dominoes, shove-ha'penny and liar dice, dining room; children welcome, terrace tables, bedrooms, open all day Sat in summer, cl Sun night and in winter all day Mon *(Bob Ellis, LYM, Ian and Sue Wells)*

STIRLINGSHIRE

STIRLING [NS7993]
2 Baker Street FK8 1BJ [Baker St]: Former Hogshead, with well kept ales such as Caledonian Deuchars IPA and Greene King Abbot, simple pubby food, friendly staff and atmosphere, stripped wood and mock gaslamps; open all day *(Tim and Ann Newell)*

SUTHERLAND

BONAR BRIDGE [NH6191]
Bridge Hotel IV24 3EB [Dornoch Rd]: Wide choice of enjoyable cheap bar food from sandwiches up, friendly service, good coffee, coal fire, small dining room *(Sarah and Peter Gooderham)*
BRORA [NC9003]
Sutherland Arms KW9 6NX [Fountain Sq]: Appealing hotel under newish management, good value food, good real ale; sensibly priced bedrooms *(Chris Evans)*
HELMSDALE [ND0215]
Bannockburn KW8 6JY [Stafford St]: Simple welcoming pub, working hard to please with its limited range of bar lunches *(Sarah and Peter Gooderham)*
LAIRG [NC5224]
☆ *Crask Inn* IV27 4AB [A836 13 miles N towards Altnaharra]: Remote inn on single-track road through peaceful moorland, good simple food cooked by landlady from soup and toasted sandwiches to their own lamb (the friendly hard-working licensees keep sheep on this working croft), comfortably basic bar with large stove to dry the sheepdogs, Black Isle organic bottled beers, pleasant separate dining room, no piped

music; dogs welcome, three or four bedrooms (lights out when the generator goes off), and simple nearby bunkhouse *(Maurice and Gill McMahon, Les and Sandra Brown)*

TAYSIDE

KINROSS [NO1102]
Green KY13 8AS [The Muirs]: Large, comfortable and civilised recently renovated bar, in old coaching inn opp golf course, good specials, friendly staff; bedrooms *(Dave Cuthbert)*

WEST LOTHIAN

QUEENSFERRY [NT1378]
Hawes EH30 9TA [Newhalls Rd]: Featured famously in *Kidnapped*, in great spot for tourists with fine views of the Forth bridges (one rail bridge support in car park), recently refurbished, with enjoyable food all day till 10pm in roomy separate dining areas, friendly staff, wide range of wines by the glass, well kept ales such as Greene King Old Speckled Hen; children welcome, tables on back lawn with play area, good bedrooms, esp Duke of Argyll suite *(LYM, Adrian Johnson)*
Rail Bridge EH30 9TA [South Queensferry]: Pleasant newish building, varied food, great views across Forth *(Christine and Neil Townend)*

WIGTOWNSHIRE

BLADNOCH [NX4254]
Bladnoch Inn DG8 9AB: Bright and neatly laid out, with enjoyable pubby food from sandwiches up using quality ingredients, friendly Irish owners, obliging service, Theakstons, dining area with dog pictures; keg beer, piped radio may obtrude; children and dogs welcome, picturesque riverside setting across from Bladnoch Distillery (tours available), newly upgraded bedrooms *(Mr Pusill, Richard J Holloway)*
PORT LOGAN [NX0940]
☆ *Port Logan Inn* DG9 9NG [Laigh St]: Lovely sea-view spot in pretty fishing harbour, welcoming and enthusiastic newish management, one or two well kept ales such as Caledonian Deuchars IPA or Greene King Abbot, enjoyable food inc local fish and game, old local photographs and lots of electronic equiment; handy for Logan Botanic Garden *(Mark O'Sullivan)*
PORTPATRICK [NW9954]
Crown DG9 8SX [North Crescent]: Waterside hotel in delightful harbourside village, good atmosphere and warm fire in rambling old-fashioned bar with cosy nooks and crannies, several dozen malt whiskies, decent wine by the glass, pleasant staff, food from good crab sandwiches up, attractively decorated early 20th-c dining room opening through conservatory into sheltered back garden; TV, games machine, piped music; children and dogs welcome, tables out in front, open all day *(LYM, Chris Smith, Mrs Pat Crabb)*

SCOTTISH ISLANDS

ARRAN

BRODICK [NS0136]
Brodick Bar KA27 8BU [Alma Rd]: Simple modern bar tucked away off seafront, friendly attentive service, Caledonian Deuchars 70/- and IPA, quite a few malt whiskies, remarkably wide choice of enjoyable food in restaurant *(Ken Richards)*

CATACOL [NR9049]
Catacol Bay KA27 8HN: Unpretentious, in wonderful setting yards from the sea with bay window looking across to Kintyre, bright décor, decent home-made food, unusual beers inc local Arran; lots of notices such as warning to leave sticks and backpacks outside; tables outside, bedrooms – the ones at the front have the view *(Andrew Wallace, Sarah and Peter Gooderham, Kay and Alistair Butler)*

LAGG [NR9521]
Lagg Hotel KA27 8PQ: Good range of bar food in pleasant lounge with log fire, comfortably refurbished restaurant; picnic-sets in extensive and interesting well kept burnside gardens, 13 well equipped bedrooms, nearby beaches *(Sarah and Peter Gooderham)*

SANNOX [NS0145]
Sannox Bay KA27 8JD [aka Ingledene Hotel]: Neat bar popular with locals and visitors, good value generous food in conservatory and restaurant, pleasant staff; garden tables, seaview bedrooms, sandy beach *(Tina and David Woods-Taylor)*

BARRA

TANGASDALE [NL6599]
Isle of Barra Hotel HS9 5XW: Great spot on sweep of sandy beach, good local seafood in restaurant, comfortable sea-view lounge, friendly public bar; 30 good value bedrooms, good breakfast, cl winter exc New Year *(Dave Braisted)*

COLL

ARINAGOUR [NM2257]
Coll Hotel PA78 6SZ: Wonderful fresh seafood cooked by landlady, good not over-costly wine range, popular with yachtsmen; simple comfortable bedrooms, great views *(Pat and Stewart Gordon)*

COLONSAY

SCALASAIG [NR3893]
☆ *Isle of Colonsay Hotel* PA61 7YP: Haven for ramblers and birders, appealing and restrained up-to-date décor with log fires, pastel walls and polished painted boards, bar with sofas and board games, enjoyable food inc fresh seafood, game and venison specialities, bottle-conditioned ales and perhaps a summer cask ale, lots of malt whiskies, informal restaurant; children and dogs welcome, comfortable bedrooms *(anon)*

CUMBRAE

MILLPORT [NS1554]
Frasers KA28 0AS [Cardiff St]: Bargain food in bar and lounge with old paddle steamer pictures, Belhaven beer; tables in yard behind *(Dave Braisted)*

HARRIS

RODEL [NG0483]
☆ *Rodel Hotel* HS5 3TW [A859 at southern tip of South Harris (hotel itself may be unsigned)]: Comfortably updated, light and contemporary, with local art in two bars and dining room, enjoyable bar lunches; keg beer; four bedrooms and self-catering, beautiful setting in small harbour *(Stephen R Holman, Dave Braisted)*

TARBERT [NB1500]
☆ *Harris Hotel* HS3 3DL [Scott Rd]: Large hotel with small panelled bar, local Skye and Hebridean real ales, lots of malt whiskies, enjoyable bar lunches from good range of sandwiches through some interesting light dishes to steak, good choice of evening restaurant meals; comfortable bedrooms *(Bob and Angela Brooks, BB)*

ISLAY

BOWMORE [NR3159]
☆ *Harbour Inn* PA43 7JR [The Square]: Fine inn with traditional local bar, lovely harbour and sea views from comfortable dining lounge, good food inc local seafood and delicious puddings, good choice of wines and local malts inc attractively priced rare ones, warmly welcoming service; bedrooms *(Alan Cole, Kirstie Bruce)*

BRIDGEND [NR3362]
Bridgend Hotel PA44 7PJ: Country house hotel with comfortable brown-décor tartan-carpet bar, interesting prints and maps, open fire, generous bar food using good local seafood, lamb, beef and game, lots of malt whiskies inc all the Islay ones; bedrooms *(Richard J Holloway)*

PORT ASKAIG [NR4369]
Port Askaig PA46 7RD: Snug and interesting carpeted original bar with good range of malt whiskies, local bottled ales, popular bar food all day, neat bistro restaurant overlooking sea; attractive garden between ferry pier and lifeboat station, eight bedrooms, open all day *(Dave Braisted)*

PORT CHARLOTTE [NR2558]
☆ *Port Charlotte Hotel* PA48 7TU [Main St]: Roaring log or peat fire and lovely sea loch views in smallish traditional bar, bright and attractive with lots of wood, piano and charcoal prints, nicely furnished back lounge with books on the area, dozens of rare Islay

and other malts, real ales such as Adnams, Black Sheep and Islay, wide choice of bar food lunchtime and evening esp good local seafood, good welcoming service, local art and sailing ship prints in comfortable restaurant, good wines; folk nights; good bedrooms, pleasing Georgian village, sandy beach – a nice spot for families *(Alan Cole, Kirstie Bruce, Richard J Holloway)*
PORTNAHAVEN [NN1652]
An Tighe Seinnse PA47 7SJ [Queen St]: Good food from pizzas to fresh local seafood in small end-of-terrace harbourside pub tucked away in remote and attractive fishing village, cosy bar and room off, good choice of malt whiskies, local Islay ales, open fire *(David Hoult)*

JURA

CRAIGHOUSE [NR5266]
Jura Hotel PA60 7XU: Superb position next to the famous distillery, looking east over the Small Isles to the mainland, enjoyable fairly priced home-made bar food, agreeable owner, good restaurant; tables and seats in garden down to water's edge, bedrooms, most with sea view – the island is great for walkers, bird-watchers and photographers *(Dave Braisted, Richard J Holloway)*

LEWIS

CARLOWAY [NB1940]
Doune Braes HS2 9AA [Doune]: Handy for the Callanish standing stones, comfortable lounge bar and restaurant, small but interesting menu strong on fresh seafood, public bar with pool and darts; 15 bedrooms *(Dave Braisted)*

MULL

CRAIGNURE [NM7236]
Craignure Inn PA65 6AY: Small 18th-c stone-built inn overlooking Sound of Mull, friendly bar with a local Isle of Mull beer on tap, several dozen malt whiskies, limited range of decent pub food, cheerful staff; good-sized bedrooms, good breakfast, handy for Oban car ferry, open all day in summer *(Dave Braisted)*
DERVAIG [NM4251]
☆ *Bellachroy* PA75 6QW: Island's oldest inn, in sleepy village, with traditional basic bar and lounge used more by residents, fine atmosphere, landlady cooks good restaurant food inc local seafood and plenty of other fresh produce, reasonable prices, children's helpings, local ales and whiskies and wide wine choice; well behaved dogs welcome, six comfortable bedrooms *(Miss E Thorne)*
FIONNPHORT [NM3023]
Keel Row PA66 6BL [Keel Row]: Interesting place with wonderful seaside atmosphere, roaring fire, friendly helpful staff, good food using local fish etc in lunchtime restaurant

(evenings too, summer) with great view over Iona, keg beer but perhaps a Tobermory bottled beer as well as the whisky; children welcome *(Ian and Sue Wells)*
TOBERMORY [NM5055]
McGochans PA75 6NR [Ledaig]: Modernised harbourside bar next to Tobermory Distillery, modestly priced enjoyable food all day, quick cheerful service, perhaps a real ale from the new nearby brewery; popular with young people – pool, games machines, piped music or juke box, quiz night; picnic-sets under cocktail parasols out on terrace facing harbour *(John Tav)*

ORKNEY

BURRAY [ND4795]
Sands KW17 2SS: Simple stone building overlooking harbour, sea and South Ronaldsay, good old-fashioned bar, good value; seaview bedrooms *(PL)*
DOUNBY [HY2902]
Smithfield KW17 2HT: Friendly family-run hotel with good atmosphere in pleasant comfortable bar used by locals, converted barn with small balcony in the eaves, good value; children welcome, bedrooms, open all day *(PL)*
STROMNESS [HY2509]
Ferry Inn KW16 3AD [John St]: Very busy from breakfast time till 1am, enjoyable generous food from pubby things to restaurant dishes (best to book at wknds), perhaps local Highland Scapa Special ale, modest wine list, lively young crowd evenings; 12 bedrooms *(J K Parry, PL)*

SKYE

ARDVASAR [NG6303]
☆ *Ardvasar Hotel* IV45 8RS [A851 at S of island, nr Armadale pier]: Lovely sea and mountain views from comfortable white stone inn in peaceful very pretty spot, with friendly owner and staff, good home-made food inc local fish (children welcome in eating areas), pleasant staff, lots of malt whiskies, two or three well kept real ales, two bars and games room; TV, piped music; tables outside, bedrooms, good walks, open all day *(Walter and Susan Rinaldi-Butcher, LYM)*
DUNVEGAN [NG2547]
Dunvegan IV55 8WA [A850/A863]: Plenty of tables in airy bar, reasonably priced food from baguettes up inc good specials, good friendly service; limited beer range *(anon)*
ISLE ORNSAY [NG7012]
☆ *Eilean Iarmain* IV43 8QR [off A851 Broadford—Armadale]: Bar adjunct to smart hotel in beautiful location, with friendly willing staff inc students at the island's gaelic college, enjoyable straightforward bar food from same kitchen as charming sea-view restaurant, an Isle of Skye real ale, good choice of vatted (blended) malt

whiskies inc its own Te Bheag, open fire; piped gaelic music; children welcome, very comfortable bedrooms *(Joan and Tony Walker, LYM, Mike and Sue Loseby)*

SLIGACHAN [NG4930]

☆ *Sligachan Hotel* IV47 8SW [A87 Broadford—Portree, junction with A863]: Remote hotel with almost a monopoly on the Cuillins, huge modern pine-clad bar (children's play area, games room) separating original basic climbers' and walkers' bar from plusher more sedate hotel side; quickly served popular food all day from home-made cakes with tea or coffee through decent straightforward bar food to fresh local seafood, fine log or coal fire, efficient pleasant staff, their own Cuillin Pinnacle and Skye ales, scottish guest beers, dozens of malt whiskies on optic, good meals in hotel restaurant; piped highlands and islands music, very

lively some nights, with summer live music and big camp site opp; children welcome, tables outside, 22 good value bedrooms, open all day *(BB, Walter and Susan Rinaldi-Butcher)*

SOUTH UIST

ERISKAY [NF7811]

Am Politician HS8 5JL [Balla]: Modern bar (only bar on the island) interesting as virtual museum to the sinking of the *Politician* of *Whisky Galore* fame – the boat is still visible at low tide; good quickly served local seafood, bottled Hebridean ale, pool table one end and conservatory the other, original bottles of the salvaged whisky on show – worth more than £1,500 at auction these days; live music some nights, pleasant outside table area *(Dave Braisted)*

Wales

This year's two new entries are both pubs which we have enjoyed in the past, and which are again finding great favour with readers: the Ty Coch at Porth Dinllaen, chosen not for its beer (it doesn't have real ale) but above all for its idyllic position on a prime lonely beach; and the Royal Oak at Gladestry, a nicely unrarefied country inn popular with local farmers and Offa's Dyke walkers, where the most recent owners have set a very welcoming tone. The excellent Brunning & Price group of pubs continues to hit the winning formula for food, drinks, service and ambience, while each remains distinctly individual. Four of their pubs feature here: the Pen-y-Bryn looking down on Colwyn Bay (very inviting inside, and with great views over the bay), the Pant-yr-Ochain in Gresford (with a long list of drinks to enjoy, in a 16th-c building that has a light, stylish atmosphere), the Corn Mill in Llangollen (a stunning conversion of a watermill looking on to the town, river, canal and steam railway, which gains its Food Award this year), and the Glasfryn opposite the theatre in Mold. A good number of our other welsh pubs are in particularly inviting waterside locations – splendid places to while away a sunny afternoon. Standing out in that category are the Harbourmaster on the quay in Aberaeron, the Nags Head at Abercych (with a lovely riverside location, own-brew beer and gargantuan food helpings), the Penhelig Arms in Aberdovey (impressive particularly for accommodation and wines), the Sloop at Porthgain (well placed for the Pembrokeshire Coast Path, and the fresh fish is really enjoyable), and the marvellously traditional and simple Cresselly Arms on a tidal creek at Cresswell Quay. Other pubs that stand out as really special are the Olde Bulls Head in Beaumaris (also a pleasant space to stay; they're adding more rooms during 2008), the Bear in Crickhowell, the Griffin at Felinfach (a classy dining pub with good bedrooms), the newly revamped Queens Head near Llandudno Junction (much enjoyed for its food in particular), the Harp at Old Radnor (in a really glorious position on a hill looking far over the Marches, and the food has generated enthusiastic reports since its most recent owners took over), the Clytha Arms near Raglan (where the beer is very well kept), the Groes at Ty'n-y-groes (a friendly hotel in the heart of Snowdonia), and the Nags Head on the edge of Usk, where the Key family keep things marvellously traditional and chatty – one of the best all-rounders we know. Some pubs here owe much of their alluring atmosphere to rather special buildings or positions, including the thatched Blue Anchor at East Aberthaw, the Pen-y-Gwryd, a climbers' haunt in the wilds of Snowdonia above Llanberris, the stone and thatch 16th-c Bush at St Hilary, the enchantingly offbeat Tafarn Sinc at Rosebush (a corrugated shed in a memorably strange location near a defunct quarry) and the simple one-room Goose & Cuckoo up in the hills at Rhyd-y-Meirch. Architecturally one of the most memorable old pubs we feature is the Plough & Harrow at Monknash, in a terrifically evocative medieval monastic building, and with an impressive selection of real ales, as well as farm cider and perry. For a good meal in memorable surroundings, our overall choice as Wales Dining Pub of the Year is the Corn Mill in Llangollen. While pub food prices in Wales are pretty much in line with the UK average, drinks prices here tend to be very slightly lower. Brains is the main brewer, and as well as brewing their own beers brew Hancocks for Coors (the international firm which now owns the former Bass combine). Tomos Watkins and Rhymney ales are well worth looking out for – good beers, and we found them as the cheapest in a couple of our main entries. There are at least two dozen other small brewers which you may come across in Wales, such as Breconshire, Felinfoel, Plassey, Conwy, Evan Evans and Bullmastiff. We have listed the Lucky Dip entries at the end of the chapter under the various regions (rather than the newer administrative areas which have replaced them). We'd particularly pick out, in Clwyd, the West Arms in Llanarmon DC; in Dyfed, the Druidstone Hotel at Broad Haven, Dyffryn Arms at Cwm Gwaun, Georges in Haverfordwest, Castle in Little Haven, Golden Lion in Newport and Stackpole Inn; in Gwent, the Hardwick near Abergavenny and Priory Hotel at Llanthony; in Gwynedd, the Black Buoy in Caernarfon; in Mid Glamorgan, the Black Cock near Caerphilly and Prince of Wales at Kenfig; in Powys, the Star in Talybont-on-Usk; and in South Glamorgan, the Cayo Arms in Cardiff.

ABERAERON

SN4562   MAP 6

Harbourmaster 🍴 ☼ 🛏

Harbour Lane; SA46 0BA

Stylish, thriving waterside dining pub/hotel, interesting food (at a price), up-to-date bedrooms

---

A useful place to know about (even though some readers have found it not pubby enough in character), this has a prime location on the yacht-filled harbour, among a charming array of colourwashed buildings. Modern rustic in style, the wine bar has dark wood panelling, sofas, and chunky blocks of wood as low tables or stools on dark wood floors; piped music. In the restaurant, new light wood furniture looks stylishly modern on light wood floors against light and dark blue walls. Buckleys Best and a guest such as Tomas Watkin on handpump, and a good wine list, with a constantly changing selection sold by the glass. The owners are chatty and welcoming, and if you stay the breakfasts are good.

🍴 **Tasty bar meals served in here might include grilled mackerel, cardigan bay crab risotto, grilled crevettes in chilli butter and mixed tapas. In the restaurant there's a choice of good, fashionable food (not cheap).** *Starters/Snacks: £4.00 to £7.50. Main Courses: £10.50 to £12.50. Puddings: £5.50*

Free house ~ Licensees Glyn and Menna Heulyn ~ Real ale ~ Bar food (12-2, 6-9; not Mon lunchtime or Sun evening) ~ Restaurant ~ (01545) 570755 ~ Children welcome ~ Open 11-11; closed 24 Dec-early Jan; Mon lunchtime, Sun evening ~ Bedrooms: £60S/£110B

Recommended by Mr and Mrs P R Thomas, Blaise Vyner, Graham and Glenis Watkins, Dr A McCormick, Andy Sinden, Louise Harrington, Geoff and Angela Jaques, Mike and Mary Carter, Di and Mike Gillam, Patrick Darley

---

Real ale to us means beer which has matured naturally in its cask –
not pressurised or filtered.

ABERCYCH

SN2539   MAP 6

Nags Head 🍺
Off B4332 Cenarth—Boncath; SA37 0HJ

Enticing riverside position, good value own-brew beer and gargantuan quantities of bar food

Though it's nicely tucked away, this riverside inn does manage to attract a wide range of customers. One thing to try here is the much-enjoyed Old Emry's beer, made in their own brewery and named after one of the regulars; others might include Greene King Abbot, Old Speckled Hen and Wadworths XXX. The dimly lit beamed and flagstoned bar has a big fireplace, clocks showing the time around the world, stripped wood tables, a piano, photographs and postcards of locals, and hundreds of beer bottles displayed around the brick and stone walls – look out for the big stuffed rat. A plainer small room leads down to a couple of big dining areas, and there's another little room behind the bar; piped music and TV. Lit by fairy lights in the evening, the pub is tucked away in a little village; tables under cocktail parasols across the quiet road look over the water, and there are nicely arranged benches, and a children's play area. Service is pleasant and efficient. They sometimes have barbecues out here in summer.

🍽 **Served in huge helpings (so you might struggle to get through a three-course meal; one reader found portions excessive), the bar food might include sandwiches, cawl (beef stew), steak and Old Emrys ale pie, mixed grill, lamb steak marinated with rosemary and redcurrant, liver, bacon and onions with mash, and cottage pie with swede mash.** *Starters/Snacks: £2.50 to £6.50. Main Courses: £6.50 to £14.95. Puddings: £1.50 to £3.75*

Own brew ~ Licensee Samantha Jamieson ~ Real ale ~ Bar food (12-2, 6-9 (not Mon)) ~ Restaurant ~ (01239) 841200 ~ Children welcome but with restrictions ~ Dogs allowed in bar ~ Open 12-3, 6-12; 12-10.30 Sun; closed Mon
Recommended by John and Enid Morris, Colin Moore, Dr and Mrs A K Clarke

ABERDOVEY

SN6196   MAP 6

Penhelig Arms 🍽 ♟ 🛏
Opposite Penhelig railway station; LL35 0LT

Impressive wine list and a most enjoyable range of fish and other dishes; fine harbourside location, a nice place to stay

This lovely 18th-c hotel has nothing in the way of fruit machines or piped music, and the setting by the harbour and the Dyfi Estuary alone justifies a visit. The knowledgeable and enthusiastic licensee has accumulated an impressive selection of some 300 wines, with around 30 sold by the glass. Good log fires in the small original beamed bar make it especially cosy in winter, and there's nothing in the way of fruit machines or piped music. On handpump are Hancocks HB as well as two chosen from Adnams Broadside, Shepherd Neame Spitfire, Timothy Taylors and Wells & Youngs Special with perhaps a guest such as Brains Rev James or Greene King Abbott; two dozen malt whiskies, fruit and peppermint teas, and various coffees; dominoes. The bedrooms are comfortable (some have balconies overlooking the estuary) but the ones nearest the road can be noisy; breakfasts are varied and good.

🍽 **In addition to lunchtime sandwiches, the daily lunch and dinner menus (which they serve in the dining area of the bar and restaurant) could include soup, grilled goats cheese with roast peppers and chutney, a good selection of fish dishes such as seared fillet of organic shetland salmon or grilled cod with king prawns, chargrilled lamb's liver and bacon with black pudding and leek mash, and chargrilled fillet steak. It's worth booking, as they can get very busy (perhaps as a result of this, one reader found the standard of service felt somewhat short).** *Starters/Snacks: £3.50 to £7.95. Main Courses: £7.95 to £17.00. Puddings: £4.50*

Free house ~ Licensees Robert and Sally Hughes ~ Real ale ~ Bar food ~ Restaurant ~ (01654) 767215 ~ Children welcome ~ Dogs allowed in bar ~ Open 11-3(4 Sat), 6-11; 12-4, 6-11 Sun; closed 25-26 Dec ~ Bedrooms: £49S/£78S

Recommended by Mike and Mary Carter, C J Pratt, David Glynne-Jones, Ian and Jane Irving, Colin Moore,
C J Fletcher, Philip Hesketh, Di and Mike Gillam, Jacquie Jones, Gerry and Rosemary Dobson

ABERGORLECH
SN5833   MAP 6

Black Lion £
B4310 (a pretty road roughly NE of Carmarthen); SA32 7SN

Delightful old pub in a super rural position, with caring staff

We've had very favourable reports this year on this happy 17th-c coaching inn, especially about the staff who really care to make their customers welcome. It's placed in a tranquil spot in the wooded Cothi Valley; the picnic-sets, wooden seats and benches have lovely views, and the garden slopes down towards the River Cothi where there's a Roman triple-arched bridge. The plain but comfortably cosy stripped-stone bar is traditionally furnished with oak tables and chairs, and high-backed black settles facing each other across the flagstones by the gas-effect log fire. There are horsebrasses and copper pans on the black beams, old jugs on shelves, fresh flowers, and paintings by a local artist. The dining extension has french windows opening on to a landscaped enclosed garden. The one or two real ales are likely to come from Merthyr Tydfil's Rhymney Brewery, and are kept under a light blanket pressure on handpump; also welsh whisky, mulled wine in winter and lots of fruit juices. Sensibly placed darts and piped music. The pub is a good place to head for if you're visiting the nearby Dolaucothi Gold Mines at Pumsaint, or the plantations of Brechfa Forest, which has excellent and challenging trails for mountain bikers.

🍴 **Good value freshly cooked bar food (there may be a wait at busy times) includes soup, sandwiches, ploughman's, curry, sirloin steak, and vegetable and stilton crumble; on some evenings (Tues-Thurs) they prepare their own pizzas, and there are one- to three-course Sunday lunches and changing specials like mushroom stroganoff and steak and kidney pudding; children's meals.** *Starters/Snacks: £2.75 to £4.75. Main Courses: £5.50 to £10.95. Puddings: £3.50*

Free house ~ Licensees Michelle and Guy Richardson ~ Real ale ~ Bar food ~ Restaurant ~ (01558) 685271 ~ Well behaved children welcome ~ Dogs allowed in bar ~ Open 12-3, 7-11; 12-11(10 Sun) Sat; closed Mon exc bank hols
Recommended by David and Lin Short, Pete Yearsley, Richard Siebert

BEAUMARIS
SH6076   MAP 6

Olde Bulls Head 🍴 ♀ 🛏
Castle Street; LL58 8AP

Interesting and much-liked historic pub; spot on for food, accommodation and wines

Readers really enjoy the food and accommodation at this 15th-c inn, and the low-beamed bar is a genuinely pubby, rambling place, with plenty of interesting reminders of the town's past: a rare 17th-c brass water clock, a bloodthirsty crew of cutlasses and even an oak ducking stool tucked among the snug alcoves. There are also lots of copper and china jugs, comfortable low-seated settles, leather-cushioned window seats, a good log fire, and Bass, Hancocks and a guest on handpump. The brasserie wine list includes a dozen available by the glass; the restaurant list runs to 120 bottles. The entrance to the pretty courtyard is closed by what is listed in *The Guinness Book of Records* as the biggest simple-hinged door in Britain (11 feet wide and 13 feet high). Named after characters in Dickens's novels, the bedrooms are very well equipped; some are traditional, and others more up to date. The pub is converting an adjacent property into upmarket, contemporary-style accommodation, planned to be completed during 2008.

🍴 **Quite a contrast, the busy brasserie behind is lively and modern, with a menu that includes sandwiches, soup, fish chowder, lemon and olive chicken kebab, braised lamb shank, vine tomato risotto, rib-eye steak, and several puddings such as rhubarb and raspberry fool; small but decent children's menu. There is also a smart restaurant upstairs.** *Starters/Snacks: £3.20 to £5.80. Main Courses: £6.95 to £14.60. Puddings: £3.70 to £5.60*

Free house ~ Licensee David Robertson ~ Real ale ~ Bar food (12-2(3 Sun), 6-9; not 25, 26 Dec or evening 1 Jan) ~ Restaurant ~ (01248) 810329 ~ Children welcome in brasserie but no under-7s in loft restaurant ~ Open 11-11; 12-10.30 Sun ~ Bedrooms: £77B/£100B

Recommended by Donald Mills, Simon Cottrell, Dr A McCormick, Clive Watkin, Neil Whitehead, Victoria Anderson, John and Enid Morris, Dave Webster, Sue Holland, W W Burke, Revd D Glover, Phil and Jane Hodson, Mrs Jane Kingsbury

CAPEL CURIG
SH7257   MAP 6

Bryn Tyrch
A5 W of village; LL24 OEL

Perfectly placed for the mountains of Snowdonia, and interesting food (all day weekends) featuring tasty vegetarian dishes

This inn has a great setting, among the high mountains of Snowdonia, with some choice and challenging walking right on its doorstep: you can take in the terrific views from the large picture windows that run the length of one wall – looking across the road to picnic-sets on a floodlit patch of grass by a stream running down to a couple of lakes, and the peaks of the Carneddau, Tryfan and Glyders in close range. Comfortably relaxed, the bar has several easy chairs round low tables, some by a coal fire with magazines and outdoor equipment catalogues piled to one side, and a pool table in the plainer hikers' bar. Flowers IPA, Greene King Old Speckled Hen, Great Orme Best and Extravaganza, and a guest like Camerons Castle Eden on handpump, and quite a few malt whiskies, including some local ones; pool, chess, draughts, cards and billiards. There are tables on a steep little garden at the side. Bedrooms are simple but clean, and some have views; £10 cleaning charge for dogs. Some readers have found the décor rather tired.

🍴 **Wholesome food, with an emphasis on vegetarian and vegan dishes, is generously served to meet the healthy appetite of anyone participating in the local outdoor attractions and the changing menu could include soup, lunchtime sandwiches, smoked salmon salad, vegetable bake, vegetarian kebabs, beef and Guinness pie, lamb and leek sausages with mash, and tiger king prawns with garlic and ginger couscous.**
Starters/Snacks: £3.95 to £5.25. Main Courses: £8.95 to £16.00. Puddings: £3.95 to £5.25

Free house ~ Licensee Rita Davis ~ Real ale ~ Bar food (12-2, 6-9; 12-9 Sat, Sun) ~ (01690) 720223 ~ Children welcome ~ Dogs allowed in bedrooms ~ Open 12-11(10.30 Sun); may be closed Tues and Weds in winter ~ Bedrooms: £40(£45B)/£56(£65S)(£65B)

Recommended by Peter Craske, Andy Sinden, Louise Harrington, Anthony Smith

COLWYN BAY
SH8478   MAP 6

Pen-y-Bryn 🍷 🍴
B5113 Llanwrst Road, on S outskirts; when you see the pub turn off into Wentworth Avenue for its car park; LL29 6DD

Modern pub in great position overlooking the bay, reliable food all day, good range of drinks, obliging staff

It might be hard to tear yourself away from this idyllically placed, civilised single-storey pub, and though it looks like a suburban bungalow from outside it has a light and airy open-plan interior. It has terrific views over the bay and the Great Orme (it's worth booking a window table). Working around the three long sides of the bar counter, the mix of seating and well spaced tables, oriental rugs on pale stripped boards, shelves of books, welcoming coal fires, profusion of pictures, big pot plants, careful lighting and dark green school radiators are all typical of the pubs in this small chain. Besides Flowers Original and Thwaites, you'll find four changing guests such as Brains SA, Harviestoun Bitter and Twisted, Phoenix White Monk and Wychwood Hobgoblin on handpump. They also have well chosen good value wines including 20 by the glass, 70 malts and several irish whiskeys, proper coffee and freshly squeezed orange juice; faint piped music. Outside there are sturdy tables and chairs on a side terrace and a lower one, by a lawn with picnic-sets.

🍴 Served all day, the reliable and much liked food from a changing menu could typically include sandwiches, ploughman's, soup, smoked haddock and salmon fishcake, pan-fried pigeon breast with black pudding and red wine sauce, braised shoulder of lamb, steakburger, fish pie and sweet potato, chickpea and spinach curry, with puddings such as lemon tart with coulis or chocolate brownie; efficient service from friendly staff. *Starters/Snacks: £4.25 to £8.95. Main Courses: £8.95 to £19.95. Puddings: £3.95 to £4.95*

Brunning & Price ~ Licensees Graham Arathoon and Graham Price ~ Real ale ~ Bar food (12-9.30(9 Sun)) ~ (01492) 533360 ~ Children under 12 welcome till 7.30pm ~ Open 11.30-11; 12-10.30 Sun; closed 25-26 Dec and 1 Jan evenings

Recommended by KC, Dr Dale Archer, William Ruxton, Paul Boot, Joan York, Donald Mills, G Robinson

CRESSWELL QUAY

SN0506 MAP 6

Cresselly Arms

Village signposted from A4075; SA68 0TE

Marvellously simple alehouse, with benches outside overlooking a tidal creek

Nothing changes from one year to the next at this simple creeper-covered alehouse. It faces a creek of the Cresswell River, and if you time the tides right, you can arrive by boat, and seats outside make the most of the view. Often full of locals, the two simple and comfortably old-fashioned communicating rooms have a relaxed and jaunty air, as well as red and black floor tiles, built-in wall benches, kitchen chairs and plain tables, an open fire in one room, a working Aga in the other, and a high beam-and-plank ceiling hung with lots of pictorial china. A third red-carpeted room is more conventionally furnished, with red-cushioned mate's chairs around neat tables. Worthington BB and a winter guest beer are tapped straight from the cask into glass jugs by the landlord, whose presence is a key ingredient of the atmosphere. No children.

🍴 No food, except filled rolls on Saturday mornings.

Free house ~ Licensees Maurice and Janet Cole ~ Real ale ~ No credit cards ~ (01646) 651210 ~ Open 12-3, 5-11; 11-11 Sat; 12-3, 5(7 winter)-10.30 Sun

Recommended by the Didler, Pete Baker

CRICKHOWELL

SO2118 MAP 6

Bear ★

Brecon Road; A40; NP8 1BW

Civilised and interesting inn with splendid old-fashioned bar area warmed by a log fire, good food and bedrooms

Several readers enjoy coming back to this comfortable old coaching inn time and time again, and although one dining area has recently been given an overhaul the main bar area hasn't changed in years. Placed right in the heart of this delightful little town, the Bear manages to blend traditional charms with efficient service, and is a welcoming place to stay – and they're modernising some bedrooms in a country style, though they will retain the antiques in the older rooms. The comfortably decorated, heavily beamed lounge has fresh flowers on tables, lots of little plush-seated bentwood armchairs and handsome cushioned antique settles, and a window seat looking down on the market square. Up by the great roaring log fire, a big sofa and leather easy chairs are spread among rugs on the oak parquet floor. Other good antiques include a fine oak dresser filled with pewter and brass, a longcase clock, and interesting prints. Bass, Brains Rev James, Greene King Ruddles Best and a guest such as Cwmbran Jones and Evans on handpump, as well as 24 malt whiskies, vintage and late-bottled ports, unusual wines (with ten by the glass) and liqueurs; disabled lavatories.

Tipping is not normal for bar meals, and not usually expected.

🍴 Good, honest bar food could include items such as sandwiches, scallops with pesto mash, welsh rarebit, steaks, cod on spinach grilled with cheddar, roast rack of welsh lamb and grilled ham with mash and parsley sauce; they do a popular three-course Sunday lunch. You can eat in the garden in summer. *Starters/Snacks: £3.75 to £6.50. Main Courses: £6.95 to £15.95. Puddings: £4.50*

Free house ~ Licensee Judy Hindmarsh ~ Real ale ~ Bar food (12-2, 6-10; 12-2, 7-9.30 Sun) ~ Restaurant ~ (01873) 810408 ~ Children welcome except in main bar ~ Dogs allowed in bar and bedrooms ~ Open 11-3, 6-11; 12-3, 7-10.30 Sun ~ Bedrooms: £65S/£80S(£90B)

Recommended by Colin McKerrow, Mr and Mrs A J Hudson, Mrs Phoebe A Kemp, Di and Mike Gillam, Roger Smith, LM, David and Sheila Pearcey, Giles and Liz Ridout, R Halsey, Colin Moore, Donna and Roger, Mrs D W Privett, David Edwards, Dr A McCormick, Dr Phil Putwain, WW Burke, Bob and Angela Brooks, Barry and Anne, Mike and Mary Carter, Peter Titcomb, Blaise Vyner, R Michael Richards, Guy Vowles, Roy Hoing, Denys Gueroult

Nantyffin Cider Mill ♀
1½ miles NW, by junction A40/A479; NP8 1LP

Foody and discerning; in a converted barn with imaginative brasserie food and interesting drinks, and meat mostly from its own farm

In a pretty rural location, this civilised L-shaped pink-washed tiled stone dining pub faces an attractive stretch of the River Usk, on the other side of a fairly busy main road, with tables on the lawn making the most of the views. Although the food is very much the focus, there's a smartly traditional pubby atmosphere too. You can see the old cider press that gives the pub its name in the raftered barn that has been converted into the striking dining room; appropriately, they still serve farm cider. With warm grey stonework, the bar has fresh flowers, good solid comfortable tables and chairs and a woodburner in a fine broad fireplace. The counter at one end of the main open-plan area has Wells & Youngs Bitter and a guest such as Wye Valley Cwrw Dewi Sant on handpump, as well as thoughtfully chosen new world wines (a few by the glass or half bottle), Pimms and home-made lemonade in summer, organic farmhouse apple juice, and hot punch and mulled wine in winter. A ramp makes disabled access easy.

🍴 Largely featuring meat and poultry from the family farm a few miles away, the seasonally changing menu could include welsh coast cheese fritters, hand-rolled open ravioli, confit of welsh mountain lamb, supreme of sasso chicken wrapped in cured ham, pork sausages and mash, vegetarian risotto cake and fresh fish specials. *Starters/Snacks: £3.95 to £8.95. Main Courses: £7.50 to £16.95. Puddings: £4.95 to £6.95*

Free house ~ Licensees Glyn Bridgeman and Sean Gerrard ~ Real ale ~ Bar food (12-2.30, 6.30-9.30) ~ Restaurant ~ (01873) 810775 ~ Children welcome ~ Dogs allowed in bar ~ Open 12-3, 6-10; 12-3, 7-9.30 Sun; closed Mon exc bank hols, and Sun evening Sept-Mar

Recommended by Bernard Stradling, Tom and Ruth Rees

EAST ABERTHAW   ST0366   MAP 6

Blue Anchor
B4265; CF62 3DD

Ancient waterside pub, loaded with character and a popular place for a beer

The snug low-beamed little rooms of this atmospheric place date back over 600 years, and friendly staff serve Brains Bitter, Theakstons Old Peculier, Wadworths 6X and Wye Valley Hereford Pale Ale on handpump, alongside a changing guest from a brewer such as Rhymney Bitter. The building has massive stone walls and tiny doorways, and open fires everywhere, including one in an inglenook with antique oak seats built into its stripped stonework. Other seats and tables are worked into a series of chatty little alcoves, and the more open front bar still has an ancient lime-ash floor; fruit machine, darts, trivia machine and dominoes. Rustic seats shelter peacefully among tubs and troughs of flowers outside, with more stone tables on a newer terrace. From here a path leads to the shingly flats of the estuary. The pub can get very full in the evenings and on summer weekends, and it's used as a base by a couple of local motorbike clubs. More reports please.

🍴 As well as lunchtime baguettes and filled baked potatoes, bar food might include soup, thai-style fishcakes, beef and ale casserole, roast butternut squash, rump steak and specials such as seared fillet of black bream or calves liver. *Starters/Snacks: £2.75 to £4.95. Main Courses: £7.50 to £10.00. Puddings: £3.75*

Free house ~ Licensee Jeremy Coleman ~ Real ale ~ Bar food (12-2, 6-8; not Sat evening, not Sun) ~ Restaurant ~ (01446) 750329 ~ Children welcome ~ Dogs allowed in bar ~ Open 11-11; 12-10.30 Sun

Recommended by J R Ringrose, Norman and Sarah Keeping

FELINFACH   SO0933   MAP 6

Griffin 🍽 🍷 🛏
A470 NE of Brecon; LD3 0UB

A classy dining pub for enjoying good, unpretentious cooking featuring lots of home-grown vegetables; upbeat rustic décor, nice bedrooms

---

Readers thoroughly enjoy the experience of eating and staying in this stylish, relaxed dining pub. The back bar is quite pubby in an up-to-date way, with three leather sofas around a low table on pitted quarry tiles, by a high slate hearth with a log fire, and behind them mixed stripped seats around scrubbed kitchen tables on bare boards, and a bright blue-and-ochre colour scheme. It has a few modern prints, and some nice photoprints of a livestock market by Victoria Upton. The acoustics are pretty lively, with so much bare flooring and uncurtained windows. The two smallish front dining rooms, linking through to the back bar, are attractive: on the left, mixed dining chairs around mainly stripped tables on flagstones, and white-painted rough stone walls, with a cream-coloured Aga in a big stripped-stone embrasure; on the right, similar furniture on bare boards, with big modern prints on terracotta walls, and good dark curtains. There may be piped radio in the bar. They have a good choice of wines including 11 by the glass, welsh spirits, cocktails and Breconshire Golden Valley and Winter Beacons, and Tomos Watkins OSB on handpump; local farm cider and perry, and local apple and pear juices. Wheelchair access is good, and there are tables outside. Bedrooms are comfortable and tastefully decorated, and the hearty breakfasts nicely informal: you make your own toast on the Aga and help yourself to home-made marmalade and jam. The licensees also own the Gurnards Head in Zennor, Cornwall.

🍴 Using organic produce from the pub's own kitchen garden (from which the surplus is often for sale), consistently good food from the lunch and evening menus might include roasted butternut squash soup, home-cured pigeon breast, seared tuna on crushed new potatoes and aubergine caviar, creamed wild mushroom risotto, sirloin steak with green peppercorn sauce, and venison stew and mash. *Starters/Snacks: £4.90 to £9.90. Main Courses: £7.90 to £17.90. Puddings: £5.00 to £8.50*

Free house ~ Licensees Charles and Edmund Inkin ~ Real ale ~ Bar food (12.30-2.30, 6.30-9.30(9 Sun); not Mon lunch (exc bank hols)) ~ Restaurant ~ (01874) 620111 ~ Children welcome ~ Dogs allowed in bar and bedrooms ~ Open 11-11 ~ Bedrooms: £67.50B/£97.50B

Recommended by K H Frostick, Euryn Jones, J P Humphery, Mrs Philippa Wilson, John and Enid Morris, Rodney and Norma Stubington

GLADESTRY   SO2355   MAP 6

Royal Oak 🍺
B4594 W of Kington; HR5 3NR

A thoroughly likeable, welcoming village local on the Offa's Dyke Path, enjoyable food and drink

---

A mixture of locals and walkers frequent this cheery village pub, and you might find hikers tackling the Offa's Dyke Path, members of the Gladestry football team and one or two farmers all enjoying a drink here. Warmed by an open fire, the simple bar has beams, stripped stone and flagstones; there's also a cosy turkey-carpeted lounge; pool room, darts, cribbage, board games and piped music. Chatty groups gather around the bar, where bar staff draw Brains Rev James and Hancocks HB, plus perhaps a guest ale such as Wye Valley Butty Bach from handpump, as well as local cider and apple juice; darts, pool, cribbage, dominoes, video game, juke box, quoits, discreet piped music.

🍴 Besides ploughman's, sandwiches and baguettes, the nice bar food includes steak and stout pie, cawl (a welsh beef stew), sirloin steak and three-bean chilli, with specials like poached trout or pork tenderloin with mustard mash and herefordshire cider sauce; puddings might include whinberry (bilberry) tart, with the fruit painstakingly picked from the nearby moors. *Starters/Snacks: £2.60 to £6.45. Main Courses: £4.50 to £12.50. Puddings: £3.35 to £3.95*

Free house ~ Licensee Mrs Amanda Evans ~ Real ale ~ Bar food (12-2, 7-9; Sun 12-3) ~ (01544) 370669 ~ Children welcome ~ Dogs allowed in bar ~ Occasional live music ~ Open 12-3, 7-11; 12-11 Sat; 12-3, 7-11 Sun; closed Mon exc bank hols ~ Bedrooms: £35S/£55S

Recommended by T B Noyes, Peter Edwards, MLR, Duncan Cameron

GRESFORD   SJ3453   MAP 6

Pant-yr-Ochain 🍴 ♀ 🍺

Off A483 on N edge of Wrexham: at roundabout take A5156 (A534) towards Nantwich, then first left towards the Flash; LL12 8TY

Thoughtfully run, gently refined dining pub with rooms, good food all day, very wide range of drinks, pretty lakeside garden

The licensees at this handsome 16th-c country house owned by the excellent Brunning & Price group pay plenty of attention to detail. It has been thoughtfully refurbished inside: the light and airy rooms are stylishly decorated, with a wide range of interesting prints and bric-a-brac on walls and on shelves, and a good mix of individually chosen country furnishings, including comfortable seats for relaxing as well as more upright ones for eating, and there's a recently rebuilt conservatory as well as a good open fire; one area is set out as a library, with floor to ceiling bookshelves. Six real ales on handpump feature Flowers Original, Timothy Taylors Landlord and Thwaites Original alongside guests such as Phoenix Arizona, Roosters Yankee and Weetwood Old Dog; they have a good range of decent wines (strong on up-front new world ones), with 21 by the glass, and around 110 malt whiskies. Disabled access is good; piped music, board games and dominoes.

🍴 Good food, from a well balanced daily changing menu, might typically include sandwiches, curried parsnip soup, roast garlic and mushroom risotto, braised lamb shank with redcurrant and rosemary gravy, duck confit leg, oriental vegetable stir fry, or smoked haddock and salmon fishcakes, with puddings like apple tart or chocolate brownie. *Starters/Snacks: £4.25 to £8.50. Main Courses: £8.95 to £15.95. Puddings: £4.95 to £6.50*

Brunning & Price ~ Licensee Lindsey Douglas ~ Real ale ~ Bar food (12-9.30(9 Sun)) ~ No credit cards ~ (01978) 853525 ~ Children welcome away from bar till 6pm ~ Open 12-11(10.30 Sun); closed 25, 26 Dec

Recommended by Ian Phillips, Bruce and Sharon Eden, L and D Webster, David Glynne-Jones, Dr R A Smye, Clive Watkin, R T and J C Moggridge, Paul Boot, David Johnson

HAY-ON-WYE   SO2342   MAP 6

Kilverts 🛏

Bullring; HR3 5AG

Civilised and enjoyable bar with decent food and drink; a comfortable place to stay

With a new owner this year, this pleasantly relaxed hotel makes a civilised stopping-off point and stays open all day. You can sit out at tables in a small front flagstoned courtyard (with outdoor heaters and shelters) or while away the hours by the fountain in a pretty terraced back garden. Calm and understated, the airy high-beamed bar has some stripped stone walls, *Vanity Fair* caricatures, a couple of standing timbers, candles on well spaced mixed old and new tables, and a pleasant variety of seating. They've an extensive wine list with about a dozen by the glass, as well as Brains Rev James and Wye Valley Butty Bach and Wye Valley on handpump, a decent choice of wines by the glass, several malt whiskies, and good coffees; piped music. There's a £5.50 cleaning charge for dogs in the comfortable bedrooms. More reports on the new regime please.

🍴 Lunchtime snacks and bar food include soup, sandwiches, filo parcel with roasted aubergine, courgettes and mozzarella, chargrilled rib-eye steak, salmon and crab fishcakes with tomato and herb salsa, and lemon chicken coriander and sesame seed salad. *Starters/Snacks: £3.90 to £6.50. Main Courses: £8.00 to £15.00. Puddings: £4.50*

Free house ~ Licensee Robert Davies ~ Real ale ~ Bar food (12-2, 6.15(6.30 Fri, Sat)-9.30) ~ Restaurant ~ (01497) 821042 ~ Children welcome ~ Dogs welcome ~ Open 10am-11pm ~ Bedrooms: £55B/£80B

Recommended by Ian Phillips, Mrs Philippa Wilson, Sue Demont, Tim Barrow, Bob and Angela Brooks, Andy and Jill Kassube, Mike and Mary Carter, Alun Howells, Jeremy Whitehorn, MMO, Peter Craske

Old Black Lion 🍴 🍺 🛏

Lion Street; HR3 5AD

Low-beamed bar with pubby atmosphere, nicely unchanged in feel; good food and drink, pleasantly old-fashioned bedrooms

Readers like the food and drink at this reassuringly unchanging hotel, which keeps things ticking over smoothly even when it's busy. Dating back in part to the 13th c, it's right in the heart of town, and has a comfortable low-beamed bar with crimson and yellow walls, nice old pine tables, and an original fireplace. As well as Old Black Lion (which is Wye Valley Butty Bach but with the pub's own label) on handpump, they have Brains Rev James and good value wines; service is polite and briskly efficient. There are tables out behind on a sheltered terrace. Comfortably creaky bedrooms make this an atmospheric place to stay.

🍴 You can eat from either the bar or restaurant menu throughout, with a typical choice including soup, lunchtime snacks and sandwiches, fresh atlantic prawn salad, moroccan lamb, steak and kidney pie, roasted monkfish with rosemary and butter cream sauce and wrapped in bacon, beef wellington, and mushroom and spinach tagliatelle. *Starters/Snacks: £4.95 to £6.55. Main Courses: £10.65 to £17.95. Puddings: £4.65*

Free house ~ Licensee Mrs Leighton ~ Real ale ~ Bar food (12-2.30, 6.30-9.30) ~ Restaurant ~ (01497) 820841 ~ Children over 5 welcome if dining ~ Open 11-11; 12-10.30 Sun; closed 24-26 Dec ~ Bedrooms: £42.50B/£85B

Recommended by Richard Marjoram, Mrs Phoebe A Kemp, Richard, David and Jean Hall, Ian Phillips, Jeremy Whitehorn, Mrs Philippa Wilson, Nick and Meriel Cox, Andy and Jill Kassube, DFL, Sue Demont, Tim Barrow

LLANARMON DYFFRYN CEIRIOG   SJ1532   MAP 6

Hand 🛏

On B4500 from Chirk; LL20 7LD

Comfortable rural hotel in a remote valley; cosy low-beamed bar area, good bedrooms

A peaceful place to stay, this former farmhouse stands at the head of the unspoilt Ceiriog Valley, beneath the Berwyn Hills, and if you want to sit outside there are tables out on a crazy-paved front terrace, with more in the garden, which has flowerbeds around another sheltered terrace. The black-beamed carpeted bar on the left of the broad-flagstoned entrance hall has a good log fire in its inglenook fireplace, a mixture of chairs and settles, and old prints on its cream walls, with bar stools along the modern bar counter, which has Weetwood Best and sometimes a guest such as Weetwood Eastgate on handpump from the modern bar counter, several malt whiskies, and reasonably priced wines by the glass; happy and welcoming staff help towards the warm atmosphere. Round the corner is the largely stripped stone dining room, with a woodburning stove and carpeted floor; TV, darts, pool and dominoes. If you are staying, they do a good country breakfast, and the residents' lounge on the right is comfortable and attractive. Pistyll Rhaeadr, the highest waterfall in Wales, is not far away, and this is fine hill-walking country. More reports please.

🍴 Besides lunchtime sandwiches and ploughman's, items from a seasonally changing menu might include braised welsh lamb shank with lemon and herb crust, sausages and mash, free-range pork cutlets, sirloin steak, a vegetarian dish such as spiced couscous with butternut squash, and grilled trout from a local trout farm in the valley. *Starters/Snacks: £4.50 to £5.00. Main Courses: £8.00 to £15.00. Puddings: £4.50 to £5.00*

Free house ~ Licensees Gaynor and Martin de Luchi ~ Bar food (12-2.15(12.30-2.45 Sun), 6-8.45) ~ Restaurant ~ (01691) 600666 ~ Children welcome away from bar ~ Dogs allowed in bar and bedrooms ~ Open 11(12 Sun)-11(12.30 Sat) ~ Bedrooms: £50B/£80B

Recommended by Patrick Renouf, Mr and Mrs J Jennings

LLANBERIS

SH6655 MAP 6

Pen-y-Gwryd £ 🛏

Nant Gwynant; at junction of A498 and A4086, ie across mountains from Llanberis – OS Sheet 115 map reference 660558; LL55 4NT

In the hands of the same family for decades, an illustrious favourite with the mountain fraternity

'What an experience, staying in this unique time warp – basic but fabulous,' remarked one reader, who 'just felt a bit of a fraud, not having ascended Snowdon!' Right at the foot of some of the highest mountains of Snowdonia National Park, this jovial family-run place is a long-standing haunt of walkers and mountaineers. The team that first climbed Everest in 1953 used it as a training base, leaving their fading signatures scrawled on the ceiling. One snug little room in the homely slate-floored log cabin bar has built-in wall benches and sturdy country chairs to let you gaze at the surrounding mountain landscapes – like precipitous Moel Siabod beyond the lake opposite. A smaller room has a worthy collection of illustrious boots from famous climbs, and a cosy panelled smoke room has more fascinating climbing mementoes and equipment; darts, pool, board games and bar billiards. There's a sociable atmosphere, and alongside Bass, they've home-made lemonade in summer, mulled wine in winter, and sherry from their own solera in Puerto Santa Maria. Staying here can be quite an experience: a gong at 7.30pm signals the prompt start of service in the evening restaurant, but they don't hang around – if you're late, you'll miss it, and there's no evening bar food. The excellent, traditional breakfast is served at 8.50am; they're not generally flexible with this; comfortable but basic bedrooms, dogs £2 a night. The inn has its own chapel (built for the millennium and dedicated by the Archbishop of Wales), sauna and outdoor natural pool.

🍴 The short choice of simple, good-value home-made lunchtime bar food (you order it through a hatch) might include soup, chicken liver pâté, fried smoked chicken and mushrooms in creamy mustard sauce, beef lasagne or four welsh cheese, cherry tomato and red onion quiche; puddings such as chocolate pudding or apple and blackberry pie. *Starters/Snacks: £3.30 to £5.50. Main Courses: £5.95 to £6.95. Puddings: £2.95*

Free house ~ Licensee Jane Pullee ~ Real ale ~ Bar food (lunchtime only) ~ Restaurant (evening) ~ (01286) 870211 ~ Children welcome ~ Dogs allowed in bar ~ Open 11-11; closed all Nov-Dec, and Mon-Thurs Jan-Feb ~ Bedrooms: £38/£76(£90B)

Recommended by Edna Jones, Andrea Rampley, John and Enid Morris, John and Joan Nash, Donald Mills

LLANDDAROG

SN5016 MAP 6

White Hart 🍺

Just off A48 E of Carmarthen, via B4310; aka Yr Hydd Gwyn; SA32 8NT

Popular thatched pub full of interest and antiques, unusual own-brew beers

Well over 600 years old, this thatched pub simply oozes historic character, and one reader records drinking here some 60 years back and seemingly not much has changed. The rooms are still packed with fascinating details and sundry bits and pieces – 17th-c welsh oak carving, a tall grandfather clock, stained glass, a collection of hats and riding boots, china, brass and copper on walls and dark beams, antique prints and even a suit of armour. The heavily carved fireside settles by the huge crackling log fire are the best place to sit. But the main attraction today is the range of beers they make using water from their own 300-foot borehole. Named after the family in charge, the small Coles brewery produces ales such as Cwrw Blasus, Golden, Llanddarog, as well as a barley stout, and a lager, and there are usually four available on handpump. There are steps down to the high-raftered dining room, also interestingly furnished. Two small niggles: the 25p charge for a pint of tap water (unless you're eating) and one reader found the service left a little to be desired. There are picnic-sets out on a terrace and a children's play area; they can put a ramp in place for disabled access. Look out for Zac the macaw.

🍴 Generous helpings of tasty bar food from the servery include sandwiches, baked potatoes, ploughman's, curries, a range of pies, pizzas, steaks, battered cod, cheese and broccoli bake, with specials such as duck breast in orange and cranberry sauce, lamb shank and whole bass. *Starters/Snacks: £4.00 to £5.95. Main Courses: £6.00 to £19.95. Puddings: £3.95 to £5.50*

Own brew ~ Licensees Marcus and Cain Coles ~ Real ale ~ Bar food (11.30-2, 6.30-10; 12-2, 7-9.30 Sun) ~ (01267) 275395 ~ Children welcome ~ Open 11.30-3, 6.30-11; 12-3, 7-10.30 Sun; closed 25, 26 Dec

Recommended by Peter Hacker, Richard and Judy Winn, Norma and Noel Thomas, Mike Pugh, R J Davies, MDN, Tom Evans, MLR, Dr and Mrs A K Clarke

LLANDUDNO JUNCTION   SH8180 MAP 6

Queens Head

Glanwydden; heading towards Llandudno on B5115 from Colwyn Bay, turn left into Llanrhos Road at roundabout as you enter the Penrhyn Bay speed limit; Glanwydden is signposted as the first left turn off this; LL31 9JP

Classy food (all day Sunday) prepared with considerable care in comfortably modern dining pub; some interesting drinks too

Strong reports from readers indicate that this modest-looking whitewashed dining pub is going from strength to strength. There's been a major refurbishment since the last edition of the *Guide* – both inside and out, featuring a new outdoor seating area, available for smokers. Despite the emphasis on eating, locals do pop in for a drink, and you'll find Adnams Bitter and guests like Greate Orme Ormes Best and Weetwood Old Dog on handpump, as well as decent wines (including some unusual ones and 15 by the glass), 20 malt whiskies and good coffee. The spaciously comfortable modern lounge bar – partly divided by a white wall of broad arches – has brown plush wall banquettes and windsor chairs around neat black tables, and there's a little public bar; unobtrusive piped music. The village location is attractive and handy for northern Snowdonia; you can rent the pretty stone cottage (which sleeps two) across the road.

🍴 With an emphasis on fresh produce, the well presented and efficiently served dishes could include soup, open sandwiches, their own burgers topped with melted cheese and sticky onions, hot foie gras with black pudding, steak, mushroom and ale pie, half a crispy roast duck with soured cherry sauce, fish dishes such as steamed fillet of bass or salmon, very good conwy mussels and various steaks; they also have a daily specials board and do Sunday roasts. *Starters/Snacks: £4.10 to £6.95. Main Courses: £8.50 to £17.95. Puddings: £4.35*

Free house ~ Licensees Robert and Sally Cureton ~ Real ale ~ Bar food (12-2, 6-9; 12-9 Sun) ~ Restaurant ~ (01492) 546570 ~ Children over 7 in restaurant ~ Open 11.30-3, 6-11; 11.30-10.30 Sun

Recommended by KC, Dodie and Cliff Rutherford, Revd D Glover, Donald Mills, GLD, Mike and Mary Carter, Dave Webster, Sue Holland, Matt Anderson

---

Post Office address codings confusingly give the impression that some pubs are in Gwent or Powys, Wales when they're really in Gloucestershire or Shropshire (which is where we list them).

LLANELIAN-YN-RHOS   SH8676   MAP 6

White Lion

Signed off A5830 (shown as B5383 on some maps) and B5381, S of Colwyn Bay; LL29 8YA

Pretty pub with friendly service, generous food, pleasantly traditional bar and roomy dining area

In pleasant rolling pastures above Colwyn Bay, this picturesque and efficiently run rural pub is well worth seeking out. It has two distinct parts, each with its own personality, linked by a broad flight of steps. Up at the top is a neat and very spacious dining area, while down at the other end is a traditional old bar, with antique high-backed settles angling snugly around a big fireplace, and flagstones by the counter where they serve Marstons Burton and Pedigree and a guest such as Smiles Heritage; on the left, another dining area has jugs hanging from the beams, and teapots above the window. Prompt service from helpful staff, good wine list and lots of malt whiskies; dominoes, cards and piped music. Outside, an attractive courtyard between the pub and the church has sheltered tables (it's also used for parking).

Ⅲ **A wide choice of good, generously served food includes sandwiches, ciabattas and hot baguettes, soup, black pudding and smoked bacon salad with honey and mustard dressing, fresh mussels, traditional roasts and roasted mediterranean vegetables on a garlic croûton topped with goats cheese, together with specials such as steak and kidney pie, roast welsh lamb shoulder or grilled salmon fillet with honey and wholegrain mustard dressing;** **they also do a children's menu.** *Starters/Snacks: £3.50 to £5.95. Main Courses: £6.95 to £13.50. Puddings: £2.50 to £3.95*

Free house ~ Licensee Simon Cole ~ Real ale ~ Bar food (12-2, 6-9) ~ Restaurant ~ (01492) 515807 ~ Children welcome ~ Live jazz every Tues evening, bluegrass Weds ~ Open 11.30-3, 6-11(11.30 Sat); 12-4, 6-10.30 Sun; closed Mon except bank hols

Recommended by GLD, Mr and Mrs B Hobden, Michael and Jenny Back, Donald Mills

LLANFERRES   SJ1860   MAP 6

Druid

A494 Mold—Ruthin; CH7 5SN

17th-c inn with beams, antique settles and a log fire in the bar; wonderful views

The scenic setting in the Alyn Valley makes this former farmhouse an ideal place to come after a walk in the Clwydian Hills: from here it's only a short drive up to the Offa's Dyke Path which makes its way to the summit of Moel Famau. You can enjoy the views from tables outside at the front and from the broad bay window in the civilised, smallish plush lounge. You can also see the hills from the bigger beamed and characterful back bar, with its two handsome antique oak settles as well as a pleasant mix of more modern furnishings. There's a quarry-tiled area by the log fire, and a three-legged cat, Chu. Marstons Burton and a guest from breweries such as Brains or Jennings are on handpump, and the pub stocks more than 30 malt whiskies. A games room has darts and pool, along with board games; piped music. More reports please.

Ⅲ **A wide range of bar food might feature soup, filled baps, steak and ale pie, swordfish with garlic butter, shoulder of welsh lamb, mixed vegetables in a creamy chilli sauce, and a few daily specials including fresh fish.** *Starters/Snacks: £3.55 to £4.95. Main Courses: £7.95 to £15.95. Puddings: £3.95 to £4.95*

Union Pub Company ~ Lease James Dolan ~ Real ale ~ Bar food (12-3, 6-9; 12-9.30 Sat; 12-9 Sun) ~ (01352) 810225 ~ Children welcome ~ Dogs allowed in bar and bedrooms ~ Open 12-3, 5.30-12; 12-12 Sat; 12-11 Sun ~ Bedrooms: £45S/£65S

Recommended by KC, Gareth Mo Owen

LLANFRYNACH

S00725 MAP 6

White Swan ♀

Village signposted from B4558, off A40 E of Brecon – take second turn to village, which is also signed to pub; LD3 7BZ

Much revamped, cosily mellow country dining pub with a pretty terrace

This substantially refurbished coaching inn, very usefully located in a village in the Brecon Beacons National Park, puts much emphasis on dining and wines. The original part of the beamed bar has stripped stone and flagstones, with sturdy oak tables and nice carver chairs in a polished country-kitchen style, a woodburning stove, and leather sofas and armchairs in groups around low tables; it opens into an apricot-walled high-ceilinged extension, light and airy, with bare boards and different sets of chairs around each table. Up to three ales on handpump feature Brains Rev James and SA, and Hancocks HB; good wines and coffees; piped music. The charming secluded back terrace has stone and wood tables with a good choice of sun or shade, and is attractively divided into sections by low plantings and climbing shrubs, with views out over peaceful paddocks. The pub is well placed for hefty hikes up the main Brecon Beacons summits, or for undemanding saunters along the towpath of the Monmouthshire and Brecon Canal. More reports please.

🍴 **The good food is very much the centre of attention, with at lunchtimes a short choice of items like braised shank of welsh mountain lamb, lasagne or chicken curry; evening food might include starters like smoked salmon and crab risotto or terrine of ham hock, and main courses like rib-eye steak or roast cherry tomato, balsamic onion and wild mushroom tart.** *Starters/Snacks: £4.25 to £5.95. Main Courses: £9.95 to £16.95. Puddings: £4.95 to £5.95*

Free house ~ Licensee Richard Griffiths ~ Real ale ~ Bar food (12-2(2.30 Sun), 7-9(8.30 Sun)) ~ Restaurant ~ (01874) 665276 ~ Children welcome ~ Open 12-3, 6.30-11: 12-11.30 Sat, Sun; closed Mon

Recommended by Norman and Sarah Keeping, Mr and Mrs R B Berry

LLANGOLLEN

SJ2142 MAP 6

Corn Mill 🍴 ♀ 🍺

Dee Lane, very narrow lane off Castle Street (A539) just S of bridge; nearby parking can be tricky, may be best to use public park on Parade Street/East Street and walk; LL20 8PN

WALES DINING PUB OF THE YEAR

A strong all-rounder, with personable young staff, super food all day, good beers, and a fascinating riverside building

Readers continue to heap praise on every aspect of this supremely well run converted watermill, which is part of the excellent Brunning & Price group. The position is really special, jutting over the River Dee which rushes over rocks below, and you look across the river to the steam trains puffing away at the nearby station and maybe a horse-drawn barge on the Llangollen Canal. An area with decking and teak tables and chairs is perfect for taking in the view. Quite a bit of the mill machinery remains – most obviously the great waterwheel, still turning – but the place has been interestingly refitted with pale pine flooring on stout beams, a striking open stairway with gleaming timber and tensioned steel rails, and mainly stripped stone walls. A lively bustling chatty feel greets you, with quick service from plenty of pleasant young staff, good-sized dining tables, big rugs, nicely chosen pictures (many to do with water) and lots of pot plants. One of the two serving bars, away from the water, has a much more local feel, with pews on dark slate flagstones, daily papers, and regulars on the bar stools. Five changing beers like Boddingtons, Caledonian Deuchars IPA, Facers DHB, Oakham JHB and Woodlands Midnight Stout on handpump, around 50 malt whiskies and a decent wine choice that includes 17 by the glass. The pub can get busy, so it might be worth booking if you're planning to eat. Note that vehicle access is difficult.

🍴 **Good food – served all day – from a daily changing menu could include sandwiches, ploughman's, soup, smoked trout potato cake with poached egg and hollandaise sauce, roast welsh beef, salmon fillet in pastry with prawns, white wine and cream sauce, sausage with cheese mash,** *Starters/Snacks: £4.25 to £5.95. Main Courses: £8.25 to £13.50. Puddings: £3.95 to £4.95*

Brunning & Price ~ Licensee Andrew Barker ~ Real ale ~ Bar food (12-9.30(9 Sun)) ~ (01978) 869555 ~ Children in eating areas till 7pm ~ Open 12-11(10.30 Sun)

Recommended by J R Ringrose, Pete Yearsley, Bruce and Sharon Eden, Mike and Mary Carter, Clive Watkin, Brian Brooks, Richard and Karen Holt, Dr K P Tucker, Gwyn and Anne Wake, Phil and Jane Hodson, Malcolm Pellatt, Kevin Jeavons, Alison Turner, Gerry and Rosemary Dobson, A Darroch Harkness

MOLD
SJ2465   MAP 6

Glasfryn 🍴 ♈ 🍺

N of the centre on Raikes Lane (parallel to the A5119), just past the well signposted Theatre Clwyd; CH7 6LR

Open-plan bistro-style pub with inventive, upmarket food available all day, nice décor, wide drinks choice

Although it's unassuming from outside, this is a really buzzing place run with considerable verve by enthusiastic and friendly staff. The great range of drinks and attractive layout are part of its appeal. Open-plan rooms have both spaciousness and nice quiet corners, with an informal and attractive mix of country furnishings, and interesting decorations. Besides a good variety of around a dozen wines by the glass and around 100 whiskies, they've eight beers on handpump, with Bryn Cyf (brewed locally), Caledonian Deuchars IPA, Flowers Original, Thwaites Original and Timothy Taylors Landlord, alongside swiftly changing guests like Greene King Abbot and Shepherd Neame Bishops Finger. Outside, sturdy timber tables on a big terrace give superb views to the Clwydian Hills – idyllic on a warm summer's evening. Theatr Clwyd is just across the road.

🍴 **From a daily changing menu, the full choice of good, well prepared food (not cheap) is available all day and might include items like sandwiches, cauliflower and brie soup, slow-roasted duck leg with cucumber and orange salad, steakburger, rump steak with blue cheese mayonnaise, chicken and avocado salad with lemon and watercress dressing, and gammon, cider, apple and potato pie; puddings such as chocolate brownie or summer fruit pudding.** *Starters/Snacks: £4.25 to £6.25. Main Courses: £8.95 to £14.95. Puddings: £4.95 to £6.25*

Brunning & Price ~ Licensee James Meakin ~ Real ale ~ Bar food (12-9.30(9 Sun)) ~ (01352) 750500 ~ Children welcome but with restrictions ~ Dogs allowed in bar ~ Open 11.30-11; 12-10.30 Sun; closed 25-26 Dec

Recommended by KC, Chris Flynn, Wendy Jones, Dodie and Cliff Rutherford, Clive Watkin, Brian Brooks, Dr Phil Putwain

MONKNASH
SS9170   MAP 6

Plough & Harrow 🍺

Signposted Marcross, Broughton off B4265 St Brides Major—Llantwit Major – turn left at end of Water Street; OS Sheet 170 map reference 920706; CF71 7QQ

Marvellously evocative old building full of history and character, with a good choice of real ales

An untouched and richly atmospheric place, this ancient cottage has a real time-warp quality. In medieval times is was part of a monastic grange, the ruined walls and dovecote of which still stand close by. Built with massively thick stone walls, its dimly lit unspoilt main bar used to be the scriptures room and mortuary; instantly welcoming and genuinely atmospheric, it seems hardly changed over the last 70 years. The heavily black-beamed ceiling has ancient ham hooks, an intriguing arched doorway to the back, and a comfortably informal mix of furnishings that includes three fine stripped pine settles on the broad flagstones. There's a log fire in a huge fireplace with a side bread oven large enough to feed a village. The room on the left has lots of Wick Rugby Club memorabilia (it's their club room); daily papers, piped music, darts and TV (for sporting events only). Up to eight well kept real ales on handpump or tapped from the cask might include Archers Golden, Bass, Shepherd Neame Spitfire and Wye Valley Hereford Pale Ale, and thoughtfully sourced guest ales from brewers such as Bank Top, Triple fff and Vale of Glamorgan, as well as farm cider and perry; helpful service from knowledgeable staff. It can get crowded at weekends, when it's popular with families (they do children's helpings). There are picnic-sets in the front garden (with a covered area available to smokers), which has a boules pitch, and they hold barbecues out here in summer. Dogs are welcome in the bar – but not while food is being served. In a peaceful spot not far from the coast near Nash Point, it's an enjoyable walk from here down to the sea, where you can pick up a fine stretch of the coastal path along the top of remarkable candy-striped cliffs full of blow holes and fissures.

🍴 Written up on blackboards, the reasonably priced daily changing lunchtime bar food could include sandwiches, leek and stilton bake, sausages and mash, moussaka and welsh faggots; children's menu; more expensive evening food could feature soup, haddock with welsh rarebit crust, and beef medallions with green pepper sauce. *Starters/Snacks: £3.50 to £6.95. Main Courses: £6.95 to £9.95. Puddings: £1.20 to £3.95*

Free house ~ Licensee Gareth Davies ~ Real ale ~ Bar food (12-2.30, 6-9; not Sun evenings) ~ Restaurant ~ (01656) 890209 ~ No children after 9pm at weekends ~ Dogs allowed in bar ~ Live music Sat or Sun evening ~ Open 12-11(10.30 Sun)

Recommended by Blaise Vyner, John and Joan Nash, Gwyn and Anne Wake, R C Vincent

OLD RADNOR

SO2459 MAP 6

Harp 🛏

Village signposted off A44 Kington—New Radnor in Walton; LD8 2RH

Delightfully placed pub with cosily cottagey bar and comfortable bedrooms; tasty food served by caring staff

The latest owners of this charming old hilltop pub, in perfect walking country and overlooking the heights of Radnor Forest, have generated consistent praise from readers. In the evening and at weekends chatty locals gather in the old-fashioned brownstone public bar, which has high-backed settles, an antique reader's chair and other elderly chairs around a log fire; cribbage, Jenga, dominoes. The snug slate-floored lounge has a handsome curved antique settle and another log fire in a fine inglenook, and there are lots of local books and guides for residents. Outside, there's plenty of seating – either under the big sycamore tree, or on the grass. They have two real ales, usually featuring Hop Back Crop Circle, Three Tuns XXX or Three 8, or Wye Valley Hereford Pale Ale, or perhaps a guest such as Shepherd Neame Spitfire or Timothy Taylors Landlord; several malt whiskies, Dunkerton's organic cider and local apple juice; friendly, helpful service. Note they don't allow large dogs in the bedrooms, which are generally much enjoyed by readers. The impressive church is worth a look for its interesting early organ case (Britain's oldest), fine rood screen and ancient font. Note they don't open weekday lunchtimes.

🍴 Well liked bar food could typically include vegetable soup, grilled feta cheese with salad, welsh black rump steak, seared parmesan-crusted salmon fillet, steak and kidney pie or gressingham duck breast with cranberry and madeira sauce, with puddings like chocolate almond brownie or apple and cinnamon crumble; it can be worth booking on busy evenings. *Starters/Snacks: £3.95 to £4.95. Main Courses: £6.95 to £14.95. Puddings: £3.95 to £4.25*

Free house ~ Licensees David and Jenny Ellison ~ Real ale ~ Bar food ~ Restaurant ~ (01544) 350655 ~ Children welcome ~ Dogs allowed in bar ~ Open 6-11; 12-3, 6-11(10.30 Sun) Sat; closed weekday lunchtimes, all day Mon (exc bank hols) ~ Bedrooms: £40B/£64B

Recommended by David and Jacque Hart, the Didler, Trevor and Janet Cooper-Tydeman, Reg Fowle, Helen Rickwood, Mike Anderson

PEMBROKE FERRY   SM9704   MAP 6

Ferry Inn

Nestled below A477 toll bridge, N of Pembroke; SA72 6UD

Right by the water, a tempting place to linger for a drink on a summer's day, food majoring on fish

This former sailors' haunt is attractively set by the Cleddau Estuary, not by the present-day ferry but below the Cleddau Bridge where the old ferry used to stop years ago. Tables on a terrace by the water make a lovely place to sit out in summer, and inside it also has quite a nautical feel, with lots of seafaring pictures and memorabilia, a lovely open fire and good sea views. Bass and a guest such as Shepherd Neame Spitfire on handpump, and Felinfoel Double Dragon is served under light blanket pressure; games machine and unobtrusive piped music. More reports please.

🍴 **With something of an emphasis on fresh fish, the bar food might include soup, prawns, spanish chorizo sausage in red wine, sausage and mash, natural smoked haddock or broccoli cream cheese bake, with fresh fish specials such as bass or turbot.** *Starters/Snacks: £4.00 to £6.50. Main Courses: £8.00 to £15.00. Puddings: £2.50 to £4.00*

Free house ~ Licensee Jayne Surtees ~ Real ale ~ Bar food (12-2, 7-9.30; 12-1.30, 7-9 Sun) ~ (01646) 682947 ~ Children welcome but with restrictions ~ Open 11.30-3, 6.30(7 Mon)-11; 12-2.30, 7-10.30 Sun; closed 25-26 Dec

Recommended by Brian McBurnie, Mayur Shah, Prof H G Allen, Jim Abbott, JJW, CMW

PORTH DINLLAEN   SH2741   MAP 6

Ty Coch

Beach car park signposted from Morfa Nefyn, then 15-minute walk; LL53 6DB

Idyllic location right on the beach, far from the roads; simple fresh lunches

This unspoilt place has a super position on a curving, shallowly shelving beach backed by low grassy hills and sand-cliffs, and overlooking an expanse of water with boats anchored in the foreground and shadowy hills beyond. The pub is said to have been used by 17th-c smugglers and pirates, and the walls and beams are hung every inch with pewter, riding lights, navigation lamps, lanterns, small fishing nets, old miners' and railway lamps, copper utensils, an ale-yard, and lots of RNLI photographs and memorabilia; there are ships in bottles, a working barometer, a Caernarfon grandfather clock, and simple furnishings. An open coal fire burns at one end of the bar. There are tables outside; the walk here along the beach is particularly nice when the tide's out (otherwise you can walk across via the golf course).

🍴 **From a short menu, simple lunchtime bar food includes filled leek and potato soup, ploughman's, filled ciabattas and baguettes, pies, baked potatoes, and local crab and mussels.** *Starters/Snacks: £3.95 to £6.95. Main Courses: £7.95 to £8.95. Puddings: £3.95*

Free house ~ Licensee Mrs Brione Webley ~ Bar food (12-2.30) ~ (01758) 720498 ~ Children welcome ~ Dogs welcome ~ Live music twice weekly in July and Aug ~ Open 11-11; 11-3 Sun; open during day in Christmas week; Sat and Sun 12-4 only in winter

Recommended by Dr K P Tucker, Tony and Maggie Harwood, Steff Clegg

---

'Children welcome' means the pub says it lets children inside without any special restriction. If it allows them in, but to restricted areas such as an eating area or family room, we specify this. Places with separate restaurants often let children use them, hotels usually let them into public areas such as lounges.
Some pubs impose an evening time limit – let us know if you find this.

PORTHGAIN

Sloop

Off A487 St Davids—Fishguard; SA62 5BN

Thoroughly nautical pub in wonderful coastal setting, fresh fish in season, efficient service even at busy times

Step from an enchanting pembrokeshire cove into this memorably placed pub and you encounter seafaring memorabilia in many forms: the walls of the plank-ceilinged bar are hung with lobster pots and fishing nets, ships' clocks and lanterns, and even relics from wrecks along this stretch of the shoreline. Down a step, another room leads round to a decent-sized eating area, with simple wooden chairs and tables, cushioned wall seats, and a freezer with ice-creams for children. There are two or three well kept real ales on handpump, usually from Bass, Brains Rev James, Greene King IPA and Worthington Draught, or perhaps a guest from a brewer such as Felinfoel, and wine by the glass in three different sized glasses. Rather than having a number for food service, many of the tables are named after a wrecked ship. There's a well segregated games room (used mainly by children) which has a couple of games machines, TV, juke box, pool, darts and Scrabble. At the height of summer they may extend food serving times. Tables on the terrace overlook the harbour, with outdoor heaters for cooler weather. They don't have bedrooms but let a cottage in the village. The pub is right next to the coastal path, and there are outstanding cliff walks from here in either direction.

🍴 **Well prepared bar food often includes fresh fish they catch themselves (they run their own fishing business) such as crab, lobster, scallops and mackerel according to season. The menu might also feature lunchtime filled baguettes, soup or welsh cawl (beef stew), steakburger, welsh black rib-eye steak or sirloin steak, and specials like roast rump of lamb or roasted butternut squash and tarragon tagliatelle; they also do breakfasts.** *Starters/Snacks: £1.55 to £6.05. Main Courses: £4.65 to £15.20. Puddings: £2.45 to £4.00*

Free house ~ Licensee Matthew Blakiston ~ Real ale ~ Bar food (9.30-11, 12-2.30, 6-9.30; not 25 Dec) ~ No credit cards ~ (01348) 831449 ~ Under-16s must be accompanied by an adult ~ Open 9.30pm-1am(1.30am Fri, Sat)

Recommended by Ian and Deborah Carrington, Blaise Vyner, Andy and Alice Jordan, Trevor and Judith Pearson, Jim Abbott, Geoff and Brigid Smithers, Norma and Noel Thomas, MDN, John and Enid Morris, Jeff Davies, Mr and Mrs A H Young, Peter and Anne Hollindale

RAGLAN

Clytha Arms   🛏

Clytha, off Abergavenny road – former A40, now declassified; NP7 9BW

Beautifully placed in parkland, a relaxing spot for enjoying good food and beer; comfortable bedrooms

This gracious old country inn combines a civilised atmosphere with a pleasantly pubby feel, and has an attractive setting in spacious grounds on the edge of Clytha Park. With long heated verandahs and diamond-paned windows, it's comfortable, light and airy, with scrubbed wood floors, pine settles, big faux fur cushions on the window seats, a good mix of old country furniture and a couple of warming fires. Don't miss the murals in the lavatories. Run by charming licensees, it's the sort of relaxed place where everyone feels welcome, from locals who've walked here for a pint, to diners in the contemporary linen-set restaurant. An impressive choice of drinks includes well kept Felinfoel Double Dragon, Hook Norton Hooky and Rhymney Bitter, three swiftly changing guest beers from brewers such as Brains, Caledonian and Otley, an extensive wine list with about a dozen or so by the glass, belgian beers and a good choice of spirits. They have occasional cider and beer festivals; darts, shove-ha'penny, boules, bar billiards, cribbage and board games. The pub has its own english setter and collie. A couple of readers this year have found the service left a little to be desired, although we understand the pub has taken on new staff and the most recent reports have been more positive; one felt the loos could still do with sprucing up. The bedrooms are comfortable, with good welsh breakfasts.

🍴 The good bar menu includes sandwiches, soup, ploughman's, a pie of the day, tapas, mussels, wild boar sausages with potato and pea cake, and lentil moussaka. The restaurant menu is pricier and more elaborate. *Starters/Snacks: £3.95 to £6.50. Main Courses: £6.00 to £12.00. Puddings: £6.00*

Free house ~ Licensees Andrew and Beverley Canning ~ Real ale ~ Bar food (12.30-2.15, 7-9.30; not Sun evening or Mon lunch) ~ Restaurant ~ (01873) 840206 ~ Children welcome ~ Dogs allowed in bar ~ Open 12-12(11 Sun); closed Mon lunchtime; 3-6 Mon-Thurs ~ Bedrooms: £80B/£100B

Recommended by Tom and Ruth Rees, Mike Pugh, Glenys and John Roberts, the Didler, R T and J C Moggridge, Donna and Roger, Pete Baker, John Bromley, June Whitworth, Mike and Mary Carter, Paul J Robinshaw, Karen Eliot, Dr W J M Gissane, Simon Jones, Colin McKerrow, Peter Dearing, Roy Hoing, William Goodhart

RED WHARF BAY
SH5281   MAP 6

Ship ♀ 🍺

Village signposted off B5025 N of Pentraeth; LL75 8RJ

Nicely old-fashioned inside, with good drinks, sweeping coastal views from benches outside

This long, whitewashed, 16th-c house stands right on Anglesey's north coast, and on fine days there are plenty of takers for tables outside that get terrific views of some ten square miles of tidal sands, fringed by dunes and headlands. Inside is old-fashioned and interesting, with lots of nautical bric-a-brac in big rooms on each side of the busy stone-built bar counter, both with long cushioned varnished pews built around the walls, glossily varnished cast-iron-framed tables and roaring fires; piped Classic FM (in lounge only). Adnams, Brains and one or two guests such as Hobgoblin on handpump, nearly 50 malt whiskies, and a wider choice of wines than is usual for the area (with about ten by the glass). If you want to run a tab they'll ask to keep your credit card behind the bar in a locked numbered box (to which you are given the key).

🍴 The bar menu (not cheap) typically includes soup, lunchtime sandwiches, sausages with mash, grilled goats cheese with creamed fennel and asparagus fettuccine, chargrilled cutlet of pork with organic cider and shallot cream, and chargrilled rib-eye of welsh beef. *Starters/Snacks: £3.50 to £6.50. Main Courses: £8.95 to £17.95. Puddings: £4.00 to £6.00*

Free house ~ Licensee Neil Kenneally ~ Real ale ~ Bar food (12-2.30, 6-9; 12-9 Sun) ~ (01248) 852568 ~ Children in family areas ~ Open 11-11

Recommended by Glenwys and Alan Lawrence, Dr K P Tucker, Piotr Chodzko-Zajko, Joan York, J R Ringrose

RHYD-Y-MEIRCH
SO2907   MAP 6

Goose & Cuckoo 🍺

Upper Llanover signposted up narrow track off A4042 S of Abergavenny; after ½ mile take first left, then keep on up (watch for hand-written Goose signs at the forks); NP7 9ER

Remote single-room pub looking over a picturesque valley just inside the Brecon Beacons National Park, good drinks range

A delightful place to arrive at, particularly on foot – many do, as there are rewarding walks around here, along the nearby Monmouthshire and Brecon Canal towpath or breezy hikes over the moors. This simple place is essentially one small rustically furnished room with a woodburner in an arched stone fireplace. A small picture-window extension makes the most of the view down the valley. They have Brains Rev James and Wells & Youngs, and often a guest on handpump, as well as more than 80 whiskies; daily papers, cribbage, darts and board games. A variety of rather ad hoc picnic-sets is out on the gravel below, and the licensees keep sheep, geese and chickens, and may have honey for sale. The pub has a self-catering cottage, sleeping four, next door.

🍴 The choice of simple food includes filled rolls, bean soup, turkey and ham pie, steak and kidney pie and liver and bacon casserole. *Starters/Snacks: £2.00 to £2.50. Main Courses: £7.00. Puddings: £2.50*

Free house ~ Licensees Michael and Carol Langley ~ Real ale ~ Bar food (12-2.30, 7-9; not Sun evening) ~ No credit cards ~ (01873) 880277 ~ Children welcome but with restrictions ~ Dogs allowed in bar ~ Open 11.30-3, 7-11; 12.30-11 Fri, Sat; 12-10.30 Sun; closed Mon except bank hols ~ Bedrooms: £30S/£60S

Recommended by Reg Fowle, Helen Rickwood, Guy Vowles, Ruth Owens, R T and J C Moggridge, MLR

ROSEBUSH   SN0729   MAP 6

Tafarn Sinc
B4329 Haverfordwest—Cardigan; SA66 7QU

Unique 19th-c curio, a slice of social and industrial history

One reader was thrilled to hear his native Welsh being spoken at this extraordinary survival, which dates from 1876. A maroon-painted corrugated iron shed, it was built as a very basic hotel for a halt for a long-defunct railway serving quarries beneath the Preseli Hills. The halt itself has been more or less re-created, even down to life-size dummy passengers waiting out on the platform; the sizeable garden is periodically enlivened by the sounds of steam trains chuffing through – actually broadcast from a replica signal box. Though not exactly elegant, inside is really interesting, almost a museum of local history, with sawdust on the floor and an appealingly buoyant feel. The bar has plank panelling, an informal mix of chairs and pews, woodburners, and Cwrw Tafarn Sinc (brewed specially for the pub), and a weekly changing guest such as Brains Rev James on handpump; piped music, darts, games machine and TV.

🍴 **Basic food includes home-made faggots with mushy peas, vegetable lasagne, lamb burgers, steaks and puddings.** *Main Courses: £8.90 to £15.90. Puddings: £3.90*

Free house ~ Licensee Brian Llewelyn ~ Real ale ~ Bar food (12-2.30, 6-9) ~ Restaurant ~ (01437) 532214 ~ Children not allowed in bar after 9pm ~ Open 12-midnight (1am Sat, 11 Sun); closed Mon

Recommended by the Didler, John and Enid Morris, Mark Flynn, Jeff Davies, Colin Moore

SHIRENEWTON   ST4894   MAP 6

Carpenters Arms
Mynydd-bach; B4235 Chepstow—Usk, about ½ mile N; NP16 6BU

Pleasantly unsophisticated former smithy, with nicely timeless décor

Originally a smithy, this unpretentious and friendly place has an enjoyably unchanged atmosphere. There's an array of chamber-pots, an attractive Victorian tiled fireplace, and a collection of chromolithographs of antique royal occasions. One of the unusual interconnecting rooms still has blacksmith's bellows hanging from the planked ceiling. Furnishings run the gamut too, from one very high-backed ancient settle to pews, kitchen chairs, a nice elm table, several sewing-machine trestle tables and so forth; darts, board games and piped pop music. They have three to five real ales on handpump – from Bass, Brains, Fullers London Pride and Shepherd Neame Spitfire or an occasional seasonal guest. There are tables outside at the front, under hanging baskets in summer.

🍴 **Straightforward bar food, written up on blackboards, takes in a wide choice, including sandwiches, soup and filled baked potatoes, fish pie, game pie and a mixed grill.** *Starters/Snacks: £3.50 to £5.00. Main Courses: £7.50 to £18.00. Puddings: £3.50*

Punch ~ Lease Gary and Sandra Hayes ~ Real ale ~ Bar food (12-2.30, 6.30-10) ~ Restaurant ~ No credit cards ~ (01291) 641231 ~ Children welcome ~ Dogs welcome ~ Open 12-3, 5.30-12; 12-midnight Sat, Sun; 12-3.30, 5.30-12 (10.30 Sun) in winter

Recommended by Dr and Mrs C W Thomas, Steve Bailey, Mrs D W Privett, Dr and Mrs A K Clarke

---

Ring the bull is an ancient pub game – you try to lob a ring on a piece of string over a hook (occasionally a bull's horn) on wall or ceiling.

SKENFRITH   SO4520   MAP 6

Bell ♀ ⇘

Just off B4521, NE of Abergavenny and N of Monmouth; NP7 8UH

Elegant but relaxed, generally much praised for classy though pricy food and excellent accommodation

Close to the impressive ruin of Skenfrith Castle and a pretty bridge over the River Monnow, this is a popular and welcoming place to enjoy a celebratory meal out. Though most readers thoroughly enjoy it, a couple have reported a few blips in the service and one found the cooking didn't come up to expectations. The big back bare-boards dining area is very neat, light and airy, with dark country-kitchen chairs and rush-seat dining chairs, church candles and flowers on the dark tables, canary walls and a cream ceiling, and brocaded curtains on sturdy big-ring rails. The flagstoned bar on the left has a rather similar décor, with old local and school photographs, and a couple of pews as well as tables and café chairs; Breconshire Golden Valley, Freeminer and Timothy Taylors Landlord as well as Broome Farm cider on handpump from an attractive bleached oak bar counter; board games. They have good wines by the glass and half-bottle, and make good coffee. The lounge bar on the right, opening into the dining area, has a nice Jacobean-style carved settle and a housekeeper's chair by a log fire in the big fireplace. The atmosphere is relaxed but smart (the lavatories are labelled Loos). There are good solid round picnic-sets as well as the usual rectangular ones out on the terrace, with steps up to a sloping lawn; it's a quiet spot. The bedrooms are comfortable, with thoughtful touches.

🍴 Using named local suppliers of carefully chosen fresh ingredients, the lunch and dinner menus might include filled baguettes, cream of spicy red pepper and tomato soup, confit of duck and artichoke terrine, glazed belly pork, roasted fillet of bass or roasted butternut squash and herb risotto, with puddings such as white chocolate mousse or fig sticky toffee pudding. *Starters/Snacks: £4.50 to £8.50. Main Courses: £13.50 to £18.00. Puddings: £5.75*

Free house ~ Licensees William and Janet Hutchings ~ Real ale ~ Bar food ~ Restaurant ~ (01600) 750235 ~ Children over 8 welcome ~ Dogs allowed in bar and bedrooms ~ Open 11-11; 12-10.30 Sun; closed all day Mon in winter; last week Jan/first week Feb ~ Bedrooms: £95B/£105B

Recommended by Tom and Ruth Rees, Mrs A J Evans, Bernard Stradling, R T and J C Moggridge, Alec and Barbara Jones, David and Sue Smith, William Goodhart, Mr and Mrs R S Ashford, Kevin Jeavons, Alison Turner

ST HILARY   ST0173   MAP 6

Bush

Village signposted from A48 E of Cowbridge; CF71 7DP

Cosily old-fashioned village pub, low beams and settles; good food served by helpful staff

The ample log fire in this ancient stone and thatch pub makes this a particularly inviting place to come to in winter. Comfortable in a quietly stylish way, it has stripped old stone walls, and farmhouse tables and chairs in the low-beamed carpeted lounge bar, while the other bar is pubbier with old settles and pews on aged flagstones, and a pleasant mix of locals and visitors. Bass, Greene King Abbot, Hancocks HB and a guest from a brewery such as Shepherd Neame or Vale of Glamorgan on handpump or tapped from the cask; TV, cribbage, dominoes and subdued piped music. There are tables and chairs in front, and more in the back garden; reasonable disabled access.

🍴 The well presented bar food might include lunchtime baguettes and ploughman's, soup, wild boar and apple sausages with mash and a pie of the day; also available in the bar, the restaurant menu has welsh rarebit, slow-braised lamb shank, fillet of welsh beef on wilted spinach, baked goats cheese pancake, with puddings such as apricot bread and butter pudding. The Sunday lunch, with organic meats and very good vegetables, is well liked. *Starters/Snacks: £3.95 to £7.95. Main Courses: £6.95 to £18.00. Puddings: £3.95*

Punch ~ Tenant Phil Thomas ~ Real ale ~ Bar food (12-2.30(3 Sun), 6.30-9.30; Sun 5.30-8) ~ Restaurant ~ (01446) 772745 ~ Children welcome ~ Dogs allowed in bar ~ Open 12-11(10.30 Sun)

Recommended by Mark and Deb Ashton, P Price, Malcolm and Faith Thomas, Donna and Roger

TINTERN

Cherry Tree 🍺

Pub signed up narrow Raglan road off A466, beside Royal George; parking very limited; NP16 6TH

Interesting extended pub handy for Tintern Abbey, with good beer; pretty garden

This sympathetically extended 16th-c cottage makes a useful stopping point in one of the most celebrated parts of the lower Wye Valley, half a mile or so from the abbey and honey-pot centre of Tintern but just far enough away to be pleasantly relaxed. Not especially smart, it's very much at the heart of the local community – the building takes in the village shop and post office. Hancocks HB and four guests like Archers Golden, Moles Molecatcher, Stonehenge Pigswill and Wye Valley Butty Bach are on handpump, and they also serve farm ciders from the barrel, along with a good few wines by the glass, and home-made country wines; warmly welcoming service. The original beamed and stone-built bar has a walnut serving counter in one area and a good open fire in another, and leads into the slate-floored extension; cribbage, darts, cards, dominoes, board games and piped music. Readers have found them reluctant to take credit cards for smaller amounts. There are tables out in a charming garden, and on a nicely refurbished terrace; disabled access is difficult. They have two beer and cider festivals a year. More reports please.

🍴 **Bar food, made with fresh ingredients, might include sandwiches, soup, omelettes, beef chilli, lamb stew with herby dumplings, paella (for two), daily specials and a choice of Sunday roasts; children's menu.** *Starters/Snacks: £3.95 to £4.95. Main Courses: £4.95 to £22.95. Puddings: £2.95 to £3.50*

Free house ~ Licensees Jill and Steve Pocock ~ Real ale ~ Bar food (12-3, 6-9(8.30 Sun); not Sun evenings) ~ Restaurant ~ (01291) 689292 ~ Children in dining areas only ~ Dogs allowed in bar ~ Occasional live music ~ Open 12-11(10.30 Sun) ~ Bedrooms: /£60B

Recommended by Tony and Wendy Hobden, John and Gloria Isaacs, Tim and Ann Newell, R T and J C Moggridge, James Read, Ginette Medland, Pete Baker, the Didler

TY'N-Y-GROES

Groes 🍴 🍷 🛏

B5106 N of village; LL32 8TN

Excelling for food and accommodation, a thoroughly welcoming hotel and bar in northern Snowdonia

With a fine setting overlooking the Vale of Conwy and the peaks of Snowdonia, this extremely well run hotel has been welcoming visitors since 1573, when it was reputedly the first welsh pub to be properly licensed. Past the hot stove in the entrance area, the spotlessly kept rambling, low-beamed and thick-walled rooms are nicely decorated with antique settles and an old sofa, old clocks, portraits, hats and tins hanging from the walls, and fresh flowers. A fine antique fireback is built into one wall, perhaps originally from the formidable fireplace in the back bar, which houses a collection of stone cats as well as cheerful winter log fires. There is also an airy and verdant conservatory. Brains Rev James, Great Orme and Marstons Burton on handpump, and they've a good few malt whiskies, kir, and a fruity Pimms in summer; piped music. The neatly kept, well equipped bedroom suites (some have terraces or balconies) have gorgeous views, and in summer it's a pleasure to sit outside in the pretty garden with its flower-filled hayricks; there are more seats on the flower-decked roadside. They also rent out a well appointed wooden cabin, idyllically placed nearby, as well as a cottage in the historic centre of Conwy.

🍴 **Using lamb and salmon from the Conwy Valley, and game birds from local shoots, and the hotel's own bread and home-grown herbs, well presented dishes might include soup, sandwiches, sausages, bacon and mash, welsh hill lamb shepherd's pie, haddock, poached salmon with hollandaise sauce and steaks, with daily specials such as game casserole; puddings could feature as white chocolate and vanilla bean panna cotta or sticky toffee pudding.** *Starters/Snacks: £4.50 to £7.90. Main Courses: £8.25 to £17.45. Puddings: £4.95 to £7.25*

Free house ~ Licensee Dawn Humphreys ~ Real ale ~ Bar food (12-2.15, 6.30-9) ~ Restaurant ~ (01492) 650545 ~ Children in family dining area ~ Dogs allowed in bedrooms ~ Open 12-3, 6.30(6 Sat)-11~ Bedrooms: £79B/£95B

Recommended by Margaret and Jeff Graham, Mike and Mary Carter, Neil Whitehead, Victoria Anderson, J F M and M West, Joan York, Sarah and Peter Gooderham, Donald Mills, Clive Watkin, Phil and Jane Hodson, Di and Mike Gillam, Rodney and Norma Stubington, Dr and Mrs P Truelove, Denys Gueroult

USK   SO3700   MAP 6

Nags Head ⑪ ♀
The Square; NP15 1BH

Spotlessly kept by the same family for many years, traditional in style, as warm a reception as could be hoped for, with good food and drinks

'Can't wait to go back', 'As good as ever' and 'Great welcome from the Key family and all the staff' are typical comments this super-friendly old coaching inn generates from happy readers. With a friendly chatty atmosphere, the beautifully kept traditional main bar has lots of well polished tables and chairs packed under its beams (some with farming tools), lanterns or horsebrasses and harness attached, as well as leatherette wall benches, and various sets of sporting prints and local pictures – look out for the original deeds to the pub. Tucked away at the front is an intimate little corner with some african masks, while on the other side of the room a passageway leads to a new dining area converted from the old coffee bar. There may be prints for sale, and perhaps a knot of sociable locals. They do 15 wines by the glass, along with three ales on handpump – from Brains Bread of Heaven, Rev James or SA and Buckleys Best. The centre of Usk is full of pretty hanging baskets and flowers in summer, and the church is well worth a look.

⑪ Popular, generously served and reasonably priced food includes soup, grilled sardines, frog legs in hot provençale sauce, usk wild boar sausages and vegetable pancake, with specials such as whole stuffed partridge cooked in port. You can book tables, some of which may be candlelit at night; nice proper linen napkins, and quiet piped classical music. *Starters/Snacks: £4.00 to £6.00. Main Courses: £7.50 to £15.00. Puddings: £3.00 to £4.30*

Free house ~ Licensees the Key family ~ Real ale ~ Bar food (11.30-2, 5.30-9.30) ~ Restaurant ~ (01291) 672820 ~ Children welcome ~ Dogs welcome ~ Open 10.30-3, 5.30-11(10.30 Sun)

Recommended by Mike Pugh, Sue and Ken Le Prevost, Terry and Linda Moseley, Peter Craske, Andrew and Sian Williams, Roy and Lindsey Fentiman, Tim and Ann Newell, Eryl and Keith Dykes, M G Hart, Donna and Roger, Andy and Jill Kassube, Graham Cooper, Mick and Carol Cordell, Roger and Anne Newbury, John and Helen Rushton, Dr and Mrs C W Thomas

LUCKY DIP

Besides the fully inspected pubs, you might like to try these Lucky Dips recommended to us and described by readers (if you do, please send us reports: www.goodguides.co.uk).

ANGLESEY

BEAUMARIS [SH6076]
☆ *Sailors Return* LL58 8AB [Church St]: Bright cheery partly divided open-plan dining pub with comfortable banquettes and open fire, all tables set for generous good value food from sandwiches and baguettes up, small helpings for OAPs, good value Sun lunch worth booking, cheerful helpful staff, decent wines, Bass and perhaps one or two other real ales (you tend to feel a bit in the way if you're just standing there for a drink); unobtrusive piped music; children welcome in eating area, dogs in bar, comfortable bedrooms *(Phil Merrin, LYM, Mr and Mrs*

H J Stephens, Neil Whitehead, Victoria Anderson, Robin and Ann Taylor, J and E Dakin)
LLANDDONA [SH5779]
Owain Glyndwr LL58 8UF [4 miles NW of Beaumaris]: Proper pub in old stone building, friendly family service, decent choice of good value food (all day Sun) from baguettes to steak, good range of beers *(Robin and Ann Taylor)*
MENAI BRIDGE [SH5572]
☆ *Liverpool Arms* LL59 5EY [St Georges Pier]: Under newish management, with young chef doing good quite inventive food using prime local fish and welsh black beef, decent wines and real ales, quick friendly service, four

low-beamed rooms with interesting mostly maritime photographs and prints, panelled dining room, popular conservatory catching evening sun; a few terrace tables *(Mr and Mrs J Roberts)*

RHOSCOLYN [SH2675]

White Eagle LL65 2NJ [off B4545 S of Holyhead]: Splendid remote setting with panoramic views towards Snowdonia from dining area, friendly welcome to all inc wet walkers, four well kept interesting changing ales, prompt service, enjoyable food (all day in summer); children welcome, good large garden, lane down to beach, open all day in summer *(Christine Shepherd)*

CLWYD

BERSHAM [SJ3149]

Black Lion LL14 4HN [Ddol]: Friendly local in former industrial area, good Hydes ales, welcoming staff and inexpensive straightforward bar food, darts, cards and pool in public bar, TV in lounge for racing; a few tables outside *(Pete Baker)*

BODFARI [SJ0970]

☆ *Dinorben Arms* LL16 4DA [off A541, near church]: Attractive black and white hillside pub nr Offa's Dyke, three well worn beamed and flagstoned rooms with open fires, old-fashioned settles, glassed-over old well, lots of hanging whisky-water jugs, over 250 malt whiskies, popular food from sandwiches and bar snacks to restaurant dishes, carvery (Fri/Sat night, Sun lunch), pleasant staff, Banks's, Marstons Pedigree and a guest beer, good wines, darts and pool, light and airy garden room; fruit machine, TV, piped classical music; children welcome, grassy play area, charming views from pretty brick terraces, open all day wknds *(KC, LYM, Donald Mills)*

BWLCHGWYN [SJ2453]

Moors LL11 5YL [Maes Maelor; A525/B5430 SW]: Friendly pub locally popular for enjoyable home cooking, well kept ales such as Thwaites Lancaster Bomber *(J Bennett)*

CARROG [SJ1143]

Grouse LL21 9AT [B5436, signed off A5 Llangollen—Corwen]: Small unpretentious pub with great views over River Dee and beyond from bay window and balcony, Lees real ales, good choice of well prepared food all day from good sandwiches up, friendly staff and regulars, local pictures, pool in games room; piped music, narrow turn into car park; wheelchair access, tables in pretty walled garden with sunny terrace, handy for Llangollen steam railway, bedrooms *(John Oates, Denise Walton, Edward Leetham)*

CILCAIN [SJ1765]

☆ *White Horse* CH7 5NN [signed from A494 W of Mold; The Square]: Homely and welcoming country local, several unspoilt rooms, low joists, mahogany and oak settles, roaring inglenook log or coal fire, quarry-tiled back bar allowing dogs and muddy boots, long-

serving landlord, interesting changing ales, home-made straightforward food, pub games; no children inside; picnic-sets outside, delightful village *(J R Ringrose, LYM, MLR, Ann and Tony Bennett-Hughes)*

COEDWAY [SJ3414]

Old Hand & Diamond SY5 9AR [B4393 W of Shrewsbury]: Friendly staff, enjoyable food from familiar favourites to interesting specials, succulent local lamb and game, a local real ale, nice wine, beams, panelling and stripped stone in carpeted bar, light and airy restaurant with local pictures; tables under cocktail parasols on side terrace, lots of climbing roses and hanging baskets, attractive beamed bedrooms *(Louise Gibbons)*

GRESFORD [SJ3455]

Griffin LL12 8RG [The Green (B5373, just off A483 Chester—Wrexham)]: Homely and unspoilt traditional village pub, well divided single bar with real ales such as Black Sheep and Everards, chatty regulars, piano in one bit, darts in another; opens at 4pm (3pm wknds) *(Pete Baker)*

GWERNYMYNYDD [SJ2162]

Rainbow CH7 5LG [Ruthin Rd (A494)]: Welcoming staff, enjoyable food inc some enterprising dishes, family bargains before 7pm; no piped music; children welcome *(KC)*

GWYTHERIN [SH8761]

Lion LL22 8UU [B5384 W of Denbigh]: Isolated much refurbished small village pub with good enterprising pub food and locally popular small restaurant area with log fire, another in friendly and attractive main bar, good wines by the glass, two real ales; poor disabled access; garden seating planned, nice walks, five good bedrooms, cl wkdy lunchtimes and Mon *(David Johnson)*

HALKYN [SJ2070]

Blue Bell CH8 8DL [Rhosesmor Rd (B5123 S)]: Good changing farm ciders and perries (perhaps their own cider too), a good value beer brewed just for them in Flint and particularly well kept changing ales, wknd lunches from light dishes to substantial meals using local supplies, warm welcome, real fires, no piped music – live Thurs/Fri, jazz Sun lunchtime; fine spot on Halkyn Mountain, remarkable views in clear weather, cl wkdy lunchtimes, open all day wknds *(anon)*

LLANARMON DYFFRYN CEIRIOG [SJ1532]

☆ *West Arms* LL20 7LD [end of B4500 W of Chirk]: 16th-c beamed and timbered inn in lovely surroundings, cosy atmosphere in picturesque upmarket lounge bar full of antique settles, sofas, even an elaborately carved confessional stall, particularly good original bar food strong on local produce and fairly priced, warm and friendly staff, good range of wines, malt whiskies and well kept ales, more sofas in old-fashioned entrance hall, comfortable back bar too, roaring log fires, good restaurant; children welcome, pretty lawn running down to River Ceiriog (fishing for residents), comfortable character bedrooms, good walks *(Mrs A J Evans, Mrs Linda Norsworthy, LYM)*

LLANDEGLA [SJ1952]

Crown LL11 3AD [Ruthin Rd (A525)]: Quickly served good value food in comfortable bar with good set of Hogarth prints, Lees real ale, good helpful service, popular restaurant; on Offa's Dyke Path *(KC)*

LLANGERNYW [SH8767]

Stag LL22 8PP: 17th-c timbered and beamed pub with three linked areas, log fire, quaint nooks, settles and bric-a-brac, good range of real ales, hearty food using local ingredients, friendly staff *(Ian Clarke)*

LLANGYNHAFAL [SJ1263]

White Horse LL16 4LL [Hendrerwydd; sign to pub off B5429 N of Ruthin]: Tucked-away village pub with three quickly changing real ales such as Conwy and Greene King, good unusual changing fresh food inc one or two lunchtime sandwiches, good range of wines, great collection of spirits, relaxed atmosphere, friendly attentive service, daily papers, armchairs, sofa, open fire and interesting bric-a-brac in small old-fashioned rustic bar, opening into three smartly mediterranean-style bare-boards eating areas; nicely done terrace with rustic views and aromas *(Roger and Anne Newbury)*

LLANNEFYDD [SH9870]

☆ *Hawk & Buckle* LL16 5ED [NW of Henllan]: Welcoming village inn, high up with a sweeping panorama over Irish Sea to Blackpool Tower; no real ale, but tasty bar food (not Sun evening), long knocked-through black-beamed lounge bar with comfortable settles, log fire, side bar with pool (and unobtrusive piped music); children welcome in restaurant, cl Mon *(Kenneth and Mary Davies, LYM, Clive Watkin, Donald Mills)*

MINERA [SJ2651]

Tyn-y-Capel LL11 3DA [Church Rd]: Enjoyable and enterprising food, real ales such as Everards Beacon, Greene King Old Speckled Hen and Shepherd Neame Spitfire, great views; open all day wknds *(Rita and Keith Pollard)*

MOLD [SJ2364]

Bryn Awel CH7 1BL [A541 Denbigh Rd nr Bailey Hill]: Hillside modern hotel with picture-window country views in comfortable good-sized dining area, welcoming attentive service, sensibly priced food inc thai dishes, cheerful bustling carpeted lounge bar; may be piped music; neat bedrooms *(KC)*

We Three Loggerheads CH7 5LH [Ruthin Rd (A494, 3 miles towards Ruthin)]: Comfortable two-level bar with well kept Wells & Youngs Bombardier, pleasant staff, decent food; picnic-sets out on side terrace overlooking river, open all day at least in summer *(LYM, Mrs Maricar Jagger)*

OVERTON BRIDGE [SJ3542]

☆ *Cross Foxes* LL13 0DR [A539 W of Overton, nr Erbistock]: Appealingly modernised and civilised waterside dining pub with food all day, linked but distinct areas with lots of pictures and a good mix of variously sized tables, big candles at night, good log fires, Banks's, Marstons and guest beers, splendid range of wines by the glass and of spirits, good coffees; children welcome, dogs allowed in bar, picnic-sets out on crazy-paved terrace above lawn to River Dee, play area, open all day *(R T and J C Moggridge, J R Ringrose, Bruce and Sharon Eden, Paul Boot, UN, LYM)*

PENLEY [SJ4139]

Dymock Arms LL13 0LS [Overton Rd (A539 Whitchurch—Ruabon)]: Ancient pub reopened after two-year restoration by landlord/chef himself, enjoyable food from sandwiches up, restaurant on right *(Noel Grundy)*

PONTBLYDDYN [SJ2761]

New Inn CH7 4HR [A5104, just S of A541 3 miles SE of Mold]: Interesting choice of good food in unassuming building's pleasant upstairs dining room, good service; piped music *(KC)*

RHEWL [SJ1744]

☆ *Sun* LL20 7YT [off A5 or A542 NW of Llangollen]: Unpretentious cottagey local with simple consistently good value generous food from sandwiches and bargain light lunches up, good Sun lunch, a well kept changing real ale, chatty landlord and friendly staff, coal fire in old open range, hatch service to back room, dark little lounge, no piped music; outside lavatories, portakabin games room – children allowed here and in eating area; dogs welcome, lovely peaceful spot, good walking country just off Horseshoe Pass, relaxing valley views from terrace and small pretty garden, cl Mon, open all day wknds *(LYM, Mike and Lynn Robinson)*

RHOS-ON-SEA [SH8480]

Rhos Fynach LL28 4NG [Rhos Rd]: Picturesque stone-built pub in own grounds opp small harbour, handsome lounge with low beams, flagstones, two open fires, prints and brassware, well kept real ales, enjoyable reasonably priced food, friendly service, upstairs restaurant; piped music *(Robin and Janice Dewhurst)*

RHYDYMWYN [SJ2166]

Antelope CH7 5HE [Denbigh Rd (A541)]: Pleasant bar and attractive restaurant, satisfying food; shame about the piped music *(KC)*

RUTHIN [SJ1258]

Wynnstay Arms LL15 1AN [Well St]: Contemporary refurbishment with real ale, good wines by the glass, wide choice of reasonably priced food from sandwiches, paninis and pubby favourites to up-to-date dishes in café/bar and brasserie; six bedrooms *(anon)*

TAL-Y-CAFN [SH7871]

☆ *Tal-y-Cafn Hotel* LL28 5RR [A470 Conway—Llanwrst]: Comfortable pub thriving under new licensees after gentle move upmarket, good choice of enjoyable food, real ales, lounge bar with jugs hanging from ceiling and log fire in big inglenook; unobtrusive piped classical music; children welcome, seats in spacious garden, pleasant surroundings, handy for Bodnant Gardens *(LYM, KC)*

DYFED

ABERYSTWYTH [SN6777]
Yr Hen Orsaf SY23 1LN [Alexandra Rd]: Rather elegant high-ceilinged Wetherspoons in concourse of Cambrian Railways station, their usual food and drink bargains, efficient service, several different areas, platform view; terrace tables by the buffer stops, open all day from breakfast *(B and M Kendall, Reg Fowle, Helen Rickwood)*

BANCYFELIN [SN3218]
Fox & Hounds SA33 5ND [off A40 W of Carmarthen; High St]: New owners doing enjoyable freshly made food, quickly changing real ales such as Cannon Royall; bedrooms *(D and M T Ayres-Regan)*

BONCATH [SN2038]
☆ **Boncath Inn** SA37 0JN [B4332 Cenarth—Eglwyswrw]: Good home-made food inc tasty specials running up to lobster in large, friendly and attractively traditional village pub, four changing real ales (not cheap), woodburner, farm tools and photographs of former railway; prominent pool table; open all day *(Colin Moore, Brian and Carole Polhill)*

BROAD HAVEN [SM8616]
☆ **Druidstone Hotel** SA62 3NE [N of village on coast rd, bear left for about 1½ miles then follow sign left to Druidstone Haven – inn a sharp left turn after another ½ mile; OS Sheet 157 map ref 862168, marked as Druidston Villa]: Cheerfully informal, the family's former country house in a grand spot above the sea, individualistic and relaxed, ruled out of the main entries only by its club licence (you can't go for just a drink and have to book to eat or stay here); terrific views, good inventive home cooking with fresh often organic ingredients, efficient service, folksy cellar bar with Worthington BB tapped from the cask, good wines, country wines and other drinks, ceilidhs and folk events, chummy dogs (dogs welcomed), all sorts of sporting activities from boules to sand-yachting; attractive high-walled garden, spacious homely bedrooms, even an eco-friendly chalet, cl Nov and Jan, restaurant cl Sun evening *(Mark Flynn, Blaise Vyner, John and Enid Morris, Colin Moore, LYM)*

CAPEL BANGOR [SN6580]
Tynllidiart Arms SY23 3LR [A44]: Quaint roadside cottage with woodburner in big stripped-stone bare-boards bar, has its own tiny brewery (in what used to be the gents') with four well kept ales inc a Stout, friendly landlord and good staff, nice atmosphere, limited good value bar food inc good crab sandwiches, also large upstairs dining room; well behaved children and dogs allowed *(Mike and Mary Carter)*

CAREW [SN0403]
☆ **Carew Inn** SA70 8SL [A4075, just off A477]: Cheerful old beamed pub with wide choice of enjoyable food, well kept Brains Rev James and another real ale, friendly service, unpretentious old-fashioned furnishings in small linked rooms with interesting prints, cosy upstairs dining room, traditional games; very busy in summer, piped music, live Thurs and summer Sun; children and dogs welcome, back garden overlooking spectacular castle ruins, outdoor heaters and summer marquee, good play area, more tables out in front, open all day wknds and summer *(Bob and Angela Brooks, LYM, the Didler, Colin Moore)*

CWM GWAUN [SN0333]
☆ **Dyffryn Arms** SA65 9SE [Cwm Gwaun and Pontfaen signed off B4313 E of Fishguard]: Classic unspoilt country tavern, virtually the social centre for this lush green valley, very relaxed, basic and idiosyncratic, with much-loved veteran landlady (her farming family have run it since 1840, and she's been in charge for well over one-third of that time); 1920s front parlour with plain deal furniture inc rocking chair and draughts boards inlaid into tables, coal fire, Bass, Carlsberg Burton or Tetleys served by jug through a sliding hatch, low prices, World War I prints and posters, darts; pretty countryside, open more or less all day (may close if no customers) *(Giles and Annie Francis, the Didler, Colin Moore, LYM)*

FELINDRE FARCHOG [SN0939]
Olde Salutation SA41 3UY [A487 Newport—Cardigan]: Stylish new conservatory restaurant (may be open only Thurs-Sat) in spacious sympathetically modernised pub with good value bar food too, from toasties and baguettes to local beef and seasonal sea trout, Brains Rev James, Felinfoel Double Dragon and a guest beer, good wines by the glass, genial landlord and friendly staff; disabled access and facilities, eight comfortable bedrooms in newish extension, good breakfast, fishing and good walks by nearby River Nevern *(Blaise Vyner, Paul A Moore, Steve Godfrey, Colin Moore)*

FISHGUARD [SM9537]
☆ **Fishguard Arms** SA65 9HJ [Main St (A487)]: Tiny front bar with changing real ales served by jug at unusually high counter, warmly friendly staff, open fire, rugby photographs, traditional games in back room; open all day Sun, cl Mon, also perhaps lunchtime Tues and Sat *(Blaise Vyner, LYM, the Didler)*
Royal Oak SA65 9HA [Market Sq, Upper Town]: Dark beams, stripped stone and panelling, big picture-window dining extension, pictures commemorating defeat here of bizarre french raid in 1797, Brains and changing guest beers from bar counter carved with welsh dragon, decent well priced generous food, woodburner; bar billiards, games machine; pleasant terrace, open all day *(Mike Pugh, the Didler, BB)*

HAVERFORDWEST [SM9515]

☆ *Georges* SA61 1NH [Market St]: Intermingled with eclectibles shop and small coffee bar/teashop area is long narrow celtic-theme bar with small stable-like booths – not a pub, but has Brains SA or Rev James and a guest beer, interesting reasonably priced wines esp new world, quick cheerful service even when busy, relaxed and idiosyncratic atmosphere underlined by fancy mirrors, glistening crystals and dangly hangings, clogs, aromatherapy and much more for sale; larger upstairs restaurant, good value interesting home-made food using good meat, their own fresh veg and good fish and vegetarian ranges; no dogs; lovely walled garden, open 10.30-5.30, all day Sat *(Mike Pugh, Richard and Judy Winn, Richard Bowen)*

HAYSCASTLE CROSS [SM9125]

Cross SA62 5PR [B4330 Haverfordwest—Fishguard]: Cosy and old-fashioned inside, with roaring log fire in bar, friendly landlady and staff, good value home cooking, Brains Rev James, separate dining room; picnic-sets in smallish sheltered garden, may be cl wkdy lunchtimes, and for sale as we go to press, so may be changes *(Helene Grygar)*

LITTLE HAVEN [SM8512]

☆ *Castle* SA62 3UF: Good value open-plan pub well placed by green looking over sandy bay (lovely sunsets), efficient cheerful service even when busy, good reasonably priced food inc great ploughman's, tasty cawl (beef stew) and local fish (best to book for meals), good choice of wines by the glass, Brains, bare-boards bar and carpeted dining area with big oak tables, beams, some stripped stone, castle prints, pool in back area; children welcome, picnic-sets on front terrace, two good sea-view bedrooms, open all day from 9.30am *(Mark Flynn, Ian and Celia Abbott, Geoff and Angela Jaques, Alan Sutton, Mr and Mrs A H Young, John Rees)*

LLANDDAROG [SN5016]

☆ *Butchers Arms* SA32 8NS: Ancient heavily black-beamed local with three smallish eating areas rambling off small central bar, cheerily welcoming atmosphere, generous reasonably priced home cooking from sandwiches through hearty country dishes to nice puddings (menu willingly adapted for children), friendly helpful staff, Felinfoel Best and Double Dragon tapped from the cask, good wines by the glass, conventional pub furniture, fairylights and candles in bottles, woodburner in biggish fireplace; piped music; tables outside, delightful window boxes, cl Mon *(A S and M E Marriott, BB, Tom Evans)*

LLANDEILO [SN6226]

☆ *Angel* SA19 7LY [Salem; unclassified rd N, off B4302]: Young chef/landlord doing good reasonably priced home-made food using fresh produce from baguettes to well filled pitta breads and lunchtime bargain specials to wide range of fish, imaginative dishes in comfortable back bistro with thriving civilised atmosphere, attractive open-plan U-shaped bar, friendly helpful young staff, Brains and local real ales; tables outside, lovely country setting opp castle *(D and C Dampier, Mike Pugh, John Stirrup, Guy and Carol Austin Potter)*

☆ *Cottage* SA19 6SD [Pentrefelin (A40 towards Carmarthen – brown sign from Llandeilo)]: Large smart open-plan beamed dining pub, comfortable and welcoming, with huge log fire and lots of horsey prints, plates and brasses, generous good value food from baguettes to good local fish and welsh black beef, Brains SA and Fullers London Pride, decent house wines, thoughtful service, well appointed back dining room; piped music *(Michael and Alison Sandy, Tom Evans)*

White Horse SA19 6EN [Rhosmaen St]: Friendly 16th-c local with several rooms, popular for its real ales inc Breconshire, occasional live music; tables outside front and back *(the Didler)*

LLANDOVERY [SN7634]

Red Lion SA20 0AA [Market Sq]: One basic welcoming room with no bar, Brains Buckleys and a guest beer tapped from the cask, jovial landlord; cl Sun, may cl early evening if no customers *(BB, the Didler)*

LLANGADOG [SN7028]

Red Lion SA19 9AA [Church St]: Well kept local Evan Evans ales and good straightforward lunches inc welsh lamb and beef in striking old stone-built inn; comfortable bedrooms *(John Rees)*

LLANYCHAER [SM9835]

Bridge End SA65 9TB [Bridge St (B4313 SE of Fishguard)]: Former watermill in attractive hamlet, friendly enthusiastic staff, one or two real ales, good choice of food from lunchtime snacks to full evening meals inc popular roast Sun lunch *(Colin Moore)*

NEWPORT [SN0539]

☆ *Golden Lion* SA42 0SY [East St (A487)]: Nicely refurbished pub with generous enjoyable well priced food from baguettes to local welsh black beef, friendly service, several well kept real ales, good local atmosphere in cosy series of linked rooms, some distinctive old settles; children welcome in popular dining rooms and games bar, good disabled access and facilities, quiet garden behind, good value comfortable bedrooms, big breakfast *(Steve Godfrey, Kevin Murphy, LYM)*

☆ *Royal Oak* SA42 0TA [West St (A487)]: Bustling and well run sizeable pub with friendly helpful landlady and staff, good choice of good generous food inc lunchtime light dishes, local lamb and lots of authentic curries, Tues OAP lunch, Greene King Old Speckled Hen and guest beers, children welcome in lounge with eating areas, separate stone and slate bar with pool and games, upstairs dining room; some tables outside, an easy walk from the beach and coast path *(Colin Moore, Blaise Vyner, John and Enid Morris)*

PEMBROKE DOCK [SM9603]
Shipwright SA72 6JX [Front St]: Good atmosphere, enjoyable food, real ales; overlooks estuary, and handy for Ireland ferry (*D and M T Ayres-Regan*)

PONTRHYDFENDIGAID [SN7366]
Black Lion SY25 6BE [B4343 Tregaron—Devils Bridge]: Informal country inn under friendly new management, enjoyable traditional food all day, beams and log fire, real ales; picnic-sets outside, five good value bedrooms, good breakfast, handy for Strata Florida abbey, open all day (*Sarah and Peter Gooderham, Bill Lockwood*)

PORTHGAIN [SM8132]
Shed SA62 5BN: Recently opened in what looks to be a seaside former boat shed, emphasis on fresh fish in upstairs evening bistro (not winter Sun-Weds), sells beer too, daytime tearoom (*MDN*)

SAUNDERSFOOT [SN1304]
☆ *Royal Oak* SA69 9HA [Wogan Terrace (B4316)]: Splendid position by harbour, friendly service, several well kept changing ales in comfortable carpeted lounge bar and small public bar, popular food (not Sun evening) in dining area – go for the fresh local fish when they have it; piped music, TV; children welcome, tables out on heated terrace making the most of the view, open all day till late (*David Eberlin, the Didler, LYM*)

SOLVA [SM8024]
☆ *Cambrian* SA62 6UU [Lower Solva; off A487 Haverfordwest—St Davids]: Attractive neatly kept civilised dining pub much enjoyed by older people, enjoyable if not cheap food all day inc authentic pasta, notable fish and chips and popular Sun lunch in bar and restaurant, decent italian wines, real ales such as Brains Revd James and local Ceredigion Red Kite, courteous efficient service, log fires; piped music, no dogs or children; nice spot nr harbour and art and crafts shops (*David and Jean Hall, Geoff and Angela Jaques, Philip Lane*)

ST DAVID'S [SM7525]
☆ *Farmers Arms* SA62 6RF [Goat St]: Bustling old-fashioned low-ceilinged pub by cathedral gate, cheerful and unpretentiously pubby, mainly drinking on the left and eating on the right, central servery with well kept Brains Rev James, wide choice of good value home-made food from baguettes and ploughman's with local cheeses to steaks and Sun lunch, lively friendly young staff, chatty landlord and locals, pool room; they may try to keep your credit card while you eat, TV for rugby; cathedral view from large tables on big back suntrap terrace, and lack of car park means no tour bus groups, open all day (*Andy and Alice Jordan, P Price, Geoff and Angela Jaques, Tim and Mark Allen*)

STACKPOLE [SR9896]
☆ *Stackpole Inn* SA71 5DF [off B4319 S of Pembroke]: Good friendly L-shaped dining pub on four levels, wide choice from baguettes up inc plenty of local produce, Brains Rev James and Felinfoel Best and Double Dragon, pleasant atmosphere, neat uncluttered décor with light oak furnishings and ash beams in low ceilings, shove-ha'penny and dominoes; piped music; children welcome, disabled access and facilities, tables out in attractive gardens, good woodland and coastal walks in the Stackpole estate, open all day (Sun afternoon break), four-bedroom annexe (*Ron Gentry, LYM, Brian McBurnie, P Price, Ian and Deborah Carrington*)

TRESAITH [SN2751]
☆ *Ship* SA43 2JL: Tastefully decorated bistro-style pub on Cardigan Bay with magnificent views of sea, beach, famous waterfall, perhaps even dolphins and seals; good value generous home-made food from ploughman's with local cheeses to local fish, speciality paella, take-away pizzas, Buckleys and two changing guest beers often from Ceredigion, good photographs, dining area, cheerful staff; they may try to keep your credit card while you eat, children welcome (back room quieter); tables with heaters out on decking stepped down to garden (*Pete Yearsley, Mark Flynn*)

GWENT

ABERGAVENNY [SO2914]
Angel NP7 5EN [Cross St, by Town Hall]: Fresh and comfortable, with good friendly staff, enjoyable food, thriving atmosphere, some big comfortable settees, lovely bevelled glass behind servery, popular restaurant (*Mary McSweeney, Graham and Glenis Watkins*)

Coliseum NP7 5PE [Lion St/Frogmore St]: Steps up to modest Wetherspoons cinema conversion, very light and spacious, with low-priced real ales and good coffee, pleasant service, their usual food, lots of panelling, raised areas one end; wheelchair lift (*Mike Pugh, Reg Fowle, Helen Rickwood*)

☆ *Hardwick* NP7 9AA [Hardwick; B4598 2 miles E]: Heavy-beamed dining pub with chef-landlord doing good enterprising food using fresh seasonal local produce as well as more usual pubby dishes, welcoming landlady and good service, comfortable mix of furnishings and some interesting artworks in two linked dining rooms, Greene King and Rhymney from small bar, good wines and coffee; cl Sun evening and Mon (*Jane McQuitty, John Bromley, June Whitworth, Joyce and Maurice Cottrell, John Smart*)

Hen & Chickens NP7 5EG [Flannel St]: Unpretentious and relaxed traditional local, Bass, Brains and guest beers from bar unusually set against street windows, special drinks offers, basic wholesome cheap lunchtime food (not Sun), mugs of tea and coffee, friendly efficient staff, interesting side areas, popular darts, cards and dominoes; Sun jazz; TV, very busy on market day; terrace tables (*Pete Baker, the Didler, Reg Fowle, Helen Rickwood*)

BRYNGWYN [SO4007]
☆ *Cripple Creek* NP15 2AA [Abergavenny Rd; off old A40 W of Raglan]: Smartly extended and civilised old country dining pub with wide range of good reasonably priced food from simple things to more elaborate meals inc fresh fish and choice of four Sun roasts, efficient cheerful staff, real ales such as Adnams Broadside, Brains and Tetleys, decent wines, teas and coffees, pleasant restaurant; country views from small terrace, play area, open all day *(Mike Pugh, Rhiannon Davies)*

CALDICOT [ST4888]
Castle NP26 4HW [Church Rd]: Attractive open-plan pub doing well under current landlord, popular food all day, well kept changing real ales; by drive of historic castle, with tables outside, play area, covered terrace for smokers *(Tim and Ann Newell)*

CHEPSTOW [ST5394]
Castle View NP16 5EZ [Bridge St]: Hotel bar with white-painted walls and some exposed stonework, plush chairs and stools, good value bar food inc good sandwich range, Wye Valley Hereford PA from main bar counter, daily papers; opp castle and its car park, tables in pretty back garden with fountain, 13 bedrooms *(BB, Dr A J and Mrs Tompsett, Rob and Penny Wakefield)*
Grape NP16 5EU [St Mary St]: Two-level bar with upper gallery, Brains ales, decent reasonably priced pubby food, pleasant service *(Neil and Anita Christopher)*

GROSMONT [SO4024]
Angel NP7 8EP: 17th-c village local owned by village co-operative, Tomos Watkins ales, range of farm ciders, good value straightforward bar food, friendly atmosphere, pool room with darts; a couple of tables and boules pitch behind, seats out by ancient market cross on attractive steep single street within sight of castle *(R T and J C Moggridge, BB, Reg Fowle, Helen Rickwood)*

LLANDEVAUD [ST3991]
Foresters Oaks NP18 2AA [A48]: More smart restaurant than pub, but does have cosy good-sized beamed bar area with soft sofas where you can have just a drink, steps down to dining areas with exemplary service, good value meals with careful up-to-date cooking *(Dr and Mrs C W Thomas)*

LLANTHONY [SO2827]
☆ *Priory Hotel* NP7 7NN [aka Abbey Hotel, Llanthony Priory; off A465, back rd Llanvihangel Crucorney—Hay]: Magical setting for plain bar in dim-lit vaulted flagstoned crypt of graceful ruined Norman abbey, lovely in summer, with lawns around and the peaceful border hills beyond; real ales such as Brains Rev James and Felinfoel, farm cider in summer, good coffee, simple lunchtime bar food (can be long queue on fine summer days, but number system then works well), evening restaurant; no dogs or children, occasional live music; bedrooms in

restored parts of abbey walls, open all day Sat and summer Sun, cl winter Mon-Thurs and Sun evening, great walks all around *(LYM, the Didler, Barry and Anne, MLR, Jenny and Brian Seller, Reg Fowle, Helen Rickwood)*

LLANTILIO CROSSENNY [SO3815]
Hogs Head NP7 8TA [Treadam, just W off B4233]: Pub opened in converted barn as farm diversification, enjoyable food and real ale, some live music *(T B Noyes, Reg Fowle, Helen Rickwood)*

MONMOUTH [SO5012]
Kings Head NP25 3DY [Agincourt Sq]: Wetherspoons in former substantial coaching inn, plenty of well spaced seating with extensive central family area, their usual good deals all day on food (using some local produce) and on drink, pleasant service, lots of books inc interesting ones *(PRT, Reg Fowle, Helen Rickwood)*
Robin Hood NP25 3EQ [Monnow St]: Ancient pub with good home cooking, well kept Bass, friendly service; tables outside with play area *(Dr D J and Mrs S C Walker)*

PANTYGELLI [SO3017]
Crown NP7 7HR [Old Hereford Rd, N of Abergavenny]: Pretty stone-built pub below Black Mountains, welcoming inside, with nice old furnishings and dark wood, affable family service, well kept real ales such as Rhymney and Shepherd Neame Spitfire, Stowford Press farm cider, good wine choice, interesting and enjoyable lunchtime food inc good plate of welsh cheeses, more extensive evening menu, Sun roasts, plenty of local produce; attractive terrace *(Reg Fowle, Helen Rickwood, Colin McKerrow, Mike Pugh)*

PONTYPOOL [ST3398]
Carpenters Arms NP4 0TH [Coedypaen, just SE of Llandegfedd reservoir]: Enjoyable and imaginative food inc fresh fish from hard-working new chef-landlord in pretty country pub with warm welcome, well kept real ales, good wine range; children welcome, pleasant seating outside, plans for small caravan site *(Gwyneth and Salvo Spadaro-Dutturi)*
Sebastopol Social Club NP4 5DU [Wern Rd, Sebastopol]: Sign in for a very small fee, at least five well kept interesting real ales at tempting prices, sandwiches and rolls, bar and lounge; big-screen sports TV; well behaved children and dogs welcome, small back terrace *(Gwyneth and Salvo Spadaro-Dutturi)*

PRINCETOWN [SO1110]
Prince of Wales NP22 3AE [Merthyr Rd]: Well run family local with bargain food, comfortable wall banquettes, friendly service, log fire *(Bill Hainsworth)*

RAGLAN [SO4107]
Beaufort Arms NP15 2DY [High St]: Old-fashioned pub/hotel (former coaching inn), attentive friendly staff, comfortable and roomy character beamed bars, well kept ales, good range of food inc local dishes and familiar favourites, log fire; piped music; children welcome, 15 bedrooms *(Graham and Glenis Watkins, David and Sue Smith)*

Ship NP15 2DY [High St]: Lively local in former coaching inn, several well kept changing ales, three open fires, simple hearty pubby food, friendly staff, games table; very busy Sat night; front terrace, open all day *(David and Sue Smith)*

ST ARVANS [ST5196]

Piercefield NP16 6EJ: Modern décor and setting, nice choice of innovative enjoyable food, friendly efficient service *(Mike and Mary Carter)*

TINTERN [SO5300]

Anchor NP16 6TE: Smart pub right by abbey arches, reasonably priced usual food, local perry and cider displayed alongside original medieval cider press in main bar, two well kept real ales, plush banquettes, lots of paintings and photographs, large restaurant and separate carvery; daytime teahouse, spacious lawn with pets corner, comfortable bedrooms *(Linda and Rob Hilsenroth, Phil and Jane Hodson)*

TRELLECK [SO5005]

☆ ***Lion*** NP25 4PA [B4293 6 miles S of Monmouth]: Open-plan bar with one or two low black beams, comfortably worn in mix of furnishings, two log fires, several changing real ales, wide food range, cribbage, dominoes, shove-ha'penny and table skittles; piped music; children and dogs welcome, picnic-sets and an aviary out on the grass, side courtyard overlooking church, bedrooms in separate cottage, cl Sun evening, open all day summer Sats *(LM, R T and J C Moggridge, Theocsbrian, LYM, David and Sue Smith)*

GWYNEDD

BANGOR [SH5873]

Boatyard LL57 2SF [Garth Rd]: Former Union, five quiet and attractively refurbished linked areas inc dining areas with pale wood tables and chairs, well kept Burtonwood, Marstons and guest beers, wide choice of food inc fish and other local produce, good service, tasteful modicum of nautical memorabilia and racehorse photographs; terrace tables overlooking bay, reasonably priced bedrooms *(Brian Kells)*

Skerries LL57 1YE [High St]: Interesting local memorabilia, good choice of guest beers, darts and pool; juke box, video games; relaxing back terrace *(David Abbot)*

BARMOUTH [SH6115]

Last LL42 1EL [Church St]: 15th-c harbourside local behind modern front with low beams, flagstones, nautical bric-a-brac and harbour mural, little waterfall down back bar's natural rock wall, wide choice of simple well presented food, friendly staff, real ale; roadside tables overlooking harbour and bay *(Mike and Mary Carter)*

BETWS-Y-COED [SH7955]

☆ ***Ty Gwyn*** LL24 0SG [A5 just S of bridge to village]: Restaurant-with-rooms rather than pub (you must eat or stay overnight to be served alcohol – disqualifying it from our main entries), but pubby feel in beamed

lounge bar with ancient cooking range, easy chairs, antiques, silver, cut glass, old prints and interesting bric-a-brac, really good interesting meals (they do sandwiches too), real ales such as Adnams, Brains Rev James and Greene King Old Speckled Hen, friendly professional service; piped music; children welcome (high chair and toys), cl Mon-Weds in Jan *(Nigel and Sheila Mackereth, LYM, Mr and Mrs P J Fisk, Jon Floyd, Revd D Glover)*

CAERNARFON [SH4762]

☆ ***Black Buoy*** LL55 1RW [Northgate St]: Busy traditional pub by castle walls, sadly renamed losing its historical connection (properly Black Boy, from King Charles II's nickname in its Kings Head days), but attractively renovated, with cheery fire, beams from ships wrecked here in 16th c, bare floors and thick walls, lots of welsh chat, hearty food all day from filled baguettes and doorstep sandwiches up, willing friendly service, well kept ales such as Brains, Conwy Honey Fayre and Purple Moose Madogs, character lounge bar, restaurant, public bar with TV; a few pavement picnic-sets, bedrooms *(Alastair Stevenson, Revd D Glover, N R White, David Crook, Neil Whitehead, Victoria Anderson, Glenwys and Alan Lawrence)*

CONWY [SH7877]

☆ ***Castle Hotel*** LL32 8DB [High St]: Plenty of well spaced tables in interesting old building's cosy sympathetically refurbished bars, good substantial food all day here and in restaurant, three real ales, decent wines, friendly atmosphere and good informed service; own car parks (which helps here), 29 bedrooms with own bathrooms *(J F M and M West, Dave Webster, Sue Holland, Keith and Sue Ward)*

DOLGELLAU [SH7318]

Royal Ship LL40 1AR [Queens Sq]: Small civilised central hotel, appealingly old-fashioned, with varied above-average food, Robinsons real ale, compact public bar, lounge with dining area, more formal restaurant (worth booking ahead); bedrooms *(Mike and Mary Carter, C J Fletcher, Prof H G Allen, Robin and Ann Taylor)*

GLANDWYFACH [SH4843]

Goat LL51 9LJ [A487]: Thick slate walls, good choice of freshly made food, reasonable prices, real ale, pleasant largely welsh-speaking atmosphere, friendly family service; garden, bedrooms *(GLD, Noel Grundy)*

LLANBEDR [SH5826]

Victoria LL45 2LD [A496 S of Harlech]: Riverside dining pub well geared to lots of summer visitors, wide choice of food all day, big lounge with snug area by old-fashioned inglenook, Robinsons real ale, roomy dining area; children welcome, attractive garden with end play area, bedrooms *(Mike and Lynn Robinson, LYM)*

LLANBEDROG [SH3231]

Glynyweddw Arms LL53 7TH: Good choice of real ales and of enjoyable food; garden with terrace tables *(Noel Grundy)*

LLANDUDNO [SH7882]
Palladium LL30 2DD [Gloddaeth St]:
Spacious Wetherspoons in beautifully
restored former theatre, boxes and seats
intact, spectacular ceilings, quick polite
helpful service, good value food and drinks,
plenty of seating *(John Tav)*

LLANDWROG [SH4556]
Harp LL54 5SY [½ mile W of A499 S of
Caernarfon]: Welcoming village pub with
with irregular layout giving cosy corners and
plenty of atmosphere, good friendly service,
local and other real ales, daily papers and
magazines, plenty of board games and
Jenga, parrot that's bilingual if it's feeling
chatty, standard food plus welsh specialities,
cheerful separate dining room; picnic-sets
among fruit trees overlooking quiet village's
imposing church, well equipped cottagey
bedrooms, good breakfast, cl Mon
(K Hutchinson, BB, N R White)

LLANENGAN [SH2826]
Sun LL53 7LG: Friendly and cosy Robinsons
pub in small village nr spectacular sandy
Hell's Mouth beach, three real ales,
enjoyable family food; large partly covered
terrace and garden (very popular with
children) with outdoor summer bar and pool
table, bedrooms *(Noel Grundy)*

LLANUWCHLLYN [SH8730]
☆ *Eagles* LL23 7UB [aka Eryrod; A494/B4403]:
Good reasonably priced food from
sandwiches to traditional and more
enterprising dishes (bilingual menu), helpful
and courteous young staff, thriving
atmosphere in small front bar and plush back
lounge, neat décor with beams and some
stripped stone, back picture-window view of
mountains with Lake Bala in distance,
Theakstons Best, limited wine list, strong
coffee, no music; disabled access, picnic-sets
under cocktail parasols on flower-filled back
terrace *(KC, Michael and Jenny Back,
Jacquie Jones)*

LLANYSTUMDWY [SH4738]
Tafarn y Plu LL52 0SH: Thoroughly welsh
beamed two-bar pub opp Lloyd George's
boyhood home and museum, real ales such
as Conwy, Felinfoel or Evan Evans, a welsh
lager, Gwynt y Ddraig farm cider and even
welsh wines, spirits and liqueurs; warmly
welcoming licensees, enjoyable bar food
from sandwiches to steaks most days, log
fire, panelled partitions, traditional rustic
décor, small restaurant; large peaceful
garden *(Ian Parri, Gwilym Prydderch)*

MAENTWROG [SH6640]
Grapes LL41 4HN [A496; village signed from
A470]: Simple rambling stripped stone inn
popular with families in summer for wide
choice of generous standard food (can be a
wait at busy times), changing ales such as St
Austell Tribute, over 30 malt whiskies and
decent wine choice, lots of stripped pine
(pews, settles, panelling, pillars and carvings),
good log fires, intriguing collection of brass
blowlamps, lovely views from conservatory
dining extension, pleasant back terrace and

walled garden; they may try to keep your
credit card while you eat, juke box in public
bar; disabled facilities, dogs welcome, open all
day *(Julian and Janet Dearden, David Crook,
LYM, Mike and Mary Carter)*

PENTIR [SH5766]
Vaynol Arms LL57 4EA [B4366, off A5 S of
Bangor]: Good food using local produce at
value prices, friendly staff, real ales,
restaurant extension; children very welcome
(G Robinson)

RHYD DDU [SH5652]
Cwellyn Arms LL54 6TL [A4085 N of
Beddgelert]: Comfortably basic 18th-c
Snowdon pub not far below Welsh Highland
Railway top terminus, from two to nine real
ales, wide choice of popular generous
straightforward food from filled rolls and
baked potatoes up, good young temporary
staff; tiled-floor bar with small woodburner,
pleasant restaurant area (not always open),
small games room with pool, darts and TV;
children and walkers welcome, spectacular
Snowdon views from garden tables with
barbecue, babbling stream just over wall, big
adventure playground, camp site and
bedrooms, usually open all day *(David Crook)*

TALYLLYN [SH7210]
☆ *Tynycornel* LL36 9AJ [B4405, off A487 S of
Dolgellau]: Hotel rather than pub, but worth
knowing for its enjoyable bar lunches and
great setting below mountains, with picture
windows overlooking attractive lake; polite
service, comfortable sofas and armchairs,
central log fire, nice pictures, extended
restaurants and conservatory; keg beer;
children welcome, prettily planted side
courtyard, open all day, boat hire for
fishermen, good bedrooms *(Mike and
Mary Carter, C J Pratt, Des and Ursula Weston,
LYM, B and M Kendall, Jacquie Jones,
Robin and Ann Taylor)*

TREFRIW [SH7863]
Old Ship LL27 0JH: Cheerful local
atmosphere, friendly staff, enjoyable
generous food, changing real ales inc
Banks's and Marstons Pedigree, warm
woodburner *(Donald Mills, Ian Clarke)*

TUDWEILIOG [SH2336]
☆ *Lion* LL53 8ND [Nefyn Rd (B4417), Lleyn
Peninsula]: Cheerfully busy village inn with
wide choice of good value straightforward
food in bar and family dining conservatory
(small helpings for children, who have a
pretty free rein here), quick friendly service,
real ales well described by helpful landlord,
dozens of malt whiskies, decent wines,
games in lively public bar; pleasant front
garden, good value bedrooms *(LYM,
Noel Grundy, J V Dadswell)*

TYWYN [SH5800]
Corbett Arms LL36 9DG [Corbett Sq]:
Georgian/Victorian hotel with cosy public
bar, Greene King Old Speckled Hen and two
other ales from small brewers, full-height
tables in one corner, low ones elsewhere,
conservatory; good big garden, bedrooms
(C J Fletcher)

MID GLAMORGAN

CAERPHILLY [ST1484]

☆ **Black Cock** CF83 1NF [Watford; Tongwynlais exit from M4 junction 32, then right just after church]: Well run country pub with large brightly lit back dining extension off neat blue-plush bar, good choice of low-priced food all day from huge baguettes up inc several pies (speciality corned beef pie), well kept Hancocks HB and Theakstons Old Peculier, neat friendly staff, open fire in pretty tiled fireplace, interesting brass-tabled public bar; children welcome, sizeable terraced garden among trees with barbecue and good play area for under-9s, up in the hills just below Caerphilly Common, bedrooms, camp site, open all day (BB, John and Helen Rushton, B M Eldridge)

COITY [SS9281]

Six Bells CF35 6BH [Heol West Plas]: Recently well upgraded, with simple choice of good value food inc popular Sun lunch, obliging licensees; tables out by road opp medieval castle (R C Vincent)

KENFIG [SS8081]

☆ **Prince of Wales** CF33 4PR [2¼ miles from M4 junction 37; A4229 towards Porthcawl, then right when dual carriageway narrows on bend, signed Maudlam and Kenfig]: Interesting ancient local among historic sand dunes, plenty of individuality, well kept Bass and a wknd guest beer tapped from the cask, good choice of malt whiskies and decent wines, enjoyable straightforward food, stripped stone and log fire, lots of wreck pictures, traditional games, small upstairs dining room for summer and busy wknds; may have big-screen TV for special sports events; children and (in non-carpet areas) dogs welcome, handy for nature-reserve walks (awash with orchids in June) (John and Joan Nash, Phil and Sally Gorton, LYM, the Didler)

MISKIN [ST0480]

Miskin Arms CF72 8JQ [handy for M4 junction 34, via A4119 and B4264]: Friendly and roomy village pub with well kept changing ales such as Hancocks HB, good value bar food, popular restaurant Sun lunch and Tues-Sat evenings (Colin Moore)

OGMORE [SS8876]

☆ **Pelican** CF32 0QP: Recently revamped old country pub in nice spot above ruined castle, attractive rambling layout, good choice of enjoyable food and of well kept ales such as Bass, Greene King Old Speckled Hen and Worthington, enjoyable food from enterprising big rolls to interesting main dishes, good cheerful service; they may try to keep your credit card while you eat; tables on side terrace, quite handy for the beaches, open all day (Martin Jeeves, LYM)

PENDERYN [SN9408]

Red Lion CF44 9JR [off A4059 at Lamb, then up Church Rd (narrow hill from T junction)]: Good range of real ales tapped from the cask in friendly old stone-built local high in good walking country, dark beams, flagstone floors, antique settles, blazing log fires; great views from big garden (S Beh, LYM)

PONTSTICILL [SO0511]

Red Cow CF48 2UN [N of Merthyr Tydfil]: Well kept Rhymney Best, good generous pub lunches, welcoming helpful landlord (John Arnold)

THORNHILL [ST1484]

Travellers Rest CF83 1LY [A469 S of Caerphilly]: Attractive thatched stone-built Vintage Inn dining pub tucked into hillside, well kept ales inc Hancocks HB, good sensibly priced wine choice, winter mulled wine, friendly helpful young staff, daily papers, reasonably priced food all day from sandwiches up, huge fireplace and nooks and crannies off low-beamed main bar; piped music; children welcome lunchtimes, open all day, plenty of tables out on grass, good walks (John and Joan Nash)

POWYS

BEGUILDY [SO1979]

Radnorshire Arms LD7 1YE [B4355 Knighton—Newtown]: Beautifully set pretty little black and white pub with wide-ranging enjoyable food using local produce and good fish (best to book Sun lunch), good-sized helpings, cheerful bustling atmosphere, friendly licensees, well kept local beers and Fullers London Pride, nice house wine, extensive comfortable eating areas, small attractive lounge (anon)

BERRIEW [SJ1800]

☆ **Lion** SY21 8PQ [B4390; village signed off A483 Welshpool—Newtown]: Black and white inn in attractive riverside village (with lively sculpture gallery), nicely old-fashioned inglenook public bar and partly stripped stone lounge bar with open fire, home-made food (not Sun evening) here or in restaurant from sandwiches and baguettes to good fresh fish choice, well organised service, Banks's and Marstons real ales, decent house wines, dominoes and cribbage; more reports on service please; children and dogs welcome, bedrooms, open all day (LYM, Jill Sparrow, Dave Cuthbert, John and Helen Rushton, J V Dadswell)

BLEDDFA [SO2068]

Hundred House LD7 1PA [A488 Knighton—Penybont]: Small relaxed lounge with log fire in huge stone fireplace, L-shaped main bar with attractively flagstoned lower games area, cosy dining room with another vast fireplace, has had good value food and real ales such as Brains Bread of Heaven; tables in peaceful garden dropping steeply behind to small stream, lovely countryside; new licensees took over end 2006 – reports on new regime please (BB)

BRECON [SO0428]

Boars Head LD3 9AL [Watergate, nr R Usk Bridge]: Big two-bar town pub serving as tap for Breconshire brewery, several of their ales and a guest beer, enjoyable bar food from toasties up, big log fireplace, basic public bar with pool and big-screen TV; terrace overlooking River Usk *(MLR, Andy and Jill Kassube, Mr and Mrs R B Berry)*

BUILTH WELLS [SO00451]

Lion LD2 3DT [Broad St]: Well kept hotel bar with good service, wide range of enjoyable lunchtime bar food, real ale; comfortable traditional bedrooms *(A and B D Craig)*

CARNO [SN9696]

Aleppo Merchant SY17 5LL [A470 Newtown—Machynlleth]: Good value popular food from good sandwiches to steaks, obliging service, Boddingtons and Marstons Pedigree, tapestries in plushly modernised stripped stone bar, peaceful lounge on right with open fire, restaurant (well behaved children allowed here), back extension with big-screen TV in games room; piped music; steps up to tables in attractively enlarged garden, bedrooms, nice countryside *(LYM, Michael and Jenny Back)*

CRICKHOWELL [SO2119]

White Hart NP8 1DL [Brecon Rd (A40 W)]: Stripped stone, beams and flagstones, friendly new landlord, enjoyable food from lunchtime sandwiches up inc several welsh specialities, Brains ales and a guest beer, bar with end eating area, sizeable restaurant, pub games; may be piped music; children in eating areas, some tables outside, open all day Sat *(LYM, Mike and Mary Carter)*

CWMDU [SO1823]

☆ *Farmers Arms* NP8 1RU [A479 NW of Crickhowell]: Friendly 18th-c country local, popular with walkers, with welcoming landlord, good hearty home cooking inc good local lamb, beef and cheeses, some bargain prices, well kept Brains ales, decent wines by the glass, unpretentious partly flagstoned bar with attractive prints, stove in big stone fireplace, plush restaurant; TV; children welcome, tables in garden, comfortable bedrooms with good breakfast, campsite nearby *(BB, Jenny and Brian Seller, Paul and Sue Dix, Mike and Mary Carter)*

DERWENLAS [SN7299]

Black Lion SY20 8TN [A487 just S of Machynlleth]: Cosy and peaceful 16th-c country pub, good range of enjoyable sensibly priced food, good staff, real ale, decent wines, heavy black beams, thick walls and black timbering, attractive pictures and lion models, tartan carpet over big slate flagstones, great log fire; piped music; garden up behind with play area and steps up into woods, bedrooms *(Mike and Mary Carter, BB)*

DINAS MAWDDWY [SH8514]

Llew Coch SY20 9JA [aka Red Lion; just off A470 E of Dolgellau]: Genuine old country local surrounded by steep fir forests (good walks), wide choice of cheap cheerful food from good sandwiches to trout or salmon from River Dovey just behind, well kept Brains Rev James and Worthington, quick friendly service, charming timbered front bar sparkling with countless brasses, good log

fire; inner family room lively with video games, pool and Sat evening live music, dining extension (popular for Sun lunch); good wheelchair access, dogs welcome, tables out on quiet lane *(B and M Kendall, LYM)*

HAY-ON-WYE [SO2039]

Hollybush HR3 5PS [SW on B4350]: Old country inn with bar recently opened up into big single room, log fire one end, bar the other with a couple of real ales such as Breconshire and Spinning Dog, food all day; bedrooms, camp site by River Wye, open all day from 8am *(MLR)*

Three Tuns HR3 5DB [Broad St]: Former favourite reopened on the very day in summer 2007 that we finished writing this chapter, so too soon to give a verdict, but must be a good omen! 2005 fire damage thoughtfully made good by new licensees, blackened beams, some stripped masonry, inglenook woodburners, ancient stairs restored to upper raftered restaurant served by new kitchen, tables out on back terrace; reports please *(BOB)*

KNIGHTON [SO2872]

Horse & Jockey LD7 1AE [Wylcwm Pl]: Several cosy and friendly areas, one with log fire, good traditional and innovative food in bar and adjoining restaurant, real ales such as Greene King Old Speckled Hen; tables in pleasant courtyard, handy for Offa's Dyke *(Joan York, Tim and Mark Allen)*

LLANAFAN FAWR [SN9655]

Red Lion LD2 3PN [B4358 SW of Llandrindod Wells]: Attractive ancient pub in interesting small village, welcoming and entertaining landlord, friendly efficient staff, good fresh food using local produce, real ales, good atmosphere in the two or three rooms off front bar; tables out by roadside *(John Joseph Smith)*

LLANBEDR [SO2320]

Red Lion NP8 1SR [off A40 at Crickhowell]: Quaint spotlessly kept old local in pretty little village set in dell, heavy beams, antique settles in lounge and snug, log fires, welcoming service, front dining area with home-made food; good walking country (porch for muddy boot removal), cl wkdy lunchtime (exc 2-5 Weds – no food then), open all day wknds *(Owen Barden)*

LLANGEDWYN [SJ1924]

☆ *Green Inn* SY10 9JW [B4396 3/4 mile E of Llangedwyn]: Ancient country dining pub with various snug alcoves, nooks and crannies, a good mix of furnishings inc oak settles and pretty fabrics, blazing log fire, Tetleys with a couple of changing winter guest beers; children and dogs welcome, attractive garden over road running down towards River Tanat (fishing permits available), open all day wknds *(LYM)*

LLANGENNY [SO2417]

Dragons Head NP8 1HD: Chatty two-room bar in pretty valley setting, friendly efficient staff, quickly changing real ales such as Brains Rev James and Shepherd Neame

Spitfire, local farm cider, reasonably priced wines, wide choice of enjoyable home-made food from sandwiches to welsh black beef, low beams, big woodburner, pews, housekeeper's chairs and a high-backed settle among other seats, two attractive dining areas; picnic-sets on heated terrace and over road by stream, nearby camp site, cl wkdy lunchtimes *(LYM, Owen Barden)*

LLANGURIG [SN9079]

Blue Bell SY18 6SG: Cheerful country inn with well kept real ales and decent food in flagstoned bar, games room with darts, dominoes and pool, small dining room; inexpensive simple bedrooms *(LYM, Colin Moore)*

LLANGYNIDR [SO1519]

☆ *Coach & Horses* NP8 1LS [Cwm Crawnon Rd (B4558 W of Crickhowell)]: Tidy and roomy flower-decked dining pub with welcoming licensees doing good value bar food from ciabattas up, real ales, comfortable banquettes and stripped stone, nice big log fire ideal for winter nights, large attractive restaurant; wait-your-turn food ordering system, no dogs now; picnic-sets across road in safely fenced pretty sloping garden by lock of Newport & Brecon Canal, lovely setting and walks, open all day *(Blaise Vyner, LYM, Mike and Mary Carter)*

Red Lion NP8 1NT [off B4558; Duffryn Rd]: Creeper-covered 16th-c inn, attractively furnished bow-windowed bar with good log fire, Breconshire real ales, bar food such as curries, lively games room; sheltered pretty garden, good value bedrooms *(Paul J Robinshaw)*

LLANGYNOG [SJ0526]

New Inn SY10 0EX [B4391 S of Bala]: Comfortable neatly kept pub with several linked areas, obliging landlord, wide choice of bargain generous food from crusty baguettes up, Flowers, restaurant; disabled access *(Michael and Jenny Back)*

LLANWDDYN [SJ0219]

Lake Vyrnwy Hotel SY10 0LY: Comfortable pub extension, well done in old tavern style, behind smart late 19th-c country hotel in remote beautiful spot with lake view from big-windowed blue-carpeted lounge and sun-struck balcony, well kept Woods Shropshire Lad, wide range of enjoyable generous food from sandwiches up, friendly young staff; quiet piped music; dogs welcome in simple public bar, bedrooms *(Dennis Jenkin)*

LLOWES [SO1941]

☆ *Radnor Arms* HR3 5JA [A438 Brecon—Hereford]: Attractive country dining pub with very wide choice of good food served in local pottery (for sale here) from good sandwiches and choice of inventive soups to fine restaurant-style dishes, fair prices, friendly staff and regulars, well kept Brains, good coffee, cottagey bar with beams and stripped stone, log fire, two small dining rooms, postcards and knick-knacks for sale, lost property section; tables in interesting garden looking out over fields towards the Wye, cl Sun pm, Mon *(Reg Fowle, Helen Rickwood)*

LLYSWEN [SO1337]

☆ *Griffin* LD3 0UR [A470, village centre]: Attractive country pub with sensible choice of enjoyable food from good home-baked open sandwiches up, Brains real ales, limited but good value wines by the glass, great coffee, attentive welcoming staff, fine log fire in easy-going cosy bar; piped music; children welcome in eating areas, tables out by road, comfortable bedrooms *(Bruce and Sharon Eden, Terry and Linda Moseley, LYM)*

MACHYNLLETH [SH7400]

Skinners Arms SY20 8AJ [Penrallt St]: Friendly two-bar local with well priced drinks inc well kept real ale, good choice of food all day at least in summer, good mix of ages; open all day *(Laura Holt)*

☆ *Wynnstay Arms* SY20 8AE [Maengwyn St]: Civilised old-fashioned market-town hotel, neatly kept, with good sandwiches and interesting hot food in busy and welcomingly pubby bare-boards annexe bar, good friendly staff, three real ales, good choice of wines by the glass, comfortable and relaxed hotel lounge and good restaurant; courtyard tables, bedrooms *(Mike and Mary Carter, A and B D Craig, J and F Gowers)*

MALLWYD [SH8612]

Brigands SY20 9HJ: Attractive and welcoming stone-built Tudor-style hotel with big sofas and woodburner in spick and span central bar, cosy snug, dining rooms either side, good range of reasonably priced food from sandwiches and chips up inc good local beef and lamb, Timothy Taylors Landlord and Worthington, good wine choice; tables on extensive neatly kept lawns with play area, nice bedrooms, lovely views, three miles of sea trout fishing on River Dovey *(John and Joan Nash)*

MONTGOMERY [SO2296]

Dragon SY15 6PA [Market Sq]: Tall timbered 17th-c hotel with attractive prints and china in pleasant beamed bar, good friendly service, enjoyable reasonably priced food, good wines and coffee, Woods Special and guest beer, board games, restaurant; unobtrusive piped music, jazz most Weds; comfortable well equipped bedrooms and swimming pool, quiet little town below ruined Norman castle, open all day *(LYM, Mark Percy, Lesley Mayoh, Dave Cuthbert, Tony and Dot Mariner)*

NEW RADNOR [SO2160]

Radnor Arms LD8 2SP [Broad St]: Unpretentious village local with enjoyable reasonably priced home cooking from baked potatoes to popular Sun carvery, children's dishes, two well kept changing ales, choice of ciders, friendly staff; open all day wknds *(MLR)*

PRESTEIGNE [SO3164]

☆ *Radnorshire Arms* LD8 2BE [High St (B4355 N of centre)]: Fine Elizabethan timbered hotel, comfortably worn in and full of rambling individuality and historical charm, recently bought by new owner and still settling down as we went to press; relaxed bar, venerable dark oak panelling, latticed windows, elegantly moulded black oak beams, polished copper pans and measures, a handful of armchairs, lovely dining room, friendly staff, a couple of changing real ales and local cider; piped music; children welcome, garden area with shelter, bedrooms; more reports on new regime please *(LYM, Ian Stafford, Reg Fowle, Helen Rickwood)*

TALGARTH [SO1729]

Castle Inn LD3 0EP [Pengenffordd, A479 3 miles S]: At the head of Rhiangoll Valley, handy for Black Mountains walks inc nearby Castell Dinas and Waun Fach, well kept changing ales such as Archers Golden, Rhymney and Wye Valley, pubby food using local meats, friendly staff, log fire; no dogs (pub dog called Spot); picnic-sets in sheltered garden, four bedrooms and neatly refurbished bunkhouse, cl Mon and wkdy lunchtimes *(MLR)*

TALYBONT-ON-USK [SO1122]

☆ *Star* LD3 7YX [B4558]: Fine choice of changing real ales inc local Breconshire, usually about four in winter and more in summer, in relaxed and unpretentious stone-built local, straightforward food from good cheap filled rolls to some tasty main dishes, friendly attentive service, good log fire in fine inglenook with bread oven, Dunkerton's farm cider, three bustling plain rooms off central servery inc brightly lit games area, lots of beermats, bank notes and coins on beams, monthly band night, winter quiz Mon; dogs and children welcome, picnic-sets in sizeable tree-ringed garden below Monmouth & Brecon Canal, bedrooms, open all day Sat and summer *(LYM, Pete Baker, the Didler, Andy and Jill Kassube, MLR, Paul J Robinshaw)*

White Hart LD3 7JD: Stone-built coaching inn with big relaxed bar divided by working fireplace from beamed dining area, enjoyable food inc all-day Sun roast, four well kept changing ales, Thatcher's farm cider, welcoming knowledgeable landlord; on Taff Trail, some tables out by Monmouth & Brecon Canal *(Jarrod and Wendy Hopkinson)*

WELSHPOOL [SJ2107]

Raven SY21 7LT [Raven Sq]: Good range of reasonably priced home-made food from baguettes and baked potatoes up in welcoming lounge bar/restaurant; handy for steam railway *(Dave Cuthbert)*

SOUTH GLAMORGAN

CARDIFF [ST1776]

☆ *Cayo Arms* CF11 9LL [Cathedral Rd]: Chatty helpful young staff, well kept Tomos Watkins ales with a guest such as Banks's, good value food all day from ciabattas and baked potatoes to full meals inc Sun lunch, daily papers, pubby front bar with

comfortable side area in Edwardian style, more modern back dining area; piped music, big-screen TV in one part, very busy wknds; tables out in front, more in yard behind (with parking), good value bedrooms, open all day *(Michael and Alison Sandy, Bruce Bird, the Didler, Dr and Mrs A K Clarke)*

Old Butchers Arms CF14 6NB [Heol Y Felin, Rhiwbina]: Enjoyable reasonably priced food inc afternoon bargains, Brains, Greene King Old Speckled Hen and changing guest beers, popular with students *(R J Collis, Dr and Mrs A K Clarke)*

Vulcan CF24 2FH [Adam St]: Largely untouched Victorian local surrounded (and perhaps soon to be swallowed) by redevelopment, good value lunches (not Sun) in sedate lounge with some original features inc ornate fireplace, well kept Brains Bitter and SA, maritime pictures in lively sawdust-floor public bar with darts, dominoes, cards and juke box; open all day, cl Sun pm *(the Didler)*

Waterguard CF10 4PA [Harbour Drive]: Pleasant if unusual pub – a sort of modernist blockhouse with a castellated gothic front half – with bargain Sam Smiths beers, good value traditional food all day, friendly staff; beautiful bay views, picnic-sets in large outside area, open all day *(B M Eldridge)*

Westgate CF11 9AD [Cowbridge Rd E]: Friendly and comfortable, with well kept Brains, good value food, caricatures, old photographs and plaques showing former Cardiff pubs *(Bruce Bird)*

Yard CF10 1AD [St Mary St]: Unusual conversion of the loading bay of Brains' original brewery (the well kept ales now come from their nearby new home in the former Hancocks' brewery), good value food esp chargrills cooked in front of you, functional décor using some original girders etc, upper gallery with Brains family portraits in comfortable 'board room'; piped music may be loud, lighting dim; courtyard tables, open all day till late *(Bruce Bird)*

LLANCARFAN [ST0570]

Fox & Hounds CF62 3AD [signed off A4226; can also be reached from A48 from Bonvilston or B4265 via Llancadle]: Good carefully cooked food using local ingredients such as fresh fish, welsh black beef and farmhouse cheeses in neat comfortably modernised village pub, friendly open-plan bar rambling through arches, coal fire, Brains Bitter and Rev James, good wine choice, traditional settles and plush banquettes, candlelit bistro, simple end family room; children welcome, unobtrusive piped music; tables out behind, pretty streamside setting by interesting church, eight comfortable bedrooms, good breakfast, open all day wknds *(Blaise Vyner, BB)*

LLANTWIT MAJOR [SS9668]

Old Swan CF61 1SB [Church St]: Unusual dark medieval building with lancet windows, candles even midday, good log fires in big stone fireplaces, both main rooms set for wide choice of attractively priced usual food from baguettes up (over 20 mash flavours), children's menu, a couple of changing ales such as Oakham JHB and St Austell; tables in back garden, open all day (LYM, Ian Phillips)

PENARTH [ST1871]

Windsor CF64 1JE [Windsor Rd]: Convivial bare-boards pub with about eight interesting changing real ales, good value end restaurant; frequent live music (Pete Baker)

PENDOYLAN [ST0576]

☆ *Red Lion* CF71 7UJ [2½ miles S of M4 junction 34]: Quiet and comfortable dining pub, unusually good interesting restaurant food, good value lunches and early evening meals, friendly professional service, pleasant bar with Marstons Pedigree; good garden with play area, next to church in pretty vale (Virginia Porter, Martin Jeeves)

WEST GLAMORGAN

CRYNANT [SN7906]

Kingfisher SA10 8PP: Hard-working newish licensees doing enjoyable food inc good Sun lunch (Gaynor Gregory)

PEN-Y-CAE [SN8413]

Pen-y-Cae SA9 1FA [Brecon Rd]: Well furnished, with enjoyable if not cheap food, great views from conservatory restaurant (glass lift for the less than able) (Gaynor Gregory)

REYNOLDSTON [SS4889]

King Arthur SA3 1AD [Higher Green, off A4118]: Cheerfully busy pub/hotel with timbered main bar and hall, back family summer dining area (games room with pool in winter), popular food from lunchtime baguettes to Sun roasts, Bass, Felinfoel Double Dragon and Worthington Best, friendly helpful staff, country-house bric-a-brac and log fire; lively local atmosphere evenings, piped music; tables outside with play area, open all day, bedrooms (Eric and Mary Barrett, LYM)

Please tell us if the décor, atmosphere, food or drink at a pub is different from our description. We rely on readers' reports to keep us up to date. No stamp needed: The Good Pub Guide, FREEPOST TN1569, Wadhurst, E Sussex TN5 7BR.

Channel Islands

The very good all-rounder, the Fleur du Jardin in King's Mills on Guernsey, continues to set the standard for pubs on the Channel Islands. With the only Food Award in this chapter, its menu offers a good cross-section of beautifully prepared dishes, from pub standards to more imaginative meals. Once again, it is the Channel Islands Dining Pub of the Year. Eating out in the islands' pubs is generally good value – given equivalent quality, pub food prices tend to be rather lower than on the mainland. The Old Portelet Inn in St Brelade has such good prices that it qualifies for a Bargain Award; there are quite a few places, such as the Old Smugglers in St Brelade and La Pulente on St Ouens Bay, that keep their prices nearly as low. Drinks prices too are comfortably below the mainland average (though some areas on the mainland are now cheaper). The islands' own breweries are Jersey and, on Guernsey, Randalls, though you may find mainland beers such as Bass, Courage and Ringwood just as cheap. Several places have lovely sea views – look out especially for the harbourside terrace at the Old Court House in St Aubin, and the beach views from La Pulente in St Ouens Bay. The Lucky Dip section at the end of this short chapter includes a few other recommendations; we'd particularly note the Harbour Lights at Newtown on Alderney – a *Guide* perennial.

KING'S MILLS   MAP 1

Fleur du Jardin 🍴 ♀ 🛏

King's Mills Road; GY5 7JT

CHANNEL ISLANDS DINING PUB OF THE YEAR

Gently upmarket hotel in attractive grounds, lovely food

This well appointed old hotel is peacefully set in good-sized gardens, with tables among colourful borders, shrubs, bright hanging baskets and flower barrels. Comfortably civilised, its cosy relaxing rooms have low beams and thick granite walls, a good log fire in the public bar (popular with locals), and individual country furnishings in the hotel lounge bar. Fullers London Pride and Guernsey Sunbeam (actually now brewed by the Jersey Brewery, specially for pubs on Guernsey) are well kept on handpump, alongside a good wine list (with around 15 by the glass) and a local cider. Service is friendly and efficient; piped music, TV. They have a large car park and there is a swimming pool for residents.

🍴 A well balanced menu includes beautifully prepared dishes such as soup, timbale of crab with spicy guacamole, seared scallops with tomato, garlic and pepper salsa, italian meat platter, game, mushroom and juniper pudding, veal sausages with red onion mash and red wine jus, lamb and coconut curry, scampi, fish and chips, and daily specials such as pork and pepper terrine, and rump steak braised in red wine, shallots and mushrooms. *Starters/Snacks: £3.50 to £4.75. Main Courses: £7.50 to £14.50. Puddings: £4.50 to £7.00*

Free house ~ Licensee Amanda Walker ~ Real ale ~ Bar food ~ Restaurant ~ (01481) 257996 ~ Children welcome ~ Dogs allowed in bedrooms ~ Open 10.30am-11.45pm ~ Bedrooms: £69B/£138B

Recommended by Theocsbrian, Stephen R Holman, Gordon Neighbour, Steve Whalley, Bob and Angela Brooks

ROZEL   MAP 1

Rozel

La Vallee De Rozel; JE3 6AJ

Traditional tucked-away pub with reasonably priced food inc fresh fish in restaurant, nice hillside garden

At the edge of a sleepy little fishing village and just out of sight of the sea, this friendly place has a very pleasant steeply terraced and partly covered hillside garden. Inside, the bar counter (with Bass, Wells & Youngs Bombardier and Courage Directors under light blanket pressure) and tables in the traditional-feeling and cosy little dark-beamed back bar are stripped to their original light wood finish, and there are dark plush wall seats and stools, an open granite fireplace, and old prints and local pictures on the cream walls. Leading off is a carpeted area with flowers on big solid square tables. Piped music, TV, juke box, darts, pool, cribbage and dominoes in the games room. The upstairs restaurant has a relaxed rustic french atmosphere.

🍴 Fairly priced bar food served in generous helpings might include soup, sandwiches, filled ciabattas, salads, thai butternut squash curry with noodles, lamb shank, fish platter, and daily specials such as scallops with mulled wine jelly, green tagliatelle with prawns and truffle oil, and fillet steak wrapped in parma ham, with puddings such as orange panna cotta with raspberry ice-cream. *Starters/Snacks: £2.95 to £6.95. Main Courses: £5.95 to £15.95. Puddings: £3.95 to £4.95*

Free house ~ Licensee Trevor Amy ~ Real ale ~ Bar food (12-2.15(3.30 Sun), 6.30-9.15; not Mon or Sun evening in winter) ~ Restaurant (not Sun evening) ~ (01534) 869801 ~ Children welcome ~ Dogs welcome ~ Open 11am-11pm

Recommended by BOB

ST AUBIN   MAP 1

Old Court House Inn 🛏

Harbour Boulevard; JE3 8AB

Fabulous harbour views from some rooms, traditional bar, food from pubby snacks to restaurant dishes; a nice place to stay

The conservatory and decking in front of this very popular 15th-c hotel have glorious views over the tranquil harbour and on past St Aubin's fort right across the bay to St Helier. Other reception rooms include the pubby downstairs bar with cushioned wooden seats built against its stripped granite walls, low black beams, joists in a white ceiling, a turkey carpet, and an open fire. A dimly lantern-lit inner room has an illuminated rather brackish-looking deep well, and beyond that is the spacious cellar room which is open in summer. The Westward Bar is elegantly constructed from the actual gig of a schooner and offers a restauranty menu with prices to match. The front rooms here were once the home of a wealthy merchant, whose cellars stored privateers' plunder alongside more legitimate cargo, and the upstairs restaurant still shows signs of its time as a courtroom. One or two well kept beers might be Bass and Jersey Special on handpump; piped music. It can be difficult to find parking near the hotel.

🍴 Bar food includes soup, ciabattas, and starters such as chicken liver parfait with apple and cranberry chutney and tempura prawns with peanut and bean sprout salad, and main courses such as vegetable lasagne, meaty lasagne, sausage and mash, fish and chips, fruits de mer cocktail, plaice and grilled dover sole. *Starters/Snacks: £5.95 to £6.75. Main Courses: £11.50 to £15.95. Puddings: £4.25*

Free house ~ Licensee Jonty Sharp ~ Real ale ~ Bar food (12.30-2.30, 7-10) ~ Restaurant ~ (01534) 746433 ~ Children welcome ~ Dogs allowed in bar ~ Open 11am-11pm ~ Bedrooms: £60B/£120B

Recommended by Phil and Helen Holt

ST BRELADE   MAP 1

Old Portelet Inn £

Portelet Bay; JE3 8AJ

Family-friendly place with good value generous pubby food (something virtually all day), and good views

There's plenty at this enjoyable 17th-c farmhouse to ensure that families have a good visit. There's a supervised indoor play area (half an hour 60p), another one outside, board games in the wooden-floored loft bar, and even summer entertainments; also TV, pool and piped music. The pub is well placed at the head of a long flight of granite steps, giving views across Portelet (Jersey's most southerly bay). There are picnic-sets on the partly covered flower-bower terrace by a wishing well, and seats in the sizeable landscaped garden, with lots of scented stocks and other flowers. The low-beamed downstairs bar has a stone bar counter (well kept Bass and a guest such as Courage Directors kept under light blanket pressure and reasonably priced house wine), a huge open fire, gas lamps, old pictures, etched glass panels from France, and a nice mixture of old wooden chairs on bare oak boards and quarry tiles. It opens into the big timber-ceilinged barn restaurant, with standing timbers and plenty of highchairs; disabled and baby-changing facilities. It can get very busy, but does have its quiet moments too.

🍽 From a short snack menu, generous helpings of food, quickly served by neatly dressed attentive staff, include sandwiches, soup, prawn cocktail, macaroni cheese, baked potatoes, fish and chips, steak and kidney pudding, roast chicken, beef balti, daily specials such as duck breast with mango and coconut sauce; puddings such as lemon meringue pie, and sundaes. *Starters/Snacks: £2.90 to £4.95. Main Courses: £5.50 to £14.95. Puddings: £1.20 to £4.30*

Randalls ~ Manager Sarah Pye ~ Real ale ~ Bar food (12-2.15, 6-9(snack menu 2.30-5.30)) ~ (01534) 741899 ~ Children in restaurant and family room ~ Dogs allowed in bar ~ Open 10am-11pm

Recommended by Stephen R Holman, Phyl and Jack Street, George Atkinson

Old Smugglers

Ouaisne Bay; OS map reference 595476; JE3 8AW

Nicely straightforward proper pub, sturdily old-fashioned, with views and bar food

The welcoming bar here has thick walls, black beams, log fires and cosy black built-in settles, with well kept Bass and two guests from brewers such as Greene King Abbot and Belhaven 80/- on handpump, and a farm cider; sensibly placed darts, cribbage and dominoes. A glassed porch running the width of the building takes in interesting views over one of the island's many defence towers.

🍽 Bar food includes soup, vegetarian spring roll with sweet chilli dip, filled baguettes, prawn cocktail, steak and Guinness pie, battered haddock, chicken curry, lasagne, duck breast with orange and brandy sauce, king prawns with garlic butter or black bean sauce and steaks. *Starters/Snacks: £3.30 to £5.95. Main Courses: £5.95 to £13.25*

Free house ~ Licensee Nigel Godfrey ~ Real ale ~ Bar food (12-2, 6-9; not winter Sun evenings) ~ Restaurant ~ (01534) 741510 ~ Children welcome ~ Dogs allowed in bar ~ Open 11-11

Recommended by BOB

Bedroom prices are for high summer. Even then you may get reductions for more than one night, or (outside tourist areas) weekends. Winter special rates are common, and many inns cut bedroom prices if you have a full evening meal.

ST HELIER

MAP 1

Town House

New Street; JE2 3RA

Big lively pub with simple bistro food, sports bar

More attractive inside than its unassuming old cinema-style exterior suggests, this spacious 1930s pub is popular with a local crowd. Its two main bars are divided by heavy glass and brass doors. The sports bar on the left has two giant TV screens, darts and pool and a juke box. To the right, the lounge area has parquet flooring, some attractive panelling and upholstered armchairs at low round glass tables. Well kept Jersey Jimmys Special on handpump, and sound house wines; piped music.

🍽 **Bar food currently includes soup, sandwiches, chicken liver parfait, burgers, fajitas, mussels cooked in various ways, fish and chips, grilled pork steak with calvados cream and mushroom sauce, rib-eye steak, and puddings such as Baileys bread and butter pudding.** *Starters/Snacks: £3.50 to £8.50. Main Courses: £7.50 to £11.95. Puddings: £2.95 to £5.50*

Jersey ~ Managers Duncan Carse and Andy James ~ Real ale ~ Bar food (12-2(1-4 Sun), 6.30-9; not Mon or Sun evening) ~ Restaurant ~ (01534) 615000 ~ Children welcome ~ DJ Fri and Sat evenings ~ Open 11am-11pm
Recommended by BOB

ST JOHN

MAP 1

Les Fontaines

Le Grand Mourier, Route du Nord; JE3 4AJ

Nicely traditional public bar, bigger family area, decent food, views from terrace, play area

The cheery bustle of happy families and locals livens up this enjoyable former farmhouse, which is in a pretty spot on the north coast, and a nice place for a pint after a walk (well kept Bass and Ringwood). As you go in, look out for a worn, unmarked door at the side of the building, or as you go down the main entry lobby towards the bigger main bar go through the tiny narrow door on your right. These entrances take you into the best part, the public bar (where you might even hear the true Jersey patois) which has very heavy beams in the low dark ochre ceiling, massively thick irregular red granite walls, cushioned settles on the quarry-tiled floor and antique prints. The big granite-columned fireplace with a log fire warming its unusual inglenook seats may date back to the 16th c, and still sports its old smoking chains and side oven. The quarry tiled main bar is a marked contrast, with plenty of wheelback chairs around neat dark tables, and a spiral staircase leading up to a wooden gallery under the high pine-raftered plank ceiling; piped music and board games. A bonus for families is Pirate Pete's, a play area for children. Seats on a terrace outside have good views.

🍽 **Bar food includes sandwiches, soup, ploughman's, battered cod and cumberland sausage, and specials such as baked lamb shank with mash, cajun salmon fillet with spinach sauce, garlic seared prawn and scallop salad and lamb chops glazed with balsamic vinegar.** *Starters/Snacks: £3.50 to £5.25. Main Courses: £7.25 to £14.95. Puddings: £3.25*

Randalls ~ Manager Hazel O'Gorman ~ Real ale ~ Bar food (12-2.15(2.45 Sun), 6-9(8.30 Sun)) ~ (01534) 862707 ~ Children welcome ~ Dogs allowed in bar ~ Open 11.30am-11pm
Recommended by Ron Gentry

If a service charge is mentioned prominently on a menu or accommodation terms, you
must pay it if service was satisfactory. If service is really bad, you are legally
entitled to refuse to pay some or all of the service charge as compensation
for not getting the service you might reasonably have expected.

ST OUENS BAY   MAP 1

La Pulente

Start of Five Mile Road; OS map reference 562488; JE3 8HG

Lovely sea views, enjoyable food, friendly atmosphere

Marvellous terrace views across the endless extent of Jersey's longest beach are reason
enough to visit this bustling seaside pub. Inside, the comfortably carpeted lounge (with
ragged walls and scrubbed wood tables) and the conservatory share the same sweeping
views. Friendly staff serve well kept Bass on handpump; piped music.

🍴 **Bar food includes sandwiches, soup, baked potatoes, ploughman's, battered cod, steak
and ale pie, thai chicken curry, swordfish steak niçoise, 8oz sirloin, and daily specials
such as monkfish and king prawn kebab, roast duck breast and grilled lemon sole or
bream.** *Starters/Snacks: £3.00 to £5.50. Main Courses: £6.95 to £13.50. Puddings: £3.00*

Randalls ~ Manager Julia Wallace ~ Real ale ~ Bar food (12-2.15(3 Sun in winter), 6-9(8.30
Sun); not Sun evening in winter) ~ Restaurant ~ (01534) 744487 ~ Children welcome ~
Open 11am-11pm

Recommended by Phil and Helen Holt, Keith Eastelow

LUCKY DIP

Besides the fully inspected pubs, you might like to try these Lucky Dips recommended to us and
described by readers (if you do, please send us reports: www.goodguides.co.uk).

ALDERNEY

NEWTOWN

☆ *Harbour Lights* GY9 3YR: Welcoming, clean
and well run pub adjoining family-run hotel
in a quieter part of this quiet island,
comfortably refurbished bar with limited
choice of good well presented bar food (not
Sun nor wkdy lunchtime) from ploughman's
with home-baked bread and home-made
pickles to top-class fresh local fish and
seafood, attractive prices, real ales such as
Badger and Courage Directors, reasonably
priced wines; caters well for families, sunny
terrace in pleasant garden, bedrooms
(Bob and Angela Brooks, Donald Godden)

GUERNSEY

GRANDE HAVRE

☆ *Houmet* GY6 8JR [part of Houmet du Nord
Hotel; Rte de Picquerel]: Friendly and well
run, with good choice of reasonably priced
food inc good fresh local fish and seafood,
big picture windows overlooking rock and
sand beach; bedrooms *(BB,
Gordon Neighbour)*

ST PETER PORT

Swan GY1 1WA [St Julians Ave]: Traditional
british pub, worth the short trip from France
for good proper british food
(Christophe Gaultier)

TORTEVAL

☆ *Imperial* GY8 0PS [Pleinmont (coast rd, nr
Pleinmont Point)]: Good choice of enjoyable
meals inc good seafood and traditional
Guernsey bean jar in dining room which like
the neat and tidy bar has a great sea view
over Rocquaine Bay, Randalls beers; tables in
suntrap garden, bedrooms in hotel part
separate from the pub, handy for good beach
(Gordon Neighbour, Theocsbrian)

JERSEY

GREVE DE LECQ

☆ *Moulin de Lecq* JE3 2DT: Black-shuttered
mill in lovely location, reopened after
refurbishment and extension to include new
back restaurant, friendly bar with chatty
staff, enjoyable reasonably priced food from
baguettes up, well kept ales such as
Belhaven St Andrews, Greene King Ruddles
Best and Wells & Youngs Bombardier;
children welcome, lots of tables outside
(LYM, George Atkinson)

ST HELIER

Lamplighter [Mulcaster St]: Interesting
façade including only Union Flag visible
during Nazi occupation, small and friendly
inside, with heavy timbers, rough panelling
and scrubbed pine tables, well kept ales inc
Ringwood, bargain simple food; sports TV;
open all day *(Reg Fowle, Helen Rickwood, LYM)*

Overseas
Lucky Dip

We're always interested to hear of good bars and pubs overseas – preferably really good examples of bars that visitors would find memorable, rather than transplanted 'British pubs'. A star marks places we would be confident would deserve a main entry.

We are considering removing this section from future editions of the printed *Guide*, and instead including an expanded version on the website – perhaps a thousand entries instead of the few dozen we can print each year. Obviously we are still keen to have your reports, whichever course we take. But we would be particularly keen to know which you would prefer – existing short book section or expanded website section (we can't do both!).

AUSTRALIA

SYDNEY

Australian [100 Cumberland St, The Rocks]: Substantial modernist 1913 Federation-style building, sturdily furnished two-level bar, a dozen beers on tap and over a hundred bottled beers, lots of wines by the glass (and a good 'bottle shop' or off licence specialising in fine wines), bar food inc unusual pizzas and kangaroo pie; roof-terrace views of opera house and Sydney Harbour Bridge, wicker chairs for terrace tables, bedrooms sharing bathrooms *(Mike and Mary Carter)*

AUSTRIA

SEEFELD

Wildmoosalm [on plateau above – short bus ride from centre]: Picturesquely tyrolean family-run bar alone in the winter snowfields, three rooms full of striking stuffed birds of prey and animals, walls festooned with football shirts, fresh flowers on the tables, good beer, enjoyable food esp the apfelstrudel, really friendly bustling atmosphere, like miniature fountain of free spirits; in summer the terrace is great, overlooking small lake *(Ian Phillips, John and Joan Nash)*

BELGIUM

ANTWERP

Het Elfde Gebod [Torfbrug/Blauwmoezelstr]: Large ivy-clad café behind cathedral, overflowing with mix of religious statues and surreal art; good beer range inc Trappist Westmalle from altar-like bar, good choice of traditional belgian food inc mussels with frites, classic beef stew and good steaks, overflow upper gallery; piped classical music, can get busy – worth the wait for a table *(Mark and Ruth Brock)*

Paters Vaetje [1 Blaumoezelstraat]: High-ceilinged narrow café-bar in 17th-c building by cathedral, interesting old interior with marble-top tables on quarry tiles, carved wood counter, old beer advertisements, good beer list with four on tap and over 100 by the bottle, friendly helpful staff, some hot snacks, small eating area in panelled back gallery up steep spiral stairs (occasionally visited by an aloof cat); lavatories clean though not for the shy; tables outside ideal for the carillon concerts *(Mark and Ruth Brock)*

Quinten Matsys [Moriaanstraat, off Wolstraat]: Claims to be oldest café here, plenty of character and interesting artefacts, good shortish beer list and limited range of light meals (no snacks) *(Mark and Ruth Brock)*

BRUGES

Brugs Beertje [Kemelstraat, off Steenstr nr cathedral]: Small friendly backstreet local known as the Beer Academy, serving 350 of the country's bottled beers, most of them strong ones, in each beer's distinctive glass, as well as five on tap; vibrant atmosphere, especially in the two front rooms, table menus, helpful english-speaking staff (and customers), good basic bar food; open from 4, cl Weds, very popular with tourists *(Joe Green)*

Cambrinus [Philipstockstraat, NE corner of Markt]: Neatly kept and civilised classic café/bar with substantial helpings of good food from sandwiches to full meals at sensible prices, efficient staff, relaxed atmosphere *(Joe Green)*

Civière d'Or [Markt 33]: Smart split-level café/restaurant behind crenellated façade, dark panelling, relaxed atmosphere, plenty of beers on tap inc Maes and Grimbergen, good coffee and wines, authentic local food from flemish stew and tasty waffles to lobsters from live tank – a civilised if pricy escape from the touristy market and the other day-tripping brits (the only blot on this delightful town with its polite locals speaking perfect english); heated and covered tables outside *(George Atkinson)*

Diligence [Hoogstraat]: Quite small, with select beers, enjoyable food inc various eel dishes, welcoming services; tables all shown as reserved, so that landlady can screen her customers *(Joe Green)*

Erasmus [Wollestraat 35, between Markt and Dyver]: Small welcoming modernish hotel bar in old building, enlivened by friendly landlord's interest in his 300-plus helpfully described beers, enjoyable traditional belgian food in partly no smoking bistro area; piped classical music; comfortable bedrooms *(Mark and Ruth Brock)*

☆ *Garre* [1 de Garre – tiny alley between Markt and Burg, off Breidelstraat]: Currently our most popular belgian entry, attractive, welcoming and airy bar in 16th-c beamed and timbered building, stripped brickwork, no smoking gallery up steep stairs, elegant and civilised but very relaxed and unstuffy, well over 100 mainly local beers inc five Trappists and its own terrific strong draught beer (each well served in its own glass with cheese nibbles), good coffees and sandwiches too, sensible prices, knowledgeable helpful staff; unobtrusive piped classical music, no standing if tables are full – get there early; children welcome *(Mrs Frances Pennell, N R White, Joe Green, Mark and Ruth Brock)*

Vlissinghe [Blekersstraat]: Panelled café dating from 1515 away from the tourist centre, old paintings and tables (legend that Rubens painted a coin on one to avoid paying), unspoilt relaxed atmosphere, friendly staff, small choice of beers and snacks; piped music; some garden seating with boules, cl Sun pm, Mon, Tues *(N R White, Joe Green, Mark and Ruth Brock)*

BRUSSELS

Bécasse [11 rue de Tabora]: Unpromising corridor opens into rather genteel brown café with ranks of tables on tiled floor, ornate highly polished scrolled brass lamps showing its dark panelling and beams well, unblended Lambic (both white and sweet, young and old) served at the table in traditional blue and grey stone pitchers, also local fruit-flavoured Gueuze and other belgian beers such as Kwak served in its distinctive glass like a mini yard of ale, good cheap food such as croques monsieur or croustades made with beer and asparagus, exemplary lavatories – down steps that seem steeper as time wears on; open all day *(Joe Green)*

Bon Vieux Temps [rue Marché aux Herbes 12]: Classy and relaxing L-shaped brown café down white-tiled passage, dating from 1695, with beautifully carved dark panelling, stained glass, several unspoiled nooks and crannies, old tables inlaid with delft tiles, eccentrically shaped stove in huge fireplace, friendly landlady and helpful staff, wide range of classic beers such as Duvel, Grimbergen Blonde and Brune, Leffe, Orval *(anon)*

Mort Subite [R Montagne aux Herbes Potagères; off Grand Place via ornate Galeries St Hubert]: Under same family since 1928, long highly traditional fin de siècle room divided by two rows of pillars into nave with double rows of small polished tables and side aisles with single row, huge mirrors on all sides, leather seats, brisk uniformed polyglot waiters and waitresses bustling from lovely mirrored serving counter on dais on right, magisterial lots of belgian beers inc Duval, Gueuze, Grimbergen, Orval, Westmalle and their own speciality Kriek and other fruit beers brewed nearby (served by the bucket if you want), good straightforward food inc big omelettes, croques monsieur or madame, and local specialities such as brawn and rice tart, no piped music *(Joe Green)*

WESTVLETEREN

In de Vrede [Donkerstraat – follow Abdij St Sixtus signs off Poperinge rd]: Airy modern café in open country opp St Sixtus monastery, Trappist beer, simple snacks, useful for lunch when visiting World War I sites; shop, cl Fri *(Mark and Ruth Brock)*

CZECH REPUBLIC

PRAGUE

Café Montmartre [Retezova 7]: Tucked nicely away in quiet street parallel to Karlova (between new town square and Charles Bridge), shabby-chic and convivial café-bar with the odd easy chair and sofa as well as bentwood tables and chairs, attractive décor and few if any brits, good drinks hot and cold inc the usual beers from long bar, friendly laid-back staff and customers – some food, but primarily a place where people spin out a drink or a coffee for hours of chat; may be live music *(BB)*

Novomestsky Pivovar [Vodickova 20, Nove Mesto]: Fine brewpub opened 1994 in unlikely spot off shopping arcade, rambling series of basement rooms (some no smoking) with interesting old copper brewing equipment, lots of substantial bric-a-brac and old posters, their own unfiltered Novomestsky light and dark beers, good promptly served cheap food esp goulash – at busy times you now can't have a drink unless you eat too; open all day *(Bruce Bird, the Didler)*

☆ *Zlateho Tygra* [Husova 17, Stare Mesto]: 13th-c cellars with superb Pilsner Urquell 12 and eponymous Golden Tiger served by white-coated waiters; sometimes a queue of locals even before 3pm opening, and no standing allowed, but worth the wait (don't be put off by Reserved signs as the seats, mainly long wooden benches, aren't usually being used till later – and they do make tourists feel welcome) *(the Didler)*

EL SALVADOR

CHALATENANGO

Rinconcitos [Plaza de Cathedrale]: Wonderful café-bar on quiet street just off main sq, well priced food esp local pupusas, friendly service, interesting display of old radios and other bric-a-brac by wall display of El Salvador; fine stepped garden with views across town *(Andrew York)*

SAN SALVADOR

Luna [Colonia Buenos Aires, off Bd de los Heroes]: Aims to celebrate art and culture, wonderful friendly atmosphere, frequent events inc films and live music, very popular with ex-pats and salvadoreans alike; wide range of good food, sensible prices *(Andrew York)*

GERMANY

BERLIN

Lemkes Spezialitatenbrauerei [Dircksenstr]: Light and airy brewpub under a pair of railway arches, three or four of their own beers inc a seasonal one, decent food inc good value wkdy lunchtime buffet, staff with good english *(John Burgan, Hilary Irving, Joe Green)*

MITTENWALD

Gasthof Gries [Im Gries]: Mainly a small restaurant-with-rooms serving local specialities, but in summer has a pleasant pavement café/bar; a few bedrooms *(Ian Phillips)*

SPANDAU

Brewbaker [Flensburgerstrasse]: True to name they bake bread and brew beers – usually four, inc an excellent Pils; huge helpings of enjoyable food from open kitchen, friendly local atmosphere, housed in arch under railway; children welcome *(Joe Green)*

Deponie No 3 [Georgenstrasse]: Under two railway arches, good mainly english-speaking staff, decent beer, huge helpings of enjoyable food inc great value Sun brunch; some live music *(Joe Green)*

Sophie 'n Eck [Grosse Hamburgerstrasse]: Interesting layout, attentive hard-working staff, good atmosphere, Jever Pils, huge helpings of enjoyable sensibly priced food inc some unusual snacks *(Joe Green)*

HUNGARY

BUDAPEST

Fekete Holló Etterem [Orszaghaz utca 10; behind castle in old town]: Pleasant place with lovely vaulted ceiling restaurant, draught beers and numerous bottled beers, traditional hungarian food inc soups and goulashes with loads of bread; plenty of tables out on front terrace *(Ian Phillips)*

Gerbeaud: Attractive décor, tea room and patisserie on ground floor, basement beer hall with stools at long counter, four house beers with brewing vats on show – brewing actually elsewhere *(Ian Phillips)*

INDIA

ARPORA

Mayonnas [N of river, upstream of Baga Bridge; Goa]: Wonderful on Sun evening, live music provided by Dr Allen and his friends from England, good barbecue patronised by an amazing array of old rockers – the 60s are still alive and well in Goa *(Mike and Lynn Robinson)*

Vishal [Anjuna—Calangute; Goa]: Well stocked friendly locals' bar frequented by long stayers, no food though the very helpful owner can arrange for it to be brought in; open lavatories round the back *(Mike and Lynn Robinson)*

IRELAND (NORTHERN)

BELFAST

☆ *Crown* [Gt Victoria St, opp Europa Hotel]: Well preserved ornate 19th-c National Trust gin palace well worth sampling quickly, lively and bustling, with pillared entrance, opulent tiles outside and in, elaborately coloured windows, almost church-like ceiling, handsome mirrors, lots of individual snug booths with little doors and bells for waiter service (some graffiti too now, alas), gas lighting, mosaic tiled floor, pricy Whitewater real ale from imposing granite-top counter with colourful tiled facing, good lunchtime meals till 5 upstairs inc oysters; can be incredibly noisy, very wide range of customers (can take their toll on the downstairs gents'), and shame about the TV; open all day *(Tracey and Stephen Groves, Roy and Lindsey Fentiman)*

Cornerhouse [Ridgeway St, between Lord St bus station and Peel Rd railway station]: Large open-plan bar with pool one side, tables for the lunchtime food, drinking area in front of bar, friendly staff; live music; open all day, useful location between bus terminus and steam railway station *(anon)*

BUSHMILLS

Bushmills [Co Antrim]: Hotel with 17th-c core (rather than pub), linked rooms in various styles inc cosy gaslit ochre-walled inner room with sofa, settles, windsor chairs and original cooking pots by huge peat fire, another in hallway inglenook, well kept beers, wide choice of wines and spirits, friendly efficient staff, good restaurant; pleasant comfortable bedrooms, handy for Giant's Causeway and the venerable Bushmills Distillery *(Roy and Lindsey Fentiman)*

ENNISKILLEN

Blakes of the Hollow [Church St]: Original Victorian bar with mezzanine, lots of bric-a-brac and barrels, leisurely back bistro, smart evening restaurant *(Roy and Lindsey Fentiman)*

IRELAND (REPUBLIC)

AVOCA
Fitzgeralds [just off R752; Co Wicklow]: Coach trips come to this small ordinary village to see this, the pub in TV's *Ballykissangel*; lots of souvenirs, reasonable drinks prices, restaurant too; seats outside *(Kevin Flack)*

BANTRY
Bantry Bay Hotel [Wolfe Tone St]: Nautical-theme traditional bar in modernised hotel, Kilkenny Bitter, enjoyable food from sandwiches up, friendly service; TV; bedrooms *(Michael Dandy)*

CORK
Hayfield Manor [Perrott Ave]: Very different from the centre's busy bars, small bar in plush hotel hidden away in residential district, good choice of drinks, good service, daily papers, comfortable lounge, two restaurants; lovely gardens, comfortable bedrooms *(Michael Dandy)*

DALKEY
Finnigans: Enjoyable food at sensible prices, good wines by the glass, Kilkenny Bitter, good coffee, smiling helpful staff *(Ryta Lyndley)*

DUBLIN
☆ *Gravity Bar* [St James Gate Guinness Brewery]: Great 360° views from huge round glass-walled tasting bar on top floor – effectively Dublin's highest vantage-point (go while you can – there's talk of redevelopment coupled to a brewery move); Guinness at its best, culmination of up-to-date exhibition on firm's history, brewing and advertising campaigns, also lower Storehouse bar with lunchtime food and gift shop *(Kevin Flack, Dr and Mrs M W A Haward, Bruce and Penny Wilkie)*

Madigans [O'Connell St/N Earl St]: Plenty of atmosphere in relaxed traditional pub very near the historic GPO of the 1916 Easter Rising, long magnificently panelled bar with seats both sides, good choice of snacks and light meals, good friendly service, usual drinks, good tea, downstairs overflow; traditional music some nights *(Bruce and Penny Wilkie, JJW, CMW)*

Messrs Maguires [O'Connell Bridge, S side]: Well restored early 19th-c splendour, four floors with huge staircase, superb woodwork and ceilings, flame-effect gas fires, tasteful décor inc contemporary irish prints and functioning library; good own-brewed keg beers inc Stout, Extra Stout, Red Ale, Rusty Ale and lager, good coffee, enjoyable reasonably priced food from interesting sandwiches through very popular lunchtime carvery to top-floor gourmet restaurant; two TVs; irish music Sun-Tues from 9.30 *(JJW, CMW, Ryta Lyndley)*

O'Neills [Suffolk St]: Hospitable and welcoming spreading early Victorian pub, lots of dark panelling and cubby-holes off big lively bar, more rooms upstairs, good lunchtime carvery (all day Sun) and good value sandwich bar, quick efficient service, well served Guinness; main tourist information centre in converted church opp *(Bruce and Penny Wilkie)*

Temple Bar [Temple Bar]: Rambling multi-levelled, many-roomed pub on corner of two cobbled streets, recently refurbished with more modern back extension, lively mix of tourists and loyal locals, throbbing on wknd nights, quick friendly service even when crowded, spirits bottles packed to the ceiling, lots of old Guinness advertisements; tables out in big yard, good live music from 4pm *(Bruce and Penny Wilkie)*

HOWTH
Abbey Tavern: Enjoyable food, helpful staff, well kept Kilkenny, good irish coffee, neat housekeeping *(Ryta Lyndley)*

KINSALE
Blue Haven [Pearse St]: Small hotel's smart low-ceilinged bar with several rooms, small cushioned sofas, low tables, inglenook woodburner, bar food from sandwiches up, good choice of wines by the glass and good coffee, pleasant service, daily papers, small daytime café, restaurant; courtyard tables, bedrooms *(Michael Dandy)*

Jim Edwards [Co Cork]: Linked rooms off sizeable bar with several wines by the glass and usual beers, good service, comfortable panelled restaurant, good value food from oysters and grilled crab claws to steaks, nice puddings; charming fishing village *(Michael Dandy)*

TULLOW
Tara Arms: Typical irish bar, good facilities for eating lunchtime and evening *(D and M T Ayres-Regan)*

Clinch's Celtic Tavern [North Quay]: Local in lovely building, three small rooms, two real ales *(Noel Grundy)*

ISLE OF MAN

DOUGLAS
British [North Quay]: Popular Okells pub with pleasant décor in three linked areas, lunchtime food *(Noel Grundy)*

Railway [Banks Circus]: Reopened after major upmarket refurbishment, three real ales, many world bottled beers, lunchtime food *(Noel Grundy)*

LAXEY
Shore [Old Laxey Hill]: Pubby atmosphere and friendly landlord, enjoyable reasonably priced food (not Sun evening) from soup or big chip baguettes to steak, Bosuns Bitter *(Dr J Barrie Jones)*

Marine [Shore Rd]: Seafront hotel with lovely views, pubby atmosphere and friendly service, good generous food from crab baguettes up, sensible prices and smaller helpings available; bedrooms *(D and M T Ayres-Regan, Dr J Barrie Jones)*

PEEL [NX2484]
Creek [Station Pl/North Quay]: Pleasantly refurbished dining pub in lovely setting on the ancient quayside opp splendid Manannan heritage centre, friendly helpful staff and welcoming relaxed atmosphere, wide choice of sensibly priced food all day inc fish, crab and lobsters fresh from the boats, good local kippers and several unusual dishes, local Okells beers, etched mirrors and mainly old woodwork; wheelchair access, tables outside, self-catering flats *(John and Joan Nash, David and Sue Smith)*
PORT ERIN [SC2069]
Bay [Shore Rd]: Three rooms with bare boards and good furniture, good fresh food, up to half a dozen well kept local Bushys beer (brewery owner lives above the bar), guest beers too, wide wine choice, friendly service, lovely spot overlooking sandy beach and across to Bradda Head, live music Fri; flexible opening times *(Derek and Sylvia Stephenson, Andrew Stephenson)*

MADEIRA

FUNCHAL
Quinta da Penha de Franca [Rua Imperatriz Da Amelia]: Charming early 1970s small cocktail bar, very welcoming to non-residents, in large comfortable seaside hotel, red and white furnishings inc pubby sewing-machine tables and Biba-style lamps, piano gallery, back garden restaurant *(Susan and John Douglas)*

MALTA

VALLETTA
The Pub [Archbishop St]: Compact room with bare rock walls, Boddingtons and local Cisk beer, lots of Oliver Reed and Royal Navy memorabilia *(David and Ruth Hollands)*

NETHERLANDS

AMSTERDAM
Arendsnest [Herengracht 90]: Neatly kept appealing panelled bar, good civilised atmosphere, helpful friendly staff, long row of bentwood high stools by mahogany counter with plenty of other drinks besides the comprehensive range of dutch beers (a dozen on tap, over a hundred by the bottle), snacks; tables out by canal, open 4pm till late *(N R White)*

SPAIN

MADRID
Casa Alberto [C/Huertas, 18]: Old-fashioned café/bar with small selection of good tapas, full meals too, bullfighting pictures *(Mark and Ruth Brock)*
Espejo [Paseo de Recoletos, 31]: Impressive Art Nouveau café-restaurant, good choice of tapas, tostas and bigger meals; tables outside, on tree-lined avenue nr museums *(Mark and Ruth Brock)*

ÓRGIVA
Semaforo [Avenida González Robles]: Big helpings of tapas in good variety offered with every drink in down-to-earth bar; lovely small mountain town, bedrooms in adjacent hostal, open mid-afternoon till early morning *(Tim and Ann Newell)*

SWITZERLAND

LES PACCOTS
Lac des Joncs [Rte des Joncs 371]: Cardinal beer on tap, particularly good coffee, enjoyable food inc fondues and trout; snowbound in winter, lovely lake in summer, bedrooms *(Ian Phillips)*

THAILAND

BANGKOK
Charlies Bar [Sukhumuit Soi 11]: Unique, basically a pavement bar on quiet side street, known locally as Cheap Charlies, usually standing room only, very few chairs or tables, bar made from bric-a-brac *(P Dawn)*
Londoner Brew Pub [591 Sukhumvit Soi 33]: Brews its own good Bitter and Pilsner, first-class service, friendly even at busy times, huge screen and 12 satellite TVs for sports, two pool tables, darts, live entertainment *(P Dawn)*

TURKEY

HISARONU
Efes: Welcoming place with excellent service, particularly good milk shakes, pool, up-to-date piped music; popular with british residents and visitors *(Mayur Shah)*
Red Lion: Quiet end of town, good pastiche of traditional english pub, british-run, civilised atmosphere *(Mayur Shah)*

USA

NEW YORK
Chumleys [86 Bedford St, between Grove St and Barrow St]: Great atmosphere in 130-year-old ex-stables and speakeasy (front door still has no indication that it's a pub – look out for the air conditioner), dark bar filled with old author photographs and book jackets, basic wooden furniture, over 20 beers inc microbrews, hearty reasonably priced pub food in second room, real fire, juke box with Sinatra and swing; tables in yard *(BB)*
McSorleys [15 East 7th St, between 2nd and 3rd Aves]: Oldest irish bar in town, really original, almost unchanged since 1854 establishment (as you can see from the

ancient photographs and clippings which pack the walls), sawdust on old-fashioned concrete floor, close-set chairs around nicely worn pub tables, top-notch swift service of their signature foaming dark ale even when it's crowded, hearty pub food in second room *(BB)*

WASHINGTON
McCormick & Schmick [F Street; DC]: Enormous light and airy modern place, long bar with good draft beer, friendly knowledgeable service, some tables for good value bar snacks, restaurant behind; handy for Spy Museum *(John Evans)*

Special Interest Lists

PUBS WITH GOOD GARDENS

The pubs listed here have bigger or more beautiful gardens, grounds or terraces than are usual for their areas. Note that in a town or city this might be very much more modest than the sort of garden that would deserve a listing in the countryside.

BEDFORDSHIRE
Bletsoe, Falcon
Bolnhurst, Plough
Milton Bryan, Red Lion
Northill, Crown
Old Warden, Hare & Hounds
Riseley, Fox & Hounds

BERKSHIRE
Aldworth, Bell
Ashmore Green, Sun in the Wood
Frilsham, Pot Kiln
Holyport, Belgian Arms
Hurst, Green Man
Inkpen, Crown & Garter
Shinfield, Magpie & Parrot
White Waltham, Beehive
Winterbourne, Winterbourne Arms

BUCKINGHAMSHIRE
Bennett End, Three Horseshoes
Bovingdon Green, Royal Oak
Denham, Swan
Dorney, Palmer Arms
Fingest, Chequers
Ford, Dinton Hermit
Grove, Grove Lock
Hawridge Common, Full Moon
Hedgerley, White Horse
Oving, Black Boy
Skirmett, Frog

CAMBRIDGESHIRE
Elton, Black Horse
Fowlmere, Chequers
Heydon, King William IV
Madingley, Three Horseshoes

CHESHIRE
Aldford, Grosvenor Arms
Bunbury, Dysart Arms
Haughton Moss, Nags Head

CORNWALL
Lostwithiel, Globe
St Kew, St Kew Inn
St Mawgan, Falcon
Tresco, New Inn

CUMBRIA
Bassenthwaite Lake, Pheasant
Bouth, White Hart
Staveley, Eagle & Child

DERBYSHIRE
Hathersage, Plough
Melbourne, John Thompson
Woolley Moor, White Horse

DEVON
Avonwick, Turtley Corn Mill
Broadhembury, Drewe Arms
Clayhidon, Merry Harriers
Clyst Hydon, Five Bells
Cornworthy, Hunters Lodge
Exeter, Imperial
Exminster, Turf Hotel
Haytor Vale, Rock
Lydford, Castle Inn
Newton Abbot, Two Mile Oak
Newton Ferrers, Dolphin
Postbridge, Warren House
Poundsgate, Tavistock Inn
Sidbury, Hare & Hounds
Stokenham, Church House
Torbryan, Old Church House

DORSET
Cerne Abbas, Royal Oak
Chideock, George
Marshwood, Bottle
Nettlecombe, Marquis of Lorne
Plush, Brace of Pheasants
Shave Cross, Shave Cross Inn
Shroton, Cricketers
Tarrant Monkton, Langton Arms

ESSEX
Castle Hedingham, Bell
Chappel, Swan
Fyfield, Queens Head
Great Henny, Henny Swan
Hastingwood, Rainbow & Dove
Mill Green, Viper
Peldon, Rose
Stock, Hoop

GLOUCESTERSHIRE
Blaisdon, Red Hart
Cheltenham, Royal Oak
Ewen, Wild Duck
Frampton on Severn, Bell
Hinton Dyrham, Bull
Kilkenny, Kilkeney Inn
Nailsworth, Egypt Mill
Nether Westcote, Westcote Inn
Northleach, Wheatsheaf
Southrop, Swan
Upper Oddington, Horse & Groom

HAMPSHIRE
Bramdean, Fox
Bransgore, Three Tuns
Dundridge, Hampshire Bowman
Exton, Shoe
Houghton, Boot
Ovington, Bush
Steep, Harrow
Stockbridge, Grosvenor
Tichborne, Tichborne Arms

HEREFORDSHIRE
Aymestrey, Riverside Inn
Hoarwithy, New Harp
Sellack, Lough Pool
Ullingswick, Three Crowns
Woolhope, Butchers Arms

HERTFORDSHIRE
Ashwell, Three Tuns
Chapmore End, Woodman
Potters Crouch, Holly Bush
Preston, Red Lion
Sarratt, Cock
Willian, Fox

ISLE OF WIGHT
Hulverstone, Sun
Shorwell, Crown

KENT
Biddenden, Three Chimneys
Bough Beech, Wheatsheaf
Boyden Gate, Gate Inn
Brookland, Woolpack
Chiddingstone, Castle Inn
Groombridge, Crown
Ivy Hatch, Plough
Newnham, George
Penshurst, Bottle House
Selling, Rose & Crown
Stowting, Tiger
Ulcombe, Pepper Box

LANCASHIRE
Whitewell, Inn at Whitewell

LEICESTERSHIRE AND RUTLAND
Barrowden, Exeter Arms
Exton, Fox & Hounds
Lyddington, Old White Hart
Peggs Green, New Inn
Stathern, Red Lion

LINCOLNSHIRE
Billingborough, Fortescue Arms
Coningsby, Lea Gate Inn
Lincoln, Victoria
Stamford, George of Stamford

NORFOLK
Brancaster Staithe, Jolly Sailors
Burnham Market, Hoste Arms
Burnham Thorpe, Lord Nelson
Holkham, Victoria
Itteringham, Walpole Arms
Ringstead, Gin Trap
Snettisham, Rose & Crown
Stanhoe, Crown
Stow Bardolph, Hare Arms
Woodbastwick, Fur & Feather

NORTHAMPTONSHIRE
Bulwick, Queens Head
East Haddon, Red Lion
Farthingstone, Kings Arms
Slipton, Samuel Pepys
Wadenhoe, Kings Head

NORTHUMBRIA
Anick, Rat
Blanchland, Lord Crewe Arms
Diptonmill, Dipton Mill Inn
Greta Bridge, Morritt Arms
Newburn, Keelman
Weldon Bridge, Anglers Arms

NOTTINGHAMSHIRE
Caunton, Caunton Beck
Colston Bassett, Martins Arms

OXFORDSHIRE
Aston Tirrold, Chequers
Clifton, Duke of Cumberlands Head
Fyfield, White Hart
Highmoor, Rising Sun
Hook Norton, Gate Hangs High
Stanton St John, Star
Swerford, Masons Arms
Tadpole Bridge, Trout

SHROPSHIRE
Bishop's Castle, Castle Hotel, Three Tuns
Chetwynd Aston, Fox
Much Wenlock, Talbot

SOMERSET
Axbridge, Lamb
Chiselborough, Cat Head
Compton Martin, Ring o' Bells
Croscombe, George
Litton, Kings Arms
Monksilver, Notley Arms
Shepton Montague, Montague Inn

STAFFORDSHIRE
Stourton, Fox
Wrinehill, Hand & Trumpet

SUFFOLK
Dennington, Queens Head
Lavenham, Angel
Laxfield, Kings Head
Long Melford, Black Lion
Newbourne, Fox
Rede, Plough
Rougham, Ravenwood Hall
Stoke-by-Nayland, Crown
Tuddenham, Fountain
Walberswick, Anchor, Bell
Waldringfield, Maybush
Westleton, Crown

SURREY
Charleshill, Donkey
Coldharbour, Plough
Compton, Withies
Eashing, Stag
Elstead, Mill at Elstead
Forest Green, Parrot
Leigh, Seven Stars
Lingfield, Hare & Hounds
Newdigate, Surrey Oaks
Ottershaw, Castle
Thursley, Three Horseshoes
West End, Inn at West End
West Horsley, Barley Mow
Worplesdon, Jolly Farmer

SUSSEX
Alfriston, George
Balls Cross, Stag
Berwick, Cricketers Arms

Blackboys, Blackboys Inn
Byworth, Black Horse
Coolham, George & Dragon
Elsted, Three Horseshoes
Eridge Station, Huntsman
Fittleworth, Swan
Fletching, Griffin
Heathfield, Star
Oving, Gribble Inn
Ringmer, Cock
Singleton, Partridge
Wineham, Royal Oak

WARWICKSHIRE
Edge Hill, Castle
Ilmington, Howard Arms
Preston Bagot, Crabmill

WILTSHIRE
Berwick St James, Boot
Brinkworth, Three Crowns
Chicksgrove, Compasses
Ebbesbourne Wake, Horseshoe
Horton, Bridge Inn
Kilmington, Red Lion
Lacock, George, Rising Sun
Norton, Vine Tree
Seend, Barge
Whitley, Pear Tree

WORCESTERSHIRE
Bretforton, Fleece
Hanley Swan, Swan

YORKSHIRE
East Witton, Blue Lion
Egton Bridge, Horseshoe
Halifax, Shibden Mill
Heath, Kings Arms
South Dalton, Pipe & Glass
Sutton upon Derwent, St Vincent Arms

LONDON
Central London, Cross Keys
East London, Prospect of Whitby
North London, Spaniards Inn
South London, Crown & Greyhound, Founders
    Arms, Old Jail, Victoria
West London, Colton Arms, Dove, Windsor
    Castle

SCOTLAND
Badachro, Badachro Inn
Edinburgh, Starbank
Gairloch, Old Inn
Gatehouse of Fleet, Masonic Arms
Glenelg, Glenelg Inn
Kilmahog, Lade
Thornhill, Lion & Unicorn

WALES
Colwyn Bay, Pen-y-Bryn
Crickhowell, Bear, Nantyffin Cider Mill
Gresford, Pant-yr-Ochain
Llanfrynach, White Swan
Llangollen, Corn Mill

Mold, Glasfryn
Old Radnor, Harp
Raglan, Clytha Arms
Rosebush, Tafarn Sinc
Skenfrith, Bell
St Hilary, Bush
Tintern, Cherry Tree
Ty'n-y-groes, Groes

CHANNEL ISLANDS
King's Mills, Fleur du Jardin
Rozel, Rozel

WATERSIDE PUBS

*The pubs listed here are right beside the sea,
a sizeable river, canal, lake or loch that
contributes significantly to their attraction.*

BEDFORDSHIRE
Bletsoe, Falcon

BUCKINGHAMSHIRE
Grove, Grove Lock

CAMBRIDGESHIRE
Peterborough, Charters
Sutton Gault, Anchor

CHESHIRE
Chester, Old Harkers Arms
Wrenbury, Dusty Miller

CORNWALL
Bodinnick, Old Ferry
Mousehole, Ship
Mylor Bridge, Pandora
Polkerris, Rashleigh
Polperro, Blue Peter
Port Isaac, Port Gaverne Inn
Porthleven, Ship
Porthtowan, Blue
Sennen Cove, Old Success
Tresco, New Inn

CUMBRIA
Brampton, New Inn
Staveley, Eagle & Child
Ulverston, Bay Horse

DERBYSHIRE
Hathersage, Plough

DEVON
Beesands, Cricket
Buckfast, Abbey Inn
Culmstock, Culm Valley
Exminster, Turf Hotel
Newton Ferrers, Dolphin
Noss Mayo, Ship
Torcross, Start Bay
Tuckenhay, Maltsters Arms

ESSEX
Burnham-on-Crouch, White Harte
Chappel, Swan
Fyfield, Queens Head
Great Henny, Henny Swan

GLOUCESTERSHIRE
Ashleworth Quay, Boat

HAMPSHIRE
Exton, Shoe
Houghton, Boot
Ovington, Bush
Portsmouth, Old Customs House
Wherwell, Mayfly
Winchester, Willow Tree

HEREFORDSHIRE
Aymestrey, Riverside Inn

ISLE OF WIGHT
Bembridge, Crab & Lobster
Cowes, Folly
Seaview, Seaview Hotel
Ventnor, Spyglass

KENT
Oare, Shipwrights Arms

LANCASHIRE
Manchester, Dukes 92
Whitewell, Inn at Whitewell

NORFOLK
Brancaster Staithe, White Horse

NORTHAMPTONSHIRE
Wadenhoe, Kings Head

NORTHUMBRIA
Newcastle upon Tyne, Cluny
Newton-by-the-Sea, Ship

NOTTINGHAMSHIRE
Ranby, Chequers

OXFORDSHIRE
Godstow, Trout
Tadpole Bridge, Trout

SHROPSHIRE
Shrewsbury, Armoury

SOMERSET
Churchill, Crown
Compton Martin, Ring o' Bells
Portishead, Windmill

SUFFOLK
Chelmondiston, Butt & Oyster
Nayland, Anchor
Southwold, Harbour Inn
Waldringfield, Maybush

SURREY
Eashing, Stag
Elstead, Mill at Elstead

WILTSHIRE
Horton, Bridge Inn
Seend, Barge

WORCESTERSHIRE
Knightwick, Talbot

YORKS
Hull, Minerva
Whitby, Duke of York

LONDON
East London, Grapes, Prospect of Whitby
South London, Cutty Sark, Founders Arms
West London, Bulls Head, Dove

SCOTLAND
Aboyne, Boat
Badachro, Badachro Inn
Edinburgh, Starbank
Elie, Ship
Gairloch, Old Inn
Glenelg, Glenelg Inn
Isle of Whithorn, Steam Packet
Kingholm Quay, Swan
Plockton, Plockton Hotel
Shieldaig, Tigh an Eilean Hotel
Stein, Stein Inn
Tayvallich, Tayvallich Inn
Ullapool, Ferry Boat

WALES
Aberaeron, Harbourmaster
Abercych, Nags Head
Aberdovey, Penhelig Arms
Abergorlech, Black Lion
Cresswell Quay, Cresselly Arms
Llangollen, Corn Mill
Pembroke Ferry, Ferry Inn
Porth Dinllaen, Ty Coch
Red Wharf Bay, Ship
Skenfrith, Bell

CHANNEL ISLANDS
St Aubin, Old Court House Inn
St Ouens Bay, La Pulente

PUBS IN ATTRACTIVE SURROUNDINGS

These pubs are in unusually attractive or interesting places – lovely countryside, charming villages, occasionally notable town surroundings. Waterside pubs are listed again here only if their other surroundings are special, too.

BEDFORDSHIRE
Old Warden, Hare & Hounds

BERKSHIRE
Aldworth, Bell
Frilsham, Pot Kiln

BUCKINGHAMSHIRE
Bovingdon Green, Royal Oak
Hawridge Common, Full Moon
Skirmett, Frog
Turville, Bull & Butcher

CAMBRIDGESHIRE
Elton, Black Horse
Reach, Dyke's End

CHESHIRE
Barthomley, White Lion
Bunbury, Dysart Arms
Willington, Boot

CORNWALL
Altarnun, Rising Sun
Blisland, Blisland Inn
Gurnards Head, Gurnards Head Hotel
Helston, Halzephron
Polperro, Blue Peter
Ruan Lanihorne, Kings Head
St Kew, St Kew Inn
St Mawgan, Falcon
Tresco, New Inn
Zennor, Tinners Arms

CUMBRIA
Askham, Punch Bowl
Bassenthwaite Lake, Pheasant
Bouth, White Hart
Broughton Mills, Blacksmiths Arms
Buttermere, Bridge Hotel
Cartmel, Kings Arms
Chapel Stile, Wainwrights
Crosthwaite, Punch Bowl
Elterwater, Britannia
Hawkshead, Drunken Duck, Kings Arms
Hesket Newmarket, Old Crown
Ings, Watermill
Langdale, Old Dungeon Ghyll
Levens, Strickland Arms
Little Langdale, Three Shires
Loweswater, Kirkstile Inn
Mungrisdale, Mill Inn
Santon Bridge, Bridge Inn
Scales, White Horse
Seathwaite, Newfield Inn
Stonethwaite, Langstrath
Threlkeld, Horse & Farrier
Troutbeck, Queens Head
Ulverston, Bay Horse

DERBYSHIRE
Alderwasley, Bear
Brassington, Olde Gate
Foolow, Bulls Head
Hathersage, Plough, Scotsmans Pack
Hayfield, Lantern Pike
Kirk Ireton, Barley Mow
Ladybower Reservoir, Yorks Bridge
Litton, Red Lion
Monsal Head, Monsal Head Hotel
Over Haddon, Lathkil
Sheldon, Cock & Pullet
Woolley Moor, White Horse

DEVON
Branscombe, Fountain Head
Buckland Monachorum, Drake Manor
Chagford, Ring o' Bells
Culmstock, Culm Valley
East Budleigh, Sir Walter Raleigh
Exminster, Turf Hotel
Haytor Vale, Rock
Holne, Church House
Horndon, Elephants Nest
Iddesleigh, Duke of York

Kingston, Dolphin
Lustleigh, Cleave
Lydford, Castle Inn
Meavy, Royal Oak
Molland, London
Parracombe, Fox & Goose
Peter Tavy, Peter Tavy Inn
Postbridge, Warren House
Rattery, Church House
Sandy Park, Sandy Park Inn
Slapton, Tower
Widecombe, Rugglestone

DORSET
Corscombe, Fox
East Chaldon, Sailors Return
Marshwood, Bottle
Nettlecombe, Marquis of Lorne
Pamphill, Vine
Plush, Brace of Pheasants
Powerstock, Three Horseshoes
Worth Matravers, Square & Compass

ESSEX
Mill Green, Viper

GLOUCESTERSHIRE
Ashleworth Quay, Boat
Bisley, Bear
Bledington, Kings Head
Chedworth, Seven Tuns
Chipping Campden, Eight Bells
Frampton on Severn, Bell
Guiting Power, Hollow Bottom
Nailsworth, Weighbridge
Newland, Ostrich
Northleach, Wheatsheaf
Sapperton, Bell

HAMPSHIRE
Fritham, Royal Oak
Hawkley, Hawkley Inn
Lymington, Kings Head
Ovington, Bush
Tichborne, Tichborne Arms

HEREFORDSHIRE
Aymestrey, Riverside Inn
Dorstone, Pandy
Hoarwithy, New Harp
Sellack, Lough Pool
Titley, Stagg
Walterstone, Carpenters Arms
Woolhope, Butchers Arms

HERTFORDSHIRE
Aldbury, Greyhound
Frithsden, Alford Arms
Sarratt, Cock

ISLE OF WIGHT
Hulverstone, Sun

KENT
Brookland, Woolpack
Chiddingstone, Castle Inn
Groombridge, Crown
Newnham, George

Selling, Rose & Crown
Stowting, Tiger

LANCASHIRE
Bury, Lord Raglan
Denshaw, Rams Head
Sawley, Spread Eagle
Tunstall, Lunesdale Arms
Uppermill, Church Inn
Whitewell, Inn at Whitewell

LEICESTERSHIRE AND RUTLAND
Barrowden, Exeter Arms
Exton, Fox & Hounds

LINCOLNSHIRE
Dry Doddington, Wheatsheaf

NORFOLK
Blakeney, White Horse
Brancaster Staithe, Jolly Sailors
Burnham Market, Hoste Arms
Holkham, Victoria
Thornham, Lifeboat
Woodbastwick, Fur & Feather

NORTHUMBRIA
Blanchland, Lord Crewe Arms
Diptonmill, Dipton Mill Inn
Great Whittington, Queens Head
Haltwhistle, Milecastle Inn
Langley on Tyne, Carts Bog Inn
Newton-by-the-Sea, Ship
Romaldkirk, Rose & Crown
Stannersburn, Pheasant
Wark, Battlesteads

NOTTINGHAMSHIRE
Halam, Waggon & Horses
Laxton, Dovecote

OXFORDSHIRE
Checkendon, Black Horse
Coleshill, Radnor Arms
Great Tew, Falkland Arms
Langford, Bell
Oxford, Turf Tavern
Swinbrook, Swan

SHROPSHIRE
Bridges, Horseshoe
Cardington, Royal Oak
Picklescott, Bottle & Glass

SOMERSET
Appley, Globe
Axbridge, Lamb
Batcombe, Three Horseshoes
Cranmore, Strode Arms
Exford, White Horse
Luxborough, Royal Oak
Simonsbath, Exmoor Forest Inn
Tarr, Tarr Farm
Triscombe, Blue Ball
Wells, City Arms

STAFFORDSHIRE
Alstonefield, George
Stourton, Fox

SUFFOLK
Dennington, Queens Head
Lavenham, Angel
Newbourne, Fox
Walberswick, Bell

SURREY
Esher, Marneys
Forest Green, Parrot
Lingfield, Hare & Hounds

SUSSEX
Alfriston, George
Burpham, George & Dragon
Chilgrove, Royal Oak, White Horse
Ditchling, Bull
Fletching, Griffin
Heathfield, Star
Rye, Mermaid
Wineham, Royal Oak

WARWICKSHIRE
Edge Hill, Castle

WILTSHIRE
Axford, Red Lion
Castle Combe, Castle Inn
Donhead St Andrew, Forester
East Knoyle, Fox & Hounds
Ebbesbourne Wake, Horseshoe
Lacock, Rising Sun
Newton Tony, Malet Arms
Stourton, Spread Eagle
Wylye, Bell

WORCESTERSHIRE
Hanley Swan, Swan
Kidderminster, King & Castle
Knightwick, Talbot
Pensax, Bell

YORKSHIRE
Beck Hole, Birch Hall
Blakey Ridge, Lion
Bradfield, Strines Inn
Byland Abbey, Abbey Inn
Chapel le Dale, Hill Inn
Cray, White Lion
East Witton, Blue Lion
Grinton, Bridge Inn
Halifax, Shibden Mill
Heath, Kings Arms
Langthwaite, Charles Bathurst
Lastingham, Blacksmiths Arms
Linton in Craven, Fountaine
Litton, Queens Arms
Lund, Wellington
Middleham, Black Swan
Osmotherley, Golden Lion
Ripley, Boars Head
Robin Hood's Bay, Laurel
Shelley, Three Acres
South Dalton, Pipe & Glass
Thornton in Lonsdale, Marton Arms

Thornton Watlass, Buck
Wath in Nidderdale, Sportsmans Arms
Widdop, Pack Horse

LONDON
Central London, Olde Mitre
North London, Spaniards Inn
South London, Crown & Greyhound

SCOTLAND
Applecross, Applecross Inn
Gairloch, Old Inn
Kilberry, Kilberry Inn
Kilmahog, Lade
Kingholm Quay, Swan
Kirk Yetholm, Border
Stein, Stein Inn

WALES
Abergorlech, Black Lion
Capel Curig, Bryn Tyrch
Crickhowell, Nantyffin Cider Mill
Llanarmon Dyffryn Ceiriog, Hand
Llanberis, Pen-y-Gwryd
Old Radnor, Harp
Porth Dinllaen, Ty Coch
Red Wharf Bay, Ship
Rhyd-y-Meirch, Goose & Cuckoo
Tintern, Cherry Tree

CHANNEL ISLANDS
St Brelade, Old Portelet Inn, Old Smugglers
St John, Les Fontaines

PUBS WITH GOOD VIEWS

*These pubs are listed for their particularly
good views, either from inside or from a
garden or terrace. Waterside pubs are listed
again here only if their view is exceptional in
its own right – not just a straightforward sea
view for example.*

BUCKINGHAMSHIRE
Oving, Black Boy

CHESHIRE
Burwardsley, Pheasant
Langley, Hanging Gate
Willington, Boot

CORNWALL
Falmouth, 5 Degrees West
Ruan Lanihorne, Kings Head
Sennen Cove, Old Success

CUMBRIA
Cartmel Fell, Masons Arms
Hawkshead, Drunken Duck
Langdale, Old Dungeon Ghyll
Loweswater, Kirkstile Inn
Mungrisdale, Mill Inn
Stonethwaite, Langstrath
Threlkeld, Horse & Farrier

Troutbeck, Queens Head
Ulverston, Bay Horse

DERBYSHIRE
Alderwasley, Bear
Foolow, Bulls Head
Monsal Head, Monsal Head Hotel
Over Haddon, Lathkil

DEVON
Brixham, Maritime
Newton Ferrers, Dolphin
Portgate, Harris Arms
Postbridge, Warren House
Sidbury, Hare & Hounds
Strete, Kings Arms

DORSET
Worth Matravers, Square & Compass

GLOUCESTERSHIRE
Cranham, Black Horse
Kilkenny, Kilkeney Inn
Woodchester, Ram

ISLE OF WIGHT
Bembridge, Crab & Lobster
Hulverstone, Sun
Ventnor, Spyglass

KENT
Bodsham, Timber Batts
Tunbridge Wells, Beacon
Ulcombe, Pepper Box

LANCASHIRE
Bury, Lord Raglan
Sawley, Spread Eagle
Uppermill, Church Inn

NORFOLK
Brancaster Staithe, White Horse

NORTHUMBRIA
Anick, Rat
Seahouses, Olde Ship

OXFORDSHIRE
Swerford, Masons Arms

SOMERSET
Portishead, Windmill
Shepton Montague, Montague Inn
Tarr, Tarr Farm

SUFFOLK
Erwarton, Queens Head

SUSSEX
Byworth, Black Horse
Elsted, Three Horseshoes
Fletching, Griffin
Icklesham, Queens Head

WILTSHIRE
Axford, Red Lion
Box, Quarrymans Arms
Donhead St Andrew, Forester

East Knoyle, Fox & Hounds
Lacock, Rising Sun
Semington, Lamb
Upper Chute, Cross Keys

WORCESTERSHIRE
Malvern, Nags Head
Pensax, Bell

YORKSHIRE
Blakey Ridge, Lion
Bradfield, Strines Inn
Hartshead, Gray Ox
Kirkham, Stone Trough
Langthwaite, Charles Bathurst
Litton, Queens Arms
Shelley, Three Acres
Whitby, Duke of York

LONDON
South London, Founders Arms

SCOTLAND
Applecross, Applecross Inn
Badachro, Badachro Inn
Edinburgh, Starbank
Glenelg, Glenelg Inn
Kilberry, Kilberry Inn
Shieldaig, Tigh an Eilean Hotel
Stein, Stein Inn
Ullapool, Ferry Boat
Weem, Ailean Chraggan

WALES
Aberdovey, Penhelig Arms
Capel Curig, Bryn Tyrch
Colwyn Bay, Pen-y-Bryn
Llanberis, Pen-y-Gwryd
Llanferres, Druid
Llangollen, Corn Mill
Mold, Glasfryn
Old Radnor, Harp
Porth Dinllaen, Ty Coch
Rhyd-y-Meirch, Goose & Cuckoo
Ty'n-y-groes, Groes

CHANNEL ISLANDS
St Aubin, Old Court House Inn

PUBS IN INTERESTING BUILDINGS

*Pubs and inns are listed here for the particular
interest of their building – something really
out of the ordinary to look at, or occasionally
a building that has an outstandingly
interesting historical background.*

BUCKINGHAMSHIRE
Aylesbury, Kings Head
Forty Green, Royal Standard of England

DERBYSHIRE
Kirk Ireton, Barley Mow

DEVON
Dartmouth, Cherub
Rattery, Church House

LANCASHIRE
Liverpool, Philharmonic Dining Rooms

LINCOLNSHIRE
Stamford, George of Stamford

NORTHUMBRIA
Blanchland, Lord Crewe Arms
Newcastle upon Tyne, Crown Posada

NOTTINGHAMSHIRE
Nottingham, Olde Trip to Jerusalem

OXFORDSHIRE
Banbury, Reindeer
Fyfield, White Hart

SOMERSET
Norton St Philip, George

SUFFOLK
Laxfield, Kings Head

SURREY
Elstead, Mill at Elstead

SUSSEX
Rye, Mermaid

WILTSHIRE
Salisbury, Haunch of Venison

WORCESTERSHIRE
Bretforton, Fleece

YORKS
Hull, Olde White Harte

LONDON
Central London, Black Friar, Cittie of Yorke,
 Red Lion (SW1)
South London, George

SCOTLAND
Edinburgh, Café Royal, Guildford Arms

PUBS THAT BREW THEIR OWN BEER

*The pubs listed here brew their own beer on
the premises; many others not listed have
beers brewed for them specially, sometimes an
individual recipe (but by a separate brewer).
We mention these in the text.*

CAMBRIDGESHIRE
Peterborough, Brewery Tap

CUMBRIA
Cockermouth, Bitter End
Hawkshead, Drunken Duck
Loweswater, Kirkstile Inn

DERBYSHIRE
Melbourne, John Thompson

DEVON
Branscombe, Fountain Head

HAMPSHIRE
Cheriton, Flower Pots

HEREFORDSHIRE
Hereford, Victory

KENT
West Peckham, Swan on the Green

LANCASHIRE
Bury, Lord Raglan
Manchester, Marble Arch
Uppermill, Church Inn
Wheelton, Dressers Arms

LEICESTERSHIRE AND RUTLAND
Barrowden, Exeter Arms
Oakham, Grainstore

LINCOLNSHIRE
South Witham, Blue Cow

NORTHUMBRIA
Diptonmill, Dipton Mill Inn
Newburn, Keelman

NOTTINGHAMSHIRE
Caythorpe, Black Horse
Nottingham, Fellows Morton & Clayton

SHROPSHIRE
Bishop's Castle, Six Bells

STAFFORDSHIRE
Burton upon Trent, Burton Bridge Inn

SUFFOLK
South Elmham, St Peters Brewery

SURREY
Coldharbour, Plough

WARWICKSHIRE
Sedgley, Beacon

WORCESTERSHIRE
Knightwick, Talbot

YORKSHIRE
Cropton, New Inn
Goose Eye, Turkey
Linthwaite, Sair
Litton, Queens Arms
Sheffield, Fat Cat

SCOTLAND
Houston, Fox & Hounds
Kilmahog, Lade
Pitlochry, Moulin

WALES
Abercych, Nags Head
Llanddarog, White Hart

OPEN ALL DAY (at least in summer)

We list here all the pubs that have told us they plan to stay open all day, even if it's only Saturday. We've included the few pubs which close just for half an hour to an hour, and the many more, chiefly in holiday areas, which open all day only in summer. The individual entries for the pubs themselves show the actual details.

BEDFORDSHIRE
Bletsoe, Falcon
Henlow, Engineers Arms
Old Warden, Hare & Hounds
Stanbridge, Five Bells
Steppingley, French Horn
Woburn, Birch

BERKSHIRE
Bray, Hinds Head
Frilsham, Pot Kiln
Hurst, Green Man
Reading, Hobgoblin
Remenham, Little Angel
Ruscombe, Royal Oak
White Waltham, Beehive
Winterbourne, Winterbourne Arms

BUCKINGHAMSHIRE
Aylesbury, Kings Head
Bennett End, Three Horseshoes
Bovingdon Green, Royal Oak
Chalfont St Giles, White Hart
Denham, Swan
Dorney, Palmer Arms
Easington, Mole & Chicken
Fingest, Chequers
Ford, Dinton Hermit
Forty Green, Royal Standard of England
Grove, Grove Lock
Hawridge Common, Full Moon
Hedgerley, White Horse
Ley Hill, Swan
Skirmett, Frog
Soulbury, Boot
Stoke Mandeville, Woolpack
Turville, Bull & Butcher
Wooburn Common, Chequers

CAMBRIDGESHIRE
Cambridge, Eagle
Elton, Black Horse
Godmanchester, Exhibition
Hemingford Grey, Cock
Huntingdon, Old Bridge Hotel
Kimbolton, New Sun
Peterborough, Brewery Tap, Charters

CHESHIRE
Aldford, Grosvenor Arms
Astbury, Egerton Arms
Aston, Bhurtpore
Barthomley, White Lion
Bunbury, Dysart Arms
Burleydam, Combermere Arms
Burwardsley, Pheasant
Chester, Albion, Old Harkers Arms

Cotebrook, Fox & Barrel
Eaton, Plough
Haughton Moss, Nags Head
Langley, Hanging Gate
Mobberley, Roebuck
Peover Heath, Dog
Prestbury, Legh Arms
Tarporley, Rising Sun
Wettenhall, Boot & Slipper
Willington, Boot
Wincle, Ship

CORNWALL
Altarnun, Rising Sun
Blisland, Blisland Inn
Bodinnick, Old Ferry
Lostwithiel, Royal Oak
Mitchell, Plume of Feathers
Mithian, Miners Arms
Mousehole, Ship
Mylor Bridge, Pandora
Polkerris, Rashleigh
Polperro, Blue Peter
Port Isaac, Port Gaverne Inn
Porthleven, Ship
Porthtowan, Blue
Sennen Cove, Old Success
Tregadillett, Eliot Arms
Tresco, New Inn
Truro, Old Ale House
Zennor, Tinners Arms

CUMBRIA
Ambleside, Golden Rule
Armathwaite, Dukes Head
Askham, Punch Bowl
Bouth, White Hart
Brampton, New Inn
Broughton Mills, Blacksmiths Arms
Buttermere, Bridge Hotel
Cartmel, Kings Arms
Cartmel Fell, Masons Arms
Chapel Stile, Wainwrights
Cockermouth, Bitter End
Crosthwaite, Punch Bowl
Elterwater, Britannia
Hawkshead, Kings Arms, Queens Head
Ings, Watermill
Keswick, Dog & Gun
Kirkby Lonsdale, Sun
Langdale, Old Dungeon Ghyll
Levens, Strickland Arms
Little Langdale, Three Shires
Loweswater, Kirkstile Inn
Mungrisdale, Mill Inn
Near Sawrey, Tower Bank Arms
Santon Bridge, Bridge Inn
Scales, White Horse
Seathwaite, Newfield Inn
Staveley, Eagle & Child
Stonethwaite, Langstrath
Threlkeld, Horse & Farrier
Troutbeck, Queens Head
Ulverston, Bay Horse, Farmers Arms
Yanwath, Gate Inn

DERBYSHIRE
Alderwasley, Bear
Ashover, Old Poets Corner
Barlow, Old Pump
Derby, Alexandra, Brunswick
Fenny Bentley, Coach & Horses
Foolow, Bulls Head
Hathersage, Plough, Scotsmans Pack
Hayfield, Lantern Pike, Royal
Holbrook, Dead Poets
Hope, Cheshire Cheese
Ladybower Reservoir, Yorkshire Bridge
Litton, Red Lion
Monsal Head, Monsal Head Hotel
Over Haddon, Lathkil
Sheldon, Cock & Pullet
Wardlow, Three Stags Heads
Woolley Moor, White Horse

DEVON
Avonwick, Turtley Corn Mill
Beesands, Cricket
Branscombe, Masons Arms
Buckfast, Abbey Inn
Buckland Monachorum, Drake Manor
Cockwood, Anchor
Culmstock, Culm Valley
Dartmouth, Cherub
Exeter, Imperial
Exminster, Turf Hotel
Haytor Vale, Rock
Holbeton, Dartmoor Union
Iddesleigh, Duke of York
Lustleigh, Cleave
Lydford, Castle Inn
Marldon, Church House
Meavy, Royal Oak
Newton Abbot, Two Mile Oak
Nomansland, Mount Pleasant
Noss Mayo, Ship
Postbridge, Warren House
Poundsgate, Tavistock Inn
Rockbeare, Jack in the Green
Sandy Park, Sandy Park Inn
Sidbury, Hare & Hounds
Stoke Gabriel, Church House
Stokenham, Church House
Torbryan, Old Church House
Torcross, Start Bay
Tuckenhay, Maltsters Arms
Widecombe, Rugglestone
Winkleigh, Kings Arms
Woodbury Salterton, Diggers Rest
Yealmpton, Rose & Crown

DORSET
Cerne Abbas, Royal Oak
East Chaldon, Sailors Return
Middlemarsh, Hunters Moon
Mudeford, Ship in Distress
Poole, Cow
Sherborne, Digby Tap
Tarrant Monkton, Langton Arms
Worth Matravers, Square & Compass

ESSEX
Burnham-on-Crouch, White Harte
Castle Hedingham, Bell

Chappel, Swan
Clavering, Cricketers
Dedham, Sun
Great Henny, Henny Swan
Langham, Shepherd & Dog
Little Walden, Crown
Mill Green, Viper
Peldon, Rose
Rickling Green, Cricketers Arms
Stock, Hoop
Stow Maries, Prince of Wales
Youngs End, Green Dragon

GLOUCESTERSHIRE
Almondsbury, Bowl
Barnsley, Village Pub
Bisley, Bear
Bledington, Kings Head
Box, Halfway House
Brimpsfield, Golden Heart
Chedworth, Seven Tuns
Cheltenham, Royal Oak
Chipping Campden, Eight Bells
Cowley, Green Dragon
Didmarton, Kings Arms
Dursley, Old Spot
Ewen, Wild Duck
Fairford, Bull
Ford, Plough
Guiting Power, Hollow Bottom
Kilkenny, Kilkeney Inn
Littleton-upon-Severn, White Hart
Lower Oddington, Fox
Nailsworth, Egypt Mill, Weighbridge
Nether Westcote, Westcote Inn
Northleach, Wheatsheaf
Oldbury-on-Severn, Anchor
Tetbury, Gumstool, Snooty Fox
Upper Oddington, Horse & Groom
Woodchester, Ram

HAMPSHIRE
Bank, Oak
Bentley, Bull
Bentworth, Sun
Braishfield, Wheatsheaf
Brambridge, Dog & Crook
Easton, Chestnut Horse
Fritham, Royal Oak
Littleton, Running Horse
Lower Wield, Yew Tree
Lymington, Kings Head
Portsmouth, Old Customs House
Rotherwick, Falcon
Rowland's Castle, Castle Inn
Southsea, Wine Vaults
Stockbridge, Grosvenor
Wherwell, Mayfly
Winchester, Willow Tree, Wykeham Arms

HEREFORDSHIRE
Bodenham, Englands Gate
Dorstone, Pandy
Hereford, Victory
Hoarwithy, New Harp
Ledbury, Feathers
Walford, Mill Race
Walterstone, Carpenters Arms

HERTFORDSHIRE
Aldbury, Greyhound, Valiant Trooper
Ashwell, Three Tuns
Batford, Gibraltar Castle
Chapmore End, Woodman
Cottered, Bull
Flaunden, Bricklayers Arms
Frithsden, Alford Arms
Hertford, White Horse
Royston, Old Bull
Sarratt, Cock
Willian, Fox

ISLE OF WIGHT
Arreton, White Lion
Bembridge, Crab & Lobster
Cowes, Folly
Hulverstone, Sun
Seaview, Seaview Hotel
Ventnor, Spyglass

KENT
Bough Beech, Wheatsheaf
Brookland, Woolpack
Chiddingstone, Castle Inn
Groombridge, Crown
Hawkhurst, Queens
Hollingbourne, Windmill
Langton Green, Hare
Newnham, George
Penshurst, Bottle House
Pluckley, Mundy Bois
Selling, Rose & Crown
Shipbourne, Chaser
Stodmarsh, Red Lion
Stowting, Tiger
Tunbridge Wells, Beacon, Sankeys
West Peckham, Swan on the Green

LANCASHIRE
Barnston, Fox & Hounds
Bay Horse, Bay Horse
Bispham Green, Eagle & Child
Brindle, Cavendish Arms
Broughton, Plough at Eaves
Bury, Lord Raglan
Chipping, Dog & Partridge
Denshaw, Rams Head
Fence, Fence Gate
Great Mitton, Three Fishes
Lancaster, Sun
Liverpool, Philharmonic Dining Rooms
Longridge, Derby Arms
Lydgate, White Hart
Lytham, Taps
Manchester, Britons Protection, Dukes 92,
    Marble Arch
Mellor, Devonshire Arms, Oddfellows Arms
Nether Burrow, Highwayman
Ribchester, White Bull
Rimington, Black Bull
Stalybridge, Station Buffet
Uppermill, Church Inn
Wheatley Lane, Old Sparrow Hawk
Wheelton, Dressers Arms
Whitewell, Inn at Whitewell
Yealand Conyers, New Inn

LEICESTERSHIRE AND RUTLAND
Ab Kettleby, Sugar Loaf
Clipsham, Olive Branch
Empingham, White Horse
Mowsley, Staff of Life
Newton Burgoland, Belper Arms
Oadby, Cow & Plough
Oakham, Grainstore
Stathern, Red Lion
Stretton, Ram Jam Inn
Swithland, Griffin
Wing, Kings Arms

LINCOLNSHIRE
Allington, Welby Arms
Barnoldby le Beck, Ship
Billingborough, Fortescue Arms
Ingham, Inn on the Green
Lincoln, Victoria, Wig & Mitre
Rothwell, Blacksmiths Arms
South Witham, Blue Cow
Stamford, George of Stamford
Surfleet, Mermaid
Woolsthorpe, Chequers

NORFOLK
Bawburgh, Kings Head
Blakeney, Kings Arms
Brancaster Staithe, Jolly Sailors, White Horse
Burnham Market, Hoste Arms
Holkham, Victoria
Larling, Angel
Morston, Anchor
Norwich, Adam & Eve, Fat Cat
Old Buckenham, Gamekeeper
Ringstead, Gin Trap
Snettisham, Rose & Crown
Swanton Morley, Darbys
Thornham, Lifeboat
Tivetshall St Mary, Old Ram
Wells-next-the-Sea, Crown
Winterton-on-Sea, Fishermans Return
Woodbastwick, Fur & Feather

NORTHAMPTONSHIRE
Badby, Windmill
East Haddon, Red Lion
Great Brington, Fox & Hounds/Althorp
Kilsby, George
Nether Heyford, Olde Sun
Oundle, Ship
Slipton, Samuel Pepys
Sulgrave, Star
Wadenhoe, Kings Head
Woodnewton, White Swan

NORTHUMBRIA
Anick, Rat
Blanchland, Lord Crewe Arms
Carterway Heads, Manor House Inn
Greta Bridge, Morritt Arms
Haltwhistle, Milecastle Inn
Langley on Tyne, Carts Bog Inn
New York, Shiremoor Farm
Newburn, Keelman
Newcastle upon Tyne, Cluny, Crown Posada
Newton-by-the-Sea, Ship
Newton-on-the-Moor, Cook & Barker Arms

Seahouses, Olde Ship
Stannington, Ridley Arms
Wark, Battlesteads
Weldon Bridge, Anglers Arms

NOTTINGHAMSHIRE
Beeston, Victoria
Caunton, Caunton Beck
Halam, Waggon & Horses
Nottingham, Bell, Cock & Hoop, Fellows
    Morton & Clayton, Keans Head,
    Lincolnshire Poacher, Olde Trip to
    Jerusalem, Vat & Fiddle
Ranby, Chequers

OXFORDSHIRE
Alvescot, Plough
Banbury, Reindeer
Chipping Norton, Chequers
Churchill, Chequers
Crowell, Shepherds Crook
Cuxham, Half Moon
East Hendred, Eyston Arms
Fyfield, White Hart
Godstow, Trout
Great Tew, Falkland Arms
Highmoor, Rising Sun
Kingston Blount, Cherry Tree
Oxford, Turf Tavern
Woodstock, Kings Arms

SHROPSHIRE
Bishop's Castle, Castle Hotel, Six Bells,
    Three Tuns
Bridges, Horseshoe
Bromfield, Clive/Cookhouse
Chetwynd Aston, Fox
Grinshill, Inn at Grinshill
Ironbridge, Malthouse
Little Stretton, Ragleth
Ludlow, Church Inn
Much Wenlock, George & Dragon, Talbot
Shrewsbury, Armoury

SOMERSET
Axbridge, Lamb
Bath, Old Green Tree, Star
Bleadon, Queens Arms
Chew Magna, Bear & Swan
Churchill, Crown
Clapton-in-Gordano, Black Horse
Exford, White Horse
Huish Episcopi, Rose & Crown
Kingsdon, Kingsdon Inn
Litton, Kings Arms
Norton St Philip, George
Portishead, Windmill
Stanton Wick, Carpenters Arms
Wells, City Arms, Crown

STAFFORDSHIRE
Abbots Bromley, Goats Head
Alstonefield, George
Hoar Cross, Meynell Ingram Arms
Lichfield, Queens Head
Stourton, Fox
Wrinehill, Hand & Trumpet

SUFFOLK
Bury St Edmunds, Nutshell
Chelmondiston, Butt & Oyster
Cotton, Trowel & Hammer
Grundisburgh, Dog
Lavenham, Angel
Long Melford, Black Lion
Nayland, Anchor
Rougham, Ravenwood Hall
South Elmham, St Peters Brewery
Southwold, Harbour Inn, Lord Nelson
Stoke-by-Nayland, Angel, Crown
Walberswick, Bell
Waldringfield, Maybush
Westleton, Crown

SURREY
Cobham, Plough
Coldharbour, Plough
Eashing, Stag
Elstead, Mill at Elstead
Esher, Marneys
Forest Green, Parrot
Leigh, Seven Stars
Lingfield, Hare & Hounds
Mickleham, Running Horses
Newdigate, Surrey Oaks
Ottershaw, Castle
Thursley, Three Horseshoes
West End, Inn at West End
West Horsley, Barley Mow
Worplesdon, Jolly Farmer

SUSSEX
Alfriston, George
Arlington, Old Oak
Berwick, Cricketers Arms
Blackboys, Blackboys Inn
Brighton, Greys
Burpham, George & Dragon
Byworth, Black Horse
Charlton, Fox Goes Free
Chiddingly, Six Bells
Coolham, George & Dragon
Ditchling, Bull
Donnington, Blacksmiths Arms
East Dean, Star & Garter
East Lavant, Royal Oak
Fletching, Griffin
Horsham, Black Jug
Icklesham, Queens Head
Lodsworth, Halfway Bridge Inn
Oving, Gribble Inn
Rye, Mermaid
Singleton, Partridge
Wilmington, Giants Rest

WARWICKSHIRE
Aston Cantlow, Kings Head
Birmingham, Old Joint Stock
Brierley Hill, Vine
Easenhall, Golden Lion
Edge Hill, Castle
Long Itchington, Duck on the Pond
Netherton, Old Swan
Preston Bagot, Crabmill
Welford-on-Avon, Bell

WILTSHIRE
Box, Quarrymans Arms
Bradford-on-Avon, Dandy Lion
Castle Combe, Castle Inn
Crockerton, Bath Arms
Devizes, Bear
Fonthill Gifford, Beckford Arms
Hindon, Lamb
Lacock, George, Red Lion
Luckington, Old Royal Ship
Norton, Vine Tree
Salisbury, Haunch of Venison
Seend, Barge
Stourton, Spread Eagle
Whitley, Pear Tree

WORCESTERSHIRE
Bewdley, Little Pack Horse
Bretforton, Fleece
Clent, Fountain
Kempsey, Walter de Cantelupe
Kidderminster, King & Castle
Knightwick, Talbot
Malvern, Nags Head
Pensax, Bell

YORKSHIRE
Asenby, Crab & Lobster
Beck Hole, Birch Hall
Beverley, White Horse
Blakey Ridge, Lion
Boroughbridge, Black Bull
Bradfield, Strines Inn
Burn, Wheatsheaf
Cray, White Lion
Crayke, Durham Ox
Cropton, New Inn
East Witton, Blue Lion
Egton Bridge, Horseshoe
Ferrensby, General Tarleton
Goose Eye, Turkey
Grinton, Bridge Inn
Halifax, Shibden Mill
Harome, Star
Hartshead, Gray Ox
Heath, Kings Arms
Hull, Minerva, Olde White Harte
Kettlesing, Queens Head
Kirkbymoorside, George & Dragon
Langthwaite, Charles Bathurst
Lastingham, Blacksmiths Arms
Ledsham, Chequers
Linthwaite, Sair
Linton, Windmill
Linton in Craven, Fountaine
Low Catton, Gold Cup
Masham, Black Sheep Brewery
Middleham, Black Swan, White Swan
Mill Bank, Millbank
Osmotherley, Golden Lion
Pickering, White Swan
Pickhill, Nags Head
Ripley, Boars Head
Ripponden, Old Bridge
Robin Hood's Bay, Laurel
Sheffield, Fat Cat, New Barrack
Skipton, Narrow Boat
South Dalton, Pipe & Glass

Thornton in Lonsdale, Marton Arms
Thornton Watlass, Buck
Whitby, Duke of York
Widdop, Pack Horse

LONDON
Central London, Admiral Codrington, Albert, Argyll Arms, Bishops Finger, Black Friar, Cittie of Yorke, Coopers Arms, Cross Keys, Dog & Duck, Eagle, Grapes, Grenadier, Guinea, Jerusalem Tavern, Lamb, Lamb & Flag, Lord Moon of the Mall, Nags Head, Old Bank of England, Olde Cheshire Cheese, Olde Mitre, Princess Louise, Red Lion (both pubs), Salisbury, Seven Stars, Star, Westminster Arms
East London, Grapes, Narrow, Prospect of Whitby
North London, Chapel, Compton Arms, Drapers Arms, Duke of Cambridge, Flask, Holly Bush, Olde White Bear, Spaniards Inn
South London, Anchor & Hope, Bo-Peep, Crown & Greyhound, Cutty Sark, Fire Station, Founders Arms, Fox & Hounds, George, Greenwich Union, Market Porter, Royal Oak, Victoria, White Cross
West London, Anglesea Arms, Atlas, Bulls Head, Churchill Arms, Dove, Fat Badger, Havelock Tavern, Portobello Gold, Warrington, White Horse, Windsor Castle

SCOTLAND
Aboyne, Boat
Applecross, Applecross Inn
Badachro, Badachro Inn
Broughty Ferry, Fishermans Tavern
Edinburgh, Abbotsford, Bow Bar, Café Royal, Guildford Arms, Kays Bar, Starbank
Elie, Ship
Gairloch, Old Inn
Glasgow, Babbity Bowster, Bon Accord, Counting House
Houston, Fox & Hounds
Innerleithen, Traquair Arms
Inveraray, George
Isle of Whithorn, Steam Packet
Kilmahog, Lade
Kingholm Quay, Swan
Kippen, Cross Keys
Kirk Yetholm, Border
Linlithgow, Four Marys
Pitlochry, Moulin
Plockton, Plockton Hotel
Shieldaig, Tigh an Eilean Hotel
Stein, Stein Inn
Swinton, Wheatsheaf
Tayvallich, Tayvallich Inn
Thornhill, Lion & Unicorn
Ullapool, Ferry Boat
Weem, Ailean Chraggan

WALES
Aberaeron, Harbourmaster
Abercych, Nags Head
Abergorlech, Black Lion
Beaumaris, Olde Bulls Head
Capel Curig, Bryn Tyrch

Colwyn Bay, Pen-y-Bryn
Cresswell Quay, Cresselly Arms
East Aberthaw, Blue Anchor
Felinfach, Griffin
Gladestry, Royal Oak
Gresford, Pant-yr-Ochain
Hay-on-Wye, Kilverts, Old Black Lion
Llanarmon Dyffryn Ceiriog, Hand
Llanberis, Pen-y-Gwryd
Llandudno Junction, Queens Head
Llanferres, Druid
Llanfrynach, White Swan
Llangollen, Corn Mill
Mold, Glasfryn
Monknash, Plough & Harrow
Porth Dinllaen, Ty Coch
Porthgain, Sloop
Raglan, Clytha Arms
Red Wharf Bay, Ship
Rhyd-y-Meirch, Goose & Cuckoo
Rosebush, Tafarn Sinc
Shirenewton, Carpenters Arms
Skenfrith, Bell
St Hilary, Bush
Tintern, Cherry Tree
Ty'n-y-groes, Groes

CHANNEL ISLANDS
King's Mills, Fleur du Jardin
Rozel, Rozel
St Aubin, Old Court House Inn
St Brelade, Old Portelet Inn, Old Smugglers
St Helier, Town House
St John, Les Fontaines
St Ouens Bay, La Pulente

PUBS CLOSE TO MOTORWAY JUNCTIONS

The number at the start of each line is the number of the junction. Detailed directions are given in the main entry for each pub. In this section, to help you find the pubs quickly before you're past the junction, we give the name of the chapter where you'll find the text.

M1
13: Woburn, Birch (Beds) 3.5 miles
16: Nether Heyford, Olde Sun (Northants) 1.8 miles
18: Crick, Red Lion (Northants) 1 mile; Kilsby, George (Northants) 2.6 miles

M3
3: West End, Inn at West End (Surrey) 2.4 miles
5: Rotherwick, Falcon (Hants) 4 miles
9: Winchester, Willow Tree (Hants) 1 mile; Easton, Chestnut Horse (Hants) 3.6 miles
10: Winchester, Black Boy (Hants) 1 mile
12: Brambridge, Dog & Crook (Hants) 2.1 miles

M4
7: Dorney, Pineapple (Bucks) 2.4 miles; Dorney, Palmer Arms (Bucks) 2.7 miles
8: Oakley Green, Olde Red Lion (Berks) 4 miles

9: Holyport, Belgian Arms (Berks)
1.5 miles; Bray, Hinds Head (Berks)
1.75 miles; Bray, Crown (Berks)
1.75 miles
11: Shinfield, Magpie & Parrot (Berks)
2.6 miles
13: Winterbourne, Winterbourne Arms
(Berks) 3.7 miles
15: Badbury, Bakers Arms (Wilts) 1 mile
17: Norton, Vine Tree (Wilts) 4 miles
18: Hinton Dyrham, Bull (Gloucs) 2.4 miles

M5

4: Holy Cross, Bell & Cross (Worcs) 4 miles
7: Kempsey, Walter de Cantelupe (Worcs)
3.75 miles
9: Bredon, Fox & Hounds (Worcs) 4.5 miles
13: Frampton on Severn, Bell (Gloucs)
3 miles
16: Almondsbury, Bowl (Gloucs) 1.25 miles
19: Portishead, Windmill (Somerset)
3.7 miles; Clapton-in-Gordano, Black
Horse (Somerset) 4 miles
26: Clayhidon, Merry Harriers (Devon)
3.1 miles
28: Broadhembury, Drewe Arms (Devon)
5 miles
30: Topsham, Bridge Inn (Devon)
2.25 miles; Woodbury Salterton, Diggers
Rest (Devon) 3.5 miles

M6

4: Shustoke, Griffin (Warks) 5 miles
16: Barthomley, White Lion (Cheshire)
1 mile
29: Brindle, Cavendish Arms (Lancs) 3 miles
33: Bay Horse, Bay Horse (Lancs) 1.2 miles
35: Yealand Conyers, New Inn (Lancs)
3 miles
36: Levens, Strickland Arms (Cumbria)
4 miles
40: Yanwath, Gate Inn (Cumbria) 2.25 miles;
Askham, Punch Bowl (Cumbria)
4.5 miles

M9

3: Linlithgow, Four Marys (Scotland)
2 miles

M11

7: Hastingwood, Rainbow & Dove (Essex)
0.25 miles; Birchanger, Three Willows
(Essex) 0.8 miles
9: Hinxton, Red Lion (Cambridgeshire)
2 miles
10: Thriplow, Green Man (Cambridgeshire)
3 miles

M20

8: Hollingbourne, Windmill (Kent) 1 mile
11: Stowting, Tiger (Kent) 3.7 miles

M25

4: South London, Bo-Peep (London)
1.7 miles
10: Cobham, Plough (Surrey) 3.2 miles
11: Ottershaw, Castle (Surrey) 2.6 miles
16: Denham, Swan (Bucks) 0.75 miles
18: Chenies, Red Lion (Bucks) 2 miles;
Flaunden, Bricklayers Arms
(Hertfordshire) 4 miles
21a: Potters Crouch, Holly Bush
(Hertfordshire) 2.3 miles

M27

1: Fritham, Royal Oak (Hants) 4 miles

M40

2: Hedgerley, White Horse (Bucks)
2.4 miles; Forty Green, Royal Standard
of England (Bucks) 3.5 miles
6: Lewknor, Olde Leathern Bottel (Oxon)
0.5 miles; Kingston Blount, Cherry Tree
(Oxon) 1.9 miles; Crowell, Shepherds
Crook (Oxon) 2 miles; Cuxham, Half
Moon (Oxon) 4 miles

M48

1: Littleton-upon-Severn, White Hart
(Gloucs) 3.5 miles

M50

1: Baughton, Jockey (Worcs) 4 miles
3: Upton Bishop, Moody Cow (Herefs)
2 miles

M53

3: Barnston, Fox & Hounds (Lancs) 3 miles

M55

1: Broughton, Plough at Eaves (Lancs)
3.25 miles

M61

8: Wheelton, Dressers Arms (Lancs)
2.1 miles

M62

22: Denshaw, Rams Head (Lancs) 2 miles
25: Hartshead, Gray Ox (Yorks) 3.5 miles

M65

13: Fence, Fence Gate (Lancs) 2.6 miles

M66

1: Bury, Lord Raglan (Lancs) 2 miles

Report Forms

Please report to us: you can use the cut-out forms on the following pages, the tear-out card in the middle of the book, or just plain paper – whichever's easiest for you, or you can report to our website, **www.goodguides.co.uk**. We need to know what you think of the pubs in this edition. We need to know about other pubs worthy of inclusion. We need to know about ones that should not be included. And we need to know that vital factor – how good the landlord or landlady is.

The atmosphere and character of the pub are the most important features – why it would, or would not, appeal to strangers, so please try to describe what is special about it. In particular, we can't consider including a pub in the Lucky Dip section unless we know something about what it looks like inside, so that we can describe it to other readers. And obviously with existing entries, we need to know about any changes in décor and furnishings, too. But the bar food and the drink are also important – please tell us about them.

If the food is really quite outstanding, tick the FOOD AWARD box on the form, and tell us about the special quality that makes it stand out – the more detail, the better. And if you have stayed there, tell us about the standard of accommodation – whether it was comfortable, pleasant, good value for money. Again, if the pub or inn is worth special attention as a place to stay, tick the PLACE-TO-STAY AWARD box.

If you're in a position to gauge a pub's suitability or otherwise for **disabled people**, do please tell us about that.

Please try to gauge whether a pub should be a main entry, or is best as a Lucky Dip (and tick the relevant box). In general, main entries need qualities that would make it worth other readers' while to travel some distance to them; Lucky Dips are the pubs that are worth knowing about if you are nearby. But if a pub is an entirely new recommendation, the Lucky Dip may be the best place for it to start its career in the *Guide* – to encourage other readers to report on it.

The more detail you can put into your description of a Lucky Dip pub that's only scantily described in the current edition (or not in at all), the better. A description of its character and even furnishings is a tremendous boon.

It helps enormously if you can give the full address for any new pub – one not yet a main entry, or without a full address in the Lucky Dip sections. In a town, we need the street name; in the country, if it's hard to find, we need directions. Even better for us is the post code. If we can't find out a pub's post code, we no longer include it in the *Guide* – and the Post Office directories we use will not yet have caught up with new pubs, or ones which have changed their names. With any pub, it always helps to let us know about prices of food (and bedrooms, if there are any); and about any lunchtimes or evenings when food is not served. We'd also like to have your views on drinks quality – beer, wine, cider and so forth, even coffee and tea; and do let us know about bedrooms.

If you know that a Lucky Dip pub is open all day (or even late into the afternoon), please tell us – preferably saying which days.

When you go to a pub, don't tell them you're a reporter for *The Good Pub Guide*; we do make clear that all inspections are anonymous, and if you declare yourself as a reporter you risk getting special treatment – for better or for worse!

Sometimes pubs are dropped from the main entries simply because very few readers have written to us about them – and of course there's a risk that people may not write if they find the pub exactly as described in the entry. You can use the forms at the front of the batch of report forms just to list pubs you've been to, found as described, and can recommend.

When you write to The Good Pub Guide, FREEPOST TN1569, WADHURST, East Sussex TN5 7BR, you don't need a stamp in the UK. We'll gladly send you more forms (free) if you wish.

Though we try to answer all letters, please understand if there's a delay (particularly in summer, our busiest period). We now edit and inspect throughout the year, so reports are valuable at any time. Obviously it's most useful of all if you write soon after a pub visit, while everything's fresh in your mind, rather than storing things up for a later batch.

We'll assume we can print your name or initials as a recommender unless you tell us otherwise.

I have been to the following pubs in *The Good Pub Guide 2008* in the last few months, found them as described, and confirm that they deserve continued inclusion:

Continued overleaf

PLEASE GIVE YOUR NAME AND ADDRESS ON THE BACK OF THIS FORM

Pubs visited continued...

Your own name and address *(block capitals please)*

Postcode

Please return to
The Good Pub Guide,
FREEPOST TN1569,
WADHURST,
East Sussex
TN5 7BR

IF YOU PREFER, YOU CAN SEND US REPORTS
THROUGH OUR WEBSITE:
www.goodguides.co.uk

I have been to the following pubs in *The Good Pub Guide 2008* in the last few months, found them as described, and confirm that they deserve continued inclusion:

Continued overleaf
PLEASE GIVE YOUR NAME AND ADDRESS ON THE BACK OF THIS FORM

Pubs visited continued...

Your own name and address *(block capitals please)*

Postcode

In returning this form I confirm my agreement that the information I provide may be used by
The Random House Group Ltd, its assignees and/or licensees in any media or medium whatsoever.

Please return to
The Good Pub Guide,
FREEPOST TN1569,
WADHURST,
East Sussex
TN5 7BR

IF YOU PREFER, YOU CAN SEND US REPORTS
THROUGH OUR WEBSITE:
www.goodguides.co.uk

REPORT ON (PUB'S NAME)

Pub's address

☐ **YES** MAIN ENTRY ☐ **YES** LUCKY DIP ☐ **NO** DON'T INCLUDE

Please tick one of these boxes to show your verdict, and give reasons and descriptive comments, prices etc

☐ DESERVES **FOOD** award ☐ DESERVES **PLACE-TO-STAY** award 2008:1

PLEASE GIVE YOUR NAME AND ADDRESS ON THE BACK OF THIS FORM

REPORT ON (PUB'S NAME)

Pub's address

☐ **YES** MAIN ENTRY ☐ **YES** LUCKY DIP ☐ **NO** DON'T INCLUDE

Please tick one of these boxes to show your verdict, and give reasons and descriptive comments, prices etc

☐ DESERVES **FOOD** award ☐ DESERVES **PLACE-TO-STAY** award 2008:2

PLEASE GIVE YOUR NAME AND ADDRESS ON THE BACK OF THIS FORM

Your own name and address *(block capitals please)*

In returning this form I confirm my agreement that the information I provide may be used by
The Random House Group Ltd, its assignees and/or licensees in any media or medium whatsoever.

DO NOT USE THIS SIDE OF THE PAGE FOR WRITING ABOUT PUBS

✂ ....

Your own name and address *(block capitals please)*

In returning this form I confirm my agreement that the information I provide may be used by
The Random House Group Ltd, its assignees and/or licensees in any media or medium whatsoever.

DO NOT USE THIS SIDE OF THE PAGE FOR WRITING ABOUT PUBS

IF YOU PREFER, YOU CAN SEND US REPORTS THROUGH OUR WEBSITE:
www.goodguides.co.uk

REPORT ON (PUB'S NAME)

Pub's address

☐ **YES** MAIN ENTRY ☐ **YES** LUCKY DIP ☐ **NO** DON'T INCLUDE
Please tick one of these boxes to show your verdict, and give reasons and descriptive comments, prices etc

☐ DESERVES **FOOD** award ☐ DESERVES **PLACE-TO-STAY** award 2008:3

PLEASE GIVE YOUR NAME AND ADDRESS ON THE BACK OF THIS FORM

✂ -

REPORT ON (PUB'S NAME)

Pub's address

☐ **YES** MAIN ENTRY ☐ **YES** LUCKY DIP ☐ **NO** DON'T INCLUDE
Please tick one of these boxes to show your verdict, and give reasons and descriptive comments, prices etc

☐ DESERVES **FOOD** award ☐ DESERVES **PLACE-TO-STAY** award 2008:4

PLEASE GIVE YOUR NAME AND ADDRESS ON THE BACK OF THIS FORM

Your own name and address *(block capitals please)*

In returning this form I confirm my agreement that the information I provide may be used by
The Random House Group Ltd, its assignees and/or licensees in any media or medium whatsoever.

DO NOT USE THIS SIDE OF THE PAGE FOR WRITING ABOUT PUBS

By returning this form, you consent to the collection, recording and use of the information you submit, by The Random House Group
Ltd. Any personal details which you provide from which we can identify you are held and processed in accordance with the
Data Protection Act 1998 and will not be passed on to any third parties. The Random House Group Ltd may wish to send
you further information on their associated products. Please tick box if you do not wish to receive any such information.

IF YOU PREFER, YOU CAN SEND US REPORTS THROUGH OUR WEBSITE:
www.goodguides.co.uk

REPORT ON (PUB'S NAME)

Pub's address

☐ **YES** MAIN ENTRY ☐ **YES** LUCKY DIP ☐ **NO** DON'T INCLUDE

Please tick one of these boxes to show your verdict, and give reasons and descriptive comments, prices etc

☐ DESERVES **FOOD** award ☐ DESERVES **PLACE-TO-STAY** award 2008:5

PLEASE GIVE YOUR NAME AND ADDRESS ON THE BACK OF THIS FORM

✂ ┄┄┄

REPORT ON (PUB'S NAME)

Pub's address

☐ **YES** MAIN ENTRY ☐ **YES** LUCKY DIP ☐ **NO** DON'T INCLUDE

Please tick one of these boxes to show your verdict, and give reasons and descriptive comments, prices etc

☐ DESERVES **FOOD** award ☐ DESERVES **PLACE-TO-STAY** award 2008:6

PLEASE GIVE YOUR NAME AND ADDRESS ON THE BACK OF THIS FORM

Your own name and address *(block capitals please)*

In returning this form I confirm my agreement that the information I provide may be used by
The Random House Group Ltd, its assignees and/or licensees in any media or medium whatsoever.

DO NOT USE THIS SIDE OF THE PAGE FOR WRITING ABOUT PUBS

✂ ....

Your own name and address *(block capitals please)*

In returning this form I confirm my agreement that the information I provide may be used by
The Random House Group Ltd, its assignees and/or licensees in any media or medium whatsoever.

DO NOT USE THIS SIDE OF THE PAGE FOR WRITING ABOUT PUBS

IF YOU PREFER, YOU CAN SEND US REPORTS THROUGH OUR WEBSITE:
www.goodguides.co.uk

REPORT ON (PUB'S NAME)

Pub's address

☐ **YES** MAIN ENTRY   ☐ **YES** LUCKY DIP   ☐ **NO** DON'T INCLUDE
Please tick one of these boxes to show your verdict, and give reasons and descriptive comments, prices etc

☐ DESERVES **FOOD** award   ☐ DESERVES **PLACE-TO-STAY** award   2008:7

PLEASE GIVE YOUR NAME AND ADDRESS ON THE BACK OF THIS FORM

--✂

REPORT ON (PUB'S NAME)

Pub's address

☐ **YES** MAIN ENTRY   ☐ **YES** LUCKY DIP   ☐ **NO** DON'T INCLUDE
Please tick one of these boxes to show your verdict, and give reasons and descriptive comments, prices etc

☐ DESERVES **FOOD** award   ☐ DESERVES **PLACE-TO-STAY** award   2008:8

PLEASE GIVE YOUR NAME AND ADDRESS ON THE BACK OF THIS FORM

Your own name and address *(block capitals please)*
In returning this form I confirm my agreement that the information I provide may be used by
The Random House Group Ltd, its assignees and/or licensees in any media or medium whatsoever.

DO NOT USE THIS SIDE OF THE PAGE FOR WRITING ABOUT PUBS

✂ ....

Your own name and address *(block capitals please)*
In returning this form I confirm my agreement that the information I provide may be used by
The Random House Group Ltd, its assignees and/or licensees in any media or medium whatsoever.

DO NOT USE THIS SIDE OF THE PAGE FOR WRITING ABOUT PUBS

IF YOU PREFER, YOU CAN SEND US REPORTS THROUGH OUR WEBSITE:
www.goodguides.co.uk

REPORT ON (PUB'S NAME)

Pub's address

☐ **YES** MAIN ENTRY ☐ **YES** LUCKY DIP ☐ **NO** DON'T INCLUDE

Please tick one of these boxes to show your verdict, and give reasons and descriptive comments, prices etc

☐ DESERVES **FOOD** award ☐ DESERVES **PLACE-TO-STAY** award 2008:9

PLEASE GIVE YOUR NAME AND ADDRESS ON THE BACK OF THIS FORM

--✂

REPORT ON (PUB'S NAME)

Pub's address

☐ **YES** MAIN ENTRY ☐ **YES** LUCKY DIP ☐ **NO** DON'T INCLUDE

Please tick one of these boxes to show your verdict, and give reasons and descriptive comments, prices etc

☐ DESERVES **FOOD** award ☐ DESERVES **PLACE-TO-STAY** award 2008:10

PLEASE GIVE YOUR NAME AND ADDRESS ON THE BACK OF THIS FORM

Your own name and address *(block capitals please)*
In returning this form I confirm my agreement that the information I provide may be used by
The Random House Group Ltd, its assignees and/or licensees in any media or medium whatsoever.

DO NOT USE THIS SIDE OF THE PAGE FOR WRITING ABOUT PUBS

✂ ....

Your own name and address *(block capitals please)*
In returning this form I confirm my agreement that the information I provide may be used by
The Random House Group Ltd, its assignees and/or licensees in any media or medium whatsoever.

DO NOT USE THIS SIDE OF THE PAGE FOR WRITING ABOUT PUBS

IF YOU PREFER, YOU CAN SEND US REPORTS THROUGH OUR WEBSITE:
www.goodguides.co.uk

REPORT ON (PUB'S NAME)

Pub's address

☐ **YES** MAIN ENTRY ☐ **YES** LUCKY DIP ☐ **NO** DON'T INCLUDE
Please tick one of these boxes to show your verdict, and give reasons and descriptive
comments, prices etc

☐ DESERVES **FOOD** award ☐ DESERVES **PLACE-TO-STAY** award 2008:11

PLEASE GIVE YOUR NAME AND ADDRESS ON THE BACK OF THIS FORM

--✂

REPORT ON (PUB'S NAME)

Pub's address

☐ **YES** MAIN ENTRY ☐ **YES** LUCKY DIP ☐ **NO** DON'T INCLUDE
Please tick one of these boxes to show your verdict, and give reasons and descriptive
comments, prices etc

☐ DESERVES **FOOD** award ☐ DESERVES **PLACE-TO-STAY** award 2008:12

PLEASE GIVE YOUR NAME AND ADDRESS ON THE BACK OF THIS FORM

Your own name and address *(block capitals please)*

In returning this form I confirm my agreement that the information I provide may be used by
The Random House Group Ltd, its assignees and/or licensees in any media or medium whatsoever.

DO NOT USE THIS SIDE OF THE PAGE FOR WRITING ABOUT PUBS

✂ ....

Your own name and address *(block capitals please)*

In returning this form I confirm my agreement that the information I provide may be used by
The Random House Group Ltd, its assignees and/or licensees in any media or medium whatsoever.

DO NOT USE THIS SIDE OF THE PAGE FOR WRITING ABOUT PUBS

IF YOU PREFER, YOU CAN SEND US REPORTS THROUGH OUR WEBSITE:
www.goodguides.co.uk

REPORT ON (PUB'S NAME)

Pub's address

☐ **YES** MAIN ENTRY ☐ **YES** LUCKY DIP ☐ **NO** DON'T INCLUDE

Please tick one of these boxes to show your verdict, and give reasons and descriptive comments, prices etc

☐ DESERVES **FOOD** award ☐ DESERVES **PLACE-TO-STAY** award 2008:13

PLEASE GIVE YOUR NAME AND ADDRESS ON THE BACK OF THIS FORM

✂ -

REPORT ON (PUB'S NAME)

Pub's address

☐ **YES** MAIN ENTRY ☐ **YES** LUCKY DIP ☐ **NO** DON'T INCLUDE

Please tick one of these boxes to show your verdict, and give reasons and descriptive comments, prices etc

☐ DESERVES **FOOD** award ☐ DESERVES **PLACE-TO-STAY** award 2008:14

PLEASE GIVE YOUR NAME AND ADDRESS ON THE BACK OF THIS FORM

✂ ....

IF YOU PREFER, YOU CAN SEND US REPORTS THROUGH OUR WEBSITE:
www.goodguides.co.uk

REPORT ON (PUB'S NAME)

Pub's address

☐ **YES** MAIN ENTRY   ☐ **YES** LUCKY DIP   ☐ **NO** DON'T INCLUDE
Please tick one of these boxes to show your verdict, and give reasons and descriptive comments, prices etc

☐ DESERVES **FOOD** award   ☐ DESERVES **PLACE-TO-STAY** award   2008:15

PLEASE GIVE YOUR NAME AND ADDRESS ON THE BACK OF THIS FORM

--✂

REPORT ON (PUB'S NAME)

Pub's address

☐ **YES** MAIN ENTRY   ☐ **YES** LUCKY DIP   ☐ **NO** DON'T INCLUDE
Please tick one of these boxes to show your verdict, and give reasons and descriptive comments, prices etc

☐ DESERVES **FOOD** award   ☐ DESERVES **PLACE-TO-STAY** award   2008:16

PLEASE GIVE YOUR NAME AND ADDRESS ON THE BACK OF THIS FORM

Your own name and address *(block capitals please)*
In returning this form I confirm my agreement that the information I provide may be used by
The Random House Group Ltd, its assignees and/or licensees in any media or medium whatsoever.

DO NOT USE THIS SIDE OF THE PAGE FOR WRITING ABOUT PUBS

✂ ....

Your own name and address *(block capitals please)*
In returning this form I confirm my agreement that the information I provide may be used by
The Random House Group Ltd, its assignees and/or licensees in any media or medium whatsoever.

DO NOT USE THIS SIDE OF THE PAGE FOR WRITING ABOUT PUBS

IF YOU PREFER, YOU CAN SEND US REPORTS THROUGH OUR WEBSITE:
www.goodguides.co.uk

REPORT ON (PUB'S NAME)

Pub's address

☐ **YES** MAIN ENTRY ☐ **YES** LUCKY DIP ☐ **NO** DON'T INCLUDE
Please tick one of these boxes to show your verdict, and give reasons and descriptive
comments, prices etc

☐ DESERVES **FOOD** award ☐ DESERVES **PLACE-TO-STAY** award 2008:17

PLEASE GIVE YOUR NAME AND ADDRESS ON THE BACK OF THIS FORM

---✂

REPORT ON (PUB'S NAME)

Pub's address

☐ **YES** MAIN ENTRY ☐ **YES** LUCKY DIP ☐ **NO** DON'T INCLUDE
Please tick one of these boxes to show your verdict, and give reasons and descriptive
comments, prices etc

☐ DESERVES **FOOD** award ☐ DESERVES **PLACE-TO-STAY** award 2008:18

PLEASE GIVE YOUR NAME AND ADDRESS ON THE BACK OF THIS FORM

Your own name and address *(block capitals please)*

In returning this form I confirm my agreement that the information I provide may be used by
The Random House Group Ltd, its assignees and/or licensees in any media or medium whatsoever.

DO NOT USE THIS SIDE OF THE PAGE FOR WRITING ABOUT PUBS

✂ ....

Your own name and address *(block capitals please)*

In returning this form I confirm my agreement that the information I provide may be used by
The Random House Group Ltd, its assignees and/or licensees in any media or medium whatsoever.

DO NOT USE THIS SIDE OF THE PAGE FOR WRITING ABOUT PUBS

IF YOU PREFER, YOU CAN SEND US REPORTS THROUGH OUR WEBSITE:
www.goodguides.co.uk

REPORT ON (PUB'S NAME)

Pub's address

☐ **YES** MAIN ENTRY   ☐ **YES** LUCKY DIP   ☐ **NO** DON'T INCLUDE
Please tick one of these boxes to show your verdict, and give reasons and descriptive comments, prices etc

☐ DESERVES **FOOD** award   ☐ DESERVES **PLACE-TO-STAY** award   2008:19

PLEASE GIVE YOUR NAME AND ADDRESS ON THE BACK OF THIS FORM

REPORT ON (PUB'S NAME)

Pub's address

☐ **YES** MAIN ENTRY   ☐ **YES** LUCKY DIP   ☐ **NO** DON'T INCLUDE
Please tick one of these boxes to show your verdict, and give reasons and descriptive comments, prices etc

☐ DESERVES **FOOD** award   ☐ DESERVES **PLACE-TO-STAY** award   2008:20

PLEASE GIVE YOUR NAME AND ADDRESS ON THE BACK OF THIS FORM

Your own name and address *(block capitals please)*

In returning this form I confirm my agreement that the information I provide may be used by
The Random House Group Ltd, its assignees and/or licensees in any media or medium whatsoever.

DO NOT USE THIS SIDE OF THE PAGE FOR WRITING ABOUT PUBS

✂ ....

Your own name and address *(block capitals please)*

In returning this form I confirm my agreement that the information I provide may be used by
The Random House Group Ltd, its assignees and/or licensees in any media or medium whatsoever.

DO NOT USE THIS SIDE OF THE PAGE FOR WRITING ABOUT PUBS

IF YOU PREFER, YOU CAN SEND US REPORTS THROUGH OUR WEBSITE:
www.goodguides.co.uk